LONDON
A-Z ®

Published by Geographers' A-Z Map Company Limited
An imprint of HarperCollins Publishers
Westerhill Road
Bishopbriggs
Glasgow G64 2QT
www.az.co.uk
a-z.maps@harpercollins.co.uk

13th edition 2020

A catalogue record for this book is available from the British Library.

ISBN 978-0-00-838799-0

10 9 8 7 6 5 4 3 2

Printed in Bosnia and Herzegovina

MIX
Paper from
responsible sources
FSC™ C007454

This book is produced from independently certified
FSC™ paper to ensure responsible forest management.

For more information visit: www.harpercollins.co.uk/green

Congestion Charging Overview Map and Information	Inside Front Cover
Key to Map Pages	2-3
Large Scale Map Pages @ 5.75" to 1 mile	4-19
Map Pages @ approx. 3" to 1 mile	20-174
Index to Streets, Places, Areas and selected Places of Interest	175-448
Index to Hospitals etc.	449-454
Index to Stations	455-457
Railway Connections Map	458-459
Underground Railway Map	460-461
West End Theatres Map	462

REFERENCE

Motorway	**M1**	
A Road	**A2**	
B Road	**B408**	
Dual Carriageway		
One-way Street Traffic flow on A Roads is also indicated by a heavy line on the drivers' left.		
Road Under Construction Opening dates are correct at the time of publication.		
Proposed Road		
Junction Name	MARBLE ARCH	
Restricted Access		
Pedestrianized Road		
Track / Footpath		
Residential Walkway		
Congestion Charging Zone See inside Front Cover for information	Zone edge. Within Zone.	
Low Emission Zone Visit www.tfl.gov.uk/modes/driving for more information on London's driving zones.	Zone edge. Within Zone.	

Railway Stations:

		Large Scale Map Pages
National Rail Network	⮆	⮆
Crossrail	⮆	⮆
Docklands Light Railway	**DLR**	**DLR**
Overground	⊖	⊖
Underground	●	⊖

Railway — Level Crossing / Tunnel

London Tramlink — Tunnel / Stop
The boarding of Tramlink trams at stops may be limited to a single direction, indicated by the arrow.

Built-up Area — EXHIBITION / ROAD

Postcode Boundary

Map Continuation	82 / Large Scale Map Pages 10
Airport	✈
Car Park (selected)	P
Church or Chapel	†
Fire Station	■
Hospital	H
House Numbers (A & B Roads only)	20 / 163
Information Centre	i
National Grid Reference	⁵30
Police Station	▲
Post Office	★
River Bus Stop	R
Toilet	▽
Educational Establishment	
Hospital or Healthcare Building	
Industrial Building	
Leisure or Recreational Facility	
Place of Interest	
Public Building	
Shopping Centre or Market	
Other Selected Buildings	

SCALE

Map Pages 4-19 1:11,000

0	⅛	¼ Mile

0	100	200	300	400	500 Metres

5.75 inches (14.63 cm) to 1 mile   9.1 cm to 1 km

Map Pages 20-174 1:22,000

0	¼	½ Mile

0	250	500	750 Metres	1 Kilometre

2.88 inches (7.31 cm) to 1 mile   4.55 cm to 1 km

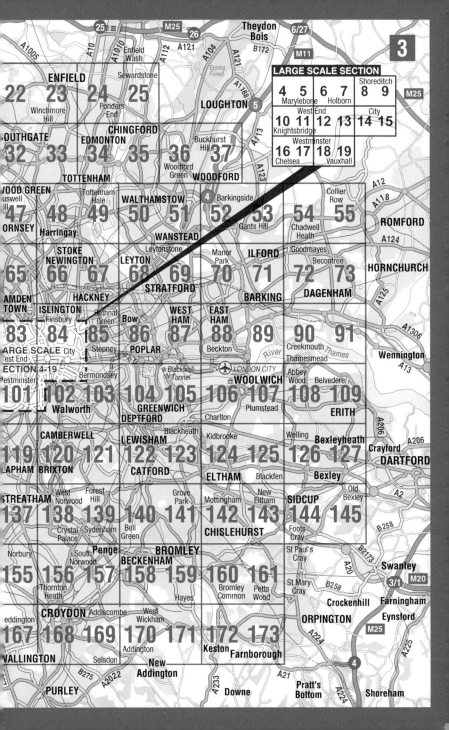

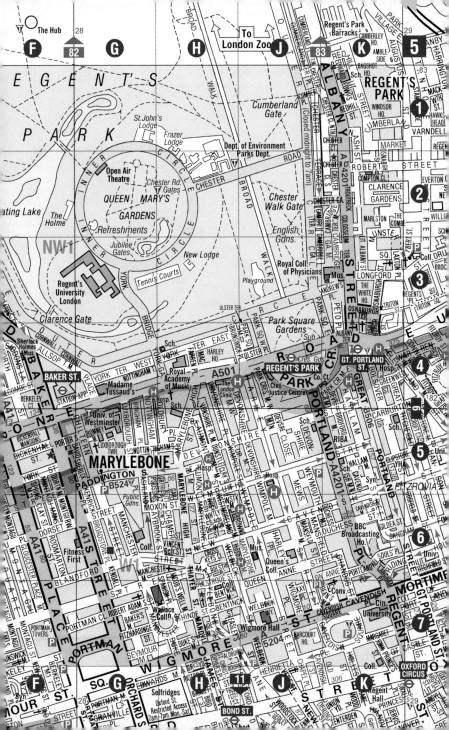

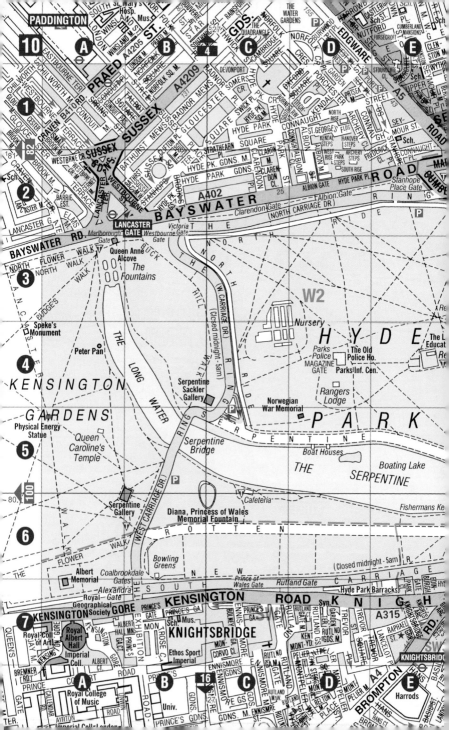

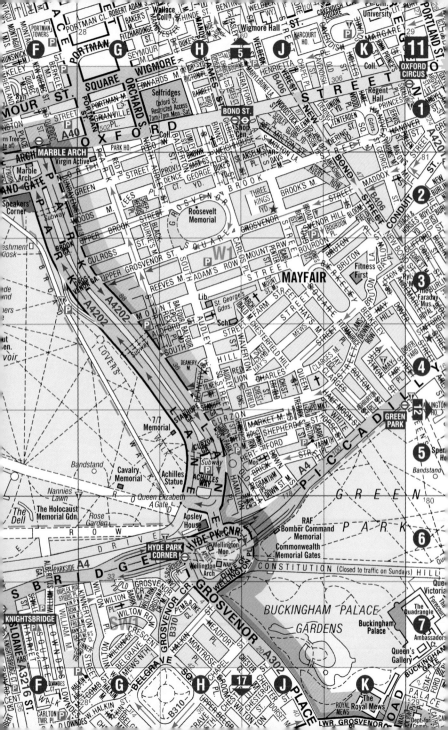

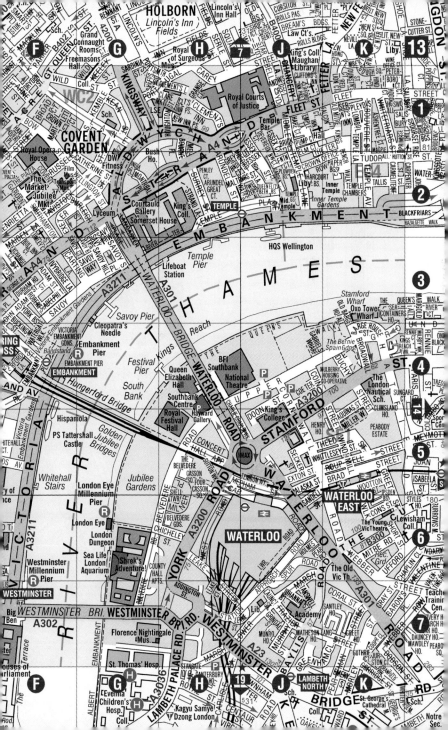

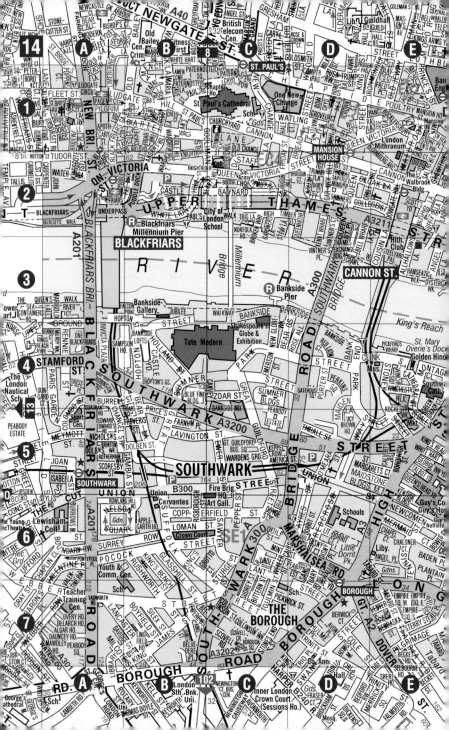

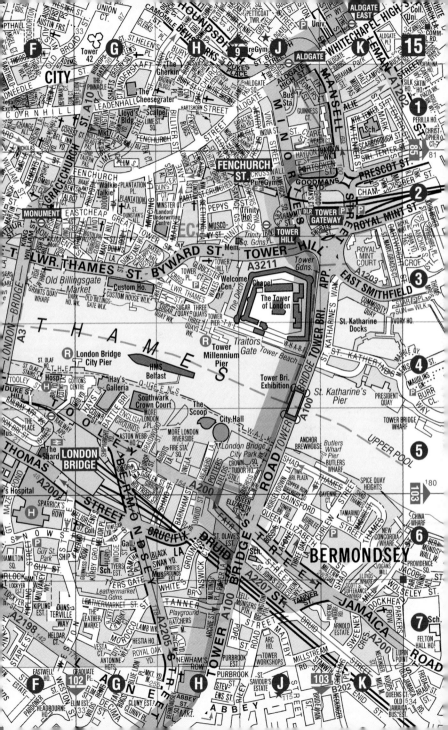

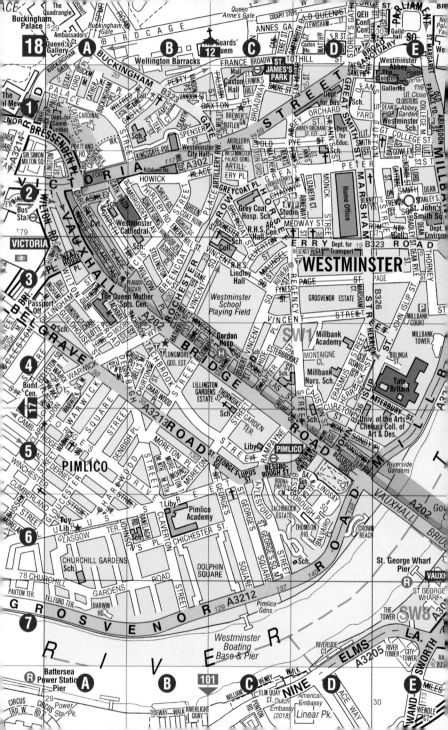

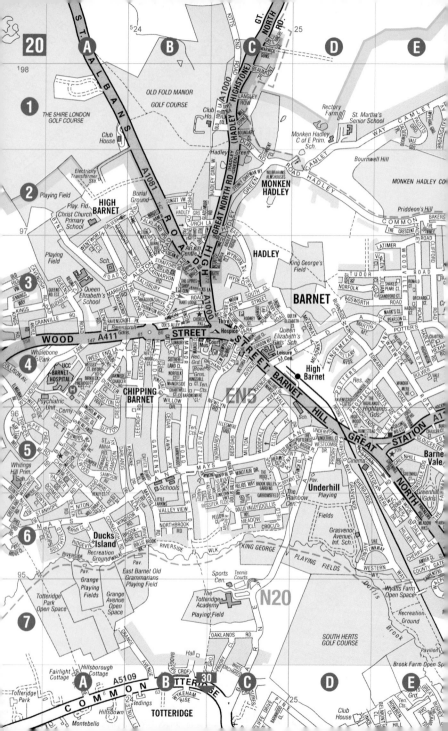

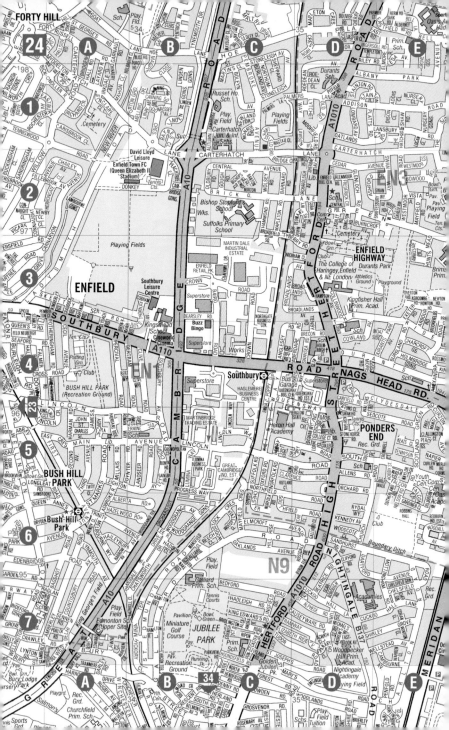

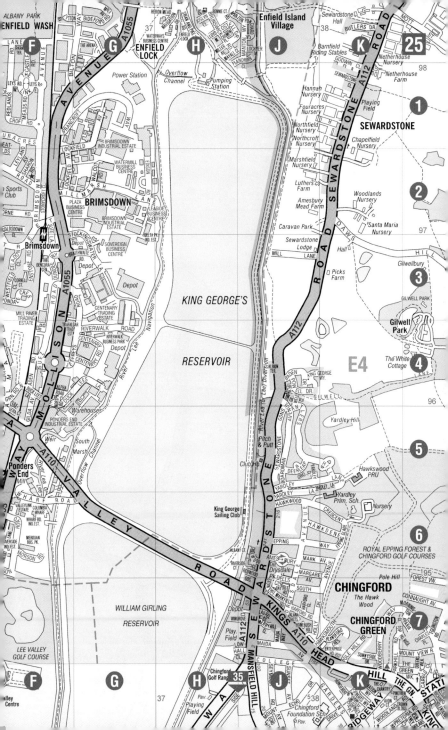

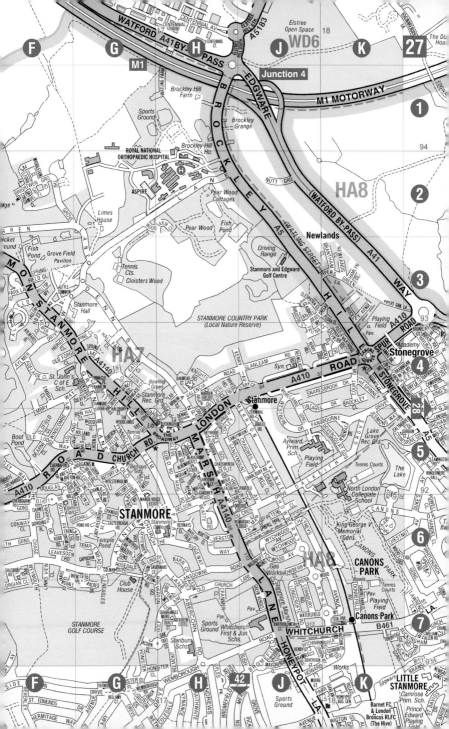

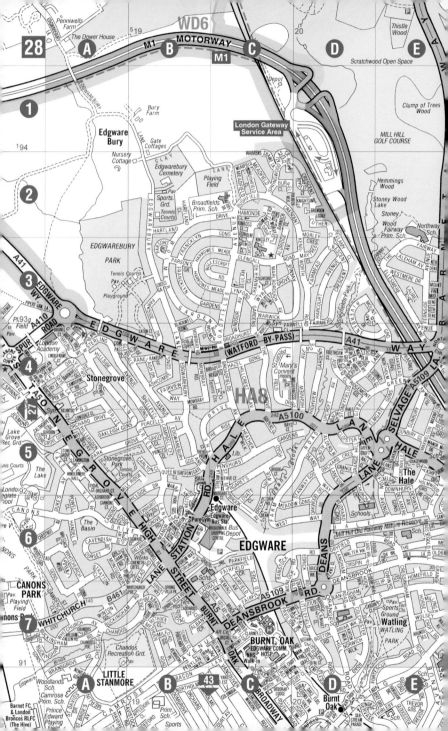

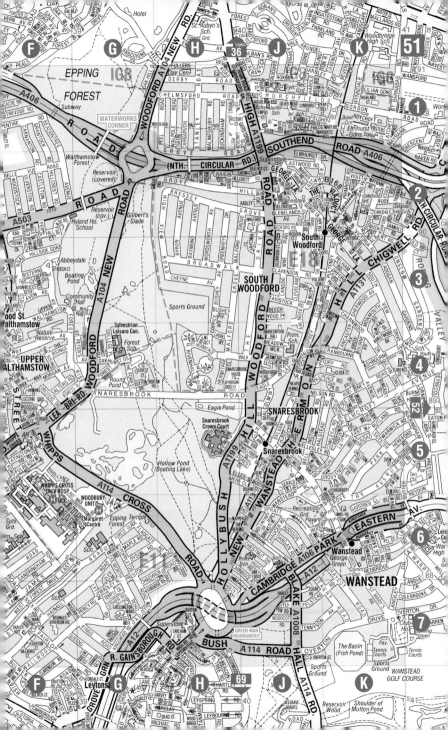

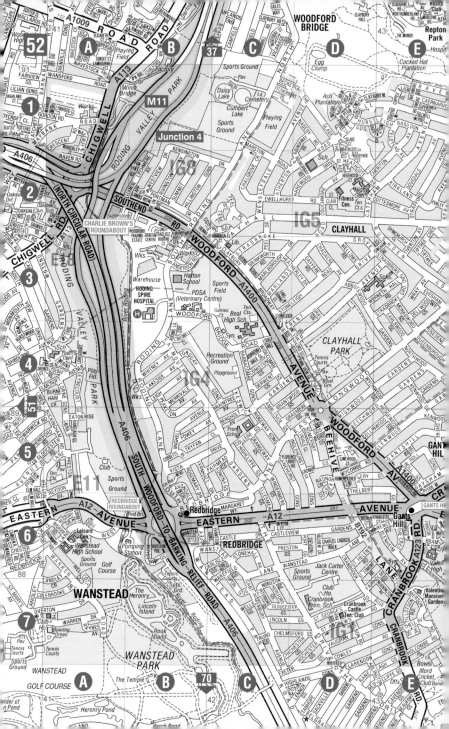

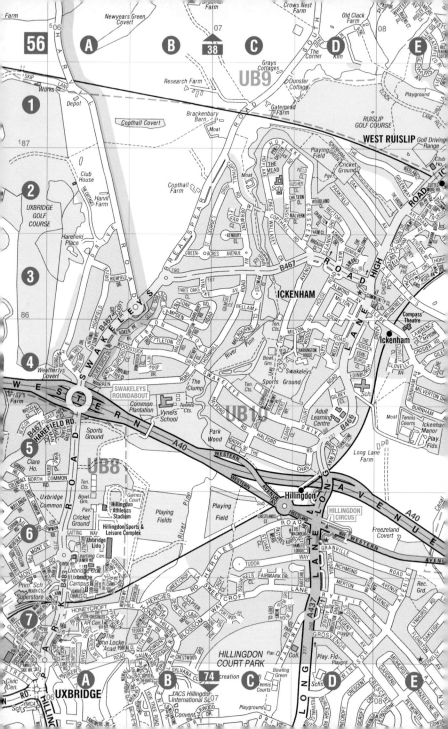

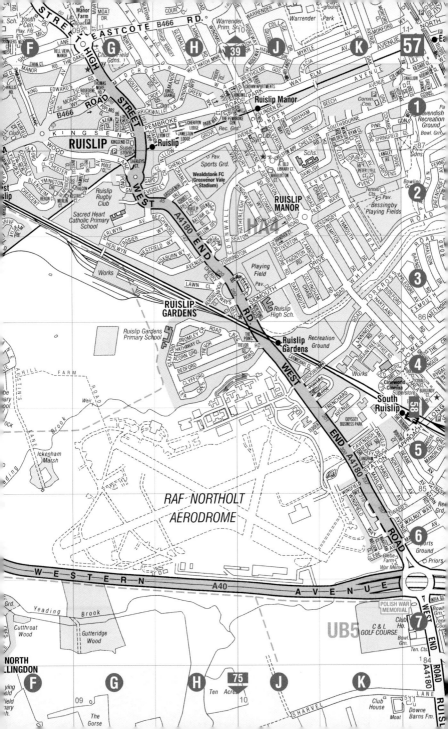

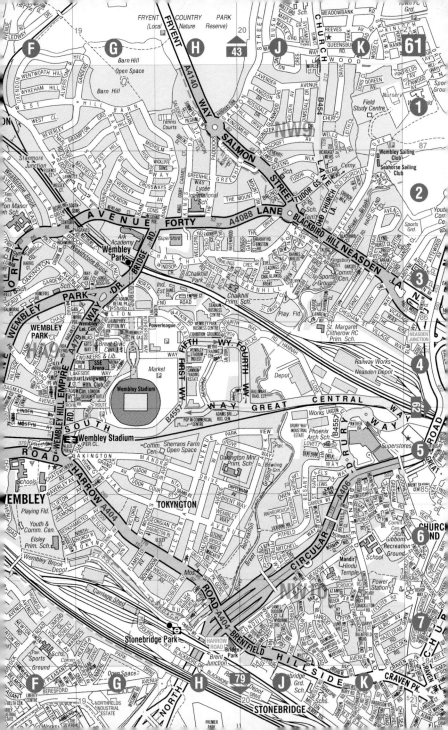

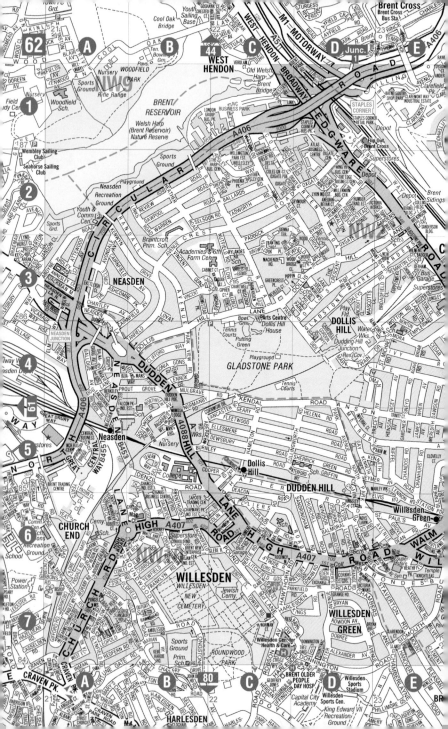

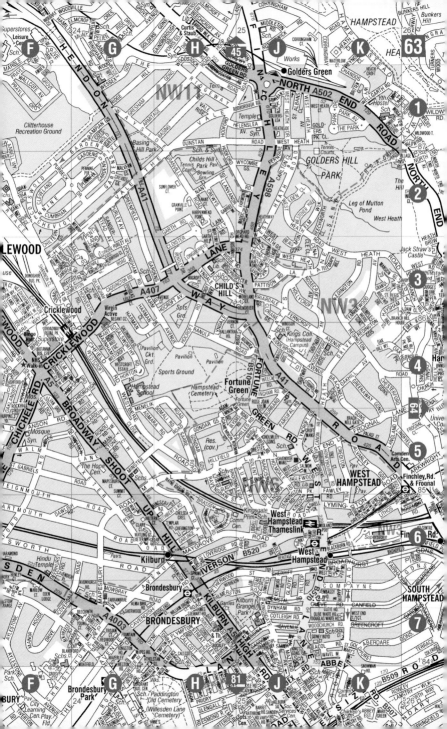

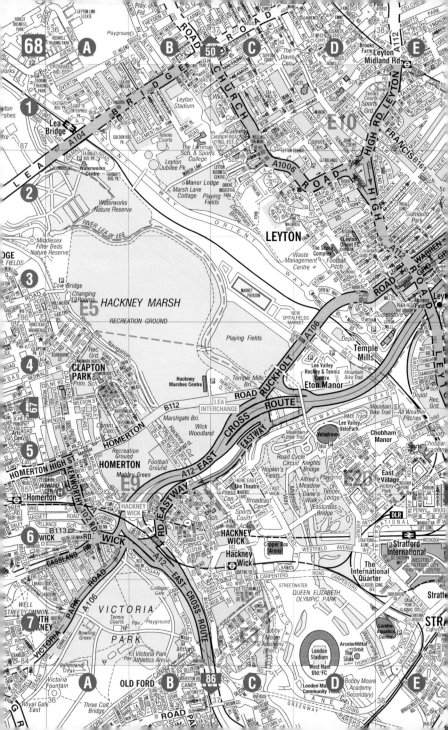

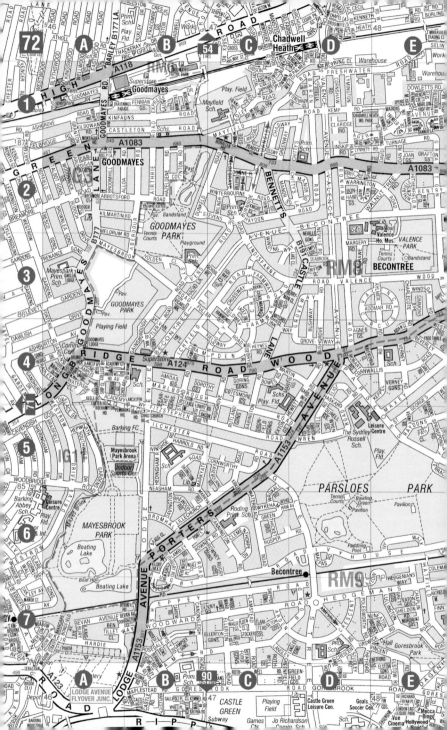

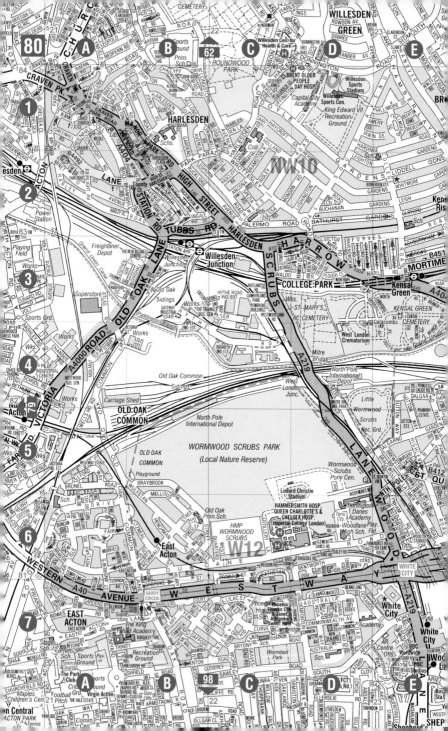

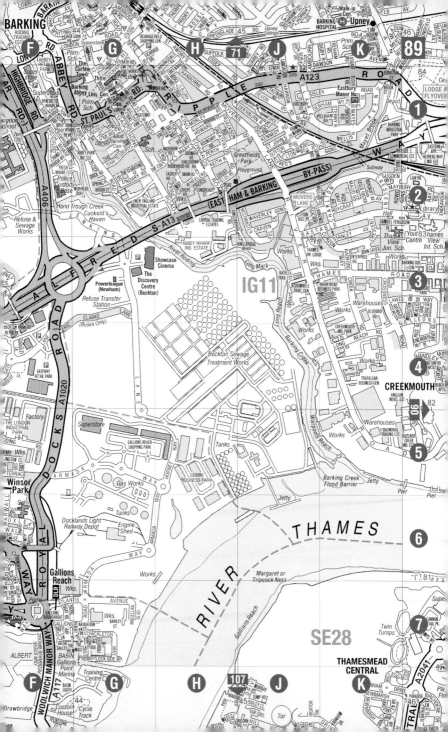

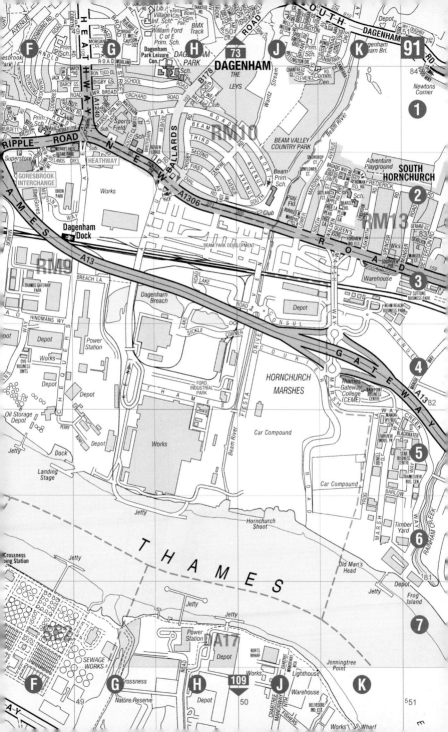

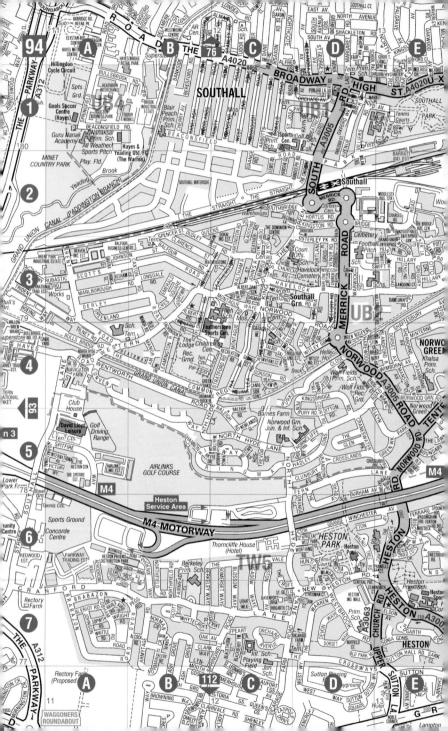

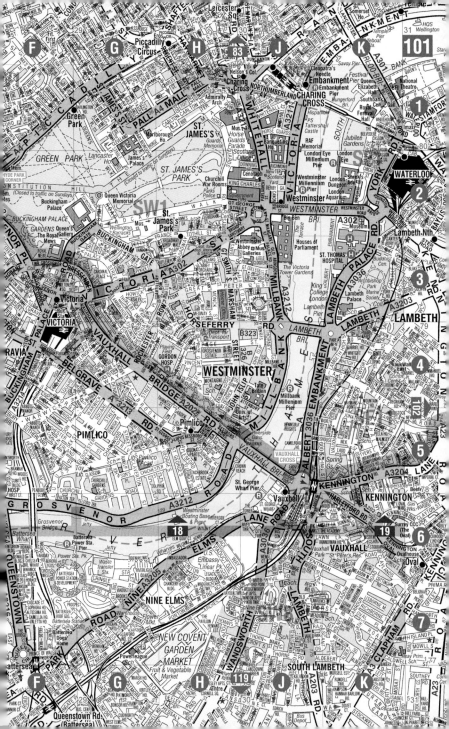

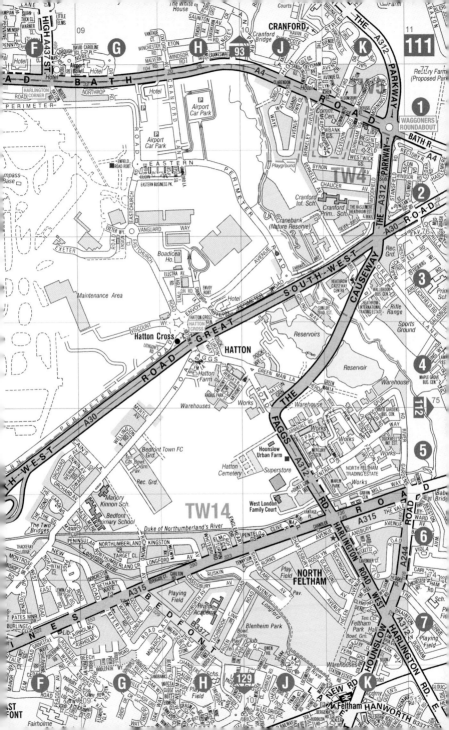

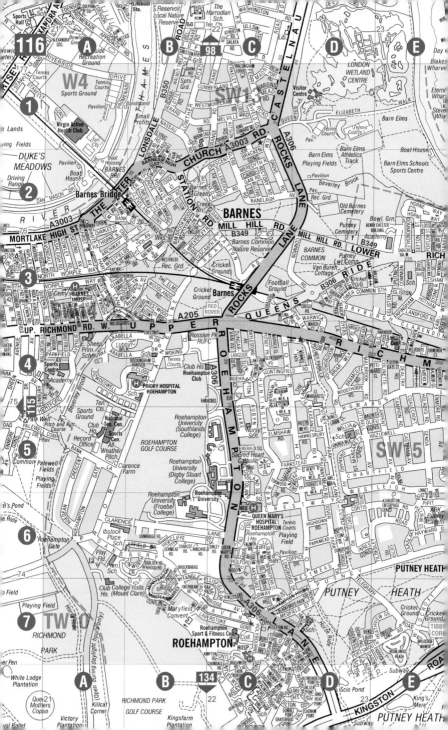

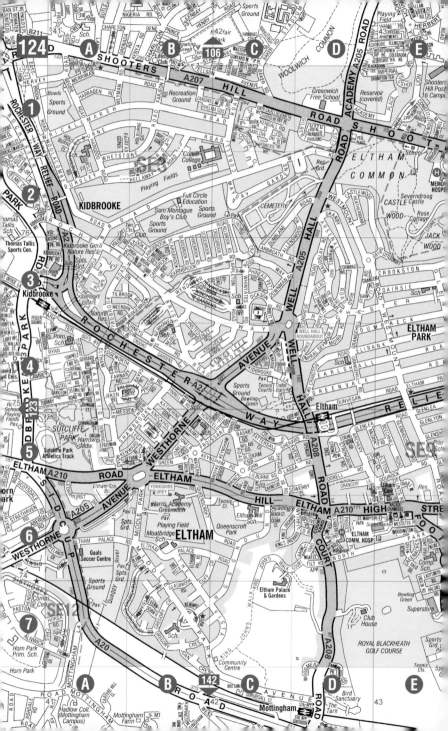

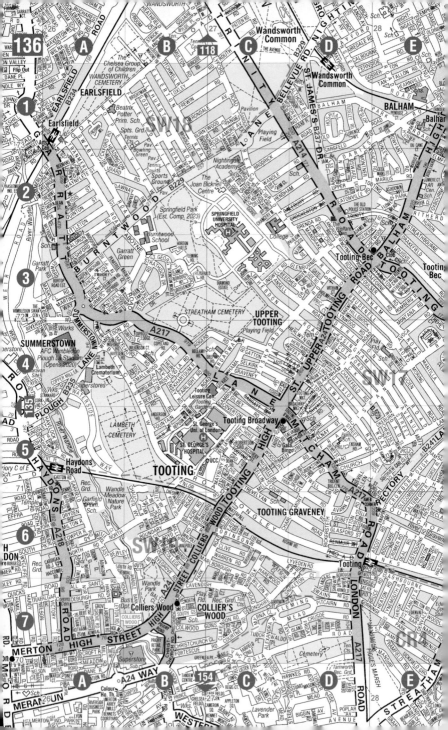

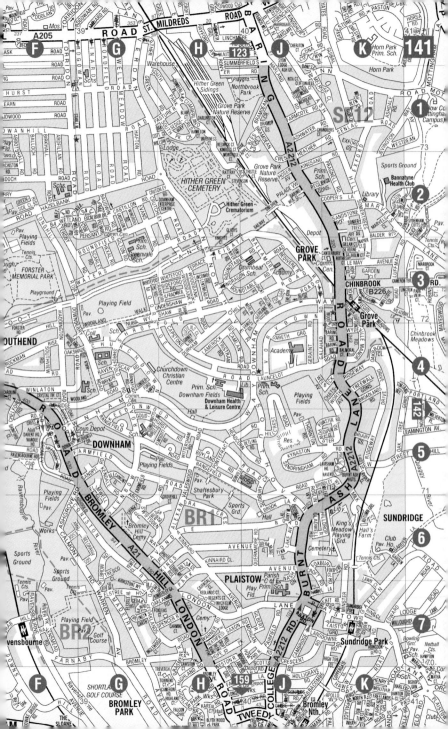

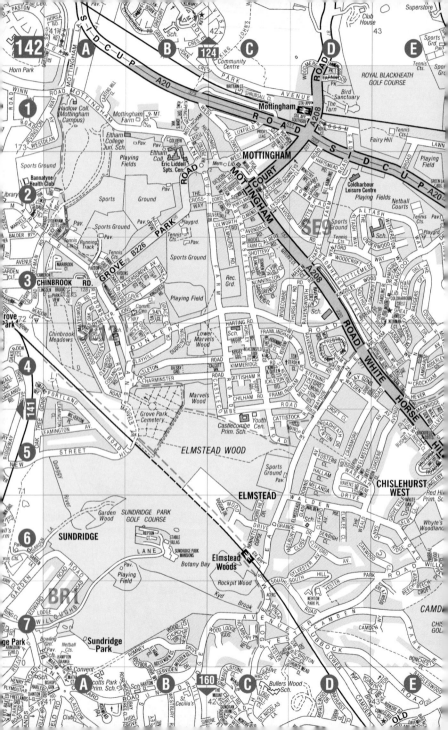

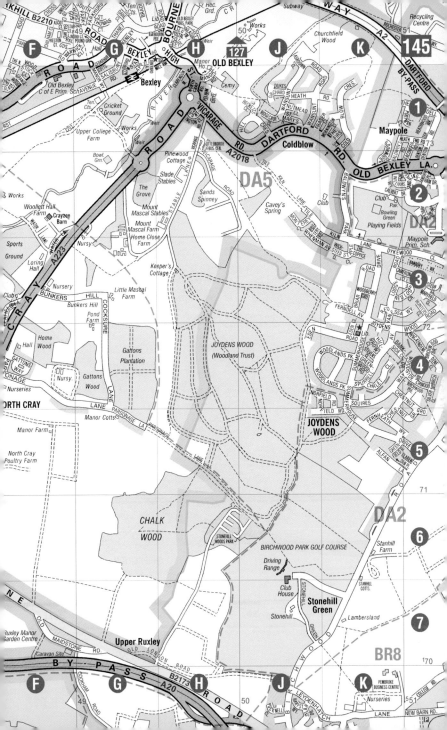

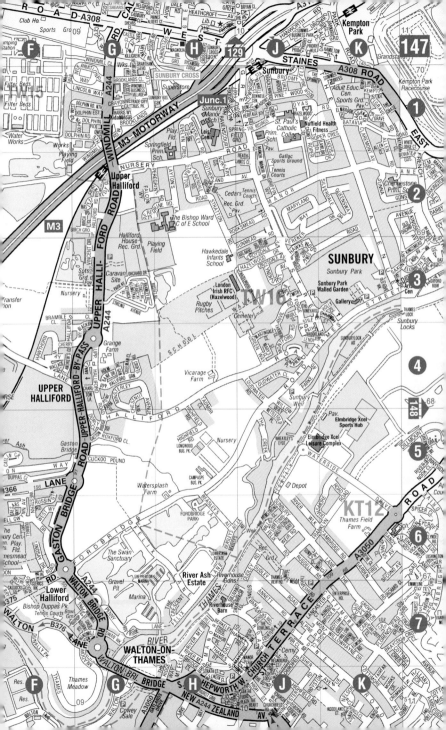

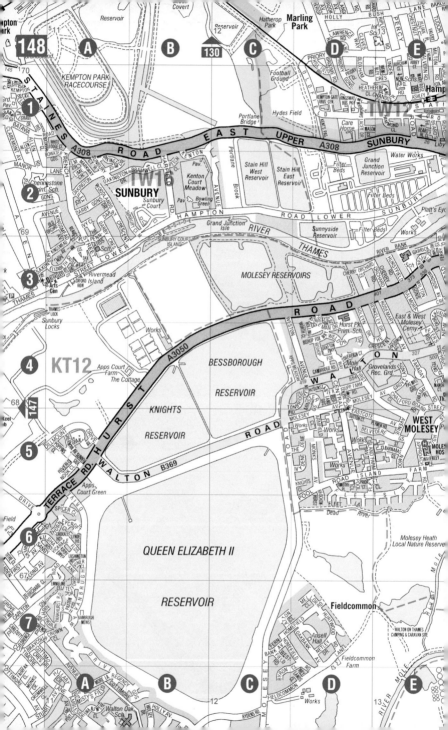

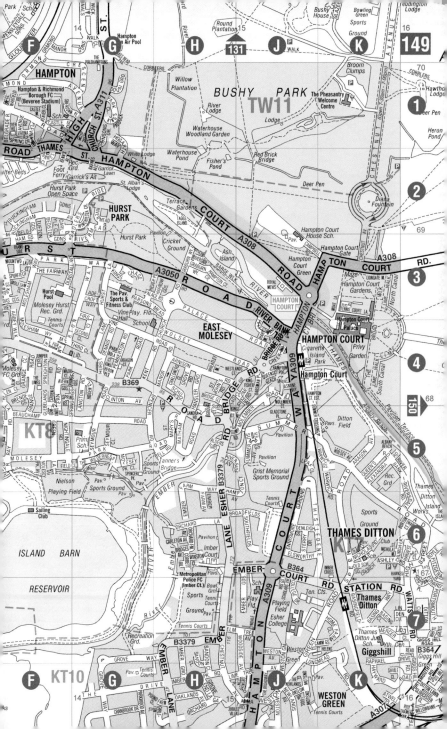

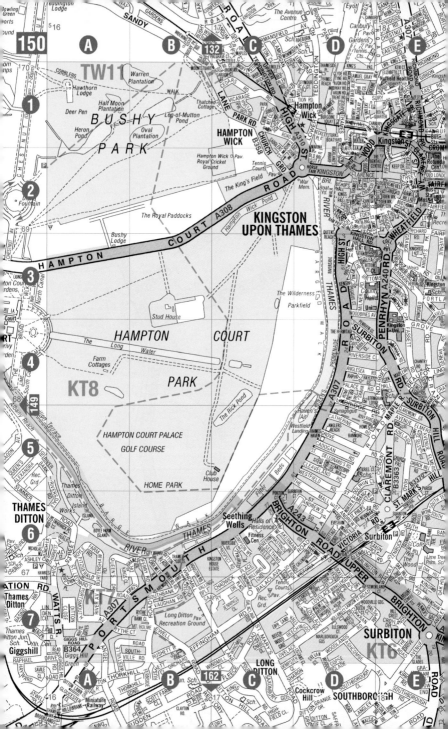

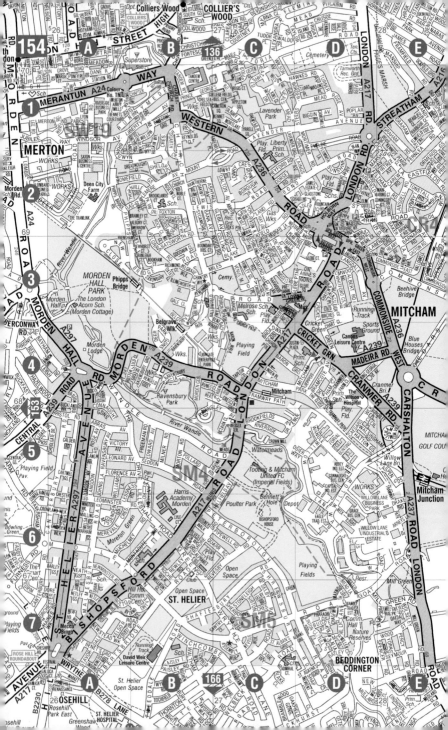

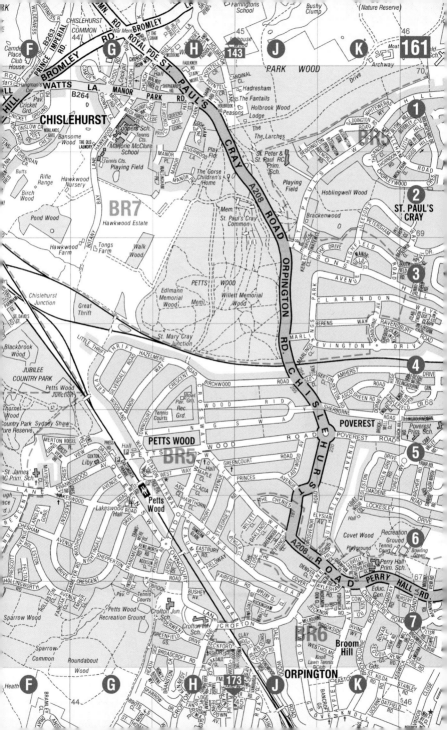

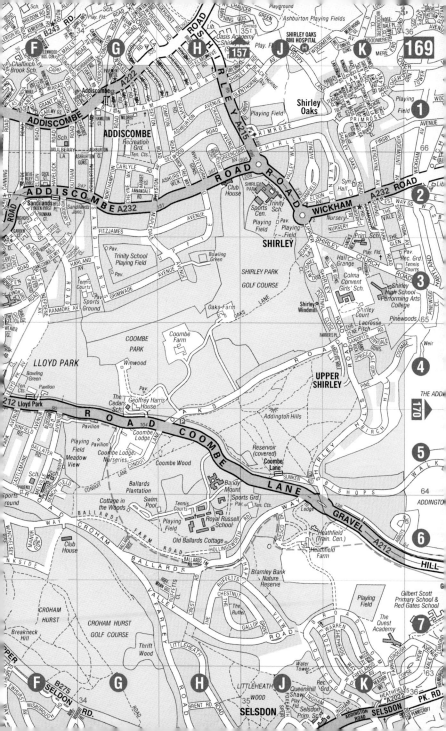

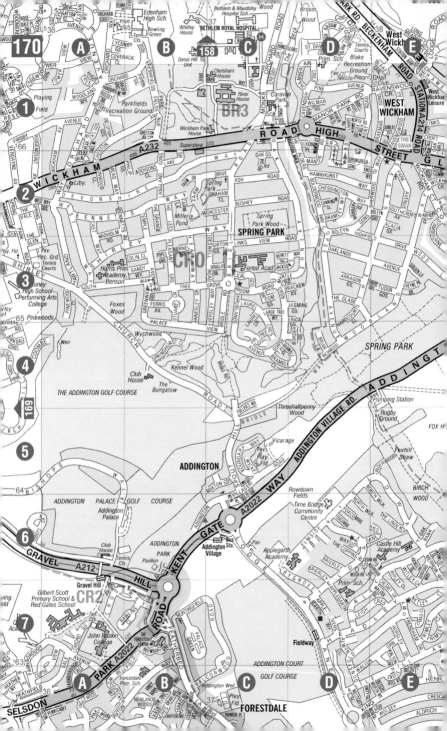

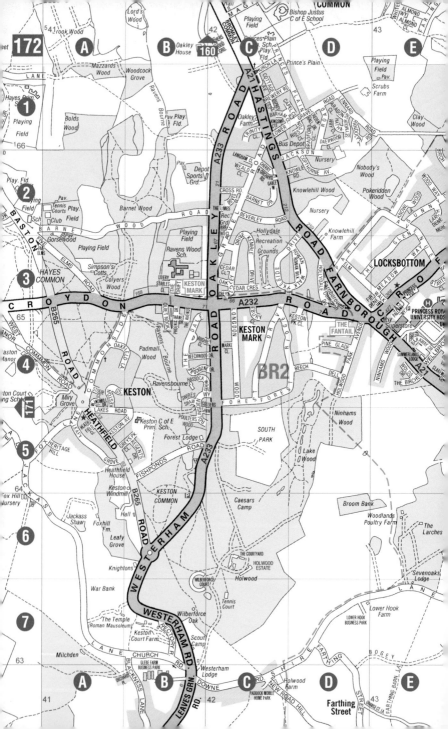

INDEX

Including Streets, Places & Areas, Industrial Estates, Selected Flats & Walkways,
Junction Names & Service Areas and Selected Places of Interest.

HOW TO USE THIS INDEX

1. Each street name is followed by its Postcode District (or, if outside the London Postcodes, by its Locality Abbreviation(s)) then by its map reference;
   e.g. **Abbey Av.** HA0: Wemb . . . . 2E **78** is in the HA0 Postcode District and the Wembley Locality and is to be found in square 2E on page **78**.
   The page number being shown in bold type.

2. A strict alphabetical order is followed in which Av., Rd., St., etc. (though abbreviated) are read in full and as part of the street name;
   e.g. **Alder M.** appears after **Aldermary Rd.** but before **Aldermoor Rd.**

3. Streets and a selection of flats and walkways that cannot be shown on the mapping, appear in the index with the thoroughfare to which they are connected shown in brackets;
   e.g. **Abbey Ct.** NW8 . . . . 2A **82** (off Abbey Rd.)

4. Addresses that are in more than one part are referred to as not continuous.

5. Places and areas are shown in the index in BLUE TYPE and the map reference is to the actual map square in which the town centre or area is located and not to the place name shown on the map; e.g. **ABBEY WOOD** 4C **108**

6. An example of a selected place of interest is **Barnet Mus.** 4B **20**

7. Junction names and Service Areas are shown in the index in BOLD CAPITAL TYPE; e.g. **ANGEL** 2A **84**

8. Map references for entries that appear on large scale pages **4-19** are shown first, with small scale map references shown in brackets;
   e.g. **Abbey Orchard St.** SW1 . . . . 1D **18** (3H **101**)

GENERAL ABBREVIATIONS

All. : Alley	**Cotts.** : Cottages	**Ind.** : Industrial	**Pct.** : Precinct
Apts. : Apartments	**Ct.** : Court	**Info.** : Information	**Prom.** : Promenade
App. : Approach	**Ctyd.** : Courtyard	**Intl.** : International	**Quad.** : Quadrant
Arc. : Arcade	**Cres.** : Crescent	**Junc.** : Junction	**Ri.** : Rise
Av. : Avenue	**Cft.** : Croft	**La.** : Lane	**Rd.** : Road
Bk. : Back	**Dpt.** : Depot	**Lit.** : Little	**Rdbt.** : Roundabout
Blvd. : Boulevard	**Dr.** : Drive	**Lwr.** : Lower	**Shop.** : Shopping
Bri. : Bridge	**E.** : East	**Mnr.** : Manor	**Sth.** : South
B'way. : Broadway	**Emb.** : Embankment	**Mans.** : Mansions	**Sq.** : Square
Bldg. : Building	**Ent.** : Enterprise	**Mkt.** : Market	**Sta.** : Station
Bldgs. : Buildings	**Est.** : Estate	**Mdw.** : Meadow	**St.** : Street
Bus. : Business	**Fld.** : Field	**Mdws.** : Meadows	**Ter.** : Terrace
Cvn. : Caravan	**Flds.** : Fields	**M.** : Mews	**Twr.** : Tower
C'way. : Causeway	**Gdn.** : Garden	**Mt.** : Mount	**Trad.** : Trading
Cen. : Centre	**Gdns.** : Gardens	**Mus.** : Museum	**Up.** : Upper
Chu. : Church	**Gth.** : Garth	**Nth.** : North	**Va.** : Vale
Circ. : Circle	**Ga.** : Gate	**No.** : Number	**Vw.** : View
Cir. : Circus	**Gt.** : Great	**Pal.** : Palace	**Vs.** : Villas
Cl. : Close	**Grn.** : Green	**Pde.** : Parade	**Vis.** : Visitors
Coll. : College	**Gro.** : Grove	**Pk.** : Park	**Wlk.** : Walk
Comn. : Common	**Hgts.** : Heights	**Pas.** : Passage	**W.** : West
Cnr. : Corner	**Ho.** : House	**Pav.** : Pavilion	**Yd.** : Yard
Cott. : Cottage	**Ho's.** : Houses	**Pl.** : Place	

LOCALITY ABBREVIATIONS

Addington: BR4,CR0 . . . . Addtn	**Claygate:** KT10 . . . . Clay	**Greenford:** UB6 . . . . G'frd	**Kew:** TW9 . . . . Kew
Arkley: EN5 . . . . Ark	**Cockfosters:** EN4-5 . . . . Cockf	**Hadley Wood:** EN4 . . . . Had W	**Kingston upon Thames:** KT1-2 . . . King T
Ashford: TW15 . . . . Ashf	**Collier Row:** RM5-7 . . . . Col R	**Ham:** TW10 . . . . Ham	**Laleham:** TW18 . . . . Lale
Banstead: SM2 . . . . Bans	**Colnbrook:** SL3 . . . . Coln	**Hampton:** TW12 . . . . Hamp	**Langley:** SL3 . . . . L'ly
Barking: IG3,IG11,RM8-9 . . . . Bark	**Cowley:** UB8 . . . . Cowl	**Hampton Hill:** TW12 . . . . Hamp H	**London Heathrow Airport:** TW6 . . H'row A
Barnet: EN4-5 . . . . Barn	**Cranford:** TW4-6,UB3 . . . . Cran	**Hampton Wick:** KT1,TW11 . . . . . . Hamp W	**Longford:** TW6,UB7 . . . . Lford
Beckenham: BR3 . . . . Beck	**Crayford:** DA1 . . . . Cray	**Hanworth:** TW13 . . . . Hanw	**Loughton:** IG9-10 . . . . Lough
Beddington: CR0,SM6 . . . . Bedd	**Croydon:** CR0 . . . . C'don	**Harefield:** UB9 . . . . Hare	**Mawney:** RM7 . . . . Mawney
Bedfont: TW14 . . . . Bedf	**Dagenham:** IG11,RM6,RM8-10 . . . . Dag	**Harlington:** UB3,UB7 . . . . Harl	**Mitcham:** CR0,CR4 . . . . Mitc
Belvedere: DA7,DA17-18 . . . . Belv	**Dartford:** DA1,DA5 . . . . Dart	**Harmondsworth:** UB7 . . . . Harm	**Morden:** SM4 . . . . Mord
Bexley: DA1,DA5,DA15 . . . . Bexl	**Downe:** BR6 . . . . Downe	**Harrow:** HA1-3 . . . . Harr	**New Addington:** CR0 . . . . New Ad
Bexleyheath: DA5-7 . . . . Bex	**East Barnet:** EN4 . . . . E Barn	**Harrow Weald:** HA3 . . . . Hrw W	**New Barnet:** EN5 . . . . New Bar
Brentford: TW7-8 . . . . Bford	**Eastcote:** HA4-5 . . . . Eastc	**Hatch End:** HA5 . . . . Hat E	**New Malden:** KT3 . . . . N Mald
Brimsdown: EN3 . . . . Brim	**East Molesey:** KT1,KT8,TW12 . . . E Mos	**Havering-Atte-Bower:** RM1 . . . . Have B	**Northolt:** UB4-5 . . . . N'olt
Bromley: BR1-2 . . . . Broml	**Edgware:** HA8 . . . . Edg	**Hayes:** BR2,BR4,UB3-4 . . . . Hayes	**Northwood:** HA6 . . . . Nwood
Buckhurst Hill: IG8-9 . . . . Buck H	**Elstree:** WD6 . . . . E'tree	**Heston:** TW5 . . . . Hest	**Orpington:** BR5-6 . . . . Orp
Bushey: WD23 . . . . Bush	**Enfield:** EN1-2 . . . . Enf	**Hextable:** BR8 . . . . Hext	**Petts Wood:** BR5-6 . . . . Pet W
Bushy Heath: WD23 . . . . B Hea	**Enfield Highway:** EN3 . . . . Enf H	**Hillingdon:** UB4,UB8,UB10 . . . . Hil	**Pinner:** HA5-6 . . . . Pinn
Carshalton: CR4,SM4-5 . . . . Cars	**Enfield Lock:** EN3 . . . . Enf L	**Hinchley Wood:** KT10 . . . . Hin W	**Ponders End:** EN3 . . . . Pond E
Chadwell Heath: RM6-7 . . . . Chad H	**Enfield Wash:** EN3 . . . . Enf W	**Hounslow:** TW3-4,TW7,TW14 . . . . Houn	**Poyle:** SL3 . . . . Poyle
Cheam: SM2-3 . . . . Cheam	**Epsom:** KT19 . . . . Eps	**Ickenham:** UB10 . . . . Ick	**Pratts Bottom:** BR6 . . . . Prat B
Chelsfield: BR6 . . . . Chels	**Erith:** DA7-8,DA17-18 . . . . Erith	**Ilford:** IG1-6,IG8,RM6 . . . . Ilf	**Purley:** CR8 . . . . Purl
Chertsey: KT16 . . . . Chert	**Esher:** KT10 . . . . Esh	**Isleworth:** TW1,TW3,TW5,TW7 . . . . Isle	**Rainham:** RM9,RM13 . . . . Rain
Chessington: KT9 . . . . Chess	**Ewell:** KT17,KT19 . . . . Ewe	**Kenton:** HA3,HA7,HA9 . . . . Kenton	**Richings Park:** SL0,SL3 . . . . Rich P
Chigwell: IG6-7 . . . . Chig	**Farnborough:** BR5-6 . . . . Farnb	**Keston:** BR2 . . . . Kes	**Richmond:** TW9-10 . . . . Rich
Chislehurst: BR7 . . . . Chst	**Feltham:** TW13-14 . . . . Felt		**Romford:** RM1,RM5,RM7 . . . . Rom

A-Z London **175**

2 Temple Place—Ability Towers

Ruislip: HA4 . . . . . Ruis
Rush Green: RM7,RM10 . . . . . Rush G
St Mary Cray: BR5-6 . . . . . St M Cry
St Pauls Cray: BR5 . . . . . St P
Sanderstead: CR2 . . . . . Sande
Selsdon: CR0,CR2 . . . . . Sels
Shepperton: TW17-18 . . . . . Shep
Sidcup: DA14-15,SE9 . . . . . Sidc
Sipson: UB7 . . . . . Sip
Southall: UB1-2 . . . . . S'hall
South Croydon: CR2 . . . . . S Croy
Staines: TW18-19 . . . . . Staines
Stanmore: HA3,HA7 . . . . . Stan
Stanwell: TW6,TW19 . . . . . Stanw
Stanwell Moor: TW19 . . . . . Stanw M
Stockley Park: UB11 . . . . . Stock P
Sunbury: TW16 . . . . . Sun
Surbiton: KT1,KT5-6,KT10 . . . . . Surb
Sutton: SM1-3 . . . . . Sutt
Swanley: BR8,DA14 . . . . . Swan
Teddington: TW1,TW11 . . . . . Tedd
Thames Ditton: KT7,KT10 . . . . . T Ditt
Thornton Heath: CR7 . . . . . Thor H
Twickenham: TW1-2,TW7,TW13 . . . . . Twick
Uxbridge: UB8,UB10 . . . . . Uxb
Waddon: CR0 . . . . . Wadd
Wallington: SM5-6 . . . . . W'gton
Walton-on-Thames: KT12 . . . . . Walt T
Wealdstone: HA3 . . . . . W'stone
Welling: DA16 . . . . . Well
Wembley: HA0,HA9,NW10 . . . . . Wemb
Wennington: RM13 . . . . . Wenn
West Drayton: UB7 . . . . . W Dray
West Molesey: KT8 . . . . . W Mole
West Wickham: BR4 . . . . . W W'ck
Weybridge: KT13 . . . . . Weyb
Whitton: TW2 . . . . . Whitt
Wilmington: DA2 . . . . . Wilm
Woodford Green: IG4,IG8-9 . . . . . Wfd G
Worcester Park: KT4,SM3 . . . . . Wor Pk
Yeading: UB4 . . . . . Yead
Yiewsley: UB7 . . . . . Yiew

2 Temple Place *2J 13*
(off Temple Pl.)
2 Willow Rd. 4C 64
7 July Memorial 5H 11 (1E 100)
10 Brock St. NW1 . . . . . 3A 6
18 Stafford Terrace *3J 99*
(off Stafford Ter.)
60 St Martins La. *WC2* *2E 12*
(off St Martin's La.)
198 Contemporary Arts & Learning *6B 120*
(off Railton Rd.)
201 Bishopsgate EC2 . . . . . 5H 9

A

Aaron Hill Rd. E6 . . . . . 5E 88
Abady Ho. *SW1* *3D 18*
(off Page St.)
Abberley M. SW4 . . . . . 3F 119
Abbess Cl. E6 . . . . . 5C 88
SW2 . . . . . 1B 138
Abbeville M. SW4 . . . . . 4H 119
Abbeville Rd. N8 . . . . . 5H 47
SW4 . . . . . 6G 119
Abbey Av. HA0: Wemb 2E 78
Abbey Cl. E5 . . . . . 4G 67
HA5: Pinn 3K 39
SW8 . . . . . 1H 119
UB3: Hayes 1K 93
UB5: N'olt 3D 76
Abbey Ct. *NW8* *2A 82*
(off Abbey Rd.)
SE6 . . . . . 6C 122
SE17 . . . . . *5C 102*
(off Macleod St.)
TW12: Hamp 7E 130
Abbey Cres. DA17: Belv 4G 109
Abbeydale Rd. HA0: Wemb 1F 79
Abbey Dr. DA2: Wilm 2K 145
SW17 . . . . . 5E 136
Abbey Est. NW8 . . . . . 1K 81
Abbeyfield Cl. CR4: Mitc 2C 154
Abbeyfield Est. SE16 . . . . . 4J 103
Abbeyfield Rd. SE16 . . . . . 4J 103
(not continuous)
Abbeyfields Cl. NW10 . . . . . 3G 79
Abbey Gdns. BR7: Chst 1E 160
NW8 . . . . . 2A 82
SE16 . . . . . 4G 103
SW1 . . . . . *1E 18*
(off Great College St.)
TW15: Ashf 5D 128
W6 . . . . . 6G 99
Abbey Gro. SE2 . . . . . 4B 108
Abbeyhill Rd. DA15: Sidc 2C 144
Abbey Ho. *E15* *2G 87*
(off Baker's Row)
NW8 . . . . . 1A 4
Abbey Ind. Est. CR4: Mitc 5D 154
HA0: Wemb 1F 79
Abbey La. BR3: Beck 7C 140
E15 . . . . . 2E 86
(not continuous)
Abbey La. Commercial Est. E15 . . . . . 2G 87
Abbey Leisure Cen.
Barking 1G 89
Abbey Life Ct. E16 . . . . . 5K 87
Abbey Lodge NW8 . . . . . 2D 4
Abbey Mansion M. SE24 . . . . . 5B 120
Abbey M. E17 . . . . . 5C 50
TW7: Isle 1B 114
Abbey Mt. DA17: Belv 5F 109
Abbey Orchard St. SW1 . . . 1D 18 (3H 101)
Abbey Orchard St. Est.
SW1 . . . . . 1D 18 (3H 101)
(not continuous)
Abbey Pde. *SW19* *7A 136*
(off Merton High St.)
W5 . . . . . 3F 79
Abbey Pk. BR3: Beck 7C 140
Abbey Pk. Ind. Est. IG11: Bark 2G 89
Abbey Retail Pk.
Barking 7F 71
Abbey Rd. CR0: C'don 3B 168
DA7: Bex 4E 126
DA17: Belv 4D 108
E15 . . . . . 2F 87
EN1: Enf 5K 23
IG2: Ilf 5H 53
IG11: Bark 1F 89
NW6 . . . . . 7K 63
NW8 . . . . . 1A 4 (7K 63)
NW10 . . . . . 1H 79
SE2 . . . . . 4D 108
SW19 . . . . . 7A 136
Abbey Rd. Apts. *NW8* *2A 82*
(off Abbey Rd.)
Abbey Sports Cen.
Barking 1G 89
Abbey St. E13 . . . . . 4J 87
SE1 . . . . . 7H 15 (3E 102)
SE16 . . . . . 7H 15 (3G 103)
Abbey Ter. SE2 . . . . . 4C 108
Abbey Trad. Est. SE26 . . . . . 5B 140
Abbey Vw. NW7 . . . . . 3G 29
Abbey Wlk. KT8: W Mole 3F 149
Abbey Wharf Ind. Est. IG11: Bark . . . 3H 89
ABBEY WOOD 4C 108
Abbey Wood Cvn. Club Site 4C 108
Abbey Wood Rd. SE2 . . . . . 4B 108
Abbot Cl. HA4: Ruis 3B 58
Abbot Ct. *SW8* *7J 101*
(off Hartington Rd.)
Abbot Ho. *E14* *7D 86*
(off Smythe St.)
Abbotsbury *NW1* *7H 65*
(off Camley St.)
Abbotsbury Cl. E15 . . . . . 2E 86
W14 . . . . . 2G 99
Abbotsbury Gdns. HA5: Eastc 7A 40
Abbotsbury Ho. W14 . . . . . 2G 99
Abbotsbury M. SE15 . . . . . 3J 121
Abbotsbury Rd. BR2: Hayes 2H 171
SM4: Mord 5K 153
W14 . . . . . 2G 99
Abbots Cl. BR5: Farnb 1G 173
Abbots Ct. *W8* *2K 99*
(off Thackeray St.)
Abbots Dr. HA2: Harr 2E 58
Abbotsford Av. N15 . . . . . 4C 48
Abbotsford Gdns. IG8: Wfd G 7D 36
Abbotsford Rd. IG3: Ilf 2A 72
Abbots Gdns. N2 . . . . . 4B 46
Abbots Grn. CR0: Addtn 6K 169
Abbotshade Rd. SE16 . . . . . 1K 103
Abbotshall Av. N14 . . . . . 3B 32
Abbotshall Rd. SE6 . . . . . 1F 141
Abbot's Ho. *W14* *3H 99*
(off St Mary Abbot's Ter.)
Abbots Lane SE1 . . . . . 5H 15
Abbots La. SE1 . . . . . 1E 102
Abbotsleigh Cl. SM2: Sutt 7K 165
Abbotsleigh Rd. SW16 . . . . . 4G 137
Abbots Mnr. SW1 . . . . . 5J 17 (4F 101)
(not continuous)
Abbots Pk. SW2 . . . . . 1A 138
Abbot's Pl. NW6 . . . . . 1K 81
Abbot's Rd. E6 . . . . . 1B 88
Abbots Rd. HA8: Edg 7D 28
Abbots Ter. N8 . . . . . 6J 47
Abbotstone Rd. SW15 . . . . . 3E 116
Abbot St. E8 . . . . . 6F 67
Abbots Wlk. W8 . . . . . 3K 99
Abbots Way BR3: Beck 5A 158
Abbotswell Rd. SE4 . . . . . 5B 122
Abbotswood Cl. DA17: Belv 3E 108
Abbotswood Gdns. IG5: Ilf 3D 52
Abbotswood Rd. SE22 . . . . . 4E 120
SW16 . . . . . 3H 137
Abbotswood Way UB3: Hayes 1K 93
Abbott Av. SW20 . . . . . 1F 153
Abbott Cl. TW12: Hamp 6C 130
UB5: N'olt 6D 58
Abbott Rd. E14 . . . . . 5E 86
(not continuous)
Abbott's Cl. UB8: Cowl 5A 74
Abbotts Cl. N1 . . . . . 6C 66
RM7: Mawney 3H 55
SE28 . . . . . 7C 90
Abbotts Cres. E4 . . . . . 4A 36
EN2: Enf 2G 23
Abbotts Dr. HA0: Wemb 2B 60
Abbotts Ho. *SW1* *6C 18*
(off Aylesford St.)
Abbotts Mead TW10: Ham 4D 132
Abbottsmede Cl. TW1: Twick 2K 131
Abbotts Pk. Rd. E10 . . . . . 7E 50
Abbotts Rd. CR4: Mitc 4G 155
EN5: New Bar 4E 20
SM3: Cheam 4G 165
UB1: S'hall 1C 94
Abbott's Wlk. DA7: Bex 7D 108
Abbott's Wharf *E14* *6C 86*
(off Stainsby Pl.)
Abbotts Wharf Moorings *E14* *6C 86*
(off Stainsby Rd.)
Abchurch La. EC4 . . . . . 2F 15 (7D 84)
(not continuous)
Abchurch Yd. EC4 . . . . . 2E 14 (7D 84)
Abdale Rd. W12 . . . . . 1D 98
Abelard Pl. W5 . . . . . 3D 96
Abel Ho. *SE11* *7K 19*
(off Kennington Rd.)
Abenglen Ind. Est. UB3: Hayes 2F 93
Aberavon Rd. E3 . . . . . 3A 86
Abercairn Rd. SW16 . . . . . 7G 137
Aberconway Rd. SM4: Mord 4K 153
Abercorn Cl. NW7 . . . . . 7B 30
NW8 . . . . . 3A 82
Abercorn Commercial Cen.
HA0: Wemb 1D 78
Abercorn Cotts. *NW8* *3A 82*
(off Abercorn Pl.)
Abercorn Cres. HA2: Harr 1F 59
Abercorn Dell WD23: B Hea 2B 26
Abercorn Gdns. HA3: Kenton 7D 42
RM6: Chad H 6B 54
Abercorn Gro. HA4: Ruis 4F 39
Abercorn Mans. *NW8* *2A 82*
(off Abercorn Pl.)
Abercorn M. TW10: Rich 5F 115
Abercorn Pl. NW8 . . . . . 3A 82
Abercorn Rd. HA7: Stan 7H 27
NW7 . . . . . 7B 30
Abercorn Wlk. NW8 . . . . . 3A 82
Abercorn Way SE1 . . . . . 5G 103
Abercrombie Dr. EN1: Enf 1B 24
Abercrombie Rd. E20 . . . . . 5D 68
Abercrombie St. SW11 . . . . . 2C 118
Aberdale Ct. *SE16* *2K 103*
(off Garter Way)
Aberdare Cl. BR4: W W'ck 2E 170
Aberdare Gdns.
NW6 . . . . . 7K 63
NW7 . . . . . 7A 30
Aberdare Rd. EN3: Pond E 4D 24
Aberdeen Cotts. HA7: Stan 7H 27
Aberdeen Ct. *W9* *4A 4*
(off Maida Vale)
Aberdeen La. N5 . . . . . 5C 66
Aberdeen Mans. *WC1* *3E 6*
(off Kenton St.)
Aberdeen Pde. *N18* *5C 34*
(off Aberdeen Rd.)
Aberdeen Pk. N5 . . . . . 5C 66
Aberdeen Pl. NW8 . . . . . 4A 4 (4B 82)
Aberdeen Rd. CR0: C'don 4C 168
HA3: W'stone 2K 41
N5 . . . . . 4C 66
N18 . . . . . 5B 34
(not continuous)
NW10 . . . . . 5B 62
Aberdeen Sq. E14 . . . . . 1B 104
Aberdeen Ter. SE3 . . . . . 2F 123
Aberdeen Wharf *E1* *1H 103*
(off Wapping High St.)
Aberdour Rd. IG3: Ilf 3B 72
Aberdour St. SE1 . . . . . 4E 102
Aberfeldy Ho. SE5 . . . . . 7B 102
(not continuous)
Aberfeldy St. E14 . . . . . 5E 86
(not continuous)
Aberford Gdns. SE18 . . . . . 1C 124
Aberfoyle Rd. SW16 . . . . . 6H 137
(not continuous)
Abergeldie Rd. SE12 . . . . . 6K 123
Abernethy Ho. *EC1* *6C 8*
(off Bartholomew Cl.)
Abernethy Rd. SE13 . . . . . 4G 123
Abersham Rd. E8 . . . . . 5F 67
Abery St. SE18 . . . . . 4J 107
Abid M. SE15 . . . . . 2G 121
Ability Pl. E14 . . . . . 2D 104
Ability Plaza *E8* *7F 67*
(off Arbutus St.)
Ability Towers *EC1* *1C 8*
(off Macclesfield Rd.)

Abingdon—Addis Ho.

Abingdon W14 4H 99
(off Kensington Village)
Abingdon Cl. KT4: Wor Pk 3D 164
NW1 6H 65
SE1 4F 103
(off Bushwood Dr.)
SW19 6A 136
UB10: Hil 1B 74
Abingdon Ct. W8 3J 99
(off Abingdon Vs.)
Abingdon Gdns. W8 3J 99
Abingdon Ho. BR1: Broml 7K 141
E2 3J 9
(off Boundary St.)
Abingdon Lodge BR2: Broml 2H 159
(off Beckenham La.)
W8 3J 99
Abingdon Mans. W8 3J 99
(off Pater St.)
Abingdon Rd. N3 2A 46
SW16 2J 155
W8 3J 99
Abingdon St. SW1 1E 18 (3J 101)
Abingdon Vs. W8 3J 99
Abinger Cl. BR1: Broml 3C 160
CR0: New Ad 6E 170
IG11: Bark 4A 72
SM6: W'gton 5J 167
Abinger Ct. SM6: W'gton 5J 167
(off Abinger Cl.)
W5 7C 78
Abinger Gdns. TW7: Isle 3J 113
Abinger Gro. SE8 6B 104
Abinger Ho. SE1 7E 14
(off Gt. Dover St.)
Abinger M. W9 4J 81
Abinger Rd. W4 3A 98
Ablett St. SE16 5J 103
Abney Gdns. N16 2F 67
Abney Pk. Cemetery
Local Nature Reserve 2E 66
Abney Pk. Ter. N16 2F 67
(off Cazenove Rd.)
Aborfield NW5 5G 65
Aboyne Dr. SW20 2C 152
Aboyne Rd. NW10 3A 62
SW17 3B 136
Abraham Fisher Ho. E12 5E 70
Abyssinia Cl. SW11 4C 118
Abyssinia Ct. N8 5K 47
Abyssinia Rd. SW11 4C 118
Acacia Av. HA4: Ruis 1J 57
HA9: Wemb 5E 60
N17 7J 33
TW8: Bford 7B 96
TW17: Shep 5C 146
UB3: Hayes 6H 75
UB7: Yiew 7B 74
Acacia Bus. Cen. E11 3G 69
Acacia Cl. BR5: Pet W 5H 161
HA7: Stan 6D 26
SE8 4A 104
SE20 2G 157
Acacia Ct. HA1: Harr 5F 41
Acacia Dr. SM3: Sutt 1H 165
Acacia Gdns. BR4: W W'ck 2E 170
NW8 2B 82
Acacia Gro. KT3: N Mald 3K 151
SE21 2D 138
Acacia Ho. N22 1A 48
(off Douglas Rd.)
Acacia M. UB7: Harm 2E 174
Acacia Pl. NW8 2B 82
Acacia Rd. BR3: Beck 3B 158
CR4: Mitc 3E 154
E11 2G 69
E17 6A 50
EN2: Enf 1J 23
N22 1A 48
NW8 2B 82
SW16 1J 155
TW12: Hamp 6E 130
W3 7J 79
The Acacias EN4: E Barn 5G 21
Acacia Wlk. SW10 7A 100
(off Tadema Rd.)
Acacia Way DA15: Sidc 1K 143
Academia Way N17 6K 33
The Academy
Middlesex County Cricket Club
2K 45
The Academy SW8 7G 19 (6K 101)
Academy Apts. E8 5H 67
(off Dalston La.)
Academy Bldgs. N1 1G 9
(off Fanshaw St.)
Academy Ct. DA5: Bexl 2K 145
(off Beaconsfield Rd.)
E2 3J 85
(off Kirkwall Pl.)
NW6 1J 81
RM8: Dag 4A 72
Academy Gdns. CR0: C'don 1F 169
UB5: N'olt 2B 76
W8 2J 99
Academy Ho. E3 5D 86
(off Violet Rd.)
Academy Pl. SE18 1D 124
TW7: Isle 1J 113
Academy Rd. SE18 1D 124
Academy Way E17 1C 50
RM8: Dag 4A 72
Acanthus Dr. SE1 5G 103
Acanthus Rd. SW11 3E 118
Accommodation La. UB7: Harm 2D 174
UB7: Lford 4B 174
Accommodation Rd. E4 3A 36
(off Ashwood Rd.)
KT17: Ewe 5C 164
NW11 1H 63
AC Court KT7: T Ditt 6A 150
Ace Pde. KT9: Chess 3E 162
Acer Av. UB4: Yead 5C 76
Acer Cl. IG8: Wfd G 6H 37
Acer Ct. EN3: Enf H 3F 25
(off Enstone Rd.)
Acer Rd. E8 7F 67
Acers BR7: Chst 7C 142
Aces Ct. TW3: Houn 2G 113
Ace Way SW11 7D 18 (6H 101)
Acfold Rd. SW6 1K 117
Achilles Cl. SE1 5G 103
Achilles Ho. E2 2H 85
(off Old Bethnal Grn. Rd.)
Achilles Rd. NW6 5J 63
Achilles Statue 5H 11 (1E 100)
Achilles St. SE14 7A 104
Achilles Way W1 5H 11 (1E 100)
Acklam Rd. W10 5G 81
(not continuous)
Acklington Dr. NW9 1A 44
Ackmar Rd. SW6 1J 117
Ackroyd Dr. E3 5B 86
Ackroyd Rd. SE23 7K 121
Acland Cl. SE18 7H 107
Acland Cres. SE5 3D 120
Acland Ho. SW9 1K 119
Acland Rd. NW2 6D 62
Acle Cl. IG6: Ilf 1F 53
Acme Studios E14 5E 86
(Gillender St.)
E14 5E 86
(off Leven Rd.)
Acock Gro. UB5: N'olt 4F 59
Acol Ct. NW6 7J 63
Acol Cres. HA4: Ruis 5K 57
Acol Rd. NW6 7J 63
Aconbury Rd.
RM9: Dag 1B 90
Acorn Cl. BR7: Chst 5G 143
E4 5J 35
EN2: Enf 1G 23
HA7: Stan 7G 27
TW12: Hamp 6F 131
Acorn Ct. E3 2C 86
(off Morville St.)
Acorn Ct. E6 7C 70
IG2: Ilf 6J 53
Acorn Gdns. SE19 1F 157
W3 5K 79
Acorn Gro. HA4: Ruis 4H 57
UB3: Harl 7H 93
Acorn Pde. SE15 7H 103
Acorn Production Cen. N7 7J 65
Acorn Wlk. SE16 1A 104
Acorn Way BR3: Beck 5E 158
BR6: Farnb 4F 173
SE23 3K 139
Acqua Ho. TW9: Kew 7H 97
Acre Dr. SE22 4G 121
Acrefield Ho. NW4 4F 45
(off Belle Vue Est.)
Acre La. SM5: Cars 4E 166
SM6: W'gton 4E 166
SW2 4J 119
Acre Path UB5: N'olt 6C 58
(off Arnold Rd.)
Acre Rd. KT2: King T 1E 150
RM10: Dag 7H 73
SW19 6B 136
Acre Way HA6: Nwood 1H 39
Acris St. SW18 5A 118
Acropolis Ho. KT1: King T 3F 151
(off Winery La.)
Actaeon Mews SE18 6F 107
ACTON 1J 97
Acton Apts. N1 1D 84
(off Branch Pl.)
Acton Central Ind. Est. W3 1H 97
Acton Cl. N9 2B 34
ACTON GREEN 3J 97
Acton Hill M. W3 1H 97
Acton Ho. E8 1F 85
(off Lee St.)
W3 6J 79
Acton La. NW10 3J 79
W3 2J 97
W4 4J 97
(not continuous)
Acton M. E8 1F 85
Acton Pk. Est. W3 2K 97
Acton St. WC1 2G 7 (3K 83)
Acton Swimming Baths 1J 97
(off Salisbury St.)
Acton Va. Ind. Pk. W3 2B 98
Acton Wlk. N20 1F 31
Acuba Rd. SW18 2K 135
Acworth Cl. N9 7D 24
Acworth Ho. SE18 6F 107
(off Barnfield Rd.)
Ada Cl. N11 3J 31
Ada Ct. N1 1C 84
(off Packington St.)
W9 2A 4 (3A 82)
Ada Gdns. E14 6F 87
E15 1H 87
Adagio Point SE8 6D 104
(off Copperas St.)
Ada Ho. E2 1G 85
(off Ada Pl.)
Adair Cl. SE25 3H 157
Adair Ho. SW3 7D 16
Adair Rd. W10 4G 81
Adair Twr. W10 4G 81
(off Appleford Rd.)
Ada Kennedy Ct. SE10 7E 104
(off Greenwich Sth. St.)
Ada Lewis Ho. HA9: Wemb 4F 61
Adam & Eve Ct. W1 7B 6
Adam & Eve M. W8 3J 99
Ada Maria Ct. E1 6H 85
(off James Voller Way)
Adam Cl. NW7 6A 30
SE6 4B 140
Adam Ct. SE11 4K 19
SW7 4A 100
(off Gloucester Rd.)
Adamfields NW3 7B 64
(off Adamson Rd.)
Adam Rd. E4 6G 35
Adams Bri. Bus. Cen. HA9: Wemb 5H 61
Adams Cl. KT5: Surb 6F 151
N3 7D 30
NW9 2H 61
RM5: Col R 1J 55
Adams Ct. E17 6A 50
EC2 7F 9 (6E 84)
Adams Gdns. Est. SE16 2J 103
Adams Ho. E14 6F 87
(off Aberfeldy St.)
Adams M. N22 7E 32
SW17 2D 136
Adamson Ct. N2 3C 46
Adamson Rd. E16 6J 87
NW3 7B 64
Adamson Way BR3: Beck 5E 158
Adams Pl. E14 1D 104
(off The Nth. Colonnade)
N7 5K 65
Adams Quarter TW8: Bford 7C 96
Adamsrill Cl. EN1: Enf 6J 23
Adamsrill Rd. SE26 4K 139
Adams Rd. BR3: Beck 5A 158
N17 2D 48
Adam's Row W1 3H 11 (7E 82)
Adams Sq. DA6: Bex 3E 126
Adams Ter. E3 3C 86
(off Rainhill Way)
Adam St. WC2 3F 13 (7J 83)
Adams Wlk. KT1: King T 2E 150
Adams Way CR0: C'don 6F 157
SE25 5H 157
Adam Wlk. SW6 7E 98
Adana SE13 2E 122
Ada Pl. E2 1G 85
Adare Wlk. SW16 3K 137
Ada Rd. HA0: Wemb 3D 60
SE5 7E 102
Adastral Ho. WC1 5G 7
(off Harpur St.)
Adastra Way SM6: W'gton 6J 167
Ada St. E8 1H 85
Adcock Wlk. BR6: Orp 4K 173
Adderley Gdns. SE9 4E 142
Adderley Gro. SW11 5E 118
Adderley Rd. HA3: W'stone 1K 41
Adderley St. E14 6E 86
Addey Ho. SE8 7B 104
ADDINGTON 5C 170
Addington Cl. UB2: S'hall 1H 95
Addington Ct. SW14 3K 115
Addington Court Golf Course 7C 170
Addington Dr. N12 6G 31
The Addington Golf Course 4B 170
Addington Gro. SE26 4A 140
Addington Ho. SW9 2K 119
(off Stockwell Rd.)
Addington Lofts SE5 7C 102
(off Bethwin Rd.)
Addington Palace Golf Course 6A 170
Addington Rd. BR4: W W'ck 4E 170
CR0: C'don 1A 168
CR2: Sande, Sels 7K 169
E3 3C 86
E16 4G 87
N4 6A 48
Addington Sq. SE5 6D 102
(not continuous)
Addington St. SE1 7H 13 (2K 101)
Addington Village Rd.
CR0: Addtn 6B 170
(not continuous)
Addis Cl. EN3: Enf H 1E 24
ADDISCOMBE 1G 169
Addiscombe Av. CR0: C'don 1G 169
Addiscombe Cl. HA3: Kenton 5C 42
Addiscombe Ct. Rd. CR0: C'don 1E 168
Addiscombe Gro. CR0: C'don 2E 168
Addiscombe Rd. CR0: C'don 2D 168
(not continuous)
Addis Ho. E1 5J 85
(off Lindley St.)

Addisland Ct. *W14* 2G **99**
   (off Holland Vs. Rd.)
Addison Av. N14 . . . .6A **22**
  TW3: Houn 1G **113**
  W11 . . . .1G **99**
Addison Bri. Pl. W14 . . . .4H **99**
Addison Cl. BR5: Pet W 6G **161**
  HA6: Nwood 1J **39**
Addison Ct. *NW6* 1J **81**
   (off Brondesbury Rd.)
Addison Cres. W14 . . . .3G **99**
   (not continuous)
Addison Dr. SE12 . . . .5K **123**
Addison Gdns. KT5: Surb 4F **151**
  W14 . . . .3G **99**
Addison Gro. W4 . . . .3A **98**
Addison Ho. NW8 . . . .1A **4**
Addison Pk. Mans. *W14* 3F **99**
   (off Richmond Way)
Addison Pl. SE25 . . . .4G **157**
  UB1: S'hall 7E **76**
  W11 . . . .1G **99**
Addison Rd. BR2: Broml 5A **160**
  E11 . . . .6J **51**
  E17 . . . .5D **50**
  EN3: Enf H 1D **24**
  IG6: Ilf 1G **53**
  SE25 . . . .4G **157**
  TW11: Tedd 6B **132**
  W14 . . . .2G **99**
Addisons Cl. CR0: C'don 2B **170**
Addison Ter. *W4* 4J **97**
   (off Chiswick Rd.)
Addison Way HA6: Nwood 1H **39**
  NW11 . . . .4H **45**
  UB3: Hayes 6J **75**
Addle Hill EC4 . . . .1B **14** (6B **84**)
Addlestone Ho. *W10* 5E **80**
   (off Sutton Way)
Addle St. EC2 . . . .7D **8** (6C **84**)
Addy Ho. SE16 . . . .4J **103**
Adecroft Way
  KT8: W Mole 3G **149**
Adela Av. KT3: N Mald 5D **152**
Adela Ho. *W6* 5E **98**
   (off Queen Caroline St.)
Adelaide Av. SE4 . . . .4B **122**
Adelaide Cl. EN1: Enf 1K **23**
  HA7: Stan 4F **27**
  SW9 . . . .4A **120**
Adelaide Community Gdn. 7D **64**
   (off Adelaide Rd.)
Adelaide Ct. BR3: Beck 7C **140**
  E9 . . . .5A **68**
   (off Kenworthy Rd.)
  NW8 . . . .2A **82**
   (off Abbey Rd.)
  W7 . . . .2K **95**
Adelaide Gdns. RM6: Chad H 5E **54**
Adelaide Gro. W12 . . . .1C **98**
Adelaide Ho. E15 . . . .2H **87**
  E17 . . . .2B **50**
  SE5 . . . .2E **120**
  W11 . . . .6H **81**
   (off Portobello Rd.)
Adelaide Rd. BR7: Chst 5F **143**
  E10 . . . .3D **68**
  IG1: Ilf 2F **71**
  KT6: Surb 5E **150**
  NW3 . . . .7B **64**
  SW18 . . . .5J **117**
  TW5: Hest 1C **112**
  TW9: Rich 4F **115**
  TW11: Tedd 6K **131**
  TW15: Ashf 5A **128**
  UB2: S'hall 4C **94**
  W13 . . . .1A **96**
Adelaide Ter. TW8: Bford 5D **96**
   (not continuous)
Adela St. W10 . . . .4G **81**
Adelina Gro. E1 . . . .5J **85**
Adelina M. SW12 . . . .1H **137**

Adelina Yd. *E1* 5J **85**
   (off Adelina Gro.)
Adeline Pl. WC1 . . . .6D **6** (5H **83**)
Adeliza Cl. IG11: Bark 7G **71**
Adelphi Ct. *E8* 4H **67**
   (off Celandine Dr.)
  SE16 . . . .2K **103**
   (off Garter Way)
  W4 . . . .6K **97**
Adelphi Cres. UB4: Hayes 3G **75**
Adelphi Ter.
  WC2 . . . .3F **13** (7J **83**)
Adelphi Theatre 3F **13**
   (off Strand)
Adelphi Way UB4: Hayes 3H **75**
Adeney Cl. W6 . . . .6F **99**
Aden Gro. N16 . . . .4D **66**
Adenmore Rd. SE6 . . . .7C **122**
Aden Rd.
  EN3: Brim 4F **25**
  IG1: Ilf 7G **53**
Aden Ter. N16 . . . .4D **66**
Adeyfield Ho. *EC1* 2F **9**
   (off Cranwood St.)
Adie Rd. W6 . . . .3E **98**
Adine Rd. E13 . . . .4K **87**
Adler Ind. Est. UB3: Hayes 2F **93**
Adler St. E1 . . . .6G **85**
Adley St. E5 . . . .5A **68**
Adlington Cl. N18 . . . .5J **33**
Admaston Rd. SE18 . . . .7G **107**
Admiral Ct. IG11: Bark 2B **90**
  SE5 . . . .1E **120**
   (off Havil St.)
  SM5: Cars 1C **166**
  SW10 . . . .1A **118**
   (off Admiral Sq.)
  W1 . . . .6G **5**
   (off Blandford St.)
Admiral Ho. *SW1* 3B **18**
   (off Willow Pl.)
  TW11: Tedd 4A **132**
Admiral Hyson Ind. Est.
  SE16 . . . .5H **103**
Admiral M. SW19 . . . .7A **136**
  W10 . . . .4F **81**
Admiral Pl. N8 . . . .4B **48**
  SE16 . . . .1A **104**
Admirals Cl. E18 . . . .4K **51**
Admirals Ct. *E6* 6F **89**
   (off Trader Rd.)
  SE1 . . . .5J **15**
   (off Horselydown La.)
Admiral Seymour Rd. SE9 . . . .4D **124**
Admiral's Ga. SE10 . . . .1D **122**
Admiral Sq. SW10 . . . .1A **118**
Admiral's Twr. *SE10* 6D **104**
   (off Dowells St.)
Admiral St. SE8 . . . .2C **122**
Admirals Wlk. NW3 . . . .3A **64**
Admirals Way E14 . . . .2C **104**
Admiralty & Commercial Court
  . . . .7J **7** (6A **84**)
Admiralty Arch 4D **12** (1H **101**)
Admiralty Av. E16 . . . .2K **105**
Admiralty Bldg. *KT2: King T* 1D **150**
   (off Down Hall Rd.)
Admiralty Cl. SE8 . . . .7C **104**
  UB7: W Dray 2A **92**
Admiralty Ho. *E1* 7G **85**
   (off Vaughan Way)
Admiralty Rd. TW11: Tedd 6K **131**
Admiralty Way TW11: Tedd 6K **131**
Admiral Wlk. W9 . . . .5J **81**
Adolf St. SE6 . . . .4D **140**
Adolphus Rd. N4 . . . .2B **66**
Adolphus St. SE8 . . . .7B **104**
Adomar Rd. RM8: Dag 3E **72**
Adpar St. W2 . . . .5A **4** (5B **82**)
Adrian Av. NW2 . . . .1D **62**
Adrian Boult Ho. *E2* 3H **85**
   (off Mansford St.)
Adrian Cl. EN5: Barn 6A **20**

Adrian Ho. *E15* 7F **69**
   (off Jupp Rd.)
  N1 . . . .1K **83**
   (off Barnsbury Est.)
  SW8 . . . .7J **101**
   (off Wyvil Rd.)
Adrian M. SW10 . . . .6K **99**
Adriatic Apts. *E16* 7J **87**
   (off Western Gateway)
Adriatic Bldg. *E14* 7A **86**
   (off Horseferry Rd.)
Adriatic Ho. *E1* 4K **85**
   (off Ernest St.)
Adrienne Av. UB1: S'hall 4D **76**
Adrienne Bus. Cen.
  UB1: S'hall 3D **76**
Adron Ho. *SE16* 4J **103**
   (off Millender Wlk.)
Adstock Ho. *N1* 7B **66**
   (off The Sutton Est.)
Advance Rd. SE27 . . . .4C **138**
Adventure Kingdom 2K **159**
   (off Stockwell Cl.)
Adventurers Ct. *E14* 7F **87**
   (off Newport Av.)
Advent Way N18 . . . .5D **34**
Adys Lawn NW2 . . . .6D **62**
Ady's Rd. SE15 . . . .3F **121**
Aegean Apts. *E16* 7J **87**
   (off Western Gateway)
Aegon Ho. *E14* 3D **104**
   (off Lanark Sq.)
Aerodrome Rd. NW9 . . . .2B **44**
Aerodrome Way TW5: Hest 6A **94**
Aeroville NW9 . . . .2A **44**
AFC Wimbledon 3G **151**
AFC Wimbledon Plough La. Stadium
  . . . .4A **136**
Affleck St. N1 . . . .1G **7** (2K **83**)
Afghan Rd. SW11 . . . .2C **118**
Afsil Ho. *EC1* 6K **7**
   (off Viaduct Bldgs.)
Aftab Ter. *E1* 4H **85**
   (off Tent St.)
Agamemnon Rd. NW6 . . . .4H **63**
Agar Cl. KT6: Surb 2F **163**
Agar Gro. NW1 . . . .7G **65**
Agar Gro. Est. NW1 . . . .7H **65**
Agar Ho. *KT1: King T* 3E **150**
   (off Denmark Rd.)
Agar Pl. NW1 . . . .7G **65**
Agar St. WC2 . . . .3E **12** (7J **83**)
Agate Cl. E16 . . . .6B **88**
  NW10 . . . .3G **79**
Agate Rd. W6 . . . .3E **98**
Agatha Cl. E1 . . . .1H **103**
Agaton Path SE9 . . . .2G **143**
Agaton Rd. SE9 . . . .2G **143**
Agave Rd. NW2 . . . .4E **62**
Agdon St. EC1 . . . .3A **8** (4B **84**)
Ager Av. RM8: Dag 1D **72**
Agincourt Rd. NW3 . . . .4D **64**
Agnes Av. IG1: Ilf 4E **70**
Agnes Cl. E6 . . . .7E **88**
Agnesfield Cl. N12 . . . .6H **31**
Agnes Gdns. RM8: Dag 4D **72**
Agnes George Wlk. E16 . . . .1B **106**
Agnes Ho. *W11* 7F **81**
   (off St Ann's Rd.)
Agnes Rd. W3 . . . .1B **98**
Agnes St. E14 . . . .6B **86**
Agnew Rd. SE23 . . . .7K **121**
Agricola Ct. *E3* 1B **86**
   (off Parnell Rd.)
Agricola Pl. EN1: Enf 5A **24**
The Ahoy Cen. 5C **104**
   (off Stretton Mans.)
Aidan Cl. RM8: Dag 4E **72**
Aigburth Mans. *SW9* 7A **102**
   (off Mowll St.)
Ailantus Ct. HA8: Edg 5A **28**
Aileen Wlk. E15 . . . .7H **69**
Ailsa Av. TW1: Twick 5A **114**

Ailsa Ho. *E16* 7E **88**
   (off University Way)
Ailsa Rd. TW1: Twick 5B **114**
Ailsa St. E14 . . . .5E **86**
Ainger M. *NW3* 7D **64**
   (off Ainger Rd.)
Ainger Rd. NW3 . . . .7D **64**
Ainsdale *NW1* 1A **6**
   (off Harrington St.)
Ainsdale Cl. BR6: Orp 1H **173**
Ainsdale Cres. HA5: Pinn 3E **40**
Ainsdale Dr. SE1 . . . .5G **103**
Ainsdale Rd. W5 . . . .4D **78**
Ainsley Av. RM7: Rom 6H **55**
Ainsley Cl. N9 . . . .1K **33**
Ainsley St. E2 . . . .3H **85**
Ainslie Cl. HA0: Wemb 2E **78**
Ainslie Wlk. SW12 . . . .7F **119**
Ainslie Wood Cres. E4 . . . .5J **35**
Ainslie Wood Gdns. E4 . . . .4J **35**
Ainslie Wood
  Local Nature Reserve 5J **35**
Ainslie Wood Rd. E4 . . . .5H **35**
Ainsty Est. SE16 . . . .2K **103**
Ainsty St. SE16 . . . .2J **103**
Ainsworth Cl. N20 . . . .2G **31**
  NW2 . . . .3C **62**
  SE15 . . . .2E **120**
Ainsworth Cl. *NW10* 3D **80**
   (off Plough Cl.)
Ainsworth Ho. *NW8* 1K **81**
   (off Ainsworth Way)
  W10 . . . .3G **81**
   (off Kilburn La.)
Ainsworth Rd. CR0: C'don 1B **168**
  E9 . . . .7J **67**
Ainsworth Way NW8 . . . .1A **82**
Aintree Av. E6 . . . .1C **88**
Aintree Cl. UB8: Hil 6D **74**
Aintree Cres. IG6: Ilf 2G **53**
Aintree Est. SW6 . . . .7G **99**
Aintree Rd. UB6: G'frd 2B **78**
Aintree St. SW6 . . . .7G **99**
Airbourne Ho. *SM6: W'gton* 4G **167**
   (off Maldon Rd.)
Air Call Bus. Cen. NW9 . . . .3K **43**
Airco Cl. NW9 . . . .3K **43**
Aird Ho. *SE1* 3C **102**
   (off Rockingham St.)
Aird Point *E16* 7G **89**
   (off Lock Side Way)
Airdrie Cl. N1 . . . .7K **65**
  UB4: Yead 5C **76**
Airedale Av. W4 . . . .4B **98**
Airedale Av. Sth. W4 . . . .5B **98**
Airedale Rd. SW12 . . . .7D **118**
  W5 . . . .3C **96**
Airlie Gdns. IG1: Ilf 1F **71**
  W8 . . . .1J **99**
Airlinks Golf Course 5A **94**
Air Links Ind. Est.
  TW13: Hanw 3C **130**
Airlinks Ind. Est. TW5: Cran 5A **94**
Air Pk. Way TW13: Felt 2K **129**
Airport Bowl 1G **111**
Airport Ga. Bus. Cen.
  UB7: Sip 7B **92**
Airport Way TW19: Stanw M 7A **174**
Air Sea M. TW2: Twick 2H **131**
Air St. W1 . . . .3B **12** (7G **83**)
Airthrie Rd. IG3: Ilf 2B **72**
Aisgill Av. W14 . . . .5H **99**
   (not continuous)
Aisher Rd. SE28 . . . .7C **90**
Aislibie Rd. SE12 . . . .4G **123**
Aiten Pl. W6 . . . .4C **98**
Aithan Ho. *E14* 6B **86**
   (off Copenhagen Pl.)
Aitken Cl. CR4: Mitc 7D **154**
  E8 . . . .1G **85**
  HA4: Eastc 6J **39**
Aitken Rd. SE6 . . . .2D **140**
  EN5: Barn 4A **20**
Aitman Dr. TW8: Bford 5G **97**

Aitons Ho. TW8: Bford 5E **96**
Aits Vw. KT8: W Mole 3F **149**
Ajax Av. NW9 . . . . .3A **44**
Ajax Ho. E2 . . . . .2H **85**
(off Old Bethnal Grn. Rd.)
Ajax Rd. NW6 . . . . .4H **63**
Akabusi Cl. CR0: C'don 6G **157**
Akbar Ho. E14 . . . . .4D **104**
(off Cahir St.)
Akehurst St. SW15 . . . . .6C **116**
Akenside Rd. NW3 . . . . .5B **64**
Akerman Rd. KT6: Surb 6C **150**
SW9 . . . . .2B **120**
Akintaro Ho. SE8 . . . . .6B **104**
(off Alverton St.)
Alabama St. SE18 . . . . .7H **107**
Alacia Ct. W3 . . . . .3J **97**
(off Bassington Rd.)
Alacross Rd. W5 . . . . .2C **96**
Alamaro Lodge SE10 . . . . .3H **105**
(off Teal St.)
Alameda Pl. E3 . . . . .2D **86**
Alana Hgts. E4 . . . . .7J **25**
Alan Coren Cl. NW2 . . . . .4E **62**
Alandale Dr. HA5: Pinn 1K **39**
Aland Ct. SE16 . . . . .3A **104**
Alander M. E17 . . . . .4E **50**
Alan Dr. EN5: Barn 6B **20**
Alan Gdns.
RM7: Rush G 7G **55**
Alan Hocken Way E15 . . . . .2G **87**
Alan Preece Ct. NW6 . . . . .7F **63**
Alan Rd. SW19 . . . . .5G **135**
Alanthus Cl. SE12 . . . . .6J **123**
Alaska Apts. E16 . . . . .7J **87**
(off Western Gateway)
Alaska Bldg. SE13 . . . . .1D **122**
(off Deal's Gateway)
Alaska Bldgs. SE1 . . . . .3F **103**
Alaska St. SE1 . . . . . .5J **13** (1A **102**)
Alastor Ho. E14 . . . . .3E **104**
(off Strattondale Ho.)
Alba Cl. UB4: Yead 4B **76**
Albacore Cres. SE13 . . . . .6D **122**
Albacore Way
UB3: Hayes 7H **75**
Alba Gdns. NW11 . . . . .6G **45**
Albain Cres. TW15: Ashf 2A **128**
Alba M. SW18 . . . . .2J **135**
Alban Highwalk EC2 . . . . .7D **8**
(not continuous)
The Albany 7C **104**
Albany N12 . . . . .6E **30**
W1 . . . . .3A **12** (7G **83**)
The Albany IG8: Wfd G 4C **36**
Albany Cl. DA5: Bexl 7C **126**
N15 . . . . .4B **48**
SW14 .4H **115**
UB10: Ick 5C **56**
Albany Ct. E7 . . . . .6G **85**
(off Plumber's Row)
E4 . . . . .6H **25**
(Chelwood Cl.)
E4 . . . . .5G **35**
(Westward Rd.)
E10 . . . . .7C **50**
HA8: Edg 1K **43**
NW8 . . . . .1A **4**
(off Abbey Rd.)
NW10 .3D **80**
(off Trenmar Gdns.)
TW15: Ashf 7E **128**
Albany Clyd. W1 . . . . . .3B **12** (7G **83**)
Albany Cres. HA8: Edg 7B **28**
Albany Mans. SW11 . . . . .7C **100**
Albany M. BR1: Broml 6J **141**
KT2: King T 6D **132**
N1 . . . . .7A **66**
SE5 . . . . .6C **102**
SM1: Sutt 5K **165**
Albany Pde. TW8: Bford 6E **96**
Albany Pk. Av. EN3: Enf W 1D **24**
Albany Pk. Rd. KT2: King T 6D **132**

Albany Pas. TW10: Rich 5E **114**
Albany Pl. TW8: Bford 6D **96**
Albany Reach KT7: T Ditt 5K **149**
Albany Rd. BR7: Chst 5F **143**
DA5: Bexl 7C **126**
DA17: Belv 6F **109**
E10 . . . . .7C **50**
E12 . . . . .4B **70**
E17 . . . . .6A **50**
KT3: N Mald 4K **151**
N4 . . . . .6A **48**
N18 . . . . .5D **34**
RM6: Chad H 6F **55**
SE5 . . . . .6C **102**
SW19 .5K **135**
TW8: Bford 6D **96**
TW10: Rich 5F **115**
W13 . . . . .7B **78**
Albany St. NW1 . . . . . . .1K **5** (2F **83**)
Albany Ter. NW1 . . . . .4K **5**
TW10: Rich 5F **115**
(off Albany Pas.)
Albany Vw. IG9: Buck H 1D **36**
Albany Works E3 . . . . .1A **86**
(off Gunmakers La.)
Alba Pl. W11 . . . . .6H **81**
Albatross NW9 . . . . .2B **44**
Albatross Cl. E6 . . . . .5D **88**
Albatross St. SE18 . . . . .7J **107**
Albatross Way SE16 . . . . .2K **103**
Albemarle SW19 . . . . .2F **135**
Albemarle App. IG2: Ilf 6F **53**
Albemarle Av. TW2: Whitt 1D **130**
Albemarle Ct. N17 . . . . .3H **49**
(off Perkyn Sq.)
Albemarle Gdns. IG2: Ilf 6F **53**
KT3: N Mald 4K **151**
Albemarle Ho. SE8 . . . . .4B **104**
(off Foreshore)
Albemarle Pk. BR3: Beck 1D **158**
HA7: Stan 5H **27**
Albemarle Rd. BR3: Beck 1D **158**
EN4: E Barn 7H **21**
Albemarle St. W1 . . . . . .3K **11** (7F **83**)
Albemarle Wlk. SW9 . . . . .3A **120**
Albemarle Way EC1 . . . . . .4A **8** (4B **84**)
Alberon Gdns. NW11 . . . . .4H **45**
Alberta Av. SM1: Sutt 4G **165**
Alberta Est. SE17 . . . . .5B **102**
(off Alberta St.)
Alberta Ho. UB4: Yead 3K **75**
(off Ayles Rd.)
Alberta Rd. DA8: Erith 1J **127**
EN1: Enf 6A **24**
Alberta St. SE17 . . . . .5B **102**
Albert Av. E4 . . . . .4H **35**
SW8 . . . . .7K **101**
Albert Barnes Ho. SE1 . . . . .3C **102**
(off New Kent Rd.)
Albert Basin 7F **89**
Albert Basin Way E16 . . . . .7G **89**
Albert Bigg Point E15 . . . . .2E **86**
(off Godfrey St.)
ALBERT BRI. 7D **16** (6C **100**)
Albert Bri. Rd. SW11 . . . . .7C **100**
Albert Carr Gdns. SW16 . . . . .5J **137**
Albert Cl. E9 . . . . .1H **85**
N22 . . . . .1H **47**
Albert Cotts. E1 . . . . .5G **85**
(off Deal St.)
Albert Ct. E7 . . . . .4J **69**
SW7 . . . . .7A **10** (3B **100**)
Albert Ct. Ga. SW1 . . . . .7E **10**
(off Knightsbridge)
Albert Cres. E4 . . . . .4H **35**
Albert Dane Cen. UB2: S'hall 3C **94**
Albert Dr. SW19 . . . . .2G **135**
Albert Emb. SE1 . . . . . . .6F **19** (5J **101**)
(Kennington La.)
SE1 . . . . .1G **19** (3K **101**)
(Lambeth Pal. Rd.)
Albert Gdns. E1 . . . . .6K **85**
Albert Ga. SW1 . . . . .6F **11** (2D **100**)

Albert Gray Ho. SW10 . . . . .7B **100**
(off Worlds End Est.)
Albert Gro. SW20 . . . . .1F **153**
Albert Hall Mans. SW7 . . .7B **10** (2B **100**)
Albert Ho. E18 . . . . .3K **51**
(off Albert Rd.)
SE28 .3G **107**
Albert Mans. CR0: C'don 1D **168**
(off Lansdowne Rd.)
SW11 .1D **118**
(off Albert Bri. Rd.)
Albert Memorial 6A **10** (2B **100**)
Albert M. E14 . . . . .7A **86**
(off Northey St.)
N4 . . . . .1K **65**
SE4 . . . . .4A **122**
W8 . . . . .3A **100**
Albert Pal. Mans. SW11 . . . . .1F **119**
(off Lurline Gdns.)
Albert Pl. N3 . . . . .1J **45**
N17 . . . . .3F **49**
W8 . . . . .3K **99**
Albert Rd. BR2: Broml 5B **160**
CR4: Mitc 3D **154**
DA5: Bexl 6G **127**
DA17: Belv 5F **109**
E10 . . . . .2E **68**
E16 . . . . .1C **106**
E17 . . . . .5C **50**
E18 . . . . .3K **51**
EN4: E Barn 4F **21**
HA2: Harr 3G **41**
IG1: Ilf 3F **71**
IG9: Buck H 2G **37**
KT1: King T 2F **151**
KT3: N Mald 4B **152**
N4 . . . . .1K **65**
N15 . . . . .6E **48**
N22 . . . . .1G **47**
NW4 . . . . .4F **45**
NW6 . . . . .2H **81**
NW7 . . . . .5G **29**
RM8: Dag 1G **73**
SE9 . . . . .3C **142**
SE20 .6K **139**
SE25 .4G **157**
SM1: Sutt 5B **166**
TW1: Twick 1K **131**
TW3: Houn 4E **112**
TW10: Rich 5E **114**
TW11: Tedd 6K **131**
TW12: Hamp H 5E **131**
TW15: Ashf 5B **128**
UB2: S'hall 3B **94**
UB3: Hayes 3G **93**
UB7: Yiew 1A **92**
W5 . . . . .4B **78**
Albert Rd. Est. DA17: Belv 5F **109**
Alberts Ct. NW1 . . . . .3D **4**
Albert Sleet Ct. N9 . . . . .3D **34**
(off Colthurst Dr.)
Albert Sq. E15 . . . . .5G **69**
SW8 . . . . .7K **101**
Albert Starr Ho. SE8 . . . . .4K **103**
(off Haddonfield)
Albert St. N12 . . . . .5F **31**
NW1 . . . . .1F **83**
Albert Studios SW11 . . . . .1D **118**
Albert Ter. IG9: Buck H 2H **37**
NW1 . . . . .1E **82**
NW10 .1J **79**
W5 . . . . .4B **78**
W6 . . . . .4E **98**
(off Beavor La.)
Albert Ter. M. NW1 . . . . .1E **82**
Albert Victoria Ho. N22 . . . . .1A **48**
Albert Wlk. E16 . . . . .2E **106**
Albert Way SE15 . . . . .7H **103**
Albert Westcott Ho. SE17 . . . . .5B **102**
Albert Whicher Ho. E17 . . . . .4E **50**
Albert Yd. SE19 . . . . .6F **139**
Albery Ct. E8 . . . . .7F **67**
(off Middleton Rd.)

Albin Av. N10 . . . . .1E **46**
SW8 . . . . .2H **119**
Albion Bldgs. N1 . . . . .2J **83**
(off Albion Yd.)
Albion Cl. RM7: Rom 6K **55**
W2 . . . . .2D **10** (7C **82**)
Albion Ct. SE10 . . . . .4G **105**
(off Azof St.)
SM2: Sutt 7B **166**
W6 . . . . .4D **98**
(off Albion Pl.)
Albion Dr. E8 . . . . .7F **67**
Albion Est. SE16 . . . . .2K **103**
Albion Gdns. W6 . . . . .4D **98**
Albion Ga. W2 . . . . .2D **10**
(not continuous)
Albion Gro. N16 . . . . .4E **66**
Albion Ho. E16 . . . . .1F **107**
(off Church St.)
SE8 . . . . .7C **104**
(off Watsons St.)
Albion M. N1 . . . . .1A **84**
NW6 . . . . .7H **63**
W2 . . . . .2D **10** (7C **82**)
W6 . . . . .4D **98**
Albion Pde. N16 . . . . .4D **66**
Albion Pl. EC1 . . . . . . .5A **8** (5B **84**)
EC2 . . . . .6F **9** (5D **84**)
W6 . . . . .4D **98**
Albion Riverside Bldg. SW11 . . . . .7C **100**
Albion Rd. DA6: Bex 4F **127**
E17 . . . . .3E **50**
KT2: King T 1J **151**
N16 . . . . .4D **66**
N17 . . . . .2G **49**
SM2: Sutt 6B **166**
TW2: Twick 1J **131**
TW3: Houn 4E **112**
UB3: Hayes 6G **75**
Albion Sq. E8 . . . . .7F **67**
(not continuous)
Albion St. CR0: C'don 1B **168**
SE16 . . . . .2J **103**
W2 . . . . .1D **10** (6C **82**)
Albion Ter. E4 . . . . .4J **25**
E8 . . . . .7F **67**
Albion Vs. Rd. SE26 . . . . .3J **139**
Albion Wlk. N1 . . . . .1F **7**
(off York Way)
Albion Way E6 . . . . .1B **88**
EC1 . . . . .6C **8** (5C **84**)
HA9: Wemb 3G **61**
SE13 . . . . .4E **122**
Albion Yd. E1 . . . . .5H **85**
N1 . . . . .2J **83**
Albon Ho. SW18 . . . . .6K **117**
(off Neville Gill Cl.)
Albrighton Rd. SE22 . . . . .3E **120**
Albuhera Cl. EN2: Enf 1F **23**
Albuhera M. NW7 . . . . .5A **30**
Albury Av. DA7: Bex 2E **126**
TW7: Isle 7K **95**
Albury Cl. TW12: Hamp 6F **131**
Albury Ct. CR0: C'don 4C **168**
(off Tanfield Rd.)
CR4: Mitc 2B **154**
SE8 . . . . .6C **104**
(off Albury St.)
SM1: Sutt 4A **166**
UB5: N'olt 3A **76**
(off Canberra Dr.)
Albury Dr. HA5: Pinn 1A **40**, 1C **40**
Albury Ho. SE1 . . . . .7B **14**
(off Boyfield St.)
Albury M. E12 . . . . .2A **70**
Albury Rd. KT9: Chess 5E **162**
Albury St. SE8 . . . . .6C **104**
Albyfield BR1: Broml 4D **160**
Albyn Rd. SE8 . . . . .1C **122**
Alcester Cl. SM6: W'gton 4F **167**
Alcester Cres. E5 . . . . .2H **67**
Alcester Rd. SM6: W'gton 4F **167**
Alcock Cl. SM6: W'gton 7H **167**

Alcock Rd. TW5: Hest 7B 94
Alconbury DA6: Bex 5H 127
Alconbury Rd. E5 . . . . 2G 67
Alcorn Cl. SM3: Sutt 2J 165
Alcott Cl. TW14: Felt 1H 129
W7 . . . . 5K 77
Alcuin Ct. HA7: Stan 7H 27
Aldam Pl. N16 . . . . 2F 67
Aldborough Ct. *IG2: Ilf* *5K 53*
(off Aldborough Rd. Nth.)
Aldborough Hall Equestrian Cen. . . . 3K 53
ALDBOROUGH HATCH 4K 53
Aldborough Rd. RM10: Dag 6J 73
Aldborough Rd. Nth. IG2: Ilf 5K 53
Aldborough Rd. Sth. IG3: Ilf 1J 71
Aldbourne Rd. W12 . . . . 1B 98
Aldbridge St. SE17 . . . . 5E 102
Aldburgh M. W1 . . . . 7H 5 (6E 82)
Aldbury Av. HA9: Wemb 7H 61
Aldbury Ho. *SW3* *5C 16*
(off Cale St.)
Aldbury M. N9 . . . . 7J 23
Aldebert Ter. SW8 . . . . 7J 101
Aldeburgh Cl. E5 . . . . 2H 67
Aldeburgh Pl. IG8: Wfd G 4D 36
SE10 . . . . *4J 105*
(off Aldeburgh St.)
Aldeburgh St. SE10 . . . . 5J 105
Alden Av. E15 . . . . 3H 87
Alden Ct. CR0: C'don 3E 168
Aldenham Dr. UB8: Hil 4D 74
Aldenham Ho. *NW1* *1B 6*
(off Aldenham St.)
Aldenham St. NW1 . . . . 1C 6 (2G 83)
Alden Ho. *E8* *1H 85*
(off Duncan Rd.)
Aldensley Rd. W6 . . . . 3D 98
Alderbrook Rd. SW12 . . . . 6F 119
Alderbury Rd. SW13 . . . . 6C 98
Alder Cl. DA18: Erith 2F 109
SE15 . . . . 6F 103
Alder Ct. E7 . . . . 5J 69
N11 . . . . 6B 32
Alder Gro. NW2 . . . . 2C 62
Aldergrove Gdns. TW3: Houn 2C 112
Alder Ho. *E3* *1B 86*
(off Hornbeam Sq.)
NW3 . . . . 6D 64
SE4 . . . . 3C 122
SE15 . . . . *6F 103*
(off Alder Cl.)
Alder Lodge SW6 . . . . 1E 116
Alderman Av. IG11: Bark 3A 90
Aldermanbury EC2 . . . . 7D 8 (6C 84)
Aldermanbury Sq. EC2 . . . . 6D 8 (5C 84)
Alderman Judge Mall
KT1: King T *2E 150*
(off Eden St.)
Aldermans Hill N13 . . . . 4D 32
Aldermans Ho. *E9* *5A 68*
(off Ward La.)
Aldermans Wlk. EC2 . . . . 6G 9 (5E 84)
Aldermary Rd. BR1: Broml 1J 159
Alder M. N19 . . . . 2G 65
Aldermoor Rd. SE6 . . . . 3B 140
Alderney Av. TW5: Hest, Isle 7F 95
Alderney Cl. NW9 . . . . 3C 44
Alderney Ct. *SE10* *6F 105*
(off Trafalgar Rd.)
Alderney Gdns. UB5: N'olt 7D 58
Alderney Ho. EN3: Enf W 1E 24
N1 . . . . *6C 66*
(off Arran Wlk.)
Alderney M. SE1 . . . . 3D 102
Alderney Rd. E1 . . . . 4K 85
Alderney St. SW1 . . . . 4K 17 (4F 101)
Alder Rd. DA14: Sidc 3K 143
SW14 . . . . 3K 115
The Alders BR4: W W'ck 1D 170
N21 . . . . 6F 23
SW16 . . . . 4G 137
TW5: Hest 6D 94
TW13: Hanw 4C 130
Alders Av. IG8: Wfd G 6B 36
ALDERSBROOK 2K 69
Aldersbrook Av. EN1: Enf 2K 23
Aldersbrook Dr. KT2: King T 6F 133
Aldersbrook La. E12 . . . . 3D 70
Aldersbrook Rd. E11 . . . . 2K 69
E12 . . . . 2K 69
Alders Cl. E11 . . . . 2K 69
HA8: Edg 5D 28
W5 . . . . 3D 96
Aldersey Gdns. IG11: Bark 6H 71
Aldersford Cl. SE4 . . . . 5K 121
Aldersgate Ct. *EC1* *6C 8*
(off Bartholomew Cl.)
Aldersgate St. EC1 . . . . 5C 8 (5C 84)
Alders Gro. KT8: E Mos 5H 149
Aldersgrove Av. SE9 . . . . 3B 142
Aldershot Rd. NW6 . . . . 1H 81
Aldershot Ter. SE18 . . . . 7E 106
Aldersmead Av. CR0: C'don 6K 157
Aldersmead Rd. BR3: Beck 7A 140
Alderson Pl. UB2: S'hall 1G 95
Alderson St. W10 . . . . 4G 81
Alders Rd. HA8: Edg 5D 28
Alderton Cl. NW10 . . . . 3K 61
Alderton Ct. *KT8: W Mole* *4D 148*
(off Dunstable Rd.)
Alderton Cres. NW4 . . . . 5D 44
Alderton Rd. CR0: C'don 7F 157
SE24 . . . . 3C 120
Alderton Way NW4 . . . . 5D 44
Alderville Rd. SW6 . . . . 2H 117
Alder Wlk. IG1: Ilf 5G 71
Alderwick Ct. *N7* *6K 65*
(off Cornelia St.)
Alderwick Dr. TW3: Houn 3H 113
Alderwood M. EN4: Had W 1F 21
Alderwood Rd. SE9 . . . . 6H 125
Aldford Ho. *W1* *4G 11*
(off Park St.)
Aldford St. W1 . . . . 4H 11 (1E 100)
ALDGATE 7J 9
Aldgate *E1* *6F 85*
(off Whitechapel High St.)
EC3 . . . . 1J 15 (6F 85)
Aldgate Av. E1 . . . . 7J 9 (6F 85)
Aldgate Barrs E1 . . . . 7K 9
Aldgate High St.
EC3 . . . . 1J 15 (6F 85)
Aldgate Pl. E1 . . . . 7K 9 (6F 85)
Aldgate Sq. EC3 . . . . 1J 15 (6F 85)
Aldgate Twr. E1 . . . . 6F 85
Aldham Ho. *SE4* *2B 122*
(off Malpas Rd.)
Aldine Ct. *W12* *2E 98*
(off Aldine St.)
Aldine Pl. W12 . . . . 2E 98
Aldine St. W12 . . . . 2E 98
Aldington Cl. RM8: Dag 1C 72
Aldington Ct. *E8* *7G 67*
(off London Flds. W. Side)
Aldington Rd. SE18 . . . . 3B 106
Aldis M. SW17 . . . . 5C 136
Aldis St. SW17 . . . . 5C 136
Aldred Rd. NW6 . . . . 5J 63
Aldren Rd. SW17 . . . . 3A 136
Aldrich Cres. CR0: New Ad 7E 170
Aldriche Way E4 . . . . 6K 35
Aldrich Gdns. SM3: Cheam 3H 165
Aldrich Ter. SW18 . . . . 2A 136
Aldrick Ho. *N1* *1K 83*
(off Barnsbury Est.)
Aldridge Av. HA4: Ruis 2A 58
HA7: Stan 1E 42
HA8: Edg 3C 28
Aldridge Ct. *W11* *5H 81*
(off Aldridge Rd. Vs.)
Aldridge Ri. KT3: N Mald 7A 152
Aldridge Rd. Vs. W11 . . . . 5H 81
Aldridge Wlk. N14 . . . . 7D 22
Aldrington Rd. SW16 . . . . 5G 137
Aldsworth Cl. W9 . . . . 4K 81
Aldwick Cl. SE9 . . . . 3H 143
Aldwick Rd. CR0: Bedd 3K 167
Aldworth Gro. SE13 . . . . 6E 122
Aldworth Rd. E15 . . . . 7G 69
Aldwych WC2 . . . . 2G 13 (6K 83)
Aldwych Av. IG6: Ilf 4G 53
Aldwych Bldgs. *WC2* *7F 7*
(off Parker M.)
Aldwych Ct. *E8* *7F 67*
(off Middleton Rd.)
Aldwych Theatre *1G 13*
(off Aldwych)
Aldwyn Ho. *SW8* *7J 101*
(off Davidson Gdns.)
Alers Rd. DA6: Bex 5D 126
Alesia Cl. N22 . . . . 7D 32
Alestan Beck Rd. E16 . . . . 6B 88
Alexa Ct. SM2: Sutt 6J 165
W8 . . . . 4J 99
Alexander Av. NW10 . . . . 7D 62
Alexander Cl. BR2: Hayes 1J 171
DA15: Sidc 6J 125
EN4: E Barn 4G 21
TW2: Twick 2J 131
UB2: S'hall 1G 95
Alexander Ct. BR3: Beck 1F 159
HA7: Stan 3F 43
TW16: Sun 6H 129
Alexander Evans M. SE23 . . . . 2K 139
Alexander Fleming Laboratory Mus.
. . . . 7B 4 (6B 82)
Alexander Ho. *E14* *3C 104*
(off Tiller Rd.)
KT2: King T *1E 150*
(off Seven Kings Way)
SE15 . . . . *2H 121*
(off Godman Rd.)
Alexander M. SW16 . . . . 5G 137
W2 . . . . 6K 81
Alexander Pl. SW7 . . . . 3C 16 (4C 100)
Alexander Rd. BR7: Chst 6F 143
DA7: Bex 2D 126
N19 . . . . 3J 65
Alexander Sq. SW3 . . . . 3C 16 (4C 100)
Alexander St. W2 . . . . 6J 81
Alexander Studios *SW11* *4B 118*
(off Haydon Way)
Alexander Ter. SE2 . . . . 5B 108
Alexandra Av. HA2: Harr 1D 58
N22 . . . . 1H 47
SM1: Sutt 3J 165
SW11 . . . . 1E 118
UB1: S'hall 7D 76
W4 . . . . 7K 97
Alexandra Cl. HA2: Harr 3E 58
SE8 . . . . 6B 104
TW15: Ashf 7F 129
Alexandra Cotts. SE14 . . . . 1B 122
Alexandra Ct. HA9: Wemb 4F 61
N14 . . . . 5B 22
SE5 . . . . *6C 102*
(off Urlwin St.)
SW7 . . . . 1A 16
TW3: Houn 2F 113
TW15: Ashf 6F 129
UB6: G'frd 2F 77
W2 . . . . *7K 81*
(off Moscow Rd.)
W9 . . . . *4A 82*
(off Maida Vale)
Alexandra Cres. BR1: Broml 6H 141
Alexandra Dr. KT5: Surb 7G 151
SE19 . . . . 5E 138
Alexandra Gdns. N10 . . . . 4F 47
SM5: Cars 7E 166
TW3: Houn 2F 113
W4 . . . . 7A 98
Alexandra Gro. N4 . . . . 1B 66
N12 . . . . 5E 30
Alexandra Ho. *E16* *1K 105*
(off Wesley Av.)
IG8: Wfd G 7K 37
W6 . . . . *5E 98*
(off Queen Caroline St.)
Alexandra Mans. *SW3* *7A 16*
(off King's Rd.)
W12 . . . . *1E 98*
(off Stanlake Rd.)
Alexandra M. N2 . . . . 3D 46
N4 . . . . 2B 66
SW19 . . . . 6H 135
Alexandra Palace 2H 47
Alexandra Palace Ice Rink 2H 47
Alexandra Palace Theatre 2H 47
Alexandra Pal. Way N8 . . . . 4G 47
N22 . . . . 4G 47
Alexandra Pde. HA2: Harr 4F 59
Alexandra Pk. Rd. N10 . . . . 2F 47
N22 . . . . 1G 47
Alexandra Pl. CR0: C'don 1E 168
NW8 . . . . 1A 82
SE25 . . . . 5D 156
Alexandra Rd. CR0: C'don 1E 168
CR4: Mitc 7C 136
E6 . . . . 3E 88
E10 . . . . 3E 68
E17 . . . . 6B 50
E18 . . . . 3K 51
EN3: Pond E 4E 24
KT2: King T 7G 133
KT7: T Ditt 5K 149
N8 . . . . 3A 48
N9 . . . . 7C 24
N10 . . . . 7A 32
N15 . . . . 5D 48
NW4 . . . . 4F 45
NW8 . . . . 1A 82
RM6: Chad H 6E 54
SE26 . . . . 6K 139
SW14 . . . . 3K 115
SW19 . . . . 6H 135
TW1: Twick 6C 114
TW3: Houn 2F 113
TW8: Bford 6D 96
TW9: Kew 2F 115
TW15: Ashf 7F 129
W4 . . . . 2K 97
Alexandra Rd. Ind. Est.
EN3: Pond E 4E 24
Alexandra Sq. SM4: Mord 5J 153
Alexandra St. E16 . . . . 5J 87
SE14 . . . . 7A 104
Alexandra Ter. *E14* *5D 104*
(off Westferry Rd.)
Alexandra Wlk. SE19 . . . . 5E 138
Alexandra Wharf *E2* *1H 85*
(off Darwen Pl.)
Alexandra Yd. E9 . . . . 1K 85
Alexandria Apts. *SE17* *4E 102*
(off Townsend St.)
Alexandria Rd. W13 . . . . 7A 78
Alex Guy Gdns. RM8: Dag 1H 73
Alexia Sq. E14 . . . . 3D 104
Alexis St. SE16 . . . . 4G 103
Alfan La. DA2: Wilm 5K 145
Alfearn Rd. E5 . . . . 4J 67
Alford Ct. *N1* *1D 8*
(off Shepherdess Wlk.)
Alford Grn. CR0: New Ad 6F 171
Alford Ho. N6 . . . . 6G 47
Alford Pl. N1 . . . . 1D 8 (2C 84)
Alford Rd. DA8: Erith 5J 109
Alfoxton Av. N15 . . . . 4B 48
Alfreda St. SW11 . . . . 1F 119
Alfred Cl. W4 . . . . 4K 97
Alfred Ct. *SE16* *4H 103*
(off Bombay St.)
Alfred Dickens Ho. *E16* *6H 87*
(off Hallsville Rd.)
Alfred Finlay Ho. N22 . . . . 2B 48
Alfred Gdns. UB1: S'hall 7C 76
Alfred Ho. *E9* *5A 68*
(off Homerton Rd.)
E12 . . . . *7C 70*
(off Tennyson Av.)
Alfred M. W1 . . . . 5C 6 (5H 83)
Alfred Nunn Ho. NW10 . . . . 1B 80

Alfred Pl.—Alscot Way

Alfred Pl. WC1 5C 6 (5H 83)
Alfred Prior Ho. E12 4E 70
Alfred Rd. DA17: Belv 5F 109
E15 5H 69
IG9: Buck H 2G 37
KT1: King T 3E 150
SE25 5G 157
SM1: Sutt 5A 166
TW13: Felt 2A 130
W2 5J 81
W3 1J 97
Alfred Salter Ho. *SE1* *4F 103*
(off Fort Rd.)
Alfred's Gdns. IG11: Bark 2J 89
Alfred St. E3 3B 86
Alfreds Way IG11: Bark 3F 89
Alfreds Way Ind. Est.
IG11: Bark 2A 90
Alfred Vs. E17 4E 50
Alfreton Cl. SW19 3F 135
Alfriston KT5: Surb 6F 151
Alfriston Av. CR0: C'don 7J 155
HA2: Harr 6E 40
Alfriston Cl. KT5: Surb 5F 151
Alfriston Rd. SW11 5D 118
Algar Cl. HA7: Stan 5E 26
TW7: Isle 3A 114
Algar Ho. SE1 7A 14
Algar Rd. TW7: Isle 3A 114
Algarve Rd. SW18 1K 135
Algernon Rd. NW4 6C 44
NW6 1J 81
SE13 4D 122
Algiers Rd. SE13 4C 122
Alibon Gdns. RM10: Dag 5G 73
Alibon Rd. RM9: Dag 5F 73
RM10: Dag 5F 73
Alice Cl. *EN5: New Bar* *4F 21*
(off Station App.)
Alice Gilliatt Ct. *W14* *6H 99*
(off Star Rd.)
Alice La. E3 1B 86
Alice M. TW11: Tedd 5K 131
Alice Owen Technology Cen. *EC1* *1A 8*
(off Goswell Rd.)
Alice Shepherd Ho. *E14* *2E 104*
(off Manchester Rd.)
Alice St. SE1 3E 102
(not continuous)
Alice Thompson Cl. SE12 2A 142
Alice Walker Cl. SE24 4B 120
Alice Way TW3: Houn 4F 113
Alicia Av. HA3: Kenton 4B 42
Alicia Cl. HA3: Kenton 4C 42
Alicia Gdns. HA3: Kenton 4B 42
Alicia Ho. DA16: Well 1B 126
Alie St. E1 1K 15 (6F 85)
Alington Cres. NW9 7J 43
Alington Gro.
SM6: W'gton 7G 167
Alison Cl. CR0: C'don 1K 169
E6 6E 88
HA5: Eastc 6K 39
Alissa Dr. EN5: New Bar 5F 21
Aliwal M. SW11 4C 118
Aliwal Rd. SW11 4C 118
Alkerden Rd. W4 5A 98
Alkham Rd. N16 2F 67
Allan Barclay Cl. N15 6F 49
Allan Cl. KT3: N Mald 5K 151
Allandale Av. N3 3G 45
Allanson Ct. *E10* *2C 68*
(off Leyton Grange Est.)
Allan Way W3 5J 79
Allard Cres. WD23: B Hea 1B 26
Allard Gdns. SW4 5H 119
Allard Ho. *NW9* *2B 44*
(off Boulevard Dr.)
Allardyce St. SW4 4K 119
Allbrook Cl. TW11: Tedd 5J 131
Allcroft Rd. NW5 5E 64
Allder Way CR2: S Croy 7B 168
Allenby Cl. UB6: G'frd 3E 76
Allenby Rd. SE23 3A 140
SE28 3G 107
UB1: S'hall 3E 76
Allen Cl. CR4: Mitc 1F 155
TW16: Sun 1K 147
Allen Ct. *E17* *6C 50*
(off Yunus Khan Cl.)
Allendale Av. UB1: S'hall 6E 76
Allendale Cl. SE5 2D 120
SE26 5K 139
Allendale Rd. HA0: Wemb 6B 60
UB6: G'frd 6B 60
Allen Edwards Dr. SW8 1J 119
Allenford Ho. *SW15* *6B 116*
(off Tunworth Cres.)
Allen Ho. *W8* *3J 99*
(off Allen St.)
Allen Mans. *W8* *3J 99*
(off Allen St.)
Allen Rd. BR3: Beck 2K 157
CR0: C'don 1A 168
E3 2B 86
N16 4E 66
TW16: Sun 1K 147
Allensbury Pl. NW1 7H 65
Allens Rd. EN3: Pond E 5D 24
Allen St. W8 3J 99
Allenswood SW19 1G 135
Allenswood Rd. SE9 3C 124
Allerford Ct. HA2: Harr 5G 41
Allerford Rd. SE6 3D 140
Allerton Ho. *N1* *1E 8*
(off Provost St.)
Allerton Rd. N16 2C 66
Allerton St. N1 1E 8 (3D 84)
Allerton Wlk. N7 2K 65
Allestree Rd. SW6 7G 99
Alleyn Cres. SE21 2D 138
Alleyndale Rd. RM8: Dag 2C 72
Alleyn Ho. *SE1* *3D 102*
(off Burbage Cl.)
Alleyn Pk. SE21 2D 138
UB2: S'hall 5E 94
Alleyn Rd. SE21 3D 138
Alley Way UB8: Uxb 7A 56
Allfarthing La. SW18 6K 117
Allgood Cl. SM4: Mord 6F 153
Allgood St. E2 1K 9 (2F 85)
All Hallows by the Tower Church
3H 15 (7E 84)
Allhallows La. EC4 3E 14 (7D 84)
All Hallows Rd. N17 1E 48
Allhallows Rd. E6 5C 88
Alliance Cl. HA0: Wemb 4D 60
TW4: Houn 5D 112
Alliance Ct. TW15: Ashf 4E 128
W3 5H 79
Alliance Rd. E13 5A 88
SE18 6A 108
W3 4H 79
Allianz Park 7K 29
Allied Ct. *N1* *7E 66*
(off Enfield Rd.)
Allied Ind. Est. W3 2A 98
Allied Way W3 2A 98
Allingham Cl. W7 7K 77
Allingham Ct. BR2: Broml 4H 159
Allingham M. *N1* *2C 84*
(off Allingham St.)
Allingham Rd. SW4 6H 119
Allingham St. N1 2C 84
Allington Av. N17 6K 33
TW17: Shep 3G 147
Allington Cl. SW19 5F 135
UB6: G'frd 7G 59
Allington Ct. *CR0: C'don* *6J 157*
(off Chart Cl.)
EN3: Pond E 5E 24
SW8 2G 119
Allington Rd. BR6: Orp 2H 173
HA2: Harr 5G 41
NW4 5D 44
W10 3G 81
Allington St. SW1 2A 18 (3F 101)
Allison Cl. SE10 1E 122
Allison Gro. SE21 1E 138
Allison Rd. N8 5A 48
W3 6J 79
Alliston Ho. *E2* *2K 9*
(off Gibraltar Wlk.)
Allitsen Rd. NW8 2C 82
(not continuous)
All Nations Ho. *E8* *7H 67*
(off Martello St.)
Allnutt Way SW4 5H 119
Alloa Rd. IG3: Ilf 2A 72
SE8 5K 103
Allom Ho. *W11* *7G 81*
(off Clarendon Rd.)
Allonby Dr. HA4: Ruis 7D 38
Allonby Gdns. HA9: Wemb 1C 60
Allotment Way NW2 3F 63
Alloway Rd. E3 3A 86
Alloy Ho. *SE14* *6B 104*
(off Moulding La.)
Allport Ho. *SE5* *3D 120*
(off Champion Pk.)
Allport M. *E1* *4J 85*
(off Hayfield Pas.)
All Saints Cl. N9 2B 34
SW8 1J 119
All Saint's Ct. *TW5: Hest* *1B 112*
(off Springwell Rd.)
All Saints Ct. *E1* *7J 85*
(off Johnson St.)
SW11 *7F 101*
(off Prince of Wales Dr.)
All Saints Dr. SE3 2G 123
(not continuous)
All Saints Ho. *W11* *5H 81*
(off All Saints Rd.)
All Saints M. HA3: Hrw W 6D 26
All Saints Pas. SW18 5J 117
All Saints Rd. SM1: Sutt 3K 165
SW19 7A 136
(not continuous)
W3 3J 97
W11 5H 81
All Saints St. N1 2K 83
All Saints Wlk. SE15 7F 103
Allsop Pl. NW1 4F 5 (4D 82)
All Souls Av. NW10 2D 80
All Souls' Pl. W1 6K 5 (5F 83)
Allum Way N20 1F 31
Alluvium Ct. *SE1* *7G 15*
(off Long La.)
Allwood Cl. SE26 4K 139
Alma Av. E4 7K 35
Alma Birk Ho. NW6 7G 63
Almack Rd. E5 4J 67
Alma Cl. N10 1F 47
Alma Ct. HA2: Harr 2H 59
Alma Cres. SM1: Sutt 5G 165
Alma Gro. SE1 4F 103
Alma Ho. N9 4B 34
TW8: Bford 6E 96
Almanza Pl. IG11: Bark 2B 90
Alma Pl. CR7: Thor H 5A 156
NW10 3D 80
SE19 7F 139
Alma Rd. DA14: Sidc 3A 144
EN3: Enf H, Pond E 5F 25
KT10: Esh 7J 149
N10 7A 32
SM5: Cars 5C 166
SW18 4A 118
UB1: S'hall 7C 76
Alma Rd. Ind. Est. EN3: Pond E 4E 24
Alma Row HA3: Hrw W 1H 41
Alma Sq. NW8 2A 82
Alma St. E15 6F 69
NW5 6F 65
Alma Ter. *E3* *1B 86*
(off Beale Rd.)
SW18 7B 118
W8 3J 99
Almeida St. N1 1B 84
Almeida Theatre *1B 84*
(off Almeida St.)
Almeric Rd. SW11 4D 118
Almer Rd. SW20 7C 134
Almington St. N4 1K 65
Almond Av. SM5: Cars 2D 166
UB7: W Dray 3C 92
UB10: Ick 3D 56
W5 3D 96
Almond Cl. BR2: Broml 7E 160
E17 4A 50
HA4: Ruis 3H 57
SE15 2G 121
TW13: Felt 1J 129
TW17: Shep 2E 146
UB3: Hayes 7G 75
Almond Gro. TW8: Bford 7B 96
Almond Ho. *E15* *3G 87*
(off Teasel Way)
Almond Rd. N17 7B 34
SE16 4H 103
Almonds Av. IG9: Buck H 2D 36
Almond Way BR2: Broml 7E 160
CR4: Mitc 5H 155
HA2: Harr 2F 41
Almorah Rd. N1 7D 66
TW5: Hest 1B 112
Almshouse La. KT9: Chess 7C 162
The Alms Ho's. IG11: Bark 6G 71
Al-Nehar Mosque *2K 83*
(off Caledonian Rd.)
Alnmouth Ct. *UB1: S'hall* *6G 77*
(off Fleming Rd.)
Alnwick N17 7C 34
Alnwick Gro. SM4: Mord 4K 153
Alnwick Rd. E16 6A 88
SE12 6K 123
ALPERTON 2E 78
Alperton La. HA0: Wemb 3C 78
UB6: G'frd 3C 78
Alperton St. W10 4H 81
Alphabet Gdns. SM5: Cars 6B 154
Alphabet M. SW9 1A 120
Alphabet Sq. E3 5C 86
Alpha Cl. NW1 2D 4 (4C 82)
Alpha Est. UB3: Hayes 2G 93
Alpha Gro. E14 2C 104
Alpha Ho. NW6 2J 81
NW8 4D 4
SW4 4K 119
Alpha Pl. NW6 2J 81
SM4: Mord 1F 165
SW3 7D 16 (6C 100)
Alpha Rd. CR0: C'don 1E 168
E4 3H 35
EN3: Pond E 4F 25
KT5: Surb 6F 151
N18 6B 34
SE14 1B 122
TW11: Tedd 5H 131
UB10: Hil 4D 74
Alpha St. SE15 2G 121
Alphea Cl. SW19 7C 136
Alpine Av. KT5: Surb 2J 163
Alpine Bus. Cen. E6 5E 88
Alpine Cl. CR0: C'don 3E 168
KT19: Ewe 5J 163
Alpine Copse BR1: Broml 2E 160
Alpine Gro. E9 7J 67
Alpine Rd. E10 2D 68
KT12: Walt T 7J 147
NW9 4G 43
SE16 5K 103
Alpine Vw. SM5: Cars 5C 166
Alpine Wlk. HA7: Stan 2D 26
Alpine Way E6 5E 88
Alric Av. KT3: N Mald 3A 152
NW10 7K 61
Alroy Rd. N4 7A 48
Alsace Rd. SE17 5E 102
Alscot Rd. SE1 4F 103
Alscot Way SE1 4F 103

Alsike Rd.—Anchor & Hope La.

Alsike Rd. DA18: Erith 3D 108
SE2 3D 108
Alsom Av. KT4: Wor Pk 4C 164
Alston Cl. KT6: Surb 7B 150
Alston Rd. EN5: Barn 3B 20
N18 5C 34
SW17 4B 136
Alston Works EN5: Barn 2B 20
Altair Cl. N17 6A 34
Altash Way SE9 2D 142
Altenburg Av. W13 3B 96
Altenburg Gdns. SW11 4D 118
Alt Gro. SW19 7H 135
Altham Ct. HA2: Harr 1F 41
Altham Rd. HA5: Pinn 1C 40
Althea St. SW6 2K 117
Althorne Gdns. E18 4H 51
Althorne Way RM10: Dag 2G 73
Althorp Cl. EN5: Ark 1H 29
Althorpe M. SW11 1B 118
Althorpe Rd. HA1: Harr 5G 41
Althorp Rd. SW17 1D 136
Altima Ct. *SE22* *4G 121*
(off E. Dulwich Rd.)
Altior Ct. N6 6G 47
Altissima Ho. SW11 7F 101
Altitude Apts. *CR0: C'don* *3D 168*
(off Altyre Rd.)
Altitude Point *E1* *6G 85*
(off Alie St.)
Altius Apts. *E3* *2C 86*
(off Wick La.)
Altius Ct. E4 6K 35
Altius Wlk. E20 6E 68
Altmore Av. E6 7D 70
Alton Av. HA7: Stan 7E 26
Alton Cl. DA5: Bexl 1E 144
TW7: Isle 2K 113
Alton Gdns. BR3: Beck 7C 140
TW2: Whitt 7H 113
Alton Ho. *E3* *3D 86*
(off Bromley High St.)
Alton Rd. CR0: Wadd 3A 168
N17 3D 48
SW15 1C 134
TW9: Rich 4E 114
Alton St. E14 5D 86
Altura Twr. SW11 2B 118
Altus Ho. SE6 4E 140
Altyre Cl. BR3: Beck 5B 158
Altyre Rd. CR0: C'don 2D 168
Altyre Way BR3: Beck 5B 158
Aluna Ct. SE15 3J 121
Alvanley Gdns. NW6 5K 63
Alverstone Av. EN4: E Barn 7H 21
SW19 2J 135
Alverstone Gdns. SE9 1G 143
Alverstone Ho. SE11 7J 19 (6A 102)
Alverstone Rd. E12 4E 70
HA9: Wemb 1F 61
KT3: N Mald 4B 152
NW2 7E 62
Alverston Gdns. SE25 5E 156
Alverton St. SE8 5B 104
(not continuous)
Alveston Av. HA3: Kenton 3B 42
Alveston Sq. E18 2J 51
Alvey St. SE17 5E 102
Alvia Gdns. SM1: Sutt 4A 166
Alvington Cres. E8 5F 67
Alway Av. KT19: Ewe 5K 163
Alwold Cres. SE12 6K 123
Alwyn Av. W4 5K 97
Alwyn Cl. CR0: New Ad 7D 170
Alwyne La. N1 7B 66
Alwyne Pl. N1 6C 66
Alwyne Rd. N1 7C 66
SW19 6H 135
W7 7J 77
Alwyne Sq. N1 6C 66
Alwyne Vs. N1 7B 66
Alwyn Gdns. NW4 4C 44
W3 6H 79
Alyth Gdns. NW11 6J 45
Alzette Ho. *E2* *2K 85*
(off Mace St.)
Amalgamated Dr. TW8: Bford 6B 96
Amanda Ct. *TW15: Ashf* *2B 128*
(off Edward Way)
Amanda M. RM7: Rom 5J 55
Amar Ct. SE18 4K 107
Amar Deep Ct. SE18 5K 107
Amarelle Apts. *CR0: C'don* *1D 168*
(off Cherry Orchard Rd.)
Amazon Bldg. N8 4K 47
Amazon St. E1 6G 85
Ambassador Bldg. SW11 6H 101
Ambassador Cl. TW3: Houn 2C 112
Ambassador Gdns. E6 5D 88
Ambassador Ho. *CR7: Lon, Thor H* *4C 156*
(off Brigstock Rd.)
NW8 1A 82
Ambassadors Court 7A 12
Ambassador's Ct. SW1 5B 12
Ambassadors Ct. *E8* *7F 67*
(off Holly St.)
Ambassador Sq. E14 4D 104
Ambassadors Theatre *1D 12*
(off West St.)
Amber Av. E17 1A 50
Amber Cl. EN5: New Bar 6E 20
Amber Ct. CR0: C'don 1E 168
E15 *1E 86*
(off Warton Rd.)
KT5: Surb 7F 151
N7 *6A 66*
(off Bride St.)
SW17 *4E 136*
(off Brudenell Rd.)
Amberden Av. N3 3J 45
Ambergate St. SE17 5B 102
Amber Gro. NW2 1F 63
Amber Ho. *E1* *6K 85*
(off Aylward St.)
Amberley Cl. BR6: Chels 5K 173
HA5: Pinn 3D 40
Amberley Ct. BR3: Beck 7B 140
DA14: Sidc 5C 144
Amberley Gdns. EN1: Enf 7K 23
KT19: Ewe 4B 164
Amberley Gro. CR0: C'don 7F 157
SE26 5H 139
Amberley Rd. E10 7C 50
EN1: Enf 7A 24
IG9: Buck H 1F 37
N13 2E 32
SE2 6D 108
W9 5J 81
Amberley Way RM7: Mawney 4H 55
SM4: Mord 7H 153
TW4: Houn 5A 112
UB10: Uxb 2A 74
Amberlith Ho. *CR7: Thor H* *5A 156*
(off Thornton Rd.)
Amber M. *N22* *3A 48*
(off High Rd.)
Amberside Cl. TW7: Isle 6H 113
Amber Way W3 2A 98
Amber Wharf *E2* *1F 85*
(off Nursery La.)
Amberwood Cl. SM6: W'gton 5J 167
Amberwood Ri. KT3: N Mald 6A 152
Amblecote Cl. SE12 3K 141
Amblecote Mdws. SE12 3K 141
Amblecote Rd. SE12 3K 141
Ambler Rd. N4 3B 66
Ambleside BR1: Broml 6F 141
NW1 1K 5
SW19 1G 135
Ambleside Av. BR3: Beck 5A 158
KT12: Walt T 7A 148
SW16 4H 137
Ambleside Cl. E9 5J 67
E10 7D 50
N17 3F 49
Ambleside Cres. EN3: Enf H 3E 24
Ambleside Dr. TW14: Felt 1H 129
Ambleside Gdns.
HA9: Wemb 1D 60
IG4: Ilf 4C 52
SM2: Sutt 6A 166
SW16 5H 137
Ambleside Point *SE15* *7J 103*
(off Tustin Est.)
Ambleside Rd. DA7: Bex 2G 127
NW10 7B 62
Ambleside Wlk. UB8: Uxb 1A 74
Ambrook Rd. DA17: Belv 3G 109
Ambrosden Av. SW1 2B 18 (3G 101)
Ambrose Av. NW11 7G 45
Ambrose Cl. BR6: Orp 3K 173
E6 5D 88
Ambrose Ct. *N18* *6A 34*
(off Cannon Rd.)
Ambrose Ho. *E14* *5C 86*
(off Selsey St.)
Ambrose M. SW11 2D 118
Ambrose St. SE16 4H 103
Ambrose Wlk. E3 2C 86
Ambulance Rd. E11 5F 51
AMC Bus. Cen. NW10 3H 79
Amelia Cl. TW4: Houn 1C 130
W3 1H 97
Amelia Ho. *E14* *6G 87*
(off Lyell St.)
NW9 *2B 44*
(off Boulevard Dr.)
TW9: Kew 7H 97
W6 *5E 98*
(off Queen Caroline St.)
Amelia Mans. *E20* *6D 68*
(off Olympic Pk. Av.)
Amelia St. SE17 5C 102
Amen Cnr. EC4 1B 14 (6B 84)
SW17 6D 136
Amen Ct. EC4 1B 14 (6B 84)
Amenity Way SM4: Mord 7E 152
The American International
University in London
Kensington Campus,
Ansdell Street *3K 99*
(off Ansdell St.)
St Albans Grove 3K 99
Young Street 2K 99
Richmond Hill Campus 7E 114
The American University of London
3K 65
America Sq. EC3 2J 15 (7F 85)
America St. SE1 5C 14 (1C 102)
Amerland Rd. SW18 5H 117
Amersham Av. N18 6J 33
Amersham Gro. SE14 7B 104
Amersham Rd. CR0: C'don 6C 156
SE14 1B 122
Amersham Va. SE14 7B 104
Amery Gdns. NW10 1E 80
Amery Ho. *SE17* *5E 102*
(off Kinglake St.)
Amery Rd. HA1: Harr 2A 60
Amesbury Av. SW2 2J 137
Amesbury Cl. KT4: Wor Pk 1E 164
Amesbury Ct. EN2: Enf 2F 23
Amesbury Dr. E4 6J 25
Amesbury Rd. BR1: Broml 3B 160
RM9: Dag 7D 72
TW13: Felt 2B 130
Amesbury Twr. SW8 2G 119
Ames Cotts. *E14* *5A 86*
(off Maroon St.)
Ames Ho. *E2* *2K 85*
(off Mace St.)
Amethyst Cl. N11 7C 32
Amethyst Ct. *BR6: Chels* *5J 173*
(off Farnborough Hill)
EN3: Enf H *3F 25*
(off Enstone Rd.)
Amethyst Rd. E15 4F 69
Amherst Av. W13 6C 78
Amherst Dr. BR5: St M Cry 4K 161
Amherst Gdns. *W13* *6C 78*
(off Amherst Rd.)
Amherst Ho. *SE16* *2K 103*
(off Wolfe Cres.)
Amherst Rd. W13 6C 78
Amhurst Gdns. TW7: Isle 2A 114
Amhurst Pde. *N16* *7F 49*
(off Amhurst Pk.)
Amhurst Pk. N16 7D 48
Amhurst Pas. E8 4G 67
Amhurst Rd. E8 5H 67
N16 4F 67
Amhurst Ter. E8 4G 67
Amhurst Wlk. SE28 1A 108
Amias Dr. HA8: Edg 4K 27
Amias Ho. *EC1* *3C 8*
(off Central St.)
Amidas Gdns. RM8: Dag 4B 72
Amiel St. E1 4J 85
Amies St. SW11 3D 118
Amigo Ho. *SE1* *1K 19*
(off Morley St.)
Amina Way SE16 3G 103
Amiot Ho. *NW9* *2B 44*
(off Heritage Av.)
Amis Av. KT19: Ewe 6H 163
Amisha Ct. *SE1* *3F 103*
(off Grange Rd.)
Amity Gro. SW20 1D 152
Amity Rd. E15 7H 69
Ammanford Grn. NW9 6A 44
Ammonite Ho. E15 7H 69
Amner Rd. SW11 6E 118
Amor Rd. W6 3E 98
Amory Ho. *N1* *1K 83*
(off Barnsbury Est.)
Amott Rd. SE15 3G 121
Amoy Pl. E14 7C 86
(not continuous)
Ampere Way CR0: Wadd 7J 155
Ampleforth Rd. SE2 2B 108
Amport Pl. NW7 6B 30
Ampthill Est. NW1 1B 6 (2G 83)
Ampthill Sq. NW1 1B 6 (2G 83)
Ampton Pl. WC1 2G 7 (3K 83)
Ampton St. WC1 2G 7 (3K 83)
Amroth Cl. SE23 1H 139
Amroth Grn. NW9 6A 44
Amstel Ct. SE15 7F 103
Amsterdam Rd. E14 3E 104
Amundsen Ct. *E14* *5C 104*
(off Napier Av.)
Amundsen Ho. *NW10* *7K 61*
(off Stonebridge Pk.)
Amwell Cl. EN2: Enf 5J 23
Amwell Ct. Est. N4 2C 66
Amwell Ho. *WC1* *1J 7*
(off Cruikshank St.)
Amwell St. EC1 1J 7 (3A 84)
Amyand Cotts. TW1: Twick 6B 114
Amyand La. TW1: Twick 7B 114
Amyand Pk. Gdns. TW1: Twick 7B 114
Amyand Pk. Rd. TW1: Twick 7A 114
Amy Cl. SM6: W'gton 7J 167
Amy Johnson Ct. HA8: Edg 2H 43
Amyruth Rd. SE4 5C 122
Amy Warne Cl. E6 4C 88
Anastasia M. N12 5E 30
Anatola Rd. N19 2G 65
Anayah Apts. *SE8* *5K 103*
(off Trundleys Rd.)
Ancaster Cres. KT3: N Mald 6C 152
Ancaster M. BR3: Beck 3K 157
Ancaster Rd. BR3: Beck 3K 157
Ancaster St. SE18 7J 107
Anchor SW18 4K 117
Anchorage Cl. SW19 5J 135
Anchorage Ho. *E14* *7F 87*
(off Clove Cres.)
Anchorage Point *E14* *2B 104*
(off Cuba St.)
Anchorage Point Ind. Est. SE7 3A 106
Anchor & Hope La. SE7 3K 105

182 A-Z London

Anchor Brewhouse—Antigua M.

Anchor Brewhouse SE1 . . . .5J 15 (1F 103)
Anchor Bus. Cen. CR0: Bedd 3J 167
Anchor Cl. IG11: Bark 3B 90
Anchor Ct. EN1: Enf 5K 23
SW1 . . . .*4C 18*
(off Vauxhall Bri. Rd.)
Anchor Dr. N15 . . . . .4E 48
Anchor Ho. *E16* *5H 87*
(off Barking Rd.)
E16 . . . .*6A 88*
(off Prince Regent La.)
EC1 . . . .*3C 8*
(off Old St.)
SW10 . . . .*6B 100*
(off Cremorne Est.)
Anchor Iron Wharf SE10 . . . . .5F 105
Anchor M. N1 . . . . .6E 66
SW12 .6F 119
Anchor Retail Pk.
Stepney Green 4J 85
Anchor St. SE16 . . . . .4H 103
Anchor Ter. E1 . . . . .4J 85
SE1 . . . .*4D 14*
(off Southwark Bri. Rd.)
Anchor Wharf *E3* *5D 86*
(off Yeo St.)
Anchor Yd. EC1 . . . . .3D 8 (4C 84)
Ancill Cl. W6 . . . . .6G 99
Ancona Rd. NW10 . . . . .2C 80
SE18 .5H 107
Andace Pk. Gdns.
BR1: Broml 1A 160
Andalus Rd. SW9 . . . . .3J 119
Ander Cl. HA0: Wemb 4D 60
Anderson Cl. N21 . . . . .5E 22
SM3: Sutt 1J 165
W3 . . . . .6K 79
Anderson Ct. NW2 . . . . .1E 62
Anderson Dr. TW15: Ashf 4E 128
Anderson Hgts. SW16 . . . . .2K 155
Anderson Ho. *E14* *7E 86*
(off Woolmore St.)
IG11: Bark 1H 89
SW17 .5B 136
Anderson Pl. TW3: Houn 4F 113
Anderson Rd. E9 . . . . .6K 67
IG8: Wfd G 3B 52
SE3 . . . . .4K 123
Anderson Sq. *N1* *1B 84*
(off Gaskin St.)
Anderson St. SW3 . . . . . . .5E 16 (5D 100)
Anderson Way DA17: Belv 2H 109
Anderton Cl. SE5 . . . . .3D 120
Anderton Ct. N22 . . . . .2H 47
Andora Ct. *NW6* *7G 63*
(off Brondesbury Pk.)
Andora Ho. E10 . . . . .1A 68
Andorra Ct. BR1: Broml 1A 160
Andover Av. E16 . . . . .6B 88
Andover Cl. TW14: Felt 1H 129
UB6: G'frd 4F 77
Andover Ct. *E2* *4H 85*
(off Thee Colts La.)
TW19: Stanw 7A 110
Andover Pl. NW6 . . . . .2K 81
Andover Rd. BR6: Orp 1H 173
N7 . . . . .2K 65
TW2: Twick 1H 131
Andoversford Ct. *SE15* *6E 102*
(off Bibury Cl.)
Andover Ter. *W6* *4D 98*
(off Raynham Rd.)
Andreck Ct. *BR3: Beck* *2E 158*
(off Crescent Rd.)
Andre St. E8 . . . . .5G 67
Andrew Cl. DA1: Cray 5K 127
Andrew Ct. SE23 . . . . .2K 139
Andrewes Gdns. E6 . . . . .6C 88
Andrewes Highwalk EC2 . . . . .6D 8
Andrewes Ho. EC2 . . . . .6D 8
SM1: Sutt 4J 165
The Andrew Gibb Memorial 1H 123
Andrew Pl. SW8 . . . . .7H 101
Andrew Reed Ho. *SW18* *7G 117*
(off Linstead Way)
Andrews Cl. HA1: Harr 7H 41
IG9: Buck H 2F 37
KT4: Wor Pk 2E 164
Andrews Crosse WC2 . . . . .1J 13
Andrews Ga. TW17: Shep 2E 146
Andrew's Ho. CR2: S Croy 6C 168
Andrews Ho. *NW3* *7D 64*
(off Fellows Rd.)
Andrews Pl. DA2: Wilm 2K 145
SE9 . . . . .6F 125
Andrew's Rd. E8 . . . . .1H 85
Andrew St. E14 . . . . .6E 86
Andrews Wlk. SE17 . . . . .6B 102
Andringham Lodge *BR1: Broml* *1K 159*
(off Palace Gro.)
Andrula Ct. N22 . . . . .1B 48
Andwell Cl. SE2 . . . . .2B 108
ANERLEY 1H 157
Anerley Gro. SE19 . . . . .7F 139
Anerley Hill SE19 . . . . .6F 139
Anerley Pk. SE20 . . . . .7G 139
Anerley Pk. Rd. SE20 . . . . .7H 139
Anerley Rd. SE19 . . . . .7G 139
SE20 .7G 139
Anerley Sta. Rd. SE20 . . . . .1H 157
Anerley St. SW11 . . . . .2D 118
Anerley Va. SE19 . . . . .7F 139
Aneurin Bevan Ct. NW2 . . . . .2D 62
Aneurin Bevan Ho. N11 . . . . .7C 32
Anfield Cl. SW12 . . . . .7G 119
ANGEL 2A 84
Angela Carter Cl. SW9 . . . . .3A 120
Angela Davies Ind. Est. SE24 . . . . .4B 120
Angela Hooper Pl. *SW1* *1B 18*
(off Victoria St.)
Angel All. E1 . . . . .7K 9
Angel Bldg. N1 . . . . .1K 7 (2A 84)
Angel Cl. N18 . . . . .5A 34
TW12: Hamp H 5G 131
Angel Cnr. Pde. N18 . . . . .4B 34
Angel Ct. E15 . . . . .6F 69
EC2 . . . . .7F 9 (6D 84)
SW1 . . . . .5B 12 (1G 101)
ANGEL EDMONTON 5B 34
Angelfield TW3: Houn 4F 113
Angel Ga. EC1 . . . . .1B 8 (3B 84)
(not continuous)
Angel Hill SM1: Sutt 3K 165
Angel Hill Dr. SM1: Sutt 3K 165
Angel Ho. *E3* *3C 86*
(off Campbell Rd.)
Angelica Cl. UB7: Yiew 6A 74
Angelica Dr. E6 . . . . .5E 88
Angelica Gdns. CR0: C'don 1K 169
Angelica Ho. *E3* *1B 86*
(off Sycamore Av.)
Angelina Ho. *SE15* *1G 121*
(off Goldsmith Rd.)
Angelis Apts. *N1* *1B 8*
(off Graham St.)
Angel La. E15 . . . . .6F 69
EC4 . . . . .3E 14 (7D 84)
UB3: Hayes 5F 75
Angell Pk. Gdns. SW9 . . . . .3A 120
Angell Rd. SW9 . . . . .3A 120
ANGELL TOWN 1A 120
Angell Town Est. SW9 . . . . .2A 120
Angel M. E1 . . . . .7H 85
N1 . . . . .2A 84
SW15 .7C 116
Angelo M. SW16 . . . . .3K 155
Angel Pl. N18 . . . . .4B 34
SE1 . . . . .6E 14 (2D 102)
Angel Rd. HA1: Harr 6J 41
KT7: T Ditt 7A 150
N18 . . . . .5B 34
Angel Rd. Works N18 . . . . .5D 34
Angel Sq. EC1 . . . . .2B 84
Angel St. EC1 . . . . .7C 8 (6C 84)
Angel Wlk. W6 . . . . .4E 98
Angel Way RM1: Rom 5K 55
Angel Wharf N1 . . . . .2C 84
Angel Yd. N6 . . . . .1E 64
Angerstein Bus. Pk. SE10 . . . . .4J 105
Angerstein La. SE3 . . . . .1H 123
Anglais M. *NW9* *4A 44*
(off Colin Cl.)
Anglebury *W2* *6J 81*
(off Talbot Rd.)
Angle Cl. UB10: Hil 1C 74
Angle Grn. RM8: Dag 1C 72
The Anglers *KT1: King T* *3D 150*
(off High St.)
Anglers Cl. TW10: Ham 4C 132
Angler's La. NW5 . . . . .6F 65
Anglers Reach KT6: Surb 5D 150
Anglesea Av. SE18 . . . . .4F 107
Anglesea Ho. *KT1: King T* *4D 150*
(off Anglesea Rd.)
Anglesea M. SE18 . . . . .4F 107
Anglesea Rd. KT1: King T 4D 150
SE18 .4F 107
Anglesea Ter. *W6* *3D 98*
(off Wellesley Av.)
Anglesey Cl. TW15: Ashf 3C 128
Anglesey Ct. Rd. SM5: Cars 6E 166
Anglesey Gdns. SM5: Cars 6E 166
Anglesey Ho. *E14* *6C 86*
(off Lindfield St.)
Anglesey Rd. EN3: Pond E 4C 24
Anglesmede Cres. HA5: Pinn 3E 40
Anglesmede Way HA5: Pinn 3E 40
Angles Rd. SW16 . . . . .4J 137
Anglia Cl. N17 . . . . .7C 34
Anglia Ct. *RM8: Dag* *1D 72*
(off Spring Cl.)
Anglia Ho. *E14* *6A 86*
(off Salmon La.)
Anglian Ind. Est. IG11: Bark 4K 89
Anglian Rd. E11 . . . . .3F 69
Anglia Wlk. *E6* *1E 88*
(off Napier Rd.)
Anglo Rd. E3 . . . . .2B 86
Angora Cl. SM6: W'gton 2E 166
Angrave Ct. *E8* *1F 85*
(off Scriven St.)
Angrave Pas. E8 . . . . .1F 85
Angus Cl. KT9: Chess 5G 163
Angus Dr. HA4: Ruis 4A 58
Angus Gdns. NW9 . . . . .1K 43
Angus Ho. SW2 . . . . .7H 119
Angus Rd. E13 . . . . .3A 88
Angus St. SE14 . . . . .7A 104
Anhalt Rd. SW11 . . . . .7C 100
Ankerdine Cres. SE18 . . . . .7F 107
Anlaby Rd. TW11: Tedd 5J 131
Anley Rd. W14 . . . . .2F 99
Anmersh Gro. HA7: Stan 1D 42
Annabel Cl. E14 . . . . .6D 86
Annabels M. W5 . . . . .4D 78
Anna Cl. E8 . . . . .1F 85
Annandale Gro. UB10: Ick 3E 56
Annandale Rd. CR0: C'don 2G 169
DA15: Sidc 7J 125
SE10 .6H 105
W4 . . . . .5A 98
Anna Neagle Cl. E7 . . . . .4J 69
Annan Way RM1: Rom 1K 55
Anne Boleyn Ct. SE9 . . . . .6G 125
Anne Boleyn's Wlk.
KT2: King T 5E 132
SM3: Cheam 7F 165
Anne Case M. KT3: N Mald 3K 151
Anne Compton M. SE12 . . . . .7H 123
Anne Goodman Ho. *E1* *6J 85*
(off Jubilee St.)
Anne Matthews Ct. *E14* *5C 86*
(off Selsey St.)
Anne M. IG11: Bark 7G 71
Anne of Cleeves Ct. SE9 . . . . .6H 125
Annes Ct. NW1 . . . . .3D 4
Annesley Apts. *E3* *5C 86*
(off Gresham Pl.)
Annesley Av. NW9 . . . . .3K 43
Annesley Cl. NW10 . . . . .3A 62
Annesley Dr. CR0: C'don 3B 170
Annesley Ho. SW9 . . . . .1A 120
Annesley Pl. BR2: Broml 6C 160
Annesley Rd. SE3 . . . . .1K 123
Annesley Wlk. N19 . . . . .2G 65
Annesmere Gdns. SE3 . . . . .3B 124
Anne St. E13 . . . . .4J 87
Anne Sutherland Ho.
BR3: Beck 7K 139
Annett Cl. TW17: Shep 4G 147
Annette Cl. HA3: W'stone 2J 41
Annette Cres. N1 . . . . .7C 66
Annette Rd. N7 . . . . .3K 65
(not continuous)
Annett Rd. KT12: Walt T 7J 147
Anne Way KT8: W Mole 4F 149
Annexe Mkt. *E1* *5J 9*
(off Spital Sq.)
Annie Besant Cl. E3 . . . . .1B 86
Annie Taylor Ho. *E12* *4E 70*
(off Walton Rd.)
Anning St. EC2 . . . . .3H 9 (4E 84)
Annington Rd. N2 . . . . .3D 46
Annis Rd. E9 . . . . .6A 68
Ann La. SW10 . . . . .6B 100
Ann Moss Way SE16 . . . . .3J 103
Ann's Cl. SW1 . . . . .7F 11
Ann's Pl. E1 .6J 9
Ann St. N1 .1C 84
SE18 .5G 107
(not continuous)
Ann Stroud Ct. SE12 . . . . .5J 123
Annsworthy Av. CR7: Thor H 3D 156
Annsworthy Cres. SE25 . . . . .2D 156
Ansar Gdns. E17 . . . . .5B 50
Ansdell Rd. SE15 . . . . .2J 121
Ansdell St. W8 . . . . .3K 99
Ansdell Ter. W8 . . . . .3K 99
Ansell Gro. SM5: Cars 1E 166
Ansell Ho. *E1* *5J 85*
(off Mile End Rd.)
Ansell Rd. SW17 . . . . .3C 136
Anselm Cl. CR0: C'don 3F 169
Anselm Rd. HA5: Hat E 1D 40
SW6 . . . . .6J 99
Ansford Rd. BR1: Broml 5E 140
Ansleigh Pl. W11 . . . . .7F 81
Anson Cl. RM7: Mawney 2H 55
Anson Ho. *E1* *4A 86*
(off Shandy St.)
SW1 . . . .*7A 18*
(off Churchill Gdns.)
Anson M. SW19 . . . . .7J 135
Anson Pl. SE28 . . . . .2H 107
Anson Rd. N7 . . . . .4G 65
NW2 . . . . .4D 62
Anson Ter. UB5: N'olt 6F 59
Anstey Ct. W3 . . . . .2H 97
Anstey Ho. *E9* *1J 85*
(off Templecombe Rd.)
Anstey Rd. SE15 . . . . .3G 121
Anstey Wlk. N15 . . . . .4B 48
Anstice Cl. W4 . . . . .7A 98
Anstridge Path SE9 . . . . .6H 125
Anstridge Rd. SE9 . . . . .6H 125
Antelope Rd. SE18 . . . . .3D 106
Antelope Wlk. KT6: Surb 5D 150
Antenor Ho. *E2* *2H 85*
(off Old Bethnal Grn. Rd.)
Anthems Way E20 . . . . .6D 68
Anthony Cl. NW7 . . . . .4F 29
Anthony Cope Ct. *N1* *1F 9*
(off Chart St.)
Anthony Ct. W3 . . . . .2A 98
Anthony Ho. *NW8* *4C 4*
(off Ashbridge St.)
Anthony Rd. DA16: Well 1A 126
SE25 .6G 157
UB6: G'frd 3J 77
Anthony St. E1 . . . . .6H 85
Anthony Way N18 . . . . .6E 34
Antigua M. E13 . . . . .3K 87

Antigua Wlk. SE19 . . . . .5D 138
Antila Ct. E1 .3K 9
(off Sclater St.)
Antilles Bay E14 . . . . .2E 104
Antill Rd. E3 . . . . .3A 86
N15 . . . . .4G 49
Antill Ter. E4 . . . . .6K 85
Antlers Hill E4 . . . . .5J 25
Antoinette M. NW2 . . . . .6C 62
Anton Cres. SM1: Sutt 3J 165
Antoneys Cl. HA5: Pinn 2B 40
Antonine Hgts. SE1 . . . . .7G 15
Anton Pl. HA9: Wemb 3H 61
Anton St. E8 . . . . .5G 67
Antony Ho. SE16 . . . . .4J 103
(off Raymouth Rd.)
Antrim Gro. NW3 . . . . .6D 64
Antrim Rd. NW3 . . . . .6D 64
Antrobus Cl. SM1: Sutt 5H 165
Antrobus Rd. W4 . . . . .4J 97
Antwerp Way E16 . . . . .2E 106
Anvil Cl. SW16 . . . . .7G 137
Anvil Rd. TW16: Sun 3J 147
Anworth Cl. IG8: Wfd G 6E 36
Apeldoorn Dr. SM6: W'gton 7J 167
Apelles St. SE18 . . . . .1C 124
(off Tellson Av.)
Apex Cl. BR3: Beck 1D 158
APEX CORNER
(Feltham) 3D 130
(Mill Hill) 4F 29
Apex Ct. W13 . . . . .7A 78
Apex Ho. E1 .3K 9
(off Bacon St.)
Apex Ind. Est. NW10 . . . . .4B 80
Apex Pde. NW7 . . . . .4E 28
(off Selvage La.)
Apex Retail Pk. 3D 130
Aphrodite Ct. E14 . . . . .4C 104
(off Homer Dr.)
E15 . . . . .1E 86
(off Warton Rd.)
Aplin Way TW7: Isle 1J 113
Apollo Av.
BR1: Broml 1K 159
Apollo Bldg. E14 . . . . .4C 104
Apollo Bus. Cen. SE8 . . . . .5K 103
Apollo Ct. E1 . . . . .7G 85
(off Thomas More St.)
E15 . . . . .1E 86
(off High St.)
SW9 . . . . .1A 120
(off Southey Rd.)
Apollo Ho. E2 . . . . .2H 85
(off St Jude's Rd.)
E3 . . . . .2C 86
(off Garrison Rd.)
N6 . . . . .7D 46
SW10 .7B 100
(off Milman's St.)
Apollo Pl. E11 . . . . .3G 69
SW10 .7B 100
Apollo Theatre 2C 12
(off Shaftesbury Av.)
Apollo Victoria Theatre 2A 18
(off Wilton Rd.)
Apollo Way DA8: Erith 4K 109
SE28 .3H 107
Apostle Ct. SE20 . . . . .7K 139
The Apostles SE23 . . . . .2K 139
(off Church Ri.)
Apostle Way CR7: Thor H 2B 156
Apothecary St. EC4 . . . . . .1A 14 (6B 84)
Appach Rd. SW2 . . . . .5A 120
Appian Ct. E3 . . . . .2B 86
(off Parnell Rd.)
Apple Blossom Ct. SW8 . . . . .7H 101
(off Pascal St.)
Appleby Cl. BR5: Pet W 7J 161
E4 . . . . .6K 35
N15 . . . . .5D 48
TW2: Twick 2H 131
UB8: Hil 6E 74

Appleby Ct. SE6 . . . . .6C 122
W3 . . . . .2J 97
(off Newport Rd.)
Appleby Gdns. TW14: Felt 1H 129
Appleby Rd. E8 . . . . .7G 67
E16 . . . . .6H 87
Appleby St. E2 . . . . .2F 85
Appledore Av. DA7: Bex 1J 127
HA4: Ruis 3K 57
Appledore Cl.
BR2: Broml 5H 159
HA8: Edg 1H 43
SW17 . . . . .2D 136
Appledore Cres. DA14: Sidc 3J 143
Appledore Way NW7 . . . . .7A 30
Appleford Ho. W10 . . . . .4G 81
(off Bosworth Rd.)
Appleford Rd. W10 . . . . .4G 81
Apple Gth. TW8: Bford 4D 96
Applegarth CRO: New Ad 7D 170
(not continuous)
KT10: Clay 5A 162
Applegarth Dr. IG2: Ilf 4K 53
Applegarth Ho. SE1 . . . . .6B 14
SE15 .7G 103
(off Bird in Bush Rd.)
Applegarth Rd. SE28 . . . . .1B 108
W14 . . . . .3F 99
Applegate Ho. E20 . . . . .5E 68
(off Victory Pde.)
Apple Gro. EN1: Enf 3K 23
HA2: Harr 1E 58
KT9: Chess 4E 162
TW1: Twick 6A 114
Apple Mkt. KT1: King T 2D 150
(off Market Pl.)
Apple Rd. E11 . . . . .3G 69
Appleshaw Ho. SE5 . . . . .3E 120
Appleton Cl. DA7: Bex 2J 127
Appleton Gdns.
KT3: N Mald 6C 152
Appleton Rd. SE9 . . . . .3C 124
Appleton Sq. CR4: Mitc 1C 154
Apple Tree Av. UB7: Yiew 5B 74
UB8: Hil 5B 74
Appletree Cl. SE20 . . . . .1H 157
Appletree Gdns. EN4: E Barn 4H 21
Apple Tree La. RM13: Rain 2K 91
APPLE TREE RDBT. 6B 74
Apple Tree Yd. E1 . . . . .3K 85
(off Longnor Rd.)
SW1 . . . . .4B 12 (1G 101)
Applewood Cl. N20 . . . . .1H 31
NW2 . . . . .3D 62
UB10: Ick 4A 56
Applewood Dr. E13 . . . . .4K 87
Apple Yd. SE20 . . . . .1H 157
Appold St. EC2 . . . . .5G 9 (5E 84)
Apprentice Gdns.
UB5: N'olt 3D 76
Apprentice Way E5 . . . . .4H 67
The Approach BR6: Orp 2K 173
EN1: Enf 2C 24
NW4 . . . . .5F 45
W3 . . . . .6K 79
Approach Cl. N16 . . . . .4E 66
Approach Rd. E2 . . . . .2J 85
EN4: E Barn 4G 21
HA8: Edg 6B 28
KT8: W Mole 5E 148
SW20 .2E 152
TW15: Ashf 6E 128
Apps Mdw. Cl. KT8: W Mole 4D 148
Aprey Gdns. NW4 . . . . .4E 44
April Cl. BR6: Chels 5K 173
TW13: Felt 3J 129
W7 . . . . .7J 77
April Ct. E2 .2G 85
(off Teale St.)
April Glen SE23 . . . . .3K 139
April St. E8 .4F 67
The Apsley Cen. NW2 . . . . .2C 62
Apsley Cl. HA2: Harr 5G 41

Apsley House 6H 11 (2E 100)
Apsley Ho. E1 . . . . .5J 85
(off Stepney Way)
NW8 . . . . .2B 82
(off Finchley Rd.)
SW15 .6C 116
(off Holford Way)
TW4: Houn 4D 112
Apsley Rd. KT3: N Mald 3J 151
SE25 . . . . .4H 157
Apsley Way NW2 . . . . .2C 62
W1 . . . . .6H 11 (2E 100)
(not continuous)
Aqua Ho. NW10 . . . . .3G 79
Aquarelle Ho. EC1 . . . . .1C 8
Aquarius TW1: Twick 1B 132
Aquarius Bus. Pk. NW2 . . . . .1C 62
(off Priestley Way)
Aquarius Ct. HA8: Edg 7B 28
Aquarius Golf Course 6J 121
Aqua Vista Sq. E3 . . . . .5C 86
(off Bow Comn. La.)
Aquila St. NW8 . . . . .2B 82
Aquinas St. SE1 . . . . .5K 13 (1A 102)
Arabella Ct. NW8 . . . . .2A 82
(off Marlborough Pl.)
Arabella Dr. SW15 . . . . .4A 116
Arabella Ho. SE16 . . . . . . .7K 15 (3G 103)
Arabia Cl. E4 . . . . .7K 25, 1A 36
Arabian Ho. E1 . . . . .4A 86
(off Ernest St.)
Arabin Rd. SE4 . . . . .4A 122
Arado Ho. NW9 . . . . .2B 44
(off Boulevard Dr.)
Aragon Av. KT7: T Ditt 5K 149
Aragon Cl. BR2: Broml 1D 172
EN2: Enf 1E 22
TW16: Sun 6H 129
Aragon Ct. KT8: E Mos 4G 149
SE11 . . . . .5J 19
(off Hotspur St.)
Aragon Dr. HA4: Ruis 1B 58
Aragon Ho. E16 . . . . .1J 105
(off Capulet M.)
Aragon Pl. SM4: Mord 7G 153
Aragon Rd. KT2: King T 5E 132
SM4: Mord 6F 153
Aragon Twr. SE8 . . . . .4B 104
Aral Ho. E1 .4K 85
(off Ernest St.)
Arandora Cres.
RM6: Chad H 7B 54
Aran Dr. HA7: Stan 4H 27
Aran Lodge NW6 . . . . .7J 63
(off Woodchurch Rd.)
Aran M. N7 .7A 66
(off St Clements St.)
Arapiles Ho. E14 . . . . .6F 87
(off Blair St.)
Arbery Rd. E3 . . . . .3A 86
Arbon Ct. N1 . . . . .1C 84
(off Linton St.)
Arbor Cl. BR3: Beck 2D 158
Arbor Ct. N16 . . . . .2D 66
Arboretum Ct. N1 . . . . .6D 66
(off Dove Rd.)
Arboretum Pl. IG11: Bark 7G 71
(off Clockhouse Av.)
Arborfield Cl. SW2 . . . . .1K 137
Arborfield Ho. E14 . . . . .7C 86
(off E. India Dock Rd.)
Arbor Ho. BR6: Orp 2H 173
(off Orchard Gro.)
SE14 .6B 104
TW8: Bford 7C 96
Arbor Rd. E4 . . . . .3A 36
Arbot Ho. SE10 . . . . .4G 105
(off Manilla Wlk.)
Arbour Ho. E1 . . . . .6K 85
(off Arbour Sq.)
Arbour Rd. EN3: Pond E 3E 24
Arbour Sq. E1 . . . . .6K 85
Arbroath Rd. SE9 . . . . .3C 124

Arbury Ter. SE26 . . . . .3G 139
Arbus Crescent
HA2: Harr 3G 41
Arbuthnot La. DA5: Bexl 6E 126
Arbuthnot Rd. SE14 . . . . .2K 121
SM4: Mord 4A 154
Arbutus St. E8 . . . . .1F 85
Arcade CRO: C'don 2C 168
The Arcade CRO: C'don 3C 168
(off High St.)
E20 . . . . .6E 68
(within Westfield Shop. Cen.)
EC2 . . . . .6G 9
N7 . . . . .4J 65
(off Macready Pl.)
SE9 . . . . .6E 124
(off High St.)
Arcade Chambers SE9 . . . . .6E 124
Arcade Pde. KT9: Chess 5D 162
Arcadia Av. N3 . . . . .2J 45
The Arcadia Cen. 7D 78
Arcadia Cl. SM5: Cars 4E 166
Arcadia Ct. E1 . . . . .7J 9
Arcadia M. KT3: N Mald 3A 152
Arcadian Av. DA5: Bexl 6E 126
Arcadian Cl. DA5: Bexl 6E 126
Arcadian Gdns. N22 . . . . .7E 32
Arcadian Pl. SW18 . . . . .7H 117
Arcadian Rd. DA5: Bexl 6E 126
Arcadia St. E14 . . . . .6C 86
Arc Ct. N11 .5A 32
RM7: Rush G 6K 55
ArcelorMittal Orbit 7D 68
Archangel St. SE16 . . . . .2K 103
Archbishop Lanfranc School Sports Cen.
. . . . .6J 155
Archbishop's Pl. SW2 . . . . .7K 119
Archdale Bus. Cen. HA2: Harr 2G 59
Archdale Cl. W12 . . . . .1D 98
Archdale Ho. SE1 . . . . .7G 15
(off Long La.)
Archdale Pl. KT3: N Mald 3H 151
Archdale Rd. SE22 . . . . .5F 121
Archel Rd. W14 . . . . .6H 99
Archer Apts. N1 . . . . .2E 84
(off Fern Cl.)
Archer Cl. EN5: Barn 6C 20
KT2: King T 7E 132
Archer Ho. N1 . . . . .1E 84
(off Whitmore Est.)
SE14 .1A 122
SW11 .1B 118
W11 . . . . .7H 81
(off Westbourne Gro.)
W13 . . . . .1B 96
(off Sherwood St.)
Archer M. SW9 . . . . .3J 119
TW12: Hamp H 6G 131
Archer Rd. BR5: St M Cry 5K 161
SE25 .4H 157
Archers Ct. CR2: S Croy 5C 168
(off Nottingham Rd.)
Archers Dr. EN3: Enf H 2D 24
Archers Lodge SE16 . . . . .5G 103
(off Culloden Cl.)
Archer Sq. SE14 . . . . .6A 104
Archer St. W1 . . . . .2C 12 (7H 83)
Archer Ter. UB7: Yiew 7A 74
Archery Cl. HA3: W'stone 3K 41
W2 . . . . .1D 10 (6C 82)
Archery Flds. Ho. WC1 . . . . .1H 7
(off Wharton St.)
Archery La. BR2: Broml 6B 160
Archery Rd. SE9 . . . . .5D 124
Archery Steps W2 . . . . .2D 10
Arches SW8 . . . . .7F 19 (6J 101)
The Arches E16 . . . . .4G 87
HA2: Harr 2F 59
NW1 . . . . .7F 65
SE8 . . . . .6A 104
SW8 . . . . .7H 101
WC2 . . . . .4F 13
(off Villiers St.)

The Arches Bus. Cen.
UB2: S'hall 2D **94**
(off Merrick Rd.)
Arches La. SW11 . . . . .6F **101**
Archgate Bus. Cen. N12 . . . . .5F **31**
Archibald M. W1 . . . . . .3J **11** (7F **83**)
Archibald Rd. N7 . . . . .4H **65**
Archibald St. E3 . . . . .3C **86**
Archie Cl. UB7: W Dray 2C **92**
Archie St. SE1 . . . . . .7H **15** (2E **102**)
Arc Ho. SE1 . . . . .7J **15**
Arch St. SE1 . . . . .3C **102**
ARCHWAY 2G **65**
Archway Bus. Cen. N19 . . . . .3H **65**
Archway Cl.
SM6: Bedd 3H **167**
SW19 . . . . .3K **135**
W10 . . . . .5F **81**
Archway Leisure Cen. 2G **65**
Archway Mall N19 . . . . .2G **65**
Archway M. SW15 . . . . .4G **117**
(off Putney Bri. Rd.)
Archway Rd. N6 . . . . .6E **46**
N19 .6E **46**
Archway St. SW13 . . . . .3A **116**
Arcola St. E8 . . . . .5F **67**
Arcola Theatre 5F **67**
Arcon Dr. UB5: N'olt 4C **76**
Arcon Ter. N9 . . . . .7B **24**
Arctic Ho. NW9 . . . . .2B **44**
(off Heritage Av.)
Arctic St. NW5 . . . . .5F **65**
Arcus Rd. BR1: Broml 6G **141**
Ardbeg Rd. SE24 . . . . .5D **120**
Arden Cl. HA1: Harr 3H **59**
SE28 . . . . .6D **90**
TW2: Whitt 7D **112**
UB4: Yead 4K **75**
Arden Ct. Gdns. N2 . . . . .6B **46**
RM9: Dag 7C **72**
Arden Cres. E14 . . . . .4C **104**
RM9: Dag 7C **72**
Arden Est. N1 . . . . .2E **84**
Arden Grange N12 . . . . .4F **31**
Arden Gro. BR6: Farnb 4F **173**
Arden Ho. N1 . . . . .1G **9**
SE11 . . . . .4G **19**
SE13 . . . . .3D **122**
(off Thurston Rd.)
SW9 . . . . .2J **119**
(off Grantham Rd.)
Arden M. E17 . . . . .5D **50**
Arden Mhor HA5: Eastc 4K **39**
Arden Rd. N3 . . . . .3H **45**
W13 . . . . .7C **78**
Ardent Cl. SE25 . . . . .3E **156**
Ardent Ho. E3 . . . . .2A **86**
(off Roman Rd.)
Ardfern Av. SW16 . . . . .3A **156**
Ardfillan Rd. SE6 . . . . .1F **141**
Ardgowan Rd. SE6 . . . . .7G **123**
Ardilaun Rd. N5 . . . . .4C **66**
Ardingly Cl. CR0: C'don 3K **169**
Ardleigh Ct. BR1: Broml 7H **141**
(off London Rd.)
Ardleigh Gdns. SM3: Sutt 7J **153**
Ardleigh Ho. IG11: Bark 1G **89**
(off Cooke St.)
Ardleigh M. IG1: Ilf 3F **71**
Ardleigh Rd. E17 . . . . .1B **50**
N1 . . . . .6E **66**
Ardleigh Ter. E17 . . . . .1B **50**
Ardley Cl. HA4: Ruis 7E **38**
NW10 . . . . .3A **62**
SE6 . . . . .3A **140**
Ardlui Rd. SE27 . . . . .2C **138**
Ardmay Gdns. KT6: Surb 5E **150**
Ardmere Ho. SE13 . . . . .6F **123**
Ardmore La. IG9: Buck H 1E **36**
Ardmore Pl. IG9: Buck H 1E **36**
Ardoch Rd. SE6 . . . . .2F **141**
Ardra Rd. N9 . . . . .3E **34**
Ardrossan Gdns.
KT4: Wor Pk 3C **164**

Ardshiel Cl. SW15 . . . . .3F **117**
Ardwell Av. IG6: Ilf 5G **53**
Ardwell Rd. SW2 . . . . .2J **137**
Ardwick Rd. NW2 . . . . .4J **63**
The Arena EN3: Enf L 1G **25**
Arena Bus. Cen. N4 . . . . .6C **48**
Arena Ho. E3 . . . . .2C **86**
(off Lefevre Wlk.)
Arena Shop. Pk. 6B **48**
Arena Sq. HA9: Wemb 4G **61**
Arena Twr. E14 . . . . .2D **104**
Ares Ct. E14 . . . . .4C **104**
(off Homer Dr.)
Arethusa Ho. E14 . . . . .4C **104**
(off Cahir St.)
Argali Ho. DA18: Erith 3E **108**
(off Kale Rd.)
Argall Av. E10 . . . . .7K **49**
Argall Way E10 . . . . .1K **67**
Argan Cl. EN5: Barn 3C **20**
Argenta Way NW10 . . . . .7H **61**
The Argent Cen.
UB3: Hayes 2J **93**
Argent Ct. E14 . . . . .5C **86**
(off Thomas Rd.)
EN5: New Bar 4F **21**
(off Leicester St.)
KT6: Surb 3G **163**
Argent Ho. IG11: Bark 4A **90**
Argenton Twr. SW18 . . . . .6K **117**
(off Mapleton Cres.)
Argo Apts. E16 . . . . .6H **87**
(off Sylvia Pankhurst St.)
Argo Bus. Cen. NW6 . . . . .3J **81**
Argonaut Pk. SL3: Poyle 4A **174**
Argon M. SW6 . . . . .7J **99**
Argon Rd. N18 . . . . .5D **34**
Argos Ct. SW9 . . . . .1A **120**
(off Caldwell St.)
Argos Ho. E2 . . . . .2H **85**
(off Old Bethnal Grn. Rd.)
Argosy Ho. SE8 . . . . .4A **104**
Argosy La. TW19: Stanw 7A **110**
Argus Cl. RM7: Mawney 1H **55**
Argus Way UB5: N'olt 3C **76**
Argyle Av. TW3: Houn 6E **112**
Argyle Cl. W13 . . . . .4A **78**
Argyle Ho. E14 . . . . .3E **104**
Argyle Pas. N17 . . . . .1F **49**
Argyle Pl. W6 . . . . .4D **98**
Argyle Rd. E1 . . . . .4K **85**
E15 . . . . .4G **69**
E16 . . . . .6K **87**
EN5: Barn 4A **20**
HA2: Harr 6F **41**
IG1: Ilf 2E **70**
N12 . . . . .5E **30**
N17 . . . . .1G **49**
N18 . . . . .4B **34**
TW3: Houn 5F **113**
UB6: G'frd 3K **77**
W13 . . . . .5A **78**
Argyle Sq. WC1 . . . . . .1F **7** (3J **83**)
(not continuous)
Argyle St. WC1 . . . . . . .1E **6** (3J **83**)
Argyle Wlk. WC1 . . . . . .2F **7** (3J **83**)
Argyle Way SE16 . . . . .5G **103**
Argyll Av. UB1: S'hall 1F **95**
Argyll Cl. SW9 . . . . .3K **119**
Argyll Ct. SW2 . . . . .7J **119**
(off New Pk. Rd.)
Argyll Gdns. HA8: Edg 2H **43**
Argyll Mans. SW3 . . . . . .7B **16** (6B **100**)
W14 .4G **99**
(off Hammersmith Rd.)
Argyll Rd. SE18 . . . . .3G **107**
W8 . . . . .2J **99**
Argyll St. W1 . . . . . . .1A **12** (6G **83**)
Argyll Ter. SW19 . . . . .7F **117**
Aria Ct. IG2: Ilf 6G **53**
Arica Ho. SE16 . . . . .3H **103**
(off Slippers Pl.)
Arica Rd. SE4 . . . . .4A **122**

Ariel Apts. E16 . . . . .6J **87**
Ariel Ct. SE11 . . . . . . .4K **19** (4B **102**)
Ariel Ho. E1 . . . . .7F **85**
(off Vaughan Way)
Ariel Rd. NW6 . . . . .6J **63**
Ariel Way TW4: Houn 3K **111**
W12 . . . . .1E **98**
Aristotle Rd. SW4 . . . . .3H **119**
Arizona Bldg. SE13 . . . . .1D **122**
(off Deal's Gateway)
The Ark W6 . . . . .5F **99**
(off Talgarth Rd.)
Arkell Gro. SE19 . . . . .7B **138**
Arkindale Rd. SE6 . . . . .3E **140**
Arklay Cl. UB8: Hil 4B **74**
Arkley Cres. E17 . . . . .5B **50**
Arkley Rd. E17 . . . . .5B **50**
Arklow Ho. SE17 . . . . .6D **102**
Arklow M. KT6: Surb 2E **162**
Arklow Rd. SE14 . . . . .6B **104**
Arkwright Rd. CR2: Sande 7F **169**
NW3 . . . . .5A **64**
Arla Pl. HA4: Ruis 4A **58**
Arlesey Cl. SW15 . . . . .5G **117**
Arlesford Rd. SW9 . . . . .3J **119**
Arlidge Ho. EC1 . . . . .5K **7**
(off Kirby St.)
Arlingford Rd. SW2 . . . . .5A **120**
Arlington N12 . . . . .3D **30**
Arlington Av. N1 . . . . .2C **84**
Arlington Bldg. E3 . . . . .2C **86**
Arlington Cl. DA15: Sidc 7J **125**
SE13 . . . . .5F **123**
SM1: Sutt 2J **165**
TW1: Twick 6C **114**
W3 .2H **97**
(off Mill Hill Rd.)
Arlington Dr. HA4: Ruis 6F **39**
SM5: Cars 2D **166**
Arlington Gdns. IG1: Ilf 1E **70**
W4 .5J **97**
Arlington Grn. NW7 . . . . .7A **30**
Arlington Ho. EC1 . . . . .1K **7**
(off Arlington Way)
SE8 . . . . .6B **104**
(off Evelyn St.)
SW1 . . . . . . .4A **12** (1G **101**)
TW9: Kew 7H **97**
UB7: W Dray 2B **92**
W12 . . . . .1D **98**
(off Tunis Rd.)
Arlington Lodge SW2 . . . . .4K **119**
Arlington M. SE13 . . . . .5F **123**
Arlington Pk. Mans. W4 . . . . .5J **97**
(off Sutton La. Nth.)
Arlington Pas. TW11: Tedd 4K **131**
Arlington Pl. SE10 . . . . .7E **104**
Arlington Rd. IG8: Wfd G 1J **51**
KT6: Surb 6D **150**
N14 . . . . .2A **32**
NW1 . . . . .1F **83**
TW1: Twick 6C **114**
TW10: Ham 2D **132**
TW11: Tedd 4K **131**
TW15: Ashf 5B **128**
W13 . . . . .6B **78**
Arlington Sq. N1 . . . . .1C **84**
Arlington St. SW1 . . . . . .4A **12** (1G **101**)
Arlington Way EC1 . . . . . .1K **7** (3A **84**)
Arliss Ho. HA1: Harr 5K **41**
Arliss Way UB5: N'olt 1A **76**
Arlow Rd. N21 . . . . .1F **33**
Armada Ct. SE8 . . . . .6C **104**
Armadale Cl. N17 . . . . .4H **49**
Armadale Rd. SW6 . . . . .7J **99**
TW14: Felt 5J **111**
Armada St. SE8 . . . . .6C **104**
Armada Way E6 . . . . .5F **89**
Armagh Rd. E3 . . . . .1B **86**
Arments Ct. SE5 . . . . .6D **102**
(off Albany Rd.)
Armfield Cl. KT8: W Mole 5D **148**
Armfield Cres. CR4: Mitc 2D **154**

Armfield Rd. EN2: Enf 1J **23**
Arminger Rd. W12 . . . . .1D **98**
Armistice Gdns. SE25 . . . . .3G **157**
Armitage Ho. NW1 . . . . .5D **4**
(off Lisson Gro.)
Armitage Rd. NW11 . . . . .1G **63**
SE10 . . . . .5H **105**
Armour Cl. N7 . . . . .6K **65**
The Armoury 4C **64**
(off Pond St.)
Armoury Ho. E3 . . . . .1A **86**
(off Gunmakers La.)
Armoury Rd. SE8 . . . . .2D **122**
Armoury Way SW18 . . . . .5J **117**
Armsby Ho. E1 . . . . .5J **85**
(off Stepney Way)
Armstead Wlk. RM10: Dag 7G **73**
Armstrong Av. IG8: Wfd G 6B **36**
Armstrong Cl. BR1: Broml 3C **160**
E6 . . . . .6D **88**
HA5: Eastc 6J **39**
KT12: Walt T 6J **147**
RM8: Dag 7D **54**
SE18 . . . . .4K **123**
Armstrong Cres. EN4: Cockf 3G **21**
Armstrong Ho. E14 . . . . .6A **86**
(off Commercial Rd.)
Armstrong Rd. NW10 . . . . .7A **62**
SE18 . . . . .3G **107**
SW7 . . . . . . .2A **16** (3B **100**)
TW13: Hanw 5C **130**
W3 .1B **98**
Armstrong Way UB2: S'hall 2F **95**
Armytage Rd. TW5: Hest 7B **94**
Arnal Cres. SW18 . . . . .7G **117**
Arncliffe NW6 . . . . .2K **81**
Arncliffe Cl. N11 . . . . .6K **31**
Arncroft Ct. IG11: Bark 3B **90**
Arndale Wlk. SW18 . . . . .5K **117**
Arne Gro. BR6: Orp 3K **173**
Arne Ho. SE11 . . . . .5G **19**
Arne St. WC2 . . . . .1F **13** (6J **83**)
Arnett Sq. E4 . . . . .6G **35**
Arne Wlk. SE3 . . . . .4H **123**
Arneways Av. RM6: Chad H 3D **54**
Arneway St. SW1 . . . . . .2D **18** (3H **101**)
Arnewood Cl. SW15 . . . . .1C **134**
Arneys La. CR4: Mitc 6E **154**
Arngask Rd. SE6 . . . . .7F **123**
Arnhem Pl. E14 . . . . .3C **104**
Arnhem Way SE22 . . . . .5E **120**
Arnhem Wharf E14 . . . . .3B **104**
Arnison Rd.
KT8: E Mos 4H **149**
Arnold Bennett Way N8 . . . . .3A **48**
Arnold Cir. E2 . . . . .2J **9** (3F **85**)
Arnold Cl. HA3: Kenton 7F **43**
Arnold Ct. N22 . . . . .7D **32**
Arnold Cres. TW7: Isle 5H **113**
Arnold Dr. KT9: Chess 6D **162**
Arnold Est. SE1 . . . . . . .7K **15** (2F **103**)
(not continuous)
Arnold Gdns. N13 . . . . .5G **33**
Arnold Ho. SE3 . . . . .3A **106**
(off Shooters Hill Rd.)
SE17 . . . . .5B **102**
(off Doddington St.)
Arnold Mans. W14 . . . . .6H **99**
(off Queen's Club Gdns.)
Arnold Rd. E3 . . . . .3C **86**
N15 . . . . .3F **49**
RM9: Dag 7F **73**
RM10: Dag 7F **73**
SW17 . . . . .7D **136**
UB5: N'olt 6B **58**
Arnold Ter. HA7: Stan 5E **26**
Arnos Gro. N14 . . . . .4C **32**
Arnos Gro. Ct. N11 . . . . .5B **32**
(off Palmer's Rd.)
Arnos Rd. N11 . . . . .5B **32**
Arnos Swimming Pool 5C **32**
Arnot Ho. SE5 . . . . .7C **102**
(off Comber Gro.)

Arnott Cl. SE28 . . . . .1C 108
 W4 . . . . .4K 97
Arnould Av. SE5 . . . . .4D 120
Arnsberg Way DA6: Bex 4G 127
 DA7: Bex 4G 127
Arnside Gdns. HA9: Wemb 1D 60
Arnside Ho. SE17 . . . . .6D 102
 (off Arnside St.)
Arnside Rd. DA7: Bex 1G 127
Arnside St. SE17 . . . . .6D 102
Arnulf St. SE6 . . . . .4D 140
Arnulls Rd. SW16 . . . . .6B 138
Arodene Rd. SW2 . . . . .6K 119
Arona Ho. BR3: Beck 2E 158
Arora Twr. SE10 . . . . .1F 105
Arosa Rd. TW1: Twick 6D 114
Arpley Sq. SE20 . . . . .7J 139
 (off High St.)
Arragon Gdns. BR4: W W'ck 3D 170
 SW16 .7J 137
Arragon Rd. E6 . . . . .1B 88
 SW18 .1J 135
 TW1: Twick 7A 114
Arran Cl. DA8: Erith 6K 109
 SM6: W'gton 4F 167
Arran Ct. NW9 . . . . .2B 44
 NW10 .3K 61
Arran Dr. E12 . . . . .1B 70
Arran Ho. E14 . . . . .1E 104
 (off Raleana Rd.)
Arran M. W5 . . . . .1F 97
Arran Rd. SE6 . . . . .2D 140
Arran Wlk. N1 . . . . .7C 66
Arras Av. SM4: Mord 5A 154
Arrival Sq. E1 . . . . .7G 85
Arrol Ho. SE1 . . . . .3C 102
Arrol Rd. BR3: Beck 3J 157
Arrow Ct. SW5 . . . . .4J 99
 (off W. Cromwell Rd.)
Arrowhead Quay E14 . . . . .2C 104
Arrow Ho. N1 . . . . .1E 84
 (off Wilmer Gdns.)
Arrow Rd. E3 . . . . .3D 86
Arrowscout Wlk. UB5: N'olt 3C 76
 (off Argus Way)
Arrows Ho. SE15 . . . . .7J 103
 (off Clifton Way)
Arrowsmith Ho. SE11 . . . . .5G 19
Arsenal FC 4A 66
Arsenal Rd. SE9 . . . . .2D 124
Arsenal Way SE18 . . . . .3G 107
Arta Ho. E1 . . . . .6J 85
 (off Devonport St.)
Artbrand Ho. SE1 . . . . .7G 15
 (off Leathermarket St.)
Artemis Ct. E14 . . . . .4C 104
 (off Homer Dr.)
Artemis Pl. SW18 . . . . .7H 117
Arterberry Rd. SW20 . . . . .7E 134
Artesian Cl. NW10 . . . . .7K 61
Artesian Gro.
 EN5: New Bar 4F 21
Artesian Ho. SE1 . . . . .3F 103
 (off Grange Rd.)
Artesian Rd. W2 . . . . .6J 81
Artesian Wlk. E11 . . . . .3G 69
Arthaus Apts. E8 . . . . .6H 67
 (off Richmond Rd.)
Arthingworth St. E15 . . . . .1G 87
Arthouse 5J 47
Arthur Ct. CR0: C'don 3E 168
 (off Fairfield Path)
 SW11 .1E 118
 W2 . . . . .6K 81
 (off Queensway)
 W10 . . . . .6F 81
 (off Silchester Rd.)
Arthur Deakin Ho. E1 . . . . .5J 9
 (off Hunton St.)
Arthurdon Rd. SE4 . . . . .5C 122
Arthur Gro. SE18 . . . . .4G 107
Arthur Henderson Ho. SW6 . . . . . .2H 117
 (off Fulham Rd.)

Arthur Horsley Wlk. E7 . . . . .5H 69
 (off Tower Hamlets Rd.)
Arthur Ho. N1 . . . . .1E 84
 (off Halcomb St.)
Arthur Lovell Ct. E14 . . . . .6B 86
 (off Lovat Cl.)
Arthur Newton Ho. SW11 . . . . .3B 118
 (off Winstanley Est.)
Arthur Rd. E6 . . . . .2D 88
 KT2: King T 7G 133
 KT3: N Mald 5D 152
 N7 . . . . .4K 65
 N9 . . . . .2A 34
 RM6: Chad H 6C 54
 SW19 .5H 135
Arthur St. EC4 . . . . .2F 15 (7D 84)
Arthur Wade Ho. E2 . . . . .1K 9
 (off Baroness Rd.)
Arthur Wallis Ho. E12 . . . . .3E 70
 (off Grantham Rd.)
Artichoke Hill E1 . . . . .7H 85
Artichoke M. SE5 . . . . .1D 120
 (off Artichoke Pl.)
Artichoke Pl. SE5 . . . . .1D 120
Artichoke Wlk. TW9: Rich 5D 114
 (off Red Lion St.)
The Artillery Bldg. E1 . . . . .6H 9
 (off Artillery La.)
Artillery Cl. IG2: Ilf 6G 53
Artillery Ho. E3 . . . . .1A 86
 (off Barge La.)
 E15 . . . . .6G 69
 SE18 .5E 106
 (off Connaught M.)
Artillery La. E1 . . . . .6H 9 (5E 84)
 W12 . . . . .6C 80
Artillery Mans. SW1 . . . . .1C 18
Artillery Pas. E1 . . . . .6J 9
Artillery Pl. HA3: Hrw W 7B 26
 SE18 .4D 106
 SW1 . . . . .2C 18 (3H 101)
Artillery Row SW1 . . . . . . .2C 18 (3G 101)
Artillery Sq. SE18 . . . . .3F 107
Artington Cl.
 BR6: Farnb 4G 173
Artisan Cl. E6 . . . . .6F 89
Artisan Ct. E8 . . . . .6G 67
Artisan M. NW10 . . . . .3F 81
 (off Warfield Rd.)
Artisan Pl. HA3: W'stone 2J 41
Artisan Quarter NW10 . . . . .3F 81
 (off Wellington Rd.)
Artizan St. E1 . . . . .7J 9
Arts Depot .5F 31
Arts La. SE16 . . . . .3F 103
Arts Sq. E1 .4A 86
Arts Theatre 2E 12
 (off Gt. Newport St.)
Arun Cl. SE25 . . . . .5G 157
Arundale KT1: King T 4D 150
 (off Anglesea Rd.)
Arundel Av. SM4: Mord 4H 153
Arundel Bldgs. SE1 . . . . .3E 102
Arundel Cl.
 CR0: Wadd 3B 168
 DA5: Bexl 6F 127
 E15 . . . . .4G 69
 SW11 .5C 118
 TW12: Hamp H 5F 131
Arundel Ct. BR2: Broml 2G 159
 HA2: Harr 4E 58
 N12 . . . . .6H 31
 N17 . . . . .1F 49
 SE16 .5H 103
 (off Verney Rd.)
 SW3 . . . . .5D 16
 (off Jubilee Pl.)
 SW13 . . . . .6D 98
 (off Arundel Ter.)
 W11 . . . . .7H 81
 (off Arundel Gdns.)
Arundel Dr. HA2: Harr 4D 58
 IG8: Wfd G 7D 36

Arundel Gdns. HA8: Edg 7E 28
 IG3: Ilf 2A 72
 N21 . . . . .1F 33
 W11 . . . . .7H 81
Arundel Gt. Ct. WC2 . . . . . .2H 13 (7K 83)
Arundel Gro. N16 . . . . .5E 66
Arundel Ho. CR0: C'don 5D 168
 (off Heathfield Rd.)
 E17 . . . . .1B 50
 W3 . . . . .2H 97
 (off Park Rd. Nth.)
Arundel Mans. SW6 . . . . .1H 117
 (off Kelvedon Rd.)
Arundel Pl. N1 . . . . .6A 66
Arundel Rd. CR0: C'don 6D 156
 EN4: Cockf 3H 21
 KT1: King T 2H 151
 SM2: Cheam, Sutt 7H 165
 (not continuous)
 TW4: Houn 3A 112
Arundel Sq. N7 . . . . .6A 66
Arundel St. WC2 . . . . .2H 13 (7K 83)
Arundel Ter. SW13 . . . . .6D 98
Arun Ho. KT2: King T 1D 150
Arvon Rd. N5 . . . . .5A 66
 (not continuous)
Asa Ct. UB3: Harl 3H 93
Asbaston Ter. IG1: Ilf 6G 71
Asbridge Ct. W6 . . . . .3D 98
 (off Dalling Rd.)
Asbury Ct. N21 . . . . .5D 22
 (off Pennington Dr.)
Ascalon Ho. SW8 . . . . .7G 101
 (off Thessaly Rd.)
Ascalon St. SW8 . . . . .7G 101
Ascensis Twr. SW18 . . . . .4A 118
Ascent Ho. NW9 . . . . .2B 44
 (off Boulevard Dr.)
Ascham Dr. E4 . . . . .7J 35
Ascham End E17 . . . . .1A 50
Ascham St. NW5 . . . . .5G 65
Aschurch Rd. CR0: C'don 7F 157
Ascot Cl. UB5: N'olt 5E 58
Ascot Ct. DA5: Bexl 7F 127
 NW8 . . . . .2A 4
Ascot Gdns. UB1: S'hall 4D 76
Ascot Ho. NW1 . . . . .1K 5
 (off Redhill St.)
 W9 . . . . .4J 81
 (off Harrow Rd.)
Ascot Lodge NW6 . . . . .1K 81
Ascot Pl. HA7: Stan 5H 27
Ascot Rd. BR5: St M Cry 4K 161
 E6 . . . . .3D 88
 N15 . . . . .5D 48
 N18 . . . . .4B 34
 SW17 .6E 136
 TW14: Bedf 1C 128
Ascott Av. W5 . . . . .2E 96
Ascott Cl. HA5: Eastc 4J 39
Ashanti M. E8 . . . . .5J 67
Ash Av. SE17 . . . . .4C 102
Ashbee Ho. E2 . . . . .3J 85
 (off Portman Pl.)
Ashbourne Av. DA7: Bex 7E 108
 E18 . . . . .4K 51
 HA2: Harr 2H 59
 N20 . . . . .2J 31
 NW11 . . . . .5H 45
Ashbourne Cl. N12 . . . . .4E 30
 W5 . . . . .5G 79
Ashbourne Ct. E5 . . . . .4A 68
 N12 . . . . .4E 30
 (off Ashbourne Cl.)
Ashbourne Gro. NW7 . . . . .5E 28
 SE22 . . . . .4F 121
 W4 . . . . .5A 98
Ashbourne Pde. NW11 . . . . .4H 45
 W5 . . . . .4F 79
Ashbourne Ri. BR6: Orp 4J 173
Ashbourne Rd. CR4: Mitc 7F 136
 W5 . . . . .4F 79
Ashbourne Ter. SW19 . . . . .7H 135

Ashbourne Way NW11 . . . . .4H 45
Ashbridge Rd. E11 . . . . .7G 51
Ashbridge St. NW8 . . . . .4C 4 (4C 82)
Ashbrook HA8: Edg 6A 28
Ashbrook Rd. N19 . . . . .1H 65
 RM10: Dag 3H 73
Ashburn Gdns. SW7 . . . . .4A 100
Ashburnham Av. HA1: Harr 6K 41
Ashburnham Cl. N2 . . . . .3B 46
Ashburnham Ct. BR3: Beck 2E 158
Ashburnham Gdns. HA1: Harr 6K 41
Ashburnham Gro. SE10 . . . . .7D 104
Ashburnham Mans. SW10 . . . . .7A 100
 (off Ashburnham Rd.)
Ashburnham M. SW1 . . . . .3D 18
 (off Regency St.)
Ashburnham Pl. SE10 . . . . .7D 104
Ashburnham Retreat SE10 . . . . .7D 104
Ashburnham Rd. DA17: Belv 4J 109
 NW10 . . . . .3E 80
 SW10 .7A 100
 TW10: Ham 3B 132
Ashburnham Twr. SW10 . . . . .7A 100
 (off Worlds End Est.)
Ashburn Pl. SW7 . . . . .4A 100
Ashburton Av. CR0: C'don 1H 169
 IG3: Ilf 5J 71
Ashburton Cl. CR0: C'don 1G 169
Ashburton Ent. Cen. SW15 . . . . . . .6E 116
Ashburton Gdns. CR0: C'don 2G 169
ASHBURTON GROVE 4A 66
Ashburton Ho. W9 . . . . .4H 81
 (off Fernhead Rd.)
Ashburton Memorial Homes
 CR0: C'don 7H 157
Ashburton Pl. W1 . . . . .4K 11 (1F 101)
Ashburton Rd. CR0: C'don 2G 169
 E16 . . . . .6J 87
 HA4: Ruis 2J 57
Ashburton Ter. E13 . . . . .2J 87
Ashburton Triangle N5 . . . . .4A 66
Ashbury Dr. UB10: Ick 3D 56
Ashbury Gdns. RM6: Chad H 5D 54
Ashbury Pl. SW19 . . . . .6A 136
Ashbury Rd. SW11 . . . . .3D 118
Ashby Av. KT9: Chess 6G 163
Ashby Cl. BR4: W W'ck 3F 171
Ashby Ct. NW8 . . . . .3B 4
 (off Pollitt Dr.)
Ashby Gro. N1 . . . . .7C 66
 (not continuous)
Ashby Ho. N1 . . . . .7C 66
 (off Essex Rd.)
 SW9 . . . . .2B 120
 UB5: N'olt 4D 76
 (off Waxlow Way)
Ashby M. SE4 . . . . .2B 122
 SW2 . . . . .5J 119
 (off Prague Pl.)
Ashby Rd. N15 . . . . .5G 49
 SE4 . . . . .2B 122
Ashbys Ct. E3 . . . . .2B 86
 (off Centurion La.)
Ashby St. EC1 . . . . .2B 8 (3B 84)
Ashby Wlk. CR0: C'don 6C 156
Ashby Way UB7: Sip 7C 92
Ashchurch Gro. W12 . . . . .3C 98
Ashchurch Pk. Vs. W12 . . . . .3C 98
Ashchurch Ter. W12 . . . . .3C 98
Ash Cl. BR5: Pet W 5H 161
 DA14: Sidc 3B 144
 HA7: Stan 6F 27
 HA8: Edg 4D 28
 KT3: N Mald 2K 151
 RM5: Col R 1H 55
 SE20 . . . . .2J 157
 SM5: Cars 2D 166
 TW7: Isle 1K 113
 UB9: Hare 1A 38
Ashcombe Av. KT6: Surb 7D 150
Ashcombe Cl. TW15: Ashf 3A 128
Ashcombe Ct. TW15: Ashf 2B 128
Ashcombe Gdns. HA8: Edg 4B 28

Ashcombe Ho. *E3* 3D *86*
    (off Bruce Rd.)
  EN3: Pond E 3E **24**
Ashcombe Pk. NW2 . . . . .3A **62**
Ashcombe Rd. SM5: Cars 6E **166**
  SW19 . . . . .5J **135**
Ashcombe Sq. KT3: N Mald 3J **151**
Ashcombe St. SW6 . . . . .2K **117**
Ash Ct. KT19: Ewe 4J **163**
  N11 . . . . .6B **32**
  SW19 . . . . .7G **135**
Ashcroft HA5: Hat E 6A **26**
  N14 . . . . .2C **32**
Ashcroft Av. DA15: Sidc 6A **126**
Ashcroft Ct. N20 . . . . .2G **31**
Ashcroft Cres. DA15: Sidc 6A **126**
Ashcroft Ho. SW8 . . . . .1G *119*
    (off Wadhurst Rd.)
Ashcroft Rd. KT9: Chess 3F **163**
Ashcroft Sq. W6 . . . . .4E **98**
Ashcroft Theatre 3D *168*
    (within Fairfield Halls)
Ashdale Cl. TW2: Whitt 7G **113**
  TW19: Stanw 2A **128**
Ashdale Gro. HA7: Stan 6E **26**
Ashdale Ho. N4 . . . . .7D **48**
Ashdale Rd. SE12 . . . . .1K **141**
Ashdale Way TW2: Whitt 7F **113**
Ashdene HA5: Pinn 3A **40**
  SE15 . . . . .7H **103**
Ashdene Cl. TW15: Ashf 7E **128**
Ashdon Cl. IG8: Wfd G 6E **36**
Ashdon Rd. NW10 . . . . .1B **80**
Ashdown *W13* 5B *78*
    (off Clivedon Ct.)
Ashdown Cl. BR3: Beck 2D **158**
  DA5: Bexl 7J **127**
Ashdown Ct. E17 . . . . .2E **50**
  IG11: Bark 6F **71**
  SM2: Sutt 6A **166**
Ashdown Cres. NW5 . . . . .5E **64**
Ashdowne Ct. N17 . . . . .1G **49**
Ashdown Pl. KT7: T Ditt 7A **150**
  KT17: Ewe 7B **164**
Ashdown Rd. EN3: Enf H 2D **24**
  KT1: King T 2E **150**
  UB10: Hil 2C **74**
Ashdown Wlk. E14 . . . . .4C **104**
  RM7: Mawney 1H **55**
Ashdown Way SW17 . . . . .2E **136**
Ashe Ho. TW1: Twick 6D **114**
Ashen E6 .6E **88**
Ashenden Rd. E5 . . . . .5A **68**
Ashen Gro. SW19 . . . . .3J **135**
Ashentree Cl. EC4 . . . . .1K **13**
Asher Loftus Way N11 . . . . .6J **31**
Asher Way E1 . . . . .7G **85**
Ashfield Av. TW13: Felt 1K **129**
  WD23: Bush 1B **26**
Ashfield Ct. BR3: Beck 7D **140**
  TW10: Ham 1E **132**
Ashfield Ct. SW9 . . . . .2J **119**
    (off Clapham Rd.)
Ashfield Ho. W14 . . . . .5H *99*
    (off W. Cromwell Rd.)
Ashfield La. BR7: Chst 6F **143**
    (not continuous)
Ashfield Pde. N14 . . . . .1C **32**
Ashfield Rd. N4 . . . . .6C **48**
  N14 . . . . .3B **32**
  W3 . . . . .1B **98**
Ashfield St. E1 . . . . .5H **85**
    (not continuous)
Ashfield Yd. E1 . . . . .5J **85**
ASHFORD .4B **128**
Ashford Av. N8 . . . . .4J **47**
  TW15: Ashf 6D **128**
  UB4: Yead 6B **76**
Ashford Bus. Complex
  TW15: Ashf 5E **128**
Ashford Cl. E17 . . . . .6B **50**
  TW15: Ashf 4A **128**
ASHFORD COMMON 7F **129**

Ashford Ct. HA8: Edg 3C **28**
  NW2 .4F **63**
Ashford Cres. EN3: Enf H 2D **24**
  TW15: Ashf 3A **128**
Ashford Ho. SE8 . . . . .6B **104**
  SW9 .4B **120**
Ashford Ind. Est. TW15: Ashf . . .4E **128**
Ashford Manor Golf Course 6B **128**
Ashford M. N17 . . . . .1G **49**
Ashford Pas. NW2 . . . . .4F **63**
Ashford Rd. E6 . . . . .7E **70**
  E18 . . . . .2K **51**
  NW2 .4F **63**
  TW13: Felt 4F **129**
  TW15: Ashf 7E **128**
  TW18: Lale, Staines 7A **128**
Ashford Tennis Club 4A **128**
Ash Gro. BR4: W W'ck 2E **170**
  E8 . . . . .1H **85**
    (not continuous)
  EN1: Enf 7K **23**
  HA0: Wemb 4A **60**
  N10 . . . . .4F **47**
  N13 . . . . .3H **33**
  NW2 .4F **63**
  SE12 . . . . .1J **141**
  SE20 . . . . .2J **157**
  TW5: Hest 1B **112**
  TW14: Felt 1G **129**
  UB1: S'hall 5E **76**
  UB3: Hayes 7F **75**
  UB7: Yiew 7B **74**
  UB9: Hare 1A **38**
  W5 . . . . .2E **96**
Ashgrove Ct. W9 . . . . .5J *81*
    (off Elmfield Way)
Ashgrove Ho. SW1 . . . . .5D *18*
    (off Lindsay Sq.)
Ashgrove Rd. BR1: Broml 6F **141**
  IG3: Ilf 1K **71**
  TW15: Ashf 5E **128**
Ash Hill Cl. WD23: Bush 1A **26**
Ash Hill Dr. HA5: Pinn 3A **40**
Ash Ho. E14 . . . . .2E *104*
    (off E. Ferry Rd.)
  SE1 . . . . .4F *103*
    (off Longfield Est.)
  W10 . . . . .4G *81*
    (off Heather Wlk.)
Ashingdon Cl. E4 . . . . .3K **35**
Ashington Ho. *E1* 4H *85*
    (off Barnsley St.)
Ashington Rd. SW6 . . . . .2H **117**
Ash Island KT8: E Mos 3H **149**
Ashlake Rd. SW16 . . . . .4J **137**
Ashland Pl. W1 . . . . .5G **5** (5E **82**)
Ashlar Pl. SE18 . . . . .4F **107**
Ashleigh Commercial Est. SE7 . .3A **106**
Ashleigh Ct. N14 . . . . .7B **22**
  W5 . . . . .4D *96*
    (off Murray Rd.)
Ashleigh Gdns. SM1: Sutt 2K **165**
Ashleigh M. SE15 . . . . .3F *121*
    (off Oglander Rd.)
Ashleigh Point SE23 . . . . .3K **139**
Ashleigh Rd. SE20 . . . . .3H **157**
  SW14 . . . . .3A **116**
Ashley Av. IG6: Ilf 2F **53**
  SM4: Mord 5J **153**
Ashley Cl. HA5: Pinn 2K **39**
  NW4 .2E **44**
Ashley Ct. *E3* 3E *86*
    (off Bolinder Way)
  EN5: New Bar 5F **21**
  NW4 .2E **44**
  SW1 . . . . .2A *18*
    (off Morpeth Ter.)
  UB5: N'olt 1C **76**
Ashley Cres. N22 . . . . .2A **48**
  SW11 . . . . .3E **118**
Ashley Dr. TW2: Whitt 7F **113**
  TW7: Isle 6J **95**

Ashley Gdns. BR6: Orp 5J **173**
  HA9: Wemb 2E **60**
  N13 . . . . .4H **33**
  SW1 . . . . .2B **18** (3G **101**)
    (not continuous)
  TW10: Ham 2D **132**
Ashley La. CR0: Wadd 4B **168**
  NW4 .2E **44**
Ashley Pl. SW1 . . . . . .2A **18** (3G **101**)
    (not continuous)
Ashley Rd. CR7: Thor H 4K **155**
  E4 . . . . .6H **35**
  E7 . . . . .7A **70**
  EN3: Enf H 2D **24**
  KT7: T Ditt 6K **149**
  N17 . . . . .3G **49**
  N19 . . . . .1J **65**
  SW19 . . . . .6K **135**
  TW9: Rich 3E **114**
  TW12: Hamp 1E **148**
Ashleys Alley N15 . . . . .4C **48**
Ashley Wlk. NW7 . . . . .7K **29**
Ashling Rd. CR0: C'don 1G **169**
Ashlin Rd. E15 . . . . .4F **69**
Ash Lodge KT12: Walt T 7J **147**
  TW16: Sun 7H *129*
    (off Forest Dr.)
Ashlone Rd. SW15 . . . . .3E **116**
Ashlyns Way KT9: Chess 6D **162**
Ashmead N14 . . . . .5B **22**
Ashmead Bus. Cen. E16 . . . . .4F **87**
Ashmead Cl. TW15: Ashf 7E **128**
Ashmead Ga. BR1: Broml 1A **160**
Ashmead Ho. *E9* 5A *68*
    (off Homerton Rd.)
  W13 . . . . .1A *96*
    (off Tewkesbury Rd.)
Ashmead M. SE8 . . . . .2C **122**
Ashmead Rd. SE8 . . . . .2C **122**
  TW14: Felt 1J **129**
Ashmere Av. BR3: Beck 2F **159**
Ashmere Cl. SM3: Cheam 5F **165**
Ashmere Gro. SW2 . . . . .4J **119**
Ash M. NW5 . . . . .5G **65**
Ashmill St. NW1 . . . . . .5C **4** (5C **82**)
Ashmole Pl. SW8 . . . . .6K **101**
Ashmole St. SW8 . . . . .6K **101**
Ashmore *NW1* 7H *65*
    (off Agar Gro.)
Ashmore Cl. SE15 . . . . .7F **103**
Ashmore Ct. N11 . . . . .6J **31**
  TW5: Hest 6E **94**
Ashmore Gro. DA16: Well 3H **125**
Ashmore Ho. *W14* 3G *99*
    (off Russell Rd.)
Ashmore Rd. SE18 . . . . .7D **106**
  W9 . . . . .2H **81**
Ashmount Est. N19 . . . . .7H **47**
Ashmount Rd. N15 . . . . .5F **49**
  N19 . . . . .7G **47**
Ashmount Ter. W5 . . . . .4D **96**
Ashmour Gdns. RM1: Rom 2K **55**
Ashneal Gdns. HA1: Harr 3H **59**
Ashness Gdns. UB6: G'frd 6B **60**
Ashness Rd. SW11 . . . . .5D **118**
Ashpark Ho. *E14* 6B *86*
    (off Norbiton Rd.)
Ashridge Cl. HA3: Kenton 6C **42**
  N3 . . . . .3J **45**
Ashridge Ct. N14 . . . . .5B **22**
  UB1: S'hall 6D *77*
    (off Redcroft Rd.)
Ashridge Cres. SE18 . . . . .7G **107**
Ashridge Gdns. HA5: Pinn 4C **40**
  N13 . . . . .5C **32**
Ashridge Way SM4: Mord 3H **153**
  TW16: Sun 6J **129**
Ash Rd. BR6: Chels 7K **173**
  CR0: C'don 2C **170**
  E15 . . . . .5G **69**
  SM3: Sutt 7G **153**
  TW17: Shep 4C **146**
Ash Row BR2: Broml 7E **160**

Ashstead Rd. E5 . . . . .7G **49**
Ashton Cl. SM1: Sutt 4J **165**
Ashton Ct. E4 . . . . .3B **36**
  HA1: Harr 3K **59**
Ashton Gdns. RM6: Chad H 6E **54**
  TW4: Houn 4D **112**
Ashton Hgts. SE23 . . . . .1J **139**
Ashton Ho. SE11 . . . . .5K **19**
  SW9 .7A **102**
Ashton Pl. KT10: Clay 7A **162**
Ashton Reach SE16 . . . . .4A **104**
Ashton Rd. E15 . . . . .5F **69**
Ashton St. E14 . . . . .7E **86**
Ashtree Av. CR4: Mitc 2B **154**
Ash Tree Cl.
  BR6: Farnb 4F **173**
  CR0: C'don 6A **158**
  KT6: Surb 2E **162**
Ash Tree Ct. TW15: Ashf 5D *128*
    (off Feltham Hill Rd.)
Ash Tree Dell NW9 . . . . .5J **43**
Ash Tree Ho. SE5 . . . . .7C *102*
    (off Pitman St.)
Ash Tree Way CR0: C'don 5K **157**
Ashurst Cl. SE20 . . . . .1H **157**
Ashurst Dr. IG2: Ilf 6F **53**
  IG6: Ilf 5G **53**
  TW17: Shep 5A **146**
Ashurst Gdns. SW2 . . . . .1A **138**
Ashurst Rd. EN4: Cockf 5J **21**
  N12 . . . . .5H **31**
Ashurst Wlk. CR0: C'don 2H **169**
Ashvale Ct. *E3* 2C *86*
    (off Matilda Gdns.)
Ashvale Rd. SW17 . . . . .5D **136**
Ashview Apts. *N4* 7C *48*
    (off Katherine Cl.)
Ashview Cl. TW15: Ashf 5A **128**
Ashview Gdns. TW15: Ashf 5A **128**
Ashville Rd. E11 . . . . .2F **69**
Ash Wlk. HA0: Wemb 4C **60**
Ashwater Rd. SE12 . . . . .1J **141**
Ash Way IG8: Wfd G 2B **52**
The Ashway Cen. KT2: King T . . .1G **150**
Ashwell Cl. E6 . . . . .6C **88**
Ashwell Ct. TW15: Ashf 2A **128**
Ashwin St. E8 . . . . .6F **67**
Ashwood Av. UB8: Hil 6C **74**
Ashwood Gdns. CR0: New Ad . . .6E **170**
  UB3: Harl 4H **93**
Ashwood Ho. *NW4* 4E *44*
    (off Belle Vue Est.)
Ashwood Rd. E4 . . . . .3A **36**
Ashworth Cl. SE5 . . . . .2D **120**
Ashworth Est. CR0: Bedd 1J **167**
Ashworth Mans. W9 . . . . .3K *81*
    (off Elgin Av.)
Ashworth Rd. W9 . . . . .3K **81**
Aske Ho. N1 . . . . .1G **9**
Asker Ho. N7 . . . . .4J **65**
Askern Cl. DA6: Bex 4D **126**
Aske St. N1 . . . . .1G **9** (3E **84**)
The Askew Bldg. *EC1* 6C *8*
    (off Bartholomew Cl.)
Askew Cres. W12 . . . . .2B **98**
Askew Rd. W12 . . . . .2B **98**
Askham Ct. W12 . . . . .1C **98**
Askham Rd. W12 . . . . .1C **98**
Askill Dr. SW15 . . . . .5G **117**
Askwith Rd.
  RM13: Rain 3K **91**
Asland Rd. E15 . . . . .1G **87**
Aslett St. SW18 . . . . .7K **117**
Asman Ho. *N1* 2B *84*
    (off Colebrooke Rd.)
Asmara Rd. NW2 . . . . .5G **63**
Asmuns Hill NW11 . . . . .5J **45**
Asmuns Pl. NW11 . . . . .5H **45**
Asolando Dr. SE17 . . . . .4C **102**
Aspect Ct. *E14* 2E *104*
    (off Manchester Rd.)
  SW6 . . . . .2A **118**
Aspects SM1: Sutt 5K **165**

Aspen Cl. KT1: Hamp W 1C **150**
  N19 ....2G **65**
  UB7: Yiew 1B **92**
  W5 ....2F **97**
Aspen Copse BR1: Broml 2D **160**
Aspen Ct. NW4 ....2G **45**
Aspen Dr. HA0: Wemb 3A **60**
Aspen Gdns. CR4: Mitc 5E **154**
  TW15: Ashf 5E **128**
  W6 ....5D **98**
Aspen Grn. DA18: Erith 3F **109**
Aspen Gro. HA5: Eastc 3H **39**
Aspen Ho. DA15: Sidc 2A **144**
  E15 ....3G **87**
    (off Teasel Way)
  SE15 ....6J **103**
    (off Sharratt St.)
Aspen La. UB5: N'olt 3C **76**
Aspenlea Rd. W6 ....6F **99**
Aspen Lodge W8 ....3K **99**
    (off Abbots Wlk.)
Aspen M. SE20 ....6J **139**
Aspen Pl. WD23: B Hea 1D **26**
Aspen Way E14 ....7D **86**
  TW13: Felt 3K **129**
Aspern Gro. NW3 ....5C **64**
Aspinall Rd. SE4 ....3K **121**
    (not continuous)
Aspinden Rd. SE16 ....4H **103**
ASPIRE National Training Cen. ...2G **27**
Aspire Sport & Fitness Cen. ..1K **33**
Aspland Gro. E8 ....6H **67**
    (off Amhurst Rd.)
Aspley Rd. SW18 ....5K **117**
Asplins Rd. N17 ....1G **49**
Asprey M. BR3: Beck 5B **158**
Asprey Pl. BR1: Broml 2C **160**
Asquith Cl. RM8: Dag 1C **72**
Asquith Ho. SW1 ....2D **18**
    (off Monck St.)
Assam St. E1 ....6G **85**
    (off White Church La.)
Assata M. N1 ....6B **66**
Assembley Ho. SE14 ....6B **104**
    (off Arklow Rd.)
Assembly Apts. SE15 ....1J **121**
    (off York Gro.)
Assembly Pas. E1 ....5J **85**
Assembly Wlk. SM5: Cars 7C **154**
Ass Ho. La. HA3: Hrw W 4A **26**
Astall Cl. HA3: Hrw W 1J **41**
Astbury Bus. Pk. SE15 ....1J **121**
Astbury Ho. SE11 ....2J **19**
Astbury Rd. SE15 ....1J **121**
Astell Ho. E14 ....6G **87**
    (off Lyell St.)
  SW3 ....5D **16**
    (off Astell St.)
Astell Rd. SE3 ....4A **124**
Astell St. SW3 ....5D **16** (5D **100**)
Asten Way RM7: Mawney 2H **55**
Aster Ct. E5 ....2J **67**
    (off Woodmill Rd.)
Asterid Hgts. E20 ....5E **68**
    (off Liberty Bri. Rd.)
Aster Pl. E9 ....7J **67**
    (off Frampton Pk. Rd.)
Aste St. E14 ....2E **104**
Astey's Row N1 ....7C **66**
Asthall Gdns. IG6: Ilf 4G **53**
Astins Ho. E17 ....4D **50**
Astleham Rd. TW17: Shep 3A **146**
Astle St. SW11 ....2E **118**
Astley Av. NW2 ....5E **62**
Astley Ho. SE1 ....5F **103**
    (off Rowcross St.)
  SW13 ....6D **98**
    (off Wyatt Dr.)
  W2 ....5J **81**
    (off Alfred Rd.)
Aston Av. HA3: Kenton 7C **42**
Aston Cl. DA14: Sidc 3A **144**
Aston Ho. IG8: Wfd G 6D **36**

Aston Grn. TW4: Cran 2A **112**
Aston Ho. EC4 ....6J **7**
    (off Furnival St.)
  RM8: Dag 4A **72**
  SW8 ....1H **119**
  W11 ....7H **81**
    (off Westbourne Gro.)
Aston M. RM6: Chad H 7C **54**
  W10 ....3F **81**
Aston Pl. SW16 ....6B **138**
Aston Rd. SW20 ....2E **152**
  W5 ....6D **78**
Aston St. E14 ....5A **86**
Aston Ter. SW12 ....6F **119**
Astonville St. SW18 ....1J **135**
Aston Webb Ho. SE1 ....5G **15**
Astor Av. RM7: Rom 6J **55**
Astor Cl. KT2: King T 6H **133**
Astor Coll. 5B **6**
    (off Charlotte St.)
Astor Ct. E16 ....6A **88**
    (off Ripley Rd.)
  SW6 ....7H **100**
    (off Maynard Cl.)
Astoria Ct. E8 ....7F **67**
    (off Queensbridge Rd.)
Astoria Ho. NW9 ....2B **44**
    (off Boulevard Dr.)
Astoria Mans. SW16 ....3J **137**
Astoria Wlk. SW9 ....3A **120**
Astra Ho. E3 ....3B **86**
    (off Alfred St.)
  SE14 ....6B **104**
    (off Arklow Rd.)
Astral Ho. E1 ....6H **9**
    (off Middlesex Rd.)
  SE6 ....4E **140**
Astrid Ho. TW13: Felt 2A **130**
Astrop M. W6 ....3E **98**
Astrop Ter. W6 ....2E **98**
Astwood Dr. HA7: Stan 2D **26**
Astwood M. SW7 ....4A **100**
Asylum Rd. SE15 ....7H **103**
Atalanta St. SW6 ....7F **99**
Atbara Rd. TW11: Tedd 6B **132**
Atcham Rd. TW3: Houn 4G **113**
Atcost Rd. IG11: Bark 5A **90**
Atcraft Cen. HA0: Wemb 1E **78**
Atelier Ct. SE8 ....7C **104**
    (off Watson's St.)
Atelier Ct. Central E14 ....5E **86**
    (off Leven St.)
Atelier Ct. Nth. E14 ....5E **86**
    (off Leven Rd.)
Atelier Ct. Sth. E14 ....5E **86**
    (off Leven Rd.)
Atheldene St. SW18 ....1K **135**
Athelney St. SE6 ....3C **140**
Athelstane Gro. E3 ....2B **86**
Athelstane M. N4 ....1A **66**
Athelstan Gdns. NW6 ....7G **63**
Athelstan Ho. E9 ....5B **68**
    (off Homerton Rd.)
  KT1: King T 4F **151**
    (off Athelstan Rd.)
Athelstan Pl. TW2: Twick 1J **131**
Athelstan Rd. KT1: King T 4F **151**
Athelstone Rd.
  HA3: W'stone 2H **41**
Athena Cl. HA2: Harr 2H **59**
  KT1: King T 3F **151**
Athena Ct. SE1 ....7G **15**
    (off City Wlk.)
Athenaeum Ct. N5 ....4C **66**
Athenaeum Lawn Tennis Club ...6K **53**
Athenaeum Pl. N10 ....3F **47**
Athenaeum Rd. N20 ....1F **31**
Athena Pl. HA6: Nwood 1H **39**
Athene Pl. EC4 ....7K **7**
    (off Thavie's Inn)
Athenia Ho. E14 ....6F **87**
    (off Blair St.)
Athenlay Rd. SE15 ....5K **121**

Athens Gdns. W9 ....4J **81**
    (off Harrow Rd.)
Atherden Rd. E5 ....4J **67**
Atherfold Rd. SW9 ....3J **119**
Atherley Way TW4: Houn 7D **112**
Atherstone Ct. W2 ....5K **81**
    (off Delamere Ter.)
Atherstone M. SW7 ....4A **100**
Atherton Dr. SW19 ....4F **135**
Atherton Hgts. HA0: Wemb ...7C **60**
Atherton Leisure Cen. 6H **69**
Atherton M. E7 ....6H **69**
Atherton Pl. HA2: Harr 3H **41**
  UB1: S'hall 7E **76**
Atherton Rd. E7 ....6H **69**
  IG5: Ilf 2C **52**
  SW13 ....7C **98**
Atherton St. SW11 ....2C **118**
Athlone Cl. E5 ....5H **67**
Athlone Ct. E17 ....3F **51**
Athlone Ho. E1 ....6J **85**
    (off Sidney St.)
Athlone Pl. W10 ....5G **81**
Athlone Rd. SW2 ....7K **119**
Athlone St. NW5 ....6E **64**
Athlon Ind. Est.
  HA0: Wemb 1D **78**
Athol Ct. HA0: Wemb 2D **78**
Athol Cl. HA5: Pinn 1K **39**
Athole Gdns. EN1: Enf 5K **23**
Athol Gdns. HA5: Pinn 1K **39**
Atholl Ho. W9 ....3A **82**
    (off Maida Vale)
Atholl Rd. IG3: Ilf 7A **54**
Athol Rd. DA8: Erith 5J **109**
Athol Sq. E14 ....6E **86**
Athol Way UB10: Hil 3C **74**
Atkin Bldg. WC1 ....5H **7**
    (off Raymond Bldgs.)
Atkins Ct. E3 ....1B **86**
    (off Willow Tree Cl.)
Atkins Dr. BR4: W W'ck 2F **171**
Atkins Lodge W8 ....2J **99**
    (off Thornwood Gdns.)
Atkinson Cl. BR6: Chels 5K **173**
  SW20 ....7C **134**
Atkinson Ct. E10 ....7D **50**
    (off Kings Cl.)
Atkinson Ho. E2 ....2G **85**
    (off Pritchards Rd.)
  E13 ....4H **87**
    (off Sutton Rd.)
  SE17 ....4D **102**
    (off Catesby St.)
  SW11 ....1E **118**
    (off Austin Rd.)
Atkinson Morley Av. SW17 ....3B **136**
Atkinson Rd. E16 ....5A **88**
Atkins Rd. E10 ....6D **50**
  SW12 ....7G **119**
Atkins Sq. E8 ....5H **67**
Atlanta Bldg. SE13 ....1D **122**
Atlanta Ct. CR7: Thor H 3C **156**
Atlanta Ho. SE16 ....3A **104**
    (off Brunswick Quay)
Atlantic Apts. E16 ....7J **87**
    (off Seagull La.)
Atlantic Bldg. E15 ....5F **69**
    (off Property Row)
Atlantic Ct. E14 ....1F **105**
    (off Jamestown Way)
  SW3 ....5E **16** (5D **100**)
Atlantic Rd. SW9 ....4A **120**
Atlantic Wharf E1 ....7K **85**
Atlas Av. E16 ....7F **89**
Atlantis Cl. IG11: Bark 3B **90**
Atlas Bus. Cen. NW2 ....1D **62**
Atlas Cres. HA8: Edg 2C **28**
Atlas Gdns. SE7 ....4A **106**
Atlas Ho. E1 ....6F **87**
  N7 ....6K **65**
  SE13 ....4F **123**

Atlas Rd. E13 ....2J **87**
  HA9: Wemb 4J **61**
  N11 ....7K **31**
  NW10 ....3A **80**
Atlas Trade Pk. DA8: Erith 5K **109**
Atlas Wharf E9 ....6C **68**
Atlip Rd. HA0: Wemb 1E **78**
Atney Rd. SW15 ....4G **117**
The Atrium IG9: Buck H 2G **37**
  W12 ....1F **99**
Atrium Apts. N1 ....1D **84**
    (off Felton St.)
Atrium Hgts. SE8 ....6D **104**
    (off Creekside)
Atrium Ho. SE8 ....7B **104**
Atterbury Rd. N4 ....6A **48**
Atterbury St. SW1 ....4D **18** (4J **101**)
Attewood Av. NW10 ....3A **62**
Attewood Rd. UB5: N'olt 6C **58**
Attfield Ct. N20 ....2G **31**
Attfield Ct. KT1: King T 1F **151**
    (off Albert Rd.)
Attilburgh Ho. SE1 ....7J **15**
    (off St Saviour's Est.)
Attleborough Ct. SE23 ....2G **139**
Attle Cl. UB10: Hil 2C **74**
Attlee Cl. CR7: Thor H 5C **156**
  UB4: Yead 3K **75**
  UB5: N'olt 3K **75**
Attlee Rd. SE28 ....7B **90**
  UB4: Yead 3J **75**
Attlee Ter. E17 ....4D **50**
Attneave St. WC1 ....2J **7** (3A **84**)
Attock M. E17 ....5D **50**
Attwood La. SE10 ....4G **105**
Atunbi Ct. NW1 ....7G **65**
    (off Farrier St.)
Atwater Cl. SW2 ....1A **138**
Atwell Cl. E10 ....6D **50**
Atwell Pl. KT7: T Ditt 7K **149**
Atwell Rd. SE15 ....2G **121**
Atwood Av. TW9: Rew 2G **115**
Atwood Ho. W14 ....4H **99**
    (off Beckford Cl.)
Atwood Rd. W6 ....4D **98**
Atwoods All. TW9: Kew 1G **115**
Aube Ho. SE6 ....4E **140**
Aubers Ridge Ct. E3 ....2B **86**
    (off Festubert Pl.)
Aubert Ct. N5 ....4B **66**
Aubert Pk. N5 ....4B **66**
Aubert Rd. N5 ....4B **66**
Aubrey Beardsley Ho. SW1 ...4B **18**
    (off Vauxhall Bri. Rd.)
Aubrey Mans. NW1 ....5C **4**
    (off Lisson St.)
Aubrey Moore Point E15 ....2E **86**
    (off Abbey La.)
Aubrey Pl. NW8 ....2A **82**
Aubrey Rd. E17 ....3C **50**
  N8 ....5J **47**
  W8 ....1H **99**
Aubrey Wlk. W8 ....1H **99**
Aubrey Way E17 ....4D **50**
Auburn Cl. SE14 ....7A **104**
Aubyn Hill SE27 ....4C **138**
Aubyn Sq. SW15 ....5C **116**
Auckland Cl. SE19 ....1F **157**
Auckland Ct. UB4: Yead 4A **76**
Auckland Gdns. SE19 ....1E **156**
Auckland Hill SE27 ....4C **138**
Auckland Ho. W12 ....7D **80**
    (off White City Est.)
Auckland Ri. SE19 ....1E **156**
Auckland Rd. E10 ....3D **68**
  IG1: Ilf 1F **71**
  KT1: King T 4F **151**
  SE19 ....1F **157**
  SW11 ....4C **118**
Auckland St. SE11 .....6G **19** (5K **101**)
Audax NW9 ....2B **44**
Auden Pl. NW1 ....1E **82**
  SM3: Cheam 4E **164**

Audleigh Pl. IG7: Chig 6K **37**
Audley Cl. N10 . . . . .7A **32**
 SW11 . . . . .3E **118**
Audley Ct. E18 . . . . .4H **51**
 HA5: Pinn 2A **40**
 TW2: Twick 3H **131**
 UB5: N'olt 3A **76**
Audley Dr. E16 . . . . .1K **105**
Audley Gdns. IG3: Ilf 2K **71**
Audley Pl. SM2: Sutt 7K **165**
Audley Rd. EN2: Enf 2G **23**
 NW4 . . . . .5C **44**
 TW10: Rich 5F **115**
 W5 .5F **79**
Audley Sq. W1 . . . . .4H **11** (1E **100**)
Audrey Cl. BR3: Beck 6D **158**
Audrey Gdns. HA0: Wemb 2B **60**
Audrey Rd. IG1: Ilf 3F **71**
Audrey St. E2 . . . . .2G **85**
Audric Cl. KT2: King T 1G **151**
Augurs La. E13 . . . . .3K **87**
Augusta Cl. KT8: W Mole 3D **148**
Augusta Rd. TW2: Twick 2G **131**
Augustas La. N1 . . . . .7A **66**
Augusta St. E14 . . . . .6D **86**
Augusta Wlk. W5 . . . . .5D **78**
Augustine Bell Twr. E3 . . . . .2C **86**
 (off Pancras Way)
Augustine Rd. HA3: Hrw W 1F **41**
 W14 .3F **99**
Augustus Bldg. E1 . . . . .6H **85**
 (off Tarling St.)
Augustus Cl. HA7: Stan 3J **27**
 TW8: Bford 7C **96**
 W12 .2D **98**
Augustus Ct. SE1 . . . . .4E **102**
 (off Old Kent Rd.)
 SW16 .2H **137**
 TW13: Hanw 4D **130**
Augustus Ho. NW1 . . . . .1A **6**
 (off Augustus St.)
Augustus La. BR6: Orp 2K **173**
Augustus Rd. SW19 . . . . .1F **135**
Augustus St. NW1 . . . . .1K **5** (2F **83**)
Aulay Ho. SE16 . . . . .3F **103**
Aultone Way SM1: Sutt 2K **165**
 SM5: Cars 3D **166**
Aultone Yd. Ind. Est.
 SM5: Cars 3D **166**
Aulton Pl. SE11 . . . . . . .6K **19** (5A **102**)
Aumonier M. N2 . . . . .4C **46**
Aura Ct. SE15 . . . . .4H **121**
Aura Ho. TW9: Kew 1H **115**
Aurelia Gdns. CR0: C'don 5K **155**
Aurelia Ho. E20 . . . . .1C **8**
 (off Sunrise Cl.)
Aurelia Rd. CR0: C'don 6J **155**
Auriel Av. RM10: Dag 6K **73**
Auriga M. N1 . . . . .5D **66**
Auriol Cl. KT4: Wor Pk 3A **164**
Auriol Dr. UB6: G'frd 7H **59**
 UB10: Hil 6C **56**
Auriol Ho. W12 . . . . .1D **98**
 (off Ellerslie Rd.)
Auriol Mans. W14 . . . . .4G **99**
 (off Edith Rd.)
Auriol Pk. Rd. KT4: Wor Pk 3A **164**
Auriol Rd. W14 . . . . .4G **99**
Aurora Apts. EC1 . . . . .1C **8**
 SW18 . . . . .5J **117**
 (off Buckhold Rd.)
Aurora Bldg. E14 . . . . .1E **104**
 (off Blackwall Way)
The Aurora Bldg. N1 . . . . .1F **9**
Aurora Gdns. 6F **101**
Aurora Ho. E14 . . . . .6D **86**
 (off Kerbey St.)
 SE6 . . . . .4E **140**
Aurora Point SE8 . . . . .4B **104**
 (off Grove St.)
Austell Gdns. NW7 . . . . .3F **29**
Austell Hgts. NW7 . . . . .3F **29**
 (off Austell Gdns.)

Austen Apts. SE20 . . . . .2H **157**
Austen Cl. SE28 . . . . .1B **108**
Austen Ho. NW6 . . . . .3J **81**
 (off Cambridge Rd.)
 SW17 . . . . .3B **136**
 (off St George's Gro.)
Austen Rd. DA8: Erith 7H **109**
 HA2: Harr 2F **59**
Austin Av. BR2: Broml 5C **160**
Austin Cl. SE23 . . . . .7A **122**
 TW1: Twick 5C **114**
Austin Ct. E6 . . . . .1A **88**
 EN1: Enf 5K **23**
 SE15 . . . . .3G **121**
 (off Peckham Rye)
Austin Friars EC2 . . . . . . .7F **9** (6D **84**)
Austin Friars Pas. EC2 . . . . .7F **9**
Austin Friars Sq. EC2 . . . . .7F **9**
 (off Austin Friars)
Austin Ho. SE14 . . . . .7B **104**
 (off Achilles St.)
Austin Rd. SW11 . . . . .1E **118**
 UB3: Hayes 2H **93**
Austin's La. HA4: Ruis 4F **57**
 UB10: Ick 3E **56**
Austin St. E2 . . . . .2J **9** (3F **85**)
Austin Ter. SE1 . . . . .1K **19**
 (off Morley St.)
Austral Cl. DA15: Sidc 3K **143**
Australia Ho. WC2 . . . . .1H **13**
 (off Aldwych)
Australian War Memorial 2E **100**
Australia Rd. W12 . . . . .7D **80**
Austral St. SE11 . . . . . . .3K **19** (4B **102**)
Austyn Gdns. KT5: Surb 1H **163**
Autumn Cl. EN1: Enf 1B **24**
 SW19 . . . . .6A **136**
Autumn Ct. RM7: Rom 6J **55**
Autumn Gro. BR1: Broml 6K **141**
Autumn Lodge CR2: S Croy 4E **168**
 (off South Pk. Hill Rd.)
Autumn St. E3 . . . . .1C **86**
Autumn Way UB7: W Dray 2B **92**
Avalon Cl. EN2: Enf 2F **23**
 SE6 . . . . .2G **141**
 SW20 . . . . .2G **153**
 W13 .5A **78**
Avalon Ct. CR0: C'don 7F **157**
Avalon Rd. SW6 . . . . .1K **117**
 W13 .4A **78**
Avante KT1: King T 3D **150**
Avantgarde Pl. E1 . . . . .3K **9**
 (off Sclater St.)
Avantgarde Twr. E1 . . . . .3J **9**
 (off Sclater St.)
Avard Gdns. BR6: Farnb 4G **173**
Avarn Rd. SW17 . . . . .6D **136**
Avebury Ct. N1 . . . . .1D **84**
 (off Imber St.)
 SE16 .4J **103**
 (off Debnams Rd.)
Avebury Pk. KT6: Surb 7D **150**
Avebury Rd. BR6: Orp 3H **173**
 E11 .1F **69**
 SW19 . . . . .1H **153**
Avebury St. N1 . . . . .1D **84**
Avedon Cl. HA2: Harr 2G **41**
Aveley Mans. IG11: Bark 7F **71**
 (off Whiting Av.)
Aveley Rd. RM1: Rom 4K **55**
Aveline St. SE11 . . . . . . .5H **19** (5A **102**)
Aveling Pk. Rd. E17 . . . . .2C **50**
Ave Maria La. EC4 . . . . . .1B **14** (6B **84**)
Avenell Mans. N5 . . . . .4B **66**
Avenell Rd. N5 . . . . .3B **66**
Avenfield Ho. W1 . . . . .2F **11**
 (off Park La.)
Avening Rd. SW18 . . . . .7J **117**
Avening Ter. SW18 . . . . .7J **117**
Avenir Ho. E15 . . . . .6F **69**
 (off Forrester Way)
Avenons Rd. E13 . . . . .4J **87**
Aventine Av. CR4: Mitc 3F **155**

The Avenue BR1: Broml 3B **160**
 BR2: Kes 4B **172**
 BR3: Beck 1D **158**
 BR4: W W'ck 7E **158**
 BR5: St P 7B **144**
 BR6: Orp 2K **173**
 CR0: C'don 3E **168**
 DA5: Bexl 7D **126**
 E3 .4D **86**
 (off Devas St.)
 E4 .6A **36**
 E11 . . . . .6K **51**
 EC2 . . . . .7H **9** (6E **84**)
 EN5: Barn 3B **20**
 HA3: Hrw W 1K **41**
 HA5: Pinn 6D **40**
 HA9: Wemb 1E **60**
 IG9: Buck H 2F **37**
 KT4: Wor Pk 2B **164**
 KT5: Surb 6F **151**
 KT17: Ewe 7D **164**
 N3 .2J **45**
 N8 .3A **48**
 N10 .2G **47**
 N11 . . . . .5A **32**
 N17 . . . . .3D **48**
 NW6 .1F **81**
 RM1: Rom 4K **55**
 SE10 . . . . .7F **105**
 SM2: Cheam 7G **165**
 SM5: Cars 7E **166**
 SW4 . . . . .4E **118**
 SW18 . . . . .7C **118**
 TW1: Twick 5B **114**
 TW3: Houn 5F **113**
 TW5: Cran 7J **93**
 TW9: Kew 2F **115**
 TW12: Hamp 6D **130**
 TW16: Sun 1K **147**
 UB10: Ick 4C **56**
 W4 .3A **98**
 W13 . . . . .6B **78**
Avenue Cl. N14 . . . . .6B **22**
 NW8 . . . . .1C **82**
 (not continuous)
 TW5: Cran 1K **111**
 UB7: W Dray 3A **92**
Avenue Ct. IG5: Ilf 3C **52**
 N14 .6B **22**
 NW2 . . . . .3H **63**
 SW3 . . . . .4E **16**
 (off Draycott Av.)
Avenue Cres. TW5: Cran 1K **111**
 W3 .2H **97**
Avenue Elmers KT6: Surb 5E **150**
Avenue Gdns. SE25 . . . . .2G **157**
 SW14 . . . . .3A **116**
 TW5: Cran 7K **93**
 TW11: Tedd 7K **131**
 W3 .2H **97**
Avenue Ho. NW6 . . . . .7G **63**
 (off The Avenue)
 NW8 .2C **82**
 (off Allitsen Rd.)
 NW10 .2D **80**
 (off All Souls Av.)
Avenue Ind. Est. E4 . . . . .6H **35**
Avenue Lodge NW8 . . . . .7B **64**
 (off Avenue Rd.)
Avenue Mans. NW3 . . . . .5K **63**
 (off Finchley Rd.)
Avenue M. N10 . . . . .3F **47**
Avenue Pde. N21 . . . . .7J **23**
 TW16: Sun 3K **147**
Avenue Pk. Rd. SE27 . . . . .2B **138**
Avenue Rd. BR3: Beck 2K **157**
 DA7: Bex 3E **126**
 DA8: Erith 7J **109**
 DA17: Belv, Erith 4J **109**
 E7 .4K **69**
 HA5: Pinn 3C **40**
 IG8: Wfd G 6F **37**
 KT1: King T 3E **150**

Avenue Rd. KT3: N Mald 4A **152**
 N6 .7G **47**
 N12 .4F **31**
 N14 .7B **22**
 N15 . . . . .5D **48**
 NW3 . . . . .7B **64**
 NW8 . . . . .7B **64**
 NW10 . . . . .2B **80**
 RM6: Chad H 7B **54**
 SE20 . . . . .1J **157**
 SE25 . . . . .2F **157**
 SM6: W'gton 7G **167**
 SW16 . . . . .2H **155**
 SW20 . . . . .2D **152**
 TW7: Isle 1K **113**
 TW8: Bford 5C **96**
 TW11: Tedd 7A **132**
 TW12: Hamp 1F **149**
 TW13: Felt 3H **129**
 UB1: S'hall 1D **94**
 W3 .2H **97**
Avenue Sth. KT5: Surb 7G **151**
Avenue Studios SW3 . . . . .4B **16**
 (off Sydney Cl.)
Avenue Ter. KT3: N Mald 3J **151**
Averill Gro. SW16 . . . . .6B **138**
Averill St. W6 . . . . .6F **99**
Avern Gdns. KT8: W Mole 4F **149**
Avern Rd. KT8: W Mole 4F **149**
Avershaw Ho. SW15 . . . . .5F **117**
Avery Cl. BR3: Beck 6B **140**
Avery Ct. NW9 . . . . .3J **43**
Avery Farm Row
 SW1 . . . . .4J **17** (4E **100**)
Avery Gdns. IG2: Ilf 5D **52**
AVERY HILL 6H **125**
Avery Hill Rd. SE9 . . . . .6H **125**
Avery Row W1 . . . . .2J **11** (7F **83**)
Avery Wlk. SW11 . . . . .3E **118**
Aviary Cl. E16 . . . . .5H **87**
Aviation Dr. NW9 . . . . .2C **44**
Aviemore Cl. BR3: Beck 5B **158**
Aviemore Way BR3: Beck 5A **158**
Avigdor M. N16 . . . . .2D **66**
Avignon Rd. SE4 . . . . .3K **121**
Avingdor Ct. W3 . . . . .1J **97**
 (off Horn La.)
Avington Ct. SE1 . . . . .4E **102**
 (off Old Kent Rd.)
Avington Gro. SE20 . . . . .7J **139**
Avion Cres. NW9 . . . . .1C **44**
Avis Sq. E1 . . . . .6K **85**
Avoca Rd. SW17 . . . . .4E **136**
Avocet Cl. SE1 . . . . .5G **103**
Avocet M. SE28 . . . . .3H **107**
Avon Cl. KT4: Wor Pk 2C **164**
 SM1: Sutt 4A **166**
 UB4: Yead 4A **76**
Avon Ct. E4 . . . . .1K **35**
 IG9: Buck H 1E **36**
 N12 .5E **30**
 SW15 . . . . .5G **117**
 UB6: G'frd 4F **77**
 W9 .5J **81**
 (off Elmfield Way)
Avondale Av. EN4: E Barn 1J **31**
 KT4: Wor Pk 1B **164**
 KT10: Hin W 3A **162**
 N12 .5E **30**
 NW2 . . . . .3A **62**
Avondale Cl. E11 . . . . .1G **69**
 E16 . . . . .5G **87**
 E18 .1K **51**
 SM2: Sutt 7A **166**
 (off Brighton Rd.)
Avondale Cres. EN3: Enf H 3F **25**
 IG4: Ilf 5B **52**
Avondale Gdns. TW4: Houn 5D **112**
Avondale Ho. SE1 . . . . .5G **103**
 (off Avondale Sq.)
Avondale Mans. SW6 . . . . .1H **117**
 (off Rostrevor Rd.)

Avondale Pk. Gdns. W11 . . . . .7G 81
Avondale Pk. Rd. W11 . . . . .7G 81
Avondale Pavement SE1 . . . . .5G 103
Avondale Ri. SE15 . . . . .3F 121
Avondale Rd.
 BR1: Broml 6G 141
 CR2: S Croy 6C 168
 DA16: Well 2C 126
 E16 .5G 87
 E17 .7C 50
 HA3: W'stone 3K 41
 N3 . . . . .1A 46
 N13 .2F 33
 N15 .5B 48
 SE9 .2C 142
 SW14 . . . . .3A 116
 SW19 . . . . .5K 135
 TW15: Ashf 3A 128
Avondale Sq. SE1 . . . . .5G 103
Avonfield Ct. E17 . . . . .3F 51
Avongrove Cl. EC1 . . . . .1D 8
 (off Bollinder Pl.)
Avon Ho. KT2: King T 1D 150
 W8 . . . . .3J 99
 (off Allen St.)
 W14 .4H 99
 (off Kensington Village)
Avonhurst Ho. NW2 . . . . .7G 63
Avonley Rd. SE14 . . . . .7J 103
Avon M. HA5: Hat E 1D 40
Avonmore Gdns. W14 . . . . .4H 99
Avonmore Mans. W14 . . . . .4G 99
 (off Avonmore Rd.)
Avonmore Pl. W14 . . . . .4G 99
Avonmore Rd. W14 . . . . .4G 99
Avonmouth Apts. SW11 . . . . .4C 118
 (off Monarch Sq.)
Avonmouth St. SE1 . . . .7C 14 (3C 102)
Avon Path CR2: S Croy 6C 168
Avon Pl. SE1 . . . . . .7D 14 (2C 102)
Avon Rd. E17 . . . . .3F 51
 SE4 .3C 122
 TW16: Sun 7H 129
 UB6: G'frd 4E 76
Avonstowe Cl. BR6: Farnb 3G 173
Avon Way E18 . . . . .3J 51
Avonwick Rd. TW3: Houn 2F 113
Avril Way E4 . . . . .5K 35
Avro Ct. E9 . . . . .5A 68
 (off Mabley St.)
Avro Ho. NW9 . . . . .2B 44
 (off Boulevard Dr.)
 SW8 . . . . .7F 101
 (off Havelock Ter.)
Avro Pl. TW5: Hest 7A 94
Avro Way SM6: W'gton 7J 167
Awfield Av. N17 . . . . .1D 48
Awliscombe Rd.
 DA16: Well 2K 125
Axe St. IG11: Bark 1G 89
 (not continuous)
Axholme Av. HA8: Edg 1G 43
Axiom Apts. BR2: Broml 4K 159
 (off Masons Hill)
Axio Way E3 . . . . .5C 86
Axis Apts. E1 . . . . .3J 9
 (off Sclater St.)
Axis Ct. SE10 . . . . .6G 105
 (off Woodland Cres.)
 SE16 . . . . .2G 103
 (off East La.)
Axis Ho. SE13 . . . . .4E 122
 (off Lewisham High St.)
Axminster Cres. DA16: Well 1C 126
Axminster Rd. N7 . . . . .3J 65
Axon Pl. IG1: IIf 2G 71
Aybrook St. W1 . . . . . .6G 5 (5E 82)
Aycliffe Cl.
 BR1: Broml 4D 160
Aycliffe Ho. SE17 . . . . .6D 102
 (off Portland St.)
Aycliffe Rd. W12 . . . . .1C 98
Ayerst Ct. E10 . . . . .7E 50

Aylands Cl. HA9: Wemb 2E 60
Aylesbury Cl. E7 . . . . .6H 69
Aylesbury Ct. SM1: Sutt 3A 166
Aylesbury Ho. HA0: Wemb 1E 78
 (off Hatton Rd.)
 SE15 . . . . .6G 103
 (off Friary Est.)
Aylesbury Rd. BR2: Broml 3J 159
 SE17 . . . . .5D 102
Aylesbury St. EC1 . . . . .4A 8 (4B 84)
 NW10 . . . . .3K 61
Aylesford Av. BR3: Beck 5A 158
Aylesford Ho. SE1 . . . . .7F 15
 (off Long La.)
Aylesford St. SW1 . . . .5C 18 (5H 101)
Aylesham Cen. 1G 121
Aylesham Ct. NW7 . . . . .7H 29
Aylesham Rd. BR6: Orp 7K 161
Aylestone Av. NW6 . . . . .7F 63
Aylett Rd. SE25 . . . . .4H 157
 TW7: Isle 2J 113
Ayley Cft. EN1: Enf 5B 24
Ayliffe Cl. KT1: King T 2G 151
Aylmer Cl. HA7: Stan 4F 27
Aylmer Ct. N2 . . . . .5D 46
Aylmer Dr. HA7: Stan 4F 27
Aylmer Ho. SE10 . . . . .5F 105
Aylmer Pde. N2 . . . . .5D 46
Aylmer Rd. E11 . . . . .1H 69
 N2 . . . . .5C 46
 RM8: Dag 3E 72
 W12 .2B 98
Ayloffe Rd. RM9: Dag 6F 73
Aylsham Dr. UB10: Ick 2E 56
Aylton Est. SE16 . . . . .2J 103
Aylward Rd. SE23 . . . . .2K 139
 SW20 . . . . .2H 153
Aylwards Ri. HA7: Stan 4F 27
Aylward St. E1 . . . . .6J 85
 (Jamaica St.)
 E1 . . . . .6J 85
 (Jubilee St.)
Aylwin Est. SE1 . . . . .3E 102
Aynhoe Mans. W14 . . . . .4F 99
 (off Aynhoe Rd.)
Aynhoe Rd. W14 . . . . .4F 99
Aynscombe Path SW14 . . . . .2J 115
Ayr Ct. W3 . . . . .5G 79
Ayres Cl. E13 . . . . .3J 87
Ayres St. SE1 . . . . . . .6D 14 (2C 102)
Ayr Grn. RM1: Rom 1K 55
Ayrsome Rd. N16 . . . . .3E 66
Ayrton Gould Ho. E2 . . . . .3K 85
 (off Roman Rd.)
Ayrton Rd. SW7 . . . . . .1A 16 (3B 100)
Ayr Way RM1: Rom 1K 55
Aysgarth Cl. SM1: Sutt 3K 165
Aysgarth Rd. SE21 . . . . .7E 120
Ayston Ho. SE16 . . . . .4K 103
 (off Plough Way)
Aytoun Pl. SW9 . . . . .2K 119
Aytoun Rd. SW9 . . . . .2K 119
Azalea Cl. IG1: IIf 5H 71
 W7 . . . . .1K 95
Azalea Ct. IG8: Wfd G 6B 36
 W7 . . . . .1K 95
Azalea Ho. SE14 . . . . .7B 104
 (off Achilles St.)
Azalea Wlk. HA5: Eastc 5K 39
Azania M. NW5 . . . . .6F 65
Azenby Rd. SE15 . . . . .2F 121
Azof St. SE10 . . . . .4G 105
Azov Ho. E1 . . . . .4A 86
 (off Commodore St.)
Aztec Ho. IG1: IIf 2H 71
 IG6: IIf 1G 53
Azura Cl. E15 . . . . .1E 86
 (off Warton Rd.)
Azure Bldg. E15 . . . . .7F 69
 (off Gt. Eastern Rd.)
Azure Ct. NW9 . . . . .5G 43

Azure Ho. E2 . . . . .3G 85
 (off Buckfast St.)
Azure Pl. TW3: Houn 4F 113

B

Baalbec Rd. N5 . . . . .5B 66
Babbacombe Cl.
 KT9: Chess 5D 162
Babbacombe Gdns. IG4: IIf 4C 52
Babbacombe Ho. BR1: Broml 1J 159
 (off Babbacombe Rd.)
Babbacombe Rd. BR1: Broml 1J 159
Babbage Ct. SE17 . . . . .6B 102
 (off Cooks Rd.)
Babbage Point SE10 . . . . .6D 104
 (off Norman Rd.)
Babell Ho. N1 . . . . .8B 66
 (off Canonbury Rd.)
Baber Bri. Cvn. Site 5A 112
Baber Bri. Pde. TW14: Felt 6A 112
Baber Dr. TW14: Felt 6A 112
Babington Ct. WC1 . . . . .5G 7
Babington Ho. SE1 . . . . .6D 14
 (off Disney St.)
Babington Ri. HA9: Wemb 6G 61
Babington Rd. NW4 . . . . .4D 44
 RM8: Dag 5C 72
 SW16 . . . . .5H 137
Babmaes St. SW1 . . . .3C 12 (7H 83)
Bache's St. N1 . . . . .2F 9 (3D 84)
Back All. EC3 . . . . .1H 15
Bk. Church La. E1 . . . . .6G 85
Bk. Hill EC1 . . . . .4K 7 (4A 84)
Backhouse Pl. SE17 . . . . .4E 102
Back La. DA5: Bexl 7G 127
 HA8: Edg 1J 43
 IG9: Buck H 2G 37
 N8 . . . . .5J 47
 NW3 . . . . .4A 64
 NW9 . . . . .2K 43
 RM6: Chad H 7D 54
 TW8: Bford 6D 96
 TW10: Ham 3C 132
Backley Gdns. SE25 . . . . .6G 157
Back Rd. DA14: Sidc 4A 144
 E11 . . . . .6G 51
 E17 . . . . .4E 50
 TW11: Tedd 7J 131
Bacon Gro. SE1 . . . . .3F 103
Bacon La. HA8: Edg 1G 43
 NW9 . . . . .4H 43
 (not continuous)
Bacon's College Sports Cen. 1A 104
Bacons La. N6 . . . . .1E 64
Bacon St. E1 . . . . .3K 9 (4F 85)
 E2 . . . . .3K 9 (4F 85)
Bacon Ter. RM8: Dag 5B 72
Bacton NW5 . . . . .5E 64
Bacton St. E2 . . . . .3J 85
Baddesley Ho. KT8: W Mole 5E 148
 (off Down St.)
Baddesley Ho. SE11 . . . . .5H 19
Baddow Cl. IG8: Wfd G 6F 37
 RM10: Dag 1G 91
Baden Dr. E4 . . . . .4J 25
Baden Pl. SE1 . . . . . . .6E 14 (2D 102)
Baden Powell Cl. KT6: Surb 2F 163
 RM9: Dag 1E 90
Baden Powell Ho. 2A 16
Baden Powell Ho. DA17: Belv 3G 109
 (off Ambrooke Rd.)
Baden Rd. IG1: IIf 5F 71
 N8 . . . . .4H 47
Bader Ct. NW9 . . . . .2B 44
 (off Runway Cl.)
Bader Way SW15 . . . . .6C 116
 UB10: Uxb 7A 56
Badger Cl. IG2: IIf 6G 53
 TW4: Houn 3A 112
 TW13: Felt 3K 129
Badger Ho. NW2 . . . . .3E 62

Badgers Cl. EN2: Enf 3G 23
 HA1: Harr 6H 41
 TW15: Ashf 5B 128
 UB3: Hayes 7G 75
Badgers Copse BR6: Orp 2K 173
 KT4: Wor Pk 2B 164
Badgers Cft. N20 . . . . .7B 20
 SE9 . . . . .3E 142
Badgers Hole CR0: C'don 4K 169
Badgers Wlk. KT3: N Mald 2A 152
Badlis Rd. E17 . . . . .3C 50
Badma Cl. N9 . . . . .3D 34
Badminton Cl. HA1: Harr 4J 41
 UB5: N'olt 6E 58
Badminton M. E16 . . . . .1J 105
Badminton Rd. SW12 . . . . .6E 118
Badric Cl. SW11 . . . . .2B 118
Badsworth Rd. SE5 . . . . .1C 120
Baffin Way E14 . . . . .1E 104
Bafton Ga. BR2: Hayes 1K 171
Bagley Cl. UB7: W Dray 2A 92
Bagley's La. SW6 . . . . .1K 117
Bagleys Spring RM6: Chad H 4E 54
Bagley Wlk. N1 . . . . .1H 83
Bagnigge Ho. WC1 . . . . .2J 7
 (off Margery St.)
Bagshot Ct. SE18 . . . . .1E 124
Bagshot Ho. NW1 . . . . .1K 5
Bagshot Rd. EN1: Enf 7A 24
Bagshot St. SE17 . . . . .5E 102
Bahram Cl. E2 . . . . .4H 85
 (off Three Colts La.)
Baildon E2 . . . . .2J 85
 (off Cyprus St.)
Baildon St. SE8 . . . . .7B 104
Bailes Pl. BR3: Beck 1A 158
Bailey Cl. E4 . . . . .4K 35
 N11 . . . . .7C 32
 SE28 .1J 107
Bailey Cotts. E14 . . . . .5A 86
 (off Maroon St.)
Bailey Ct. NW9 . . . . .3A 44
 (off Lingard Av.)
Bailey Cres. KT9: Chess 7D 162
Bailey Ho. E3 . . . . .3D 86
 (off Talwin St.)
 SW10 .7K 99
 (off Coleridge Gdns.)
Bailey M. SW2 . . . . .5A 120
 W4 . . . . .6H 97
Bailey Pl. N16 . . . . .5E 66
 SE26 .6K 139
Baileys Ho. SW11 . . . . .7H 101
 (off Charles Clowes Wl.k)
Bailey St. SE8 . . . . .4A 104
Bailey Twr. E1 . . . . .7H 85
Baillies Wlk. W5 . . . . .2D 96
Bainbridge Cl. TW10: Ham 5E 132
Bainbridge Court SE10 . . . . .3J 105
 (off Rennie Street)
Bainbridge Rd. RM9: Dag 4F 73
 (off Charlton King's Rd.)
Baird Cl. NW1 . . . . .7D 6 (6H 83)
Baird Av. UB1: S'hall 7F 77
Baird Cl. E10 . . . . .1C 68
 NW9 . . . . .6J 43
Baird Gdns. SE19 . . . . .4E 138
Baird Ho. W12 . . . . .7D 80
 (off White City Est.)
Baird Memorial Cotts. N14 . . . . . . .2C 32
 (off Balaams La.)
Baird Rd. EN1: Enf 3C 24
Baird St. EC1 . . . . .3D 8 (4C 84)
Bairny Wood App.
 IG8: Wfd G 6E 36
Baizdon Rd. SE3 . . . . .2G 123
Bakehouse M. TW12: Hamp 7E 130
Baker Beal Ct. DA7: Bex 3H 127
Baker Ho. E3 . . . . .3D 86
 (off Bromley High St.)
 W7 . . . . .1K 95
 WC1 . . . . .4F 7
 (off Colonnade)

Baker La.—Bankside

Baker La. CR4: Mitc . . . 2E 154
Baker Pas. NW10 . . . 1A 80
Baker Pl. KT19: Ewe . . . 6J 163
Baker Rd. NW10 . . . 1A 80
SE18 . . . 7C 106
Bakers Av. E17 . . . 6D 50
Bakers Ct. SE25 . . . 3E 156
Bakers End SW20 . . . 2G 153
Baker's Fld. N7 . . . 4H 65
Bakers Field Cl. KT19: Ewe . . . 7K 163
Bakers Gdns. SM5: Cars . . . 2C 166
Bakers Hall Ct. EC3 . . . 3G 15
Bakers Hill E5 . . . 1J 67
EN5: New Bar . . . 2E 20
Bakers Ho. W5 . . . 1D 96
(off The Grove)
Bakers La. N6 . . . 6D 46
Baker's M. W1 . . . 7G 5 (6E 82)
Bakers M. BR6: Chels . . . 6K 173
Bakers Pas. NW3 . . . 4A 64
(off Heath St.)
Baker's Rents E2 . . . 2J 9 (3F 85)
Baker's Row E15 . . . 2G 87
EC1 . . . 4J 7 (4A 84)
BAKER STREET . . . 5D 82
Baker St. EN1: Enf . . . 3J 23
NW1 . . . 4F 5 (4D 82)
W1 . . . 4F 5 (4D 82)
Baker's Yd. EC1 . . . 4J 7
Bakery Cl. RM6: Chad H . . . 3E 54
SW9 . . . 7K 101
Bakery M. KT6: Surb . . . 1G 163
Bakery Path HA8: Edg . . . 5C 28
(off St Margaret's Rd.)
Bakery Pl. SW11 . . . 4D 118
Bakery St. SE16 . . . 3F 103
Bakewell Way KT3: N Mald . . . 2A 152
Balaam Ho. SM1: Sutt . . . 4J 165
Balaam Leisure Cen. . . . 4J 87
Balaams La. N14 . . . 2C 32
Balaam St. E13 . . . 4J 87
Balaclava Rd. KT6: Surb . . . 7C 150
SE1 . . . 4F 103
Bala Grn. NW9 . . . 6A 44
(off Ruthin Cl.)
Balboa Court E14 . . . 5A 86
(off Pechora Way)
Balcaskie Rd. SE9 . . . 5D 124
Balchen Rd. SE3 . . . 2B 124
Balchier Rd. SE22 . . . 6H 121
Balcombe Cl. DA6: Bex . . . 4D 126
Balcombe Ho. NW1 . . . 3E 4
(off Taunton Pl.)
Balcombe St. NW1 . . . 3E 4 (4D 82)
Balcon Ct. W5 . . . 6F 79
The Balcony W12 . . . 1F 99
Balcorne St. E9 . . . 7J 67
Balder Ri. SE12 . . . 2K 141
Balderton Flats W1 . . . 1H 11
(off Balderton St.)
Balderton St. W1 . . . 1H 11 (6E 82)
Baldewyne Ct. N17 . . . 1G 49
Baldock St. E3 . . . 2D 86
Baldrey Ho. SE10 . . . 5H 105
(off Blackwall La.)
Baldry Gdns. SW16 . . . 6J 137
Baldwin Cres. SE5 . . . 1C 120
Baldwin Gdns. TW3: Houn . . . 1G 113
Baldwin Ho. SW2 . . . 1A 138
Baldwin Rd. SW11 . . . 6E 118
Baldwins Gdns. EC1 . . . 5J 7 (5A 84)
Baldwin St. EC1 . . . 2E 8 (3D 84)
Baldwin Ter. N1 . . . 2C 84
Baldwyn Gdns. W3 . . . 7K 79
Baldwyn's Pk. DA5: Bexl . . . 2K 145
Baldwyn's Rd. DA5: Bexl . . . 2K 145
Balearic Apts. E16 . . . 7J 87
(off Western Gateway)
Bale Rd. E1 . . . 5A 86
Bales Ter. N9 . . . 3A 34
Balfern Gro. W4 . . . 5A 98
Balfern St. SW11 . . . 2C 118
Balfe St. N1 . . . 2J 83
Balfour Av. W7 . . . 1K 95
Balfour Bus. Cen.
UB2: S'hall . . . 3A 94
Balfour Gro. N20 . . . 3J 31
Balfour Ho. SW11 . . . 1E 118
(off Forfar Rd.)
W10 . . . 5F 81
(off St Charles Sq.)
Balfour M. N9 . . . 3B 34
W1 . . . 4H 11 (1E 100)
Balfour Pl. SW15 . . . 4D 116
W1 . . . 3H 11 (7E 82)
Balfour Rd. BR2: Broml . . . 5B 160
HA1: Harr . . . 5H 41
IG1: Ilf . . . 2F 71
N5 . . . 4C 66
SE25 . . . 5G 157
SM5: Cars . . . 7D 166
SW19 . . . 7K 135
TW3: Houn . . . 3F 113
UB2: S'hall . . . 3B 94
W3 . . . 5J 79
W13 . . . 2A 96
Balfour St. SE17 . . . 4D 102
Balfour Ter. N3 . . . 2K 45
Balfron Twr. E14 . . . 6E 86
Balgonie Rd. E4 . . . 1A 36
Balgove Ct. NW10 . . . 6D 62
(off Eden Gro.)
Balgowan Cl. KT3: N Mald . . . 5A 152
Balgowan Rd. BR3: Beck . . . 3A 158
Balgowan St. SE18 . . . 4K 107
BALHAM . . . 1E 136
Balham Gro. SW12 . . . 7E 118
Balham High Rd. SW12 . . . 3E 136
SW17 . . . 3E 136
Balham Hill SW12 . . . 7F 119
Balham Leisure Cen. . . . 2F 137
Balham New Rd. SW12 . . . 7F 119
Balham Pk. Rd. SW12 . . . 1D 136
Balham Rd. N9 . . . 2B 34
Balham Sta. Rd. SW12 . . . 1F 137
Balin Ho. SE1 . . . 6E 14
(off Long La.)
Balladier Wlk. E14 . . . 5D 86
Ballamore Rd.
BR1: Broml . . . 3J 141
Ballance Rd. E9 . . . 6K 67
Ballantine St. SW18 . . . 4A 118
Ballantrae Ho. NW2 . . . 4H 63
Ballantyne Cl. SE9 . . . 4C 142
Ballard Cl. KT2: King T . . . 7K 133
Ballard Ho. SE10 . . . 6D 104
(off Thames St.)
Ballards Cl. RM10: Dag . . . 1H 91
Ballards Farm Rd.
CR0: C'don . . . 6G 169
CR2: S Croy . . . 6G 169
Ballards La. N3 . . . 1J 45
N12 . . . 1J 45
Ballards M. HA8: Edg . . . 6B 28
Ballards Ri. CR2: Sels . . . 6G 169
Ballards Rd. NW2 . . . 2C 62
RM10: Dag . . . 2H 91
Ballards Way CR0: C'don . . . 6G 169
CR2: Sels . . . 6G 169
Ballast Quay SE10 . . . 5F 105
Ballater Rd. CR2: S Croy . . . 5F 169
SW2 . . . 4J 119
Ball Ct. EC3 . . . 1F 15
(off Birchin La.)
Balletica Apts. WC2 . . . 1F 13
(off Long Acre)
Ball Ho. NW9 . . . 3B 44
(off Aerodrome Rd.)
Ballie Apts. E16 . . . 7G 89
(off Lock Side Way)
Ballina St. SE23 . . . 7K 121
Ballin Ct. E14 . . . 2E 104
(off Stewart St.)
Ballingdon Rd. SW11 . . . 6E 118
Ballinger Point E3 . . . 3D 86
(off Bromley High St.)
Ballinger Way UB5: N'olt . . . 4C 76
Balliol Av. E4 . . . 4B 36
Balliol Rd.
DA16: Well . . . 2B 126
N17 . . . 1E 48
W10 . . . 6E 80
Balloch Rd. SE6 . . . 1F 141
Ballogie Av. NW10 . . . 4A 62
Ballow Cl. SE5 . . . 7E 102
Balls Pond Pl. N1 . . . 6D 66
Balls Pond Rd. N1 . . . 6D 66
Balmain Cl. W5 . . . 1D 96
Balmain Ct. TW3: Houn . . . 1F 113
Balmain Lodge KT5: Surb . . . 4E 150
(off Cranes Pk. Av.)
Balman Ho. SE16 . . . 4K 103
(off Rotherhithe New Rd.)
Balmer Rd. E3 . . . 2B 86
Balmes Rd. N1 . . . 1D 84
Balmoral Apts. W2 . . . 6C 4
(off Praed St.)
Balmoral Av. BR3: Beck . . . 4A 158
N11 . . . 6K 31
Balmoral Cl. SW15 . . . 6F 117
Balmoral Ct. BR3: Beck . . . 1E 158
(off The Avenue)
HA9: Wemb . . . 3F 61
KT4: Wor Pk . . . 2D 164
NW8 . . . 2B 82
(off Queen's Ter.)
SE12 . . . 4K 141
SE16 . . . 1K 103
(off King & Queen Wharf)
SE17 . . . 5D 102
(off Merrow St.)
SE27 . . . 4C 138
SM2: Sutt . . . 7J 165
Balmoral Cres.
KT8: W Mole . . . 3E 148
Balmoral Dr. UB1: S'hall . . . 4D 76
UB4: Hayes . . . 4G 75
Balmoral Gdns. DA5: Bexl . . . 7F 127
IG3: Ilf . . . 1K 71
W13 . . . 3A 96
Balmoral Ho. E14 . . . 3D 104
(off Lanark Sq.)
E16 . . . 1K 105
(off Keats Av.)
SE1 . . . 1F 103
(off Duchess Wlk.)
W14 . . . 4G 99
(off Windsor Way)
Balmoral M. W12 . . . 3B 98
Balmoral Rd. E7 . . . 4A 70
E10 . . . 2D 68
HA2: Harr . . . 4E 58
KT1: King T . . . 4F 151
KT4: Wor Pk . . . 3D 164
NW2 . . . 6D 62
Balmoral Trad. Est.
IG11: Bark . . . 5K 89
Balmore Cl. E14 . . . 6E 86
Balmore Cres. EN4: Cockf . . . 5K 21
Balmore St. N19 . . . 2F 65
Balmuir Gdns. SW15 . . . 4E 116
Balnacraig Av. NW10 . . . 4A 62
Balniel Ga. SW1 . . . 5D 18 (5H 101)
Balsam Ho. E14 . . . 7D 86
(off E. India Dock Rd.)
Baltic Apts. E16 . . . 7J 87
(off Western Gateway)
Baltic Av. TW8: Bford . . . 5D 96
Baltic Cl. SW19 . . . 7B 136
Baltic Ct. E1 . . . 1J 103
(off Clave St.)
SE16 . . . 2K 103
Baltic Ho. SE5 . . . 2C 120
Baltic Pl. N1 . . . 1E 84
Baltic St. E. EC1 . . . 4C 8 (4C 84)
Baltic St. W. EC1 . . . 4C 8 (4C 84)
Baltimore Cl. DA17: Belv . . . 2H 109
Baltimore Ct. SW1 . . . 4C 18
(off Vauxhall Bri. Rd.)
Baltimore Ho. SE11 . . . 5J 19
SW18 . . . 3A 118
Baltimore Pl. DA16: Well . . . 2K 125
Baltimore Wharf E14 . . . 3D 104
Balvaird Pl. SW1 . . . 6D 18 (5H 101)
Balvernie Gro. SW18 . . . 7H 117
Balvernie M. SW18 . . . 7J 117
Bamber Ho. IG11: Bark . . . 1G 89
Bamber Rd. SE15 . . . 1F 121
Bamboo Ct. E5 . . . 2J 67
(off Woodmill Rd.)
Bamborough Gdns. W12 . . . 2E 98
Bamburgh N17 . . . 7C 34
Bamford Av. HA0: Wemb . . . 1F 79
Bamford Rd. BR1: Broml . . . 5E 140
IG11: Bark . . . 6G 71
Bampfylde Cl. SM6: W'gton . . . 3G 167
Bampton Ct. W5 . . . 6D 78
Bampton Dr. NW7 . . . 7H 29
Bampton Rd. SE23 . . . 3K 139
Banavie Gdns. BR3: Beck . . . 1E 158
Banbury Cl. EN2: Enf . . . 1G 23
Banbury Ct. SM2: Sutt . . . 7J 165
WC2 . . . 2E 12
Banbury Ho. E9 . . . 7K 67
Banbury Rd. E9 . . . 7K 67
E17 . . . 7E 34
Banbury St. SW11 . . . 2C 118
Banbury Wlk. UB5: N'olt . . . 2E 76
(off Brabazon Rd.)
Banchory Rd. SE3 . . . 7K 105
Bancroft Av. IG9: Buck H . . . 2D 36
N2 . . . 5C 46
Bancroft Cl. TW15: Ashf . . . 5C 128
Bancroft Ct. SW8 . . . 7J 101
(off Allen Edwards Dr.)
UB5: N'olt . . . 1A 76
Bancroft Gdns. BR6: Orp . . . 1K 173
HA3: Hrw W . . . 1G 41
Bancroft Ho. E1 . . . 4J 85
(off Cephas St.)
Bancroft Rd. E1 . . . 3J 85
HA3: Hrw W . . . 2G 41
Bandon Cl. UB10: Uxb . . . 2B 74
BANDONHILL . . . 5H 167
Bandon Ri. SM6: W'gton . . . 5H 167
Banfield Rd. SE15 . . . 3H 121
Banfor Ct. SM6: W'gton . . . 5G 167
Bangalore St. SW15 . . . 3E 116
Bangla Ho. E8 . . . 1F 85
(off Clarissa St.)
Bangor Cl. UB5: N'olt . . . 5F 59
Banim St. W6 . . . 4D 98
Banister Ho. E9 . . . 5K 67
SW8 . . . 1G 119
(off Wadhurst Rd.)
W10 . . . 3G 81
(off Bruckner St.)
Banister M. NW6 . . . 7K 63
Banister Rd. W10 . . . 3F 81
The Bank N6 . . . 1F 65
Bank Av. CR4: Mitc . . . 2B 154
Bank Bldgs. E4 . . . 6A 36
(off The Avenue)
Bank Ct. E17 . . . 4E 50
Bank End SE1 . . . 4D 14 (1C 102)
Bankfoot Rd. BR1: Broml . . . 4G 141
Bankhurst Rd. SE6 . . . 7B 122
Bank La. KT2: King T . . . 7E 132
SW15 . . . 5A 116
Bank M. SM1: Sutt . . . 6A 166
Bank of England . . . 1E 14 (6D 84)
Bank of England Museum . . . 1F 15
Bank of England Sports Cen. . . . 5A 116
Banks Ho. SE1 . . . 3C 102
(off Rockingham St.)
Banksian Wlk. TW7: Isle . . . 1J 113
Banksia Rd. N18 . . . 5E 34
Bankside CR2: S Croy . . . 6F 169
EN2: Enf . . . 1G 23
SE1 . . . 3C 14 (7C 84)
(not continuous)
UB1: S'hall . . . 1B 94

Bankside Av. SE13 . . . . .3E **122**
UB5: N'olt 2J **75**
Bankside Cl. DA5: Bexl 4K **145**
SM5: Cars 6C **166**
TW7: Isle 4K **113**
Bankside Dr. KT7: T Ditt 1B **162**
Bankside Gallery **3B 14** (7B **84**)
Bankside Lofts SE1 . . . . .4B **14**
Bankside Mix 4C **14** (1C **102**)
Bankside Pk.
IG11: Bark 3A **90**
Bankside Pl. N4 . . . . .6C **48**
Bankside Rd. IG1: Ilf 5G **71**
Bankside Way SE19 . . . . .6E **138**
Banks La. DA6: Bex 4F **127**
Bank St. E14 . . . . .1D **104**
Banks Way E12 . . . . .4E **70**
Banks Yd. TW5: Hest 6D **94**
Bankton Rd. SW2 . . . . .4A **120**
Bankwell Rd. SE13 . . . . .4G **123**
Bannatyne Health Club
Chingford 6H **35**
Grove Park 2K **141**
Maida Vale 2K **81**
(off Greville Rd.)
Orpington 7D **144**
Russell Square 3D **6**
(off Woburn Pl.)
Banner Ct. SE16 . . . . .4J **103**
(off Rotherhithe New Rd.)
Banner Ho. EC1 . . . . .4D **8**
(off Roscoe St.)
Banner La. RM8: Dag 1E **72**
Bannerman Ho. SW8 . . .7G **19** (6K **101**)
Banner St. EC1 . . . . .4D **8** (4C **84**)
Banning St. SE10 . . . . .5G **105**
Bannister Cl. SW2 . . . . .1A **138**
UB6: G'frd 5H **59**
Bannister Ho. HA3: W'stone 3J **41**
(off Headstone Dr.)
SE14 . . . . .6K **103**
(off John Williams Cl.)
Bannister Sports Cen. 6B **26**
Bannockburn Rd. SE18 . . . . . . .4J **107**
Bannon Ct. SW6 . . . . .1K **117**
(off Michael Rd.)
Bannow Cl. KT19: Ewe 4A **164**
Banqueting House 5E **12** (1J **101**)
Banstead Ct. W12 . . . . .7B **80**
Banstead Gdns. N9 . . . . .3K **33**
Banstead Rd. SM5: Cars 7B **166**
Banstead Rd. Sth. SM2: Sutt 7B **166**
Banstead St. SE15 . . . . .3J **121**
Banstead Way SM6: W'gton 5J **167**
Banstock Rd. HA8: Edg 6C **28**
Bantam Ho. NW9 . . . . .2B **44**
(off Heritage Av.)
Banting Dr. N21 . . . . .5E **22**
Banting Ho. NW2 . . . . .3C **62**
Bantock Ho. W10 . . . . .3G **81**
(off Third Av.)
Banton Cl. EN1: Enf 2C **24**
Bantry Ho. E1 . . . . .4K **85**
(off Ernest St.)
Bantry St. SE5 . . . . .7D **102**
Banwell Rd. DA5: Bexl 6D **126**
Banyan Court E16 . . . . .1K **105**
(off Regalia Close)
Banyard Rd. SE16 . . . . .3H **103**
Baptist Gdns. NW5 . . . . .6E **64**
Baquba SE13 . . . . .2D **122**
Barandon Rd. W11 . . . . .7F **81**
(off Grenfell Rd.)
Baranbel Ho. E1 . . . . .4J **85**
(off Cephas St.)
Barbara Brosnan Ct. NW8 . .1A **4** (2B **82**)
Barbara Castle Cl. SW6 . . . . .6H **99**
Barbara Cl. TW17: Shep 5D **146**
Barbara Hucklesby Cl. N22 . . . . .2B **48**
Barbauld Rd. N16 . . . . .3E **66**
Barber Beaumont Ho. E1 . . . . . . .3K **85**
(off Bancroft Rd.)

Barber Cl. N21 . . . . .7F **23**
Barberry Ct. E15 . . . . .6G **69**
Barbers All. E13 . . . . .3K **87**
Barbers Rd. E15 . . . . .2D **86**
Barbican EC2 . . . . .5D **8**
Barbican Art Gallery 5C **84**
Barbican Arts Centre 5D **8** (5C **84**)
Barbican Cinema 1 . . . . .5D **8**
(within Arts Cen.)
Barbican Cinema 2 & 3 . . . . . . .5D **8**
(off Whitecross St.)
Barbican Rd. UB6: G'frd 6F **77**
Barbican Theatre 5D **8**
(within Arts Cen.)
Barb M. W6 . . . . .3E **98**
Barbon Cl. WC1 . . . . . . .5F **7** (5K **83**)
Barbot Cl. N9 . . . . .3B **34**
Barchard St. SW18 . . . . .5K **117**
Barchester Cl. W7 . . . . .1K **95**
Barchester Rd. HA3: Hrw W 2H **41**
Barchester St. E14 . . . . .5D **86**
Barclay Cl. SW6 . . . . .7J **99**
Barclay Ho. E9 . . . . .7J **67**
(off Well St.)
Barclay Oval IG8: Wfd G 4D **36**
Barclay Path E17 . . . . .5E **50**
Barclay Rd. CR0: C'don 3D **168**
E11 . . . . .1H **69**
E13 . . . . .4A **88**
E17 . . . . .5E **50**
N18 . . . . .6J **33**
SW6 .7J **99**
Barcombe Av. SW2 . . . . .2J **137**
Barcombe Cl. BR5: St P 3K **161**
Bardell Ho. SE1 . . . . .7K **15**
(off Parkers Row)
Barden St. SE18 . . . . .7J **107**
Bardfield Av. RM6: Chad H 3D **54**
Bardney Rd. SM4: Mord 4K **153**
Bardolph Rd. N7 . . . . .4J **65**
TW9: Rich 3F **115**
Bard Rd. W10 . . . . .7F **81**
Bardsey Pl. E1 . . . . .4J **85**
Bardsey Wlk. N1 . . . . .6C **66**
(off Douglas Rd. Nth.)
Bardsley Cl. CR0: C'don 3E **168**
Bardsley Ho. SE10 . . . . .6E **104**
(off Bardsley La.)
Bardsley La. SE10 . . . . .6E **104**
Barents Ho. E1 . . . . .4K **85**
(off White Horse La.)
Barfett St. W10 . . . . .4H **81**
Barfield Av. N20 . . . . .2J **31**
Barfield Rd. BR1: Broml 3E **160**
E11 . . . . .1H **69**
Barfleur La. SE8 . . . . .4B **104**
Barford Cl. NW4 . . . . .2C **44**
Barford Ho. E3 . . . . .2B **86**
(off Tredegar Rd.)
Barford St. N1 . . . . .1A **84**
Barforth Rd. SE15 . . . . .3H **121**
Barfreston Way SE20 . . . . .1H **157**
Bargate Cl. KT3: N Mald 7C **152**
SE18 .5K **107**
Barge Dr. UB2: S'hall 3F **95**
Barge Ho. Rd. E16 . . . . .2F **107**
Barge Ho. St. SE1 . . . . . .4K **13** (1A **102**)
Barge La. E3 . . . . .1A **86**
Bargery Rd. SE6 . . . . .1D **140**
Barge Wlk.
KT1: Hamp W 1D **150**
KT2: King T 1D **150**
KT8: E Mos 6A **150**
(Boyle Farm Island)
KT8: E Mos 3H **149**
(Hampton Ct. Cres.)
SE10 .3H **105**
Bargrove Cl. SE20 . . . . .6H **139**
Bargrove Cres. SE6 . . . . .2B **140**
Barham Cl. BR2: Broml 1C **172**
BR7: Chst 5F **143**
HA0: Wemb 6B **60**
RM7: Mawney 2H **55**

Barham Ct. CR2: S Croy 4C **168**
(off Barham Rd.)
Barham Ho. SE17 . . . . .5E **102**
(off Kinglake Est.)
Barham Rd. BR7: Chst 5F **143**
CR2: S Croy 4C **168**
SW20 . . . . .7C **134**
Baring Cl. SE12 . . . . .2J **141**
Baring Ct. N1 . . . . .1D **84**
(off Baring St.)
Baring Ho. E14 . . . . .6C **86**
(off Canton St.)
Baring Rd. CR0: C'don 1G **169**
EN4: Cockf 4G **21**
SE12 . . . . .7J **123**
Baring St. N1 . . . . .1D **84**
Baritone Ct. E15 . . . . .1H **87**
(off Church St.)
Barker Cl. HA6: Nwood 1H **39**
KT3: N Mald 4H **151**
TW9: Kew 2H **115**
Barker Dr. NW1 . . . . .7G **65**
Barker Ho. SE17 . . . . .4E **102**
(off Congreve St.)
Barker M. SW4 . . . . .4F **119**
Barker's Arc. 2K **99**
Barker St. SW10 . . . . .6A **100**
Barker Wlk. SW16 . . . . .3H **137**
Barkham Rd. N17 . . . . .7J **33**
Barkham Ter. SE1 . . . . .1K **19**
BARKING 7G **71**
Barking Abbey 1G **89**
Barking Abbey School Leisure Cen.
. . . . .6A **72**
Barking Bus. Cen. IG11: Bark . . .3A **90**
Barking Ind. Pk. IG11: Bark 1K **89**
Barking Northern Relief Rd.
IG11: Bark 7F **71**
Barking Park Miniature Railway . .6H **71**
BARKING RIVERSIDE 3B **90**
Barking Rd. E6 . . . . .2A **88**
E13 . . . . .4J **87**
E16 . . . . .5G **87**
BARKINGSIDE 3G **53**
Barking Splash Pk. 5H **71**
Barkis Ho. W11 . . . . .1F **99**
Bark Pl. W2 . . . . .7K **81**
Barkston Gdns. SW5 . . . . .4K **99**
Barkway Ct. N4 . . . . .2C **66**
Barkway Dr. BR6: Farnb 4E **172**
Barkwith Ho. SE14 . . . . .6K **103**
(off Cold Blow La.)
Barkwood Cl. RM7: Rom 5J **55**
Barkworth Rd. SE16 . . . . .5H **103**
Barlborough St. SE14 . . . . .7K **103**
Barlby Gdns. W10 . . . . .4F **81**
Barlby Rd. W10 . . . . .5E **80**
Barley Cl. HA0: Wemb 4D **60**
Barleycorn Way E14 . . . . .7B **86**
(not continuous)
Barley Ct. E5 . . . . .2J **67**
RM13: Rain 5K **91**
(off Lwr Mardyke Av.)
Barleyfields Cl. RM6: Chad H 6B **54**
Barley La. IG3: Ilf 7A **54**
RM6: Chad H 7A **54**
Barley Mow Pas. EC1 . . . . .6B **8**
W4 . . . . .5K **97**
Barley Mow Way
TW17: Shep 4C **146**
Barley Shotts Bus. Pk. W10 . . . . .5H **81**
Barley Wlk. SW18 . . . . .5K **117**
Barling NW1 . . . . .6F **65**
(off Castlehaven Rd.)
Barlow Cl. SM6: W'gton 6J **167**
Barlow Dr. SE18 . . . . .1C **124**
Barlow Ho. N1 . . . . .1E **8**
(off Provost St.)
SE16 . . . . .4H **103**
(off Rennie Est.)
W11 .7G **81**
(off Walmer Rd.)
Barlow Pl. W1 . . . . .3K **11** (7F **83**)

Barlow Rd. NW6 . . . . .6H **63**
TW12: Hamp 7E **130**
W3 . . . . .1H **97**
Barlow St. SE17 . . . . .4D **102**
Barlow Way RM13: Rain 5K **91**
Barmeston Rd. SE6 . . . . .2D **140**
Barmor Cl. HA2: Harr 2F **41**
Barmouth Av. UB6: G'frd 2K **77**
Barmouth Rd. CR0: C'don 2K **169**
SW18 . . . . .6A **118**
Barnabas Ct. EN2: Enf 4F **23**
Barnabas Ho. EC1 . . . . .2C **8**
Barnabas Lodge SW8 . . . . .1J **119**
(off Guildford Rd.)
Barnabas Rd. E9 . . . . .5K **67**
Barnaby Cl. HA2: Harr 3A **59**
Barnaby Ct. NW9 . . . . .3A **44**
SE16 . . . . .2G **103**
(off Scott Lidgett Cres.)
Barnaby Ho. SE15 . . . . .6J **103**
Barnaby Pl. SW7 . . . . .4A **16**
Barnaby Way IG7: Chig 3K **37**
Barnard Cl. BR7: Chst 1H **161**
SE18 .3E **106**
SM6: W'gton 7H **167**
TW16: Sun 7H **129**
Barnard Gdns. KT3: N Mald 4C **152**
UB4: Yead 4K **75**
Barnard Gro. E15 . . . . .7H **69**
Barnard Hill N10 . . . . .1F **47**
Barnard Ho. E2 . . . . .3H **85**
(off Ellsworth St.)
Barnard Lodge EN5: New Bar 4F **21**
W9 . . . . .5J **81**
(off Admiral Wlk.)
Barnard M. SW11 . . . . .4C **118**
Barnardo Dr. IG6: Ilf 4G **53**
Barnardo Gdns. E1 . . . . .7K **85**
Barnardo St. E1 . . . . .6K **85**
Barnardo Village Wlk. IG6: Ilf 3G **53**
Barnard Rd. CR4: Mitc 3E **154**
EN1: Enf 1C **24**
SW11 . . . . .4C **118**
Barnards Ho. SE16 . . . . .2B **104**
(off Wyatt Cl.)
Barnard's Inn EC1 . . . . .6J **7**
Barnborough NW1 . . . . .1G **83**
(off Camden St.)
Barnby Sq. E15 . . . . .1G **87**
Barnby St. E15 . . . . .1G **87**
NW1 . . . . .1B **6** (2G **83**)
Barn Cl. NW5 . . . . .5H **65**
(off Torriano Av.)
TW15: Ashf 5D **128**
UB5: N'olt 2A **76**
Barn Cres. HA7: Stan 6H **27**
Barncroft Cl. UB8: Hil 5D **74**
Barneby Cl. TW2: Twick 1J **131**
BARNEHURST 3J **127**
Barnehurst Av. DA7: Bex 1J **127**
DA8: Erith 1J **127**
Barnehurst Cl. DA8: Erith 1J **127**
Barnehurst Golf Course 3K **127**
Barnehurst Rd. DA7: Bex 2J **127**
Barn Elms Athletics Track 2D **116**
Barn Elms Cl. KT4: Wor Pk 3B **164**
Barn Elms Pk. SW15 . . . . .3E **116**
BARNES 2B **116**
Barnes All. TW12: Hamp 2G **149**
Barnes Av. SW13 . . . . .7C **98**
UB2: S'hall 4D **94**
BARNES BRI. 2A **116**
Barnes Cl. E12 . . . . .4B **70**
HA8: Edg 4A **28**
Barnes Common
Nature Reserve 3C **116**
Barnes Ct. CR7: Thor H 3C **156**
E16 . . . . .5A **88**
EN5: New Bar 4E **20**
IG8: Buck H, Wfd G 5G **37**
N1 . . . . .7A **66**
Barnes End KT3: N Mald 5C **152**
Barnes High St. SW13 . . . . .2B **116**

Barnes Ho.—Bashley Rd.

Barnes Ho. E2 2J 85
(off Wadeson St.)
NW1 7F 65
(off Camden Rd.)
SE14 6K 103
(off John Williams Cl.)
Barnes Pikle W5 7D 78
Barnes Rd. IG1: Ilf 5G 71
N18 4D 34
Barnes St. E14 6A 86
Barnes Ter. SE8 5B 104
Barnes Wallis Ct. HA9: Wemb 3J 61
BARNET 3B 20
Barnet Burnt Oak Leisure Cen. 1K 43
Barnet Bus. Cen. EN5: Barn 3B 20
Barnet By-Pass NW7 6G 29
Barnet Copthall Leisure Cen. 7J 29
Barnet Copthall Sports Cen. 1D 44
Barnet Dr. BR2: Broml 2C 172
Barnet FC 1E 42
Barnet Ga. La. EN5: Ark 1H 29
Barnet Gro. E2 1K 9 (3G 85)
Barnet Hill EN5: Barn 4C 20
Barnet Ho. N20 2F 31
Barnet La. EN5: Barn 1C 30
N20 1C 30
Barnet Mus. 4B 20
Barnetts Ct. HA2: Harr 3F 59
Barnett St. E1 6H 85
BARNET VALE 5E 20
Barnet Way NW7 3E 28
Barnet Wood Rd. BR2: Broml 2A 172
Barney Cl. SE7 5A 106
Barn Fld. NW3 5D 64
Barnfield KT3: N Mald 6A 152
Barnfield Av. CR0: C'don 2J 169
CR4: Mitc 4F 155
KT2: King T 4D 132
Barnfield Cl. N4 7J 47
SW17 3B 136
Barnfield Gdns. KT2: King T 4E 132
SE18 6F 107
Barnfield Pl. E14 4C 104
Barnfield Rd. CR2: Sande 7E 168
DA17: Belv 6F 109
HA8: Edg 1J 43
SE18 6F 107
(not continuous)
W5 4C 78
Barnfield Wood Cl. BR3: Beck 6F 159
Barnfield Wood Rd. BR3: Beck 6F 159
Barnham Dr. SE28 1K 107
(not continuous)
Barnham Rd. UB6: G'frd 3G 77
Barnham St. SE1 6H 15 (2E 102)
Barn Hill HA9: Wemb 1G 61
Barnhill HA5: Eastc 5A 40
Barnhill Av. BR2: Broml 5H 159
Barnhill La. UB4: Yead 3K 75
Barnhill Rd. HA9: Wemb 3J 61
UB4: Yead 3K 75
Barningham Way NW9 6K 43
Barnlea Cl. TW13: Hanw 2C 130
Barnmead Ct. RM9: Dag 5F 73
Barnmead Gdns. RM9: Dag 5F 73
Barnmead Rd. BR3: Beck 1K 157
RM9: Dag 5F 73
Barn M. HA2: Harr 3E 58
Barn Ri. HA9: Wemb 1G 61
BARNSBURY 7K 65
Barnsbury Cl. KT3: N Mald 4J 151
Barnsbury Cres. KT5: Surb 1J 163
Barnsbury Est. N1 1K 83
(not continuous)
Barnsbury Gro. N7 7K 65
Barnsbury Ho. SW4 6H 119
Barnsbury La. KT5: Surb 2H 163
Barnsbury Pk. N1 7A 66
Barnsbury Rd. N1 2A 84
Barnsbury Sq. N1 7A 66
Barnsbury St. N1 7A 66
Barnsbury Ter. N1 7K 65
Barnscroft SW20 3D 152
Barnsdale Av. E14 4D 104
Barnsdale Rd. W9 4H 81
Barnsley St. E1 4H 85
Barnstaple Ho. SE10 7D 104
(off Devonshire Dr.)
SE12 5H 123
(off Taunton Rd.)
Barnstaple La. SE13 4E 122
Barnstaple Rd. HA4: Ruis 3A 58
Barnston Wlk. N1 1C 84
(off Popham St.)
Barn St. N16 2E 66
The Barn Theatre
Sidcup 1A 144
West Molesey 4E 148
Barn Way HA9: Wemb 1G 61
Barnwell Cl. HA8: Edg 4A 28
Barnwell Ho. SE5 1E 120
(off St Giles Rd.)
Barnwell Rd. SW2 5A 120
Barnwood Cl. HA4: Ruis 2F 57
N20 1C 30
W9 4K 81
Baron Cl. N1 2A 84
N11 5K 31
Baroness Rd. E2 1K 9 (3F 85)
Baronet Gro. N17 1G 49
Baronet Rd. N17 1G 49
Baron Gdns. IG6: Ilf 3G 53
Baron Gro. CR4: Mitc 4C 154
Baron Ho. SW19 1B 154
Baron Rd. RM8: Dag 1D 72
The Barons TW1: Twick 6B 114
Baronsclere Ct. N6 7G 47
BARONS COURT 5G 99
Barons Ct. IG1: Ilf 2H 71
NW9 6K 43
SM6: Bedd 3H 167
Baron's Ct. Rd. W14 5G 99
Barons Court Theatre 5G 99
(off Comeragh Rd.)
Baronsfield Rd. TW1: Twick 6B 114
Barons Ga. EN4: E Barn 6H 21
W4 3J 97
Barons Keep W14 5G 99
Barons Lodge E14 4F 105
(off Manchester Rd.)
Barons Mead HA1: Harr 4J 41
Baronsmead Rd. SW13 1C 116
Baronsmede W5 2F 97
Baronsmere Ct. EN5: Barn 4B 20
Baronsmere Rd. N2 4C 46
Baron's Pl. SE1 7K 13 (2A 102)
Baron St. N1 2A 84
Baron's Wlk. CR0: C'don 6A 158
Baron Wlk. CR4: Mitc 4C 154
E16 5H 87
Baroque Ct. TW3: Houn 3F 113
Baroque Gdns. SE8 4A 104
(off Grand Canal Av.)
Barque M. SE8 6C 104
Barquentine Hgts. SE10 3J 105
Barrack Rd. TW4: Houn 4B 112
Barracks La. EN5: Barn 3B 20
Barracouta Ho. SE18 6K 107
Barra Hall Cir. UB3: Hayes 7G 75
Barra Hall Rd. UB3: Hayes 7G 75
Barratt Av. N22 2K 47
Barratt Ho. N1 7B 66
(off Sable St.)
Barratt Ind. Est. UB1: S'hall 2E 94
Barratt Ind. Pk. E3 4E 86
Barratt Way HA3: W'stone 2H 41
Barra Wood Cl. UB3: Hayes 6G 75
Barrenger Rd. N10 1D 46
Barret Ho. NW6 1J 81
SW9 3K 119
(off Benedict Rd.)
Barrett Ct. SE5 7D 102
(off Dobson Wlk.)
Barrett Ho. SE17 5C 102
(off Browning St.)
Barrett Pl. UB10: Uxb 1A 74
Barrett Rd. E17 4E 50
Barrett's Grn. Rd. NW10 3J 79
Barrett's Gro. N16 5E 66
Barrett St. W1 1H 11 (6E 82)
Barrhill Rd. SW2 2J 137
Barrie Ct. EN5: New Bar 5F 21
(off Lyonsdown Rd.)
Barriedale SE14 2A 122
Barrie Est. W2 2A 10 (7B 82)
Barrie Ho. NW8 1C 82
(off St Edmund's Ter.)
W2 7A 82
(off Lancaster Ga.)
Barrier App. SE7 3B 106
Barrier Point Rd. E16 1A 106
Barringers Ct. HA4: Ruis 7F 39
Barringer Sq. SW17 4E 136
Barrington Cl. IG5: Ilf 1D 52
NW5 5E 64
Barrington Ct. N10 2E 46
SW4 2J 119
W3 2H 97
(off Cheltenham Pl.)
Barrington Rd. DA7: Bex 2D 126
E12 6E 70
N8 5H 47
SM3: Sutt 2J 165
SW9 3B 120
Barrington Vs. SE18 1E 124
Barrington Wlk. SE19 6E 138
Barrons Chase TW10: Ham 5F 133
Barrow Av. SM5: Cars 7D 166
Barrow Cl. N21 3G 33
Barrow Ct. SE6 1H 141
(off Cumberland Pl.)
Barrowdene Cl. HA5: Pinn 2C 40
Barrowell Grn. N21 2G 33
Barrowfield Cl. N9 3C 34
Barrowgate Rd. W4 5J 97
Barrow Hedges Cl. SM5: Cars 7C 166
Barrow Hedges Way SM5: Cars 7C 166
Barrow Hill KT4: Wor Pk 2A 164
Barrow Hill Cl. KT4: Wor Pk 2A 164
Barrow Hill Est. NW8 2C 82
(off Barrow Hill Rd.)
Barrow Hill Rd. NW8 1C 4 (2C 82)
Barrow Point Av. HA5: Pinn 2C 40
Barrow Point La. HA5: Pinn 2C 40
Barrow Rd. CR0: Wadd 5A 168
SW16 6H 137
Barrow Store Ct. SE1 7G 15
(off Decima St.)
Barrow Wlk. TW8: Bford 6C 96
Barrs Rd. NW10 7K 61
Barry Av. DA7: Bex 7E 108
N15 6F 49
Barry Blandford Way E3 4D 86
Barry Cl. BR6: Orp 3J 173
Barrydene N20 1G 31
Barry Ho. SE16 4H 103
(off Rennie Est.)
Barry Pde. SE22 5G 121
Barry Rd. E6 6C 88
NW10 7J 61
SE22 6G 121
Barry Ter. TW15: Ashf 2B 128
(off Orchard Way)
Barset Rd. SE15 3J 121
(not continuous)
Barson Cl. SE20 7J 139
Barston Rd. SE27 3C 138
Barstow Cres. SW2 1K 137
Barter St. WC1 6F 7 (5J 83)
Barters Wlk. HA5: Pinn 3C 40
Barth M. SE18 4J 107
Bartholomew Cl. EC1 6B 8 (5C 84)
(not continuous)
SW18 4A 118
Bartholomew Ct. E14 7F 87
(off Newport Av.)
EC1 3D 8
(off Old St.)
HA8: Edg 7J 27
Bartholomew Ho.
IG8: Wfd G 1F 53, 7K 37
W10 4G 81
(off Appleford Rd.)
Bartholomew La. EC2 1F 15 (6D 84)
Bartholomew Pl. EC1 6C 8
Bartholomew Rd. NW5 6G 65
Bartholomew Sq. E1 4H 85
EC1 3D 8 (3C 84)
Bartholomew St. SE1 3D 102
Bartholomew Vs. NW5 6G 65
Barth Rd. SE18 4J 107
Bartle Av. E6 2C 88
Bartle Rd. W11 6G 81
Bartlett Cl. E14 6C 86
Bartlett Ct. EC4 7K 7 (6A 84)
Bartlett Ho. KT4: Wor Pk 2B 164
(off The Avenue)
Bartlett Ho's. RM10: Dag 7H 73
(off Vicarage Rd.)
Bartlett M. E14 5D 104
Bartletts Pas. EC4 7K 7
(off Fetter La.)
Bartlett St. CR2: S Croy 5D 168
Bartlow Gdns. RM5: Col R 1K 55
Bartok Ho. W11 1H 99
(off Lansdowne Wlk.)
Barton Av. RM7: Rush G 1H 73
Barton Cl. DA6: Bex 5E 126
E6 6D 88
E9 5J 67
NW4 5C 44
SE15 3H 121
TW17: Shep 6D 146
Barton Ct. W14 5G 99
(off Baron's Ct. Rd.)
Barton Grn. KT3: N Mald 2K 151
Barton Ho. E3 3D 86
(off Bow Rd.)
N1 7B 66
(off Sable St.)
SW6 3K 117
(off Wandsworth Bri. Rd.)
Barton Mdws. IG6: Ilf 4F 53
Barton M. E14 2D 104
SW19 6A 136
Barton Rd. DA14: Sidc 6E 144
W14 5G 99
Barton St. SW1 1E 18 (3J 101)
Bartonway NW8 1B 82
(off Queen's Ter.)
Bartram Cl. UB8: Hil 4D 74
Bartram Rd. SE4 5A 122
Bartrams La. EN4: Had W 1F 21
Bartrip St. E9 6B 68
Barts & The London School of
Medicine & Dentistry
Whitechapel Campus 5H 85
(off Turner St.)
Barts Cl. BR3: Beck 5C 158
Barville Cl. SE4 4A 122
Barwell Bus. Pk. KT9: Chess 7D 162
Barwell Ct. KT9: Chess 7B 162
Barwell Ho. E2 4G 85
(off Menotti St.)
Barwell La. KT9: Chess 7C 162
Barwick Dr. UB8: Hil 5D 74
Barwick Ho. W3 2J 97
(off Strafford Rd.)
Barwick Rd. E7 4K 69
Barwood Av. BR4: W W'ck 1D 170
Bascombe Gro.
DA1: Bexl, Cray 7K 127
Bascombe St. SW2 6A 120
Basden Gro. TW13: Hanw 2E 130
Basden Ho. TW13: Hanw 2E 130
Basedale Rd. RM9: Dag 7B 72
Baseing Cl. E6 7E 88
Baseline Bus. Studios W11 7F 81
(off Barandon Wlk.)
Basepoint Bus. Cen. RM13: Rain 4K 91
Basevi Way SE8 6D 104
Bashley Rd. NW10 4K 79

A-Z London 193

Basil Av. E6 . . . . .3C **88**
Basildene Rd. TW4: Houn 3B **112**
Basildon Av. IG5: Ilf 1E **52**
Basildon Cl. SM2: Sutt 7K **165**
Basildon Ct. W1 . . . . .5H **5**
(off Devonshire St.)
Basildon Rd. SE2 . . . . .5A **108**
Basil Gdns. CRO: C'don 1K **169**
SE27 . . . . .5C **138**
Basil Ho. E1 . . . . .6B **85**
(off Henriques St.)
SW8 . . . . .7J **101**
(off Wyvil Rd.)
Basilica M. SW12 . . . . .6E **118**
Basilica Pl. E3 . . . . .2B **86**
Basil Mans. SW3 . . . . .7E **10**
(off Basil St.)
Basilon Rd. DA7: Bex 2E **126**
Basil Spence Ho. N22 . . . . .1K **47**
Basil St. SW3 . . . . . . .1E **16** (3D **100**)
Basin App. E14 . . . . .6A **86**
E16 . . . . .7F **89**
Basing Cl. KT7: T Ditt 7K **149**
Basing Ct. SE15 . . . . .1F **121**
Basingdon Way SE5 . . . . .4D **120**
Basing Dr. DA5: Bexl 6F **127**
Basingfield Rd. KT7: T Ditt 7K **149**
Basinghall Av. EC2 . . . . . .7E **8** (6D **84**)
Basinghall Gdns.
SM2: Sutt 7K **165**
Basinghall St. EC2 . . . . . . .7E **8** (6D **84**)
Basing Hill HA9: Wemb 2F **61**
NW11 .1H **63**
Basing Ho. Yd. E2 . . . . .1H **9**
Basing Pl. E2 . . . . .1H **9** (3E **84**)
Basing St. W11 . . . . .6H **81**
Basing Way KT7: T Ditt 7K **149**
N3 . . . . .3J **45**
Basin Mill Apts. E2 . . . . .1F **85**
(off Laburnum St.)
Basire St. N1 . . . . .1C **84**
Baskerville Gdns. NW10 . . . . .4A **62**
Baskerville Rd. SW18 . . . . .7C **118**
Basket Gdns. SE9 . . . . .5C **124**
Baslow Cl. HA3: Hrw W 1H **41**
Baslow Wlk. E5 . . . . .4K **67**
Basnett Rd. SW11 . . . . .3E **118**
Basque Ct. SE16 . . . . .2K **103**
(off Garter Way)
Bassano St. SE22 . . . . .5F **121**
Bassant Rd. SE18 . . . . .6K **107**
Bass Ct. E15 . . . . .1H **87**
(off Plaistow Rd.)
Bassein Pk. Rd. W12 . . . . .2B **98**
Bassett Gdns. TW7: Isle 7G **95**
Bassett Ho. SW19 . . . . .5K **135**
Bassett Rd. W10 . . . . .6F **81**
Bassett's Cl. BR6: Farnb 4F **173**
Bassetts Ho. BR6: Farnb 4F **173**
Bassett St. NW5 . . . . .6E **64**
Bassett's Way BR6: Farnb 4F **173**
Bassett Way UB6: G'frd 6F **77**
(off The Sutton Est.)
Bassingbourn Ho. N1 . . . . .7A **66**
(off The Sutton Est.)
Bassingham Rd. HA0: Wemb 6D **60**
SW18 . . . . .7A **118**
Bassington Rd. W3 . . . . .3J **97**
Bassishaw Highwalk EC2 . . . . . . .6E **8**
Bass M. SE22 . . . . .4G **121**
Basswood Cl. SE15 . . . . .3H **121**
Bastable Av. IG11: Bark 2J **89**
Basterfield Ho. EC1 . . . . .4C **8**
(off Golden La. Est.)
Bastion Highwalk EC2 . . . . .6C **8**
Bastion Ho. EC2 . . . . .6D **8**
(off London Wall)
Bastion Rd. SE2 . . . . .5A **108**
Bastion Mnr. Rd.
BR2: Hayes, Kes 3K **171**
Baston Rd. BR2: Hayes 2K **171**
Bastwick St. EC1 . . . . . .3C **8** (4C **84**)
Basuto Rd. SW6 . . . . .1J **117**

Batavia Cl. TW16: Sun 1K **147**
Batavia Ho. SE14 . . . . .7A **104**
(off Batavia Rd.)
Batavia M. SE14 . . . . .7A **104**
Batavia Rd. SE14 . . . . .7A **104**
TW16: Sun 1K **147**
Batchelor St. N1 . . . . .1A **84**
Bateman Cl. IG11: Bark 6G **71**
Bateman Ho. SE17 . . . . .6B **102**
(off Otto St.)
Bateman M. SW4 . . . . .6H **119**
Bateman Rd. E4 . . . . .6H **35**
Bateman's Bldgs. W1 . . . . .1C **12**
Bateman's Row EC2 . . . .3H **9** (4E **84**)
Bateman St. W1 . . . . . .1C **12** (6H **83**)
Bates Cres. CRO: Wadd 5A **168**
SW16 . . . . .7G **137**
Bateson St. SE18 . . . . .4J **107**
Bate St. E14 . . . . .7B **86**
Bat Gdns. KT2: King T 6F **133**
Bath Cl. SE15 . . . . .7H **103**
Bath Ct. EC1 . . . . .2E **8**
(St Luke's Est.)
EC1 . . . . .4J **7**
(Warner St.)
SE26 . . . . .3C **160**
(off Droitwich Cl.)
Bathgate Ho. SW9 . . . . .1B **120**
(off Lothian Rd.)
Bathgate Rd. SW19 . . . . .3F **135**
Bath Gro. E2 . . . . .2G **85**
(off Horatio St.)
Bath Ho. E2 . . . . .4G **85**
(off Ramsey St.)
IG11: Bark 7G **71**
SE1 . . . . .3C **102**
(off Bath Ter.)
Bath Ho. Rd. CRO: Bedd 1J **167**
Bath Pas. KT1: King T 2D **150**
Bath Pl. EC2 . . . . .2G **9** (3E **84**)
EN5: Barn 3C **20**
W6 . . . . .5E **98**
(off Peabody Est.)
Bath Rd. E7 . . . . .7B **70**
N9 . . . . .2C **34**
RM6: Chad H 6E **54**
SL3: Coln, Poyle 4A **174**
TW3: Houn 3F **113**
TW4: Houn 2B **112**
TW5: Cran 1G **111**
TW6: H'row A 1G **111**
UB3: Harl 1G **111**
UB7: Lford, Harm, Sip 4C **174**
W4 . . . . .4A **98**
Baths Cl. W12 . . . . .2D **98**
Baths Rd. BR2: Broml 4B **160**
Bath St. EC1 . . . . .2D **8** (3C **84**)
Bath Ter. SE1 . . . . .3C **102**
Bathurst Av. SW19 . . . . .1K **153**
Bathurst Gdns. NW10 . . . . .2D **80**
Bathurst Ho. W12 . . . . .7D **80**
(off White City Est.)
Bathurst M. W2 . . . . .2B **10** (6B **82**)
Bathurst Rd. IG1: Ilf 1F **71**
Bathurst Sq. N15 . . . . .4E **48**
Bathurst St. W2 . . . . . . .2B **10** (7B **82**)
Bathway SE18 . . . . .4E **106**
Batley Cl. CR4: Mitc 7D **154**
Batley Pl. N16 . . . . .3F **67**
Batley Rd. EN2: Enf 1H **23**
N16 . . . . .3F **67**
Batman Cl. W12 . . . . .1D **98**
Batoum Gdns. W6 . . . . .3E **99**
Batsford Ho. SW19 . . . . .4K **135**
(off Durnsford Rd.)
Batson Ho. E1 . . . . .6G **85**
(off Fairclough St.)
Batson St. W12 . . . . .2C **98**
Batsworth Rd. CR4: Mitc 3B **154**
Battalion Ho. NW9 . . . . .2B **44**
(off Heritage Av.)
Battenberg Wlk. SE19 . . . . .6E **138**
Batten Cl. E6 . . . . .6D **88**

Batten Cotts. E14 . . . . .5A **86**
(off Maroon St.)
Batten Ho. SW4 . . . . .5G **119**
W10 . . . . .3G **81**
(off Third Av.)
Batten St. SW11 . . . . .3C **118**
Battersby Rd. SE6 . . . . .2F **141**
BATTERSEA 1E **118**
Battersea Arts Cen. 3D **118**
(off Lavender Hill)
BATTERSEA BRI. 7B **100**
Battersea Bri. Rd. SW11 . . . . . . .7C **100**
Battersea Bus. Cen. SW11 . . . . .3E **118**
Battersea Bus. Pk. SW8 . . . . . . .1G **119**
Battersea Church Rd. SW11 . . . .1B **118**
Battersea Dogs' Home 7F **101**
Battersea Evolution 7E **100**
Battersea High St. SW11 . . . . . . .1B **118**
(not continuous)
BATTERSEA PARK 7F **101**
Battersea Pk. 7D **100**
Battersea Pk. Children's Zoo 7E **100**
Battersea Pk. Millennium Arena
. . . . .7E **100**
Battersea Pk. Rd. SW8 . . . . .1E **118**
SW11 . . . . .2C **118**
Battersea Power Stn. Development
SW11 . . . . .6F **101**
Battersea Ri. SW11 . . . . .5C **118**
Battersea Roof Gdns. SW11 . . . . .7F **101**
Battersea Sports Cen. 3B **118**
Battersea Sq. SW11 . . . . .1B **118**
Battery Rd. SE28 . . . . .2J **107**
Battishill St. N1 . . . . .7B **66**
Battlebridge Ct. N1 . . . . .2J **83**
(off Wharfdale Rd.)
Battle Bri. La. SE1 . . . . . .5G **15** (1E **102**)
Battle Cl. SW19 . . . . .6A **136**
Battledean Rd. N5 . . . . .5B **66**
Battle Ho. SE15 . . . . .6G **103**
(off Haymerle Rd.)
Battle Rd. DA8: Erith 4J **109**
DA17: Belv, Erith 4J **109**
Batty St. E1 . . . . .6G **85**
Batwa Ho. SE16 . . . . .5H **103**
Baudwin Rd. SE6 . . . . .2G **141**
Baugh Rd. DA14: Sidc 5C **144**
The Baulk SW18 . . . . .7J **117**
Bavant Rd. SW16 . . . . .2J **155**
Bavaria Rd. N19 . . . . .2J **65**
Bavdene M. NW4 . . . . .4D **44**
(off The Burroughs)
Bavent Rd. SE5 . . . . .2C **120**
Bawdale Rd. SE22 . . . . .5F **121**
Bawdsey Av. IG2: Ilf 4K **53**
Bawley Ct. E16 . . . . .7G **89**
Bawley Ter. E15 . . . . .1F **87**
(off Rick Roberts Way)
Bawtree Rd. SE14 . . . . .7A **104**
Bawtry Rd. N20 . . . . .3J **31**
Baxendale N20 . . . . .2F **31**
Baxendale St. E2 . . . . .3G **85**
Baxter Cl. BR1: Broml 3F **161**
UB2: S'hall 3F **95**
UB10: Hil 3D **74**
Baxter Ho. E3 . . . . .3D **86**
(off Bromley High St.)
Baxter Rd. E16 . . . . .6A **88**
IG1: Ilf 5F **71**
N1 . . . . .6D **66**
N18 . . . . .4C **34**
Baxter Wlk. SW16 . . . . .2H **137**
Bayard Ct. DA6: Bex 4H **127**
Bay Cl. E1 . . . . .4K **85**
(off Frimley Way)
W5 . . . . .3E **96**
Baycroft Cl. HA5: Eastc 3A **40**
Baydon Ct. BR2: Broml 3H **159**
Bayer Ho. EC1 . . . . .4C **8**
(off Golden La. Est.)
Bayes Cl. SE26 . . . . .5J **139**
Bayes Ct. NW3 . . . . .7D **64**
(off Primrose Hill Rd.)

Bayes Ho. N1 . . . . .7A **66**
(off Augustas La.)
Bayfield Ho. SE4 . . . . .4K **121**
(off Coston Wlk.)
Bayfield Rd. SE9 . . . . .4B **124**
Bayford M. E8 . . . . .7H **67**
(off Bayford St.)
Bayford Rd. NW10 . . . . .3F **81**
Bayford St. E8 . . . . .7H **67**
Bayford St. Bus. Cen. E8 . . . . .7H **67**
(off Sidworth St.)
Baygrove M. KT1: Hamp W 1C **150**
Bayham Pl. NW1 . . . . .1G **83**
Bayham Rd. SM4: Mord 4K **153**
W4 . . . . .3K **97**
W13 . . . . .7B **78**
Bayham St. NW1 . . . . .1G **83**
Bay Ho. SE16 . . . . .3A **104**
Bayhurst Wood Country Pk. 5B **38**
Bayleaf Cl. TW12: Hamp H 5H **131**
Bayley St. WC1 . . . . .6C **6** (5H **83**)
Bayley Wlk. SE2 . . . . .6E **108**
Baylis Hgts. SE10 . . . . .4J **105**
(off Horn Link Way)
Baylis M. TW1: Twick 7A **114**
Baylis Pl. BR1: Broml 2C **160**
Baylis Rd. SE1 . . . . .7J **13** (2A **102**)
Bayliss Av. SE28 . . . . .7D **90**
Bayliss Cl. N21 . . . . .5D **22**
UB1: S'hall 6C **76**
(off Whitecote Rd.)
Baynard Ho. EC4 . . . . .2B **14**
(off Queen Victoria St.)
Bayne Cl. E6 . . . . .6D **88**
Baynes Cl. EN1: Enf 1B **24**
Baynes Cres. RM10: Dag 7J **73**
Baynes M. NW3 . . . . .6B **64**
Baynes St. NW1 . . . . .7G **65**
Baynham Cl. DA5: Bexl 6F **127**
Bayonne Rd. W6 . . . . .6G **99**
Bays Ct. HA8: Edg 5C **28**
Bays Farm Ct. UB7: Lford 4D **174**
Bayshill Ri. UB5: N'olt 6F **59**
Baysixty6 Skate Pk. 5H **81**
(off Acklam Rd.)
Bayston Rd. N16 . . . . .3F **67**
BAYSWATER 7A **82**
Bayswater Cl. N13 . . . . .4G **33**
Bayswater Rd. W2 . . . . . .3A **10** (7K **81**)
Baythorne Ho. E16 . . . . .6H **87**
(off Turner St.)
Baythorne St. E3 . . . . .5B **86**
Bayton Ct. E8 . . . . .7G **67**
(off Lansdowne Dr.)
Bay Tree Cl. BR1: Broml 1B **160**
Baytree Cl. DA15: Sidc 1K **143**
Baytree Ct. SW2 . . . . .4K **119**
Bay Tree Ho. EC1 . . . . .4J **7**
(off Baker's Row)
Baytree Ho. E4 . . . . .7J **25**
Baytree M. SE17 . . . . .4D **102**
Baytree Rd. SW2 . . . . .4K **119**
Baywillow Av. SM5: Cars 1D **166**
Bazalgette Cl. KT3: N Mald 5K **151**
Bazalgette Gdns. KT3: N Mald 5K **151**
Bazalgette Ho. NW8 . . . . .3B **4**
(off Orchardson St.)
Bazalgette Wlk. EC4 . . . . .7A **84**
Bazalgette Way SE2 . . . . .1C **108**
Bazeley Ho. SE1 . . . . .7A **14**
(off Library St.)
Bazely St. E14 . . . . .7E **86**
Bazile Rd. N21 . . . . .6F **23**
BBC Broadcasting House
. . . . .6K **5** (5F **83**)
BBC Maida Vale Studios 4K **81**
(off Delaware Rd.)
BBC Studios 1E **98**
BBC Worldwide 7E **80**
BDA Dental Mus. 6J **5** (5F **83**)
Beacham Cl. SE7 . . . . .5B **106**
Beachborough Rd. BR1: Broml . . .4E **140**
Beach Ct. SE9 . . . . .6C **124**

Beachcroft Av. UB1: S'hall 1C 94
Beachcroft Rd. E11 . . . . .3G 69
Beachcroft Way N19 . . . . .1H 65
Beach Gro. TW13: Hanw 2E 130
Beach Ho. SW5 . . . . .5J 99
(off Philbeach Gdns.)
TW13: Hanw 2E 130
Beach Ho. Apts. IG11: Bark 4A 90
Beachy Rd. E3 . . . . .7C 68
Beacon Bingo
Cricklewood 4F 63
Beacon Cl. UB8: Uxb 5A 56
Beacon Ga. SE14 . . . . .3K 121
Beacon Hill N7 . . . . .5J 65
Beacon Ho. E14 . . . . .5D 104
(off Burrells Wharf Sq.)
SE5 .7E 102
(off Southampton Way)
Beacon Pl. CR0: Bedd 3J 167
Beacon Point SE10 . . . . .6D 104
(off Dowells St.)
Beacon Rd. SE13 . . . . .6F 123
TW6: H'row A 6C 110
Beacons Cl. E6 . . . . .5C 88
Beaconsfield WC1 . . . . .6G 7
(off Red Lion St.)
Beaconsfield Cl. N11 . . . . .5K 31
SE3 .6J 105
W4 . . . . .5J 97
Beaconsfield Pde. SE9 . . . . .4C 142
Beaconsfield Rd. BR1: Broml 3B 160
CR0: C'don 6D 156
DA5: Bexl 2K 145
E10 .2E 68
E16 . . . . .4H 87
E17 .6B 50
KT3: N Mald 2K 151
KT5: Surb 7F 151
N9 . . . . .3B 34
N11 .3K 31
N15 .4E 48
NW10 . . . . .6B 62
SE3 . . . . .7H 105
SE9 . . . . .2C 142
SE17 . . . . .5D 102
TW1: Twick 6B 114
UB1: S'hall 1B 94
UB4: Yead 1A 76
W4 . . . . .3K 97
W5 . . . . .2C 96
Beaconsfield St. N1 . . . . .1J 83
Beaconsfield Ter. RM6: Chad H . . .6D 54
Beaconsfield Ter. Rd. W14 . . . . .3G 99
Beaconsfield Wlk. E6 . . . . .6E 88
SW6 . . . . .1H 117
Beacontree Av. E17 . . . . .1F 51
BEACONTREE HEATH 1G 73
Beacontree Rd. E11 . . . . .1H 69
Beadle's Pde. RM10: Dag 6J 73
Beadlow Cl. SM5: Cars 6B 154
Beadman Pl. SE27 . . . . .4B 138
Beadman St. SE27 . . . . .4B 138
Beadnell Ct. E1 . . . . .7G 85
(off Cable St.)
Beadnell Rd. SE23 . . . . .1K 139
Beadon Rd. BR2: Broml 4J 159
W6 . . . . .4E 98
Beaford Gro. SW20 . . . . .3G 153
Beagle Cl. TW13: Felt 4K 129
Beak St. W1 . . . . .2B 12 (7G 83)
Beal Cl. DA16: Well 1A 126
The Beale Arboretum 1J 21
Beale Cl. N13 . . . . .5G 33
Beale Pl. E3 . . . . .2B 86
Beale Rd. E3 . . . . .1B 86
Beal Rd. IG1: Ilf 2E 70
Beam Av. RM10: Dag 1K 91
Beames Rd. NW10 . . . . .1A 79
Beaminster Gdns. IG6: Ilf 2F 53
Beaminster Ho. SW8 . . . . .7K 101
(off Dorset Rd.)
Beamish Dr. WD23: B Hea 1B 26

Beamish Ho. SE16 . . . . .4H 103
(off Rennie Est.)
Beamish Rd. N9 . . . . .1B 34
Beam Pk. Development
RM9: Dag 3H 91
Beam Reach Bus. Pk.
RM13: Rain 3K 91
Beam Valley Country Pk. 1J 91
Beamway RM10: Dag 7K 73
Beanacre Cl. E9 . . . . .6B 68
Bean Rd. DA6: Bex 4D 126
Beanshaw SE9 . . . . .4E 142
Beansland Gro. RM6: Chad H 3E 54
Beardow Gro. N14 . . . . .6B 22
Beard Rd. KT2: King T 5F 133
Beardsfield E13 . . . . .2J 87
Beard's Hill TW12: Hamp 1E 148
Beard's Hill Cl. TW12: Hamp 1E 148
Beardsley Ter. RM8: Dag 5B 72
(off Stonard Rd.)
Beardsley Way W3 . . . . .2K 97
Beard's Rd. TW15: Ashf 6G 129
Bearfield Rd. KT2: King T 7E 132
Bear Gdns. SE1 . . . . .4C 14 (1C 102)
Bear La. SE1 . . . . .4B 14 (1B 102)
Bear Pit Apts. SE1 . . . . .4C 14
(off New Globe Wlk.)
Bear Rd. TW13: Hanw 4B 130
Bearstead Ri. SE4 . . . . .5B 122
Bearsted Ter. BR3: Beck 1C 158
Bear St. WC2 . . . . .2D 12 (7H 83)
Beasley's Ait TW16: Sun 6H 147
Beasley's Ait La. TW16: Sun 6H 147
Beaton Cl. SE15 . . . . .1F 121
Beatrice Av. HA9: Wemb 5E 60
SW16 . . . . .3K 155
Beatrice Cl. E13 . . . . .4J 87
HA5: Eastc 4J 39
Beatrice Cl. IG9: Buck H 2G 37
Beatrice Ho. W6 . . . . .5E 98
(off Queen Caroline St.)
Beatrice Pl. SW19 . . . . .7F 117
W8 . . . . .3K 99
Beatrice Rd. E17 . . . . .5C 50
N4 . . . . .7A 48
N9 . . . . .7D 24
SE1 .4G 103
TW10: Rich 5F 115
UB1: S'hall 1D 94
Beatrice Webb Ho. E3 . . . . .2A 86
(off Chisenhale Rd.)
Beatrix Apts. E3 . . . . .4B 86
(off English St.)
Beatrix Ho. SW5 . . . . .5K 99
(off Old Brompton Rd.)
Beatson Wlk. SE16 . . . . .1A 104
(not continuous)
Beattie Cl. TW14: Felt 7H 111
Beattie Ho. SW8 . . . . .1G 119
Beattock Ri. N10 . . . . .4F 47
Beatty Ho. E14 . . . . .2C 104
(off Admirals Way)
SW1 .6B 18
(off Dolphin Sq.)
Beatty Rd. HA7: Stan 6H 27
N16 .4E 66
Beatty St. NW1 . . . . .2G 83
Beattyville Gdns. IG6: Ilf 4E 52
Beauchamp Cl. W4 . . . . .3J 97
Beauchamp Ct. EN5: Barn 4C 20
(off Victors Way)
HA7: Stan 5H 27
Beauchamp Pl. SW3 . . . . . .1D 16 (3C 100)
Beauchamp Rd. E7 . . . . .7K 69
KT8: W Mole, E Mos 5F 149
SE19 . . . . .1D 156
SM1: Sutt 4J 165
SW11 . . . . .4C 118
TW1: Twick 7A 114
Beauchamp St. EC1 . . . . . . .6J 7 (5A 84)

Beauchamp Ter. SW15 . . . . .3D 116
Beauclerc Ct. TW16: Sun 2A 148
Beauclerc Rd. W6 . . . . .3D 98
Beauclere Ho. SM2: Sutt 6A 166
Beauclerk Cl. TW13: Felt 1K 129
Beauclerk Ho. SW16 . . . . .3J 137
Beau Ct. HA7: Stan 7J 27
(off Hitchin La.)
Beaudesert M. UB7: W Dray 2A 92
Beaufort E5 .5E 88
Beaufort Av. HA3: Kenton 4A 42
Beaufort Cl. E4 . . . . .6J 35
RM7: Mawney 4J 55
SW15 . . . . .7D 116
W5 . . . . .5F 79
Beaufort Ct. E14 . . . . .2C 104
(off Admirals Way)
EN5: New Bar 5F 21
N11 .3A 32
(off The Limes Av.)
SW6 .6J 99
TW10: Ham 4C 132
Beaufort Dr. NW11 . . . . .4J 45
Beaufort Gdns. E1 . . . . .5K 85
IG1: Ilf 1E 70
NW4 .6E 44
SW3 . . . . .1D 16 (3C 100)
SW16 . . . . .7K 137
TW5: Hest 1C 112
Beaufort Ho. E16 . . . . .1K 105
(off Fairfax M.)
SW1 .6C 18
(off Aylesford St.)
SW3 .7B 16
(off Beaufort St.)
Beaufort Mans. SW3 . . . . . .7B 16 (6B 100)
Beaufort M. SW6 . . . . .6H 99
Beaufort Pk. NW11 . . . . .4J 45
Beaufort Rd. HA4: Ruis 2F 57
KT1: King T 4E 150
TW1: Twick 7C 114
TW10: Ham 4C 132
W5 . . . . .5F 79
Beaufort Sq. NW9 . . . . .2C 44
Beaufort St. SW3 . . . . . . .7A 16 (6B 100)
Beaufort Ter. E14 . . . . .5E 104
(off Ferry St.)
Beaufort Way KT17: Ewe 7C 164
Beaufoy Ho. SE27 . . . . .3B 138
SW8 .7K 101
(off Rita Rd.)
Beaufoy Rd. N17 . . . . .7K 33
(not continuous)
Beaufoy Wlk. SE11 . . . . . .4H 19 (4K 101)
Beaulieu Av. E16 . . . . .1K 105
SE26 . . . . .4H 139
Beaulieu Cl. CR4: Mitc 1E 154
NW9 .4A 44
SE5 .3D 120
TW1: Twick 6D 114
TW4: Houn 5D 112
Beaulieu Ct. W5 . . . . .5E 78
Beaulieu Dr. HA5: Pinn 6B 40
Beaulieu Gdns. N21 . . . . .7H 23
Beaulieu Hgts. SE25 . . . . .1E 156
Beaulieu Lodge E14 . . . . .3F 105
(off Schooner Cl.)
Beaulieu Pl. W4 . . . . .3J 97
Beaumanor Gdns. SE9 . . . . .4E 142
Beaumanor Mans. W2 . . . . .7K 81
(off Queensway)
Beaumaris Dr. E17 . . . . .1B 50
Beaumaris Dr. IG8: Wfd G 7G 37
Beaumaris Gdns. SE19 . . . . .7C 138
Beaumaris Grn. NW9 . . . . .6A 44
Beaumaris Twr. W3 . . . . .2J 97
(off Park Rd. Nth.)
Beaumont W14 . . . . .4H 99
(off Kensington Village)
Beaumont Av. HA0: Wemb 5C 60
HA2: Harr 6F 41
TW9: Rich 3F 115
W14 .5H 99

Beaumont Bldgs. WC2 . . . . .1F 13
(off Martlett Ct.)
Beaumont Cl. KT2: King T 7G 133
N2 . . . . .4C 46
Beaumont Ct. E1 . . . . .3K 85
E5 . . . . .3H 67
HA0: Wemb 5C 60
NW1 .1H 83
NW9 . . . . .2B 44
(off Cherry Cl.)
W1 . . . . .5H 5
(off Beaumont St.)
W4 . . . . .5J 97
Beaumont Cres. W14 . . . . .5H 99
Beaumont Dr. KT4: Wor Pk 7D 152
TW15: Ashf 5F 129
Beaumont Gdns. NW3 . . . . .3J 63
Beaumont Gro. E1 . . . . .4K 85
Beaumont Ho. E10 . . . . .7D 50
(off Skelton's La.)
W9 . . . . .3H 81
(off Fernhead Rd.)
Beaumont Lodge E8 . . . . .6G 67
(off Greenwood Rd.)
Beaumont M. HA5: Pinn 3C 40
NW5 .5H 65
(off Charlton King's La.)
W1 . . . . .5H 5 (5E 82)
Beaumont Pl. EN5: Barn 1C 20
TW7: Isle 5K 113
UB10: Ick 5C 56
W1 . . . . .3B 6 (4G 83)
Beaumont Ri. N19 . . . . .1H 65
Beaumont Rd. BR5: Pet W 6H 161
E10 . . . . .7D 50
(not continuous)
E13 . . . . .3K 87
SE19 . . . . .6C 138
SW19 . . . . .7G 117
W4 . . . . .3J 97
Beaumont Sq. E1 . . . . .5K 85
Beaumont St. W1 . . . . .5H 5 (5E 82)
Beaumont Ter. SE13 . . . . .7G 123
(off Wellmeadow Rd.)
Beaumont Wlk. NW3 . . . . .7D 64
Beauvais Ter. UB5: N'olt 3B 76
Beauvale NW1 . . . . .7E 64
(off Ferdinand St.)
Beauval Rd. SE22 . . . . .6F 121
The Beaux Arts Bldg. N7 . . . . .3J 65
Beaverbank Rd. SE9 . . . . .1H 143
Beaver Cl. SE20 . . . . .7G 139
Beaver Gro. UB5: N'olt 3C 76
Beaver Ind. Est. UB2: S'hall 3A 94
Beavers Cres. TW4: Houn 4A 112
Beavers La. TW4: Houn 2A 112
Beavers La. Campsite 4B 112
Beavers Lodge DA14: Sidc 4K 143
Beaverwood Rd. BR7: Chst 6J 143
Beavor Gro. W6 . . . . .5C 98
(off Beavor La.)
Beavor La. W6 . . . . .5C 98
Bebbington Rd. SE18 . . . . .4J 107
Beblets Cl. BR6: Chels 5K 173
Beccles Dr. IG11: Bark 6J 71
Beccles St. E14 . . . . .6B 86
Bec Cl. HA4: Ruis 3B 58
Bechervaise Ct. E10 . . . . .1D 68
(off Leyton Grange Est.)
Bechtel Ho. W6 . . . . .4F 99
(off Hammersmith Rd.)
Beck Cl. SE13 . . . . .1D 122
Beck Ct. BR3: Beck 3K 157
BECKENHAM 2C 158
Beckenham Bus. Cen.
BR3: Beck 6A 140
Beckenham Crematorium 3J 157
Beckenham Gdns. N9 . . . . .3K 33
Beckenham Gro. BR2: Broml 2F 159
Beckenham Hill Est. BR3: Beck . . .5D 140

Beckenham Hill Rd.
BR3: Beck 6D 140
SE6 . . . . . . .6D 140
Beckenham La. BR2: Broml . . .2G 159
Beckenham Place Park 6E 140
Beckenham Pl. Pk.
BR3: Beck 7D 140
Beckenham Rd. BR3: Beck . . .1K 157
BR4: W W'ck 7D 158
The Beckenham Theatre Cen. 2D 158
The Beckers N16 . . . . . . .4G 67
Becket Av. E6 . . . . . . .3E 88
Becket Cl. IG8: Wfd G 1C 52
SE25 . . . . . . .6G 157
SW19 . . . . . . .1K 153
(off High Path)
Becket Fold HA1: Harr 5K 41
Becket Ho. E16 . . . . . . .1K 105
(off Constable Av.)
SE1 . . . . . . .7E 14
WC1 . . . . . . .3F 7
Becket Rd. N18 . . . . . . .4D 34
Becket St. SE1 . . . .7E 14 (3D 102)
Beckett Cl. DA17: Belv 3F 109
NW10 . . . . . . .6A 62
SW16 . . . . . . .2H 137
Beckett Ho. E1 . . . . . . .5J 85
(off Jubilee St.)
SW9 . . . . . . .2J 119
Becketts Cl. BR6: Orp 3K 173
DA5: Bexl 1J 145
TW14: Felt 6K 111
Becketts Ho. IG1: Ilf 3E 70
Becketts Pl. KT1: Hamp W 1D 150
Becketts Wharf KT1: Hamp W . . .1D 150
(off Lwr. Teddington Rd.)
Beckett Wlk. BR3: Beck 6A 140
Beckfoot NW1 . . . . . . .1B 6
(off Ampthill Est.)
Beckford Cl. W14 . . . . . . .4H 99
Beckford Dr. BR5: Orp 7H 161
Beckford Ho. N16 . . . . . . .5E 66
Beckford Pl. SE17 . . . . . . .5C 102
Beckford Rd. CR0: C'don 6F 157
Beckham Ho. SE11 . . .4H 19 (4K 101)
(off Gilbert Rd.)
Beckhaven Ho. SE11 . . . . . . .4K 19
(off Gilbert Rd.)
Beck Ho. N18 . . . . . . .5C 34
(off Upton Rd.)
Beck La. BR3: Beck 3K 157
Beckley Ho. E3 . . . . . . .4B 86
(off Hamlets Way)
Becklow Gdns. W12 . . . . . . .2C 98
(off Becklow Rd.)
Becklow M. W12 . . . . . . .2C 98
(off Becklow Rd.)
Becklow Rd. W12 . . . . . . .2B 98
Beck River Pk. BR3: Beck . . .1B 158
Beck Rd. CR4: Mitc 6D 154
E8 . . . . . . .1H 85
Becks Sq. E10 . . . . . . .1A 68
Becks Rd. DA14: Sidc 3A 144
The Beck Theatre 6H 75
BECKTON 5E 88
BECKTON ALPS 4D 88
BECKTON PARK 6D 88
Beckton Retail Pk. 5E 88
Beckton Rd. E16 . . . . . . .5H 87
Beckton Triangle Retail Pk. 4F 89
Beck Way BR3: Beck 3B 158
Beckway Rd. SW16 . . . . . .2H 155
Beckway St. SE17 . . . . . . .4E 102
(not continuous)
Beckwith Cl. EN2: Enf 1G 23
Beckwith Ho. E2 . . . . . . .2H 85
(off Wadeson St.)
Beckwith Rd. SE24 . . . . . . .5D 120
Beclands Rd. SW17 . . . . . . .6E 136
Becmead Av. HA3: Kenton 5B 42
SW16 . . . . . . .4H 137
Becondale Rd. SE19 . . . . . .5E 138
BECONTREE 4D 72
Becontree Av. RM8: Dag 4B 72

Becontree Heath Leisure Cen. 2G 73
Becquerel Cl. SE10 . . . . . . .3H 105
(off West Parkside)
Bective Pl. SW15 . . . . . . .4H 117
Bective Rd. E7 . . . . . . .4J 69
SW15 . . . . . . .4H 117
Becton Pl. DA8: Erith 7H 109
Bedale Rd. EN2: Enf 1H 23
Bedale St. SE1 . . . .5E 14 (1D 102)
Beddalls Farm Ct. E6 . . . . . .5B 88
BEDDINGTON 4J 167
BEDDINGTON CORNER 7E 154
Beddington Cross CR0: Bedd . . .7H 155
Beddington Farm Rd.
CR0: Bedd, Wadd 7J 155
Beddington Gdns. SM5: Cars . . .6E 166
SM6: W'gton 6E 166
Beddington Grn. BR5: St P 1K 161
Beddington Gro. SM6: W'gton . . .5H 167
Beddington La.
CR0: Bedd, C'don 1G 155
Beddington Pk. 3F 167
Beddington Pk. Cotts.
SM6: Bedd 3H 167
Beddington Path BR5: St P 1K 161
Beddington Rd. BR5: St P 2J 161
IG3: Ilf 7K 53
Beddington Ter. CR0: C'don . . .7K 155
Beddington Trad. Est. CR0: Bedd . .1J 167
Bede Cl. HA5: Pinn 1B 40
Bedefield WC1 . . . . . .2F 7 (3J 83)
Bede Ho. SE14 . . . . . . .1B 122
(off Clare Rd.)
Bede Sq. E3 . . . . . . .4B 86
(off Joseph St.)
Bedevere Rd. N9 . . . . . . .3B 34
Bedfont Cl. CR4: Mitc 2E 154
TW14: Bedf 6E 110
Bedfont Ct. TW19: Stanw M 6B 174
Bedfont Ct. Est.
TW19: Stanw M 7C 174
Bedfont Grn. Cl. TW14: Bedf . . .1E 128
Bedfont Ind. Pk. TW15: Ashf . . .3E 128
Bedfont Ind. Pk. Nth.
TW15: Ashf 3E 128
Bedfont Lakes Country Pk. 2E 128
Bedfont Lakes Country Pk. Vis. Cen.
. . . . . . .3D 128
Bedfont La. TW13: Felt 7G 111
TW14: Felt 7G 111
Bedfont Rd. TW13: Felt 1E 128
TW14: Bedf 1E 128
TW19: Stanw 6A 110
Bedfont Trad. Est. TW14: Bedf . . .2F 129
Bedford Av. EN5: Barn 5C 20
UB4: Yead 6K 75
WC1 . . . . . .6D 6 (5H 83)
Bedfordbury WC2 . . . .2E 12 (7J 83)
(not continuous)
Bedford Cl. N10 . . . . . . .7K 31
W4 . . . . . . .6A 98
Bedford Cnr. W4 . . . . . . .4A 98
(off South Pde.)
Bedford Ct. CR0: C'don 1D 168
(off Tavistock Rd.)
WC2 . . . . . .3E 12 (7J 83)
Bedford Ct. Mans. WC1 . . . . . .6D 6
Bedford Gdns. W8 . . . . . . .1J 99
Bedford Gdns. Ho. W8 . . . . . .1J 99
(off Bedford Gdns.)
Bedford Hill SW12 . . . . . . .1F 137
SW16 . . . . . . .1F 137
Bedford Ho. CR0: C'don 7B 156
SW4 . . . . . . .4J 119
(off Solon New Rd. Est.)
Bedford M. N2 . . . . . . .3C 46
SE6 . . . . . . .2D 140
BEDFORD PARK 3K 97
Bedford Pk. CR0: C'don 1C 168
Bedford Pk. Cnr. W4 . . . . . .4A 98
Bedford Pk. Mans. W4 . . . . . .4K 97

Bedford Pas. SW6 . . . . . . .7G 99
(off Dawes Rd.)
W1 . . . . . .5B 6 (5G 83)
Bedford Pl. CR0: C'don 1D 168
WC1 . . . . . .5E 6 (5J 83)
Bedford Rd. DA15: Sidc 3J 143
E6 . . . . . . .1E 88
E17 . . . . . . .2C 50
E18 . . . . . . .2J 51
HA1: Harr 6G 41
HA4: Ruis 4H 57
IG1: Ilf 3F 71
KT4: Wor Pk 2E 164
N2 . . . . . . .3C 46
N8 . . . . . . .6H 47
N9 . . . . . . .7C 24
N15 . . . . . . .4E 48
N22 . . . . . . .2J 47
NW7 . . . . . . .2F 29
SW4 . . . . . . .4J 119
TW2: Twick 3H 131
W4 . . . . . . .3K 97
W13 . . . . . . .7B 78
Bedford Row SE1 . . . .7D 14 (3C 102)
WC1 . . . . . .5H 7 (5K 83)
Bedford Sq. WC1 . . . . . .6D 6 (5H 83)
Bedford St. WC2 . . . .2E 12 (7J 83)
Bedford Ter. SM2: Sutt 6A 166
SW2 . . . . . . .5J 119
Bedford Way WC1 . . . .4D 6 (4H 83)
Bedgebury Cl. E17 . . . . . . .2E 50
Bedgebury Gdns. SW19 . . . . .2G 135
Bedgebury Rd. SE9 . . . . . . .4B 124
Bedivere Rd. BR1: Broml 3J 141
Bedlam M. SE11 . . . . . . .3J 19
Bedlow Way CR0: Bedd 4K 167
Bedmond Ho. SW3 . . . . . . .5C 16
(off Cale St.)
Bedonwell Rd.
DA7: Belv, Bex, Erith 6F 109
DA17: Belv 6E 108
Bedser Cl. CR7: Thor H 3C 156
SE11 . . . . . .7H 19 (6K 101)
Bedser Dr. UB6: G'frd 5H 59
Bedster Gdns.
KT8: W Mole 2F 149
Bedwardine Rd. SE19 . . . . . .7E 138
Bedwell Cl. CR0: C'don 5D 156
Bedwell Ct. RM6: Chad H 7D 54
(off Chapel La.)
Bedwell Gdns. UB3: Harl 5G 93
(not continuous)
Bedwell Ho. SW9 . . . . . . .2A 120
Bedwell Rd. DA17: Belv 5G 109
N17 . . . . . . .1E 48
Beeby Rd. E16 . . . . . . .5K 87
Beech Av. DA15: Sidc 7A 126
HA4: Ruis 1K 57
IG9: Buck H 2E 36
N20 . . . . . . .1H 31
TW8: Bford 7B 96
W3 . . . . . . .1A 98
Beech Cl. N9 . . . . . . .6B 24
SE8 . . . . . . .6C 104
SM5: Cars 2D 166
SW15 . . . . . . .7C 116
SW19 . . . . . . .6E 134
TW15: Ashf 5F 129
TW16: Sun 2B 148
UB7: W Dray 3C 92
Beech Copse BR1: Broml 1D 160
CR2: S Croy 5E 168
Beech Ct. BR1: Broml 1H 159
(off Blyth Rd.)
BR3: Beck 7B 140
E17 . . . . . . .3F 51
IG1: Ilf 3E 70
(off Riverdene Rd.)
KT6: Surb 7D 150
UB5: N'olt 1C 76
W9 . . . . . . .5J 81
(off Elmfield Way)

Beech Cres. Ct. N5 . . . . . . .4B 66
Beechcroft BR7: Chst 7E 142
Beechcroft Av. DA7: Bex 1K 127
HA2: Harr 7E 40
KT3: N Mald 1J 151
NW11 . . . . . . .7H 45
Beechcroft Cl. BR6: Orp 4H 173
SW16 . . . . . . .5K 137
TW5: Hest 7C 94
Beechcroft Ct. N12 . . . . . . .4E 30
NW11 . . . . . . .7H 45
(off Beechcroft Av.)
Beechcroft Gdns. HA9: Wemb . . .3F 61
Beechcroft Ho. W5 . . . . . . .5E 78
Beechcroft Lodge SM2: Sutt . . .7A 166
Beechcroft Rd. BR6: Orp 4H 173
E18 . . . . . . .2K 51
KT9: Chess 3F 163
SW14 . . . . . . .3J 115
SW17 . . . . . . .2C 136
Beechdale N21 . . . . . . .2E 32
Beechdale Rd. SW2 . . . . . . .6K 119
Beech Dell BR2: Kes 4D 172
Beechdene SE15 . . . . . . .1H 121
(off Carlton Gro.)
Beech Dr. N2 . . . . . . .2D 46
Beechen Cliff Way TW7: Isle . . .2K 113
Beechen Gro. HA5: Pinn 3D 40
Beechen Pl. SE23 . . . . . . .2K 139
The Beeches CR2: S Croy 5D 168
(off Blunt Rd.)
E12 . . . . . . .7C 70
TW3: Houn 1F 113
Beeches Av. SM5: Cars 7C 166
Beeches Cl. SE20 . . . . . . .1J 157
Beeches Rd. SM3: Sutt 1G 165
SW17 . . . . . . .3C 136
Beeches Wlk. SM5: Cars 7B 166
Beechey Ho. E1 . . . . . . .1H 103
(off Watts St.)
Beechfield Cotts. BR1: Broml . . .1A 160
Beechfield Ct. CR2: S Croy 4C 168
(off Bramley Hill)
Beechfield Gdns. RM7: Rush G . . .7J 55
Beechfield Rd. BR1: Broml 2A 160
DA8: Erith 7K 109
N4 . . . . . . .6C 48
SE6 . . . . . . .1B 140
Beech Gdns. EC2 . . . . . . .5C 8
(off Beech St.)
RM10: Dag 7J 73
W5 . . . . . . .2E 96
Beech Gro. CR4: Mitc 5H 155
KT3: N Mald 3K 151
Beech Hall Cres. E4 . . . . . . .7A 36
Beech Hall Rd. E4 . . . . . . .7K 35
Beech Haven Ct. DA1: Cray 5K 127
(off London Rd.)
Beech Hill EN4: Had W 1G 21
Beech Hill Av. EN4: Had W 1F 21
Beechhill Rd. SE9 . . . . . . .5E 124
Beech Ho. CR0: New Ad 6D 170
SE16 . . . . . . .2J 103
(off Ainsty Est.)
Beech Ho. Rd. CR0: C'don 3D 168
Beech Hurst Cl. BR7: Chst 1G 161
Beeching Ct. W3 . . . . . . .3J 97
(off Bollo Bri. Rd.)
Beech La. IG9: Buck H 2E 36
Beech Lawns N12 . . . . . . .5G 31
Beechmont Cl. BR1: Broml 5G 141
Beechmore Gdns. SM3: Cheam . .2F 165
Beechmore Rd. SW11 . . . . . .1D 118
Beechmount Av. W7 . . . . . . .5H 77
Beecholme N12 . . . . . . .5E 30
Beecholme Av. CR4: Mitc 1F 155
Beecholme Est. E5 . . . . . . .3H 67
Beech Rd. N11 . . . . . . .6D 32
SW16 . . . . . . .2J 155
TW14: Bedf 7G 111
Beechrow TW10: Ham 4E 132
Beech St. EC2 . . . . .5C 8 (5C 84)
RM7: Rom 4J 55

Beech Tree Cl.—Belmont St.

Beech Tree Cl. HA7: Stan 5H **27**
N1 . . . . .7A **66**
Beech Tree Glade E4 . . . . .1C **36**
Beech Tree Pl. SM1: Sutt 5K **165**
Beechvale Cl. N12 . . . . .5H **31**
Beech Wlk. N17 . . . . .3F **49**
NW7 . . . . .6F **29**
Beech Way NW10 . . . . .7K **61**
TW2: Twick 3E **130**
Beechway DA5: Bexl 6D **126**
Beechwood Av. BR6: Chels 5J **173**
CR7: Thor H 4B **156**
HA2: Harr 3F **59**
HA4: Ruis 2H **57**
N3 . . . . .3H **45**
TW9: Kew 1G **115**
TW16: Sun 6J **129**
UB3: Hayes 7F **75**
UB6: G'frd 3F **77**
UB8: Hil 6C **74**
The Beechwood Cen.
BR2: Broml 1D 172
(off Lwr. Gravel Rd.)
Beechwood Circ. HA2: Harr 3F **59**
Beechwood Cl. KT6: Surb 7C **150**
N2 . . . . .3D **46**
NW7 . . . . .5F **29**
Beechwood Ct. SM5: Cars 4D **166**
TW16: Sun 6J **129**
W4 . . . . .6K **97**
Beechwood Cres. DA7: Bex 3D **126**
Beechwood Dr. BR2: Kes 4B **172**
IG8: Wfd G 5C **36**
Beechwood Gdns. HA2: Harr 3F **59**
IG5: Ilf .5D **52**
NW10 . . . . .3F **79**
Beechwood Gro. KT6: Surb 7C **150**
W3 . . . . .7A **80**
Beechwood Hall N3 . . . . .3H **45**
Beechwood Ho. *E2 . . . . .2G 85*
(off Teale St.)
Beechwood M. N9 . . . . .2B **34**
Beechwood Pk. E18 . . . . .3J **51**
Beechwood Pl. SE10 . . . . .1E **122**
Beechwood Ri. BR7: Chst 4F **143**
Beechwood Rd. CR2: Sande 7E **168**
E8 . . . . .6F **67**
N8 . . . . .4H **47**
Beechwoods Ct. SE19 . . . . .5F **139**
Beechworth NW6 . . . . .7G **63**
Beechworth Cl. NW3 . . . . .2J **63**
Beecroft La. SE4 . . . . .5A **122**
Beecroft M. SE4 . . . . .5A **122**
Beecroft Rd. SE4 . . . . .5A **122**
Beefeater Distillery 6J **19** (5A **102**)
Beehive Cl. E8 . . . . .7F **67**
UB10: Uxb 7B **56**
Beehive Ct. HA8: Edg 5C **28**
IG1: Ilf .6D **52**
Beehive La. IG1: Ilf 5D **52**
IG4: Ilf .5D **52**
Beehive Pl. SW9 . . . . .3A **120**
Beeken Dene BR6: Farnb 4G **173**
Beeleigh Rd. SM4: Mord 4K **153**
Beemans Row SW18 . . . . .2A **136**
Beeston Cl. E8 . . . . .5G **67**
Beeston Ho. *SE1 . . . . .3D 102*
(off Burbage Cl.)
Beeston Pl. SW1 . . . . .1K **17** (3F **101**)
Beeston Rd. EN4: E Barn 6G **21**
Beeston Way TW14: Felt 6A **112**
Beethoven St. W10 . . . . .3G **81**
Beeton Cl. HA5: Hat E 1E **40**
Beeton Way SE27 . . . . .4D **138**
Begbie Rd. SE3 . . . . .1A **124**
BEGGAR'S HILL **6B 164**
Beggar's Hill KT17: Ewe 7B **164**
Beggars Roost La.
SM1: Sutt 6J **165**
Begonia Cl. E6 . . . . .5D **88**
Begonia Pl.
TW12: Hamp 6E **130**
Begonia Wlk. W12 . . . . .6B **80**
Beirach Moshe Sq. E5 . . . . .2H **67**
Beira St. SW12 . . . . .7F **119**
Bejun Ct. EN5: New Bar 4F **21**
Bekesbourne St. E14 . . . . .6A **86**
Belcroft Cl. BR1: Broml 7H **141**
Beldam Way TW3: Houn 3D **112**
Beldanes Lodge NW10 . . . . .7C **62**
Beldham Gdns.
KT8: W Mole 2F **149**
Belfairs Dr. RM6: Chad H 7C **54**
Belfast Rd. N16 . . . . .2F **67**
SE25 .4H **157**
Belfield Rd. KT19: Ewe 7K **163**
Belfont Wlk. N7 . . . . .4J **65**
(not continuous)
Belford Gro. SE18 . . . . .4E **106**
Belford Ho. E8 . . . . .1F **85**
Belfort Rd. SE15 . . . . .2J **121**
Belfry Cl. BR1: Broml 4F **161**
SE16 .5H **103**
Belgrade Rd. N16 . . . . .4E **66**
TW12: Hamp 1F **149**
Belgrave Cl. N14 . . . . .5B **22**
NW7 . . . . .5E **28**
W3 . . . . .2H **97**
Belgrave Ct. *E2 . . . . .2H 85*
(off Temple St.)
E13 . . . . .4A **88**
E14 . . . . .7B 86
(off Westferry Cir.)
SW8 . . . . .7G 101
(off Ascalon St.)
W4 . . . . .5J **97**
Belgrave Cres. TW16: Sun 1K **147**
Belgrave Gdns. HA7: Stan 5H **27**
N14 . . . . .5C **22**
NW8 . . . . .1K **81**
Belgrave Hgts. E11 . . . . .1J **69**
Belgrave Ho. SW9 . . . . .7A **102**
Belgrave Mans. *NW8 . . . . .1K 81*
(off Belgrave Gdns.)
Belgrave M. Nth. SW1 . . . .7G **11** (2E **100**)
Belgrave M. Sth.
SW1 . . . . .1H **17** (3E **100**)
Belgrave M. W. SW1 . . . . .1G **17** (3E **100**)
Belgrave Pl. SW1 . . . . .1H **17** (3E **100**)
Belgrave Rd. CR4: Mitc 3B **154**
E10 . . . . .1E **68**
E11 . . . . .2J **69**
E13 . . . . .4A **88**
E17 . . . . .5C **50**
IG1: Ilf .1D **70**
SE25 .4F **157**
SW1 . . . . .3K **17** (4F **101**)
SW13 . . . . .7B **98**
TW4: Houn 3D **112**
TW16: Sun 1K **147**
Belgrave Sq. SW1 . . . . . . .1G **17** (3E **100**)
Belgrave St. E1 . . . . .5K **85**
Belgrave Ter. IG8: Wfd G 3D **36**
Belgrave Wlk. CR4: Mitc 3B **154**
Belgrave Yd. SW1 . . . . .2J **17**
BELGRAVIA . . . .**2H 17 (3E 100)**
Belgravia Cl. EN5: Barn 3C **20**
Belgravia Ct. SW1 . . . . .2J **17**
Belgravia Gdns. BR1: Broml 6G **141**
Belgravia Ho. *SW1 . . . . .1G 17*
(off Halkin Pl.)
SW4 . . . . .6H **119**
Belgravia M. KT1: King T 4D **150**
Belgravia Workshops *N19 . . . . .2J 65*
(off Marlborough Rd.)
Belgrove St. WC1 . . . . .1F **7** (3J **83**)
Belham Wlk. SE5 . . . . .1D **120**
Belinda Rd. SW9 . . . . .3B **120**
Belitha Vs. N1 . . . . .7K **65**
THE BELL **3C 50**
Bella Best Ho. *SW1 . . . . .5K 17*
(off Westmoreland Ter.)
Bellamy Cl. E14 . . . . .2C **104**
HA8: Edg 2D **28**
UB10: Ick 3C **56**
W14 . . . . .5H **99**
Bellamy Ct. HA7: Stan 1B **42**
Bellamy Dr. HA7: Stan 1B **42**
Bellamy Ho. SW17 . . . . .4B **136**
TW5: Hest 6E **94**
Bellamy Rd. E4 . . . . .6J **35**
EN2: Enf 2J **23**
Bellamy's Ct. *SE16 . . . . .1K 103*
(off Abbotshade Rd.)
Bellamy St. SW12 . . . . .7F **119**
Bel La. TW13: Hanw 3C **130**
Bellarmine Cl. SE28 . . . . .1K **107**
Bellasis Av. SW2 . . . . .2J **137**
Bell Av. UB7: W Dray 4B **92**
Bell Brook Ri. N11 . . . . .4A **32**
Bell Cl. HA4: Ruis 3H **57**
HA5: Pinn 2A **40**
Bellclose Rd.
UB7: W Dray 2A **92**
Bell Ct. NW4 . . . . .4E **44**
Bell Dr. SW18 . . . . .7G **117**
Bellefields Rd. SW9 . . . . .3K **119**
Bellegrove Cl. DA16: Well 2K **125**
Bellegrove Pde. DA16: Well 3K **125**
Bellegrove Rd. DA16: Well 2H **125**
Bellenden Rd. SE15 . . . . .1F **121**
Bellenden Rd. Retail Pk. 1G **121**
Bellestaines Pleasaunce E4 . . . . . . .2H **35**
Belleville Ho. *SE10 . . . . .7D 104*
(off Norman Rd.)
Belleville Rd. SW11 . . . . .5C **118**
Belle Vue UB6: G'frd 1H **77**
Bellevue Ct. TW3: Houn 4E **112**
Belle Vue Est. NW4 . . . . .4F **45**
Belle Vue La. WD23: B Hea 1C **26**
Bellevue M. N11 . . . . .5K **31**
Bellevue Pde. SW17 . . . . .1D **136**
Belle Vue Pk. CR7: Thor H 3C **156**
Bellevue Pl. E1 . . . . .4J **85**
Belle Vue Rd. E17 . . . . .2F **51**
NW4 . . . . .4E **44**
Bellevue Rd. DA6: Bex 5F **127**
KT1: King T 3E **150**
(not continuous)
N11 . . . . .4K **31**
SW13 .2C **116**
SW17 .1C **136**
W13 . . . . .4B **78**
Bellew St. SW17 . . . . .3A **136**
Bell Farm Av. RM10: Dag 3J **73**
Bellfield CR0: Sels 7A **170**
Bellfield Av.
HA3: Hrw W 6C **26**
Bellfield Cl. SE3 . . . . .7K **105**
Bellflower Cl. E6 . . . . .5C **88**
Bell Gdns. *E10 . . . . .1C 68*
(off Church Rd.)
Bellgate M. NW5 . . . . .4F **65**
BELL GREEN **4B 140**
Bell Grn. SE26 . . . . .4B **140**
Bell Grn. La. SE26 . . . . .5B **140**
Bell Grn. Retail Pk. 3B **140**
Bell Grn. Trade City SE6 . . . . .3B **140**
Bellhaven E15 . . . . .6F **69**
Bell Hill CR0: C'don 2C **168**
Bell Ho. HA9: Wemb 3E **60**
SE10 . . . . .6E 104
(off Haddo St.)
Bellhouse Cotts. UB3: Hayes 7G **75**
Bell Ho. Rd. RM7: Rush G 1J **73**
Bellina M. NW5 . . . . .4F **65**
Bell Ind. Est. W4 . . . . .4J **97**
Belling Cres. EN3: Pond E 5D **24**
BELLINGHAM **3D 140**
Bellingham *N17 . . . . .7C 34*
(off Park La.)
Bellingham Ct. IG11: Bark 3B **90**
Bellingham Grn. SE6 . . . . .3C **140**
Bellingham Leisure & Lifestyle Cen.
. . . . **3D 140**
Bellingham Rd. SE6 . . . . .3D **140**
Bellingham Trad. Est.
SE6 . . . . .3D **140**
Bell Inn Yd. EC3 . . . . .1F **15** (6D **84**)
Bell La. E1 . . . . .6J **9** (5F **85**)
E16 . . . . .1H **105**
EN3: Enf H, Enf W 1E **24**
HA9: Wemb 2D **60**
NW4 . . . . .4F **45**
TW1: Twick 1A **132**
TW14: Bedf 7F **111**
Bellmaker Ct. E3 . . . . .5C **86**
Bell Mdw. SE19 . . . . .5E **138**
Bell Moor NW3 . . . . .3A **64**
Bello Cl. SE24 . . . . .7B **120**
Bellot Gdns. *SE10 . . . . .5G 105*
(off Bellot St.)
Bellot St. SE10 . . . . .5G **105**
Bell Pde. BR4: W W'ck 2E **170**
Bellring Cl. DA17: Belv 6G **109**
Bell Rd. EN1: Enf 1J **23**
KT8: E Mos 5H **149**
TW3: Houn 3F **113**
Bells All. SW6 . . . . .2J **117**
Bells Hill EN5: Barn 5A **20**
Bellsize Ct. NW3 . . . . .5B **64**
Bell St. NW1 . . . . .5C **4** (5C **82**)
SE18 . . . . .1C **124**
Belltrees Gro. SW16 . . . . .5K **137**
Bellview Ct. TW3: Houn 4F **113**
Bell Vw. Mnr. HA4: Ruis 7F **39**
Bell Water Ga. SE18 . . . . .3E **106**
Bellwether La. *SW18 . . . . .5K 117*
(off Ryland Blvd.)
Bell Wharf La. EC4 . . . . . .3D **14** (7C **84**)
Bellwood Rd. SE15 . . . . .4K **121**
Bell Yd. WC2 . . . . .1J **13** (6A **84**)
Bell Yd. M. SE1 . . . . .7H **15** (2E **102**)
Belmarsh Rd. SE28 . . . . .2J **107**
BELMONT
HA3 . . . . **2A 42**
SM2 . . . . **7J 165**
Belmont Av. DA16: Well 3J **125**
EN4: Cockf 5J **21**
HA0: Wemb 1F **79**
KT3: N Mald 5C **152**
N9 . . . . .1B **34**
N13 . . . . .5E **32**
N17 . . . . .3C **48**
UB2: S'hall 3C **94**
Belmont Circ. HA3: Kenton 1B **42**
Belmont Cl. E4 . . . . .5A **36**
EN4: Cockf 4J **21**
IG8: Wfd G 4E **36**
N20 . . . . .1E **30**
SW4 . . . . .3G **119**
UB8: Uxb 6A **56**
Belmont Ct. N5 . . . . .4C **66**
NW11 . . . . .5H **45**
Belmont Gro. SE13 . . . . .3F **123**
W4 . . . . .4K **97**
Belmont Hall Ct. SE13 . . . . .3F **123**
Belmont Hill SE13 . . . . .3F **123**
Belmont La. BR7: Chst 5G **143**
HA7: Stan 1C **42**
Belmont Lodge HA3: Hrw W 7C **26**
Belmont M. SW19 . . . . .2F **135**
Belmont Pde. BR7: Chst 5G **143**
NW11 . . . . .5H **45**
Belmont Pk. SE13 . . . . .4F **123**
Belmont Pk. Cl. SE13 . . . . .4G **123**
Belmont Pk. Rd. E10 . . . . .6D **50**
Belmont Ri. SM2: Sutt 6H **165**
Belmont Rd. BR3: Beck 2A **158**
BR7: Chst 5F **143**
DA8: Erith 7G **109**
HA3: W'stone 3K **41**
IG1: Ilf .3G **71**
N15 . . . . .4C **48**
N17 . . . . .4C **48**
SE25 .5H **157**
SM6: W'gton 5F **167**
SW4 . . . . .3G **119**
TW2: Twick 2H **131**
UB8: Uxb 7A **56**
W4 . . . . .4K **97**
Belmont St. NW1 . . . . .7E **64**

Belmont Ter. W4 4K **97**
Belmore Av. UB4: Hayes 6J **75**
Belmore Ho. N7 5H **65**
Belmore La. N7 5H **65**
Belmore St. SW8 1H **119**
Beloe Cl. SW15 4C **116**
Belsham St. E9 6J **67**
Belsize Av. N13 6E **32**
NW3 6B **64**
W13 3B **96**
Belsize Ct. SM1: Sutt 4K **165**
Belsize Ct. Garages *NW3* *5B* ***64***
(off Belsize La.)
Belsize Cres. NW3 5B **64**
Belsize Gdns. SM1: Sutt 4K **165**
Belsize Gro. NW3 6C **64**
Belsize La. NW3 6B **64**
Belsize M. NW3 6B **64**
Belsize Pk. NW3 6B **64**
Belsize Pk. Gdns. NW3 6B **64**
Belsize Pk. M. NW3 6B **64**
Belsize Pl. NW3 5B **64**
Belsize Rd. HA3: Hrw W 7C **26**
NW6 1K **81**
Belsize Sq. NW3 6B **64**
Belsize Ter. NW3 6B **64**
Belson Rd. SE18 4D **106**
Beltane Dr. SW19 3F **135**
Belthorn Cres. SW12 7G **119**
Belton Rd. DA14: Sidc 4A **144**
E7 7K **69**
E11 4G **69**
N17 3E **48**
NW2 6C **62**
Belton Way E3 5C **86**
Beltran Rd. SW6 2K **117**
Beltwood Rd. DA17: Belv 4J **109**
BELVEDERE 4G **109**
The Belvedere SE1 1K **101**
SW10 *1A* ***118***
(off Chelsea Harbour)
Belvedere Av. IG5: Ilf 2F **53**
SW19 5G **135**
Belvedere Bldgs. SE1 7B **14** (2B **102**)
Belvedere Bus. Pk. DA17: Belv 2H **109**
Belvedere Cl. TW11: Tedd 5J **131**
Belvedere Ct. DA17: Belv 3F **109**
N1 *1E* ***84***
(off De Beauvoir Cres.)
N2 5B **46**
NW2 *6F* ***63***
(off Willesden La.)
SW15 4E **116**
Belvedere Dr. SW19 5G **135**
Belvedere Gdns. KT8: W Mole 5D **148**
SE1 6H **13** (2K **101**)
Belvedere Gro. SW19 5G **135**
Belvedere Ho. *TW13: Felt* *1J* ***129***
(off Lemon Gro.)
Belvedere Ind. Est. DA17: Belv 1J **109**
Belvedere Link Bus. Pk. DA8: Erith 3J **109**
Belvedere M. SE3 7K **105**
SE15 3J **121**
Belvedere Pl. SE1 7B **14** (2B **102**)
SW2 4K **119**
Belvedere Rd. DA7: Bex 3F **127**
E10 1A **68**
SE1 7G **13** (2K **101**)
SE19 7F **139**
W7 3K **95**
Belvedere Row Apartments *W12* *7E* ***80***
(off Fountain Park Way)
Belvedere Sq. SW19 5G **135**
Belvedere Strand NW9 2B **44**
Belvedere Way HA3: Kenton 6E **42**
Belvoir Cl. SE9 3C **142**
Belvoir Ho. SW1 4G **101**
Belvoir Rd. SE22 7G **121**
Belvue Bus. Cen. UB5: N'olt 7F **59**
Belvue Cl. UB5: N'olt 7E **58**
Belvue Rd. UB5: N'olt 7E **58**
Belz Dr. N15 4E **48**
Belz Ter. E5 7G **49**

Bembridge Cl. NW6 7G **63**
Bembridge Gdns. HA4: Ruis 2F **57**
Bembridge Ho. *KT2: King T* *2G* ***151***
(off Coombe Rd.)
SE8 *4B* ***104***
(off Longshore)
SW18 *6K* ***117***
(off Iron Mill Rd.)
Bemersyde Point *E13* *3K* ***87***
(off Dongola Rd. W.)
Bemerton Est. N1 7J **65**
Bemerton St. N1 1K **83**
Bemish Rd. SW15 3F **117**
Bempton Dr. HA4: Ruis 2K **57**
Bemsted Rd. E17 3B **50**
Benares Rd. SE18 4K **107**
Benbow Ct. *W6* *3E* ***98***
(off Benbow Rd.)
Benbow Ho. *SE8* *6C* ***104***
(off Benbow St.)
Benbow M. *E3* *3B* ***86***
(off Tredegar Sq.)
Benbow Rd. W6 3D **98**
Benbow St. SE8 6C **104**
Benbury Cl. BR1: Broml 5E **140**
Bence Ho. *SE8* *4A* ***104***
(off Rainsborough Av.)
The Bench TW10: Ham 3C **132**
Bench Fld. CR2: S Croy 6F **169**
Bencroft Rd. SW16 7G **137**
Bencurtis Pk. BR4: W W'ck 3F **171**
Bendall Ho. *NW1* *5D* ***4***
(off Penfold St.)
Bendall M. NW1 5D **4**
Bendemeer Rd. SW15 3F **117**
Benden Ho. *SE13* *5E* ***122***
(off Monument Gdns.)
Bendish Point SE28 2G **107**
Bendish Rd. E6 7C **70**
Bendmore Av. SE2 5A **108**
Bendon Valley SW18 7K **117**
Benedict Cl. BR6: Orp 3J **173**
DA17: Belv 3E **108**
Benedict Ct. RM6: Chad H 6F **55**
Benedict Dr. TW14: Bedf 7F **111**
Benedict Rd. CR4: Mitc 3B **154**
SW9 3K **119**
Benedicts Wharf IG11: Bark 1F **89**
Benedict Way N2 3A **46**
Benedict Wharf CR4: Mitc 3C **154**
Benenden Grn. BR2: Broml 5J **159**
Benenden Ho. *SE17* *5E* ***102***
(off Mina Rd.)
Benett Gdns. SW16 2J **155**
Ben Ezra Ct. *SE17* *4C* ***102***
(off Asolando Dr.)
Benfleet Cl. SM1: Sutt 3A **166**
Benfleet Ct. E8 1F **85**
Benfleet Way N11 2K **31**
Bengal Ct. *EC3* *1F* ***15***
(off Birchin La.)
Bengal Rd. IG1: Ilf 4F **71**
Bengarth Dr. HA3: Hrw W 2H **41**
Bengarth Rd. UB5: N'olt 1C **76**
Bengeo Gdns. RM6: Chad H 6C **54**
Bengeworth Rd. HA1: Harr 2A **60**
SE5 3C **120**
Ben Hale Cl. HA7: Stan 5G **27**
Benham Cl. KT9: Chess 6C **162**
SW11 3B **118**
Benham Gdns. TW4: Houn 5D **112**
Benham Ho. *SW10* *7K* ***99***
(off Coleridge Gdns.)
Benham Rd. W7 5J **77**
Benham's Pl. NW3 4A **64**
Benhill Av. SM1: Sutt 4K **165**
(not continuous)
Benhill Rd. SE5 7D **102**
SM1: Sutt 3A **166**
Benhill Wood Rd. SM1: Sutt 3A **166**
BENHILTON 2K **165**
Benhilton Gdns. SM1: Sutt 3K **165**
Benhurst Ct. SW16 5A **138**

Benhurst La. SW16 5A **138**
Benina Cl. IG2: Ilf 5K **53**
Benin Ho. *WC1* *6G* ***7***
(off Procter St.)
Benin St. SE13 7F **123**
Benjafield Cl. N18 4C **34**
Benjamin Cl. E8 1G **85**
Benjamin Ct. DA17: Belv 6F **109**
TW15: Ashf 7E **128**
Benjamin Franklin House *4E* ***12***
(off Craven St.)
Benjamin M. SW12 7G **119**
Benjamin St. EC1 5A **8** (5B **84**)
Benjamin Truman Cl. E1 4G **85**
Ben Jonson Ct. N1 2E **84**
Ben Jonson Ho. EC2 5D **8**
Ben Jonson Pl. EC2 5D **8**
Ben Jonson Rd. E1 5K **85**
Benkart M. SW15 6C **116**
Benledi Rd. E14 6F **87**
Benlow Works *UB3: Hayes* *2H* ***93***
(off Silverdale Rd.)
Bennelong Cl. W12 7D **80**
Bennerley Rd. SW11 5C **118**
Bennet Cl. KT1: Hamp W 1C **150**
Bennet M. *N19* *3H* ***65***
(off Wedmore St.)
Bennets Ctyd. SW19 1A **154**
Bennets Fld. Rd.
UB11: Stock P 1D **92**
Bennet's Hill EC4 2B **14** (7C **84**)
Bennets Lodge EN2: Enf 3G **23**
Bennet St. SW1 4A **12** (1G **101**)
Bennett Cl. DA16: Well 2A **126**
HA6: Nwood 1H **39**
TW4: Houn 5C **112**
Bennett Ct. N7 3K **65**
Bennett Gro. SE13 1D **122**
Bennett Ho. *SW1* *3D* ***18***
(off Page St.)
Bennett Pk. SE3 3H **123**
Bennett Rd. E13 4A **88**
N16 4E **66**
RM6: Chad H 6E **54**
SW9 2A **120**
Bennetts Av. CR0: C'don 2A **170**
UB6: G'frd 1J **77**
Bennett's Castle La. RM8: Dag 2C **72**
Bennetts Cl. CR4: Mitc 1F **155**
N17 6A **34**
Bennetts Copse BR7: Chst 6C **142**
Bennett St. W4 6A **98**
Bennetts Way CR0: C'don 2A **170**
Bennett's Yd.
SW1 2D **18** (3H **101**)
Benning Dr. RM8: Dag 1E **72**
Benningholme Rd.
HA8: Edg 6F **29**
Bennington Cl. CR7: Thor H 4C **156**
Bennington Rd. IG8: Wfd G 7B **36**
N17 1E **48**
Benn's All. TW12: Hamp 2F **149**
Benn St. E9 6A **68**
Benns Wlk. *TW9: Rich* *4E* ***114***
(off Michelsdale Dr.)
Benrek Cl. IG6: Ilf 1G **53**
Bensbury Cl. SW15 7D **116**
Bensham Cl. CR7: Thor H 4C **156**
Bensham Gro. CR7: Thor H 2C **156**
Bensham La. CR0: C'don 7B **156**
CR7: Thor H 5B **156**
Bensham Mnr. Rd.
CR7: Thor H 4C **156**
Bensham Mnr. Rd. Pas.
CR7: Thor H 4C **156**
Bensley Cl. N11 5J **31**
Ben Smith Way SE16 3G **103**
Benson Av. E6 2A **88**
Benson Cl. EN5: Barn 5C **20**
TW3: Houn 4E **112**
UB8: Hil 5A **74**
Benson Ct. *SW8* *1J* ***119***
(off Hartington Rd.)

Benson Ho. *E2* *3J* ***9***
(off Ligonier St.)
SE1 *5K* ***13***
(off Hatfields)
W14 *4H* ***99***
(off Radnor Ter.)
Benson Mews BR7: Chst 5E **142**
Benson Quay E1 7J **85**
Benson Rd. CR0: Wadd 3A **168**
SE23 1J **139**
The Bentall Cen. 2D **150**
Bentfield Gdns. SE9 3B **142**
Bentfield Ho. *NW9* *3B* ***44***
(off Heritage Av.)
Benthal Rd. N16 2G **67**
Bentham Ct. *N1* *7C* ***66***
(off Ecclesbourne Rd.)
Bentham Ho. *SE1* *3D* ***102***
(off Falmouth Rd.)
SE18 3F **107**
Bentham Rd. E9 6K **67**
SE28 7B **90**
Bentham Wlk. NW10 5J **61**
Ben Tillet Cl. E16 1D **106**
IG11: Bark 7A **72**
Ben Tillet Ho. N15 3B **48**
Bentinck Cl. NW8 2C **82**
Bentinck Ho. *SW1* *2D* ***18***
(off Monck St.)
W12 *7D* ***80***
(off White City Est.)
Bentinck Mans. *W1* *7H* ***5***
(off Bentinck St.)
Bentinck M. W1 7H **5** (6E **82**)
Bentinck Rd.
UB7: Yiew 1A **92**
Bentinck St. W1 7H **5** (6E **82**)
Bentley Cl. SW19 3J **135**
W7 1K **95**
Bentley Ct. *SE13* *4E* ***122***
(off Whitburn Rd.)
Bentley Dr. IG2: Ilf 6G **53**
NW2 3H **63**
Bentley Ho. *E3* *4C* ***86***
(off Wellington Way)
SE5 *1E* ***120***
(off Peckham Rd.)
Bentley Lodge WD23: B Hea 2D **26**
Bentley M. EN1: Enf 6J **23**
Bentley Priory
Local Nature Reserve 4D **26**
Bentley Priory Mus. 3D **26**
Bentley Rd. N1 6E **66**
Bentley Way
EN5: New Bar 4F **21**
HA7: Stan 5F **27**
IG8: Buck H, Wfd G 2D **36**
Benton Rd. IG1: Ilf 1H **71**
Bentons La. SE27 4C **138**
Benton's Ri. SE27 5D **138**
Bentry Cl. RM8: Dag 2E **72**
Bentry Rd. RM8: Dag 2E **72**
Bentworth Ct. *E2* *3K* ***9***
(off Granby St.)
Bentworth Rd. W12 6D **80**
Ben Uri Gallery 1K **81**
Benville Ho. *SW8* *7K* ***101***
(off Dorset Rd.)
Benwell Cen. TW16: Sun 1J **147**
Benwell Ct. TW16: Sun 1J **147**
Benwell Rd. N7 4A **66**
Benwick Cl. SE16 4H **103**
Benwick M. SE20 1J **157**
Benwood Ct.
SM1: Sutt 3A **166**
Benworth St. E3 3B **86**
Benyon Ct. *N1* *1E* ***84***
(off De Beauvoir Est.)
Benyon Ho. *EC1* *1K* ***7***
(off Myddelton Pas.)
Benyon Rd. N1 1D **84**
Benyon Wharf *E8* *1E* ***84***
(off Kingsland Rd.)

Berberis Ct. IG1: Ilf 6F **71**
Berberis Ho. *E3* 5C **86**
(off Gale Rd.)
TW13: Felt 2J **129**
Berberis Wlk.
UB7: W Dray 4A **92**
Berber Pde. SE18 . . . . .1C **124**
Berber Pl. E14 . . . . .7C **86**
Berber Rd. SW11 . . . . .5D **118**
Berberry Cl. HA8: Edg 4D **28**
Bercta Rd. SE9 . . . . .2G **143**
Berebinder Ho. *E3* 2B **86**
(off Tredegar Rd.)
Beregaria Ct. *SE11* 7K **19**
(off Kennington Pk. Rd.)
Berengers Ct. RM6: Chad H 7F **55**
(off Whalebone La. Sth.)
Berengers Pl.
RM9: Dag 6B **72**
Berenger Twr. SW10 . . . . .7B **100**
(off Worlds End Est.)
Berenger Wlk. SW10 . . . . .7B **100**
(off Worlds End Est.)
Berens Ct. DA14: Sidc 4K **143**
Berens Rd. NW10 . . . . .3F **81**
Berens Way BR7: Chst 3K **161**
Beresford Av.
HA0: Wemb . . . .
KT5: Surb 1H **163**
N20 . . . . .2J **31**
TW1: Twick 6C **114**
W7 .5H **77**
Beresford Ct. E9 . . . . .5A **68**
(off Mabley St.)
Beresford Dr. BR1: Broml 3C **160**
IG8: Wfd G 4F **37**
Beresford Gdns. EN1: Enf 4K **23**
RM6: Chad H 5E **54**
TW4: Houn 5D **112**
Beresford Rd. E4 . . . . .1B **36**
E17 . . . . .1D **50**
HA1: Harr 5H **41**
KT2: King T 1F **151**
KT3: N Mald 4J **151**
N2 . . . . .3C **46**
N5 .5D **66**
N8 .5A **48**
SM2: Sutt 7H **165**
UB1: S'hall 1B **94**
Beresford Sq. SE18 . . . . .4F **107**
Beresford St. SE18 . . . . .3F **107**
Beresford Ter. N5 . . . . .5C **66**
Berestede Rd. W6 . . . . .5B **98**
Bere St. E1 . . . . .7K **85**
Bergen Ho. *SE5* 2C **120**
(off Carew St.)
Bergenia Ho. TW13: Felt 1J **129**
Bergen Sq. SE16 . . . . .3A **104**
Berger Cl. BR5: Pet W 6H **161**
Berger Ct. *E3* 3E **86**
(off Bolinder Way)
Berger Rd. E9 . . . . .6K **67**
Berghem M. W14 . . . . .3F **99**
Bergholt Av. IG4: Ilf 5C **52**
Bergholt Cres. N16 . . . . .7E **48**
Bergholt M. NW1 . . . . .7H **65**
Berglen Ct. E14 . . . . .6A **86**
Bergman Ho. *E17* 4C **50**
(off Hoe St.)
Bering Sq. E14 . . . . .5C **104**
Bering Wlk. E16 . . . . .6B **88**
Berisford M. SW18 . . . . .6A **118**
Berkeley Av.
DA7: Bex 1D **126**
IG5: Ilf 2E **52**
RM5: Col R 1J **55**
TW4: Cran 1J **111**
UB6: G'frd 6H **59**
(not continuous)
Berkeley Cl.
BR5: Pet W 7J **161**
HA4: Ruis 3J **57**
KT2: King T 7E **132**

Berkeley Ct. BR2: Broml 4K **159**
CR0: C'don 4D **168**
(off Coombe Rd.)
KT6: Surb 7D **150**
N3 .1K **45**
N14 . . . . .6B **22**
NW1 . . . . .4F **5**
NW10 . . . . .4A **62**
NW11 . . . . .7H **45**
(off Ravenscroft Av.)
SM6: W'gton 3G **167**
W5 .7C **78**
Berkeley Cres. EN4: E Barn 5G **21**
Berkeley Dr. KT8: W Mole 3D **148**
Berkeley Gdns. KT10: Clay 6A **162**
KT12: Walt T 7H **147**
N21 . . . . .7J **23**
W8 .1J **99**
Berkeley Ho. *E3* 3C **86**
(off Wellington Way)
SE8 . . . . .5B **104**
(off Grove St.)
TW8: Bford 6D **96**
(off Albany Rd.)
Berkeley M. TW16: Sun 3A **148**
W1 . . . . .1F **11** (6D **82**)
Berkeley Pl. SW19 . . . . .6F **135**
Berkeley Rd. E12 . . . . .5C **70**
N8 .5H **47**
N15 . . . . .6D **48**
NW9 . . . . .4G **43**
SW13 . . . . .1C **116**
UB10: Hil 7E **56**
The Berkeleys SE25 . . . . .4G **157**
Berkeley Sq. W1 . . . . .3K **11** (7F **83**)
Berkeley St. W1 . . . . . .3K **11** (7F **83**)
Berkeley Twr. *E14* 1B **104**
(off Westferry Cir.)
Berkeley Wlk. *N7* 2K **65**
(off Durham Rd.)
Berkeley Waye TW5: Hest 6B **94**
Berkhampstead Rd.
DA17: Belv 5G **109**
Berkhamsted Av. HA9: Wemb 6F **61**
Berkley Cl. *TW2: Twick* 3J **131**
(off Wellesley Rd.)
Berkley Gro. NW1 . . . . .7E **64**
Berkley Rd. NW1 . . . . .7D **64**
Berkshire Ct. *W7* 4K **77**
(off Copley Cl.)
Berkshire Gdns. N13 . . . . .6F **33**
N18 . . . . .5C **34**
Berkshire Ho. SE6 . . . . .4C **140**
Berkshire Rd. E9 . . . . .6B **68**
Berkshire Way CR4: Mitc 4J **155**
Berley Rd. E17 . . . . .1B **50**
Berlin Ter. E15 . . . . .5G **69**
Bermans Way NW10 . . . . .4A **62**
BERMONDSEY 7K **15** (2G **103**)
Bermondsey Exchange *SE1* 7H **15**
(off Bermondsey St.)
Bermondsey Sq. SE1 . . . . .7H **15** (3E **102**)
Bermondsey St. SE1 . . . .5G **15** (1E **102**)
Bermondsey Trad. Est. SE16 . . . . .5J **103**
Bermondsey Wall E. SE16 . . . . . . .2G **103**
Bermondsey Wall W.
SE16 . . . . .6K **15** (2G **103**)
Bermuda Way *E1* 5A **86**
(off Dongola Rd.)
Bernal Cl. SE28 . . . . .7D **90**
Bernard Angell Ho. *SE10* 6F **105**
(off Trafalgar Rd.)
Bernard Ashley Dr. SE7 . . . . . . .5K **105**
Bernard Av. W13 . . . . .3B **96**
Bernard Cassidy St. E16 . . . . . . .5H **87**
Bernard Gdns. SW19 . . . . .5H **135**
Bernard Hegarty Lodge *E8* 7G **67**
(off Lansdowne St.)
Bernard Ho. E1 . . . . .6J **9**
Bernard Mans. *WC1* 4E **6**
(off Bernard St.)
Bernard Myers Ho. SE5 . . . . .7E **102**
(off Havil St.)

Bernard Rd. N15 . . . . .5F **49**
RM7: Rush G 7J **55**
SM6: W'gton 4F **167**
Bernard Shaw Ct. *NW1* 7G **65**
(off St Pancras Way)
Bernard Shaw Ho. *NW10* 1K **79**
(off Knatchbull Rd.)
Bernard St. WC1 . . . . . .4E **6** (4J **83**)
Bernard Sunley Ho. SW9 . . . . . . .7A **102**
(off Sth. Island Pl.)
Bernays Cl. HA7: Stan 6H **27**
Bernays Gro. SW9 . . . . .4K **119**
Bernel Dr. CR0: C'don 3B **170**
Berne Rd. CR7: Thor H 5C **156**
Berners Dr. W13 . . . . .7A **78**
Berners Ho. *N1* 2A **84**
(off Barnsbury Est.)
Berners M. W1 . . . . .6B **6** (5G **83**)
Berners Pl. W1 . . . . .7B **6** (6G **83**)
Berners Rd. N1 . . . . .1B **84**
N22 . . . . .1A **48**
Berners St. W1 . . . . .6B **6** (5G **83**)
Berner Ter. *E1* 6G **85**
(off Fairclough St.)
Berney Ho. BR3: Beck 5A **158**
Berney Rd. CR0: C'don 7D **156**
Bernhard Baron Ho. *E1* 6G **85**
(off Henriques St.)
Bernhardt Cres. NW8 . . . .3C **4** (4C **82**)
Bernhart Cl. HA8: Edg 7D **28**
Bernie Grant Arts Cen. 4F **49**
Bernville Way HA3: Kenton 5F **43**
Bernwell Rd. E4 . . . . .3B **36**
Berridge Grn. HA8: Edg 7B **28**
Berridge M. NW6 . . . . .5J **63**
Berridge Rd. SE19 . . . . .5D **138**
Berriman Rd. N7 . . . . .3K **65**
Berrington Ho. *W2* 7J **81**
(off Herrington Rd.)
Berriton Rd. HA2: Harr 1D **58**
Berrybank Cl. E4 . . . . .2K **35**
Berry Cl. N21 . . . . .1G **33**
RM10: Dag 5G **73**
Berry Cotts. *E14* 6A **86**
(off Maroon St.)
Berry Ct. TW4: Houn 5D **112**
Berrydale Rd. UB4: Yead 4C **76**
Berryfield Cl.
BR1: Broml 1C **160**
E17 . . . . .4D **50**
Berryfield Rd. SE17 . . . . .5B **102**
Berry Hill HA7: Stan 4J **27**
Berryhill SE9 . . . . .4F **125**
Berryhill Gdns. SE9 . . . . .4F **125**
Berry Ho. *E1* 4H **85**
(off Headlam St.)
SW11 . . . . .2D **118**
(off Culvert Rd.)
BERRYLANDS 6G **151**
Berrylands KT5: Surb 6F **151**
SW20 . . . . .3E **152**
Berrylands Rd. KT5: Surb 6F **151**
Berry La. SE21 . . . . .4D **138**
Berryman Cl. RM8: Dag 3C **72**
Berryman's La. SE26 . . . . .4K **139**
Berrymead Gdns. W3 . . . . .1J **97**
Berrymede Rd. W4 . . . . .3K **97**
Berry Pl. EC1 . . . . .2B **8** (3B **84**)
Berryside Apts. *N4* 1C **66**
(off Swan La.)
Berry St. EC1 . . . . .3B **8** (4B **84**)
Berry Way W5 . . . . .3E **96**
Bertal Rd. SW17 . . . . .4B **136**
Bertelli Pl. TW13: Felt 1K **129**
Bertha Hollamby Ct. *DA14: Sidc* . . .5C **144**
(off Sidcup Hill)
Bertha James Ct. BR2: Broml 4K **159**
Berthons Gdns. *E17* 5F **51**
(off Wood St.)
Berthon St. SE8 . . . . .7C **104**
Bertie Rd. NW10 . . . . .6C **62**
SE26 . . . . .6K **139**
Bertram Cotts. SW19 . . . . .7J **135**

Bertram Rd. EN1: Enf 4B **24**
KT2: King T 7G **133**
NW4 . . . . .6C **44**
Bertram St. N19 . . . . .2F **65**
Bertrand Ho. *E16* 6K **87**
(off Russell Rd.)
SW16 . . . . .3J **137**
(off Leigham Av.)
Bertrand St. SE13 . . . . .3D **122**
Bertrand Way SE28 . . . . .7B **90**
Bert Way EN1: Enf 4A **24**
Berwick Av. UB4: Yead 6B **76**
Berwick Cl. HA7: Stan 6E **26**
TW2: Whitt 1E **130**
Berwick Ct. SE1 . . . . .7D **14**
Berwick Cres. DA15: Sidc 7J **125**
Berwick Gdns. SM1: Sutt 3A **166**
Berwick Ho. BR6: Orp 1K **173**
N2 .2B **46**
Berwick Rd. DA16: Well 1B **126**
E16 . . . . .6K **87**
N22 . . . . .1B **48**
Berwick St. W1 . . . . . . .7B **6** (6G **83**)
Berwick Way BR6: Orp 1K **173**
Berwyn Av. TW3: Houn 1F **113**
Berwyn Rd. SE24 . . . . .1B **138**
TW10: Rich 4H **115**
Beryl Av. E6 . . . . .5C **88**
Beryl Ho. SE18 . . . . .5K **107**
(off Spinel Cl.)
Beryl Rd. W6 . . . . .5F **99**
Berystede KT2: King T 7H **133**
Besant Cl. NW2 . . . . .3G **63**
Besant Ct. N1 . . . . .5D **66**
SE28 . . . . .1B **108**
(off Titmuss Av.)
Besant Ho. *NW8* 1A **82**
(off Boundary Rd.)
Besant Pl. SE22 . . . . .4F **121**
Besant Rd. NW2 . . . . .4G **63**
Besant Wlk. N7 . . . . .2K **65**
Besant Way NW10 . . . . .5J **61**
Besford Ho. *E2* 2G **85**
(off Pritchard's Rd.)
Besley St. SW16 . . . . .6G **137**
Bessant Dr. TW9: Kew 1H **115**
Bessborough Gdns. SW1 . . .5D **18** (5H **101**)
Bessborough Pl. SW1 . . . . .5D **18** (5H **101**)
Bessborough Rd. HA1: Harr 1H **59**
SW15 . . . . .1C **134**
Bessborough St. SW1 . . . .5C **18** (5H **101**)
Bessemer Ct. *NW1* 7G **65**
(off Rochester Sq.)
Bessemer Pk. Ind. Est. SE24 . . . .4B **120**
Bessemer Pl. SE10 . . . . .3H **105**
Bessemer Rd. SE5 . . . . .2C **120**
Bessie Lansbury Cl. E6 . . . . .6E **88**
Bessingby Rd. HA4: Ruis 2K **57**
Bessingham Wlk. *SE4* 4K **121**
(off Aldersford Cl.)
Besson St. SE14 . . . . .1J **121**
Bessy St. E2 . . . . .3J **85**
Bestwood St. SE8 . . . . .4K **103**
Beswick M. NW6 . . . . .6K **63**
Beta Ct. *CR0: C'don* 1D **168**
(off Sydenham Rd.)
Betam Rd. UB3: Hayes 2F **93**
Beta Pl. SW4 . . . . .4K **119**
Betchworth Cl. SM1: Sutt 5B **166**
Betchworth Rd. IG3: Ilf 2J **71**
Betchworth Way CR0: New Ad 7E **170**
Betham Rd. UB6: G'frd 3H **77**
Bethany Waye TW14: Bedf 7G **111**
Bethecar Rd. HA1: Harr 5J **41**
Bethell Av. E16 . . . . .4H **87**
IG1: Ilf 7E **52**
Bethel Rd. DA16: Well 3C **126**
Bethersden Cl. BR3: Beck 7B **140**
Bethersden Ho. *SE17* 5E **102**
(off Kinglake Est.)
Bethlehem Cl. UB6: G'frd 2C **78**

Bethlehem Ho. *E14* 7B **86**
                 (off Limehouse C'way.)
BETHNAL GREEN 3H **85**
Bethnal Green Cen. for
   Sports & Performing Arts
               .2K **9** (3F **85**)
Bethnal Grn. Rd. E1 . . . . . .3J **9** (4F **85**)
  E2 . . . . .3J **9** (4F **85**)
Bethune Av. N11 . . . . .4J **31**
Bethune Rd. N16 . . . . .7D **48**
  NW10 . . . . .4K **79**
Bethwin Rd. SE5 . . . . .7B **102**
Betjeman Cl. HA5: Pinn 4E **40**
Betjeman Ct. UB7: Yiew 1A **92**
Betjeman M. N5 . . . . .4C **66**
Betony Cl. CRO: C'don 1K **169**
Betoyne Av. E4 . . . . .4B **36**
Betsham Ho. *SE1* 6E **14**
              (off Newcomen St.)
BETSTYLE CIR. 4A **32**
Betstyle Ho. N10 . . . . .7K **31**
Betstyle Rd. N11 . . . . .4A **32**
Bettenson Cl. BR7: Chst 5D **142**
Better Gym
  East Village 6E **68**
  Greenwich 2G **105**
  Harrow 6J **41**
  (within St George's Shop. & Leisure Cen.)
  Pinner 3B **40**
  Woolwich 3F **107**
Betterton Dr. DA14: Sidc 2E **144**
Betterton Ho. *WC2* 1F **13**
                (off Betterton St.)
Betterton Rd. RM13: Rain 3K **91**
Betterton St. WC2 . . . . . .1E **12** (6J **83**)
Bettons Pk. E15 . . . . .1G **87**
Bettridge Rd. SW6 . . . . .2H **117**
Betts Cl. BR3: Beck 2A **158**
Betts Ho. *E1* 7H **85**
                  (off Betts St.)
Betts M. E17 . . . . .6B **50**
Betts Rd. E16 . . . . .7K **87**
Betts St. E1 . . . . .7H **85**
Betts Way KT6: Surb 1B **162**
  SE20 . . . . .1H **157**
Betty Brooks Ho. E11 . . . . .3F **69**
Betty May Gray Ho. *E14* 4E **104**
                   (off Pier St.)
Beulah Av. CR7: Thor H 2C **156**
Beulah Cl. HA8: Edg 3C **28**
Beulah Cres. CR7: Thor H 2C **156**
Beulah Gro. CRO: C'don 6C **156**
Beulah Hill SE19 . . . . .6B **138**
Beulah Path E17 . . . . .5E **50**
Beulah Rd. CR7: Thor H 3C **156**
  E17 . . . . .5D **50**
  SM1: Sutt 4J **165**
  SW19 . . . . .7H **135**
Bevan Av. IG11: Bark 7A **72**
Bevan Ct. CRO: Wadd 5A **168**
  E3 . . . . .2C **86**
                 (off Tredegar Rd.)
  TW1: Twick 6D **114**
Bevan Ho IG11: Bark 7B **72**
  N1 . . . . .2C **84**
                  (off Halcomb St.)
  WC1 . . . . .5F **7**
                  (off Boswell St.)
Bevan M. W12 . . . . .2C **98**
Bevan Rd. EN4: Cockf 4J **21**
  SE2 .5B **108**
Bevans Ho. *SW18* 4A **118**
              (off Eltringham St.)
Bevan St. N1 . . . . .1C **84**
Bev Callender Cl. SW8 . . . . .3F **119**
Bevenden St. N1 . . . . . . .1F **9** (3D **84**)
Bevercote Wlk. *DA17: Belv* 6F **109**
               (off Osborne Rd.)
Beveree Stadium 1F **149**
Beveridge Ct. *N21* 5D **22**
               (off Pennington St.)
  SE28 . . . . .7B **90**
               (off Saunders Way)

Beveridge M. E1 . . . . .5J **85**
Beveridge Rd. NW10 . . . . .7A **62**
Beverley Av. DA15: Sidc 7K **125**
  SW20 . . . . .1B **152**
  TW4: Houn 4D **112**
Beverley Cl. EN1: Enf 4K **23**
  KT9: Chess 4C **162**
  N21 .1H **33**
  SW11 . . . . .4B **118**
  SW13 . . . . .2C **116**
Beverley Cotts. SW15 . . . . .3A **134**
Beverley Ct. HA2: Harr 3H **41**
  HA3: Kenton 4C **42**
  N2 . . . . .4D **46**
                 (off Western Rd.)
  N14 . . . . .7B **22**
  NW6 .7A **64**
                 (off Fairfax Rd.)
  SE4 .2B **122**
                 (not continuous)
  TW4: Houn 4D **112**
  W4 . . . . .5J **97**
Beverley Cres. IG8: Wfd G 1K **51**
Beverley Dr. HA8: Edg 3G **43**
Beverley Gdns. HA7: Stan 1A **42**
  HA9: Wemb 1F **61**
  KT4: Wor Pk 1C **164**
  NW11 . . . . .7G **45**
  SW13 . . . . .3B **116**
Beverley Ho. *BR1: Broml* 5F **141**
             (off Brangbourne Rd.)
Beverley Hyrst CRO: C'don 2F **169**
Beverley La. KT2: King T 7A **134**
  SW15 . . . . .3B **134**
Beverley Meads &
  Fishponds Wood Nature Reserve
                .6B **134**
Beverley M. E4 . . . . .6A **36**
Beverley Path SW13 . . . . .2B **116**
Beverley Rd. BR2: Broml 2C **172**
  CR4: Mitc 4H **155**
  DA7: Bex 2J **127**
  E4 . . . . .6A **36**
  E6 . . . . .3B **88**
  HA4: Ruis 2J **57**
  KT1: Hamp W 1C **150**
  KT3: N Mald 4C **152**
  KT4: Wor Pk 2E **164**
  RM9: Dag 4E **72**
  SE20 . . . . .2H **157**
  SW13 . . . . .3B **116**
  TW16: Sun 1H **147**
  UB2: S'hall 4C **94**
  W4 . . . . .5B **98**
Beverley Trad. Est. SM4: Mord 7F **153**
Beverley Way KT3: N Mald 1B **152**
  SW20 . . . . .1B **152**
Beversbrook Rd. N19 . . . . .3H **65**
Beverstone Rd. CR7: Thor H 4A **156**
  SW2 .5K **119**
Beverston M. W1 . . . . .6E **4**
Bevill Allen Cl. SW17 . . . . .5D **136**
Bevill Cl. SE25 . . . . .3G **157**
Bevin Cl. SE16 . . . . .1A **104**
Bevin Ct. WC1 . . . . .1H **7** (3K **83**)
Devington Path SE1 . . . . .7J **15**
Bevington Rd. BR3: Beck 2D **158**
  W10 .5G **81**
Bevington St. SE16 . . . . .2G **103**
Bevin Ho. E2 . . . . .3J **85**
                 (off Butler St.)
  E3 . . . . .3C **86**
                 (off Alfred St.)
Bevin Rd. UB4: Yead 3J **75**
Bevin Sq. SW17 . . . . .3D **136**
Bevin Way WC1 . . . . .1J **7** (2A **84**)
Bevis Marks EC3 . . . . .7H **9** (6E **84**)
Bevis Marks Synagogue . . .7H **9** (6E **84**)
Bewcastle Gdns. EN2: Enf 4D **22**
Bew Ct. SE22 . . . . .7G **121**
Bewick M. SE15 . . . . .7H **103**
Bewick St. SW8 . . . . .2F **119**

Bewley Ho. *E1* 7H **85**
                  (off Bewley St.)
Bewley St. E1 . . . . .7J **85**
  SW19 . . . . .6A **136**
Bewlys Rd. SE27 . . . . .5B **138**
Bexhill Cl. TW13: Felt 2C **130**
Bexhill Cl. TW13: Felt 5C **32**
Bexhill Rd. N11 . . . . .5C **32**
  SE4 .6B **122**
  SW14 . . . . .3J **115**
Bexhill Wlk. E15 . . . . .1G **87**
BEXLEY 7G **127**
Bexley Gdns. N9 . . . . .3J **33**
  RM6: Chad H 5B **54**
BEXLEYHEATH 4G **127**
Bexleyheath Golf Course 5E **126**
Bexleyheath Sports Club 4C **126**
Bexley High St. DA5: Bexl 7G **127**
Bexley Ho. SE4 . . . . .4A **122**
Bexley La. DA1: Cray 5K **127**
  DA14: Sidc 4C **144**
Bexley Lawn Tennis,
  Squash & Racketball Club . . .7G **127**
Bexley Local Studies & Archive Cen.
                .4G **127**
                 (off Townley Rd.)
The Bexley Mus. Collection 6J **127**
Bexley Music & Dance Cen. 4A **144**
                 (off Station Rd.)
Bexley Rd. DA8: Erith 1J **127**
  SE9 .5F **125**
Bexley Tourist Information Centre
                .4F **127**
Beynon Rd. SM5: Cars 5D **166**
Bezier Apts. EC2 . . . . .3F **9** (4D **84**)
BFI Southbank 4H **13**
Bianca Ho. *N1* 1G **9**
                 (off Crondall St.)
Bianca Rd. SE15 . . . . .6G **103**
Bibsworth Rd. N3 . . . . .2J **45**
Bibury Cl. SE15 . . . . .6E **102**
                 (not continuous)
Bicester Rd. TW9: Rich 3G **115**
Bickels Yd. SE1 . . . . .2E **102**
Bickenhall Mans. W1 . . . . .5F **5**
                 (not continuous)
Bickenhall St. W1 . . . . .5F **5** (5D **82**)
Bickersteth Rd. SW17 . . . . .6D **136**
Bickerton Rd. N19 . . . . .2G **65**
BICKLEY .3C **160**
Bickley Cres. BR1: Broml 4C **160**
Bickley Pk. Rd. BR1: Broml 3C **160**
Bickley Rd. BR1: Broml 2B **160**
  E10 . . . . .7D **50**
Bickley St. SW17 . . . . .5C **136**
Bicknell Ho. *E1* 6G **85**
                 (off Ellen St.)
Bicknell Rd. SE5 . . . . .3C **120**
Bicknoller Rd. EN1: Enf 1K **23**
Bicknor Rd. BR6: Orp 7J **161**
Bicycle M. SW4 . . . . .3H **119**
Bidborough Cl. BR2: Broml 5H **159**
Bidborough St. WC1 . . . . . .2E **6** (3J **83**)
Biddenden Way SE9 . . . . .4E **142**
Biddenham Ho. *SE16* 4K **103**
               (off Plough Way)
Bidder St. E16 . . . . .5G **87**
                 (not continuous)
Biddesden Ho. *SW3* 4E **16**
                (off Cadogan St.)
Biddestone Rd. N7 . . . . .4K **65**
Biddulph Ho. SE18 . . . . .4D **106**
Biddulph Mans. W9 . . . . .3K **81**
                 (off Elgin Av.)
Biddulph Rd. W9 . . . . .3K **81**
Bideford Av. UB6: G'frd 2B **78**
Bideford Cl. HA8: Edg 1G **43**
  TW13: Hanw 3D **130**
Bideford Gdns. EN1: Enf 7K **23**
Bideford Rd. BR1: Broml 3H **141**
  DA16: Well 7B **108**
  EN3: Enf L 1G **25**
  HA4: Ruis 3K **57**
Bidwell Gdns. N11 . . . . .7B **32**

Bidwell St. SE15 . . . . .1H **121**
Big Ben 7F **13** (2J **101**)
Biggerstaff Rd. E15 . . . . .1E **86**
Biggerstaff St. N4 . . . . .2A **66**
Biggin Av. CR4: Mitc 1D **154**
Biggin Hill SE19 . . . . .7B **138**
Biggin Hill Cl. KT2: King T 5C **132**
Biggin Way SE19 . . . . .7B **138**
Bigginwood Rd. SW16 . . . . .7B **138**
Biggs Ct. *NW9* 2A **44**
                 (off Harvey Cl.)
Biggs Row SW15 . . . . .3F **117**
Biggs Sq. E9 . . . . .6B **68**
Big Hill E5 .1H **67**
Bigland Cl. E1 . . . . .6H **85**
Bignell Rd. SE18 . . . . .5F **107**
Bignold Rd. E7 . . . . .4J **69**
Bigsworth Ct. SE20 . . . . .1H **157**
Bigwood Ct. NW11 . . . . .5K **45**
Bigwood Rd. NW11 . . . . .5K **45**
Bilberry Ho. *E3* 5C **86**
                 (off Watts Gro.)
Billet Cl. RM6: Chad H 3D **54**
Billet Rd. E17 . . . . .1K **49**
  RM6: Chad H 3B **54**
Billets Hart Cl. W7 . . . . .2J **95**
Bill Hamling Cl. SE9 . . . . .2D **142**
Billingford Cl. SE4 . . . . .4K **121**
Billing Ho. *E1* 6K **85**
                 (off Bower St.)
Billinghurst Way SE10 . . . . .3J **105**
Billingley *NW1* 1G **83**
                  (off Pratt St.)
Billing Pl. SW10 . . . . .7K **99**
Billing Rd. SW10 . . . . .7K **99**
Billings Cl. RM9: Dag 7C **72**
Billingsgate Market 1D **104**
Billing St. SW10 . . . . .7K **99**
Billington M. *W3* 1H **97**
                  (off High St.)
Billington Rd. SE14 . . . . .7K **103**
Billinton Hill CRO: C'don 2D **168**
Billiter St. EC3 . . . . .1H **15** (6E **84**)
Bill Voisey Ct. *E14* 6A **86**
                 (off Repton St.)
Bilsby Gro. SE9 . . . . .4B **142**
Bilsby Lodge *HA9: Wemb* 3J **61**
                 (off Chalklands)
The Bilton Cen. UB6: G'frd 1B **78**
Bilton Rd. UB6: G'frd 1A **78**
Bilton Towers *W1* 1F **11**
             (off Gt. Cumberland Pl.)
Bilton Way EN3: Enf L 1F **25**
  UB3: Hayes 2K **93**
Bina Gdns. SW5 . . . . .4A **100**
Binbrook Ho. *W10* 5E **80**
                 (off Sutton Way)
Bincote Rd. EN2: Enf 3E **22**
Binden Rd. W12 . . . . .3B **98**
Bindon Grn. SM4: Mord 4K **153**
Binfield Rd. CR2: S Croy 5F **169**
  SW4 .1J **119**
Bingfield St. N1 . . . . .1J **83**
                 (not continuous)
Bingham Ct. *N1* 7B **66**
                 (off Halton Rd.)
Bingham Pl. W1 . . . . .5G **5** (5E **82**)
Bingham Point *SE18* 4F **107**
                 (off Wilmount St.)
Bingham Rd. CRO: C'don 1G **169**
Bingham St. N1 . . . . .6C **66**
Bingley Rd. E16 . . . . .6A **88**
  TW16: Sun 7J **129**
  UB6: G'frd 4G **77**
Binley Ho. SW15 . . . . .6C **116**
Binnacle Ho. *E1* 1H **103**
              (off Cobblestone Sq.)
Binney St. W1 . . . . .1H **15** (6E **82**)

Binnie Ho.—Blackberry Cl.

Binnie Ho. *SE1* 3C 102
(off Bath Ter.)
Binnington Twr. BR2: Broml 6C 160
Binns Rd. W4 5A 98
Binns Ter. W4 5A 98
Binsey Wlk. SE2 2C 108
(not continuous)
Binstead Cl. UB4: Yead 6C 76
Binyon Cres. HA7: Stan 5E 26
Bioko Ct. *E1* 5A 86
(off Ocean Est.)
Biraj Ho. E6 1D 88
Birbetts Rd. SE9 2D 142
Bircham Path *SE4* 4K 121
(off Aldersford Cl.)
Birchanger Rd. SE25 5G 157
Birch Av. N13 3H 33
UB7: Yiew 6B 74
Birch Cl. E16 5G 87
IG9: Buck H 3G 37
N19 2G 65
RM7: Mawney 3H 55
SE15 2G 121
TW3: Houn 2H 113
TW8: Bford 7B 96
TW11: Tedd 5A 132
TW17: Shep 2G 147
Birch Ct. N12 4E 30
RM6: Chad H 6C 54
SM1: Sutt 4A 166
SM6: W'gton 4F 167
Birch Cres. UB10: Uxb 1B 74
Birchdale Gdns.
RM6: Chad H 7D 54
Birchdale Rd. E7 5A 70
Birchdene Dr. SE28 1A 108
Birchdown Ho. *E3* 3D 86
(off Rainhill Way)
Birchen Cl. NW9 2K 61
Birchend Cl. CR2: S Croy 6D 168
Birchen Gro. NW9 2K 61
The Birches *BR2: Broml* 4H 159
(off Durham Rd.)
BR6: Farnb 4E 172
E12 4C 70
N21 6E 22
SE5 2E 120
SE7 6K 105
TW4: Houn 7D 112
Birches Cl. CR4: Mitc 3D 154
HA5: Pinn 5C 40
N17 7B 34
Birchfield Ct. *KT12: Walt T* 7K 147
(off Grove Cres.)
Birchfield Ho. *E14* 7C 86
(off Birchfield St.)
Birchfield St. E14 7C 86
Birch Gdns. RM10: Dag 3J 73
Birch Grn. NW9 7F 29
Birch Gro. DA16: Well 4A 126
E11 4G 69
SE12 7H 123
TW17: Shep 2G 147
W3 1G 97
Birchgrove Ho. TW9: Kew 7H 97
Birch Hill CR0: C'don 5K 169
Birch Ho. *N22* 1A 48
(off Acacia Rd.)
SE14 1B 122
SW2 6A 120
UB7: W Dray 2B 92
(off Park Lodge Av.)
W10 4G 81
(off Droop St.)
Birchington Cl. DA7: Bex 1H 127
Birchington Ct. *NW6* 1K 81
(off West End La.)
Birchington Ho. E5 5H 67
Birchington Rd. KT5: Surb 7F 151
N8 6H 47
NW6 1J 81
Birchin La. EC3 1F 15 (6D 84)
Birchlands Av. SW12 7D 118
Birch Mead BR6: Farnb 2E 172
Birchmead Av. HA5: Pinn 4A 40
Birchmere Bus. Pk. SE28 2A 108
Birchmere Lodge *SE16* 5H 103
(off Sherwood Gdns.)
Birchmere Row SE3 2H 123
Birchmore Hall N5 3C 66
Birchmore Wlk. N5 3C 66
(not continuous)
Birch Pk. HA3: Hrw W 7B 26
Birch Rd. RM7: Mawney 3H 55
TW13: Hanw 5B 130
Birch Row BR2: Broml 7E 160
Birchside Apts. NW6 2H 81
Birch Tree Av. BR4: W W'ck 5H 171
Birch Tree Way CR0: C'don 2H 169
Birch Va. Ct. *NW8* 3B 4
(off Pollitt Dr.)
Birch Vw. HA1: Harr 5H 41
Birchville Ct. WD23: B Hea 1D 26
Birch Wlk. CR4: Mitc 1F 155
DA8: Erith 6J 109
IG3: Ilf 4J 71
(off Loxford La.)
Birchway UB3: Hayes 1J 93
Birchwood Apts. *N4* 7C 48
(off Woodberry Gro.)
Birchwood Av. BR3: Beck 4B 158
DA14: Sidc 2B 144
N10 3E 46
SM6: W'gton 3E 166
Birchwood Cl. SM4: Mord 4K 153
Birchwood Ct. HA8: Edg 2J 43
N13 5G 33
Birchwood Dr. DA2: Wilm 4K 145
NW3 3K 63
Birchwood Gro. TW12: Hamp 6E 130
Birchwood Pde. DA2: Wilm 4K 145
Birchwood Pk. Golf Course 7J 145
Birchwood Rd. BR5: Pet W 4H 161
BR8: Swan 7J 145
DA2: Wilm 7J 145
SW17 5F 137
Birdbrook Cl. RM10: Dag 7J 73
Birdbrook Ho. *N1* 7C 66
(off Popham Rd.)
Birdbrook Rd. SE3 4A 124
Birdcage Wlk. SW1 7A 12 (2G 101)
Birdham Cl. BR1: Broml 5C 160
Birdhurst Av. CR2: S Croy 4D 168
Birdhurst Ct. *SM6: W'gton* 7G 167
(off Woodcote Av.)
Birdhurst Gdns. CR2: S Croy 4D 168
Birdhurst Ri. CR2: S Croy 5E 168
Birdhurst Rd. CR2: S Croy 5E 168
SW18 5A 118
SW19 6C 136
Bird in Bush BMX Track 7H 103
(off Bird in Bush Rd.)
Bird in Bush Rd. SE15 7G 103
Bird in Hand La. BR1: Broml 2B 160
Bird in Hand M. *SE23* 2J 139
(off Bird-in-Hand Pas.)
Bird in Hand Pas. SE23 2J 139
Bird in Hand Yd. NW3 4A 64
Birdsall Ho. SE5 3E 120
Birds Farm Av. RM5: Col R 1H 55
Birdsfield La. E3 1B 86
Birdsmouth Ct. *N15* 4E 48
(off Bathurst Sq.)
Bird St. W1 1H 11 (6E 82)
Bird Wlk. TW2: Whitt 1D 130
Birdwood Av. SE13 6F 123
Birdwood Cl. TW11: Tedd 4J 131
Birkbeck Av. UB6: G'frd 1G 77
W3 7J 79
Birkbeck Ct. W3 1K 97
Birkbeck Gdns. IG8: Wfd G 2D 36
Birkbeck Gro. W3 2K 97
Birkbeck Hill SE21 1B 138
Birkbeck M. E8 5F 67
W3 1K 97
Birkbeck Pl. SE21 2C 138
Birkbeck Rd. BR3: Beck 2J 157
DA14: Sidc 3A 144
E8 5F 67
EN2: Enf 1J 23
IG2: Ilf 5H 53
N8 4J 47
N12 5F 31
N17 1F 49
NW7 5G 29
RM7: Rush G 1K 73
SW19 5K 135
W3 1K 97
W5 4C 96
Birkbeck St. E2 3H 85
Birkbeck Way UB6: G'frd 1H 77
Birkdale Av. HA5: Pinn 3E 40
Birkdale Cl. BR6: Orp 7H 161
SE16 5H 103
SE28 6D 90
Birkdale Ct. *UB1: S'hall* 6G 77
(off Redcroft Rd.)
Birkdale Gdns. CR0: C'don 4K 169
Birkdale Ho. *E14* 6B 86
(off Keymer Pl.)
Birkdale Rd. SE2 4A 108
W5 4E 78
Birkenhead Av. KT2: King T 2F 151
Birkenhead St. WC1 1F 7 (3J 83)
Birkhall Rd. SE6 1F 141
Birkwood Cl. SW12 7H 119
Birley Lodge *NW8* 2B 82
(off Acacia Rd.)
Birley Rd. N20 2F 31
Birley St. SW11 2E 118
Birling Rd. DA8: Erith 7K 109
Birnam Rd. N4 2K 65
Birnbeck Ct. EN5: Barn 4A 20
NW11 5H 45
Birrell Ho. *SW9* 2K 119
(off Stockwell Rd.)
Birse Cres. NW10 3A 62
Birstall Rd. N15 5E 48
Birtwhistle Ho. *E3* 1B 86
(off Parnell Rd.)
Biscay Ho. *E1* 4K 85
(off Mile End Rd.)
Biscayne Av. E14 1F 105
Biscay Rd. W6 5F 99
Biscoe Cl. TW5: Hest 6E 94
Biscoe Way SE13 3F 123
Biscott Ho. E3 4D 86
Bisenden Rd. CR0: C'don 2E 168
Bisham Cl. SM5: Cars 1D 166
Bisham Gdns. N6 1E 64
Bishop Butt Cl. BR6: Orp 3K 173
Bishop Ct. TW9: Rich 3E 114
Bishop Duppas Pk.
TW17: Shep 7G 147
Bishop Fox Way
KT8: W Mole 4D 148
Bishop Ken Rd.
HA3: W'stone 2K 41
Bishop King's Rd. W14 4G 99
Bishop Ramsey Cl.
HA4: Ruis 7H 39
Bishop Rd. N14 7A 22
Bishop's Av. E13 1K 87
SW6 2F 117
Bishops Av. BR1: Broml 2A 160
RM6: Chad H 6C 54
The Bishops Av. N2 7B 46
Bishop's Bri. Rd. W2 6A 4 (6K 81)
Bishop's Cl. N19 3G 65
SE9 2G 143
SM1: Sutt 3J 165
Bishops Cl. E17 4D 50
EN1: Enf 2C 24
EN5: Barn 6A 20
TW10: Ham 3D 132
UB10: Hil 2C 74
W4 5J 97
Bishop's Ct. EC4 7A 8
WC2 7J 7
Bishops Ct. CR0: C'don 2F 169
HA0: Wemb 4B 60
N2 5C 46
W2 6K 81
(off Bishop's Bri. Rd.)
Bishopsdale Ho. *NW6* 1J 81
(off Kilburn Vale)
Bishop's Dr. TW14: Bedf 6F 111
Bishops Dr. UB5: N'olt 1C 76
Bishopsford Ho. SM5: Cars 6C 154
Bishopsford Rd. SM4: Mord 7A 154
Bishopsgate EC2 1G 15 (6E 84)
Bishopsgate Arc. EC2 6H 9
Bishopsgate Churchyard
EC2 7G 9 (5E 84)
Bishopsgate Plaza EC3 6H 9
Bishops Grn. BR1: Broml 1A 160
Bishop's Gro. TW12: Hamp 4D 130
Bishops Gro. N2 6C 46
Bishops Gro. Cvn. Site 4E 130
Bishop's Hall KT1: King T 2D 150
Bishops Hill KT12: Walt T 7J 147
Bishops Ho. *SW8* 7J 101
(off Sth. Lambeth Rd.)
Bishop's Mans. SW6 2F 117
Bishops Mead *SE5* 7C 102
(off Camberwell Rd.)
Bishop's Pk. Rd. SW6 2F 117
Bishops Pk. Rd. SW16 1J 155
Bishops Pl. SM1: Sutt 5A 166
Bishop's Rd. CR0: C'don 7B 156
SW11 7C 100
UB3: Hayes 6E 74
Bishops Rd. N6 6E 46
SW6 1G 117
W7 2J 95
Bishops Sq. E1 5H 9 (5E 84)
Bishop's Ter. SE11 3K 19 (4A 102)
Bishopsthorpe Rd. SE26 4K 139
Bishop St. N1 1C 84
Bishops Vw. Ct. N10 4F 47
Bishops Wlk. BR7: Chst 1G 161
CR0: Addtn 5K 169
HA5: Pinn 3C 40
Bishop's Way E2 2H 85
Bishops Wharf Ho. *SW11* 7C 100
(off Parkgate Rd.)
Bishops Wood Almshouses *E5* 4H 67
(off Lwr. Clapton Rd.)
Bishopswood Rd. N6 7D 46
Bishop Way NW10 7A 62
Bishop Wilfred Wood Cl. SE15 2G 121
Bishop Wilfred Wood Ct. *E13* 2A 88
(off Pragel St.)
Bisley Cl. KT4: Wor Pk 1E 164
Bisley Pl. TW3: Houn 2F 113
Bison Ct. TW14: Felt 7K 111
Bispham Rd. NW10 3F 79
Bissagos Ct. *E1* 5A 86
(off Ocean Est.)
Bissextile Ho. SE13 2D 122
Bisson Rd. E15 2E 86
Bisterne Av. E17 3F 51
Bittacy Bus. Cen. NW7 7B 30
Bittacy Cl. NW7 6A 30
Bittacy Ct. NW7 7B 30
Bittacy Hill NW7 6A 30
Bittacy Pk. Av. NW7 5A 30
Bittacy Ri. NW7 6K 29
Bittacy Rd. NW7 6A 30
Bittern Cl. UB4: Yead 5B 76
Bittern Ct. NW9 2A 44
SE8 6C 104
Bittern Ho. *SE1* 7C 14
(off Gt. Suffolk St.)
Bittern Pl. N22 2K 47
Bittern St. SE1 7C 14 (2C 102)
The Bittoms KT1: King T 3D 150
Bittoms Ct. KT1: King T 3D 150
Bixley Cl. UB2: S'hall 4D 94
Blackall St. EC2 3G 9 (4E 84)
Blackberry Cl. E17 3D 50
TW17: Shep 4G 147

Blackberry Ct. HA3: Kenton 7E 42
Blackberry Farm Cl. TW5: Hest 7C 94
Blackberry Fld. BR5: St P 7A 144
Blackbird Ct. NW9 . . . . .3K 61
Blackbird Hill NW9 . . . . .2J 61
Blackbird Yd. E2 . . . . .1K 9 (3F 85)
Blackborne Rd. RM10: Dag 6G 73
Blackborough Ho. IG9: Buck H 2G 37
                              (off Beatrice Ct.)
Black Boy La. N15 . . . . .5C 48
Blackbrook La. BR1: Broml 5E 160
    BR2: Broml 5E 160
Black Bull Yd. EC1 . . . . .5K 7
                              (off Hatton Wall)
Blackburn NW9 . . . . .2B 44
Blackburne's M. W1 . . . . .2G 11 (7E 82)
Blackburn Rd. NW6 . . . . .6K 63
Blackburn Trad. Est.
    TW19: Stanw 6B 110
Blackburn Way TW4: Houn 5C 112
Blackbush Av. RM6: Chad H 5D 54
Blackbush Cl. SM2: Sutt 7K 165
Blackdown Cl. N2 . . . . .2A 46
Blackdown Ter. SE18 . . . . .1D 124
Blackett Apts. E3 . . . . .4B 86
                              (off Hamlets Way)
Blackett St. SW15 . . . . .3F 117
Black Fan Cl. EN2: Enf 1H 23
BLACKFEN 6A 126
Blackfen Pde. DA15: Sidc 6A 126
Blackfen Rd. DA15: Sidc 5J 125
Blackford Cl. CR2: S Croy 7B 168
Blackford's Path SW15 . . . . .7C 116
Blackfriars Bri. EC4 . . . . . .2A 14 (7B 84)
Blackfriars Ct. EC4 . . . . .2A 14
Black Friars La. EC4 . . . . . .2A 14 (6B 84)
                              (not continuous)
Blackfriars Pas. EC4 . . . . . .2A 14 (7A 84)
Blackfriars Rd. SE1 . . . . .4A 14 (2B 102)
Blackfriars Underpass
    EC4 . . . . .2A 14 (7A 84)
Black Gates HA5: Pinn 3D 40
BLACKHEATH 2H 123
Blackheath Av. SE10 . . . . .7F 105
Blackheath Bus. Cen. SE10 . . . . . .1E 122
Blackheath Bus. Est. SE10 . . . . .1E 122
                              (off Blackheath Hill)
Blackheath Concert Halls 3H 123
Blackheath Gro. SE3 . . . . .2H 123
Blackheath Hill SE10 . . . . .1E 122
BLACKHEATH PARK 3J 123
Blackheath Pk. SE3 . . . . .3H 123
Blackheath Ri. SE13 . . . . .2E 122
                              (not continuous)
Blackheath Rd. SE10 . . . . .1D 122
Blackheath RUFC 7K 105
BLACKHEATH VALE 2H 123
Blackheath Va. SE3 . . . . .2G 123
Blackheath Village SE3 . . . . .2H 123
Black Horse Ct. SE1 . . . . .3D 102
Blackhorse La. CR0: C'don 7G 157
    E17 . . . . .2K 49
Blackhorse M. E17 . . . . .3K 49
Black Horse Pde. HA5: Eastc 5K 39
BLACKHORSE ROAD 4K 49
Blackhorse Rd. DA14: Sidc 4A 144
    E17 . . . . .4K 49
    SE8 .6A 104
Blacklands Dr. UB4: Hayes 4E 74
Blacklands Rd. SE6 . . . . .4E 140
Blacklands Ter. SW3 . . . .4E 16 (4D 100)
Black Lion La. W6 . . . . .4C 98
Black Lion M. W6 . . . . .4C 98
Blackmans Yd. E2 . . . . .4G 85
Blackmore Av. UB1: S'hall 1H 95
Blackmore Dr. NW10 . . . . .7H 61
Blackmore Ho. N1 . . . . .1K 83
                              (off Barnsbury Est.)
Blackmore Rd. IG9: Buck H 1H 37
Blackmore's Gro. TW11: Tedd 6A 132
Blackness La. BR2: Kes 7B 172
Black Path E10 . . . . .7A 50
Blackpool Gdns. UB4: Hayes 4G 75

Blackpool Rd. SE15 . . . . .2H 121
BLACK PRINCE INTERCHANGE . . .6H 127
Black Prince Rd. SE1 . . . .4G 19 (4K 101)
    SE11 . . . . .4G 19 (4K 101)
Black Prince St. SE18 . . . . .6A 108
Black Rod Cl. UB3: Hayes 3H 93
Blackshaw Rd. SW17 . . . . .4A 136
Blacksmith Ho. RM6: Chad H 6C 54
    TW16: Sun 3J 147
Blacksmiths Ho. E14 . . . . .4B 87
                              (off Valencia Cl.)
    E17 . . . . .4C 50
                              (off Gillards M.)
Blacks Rd. W6 . . . . .5E 98
Blackstock M. N4 . . . . .2B 66
Blackstock Rd. N4 . . . . .2B 66
    N5 . . . . .2B 66
Blackstone Est. E8 . . . . .7G 67
Blackstone Ho. SW1 . . . . .6A 18
                              (off Churchill Gdns.)
Blackstone Rd. NW2 . . . . .5E 62
Black Swan Yd. SE1 . . . .6H 15 (2E 102)
Blackthorn Av. N7 . . . . .6A 66
    W7: W Dray 4C 92
Blackthorn Ct. E15 . . . . .4F 69
                              (off Hall Rd.)
    TW5: Hest 7C 94
Blackthorne Av. CR0: C'don 1J 169
Blackthorne Ct. SE15 . . . . .7F 103
                              (off Cator St.)
    TW15: Ashf 7E 128
    UB1: S'hall 1F 95
                              (off Dormer's Wells La.)
Blackthorne Cres. SL3: Poyle 5A 174
Blackthorne Dr. E4 . . . . .4A 36
Blackthorne Ind. Est. SL3: Poyle . . .6A 174
Blackthorne Rd. SL3: Poyle 5A 174
Blackthorn Gro. DA7: Bex 3E 126
Blackthorn Ho. SE16 . . . . .2A 104
                              (off Blondin Way)
Blackthorn Rd. IG1: Ilf 5H 71
Blackthorn St. E3 . . . . .4C 86
Blacktree M. SW9 . . . . .3A 120
BLACKWALL 1E 104
Blackwall La. SE10 . . . . .5G 105
Blackwall Trad. Est. E14 . . . . .5F 87
BLACKWALL TUNNEL 1F 105
Blackwall Tunnel App. E14 . . . . . . .7E 86
Blackwall Tunnel Northern App.
    E3 . . . . .2C 86
Blackwall Tunnel Southern App.
    SE10 . . . . .3G 105
Blackwall Way E14 . . . . .1E 104
Blackwater Cl. E7 . . . . .4H 69
    RM13: Rain 5K 91
Blackwater Ho. NW8 . . . . .5B 4
                              (off Church St.)
Blackwater St. SE22 . . . . .5F 121
Blackwell Cl. E5 . . . . .4K 67
    HA3: Hrw W 7C 26
    N21 .5D 22
Blackwell Gdns. HA8: Edg 4B 28
Blackwell Ho. SW4 . . . . .6H 119
Blackwood Ho. E1 . . . . .4H 85
                              (off Collingwood St.)
Blackwood St. SE17 . . . . .5D 102
Blade M. SW15 . . . . .4H 117
Bladen Ho. E1 . . . . .6K 85
                              (off Dunelm St.)
Blades Cl. SW15 . . . . .4H 117
    W6 . . . . .5D 98
                              (off Lower Mall)
Blades Ho. SE11 . . . . .7J 19
                              (off Kennington Oval)
Blandindon Dr. DA5: Bexl 7C 126
Bladon Cl. SW16 . . . . .6J 137
Bladon Gdns. HA2: Harr 6F 41
Blagdens Cl. N14 . . . . .2C 32
Blagdens La. N14 . . . . .2B 32
Blagdon Cl. W7 . . . . .7J 77
Blagdon Rd. KT3: N Mald 4B 152
    SE13 . . . . .6D 122
Blagdon Wlk. TW11: Tedd 6C 132

Blagrove Cres. HA4: Eastc 6K 39
Blagrove Rd. TW11: Hamp W 7B 132
    W10 . . . . .5G 81
Blair Av. NW9 . . . . .7A 44
Blair Cl. DA15: Sidc 5J 125
    N1 . . . . .6C 66
    UB3: Harl 4J 93
Blair Ct. BR3: Beck 1D 158
    NW8 . . . . .1B 82
    SE6 .1H 141
Blairderry Rd. SW2 . . . . .2J 137
Blairgowrie Ct. E14 . . . . .6F 87
                              (off Blair St.)
Blair Ho. SW9 . . . . .2K 119
Blair St. E14 . . . . .6E 86
Blake Av. IG11: Bark 1J 89
Blake Bldg. N8 . . . . .3K 47
Blake Cl. DA16: Well 1J 125
    SM5: Cars 1C 166
    UB4: Hayes 2F 75
    W10 . . . . .5E 80
Blake Ct. N21 . . . . .5E 22
    NW6 . . . . .3J 81
                              (off Malvern Rd.)
    SE16 .5H 103
                              (off Stubbs Dr.)
Blakeden Dr. KT10: Clay 6A 162
Blake Gdns. SW6 . . . . .1K 117
Blake Hall Cres. E11 . . . . .1J 69
Blake Hall Rd. E11 . . . . .7J 51
Blakehall Rd. SM5: Cars 6D 166
Blake Ho. E14 . . . . .2C 104
                              (off Admirals Way)
    SE1 . . . . .1J 19 (3A 102)
    SE8 . . . . .6C 104
                              (off New King St.)
Blake M. TW9: Kew 1G 115
Blakemore Gdns. SW13 . . . . .6D 98
Blakemore Rd. CR7: Thor H 5K 155
    SW16 . . . . .3J 137
Blakemore Way DA17: Belv 3E 108
Blakeney Av. BR3: Beck 1B 158
Blakeney Cl. E8 . . . . .5G 67
    N20 . . . . .1G 31
    NW1 . . . . .7H 65
Blakeney Rd. BR3: Beck 7B 140
Blakenham Rd. SW17 . . . . .4D 136
Blaker Ct. SE7 . . . . .7A 106
                              (not continuous)
Blake Rd. CR0: C'don 2E 168
    CR4: Mitc 3C 154
    E16 . . . . .4H 87
    N11 . . . . .7B 32
Blaker Rd. E15 . . . . .2E 86
Blakes Av. KT3: N Mald 5B 152
Blake's Grn. BR4: W W'ck 1E 170
Blakes La. KT3: N Mald 5B 152
Blakesley Av. W5 . . . . .6C 78
Blakesley Ho. E12 . . . . .3E 70
                              (off Grantham Rd.)
Blakesley Wlk. SW20 . . . . .2H 153
Blakes Rd. SE15 . . . . .7E 102
Blakes Ter. KT3: N Mald 5C 152
Blakesware Gdns. N9 . . . . .7J 23
Blake Twr. EC2 . . . . .5C 8
                              (off Fann St.)
Blakewood Cl. TW13: Hanw 4A 130
Blakewood Ct. SE20 . . . . .7H 139
                              (off Anerley Pk.)
Blanchard Cl. SE9 . . . . .3C 142
Blanchard Ho. TW1: Twick 6D 114
                              (off Clevedon Rd.)
Blanchard Way E8 . . . . .6G 67
Blanch Cl. SE15 . . . . .7J 103
Blanchedowne SE5 . . . . .4D 120
Blanche St. E16 . . . . .4H 87
Blanchland Rd. SM4: Mord 5K 153
Blandfield Rd. SW12 . . . . .7E 118
Blandford Av. BR3: Beck 2A 158
    TW2: Whitt 1F 131
Blandford Cl. CR0: Bedd 3J 167
    N2 . . . . .4A 46
    RM7: Mawney 4H 55

Blandford Ct. N1 . . . . .7E 66
                              (off St Peter's Way)
    NW6 . . . . .7F 63
Blandford Cres. E4 . . . . .7K 25
Blandford Ho. SW8 . . . . .7K 101
                              (off Richborne Ter.)
Blandford Rd. BR3: Beck 2J 157
    TW11: Tedd 5H 131
    UB2: S'hall 4E 94
    W4 . . . . .3A 98
    W5 . . . . .2D 96
Blandford Sq. NW1 . . . . . . .4D 4 (4C 82)
Blandford St. W1 . . . . .7F 5 (6D 82)
Blandford Waye
    UB4: Yead 6A 76
Bland Ho. SE11 . . . . .5H 19
Bland St. SE9 . . . . .4B 124
Blaney Cres. E6 . . . . .3F 89
Blanmerle Rd. SE9 . . . . .1F 143
Blann Cl. SE9 . . . . .6B 124
Blantyre St. SW10 . . . . .7B 100
Blantyre Twr. SW10 . . . . .7B 100
                              (off Worlds End Est.)
Blantyre Wlk. SW10 . . . . .7B 100
                              (off Worlds End Est.)
Blashford NW3 . . . . .7D 64
                              (off Adelaide Rd.)
Blashford St. SE13 . . . . .7F 123
Blashill Ct. E14 . . . . .7E 86
                              (off Bullivant St.)
Blasker Wlk. E14 . . . . .5D 104
Blaven Path E16 . . . . .4H 87
Blawith Rd. HA1: Harr 4J 41
Blaxland Ho. W12 . . . . .7D 80
                              (off White City Est.)
Blaydon Cl. HA4: Ruis 7G 39
    N17 . . . . .7C 34
Blaydon Ct. UB5: N'olt 6E 58
Blaydon Wlk. N17 . . . . .7C 34
Blazer Ct. NW8 . . . . .2B 4
Bleak Hill La. SE18 . . . . .6K 107
Bleak Ho. La. W4 . . . . .4K 97
                              (off Chiswick High Rd.)
Blean Gro. SE20 . . . . .7J 139
Bleasdale Av. UB6: G'frd 2A 78
Blechynden Ho. W10 . . . . .6F 81
                              (off Kingsdown Cl.)
Blechynden St. W10 . . . . .7F 81
Bledlow Cl.
    NW8 . . . . .4B 4 (4B 82)
    SE28 .7C 90
Bledlow Ri. UB6: G'frd 2G 77
Bleeding Heart Yd. EC1 . . . . .6K 7
Blegborough Rd. SW16 . . . . .6G 137
Blemundsbury WC1 . . . . .5G 7
                              (off Dombey St.)
BLENDON 6D 126
Blendon Dr. DA5: Bexl 6D 126
Blendon Path
    BR1: Broml 7H 141
Blendon Rd. DA5: Bexl 6D 126
Blendon Row SE17 . . . . .4D 102
                              (off Orb St.)
Blendon Ter. SE18 . . . . .5G 107
Blendworth Point SW15 . . . . .1D 134
Blenheim Av. IG2: Ilf 6E 52
Blenheim Bus. Cen. CR4: Mitc . . .2D 154
                              (off London Rd.)
The Blenheim Cen. 3F 113
Blenheim Cl. N21 . . . . .1H 33
    RM7: Mawney 4J 55
    SE12 . . . . .1K 141
    SM6: W'gton 7G 167
    SW20 . . . . .3E 152
    UB6: G'frd 2H 77
Blenheim Ct. BR2: Broml 4H 159
    DA14: Sidc 3H 143
    HA3: Kenton 6A 42
    IG8: Wfd G 7E 36
    N7 . . . . .6J 65
    N19 . . . . .2J 65
    RM13: Rain 2K 91
                              (off Lowen Rd.)

Blenheim Ct.—Boleyn Dr.

Blenheim Ct. SE10 . . . . 5J 105
(off Denham St.)
SE16 . . . . 1K 103
(off King & Queen Wharf)
SM2: Sutt 6A 166
Blenheim Cres. CR2: S Croy 7C 168
HA4: Ruis 2F 57
W11 . . . . 7G 81
Blenheim Dr. DA16: Well 1K 125
Blenheim Gdns. HA9: Wemb 3E 60
KT2: King T 7H 133
NW2 . . . . 6E 62
SM6: W'gton 6G 167
SW2 . . . . 6K 119
Blenheim Gro. SE15 . . . . 2G 121
Blenheim Ho. E16 . . . . 1K 105
(off Constable Av.)
SE18 . . . . 3G 107
SW3 . . . . 6D 16
(off Kings Rd.)
TW3: Houn 3E 112
Blenheim Pde. UB10: Hil 4D 74
Blenheim Pk. Rd. CR2: S Croy 7C 168
Blenheim Pas. NW8 . . . . 2A 82
Blenheim Pl. TW11: Tedd 5K 131
Blenheim Ri. N15 . . . . 4F 49
Blenheim Rd. BR1: Broml 4C 160
DA15: Sidc 1C 144
E6 . . . . 3B 88
E15 . . . . 4G 69
E17 . . . . 3K 49
EN5: Barn 3A 20
HA2: Harr 6F 41
NW8 . . . . 2A 82
SE20 . . . . 7J 139
SM1: Sutt 3J 165
SW20 . . . . 3E 152
UB5: N'olt 6F 59
W4 . . . . 3A 98
Blenheim Shop. Cen. 7J 139
Blenheim St. W1 . . . . 1J 11 (6F 83)
Blenheim Ter. NW8 . . . . 2A 82
Blenheim Twr. SE14 . . . . 7A 104
(off Batavia Rd.)
Blenheim Way TW7: Isle 1A 114
Blenkarne Rd. SW11 . . . . 6D 118
Bleriot Rd. TW5: Hest 7A 94
Blessbury Rd. HA8: Edg 1J 43
Blessington Cl. SE13 . . . . 3F 123
Blessington Rd. SE13 . . . . 3F 123
Blessing Way IG11: Bark 3C 90
Bletchingley Cl. CR7: Thor H 4B 156
Bletchley Ct. HA7: Stan 7K 27
(off Hitchin Way)
N1 . . . . 1E 8
Bletchley St. N1 . . . . 1D 8 (2D 84)
Bletchmore Cl. UB3: Harl 5F 93
Bletsoe Wlk. N1 . . . . 2C 84
Blewbury Ho. SE2 . . . . 2C 108
(not continuous)
Blick Ho. SE16 . . . . 3J 103
(off Neptune St.)
Blincoe Cl. SW19 . . . . 2F 135
Bliss Cres. SE13 . . . . 2D 122
Blissett St. SE10 . . . . 1E 122
Bliss Ho. EN1: Enf 1B 24
Bliss M. W10 . . . . 3G 81
Blisworth Cl. UB4: Yead 4C 76
Blisworth Ho. E2 . . . . 1G 85
(off Whiston Rd.)
Blithbury Rd. RM9: Dag 6B 72
Blithdale Rd. SE2 . . . . 4A 108
Blithehale Ct. E2 . . . . 3H 85
(off Withan St.)
Blithfield St. W8 . . . . 3K 99
Blockley Rd. HA0: Wemb 2B 60
Block Wharf E14 . . . . 2C 104
(off Cuba St.)
Bloemfontein Av. W12 . . . . 1D 98
Bloemfontein Rd. W12 . . . . 7D 80
Bloemfontein Way W12 . . . . 1D 98
Blomfield Ct. W9 . . . . 3A 4
(off Maida Vale)
Blomfield Mans. W12 . . . . 1E 98
(off Stanlake Rd.)
Blomfield Rd. W9 . . . . 4A 4 (5K 81)
Blomfield St. EC2 . . . . 6F 9 (5D 84)
Blomfield Vs. W2 . . . . 5K 81
Blomville Rd. RM8: Dag 3E 72
Blondell Cl. UB7: Harm 2E 174
Blondel St. SW11 . . . . 2E 118
Blondin Av. W5 . . . . 4C 96
Blondin Pk. & Nature Area 4B 96
Blondin St. E3 . . . . 2C 86
Blondin Way SE16 . . . . 2A 104
Bloomberg Arc. EC4 . . . . 6D 84
Bloomberg Ct. SW1 . . . . 4C 18
(off Vauxhall Bri. Rd.)
Bloomburg St. SW1 . . . . 4B 18 (4H 101)
Bloomfield Ct. E10 . . . . 3D 68
(off Brisbane Rd.)
N6 . . . . 6E 46
Bloomfield Cres. IG2: Ilf 6F 53
Bloomfield Ho. E1 . . . . 5G 85
(off Old Montague St.)
Bloomfield Pl. W1 . . . . 2K 11
Bloomfield Rd. BR2: Broml 5B 160
KT1: King T 4E 150
N6 . . . . 6E 46
SE18 . . . . 6F 107
Bloomfield Ter. SW1 . . . . 5H 17 (5E 100)
Bloom Gro. SE27 . . . . 3B 138
Bloomhall Rd. SE19 . . . . 5D 138
Bloom Ho. E3 . . . . 2D 86
(off Alameda Pl.)
Bloom Pk. Rd. SW6 . . . . 7H 99
BLOOMSBURY 5E 6 (5J 83)
Bloomsbury Cl. NW7 . . . . 7H 29
W5 . . . . 7F 79
Bloomsbury Ct. HA5: Pinn 3D 40
TW5: Cran 1K 111
WC1 . . . . 6F 7
Bloomsbury Ho. SW4 . . . . 6H 119
Bloomsbury Mans. BR1: Broml 1K 159
(off Widmore Rd.)
Bloomsbury M. IG8: Wfd G 6H 37
Bloomsbury Pl. SW18 . . . . 5A 118
WC1 . . . . 5F 7 (5J 83)
Bloomsbury Sq. WC1 . . . . 6F 7 (5J 83)
Bloomsbury St. WC1 . . . . 6D 6 (5H 83)
Bloomsbury Theatre 3C 6
Bloomsbury Way WC1 . . . . 6E 6 (5J 83)
Blore Cl. SW8 . . . . 1H 119
Blore Ct. W1 . . . . 1C 12
Blore Ho. SW10 . . . . 7K 99
(off Coleridge Gdns.)
Blossom Av. HA2: Harr 2F 59
Blossom Cl. CR2: S Croy 5F 169
RM9: Dag 1F 91
W5 . . . . 2E 96
Blossom Ct. SE15 . . . . 7F 103
(off All Saints Walk)
Blossom Dr. BR6: Orp 2K 173
Blossom La. EN2: Enf 1H 23
Blossom Pl. SE28 . . . . 3G 107
Blossom St. E1 . . . . 4H 9 (4E 84)
Blossom Way UB7: W Dray 4C 92
UB10: Hil 7B 56
Blossom Waye TW5: Hest 6C 94
Blount M. UB10: Uxb 2A 74
Blount St. E14 . . . . 6A 86
Bloxam Gdns. SE9 . . . . 5C 124
Bloxhall Rd. E10 . . . . 1B 68
Bloxham Cres. TW12: Hamp 7D 130
Bloxworth Cl. SM6: W'gton 3G 167
Blucher Rd. SE5 . . . . 7C 102
Blue Anchor All. TW9: Rich 4E 114
Blue Anchor La. SE16 . . . . 4G 103
Blue Anchor Yd. E1 . . . . 2K 15 (7G 85)
Blue Ball Yd. SW1 . . . . 5A 12 (1G 101)
Bluebell Apts. N4 . . . . 1C 66
(off Swan La.)
Bluebell Av. E12 . . . . 5B 70
Bluebell Cl. BR6: Farnb 2G 173
E9 . . . . 1J 85
RM7: Rush G 2K 73
Bluebell Cl. SE26 . . . . 4F 139
SM6: W'gton 1F 167
UB5: N'olt 6D 58
Bluebell Ct. NW9 . . . . 1A 44
(off Heybourne Cres.)
Bluebell Ho. SE16 . . . . 2A 104
(off Bondin Way)
Bluebell Ter. UB7: W Dray 2B 92
Bluebell Way IG1: Ilf 6F 71
Blueberry Cl. IG8: Wfd G 6D 36
Bluebird Cl. SW20 . . . . 2E 152
Bluebird Ho. IG11: Bark 3K 89
Bluebird La. RM10: Dag 7G 73
Bluebird Way SE28 . . . . 2H 107
Blue Boar All. EC3 . . . . 7J 9
(off Aldgate High St.)
Blue Bldg. SE10 . . . . 5H 105
(off Glenforth St.)
Blue Ct. N1 . . . . 1D 84
(off Sherborne St.)
Blue Elephant Theatre 7C 102
(off Bethwin Rd.)
Bluefield Cl. TW12: Hamp 5E 130
Blue Fin Bldg. SE1 . . . . 4B 14
Bluegate M. E1 . . . . 7H 85
Bluegates KT17: Ewe 7C 164
Bluehouse Rd. E4 . . . . 2B 36
Blue Lion Pl. SE1 . . . . 7G 15 (3E 102)
Blueprint Apts. SW12 . . . . 7F 119
(off Balham Gro.)
Blue Riband Ind. Est.
CR0: C'don 2B 168
Blues St. E8 . . . . 6F 67
Blue Water SW18 . . . . 4K 117
Blumenthal Cl. TW7: Isle 7H 95
Blundell Cl. E8 . . . . 5G 67
Blundell Rd. HA8: Edg 1K 43
Blundell St. N7 . . . . 7J 65
Blunden Cl. RM8: Dag 1C 72
Blunden Ct. SW6 . . . . 7J 99
(off Farm La.)
Blunt Rd. CR2: S Croy 5D 168
Blunts Av. UB7: Sip 7C 92
Blunts Rd. SE9 . . . . 5E 124
Blurton Rd. E5 . . . . 4J 67
Blydon Ct. N21 . . . . 5E 22
(off Chaseville Pk. Rd.)
Blyth Cl. E14 . . . . 4F 105
TW1: Twick 6K 113
Blyth Ct. BR1: Broml 1H 159
(off Blyth Rd.)
Blythe Cl. SE6 . . . . 7B 122
BLYTHE HILL 7B 122
Blythe Hill BR5: St P 1K 161
SE6 . . . . 7B 122
Blythe Hill La. SE6 . . . . 7B 122
Blythe Hill Pl. SE23 . . . . 7A 122
Blythe Ho. SE11 . . . . 7J 19 (6A 102)
Blythe M. W14 . . . . 3F 99
Blythendale Ho. E2 . . . . 2G 85
(off Mansford St.)
Blythe Rd. W14 . . . . 3F 99
Blythe St. E2 . . . . 3H 85
Blytheswood Pl. SW16 . . . . 4K 137
Blythe Va. SE6 . . . . 1B 140
Blyth Hill Pl. SE23 . . . . 7A 122
(off Brockley Pk.)
Blyth Ho. DA8: Erith 5K 109
Blyth Rd. BR1: Broml 1H 159
E17 . . . . 7B 50
SE28 . . . . 7C 90
UB3: Hayes 2G 93
Blyth's Wharf E14 . . . . 7A 86
Blythswood Rd. IG3: Ilf 1A 72
Blyth Wood Pk. BR1: Broml 1H 159
Blythwood Rd. HA5: Pinn 1B 40
N4 . . . . 7J 47
The BMX Track
London 6D 102
Boades M. NW3 . . . . 4B 64
Boadicea St. N1 . . . . 1K 83
Boakes Cl. NW9 . . . . 4J 43
Boardman Av. E4 . . . . 5J 25
Boardman Cl. EN5: Barn 5B 20
Boardwalk Pl. E14 . . . . 1E 104
Boarley Ho. SE17 . . . . 4E 102
(off Massinger St.)
Boars Head Yd. TW8: Bford 7D 96
Boatemah Wlk. SW9 . . . . 2A 120
(off Peckford Pl.)
Boaters Av. TW8: Bford 7C 96
The Boathouse E14 . . . . 6C 86
The Boathouse Cen. W10 . . . . 4F 81
(off Canal Cl.)
Boathouse Wlk. SE15 . . . . 7F 103
(not continuous)
Boat La. E2 . . . . 1F 85
Boat Lifter Way SE16 . . . . 4A 104
Boat Quay E16 . . . . 7A 88
Boatyard Apts. E14 . . . . 5D 104
Bob Anker Cl. E13 . . . . 3J 87
Bobbin Cl. SM6: W'gton 2E 166
SW4 . . . . 3G 119
Bobby Moore Way IG11: Bark 1G 89
N10 . . . . 7J 31
The Bob Hope Theatre 6D 124
Bob Marley Way SE24 . . . . 4A 120
Bockhampton Rd. KT2: King T 7F 133
Bocking St. E8 . . . . 1H 85
Boddicott Cl. SW19 . . . . 2G 135
Boddington Gdns. W3 . . . . 2G 97
Boddington Ho. SE14 . . . . 1J 121
(off Pomeroy St.)
SW13 . . . . 6D 98
(off Wyatt Dr.)
Bodeney Ho. SE5 . . . . 1E 120
(off Peckham Rd.)
Boden Ho. E1 . . . . 5K 9
(off Woodseer St.)
Bodiam Cl. EN1: Enf 2K 23
Bodiam Rd. SW16 . . . . 7H 137
Bodiam Way NW10 . . . . 3F 79
Bodicea M. TW4: Houn 6D 112
Bodington Ct. W12 . . . . 2F 99
Bodium Ct. E17 . . . . 1B 50
(off Thornbury Way)
Bodleian Ho. SE20 . . . . 1G 157
Bodley Cl. KT3: N Mald 5A 152
Bodley Mnr. Way SW2 . . . . 7A 120
Bodley Rd. KT3: N Mald 6K 151
Bodley Way SE17 . . . . 4C 102
Bodmin Cl. HA2: Harr 3D 58
Bodmin Gro. SM4: Mord 5K 153
Bodmin St. SW18 . . . . 1J 135
Bodnant Gdns. SW20 . . . . 3C 152
Bodney Rd. E8 . . . . 5H 67
Boeing Way UB2: S'hall 3K 93
Boevey Path DA17: Belv 5F 109
Bogart Ct. E14 . . . . 7C 86
(off Premiere Pl.)
Bogey La. BR6: Downe 7E 172
Bognor Rd. DA16: Well 1D 126
Bohemia Pl. E8 . . . . 6J 67
Bohn Rd. E1 . . . . 5A 86
Bohun Gro. EN4: E Barn 6H 21
Boileau Pde. W5 . . . . 6F 79
(off Boileau Rd.)
Boileau Rd. SW13 . . . . 7C 98
W5 . . . . 6F 79
The Boiler Ho. UB3: Hayes 2G 93
(off Material Wlk.)
Boisseau Ho. E1 . . . . 5J 85
(off Stepney Way)
Bolanachi Bldg. SE16 . . . . 3F 103
Bolander Gro. SW6 . . . . 6J 99
Bolden St. SE8 . . . . 2D 122
Boldero Pl. NW8 . . . . 4C 4
Bolderwood Way BR4: W W'ck 2D 170
Boldmere Rd. HA5: Eastc 7A 40
Boleyn Av. EN1: Enf 1C 24
Boleyn Cl. E17 . . . . 4C 50
Boleyn Ct. IG9: Buck H 1D 36
KT8: E Mos 4H 149
(off Bridge Rd.)
Boleyn Dr. HA4: Ruis 2B 58
KT8: W Mole 3D 148

A-Z London 203

Boleyn Gdns. BR4: W W'ck 2D 170
RM10: Dag 7J 73
Boleyn Gro. BR4: W W'ck 2E 170
Boleyn Ho. E16 . . . . .1J 105
(off Southey M.)
Boleyn Rd. E6 . . . . .2B 88
E7 . . . . .7J 69
N16 . . . . .5E 66
Boleyn Way EN5: New Bar 3F 21
Bolina Rd. SE16 . . . . .5J 103
Bolinder Way E3 . . . . .3E 86
Bolingbroke Cl. EN4: Cockf 3J 21
Bolingbroke Gro. SW11 . . . . .4C 118
Bolingbroke Rd. W14 . . . . .3F 99
Bolingbroke Wlk. SW11 . . . . .1B 118
Bolingbroke Way
UB3: Hayes 1F 93
Bolliger Ct. NW10 . . . . .4J 79
Bollinder Pl. EC1 . . . . .1C 8 (3C 84)
Bollo Bri. Rd. W3 . . . . .3H 97
Bollo La. W3 . . . . .2H 97
W4 . . . . .4J 97
Bolney Ga. SW7 . . . . . . .7C 10 (2C 100)
Bolney St. SW8 . . . . .7K 101
Bolney Way TW13: Hanw 3C 130
Bolsover St. W1 . . . . . . .4K 5 (4F 83)
Bolstead Rd. CR4: Mitc 1F 155
Bolster Gro. N22 . . . . .7C 32
Bolt Cl. EC4 . . . . .6A 84
Bolt Ho. N1 . . . . .1E 84
(off Phillipp St.)
Boltmore Cl. NW4 . . . . .3F 45
Bolton Cl. KT9: Chess 6D 162
SE20 . . . . .2G 157
Bolton Cres. SE5 . . . . .7B 102
SE11 . . . . .7A 102
Bolton Dr. SM4: Mord 7A 154
Bolton Gdns. BR1: Broml 6H 141
NW10 . . . . .2F 81
SW5 .5K 99
TW11: Tedd 6A 132
Bolton Gdns. M. SW10 . . . . .5A 100
Bolton Ho. SE10 . . . . .5G 105
(off Trafalgar Rd.)
SE11 . . . . .4B 102
(off George Mathers Rd.)
Bolton Pl. NW8 . . . . .1K 81
(off Bolton Rd.)
Bolton Rd. E15 . . . . .6H 69
HA1: Harr 4G 41
KT9: Chess 6D 162
N18 .5A 34
NW8 .1K 81
NW10 . . . . .1A 80
W4 . . . . .7J 97
The Boltons HA0: Wemb 4K 59
IG8: Wfd G 4D 36
SW10 . . . . .5A 100
Boltons Ct. SW5 . . . . .5K 99
(off Old Brompton Rd.)
Bolton's La. UB3: Harl 1E 110
Boltons Pl. SW5 . . . . .5A 100
Bolton St. W1 . . . . .4K 11 (1F 101)
Bolton Studios SW10 . . . . .5A 100
Bolton Wlk. N7 . . . . .2K 65
(off Durham Rd.)
Bombay Ct. SE16 . . . . .2J 103
(off St Marychurch St.)
Bombay St. SE16 . . . . .4H 103
Bomer Cl. UB7: Sip 7C 92
Bomore Rd. W11 . . . . .7G 81
Bonar Pl. BR7: Chst 7C 142
Bonar Rd. SE15 . . . . .7G 103
Bonchester Cl. BR7: Chst 7E 142
Bonchurch Cl. SM2: Sutt 7K 165
Bonchurch Rd. W10 . . . . .5G 81
W13 .1B 96
Bond Cl. DA16: Well 2J 125
UB7: Yiew 6B 74
Bond Ct. EC4 . . . . .2E 14 (7D 84)
Bondfield Av. UB4: Yead 3J 75
Bondfield Rd. E6 . . . . .5D 88
Bond Gdns. SM6: W'gton 4G 167

Bond Ho. NW6 . . . . .2H 81
(off Rupert Rd.)
SE14 . . . . .7A 104
(off Goodwood Rd.)
TW8: Bford 5D 96
Bonding Yd. Wlk. SE16 . . . . .3A 104
Bond Rd. CR4: Mitc 2C 154
KT6: Surb 2F 163
Bond St. E15 . . . . .5G 69
W4 . . . . .4K 97
W5 . . . . .7D 78
Bondway SW8 . . . . .7F 19 (6J 101)
Bonesgate Open Space
Local Nature Reserve 6G 163
Boneta Rd. SE18 . . . . .3D 106
Bonfield Rd. SE13 . . . . .4E 122
Bonham Rd. SW2 . . . . .5F 109
Bonham Gdns. RM8: Dag 2D 72
Bonham Ga. KT12: Walt T 7H 147
(off New Zealand Av.)
Bonham Ho. W11 . . . . .1H 99
(off Boyne Ter. M.)
Bonham Rd. RM8: Dag 2D 72
SW2 .5K 119
Bonheur Rd. W4 . . . . .2K 97
Bonhill St. EC2 . . . . .4F 9 (4D 84)
Boniface Gdns. HA3: Hrw W 7A 26
Boniface Rd. UB10: Ick 3D 56
Boniface Wlk. HA3: Hrw W 7A 26
Bonington Ho. EN1: Enf 5B 24
Bonington Sq. SW8 . . . . .7G 19 (6K 101)
Bonita M. SE4 . . . . .3K 121
Bon Marche M. SE27 . . . . .4E 138
Bonner Hill Rd. KT1: King T 2F 151
Bonner Rd. E2 . . . . .2J 85
Bonnersfield Cl. HA1: Harr 6K 41
Bonnersfield La. HA1: Harr 6K 41
(not continuous)
Bonner St. E2 . . . . .2J 85
Bonnet St. E16 . . . . .2K 105
Bonneville Gdns. SW4 . . . . .6G 119
Bonnington Ct. UB5: N'olt 2B 76
(off Gallery Gdns.)
Bonnington Ho. N1 . . . . .2K 83
Bonnington Sq. SW8 . . . . .7G 19 (6K 101)
Bonny St. NW1 . . . . .7G 65
Bonser Rd. TW1: Twick 2K 131
Bonsor Ho. SW8 . . . . .1G 119
Bonsor St. SE5 . . . . .7E 102
Bonville Gdns. NW4 . . . . .4D 44
Bonville Rd. BR1: Broml 5H 141
Bookbinders Cott. Homes N20 . . . .3J 31
Bookbinders Ct. E1 . . . . .4H 85
(off Cudworth St.)
Booker Cl. E14 . . . . .5B 86
Booker Rd. N18 . . . . .5B 34
Bookham Cl. CR4: Mitc 3B 154
Book Ho. N1 . . . . .1C 8 (2C 84)
Book M. WC2 . . . . .6H 83
Booth's Pl. W1 . . . . .6B 6 (5G 83)
Boot Pde. HA8: Edg 6B 28
(off High St.)
Boot St. N1 . . . . .2G 9 (3E 84)
Bordars Rd. W7 . . . . .5J 77
Bordars Wlk. W7 . . . . .5J 77
Bordeaux Ho. E15 . . . . .5G 69
(off Luxembourg M.)

Borden Av. EN1: Enf 6J 23
Border Cres. SE26 . . . . .5H 139
Border Gdns. CRO: C'don 4D 170
Bordergate CR4: Mitc 1D 154
Border Rd. SE26 . . . . .5H 139
Bordesley Rd. SM4: Mord 5K 153
Bordeston Ct. TW8: Bford 7C 96
(off The Ham)
Bordon Wlk. SW15 . . . . .7C 116
Boreas Wlk. N1 . . . . .1B 8
Boreham Av. E16 . . . . .6J 87
Boreham Cl. E11 . . . . .1E 68
Boreham Rd. N22 . . . . .2C 48
Boreman Ho. SE10 . . . . .6E 104
(off Thames St.)
Borgard Rd. SE18 . . . . .4D 106
Borkwood Pk. BR6: Orp 4K 173
Borkwood Way BR6: Orp 4J 173
Borland Rd. SE15 . . . . .4J 121
TW11: Tedd 7B 132
Borley Ct. TW19: Stanw 1A 128
Borneo St. SW15 . . . . .3E 116
THE BOROUGH 7D 14 (2D 102)
Borough High St. SE1 . . .7D 14 (2C 102)
Borough Hill CRO: Wadd 3B 168
Borough Mkt. SE1 . . . . .5E 14
Borough Rd. CR4: Mitc 2C 154
KT2: King T 1G 151
SE1 . . . . .7B 14 (3B 102)
TW7: Isle 1J 113
Borough Sq. SE1 . . . . .7C 14
Borrett Cl. SE17 . . . . .5C 102
Borrodaile Rd. SW18 . . . . .6K 117
Borrowdale NW1 . . . . .2A 6
(off Robert St.)
Borrowdale Av. HA3: W'stone 2A 42
Borrowdale Cl. IG4: Ilf 4C 52
N2 . . . . .2A 46
Borthwick Ct. EN2: Enf 1H 23
Borthwick M. E15 . . . . .4G 69
Borthwick Rd. E15 . . . . .4G 69
NW9 .6B 44
Borthwick St. SE8 . . . . .5C 104
Borwick Av. E17 . . . . .3B 50
Bosanquet Cl. UB8: Cowl 4A 74
Bosbury Rd. SE6 . . . . .3E 140
Boscastle Rd. NW5 . . . . .3F 65
Boscobel Cl. BR1: Broml 2D 160
Boscobel Ho. E8 . . . . .6H 67
Boscobel Pl. SW1 . . . . . .3H 17 (4E 100)
Boscobel St. NW8 . . . . . .4B 4 (4B 82)
Bosco Cl. BR6: Orp 4K 173
Boscombe Av. E10 . . . . .7F 51
Boscombe Cir. NW9 . . . . .1K 43
Boscombe Cl. E5 . . . . .5A 68
Boscombe Gdns. SW16 . . . . .6J 137
Boscombe Ho. CRO: C'don 1D 168
(off Sydenham Rd.)
Boscombe Rd. KT4: Wor Pk 1E 164
SW17 . . . . .6E 136
SW19 . . . . .1K 153
W12 .1C 98
Bose Cl. N3 . . . . .1G 45
Bosgrove E4 . . . . .2K 35
Boss Ho. SE1 . . . . .6J 15
(off Boss St.)
Boss St. SE1 . . . . .6J 15 (2F 103)
Bostall Heath SE2 . . . . .5C 108
Bostall Hill SE2 . . . . .5A 108
Bostall La. SE2 . . . . .4B 108
Bostall Mnr. Way SE2 . . . . .4B 108
Bostall Pk. Av. DA7: Bex 7E 108
Bostall Rd. BR5: St P 7B 144
Bostock Ho. TW5: Hest 6E 94
Boston Bus. Pk. W7 . . . . .3J 95
Boston Cl. SE25 . . . . .4F 157
SM2: Sutt 7A 166
Boston Gdns. TW8: Bford 4A 96
W4 . . . . .6A 98
W7 . . . . .3J 95
Boston Gro. HA4: Ruis 6E 38
Boston Ho. SW5 . . . . .4K 99
(off Collingham Rd.)

BOSTON MANOR 4A 96
Boston Manor House 5B 96
Boston Mnr. Rd. TW8: Bford 4B 96
Boston Pde. W7 . . . . .3A 96
Boston Pk. Rd.
TW8: Bford 5C 96
Boston Pl. NW1 . . . . . . .4E 4 (4D 82)
Boston Rd. CRO: C'don 6K 155
E6 . . . . .3C 88
E17 . . . . .6C 50
HA8: Edg 7D 28
W7 . . . . .1J 95
Bostonthorpe Rd. W7 . . . . .2J 95
Boston Va. W7 . . . . .4A 96
Bosun Cl. E14 . . . . .2C 104
Boswell Ct. KT2: King T 1F 151
(off Clifton Rd.)
NW9 . . . . .2A 44
(off Charcot Rd.)
W14 . . . . .3F 99
(off Blythe Rd.)
WC1 . . . . .5F 7 (5J 83)
Boswell Ho. WC1 . . . . .5F 7
(off Boswell St.)
Boswell Path UB3: Harl 4H 93
Boswell Rd. CR7: Thor H 4C 156
Boswell St. WC1 . . . . . . .5F 7 (5J 83)
Boswood Ct. TW3: Houn 3D 112
Bosworth Cl. E17 . . . . .1B 50
Bosworth Ho. W10 . . . . .4G 81
(off Bosworth Rd.)
Bosworth Rd. EN5: New Bar 3D 20
N11 . . . . .6C 32
RM10: Dag 3G 73
W10 . . . . .4G 81
Botanic Sq. E14 . . . . .6G 87
Botany Bay La.
BR7: Chst 3G 161
Botany Cl. EN4: E Barn 4H 21
Boteley Cl. E4 . . . . .2A 36
Botham Cl. HA8: Edg 7D 28
Botha Rd. E13 . . . . .5K 87
Bothwell Cl. E16 . . . . .5H 87
Bothwell St. W6 . . . . .6F 99
Botolph All. EC3 . . . . .2G 15
Botolph La. EC3 . . . . . . .3G 15 (7E 84)
Botsford Rd. SW20 . . . . .2G 153
Botts M. W2 . . . . .6J 81
Botwell Comn. Rd.
UB3: Hayes 7F 75
Botwell Cres. UB3: Hayes 6G 75
Botwell Green Sports & Leisure Cen.
. . . . .1H 93
Botwell La. UB3: Hayes 7G 75
Boucher Cl. TW11: Tedd 5K 131
Bouchier Ho. N2 . . . . .2B 46
(off The Grange)
Boughton Av. BR2: Hayes 7H 159
Boughton Ho. SE1 . . . . .6E 14
(off Tennis St.)
Boughton Rd. SE28 . . . . .3J 107
Boulcott St. E1 . . . . .6K 85
The Boulevard IG8: Wfd G 6K 37
SW6 .1A 118
SW17 . . . . .2E 136
SW18 . . . . .4K 117
Boulevard Dr. NW9 . . . . .2B 44
Boulevard Walkway E1 . . .1K 15 (6G 85)
Boulogne Ho. SE1 . . . . .7G 15
Boulogne Rd. CRO: C'don 6C 156
Boulter Cl. BR1: Broml 3E 160
Boulter Ho. SE14 . . . . .1J 121
(off Kender St.)
Boulton Ho. TW8: Bford 5C 96
Boulton Rd. RM8: Dag 2E 72
Boultwood Rd. E6 . . . . .6D 88
Bounces La. N9 . . . . .2C 34
Bounces Rd. N9 . . . . .2C 34
Boundaries Rd. SW12 . . . . .2D 136
TW13: Felt 1A 130
Boundary Av. E17 . . . . .7B 50
Boundary Bus. Ct.
CR4: Mitc 3B 154

Boundary Cl. EN5: Barn 1C **20**
  IG3: Ilf 4J **71**
  KT1: King T 3H **151**
  SE20 .2G **157**
  UB2: S'hall 5E **94**
Boundary Ct. N18 . . . . .6A **34**
               (off Snells Pk.)
Boundary Ho. SE5 . . . . .7C **102**
  W11 .1F **99**
        (off Queensdale Cres.)
Boundary La. E13 . . . . .3B **88**
  SE17 .6C **102**
Boundary Pas. E2 . . . . .3J **9** (4F **85**)
Boundary Rd. DA15: Sidc 5J **125**
  E13 . . . . .2A **88**
  E17 . . . . .7B **50**
  HA5: Eastc 7B **40**
  HA9: Wemb 3E **60**
  IG11: Bark 2G **89**
           (The Clarksons)
  IG11: Bark 4H **71**
        (King Edwards Rd.)
  N2 . . . . .1B **46**
  N9 . . . . .6D **24**
  N22 . . . . .3B **48**
  NW8 . . . . .1K **81**
  SM5: W'gton, Cars 6F **167**
  SM6: W'gton 6F **167**
  SW19 . . . . .6B **136**
Boundary Row SE1 . . . . .6A **14** (2B **102**)
Boundary St. E2 . . . . .2J **9** (3F **85**)
Boundary Way
  CR0: Addtn 5C **170**
BOUNDS GREEN 6C **32**
Bounds Grn. Ct. N11 . . . . .6C **32**
        (off Bounds Grn. Rd.)
Bounds Grn. Ind. Est. N11 . . . . . .6B **32**
Bounds Grn. Rd. N11 . . . . .6B **32**
  N22 . . . . .6B **32**
Bourbon Ho. SE6 . . . . .5E **140**
Bourbon La. W12 . . . . .1F **99**
Bourbon Rd. SW9 . . . . .1A **120**
Bourchier St. W1 . . . . .2C **12** (7H **83**)
Bourdon Pl. W1 . . . . .2K **11**
Bourdon Rd. SE20 . . . . .2J **157**
Bourdon St. W1 . . . . . . .3J **11** (7F **83**)
Bourke Cl. NW10 . . . . .6A **62**
  SW4 .6J **119**
Bourlet Cl. W1 . . . . .6A **6** (5G **83**)
Bourn Av. EN4: E Barn 5G **21**
  N15 . . . . .4D **48**
  UB8: Hil 4C **74**
Bournbrook Rd. SE3 . . . . .3B **124**
The Bourne N14 . . . . .1C **32**
Bourne Av. HA4: Ruis 5A **58**
  N14 . . . . .2D **32**
  UB3: Harl 3E **92**
Bournebrook Gro. RM7: Rush G . .6K **55**
Bourne Cir. UB3: Harl 3E **92**
Bourne Cl. TW7: Isle 3J **113**
Bourne Ct. E11 . . . . .5J **51**
  HA4: Ruis 5K **57**
  IG8: Wfd G 3B **52**
  W4 . . . . .6J **97**
Bourne Dr. CR4: Mitc 2B **154**
Bourne Est. EC1 . . . . . . .5J **7** (5A **84**)
Bourne Gdns. E4 . . . . .4J **35**
Bourne Hall Mus. 7B **164**
Bourne Hill N13 . . . . .2D **32**
Bourne Hill Cl. N13 . . . . .2E **32**
Bourne Ho. IG9: Buck H 3G **37**
  TW15: Ashf 5C **128**
Bourne Ind. Pk. DA1: Cray 5K **127**
Bourne Mead DA5: Bexl 5K **127**
Bournemead Av. UB5: N'olt 2J **75**
Bournemead Cl. UB5: N'olt 3J **75**
Bournemead Way UB5: N'olt 2K **75**
Bourne M. W1 . . . . . . .1H **11** (6E **82**)
Bournemouth Cl. SE15 . . . . .2G **121**
Bournemouth Rd. SE15 . . . . .2G **121**
  SW19 . . . . .1J **153**
Bourne Pde. DA5: Bexl 7H **127**

Bourne Pl. W4 . . . . .5K **97**
Bourne Rd. BR2: Broml 4B **160**
  DA1: Cray 6J **127**
  DA5: Bexl, Dart 7H **127**
  E7 . . . . .3H **69**
  N8 . . . . .6J **47**
Bournes Ho. N15 . . . . .6E **48**
           (off Chisley Rd.)
Bourneside Cres. N14 . . . . .1C **32**
Bourneside Gdns. SE6 . . . . .5E **140**
Bourne St. CR0: C'don 2B **168**
  SW1 . . . . .4G **17** (4E **100**)
Bourne Ter. W2 . . . . .5K **81**
Bourne Va. BR2: Hayes 1H **171**
Bournevale Rd. SW16 . . . . .4J **137**
Bourne Vw. UB6: G'frd 6K **59**
Bourne Way BR2: Hayes 2H **171**
  KT19: Ewe 4J **163**
  SM1: Sutt 5H **165**
Bournewood Rd. SE18 . . . . .7A **108**
Bournville Rd. SE6 . . . . .7C **122**
Bournwell Cl. EN4: Cockf 3J **21**
Bourton Cl. UB3: Hayes 1J **93**
Bousfield Rd. SE14 . . . . .2K **121**
Boutflower Rd. SW11 . . . . .4C **118**
Boutique Hall SE13 . . . . .4E **122**
Bouton Pl. N1 . . . . .7B **66**
        (off Waterloo Ter.)
Bouverie Gdns. HA3: Kenton 6D **42**
Bouverie M. N16 . . . . .2E **66**
Bouverie Pl. W2 . . . . . . .7B **4** (6B **82**)
Bouverie Rd. HA1: Harr 6G **41**
  N16 . . . . .2E **66**
Bouverie St. EC4 . . . . . .1K **13** (6A **84**)
Bouvier Rd. EN3: Enf W 1D **24**
Boveney Cl. SE23 . . . . .6K **121**
Boveney Rd. SE23 . . . . .7K **121**
Bovet Cl. E1 . . . . .5A **86**
        (off Ocean Est.)
Bovill Rd. SE23 . . . . .7K **121**
Bovingdon Av. HA9: Wemb 6G **61**
Bovingdon Cl. N19 . . . . .2G **65**
Bovingdon La. NW9 . . . . .1A **44**
Bovingdon Rd. SW6 . . . . .1K **117**
Bovril Cl. SW6 . . . . .7K **99**
        (off Fulham Rd.)
BOW 3B **86**
Bowater Cl. NW9 . . . . .5K **43**
  SW2 .6J **119**
Bowater Gdns. TW16: Sun 2A **148**
Bowater Ho. EC1 . . . . .4C **8**
        (off Golden La. Est.)
Bowater Pl. SE3 . . . . .7K **105**
Bowater Rd. HA9: Wemb 3H **61**
  SE18 .3B **106**
Bow Bell Twr. E3 . . . . .1C **86**
        (off Pancras Way)
Bow Bri. Est. E3 . . . . .3D **86**
The Bow Brook E2 . . . . .2K **85**
        (off Mace St.)
Bow Churchyard EC4 . . . . .1D **14**
BOW COMMON 5C **86**
Bow Comn. La. E3 . . . . .4B **86**
Bow Creek Ecology Ps. 6G **87**
Bowden Cl. TW14: Bedf 1G **129**
Bowden Ho. E3 . . . . .3D **86**
        (off Rainhill Way)
Bowden St. SE11 . . . . . .6K **19** (5A **102**)
Bowditch SE8 . . . . .4B **104**
Bowdon Rd. E17 . . . . .7C **50**
Bowen Ct. SE16 . . . . .4J **103**
        (off Debnams Rd.)
Bowen Dr. SE21 . . . . .3E **138**
Bowen Rd. HA1: Harr 7G **41**
Bowen St. E14 . . . . .6D **86**
Bower Av. SE10 . . . . .1G **123**
Bower Cl. RM5: Col R 1K **55**
  UB5: N'olt 2A **76**
Bower Ct. E4 . . . . .1K **35**
        (off The Ridgeway)
Bowerdean St. SW6 . . . . .1K **117**
Bowerden Ct. NW10 . . . . .2D **80**
Bowerman Av. SE14 . . . . .6A **104**

Bowerman Ct. N19 . . . . .2H **65**
        (off St John's Way)
Bower St. E1 . . . . .6K **85**
Bowers Wlk. E6 . . . . .6D **88**
Bowery Apartments W12 . . . . .7E **80**
      (off Fountain Park Way)
Bowery Ct. RM10: Dag 6H **73**
Bowes Cl. DA15: Sidc 6B **126**
Bowe's Ho. IG11: Bark 7F **71**
Bowes-Lyon Hall E16 . . . . .1J **105**
        (off Wesley Av.)
BOWES PARK 6D **32**
Bowes Rd. N11 . . . . .5B **32**
  N13 . . . . .5B **32**
  RM8: Dag 4C **72**
  W3 . . . . .7A **80**
Bow Exchange E3 . . . . .3C **86**
        (off Yeo St.)
Bow Fair E3 . . . . .2C **86**
        (off Fairfield Rd.)
Bowfell Rd. W6 . . . . .6E **98**
Bowford Av. DA7: Bex 1E **126**
Bowhill Cl. SW9 . . . . .7A **102**
Bow Ho. N1 . . . . .1E **84**
        (off Wilmer Gdns.)
Bowie Cl. SW4 . . . . .7H **119**
Bowland Rd. IG8: Wfd G 6F **37**
  SW4 .4H **119**
Bowland Yd. SW1 . . . . .7F **11**
Bow La. EC4 . . . . .1D **14** (6C **84**)
  N12 . . . . .7F **31**
  NW4 .6G **153**
Bowlby Ho. SE4 . . . . .4K **121**
        (off Frendsbury Rd.)
Bowl Ct. EC2 . . . . .4H **9** (4E **84**)
Bowles Cl. N12 . . . . .7H **31**
Bowles Rd. SE1 . . . . .6G **103**
Bowley Cl. SE19 . . . . .6F **139**
Bowley Ho. SE16 . . . . .3G **103**
Bowley La. SE19 . . . . .5F **139**
Bowling Cl. SE10 . . . . .4G **105**
  TW8: Bford 7C **96**
        (off Durham Wharf Dr.)
The Bowling KT12: Walt T 7J **147**
Bowling Cl. UB10: Uxb 1B **74**
Bowling Grn. Cl. SW15 . . . . .7D **116**
Bowling Grn. Ct.
  HA9: Wemb 2F **61**
Bowling Grn. Ho. SW10 . . . . .7B **100**
        (off Riley St.)
Bowling Grn. La. EC1 . . . . . .3K **7** (4A **84**)
Bowling Grn. Pl. SE1 . . .6E **14** (2D **102**)
Bowling Grn. Row SE18 . . . . .3D **106**
Bowling Grn. St. SE11 . . . .7J **19** (6A **102**)
Bowling Grn. Wlk. N1 . . . . .1G **9** (3E **84**)
Bow Locks E3 . . . . .4E **86**
Bowls Cl. HA7: Stan 5G **27**
Bowman Av. E16 . . . . .7H **87**
Bowman Ho. N1 . . . . .1E **84**
        (off Nuttall St.)
Bowman M. SW18 . . . . .1H **135**
Bowman's Bldgs. NW1 . . . . .5C **4**
        (off Penfold Pl.)
Bowmans Cl. W13 . . . . .1B **96**
Bowmans Lea SE23 . . . . .7J **121**
Bowmans Mdw. SM6: W'gton 3F **167**
Bowman's M. E1 . . . . .6G **85**
  N7 . . . . .3J **65**
Bowman's Pl. N7 . . . . .3J **65**
Bowman Trad. Est. NW9 . . . . .3G **43**
Bowmead SE9 . . . . .2D **142**
Bowmore Wlk. NW1 . . . . .7H **65**
Bowness Cl. E8 . . . . .6F **67**
        (off Beechwood Rd.)
Bowness Cres. SW15 . . . . .5A **134**
Bowness Dr. TW4: Houn 4C **112**
Bowness Ho. SE15 . . . . .7J **103**
        (off Hillbeck Cl.)
Bowness Rd. DA7: Bex 2H **127**
  SE6 . . . . .7D **122**
Bowood Rd. EN3: Enf H 2E **24**
  SW11 . . . . .5E **118**

Bow River Village E3 . . . . .2E **86**
        (off Global App.)
Bow Rd. E3 . . . . .3B **86**
Bowrons Av. HA0: Wemb 7D **60**
Bowry Ho. E14 . . . . .5B **86**
        (off Wallwood St.)
Bowsley Ct. TW13: Felt 2J **129**
Bowspirit Apts. SE8 . . . . .7D **104**
Bowsprit Point E14 . . . . .3C **104**
        (off Westferry Rd.)
Bow St. E15 . . . . .5G **69**
  WC2 . . . . .1F **13** (6J **83**)
Bowstring Plaza E3 . . . . .3B **86**
        (off St Clements Av.)
Bow Triangle Bus. Cen. E3 . . . . . .4C **86**
        (not continuous)
Bowyer Cl. E6 . . . . .5D **88**
Bowyer Ho. N1 . . . . .1E **84**
        (off Whitmore Est.)
Bowyer Pl. SE5 . . . . .7C **102**
Bowyer Plaza E3 . . . . .3B **86**
        (off St Clements Av.)
Bowyers Ct. TW1: Isle 4B **114**
Bowyer St. SE5 . . . . .7C **102**
Boxall Rd. SE21 . . . . .6E **120**
Boxelder Cl. HA8: Edg 5D **28**
Boxgrove Rd. SE2 . . . . .3C **108**
Box La. IG11: Bark 2B **90**
Boxley Rd. SM4: Mord 4A **154**
Boxley St. E16 . . . . .1K **105**
Boxmoor Ho. E2 . . . . .1G **85**
  W11 .1F **99**
        (off Queensdale Cres.)
Boxmoor Rd. HA3: Kenton 4B **42**
Boxoll Rd. RM9: Dag 4F **73**
Box Park .2D **168**
Box Tree Ho. SE8 . . . . .6A **104**
Boxtree La. HA3: Hrw W 1G **41**
Boxtree Rd. HA3: Hrw W 7C **26**
Boxwood Cl. UB7: W Dray 2B **92**
Boxworth Cl. N12 . . . . .5G **31**
Boxworth Gro. N1 . . . . .1K **83**
Boyce Ho. SW16 . . . . .5G **137**
  W10 . . . . .3H **81**
        (off Bruckner St.)
Boyce Way E13 . . . . .4J **87**
Boycroft Av. NW9 . . . . .6J **43**
Boyd Av. UB1: S'hall 1D **94**
Boyd Bldg. E16 . . . . .7D **87**
        (off Frobisher Yd.)
Boyd Cl. KT2: King T 7G **133**
Boydell Ct. NW8 . . . . .7B **64**
        (not continuous)
Boyden Ho. E17 . . . . .3E **50**
Boyd Rd. SW19 . . . . .6B **136**
Boyd St. E1 . . . . .6G **85**
Boyd Way SE3 . . . . .4A **124**
Boyfield St. SE1 . . . . . . .7B **14** (2B **102**)
Boyland Rd. BR1: Broml 5H **141**
Boyle Av. HA7: Stan 6F **27**
Boyle Cl. UB10: Uxb 2B **74**
Boyle Farm Island
  KT7: T Ditt 6A **150**
Boyle Farm Rd. KT7: T Ditt 6A **150**
Boyle St. W1 . . . . .2A **12** (7G **83**)
Boyne Av. NW4 . . . . .4F **45**
Boyne Rd. RM10: Dag 3G **73**
  SE13 .3E **122**
Boyne Ter. M. W11 . . . . .1H **99**
Boyseland Ct. HA8: Edg 2D **28**
Boyson Rd. SE17 . . . . .6C **102**
        (not continuous)
Boyson Wlk. SE17 . . . . .6D **102**
Boyton Cl. E1 . . . . .4J **85**
  N8 . . . . .3J **47**
Boyton Ho. NW8 . . . . .2B **82**
        (off Wellington Rd.)
  N8 . . . . .3J **47**
Boyton Rd. N8 . . . . .3J **47**
Brabant Ct. EC3 . . . . .2G **15**
Brabant Rd. N22 . . . . .2K **47**
Brabazon Av. SM6: W'gton 7J **167**

Brabazon Ct. SW1 . . . .5C **18**
   (off Moreton St.)
Brabazon Rd. TW5: Hest 7A **94**
  UB5: N'olt 2E **76**
Brabazon St. E14 . . . .6D **86**
Brabner Ho. E2 . . . .1K **9**
   (off Wellington Row)
Brabourne Cl. SE19 . . . .5E **138**
Brabourne Cres. DA7: Bex 6F **109**
Brabourne Hgts. NW7 . . . .3F **29**
Brabourne Ri. BR3: Beck 5E **158**
Brabourn Gro. SE15 . . . .2J **121**
Brabrook Ct. SM6: W'gton 4F **167**
Brabstone Ho. UB6: G'frd 2K **77**
Bracer Ho. N1 . . . .2E **84**
   (off Whitmore Est.)
Bracewell Av. UB6: G'frd 5K **59**
Bracewell Rd. W10 . . . .5E **80**
Bracewood Gdns. CRO: C'don 3F **169**
Bracey M. N4 . . . .2J **65**
Bracey St. N4 . . . .2J **65**
The Bracken E4 . . . .2K **35**
Bracken Av. CRO: C'don 3D **170**
  SW12 . . . .6E **118**
Brackenbridge Dr. HA4: Ruis 3B **58**
Brackenbridge Ho. HA4: Ruis 4C **58**
   (off Brackenhill)
Brackenbury N4 . . . .1A **66**
   (off Osborne Rd.)
Brackenbury Gdns. W6 . . . .3D **98**
Brackenbury Rd. N2 . . . .3A **46**
  W6 . . . .3D **98**
Bracken Cl. E6 . . . .5D **88**
  TW2: Whitt 7E **112**
  TW16: Sun 6H **129**
Brackendale N21 . . . .2E **32**
Brackendale Cl. TW3: Houn 1F **113**
Brackendene DA2: Wilm 4K **145**
Bracken End TW7: Isle 5H **113**
Brackenfield Cl. E5 . . . .3H **67**
Bracken Gdns. SW13 . . . .2C **116**
Brackenhill HA4: Ruis 4C **58**
Bracken Hill Cl. BR1: Broml 1H **159**
Bracken Hill La. BR1: Broml 1H **159**
Bracken Ho. E3 . . . .5C **86**
   (off Devons Rd.)
Bracken Ind. Est. IG6: Ilf 1J **53**
Bracken M. E4 . . . .1K **35**
  RM7: Rom 6H **55**
Brackens BR3: Beck 7C **140**
The Brackens EN1: Enf 7K **23**
Brackenwood TW16: Sun 1J **147**
Brackenwood Lodge EN5: New Bar 4D **20**
   (off Prospect Rd.)
Brackley Av. SE15 . . . .3J **121**
Brackley Cl. SM6: W'gton 7J **167**
Brackley Cl. NW8 . . . .3B **4**
   (off Pollitt Dr.)
Brackley Rd. BR3: Beck 7B **140**
  W4 . . . .5A **98**
Brackley Sq. IG8: Wfd G 7G **37**
Brackley St. EC1 . . . .5D **8** (4C **84**)
Brackley Ter. W4 . . . .7C **28**
Bracklyn Ct. N1 . . . .2D **84**
   (not continuous)
Bracklyn St. N1 . . . .2D **84**
Bracknell Cl. N22 . . . .1A **48**
Bracknell Gdns. NW3 . . . .4K **63**
Bracknell Ga. NW3 . . . .5K **63**
Bracknell Way NW3 . . . .4K **63**
Bracondale Rd. SE2 . . . .4A **108**
Bradbeer Ho. E2 . . . .3J **85**
   (off Cornwall Av.)
Bradbourne Rd. DA5: Bexl 7G **127**
Bradbourne St. SW6 . . . .2J **117**
Bradbury Cl. UB2: S'hall 4D **94**
Bradbury M. N16 . . . .5E **66**
Bradbury St. N16 . . . .5E **66**
Bradby Ho. NW8 . . . .2C **4**
   (off Hamilton Ter.)
Bradby's HA1: Harr 1J **59**
   (off High St.)

Braddock Cl. TW7: Isle 2K **113**
Braddon Ct. EN5: Barn 3B **20**
Braddon Rd. TW9: Rich 3F **115**
Braddyll St. SE10 . . . .5G **105**
Bradenham Av. DA16: Well 4A **126**
Bradenham Cl. SE17 . . . .6D **102**
Bradenham Rd.
  HA3: Kenton 4B **42**
  UB4: Hayes 3G **75**
Braden St. W9 . . . .4K **81**
Bradfield Cl. NW1 . . . .7F **65**
   (off Hawley Rd.)
Bradfield Dr. IG11: Bark 5A **72**
Bradfield Ho. IG8: Wfd G 6K **37**
Bradfield Rd. E16 . . . .2J **105**
  HA4: Ruis 5C **58**
Bradford Cl. BR2: Broml 1D **172**
  N17 . . . .6A **34**
  SE26 . . . .4H **139**
Bradford Dr. KT19: Ewe 6B **164**
Bradford Ho. W14 . . . .3F **99**
   (off Spring Va. Ter.)
Bradford Rd. IG1: Ilf 1H **71**
  W3 . . . .2A **98**
Bradfords Cl. IG9: Buck H 4G **37**
Bradgate SE6 . . . .6D **122**
Brading Cres. E11 . . . .2K **69**
Brading Rd. CRO: C'don 6K **155**
  SW2 . . . .7K **119**
Brading Ter. W12 . . . .3C **98**
Bradiston Rd. W9 . . . .3H **81**
Bradley Cl. N7 . . . .6J **65**
Bradley Gdns. W13 . . . .6B **78**
Bradley Ho. E3 . . . .3D **86**
   (off Bromley High St.)
  IG8: Wfd G 7D **36**
  SE16 . . . .4J **103**
   (off Raymouth Rd.)
Bradley M. SW17 . . . .1D **136**
Bradley Rd. N22 . . . .2K **47**
  SE19 . . . .6C **138**
Bradley's Cl. N1 . . . .2A **84**
Bradley Stone Rd. E6 . . . .5D **88**
Bradman Ho. NW8 . . . .3A **82**
   (off Abercorn Pl.)
Bradman Row HA8: Edg 7D **28**
Bradmead SW8 . . . .7F **101**
Bradmore Ct. EN3: Enf H 3F **25**
   (off Enstone Rd.)
Bradmore Pk. Rd. W6 . . . .4D **98**
Bradshaw Cl. SW19 . . . .6J **135**
Bradshaw Cotts. E14 . . . .6A **86**
   (off Repton St.)
Bradshaw Dr. NW7 . . . .7A **30**
Bradshaw Waye UB8: Hil 5B **74**
Bradshaws Cl. SE25 . . . .3G **157**
Bradstock Ho. E9 . . . .7A **68**
Bradstock Rd. E9 . . . .6K **67**
  KT17: Ewe 5C **164**
Brad St. SE1 . . . .5K **13** (1A **102**)
Bradwell Av. RM10: Dag 2G **73**
Bradwell Cl. E18 . . . .4H **51**
Bradwell Ho. NW6 . . . .1K **81**
   (off Mortimer Cres.)
Bradwell M. N18 . . . .4B **34**
Bradwell Rd. IG9: Buck H 1H **37**
Bradwell St. E1 . . . .3K **85**
Brady Ct. RM8: Dag 1D **72**
Brady Dr. BR1: Broml 3E **160**
Brady Ho. SW8 . . . .1G **119**
   (off Corunna Rd.)
Bradymead E6 . . . .6E **88**
Brady St. E1 . . . .4H **85**
Braeburn Ct. BR6: Orp 2K **173**
   (off Blossom Dr.)
  EN4: E Barn 4G **21**
  RM13: Rain 2K **91**
   (off Broadis Way)
Brae Ct. KT2: King T 1G **151**
Braemar SW15 . . . .6F **117**
Braemar Av. CR2: S Croy 7C **168**
  CR7: Thor H 3A **156**
  DA7: Bex 4J **127**

Braemar Av. HA0: Wemb 7D **60**
  N22 . . . .1J **47**
  NW10 . . . .3K **61**
  SW18 . . . .2J **135**
  SW19 . . . .2J **135**
Braemar Cl. SE16 . . . .5H **103**
   (off Masters Dr.)
Braemar Ct. SE6 . . . .1H **141**
   (off Cumberland Pl.)
Braemar Gdns. BR4: W W'ck 1E **170**
  DA15: Sidc 3H **143**
  NW9 . . . .1K **43**
Braemar Ho. W9 . . . .3A **82**
   (off Maida Vale)
Braemar Mans. SW7 . . . .3K **99**
   (off Cornwall Gdns.)
Braemar Rd. E13 . . . .4H **87**
  KT4: Wor Pk 3D **164**
  N15 . . . .5E **48**
  TW8: Bford 6D **96**
Braeside BR3: Beck 5C **140**
Braeside Av. SW19 . . . .1G **153**
Braeside Cres. DA7: Bex 4J **127**
Braeside Rd. SW16 . . . .7G **137**
Braes St. N1 . . . .7B **66**
Braesyde Cl. DA17: Belv 4F **109**
Brafferton Rd. CRO: C'don 4C **168**
Braganza St. SE17 . . . .5B **102**
Bragg Rd. RM8: Dag 6B **72**
Braham Ct. E2 . . . .4H **85**
   (off Three Colts La.)
Braham Ho. SE11 . . . .6H **19** (5K **101**)
Braham St. E1 . . . .1K **15** (6F **85**)
Braid Av. W3 . . . .6A **80**
Braid Cl. TW13: Hanw 2D **130**
Braidwood Pas. EC1 . . . .5C **8**
   (off Aldersgate St.)
Braidwood Rd. SE6 . . . .1F **141**
Braidwood St. SE1 . . . .5G **15** (1E **102**)
Brailsford Cl. CR4: Mitc 7C **136**
Brailsford Rd. SW2 . . . .5A **120**
Brainton Av. TW14: Felt 7K **111**
Braintree Av. IG4: Ilf 4C **52**
Braintree Ho. E1 . . . .4J **85**
   (off Malcolm Rd.)
Braintree Rd. HA4: Ruis 4K **57**
  RM10: Dag 3G **73**
Braintree St. E2 . . . .3J **85**
Braithwaite Av. RM7: Rush G 7G **55**
Braithwaite Gdns. HA7: Stan 1C **42**
Braithwaite Ho. E15 . . . .6F **69**
   (off Forrester Way)
  EC1 . . . .3E **8**
   (off Bunhill Row)
Braithwaite Rd. EN3: Brim 3G **25**
Braithwaite St. E1 . . . .4J **9** (4F **85**)
Braithwaite Twr. W2 . . . .5B **4**
Bramah Grn. SW9 . . . .1A **120**
Bramah Ho. SW1 . . . .6J **17** (5F **101**)
Bramah Rd. SW9 . . . .1A **120**
Bramalea Cl. N6 . . . .6E **46**
Bramall Cl. E15 . . . .5H **69**
Bramber Ct. TW8: Bford 4E **96**
  W14 . . . .6H **99**
   (off Bramber Rd.)
Bramber Ho. KT2: King T 1E **150**
   (off Seven Kings Way)
Bramber Rd. N12 . . . .5H **31**
  W14 . . . .6H **99**
Brambleacres Cl. SM2: Sutt 7J **165**
Bramblebury Rd. SE18 . . . .5G **107**
Bramble Cl. BR3: Beck 5E **158**
  CRO: C'don 4C **170**
  HA7: Stan 7J **27**
  N15 . . . .4G **49**
  SE19 . . . .1D **156**
  TW17: Shep 3F **147**
Bramble Cft. DA8: Erith 4J **109**

Brambledown Cl.
  BR4: W W'ck 5G **159**
Brambledown Rd.
  CR2: Sande 7E **168**
  SM5: Cars 7E **166**
  SM6: W'gton 7E **166**
Bramble Gdns. W12 . . . .7B **80**
Bramble Ho. E3 . . . .5C **86**
   (off Devons Rd.)
Bramble La. TW12: Hamp 6D **130**
The Brambles SM1: Sutt 2B **166**
  SW19 . . . .5H **135**
   (off Woodside)
  UB7: W Dray 4A **92**
Brambles Cl. TW7: Isle 7B **96**
Brambles Farm Dr. UB10: Hil 3C **74**
Bramblewood Cl. SM5: Cars 1C **166**
Brambling Ct. SE8 . . . .6B **104**
   (off Abinger Gro.)
The Bramblings E4 . . . .4A **36**
Bramcote Av. CR4: Mitc 4D **154**
Bramcote Cl. CR4: Mitc 4D **154**
   (off Bramcote Av.)
Bramcote Gro. SE16 . . . .5J **103**
Bramcote Rd. SW15 . . . .4D **116**
Bramdean Cres. SE12 . . . .1J **141**
Bramdean Gdns. SE12 . . . .1J **141**
Bramerton NW6 . . . .7F **63**
   (off Willesden La.)
Bramerton Rd. BR3: Beck 3B **158**
Bramerton St. SW3 . . . .7C **16** (6C **100**)
Bramfield Ct. N4 . . . .2C **66**
   (off Queen's Dr.)
Bramfield Rd. SW11 . . . .6C **118**
Bramford Ct. N14 . . . .2C **32**
Bramford Rd. SW18 . . . .4A **118**
Bramham Gdns. KT9: Chess 4D **162**
  SW5 . . . .5K **99**
Bramhope La. SE7 . . . .6K **105**
Bramlands Cl. SW11 . . . .3C **118**
Bramley Av. TW17: Shep 3G **147**
Bramley Ban
  Local Nature Reserve 6J **169**
Bramley Cl. BR6: Farnb 1F **173**
  CR2: S Croy 5C **168**
  E17 . . . .2A **50**
  HA5: Eastc 3H **39**
  IG8: Wfd G 7F **37**
  N14 . . . .5A **22**
  NW7 . . . .3F **29**
  TW2: Whitt 6G **113**
  UB3: Hayes 7J **75**
Bramley Ct. BR6: Orp 2K **173**
   (off Blossom Dr.)
  CR4: Mitc 2B **154**
  DA16: Well 1B **126**
  E4 . . . .
   (off The Ridgeway)
  EN4: E Barn 4H **21**
  RM13: Rain 2K **91**
   (off Broadis Way)
  UB1: S'hall 7G **77**
   (off Haldane Rd.)
Bramley Cres. IG2: Ilf 6E **52**
  SW8 . . . .7H **101**
Bramley Hill CR2: S Croy 5B **168**
Bramley Ho. SW15 . . . .6B **116**
   (off Tunworth Cres.)
  TW4: Houn 4D **112**
  W10 . . . .6F **81**
Bramley Hyrst CR2: S Croy 5C **168**
Bramley Lodge HA0: Wemb 4D **60**
Bramley Pde. N14 . . . .4C **22**
Bramley Rd. N14 . . . .5K **21**
  SM1: Sutt 5A **166**
  SM2: Cheam 7F **165**
  W5 . . . .3C **96**
  W10 . . . .6F **81**
Bramley Sports Ground 5K **21**
Bramley Way BR4: W W'ck 2D **170**
  TW4: Houn 5D **112**
Brampton WC1 . . . .6G **7**
   (off Red Lion Sq.)

Brampton Cl. E5 . . . . .2H 67
Brampton Ct. NW4 . . . . .4D 44
   RM7: Rush G 6K 55
           (off Union Rd.)
Brampton Gro. HA3: Kenton 4A 42
   HA9: Wemb 1G 61
   NW4 . . . . .4D 44
Brampton Ho. SE16 . . . . .2J 103
        (off Albatross Way)
Brampton La. NW4 . . . . .4E 44
Brampton Pk. Rd. N22 . . . . .3A 48
Brampton Rd. CRO: C'don 7F 157
   DA7: Bex 3D 126
   E6 . . . . .3B 88
   N15 . . . . .5C 48
   NW9 .4G 43
   SE2 .6C 108
   UB10: Hil 2D 74
Bramshaw Ri. KT3: N Mald 6A 152
Bramshaw Rd. E9 . . . . .6K 67
Bramshill Gdns. NW5 . . . . .3F 65
Bramshill Rd. NW10 . . . . .2B 80
Bramshot Av. SE7 . . . . .6J 105
Bramshurst NW8 . . . . .1K 81
         (off Abbey Rd.)
Bramston Rd. NW10 . . . . .2C 80
   SW17 . . . . .3A 136
Bramwell Cl. TW16: Sun 2B 148
Bramwell Ho. SE1 . . . . .3C 102
   SW1 . . . . .6A 18
      (off Churchill Gdns.)
Bramwell M. N1 . . . . .1K 83
Bramwell Way E16 . . . . .1A 106
Brancaster Dr. NW7 . . . . .7H 29
Brancaster Ho. E1 . . . . .3K 85
        (off Moody St.)
Brancaster Rd. E12 . . . . .4D 70
   IG2: Ilf 6J 53
   SW16 . . . . .3J 137
Brancepeth Gdns. IG9: Buck H . . .2D 36
Branch Hill NW3 . . . . .3A 64
Branch Hill Ho. NW3 . . . . .3K 63
Branch Pl. N1 . . . . .1D 84
Branch Rd. E14 . . . . .7A 86
Branch St. SE15 . . . . .7E 102
Brancker Rd. HA3: Kenton 3D 42
Brancroft Way EN3: Brim 1F 25
Brand Av. UB10: Uxb 2A 74
Brand Cl. N4 . . . . .1B 66
Brandesbury Sq. IG8: Wfd G 7K 37
Brandlehow Rd. SW15 . . . . .4H 117
Brandon Cl. E16 . . . . .4H 87
Brandon Est. SE17 . . . . .5B 102
Brandon Ho. BR3: Beck 5D 140
     (off Beckenham Hill Rd.)
Brandon Mans. W14 . . . . .6G 99
     (off Queen's Club Gdns.)
Brandon M. EC2 . . . . .6E 8
   SE17 . . . . .4C 102
Brandon Rd. E17 . . . . .4E 50
   N7 . . . . .7J 65
   SM1: Sutt 4K 165
   UB2: S'hall 5D 94
Brandon St. SE17 . . . . .4C 102
       (not continuous)
Brandram M. SE13 . . . . .4G 123
      (off Brandram Rd.)
Brandram Rd. SE13 . . . . .3G 123
Brandrams Wharf SE16 . . . . .2J 103
Brandreth Ct. HA1: Harr 6K 41
Brandreth Rd. E6 . . . . .6D 88
   SW17 . . . . .2F 137
The Brandries SM6: Bedd 3H 167
Brands Ho. NW6 . . . . .1H 81
      (off Lincoln M.)
Brand St. SE10 . . . . .7E 104
Brandville Gdns. IG6: Ilf 4F 53
Brandville Rd. UB7: W Dray 2A 92
Brandy Way SM2: Sutt 7J 165
Brangbourne Rd. BR1: Broml 5E 140
Brangton Rd. SE11 . . . . . .6H 19 (5K 101)
Brangwyn Ct. W14 . . . . .3G 99
      (off Blythe Rd.)

Brangwyn Cres. SW19 . . . . .1A 154
Branksea St. SW6 . . . . .7G 99
Branksome Av. N18 . . . . .6A 34
Branksome Cl. TW11: Tedd 4H 131
Branksome Ho. SW8 . . . . .7K 101
      (off Meadow Rd.)
Branksome Rd. SW2 . . . . .5J 119
   SW19 . . . . .1J 153
Branksome Way HA3: Kenton 6F 43
   KT3: N Mald 1J 151
Branksone Ct. N2 . . . . .3A 46
Brannigan Way HA8: Edg 4K 27
Bransby Rd. KT9: Chess 6E 162
Branscombe NW1 . . . . .1G 83
      (off Plender St.)
Branscombe Ct. BR2: Broml 5H 159
Branscombe Gdns. N21 . . . . .7F 23
Branscombe St. SE13 . . . . .3D 122
Bransdale Cl. NW6 . . . . .1J 81
Bransgrove Rd. HA8: Edg 1F 43
Branston Cres. BR5: Pet V 1H 173
Branstone Rd. TW9: Kew 1F 115
Brants Wlk. W7 . . . . .4J 77
Brantwood Av. DA8: Erith 7J 109
   TW7: Isle 4A 114
Brantwood Cl. E17 . . . . .3D 50
Brantwood Gdns. EN2: Enf 4D 22
   IG4: Ilf 4C 52
Brantwood Ho. SE5 . . . . .7C 102
     (off Wyndam Est.)
Brantwood Rd. CR2: S Croy 7C 168
   DA7: Bex 2H 127
   N17 . . . . .6B 34
   SE24 . . . . .5C 120
Branxholme Ct. BR1: Broml 1H 159
Braque Bldg. SE1 . . . . .5C 14
      (off Union St.)
Brasenose Dr. SW13 . . . . .6E 98
Brasher Cl. UB6: G'frd 5H 59
Brassett Point E15 . . . . .1G 87
      (off Abbey Rd.)
Brassey Cl. TW14: Felt 1J 129
Brassey Ho. E14 . . . . .4D 104
      (off Cahir St.)
Brassey Rd. NW6 . . . . .6H 63
Brassey Sq. SW11 . . . . .3E 118
Brassie Av. W3 . . . . .6A 80
Bass Talley All. SE16 . . . . .2K 103
Brasted Cl. BR6: Orp 2K 173
   DA6: Bex 5D 126
   SE26 . . . . .4J 139
Brasted Lodge BR3: Beck 7C 140
Brathay NW1 . . . . .1B 6
      (off Ampthill Est.)
Brathway Rd. SW18 . . . . .7J 117
Bratley St. E1 . . . . .4G 85
Bratten Ct. CRO: C'don 6D 156
Braund Av. UB6: G'frd 4F 77
Braundton Av. DA15: Sidc 1K 143
Braunston Dr. UB4: Yead 4C 76
Braunston Ho. HA0: Wemb 1E 78
Bravington Cl. TW17: Shep 5B 146
Bravington Pl. W9 . . . . .4H 81
Bravington Rd. W9 . . . . .2H 81
Bravingtons Wlk. N1 . . . . .1F 7
      (off York Way)
Brawne Ho. SE17 . . . . .6B 102
     (off Brandon St.)
Braxfield Rd. SE4 . . . . .4A 122
Braxted Pk. SW16 . . . . .6K 137
Bray NW3 .7C 64
Brayards Rd. SE15 . . . . .2H 121
Brayards Rd. Est. SE15 . . . . .2H 121
      (off Caulfield Rd.)
Braybourne Dr. TW7: Isle 7K 95
Braybrooke Gdns. SE19 . . . . . . .7E 138
Braybrook St. W12 . . . . .5B 80
Brayburne Av. SW4 . . . . .2G 119
Bray Ct. E2 . . . . .3K 85
     (off Meath Cres.)
   SW16 . . . . .5J 137
Braycourt Av. KT12: Walt T 7K 147

Bray Cres. SE16 . . . . .2K 103
Braydon Rd. N16 . . . . .1G 67
Bray Dr. E16 . . . . .7H 87
Brayfield Ter. N1 . . . . .7A 66
Brayford Sq. E1 . . . . .6J 85
Bray Pas. E16 . . . . .7J 87
Bray Pl. SW3 . . . . .4E 16 (4D 100)
Bray Rd. NW7 . . . . .6A 30
Brays Gdns. SE6 . . . . .7D 122
   SE13 . . . . .6E 122
Brayton Gdns. EN2: Enf 4C 22
Braywood Rd. SE9 . . . . .4H 125
Brazier Cres. UB5: N'olt 4D 76
Brazil Cl. CRO: Bedd 7J 155
Breacher Ho. Apts. IG11: Bark . . .4A 90
Breach La. RM9: Dag 3G 91
Bread St. EC4 . . . . .1D 14 (6C 84)
      (not continuous)
Breakspear Crematorium 5E 38
Breakspear Ho. UB9: Hare 3A 38
Breakspear M. UB9: Hare 3A 38
Breakspear Rd. HA4: Ruis 7D 38
Breakspear Rd. Nth. UB9: Hare . . .3A 38
Breakspear Rd. Sth. UB9: Hare . . .3B 56
   UB10: Ick 3B 56
Breakspears Dr.
   BR5: St P 7A 144, 1K 161
Breakspears M. SE4 . . . . .2B 122
Breakspears Rd. SE4 . . . . .4B 122
      (not continuous)
Breakwell Ct. W10 . . . . .4G 81
     (off Wornington Rd.)
Bream Cl. N17 . . . . .4H 49
Bream Gdns. E6 . . . . .3E 88
Breamore Cl. SW15 . . . . .1C 134
Breamore Ct. IG3: Ilf 2A 72
Breamore Ho. SE15 . . . . .7G 103
      (off Friary Est.)
Breamore Rd. IG3: Ilf 2K 71
Bream's Bldgs. EC4 . . . . .7J 7 (6A 84)
Bream St. E3 . . . . .7C 68
Breamwater Gdns. TW10: Ham . . .3B 132
Brearley Cl. HA8: Edg 7D 28
   UB8: Uxb 6A 56
Breasley Cl. SW15 . . . . .4D 116
Breasy Pl. NW4 . . . . .4D 44
     (off Burroughs Gdns.)
Brechin Pl. SW7 . . . . .4A 100
Brecknock Rd. N7 . . . . .5H 65
   N19 .4G 65
Brecknock Rd. Est. N19 . . . . .4G 65
Brecon Cl. CR4: Mitc 3J 155
   KT4: Wor Pk 2E 164
Brecon Grn. NW9 . . . . .6A 44
Brecon Ho. E3 . . . . .2B 86
      (off Ordell Rd.)
   UB5: N'olt 3D 76
      (off Taywood Rd.)
   W2 . . . . .6A 82
      (off Hallfield Est.)
Brecon Lodge UB7: W Dray 2B 92
Brecon M. N7 . . . . .5H 65
Brecon Rd. EN3: Pond E 4D 24
   W6 . . . . .6G 99
Brede Cl. E6 . . . . .3E 88
Bredel Ho. E14 . . . . .5C 86
      (off St Paul's Way)
Brede M. E6 . . . . .3E 88
Bredgar SE13 . . . . .5D 122
Bredgar Rd. N19 . . . . .2H 65
Bredhurst Cl. SE20 . . . . .6J 139
Bredinghurst SE22 . . . . .7G 121
Bredin Ho. SW10 . . . . .7K 99
     (off Coleridge Gdns.)
Bredon Rd. CRO: C'don 7F 157
Bree Cl. NW9 . . . . .3J 43
Breer St. SW6 . . . . .3K 117
Breezers Ct. E1 . . . . .7G 85
      (off The Highway)
Breezer's Hill E1 . . . . .7G 85
Brember Rd. HA2: Harr 2G 59
Bremer M. E17 . . . . .4D 50

Bremner Rd. SW7 . . . . .1A 16 (3A 100)
Brenchley Cl. BR2: Broml 6H 159
   BR7: Chst 1E 160
Brenchley Gdns. SE23 . . . . .6J 121
Brenchley Rd. BR5: St P 2K 161
Brenda Rd. SW17 . . . . .2D 136
Brende Gdns. KT8: W Mole 4F 149
Brendon Av. NW10 . . . . .4A 62
Brendon Cl. UB3: Harl 7E 92
   UB3: S'hall 4F 95
Brendon Gdns. HA2: Harr 4F 59
   IG2: Ilf 5J 53
Brendon Gro. N2 . . . . .2A 46
Brendon Rd. RM8: Dag 1F 73
   SE9 .2H 143
Brendon St. W1 . . . . .7D 4 (6C 82)
Brendon Vs. N21 . . . . .1H 33
Brendon Way EN1: Enf 7K 23
Brenley Cl. CR4: Mitc 3E 154
Brenley Gdns. SE9 . . . . .4B 124
Brenley Ho. SE1 . . . . .6E 14
      (off Tennis St.)
Brennand Ct. N19 . . . . .3G 65
Brent Cl. DA5: Bexl 1E 144
Brentcot Cl. W13 . . . . .4B 78
Brent Ct. NW11 . . . . .7F 45
   W7 . . . . .7H 77
Brent Cres. NW10 . . . . .2F 79
BRENT CROSS 7E 44
Brent Cross Fly-Over NW4 . . . . . .7F 45
Brent Cross Gdns. NW4 . . . . .7F 45
BRENT CROSS INTERCHANGE . . .6E 44
Brent Cross Shop. Cen. 7E 44
Brentfield NW10 . . . . .7H 61
Brentfield Cl. NW10 . . . . .6K 61
Brentfield Gdns. NW2 . . . . .7F 45
Brentfield Ho. NW10 . . . . .7K 61
Brentfield Rd. NW10 . . . . .6K 61
BRENTFORD 6D 96
Brentford Bus. Cen. TW8: Bford . . .7C 96
Brentford Cl. UB4: Yead 4B 76
BRENTFORD END 7C 96
Brentford FC 6D 96
Brentford Fountain Leisure Cen. . . .5G 97
Brentford Ho. TW1: Twick 7B 114
Brent Grn. NW4 . . . . .5E 44
Brent Grn. Wlk. HA9: Wemb 3J 61
Brentham Club 3C 78
Brentham Way W5 . . . . .4D 78
Brent Ho. E9 . . . . .6J 67
     (off Brenthouse Rd.)
Brenthouse Rd. E9 . . . . .7J 67
Brenthurst Rd. NW10 . . . . .6B 62
Brent Lea TW8: Bford 7C 96
Brentmead Cl. W7 . . . . .7J 77
Brentmead Gdns. NW10 . . . . .2F 79
Brentmead Pl. NW11 . . . . .6F 45
Brent Mus. 6B 62
Brent New Ent. Cen. NW10 . . . . . .6B 62
Brenton Ct. E9 . . . . .5A 68
      (off Mabley St.)
Brenton St. E14 . . . . .6A 86
Brent Pk. Ind. Est. UB2: S'hall . . .3K 93
Brent Pk. Rd. NW4 . . . . .7D 44
   NW9 .7D 44
Brent Pl. EN5: Barn 5C 20
Brent Reservoir 1B 62
Brent Rd. CR2: Sels 7H 169
   E16 . . . . .6J 87
   SE18 . . . . .7F 107
   TW8: Bford 6C 96
   UB2: S'hall 3A 94
Brent Side TW8: Bford 6C 96
Brentside Cl. W13 . . . . .4A 78
Brentside Executive Cen.
   TW8: Bford 6D 96
Brent Sth. Shop. Pk. 1E 62
Brent St. NW4 . . . . .4E 44
Brent Ter. NW2 . . . . .1E 62
      (not continuous)
Brent Trad. Cen. NW10 . . . . .5A 62
Brentvale Av. HA0: Wemb 1F 79
   UB1: S'hall 1H 95

Brent Valley Golf Course 7J 77
Brent Vw. Rd. NW9 . . . . .6C 44
Brentwaters Bus. Pk.
   TW8: Bford 7C 96
Brent Way HA9: Wemb 6H 61
   N3 . . . . .6D 30
   TW8: Bford 7D 96
Brentwick Gdns. TW8: Bford 4E 96
Brentwood Cl. SE9 . . . . .1G 143
Brentwood Ho. SE18 . . . . .7B 106
   (off Portway Gdns.)
Brentwood Lodge NW4 . . . . .5F 45
   (off Holmdale Gdns.)
Brereton Rd. N17 . . . . .7A 34
Bressay Dr. NW7 . . . . .7H 29
Bressenden Pl. SW1 . . .1K 17 (3F 101)
Bressey Av. EN1: Enf 1B 24
Bressey Gro. E18 . . . . .2H 51
Bresslaw Ct. E3 . . . . .5B 86
   (off Wager St.)
Breton Highwalk EC2 . . . . .5D 8
   (off Golden La.)
Breton Ho. EC2 . . . . .5D 8
   SE1 . . . . .7J 15
   (off St Saviour's Est.)
Brett Cl. N16 . . . . .2E 66
   UB5: N'olt 3B 76
Brett Ct. N9 . . . . .2D 34
Brettell St. SE17 . . . . .5D 102
Brettenham Av. E17 . . . . .1C 50
Brettenham Rd. E17 . . . . .2C 50
   N18 . . . . .4B 34
Brett Gdns. RM9: Dag 7E 72
Brett Ho. Cl. SW15 . . . . .7F 117
Brettinghurst SE1 . . . . .5G 103
   (off Avondale Sq.)
Brett Pas. E8 . . . . .5H 67
Brett Rd. E8 . . . . .5H 67
Brewers Bldgs. EC1 . . . . .1A 8
   (off Rawstorne St.)
Brewers Ct. W2 . . . . .5A 82
Brewer's Grn. SW1 . . . . .1C 18
Brewer's Hall Gdn. EC2 . . . . .6D 8
   (off Aldermanbury Sq.)
Brewers La. E20 . . . . .5D 68
   TW9: Rich 5D 114
Brewer St. W1 . . . . .2B 12 (7G 83)
The Brewery EC2 . . . . . . .5E 8 (5C 84)
   RM1: Rom 5K 55
Brewery Cl. HA0: Wemb 5A 60
The Brewery Ind. Est. N1 . . . . .1D 8
   (off Wenlock Rd.)
Brewery La. TW1: Twick 7K 113
Brewery M. Cen. TW7: Isle 3A 114
Brewery Rd. BR2: Broml 1C 172
   N7 . . . . .7J 65
   SE18 . . . . .5H 107
Brewery Sq. EC1 . . . . .3B 8 (4B 84)
   SE1 . . . . .5J 15
Brewery Wlk. RM1: Rom 5K 55
Brewhouse La. E1 . . . . .1H 103
   SW15 .3G 117
Brewhouse Rd. SE18 . . . . .4D 106
Brewhouse Wlk. SE16 . . . . .1A 104
Brewhouse Yd. EC1 . . . . . .3A 8 (4B 84)
Brewin Ter. UB4: Yead 5A 76
   (off Larch Cres.)
Brewood Rd. RM8: Dag 6B 72
Brewster Gdns. W10 . . . . .5E 80
Brewster Ho. E14 . . . . .7B 86
   (off Three Colt St.)
   SE1 . . . . .4F 103
   (off Dunton Rd.)
Brewster Pl. KT1: King T 2J 151
Brewster Rd. E10 . . . . .1D 68
The Breyer Group Stadium 5D 68
   (shown as Leyton Orient FC)
Brian Rd. RM6: Chad H 5C 54
Brian Ho. SE1 . . . . .2J 19
Briants Cl. HA5: Pinn 2D 40
Briant St. SE14 . . . . .1K 121
Briar Av. SW16 . . . . .7K 137
Briarbank Rd. W13 . . . . .6A 78

Briar Cl. IG9: Buck H 2G 37
   N2 . . . . .3K 45
   N13 . . . . .3H 33
   TW7: Isle 5K 113
   TW12: Hamp 5D 130
Briar Ct. E3 . . . . .2C 86
   (off Morville St.)
   SM3: Cheam 4E 164
   SW15 .4D 116
Briar Cres. UB5: N'olt 6F 59
Briardale HA8: Edg 4E 28
Briardale Gdns. NW3 . . . . .3J 63
Briarfield Av. N3 . . . . .2K 45
   (not continuous)
Briarfield Cl. DA7: Bex 2G 127
Briar Gdns. BR2: Hayes 1H 171
Briaris Cl. N17 . . . . .7C 34
Briar La. BR4: Addtn 4D 170
Briar Rd. DA5: Bexl 3K 145
   HA3: Kenton 5C 42
   NW2 . . . . .4E 62
   SW16 .3J 155
   TW2: Twick 1J 131
   TW17: Shep 5B 146
The Briars TW19: Stanw M 7B 174
   WD23: B Hea 1D 26
Briarswood Way BR6: Chels 5K 173
Briar Wlk. HA8: Edg 7D 28
   SW15 .4D 116
   W10 . . . . .4G 81
Briar Way UB7: W Dray 2C 92
Briar Wood Cl. BR2: Broml 2C 172
Briarwood Cl. NW9 . . . . .6J 43
   TW13: Felt 4G 129
Briarwood Ct. KT4: Wor Pk 1C 164
   (off The Avenue)
Briarwood Dr. HA6: Nwood 2J 39
Briarwood Rd.
   KT17: Ewe 6C 164
   SW4 . . . . .5H 119
Briary Cl. NW3 . . . . .7C 64
Briary Ct. DA14: Sidc 5B 144
   E16 . . . . .6H 87
Briary Gdns. BR1: Broml 5K 141
Briary Gro. HA8: Edg 2H 43
Briary La. N9 . . . . .3A 34
Briary Lodge BR3: Beck 1E 158
Brickbarn Cl. SW10 . . . . .7A 100
   (off King's Barn)
Brick Ct. EC4 . . . . .1J 13 (6A 84)
Brickett Cl. HA4: Ruis 5E 38
Brick Farm Cl. TW9: Kew 1H 115
Brickfield Cl. E9 . . . . .6J 67
   TW8: Bford 7C 96
Brickfield Cotts. BR7: Chst 5E 142
   SE18 . . . . .6K 107
Brickfield Farm Gdns.
   BR6: Farnb 4G 173
Brickfield Ho. N1 . . . . .1E 84
   (off Hertford Rd.)
Brickfield La. UB3: Harl 6F 93
Brickfield Rd. CR4: Mitc 3C 154
   CR7: Thor H 1B 156
   E3 . . . . .4D 86
   SW4 . . . . .6H 119
   (off Parkfield Rd.)
   SW19 .4K 135
Brickfields HA2: Harr 2H 59
   (not continuous)
Brickfields Way UB7: W Dray 3B 92
Brick Kiln One SE13 . . . . .3E 122
   (off Station Rd.)
Brick Kiln Two SE13 . . . . .3E 122
   (off Station Rd.)
Brick La. E1 . . . . .3K 9 (4F 85)
   E2 . . . . .2K 9 (3F 85)
   EN1: Enf 2C 24
   EN3: Enf H 2C 24
   HA7: Stan 7J 27
   UB5: N'olt 3D 76
Brick Lane Mosque 5K 9
Brick Lane Music Hall 1B 106
BRICKLAYER'S ARMS 4D 102

Bricklayers Arms Distribution Cen.
   SE1 . . . . .4E 102
   (not continuous)
Bricklayers St. SE11 . . . . .4A 102
Brick St. W1 . . . . .5J 11 (1F 101)
Brickwall La. HA4: Ruis 1G 57
Brickwood Cl. SE26 . . . . .3H 139
Brickwood Rd.
   CR0: C'don 2E 168
Brideale Cl. SE15 . . . . .6F 103
Bride Ct. EC4 . . . . .1A 14
Bride La. EC4 . . . . .1A 14 (6B 84)
Bridel M. N1 . . . . .1B 84
   (off Colebrook Row)
Brides M. N7 . . . . .6K 65
Brides Pl. N1 . . . . .7E 66
Bridewain St. SE1 . . . . . . .7J 15 (3F 103)
Bridewell Pl. E1 . . . . .1H 103
   EC4 . . . . .1A 14 (6B 84)
Bridford M. W1 . . . . .5K 5 (5F 83)
The Bridge HA3: W'stone 4K 41
   SW11 .7F 101
Bridge App. NW1 . . . . .7E 64
Bridge Av. W6 . . . . .4E 98
   W7 . . . . .5H 77
Bridge Av. Mans. W6 . . . . .5E 98
   (off Bridge Av.)
The Bridge Bus. Cen. DA2: S'hall . . .2E 94
Bridge Cl. EN1: Enf 2C 24
   KT12: Walt T 7H 147
   TW11: Tedd 4K 131
   W10 . . . . .6F 81
Bridge Ct. E10 . . . . .1B 68
   E14 . . . . .7F 87
   (off Newport Av.)
   HA2: Harr 2G 59
   KT12: Walt T 7H 147
   (off Bridge St.)
Bridge Dr. N13 . . . . .4E 32
Bridge End E17 . . . . .1E 50
Bridge End Cl. KT2: King T 1G 151
Bridgefield Ho. W2 . . . . .6K 81
   (off Queensway)
Bridgefield Rd. SM1: Sutt 6J 165
Bridgefoot SE1 . . . . .6F 19 (5J 101)
   TW16: Sun 1H 147
Bridge Gdns. KT8: E Mos 4H 149
   N16 . . . . .4D 66
   TW15: Ashf 7E 128
Bridge Ga. N21 . . . . .7H 23
Bridgehill Cl. HA0: Wemb 1D 78
Bridge Ho. CR0: C'don 3C 168
   (off Surrey St.)
   E9 . . . . .7A 68
   (off Shepherds La.)
   NW3 . . . . .7E 64
   (off Adelaide Rd.)
   NW10 .2F 81
   (off Chamberlayne Rd.)
   SE4 . . . . .4B 122
   SM2: Sutt 6K 165
   (off Bridge Rd.)
   SW1 . . . . .5J 17
   (off Ebury Br.)
   UB7: W Dray 1A 92
Bridgehouse Ct. SE1 . . . . .7A 14
   (off Blackfriars Rd.)
Bridge Ho. Quay E14 . . . . .1E 104
Bridgeland Rd. E16 . . . . .7J 87
Bridgelands Cl. BR3: Beck 7B 140
Bridge La. NW11 . . . . .4G 45
   SW11 .1C 118
The Bridge Leisure Cen. 4B 140
Bridgeman Ho. E9 . . . . .7J 67
   (off Frampton Pk. Rd.)
   W14 . . . . .4H 99
   (off Radnor Ter.)
Bridgeman Rd. N1 . . . . .7K 65
   TW11: Tedd 6A 132
Bridgeman St. NW8 . . . . .2C 82
Bridge Mdws. SE14 . . . . .6K 103
Bridge M. NW10 . . . . .6A 62

Bridgemount M. N4 . . . . .7K 47
BRIDGEN 7E 126
Bridgend Rd. SW18 . . . . .4A 118
Bridgenhall Rd. EN1: Enf 1A 24
Bridgen Ho. E1 . . . . .6H 85
   (off Nelson St.)
Bridgen Rd. DA5: Bexl 7E 126
Bridge Pde. N21 . . . . .7H 23
   (off Ridge Av.)
Bridgepark SW18 . . . . .5H 117
Bridge Pk. Community Leisure Cen.
   . . . . .7H 61
Bridge Pl. CR0: C'don 1D 168
   SW1 . . . . .3K 17 (4F 101)
Bridgepoint Lofts E7 . . . . .7A 70
Bridgepoint Pl. N6 . . . . .1G 65
   (off Hornsey La.)
Bridgeport Pl. E1 . . . . .1G 103
Bridge Rd. BR3: Beck 7B 140
   DA7: Bex 2E 126
   E6 . . . . .7D 70
   E11 . . . . .6F 51
   E15 . . . . .7F 69
   E17 . . . . .7B 50
   HA9: Wemb 3G 61
   KT8: E Mos 4H 149
   KT9: Chess 5E 162
   N9 . . . . .3B 34
   N22 . . . . .1J 47
   NW10 .6A 62
   SM2: Sutt 6K 165
   SM6: W'gton 5F 167
   TW1: Twick 6B 114
   TW3: Houn, Isle 3H 113
   TW7: Isle 3H 113
   UB2: S'hall 2D 94
Bridge Rd. Dpt. E15 . . . . .1G 87
Bridge Row CR0: C'don 1D 168
Bridges Av. KT8: E Mos 6H 149
Bridges Ct. Rd. SW11 . . . . .3B 118
Bridges Ho. SE5 . . . . .7D 102
   (off Elmington Est.)
Bridgeside Lodge N1 . . . . .2C 84
   (off Wharf Rd.)
Bridges La. CR0: Bedd 4J 167
Bridges Pl. SW6 . . . . .1H 117
Bridges Rd. HA7: Stan 5E 26
   SW19 .6K 135
Bridges Rd. M. SW19 . . . . .6K 135
Bridge St. HA5: Pinn 3C 40
   KT12: Walt T 7G 147
   SW1 . . . . .7E 12 (2J 101)
   TW9: Rich 5D 114
   W4 . . . . .4K 97
Bridges Wharf SW11 . . . . .3B 118
Bridge Ter. E15 . . . . .7F 69
Bridge Theatre 5J 15
   (off Tower Bri. Rd.)
Bridgetown Cl. SE19 . . . . .5E 138
Bridge Vw. W6 . . . . .5E 98
Bridge Vw. Ct. SE1 . . . . .3E 102
   (off Grange Rd.)
Bridge Wlk. SE8 . . . . .6D 104
   (off Copperas St.)
Bridgewalk Hgts. SE1 . . . . .6F 15
   (off Weston St.)
Bridgewater Cl. BR7: Chst 3J 161
Bridgewater Gdns.
   HA8: Edg 2F 43
Bridgewater Highwalk EC2 . . . . .5C 8
Bridgewater House E14 . . . . .6D 87
   (off Lookout Lane)
Bridgewater Rd. E15 . . . . .1E 86
   HA0: Wemb 6C 60
Bridgewater Sq. EC2 . . . . .5C 8 (5C 84)
Bridgewater St. EC2 . . . . . .5C 8 (5C 84)
Bridge Way N11 . . . . .3B 32
   NW11 .5H 45
   TW2: Whitt 7G 113
   UB10: Ick 5D 56
Bridgeway HA0: Wemb 7E 60
   IG11: Bark 7K 71
Bridgeway St. NW1 . . . . .2G 83

Bridge Wharf E2	.2K 85
N1	.2K 83
	(off Calshot St.)
Bridge Wharf Rd. TW7: Isle	.3B 114
Bridgewood Cl. SE20	.7H 139
Bridgewood Rd. KT4: Wor Pk	.4C 164
SW16	.7H 137
Bridge Yd. SE1	.4F 15 (1D 102)
Bridgford St. SW18	.3A 136
Bridgman Rd. W4	.3J 97
Bridgnorth Ho. SE15	.6G 103
	(off Friary Est.)
Bridgwater Ho. W2	.6A 82
	(off Hallfield Est.)
Bridgwater Rd. HA4: Ruis	.4J 57
Bridle Cl. KT1: King T	.4D 150
KT19: Ewe	.5K 163
TW16: Sun	.3J 147
Bridle La. TW1: Twick	.6B 114
W1	.2B 12 (7G 83)
Bridle M. E1	.6G 85
	(off Boulevard Walkway)
EN5: Barn	.4C 20
Bridle Path CRO: Bedd	.3J 167
The Bridle Path IG8: Wfd G	.7B 36
Bridlepath Way TW14: Bedf	.7G 111
Bridle Rd. CRO: C'don	.3C 170
CR2: Sande	.7G 169
HA5: Eastc	.6K 39
KT10: Clay	.6B 162
Bridle Way BR6: Farnb	.4G 173
CRO: C'don	.5C 170
The Bridle Way SM6: W'gton	.4G 167
Bridlington Rd. N9	.7C 24
Bridport SE17	.5D 102
	(off Cadiz St.)
Bridport Av. RM7: Rom	.6H 55
Bridport Ho. N1	.1D 84
	(off Bridport Pl.)
N18	.5A 34
	(off College Gdns.)
Bridport Pl. N1	.1D 84
	(not continuous)
Bridport Rd. CR7: Thor H	.3A 156
N18	.5K 33
UB6: G'frd	.1F 77
Bridport Ter. SW8	.1H 119
	(off Deeley Rd.)
Bridstow Pl. W2	.6J 81
Brief St. SE5	.1B 120
Brierfield NW1	.1G 83
	(off Arlington Rd.)
Brierley CRO: New Ad	.6D 170
	(not continuous)
Brierley Av. N9	.1D 34
Brierley Cl. SE25	.4G 157
Brierley Ct. W7	.7J 77
Brierley Rd. E11	.4F 69
SW12	.2G 137
Brierly Gdns. E2	.2J 85
Brigade Cl. HA2: Harr	.2H 59
Brigade St. SE3	.2H 123
	(off Tranquil V.)
Brigadier Av. EN2: Enf	.1H 23
Brigadier Hill EN2: Enf	.1H 23
Brigadier Ho. NW9	.2B 44
	(off Heritage Av.)
Briggeford Cl. E5	.2G 67
Briggs Cl. CR4: Mitc	.1F 155
Briggs Ho. E2	.1K 9
	(off Chambord St.)
Bright Cl. DA17: Belv	.4D 108
Brightfield Rd. SE12	.5G 123
Bright Ho. KT1: King T	.3D 150
	(off Kingston Hall Rd.)
Brightling Rd. SE4	.6B 122
Brightlingsea Pl. E14	.7B 86
Brightman Rd. SW18	.1B 136
Brighton Av. E17	.5B 50
Brighton Bldgs. SE1	.3E 102
	(off Tower Bri. Rd.)
Brighton Cl. UB10: Hil	.7D 56
Brighton Dr. UB5: N'olt	.6E 58

Brighton Gro. SE14	.1A 122
Brighton Ho. SE5	.1D 120
	(off Camberwell Grn.)
Brighton Rd. CR2: S Croy	.5C 168
E6	.3E 88
	(not continuous)
KT6: Surb	.6C 150
N2	.2A 46
N16	.4E 66
SM2: Sutt	.7K 165
Brighton Ter. SW9	.4K 119
The Brightside EN3: Enf H	.1E 24
Brightside Rd. SE13	.6F 123
Bright St. E14	.5D 86
Brightwell Cl. CRO: C'don	.1A 168
Brightwell Ct. N7	.5K 65
	(off Mackenzie Rd.)
Brightwell Cres. SW17	.5D 136
Brightwen Gro.	
HA7: Stan	.2F 27
Brig M. SE8	.6C 104
Brigstock Ho. SE5	.2C 120
Brigstock Rd.	
CR7: Thor H	.5A 156
DA17: Belv	.4H 109
Brill Pl. NW1	.1D 6 (2H 83)
Brim Hill N2	.4A 46
Brimpsfield Cl. SE2	.3B 108
	(not continuous)
BRIMSDOWN	.2G 25
Brimsdown Av. EN3: Enf H	.2F 25
Brimsdown Ho. E3	.4D 86
Brimsdown Ind. Est. EN3: Brim	.1G 25
	(Lockfield Av.)
EN3: Brim	.2G 25
	(Stockingswater La.)
Brimstone Ho. E15	.7G 69
	(off Victoria St.)
Brindle Ga. DA15: Sidc	.1J 143
Brindlewick Gdns.	
BR3: Beck	.6C 140
Brindley Cl. DA7: Bex	.3H 127
HA0: Wemb	.1D 78
Brindley Ct. HA7: Stan	.7J 27
Brindley Ho. W2	.5J 81
	(off Alfred Rd.)
Brindley St. SE14	.1B 122
Brindley Way BR1: Broml	.5J 141
UB1: S'hall	.7F 77
Brindwood Rd. E4	.3G 35
Brine Ho. E3	.2A 86
	(off St Stephen's Rd.)
Brinkburn Cl. HA8: Edg	.3H 43
SE2	.4A 108
Brinkburn Gdns. HA8: Edg	.3G 43
Brinkley KT1: King T	.2G 151
Brinkley Rd. KT4: Wor Pk	.2D 164
Brinklow Cres. SE18	.7F 107
Brinklow Ho. W2	.5K 81
	(off Torquay St.)
Brinkworth Rd. IG5: Ilf	.3C 52
Brinkworth Way E9	.6B 68
Brinsdale Rd. NW4	.3F 45
Brinsley Ho. E1	.6J 85
	(off Tarling St.)
Brinsley Rd. HA3: Hrw W	.2H 41
Brinsworth Cl. TW2: Twick	.1H 131
Brinsworth Ho. TW2: Twick	.2H 131
Brinton Wlk. SE1	.5A 14
Brion Pl. E14	.5E 86
Brisbane Av. SW19	.1K 153
Brisbane Ho. W12	.7D 80
	(off White City Est.)
Brisbane Rd. E10	.2D 68
IG1: Ilf	.7F 53
W13	.2A 96
Brisbane St. SE5	.7D 102
Briscoe Cl. E11	.3H 69
Briscoe M. TW2: Twick	.2H 131
Briscoe Rd. SW19	.6B 136
Briset Rd. SE9	.3B 124
Briset St. EC1	.5A 8 (4B 84)
Briset Way N7	.2K 65

Bristol Av. NW9	.1B 44
Bristol Cl. SM6: W'gton	.7J 167
TW4: Houn	.7E 112
TW19: Stanw	.6A 110
Bristol Ct. TW19: Stanw	.6A 110
Bristol Gdns. SW15	.7E 116
W9	.4K 81
Bristol Ho. IG11: Bark	.7A 72
	(off Margaret Bondfield Av.)
SE11	.2J 19
SW1	.5G 17
	(off Lwr. Sloane St.)
WC1	.5F 7
	(off Southampton Row)
Bristol M. W9	.4K 81
Bristol Pk. Rd. E17	.4A 50
Bristol Rd. E7	.6A 70
SM4: Mord	.5A 154
UB6: G'frd	.1F 77
Bristol Wlk. NW6	.2J 81
	(off Alpha Pl.)
Briston Gro. N8	.6J 47
Briston M. NW7	.7H 29
Bristow Ct. E8	.1H 85
	(off Triangle Rd.)
Bristowe Cl. SW2	.6A 120
Bristow Rd. CRO: Bedd	.4J 167
DA7: Bex	.1E 126
SE19	.5E 138
TW3: Houn	.3G 113
Britannia Bldg. N1	.1E 8
	(off Ebenezer St.)
Britannia Bus. Cen. NW2	.4F 63
Britannia Cl. SW4	.4H 119
UB5: N'olt	.3B 76
Britannia Ct. KT2: King T	.1D 150
	(off Skerne Wlk.)
Britannia Ga. E16	.1J 105
BRITANNIA JUNC.	.1F 83
Britannia La. TW2: Whitt	.7G 113
Britannia Leisure Cen.	.1D 84
Britannia Rd. E14	.4C 104
IG1: Ilf	.3F 71
KT5: Surb	.7F 151
N12	.3F 31
SW6	.7K 99
Britannia Row N1	.1B 84
Britannia St. WC1	.1G 7 (3K 83)
Britannia Wlk. N1	.1E 8 (2D 84)
	(not continuous)
Britannia Way NW10	.4H 79
SW6	.7K 99
	(off Britannia Rd.)
TW19: Stanw	.7A 110
Britannic Highwalk EC2	.6E 8
	(off Moor La.)
British Gro. W4	.5B 98
British Gro. Nth. W4	.5B 98
British Gro. Pas. W4	.5B 98
British Gro. Sth. W4	.5B 98
British Legion Rd. E4	.2C 36
British Library	.1D 6 (3H 83)
British Mus.	.6D 6 (5J 83)
British St. E3	.3B 86
British Telecom Cen.	.7C 8
British Wharf Ind. Est. SE14	.5K 103
Britley Ho. E14	.6B 86
	(off Copenhagen Pl.)
Brittain Ct. SE9	.1C 142
Brittain Rd. RM8: Dag	.3E 72
Brittany Ho. EN2: Enf	.1H 23
Brittany Point SE11	.4J 19
Britten Cl. NW11	.1K 63
Britten Ct. E15	.2F 87
Brittenden Cl. BR6: Chels	.6K 173
Brittenden Pde. BR6: Chels	.6K 173
Britten Dr. UB1: S'hall	.6E 76
Britten Ho. SW3	.5D 16
	(off Britten St.)
Britten St. SW3	.6C 16 (5C 100)
Britten Theatre	.1A 16
	(off Prince Consort Rd.)

Brittidge Rd. NW10	.7A 62
Britton Cl. SE6	.7F 123
Britton St. EC1	.4A 8 (4B 84)
Brixham Cres. HA4: Ruis	.1J 57
Brixham Gdns. IG3: Ilf	.5J 71
Brixham Rd. DA16: Well	.1D 126
Brixham St. E16	.1E 106
BRIXTON	.4K 119
Brixton Hill SW2	.7J 119
Brixton Hill Ct. SW2	.5K 119
Brixton Hill Pl. SW2	.7J 119
Brixton Oval SW2	.4A 120
Brixton Recreation Cen.	.3A 120
	(off Brixton Sta. Rd.)
Brixton Rd. SE11	.7J 19 (6A 102)
SW9	.4A 120
Brixton Sta. Rd. SW9	.3A 120
Brixton Water La. SW2	.5K 119
Broadacre Cl. UB10: Ick	.3D 56
Broadash Cl. SW16	.3A 138
Broadbent Cl. N6	.1F 65
Broadbent St. W1	.2J 11 (7F 83)
Broadberry Cl. N18	.6C 34
Broadbridge Cl. SE3	.7J 105
Broad Comn. Est. N16	.1G 67
	(off Osbaldeston Rd.)
Broadcoombe CR2: Sels	.7J 169
Broadcroft Av. HA7: Stan	.2D 42
Broadcroft Rd. BR5: Pet W	.7H 161
Broadeaves Cl. CR2: S Croy	.5E 168
Broadfield NW6	.6K 63
Broadfield Cl. CRO: Wadd	.2K 167
NW2	.3E 62
Broadfield Ct. HA2: Harr	.1F 41
	(off Broadfields)
WD23: B Hea	.2D 26
Broadfield La. NW1	.7J 65
Broadfield Pde. HA8: Edg	.3C 28
	(off Glengall Rd.)
Broadfield Rd. SE6	.7G 123
Broadfields HA2: Harr	.2F 41
KT8: E Mos	.6J 149
Broadfields Av. HA8: Edg	.4C 28
N21	.6F 23
Broadfields Hgts. HA8: Edg	.4C 28
Broadfield Sq. EN1: Enf	.2C 24
Broadfields Way NW10	.5B 62
Broadfield Way IG9: Buck H	.3F 37
Broadford Ho. E1	.4A 86
	(off Commodore St.)
Broadgate EC2	.6F 9
Broadgate Circle	.6G 9 (5E 84)
Broadgate Circ. EC2	.5G 9 (5E 84)
Broadgate Plaza EC2	.5E 84
Broadgate Rd. E16	.6B 88
Broadgates Av. EN4: Had W	.1E 20
Broadgates Ct. SE11	.6K 19
	(off Cleaver St.)
Broadgates Rd. SW18	.1B 136
Broadgate Twr. EC2	.4H 9 (4E 84)
BROAD GREEN	.7B 156
Broad Grn. Av. CRO: C'don	.7B 156
Broadhead Apts. E3	.3B 86
	(off St Clements Av.)
Broadhead Strand NW9	.1B 44
Broadheath Dr. BR7: Chst	.5D 142
Broadhinton Rd. SW4	.3F 119
Broadhurst Av. HA8: Edg	.4C 28
IG3: Ilf	.4K 71
Broadhurst Cl. NW6	.6A 64
TW10: Rich	.5F 115
Broadhurst Gdns. HA4: Ruis	.2A 58
NW6	.6K 63
Broadis Way RM13: Rain	.2K 91
Broadlands E17	.3A 50
TW13: Hanw	.3E 130
Broadlands Av. EN3: Enf H	.3C 24
SW16	.2J 137
TW17: Shep	.6E 146
Broadlands Cl. EN3: Enf H	.3D 24
N6	.7E 46
SW16	.2J 137

Broadlands Ct. *TW9:* Kew 7G **97**
   (off Kew Gdns. Rd.)
Broadlands Lodge N6 . . . . .7D **46**
Broadlands Rd. BR1: Broml 4K **141**
   N6 . . . . .7D **46**
Broadlands Way KT3: N Mald 6B **152**
Broad La. EC2 . . . . .5G **9** (5E **84**)
   N8 . . . . .5K **47**
   N15 . . . . .4F **49**
   N17 . . . . .4G **49**
   TW12: Hamp 7D **130**
Broad Lawn SE9 . . . . .2E **142**
Broadlawns Ct. HA3: Hrw W 1K **41**
Broadley St. NW8 . . . . .5B **4** (5B **82**)
Broadley Ter. NW1 . . . . . .4D **4** (4C **82**)
Broadmayne SE17 . . . . .5D **102**
   (off Portland St.)
Broadmead SE6 . . . . .3C **140**
   W14 . . . . .5G **99**
Broadmead Av. KT4: Wor Pk 7C **152**
   (off Navestock Cres.)
Broadmead Cl. HA5: Hat E 1C **40**
   TW12: Hamp 6E **130**
Broadmead Ct. IG8: Wfd G 6D **36**
Broadmead Rd. IG8: Wfd G 6D **36**
   (not continuous)
   UB4: Yead 4C **76**
   UB5: N'olt 4C **76**
Broad Oak IG8: Wfd G 5E **36**
   TW16: Sun 6H **129**
Broad Oak Cl. E4 . . . . .5H **35**
Broadoak Ct. SW9 . . . . .3A **120**
   (off Gresham Rd.)
Broadoak Ho. NW6 . . . . .1K **81**
   (off Mortimer Cres.)
Broadoak Rd. DA8: Erith 7K **109**
Broadoaks KT6: Surb 2H **163**
Broadoaks Way BR2: Broml 5H **159**
Broad Pas. W3 . . . . .1B **98**
Broad Sanctuary SW1 . . . .7D **12** (2H **101**)
Broadstone NW1 . . . . .7H **65**
   (off Agar Gro.)
Broadstone Ho. SW8 . . . . .7K **101**
   (off Dorset Rd.)
Broadstone Pl. W1 . . . . .6G **5** (5E **82**)
Broad St. RM10: Dag 7G **73**
   TW11: Tedd 6K **131**
Broad St. Av. EC2 . . . . .6G **9** (5E **84**)
Broad St. Mkt.
   RM10: Dag 7G **73**
Broad St. Pl. EC2 . . . . .6F **9**
Broadview NW9 . . . . .6G **43**
Broadview Pl. E5 . . . . .1J **67**
Broadview Rd. SW16 . . . . .7H **137**
Broad Wlk. N21 . . . . .2E **32**
   NW1 . . . . .1H **5** (1E **82**)
   SE3 . . . . .2A **124**
   TW5: Hest 1B **112**
   TW9: Kew 7F **97**
   W1 . . . . .3F **11** (7D **82**)
Broadwalk E18 . . . . .3H **51**
   HA2: Harr 5E **40**
The Broad Wlk. KT8: E Mos 4K **149**
   W8 . . . . .1K **99**
The Broadwalk HA6: Nwood 2E **38**
Broadwalk Ct. W8 . . . . .1J **99**
   (off Palace Gdns. Ter.)
Broadwalk Ho. EC2 . . . . .5G **9**
   SW7 . . . . .2A **100**
   (off Hyde Pk. Ga.)
Broad Wlk. La. NW11 . . . . .7H **45**
Broadwalk Shop. Cen.
   Edgware 6C **28**
Broadwall SE1 . . . . .4K **13** (1A **102**)
Broadwater Farm Est. N17 . . . . .2D **48**
Broadwater Gdns. BR6: Farnb 4F **173**
Broadwater Rd. N17 . . . . .1E **48**
   SE28 . . . . .3H **107**
   SW17 . . . . .4C **136**
Broadway DA6: Bex 4E **126**
   (not continuous)
   DA7: Bex 4H **127**

Broadway E15 . . . . .7F **69**
   IG11: Bark 1G **89**
   SW1 . . . . .7C **12** (3H **101**)
   W7 . . . . .1J **95**
   W13 . . . . .1A **96**
The Broadway CR0: Bedd 4J **167**
   E4 . . . . .6A **36**
   E13 . . . . .2K **87**
   HA2: Harr 2H **59**
   HA3: W'stone 2J **41**
   HA6: Nwood 2J **39**
   HA7: Stan 7F **27**
   HA9: Wemb 3E **60**
   IG8: Wfd G 6E **36**
   KT7: T Ditt 7J **149**
   N8 . . . . .6J **47**
   N9 . . . . .3B **34**
   N11 . . . . .5J **31**
   N14 . . . . .1C **32**
   (off The Bourne)
   N22 . . . . .2A **48**
   NW7 . . . . .5F **29**
   RM8: Dag 1F **73**
   SM1: Sutt 5A **166**
   SM3: Cheam 6G **165**
   SW13 . . . . .2A **116**
   SW19 . . . . .6H **135**
   UB1: S'hall 7B **76**
   UB6: G'frd 4G **77**
   W3 . . . . .2G **97**
   (off Ridgeway Dr.)
   W5 . . . . .7D **78**
   (off Hammersmith B'way.)
Broadway Arc. W6 . . . . .4E **98**
   (off Hammersmith B'way.)
Broadway Av. CR0: C'don 5D **156**
   TW1: Twick 6B **114**
The Broadway Cen. 4E **98**
Broadway Chambers W6 . . . . .4E **98**
   (off Hammersmith B'way.)
Broadway Cl. IG8: Wfd G 6E **36**
Broadway Ct. BR3: Beck 3E **158**
   SW19 . . . . .6J **135**
Broadway Gdns. CR4: Mitc 4C **154**
   IG8: Wfd G 6E **36**
Broadway Ho. BR1: Broml 5F **141**
   (off Bromley Rd.)
   BR1: Broml 3J **159**
   (High St.)
   E8 . . . . .1H **85**
   (off Ada St.)
Broadway Mans. SW6 . . . . .7J **99**
   (off Fulham Rd.)
Broadway Mkt. E8 . . . . .1H **85**
   (not continuous)
   IG6: Ilf 1H **53**
   (not continuous)
   SW17 . . . . .4D **136**
Broadway Mkt. M. E8 . . . . .1G **85**
Broadway M. E5 . . . . .7F **49**
   N13 . . . . .5E **32**
   N21 . . . . .1G **33**
Broadway Pde. E4 . . . . .6K **35**
   (off The Broadway)
   HA2: Harr 5F **41**
   N8 . . . . .6J **47**
   UB3: Hayes 1J **93**
Broadway Pl. SW19 . . . . .6H **135**
Broadway Retail Pk. 4F **63**
Broadway Shop. Cen.
   Bexleyheath 4G **127**
Broadway Shop. Mall
   St James's Park 1C **18** (3H **101**)
Broadway Sq. DA6: Bex 4G **127**
The Broadway Theatre
   Barking 1G **89**
   Catford 7D **122**
Broadway Wlk. E14 . . . . .2C **104**
Broadwell Ct. TW5: Hest 1B **112**
   (off Springwell Rd.)
Broadwell Pde. NW6 . . . . .6K **63**
   (off Broadhurst Gdns.)
Broadwick St. W1 . . . . .2B **12** (7G **83**)
Broadwood Av. HA4: Ruis 6F **39**

Broadwood Ter. W8 . . . . .4H **99**
Broad Yd. EC1 . . . . .4A **8** (4B **84**)
Brocade Cl. SM6: W'gton 2F **167**
Brocas Cl. NW3 . . . . .7C **64**
Brockbridge Ho. SW15 . . . . .6B **116**
Brockdene Dr. BR2: Kes 4B **172**
Brockdish Av. IG11: Bark 5K **71**
Brockhurst KT8: W Mole 5D **148**
Brockenhurst Av. KT4: Wor Pk . . .1A **164**
Brockenhurst Gdns. IG1: Ilf 5G **71**
   NW7 . . . . .7F **29**
Brockenhurst M. N18 . . . . .4B **34**
Brockenhurst Rd. CR0: C'don . . .7H **157**
Brockenhurst Way SW16 . . . . . . .2H **155**
Brocket Ho. SW8 . . . . .2H **119**
Brockham Cl. SW19 . . . . .5H **135**
Brockham Ct. CR2: S Croy 5C **168**
Brockham Cres. CR0: New Ad . . .7F **171**
Brockham Dr. IG2: Ilf 6F **53**
   SW2 . . . . .7K **119**
Brockham Ho. NW1 . . . . .1G **83**
   (off Bayham Pl.)
   SW2 . . . . .7K **119**
   (off Brockham Dr.)
Brockham St. SE1 . . . . . .7D **14** (3C **102**)
Brockhurst Cl. HA7: Stan 6E **26**
Brockill Cres. SE4 . . . . .4A **122**
Brocklebank Ho. E16 . . . . .1E **106**
   (off Glenister St.)
Brocklebank Retail Park 4K **105**
Brocklebank Rd. SE7 . . . . .4K **105**
   SW18 . . . . .7A **118**
Brocklehurst St. SE14 . . . . .7K **103**
Brocklesby Rd. SE25 . . . . .4H **157**
BROCKLEY 4K **121**
Brockley Av. HA7: Stan 3K **27**
Brockley Cl. HA7: Stan 4K **27**
Brockley Cres. RM5: Col R 1J **55**
Brockley Cross SE4 . . . . .3A **122**
Brockley Cross Bus. Cen. SE4 . . .3A **122**
Brockley Footpath SE15 . . . . .3J **121**
   (not continuous)
Brockley Gdns. SE4 . . . . .2B **122**
Brockley Gro. SE4 . . . . .5A **122**
Brockley Hall Rd. SE4 . . . . .5A **122**
Brockley Hill HA7: Stan 1H **27**
Brockley Jack Theatre 5A **122**
Brockley M. SE4 . . . . .5A **122**
Brockley Pk. SE23 . . . . .7A **122**
Brockley Ri. SE23 . . . . .1A **140**
Brockley Rd. SE4 . . . . .3B **122**
Brockleyside HA7: Stan 4K **27**
Brockley Vw. SE23 . . . . .7A **122**
Brockley Way SE4 . . . . .5K **121**
Brockman Ri. BR1: Broml 4F **141**
Brockmer Ho. E1 . . . . .7H **85**
   (off Crowder St.)
Brock Pl. E3 . . . . .4D **86**
Brock Rd. E13 . . . . .5K **87**
Brocks Dr. SM3: Cheam 3G **165**
Brockshot Cl. TW8: Bford 5D **96**
Brock St. NW1 . . . . .3A **6**
   (off Triton Sq.)
   SE15 . . . . .3J **121**
Brockway Cl. E11 . . . . .2G **69**
Brockweir E2 . . . . .2J **85**
   (off Cyprus St.)
Brockwell Av. BR3: Beck 5D **158**
Brockwell Cl.
   BR5: St M Cry 5K **161**
Brockwell Ho. SE11 . . . . .7H **19**
   (off Vauxhall St.)
Brockwell Pk. 6B **120**
Brockwell Pk. Gdns. SE24 . . . . . . .7A **120**
Brockwell Pk. Lido 6B **120**
Brockwell Pk. Row SW2 . . . . .7A **120**
Brockwell Pas. SE24 . . . . .6B **120**
Brodia Rd. N16 . . . . .3E **66**
Brodick Ho. E3 . . . . .2B **86**
   (off Saxon Rd.)
Brodie Ho. SE1 . . . . .5F **103**
   (off Cooper's Rd.)

Brodie Rd. E4 . . . . .1K **35**
   EN2: Enf 1H **23**
Brodie St. SE1 . . . . .5F **103**
Brodlove La. E1 . . . . .7K **85**
Brodrick Gro. SE2 . . . . .4B **108**
Brodrick Rd. SW17 . . . . .2C **136**
Brody Ho. E1 . . . . .6J **9**
   (off Strype St.)
Brograve Gdns. BR3: Beck 2D **158**
Broken Wharf EC4 . . . . . .2C **14** (7C **84**)
Brokesley St. E3 . . . . .3B **86**
Broke Wlk. E8 . . . . .1F **85**
Bromar Rd. SE5 . . . . .3E **120**
Bromefield HA7: Stan 1C **42**
Bromehead St. E1 . . . . .6J **85**
Bromell's Rd. SW4 . . . . .4G **119**
Brome Rd. SE9 . . . . .3D **124**
Bromfelde Rd. SW4 . . . . .3H **119**
Bromfelde Wlk. SW4 . . . . .2H **119**
Bromfield St. SE16 . . . . .3G **103**
   (off Ben Smith Way)
Bromfield St. N1 . . . . .1A **84**
Bromhall Rd. RM8: Dag 6B **72**
   RM9: Dag 6B **72**
Bromhead Rd. E1 . . . . .6J **85**
   (off Jubilee St.)
Bromhedge SE9 . . . . .3D **142**
Bromholm Rd. SE2 . . . . .3B **108**
Bromleigh Ct. SE23 . . . . .2G **139**
Bromleigh Ho. SE1 . . . . .7J **15**
   (off St Saviour's Est.)
BROMLEY
   BR1 . . . . .2J **159**
   E3 . . . . .3D **86**
Bromley Av. BR1: Broml 7G **141**
Bromley Coll. BR1: Broml 1J **159**
BROMLEY COMMON 7C **160**
Bromley Comn. BR2: Broml 4A **160**
Bromley Cres. BR2: Broml 3H **159**
   HA4: Ruis 4H **57**
Bromley FC 5K **159**
Bromley Gdns. BR2: Broml 3H **159**
Bromley Gro. BR2: Broml 2F **159**
Bromley Hall Rd. E14 . . . . .5E **86**
Bromley High St. E3 . . . . .3D **86**
Bromley Hill BR1: Broml 6G **141**
Bromley Ho. BR1: Broml 1J **159**
   (off North St.)
Bromley Ind. Cen. BR1: Broml . . .3B **160**
Bromley La. BR7: Chst 7G **143**
Bromley Little Theatre 1J **159**
BROMLEY PARK 1G **159**
Bromley Pk. BR1: Broml 1H **159**
Bromley Pl. W1 . . . . .5A **6** (5G **83**)
Bromley Rd. BR1: Broml 1D **140**
   BR2: Broml 2D **158**
   BR3: Beck 1D **158**
   BR7: Chst 1F **161**
   E10 . . . . .6D **50**
   E17 . . . . .3C **50**
   N17 . . . . .1F **49**
   N18 . . . . .3J **33**
   SE6 . . . . .1D **140**
Bromley St. E1 . . . . .5K **85**
Bromley Tennis Cen. 3H **173**
BROMPTON 2D **16** (3C **100**)
Brompton Arc. SW3 . . . . .7E **10**
Brompton Cemetery 6K **99**
Brompton Cl. SE20 . . . . .2G **157**
   TW4: Houn 5D **112**
Brompton Cotts. SW10 . . . . .6A **100**
   (off Hollywood Rd.)
Brompton Ct. BR1: Broml 1J **159**
   (off Tweedy Rd.)
Brompton Gro. N2 . . . . .4C **46**
Brompton M. N12 . . . . .6F **31**
Brompton Oratory 2C **16** (3C **100**)
Brompton Pk. Cres. SW6 . . . . .6K **99**
Brompton Pl. SW3 . . . . . .1D **16** (3G **100**)
Brompton Rd. SW1 . . . . . .3C **16** (4C **100**)
   SW3 . . . . .3C **16** (4C **100**)
   SW7 . . . . .4C **100**

Brompton Sq. SW3 . . . . . . .1C **16** (3C **100**)
Brompton Ter. SE18 . . . . .1D **124**
Brompton Vs. SW6 . . . . .6J **99**
(off Lillie Rd.)
Bromwich Av. N6 . . . . .2E **64**
Bromyard Av. W3 . . . . .7A **80**
Bromyard Ho. SE15 . . . . .7H **103**
(off Commercial Way)
Bromyward Ho. W3 . . . . .1B **98**
Bron Ct. NW6 . . . . .1J **81**
BRONDESBURY 7H **63**
Brondesbury Ct. NW2 . . . . .6F **63**
Brondesbury M. NW6 . . . . .7J **63**
BRONDESBURY PARK 1E **80**
Brondesbury Pk. NW2 . . . . .6E **62**
NW6 .6E **62**
Brondesbury Pk. Mans. NW6 . . . . .5E **42**
(off Salusbury Rd.)
Brondesbury Rd. NW6 . . . . .2H **81**
Brondesbury Vs. NW6 . . . . .2H **81**
Bronhill Ter. N17 . . . . .1G **49**
Bronsart Rd. SW6 . . . . .7G **99**
Bronson Rd. SW20 . . . . .2F **153**
Bronte Cl. DA8: Erith 7H **109**
E7 . . . . .4J **69**
IG2: Ilf 4E **52**
Bronte Ct. W3 . . . . .2G **97**
W14 . . . . .3F **99**
(off Girdler's Rd.)
Bronte Ho. N16 . . . . .5E **66**
SW4 .7G **119**
SW17 . . . . .3B **136**
(off Grosvenor Way)
Bronti Cl. SE17 . . . . .5C **102**
Bronwen Ct. NW8 . . . . .2A **4**
(off Grove End Rd.)
Bronze Age Way DA8: Erith 2H **109**
DA17: Belv 2H **109**
Bronze St. SE8 . . . . .7C **104**
Bronze Wlk. W12 . . . . .7F **81**
Brook Av. HA8: Edg 6C **28**
HA9: Wemb 2F **61**
RM10: Dag 7H **73**
Brookbank Av. W7 . . . . .5H **77**
Brookbank Rd. SE13 . . . . .3C **122**
Brook Cl. HA4: Ruis 7G **39**
NW7 .7B **30**
SW17 . . . . .2E **136**
SW20 . . . . .3D **152**
TW19: Stanw 7B **110**
W3 . . . . .1G **97**
Brook Ct. BR3: Beck 1B **158**
E11 . . . . .3G **69**
E17 . . . . .3A **50**
EC4 . . . . .2E **14**
(off Laurence Pountney La.)
HA8: Edg 5C **28**
IG11: Bark 1H **89**
(Sebastian Ct.)
IG11: Bark 2G **89**
(Spring Pl.)
SE12 .3A **142**
Brook Cres. E4 . . . . .4H **35**
N9 . . . . .4C **34**
Brookdale N11 . . . . .4B **32**
Brookdale Rd. DA5: Bexl 6E **126**
E17 . . . . .3C **50**
SE6 . . . . .7D **122**
(Catford Bway.)
SE6 . . . . .6D **122**
(Medusa Rd.)
Brookdales NW11 . . . . .4G **45**
Brookdene Rd. SE18 . . . . .4J **107**
Brook Dr. HA1: Harr 4G **41**
HA4: Ruis 7G **39**
SE11 . . . . .2K **19** (3A **102**)
Brooke Av. HA2: Harr 3G **59**
Brooke Cl. WD23: Bush 1B **26**
Brooke Ct. W10 . . . . .2G **81**
(off Kilburn La.)
Brooke Ho. SE14 . . . . .1A **122**
WD23: Bush 1B **26**
Brookehowse Rd. SE6 . . . . .2C **140**

Brookend Rd. DA15: Sidc 1J **143**
Brooke Rd. E5 . . . . .3G **67**
E17 . . . . .4E **50**
N16 . . . . .3F **67**
Brooke's Ct. EC1 . . . . . .6J **7** (5A **84**)
Brooke's Mkt. EC1 . . . . .5K **7**
Brooke St. EC1 . . . . . . .6J **7** (5A **84**)
Brooke Way WD23: Bush 1B **26**
Brookfield N6 . . . . .3E **64**
Brookfield Av. E17 . . . . .4E **50**
NW7 .6J **29**
SM1: Sutt 4B **166**
W5 . . . . .4D **78**
Brookfield Cl. NW7 . . . . .6J **29**
Brookfield Ct. N12 . . . . .4E **30**
UB6: G'frd 3G **77**
Brookfield Cres. HA3: Kenton 5E **42**
NW7 .6J **29**
Brookfield Gdns. KT10: Clay 6A **162**
Brookfield Pk. NW5 . . . . .3F **65**
Brookfield Path IG8: Wfd G 6B **36**
Brookfield Rd. E9 . . . . .6A **68**
N9 . . . . .3B **34**
W4 . . . . .2K **97**
Brookfields EN3: Pond E 4E **24**
Brookfields Av. CR4: Mitc 5C **154**
Brook Gdns. E4 . . . . .4J **35**
KT2: King T 1J **151**
SW13 . . . . .3B **116**
Brook Ga. W1 . . . . .3F **11** (7D **82**)
BROOK GREEN 4F **99**
Brook Grn. W6 . . . . .3F **99**
Brook Grn. Flats W14 . . . . .3F **99**
(off Dunsany Rd.)
Brookhill Cl. EN4: E Barn 5H **21**
SE18 .5F **107**
Brookhill Rd. EN4: E Barn 5H **21**
SE18 .6F **107**
Brook Ho. E1 . . . . .7G **85**
(off Fletcher St.)
W6 . . . . .4E **98**
(off Shepherd's Bush Rd.)
Brookhouse Gdns. E4 . . . . .4B **36**
Brook Ho's. NW1 . . . . .2G **83**
(off Cranleigh St.)
Brook Ind. Est. UB4: Yead 1B **94**
Brooking Cl. RM8: Dag 3C **72**
Brooking Rd. E7 . . . . .5J **69**
Brookland Cl. NW11 . . . . .4J **45**
Brookland Gth. NW11 . . . . .4J **45**
Brookland Hill NW11 . . . . .4K **45**
Brookland Ri. NW11 . . . . .4J **45**
The Brooklands TW7: Isle 1H **113**
Brooklands App. RM1: Rom 4K **55**
Brooklands Av. DA15: Sidc 2H **143**
SW19 . . . . .2K **135**
Brooklands Cl. RM7: Rom 4K **55**
TW16: Sun 1G **147**
Brooklands Ct. CR4: Mitc 2B **154**
KT1: King T 4D **150**
(off Surbiton Rd.)
N21 . . . . .5J **23**
NW6 .7H **63**
Brooklands Dr. UB6: G'frd 1C **78**
Brooklands La. RM7: Rom 4K **55**
(not continuous)
Brooklands Pk. SE3 . . . . .3J **123**
Brooklands Pas. SW8 . . . . .1H **119**
Brooklands Pl. TW12: Hamp H 5F **131**
Brooklands Rd. KT7: T Ditt 1A **162**
RM7: Rom 4K **55**
Brooklands Ter. TW16: Sun 4J **147**
Brook La. BR1: Broml 6J **141**
DA5: Bexl, Bex 6D **126**
SE3 .2K **123**
Brook La. Bus. Cen. TW8: Bford . . .5D **96**
Brook La. Nth. TW8: Bford 5D **96**
(not continuous)
Brooklea Cl. NW9 . . . . .1A **44**
Brook Lodge NW11 . . . . .5F **45**
(off Nth. Circular Rd.)
RM7: Rom 4K **55**
(off Brooklands Rd.)

Brooklyn SE20 . . . . .7G **139**
Brooklyn Av. SE25 . . . . .4H **157**
Brooklyn Cl. SM5: Cars 2C **166**
Brooklyn Ct. W12 . . . . .1E **98**
(off Frithville Gdns.)
Brooklyn Gro. SE25 . . . . .4H **157**
Brooklyn Rd. BR2: Broml 5B **160**
SE25 . . . . .4H **157**
Brookman Ho. E3 . . . . .2B **86**
Brook Va. DA8: Erith 1H **127**
(off Mostyn Gro.)
Brookmarsh Ind. Est. SE10 . . . . . .7D **104**
Brook Mead KT19: Ewe 6A **164**
Brookmead CR0: Bedd 6G **155**
Brookmead Av.
BR1: Broml 5D **160**
Brookmead Ind. Est.
CR0: Bedd 6G **155**
Brook Mdw. N12 . . . . .3E **30**
Brook Mdw. Cl. IG8: Wfd G 6B **36**
Brookmead Rd.
CR0: C'don 6G **155**
Brook M. IG7: Chig 3K **37**
N13 . . . . .5F **33**
Brook M. Nth. W2 . . . . .2A **10** (7A **82**)
Brookmill Rd. SE8 . . . . .1C **122**
Brook Pde. IG7: Chig 3K **37**
Brook Pk. Cl. N21 . . . . .5G **23**
Brook Pl. EN5: Barn 5D **20**
Brook Retail Pk.
South Ruislip 5B **58**
Brook Ri. IG7: Chig 3K **37**
Brook Rd. CR7: Thor H 4C **156**
IG2: Ilf 6J **53**
IG9: Buck H, Wfd G 2D **36**
KT6: Surb 2E **162**
N8 . . . . .4J **47**
N22 . . . . .3K **47**
NW2 .2B **62**
TW1: Twick 6A **114**
Brook Rd. Sth. TW8: Bford 6D **96**
Brooks Apts. E3 . . . . .5C **86**
(off Geoff Cade Way)
Brooks Av. E6 . . . . .4D **88**
Brooksbank Ho. E9 . . . . .6J **67**
(off Retreat Pl.)
Brooksbank St. E9 . . . . .6J **67**
Brooksby Ho. N1 . . . . .7A **66**
(off Liverpool Rd.)
Brooksby M. N1 . . . . .7A **66**
Brooksby St. N1 . . . . .7A **66**
Brooksby's Wlk. E9 . . . . .5K **67**
Brooks Cl. SE9 . . . . .2E **142**
Brooks Ct. SW11 . . . . .7G **101**
Brookscroft E17 . . . . .3D **50**
Brookscroft Rd. E17 . . . . .1D **50**
(not continuous)
Brooks Farm 7D **50**
Brookshill HA3: Hrw W 5C **26**
Brookshill Av. HA3: Hrw W 5C **26**
Brookshill Dr. HA3: Hrw W 5C **26**
Brookshill Ga. HA3: Hrw W 5C **26**
Brookside BR6: Orp 7K **161**
EN4: E Barn 6H **21**
N21 . . . . .6E **22**
SM5: Cars 5E **166**
UB10: Uxb 7B **56**
Brookside Cl. EN5: Barn 6B **20**
HA2: Harr 4C **58**
HA3: Kenton 5D **42**
TW13: Felt 3J **129**
Brookside Cres. KT4: Wor Pk 1C **164**
Brookside Rd. N9 . . . . .4C **34**
(not continuous)
N19 . . . . .2G **65**
NW11 . . . . .6G **45**
UB4: Yead 7A **76**
Brookside Sth. EN4: E Barn 7K **21**
Brookside Wlk. N3 . . . . .3G **45**
Brookside Way CR0: C'don 6K **157**
Brooks La. W4 . . . . .6G **97**
Brooks Lodge N1 . . . . .2E **84**
Brook's M. W1 . . . . .2J **11** (7F **83**)
Brook Sq. SE18 . . . . .1C **124**

Brooks Rd. E13 . . . . .1J **87**
W4 . . . . .5G **97**
Brook St. DA8: Erith 5H **109**
DA17: Belv, Erith 5H **109**
KT1: King T 2E **150**
N17 . . . . .2F **49**
W1 . . . . .2H **11** (7F **83**)
W2 . . . . .2B **10** (7B **82**)
Brooksville Av. NW6 . . . . .1G **81**
Brook Valley Gdns. EN5: Barn 5C **20**
Brookview Ct. EN1: Enf 5K **23**
Brookview Rd. SW16 . . . . .5G **137**
Brookville Rd. SW6 . . . . .7H **99**
Brook Wlk. HA8: Edg 6E **28**
N2 . . . . .1B **46**
Brook Way IG7: Chig 3K **37**
Brookway SE3 . . . . .3J **123**
Brookwell Ho. E17 . . . . .4K **49**
Brookwood Av. SW13 . . . . .2B **116**
Brookwood Cl. BR2: Broml 4H **159**
Brookwood Ho. SE1 . . . . .7B **14**
(off Webber St.)
Brookwood Rd. SW18 . . . . .1H **135**
TW3: Houn 2F **113**
Broom Cl. BR2: Broml 6C **160**
TW11: Tedd 7D **132**
Broomcroft Av. UB5: N'olt 3A **76**
Broome Rd. TW12: Hamp 7D **130**
Broome Way SE5 . . . . .7D **102**
Broomfield E17 . . . . .7B **50**
NW1 .7E **64**
(off Ferdinand St.)
TW16: Sun 1J **147**
Broomfield Av. N13 . . . . .5E **32**
Broomfield Ct. N2 . . . . .4C **46**
(off Stanmore Hill)
SE17 . . . . .4E **102**
(off Massinger St.)
Broomfield La. N13 . . . . .4D **32**
Broomfield Pl. W13 . . . . .1B **96**
Broomfield Rd. BR3: Beck 3A **158**
DA6: Bex 5G **127**
KT5: Surb 1F **163**
N13 . . . . .5D **32**
RM6: Chad H 7D **54**
TW9: Kew 1F **115**
TW11: Tedd 6C **132**
W13 .1B **96**
Broomfield St. E14 . . . . .5C **86**
Broom Gdns. CR0: C'don 3C **170**
Broomgrove Gdns. HA8: Edg 1G **43**
Broomgrove Rd. SW9 . . . . .2K **119**
Broomhall Rd. CR2: Sande 7D **168**
BROOM HILL 7K **161**
Broomhill Cl. IG8: Wfd G 6D **36**
Broomhill Ri. DA6: Bex 5G **127**
Broomhill Rd. BR6: Orp 7K **161**
IG3: Ilf 2A **72**
IG8: Wfd G 6D **36**
(not continuous)
SW18 . . . . .5J **117**
Broomhill Wlk. IG8: Wfd G 6C **36**
Broomhouse La. SW6 . . . . .2J **117**
Broomhouse Rd. SW6 . . . . .2J **117**
Broomloan La. SM1: Sutt 3J **165**
Broom Lock TW11: Tedd 6C **132**
Broom Mead DA6: Bex 6G **127**
Broom Pk. TW11: Tedd 7D **132**
Broom Rd. CR0: C'don 3C **170**
TW11: Tedd 5C **132**
Broomsleigh Bus. Pk. SE26 . . . . . .5B **140**
Broomsleigh St. NW6 . . . . .5H **63**
Broom Water TW11: Tedd 6C **132**
Broom Water W. TW11: Tedd 5C **132**
Broomwood Cl.
CR0: C'don 5K **157**
DA5: Bexl 2K **145**
Broomwood Rd. SW11 . . . . .6D **118**
Broseley Gro. SE26 . . . . .5A **140**
Brosse Way BR2: Broml 6C **160**
Broster Gdns. SE25 . . . . .3F **157**

Brotherstone Wlk.
TW9: Kew 1H 115
Brouard Ct. BR1: Broml 3J 159
Brougham Rd. E8 . . . . .1G 85
W3 .6J 79
Brougham St. SW11 . . . . .2D 118
Brough Cl. KT2: King T 5D 132
SW8 . . . . .7J 101
Broughton Av. N3 . . . . .3G 45
TW10: Ham 3B 132
Broughton Ct. W13 . . . . .7B 78
Broughton Dr. SW9 . . . . .4A 120
Broughton Gdns. N6 . . . . .6G 47
Broughton Pl. E17 . . . . .1B 50
Broughton Rd. BR6: Orp 2H 173
CR7: Thor H 6A 156
SW6 . . . . .2K 117
W13 . . . . .7B 78
Broughton Rd. App. SW6 . . . . . .2K 117
Broughton St. SW8 . . . . .2E 118
Broughton St. Ind. Est. SW11 . . .2E 118
Brouncker Rd. W3 . . . . .2J 97
Browells La. TW13: Felt 2K 129
(not continuous)
Brown Bear Ct. TW13: Hanw 4B 130
Brown Cl. SM6: W'gton 7J 167
Browne Ho. SE8 . . . . .7C 104
(off Deptford Chu. St.)
Brownell Pl. W7 . . . . .2K 95
Brownfield Area E14 . . . . .6D 86
Brownfield St. E14 . . . . .6D 86
Browngraves Rd.
UB3: Harl 7E 92
Brown Hart Gdns. W1 . . . .2H 11 (7E 82)
Brownhill Rd. SE6 . . . . .7D 122
Browning Apts. E3 . . . . .4B 86
(off Hamlets Way)
Browning Av. KT4: Wor Pk 1D 164
SM1: Sutt 4C 166
W7 .6K 77
Browning Cl. DA16: Well 1J 125
E17 .4E 50
RM5: Col R 1F 55
TW12: Hamp 4D 130
W9 . . . . .4A 4 (4A 82)
Browning Ct. W14 . . . . .6H 99
(off Turneville Rd.)
Browning Ho. N16 . . . . .4E 66
(off Shakspeare Wlk.)
SE14 . . . . .1A 122
(off Loring Rd.)
W12 .6E 80
(off Wood La.)
Browning M. W1 . . . . .6H 5 (5F 83)
Browning Rd. E11 . . . . .7H 51
E12 . . . . .5D 70
EN2: Enf 1J 23
Browning St. SE17 . . . . .5C 102
Browning Way TW5: Hest 1B 112
Brownlea Gdns. IG3: Ilf 2A 72
Brownlow Cl. EN4: E Barn 5G 21
Brownlow Ct. N2 . . . . .5A 46
N11 . . . . .6D 32
(off Brownlow Rd.)
Brownlow Ho. SE16 . . . . .2G 103
(off George Row)
Brownlow M. WC1 . . . . . . .4H 7 (4K 83)
Brownlow Rd. CR0: C'don 4E 168
E7 . . . . .4J 69
E8 . . . . .1F 85
N3 . . . . .7E 30
N11 . . . . .6D 32
NW10 . . . . .7A 62
W13 . . . . .1A 96
Brownlow St. WC1 . . . . . . .6H 7 (5K 83)
Browngrigg Rd.
TW15: Ashf 4C 128
Brown's Bldgs. EC3 . . .1H 15 (6E 84)
Brownsea Wlk. NW7 . . . . .6A 30
Browns La. NW5 . . . . .5F 65
Brownspring Dr. SE9 . . . . .4F 143
Brown's Rd. KT5: Surb 7F 151
Browns Rd. E17 . . . . .3C 50

Brown St. W1 . . . . .7E 4 (6D 82)
Brownswell Rd. N2 . . . . .2B 46
BROWNSWOOD PARK 2B 66
Brownswood Rd. N4 . . . . .3B 66
Broxash Rd. SW11 . . . . .6E 118
Broxbourne Av. E18 . . . . .4K 51
Broxbourne Ho. E3 . . . . .4D 86
(off Empson St.)
Broxbourne Rd. BR6: Orp 1K 173
E7 . . . . .3J 69
Broxholme Cl. SE25 . . . . .4D 156
Broxholme Ho. SW6 . . . . .1K 117
(off Harwood Rd.)
Broxholm Rd. SE27 . . . . .3A 138
Broxted Rd. SE6 . . . . .2B 140
Broxwood Way NW8 . . . . .1C 82
Bruce Av. TW17: Shep 6E 146
Bruce Castle Ct. N17 . . . . .1F 49
(off Lordship La.)
Bruce Castle Mus. 1E 48
Bruce Castle Rd. N17 . . . . .1F 48
Bruce Cl. DA16: Well 1B 126
W10 . . . . .5F 81
Bruce Ct. DA15: Sidc 4K 143
Bruce Gdns. N20 . . . . .3J 31
Bruce Gro. N17 . . . . .1E 48
Bruce Hall M. SW17 . . . . .4E 136
Bruce Ho. W10 . . . . .5F 81
Bruce Rd. CR4: Mitc 7E 136
E3 .3D 86
EN5: Barn 3B 20
HA3: W'stone 2J 41
NW10 . . . . .7K 61
SE25 . . . . .4D 156
Bruckner St. W10 . . . . .3G 81
Brudenell Rd. SW17 . . . . .3D 136
Bruffs Mdw. UB5: N'olt 6C 58
Bruford Ct. SE8 . . . . .6C 104
Bruges Pl. NW1 . . . . .7G 65
(off Randolph St.)
Brumfield Rd. KT19: Ewe 5J 163
Brummel Cl. DA7: Bex 3J 127
Brumwell Av. SE18 . . . . .5E 106
Brune Ho. E1 . . . . .6J 9
(off Bell La.)
Brunei Gallery 5D 6 (5H 83)
Brunel Bldg. W2 . . . . .6A 4
Brunel Cl. SE19 . . . . .6F 139
TW5: Cran 7K 93
UB5: N'olt 3D 76
Brunel Ct. HA8: Edg 4A 28
SE16 . . . . .2J 103
(off Canon Beck Rd.)
SW13 . . . . .2B 116
(off Westfields Av.)
Brunel Est. W2 . . . . .5J 81
Brunel Ho. BR2: Broml 6C 160
(off Wells Vw. Dr.)
E14 . . . . .5D 104
(off Ship Yd.)
RM8: Dag 4A 72
SW10 . . . . .7B 100
(off Cheyne Rd.)
Brunel M. W10 . . . . .3F 81
Brunel Pl. UB1: S'hall 6F 77
Brunel Rd. E17 . . . . .6A 50
IG8: Wfd G 5J 37
SE16 . . . . .2J 103
W3 .5A 80
Brunel Science Pk. UB8: Cowl . . .3A 74
Brunel St. E16 . . . . .6H 87
Brunel University
Indoor Athletics Cen. 3A 74
Sports Pk. 4B 74
Brunel University
Uxbridge Campus 3A 74
Brunel Wlk. N15 . . . . .5E 48
TW2: Whitt 7E 112
Brune St. E1 . . . . .6J 9 (5F 85)
Brunlees Ho. SE1 . . . . .3C 102
(off Bath Ter.)
Brunner Cl. NW11 . . . . .5K 45
Brunner Ho. SE6 . . . . .4E 140

Brunner Rd. E17 . . . . .5A 50
W5 .4D 78
Bruno Pl. NW9 . . . . .2J 61
Brunswick Av. N11 . . . . .3K 31
Brunswick Cen. 3E 6 (4J 83)
Brunswick Cl. DA6: Bex 4D 126
HA5: Pinn 6C 40
KT7: T Ditt 1A 162
TW2: Twick 3H 131
Brunswick Cl. Est.
EC1 . . . . .2A 8 (3B 84)
(off Tompion St.)
EN4: E Barn 5G 21
SE1 . . . . .7H 15 (2E 102)
SM1: Sutt 4K 165
SW1 . . . . .4D 18
(off Regency St.)
Brunswick Cres. N11 . . . . .3K 31
Brunswick Flats W11 . . . . .6J 81
(off Westbourne Gro.)
Brunswick Gdns. IG6: Ilf 1G 53
W5 .4E 78
W8 .1J 99
Brunswick Gro. N11 . . . . .3K 31
Brunswick Ho. E2 . . . . .2F 85
(off Thurtle Rd.)
N3 .1H 45
SE16 . . . . .3A 104
(off Brunswick Quay)
W6 .5E 98
(off Parrs Way)
Brunswick Ind. Pk. N11 . . . . .4A 32
Brunswick Mans. WC1 . . . . .3F 7
(off Handel St.)
Brunswick M. SW16 . . . . .6H 137
W1 . . . . .7F 5 (6D 82)
BRUNSWICK PARK 3J 31
Brunswick Pk. SE5 . . . . .1E 120
Brunswick Pk. Gdns. N11 . . . . . . .2K 31
Brunswick Pk. Rd. N11 . . . . .2K 31
Brunswick Pl. N1 . . . . . . .2F 9 (3D 84)
NW1 . . . . .4H 5 (4E 82)
(not continuous)
SE19 . . . . .7G 139
Brunswick Quay SE16 . . . . .3K 103
Brunswick Rd. DA6: Bex 4D 126
E10 .1E 68
E14 .6E 86
EN3: Enf L 1H 25
KT2: King T 1G 151
N15 .5E 48
SM1: Sutt 4K 165
W5 .4D 78
Brunswick Sq. N17 . . . . .6A 34
WC1 . . . . .3F 7 (4J 83)
(not continuous)
Brunswick St. E17 . . . . .5E 50
Brunswick Ter. BR3: Beck 1D 158
Brunswick Vs. SE5 . . . . .1E 120
Brunswick Way N11 . . . . .4A 32
Brunton Pl. E14 . . . . .6A 86
Brushfield St. E1 . . . . .5H 9 (5E 84)
Brushwood Cl. E14 . . . . .5D 86
Brussels Rd. SW11 . . . . .4B 118
Bruton Cl. BR7: Chst 7D 142
Bruton La. W1 . . . . .3K 11 (7F 83)
Bruton Pl. W1 . . . . .3K 11 (7F 83)
Bruton Rd. SM4: Mord 4A 154
Bruton St. W1 . . . . .3K 11 (7F 83)
Bruton Way W13 . . . . .5A 78
Brutus Ct. SE11 . . . . .4B 102
(off Kennington La.)
Bryan Av. NW10 . . . . .7D 62
Bryan Cl. TW16: Sun 7J 129
Bryan Ho. NW10 . . . . .7D 62
SE16 . . . . .2B 104
Bryan Rd. SE16 . . . . .2B 104
Bryan's All. SW6 . . . . .2K 117
Bryanston Av. TW2: Whitt 1F 131
Bryanston Cl. UB2: S'hall 4D 94
Bryanston Ct. W1 . . . . .7E 4
(not continuous)

Bryanstone Ct. SM1: Sutt 3A 166
Bryanstone Rd. N8 . . . . .5H 47
Bryanston Mans. W1 . . . . .5E 4
(off York St.)
Bryanston M. E. W1 . . . . . .6E 4 (5D 82)
Bryanston M. W. W1 . . . . . .6E 4 (5D 82)
Bryanston Pl. W1 . . . . .6E 4 (5D 82)
Bryanston Sq. W1 . . . . .6E 4 (6D 82)
Bryanston St. W1 . . . . . . .1E 10 (6D 82)
Bryan St. N1 . . . . .1K 83
Bryant Av. RM10: Dag 7J 73
Bryant Cl. EN5: Barn 5C 20
Bryant Ct. E2 . . . . .1F 85
(off Whiston Rd.)
W3 .1K 97
Bryant Ho. E3 . . . . .2C 86
(off Thomas Fyre Dr.)
Bryant Rd. UB5: N'olt 3A 76
Bryant St. E2 . . . . .1F 85
E15 .7F 69
Bryantwood Rd. N7 . . . . .5A 66
Brycedale Cres. N14 . . . . .4C 32
Bryce Ho. SE14 . . . . .6K 103
(off John Williams Cl.)
Bryce Rd. RM8: Dag 4C 72
Brydale Ho. SE16 . . . . .4K 103
(off Rotherhithe New Rd.)
Bryden Cl. SE26 . . . . .5A 140
Brydges Pl. WC2 . . . . . . .3E 12 (7J 83)
Brydges Rd. E15 . . . . .5F 69
Brydon Wlk. N1 . . . . .1J 83
Bryer Ct. EC2 . . . . .5C 8
Bryett Rd. N7 . . . . .3J 65
Bryher Ct. SE11 . . . . .5J 19
Brymay Cl. E3 . . . . .2C 86
Brymcourt W9 . . . . .2K 81
Brynford Rd. SW11 . . . . .1D 118
Bryn-y-mawr Rd. EN1: Enf 4A 24
Bryony Cl. UB8: Hil 5B 74
Bryony Rd. W12 . . . . .7C 80
Bryony Way TW16: Sun 6J 129
Bubbling Well Sq. SW18 . . . . . . .5K 117
(off Ryland Blvd.)
Buccleugh Ho. E5 . . . . .7G 49
Buchanan Cl. N21 . . . . .5E 22
Buchanan Ct. SE16 . . . . .4K 103
(off Worgan St.)
Buchanan Gdns. NW10 . . . . .2D 80
Buchan Ho. W3 . . . . .2H 97
(off Hanbury Rd.)
Buchan Rd. SE15 . . . . .3J 121
Bucharest Rd. SW18 . . . . .7A 118
Buckden Cl. N2 . . . . .4D 46
SE12 . . . . .6J 123
Buckfast Cl. W13 . . . . .7A 78
(off Romsey Rd.)
Buckfast Ho. N14 . . . . .5B 22
Buckfast Rd. SM4: Mord 4K 153
Buckfast St. E2 . . . . .3G 85
Buck Hill Wlk. W2 . . . . . .3B 10 (7B 82)
Buckhold Rd. SW18 . . . . .6J 117
Buckhurst Av. SM5: Cars 1C 166
Buckhurst Ct. IG9: Buck H 1G 37
BUCKHURST HILL 2G 37
Buckhurst Hill Ho.
IG9: Buck H 2E 36
Buckhurst Ho. N7 . . . . .5H 65
Buckhurst St. E1 . . . . .4H 85
E2 .4H 85
Buckhurst Way IG9: Buck H 4G 37
Buckingham Arc. WC2 . . . . .3E 12
Buckingham Av. CR7: Thor H 1A 156
DA16: Well 4J 125
KT8: W Mole 2F 149
N20 .7F 21
TW14: Felt 6K 111
UB6: G'frd 1A 78
Buckingham Chambers SW1 . . . . .3B 18
(off Greencoat Pl.)
Buckingham Cl. BR5: Pet W 7J 161
EN1: Enf 2K 23
TW12: Hamp 5D 130
W5 .5C 78

Buckingham Ct. NW4 ....3C 44
UB5: N'olt 2C 76
W7 ....4K 77
  (off Copley Cl.)
W11 ....7J 81
  (off Kensington Pk. Rd.)
Buckingham Dr. BR7: Chst 4G 143
Buckingham Gdns.
CR7: Thor H 2A 156
HA8: Edg 7K 27
KT8: W Mole 2F 149
Buckingham Ga. SW1 ....1A 18 (3G 101)
Buckingham Gro. UB10: Hil 2C 74
Buckingham La. SE23 ....7A 122
Buckingham Mans. NW6 ....5K 63
  (off West End La.)
Buckingham M. N1 ....6E 66
NW10 ....2B 80
SW1 ....1A 18
Buckingham Palace 7K 11 (2F 101)
Buckingham Pal. Rd.
SW1 ....4J 17 (4F 101)
Buckingham Pde. HA7: Stan 5H 27
Buckingham Pl. SW1 ....1A 18 (3G 101)
Buckingham Rd. CR4: Mitc 4J 155
E10 ....3D 68
E11 ....4A 52
E15 ....5H 69
E18 ....1H 51
HA1: Harr 5H 41
HA8: Edg 7A 28
IG1: Ilf 2H 71
KT1: King T 4F 151
N1 ....6E 66
N22 ....1J 47
NW10 ....2B 80
TW10: Ham 2D 132
TW12: Hamp 7D 130
Buckingham St. WC2 ....4F 13 (7J 83)
Buckingham Way SM6: W'gton ...7G 167
Buckland Cl. NW7 ....4H 29
Buckland Ct. N1 ....2E 84
  (off St John's Est.)
UB10: Ick 2E 56
Buckland Cres. NW3 ....7B 64
Buckland Ho. SW1 ....5J 17
  (part of Abbots Mnr.)
Buckland Ri. HA5: Pinn 1A 40
Buckland Rd. BR6: Orp 4J 173
E10 ....2E 68
KT9: Chess 5F 163
Bucklands Rd. TW11: Tedd 6C 132
Buckland St. N1 ....2D 84
Buckland's Wharf KT1: King T ..2D 150
Buckland Wlk. SM4: Mord 4A 154
W3 ....2J 97
Buckland Way KT4: Wor Pk 1E 164
Buck La. NW9 ....5K 43
Bucklebury NW1 ....3A 6
  (off Stanhope St.)
Buckleigh Av. SW20 ....3G 153
Buckleigh Rd. SW16 ....6H 137
Buckleigh Way SE19 ....7F 139
Buckler Cl. N7 ....5K 65
Buckler Gdns. SE9 ....3D 142
Bucklers All. SW6 ....6H 99
Bucklersbury EC4 ......1E 14 (6D 84)
Bucklersbury Pas. EC4 ......6D 84
Buckler's Way SM5: Cars 3D 166
Buckles Ct. DA17: Belv 4D 108
Buckle St. E1 ....7K 9 (6E 85)
Buckley Cl. SE23 ....7H 121
Buckley Ct. NW6 ....7H 63
SE1 ....3F 103
Buckley Ho. W14 ....2G 99
  (off Holland Pk. Av.)
Buckley Rd. NW6 ....7H 63
Buckmaster Cl. SW9 ....3A 120
  (off Stockwell Pk. Rd.)
Buckmaster Ho. N7 ....4K 65
Buckmaster Rd. SW11 ....4C 118
Bucknall St. WC2 ......7D 6 (6J 83)
Bucknall Way BR3: Beck 4D 158

Bucknell Cl. SW2 ....4K 119
Buckner Rd. SW2 ....4K 119
Bucknill Ho. SW1 ....5J 17
  (off Ebury Bri. Rd.)
Buckrell Rd. E4 ....2A 36
Buckridge Ho. EC1 ....5J 7
  (off Portpool La.)
Buckshead Ho. W2 ....5J 81
  (off Gt. Western Rd.)
Buckstone Cl. SE23 ....6J 121
Buckstone Rd. N18 ....5B 34
Buck St. NW1 ....7F 65
Buckters Rents SE16 ....1A 104
Buckthorne Rd. SE4 ....5A 122
Buckthorn Ho. DA15: Sidc ...3K 143
  (off Longlands Rd.)
E15 ....3G 87
  (off Manor Rd.)
Buck Wlk. E17 ....4F 51
Buckwheat Ct. DA18: Erith ...3D 108
Budd Cl. N12 ....4E 30
The Buddhapadipa Temple ...4F 135
Buddings Circ. HA9: Wemb ...3J 61
Buddleia Ho. TW13: Felt ...1J 129
Budd's All. TW1: Twick ...5C 114
Budé Cl. E17 ....5B 50
Budge La. CR4: Mitc 7D 154
Budge's Wlk. W2 ....3A 10
Budleigh Cres. DA16: Well ...1C 126
Budleigh Ho. SE15 ....7G 103
  (off Bird in Bush Rd.)
Budoch Cl. IG3: Ilf 2A 72
Budoch Dr. IG3: Ilf 2A 72
Buer Rd. SW6 ....2G 117
Bugsby's Way SE7 ....4H 105
SE10 ....4H 105
Buick Ho. E3 ....4C 86
  (off Wellington Way)
KT2: King T 2F 151
Building 50 SE18 ....3G 107
Bulbarrow NW8 ....1K 81
  (off Abbey Rd.)
Bulganak Rd. CR7: Thor H ...4C 156
Bulinga St. SW1 ....4E 18
Bullace Row SE5 ....1D 120
Bull All. DA16: Well 3B 126
Bullard's Pl. E2 ....3K 85
Bullbanks Rd. DA17: Belv ...4J 109
Bulleid Way SW1 ....4K 17 (4F 101)
Bullen Ho. E1 ....4H 85
  (off Collingwood St.)
Bullen St. SW11 ....2C 118
Buller Cl. SE15 ....7G 103
Buller Rd. CR7: Thor H ...2D 156
IG11: Bark 7J 71
N17 ....2G 49
N22 ....2A 48
NW10 ....3F 81
Bullers Cl. DA14: Sidc ...5E 144
Bullers Wood Dr. BR7: Chst ...7D 142
Bullescroft Rd. HA8: Edg ...3B 28
Bullfinch Ho. NW9 ....6B 44
  (off Perryfield Way)
Bullingham Mans. W8 ......2J 99
  (off Pitt St.)
Bull Inn Ct. WC2 ....3F 13
Bullivant St. E14 ....7E 86
Bull La. BR7: Chst 7H 143
N18 ....5K 33
RM10: Dag 3H 73
Bullman Cl. DA7: Bex 3H 127
Bull Rd. E15 ....2H 87
Bullrush Cl. CR0: C'don ...6E 156
SM5: Cars 2C 166
Bull's All. SW14 ....2K 115
Bulls Bri. Cen. UB3: Hayes ...3J 93
Bullsbridge Ind. Est. UB2: S'hall ...4K 93
Bulls Bri. Rd. UB2: S'hall ...4A 94
UB3: Hayes 3K 93
Bullsbrook Rd. UB4: Yead ...1A 94
Bulls Gdns. SW3 ....3D 16 (4C 100)
Bulls Head Pas. EC3 .....1G 15
The Bull Theatre 4C 20

Bull Yd. SE15 ....1G 121
Bulmer Gdns. HA3: Kenton ...7D 42
Bulmer M. W11 ....7J 81
Bulmer Pl. W11 ....1J 99
Bulstrode Av. TW3: Houn ...2D 112
Bulstrode Gdns.
TW3: Houn 3E 112
Bulstrode Pl. W1 ....6H 5 (5E 82)
Bulstrode Rd. TW3: Houn ...3E 112
Bulstrode St. W1 ....7H 5 (6E 82)
Bulwark Ct. E14 ....4E 104
  (off Parkside Sq.)
Bulwer Ct. E11 ....1F 69
Bulwer Ct. Rd. E11 ......1F 69
Bulwer Gdns. EN5: New Bar ...4F 21
Bulwer Rd. E11 ....7F 51
EN5: New Bar 4C 20
N18 ....4K 33
Bulwer St. W12 ....1E 98
Bunbury Ho. SE15 ....7G 103
  (off Fenham Rd.)
Bunce's La. IG8: Wfd G ...7C 36
Bungalow Rd. SE25 ....4E 156
The Bungalows E10 ....6E 50
HA2: Harr 4D 58
IG6: Ilf 1J 53
SM6: W'gton 5F 167
SW16 ....7F 137
UB4: Yead 4B 76
Bunhill Row EC1 ....3E 8 (4D 84)
Bunhouse Pl. SW1 ....5H 17 (5E 100)
Bunkers Hill DA14: Sidc ...3F 145
DA17: Belv 4G 109
NW11 ....7A 46
Bunning Way N7 ....7J 65
Bunns La. NW7 ....6F 29
  (not continuous)
Bunsen Ho. E3 ....2A 86
  (off Grove Rd.)
Bunsen St. E3 ....2A 86
Buntingbridge Rd. IG2: Ilf ...5H 53
Bunting Cl. CR4: Mitc ...5D 154
N9 ....1E 34
Bunting Ct. NW9 ....2A 44
Bunting Ho. UB10: Ick ...2E 56
  (off Coyle Dr.)
Bunton St. SE18 ....3E 106
Bunwell Ho. E3 ....4B 86
  (off William Whiffin Sq.)
Bunyan Ct. EC2 ....5C 8
Bunyan Rd. E17 ....3A 50
Buonaparte M. SW1 ....5C 18 (5H 101)
Burbage Ho. N1 ....1D 84
  (off Poole St.)
SE14 ....6K 103
  (off Samuel Cl.)
Burbage Rd. SE21 ....6C 120
SE24 ....6C 120
Burberry Cl. KT3: N Mald ...2A 152
Burbidge Rd. TW17: Shep ...4C 146
Burbridge Gdns. UB10: Uxb ...2A 74
Burbridge Way N17 ......2G 49
Burcham St. TW12: Hamp ...7E 130
Burcham St. E14 ....6D 86
Burcharbro Rd. SE2 .....6D 108
Burchell Ct. WD23: Bush ...1B 26
Burchell Ho. SE11 ......5H 19
  (off Jonathan St.)
Burchell Rd. E10 ....1D 68
SE15 ....1H 121
Burcher Gale Gro. SE15 ...7F 103
Burchetts Way
TW17: Shep 6D 146
Burchett Way RM6: Chad H ...6E 55
Burchwall Cl. RM5: Col R ...1J 55
Burcote Rd. SW18 ....7B 118
Burden Cl. TW8: Bford ...5C 96
Burden Ho. SW8 ....7J 101
  (off Thorncroft St.)
Burdenshott Av. TW10: Rich ...4H 115
Burden Way E11 ....2K 69

Burder Cl. N1 ....6E 66
Burder Rd. N1 ....6E 66
Burdett Av. SW20 ....1C 152
Burdett Cl. DA14: Sidc ...5E 144
W7 ....1K 95
Burdett M. NW3 ....6B 64
W2 ....6K 81
Burdett Rd. CR0: C'don ...6D 156
E3 ....4A 86
E14 ....4A 86
TW9: Rich 2F 115
Burdetts Rd. RM9: Dag ...1F 91
Burdock Cl. CR0: C'don ...1K 169
Burdock Rd. N17 ....3G 49
Burdon La. SM2: Cheam ...7G 165
Burdon Pk. SM2: Cheam ...7H 165
Bure Ct. EN5: New Bar ...5E 20
Burfield Cl. SW17 ......4B 136
Burford Cl. IG6: Ilf 4G 53
RM8: Dag 3C 72
UB10: Ick 4A 56
Burford Gdns. N13 ......3E 32
Burford Ho. TW8: Bford ...5D 96
Burford Rd. BR1: Broml ...4C 160
E6 ....3C 88
E15 ....1F 87
KT4: Wor Pk 7B 152
SE6 ....2B 140
SM1: Sutt 2J 165
TW8: Bford 5E 96
Burford Wlk. SW6 ....7A 100
Burford Way CR0: New Ad ...6E 170
Burford Wharf Apts. E15 ....1F 87
  (off Cam Rd.)
Burges Gro. SW13 ....7D 98
Burges Rd. E6 ....7C 70
Burgess Av. NW9 ....6K 43
Burgess Bus. Pk. SE5 ...7D 102
Burgess Cl. TW13: Hanw ...4C 130
Burgess Ct. E6 ....7E 70
SE6 ....7C 122
UB1: S'hall 6F 77
  (off Fleming Rd.)
Burgess Hill NW2 ....4J 63
Burgess Ho. SE5 ....7C 102
  (off Bethwin Rd.)
Burgess Lofts SE5 ......7C 102
  (off Bethwin Rd.)
Burgess M. SW19 ....6K 135
Burgess Pk. 6D 102
Burgess Rd. E6 ....7E 70
E15 ....4G 69
SM1: Sutt 4K 165
Burgess St. E14 ....5C 86
SW8 ....3D 102
Burgh House 4B 64
Burgh St. N1 ....2B 84
Burghley Av.
KT3: N Mald 1K 151
Burghley Hall Cl. SW19 ...1G 135
Burghley Ho. SW19 ......3G 135
Burghley Pl. CR4: Mitc ...5D 154
Burghley Rd. E11 ....1G 69
N8 ....3A 48
NW5 ....4F 65
SW19 ....4F 135
Burghley Twr. W3 ....7B 80
Burgh St. N1 ....2B 84
Burgoine Quay
KT1: Hamp W 1D 150
Burgon St. EC4 ....1B 14 (6B 84)
Burgos Cl. CR0: Wadd ...6A 168
Burgos Gro. SE10 ......1D 122
Burgoyne Ho. TW8: Bford ...5D 96
  (off Ealing Rd.)
Burgoyne Rd. N4 ....6B 48
SE25 ....4F 157
SW9 ....3K 119
TW16: Sun 6H 129
Burgundy Ct. HA4: Ruis ...1A 58
Burgundy Ho. E20 ......5E 68
  (off Liberty Bri. Rd.)
Burgundy Pl. W12 ......1F 99

Burham Cl. SE20 . . . . .7J **139**
Burhill Gro. HA5: Pinn 2C **40**
Burke Cl. SW15 . . . . .4A **116**
Burke Lodge E13 . . . . .3K **87**
Burke St. E16 . . . . .5H **87**
(not continuous)
Burket Cl. UB2: S'hall 4C **94**
Burland Rd. SW11 . . . . .5D **118**
Burleigh Av. DA15: Sidc 5K **125**
SM6: W'gton 3E **166**
Burleigh Cl. RM7: Mawney 4H **55**
Burleigh Gdns. N14 . . . . .1B **32**
TW15: Ashf 5E **128**
Burleigh Ho. SW3 . . . . .7B **16**
W10 . . . . .5G **81**
(off St Charles Sq.)
WC1 . . . . .2F **7**
Burleigh Pde. N14 . . . . .1C **32**
Burleigh Pl. SW15 . . . . .5F **117**
Burleigh Rd. EN1: Enf 4K **23**
SM3: Sutt 1G **165**
UB10: Hil 1D **74**
Burleigh St. WC2 . . . .2G **13** (7K **83**)
Burleigh Wlk. SE6 . . . . .1E **140**
Burleigh Way EN2: Enf 3J **23**
Burley Cl. E4 . . . . .5H **35**
SW16 . . . . .2H **155**
Burley Ho. E1 . . . . .6K **85**
(off Chudleigh St.)
Burley Rd. E16 . . . . .6A **88**
Burlington Arc. W1 . . . .3A **12** (7G **83**)
Burlington Av. RM7: Rom 6H **55**
TW9: Kew 1G **115**
Burlington Cl. BR6: Farnb 2F **173**
E6 . . . . .6C **88**
HA5: Eastc 3K **39**
TW14: Bedf 7F **111**
W9 . . . . .4J **81**
Burlington Cnr. NW1 . . . . .7G **65**
(off Camden Rd.)
Burlington Ct. E1 . . . . .7G **85**
(off Cable St.)
UB7: W Dray 2B **92**
(off Park Lodge Av.)
Burlington Gdns. RM6: Chad H . .7E **54**
SW6 . . . . .2G **117**
W1 . . . . .3A **12** (7G **83**)
W3 . . . . .1J **97**
W4 . . . . .5J **97**
Burlington Ho. N15 . . . . .6D **48**
(off Tewkesbury Rd.)
SE16 . . . . .2K **103**
(off Province Dr.)
Burlington La. W4 . . . . .7J **97**
Burlington M. SW15 . . . . .5H **117**
W3 . . . . .1J **97**
Burlington Pl. IG8: Wfd G 3E **36**
SW6 . . . . .2G **117**
Burlington Ri. EN4: E Barn 1H **31**
Burlington Rd. CR7: Thor H 2C **156**
EN2: Enf 1J **23**
KT3: N Mald 4B **152**
N10 . . . . .3E **46**
N17 . . . . .1G **49**
SW6 . . . . .2G **117**
TW7: Isle 1H **113**
W4 . . . . .5J **97**
Burma M. N16 . . . . .4D **66**
Burma Rd. N16 . . . . .4D **66**
Burmarsh NW5 . . . . .6E **64**
Burmarsh Ct. SE20 . . . . .1J **157**
Burma Ter. SE19 . . . . .5E **138**
Burmester Rd. SW17 . . . . .3A **136**
Burnaby Cres. W4 . . . . .6J **97**
Burnaby Gdns. W4 . . . . .6H **97**
Burnaby St. SW10 . . . . .7A **100**
Burnand Ho. W14 . . . . .3F **99**
(off Redan St.)
Burnbrae Cl. N12 . . . . .6E **30**
Burnbury Rd. SW12 . . . . .1G **137**
Burncroft Av. EN3: Enf H 2D **24**
Burndell Way UB4: Yead 5B **76**
Burne Jones Ho. W14 . . . . .4G **99**

Burnell Av. DA16: Well 2A **126**
TW10: Ham 5C **132**
Burnell Bldg. NW2 . . . . .2E **62**
Burnell Gdns. HA7: Stan 2D **42**
Burnell Ho. E20 . . . . .5D **68**
(off Peloton Av.)
Burnelli Bldg. SW11 . . . . .7F **101**
(off Sopwith Way)
Burnell Rd. SM1: Sutt 4K **165**
Burnell Wlk. SE1 . . . . .5F **103**
(off Cadet Dr.)
Burnels Av. E6 . . . . .3E **88**
Burness Cl. N7 . . . . .6K **65**
Burne St. NW1 . . . . . .5C **4** (5C **82**)
Burnett Cl. E9 . . . . .5J **67**
Burnett Ho. SE13 . . . . .2E **122**
(off Lewisham Hill)
Burnett Rd. IG6: Ilf 7K **37**
Burney Av. KT5: Surb 5F **151**
Burney St. SE10 . . . . .7E **104**
Burnfoot Av. SW6 . . . . .1G **117**
Burnham NW3 . . . . .7C **64**
Burnham Av. UB10: Ick 4E **56**
Burnham Cl. EN1: Enf 1K **23**
HA3: W'stone 4A **42**
NW7 . . . . .7H **29**
SE1 . . . . .4F **103**
Burnham Ct. NW4 . . . . .4E **44**
(off Brent St.)
NW6 . . . . .7A **64**
(off Fairhazel Gdns.)
W2 . . . . .7K **81**
(off Moscow Rd.)
Burnham Cres. E11 . . . . .4A **52**
Burnham Dr. KT4: Wor Pk 2E **165**
Burnham Est. E2 . . . . .3J **85**
(off Burnham St.)
Burnham Gdns. CR0: C'don 7F **157**
TW4: Cran 1K **111**
UB3: Harl 3F **93**
Burnham Rd. DA14: Sidc 2E **144**
E4 . . . . .5G **35**
RM7: Rom 3K **55**
RM9: Dag 7B **72**
SM4: Mord 4K **153**
Burnham St. E2 . . . . .3J **85**
KT2: King T 1G **151**
Burnham Way SE26 . . . . .5B **140**
W13 . . . . .3B **96**
Burnhill Cl. SE15 . . . . .7H **103**
Burnhill Ho. EC1 . . . . .2C **8**
(off Norman St.)
Burnhill Rd. BR3: Beck 2C **158**
Burnley Rd. NW10 . . . . .5B **62**
SW9 . . . . .2K **119**
Burnsall St. SW3 . . . .6D **16** (5C **100**)
Burns Av. DA15: Sidc 6B **126**
RM6: Chad H 7C **54**
TW14: Felt 6J **111**
UB1: S'hall 7E **76**
Burns Cl. DA16: Well 1K **125**
E17 . . . . .4E **50**
SM5: Cars 7E **166**
SW19 . . . . .6B **136**
UB4: Hayes 5H **75**
Burns Ho. E2 . . . . .3J **85**
(off Cornwall Av.)
SE17 . . . . .5B **102**
(off Doddington Gro.)
Burnside Av. E4 . . . . .6G **35**
Burnside Cl. EN5: New Bar 3D **20**
SE16 . . . . .1K **103**
TW1: Twick 6A **114**
Burnside Ct. SM5: Cars 3E **166**
Burnside Cres. HA0: Wemb 1D **78**
Burnside Rd. RM8: Dag 2C **72**
Burns Rd. HA0: Wemb 2E **78**
NW10 . . . . .1B **80**
SW11 . . . . .2D **118**
W13 . . . . .2B **96**
Burns Way TW5: Hest 2B **112**
Burnt Ash Hgts. BR1: Broml 5K **141**
Burnt Ash Hill SE12 . . . . .6H **123**

Burnt Ash La. BR1: Broml 7J **141**
Burnt Ash Rd. SE12 . . . . .5H **123**
Burnthwaite M. SW6 . . . . .7J **99**
(off Burnthwaite Rd.)
Burnthwaite Rd. SW6 . . . . .7H **99**
BURNT OAK 1H **43**
Burnt Oak Apts. E16 . . . . .6J **87**
(off Pacific Rd.)
Burnt Oak B'way. HA8: Edg 7B **28**
Burnt Oak Flds. HA8: Edg 1J **43**
Burnt Oak La. DA15: Sidc 6A **126**
(not continuous)
Burntwood Cl. SW18 . . . . .1C **136**
Burntwood Grange Rd.
SW18 . . . . .1B **136**
Burntwood La. SW17 . . . . .3A **136**
Burntwood Vw. SE19 . . . . .5F **139**
Buross St. E1 . . . . .6H **85**
Burpham Cl. UB4: Yead 5B **76**
Burrage Ct. SE16 . . . . .4K **103**
(off Worgan St.)
Burrage Gro. SE18 . . . . .4G **107**
Burrage Pl. SE18 . . . . .5F **107**
Burrage Rd. SE18 . . . . .5G **107**
Burrard Ho. E2 . . . . .2J **85**
(off Bishop's Way)
Burrard Rd. E16 . . . . .6K **87**
NW6 . . . . .5J **63**
Burr Cl. DA7: Bex 3F **127**
E1 . . . . .4K **15** (1G **103**)
Burreed M. RM13: Rain 2J **91**
Burrell Cl. CR0: C'don 6A **158**
HA8: Edg 2C **28**
Burrell Row BR3: Beck 2C **158**
Burrell St. SE1 . . . . . .4A **14** (1B **102**)
Burrells Wharf Sq. E14 . . . . . . .5D **104**
Burrell Towers E10 . . . . .7C **50**
Burrhill Ct. SE16 . . . . .3K **103**
(off Worgan St.)
Burritt Rd. KT1: King T 2G **151**
The Burroughs NW4 . . . . .4D **44**
The Burroughs Club 4D **44**
Burroughs Cotts. E14 . . . . .5A **86**
(off Halley St.)
Burroughs Gdns. NW4 . . . . .4D **44**
Burroughs Pde. NW4 . . . . .4D **44**
Burrow Ho. SW9 . . . . .2A **120**
(off Stockwell Pk. Rd.)
Burrow Rd. SE22 . . . . .4E **120**
Burrows M. SE1 . . . . .6A **14** (2B **102**)
Burrows Rd. NW10 . . . . .3E **80**
Burrow Wlk. SE21 . . . . .7C **120**
Burr Rd. SW18 . . . . .1J **135**
Bursar St. SE1 . . . . . .5G **15** (1E **102**)
Bursdon Cl. DA15: Sidc 2K **143**
Bursland Rd. EN3: Pond E 4E **24**
Burslem St. E1 . . . . .6G **85**
Burstock Rd. SW15 . . . . .4G **117**
Burston Rd. SW15 . . . . .5F **117**
Burston Vs. SW15 . . . . .5F **117**
(off St John's Av.)
Burstow Rd. SW20 . . . . .1G **153**
Burtenshaw Rd.
KT7: T Ditt 7A **150**
Burtley Cl. N4 . . . . .1C **66**
Burton Bank N1 . . . . .7D **66**
(off Yeate St.)
Burton Cl. CR7: Thor H 3D **156**
KT9: Chess 7D **162**
Burton Ct. KT7: T Ditt 6A **150**
SE20 . . . . .2J **157**
SW3 . . . . .5F **17**
(not continuous)
Burton Gdns. TW5: Hest 1D **112**
Burton Gro. SE17 . . . . .5D **102**
Burton Ho. CL NW7 . . . . .4A **30**
Burtonhole La. N12 . . . . .4B **30**
NW7 . . . . .5K **29**
Burton Ho. SE16 . . . . .2H **103**
(off Cherry Gdn. St.)
Burton La. SW9 . . . . .2A **120**
(not continuous)
Burton M. SW1 . . . . .4H **17** (4E **100**)

Burton Pl. WC1 . . . . . . .2D **6** (3H **83**)
Burton Ridge Ct. E3 . . . . .2B **86**
(off Festubert Pl.)
Burton Rd. E18 . . . . .3K **51**
KT2: King T 7E **132**
NW6 . . . . .7H **63**
SW9 . . . . .2B **120**
(Akerman Rd.)
SW9 . . . . .2A **120**
(Evesham Wlk.)
Burtons Ct. E15 . . . . .7F **69**
Burton's Rd. TW12: Hamp H 4F **131**
Burton St. WC1 . . . . . .2D **6** (3H **83**)
Burtonwood Ho. N4 . . . . .7D **48**
Burtop Rd. Est. SW17 . . . . .3A **136**
Burt Rd. E16 . . . . .1A **106**
Burt's Wharf DA17: Belv 7J **91**
Burtt Ho. N1 . . . . .1G **9**
(off Aske St.)
Burtwell La. SE27 . . . . .4D **138**
Burwash Ho. SE1 . . . . .7F **15**
(off Kipling Est.)
Burwash Rd. SE18 . . . . .5H **107**
Burway Cl. CR2: S Croy 6E **168**
Burwell Cl. E1 . . . . .2G **151**
(off Excelsior Cl.)
Burwell Av. UB6: G'frd 6J **59**
Burwell Cl. E1 . . . . .6H **85**
Burwell Rd. E10 . . . . .1A **68**
Burwell Wlk. E3 . . . . .4C **86**
Burwood Av. BR2: Hayes 2K **171**
HA5: Eastc 5K **39**
Burwood Cl. KT6: Surb 1G **163**
Burwood Ho. SW9 . . . . .4B **120**
Burwood Pl. EN4: Had W 1F **21**
W2 . . . . .7D **4** (6C **82**)
Bury Av. HA4: Ruis 6E **38**
UB4: Hayes 2G **75**
Bury Cl. SE16 . . . . .1K **103**
Bury Ct. EC3 . . . . .7H **9** (6E **84**)
Buryfield Ct. SE8 . . . . .4K **103**
(off Lower Rd.)
Bury Gro. SM4: Mord 5K **153**
Bury Hall Vs. N9 . . . . .7A **24**
Bury Pl. WC1 . . . . .6E **6** (5J **83**)
Bury Rd. E4 . . . . .1B **36**
N22 . . . . .2A **48**
RM10: Dag 5H **73**
Burnside Cl. IG2: Ilf 4K **53**
Bury St. EC3 . . . . .1H **15** (6E **84**)
HA4: Ruis 5E **38**
N9 . . . . .7A **24**
SW1 . . . . .4B **12** (1G **101**)
Bury St. W. N9 . . . . .7J **23**
Bury Wlk. SW3 . . . . . .4C **16** (4C **100**)
Busbridge Ho. E14 . . . . .5C **86**
(off Brabazon St.)
Busby Ho. SW16 . . . . .4G **137**
Busby M. NW5 . . . . .6H **65**
Busby Pl. NW5 . . . . .6H **65**
Busch Cl. TW7: Isle 1B **114**
Bushbaby Cl. SE1 . . . . .3E **102**
Bushberry Rd. E9 . . . . .6A **68**
Bush Cl. IG2: Ilf 5H **53**
Bush Cotts. SW18 . . . . .5J **117**
Bush Ct. N14 . . . . .1B **32**
W12 . . . . .2F **99**
Bushell Cl. SW2 . . . . .2K **137**
Bushell Grn. WD23: B Hea 2C **26**
Bushell St. E1 . . . . .1G **103**
Bushell Way BR7: Chst 5E **142**
BUSHEY 1C **26**
Bushey Av. BR5: Pet W 7H **161**
E18 . . . . .3H **51**
Bushey Cl. E4 . . . . .3K **35**
UB10: Ick 2C **56**
Bushey Ct. SW20 . . . . .3D **152**
Bushey Down SW12 . . . . .2F **137**
BUSHEY HEATH 1C **26**
Bushey Hill Rd. SE5 . . . . .1E **120**
Bushey La. SM1: Sutt 4J **165**
Bushey Lees DA15: Sidc 6K **125**
BUSHEY MEAD 2F **153**

Bushey Rd. CR0: C'don 2C 170
  E13 . . . . .2A 88
  N15 . . . . .6E 48
  SM1: Sutt 4J 165
  (not continuous)
  SW20 .3D 152
  UB3: Harl 4G 93
  UB10: Ick 2C 56
Bushey Way BR3: Beck 6F 159
Bush Fair Ct. N14 . . . . .6A 22
Bushfield Cl. HA8: Edg 2C 28
Bushfield Cres. HA8: Edg 2C 28
Bush Gro. HA7: Stan 1D 42
  NW9 . . . . .7J 43
Bushgrove Rd. RM8: Dag 4D 72
Bush Hill N21 . . . . .7H 23
Bush Hill Pde. EN1: Enf 7J 23
  N9 . . . . .7J 23
BUSH HILL PARK 6A 24
Bush Hill Pk. Golf Course 5H 23
Bush Hill Rd. HA3: Kenton 6F 43
  N21 . . . . .6J 23
Bush House 2G 13
  NW10 . . . . .4K 79
Bush La. EC4 . . . . .2E 14 (7D 84)
Bushmead Cl. N15 . . . . .4F 49
Bushmoor Cres. SE18 . . . . .7F 107
Bushnell Rd. SW17 . . . . .2F 137
Bush Rd. E8 . . . . .1H 85
  E11 . . . . .7H 51
  IG9: Buck H 4G 37
  SE8 . . . . .4K 103
  TW9: Kew 6F 97
  TW17: Shep 5B 146
Bush Theatre 2E 98
Bushway RM8: Dag 4D 72
Bushwood E11 . . . . .7H 51
Bushwood Dr. SE1 . . . . .4F 103
Bushwood Rd. TW9: Kew 6G 97
Bushy Ct. KT1: Hamp W 1C 150
  (off Beverley Rd.)
Bushy Pk. 7H 131
Bushy Pk. Gdns.
  TW11: Tedd 5H 131
Bushy Pk. Rd. TW11: Tedd 7B 132
  (not continuous)
Bushy Rd. TW11: Tedd 6K 131
Business Design Centre 1A 84
  (off Upper St.)
Buspace Studios W10 . . . . .4G 81
  (off Conlan St.)
Butcher Row E14 . . . . .7K 85
Butchers M. UB3: Hayes 7H 75
  (off Hemmen La.)
Butchers Rd. E16 . . . . .6J 87
Bute Av. TW10: Ham 2E 132
Bute Cl. SM6: W'gton 5G 167
Bute Gdns.
  SM6: W'gton 5G 167
  TW10: Ham 1E 132
  W6 . . . . .4F 99
Bute Gdns. W. SM6: W'gton 5G 167
Bute M. NW11 . . . . .5A 46
Bute Rd. CR0: C'don 1A 168
  IG6: Ilf 5F 53
  SM6: W'gton 4G 167
Bute St. SW7 . . . . .3A 16 (4B 100)
Bute Wlk. N1 . . . . .6D 66
Butfield Ho. E9 . . . . .6J 67
  (off Stevens Av.)
Butler Av. HA1: Harr 7H 41
Butler Cl. HA8: Edg 2H 43
Butler Ct. HA0: Wemb 4A 60
  RM8: Dag 2G 73
  (off Gosfield Rd.)
  SW11 .1C 118
  (off Hyde La.)
Butler Farm Cl. TW10: Ham 4D 132
Butler Ho. E2 . . . . .3J 85
  (off Bacton St.)
  E3 . . . . .5B 86
  (off Geoffrey Chaucer Way)

Butler Ho. E14 . . . . .6B 86
  (off Burdett St.)
  SW9 . . . . .1B 120
  (off Lothian Rd.)
Butler Pl. SW1 . . . . . .1C 18 (3H 101)
Butler Rd. HA1: Harr 7G 41
  NW10 . . . . .7B 62
  RM8: Dag 4B 72
Butlers & Colonial Wharf SE1 . . . .6K 15
  (off Shad Thames)
Butlers Cl. TW4: Houn 3D 112
Butlers Dr. E4 . . . . .1K 25
Butler St. E2 . . . . .3J 85
  UB10: Hil 4D 74
Butlers Wharf SE1 . . . . . .5K 15 (1F 103)
Butlers Wharf W. SE1 . . . . .5J 15
  (off Shad Thames)
Butley Ct. E3 . . . . .2A 86
  (off Ford St.)
Buttercup Cl. UB5: N'olt 6D 58
Butterfield Cl. N17 . . . . .6H 33
  SE16 .2H 103
  TW1: Twick 6K 113
Butterfields E17 . . . . .5E 50
Butterfield Sq. E6 . . . . .6D 88
Butterfly Apts. SW11 . . . . .4C 118
  (off Comyn Rd.)
Butterfly Ct. E6 . . . . .3D 88
  N15 . . . . .4E 48
  (off Bathurst Sq.)
  NW9 . . . . .1A 44
Butterfly La. SE9 . . . . .6F 125
Butterfly Wlk. SE5 . . . . .1D 120
  (off Denmark Hill)
Butter Hill SM5: Cars 3E 166
  SM6: W'gton 3E 166
Butteridges Cl. RM9: Dag 1F 91
Buttermere NW1 . . . . .1K 5
  (off Augustus St.)
Buttermere Cl. E15 . . . . .4F 69
  SE1 . . . . .4F 103
  SM4: Mord 6G 153
  TW14: Felt 1H 129
Buttermere Ct. NW8 . . . . .1B 82
  (off Boundary Rd.)
Buttermere Dr. SW15 . . . . .5G 117
Buttermere Ho. E3 . . . . .3B 86
  (off Mile End Rd.)
Buttermere Wlk. E8 . . . . .6F 67
Butterwick W6 . . . . .4F 99
Butterworth Gdns. IG8: Wfd G 6D 36
Butterworth Ter. SE17 . . . . .5C 102
  (off Sutherland Wlk.)
Buttery M. N14 . . . . .3D 32
Buttesland St. N1 . . . . . . .1F 9 (3D 84)
Buttfield Cl. RM10: Dag 6H 73
Buttmarsh Cl. SE18 . . . . .5F 107
Button Lodge E17 . . . . .4C 50
Buttonscroft Cl.
  CR7: Thor H 3C 156
The Butts TW8: Bford 6C 96
  TW16: Sun 3A 148
Buttsbury Rd. IG1: Ilf 5G 71
Butts Cotts. TW13: Hanw 3C 130
Butts Cres. TW13: Hanw 3E 130
Butts Piece UB5: N'olt 2K 75
Butts Rd. BR1: Broml 5G 141
Buxhall Cres. E9 . . . . .6B 68
Buxted Rd. E8 . . . . .7F 67
  N12 . . . . .5H 31
  SE22 . . . . .4E 120
Buxton Cl. IG8: Wfd G 6G 37
  N9 . . . . .2D 34
Buxton Ct. E11 . . . . .7H 51
  N1 . . . . .1D 8
  (not continuous)
Buxton Cres. SM3: Cheam 4G 165
Buxton Dr. E11 . . . . .4G 51
  KT3: N Mald 2K 151
Buxton Gdns. W3 . . . . .7H 79
Buxton Ho. E11 . . . . .4G 51
Buxton M. SW4 . . . . .2H 119

Buxton Rd. CR7: Thor H 5B 156
  DA8: Erith 7K 109
  E4 . . . . .1A 36
  E6 . . . . .3C 88
  E15 . . . . .5G 69
  E17 . . . . .4A 50
  (not continuous)
  IG2: Ilf 6J 53
  N19 . . . . .1H 65
  NW2 . . . . .6D 62
  SW14 .3A 116
  TW15: Ashf 5A 128
Buxton St. E1 . . . . .4K 9 (4G 85)
Buzzard Creek Ind. Est.
  IG11: Bark 5A 90
Buzz Bingo
  Bexleyheath 4H 127
  Enfield 4B 24
  Feltham 2K 129
  Stratford 1F 87
Byam St. SW6 . . . . .2A 118
Byards Cl. SE16 . . . . .4K 103
  (off Worgan St.)
Byards Cft. SW16 . . . . .1H 155
Byas Ho. E3 . . . . .3B 86
  (off Benworth St.)
Byatt Wlk. TW12: Hamp 6C 130
Bychurch End TW11: Tedd 5K 131
Bycroft Rd. UB1: S'hall 4E 76
Bycroft St. SE20 . . . . .7K 139
Bycullah Av. EN2: Enf 3G 23
Bycullah Rd. EN2: Enf 2G 23
The Bye W3 . . . . .6A 80
Byegrove Rd. SW19 . . . . .6B 136
Byelands Cl. SE16 . . . . .1K 103
The Bye Way
  HA3: W'stone 1J 41
The Byeway SW14 . . . . .3J 115
Byeways TW2: Twick 3F 131
The Byeways KT5: Surb 5G 151
Byfeld Gdns. SW13 . . . . .1C 116
Byfield Cl. SE16 . . . . .2B 104
Byfield Rd. TW7: Isle 3A 114
Byford Cl. E15 . . . . .7G 69
Byford Ho. EN5: Barn 4A 20
  HA2: Harr 1E 58
Bygrove CR0: New Ad 6D 170
Bygrove St. E14 . . . . .6D 86
  (not continuous)
Byland Cl. N21 . . . . .7E 22
  SE2 . . . . .3B 108
  SM4: Mord 7A 154
Byne Rd. SE26 . . . . .6J 139
Bynes Rd. CR2: S Croy 7D 168
Byng Pl. WC1 . . . . .4D 6 (4H 83)
Byng Rd. EN5: Barn 2A 20
Byng St. E14 . . . . .2C 104
Bynon Av. DA7: Bex 3F 127
Byre Rd. N14 . . . . .6A 22
Byrne Cl. CR0: C'don 6C 156
Byrne Rd. SW12 . . . . .1F 137
Byron Av. E12 . . . . .6C 70
  E18 . . . . .3H 51
  KT3: N Mald 5C 152
  NW9 . . . . .4H 43
  SM1: Sutt 4B 166
  TW4: Cran 2J 111
Byron Av. E. SM1: Sutt 4B 166
Byron Cl. E8 . . . . .1G 85
  KT12: Walt T 7C 148
  SE20 . . . . .3H 157
  SE26 . . . . .4A 140
  SE28 . . . . .1C 108
  SW16 . . . . .6J 137
  TW12: Hamp 4D 130
Byron Ct. E11 . . . . .4K 51
  (off Makepeace Rd.)
  EN2: Enf 2G 23
  HA1: Harr 6J 41
  NW6 . . . . .7A 64
  (off Fairfax Rd.)
  SE22 . . . . .1G 139

Byron Ct. SW3 . . . . .4D 16
  (off Elystan St.)
  W7 . . . . .5J 61
  (off Boston Rd.)
  W9 . . . . .4J 81
  (off Lanhill Rd.)
  WC1 . . . . .3G 7
  (off Mecklenburgh Sq.)
Byron Dr. DA8: Erith 7H 109
  N2 . . . . .6B 46
Byron Gdns. SM1: Sutt 4B 166
Byron Hill Rd. HA2: Harr 1H 59
Byron Ho. DA1: Cray 5K 127
Byron M. NW3 . . . . .4C 64
  W9 . . . . .4J 81
Byron Pde. UB10: Hil 4E 74
Byron Rd. E10 . . . . .1D 68
  E17 . . . . .3C 50
  HA0: Wemb 2C 60
  HA1: Harr 6J 41
  HA3: W'stone 2K 41
  NW2 . . . . .2D 62
  NW7 . . . . .5H 29
  W5 . . . . .1F 97
Byron St. E14 . . . . .6E 86
Byron Ter. N9 . . . . .6D 24
  SE7 . . . . .7A 106
Byron Way UB4: Hayes 4H 75
  UB5: N'olt 3C 76
  UB7: W Dray 4B 92
Bysouth Cl. IG5: Ilf 1F 53
  N15 . . . . .4D 48
Bythorn St. SW9 . . . . .3K 119
Byton Rd. SW17 . . . . .6D 136
Byward Av. TW14: Felt 6A 112
Byward St. EC3 . . . . . . .3H 15 (7E 84)
Bywater Ho. SE18 . . . . .3C 106
Bywater Pl. SE16 . . . . .1A 104
Bywater St. SW3 . . . . . . .5E 16 (5D 100)
The Byway KT19: Ewe 4B 164
  SM2: Sutt 7B 166
Bywell Pl. E16 . . . . .5H 87
  W1 . . . . .6A 6
Bywood Av. CR0: C'don 6J 157
Byworth Wlk. N19 . . . . .1J 65

C

Cabanel Pl. SE11 . . . . . . .4H 19 (4A 102)
Cabbell St. NW1 . . . . . . .6C 4 (5C 82)
Cabinet Ct. NW2 . . . . .3B 62
Cabinet Way E4 . . . . .6G 35
Cable Cl. SE16 . . . . .4A 104
  (off Rope St.)
Cable Ho. WC1 . . . . .1J 7
  (off Gt. Percy St.)
Cable Pl. SE10 . . . . .1E 122
Cable St. E1 . . . . .7G 85
  E16 . . . . .2K 105
Cable Trade Pk. SE7 . . . . .4A 106
Cable Wlk. SE10 . . . . .4G 105
Cabot Cl. CR0: Wadd 3A 168
Cabot Ct. SE16 . . . . .4K 103
  (off Worgan St.)
Cabot Sq. E14 . . . . .1C 104
Cabot Way E6 . . . . .1B 88
Cabrail Court E14 . . . . .5A 86
  (off Aston Street)
Cab Rd. SE1 . . . . .5H 13
Cabul Rd. SW11 . . . . .2C 118
Caci Ho. W14 . . . . .4H 99
  (off Kensington Village)
Cactus Cl. SE15 . . . . .2E 120
Cactus Wlk. W12 . . . . .6B 80
Cadbury Cl. N20 . . . . .1F 31
  TW7: Isle 1A 114
  TW16: Sun 7G 129
Cadbury Rd. TW16: Sun 7G 129
Cadbury Way SE16 . . . . .3F 103
Caddington Cl. EN4: E Barn 5H 21
Caddington Rd. NW2 . . . . .3G 63
Caddis Cl. HA7: Stan 7E 26

Cadell Cl. E2 . . . 1K **9** (2F **85**)
Cade Rd. SE10 . . . 1F **123**
Cader Rd. SW4 . . . 6A **118**
Cadet Dr. SE1 . . . 4F **103**
Cadet Ho. SE18 . . . 3F **107**
Cadiz Ct. RM10: Dag . . . 7K **73**
Cadiz Rd. RM10: Dag . . . 7J **73**
Cadiz St. SE17 . . . 5C **102**
Cadley Ter. SE23 . . . 2J **139**
Cadman Cl. SW9 . . . 7B **102**
Cadman Ct. W4 . . . 5H **97**
(off Chaseley Dr.)
Cadmer Cl. KT3: N Mald . . . 4A **152**
Cadmium Sq. E2 . . . 3K **85**
(off Palmer's Rd.)
Cadmore Ho. N1 . . . 7B **66**
(off The Sutton Est.)
Cadmus Cl. SW4 . . . 3H **119**
Cadmus Cl. SE16 . . . 4A **104**
(off Seafarer Way)
SW9 . . . 1A **120**
(off Southey Rd.)
Cadnam Lodge E14 . . . 3E **104**
(off Schooner Cl.)
Cadnam Point SW15 . . . 1D **134**
Cadogan Cl. BR3: Beck . . . 1F **159**
E9 . . . 7B **68**
HA2: Harr . . . 4F **59**
TW11: Tedd . . . 5J **131**
Cadogan Ct. E9 . . . 7B **68**
(off Cadogan Ter.)
SM2: Sutt . . . 6K **165**
SW3 . . . 4E **16**
(off Draycott Av.)
Cadogan Ct. Gdns. SW1 . . . 3G **17**
(off D'Oyley St.)
Cadogan Gdns. E18 . . . 3K **51**
N3 . . . 1K **45**
N21 . . . 5F **23**
SW3 . . . 3F **17** (4D **100**)
Cadogan Ga. SW1 . . . 3F **17** (4D **100**)
Cadogan Hall . . . 3G **17**
(off Sloane Ter.)
Cadogan Ho. IG8: Wfd G . . . 7K **37**
SW3 . . . 7B **16**
Cadogan La. SW1 . . . 2G **17** (3E **100**)
Cadogan Mans. SW3 . . . 4F **17**
(off Cadogan Gdns.)
Cadogan Pl. SW1 . . . 1F **17** (3D **100**)
Cadogan Rd. KT6: Surb . . . 5D **150**
SE18 . . . 3G **107**
Cadogan Sq. SW1 . . . 2E **16** (3D **100**)
Cadogan St. SW3 . . . 4E **16** (4D **100**)
Cadogan Ter. E9 . . . 6B **68**
Cadoxton Av. N15 . . . 6F **49**
Cadwal Apts. N1 . . . 7J **65**
(off Caledonian Rd.)
Cadwallon Rd. SE9 . . . 2F **143**
Caedmon Rd. N7 . . . 4K **65**
Caerleon Cl. DA14: Sidc . . . 5C **144**
KT10: Clay . . . 7B **162**
Caerleon Ter. SE2 . . . 4B **108**
Caernarfon Ho. HA7: Stan . . . 5F **27**
Caernarvon Cl. CR4: Mitc . . . 3J **155**
Caernarvon Dr. IG5: Ilf . . . 1E **52**
Caernarvon Ho. E16 . . . 1K **105**
(off Audley Dr.)
W2 . . . 6A **82**
(off Hallfield Est.)
Caesar Ct. E2 . . . 2K **85**
(off Palmer's Rd.)
Caesars Wlk. CR4: Mitc . . . 5D **154**
Caesars Way TW17: Shep . . . 6F **147**
Cagney Ho. TW16: Sun . . . 1J **147**
Cagni Ho. SM1: Sutt . . . 4K **165**
Cahill St. EC1 . . . 4D **8** (4C **84**)
Cahir St. E14 . . . 4D **104**
Cain Ct. W5 . . . 5C **78**
(off Castlebar M.)
Caine Ho. W3 . . . 2H **97**
(off Hanbury Rd.)
Cain's La. TW14: Felt . . . 5G **111**
Caird St. W10 . . . 3G **81**

Cairn Av. W5 . . . 1D **96**
Cairncross M. N8 . . . 6J **47**
Cairndale Cl. BR1: Broml . . . 7H **141**
Cairnfield Av. NW2 . . . 3A **62**
Cairngorm Cl. TW11: Tedd . . . 5A **132**
Cairns Av. IG8: Wfd G . . . 6H **37**
SW16 . . . 3G **155**
Cairns M. SE18 . . . 1C **124**
Cairns Pl. SW16 . . . 2G **155**
Cairns Rd. SW11 . . . 5C **118**
Cairn Way HA7: Stan . . . 6E **26**
Cairo New Rd. CR0: C'don . . . 2B **168**
Cairo Rd. E17 . . . 4C **50**
Caisson Moor Ct. E3 . . . 4E **86**
(off Navigation Rd.)
Caister Ho. N7 . . . 6K **65**
Caister Cl. E15 . . . 1H **87**
(off Caistor Pk. Rd.)
Caistor M. SW12 . . . 7F **119**
Caistor Rd. SW12 . . . 7F **119**
Caithness Gdns. DA15: Sidc . . . 6K **125**
Caithness Ho. N1 . . . 1K **83**
(off Twyford St.)
Caithness Rd. CR4: Mitc . . . 7F **137**
W14 . . . 3F **99**
Caithness Wlk. CR0: C'don . . . 2D **168**
Calais Ga. SE5 . . . 1B **120**
Calais St. SE5 . . . 1B **120**
Calbourne Rd. SW12 . . . 7D **118**
Calcott Ct. W14 . . . 3G **99**
(off Blythe Rd.)
Calcott Wlk. SE9 . . . 4C **142**
Calcraft Ho. E2 . . . 2J **85**
(off Bonner Rd.)
Caldbeck Av. KT4: Wor Pk . . . 2C **164**
Caldecote KT1: King T . . . 2G **151**
(off Excelsior Cl.)
Caldecote Gdns. WD23: Bush . . . 1D **26**
CALDECOTE HILL . . . 1E **26**
Caldecote Rd. SE5 . . . 2C **120**
Caldecott Way E5 . . . 3K **67**
Calder Av. UB6: G'frd . . . 2K **77**
Calder Cl. EN1: Enf . . . 3K **23**
Calder Ct. SE16 . . . 1B **104**
Calder Gdns. HA8: Edg . . . 3G **43**
Calderon Ho. NW8 . . . 2C **82**
(off Townshend Est.)
Calderon Pl. W10 . . . 5E **80**
Calderon Rd. E11 . . . 4F **68**
Caldervale Rd. SW4 . . . 5H **119**
Calder Way SL3: Poyle . . . 6A **174**
Caldew St. SE5 . . . 7D **102**
Caldicot Grn. NW9 . . . 6A **44**
Caldon Ho. UB5: N'olt . . . 4D **76**
Caldwell Cl. SE18 . . . 5E **106**
Caldwell Ho. SW13 . . . 7E **98**
(off Trinity Chu. Rd.)
Caldwell St. SW9 . . . 7A **102**
Caldy Rd. DA17: Belv . . . 3H **109**
Caldy Wlk. N1 . . . 7C **66**
Caleb St. SE1 . . . 6C **14** (2C **102**)
Caledonia Ct. IG11: Bark . . . 2C **90**
(off Keel Cl.)
Caledonia Ho. E14 . . . 6A **86**
(off Salmon La.)
Caledonian Cl. IG3: Ilf . . . 1B **72**
Caledonian Ct. BR2: Broml . . . 6C **160**
(off Wells Vw. Dr.)
UB5: N'olt . . . 4C **76**
Caledonian Point SE10 . . . 6D **104**
(off Norman Rd.)
Caledonian Rd. N1 . . . 1F **7** (2J **83**)
N7 . . . 4K **65**
Caledonian Sq. NW1 . . . 6H **65**
Caledonian Wharf E14 . . . 4F **105**
Caledonia Rd. TW19: Stanw . . . 1A **128**
Caledonia St. N1 . . . 1F **7** (2J **83**)

Caledon Rd. E6 . . . 1D **88**
SM6: W'gton . . . 4E **166**
Caledonia M. KT6: Surb . . . 6D **150**
Cale St. SW3 . . . 5C **16** (5C **100**)
Caletock Way SE10 . . . 5H **105**
Calgarth NW1 . . . 1B **6**
(off Ampthill Est.)
Calgary Ct. RM7: Mawney . . . 4H **55**
SE16 . . . 2J **103**
(off Canada Est.)
Calia Ho. E20 . . . 6E **68**
(off Anthems Way)
Caliban Twr. N1 . . . 2E **84**
(off Arden Est.)
Calico Av. SM6: W'gton . . . 2E **166**
Calico Ct. SE16 . . . 3G **103**
(off Marine St.)
Calico Ho. E20 . . . 6E **68**
(off Mirabelle Gdns.)
EC4 . . . 1D **14**
(off Well Ct.)
SE1 . . . 7G **15**
(off Long La.)
Calico Row SW11 . . . 3A **118**
Calidore Cl. SW2 . . . 6K **119**
California Bldg. SE13 . . . 1D **122**
(off Deal's Gateway)
California Ct. WD23: B Hea . . . 1E **26**
(off High Rd.)
California La. WD23: B Hea . . . 1C **26**
California Rd. KT3: N Mald . . . 4H **151**
Callaby Ter. N1 . . . 6D **66**
Callaghan Cl. SE13 . . . 4G **123**
Callahan Cotts. E1 . . . 5J **85**
(off Lindley St.)
Callander Rd. SE6 . . . 2D **140**
The Callanders WD23: B Hea . . . 1D **26**
Callard Av. N13 . . . 4G **33**
Callcott Cl. W2 . . . 4A **4**
Callcott Ct. NW6 . . . 7H **63**
Callcott Rd. NW6 . . . 7H **63**
Callcott St. W8 . . . 1J **99**
Callendar Rd. SW7 . . . 1A **16** (3B **100**)
Callender Ct. CR0: C'don . . . 6C **156**
(off Harry Cl.)
Callingham Cl. E14 . . . 5B **86**
Callington M. TW2: Twick . . . 2J **131**
Callis Close SE18 . . . 3E **106**
Callis Farm Cl. TW19: Stanw . . . 6A **110**
Callisons Pl. SE10 . . . 5G **105**
Callis Rd. E17 . . . 6B **50**
Calliston Ct. E16 . . . 5J **87**
(off Hammersley Rd.)
Callow St. SW3 . . . 7A **16** (6B **100**)
Cally Pool & Gym . . . 1K **83**
Calmont Rd. BR1: Broml . . . 6F **141**
Calne Av. IG5: Ilf . . . 1F **53**
Calonne Rd. SW19 . . . 4F **135**
Calshot Ho. N1 . . . 2K **83**
(off Calshot St.)
Calshot Rd. TW6: H'row A . . . 2C **110**
Calshot St. N1 . . . 1G **7** (2K **83**)
Calshot Way EN2: Enf . . . 3G **23**
TW6: H'row A . . . 2C **110**
Calstock Ho. SE11 . . . 5K **19**
Calstock Rd. SE11 . . . 5K **19**
Calthorpe Gdns. HA8: Edg . . . 5K **27**
SM1: Sutt . . . 3A **166**
Calthorpe St. WC1 . . . 3H **7** (4K **83**)
Calton Av. SE21 . . . 6E **120**
Calton Rd. EN5: New Bar . . . 6F **21**
Calverley Cl. BR3: Beck . . . 6D **140**
Calverley Cres. RM10: Dag . . . 2G **73**
Calverley Gdns. HA3: Kenton . . . 7D **42**
Calverley Gro. N19 . . . 1H **65**
Calverley Rd. KT17: Ewe . . . 6C **164**
Calvert Av. E2 . . . 2H **9** (3E **84**)
Calvert Cl. DA14: Sidc . . . 6E **144**
DA17: Belv . . . 4G **109**
Calvert Ct. TW9: Rich . . . 4F **115**

Calvert Dr. DA2: Wilm . . . 2K **145**
Calvert Ho. W12 . . . 7D **80**
(off White City Est.)
Calvert M. RM8: Dag . . . 1E **72**
Calverton SE5 . . . 6E **102**
(off Albany Rd.)
Calverton Pl. UB6: G'frd . . . 6K **59**
Calverton Rd. E6 . . . 1E **88**
Calvert Rd. EN5: Barn . . . 2A **20**
SE10 . . . 5H **105**
Calvert's Bldgs. SE1 . . . 5E **14** (1D **102**)
Calvert St. NW1 . . . 1E **82**
Calvin St. E1 . . . 4J **9** (4F **85**)
Calydon Rd. SE7 . . . 5K **105**
Calypso Cres. SE15 . . . 7F **103**
Calypso Way SE16 . . . 3B **104**
Camac Rd. TW2: Twick . . . 1H **131**
Camarthen Grn. NW9 . . . 5A **44**
Cambalt Rd. SW15 . . . 5F **117**
Cambay Ho. E1 . . . 4A **86**
(off Harford St.)
Camber Ho. SE15 . . . 6J **103**
Camberley Av. EN1: Enf . . . 4K **23**
SW20 . . . 2D **152**
Camberley Cl. SM3: Cheam . . . 3F **165**
Camberley Ho. NW1 . . . 1K **5**
Camberley Rd.
TW6: H'row A . . . 3C **110**
Cambert Way SE3 . . . 4K **123**
CAMBERWELL . . . 1D **120**
Camberwell Bus. Cen. SE5 . . . 7D **102**
Camberwell Chu. St. SE5 . . . 1D **120**
Camberwell Glebe SE5 . . . 1E **120**
CAMBERWELL GREEN . . . 1C **120**
Camberwell Grn. SE5 . . . 1D **120**
Camberwell Gro. SE5 . . . 1D **120**
Camberwell Leisure Cen. . . . 1D **120**
Camberwell New Rd. SE5 . . . 6A **102**
Camberwell Pas. SE5 . . . 1C **120**
Camberwell Rd. SE5 . . . 6C **102**
Camberwell Sta. Rd. SE5 . . . 1C **120**
Camberwell Trad. Est. SE5 . . . 1B **120**
Cambeys Rd. RM10: Dag . . . 5H **73**
Cambisgate SW19 . . . 5G **135**
Cambium Apts. SW19 . . . 7F **117**
(off Beatrice Pl.)
W8 . . . 3K **99**
(off Beatrice Pl.)
Cambium Ho. HA9: Wemb . . . 4G **61**
(off Palace Arts Way)
Camborne Av. W13 . . . 2B **96**
Camborne Cl. TW6: H'row A . . . 3C **110**
Camborne Cres. TW6: H'row A . . . 3C **110**
(off Camborne Rd.)
Camborne M. SW18 . . . 7J **117**
W11 . . . 6G **81**
Camborne Rd. CR0: C'don . . . 7G **157**
DA14: Sidc . . . 3D **144**
DA16: Well . . . 2K **125**
HA8: Edg . . . 4A **28**
SM2: Sutt . . . 7J **165**
SM4: Mord . . . 5F **153**
SW18 . . . 7J **117**
Camborne Way TW5: Hest . . . 1E **112**
Cambourne Av. N9 . . . 7E **24**
Cambourne Wlk. TW10: Rich . . . 6D **114**
Cambrai Ct. N13 . . . 3D **32**
Cambray Rd. BR6: Orp . . . 7K **161**
SW12 . . . 1G **137**
Cambria Cl. DA15: Sidc . . . 1H **143**
TW3: Houn . . . 4E **112**
Cambria Ct. E17 . . . 3A **50**
TW14: Felt . . . 7K **111**
Cambria Gdns. TW19: Stanw . . . 7A **110**
(not continuous)
Cambria Ho. E14 . . . 6A **86**
(off Salmon La.)
SE26 . . . 4G **139**
(off High Level Dr.)
Cambrian Av. IG2: Ilf . . . 5J **53**
Cambrian Cl. SE27 . . . 3B **138**
Cambrian Grn. NW9 . . . 5A **44**
(off Snowdon Dr.)

Cambrian Rd. E10 . . . . .7C **50**
TW10: Rich 6F **115**
Cambria Rd. SE5 . . . . .3C **120**
Cambria St. SW6 . . . . .7K **99**
Cambridge Av. DA16: Well 4K **125**
KT3: N Mald 3A **152**
(not continuous)
NW6 . . . . .2J **81**
UB6: G'frd 5K **59**
Cambridge Barracks Rd.
SE18 .4D **106**
Cambridge Cir. WC2 . . . . .1D **12** (6H **83**)
Cambridge Cl. E17 . . . . .6B **50**
EN4: E Barn 1K **31**
N22 . . . . .1A **48**
NW10 . . . . .3J **61**
SW20 . . . . .1D **152**
TW4: Houn 4C **112**
UB7: Harm 2E **174**
Cambridge Cotts. TW9: Kew 6G **97**
Cambridge Ct. E2 . . . . .2H **85**
(off Cambridge Heath Rd.)
N16 . . . . .7E **48**
(off Amhurst Pk.)
NW6 . . . . .2J **81**
(not continuous)
W2 . . . . .6C **4**
(off Edgware Rd.)
W6 . . . . .4E **98**
(off Shepherd's Bush Rd.)
Cambridge Cres. E2 . . . . .2H **85**
TW11: Tedd 5A **132**
Cambridge Dr. HA4: Ruis 2A **58**
SE12 .5J **123**
Cambridge Gdns. EN1: Enf 2B **24**
KT1: King T 2G **151**
N10 . . . . .1E **46**
N17 . . . . .7J **33**
N21 . . . . .7J **23**
NW6 . . . . .2J **81**
W10 . . . . .6F **81**
Cambridge Ga. NW1 . . . . . .3J **5** (4F **83**)
Cambridge Ga. M. NW1 . . . .3K **5** (4F **83**)
Cambridge Grn. SE9 . . . . .1F **143**
Cambridge Gro. SE20 . . . . .1H **157**
W6 . . . . .4D **98**
Cambridge Gro. Rd. KT1: King T . .3G **151**
(not continuous)
Cambridge Heath Rd. E1 . . . . . . .5H **85**
E2 . . . . .5H **85**
Cambridge Ho. W6 . . . . .4D **98**
(off Cambridge Gro.)
W13 . . . . .6A **78**
Cambridge Pde. EN1: Enf 1B **24**
Cambridge Pk. E11 . . . . .7J **51**
TW1: Twick 6C **114**
Cambridge Pk. Ct. TW1: Twick . . .7D **114**
Cambridge Pk. Rd. E11 . . . . .7J **51**
(off Lonsdale Rd.)
Cambridge Pas. E9 . . . . .7J **67**
Cambridge Pl. W8 . . . . .2K **99**
Cambridge Rd. BR1: Broml 7J **141**
CR4: Mitc 3G **155**
DA14: Sidc 4A **144**
E4 . . . . .1A **36**
E11 . . . . .6H **51**
HA2: Harr 5E **40**
IG3: Ilf .1J **71**
IG11: Bark 7G **71**
KT1: King T 2F **151**
KT2: King T 2F **151**
KT3: N Mald 4K **151**
KT8: W Mole 4D **148**
KT12: Walt T 6K **147**
NW6 . . . . .2J **81**
(not continuous)
SE20 .3H **157**
SM5: Cars 6C **166**
SW11 .1D **118**
SW13 . . . . .2B **116**
SW20 . . . . .1C **152**
TW1: Twick 6D **114**
TW4: Houn 4C **112**

Cambridge Rd. TW9: Kew 7G **97**
TW11: Tedd 4K **131**
TW12: Hamp 7D **130**
TW15: Ashf 7E **128**
UB1: S'hall 1D **94**
W7 . . . . .2K **95**
Cambridge Rd. Nth. W4 . . . . .5H **97**
Cambridge Rd. Sth. W4 . . . . .5H **97**
Cambridge Row SE18 . . . . .5F **107**
Cambridge Sq. W2 . . . . . . .7C **4** (6C **82**)
Cambridge St. SW1 . . . .4K **17** (4F **101**)
Cambridge Ter. N9 . . . . .7K **23**
NW1 . . . . .2J **5** (3F **83**)
Cambridge Ter. M. NW1 . . . .2K **5** (3F **83**)
Cambridge Theatre 1E **12**
(off Earlham St.)
Cambstone Cl. N11 . . . . .2K **31**
Cambus Cl. UB4: Yead 5C **76**
Cambus Rd. E16 . . . . .5J **87**
Cam Ct. SE15 . . . . .6F **103**
Camdale Rd. SE18 . . . . .7K **107**
Camden Arts Cen. 5K **63**
Camden Av. TW13: Felt 1A **130**
UB4: Yead 7B **76**
Camden Cl. BR7: Chst 1G **161**
Camden Cl. DA17: Belv 5G **109**
NW1 . . . . .7G **65**
(off Rousden St.)
Camden Gdns. CR7: Thor H 3B **156**
NW1 . . . . .7F **65**
SM1: Sutt 5K **165**
Camden Gro. BR7: Chst 6F **143**
Camden High St. NW1 . . . . .7F **65**
Camden Hill Rd. SE19 . . . . .6E **138**
Camden Ho. SE8 . . . . .5B **104**
Camdenhurst St. E14 . . . . .6A **86**
Camden La. N7 . . . . .5H **65**
Camden Lock Market 7F **65**
Camden Lock Pl. NW1 . . . . .7F **65**
Camden Markets 7F **65**
Camden M. NW1 . . . . .7G **65**
Camden Pk. Rd. BR7: Chst 7D **142**
NW1 . . . . .6H **65**
Camden Pas. N1 . . . . .2B **84**
Camden People's Theatre 3A **6**
(off Hampstead Rd.)
Camden Rd. DA5: Bexl 1E **144**
E11 . . . . .6K **51**
E17 . . . . .6B **50**
N7 . . . . .4J **65**
NW1 . . . . .7G **65**
SM1: Sutt 5K **165**
SM5: Cars 4D **166**
Camden Row HA5: Pinn 3A **40**
SE3 .2G **123**
Camden Sq. NW1 . . . . .5H **65**
(not continuous)
SE15 .1F **121**
Camden St. NW1 . . . . .7G **65**
Camden Studios NW1 . . . . .1G **83**
(off Camden St.)
Camden Ter. NW1 . . . . .6H **65**
CAMDEN TOWN 1F **83**
Camden Wlk. N1 . . . . .1B **84**
Camden Way BR7: Chst 7D **142**
CR7: Thor H 3B **156**
Cameford Ct. SW2 . . . . .7J **119**
Camelford NW1 . . . . .1G **83**
(off Royal Coll. St.)
Camelford Ct. W11 . . . . .6G **81**
Camelford Ho. SE1 . . . . .5F **19** (5J **101**)
Camelford Wlk. W11 . . . . .6G **81**
Camel Gro. KT2: King T 5D **132**
Camellia Cl. E10 . . . . .2C **68**
Camellia Ho. SE8 . . . . .7B **104**
(off Idonia St.)
SW11 .7F **101**
TW13: Felt 1J **129**
(off Bedfont La.)
Camellia La. KT5: Surb 4H **151**
Camellia Pl. TW2: Whitt 7F **113**
Camellia St. SW8 . . . . .7J **101**
(not continuous)

Camelot Cl. SE28 . . . . .2H **107**
SW19 .4H **135**
Camelot Ho. NW1 . . . . .6H **65**
Camel Rd. E16 . . . . .1C **106**
Camera Pl. SW10 . . . . . .7A **16** (6B **100**)
The Camera Press Gallery 6J **15**
(off Queen Elizabeth St.)
Cameret Ct. W11 . . . . .2F **99**
(off Holland Rd.)
Cameron Cl. DA5: Bexl 3K **145**
N18 . . . . .4C **34**
N20 . . . . .2G **31**
N22 . . . . .7E **32**
Cameron Cres. HA8: Edg 1H **43**
Cameron Ho. BR1: Broml 1H **159**
NW8 . . . . .2C **82**
(off St John's Wood Ter.)
SE5 . . . . .7C **102**
Cameron Pl. E1 . . . . .6H **85**
SW16 .2A **138**
Cameron Rd. BR2: Broml 5J **159**
CR0: C'don 6B **156**
IG3: Ilf .1J **71**
SE6 . . . . .2B **140**
Cameron Sq. CR4: Mitc 1C **154**
Cameron Ter. SE12 . . . . .3K **141**
Camerton Cl. E8 . . . . .6F **67**
The Camgate Cen.
TW19: Stanw 6B **110**
Camgate Mans. SE5 . . . . .6C **102**
(off Camberwell Rd.)
Camilla Cl. TW16: Sun 6H **129**
Camilla Rd. SE16 . . . . .4H **103**
Camille Cl. SE25 . . . . .3G **157**
Camlan Rd. BR1: Broml 4H **141**
Camlet St. E2 . . . . .3J **9** (4F **85**)
Camlet Way EN4: Barn, Had W 2D **20**
Camley St. N1 . . . . .7H **65**
Camley Street Natural Pk. 2J **83**
Camley Street Natural Pk. Vis. Cen.
. . . . .2H **83**
Camm Gdns. KT1: King T 2F **151**
KT7: T Ditt 7K **149**
Camms Ter. RM10: Dag 5J **73**
(off Cambeys Rd.)
Camomile Av. CR4: Mitc 1D **154**
Camomile Rd. RM7: Rush G 2K **73**
Camomile St. EC3 . . . . . .7H **9** (6E **84**)
Camomile Way UB7: Yiew 6A **74**
Campaign Ct. W9 . . . . .4H **81**
(off Chantry Cl.)
Campana Rd. SW6 . . . . .1J **117**
Campania Bldg. E1 . . . . .7K **85**
(off Jardine Rd.)
Campaspe Bus. Pk. TW16: Sun . . .5H **147**
Campbell Av. IG6: Ilf 4F **53**
Campbell Cl. HA4: Ruis 6J **39**
SE18 .1E **124**
SW16 .4H **137**
TW2: Twick 1H **131**
Campbell Ct. N17 . . . . .1F **49**
NW9 . . . . .6J **43**
SE22 .1G **139**
SW7 . . . . .3A **100**
(off Gloucester Rd.)
Campbell Cft. HA8: Edg 5B **28**
Campbell Gordon Way NW2 . . . . . .4D **62**
Campbell Ho. 3C **6** (4H **83**)
Campbell Ho. SW1 . . . . .6A **18**
(off Churchill Gdns.)
W2 . . . . .4A **4**
(off Hall Pl.)
W12 . . . . .7D **80**
(off White City Est.)
Campbell Rd. CR0: C'don 7B **156**
E3 . . . . .3C **86**
E6 . . . . .1C **88**
E15 . . . . .4H **69**
E17 . . . . .4B **50**
KT8: E Mos 3J **149**
N17 . . . . .1F **49**
TW2: Twick 2H **131**
W7 . . . . .7J **77**

Campbell Wlk. N1 . . . . .1J **83**
(off Outram Pl.)
Campdale Rd. N7 . . . . .3H **65**
Campden Cres. HA0: Wemb 3B **60**
RM8: Dag 4B **72**
Campden Gro. W8 . . . . .2J **99**
Campden Hill W8 . . . . .2J **99**
Campden Hill Ct. W8 . . . . .2J **99**
Campden Hill Gdns. W8 . . . . .1J **99**
Campden Hill Mans. W8 . . . . .1J **99**
(off Edge St.)
Campden Hill Pl. W11 . . . . .1H **99**
Campden Hill Rd. W8 . . . . .1J **99**
Campden Hill Sq. W8 . . . . .1H **99**
Campden Hill Towers W11 . . . . .1J **99**
Campden Ho. NW6 . . . . .7B **64**
(off Harben Rd.)
W8 . . . . .2J **99**
(off Sheffield Ter.)
Campden Ho. Cl. W8 . . . . .2J **99**
Campden Ho's. W8 . . . . .1J **99**
Campden Ho. Ter. W8 . . . . .1J **99**
(off Kensington Chu. St.)
Campden Mans. W8 . . . . .1J **99**
(off Kensington Mall)
Campden Rd. CR2: S Croy 5E **168**
UB10: Ick 3B **56**
Campden St. W8 . . . . .1J **99**
Campden Way RM8: Dag 4B **72**
Campe Ho. N10 . . . . .7K **31**
Campen Cl. SW19 . . . . .2G **135**
Camperdown St. E1 . . . .1K **15** (6F **85**)
Campfield Rd. SE9 . . . . .7B **124**
Campion Cl. CR0: C'don 4E **168**
E6 . . . . .7D **88**
HA3: Kenton 6F **43**
RM7: Rush G 2K **73**
UB8: Hill 5B **74**
Campion Ct. HA0: Wemb 2E **78**
Campion Gdns. IG8: Wfd G 5D **36**
Campion Ho. E14 . . . . .4D **86**
(off Frances Wharf)
SE16 .2A **104**
(off Blondin Way)
Campion Pl. SE28 . . . . .1A **108**
Campion Rd. E10 . . . . .7D **50**
SW15 .4E **116**
TW7: Isle 1K **113**
Campion Ter. NW2 . . . . .3F **63**
Campion Way HA8: Edg 4D **28**
Camplin Rd. HA3: Kenton 5E **42**
Camplin St. SE14 . . . . .7K **103**
Camp Rd. SW19 . . . . .5D **134**
The Campsbourne N8 . . . . .4J **47**
Campsbourne Ho. N8 . . . . .4J **47**
(off Pembroke Rd.)
Campsbourne Pde. N8 . . . . .4J **47**
(off High St.)
Campsbourne Rd. N8 . . . . .3J **47**
(not continuous)
Campsey Gdns. RM9: Dag 7B **72**
Campsey Rd. RM9: Dag 7B **72**
Campsfield Ho. N8 . . . . .3J **47**
(off Campsfield Rd.)
Campsfield Rd. N8 . . . . .3J **47**
Camphill Pl. SE13 . . . . .5E **122**
Camphill Rd. SE13 . . . . .5E **122**
Campus Av. RM8: Dag 4A **72**
Campus Ho. TW7: Isle 7J **95**
Campus Rd. E17 . . . . .6B **50**
Campus Way NW4 . . . . .3D **44**
Camp Vw. SW19 . . . . .5D **134**
Cam Rd. E15 . . . . .1F **87**
Camrose Av. DA8: Erith 6H **109**
HA8: Edg 2E **42**
TW13: Felt 4A **130**
Camrose Cl. CR0: C'don 7A **158**
SM4: Mord 4J **153**
Camrose St. SE2 . . . . .5A **108**
Camwal Cl. CR4: Mitc 2C **154**
Canada Av. N18 . . . . .6H **33**
Canada Cres. W3 . . . . .5J **79**

Canada Est.—Capstan Cl.

Canada Est. SE16 ... 3J 103
Canada Gdns. SE13 ... 5E 122
Canada House ... *3A 104*
(off Brunswick Quay)
Canada House ... 4D 12
Canada Memorial ... 2G 101
Canada Pl. *E14* ... *1D 104*
(off Canada Sq.)
Canada Rd. W3 ... 5J 79
Canada Sq. E14 ... 1D 104
Canada St. SE16 ... 2K 103
Canada Way W12 ... 7D 80
Canada Wharf SE16 ... 1B 104
Canadian Av. SE6 ... 1D 140
Canal App. SE8 ... 5A 104
Canal Blvd. NW1 ... 6H 65
CANAL BRIDGE ... 6G 103
Canal Bldg. N1 ... 2C 84
Canal Cl. E1 ... 4A 86
W10 ... 4F 81
Canal Cotts. *E3* ... *1B 86*
(off Parnell Rd.)
Canaletto *EC1* ... *1C 8*
(off City Rd.)
Canal Gro. SE15 ... 6H 103
Canal Market ... *7F 65*
(off Castlehaven Rd.)
Canal Mill Apts. *E2* ... *1F 85*
(off Boat La.)
Canal Path E2 ... 1F 85
Canal Reach N1 ... 1H 83
Canalside Activity Cen. ... 4F 81
Canalside Gdns. UB2: S'hall ... 4C 94
Canalside Sq. N1 ... 1C 84
Canal Side Studios *NW1* ... *1H 83*
(off St Pancras Way)
Canalside Studios *N1* ... *1E 84*
(off Orsman Rd.)
Canalside Wlk. W2 ... 6A 4 (5B 82)
Canal St. SE5 ... 6D 102
Canal Wlk. CR0: C'don ... 6E 156
E17 ... 3K 49
N1 ... 1D 84
NW10 ... *7J 61*
(off Westend Cl.)
SE26 ... 5J 139
Canal Way W10 ... 4F 81
Canal Wharf *E8* ... *1E 84*
(off Kingsland Rd.)
UB6: G'frd ... 1A 78
Canal Yd. UB2: S'hall ... 4K 93
Canary Vw. *SE10* ... *6D 104*
(off Dowells St.)
Canary Wharf Tower ... 1D 104
Canberra Cl. NW4 ... 3C 44
RM10: Dag ... 1K 91
Canberra Cres. RM10: Dag ... 7K 73
Canberra Dr. UB4: N'olt ... 3A 76
UB5: N'olt ... 3A 76
Canberra Path *E10* ... *7D 50*
(off Whitney Rd.)
Canberra Pl. TW9: Rich ... 3G 115
Canberra Rd. DA7: Bex ... 6D 108
E6 ... 1D 88
SE7 ... 6A 106
TW6: H'row A ... 3C 110
W13 ... 1A 96
Canbury Av. KT2: King T ... 1F 151
Canbury Bus. Cen. KT2: King T ... 1E 150
Canbury Bus. Pk. *KT2: King T* ... *1E 150*
(off Canbury Pk. Rd.)
Canbury Ct. KT2: King T ... 7D 132
Canbury M. SE26 ... 3G 139
Canbury Pk. Rd. KT2: King T ... 1E 150
Canbury Pas. KT2: King T ... 1D 150
Cancell Rd. SW9 ... 1A 120
Candahar Rd. SW11 ... 2C 118
Candida Ct. NW1 ... 7F 65
Candid Ho. *NW10* ... *3D 80*
(off Trenmar Gdns.)
Candle Gro. SE15 ... 3H 121
Candlelight Ct. *E15* ... *6H 69*
(off Romford Rd.)
Candler M. TW1: Twick ... 7A 114
Candler St. N15 ... 6D 48
Candle St. E1 ... 5A 86
Candover Cl. UB7: Harm ... 3E 174
Candover St. W1 ... 6A 6 (5G 83)
Candy St. E3 ... 1B 86
Candy Wharf E3 ... 4A 86
Caney M. NW2 ... 2F 63
Canfield Dr. HA4: Ruis ... 5K 57
Canfield Gdns. NW6 ... 7K 63
Canfield Ho. *N15* ... *6E 48*
(off Albert Rd.)
Canfield Pl. NW6 ... 6A 64
Canfield Rd. IG8: Wfd G ... 7H 37
Canford Av. UB5: N'olt ... 1D 76
Canford Cl. EN2: Enf ... 2F 23
Canford Gdns. KT3: N Mald ... 6A 152
Canford Pl. TW11: Tedd ... 6C 132
Canford Rd. SW11 ... 5E 118
Canham Gdns. TW4: Houn ... 7D 112
Canham Rd. SE25 ... 3E 156
W3 ... 2A 98
Canius Ho. *CR0: C'don* ... *3C 168*
(off Scarbrook Rd.)
Canmore Gdns. SW16 ... 7G 137
CANN HALL ... 4G 69
Cann Hall Rd. E11 ... 4G 69
Cann Ho. *W14* ... *3G 99*
(off Russell Rd.)
Canning Cres. N22 ... 1K 47
Canning Cross SE5 ... 2E 120
Canning Ho. *W12* ... *7D 80*
(off Australia Rd.)
Canning Pas. W8 ... 3A 100
Canning Pl. W8 ... 3A 100
Canning Pl. M. *W8* ... *3A 100*
(off Canning Pl.)
Canning Rd. CR0: C'don ... 2F 169
E15 ... 2G 87
E17 ... 4A 50
HA3: W'stone ... 3J 41
N5 ... 3B 66
Canning Sq. EN1: Enf ... 1B 24
Cannington Rd. RM9: Dag ... 6C 72
CANNING TOWN ... 6H 87
CANNING TOWN ... 5G 87
Cannizaro Rd. SW19 ... 6E 134
Cannock Ct. E17 ... 2E 50
Cannock Ho. N4 ... 7C 48
Cannonbury Av. HA5: Pinn ... 6B 40
Cannon Cl. SW20 ... 3E 152
TW12: Hamp ... 6F 131
Cannon Ct. *EC1* ... *3B 8*
(off Brewhouse Yd.)
Cannon Dr. E14 ... 7C 86
Cannon Hill N14 ... 3D 32
NW6 ... 5J 63
Cannon Hill La. SW20 ... 5F 153
Cannon Hill M. N14 ... 3D 32
Cannon Ho. SE11 ... 4H 19
Cannon La. HA5: Pinn ... 5C 40
NW3 ... 3B 64
Cannon Pl. NW3 ... 3B 64
SE7 ... 5C 106
Cannon Retail Pk. ... 7A 90
Cannon Rd. DA7: Bex ... 1E 126
N14 ... 3D 32
N17 ... 6A 34
Cannon St. EC4 ... 1C 14 (6C 84)
Cannon St. Rd. E1 ... 6H 85
Cannon Trad. Est.
HA9: Wemb ... 4H 61
Cannon Way KT8: W Mole ... 4E 148
Cannon Wharf Bus. Cen. *SE8* ... *4A 104*
(off Pell St.)
Cannon Wharf Development *SE8* ... *4A 104*
(off Yeoman St.)
Cannon Workshops *E14* ... *7C 86*
(off Cannon Dr.)
Canoe Wlk. E14 ... 6B 86
Canon All. *EC4* ... *1C 14*
(off Queen's Head Pas.)
Canon Av. RM6: Chad H ... 5C 54
Canon Beck Rd. SE16 ... 2J 103
Canonbie Rd. SE23 ... 7J 121
CANONBURY ... 6C 66
Canonbury Bus. Cen. N1 ... 1C 84
Canonbury Cotts. EN1: Enf ... 1K 23
Canonbury Ct. *N1* ... *7B 66*
(off Hawes St.)
Canonbury Cres. N1 ... 7C 66
Canonbury Gro. N1 ... 7C 66
Canonbury Hgts. *N1* ... *6D 66*
(off Dove Rd.)
Canonbury La. N1 ... 7B 66
Canonbury Pk. Nth. N1 ... 6C 66
Canonbury Pk. Sth. N1 ... 6C 66
Canonbury Pl. N1 ... 6B 66
(not continuous)
Canonbury Rd. EN1: Enf ... 1K 23
N1 ... 6B 66
Canonbury Sq. N1 ... 7B 66
Canonbury St. N1 ... 7C 66
Canonbury Vs. N1 ... 7B 66
Canon Ho. *W10* ... *3H 81*
(off Bruckner St.)
Canon Mohan Cl. N14 ... 6K 21
Canon Rd. BR1: Broml ... 3A 160
Canon Row SW1 ... 7E 12 (2J 101)
(not continuous)
Canon's Cl. N2 ... 7B 46
Canons Cl. CR4: Mitc ... 4D 154
HA8: Edg ... 6A 28
Canons Cnr. HA8: Edg ... 4K 27
Canons Ct. E15 ... 4G 69
HA8: Edg ... 6A 28
Canons Dr. HA8: Edg ... 6K 27
Canonsleigh Rd. RM9: Dag ... 7B 72
Canons Leisure Cen.
Mitcham ... 4D 154
CANONS PARK ... 7J 27
Canons Pk. ... 6J 27
Canons Pk. Cl. HA8: Edg ... 7K 27
Canons Row HA8: Edg ... 4K 27
Canon St. N1 ... 1C 84
Canon's Wlk. CR0: C'don ... 3K 169
Canons Way HA8: Edg ... 4A 28
Canopus Way TW19: Stanw ... 7A 110
Canrobert St. E2 ... 2H 85
Cantelowes Rd. NW1 ... 6H 65
Canterbury Av. DA15: Sidc ... 2B 144
IG1: Ilf ... 7C 52
Canterbury Cl. BR3: Beck ... 1D 158
E6 ... 6D 88
KT4: Wor Pk ... 2F 165
SE5 ... *2C 120*
(off Lilford Rd.)
UB6: G'frd ... 5F 77
Canterbury Ct. *CR2: S Croy* ... *7C 168*
(off St Augustine's Av.)
NW6 ... *2J 81*
(off Canterbury Rd.)
NW9 ... 2A 44
SE5 ... 7A 102
SE12 ... 3K 141
TW15: Ashf ... 4B 128
Canterbury Cres. SW9 ... 3A 120
Canterbury Gro. SE27 ... 4A 138
Canterbury Hall KT4: Wor Pk ... 7D 152
Canterbury Ho. *CR0: C'don* ... *1D 168*
(off Sydenham Rd.)
E3 ... *3D 86*
(off Bow Rd.)
IG11: Bark ... *7A 72*
(off Margaret Bondfield Av.)
RM8: Dag ... *4A 72*
(off Academy Way)
SE1 ... 1H 19 (3K 101)
SE8 ... *5C 104*
(off Wharf St.)
Canterbury Ind. Pk. SE15 ... 6J 103
Canterbury Pl. SE17 ... 5B 102
Canterbury Rd. CR0: C'don ... 7K 155
E10 ... 7E 50
HA1: Harr ... 5F 41
HA2: Harr ... 5F 41
Canterbury Rd. NW6 ... 2H 81
(Carlton Va.)
NW6 ... 2J 81
(Princess Rd.)
SM4: Mord ... 7K 153
TW13: Hanw ... 2C 130
Canterbury Ter. NW6 ... 2J 81
Canter Way E1 ... 1K 15 (6G 85)
Cantium Retail Pk. ... 6G 103
Cantley Gdns. IG2: Ilf ... 6G 53
SE19 ... 1F 157
Cantley Rd. W7 ... 3A 96
Canto Ct. *EC1* ... *3D 8*
(off Old St.)
Canton St. E14 ... 6C 86
Cantrell Rd. E3 ... 4B 86
Cantwell Rd. SE18 ... 7F 107
Canute Gdns. SE16 ... 4K 103
Canvey St. SE1 ... 4C 14 (1C 102)
Canyon Gdn. *E3* ... *3B 86*
(off St Clements Av.)
Cape Cl. IG11: Bark ... 7F 71
Cape Henry Ct. *E14* ... *7F 87*
(off Jamestown Way)
Cape Ho. *E8* ... *6F 67*
(off Dalston La.)
E16 ... *1K 105*
(off Cunningham Av.)
Capel Av. SM6: W'gton ... 5K 167
Capel Cl. BR2: Broml ... 1C 172
N20 ... 3F 31
Capel Ct. *EC2* ... *1F 15*
(off Bartholomew La.)
SE20 ... 1J 157
Capel Cres. HA7: Stan ... 2F 27
Capel Gdns. HA5: Pinn ... 4D 40
IG3: Bark, Ilf ... 4K 71
Capel Ho. *E9* ... *7J 67*
(off Loddiges Rd.)
Capel Rd. E7 ... 4K 69
E12 ... 4K 69
EN4: E Barn ... 6H 21
Capener's Cl. SW1 ... 7F 11
Capern Rd. SW18 ... 1A 136
Cape Rd. N17 ... 3G 49
Cape Yd. E1 ... 1G 103
Capital Bus. Cen.
CR2: S Croy ... 7D 168
HA0: Wemb ... 2D 78
Capital E. Apts. *E16* ... *7J 87*
(off Western Gateway)
Capital Ho. *SW15* ... *5G 117*
(off Plaza Gdns.)
Capital Ind. Est. CR4: Mitc ... 5D 154
DA17: Belv ... 3H 109
Capital Interchange Way
TW8: Bford ... 5G 97
Capital Mill Apts. *E2* ... *1F 85*
(off Whiston Rd.)
Capital Trad. Est. IG11: Bark ... 2H 89
Capital Wharf E1 ... 1G 103
Capitol Bldg. *SW11* ... *6H 101*
(off New Union Sq.)
Capitol Ind. Pk. NW9 ... 3J 43
Capitol Wlk. *SE23* ... *2J 139*
(off London Rd.)
Capitol Way NW9 ... 3J 43
Capland Ho. *NW8* ... *3B 4*
(off Capland St.)
Capland St. NW8 ... 3B 4 (4B 82)
Caple Ho. *SW10* ... *7A 100*
(off King's Rd.)
Caple Rd. NW10 ... 2B 80
Capper St. WC1 ... 4B 6 (4G 83)
Caprea Cl. UB4: Yead ... 5B 76
Capricorn Cen. RM8: Dag ... 7F 55
Capricorn Ct. *HA8: Edg* ... *7B 28*
(off Zodiac Cl.)
Capri Ho. E17 ... 2B 50
NW9 ... *3B 44*
(off Caversham Rd.)
Capri Rd. CR0: C'don ... 1F 169
Capstan Cl. RM6: Chad H ... 6B 54

218 A-Z London

Capstan Ct. *E1* 7J **85**
  (off Wapping Wall)
Capstan Ho. *E14* 7F **87**
  (off Clove Cres.)
E14 . . . . .4E **104**
  (off Stebondale St.)
Capstan Ride EN2: Enf 2F **23**
Capstan Rd. SE8 . . . . .4B **104**
Capstan Sq. E14 . . . . .2E **104**
Capstan Way SE16 . . . . .1A **104**
Capstone Rd. BR1: Broml 4H **141**
Captain St. *SE18* 1C **124**
  (off Tellson Av.)
Capthorne Av. HA2: Harr 1C **58**
Capuchin Cl. HA7: Stan 6G **27**
Capulet M. E16 . . . . .1J **105**
Capulet Sq. *E3* 3D **86**
  (off Talwin St.)
Capworth St. E10 . . . . .1C **68**
Caraclo Cl. W2 . . . . .6J **81**
Caracdo Evans Cl. *N11* 5A **32**
  (off Springfield Rd.)
Caracdo St. SE10 . . . . .5G **105**
Caracdon Cl. E11 . . . . .1G **69**
Caracdon Way N15 . . . . .4D **48**
Caragh Mews UB2: S'hall 4C **94**
Cara Ho. *N1* 7A **66**
  (off Liverpool Rd.)
NW9 . . . . .3J **43**
Caramel Ct. *E3* 2D **86**
  (off Taylor Pl.)
Caranday Vs. *W11* 1F **99**
  (off Norland Rd.)
Carat Ho. *E14* 5C **86**
  (off Ursula Gould Way)
Caravel Cl. E14 . . . . .3C **104**
Caravel House *E16* 2K **105**
  (off Regalia Close)
Caravelle Gdns. UB5: N'olt 3B **76**
Caravel M. SE8 . . . . .6C **104**
Caraway Apts. *SE1* 6K **15**
  (off Cayenne St.)
Caraway Cl. E13 . . . . .5K **87**
Caraway Hgts. *E14* 7E **86**
  (off Poplar High St.)
Caraway Pl. SM6: W'gton 3F **167**
Carberry Rd. SE19 . . . . .6E **138**
Carbery Av. W3 . . . . .2F **97**
Carbis Cl. E4 . . . . .1A **36**
Carbis Rd. E14 . . . . .6B **86**
Carbrooke Ho. *E9* 1J **85**
  (off Templecombe Rd.)
Carbuncle Pas. N17 . . . . .2G **49**
Carburton St. W1 . . . . .5K 5 (5F **83**)
Cardale St. E14 . . . . .2E **104**
Cardamon Bldg. *SE1* 5K **15**
  (off Shad Thames)
Carden Ct. KT8: W Mole 4F **149**
Carden Rd. SE15 . . . . .3H **121**
Cardiff Ho. *SE15* 6G **103**
  (off Friary Est.)
Cardiff Rd. EN3: Pond E 4E **25**
W7 . . . . .3A **96**
Cardiff St. SE18 . . . . .7J **107**
Cardigan Ct. *W7* 4K **77**
  (off Copley Cl.)
Cardigan Gdns. IG3: Ilf 2A **72**
Cardigan Pl. SE3 . . . . .2F **123**
Cardigan Rd. E3 . . . . .2B **86**
SW13 . . . . .2C **116**
SW19 . . . . .6A **136**
TW10: Rich 6E **114**
Cardigan St. SE11 . . . . . .5J 19 (5A **102**)
Cardigan Wlk. *N1* 7C **66**
  (off Ashby Gro.)
Cardinal Av. KT2: King T 5E **132**
SM4: Mord 6G **153**
Cardinal Bourne St. SE1 . . . . .3D **102**
Cardinal Cap All. SE1 . . . . .1C **102**
Cardinal Cl. BR7: Chst 1J **161**
HA8: Edg 7D **28**
KT4: Wor Pk 4C **164**
SM4: Mord 6G **153**

Cardinal Ct. *E1* 7G **85**
  (off Thomas More St.)
Cardinal Cres. KT3: N Mald 2J **151**
Cardinal Hinsley Cl. NW10 . . . . .2C **80**
Cardinal Mans. *SW1* 3A **18**
  (off Carlisle Pl.)
Cardinal Pl. SW1 . . . . .1A 18 (3G **101**)
  (not continuous)
SW15 . . . . .4F **117**
Cardinal Rd. HA4: Ruis 1B **58**
TW13: Felt 1K **129**
Cardinals Wlk. TW12: Hamp 7G **131**
TW16: Sun 6G **129**
Cardinals Way N19 . . . . .1H **65**
Cardinal Wlk. SW1 . . . . .2A **18**
Cardinal Way HA3: W'stone 3J **41**
Cardine M. SE15 . . . . .7H **103**
Cardington Sq.
TW4: Houn 4B **112**
Cardington St. NW1 . . . . . .1B 6 (3G **83**)
Cardinham Rd.
BR6: Chels 4K **173**
Cardozo Rd. N7 . . . . .5J **65**
Cardrew Av. N12 . . . . .5G **31**
Cardrew Cl. N12 . . . . .5H **31**
Cardrew Ct. N12 . . . . .5G **31**
Cardross Ho. *W6* 3D **98**
  (off Cardross St.)
Cardross St. W6 . . . . .3D **98**
Cardwell Rd. N7 . . . . .4J **65**
Cardwell Ter. *N7* 4J **65**
  (off Cardwell Rd.)
Career Ct. *SE16* 2K **103**
  (off Christopher Cl.)
Carew Cl. N7 . . . . .2K **65**
Carew Ct. RM6: Chad H 6B **54**
  (off Quarles Pk. Rd.)
SE14 . . . . .6K **103**
  (off Samuel Cl.)
SM2: Sutt 7K **165**
Carew Manor & Dovecote 3H **167**
Carew Mnr. Cotts.
SM6: Bedd 3H **167**
Carew Rd. CR4: Mitc 2E **154**
CR7: Thor H 4B **156**
N17 . . . . .2G **49**
SM6: W'gton 6G **167**
TW15: Ashf 6E **128**
W13 . . . . .2C **96**
Carew St. SE5 . . . . .2C **120**
Carey Cl. DA6: Bex 5H **127**
SE5 . . . . .7C **102**
Carey Gdns. SW8 . . . . .1G **119**
Carey La. EC2 . . . . .7C 8 (6C **84**)
Carey Mans. *SW1* 3C **18**
  (off Rutherford St.)
Carey Pl. SW1 . . . . .4C 18 (4H **101**)
Carey Rd. RM9: Dag 4E **72**
Carey St. WC2 . . . . .1H 13 (6K **83**)
Carey Way HA9: Wemb 4H **61**
Carfax Ho. SE20 . . . . .1G **157**
Carfax Pl. SW4 . . . . .4H **119**
Carfax Rd. UB3: Harl 5H **93**
Carfree Cl. N1 . . . . .7A **66**
Cargill Rd. SW18 . . . . .1K **135**
Cargo Point TW19: Stanw 6B **110**
Cargreen Pl. *SE25* 4F **157**
  (off Cargreen Rd.)
Cargreen Rd. SE25 . . . . .4F **157**
Cargrey Ho. HA7: Stan 5H **27**
Carholme Rd. SE23 . . . . .1B **140**
Carillon Ct. *E1* 5G **85**
  (off Grealorex St.)
W5 . . . . .7D **78**
Carina Ho. E20 . . . . .5E **68**
  (off Cheering La.)
Carinthia Ct. *SE16* 4A **104**
  (off Plough Way)
Carisbrook N10 . . . . .2F **47**
Carisbrook Cl. EN1: Enf 1A **24**
Carisbrooke Av. DA5: Bexl 1D **144**
Carisbrooke Cl. HA7: Stan 2D **42**
TW4: Houn 7C **112**

Carisbrooke Ct. SM2: Cheam 7H **165**
UB5: N'olt 1D **76**
  (off Eskdale Av.)
W1 . . . . .6H **5**
  (off Weymouth St.)
W3 . . . . .2J **97**
  (off Brouncker Rd.)
Carisbrooke Gdns. SE15 . . . . .7F **103**
Carisbrooke Ho. KT2: King T 1E **150**
  (off Seven Kings Way)
TW10: Rich 5G **115**
UB7: W Dray 2B **92**
  (off Park Lodge Av.)
Carisbrooke Rd. BR2: Broml 4A **160**
CR4: Mitc 4H **155**
E17 . . . . .4A **50**
Carker's La. NW5 . . . . .5F **65**
Carlcott Cl. KT12: Walt T 7K **147**
Carleton Av. KT8: E Mos 6H **149**
SM6: W'gton 7H **167**
Carleton Cl. KT10: Esh 7H **149**
Carleton Gdns. N19 . . . . .5G **65**
Carleton Ho. *NW9* 3B **44**
  (off Boulevard Dr.)
Carleton Rd. N7 . . . . .5H **65**
N19 . . . . .5H **65**
Carleton Vs. NW5 . . . . .5G **65**
Carlile Cl. E3 . . . . .2B **86**
Carlile Ho. *SE1* 3D **102**
  (off Tabard St.)
Carlile Pl. TW10: Rich 6F **115**
Carlina Gdns. IG8: Wfd G 5E **36**
Carlingford Gdns. CR4: Mitc 7D **136**
Carlingford Rd. N15 . . . . .3B **48**
NW3 . . . . .4B **64**
SM4: Mord 6F **153**
Carlisle Av. EC3 . . . . .1J 15 (6E **84**)
W3 . . . . .6A **80**
Carlisle Cl. HA5: Pinn 7C **40**
KT2: King T 1G **151**
Carlisle Gdns. HA3: Kenton 7D **42**
IG1: Ilf .6C **52**
Carlisle La. SE1 . . . . .2H 19 (3K **101**)
Carlisle Mans. *SW1* 3A **18**
  (off Carlisle Pl.)
Carlisle M. KT2: King T 1G **151**
Carlisle Pl. N11 . . . . .4A **32**
SW1 . . . . .2A 18 (3G **101**)
Carlisle Rd. E10 . . . . .1C **68**
N4 . . . . .7A **48**
NW6 . . . . .1G **81**
NW9 . . . . .3J **43**
SM1: Sutt 6H **165**
TW12: Hamp 7F **131**
Carlisle St. W1 . . . . .1C 12 (6H **83**)
Carlisle Wlk. E8 . . . . .6F **67**
Carlisle Way SW17 . . . . .5E **136**
Carlos Pl. W1 . . . . .3H 11 (7E **82**)
Carlow St. NW1 . . . . .2G **83**
Carlson Ct. SW15 . . . . .4H **117**
Carlton Av. CR2: S Croy 7E **168**
HA3: Kenton 5B **42**
N14 . . . . .5C **22**
TW14: Felt 6A **112**
UB3: Harl 4G **93**
Carlton Av. E. HA9: Wemb 2D **60**
Carlton Av. W. HA0: Wemb 2B **60**
Carlton Cl. HA8: Edg 5B **28**
KT9: Chess 6D **162**
NW3 . . . . .2J **63**
UB5: N'olt 5G **59**
Carlton Ct. IG6: Ilf 3H **53**
N3 . . . . .7D **30**
SE20 . . . . .1H **157**
UB8: Cowl 5A **74**
W9 . . . . .2K **81**
  (off Maida Vale)
Carlton Cres. SM3: Cheam 4G **165**
Carlton Dr. IG6: Ilf 3H **53**
SW15 . . . . .5F **117**
Carlton Gdns. SW1 . . . . . . .5C 12 (1H **101**)
W5 . . . . .6C **78**

Carlton Grn. DA14: Sidc 4K **143**
Carlton Gro. SE15 . . . . .1H **121**
Carlton Hill NW8 . . . . .2K **81**
Carlton Ho. NW6 . . . . .2J **81**
  (off Canterbury Ter.)
SE16 . . . . .2K **103**
  (off Wolfe Cres.)
TW3: Houn 6E **112**
TW14: Felt 6H **111**
Carlton Ho. Ter. SW1 . . . .5C 12 (1H **101**)
Carlton Lodge *N4* 7A **48**
  (off Carlton Rd.)
Carlton Mans. N16 . . . . .1F **67**
NW6 . . . . .7J **63**
  (off West End La.)
W9 . . . . .3K **81**
W14 . . . . .2G **99**
  (off Holland Pk. Gdns.)
Carlton M. NW6 . . . . .5J **63**
  (off West Cotts.)
Carlton Pde. HA9: Wemb 2E **60**
Carlton Pk. Av. SW20 . . . . .2F **153**
Carlton Rd. CR2: S Croy 6D **168**
DA8: Erith 6H **109**
DA14: Sidc 5K **143**
DA16: Well 3B **126**
E11 . . . . .1H **69**
E12 . . . . .4B **70**
E17 . . . . .1A **50**
KT3: N Mald 2A **152**
KT12: Walt T 7K **147**
N4 . . . . .7A **48**
N11 . . . . .5K **31**
SW14 . . . . .3J **115**
TW16: Sun 7H **129**
W4 . . . . .2K **97**
W5 . . . . .7C **78**
Carlton Sq. E1 . . . . .4K **85**
  (not continuous)
Carlton St. SW1 . . . . .3C 12 (7H **83**)
Carlton Ter. E7 . . . . .7A **70**
E11 . . . . .5K **51**
  (not continuous)
N18 . . . . .3J **33**
SE26 . . . . .3J **139**
Carlton Twr. Pl. SW1 . . . . .1F 17 (3D **100**)
Carlton Towers SM5: Cars 3D **166**
Carlton Va. NW6 . . . . .2H **81**
Carlton Vs. SW15 . . . . .5G **117**
The Carlton Works *SE15* 7H **103**
  (off Asylum Rd.)
Carlwell St. SW17 . . . . .5C **136**
Carlyle Av. BR1: Broml 3B **160**
UB1: S'hall 7D **76**
Carlyle Cl. KT8: W Mole 2F **149**
N2 . . . . .6A **46**
Carlyle Ct. *SW6* 1K **117**
  (off Imperial Rd.)
SW10 . . . . .1A **118**
  (off Chelsea Harbour Dr.)
Carlyle Gdns. UB1: S'hall 7D **76**
Carlyle Ho. KT8: W Mole 5E **148**
  (off Down St.)
N16 . . . . .3E **66**
SE5 . . . . .7C **102**
  (off Bethwin Rd.)
SW3 . . . . .7B **16**
  (off Old Church St.)
Carlyle Mans. SW3 . . . . .7C **16**
  (off Cheyne Wlk.)
W8 . . . . .1J **99**
  (off Kensington Mall)
Carlyle M. E1 . . . . .4K **85**
Carlyle Pl. SW15 . . . . .4F **117**
Carlyle Rd. CR0: C'don 2G **169**
E12 . . . . .4C **70**
NW10 . . . . .1K **79**
SE28 . . . . .7B **90**
W5 . . . . .4C **96**
Carlyle's House 7C **16**
Carlyle Sq. SW3 . . . . .6B 16 (5B **100**)
Carly M. *E2* 3G **85**
  (off Barnet Gro.)

Carlyon Av. HA2: Harr 4D **58**
Carlyon Cl. HA0: Wemb 1E **78**
Carlyon Rd. HA0: Wemb 2E **78**
UB4: Yead 5A **76**
(not continuous)
Carlys Cl. BR3: Beck 2K **157**
Carmalt Gdns. SW15 . . . . .4E **116**
Carmarthen Ct. W7 . . . . .4K **77**
(off Copley Cl.)
Carmarthen Pl. SE1 . . . . . .6G 15 (2E **102**)
Carmel Ct. HA9: Wemb 2H **61**
W8 . . . . .2K **99**
(off Holland St.)
Carmelite Cl. HA3: Hrw W 1G **41**
Carmelite Rd. HA3: Hrw W 1G **41**
Carmelite St. EC4 . . . . . . .2K 13 (7A **84**)
Carmelite Wlk. HA3: Hrw W 1G **41**
Carmelite Way HA3: Hrw W 2G **41**
Carmel Lodge SW6 . . . . .6J **99**
(off Lillie Rd.)
Carmelo M. E1 . . . . .5K **85**
(off Maria Ter.)
Carmel Way TW9: Rich 2H **115**
Carmen St. E14 . . . . .6D **86**
Carmichael Cl. HA4: Ruis 4J **57**
SW11 .3B **118**
Carmichael Ct. SW13 . . . . .2B **116**
(off Grove Rd.)
Carmichael Ho. E14 . . . . .7E **86**
(off Poplar High St.)
Carmichael M. SW18 . . . . .7B **118**
Carmichael Rd. SE25 . . . . .5F **157**
Carmine W2 . . . . .6B **4**
Carmine Cl. BR1: Broml 7H **141**
Carmine Wharf E14 . . . . .6B **86**
Carminia Rd. SW17 . . . . .2F **137**
Carnaby St. W1 . . . . . . .1A 12 (6G **83**)
Carnac St. SE27 . . . . .4D **138**
Carnanton Rd. E17 . . . . .1F **51**
Carnarvon Av. EN1: Enf 3A **24**
Carnarvon Dr. UB3: Harl 3E **92**
Carnarvon Rd. E10 . . . . .5E **50**
E15 . . . . .6H **69**
E18 . . . . .1H **51**
EN5: Barn 3B **20**
Carnation Cl. RM7: Rush G 2K **73**
Carnation St. SE2 . . . . .5B **108**
Carnbrook M. SE3 . . . . .3B **124**
Carnbrook Rd. SE3 . . . . .3B **124**
Carnecke Gdns. SE9 . . . . .5C **124**
Carnegie Cl. KT6: Surb 2F **163**
Carnegie Pl. SW19 . . . . .3F **135**
Carnegie Rd. HA1: Harr 7K **41**
Carnegie St. N1 . . . . .1K **83**
Carnell Apts. E14 . . . . .6B **86**
(off St Anne's Row)
Carney Pl. SW9 . . . . .4A **120**
Carnforth Cl. KT19: Ewe 6H **163**
Carnforth Rd. SW16 . . . . .7H **137**
(not continuous)
Carnie Lodge SW17 . . . . .3F **137**
Carnival Ho. SE1 . . . . .6K **15**
(off Gainsford St.)
Carnoustie Cl. SE28 . . . . .6D **90**
Carnoustie Dr. N1 . . . . .7K **65**
(not continuous)
Carnwath Rd. SW6 . . . . .3J **117**
Caroe Ct. N9 . . . . .1C **34**
Carol Cl. NW4 . . . . .4F **45**
Carolean Cres. SE8 . . . . .4A **104**
Carole Ho. NW1 . . . . .1D **82**
(off Regent's Pk. Rd.)
Carolina Cl. E15 . . . . .5G **69**
Carolina Rd. CR7: Thor H 2B **156**
Caroline Cl. CR0: C'don 4E **168**
N10 . . . . .2F **47**
SW16 .3K **137**
TW7: Isle 7H **95**
UB7: W Dray 2A **92**
W2 . . . . .7K **81**
Caroline Ct. HA7: Stan 6F **27**
SE6 . . . . .4F **141**
TW15: Ashf 6D **128**

Caroline Gdns. E2 . . . . .1H 9 (3E **84**)
SE15 . . . . .7H **103**
(not continuous)
Caroline Ho. W2 . . . . .7K **81**
(off Bayswater Rd.)
W6 . . . . .5E **98**
(off Queen Caroline St.)
Caroline Pl. SW11 . . . . .2E **118**
UB3: Harl 7G **93**
W2 . . . . .7K **81**
Caroline Pl. M. W2 . . . . .7K **81**
Caroline Rd. SW19 . . . . .7H **135**
Caroline St. E1 . . . . .6K **85**
Caroline Ter. SW1 . . . . . .4G 17 (4E **100**)
Caroline Wlk. W6 . . . . .6G **99**
(off Lillie Rd.)
Carol St. NW1 . . . . .1G **83**
Caronia Ct. SE16 . . . . .4A **104**
(off Plough Way)
Caro Pl. KT3: N Mald 4B **152**
Carpenter Gdns. N21 . . . . .2G **33**
Carpenter Ho. E1 . . . . .5K **85**
(off Trafalgar Gdns.)
E14 . . . . .5C **86**
(off Burgess St.)
NW11 .6A **46**
Carpenters Arms Apts. SE1 . . . . . .4G **103**
(off Welsford St.)
Carpenters Cl. EN5: New Bar 6E **20**
Carpenters Ct. BR1: Broml 2B **160**
NW1 . . . . .1G **83**
(off Pratt St.)
TW2: Twick 2J **131**
Carpenters M. N7 . . . . .5J **65**
Carpenters Pl. SW4 . . . . .4H **119**
Carpenter's Rd. E15 . . . . .7E **68**
E20 . . . . .6C **68**
Carpenter St. W1 . . . . . . .3J 11 (7F **83**)
Carp Ho. E3 . . . . .1B **86**
(off Old Ford Rd.)
Carradale Ho. E14 . . . . .6E **86**
(off St Leonard's Rd.)
Carrara Cl. SE24 . . . . .4A **120**
SW9 . . . . .4B **120**
Carrara M. E8 . . . . .6G **67**
(off Dalston La.)
Carrara Wharf SW6 . . . . .3G **117**
Carr Cl. HA7: Stan 6F **27**
Carre M. SE5 . . . . .1B **120**
(off Calais St.)
Carrera Twr. EC1 . . . . .1C **8**
Carr Gro. SE18 . . . . .4C **106**
Carr Ho. DA1: Cray 5K **127**
Carriage Dr. E. SW11 . . . . .7E **100**
Carriage Dr. Nth. SW11 . . .7H 17 (6E **100**)
(Carriage Dr. E.)
SW11 .7D **100**
(The Parade)
Carriage Dr. Sth. SW11 . . . . .1D **118**
(not continuous)
Carriage Dr. W. SW11 . . . . .7D **100**
Carriage Ho. E15 . . . . .6F **69**
(off Leyton St.)
N4 . . . . .2A **66**
Carriage M. IG1: IIf 2G **71**
Carriage Pl. N16 . . . . .3D **66**
SW16 .5G **137**
Carriage St. SE18 . . . . .3F **107**
Carriage Way SE8 . . . . .7C **104**
(off Deptford High St.)
Carrick Cl. TW7: Isle 3A **114**
Carrick Ct. E3 . . . . .3E **86**
(off Bolinder Way)
Carrick Dr. IG6: IIf 1G **53**
Carrick Gdns. N17 . . . . .7K **33**
Carrick Ho. N7 . . . . .6K **65**
(off Caledonian Rd.)
SE11 . . . . .5K 19 (5A **102**)
Carrick M. SE8 . . . . .6C **104**
Carrick Sq. TW8: Bford 7F **97**
(off Narrowboat Av.)
Carrill Way DA17: Belv 3D **108**
Carrington Av. TW3: Houn 5F **113**

Carrington Cl. CR0: C'don 7A **158**
KT2: King T 5J **133**
Carrington Ct. SW11 . . . . .4C **118**
(off Barnard Rd.)
Carrington Gdns. E7 . . . . .4J **69**
Carrington Ho. W1 . . . . .5J **11**
(off Carrington St.)
Carrington Rd. TW10: Rich 4G **115**
Carrington Sq. HA3: Hrw W 6B **26**
Carrington St. W1 . . . . . .5J 11 (1F **101**)
Carrock Ct. RM7: Rush G 6K **55**
(off Union Rd.)
Carrol Cl. NW5 . . . . .4F **65**
Carroll Cl. E15 . . . . .5H **69**
Carroll Ho. W2 . . . . .2A **10**
(off Craven Ter.)
Carron Cl. E14 . . . . .6D **86**
Carroun Rd. SW8 . . . . .7K **101**
Carroway La. UB6: G'frd 3H **77**
Carrow Rd. RM9: Dag 7B **72**
Carr Rd. E17 . . . . .2B **50**
UB5: N'olt 6E **58**
Carrs La. N21 . . . . .5H **23**
Carr St. E14 . . . . .5A **86**
CARSHALTON 4E **166**
Carshalton Athletic FC 4C **166**
CARSHALTON BEECHES 7C **166**
Carshalton Boys Sports Coll. Cen.
. . . . .2C **166**
Carshalton Gro. SM1: Sutt 4B **166**
Carshalton Ho. SE12 . . . . .5H **123**
CARSHALTON ON THE HILL 7E **166**
Carshalton Pk. Rd. SM5: Cars 5D **166**
Carshalton Pl. SM5: Cars 5E **166**
Carshalton Rd. CR4: Mitc 4E **154**
SM1: Sutt 5A **166**
SM5: Cars 5A **166**
Carslake Rd. SW15 . . . . .6E **116**
Carson Rd. E16 . . . . .4J **87**
EN4: Cockf 4J **21**
SE21 .2D **138**
Carson Ter. W11 . . . . .1G **99**
(off Princes Pl.)
Carstairs Rd. SE6 . . . . .3E **140**
Carston Cl. SE12 . . . . .5H **123**
Carswell Cl. IG4: IIf 4B **52**
Carswell Rd. SE6 . . . . .7E **122**
Carter Cl. EN5: Barn 5B **20**
NW9 . . . . .6K **43**
Carter Ct. EC4 . . . . .1A **14**
Carter Dr. RM5: Col R 1H **55**
Carteret Ho. W12 . . . . .7D **80**
(off White City Est.)
Carteret St. SW1 . . . . . . .7C 12 (2H **101**)
Carteret Way SE8 . . . . .4A **104**
Carterhatch La. EN1: Enf 1A **24**
Carterhatch Rd. EN3: Enf H 1D **24**
Carter Ho. E1 . . . . .6J **9**
(off Brick La.)
Carter Pl. SE17 . . . . .5C **102**
Carter Rd. E13 . . . . .1K **87**
SW19 .6B **136**
Carters Cl. KT4: Wor Pk 2F **165**
NW5 . . . . .5H **65**
(off Torriano Av.)
Carters Hill Cl. SE9 . . . . .1A **142**
Carters La. SE23 . . . . .2A **140**
Carter Sq. E14 . . . . .6D **86**
(off Bowen St.)
Carter's Yd. SW18 . . . . .5J **117**
Cartier Circ. E14 . . . . .1D **104**
Carting La. WC2 . . . . .3F 13 (7J **83**)
Cart La. E4 . . . . .1B **36**
Cart Lodge M. CR0: C'don 1E **168**
Cartmel NW1 . . . . .1A **6**
(off Harrington St.)

Cartmel Cl. N17 . . . . .7C **34**
Cartmel Ct. UB5: N'olt 6C **58**
Cartmel Gdns. SM4: Mord 5A **154**
Cartmel Rd. DA7: Bex 1G **127**
Carton Ho. W11 . . . . .7F **81**
(off St Ann's Rd.)
Cartoon Mus. 6A 6 (6G **83**)
Cartridge Pl. SE18 . . . . .3F **107**
Cartwright Gdns. WC1 . . . . .2E 6 (3J **83**)
Cartwright Ho. SE1 . . . . .3C **102**
(off County St.)
Cartwright Rd. RM9: Dag 7F **73**
Cartwright St. E1 . . . . .2K 15 (7F **85**)
Cartwright Way SW13 . . . . .7D **98**
Carvel Ho. E14 . . . . .5E **104**
(off Manchester Rd.)
Carvell Ho. NW9 . . . . .3B **44**
(off Aerodrome Rd.)
Carver Cl. W4 . . . . .3J **97**
Carver Rd. SE24 . . . . .6C **120**
Carville Cres. TW8: Bford 4E **96**
Carville Hall Pk. TW8: Bford 5E **96**
(off Claybonds La.)
Carville St. N4 . . . . .2C **66**
Cary Av. SE16 . . . . .4A **104**
Cary Rd. E11 . . . . .4G **69**
Carysfort Rd. N8 . . . . .5H **47**
N16 . . . . .3D **66**
Casbeard St. N4 . . . . .2C **66**
Casby Ho. SE16 . . . . .3G **103**
(off Marine St.)
Cascade Av. N10 . . . . .4G **47**
Cascade Cl. IG9: Buck H 2G **37**
Cascade Ct. SW11 . . . . .7F **101**
Cascade Rd. IG9: Buck H 2G **37**
Cascades Cl. SW19 . . . . .7H **135**
Cascades Twr. E14 . . . . .1B **104**
Casel Ct. HA7: Stan 2F **27**
(off Brightwen Gro.)
Casella Rd. SE14 . . . . .7K **103**
Casewick Rd. SE27 . . . . .5A **138**
Casey Av. UB5: N'olt 2D **76**
Casey Cl. NW8 . . . . .2C 4 (3C **82**)
Casey Ct. SE14 . . . . .1K **121**
(off Besson St.)
Cashmere Ho. E8 . . . . .1F **85**
(off Pamela St.)
Casia Point E20 . . . . .7E **68**
Casina Rd. E5 . . . . .2J **67**
Casings Way E3 . . . . .7C **68**
Casino Av. SE24 . . . . .5C **120**
Caspian Cl. SE5 . . . . .7D **102**
Caspian Wlk. E16 . . . . .6B **88**
Caspian Wharf E3 . . . . .5D **86**
(off Violet Rd.)
Cassander Pl. HA5: Pinn 1C **40**
(off Holly Gro.)
Cassandra Cl. UB5: N'olt 4H **59**
Casselden Rd. NW10 . . . . .7K **61**
Cassell Ho. SW9 . . . . .2K **119**
(off Stockwell Gdns. Est.)
Cass Ho. E9 . . . . .6K **67**
(off Harrowgate Rd.)
Cassia Ho. E1 . . . . .6G **85**
(off Piazza Wlk.)
Cassidy Rd. SW6 . . . . .7J **99**
(not continuous)
Cassilda Rd. SE2 . . . . .4A **108**
Cassilis Rd. E14 . . . . .2C **104**
TW1: Twick 5B **114**
Cassini Apts. E16 . . . . .6J **87**
Cassiobury Av. TW14: Felt 7H **111**
Cassiobury Rd. E17 . . . . .5A **50**
Cassland Rd. CR7: Thor H 4D **156**
E9 . . . . .7K **67**
Casslee Rd. SE6 . . . . .7B **122**
Cassocks Sq. TW17: Shep 7F **147**
Casson Apts. E14 . . . . .6C **86**
(off Upper Nth. St.)
Casson Ho. E1 . . . . .5K **9**
(off Hanbury St.)
Casson Sq. SE1 . . . . .5H 13 (1K **101**)
Casson St. E1 . . . . .5G **85**

Castalia Sq. E14 . . . . 2E **104**
Castellain Mans. *W9* 4K **81**
(off Castellain Rd.)
Castellain Rd. W9 . . . . 4K **81**
Castellane Cl. HA7: Stan 7E **26**
Castell Ho. SE8 . . . . 7C **104**
Castello Av. SW15 . . . . 5E **116**
CASTELNAU 6D **98**
Castelnau SW13 . . . . 1C **116**
Castelnau Gdns. SW13 . . . . 6D **98**
Castelnau Mans. *SW13* 6D **98**
(off Castelnau)
Castelnau Row SW13 . . . . 6D **98**
Casterbridge *NW6* 1K **81**
(off Abbey Rd.)
W11 . . . . 6H **81**
(off Dartmouth Cl.)
Casterbridge Rd. SE3 . . . . 3J **123**
Casterton St. E8 . . . . 6H **67**
Castile Rd. SE18 . . . . 4E **106**
Castillon Rd. SE6 . . . . 2G **141**
Casting Ho. SE14 . . . . 6B **104**
Castlands Rd. SE6 . . . . 2B **140**
Castleacre *W2* 1C **10**
(off Hyde Pk. Cres.)
Castle Av. E4 . . . . 5A **36**
KT17: Ewe 7D **164**
UB7: Yiew 7A **74**
Castlebar Ct. W5 . . . . 5C **78**
Castlebar Hill W5 . . . . 5C **78**
Castlebar M. W5 . . . . 5C **78**
Castlebar Pk. W5 . . . . 5B **78**
Castlebar Rd. W5 . . . . 5C **78**
Castle Baynard St.
EC4 . . . . 2B **14** (7B **84**)
Castlebrook Cl. SE11 . . . . 4B **102**
Castle Bus. Cen. *TW12: Hamp* . . 1F **149**
(off Castle M.)
The Castle Cen. 4B **102**
The Castle Cinema 5K **67**
The Castle Climbing Cen. 2C **66**
Castle Cl. BR2: Broml 3G **159**
E9 . . . . 5A **68**
SW19 . . . . 3F **135**
TW16: Sun 7G **129**
W3 . . . . 2H **97**
Castlecombe Dr. SW19 . . . . 7F **117**
Castlecombe Rd. SE9 . . . . 4C **142**
Castle Ct. *EC3* 1F **15**
(off Birchin La.)
SE26 . . . . 4A **140**
SW15 . . . . 3G **117**
(off Brewhouse La.)
Castleden Ho. *NW3* 7B **64**
(off Hilgrove Rd.)
Castledine Rd. SE20 . . . . 7H **139**
Castle Dr. IG4: Ilf 6C **52**
Castleford Av. SE9 . . . . 1F **143**
Castleford Cl. N17 . . . . 6A **34**
Castleford Ct. *NW8* 3B **4**
(off Henderson Dr.)
Castlegate TW9: Rich 3F **115**
Castle Green Leisure Cen. 1D **90**
Castlehaven Rd. NW1 . . . . 7F **65**
Castle Hgts. RM9: Dag 1B **90**
Castle Hill Av. CRO: New Ad 7D **170**
Castle Hill
Local Nature Reserve 6G **163**
Castle Hill Pde. *W13* 7B **78**
(off The Avenue)
Castle Ho. SM2: Sutt 6J **165**
SW8 . . . . 7J **101**
(off Sth. Lambeth Rd.)
Castle La. SW1 . . . . 1B **18** (3G **101**)
Castleleigh Ct. EN2: Enf 5J **23**
Castlemaine SW11 . . . . 2D **118**
Castlemaine Av.
CR2: S Croy 5F **169**
KT17: Ewe 7D **164**
Castlemain St. E1 . . . . 5H **85**
Castle Mead SE5 . . . . 7C **102**
Castle M. N12 . . . . 5F **31**
NW1 . . . . 6F **65**

Castle M. SW17 . . . . 4C **136**
TW12: Hamp 1F **149**
(not continuous)
Castle Pde. KT17: Ewe 7C **164**
Castle Pl. NW1 . . . . 6F **65**
W4 . . . . 4A **98**
Castle Point *E13* 2A **88**
(off Boundary Rd.)
Castlereagh Ho. HA7: Stan 6G **27**
Castlereagh St. W1 . . . . . 7E **4** (6D **82**)
Castle Rd. EN3: Enf H 1F **25**
N12 . . . . 5F **31**
NW1 . . . . 6F **65**
RM9: Dag 1B **90**
TW7: Isle 2K **113**
UB2: S'hall 3D **94**
UB5: N'olt 6F **59**
Castle Row W4 . . . . 5K **97**
Castle Sq. SE17 . . . . 4C **102**
Castle St. E6 . . . . 2A **88**
E13 . . . . 2A **88**
KT1: King T 2E **150**
Castleton Av. DA7: Bex 1K **127**
HA9: Wemb 4E **60**
Castleton Cl. CRO: C'don 6A **158**
Castleton Gdns. HA9: Wemb 3E **60**
Castleton Ho. *E14* 4E **104**
(off Pier St.)
Castleton Rd. CR4: Mitc 4H **155**
E17 . . . . 2F **51**
HA4: Ruis 1B **58**
IG3: Ilf 1A **72**
SE9 . . . . 4B **142**
Castletown Rd. W14 . . . . 5G **99**
Castleview Cl. N4 . . . . 2C **66**
Castleview Gdns. IG1: Ilf 6C **52**
Castle Wlk. TW16: Sun 3A **148**
Castle Way SW19 . . . . 3F **135**
TW13: Hanw 4A **130**
Castle Wharf *E14* 7G **87**
(off Orchard Pl.)
Castlewood Dr. SE9 . . . . 2D **124**
Castlewood Rd. EN4: Cockf 3G **21**
N15 . . . . 6G **49**
N16 . . . . 6G **49**
Castle Yd. N6 . . . . 7E **46**
SE1 . . . . 4B **14** (1B **102**)
TW10: Rich 5D **114**
Castor La. E14 . . . . 7D **86**
Catalina Ho. E1 . . . . 1K **15**
Catalina Rd. TW6: H'row A 2D **110**
Catalpa Ct. SE13 . . . . 6F **123**
Caterham Av. IG5: Ilf 2D **52**
Caterham High School Fitness Cen.
. . . . 2D **52**
Caterham Rd. SE13 . . . . 3F **123**
Catesby Ho. *E9* 7J **67**
(off Frampton Pk. Rd.)
Catesby St. SE17 . . . . 4D **102**
CATFORD 7D **122**
Catford B'way. SE6 . . . . 7D **122**
CATFORD GYRATORY 7D **122**
Catford Hill SE6 . . . . 1B **140**
Catford Island SE6 . . . . 7D **122**
Catford M. SE6 . . . . 7D **122**
Catford Rd. SE6 . . . . 7C **122**
Catford Trad. Est. SE6 . . . . 2D **140**
Cathall Rd. E11 . . . . 2F **69**
Cathay Ho. SE16 . . . . 2H **103**
Cathay St. SE16 . . . . 2H **103**
Cathay Wlk. UB5: N'olt 2E **76**
(off Brabazon Rd.)
Cathcart Dr. BR6: Orp 2J **173**
Cathcart Hill N19 . . . . 3G **65**
Cathcart Ho. *SW10* 5A **100**
(off Cathcart Rd.)
Cathcart Rd. SW10 . . . . 6K **99**
Cathcart St. NW5 . . . . 6F **65**
Cathedral Lodge *EC1* 5C **8**
(off Aldersgate St.)
Cathedral Mans. *SW1* 3A **18**
(off Vauxhall Bri. Rd.)
Cathedral Piazza SW1 . . . 2A **18** (3G **101**)

Cathedral St. SE1 . . . . . . 4E **14** (1D **102**)
Cathedral Wlk. SW1 . . . . . 1A **18** (3G **101**)
Catherall Rd. N5 . . . . 3C **66**
Catherine Cl. NW4 . . . . 4D **44**
Catherine Ct. IG2: Ilf 5G **53**
N14 . . . . 5B **22**
SW3 . . . . 7A **16**
(off Callow St.)
SW19 . . . . 5H **135**
Catherine Dr. TW9: Rich 4E **114**
TW16: Sun 6H **129**
Catherine Gdns. TW3: Houn 4H **113**
Catherine Griffiths Ct. *EC1* 3K **7**
(off Northampton Rd.)
Catherine Gro. SE10 . . . . 1D **122**
Catherine Ho. *E3* 2C **86**
(off Thomas Fyre Dr.)
N1 . . . . 1E **84**
(off Whitmore Est.)
Catherine Howard Ct. SE9 . . . . . . 6H **125**
Catherine of Aragon Ct. SE9 . . . . 6G **125**
Catherine Parr Ct. SE9 . . . . 6H **125**
Catherine Pl. HA1: Harr 5K **41**
SW1 . . . . 1A **18** (3G **101**)
Catherine Rd. KT6: Surb 5D **150**
Catherine St. WC2 . . . . . . 2G **13** (7K **83**)
Catherine Wheel All. E1 . . . 6H **9** (5E **84**)
Catherine Wheel Rd. TW8: Bford . . 7D **96**
Catherine Wheel Yd. SW1 . . . . . . 5A **12**
Catherwood Ct. N1 . . . . 1E **8**
Cat Hill EN4: E Barn 6H **21**
Cathies Rd. SW12 . . . . 6F **119**
Cathnor Rd. W12 . . . . 2D **98**
Catkin Cl. E14 . . . . 6F **87**
Catlin Cres. TW17: Shep 5F **147**
Catling Cl. SE23 . . . . 3J **139**
Catlin's La. HA5: Eastc 3K **39**
Catlin St. SE16 . . . . 5G **103**
Cator La. BR3: Beck 1B **158**
Cato Rd. SW4 . . . . 3H **119**
Cator Rd. SE26 . . . . 6K **139**
SM5: Cars 5D **166**
Cator St. SE15 . . . . 7F **103**
(Commercial Way)
SE15 . . . . 6E **103**
(Ebley Cl.)
Cato St. W1 . . . . 6D **4** (5C **82**)
Catsey La. WD23: Bush 1B **26**
Catsey Woods WD23: Bush 1B **26**
Catterick Cl. N11 . . . . 6K **31**
Cattistock Rd. SE9 . . . . 5C **142**
Cattley Cl. EN5: Barn 4B **20**
Cattle Mkt. SW1 . . . . 6G **7** (5K **83**)
Catwalk Pl. N15 . . . . 6D **48**
Caudwell Ter. SW18 . . . . 6B **118**
Caughley Ho. SE11 . . . . 2J **19**
Caulfield Ct. *NW1* 7G **65**
(off Baynes St.)
Caulfield Gdns. HA5: Pinn 2A **40**
Caulfield Rd. E6 . . . . 1C **88**
SE15 . . . . 2H **121**
W3 . . . . 3J **97**
The Causeway KT9: Chess 4E **162**
KT10: Clay 7A **162**
N2 . . . . 4C **46**
N18 . . . . 6D **34**
SM2: Sutt 7A **166**
SM5: Cars 3E **166**
SW18 . . . . 5K **117**
SW19 . . . . 5E **134**
TW11: Tedd 6K **131**
TW14: Felt, Houn 4J **111**
Causeyware Rd. N9 . . . . 7D **24**
Causton Cotts. *E14* 6A **86**
(off Galsworthy Av.)
Causton Ho. SE5 . . . . 6C **102**
SW9 . . . . 1K **119**
Causton Rd. N6 . . . . 7F **47**
Causton Sq. RM10: Dag 7G **73**
Causton St. SW1 . . . . . . 4D **18** (4H **101**)
Cautley Av. SW4 . . . . 5G **119**
Cavalier Cl. RM6: Chad H 4D **54**
SM6: W'gton 6G **167**

Cavalier Ct. KT5: Surb 6F **151**
Cavalier Gdns. UB3: Hayes 6F **75**
Cavalier Ter. SE7 . . . . 6A **106**
Cavalry Cres. TW4: Houn 4B **112**
Cavalry Gdns. SW15 . . . . 5H **117**
Cavalry Memorial 5G **11**
Cavalry Pl. E17 . . . . 2K **49**
Cavalry Sq.
SW3 . . . . 5F **17** (5D **100**)
Cavan Pl. HA5: Hat E 1D **40**
Cavatina Point *SE8* 6D **104**
(off Copperas St.)
Cavaye Ho. SW10 . . . . 7A **16**
(off Cavaye Pl.)
Cavaye Pl. SW10 . . . . . . 6A **16** (5A **100**)
Cavell Dr. EN2: Enf 2F **23**
Cavell Ho. *N1* 1E **84**
(off Colville Est.)
Cavell Rd. N17 . . . . 7J **33**
Cavell St. E1 . . . . 5H **85**
Cavendish Av. DA8: Erith 6J **109**
DA15: Sidc 7A **126**
DA16: Well 3K **125**
HA1: Harr 4H **59**
HA4: Ruis 5K **57**
IG8: Wfd G 1K **51**
KT3: N Mald 5C **152**
N3 . . . . 2J **45**
NW8 . . . . 1B **4** (2B **82**)
W13 . . . . 5A **78**
Cavendish Cl. N18 . . . . 5C **34**
NW6 . . . . 6H **63**
NW8 . . . . 1B **4** (3B **82**)
TW16: Sun 6H **129**
UB4: Hayes 5G **75**
Cavendish Ct. EC3 . . . . 7H **9**
SE6 . . . . 1E **140**
(off Bromley Rd.)
SM6: W'gton 6F **167**
TW16: Sun 6H **129**
Cavendish Dr. E11 . . . . 1F **69**
HA8: Edg 6A **28**
Cavendish Gdns. IG1: Ilf 1E **70**
IG11: Bark 5J **71**
RM6: Chad H 5E **54**
SW4 . . . . 6G **119**
Cavendish Ho. CRO: C'don 1D **168**
(off Tavistock Rd.)
NW8 . . . . 1B **4**
(off Wellington Rd.)
NW9 . . . . 3B **44**
SW1 . . . . 2D **18**
(off Monck St.)
UB7: W Dray 2B **92**
(off Park Lodge Av.)
W1 . . . . 6A **6**
(off Mortimer St.)
Cavendish Mans. *EC1* 4J **7**
(off Rosebery Av.)
NW6 . . . . 5J **63**
Cavendish M. Nth. W1 . . . . 5K **5** (5F **83**)
Cavendish M. Sth. W1 . . . . 6K **5** (5F **83**)
Cavendish Pde. *SW4* 6F **119**
(off Clapham Comn. Sth. Side)
TW4: Houn 2C **112**
Cavendish Pl. BR1: Broml 4D **160**
NW2 . . . . 6F **63**
SW4 . . . . 5H **119**
W1 . . . . 7K **5** (6F **83**)
Cavendish Rd. CRO: C'don 1B **168**
E4 . . . . 6K **35**
EN5: Barn 3A **20**
KT3: N Mald 4B **152**
N4 . . . . 6B **48**
N18 . . . . 5C **34**
NW6 . . . . 7G **63**
SM2: Sutt 7A **166**
SW12 . . . . 6F **119**
SW19 . . . . 7B **136**
TW16: Sun 6H **129**
W4 . . . . 1J **115**
Cavendish Sq. W1 . . . . . . 7K **5** (6F **83**)
Cavendish St. N1 . . . . 2D **84**

Cavendish Ter. E3 . . . . .3B 86
  TW13: Felt 2J 129
Cavendish Way BR4: W W'ck 1D 170
Cavenham Gdns. IG1: Ilf 3H 71
Caverleigh Pl. BR1: Broml 2A 160
Caverleigh Way KT4: Wor Pk 1C 164
Cave Rd. E13 . . . . .3K 87
  TW10: Ham 4C 132
Caversham Av. N13 . . . . . . .3F 33
  SM3: Cheam 2G 165
Caversham Ct. N11 . . . . . . .3K 31
  (off Brunswick Pk. Rd.)
Caversham Ho. KT1: King T 2E 150
  (off Lady Booth Rd.)
  N15 . . . . .4C 48
  (off Caversham Rd.)
  SE15 . . . . .6G 103
  (off Haymerle Rd.)
Caversham M. SW3 . . . . . . .7E 16
Caversham Rd. KT1: King T 2F 151
  N15 . . . . .4C 48
  NW5 . . . . .6G 65
  NW9 . . . . .3C 44
Caversham St. SW3 . . . .7E 16 (6D 100)
Caverswall St. W12 . . . . . . .6E 80
Caveside Cl. BR7: Chst 1E 160
Cavesson Ho. E20 . . . . . . .5E 68
  (off Ribbons Wlk.)
Cavour Ho. SE17 . . . . . . .5B 102
  (off Alberta Est.)
Cawdor Cres. W7 . . . . . . .4A 96
Cawdor Wlk. E14 . . . . . . .6E 86
Cawnpore St. SE19 . . . . . .5E 138
Cawston Ct. BR1: Broml 7H 141
Cawston M. SW16 . . . . . . .5B 138
Caxton Ct. SW11 . . . . . . .2C 118
Caxton Gro. E3 . . . . .3C 86
Caxton Hall SW1 . . . . . . .1C 18
Caxton Ho. 7D 12
Caxton M. TW8: Bford 6D 96
Caxton Pl. IG1: Ilf 3E 70
Caxton Rd. N22 . . . . . . .2K 47
  SW19 . . . . .5A 136
  UB2: S'hall 3B 94
  W12 . . . . .2F 99
The Caxtons SW9 . . . . . . .7B 102
  (off Langton Rd.)
Caxton St. SW1 . . . .1C 18 (3G 101)
Caxton St. Nth. E16 . . . . . . .6H 87
Caxton Trad. Est. UB3: Hayes 2G 93
Caxton Wlk. WC2 . . . .1D 12 (6H 83)
Cayenne Ct. SE1 . . . .6K 15 (2F 103)
Caygill Cl. BR2: Broml 4H 159
Cayley Rd. TW6: H'row A 3D 110
  UB2: S'hall 3F 95
Cayton Pl. EC1 . . . . .2E 8
Cayton Rd. UB6: G'frd 2J 77
Cayton St. EC1 . . . .2E 8 (3D 84)
Cazenove Rd. E17 . . . . . . .1C 50
  N16 . . . . .2F 67
Cearns Ho. E6 . . . . .1B 88
Cecil Av. EN1: Enf 4A 24
  HA9: Wemb 5F 61
  IG11: Bark 7H 71
Cecil Cl. KT9: Chess 4D 162
  TW15: Ashf 7E 128
  W5 . . . . .5D 78
Cecil Ct. CR0: C'don 2F 169
  EN2: Enf 4J 23
  EN5: Barn 3A 20
  NW6 . . . . .7K 63
  SW10 . . . . .6A 100
  (off Fawcett St.)
  WC2 . . . . . . .3E 12 (7J 83)
Cecile Pk. N8 . . . . .6J 47
Cecil Gro. NW8 . . . . .1C 82
The Cecil Hepworth Playhouse . . .7H 147
  (off Hepworth Way)
Cecil Ho. E17 . . . . .1C 50
Cecilia Cl. N2 . . . . .3A 46
Cecilia Rd. E8 . . . . .5F 67
Cecil Manning Cl. UB6: G'frd 1A 78
Cecil Mans. SW17 . . . . . . .2E 136

Cecil Pk. HA5: Pinn 4C 40
Cecil Pl. CR4: Mitc 5D 154
Cecil Rhodes Ho. NW1 . . . . . . .2H 83
  (off Goldington St.)
Cecil Rd. CR0: C'don 6J 155
  E11 . . . . .3H 69
  E13 . . . . .1J 87
  E17 . . . . .1C 50
  EN2: Enf 3H 23
  HA3: W'stone 3J 41
  IG1: Ilf 4F 71
  N10 . . . . .2F 47
  N14 . . . . .1B 32
  NW9 . . . . .3A 44
  NW10 . . . . .1A 80
  RM6: Chad H 7D 54
  SM1: Sutt 6H 165
  SW19 . . . . .7K 135
  TW3: Houn 2G 113
  TW15: Ashf 7E 128
  W3 . . . . .5J 79
Cecil Rosen Ct. HA0: Wemb 3B 60
  WD23: B Hea 1D 26
Cecil Sharp House 1E 82
  (off Gloucester Av.)
Cecil Way BR2: Hayes 1J 171
Cedar Av. DA15: Sidc 7A 126
  EN3: Enf H 2D 24
  EN4: E Barn 7H 21
  HA4: Ruis 5A 58
  RM6: Chad H 5E 54
  TW2: Whitt 6F 113
  UB3: Hayes 6J 75
  UB7: Yiew 7B 74
Cedar Cl. BR2: Broml 3C 172
  E3 . . . . .1B 86
  IG1: Ilf 5H 71
  IG9: Buck H 2G 37
  KT8: E Mos 4J 149
  RM7: Rom 4J 55
  SE21 . . . . .1C 138
  SM5: Cars 6D 166
  SW15 . . . . .4K 133
Cedar Copse BR1: Broml 2D 160
Cedar Ct. E11 . . . . .5K 51
  E18 . . . . .1J 51
  N1 . . . . .7C 66
  N10 . . . . .2E 46
  N11 . . . . .5B 32
  N20 . . . . .1G 31
  SE1 . . . . .7G 15
  (off Royal Oak Yd.)
  SE7 . . . . .6A 106
  SE9 . . . . .6C 124
  SE13 . . . . .4F 123
  SM2: Sutt 6A 166
  SW19 . . . . .3F 135
  TW8: Bford 6C 96
Cedar Cres. BR2: Broml 3C 172
Cedarcroft Rd. KT9: Chess 4F 163
Cedar Dr. HA5: Hat E 6A 26
  N2 . . . . .4C 46
Cedar Gdns. SM2: Sutt 6A 166
Cedar Grange EN1: Enf 5K 23
Cedar Gro. DA5: Bexl 6D 126
  UB1: S'hall 5E 76
  W5 . . . . .3E 96
Cedar Hgts. NW2 . . . . . . .6H 63
  TW10: Ham 1E 132
Cedar Ho. CR0: New Ad 6D 170
  E2 . . . . .2E 104
  (off Mowlem St.)
  E14 . . . . .2E 104
  (off Manchester Rd.)
  HA9: Wemb 4G 61
  (off Engineers Way)
  N22 . . . . .1A 48
  (off Acacia Rd.)
  SE14 . . . . .1K 121
  SE16 . . . . .2K 103
  (off Woodland Cres.)
  SW6 . . . . .2A 118
  (off Lensbury Av.)

Cedar Ho. TW9: Kew 1H 115
  TW16: Sun 7H 129
  (off Spelthorne Gro.)
  UB4: Yead 4A 76
  W8 . . . . .3K 99
  (off Marloes Rd.)
Cedarhurst BR1: Broml 7G 141
Cedarhurst Cotts. DA5: Bexl 7G 127
Cedarhurst Dr. SE9 . . . . . . .5A 124
Cedarland Ter. SW20 . . . . . . .7D 134
Cedar Lawn Av. EN5: Barn 5B 20
Cedar Mt. SE4 . . . . .3B 122
  SW15 . . . . .5F 117
Cedarne Rd. SW6 . . . . . . .7K 99
Cedar Pk. IG7: Chig 4K 37
Cedar Pk. Gdns. RM6: Chad H 7D 54
  SW19 . . . . .5D 134
Cedar Pk. Rd. EN2: Enf 1H 23
Cedar Pl. SE7 . . . . .5A 106
Cedar Ri. N14 . . . . .7K 21
Cedar Rd. BR1: Broml 2A 160
  CR0: C'don 2D 168
  EN2: Enf 1G 23
  KT8: E Mos 4J 149
  N17 . . . . .1F 49
  NW2 . . . . .4E 62
  RM7: Rom 4J 55
  SM2: Sutt 6A 166
  TW4: Cran 2A 112
  TW11: Tedd 5A 132
  TW14: Bedf 1F 129
The Cedars E9 . . . . .7K 67
  (off Banbury Rd.)
  E15 . . . . .7H 69
  IG9: Buck H 1D 36
  SM6: W'gton 4G 167
  TW11: Tedd 6K 131
  W13 . . . . .6C 78
Cedars Av. CR4: Mitc 4E 154
  E17 . . . . .5C 50
Cedars Cl. NW4 . . . . .3F 45
  SE13 . . . . .3F 123
Cedars Ct. N9 . . . . .2K 33
Cedars Dr. UB10: Hil 2B 74
Cedars Ho. E17 . . . . .3D 50
Cedarside Apts. NW6 . . . . . . .2H 81
Cedars M. SW4 . . . . .4F 119
  (not continuous)
Cedars Rd. BR3: Beck 2A 158
  CR0: Bedd 3D 167
  E15 . . . . .6G 69
  KT1: Hamp W 1C 150
  N9 . . . . .2B 34
  N21 . . . . .2G 33
  SM4: Mord 4J 153
  SW4 . . . . .3F 119
  SW13 . . . . .2C 116
  W4 . . . . .5J 97
Cedar Ter. TW9: Rich 4E 114
Cedar Tree Gro. SE27 . . . . . . .5B 138
Cedar Vw. KT1: King T 3D 150
  (off Milner Rd.)
Cedarville Gdns. SW16 . . . . . .6K 137
Cedar Way N1 . . . . .7H 65
  TW16: Sun 7G 129
Cedar Way Ind. Est. N1 . . . . . .7H 65
Cedarwood Pl. DA14: Sidc 2D 144
Cedra Ct. N16 . . . . .1G 67
Cedric Chambers NW8 . . . . . .3A 4
  (off Northwick Cl.)
Cedric Rd. SE9 . . . . .3G 143
Celadon Cl. EN3: Enf H 3F 25
Celandine Cl. E14 . . . . .5C 86
Celandine Cl. E4 . . . . .3J 35
Celandine Dr. E8 . . . . .7F 67
  SE28 . . . . .1B 108
Celandine Gro. N14 . . . . . . .5B 22
Celandine Way E15 . . . . .3G 87
Celbridge M. W2 . . . . .5K 81
Celebration Av. E20 . . . . . . .5E 68
Celebration Way E4 . . . . .6K 35
Celestial Gdns. SE13 . . . . . . .4F 123

Celia Cres. TW15: Ashf 6A 128
Celia Ho. N1 . . . . .2E 84
  (off Arden Est.)
Celia Rd. N19 . . . . .4G 65
Cellini St. SW8 . . . . .7H 101
Celtic Av. BR2: Broml 3G 159
Celtic St. E14 . . . . .5D 86
Cemetery La. SE7 . . . . .6C 106
  TW17: Shep 7D 146
Cemetery Rd. E7 . . . . .5H 69
  N17 . . . . .7K 33
  SE2 . . . . .7B 108
Cemetery Way E4 . . . . .3H 35
Cenacle Cl. NW3 . . . . .3J 63
Cenotaph 6E 12 (2J 101)
Centaur Ct. TW8: Bford 5E 96
Centaurs Bus. Pk. TW7: Isle 6A 96
Centaur St. SE1 . . . .1H 19 (3K 101)
Centenary Rd. EN3: Brim 4G 25
Centenary Trad. Est.
  EN3: Brim 3G 25
Centennial Av. WD6: E'tree 1H 27
Centennial Ct. WD6: E'tree 1H 27
Centennial Pk. WD6: E'tree 1H 27
Central Apts. HA9: Wemb 5E 60
Central Arc. TW15: Ashf 4B 128
  (off Woodthorpe Rd.)
Central Av. DA16: Well 2K 125
  E11 . . . . .2F 69
  EN1: Enf 2C 24
  HA5: Pinn 6D 40
  KT8: W Mole 4D 148
  N2 . . . . .2B 46
  N9 . . . . .3K 33
  SM6: W'gton 5J 167
  SW6 . . . . .3A 118
  SW11 . . . . .7D 100
  TW3: Houn 4G 113
  UB3: Hayes 1H 93
Central Bus. Cen. NW10 . . . . . .5A 62
Central Cir. NW4 . . . . .5D 44
Central Ctyd. EC2 . . . . .7H 9
  (off Cutlers Gdns.)
Central Criminal Court
  Old Bailey 7B 8 (6B 84)
Central Cross Apts. CR0: C'don . . .4C 168
  (off South End)
Centrale Shop. Cen. 2C 168
Central Gdns. SM4: Mord 5K 153
Central Gurdwara (Khalsa Jatha) . . .1F 99
Central Hill SE19 . . . . .5D 138
Central Ho. E15 . . . . .2D 86
  IG11: Bark 7G 71
Central Lawn RM8: Dag 1E 72
  (off Ager Av.)
Central Mall SW18 . . . . . . .6K 117
  (within Southside Shop. Cen.)
Central Mans. NW4 . . . . . . .5D 44
  (off Watford Way)
Central Mill Apts. E8 . . . . . . .1F 85
  (off Samuel St.)
Central Pde. DA15: Sidc 3A 144
  E17 . . . . .4C 50
  EN3: Enf H 2D 24
  HA1: Harr 5K 41
  IG2: Ilf 6H 53
  KT6: Surb 6E 150
  KT8: W Mole 4D 148
  SE20 . . . . .7K 139
  (off High St.)
  TW5: Hest 7D 94
  TW14: Felt 7A 112
  UB6: G'frd 3A 78
  W3 . . . . .2H 97
Central Pk. NW10 . . . . .3J 79
Central Pk. Av. RM10: Dag 3H 73
Central Pk. Est. TW4: Houn 5B 112
Central Pk. Rd. E6 . . . . .2B 88
Central Pl. SE25 . . . . .5G 157
Central Rd. HA0: Wemb 5B 60
  KT4: Wor Pk 1C 164
  SM4: Mord 6J 153
Central St Giles Piazza WC2 . . . . .7E 6

Central St Martins College of Art & Design
   Back Hill Site 4K 7
   Byam Shaw Campus 2H 65
The Central School of Speech & Drama
   . . . . .7B 64
Central School Path SW14 . . . . .3J 115
Central Sq. HA9: Wemb 5E 60
   (off High Rd.)
   KT8: W Mole 5D 148
   N18 . . . . .6D 34
   NW11 . . . . .6K 45
Central St. EC1 . . . . .1C 8 (3C 84)
Central Synagogue 5K 5 (5F 83)
Central Ter. BR3: Beck 3K 157
Central Walkway N19 . . . . .4H 65
   (off Pleshey Rd.)
Central Way NW10 . . . . .3J 79
   SE28 .1A 108
   SM5: Cars 7C 166
   TW14: Felt 5J 111
Central W. UB6: G'frd 4G 77
The Centre KT12: Walt T 7J 147
   TW3: Houn 3F 113
   TW13: Felt 1K 129
Centre Av. W3 . . . . .1K 97
Centre Comm. Rd. BR7: Chst 6G 143
Centre Cl. Shop. Cen. 6H 135
Cen. for Wildlife Gardening Vis. Cen.
   . . . . .3F 121
Centre Hgts. NW3 . . . . .7B 64
   (off Finchley Rd.)
Cen. Point SE1 . . . . .5G 103
Centrepoint WC2 . . . . .7D 6
Cen. Point Ho. WC2 . . . . .7D 6
   (off St Giles High St.)
Centre Rd. E7 . . . . .2J 69
   E11 . . . . .2J 69
   RM10: Dag 2H 91
Centre Square KT1: King T 2E 150
   (off Eden Walk Shop. Cen.)
Centre St. E2 . . . . .2H 85
Centre Vw. Apts. CR0: C'don 3C 168
   (off Whitgift St.)
Centre Way E17 . . . . .7K 35
   N9 . . . . .2D 34
Centreway IG1: Ilf 2G 71
   (off High Rd.)
Centreway Apts. IG1: Ilf 2G 71
   (off Axon Pl.)
Centric Cl. NW1 . . . . .1E 82
Centrillion Point CR0: C'don 4C 168
   (off Mason's Av.)
Centro Cl. E6 . . . . .4D 88
Centurion Sq. SE18 . . . . .1C 124
Centurion Bldg. SW11 . . . . .7J 17 (6F 101)
Centurion Cl. N7 . . . . .7K 65
Centurion Cl. SE18 . . . . .4E 106
   SM6: W'gton 2F 167
Centurion Ho. UB3: Hayes 6F 75
Centurion La. E3 . . . . .1B 86
Centurion Way DA18: Erith 3F 109
Century Cl. NW4 . . . . .5F 45
Century Ct. NW8 . . . . .2B 4
Century Ho. HA9: Wemb 2F 61
   SW15 . . . . .4F 117
Century M. E5 . . . . .4J 67
   N5 . . . . .3B 66
   (off Conewood St.)
Century Plaza HA8: Edg 6B 28
   (off Station Rd.)
Century Rd. E17 . . . . .3A 50
Century Way BR3: Beck 6B 140
Century Yd. SE23 . . . . .2J 139
   (not continuous)
Cephas Av. E1 . . . . .4J 85
Cephas Ho. E1 . . . . .4J 85
   (off Doveton St.)
Cephas St. E1 . . . . .4J 85
Ceres Rd. SE18 . . . . .4K 107
Cerise Apts. E3 . . . . .1A 86
   (off Gunmaker's La.)
Cerise Rd. SE15 . . . . .1G 121
Cerne Cl. UB4: Yead 7A 76

Cerne Rd. SM4: Mord 6A 154
Cerney M. W2 . . . . .2A 10
Cervantes Ct. W2 . . . . .6K 81
   W11 .6G 81
   (off Rushton M.)
Cervantes Theatre 6B 14 (2B 102)
Cester St. E2 . . . . .1G 85
Ceylon Ho. E1 . . . . .1K 15
   (off Alie St.)
Ceylon Rd. W14 . . . . .3F 99
Ceylon Wharf Apts. SE16 . . . . . .2J 103
   (off St Marychurch St.)
CFGS Community Performing
   Arts & Sports Cen. 3B 86
Chadd Dr. SE15 . . . . .3H 121
Chadacre Av. IG5: Ilf 3D 52
Chadacre Cl. E15 . . . . .1J 87
   (off Vicars Cl.)
Chadacre Ho. SW9 . . . . .4B 120
   (off Loughborough Pk.)
Chadacre Rd. KT17: Ewe 6D 164
Chadbourn St. E14 . . . . .5D 86
Chadbury Cl. NW7 . . . . .1C 44
Chad Cres. N9 . . . . .3D 34
Chadd Dr. BR1: Broml 3C 160
Chadd Grn. E13 . . . . .1J 87
   (not continuous)
Chadston Ho. N1 . . . . .7B 66
   (off Halton Rd.)
Chadswell WC1 . . . . .2F 7
   (off Cromer St.)
Chadview Cl. RM6: Chad H 7D 54
Chadville Gdns. RM6: Chad H 5D 54
Chadway RM8: Dag 1C 72
Chadway Ho. RM6: Chad H 7B 54
CHADWELL HEATH 7D 54
Chadwell Heath Ind. Pk.
   RM8: Dag 1D 72
Chadwell Heath La.
   RM6: Chad H 4B 54
Chadwell Ho. SE17 . . . . .5D 102
   (off Inville Rd.)
Chadwell La. N8 . . . . .3K 47
Chadwell St. EC1 . . . . .1K 7 (3A 84)
Chadwick Av. E4 . . . . .4A 36
   N21 . . . . .5E 22
   SW19 . . . . .6J 135
Chadwick Cl. SW15 . . . . .7B 116
   TW11: Tedd 6A 132
   W7 . . . . .5K 77
Chadwick Ct. E14 . . . . .6B 86
   (off Jonzen Wlk.)
Chadwick Gdns. UB8: Uxb 7A 56
Chadwick M. W4 . . . . .6H 97
Chadwick Pl. KT6: Surb 7C 150
Chadwick Rd. E11 . . . . .6G 51
   IG1: Ilf 3F 71
   NW10 . . . . .1B 80
   SE15 . . . . .2F 121
Chadwick St. SW1 . . . . . .2C 18 (3H 101)
Chadwick Way SE28 . . . . .7D 90
Chadwin Rd. E13 . . . . .5K 87
Chadworth Ho. EC1 . . . . .2C 8
   (off Lever St.)
   N4 . . . . .1C 66
Chaffinch Av. CR0: C'don 6K 157
Chaffinch Bus. Pk. BR3: Beck 4K 157
Chaffinch Cl. CR0: C'don 5K 157
   KT6: Surb 3G 163
   N9 . . . . .1E 34
Chaffinch Rd. BR3: Beck 1A 158
Chafford Way RM6: Chad H 4C 54
Chagford Ho. E3 . . . . .3D 86
   (off Talwin St.)
Chagford St. NW1 . . . . .4E 4 (4D 82)
Chailey Av. EN1: Enf 2A 24
Chailey Cl. TW5: Hest 1B 112
Chailey Ind. Est. UB3: Hayes 2J 93
Chailey St. E5 . . . . .3J 67
Chainmakers Ho. E14 . . . . .6F 87
   (off Blair St.)
Chalbury Wlk. N1 . . . . .2K 83
Chalcombe Rd. SE2 . . . . .3B 108

Chalcot Cl. SM2: Sutt 7J 165
Chalcot Cres. NW1 . . . . .1D 82
Chalcot Gdns. NW3 . . . . .6D 64
Chalcot M. SW16 . . . . .3J 137
Chalcot Rd. NW1 . . . . .7E 64
Chalcot Sq. NW1 . . . . .7E 64
   (not continuous)
Chalcott Gdns. KT6: Surb 1C 162
Chalcroft Rd. SE13 . . . . .5G 123
Chaldon Cl. SE19 . . . . .2D 156
Chaldon Path
   CR7: Thor H 4B 156
Chaldon Rd. SW6 . . . . .7G 99
Chale Rd. SW2 . . . . .6J 119
Chalet Cl. DA5: Bexl 4K 145
   TW15: Ashf 6F 129
Chalet Ct. CR7: Thor H 5C 156
Chalet Est. NW7 . . . . .4H 29
Chalfont Av. HA9: Wemb 6H 61
Chalfont Cl. HA1: Harr 6K 41
   (off Northwick Pk. Rd.)
   NW1 . . . . .4F 5
   (off Baker St.)
   NW9 . . . . .3B 44
Chalfont Grn. N9 . . . . .3K 33
Chalfont Ho. SE16 . . . . .3H 103
   (off Keetons Rd.)
Chalfont M. SW19 . . . . .1H 135
   UB10: Hil 7D 56
Chalfont Rd. N9 . . . . .3K 33
   SE25 .3F 157
   UB3: Hayes 2J 93
Chalfont Wlk. HA5: Pinn 2A 40
Chalfont Way W13 . . . . .3B 96
Chalfont NW6 . . . . .6A 64
   (off Finchley Rd.)
Chalford Cl. KT8: W Mole 4E 148
Chalford Rd. SE21 . . . . .4D 138
Chalford Wlk. IG8: Wfd G 1B 52
Chalgrove Av. SM4: Mord 5J 153
Chalgrove Cres. IG5: Ilf 2C 52
Chalgrove Gdns. N3 . . . . .3G 45
Chalgrove Rd. N17 . . . . .1H 49
   SM2: Sutt 7B 166
Chalice Cl. SM6: W'gton 6H 167
Chalice Ct. N2 . . . . .4C 46
   SE19 . . . . .6D 138
Chalkenden Cl. SE20 . . . . .7H 139
CHALKER'S CORNER 3H 115
CHALK FARM 7E 64
Chalk Farm Pde. NW3 . . . . .7E 64
   (off Adelaide Rd.)
Chalk Farm Rd. NW1 . . . . .7E 64
Chalk Hill Rd. W6 . . . . .4F 99
Chalkhill Rd. HA9: Wemb 3H 61
Chalklands HA9: Wemb 3J 61
Chalk La. EN4: Cockf 3J 21
Chalkley Cl. CR4: Mitc 2D 154
Chalkmill Dr. EN1: Enf 3C 24
Chalk Pit Way SM1: Sutt 5A 166
Chalk Rd. E13 . . . . .5K 87
Chalkstone Cl. DA16: Well 1A 126
Chalkwell Ho. E1 . . . . .6K 85
   (off Pitsea St.)
Chalkwell Pk. Av. EN1: Enf 4K 23
Challenge Cl. NW10 . . . . .1A 80
Challenge Ct. TW2: Twick 7J 113
Challenger Ho. E14 . . . . .7A 86
   (off Victory Pl.)
Challenge Rd. TW15: Ashf 3F 129
Challice Way SW2 . . . . .1K 137
Challin St. SE20 . . . . .1J 157
Challis Ho. SW11 . . . . .2D 118
Challis Rd. TW8: Bford 5D 96
Challoner Cl. N2 . . . . .2B 46
Challoner Ct. BR2: Broml 2F 159
   W14 . . . . .5H 99
   (off Challoner St.)
Challoner Cres. W14 . . . . .5H 99
Challoner Mans. W14 . . . . .5H 99
   (off Challoner St.)
Challoners Cl. KT8: E Mos 4H 149
Challoner St. W14 . . . . .5H 99

Challoner Wlk. E1 . . . . .6G 85
   (off Christian St.)
Chalmers Ho. E17 . . . . .5D 50
Chalmers Rd. TW15: Ashf 5D 128
Chalmers Rd. E. TW15: Ashf 4D 128
Chalmers Wlk. SE17 . . . . .6B 102
   (off Hillingdon St.)
Chalmers Way TW1: Isle 4B 114
   TW14: Felt 5K 111
Chaloner Cl. SE1 . . . . .6E 14
Chalsey Rd. SE4 . . . . .4B 122
Chalton Dr. N2 . . . . .6B 46
Chalton Ho. NW1 . . . . .1C 6
   (off Chalton St.)
Chalton St. NW1 . . . . .1C 6 (2G 83)
   (not continuous)
Chamberlain Cl. IG1: Ilf 3G 71
   SE28 .3H 107
   UB3: Hayes 7H 75
Chamberlain Cotts. SE5 . . . . .1D 120
Chamberlain Cl. SE16 . . . . .4J 103
   (off Silwood St.)
Chamberlain Cres.
   BR4: W W'ck 1D 170
Chamberlain Gdns. TW3: Houn . . .1G 113
Chamberlain Ho. E1 . . . . .7J 85
   (off Cable St.)
   EC2 . . . . .3G 9
   (off Blackall St.)
   NW1 . . . . .2A 6
   SE1 . . . . .7J 13
   (off Westminster Bri. Rd.)
Chamberlain La. HA5: Eastc 3J 39
Chamberlain Pl. E17 . . . . .3A 50
Chamberlain Rd. N2 . . . . .2A 46
   W13 . . . . .2A 96
Chamberlain St. NW1 . . . . .7D 64
Chamberlain Wlk. TW13: Hanw . . .4C 130
Chamberlain Way HA5: Eastc 3K 39
   KT6: Surb 7E 150
Chamberlayne Av. HA9: Wemb 3E 60
Chamberlayne Mans. NW10 . . . . .3F 81
   (off Chamberlayne Rd.)
Chamberlayne Rd. NW10 . . . . . . .1E 80
Chamberlens Garages W6 . . . . . . .4D 98
   (off Dalling Rd.)
The Chambers SW10 . . . . .1A 118
   (off Chelsea Harbour Dr.)
Chambers Av. DA14: Sidc 6E 144
Chambers Bus. Pk. UB7: Sip 6C 92
Chambers Gdns. N2 . . . . .1B 46
Chambers La. NW10 . . . . .7D 62
Chambers Pk. Hill SW20 . . . . . . .7D 134
Chambers Rd. N7 . . . . .4J 65
Chambers St. SE16 . . . . .2G 103
Chamber St. E1 . . . . .2K 15 (7F 85)
Chambers Wlk. HA7: Stan 5G 27
Chambers Wharf SE16 . . . . .2G 103
Chambon Pl. W6 . . . . .4C 98
Chambord Ho. E2 . . . . .2K 9
   (off Charlbord St.)
Chambord St. E2 . . . . .2K 9 (3F 85)
Chamomile Ct. E17 . . . . .6C 50
   (off Yunus Khan Cl.)
Champa Cl. N17 . . . . .2F 49
Champion Cres. SE26 . . . . .4A 140
Champion Gro. SE5 . . . . .3D 120
Champion Hill SE5 . . . . .3D 120
Champion Hill Est. SE5 . . . . .3E 120
Champion Hill Stadium 4E 120
Champion Ho. SE7 . . . . .6A 106
   (off Charlton Rd.)
Champion Pk. SE5 . . . . .2D 120
Champion Rd. SE26 . . . . .4A 140
Champions Wlk. E20 . . . . .5E 68
Champions Way NW4 . . . . .1D 44
   NW7 . . . . .1D 44
Champlain Ho. W12 . . . . .7D 80
   (off White City Est.)
Champness Cl. SE17 . . . . .3K 49
   SE27 .4D 138
Champness Rd. IG11: Bark 6K 71

Champneys Cl. SM2: Cheam 7H 165
Chancel Ct. W1 . . . . .2C 12
    (off Old Compton St.)
Chancel Ind. Est. NW10 . . . . .5B 62
Chancellor Gdns. CR2: S Croy 7B 168
Chancellor Gro. SE21 . . . . .2C 138
Chancellor Ho. E1 . . . . .1H 103
    (off Green Bank)
  SW7 . . . . .3A 100
    (off Hyde Pk. Ga.)
Chancellor Pas. E14 . . . . .1C 104
Chancellor Pl. NW9 . . . . .2B 44
Chancellors Cl. BR3: Beck 7C 158
Chancellors Ct. WC1 . . . . .5G 7
Chancellor's Rd. W6 . . . . .5E 98
Chancellor's St. W6 . . . . .5E 98
Chancellors Wharf W6 . . . . .5E 98
Chancellor Way RM8: Dag 4A 72
Chancelot Rd. SE2 . . . . .4B 108
Chancel St. SE1 . . . . .5A 14 (1B 102)
Chancery Bldg. SW11 . . . . .7H 101
Chancery Bldgs. E1 . . . . .7H 85
    (off Lowood St.)
Chancerygate UB7: Yiew 1C 92
Chancerygate Bus. Cen.
  HA4: Ruis 4C 58
Chancery Ga. Bus. Pk.
  KT6: Surb 2F 163
Chancerygate Ind. Pk.
  DA14: Sidc 7D 144
Chancery La. BR3: Beck 2D 158
  WC2 . . . . .6H 7 (6A 84)
Chancery M. SW17 . . . . .2C 136
Chance St. E1 . . . . .3J 9 (4F 85)
  E2 .3J 9 (4F 85)
Chanctonbury Cl. SE9 . . . . .3F 143
Chanctonbury Gdns. SM2: Sutt . . .7K 165
Chanctonbury Way N12 . . . . .4C 30
Chandaria Ct. CR0: C'don 3C 168
    (off Church Rd.)
Chandler Av. E16 . . . . .5J 87
Chandler Cl. TW12: Hamp 1E 148
Chandler Ct. TW14: Felt 6J 111
Chandler Ho. NW6 . . . . .1H 81
    (off Willesden La.)
  WC1 . . . . .4F 7
    (off Colonnade)
Chandlers Av. SE10 . . . . .2H 105
Chandlers Cl. KT8: W Mole 5F 149
  TW14: Felt 7H 111
Chandlers Ct. SE12 . . . . .1K 141
Chandlers Dr. DA8: Erith 4K 109
Chandlers M. E14 . . . . .2C 104
Chandler St. E1 . . . . .1H 103
Chandlers Way SW2 . . . . .7A 120
Chandler Way SE15 . . . . .6E 102
The Chandlery SE1 . . . . .1K 19
    (off Gerridge St.)
Chandlery Ho. E1 . . . . .6G 85
    (off Gower's Wlk.)
Chandon Lodge SM2: Sutt 7A 166
Chandos Av. E17 . . . . .2C 50
  N14 . . . . .3B 32
  N20 . . . . .1F 31
  W5 . . . . .4C 96
Chandos Cl. IG9: Buck H 2E 36
Chandos Ct. HA7: Stan 6G 27
  HA8: Edg 7A 28
  N14 . . . . .2C 32
Chandos Cres. HA8: Edg 7A 28
Chandos Pde. HA8: Edg 7A 28
Chandos Pl. WC2 . . . . . .3E 12 (7J 83)
Chandos Rd. E15 . . . . .5F 69
  HA1: Harr 5G 41
  HA5: Eastc 7B 40
  N2 . . . . .2B 46
  N17 . . . . .2E 48
  NW2 . . . . .5E 62
  NW10 . . . . .4A 80
Chandos St. W1 . . . . .6K 5 (5F 83)
Chandos Way NW11 . . . . .1K 63
Change All. EC3 . . . . . . .1F 15 (6D 84)
Chanin M. NW2 . . . . .5E 62

Channel 4 TV 2C 18
Channel Cl. TW5: Hest 1E 112
Channel Ga. Rd. NW10 . . . . .3A 80
Channel Ho. SE16 . . . . .2K 103
    (off Water Gdns. Sq.)
Channel Islands Est. N1 . . . . .6C 66
Channelsea Ho. E15 . . . . .2F 87
Channelsea Path E15 . . . . .1F 87
Channelsea Rd. E15 . . . . .1F 87
Channon Ct. KT6: Surb 5E 150
    (off Maple Rd.)
Chantrelle Ct. SE8 . . . . .4A 104
    (off Yeoman St.)
Chantress Cl. RM10: Dag 1J 91
Chantry Ho. SW1 . . . . .3K 17
Chantry Rd. SW9 . . . . .3K 119
The Chantry E4 . . . . .1K 35
  UB8: Hil .3B 74
Chantry Cl. DA14: Sidc 5E 144
  EN2: Enf 1H 23
  HA3: Kenton 5C 42
  SE2 . . . . .3C 108
  TW16: Sun 7J 129
  UB7: Yiew 7A 74
  W9 . . . . .4J 81
Chantry Ct. SM5: Cars 3C 166
Chantry Cres. NW10 . . . . .6B 62
Chantry Ho. KT1: King T 4E 150
Chantry La. BR2: Broml 5B 160
Chantry Pl. HA3: Hrw W 1F 41
Chantry Rd. HA3: Hrw W 1F 41
  KT9: Chess 5F 163
Chantry Sq. W8 . . . . .3K 99
Chantry St. N1 . . . . .1B 84
Chantry Way CR4: Mitc 3B 154
Chant Sq. E15 . . . . .7F 69
Chant St. E15 . . . . .7F 69
    (not continuous)
The Chapel SW15 . . . . .6G 117
Chapel Cl. DA1: Cray 5K 127
  NW10 . . . . .5B 62
Chapel Ct. E10 . . . . .2D 68
    (off Rosedene Ter.)
  N2 . . . . .3C 46
  RM7: Rush G 6K 55
    (off Bournebrook Gro.)
  SE1 . . . . .5E 14 (2D 102)
  SE18 . . . . .6A 108
  UB3: Hayes 7H 75
CHAPEL END 1D 50
Chapel Farm Rd. SE9 . . . . .3D 142
Chapel Ga. M. SW4 . . . . .3J 119
    (off Bedford Rd.)
Chapel Ga. Pl. BR7: Chst 6F 143
Chapel Hill DA1: Cray 5K 127
Chapel Ho. E14 . . . . .5D 104
Chapelier Ho. SW18 . . . . .4J 117
Chapel La. HA5: Pinn 3B 40
  RM6: Chad H 7D 54
  UB8: Hil .6C 74
Chapel Mkt. N1 . . . . .2A 84
Chapel M. IG8: Wfd G 6K 37
Chapel Mill Rd. KT1: King T 3F 151
Chapelmount Rd. IG8: Wfd G 6J 37
Chapel of St John the Evangelist . . .3J 15
    (within The Tower of London)
Chapel of St Peter & St Paul 6F 105
    (within University of Greenwich)
Chapel Pl. EC2 . . . . .2G 9 (3E 84)
  N1 . . . . .2A 84
  N17 . . . . .7A 34
  W1 . . . . .1J 11 (6F 83)
Chapel Rd. DA7: Bex 4G 127
  IG1: Ilf 3E 70
  SE27 . . . . .4B 138
  TW1: Twick 7B 114
  TW3: Houn 3F 113
  W13 . . . . .1B 96
Chapel Side W2 . . . . .7K 81
Chapel Stones N17 . . . . .1F 49
Chapel St. EN2: Enf 3H 23
  NW1 . . . . .6C 4 (5C 82)
  SW1 . . . . .1H 17 (3E 100)

Chapel Vw. CR2: Sels 6J 169
Chapel Wlk. CR0: C'don 2C 168
  NW4 . . . . .4D 44
    (not continuous)
Chapel Way N7 . . . . .3K 65
Chapel Yd. SW18 . . . . .5K 117
    (off Wandsworth High St.)
Chaplin Cl. HA0: Wemb 6D 60
  SE1 . . . . .6K 13 (2A 102)
Chaplin Ct. E3 . . . . .4B 86
    (off Joseph St.)
  SE14 . . . . .1K 121
    (off Besson St.)
  SE17 . . . . .6B 102
    (off Royal Rd.)
Chaplin Cres. TW16: Sun 6G 129
Chaplin Ho. DA14: Sidc 4A 144
    (off Sidcup High St.)
  E17 . . . . .4C 50
    (off Hoe St.)
  N1 . . . . .1D 84
    (off Shepperton Rd.)
  W3 . . . . .3J 97
    (off All Saints Rd.)
Chaplin Rd. E15 . . . . .2H 87
  HA0: Wemb 6C 60
  N17 . . . . .3F 49
  NW2 . . . . .6C 62
  RM9: Dag 7E 72
Chaplin Sq. N12 . . . . .7G 31
Chapman Cl. UB7: W Dray 3B 92
Chapman Cres. HA3: Kenton 6E 42
Chapman Grn. N22 . . . . .1A 48
Chapman Ho. E1 . . . . .6H 85
    (off Bigland St.)
  NW9 . . . . .3B 44
    (off Aerodrome Rd.)
Chapman Pl. N4 . . . . .2B 66
Chapman Rd. CR0: C'don 1A 168
  DA17: Belv 5G 109
  E9 . . . . .6B 68
Chapman's La. DA17: Belv 4D 108
  SE2 . . . . .4C 108
Chapmans Pk. Ind. Est. NW10 . . . . .6B 62
Chapman Sq. SW19 . . . . .2F 135
Chapman's Ter. N22 . . . . .1B 48
Chapman St. E1 . . . . .7H 85
Chapone Pl. W1 . . . . .1C 12 (6H 83)
Chapter Chambers SW1 . . . . .4C 18
    (off Chapter St.)
Chapter Cl. UB10: Hil 7B 56
  W4 . . . . .3J 97
Chapter House 1C 14
Chapter Ho. E2 . . . . .4G 85
    (off Dunbridge St.)
Chapter Rd. NW2 . . . . .5C 62
  SE17 . . . . .5B 102
Chapter St. SW1 . . . . . . .4C 18 (4H 101)
Chapter Way SW19 . . . . .1B 154
  TW12: Hamp 4E 130
Chara Pl. W4 . . . . .6K 97
Charcot Ho. SW15 . . . . .6B 116
Charcot Rd. NW9 . . . . .2A 44
Charcroft Ct. W14 . . . . .2F 99
    (off Minford Gdns.)
Charcroft Gdns. EN3: Pond E 4E 24
Chardin Ho. SW9 . . . . .1A 120
    (off Gosling Way)
Chardin Rd. W4 . . . . .4A 98
Chardmore Rd. N16 . . . . .1G 67
Chard Rd. TW6: H'row A 2D 110
Chardwell Cl. E6 . . . . .6D 88
Charecroft Way W14 . . . . .2F 99
Charfield Ct. W9 . . . . .4K 81
    (off Shirland Rd.)
Charford Rd. E16 . . . . .5J 87
Chargeable La. E13 . . . . .4H 87
Chargeable St. E16 . . . . .4H 87
Chargrove Cl. SE16 . . . . .2K 103
Charing Cl. BR6: Orp 4K 173
Charing Ct. BR2: Broml 2G 159
Charing Cross SW1 . . . . .4E 12
Charing Cross Rd. WC2 . . . . . .7D 6 (6H 83)

Charing Cross Sports Club 6F 99
Charing Cross Theatre 4F 13
    (off Villiers St.)
Charing Cross Underground Shop. Cen.
  . . . . .3E 12
Charing Ho. SE1 . . . . .6K 13
    (off Windmill Wlk.)
Chariot Cl. E3 . . . . .1C 86
Charis Ho. E3 . . . . .3D 86
    (off Grace St.)
Charlbert Ct. NW8 . . . . .2C 82
    (off Charlbert St.)
Charlbert St. NW8 . . . . .2C 82
Charlbury Av. HA7: Stan 5J 27
Charlbury Gdns. IG3: Ilf 2K 71
Charlbury Gro. W5 . . . . .6C 78
Charlbury Rd. UB10: Ick 3B 56
Charldane Rd. SE9 . . . . .3F 143
Charlecote Gro. SE26 . . . . .3H 139
Charlecote Rd. RM8: Dag 3E 72
Charlemont Rd. E6 . . . . .4D 88
Charles II Pl. SW3 . . . . . .6E 16 (5D 100)
Charles II St. SW1 . . . . . .4C 12 (1H 101)
Charles Auffray Ho. E1 . . . . .5J 85
    (off Smithy St.)
Charles Babbage Cl.
  KT9: Chess 7C 162
Charles Baker Pl. SW17 . . . . .1C 136
Charles Barry Cl. SW4 . . . . .3G 119
Charles Bradlaugh Ho. N17 . . . . . . .7C 34
    (off Haynes Cl.)
Charles Burton Ct. E5 . . . . .5A 68
    (off Ashenden Rd.)
Charles Chu. Wlk. IG1: Ilf 6D 52
Charles Cl. DA14: Sidc 4B 144
Charles Clowes Wlk. SW11 . . . . . . .7H 101
Charles Cobb Gdns. CR0: Wadd . . .5A 168
Charles Coveney Rd. SE15 . . . . .1F 121
Charles Cres. HA1: Harr 7H 41
    (not continuous)
The Charles Cryer Studio Theatre
  . . . . .4E 166
Charles Darwin Ho. E2 . . . . .3H 85
    (off Canrobert St.)
  E16 . . . . .6H 87
    (off Minnie Baldock St.)
Charles Dickens Ho. E2 . . . . .3G 85
    (off Mansford St.)
The Charles Dickens Mus. 4H 7
Charlesfield SE9 . . . . .3A 142
Charles Flemwell M. E16 . . . . .1J 105
Charles Gardner Ct. N1 . . . . .1F 9
    (off Haberdasher St.)
Charles Grinling Wlk. SE18 . . . . .4E 106
Charles Gro. N14 . . . . .1B 32
Charles Haller St. SW2 . . . . .7A 120
Charles Harrod Ct. SW13 . . . . .6E 98
    (off Somerville Av.)
Charles Hocking Ho. W3 . . . . .2J 97
    (off Bollo Bri. Rd.)
Charles Ho. N17 . . . . .7A 34
    (off Love La.)
  UB2: S'hall 2E 94
  W14 . . . . .4H 99
Charles Lamb Ct. N1 . . . . .2B 84
    (off Gerrard Rd.)
Charles La. NW8 . . . . .2C 82
Charles Lesser Ho. KT9: Chess 5D 162
Charles Mackenzie Ho. SE16 . . . . . .4G 103
    (off Linsey St.)
Charlesmere Gdns. SE28 . . . . .2J 107
    (off Thames Reach)
Charles Nex M. SE21 . . . . .2C 138
Charles Pl. E4 . . . . .7K 25, 1A 36
  NW1 . . . . .2B 6 (3G 83)
Charles Rd. E7 . . . . .7A 70
  RM6: Chad H 6D 54
  RM10: Dag 7H 73
  SW19 . . . . .1J 153
  TW18: Staines 6A 128
  W13 . . . . .6A 78
Charles Rowan Ho. WC1 . . . . .2J 7
    (off Margery St.)

Charles Sevright Way NW7 . . . . .5A **30**
Charles Simmons Ho. *WC1* 2J **7**
    (off Margery St.)
Charles Sq. N1 . . . . .2F **9** (3D **84**)
Charles Sq. Est. N1 . . . . .2F **9**
Charles St. CRO: C'don 3C **168**
  E16 .1A **106**
  EN1: Enf 5A **24**
  N19 . . . . .1J **65**
  SW13 . . . . .2A **116**
  TW3: Houn 2D **112**
  UB10: Hil 4D **74**
  W1 . . . . .4J **11** (1F **101**)
Charles Talbot M. SE22 . . . . . . .1H **139**
Charleston Cl. TW13: Felt 3J **129**
Charleston St. SE17 . . . . .4C **102**
Charles Townsend Ho. *EC1* 3A **8**
    (off Skinner St.)
Charles Uton Ct. E8 . . . . .4G **67**
Charles Whincup Rd. E16 . . . . . .1K **105**
Charlesworth Ho. *E14* 6C **86**
    (off Dod St.)
Charlesworth Ho. SW13 . . . . . . .3A **116**
Charleville Cir. SE26 . . . . .5G **139**
Charleville Ct. *W14* 5H **99**
    (off Charleville Rd.)
Charleville Mans. *W14* 5G **99**
    (off Charleville Rd.)
Charleville M. TW7: Isle 4B **114**
Charleville Rd. W14 . . . . .5G **99**
CHARLIE BROWN'S RDBT. 2A **52**
Charlie Chaplin Wlk.
  SE1 . . . . .4H **13** (1K **101**)
Charlieville Rd. DA8: Erith 7J **109**
Charlmont Rd. SW17 . . . . .6C **136**
Charlotte Cl. DA6: Bex 5E **126**
  IG6: Ilf .1G **53**
Charlotte Ct. IG2: Ilf 6E **52**
  N8 . . . . .6H **47**
  SE1 . . . . .4E **102**
    (off Old Kent Rd.)
  W6 . . . . .4C **98**
Charlotte Despard Av. SW11 . . . .1E **118**
Charlotte Ho. *E16* 1H **105**
    (off Fairfax M.)
  W6 . . . . .5F **99**
    (off Queen Caroline St.)
Charlotte M. W1 . . . . .5B **6** (5G **83**)
  W10 . . . . .6F **81**
  W14 . . . . .4G **99**
Charlotte Pk. Av. BR1: Broml 3C **160**
Charlotte Pl. NW9 . . . . .5J **43**
  SW1 . . . . .4A **18** (4G **101**)
  W1 . . . . .6B **6** (5G **83**)
Charlotte Rd. EC2 . . . . .2G **9** (3E **84**)
  RM10: Dag 6H **73**
  SM6: W'gton 6G **167**
  SW13 . . . . .1B **116**
Charlotte Row SW4 . . . . .3G **119**
Charlotte Sq. TW10: Rich 6F **115**
Charlotte St. W1 . . . . .5B **6** (5G **83**)
Charlotte Ter. N1 . . . . .1K **83**
Charlow Cl. SW6 . . . . .2A **118**
CHARLTON
  SE7 .7B **106**
  TW17 . . . . .3E **146**
Charlton Athletic FC 5A **106**
Charlton Chu. La. SE7 . . . . .5A **106**
Charlton Cl. UB10: Ick 2D **56**
Charlton Ct. E2 . . . . .1F **85**
  NW5 .5H **65**
Charlton Cres. IG11: Bark 2K **89**
Charlton Dene SE7 . . . . .7A **106**
Charlton Ga. Bus. Pk. SE7 . . . . .4A **106**
Charlton Ho. TW8: Bford 6E **96**
Charlton King's Rd. NW5 . . . . . . .5H **65**
Charlton La. SE7 . . . . .4B **106**
  TW17: Shep 3E **146**
    (not continuous)
Charlton Lido 7B **106**
Charlton Pk. La. SE7 . . . . .7B **106**
Charlton Pk. Rd. SE7 . . . . .6B **106**
Charlton Pl. N1 . . . . .2B **84**

Charlton Riverside Pl. SE7 . . . . . .4K **105**
Charlton Rd. HA3: Kenton 4D **42**
  HA9: Wemb 1F **61**
  N9 . . . . .1E **34**
  NW10 . . . . .1A **80**
  SE3 .7J **105**
  SE7 .7J **105**
  TW17: Shep 3E **146**
Charlton Ter. SE11 . . . . .6A **102**
Charlton Way SE3 . . . . .1G **123**
Charlwood CRO: Sels 7B **170**
Charlwood Cl. HA3: Hrw W 6D **26**
Charlwood Ho. SW1 . . . . .4C **18**
    (off Vauxhall Bri. Rd.)
  TW9: Kew 7H **97**
Charlwood Ho's. *WC1* 2F **7**
    (off Midhope St.)
Charlwood Pl. SW1 . . . . .4B **18** (4G **101**)
Charlwood Rd. SW15 . . . . .4F **117**
Charlwood St. SW1 . . . . . .6A **18** (5G **101**)
    (not continuous)
Charlwood Ter. SW15 . . . . .4F **117**
Charmans Ho. *SW8* 7J **101**
    (off Wandsworth Rd.)
Charmeuse Ct. *E2* 2H **85**
    (off Silk Weaver Way)
Charmian Av. HA7: Stan 3D **42**
Charmian Ho. *N1* 1G **9**
    (off Crondall St.)
Charmille Av. NW9 . . . . .1B **44**
Charminster Av. SW19 . . . . .2J **153**
Charminster Ct. KT6: Surb 7D **150**
Charminster Rd. KT4: Wor Pk 1F **165**
  SE9 .8B **142**
Charmouth Ct. TW10: Rich 5F **115**
Charmouth Ho. SW8 . . . . .7K **101**
Charmouth Rd. DA16: Well 1C **126**
Charnock Ho. *W12* 7D **80**
    (off White City Est.)
Charnock Rd. E5 . . . . .3H **67**
Charnwood Av. SW19 . . . . .2J **153**
Charnwood Cl. KT3: N Mald 4A **152**
Charnwood Dr. E18 . . . . .3K **51**
Charnwood Gdns. E14 . . . . .4C **104**
Charnwood Pl. N20 . . . . .2F **31**
Charnwood Rd. SE25 . . . . .5D **156**
  UB10: Hil 2C **74**
Charnwood St. E5 . . . . .2H **67**
Charrington Rd. CRO: C'don 2C **168**
Charrington St. NW1 . . . . .2H **83**
    (not continuous)
Charsley Rd. SE6 . . . . .2D **140**
Chart Cl. BR2: Broml 1G **159**
  CRO: C'don 6J **157**
  CR4: Mitc 4D **154**
Charter Av. IG2: Ilf 1H **71**
Charter Bldgs. *SE10* 1D **122**
    (off Catherine Gro.)
Charter Ct. KT3: N Mald 3A **152**
  N4 . . . . .1A **66**
  N22 . . . . .1H **47**
  UB1: S'hall 1E **94**
Charter Cres. TW4: Houn 4C **112**
Charter Dr. DA5: Bexl 7E **126**
Charterhouse 4B **8** (4B **84**)
Charter Ho. *SM2: Sutt* 6K **165**
    (off Mulgrave Rd.)
  WC2 . . . . .1F **13**
    (off Crown Ct.)
Charterhouse Apts. SW18 . . . . . .4A **118**
Charterhouse Av. HA0: Wemb 4C **60**
Charterhouse Bldgs. EC1 . . .4B **8** (4C **84**)
Charterhouse M. EC1 . . . . . .5B **8** (5B **84**)
Charterhouse Museum 5B **8**
Charterhouse Rd. BR6: Chels 3K **173**
  E8 . . . . .4G **67**
Charterhouse Sq. EC1 . . . . .5B **8** (5B **84**)
Charterhouse St. EC1 . . . . . .6K **7** (5A **84**)
Charteris Community Sports Cen.
  . . . . .1J **81**
Charteris Rd. IG8: Wfd G 7F **36**
  N4 . . . . .1A **66**
  NW6 .1H **81**

Charter Quay KT1: King T 2D **150**
    (off Wadbrook St.)
Charter Rd. KT1: King T 3H **151**
The Charter Rd. IG8: Wfd G 6B **36**
Charters Cl. SE19 . . . . .5E **138**
Charter Sq. KT1: King T 2H **151**
Charter Way N3 . . . . .4H **45**
  N14 . . . . .6B **22**
Chartes Ho. *SE1* 7H **15**
    (off Stevens St.)
Chartfield Av. SW15 . . . . .5D **116**
Chartfield Sq. SW15 . . . . .5F **117**
Chartham Ct. SW9 . . . . .3A **120**
    (off Canterbury Cres.)
Chartham Gro. SE27 . . . . .3B **138**
Chartham Ho. *SE1* 7F **15**
    (off Weston St.)
Chartham Rd. SE25 . . . . .3H **157**
Chart Hills Cl. SE28 . . . . .6E **90**
Chart Ho. CR4: Mitc 2D **154**
  E14 . . . . .5D **104**
    (off Burrells Wharf Sq.)
Chartley Av. HA7: Stan 5E **26**
  NW2 .3A **62**
Charton Cl. DA17: Belv 6F **109**
Chartres Ct. UB6: G'frd 2H **77**
Chartridge *SE17* 6D **102**
    (off Westmoreland Rd.)
Chart St. N1 . . . . .1F **9** (3D **84**)
Chartwell Bus. Cen. BR1: Broml . .3B **160**
Chartwell Cl. CRO: C'don 1D **168**
  SE9 .2H **143**
  UB6: G'frd 1F **77**
Chartwell Ct. EN5: Barn 4B **20**
  IG8: Wfd G 7C **36**
  NW2 .3C **62**
  UB3: Hayes 7H **75**
Chartwell Dr. BR6: Farnb 5H **173**
Chartwell Gdns. SM3: Cheam 4G **165**
Chartwell Ho. SW10 . . . . .1A **118**
  W11 . . . . .1H **99**
    (off Ladbroke Rd.)
Chartwell Lodge BR3: Beck 7C **140**
Chartwell Pl. HA2: Harr 2H **59**
  SM3: Cheam 4G **165**
Chartwell Way SE20 . . . . .1H **157**
Charville Ct. HA1: Harr 6K **41**
    (off Gayton Rd.)
  SE10 .6F **105**
    (off Trafalgar Gro.)
Charville La. UB4: Hayes 3E **74**
Charville La. W. UB10: Hil 3D **74**
    (not continuous)
Charwood SW16 . . . . .4A **138**
The Chase BR1: Broml 3K **159**
  DA7: Bex 3H **127**
  E12 . . . . .4B **70**
  HA5: Eastc 6A **40**
  HA5: Pinn 4D **40**
  HA7: Stan 6F **27**
  HA8: Edg 1H **43**
  RM1: Rom 3K **55**
  RM6: Chad H 6E **54**
  RM7: Rush G 3K **73**
  SM6: W'gton 5J **167**
  SW4 .3F **119**
  SW16 . . . . .7K **137**
  SW20 . . . . .1G **153**
  TW16: Sun 1K **147**
  UB10: Ick 5C **56**
Chase Bank Ct. *N14* 6B **22**
    (off Avenue Rd.)
The Chase Cen. NW10 . . . . .3K **79**
Chase Ct. *SW3* 2E **16**
    (off Beaufort Gdns.)
  SW20 . . . . .2G **153**
  TW7: Isle 2A **114**
Chase Ct. Gdns. EN2: Enf 2H **23**
Chase Cross Rd. RM5: Col R 1J **55**
Chasefield Rd. SW17 . . . . .4D **136**
Chase Gdns. E4 . . . . .4H **35**
  TW2: Whitt 7H **113**
Chase Grn. EN2: Enf 3H **23**

Chase Grn. Av. EN2: Enf 2G **23**
Chase Hill EN2: Enf 3H **23**
Chase Ho. *NW6* 3J **81**
    (off Hansel Rd.)
Chase La. IG2: Ilf 5H **53**
  IG6: Ilf .5H **53**
Chaseley Dr. W4 . . . . .5H **97**
Chaseley St. E14 . . . . .6A **86**
Chasemore Cl. CR4: Mitc 7D **154**
Chasemore Gdns. CRO: Wadd . . .5A **168**
Chasemore Ho. *SW6* 7G **99**
    (off Williams Cl.)
Chase Ridings EN2: Enf 2F **23**
Chase Rd. N14 . . . . .5B **22**
  NW10 .4K **79**
Chase Rd. Trad. Est. NW10 . . . . . .4K **79**
CHASE SIDE 1J **23**
Chase Side EN2: Enf 3H **23**
  N14 . . . . .5K **21**
Chase Side Av. EN2: Enf 2H **23**
  SW20 . . . . .1G **153**
Chase Side Cres. EN2: Enf 1H **23**
Chase Side Pl. EN2: Enf 2H **23**
Chaseville Pde. N21 . . . . .5E **22**
Chaseville Pk. Rd. N21 . . . . .5D **22**
Chase Way N14 . . . . .2A **32**
Chaseway Lodge E16 . . . . .6J **87**
    (off Butchers Rd.)
Chaseways Vs. RM5: Col R 1F **55**
Chasewood Av. EN2: Enf 2G **23**
Chasewood Ct. NW7 . . . . .5E **28**
Chasewood Pk. HA1: Harr 3K **59**
Chaston Pl. NW5 . . . . .5F **65**
    (off Grafton Ter.)
Chater Ho. *E2* 3K **85**
    (off Roman Rd.)
Chatfield Rd. CRO: C'don 1B **168**
  SW11 . . . . .3A **118**
Chatham Av. BR2: Hayes 7H **159**
Chatham Cl. NW11 . . . . .5J **45**
  SE18 .3F **107**
  SM3: Sutt 7H **153**
Chatham Ho. *SM6: W'gton* 5F **167**
    (off Melbourne Rd.)
Chatham Pl. E9 . . . . .6J **67**
Chatham Rd. E17 . . . . .3A **50**
  E18 . . . . .2H **51**
  KT1: King T 2G **151**
  SW11 . . . . .6D **118**
Chatham St. SE17 . . . . .4D **102**
Chatsfield Pl. W5 . . . . .6E **78**
Chats Palace Arts Cen. 5K **67**
Chatswood M. DA14: Sidc 4K **143**
  DA15: Sidc 1A **144**
  HA9: Wemb 5F **61**
  NW4 . . . . .2E **44**
  SW20 . . . . .1G **153**
Chatsworth Cl. BR4: W W'ck 2H **171**
  NW4 . . . . .2E **44**
  W4 . . . . .6J **97**
Chatsworth Ct. HA7: Stan 5H **27**
  SW16 . . . . .3K **155**
  W8 . . . . .4J **99**
    (off Pembroke Rd.)
Chatsworth Cres. TW3: Houn 4H **113**
Chatsworth Dr. EN1: Enf 7B **24**
Chatsworth Est. E5 . . . . .4K **67**
Chatsworth Gdns. HA2: Harr 1F **59**
  KT3: N Mald 5B **152**
  W3 . . . . .1H **97**
Chatsworth Ho. *BR2: Broml* 4J **159**
    (off Westmoreland Rd.)
  E16 . . . . .1K **105**
    (off Wesley Av.)
  SE1 . . . . .5J **15**
    (off Duchess Wlk.)
Chatsworth Lodge *W4* 5K **97**
    (off Bourne Pl.)
Chatsworth Pde. BR5: Pet W 5G **161**
Chatsworth Pl. CR4: Mitc 3D **154**
  TW11: Tedd 4A **132**
Chatsworth Ri. W5 . . . . .4F **79**

Chatsworth Rd. CR0: C'don 4D **168**
  E5 . . . . .3J **67**
  E15 . . . . .5H **69**
  NW2 . . . . .6E **62**
  SM3: Cheam 5F **165**
  UB4: Yead 4K **75**
  W4 . . . . .6J **97**
  W5 . . . . .4F **79**
Chatsworth Way SE27 . . . . .3B **138**
CHATTERN HILL 4D **128**
Chattern Hill TW15: Ashf 4D **128**
Chattern Rd. TW15: Ashf 4E **128**
Chatterton Cl. TW9: Kew 2F **115**
Chatterton M. N4 . . . . .3B **66**
    (off Chatterton Rd.)
Chatterton Rd. BR2: Broml 4B **160**
  N4 . . . . .3B **66**
Chatto Rd. SW11 . . . . .5D **118**
Chaucer Av. TW4: Cran 2K **111**
  TW9: Rich 3G **115**
  UB4: Hayes 5J **75**
Chaucer Cl. N11 . . . . .5B **32**
Chaucer Ct. BR2: Broml 5A **160**
  EN5: New Bar 5E **20**
  N16 . . . . .4E **66**
  SW17 . . . . .3B **136**
    (off Lanesborough Way)
Chaucer Dr. SE1 . . . . .4F **103**
Chaucer Gdns. E1 . . . . .1K **15**
    (off Piazza Wlk.)
  SM1: Sutt 3J **165**
Chaucer Grn. CR0: C'don 7H **157**
Chaucer Ho. EN5: Barn 4A **20**
  SM1: Sutt 3J **165**
    (off Chaucer Gdns.)
  SW1 . . . . .6A **18**
    (off Churchill Gdns.)
Chaucer Mans. W14 . . . . .6G **99**
    (off Queen's Club Gdns.)
Chaucer Rd. DA15: Sidc 1C **144**
  DA16: Well 1J **125**
  E7 . . . . .6J **69**
  E11 . . . . .6J **51**
  E17 . . . . .2E **50**
  SE24 .5A **120**
  SM1: Sutt 4J **165**
  TW15: Ashf 4A **128**
  W3 . . . . .1J **97**
Chaucer Way SW19 . . . . .6B **136**
Chaulden Ho. EC1 . . . . .2F **9**
    (off Cranwood St.)
Chauncey Cl. N9 . . . . .3B **34**
Chaundrye Cl. SE9 . . . . .6D **124**
Chauntler Cl. E16 . . . . .6K **87**
Chaville Cl. N11 . . . . .4K **31**
Chaville Way N3 . . . . .1J **45**
Cheadle Cl. NW8 . . . . .3B **4**
    (off Henderson Dr.)
Cheadle Ho. E14 . . . . .6B **86**
    (off Copenhagen Pl.)
CHEAM 6G **165**
Cheam Comn. Rd. KT4: Wor Pk . .2D **164**
Cheam Leisure Cen. 4F **165**
Cheam Mans. SM3: Cheam 7G **165**
Cheam Pk. Way SM3: Cheam . . .6G **165**
Cheam Rd. SM1: Sutt 6H **165**
  SM2: Cheam 7F **165**
Cheam St. SE15 . . . . .3J **121**
CHEAM VILLAGE 6G **165**
Cheapside EC2 . . . . .1D **14** (6C **84**)
  N13 . . . . .4J **33**
  N22 . . . . .3A **48**
Cheapside Pas. EC2 . . . . .1C **14**
    (off One New Change)
Cheddar Cl. N11 . . . . .6J **31**
Cheddar Waye UB4: Yead 6K **75**
Cheddington Ho. E2 . . . . .1G **85**
    (off Whiston Rd.)
Cheddington Rd. N18 . . . . .3K **33**
Chedworth Cl. E16 . . . . .6H **87**
    (off Wouldham Rd.)
Chedworth Ho. N15 . . . . .4D **48**
    (off West Grn. Rd.)

Cheering La. E20 . . . . .5E **68**
The Cheesegrater 1G **15**
Cheeseman Cl. TW12: Hamp 6C **130**
Cheesemans Ter. W14 . . . . .5H **99**
    (not continuous)
Cheffery Ct. TW15: Ashf 6D **128**
Cheldon Av. NW7 . . . . .7A **30**
Chelford Rd. BR1: Broml 5F **141**
Chelmer Cres. IG11: Bark 2B **90**
Chelmer Rd. E9 . . . . .5K **67**
Chelmsford Cl. E6 . . . . .6D **88**
  W6 . . . . .6F **99**
Chelmsford Ct. N14 . . . . .7C **22**
    (off Chelmsford Rd.)
Chelmsford Gdns. IG1: Ilf 7C **52**
Chelmsford Ho. N7 . . . . .4K **65**
    (off Holloway Rd.)
Chelmsford Rd. E11 . . . . .1F **69**
  E17 . . . . .6C **50**
  E18 . . . . .1H **51**
  N14 . . . . .7B **22**
Chelmsford Sq. NW10 . . . . .1E **80**
Chelmsine Cl. HA4: Ruis 5E **38**
CHELSEA 6D **16** (5C **100**)
CHELSEA BRI. 7J **17** (6F **101**)
Chelsea Bri. Rd.
  SW1 . . . . .5G **17** (5E **100**)
Chelsea Bri. Wharf SW11 . . . . . . .6F **101**
Chelsea Cloisters SW3 . . .4D **16** (4C **100**)
Chelsea Cl. HA8: Edg 2G **43**
  KT4: Wor Pk 7C **152**
  NW10 . . . . .1K **79**
  TW12: Hamp H 5G **131**
Chelsea Ct. BR1: Broml 3C **160**
    (off Holmdene Ct.)
  SW3 . . . . .7G **17**
    (off Embankment Gdns.)
Chelsea Cres. NW2 . . . . .6H **63**
  SW10 . . . . .1A **118**
Chelsea Emb. SW3 . . . . .7D **16** (6C **100**)
Chelsea Farm Ho. Studios
  SW10 . . . . .6B **100**
    (off Cremorne Est.)
Chelsea FC 7K **99**
Chelsea Flds. SW19 . . . . .1B **154**
Chelsea Gdns. SM3: Cheam 4G **165**
  SW1 . . . . .6H **17** (5E **100**)
  W13 . . . . .5K **77**
Chelsea Ga. SW1 . . . . .6H **17**
Chelsea Harbour SW10 . . . . .1A **118**
Chelsea Harbour Design Cen.
  SW10 . . . . .1A **118**
    (off Chelsea Harbour Dr.)
Chelsea Harbour Dr. SW10 . . . . .1A **118**
Chelsea Lodge SW3 . . . . .7F **17**
    (off Tite St.)
Chelsea Mnr. Ct. SW3 . . .7D **16** (6C **100**)
Chelsea Mnr. Gdns.
  SW3 . . . . .6D **16** (5C **100**)
Chelsea Mnr. St. SW3 . . . .6D **16** (5C **100**)
Chelsea Mnr. Studios SW3 . . . . . .6D **16**
    (off Flood St.)
Chelsea Pk. Gdns. SW3 . .7A **16** (6B **100**)
Chelsea Physic Garden . . .7E **16** (6D **100**)
Chelsea Reach Twr. SW10 . . . . . .7B **100**
    (off Worlds End Est.)
Chelsea Sports Cen. 5B **16** (5B **100**)
Chelsea Sq. SW3 . . . . . . .5B **16** (5B **100**)
Chelsea Studios SW6 . . . . .7K **99**
    (off Fulham Rd.)
The Chelsea Theatre 7A **100**
Chelsea Towers SW3 . . . . .7D **16**
Chelsea Village SW6 . . . . .7K **99**
    (off Fulham Rd.)
Chelsea Vista SW6 . . . . .1A **118**
Chelsea Wharf SW10 . . . . .7B **100**
    (off Lots Rd.)
Chelsfield Av. N9 . . . . .7E **24**
Chelsfield Gdns. SE26 . . . . .3J **139**
Chelsfield Grn. N9 . . . . .7E **24**
    (not continuous)
Chelsfield Ho. SE17 . . . . .4E **102**
    (off Massinger St.)

Chelsfield Point E9 . . . . .7K **67**
    (off Penshurst Rd.)
Chelsham Rd. CR2: S Croy 7D **168**
  SW4 . . . . .3H **119**
Chelsiter Ct. DA14: Sidc 4K **143**
Chelston App. HA4: Ruis 2J **57**
Chelston Ct. E11 . . . . .5K **51**
Chelston Rd. HA4: Ruis 1J **57**
Chelsworth Dr. SE18 . . . . .6H **107**
Cheltenham Av. TW1: Twick 7A **114**
Cheltenham Cl.
  KT3: N Mald 3J **151**
  UB5: N'olt 6F **59**
Cheltenham Ct. HA7: Stan 5H **27**
    (off Marsh La.)
Cheltenham Gdns. E6 . . . . .2C **88**
Cheltenham Ho. IG8: Wfd G 6K **37**
  UB3: Harl 3E **92**
    (off Skipton Dr.)
Cheltenham Pl. HA3: Kenton 4E **42**
  W3 . . . . .1H **97**
Cheltenham Rd. BR6: Chels 3K **173**
  E10 . . . . .6E **50**
  SE15 .4J **121**
Cheltenham Ter. SW3 . . . .5F **17** (5D **100**)
Chelverton Rd. SW15 . . . . .4F **117**
Chelwood N20 . . . . .2G **31**
Chelwood Cl. E4 . . . . .6J **25**
Chelwood Ct. CR2: S Croy 5C **168**
  SW11 .1B **118**
    (off Westbridge Rd.)
Chelwood Gdns. TW9: Kew 2G **115**
Chelwood Gdns. Pas.
  TW9: Kew 2G **115**
Chelwood Ho. W2 . . . . .1B **10**
    (off Gloucester Sq.)
Chelwood Wlk. SE4 . . . . .4A **122**
Chenappa Cl. E13 . . . . .3J **87**
Chenduit Way HA7: Stan 5E **26**
Cheney Ct. SE23 . . . . .1K **139**
Cheney Row E17 . . . . .1B **50**
Cheneys Rd. E11 . . . . .3G **69**
Cheney St. HA5: Eastc 4A **40**
The Chenies BR6: Pet W 6J **161**
  NW1 . . . . .2H **83**
    (off Pancras Rd.)
Chenies Ho. W2 . . . . .7K **81**
    (off Moscow Rd.)
  W4 . . . . .7B **98**
    (off Corney Reach Way)
Chenies M. WC1 . . . . .4C **6** (4H **83**)
Chenies Pl. NW1 . . . . .2H **83**
Chenies St. WC1 . . . . .5C **6** (5H **83**)
Cheniston Gdns. W8 . . . . .3K **99**
Chenla SE13 . . . . .2D **122**
Chenneston Cl. TW16: Sun 1J **147**
Cheping Ho. W10 . . . . .4F **81**
    (off Shalfleet Dr.)
Chepstow Cl. SW15 . . . . .5G **117**
Chepstow Cnr. W2 . . . . .6J **81**
    (off Chepstow Pl.)
Chepstow Ct. W11 . . . . .7J **81**
    (off Chepstow Vs.)
Chepstow Cres. IG3: Ilf 6J **53**
  W11 . . . . .7J **81**
Chepstow Gdns. UB1: S'hall 6D **76**
Chepstow Pl. W2 . . . . .6J **81**
Chepstow Ri. CR0: C'don 3E **168**
Chepstow Rd. CR0: C'don 3E **168**
  W2 . . . . .6J **81**
  W7 . . . . .3A **96**
Chepstow Vs. W11 . . . . .7H **81**
The Chequers HA5: Pinn 3B **40**
Chequers Cl. BR5: St P 4K **161**
  NW9 . . . . .2A **44**
Chequers Ct. DA17: Belv 4G **109**
  EC1 . . . . .4D **8**
    (off Chequer St.)
Chequers Ho. NW8 . . . . .3C **4**
    (off Jerome Cres.)
Chequers La. RM9: Dag 4F **91**
    (not continuous)

Chequers Pde. N13 . . . . .5H **33**
  RM9: Dag 1F **91**
  SE9 . . . . .6D **124**
    (off Eltham High St.)
Chequer St. EC1 . . . . .4D **8** (4C **84**)
    (not continuous)
Chequers Way N13 . . . . .5G **33**
Cherbury Cl. SE28 . . . . .6D **90**
Cherbury Ct. N1 . . . . .2D **84**
    (off St John's Est.)
Cherbury St. N1 . . . . .2D **84**
Cherchefelle M. HA7: Stan 5G **27**
Cherimoya Gdns. KT8: W Mole . . .3F **149**
Cherington Rd. W7 . . . . .1J **95**
Cheriton Av. BR2: Broml 5H **159**
  IG5: Ilf .2D **52**
Cheriton Cl. EN4: Cockf 3J **21**
  W5 . . . . .5C **78**
Cheriton Ct. SE12 . . . . .7J **123**
  SE25 .5E **156**
Cheriton Dr. SE18 . . . . .7H **107**
Cheriton Lodge HA4: Ruis 1H **57**
Cheriton Sq. SW17 . . . . .2E **136**
Cherry Av. UB1: S'hall 1B **94**
Cherry Blossom Cl. N13 . . . . .5G **33**
Cherry Cl. E17 . . . . .5D **50**
  HA0: Wemb 3D **60**
  HA4: Ruis 3H **57**
  NW9 . . . . .2A **44**
  SM4: Mord 4G **153**
  SM5: Cars 2D **166**
  SW2 . . . . .7A **120**
  W5 . . . . .3D **96**
Cherrycot Hill BR6: Farnb 4G **173**
Cherrycot Ri. BR6: Farnb 4G **173**
Cherry Ct. HA5: Pinn 2B **40**
  IG6: Ilf .3F **53**
  W3 . . . . .1A **98**
Cherry Cres. TW8: Bford 7B **96**
Cherrydown Av. E4 . . . . .3G **35**
Cherrydown Cl. E4 . . . . .3H **35**
Cherrydown Rd. DA14: Sidc 2D **144**
Cherrydown Wlk. RM7: Mawney . .2H **55**
Cherry Gdn. Ho. SE16 . . . . .2H **103**
    (off Cherry Gdn. St.)
Cherry Gdns. RM9: Dag 5F **73**
  UB5: N'olt 7F **59**
Cherry Gdn. St. SE16 . . . . .2H **103**
Cherry Gth. TW8: Bford 5D **96**
Cherry Gro. UB3: Hayes 1K **93**
  UB8: Hil 5D **74**
Cherry Hill EN5: New Bar 6E **20**
  HA3: Hrw W 6E **26**
Cherry Hill Gdns. CR0: Wadd 4K **167**
Cherrylands Cl. NW9 . . . . .2J **61**
Cherry La. UB7: W Dray 4B **92**
Cherry Laurel Wlk. SW2 . . . . .6K **119**
Cherry Orchard SE7 . . . . .6A **106**
  UB7: W Dray 2A **92**
Cherry Orchard Gdns.
  CR0: C'don 1D **168**
  KT8: W Mole 3D **148**
Cherry Orchard Rd.
  BR2: Broml 2C **172**
  CR0: C'don 2D **168**
  KT8: W Mole 3E **148**
Cherry Pk. La. E20 . . . . .7E **68**
Cherry Red Records Stadium 3H **151**
Cherry Rd. EN3: Enf W 1D **24**
Cherry St. RM7: Rom 5K **55**
Cherry Tree Av. UB7: Yiew 6B **74**
Cherry Tree Cl. E9 . . . . .1J **85**
  HA0: Wemb 4A **60**
Cherry Tree Ct. NW1 . . . . .7G **65**
    (off Camden Rd.)
  NW9 . . . . .4J **43**
  SE7 . . . . .6A **106**
Cherry Tree Dr. SW16 . . . . .3J **137**
Cherry Tree Hill N2 . . . . .5C **46**
Cherry Tree Ho. N22 . . . . .7D **32**
Cherry Tree Ri. IG9: Buck H 4F **37**
Cherry Tree Rd. E15 . . . . .5G **69**
  N2 . . . . .4D **46**

Cherry Tree Ter. SE1 . . . . .7H 15
    (off Whites Grounds)
Cherry Tree Wlk. BR3: Beck 4B 158
  BR4: W W'ck 4H 171
  EC1 . . . . .4D 8 (4C 84)
Cherry Tree Way E13 . . . . .4B 88
  HA7: Stan 6G 27
Cherry Wlk. BR2: Hayes 1J 171
Cherry Way KT19: Ewe 6K 163
  TW17: Shep 4F 147
Cherrywood Cl. E3 . . . . .3A 86
  KT2: King T 7G 133
Cherrywood Cl. TW11: Tedd 5A 132
Cherrywood Dr. SW15 . . . . .5F 117
Cherrywood La. SM4: Mord 4G 153
Cherrywood Lodge SE13 . . . . .6F 123
    (off Birdwood Av.)
Cherry Wood Way W5 . . . . .5G 79
Chertsey Bri. Rd. KT16: Chert 7A 146
Chertsey Ct. SW14 . . . . .3H 115
Chertsey Dr. SM3: Cheam 2G 165
Chertsey Ho. E2 . . . . .2J 9
    (off Arnold Cir.)
CHERTSEY MEADS 7A 146
Chertsey Meads
  Local Nature Reserve 7A 146
Chertsey Rd. E11 . . . . .2F 69
  IG1: Ilf .4H 71
  TW1: Twick 6K 113
  TW2: Twick 2F 131
  TW13: Felt 3G 129
  TW15: Ashf 7F 129
  TW16: Sun 7F 129
  TW17: Shep 7A 146
Chertsey St. SW17 . . . . .5E 136
Chervil Cl. TW13: Felt 3J 129
Chervil M. SE28 . . . . .1B 108
Cherwell Ct. KT19: Ewe 4J 163
Cherwell Ho. NW8 . . . . .4B 4
Cherwell M. SW11 . . . . .4C 118
Cherwell Way HA4: Ruis 6E 38
Cheryls Cl. SW6 . . . . .1K 117
Cheseman St. SE26 . . . . .3H 139
Chesfield Rd. KT2: King T 7E 132
Chesham Apts. E4 . . . . .7J 35
Chesham Av. BR5: Pet W 6F 161
Chesham Cl. NW7 . . . . .4F 29
  RM7: Rom 4K 55
  SW1 . . . . .2G 17
Chesham Cres. SE20 . . . . .1J 157
Chesham Flats W1 . . . . .2H 11
    (off Brown Hart Gdns.)
Chesham Ho. SE8 . . . . .1C 122
    (off Brookmill Rd.)
Chesham M. SW1 . . . . .1K 16
Chesham Pl. SW1 . . . . .2G 17 (3E 100)
    (not continuous)
Chesham Rd. KT1: King T 2G 151
  SE20 . . . . .2J 157
  SW19 .5B 136
Chesham St. NW10 . . . . .3K 61
  SW1 . . . . .2G 17 (3E 100)
Chesham Ter. W13 . . . . .2B 96
Cheshire Cl. CR4: Mitc 3J 155
  E17 . . . . .1D 50
  SE4 . . . . .2B 122
Cheshire Ct. EC4 . . . . .1K 13
    (off Fleet St.)
Cheshire Gdns. KT9: Chess 6D 162
Cheshire Ho. N18 . . . . .4C 34
  SM4: Mord 7K 153
Cheshire Rd. N22 . . . . .7E 32
Cheshire St. E2 . . . . .3K 9 (4F 85)
Cheshir Ho. NW4 . . . . .4E 44
Chesholm Rd. N16 . . . . .3E 66
Chesnut Ho. NW6 . . . . .1K 81
    (off Mortimer Cres.)
Chesnut Rd. DA17: Belv 5G 109
  E7 . . . . .6K 69
Chesil Ct. E2 . . . . .2J 9
  SW3 . . . . .7D 16 (6C 100)
Chesilton Rd. SW6 . . . . .1H 117
Chesil Way UB4: Hayes 3H 75

Chesley Gdns. E6 . . . . .2B 88
Chesney Ct. W9 . . . . .4J 81
    (off Shirland Rd.)
Chesney Cres. CR0: New Ad 7E 170
Chesney Ho. SE13 . . . . .4F 123
    (off Mercator Rd.)
Chesney St. SW11 . . . . .1E 118
Chesnut Gro. N17 . . . . .3F 49
Chesnut Rd. N17 . . . . .3F 49
Chesnut Row N3 . . . . .7D 30
    (off Nether St.)
Chessell Cl. CR7: Thor H 4B 156
Chessholme Ct. TW16: Sun 7G 129
    (off Scotts Av.)
Chessholme Rd. TW15: Ashf 6E 128
Chessing Ct. N2 . . . . .3D 46
    (off Fortis Grn.)
CHESSINGTON 5E 162
Chessington Av. DA7: Bex 7E 108
  N3 . . . . .3G 45
Chessington Cl. KT19: Ewe 6J 163
Chessington Ct. HA5: Pinn 4D 40
  N3 . . . . .3H 45
    (off Charter Way)
Chessington Hall Gdns.
  KT9: Chess 7D 162
Chessington Hill Pk.
  KT9: Chess 5G 163
Chessington Ho. SW8 . . . . .2H 119
Chessington Lodge N3 . . . . .3H 45
Chessington Mans. E10 . . . . .7C 50
  E11 . . . . .7G 51
Chessington Pde. KT9: Chess 6D 162
Chessington Pk. KT9: Chess 4G 163
Chessington Rd. KT17: Ewe 7B 164
  KT19: Ewe 6G 163
Chessington Sports Cen. 7D 162
Chessington Trade Pk.
  KT9: Chess 4G 163
Chessington Way BR4: W W'ck . . .2D 170
Chesson Rd. W14 . . . . .6H 99
Chesswood Way HA5: Pinn 2B 40
Chestbrook Ct. EN1: Enf 5K 23
    (off Forsyth Pl.)
Chester Av. TW2: Whitt 1D 130
  TW10: Rich 6F 115
Chester Cl. SM1: Sutt 2J 165
  SW1 . . . . .7J 11 (2F 101)
  SW13 .3D 116
  TW10: Rich 6F 115
  TW15: Ashf 5F 129
  UB8: Hil 6D 74
Chester Cl. Nth. NW1 . . . . . .1K 5 (3F 83)
Chester Cl. Sth. NW1 . . . . . .2K 5 (3F 83)
Chester Cotts. SW1 . . . . .4G 17
Chester Ct. BR2: Broml 4H 159
    (off Durham Rd.)
  NW1 . . . . .1K 5 (3F 83)
    (not continuous)
  SE5 . . . . .7D 102
    (off Lomond Gro.)
  SE8 . . . . .5K 103
  W6 . . . . .4F 99
    (off Wolverton Gdns.)
Chester Cres. E8 . . . . .5F 67
Chester Dr. HA2: Harr 6D 40
Chesterfield Cl. SE13 . . . . .2F 123
Chesterfield Ct. KT5: Surb 5E 150
    (off Cranes Pk.)
Chesterfield Dr. KT10: Hin W 2A 162
Chesterfield Flats EN5: Barn 5A 20
    (off Bells Hill)
Chesterfield Gdns. N4 . . . . .5B 48
  SE10 . . . . .7F 105
  W1 . . . . .4J 11 (1F 101)
Chesterfield Gro. SE22 . . . . .5F 121
Chesterfield Hill W1 . . . . . .4J 11 (1F 101)
Chesterfield Ho. W1 . . . . .4H 11
    (off Chesterfield Gdns.)
Chesterfield Lodge N21 . . . . .7E 22
    (off Church Hill)
Chesterfield M. N4 . . . . .5B 48
  TW15: Ashf 4A 128

Chesterfield Rd. E10 . . . . .6E 50
  EN5: Barn 5A 20
  KT19: Ewe 7K 163
  N3 . . . . .6D 30
  TW15: Ashf 4A 128
  W4 . . . . .6J 97
Chesterfield St. W1 . . . . . .4J 11 (1F 101)
Chesterfield Wlk. SE10 . . . . .1F 123
Chesterfield Way SE15 . . . . .7J 103
  UB3: Hayes 2J 93
Chesterford Gdns. NW3 . . . . .4K 63
Chesterford Ho. SE18 . . . . .1B 124
    (off Tellson Av.)
Chesterford Rd. E12 . . . . .5D 70
Chester Gdns. EN3: Pond E 6C 24
  SM4: Mord 6A 154
  W13 . . . . .6B 78
Chester Ga. NW1 . . . . .2J 5 (3F 83)
Chester Ho. N10 . . . . .2F 47
  SE8 . . . . .6B 104
  SW1 . . . . .3J 17
    (off Eccleston Pl.)
  SW9 . . . . .7A 102
    (off Cranmer Rd.)
Chesterman Ct. W4 . . . . .7A 98
    (off Corney Reach Way)
Chester M. E17 . . . . .2C 50
  SW1 . . . . .1J 17 (3F 101)
Chester Pl. NW1 . . . . .1J 5 (3F 83)
Chester Rd. DA15: Sidc 5J 125
  E7 . . . . .7B 70
  E11 . . . . .6K 51
  E16 . . . . .4G 87
  E17 . . . . .5K 49
  HA6: Nwood 1H 39
  IG3: Ilf .1K 71
  IG7: Chig 3K 37
  N9 . . . . .1C 34
  N17 . . . . .3D 48
  N19 . . . . .2F 65
  NW1 . . . . .2H 5 (3E 82)
  SW19 .6E 134
  TW4: Houn 3K 111
  TW6: H'row A 3C 110
Chester Row SW1 . . . . . . .4G 17 (4E 100)
The Chesters KT3: N Mald 1A 152
Chester Sq. SW1 . . . . .3H 17 (4E 100)
Chester Sq. M. SW1 . . . . .2J 17
Chester St. E2 . . . . .4G 85
  SW1 . . . . .1H 17 (3E 100)
Chester Ter. IG11: Bark 6H 71
  NW1 . . . . .1J 5 (3F 83)
    (not continuous)
Chesterton Cl. SW18 . . . . .5J 117
  UB6: G'frd 2F 77
Chesterton Ct. W5 . . . . .5D 78
Chesterton Dr. TW19: Stanw 1B 128
Chesterton Ho. CR0: C'don 4D 168
    (off Heathfield Rd.)
  SW11 . . . . .3B 118
    (off Ingrave St.)
  W10 . . . . .5G 81
    (off Portobello Rd.)
Chesterton Rd. E13 . . . . .3J 87
  W10 . . . . .5F 81
Chesterton Sq. W8 . . . . .4J 99
Chesterton Ter. E13 . . . . .3J 87
  KT1: King T 2G 151
Chester Way SE11 . . . . . .4K 19 (4A 102)
Chesthunte Rd. N17 . . . . .1C 48
Chestlands Cl. UB10: Hil 6C 56
Chestnut All. SW6 . . . . .6H 99
Chestnut Apts. E3 . . . . .2D 86
    (off Alameda Pl.)
Chestnut Av. BR4: W W'ck 5G 171
  E7 . . . . .4K 69
  HA0: Wemb 5B 60
  HA6: Nwood 2H 39
  HA8: Edg 6K 27
  IG9: Buck H 3G 37
  KT8: E Mos 3K 149
  KT10: Esh 7H 149
  KT19: Ewe 4A 164

Chestnut Av. N8 . . . . .5J 47
  SW14 .3K 115
  TW8: Bford 4D 96
  TW11: Tedd 2K 149
  TW12: Hamp 7E 130
  UB7: Yiew 7B 74
Chestnut Av. Nth. E17 . . . . .4F 51
Chestnut Av. Sth. E17 . . . . .5E 50
Chestnut Cl. BR6: Chels 5K 173
  DA15: Sidc 1A 144
  IG9: Buck H 3G 37
  N14 . . . . .5B 22
  N16 . . . . .2D 66
  SE6 . . . . .5E 140
  SE14 . . . . .1B 122
  SM5: Cars 1D 166
  SW16 .4A 138
  TW15: Ashf 4D 128
  TW16: Sun 6H 129
  UB3: Hayes 7G 75
  UB7: Harl, Sip 5B 92
Chestnut Ct. CR2: S Croy 4C 168
    (off Bramley Hill)
  N8 . . . . .5J 47
  SW6 . . . . .6H 99
  TW13: Hanw 5B 130
  TW19: Stanw 1A 128
    (off Mulberry Av.)
  W8 . . . . .3K 99
    (off Abbots Wlk.)
Chestnut Dr. DA7: Bex 3D 126
  E11 . . . . .6J 51
  HA3: Hrw W 7E 26
  HA5: Pinn 6B 40
Chestnut Gro. CR2: Sels 7H 169
  CR4: Mitc 5H 155
  DA2: Wilm 4K 145
  EN4: E Barn 5J 21
  HA0: Wemb 5B 60
  KT3: N Mald 3K 151
  SE20 . . . . .7H 139
  SW12 .7E 118
  TW7: Isle 4A 114
  W5 . . . . .3D 96
Chestnut Ho. E3 . . . . .1B 86
    (off Sycamore Av.)
  SW15 .4B 116
  W4 . . . . .4A 98
    (off The Orchard)
Chestnut La. N20 . . . . .1B 30
Chestnut M. SW14 . . . . .4J 115
Chestnut Pl. SE26 . . . . .4F 139
Chestnut Plaza E20 . . . . .6E 68
    (within Westfield Shop. Cen.)
Chestnut Ri. SE18 . . . . .6H 107
  WD23: Bush 1A 26
Chestnut Rd. KT2: King T 7E 132
  SE27 . . . . .3B 138
  SW20 .2F 153
  TW2: Twick 2J 131
  TW15: Ashf 4D 128
The Chestnuts BR3: Beck 3K 157
  HA5: Hat E 1D 40
  N5 . . . . .4C 66
    (off Highbury Grange)
  UB10: Uxb 7A 56
Chestnuts Ho. E17 . . . . .6C 50
    (off Hoe St.)
Chestnut Ter. SM1: Sutt 4K 165
Chestnut Wlk. IG8: Wfd G 5D 36
  TW17: Shep 4G 147
Chestnut Way TW13: Felt 3K 129
Cheston Av. CR0: C'don 2A 170
Chestwood Gro. UB10: Hil 7B 56
Chesworth Ct. E1 . . . . .5J 85
    (off Fulneck Pl.)
Chettle Cl. SE1 . . . . .3D 102
    (off Spurgeon St.)
Chettle Ct. N8 . . . . .6A 48
Chetwode Ho. NW8 . . . . .3C 4
Chetwode Rd. SW17 . . . . .3D 136
Chetwood Wlk. E6 . . . . .5C 88
    (off Greenwich Cres.)

Chetwynd Av. EN4: E Barn 1J **31**
Chetwynd Dr. UB10: Hil 2B **74**
Chetwynd Rd. NW5 . . . . .4F **65**
Chetwynd Vs. NW5 . . . . .4F **65**
   (off Chetwynd Rd.)
Chevalier Cl. HA7: Stan 4K **27**
Cheval Pl. SW7 . . . . . .1D **16** (3C **100**)
Cheval St. E14 . . . . .3C **104**
Cheveney Wlk. BR2: Broml 3J **159**
Chevening Rd. NW6 . . . . .2F **81**
  SE10 . . . . .5H **105**
  SE19 . . . . .6D **138**
The Chevenings DA14: Sidc 3C **144**
Cheverell Ho. E2 . . . . .2G **85**
   (off Pritchard's Rd.)
Cheverton Rd. N19 . . . . .1H **65**
Chevet St. E9 . . . . .5A **68**
Chevington NW2 . . . . .6H **63**
Cheviot N17 . . . . .7C **34**
   (off Northumberland Gro.)
Cheviot Cl. DA7: Bex 2K **127**
  EN1: Enf 2J **23**
  UB3: Harl 7F **93**
Cheviot Cl. SE14 . . . . .6J **103**
   (off Avonley Rd.)
  UB2: S'hall 4F **95**
Cheviot Gdns. NW2 . . . . .2F **63**
  SE27 . . . . .4B **138**
Cheviot Ga. NW2 . . . . .2G **63**
Cheviot Ho. E1 . . . . .6H **85**
   (off Commercial Rd.)
Cheviot Rd. SE27 . . . . .5A **138**
Cheviot Way IG2: Ilf 4J **53**
Chevron Cl. E16 . . . . .6J **87**
Chevy Rd. UB2: S'hall 2G **95**
Chewton Rd. E17 . . . . .4A **50**
Cheylesmore Ho. SW1 . . . . .5J **17**
   (off Ebury Bri. Rd.)
Cheyne Av. E18 . . . . .3H **51**
  TW2: Whitt 1D **130**
Cheyne Cl. BR2: Broml 3C **172**
  NW4 . . . . .5E **44**
Cheyne Ct. SW3 . . . . . .7E **16** (6D **100**)
Cheyne Gdns. SW3 . . . . .7D **16** (6C **100**)
Cheyne Hill KT5: Surb 4F **151**
Cheyne Ho. SW3 . . . . .7E **16**
   (off Chelsea Emb.)
Cheyne M. SW3 . . . . . . .7D **16** (6C **100**)
Cheyne Pk. Dr. BR4: W W'ck 3E **170**
Cheyne Path W7 . . . . .5K **77**
Cheyne Pl. SW3 . . . . . . .7E **16** (6D **100**)
Cheyne Rd. TW15: Ashf 7F **129**
Cheyne Row SW3 . . . . . .7C **16** (6C **100**)
Cheyne Wlk. CR0: C'don 2G **169**
  N21 . . . . .5G **23**
  NW4 . . . . .6E **44**
  SW3 . . . . .7C **16** (7B **100**)
  SW10 . . . . .7B **100**
Cheyneys Av. HA8: Edg 6J **27**
Chichele Gdns. CR0: C'don 4E **168**
Chichele Rd. NW2 . . . . .5F **63**
Chicheley Gdns. HA3: Hrw W 7B **26**
   (not continuous)
Chicheley Rd. HA3: Hrw W 7B **26**
Chicheley St. SE1 . . . . . .6H **13** (2K **101**)
Chichester Av. HA4: Ruis 2F **57**
Chichester Cl. E6 . . . . .6C **88**
  SE3 . . . . .7A **106**
  TW12: Hamp 6D **130**
Chichester Cl. HA7: Stan 3E **42**
  HA8: Edg 6B **28**
   (off Whitchurch La.)
  KT17: Ewe 7B **164**
  NW1 . . . . .7G **65**
   (off Royal Coll. St.)
  TW19: Stanw 1A **128**
  UB5: N'olt 1D **76**
Chichester Gdns. IG1: Ilf 7C **52**
Chichester Ho. NW6 . . . . .2J **81**
  SW9 . . . . .7A **102**
   (off Cranmer Rd.)
Chichester Lodge SE10 . . . . .4J **105**
   (off Peartree Way)

Chichester M. SE27 . . . . .4A **138**
Chichester Rents WC2 . . . . .7J **7**
Chichester Rd. CR0: C'don 3E **168**
  E11 . . . . .3G **69**
  N9 . . . . .1B **34**
  NW6 . . . . .2J **81**
  W2 . . . . .5K **81**
Chichester St. SW1 . . . . .6B **18** (5G **101**)
Chichester Way E14 . . . . .4F **105**
  TW14: Felt 7A **112**
Chickenshed Theatre 5K **21**
Chicksand Ho. E1 . . . . .5K **9**
   (off Chicksand St.)
Chicksand St. E1 . . . . . . .6K **9** (5F **85**)
   (not continuous)
Chiddingfold N12 . . . . .3D **30**
Chiddingstone SE13 . . . . .5E **122**
Chiddingstone Av. DA7: Bex 7F **109**
Chiddingstone St. SW6 . . . . .2J **117**
Chieveley Pde. DA7: Bex 3H **127**
Chieveley Rd. DA7: Bex 4H **127**
Chignell Pl. W13 . . . . .1A **96**
CHIGWELL 3K **37**
Chigwell Ct. E9 . . . . .6A **68**
   (off Ballance Rd.)
Chigwell Golf Course 1H **37**
Chigwell Hill E1 . . . . .7H **85**
Chigwell Hurst Ct. HA5: Pinn 3B **40**
Chigwell Pk. IG7: Chig 4K **37**
Chigwell Pk. Dr. IG7: Chig 4K **37**
Chigwell Ri. IG7: Chig 2K **37**
Chigwell Rd. E18 . . . . .3K **51**
  IG8: Wfd G 2A **52**
Chilcombe Ho. SW15 . . . . .7C **116**
   (off Fontley Way)
Chilcot Cl. E14 . . . . .6D **86**
Chilcott Cl. HA0: Wemb 4C **60**
Childebert Rd. SW17 . . . . .2F **137**
Childeric Rd. SE14 . . . . .7A **104**
Childerley KT1: King T 3G **151**
   (off Burritt Rd.)
Childerley St. SW6 . . . . .1G **117**
The Childers IG8: Wfd G 5J **37**
Childers St. SE8 . . . . .6A **104**
Child La. SE10 . . . . .3H **105**
Childs Cl. UB3: Hayes 7J **75**
CHILD'S HILL 3H **63**
Childs Hill Wlk. NW2 . . . . .3H **63**
   (off Cricklewood La.)
Child's La. SE19 . . . . .6E **138**
Child's M. SW5 . . . . .4J **99**
   (off Child's Pl.)
Child's Pl. SW5 . . . . .4J **99**
Child's St. SW5 . . . . .4J **99**
Child's Wlk. SW5 . . . . .4J **99**
   (off Child's St.)
Childs Way NW11 . . . . .5H **45**
Chilham Cl. DA5: Bexl 7F **127**
Chilham Ho. SE1 . . . . .3D **102**
  SE15 . . . . .6J **103**
Chilham Rd. SE9 . . . . .4C **142**
Chilham Way BR2: Hayes 7J **159**
Chilianwallah Memorial
   . . . . .7G **17** (6E **100**)
Chillerton Rd. SW17 . . . . .5E **136**
Chillingford Ho. SW17 . . . . .4A **136**
Chillington Dr. SW11 . . . . .4B **118**
Chillingworth Gdns. TW1: Twick 3K **131**
Chillingworth Rd. N7 . . . . .5A **66**
Chill La. N1 . . . . .1H **83**
Chilmark Gdns. KT3: N Mald 6C **152**
Chilmark Rd. SW16 . . . . .2H **155**
Chiltern Av. TW2: Whitt 1E **130**
Chiltern Cl. CR0: C'don 3E **168**
  DA7: Bex 1K **127**
  KT4: Wor Pk 1E **164**
  UB10: Ick 2C **56**
Chiltern Cl. BR2: Broml 2C **172**
   (off Gravel Rd.)
  EN5: New Bar 5K **21**
  HA1: Harr 5H **41**
  N10 . . . . .2E **46**

Chiltern Ct. NW1 . . . . .4F **5**
   (off Baker St.)
  SE14 . . . . .7J **103**
   (off Avonley Rd.)
  UB8: Hil 4D **74**
Chiltern Dene EN2: Enf 4E **22**
Chiltern Dr. KT5: Surb 6G **151**
Chiltern Gdns. BR2: Broml 4H **159**
  NW2 . . . . .3F **63**
Chiltern Hgts. N1 . . . . .7K **65**
   (off Caledonian Rd.)
Chiltern Ho. N9 . . . . .3B **34**
  SE17 . . . . .6D **102**
   (off Portland St.)
  W5 . . . . .5E **78**
  W10 . . . . .5G **81**
   (off Telford Rd.)
Chiltern Rd. E3 . . . . .4C **86**
  HA5: Eastc 5A **40**
  IG2: Ilf 5J **53**
The Chilterns BR1: Broml 2K **159**
   (off Murray Av.)
Chiltern St. W1 . . . . .5G **5** (5E **82**)
Chiltern Way IG8: Wfd G 3D **36**
Chilthorne Cl. SE6 . . . . .7B **122**
Chilton Av. W5 . . . . .4D **96**
Chilton Cl. N22 . . . . .7D **32**
   (off Truro Rd.)
Chilton Gro. SE8 . . . . .4K **103**
Chilton Ind. Est. SE12 . . . . .6H **123**
Chiltonian Ind. Est. SE13 . . . . .5F **123**
Chilton Rd. HA8: Edg 6B **28**
  TW9: Rich 3G **115**
The Chiltons E18 . . . . .2J **51**
Chilton St. E2 . . . . .3K **9** (4F **85**)
Chilvers Cl. TW2: Twick 2J **131**
Chilver St. SE10 . . . . .5H **105**
Chilworth Ct. SW19 . . . . .1F **135**
Chilworth Gdns. SM1: Sutt 3A **166**
Chilworth M. W2 . . . . . . .1A **10** (6B **82**)
Chilworth Pl. IG11: Bark 4A **90**
Chilworth St. W2 . . . . . . .1A **10** (6A **82**)
Chimes Av. N13 . . . . .5F **33**
Chimes Ct. BR3: Beck 1A **158**
Chimes Ter. N8 . . . . .5J **47**
Chimney Ct. E1 . . . . .1H **103**
   (off Brewhouse La.)
China Ct. E1 . . . . .1H **103**
   (off Asher Way)
China Hall M. SE16 . . . . .3J **103**
China M. SW2 . . . . .7K **119**
China Wharf SE1 . . . . . . .6K **15** (2G **103**)
Chinbrook Cres. SE12 . . . . .3K **141**
Chinbrook Rd. SE12 . . . . .3K **141**
Chinchilla Dr. TW4: Houn 2A **112**
The Chine HA0: Wemb 5B **60**
  N10 . . . . .4G **47**
  N21 . . . . .6G **23**
Ching Ct. WC2 . . . . .1E **12**
   (off Monmouth St.)
Chingdale Rd. E4 . . . . .3B **36**
CHINGFORD 1K **35**
Chingford Av. E4 . . . . .3H **35**
Chingford Golf Course 1B **36**
Chingford Golf Range 1H **35**
CHINGFORD GREEN 1A **36**
CHINGFORD HATCH 4A **36**
Chingford Ind. Cen. E4 . . . . .5F **35**
Chingford La. IG8: Wfd G 4B **36**
Chingford Leisure Cen. 4K **35**
CHINGFORD MOUNT 4H **35**
Chingford Mt. Rd. E4 . . . . .4H **35**
Chingford Rd. E4 . . . . .6H **35**
  E17 . . . . .1D **50**
Chingley Cl. BR1: Broml 6G **141**
Chingstone Ter. E4 . . . . .5K **35**
Ching Way E4 . . . . .6G **35**
   (not continuous)
Chinnery Cl. EN1: Enf 1A **24**
Chinnock's Wharf E14 . . . . .7A **86**
   (off Narrow St.)
Chinnor Cres. UB6: G'frd 2F **77**

Chipka St. E14 . . . . .2E **104**
   (not continuous)
Chipley St. SE14 . . . . .6A **104**
Chipmunk Gro. UB5: N'olt 3C **76**
Chippendale All. UB8: Uxb 7A **56**
Chippendale Ho. SW1 . . . . .6K **17**
   (off Churchill Gdns.)
Chippendale St. E5 . . . . .3K **67**
Chippendale Waye UB8: Uxb 7A **56**
Chippenham KT1: King T 2F **151**
   (off Excelsior Cl.)
Chippenham Av. HA9: Wemb 5H **61**
Chippenham Cl. HA5: Eastc 4H **39**
Chippenham Gdns. NW6 . . . . .3J **81**
Chippenham M. W9 . . . . .4J **81**
Chippenham Rd. W9 . . . . .4J **81**
Chipperfield Ho. SW3 . . . . .5C **16**
   (off Cale St.)
Chipperfield Rd. BR5: St P 7A **144**
   (not continuous)
CHIPPING BARNET 4B **20**
Chipping Cl. EN5: Barn 3B **20**
Chipstead Av. CR7: Thor H 4B **156**
Chipstead Cl. SE19 . . . . .7F **139**
  SM2: Sutt 7K **165**
Chipstead Gdns. NW2 . . . . .2D **62**
Chipstead Rd. TW6: H'row A 3C **110**
Chipstead St. SW6 . . . . .1J **117**
Chip St. SW4 . . . . .3H **119**
Chirk Cl. UB4: Yead 4C **76**
Chisenhale Rd. E3 . . . . .2A **86**
Chisholm Ct. W6 . . . . .5C **98**
Chisholm Rd. CR0: C'don 2E **168**
  TW10: Rich 6F **115**
Chisledon Wlk. E9 . . . . .6B **68**
   (off Osborne Rd.)
CHISLEHURST 6F **143**
Chislehurst Av. N12 . . . . .7F **31**
Chislehurst Caves 1E **160**
Chislehurst Golf Course 7F **143**
Chislehurst Rd. BR1: Broml 2B **160**
  BR5: Pet W 4J **161**
  BR6: Orp, Pet W, St M Cry 4J **161**
  BR7: Chst 2B **160**
  DA14: Sidc 5A **144**
  TW10: Rich 5E **114**
CHISLEHURST WEST 6E **142**
Chislet Cl. BR3: Beck 7C **140**
Chisley Rd. N15 . . . . .6E **48**
Chiswell Sq. SE3 . . . . .2K **123**
Chiswell St. EC1 . . . . . . .5E **8** (5C **84**)
  SE5 . . . . .7D **102**
   (off Edmund St.)
CHISWICK 5K **97**
CHISWICK BRI. 2J **115**
Chiswick Cl. CR0: Bedd 3K **167**
Chiswick Comm. Rd. W4 . . . . .4K **97**
Chiswick Community Sports Hall 7K **97**
Chiswick Ct. HA5: Pinn 3D **40**
  W4 . . . . .4H **97**
Chiswick High Rd. TW8: Bford 5G **97**
  W4 . . . . .5G **97**
Chiswick House & Gdns. 6K **97**
Chiswick Ho. Grounds W4 . . . . .6A **98**
Chiswick La. W4 . . . . .5A **98**
Chiswick La. Sth. W4 . . . . .6B **98**
Chiswick Lifeboat Station 7B **98**
Chiswick Mall W4 . . . . .6B **98**
  W6 . . . . .6B **98**
Chiswick Pk. W4 . . . . .4H **97**
Chiswick Pier 7B **98**
Chiswick Plaza W4 . . . . .6J **97**
Chiswick Quay W4 . . . . .1J **115**
Chiswick Rd. N9 . . . . .2B **34**
  W4 . . . . .4J **97**
CHISWICK RDBT. 5G **97**
Chiswick Sq. W4 . . . . .6A **98**
Chiswick Staithe W4 . . . . .1J **115**
Chiswick Ter. W4 . . . . .4J **97**
   (off Chiswick High Rd.)
Chiswick Village W4 . . . . .6G **97**
Chiswick Wharf W4 . . . . .6B **98**
Chitterfield Ga. UB7: Sip 7C **92**

Chitty's La. RM8: Dag 2D **72**
Chitty St. W1 . . . . .5B **6** (5G **83**)
Chivalry Rd. SW11 . . . . .5C **118**
Chivelston SW19 . . . . .1F **135**
Chivenor Gro. KT2: King T 5D **132**
Chivers Pas. SW18 . . . . .5K **117**
Chivers Rd. E4 . . . . .3J **35**
Choats Mnr. Way RM9: Dag 2E **90**
Choats Rd. IG11: Bark 2C **90**
   RM9: Dag 2C **90**
Chobham Academy Sports Cen. . .5E **68**
Chobham Gdns. SW19 . . . . .2F **135**
CHOBHAM MANOR 5D **68**
Chobham Rd. E15 . . . . .5F **69**
The Chocolate Factory 1 N22 . . . .2K **47**
   (off Clarendon Rd.)
The Chocolate Factory 2 N22 . . . .2K **47**
   (off Coburg Rd.)
Chocolate Studios N1 . . . . .1E **8**
   (off Shepherdess Pl.)
Choice Vw. IG1: Ilf 2G **71**
   (off Axon Pl.)
Cholmeley Cl. N6 . . . . .7F **47**
Cholmeley Cres. N6 . . . . .7F **47**
Cholmeley Lodge N6 . . . . .1F **65**
Cholmeley Pk. N6 . . . . .1F **65**
Cholmeley Gdns. NW6 . . . . .5J **63**
Cholmley Rd. KT7: T Ditt 6B **150**
Cholmley Ter. KT7: T Ditt 7B **150**
   (off Portsmouth Rd.)
Cholmley Vs. KT7: T Ditt 6B **150**
   (off Portsmouth Rd.)
Cholmondeley Av. NW10 . . . . .2C **80**
Cholmondeley Wlk. TW9: Rich 5C **114**
Choppin's Ct. E1 . . . . .1H **103**
Chopwell Cl. E15 . . . . .7F **69**
Chorleywood Cres. BR5: St P 2K **161**
Choudhury Mans. N1 . . . . .7J **65**
   (off Pembroke St.)
Choumert Gro. SE15 . . . . .2G **121**
Choumert M. SE15 . . . . .2G **121**
Choumert Rd. SE15 . . . . .3F **121**
Choumert Sq. SE15 . . . . .2G **121**
Chow Sq. E8 . . . . .5F **67**
Chrislea Cl. TW5: Hest 6D **94**
Chrisp Ho. SE10 . . . . .6G **105**
   (off Maze Hill)
Chrisp St. E14 . . . . .5D **86**
   (not continuous)
Chris Pullen Way N7 . . . . .6J **65**
Christabel Cl. TW7: Isle 3J **113**
Christabel Pankhurst Ct. SE5 . . . .7D **102**
   (off Brisbane St.)
Christchurch Av. DA8: Erith 6K **109**
   HA0: Wemb 6E **60**
   HA3: Kenton, W'stone 4K **41**
   N12 .6F **31**
   NW6 .1F **81**
   TW11: Tedd 5A **132**
Christchurch Cl. EN2: Enf 2H **23**
   N12 .7G **31**
   SW19 . . . . .7B **136**
Christ Church Cl. NW10 . . . . .1A **80**
Christchurch Ct. EC4 . . . . .7B **8**
   (off Warwick La.)
   NW6 .7G **63**
   (off Willesden La.)
   UB4: Yead 4A **76**
   (off Dunedin Way)
Christchurch Flats TW9: Rich 3E **114**
Christchurch Gdns. HA3: W'stone . .4A **42**
Christchurch Grn. HA0: Wemb 6E **60**
Christchurch Hill NW3 . . . . .3B **64**
Christchurch Ho. RM8: Dag 5B **72**
   SW2 .1K **137**
   (off Christchurch Rd.)
Christchurch La. EN5: Barn 2B **20**
Christchurch Lodge EN4: Cockf . . .4J **21**
Christchurch Pk. SM2: Sutt 7A **166**
Christchurch Pas. EN5: Barn 2B **20**
   NW3 .3A **64**
Christchurch Path UB3: Harl 3E **92**
Christchurch Pl. SW8 . . . . .2H **119**

Christ Chu. Rd. BR3: Beck 2C **158**
   KT5: Surb 6F **151**
Christchurch Rd. DA15: Sidc 4K **143**
   IG1: Ilf 1F **71**
   N8 . . . . .6J **47**
   SW2 .1K **137**
   SW14 . . . . .5H **115**
   SW19 . . . . .7B **136**
   TW6: H'row A 3C **110**
Christ Church Spitalfields . . .5J **9** (5F **85**)
Christchurch Sq. E9 . . . . .1J **85**
Christchurch St. SW3 . . .7E **16** (6D **100**)
Christchurch Ter. SW3 . . . . .7E **16**
Christian Cl. SE16 . . . . .1B **104**
Christian Flds. SW16 . . . . .7A **138**
Christian Pl. E1 . . . . .6G **85**
   (off Burslem St.)
Christian St. E1 . . . . .6G **85**
Christie Ct. N19 . . . . .2J **65**
Christie Dr. CRO: C'don 5G **157**
Christie Gdns. RM6: Chad H 6B **54**
Christie Ho. E16 . . . . .5J **87**
   (off Hammersley Rd.)
   SE10 . . . . .5H **105**
   (off Blackwall La.)
   W12 .6D **80**
   (off Du Cane Rd.)
Christie Rd. E9 . . . . .6A **68**
Christina Sq. N4 . . . . .1B **66**
Christina St. EC2 . . . . .3G **9** (4E **84**)
Christine Worsley Cl. N21 . . . . . .1G **33**
Christopher Av. W7 . . . . .3A **96**
Christopher Bell Twr. E3 . . . . .2C **86**
   (off Pancras Way)
Christopher Boones Ct. SE13 . . . .4F **123**
   (off Bessington Rd.)
Christopher Cl. DA15: Sidc 5K **125**
   SE16 . . . . .2K **103**
Christopher Ct. DA15: Sidc 2A **144**
   (off Station Rd.)
   E1 . . . . .1K **15**
   TW15: Ashf 5A **128**
Christopher Gdns. RM9: Dag 5D **72**
Christopher Pl. N22 . . . . .7D **32**
   (off Myddleton Rd.)
   NW1 . . . . .1D **6** (3H **83**)
Christopher Rd. UB2: S'hall 4K **93**
Christophers M. W11 . . . . .1G **99**
Christopher St. EC2 . . . .4F **9** (4D **84**)
Chroma Mans. E20 . . . . .6E **68**
   (off Penny Brookes St.)
Chronicle Av. NW9 . . . . .3A **44**
Chronicle Twr. N1 . . . . .1C **8**
Chryssell Rd. SW9 . . . . .7A **102**
Chudworthy St. SE14 . . . . .6A **104**
Chudleigh DA14: Sidc 4B **144**
Chudleigh Cres. IG3: Ilf 4J **71**
Chudleigh Gdns. SM1: Sutt 3A **166**
Chudleigh Rd. NW6 . . . . .7F **63**
   SE4 .5B **122**
   TW2: Twick 6J **113**
Chudleigh St. E1 . . . . .6K **85**
Chudleigh Way HA4: Ruis 1J **57**
Chulsa Rd. SE26 . . . . .5H **139**
Chumleigh Gdns. SE5 . . . . .6E **102**
   (off Chumleigh St.)
Chumleigh St. SE5 . . . . .6E **102**
Chumleigh Wlk. KT5: Surb 4F **151**
Chumleigh All. CRO: C'don 1A **168**
Church App. SE21 . . . . .3D **138**
Church Av. BR3: Beck 1C **158**
   DA14: Sidc 5A **144**
   E4 . . . . .6A **36**
   (not continuous)
   HA4: Ruis 1F **57**
   HA5: Pinn 6C **40**
   NW1 .7F **65**
   SW14 . . . . .3K **115**
   UB2: S'hall 3C **94**
   UB5: N'olt 7D **58**
Churchbank E17 . . . . .4C **50**
   (off Eastfield Rd.)

Churchbury Cl. EN1: Enf 2K **23**
Churchbury La. EN1: Enf 3J **23**
Churchbury Rd. EN1: Enf 2K **23**
   SE9 .7B **124**
Church Cloisters EC3 . . . . .3G **15**
Church Cl. HA6: Nwood 1H **39**
   HA8: Edg 5D **28**
   N20 .3H **31**
   TW3: Houn 2C **112**
   UB4: Hayes 5F **75**
   UB7: W Dray 3A **92**
   W8 . . . . .2K **99**
Church Ct. EC4 . . . . .6A **84**
   SE16 . . . . .2B **104**
   (off Rotherhithe St.)
   TW9: Rich 5D **114**
Church Cres. E9 . . . . .7K **67**
   N3 . . . . .1H **45**
   N10 . . . . .4F **47**
   N20 .3H **31**
Churchcroft Cl. SW12 . . . . .7E **118**
Churchdown BR1: Broml 4G **141**
Church Dr. BR4: W W'ck 3G **171**
   HA2: Harr 6E **40**
   NW9 .1K **61**
Church Elm La. RM10: Dag 6G **73**
CHURCH END
   N3 . . . . .1H **45**
   NW10 . . . . .7A **62**
Church End E17 . . . . .4D **50**
   NW4 .3D **44**
Church Entry EC4 . . . . .1B **14**
Church Est. Almshouses
   TW9: Rich 4F **115**
   (off Sheen Rd.)
Church Farm La. SM3: Cheam . . .6G **165**
Church Farm Leisure Cen. 7J **21**
Churchfield Av. N12 . . . . .6G **31**
Churchfield Cl. HA2: Harr 4G **41**
   UB3: Hayes 7H **75**
Churchfield Ho. KT12: Walt T 7J **147**
   W2 . . . . .4A **4**
   (off Hall Pl.)
Churchfield Mans. SW6 . . . . .2H **117**
   (off New Kings Rd.)
Churchfield Pl. TW17: Shep 7D **146**
Churchfield Rd. DA16: Well 3A **126**
   KT12: Walt T 7J **147**
   W3 . . . . .1J **97**
   W7 . . . . .2J **95**
   W13 .1B **96**
Churchfields E18 . . . . .1J **51**
   KT8: W Mole 3E **148**
   SE10 . . . . .6E **104**
Churchfields Av. TW13: Hanw 3D **130**
Churchfields Rd. BR3: Beck 2K **157**
Churchfield Way N12 . . . . .6F **31**
Church Gdns. HA0: Wemb 4A **60**
   W5 . . . . .2D **96**
Church Gth. N19 . . . . .2H **65**
   (off St John's Gro.)
Church Ga. SW6 . . . . .3G **117**
Church Grn. SW9 . . . . .1A **120**
   UB3: Hayes 6H **75**
Church Gro. KT1: Hamp W 1C **150**
   SE13 . . . . .5D **122**
Church Hill DA1: Cray 4K **127**
   E17 . . . . .4C **50**
   HA1: Harr 1J **59**
   N21 .7E **22**
   SE18 . . . . .3D **106**
   SM5: Cars 5D **166**
   SW19 . . . . .5H **135**
Church Hill Rd. E17 . . . . .4D **50**
   EN4: E Barn 6H **21**
   KT6: Surb 5E **150**
   SM3: Cheam 3F **165**
Church Hill Wood
   BR5: St M Cry 5K **161**
Church Ho. EC1 . . . . .3B **8**
   (off Compton St.)
   SW1 .1D **18**
   (off Gt. Smith St.)

Church Hyde SE18 . . . . .6J **107**
Churchill Av. HA3: Kenton 6B **42**
   UB10: Hil 3D **74**
Churchill Cl. TW14: Felt 1H **129**
   UB10: Hil 3D **74**
Churchill Ct. BR6: Farnb 5G **173**
   HA2: Harr 2F **59**
   (Eastcote Av.)
   HA2: Harr 5F **41**
   (Montrose Ct.)
   HA5: Hat E 1C **40**
   N4 . . . . .7A **48**
   N9 . . . . .1K **33**
   SE18 . . . . .4D **106**
   UB5: N'olt 5E **58**
   (off Newmarket Av.)
   W5 . . . . .4F **79**
Churchill Gdns. SW1 . . . . .6A **18**
   (not continuous)
   W3 . . . . .6G **79**
Churchill Gdns. Rd.
   SW1 . . . . .6K **17** (5F **101**)
Churchill Lodge IG6: Ilf 4G **53**
Churchill Pl. E14 . . . . .1D **104**
   HA1: Harr 4J **41**
Churchill Rd. CR2: S Croy 7C **168**
   E16 . . . . .6A **88**
   HA8: Edg 6A **28**
   NW2 .6D **62**
   NW5 .4F **65**
   UB10: Uxb 2A **74**
Churchills M. IG8: Wfd G 6C **36**
Churchill Ter. E4 . . . . .4H **35**
Churchill Theatre 2J **159**
Churchill Wlk. E9 . . . . .5J **67**
Churchill War Rooms 6D **12** (2H **101**)
Churchill Way BR1: Broml 2J **159**
   TW16: Sun 5J **129**
Churchlands Way KT4: Wor Pk . . .2F **165**
Church La. BR2: Broml 1C **172**
   BR7: Chst 1G **161**
   E11 . . . . .1G **69**
   E17 . . . . .4D **50**
   EN1: Enf 3J **23**
   HA3: W'stone 1K **41**
   HA5: Pinn 3C **40**
   KT7: T Ditt 6K **149**
   KT9: Chess 6F **163**
   N2 . . . . .3B **46**
   N8 . . . . .4K **47**
   N9 . . . . .2B **34**
   N17 . . . . .1E **48**
   NW9 .6J **43**
   RM10: Dag 7J **73**
   SM6: Bedd 3H **167**
   (not continuous)
   SW17 . . . . .5D **136**
   SW19 . . . . .1H **153**
   TW1: Twick 1A **132**
   TW10: Ham 1E **132**
   TW11: Tedd 5K **131**
   W5 . . . . .2C **96**
Churchley Rd. SE26 . . . . .4H **139**
Church Manorway DA8: Erith 4K **109**
   DA17: Belv 2J **109**
   SE2 .5A **108**
Church Mead SE5 . . . . .7C **102**
   (off Camberwell Rd.)
Churchmead Cl. EN4: E Barn 6H **21**
Church Mdw. KT6: Surb 2C **162**
Churchmead Rd. NW10 . . . . .6C **62**
Churchmore Rd. SW16 . . . . .1G **155**
Church Mt. N2 . . . . .5B **46**
Church Paddock Ct.
   SM6: Bedd 3H **167**
Church Pde. TW15: Ashf 4B **128**
Church Pas. EN5: Barn 3B **20**
   KT6: Surb 5E **150**
   TW1: Twick 1B **132**
Church Path CRO: C'don 2C **168**
   CR4: Mitc 3C **154**
   (not continuous)
   E11 . . . . .5J **51**

Church Path E17 . . . . .4D **50**
N5 . . . . .5B **66**
N12 . . . . .3F **31**
(Woodside La.)
N12 . . . . .4F **31**
(Woodside Pk. Rd.)
N17 . . . . .7K **33**
NW10 . . . . .7A **62**
SM6: Bedd 3H **167**
SW14 . . . . .3K **115**
(not continuous)
SW19 .2H **153**
UB1: S'hall 1E **94**
UB2: S'hall 3D **94**
(not continuous)
W3 . . . . .2J **97**
(not continuous)
W4 . . . . .3J **97**
Church Pl. CR4: Mitc 3C **154**
SW1 . . . . .3B **12** (7G **83**)
UB10: Ick 3E **56**
W3 . . . . .2D **96**
Church Ri. KT9: Chess 6F **163**
SE23 . . . . .2K **139**
Church Rd. BR2: Broml 2J **159**
(Edison Rd.)
BR2: Broml 3G **159**
(Hazelwood Ho's.)
BR2: Kes 7B **172**
BR6: Farnb 5G **173**
CR0: C'don 3C **168**
(not continuous)
CR4: Mitc 1B **154**
DA7: Bex 2F **127**
DA8: Erith 5K **109**
DA14: Sidc 4A **144**
DA16: Well 2B **126**
E10 . . . . .1C **68**
E12 . . . . .5C **70**
E17 . . . . .2A **50**
EN3: Pond E 6D **24**
HA6: Nwood 1H **39**
HA7: Stan 5G **27**
IG2: Ilf .6J **53**
IG9: Buck H 1E **36**
IG11: Bark 6G **71**
KT1: King T 2F **151**
KT4: Wor Pk 1A **164**
KT6: Surb 1C **162**
KT8: E Mos 4H **149**
KT10: Clay 7A **162**
KT19: Ewe 7K **163**
N1 . . . . .6C **66**
N6 . . . . .6E **46**
N17 . . . . .1E **48**
(not continuous)
NW4 . . . . .4D **44**
NW10 . . . . .7A **62**
SE19 . . . . .1E **156**
SM3: Cheam 6G **165**
SM6: Bedd 3H **167**
SW13 .2B **116**
SW19 .5G **135**
(Courthorpe Rd.)
SW19 .1B **154**
(Reynolds Cl.)
TW5: Cran 5K **93**
TW5: Hest 7E **94**
TW7: Isle 1H **113**
TW9: Rich 4E **114**
TW10: Ham 4D **132**
TW10: Rich 5E **114**
TW11: Tedd 4J **131**
TW13: Hanw 5B **130**
TW15: Ashf 3B **128**
TW17: Shep 7D **146**
UB2: S'hall 3D **94**
UB3: Hayes 1H **93**
UB5: N'olt 2B **76**
UB7: W Dray 3A **92**
UB8: Cowl 4A **74**
W3 . . . . .1J **97**
W7 . . . . .7H **77**

Church Rd. Almshouses E10 . . . .2D **68**
(off Church Rd.)
Church Rd. Ind. Est. E10 . . . . . . .1C **68**
Church Row BR7: Chst 1G **161**
NW3 . . . . .4A **64**
SW6 . . . . .7J **99**
(off Moore Pk. Rd.)
SW18 .5K **117**
Church Row M. BR7: Chst 7G **143**
Church Sq. TW17: Shep 7D **146**
Church St. CR0: C'don 3B **168**
E15 . . . . .1G **87**
E16 . . . . .1F **107**
EN2: Enf 3H **23**
KT1: King T 2D **150**
KT12: Walt T 7J **147**
KT17: Ewe 7C **164**
N9 . . . . .7J **23**
NW8 . . . . .5B **4** (5B **82**)
RM10: Dag 6H **73**
SM1: Sutt 5K **165**
TW1: Twick 1A **132**
TW7: Isle 3B **114**
TW12: Hamp 1G **149**
TW16: Sun 3K **147**
W2 . . . . .5B **4** (5B **82**)
(not continuous)
Church St. Est. NW8 . . . . . .4B **4** (4B **82**)
Church St. Nth. E15 . . . . .1G **87**
Church Stretton Rd.
TW3: Houn 5G **113**
Church Ter. NW4 . . . . .3D **44**
SE13 . . . . .3G **123**
TW10: Rich 5D **114**
Church Va. N2 . . . . .3D **46**
SE23 . . . . .2K **139**
Church Vw. TW10: Rich 5E **114**
Church Vw. Gro. SE26 . . . . .6K **139**
Churchview Rd. TW2: Twick 1H **131**
Church Wlk. EN2: Enf 3J **23**
KT7: T Ditt 6K **149**
KT12: Walt T 7J **147**
(not continuous)
N6 . . . . .3E **64**
N16 . . . . .3D **66**
(not continuous)
NW2 . . . . .3H **63**
NW4 . . . . .3E **44**
NW9 . . . . .2K **61**
SW13 .1C **116**
SW15 .5D **116**
SW16 .2J **155**
SW20 .3E **152**
TW8: Bford 6C **96**
(not continuous)
TW9: Rich 5D **114**
UB3: Hayes 6G **75**
Churchward Ho. SE17 . . . . .6B **102**
(off Lorrimore Sq.)
W14 . . . . .5H **99**
(off Ivatt Pl.)
Church Way EN4: Cockf 4J **21**
HA8: Edg 6B **28**
N20 . . . . .3H **31**
Churchway NW1 . . . . .1D **6** (3H **83**)
(not continuous)
Churchwell Path E9 . . . . .5J **67**
Churchwood Gdns. IG8: Wfd G . .4D **36**
SE23 . . . . .7J **121**
Churchyard Pas. SE5 . . . . .2D **120**
Churchyard Row SE11 . . . . .4B **102**
Churston Av. E13 . . . . .1K **87**
Churston Cl. SW2 . . . . .1A **138**
Churston Dr. SM4: Mord 5F **153**
Churston Gdns. N11 . . . . .6B **32**
Churston Mans. WC1 . . . . .4H **7**
(off Gray's Inn Rd.)
Churton Pl. SW1 . . . . . .4B **18** (4G **101**)
W4 . . . . .6H **97**
(off Chiswick Village)
Churton St. SW1 . . . . . .4B **18** (4G **101**)
Chusan Pl. E14 . . . . .6B **86**

Chute Ho. SW9 . . . . .2A **120**
(off Stockwell Pk. Rd.)
Chuter Ede Ho. SW6 . . . . .6H **99**
(off Clem Attlee Ct.)
Chyngton Cl. DA15: Sidc 3K **143**
Cibber Rd. SE23 . . . . .2K **139**
Cicada Rd. SW18 . . . . .6A **118**
Cicely Ct. CR0: Wadd 5A **168**
Cicely Ho. NW8 . . . . .2B **82**
(off Cochrane St.)
Cicely Rd. SE15 . . . . .1G **121**
Cinderella Path NW11 . . . . .1K **63**
Cinderford Way BR1: Broml 4G **141**
Ciné Lumière 3A **16**
(off Queensberry Pl.)
Cineworld Cinema
Bexleyheath 4H **127**
Chelsea, Fulham Rd. 5A **100**
Enfield .4B **24**
Feltham 2K **129**
Ilford 3F **71**
(off Clements Rd.)
Leicester Sq. 2D **12**
(off Leicester Sq.)
The O2 . . . . .1G **105**
(within The O2)
South Ruislip 4K **57**
Wandsworth 5K **117**
Wembley 4G **61**
West India Quay 7C **86**
Wood Green 2A **48**
(within Wood Green Shop. City)
Cinnabar Wharf Central E1 . . . .1G **103**
(off Wapping High St.)
Cinnabar Wharf E. E1 . . . . .1G **103**
(off Wapping High St.)
Cinnabar Wharf W. E1 . . . . .1G **103**
(off Wapping High St.)
Cinnamon Cl. CR0: C'don 7J **155**
SE15 . . . . .7F **103**
Cinnamon M. N13 . . . . .2F **33**
Cinnamon Row SW11 . . . . .3A **118**
Cinnamon St. E1 . . . . .1H **103**
Cinnamon Wharf SE1 . . . . .6K **15**
(off Shad Thames)
Cintra Pk. SE19 . . . . .7F **139**
Cipher Ct. NW2 . . . . .3C **62**
Circa Apts. NW1 . . . . .7E **64**
The Circle NW2 . . . . .3A **62**
NW7 . . . . .6E **28**
SE1 . . . . .6J **15**
(off Queen Elizabeth St.)
Circle Gdns. SW19 . . . . .2J **153**
The Circuits HA5: Pinn 4A **40**
Circular Rd. N17 . . . . .3F **49**
Circular Way SE18 . . . . .6D **106**
Circus Lodge NW8 . . . . .1A **4**
Circus M. W1 . . . . .5E **4**
Circus Pl. EC2 . . . . .6F **9** (5D **84**)
Circus Rd. NW8 . . . . .1A **4** (3B **82**)
Circus Rd. E. SW11 . . . . .7K **17** (7F **101**)
Circus Rd. W. SW11 . . . . .7F **101**
Circus St. SE10 . . . . .7E **104**
Circus W. SW11 . . . . . .7K **17** (6F **101**)
Cirencester St. W2 . . . . .5K **81**
Cirrus Apts. E1 . . . . .3K **9**
(off Bacon St.)
Cirrus Cl. SM6: W'gton 7J **167**
Cissbury Ho. SE26 . . . . .3G **139**
Cissbury Rd. N15 . . . . .5D **48**
Cissbury Ring Nth. N12 . . . . .5C **30**
Cissbury Ring Sth. N12 . . . . .5C **30**
Citadel Pl. SE11 . . . . .5G **19** (5K **101**)
Citius Apts. E3 . . . . .2K **86**
(off Tredegar La.)
Citius Ho. E14 . . . . .6K **35**
Citius Wlk. E20 . . . . .6E **68**
Citizen Ho. N7 . . . . .4A **66**
Citizen Rd. N7 . . . . .4A **66**
Citrine Apts. E3 . . . . .1A **86**
(off Gunmaker's La.)
Citrus Ho. SE8 . . . . .5B **104**
(off Alverton St.)

City Apts. E1 . . . . .7K **9**
(off White Church La.)
City Bus. Cen. SE16 . . . . .3J **103**
City Ct. CR0: C'don 7B **156**
City Cross Bus. Pk. SE10 . . . . . .4G **105**
City E. Bldg. E1 . . . . .7H **85**
(off Cable St.)
City Forum EC1 . . . . .1C **8** (3C **84**)
City Gdn. Row EC1 . . . . .3C **84**
N1 . . . . .1C **8** (2B **84**)
City Ga. Ho. IG2: Ilf 6E **52**
(off Eastern Av.)
City Gateway E1 . . . . .7G **85**
(off Ensign St.)
City Hall
Southwark 5H **15** (1E **102**)
City Harbour E14 . . . . .3D **104**
(off Selsdon Way)
City Hgts. E8 . . . . .1F **85**
(off Kingsland Rd.)
City Ho. BR2: Broml 6C **160**
City Island E14 . . . . .6G **87**
City Island Way E14 . . . . .6G **87**
City Lights Ct. SE11 . . . . .5K **19**
(off Bowden St.)
City Mill Apts. E8 . . . . .1F **85**
(off Lovelace St.)
City Mill River Path E15 . . . . .1E **86**
City Nth. E. Twr. N4 . . . . .2A **66**
(off City Nth. Pl.)
City Nth. Pl. N4 . . . . .2A **66**
City Nth. W. Twr. N4 . . . . .2A **66**
CITY OF LONDON 1E **14** (6D **84**)
City of London Almshouses
SW9 . . . . .4K **119**
City of London Crematorium 3C **70**
City of London Distillery 6B **84**
City of London Point N7 . . . . .6H **65**
(off York Way)
City of London Police Mus. 6E **9**
City of London Tourist Info. Cen.
. . . . .1C **14** (6C **84**)
The City Pavilion
Marks Gate 2F **55**
City Pav. EC1 . . . . .5A **8**
(off Britton St.)
City Pl. Ho. EC2 . . . . .6D **8**
(off Basinghall St.)
Citypoint EC2 . . . . .5E **8**
City Pride Development E14 . . . .1C **104**
City Rd. EC1 . . . . .1A **8** (2B **84**)
City Twr. EC2 . . . . .6E **8**
(off Basinghall St.)
SW8 . . . . .7E **18** (6J **101**)
City University London
The Saddlers Sports Cen.
. . . . .3B **8** (4B **84**)
City University London
Goswell Pl. 3B **84**
Northampton Square Campus
. . . . .2A **8** (3B **84**)
City Vw. IG1: Ilf 2G **71**
(off Axon Pl.)
Cityview SE7 . . . . .6A **106**
City Vw. Apts. N1 . . . . .7C **66**
(off Essex Rd.)
N4 . . . . .7D **48**
(off Devan Gro.)
City Vw. Ct. SE22 . . . . .7G **121**
City Wlk. SE1 . . . . .7G **15** (2E **102**)
City Wlk. Apts. EC1 . . . . .2C **8**
(off Seward St.)
City Wharf Ho. KT7: T Ditt 6B **150**
Civic Way
HA4: Ruis 5B **58**
IG6: Ilf .4G **53**
Civil & Family Court
Barnet .1J **45**
Civil Justice Cen.
Central London 4J **5**
Clabon M. SW1 . . . . . . .2E **16** (3D **100**)
Clack La. HA4: Ruis 1E **56**
Clack St. SE16 . . . . .2J **103**

Clacton Rd. E6 . . . 3B 88
 E17 . . . 6A 50
 N17 . . . 2F 49
Claigmas Gdns. N3 . . . 1K 45
Claire Ct. HA5: Hat E . . . 1D 40
 N12 . . . 3F 31
 NW2 . . . 6G 63
 WD23: B Hea . . . 1C 26
Claire Gdns. HA7: Stan . . . 5H 27
Claire Ho. IG1: Ilf . . . 4F 71
Claire Pl. E14 . . . 3C 104
Clairvale Rd. TW5: Hest . . . 1B 112
Clairview Rd. SW16 . . . 5F 137
Clairville Gdns. W7 . . . 1J 95
Clairville Point SE23 . . . 3K 139
(off Dacres Rd.)
Clamp Hill HA7: Stan . . . 4C 26
Clancarty Rd. SW6 . . . 2J 117
Clandon Cl. KT17: Ewe . . . 6B 164
 W3 . . . 2H 97
Clandon Gdns. N3 . . . 3J 45
Clandon Ho. SE1 . . . 7B 14
(off Webber St.)
Clandon Rd. IG3: Ilf . . . 2J 71
Clandon St. SE8 . . . 2C 122
Clandon Ter. SW20 . . . 2F 153
Clanricarde Gdns. W2 . . . 7J 81
CLAPHAM . . . 4G 119
CLAPHAM COMMON . . . 4H 119
Clapham Comn. Nth. Side SW4 . . . 4D 118
Clapham Comn. Northside SW4 . . . 4G 119
(off Rookery Rd.)
Clapham Comn. Sth. Side SW4 . . . 6F 119
Clapham Comn. W. Side SW4 . . . 4D 118
(not continuous)
Clapham Cres. SW4 . . . 4H 119
Clapham High St. SW4 . . . 4H 119
CLAPHAM JUNCTION . . . 3C 118
Clapham Leisure Cen. . . . 3H 119
Clapham Mnr. Ct. SW4 . . . 3G 119
Clapham Mnr. St. SW4 . . . 3G 119
CLAPHAM PARK . . . 5H 119
Clapham Pk. Est. SW4 . . . 6H 119
Clapham Pk. Rd. SW4 . . . 4G 119
Clapham Pk. Ter. SW2 . . . 5J 119
(off Lyham Rd.)
Clapham Picturehouse . . . 4G 119
Clapham Rd. SW9 . . . 3J 119
Clapham Rd. Est. SW4 . . . 3J 119
Clap La. RM10: Dag, Rush G . . . 2H 73
Claps Ga. La. E6 . . . 4E 88
Clapton Comn. E5 . . . 7F 49
(not continuous)
CLAPTON PARK . . . 4K 67
Clapton Pk. Est. E5 . . . 4K 67
Clapton Pas. E5 . . . 5J 67
Clapton Sq. E5 . . . 5J 67
Clapton Ter. E5 . . . 1G 67
Clapton Way E5 . . . 4G 67
Clara Grant Ho. E14 . . . 3C 104
(off Mellish St.)
Clara Nehab Ho. NW11 . . . 5H 45
(off Leeside Cres.)
Clara Pl. SE18 . . . 4E 106
Clare Cl. N2 . . . 3A 46
Clare Cnr. SE9 . . . 7F 125
Clare Ct. W11 . . . 7G 81
(off Clarendon Rd.)
 WC1 . . . 2F 7
(off Judd St.)
Claredale Ho. E2 . . . 2H 85
(off Claredale St.)
Claredale St. E2 . . . 2G 85
Clare Gdns. E7 . . . 4J 69
 IG11: Bark . . . 6K 71
 W11 . . . 6G 81
Clare Ho. E3 . . . 1B 86
 E16 . . . 7E 88
(off University Way)
 HA8: Edg . . . 2C 28
(off Burnt Oak B'way.)
 SE1 . . . 5F 103
(off Cooper's Rd.)

Clare La. N1 . . . 7C 66
Clare Lawn Av. SW14 . . . 5K 115
Clare Mkt. WC2 . . . 1H 13 (6K 83)
Clare M. SW6 . . . 7K 99
Claremont TW17: Shep . . . 6D 146
(off Laleham Rd.)
Claremont Av. HA3: Kenton . . . 5E 42
 KT3: N Mald . . . 5C 152
 TW16: Sun . . . 1K 147
Claremont Cl. BR6: Farnb . . . 4E 172
 E16 . . . 1E 106
 N1 . . . 1K 7 (2A 84)
 SW2 . . . 1J 137
Claremont Ct. E2 . . . 2H 85
(off Cambridge Heath Rd.)
 E2 . . . 2G 85
(off Claredale St.)
 W2 . . . 6K 81
(off Queensway)
 W9 . . . 2H 81
(off Claremont Rd.)
Claremont Dr. TW17: Shep . . . 6D 146
Claremont Gdns. IG3: Ilf . . . 2J 71
 KT6: Surb . . . 5E 150
Claremont Gro. IG8: Wfd G . . . 6F 37
 W4 . . . 7A 98
Claremont Ho. NW9 . . . 3B 44
 SE16 . . . 2A 104
 SM2: Sutt . . . 7K 165
Claremont Pk. N3 . . . 1G 45
Claremont Pl. KT10: Clay . . . 6A 162
Claremont Rd. BR1: Broml . . . 4C 160
 CR0: C'don . . . 1G 169
 E7 . . . 5K 69
 E11 . . . 3F 69
 E17 . . . 2A 50
 HA3: W'stone . . . 2J 41
 KT6: Surb . . . 5E 150
 N6 . . . 7G 47
 NW2 . . . 7F 45
 TW1: Twick . . . 6B 114
 TW11: Tedd . . . 5K 131
 W9 . . . 2G 81
 W13 . . . 5A 78
Claremont Sq. N1 . . . 1J 7 (2A 84)
Claremont St. E16 . . . 2E 106
 N18 . . . 6B 34
 SE10 . . . 6D 104
Claremont Ter. KT7: T Ditt . . . 7B 150
Claremont Vs. SE5 . . . 7D 102
(off Southampton Way)
Claremont Way NW2 . . . 1E 62
(not continuous)
Claremont Way Ind. Est. NW2 . . . 1E 62
Clarence Av. BR1: Broml . . . 4C 160
 IG2: Ilf . . . 6E 52
 KT3: N Mald . . . 2J 151
 SW4 . . . 7H 119
Clarence Cl. EN4: E Barn . . . 5G 21
 WD23: B Hea . . . 1E 26
Clarence Ct. NW7 . . . 5F 29
 W6 . . . 4D 98
(off Cambridge Gro.)
Clarence Cres. DA14: Sidc . . . 3B 144
 SW4 . . . 6H 119
Clarence Gdns. NW1 . . . 2K 5 (3F 83)
Clarence Ga. IG8: Ilf, Wfd G . . . 6K 37
Clarence Ga. Gdns. NW1 . . . 4F 5
(off Glentworth St.)
Clarence House . . . 6B 12
Clarence Ho. SE17 . . . 6D 102
(off Merrow St.)
Clarence La. SW15 . . . 6A 116
Clarence M. E5 . . . 5H 67
 SE16 . . . 1K 103
 SW12 . . . 7F 119
Clarence Pk. Cres. HA7: Stan . . . 3D 26
Clarence Pl. E5 . . . 5H 67
Clarence Rd. BR1: Broml . . . 3B 160
 CR0: C'don . . . 7D 156
 DA6: Bex . . . 4E 126
 DA14: Sidc . . . 3B 144
 E5 . . . 4H 67

Clarence Rd. E12 . . . 4A 70
 E16 . . . 4G 87
 E17 . . . 2K 49
 EN3: Pond E . . . 5C 24
 N15 . . . 5C 48
 N22 . . . 7D 32
 NW6 . . . 7H 63
 SE8 . . . 6D 104
 SE9 . . . 2C 142
 SM1: Sutt . . . 5K 165
 SM6: W'gton . . . 5F 167
 SW19 . . . 6K 135
 TW9: Kew . . . 1F 115
 TW11: Tedd . . . 6K 131
 W4 . . . 5G 97
Clarence St. KT1: King T . . . 2D 150
 TW9: Rich . . . 4E 114
 UB2: S'hall . . . 3B 94
Clarence Ter. NW1 . . . 3F 5 (4D 82)
 TW3: Houn . . . 4F 113
Clarence Wlk. SW4 . . . 2J 119
Clarence Way NW1 . . . 7F 65
Clarendon Cl. DA2: Wilm . . . 5K 145
 E9 . . . 7J 67
 W2 . . . 2C 10 (7C 82)
Clarendon Ct. BR3: Beck . . . 1D 158
(off Albemarle Rd.)
 EC1 . . . 4D 8
 NW2 . . . 7E 62
 NW11 . . . 4H 45
 TW5: Cran . . . 1J 111
 TW9: Kew . . . 1F 115
 W9 . . . 3A 4
(off Maida Va.)
Clarendon Cres. TW2: Twick . . . 3H 131
Clarendon Cross W11 . . . 7G 81
Clarendon Dr. SW15 . . . 4E 116
Clarendon Flats W1 . . . 1H 11
(off Balderton St.)
Clarendon Gdns. HA9: Wemb . . . 3D 60
 IG1: Ilf . . . 7D 52
 NW4 . . . 3C 44
 W9 . . . 4A 82
Clarendon Grn. BR5: St P . . . 4K 161
Clarendon Gro. CR4: Mitc . . . 3D 154
 NW1 . . . 1C 6 (3H 83)
Clarendon Ho. KT2: King T . . . 1E 150
(off Cowleaze Rd.)
 NW1 . . . 1B 6
(off Werrington St.)
 W2 . . . 2C 10
(off Strathearn Pl.)
Clarendon Lodge W11 . . . 7G 81
(off Clarendon Rd.)
Clarendon Path BR5: St P . . . 4K 161
(not continuous)
Clarendon Pl. W2 . . . 2C 10 (7C 82)
Clarendon Ri. SE13 . . . 4E 122
Clarendon Rd. CR0: C'don . . . 2B 168
 E11 . . . 1F 69
 E17 . . . 6D 50
 E18 . . . 3J 51
 HA1: Harr . . . 6J 41
 N8 . . . 3K 47
 N15 . . . 4C 48
 N18 . . . 6B 34
 N22 . . . 2K 47
 SM6: W'gton . . . 6G 167
 SW19 . . . 7C 136
 TW15: Ashf . . . 4B 128
 UB3: Hayes . . . 2H 93
 W5 . . . 3E 78
 W11 . . . 7G 81
Clarendon St. SW1 . . . 5K 17 (5F 101)
Clarendon Ter. W9 . . . 3A 4 (4A 82)
Clarendon Wlk. W11 . . . 6G 81
Clarendon Way BR5: St P . . . 3K 161
 BR7: Chst . . . 3K 161
 N21 . . . 6H 23
Clarens St. SE6 . . . 2B 140

Clare Pl. SW15 . . . 7B 116
Clare Point NW2 . . . 1F 63
(off Whitefield Av.)
Clare Rd. E11 . . . 6F 51
 NW10 . . . 7C 62
 SE14 . . . 1B 122
 TW4: Houn . . . 3D 112
 TW19: Stanw . . . 1A 128
 UB6: G'frd . . . 6H 59
Clare St. E2 . . . 2H 85
Claret Gdns. SE25 . . . 3E 156
Clareville Ct. SW7 . . . 4A 16
(off Clareville St.)
Clareville Gro. SW7 . . . 4A 16 (4A 100)
Clareville Gro. M. SW7 . . . 4A 16 (4A 100)
Clareville Rd. BR5: Farnb . . . 2G 173
Clareville St. SW7 . . . 4A 16 (4A 100)
Clare Way DA7: Bex . . . 1E 126
Clarewood Ct. W1 . . . 6E 4
(off Seymour Pl.)
Clarewood Wlk. SW9 . . . 4A 120
Clarges M. W1 . . . 4J 11 (1F 101)
Clarges St. W1 . . . 4K 11 (1F 101)
Claribel Rd. SW9 . . . 2B 120
Clarice Way SM6: W'gton . . . 7J 167
Claridge Ho. SW6 . . . 2H 117
Claridge Ct. SW6 . . . 2H 117
Claridge Rd. RM8: Dag . . . 1D 72
Clarinet Cl. HA8: Edg . . . 7C 28
Clarion Ho. E3 . . . 2A 86
(off Roman Rd.)
 SW1 . . . 5B 18
(off Moreton Pl.)
 W1 . . . 1C 12
(off St Anne's Ct.)
Clarissa Ho. E14 . . . 6D 86
(off Cordela St.)
Clarissa Rd. RM6: Chad H . . . 7D 54
Clarissa St. E8 . . . 1F 85
Clarke Apts. E3 . . . 4B 86
(off Heath Pl.)
Clarke Cl. CR0: C'don . . . 6C 156
Clarke Mans. IG11: Bark . . . 7K 71
(off Upney La.)
Clarke M. N9 . . . 3C 34
Clarke Path N16 . . . 1G 67
Clarkes Av. KT4: Wor Pk . . . 1F 165
Clarkes Dr. UB8: Hil . . . 5A 74
Clarke's M. W1 . . . 5H 5 (5E 82)
Clark Gro. IG3: Ilf . . . 4J 71
Clark Ho. SW10 . . . 7A 100
(off Coleridge Gdns.)
Clarks Mead WD23: Bush . . . 1B 26
Clarkson Rd. E16 . . . 6H 87
Clarkson Row NW1 . . . 2G 83
(off Mornington Ter.)
The Clarksons IG11: Bark . . . 2G 89
Clarkson St. E2 . . . 3H 85
Clarks Rd. IG1: Ilf . . . 2H 71
Clark St. E1 . . . 5H 85
(not continuous)
Clark Way TW5: Hest . . . 7B 94
Clarnico Rd. E20 . . . 6C 68
Clarson Ho. SE5 . . . 7B 102
(off Midnight Av.)
 SE8 . . . 6A 104
Classic Mans. E9 . . . 7H 67
(off Wells St.)
Classon Cl. UB7: W Dray . . . 2A 92
Claude Av. NW9 . . . 1B 44
Claude Rd. E10 . . . 2E 68
 E13 . . . 1K 87
 SE15 . . . 2H 121
Claude St. E14 . . . 4C 104
Claudia Jones Ho. N17 . . . 1C 48
Claudia Jones Way SW2 . . . 6J 119
Claudia Pl. SW19 . . . 1G 135
Claudius Cl. HA7: Stan . . . 3J 27
Claughton Rd. E13 . . . 2A 88
Clauson Av. UB5: N'olt . . . 5F 59
Clavell St. SE10 . . . 6E 104
Claverdale Rd. SW2 . . . 7K 119
Clavering Av. SW13 . . . 6D 98
Clavering Cl. TW1: Twick . . . 4A 132

Clavering Ho. *SE13* *4F 123*
    (off Blessington Rd.)
Clavering Pl. SW12 . . . . .6E **118**
Clavering Rd. E12 . . . . .1B **70**
Claverings Ind. Est. *N9* *2D 34*
    (off Centre Way)
Claverley Gro. N3 . . . . .1K **45**
Claverley Vs. N3 . . . . .7E **30**
Claverton St. SW1 . . . . .6B **18** (5G **101**)
Clave St. E1 . . . . .1J **103**
Claxton Gro. W6 . . . . .5F **99**
Claxton Path *SE4* *4K 121*
    (off Coston Wlk.)
Clay Av. CR4: Mitc 2F **155**
Claybank Gro. SE13 . . . . .3D **122**
Claybourne M. SE19 . . . . .7E **138**
Claybridge Rd. SE12 . . . . .4A **142**
Claybrook Cl. N2 . . . . .3B **46**
Claybrook Rd. W6 . . . . .6F **99**
Claybury WD23: Bush 1A **26**
Claybury B'way. IG5: Ilf 3C **52**
Claybury Hall IG8: Wfd G 7J **37**
Claybury M. IG5: Ilf 1D **52**
Claybury Rd. IG8: Wfd G 7H **37**
Clay Ct. E17 . . . . .3F **51**
  SE1 . . . .*7G 15*
    (off Long La.)
Claydon Dr. CR0: Bedd 4J **167**
Claydon Ho. *NW4* *2F 45*
    (off Holders Hill Rd.)
  SW10 . . . . .1A **118**
Claydown M. SE18 . . . . .5E **106**
Clayfarm Rd. SE9 . . . . .2G **143**
CLAYGATE 7A **162**
Claygate Common 7A **162**
Claygate Cres. CR0: New Ad 6E **170**
Claygate La. KT7: T Ditt 1A **162**
  KT10: Clay, Hin W 2A **162**
Claygate Rd. W13 . . . . .3B **96**
CLAYHALL 3C **52**
Clayhall Av. IG5: Ilf 3C **52**
Clayhall Ct. *E3* *2B 86*
    (off St Stephen's Rd.)
Clay Hill EN2: Enf 1K **23**
Clayhill KT5: Surb 5G **151**
Clayhill Cres. SE9 . . . . .4B **142**
Claylands Pl. SW8 . . . . .7A **102**
Claylands Rd. SW8 . . . .7H **19** (6K **101**)
Clay La. HA3: Kenton 4D **42**
  HA8: Edg 2B **28**
  TW19: Stanw 7B **110**
  WD23: B Hea 1D **26**
Claymill Ho. SE18 . . . . .5G **107**
Claymore Cl. SM4: Mord 7J **153**
Clay Path E17 . . . . .2C **50**
Claypole Ct. *E17* *5C 50*
    (off Yunus Khan Cl.)
Claypole Dr. TW5: Hest 1C **112**
Claypole Rd. E15 . . . . .2E **86**
Clayponds Av. TW8: Bford 4D **96**
Clayponds Gdns. W5 . . . . .4D **96**
    (not continuous)
Clayponds La. TW8: Bford 5E **96**
    (not continuous)
Clay St. W1 . . . . .6F **5** (5D **82**)
Clayton Av. HA0: Wemb 7E **60**
Clayton Bus. Cen. UB3: Hayes 2G **93**
Clayton Cl. E6 . . . . .6D **88**
Clayton Cres. N1 . . . . .1J **83**
  TW8: Bford .5D **96**
Clayton Dr. SE8 . . . . .5A **104**
Clayton Fld. NW9 . . . . .7F **29**
Clayton Ho. *E9* *7J 67*
    (off Frampton Pk. Rd.)
  KT7: T Ditt .1B **162**
  SW13 . . . .*7E 98*
    (off Trinity Chu. Rd.)
Clayton M. SE10 . . . . .1F **123**
Clayton Rd. KT9: Chess 4C **162**
  RM7: Rush G 1J **73**
  SE15 . . . . .1G **121**
  TW7: Isle 3J **113**
  UB3: Hayes 2G **93**

Clayton St. SE11 . . . . .7J **19** (6A **102**)
Clayton Ter. UB4: Yead 5C **76**
Claytonville Ter. DA17: Belv 2J **109**
Clay Wood Cl. BR6: Orp 7J **161**
Clayworth Cl. DA15: Sidc 6B **126**
Cleanthus Cl. SE18 . . . . .1F **125**
Cleanthus Rd. SE18 . . . . .2F **125**
    (not continuous)
Clearbrook Way E1 . . . . .6J **85**
Clearwater Pl. KT6: Surb 6C **150**
Clearwater Ter. W11 . . . . .2F **99**
Clearwater Yd. *NW1* *1F 83*
    (off Inverness St.)
Clearwell Dr. W9 . . . . .4K **81**
Cleave Av. BR6: Chels 6J **173**
  UB3: Harl 4G **93**
Cleaveland Rd. KT6: Surb 5D **150**
Cleaverholme Cl. SE25 . . . . .6H **157**
Cleaver Ho. *NW3* *7D 64*
    (off Adelaide Rd.)
Cleaver Sq. SE11 . . . . .6K **19** (5A **102**)
Cleaver St. SE11 . . . . .5K **19** (5A **102**)
Cleaves Almshouses
  KT2: King T *2E 150*
    (off London Rd.)
Cleave Ct. TW14: Bedf 1G **129**
Cleeve Hill SE23 . . . . .1H **139**
Cleeve Ho. *E2* *2H 9*
    (off Calvert Av.)
Cleeve Pk. Gdns. DA14: Sidc 2B **144**
Cleeve Way SM1: Sutt 1K **165**
  SW15 . . . . .7B **116**
Cleeve Workshops *E2* *2H 9*
    (off Boundary Rd.)
Clegg Ho. *SE16* *3J 103*
    (off Moodkee St.)
Clegg St. E1 .1H **103**
  E13 . . . . .2J **87**
Cleland Ho. *E2* *2J 85*
    (off Sewardstone Rd.)
Clematis Apts. *E3* *3B 86*
    (off Merchant St.)
Clematis Gdns. IG8: Wfd G 5D **36**
Clematis St. W12 . . . . .7C **80**
Clem Attlee Ct. SW6 . . . . .6H **99**
Clem Attlee Pde. *SW6* *6H 99*
    (off North End Rd.)
Clemence Rd. RM10: Dag 1J **91**
Clemence St. E14 . . . . .5B **86**
Clement Av. SW4 . . . . .4H **119**
Clement Cl. NW6 . . . . .7E **62**
  W4 . . . . .4K **97**
Clement Danes Ho. W12 . . . . .6D **80**
Clement Gdns. UB3: Harl 4G **93**
Clementhorpe Rd. RM9: Dag 6C **72**
Clement Ho. SE8 . . . . .4A **104**
  W10 . . . .*5E 80*
    (off Dalgarno Gdns.)
Clementina Ct. *E3* *4A 86*
    (off Copperfield Rd.)
Clementina Rd. E10 . . . . .1B **68**
Clementine Cl. W13 . . . . .2B **96**
Clementine Wlk. IG8: Wfd G 7D **36**
Clement Rd. BR3: Beck 2K **157**
  SW19 . . . . .5G **135**
Clement's Av. E16 . . . . .7J **87**
Clements Cl. N12 . . . . .4E **30**
Clements Ct. IG1: Ilf 3F **71**
  TW4: Houn .4B **112**
Clement's Inn WC2 . . . . . . .1H **13** (6K **83**)
Clement's Inn Pas. WC2 . . . . .1H **13**
Clements La. EC4 . . . . . . .2F **15** (7D **84**)
  IG1: Ilf 3F **71**
Clements Pl. TW8: Bford 5D **96**
Clements Rd. E6 . . . . .7C **70**
  IG1: Ilf 3F **71**
  SE16 . . . . .3G **103**
Clemson Ho. E8 . . . . .1F **85**
Clendon Way SE18 . . . . .4H **107**
Clennam St. SE1 . . . . . . .6D **14** (2C **102**)
Clensham Ct. SM1: Sutt 2J **165**
Clensham La. SM1: Sutt 2J **165**
Clenston M. W1 . . . . .7E **4** (6D **82**)

Cleopatra Cl. HA7: Stan 3J **27**
Cleopatra's Needle 3G **13** (7K **83**)
Clephane Rd. N1 . . . . .6C **66**
Clephane Rd. Nth. N1 . . . . .6C **66**
Clere Pl. EC2 . . . . .3F **9** (4D **84**)
Clere St. EC2 . . . . .3F **9** (4D **84**)
Clerics Wlk. TW17: Shep 7F **147**
CLERKENWELL 4K **7** (4A **84**)
Clerkenwell Cl. EC1 . . . . . .3K **7** (4A **84**)
    (not continuous)
Clerkenwell Ct. *N1* *2B 84*
    (off Duncan St.)
Clerkenwell Grn. EC1 . . . . .4K **7** (4A **84**)
Clerkenwell Rd. EC1 . . . . . .4J **7** (4A **84**)
Clerks Pl. EC3 . . . . .7G **9** (6E **84**)
Clermont Rd. E9 . . . . .1J **85**
Clevedon Cl. N16 . . . . .3F **67**
Clevedon Ct. CR2: S Croy 5E **168**
  SW11 . . . .*1C 118*
    (off Bolingbroke Wlk.)
Clevedon Gdns. TW5: Cran 1K **111**
  UB3: Harl 3F **93**
Clevedon Ho. SM1: Sutt 4A **166**
Clevedon Mans. NW5 . . . . .4E **64**
Clevedon Pas. N16 . . . . .2F **67**
Clevedon Rd. KT1: King T 2G **151**
  SE20 . . . . .1K **157**
  TW1: Twick .6D **114**
Cleve Ho. NW6 . . . . .7K **63**
Cleveland Av. SW20 . . . . .2H **153**
  TW12: Hamp 7D **130**
  W4 . . . . .4B **98**
Cleveland Ct. W13 . . . . .5B **78**
Cleveland Gdns. KT4: Wor Pk 2A **164**
  N4 . . . . .5C **48**
  NW2 . . . . .2F **63**
  SW13 . . . . .2B **116**
  W2 . . . . .6A **82**
Cleveland Gro. E1 . . . . .4J **85**
Cleveland Ho. *N2* *2B 46*
    (off The Grange)
Cleveland Mans. *NW6* *7H 63*
    (off Willesden La.)
  SW9 . . . .*7A 102*
    (off Mowll St.)
  W9 . . . . .4J **81**
Cleveland M. W1 . . . . .5A **6** (5G **83**)
Cleveland Pk. TW19: Stanw 6A **110**
Cleveland Pk. Av. E17 . . . . .4C **50**
Cleveland Pk. Cres. E17 . . . . .4C **50**
Cleveland Pl.
  SW1 . . . . .4B **12** (1G **101**)
Cleveland Ri. SM4: Mord 7F **153**
Cleveland Rd. DA16: Well 2K **125**
  E18 . . . . .3J **51**
  IG1: Ilf 3F **71**
  KT3: N Mald 4A **152**
  KT4: Wor Pk 2A **164**
  N1 . . . . .7D **66**
  N9 . . . . .7C **24**
  SW13 . . . . .2B **116**
  TW7: Isle 4A **114**
  W4 . . . . .3J **97**
  W13 . . . . .5A **78**
Cleveland Row SW1 . . . .5A **12** (1G **101**)
Cleveland Sq. W2 . . . . .6A **82**
Cleveland St. W1 . . . . . . .4K **5** (4F **83**)
Cleveland Ter. W2 . . . . .6A **82**
Cleveland Way E1 . . . . .4J **85**
Cleveley Cl. SE7 . . . . .4B **106**
Cleveley Ct. *SE16* *4A 104*
    (off Ashton Reach)
Cleveley Cres. W5 . . . . .2E **78**
Cleveleys Rd. E5 . . . . .3H **67**
Cleverly Est. W12 . . . . .1C **98**
Cleve Rd. DA14: Sidc 3D **144**
  NW6 . . . . .7J **63**
Cleves Av. KT17: Ewe 7D **164**
Cleves Ho. *E16* *1J 105*
    (off Southey M.)
Cleves Rd. E6 . . . . .1B **88**
  TW10: Ham .3C **132**
Cleves Wlk. IG6: Ilf 1G **53**

Cleves Way HA4: Ruis 1B **58**
  TW12: Hamp 7D **130**
  TW16: Sun .6H **129**
Clewer Ct. *E10* *1C 68*
    (off Leyton Grange Est.)
Clewer Cres. HA3: Hrw W 1H **41**
Clewer Ho. *SE2* *2D 108*
    (off Wolvercote Rd.)
Cley Ho. SE4 .4K **121**
C&L Golf Course 7K **57**
Clichy Est. E1 .5J **85**
Clichy Ho. *E1* *5J 85*
    (off Stepney Way)
Clifden M. E5 .4K **67**
Clifden Rd. E5 . . . . .5J **67**
  TW1: Twick .1K **131**
  TW8: Bford .6D **96**
Cliffe Ho. *SE10* *5H 105*
    (off Blackwall La.)
Cliffe Rd. CR2: S Croy 5D **168**
Cliffe Wlk. *SM1: Sutt* *5A 166*
    (off Greyhound Rd.)
Clifford Av. BR7: Chst 6D **142**
  IG5: Ilf 1F **53**
  SM6: W'gton 4G **167**
  SW14 . . . . .3H **115**
Clifford Cl. UB5: N'olt 1C **76**
Clifford Ct. *W2* *5K 81*
    (off Westbourne Pk. Vs.)
Clifford Dr. SW9 . . . . .4B **120**
Clifford Gdns. NW10 . . . . .2E **80**
  UB3: Harl 4G **93**
Clifford Gro. TW15: Ashf 4C **128**
Clifford Haigh Ho. SW6 . . . . .7F **99**
Clifford Ho. *BR3: Beck* *6D 140*
    (off Calverley Cl.)
  W14 . . . .*4H 99*
    (off Edith Vs.)
Clifford Rd. E16 . . . . .4H **87**
  E17 . . . . .2E **50**
  EN5: New Bar 3E **20**
  HA0: Wemb .7D **60**
  N1 . . . . .6D **24**
  N9 . . . . .6D **24**
  SE25 . . . . .4G **157**
  TW4: Houn .3B **112**
  TW10: Ham .2D **132**
Clifford's Inn EC4 . . . . .1J **13**
Clifford's Inn Pas. EC4 . . . . .1J **13** (6A **84**)
Clifford St. W1 . . . . .3A **12** (7G **83**)
Clifford Way NW10 . . . . .4B **62**
Cliff Rd. NW1 .6H **65**
Cliffsend Ho. *SW9* *1A 120*
    (off Cowley Rd.)
Cliff Ter. SE8 .2C **122**
Cliffview Rd. SE13 . . . . .3C **122**
Cliff Vs. NW1 .6H **65**
Cliff Wlk. E16 .5H **87**
Clifton Av. E17 . . . . .3K **49**
  HA7: Stan 2B **42**
  HA9: Wemb .6F **61**
  N3 . . . . .1H **45**
  TW13: Felt 3A **130**
  W12 . . . . .1B **98**
Clifton Cl. BR6: Farnb 5G **173**
Clifton Ct. BR3: Beck 1D **158**
  IG8: Wfd G 6D **36**
  KT5: Surb 7F **151**
  N4 . . . . .2A **66**
  NW8 . . . . .3A **4**
  SE15 . . . . .7H **103**
  TW19: Stanw 6A **110**
Clifton Cres. SE15 . . . . .7H **103**
Clifton Est. SE15 . . . . .1H **121**
Clifton Gdns. EN2: Enf 4D **22**
  N15 . . . . .6F **49**
  NW11 . . . . .6H **45**
  UB10: Hil 2D **74**
  W4 . . . . .4K **97**
    (not continuous)
  W9 . . . . .4A **82**
Clifton Ga. SW10 . . . . .6A **100**
Clifton Gro. E8 . . . . .6G **67**

Clifton Hill NW8 . . . . .2K 81
Clifton Hill Studios NW8 . . . . . .2A 82
Clifton Ho. E2 . . . . .3J 9
  (off Club Row)
  E11 . . . . .2G 69
Clifton M. SE25 . . . . .4E 156
Clifton Pde. TW13: Felt 3A 130
Clifton Pk. Av. SW20 . . . . . . .2E 152
Clifton Pl. SE16 . . . . .2J 103
  SW10 . . . . .6A 100
  (off Hollywood Rd.)
  W2 . . . . .1B 10 (6B 82)
Clifton Ri. SE14 . . . . .7A 104
  (not continuous)
Clifton Rd. DA14: Sidc 4J 143
  DA16: Well 3C 126
  E7 . . . . .6B 70
  E16 . . . . .5G 87
  HA3: Kenton 4F 43
  IG2: Ilf 6H 53
  KT2: King T 7F 133
  N1 . . . . .6C 66
  N3 . . . . .1A 46
  N8 . . . . .6H 47
  N22 . . . . .1G 47
  NW10 . . . . .2C 80
  SE25 . . . . .4E 156
  SM6: W'gton 5F 167
  SW19 . . . . .6F 135
  TW7: Isle 2J 113
  TW11: Tedd 4J 131
  UB2: S'hall 4C 94
  UB6: G'frd 4G 77
  W9 . . . . .3A 4 (4A 82)
Clifton St. EC2 . . . . .4G 9 (4E 84)
Clifton Ter. N4 . . . . .2A 66
Clifton Vs. W9 . . . . .5A 82
Cliftonville Ct. SE12 . . . . .1J 141
Clifton Wlk. W6 . . . . .4D 98
  (off King St.)
Clifton Way HA0: Wemb 1E 78
  SE15 . . . . .7H 103
Climsland Ho. SE1 . . .4K 13 (1A 102)
Cline Rd. N11 . . . . .6B 32
Clinger Ct. N1 . . . . .1E 84
  (off Hobbs Pl. Est.)
Clink Prison Mus. 4E 14
Clink St. SE1 . . . . . . .4D 14 (1D 102)
Clink Wharf SE1 . . . . .4E 14
  (off Clink St.)
Clinton Av. DA16: Well 4A 126
  KT8: E Mos 4G 149
Clinton Ho. KT6: Surb 7D 150
  (off Lovelace Gdns)
Clinton Rd. E3 . . . . .3A 86
  E7 . . . . .4J 69
  N15 . . . . .4D 48
Clinton Ter. SE8 . . . . .6C 104
  (off Watergate St.)
  SM1: Sutt 4A 166
Clipper Apts. SE10 . . . . .6E 104
  (off Welland St.)
Clipper Cl. SE16 . . . . .2K 103
Clipper Ho. E14 . . . . .5E 104
  (off Manchester Rd.)
Clipper Way SE13 . . . . .4E 122
Clippesby Cl. KT9: Chess 6F 163
Clipstone M. W1 . . . . . .5A 6 (5G 83)
Clipstone Rd.
  TW3: Houn 3E 112
Clipstone St. W1 . . . . . .5K 5 (5B 83)
Clissold Cl. N2 . . . . .3D 46
Clissold Ct. N4 . . . . .2C 66
Clissold Cres. N16 . . . . .3D 66
Clissold Leisure Cen. 3D 66
Clissold Rd. N16 . . . . .3D 66
Clitheroe Av. HA2: Harr 1E 58
Clitheroe Rd. SW9 . . . . .2J 119
Clitherow Av. W7 . . . . .3A 96
Clitherow Ct. TW8: Bford 5C 96
Clitherow Pas. TW8: Bford 5C 96
Clitherow Rd. TW8: Bford 5B 96
Clitterhouse Cres. NW2 . . . . . .1E 62

Clitterhouse Rd. NW2 . . . . .1E 62
Clive Av. N18 . . . . .6B 34
Clive Ct. W9 . . . . .4A 82
Cliveden Cl. N12 . . . . .4F 31
Cliveden Ho. E16 . . . . .1J 105
  (off Fitzwilliam M.)
  SW1 . . . . .3G 17
  (off Cliveden Pl.)
Cliveden Pl. SW1 . . .3G 17 (4E 100)
  TW17: Shep 6E 146
Cliveden Rd. SW19 . . . . .1H 153
Clivedon Ct. W13 . . . . .5B 78
Clivedon Rd. E4 . . . . .5B 36
Clive Ho. SE10 . . . . .6E 104
  (off Haddo St.)
Clive Lloyd Ho. N15 . . . . .5C 48
  (off Woodlands Pk. Rd.)
Clive Lodge NW4 . . . . .6F 45
Clive Pas. SE21 . . . . .3D 138
Clive Rd. DA17: Belv 4G 109
  EN1: Enf 4B 24
  SE21 . . . . .3D 138
  SW19 . . . . .6C 136
  TW1: Twick 4K 131
  TW14: Felt 6J 111
Clivesdale Dr. UB3: Hayes 1K 93
Clive Way EN1: Enf 4B 24
Cloak La. EC4 . . . . . . .2D 14 (7C 84)
Clochar Ct. NW10 . . . . .1B 80
Clock Cl. E11 . . . . .4K 51
Clock Ho. E3 . . . . .3E 86
  E17 . . . . .4F 51
  (off Wood St.)
The Clockhouse SW19 . . . . .3E 134
Clockhouse Av. IG11: Bark 1G 89
Clockhouse Cl. SW19 . . . . .2E 134
Clockhouse Ct. BR3: Beck 2A 158
CLOCKHOUSE JUNC. 5E 32
Clockhouse La.
  RM5: Col R 1H 55
  TW14: Bedf 4C 128
  TW15: Ashf 4C 128
Clock Ho. Pde. E11 . . . . .6K 51
Clockhouse Pde. N13 . . . . .5F 33
Clockhouse Pl. SW15 . . . . .6G 117
Clock Ho. Rd. BR3: Beck 3A 158
CLOCKHOUSE RDBT. 1D 128
Clock Pde. EN2: Enf 5J 23
Clock Pl. SE1 . . . . .4B 102
  (off Newington Butts)
Clock Twr. Ind. Est. TW7: Isle . . .3K 113
Clock Twr. M. N1 . . . . .1C 84
  SE28 . . . . .7B 90
  W7 . . . . .1J 95
Clock Twr. Pl. TW7: Isle 3K 113
Clock Vw. Cres. N7 . . . . .6J 65
  (not continuous)
Clockwork Apts. EC4 . . . . .1B 14
  (off Ludgate Sq.)
Clockwork M. E5 . . . . .5K 67
Cloister Cl. TW11: Tedd 5B 132
Cloister Gdns. HA8: Edg 5D 28
  SE25 . . . . .6H 157
Cloister Rd. NW2 . . . . .3H 63
  W3 . . . . .5J 79
The Cloisters 1E 18
The Cloisters E1 . . . . .4J 9
  SW9 . . . . .1A 120
Cloisters Av. BR2: Broml 5D 160
Cloisters Bus. Cen. SW8 . . . . . .7F 101
  (off Battersea Pk. Rd.)
Cloisters Ct. DA7: Bex 3H 127
Cloisters Mall KT1: King T 2E 150
Clonard Way HA5: Hat E 6A 26
Clonbrock Rd. N16 . . . . .4E 66
Cloncurry St. SW6 . . . . .2F 117
Clonmel Cl. HA2: Harr 2H 59
Clonmell Rd. N17 . . . . .3D 48
Clonmel Rd. SW6 . . . . .7H 99
  TW11: Tedd 4H 131
Clonmore St. SW18 . . . . .1H 135
Cloonmore Av. BR6: Chels 4K 173
Clorane Gdns. NW3 . . . . .3J 63

The Close BR3: Beck 4A 158
  BR5: Pet W 6J 161
  CR4: Mitc 4D 154
  DA5: Bexl 6G 127
  DA14: Sidc 4B 144
  E4 . . . . .7K 35
  EN4: E Barn 6J 21
  HA0: Wemb 6E 60
  HA2: Harr 2G 41
  HA5: Eastc 7A 40
  HA5: Pinn 7D 40
  HA9: Wemb 3J 61
  IG2: Ilf 6J 53
  KT3: N Mald 2J 151
  KT6: Surb 6E 150
  N10 . . . . .2F 47
  N14 . . . . .2C 32
  N20 . . . . .2C 30
  RM6: Chad H 6E 54
  SE3 . . . . .2F 123
  SE25 . . . . .6G 157
  SM3: Sutt 7H 153
  SM5: Cars 7C 166
  TW2: Twick 2H 131
  TW9: Rich 3H 115
  UB10: Hil 1C 74
Cloth Cl. EC1 . . . . .6B 8
Cloth Fair EC1 . . . . . . .6B 8 (5B 84)
Cloth Ho. EC1 . . . . .5C 8
  (off Cloth St.)
Clothier St. E1 . . . . . . .7H 9 (6E 84)
Cloth St. EC1 . . . . .5C 8 (5C 84)
Clothworkers Rd. SE18 . . . . . . .7H 107
Cloudesdale Rd. SW17 . . . . . . .2F 137
Cloudesley Cl. DA14: Sidc 4K 143
Cloudesley Ho. N1 . . . . .1A 84
  (off Cloudesley St.)
Cloudesley Mans. N1 . . . . .1A 84
  (off Cloudesley Pl.)
Cloudesley Pl. N1 . . . . .1A 84
Cloudesley Rd. DA7: Bex 1F 127
  N1 . . . . .1A 84
  (not continuous)
Cloudesley Sq. N1 . . . . .1A 84
Cloudesley St. N1 . . . . .1A 84
Cloud Way TW6: H'row A 3D 110
Clouston Cl. SM6: W'gton 5J 167
Clova Rd. E7 . . . . .6H 69
Clove Cres. E14 . . . . .7E 86
Clove Hitch Quay SW11 . . . . . . .3A 118
Clovelly Av. NW9 . . . . .4B 44
  UB10: Ick 4E 56
Clovelly Cl. HA5: Eastc 3K 39
  UB10: Ick 4E 56
Clovelly Ct. NW2 . . . . .5E 62
  RM7: Mawney 1H 55
  SE19 . . . . .1F 157
Clovelly Ho. W2 . . . . .6A 82
  (off Hallfield Est.)
Clovelly Rd. DA7: Bex 6E 108
  N8 . . . . .4H 47
  TW3: Houn 2E 112
  W4 . . . . .2K 97
  W5 . . . . .2C 96
Clovelly Way HA6: St M Cry 6K 161
  E1 . . . . .6J 85
  HA2: Harr 2D 58
Clover Court E14 . . . . .3D 104
  (off Watergate Walk)
Cloverdale Cl. SM6: W'gton 6F 167
Cloverdale Gdns. DA15: Sidc . . .6K 125
Clover M. SW3 . . . . . .7F 17 (6D 100)
Clover Way SM6: W'gton 1E 166
Clove St. E13 . . . . .4J 87
  RM9: Dag 3E 90
Clowders Rd. SE6 . . . . .3B 140
Clowser Cl. SM1: Sutt 5A 166
Cloysters Grn. E1 . . . . .1G 103
Cloyster Wood HA8: Edg 7J 27
Club Gdns. Rd. BR2: Hayes 7J 159
The Clubhouse E14 . . . . .6C 86

Clubhouse La. UB10: Ick 4C 56
Club Row E1 . . . . .3J 9 (4F 85)
  E2 . . . . .3J 9 (4F 85)
The Clumps TW15: Ashf 4F 129
Clunbury Av. UB2: S'hall 5D 94
Clunbury St. N1 . . . . .2D 84
Clunie Ho. SW1 . . . . .1F 17
  (off Hans Pl.)
Cluny Est. SE1 . . . . . . .7G 15 (3E 102)
Cluny M. SW5 . . . . .4J 99
Cluny Pl. SE1 . . . . . . .7G 15 (3E 102)
Cluse Ct. N1 . . . . .2C 84
  (off St Peters St.)
Cluster Ho. W3 . . . . .1B 98
Clutton St. E14 . . . . .5D 86
Clydach Rd. EN1: Enf 4A 24
Clyde Cir. N15 . . . . .4E 48
Clyde Ct. NW1 . . . . .2H 83
  (off Hampden Cl.)
Clyde Flats SW6 . . . . .7H 99
  (off Rylston Rd.)
Clyde Ho. KT2: King T 1D 150
  SW18 . . . . .4J 117
  (off Enterprise Way)
Clyde Pl. E10 . . . . .7D 50
Clyde Rd. CR0: C'don 2F 169
  N15 . . . . .4E 48
  (not continuous)
  N22 . . . . .1H 47
  SM1: Sutt 5J 165
  SM6: W'gton 6G 167
  TW19: Stanw 1A 128
Clydesdale EN3: Pond E 4E 24
Clydesdale Av. HA7: Stan 3D 42
Clydesdale Cl. TW7: Isle 3K 113
Clydesdale Ct. N20 . . . . .1G 31
Clydesdale Gdns. TW10: Rich . . .4H 115
Clydesdale Ho. DA18: Erith 2E 108
  (off Kale Rd.)
  W11 . . . . .6H 81
  (off Clydesdale Rd.)
Clydesdale Rd. W11 . . . . .6H 81
Clydesdale Way DA17: Belv 2H 109
Clyde Sq. E14 . . . . .6B 86
Clyde St. SE8 . . . . .6B 104
Clyde Ter. SE23 . . . . .2J 139
Clyde Va. SE23 . . . . .2J 139
Clyde Way RM1: Rom 1K 55
Clyde Wharf E16 . . . . .1J 105
Clydon Cl. DA8: Erith 6K 109
Clyfford Rd. HA4: Ruis 4K 57
Clymping Dene TW14: Felt 7K 111
Clynes Ho. E2 . . . . .3K 85
  (off Knottisford St.)
  RM10: Dag 3G 73
  (off Uvedale Rd.)
Clyston St. SW8 . . . . .2G 119
Coach & Horses Yd. W1 . . .2K 11 (7G 83)
Coach Ho. La. N5 . . . . .4B 66
  SW19 . . . . .4F 135
Coach Ho. M. SE1 . . . . .7G 15
  (off Long La.)
  SE14 . . . . .2K 121
  SE23 . . . . .6K 121
  SM2: Sutt 6K 165
Coachhouse M. SE20 . . . . .7H 139
Coach Ho. Yd. NW3 . . . . .4A 64
  (off Heath St.)
  SW18 . . . . .4K 117
Coachmaker M. SW4 . . . . .3J 119
  (off Bedford Rd.)
  W4 . . . . .3K 97
  (off Berrymede Rd.)
Coach Yd. M. N19 . . . . .1J 65
Coalbrookdale Gates 6A 10 (2B 100)
Coaldale Wlk. SE21 . . . . .7C 120
Coal Drops Yard 1J 83
Coalecroft Rd. SW15 . . . . .4E 116
Coal Lane SW9 . . . . .4A 120
Coalmakers Wharf E14 . . . . .6C 86
Coalport Ho. SE11 . . . . .2J 19
Coal Post Cl. BR6: Chels 6K 173
Coalstore Ct. E1 . . . . .5A 86

Coatbridge Ho. N1 . . . . .7K 65
    (off Carnoustie Dr.)
Coates Av. SW18 . . . . .6C 118
Coates Cl. CR7: Thor H 3C 156
Coates Hill Rd. BR1: Broml . . .2E 160
Coate St. E2 . . . . .2G 85
Coates Wlk. TW8: Bford 6E 96
Cobalt SE28 . . . . .2A 108
The Cobalt Bldg. EC2 . . . . .5C 8
    (off Bridgewater Sq.)
Cobalt Cl. BR3: Beck 4K 157
NW9 . . . . .1B 44
Cobalt Ct. HA4: Ruis 4A 58
Cobalt Pl. SW11 . . . . .1B 118
Cobalt Sq. SW8 . . . . .7G 19
Cobalt Twr. SE14 . . . . .6A 104
Cobbett Rd. SE9 . . . . .3C 124
  TW2: Whitt 1E 130
Cobbetts Av. IG4: Ilf 5B 52
Cobbett St. SW8 . . . . .7K 101
Cobble La. N1 . . . . .7B 66
Cobble M. N5 . . . . .3C 66
  N6 .1E 64
    (off Highgate West Hill)
Cobbie Path E17 . . . . .5C 50
    (off Cedars Av.)
Cobblestone Pl. CR0: C'don 1C 168
Cobblestone Sq. E1 . . . . .1H 103
Cobbold Ct. SW1 . . . . .3C 18
    (off Elverton St.)
Cobbold Ind. Est. NW10 . . . . .6B 62
Cobbold M. W12 . . . . .2B 98
Cobbold Rd. E11 . . . . .3H 69
  NW10 . . . . .6B 62
  W12 . . . . .2A 98
Cobb's Ct. EC4 . . . . .1B 14
Cobb's Hall SW6 . . . . .6F 99
    (off Fulham Pal. Rd.)
Cobb's Rd. TW4: Houn 4D 112
Cobbsthorpe Vs. SE26 . . . . .4K 139
Cobb St. E1 . . . . .6J 9 (5F 85)
Cobden Bldgs. WC1 . . . . .1G 7
    (off King's Cross Rd.)
Cobden Ct. BR2: Broml 4A 160
Cobden Ho. E2 . . . . .3G 85
    (off Nelson Gdns.)
  NW1 . . . . .2G 83
    (off Arlington Rd.)
Cobden M. SE26 . . . . .5H 139
Cobden Rd. BR6: Farnb 4H 173
  E11 . . . . .3G 69
  SE25 . . . . .5G 157
Cobham Av. KT3: N Mald 5C 152
Cobham Cl. BR2: Broml 7C 160
  DA15: Sidc 6B 126
  EN1: Enf 3B 24
  HA8: Edg 2H 43
  SM6: W'gton 6J 167
  SW11 . . . . .6C 118
Cobham Ct. CR4: Mitc 2B 154
Cobham M. NW1 . . . . .7H 65
Cobham Pl. DA6: Bex 5E 126
Cobham Rd. E17 . . . . .1E 50
  IG3: Ilf 2J 71
  KT1: King T 2G 151
  N22 . . . . .3B 48
  TW5: Hest 7A 94
Cobland Rd. SE12 . . . . .4A 142
Coborn M. E3 . . . . .3B 86
    (off Coborn St.)
Coborn Rd. E3 . . . . .2B 86
Coborn St. E3 . . . . .3B 86
Cobourg Rd. SE5 . . . . .6F 103
Cobourg St. NW1 . . . . . . .2B 6 (3G 83)
    (off Fleming Rd.)
Cobtree Ct. UB1: S'hall 6G 77
Coburg Cl. SW1 . . . . . .3B 18 (4G 101)
Coburg Cres. SW2 . . . . .1K 137
Coburg Dwellings E1 . . . . .6J 85
    (off Hardinge St.)
Coburg Gdns. IG5: Ilf 2B 52
Coburg Rd. N22 . . . . .3K 47
Cochrane Cl. NW8 . . . . .1B 4

Cochrane Ct. E10 . . . . .1C 68
    (off Leyton Grange Est.)
Cochrane Ho. E14 . . . . .2C 104
    (off Admirals Way)
Cochrane M. NW8 . . . . .2B 82
Cochrane Rd. SW19 . . . . .7G 135
Cochrane St. NW8 . . . . . . .1B 4 (2B 82)
Cockburn Ho. SW1 . . . . .6D 18
    (off Aylesford St.)
COCKCROW HILL 1D 162
Cockerell Rd. E17 . . . . .7A 50
COCKFOSTERS 4J 21
Cockfosters Pde. EN4: Cockf 4K 21
Cockfosters Rd.
  EN4: Cockf, Had W 1H 21
Cock Hill E1 . . . . .6H 9 (5E 84)
Cock La. EC1 . . . . .6A 8 (5B 84)
Cockpit Steps SW1 . . . . .7C 12
Cockpit Theatre 4C 4
    (off Gateforth St.)
Cockpit Yd. WC1 . . . . .5H 7 (5K 83)
Cocks Cres. KT3: N Mald 4B 152
Cocksett Av. BR6: Chels 6J 173
Cockspur Ct. SW1 . . . .4D 12 (1H 101)
Cockspur St. SW1 . . . . .4D 12 (1H 101)
Cocksure La. DA14: Sidc 3G 145
The Coda Cen. SW6 . . . . .7G 99
Coda Residences SW11 . . . . .3B 118
    (of York Place)
Code Cl. NW2 . . . . .3C 62
Code St. E1 . . . . .4K 9
Codicote Ho. SE8 . . . . .4K 103
    (off Chilton Gro.)
Codling Cl. E1 . . . . .1G 103
Codling Way HA0: Wemb 4D 60
Codrington Ct. E1 . . . . .4H 85
  SE16 . . . . .7A 86
Codrington Hill SE23 . . . . .7A 122
Codrington M. W11 . . . . .6G 81
Cody Cl. HA3: Kenton 3D 42
  SM6: W'gton 7H 167
Cody Rd. E16 . . . . .4F 87
Coe Av. SE25 . . . . .6G 157
Coe's All. EN5: Barn 4B 20
Cofferdam Way SE8 . . . . .7D 104
Coffey St. SE8 . . . . .7C 104
Cogan Av. E17 . . . . .1A 50
Coin St. SE1 . . . . .4J 13 (1A 102)
    (not continuous)
Coity Rd. NW5 . . . . .6E 64
Cokers La. SE21 . . . . .1D 138
Coke St. E1 . . . . .6G 85
Colas M. NW6 . . . . .1J 81
Colbeck M. SE6 . . . . .7F 123
  SW7 . . . . .4K 99
Colbeck Rd. HA1: Harr 7G 41
Colberg Pl. N16 . . . . .7F 49
Colbert SE5 . . . . .1E 120
    (off Sceaux Gdns.)
Colborne Cl. KT17: Ewe 6B 164
Colborne Ho. E14 . . . . .7C 86
    (off E. India Dock Rd.)
Colborne Way KT4: Wor Pk 3E 164
Colbrook Av. UB3: Harl 3F 93
Colbrook Cl. UB3: Harl 3F 93
Colburn Way SM1: Sutt 3B 166
Colby M. SE19 . . . . .5E 138
Colby Rd. KT12: Walt T 7J 147
  SE19 . . . . .5E 138
Colchester Av. E12 . . . . .4D 70
Colchester Dr. HA5: Pinn 5B 40
Colchester Ho. E3 . . . . .1B 86
    (off Parnell Rd.)
Colchester Rd. E10 . . . . .7E 50
  E17 . . . . .6C 50
  HA6: Nwood 2J 39
  HA8: Edg 7D 28
Colclough Cl. CR0: C'don 6C 156
    (off Simpson Cl.)
Coldbath Sq. EC1 . . . . . .3J 7 (4A 84)
Coldbath St. SE13 . . . . .1D 122
COLDBLOW 1J 145
Cold Blow Cres. DA5: Bexl 1K 145

Cold Blow La. SE14 . . . . .7K 103
    (not continuous)
Cold Blows CR4: Mitc 3D 154
Coldershaw Rd. W7 . . . . .1A 96
  W13 . . . . .1A 96
Coldfall Av. N10 . . . . .2E 46
Coldham Ct. N22 . . . . .1B 48
Coldharbour E14 . . . . .2E 104
Coldharbour Crest SE9 . . . . .3E 142
Coldharbour Ind. Est. SE5 . . . . . . .2C 120
Coldharbour La. SE5 . . . . .3C 120
  SW9 . . . . .4A 120
  UB3: Hayes 1J 93
Coldharbour Leisure Cen. 2D 142
Coldharbour Pl. SE5 . . . . .2C 120
Coldharbour Rd. CR0: Wadd 5A 168
Coldharbour Way
  CR0: Wadd 5A 168
Coldstream Gdns. SW18 . . . . .6H 117
Colebeck M. N1 . . . . .6B 66
Colebert Av. E1 . . . . .4J 85
Colebert Ho. E1 . . . . .4J 85
    (off Colebert Av.)
Colebrook Cl. NW7 . . . . .6A 30
  SW15 . . . . .7F 117
Colebrook Ct. SW3 . . . . .4D 16
    (off Makins St.)
Colebrooke Av. W13 . . . . .6B 78
Colebrooke Ct. DA14: Sidc 3B 144
Colebrooke Dr. E11 . . . . .7A 52
Colebrooke Pl. N1 . . . . .1B 84
Colebrooke Ri. BR2: Broml 2G 159
Colebrooke Row N1 . . . . .2B 84
Colebrook Ho. E14 . . . . .6D 86
    (off Ellesmere St.)
  SE18 . . . . .7E 106
Colebrook Rd. SW16 . . . . .1J 155
Colebrook Way N11 . . . . .5A 32
Colebury Path SE5 . . . . .7D 102
Colechurch Ho. SE1 . . . . .5G 103
    (off Avondale Sq.)
Cole Cl. SE28 . . . . .1B 108
Cole Ct. TW1: Twick 7A 114
Coledale Dr. HA7: Stan 1C 42
Colefax Bldgs. E1 . . . . .6G 85
    (off Plumber's Row)
Coleford Rd. SW18 . . . . .5A 118
Cole Gdns. TW5: Cran 7J 93
Colegrave Rd. E15 . . . . .5F 69
Colegrove Rd. SE15 . . . . .6F 103
Coleherne Ct. SW5 . . . . .5K 99
Coleherne Mans. SW5 . . . . .5K 99
    (off Old Brompton Rd.)
Coleherne M. SW10 . . . . .5K 99
Coleherne Rd. SW10 . . . . .5K 99
Colehill Gdns. SW6 . . . . .2G 117
Colehill La. SW6 . . . . .1G 117
Cole Ho. SE1 . . . . .7K 13
    (off Baylis Rd.)
Coleman Cl. SE25 . . . . .2G 157
Coleman Ct. SW18 . . . . .7J 117
Coleman Flds. N1 . . . . .1C 84
Coleman Mans. N8 . . . . .7J 47
Coleman Rd. DA17: Belv 4G 109
  RM9: Dag 6E 72
  SE5 . . . . .7E 102
Colemans Heath SE9 . . . . .3E 142
Coleman St. EC2 . . . . .7E 8 (6D 84)
Coleman St. Bldgs. EC2 . . . . .7E 8
Colenso Dr. NW7 . . . . .7H 29
Colenso Rd. E5 . . . . .4J 67
  IG2: Ilf 1J 71
COLE PARK 6A 114
Cole Pk. Gdns.
  TW1: Twick 5A 114
Cole Pk. Rd. TW1: Twick 6A 114
Cole Pk. Vw. TW1: Twick 6A 114
Colepits Wood Rd. SE9 . . . . .5H 125
Coleraine Rd. N8 . . . . .3A 48
  SE3 . . . . .6H 105
Coleridge Av. E12 . . . . .6C 70
  SM1: Sutt 4C 166
Coleridge Cl. SW8 . . . . .2F 119

Coleridge Ct. EN5: New Bar 5E 20
    (off Station Rd.)
  N1 . . . . .1C 84
    (off Dibden St.)
  SW1 . . . . .3C 18
    (off Regency St.)
  W14 . . . . .3F 99
    (off Blythe Rd.)
Coleridge Cres. SL3: Poyle 4A 174
Coleridge Dr. HA4: Ruis 6K 39
Coleridge Gdns. NW6 . . . . .7A 64
  SW10 . . . . .7K 99
Coleridge Ho. SE17 . . . . .5C 102
    (off Browning St.)
  SW1 . . . . .6B 18
    (off Churchill Gdns.)
Coleridge La. N8 . . . . .6J 47
Coleridge Rd. CR0: C'don 7J 157
  E17 . . . . .4B 50
  N4 . . . . .2A 66
  N8 . . . . .6H 47
  N12 . . . . .5F 31
  TW15: Ashf 4A 128
Coleridge Sq. SW10 . . . . .7A 100
    (off Coleridge Gdns.)
  W13 . . . . .6A 78
Coleridge Wlk. NW11 . . . . .4J 45
Coleridge Way UB4: Hayes 6J 75
  UB7: W Dray 4A 92
Cole Rd. TW1: Twick 6A 114
Colesburg Rd. BR3: Beck 3B 158
Coles Cres. HA2: Harr 2F 59
Coles Grn. WD23: B Hea 1B 26
Coles Grn. Ct. NW2 . . . . .2C 62
Coles Grn. Rd. NW2 . . . . .1C 62
Coleshill Flats SW1 . . . . .4H 17
Coleshill Rd. TW11: Tedd 6J 131
Colestown St. SW11 . . . . .2C 118
Cole St. SE1 . . . . .7D 14 (2C 102)
Colesworth Ho. HA8: Edg 2J 43
    (off Burnt Oak B'way.)
Colet Cl. N13 . . . . .6G 33
Colet Ct. W6 . . . . .4F 99
    (off Hammersmith Rd.)
Colet Flats E1 . . . . .6A 86
    (off Troon St.)
Colet Gdns. W14 . . . . .4F 99
Colet Ho. SE17 . . . . .5B 102
    (off Doddington Gro.)
Colette Ct. SE16 . . . . .2K 103
    (off Eleanor Cl.)
Coley St. WC1 . . . . .4H 7 (4K 83)
Colfe & Hatcliffe Glebe SE13 . . . .5D 122
    (off Lewisham High St.)
Colfe Rd. SE23 . . . . .1A 140
Colfe's Leisure Cen. 6J 123
Colgate Ct. EN5: Barn 5B 20
    (off Leecroft Rd.)
Colham Av. UB7: Yiew 1A 92
COLHAM GREEN 5C 74
Colham Grn. Rd. UB8: Hil 5C 74
Colham Mill Rd. UB7: W Dray 2A 92
Colham Rd. UB8: Hil 4B 74
COLHAM RDBT. 6C 74
Colina M. N15 . . . . .4B 48
Colina Rd. N15 . . . . .5B 48
Colin Cl. BR4: W W'ck 3H 171
  CR0: C'don 3B 170
  NW9 . . . . .4A 44
Colin Ct. SE6 . . . . .7B 122
Colin Cres. NW9 . . . . .4B 44
COLINDALE 3K 43
Colindale Av. NW9 . . . . .3K 43
Colindale Bus. Pk. NW9 . . . . .3J 43
Colindale Gdns. NW9 . . . . .3B 44
Colindale Retail Pk. 4K 43
Colindeep Gdns. NW4 . . . . .4C 44
Colindeep La. NW4 . . . . .3A 44
  NW9 . . . . .3A 44
Colin Dr. NW9 . . . . .5B 44
Colinette Rd. SW15 . . . . .4E 116
Colin Gdns. NW9 . . . . .4B 44
Colin Pde. NW9 . . . . .4A 44

Colin Pk. Rd. NW9 . . . . .4A 44
Colin Pond Ct. RM6: Chad H . . .4D 54
Colin Rd. NW10 . . . . .6C 62
Colinsdale N1 . . . . .1B 84
　　　　　　　　(off Camden Wlk.)
Colinton Rd. IG3: Ilf 2B 72
Colin Winter Ho. E1 . . . . .4J 85
　　　　　　　　(off Nicholas Rd.)
Coliseum Theatre 3E 12
　　　　　　　　(off St Martin's La.)
Coliston Pas. SW18 . . . . .7J 117
　　　　　　　　(off Coliston Rd.)
Coliston Rd. SW18 . . . . .7J 117
Collamore Av. SW18 . . . . .1C 136
Collapit Cl. HA1: Harr 6F 41
Collard Pl. NW1 . . . . .7F 65
Collards Almshouses E17 . . . . . .5E 50
　　　　　　　　(off Maynard Rd.)
Collection Pl. NW8 . . . . .1K 81
　　　　　　　　(off Bolton Pl.)
College App. SE10 . . . . .6E 104
College Av. HA3: Hrw W 1J 41
College Cl. E9 . . . . .5J 67
　　HA3: Hrw W 7D 26
　　N18 .5A 34
　　TW2: Twick 1H 131
College Ct. EN3: Pond E 5D 24
　　NW3 .6B 64
　　　　　　　　(off College Cres.)
　　SW3 .6F 17
　　W5 . . . . .7E 78
　　W6 . . . . .5E 98
　　　　　　　　(off Queen Caroline St.)
College Ct. Rd. EN3: Pond E 5D 24
College Cres. NW3 . . . . .6A 64
College Cross N1 . . . . .7A 66
College Dr. HA4: Ruis 7J 39
　　KT7: T Ditt 7J 149
College E. E1 . . . . .6K 9 (5F 85)
College Flds. Bus. Cen. SW19 . . .1C 154
College Gdns. E4 . . . . .7J 25
　　EN2: Enf 1J 23
　　IG4: Ilf 5C 52
　　KT3: N Mald 5B 152
　　N18 .5B 34
　　SE21 . . . . .1E 138
　　SW17 . . . . .2C 136
College Grn. SE19 . . . . .7E 138
College Gro. NW1 . . . . .1G 83
College Hall 4C 6 (4H 83)
College Hill EC4 . . . . . .2D 14 (7C 84)
College Hill Rd. HA3: Hrw W 7D 26
College Ho. SW15 . . . . .5F 117
　　TW7: Isle 7J 95
College La. NW5 . . . . .4F 65
College Mans. NW6 . . . . .1G 81
　　　　　　　　(off Salusbury Rd.)
College M. N1 . . . . .7A 66
　　　　　　　　(off College Cross)
　　SW1 . . . . .1E 18
　　SW18 . . . . .5K 117
College of Arms 2C 14
College Pde. NW6 . . . . .1G 81
　　　　　　　　(off Salusbury Rd.)
COLLEGE PARK 3D 80
College Pk. Cl. SE13 . . . . .4F 123
College Pk. Rd. N17 . . . . .6A 34
College Pl. E17 . . . . .4G 51
　　NW1 .1G 83
　　SW10 . . . . .7A 100
College Point E15 . . . . .6H 69
College Rd. BR1: Broml 1J 159
　　BR8: Hext 7K 145
　　CR0: C'don 2D 168
　　E17 .5E 50
　　EN2: Enf 2J 23
　　HA1: Harr 6J 41
　　HA3: Hrw W 1J 41
　　HA9: Wemb 1D 60
　　N17 .6A 34
　　N21 .2F 33
　　NW10 . . . . .2E 80
　　SE19 . . . . .5F 139

College Rd. SE21 . . . . .7E 120
　　SW19 . . . . .6B 136
　　TW7: Isle 1K 113
　　W13 .6B 78
COLLEGE RDBT. 3E 150
College Row E9 . . . . .5K 67
　　　　　　　　(off Homerton Gro.)
College Slip BR1: Broml 1J 159
College St. EC4 . . . . . . .2D 14 (7C 84)
College Ter. E3 . . . . .3B 86
　　N3 . . . . .2H 45
College Vw. SE9 . . . . .1B 142
College Wlk. KT1: King T 3E 150
College Way RM8: Dag 4A 72
　　TW15: Ashf 4B 128
　　UB3: Hayes 7J 75
College Yd. NW5 . . . . .4F 65
　　NW6 .1G 81
Collendale Rd. E17 . . . . .3K 49
Collett St. E9 . . . . .6J 67
Colleton Ho. SE10 . . . . .5H 105
　　　　　　　　(off Armitage Rd.)
Collett Rd. N15 . . . . .5F 49
Collett SE16 . . . . .3G 103
Collett Way UB2: S'hall 2F 95
Collier Cl. E6 . . . . .7F 89
　　KT19: Ewe 6G 163
Collier Dr. HA8: Edg 2G 43
COLLIER ROW 1H 55
Collier Row La. RM5: Col R 1H 55
Collier Row Rd. RM5: Col R 1F 55
Colliers Cl. CR0: C'don 4D 168
　　　　　　　　(off St Peter's Rd.)
Colliers Shaw BR2: Kes 4B 172
Collier St. N1 . . . . .2K 83
Colliers Water La. CR7: Thor H . .5A 156
COLLIERS WOOD 7B 136
Colliers Wood (Underground) . . .7B 136
Colliford Ct. HA8: Edg 4A 28
　　　　　　　　(off King's Dr.)
Collindale Av. DA8: Erith 7H 109
　　DA15: Sidc 1A 144
Collingbourne Rd. W12 . . . . .1D 98
Collingham Gdns. SW5 . . . . .4K 99
Collingham Pl. SW5 . . . . .4K 99
Collingham Rd. SW5 . . . . .4K 99
Collings Cl. N22 . . . . .6E 32
Collington St. SE10 . . . . .5F 105
Collingtree Rd. SE26 . . . . .4J 139
Collingwood Av. KT5: Surb 1J 163
　　N10 .3E 46
Collingwood Cl. SE20 . . . . .1H 157
　　TW2: Whitt 7E 112
Collingwood Ho. E1 . . . . .4H 85
　　　　　　　　(off Darling Row)
　　SE16 . . . . .2H 103
　　　　　　　　(off Cherry Gdn. St.)
　　SW1 . . . . .6C 18
　　　　　　　　(off Dolphin Sq.)
　　W1 . . . . .5A 6
　　　　　　　　(off Clipstone St.)
Collingwood Rd. CR4: Mitc 3C 154
　　E17 .6C 50
　　N15 .4E 48
　　SM1: Sutt 3J 165
　　UB8: Hil 4D 74
Collingwood St. E1 . . . . .4H 85
Collins Av. HA7: Stan 2E 42
Collins Bldg. NW2 . . . . .2E 62
Collins Ct. E8 . . . . .6G 67
　　DA4: Ruis 2A 58
Collins Ho. E14 . . . . .7E 86
　　　　　　　　(off Newby Pl.)
　　SE10 . . . . .5H 105
　　　　　　　　(off Armitage Rd.)
Collinson Ct. SE1 . . . . .7C 14
　　　　　　　　(off Gt. Suffolk St.)
Collinson Ho. SE3 . . . . .4K 123
　　　　　　　　(off Wallace Ct.)
　　SE15 . . . . .7G 103
　　　　　　　　(off Peckham Pk. Rd.)

Collinson St. SE1 . . . . . . .7C 14 (2C 102)
Collinson Wlk. SE1 . . . . . .7C 14 (2C 102)
Collins Path TW12: Hamp 6D 130
Collins Rd. N5 . . . . .4C 66
Collins Sq. SE3 . . . . .2H 123
Collins St. SE3 . . . . .2G 123
　　　　　　　　(not continuous)
Collin's Yd. N1 . . . . .1B 84
Collinwood Av. EN3: Enf H 3D 24
Collinwood Gdns. IG5: Ilf 5D 52
Collis All. TW2: Twick 1J 131
Collison Pl. N16 . . . . .1E 66
Coll's Rd. SE15 . . . . .1J 121
Collyer Av. CR0: Bedd 4J 167
Collyer Pl. SE15 . . . . .1G 121
Collyer Rd. CR0: Bedd 4J 167
Colman Ct. HA7: Stan 6G 27
　　N12 .6F 31
Colman Pde. EN1: Enf 3K 23
Colman Rd. E16 . . . . .5A 88
Colmans Wharf E14 . . . . .5D 86
　　　　　　　　(off Morris Rd.)
Colmar Cl. E1 . . . . .4K 85
Colmer Pl. HA3: Hrw W 7C 26
Colmer Rd. SW16 . . . . .1J 155
Colmore M. SE15 . . . . .1H 121
Colmore Rd. EN3: Pond E 4D 24
Colnbrook Cl. SL3: Poyle 4A 174
Colnbrook St. SE1 . . . . .3B 102
Colne Ct. KT19: Ewe 4J 163
　　W7 . . . . .6H 77
　　　　　　　　(off High La.)
Colnedale Rd. UB8: Uxb 5A 56
Colne Ho. IG11: Bark 7F 71
　　NW8 .4B 4
　　　　　　　　(off Penfold St.)
Colne Pk. Cvn. Site 1D 174
Colne Reach TW19: Stanw M 7A 174
Colne Rd. E5 . . . . .4A 68
　　N21 .7J 23
　　TW1: Twick 1J 131
　　TW2: Twick 1J 131
　　Colne. St. E13 . . . . .3J 87
Colne Valley 5A 14
Colney Hatch La. N10 . . . . .6J 31
　　N11 .6J 31
Colnmore Ct. E2 . . . . .3K 85
　　　　　　　　(off Meath Cres.)
Coln Trad. Est. SL3: Poyle 4A 174
Cologne Rd. SW11 . . . . .4B 118
Coloma Ct. BR4: W W'ck 4G 171
Colombo Centre 5A 14
Colombo Rd. IG1: Ilf 1G 71
Colombo St. SE1 . . . . . .5A 14 (1B 102)
Colomb St. SE10 . . . . .5G 105
Colonel's Wlk. EN2: Enf 3G 23
Colonial Av. TW2: Whitt 6G 113
Colonial Ct. N7 . . . . .3K 65
Colonial Dr. W4 . . . . .4J 97
Colonial Rd. TW14: Felt 7G 111
Colonnade WC1 . . . . . . .4F 7 (4J 83)
The Colonnade SE1 . . . . .6J 13
　　　　　　　　(off Waterloo Rd.)
　　SE8 .4B 104
Colonnade Gdns. W3 . . . . .1B 98
The Colonnades W2 . . . . .6K 81
The Colonnades Leisure Pk. 6A 168
Colonnade Wlk. SW1 . . .4J 17 (4F 101)
Colony Mans. SW5 . . . . .5K 99
　　　　　　　　(off Earl's Ct. Rd.)
Colony M. N1 . . . . .6D 66
　　　　　　　　(off Mildmay Gro. Nth.)
Colorado Apts. N8 . . . . .2K 47
　　　　　　　　(off Gt. Amwell La.)
Colorado Bldg. SE13 . . . . .1D 122
　　　　　　　　(off Deal's Gateway)
Colosseum Apts. E2 . . . . .2K 85
　　　　　　　　(off Palmers Rd.)
Colosseum Ter. NW1 . . . . .2K 5
Colour Ho. SW1 . . . . .5B 12
Colour Ho. SE1 . . . . .7H 15
　　　　　　　　(off Bell Yd M.)
Colour House Theatre 1A 154

Colroy Ct. NW11 . . . . .5G 45
Colson Rd. CR0: C'don 2E 168
Colson Way SW16 . . . . .4G 137
Colstead Ho. E1 . . . . .6H 85
　　　　　　　　(off Watney Mkt.)
Colsterworth Rd. N15 . . . . .4F 49
　　　　　　　　(not continuous)
Colston Av. SM5: Cars 4C 166
Colston Cl. SM5: Cars 4D 166
Colston Rd. E7 . . . . .6B 70
　　SW14 . . . . .4J 115
Coltash Ct. EC1 . . . . .3D 8
　　　　　　　　(off Whitecross St.)
Colthurst Cres. N4 . . . . .2B 66
Colthurst Dr. N9 . . . . .3C 34
Coltman Ho. SE10 . . . . .6E 104
　　　　　　　　(off Welland St.)
Coltman St. E14 . . . . .5A 86
Coltness Cres. SE2 . . . . .5B 108
Colton Gdns. N17 . . . . .3C 48
Colton Rd. HA1: Harr 5J 41
Coltsfoot Dr. UB7: Yiew 6A 74
Columbas Dr. NW3 . . . . .1B 64
Columbia Av. HA4: Ruis 1K 57
　　HA8: Edg 1H 43
　　KT4: Wor Pk 7B 152
Columbia Gdns. SW6 . . . . .6J 99
　　　　　　　　(off One Lillie Sq.)
Columbia Gdns. Nth. SW6 . . . . . .6J 99
　　　　　　　　(off Rickett St.)
Columbia Gdns. Sth. SW6 . . . . . .6J 99
　　　　　　　　(off Rickett St.)
Columbia Ho. E3 . . . . .4B 86
　　　　　　　　(off Hamlets Way)
Columbia Point SE16 . . . . .3J 103
　　　　　　　　(off Canada Est.)
Columbia Rd. E2 . . . . . . .1J 9 (3F 85)
　　E13 .4H 87
Columbia Rd. Flower Market 1K 9
　　　　　　　　(off Columbia Rd.)
Columbia Sq. SW14 . . . . .4J 115
Columbia Wharf EN3: Pond E 6F 25
Columbine Av. CR2: S Croy 7B 168
　　E6 . . . . .5C 88
Columbine Way SE13 . . . . .2E 122
Columbus Ct. SE16 . . . . .1J 103
　　　　　　　　(off Rotherhithe St.)
Columbus Ctyd. E14 . . . . .1C 104
Columbus Gdns. HA6: Nwood . . .1J 39
Colva Wlk. N19 . . . . .2F 65
Colvern Ho. RM7: Rom 5J 55
Colverson Ho. E1 . . . . .5J 85
　　　　　　　　(off Lindley St.)
Colvestone Cres. E8 . . . . .5F 67
Colville Ct. SE9 . . . . .1B 142
Colville Est. N1 . . . . .1E 84
Colville Est. W. E2 . . . . .2K 9
Colville Gdns. W11 . . . . .6H 81
　　　　　　　　(not continuous)
Colville Ho. E2 . . . . .2J 85
　　　　　　　　(off Waterloo Gdns.)
　　W11 .6H 81
Colville Ho's. W11 . . . . .6H 81
Colville Mans. E20 . . . . .5D 68
　　　　　　　　(off Victory Pde.)
Colville M. W11 . . . . .6H 81
Colville Pl. W1 . . . . .6B 6 (5H 83)
Colville Rd. E11 . . . . .3E 68
　　E17 .2A 50
　　N9 . . . . .1C 34
　　W3 . . . . .3H 97
　　W11 .6H 81
Colville Sq. W11 . . . . .6H 81
Colville Ter. W11 . . . . .6H 81
Colvin Cl. SE26 . . . . .5J 139
Colvin Gdns. E4 . . . . .3K 35
　　E11 .4K 51
　　IG6: Ilf 1G 53
Colvin Ho. W10 . . . . .6F 81
　　　　　　　　(off Kingsdown Cl.)
Colvin Rd. CR7: Thor H 5A 156
　　E6 . . . . .7C 70
Colwall Gdns. IG8: Wfd G 5D 36
Colwell Cres. EN3: Pond E 5D 24

Colwell Ho. KT12: Walt T 7H 147
(off Hepworth Way)
Colwell Rd. SE22 ....5F 121
Colwick Cl. N6 ....7H 47
Colwith Rd. W6 ....6E 98
Colwood Gdns. SW19 ....7B 136
Colworth Gro. SE17 ....4C 102
Colworth Rd. CRO: C'don 1G 169
E11 ....6G 51
Colwyn Av. UB6: G'frd 2K 77
Colwyn Cl. SW16 ....5G 137
Colwyn Cres. TW3: Houn 1G 113
Colwyn Grn. NW9 ....6A 44
(off Snowdon Dr.)
Colwyn Ho. SE1 ......2J 19 (3A 102)
Colwyn Rd. NW2 ....3D 62
Colyer Cl. SE9 ....2F 143
Colyers Cl. DA8: Erith 1K 127
Colyers La. DA8: Erith 1J 127
Colyers Wlk. DA8: Erith 1K 127
Colyton Cl. DA16: Well 1D 126
HAO: Wemb 6C 60
Colyton La. SW16 ....5A 138
Colyton Rd. SE22 ....5H 121
Colyton Way N18 ....5B 34
The Combe NW1 ......2K 5 (3F 83)
Combe Av. SE3 ....7H 105
Combedale Rd. SE10 ....5J 105
Combe Ho. W2 ....5J 81
(off Gt. Western Rd.)
Combemartin Rd. SW18 ......7G 117
Combe M. SE3 ....7H 105
Comber Cl. NW2 ....3D 62
Comber Gro. SE5 ....7C 102
Comber Ho. SE5 ....7C 102
Combermere Rd. SM4: Mord ...6K 153
SW9 ....3K 119
Comberton KT1: King T 2G 151
(off Eureka Rd.)
Comberton Rd. E5 ....2H 67
Combeside SE18 ....7K 107
Combwell Cres. SE2 ....3A 108
Comedy Store 3C 12
(off Oxendon St.)
Comely Bank Rd. E17 ....5E 50
Comeragh M. W14 ....5G 99
Comeragh Rd. W14 ....5G 99
Comer Cres. UB2: S'hall 2G 95
(off Windmill Av.)
Comerford Rd. SE4 ....4A 122
Comer Ho. EN5: New Bar 4F 21
Comet Cl. E12 ....4B 70
Comet Ho. UB3: Harl 7E 92
Comet Pl. SE8 ....7C 104
(not continuous)
Comet Rd. TW19: Stanw 7A 110
Comet St. SE8 ....7C 104
Comfort St. SE15 ....6E 102
Commander Av. NW9 ....3C 44
Commerce Pk. CRO: Wadd 2K 167
Commerce Rd. N22 ....1K 47
TW8: Bford 6C 96
Commerce Way CRO: Wadd ...2K 167
Commercial Rd. E1 ....7K 9 (6G 85)
E14 ....6G 85
N18 ....5K 33
Commercial Rd. Ind. Est. N18 ...6A 34
Commercial St. E1 .....4J 9 (4F 85)
Commercial Way NW10 ......2H 79
SE10 ....4H 105
SE15 ....7F 103
Commercial Wharf E8 ....1E 84
(off Kingsland Rd.)
Commerell Pl. SE10 ....5H 105
Commerell St. SE10 ....5G 105
Commodity Quay E1 ..3K 15 (7F 85)
Commodore Cl. SE8 ....1C 122
(off Albyn Rd.)
Commodore Ho. E14 ....7E 86
(off Poplar High St.)
E16 ....2K 105
(off Royal Crest Av.)
SW18 ....3A 118

Commodore St. E1 ....4A 86
The Common E15 ....6G 69
HA7: Stan 2D 26
UB2: S'hall 4A 94
UB7: W Dray 1D 174
W5 ....7E 78
(not continuous)
Commondale SW15 ....2E 116
Commonfield La. SW17 ......5C 136
Common La. KT10: Clay 7A 162
Common Mile Cl. SW4 ....5H 119
Common Rd. HA7: Stan 4C 26
KT10: Clay 6A 162
SW13 ....3D 116
Commonside BR2: Kes 4A 172
Commonside E. CR4: Mitc ...3E 154
Commonside W. CR4: Mitc ...3D 154
Commonwealth Av.
UB3: Hayes 6F 75
W12 ....7D 80
(not continuous)
Commonwealth Memorial Gates
...............6J 11 (2F 101)
Commonwealth Rd. N17 .....7B 34
Commonwealth Secretariat ...5B 12
Commonwealth Way SE2 .....5B 108
Community Cl. TW5: Cran 1K 111
UB10: Ick 3D 56
Community La. N7 ....5H 65
Community Rd. E15 ....5F 69
UB6: G'frd 1G 77
Como Rd. SE23 ....2A 140
Como St. RM7: Rom 5K 55
Compass Bus. Pk.
KT9: Chess 4G 163
Compass Cl. HA8: Edg 4A 28
TW15: Ashf 7E 128
Compass Ct. SE1 ....5J 15
(off Shad Thames)
Compass Hill TW10: Rich 6D 114
Compass Ho. E1 ....1J 103
(off Raine St.)
SW18 ....4K 117
Compass La. BR1: Broml 1J 159
(off North St.)
Compass Point E14 ....7B 86
(off Grenade St.)
Compass Theatre 3E 56
Compayne Gdns. NW6 ....7K 63
Compayne Mans. NW6 ......6K 63
(off Fairhazel Gdns.)
Compter Pas. EC2 ....1D 14
Compton Av. E6 ....2B 88
HA0: Wemb 4C 60
N1 ....6B 66
N6 ....7C 46
Compton Cl. E3 ....5C 86
HA8: Edg 7D 28
NW1 ....2K 5
NW11 ....3F 63
SE15 ....7G 103
W13 ....6A 78
Compton Ct. SE19 ....6E 138
SM1: Sutt 4A 166
Compton Cres. KT9: Chess ...5E 162
N17 ....7H 33
UB5: N'olt 1B 76
W4 ....6J 97
Compton Ho. E20 ....5D 68
(off Peloton Av.)
SW10 ....1A 118
SW11 ....1C 118
Compton Leisure Cen. 4C 108
Compton Pas. EC1 ....3B 8 (4B 84)
Compton Pl. WC1 ......3E 6 (4J 83)
Compton Ri. HA5: Pinn 5C 40
Compton Rd. CRO: C'don 1H 169
N1 ....6B 66
N21 ....1G 33
NW10 ....3F 81
SW19 ....6H 135
UB3: Hayes 7G 75
Compton St. EC1 .....3A 8 (4B 84)

Compton Ter. N1 ....6B 66
N4 ....6C 48
N21 ....1F 33
Comreddy Cl. EN2: Enf 1G 23
Comus Ho. SE17 ....4E 102
(off Comus Pl.)
Comus Pl. SE17 ....4E 102
Comyn Rd. SW11 ....4C 118
The Comyns WD23: B Hea ...1B 26
Comyns Cl. E16 ....5H 87
Comyns Rd. RM9: Dag 7G 73
Conant Ho. SE11 ....7A 19
(off St Agnes Pl.)
Conant M. E1 ....7G 85
Concanon Rd. SW2 ....4K 119
Concert Hall App. SE1 ...5H 13 (1K 101)
Concord Bus. Cen. W3 ......4H 79
Concord Cl. UB5: N'olt 3B 76
Concord Ct. KT1: King T 3F 151
(off Winery La.)
Concorde Cl. TW3: Houn 2F 113
UB10: Uxb 2A 74
Concorde Dr. E6 ....5D 88
Concord Ho. CRO: C'don 6B 156
KT3: N Mald 3A 152
N17 ....7A 34
(off Park La.)
Concordia Wharf E14 ....1E 104
(off Coldharbour)
Concord Rd. EN3: Pond E 5C 24
W3 ....4H 79
Concord Ter. HA2: Harr 2F 59
(off Coles Cres.)
The Concourse N9 ....2B 34
(within Edmonton Grn. Shop. Cen.)
NW9 ....1B 44
(off Quakers Course)
Condell Rd. SW8 ....1G 119
Conder St. E14 ....6A 86
Condor Ho. E13 ....1J 87
(off Brooks Rd.)
Condor Path UB5: N'olt 2E 76
(off Union Rd.)
Condor Way TW6: H'row A ...3C 110
Condover Cres. SE18 ....7F 107
Condray Pl. SW11 ....7C 100
Conduit Av. SE10 ....1F 123
Conduit Ct. WC2 ....2E 12
Conduit La. CRO: C'don 5G 169
CR2: S Croy 5G 169
EN3: Pond E 6F 25
N18 ....5D 34
Conduit M. SE18 ....5F 107
W2 ....1A 10 (6B 82)
Conduit Pas. W2 ....1A 10
Conduit Pl. W2 ......1A 10 (6B 82)
Conduit Rd. SE18 ....5F 107
Conduit St. W1 ....2K 11 (7F 83)
Conduit Way NW10 ....7J 61
Conewood St. N5 ....3B 66
Coney Acre SE21 ....1C 138
Coneybeare Point SE10 .....4J 105
Coney Burrows E4 ....2B 36
Coney Gro. UB8: Hil 3C 74
Coneygrove Path UB5: N'olt ...6C 58
(off Arnold Rd.)
CONEY HALL 3G 171
Coney Hall Pde. BR4: W W'ck ...3G 171
Coney Hill Rd. BR4: W W'ck ...2G 171
Coney Way SW8 ....6K 101
Conference Cl. E4 ....2K 35
Conference Rd. SE2 ....4C 108
Confluence Plaza SE13 .....3E 122
(off Station Rd.)
Congers Ho. SE8 ....7C 104
Congleton Gro. SE18 ....5G 107
Congo Dr. N9 ....3D 34
Congo Rd. SE18 ....5H 107
Congress Rd. SE2 ....4C 108
Congreve Ho. N16 ....5E 66
Congreve Rd. SE9 ....3D 124
Congreve St. SE17 ....4E 102

Congreve Wlk. E16 ....5B 88
(off Fulmer Rd.)
Conical Cnr. EN2: Enf 2H 23
Conifer Cl. BR6: Orp 4H 173
Conifer Ct. TW15: Ashf 5B 128
(off The Crescent)
Conifer Gdns. EN1: Enf 6K 23
SM1: Sutt 2K 165
SW16 ....3K 137
Conifer Ho. SE4 ....4B 122
(off Brockley Rd.)
Conifers Cl. TW11: Tedd 7B 132
Conifer Way HA0: Wemb 3C 60
UB3: Hayes 7J 75
Coniger Rd. SW6 ....2J 117
Coningham Ct. SW10 ....2H 118
(off King's Rd.)
Coningham M. W12 ....1C 98
Coningham Rd. W12 ....2D 98
Coningsby Av. NW9 ....2A 44
Coningsby Cotts. W5 ....2D 96
Coningsby Ct. CR4: Mitc 2E 154
Coningsby Gdns. E4 ....6J 35
Coningsby Rd. CR2: S Croy ...7C 168
N4 ....7B 48
W5 ....2D 96
Conington Rd. SE13 ....2D 122
Conisbee Ct. N14 ....5B 22
Conisborough Cres. SE6 ....3E 140
Conisbrough NW1 ....1G 83
(off Bayham St.)
Coniscliffe Cl. BR7: Chst 1E 160
Coniscliffe Rd. N13 ....3H 33
Coniston NW1 ....1A 6
(off Harrington St.)
Coniston Av. DA16: Well 3J 125
IG11: Bark 7J 71
UB6: G'frd 3B 78
Coniston Cl. DA7: Bex 1J 127
DA8: Erith 7K 109
IG11: Bark 7J 71
N20 ....3F 31
SW13 ....2B 116
SW20 ....6F 153
W4 ....7J 97
Coniston Ct. NW7 ....7B 30
(off Langstone Way)
SE16 ....2K 103
(off Eleanor Cl.)
SM6: W'gton 4F 167
TW15: Ashf 3A 128
W2 ....1D 10
(off Kendal St.)
Conistone Way N7 ....7J 65
Coniston Gdns. HA5: Eastc ...4J 39
HA9: Wemb 1C 60
IG4: Ilf 4C 52
N9 ....1D 34
NW9 ....5K 43
SM2: Sutt 6B 166
Coniston Ho. E3 ....4B 86
(off Southern Gro.)
SE5 ....7C 102
(off Wyndham Rd.)
Coniston Rd. BR1: Broml 6G 141
CRO: C'don 7G 157
DA7: Bex 1J 127
N10 ....2F 47
N17 ....6B 34
TW2: Whitt 6F 113
Coniston Wlk. E9 ....5J 67
Coniston Way
KT9: Chess 3E 162
Conlan St. W10 ....4G 81
Conley Rd. NW10 ....6A 62
Conley St. SE10 ....5G 105
Connaught Av. E4 .....7K 25, 1A 36
E11 ....2K 23
EN4: E Barn 1J 31
SW14 ....3J 115
TW4: Houn 4C 112
TW15: Ashf 4A 128
Connaught Bri. E16 ....1B 106

Connaught Bus. Cen.
CRO: Wadd 6K 167
CR4: Mitc 5D 154
NW9 . . . . .5B 44
Connaught Cl. E10 . . . . .2A 68
EN1: Enf 2K 23
SM1: Sutt 2B 166
UB8: Hil 4E 74
W2 . . . . .1D 10 (6C 82)
The Connaught Club 1C 36
Connaught Ct. E17 . . . . .4D 50
(off Orford Rd.)
W2 . . . . .1E 10
(off Connaught St.)
Connaught Dr. NW11 . . . . .4J 45
Connaught Gdns. N10 . . . . .5F 47
N13 .4G 33
SM4: Mord 4A 154
Connaught Hall 3D 6 (4H 83)
Connaught Hgts. E16 . . . . .1B 106
(off Agnes George Wlk.)
UB10: Hil 4E 74
(off Uxbridge Rd.)
Connaught Ho. NW10 . . . . .3D 80
(off Trenmar Gdns.)
W1 . . . . .3J 11
(off Davies St.)
Connaught La. IG1: Ilf 2G 71
Connaught Lodge N4 . . . . .7A 48
(off Connaught Rd.)
Connaught M. NW3 . . . . .4C 64
SE18 . . . . .5E 106
SW6 . . . . .1G 117
Connaught Pl. W2 . . . . .2E 10 (7D 82)
Connaught Rd. E4 . . . . .1B 36
E11 .1F 69
E16 . . . . .1B 106
E17 .5C 50
EN5: Barn 6A 20
HA3: W'stone 1K 41
IG1: Ilf 2H 71
KT3: N Mald 4A 152
N4 . . . . .7A 48
NW10 . . . . .1A 80
SM1: Sutt 2B 166
TW10: Rich 5F 115
TW11: Tedd 5H 131
W13 . . . . .7B 78
CONNAUGHT RDBT. 7B 88
(off Victoria Dock Rd.)
Connaught Sq. W2 . . . .1D 10 (6D 82)
Connaught St. W2 . . . .1D 10 (6C 82)
Connaught Way N13 . . . . .4G 33
Connaught Works E3 . . . . .1A 86
(off Old Ford Rd.)
Connect La. IG6: Ilf 2G 53
Connell Ct. SE14 . . . . .6K 103
(off Myers La.)
Connell Cres. W5 . . . . .4F 79
Connersville Way CRO: Wadd . . .3A 168
Conniffe Ct. SE9 . . . . .5F 125
Conningham St. SE9 . . . . .5A 124
Connington Cres. E4 . . . . .3A 36
Connolly Ct. RM7: Rush G 6K 55
(off Union Rd.)
Connor Cl. E11 . . . . .7G 51
IG6: Ilf 1G 53
Connor Ct. SW11 . . . . .1F 119
Connor Rd. RM9: Dag 4F 73
Connor St. E9 . . . . .1K 85
Conolly Rd. W7 . . . . .1J 95
Conrad Cl. NW9 . . . . .2A 44
(off Needleman Cl.)
SE16 . . . . .4A 104
(off Cary Av.)
Conrad Dr. KT4: Wor Pk 1E 164
Conrad Ho. E8 . . . . .6G 67
E14 . . . . .1D 104
(off Victory Pl.)
E16 . . . . .1K 105
(off Wesley Av.)
N16 . . . . .5E 66
(off Matthias Rd.)

Conrad Ho. SW8 . . . . .7J 101
(off Wyvil Rd.)
Consfield Av. KT3: N Mald 4C 152
Consort Cl. W8 . . . . .3K 99
(off Wright's La.)
Consort Ho. E14 . . . . .5D 104
(off St Davids Sq.)
SW6 . . . . .2A 118
(off Lensbury Av.)
W2 . . . . .7K 81
(off Queensway)
Consort Lodge NW8 . . . . .1D 82
(off Prince Albert Rd.)
Consort M. TW7: Isle 5H 113
Consort Rd. SE15 . . . . .1H 121
Cons St. SE1 . . . . .6K 13 (2A 102)
Constable Av. E16 . . . . .1K 105
Constable Cl. N11 . . . . .5J 31
NW11 . . . . .6K 45
UB4: Hayes 2E 74
Constable Ct. SE16 . . . . .5H 103
(off Stubbs Dr.)
W4 . . . . .5H 97
(off Chaseley Dr.)
Constable Cres. N15 . . . . .5G 49
Constable Gdns. HA8: Edg 1G 43
TW7: Isle 5H 113
Constable Ho. E14 . . . . .2C 104
(off Cassilis Rd.)
NW3 . . . . .7D 64
UB5: N'olt 2B 76
(off Gallery Gdns.)
Constable M. BR1: Broml 2K 159
RM8: Dag 4B 72
Constable Wlk. SE21 . . . . .3E 138
Constabulary Cl. UB7: W Dray 3A 92
Constance Allen Ho. W10 . . . . .6F 81
(off Bridge Cl.)
Constance Cl. SW15 . . . . .4K 133
Constance Cres. BR2: Hayes 7H 159
Constance Rd. CRO: C'don 7B 156
EN1: Enf 6K 23
SM1: Sutt 4A 166
TW2: Whitt 7F 113
Constance St. E16 . . . . .1C 106
Constant Ho. E14 . . . . .7D 86
(off Harrow La.)
Constantine Ct. E1 . . . . .6G 85
(off Fairclough St.)
Constantine Ho. NW9 . . . . .3B 44
(off Boulevard Dr.)
UB3: Hayes 6F 75
Constantine Pl. UB10: Hil 1B 74
Constantine Rd. NW3 . . . . .4C 64
Constellation Way TW6: H'row A . .3D 110
Constitution Hill SW1 . . . .6J 11 (2F 101)
Constitution Ri. SE18 . . . . .1E 124
Consul Av. RM9: Dag, Rain 3J 91
RM13: Rain 3J 91
Consul Ho. E3 . . . . .4C 86
(off Wellington Way)
Container City 1 E14 . . . . .7G 87
Container City 2 E14 . . . . .7G 87
Contemporary Applied Arts 5B 14
(off Southwark St.)
Content St. SE17 . . . . .4D 102
Contessa Cl. BR6: Farnb 5J 173
Contrail Way TW6: H'row A 3D 110
Convair Wlk. UB5: N'olt 3B 76
Convent Cl. BR3: Beck 7E 140
EN5: Barn 2C 20
Convent Gdns. W5 . . . . .4C 96
W11 .6G 81
Convent Hill SE19 . . . . .6C 138
Convent Rd. TW15: Ashf 5D 128
Convent Way UB2: S'hall 4A 94
Conway Cl. BR3: Beck 1A 158
HA7: Stan 7F 27
Conway Cres. RM6: Chad H 6C 54
UB6: G'frd 2J 77
Conway Dr. SM2: Sutt 6K 165
TW15: Ashf 6E 128
UB3: Harl 3E 92

Conway Gdns. CR4: Mitc 4J 155
EN2: Enf 1K 23
HA9: Wemb 7C 42
Conway Gro. W3 . . . . .5K 79
Conway Ho. E14 . . . . .4C 104
(off Cahir St.)
SW3 .6F 17
(off Ormonde Ga.)
Conway M. W1 . . . . .4A 6
Conway Rd. N14 . . . . .3D 32
N15 .5B 48
NW2 . . . . .2E 62
SE18 . . . . .4H 107
SW20 . . . . .1E 152
TW4: Houn 7D 112
TW13: Hanw 5B 130
Conway St. W1 . . . . . .4A 6 (4G 83)
(not continuous)
Conway Wlk. TW12: Hamp 6D 130
Conybeare NW3 . . . . .7C 64
Conyers Cl. IG8: Wfd G 6B 36
Conyer's Rd. SW16 . . . . .5H 137
Conyer St. E3 . . . . .2A 86
Cooden Cl. BR1: Broml 7K 141
Cook Ct. SE8 . . . . .5A 104
(off Evelyn St.)
SE16 .1J 103
(off Rotherhithe St.)
Cooke Cl. SE2 . . . . .3C 108
Cookes Cl. E11 . . . . .2H 69
Cookes La. SM3: Cheam 6G 165
Cooke St. IG11: Bark 1G 89
(not continuous)
Cookham Cl. UB2: S'hall 3F 95
Cookham Cres. SE16 . . . . .2K 103
Cookham Dene Cl. BR7: Chst 1H 161
Cookham Ho. E2 . . . . .3J 9
(off Montclare St.)
Cookham Rd. BR8: Swan 7G 145
Cookhill Rd. SE2 . . . . .2B 108
Cook Rd. RM9: Dag 1E 90
Cook's Cl. RM5: Col R 1J 55
Cook's Ct. E14 . . . . .1C 104
(off Cabot Sq.)
Cooks Hole Rd. EN2: Enf 1H 23
Cookson Gro. DA8: Erith 7H 109
Cook's Rd. E15 . . . . .2D 86
Cooks Rd. SE17 . . . . .6B 102
Coolfin Rd. E16 . . . . .6J 87
Coolgardie Av. E4 . . . . .5A 36
IG7: Chig 3K 37
Coolgardie Rd. TW15: Ashf 5E 128
Coolhurst Rd. N8 . . . . .6H 47
Coolhurst Tennis & Squash Club . .6H 47
Cool Oak La. NW9 . . . . .7A 44
Coomassie Rd. W9 . . . . .4H 81
COOMBE 7J 133
Coombe Av. CRO: C'don 4E 168
Coombe Bank KT2: King T 1A 152
Coombe Cl. HA8: Edg 2F 43
TW3: Houn 4E 112
Coombe Cnr. N21 . . . . .1G 33
Coombe Ct. CRO: C'don 4D 168
(off Coombe Rd.)
Coombe Cres. TW12: Hamp 7D 130
Coombe Dene BR2: Broml 4H 159
(off Cumberland Rd.)
Coombe Dr. HA4: Ruis 1K 57
KT2: King T 7K 133
Coombe End KT2: King T 7K 133
Coombefield Cl. KT3: N Mald 5A 152
Coombe Gdns. KT3: N Mald 4B 152
SW20 . . . . .2C 152
Coombe Hill Glade KT2: King T . .7A 134
Coombe Hill Golf Course 7K 133
Coombe Hill Rd. KT2: King T 7A 134
Coombe Ho. N7 . . . . .5K 65
Coombe Ho. Chase KT3: N Mald . .1K 151
COOMBE LANE 1B 152
Coombe La. CRO: C'don 5H 169
SW20 . . . . .1B 152
Coombe La. Flyover SW20 . . . . . .1B 152
Coombe La. W. KT2: King T 1H 151

Coombe Lea BR1: Broml 3C 160
Coombe Lodge SE7 . . . . .6A 106
Coombe Neville KT2: King T 7K 133
Coombe Pk. KT2: King T 5J 133
Coombe Pl. KT2: King T 5J 133
Coomber Ho. SW6 . . . . .3K 117
(off Wandsworth Bri. Rd.)
Coombe Ridings KT2: King T 5J 133
Coombe Ri. KT2: King T 1J 151
Coombe Rd. CRO: C'don 4D 168
KT2: King T 1G 151
KT3: N Mald 2A 152
N22 . . . . .2A 48
NW10 . . . . .3K 61
SE26 . . . . .4H 139
TW12: Hamp 6D 130
W4 . . . . .5A 98
W13 .3B 96
Coomber Way CRO: Bedd 7H 155
Coombes Rd. RM9: Dag 1F 91
Coombe Wlk. SM1: Sutt 3K 165
Coombewood Dr. RM6: Chad H . . .6F 55
Coombe Wood Golf Course 7H 133
Coombe Wood
  Local Nature Reserve 7B 134
Coombe Wood Rd. KT2: King T . . .5J 133
Coombrook Ct. SE16 . . . . .2A 104
(off Elgar St.)
Coombs St. N1 . . . . .1B 8 (2B 84)
Coomer M. SW6 . . . . .6H 99
Coomer Pl. SW6 . . . . .6H 99
Coomer Rd. SW6 . . . . .6H 99
Cooms Wlk. HA8: Edg 1J 43
Coope Cl. RM7: Rush G 6K 55
(off Union Rd.)
The Cooperage SE1 . . . . .6J 15
(off Gainsford St.)
SW8 . . . . .7K 101
(off Regent's Bri. Gdns.)
Cooperage Cl. N17 . . . . .6A 34
Cooperage Yd. E15 . . . . .2E 86
Co-operative Ho. SE15 . . . . .3G 121
Cooper Av. E17 . . . . .1A 50
Cooper Cl. SE1 . . . . . . .7K 13 (2A 102)
Cooper Ct. SE18 . . . . .6F 107
Cooper Cres. SM5: Cars 3D 166
Cooper Ho. NW8 . . . . .4A 4
(off Lyons Pl.)
SE4 . . . . .5K 121
(off St Norbert Rd.)
TW4: Houn 3D 112
NW4 .5C 44
NW10 . . . . .5C 62
Coopersale Cl. IG8: Wfd G 7F 37
Coopersale Rd. E9 . . . . .5K 67
Coopers Cl. E1 . . . . .4J 85
RM10: Dag 6H 73
Coopers Ct. E3 . . . . .4B 86
(off Eric St.)
TW7: Isle 2K 113
(off Woodlands Rd.)
W3 . . . . .1J 97
(off Church Rd.)
Cooper's La. SE12 . . . . .2K 141
Coopers La. E10 . . . . .1D 68
E20 .5D 68
NW1 .2H 83
Coopers Lodge SE1 . . . . .6J 15
(off Tooley St.)
Cooper's M. BR3: Beck 2C 158
Cooper's Rd. SE1 . . . . .5F 103
Coopers Row EC3 . . . . . .2J 15 (7F 85)
Cooper St. E16 . . . . .5H 87
Coopers Wlk. E15 . . . . .5G 69
Coopers Yd. SE19 . . . . .6E 138
Cooper's Yd. N1 . . . . .7B 66
(off Upper St.)
Coote Gdns. RM8: Dag 3F 73
Coote Rd. DA7: Bex 1F 127
RM8: Dag 3F 73
Cope Ho. EC1 . . . . .2D 8
Copeland Dr. E14 . . . . .4C 104

Copeland Ho. SE11 . . . 2H 19
  SW17 . . . 4B 136
Copeland Rd. E17 . . . 6D 50
  SE15 . . . 2G 121
Copeman Cl. SE26 . . . 5J 139
Copenhagen Ct. SE8 . . . 4A 104
  (off Pell St.)
Copenhagen Gdns. W4 . . . 2K 97
Copenhagen Ho. N1 . . . 1K 83
  (off Barnsbury Est.)
Copenhagen Pl. E14 . . . 6B 86
  (not continuous)
Copenhagen St. N1 . . . 1J 83
Cope Pl. W8 . . . 3J 99
Copers Cope Rd. BR3: Beck . . . 7B 140
Cope St. SE16 . . . 4K 103
Copford Cl. IG8: Wfd G . . . 6H 37
Copford Wlk. N1 . . . 1C 84
  (off Popham St.)
Copgate Path SW16 . . . 6K 137
Copinger Wlk. HA8: Edg . . . 1H 43
Copland Av. HA0: Wemb . . . 5D 60
Copland Cl. HA0: Wemb . . . 5C 60
Copland M. HA0: Wemb . . . 6E 60
Copland Rd. HA0: Wemb . . . 6E 60
Copleston M. SE15 . . . 2F 121
Copleston Pas. SE5 . . . 2F 121
Copleston Rd. SE15 . . . 3F 121
Copley Cl. SE17 . . . 6C 102
  W7 . . . 4K 77
Copley Dene BR1: Broml . . . 1B 160
Copley Pk. SW16 . . . 6K 137
Copley Rd. HA7: Stan . . . 5H 27
Copley St. E1 . . . 5K 85
Coppard Gdns. KT9: Chess . . . 6C 162
Coppelia Rd. SE3 . . . 4H 123
Coppen Rd. RM8: Dag . . . 7F 55
Copperas St. SE8 . . . 6D 104
Copper Beech Cl. IG5: Ilf . . . 1E 52
Copperbeech Cl. NW3 . . . 5B 64
Copper Beeches TW7: Isle . . . 1H 113
Copper Box Arena . . . 6C 68
Copper Cl. N17 . . . 7C 34
  SE19 . . . 7F 139
Copper Ct. E5 . . . 2J 67
Copperdale Rd. UB3: Hayes . . . 2J 93
Copperfield Av. UB8: Hil . . . 5C 74
Copperfield Dr. N15 . . . 4F 49
Copperfield Ho. SE1 . . . 7K 15
  W1 . . . 5H 5
  (off Marylebone High St.)
  W11 . . . 1F 99
  (off St Ann's Rd.)
Copperfield M. E2 . . . 2G 85
  (off Claredale St.)
  N18 . . . 4K 33
Copperfield Rd. E3 . . . 4A 86
  SE28 . . . 6C 90
Copperfields BR3: Beck . . . 1E 158
  HA1: Harr . . . 7J 41
  TW16: Sun . . . 6H 129
Copperfields Ct. W3 . . . 2G 97
Copperfield St. SE1 . . . 6B 14 (2B 102)
Copperfield Way BR7: Chst . . . 6G 143
  HA5: Pinn . . . 4D 40
Coppergate Cl. BR1: Broml . . . 1K 159
Copper La. N16 . . . 4D 66
Copperlight Apts. SW18 . . . 5J 117
  (off Buckhold Rd.)
Coppermead Cl. NW2 . . . 3E 62
Copper M. W4 . . . 3J 97
Copper Mill Dr. TW7: Isle . . . 2K 113
Coppermill Hgts. N17 . . . 3H 49
  (off Daneland Wlk.)
Copper Mill La. SW17 . . . 4A 136
Coppermill La. E17 . . . 6J 49
Copper Row SE1 . . . 5J 15
Copperwood Pl. SE10 . . . 1E 122
The Copperworks N1 . . . 2J 83
  (off Railway St.)
Coppetts Cen. . . . 7J 31
Coppetts Cl. N12 . . . 7H 31

Coppetts Rd. N10 . . . 7J 31
Coppetts Wood & Glebelands
  Local Nature Reserve . . . 6J 31
The Coppice DA5: Bexl . . . 3K 145
  EN2: Enf . . . 4G 23
  EN5: New Bar . . . 6E 20
  (off Great Nth. Rd.)
  TW15: Ashf . . . 6D 128
  UB7: Yiew . . . 6A 74
Coppice Cl. BR3: Beck . . . 4D 158
  HA4: Ruis . . . 6F 39
  HA7: Stan . . . 6E 26
  SW20 . . . 3E 152
Coppice Dr. SW15 . . . 6D 116
Coppice Wlk. N20 . . . 3D 30
Coppice Way E18 . . . 4H 51
Coppies Gro. N11 . . . 4A 32
Copping Cl. CR0: C'don . . . 4E 168
The Coppins CR0: New Ad . . . 6D 170
  HA3: Hrw W . . . 6D 26
Coppock Cl. SW11 . . . 2C 118
Coppsfield KT8: W Mole . . . 3E 148
The Copse E4 . . . 1C 36
  N2 . . . 3D 46
Copse Av. BR4: W W'ck . . . 2D 170
Copse Cl. HA6: Nwood . . . 2E 38
  SE7 . . . 6K 105
Copse Glade KT6: Surb . . . 7D 150
COPSE HILL . . . 7C 134
Copse Hill SM2: Sutt . . . 7K 165
  SW20 . . . 1C 152
Copse Vw. CR2: Sels . . . 7K 169
Copsewood Cl. DA15: Sidc . . . 6J 125
Captain Ho. SW18 . . . 4J 117
Coptefield Dr. DA17: Belv . . . 3D 108
Copthall Av. EC2 . . . 7F 9 (6D 84)
  (not continuous)
Copthall Bldgs. EC2 . . . 7F 9
Copthall Cl. EC2 . . . 7E 8 (6D 84)
Copthall Dr. NW7 . . . 7H 29
Copthall Gdns. NW7 . . . 7H 29
  TW1: Twick . . . 1K 131
Copthall Rd. E. UB10: Ick . . . 2C 56
Copthall Rd. W. UB10: Ick . . . 2C 56
Copthorne Av. BR2: Broml . . . 2D 172
  SW12 . . . 7H 119
Copthorne Chase TW15: Ashf . . . 4B 128
Copthorne Ct. TW17: Shep . . . 6E 146
Copthorne M. UB3: Harl . . . 4G 93
Coptic St. WC1 . . . 6E 6 (5J 83)
Copt Pl. NW7 . . . 6B 30
Copwood Cl. N12 . . . 4G 31
Coral Apts. E16 . . . 7J 87
  (off Western Gateway)
Coral Cl. RM6: Chad H . . . 3D 54
Coral Ho. E1 . . . 4A 86
  (off Harford St.)
  NW10 . . . 3G 79
Coraline Cl. UB1: S'hall . . . 3D 76
Coraline Wlk. SE2 . . . 3C 108
Coral Mans. NW6 . . . 1J 81
  (off Kilburn High Rd.)
Coral Row SW11 . . . 3J 118
Coral St. SE1 . . . 7K 13 (2A 102)
Coram Ho. W4 . . . 5A 98
  (off Wood St.)
  WC1 . . . 3E 6
Coram Mans. WC1 . . . 4G 7
  (off Millman St.)
Coram St. WC1 . . . 4E 6 (4J 83)
Coran Cl. N9 . . . 7E 24
Corban Rd. TW3: Houn . . . 3E 112
Corbar Cl. EN4: Had W . . . 1G 21
Corbden Cl. SE15 . . . 1F 121
Corben M. SW8 . . . 2G 119
Corbet Cl. SM6: W'gton . . . 2E 166
Corbet Ct. EC3 . . . 1F 15 (6D 84)
Corbet Ho. N1 . . . 2A 84
  (off Barnsbury Est.)
  SE5 . . . 7C 102
  (off Wyndham Rd.)
Corbet Pl. E1 . . . 5J 9 (5F 85)

Corbett Av. KT8: E Mos . . . 6H 149
Corbett Ct. SE26 . . . 4B 140
Corbett Gro. N22 . . . 7D 32
Corbett Ho. SW10 . . . 6A 100
  (off Cathcart Rd.)
Corbett Rd. E11 . . . 6A 52
  E17 . . . 3E 50
Corbetts La. SE16 . . . 4J 103
  (not continuous)
Corbetts Pas. SE16 . . . 4J 103
  (off Corbetts La.)
Corbetts Wharf SE16 . . . 2H 103
  (off Bermondsey Wall E.)
Corbicum E11 . . . 7G 51
Corbidge Cl. SE8 . . . 6D 104
Corbiere Ct. SW19 . . . 6F 135
Corbiere Ho. N1 . . . 1D 84
  (off De Beauvoir Est.)
Corbin Ho. E3 . . . 3D 86
  (off Bromley High St.)
Corbins La. HA2: Harr . . . 3F 59
Corbould Cl. SM5: Cars . . . 6D 166
Corbridge N17 . . . 2C 34
Corbridge Cres. E2 . . . 2H 85
Corbylands Rd. DA15: Sidc . . . 7J 125
Corbyn St. N4 . . . 1J 65
Corby Cres. EN2: Enf . . . 4D 22
Corby Rd. NW10 . . . 2K 79
Corby Way E3 . . . 4C 86
Cordage Ho. E1 . . . 1H 103
  (off Cobblestone Sq.)
Cordelia Cl. SE24 . . . 4B 120
Cordelia Gdns. TW19: Stanw . . . 7A 110
Cordelia Ho. N1 . . . 2E 84
  (off Arden Est.)
Cordelia Rd. TW19: Stanw . . . 7A 110
Cordelia St. E14 . . . 6D 86
Cordell Ho. N15 . . . 5F 49
  (off Newton Rd.)
Cordingley Rd. HA4: Ruis . . . 2F 57
Cording St. E14 . . . 5D 86
Cordwainer Ho. E8 . . . 1H 85
Cordwainers Ct. E9 . . . 7J 67
  (off St Thomas's Sq.)
Cordwainers Wlk. E13 . . . 2J 87
Cord Way E14 . . . 3C 104
Cordwell Rd. SE13 . . . 5G 123
Corefield Cl. N11 . . . 2K 31
Corelli Ct. SE1 . . . 4H 103
  SW5 . . . 4J 99
  (off W. Cromwell Rd.)
Corelli Rd. SE3 . . . 2C 124
Corfe Av. HA2: Harr . . . 4E 58
Corfe Cl. TW4: Houn . . . 1C 130
  UB4: Yead . . . 6A 76
Corfe Ho. SW8 . . . 7K 101
  (off Dorset Rd.)
Corfe Twr. W3 . . . 2H 97
Corfield Rd. N21 . . . 5E 22
Corfield St. E2 . . . 3H 85
Corfton Lodge W5 . . . 5E 78
Corfton Rd. W5 . . . 6E 78
Coriander Av. E14 . . . 6E 87
Coriander Ct. SE1 . . . 6K 15
  (off Gainsford St.)
Cories Cl. RM8: Dag . . . 2D 72
Corinium Cl. HA9: Wemb . . . 4F 61
Corinne Rd. N19 . . . 4G 65
Corinthian Manorway DA8: Erith . . . 4K 109
Corinthian Rd. DA8: Erith . . . 4K 109
Corinthian Way TW19: Stanw . . . 7A 110
Corkers Path IG1: Ilf . . . 2G 71
Cork Ho. SW19 . . . 4K 135
Cork Rd. KT6: Surb . . . 7D 150
Corkscrew Hill BR4: W W'ck . . . 2E 170
Cork Sq. E1 . . . 1H 103
Cork St. M. W1 . . . 3A 12 (7G 83)
Cork St. M. W1 . . . 3A 12
Cork Tree Ho. SE27 . . . 5B 138
  (off Lakeview Rd.)
Cork Tree Retail Pk. . . . 5F 35
Cork Tree Way E4 . . . 5F 35

Corlett St. NW1 . . . 5C 4 (5C 82)
Cormont Rd. SE5 . . . 1B 120
Cormorant Cl. E17 . . . 7F 35
Cormorant Ct. SE8 . . . 6B 104
  (off Pilot Cl.)
Cormorant Ho. EN3: Pond E . . . 5E 24
Cormorant Lodge E1 . . . 1G 103
  (off Thomas More St.)
Cormorant Pl. SM1: Sutt . . . 5H 165
Cormorant Rd. E7 . . . 5H 69
Cornbury Ho. SE8 . . . 6B 104
  (off Evelyn St.)
Cornbury Rd. HA8: Edg . . . 7J 27
Cornel Ho. DA15: Sidc . . . 3A 144
Cornelia Dr. UB4: Yead . . . 4A 76
Cornelia Ho. TW1: Twick . . . 6D 114
  (off Denton Rd.)
Cornelia St. N7 . . . 6K 65
Cornell Bldg. E1 . . . 6G 85
  (off Coke St.)
Cornell Cl. DA14: Sidc . . . 6E 144
Cornell Ct. EN3: Enf H . . . 3F 25
Cornell Gdns. EN4: E Barn . . . 5K 21
Cornell Ho. HA2: Harr . . . 3D 58
Cornell Sq. SW8 . . . 1H 119
The Corner W5 . . . 1E 96
Corner Ct. E2 . . . 4H 85
  (off Three Colts La.)
Cornercroft SM3: Cheam . . . 5F 165
  (off Wickham Av.)
Corner Fielde SW2 . . . 1K 137
Corner Grn. SE3 . . . 2J 123
Corner Ho. NW6 . . . 2K 81
  (off Oxford Rd.)
The Corner HOUSE Arts Cen. . . . 1F 163
Corner Ho. St. WC2 . . . 4E 12
Corner Mead NW9 . . . 7G 29
Cornerside TW15: Ashf . . . 7E 128
Corney Reach Way W4 . . . 7A 98
Corney Rd. W4 . . . 6A 98
Cornfield Cl. UB8: Uxb . . . 2A 74
Cornflower La. CR0: C'don . . . 1K 169
Cornflower Ter. SE22 . . . 6H 121
Cornford Cl. BR2: Broml . . . 5J 159
Cornford Gro. SW12 . . . 2F 137
Cornhill EC3 . . . 1F 15 (6D 84)
Cornick Ho. SE16 . . . 3H 103
  (off Slippers Pl.)
Cornish Ct. N9 . . . 7C 24
Cornish Gro. SE20 . . . 1H 157
Cornish Ho. SE17 . . . 6B 102
  (off Brandon Est.)
  TW8: Bford . . . 5F 97
Corn Mill Dr. BR6: Orp . . . 7K 161
Cornmill Ho. RM7: Rom . . . 6J 55
  SE8 . . . 5C 104
  (off Wharf St.)
Cornmill La. SE13 . . . 3E 122
Cornshaw Rd. RM8: Dag . . . 1D 72
Cornthwaite Rd. E5 . . . 3J 67
Cornwall Av. DA16: Well . . . 3J 125
  E2 . . . 3J 85
  KT10: Clay . . . 7A 162
  N3 . . . 7D 30
  N22 . . . 1J 47
  UB1: S'hall . . . 5D 76
Cornwall Cl. IG11: Bark . . . 6K 71
Cornwall Cl. HA5: Hat E . . . 1D 40
  W7 . . . 4K 77
  (off Copley Cl.)
Cornwall Cres. W11 . . . 6G 81
Cornwall Dr. BR5: St P . . . 7C 144
Cornwall Gdns. NW10 . . . 6D 62
  SE25 . . . 4F 157
  SW7 . . . 3K 99
Cornwall Gdns. Wlk. SW7 . . . 3K 99
Cornwall Gro. W4 . . . 5A 98
Cornwall Ho. SW7 . . . 3K 99
  (off Cornwall Gdns.)
Cornwallis Av. N9 . . . 2C 34
  SE9 . . . 2H 143

Cornwallis Ct. *SW8* *1J* **119**
(off Lansdowne Grn.)
Cornwallis Gro. N9 . . . .*2C* **34**
Cornwallis Ho. *SE16* *2H* **103**
(off Cherry Gdn. St.)
W12 . . . .*7D* **80**
(off India Way)
Cornwallis Rd. E17 . . . .*4K* **49**
N9 . . . .*2C* **34**
N19 . . . .*2J* **65**
RM9: Dag *4D* **72**
SE18 . . . .*3G* **107**
(Gunnery Ter.)
SE18 . . . .*3F* **107**
(Warren La.)
Cornwallis Sq. N19 . . . .*2J* **65**
Cornwallis Wlk. SE9 . . . .*3D* **124**
Cornwall Mans. *SW10* *7A* **100**
(off Cremorne Rd.)
W8 . . . .*2K* **99**
(off Kensington Ct.)
W14 . . . .*3F* **99**
(off Blythe Rd.)
Cornwall M. Sth. SW7 . . . .*3A* **100**
Cornwall M. W. SW7 . . . .*3K* **99**
Cornwall Pl. E4 . . . .*4J* **25**
Cornwall Rd. CRO: C'don *2B* **168**
HA1: Harr *6G* **41**
HA4: Ruis *3H* **57**
HA5: Hat E *1D* **40**
N4 . . . .*7A* **48**
N15 . . . .*5D* **48**
N18 . . . .*5B* **34**
SE1 . . . .*4J* **13** (1A **102**)
SM2: Sutt *7H* **165**
TW1: Twick *7A* **114**
UB8: Uxb *6A* **56**
Cornwall Sq. SE11 . . . .*5K* **19**
Cornwall St. E1 . . . .*7H* **85**
Cornwall Ter. NW1 . . . . .*4F* **5** (4D **82**)
Cornwall Ter. M. NW1 . . . .*4F* **5**
Corn Way E11 . . . .*3F* **69**
Cornwell Gdns. E10 . . . .*7C* **50**
Cornwood Cl. N2 . . . .*5B* **46**
Cornwood Dr. E1 . . . .*6J* **85**
Cornworthy Rd. RM8: Dag *5C* **72**
Corona Bldg. *E14* *1E* **104**
(off Blackwall Way)
Corona Rd. SE12 . . . .*7J* **123**
Coronation Av. N16 . . . .*4F* **67**
Coronation Cl. DA5: Bexl *6D* **126**
IG6: Ilf *4G* **53**
Coronation Ct. DA8: Erith *7K* **109**
E15 . . . .*6H* **69**
KT1: King T *4E* **150**
(off Surbiton Rd.)
W10 . . . .*5E* **80**
(off Brewster Gdns.)
Coronation Rd. E13 . . . .*3A* **88**
NW10 . . . .*3G* **79**
UB3: Harl *4H* **93**
Coronation Vs. NW10 . . . .*4H* **79**
Coronation Wlk. TW2: Whitt *1E* **130**
Coroner's Court
City of London *2E* **14** (7D **84**)
North London *4C* **20**
Poplar *7D* **86**
(off Poplar High St.)
St Pancras *1H* **83**
South London *3D* **168**
(off Barclay Rd.)
Southwark *2D* **102**
West London *1A* **118**
Westminster *3D* **18** (4H **101**)
Coronet Pde. HA0: Wemb *6E* **60**
Coronet St. N1 . . . .*2G* **9** (3E **84**)
Corporate Dr. TW13: Felt *3K* **129**
Corporate Ho. HA3: Hrw W *1H* **41**
Corporation Av.
TW4: Houn *4C* **112**
Corporation Row EC1 . .*3K* **7** (4A **84**)
Corporation St. E15 . . . .*2G* **87**
N7 . . . .*5J* **65**

Corrance Rd. SW2 . . . .*4J* **119**
Corri Av. N14 . . . .*4C* **32**
Corrib Cl. N13 . . . .*3E* **32**
Corrib Dr. SM1: Sutt *5C* **166**
Corrigan Cl. NW4 . . . .*3E* **44**
Corringham Ct. NW11 . . . .*7J* **45**
Corringham Ho. *E1* *6K* **85**
(off Pitsea St.)
Corringham Rd. HA9: Wemb *2G* **61**
NW11 . . . .*7J* **45**
Corringway NW11 . . . .*7K* **45**
W5 . . . .*4G* **79**
Corris Grn. NW9 . . . .*5A* **44**
Corry Dr. SW9 . . . .*4B* **120**
Corry Ho. *E14* *7D* **86**
(off Wade's Pl.)
Corsair Cl. TW19: Stanw *7A* **110**
Corsair Ho. *E16* *2A* **106**
(off Starboard Way)
Corsair Rd. TW19: Stanw *7A* **110**
Corscombe Cl. KT2: King T *5J* **133**
Corsehill St. SW16 . . . .*6G* **137**
Corsellis Sq. *TW1: Isle* *4B* **114**
(off Varley Dr.)
Corsham St. N1 . . . .*2F* **9** (3D **84**)
Corsica St. N5 . . . .*6B* **66**
Corsley Way E9 . . . .*6B* **68**
Cortayne Ct. TW2: Twick *2J* **131**
Cortayne Rd. SW6 . . . .*2H* **117**
Cortis Rd. SW15 . . . .*6D* **116**
Cortis Ter. SW15 . . . .*6D* **116**
Cortland Cl. IG8: Wfd G *1A* **52**
Corunna Rd. SW8 . . . .*1G* **119**
Corunna Ter. SW8 . . . .*1G* **119**
Corvette Sq. SE10 . . . .*6F* **105**
Corwell Gdns. UB8: Hil *6E* **74**
Corwell La. UB8: Hil *6E* **74**
Coryton Path *W9* *4H* **81**
(off Ashmore Rd.)
Cosbycote Av. SE24 . . . .*5C* **120**
Cosdach Av. SM6: W'gton *7H* **167**
Cosedge Cres. CRO: Wadd *5A* **168**
Cosgrove Cl. N21 . . . .*2H* **33**
UB4: Yead *4B* **76**
Cosgrove Ho. *E2* *1G* **85**
(off Whiston Rd.)
HA0: Wemb *1E* **78**
(off Hatton Rd.)
Cosmo Pl. WC1 . . . .*5F* **7** (5J **83**)
Cosmopolitan Ct. EN1: Enf *5B* **24**
Cosmopolitan Way
TW6: H'row A *3D* **110**
Cosmur Cl. W12 . . . .*3B* **98**
Cossall Wlk. SE15 . . . .*2H* **121**
Cossar M. SW2 . . . .*5A* **120**
Cosser St. SE1 . . . .*1J* **19** (3A **102**)
Costa St. SE15 . . . .*2G* **121**
Costemonger Bldg. *SE16* *3F* **103**
(off Arts La.)
Coster Av. N4 . . . .*1C* **66**
Costons Av. UB6: G'frd *3H* **77**
Costons La. UB6: G'frd *3H* **77**
(not continuous)
Coston Wlk. SE4 . . . .*4K* **121**
Cosway Mans. *NW1* *5D* **4**
(off Shroton St.)
Cosway St. NW1 . . . .*5D* **4** (5C **82**)
Cotall St. E14 . . . .*5C* **86**
Coteford Cl. HA5: Eastc *5J* **39**
Coteford St. SW17 . . . .*4D* **136**
Cotelands CRO: C'don *3E* **168**
Cotesbach Rd. E5 . . . .*3J* **67**
Cotes Ho. *NW8* *4C* **4**
(off Broadley St.)
Cotesmore Gdns. RM8: Dag *4C* **72**
Cotford Rd. CR7: Thor H *4C* **156**
Cotham St. SE17 . . . .*4C* **102**
Cotherstone Ct. *E2* *4H* **85**
(off Three Colts La.)
Cotherstone Rd. SW2 . . . .*1K* **137**
Cotleigh Av. DA5: Bexl *2D* **144**
Cotleigh Rd. NW6 . . . .*7J* **63**
RM7: Rom *6K* **55**

Cotman Cl. NW11 . . . .*6A* **46**
SW15 . . . .*6F* **117**
Cotman Gdns. HA8: Edg *2G* **43**
Cotman Ho. *NW8* *2C* **82**
(off Townshend Est.)
UB5: N'olt *2B* **76**
(off Academy Gdns.)
Cotman M. RM8: Dag *5C* **72**
(off Highgrove Rd.)
Cotmans Cl. UB3: Hayes *1J* **93**
Coton Dr. UB10: Ick *3E* **56**
Coton Rd. DA16: Well *3A* **126**
Cotsford Av. KT3: N Mald *5J* **151**
Cotswold Cl. DA7: Bex *2K* **127**
KT2: King T *6J* **133**
KT10: Hin W *2A* **162**
N11 . . . .*4K* **31**
Cotswold Ct. EC1 . . . .*3C* **8**
UB6: G'frd *2A* **77**
(off Hodder Dr.)
Cotswold Gdns. E6 . . . .*3B* **88**
IG2: Ilf *7H* **53**
NW2 . . . .*2F* **63**
Cotswold Ga. NW2 . . . .*1G* **63**
Cotswold M. SW11 . . . .*1B* **118**
Cotswold Ri. BR6: St M Cry *6K* **161**
Cotswold Rd. TW12: Hamp *5E* **130**
Cotswold St. SE27 . . . .*4B* **138**
Cotswold Way EN2: Enf *3E* **22**
KT4: Wor Pk *2E* **164**
Cottage Av. BR2: Broml *1C* **172**
Cottage Cl. *E1* *4J* **85**
(off Mile End Rd.)
HA2: Harr *2H* **59**
HA4: Ruis *1F* **57**
Cottage Fld. Cl. DA14: Sidc *1C* **144**
Cottage Grn. SE5 . . . .*7D* **102**
Cottage Gro. KT6: Surb *6D* **150**
SW9 . . . .*3J* **119**
Cottage Pl. SW3 . . . .*1C* **16** (3C **100**)
Cottage Rd. KT19: Ewe *7K* **163**
N7 . . . .*5K* **65**
(not continuous)
The Cottages UB10: Ick *2A* **56**
Cottage St. E14 . . . .*7D* **86**
Cottage Wlk. N16 . . . .*3F* **67**
Cotton Dr. NW9 . . . .*3B* **44**
SW20 . . . .*7D* **134**
Cottenham Pde. SW20 . . . .*2D* **152**
COTTENHAM PARK *1D* **152**
Cottenham Pk. Rd. SW20 . . . .*1C* **152**
(not continuous)
Cottenham Pl. SW20 . . . .*7D* **134**
Cottenham Rd. E17 . . . .*4B* **50**
Cotterill Rd. KT6: Surb *2E* **162**
Cottesbrook St. SE14 . . . .*7A* **104**
Cottesloe Ho. NW8 . . . .*3C* **4**
Cottesloe M. *SE1* *1K* **19**
(off Emery St.)
Cottesmore Av. IG5: Ilf *2E* **52**
Cottesmore Ct. *W8* *3K* **99**
(off Stanford Rd.)
Cottesmore Gdns. W8 . . . .*3K* **99**
Cottesmore Ho. UB10: Ick *2E* **56**
Cottimore Av. KT12: Walt T *7K* **147**
Cottimore Cres. KT12: Walt T *7K* **147**
Cottimore La. KT12: Walt T *7K* **147**
Cottimore Ter. KT12: Walt T *7K* **147**
Cottingham Chase HA4: Ruis *3J* **57**
Cottingham Rd. SE20 . . . .*7H* **139**
SW8 . . . .*7K* **101**
Cottington Rd. TW13: Hanw *4B* **130**
Cottington St. SE11 . . . . .*5K* **19** (5A **102**)
Cottle Way *SE16* *2H* **103**
(off Paradise St.)
Cotton Apts. *E1* *5K* **85**
(off Killick Way)
Cotton Av. W3 . . . .*6K* **79**
Cotton Cl. CR4: Mitc *3C* **154**
E11 . . . .*2G* **69**
RM9: Dag *7C* **72**
Cottongrass Cl. CRO: C'don *1K* **169**

Cottonham Cl. N12 . . . .*5G* **31**
Cotton Hill BR1: Broml *4E* **140**
Cotton Ho. SW2 . . . .*7J* **119**
Cotton Row SW11 . . . .*3A* **118**
Cottons App. RM7: Rom *5K* **55**
Cottons Cen.
SE1 . . . .*4G* **15** (1E **102**)
Cottons Ct. RM7: Rom *5K* **55**
Cotton's Gdns. E2 . . . .*1H* **9** (3E **84**)
Cottons La. SE1 . . . .*4F* **15** (1D **102**)
Cotton St. E14 . . . .*7E* **86**
Cotton Way SM6: W'gton *2E* **166**
Cottonworks Ho. N7 . . . .*3K* **65**
(off Seven Sisters Rd.)
Cottrell Ct. SE10 . . . .*4H* **105**
(off Hop St.)
Cottrill Gdns. E8 . . . .*6H* **67**
Cotts Cl. W7 . . . .*5K* **77**
Couchmore Av. IG5: Ilf *2D* **52**
Coulgate St. SE4 . . . .*3A* **122**
Coulson Cl. RM8: Dag *1C* **72**
Coulson St. SW3 . . . .*5E* **16** (5D **100**)
Coulter Cl. UB4: Yead *4C* **76**
Coulter Rd. W6 . . . .*3D* **98**
Coulthurst Ct. SW16 . . . .*7J* **137**
(off Heybridge Av.)
Councillor St. SE5 . . . .*7C* **102**
Counter Cl. SE1 . . . .*5E* **14**
(off Borough High St.)
Counter Ho. E1 . . . .*7G* **85**
Counters Ct. W14 . . . .*3G* **99**
(off Holland Rd.)
Counter St. SE1 . . . .*5G* **15** (1E **102**)
Countess Rd. NW5 . . . .*5G* **65**
Countisbury Av. EN1: Enf *7A* **24**
Country Way TW13: Hanw *6K* **129**
County Court
Brentford *6D* **96**
Bromley *1J* **159**
Central London *4J* **5**
Clerkenwell & Shoreditch
. . . .*3C* **8** (4C **84**)
Croydon *2D* **168**
Edmonton *6B* **34**
Kingston upon Thames *2D* **150**
Uxbridge *5H* **75**
Wandsworth *5G* **117**
West London *5F* **99**
(off Talgarth Rd.)
Willesden *2B* **80**
County Gdns. TW7: Isle *4H* **113**
County Ga. EN5: New Bar *6E* **20**
SE9 . . . .*3G* **143**
The County Ground
Beckenham *6C* **140**
County Gro. SE5 . . . .*1C* **120**
County Hall Apts. SE1 . . . .*6G* **13**
County Hall (Former) *6G* **13**
(off Westminster Bri. Rd.)
County Ho. BR3: Beck *1A* **158**
SW9 . . . .*1A* **120**
(off Brixton Rd.)
County Pde. TW8: Bford *7D* **96**
County Rd. CR7: Thor H *2B* **156**
E6 . . . .*5F* **89**
County Sq. SE1 . . . .*3C* **102**
Coupland Pl. SE18 . . . .*5G* **107**
Courage Stadium *5K* **159**
Courcy Rd. N8 . . . .*3A* **48**
Courier Rd. RM9: Dag *4J* **91**
Courland Gro. SW8 . . . .*1H* **119**
Courland St. SW8 . . . .*1H* **119**
The Course SE9 . . . .*3E* **142**
The Court HA4: Ruis *4C* **58**
Court Annexe *7D* **14** (2C **102**)
Courtauld Cl. SE28 . . . .*1A* **108**
Courtauld Gallery *2G* **13**
Courtauld Ho. *E2* *1G* **85**
(off Goldsmiths Row)
The Courtauld Institute of Art *7K* **83**
(off Strand)
Courtauld Rd. N19 . . . .*1J* **65**
Court Av. DA17: Belv *5F* **109**

Court Cl. HA3: Kenton 3E 42
NW8 . . . . .7B 64
(off Boydell Ct.)
SM6: W'gton 7H 167
TW2: Twick 3F 131
Court Cl. Av. TW2: Twick 3F 131
Court Cres. KT9: Chess 5D 162
Court Downs Rd. BR3: Beck 2D 158
Court Dr. CRO: Wadd 4K 167
HA7: Stan .4K 27
SM1: Sutt .4C 166
UB10: Hil 1B 74
Courtenay Av. HA3: Hrw W 7B 26
N6 . . . . .7C 46
SM2: Sutt .7J 165
Courtenay Dr. BR3: Beck 2F 159
Courtenay Gdns. HA3: Hrw W 2G 41
Courtenay H. CRO: C'don 7C 156
(off Oakfield Rd.)
Courtenay M. E17 . . . . .5A 50
Courtenay Pl. E17 . . . . .5A 50
Courtenay Rd. E11 . . . . .3H 69
E17 . . . . .4K 49
HA9: Wemb 3D 60
KT4: Wor Pk 3E 164
SE20 . . . . .6K 139
Courtenay Sq. SE11 . . . . . .6J 19 (5A 102)
Courtenay St. SE11 . . . . . .5J 19 (5A 102)
Courtens M. HA7: Stan 7H 27
Court Farm Av. KT19: Ewe 5K 163
Court Farm La. UB5: N'olt 7E 58
Court Farm Rd. SE9 . . . . .2B 142
UB5: N'olt .7E 58
Courtfield W5 . . . . .5C 78
Courtfield Av. HA1: Harr 5K 41
Courtfield Cres. HA1: Harr 5K 41
Courtfield Gdns. HA4: Ruis 2H 57
SW5 . . . . .4K 99
W13 . . . . .6A 78
Courtfield Ho. EC1 . . . . .5J 7
(off Baldwins Gdns.)
Courtfield M. SW5 . . . . .4A 100
Courtfield Ri. BR4: W W'ck 3F 171
Courtfield Rd. SW7 . . . . .4A 100
TW15: Ashf 6D 128
Court Gdns. N1 . . . . .6A 66
N7 . . . . .6A 66
Courtgate Cl. NW7 . . . . .6G 29
Courthill Rd. SE13 . . . . .4E 122
Courthope Ho. SE16 . . . . .3J 103
(off Lower Rd.)
SW8 . . . . .7J 101
(off Hartington Rd.)
Courthope Rd. NW3 . . . . .4D 64
SW19 . . . . .5G 135
UB6: G'frd .2H 77
Courthope Vs. SW19 . . . . .7G 135
The Courthouse SW1 . . . . .2D 18
(off Horseferry Rd.)
Courthouse Gdns. N3 . . . . .6D 30
Courthouse La. N16 . . . . .4F 67
Courthouse Rd. N12 . . . . .6E 30
Courthouse Way SE18 . . . . .5K 117
Courtland Av. E4 . . . . .2C 36
IG1: Ilf 2D 70
NW7 . . . . .3E 28
SW16 . . . . .7K 137
Courtland Gro. SE28 . . . . .6D 90
Courtland Ho. SE20 . . . . .1G 157
Courtland Rd. E6 . . . . .1C 88
Courtlands KT12: Walt T 7J 147
TW10: Rich 5G 115
Courtlands Av. BR2: Hayes 1G 171
SE12 . . . . .5K 123
TW9: Kew .2H 115
TW12: Hamp 6D 130
Courtlands Cl. HA4: Ruis 7H 39
Courtlands Dr. KT19: Ewe 6A 164
Courtlands Rd. KT5: Surb 7G 151
Court La. SE21 . . . . .6E 120
Court La. Gdns. SE21 . . . . .7E 120
Courtleet Dr. DA8: Erith 1H 127
Courtleigh NW11 . . . . .5H 45

Courtleigh Gdns. NW11 . . . . .4G 45
Court Lodge DA17: Belv 5G 109
SW1 . . . . .4G 17
(off Sloane Sq.)
Courtman Rd. N17 . . . . .7H 33
Court Mead UB5: N'olt 3D 76
Courtmead Cl. SE24 . . . . .6C 120
Court M. SE13 . . . . .6G 123
Courtnell St. W2 . . . . .6J 81
Courtney Cl. SE19 . . . . .6E 138
Courtney Ct. N7 . . . . .5A 66
Courtney Cres. SM5: Cars 7D 166
Courtney Ho. NW4 . . . . .3E 44
(off Mulberry Cl.)
W14 . . . . .3G 99
(off Russell Rd.)
Courtney Pl. CRO: Wadd 3A 168
Courtney Rd. CRO: Wadd 3A 168
N7 . . . . .5A 66
SW19 . . . . .7C 136
TW6: H'row A 3C 110
Courtney Way
TW6: H'row A 2C 110
Court Pde. HA0: Wemb 3B 60
Courtrai Rd. SE23 . . . . .6A 122
Court Rd. SE9 . . . . .6D 124
SE25 . . . . .2F 157
UB2: S'hall 4D 94
UB10: Ick 5D 56
Ct. Royal SW15 . . . . .5G 117
Courtside N8 . . . . .6H 47
SE26 . . . . .3H 139
Court St. BR1: Broml 2J 159
E1 . . . . .5H 85
Courtville Ho. W10 . . . . .3G 81
(off Third Av.)
Court Way NW9 . . . . .4A 44
TW2: Twick 7K 113
W3 . . . . .5J 79
Courtway IG6: Ilf 3G 53
IG8: Wfd G .5F 37
The Courtyard BR2: Kes 6C 172
E2 . . . . .1K 9
(off Ezra St.)
EC3 . . . . .1F 15
(within Royal Exchange)
N1 . . . . .7K 65
NW1 . . . . .7E 64
SE14 . . . . .1K 121
(off Besson St.)
SW3 . . . . .7B 16
(off Trident Pl.)
Courtyard Apts. E1 . . . . .3K 9
(off Sclater St.)
Courtyard Ho. SW6 . . . . .2A 118
(off Lensbury Av.)
Courtyard M. BR5: St P 7A 144
Courtyard Theatre 2G 9 (3E 84)
Cousin La. EC4 . . . . .3E 14 (7D 84)
Cousins Cl. UB7: Yiew 7A 74
Couthurst Rd. SE3 . . . . .6K 105
Coutts Av. KT9: Chess 5E 162
Coutt's Cres. NW5 . . . . .3E 64
Couzens Ho. E3 . . . . .5B 86
(off Weatherley Cl.)
Coval Gdns. SW14 . . . . .4H 115
Coval La. SW14 . . . . .4H 115
Coval Pas. SW14 . . . . .4J 115
Coval Rd. SW14 . . . . .4H 115
Coveleees Wall E6 . . . . .6E 88
Covell Ct. EN2: Enf 1E 22
(off The Ridgeway)
SE8 . . . . .7C 104
COVENT GARDEN 2F 13 (7J 83)
Covent Gdn. WC2 . . . . .2F 13 (7J 83)
Covent Garden Piazza WC2 . . . . .2F 13
Coventry Cl. E6 . . . . .6D 88
NW6 . . . . .2J 81
Coventry Hall SW16 . . . . .5J 137

Coventry Rd. E1 . . . . .4H 85
E2 . . . . .4H 85
IG1: Ilf 2F 71
SE25 . . . . .4G 157
Coventry St. W1 . . . . . . .3C 12 (7H 83)
Coverack Cl. CRO: C'don 7A 158
N14 . . . . .6B 22
Coverdale Cl. HA7: Stan 5G 27
Coverdale Gdns. CRO: C'don 3F 169
Coverdale Rd. N11 . . . . .6K 31
NW2 . . . . .7F 63
W12 . . . . .2D 98
The Coverdales IG11: Bark 2H 89
Coverham Ho. SE4 . . . . .4K 121
(off Billingford Cl.)
Coverley Cl. E1 . . . . .5G 85
Coverley Point SE11 . . . . .4G 19
The Covert BR6: Pet W 6J 161
HA6: Nwood 1E 38
SE19 . . . . .7F 139
(off Fox Hill)
Coverton Rd. SW17 . . . . .5C 136
Covert Way EN4: Had W 2F 21
Covet Wood Cl. BR5: St M Cry 6K 161
Covey Cl. SW19 . . . . .2K 153
Covey Rd. KT4: Wor Pk 2E 164
Covington Gdns. SW16 . . . . .7B 138
Covington Way SW16 . . . . .6K 137
(not continuous)
Cowan Cl. E6 . . . . .5C 88
Cowbridge La. IG11: Bark 7F 71
Cowbridge Rd. HA3: Kenton 4F 43
Cowcross St. EC1 . . . . .5A 8 (5B 84)
Cowdenbeath Path N1 . . . . .1K 83
Cowden Rd. BR6: Orp 7K 161
Cowden St. SE6 . . . . .4C 140
Cowdray Rd. UB10: Hil 1E 74
Cowdrey Cl. EN1: Enf 2K 23
Cowdrey M. SE6 . . . . .4C 140
Cowdrey Rd. SW19 . . . . .5K 135
Cowen Av. HA2: Harr 2H 59
Cowgate Rd. UB6: G'frd 3H 77
Cowick Rd. SW17 . . . . .4D 136
Cowings Mead UB5: N'olt 6C 58
Cowland Av. EN3: Pond E 4D 24
Cow La. UB6: G'frd 2H 77
Cow Leaze E6 . . . . .6E 88
Cowleaze Rd. KT2: King T 1E 150
COWLEY 4A 74
Cowley La. E11 . . . . .3G 69
COWLEY PEACHEY 6A 74
Cowley Pl. NW4 . . . . .5E 44
Cowley Rd. E11 . . . . .5K 51
IG1: Ilf 7D 52
SW9 . . . . .1A 120
(not continuous)
SW14 . . . . .3A 116
W3 . . . . .1B 98
Cowley St. SW1 . . . . . . .1E 18 (3J 101)
Cowling Cl. W11 . . . . .1G 99
Cowper Av. E6 . . . . .7C 70
SM1: Sutt .4B 166
Cowper Cl. BR2: Broml 4B 160
DA16: Well .5A 126
Cowper Gdns. N14 . . . . .6A 22
SM6: W'gton 6G 167
Cowper Ho. SE17 . . . . .5C 102
(off Browning St.)
SW1 . . . . .6C 18
(off Aylesford St.)
Cowper Rd. BR2: Broml 4B 160
DA17: Belv 4G 109
KT2: King T 5F 133
N14 . . . . .1A 32
N16 . . . . .5E 66
N18 . . . . .5B 34
SW19 . . . . .6A 136
W3 . . . . .1K 97
W7 . . . . .7K 77
Cowper's Ct. EC3 . . . . .1F 15
(off Birchin La.)
Cowper St. EC2 . . . . .3F 9 (4D 84)
Cowper Ter. W10 . . . . .5F 81

Cowslip Cl. UB10: Uxb 7A 56
Cowslip Rd. E18 . . . . .2K 51
Cowthorpe Rd. SW8 . . . . .1H 119
Cox Ct. EN4: E Barn 4H 21
Coxe Pl. HA3: W'stone 4A 42
Cox Ho. W6 .6G 99
(off Field Rd.)
Cox La. KT9: Chess 4F 163
KT19: Ewe 5H 163
(not continuous)
Coxmount Rd. SE7 . . . . .5B 106
Coxs Av. TW17: Shep 3G 147
Coxson Way SE1 . . . . . . .7J 15 (2F 103)
Cox's Wlk. SE21 . . . . .1G 139
Coxwell Blvd. NW9 . . . . .7G 29
Coxwell Rd. SE18 . . . . .5H 107
SE19 . . . . .7E 138
Coxwold Path KT9: Chess 7E 162
Coyle Dr. UB10: Ick 2E 56
Crabbs Cft. Cl. BR6: Farnb 5G 173
Crab Hill BR3: Beck 7F 141
Crabtree Av. HA0: Wemb 2E 78
RM6: Chad H 4D 54
Crabtree Cl. E2 . . . . .2F 85
Crabtree Ct. EN5: New Bar 4E 20
Crabtree Hall SW6 . . . . .7E 98
(off Crabtree La.)
Crabtree La. SW6 . . . . .7E 98
(not continuous)
Crabtree Manorway Nth.
DA17: Belv, Erith 2J 109
Crabtree Manorway Sth.
DA17: Belv 3J 109
Crabtree Pl. W1 . . . . .6C 6 (5G 83)
Crabtree Wlk.
CRO: C'don 1G 169
Crace St. NW1 . . . . .1C 6 (3H 83)
Craddock Rd. EN1: Enf 3A 24
Craddock St. NW5 . . . . .6E 64
Cradford Ho. Nth. E2 . . . . .3K 85
Cradford Ho. Sth. E2 . . . . .3K 85
Cradley Rd. SE9 . . . . .1H 143
Crafts Council & Gallery 2A 84
Cragie Ho. SE1 . . . . .4F 103
(off Balaclava Rd.)
Craig Dr. UB8: Hil 6D 74
Craigen Av. CRO: C'don 1H 169
Craigen Gdns. IG3: Ilf 4J 71
Craigerne Rd. SE3 . . . . .7K 105
Craig Gdns. E18 . . . . .2H 51
Craigholm SE18 . . . . .2E 124
Craig Ho. E17 . . . . .4C 50
(off High St.)
Craigmore Ct. HA6: Nwood 1G 39
Craigmuir Pk. HA0: Wemb 1F 79
Craignair Rd. SW2 . . . . .7A 120
Craignish Av. SW16 . . . . .2K 155
Craig Pk. Rd. N18 . . . . .4C 34
Craig Rd. TW10: Ham 4C 132
Craig's Ct. SW1 . . . . .4E 12 (1J 101)
Craigton Rd. SE9 . . . . .4D 124
Craigweil Cl. HA7: Stan 5J 27
Craigweil Dr. HA7: Stan 5J 27
Craigwell Av. TW13: Felt 3J 129
Craik Ct. NW6 . . . . .2H 81
(off Carlton Vale)
Crail Row SE17 . . . . .4D 102
Crales Ho. SE18 . . . . .3C 106
Cramer St. W1 . . . . .6H 5 (5E 82)
Crammond Cl. W6 . . . . .6G 99
Cramond Ct. TW14: Bedf 1G 129
Cramonde Ct. DA16: Well 2A 126
Crampton Ho. SW8 . . . . .1G 119
Crampton Rd. SE20 . . . . .6J 139
Crampton St. SE17 . . . . .4C 102
Cranberry Cl. NW7 . . . . .6G 29
UB5: N'olt .2B 76
Cranberry Ent. Pk. N17 . . . . .7A 34
(off White Hart La.)
Cranberry La. E16 . . . . .4G 87
Cranbourn Cl. KT6: Surb 3G 163
UB2: S'hall 4E 94
Cranborne Rd. IG11: Bark 1H 89

Cranborne Waye UB4: Yead 6K 75
   (not continuous)
Cranbourn All. WC2 . . . . .2D 12
   (off Cranbourn St.)
Cranbourne WC1 . . . . .1G 83
   (off Agar Gro.)
Cranbourne Av. E11 . . . . .4K 51
Cranbourne Cl. SW16 . . . . .3J 155
Cranbourne Ct. SW11 . . . . .7C 100
   (off Albert Bri. Rd.)
Cranbourne Dr. HA5: Pinn 5B 40
Cranbourne Gdns. IG6: Ilf 3G 53
  NW11 . . . . .5G 45
Cranbourne Rd. E12 . . . . .5C 70
  E15 . . . . .4E 68
  HA6: Nwood 3H 39
  N10 . . . . .2F 47
Cranbourne Ho. SE16 . . . . .2H 103
   (off Marigold St.)
Cranbourne Pas. SE16 . . . . .2H 103
Cranbourn St. WC2 . . . . .2D 12 (7H 83)
CRANBROOK 1D 70
Cranbrook NW1 . . . . .1G 83
   (off Camden St.)
Cranbrook Castle Tennis Club 7D 52
Cranbrook Cl. BR2: Hayes 6J 159
Cranbrook Cl. CR2: S Croy 5E 168
  TW8: Bford 6C 96
Cranbrook Dr. KT10: Esh 7G 149
  TW2: Whitt 1F 131
Cranbrook Est. E2 . . . . .2K 85
Cranbrook La. N11 . . . . .4A 32
Cranbrook M. E17 . . . . .5B 50
Cranbrook Pk. N22 . . . . .1A 48
Cranbrook Ri. IG1: Ilf 6D 52
Cranbrook Rd. CR7: Thor H 2C 156
  DA7: Bex 1F 127
  EN4: E Barn 6G 21
  IG1: Ilf 7E 52
  IG2: Ilf 6E 52
  IG6: Ilf 6E 52
  SE8 . . . . .1C 122
  SW19 . . . . .7G 135
  TW4: Houn 4D 112
  W4 . . . . .5A 98
Cranbrook St. E2 . . . . .2K 85
Cranbury Rd. SW6 . . . . .2K 117
Crandley Ct. SE8 . . . . .4A 104
   (not continuous)
Crane Av. TW7: Isle 5A 114
  W3 . . . . .7J 79
Cranebank .2J 111
Cranebank M. TW1: Twick 4A 114
Cranebrook TW2: Twick 2G 131
Crane Cl. HA2: Harr 3G 59
  RM10: Dag 6G 73
Crane Ct. EC4 . . . . .6A 84
  KT19: Ewe 4J 163
  SW14 . . . . .4J 115
Craneford Cl. TW2: Twick 7K 113
Craneford Way TW2: Twick 7J 113
Crane Gdns. UB3: Harl 4H 93
Crane Gro. N7 . . . . .6A 66
Crane Hgts. N17 . . . . .3H 49
   (off Waterside Way)
Crane Ho. E3 . . . . .2A 86
   (off Roman Rd.)
  SE15 . . . . .1F 121
  TW13: Hanw 3E 130
Crane Lodge Rd. TW5: Cran 6K 93
Crane Mead SE16 . . . . .5J 103
Crane Mead Ct. TW1: Twick 7K 113
Crane Pk. Island Nature Reserve
  . . . . .2D 130
Crane Pk. Rd. TW2: Whitt 2F 131
Crane Rd. TW2: Twick 1J 131
  TW19: Stanw 6C 110
Cranesbill Cl. NW9 . . . . .3K 43
  SW16 . . . . .2H 155
Cranes Dr. KT5: Surb 4E 150
Cranes Pk. KT5: Surb 4E 150
Cranes Pk. Av. KT5: Surb 4E 150
Cranes Pk. Cres. KT5: Surb 4F 151

Crane St. SE10 . . . . .5F 105
  SE15 . . . . .1F 121
Craneswater UB3: Harl 7H 93
Craneswater Pk. UB2: S'hall 5D 94
Crane Way TW2: Whitt 7G 113
Cranfield Cl. SE27 . . . . .3C 138
Cranfield Ct. W1 . . . . .6D 4
Cranfield Dr. NW9 . . . . .7F 29
Cranfield Ho. WC1 . . . . .5E 6
Cranfield Rd. SE4 . . . . .3B 122
Cranfield Rd. E. SM5: Cars 7E 166
Cranfield Rd. W. SM5: Cars 7E 166
Cranfield Row SE1 . . . . .1K 19
Cranfield Wlk. SE3 . . . . .3K 123
CRANFORD .7J 93
Cranford Av. N13 . . . . .5D 32
  TW19: Stanw 7A 110
Cranford Cl. SW20 . . . . .7D 134
  TW19: Stanw 7A 110
Cranford Community College Sports Cen.
  . . . . .6K 93
Cranford Cotts. E1 . . . . .7K 85
   (off Cranford St.)
Cranford Dr. UB3: Harl 4H 93
Cranford La. TW5: Cran, Hest 7K 93
  TW6: H'row A 1H 111
   (Bath Rd.)
  TW6: H'row A 3H 111
   (Elmdon Rd.)
  UB3: Cran, Harl 6F 93
Cranford M. BR2: Broml 5C 160
Cranford Pk. Rd. UB3: Harl 4H 93
Cranford St. E1 . . . . .7K 85
Cranford Way N8 . . . . .4K 47
Cranhurst Rd. NW2 . . . . .5E 62
Cranleigh W11 . . . . .1H 99
   (off Ladbroke Rd.)
Cranleigh Cl. BR6: Chels 3K 173
  DA5: Bexl 6H 127
  SE20 . . . . .2H 157
Cranleigh Ct. CR4: Mitc 3B 154
  TW9: Rich 3G 115
  UB1: S'hall 6D 76
Cranleigh Gdns. HA3: Kenton 5E 42
  IG11: Bark 7H 71
  KT2: King T 6F 133
  N21 . . . . .5F 23
  SE25 . . . . .3E 156
  SM1: Sutt 2K 165
  UB1: S'hall 6D 76
Cranleigh Gdns. Ind. Est.
  UB1: S'hall 6D 76
Cranleigh Ho's. NW1 . . . . .2G 83
   (off Cranleigh St.)
Cranleigh M. SW11 . . . . .2C 118
Cranleigh Rd. N15 . . . . .5C 48
  SW19 . . . . .3J 153
  TW13: Felt 4H 129
Cranleigh St. NW1 . . . . .2G 83
Cranley Dene Ct. N10 . . . . .4F 47
Cranley Dr. HA4: Ruis 2H 57
  IG2: Ilf 7G 53
CRANLEY GARDENS 4F 47
Cranley Gdns. N10 . . . . .4F 47
  N13 . . . . .3E 32
  SM6: W'gton 7G 167
  SW7 . . . . .5A 16 (5A 100)
Cranley M. SW7 . . . . . .5A 16 (5A 100)
Cranley Pde. SE9 . . . . .4C 142
   (off Beaconsfield Rd.)
Cranley Pl. SW7 . . . . . .4A 16 (4B 100)
Cranley Rd. E13 . . . . .5K 87
  IG2: Ilf 6G 53
Cranmer Av. W13 . . . . .3B 96
Cranmer Cl. HA4: Ruis 1B 58
  HA7: Stan 7H 27
  SM4: Mord 6F 153
Cranmer Ct. N3 . . . . .2G 45
  SW3 . . . . .4D 16 (4C 100)
  SW4 . . . . .3H 119
  TW12: Hamp H 5F 131
Cranmere Ct. EN2: Enf 2F 23
Cranmer Farm Cl. CR4: Mitc 4D 154

Cranmer Gdns. RM10: Dag 4J 73
Cranmer Ho. SW9 . . . . .7A 102
   (off Cranmer Rd.)
  SW11 . . . . .1C 118
   (off Surrey La. Est.)
Cranmer Rd. CR0: C'don 3B 168
  CR4: Mitc 4D 154
  E7 . . . . .4K 69
  HA8: Edg 3C 28
  KT2: King T 5E 132
  SW9 . . . . .7A 102
  TW12: Hamp H 5F 131
  UB3: Hayes 6F 75
Cranmer Ter. SW17 . . . . .5B 136
Cranmore Av. TW7: Isle 7G 95
Cranmore Rd. BR1: Broml 3H 141
  BR7: Chst 5D 142
Cranmore Way N10 . . . . .4G 47
Cranston Cl. TW3: Houn 2C 112
  UB10: Ick 2C 57
Cranston Est. N1 . . . . .2D 84
Cranston Gdns. E4 . . . . .6J 35
Cranston Rd. SE23 . . . . .1A 140
Cranswick Rd. SE16 . . . . .5H 103
Crantock Rd. SE6 . . . . .2D 140
Cranwell Cl. E3 . . . . .4D 86
Cranwell Gro. TW17: Shep 4B 146
Cranwell Rd. TW6: H'row A 2D 110
Cranwich Av. N21 . . . . .7J 23
Cranwich Rd. N16 . . . . .7D 48
Cranwood Ct. EC1 . . . . .2F 9
Cranwood St. EC1 . . . . . . .2E 8 (3D 84)
Cranworth Cres. E4 . . . . .1A 36
Cranworth Gdns. SW9 . . . . .1A 120
Craster Rd. SW2 . . . . .7K 119
Crathie Rd. SE12 . . . . .6K 123
Cravan Av. TW13: Felt 2J 129
Craven Av. UB1: S'hall 5D 76
  W5 . . . . .7C 78
Craven Cl. N16 . . . . .7G 49
  UB4: Hayes 6J 75
Craven Cottage 2F 117
Craven Ct. NW10 . . . . .1A 80
  RM6: Chad H 6E 54
Craven Gdns. IG6: Ilf 2H 53
  IG11: Bark 2J 89
  SW19 . . . . .5J 135
Craven Hill W2 . . . . .7A 82
Craven Hill Gdns. W2 . . . . .7A 82
   (not continuous)
Craven Hill M. W2 . . . . .7A 82
Craven Ho. N2 . . . . .2B 46
   (off High Rd. E. Finchley)
Craven Lodge SW6 . . . . .1F 117
   (off Harbord St.)
  W2 . . . . .7A 82
   (off Craven Hill)
Craven M. SW11 . . . . .3E 118
Craven Pk. NW10 . . . . .1K 79
Craven Pk. M. NW10 . . . . .7A 62
Craven Pk. Rd. N15 . . . . .6F 49
  NW10 . . . . .1A 80
Craven Pas. WC2 . . . . .4E 12
   (off Craven St.)
Craven Rd. CR0: C'don 1H 169
  KT2: King T 1F 151
  NW10 . . . . .1K 79
  W2 . . . . .1A 10 (7A 82)
  W5 . . . . .7C 78
Craven St. WC2 . . . . . . .4E 12 (1J 101)
Craven Ter. W2 . . . . .2A 10 (7A 82)
Craven Wlk. N16 . . . . .7G 49
Crawford Av. HA0: Wemb 5D 60
Crawford Bldgs. W1 . . . . .6D 4
   (off Homer St.)
Crawford Cl. TW7: Isle 2J 113
Crawford Ct. NW9 . . . . .3A 44
   (off Charcot Rd.)
Crawford Est. SE5 . . . . .2C 120
Crawford Gdns. N13 . . . . .3G 33
  UB5: N'olt 3D 76
Crawford Mans. W1 . . . . .6D 4
   (off Crawford St.)

Crawford M. SW20 . . . . .7D 134
  W1 . . . . .6E 4 (5D 82)
Crawford Pas. EC1 . . . . . .4K 7 (4A 84)
Crawford Pl. W1 . . . . .7D 4 (6C 82)
Crawford Rd. SE5 . . . . .1C 120
Crawford St. NW10 . . . . .7K 61
  W1 . . . . .6E 4 (5C 82)
Crawley Rd. E10 . . . . .1D 68
  EN1: Enf 7K 23
  N22 . . . . .2C 48
Crawshay Rd. SW9 . . . . .1A 120
Crawthew Gro. SE22 . . . . .4F 121
Craybrooke Rd. DA14: Sidc 4B 144
Craybury End SE9 . . . . .2G 143
Crayfields Bus. Pk. BR5: St P 7C 144
CRAYFORD .5K 127
Crayford Cl. E6 . . . . .6C 88
Crayford Ct. W3 . . . . .3J 97
   (off Bollo Bri. Rd.)
Crayford Ho. SE1 . . . . .7F 15
   (off Long La.)
Crayford M. N7 . . . . .4J 65
Crayford Rd. N7 . . . . .4H 65
Cray Ho. NW8 . . . . .5B 4
   (off Penfold St.)
Crayke Hill KT9: Chess 7E 162
Crayle Ho. EC1 . . . . .3B 8
   (off Malta St.)
Crayleigh Ter. DA14: Sidc 6C 144
Crayonne Cl. TW16: Sun 1G 147
Cray Rd. DA14: Sidc 6C 144
  DA17: Belv 6G 109
Cray Valley Rd.
  BR5: St M Cry 5K 161
Cray Wanderers FC 5K 159
Crayzee Barn 2F 145
Crealock Gro. IG8: Wfd G 5C 36
Crealock St. SW18 . . . . .6K 117
Creasy Est. SE1 . . . . .3E 102
Creative Ho. SW8 . . . . .7F 101
   (off Prince of Wales Dr.)
Creative Rd. SE8 . . . . .7D 104
Crebor St. SE22 . . . . .6G 121
Crecy Ct. SE11 . . . . .5J 19
   (off Hotspur St.)
Credenhall Dr. BR2: Broml 1D 172
Credenhill Ho. SE15 . . . . .7H 103
Credenhill St. SW16 . . . . .6G 137
Crediton Hgts. NW10 . . . . .1F 81
   (off Okehampton Rd.)
Crediton Hill NW6 . . . . .5K 63
Crediton Rd. E16 . . . . .6J 87
  NW10 . . . . .1F 81
Crediton Way KT10: Clay 5A 162
Credon Rd. E13 . . . . .2A 88
  SE16 . . . . .5H 103
Creechurch La. EC3 . . . . .1H 15 (6E 84)
   (not continuous)
Creechurch Pl. EC3 . . . . .1H 15
Creed Ct. E1 . . . . .3A 86
  EC4 . . . . .1B 14
Creed La. EC4 . . . . .1B 14 (6B 84)
Creed Pas. SE10 . . . . .5G 105
   (off Hoskins St.)
The Creek TW16: Sun 5J 147
Creek Cotts. KT8: E Mos 4J 149
   (off Creek Rd.)
Creek Ho. W14 . . . . .3G 99
   (off Russell Rd.)
CREEKMOUTH 4K 89
Creekmouth Ind. Pk. IG11: Bark . . .4K 89
Creek Rd. IG11: Bark 3K 89
  KT8: E Mos 4J 149
  SE8 . . . . .6C 104
  SE10 . . . . .6C 104
Creekside SE8 . . . . .7D 104
Creekside Foyer SE8 . . . . .6D 104
   (off Stowage)
Creek Way RM13: Rain 5K 91
Creeland Gro. SE6 . . . . .1B 140
Crefeld Cl. W6 . . . . .6G 99
Creffield Rd. W3 . . . . .7F 79
  W5 . . . . .7F 79

Creighton Av. E6 . . . . .2B **88**
  N2 . . . . .3C **46**
  N10 . . . . .3C **46**
Creighton Cl. W12 . . . . .7C **80**
Creighton Rd. N17 . . . . .7K **33**
  NW6 . . . . .2F **81**
  W5 . . . . .3D **96**
Cremer Bus. Cen. E2 . . . . .1J **9**
             (off Cremer St.)
Cremer Ho. SE8 . . . . .4D **106**
        (off Deptford Chu. St.)
Cremer St. E2 . . . . .1J **9** (2F **85**)
Cremorne Est. SW10 . . . . .6B **100**
          (not continuous)
Cremorne Riverside Cen. 7B **100**
Cremorne Rd. SW10 . . . . .7A **100**
Creon Ct. SW9 . . . . .7A **102**
          (off Caldwell St.)
Crescent EC3 . . . . .2J **15** (7F **85**)
The Crescent BR3: Beck 1C **158**
  BR4: W W'ck 6G **159**
  CR0: C'don 5D **156**
  DA5: Bexl 7C **126**
  DA14: Sidc 4K **143**
  E17 . . . . .6A **50**
  EN5: New Bar 2E **20**
  HA0: Wemb 2B **60**
  HA2: Harr 1G **59**
  IG2: Ilf 6E **52**
  KT3: N Mald 3J **151**
  KT6: Surb 5E **150**
  KT8: W Mole 4E **148**
  N11 . . . . .4J **31**
  NW2 . . . . .3D **62**
  SE8 . . . . .1C **122**
             (off Seager Pl.)
  SM1: Sutt 5B **166**
  SW13 . . . . .2B **116**
  SW19 . . . . .3J **135**
  TW15: Ashf 5B **128**
  TW17: Shep 7H **147**
  UB1: S'hall 2D **94**
  UB3: Harl 7E **92**
  W3 . . . . .6A **80**
  W12 . . . . .1E **98**
Crescent Arc. SE10 . . . . .6E **104**
           (off Creek Rd.)
Crescent Ct. KT6: Surb 5D **150**
  SW4 . . . . .5H **119**
           (off Park Hill)
Crescent Ct. Bus. Cen. E16 . . . . .4F **87**
Crescent Dr. BR5: Pet W 5F **161**
Crescent E. EN4: Had W 1F **21**
Crescent Gdns. HA4: Ruis 7K **39**
  SW19 . . . . .3J **135**
Crescent Gro. CR4: Mitc 4C **154**
  SW4 . . . . .4G **119**
Crescent Ho. EC1 . . . . .4C **8**
        (off Golden La. Est.)
  SE13 . . . . .2D **122**
Crescent La. SW4 . . . . .4G **119**
Crescent Mans. SW3 . . . . .4C **16**
         (off Fulham Rd.)
  W11 . . . . .7G **81**
         (off Elgin Cres.)
Crescent M. N22 . . . . .1J **47**
Crescent Pde. UB10: Hil 3C **74**
Crescent Pl. SW3 . . . . . . .3D **16** (4C **100**)
Crescent Ri. EN4: E Barn 5H **21**
  N3 . . . . .1H **45**
  N22 . . . . .1H **47**
Crescent Rd.
  BR1: Broml 7J **141**
  BR3: Beck 2D **158**
  DA15: Sidc 3K **143**
  E4 . . . . .1B **36**
  E6 . . . . .1A **88**
  E10 . . . . .2D **68**
  E13 . . . . .1J **87**
  E18 . . . . .1A **52**
  EN2: Enf 4G **23**
  EN4: E Barn 4G **21**
  KT2: King T 7G **133**

Crescent Rd. N3 . . . . .1H **45**
  N8 . . . . .6H **47**
  N9 . . . . .1B **34**
  N11 . . . . .4J **31**
  N15 . . . . .3B **48**
  N22 . . . . .1H **47**
  RM10: Dag 3H **73**
  SE18 . . . . .5F **107**
  SW20 . . . . .1F **153**
  TW17: Shep 5E **146**
Crescent Row EC1 . . . . . .4C **8** (4C **84**)
Crescent Stables SW15 . . . . .5G **117**
Crescent St. N1 . . . . .7K **65**
Cres. Way BR6: Orp 5J **173**
  N12 . . . . .6H **31**
  SE4 . . . . .3C **122**
  SW16 . . . . .6K **137**
Crescent W. EN4: Had W 1F **21**
Crescent Wood Rd. SE26 . . . . .3G **139**
Cresford Rd. SW6 . . . . .1K **117**
Crespigny Rd. NW4 . . . . .6D **44**
Cressage Cl. UB1: S'hall 4E **76**
Cressage Ho. TW8: Bford 6E **96**
          (off Ealing Rd.)
Cressal Ho. E14 . . . . .3C **104**
           (off Tiller Rd.)
Cresset Ho. E9 . . . . .6J **67**
Cresset Rd. E9 . . . . .6J **67**
Cresset St. SW4 . . . . .3H **119**
Cressfield Cl. NW5 . . . . .5E **64**
Cressida Rd. N19 . . . . .1G **65**
Cressingham Gro. SM1: Sutt 4A **166**
Cressingham Rd. HA8: Edg 6E **28**
  SE13 . . . . .3E **122**
Cressington Cl. N16 . . . . .5E **66**
Cress M. BR1: Broml 5F **141**
Cresswell Gdns. SW5 . . . . .5A **100**
Cresswell Ho. HA9: Wemb 3E **60**
  TW19: Stanw 6A **110**
         (off Douglas Rd.)
Cresswell Pk. SE3 . . . . .3H **123**
Cresswell Pl. SW10 . . . . .5A **100**
Cresswell Rd. SE25 . . . . .4G **157**
  TW1: Twick 6D **114**
  TW13: Hanw 3C **130**
Cresswell Way N21 . . . . .7F **23**
Cressy Ct. E1 . . . . .5J **85**
  W6 . . . . .3D **98**
Cressy Ho. SW15 . . . . .3D **116**
Cressy Ho's. E1 . . . . .5J **85**
         (off Hannibal Rd.)
Cressy Pl. E1 . . . . .5J **85**
Cressy Rd. NW3 . . . . .5D **64**
The Crest KT5: Surb 5G **151**
  N13 . . . . .4F **33**
  NW4 . . . . .5E **44**
Cresta Ct. W5 . . . . .4F **79**
Cresta Ho. E3 . . . . .4C **86**
        (off Dimson Cres.)
  NW3 . . . . .7B **64**
         (off Finchley Rd.)
Crestbrook Av. N13 . . . . .3G **33**
Crestbrook Pl. N13 . . . . .3G **33**
         (off Green Lanes)
Crest Ct. NW4 . . . . .5E **44**
Crest Dr. EN3: Enf W 1D **24**
Crested Ct. NW9 . . . . .7B **44**
Crestfield St. WC1 . . . . . . .1F **7** (3J **83**)
Creston Av. HA4: Ruis 3A **58**
Creston House SW11 . . . . .3B **118**
        (off Gartons Way)
Creston Way KT4: Wor Pk 1F **165**
Crest Rd. BR2: Hayes 7H **159**
  CR2: Sels 7H **169**
  NW2 . . . . .2B **62**
Crest Vw. HA5: Pinn 4B **40**
Crest Vw. Dr. BR5: Pet W 5F **161**
Crest Wlk. E18 . . . . .2A **52**
Crestway SW15 . . . . .6C **116**
Crestwood Way TW4: Houn 5C **112**
Creswell Dr. BR3: Beck 5D **158**
Creswick Ct. W3 . . . . .7H **79**
Creswick Rd. W3 . . . . .7H **79**

Creswick Wlk. E3 . . . . .3C **86**
  NW11 . . . . .4H **45**
Creton St. SE18 . . . . .3E **106**
Creukhorne Rd. NW10 . . . . .7A **62**
Crewdson Rd. SW9 . . . . .7A **102**
Crewe Pl. NW10 . . . . .3B **80**
Crewkerne Ct. SW11 . . . . .1B **118**
        (off Bolingbroke Wlk.)
Crews St. E14 . . . . .4C **104**
Crewys Rd. NW2 . . . . .2H **63**
  SE15 . . . . .2H **121**
Crichton Av. SM6: Bedd 5H **167**
Crichton Rd. DA14: Sidc 6D **144**
Crichton Rd. SM5: Cars 6D **166**
Crichton St. SW8 . . . . .2G **119**
Crick Cl. IG11: Bark 2A **90**
         (off Spring Pl.)
Cricketers Arms Rd. EN2: Enf 2H **23**
Cricketers Cl. DA8: Erith 5K **109**
  KT9: Chess 4D **162**
  N14 . . . . .7B **22**
Cricketers Ct. SE11 . . . . .4B **102**
        (off Kennington La.)
Cricketers M. SW18 . . . . .5K **117**
Cricketers Ter. SM5: Cars 3C **166**
Cricketers Wlk. SE26 . . . . .5J **139**
Cricketfield Rd. E5 . . . . .4H **67**
Cricket Grn. CR4: Mitc 3D **154**
Cricket Ground Rd. BR7: Chst 1F **161**
Cricket La. BR3: Beck 6A **140**
  TW12: Hamp H 6G **131**
Cricklade Av. SW2 . . . . .2J **137**
Cricklefield Pl. IG1: Ilf 2J **71**
CRICKLEWOOD 4F **63**
Cricklewood B'way. NW2 . . . . .3E **62**
Cricklewood La. NW2 . . . . .4F **63**
Cridland St. E15 . . . . .1H **87**
Crieff Ct. TW11: Tedd 7C **132**
Crieff Rd. SW18 . . . . .6A **118**
Criffel Av. SW2 . . . . .2H **137**
Crimscott St. SE1 . . . . .3E **102**
Crimsworth Rd. SW8 . . . . .1H **119**
Crinan St. N1 . . . . .2J **83**
Cringle St. SW11 . . . . .7G **101**
Crinoline M. E1 . . . . .6J **9** (5F **85**)
Cripplegate St. EC2 . . . . . .5D **8** (5C **84**)
Cripps Cl. IG6: Ilf 3G **53**
Cripps Grn. UB4: Yead 4K **75**
Crispe Ho. IG11: Bark 2H **89**
  N1 . . . . .1K **83**
        (off Barnsbury Est.)
Crispen Rd. TW13: Hanw 4C **130**
Crispian Cl. NW10 . . . . .4A **62**
Crispin Cl. CR0: Bedd 2J **167**
Crispin Cl. SE17 . . . . .4E **102**
Crispin Cres. CR0: Bedd 3H **167**
Crispin Ind. Cen. N18 . . . . .5D **34**
Crispin Lodge N11 . . . . .5J **31**
Crispin M. NW11 . . . . .5H **45**
Crispin Pl. E1 . . . . .5J **9** (5F **85**)
Crispin Rd. HA8: Edg 6D **28**
Crispin St. E1 . . . . .6J **9** (5F **85**)
Crispin Way UB8: Hil 4B **74**
Crisp Rd. W6 . . . . .5E **98**
Cristie Ct. E16 . . . . .4H **87**
Crittenden Rd. SW6 . . . . .2H **117**
Crockerton Rd. SW17 . . . . .2D **136**
Crockham Way SE9 . . . . .4E **142**
Crocus Cl. CR0: C'don 1K **169**
Crocus Fld. EN5: Barn 6C **20**
The Croft CR0: C'don 3F **169**
  E4 . . . . .2B **36**
  EN5: Barn 4B **20**

The Croft HA0: Wemb 5C **60**
  HA4: Ruis 4A **58**
  HA5: Pinn 7D **40**
  HA8: Edg 7C **28**
  NW10 . . . . .2B **80**
  TW5: Hest 6C **94**
  W5 . . . . .5E **78**
Croft Av. BR4: W W'ck 1E **170**
Croft Cl. BR7: Chst 5D **142**
  DA17: Belv 5F **109**
  NW7 . . . . .3F **29**
  UB3: Harl 7E **92**
  UB10: Hil 7C **56**
Croft Ct. HA4: Ruis 1H **57**
  SE13 . . . . .6E **122**
  SM1: Sutt 2B **166**
Croftdown Rd. NW5 . . . . .3E **64**
Croft End Cl. KT9: Chess 3F **163**
Crofters Cl. TW7: Isle 5H **113**
Crofters Ct. SE8 . . . . .4A **104**
         (off Croft St.)
Crofters Mead CR0: Sels 7B **170**
Crofters Way NW1 . . . . .1H **83**
Croft Gdns. HA4: Ruis 1H **57**
  W7 . . . . .2A **96**
Croft Ho. E17 . . . . .4D **50**
  NW9 . . . . .2B **44**
  W10 . . . . .3G **81**
         (off Third Av.)
Croft Lodge Cl. IG8: Wfd G 6E **36**
Croft M. N12 .3F **31**
CROFTON 2G **173**
Crofton Albion Sports Ground 4J **123**
Crofton Av. BR6: Farnb 2G **173**
  DA5: Bexl 7D **126**
  W4 . . . . .7J **97**
Croftongate Way SE4 . . . . .5A **122**
Crofton Gro. E4 . . . . .4A **36**
Crofton Ho. SW3 . . . . .7C **16**
        (off Old Church St.)
Crofton La.
  BR5: Farnb, Orp, Pet W 2H **173**
  BR6: Pet W 7H **161**
CROFTON PARK 5B **122**
Crofton Pk. Rd. SE4 . . . . .6B **122**
Crofton Rd. BR6: Farnb, Orp 3E **172**
  E13 . . . . .4K **87**
  SE5 . . . . .1E **120**
Crofton Roman Villa 2J **173**
Crofton Ter. E5 . . . . .5A **68**
  TW9: Rich 4F **115**
Crofton Way EN2: Enf 2F **23**
  EN5: New Bar 6E **20**
Croft Rd. BR1: Broml 6J **141**
  EN3: Enf H 1F **25**
  SM1: Sutt 5C **166**
  SW16 . . . . .1A **156**
  SW19 . . . . .7A **136**
The Crofts TW17: Shep 4G **147**
Crofts Ho. E2 . . . . .2G **85**
         (off Teale St.)
The Croftside SE25 . . . . .3G **157**
Crofts La. N22 . . . . .7F **33**
Crofts Rd. HA1: Harr 6A **42**
Crofts St. E1 . . . . .3K **15** (7G **85**)
Croft St. SE8 . . . . .4A **104**
Crofts Vs. HA1: Harr 6A **42**
Cft. Way DA15: Sidc 3J **143**
  TW10: Ham 3B **132**
Croftway NW3 . . . . .4J **63**
  TW10: Ham 7E **64**
Croham Cl. CR2: S Croy 7E **168**
Croham Hurst Golf Course 6F **169**
Croham Mnr. Rd. CR2: S Croy 7E **168**
Croham Mt. CR2: S Croy 7E **168**
Croham Pk. Av. CR2: S Croy 5D **168**
Croham Rd. CR2: S Croy 5D **168**
Croham Valley Rd. CR2: Sels 6G **169**
Croindene Rd. SW16 . . . . .1J **155**
Crokesley Ho. HA8: Edg 2J **43**
      (off Burnt Oak B'way.)
Cromartie Rd. N19 . . . . .7H **47**
Cromarty Ct. SW2 . . . . .5K **119**

Cromarty Ho. *E1* *5A 86*
(off Ben Jonson Rd.)
Cromarty Rd. HA8: Edg 2C 28
Cromberdale Ct. *N17* *1G 49*
(off Spencer Rd.)
Crombie Cl. IG4: Ilf 5D 52
Crombie M. SW11 . . . . .2C 118
Crombie Rd. DA15: Sidc 1H 143
Crome Ho. *UB5: N'olt* *2C 76*
(off Parkfield Dr.)
Cromer Cl. UB8: Hil 6E 74
Cromer Hyde SM4: Mord 5K 153
Crome Rd. NW10 . . . . .6A 62
Cromer Pl. BR6: Orp 1J 173
Cromer Rd. E10 . . . . .7F 51
EN5: New Bar 4F 21
IG8: Wfd G 4D 36
N17 . . . . .2G 49
RM6: Chad H 6E 54
RM7: Rom 6K 55
SE25 .3H 157
SW17 . . . . .6E 136
TW6: H'row A 2C 110
Cromer St. WC1 . . . . .2E 6 (3J 83)
Cromer Ter. E8 . . . . .5G 67
RM6: Chad H 5J 55
Cromer Vs. Rd. SW18 . . . . . . .6H 117
Cromford Cl. BR6: Orp 3J 173
Cromford Path E5 . . . . .4K 67
Cromford Rd. SW18 . . . . .5J 117
Cromford Way KT3: N Mald 1K 151
Cromie Cl. N13 . . . . .3F 33
Cromlix Cl. BR7: Chst 2F 161
Crompton Ct. *BR2: Broml* *3J 159*
(off St Mark's Sq.)
SW3 . . . . .3C 16 (4C 100)
Crompton Ho. *SE1* *3C 102*
(off County St.)
W2 . . . .*4A 4*
(off Hall Pl.)
Crompton Pl. EN3: Enf L 1H 25
Crompton St. W2 . . . . . . .4A 4 (4B 82)
Cromwell Av. BR2: Broml 4K 159
KT3: N Mald 5B 152
N6 . . . . .1F 65
W6 . . . . .5D 98
Cromwell Cen. IG11: Bark 3A 90
NW10 .3K 79
The Cromwell Cen. *RM8: Dag* *7F 55*
(off Coppen Rd.)
E1 . . . . .1G 103
KT12: Walt T 7K 147
N2 . . . . .4B 46
W3 . . . . .1J 97
(not continuous)
W4 . . . .*5H 97*
(off Harvard Rd.)
Cromwell Ct. EN3: Pond E 5E 24
Cromwell Cres. SW5 . . . . .4J 99
Cromwell Gdns. SW7 . . .2B 16 (3B 100)
Cromwell Gro. W6 . . . . .3E 98
Cromwell Highwalk EC2 . . . . .5D 8
Cromwell Ho. CR0: C'don 3B 168
SW11 . . . .*1E 118*
(off Charlotte Despard Av.)
Cromwell Ind. Est. E10 . . . . .1A 68
Cromwell Lodge DA6: Bex 5E 126
E1 . . . .*4J 85*
(off Cleveland Gro.)
IG11: Bark 5J 71
Cromwell Mans. *SW5* *4J 99*
(off Cromwell Rd.)
Cromwell M. SW7 . . . . .3B 16 (4B 100)
Cromwell Pl. EC2 . . . .*5D 8*
(off Silk St.)
N6 . . . . .1F 65
SW7 . . . . .3B 16 (4B 100)
SW14 . . . . .3J 115
Cromwell Rd. BR3: Beck 2A 158
CR0: C'don 7D 156
E7 . . . . .7A 70
E17 . . . . .5E 50

Cromwell Rd. HA0: Wemb 2E 78
KT2: King T 1E 150
KT4: Wor Pk 3K 163
N3 . . . . .1A 46
N10 . . . . .7K 31
(not continuous)
SW5 . . . . .4J 99
SW7 . . . . .3A 16 (4J 99)
SW9 .1A 120
SW19 . . . . .5J 135
TW3: Houn 4E 112
TW11: Tedd 6A 132
TW13: Felt 1K 129
UB3: Hayes 6F 75
Cromwell St. TW3: Houn 4E 112
Cromwell Twr. EC2 . . . . .5D 8
Cromwell Trad. Cen. IG11: Bark . . .3J 89
Crondace Rd. SW6 . . . . .1J 117
Crondall Ct. N1 . . . . .1F 9
Crondall Ho. SW15 . . . . .7C 116
Crondall St. N1 . . . . . . .1F 9 (2D 84)
Crone Ct. *NW6* *2H 81*
(off Denmark Rd.)
Cronin St. SE15 . . . . .7F 103
CROOKED BILLET 1C 50
Crooked Billet SW19 . . . . .6E 134
Crooked Billet Yd. E2 . . . . .1H 9
Crooked Usage N3 . . . . .3G 45
Crooke Rd. SE8 . . . . .5A 104
Crookham Rd. SW6 . . . . .1H 117
Crook Log DA6: Bex 3D 126
Crook Log Leisure Cen. 3D 126
Crookston Rd. SE9 . . . . .3E 124
Croombs Rd. E16 . . . . .5A 88
Croom's Hill SE10 . . . . .7E 104
Croom's Hill Gro. SE10 . . . . . . .7E 104
Cropley Ct. *N1* *2D 84*
(off Cropley St.)
Cropley St. N1 . . . . .1E 8 (2D 84)
Croppath Rd. RM10: Dag 4G 73
Cropthorne Ct. W9 . . . . .3A 82
Crosbie Ho. *E17* *3E 50*
(off Prospect Hill)
Crosby Cl. TW13: Hanw 3C 130
Crosby Ct. SE1 . . . . . . .6E 14 (2D 102)
Crosby Gdns. UB8: Uxb 7A 56
Crosby Ho. *BR1: Broml* *2J 159*
(off Elmfield Rd.)
E7 . . . . .6J 69
E14 . . . . .3E 104
(off Manchester Rd.)
Crosby Rd. E7 . . . . .6J 69
RM10: Dag 2H 91
Crosby Row SE1 . . . . . .7E 14 (2D 102)
Crosby Sq. EC3 . . . . . .1G 15 (6E 84)
Crosby Wlk. E8 . . . . .6F 67
SW2 .7A 120
Crosby Way SW2 . . . . .7A 120
Crosier Cl. SE3 . . . . .1C 124
Crosier Rd. UB10: Ick 4E 56
Crosier Way HA4: Ruis 3G 57
Crosland Pl. SW11 . . . . .3E 118
Cross Av. SE10 . . . . .6F 105
Crossbones Graveyard *5D 14*
(off Redcross Way)
Crossbow Ho. *N1* *1E 84*
(off Whitmore Est.)
W13 . . . .*1B 96*
(off Sherwood Cl.)
Crossbrook Rd. SE3 . . . . .2C 124
Cross Cl. SE15 . . . . .2H 121
Cross Ct. *SE28* *7B 90*
(off Titmuss Av.)
Cross Deep TW1: Twick 2K 131
Cross Deep Gdns. TW1: Twick . . .2K 131
Crossfield Ct. *W10* *6F 81*
(off Cambridge Gdns.)
Crossfield Ho. *W11* *6F 81*
(off Mary Pl.)
Crossfield Rd. N17 . . . . .3C 48
NW3 .6B 64
Crossfield St. SE8 . . . . .7C 104
(not continuous)

Crossford St. SW9 . . . . .2K 119
Cross Ga. HA8: Edg 3B 28
Crossgate UB6: G'frd 6B 60
Crossharbour Plaza E14 . . . . . . .3D 104
Cross Keys Cl. N9 . . . . .2C 34
W1 . . . . .6H 5 (5E 82)
Cross Keys Sq. *EC1* *6C 8*
(off Little Britain)
Cross Lances Rd. TW3: Houn 4F 113
Crossland Rd. CR7: Thor H 6B 156
Crosslands Av. UB2: S'hall 5D 94
W5 . . . . .1F 97
Crosslands Pde. UB2: S'hall 5E 94
Crosslands Rd. KT19: Ewe 6K 163
Cross La. DA5: Bexl 7F 127
EC3 . . . . .3G 15 (7E 84)
(not continuous)
N8 . . . . .3K 47
(not continuous)
Crossleigh Ct. *SE14* *7B 104*
(off New Cross Rd.)
Crosslet St. SE17 . . . . .4D 102
Crosslet Va. SE10 . . . . .1D 122
Crossley St. N7 . . . . .6A 66
Crossmead SE9 . . . . .1D 142
Crossmead Av. UB6: G'frd 3E 76
Crossmount Ho. *SE5* *7C 102*
(off Bowyer St.)
Crossness Footpath DA18: Erith . . .1F 109
Crossness La. SE2 . . . . .7E 90
Crossness Nature Reserve 1G 109
The Crossness Pumping Station
. . . . .6F 91
Crossness Rd. IG11: Bark 3K 89
Crosspoint Ho. *SE8* *7C 104*
(off Watson's St.)
Crossrail Pl. E14 . . . . .1D 104
Crossrail Wlk. E14 . . . . .1D 104
Cross Rd. BR2: Broml 2C 172
CR0: C'don 1D 168
DA14: Sidc 4B 144
E4 . . . . .1A 36
EN1: Enf 4K 23
HA1: Harr 4H 41
HA2: Harr 3F 59
HA3: W'stone 2A 42
IG8: Wfd G 6J 37
KT2: King T 7F 133
N11 . . . . .5A 32
N22 . . . . .7F 33
RM6: Chad H 7C 54
RM7: Mawney 4G 55
SE5 . . . . .2E 120
SM1: Sutt 5B 166
SW19 . . . . .7J 135
TW13: Hanw 4C 130
Cross St. N1 . . . . .1B 84
N18 . . . . .5B 34
SE5 . . . . .3D 120
SW13 . . . . .2A 116
TW12: Hamp H 5G 131
Crossthwaite Av. SE5 . . . . .4D 120
Crosstrees Ho. *E14* *3C 104*
(off Cassilis Rd.)
Crosswall EC3 . . . . . . .2J 15 (7F 85)
Cross Way NW10 . . . . .7C 62
Crossway BR5: Pet W 4H 161
EN1: Enf 7K 23
HA4: Ruis 4A 58
HA5: Pinn 2K 39
IG8: Wfd G 4F 37
N12 . . . . .6G 31
N16 . . . . .5E 66
NW9 .4B 44
RM8: Dag 3C 72
SE28 .6B 90
SW20 . . . . .4E 152
UB3: Hayes 1J 93
W13 .4A 78
The Cross Way HA3: W'stone 2J 41
The Crossway N22 . . . . .7G 33
SE9 . . . . .2B 142
UB10: Hil 2B 74

Crossway Ct. SE4 . . . . .2A 122
Crossway Pde. *N22* *7G 33*
(off The Crossway)
Crossways CR2: Sels 7A 170
N21 . . . . .6H 23
SM2: Sutt 7B 166
TW16: Sun 7H 129
The Crossways HA9: Wemb 2G 61
KT5: Surb 1H 163
TW5: Hest 7D 94
Crossways Rd. BR3: Beck 4C 158
CR4: Mitc 3F 155
Crossways Ter. E5 . . . . .4J 67
Crosswell Cl. TW17: Shep 2E 146
Croston St. E8 . . . . .1G 85
Crothall Cl. N13 . . . . .3E 32
Crouch Av. IG11: Bark 2B 90
Crouch Cl. BR3: Beck 6C 140
Crouch Cft. SE9 . . . . .3E 142
CROUCH END 7H 47
Crouch End Hill N8 . . . . .7H 47
Crouch Hall Ct. N19 . . . . .1J 65
Crouch Hall Rd. N8 . . . . .6H 47
Crouch Hill N4 . . . . .6J 47
N8 . . . . .6J 47
Crouchman's Cl. SE26 . . . . .3F 139
Crouch Rd. NW10 . . . . .7K 61
Crowborough Rd. SW17 . . . . . . .6E 136
Crowden Way SE28 . . . . .7C 90
Crowder Cl. N12 . . . . .1A 46
Crowder St. E1 . . . . .7H 85
Crowfield Ho. N5 . . . . .4C 66
Crowfoot Cl. E9 . . . . .5B 68
SE28 .1J 107
Crossness Rd. IG11: Bark 3K 89
Crowhurst Cl. SW9 . . . . .2A 120
Crowhurst Ho. *SW9* *2K 119*
(off Aytoun Rd.)
Crowland Av. UB3: Harl 4G 93
Crowland Gdns. N14 . . . . .7D 22
Crowland Ho. *NW8* *1A 82*
(off Springfield Rd.)
Crowland Rd. CR7: Thor H 4D 156
N15 . . . . .5F 49
CROWLANDS 7H 55
Crowlands Av. RM7: Rom 6H 55
Crowlands Heath Golf Course 1H 73
Crowland Ter. N1 . . . . .7D 66
Crowland Wlk.
SM4: Mord 6K 153
Crow La. RM7: Rush G 7F 55
Crowley Cres.
CR0: Wadd 5A 168
Crowley M. SW16 . . . . .3G 155
Crowline Wlk. N1 . . . . .6C 66
Crowmarsh Gdns. SE23 . . . . .7J 121
Crown All. *SE9* *6D 124*
(off Court Yd.)
Crown Apts. HA4: Ruis 1J 57
Crown Arc. KT1: King T 2D 150
Crownbourne Ct. *SM1: Sutt* *4K 165*
(off St Nicholas Way)
Crown Bldgs. E4 . . . . .1K 35
Crown Cl. E3 . . . . .1C 86
IG9: Buck H 1E 36
KT12: Walt T 7A 148
N22 . . . . .1A 48
NW6 .6K 63
NW7 .2G 29
UB3: Hayes 2H 93
Crown Cl. Bus. Cen. *E3* *1C 86*
(off Crown Cl.)
Crown Cotts. RM5: Col R 1G 55
Crown Court
Blackfriars 6B 14 (2B 102)
Croydon 2D 168
Harrow 3H 41
Inner London 7C 14 (3C 102)
Isleworth 1J 113
Kingston upon Thames 3D 150
Snaresbrook 5H 51
Southwark 4G 15 (1E 102)
Wood Green 1A 48
Woolwich 2J 107

Crown Ct. EC2 . . . . .1D **14**
  N10 . . . . .7K **31**
  NW8 . . . . .2D **4**
    (off Park Rd.)
  SE12 . . . . .6K **123**
  WC2 . . . . .1F **13** (6J **83**)
Crown Dale SE19 . . . . .6B **138**
  (not continuous)
Crowndale Ct. NW1 . . . . .2H **83**
    (off Crowndale Rd.)
Crowndale Pl. E17 . . . . .2E **50**
Crowndale Rd. NW1 . . . . .2G **83**
Crown Dr. RM7: Rush G 6K **55**
Crownfield Av. IG2: Ilf 6J **53**
Crownfield Rd. E15 . . . . .4F **69**
Crowngate Ho. E3 . . . . .2B **86**
    (off Hereford Rd.)
Crown Grn. M. HA9: Wemb 2E **60**
Crown Hill CR0: C'don 2C **168**
Crownhill Rd. IG8: Wfd G 7H **37**
  NW10 . . . . .1B **80**
  NW10 . . . . .2G **79**
Crown Ho. KT3: N Mald 3J **151**
Crown La. BR2: Broml 5B **160**
  BR7: Chst 1G **161**
  N14 . . . . .1B **32**
  SM4: Mord 4J **153**
  SW16 . . . . .5A **138**
Crown La. Gdns. SW16 . . . . . . .5A **138**
Crown La. Spur BR2: Broml 6B **160**
Crown Lodge SW3 . . . . .4D **16**
Crown Mdw. Ct. BR2: Broml 6C **160**
Crownmead Way
  RM7: Mawney 4H **55**
Crown M. E1 . . . . .5K **85**
    (off White Horse La.)
  E13 . . . . .1A **88**
  TW13: Felt 1K **129**
  W6 . . . . .4C **98**
Crown Mill CR4: Mitc 5C **154**
Crown Office Row EC4 . . .2J **13** (7A **84**)
Crown Pde. N14 . . . . .1B **32**
  SM4: Mord 3J **153**
Crown Pas. KT1: King T 2D **150**
    (off Church St.)
  SW1 . . . . .5B **12** (1G **101**)
  NW5 . . . . .6F **65**
  SE16 . . . . .5H **103**
Crown Point SE19 . . . . .6B **138**
Crown Point Pde. SE19 . . . . . . .6B **138**
    (off Crown Dale)
Crown Reach SW1 . . . . .6D **18** (5H **101**)
Crown Rd. EN1: Enf 3B **24**
  HA4: Ruis 5B **58**
  (not continuous)
  IG6: Ilf 4H **53**
  KT3: N Mald 1J **151**
  N10 . . . . .7K **31**
  SM1: Sutt 4K **165**
  SM4: Mord 4K **153**
  TW1: Twick 6B **114**
Crown Sq. SE1 . . . . .5H **15**
Crownstone Ct. SW2 . . . . .5A **120**
Crownstone Rd. SW2 . . . . .5A **120**
Crown St. HA2: Harr 1H **59**
  RM10: Dag 6J **73**
  (not continuous)
  SE5 . . . . .7C **102**
  W3 . . . . .1H **97**
Crown Ter. N14 . . . . .1C **32**
    (off Crown La.)
  TW9: Rich 4F **115**
Crown Trad. Cen. UB3: Hayes . . .2G **93**
Crowntree Cl. TW7: Isle 6K **95**
Crown Wlk. HA9: Wemb 3F **61**
Crown Way UB7: Yiew 1B **92**
Crown Wharf E14 . . . . .1E **104**
    (off Coldharbour)
  SE8 . . . . .5B **104**
    (off Grove St.)
Crown Woods La. SE18 . . . . . . .2F **125**
Crown Woods Way SE9 . . . . . . .5H **125**

Crown Yd. E2 . . . . .2H **85**
  SW6 . . . . .2J **117**
  TW3: Houn 3G **113**
Crowshott Av. HA7: Stan 2C **42**
Crows Rd. E3 . . . . .3F **87**
  IG11: Bark 6F **71**
Crowther Av. TW8: Bford 4E **96**
Crowther Cl. SW6 . . . . .6H **99**
    (off Bucklers All.)
Crowther Rd. SE25 . . . . .5G **157**
Crowthorne Cl. SW18 . . . . .7H **117**
Crowthorne Rd. W10 . . . . .6F **81**
Croxall Ho. KT12: Walt T 6A **148**
Croxden Cl. HA8: Edg 3G **43**
Croxden Wlk. SM4: Mord 6A **154**
Croxford Gdns. N22 . . . . .7G **33**
Croxford Way RM7: Rush G 1K **73**
Croxley Grn. BR5: St P 7B **144**
Croxley Rd. W9 . . . . .3H **81**
Croxted Cl. SE21 . . . . .7C **120**
Croxted M. SE24 . . . . .6C **120**
Croxted Rd. SE21 . . . . .7C **120**
  SE24 . . . . .7C **120**
Croxteth Ho. SW8 . . . . .2H **119**
Croyde Av. UB3: Harl 4G **93**
  UB6: G'frd 3G **77**
Croyde Cl. DA15: Sidc 7H **125**
CROYDON 2C **168**
Croydon N17 . . . . .2D **48**
    (off Gloucester Rd.)
Croydon Airport Ind. Est.
  CR0: Wadd 6K **167**
Croydon Airport Vis. Cen. 6A **168**
Croydon Clocktower 3C **168**
    (off Katharine St.)
Croydon Crematorium 5K **155**
The Croydon Flyover CR0: C'don . .4B **168**
Croydon Gro. CR0: C'don 1B **168**
Croydon Ho. SE1 . . . . .5H **15**
    (off Wootton St.)
Croydon Rd. BR2: Hayes, Kes . . .3G **171**
  BR3: Beck 4K **157**
  BR4: Hayes, W W'ck 3G **171**
  CR0: Bedd, Wadd 4F **167**
  CR0: C'don 4E **154**
  CR4: Mitc 4E **154**
  E13 . . . . .4H **87**
  SE20 . . . . .2H **157**
  SM6: Bedd, W'gton 4F **167**
  TW6: H'row A 2D **110**
Croydon Rd. Ind. Est. BR3: Beck . .4K **157**
Croydon Sailing Club 2F **157**
Croydon Sports Arena 5J **157**
Croydon Valley Trade Pk.
  CR0: Bedd 7J **155**
    (off Therapia La.)
Croyland Rd. N9 . . . . .1B **34**
Croylands Dr. KT6: Surb 7E **150**
Croysdale Av. TW16: Sun 3J **147**
Crozier Ho. SW8 . . . . .7K **101**
    (off Wilkinson St.)
Crozier Ter. E9 . . . . .5K **67**
  (not continuous)
Crucible Cl. RM6: Chad H 6B **54**
Crucifix La. SE1 . . . . .6H **15** (2E **102**)
Cruden Ho. E3 . . . . .2B **86**
    (off Vernon Rd.)
  SE17 . . . . .6B **102**
    (off Brandon Est.)
Cruden St. N1 . . . . .1B **84**
Cruikshank Ho. NW8 . . . . .2C **82**
    (off Townshend Rd.)
Cruikshank Rd. E15 . . . . .4G **68**
Cruikshank St. WC1 . . . .1J **7** (3A **84**)
Crummock Gdns. NW9 . . . . .5A **44**
Crumpsall St. SE2 . . . . .4C **108**
Crundale Av. NW9 . . . . .5G **43**
Crunden Rd. CR2: S Croy 7D **168**
Crusader Gdns. CR0: C'don 3E **168**
Crusader Ind. Est. N4 . . . . .6D **48**
Crusoe M. N16 . . . . .2D **66**
Crusoe Rd. CR4: Mitc 7D **136**
  DA8: Erith 5K **109**

Crutched Friars EC3 . . . .2H **15** (7E **84**)
Crutchley Rd. SE6 . . . . .2G **141**
The Crypt 1D **120**
The Crystal 7J **87**
Crystal Ct. E8 . . . . .1H **85**
  N14 . . . . .5B **22**
  SE19 . . . . .5F **139**
    (off College Rd.)
Crystal Ho. SE18 . . . . .5K **107**
CRYSTAL PALACE 6F **139**

                . . . . .6G **139**
Crystal Palace Athletics Stadium

                . . . . .6G **139**
Crystal Pal. Caravan Club Site . . .5G **139**
Crystal Palace Dinosaurs 6G **139**
Crystal Palace FC 4E **156**
Crystal Palace Indoor Bowling Club

                . . . . .1H **157**
Crystal Palace Mus. 6F **139**
Crystal Palace National Sports Cen.

                . . . . .5G **139**
Crystal Palace Pde. SE19 . . . . . .6F **139**
Crystal Palace Pk. 5G **139**
Crystal Palace Pk. Farm 6G **139**
Crystal Palace Pk. Rd. SE26 . . . .5G **139**
Crystal Palace Rd. SE22 . . . . . . .6F **121**
Crystal Palace Sta. Rd.

            SE19 . . . . .6G **139**
Crystal Ter. SE19 . . . . .6D **138**
Crystal Vw. Ct. BR1: Broml 4F **141**
Crystal Way HA1: Harr 5K **41**
  RM8: Dag 1C **72**
Crystal Wharf N1 . . . . .2B **84**
Cuba Dr. EN3: Enf H 2D **24**
Cuba St. E14 . . . . .2C **104**
The Cube

  North East London Gymnastic Club

                . . . . .4D **66**
Cube Ho. SE16 . . . . .3F **103**
Cubitt Apts. SW11 . . . . .3A **118**
    (off Chatfield Rd.)
Cubitt Bldg. SW1 . . . . . .7J **17** (5F **101**)
Cubitt Cl. NW1 . . . . .1A **6**
    (off Park Village E.)
Cubitt Ho. SW4 . . . . .6G **119**
Cubitt Sq. UB2: S'hall 1G **95**
Cubitt Steps E14 . . . . .1C **104**
Cubitt St. WC1 . . . . . . .2H **7** (3K **83**)
Cubitt Ter. SW4 . . . . .3G **119**
CUBITT TOWN 4E **104**
Cuckoo Av. W7 . . . . .4J **77**
Cuckoo Dene W7 . . . . .5H **77**
Cuckoo Hall La. N9 . . . . .7D **24**
Cuckoo Hall Rd. N9 . . . . .7D **24**
Cuckoo Hill HA5: Eastc, Pinn 3A **40**
Cuckoo Hill Dr. HA5: Pinn 3A **40**
Cuckoo Hill Rd. HA5: Pinn 4A **40**
Cuckoo La. W7 . . . . .7J **77**
Cuckoo Pound TW17: Shep 5G **147**
Cudas Cl. KT19: Ewe 4B **164**
Cuddington Av. KT4: Wor Pk 3B **164**
Cudham La. Nth.

  BR6: Downe 7J **173**
Cudham St. SE6 . . . . .7E **122**
Cudweed Court E14 . . . . .3D **104**
    (off Watergate Walk)
Cudworth Ho. SW8 . . . . .1G **119**
Cudworth St. E1 . . . . .4H **85**
Cuff Cres. SE9 . . . . .6B **124**
Cuff Point E2 . . . . .1J **9**
    (off Columbia Rd.)
Culand Ho. SE17 . . . . .4E **102**
    (off Congreve St.)
Culford Gdns. SW3 . . . . .4F **17** (4D **100**)
Culford Gro. N1 . . . . .6E **66**
Culford Mans. SW3 . . . . .4F **17**
    (off Culford Gdns.)
Culford M. N1 . . . . .6E **66**
Culford Rd. N1 . . . . .7E **66**
Culford Ter. N1 . . . . .6E **66**
    (off Balls Pond Rd.)

Culgaith Gdns. EN2: Enf 4D **22**
Culham Ho. E2 . . . . .2J **9**
    (off Palissy St.)
  W2 . . . . .5J **81**
    (off Gt. Western Rd.)
Cullen Way NW10 . . . . .4J **79**
Culling Rd. DA17: Belv 3J **109**
Cullingham Rd. SE16 . . . . .3J **103**
Cullington Cl.
  HA3: W'stone 4A **42**
Cullingworth Rd. NW10 . . . . .5C **62**
Culloden Cl. SE7 . . . . .6K **105**
  SE16 . . . . .5G **103**
Culloden Ho. SE14 . . . . .7A **104**
    (off Batavia Rd.)
Culloden Rd. EN2: Enf 2G **23**
Cullum St. EC3 . . . . . . .2G **15** (7E **84**)
Cullum Welch Ct. N1 . . . . .1F **9**
    (off Haberdasher St.)
Cullum Welch Ho. EC1 . . . . .4C **8**
    (off Golden La. Est.)
Culmington Pde. W13 . . . . .1C **96**
    (off Uxbridge Rd.)
Culmington Rd. CR2: S Croy 7C **168**
  W13 . . . . .1C **96**
Culmore Rd. SE15 . . . . .7H **103**
Culmstock Rd. SW11 . . . . .5E **118**
Culpepper Cl. N18 . . . . .5C **34**
Culpepper Ct. SE11 . . . . .3J **19**
Culross Cl. N15 . . . . .4C **48**
Culross Ho. W10 . . . . .6F **81**
    (off Bridge Cl.)
Culross St. W1 . . . . . . .3G **11** (7E **82**)
Culsac Rd. KT6: Surb 2E **162**
Culverden Rd. SW12 . . . . .2G **137**
Culver Gro. HA7: Stan 2C **42**
Culverhouse WC1 . . . . .6G **7**
    (off Red Lion Sq.)
Culverhouse Gdns. SW16 . . . . . .3K **137**
Culverlands Cl. HA7: Stan 4G **27**
Culverley Rd. SE6 . . . . .1D **140**
Culvers Av. SM5: Cars 2D **166**
Culvers Retreat SM5: Cars 1D **166**
Culverstone Cl.
  BR2: Broml 6H **159**
Culvers Way SM5: Cars 2D **166**
Culvert Dr. E3 . . . . .3E **86**
Culvert Pl. SW11 . . . . .2E **118**
Culvert Rd. N15 . . . . .5E **48**
  (not continuous)
  SW11 . . . . .2D **118**
Culworth Ho. NW8 . . . . .2C **82**
    (off Allitsen Rd.)
Culworth St. NW8 . . . . .2C **82**
Culzean Cl. SE27 . . . . .3B **138**
Cumberland Av. DA16: Well 3J **125**
  NW10 . . . . .3H **79**
Cumberland Basin 1E **82**
Cumberland Basin NW1 . . . . . . .1E **82**
Cumberland Bus. Pk. NW10 . . . . .3H **79**
Cumberland Cl. E8 . . . . .6F **67**
  IG6: Ilf 1G **53**
  SW20 . . . . .7F **135**
  TW1: Twick 6B **114**
Cumberland Ct. CR0: C'don 1D **168**
  DA16: Well 2J **125**
  HA1: Harr 3J **41**
    (off Princes Dr.)
  SW1 . . . . .5K **17**
    (off Cumberland St.)
  W1 . . . . .1F **11**
    (off Gt. Cumberland Pl.)
Cumberland Cres. W14 . . . . .4G **99**
  (not continuous)
Cumberland Dr. DA7: Bex 7E **108**
  KT9: Chess 3E **162**
  KT10: Hin W 2A **162**
Cumberland Gdns. NW4 . . . . . . .2G **45**
  WC1 . . . . .1J **7** (3A **84**)
Cumberland Ga. W1 . . . .2E **10** (7D **82**)
Cumberland Ho. E16 . . . . .1J **105**
    (off Wesley Av.)
  KT2: King T 7H **133**

Cumberland Ho. *N9* *1D 34*
        (off Cumberland Rd.)
  SE28 . . . .*2G 107*
Cumberland Ho. *W8* *2K 99*
        (off Kensington Ct.)
Cumberland Mans. *W1* *7E 4*
Cumberland Mkt. *NW1* . . .*1K 5 (3F 83)*
Cumberland M.
  SE11 . . . .*6K 19 (5A 102)*
Cumberland Mills Sq. *E14* *5F 105*
Cumberland Pk. *NW10* *3C 80*
  W3 . . . .*7J 79*
Cumberland Pl. *NW1* . . . . .*1J 5 (3F 83)*
  SE6 . . . .*1H 141*
  TW16: Sun *4J 147*
Cumberland Rd. *BR2: Broml* *4G 159*
  E12 . . . .*4B 70*
  E13 . . . .*5K 87*
  E17 . . . .*2A 50*
  HA1: Harr *5F 41*
  HA7: Stan *3F 43*
  N9 . . . .*1D 34*
  N22 . . . .*2K 47*
  SE25 . . . .*6H 157*
  SW13 . . . .*1B 116*
  TW9: Kew *7G 97*
  TW15: Ashf *3A 128*
  W3 . . . .*7J 79*
  W7 . . . .*2K 95*
Cumberland St. *SW1* . . . . .*5K 17 (5F 101)*
Cumberland Ter. *NW1* . . . . .*1J 5 (2F 83)*
Cumberland Ter. M. *NW1* *1J 5*
        (not continuous)
Cumberland Vs. *W3* *7J 79*
        (off Cumberland Rd.)
Cumberland Wharf *SE16* *2J 103*
        (off Rotherhithe St.)
Cumberlow Av. *SE25* *3F 157*
Cumbernauld Gdns. *TW16: Sun* . .*5H 129*
Cumberton Rd. *N17* *1D 48*
Cumbrae Gdns. *KT6: Surb* *2D 162*
Cumbrian Gdns. *NW2* *2F 63*
Cumbrian Way *UB8: Uxb* *7A 56*
Cumming St. *N1* . . . .*1H 7 (2K 83)*
Cumnor Cl. *SW9* *2K 119*
        (off Robsart St.)
Cumnor Gdns. *KT17: Ewe* *6C 164*
Cumnor Rd. *SM2: Sutt* *6A 166*
Cunard Ct. *HA7: Stan* *2F 27*
        (off Brightwen Gro.)
Cunard Cres. *N21* *6J 23*
Cunard Pl. *EC3* . . . .*1H 15 (6E 84)*
Cunard Rd. *NW10* *3K 79*
Cunard Wlk. *SE16* *4K 103*
Cundy Rd. *E16* *6A 88*
Cundy St. *SW1* . . . .*4H 17 (4E 100)*
Cuneo Mews *NW7* *5B 30*
Cunliffe Pde. *KT19: Ewe* *4B 164*
Cunliffe Rd. *KT19: Ewe* *4B 164*
Cunliffe St. *SW16* *6G 137*
Cunningham Av. *E16* *2K 105*
Cunningham Cl.
  BR4: W W'ck *2D 170*
  RM6: Chad H *5C 54*
Cunningham Ct. *E10* *3D 68*
        (off Oliver Rd.)
  W9 . . . .*4A 4*
        (off Maida Vale)
Cunningham Dr. *UB10: Ick* *2E 56*
Cunningham Ho. *SE5* *7D 102*
        (off Elmington Est.)
Cunningham Pk. *HA1: Harr* *5G 41*
Cunningham Pl. *NW8* . . . .*3A 4 (4B 82)*
Cunningham Rd. *N15* *4G 49*
Cunnington St. *W4* *3J 97*
Cupar Rd. *SW11* *1E 118*
Cupola Cl. *BR1: Broml* *5K 141*
Cureton St. *SW1* . . . . .*4D 18 (4H 101)*
Curfew Ho. *IG11: Bark* *1G 89*
The Curfew Tower *1G 89*
Curie Ct. *HA1: Harr* *7B 42*
Curie Gdns. *NW9* *2A 44*
Curlew Cl. *SE28* *7D 90*

Curlew Ct. *KT6: Surb* *3G 163*
  W13 . . . .*4K 77*
Curlew Ho. *EN3: Pond E* *5E 24*
  SE4 . . . .*4A 122*
        (off St Norbert Rd.)
  SE15 . . . .*1F 121*
Curlew St. *SE1* . . . .*6K 15 (2F 103)*
  SE18 . . . .*1C 124*
        (off Tellson Av.)
Curlew Way *UB4: Yead* *5B 76*
Curness St. *SE13* *4E 122*
Curnick's La. *SE27* *4C 138*
Curran Av. *DA15: Sidc* *5K 125*
  SM6: W'gton *3E 166*
Curran Ho. *SW3* *4C 16*
        (off Lucan Pl.)
Currey Rd. *UB6: G'frd* *6H 59*
Curricle St. *W3* *1A 98*
Currie Hill Cl. *SW19* *4H 135*
Curry Ri. *NW7* *6A 30*
Cursitor St. *EC4* . . . .*7J 7 (6A 84)*
Curtain Pl. *EC2* . . . .*3H 9 (3E 84)*
Curtain Rd. *EC2* . . . .*2H 9 (4E 84)*
Curthwaite Gdns. *EN2: Enf* *4C 22*
Curtis & Staub Health Club
  Golders Green *7H 45*
Curtis Dr. *W3* *6K 79*
Curtis Fld. Rd. *SW16* *4K 137*
Curtis Ho. *SE17* *5D 102*
        (off Morecambe St.)
Curtis La. *HA0: Wemb* *6E 60*
Curtis Rd. *KT19: Ewe* *4J 163*
  TW4: Houn *7D 112*
Curtiss Ho. *NW9* *3B 44*
Curtis St. *SE1* *4F 103*
Curtis Way *SE1* *4F 103*
  SE28 . . . .*7B 90*
Curtlington Ho. *HA8: Edg* *2J 43*
        (off Burnt Oak B'way)
The Curve *W12* *7C 80*
Curwen Av. *E7* *4K 69*
Curwen Rd. *W12* *2C 98*
Curzon Av. *EN3: Pond E* *5E 24*
  HA7: Stan *1A 42*
Curzon Cinema
  Bloomsbury . . . .*4F 7 (4J 83)*
  Mayfair *5J 11*
        (off Curzon St.)
  Richmond *5D 114*
  Soho *2D 12*
        (off Shaftesbury Av.)
  Victoria *1B 18*
        (off Victoria St.)
Curzon Cl. *BR6: Orp* *4H 173*
Curzon Ct. *SW6* *1A 118*
        (off Imperial Rd.)
Curzon Cres. *IG11: Bark* *2K 89*
  NW10 . . . .*7A 62*
Curzon Ga. *W1* . . . .*5H 11 (1E 100)*
Curzon Pl. *HA5: Eastc* *5A 40*
Curzon Rd. *CR7: Thor H* *6A 156*
  N10 . . . .*2F 47*
  W5 . . . .*4B 78*
Curzon Sq. *W1* . . . .*5H 11 (1E 100)*
Curzon St. *W1* . . . .*5H 11 (1E 100)*
Cusack Cl. *TW1: Tedd* *4K 131*
Custance Ho. *N1* *1E 8*
        (off Provost St.)
Custance St. *N1* . . . .*1E 8 (3D 84)*
CUSTOM HOUSE *6A 88*
Custom Ho. *EC3* . . . .*3G 15 (7E 84)*
Custom Ho. Reach *SE16* *2B 104*
Custom Ho. Wlk.
  EC3 . . . .*3G 15 (7E 84)*
The Cut *SE1* . . . .*6K 13 (2A 102)*
Cutbush Ho. *N7* *5H 65*
Cutcombe Rd. *SE5* *2C 120*
Cuthberga Cl. *IG11: Bark* *7G 71*
Cuthbert Bell Twr. *E3* *2C 86*
        (off Pancras Way)
Cuthbert Gdns. *SE25* *3E 156*
Cuthbert Harrowing Ho. *EC1* *4C 8*
        (off Golden La. Est.)

Cuthbert Ho. *W2* *5A 4*
        (off Hall Pl.)
Cuthbert Rd. *CR0: C'don* *2B 168*
  E17 . . . .*3E 50*
  N18 . . . .*5B 34*
Cuthbert St. *W2* . . . .*5A 4 (5B 82)*
Cuthill Wlk. *SE5* *1D 120*
Cutlers Gdns. *EC2* . . . .*6H 9 (5E 84)*
Cutlers Gdns. Arc. *EC2* *7H 9*
        (off Devonshire Sq.)
Cutlers Sq. *E14* *4C 104*
Cutlers Ter. *N1* *6E 66*
        (off Balls Pond Rd.)
Cutler St. *E1* . . . .*7H 9 (6E 84)*
Cutter Ho. *DA8: Erith* *4K 109*
  E16 . . . .*2K 105*
        (off Admiralty Av.)
Cutter La. *SE10* *2G 105*
Cutthroat All. *TW10: Ham* *2C 132*
Cutty Sark *6E 104*
Cutty Sark Gdns. *SE10* *6E 104*
        (off King William Wlk.)
Cutty Sark Hall *SE10* *6E 104*
        (off Welland St.)
Cuxton *BR5: Pet W* *5G 161*
Cuxton Cl. *DA6: Bex* *5E 126*
Cuxton Ho. *SE17* *5E 102*
        (off Mina Rd.)
Cyan Apts. *E3* *1A 86*
        (off Gunmaker's La.)
Cyclamen Cl. *TW12: Hamp* *6E 130*
Cyclamen Way *KT19: Ewe* *5J 163*
Cyclops M. *E14* *4C 104*
Cygnet Av. *TW14: Felt* *7A 112*
Cygnet Cl. *NW10* *5K 61*
Cygnet Ho. *CR0: C'don* *1D 168*
  SE15 . . . .*6G 103*
  SW3 . . . .*6D 16*
        (off King's Rd.)
Cygnet Ho. Nth. *E14* *6D 86*
        (off Chrisp St.)
Cygnet Ho. Sth. *E14* *6D 86*
        (off Chrisp St.)
The Cygnets *TW13: Hanw* *4C 130*
Cygnet St. *E1* . . . .*3K 9 (4F 85)*
Cygnet Way *UB4: Yead* *5B 76*
Cygnus Bus. Cen. *NW10* *5B 62*
Cymbeline Ct. *HA1: Harr* *6K 41*
Cynthia St. *N1* . . . .*1H 7 (2K 83)*
Cyntra Pl. *E8* *7H 67*
Cypress Av. *TW2: Whitt* *7G 113*
Cypress Cl. *E5* *2G 67*
  KT19: Eps *7K 163*
Cypress Ct. *NW9* *4G 43*
        (off Alpine Rd.)
  SM1: Sutt *5J 165*
Cypress Gdns. *SE4* *5A 122*
Cypress Ho. *SE14* *1K 121*
  SE16 . . . .*2K 103*
        (off Woodland Cres.)
Cypress Pl. *W1* . . . .*4B 6 (4G 83)*
Cypress Rd. *HA3: Hrw W* *2H 41*
  SE25 . . . .*2E 156*
Cypress Tree Cl.
  DA15: Sidc *1K 143*
CYPRUS *7E 88*
Cyprus Av. *N3* *2G 45*
Cyprus Cl. *N4* *6B 48*
Cyprus Gdns. *N3* *2G 45*
Cyprus Pl. *E2* *2J 85*
  E6 . . . .*7E 88*
Cyprus Rd. *N3* *2H 45*
  N9 . . . .*2A 34*
Cyprus St. *E2* *2J 85*
        (not continuous)
Cyrena Rd. *SE22* *6F 121*
Cyril Lodge *DA14: Sidc* *4A 144*
Cyril Mans. *SW11* *1D 118*
Cyril Rd. *BR6: Orp* *7K 161*
  DA7: Bex *2E 126*
Cyrus Fld. St. *SE10* *4G 105*
Cyrus Ho. *EC1* *3B 8*
Cyrus St. *EC1* *3B 8*

Cyrus Ter. *UB10: Ick* *3E 56*
        (off Pentland Way)
Czar St. *SE8* *6C 104*

D

Dabbs Hill La. *UB5: N'olt* *6D 58*
        (not continuous)
Dabbs La. *EC1* *4K 7*
        (off Farringdon Rd.)
Dabin Cres. *SE10* *1E 122*
Dacca St. *SE8* *6B 104*
Dace Rd. *E3* *1C 86*
Dacre Av. *IG5: Ilf* *2E 52*
Dacre Cl. *UB6: G'frd* *2F 77*
Dacre Gdns. *SE13* *4G 123*
Dacre Ho. *SW3* *7B 16*
Dacre Pk. *SE13* *3G 123*
Dacre Pl. *SE13* *3G 123*
Dacre Rd. *CR0: C'don* *7J 155*
  E11 . . . .*1H 69*
  E13 . . . .*1K 87*
Dacres Est. *SE23* *3K 139*
Dacres Ho. *SW4* *3F 119*
Dacres Rd. *SE23* *2K 139*
Dacre St. *SW1* . . . .*1C 18 (3H 101)*
Dade Way *UB2: S'hall* *5D 94*
Daerwood Cl. *BR2: Broml* *1D 172*
Daffodil Cl. *CR0: C'don* *1K 169*
Daffodil Gdns. *IG1: Ilf* *5F 71*
Daffodil Pl. *TW12: Hamp* *6E 130*
Daffodil St. *W12* *7B 80*
Dafforne Rd. *SW17* *3E 136*
Da Gama Pl. *E14* *5C 104*
DAGENHAM *6G 73*
Dagenham & Redbridge FC *5H 73*
Dagenham Av. *RM9: Dag* *1E 90*
        (not continuous)
Dagenham Pk. Leisure Cen. *7G 73*
Dagenham Rd. *E10* *1B 68*
  RM7: Rush G *7K 55*
  RM10: Dag *4J 73*
  RM13: Rain *7K 73*
Dagmar Av. *HA9: Wemb* *4F 61*
Dagmar Ct. *E14* *3E 104*
Dagmar Gdns. *NW10* *2F 81*
Dagmar M. *UB2: S'hall* *3C 94*
        (off Dagmar Rd.)
Dagmar Pas. *N1* *1B 84*
        (off Cross St.)
Dagmar Rd. *KT2: King T* *1F 151*
  N4 . . . .*7A 48*
  N15 . . . .*4D 48*
  N22 . . . .*1H 47*
  RM10: Dag *7J 73*
  SE5 . . . .*1E 120*
  SE25 . . . .*5E 156*
  UB2: S'hall *3C 94*
Dagmar Ter. *N1* *1B 84*
Dagnall Pk. *SE25* *6E 156*
Dagnall Rd. *SE25* *5E 156*
Dagnall St. *SW11* *2D 118*
Dagnan Rd. *SW12* *7F 119*
Dagobert Ho. *E1* *5J 85*
        (off Smithy St.)
Dagonet Gdns. *BR1: Broml* *3J 141*
Dagonet Rd. *BR1: Broml* *3J 141*
Dahlia Gdns. *CR4: Mitc* *4H 155*
  IG1: Ilf *6F 71*
Dahlia Rd. *SE2* *4B 108*
Dahomey Rd. *SW16* *6G 137*
Daimler Ho. *E3* *4C 86*
        (off Wellington Way)
Daimler Way *SM6: W'gton* *7J 167*
Dain Ct. *W8* *4J 99*
        (off Lexham Gdns.)
Daines Cl. *E12* *3D 70*
Dainford Cl. *BR1: Broml* *5F 141*
Dainton Cl. *BR1: Broml* *1K 159*
Dainton Ho. *W2* *5J 81*
        (off Gt. Western Rd.)
Daintry Cl. *HA3: W'stone* *4A 42*

Daintry Way E9 . . . . .6B 68
Dairsie Ct. BR1: Broml 1A 160
Dairsie Rd. SE9 . . . . .3E 124
Dairy Cl. BR1: Broml 7K 141
　CR7: Thor H 2C 156
　NW10 .1C 80
　SW6 .1J 117
　UB6: G'frd 2H 77
Dairy Farm Pl. SE15 . . . . .1J 121
Dairy La. SE18 . . . . .4D 106
Dairyman Cl. NW2 . . . . .3F 63
Dairy M. N2 . . . . .4C 46
　RM6: Chad H 7D 54
　SW9 .3J 119
Dairy Wlk. SW19 . . . . .4G 135
Daisy Cl. CR0: C'don 1K 169
　NW9 . . . . .2J 61
Daisy Dobbins Wlk. N19 . . . . .7J 47
　　　　　　(off Jessie Blythe La.)
Daisy La. SW6 . . . . .3J 117
Daisy Rd. E16 . . . . .4G 87
　E18 . . . . .2K 51
Dakin Pl. E1 . . . . .5A 86
Dakota Bldg. SE13 . . . . .1D 122
　　　　　　(off Deal's Gateway)
Dakota Cl. SM6: W'gton 7K 167
Dakota Gdns. E6 . . . . .4C 88
　UB5: N'olt 3C 76
Dakota Ho. CR7: Thor H 6B 156
Dalberg Rd. SW2 . . . . .4A 120
　　　　　　(not continuous)
Dalberg Way SE2 . . . . .3D 108
Dalby Rd. SW18 . . . . .4A 118
Dalby St. NW5 . . . . .6F 65
Dalcross Rd. TW4: Houn 2C 112
The Dale BR2: Kes 4B 172
Dale Av. HA8: Edg 1F 43
　TW4: Houn 3C 112
Dalebury Pl. TW5: Hest 5E 94
Dalebury Rd. SW17 . . . . .2D 136
Dale Cl. E4 . . . . .3K 35
　EN5: New Bar 6E 20
　HA5: Pinn 1K 39
　SE3 .3J 123
Dale Cl. EN2: Enf 1H 23
　KT2: King T 7F 133
　　　　　　(off York Rd.)
Dale Dr. UB4: Hayes 4H 75
Dalefield IG9: Buck H 1F 37
　　　　　　(off Roebuck La.)
Dale Gdns. IG8: Wfd G 4E 36
Dale Grn. Rd. N11 . . . . .3A 32
Dale Gro. N12 . . . . .5F 31
Daleham Dr. UB8: Hil 6D 74
Daleham Gdns. NW3 . . . . .5B 64
Daleham M. NW3 . . . . .6B 64
Dalehead NW1 . . . . .1A 6
　　　　　　(off Hampstead Rd.)
Dale Ho. N1 . . . . .1E 84
　　　　　　(off Halcomb St.)
　NW8 .1A 82
　　　　　　(off Boundary Rd.)
　SE4 .4A 122
Dale Lodge N6 . . . . .6G 47
Dalemain M. E16 . . . . .1J 105
Dale Pk. Av. SM5: Cars 2D 166
Dale Pk. Rd. SE19 . . . . .1C 156
Dale Rd. KT12: Walt T 7H 147
　NW5 .5E 64
　SE17 . . . . .6B 102
　SM1: Sutt 4H 165
　TW16: Sun 7H 129
　UB6: G'frd 5F 77
Dale Row W11 . . . . .6G 81
Daleside Rd. KT19: Ewe 6K 163
　SW16 . . . . .5F 137
Dale St. W4 . . . . .5A 98
Dale Vw. Av. E4 . . . . .2K 35
Dale Vw. Cres. E4 . . . . .2K 35
Dale Vw. Gdns. E4 . . . . .3A 36
Daleview Rd. N15 . . . . .6E 48
Dalewood Gdns. KT4: Wor Pk 2D 164

Dale Wood Rd. BR6: Orp 7J 161
Daleworth Cl. BR3: Beck 6C 140
Daley Ho. W12 . . . . .6D 80
Daley St. E9 . . . . .6K 67
Daley Thompson Way SW8 . . . . . .2F 119
Dalgarno Gdns. W10 . . . . .5E 80
Dalgarno Way W10 . . . . .4E 80
Dalgleish St. E14 . . . . .6A 86
Daling Way E3 . . . . .1A 86
Dalkeith Ct. SW1 . . . . .3D 18
　　　　　　(off Vincent St.)
Dalkeith Gro. HA7: Stan 5J 27
Dalkeith Ho. SW9 . . . . .1B 120
　　　　　　(off Lothian Rd.)
Dalkeith Rd. IG1: Ilf 3G 71
　SE21 . . . . .1C 138
Dallas Rd. NW4 . . . . .7C 44
　SE26 .3H 139
　SM3: Cheam 6G 165
　W5 . . . . .5F 79
Dallas Ter. UB3: Harl 3H 93
Dallega Cl. UB3: Hayes 7F 75
Dallinger Rd. SE12 . . . . .6H 123
Dalling Rd. W6 . . . . .4D 98
Dallington Sq. EC1 . . . . .3B 8
　　　　　　(off Dallington St.)
Dallington St. EC1 . . . . .3B 8 (4B 84)
Dallin Rd. DA6: Bex 4D 126
　SE18 .7F 107
Dalmain Rd. SE23 . . . . .1K 139
Dalmany Pas. CR0: C'don 7F 157
Dalmeny Av. N7 . . . . .4H 65
　SW16 . . . . .2A 156
Dalmeny Cl. HA0: Wemb 6C 60
Dalmeny Cres. TW3: Houn 4H 113
Dalmeny Rd. DA8: Erith 1H 127
　EN5: New Bar 6F 21
　KT4: Wor Pk 3D 164
　N7 . . . . .3H 65
　　　　　　(not continuous)
　SM5: Cars 7E 166
Dalmeyer Rd. NW10 . . . . .6B 62
Dalmore Rd. SE21 . . . . .2C 138
Dalo Lodge E3 . . . . .5C 86
　　　　　　(off Gale St.)
Dalrymple Cl. N14 . . . . .7C 22
Dalrymple Rd. SE4 . . . . .4A 122
DALSTON 6F 67
Dalston Gdns. HA7: Stan 1E 42
Dalston La. E8 . . . . .6F 67
Dalston Sq. E8 . . . . .6F 67
　　　　　　(not continuous)
Dalton Av. CR4: Mitc 2C 154
Dalton Cl. BR6: Orp 3J 173
　UB4: Hayes 4F 75
Dalton Ho. E3 . . . . .2A 86
　　　　　　(off Ford St.)
　HA7: Stan 5F 27
　SE14 . . . . .6K 103
　　　　　　(off John Williams Cl.)
　SW1 .5J 17
　　　　　　(off Ebury Bri. Rd.)
Dalton Ho. Apts. IG11: Bark 4A 90
Dalton Rd. HA3: W'stone 2H 41
Dalton St. SE27 . . . . .3B 138
Dalwood St. SE5 . . . . .1E 120
Daly Dr. BR1: Broml 3E 160
Dalyell Rd. SW9 . . . . .3K 119
Damascene Wlk. SE21 . . . . .1C 138
Damask Cl. SM1: Sutt 1K 165
Damask Cres. E16 . . . . .4G 87
Damer Ter. SW10 . . . . .7A 100
Dames Rd. E7 . . . . .3J 69
Dame St. N1 . . . . .2C 84
Damien Ct. E1 . . . . .6H 85
　　　　　　(off Damien St.)
Damien St. E1 . . . . .6H 85
Damon Cl. DA14: Sidc 3B 144
Damory Ho. SE16 . . . . .4H 103
　　　　　　(off Abbeyfield Est.)
Damsel Ho. SE4 . . . . .3A 122
　　　　　　(off Dragonfly Pl.)

Damsel Wlk. NW9 . . . . .6C 44
　　　　　　(off Perryfield Way)
Damson Dr. UB3: Hayes 7J 75
Damson Way SM5: Cars 7D 166
Damsonwood Rd. UB2: S'hall 3E 94
Danbrook Rd. SW16 . . . . .1J 155
Danbury Cl. RM6: Chad H 3D 54
Danbury Mans. IG11: Bark 7F 71
　　　　　　(off Whiting Av.)
Danbury M. SM6: W'gton 4F 167
Danbury St. N1 . . . . .2B 84
Danbury Way IG8: Wfd G 6F 37
Danby Cl. EN2: Enf 3H 23
Danby Ho. E9 . . . . .7J 67
　　　　　　(off Frampton Pk. Rd.)
　W10 . . . . .3G 81
　　　　　　(off Bruckner St.)
Danby St. SE15 . . . . .3F 121
Dance Ho. SE4 . . . . .5K 121
　　　　　　(off St Norbert Rd.)
Dancer Rd. SW6 . . . . .1H 117
　TW9: Rich 3G 115
Dando Cres. SE3 . . . . .3J 123
Dancer Way SE8 . . . . .6D 104
Dance Sq. EC1 . . . . .2C 8 (3C 84)
Dan Ct. NW10 . . . . .3G 79
Dandelion Court E14 . . . . .3D 104
　　　　　　(off Watergate Walk)
Dandridge Cl. SE10 . . . . .5H 105
Dandridge Ho. E1 . . . . .5J 9
　　　　　　(off Lamb St.)
Danebury CR0: New Ad 6E 170
Danebury Av. SW15 . . . . .6A 116
Daneby Rd. SE6 . . . . .3D 140
Dane Cl. BR6: Farnb 5H 173
　DA5: Bexl 7G 127
Danecourt Gdns. CR0: C'don 3F 169
Danecroft Rd. SE24 . . . . .5C 120
Danehill Wlk. DA14: Sidc 3A 144
Danehurst TW8: Bford 7C 96
Danehurst Gdns. IG4: Ilf 5C 52
Danehurst St. SW6 . . . . .1G 117
Daneland EN4: E Barn 6J 21
Daneland Wlk. N17 . . . . .3H 49
Danemead Gro. UB5: N'olt 5F 59
Danemere St. SW15 . . . . .3E 116
Dane Pl. E3 . . . . .2A 86
Dane Rd. IG1: Ilf 5G 71
　N18 . . . . .3D 34
　SW19 . . . . .1A 154
　TW15: Ashf 6E 128
　UB1: S'hall 7C 76
　W13 . . . . .1C 96
Danesbury Rd. TW13: Felt 1K 129
Danescombe SE12 . . . . .1J 141
Danes Cl. HA9: Wemb 3H 61
　NW8 .1D 82
　　　　　　(off St Edmund's Ter.)
Danescourt Cres. SM1: Sutt 2A 166
Danescroft NW4 . . . . .5F 45
Danescroft Av. NW4 . . . . .5F 45
Danescroft Gdns. NW4 . . . . .5F 45
Danesdale Rd. E9 . . . . .6A 68
Danesfield SE5 . . . . .6E 102
　　　　　　(off Albany Rd.)
Danes Ga. HA1: Harr 3J 41
Danes Ho. W10 . . . . .5E 80
　　　　　　(off Sutton Way)
Danes Rd. RM7: Rush G 7J 55
Dane St. WC1 . . . . .6G 7 (5K 83)
Daneswood Av. SE6 . . . . .3E 140
Dane's Yd. E15 . . . . .2E 86
Danethorpe Rd.
　HA0: Wemb 6D 60
Danetree Cl. KT19: Ewe 7J 163
Danetree Rd. KT19: Ewe 7J 163
Danette Gdns. RM10: Dag 2G 73
Daneville Rd. SE5 . . . . .1D 120
Danewood Dr. N2 . . . . .7B 46
Dangan Rd. E11 . . . . .6J 51
Daniel Bolt Cl. E14 . . . . .5D 86
Daniel Cl. N18 . . . . .4D 34
　SW17 . . . . .6C 136
　TW4: Houn 7D 112

Daniel Ct. BR3: Beck 7C 140
　　　　　　(off Brackley Rd.)
　NW9 . . . . .1A 44
Daniel Gdns. SE15 . . . . .7F 103
Daniell Ho. N1 . . . . .2D 84
　　　　　　(off Cranston Est.)
Daniell Way CR0: Wadd 1J 167
Daniel Pl. NW4 . . . . .7D 44
Daniel Rd. W5 . . . . .7F 79
Daniels Rd. SE15 . . . . .3J 121
Danleigh Ct. N14 . . . . .7C 22
Dan Leno Wlk. SW6 . . . . .7K 99
Dan Mason Dr. W4 . . . . .2J 115
Dannatt Cl. N2 . . . . .2G 31
DANNY FISZMAN BRI. 4A 66
Dansey Pl. W1 . . . . .2C 12
Dansington Rd. DA16: Well 4A 126
Danson Cres. DA16: Well 3B 126
Danson House 4C 126
DANSON INTERCHANGE 5C 126
Danson La. DA16: Well 4B 126
Danson Mead DA16: Well 3C 126
Danson Pk. 5C 126
Danson Pk. Watersports Cen. 4C 126
Danson Rd. DA5: Bexl, Bex 6C 126
　DA6: Bex 5D 126
　SE17 .5B 102
Danson Underpass
　DA15: Sidc 6C 126
Dante Pl. SE11 . . . . .4B 102
Dante Rd. SE11 . . . . .4B 102
Danube Apts. N8 . . . . .3K 47
　　　　　　(off Gt. Amwell La.)
Danube Cl. N9 . . . . .3D 34
Danube Ct. SE15 . . . . .7F 103
　　　　　　(off Daniel Gdns.)
Danube St. SW3 . . . . .5D 16 (5C 100)
Danvers St. SW11 . . . . .4C 118
Danvers Ho. E1 . . . . .6G 85
　　　　　　(off Christian St.)
Danvers Rd. N8 . . . . .4H 47
Danvers St. SW3 . . . . .7B 16 (6B 100)
Dao Ct. E13 . . . . .1K 87
Da Palma Ct. SW6 . . . . .6J 99
　　　　　　(off Anselm Rd.)
Daphne Ct. KT4: Wor Pk 2A 164
Daphne Gdns. E4 . . . . .3K 35
Daphne Ho. N22 . . . . .1A 48
　　　　　　(off Acacia Rd.)
Daphne St. SW18 . . . . .6A 118
Daplyn St. E1 . . . . .5K 9 (5G 85)
Dara Ho. NW9 . . . . .3K 43
Darbishire Pl. E1 . . . . .2K 15
D'Arblay St. W1 . . . . .1B 12 (6G 83)
Darby Cres. TW16: Sun 2A 148
Darby Gdns. TW16: Sun 2A 148
Darcies M. N8 . . . . .6J 47
Darcy Av. SM6: W'gton 4G 167
Darcy Cl. N20 . . . . .2G 31
D'Arcy Dr. HA3: Kenton 4D 42
D'Arcy Gdns. HA3: Kenton 4D 42
Darcy Gdns. RM9: Dag 1F 91
Darcy Ho. E8 . . . . .1H 85
　　　　　　(off London Flds. E. Side)
　RM9: Dag 1G 91
D'Arcy Pl. BR2: Broml 4J 159
D'Arcy Rd. SM3: Cheam 4F 165
Darcy Rd. SW16 . . . . .2J 155
　TW7: Isle 1A 114
Dare Gdns. RM8: Dag 3E 72
Darent Rd. TW9: Rich 3G 115
Darent Ho. BR1: Broml 5F 141
　NW8 . . . . .5B 4
　　　　　　(off Church St. Est.)
Darenth Rd. DA16: Well 1A 126
　N16 . . . . .7F 49
Darfield NW1 . . . . .1G 83
　　　　　　(off Bayham St.)
Darfield Rd. SE4 . . . . .5B 122
Darfield Way W10 . . . . .6F 81
Darfur St. SW15 . . . . .3F 117
Dargate Cl. SE19 . . . . .7F 139
Darien Rd. SW11 . . . . .3B 118

Daring Ho. *E3* 2A **86**
(off Roman Rd.)
Dark Ho. Wlk. EC3 . . . . . . .3F **15** (7D **84**)
Darlands Dr. EN5: Barn 5A **20**
Darlan Rd. SW6 . . . . .7H **99**
Darlaston Rd. SW19 . . . . .7F **135**
Darley Cl. CR0: C'don 6A **158**
Darley Dr. KT3: N Mald 2K **151**
Darley Gdns. SM4: Mord 6A **154**
Darley Ho. SE11 . . . . .6G **19**
Darley Rd. N9 . . . . .1A **34**
SW11 . . . . .6D **118**
Darling Ho. TW1: Twick 6D **114**
Darling Rd. SE4 . . . . .3C **122**
Darling Row E1 . . . . .4H **85**
Darlington Ct. SE6 . . . . .1H **141**
Darlington Ho. *SW8* 7H **101**
(off Hemans St.)
Darlington Rd. SE27 . . . . .5B **138**
Darmaine Cl. CR2: S Croy 7C **168**
Darnall Ho. *SE10* 1E **122**
(off Royal Hill)
Darnaway Pl. *E14* 5E **86**
(off Aberfeldy St.)
Darndale Cl. E17 . . . . .2B **50**
Darnley Cl. DA15: Sidc 5K **125**
Darnley Ho. *E14* 6A **86**
(off Camdenhurst St.)
Darnley Rd. E9 . . . . .6J **67**
IG8: Wfd G 1J **51**
Darnley Ter. W11 . . . . .1F **99**
Darrell Charles Ct.
UB8: Uxb 7A **56**
Darrell Rd. SE22 . . . . .5G **121**
Darren Cl. N4 . . . . .7K **47**
Darren Ct. N7 . . . . .4J **65**
Darrick Wood Rd. BR6: Orp 2H **173**
Darrick Wood Sports Cen. 3G **173**
Darrick Wood Swimming Pool . .3G **173**
Darris Cl. UB4: Yead 4C **76**
Darsley Dr. SW8 . . . . .1H **119**
Dartford Av. N9 . . . . .6D **24**
Dartford By-Pass DA5: Bexl 7K **127**
Dartford Gdns. RM6: Chad H 5B **54**
Dartford Ho. *SE1* 4F **103**
(off Longfield Est.)
Dartford Rd. DA5: Bexl 1J **145**
Dartford St. SE17 . . . . .6C **102**
Dartington *NW1* 1G **83**
(off Plender St.)
Dartington Ho. *SW8* 2H **119**
(off Union Gro.)
W2 .5K **81**
(off Senior St.)
Dartle Ct. *SE16* 2G **103**
(off Scott Lidgett Cres.)
Dartmoor Wlk. *E14* 4C **104**
(off Severnake Cl.)
Dartmouth Cl. W11 . . . . .6H **81**
Dartmouth Ct. SE10 . . . . .1E **122**
Dartmouth Gro. SE10 . . . . .1E **122**
Dartmouth Hill SE10 . . . . .1E **122**
Dartmouth Ho. *KT2: King T* 1E **150**
(off Seven Kings Way)
SE10 . . . . .1D **122**
(off Catherine Gro.)
DARTMOUTH PARK 3F **65**
Dartmouth Pk. Av. NW5 . . . . .3F **65**
Dartmouth Pk. Hill N19 . . . . .1F **65**
NW5 . . . . .1F **65**
Dartmouth Pk. Rd. NW5 . . . . . . .4F **65**
Dartmouth Pl. SE23 . . . . .2J **139**
W4 .6A **98**
Dartmouth Rd. BR2: Hayes 7J **159**
HA4: Ruis 3J **57**
NW2 . . . . .6F **63**
NW4 . . . . .6C **44**
SE23 . . . . .3H **139**
SE26 . . . . .3H **139**
Dartmouth Row SE10 . . . . .2E **122**
Dartmouth St. SW1 . . . . .7D **12** (2H **101**)
Dartmouth Ter. SE10 . . . . .1F **123**

Dartnell Rd. CR0: C'don 7F **157**
Darton Ct. W3 . . . . .1J **97**
Dartrey Twr. *SW10* 7A **100**
(off Worlds End Est.)
Dartrey Wlk. SW10 . . . . .7A **100**
Dart St. W10 . . . . .3G **81**
Darvell Ho. *SE17* 5D **102**
(off Inville Rd.)
Darville Rd. N16 . . . . .3F **67**
Darwell Cl. E6 . . . . .2E **88**
Darwell M. E6 . . . . .2E **88**
Darwen Pl. E2 . . . . .2H **85**
Darwin Cl. BR6: Farnb 5H **173**
N11 .3A **32**
Darwin Ct. *CR2: S Croy* 5B **168**
(off Warham Rd.)
E13 .3K **87**
NW1 . . . . .1F **83**
(not continuous)
SE17 . . . . .4D **102**
(off Barlow St.)
Darwin Dr. UB1: S'hall 6F **77**
Darwin Ho. SE20 . . . . .1G **157**
SW1 . . . . .7A **18**
Darwin Rd. DA16: Well 3K **125**
N22 .1B **48**
W5 .5C **96**
Darwin St. SE17 . . . . .4D **102**
(not continuous)
Darwood Ct. *NW6* 7A **64**
(off Belsize Rd.)
Daryngton Dr. UB6: G'frd 2H **77**
Daryngton Ho. *SE1* 7F **15**
(off Hankey Pl.)
SW8 . . . . .7J **101**
(off Hartington Rd.)
Dashwood Cl. DA6: Bex 5G **127**
Dashwood Rd. N8 . . . . .6K **47**
Dashwood Studios *SE17* 4C **102**
(off Walworth Rd.)
Dassett Rd. SE27 . . . . .5B **138**
Data Point Bus. Cen. E16 . . . . . . .4F **87**
Datchelor Pl. SE5 . . . . .1D **120**
Datchet Ho. *E2* 2J **9**
(off Virginia Rd.)
NW1 . . . . .1K **5**
(off Augustus St.)
Datchet Rd. SE6 . . . . .2B **140**
Datchworth Ct. EN1: Enf 5K **23**
Datchworth Ho. *N1* 7B **66**
(off The Sutton Est.)
Date St. SE17 . . . . .5D **102**
Daubeney Gdns. N17 . . . . .7H **33**
Daubeney Pl. *TW12: Hamp* 1G **149**
(off High St.)
Daubeney Rd. E5 . . . . .4A **68**
N17 .7H **33**
Daubeney Twr. *SE8* 5B **104**
(off Bowditch)
Dault Rd. SW18 . . . . .6A **118**
Dauncey Ho. SE1 . . . . .7A **14**
Dave Adams Ho. *E3* 2B **86**
(off Norman Gro.)
Davema Cl. BR7: Chst 1E **160**
Davenant Ho. *E1* 5G **85**
(off Old Montague St.)
Davenant Pl. SE26 . . . . .5H **139**
Davenant Rd. CR0: C'don 4B **168**
N19 .2H **65**
Davenant St. E1 . . . . .5G **85**
Davenport Cen. IG11: Bark 1B **90**
Davenport Cl. TW11: Tedd 6A **132**
Davenport Ct. CR0: C'don 7B **156**
Davenport Ho. *SE11* 3J **19**
(off Walnut Tree Wlk.)
UB7: W Dray 2B **92**
Davenport Lodge TW5: Hest 7C **94**
Davenport Rd. DA14: Sidc 2E **144**
SE6 . . . . .6D **122**
Daventer Dr. HA7: Stan 7E **26**
Daventry Cl. SL3: Poyle 4A **174**
Daventry St. NW1 . . . . . .5C **4** (5C **82**)

Daver Ct. SW3 . . . . .5D **16** (5C **100**)
W5 .4D **78**
Davern Cl. SE10 . . . . .4H **105**
Davey Cl. N7 . . . . .6K **65**
N13 .5E **32**
Davey Gdns. IG11: Bark 4A **90**
Davey Rd. E9 . . . . .7C **68**
Davey's Ct. WC2 . . . . .2E **12**
Davey St. SE15 . . . . .6F **103**
David Av. UB6: G'frd 3J **77**
David Cl. UB3: Harl 7G **93**
David Coffer Ct. DA17: Belv 4H **109**
David Ct. *E14* 5D **86**
(off Hillary M.)
N20 .3F **31**
Davidge Ho. *SE1* 7K **13**
(off Coral St.)
Davidge St. SE1 . . . . . . .7A **14** (2B **102**)
David Hewitt Ho. *E3* 5D **86**
(off Watts Gro.)
David Ho. DA15: Sidc 3A **144**
SW8 . . . . .7J **101**
(off Wyvil Rd.)
David Lean Cinema 3D **168**
(within Fairfield Halls)
David Lee Point E15 . . . . .1E **87**
(off Leather Gdns.)
David Lloyd Leisure
Barnet 7G **31**
Beckenham 4B **158**
Cheam 7F **165**
Chigwell 1J **37**
Enfield 2B **24**
Fulham 7J **99**
(within Fulham Broadway Shop. Cen.)
Hampton 3E **130**
Heston 5A **94**
Kidbrooke 4K **123**
Kingston upon Thames 2E **150**
(within The Rotunda Cen.)
Purley 6K **167**
Raynes Park 3F **153**
Sidcup 5C **144**
Sudbury Hill 5H **59**
David M. SE10 . . . . .7E **104**
W1 . . . . .5F **5** (5D **82**)
David Rd. RM8: Dag 2E **72**
SL3: Poyle 5A **174**
Davidson Gdns. SW8 . . . . .7J **101**
Davidson La. HA1: Harr 7K **41**
Davidson Rd. CR0: C'don 1E **168**
Davidson Terraces *E7* 5K **69**
(off Claremont Rd.)
David's Rd. SE23 . . . . .1J **139**
David St. E15 . . . . .6F **69**
David Twigg Cl. KT2: King T 1E **150**
David Weir Leisure Cen. 7B **154**
David Wildman La. NW7 . . . . .6B **30**
Davies Cl. CR0: C'don 6G **157**
Davies La. E11 . . . . .2G **69**
Davies M. W1 . . . . .2J **11** (7F **83**)
Davies St. W1 . . . . .1J **11** (6F **83**)
Davies Wlk. TW7: Isle 1H **113**
Da Vinci Ct. *SE16* 5H **103**
(off Rossetti Rd.)
Da Vinci Lodge *SE10* 3H **105**
(off W. Parkside)
Da Vinci Torre *SE13* 3D **122**
(off Loampit Va.)
Davington Gdns. RM8: Dag 5B **72**
Davington Rd. RM8: Dag 6B **72**
Davinia Cl. IG8: Wfd G 6J **37**
Davis Ho. *W12* 7D **80**
(off White City Est.)
Davis Rd. KT9: Chess 4G **163**
W3 .1A **98**
Davis Rd. Ind. Pk. KT9: Chess . . .4G **163**
Davis St. E13 . . . . .2K **87**
Davisville Rd. W12 . . . . .2C **98**
Davis Way DA14: Sidc 6E **144**
Davmor Ct. TW8: Bford 5C **96**
Dawburn Pl. TW5: Hest 7B **94**
Dawes Av. TW7: Isle 5A **114**

Dawes Cl. UB10: Uxb 2A **74**
Dawes Ho. *SE17* 4D **102**
(off Orb St.)
Dawe's Rd. UB10: Uxb 2A **74**
Dawes Rd. SW6 . . . . .7G **99**
Dawes St. SE17 . . . . .5D **102**
Dawkins Ct. SE1 . . . . .3D **102**
Dawley Av. UB8: Hil 5E **74**
Dawley Pde. UB3: Hayes 7E **74**
Dawley Pk. UB3: Hayes 2F **93**
Dawley Rd. UB3: Harl, Hayes 7E **74**
Dawlish Av. N13 . . . . .4D **32**
SW18 . . . . .2K **135**
Dawlish Dr. IG1: Ilf 2A **78**
HA4: Ruis 2J **57**
HA5: Pinn 5C **40**
IG3: Ilf 4J **71**
Dawlish Rd. E10 . . . . .1E **68**
N17 .3G **49**
NW2 . . . . .6F **63**
Dawnay Gdns. SW18 . . . . .2B **136**
Dawnay Rd. SW18 . . . . .2A **136**
Dawn Cl. TW4: Houn 3C **112**
Dawn Cres. E15 . . . . .1F **87**
Dawpool Rd. NW2 . . . . .2B **62**
Daws Hill E4 . . . . .2K **25**
Daws La. NW7 . . . . .5G **29**
Dawson Av. IG11: Bark 7K **71**
Dawson Ct. SE18 . . . . .4G **107**
UB3: Hayes 5F **75**
Dawson Ct. *W3* 3J **97**
(off Palmerston Rd.)
Dawson Gdns. IG11: Bark 7K **71**
Dawson Ho. *E2* 3J **85**
(off Sceptre Rd.)
Dawson Pl. W2 . . . . .7J **81**
Dawson Rd. KT1: King T 3F **151**
NW2 . . . . .5E **62**
Dawson St. E2 . . . . .1K **9** (2F **85**)
Dawson Ter. N9 . . . . .7D **24**
Dax Ct. TW16: Sun 3A **148**
Daybrook Rd. SW19 . . . . .2K **153**
Day Dr. RM8: Dag 1D **72**
Day Ho. *SE5* 7C **102**
(off Bethwin Rd.)
Daylesford Av. SW15 . . . . .4C **116**
Daymer Gdns. HA5: Eastc 4K **39**
Daynor Ho. *NW6* 1J **81**
(off Quex Ho.)
Daysbrook Rd. SW2 . . . . .1K **137**
Days La. DA15: Sidc 7J **125**
Dayton Gro. SE15 . . . . .1J **121**
Deaconess Ct. N15 . . . . .4F **49**
(off Tottenham Grn. E.)
The Deacon Est. E4 . . . . .6G **35**
Deacon Ho. *SE11* 4H **19**
(off Black Prince Rd.)
Deacon M. N1 . . . . .7D **66**
Deacon Rd. KT2: King T 1F **151**
NW2 . . . . .5C **62**
Deacons Cl. HA5: Pinn 2K **39**
Deacons Ct. TW1: Twick 2K **131**
Deacons Leas BR6: Orp 4H **173**
Deacon's Ri. N2 . . . . .5B **46**
Deacons Ter. *N1* 6C **66**
(off Harecourt Rd.)
Deacons Wlk. TW12: Hamp 4E **130**
Deacon Way IG8: Wfd G 7J **37**
Deal Ct. *NW9* 2B **44**
(off Hazel Cl.)
UB1: S'hall 6G **77**
(off Haldane Rd.)
Deal Ho. *SE15* 6K **103**
(off Lovelinch La.)
SE17 . . . . .5E **102**
(off Mina Rd.)
Deal M. W5 . . . . .4D **96**
Deal Porters Wlk. SE16 . . . . .2K **103**
Deal Porters Way SE16 . . . . .3J **103**
Deal Rd. SW17 . . . . .6E **136**
Deal's Gateway SE10 . . . . .1C **122**
SE13 . . . . .1C **122**
Deal St. E1 . . . . .5G **85**

Dealtry Rd. SW15 . . . . .4E 116
Deal Wlk. SW9 . . . . .7A 102
Dean Abbott Ho. SW1 . . . . .3C 18
(off Vincent St.)
Dean Bradley St. SW1 . . .2E 18 (3J 101)
Dean Cl. E9 . . . . .5J 67
SE16 . . . . .1K 103
UB10: Hil 7B 56
Dean Ct. HA0: Wemb 3B 60
HA8: Edg 6C 28
RM7: Rom 5K 55
SW8 . . . . .7J 101
(off Thorncroft St.)
W3 . . . . .6K 79
Deancross St. E1 . . . . .6J 85
Dean Dr. HA7: Stan 2E 42
Deane Av. HA4: Ruis 5A 58
Deane Ct. HA6: Nwood 1G 39
Deane Cft. Rd. HA5: Eastc 6A 40
Deanery Cl. N2 . . . . .4C 46
Deanery M. W1 . . . . .4H 11
Deanery Rd. E15 . . . . .6G 69
Deanery St. W1 . . . . .4H 11 (1E 100)
Deane Way HA4: Ruis 6K 39
Dean Farrar St. SW1 . . .1D 18 (3H 101)
Deanfield Gdns. CR0: C'don 4D 168
Dean Gdns. E17 . . . . .4F 51
Deanhill Ct. SW14 . . . . .4H 115
Deanhill Rd. SW14 . . . . .4H 115
Dean Ho. E1 . . . . .6J 85
(off Tarling St.)
SE14 . . . . .7A 104
(off New Cross Rd.)
Dean Path RM8: Bark 4A 72
Dean Rd. CR0: C'don 4D 168
NW2 . . . . .6E 62
SE28 . . . . .1A 108
TW3: Houn 5F 113
TW12: Hamp 5H 131
Dean Ryle St. SW1 . . . . .3E 18 (4J 101)
Deansbrook Cl. HA8: Edg 7D 28
Deansbrook Rd. HA8: Edg 7C 28
Dean's Bldgs. SE17 . . . . .4D 102
Deans Cl. CR0: C'don 3F 169
HA8: Edg 6D 28
W4 . . . . .6H 97
Dean's Ct. EC4 . . . . . .1B 14 (6B 84)
Deanscroft Av. NW9 . . . . .1J 61
Deans Dr. HA8: Edg 5E 28
N13 . . . . .6G 33
Deans Ga. SE23 . . . . .3K 139
Deanshanger Ho. SE8 . . . . .4K 103
(off Chilton Gro.)
Deans La. HA8: Edg 6D 28
W4 . . . . .6H 97
(off Deans Cl.)
Dean's M. W1 . . . . .7K 5 (6F 83)
Deans Rd. SM1: Sutt 3K 165
W7 . . . . .1K 95
Dean Stanley St. SW1 . . .2E 18 (3J 101)
Deanston Wharf E16 . . . . .2K 105
(not continuous)
Dean St. E7 . . . . .5J 69
W1 . . . . .7C 6 (6H 83)
Deans Way HA8: Edg 5D 28
Deansway N2 . . . . .4B 46
N9 . . . . .3K 33
Deanswood N11 . . . . .6C 32
Dean's Yd. SW1 . . . . . .1D 18 (3H 101)
Dean Trench St. SW1 . . .2E 18 (3J 101)
Dean Wlk. HA8: Edg 6D 28
Dean Way UB2: S'hall 2F 95
Dearne Cl. HA7: Stan 5F 27
De'Arn Gdns. CR4: Mitc 3C 154
Dearsley Ho. RM13: Rain 2K 91
Dearsley Rd. EN1: Enf 3B 24
Deauville Cl. E14 . . . . .6F 87
Deauville Ct. SE16 . . . . .2F 103
(off Eleanor Cl.)
SW4 . . . . .6G 119
De Barowe M. N5 . . . . .4B 66
Debdale Ho. E2 . . . . .1G 85
(off Whiston Rd.)

Debden N17 . . . . .2D 48
(off Gloucester Rd.)
Debden Cl. IG8: Wfd G 7G 37
KT2: King T 5D 132
NW9 . . . . .1A 44
Debden Pl. UB10: Uxb 1A 74
De Beauvoir Ct. N1 . . . . .7D 66
(off Northchurch Rd.)
De Beauvoir Cres. N1 . . . . .1E 84
De Beauvoir Est. N1 . . . . .1E 84
De Beauvoir Pl. N1 . . . . .6E 66
De Beauvoir Rd. N1 . . . . .1E 84
De Beauvoir Sq. N1 . . . . .7E 66
DE BEAUVOIR TOWN 1E 84
De Beauvoir Wharf N1 . . . . .1E 84
(off Hertford Rd.)
Debenham Ct. E8 . . . . .1G 85
(off Pownall Rd.)
Debham Ct. NW2 . . . . .3E 62
Deblin Dr. UB10: Uxb 2A 74
Debnams Rd. SE16 . . . . .4J 103
De Bohun Av. N14 . . . . .6A 22
Deborah Cl. TW7: Isle 1J 113
Deborah Ct. E18 . . . . .3K 51
(off Victoria Rd.)
Deborah Cres. HA4: Ruis 7F 39
Deborah Lodge HA8: Edg 1H 43
Debrabant Cl. DA8: Erith 6K 109
De Brome Rd. TW13: Felt 1A 130
De Bruin Ct. E14 . . . . .5E 104
(off Ferry St.)
Deburgh Rd. SW19 . . . . .7A 136
Debussy NW9 . . . . .2B 44
Decapod St. E15 . . . . .5F 69
Decima St. SE1 . . . . . . .7G 15 (3E 102)
Decima Studios SE1 . . . . .7G 15
(off Decima St.)
Decimus Cl. CR7: Thor H 4D 156
Deck Cl. SE16 . . . . .1K 103
De Coubertin St. E20 . . . . .6E 68
Decoy Av. NW11 . . . . .5G 45
De Crespigny Pk. SE5 . . . . .2D 120
Dee Ct. W7 . . . . .6H 77
(off Hobbayne Rd.)
Dee Ho. KT2: King T 1D 150
(off May Bate Av.)
Deeley Rd. SW8 . . . . .1H 119
Deena Cl. W3 . . . . .6F 79
Deen City Farm 2A 154
Deepak Ho. SW17 . . . . .4C 136
Deepdale SW19 . . . . .4F 135
Deepdale Av. BR2: Broml 4H 159
Deepdale Cl. N11 . . . . .6K 31
Deepdale Cl. CR2: S Croy 4D 168
(off Birdhurst Av.)
Deep Dene W5 . . . . .4F 79
Deepdene Av. CR0: C'don 3F 169
Deepdene Cl. E11 . . . . .4J 51
Deepdene Ct. BR2: Broml 3G 159
N21 . . . . .6G 23
Deepdene Gdns. SW2 . . . . .7K 119
Deepdene Mans. SW6 . . . . .1H 117
(off Rostrevor Rd.)
Deepdene Point SE23 . . . . .3K 139
Deepdene Rd. DA16: Well 3A 126
SE5 . . . . .4D 120
Deepwell Cl. TW7: Isle 1A 114
Deepwood La. UB6: G'frd 3H 77
Deerbrook Rd. SE24 . . . . .1B 138
Deerdale Rd. SE24 . . . . .4C 120
Deerfield Cl. NW9 . . . . .5B 44
Deerfield Cotts. NW9 . . . . .5B 44
Deerhurst Cl. TW13: Felt 4K 129
Deerhurst Ct. CR0: C'don 1B 168
(off Parson's Mead)
Deerhurst Cres. TW12: Hamp H . . .5G 131
Deerhurst Ho. SE15 . . . . .6G 103
(off Haymerle Rd.)
Deerhurst Rd. NW2 . . . . .6F 63
SW16 .5K 137
Deering Ho. SE3 . . . . .4A 124
Deerings Dr. HA5: Eastc 5J 39
Deerleap Gro. E4 . . . . .5J 25

Dee Rd. TW9: Rich 4F 115
Deer Pk. Cl. KT2: King T 7H 133
Deer Pk. Gdns. CR4: Mitc 4B 154
Deer Pk. Rd. SW19 . . . . .2K 153
Deer Pk. Way BR4: W W'ck 2H 171
Deeside Rd. SW17 . . . . .3B 136
Dee St. E14 . . . . .6E 86
Defence Cl. SE28 . . . . .1J 107
Defiance Wlk. SE18 . . . . .3D 106
Defiant Way SM6: W'gton 7J 167
Defoe Av. TW9: Kew 7G 97
Defoe Cl. SE16 . . . . .2B 104
SW17 .6C 136
Defoe Ho. EC2 . . . . .5D 8
(off Beech St.)
SW17 .4D 136
Defoe Rd. N16 . . . . .3E 66
De Frene Rd. SE23 . . . . .4K 139
Degema Rd. BR7: Chst 5F 143
Dehar Cres. NW9 . . . . .7B 44
Dehavilland Cl. UB5: N'olt 3B 76
De Havilland Ct. N17 . . . . .3H 49
De Havilland Dr. SE18 . . . . .6F 107
De Havilland Rd. HA8: Edg 2G 43
TW5: Hest 7A 94
Dehavilland Studios E5 . . . . .2J 67
(off Cale St.)
De Havilland Way TW19: Stanw . . .6A 110
Dekker Cl. RM5: Col R 1G 55
Dekker Ho. SE5 . . . . .7D 102
(off Elmington St.)
Dekker Rd. SE21 . . . . .6E 120
Dekota HA9: Wemb 4G 61
(off Engineers Way)
Delacourt Rd. SE3 . . . . .7K 105
Delafield Ho. E1 . . . . .6G 85
(off Christian St.)
Delafield Rd. SE7 . . . . .5K 105
Delaford Rd. SE16 . . . . .5H 103
Delaford St. SW6 . . . . .7G 99
Delahay Ho. SW3 . . . . .7E 16
(off Chelsea Emb.)
Delamare St. SE6 . . . . .3D 140
Delamere Cres. CR0: C'don 6J 157
Delamere Ct. E17 . . . . .2E 50
Delamere Gdns. NW7 . . . . .6E 28
Delamere Rd. SW20 . . . . .1F 153
UB4: Yead 7B 76
W5 . . . . .2E 96
Delamere St. W2 . . . . .5K 81
Delamere Ter. W2 . . . . .5K 81
Delancey Pas. NW1 . . . . .1F 83
(off Delancey St.)
Delancey St. NW1 . . . . .1F 83
Delancey Studios NW1 . . . . .1F 83
Delany Ho. SE10 . . . . .6E 104
(off Thames St.)
Delarch Ho. SE1 . . . . .7A 14
De Laune St. SE17 . . . . .6K 19 (5B 102)
Delaware Mans. W9 . . . . .4K 81
(off Delaware Rd.)
Delaware Rd. W9 . . . . .4K 81
Delawyk Cres. SE24 . . . . .6C 120
Delcombe Av. KT4: Wor Pk 1E 164
Delderfield Ho. RM1: Rom 2K 55
(off Portnoi Cl.)
Delft Ho. KT2: King T 7F 133
(off Acre Rd.)
Delft Way SE22 . . . . .5E 120
Delhi Rd. EN1: Enf 7A 24
Delhi St. N1 . . . . .1J 83
Delia St. SW18 . . . . .7K 117
Delisle Rd. SE28 . . . . .1J 107
Delius Gro. E15 . . . . .2F 87
The Dell DA5: Bexl 1K 145
HA0: Wemb 5B 60
HA5: Pinn 2B 40
IG8: Wfd G 3E 36
SE2 . . . . .5A 108
SE19 . . . . .1F 157
TW8: Bford 6C 96
TW14: Felt 7K 111

Della Path E5 . . . . .3G 67
Dellbow Rd. TW14: Felt 5K 111
Dell Cl. E15 . . . . .1F 87
IG8: Wfd G 3E 36
SM6: W'gton 4G 167
Dell Farm Rd. HA4: Ruis 5F 39
Dellfield Cl. BR3: Beck 1E 158
Dell La. KT17: Ewe 5C 164
Dellors Cl. EN5: Barn 5A 20
Dellow Cl. IG2: Ilf 7H 53
Dellow Ho. E1 . . . . .7H 85
(off Dellow St.)
Dellow St. E1 . . . . .7H 85
Dell Rd. KT17: Ewe 6C 164
UB7: W Dray 4B 92
Dells Cl. E4 . . . . .7J 25
TW11: Tedd 6K 131
Dell's M. SW1 . . . . .4B 18
Dell Wlk. KT3: N Mald 2A 152
Dell Way W13 . . . . .6C 78
Dellwood Gdns. IG5: Ilf 3E 52
Delmare Cl. SW9 . . . . .4K 119
Delme Cres. SE3 . . . . .2K 123
Delmerend Ho. SW3 . . . . .5C 16
(off Cale St.)
Delmey Cl. CR0: C'don 3F 169
Deloraine Ho. SE8 . . . . .1C 122
Delorme St. W6 . . . . .6F 99
Delroy Ct. N20 . . . . .7F 21
Delta Bldg. E14 . . . . .6E 86
(off Ashton St.)
The Delta Bldg. RM7: Rush G 6K 55
Delta Cen. HA0: Wemb 1F 79
Delta Cl. KT4: Wor Pk 3B 164
Delta Ct. NW2 . . . . .2C 62
SE8 . . . . .6A 104
(off Trundleys Rd.)
Delta Gro. UB5: N'olt 3B 76
Delta Ho. N1 . . . . .1C 8
(off Nile St.)
Delta Mews NW7 . . . . .5B 30
Delta Pk. SW18 . . . . .4K 117
Delta Pk. Ind. Est. EN3: Brim 3G 25
Delta Point CR0: C'don 1C 168
(off Wellesley Rd.)
E2 . . . . .3G 85
(off Delta St.)
Delta Rd. KT4: Wor Pk 3A 164
Delta St. E2 . . . . .3G 85
De Luci Rd. DA8: Erith 5J 109
De Lucy St. SE2 . . . . .4B 108
Delvan Cl. SE18 . . . . .7E 106
Delvers Mead RM10: Dag 4J 73
Delverton Ho. SE17 . . . . .5B 102
(off Delverton Rd.)
Delverton Rd. SE17 . . . . .5B 102
Delvino Rd. SW6 . . . . .1J 117
Demesne Rd. SM6: W'gton 4H 167
Demeta Cl. HA9: Wemb 3J 61
De Montfort Pde. SW16 . . . . .3J 137
De Montfort Rd. SW16 . . . . .3J 137
De Morgan Rd. SW6 . . . . .3K 117
Dempsey Cl. SE6 . . . . .7C 122
Dempster Cl. KT6: Surb 1C 162
Dempster Rd. SW18 . . . . .5A 118
The Den 5J 103
Denbar Pde. RM7: Rom 4K 55
Denberry Dr. DA14: Sidc 3B 144
Denbigh Cl. BR7: Chst 6D 142
HA4: Ruis 2H 57
SM1: Sutt 5J 165
UB1: S'hall 6D 76
W11 . . . . .7H 81
Denbigh Ct. E6 . . . . .3B 88
W7 . . . . .5K 77
(off Copley Cl.)
Denbigh Dr. UB3: Harl 2E 92
Denbigh Gdns. TW10: Rich 5F 115
Denbigh Ho. SW1 . . . . .1F 17
(off Hans Pl.)
W11 . . . . .7H 81
(off Westbourne Gro.)
Denbigh M. SW1 . . . . .4A 18

Denbigh Pl. SW1 . . . . . .5A **18** (5G **101**)
Denbigh Rd. E6 . . . . .3B **88**
  TW3: Houn 2F **113**
  UB1: S'hall 6D **76**
  W11 .7H **81**
  W13 .7B **78**
Denbigh St. SW1 . . . . . .4A **18** (4G **101**)
  (not continuous)
Denbigh Ter. W11 . . . . .7H **81**
Denbridge Rd. BR1: Broml . . .2D **160**
Denbury Ho. E3 . . . . .3D **86**
  (off Talwin St.)
Denby Ct. SE11 . . . . .3H **19**
Dence Ho. E2 . . . . .2K **9**
  (off Turin St.)
Denchworth Ho. SW9 . . . . .2A **120**
Dencliffe TW15: Ashf 5C **128**
Den Cl. BR3: Beck 3F **159**
The Dencora Cen.
  EN3: Brim 3F **25**
The Dene CR0: C'don 4K **169**
  HA9: Wemb 4E **60**
  KT8: W Mole 5D **148**
  W13 .5B **78**
Dene Av. DA15: Sidc 7B **126**
  TW3: Houn 3D **112**
Dene Cl. BR2: Hayes 1H **171**
  DA2: Wilm 4K **145**
  E10 . . . . .2D **68**
  KT4: Wor Pk 2B **164**
  SE4 .3A **122**
Dene Ct. CR2: S Croy 5C **168**
  (off Warham Rd.)
  W5 . . . . .5C **78**
Denecroft Cres. UB10: Hil 1D **74**
Dene Gdns. HA7: Stan 5H **27**
  KT7: T Ditt 2A **162**
Dene Ho. N14 . . . . .7C **22**
Denehurst Gdns. IG8: Wfd G . . .4E **36**
  NW4 .6E **44**
  TW2: Twick 7H **113**
  TW10: Rich 4G **115**
  W3 . . . . .1H **97**
Dene Rd. IG9: Buck H 1G **37**
  N11 . . . . .1J **31**
Denesmead SE24 . . . . .5C **120**
Denewood EN5: New Bar 5F **21**
Denewood Rd. N6 . . . . .6D **46**
Denford St. SE10 . . . . .5H **105**
  (off Glenforth St.)
Dengie Wlk. N1 . . . . .1C **84**
  (off Basire St.)
Denham Cl. DA16: Well 3C **126**
Denham Ct. NW6 . . . . .7A **64**
  (off Fairfax Rd.)
  SE26 . . . . .3H **139**
  (off Kirkdale)
  UB1: S'hall 7G **77**
  (off Baird St.)
Denham Cres. CR4: Mitc 4D **154**
Denham Dr. IG2: Ilf 6G **53**
Denham Ho. UB7: W Dray 2B **92**
  (off Park Lodge Av.)
  W12 .7D **80**
  (off White City Est.)
Denham Rd. N20 . . . . .3J **31**
  TW14: Felt 7A **112**
Denham St. SE10 . . . . .5J **105**
Denham Way
  IG11: Bark 1J **89**
Denholme Rd. W9 . . . . .3H **81**
Denison Cl. N2 . . . . .3A **46**
Denison Ho. E14 . . . . .3D **104**
Denison Rd. SW19 . . . . .6B **136**
  TW13: Felt 4H **129**
  W5 . . . . .4C **78**
Deniston Av. DA5: Bexl 1E **144**
Denis Way SW4 . . . . .3H **119**
Denland Ho. SW8 . . . . .7K **101**
  (off Dorset Rd.)
Denleigh Gdns. KT7: T Ditt 6J **149**
  N21 . . . . .1F **33**
Denman Av. UB2: S'hall 1H **95**

Denman Dr. KT10: Clay 5A **162**
  NW11 . . . . .5J **45**
  TW15: Ashf 6D **128**
Denman Dr. Nth. NW11 . . . . .5J **45**
Denman Dr. Sth. NW11 . . . . .5J **45**
Denman Ho. N16 . . . . .2E **66**
Denman Pl. W1 . . . . .2C **12**
Denman Rd. SE15 . . . . .1F **121**
Denman St. W1 . . . . . .3C **12** (7H **83**)
Denmark Av. SW19 . . . . .7G **135**
Denmark Ct. SM4: Mord 6J **153**
Denmark Gdns. SM5: Cars 3D **166**
Denmark Gro. N1 . . . . .2A **84**
DENMARK HILL 3C **120**
Denmark Hill SE5 . . . . .1D **120**
Denmark Hill Dr. NW9 . . . . .3C **44**
Denmark Hill Est. SE5 . . . . .4D **120**
Denmark Ho. SE7 . . . . .4C **106**
Denmark Mans. SE5 . . . . .2C **120**
  (off Coldharbour La.)
Denmark Path SE25 . . . . .5H **157**
Denmark Pl. E3 . . . . .3C **86**
  WC2 . . . . .7D **6** (6H **83**)
Denmark Rd. BR1: Broml 1K **159**
  KT1: King T 3E **150**
  N8 . . . . .4A **48**
  NW6 .2H **81**
  SE5 .1C **120**
  SE25 . . . . .5G **157**
  SM5: Cars 3D **166**
  SW19 . . . . .6F **135**
  TW2: Twick 3H **131**
  W13 .7B **78**
Denmark St. E11 . . . . .3G **69**
  E13 . . . . .5K **87**
  N17 . . . . .1H **49**
  WC2 . . . . .7D **6** (6H **83**)
Denmark Ter. N2 . . . . .3D **46**
Denmark Wlk. SE27 . . . . .4C **138**
Denmead Ho. SW15 . . . . .6B **116**
Denmead Rd. CR0: C'don 1B **168**
Denmore Ct. SM6: W'gton 5F **167**
Dennard Way BR6: Farnb 4F **173**
Denner Rd. E4 . . . . .2H **35**
Denne Ter. E8 . . . . .1F **85**
Dennett Rd. CR0: C'don 1A **168**
Dennett's Gro. SE14 . . . . .2K **121**
Dennett's Rd. SE14 . . . . .1J **121**
Denning Av. CR0: Wadd 4A **168**
Denning Cl. NW8 . . . . . . .1A **4** (3A **82**)
  TW12: Hamp 5D **130**
Denning M. SW12 . . . . .6E **118**
Denning Point E1 . . . . .7K **9**
  (off Commercial St.)
Denning Rd. NW3 . . . . .4B **64**
Dennington Cl. E5 . . . . .2J **67**
Dennington Pk. Rd. NW6 . . . . . . .6J **63**
The Denningtons KT4: Wor Pk . . .2A **164**
Dennis Av. HA9: Wemb 5F **61**
Dennis Cl. TW15: Ashf 7F **129**
Dennis Gdns. HA7: Stan 5H **27**
Dennis Ho. E3 . . . . .2B **86**
  (off Roman Rd.)
  SM1: Sutt 4K **165**
Dennis La. HA7: Stan 3G **27**
Dennison Point E15 . . . . .7E **68**
Dennis Pde. N14 . . . . .1C **32**
Dennis Pk. Cres. SW20 . . . . . . .1G **153**
Dennis Reeve Cl. CR4: Mitc 1D **154**
Dennis Rd. KT8: E Mos 4G **149**
Dennis Severs' House 5H **9** (5E **84**)
Dennis Way SW4 . . . . .3H **119**
Denny Cl. E6 . . . . .5C **88**
Denny Cres. SE11 . . . . . . .5K **19** (5A **102**)
Denny Gdns. RM9: Dag 7B **72**
Denny Rd. N9 . . . . .1C **34**
Denny St. SE11 . . . . . . .5K **19** (5A **102**)
Den Rd. BR2: Broml 3F **159**
Densham Ho. NW8 . . . . .1B **4**
  (off Cochrane St.)
Densham Rd. E15 . . . . .1G **87**
Densole Cl. BR3: Beck 1A **158**

Denstone Ho. SE15 . . . . .6G **103**
  (off Haymerle Rd.)
Densworth Gro. N9 . . . . .2D **34**
Dent Ho. SE17 . . . . .4E **102**
  (off Peacock St.)
Denton NW1 . . . . .6E **64**
Denton Ho. N1 . . . . .7B **66**
  (off Halton Rd.)
Denton Rd. DA5: Bexl 2K **145**
  DA16: Well 7C **108**
  N8 . . . . .5K **47**
  N18 .4K **33**
  TW1: Twick 6D **114**
Denton St. SW18 . . . . .6K **117**
Denton Ter. DA5: Bexl 2K **145**
Denton Way E5 . . . . .3K **67**
Dents Rd. SW11 . . . . .6D **118**
Denver Cl. BR6: Pet W 6J **161**
Denver Rd. N16 . . . . .7E **48**
Denwood SE23 . . . . .3K **139**
Denyer St. SW3 . . . . . .4D **16** (4C **100**)
Denys Ho. EC1 . . . . .5J **7**
  (off Bourne Est.)
Denziloe Av. UB10: Hil 3D **74**
Denzil Rd. NW10 . . . . .5B **62**
Deodar Rd. SW15 . . . . .4G **117**
Deodora Cl. N20 . . . . .3H **31**
Department for Business, Energy &
  Industrial Strategy . . .1D **18** (3H **101**)
Department for Communities 1A **18**
Department for Education 1D **18**
Department for Energy & Climate Change
   . . . . .5E **12**
Department for Transport
   . . . . .3D **18** (4H **101**)
Department for Work & Pensions
   . . . . .7D **12**
Department of Environment
  Parks Department 1J **5** (3E **82**)
De Pass Gdns. IG11: Bark 4A **90**
Depot App. NW2 . . . . .4F **63**
  NW10: Wemb 6G **61**
Depot Rd. TW3: Houn 3H **113**
  W12 .7E **80**
Depot St. SE5 . . . . .6D **102**
DEPTFORD 7C **104**
Deptford Bri. SE8 . . . . .1C **122**
Deptford B'way. SE8 . . . . .1C **122**
Deptford Bus. Pk. SE15 . . . . . . .6J **103**
Deptford Chu. St. SE8 . . . . .6C **104**
Deptford Ferry Rd. E14 . . . . .4C **104**
Deptford Grn. SE8 . . . . .6C **104**
Deptford High St. SE8 . . . . .6C **104**
Deptford Pk. Bus. Cen. SE8 . . . .5A **104**
Deptford Strand SE8 . . . . .4B **104**
Deptford Trad. Est. SE8 . . . . . . .6A **104**
Deptford Wharf SE8 . . . . .4B **104**
De Quincey Ho. SW1 . . . . .6A **18**
  (off Lupus St.)
De Quincey M. E16 . . . . .1J **105**
De Quincey Rd. N17 . . . . .1D **48**
Derby Av. HA3: Hrw W 1H **41**
  N12 .5F **31**
  RM7: Rom 6J **55**
Derby Ga. SW1 . . . . . . .6E **12** (2J **101**)
  (not continuous)
Derby Hill SE23 . . . . .2J **139**
Derby Hill Cres. SE23 . . . . .2J **139**
Derby Ho. HA5: Pinn 2B **40**
  SE11 . . . . .3J **19**
Derby Lodge N3 . . . . .2H **45**
  WC1 . . . . .1G **7**
  (off Britannia St.)
Derby Rd. CR0: C'don 1B **168**
  E7 . . . . .7B **70**
  E9 . . . . .1K **85**
  E18 .1H **51**
  EN3: Pond E 5C **24**
  KT5: Surb 1G **163**
  N18 .5D **34**
  SM1: Sutt 6H **165**
  SW14 . . . . .4H **115**
  SW19 . . . . .7J **135**

Derby Rd. TW3: Houn 4F **113**
  UB6: G'frd 1F **77**
Derby Rd. Ind. Est. TW3: Houn . . .4F **113**
Derbyshire St. E2 . . . . .3G **85**
  (not continuous)
Derby St. W1 . . . . .5H **11** (1E **100**)
Dere Cl. SW6 . . . . .1G **117**
Dereham Ho. SE4 . . . . .4K **121**
  (off Frendsbury Rd.)
Dereham Pl. EC2 . . . . . . .2H **9** (3E **84**)
Dereham Rd. IG11: Bark 5K **71**
Derek Av. HA9: Wemb 7H **61**
  KT19: Ewe 6G **163**
  SM6: W'gton 4F **167**
Derek Cl. KT19: Ewe 5H **163**
Derek Walcott Cl. SE24 . . . . . . .5B **120**
Dericote St. E8 . . . . .1H **85**
Deridene Cl. TW19: Stanw 6A **110**
Derifall Cl. E6 . . . . .5D **88**
Dering Pl. CR0: C'don 4C **168**
Dering Rd. CR0: C'don 4C **168**
Dering St. W1 . . . . .1K **11** (6F **83**)
Dering Yd. W1 . . . . .1K **11** (6F **83**)
Derinton Rd. SW17 . . . . .4D **136**
Derley Rd. UB2: S'hall 3A **94**
Dermody Gdns. SE13 . . . . .5F **123**
Dermody Rd. SE13 . . . . .5F **123**
Derny Av. E20 . . . . .5D **68**
Deronda Rd. SE24 . . . . .1B **138**
Deroy Cl. SM5: Cars 6D **166**
Derrick Gdns. SE7 . . . . .3A **106**
Derrick Rd. BR3: Beck 3B **158**
Derrycombe Ho. W2 . . . . .5J **81**
  (off Gt. Western Rd.)
Derry Ho. NW8 . . . . .4B **4**
  (off Church St. Est.)
Derry M. N19 . . . . .2J **65**
Derry St. W8 . . . . .2K **99**
Dersingham Av. E12 . . . . .4D **70**
Dersingham Rd. NW2 . . . . .3G **63**
Derwent NW1 . . . . .2A **6**
  (off Robert St.)
Derwent Av. EN4: E Barn 1J **31**
  N18 .5J **33**
  NW7 .6E **28**
  NW9 .5A **44**
  SW15 . . . . .4A **134**
  UB10: Ick 2C **56**
Derwent Cl. TW14: Felt 1H **129**
Derwent Ct. SE16 . . . . .2K **103**
  (off Eleanor Cl.)
Derwent Cres. DA7: Bex 2G **127**
  HA7: Stan 2C **42**
  N20 .3F **31**
Derwent Dr. BR5: Pet W 7H **161**
  UB4: Hayes 5G **75**
Derwent Gdns. HA9: Wemb 7C **42**
  IG4: Ilf 4C **52**
Derwent Gro. SE22 . . . . .4F **121**
Derwent Ho. E3 . . . . .4B **86**
  (off Southern Gro.)
  KT2: King T 1D **150**
  (off May Bate Av.)
  SW7 .3A **16**
  (off Cromwell Rd.)
Derwent Lodge KT4: Wor Pk 2D **164**
  TW7: Isle 2H **113**
Derwent Point EC1 . . . . .1A **8**
  (off Goswell Rd.)
Derwent Ri. NW9 . . . . .6A **44**
Derwent Rd. N13 . . . . .4E **32**
  SE20 . . . . .2G **157**
  SW20 . . . . .6F **153**
  TW2: Whitt 6F **113**
  UB1: S'hall 6D **76**
  W5 . . . . .3C **96**
Derwent St. SE10 . . . . .5G **105**
Derwent Wlk. SM6: W'gton 7F **167**
Derwentwater Rd. W3 . . . . .1J **97**
Derwent Yd. W5 . . . . .3C **96**
  (off Derwent Rd.)
De Salis Rd. UB10: Hil 4E **74**

Des Barres Ct. *SE10* 3J *105*
    (off Peartree Way)
Desborough Cl. TW17: Shep 7C 146
W2 . . . . .5K 81
Desborough Ho. *W14* 6H *99*
    (off North End Rd.)
Desborough Sailing Club 7D 146
Desborough St. *W2* 5K *81*
    (off Cirencester St.)
Desenfans Rd. SE21 . . . . .6E 120
Desford Rd. E16 . . . . .4G 87
Desford Way TW15: Ashf 2B 128
Design Museum 3H 99
Desmond Ho. EN4: E Barn 6H 21
Desmond St. SE14 . . . . .6A 104
Desmond Tutu Dr. SE23 . . . . . .1B 140
Despard Rd. N19 . . . . .1G 65
Desvignes Dr. SE13 . . . . .6F 123
Dethick Ct. E3 . . . . .1A 86
Detling Ho. *SE17* 4E *102*
    (off Congreve St.)
Detling Rd. BR1: Broml 5J 141
DA8: Erith 7K 109
Detmold Rd. E5 . . . . .2J 67
Dettingen Pl. IG11: Bark 2B 90
Devalls Cl. E6 . . . . .7F 89
Devana End SM5: Cars 3D 166
Devane Way SE27 . . . . .3B 138
Devan Gro. N4 . . . . .7D 48
Devas Rd. SW20 . . . . .1E 152
Devas St. E3 . . . . .4D 86
Devenay Rd. E15 . . . . .7H 69
Devenish Rd. SE2 . . . . .2A 108
Deventer Cres. SE22 . . . . .5E 120
Deveraux Cl. BR3: Beck 5E 158
De Vere M. *W8* 3A *100*
    (off Canning Pl.)
De Vere Cl. SM6: W'gton 7J 167
De Vere Cotts. *W8* 3A *100*
    (off Canning Pl.)
De Vere Gdns. IG1: Ilf 2D 70
W8 . . . . .2A 100
Deverill St. SE1 . . . . .3D 102
De Vere M. *W8* 3A *100*
    (off Canning Pl.)
Devereux Ct. WC2 . . . . .1J 13
Devereux La. SW13 . . . . .7D 98
Devereux Rd. SW11 . . . . .6D 118
Deveron Way RM1: Rom 1K 55
Devey Cl. KT2: King T 7B 134
Devitt Ho. E14 . . . . .7D *86*
    (off Wade's Pl.)
Devizes St. N1 . . . . .1D 84
Devon Av. TW2: Twick 1G 131
Devon Cl. IG9: Buck H 2E 36
N17 . . . . .3F 49
UB6: G'frd 1C 78
Devon Ct. TW12: Hamp 7E 130
W7 . . . . .7J 77
    (off Copley Cl.)
Devoncroft Gdns. TW1: Twick 7A 114
Devon Gdns. N4 . . . . .6B 48
Devon Ho. E17 . . . . .2B 50
N1 . . . . .2B *84*
    (off Upper St.)
Devonhurst Pl. W4 . . . . .5K 97
Devonia Gdns. N18 . . . . .6H 33
Devonia Rd. N1 . . . . .2B 84
Devon Mans. *HA3: Kenton* 5C *42*
    (off Woodcock Hill)
SE1 . . . . .6J *15*
    (off Tooley St.)
Devon Pde. HA3: Kenton 5C 42
Devonport W2 . . . . .1C 10 (6C 82)
Devonport Gdns. IG1: Ilf 6D 52
Devonport Ho. *W2* 5J *81*
    (off Gt. Western Rd.)
Devonport M. W12 . . . . .2D 98
Devonport Rd. W12 . . . . .1D 98
    (not continuous)
Devonport St. E1 . . . . .6J 85
Devon Ri. N2 . . . . .4B 46
Devon Rd. IG11: Bark 1J 89
SM2: Cheam 7G 165
Devons Est. E3 . . . . .3D 86

Devonshire Av. SM2: Sutt 7A 166
Devonshire Cl. E15 . . . . .4G 69
N13 . . . . .3F 33
W1 . . . . .5J 5 (5F *83*)
Devonshire Ct. *E1* 3J *85*
    (off Bancroft Rd.)
HA5: Hat E 1D *40*
    (off Devonshire Rd.)
N17 . . . . .6H 33
TW13: Felt 2K 129
WC1 .5F 7
    (off Boswell St.)
Devonshire Cres. NW7 . . . . .7A 30
Devonshire Dr. KT6: Surb 1D 162
SE10 . . . . .7D 104
Devonshire Gdns. N17 . . . . .6H 33
N21 . . . . .7H 23
W4 . . . . .7J 97
Devonshire Gro. SE15 . . . . .6H 103
Devonshire Hall *E9* 6J *67*
    (off Frampton Pk. Rd.)
Devonshire Hill La. N17 . . . . .6G 33
Devonshire Ho. *E14* 4C *104*
    (off Westferry Rd.)
IG8: Wfd G 7K 37
NW6 .6H *63*
    (off Kilburn High Rd.)
SE1 .3C *102*
    (off Bath Ter.)
SM2: Sutt 7A 166
SW1 .5D *18*
    (off Lindsay Sq.)
SW15 . . . . .5F 117
W2 . . . . .5B *4*
    (off Admiral Wlk.)
Devonshire Ho. Bus. Cen.
BR2: Broml 4K *159*
    (off Devonshire Sq.)
Devonshire M. N13 . . . . .4F 33
SW10 . . . . .7A *16*
    (off Park Wlk.)
W4 . . . . .5A 98
Devonshire M. Nth. W1 . . . .5J 5 (5F *83*)
Devonshire M. Sth. W1 . . . .5J 5 (5F *83*)
Devonshire M. W. W1 . . . .4H 5 (4E *82*)
Devonshire Pas. W4 . . . . .5A 98
Devonshire Pl. NW2 . . . . .3J 63
W1 . . . . .4H 5 (4E *82*)
W8 . . . . .3K 99
Devonshire Pl. M. W1 . . . .4H 5 (5E *82*)
Devonshire Point TW15: Ashf 3E *128*
Devonshire Rd. BR6: Orp 7K 161
CR0: C'don 7D 156
DA6: Bex 4E 126
E16 . . . . .6H 87
E17 . . . . .6C 50
HA1: Harr 6H 41
HA5: Eastc 6A 40
HA5: Hat E 1D 40
IG2: Ilf 7G 53
N9 . . . . .1D 34
N13 .4E 32
N17 .6H 33
NW7 .7A 30
SE9 .2C 142
SE23 . . . . .1J 139
SM2: Sutt 7A 166
SM5: Cars 4E 166
SW19 . . . . .7C 136
TW13: Hanw 3C 130
UB1: S'hall 5E 76
W4 . . . . .5A 98
W5 . . . . .3C 96
Devonshire Road Nature Reserve
. . . . .7K 121
Devonshire Road Nature Reserve
Vis. Cen. 7K 121
Devonshire Row EC2 . . . . . .6H 9 (5E *84*)
Devonshire Row M. W1 . . . . .4K 5
Devonshire Sq. BR2: Broml 4K *159*
EC2 . . . . .6H 9 (6E *84*)
Devonshire St. W1 . . . . . . .5H 5 (5E *82*)
W4 . . . . .5A 98

Devonshire Ter. W2 . . . . .6A *82*
Devonshire Way CR0: C'don 2A *170*
UB4: Yead 6K 75
Devons Rd. E3 . . . . .3D 86
Devon St. SE15 . . . . .6H 103
Devon Way KT9: Chess 5C 162
KT19: Ewe 5H 163
UB10: Hil 2B 74
Devon Waye TW5: Hest 7D 94
De Walden Ho. *NW8* 2C *82*
    (off Allitsen Rd.)
De Walden St. W1 . . . . . .6H 5 (5E *82*)
Dewar St. SE15 . . . . .3G 121
Dewberry Gdns. E6 . . . . .5C 88
Dewberry St. E14 . . . . .5E 86
Dewey Ct. BR1: Broml 3J 159
Dewey La. *SW2* 6A *120*
    (off Tulse Hill)
Dewey Rd. N1 . . . . .2A 84
RM10: Dag 6H 73
Dewey St. SW17 . . . . .5D 136
Dewhurst Ct. TW3: Houn 4E 112
Dewhurst Rd. W14 . . . . .3F 99
Dewsbury Cl. HA5: Pinn 6C 40
Dewsbury Ct. W4 . . . . .4J 97
Dewsbury Gdns. KT4: Wor Pk 3C 164
Dewsbury Rd. NW10 . . . . .5C 62
Dewsbury Ter. NW1 . . . . .1F 83
Dews Farm Sand Pits Nature Reserve
. . . . .6A 38
De Wyndsor Ct. *SE16* 3G *103*
    (off Jamaica Rd.)
Dexter Apts. *SE15* 1H *121*
    (off Queen's Rd.)
Dexter Ho. *DA18: Erith* 3E *108*
    (off Kale Rd.)
Dexter Rd. EN5: Barn 6A 20
Deyncourt Rd. N17 . . . . .1C 48
Deynecourt Gdns. E11 . . . . .4A 52
D'Eynsford Rd. SE5 . . . . .1D 120
Dhonau Ho. *SE1* 4F *103*
    (off Longfield Est.)
Diadem Ct. W1 . . . . .7C 6
The Dial Wlk. W8 . . . . .2K 99
Diameter Rd. BR5: Pet W 7F 161
Diamond Cl. RM8: Dag 1C 72
Diamond Est. SW17 . . . . .3C 136
Diamond Gdns. E3 . . . . .5B 86
Diamond Ho. *E3* 2A *86*
    (off Roman Rd.)
Diamond Jubilee Way SM5: Cars . .7D 166
Diamond Rd. HA4: Ruis 4B 58
Diamond St. NW10 . . . . .7K 61
SE15 . . . . .7E 102
Diamond Ter. SE10 . . . . .1E 122
Diamond Way E3 . . . . .6C 104
Diana Cl. DA14: Sidc 2E 144
Dianne Cl. SE12 . . . . .1J 141
Dianthus Cl. SE2 . . . . .5B 108
Diana Ho. SW13 . . . . .1B 116
Diana, Princess of Wales
Memorial Fountain 6C 10 (2C 100)
Diana, Princess of Wales
Memorial Playground 1K 99
Diana, Princess of Wales Memorial Wlk.
Kensington Gdns. 1K 99
Diana Rd. E17 . . . . .3B 50
Dianne Way EN4: E Barn 4H 21
Dibden Ho. SE5 . . . . .7E 102
Dibden St. N1 . . . . .1C 84
Dibdin Cl. SM1: Sutt 3J 165
Dibdin Ho. W9 . . . . .2K 81
Dibdin Rd. SM1: Sutt 3J 165
Dibdin Row *SE1* 1K 19 (3A *102*)
Dicey Av. NW2 . . . . .4E 62
Dickens Av. N3 . . . . .1A 46
UB8: Hil 6D 74
Dickens Cl. DA8: Erith 7H 109
TW10: Ham 2E 132
UB3: Harl 4G 93

Dickens Ct. *E11* 4J *51*
    (off Makepeace Rd.)
SW17 . . . . .3B *136*
    (off Grosvenor Way)
Dickens Dr. BR7: Chst 6G 143
Dickens Est. SE1 . . . . .2G 103
SE16 . . . . .3G 103
Dickens Ho. *NW6* 3J *81*
    (off Malvern Rd.)
NW8 .3B *4*
SE17 . . . . .5B *102*
    (off Doddington Gro.)
SE19 . . . . .7E 138
WC1 .3E 6
Dickens La. N18 . . . . .5K 33
Dickens M. *EC1* 5A *8*
    (off Turnmill St.)
Dickenson Cl. N9 . . . . .1B 34
Dickenson Rd. N8 . . . . .7J 47
TW13: Hanw 5A 130
Dickenson's La. SE25 . . . . .6G 157
Dickensons La. SE25 . . . . .5G 157
    (not continuous)
Dickensons Pl. SE25 . . . . .6G 157
Dickens Pl. SL3: Poyle 4A 174
Dickens Ri. IG7: Chig 3K 37
Dickens Rd. E6 . . . . .2B 88
Dickens Sq. SE1 . . . . . . .7D 14 (3C 102)
Dickens St. SW8 . . . . .2F 119
Dickenswood Cl. SE19 . . . . .7B 138
Dickerage La. KT3: N Mald 3J 151
Dickerage Rd. KT1: King T 1J 151
KT3: N Mald 1J 151
Dickinson Ct. *EC1* 3B *8*
    (off Brewhouse Yd.)
Dicksee Ho. *NW8* 4A *4*
    (off Lyons Pl.)
Dickson Fold HA5: Pinn 4B 40
Dickson Ho. *E1* 6H *85*
    (off Philpot St.)
N1 . . . . .7A *66*
    (off Drummond Way)
Dickson Rd. SE9 . . . . .3C 124
Dick Turpin Way TW14: Felt 4H 111
Didsbury Cl. E6 . . . . .1D 88
Dieppe Cl. W14 . . . . .5H 99
Digby Bus. Cen. *E9* 6K *67*
    (off Digby Rd.)
Digby Cres. N4 . . . . .2C 66
Digby Gdns. RM10: Dag 1G 91
Digby Mans. *W6* 5D *98*
    (off Hammersmith Bri. Rd.)
Digby Pl. CR0: C'don 3F 169
Digby Rd. E9 . . . . .6K 67
IG11: Bark 7K 71
Digby St. E2 . . . . .3J 85
Digby Stuart College
Roehampton University 5C 116
Diggon St. E1 . . . . .5K 85
Dighton Cl. SE5 . . . . .6C 102
Dighton Rd. SW18 . . . . .5A 118
Dignum St. N1 . . . . .2A 84
Digswell St. N7 . . . . .6A 66
Dilhorne Cl. SE12 . . . . .3K 141
Dilke St. SW3 . . . . .7F 17 (6D 100)
Dillmount Dr. KT12: Walt T 5A 148
Dilloway La. UB2: S'hall 2C 94
Dillwyn Cl. SE26 . . . . .4A 140
Dilston Cl. UB5: N'olt 3A 76
Dilston Gro. SE16 . . . . .4J 103
Dilton Gdns. SW15 . . . . .1C 134
Dilwyn Ct. E17 . . . . .2A 50
Dimes Pl. W6 . . . . .4D 98
Dimmock Dr. UB6: G'frd 5H 59
Dimond Cl. E7 . . . . .4J 69
Dimsdale Dr. EN1: Enf 7B 24
NW9 .1J 61
Dimsdale Hgts. *E1* 6H *85*
    (off Spencer Way)
Dimsdale Wlk. E13 . . . . .2J 87
Dimson Cres. E3 . . . . .3C 86
Dinerman Ct. NW8 . . . . .1A 82
The Dingle UB10: Hil 3D 74

Dingle Gdns. E14 . . . . .7C **86**
Dingle Rd. TW15: Ashf 5D **128**
Dingles Ct. HA5: Pinn 1B **40**
Dingley La. SW16 . . . . .2H **137**
Dingley Pl. EC1 . . . . .1D 8 (3C **84**)
Dingley Rd. EC1 . . . . .2C 8 (3C **84**)
Dingwall Av. CRO: C'don 2C **168**
Dingwall Gdns. NW11 . . . . .6J **45**
Dingwall Rd. CRO: C'don 1D **168**
SM5: Cars 7D **166**
SW18 . . . . .7A **118**
Dinmont Est. E2 . . . . .2G **85**
Dinmont Ho. E2 . . . . .2G **85**
(off Pritchard's Rd.)
Dinmont St. E2 . . . . .2H **85**
Dinmore Ho. E9 . . . . .1J **85**
(off Templecombe Rd.)
Dinnington Ho. E1 . . . . .4H **85**
(off Coventry Rd.)
Dinosaur Escape Adventure Golf . . .1A **76**
Dinsdale Gdns. EN5: New Bar 5E **20**
SE25 . . . . .5E **156**
Dinsdale Rd. SE3 . . . . .6H **105**
Dinsmore Rd. SW12 . . . . .7F **119**
Dinton Ho. NW8 . . . . .3D **4**
(off Lilestone St.)
Dinton Rd. KT2: King T 7F **133**
SW19 . . . . .6B **136**
Diploma Av. N2 . . . . .4C **46**
Diploma Ct. N2 . . . . .4C **46**
Diprose Lodge SW17 . . . . .4B **136**
Dirleton Rd. E15 . . . . .1H **87**
Dirty La. SE1 . . . . .1C **102**
Disbrowe Rd. W6 . . . . .6G **99**
Discover
Stratford 7F **69**
Discover Greenwich Visitor Cen. . . .6E **104**
Discovery Bus. Pk. SE16 . . . . .3G **103**
(off St James's Rd.)
The Discovery Centre
Becton 3G **89**
Discovery Dock Apts. E. E14 . . . .2D **104**
(off Sth. Quay Sq.)
Discovery Dock Apts. W. E14 . . . .2D **104**
(off Sth. Quay Sq.)
Discovery Ho. E14 . . . . .6H **87**
(off Newby Pl.)
Discovery Twr. E16 . . . . .6H **87**
(off Minnie Baldock St.)
Discovery Wlk. E1 . . . . .1H **103**
Dishforth La. NW9 . . . . .7F **29**
Disley Ct. UB1: S'hall 6F **77**
(off Howard Rd.)
Disney Pl. SE1 . . . . .6D **14** (2C **102**)
Disney St. SE1 . . . . .6D **14** (2C **102**)
Dison Cl. EN3: Enf H 1E **24**
Dispensary La. E8 . . . . .5H **67**
Disraeli Cl. SE28 . . . . .1C **108**
W4 .3K **97**
Disraeli Gdns. SW15 . . . . .4H **117**
Disraeli Rd. E7 . . . . .6J **69**
NW10 . . . . .2K **79**
SW15 . . . . .4G **117**
W5 .1D **96**
Diss St. E2 . . . . .1J 9 (3F **85**)
Distaff La. EC4 . . . . .2C **14** (7C **84**)
Distel Apts. SE10 . . . . .4G **105**
(off Telegraph Av.)
Distillery La. W6 . . . . .5E **98**
Distillery Rd. W6 . . . . .5E **98**
Distillery Twr. SE8 . . . . .1C **122**
Distillery Wlk. TW8: Bford 6E **96**
Distillery Wharf W6 . . . . .6E **98**
Distin St. SE11 . . . . .4J **19** (4A **102**)
District Rd. HA0: Wemb 5B **60**
Ditch All. SE13 . . . . .1D **122**
Ditchburn St. E14 . . . . .7E **86**
Ditchfield Rd. UB4: Yead 4C **76**
Ditchley Ct. W7 . . . . .5K **77**
(off Templeman Rd.)
Dittisham Rd. SE9 . . . . .4C **142**
Ditton Cl. KT7: T Ditt 7A **150**
Dittoncroft Cl. CRO: C'don 4E **168**

Ditton Grange Cl. KT6: Surb 1D **162**
Ditton Grange Dr. KT6: Surb 1D **162**
Ditton Hill KT6: Surb 1C **162**
Ditton Hill Rd. KT6: Surb 1C **162**
Ditton Lawn KT7: T Ditt 1A **162**
Ditton Pl. SE20 . . . . .1H **157**
Ditton Reach KT7: T Ditt 6B **150**
Ditton Rd. DA6: Bex 5D **126**
KT6: Surb 2D **162**
UB2: S'hall 5D **94**
Diversity Av. RM13: Rain 2K **91**
Divine Way UB3: Hayes 6F **75**
Divis Way SW15 . . . . .6D **116**
(off Dover Pk. Dr.)
Dixie Ct. SE6 . . . . .6C **122**
Dixon Butler M. W9 . . . . .4J **81**
Dixon Clark Ct. N1 . . . . .6B **66**
Dixon Cl. E6 . . . . .6D **88**
Dixon Ho. W10 . . . . .6F **81**
(off Darfield Way)
Dixon Pl. BR4: W W'ck 1D **170**
Dixon Rd. SE14 . . . . .1A **122**
SE25 . . . . .3E **156**
Dixon's All. SE16 . . . . .2H **103**
Dixon Way NW10 . . . . .7A **62**
Dobbin Cl. HA3: Kenton 2A **42**
Dobell Rd. SE9 . . . . .5D **124**
Dobree Av. NW10 . . . . .7D **62**
Dobson Cl. NW6 . . . . .7B **64**
Dobson Ho. SE14 . . . . .6K **103**
(off John Williams Cl.)
Dobson Wlk. SE5 . . . . .7D **102**
Doby Ct. EC4 . . . . .2D **14**
The Dock E1 . . . . .7H **85**
Dock Cotts. E1 . . . . .7J **85**
(off The Highway)
Dockers Tanner Rd. E14 . . . . .3C **104**
Dockett Eddy KT16: Chert 7A **146**
Dockett Eddy La. TW17: Shep 7B **146**
Dockett Moorings KT16: Chert 7A **146**
Dockhead SE1 . . . . .7K **15** (2F **103**)
Dockhead Wharf SE1 . . . . .7K **15**
(off Shad Thames)
Dock Hill Av. SE16 . . . . .1K **103**
Docklands Ct. E14 . . . . .6B **86**
(off Wharf La.)
The Docklands Equestrian Cen. 4E **88**
Docklands Sailing & Watersports Cen.
. . . . .3C **104**
Dockland St. E16 . . . . .1E **106**
(not continuous)
Dockley Rd. SE16 . . . . .3G **103**
Dockley Rd. Ind. Est. SE16 . . . . . .3G **103**
(off Dockley Rd.)
Dock Mdw. Reach W7 . . . . .3J **95**
Dock Offices SE16 . . . . .3J **103**
(off Surrey Quays Rd.)
Dock Rd. E16 . . . . .7H **87**
IG11: Bark 2G **89**
TW8: Bford 7D **96**
Dockside Ct. E5 . . . . .2J **67**
Dockside Rd. E16 . . . . .7B **88**
Dock St. E1 . . . . .7G **85**
Dockw.eed Court E14 . . . . .3D **104**
(off Watergate Walk)
Dockwell Cl. TW14: Felt 4J **111**
Dockwell's Ind. Est. TW14: Felt . . .5K **111**
Dockyard La. E14 . . . . .2D **104**
Dr Johnson Av. SW17 . . . . .3F **137**
Dr Johnson's House 1K **13**
(off Pemberton Row)
Doctors Cl. SE26 . . . . .5J **139**
Docura Ho. N7 . . . . .2K **65**
Docwra's Bldgs. N1 . . . . .6E **66**
Dodbrooke Rd. SE27 . . . . .3A **138**
Dodd Ho. SE16 . . . . .4H **103**
(off Rennie Est.)
Doddington Gro. SE17 . . . . .6B **102**
Doddington Pl. SE17 . . . . .6B **102**
Dodds Ho. SE10 . . . . .3J **105**
(off Peartree Way)
Dodsley Pl. N9 . . . . .3D **34**
Dodson St. SE1 . . . . .7K **13** (2A **102**)

Dod St. E14 . . . . .6B **86**
Doebury Wlk. SE18 . . . . .7A **108**
(off Prestwood Cl.)
Doel Cl. SW19 . . . . .7A **136**
Dog & Duck Yd. WC1 . . . . .5H **7**
Doggett Rd. SE6 . . . . .7C **122**
Doggetts Cl. EN4: E Barn 5H **21**
Doghurst Av. UB3: Harl 7D **92**
Doghurst Dr. UB7: Sip 7D **92**
Dog Kennel Hill SE22 . . . . .3E **120**
Dog Kennel Hill Est. SE22 . . . . .3E **120**
(off Albrighton Rd.)
Dog La. NW10 . . . . .4A **62**
Doherty Rd. E13 . . . . .4J **87**
Dokal Ind. Est. UB2: S'hall 2C **94**
Dolben Ct. SW1 . . . . .4D **18**
(off Montaigne Cl.)
Dolben St. SE1 . . . . .5A **14** (1B **102**)
(not continuous)
Dolby Rd. SW6 . . . . .2H **117**
Dolland Ho. SE11 . . . . .6H **19**
Dolland St. SE11 . . . . .6H **19** (5K **101**)
Dollar Bay Pl. E14 . . . . .2E **104**
Dollary Pde. KT1: King T 3H **151**
(off Kingston Rd.)
Dolliffe Cl. CR4: Mitc 2C **154**
Dollis Av. N3 . . . . .1H **45**
Dollis Brook Wlk. EN5: Barn 6B **20**
Dollis Cres. HA4: Ruis 1A **58**
Dolliscroft NW7 . . . . .7B **30**
DOLLIS HILL 2D **62**
Dollis Hill Av. NW2 . . . . .3D **62**
Dollis Hill Est. NW2 . . . . .3C **62**
Dollis Hill La. NW2 . . . . .4B **62**
Dollis Pk. N3 . . . . .1H **45**
Dollis Rd. N3 . . . . .7B **30**
NW7 .7B **30**
Dollis Valley Dr. EN5: Barn 6C **20**
Dollis Valley Way EN5: Barn 6C **20**
Dolman Cl. N3 . . . . .2A **46**
Dolman Rd. W4 . . . . .4K **97**
Dolman St. SW4 . . . . .4K **119**
Dolomite Ct. HA4: Ruis 4A **58**
Dolphin Cl. KT6: Surb 5D **150**
SE16 . . . . .2K **103**
SE28 . . . . .6D **90**
Dolphin Ct. NW11 . . . . .6G **45**
Dolphin Est. TW16: Sun 1G **147**
Dolphin Ho. SW6 . . . . .2A **118**
(off Lensbury Av.)
SW18 . . . . .4K **117**
TW16: Sun 1G **147**
(off Windmill Rd.)
Dolphin La. E14 . . . . .7D **86**
Dolphin Rd. TW16: Sun 1G **147**
UB5: N'olt 2D **76**
Dolphin Rd. Nth. TW16: Sun 1G **147**
Dolphin Rd. Sth. TW16: Sun 1G **147**
Dolphin Rd. W. TW16: Sun 1G **147**
Dolphin Sq. SW1 . . . . .6B **18** (5G **101**)
W4 .7A **98**
Dolphin St. KT1: King T 2E **150**
Dolphin Twr. SE8 . . . . .6B **104**
(off Abinger Gro.)
Dombey Ho. SE1 . . . . .7K **15**
(off Wolseley St.)
W11 .1F **99**
Dombey St. WC1 . . . . .5G **7** (5K **83**)
(not continuous)
Domecq Ho. EC1 . . . . .3B **8**
(off Dallington St.)
Dome Hill Pk. SE26 . . . . .4F **139**
Domelton Ho. SW18 . . . . .6K **117**
(off Iron Mill Rd.)
Domett Cl. SE5 . . . . .4D **120**
Domfe Pl. E5 . . . . .4J **67**
Domingo St. EC1 . . . . .3C **8** (4C **84**)
Dominica Cl. E13 . . . . .2B **88**
Dominion Apartments E17 . . . . . . .5B **50**
Dominion Bus. Pk. N9 . . . . .2E **34**
The Dominion Cen. UB2: S'hall 2C **94**

Dominion Cl. TW3: Houn 2H **113**
Dominion Ct. E8 . . . . .7F **67**
(off Middleton Rd.)
Dominion Dr. SE16 . . . . .2K **103**
Dominion Ho. E14 . . . . .5D **104**
(off St Davids Sq.)
EC1 .6C **8**
(off Bartholomew Cl.)
Dominion Ind. Est. UB2: S'hall 2C **94**
(off Feather Rd.)
Dominion Pde. HA1: Harr 5K **41**
Dominion Rd. CRO: C'don 7F **157**
UB2: S'hall 2C **94**
Dominion St. EC2 . . . . .5F 9 (5D **84**)
Dominion Theatre 7D **6**
(off Tottenham Ct. Rd.)
Dominion Wlk. E14 . . . . .7F **87**
(off Fairmont Av.)
Domonic Dr. SE9 . . . . .4F **143**
Domville Cl. N20 . . . . .2G **31**
Domville Ct. SE17 . . . . .5E **102**
(off Bagshott St.)
Donald Dr. RM6: Chad H 5C **54**
Donald Hunter Ho. E7 . . . . .5K **69**
(off Woodgrange Rd.)
Donald Rd. CRO: C'don 7A **156**
E13 .1K **87**
Donaldson Rd. NW6 . . . . .1H **81**
SE18 . . . . .1E **124**
Donald Woods Gdns. KT5: Surb . . .2H **163**
Donato Dr. SE15 . . . . .6E **102**
Doncaster Dr. UB5: N'olt 5D **58**
Doncaster Gdns. N4 . . . . .6C **48**
UB5: N'olt 5D **58**
Doncaster Rd. N9 . . . . .7C **24**
Donegal Ho. E1 . . . . .4H **85**
(off Cambridge Heath Rd.)
Donegal St. N1 . . . . .2K **83**
Doneraile Ho. SW1 . . . . .5J **17**
(off Ebury Bri. Rd.)
Doneraile St. SW6 . . . . .2F **117**
Dongola Rd. E1 . . . . .5A **86**
E13 .3K **87**
N17 .3E **48**
Dongola Rd. W. E13 . . . . .3K **87**
Don Gratton Ho. E1 . . . . .5G **85**
(off Old Montague St.)
Donington Av. IG2: Ilf 5G **53**
IG6: Ilf 5G **53**
Donkey All. SE22 . . . . .7G **121**
Donkey La. EN1: Enf 2B **24**
UB7: W Dray 1D **174**
Donkin Ho. SE16 . . . . .4H **103**
(off Rennie Est.)
Donmar Warehouse Theatre 1E **12**
(off Earlham St.)
Donnatt's Rd. SE14 . . . . .1B **122**
Donne Ct. SE24 . . . . .6C **120**
Donne Ho. E14 . . . . .6C **86**
(off Dod St.)
SE14 . . . . .6K **103**
(off Samuel Cl.)
Donnelly Ct. SW6 . . . . .7G **99**
(off Dawes Rd.)
Donnelly Ho. SE1 . . . . .1J **19**
(off McAuley Cl.)
Donne Pl. CR4: Mitc 4F **155**
SW3 . . . . .3D **16** (4C **100**)
Donne Rd. RM8: Dag 2C **72**
Donnington Ct. NW1 . . . . .7F **65**
(off Castlehaven Rd.)
NW10 . . . . .7D **62**
(off Donnington Rd.)
Donnington Mans. NW10 . . . . .1E **80**
(off Donnington Rd.)
Donnington Rd. HA3: Kenton 5D **42**
KT4: Wor Pk 2C **164**
NW10 . . . . .7D **62**
Donnybrook Ct. E3 . . . . .3A **86**
(off Old Ford Rd.)
Donnybrook Rd. SW16 . . . . .7G **137**
Donoghue Bus. Pk. NW2 . . . . .3F **63**

Donoghue Cotts. *E14* 5A **86**
   (off Galsworthy Av.)
Donoghue Ct. *E3* 4D **86**
   (off Barry Blandford Way)
Donovan Av. N10 . . . . .2F **47**
Donovan Ct. *SW10* 6A **16**
   (off Drayton Gdns.)
Donovan Ho. *E1* 7J **85**
   (off Cable St.)
Donovan Pl. N21 . . . . .5E **22**
Don Phelan Cl. SE5 . . . . .1D **120**
Dons Ct. *BR1: Broml* 1H **159**
   (off London Rd.)
Doone Cl. TW11: Tedd 6A **132**
Doon St. SE1 . . . . . .5J **13** (1A **102**)
Dora Ho. *E14* 6B **86**
   (off Rhodeswell Rd.)
W11 . . . . .7F **81**
   (off St Ann's Rd.)
Doral Way SM5: Cars 5D **166**
Doran Cl. E6 . . . . .2D **88**
Dorando Cl. W12 . . . . .7D **80**
Doran Gro. SE18 . . . . .7J **107**
Doran Mnr. *N2* 5D **46**
   (off Great Nth. Rd.)
Doran Wlk. E15 . . . . .7E **68**
Dora Rd. SW19 . . . . .5J **135**
Dora St. E14 . . . . .6B **86**
Dora Way SW9 . . . . .2A **120**
Dorchester Av. DA5: Bexl 1D **144**
  HA2: Harr 6G **41**
  N13 .4H **33**
Dorchester Cl. BR5: St P 7B **144**
  KT10: Hin W 2A **162**
  UB5: N'olt 5F **59**
Dorchester Ct. *E18* 1H **51**
   (off Buckingham Rd.)
N1 . . . . .7E **66**
   (off Englefield Rd.)
  N10 .3F **47**
  N14 .7A **22**
  NW2 . . . . .3F **63**
  SE24 . . . . .5C **120**
  SW1 .2F **17**
   (off Sloane St.)
Dorchester Dr. SE24 . . . . .5C **120**
  TW14: Bedf 6G **111**
Dorchester Gdns. E4 . . . . .4H **35**
  NW11 . . . . .4J **45**
Dorchester Gro. W4 . . . . .5A **98**
Dorchester Ho. TW9: Kew 7H **97**
  TW1: Twick 6C **114**
Dorchester Rd. KT4: Wor Pk 1E **164**
  SM4: Mord 7K **153**
  UB5: N'olt 5F **59**
Dorchester Ter. *NW2* 3F **63**
   (off Needham Ter.)
Dorchester Way HA3: Kenton 6F **43**
Dorchester Waye UB4: Yead 6K **75**
   (not continuous)
Dorcis Av. DA7: Bex 2E **126**
Dordrecht Rd. W3 . . . . .1A **98**
Dore Av. E12 . . . . .5E **70**
Doreen Av. NW9 . . . . .1K **61**
Doreen Capstan Ho. E11 . . . . .3G **69**
   (off Apollo Pl.)
Dore Gdns. SM4: Mord 7K **153**
Dorell Cl. UB1: S'hall 5D **76**
Dorey Ho. *TW8: Bford* 7C **96**
   (off High St.)
Dorfman Theatre 4H **13**
   (within National Theatre)
Doria Rd. SW6 . . . . .2H **117**
Doric Ho. *E2* 2K **85**
   (off Mace St.)
Doric Way NW1 . . . . .1C **6** (3H **83**)
Dorie M. *N12* 4E **30**
   (off Ashbourne Cl.)
Dorien Rd. SW20 . . . . .2F **153**
Doris Ashby Cl. UB6: G'frd 1A **78**
Doris Av. DA8: Erith 1J **127**
Doris Emmerton Ct. SW11 . . . . . .4A **118**

Doris Rd. E7 . . . . .7J **69**
  TW15: Ashf 6F **129**
Dorking Cl. KT4: Wor Pk 2F **165**
  SE8 . . . . .6B **104**
Dorking Ct. *N17* 1G **49**
   (off Hampden La.)
Dorking Ho. SE1 . . . . .3D **102**
Dorlcote Rd. SW18 . . . . .7C **118**
Dorly Cl. TW17: Shep 5G **147**
Dorman Pl. N9 . . . . .2B **34**
Dormans Cl. HA6: Nwood 1F **39**
Dorman Wlk. NW10 . . . . .5K **61**
Dorman Way NW8 . . . . .1B **82**
Dorma Trad. Pk. E10 . . . . .1H **87**
Dormay St. SW18 . . . . .5K **117**
Dormer Cl. E15 . . . . .6H **69**
  EN5: Barn 5A **20**
Dormer's Av. UB1: S'hall 6E **76**
Dormers Ri. UB1: S'hall 7F **77**
DORMER'S WELLS 6E **76**
Dormer's Wells La. UB1: S'hall . . .6E **76**
Dormers Wells Leisure Cen. 6F **77**
Dormstone Ho. *SE17* 4E **102**
   (off Congreve St.)
Dormywood HA4: Ruis 5H **39**
Dornberg Cl. SE3 . . . . .7J **105**
Dornberg Rd. SE3 . . . . .7K **105**
Dorncliffe Rd. SW6 . . . . .2G **117**
Dorney NW3 . . . . .7C **64**
Dorney Ri. BR5: St M Cry 4K **161**
Dorney Way TW4: Houn 5C **112**
Dornfell St. NW6 . . . . .5J **63**
Dornoch Ho. *E3* 2B **86**
   (off Anglo Rd.)
Dornton Rd. CR2: S Croy 5D **168**
  SW12 . . . . .2F **137**
Dorothy Av. HA0: Wemb 7E **60**
Dorothy Gdns. RM8: Dag 4B **72**
Dorothy Evans Cl. DA7: Bex 4H **127**
Dorothy Pettingell Ho. *SM1: Sutt* . .3K **165**
   (off Vermont Rd.)
Dorothy Rd. SW11 . . . . .3D **118**
Dorothy Smith La. N17 . . . . .7J **33**
Dorrell Pl. SW9 . . . . .3A **120**
Dorrien Wlk. SW16 . . . . .2H **137**
Dorrington Cl. IG11: Bark 7A **72**
Dorrington Ct. SE25 . . . . .2E **156**
Dorrington Point *E3* 3D **86**
   (off Bromley High St.)
Dorrington St. EC1 . . . . . . .5J **7** (5A **84**)
Dorrington Way BR3: Beck 5E **158**
Dorrit Ho. *W11* 1F **99**
   (off St Ann's Rd.)
Dorrit M. N18 . . . . .5K **33**
Dorrit St. SE1 . . . . .6D **14** (2C **102**)
Dorrit Way BR7: Chst 6G **143**
Dorryn Ct. SE26 . . . . .5K **139**
Dors Cl. NW9 . . . . .1K **61**
Dorset Av. DA16: Well 4K **125**
  RM1: Rom 4K **55**
  UB2: S'hall 4E **94**
  UB4: Hayes 3G **75**
Dorset Bldgs. EC4 . . . . . .1A **14** (6B **84**)
Dorset Cl. KT9: Chess 4D **162**
  NW1 . . . . .5E **4** (5D **82**)
  UB4: Hayes 3G **75**
Dorset Ct. HA6: Nwood 1H **39**
  N1 . . . . .7E **66**
   (off Hertford Rd.)
  UB5: N'olt 3C **76**
  W7 . . . . .5K **77**
Dorset Dr. HA8: Edg 6A **28**
Dorset Gdns. CR4: Mitc 4K **155**
  HA0: Wemb 5C **60**
Dorset Ho. *NW1* 5F **5**
   (off Gloucester Pl.)
Dorset Mans. *SW6* 6F **99**
   (off Lille Rd.)
Dorset M. N3 . . . . .1J **45**
  SW1 . . . . .1J **17** (3F **101**)
Dorset Pl. E15 . . . . .6F **69**
Dorset Ri. EC4 . . . . .1A **14** (6B **84**)

Dorset Rd. BR3: Beck 3K **157**
  CR4: Mitc 2C **154**
  E7 . . . . .7A **70**
  HA1: Harr 6G **41**
  N15 .4D **48**
  N22 .1J **47**
  SE9 . . . . .2C **142**
  SW8 . . . . .7J **101**
  SW19 . . . . .1J **153**
  TW15: Ashf 3A **128**
  W5 . . . . .3C **96**
Dorset Sq. NW1 . . . . . . .4E **4** (4D **82**)
Dorset St. W1 . . . . .6F **5** (5D **82**)
Dorset Way TW2: Twick 1H **131**
  UB10: Hil 2B **74**
Dorset Waye TW5: Hest 7D **94**
Dorset Wharf *W6* 7F **98**
   (off Rainville Rd.)
Dorsey Ho. *N1* 6B **66**
   (off Canonbury Rd.)
Dorton Cl. SE15 . . . . .7E **102**
Dorton Vs. UB7: Sip 7C **92**
Dorville Cres. W6 . . . . .3D **98**
Dorville Rd. SE12 . . . . .5H **123**
Dothill Rd. SE18 . . . . .7G **107**
Douai Gro. TW12: Hamp 1G **149**
Doughty Ct. *E1* 1H **103**
   (off Prusom St.)
Doughty Ho. *SW10* 6A **100**
   (off Netherton Gro.)
Doughty M. WC1 . . . . .4G **7** (4K **83**)
Doughty St. WC1 . . . . .3G **7** (4K **83**)
Douglas Av. E17 . . . . .1B **50**
  HA0: Wemb 7E **60**
  KT3: N Mald 4D **152**
Douglas Bader Ho. TW7: Isle 3H **113**
Douglas Cl. HA7: Stan 5F **27**
  IG6: Ilf 7K **37**
  SM6: W'gton 6J **167**
Douglas Ct. *KT1: King T* 4E **150**
   (off Geneva Rd.)
  N3 . . . . .2K **45**
  NW6 .7J **63**
   (off Quex Rd.)
Douglas Cres. UB4: Yead 4A **76**
Douglas Dr. CR0: C'don 3C **170**
Douglas Eyre Sports Cen. 5K **49**
Douglas Ho. KT6: Surb 1F **163**
Douglas Johnstone Ho. *SW6* 6H **99**
   (off Clem Attlee Ct.)
Douglas Mans. TW3: Houn 3F **113**
Douglas M. NW2 . . . . .3G **63**
Douglas Path *E14* 5E **104**
   (off Manchester Rd.)
Douglas Rd. DA16: Well 1B **126**
  E4 . . . . .1B **36**
  E16 .5J **87**
  IG3: Ilf 7A **54**
  KT1: King T 2H **151**
  KT6: Surb 2F **163**
  N1 . . . . .7C **66**
  N22 .1A **48**
  NW6 . . . . .1H **81**
  TW3: Houn 3F **113**
  TW19: Stanw 6A **110**
Douglas Rd. Nth. N1 . . . . .6C **66**
Douglas Rd. Sth. N1 . . . . .6C **66**
Douglas Robinson Ct. *SW16* 7J **137**
   (off Streatham High Rd.)
Douglas Sq. SM4: Mord 6J **153**
Douglas St. SW1 . . . . . .4C **18** (4H **101**)
Douglas Ter. E17 . . . . .1B **50**
Douglas Waite Ho. NW6 . . . . .7J **63**
Douglas Way SE8 . . . . .7B **104**
   (Stanley St.)
SE8 . . . . .7C **104**
   (Watsons St.)
Doulton Ho. SE11 . . . . .2H **19**
Doulton M. NW6 . . . . .6K **63**
Doungsforth Gdns. SW18 . . . . . .1K **135**
Douro Pl. W8 . . . . .3K **99**
Douro St. E3 . . . . .2C **86**
Douthwaite Sq. E1 . . . . .1G **103**

Dove App. E6 . . . . .5C **88**
Dove Cl. NW7 . . . . .7G **29**
  SM6: W'gton 7K **167**
  UB5: N'olt 4B **76**
Dove Commercial Cen. NW5 . . . . .5G **65**
Dovecot Cl. HA5: Eastc 5A **40**
Dovecote Av. N22 . . . . .3A **48**
Dovecote Gdns. SW14 . . . . .3K **115**
Dovecote Ho. *SE16* 2K **103**
   (off Water Gdns. Sq.)
Dovecote M. UB9: Hare 3A **3**
Dove Cl. TW19: Stanw 7A **110**
Dovedale Av. HA3: Kenton 6C **42**
  IG5: Ilf 2E **52**
Dovedale Bus. Est. SE15 . . . . . . .2G **121**
   (off Blenheim Gro.)
Dovedale Cl. DA16: Well 2A **126**
Dovedale Ri. CR4: Mitc 7D **136**
Dovedale Rd. SE22 . . . . .5H **121**
Dovedale Cl. N14 . . . . .2D **32**
Dovehouse Ct. *UB5: N'olt* 3B **76**
   (off Delta Gro.)
Dove Ho. Gdns. E4 . . . . .2H **35**
Dovehouse Mead IG11: Bark 2H **89**
Dovehouse St. SW3 . . . . .5B **16** (5B **100**)
Dove M. SW5 . . . . .4A **100**
Dove Pk. HA5: Hat E 1E **40**
Dover Cl. NW2 . . . . .2F **63**
  RM5: Col R 2J **55**
Dover Ct. *EC1* 3A **8**
   (off St John St.)
  N1 . . . . .7D **66**
   (off Southgate Rd.)
Dovercourt Av. CR7: Thor H 5A **156**
Dovercourt Est. N1 . . . . .6D **66**
Dovercourt Gdns. HA7: Stan 5K **27**
Dovercourt La. SM1: Sutt 3A **166**
Dovercourt Rd. SE22 . . . . .6E **120**
Doverfield Rd. SW2 . . . . .7J **119**
Dover Flats SE1 . . . . .4E **102**
Dover Gdns. SM5: Cars 3D **166**
Dover Ho. N18 . . . . .4C **34**
  SE15 . . . . .6J **103**
Dover Ho. Rd. SW15 . . . . .4C **116**
Doveridge Gdns. N13 . . . . .4G **33**
Dove Rd. N1 . . . . .6D **66**
Dove Row E2 . . . . .1G **85**
Dover Pk. Dr. SW15 . . . . .6D **116**
Dover Patrol SE3 . . . . .2K **123**
Dover Rd. E12 . . . . .2A **70**
  N9 . . . . .2D **34**
  RM6: Chad H 6E **54**
  SE19 . . . . .6D **138**
Dover St. W1 . . . . .3K **11** (7F **83**)
Dover Ter. *TW9: Rich* 2F **115**
   (off Sandycombe Rd.)
Dover Yd. W1 . . . . .4A **12**
Doves Cl. BR2: Broml 2C **172**
Doves Yd. N1 . . . . .1A **84**
Dovet Ct. SW9 . . . . .1K **119**
Doveton Ho. *E1* 4J **85**
   (off Doveton St.)
Doveton Rd. CR2: S Croy 5D **168**
Doveton St. E1 . . . . .4J **85**
Dove Wlk. SW1 . . . . .5G **17** (5E **100**)
Dovey Lodge *N1* 7A **66**
   (off Bewdley St.)
Dovill Ct. *SE16* 3G **103**
   (off Old Jamaica Rd.)
Dowanhill Rd. SE6 . . . . .1F **141**
Dowd Cl. N11 . . . . .2K **31**
Dowdeswell Cl. SW15 . . . . .4A **116**
Dowding Dr. SE9 . . . . .5A **124**
Dowding Ho. N6 . . . . .7E **46**
   (off Hillcrest)
Dowding Pl. HA7: Stan 6F **27**
Dowding Rd. UB10: Uxb 7B **56**
Dowells St. SE10 . . . . .6D **104**
Dowgate Hill EC4 . . . . . . .2E **14** (7D **84**)
Dowland St. W10 . . . . .3G **81**
Dowlas St. SE5 . . . . .7E **102**
Dowler Ct. *KT2: King T* 1E **150**
   (off Bovingdon Rd. — text truncated)
Dowells Av. SM6: W'gton 7F **167**
Dower Ct. *SE16* 4J **103**
   (off Silwood Rd.)

Dowes Ho. SW16 . . . . .3J 137
Dowgate Hill EC4 . . . . . . .2E 14 (7D 84)
Dowland St. W10 . . . . .3G 81
Dowlas St. SE5 . . . . .7E 102
Dowler Ct. KT2: King T 1E 150
Dowler Ho. E1 . . . . .6G 85
(off Burslem St.)
Dowlerville Rd. BR6: Chels 6K 173
Dowletts Rd. RM8: Dag 1E 72
Dowling Ho. DA17: Belv 3F 109
Dowman Cl. SW19 . . . . .7K 135
Downage NW4 . . . . .3E 44
(not continuous)
Downalong WD23: B Hea 1C 26
Downbank Av. DA7: Bex 1K 127
Down Barns Rd. HA4: Ruis 3B 58
Downbarton Ho. SW9 . . . . .1A 120
(off Gosling Way)
Downbury M. SW18 . . . . .5J 117
Down Cl. UB5: N'olt 2K 75
Downderry Rd. BR1: Broml 3F 141
Downe Cl. DA16: Well 7C 108
Downend SE18 . . . . .7F 107
Downend Ct. SE15 . . . . .6E 102
(off Bibury Cl.)
Downe Rd. BR2: Kes 7C 172
CR4: Mitc 2D 154
Downer's Cott. SW4 . . . . .4G 119
Downesbury NW3 . . . . .6D 64
(off Steele's Rd.)
Downes Cl. TW1: Twick 6B 114
Downes Ct. N21 . . . . .1F 33
Downes Ho. CR0: Wadd 4B 168
(off Violet La.)
Downe Ter. TW10: Rich 6E 114
Downey Ho. E1 . . . . .4K 85
(off Globe Rd.)
Downfield KT4: Wor Pk 1B 164
Downfield Cl. W9 . . . . .4K 81
Down Hall Rd. KT2: King T 1D 150
DOWNHAM 5F 141
Downham Cl. RM5: Col R 1G 55
Downham Ct. N1 . . . . .7D 66
(off Downham Rd.)
Downham Ent. Cen. SE6 . . . . . . .2H 141
Downham Health & Leisure Cen.
. . . . .4H 141
Downham La. BR1: Broml 5F 141
Downham Rd. N1 . . . . .7D 66
Downham Way BR1: Broml 5F 141
Downham Wharf N1 . . . . .1E 84
(off Downham Rd.)
Downhills Av. N17 . . . . .3D 48
Downhills Pk. Rd. N17 . . . . .3C 48
Downhills Way N17 . . . . .3C 48
Downhurst Av. NW7 . . . . .5E 28
Downhurst Ct. NW4 . . . . .3E 44
Downie Wlk. SE18 . . . . .5F 107
(off Brunwell Av.)
Downing Cl. HA2: Harr 3G 41
Downing Ct. WC1 . . . . .4F 7
(off Grenville St.)
Downing Dr. UB6: G'frd 1H 77
Downing Ho. W10 . . . . .6F 81
(off Cambridge Gdns.)
Downing Rd. RM9: Dag 7F 73
Downings E6 . . . . .6E 88
Downing St. SW1 . . . . .6E 12 (2J 101)
Downland Cl. N20 . . . . .1F 31
Downland Ct. E11 . . . . .2G 69
Downleys Cl. SE9 . . . . .2C 142
Downman Rd. SE9 . . . . .3C 124
Down Pl. W6 . . . . .4D 98
Down Rd. TW11: Tedd 6B 132
The Downs SW20 . . . . .7F 135
Downs Av. BR7: Chst 5D 142
HA5: Pinn 6C 40
Downs Bri. Rd. BR3: Beck 1F 158
Downs Ct. UB6: G'frd 3A 78
Downs Ct. Pde. E8 . . . . .5H 67
(off Amhurst Rd.)
Downsell Rd. E15 . . . . .4E 68
Downsfield Rd. E17 . . . . .6A 50

Downshall Av. IG3: Ilf 6J 53
Downs Hill BR3: Beck 7F 141
Downshire Hill NW3 . . . . .4B 64
Downside TW1: Twick 3K 131
TW16: Sun 1J 147
Downside Cl. SW19 . . . . .6A 136
Downside Cres. NW3 . . . . .5C 64
W13 . . . . .4A 78
Downside Rd. SM2: Sutt 6B 166
Downside Wlk. TW8: Bford 6D 96
(off Windmill Rd.)
UB5: N'olt 3D 76
Downs La. E5 . . . . .4H 67
Downs Pk. Rd. E5 . . . . .5F 67
E8 . . . . .5F 67
Downs Rd. BR3: Beck 2D 158
CR7: Thor H 1C 156
E5 . . . . .4G 67
EN1: Enf 4K 23
Down St. KT8: W Mole 5E 148
W1 . . . . .5J 11 (1F 101)
Down St. M. W1 . . . . . .5J 11 (1F 101)
Downs Vw. TW7: Isle 1K 113
Downsview Gdns. SE19 . . . . .7B 138
Downsview Rd. SE19 . . . . .7C 138
Downsway BR6: Orp 5J 173
The Downsway SM2: Sutt 7A 166
Downton Av. SW2 . . . . .2J 137
Downton Rd. SE16 . . . . .2A 104
Down Way UB5: N'olt 3K 75
Downy Ho. W3 . . . . .1A 98
Downey St. N1 . . . . .1A 84
Dowsett Rd. N17 . . . . .2F 49
Dowson Cl. SE5 . . . . .4D 120
Dowson Ho. E1 . . . . .6K 85
(off Bower St.)
Doyce St. SE1 . . . . . . .6C 14 (2C 102)
Doyle Gdns. NW10 . . . . .1C 80
Doyle Ho. SW13 . . . . .7E 98
(off Trinity Chu. Rd.)
Doyle Rd. SE25 . . . . .4G 157
D'Oyley St. SW1 . . . . . .3G 17 (4E 100)
Doynton St. N19 . . . . .2F 65
Draco Ga. SW15 . . . . .3E 116
Draco St. SE17 . . . . .6C 102
Dragmore St. SW4 . . . . .6H 119
Dragonfly Cl. E13 . . . . .3K 87
KT5: Surb 1J 163
Dragonfly Ct. NW9 . . . . .1A 44
(off Heybourne Cres.)
Dragonfly Pl. SE4 . . . . .3A 122
Dragon Rd. SE15 . . . . .6E 102
Dragons Way EN5: Barn 5C 20
Dragon Yd. WC1 . . . . . . .7F 7 (6J 83)
Dragon Rd. SE8 . . . . .5B 104
Dragor Rd. NW10 . . . . .4J 79
Drake Cl. IG11: Bark 4A 90
SE16 . . . . .2K 103
Drake Ct. KT5: Surb 4E 150
(off Cranes Pk. Av.)
SE1 . . . . .7D 14
(off Swan St.)
SE19 . . . . .5F 139
W12 . . . . .2E 98
(off Scott's Rd.)
Drake Cres. SE28 . . . . .6C 90
Drakefell Rd. SE4 . . . . .2K 121
SE14 . . . . .2K 121
Drakefield Rd. SW17 . . . . .3E 136
Drake Hall E16 . . . . .1K 105
(off Wesley Av.)
Drake Ho. E1 . . . . .5J 85
(off Stepney Way)
E14 . . . . .7A 86
(off Victory Pl.)
SW1 . . . . .7C 18
(off Dolphin Sq.)
Drakeland Ho. W9 . . . . .4H 81
(off Fernhead Rd.)
Drakeley Ct. N5 . . . . .4B 66
Drake M. BR2: Broml 4A 160
Drake Rd. CR0: C'don 7K 155
CR4: Mitc 6E 154

Drake Rd. HA2: Harr 2D 58
KT9: Chess 5G 163
SE4 . . . . .3C 122
The Drakes SE8 . . . . .6C 104
Drakes Ct. SE23 . . . . .1J 139
Drakes Clyd. NW6 . . . . .7H 63
Drakes Dr. HA6: Nwood 1D 38
Drake St. EN2: Enf 1J 23
WC1 . . . . .6G 7 (5K 83)
Drakes Wlk. E6 . . . . .1D 88
Drakewood Rd. SW16 . . . . .7H 137
Draper Cl. DA17: Belv 4F 109
TW7: Isle 2H 113
Draper Ct. BR1: Broml 4C 160
Draper Ho. SE1 . . . . .4B 102
(off Newington Butts)
Draper Pl. N1 . . . . .1B 84
(off Dagmar Ter.)
Drapers Almshouses E3 . . . . .3D 86
(off Rainhill Way)
Drapers Cott. Homes NW7 . . . . . .4G 29
(not continuous)
Draper's Ct. SW11 . . . . .1E 118
(off Battersea Pk. Rd.)
Drapers Gdns. EC2 . . . . . .7F 9 (6D 84)
Drapers Rd. E15 . . . . .4F 69
EN2: Enf 2G 23
N17 . . . . .3F 49
Drapers Yd. SW18 . . . . .5K 117
(off Ryland Blvd.)
Drappers Way SE16 . . . . .4G 103
Draven Cl. BR2: Hayes 7H 159
Drawbrook Rd. SE10 . . . . .2F 105
Drawell Cl. SE18 . . . . .5J 107
Drax Av. SW20 . . . . .7C 134
Draxmont SW19 . . . . .6G 135
Draycot Rd. E11 . . . . .6K 51
KT6: Surb 1G 163
Draycott Av. HA3: Kenton 6B 42
SW3 . . . . .3D 16 (4C 100)
Draycott Cl. HA3: Kenton 6B 42
NW2 . . . . .3F 63
SE5 . . . . .7D 102
(not continuous)
Draycott M. SW6 . . . . .2H 117
(off Laurel Bank Gdns.)
Draycott Pl. SW3 . . . . . .4E 16 (4D 100)
Draycott Ter. SW3 . . . . .4F 17 (4D 100)
Dray Ct. HA0: Wemb 5A 60
(off Brewery Cl.)
Drayford Cl. W9 . . . . .4H 81
Dray Gdns. SW2 . . . . .5K 119
Draymans M. SE15 . . . . .2F 121
Draymans Way TW7: Isle 3K 113
Drayside M. UB2: S'hall 2D 94
Drayson M. W8 . . . . .2J 99
Drayton Av. BR6: Farnb 1F 173
W13 . . . . .7A 78
Drayton Bri. Rd. W7 . . . . .7K 77
W13 . . . . .7K 77
Drayton Cl. IG1: Ilf 1H 71
TW4: Houn 5D 112
Drayton Ct. UB7: W Dray 4B 92
Drayton Gdns. N21 . . . . .7G 23
SW10 . . . . .6A 16 (5A 100)
UB7: W Dray 2A 92
W13 . . . . .7A 78
Drayton Grn. W13 . . . . .7A 78
Drayton Grn. Rd. W13 . . . . .7B 78
Drayton Gro. W13 . . . . .7A 78
Drayton Ho. E11 . . . . .1G 69
SE5 . . . . .7D 102
(off Elmington Rd.)
Drayton Pk. N5 . . . . .4A 66
Drayton Pk. M. N5 . . . . .5A 66
Drayton Rd. CR0: C'don 2B 168
E11 . . . . .1F 69
N17 . . . . .2E 48
NW10 . . . . .1B 80
W13 . . . . .7A 78
Drayton Waye HA3: Kenton 6B 42

Dray Wlk. E1 . . . . .4K 9 (4F 85)
Dreadnought Cl. SW19 . . . . .2B 154
Dreadnought St. SE10 . . . . .3G 105
Dreadnought Wlk. SE10 . . . . .6D 104
Drenon Sq. UB3: Hayes 7H 75
Dresden Cl. NW6 . . . . .6K 63
Dresden Ho. SE11 . . . . .3H 19
SW11 . . . . .2E 118
(off Dagnall St.)
Dresden Rd. N19 . . . . .1G 65
Dressington Av. SE4 . . . . .6C 122
Drewery Cl. SE3 . . . . .3G 123
Drewett Ho. E1 . . . . .6G 85
(off Christian St.)
Drew Gdns. UB6: G'frd 6K 59
Drew Ho. SE8 . . . . .5C 104
SW16 . . . . .3J 137
Drew Rd. E16 . . . . .1B 106
(not continuous)
Drewstead La. SW16 . . . . .2H 137
Drewstead Rd. SW16 . . . . .2H 137
Drey Cl. KT4: Wor Pk 2C 164
(off The Avenue)
Driffield Ct. NW9 . . . . .1A 44
(off Pageant Av.)
Driffield Rd. E3 . . . . .2A 86
The Drift BR2: Broml 3B 172
Drift Cl. E16 . . . . .7F 89
The Driftway CR4: Mitc 1E 154
Driftway Ho. E3 . . . . .2B 86
(off Stafford Rd.)
Drinkwater Ho. SE5 . . . . .7D 102
(off Picton St.)
Drinkwater Rd. HA2: Harr 2F 59
The Drive BR3: Beck 2C 158
BR4: W W'ck 7F 159
BR6: Orp 2K 173
BR7: Chst 3K 161
CR7: Thor H 4D 156
DA5: Bexl 6C 126
DA8: Erith 7H 109
DA14: Sidc 3B 144
E4 . . . . .1A 36
E17 . . . . .3D 50
E18 . . . . .4J 51
EN2: Enf 1J 23
EN5: Barn 3B 20
EN5: New Bar 6F 21
HA2: Harr 7E 40
HA6: Nwood 2G 39
HA8: Edg 5B 28
HA9: Wemb 2J 61
IG1: Ilf 6C 52
IG9: Buck H 1F 37
IG11: Bark 7K 71
KT2: King T 7J 133
KT6: Surb 7E 150
KT10: Esh 7G 149
KT19: Ewe 6B 164
N3 . . . . .7D 30
N6 . . . . .5D 46
N7 . . . . .6K 65
(not continuous)
N11 . . . . .6B 32
NW10 . . . . .1B 80
NW11 . . . . .2H 45
RM5: Col R 1J 55
SM4: Mord 5A 154
SW6 . . . . .2G 117
SW20 . . . . .7E 134
TW3: Houn 2H 113
TW7: Isle 2H 113
TW14: Felt 7A 112
TW15: Ashf 7F 129
UB10: Ick 4A 56
W3 . . . . .6J 79
Drive Ct. HA8: Edg 5B 28
Drive Mans. SW6 . . . . .2G 117
(off Fulham Rd.)
Droitwich Cl. SE26 . . . . .3G 139
Dromey Gdns. HA3: Hrw W 7E 26
Dromore Rd. SW15 . . . . .6G 117
Dronfield Gdns. RM8: Dag 5C 72

Dron Ho. E1 . . . . .5J 85
(off Adelina Gro.)
Droop St. W10 . . . . .3F 81
Drovers Ct. KT1: King T 2E 150
(off Fairfield E.)
Drovers Pl. SE15 . . . . .7J 103
Drovers Rd. CR2: S Croy 5D 168
Drovers Way N7 . . . . .6J 65
Druce Rd. SE21 . . . . .6E 120
Druid St. SE1 . . . . .6H 15 (2E 102)
(not continuous)
Druids Way BR2: Broml 4F 159
Drumaline Ridge KT4: Wor Pk 2A 164
Drum Ct. N1 . . . . .7J 65
(off Gifford St.)
Drummer Stagpole M. NW7 . . . . . . .5B 30
Drummond Av. RM7: Rom 4K 55
Drummond Ct. N12 . . . . .7H 31
W3 . . . . .3J 97
(off Palmerston Rd.)
Drummond Cres. NW1 . . . . . .1C 6 (3H 83)
Drummond Dr. HA7: Stan 7E 26
Drummond Ga. SW1 . . . . . .5D 18 (5H 101)
Drummond Ho. E2 . . . . .2G 85
(off Goldsmiths Row)
N2 . . . . .2A 46
(off Font Hills)
Drummond Pl. TW1: Twick 7B 114
Drummond Rd. CR0: C'don 2C 168
E11 . . . . .6A 52
RM7: Rom 4K 55
SE16 .3H 103
The Drummonds IG9: Buck H 2E 36
Drummonds Pl. TW9: Rich 4E 114
Drummond St. NW1 . . . . .3A 6 (4G 83)
Drummond Way N1 . . . . .7A 66
Druries HA1: Harr 1J 59
(off High St.)
Drury Cl. SW15 . . . . .6C 116
Drury Cres. CR0: Wadd 2A 168
Drury Ho. SW8 . . . . .1G 119
Drury La. WC2 . . . . .7F 7 (6J 83)
Drury Lane Theatre Royal 2G 13
(off Catherine St.)
Drury Rd. HA1: Harr 7G 41
Drury Way NW10 . . . . .5K 61
Drury Way Ind. Est. NW10 . . . . . . .5J 61
Dryad St. SW15 . . . . .3F 117
Dryburgh Gdns. NW9 . . . . .3G 43
Dryburgh Ho. SW1 . . . . .5K 17
(part of Abbots Mnr.)
Dryburgh Rd. SW15 . . . . .3D 116
Dryden Av. W7 . . . . .6K 77
Dryden Bldg. E1 . . . . .6G 85
(off Commercial Rd.)
Dryden Cl. SW4 . . . . .5H 119
Dryden Ct. SE11 . . . . .4K 19 (4A 102)
Dryden Mans. W14 . . . . .6G 99
(off Queen's Club Gdns.)
Dryden Rd. DA16: Well 1K 125
EN1: Enf 6K 23
HA3: W'stone 1K 41
SW19 .6A 136
Dryden St. WC2 . . . . .1F 13 (6J 83)
Dryfield Cl. NW10 . . . . .6J 61
Dryfield Rd. HA8: Edg 6D 28
Dryfield Wlk. SE8 . . . . .6C 104
Dryhill Rd. DA17: Belv 6F 109
Dryland Av. BR6: Orp 4K 173
Drylands Rd. N8 . . . . .6J 47
Drysdale Av. E4 . . . . .7J 25
Drysdale Dwellings E8 . . . . .5F 67
(off Dunn St.)
Drysdale Pl. N1 . . . . .1H 9 (3E 84)
Drysdale St. N1 . . . . .1H 9 (3E 84)
Dublin Av. E8 . . . . .1G 85
Dublin Cl. HA2: Harr 2H 59
(off Northolt Rd.)
Du Burstow Ter. W7 . . . . .2J 95
Ducaine Apts. E3 . . . . .3B 86
(off Merchant St.)
Ducal St. E2 . . . . .2K 9 (3F 85)
Du Cane Av. W12 . . . . .6E 80

Du Cane Ct. SW17 . . . . .1E 136
Du Cane Rd. W12 . . . . .6B 80
Ducavel Ho. SW2 . . . . .1K 137
Duchess Cl. N11 . . . . .5A 32
SM1: Sutt 4A 166
Duchess Cres. HA7: Stan 3E 26
Duchess Dr. E13 . . . . .4K 87
Duchess Gro. IG9: Buck H 2E 36
Duchess M. W1 . . . . .6K 5 (5F 83)
W3 . . . . .1G 97
Duchess of Bedford Ho. W8 . . . . . .2J 99
(off Duchess of Bedford's Wlk.)
Duchess of Bedford's Wlk.
W8 . . . . .2J 99
Duchess St. W1 . . . . .6K 5 (5F 83)
Duchess Theatre 2G 13
(off Catherine St.)
Duchess Wlk. SE1 . . . . . . .5J 15 (1F 103)
Duchy Rd. EN4: Had W 1G 21
Duchy St. SE1 . . . . .4K 13 (1A 102)
(not continuous)
Ducie St. SW4 . . . . .4K 119
Duckett M. N4 . . . . .6B 48
Duckett Rd. N4 . . . . .6B 48
Duckett's Apts. E3 . . . . .7B 68
(off Wick La.)
Duckett St. E1 . . . . .4K 85
Duckham Ct. E14 . . . . .4D 104
(off Nauticus Wlk.)
Duck La. W1 . . . . .1C 12
Duck Lees La. EN3: Pond E 4F 25
Duck's Hill Rd. HA4: Ruis 2D 38
HA6: Nwood 1D 38
DUCKS ISLAND 6A 20
Ducks Wlk. TW1: Twick 5C 114
Du Cros Dr. HA7: Stan 6J 27
Du Cros Rd. W3 . . . . .1A 98
DUDDEN HILL 5D 62
Dudden Hill La. NW10 . . . . .4B 62
Dudden Hill Pde. NW10 . . . . .4B 62
Duddington Cl. SE9 . . . . .4B 142
Dudley Av. HA3: Kenton 3C 42
Dudley Ct. NW11 . . . . .4H 45
W1 . . . . .1E 10
(off Up. Berkeley St.)
WC2 . . . . .7E 6 (6J 83)
Dudley Dr. HA4: Ruis 5K 57
SM4: Mord 1G 165
Dudley Gdns. HA2: Harr 1H 59
W13 . . . . .2B 96
Dudley M. SW2 . . . . .6A 120
Dudley Pl. TW19: Stanw 6B 110
UB3: Harl 4F 93
Dudley Rd. E17 . . . . .2C 50
HA2: Harr 2G 59
IG1: Ilf .4F 71
KT1: King T 3F 151
KT12: Walt T 6J 147
N3 . . . . .2K 45
NW6 . . . . .2G 81
SW19 .6J 135
TW9: Rich 2F 115
TW14: Bedf 1E 128
TW15: Ashf 5B 128
UB2: S'hall 2B 94
Dudley St. W2 . . . . .6A 4 (5B 82)
Dudlington Rd. E5 . . . . .2J 67
Dudmaston M. SW3 . . . . .5B 16
Dudrich Cl. N11 . . . . .6J 31
Dudrich M. EN2: Enf 1F 23
Dudsbury Rd. DA14: Sidc 6B 144
Dudsel La. TW5: Cran 1J 111
Duett Ct. TW5: Hest 7C 94
Duffell Ho. SE11 . . . . .6H 19
Dufferin Av. EC1 . . . . .4E 8
Dufferin Cl. EC1 . . . . .4E 8
(off Dufferin St.)
Dufferin St. EC1 . . . . .4D 8 (4C 84)
Duffield Cl. HA1: Harr 5K 41
Duffield Dr. N15 . . . . .4F 49
Duff St. E14 . . . . .6D 86
Dufour's Pl. W1 . . . . .1B 12 (6G 83)

Dufton Dwellings E15 . . . . .4G 69
(off High Rd. Leyton)
Dugard Way SE11 . . . . .4B 102
Dugdale Cen. 4J 23
Dugdale Ct. NW10 . . . . .3D 80
(off Harrow Rd.)
Duggan Dr. BR7: Chst 6C 142
Dugolly Av. HA9: Wemb 3H 61
Dujardin M. EN3: Pond E 6E 24
Duke Cl. TW3: Houn 4D 112
Duke Gdns. IG6: Ilf 4H 53
Duke Humphrey Rd. SE3 . . . . .1G 123
Duke of Cambridge Cl.
TW2: Whitt 6H 113
Duke of Clarence Ct. SE17 . . . . . . .5C 102
(off Manor Pl.)
Duke of Edinburgh Rd. SM1: Sutt ..2B 166
Duke of Wellington Av. SE18 . . . . . .3F 107
Duke of Wellington Pl.
SW1 . . . . .6H 11 (2E 100)
Duke of York Column 5D 12 (1H 101)
Duke of York Sq. SW3 . . . .4F 17 (5D 100)
Duke of York's Theatre 3E 12
(off St Martin's La.)
Duke of York St. SW1 . . . .4B 12 (1G 101)
Duke Rd. IG6: Ilf 4H 53
W4 . . . . .5K 97
Duke's Av. HA8: Edg 6A 28
N10 . . . . .3F 47
N14 . . . . .5K 97
Dukes Av. HA1: Harr 4J 41
HA2: Harr 6D 40
KT2: King T 4C 132
KT3: N Mald 3A 152
N3 . . . . .1K 45
TW4: Houn 4C 112
TW10: Ham 3C 132
UB5: N'olt 7C 58
Dukes Cl. TW12: Hamp 5D 130
TW15: Ashf 4E 128
Dukes Ct. E6 . . . . .1E 88
(not continuous)
SE13 .2E 122
SW14 .2K 115
W2 . . . . .7K 81
(off Moscow Rd.)
Dukes Ga. W4 . . . . .4J 97
Dukes Grn. Av. TW14: Felt 5J 111
Dukes Head Pas. TW12: Hamp . . .7G 131
Duke's Head Yd. N6 . . . . .1F 65
Duke Shore Wharf E14 . . . . .7B 86
Duke's Ho. SW1 . . . . .3D 18
(off Vincent St.)
Dukes La. W8 . . . . .2K 99
Duke's La. Chambers W8 . . . . .2K 99
(off Dukes La.)
Duke's La. Mans. W8 . . . . .2K 99
(off Dukes La.)
Dukes Lodge W8 . . . . .1H 99
(off Holland Wlk.)
Dukes Meadow Golf & Tennis 2K 115
Duke's Meadow Golf Course 2K 115
Duke's Meadows 2K 115
Duke's M. N10 . . . . .3F 47
Duke's M. W1 . . . . .7H 5
Dukes Orchard DA5: Bexl 1J 145
Duke's Pas. E17 . . . . .4E 50
Duke's Pl. EC3 . . . . .1H 15 (6E 84)
Dukes Point N6 . . . . .1F 65
(off Dukes Head Yd.)
Dukes Ride UB10: Ick 4A 56
Duke's Rd. WC1 . . . . .2D 6 (3H 83)
Dukes Rd. E6 . . . . .1E 88
W3 . . . . .4G 79
Dukesthorpe Rd. SE26 . . . . .4K 139
Duke St. SM1: Sutt 4B 166
TW9: Rich 4D 114
W1 . . . . .7H 5 (6E 82)
Duke St. Hill SE1 . . . . .4F 15 (1D 102)
Duke St. Mans. W1 . . . . .1H 11
(off Duke St.)
Duke St. St James's
SW1 . . . . .4B 12 (1G 101)

Dukes Way BR4: W W'ck 3G 171
HA9: Wemb 5E 60
Dukes Yd. W1 . . . . .2H 11 (7E 82)
Dulas St. N4 . . . . .1K 65
Dulford St. W11 . . . . .7G 81
Dulka Rd. SW11 . . . . .5D 118
Dulverton NW1 . . . . .1G 83
(off Royal College St.)
Dulverton Mans. WC1 . . . . .4H 7
Dulverton Rd. HA4: Ruis 1J 57
SE9 .2G 143
DULWICH .1B 138
Dulwich & Sydenham Hill Golf Course
. . . . .2F 139
Dulwich Bus. Cen. SE23 . . . . .1K 139
Dulwich Comn. SE21 . . . . .1E 138
SE22 .1E 138
Dulwich Hamlet FC 4E 120
Dulwich Lawn Cl. SE22 . . . . .5F 121
Dulwich Leisure Cen. 4G 121
The Dulwich Oaks SE21 . . . . .3F 139
Dulwich Picture Gallery 7D 120
Dulwich Ri. Gdns. SE22 . . . . .5F 121
Dulwich Rd. SE24 . . . . .5A 120
Dulwich Upper Wood Nature Pk.
. . . . .5F 120
DULWICH VILLAGE 7E 120
Dulwich Village SE21 . . . . .6D 120
Dulwich Wood Av. SE19 . . . . .4E 138
Dulwich Wood Pk. SE19 . . . . .4E 138
Dumain Ct. SE11 . . . . .4B 102
(off Opal St.)
Dumbarton Ct. SW2 . . . . .6J 119
Dumbarton Rd. SW2 . . . . .6J 119
Dumbleton Cl. KT1: King T 1H 151
Dumbreck Rd. SE9 . . . . .4D 124
Dumont Rd. N16 . . . . .3E 66
Dumpton Pl. NW1 . . . . .7E 64
Dumsey Eyot KT16: Chert 7A 146
Dunally Pk. TW17: Shep 7F 147
Dunbar Av. BR3: Beck 4A 158
RM10: Dag 3G 73
SW16 .2A 156
Dunbar Cl. UB4: Hayes 5K 75
Dunbar Ct. BR2: Broml 3H 159
(off Durham Rd.)
SM1: Sutt 5B 166
Dunbar Gdns. RM10: Dag 5G 73
Dunbar Rd. E7 . . . . .6J 69
KT3: N Mald 4J 151
N22 . . . . .1A 48
Dunbar St. SE27 . . . . .3C 138
Dunbar Twr. E8 . . . . .6F 67
(off Dalston Sq.)
Dunbar Wharf E14 . . . . .7B 86
(off Narrow St.)
Dunblane Cl. HA8: Edg 2C 28
Dunblane Rd. SE9 . . . . .3C 124
Dunboe Pl. TW17: Shep 7E 146
Dunboyne Rd. NW3 . . . . .5D 64
Dunbridge Ho. SW15 . . . . .6B 116
Dunbridge St. E2 . . . . .4G 85
Duncan Cl. EN5: New Bar 4F 21
Duncan Ct. E14 . . . . .5E 86
(off Teviot St.)
N21 . . . . .1G 33
Duncan Gro. W3 . . . . .6A 80
Duncan Ho. E15 . . . . .1F 87
NW3 . . . . .7D 64
(off Fellows Rd.)
SW1 . . . . .6B 18
(off Dolphin Sq.)
Duncannon Ho. SW1 . . . . .6D 18
(off Lindsay Sq.)
Duncannon St. WC2 . . . . .3E 12 (7J 83)
Duncan Rd. E8 . . . . .1H 85
TW9: Rich 4E 114
Duncan St. N1 . . . . .2B 84
Duncan Ter. N1 . . . . .2B 84
(not continuous)
Dunch St. E1 . . . . .6H 85
Dunchurch Ho. RM10: Dag 7G 73
Duncombe Hill SE23 . . . . .7A 122

Duncombe Rd. N19 . . . . .1H 65
Duncrievie Rd. SE13 . . . . .6F 123
Duncroft SE18 . . . . .7J 107
Dundalk Ho. E1 . . . . .6J 85
　　　　　　　　　　　　　(off Clark St.)
Dundalk Rd. SE4 . . . . .3A 122
Dundas Ct. SE10 . . . . .6D 104
　　　　　　　　　　　　　(off Dowells St.)
Dundas Gdns. KT8: W Mole 3F 149
Dundas Ho. E2 . . . . .2J 85
　　　　　　　　　　　　　(off Bishop's Way)
Dundas Rd. SE15 . . . . .2J 121
　SW9 . . . . .1A 120
Dundee Ct. E1 . . . . .7G 15
　　　　　　　　　(off Wapping High St.)
　SE1 . . . . .7G 15
　　　　　　　　　　　　　(off Long La.)
Dundee Ho. W9 . . . . .3A 82
　　　　　　　　　　　　(off Maida Vale)
Dundee Rd. E13 . . . . .2K 87
　SE25 . . . . .5H 157
Dundee St. E1 . . . . .1H 103
Dundee Way EN3: Brim 3F 25
Dundee Wharf E14 . . . . .7B 86
Dundela Gdns. KT4: Wor Pk 4D 164
Dundonald Cl. E6 . . . . .6C 88
Dundonald Rd. NW10 . . . . .1F 81
　SW19 . . . . .7G 135
Dundry Ho. SE26 . . . . .3G 139
Dunedin Ho. E16 . . . . .1D 106
　　　　　　　　　　　　(off Manwood St.)
Dunedin M. SW2 . . . . .1J 137
Dunedin Rd. E10 . . . . .4E 68
　IG1: Ilf 1G 71
Dunedin Way UB4: Yead 4A 76
Dunelm Gro. SE27 . . . . .3C 138
Dunelm St. E1 . . . . .6K 85
Dunfield Gdns. SE6 . . . . .5D 140
Dunfield Rd. SE6 . . . . .5D 140
　　　　　　　　　　　　(not continuous)
Dunford Cl. HA5: Hat E 1D 40
Dunford Rd. N7 . . . . .4K 65
Dungannon Ho. SW6 . . . . .7J 99
　　　　　　　　　　　　(off Vanston Pl.)
Dungarvan Av. SW15 . . . . .4C 116
Dunheved Cl. CR7: Thor H 6A 156
Dunheved Rd. Nth. CR7: Thor H 6A 156
Dunheved Rd. Sth. CR7: Thor H 6A 156
Dunheved Rd. W. CR7: Thor H 6A 156
Dunhill Point SW15 . . . . .1C 134
Dunholme Grn. N9 . . . . .3A 34
Dunholme La. N9 . . . . .3A 34
Dunholme Rd. N9 . . . . .3A 34
Dunkeld Rd. RM8: Dag 2B 72
　SE25 . . . . .4D 156
Dunkery Rd. SE9 . . . . .4B 142
Dunkirk Ho. SE1 . . . . .2D 102
Dunkirk St. SE27 . . . . .4C 138
Dunlace Rd. E5 . . . . .4J 67
Dunleary Cl. TW4: Houn 7D 112
Dunley Dr. CR0: New Ad 7D 170
Dunlin Ho. SE16 . . . . .4K 103
　　　　　　　　　　　　(off Tawny Way)
Dunloe Av. N17 . . . . .3D 48
Dunloe Cl. E2 . . . . .2F 85
Dunloe St. E2 . . . . .2F 85
Dunlop Pl. SE16 . . . . .3F 103
Dunmore Point E2 . . . . .2J 9
　　　　　　　　　　　(off Gascoigne Pl.)
Dunmore Rd. NW6 . . . . .1G 81
　SW20 . . . . .1E 152
Dunmow Cl. RM6: Chad H 5C 54
　TW13: Hanw 3C 130
Dunmow Ho. SE11 . . . . .5H 19
　　　　　　　　　　　(off Newburn St.)
Dunmow Rd. E15 . . . . .4F 69
Dunmow Wlk. N1 . . . . .1C 84
　　　　　　　　　　　　(off Popham St.)
Dunnage Cres. SE16 . . . . .4A 104
　　　　　　　　　　　　(not continuous)
Dunnell Cl. TW16: Sun 1J 147
Dunnett Ho. E3 . . . . .2B 86
　　　　　　　　　　　　(off Vernon Rd.)

Dunnico Ho. SE17 . . . . .5E 102
　　　　　　　　　　　　　(off East St.)
Dunn Mead NW9 . . . . .7G 29
Dunnock Cl. N9 . . . . .1E 34
Dunnock Dr. HA7: Stan 5E 26
Dunnock Ho. NW9 . . . . .6B 44
Dunnock M. E5 . . . . .3G 67
Dunnock Rd. E6 . . . . .6C 88
Dunn's Pas. WC1 . . . . .7F 7
Dunnose Ct. E18 . . . . .5F 67
Dunollie Pl. NW5 . . . . .5G 65
Dunollie Rd. NW5 . . . . .5G 65
Dunoon Gdns. SE23 . . . . .7K 121
Dunoon Ho. N1 . . . . .1K 83
　　　　　　　　　　　(off Bemerton Est.)
Dunoon Rd. SE23 . . . . .7J 121
Dunoran Home BR1: Broml 1C 160
Dunraven Dr. EN2: Enf 2F 23
Dunraven Rd. W12 . . . . .1C 98
Dunraven St. W1 . . . . .2F 11 (7D 82)
Dunsany Rd. W14 . . . . .3F 99
Dunsfold Cl. SM2: Sutt 7K 165
　　　　　　　　　　　(off Blackbush Cl.)
Dunsfold Way CR0: New Ad 7D 170
Dunsford Way SW15 . . . . .6D 116
Dunsmore Cl. UB4: Yead 4B 76
Dunsmore Rd. KT12: Walt T 6K 147
Dunsmure Rd. N16 . . . . .1E 66
Dunspring La. IG5: Ilf 2F 53
Dunstable M. W1 . . . . .5H 5 (5E 82)
Dunstable Rd. KT8: W Mole 4D 148
　TW9: Rich 4E 114
Dunstall Rd. SW20 . . . . .6D 134
Dunstall Way KT8: W Mole 3F 149
Dunstall Welling Est.
　DA16: Well 2B 126
Dunstan Cl. N2 . . . . .3A 46
Dunstan Glade BR5: Pet W 6H 161
Dunstan Rd. SE20 . . . . .7H 139
Dunstan Ho's. E1 . . . . .5J 85
　　　　　　　　　　　(off Stepney Grn.)
Dunstan M. EN1: Enf 3K 23
Dunstan Rd. NW11 . . . . .1H 63
Dunstan's Gro. SE22 . . . . .6H 121
Dunstan's Rd. SE22 . . . . .7G 121
Dunster Av. SM4: Mord 1F 165
Dunster Cl. EN5: Barn 4A 20
　RM5: Col R 2J 55
Dunster Ct. EC3 . . . . .2H 15 (7E 84)
Dunster Dr. NW9 . . . . .1J 61
Dunster Gdns. NW6 . . . . .7H 63
Dunster Ho. SE6 . . . . .3E 140
Dunsterville Way SE1 . . . . .7F 15 (2D 102)
Dunston Ct. SE6 . . . . .7C 122
Dunston Rd. E8 . . . . .1F 85
　SW11 . . . . .2E 118
Dunston St. E8 . . . . .1E 84
Dunton Cl. KT6: Surb 1E 162
Dunton Cl. SE23 . . . . .2H 139
Dunton Rd. E10 . . . . .7D 50
　RM1: Rom 4K 55
　SE1 . . . . .5F 103
Dunthshill Rd. SW18 . . . . .1K 135
Dunton Rd. KT8: W Mole 4E 148
Dunvegan Rd. SE9 . . . . .4D 124
Dunwich Ct. RM6: Chad H 5B 54
　　　　　　　　　　　(off Glandford Way)
Dunwich Rd. DA7: Bex 1F 127
Dunworth M. W11 . . . . .6H 81
Duplex Ride SW1 . . . . .7F 11 (2D 100)
Dupont Rd. SW20 . . . . .2F 153
Duppas Av. CR0: Wadd 4B 168
Duppas Cl. TW17: Shep 5F 147
Duppas Ct. CR0: C'don 3B 168
　　　　　　　　　　　(off Duppas Hill Ter.)
Duppas Hill La. CR0: C'don 4B 168
Duppas Hill Rd. CR0: Wadd 4A 168
Duppas Hill Ter. CR0: C'don 3B 168
Duppas Rd. CR0: Wadd 3A 168
Dupree Rd. SE7 . . . . .5K 105
Dura Den Cl. BR3: Beck 7D 140

Durand Gdns. SW9 . . . . .1K 119
Durands Wlk. SE16 . . . . .2B 104
Durand Way NW10 . . . . .7J 61
Durants Pk. .3D 24
Durants Pk. Av.
　EN3: Pond E 4E 24
Durants Rd. EN3: Pond E 4D 24
Durant St. E2 . . . . .2G 85
Durban Ct. E7 . . . . .7B 70
Durban Gdns. RM10: Dag 7J 73
Durban Ho. W12 . . . . .7D 80
　　　　　　　　　　　(off White City Est.)
Durban Rd. BR3: Beck 2B 158
　E15 . . . . .3G 87
　E17 . . . . .1B 50
　IG2: Ilf 1J 71
　N17 . . . . .6K 33
　SE27 . . . . .4C 138
Durbin Rd. KT9: Chess 4E 162
Durban Cotts. UB1: S'hall 6D 76
　　　　　　　　　　　(off Denbigh Rd.)
Durdans Ho. NW1 . . . . .7F 65
　　　　　　　　　　　　(off Farrier St.)
Durdans Rd. UB1: S'hall 6D 76
Durell Gdns. RM9: Dag 5D 72
Durell Ho. SE16 . . . . .2K 103
　　　　　　　　　　　　(off Wolfe Cres.)
Durell Rd. RM9: Dag 5D 72
Durfey Pl. SE5 . . . . .7D 102
Durford Cres. SW15 . . . . .1D 134
Durham Av. BR2: Broml 4H 159
　IG8: Buck H, Wfd G 5G 37
　TW5: Hest 5D 94
Durell Rd. RM9: Dag 5D 72
Durfey Pl. SE5 . . . . .7D 102
Durham Cl. SW20 . . . . .2D 152
Durham Ct. NW6 . . . . .2J 81
　　　　　　　　　　　(off Kilburn Pk. Rd.)
　TW11: Tedd 4J 131
Durham Hill BR1: Broml 4H 141
Durham Ho. BR2: Broml 4G 159
　IG11: Bark 7A 72
　　　　　　　　　(off Margaret Bondfield Av.)
　NW8 . . . . .2D 4
　　　　　　　　　　　　(off Lorne Cl.)
　RM10: Dag 5J 73
Durham Ho. St. WC2 . . . . .3F 13
Durham Pl. IG1: Ilf 4G 71
　SW3 . . . . .6E 16 (5D 100)
Durham Ri. SE18 . . . . .5G 107
Durham Rd. BR2: Broml 3H 159
　DA14: Sidc 5B 144
　E12 . . . . .4B 70
　E16 . . . . .4G 87
　HA1: Harr .5F 41
　N2 . . . . .3C 46
　N7 . . . . .2K 65
　N9 . . . . .2B 34
　RM10: Dag 5J 73
　SW20 . . . . .1D 152
　TW14: Felt 7A 112
　W5 . . . . .3D 96
Durham Row E1 . . . . .5A 86
Durham St. SE11 . . . . .6G 19 (5K 101)
Durham Ter. W2 . . . . .6K 81
Durham Wharf Dr. T
　W8: Bford .7C 96
Durham Yd. E2 . . . . .3H 85
Durley Av. HA5: Pinn 7C 40
Durley Rd. N16 . . . . .7E 48
Durlston Rd. E5 . . . . .2G 67
　KT2: King T 6E 132
Durnford Ho. SE6 . . . . .3E 140
Durnford St. N15 . . . . .5E 48
　SE10 . . . . .6E 104
Durning Rd. SE19 . . . . .5D 138
Durnsford Av. SW19 . . . . .2J 135
Durnsford Ct. EN3: Enf H 3F 25
　　　　　　　　　　　　(off Enstone Rd.)
Durnsford Rd. N11 . . . . .1H 47
　SW19 . . . . .2J 135
Durrant Cl. HA3: Hrw W 2J 41
Durrant Ho. EC1 . . . . .5E 8
　　　　　　　　　　　(off Chiswell St.)
Durrant Way BR6: Farnb 5H 173

Durrell Rd. SW6 . . . . .1H 117
Durrell Way TW17: Shep 6F 147
Durrels Ho. W14 . . . . .4H 99
　　　　　　　　　　　(off Warwick Gdns.)
Durrington Av. SW20 . . . . .7E 134
Durrington Pk. Rd. SW20 . . . . .1E 152
Durrington Rd. E5 . . . . .4A 68
Durrington Twr. SW8 . . . . .2G 119
Durrisdeer Ho. NW2 . . . . .4H 63
　　　　　　　　　　　　　(off Lyndale)
Dursley Cl. SE3 . . . . .2A 124
Dursley Gdns. SE3 . . . . .1B 124
Dursley Rd. SE3 . . . . .2A 124
Durward Ho. W8 . . . . .2K 99
　　　　　　　　　　　(off Kensington Ct.)
Durward St. E1 . . . . .5H 85
Durweston M. W1 . . . . .5F 5
Durweston St. W1 . . . . .6F 5 (5D 82)
Dury Falls Cl. RM5: Col R 2J 55
Dury Rd. EN5: Barn 1C 20
Dutch Barn Cl.
　TW19: Stanw 6A 110
Dutch Gdns. KT2: King T 6H 133
Dutch Yd. SW18 . . . . .5J 117
Dutton St. SE10 . . . . .1E 122
Duval Ho. N19 . . . . .2H 65
　　　　　　　　　　　(off Ashbrook Rd.)
　SW11 . . . . .3C 118
Duxberry Av. TW13: Felt 3A 130
Duxberry Cl. BR2: Broml 5C 160
Duxford Ho. SE2 . . . . .2D 108
　　　　　　　　　　　(off Wolvercote Rd.)
DW Fitness
　Waldorf Hotel 2G 13
Dyas Rd. TW16: Sun 1J 147
Dye Ho. La. E3 . . . . .1C 86
Dyer Ho. TW12: Hamp 1F 149
Dyer's Bldgs. EC1 . . . . .6J 7 (5A 84)
Dyers Hall Rd. E11 . . . . .1G 69
Dyers Hall Rd. Sth. E11 . . . . .2F 69
Dyers La. SW15 . . . . .4D 116
Dykes Way BR2: Broml 3H 159
Dykewood Cl. DA5: Bexl 3K 145
Dylan Rd. DA17: Belv 3G 109
　SE24 . . . . .4B 120
Dylways SE5 . . . . .4D 120
Dymchurch Cl. BR6: Orp 4J 173
　IG5: Ilf 2E 52
Dymes Path SW19 . . . . .2F 135
Dymock St. SW6 . . . . .3K 117
Dyneley Rd. SE12 . . . . .3A 142
Dyne Rd. NW6 . . . . .7G 63
Dynevor Rd. N16 . . . . .3E 66
　TW10: Rich 5E 114
Dynham Rd. NW6 . . . . .7J 63
Dyott St. WC1 . . . . .7D 6 (6H 83)
Dysart Av. KT2: King T 5C 132
Dysart St. EC2 . . . . .4G 9 (4D 84)
Dyson Ct. HA0: Wemb 4A 60
　NW2 . . . . .1E 62
Dyson Dr. UB10: Uxb 1A 74
Dyson Ho. SE10 . . . . .5H 105
　　　　　　　　　　　(off Blackwall La.)
Dyson Rd. E11 . . . . .6G 51
　E15 . . . . .6H 69
Dysons Rd. N18 . . . . .5C 34

E

Eade Rd. N4 .7C 48
Eagans Cl. N2 . . . . .3B 46
Eagle Av. RM6: Chad H 6E 54
Eagle Cl. EN3: Pond E 4D 24
　SE16 . . . . .5J 103
　SM6: W'gton 6J 167
Eagle Ct. E11 . . . . .4J 51
　EC1 . . . . .5A 8 (5B 84)
Eagle Dr. NW9 . . . . .2A 44
Eagle Dwellings EC1 . . . . .1D 8
　　　　　　　　　　　　　(off City Rd.)
Eagle Hgts. SW11 . . . . .3C 118
Eagle Hill SE19 . . . . .6D 138

Eagle Ho. E1 . . . 4H 85
(off Headlam St.)
EC1 . . . 2E 8
(off City Rd.)
N1 . . . 2D 84
(off Eagle Wharf Rd.)
Eagle Ho. M. SW4 . . . 5G 119
Eagle La. E11 . . . 4J 51
Eagle Lodge NW11 . . . 7H 45
Eagle Mans. N16 . . . 5F 67
(off Salcombe Rd.)
Eagle M. N1 . . . 6E 66
Eagle Pl. SW1 . . . 3B 12
SW7 . . . 5A 100
Eagle Point EC1 . . . 2E 8
(off City Rd.)
Eagle Rd. HA0: Wemb . . . 7D 60
TW6: H'row A . . . 3H 111
Eaglesfield Rd. SE18 . . . 1F 125
Eagle St. WC1 . . . 6G 7 (5K 83)
Eagle Ter. IG8: Wfd G . . . 7E 36
Eagle Trad. Est. CR4: Mitc . . . 6D 154
Eagle Wharf Ct. SE1 . . . 5J 15
(off Lafone St.)
Eagle Wharf E. E14 . . . 7A 86
(off Narrow St.)
Eagle Wharf Rd. N1 . . . 2C 84
Eagle Wharf W. E14 . . . 7A 86
(off Narrow St.)
Eagle Works E. E1 . . . 4K 9
Eagle Works W. E1 . . . 4J 9
Eagling Cl. E3 . . . 3C 86
Ealdham Sq. SE9 . . . 4A 124
EALING . . . 7D 78
Ealing B'way. Cen. . . . 7D 78
EALING COMMON . . . 7F 79
Ealing Golf Course . . . 3B 78
Ealing Grn. W5 . . . 1D 96
Ealing Lawn Tennis Club &
Indoor Tennis Cen. . . . 7F 79
Ealing Pk. Gdns. W5 . . . 4C 96
Ealing Pk. Mans. W5 . . . 3D 96
(off Sth. Ealing Rd.)
Ealing Rd. HA0: Wemb . . . 6E 60
TW8: Bford . . . 5D 96
UB5: N'olt . . . 1E 76
Ealing Squash & Fitness Club . . . 6E 78
Ealing Studios . . . 1D 96
Ealing Village W5 . . . 6E 78
Eamont Cl. HA4: Ruis . . . 7D 38
Eamont Ct. NW8 . . . 2C 82
(off Eamont St.)
Eamont St. NW8 . . . 2C 82
Eardley Cres. SW5 . . . 5J 99
Eardley Point SE18 . . . 4F 107
(off Wilmount St.)
Eardley Rd. DA17: Belv . . . 5G 109
SW16 . . . 5G 137
Earhart Ho. NW9 . . . 3C 44
(off East Dr.)
Earhart Way TW6: Cran, H'row A . . . 3J 111
Earl Cl. N11 . . . 5A 32
Earldom Rd. SW15 . . . 4E 116
Earle Gdns. KT2: King T . . . 7E 132
Earle Ho. SW1 . . . 4D 18
(off Montaigne Cl.)
Earlham Ct. E11 . . . 7H 51
Earlham Gro. E7 . . . 5H 69
N22 . . . 7E 32
Earlham St. WC2 . . . 1D 12 (6J 83)
Earl Ho. NW1 . . . 4D 4
(off Lisson Gro.)
Earlom Ho. WC1 . . . 2J 7
(off Margery St.)
Earl Ri. SE18 . . . 5H 107
Earl Rd. SW14 . . . 4J 115
Earlsbury Gdns. HA8: Edg . . . 4B 28
EARL'S COURT . . . 4K 99
Earl's Ct. Gdns. SW5 . . . 4K 99
Earl's Ct. Rd. SW5 . . . 3J 99
W8 . . . 3J 99
Earl's Ct. Sq. SW5 . . . 5K 99
Earls Cres. HA1: Harr . . . 4J 41

Earlsdown Ho. IG11: Bark . . . 2H 89
Earlsferry Way N1 . . . 7J 65
(not continuous)
EARLSFIELD . . . 1A 136
Earlsfield Ho. KT2: King T . . . 1D 150
(off Seven Kings Way)
Earlsfield Rd. SW18 . . . 1A 136
Earlshall Rd. SE9 . . . 4D 124
Earls Ho. TW9: Kew . . . 7H 97
Earlsmead HA2: Harr . . . 4D 58
Earlsmead Rd. N15 . . . 5F 49
NW10 . . . 3E 80
Earlsmead Stadium . . . 4D 58
Earls Ter. W8 . . . 3H 99
Earlsthorpe M. SW12 . . . 6E 118
Earlsthorpe Rd. SE26 . . . 4K 139
Earlston Gro. E9 . . . 1H 85
Earl St. EC2 . . . 5G 9 (5D 84)
Earl's Wlk. W8 . . . 3J 99
Earls Wlk. W8 . . . (off Queen Elizabeth St.)
Earlswood Av. CR7: Thor H . . . 5A 156
Earlswood Cl. SE10 . . . 6G 105
Earlswood Gdns. IG5: Ilf . . . 3E 52
Earlswood St. SE10 . . . 5G 105
Early M. NW1 . . . 1F 83
Early Rivers Ho. E20 . . . 5E 68
(off Ellis Way)
Earnshaw Ho. EC1 . . . 2B 8
(off Percival St.)
Earnshaw St. WC2 . . . 7D 6 (6H 83)
Earsby St. W14 . . . 4G 99
(not continuous)
Easby Cres. SM4: Mord . . . 6K 153
Easebourne Rd. RM8: Dag . . . 5C 72
Easedale Ho. TW7: Isle . . . 5K 113
Eashing Point SW15 . . . 1D 134
(off Wanborough Dr.)
Easleys M. W1 . . . 7H 5 (6E 82)
East 10 Ent. Pk. E10 . . . 1A 68
EAST ACTON . . . 7B 80
E. Acton Arc. W3 . . . 6A 80
E. Acton Ct. W3 . . . 7A 80
E. Acton La. W3 . . . 1A 98
E. Arbour St. E1 . . . 6K 85
East Av. E12 . . . 7C 70
E17 . . . 4D 50
SM6: W'gton . . . 5K 167
UB1: S'hall . . . 7D 76
UB3: Hayes . . . 1H 93
E. Bank N16 . . . 7E 48
Eastbank Cl. E17 . . . 5D 50
Eastbank Rd. TW12: Hamp H . . . 5G 131
EAST BARNET . . . 6H 21
E. Barnet Rd. EN4: E Barn . . . 4G 21
E. Bay La. E20 . . . 5C 68
E. Beckton District Cen. . . . 5D 88
EAST BEDFONT . . . 7G 111
E. Block SE1 . . . 6H 13
(off York Rd.)
Eastbourne Av. W3 . . . 6K 79
Eastbourne Gdns. SW14 . . . 3J 115
Eastbourne M. W2 . . . 7A 4 (6A 82)
Eastbourne Rd. E6 . . . 3E 88
(not continuous)
E15 . . . 1G 87
N15 . . . 6E 48
SW17 . . . 6E 136
TW8: Bford . . . 5C 96
TW13: Felt . . . 2B 130
W4 . . . 6J 97
Eastbourne Ter. W2 . . . 7A 4 (6A 82)
Eastbournia Av. N9 . . . 3C 34
Eastbrook Av. N9 . . . 7D 24
RM10: Dag . . . 4J 73
Eastbrook Cl. RM10: Dag . . . 4J 73
Eastbrook Dr. RM7: Rush G . . . 3K 73
Eastbrookend Country Pk. . . . 3K 73
Eastbrook Rd. SE3 . . . 1K 123
Eastbury Av. EN1: Enf . . . 1A 24
IG11: Bark . . . 1J 89

Eastern Ct. EN5: New Bar . . . 5F 21
(off Lyonsdown Rd.)
IG11: Bark . . . 1J 89
Eastbury Gro. W4 . . . 5A 98
Eastbury Manor House . . . 1K 89
Eastbury Rd. BR5: Pet W . . . 6H 161
E6 . . . 4E 88
KT2: King T . . . 7E 132
RM7: Rom . . . 6K 55
Eastbury Sq. IG11: Bark . . . 1K 89
Eastbury Ter. E1 . . . 4K 85
E. Carriage Ho. SE18 . . . 3F 107
(off Royal Carriage M.)
Eastcastle St. W1 . . . 7A 6 (6G 83)
Eastcheap EC3 . . . 2G 15 (7E 84)
E. Churchfield Rd. W3 . . . 1K 97
Eastchurch Rd. TW6: H'row A . . . 2G 111
East Cl. EN4: Cockf . . . 4K 21
UB6: G'frd . . . 2G 77
W5 . . . 4G 79
Eastcombe Av. SE7 . . . 6K 105
EASTCOTE . . . 7K 39
Eastcote BR6: Orp . . . 1K 173
Eastcote Av. HA2: Harr . . . 2F 59
KT8: W Mole . . . 5D 148
UB6: G'frd . . . 5A 60
Eastcote Hockey & Badminton Club
. . . 6H 39
Eastcote Ind. Est. HA4: Ruis . . . 7A 40
Eastcote La. HA2: Harr . . . 4C 58
UB5: N'olt . . . 5D 58
(not continuous)
Eastcote La. Nth. UB5: N'olt . . . 6D 58
Eastcote Pl. HA5: Eastc . . . 6K 39
Eastcote Rd. DA16: Well . . . 2H 125
HA2: Harr . . . 3G 59
HA4: Ruis . . . 7G 39
HA5: Pinn . . . 5B 40
Eastcote St. SW9 . . . 2K 119
Eastcote Vw. HA5: Pinn . . . 4A 40
EASTCOTE VILLAGE . . . 5K 39
Eastcott Cl. KT2: King T . . . 5J 133
East Ct. HA0: Wemb . . . 2C 60
East Cres. EN1: Enf . . . 5A 24
N11 . . . 4J 31
East Cft. Ho. HA2: Harr . . . 2G 59
Eastcroft Rd. KT19: Ewe . . . 7A 164
E. Cross Route E9 . . . 5B 68
(Crowfoot Cl.)
E9 . . . 7B 68
(Wansbeck Rd.)
Eastdown Ct. SE13 . . . 4F 123
Eastdown Ho. E8 . . . 4G 67
Eastdown Pk. SE13 . . . 4F 123
East Dr. NW9 . . . 3C 44
SM5: Cars . . . 7C 166
E. Duck Lees La. EN3: Pond E . . . 4F 25
EAST DULWICH . . . 4F 121
East Dulwich Est. SE22 . . . 3E 120
(off Albrighton Rd.)
E. Dulwich Gro. SE22 . . . 5E 120
E. Dulwich Rd. SE15 . . . 4F 121
SE22 . . . 4F 121
(not continuous)
E. End Farm HA5: Pinn . . . 3D 40
E. End Rd. N2 . . . 3K 45
N3 . . . 2J 45
E. End Way HA5: Pinn . . . 3D 40
East Entrance RM10: Dag . . . 2H 91
Eastern App. IG11: Bark . . . 1A 90
Eastern Av. E11 . . . 6K 51
HA5: Pinn . . . 7B 40
IG2: Ilf . . . 6F 53
IG4: Ilf . . . 6C 52
RM6: Chad H . . . 4A 54
Eastern Av. E. RM1: Rom . . . 3K 55
Eastern Av. Retail Pk.
Romford . . . 4J 55
Eastern Av. W. RM1: Rom . . . 4J 55
RM6: Chad H . . . 4A 54
RM7: Chad H, Mawney, Rom . . . 4E 54
Eastern Bus. Pk.
TW6: H'row A . . . 2G 111

Eastern Ct. E15 . . . 6G 69
(off Gt. Eastern Rd.)
Eastern Gateway E16 . . . 7A 88
Eastern Ho. E2 . . . 3H 85
(off Bethnal Grn. Rd.)
Eastern Ind. Est. DA18: Erith . . . 2G 109
Eastern Perimeter Rd.
TW6: H'row A . . . 2H 111
Eastern Quay Apts. E16 . . . 1K 105
(off Portsmouth M.)
Eastern Rd. E13 . . . 2K 87
E17 . . . 5E 50
N2 . . . 3D 46
N22 . . . 1J 47
SE4 . . . 4C 122
EASTERN RDBT. . . . 2G 71
Eastern Way DA17: Belv . . . 2A 108
DA18: Erith . . . 2A 108
SE2 . . . 2A 108
SE28 . . . 2A 108
E. Ferry Rd. E14 . . . 4D 104
Eastfield Gdns. RM10: Dag . . . 4G 73
Eastfield Rd. E17 . . . 4C 50
EN3: Enf W . . . 1E 24
N8 . . . 3J 47
RM9: Dag . . . 4F 73
RM10: Dag . . . 4F 73
Eastfields HA5: Eastc . . . 5A 40
Eastfields Av. SW18 . . . 4J 117
Eastfields Rd. CR4: Mitc . . . 2E 154
W3 . . . 5J 79
Eastfield St. E14 . . . 5A 86
EAST FINCHLEY . . . 4C 46
East Gdns. SW17 . . . 6C 136
Eastgate Bus. Pk. E10 . . . 1A 68
Eastgate Cl. SE28 . . . 6D 90
Eastglade HA5: Pinn . . . 3D 40
East Gro. SE17 . . . 4C 102
EAST HAM . . . 2D 88
East Ham & Barking By-Pass
IG11: Bark . . . 2H 89
Eastham Cl. EN5: Barn . . . 5B 20
East Ham Ind. Est. E6 . . . 4C 88
East Ham Leisure Cen. . . . 1D 88
East Ham Mnr. Way E6 . . . 6E 88
East Ham Nature Reserve . . . 4D 88
East Ham Nature Reserve Vis. Cen.
. . . 4D 88
E. Handyside Canopy . . . 1J 83
E. Harding St. EC4 . . . 7K 7 (6A 84)
E. Heath Rd. NW3 . . . 3A 64
E. Hill HA9: Wemb . . . 2G 61
SW18 . . . 5K 117
Eastholm NW11 . . . 4K 45
East Holme DA8: Erith . . . 1K 127
Eastholme UB3: Hayes . . . 1J 93
E. India Bldgs. E14 . . . 7C 86
(off Saltwell St.)
E. India Ct. SE16 . . . 2J 103
(off St Marychurch St.)
East India Dock Basin
Local Nature Reserve . . . 7G 87
E. India Dock Ho. E14 . . . 6E 86
E. India Dock Rd. E14 . . . 6C 86
E. India Way CRO: C'don . . . 1F 169
Eastlake Ho. NW8 . . . 4B 4
Eastlake Rd. SE5 . . . 2C 120
Eastlands Cres. SE21 . . . 6F 121
East La. HA0: Wemb . . . 3B 60
HA9: Wemb . . . 3B 60
KT1: King T . . . 3D 150
SE16 . . . 2G 103
(Chambers St.)
SE16 . . . 2G 103
(Scott Lidgett Cres.)
East La. Bus. Pk. HA9: Wemb . . . 2D 60
Eastlea M. E16 . . . 4G 87
Eastleigh Av. HA2: Harr . . . 2F 59
Eastleigh Cl. NW2 . . . 3A 62
SM2: Sutt . . . 7K 165
Eastleigh Rd. DA7: Bex . . . 3J 127
E17 . . . 2B 50

Eastleigh Wlk. SW15 . . . . .7C 116
Eastleigh Way TW14: Felt 1J 129
E. Lodge E16 . . . . .1J 105
(off Wesley Av.)
E. London Crematorium 3H 87
East London Gymnastic Cen. . . .6D 88
E. London Markazi Mosque 7G 85
E. London Mosque 5G 85
Eastman Ho. SW4 . . . . .6G 119
Eastman Rd. W3 . . . . .2K 97
E. Mead HA4: Ruis 3B 58
Eastmead Av. UB6: G'frd 3F 77
Eastmead Cl. BR1: Broml 2C 160
Eastmearn Rd. SE21 . . . . .2C 138
EAST MOLESEY 4H 149
Eastmoor Pl. SE7 . . . . .3B 106
Eastmoor St. SE7 . . . . .3B 106
East Mt. St. E1 . . . . .5H 85
(not continuous)
Eastney Rd. CR0: C'don 1B 168
Eastney St. SE10 . . . . .5F 105
Eastnor Rd. SE9 . . . . .1G 143
Eastone Apts. E1 . . . . .6K 9
(off Lolesworth Cl.)
Easton St. WC1 . . . . .3J 7 (4A 84)
East Pk. Cl. RM6: Chad H 5E 54
E. Parkside SE10 . . . . .2G 105
E. Park Wlk. E20 . . . . .5E 68
East Pas. EC1 . . . . .5C 8
East Pl. SE27 . . . . .4C 138
E. Point SE1 . . . . .5G 103
E. Pole Cotts. N14 . . . . .4C 22
E. Poultry Av. EC1 . . . . .6A 8 (5B 84)
East Ramp TW6: H'row A 1D 110
East Rd. DA16: Well 2B 126
E15 . . . . .1J 87
EN3: Enf W 1D 24
EN4: E Barn 1K 31
HA1: Harr 7B 42
HA8: Edg 1H 43
KT2: King T 1F 150
N1 . . . . .2E 8 (3D 84)
RM6: Chad H 5E 54
RM7: Rush G 7K 55
SW3 . . . . .6G 17 (5E 100)
SW19 . . . . .6A 136
TW14: Bedf 7F 111
UB7: W Dray 4B 92
E. Rochester Way DA5: Bexl 6F 127
DA15: Sidc 5J 125
E. Row E11 . . . . .6J 51
W10 . . . . .4G 81
Eastry Av. BR2: Hayes 6H 159
Eastry Ho. SW8 . . . . .7J 101
(off Hartington Rd.)
W11 . . . . .7G 81
(off Walmer Rd.)
Eastry Rd. DA8: Erith 7G 109
EAST SHEEN 4J 115
E. Sheen Av. SW14 . . . . .5K 115
East Shop. Cen. 7K 69
E. Side W12 . . . . .2E 98
(off Shepherd's Bush Mkt.)
Eastside Halls SW7 . . . . .1B 16
(off Prince's Gdns.)
Eastside M. E3 . . . . .2C 86
(off Morville St.)
Eastside Rd. NW11 . . . . .4H 45
E. Smithfield E1 . . . . . . .3K 15 (7F 85)
E. Stand N5 . . . . .3B 66
East St. BR1: Broml 2J 159
DA7: Bex 4G 127
IG11: Bark 1G 89
SE17 . . . . .5C 102
(not continuous)
E. Surrey Gro. SE15 . . . . .7F 103
E. Tenter St. E1 . . . . .1K 15 (6F 85)
East Ter. DA15: Sidc 1J 143
E. Thamesmead Bus. Pk.
DA18: Erith 2F 109
East Twr. E14 . . . . .2D 104
(off Pan Peninsula Sq.)
SW10 . . . . .7B 100

East Towers HA5: Pinn 5B 40
East Va. W3 . . . . .1B 98
East Vw. E4 . . . . .5K 35
EN5: Barn 2C 20
Eastview Av. SE18 . . . . .7J 107
Eastville Av. NW11 . . . . .6H 45
East Wlk. EN4: E Barn 7K 21
UB3: Hayes 1J 93
E. Way BR2: Hayes 7J 159
CR0: C'don 2A 170
E11 . . . . .4H 51
HA4: Ruis 1J 57
UB3: Hayes 1J 93
Eastway E9 . . . . .6B 68
(not continuous)
SM4: Mord 5F 153
SM6: W'gton 4G 167
Eastway Cres. HA2: Harr 2F 59
Eastwell Cl. BR3: Beck 7A 140
Eastwell Ho. SE1 . . . . .7F 15
E. Wick E20 . . . . .5C 68
EAST WICKHAM 1C 126
East Wintergarden 1D 104
(off Bank St.)
Eastwood Cl. E18 . . . . .2J 51
N7 . . . . .5A 66
N17 . . . . .7C 34
Eastwood Ho. E3 . . . . .5C 86
(off Bow Comn. La.)
Eastwood Rd. E18 . . . . .2J 51
IG3: Ilf .1A 72
N10 . . . . .2E 46
UB7: W Dray 2C 92
East Woodside DA5: Bexl 7E 126
Eastwood St. SW16 . . . . .6G 137
easyGym
Fulham 6H 99
Eatington Rd. E10 . . . . .5F 51
Eaton Cl. HA7: Stan 4G 27
SW1 . . . . .4G 17 (4E 100)
Eaton Ct. E18 . . . . .2J 51
HA8: Edg 4B 28
Eaton Dr. KT2: King T 7G 133
RM5: Col R 1H 55
SW9 . . . . .4B 120
Eaton Gdns. RM9: Dag 7E 72
Eaton Ga. SW1 . . . . . .3G 17 (4E 100)
Eaton Ho. E14 . . . . .7B 86
(off Westferry Cir.)
SW11 .1B 118
Eaton La. SW1 . . . . . . .2K 17 (3F 101)
Eaton Mans. SW1 . . . . .4G 17
(off Bourne St.)
Eaton M. Nth. SW1 . . . .3G 17 (4E 100)
Eaton M. Sth. SW1 . . . .3H 17 (4E 100)
Eaton M. W. SW1 . . . . .3H 17 (4E 100)
Eaton Pk. Rd. N13 . . . . .2F 33
Eaton Pl. SW1 . . . . . . .2G 17 (4E 100)
Eaton Ri. E11 . . . . .5A 52
W5 . . . . .5D 78
Eaton Rd. DA14: Sidc 2D 144
EN1: Enf 4K 23
NW4 . . . . .5E 44
SM2: Sutt 6B 166
TW3: Houn 4H 113
Eaton Row SW1 . . . . . .2J 17 (3F 101)
Eatons Mead E4 . . . . .2H 35
Eaton Sq. SW1 . . . . . . .3G 17 (4E 100)
Eaton Ter. E3 . . . . .3A 86
SW1 . . . . .3G 17 (4E 100)
Eaton Ter. M. SW1 . . . . .3G 17
Eatonville Rd. SW17 . . . . .2D 136
Eatonville Vs. SW17 . . . . .2D 136
Ebb Ct. E16 . . . . .7G 89
Ebbett Ct. W3 . . . . .5K 79
Ebbisham Dr. SW8 . . . . .7G 19 (6K 101)
Ebbisham Rd. KT4: Wor Pk 2E 164
Ebbsfleet Rd. NW2 . . . . .5G 63
Ebdon Way SE3 . . . . .3K 123
Ebenezer Ho. SE11 . . . . .4K 19 (4B 102)
Ebenezer Mussel Ho. E2 . . . . .2J 85
(off Patriot Sq.)

Ebenezer St. N1 . . . . .1E 8 (3D 84)
Ebenezer Wlk. SW16 . . . . .1G 155
Ebley Cl. SE15 . . . . .6F 103
Ebner St. SW18 . . . . .5K 117
Ebony Cres. EN4: E Barn 5K 21
Ebony Ho. E2 . . . . .3G 85
(off Buckfast St.)
Ebor Cotts. SW15 . . . . .3A 134
Ebor St. E1 . . . . .3J 9 (4F 85)
Ebrington Rd. HA3: Kenton 6D 42
Ebsworth St. SE23 . . . . .7K 121
Eburne Rd. N7 . . . . .3J 65
Ebury Bri. SW1 . . . . . . .5J 17 (5F 101)
Ebury Bri. Est. SW1 . . . .5J 17 (5F 100)
Ebury Bri. Rd. SW1 . . . .6H 17 (5E 100)
Ebury M. BR2: Kes 3C 172
Ebury M. N5 . . . . .3C 66
SW1 . . . . .3J 17 (4F 101)
SE27 .3B 138
Ebury M. E. SW1 . . . . . .2J 17 (3F 101)
Ebury Sq. SW1 . . . . . . .4H 17 (4E 100)
Ebury St. SW1 . . . . .4H 17 (4E 100)
Ecclesbourne Apts. N1 . . . . .7D 66
(off Ecclesbourne Rd.)
Ecclesbourne Cl. N13 . . . . .5F 33
Ecclesbourne Gdns. N13 . . . . . . .5F 33
Ecclesbourne Rd. CR7: Thor H . . .5C 156
N1 . . . . .7C 66
Eccleshill BR2: Broml 4H 159
(off Durham Rd.)
Eccles Rd. SW11 . . . . .4D 118
Eccleston Bri. SW1 . . . . .3K 17 (4F 101)
Eccleston Cl. BR6: Orp 1H 173
EN4: Cockf 4J 21
Eccleston Cres. RM6: Chad H 7B 54
Eccleston Ct. HA9: Wemb 5E 60
Ecclestone M. HA9: Wemb 5E 60
Ecclestone Pl. HA9: Wemb 5F 61
Eccleston Ho. SW2 . . . . .6A 120
Eccleston M. SW1 . . . . .2H 17 (3E 100)
Eccleston Pl. SW1 . . . . . .3J 17 (4F 101)
Eccleston Rd. W13 . . . . .7A 78
(not continuous)
Eccleston Sq. SW1 . . . . .4K 17 (4F 101)
Eccleston Sq. M. SW1 . . .4A 18 (4F 101)
Eccleston St. SW1 . . . . . .2J 17 (3F 101)
Eccleston Yard SW1 . . . . .3J 17
Echelforde Dr. TW15: Ashf 4C 128
Echo Ct. E16 . . . . .2A 106
(off Admiralty Av.)
Echo Hgts. E4 . . . . .1J 35
Eckford St. N1 . . . . .2A 84
Eckington Cl. SE14 . . . . .7K 103
Eckington Ho. N15 . . . . .6D 48
(off Fladbury Rd.)
Eckington La. SE14 . . . . .7K 103
Eckstein Rd. SW11 . . . . .4C 118
Eclipse Bldg. N1 . . . . .6A 66
(off Laycock St.)
Eclipse Ho. N22 . . . . .2K 47
(off Station Rd.)
Eclipse Rd. E13 . . . . .5K 87
Ecology Cen. & Arts Pavilion 3A 86
Eco Va. SE23 . . . . .6H 121
Ector Rd. SE6 . . . . .2G 141
Edam Ct. DA15: Sidc 3A 144
Edans Ct. W12 . . . . .2B 98
Edbrooke Rd. W9 . . . . .4J 81
Eddington Ct. E16 . . . . .4D 88
(off Silvertown Sq.)
Eddinton Cl. CR0: New Ad 6E 170
Eddisbury Ho. SE26 . . . . .3G 139
Eddiscombe Rd. SW6 . . . . .2H 117
Eddy Cl. RM7: Rom 6H 55
Eddystone Rd. SE4 . . . . .5A 122
Eddystone Twr. SE8 . . . . .5A 104
Eddystone Wlk. TW19: Stanw 7A 110
Eden Apts. E14 . . . . .4C 104
(off Glengarnock Av.)
Edenbridge Cl. SE16 . . . . .5H 103
(off Masters Dr.)

Edenbridge Rd. E9 . . . . .7K 67
EN1: Enf 6K 23
Eden Cl. DA5: Bexl 4K 145
HA0: Wemb 1D 78
NW3 . . . . .2J 63
W8 . . . . .3J 99
Eden Ct. IG6: Ilf 1H 53
Edencourt Rd. SW16 . . . . .6F 137
Edendale W3 . . . . .7H 79
Edendale Rd. DA7: Bex 1K 127
Edenfield Gdns. KT4: Wor Pk 3B 164
Eden Gro. E17 . . . . .5D 50
N7 . . . . .5K 65
NW10 .6D 62
Edenham Way W10 . . . . .4H 81
Eden Ho. NW8 . . . . .4C 4
(off Church St.)
SE8 . . . . .7C 104
(off Deptford High St.)
SE16 . . . . .2K 103
(off Water Gdns. Sq.)
Edenhurst Av. SW6 . . . . .3H 117
Eden Lodge NW6 . . . . .7F 63
Eden M. SW17 . . . . .3A 136
EDEN PARK 5C 158
Eden Pk. Av. BR3: Beck 4A 158
Eden Rd. BR3: Beck 4A 158
CR0: C'don 4D 168
DA5: Bexl 4J 145
E17 . . . . .5D 50
SE27 .4B 138
Edensor Gdns. W4 . . . . .7A 98
Edensor Rd. W4 . . . . .7A 98
Eden St. KT1: King T 2D 150
Edenvale Cl. CR4: Mitc 7E 136
Edenvale Rd. CR4: Mitc 7E 136
Edenvale St. SW6 . . . . .2A 118
Eden Wlk. KT1: King T 2E 150
Eden Walk Shopping Centre 2E 150
Eden Way BR3: Beck 5B 158
E3 . . . . .1B 86
Ederline Av. SW16 . . . . .3K 155
Edgar Ct. KT3: N Mald 2A 152
Edgar Ho. E9 . . . . .5A 68
(off Homerton Rd.)
E11 . . . . .7J 51
SW8 . . . . .7J 101
(off Wyvil Rd.)
Edgar Kail Way SE22 . . . . .4E 120
Edgarley Ter. SW6 . . . . .1G 117
Edgar Myles Ho. E16 . . . . .5H 87
(off Ordnance Rd.)
Edgar Rd. E3 . . . . .3D 86
RM6: Chad H 7D 54
TW4: Houn 7D 112
UB7: Yiew 7A 74
Edgar Wallace Cl. SE15 . . . . .7E 102
Edgar Wright Ct. SW6 . . . . .7H 99
(off Dawes Rd.)
Edgcott Ho. W10 . . . . .5E 80
(off Sutton Way)
The Edge
Finsbury 7C 48
The Edge SE8 . . . . .7B 104
(off Glenville Gro.)
Edge Apts. E15 . . . . .7F 69
Edgeborough Way BR1: Broml 7B 142
Edgebury BR7: Chst 4F 143
Edgebury Wlk. BR7: Chst 4G 143
The Edge Bus. Cen. NW2 . . . . . . .2D 62
Edgecombe Ho. SE5 . . . . .2E 120
SW19 .1G 135
Edgecoombe CR2: Sels 7J 169
Edgecoombe Cl. KT2: King T 7K 133
Edgecote Cl. W3 . . . . .1J 97
Edgecot Gro. N15 . . . . .5E 48
Edgecumbe Av. NW9 . . . . .1B 44
Edgefield Av. IG11: Bark 7K 71
Edgefield Cl. BR3: Beck 6C 140
Edgefield Ct. IG11: Bark 7K 71
(off Edgefield Av.)
Edge Hill SE18 . . . . .6F 107
SW19 .7F 135

Edge Hill Av. N3 . . . . .4J 45
Edge Hill Ct. DA14: Sidc 4K 143
SW19 .7F 135
Edgehill Gdns. RM10: Dag 4G 73
Edgehill Ho. SW9 . . . . .2B 120
Edgehill Rd. BR7: Chst 3G 143
CR4: Mitc 1F 155
W13 . . . . .5C 78
Edgeley La. SW4 . . . . .3H 119
Edgeley Rd. SW4 . . . . .3H 119
Edgel St. SW18 . . . . .4K 117
Edge Point Cl. SE27 . . . . .5B 138
Edge St. W8 . . . . .1J 99
Edgewood Dr. BR6: Chels 5K 173
Edgewood Grn. CRO: C'don 1K 169
Edgeworth Av. NW4 . . . . .5C 44
Edgeworth Cl. NW4 . . . . .5C 44
Edgeworth Ct. EN4: Cockf 4H 21
(off Fordham Rd.)
Edgeworth Cres. NW4 . . . . .5C 44
Edgeworth Ho. NW8 . . . . .1A 82
(off Boundary Rd.)
Edgeworth Rd. EN4: Cockf 4H 21
SE9 .4A 124
The Edge Youth Cen. 4J 163
Edgington Rd. SW16 . . . . .6H 137
Edgington Way DA14: Sidc 7C 144
Edgson Ho. SW1 . . . . .5J 17
(off Ebury Bri. Rd.)
EDGWARE 6B 28
EDGWARE BURY 1A 28
Edgwarebury Gdns. HA8: Edg . .5B 28
Edgwarebury La. HA8: Edg 1A 28
(not continuous)
WD6: E'tree 1A 28
Edgware Ct. HA8: Edg 6B 28
Edgware Rd. NW2 . . . . .1D 62
NW9 .2J 43
W2 . . . . .4A 4 (4B 82)
Edgware Way HA8: Edg 4A 28
NW7 .4A 28
WD6: E'tree 1J 27
Edicule Sq. E3 . . . . .3A 86
Edinburgh Cl. E2 . . . . .2J 85
HA5: Pinn 7B 40
UB10: Ick 4D 56
Edinburgh Ct. DA8: Erith 7K 109
KT1: King T 3E 150
(off Watersplash Cl.)
SE16 . . . . .1K 103
(off Rotherhithe St.)
SW20 . . . . .5F 153
Edinburgh Dr. UB10: Ick 4D 56
Edinburgh Ga. SW1 . . . . .7E 10 (2D 100)
Edinburgh Ho. NW4 . . . . .3E 44
W9 . . . . .3K 81
(off Maida Vale)
Edinburgh Rd. E13 . . . . .2K 87
E17 .5C 50
N18 .5B 34
SM1: Sutt 2A 166
W7 . . . . .2K 95
Edington NW5 . . . . .6E 64
Edington Rd. EN3: Enf H 2D 24
SE2 .3B 108
Edison Bldg. E14 . . . . .2C 104
Edison Cl. E17 . . . . .5C 50
UB7: W Dray 2B 92
Edison Ct. CRO: C'don 7B 156
(off Campbell Rd.)
SE10 . . . . .3H 105
(off Schoolbank Rd.)
W3 . . . . .2A 98
Edison Dr. HA9: Wemb 3E 60
UB1: S'hall 6F 77
Edison Gro. SE18 . . . . .7K 107
Edison Hgts. E1 . . . . .3K 9
(off Cygnet St.)
Edison Ho. HA9: Wemb 3J 61
(off Barnhill Rd.)
SE1 .4D 102
(off New Kent Rd.)
Edison M. SW18 . . . . .6K 117

Edison Rd. BR2: Broml 2J 159
DA16: Well 1K 125
EN3: Brim 2G 25
N8 . . . . .6H 47
Edis St. NW1 . . . . .1E 82
Ediswan Way EN3: Pond E 5D 24
Editha Mans. SW10 . . . . .6A 100
(off Edith Gro.)
Edith Brinson Ho. E14 . . . . .6F 87
(off Oban St.)
Edith Cavell Cl. N19 . . . . .7J 47
Edith Cavell Ho. E14 . . . . .6D 86
(off Sturry St.)
Edith Cavell Way SE18 . . . . . . .1C 124
Edith Gdns. KT5: Surb 7H 151
Edith Gro. SW10 . . . . .6A 100
Edith Ho. W6 . . . . .5E 98
(off Queen Caroline St.)
Edithna St. SW9 . . . . .3J 119
Edith Nesbit Wlk. SE9 . . . . .5D 124
Edith Neville Cotts. NW1 . . . . . . .1C 6
(off Drummond Cres.)
Edith Ramsay Ho. E1 . . . . .5A 86
(off Duckett St.)
Edith Rd. E6 . . . . .7B 70
E15 .5F 69
N11 .7C 32
RM6: Chad H 7D 54
SE25 . . . . .5D 156
SW19 . . . . .6K 135
W14 .4G 99
Edith Row SW6 . . . . .1K 117
Edith St. E2 . . . . .2G 85
Edith Summerskill Ho. SW6 . . . . . .7H 99
(off Clem Attlee Ct.)
Edith Ter. SW10 . . . . .7A 100
Edith Vs. W14 . . . . .4H 99
Edith Yd. SW10 . . . . .7A 100
Edmansons Cl. N17 . . . . .1F 49
Edmeston Cl. E9 . . . . .6A 68
Edmond Ct. SE14 . . . . .1J 121
Edmonds Ct. KT8: W Mole 5F 149
Edmonscote W13 . . . . .5A 78
EDMONTON 3B 34
Edmonton Ct. SE16 . . . . .3J 103
(off Canada Est.)
Edmonton Grn. Shop. Cen. 2B 34
Edmonton Leisure Cen. 3B 34
Edmund Gro. TW13: Hanw 2D 130
Edmund Halley Way SE10 . . . . . .2G 105
Edmund Ho. SE17 . . . . .6B 102
(off Haymerle Rd.)
Edmund Hurst Dr. E6 . . . . .5F 89
Edmund Rd. CR4: Mitc 3C 154
DA16: Well 3A 126
Edmundsbury Ct. Est.
SW9 . . . . .4K 119
Edmunds Cl. UB4: Yead 5A 76
Edmund St. SE5 . . . . .7D 102
Edmunds Wlk. N2 . . . . .4C 46
Edna Ho. SE15 . . . . .6G 103
(off Haymerle Rd.)
Edna Rd. SW20 . . . . .2F 153
Edna St. SW11 . . . . .1C 118
Edred Ho. E9 . . . . .4A 68
(off Lindisfarne Way)
Edrich Ho. SW4 . . . . .1J 119
Edric Ho. SW1 . . . . .3D 18
(off Page St.)
Edrick Rd. HA8: Edg 6D 28
Edrick Wlk. HA8: Edg 6D 28
Edric Rd. SE14 . . . . .7K 103
Edridge Rd. CRO: C'don 3C 168
Education Sq. E1 . . . . .6G 85
(off Alder St.)
Edward VII Mans. NW10 . . . . .3F 81
(off Chamberlayne Rd.)
Edward Alderton Theatre 3D 126
Edward Av. E4 . . . . .6J 35
SM4: Mord 5B 154
Edward Bond Ho. WC1 . . . . .2F 7
(off Cromer St.)
Edward Clifford Ho. SE17 . . . . . . .4D 102
(off Elsted St.)

Edward Cl. N9 . . . . .7A 24
NW2 .4F 63
TW12: Hamp H 5G 131
Edward Ct. E16 . . . . .5J 87
Edward Dodd Ct. N1 . . . . .1F 9
(off Chart St.)
Edward Edward's Ho. SE1 . . . . . . .5A 14
Edwardes Pl. W8 . . . . .3H 99
Edwardes Sq. W8 . . . . .3H 99
Edward Gro. EN4: E Barn 5G 21
Edward Heylin Ct. E15 . . . . .2D 86
(off High St.)
Edward Heylin Ho. E3 . . . . .2C 86
(off Thomas Fyre Dr.)
Edward Ho. SE11 . . . . .5H 19
W2 . . . . .4A 4
(off Hall Pl.)
Edward Kennedy Ho. W10 . . . . . . .4G 81
(off Wornington Rd.)
Edward Mann Cl. E. E1 . . . . .6K 85
(off Pitsea St.)
Edward Mann Cl. W. E1 . . . . .6K 85
(off Pitsea St.)
Edward M. NW1 . . . . .1K 5 (3F 83)
Edward Mills Way E14 . . . . .6C 86
Edward Pl. SE8 . . . . .6B 104
Edward Rd. BR1: Broml 7K 141
BR7: Chst 5F 143
CRO: C'don 7E 156
E17 .4K 49
EN4: E Barn 5G 21
HA2: Harr 3G 41
RM6: Chad H 6E 54
SE20 . . . . .7K 139
TW12: Hamp H 5G 131
TW14: Felt 5F 111
UB5: N'olt 2A 76
Edward's Av. HA4: Ruis 6K 57
Edwards Cl. KT4: Wor Pk 2F 165
Edward's Cotts. N1 . . . . .6B 66
Edwards Ct. CRO: C'don 4E 168
(off South Pk. Hill Rd.)
Edwards Dr. N11 . . . . .7C 32
Edward's La. N16 . . . . .2E 66
Edwards Mans. IG11: Bark 7K 71
(off Upney La.)
Edwards M. N1 . . . . .7B 66
W1 . . . . .1G 11 (6E 82)
Edwards Pas. E1 . . . . .5J 85
(off Trinity Grn.)
Edwards Pl. KT12: Walt T 7J 147
Edward Sq. N1 . . . . .1K 83
SE16 . . . . .1A 104
Edwards Rd. DA17: Belv 4G 109
Edward St. E16 . . . . .4J 87
(not continuous)
SE8 .6B 104
SE14 . . . . .7A 104
Edwards Way SE4 . . . . .5C 122
Edwards Yd. HA0: Wemb 1E 78
Edward Temme Av. E15 . . . . .7H 69
Edward Tyler Rd. SE12 . . . . .2A 142
Edward Way TW15: Ashf 2B 128
Edwina Gdns. IG4: Ilf 5C 52
Edwin Arnold Ct. DA14: Sidc 4K 143
Edwin Av. E6 . . . . .2E 88
(not continuous)
Edwin Cl. DA7: Bex 6F 109
Edwin Hall Pl. SE13 . . . . .6F 123
Edwin Ho. SE15 . . . . .7G 103
Edwin Pl. CRO: C'don 1E 168
(off Cross Rd.)
Edwin Rd. HA8: Edg 6E 28
TW1: Twick 1K 131
TW2: Twick 1J 131
Edwin's Mead E9 . . . . .4A 68
Edwin Stray Ho. TW13: Hanw 2E 130
Edwin St. E1 . . . . .4J 85
E16 .5J 87
Edwin Ware Ct. HA5: Pinn 2A 40
Edwy Ho. E9 . . . . .4B 68
(off Homerton Rd.)
Edwyn Cl. EN5: Barn 6A 20

Edwyn Ho. SW18 . . . . .6K 117
(off Neville Gill Cl.)
Eel Brook Cl. SW6 . . . . .1K 117
Eel Pie Island TW1: Twick 1A 132
Effie Pl. SW6 . . . . .7J 99
Effie Rd. SW6 . . . . .7J 99
Effingham Cl. SM2: Sutt 7K 165
Effingham Lodge KT1: King T 4D 150
Effingham Rd. CRO: C'don 7K 155
KT6: Surb 7B 150
N8 . . . . .5A 48
SE12 . . . . .5G 123
Effort St. SW17 . . . . .5C 136
Effra Cl. SW19 . . . . .6K 135
Effra Ct. SW2 . . . . .5K 119
(off Brixton Hill)
Effra Pde. SW2 . . . . .5A 120
Effra Rd. SW2 . . . . .4A 120
SW19 . . . . .6K 135
Effra Rd. Retail Pk. 5A 120
Egan Way UB3: Hayes 7G 75
Egbert Ho. E9 . . . . .5A 68
(off Homerton Rd.)
Egbert St. NW1 . . . . .1E 82
Egbury Ho. SW15 . . . . .6B 116
(off Tangley Gro.)
Egeremont Rd. SE13 . . . . .2D 122
Egerton Cl. DA17: Belv 5J 109
HA5: Eastc 4J 39
Egerton Cl. E11 . . . . .7F 51
Egerton Cres. SW3 . . . . .3D 16 (4C 100)
Egerton Dr. SE10 . . . . .1D 122
TW7: Isle 3B 114
Egerton Gdns. IG3: Ilf 3K 71
NW4 .4D 44
NW10 . . . . .1E 80
SW3 . . . . .2C 16 (4C 100)
W13 .6B 78
Egerton Gdns. M. SW3 . . .2D 16 (3C 100)
Egerton Pl. SW3 . . . . . . .2D 16 (3C 100)
Egerton Rd. HA0: Wemb 7F 61
KT3: N Mald 4B 152
N16 .7F 49
SE25 . . . . .3E 156
TW2: Twick 7J 113
Egerton Ter. SW3 . . . . . .2D 16 (3C 100)
Egerton Way UB3: Harl 7D 92
Eggardon Cl. UB5: N'olt 6F 59
Egham Cl. SM3: Cheam 2G 165
SW19 . . . . .2G 135
Egham Cres. SM3: Cheam 3G 165
Egham Rd. E13 . . . . .5K 87
Eglantine Rd. SW18 . . . . .5A 118
Egleston Rd. SM4: Mord 6K 153
Egleton Ho. SW15 . . . . .7C 116
Eglington Ct. SE17 . . . . .6C 102
Eglington Rd. E4 . . . . .7K 25
Eglinton Hill SE18 . . . . .6E 107
Eglinton Rd. SE18 . . . . .6E 106
Eglston Rd. SW15 . . . . .3E 116
Eglston Rd. SW15 . . . . .3E 116
Eglon M. NW1 . . . . .7D 64
Egmont Av. KT6: Surb 1F 163
Egmont Ct. KT12: Walt T 7K 147
(off Egmont Rd.)
Egmont M. KT19: Ewe 4K 163
Egmont Rd. KT3: N Mald 4B 152
KT6: Surb 1F 163
KT12: Walt T 7K 147
SM2: Sutt 7K 165
Egmont St. SE14 . . . . .7K 103
Egremont Ho. E20 . . . . .5E 68
(off Medals Way)
SE13 . . . . .2D 122
(off Russett Way)
Egremont Rd. SE27 . . . . .3A 138
Egret Hgts. N17 . . . . .3H 49
(off Waterside Way)
Egret Ho. SE16 . . . . .4K 103
(off Tawny Way)
Egret Way UB4: Yead 5B 76
Eider Cl. E7 . . . . .5H 69
UB4: Yead 5B 76

Eider Ct. *SE8* 6B **104**
Eighteenth Rd. CR4: Mitc 4J **155**
Eighth Av. E12 . . . . .4D **70**
  UB3: Hayes 1J **93**
Eileen Lenton Ct. *N15* 4F **49**
  (off Tottenham Grn. E.)
Eileen Rd. SE25 . . . . .5D **156**
Eindhoven Cl. SM5: Cars 1E **166**
Einstein Ho. HA9: Wemb 3J **61**
Eisenhower Dr. E6 . . . . .5C **88**
Ekarro Ho. *SW8* 1J **119**
  (off Guildford Rd.)
Elaine Gro. NW5 . . . . .5E **64**
Elam Cl. SE5 . . . . .2B **120**
Elam St. SE5 . . . . .2B **120**
Elan Ct. E1 . . . . .5H **85**
Eland Pl. CR0: Wadd 3B **168**
Eland Rd. CR0: Wadd 3B **168**
  SW11 .3D **118**
Elba Pl. SE17 . . . . .4C **102**
Elberon Av. CR0: Bedd 6G **155**
Elbe St. SW6 . . . . .2A **118**
Elborough Rd. SE25 . . . . .5G **157**
Elborough St. SW18 . . . . .1J **135**
Elbourne Ct. *SE16* 3K **103**
  (off Worgan St.)
Elbourne Trad. Est. DA17: Belv 3H **109**
Elbourn Ho. *SW3* 5C **16**
  (off Cale St.)
Elbow Mdw. SL3: Poyle 4A **174**
Elbury Dr. E16 . . . . .6J **87**
Elcho St. SW11 . . . . .7C **100**
Elcot Av. SE15 . . . . .7H **103**
Elden Ho. *SW3* 3C **16**
  (off Sloane Av.)
Eldenwall Ind. Est. RM8: Dag 1F **73**
Elder Av. N8 . . . . .5J **47**
Elderberry Gro. SE27 . . . . .4C **138**
Elderberry Rd. W5 . . . . .2E **96**
Elderberry Way E6 . . . . .3D **88**
Elder Cl. DA15: Sidc 1K **143**
  N20 . . . . .2E **30**
  UB7: Yiew 7A **74**
Elder Ct. WD23: B Hea 2D **26**
Elderfield Ho. *E14* 7C **86**
  (off Pennyfields)
Elderfield Pl. SW17 . . . . .4F **137**
Elderfield Rd. E5 . . . . .4K **67**
Elderfield Wlk. E11 . . . . .5K **51**
Elderflower Way E15 . . . . .7G **69**
Elder Gdns. SE27 . . . . .5C **138**
Elder Ho. *E15* 3G **87**
  (off Manor Rd.)
  KT1: King T 1D **150**
  (off Water La.)
  SE16 . . . . .3A **104**
Elder Oak Cl. SE20 . . . . .1H **157**
Elder Oak Ct. *SE20* 1H **157**
  (off Anerley Rd.)
Elder Pl. CR2: S Croy 6B **168**
Elder Rd. SE27 . . . . .5C **138**
Elderslie Cl. BR3: Beck 5C **158**
Elderslie Rd. SE9 . . . . .5E **124**
Elder St. E1 . . . . .5J **9** (4F **85**)
  (not continuous)
Elderton Rd. SE26 . . . . .4A **140**
Eldertree Pl. CR4: Mitc 1G **155**
Eldertree Way CR4: Mitc 1G **155**
Elder Wlk. *N1* 1B **84**
  (off Popham St.)
  SE13 . . . . .3E **122**
Elderwood Pl. SE27 . . . . .5C **138**
Eldon Av. CR0: C'don 2J **169**
  TW5: Hest 7E **94**
Eldon Ct. NW6 . . . . .1J **81**
Eldon Gro. NW3 . . . . .5B **64**
Eldon Ho. *NW9* 3C **44**
  (off East Dr.)
Eldon Pk. SE25 . . . . .4H **157**
Eldon Rd.
  E17 . . . . .4B **50**
  N9 . . . . .1D **34**

Eldon Rd. N22 . . . . .1B **48**
  W8 . . . . .3K **99**
Eldons Pas. *E1* 7G **85**
  (off Cable St.)
Eldon St. EC2 . . . . .6F **9** (5D **84**)
Eldon Way NW10 . . . . .3H **79**
Eldred Rd. IG11: Bark 1J **89**
Eldrick Ct. TW14: Bedf 1F **129**
Eldridge Cl. TW14: Felt 1J **129**
Eldridge Ct. RM10: Dag 6H **73**
  SE16 . . . . .3G **103**
Eleanor Cl. N15 . . . . .3F **49**
  SE16 . . . . .2K **103**
Eleanor Ct. *E2* 1G **85**
  (off Whiston Rd.)
Eleanor Cres. NW7 . . . . .5A **30**
Eleanor Gdns. EN5: Barn 5A **20**
  RM8: Dag 2F **73**
Eleanor Gro. SW13 . . . . .3A **116**
  UB10: Ick 3D **56**
Eleanor Ho. *W6* 5E **98**
  (off Queen Caroline St.)
Eleanor Rathbone Ho. *N6* 7H **47**
  (off Avenue Rd.)
Eleanor Rd. E8 . . . . .6H **67**
  E15 . . . . .6H **69**
  N11 . . . . .6D **32**
  SW9 .1A **120**
Eleanor St. E3 . . . . .3C **86**
Eleanor Wlk. SE18 . . . . .4C **106**
Electra Av. TW6: H'row A 3H **111**
Electra Bus. Pk. E16 . . . . .5F **87**
Electric Av. SW9 . . . . .4A **120**
Electric Cinema
  Portobello 6H **81**
  Shoreditch 4F **85**
  (off Club Row)
The Electric Empire *SE14* 1K **121**
  (off New Cross Rd.)
Electric Ho. *E3* 3C **86**
  (off Bow Rd.)
Electric La. SW9 . . . . .4A **120**
  (not continuous)
Electric Pde. E18 . . . . .2J **51**
  (off George La.)
  IG3: Ilf .2J **71**
  KT6: Surb 6D **150**
Elektron Twr. E14 . . . . .7F **87**
Eleonora Ter. SM1: Sutt 5A **166**
  (off Lind Rd.)
ELEPHANT & CASTLE 3B **102**
Elephant & Castle SE1 . . . . .4B **102**
Elephant La. SE16 . . . . .2J **103**
Elephant Pk. Development SE17 . . .4C **102**
Elephant Rd. SE17 . . . . .4C **102**
Elers Rd. UB3: Harl 4F **93**
  W13 . . . . .2C **96**
Eley Rd. N18 . . . . .4E **34**
Eley Rd. Retail Pk. 5D **34**
Eleys Est. N18 . . . . .4E **34**
  (not continuous)
Elfindale Rd. SE24 . . . . .5C **120**
Elfin Gro. TW11: Tedd 5K **131**
Elfin Oak .1K **99**
Elford Cl. SE3 . . . . .4A **124**
Elford M. SW4 . . . . .5G **119**
Elfort Rd. N5 . . . . .4A **66**
Elfrida Cl. IG8: Wfd G 7D **36**
Elfrida Cres. SE6 . . . . .4C **140**
Elf Row E1 . . . . .7J **85**
Elfwine Rd. W7 . . . . .5J **77**
Elgal Cl. BR6: Farnb 5F **173**
Elgar *N8* 3J **47**
  (off Boyton Cl.)
Elgar Av. KT5: Surb 1G **163**
  NW10 . . . . .6K **61**
  (not continuous)
  SW16 .3J **155**
  W5 . . . . .2E **96**
Elgar Cl. E13 . . . . .2A **88**
  IG9: Buck H 2G **37**
  SE8 . . . . .7C **104**
  UB10: Ick 2C **56**

Elgar Ct. NW6 . . . . .3J **81**
  W14 . . . . .3G **99**
  (off Blythe Rd.)
Elgar Ho. *NW6* 7A **64**
  (off Fairfax Rd.)
  SW1 . . . . .6K **17**
  (off Churchill Gdns.)
Elgar St. SE16 . . . . .3A **104**
Elgin Av. HA3: Kenton 2B **42**
  TW15: Ashf 6E **128**
  W9 . . . . .4H **81**
  W12 . . . . .2C **98**
Elgin Cl. W12 . . . . .2D **98**
Elgin Ct. CR2: S Croy 4C **168**
  (off Bramley Hill)
  W9 . . . . .4K **81**
Elgin Cres. TW6: H'row A 2G **111**
  W11 . . . . .7G **81**
Elgin Dr. HA6: Nwood 1G **39**
Elgin Est. *W9* 4J **81**
  (off Elgin Av.)
Elgin Ho. E14 . . . . .6D **86**
  (off Ricardo St.)
  RM6: Chad H 6F **55**
  (off High Rd.)
Elgin Mans. W9 . . . . .3K **81**
Elgin M. W11 . . . . .6G **81**
Elgin M. Nth. W9 . . . . .3K **81**
Elgin M. Sth. W9 . . . . .3K **81**
Elgin Rd. CR0: C'don 2F **169**
  IG3: Ilf .1J **71**
  N22 . . . . .2G **47**
  SM1: Sutt 3A **166**
  SM6: W'gton 6G **167**
Elgood Cl. W11 . . . . .7G **81**
Elgood Ho. NW8 . . . . .2B **82**
  (off Wellington Rd.)
  SE1 . . . . .7E **14**
  (off Tabard St.)
Elham Cl. BR1: Broml 7B **142**
Elham Ho. E5 . . . . .5H **67**
Elia M. N1 . . . . .1A **8** (2B **84**)
Elias Pl. SW8 . . . . .6A **102**
Elia St. N1 . . . . .1B **8** (2B **84**)
Elibank Rd. SE9 . . . . .4D **124**
Elim Est. SE1 . . . . .7G **15** (3E **102**)
Elim St. SE1 . . . . .7G **15** (3D **102**)
  (not continuous)
Elim Way E13 . . . . .3H **87**
Eliot Bank SE23 . . . . .2H **139**
Eliot Cotts. SE3 . . . . .2G **123**
Eliot Ct. SW18 . . . . .6K **117**
Eliot Dr. HA2: Harr 2F **59**
Eliot Gdns. SW15 . . . . .4C **116**
Eliot Hill SE13 . . . . .2E **122**
Eliot M. NW8 . . . . .2A **82**
Eliot Pk. SE13 . . . . .2E **122**
Eliot Pl. SE3 . . . . .2G **123**
Eliot Rd. RM9: Dag 4D **72**
Eliot Va. SE3 . . . . .2F **123**
Elis David Almshouses
  CR0: C'don 3B **168**
Elis Way E20 . . . . .5E **68**
Elizabethan Cl. TW19: Stanw 7A **110**
Elizabethan Way TW19: Stanw . . .7A **110**
Elizabeth Av. EN2: Enf 3G **23**
  IG1: Ilf .2H **71**
  N1 . . . . .1C **84**
  TW18: Staines 7A **128**
Elizabeth Barnes Ct. *SW6* 2K **117**
  (off Marinefield Rd.)
Elizabeth Bates Ct. *E1* 5J **85**
  (off Fulneck Pl.)
Elizabeth Blackwell Ho. N22 . . . . .1A **48**
  (off Progress Way)
Elizabeth Blount Ct. *E14* 6A **86**
  (off Carr St.)
Elizabeth Bri. SW1 . . . . . .4J **17** (4F **101**)
Elizabeth Cl. E14 . . . . .6D **86**
  EN5: Barn 3A **20**
  RM7: Mawney 1H **55**
  SM1: Sutt 4H **165**
  W9 . . . . .4A **82**

Elizabeth Clyde Cl. N15 . . . . .4E **48**
Elizabeth Cotts.
  TW9: Kew 1F **115**
Elizabeth Ct. BR1: Broml 1H **159**
  (off Highland Rd.)
  CR0: C'don 3E **168**
  (off The Avenue)
  E4 . . . . .5G **35**
  E10 . . . . .7D **50**
  IG8: Wfd G 7F **37**
  KT2: King T 1E **150**
  NW1 . . . . .3D **4**
  SW1 . . . . .2D **18**
  SW10 .6B **100**
  (off Milman's St.)
  TW11: Tedd 5J **131**
  TW16: Sun 3A **148**
  (off Elizabeth Gdns.)
Elizabeth Croll Ho. *WC1* 1H **7**
  (off Penton Ri.)
Elizabeth Fry Apts. IG11: Bark 7G **71**
  (off Kings Rd.)
Elizabeth Fry Ho. UB3: Harl 4H **93**
Elizabeth Fry M. E8 . . . . .7H **67**
Elizabeth Fry Pl. SE18 . . . . .1C **124**
Elizabeth Gdns.
  HA7: Stan 6H **27**
  TW7: Isle 4A **114**
  TW16: Sun 3A **148**
  W3 . . . . .1B **98**
Elizabeth Garrett Anderson Ho.
  DA17: Belv 3G **109**
  (off Ambrooke Rd.)
Elizabeth Ho. *E3* 3D **86**
  (off St Leonard's St.)
  SE11 . . . . .4K **19**
  (off Reedworth St.)
  SM3: Cheam 6G **165**
  (off Park La.)
  W6 . . . . .5E **98**
  (off Queen Caroline St.)
Elizabeth Ind. Est. SE14 . . . . .6K **103**
Elizabeth M. *E2* 2G **85**
  (off Kay St.)
  E10 . . . . .1E **68**
  HA1: Harr 6J **41**
  NW3 . . . . .6C **64**
Elizabeth Newcomen Ho. *SE1* . . .6E **14**
  (off Newcomen St.)
Elizabeth Pl. N15 . . . . .4D **48**
Elizabeth Ride N9 . . . . .7C **24**
Elizabeth Rd. E6 . . . . .1B **88**
  N15 . . . . .5E **48**
Elizabeth Sq. *SE16* 7A **86**
  (off Sovereign Cres.)
Elizabeth St. SW1 . . . . . . .3H **17** (4E **100**)
Elizabeth Ter. SE9 . . . . .6D **124**
Elizabeth Way SE19 . . . . .7D **138**
  TW13: Hanw 4A **130**
Elkanette M. N20 . . . . .2F **31**
Elkington Point SE11 . . . . .4J **19**
Elkington Rd. E13 . . . . .4K **87**
Elkstone Rd. W10 . . . . .5H **81**
Ella Cl. BR3: Beck 2C **158**
Ellacott M. SW16 . . . . .2H **137**
Ellaline Rd. W6 . . . . .6F **99**
Ella M. NW3 . . . . .4D **64**
Ellanby Cres. N18 . . . . .4C **34**
Elland Cl. EN5: New Bar 5G **21**
Elland Ho. *E14* 6B **86**
  (off Copenhagen Pl.)
Elland Rd. SE15 . . . . .4J **121**
Ella Rd. N8 . . . . .7J **47**
Ellement Cl. HA5: Pinn 5B **40**
Ellena Ct. N14 . . . . .3D **32**
  (off Conway Rd.)
Ellenborough Ho. *W12* 7D **80**
  (off White City Est.)
Ellenborough Pl. SW15 . . . . .4C **116**
Ellenborough Rd. DA14: Sidc 5D **144**
  N22 . . . . .1C **48**
Ellenbridge Way CR2: Sande 7E **168**
Ellen Cl. BR1: Broml 3B **160**

Ellen Ct. *E4* .1K **35**
   (off The Ridgeway)
N9 . . . . .2D **34**
Ellen Julia Ct. *E1* 6J **85**
   (off James Voller Way)
Ellen Phillips La. *E2* 2G **85**
Ellen St. *E1* 6G **85**
Ellen Terry Ct. *NW1* 7F **65**
   (off Farrier St.)
Ellen Webb Dr. HA3: W'stone 3J **41**
Ellen Wilkinson Ho. *E2* 3K **85**
   (off Usk St.)
RM10: Dag 3G **73**
SW6 . . . . .6H **99**
   (off Clem Attlee Ct.)
Elleray Rd. TW11: Tedd 6K **131**
Ellerby St. SW6 . . . . .1F **117**
Ellerdale Cl. NW3 . . . . .4A **64**
Ellerdale Rd. NW3 . . . . .5A **64**
Ellerdale St. SE13 . . . . .4D **122**
Ellerdine Rd. TW3: Houn 4G **113**
Ellerker Gdns. TW10: Rich 6E **114**
Ellerman Av. TW2: Whitt 1D **130**
Ellerslie Gdns. NW10 . . . . .1C **80**
Ellerslie Rd. W12 . . . . .1D **98**
Ellerslie Sq. Ind. Est. SW2 . . . . . . .5J **119**
Ellerton Gdns. RM9: Dag 7C **72**
Ellerton Lodge N3 . . . . .2J **45**
Ellerton Rd. KT6: Surb 2F **163**
RM9: Dag .7C **72**
SW13 . . . . .1C **116**
SW18 . . . . .1B **136**
SW20 . . . . .7C **134**
Ellery Ho. SE17 . . . . .4D **102**
Ellery Rd. SE19 . . . . .7D **138**
Ellery St. SE15 . . . . .2H **121**
Ellesmere Av. BR3: Beck 2E **158**
NW7 . . . . .3E **28**
Ellesmere Cl. E11 . . . . .5H **51**
HA4: Ruis .7E **38**
Ellesmere Ct. SE12 . . . . .1J **141**
W4 . . . . .5K **97**
Ellesmere Gdns. IG4: Ilf 5C **52**
Ellesmere Gro. EN5: Barn 5C **20**
Ellesmere Ho. SW10 . . . . .6A **100**
   (off Fulham Rd.)
Ellesmere Mans. NW6 . . . . .6A **64**
   (off Canfield Gdns.)
Ellesmere Rd. E3 . . . . .2A **86**
NW10 . . . . .5C **62**
TW1: Twick 6C **114**
UB6: G'frd 4G **77**
W4 . . . . .6K **97**
Ellesmere St. E14 . . . . .6D **86**
Ellie M. E13 .2A **88**
TW15: Ashf 2A **128**
Ellingfort Rd. E8 . . . . .7H **67**
Ellingham Rd. E15 . . . . .4F **69**
KT9: Chess 6D **162**
W12 . . . . .2C **98**
Ellington Ct. N14 . . . . .2C **32**
Ellington Ho. SE1 . . . . .3C **102**
SE18 . . . . .7E **106**
Ellington Rd. N10 . . . . .4F **47**
TW3: Houn 2F **113**
TW13: Felt 4H **129**
Ellington St. N7 . . . . .6A **66**
Elliot Cl. E15 . . . . .7G **69**
IG8: Wfd G 6G **37**
Elliot Ho. SW17 . . . . .3B **136**
   (off Grosvenor Way)
W1 . . . . .6D **4**
   (off Cato St.)
Elliot Rd. NW4 . . . . .6D **44**
Elliott Av. HA4: Ruis 2K **57**
Elliott Cl. HA9: Wemb 3F **61**
Elliott Gdns. TW17: Shep 4C **146**
Elliott Rd. BR2: Broml 4B **160**
CR7: Thor H 4B **156**
HA7: Stan 6F **27**
SW9 . . . . .1B **120**
W4 . . . . .4A **98**
Elliott's Pl. N1 . . . . .1B **84**

Elliott Sq. NW3 . . . . .7C **64**
Elliotts Row SE11 . . . . .4B **102**
Ellis Av. RM8: Dag 1E **72**
Ellis Cl. HA4: Eastc 6J **39**
HA8: Edg 6F **29**
NW10 . . . . .6D **62**
SE9 . . . . .2G **143**
Elliscombe Mt. SE7 . . . . .6A **106**
Elliscombe Rd. SE7 . . . . .6A **106**
Ellis Ct. *E1* 6J **85**
   (off James Voller Way)
W7 . . . . .5K **77**
Ellisfield Dr. SW15 . . . . .7C **116**
Ellis Franklin Ct. NW8 . . . . .2A **82**
   (off Abbey Rd.)
Ellis Ho. SE17 . . . . .5D **102**
   (off Brandon St.)
Ellison Apts. *E3* 3C **86**
   (off Merchant St.)
Ellison Gdns. UB2: S'hall 4D **94**
Ellison Ho. SE13 . . . . .2D **122**
   (off Lewisham Rd.)
Ellison Rd. DA15: Sidc 1H **143**
SW13 . . . . .2B **116**
SW16 . . . . .7H **137**
Ellis Rd. CR4: Mitc 6D **154**
UB2: S'hall 1G **95**
Ellis St. SW1 . . . . .3F **17** (4E **100**)
Ellis Ter. SE11 . . . . .7A **102**
Elliston Ho. SE18 . . . . .4E **106**
   (off Wellington St.)
Ellora Rd. SW16 . . . . .5H **137**
Ellswood Ct. KT6: Surb 7D **150**
Ellsworth St. E2 . . . . .3H **85**
Ellwood Ct. W9 . . . . .4K **81**
   (off Clearwell Dr.)
Elmar Rd. N15 . . . . .4D **48**
Elm Av. HA4: Ruis 1J **57**
TW19: Stanw 2A **128**
W5 . . . . .1E **96**
Elmbank N14 . . . . .7D **22**
Elmbank Av. EN5: Barn 4A **20**
Elm Bank Dr. BR1: Broml 2B **160**
Elm Bank Gdns. SW13 . . . . .2A **116**
Elmbank Way W7 . . . . .5H **77**
Elmbourne Dr. DA17: Belv 4G **109**
Elmbourne Rd. SW17 . . . . .3F **137**
Elmbridge Av. KT5: Surb 5H **151**
Elmbridge Cl. HA4: Ruis 6J **39**
Elmbridge Dr. HA4: Ruis 5H **39**
Elmbridge Wlk. E8 . . . . .7G **67**
Elmbridge Xcel Leisure Complex . .5K **147**
Elmbridge Xcel Sports Hub 5K **147**
Elmbrook Cl. TW16: Sun 1K **147**
Elmbrook Gdns. SE9 . . . . .4C **124**
Elmbrook Rd. SM1: Sutt 4H **165**
Elm Cl. CR2: S Croy 6K **49**
E11 . . . . .6K **51**
HA2: Harr 6F **41**
IG9: Buck H 2G **37**
KT5: Surb 7J **151**
N19 . . . . .2G **65**
NW4 . . . . .5F **45**
RM7: Mawney 1H **55**
SM5: Cars 1D **166**
SW20 . . . . .4E **152**
TW2: Twick 2F **131**
UB3: Hayes 6J **75**
Elmcote HA5: Pinn 2B **40**
Elm Cotts. CR4: Mitc 2D **154**
Elm Ct. CR4: Mitc 2D **154**
EC4 . . . . .1J **13**
EN4: E Barn 7H **21**
KT8: W Mole 4F **149**
SE1 . . . . .7G **15**
   (off Royal Oak Yd.)
SE13 . . . . .3F **123**
SW9 . . . . .1A **120**
   (off Cranworth Gdns.)
TW16: Sun 7H **129**
   (off Grangewood Dr.)
W9 . . . . .5J **81**
   (off Admiral Wlk.)

Elmcourt Rd. SE27 . . . . .2B **138**
Elm Cres. KT2: King T 1E **150**
W5 . . . . .1E **96**
Elmcroft N6 .7G **47**
N8 . . . . .5K **47**
Elmcroft Av. DA15: Sidc 7K **125**
E11 . . . . .5K **51**
N9 . . . . .6C **24**
NW11 . . . . .7H **45**
Elmcroft Cl. E11 . . . . .4K **51**
KT9: Chess 3E **162**
TW14: Felt 6H **111**
W5 . . . . .6D **78**
Elmcroft Cres. HA2: Harr 3E **40**
NW11 . . . . .7G **45**
Elmcroft Dr. KT9: Chess 3E **162**
TW15: Ashf 5C **128**
Elmcroft Gdns. NW9 . . . . .4G **43**
Elmcroft St. E5 . . . . .4J **67**
Elmcroft Ter. UB8: Hil 6C **74**
Elmdale Rd. N13 . . . . .5E **32**
Elmdene KT5: Surb 1J **163**
Elmdene Cl. BR3: Beck 6B **158**
Elmdene Rd. SE18 . . . . .5F **107**
Elmdon Rd. TW4: Houn 2B **112**
TW6: H'row A 3H **111**
Elm Dr. HA2: Harr 6F **41**
TW16: Sun 2K **147**
Elmer Cl. EN2: Enf 3E **22**
Elmer Gdns. HA8: Edg 7C **28**
TW7: Isle 3H **113**
Elmer Ho. NW8 . . . . .5C **4**
   (off Penfold St.)
Elmer Rd. SE6 . . . . .7E **122**
Elmers Dr. TW11: Tedd 6B **132**
ELMERS END 4A **158**
Elmers End Rd. BR3: Beck 2J **157**
SE20 . . . . .2J **157**
Elmerside Rd. BR3: Beck 4A **158**
Elmers Lodge BR3: Beck 4K **157**
Elmer's End SE25 . . . . .7G **157**
Elmfield HA1: Harr 7K **41**
Elmfield Av. CR4: Mitc 1E **154**
N8 . . . . .5J **47**
TW11: Tedd 5K **131**
Elmfield Cl. HA1: Harr 2J **59**
Elmfield Ct. DA16: Well 1B **126**
Elmfield Ho. N2 . . . . .3E **46**
   (off The Grange)
NW8 . . . . .2K **81**
   (off Carlton Hill)
W9 . . . . .4J **81**
   (off Goldney Rd.)
Elmfield Pk. BR1: Broml 3J **159**
Elmfield Rd. BR1: Broml 2J **159**
E4 . . . . .2K **35**
E17 . . . . .6K **49**
N2 . . . . .3B **46**
SW17 . . . . .2E **136**
UB2: S'hall 3C **94**
Elmfield Way CR2: Sande 7F **169**
W9 . . . . .5J **81**
Elm Friars Wlk. NW1 . . . . .7H **65**
Elm Gdns. CR4: Mitc 4H **155**
KT10: Clay 6A **162**
N2 . . . . .3A **46**
Elmgate Av. TW13: Felt 3K **129**
Elmgate Gdns. HA8: Edg 5D **28**
Elm Grn. W3 . . . . .6A **80**
Elmgreen Cl. E15 . . . . .1G **87**
Elm Gro. BR6: Orp 1K **173**
DA8: Erith 7K **109**
HA2: Harr 7E **40**
IG8: Wfd G 5C **36**
KT2: King T 1E **150**
N8 . . . . .6J **47**
NW2 . . . . .4F **63**
SE15 . . . . .2F **121**
SM1: Sutt 4K **165**
SW19 . . . . .7H **135**
UB7: Yiew 7B **74**
Elmgrove Cres. HA1: Harr 5K **41**
Elmgrove Gdns. HA1: Harr 5A **42**

Elm Gro. Pde. SM6: W'gton 3E **166**
Elmgrove Point SE18 . . . . .4H **107**
Elm Gro. Rd. SW13 . . . . .1C **116**
W5 . . . . .2E **96**
Elmgrove Rd. CR0: C'don 7H **157**
HA1: Harr 5K **41**
Elm Hall Gdns. E11 . . . . .5K **51**
   (not continuous)
Elm Ho. *E3* 1B **86**
   (off Sycamore Av.)
E14 . . . . .6C **104**
   (off E. Ferry Rd.)
KT2: King T 7F **133**
   (off Elm Rd.)
W10 . . . . .4G **81**
   (off Briar Wlk.)
Elmhurst DA17: Belv 6E **108**
Elmhurst Av. CR4: Mitc 7F **137**
N2 . . . . .3B **46**
Elmhurst Ct. CR0: C'don 4D **168**
Elmhurst Dr. E18 . . . . .2J **51**
Elmhurst Lodge SM2: Sutt 7A **166**
Elmhurst Mans. SW4 . . . . .3H **119**
Elmhurst Rd. E7 . . . . .7K **69**
N17 . . . . .2F **49**
SE9 . . . . .2C **142**
Elmhurst St. SW4 . . . . .3H **119**
Elmington Cl. DA5: Bexl 6H **127**
Elmington Est. SE5 . . . . .7D **102**
Elmington Rd. SE5 . . . . .7D **102**
Elmira St. SE13 . . . . .3D **122**
Elm La. SE6 . . . . .2B **140**
Elm Lawn Cl. UB8: Uxb 7A **56**
Elmlea Dr. UB3: Hayes 5G **75**
Elm Lea Trad. Est. N17 . . . . .6C **34**
Elmlee Cl. BR7: Chst 6D **142**
Elmley Cl. E6 . . . . .5C **88**
Elmley St. SE18 . . . . .5H **107**
   (not continuous)
Elm Lodge SW6 . . . . .1E **116**
Elmore Cl. HA0: Wemb 2E **78**
HA3: Kenton 2B **42**
Elmore Dr. HA3: Kenton 2B **42**
Elmore Ho. N1 . . . . .7D **66**
   (off Elmore St.)
SW9 . . . . .2B **120**
Elmore Rd. E11 . . . . .3E **68**
EN3: Enf W 1E **24**
Elmore St. N1 . . . . .7C **66**
Elm Pde. DA14: Sidc 4A **144**
Elm Pk. HA7: Stan 5G **27**
SW2 . . . . .6K **119**
Elm Pk. Av. N15 . . . . .5F **49**
Elm Pk. Chambers SW10 . . . . .6A **16**
   (off Fulham Rd.)
Elm Pk. Ct. HA5: Pinn 3A **40**
Elm Pk. Gdns. NW4 . . . . .5E **45**
SW10 . . . . .6A **16** (5B **100**)
Elm Pk. Ho. SW10 . . . . . . .6A **16** (6A **100**)
Elm Pk. La. SW3 . . . . .6A **16** (5B **100**)
Elm Pk. Mans. SW10 . . . . .7A **16** (6A **100**)
Elm Pk. Rd. E10 . . . . .1A **68**
HA5: Pinn 2A **40**
N3 . . . . .7C **30**
N21 . . . . .7H **23**
SE25 . . . . .3F **157**
SW3 . . . . .7A **16** (6B **100**)
Elm Pas. EN5: Barn 4C **20**
Elm Pl. SW7 . . . . .5A **16** (5B **100**)
TW15: Ashf 5C **128**
Elm Quay Ct. SW11 . . . .7C **18** (6H **101**)
Elm Rd. BR3: Beck 2B **158**
BR6: Chels 7K **173**
CR7: Thor H 4D **156**
DA14: Sidc 4A **144**
E7 . . . . .6H **69**
E11 . . . . .2F **69**
E17 . . . . .5E **50**
EN5: Barn 4C **20**
HA9: Wemb 5E **60**
KT2: King T 1F **151**
KT3: N Mald 2K **151**
KT9: Chess 4E **162**

Elm Rd. KT17: Ewe 6B **164**
  N22 . . . . .1B **48**
  RM7: Mawney 2H **55**
  SM6: W'gton 1E **166**
  SW14 . . . . .3J **115**
  TW14: Bedf 1F **129**
Elm Rd. W. SM3: Sutt 7H **153**
Elm Row NW3 . . . . .3A **64**
The Elms CR0: C'don 1C **168**
  (off Tavistock Rd.)
  E12 . . . . .6B **70**
  KT10: Clay 7A **162**
  SW13 . . . . .3B **116**
  TW15: Ashf 5C **128**
Elms Av. N10 . . . . .3A **4**
  NW4 . . . . .5F **45**
Elmscott Gdns. N21 . . . . .6H **23**
Elmscott Rd. BR1: Broml 5G **141**
Elms Cl. HA0: Wemb 4A **60**
Elms Cres. SW4 . . . . .6G **119**
Elmsdale Rd. E17 . . . . .4B **50**
Elms Gdns. HA0: Wemb 4A **60**
  RM9: Dag 4F **73**
Elmshaw Rd. SW15 . . . . .5C **116**
Elmshurst Cres. N2 . . . . .4B **46**
Elmside CR0: New Ad 6D **170**
Elmside Rd. HA9: Wemb 3G **61**
Elms La. HA0: Wemb 3A **60**
Elmsleigh Av. HA3: Kenton 4B **42**
Elmsleigh Ct. SM1: Sutt 3K **165**
Elmsleigh Ho. TW2: Twick 2H **131**
  (off Staines Rd.)
Elmsleigh Rd. TW2: Twick 2H **131**
Elmslie Cl. IG8: Wfd G 6J **37**
Elmslie Point E3 . . . . .5B **86**
  (off Leopold St.)
Elms M. W2 . . . . .2A **10** (7B **82**)
Elms Pk. Av. HA0: Wemb 4A **60**
Elms Rd. HA3: Hrw W 7D **26**
  SW4 . . . . .5G **119**
ELMSTEAD .6D **142**
Elmstead Av. BR7: Chst 5D **142**
  HA9: Wemb 1E **60**
Elmstead Cl. KT19: Ewe 5A **164**
  N20 . . . . .2D **30**
Elmstead Gdns. KT4: Wor Pk 3C **164**
Elmstead Glade BR7: Chst 6D **142**
Elmstead La. BR7: Chst 7C **142**
Elmstead Rd. DA8: Erith 1K **127**
  IG3: Ilf 2J **71**
Elmsted Cres. DA16: Well 6C **108**
Elmstone Rd. SW6 . . . . .1J **117**
Elm St. WC1 . . . . .4H **7** (4K **83**)
Elmsway TW15: Ashf 5C **128**
Elmsworth Av. TW3: Houn 2F **113**
Elm Ter. HA3: Hrw W 1H **41**
  NW2 . . . . .3J **63**
  NW3 . . . . .4C **64**
  SE9 . . . . .6E **124**
Elmton Ct. NW8 . . . . .3A **4**
  (off Cunningham Pl.)
Elm Tree Rd. KT10: Esh 7H **149**
Elm Tree Cl. NW8 . . . . .1A **4** (3B **82**)
  TW15: Ashf 5D **128**
  UB5: N'olt .2D **76**
Elm Tree Ct. NW8 . . . . .1A **4**
  SE7 . . . . .6A **106**
Elm Tree Rd. NW8 . . . . . . .1A **4** (3B **82**)
Elmtree Rd. TW11: Tedd 4J **131**
Elm Vw. Ct. UB2: S'hall 4E **94**
Elm Vw. Ho. UB3: Harl 4F **93**
Elm Wlk. BR6: Farnb 3D **172**
  NW3 . . . . .2J **63**
  SW20 . . . . .4E **152**
Elm Way KT4: Wor Pk 3E **164**
  KT19: Ewe 5K **163**
  N11 . . . . .6K **31**
  NW10 . . . . .4A **62**
Elmwood Av. HA3: Kenton 5A **42**
  N13 . . . . .5D **32**
  TW13: Felt, Hanw 2J **129**
Elmwood Cl. KT17: Ewe 7C **164**
  SM6: W'gton 2F **167**

Elmwood Ct. E10 . . . . .1C **68**
  (off Goldsmith Rd.)
  HA0: Wemb 3A **60**
  SW11 . . . . .1F **119**
Elmwood Cres. NW9 . . . . .4J **43**
Elmwood Dr. DA5: Bexl 7E **126**
  KT17: Ewe 6C **164**
Elmwood Gdns. W7 . . . . .6J **77**
Elmwood Ho. NW10 . . . . .2D **80**
  (off All Souls Av.)
Elmwood Rd. CR0: C'don 7B **156**
  CR4: Mitc 3D **154**
  SE24 . . . . .5D **120**
  W4 . . . . .6J **97**
Elmworth Gro. SE21 . . . . .2D **138**
Elnathan M. W9 . . . . .4K **81**
Elphinstone Ct. SW16 . . . . .6J **137**
Elphinstone Rd. E17 . . . . .2B **50**
Elphinstone St. N5 . . . . .4B **66**
Elrington Rd. E8 . . . . .6G **67**
  IG8: Wfd G 5D **36**
Elsa Cotts. E14 . . . . .5A **86**
  (off Halley St.)
Elsa Ct. BR3: Beck 1B **158**
Elsa Rd. DA16: Well 2B **126**
Elsa St. E1 . . . . .5A **86**
Elsdale St. E9 . . . . .6J **67**
Elsden M. E2 . . . . .2J **85**
Elsden Rd. N17 . . . . .1F **49**
Elsenham Rd. E12 . . . . .5E **70**
Elsenham St. SW18 . . . . .1H **135**
Elsham Rd. E11 . . . . .3G **69**
  W14 . . . . .2G **99**
Elsham Ter. W14 . . . . .3G **99**
  (off Elsham Rd.)
Elsiedene Rd. N21 . . . . .7H **23**
Elsie La. Ct. W2 . . . . .5J **81**
  (off Westbourne Pk. Vs.)
Elsinge Rd. SE4 . . . . .5B **122**
Elsie Rd. SE22 . . . . .4F **121**
Elsinore Av. TW19: Stanw 7A **110**
Elsinore Gdns. NW2 . . . . .3G **63**
Elsinore Ho. N1 . . . . .1A **84**
  (off Denmark Gro.)
  SE5 . . . . .2C **120**
  (off Denmark Rd.)
  SE7 . . . . .4C **106**
  W6 . . . . .5F **99**
  (off Fulham Pal. Rd.)
Elsinore Rd. SE23 . . . . .1A **140**
Elsinore Way TW9: Rich 3H **115**
Elsley Cl. HA9: Wemb 6H **61**
Elsley Rd. SW11 . . . . .3D **118**
Elspeth Rd. HA0: Wemb 5E **60**
  SW11 . . . . .4D **118**
Elsrick Av. SM4: Mord 5J **153**
Elstan Way CR0: C'don 7A **158**
Elstar Ct. RM13: Rain 2K **91**
  (off Lowen Rd.)
Elstead Ct. SM3: Sutt 1G **165**
Elstead Ho. SW2 . . . . .7K **119**
  (off Redlands Way)
Elsted St. SE17 . . . . .4D **102**
Elstow Cl. HA4: Ruis 7B **40**
  SE9 . . . . .5D **124**
  (not continuous)
Elstow Gdns. RM9: Dag 1E **90**
Elstow Grange NW6 . . . . .7F **63**
Elstow Rd. RM9: Dag 1E **90**
Elstree Gdns. DA17: Belv 4E **108**
  IG1: Ilf 5G **71**
  N9 . . . . .1C **34**
Elstree Hill BR1: Broml 7G **141**
Elstree Hill Sth. WD6: E'tree 1H **27**
Elstree Rd. WD23: B Hea 1D **26**
Elswick Rd. SE13 . . . . .2D **122**
Elswick St. SW6 . . . . .2A **118**
Elsworthy KT7: T Ditt 7A **150**
Elsworthy Ct. NW3 . . . . .7D **64**
  (off Primrose Hill Rd.)
Elsworthy Ri. NW3 . . . . .7C **64**
Elsworthy Rd. NW3 . . . . .1C **82**

Elsworthy Ter. NW3 . . . . .7C **64**
Elsynge Rd. SW18 . . . . .5B **118**
ELTHAM 6D **124**
Eltham Cen. 5E **124**
Eltham Crematorium 4H **125**
Eltham Grn. SE9 . . . . .5B **124**
Eltham Grn. Rd. SE9 . . . . .4A **124**
Eltham High St. SE9 . . . . .6D **124**
Eltham Hill SE9 . . . . .5B **124**
Eltham Palace & Gdns. 7C **124**
Eltham Pal. Rd. SE9 . . . . .6A **124**
ELTHAM PARK 4E **124**
Eltham Pk. Gdns. SE9 . . . . .4E **124**
Eltham Rd. SE9 . . . . .5H **123**
  SE12 . . . . .5H **123**
Eltham Warren Golf Course 5F **125**
Elthiron Rd. SW6 . . . . .1J **117**
Elthorne Av. W7 . . . . .2K **95**
Elthorne Ct. TW13: Felt 1A **130**
ELTHORNE HEIGHTS 5J **77**
Elthorne Pk. Rd. W7 . . . . .2K **95**
Elthorne Rd. N19 . . . . .2H **65**
  NW9 . . . . .7K **43**
Elthorne Sports Cen. 3K **95**
Elthorne Way NW9 . . . . .6K **43**
Elthruda Rd. SE13 . . . . .6F **123**
Eltisley Rd. IG1: Ilf 4F **71**
Elton Av. EN5: Barn 5C **20**
  HA0: Wemb 5B **60**
  UB6: G'frd .6J **59**
Elton Cl. KT1: Hamp W 7C **132**
Elton Ho. E3 . . . . .1B **86**
  (off Candy St.)
Elton Pl. N16 . . . . .5E **66**
Elton Rd. KT2: King T 1F **151**
Eltringham St. SW18 . . . . .4A **118**
Eluna Apts. E1 . . . . .7H **85**
  (off Wapping La.)
Elvaston M. SW7 . . . . .2A **16** (3A **100**)
Elvaston Pl. SW7 . . . . .2A **16** (3A **100**)
Elveden Ho. SE24 . . . . .5B **120**
Elveden Pl. NW10 . . . . .2G **79**
Elveden Rd. NW10 . . . . .2G **79**
Elvedon Rd. TW13: Felt 3H **129**
Elvendon Rd. N13 . . . . .6D **32**
Elver Gdns. E2 . . . . .2G **85**
Elverson M. SE14 . . . . .1J **121**
Elverson Rd. SE8 . . . . .2D **122**
Elverton St. SW1 . . . . . .3C **18** (4H **101**)
Elvin Ct. NW9 . . . . .7J **43**
Elvin Gardens HA9: Wemb 4G **61**
Elvington Grn. BR2: Broml 5H **159**
Elvington La. NW9 . . . . .1A **44**
Elvino Rd. SE26 . . . . .5A **140**
Elwell Cl. NW2 . . . . .6E **62**
Elwill Way BR3: Beck 4E **158**
Elwin St. E2 . . . . .1K **9** (3G **85**)
Elwood Cl. EN5: New Bar 4F **21**
Elwood St. N5 . . . . .3B **66**
Elworth Ho. SW8 . . . . .7K **101**
  (off Oval Pl.)
Ely Gdns. RM9: Dag 7J **123**
Ely Cl. KT3: N Mald 2B **152**
Ely Ct. EC1 . . . . .6K **7**
  KT1: King T 2G **151**
Ely Gdns. IG1: Ilf 7C **52**
  RM10: Dag 3J **73**
Ely Ho. SE15 . . . . .7G **103**
  (off Friary Est.)
Elyne Rd. N4 . . . . .6A **48**
Ely Pl. EC1 . . . . .6K **7** (5A **84**)
  IG8: Wfd G 6K **37**
  SW8 . . . . .7K **101**
Ely Rd. CR0: C'don 5D **156**
  E10 . . . . .6E **50**
  TW4: Houn 3A **112**
  TW6: H'row A 2H **111**
  (off Esher Clo.)
Elysian Av. BR5: St M Cry 6K **161**
Elysian M. N7 . . . . .6K **65**
Elysian Pl. CR2: S Croy 7C **168**
Elysium Apts. E1 . . . . .4J **85**
  (off Theven St.)

Elysium Pl. SW6 . . . . .2H **117**
  (off Elysium St.)
Elysium St. SW6 . . . . .2H **117**
Elystan Bus. Cen. UB4: Yead 7A **76**
Elystan Cl. SM6: W'gton 7G **167**
Elystan Ho. SW3 . . . . .4C **16**
  (off Elystan St.)
Elystan Pl. SW3 . . . . .5D **16** (5C **100**)
Elystan St. SW3 . . . . .4C **16** (4C **100**)
Elystan Wlk. N1 . . . . .1A **84**
Ely's Yd. E1 . . . . .5K **9** (5F **85**)
Emanuel Av. W3 . . . . .6J **79**
Emanuel Dr. TW12: Hamp 5D **130**
Emanuel Ho. SW1 . . . . .3H **101**
Embankment SW15 . . . . .2F **117**
The Embankment TW1: Twick 1A **132**
Embankment Galleries 2H **13**
  (within Somerset House)
Embankment Gdns. SW3 . .7F **17** (6D **100**)
Embankment Pier WC2 . .4F **13** (1J **101**)
Embankment Pl. WC2 . . . .4F **13** (1J **101**)
Embassy Apts. SE5 . . . . .2C **120**
  (off Coldharbour La.)
Embassy Ct. DA14: Sidc 3B **144**
  DA16: Well 3B **126**
  E2 . . . . .4H **85**
  (off Brady St.)
  N11 . . . . .6C **32**
  (off Bounds Grn. Rd.)
  NW8 . . . . .1B **4**
  SM6: W'gton 6F **167**
  W5 . . . . .7F **79**
Embassy Gdns. BR3: Beck 1B **158**
Embassy Ho. NW6 . . . . .7K **63**
Embassy Lodge N3 . . . . .2H **45**
  (off Cyprus Rd.)
Embassy of United States of America
  . . . . .7D **18** (6H **101**)
Embassy Theatre 7B **64**
Embassy Way SW11 . . . . .6H **101**
Emba St. SE16 . . . . .2G **103**
Ember Cl. BR5: Pet W 7G **161**
Ember Ct. NW9 . . . . .2B **44**
Embercourt Rd. KT7: T Ditt 6J **149**
Ember Farm Av. KT8: E Mos 6H **149**
Ember Farm Way KT8: E Mos 6H **149**
Ember Gdns. KT7: T Ditt 7J **149**
Ember La. KT8: E Mos 7H **149**
  KT10: Esh 7H **149**
Emberton SE5 . . . . .6E **102**
  (off Albany Rd.)
Emberton Ct. EC1 . . . . .2A **8**
  (off Tompion St.)
Embleton Rd. SE13 . . . . .4D **122**
Embleton Wlk. TW12: Hamp 5D **130**
Embroidery World Bus. Cen.
  IG8: Wfd G 2B **52**
Embry Cl. HA7: Stan 4F **27**
Embry Dr. HA7: Stan 6F **27**
Embry Rd. SE9 . . . . .4A **124**
Embry Way HA7: Stan 5F **27**
Emden Cl. UB7: W Dray 2C **92**
Emden St. SW6 . . . . .1K **117**
Emerald Cl. E16 . . . . .6B **88**
Emerald Ct. HA4: Ruis 4A **58**
Emerald Gdns. RM8: Dag 1G **73**
Emerald Rd. NW10 . . . . .1K **79**
Emerald Sq. SW15 . . . . .5C **116**
  UB2: S'hall 3B **94**
Emerald St. WC1 . . . . .5G **7** (5K **83**)
Emerson Apts. N8 . . . . .3K **47**
Emerson Gdns. HA3: Kenton 6F **43**
Emerson M. KT3: N Mald 4A **152**
Emerson Rd. IG1: Ilf 7E **52**
Emerson St. SE1 . . . . . .4C **14** (1C **102**)
Emerton Cl. DA6: Bex 4E **126**
Emery Hill St. SW1 . . . . . .2B **18** (3G **101**)
Emery St. SE1 . . . . .1K **19** (3A **102**)
Emery Walker Trust 5C **98**
  (off Hammersmith Ter.)
Emes Rd. DA8: Erith 7J **109**
Emilia Cl. EN3: Pond E 5C **24**
Emily Bowes Ct. N17 . . . . .3H **49**

Emily Ct. *SE1* 7C *14*
  (off Sudrey St.)
Emily Duncan Pl. E7 . . . . .4K *69*
Emily Ho. *W10* 4G *81*
  (off Kensal Rd.)
Emily St. *E16* 6H *87*
  (off Jude St.)
Emirates Stadium 4A *66*
Emlyn Gdns. W12 . . . . .2A *98*
Emlyn Rd. W12 . . . . .2A *98*
Emma Ho. RM1: Rom 4K *55*
Emmanuel Ct. E10 . . . . .7D *50*
Emmanuel Ho. SE11 . . . .4J *19* (4A *102*)
Emmanuel Rd. HA6: Nwood 1H *39*
  SW12 . . . . .1G *137*
Emma Rd. E13 . . . . .2H *87*
Emma St. E2 . . . . .2H *85*
Emmaus Way IG7: Chig 5K *37*
Emmeline Ct. KT12: Walt T 7A *148*
Emminster Ho. NW6 . . . . .1K *81*
  (off Abbey Rd.)
Emmott Av. IG6: Ilf 5G *53*
Emmott Cl. E1 . . . . .4A *86*
  NW11 . . . . .6A *46*
Emms Pas. KT1: King T 2D *150*
Emperor Ho. E20 . . . . .5E *68*
  (off Napa Cl.)
  SE4 . . . . .3A *122*
  (off Dragonfly Pl.)
Emperor's Ga. SW7 . . . . .3A *100*
Empingham Ho. SE8 . . . . .4K *103*
  (off Chilton Gro.)
Empire Av. N18 . . . . .5H *33*
Empire Cinema
  Haymarket 3C *12*
  (off Haymarket)
  Sutton 5K *165*
  Walthamstow 4C *50*
Empire Cl. SE7 . . . . .6K *105*
Empire Ct. HA9: Wemb 3H *61*
Empire Ho. N18 . . . . .6J *33*
  SW7 . . . . .2C *16*
Empire Pde. HA9: Wemb 3G *61*
  N18 . . . . .6J *33*
Empire Reach SE10 . . . . .6D *104*
  (off Dowells St.)
Empire Rd. UB6: G'frd 1B *78*
Empire Sq. N7 . . . . .3J *65*
  SE1 . . . . .7E *14*
  (off Tabard St.)
  SE20 . . . . .7K *139*
  (off High St.)
Empire Sq. E. SE1 . . . . .7E *14*
Empire Sq. Sth. SE1 . . . . .7E *14*
Empire Sq. W. SE1 . . . . .7E *14*
Empire Way HA9: Wemb 4F *61*
Empire Wharf E3 . . . . .1A *86*
  (off Old Ford Rd.)
Empire Wharf Rd. E14 . . . . .4F *105*
Empress App. SW6 . . . . .5J *99*
Empress Av. E4 . . . . .7J *35*
  E12 . . . . .2A *70*
  IG1: Ilf 2D *70*
  IG8: Wfd G 7C *36*
Empress Dr. BR7: Chst 6F *143*
Empress M. SE5 . . . . .2C *120*
Empress Pde. E4 . . . . .7H *35*
Empress Pl. SW6 . . . . .5J *99*
Empress State Bldg. SW6 . . . . . . .5J *99*
Empress St. SE17 . . . . .6C *102*
Empson St. E3 . . . . .4D *86*
Emsworth Cl. N9 . . . . .1D *34*
Emsworth Ct. SW16 . . . . .3J *137*
Emsworth Rd. IG6: Ilf 2F *53*
Emsworth St. SW2 . . . . .2K *137*
EMT Ho. E6 . . . . .5E *88*
Emu Rd. SW8 . . . . .2F *119*
Enard Ho. E3 . . . . .2B *86*
  (off Cardigan Rd.)
Ena Rd. SW16 . . . . .3J *155*
Enbrook St. W10 . . . . .3G *81*
The Enclave SW13 . . . . .2B *116*

Enclave Ct. EC1 . . . . .3B *8*
  (off Dallington St.)
Endale Cl. SM5: Cars 2D *166*
Endeavour Ho. E14 . . . . .2C *104*
  (off Cuba St.)
  SE16 . . . . .4A *104*
  (off Ashton Reach)
Endeavour Sq. E20 . . . . .7E *68*
Endeavour Way CRO: Bedd 7J *155*
  IG11: Bark 2A *90*
  SW19 . . . . .4K *135*
Endell St. WC2 . . . . .7E *6* (6J *83*)
Enderby St. SE10 . . . . .5F *105*
Enderley Cl. HA3: Hrw W 2J *41*
Enderley Rd. HA3: Hrw W 1J *41*
Enders Cl. EN2: Enf 1F *23*
Endersleigh Gdns. NW4 . . . . .4C *44*
Endlebury Rd. E4 . . . . .2K *35*
Endlesham Rd. SW12 . . . . .7E *118*
Endsleigh Ct. WC1 . . . . .3D *6*
Endsleigh Gdns. IG1: Ilf 2D *70*
  KT6: Surb 6C *150*
  WC1 . . . . .3D *6* (4H *83*)
Endsleigh Ind. Est. UB2: S'hall 4C *94*
Endsleigh Pl. WC1 . . . . . . .3D *6* (4H *83*)
Endsleigh Rd. UB2: S'hall 4C *94*
  W13 . . . . .7A *78*
Endsleigh St. WC1 . . . . . . .3D *6* (4H *83*)
Endway KT5: Surb 7H *151*
Endwell Rd. SE4 . . . . .2A *122*
Endymion Rd. N4 . . . . .7A *48*
  SW2 . . . . .6K *119*
Energen Cl. NW10 . . . . .6A *62*
énergie Fitness
  Old Street 4D *84*
The Energy Cen. N1 . . . . .1G *9*
  (off Bowling Grn. Wlk.)
ENFIELD 3J *23*
Enfield Bus. Cen. EN3: Enf H 2D *24*
Enfield Cloisters N1 . . . . .1G *9*
  (off Fanshaw St.)
Enfield Golf Course 4G *23*
ENFIELD HIGHWAY 3D *24*
Enfield Ho. SW9 . . . . .2J *119*
  (off Stockwell Rd.)
ENFIELD ISLAND VILLAGE 1H *25*
ENFIELD LOCK 1G *25*
Enfield Lock EN3: Enf L 1H *25*
Enfield Mus. 4J *23*
  (off London Rd.)
Enfield Retail Pk. 3B *24*
Enfield Rd. EN2: Enf 4C *22*
  N1 . . . . .7D *66*
  TW6: H'row A 2G *111*
  TW8: Bford 5D *96*
  W3 . . . . .2H *97*
ENFIELD ROAD RDBT. 2G *111*
ENFIELD TOWN 4J *23*
Enfield Town FC 2A *24*
Enfield Wlk. TW8: Bford 5D *96*
ENFIELD WASH 1F *25*
Enford St. W1 . . . . .5E *4* (5D *82*)
Engadine Cl. CRO: C'don 3F *169*
Engadine St. SW18 . . . . .1H *135*
Engate St. SE13 . . . . .4E *122*
Engel Pk. NW7 . . . . .6K *29*
Engine Cl. SW1 . . . . .5B *18*
  (off Ambassador's Ct.)
Engineer Cl. SE18 . . . . .6E *106*
Engineers Row SE18 . . . . .4E *106*
  (off Woolwich New Rd.)
Engineers Way HA9: Wemb 4G *61*
Englands La. NW3 . . . . .6D *64*
England Way KT3: N Mald 4H *151*
Englefield NW1 . . . . .2A *6*
  (off Clarence Gdns.)
Englefield Cl. BR5: St M Cry 5K *161*
  CRO: C'don 6C *156*
  EN2: Enf 2F *23*
Englefield Cres. BR5: St M Cry 4K *161*
Englefield Path BR5: St M Cry 4K *161*
Englefield Rd. N1 . . . . .7D *66*

Engleheart Dr. TW14: Felt 6H *111*
Engleheart Rd. SE6 . . . . .7D *122*
Englewood Rd. SW12 . . . . .6F *119*
English Grounds SE1 . . . .5G *15* (1E *102*)
English St. E3 . . . . .4B *86*
Enid St. SE16 . . . . .7K *15* (3F *103*)
Enmore Av. SE25 . . . . .5G *157*
Enmore Gdns. SW14 . . . . .5K *115*
Enmore Rd. SE25 . . . . .5G *157*
  SW15 . . . . .4E *116*
  UB1: S'hall 4E *76*
Ennerdale NW1 . . . . .1A *6*
  (off Varndell St.)
Ennerdale Av. HA7: Stan 3C *42*
Ennerdale Cl. SM1: Sutt 4H *165*
  TW14: Felt 1H *129*
Ennerdale Ct. E11 . . . . .7J *51*
  (off Cambridge Rd.)
Ennerdale Dr. NW9 . . . . .5A *44*
Ennerdale Gdns. HA9: Wemb 1C *60*
Ennerdale Ho. E3 . . . . .4B *86*
Ennerdale Rd. DA7: Bex 1G *127*
  TW9: Kew, Rich 2F *115*
Ennersdale Rd. SE13 . . . . .5F *123*
Ennis Ho. E14 . . . . .6D *86*
  (off Vesey Path)
Ennismore Av. UB6: G'frd 6J *59*
  W4 . . . . .4A *98*
Ennismore Gdns. KT7: T Ditt 6J *149*
  SW7 . . . . .7C *10* (2C *100*)
Ennismore Gdns. M. SW7 . .1C *16* (3C *100*)
Ennismore M. SW7 . . . . . . .7C *10* (3C *100*)
Ennismore St. SW7 . . . . . . .1C *16* (3C *100*)
Ennis Rd. N4 . . . . .1A *66*
  SE18 . . . . .6G *107*
Ennor Ct. SM3: Cheam 4E *164*
Ensbury Ho. SW8 . . . . .7K *101*
  (off Carroun Rd.)
Ensham Ho. SW17 . . . . .5D *136*
Ensign Cl. TW6: H'row A 3G *111*
  TW19: Stanw 1A *128*
Ensign Dr. N13 . . . . .3H *33*
Ensign Ho. E14 . . . . .2C *104*
  (off Admirals Way)
  NW9 . . . . .3C *44*
  (off East Dr.)
  SW18 . . . . .3A *118*
Ensign St. E1 . . . . .7G *85*
Ensign Way SM6: W'gton 7J *167*
  TW19: Stanw 1A *128*
Enslin Rd. SE9 . . . . .6E *124*
Ensor M. SW7 . . . . .5A *16* (5B *100*)
Enstone Rd. EN3: Enf H 3F *25*
  UB10: Ick .3B *56*
Enterprise Bus. Pk. E14 . . . . .2D *104*
The Enterprise Cen. BR3: Beck 5A *140*
  (off Cricket La.)
Enterprise Cl. CRO: C'don 1A *168*
Enterprise Ho. E4 . . . . .7K *25*
  E9 . . . . .7J *67*
  (off Tudor Gro.)
  E14 . . . . .5D *104*
  (off St Davids Sq.)
  IG11: Bark 3K *89*
  KT12: Walt T 7K *147*
Enterprise Ind. Est. SE16 . . . . .5J *103*
Enterprise Trad. Est. UB2: S'hall . . .2F *95*
Enterprise Way NW10 . . . . .3B *80*
  SW18 . . . . .4J *117*
  TW11: Tedd 6K *131*
Enterprize Way SE8 . . . . .4B *104*
Entertainment Av. SE10 . . . . .1G *105*
Envoy Av. TW6: H'row A 3H *111*
Envoy Ho. NW9 . . . . .3C *44*
  (off East Dr.)
ENVOY RDBT. 3H *111*
Epirus M. SW6 . . . . .7J *99*
Epirus Rd. SW6 . . . . .7H *99*
Epping Cl. E14 . . . . .4C *104*
  RM7: Mawney 3H *55*

Epping Glade E4 . . . . .6K *25*
Epping New Rd. IG9: Buck H 3D *36*
Epping Pl. N1 . . . . .6A *66*
Epping Way E4 . . . . .6J *25*
Epple Rd. SW6 . . . . .1H *117*
Epsom Cl. DA7: Bex 3H *127*
  UB5: N'olt 5D *58*
Epsom Rd. CRO: Wadd 4A *168*
  E10 . . . . .6E *50*
  IG3: Ilf 6K *53*
  SM3: Sutt 7H *153*
  SM4: Mord 7H *153*
Epsom Sq. TW6: H'row A 2H *111*
Epstein Ct. N1 . . . . .1B *84*
  (off Gaskin St.)
Epstein Rd. SE28 . . . . .1A *108*
Epstein Sq. E14 . . . . .6C *86*
  (off Upper Nth. St.)
Epworth Rd. TW7: Isle 7B *96*
Epworth St. EC2 . . . . .4F *9* (4D *84*)
Equana Apts. SE8 . . . . .5A *104*
  (off Evelyn St.)
Equiano Ho. SW9 . . . . .1K *119*
  (off Lett Rd.)
Equinox Ct. IG2: Ilf 5F *53*
Equinox Ho. IG11: Bark 6G *71*
  (off Wakering Rd.)
Equinox Sq. E14 . . . . .6D *86*
Equity M. W5 . . . . .1D *96*
Equity Sq. E2 . . . . .2K *9*
  (off Shacklewell St.)
Erasmus St. SW1 . . . . .4D *18* (4H *101*)
Erconwald St. W12 . . . . .6B *80*
Erebus Dr. SE28 . . . . .3G *107*
Eresby Dr. BR3: Beck 1C *170*
Eresby Ho. SW7 . . . . .7D *10*
  (off Rutland Ga.)
Eresby Pl. NW6 . . . . .7J *63*
Erica Gdns. CRO: C'don 3D *170*
Erica Ho. N22 . . . . .1A *48*
  (off Acacia Rd.)
  SE4 . . . . .3B *122*
Erica St. W12 . . . . .7C *80*
Eric Clarke La. IG11: Bark 4F *89*
Eric Cl. E7 .4J *69*
Ericcson Cl. SW18 . . . . .5J *117*
Eric Fletcher Ct. N1 . . . . .7C *66*
  (off Essex Rd.)
Erickson Gdns. BR2: Broml 6C *160*
Eric Liddell Sports Cen. 2B *142*
Eric Rd. E7 .4J *69*
  NW10 . . . . .6B *62*
  RM6: Chad H 7D *54*
Eric Shipman Ter. E13 . . . . .4J *87*
  (off Balaam St.)
Ericson Ho. SE13 . . . . .4F *123*
  (off Blessington Rd.)
Eric St. E3 .4B *86*
  (not continuous)
Eric Wilkins Ho. SE1 . . . . .5G *103*
  (off Old Kent Rd.)
Eridge Rd. W4 . . . . .3K *97*
Erin Cl. BR1: Broml 7G *141*
  IG3: Ilf 6A *54*
  SW6 . . . . .7J *99*
Erin Ct. NW2 . . . . .6E *62*
Erindale SE18 . . . . .6H *107*
Erindale Ter. SE18 . . . . .6H *107*
Erin M. N22 . . . . .1B *48*
Erin's Vs. SE14 . . . . .1K *121*
  (off New Cross Rd.)
ERITH 5K *109*
Erith Cres. RM5: Col R 1J *55*
Erith Quarry DA8: Erith 6J *109*
Erith Rd. DA7: Bex 4H *127*
  DA8: Erith 5G *109*
  (Picardy Rd.)
  DA8: Erith 5G *109*
  (Watling St.)
  DA17: Belv, Erith 5G *109*
Erith School Community Sports Cen.
  . . . . .7J *109*
Erlanger Rd. SE14 . . . . .1K *121*

Erlesmere Gdns. W13 . . . . .3A 96
Erlich Cotts. E1 . . . . .5J 85
        (off Sidney St.)
Ermine Cl. TW4: Houn 2A 112
Ermine Ho. E3 . . . . .1B 86
        (off Parnell Rd.)
N17 . . . . .7A 34
        (off Moselle St.)
Ermine M. E2 . . . . .1F 85
Ermine Rd. N15 . . . . .6F 49
SE13 .4D 122
Ermine Side EN1: Enf 5B 24
Ermington Rd. SE9 . . . . .2G 143
Ernald Av. E6 . . . . .2C 88
Erncroft Way TW1: Twick 6K 113
Ernest Av. SE27 . . . . .4B 138
Ernest Cl. BR3: Beck 5C 158
Ernest Cotts. KT17: Ewe 7B 164
Ernest Gdns. W4 . . . . .6H 97
Ernest Gro. BR3: Beck 5B 158
Ernest Harriss Ho. W9 . . . . .4J 81
        (off Elgin Av.)
Ernest Rd. KT1: King T 2H 151
Ernest Shackleton Lodge SE10 . . .4G 105
        (off Christchurch Way)
Ernest Sq. KT1: King T 2H 151
Ernest St. E1 . . . . .4K 85
Ernle Rd. SW20 . . . . .7D 134
Ernshaw Pl. SW15 . . . . .5G 117
Ernst Bldg. SE1 . . . . .5C 14
        (off Union St.)
Eros 3C 12 (7H 83)
Eros Ho. Shops SE6 . . . . .7D 122
        (off Brownhill Rd.)
Erpingham Rd. SW15 . . . . .3E 116
Erridge Rd. SW19 . . . . .2J 153
Errington Rd. W9 . . . . .4H 81
Errol Gdns. KT3: N Mald 4C 152
UB4: Yead 4K 75
Errol St. EC1 . . . . .4D 8 (4C 84)
Erskine Cl. SM1: Sutt 3C 166
Erskine Cres. N17 . . . . .4H 49
Erskine Hill NW11 . . . . .4J 45
Erskine Ho. SW1 . . . . .6A 18
        (off Churchill Gdns.)
Erskine M. NW3 . . . . .7D 64
        (off Erskine Rd.)
Erskine Rd. E17 . . . . .4B 50
NW3 . . . . .7D 64
SM1: Sutt 4B 166
Erwin Ho. NW9 . . . . .3C 44
        (off Commander Av.)
Erwood Rd. SE7 . . . . .5C 106
Esam Way SW16 . . . . .5A 138
Escot Rd. TW16: Sun 7G 129
Escott Gdns. SE9 . . . . .4C 142
Escreet Gro. SE18 . . . . .4E 106
Esher Av. KT12: Walt T 7J 147
RM7: Rom 6J 55
SM3: Cheam 3F 165
Esher Cl. DA5: Bexl 1E 144
Esher Cres. TW6: H'row A 2H 111
Esher Gdns. SW19 . . . . .2F 135
Esher M. CR4: Mitc 3E 154
Esher Rd. IG3: IIf 3J 71
KT8: E Mos 6H 149
Eskdale NW1 . . . . .1A 6
        (off Stanhope St.)
Eskdale Av. UB5: N'olt 1D 76
Eskdale Cl. HA9: Wemb 2D 60
Eskdale Rd. DA7: Bex 2G 127
Esker Pl. E2 . . . . .2H 85
Esk Ho. E3 . . . . .4B 86
        (off British St.)
Eskmont Ridge SE19 . . . . .7D 138
Esk Rd. E13 . . . . .4J 87
Esk Way RM1: Rom 1K 55
Esmar Cres. NW9 . . . . .7C 44
Esmat Cl. E11 . . . . .5K 51
Esmeralda Rd. SE1 . . . . .4G 103
Esmond Ct. W8 . . . . .3K 99
        (off Thackeray St.)
Esmond Gdns. W4 . . . . .4K 97

Esmond Rd. NW6 . . . . .1H 81
W4 . . . . .4K 97
Esmond St. SW15 . . . . .4G 117
Esparto St. SW18 . . . . .7K 117
Esprit Ct. E1 . . . . .6J 9
        (off Brune St.)
Esquiline La. CR4: Mitc 3F 155
Essan Ho. W5 . . . . .5B 78
Essence E3 . . . . .2B 86
        (off Cardigan Rd.)
Essence Ct. HA9: Wemb 2F 61
Essenden Rd. CR2: S Croy 7E 168
DA17: Belv 5G 109
Essendine Mans. W9 . . . . .3J 81
Essendine Rd. W9 . . . . .3J 81
Essex Av. TW7: Isle 3J 113
Essex Cl. E17 . . . . .4A 50
HA4: Ruis 1B 58
RM7: Mawney 4H 55
SM4: Mord 7F 153
Essex Ct. EC4 . . . . .1J 13
SW13 .2B 116
W6 . . . . .3E 98
        (off Hammersmith Gro.)
Essex Gdns. N4 . . . . .6B 48
Essex Gro. SE19 . . . . .6D 138
Essex Hall E17 . . . . .1K 49
Essex Ho. E14 . . . . .6D 86
        (off Giraud St.)
Essex Mans. E11 . . . . .7F 51
Essex M. SE19 . . . . .6E 138
Essex Pk. N3 . . . . .6E 30
Essex Pk. M. W3 . . . . .1A 98
Essex Pl. W4 . . . . .4J 97
        (not continuous)
Essex Pl. Sq. W4 . . . . .4K 97
Essex Rd. E4 . . . . .1B 36
E10 . . . . .6E 50
E12 . . . . .5C 70
E17 . . . . .6A 50
E18 . . . . .2K 51
EN2: Enf 4J 23
IG11: Bark 7H 71
N1 . . . . .1B 84
NW10 . . . . .7A 62
RM6: Chad H 7C 54
RM7: Mawney 4H 55
RM10: Dag 5J 73
W3 . . . . .7J 79
W4 . . . . .4K 97
Essex Rd. Sth. E11 . . . . .7F 51
Essex St. E7 . . . . .5J 69
WC2 . . . . .1J 13 (6A 84)
Essex Twr. SE20 . . . . .1H 157
        (off Jasmine Gro.)
Essex Vs. W8 . . . . .2J 99
Essex Wharf E5 . . . . .2K 67
Essian St. E1 . . . . .5A 86
Essoldo Way HA8: Edg 3F 43
Estate Way E10 . . . . .1B 68
Estcourt Rd. SE25 . . . . .6H 157
SW6 . . . . .7H 99
Estella Apts. E15 . . . . .6F 69
        (off Grove Cres. Rd.)
Estella Av. KT3: N Mald 4D 152
Estella Ho. W11 . . . . .7F 81
        (off St Ann's Rd.)
Estelle Rd. NW3 . . . . .4D 64
Esterbrooke St. SW1 . . . . . .4C 18 (4H 101)
Este Rd. SW11 . . . . .3C 118
Esther Anne Pl. N1 . . . . .1B 84
Esther Cl. N21 . . . . .7F 23
Esther M. BR1: Broml 1K 159
        (off Freelands Rd.)
Esther Randall Ct. NW1 . . . . .3K 5
        (off Lit. Albany St.)
Esther Rd. E11 . . . . .7G 51
Estoria Cl. SW2 . . . . .7A 120
Estorick Collection of Modern Italian Art
        . . . . .6B 66
Estreham Rd. SW16 . . . . .6H 137
Estridge Cl. TW3: Houn 4E 112
Estuary Cl. IG11: Bark 3B 90

Estuary Ho. E16 . . . . .1B 106
        (off Agnes George Wlk.)
Eswyn Rd. SW17 . . . . .4D 136
Etal Ho. N1 . . . . .7B 66
        (off The Sutton Est.)
Etcetera Theatre 7F 65
        (off Camden High St.)
Etchingham Ct. N3 . . . . .7E 30
Etchingham Pk. Rd. N3 . . . . .7E 30
Etchingham Rd. E15 . . . . .4E 68
Eternit Wlk. SW6 . . . . .1E 116
Etfield Gro. DA14: Sidc 5B 144
Ethan Dr. N2 . . . . .3K 45
Ethelbert Cl. BR1: Broml 2J 159
Ethelbert Ct. BR1: Broml 3J 159
        (off Ethelbert Rd.)
Ethelbert Gdns. IG2: IIf 5D 52
Ethelbert Ho. E9 . . . . .4A 68
        (off Homerton Rd.)
Ethelbert Rd. BR1: Broml 3J 159
DA8: Erith 7J 109
SW20 .1F 153
Ethelbert St. SW12 . . . . .1F 137
Ethel Brooks Ho. SE18 . . . . .6F 107
Ethelburga St. SW11 . . . . .1C 118
Ethelburga Twr. SW11 . . . . .1C 118
        (off Rosenau Rd.)
Etheldene Av. N10 . . . . .4G 47
Ethelden Rd. W12 . . . . .1D 98
Ethelred Ct. HA3: Kenton 5G 43
Ethel Rd. E16 . . . . .6K 87
TW15: Ashf 5A 128
Ethel St. SE17 . . . . .4C 102
Etheridge Rd. NW4 . . . . .7E 44
        (not continuous)
Etherley Rd. N15 . . . . .5C 48
Etherow St. SE22 . . . . .7G 121
Etherstone Grn. SW16 . . . . .4A 138
Etherstone Rd. SW16 . . . . .4A 138
Ethnard Rd. SE15 . . . . .6H 103
Ethos Sport Imperial 7B 10 (2B 100)
Ethronvi Rd. DA7: Bex 3E 126
Etloe Ho. E10 . . . . .1C 68
Etloe Rd. E10 . . . . .2C 68
Eton Av. EN4: E Barn 6H 21
HA0: Wemb 4B 60
KT3: N Mald 5K 151
N12 . . . . .7F 31
NW3 . . . . .7B 64
TW5: Hest 6D 94
Eton Cl. SW18 . . . . .7K 117
Eton Coll. Rd. NW3 . . . . .6D 64
Eton Ct. HA0: Wemb 4C 60
NW3 . . . . .7B 64
Eton Garages NW3 . . . . .6C 64
Eton Gro. NW9 . . . . .3G 43
SE13 . . . . .3G 123
Eton Hall NW3 . . . . .6D 64
Eton Ho. N5 . . . . .4B 66
        (off Leigh Rd.)
UB7: W Dray 2B 92
ETON MANOR 4D 68
Eton Mnr. Ct. E10 . . . . .2C 68
        (off Leyton Grange Est.)
Eton M. N1 . . . . .7K 65
Eton Pl. NW3 . . . . .7E 64
Eton Ri. NW3 . . . . .6D 64
Eton Rd. IG1: IIf 4G 71
NW3 . . . . .7D 64
UB3: Harl 7H 93
Eton St. TW9: Rich 5E 114
Eton Vs. NW3 . . . . .6D 64
Etta St. SE8 . . . . .6A 104
Ettrick St. E14 . . . . .6E 86
        (not continuous)
Etwell Pl. KT5: Surb 6F 151
Eucalyptus M. SW16 . . . . .6H 137
Euesden Cl. N9 . . . . .3C 34
Eugene Cotter Ho. SE17 . . . . .4D 102
        (off Tatum St.)
Eugenia Rd. SE16 . . . . .4J 103
Eugenie M. BR7: Chst 1F 161
Eureka Rd. KT1: King T 2G 151

Euro Cl. NW10 . . . . .6C 62
Eurolink Bus. Cen. SW2 . . . . .4A 120
Europa Pl. EC1 . . . . .2C 8 (3C 84)
Europa Trade Pk. E16 . . . . .4G 87
Europa Trad. Est.
   DA8: Erith 5K 109
European Bus. Cen. NW9 . . . . .3J 43
        (not continuous)
European Design Cen. NW9 . . . . . . .3K 43
Europe Rd. SE18 . . . . .3D 106
Euro Trade Cen.
   DA17: Belv 2J 109
Eustace Bldg. SW11 . . . . .6F 101
Eustace Ho. SE11 . . . . .3G 19
Eustace Pl. SE18 . . . . .4D 106
Eustace Rd. E6 . . . . .3C 88
   RM6: Chad H 7D 54
   SW6 . . . . .7J 99
Euston Cir. NW1 . . . . .3B 6 (4G 83)
Euston Gro. NW1 . . . . .2C 6
Euston Rd. CR0: C'don 1A 168
N1 . . . . .4A 6 (3H 83)
NW1 . . . . .4A 6 (4F 83)
Euston Sq. NW1 . . . . .2C 6 (3H 83)
        (not continuous)
Euston Sta. Colonnade
   NW1 . . . . .2C 6 (3H 83)
Euston Twr. NW1 . . . . .2B 6 (3G 83)
Euston Twr. NW1 . . . . .3A 6 (4G 83)
EUSTON UNDERPASS 4G 83
Eva Ct. CR2: S Croy 6E 168
Evan Cook Cl. SE15 . . . . .1J 121
Evandale Rd. SW9 . . . . .2A 120
Evangelist Ho. EC4 . . . . .1A 14
        (off Black Friars La.)
Evangelist Rd. NW5 . . . . .4F 65
Evan Ho. E16 . . . . .5J 87
        (off Exeter Rd.)
Evans Apts. E2 . . . . .3K 85
Evans Cl. E8 . . . . .6F 67
Evans Gro. TW13: Hanw 2E 130
Evans Ho. SW8 . . . . .7H 101
        (off Wandsworth Rd.)
   TW13: Hanw 2E 130
   W12 . . . . .7D 80
        (off White City Est.)
Evans Rd. SE6 . . . . .2G 141
Evanston Av. E4 . . . . .7K 35
Evanston Gdns. IG4: IIf 6C 52
Eva Rd. RM6: Chad H 7C 54
Evedon Ho. N1 . . . . .1E 84
        (off Halcomb St.)
Evelina Cl. W6 . . . . .3D 98
        (off Vinery Way)
Evelina Mans. SE5 . . . . .7D 102
Evelina Rd. SE15 . . . . .3J 121
SE20 . . . . .7J 139
Eveline Lowe Est. SE16 . . . . .3G 103
Eveline Rd. CR4: Mitc 1D 154
Evelyn Av. HA4: Ruis 7G 39
NW9 . . . . .4K 43
Evelyn Cl. TW2: Whitt 7F 113
Evelyn Ct. E3 . . . . .5B 86
        (off Burdett Rd.)
E8 . . . . .4G 67
N1 . . . . .1E 8
        (off Evelyn Wlk.)
Evelyn Cres. TW16: Sun 1H 147
Evelyn Denington Ct. N1 . . . . .7B 66
        (off The Sutton Est.)
Evelyn Denington Rd. E6 . . . . .4C 88
Evelyn Dr. HA5: Pinn 1B 40
Evelyn Fox Ct. W10 . . . . .5E 80
Evelyn Gdns. SW7 . . . . . . .6A 16 (5A 100)
TW9: Rich 4E 114
Evelyn Gro. UB1: S'hall 6D 76
W5 . . . . .1F 97
Evelyn Ho. SE14 . . . . .1A 122
        (off Loring Rd.)
W8 . . . . .2K 99
        (off Hornton Pl.)
W12 . . . . .2B 98
        (off Cobbold Rd.)

Evelyn Mans. *SW1* 2A **18**
   (off Carlisle Pl.)
W14 . . . . .6G **99**
   (off Queen's Club Gdns.)
Evelyn Rd. E16 . . . . .1J **105**
E17 . . . . .4E **50**
EN4: Cockf 4J **21**
SW19 . . . . .5K **135**
TW9: Rich 3E **114**
TW10: Rich 3C **132**
W4 . . . . .3K **97**
Evelyns Cl. UB8: Hil 6C **74**
Evelyn St. SE8 . . . . .4A **104**
Evelyn Ter. TW9: Rich 3E **114**
Evelyn Way SM6: Bedd 4H **167**
TW16: Sun 1H **147**
Evelyn Yd. *W1* 7C **6** (6H **83**)
Eve Martin Ct. *EC1* 2B **8**
   (off Goswell Road)
Evening Hill BR3: Beck 7E **140**
Evenlode Ho. SE2 . . . . .2C **108**
Evenwood Cl. SW15 . . . . .5G **117**
Everall Ct. E4 . . . . .6G **35**
Everard Av. BR2: Hayes 1J **171**
Everard Ct. N13 . . . . .3E **32**
Everard Ho. *E1* 6G **85**
   (off Boyd St.)
Everard Way HA9: Wemb 3E **60**
Everatt Cl. SW18 . . . . .6H **117**
Everdon Rd. SW13 . . . . .6C **98**
Everest Pl. E14 . . . . .5E **86**
Everest Rd. SE9 . . . . .5D **124**
TW19: Stanw 7A **110**
Everett Cl. HA5: Eastc 3H **39**
WD23: B Hea 1D **26**
Everett Ho. *SE17* 5D **102**
   (off East St.)
Everett Wlk. *DA17: Belv* 5F **109**
   (off Osborne Rd.)
Everglade Ho. E17 . . . . .2B **50**
The Everglades TW3: Houn 3G **113**
Everglade Strand NW9 . . . . . . .1B **44**
Evergreen Apts. *IG8: Wfd G* . . .1H **51**
   (off High Rd. Woodford Grn.)
Evergreen Cl. SE20 . . . . .7J **139**
Evergreen Dr. UB7: W Dray 2B **92**
UB10: Hil 2D **74**
Evergreen Sq. E8 . . . . .7F **67**
Evergreen Way UB3: Hayes 7H **75**
Everilda St. N1 . . . . .1K **83**
Evering Rd. E5 . . . . .3F **67**
N16 . . . . .3F **67**
Everington Rd. N10 . . . . .2D **46**
Everington St. W6 . . . . .6F **99**
Everitt Rd. NW10 . . . . .3K **79**
Everleigh St. N4 . . . . .1K **65**
Eve Rd. E11 . . . . .4G **69**
E15 . . . . .2G **87**
N17 . . . . .3E **48**
TW7: Isle 4A **114**
Eversfield Gdns. NW7 . . . . .6F **29**
Eversfield Rd. TW9: Kew 2F **115**
Evershed Ho. *E1* 7K **9**
   (off Old Castle St.)
Evershed Wlk. W4 . . . . .3J **97**
Eversholt Ct. EN5: New Bar 5F **21**
Eversholt St. NW1 . . . . .1B **6** (2G **83**)
Evershot Rd. N4 . . . . .1K **65**
Eversleigh Ct. N3 . . . . .7C **30**
Eversleigh Pl. BR3: Beck 6C **140**
Eversleigh Rd. E6 . . . . .1B **88**
EN5: New Bar 5F **21**
N3 . . . . .7C **30**
SW11 . . . . .3D **118**
Eversley Av. DA7: Bex 2K **127**
HA9: Wemb 2G **61**
Eversley Cl. N21 . . . . .6E **22**
Eversley Cres. HA4: Ruis 2G **57**
N21 . . . . .6F **23**
TW7: Isle 1H **113**
Eversley Ho. *E2* 2K **9**
   (off Gosset St.)

Eversley Mt. N21 . . . . .6E **22**
Eversley Pk. SW19 . . . . .6D **134**
Eversley Pk. Rd. N21 . . . . .6E **22**
Eversley Rd. KT5: Surb 4F **151**
SE7 . . . . .6K **105**
SE19 . . . . .7D **138**
Eversley Way CR0: C'don 3C **170**
Everthorpe Rd. SE15 . . . . .3F **121**
Everton Ct. *HA7: Stan* 3E **42**
   (off Honeypot La.)
Everton Dr. HA7: Stan 3E **42**
Everton M. NW1 . . . . . . .2A **6** (3G **83**)
Everton Rd. CR0: C'don 1G **169**
Everyman Cinema
   Baker St. 5F **5**
   (off Baker St.)
   Barnet 5D **20**
   Belsize Pk. 5C **64**
   King's Cross 1J **83**
   Muswell Hill 4F **47**
Everyman on the Corner Cinema 1H **83**
Everyman Screen on the Green Cinema
 . . . . .1B **84**
   (off Upper St.)
Evesham Av. E17 . . . . .2C **50**
Evesham Cl. SM2: Sutt 7J **165**
UB6: G'frd 2F **77**
Evesham Ct. TW10: Rich 6F **115**
W13 . . . . .1A **96**
   (off Tewkesbury Rd.)
Evesham Grn. SM4: Mord 6K **153**
Evesham Ho. *E2* 2J **85**
   (off Old Ford Rd.)
NW8 . . . . .1A **82**
   (off Abbey Rd.)
SW1 . . . . .5K **17**
   (part of Abbots Mnr.)
Evesham Rd. E15 . . . . .7H **69**
N11 . . . . .5B **32**
SM4: Mord 6K **153**
Evesham Ter. KT6: Surb 6D **150**
Evesham Wlk. SE5 . . . . .2D **120**
SW9 .2A **120**
Evesham Way IG5: Ilf 3E **52**
SW11 . . . . .3E **118**
Evette M. IG5: Ilf 1E **52**
Evry Rd. DA14: Sidc 6C **144**
Ewald Rd. SW6 . . . . .2H **117**
Ewanrigg Ter. IG8: Wfd G 5F **37**
Ewart Gro. N22 . . . . .1K **47**
Ewart Ho. *HA1: Harr* 5A **42**
Ewart Pl. E3 . . . . .2B **86**
Ewart Rd. SE23 . . . . .7K **121**
Ewe Cl. N7 . . . . .6J **65**
EWELL 7C **164**
Ewell By-Pass KT17: Ewe 7C **164**
Ewell Ct. Av. KT19: Ewe 5A **164**
Ewellhurst Rd. IG5: Ilf 2C **52**
Ewell Pk. Gdns. KT17: Ewe 7C **164**
Ewell Pk. Way KT17: Ewe 6C **164**
Ewell Rd. KT6: Surb 7B **150**
   (Mount Holme)
   KT6: Surb 6E **150**
   (South Ter.)
   SM3: Cheam 6F **165**
Ewelme Rd. SE23 . . . . .1J **139**
Ewen Cres. SW2 . . . . .7A **120**
Ewen Henderson Ct. *SE14* 7A **104**
   (off Goodwood Rd.)
Ewen Ho. *N1* 1K **83**
   (off Barnsbury Est.)
Ewer St. SE1 . . . . . . .5C **14** (1C **102**)
Ewhurst Av. CR2: Sande 7F **169**
Ewhurst Cl. E1 . . . . .5J **85**
Ewhurst Ct. CR4: Mitc 3B **154**
Ewhurst Rd. SE4 . . . . .6B **122**
Exbury Ho. E9 . . . . .6J **67**
SW1 . . . . .5C **18**
   (off Rampayne St.)
Exbury Rd. SE6 . . . . .2C **140**
Excalibur Dr. SE6 . . . . .2G **141**
ExCeL .7K **87**

Excel Ct. WC2 . . . . .3D **12**
Excel Marina E16 . . . . .7J **87**
Excelsior Cl. KT1: King T 2G **151**
Excelsior Gdns. SE13 . . . . .2E **122**
Excelsior Ind. Est. SE15 . . . . . .6J **103**
Excel Waterfront E16 . . . . .7K **87**
The Exchange *CR0: C'don* 3C **168**
   (off Surrey St.)
IG1: Ilf .2F **71**
Exchange Apts. *BR2: Broml* . . .4K **159**
   (off Sparkes Cl.)
Exchange Arc. EC2 . . . . .5H **9** (5E **84**)
Exchange Bldg. *E1* 4J **9**
   (off Commercial St.)
Exchange Cl. N11 . . . . .2K **31**
Exchange Ct. *CR0: C'don* 1C **168**
   (off Bedford Pk.)
WC2 . . . . .3F **13** (7J **83**)
Exchange Garages N13 . . . . . . .4F **33**
Exchange Gdns. SW8 . . . . .6J **101**
Exchange Ho. EC2 . . . . .5H **9**
NW10 . . . . .7D **62**
SW1 . . . . .4C **18**
   (off Vauxhall Bri. Rd.)
Exchange Mans. NW11 . . . . . . .7H **45**
Exchange Pl. EC2 . . . . . .5G **9** (5E **84**)
Exchange Sq. EC2 . . . . . .5G **9** (5E **84**)
Exchange St. EC1 . . . . . .2C **8** (3C **84**)
RM1: Rom 5K **55**, 6K **55**
Exchange Wlk. HA5: Pinn 7C **40**
Exforde Av. TW15: Ashf 4C **128**
Exeter Cl. E6 . . . . .6D **88**
Exeter Ct. *KT6: Surb* 5E **150**
   (off Maple Rd.)
NW6 . . . . .2J **81**
   (off Cambridge Rd.)
Exeter Gdns. IG1: Ilf 1C **70**
Exeter Ho. *E14* 5E **86**
   (off St Ives Pl.)
IG11: Bark 7A **72**
   (off Margaret Bondfield Av.)
N1 . . . . .1E **84**
   (off New Era Est.)
RM8: Dag 4A **72**
SE15 .6G **103**
   (off Friary Est.)
SW15 . . . . .6E **116**
TW13: Hanw 2B **130**
W2 . . . . .6A **82**
   (off Hallfield Est.)
Exeter Mans. NW2 . . . . .6G **63**
Exeter M. NW6 . . . . .6K **63**
SW6 . . . . .7J **99**
Exeter Pl. SE26 . . . . .3G **139**
Exeter Rd. CR0: C'don 7E **156**
DA16: Well 2K **125**
E16 . . . . .5J **87**
E17 . . . . .5C **50**
EN3: Pond E 3E **24**
HA2: Harr 2C **58**
N9 . . . . .2D **34**
N14 . . . . .1A **32**
NW2 . . . . .5G **63**
RM10: Dag 6H **73**
TW6: H'row A 3D **110**
TW13: Hanw 3D **130**
Exeter St. WC2 . . . . .2F **13** (7J **83**)
Exeter Way SE14 . . . . .7B **104**
TW6: H'row A 2G **111**
Exford Cl. *SW11* 1B **118**
   (off Bolingbroke Wlk.)
Exford Gdns. SE12 . . . . .1K **141**
Exford Rd. SE12 . . . . .2K **141**
Exhibition Cl. W12 . . . . .7E **80**
Exhibition Grounds HA9: Wemb . .4H **61**
Exhibition Rd. SW7 . . . .7B **10** (2B **100**)
Exhibition Way HA9: Wemb 4G **61**
Exit Rd. N2 . . . . .2B **46**
Exmoor Cl. IG6: Ilf 1G **53**
Exmoor Ho. *DA17: Belv* 2H **109**
E3 . . . . .2A **86**
   (off Gernon Rd.)

Exmoor St. W10 . . . . .4F **81**
Exmouth Ho. *E14* 4D **104**
   (off Cahir St.)
EC1 . . . . .3J **7**
   (off Pine St.)
Exmouth Mkt. EC1 . . . . . .3J **7** (4A **84**)
Exmouth M. NW1 . . . . . . .2B **6** (3G **83**)
Exmouth Pl. E8 . . . . .7H **67**
Exmouth Rd. DA16: Well 1C **126**
E17 . . . . .5B **50**
HA4: Ruis 3A **58**
UB4: Hayes 3G **75**
Exmouth St. E1 . . . . .6J **85**
Exning Rd. E16 . . . . .4H **87**
Exonbury NW8 . . . . .1K **81**
   (off Abbey Rd.)
Exon St. SE17 . . . . .5E **102**
Explorer Av. TW19: Stanw 1A **128**
Explorers Ct. *E14* 7F **87**
   (off Newport Av.)
Export Ho. *SE1* 7H **15**
   (off Tower Bri. Rd.)
Express Dr. IG3: Ilf 1B **72**
Express Ho. *SE8* 6A **104**
   (off Rolt St.)
Express Newspapers *SE1* 4A **14**
   (off Blackfriars Rd.)
Express Wharf *E14* 2C **104**
   (off Hutchings St.)
Exton Gdns. RM8: Dag 5C **72**
Exton Rd. NW10 . . . . .7J **61**
Exton St. SE1 . . . . .5J **13** (1A **102**)
Eyebright Cl. CR0: C'don 1K **169**
Eyhurst Cl. NW2 . . . . .2C **62**
Eylewood Rd. SE27 . . . . .5C **138**
Eynella Rd. SE22 . . . . .7F **121**
Eynham Rd. W12 . . . . .6E **80**
Eynsford Cl. BR5: Pet W 7G **161**
Eynsford Cres. DA5: Bexl 1C **144**
Eynsford Ho. *SE1* 7E **14**
   (off Crosby Row)
SE15 .6J **103**
SE17 .4E **102**
   (off East St.)
Eynsford Rd. IG3: Ilf 2J **71**
Eynsford Ter. UB7: Yiew 6B **74**
Eynsham Dr. SE2 . . . . .4A **108**
Eynswood Dr. DA14: Sidc 5B **144**
Eyot Gdns. W6 . . . . .5B **98**
Eyot Grn. W4 . . . . .5B **98**
Eyot Ho. *SE16* 3G **103**
   (off Frean St.)
Eyre Ct. NW8 . . . . .2B **82**
Eyre Rd. NW8 . . . . .3A **82**
Eyre St. Hill EC1 . . . . . . .4J **7** (4A **84**)
Eysham Cl. EN5: New Bar 5E **20**
Eythorne Rd. SW9 . . . . .1A **120**
Ezra St. E2 . . . . .1K **9** (3F **85**)

F

Faber Gdns. NW4 . . . . .5C **44**
Fabian Bell Twr. *E3* 2C **86**
   (off Pancras Way)
Fabian Rd. SW6 . . . . .7H **99**
Fabian St. E6 . . . . .4D **88**
Fable Apts. N1 . . . . .1C **8**
The Facade SE23 . . . . .2J **139**
Factory La. CR0: C'don 1A **168**
N17 . . . . .2F **49**
Factory Rd. E16 . . . . .1B **106**
Factory Yd. W7 . . . . .1J **95**
Faggs Rd. TW14: Felt 4H **111**
Fairacre HA5: Eastc 4J **39**
   KT3: N Mald 3A **152**
Fairacre Ct. HA6: Nwood 1G **39**
Fair Acres BR2: Broml 5J **159**
CR0: Sels 7B **170**
Fairacres HA4: Ruis 7H **39**
SW15 . . . . .4B **116**
Fairbairn Grn. SW9 . . . . .1B **120**
Fairbank Av. BR6: Farnb 2F **173**

Fairbank Est. N1 . . . . .1F **9** (2D **84**)
Fairbanks Ct. HA0: Wemb 1E **78**
Fairbanks Rd. N17 . . . . .3F **49**
Fairbourne Ho. UB3: Harl 3E **92**
Fairbourne Rd. N17 . . . . .3E **48**
  SW4 . . . . .6H **119**
Fairbriar Residence SW7 . . . . . .4A **100**
        (off Stanhope Gdns.)
Fairbridge Rd. N19 . . . . .2H **65**
Fairbrook Cl. N13 . . . . .5F **33**
Fairbrook Rd. N13 . . . . .6F **33**
Fairburn Ct. SW15 . . . . .5G **117**
Fairburn Ho. W14 . . . . .5H **99**
           (off Ivatt Pl.)
Fairby Ho. SE1 . . . . .4F **103**
        (off Longfield Est.)
Fairby Rd. SE12 . . . . .5K **123**
Fairchild Cl. SW11 . . . . .2B **118**
Fairchild Ho. E2 . . . . .2H **85**
       (off Cambridge Cres.)
  E9 . . . . .7J **67**
       (off Frampton Pk. Rd.)
  N1 . . . . .1G **9**
         (off Fanshaw St.)
  N3 . . . . .1J **45**
Fairchild Pl. EC2 . . . . .4H **9**
Fairchild St. EC2 . . . . . .3H **9** (4E **84**)
Fair Cl. WD23: Bush 1A **26**
Fairclough Cl. UB5: N'olt 4D **76**
Fairclough St. E1 . . . . .6G **85**
Faircroft Ct. TW11: Tedd 6A **132**
FAIR CROSS 5J **71**
Faircross Av. IG11: Bark 6G **71**
  RM5: Col R 1K **55**
Faircross Pde. IG11: Bark 5J **71**
Fairdale Gdns. SW15 . . . . .4D **116**
  UB3: Hayes 2J **93**
Fairey Av. UB3: Harl 4H **93**
Fairfax Av. KT17: Ewe 7D **164**
Fairfax Cl. KT12: Walt T 7K **147**
Fairfax Ct. NW6 . . . . .7A **64**
         (off Fairfax Rd.)
Fairfax Gdns. SE3 . . . . .1A **124**
Fairfax Ho. KT1: King T 5F **151**
        (off Livesey Cl.)
Fairfax Mans. NW6 . . . . .7A **64**
        (off Finchley Rd.)
Fairfax M. E16 . . . . .1K **105**
  N8 . . . . .4B **48**
  SW15 . . . . .4E **116**
Fairfax Pl. NW6 . . . . .7A **64**
  W14 .3G **99**
Fairfax Rd. N8 . . . . .4A **48**
  NW6 .7A **64**
  TW11: Tedd 6A **132**
  W4 . . . . .3A **98**
Fairfax Way N10 . . . . .7K **31**
Fairfield E1 . . . . .5J **85**
        (off Redman's Rd.)
  KT1: King T 2F **151**
  N20 .7G **21**
  NW1 .1G **83**
        (off Arlington Rd.)
Fairfield Av. HA4: Ruis 7E **38**
  HA8: Edg 6C **28**
  NW4 .6D **44**
  TW2: Whitt 1F **131**
Fairfield Cl. CR4: Mitc 7C **136**
  DA15: Sidc 6K **125**
  EN3: Pond E 4E **24**
  KT19: Ewe 5A **164**
  N12 .4F **31**
Fairfield Ct. HA4: Ruis 1F **57**
  HA6: Nwood 2J **39**
  NW10 . . . . .1C **80**
Fairfield Cres. HA8: Edg 6C **28**
Fairfield Dr. HA2: Harr 3G **41**
  SW18 . . . . .5K **117**
  UB6: G'frd 1C **78**
Fairfield E. KT1: King T 2E **150**
Fairfield Gdns. N8 . . . . .5J **47**
Fairfield Gro. SE7 . . . . .6B **106**
Fairfield Halls 3D **168**

Fairfield Nth. KT1: King T 2E **150**
Fairfield Path CR0: C'don 3D **168**
Fairfield Pl. KT1: King T 3E **150**
Fairfield Rd. BR1: Broml 7J **141**
  BR3: Beck 2C **158**
  BR5: Pet W 6H **161**
  CR0: C'don 3D **168**
  DA7: Bex 2F **127**
  E3 . . . . .2C **86**
  E17 . . . . .2A **50**
  IG1: Ilf 6F **71**
  IG8: Wfd G 6D **36**
  KT1: King T 2E **150**
  N8 . . . . .5J **47**
  N18 .4B **34**
  UB1: S'hall 6D **76**
  UB7: Yiew 7A **74**
  UB8: Uxb 6A **56**
Fairfields Cl. NW9 . . . . .5J **43**
Fairfields Cres. NW9 . . . . .4J **43**
Fairfield Sth. KT1: King T 2E **150**
Fairfields Rd. TW3: Houn 3G **113**
Fairfield St. SW18 . . . . .5K **117**
Fairfield Trade Pk. KT1: King T . .3F **151**
Fairfield Way EN5: Barn 5D **20**
  KT19: Ewe 5A **164**
Fairfield W. KT1: King T 2E **150**
Fairfoot Rd. E3 . . . . .4C **86**
Fairford SE6 . . . . .1C **140**
Fairford Av. CR0: C'don 5K **157**
  DA7: Bex 1K **127**
Fairford Cl. CR0: C'don 5A **158**
Fairford Ct. SM2: Sutt 7K **165**
Fairford Gdns. KT4: Wor Pk 2B **164**
Fairford Ho.
  SE11 . . . . .4K **19** (4A **102**)
Fairgreen EN4: Cockf 3J **21**
Fairgreen Ct. EN4: Cockf 3J **21**
Fairgreen E. EN4: Cockf 3J **21**
Fairgreen Rd. CR7: Thor H 5B **156**
Fairhall Ct. KT5: Surb 7F **151**
Fairhaven Av. CR0: C'don 6K **157**
Fairhaven Ct. CR2: S Croy 5C **168**
        (off Warham Rd.)
Fairhazel Gdns. NW6 . . . . .6K **63**
Fairhazel Mans. NW6 . . . . .7A **64**
        (off Fairhazel Gdns.)
Fairholme TW14: Bedf 7F **111**
Fairholme Cl. N3 . . . . .4G **45**
Fairholme Cres. UB4: Hayes 4H **75**
Fairholme Gdns. N3 . . . . .3G **45**
Fairholme Rd. CR0: C'don 7A **156**
  HA1: Harr 5K **41**
  IG1: Ilf 7D **52**
  SM1: Sutt 6H **165**
  TW15: Ashf 5A **128**
  W14 .5G **99**
Fairholt Cl. N16 . . . . .1E **66**
Fairholt Rd. N16 . . . . .1D **66**
Fairholt St. SW7 . . . . . .1D **16** (3C **100**)
Fairland Ho. BR2: Broml 4K **159**
Fairland Rd. E15 . . . . .6H **69**
Fairlands Av. CR7: Thor H 4K **155**
  IG9: Buck H 2D **36**
  SM1: Sutt 2J **165**
Fairlands Ct. SE9 . . . . .6E **124**
Fairlawn KT2: King T 6J **133**
  SE7 .7A **106**
Fairlawn Av. DA7: Bex 2D **126**
  N2 . . . . .4C **46**
  W4 . . . . .4J **97**
Fairlawn Cl. KT2: King T 6J **133**
  KT10: Clay 6A **162**
  N14 .6B **22**
  TW13: Hanw 4D **130**
Fairlawn Ct. SE7 . . . . .7A **106**
        (not continuous)
  W4 . . . . .4J **97**
Fairlawn Dr. IG8: Wfd G 7D **36**
Fairlawnes SM6: W'gton 5F **167**
Fairlawn Gro. W4 . . . . .4J **97**
Fairlawn Mans. SE14 . . . . .1K **121**

Fairlawn Pk. SE26 . . . . .5A **140**
Fairlawn Rd. SW19 . . . . .7H **135**
Fairlawns HA5: Pinn 2B **40**
  TW1: Twick 6C **114**
  TW16: Sun 3J **147**
Fairlead Ho. E14 . . . . .3C **104**
        (off Alpha Gro.)
Fairleads Ho. E17 . . . . .4K **49**
        (off Wickford Way)
Fairlea Pl. W5 . . . . .4C **78**
Fairlie Ct. E3 . . . . .3D **86**
       (off Stroudley Wlk.)
Fairlie Gdns. SE23 . . . . .7J **121**
Fairlight TW12: Hamp H 5F **131**
Fairlight Av. E4 . . . . .2A **36**
  IG8: Wfd G 6D **36**
  NW10 . . . . .2A **80**
Fairlight Cl. E4 . . . . .2A **36**
  KT4: Wor Pk 4E **164**
Fairlight Ct. NW10 . . . . .2A **80**
  UB6: G'frd 2G **77**
Fairlight Rd. SW17 . . . . .4B **136**
Fairline Ct. BR3: Beck 2E **158**
FAIRLOP 1J **53**
Fairlop Cl. E11 . . . . .1F **69**
Fairlop Gdns. IG6: Ilf 1G **53**
Fairlop Outdoor Activity Cen. 1K **53**
Fairlop Rd. E11 . . . . .7F **51**
  IG6: Ilf 2G **53**
Fairlop Waters Country Pk. 2K **53**
Fairlop Waters Golf Course 1J **53**
Fairmark Dr. UB10: Hil 6C **56**
Fairmead BR1: Broml 4D **160**
  KT5: Surb 1H **163**
Fairmead Cl.
  BR1: Broml 4D **160**
  KT3: N Mald 3K **151**
  TW5: Hest 7B **94**
Fairmead Ct. TW9: Rich 2H **115**
Fairmead Cres. HA8: Edg 3D **28**
Fairmead Gdns. IG4: Ilf 5C **52**
Fairmead Ho. E9 . . . . .4A **68**
Fairmead Rd. CR0: C'don 7K **155**
  N19 .3H **65**
Fairmile Av. SW16 . . . . .5H **137**
Fairmile Ho. TW11: Tedd 4A **132**
Fairmont Av. E14 . . . . .1F **105**
Fairmont Cl. DA17: Belv 5F **109**
Fairmont Ho. E3 . . . . .4C **86**
       (off Wellington Way)
  SE16 . . . . .2K **103**
        (off Needleman St.)
Fairmont M. NW2 . . . . .2J **63**
Fairmount Rd. SW2 . . . . .6K **119**
Fairoak Cl. BR5: Pet W 7F **161**
Fairoak Dr. SE9 . . . . .5H **125**
Fairoak Gdns. RM1: Rom 2K **55**
Fair Oak Pl. IG6: Ilf 2G **53**
Fairseat Cl. WD23: B Hea 2D **26**
Fairstead Lodge IG8: Wfd G 6D **36**
       (off Snakes La. W.)
Fairstead Wlk. N1 . . . . .1C **84**
        (off Popham St.)
Fair St. SE1 . . . . .6H **15** (2E **102**)
  TW3: Houn 3G **113**
Fairthorne Vs. SE7 . . . . .5J **105**
        (off Felltram Way)
Fairthorn Rd. SE7 . . . . .5J **105**
Fairview HA4: Ruis 4A **58**
Fairview Av. HA0: Wemb 6D **60**
Fairview Cl. E17 . . . . .1A **50**
  SE26 . . . . .5A **140**
Fairview Ct. NW4 . . . . .2F **45**
  TW15: Ashf 5C **128**
Fairview Cres. HA2: Harr 1E **58**
Fairview Dr. BR6: Orp 4H **173**
  TW17: Shep 5B **146**
Fairview Est. NW10 . . . . .3J **79**
Fairview Gdns. IG8: Wfd G 1K **51**
Fairview Ho. SW2 . . . . .7K **119**
Fairview Ind. Pk.
  RM13: Rain 5K **91**
Fairview Pl. SW2 . . . . .7K **119**

Fairview Rd. EN2: Enf 1F **23**
  N15 .5F **49**
  SM1: Sutt 5B **166**
  SW16 . . . . .1K **155**
Fairview Vs. E4 . . . . .7H **35**
Fairview Way HA8: Edg 4B **28**
Fairwall Ho. SE5 . . . . .1E **120**
Fairwater Av. DA16: Well 4A **126**
Fairwater Dr. TW17: Shep 5E **146**
Fairweather Ho. E16 . . . . .2K **105**
        (off Bonnet St.)
  TW11: Tedd 4A **132**
Fairway BR5: Pet W 5H **161**
  DA6: Bex 5E **126**
  IG8: Wfd G 5F **37**
  SW20 . . . . .3E **152**
The Fairway BR1: Broml 5D **160**
  EN5: New Bar 6E **20**
  HA0: Wemb 3B **60**
  HA4: Ruis 4A **58**
  KT3: N Mald 1K **151**
  KT8: W Mole 3F **149**
  N13 .3H **33**
  N14 .6A **22**
  NW7 .3E **28**
  UB5: N'olt 6G **59**
  UB10: Hil 3B **74**
  W3 . . . . .6A **80**
Fairway Av. NW9 . . . . .3H **43**
Fairway Cl. CR0: C'don 5A **158**
  KT10: Surb 3B **162**
  KT19: Ewe 4J **163**
  NW11 . . . . .7A **46**
  TW4: Houn 5A **112**
       (Amberley Way)
  TW4: Houn 5B **112**
        (Islay Gdns.)
Fairway Ct. E3 . . . . .3E **86**
        (off Culvert Dr.)
  EN5: New Bar 6E **20**
  NW7 .3E **28**
  SE16 . . . . .2K **103**
        (off Christopher Cl.)
Fairway Dr. SE28 . . . . .6D **90**
  UB6: G'frd 7F **59**
Fairway Gdns. BR3: Beck 6F **159**
  IG1: Ilf 5G **71**
Fairways E17 . . . . .4E **50**
  HA7: Stan 2E **42**
  TW7: Isle 1H **113**
  TW11: Tedd 7D **132**
  TW15: Ashf 6D **128**
Fairways Bus. Pk. E10 . . . . .2A **68**
Fairway Trad. Est. TW4: Houn . . .5A **112**
Fairweather Cl. DA16: Well 5A **126**
  N15 .4E **48**
Fairweather Ct. N13 . . . . .3E **32**
Fairweather Ho. N7 . . . . .4J **65**
Fairweather Rd. N16 . . . . .6G **49**
Fairwyn Rd. SE26 . . . . .4A **140**
Faith Ct. E3 . . . . .2C **86**
        (off Lefevre Wlk.)
  SE1 .5F **103**
        (off Cooper's Rd.)
Faith M. E12 . . . . .4B **70**
Fakenham Cl. NW7 . . . . .7H **29**
  UB5: N'olt 6D **58**
Fakruddin St. E1 . . . . .4G **85**
Falcon WC1 . . . . .5F **7**
       (off Old Gloucester St.)
Falcon Av. BR1: Broml 4C **160**
Falconberg M. W1 . . . . . . .7D **6** (6H **83**)
Falcon Cl. HA6: Nwood 1G **39**
  W4 . . . . .6J **97**
Falcon Ct. E18 . . . . .3K **51**
        (off Albert Rd.)
  EC4 . . . . .1K **13** (6A **84**)
  EN5: New Bar 4F **21**
  HA4: Ruis 2G **57**
  N1 . . . . .1E **8**
       (off City Gdn. Row)
Falcon Cres. EN3: Pond E 5E **24**
Falcondal Ct. NW10 . . . . .3G **79**

Falcon Dr.—Farrow Pl.

Falcon Dr. TW19: Stanw 6A 110
Falconer Ct. *N17* *7H 33*
(off Compton Cres.)
Falconer Wlk. N7 . . . . 2K 65
Falconet Ct. *E1* *1H 103*
(off Wapping High St.)
Falcon Gro. SW11 . . . . 3C 118
Falcon Highwalk EC2 . . . . 6C 8
Falcon Ho. BR1: Broml 1H 159
E14 . . . . *5D 104*
(off St Davids Sq.)
NW6 . . . . *1K 81*
(off Springfield Wlk.)
SW5 . . . . *5K 99*
(off Old Brompton Rd.)
Falcon La. SW11 . . . . 3C 118
Falcon Lodge *W9* *5J 81*
(off Admiral Wlk.)
Falcon Park Community Sports Centre
. . . . 2D 118
Falcon Pk. Ind. Est. NW10 . . . . 4A 62
Falcon Point SE1 . . . . 3B 14 (7B 84)
Falcon Rd. EN3: Pond E 5E 24
SW11 . . . . 2C 118
TW12: Hamp 7D 130
Falconry Ct. *KT1: King T* *3E 150*
(off Fairfield Sth.)
Falcon St. E13 . . . . 4J 87
Falcon Ter. SW11 . . . . 3C 118
Falcon Way E11 . . . . 4J 51
E14 . . . . 4D 104
HA3: Kenton 5E 42
NW9 . . . . 2A 44
TW14: Felt 5K 111
TW16: Sun 2G 147
Falcon Wharf SW11 . . . . 2B 118
FALCONWOOD 4K 125
FALCONWOOD 4H 125
Falconwood Av. DA16: Well 2H 125
Falconwood Ct. *SE3* *2H 123*
(off Montpelier Row)
Falconwood Pde. DA16: Well 4J 125
Falconwood Rd. CR0: Sels 7B 170
Falcourt Cl. SM1: Sutt 5K 165
Falkirk Ct. *SE16* *1K 103*
(off Rotherhithe St.)
Falkirk Ho. *W9* *2K 81*
(off Maida Vale)
Falkirk St. N1 . . . . 1H 9 (2E 84)
Falkland Av. N3 . . . . 7D 30
N11 . . . . 4A 32
Falkland Ho. SE6 . . . . 4E 140
W8 . . . . 3K 99
W14 . . . . *5H 99*
(off Edith Vs.)
Falkland Pk. Av. SE25 . . . . 3E 156
Falkland Pl. NW5 . . . . 5G 65
Falkland Rd. EN5: Barn 2B 20
N8 . . . . 4A 48
NW5 . . . . 5G 65
Fallaize Av. IG1: Ilf 4F 71
Falling La. UB7: Yiew 7A 74
Falloden Way NW11 . . . . 4J 45
Fallodon Ho. *W11* *5H 81*
(off Tavistock Cres.)
FALLOW CORNER 7F 31
Fallow Ct. *SE16* *5G 103*
(off Argyle Way)
Fallow Ct. Av. N12 . . . . 7F 31
Fallowfield HA7: Stan 4F 27
Fallowfield Ct. HA7: Stan 3F 27
Fallowfields Dr. N12 . . . . 6H 31
Fallowhurst Path N3 . . . . 7F 31
Fallow Pl. TW11: Tedd 5J 131
Fallows Cl. N2 . . . . 2B 46
Fallsbrook Rd. SW16 . . . . 6F 137
Falman Cl. N9 . . . . 1B 34
Falmer Rd. E17 . . . . 3D 50
EN1: Enf 4K 23
N15 . . . . 5C 48
Falmouth Av. E4 . . . . 5A 36
Falmouth Cl. N22 . . . . 7E 32
SE12 . . . . 5H 123
Falmouth Gdns. IG4: Ilf 4B 52
Falmouth Ho. HA5: Hat E 1D 40
KT2: King T *1D 150*
(off Skerne Rd.)
SE11 . . . . *5K 19*
(off Seaton Cl.)
W2 . . . . *2C 10*
(off Clarendon Pl.)
Falmouth Rd. SE1 . . . . . . 7E 14 (3C 102)
Falmouth St. E15 . . . . 5F 69
Falmouth Wlk. SW15 . . . . 6C 116
Falmouth Way E17 . . . . 5B 50
Falstaff Bldg. *E1* *7H 85*
(off Cannon St. Rd.)
Falstaff Cl. DA1: Cray 7K 127
Falstaff Ct. *SE11* *4B 102*
(off Opal St.)
Falstaff Ho. *N1* *1G 9*
(off Regan Way)
Falstaff M. *TW12: Hamp H* *5H 131*
(off High St.)
Fambridge Cl. SE26 . . . . 4B 140
Fambridge Ct. *RM7: Rom* *5K 55*
(off Marks Rd.)
Fambridge Rd. RM8: Dag 1G 73
Family Court
East London 1C 104
West London 6J 111
Fancourt M. BR1: Broml 3E 160
Fane St. W14 . . . . 6H 99
The Fan Mus. 7E 104
Fann St. EC1 . . . . 4C 8 (4C 84)
EC2 . . . . 4C 8 (4C 84)
(not continuous)
Fanshawe Av. IG11: Bark 6G 71
Fanshawe Cres. RM9: Dag 5E 72
Fanshawe Rd. TW10: Ham 4C 132
Fanshaw St. N1 . . . . 1G 9 (3E 84)
THE FANTAIL 3D 172
Fantail Cl. SE28 . . . . 6C 90
Fanthorpe St. SW15 . . . . 3E 116
Faraday Av. DA14: Sidc 2A 144
Faraday Cl. N7 . . . . 6K 65
Faraday Ho. *E14* *7B 86*
(off Brightlingsea Pl.)
HA9: Wemb 3J 61
SE1 . . . . *7E 14*
(off Cole St.)
SW11 . . . . 7K 17 (6F 101)
Faraday Lodge SE10 . . . . 3H 105
Faraday Mans. *W14* *6G 99*
(off Queen's Club Gdns.)
The Faraday Mus. 3A 12 (7G 83)
Faraday Pl. KT8: W Mole 4E 148
Faraday Rd. DA16: Well 3A 126
E15 . . . . 6H 69
KT8: W Mole 4E 148
SW19 . . . . 6J 135
UB1: S'hall 7F 77
W3 . . . . 7J 79
W10 . . . . 5G 81
Faraday Way CR0: Wadd 1K 167
SE18 . . . . 3B 106
Fareham Rd. TW14: Felt 7A 112
Farewell Pl. CR4: Mitc 1C 154
Fari Ct. *E17* *4C 50*
(off Tower M.)
Faringdon Av. BR2: Broml 7E 160
Faringford Rd. E15 . . . . 7G 69
Farjeon Ho. *NW6* *7B 64*
(off Hilgrove Rd.)
Farjeon Rd. SE3 . . . . 1B 124
Farleigh Av. BR2: Hayes 7H 159
Farleigh Ct. CR2: S Croy 5C 168
Farleigh Ho. *N1* *7B 66*
(off Halton Rd.)
Farleigh Pl. N16 . . . . 4F 67
Farleigh Rd. N16 . . . . 4F 67
Farley Ct. *NW1* *4G 5*
(off Allsop Pl.)
W14 . . . . 3H 99
Farley Dr. IG3: Ilf 1J 71
Farley Ho. SE26 . . . . 3H 139
Farley M. SE6 . . . . 7E 122
Farley Pl. SE25 . . . . 4G 157
Farley Rd. CR2: Sels 7H 169
SE6 . . . . 7D 122
Farlington Pl. SW15 . . . . 7D 116
Farlow Rd. SW15 . . . . 3F 117
Farlton Rd. SW18 . . . . 1K 135
Farman Gro. UB5: N'olt 3B 76
Farman Ter. HA3: Kenton 4D 42
Farm Av. HA0: Wemb 6C 60
HA2: Harr 7D 40
NW2 . . . . 3G 63
SW16 . . . . 4J 137
Farmborough Cl. HA1: Harr 7H 41
Farm Cl. BR4: W W'ck 3H 171
IG9: Buck H 3F 37
RM10: Dag 7J 73
SM2: Sutt 7B 166
SW6 . . . . 7J 99
TW17: Shep 7C 146
UB1: S'hall 7F 77
UB10: Ick 2D 56
Farmcote Rd. SE12 . . . . 1J 141
Farm Ct. NW4 . . . . 3C 44
Farmdale Rd. SE10 . . . . 5J 105
SM5: Cars 7C 166
Farm Dr. CR0: C'don 2B 170
Farm End HA6: Nwood 1D 38
Farmer Rd. E10 . . . . 1D 68
Farmer's Rd. SE5 . . . . 7B 102
Farmer St. W8 . . . . 1J 99
Farmfield Rd. BR1: Broml 5G 141
Farm Ho. Ct. NW7 . . . . 7H 29
Farmhouse Rd. SW16 . . . . 7G 137
Farmilo Rd. E17 . . . . 7B 50
Farmington Av. SM1: Sutt 3B 166
Farmlands EN2: Enf 1F 23
HA5: Eastc 4J 39
The Farmlands UB5: N'olt 6D 58
Farmland Wlk. BR7: Chst 5F 143
Farm La. CR0: C'don 2B 170
N14 . . . . 7A 22
SW6 . . . . 6J 99
Farmleigh N14 . . . . 7B 22
Farmleigh Ho. SW9 . . . . 5B 120
Farm M. CR4: Mitc 2F 155
Farm Pl. W8 . . . . 1J 99
Farm Rd. HA8: Edg 6C 28
N21 . . . . 1H 33
NW10 . . . . 1K 79
SM2: Sutt 7B 166
SM4: Mord 5K 153
TW4: Houn 1C 130
Farmstead Ct. *SM6: W'gton* *5F 167*
(off Melbourne Rd.)
Farmstead Rd. HA3: Hrw W 1H 41
SE6 . . . . 4D 140
Farm St. W1 . . . . 3J 11 (7F 83)
Farm Va. DA5: Bexl 6H 127
Farm Wlk. NW11 . . . . 5H 45
Farm Way IG9: Buck H 4F 37
KT4: Wor Pk 3E 164
Farmway RM8: Dag 3C 72
Farnaby Ho. *W10* *3H 81*
(off Bruckner St.)
Farnaby Rd. BR1: Broml 7F 141
BR2: Broml 7F 141
SE9 . . . . 4A 124
Farnan Av. E17 . . . . 2C 50
Farnan Lodge SW16 . . . . 5J 137
Farnan Rd. SW16 . . . . 5J 137
FARNBOROUGH 5G 173
Farnborough Av. CR2: Sels 7K 169
E17 . . . . 3A 50
Farnborough Cl. HA9: Wemb 2H 61
Farnborough Comn. BR6: Farnb . . . 3D 172
Farnborough Cres. BR2: Hayes 1H 171
CR2: Sels 7A 170
Farnborough Hill
BR6: Chels, Farnb 5H 173
Farnborough Ho. SW15 . . . . 1C 134
Farnborough Way
BR6: Chels, Farnb 5G 173
Farncombe St. SE16 . . . . 2G 103
Farndale Av. N13 . . . . 2G 33
Farndale Ct. SE18 . . . . 7C 106
Farndale Cres. UB6: G'frd 3G 77
Farndale Ho. *NW6* *1K 81*
(off Kilburn Vale)
Farnell M. SW5 . . . . 5K 99
Farnell Pl. W3 . . . . 7H 79
Farnell Rd. TW7: Isle 3H 113
Farnfield Ct. CR2: S Croy 5B 168
Farnham Cl. N20 . . . . 7F 21
Farnham Ct. SM3: Cheam 6G 165
UB1: S'hall *7G 77*
(off Redcroft Rd.)
Farnham Gdns. SW20 . . . . 2D 152
Farnham Ho. NW1 . . . . 4D 4
SE1 . . . . *5C 14*
(off Union St.)
Farnham Pl. SE1 . . . . 5B 14 (1B 102)
Farnham Rd. DA16: Well 2C 126
IG3: Ilf 7K 53
Farnham Royal SE11 . . . . 6H 19 (5K 101)
Farningham Ct. SW16 . . . . 7H 137
Farningham Ho. N4 . . . . 7D 48
Farningham Rd. N17 . . . . 7B 34
Farnley Ho. SW8 . . . . 2H 119
Farnley Rd. E4 . . . . 1B 36
SE25 . . . . 4D 156
Farnsworth Ct. *SE10* *3H 105*
(off West Parkside)
Farnsworth Dr. HA8: Edg 4K 27
Farnworth Ho. *E14* *4F 105*
(off Manchester Rd.)
Faro Cl. BR1: Broml 2E 160
Faroe Rd. W14 . . . . 3F 99
Farorna Wlk. EN2: Enf 1F 23
Farquhar Rd. SE19 . . . . 5F 139
SW19 . . . . 3J 135
Farquharson Rd. CR0: C'don 1C 168
Farrance Rd. RM6: Chad H 7E 54
Farrance St. E14 . . . . 6C 86
Farrans Ct. HA3: Kenton 7B 42
Farrant Av. N22 . . . . 2A 48
Farrant Cl. BR6: Chels 7K 173
Farr Av. IG11: Bark 2A 90
Farrell Ho. *E1* *6J 85*
(off Ronald St.)
Farren Rd. SE23 . . . . 2A 140
Farrer Ct. TW1: Twick 7D 114
Farrer Ho. SE8 . . . . 7C 104
Farrer M. N8 . . . . 4G 47
Farrer Rd. HA3: Kenton 5E 42
N8 . . . . 4G 47
Farrer's Pl. CR0: C'don 4K 169
Farrier Cl. BR1: Broml 3B 160
TW16: Sun 4J 147
UB8: Hil 6C 74
Farrier Ct. *E1* *5K 85*
(off White Horse La.)
RM13: Rain *2K 91*
(off Lowen Rd.)
Farrier Pl. SM1: Sutt 3K 165
Farrier Rd. UB5: N'olt 2E 76
Farriers Ho. *EC1* *4D 8*
(off Errol St.)
Farriers M. SE15 . . . . 3J 121
SW9 . . . . 4A 120
Farrier St. NW1 . . . . 7F 65
Farriers Yd. *W6* *5F 99*
(off Smiths Sq.)
Farrier Wlk. SW10 . . . . 6A 100
Farringdon Ho. TW9: Kew 7H 97
UB7: W Dray 2B 92
Farringdon La. EC1 . . . . 4K 7 (4A 84)
Farringdon Rd. EC1 . . . . 3J 7 (4A 84)
Farringdon St. EC4 . . . . 6A 8 (5B 84)
Farrington Ct. *BR1: Broml* *2K 159*
(off Widmore Rd.)
Farrington Pl. BR7: Chst 7H 143
Farrins Rents SE16 . . . . 1A 104
Farrow Ho. NW9 . . . . 3C 44
Farrow La. SE14 . . . . 7J 103
Farrow Pl. SE16 . . . . 3A 104

266 A-Z London

Farr Rd. EN2: Enf 1J **23**
Farsby Ho. Apts. IG11: Bark 4A **90**
    (off Manwell La.)
Farthingale Wlk. E15 . . . . .7F **69**
Farthing All. SE1 . . . . . .7K **15** (2G **103**)
Farthing Barn La. BR6: Downe . . .7E **172**
Farthing Flds. E1 . . . . .1H **103**
The Farthings KT2: King T 1G **151**
Farthings Cl. E4 . . . . .3B **36**
    HA5: Eastc 6K **39**
FARTHING STREET 7D **172**
Farthing St. BR6: Downe 7D **172**
Farwell Rd. DA14: Sidc 4B **144**
Farwig La. BR1: Broml 1H **159**
Fashion & Textile Mus. . . .6H **15** (2E **102**)
Fashion St. E1 . . . . .6K **9** (5F **85**)
Fashoda Rd. BR2: Broml 4B **160**
Fassett Rd. E8 . . . . .6G **67**
    KT1: King T 4E **150**
Fassett Sq. E8 . . . . .6G **67**
Fathom Cl. E16 . . . . .7F **89**
    (off Basin App.)
Fauconberg Ct. W4 . . . . .6J **97**
    (off Fauconberg Rd.)
Fauconberg Rd. W4 . . . . .6J **97**
Faulkner Cl. RM8: Dag 7D **54**
Faulkner Ho. BR7: Chst 7H **143**
    W6 . . . . .6E **98**
Faulkner M. E17 . . . . .1A **50**
Faulkners All. EC1 . . . . . .5A **8** (5B **84**)
Faulkner St. SE14 . . . . .1J **121**
Fauna Cl. HA7: Stan 4J **27**
    RM6: Chad H 6C **54**
Faunce Ho. SE17 . . . . .6B **102**
    (off Doddington Gro.)
Faunce St. SE17 . . . . .5B **102**
Favart Rd. SW6 . . . . .1J **117**
Faversham Av. E4 . . . . .1B **36**
    EN1: Enf 6J **23**
Faversham Ho. NW1 . . . . .1G **83**
    (off Bayham Pl.)
    SE17 .5E **102**
    (off Kinglake St.)
Faversham Rd. BR3: Beck 2B **158**
    SE6 . . . . .7B **122**
    SM4: Mord 6K **153**
Fawcett Cl. SW11 . . . . .2B **118**
    SW16 . . . . .5A **138**
Fawcett Cl. SW10 . . . . .6A **100**
    (off Fawcett St.)
Fawcett Est. E5 . . . . .1G **67**
Fawcett Rd. CRO: C'don 3C **168**
    NW10 . . . . .7B **62**
Fawcett St. SW10 . . . . .6A **100**
Fawe Pk. M. SW15 . . . . .4H **117**
Fawe Pk. Rd. SW15 . . . . .4H **117**
Fawe St. E14 . . . . .5D **86**
Fawkham Ho. SE1 . . . . .4F **103**
    (off Longfield Est.)
Fawley Lodge E14 . . . . .4F **105**
    (off Millennium Dr.)
Fawley Rd. NW6 . . . . .5K **63**
Fawnbrake Av. SE24 . . . . .5B **120**
Fawn Hgts. IG9: Buck H 2E **36**
    (off Stag La.)
Fawn Rd. E13 . . . . .2A **88**
Fawns Mnr. Cl. TW14: Bedf 1E **128**
Fawns Mnr. Rd. TW14: Bedf 1F **129**
Fawood Av. NW10 . . . . .7J **61**
Faygate Cres. DA6: Bex 5G **127**
Faygate Rd. SW2 . . . . .2K **137**
Fayland Av. SW16 . . . . .5G **137**
Fazeley Ct. W9 . . . . .5J **81**
    (off Elmfield Way)
Fazeley Ho. UB5: N'olt 3D **76**
    (off Taywood Rd.)
Fearnley Cres. TW12: Hamp 5C **130**
Fearnley Ho. SE5 . . . . .2E **120**
Fearns Ho. W13 . . . . .1A **96**
Fearon St. SE10 . . . . .5J **105**
Featherbed La. CRO: Sels 7B **170**
Feather M. E1 . . . . .5G **85**

Feathers Pl. SE10 . . . . .6F **105**
Featherstone Av. SE23 . . . . .2H **139**
Featherstone Ct. UB2: S'hall 3B **94**
Featherstone Ho. UB4: Yead 5A **76**
Featherstone Ind. Est. UB2: S'hall . .3C **94**
    (off Feather Rd.)
Featherstone Rd. NW7 . . . . .6J **29**
    UB2: S'hall 3C **94**
Featherstone Sports Cen. 4B **94**
Featherstone St. EC1 . . . .3E **8** (4D **84**)
Featherstone Ter. UB2: S'hall 3C **94**
Featley Rd. SW9 . . . . .3B **120**
Federal Rd. UB6: G'frd 1C **78**
Federation Rd. SE2 . . . . .4B **108**
Fee Farm Rd. KT10: Clay 7A **162**
Feeny Cl. NW10 . . . . .4B **62**
Felbridge Av. HA7: Stan 1A **42**
Felbridge Cl. SM2: Sutt 7K **165**
    SW16 . . . . .4A **138**
Felbridge Ct. TW13: Felt 1K **129**
    (off High St.)
    UB3: Harl 6F **93**
Felbridge Ho. SE22 . . . . .3E **120**
Felbrigge Rd. IG3: Ilf 2K **71**
Felday Rd. SE13 . . . . .6D **122**
Felden Cl. HA5: Hat E 1C **40**
Felden St. SW6 . . . . .1H **117**
Feldman Cl. N16 . . . . .1G **67**
Feldspar Ct. EN3: Enf H 3F **25**
    (off Enstone Rd.)
Feldspar M. N13 . . . . .5G **33**
Felgate M. W6 . . . . .4D **98**
Felhampton Rd. SE9 . . . . .2F **143**
Felhurst Cres. RM10: Dag 4H **73**
Feline Ct. EN4: E Barn 6H **21**
Felix Av. N8 . . . . .6J **47**
Felix Cl. E17 . . . . .5D **50**
    NW9 . . . . .2A **44**
Felix Ho. E16 . . . . .7E **88**
    (off University Way)
Felix La. TW17: Shep 6G **147**
Felix Mnr. BR7: Chst 6J **143**
Felix Neubergh Ho. EN1: Enf 4K **23**
Felix Pl. SW2 . . . . .5A **120**
    (off Talma Rd.)
Felix Point E14 . . . . .6C **86**
    (off Upper Nth. St.)
Felix Rd. KT12: Walt T 6J **147**
    W13 . . . . .7A **78**
Felixstowe Ct. E16 . . . . .1F **107**
Felixstowe Rd. N9 . . . . .3B **34**
    N17 . . . . .3F **49**
    NW10 . . . . .3D **80**
    SE2 . . . . .3B **108**
Felix St. E2 . . . . .2H **85**
Fellbrigg Rd. SE22 . . . . .5F **121**
Fellbrigg St. E1 . . . . .4H **85**
Fellbrook TW10: Ham 3B **132**
Fellmongers Path SE1 . . . . .7J **15**
Fellmongers Yd. CRO: C'don 3C **168**
Fellowes Cl. UB4: Yead 4B **76**
Fellowes Rd. SM5: Cars 3C **166**
Fellows Ct. E2 . . . . .1J **9** (2F **85**)
    (not continuous)
Fellowship Cl. RM8: Dag 4A **72**
Fellowship Ho. E6 . . . . .2C **88**
    (off St Bartholomew's Rd.)
Fellows Rd. NW3 . . . . .7B **64**
Fell Rd. CRO: C'don 3C **168**
Feltram M. SE7 . . . . .5J **105**
Feltram Way SE7 . . . . .5J **105**
Fell Wlk. HA8: Edg 1J **43**
Felmersham Cl. SW4 . . . . .4J **119**
Felmingham Rd. SE20 . . . . .2J **157**
Felnex Av. SM6: W'gton 2E **166**
Felnex Trad. Est. NW10 . . . . .2K **79**
    SM6: W'gton 2E **166**
Felsberg Rd. SW2 . . . . .6J **119**
Fels Cl. RM10: Dag 3H **73**
Fels Farm Av. RM10: Dag 3J **73**
Felsham Rd. SW15 . . . . .3E **116**
Felspar Cl. SE18 . . . . .5K **107**
Felstead Av. IG5: Ilf 1E **52**

Felstead Cl. N13 . . . . .5F **33**
Felstead Gdns. E14 . . . . .5E **104**
Felstead Rd. E9 . . . . .6B **68**
    E11 . . . . .7J **51**
Felstead St. E9 . . . . .6B **68**
Felstead Wharf E14 . . . . .5E **104**
Felsted Rd. E16 . . . . .6B **88**
FELTHAM 1K **129**
Feltham Av. KT8: E Mos 4J **149**
Felthambrook Ind. Est.
    TW13: Felt 3K **129**
Felthambrook Way TW13: Felt . . .3K **129**
Feltham Bus. Complex
    TW13: Felt 2K **129**
Feltham Corporate Cen.
    TW13: Felt 3K **129**
FELTHAMHILL 5H **129**
Feltham Hill Rd. TW15: Ashf 5C **128**
    TW13: Felt, CR4: Mitc 2D **154**
    TW15: Ashf 4C **128**
Felton Cl. BR5: Pet W 6F **161**
Felton Hall Ho. SE16 . . . . .7K **15**
Felton Ho. N1 . . . . .1D **84**
    (off Colville Est.)
Felton Lea DA14: Sidc 5K **143**
Felton Rd. IG11: Bark 2J **89**
    W13 . . . . .2C **96**
Felton St. N1 . . . . .1D **84**
Fencepiece Rd. IG6: Chig, Ilf 1G **53**
Fenchurch Av. EC3 . . . . . .1G **15** (6E **84**)
Fenchurch Bldgs. EC3 . . .1H **15** (6E **84**)
Fenchurch Ho. EC3 . . . . .2J **15**
    (off Minories)
Fenchurch M. E3 . . . . .5B **86**
    (off St Paul's Way)
Fenchurch Pl. EC3 . . . . . .2H **15** (6E **84**)
Fenchurch St. EC3 . . . . . .2G **15** (7E **84**)
Fen Ct. EC3 . . . . .2G **15** (6E **84**)
Fendall Rd. KT19: Ewe 5J **163**
Fendall St. SE1 . . . . .3E **102**
    (not continuous)
Fendt Cl. E16 . . . . .6H **87**
Fendyke Rd. DA17: Belv 4D **108**
Fenelon Pl. W14 . . . . .4H **99**
Fengate Cl. KT9: Chess 6D **162**
Fen Gro. DA15: Sidc 5K **125**
Fenham Rd. SE15 . . . . .7G **103**
Fenland Ho. E5 . . . . .2J **67**
Fen La. SW13 . . . . .1D **116**
Fenman Ct. N17 . . . . .1H **49**
Fenman Gdns. IG3: Ilf 1B **72**
Fenn Cl. BR1: Broml 6J **141**
Fennel Apts. SE1 . . . . .5J **15**
    (off Cayenne Ct.)
Fennel Cl. CRO: C'don 1K **169**
    E16 . . . . .4G **87**
Fennells Mead KT17: Ewe 7B **164**
Fennell St. SE18 . . . . .6E **106**
Fenner Cl. SE16 . . . . .4H **103**
Fenner Ho. E1 . . . . .1H **103**
    (off Watts St.)
Fenner Sq. SW11 . . . . .3B **118**
Fenn Ho. TW7: Isle 1B **114**
Fennings Rd. SW4 . . . . .6H **119**
Fenning St. SE1 . . . . . . .6G **15** (2E **102**)
Fenn St. E9 . . . . .5K **67**
Fenstanton N4 . . . . .1K **65**
    (off Marquis Rd.)
Fenstanton Av. N12 . . . . .6G **31**
Fen St. E16 . . . . .7H **87**
Fenswood Cl. DA5: Bexl 6G **127**
Fentiman Rd. SW8 . . . . . .7F **19** (6J **101**)
Fentiman Way HA2: Harr 2F **59**
Fenton Cl. BR7: Chst 5D **142**
    E8 . . . . .6F **67**
    SW9 . . . . .2K **119**
Fenton House 4B **64**
    (off Hampstead Gro.)
Fenton Ho. SE14 . . . . .7A **104**
    TW5: Hest 6E **94**
Fenton Pde. SE10 . . . . .5H **105**
    (off Woolwich Rd.)

Fenton Rd. HA2: Harr 3G **41**
    N17 . . . . .7H **33**
Fentons Av. E13 . . . . .3K **87**
Fenton St. E1 . . . . .6H **85**
Fenwick Cl. SE18 . . . . .6E **106**
Fenwick Gro. SE15 . . . . .3G **121**
Fenwick Ho. EC1 . . . . .5B **84**
    (off Little Britain)
Fenwick Pl. CR2: S Croy 7B **168**
    SW9 . . . . .3J **119**
Fenwick Rd. SE15 . . . . .3G **121**
Ferby Ct. DA14: Sidc 4K **143**
    (off Main Rd.)
Ferdinand Ct. SE6 . . . . .7C **122**
    (off Adenmore Rd.)
Ferdinand Dr. SE15 . . . . .7E **102**
Ferdinand Ho. NW1 . . . . .7E **64**
    (off Ferdinand Pl.)
Ferdinand Magellan Court E16 . . .2K **105**
    (Ferdinand Magellan Court)
Ferdinand Pl. NW1 . . . . .7E **64**
Ferdinand St. NW1 . . . . .7E **64**
Ferguson Av. KT5: Surb 5F **151**
Ferguson Cl. BR2: Broml 3F **159**
    E14 . . . . .4C **104**
Ferguson Dr. W3 . . . . .6K **79**
Fergus Rd. N5 . . . . .5B **66**
Fergusson M. SW4 . . . . .2J **119**
Fergus St. SE10 . . . . .3J **105**
Ferial Ct. SE15 . . . . .7G **103**
    (off Fenham Rd.)
Fermain Ct. E. N1 . . . . .1E **84**
    (off Hertford Rd.)
Fermain Ct. Nth. N1 . . . . .1E **84**
    (off De Beauvoir Est.)
Fermain Ct. W. N1 . . . . .1E **84**
    (off De Beauvoir Est.)
Ferme Pk. Rd. N4 . . . . .5J **47**
    N8 . . . . .5J **47**
Fermor Rd. SE23 . . . . .1A **140**
Fermoy Ho. W9 . . . . .4H **81**
    (off Fermoy Rd.)
Fermoy Rd. UB6: G'frd 4F **77**
    W9 . . . . .4H **81**
    (not continuous)
Fern Av. CR4: Mitc 4H **155**
Fernbank IG9: Buck H 1E **36**
Fernbank Av. HA0: Wemb 4K **59**
    KT12: Walt T 7C **148**
Fernbank M. SW12 . . . . .6G **119**
Fernbrook Av. DA15: Sidc 5J **125**
Fernbrook Cres. SE13 . . . . .6G **123**
    (off Leaharst Rd.)
Fernbrook Dr. HA2: Harr 7F **41**
Fernbrook Rd. SE13 . . . . .5G **123**
Ferncliff Rd. E8 . . . . .5G **67**
Fern Cl. N1 . . . . .2E **84**
Fern Ct. DA7: Bex 4G **127**
    RM7: Rom 5K **55**
    SE14 .2K **121**
Ferncroft Av. HA4: Ruis 2A **58**
    N12 . . . . .6J **31**
    NW3 . . . . .3J **63**
Ferndale BR1: Broml 2A **160**
Ferndale Av. E17 . . . . .5F **51**
    TW4: Houn 3C **112**
Ferndale Cl. DA7: Bex 1E **126**
Ferndale Community Sports Cen.
    . . . . .3K **119**
Ferndale Cres. SM5: Cars 1D **166**
Ferndale Rd. E7 . . . . .7K **69**
    E11 . . . . .2G **69**
    N15 . . . . .6F **49**
    RM5: Col R 2J **55**
    SE25 . . . . .5H **157**
    SW4 . . . . .4J **119**
    SW9 . . . . .4J **119**
    TW15: Ashf 5A **128**
Ferndale St. E6 . . . . .7F **89**
Ferndale Ter. HA1: Harr 4K **41**
Ferndale Way BR6: Farnb 5H **173**
Ferndell Av. DA5: Bexl 3K **145**
Fern Dene W13 . . . . .5B **78**

Ferndene Rd. SE24 . . . . .4C 120
Ferndn Way RM7: Rom 6H 55
Ferndown HA6: Nwood 2J 39
NW1 . . . . .7H 65
(off Camley St.)
Ferndown Av. BR6: Orp 1H 173
Ferndown Cl. HA5: Pinn 1C 40
SM2: Sutt 6B 166
Ferndown Ct. UB1: S'hall 6G 77
(off Haldane Rd.)
Ferndown Lodge E14 . . . . .3E 104
(off Manchester Rd.)
Ferndown Rd. SE9 . . . . .7B 124
Ferney Meade Way TW7: Isle 2A 114
Ferney Rd. EN4: E Barn 7K 21
Fern Gro. TW14: Felt 7K 111
Fernhall Dr. IG4: Ilf 5B 52
Fernham Rd. CR7: Thor H 3C 156
Fernhead Rd. W9 . . . . .3H 81
Fernheath Way DA2: Wilm 5K 145
Fernhill Ct. E17 . . . . .2F 51
Fernhill Gdns. KT2: King T 5D 132
Fern Hill Pl. BR6: Farnb 5G 173
Fernhill St. E16 . . . . .1D 106
Fernholme Rd. SE15 . . . . .5K 121
Fernhurst Gdns. HA8: Edg 6B 28
Fernhurst Rd. CR0: C'don 7H 157
SW6 . . . . .1G 117
TW15: Ashf 4E 128
Fern La. TW5: Hest 5D 94
Fernlea Rd. CR4: Mitc 2E 154
SW12 .1F 137
Fernleigh Cl. CR0: Wadd 4A 168
W9 . . . . .3H 81
Fernleigh Cl. HA2: Harr 2F 41
HA9: Wemb 2E 60
RM7: Rom 5J 55
Fernleigh Rd. N21 . . . . .2F 33
Fernly Cl. HA5: Eastc 4A 40
Fernsbury St. WC1 . . . . . .2J 7 (3A 84)
Fernshaw Cl. SW10 . . . . .6A 100
Fernshaw Mans. SW10 . . . . .6A 100
(off Fernshaw Rd.)
Fernshaw Rd. SW10 . . . . .6A 100
Fernside IG9: Buck H 1E 36
KT7: T Ditt 1B 162
NW11 .2J 63
Fernside Av. NW7 . . . . .3E 28
TW13: Felt 4K 129
Fernside Cl. NW4 . . . . .2F 45
Fernside Rd. SW12 . . . . .1D 136
Ferns Rd. E15 . . . . .6H 69
Fern St. E3 . . . . .4C 86
Fernthorpe Rd. SW16 . . . . .6G 137
Ferntower Rd. N5 . . . . .5D 66
Fern Wlk. SE16 . . . . .5G 103
TW15: Ashf 5A 128
Fernways IG1: Ilf 4F 71
Fernwood SW19 . . . . .1H 135
Fernwood Av. HA0: Wemb 6C 60
SW16 .4H 137
Fernwood Cl. BR1: Broml 2A 160
Fernwood Cl. N14 . . . . .7B 22
Fernwood Cres. N20 . . . . .3J 31
Fernwood Pl. KT10: Hin W 2A 162
Ferny Hill EN4: Had W 1J 21
Ferranti Cl. SE18 . . . . .3B 106
Ferrard Cl. TW5: Hest 6E 94
Ferrers Av. SM6: Bedd 4H 167
UB7: W Dray 2A 92
Ferrers Rd. SW16 . . . . .5H 137
Ferrestone Rd. N8 . . . . .4K 47
Ferrey M. SW9 . . . . .2A 120
Ferriby Cl. N1 . . . . .7A 66
Ferrie Cl. NW9 . . . . .1B 44
Ferrier Ind. Est. SW18 . . . . .4K 117
(off Ferrier St.)
Ferrier Point E16 . . . . .5J 87
(off Forty Acre La.)
Ferrier St. SW18 . . . . .4K 117
Ferring Cl. HA2: Harr 1G 59
Ferrings SE21 . . . . .3E 138
Ferris Av. CR0: C'don 3B 170

Ferris Rd. SE22 . . . . .4G 121
Ferron Rd. E5 . . . . .3H 67
Ferrybridge Ho. SE11 . . . . .2H 19
Ferrydale Lodge NW4 . . . . .4E 44
(off Parson St.)
Ferry Ho. E5 . . . . .1H 67
(off Harrington Hill)
Ferry Island Retail Pk. 3G 49
Ferry La. N17 . . . . .4G 49
SW13 .6B 98
TW8: Bford 6E 96
TW9: Kew 6F 97
TW17: Shep 7C 146
Ferryman's Quay SW6 . . . . .2A 118
Ferrymead Av. UB6: G'frd 3E 76
Ferrymead Dr. UB6: G'frd 2E 76
Ferrymead Gdns. UB6: G'frd 2G 77
Ferrymoor TW10: Ham 3B 132
Ferry Pl. SE18 . . . . .3E 106
Ferry Quays TW8: Bford 6E 96
(Ferry La.)
TW8: Bford 7D 96
(off Point Wharf La.)
Ferry Rd. KT7: T Ditt 6B 150
KT8: W Mole 3E 148
SW13 .7C 98
TW1: Twick 1B 132
TW11: Tedd 5B 132
Ferry Sq. TW8: Bford 7E 96
Ferry St. E14 . . . . .5E 104
Ferry Wharf TW8: Bford 7E 96
Festing Rd. SW15 . . . . .3F 117
Festival Cl. DA5: Bexl 1D 144
UB10: Hil 1D 74
Festival Ct. E8 . . . . .7F 67
(off Holly St.)
SM1: Sutt 7K 153
Festival Wlk. SM5: Cars 4D 166
Festival Way E4 . . . . .6K 35
Festive Mans. E20 . . . . .5E 68
(off Napa Cl.)
Festive Wlk. SW15 . . . . .2F 117
Festoon Way E16 . . . . .7B 88
Festubert Pl. E3 . . . . .2B 86
Festuca Ho. E20 . . . . .5E 68
(off Mirabelle Gdns.)
Fetherstone Ct. RM6: Chad H 6F 55
(off High Rd.)
Fetherton Ct. IG11: Bark 2G 89
(off Spring Pl.)
Fetter La. EC4 . . . . . . .1K 13 (6A 84)
Fetter La. Apts. EC4 . . . . .1J 13
(off Fetter La.)
Fettes Ho. NW8 . . . . .2B 82
(off Wellington Rd.)
Fettle Ct. SE14 . . . . .6A 104
(off Moulding La.)
Fews Lodge RM6: Chad H 4D 54
Ffinch St. SE8 . . . . .7C 104
Fiador Apts. SE10 . . . . .4G 105
(off Telegraph Av.)
Fidelis Ho. E1 . . . . .6J 9
(off Gun St.)
Fidgeon Cl. BR1: Broml 3E 160
Field Cl. BR1: Broml 2A 160
E4 . . . . .6J 35
HA4: Ruis 1E 56
IG9: Buck H 3F 37
KT8: W Mole 5F 149
KT9: Chess 5C 162
NW2 .2C 62
TW4: Cran 1K 111
UB3: Harl 7F 92
UB10: Ick 2D 56
FIELDCOMMON 7D 148
Fieldcommon La. KT12: Walt T 7C 148
Field Ct. SW19 . . . . .3J 135
WC1 . . . . .6H 7 (5K 83)
Field End HA4: Ruis 6A 58
UB5: N'olt 6B 58
Fieldend TW1: Twick 4K 131
Fld. End Rd. HA4: Ruis 5K 39
HA5: Eastc 5K 39

Fieldend Rd. SW16 . . . . .1G 155
Fielder Apts. E3 . . . . .4B 86
(off Heath Pl.)
Fielders Cl. EN1: Enf 4K 23
HA2: Harr 1G 59
Fielders Cres. IG11: Bark 4C 90
Fieldfare Rd. SE28 . . . . .7C 90
Fieldgate La. CR4: Mitc 2C 154
Fieldgate Mans. E1 . . . . .5G 85
(off Fieldgate St.)
Fieldgate St. E1 . . . . .5G 85
Field Ho. NW6 . . . . .3F 81
(off Harvist Rd.)
SM4: Mord 5K 153
(off School Ga. Dr.)
Fieldhouse Cl. E18 . . . . .1J 51
Fieldhouse Rd. SW12 . . . . .1G 137
Fielding Av. TW2: Twick 3G 131
Fielding Ct. WC2 . . . . .1E 12
(off Earlham St.)
Fielding Ho. NW8 . . . . .1A 82
(off Ainsworth Way)
W4 . . . . .6A 98
(off Devonshire Rd.)
Fielding La. BR2: Broml 4A 160
Fielding M. SW13 . . . . .6D 98
Fielding Rd. W4 . . . . .3K 97
W14 . . . . .3F 99
The Fieldings SE23 . . . . .1J 139
Fielding St. SE17 . . . . .6C 102
Fielding Ter. W5 . . . . .7F 79
Fielding Wlk. W13 . . . . .3B 96
Field La. TW8: Bford 7C 96
TW11: Tedd 5A 132
Fld. Maple M. RM5: Col R 1G 55
Field Mead NW7 . . . . .7F 29
NW9 .7F 29
Fieldpark Gdns. CR0: C'don 1A 170
Field Pl. KT3: N Mald 6B 152
SW19 .1B 154
Field Point E7 . . . . .4J 69
Field Rd. E7 . . . . .4H 69
N17 . . . . .3D 48
TW14: Felt 6K 111
W6 . . . . .5G 99
Fields Est. E8 . . . . .7G 67
Fieldside Cl. BR6: Farnb 4G 173
Fieldside Rd. BR1: Broml 5F 141
Fields Pk. Cres. RM6: Chad H 5D 54
Field St. WC1 . . . . .1G 7 (3K 83)
Fields Wlk. SW11 . . . . .7F 101
Fieldsway Ho. N5 . . . . .5A 66
Field Vw. TW13: Felt 4F 129
Field Vw. Cl. RM7: Mawney 3G 55
Fieldview Cotts. N14 . . . . .2C 32
(off Balaams La.)
Field Way BR5: Pet W 6H 161
CR0: New Ad 7D 170
RM8: Dag 3C 72
Fieldway Cres. N5 . . . . .5A 66
Fiennes Cl. RM8: Dag 1C 72
Fiesta Dr. RM9: Dag 4J 91
Fifehead Cl. TW15: Ashf 6A 128
Fife Rd. E16 . . . . .5J 87
KT1: King T 2E 150
N22 . . . . .7G 33
SW14 .5J 115
Fife Ter. N1 . . . . .2K 83
Fifield Path SE23 . . . . .3K 139
Fifth Av. E12 . . . . .4D 70
UB3: Hayes 1H 93
W10 . . . . .3G 81
Fifth Cross Rd. TW2: Twick 2H 131
Fifth Way HA9: Wemb 4H 61
Figges Rd. CR4: Mitc 7E 136
Fight for Peace Academy 1E 106
Fig Tree Cl. NW10 . . . . .1A 80
Figure Ct. SW3 . . . . .6F 17

Filament Wlk. SW18 . . . . .5J 117
(off Spectrum Way)
Filanco Ct. W7 . . . . .1K 95
Filby Cl. DA8: Erith 7K 109
Filby Rd. KT9: Chess 6F 163
Filey Av. N16 . . . . .1G 67
Filey Cl. SM2: Sutt 7A 166
Filey Waye HA4: Ruis 2J 57
Filigree Ct. SE16 . . . . .1B 104
Fillebrook Av. EN1: Enf 2K 23
Fillebrook Rd. E11 . . . . .1F 69
Filmer Chambers SW6 . . . . .1G 117
(off Filmer Rd.)
Filmer Ho. SW6 . . . . .1H 117
(off Filmer Rd.)
Filmer M. SW6 . . . . .1H 117
Filston Rd. DA8: Erith 5J 109
Filton Cl. NW9 . . . . .1A 44
Filton Ct. SE14 . . . . .7J 103
(off Farrow La.)
Finborough Ho. SW10 . . . . .6A 100
(off Finborough Rd.)
Finborough Rd. SW10 . . . . .5K 99
SW17 .6D 136
The Finborough Theatre 6K 99
(off Finborough Rd.)
Finchale Rd. SE2 . . . . .3A 108
Fincham Cl. UB10: Ick 3E 56
Finch Av. SE27 . . . . .4D 138
Finch Cl. EN5: Barn 5D 20
NW10 .6K 61
Finch Ct. DA14: Sidc 3B 144
Finchdean Ho. SW15 . . . . .7B 116
Finch Dr. TW14: Felt 7B 112
Finch Gdns. E4 . . . . .5H 35
Finch Ho. E3 . . . . .1B 86
(off Jasmine Sq.)
SE8 . . . . .7C 104
(off Bronze St.)
Finchingfield Av. IG8: Wfd G 7F 37
Finch La. EC3 . . . . .1F 15 (6D 84)
FINCHLEY 1J 45
Finchley Cl. N3 . . . . .6E 30
Finchley Golf Course 6C 30
Finchley Ind. Est. N12 . . . . .4F 31
Finchley La. NW4 . . . . .4E 44
Finchley Lido Leisure Cen. 7G 31
Finchley Manor Club 1H 45
Finchley Pk. N12 . . . . .4F 31
Finchley Pl. NW8 . . . . .2B 82
Finchley Rd. NW2 . . . . .4H 45
NW3 .4H 45
NW8 . . . . .1B 82
NW11 .4H 45
Finchley Way N3 . . . . .7D 30
Finch Lodge W9 . . . . .5J 81
(off Admiral Wlk.)
Finch M. SE15 . . . . .1F 121
Finch's Ct. E14 . . . . .7D 86
Finch's Ct. M. E14 . . . . .7D 86
(off Finch's Ct.)
Finden Rd. E7 . . . . .5K 69
Findhorn Av. UB4: Yead 5K 75
Findhorn St. E14 . . . . .6E 86
Findlay Ho. E3 . . . . .3C 86
(off Trevithick Way)
Findon Cl. HA2: Harr 3F 59
SW18 .6J 117
Findon Rd. N9 . . . . .1C 34
W12 . . . . .2C 98
Fine Bush La. UB9: Hare 6D 38
Fingal St. SE10 . . . . .5H 105
Fingest Ho. NW8 . . . . .3C 4
(off Lilestone St.)
Finians Cl. UB10: Uxb 7B 56
Finland Rd. SE4 . . . . .3A 122
Finland St. SE16 . . . . .3A 104
Finlays Cl. KT9: Chess 5G 163
Finlay St. SW6 . . . . .1F 117
Finley Ct. SE5 . . . . .7C 102
(off Redcar St.)
Finmere Ho. N4 . . . . .7C 48

Finnemore Ho. *N1* *1C 84*
   (off Britannia Row)
Finney La. TW7: Isle 1A 114
Finn Ho. *N1* *1F 9*
   (off Bevenden St.)
Finnis St. E2 . . . . .3H 85
Finnymore Rd. RM9: Dag 7E 72
FINSBURY 3C 8 (3A 84)
Finsbury Av. EC2 . . . . . .6F 9 (5D 84)
Finsbury Av. Sq. EC2 . . . .5G 9 (5E 84)
Finsbury Cir. EC2 . . . . . .6F 9 (5D 84)
Finsbury Cotts. N22 . . . . .7D 32
Finsbury Est. EC1 . . . . . .2K 7 (3A 84)
Finsbury Ho. N22 . . . . .1J 47
Finsbury Leisure Cen. . . .3C 8 (3C 84)
Finsbury Mkt. EC2 . . . . . . .4G 9 (4E 84)
   (not continuous)
FINSBURY PARK 1A 66
Finsbury Pk. Av. N4 . . . . .6C 48
Finsbury Pk. Rd. N4 . . . . .2B 66
Finsbury Pavement EC2 . .5F 9 (5D 84)
Finsbury Rd. N22 . . . . .7E 32
   (not continuous)
Finsbury Sq. EC2 . . . . . . .4F 9 (4D 84)
Finsbury St. EC2 . . . . . . .5E 8 (5D 84)
Finsbury Way DA5: Bexl 6F 127
Finsen Rd. SE5 . . . . .4C 120
Finstock Rd. W10 . . . . .6F 81
Finucane Ct. TW9: Rich *3F 115*
   (off Lwr. Mortlake Rd.)
Finucane Ri. WD23: B Hea 2B 26
Finwhale Ho. E14 . . . .*3D 104*
   (off Glengall Gro.)
Fiona Ct. EN2: Enf 3G 23
   NW6 . . . . .2J 81
Firbank Cl. E16 . . . . .5B 88
   EN2: Enf 4H 23
Firbank Rd. SE15 . . . . .2H 121
Fir Cl. KT12: Walt T 7J 147
Fircroft Gdns. HA1: Harr 3J 59
Fircroft Rd. KT9: Chess 4F 163
   SW17 .2D 136
Fir Dene BR6: Farnb 3D 172
Firdene KT5: Surb 1J 163
Fire Bell All. KT6: Surb 6E 150
Firecrest Dr. NW3 . . . . .3K 63
Firefly Cl. UB3: Hayes 7H 75
   UB5: N'olt 3B 76
Firefly Gdns. E6 . . . . .4C 88
Firehorn Ho. E15 . . . .*3G 87*
   (off Teasel Way)
Firemans Flats N22 . . . . .7D 32
Fire Station All. EN5: Barn 3B 20
Fire Station M. BR3: Beck 1C 158
Fire Station Square SE1 . . . . .5H 15
Firestone Ho. TW8: Bford 5E 96
Firethorn Cl. HA8: Edg 4D 28
Firewatch Ct. E1 . . . .*5A 86*
   (off Candle St.)
Fir Gro. KT3: N Mald 6B 152
Firgrove Ct. SE6 . . . . .7C 122
Fir Gro. Rd. SW9 . . . . .2A 120
Firhill Rd. SE6 . . . . .4C 140
Fir Ho. W10 . . . .*5E 80*
   (off Droop St.)
Firle Ho. W10 . . . .*5E 80*
   (off Sutton Way)
Firman Cl. KT3: N Mald 4A 152
Firmans Ct. E17 . . . . .4F 51
Fir Rd. SM3: Sutt 1H 165
   TW13: Hanw 5B 130
The Firs DA5: Bexl 1K 145
   DA15: Sidc 2K 143
   E6 . . . . .7C 70
   HA8: Edg 4E 28
   (off Stoneyfields La.)
   IG8: Wfd G 7F 37
   N20 . . . . .1G 31
   SE26 . . . . .5H 139
   (Border Rd.)
   SE26 . . . . .5J 139
   (Waverley Ct.)
   W5 . . . . .5D 78

Firs Av. N10 . . . . .3E 46
   N11 . . . . .6J 31
   SW14 . . . . .4J 115
Firsby Av. CR0: C'don 1K 169
Firsby Rd. N16 . . . . .1G 67
Firs Cl. CR4: Mitc 2F 155
   N10 . . . . .4E 46
   SE23 . . . . .7A 122
Firscroft N13 . . . . .3H 33
Firs Dr. TW5: Cran 7K 93
Firs Ho. N22 . . . . .1A 48
   (off Acacia Rd.)
Firside Gro. DA15: Sidc 1K 143
Firs La. N13 . . . . .3H 33
   N21 . . . . .7H 23
Firs Pk. Av. N21 . . . . .1J 33
Firs Pk. Gdns. N21 . . . . .1H 33
First Av. DA7: Bex 7C 108
   E12 . . . . .4C 70
   E13 . . . . .3J 87
   E17 . . . . .5C 50
   EN1: Enf 5A 24
   HA9: Wemb 2D 60
   KT8: W Mole 4D 148
   KT12: Walt T 6K 147
   KT19: Ewe 7A 164
   N18 . . . . .4D 34
   NW4 . . . . .4E 44
   RM6: Chad H 5C 54
   RM10: Dag 2H 91
   SW14 . . . . .3A 116
   UB3: Hayes 1H 93
   W3 . . . . .1B 98
   W10 . . . . .4H 81
First Central Bus. Pk. NW10 . . . . .3F 79
First Cl. KT8: W Mole 3G 149
First Cross Rd. TW2: Twick 2J 131
First Dr. NW10 . . . . .7J 61
First St. SW3 . . . . .3D 16 (4C 100)
Firstway SW20 . . . . .2E 152
Firs Wlk. IG8: Wfd G 5D 36
Firswood Av. KT19: Ewe 5A 164
Firth Gdns. SW6 . . . . .1G 117
Firth Ho. E2 . . . .*3G 85*
   (off Turin St.)
Fir Tree Av. UB7: W Dray 3C 92
Firtree Av. CR4: Mitc 2E 154
Fir Tree Cl. BR6: Chels 5K 173
   KT19: Ewe 4B 164
   RM1: Rom 3K 55
   SW16 . . . . .5G 137
   W5 . . . . .6E 78
Fir Tree Gdns. CR0: C'don 4C 170
Fir Tree Gro. SM5: Cars 7D 166
Firtree Ho. SE13 . . . .*7F 123*
   (off Birdwood Av.)
Fir Tree Pl. TW15: Ashf 5C 128
Fir Trees Cl. SE16 . . . . .1A 104
Fir Tree Wlk. EN1: Enf 3J 23
   RM10: Dag 3J 73
Fir Wlk. SM3: Cheam 6F 165
Fisher Cl. CR0: C'don 1F 169
   E9 . . . . .5K 67
   SE16 . . . . .1K 103
   UB6: G'frd 3E 76
Fisher Ho. E1 . . . .*7J 85*
   (off Cable St.)
   N1 . . . .*1A 84*
   (off Barnsbury Est.)
Fisherman Cl. TW10: Ham 4B 132
Fishermans Dr. SE16 . . . . .2K 103
Fisherman's Pl. W4 . . . . .6B 98
Fisherman's Wlk. E14 . . . . .1C 104
Fishermans Wlk. SE28 . . . . .2J 107
Fisher Rd. HA3: W'stone 2K 41
Fisher's Cl. SW16 . . . . .3H 137
Fishers Ct. SE14 . . . . .1K 121
Fishersdene KT10: Clay 7A 162
Fisher's La. W4 . . . . .4K 97
Fisher St. E16 . . . . .5J 87
   WC1 . . . . .6G 7 (5K 83)

Fishers Way DA17: Belv 1J 109
   HA0: Wemb 5B 60
Fishers Wood Gro.
   BR2: Broml 7C 160
Fisherton St. NW8 . . . . . . .4A 4 (4B 82)
Fishguard Way E16 . . . . .1F 107
Fishmongers Hall Wharf EC4 . . . . .3E 14
Fishponds Rd. BR2: Kes 5B 172
   SW17 . . . . .4C 136
Fish St. Hill EC3 . . . . . . .3F 15 (7D 84)
Fish Wharf EC3 . . . . .3F 15 (7D 84)
Fisk Cl. TW16: Sun 6H 129
Fiske Ct. IG11: Bark 2H 89
   N17 . . . . .1G 49
   SM2: Sutt 7A 166
Fitch Ct. SW2 . . . . .5A 120
Fitness4Less
   Canning Town 5H 87
   Sutton 6J 165
Fitness First
   Angel 1A 8 (2B 84)
   Baker Street 6F 5 (5D 82)
   Beckenham 6C 140
   Berkeley Square 3K 11 (7F 83)
   Brixton 3A 120
   Camden 1F 83
   Clapham Junction 4C 118
   Covent Garden 3F 13
   (off Bedford St.)
   Fetter Lane 1K 13
   (off Fetter La.)
   Gracechurch Street 2F 15
   (off Gracechurch St.)
   Great Marlborough Street 1A 12
   Hammersmith 4E 98
   Harringay 6B 48
   (off Arena Shop. Pk.)
   Highbury 3B 66
   High Holborn 6G 7
   (off High Holborn)
   Ilford .2G 71
   Kilburn 1H 81
   Kingly Street 2A 12
   Leyton Mills 3E 68
   London Bridge 5F 15
   (off London Bri. St.)
   London Bridge, Cottons 4F 15
   (off Tooley St.)
   Paternoster Square 7B 8
   Queen Victoria Street 2C 14
   (off Queen Victoria St.)
   Streatham 2J 137
   Thomas More Square 7G 85
   (off Thomas More Sq.)
   Tooting Bec 3E 136
Fittleton Gdns. E3 . . . . .4D 86
Fitzalan Rd. N3 . . . . .3G 45
Fitzalan St. SE11 . . . . . .3H 19 (4A 102)
Fitzclarence Ho. W11 . . . . .2G 99
   (off Holland Park Av.)
Fitzgeorge Av. KT3: N Mald 1K 151
   W14 . . . . .4G 99
Fitzgerald Av. SW14 . . . . .3A 116
Fitzgerald Ct. E10 . . . . .1D 68
   (off Leyton Grange Est.)
Fitzgerald Ho. E14 . . . . .6D 86
   (off E. India Dock Rd.)
   SW9 .2A 120
   SW17 .3B 136
   UB3: Hayes 1K 93
Fitzgerald Rd. E11 . . . . .5J 51
   SW14 . . . . .3K 115
Fitzhardinge Ho. W1 . . . . .7G 5
   (off Portman Sq.)
Fitzhardinge St. W1 . . . . . .7G 5 (6E 82)
Fitzherbert Cl. IG8: Ilf, Wfd G 1C 52
Fitzherbert Wlk. UB1: S'hall 2H 95
Fitzhugh Gro. SW18 . . . . .6B 118
Fitzjames Av. CR0: C'don 2G 169
   W14 . . . . .4G 99
Fitzjohn Av. EN5: Barn 5B 20
Fitzjohn's Av. NW3 . . . . .4A 64

Fitzmaurice Ho. SE16 . . . .*4H 103*
   (off Rennie Est.)
Fitzmaurice Pl. W1 . . . . . .4K 11 (1F 101)
Fitzneal St. W12 . . . . .6B 80
Fitzpatrick Rd. SW9 . . . . .1B 120
FITZROVIA 5K 5
Fitzrovia Apts. W1 . . . . .4K 5
   (off Bolsover St.)
FITZROY BRI. 1E 82
Fitzroy Bus. Pk. BR5: St P 7D 144
Fitzroy Cl. N6 . . . . .1D 64
Fitzroy Ct. CR0: C'don 7D 156
   N6 . . . . .6G 47
   W1 . . . . .4B 6
Fitzroy Cres. W4 . . . . .7K 97
Fitzroy Gdns. SE19 . . . . .7E 138
Fitzroy Ho. E14 . . . .*5B 86*
   (off Wallwood St.)
   SE1 . . . .*5F 103*
   (off Cooper's La.)
Fitzroy House Mus. 4A 6 (4G 83)
Fitzroy M. W1 . . . . .4A 6
Fitzroy Pk. N6 . . . . .1D 64
Fitzroy Rd. NW1 . . . . .1E 82
Fitzroy Sq. W1 . . . . .4A 6 (4G 83)
Fitzroy St. W1 . . . . .4A 6 (4G 83)
   (not continuous)
Fitzroy Yd. NW1 . . . . .1E 82
Fitzstephen Rd. RM8: Dag 5B 72
Fitzwarren Gdns. N19 . . . . .1G 65
Fitzwilliam Av. TW9: Rich 2F 115
Fitzwilliam Cl. N20 . . . . .1K 31
Fitzwilliam Hgts. SE23 . . . . .2J 139
Fitzwilliam Ho. TW9: Rich 4D 114
Fitzwilliam M. E16 . . . . .1J 105
Fitzwilliam Rd. SW4 . . . . .3G 119
Fitz Wygram Cl. TW12: Hamp H . .5G 131
Five Acre NW9 . . . . .2B 44
Fiveacre Cl. CR7: Thor H 6A 156
Five Arches Bus. Pk.
   DA14: Sidc 5D 144
Five Bell All. E14 . . . .*6B 86*
   (off Three Colt St.)
Five Elms BR2: Hayes 3K 171
Five Elms Rd. BR2: Hayes 3K 171
   RM9: Dag 3F 73
Five Oaks M. BR1: Broml 3J 141
Fives Ct. SE11 . . . . .3B 102
FIVEWAYS 2F 143
Five Ways Bus. Cen. TW13: Felt . . .3K 129
FIVEWAYS CORNER
   (Croydon) 4A 168
   (Hendon) 1C 44
Fiveways Rd. SW9 . . . . .2A 120
Fixie Bldg. E17 . . . .*5B 50*
   (off Track St.)
Flack Ct. E10 . . . . .7D 50
Fladbury Rd. N15 . . . . .6D 48
Fladgate Rd. E11 . . . . .6G 51
Flag Cl. CR0: C'don 1K 169
Flagon Cl. CR0: C'don 4C 168
   (off St Andrew's Rd.)
Flagship Ho. E16 . . . .*2K 105*
   (off Royal Crest Av.)
Flag Wlk. HA5: Eastc 6J 39
Flambard Rd. HA1: Harr 6A 42
Flamborough Ho. SE15 . . . .*1G 121*
   (off Clayton Rd.)
Flamborough Rd. HA4: Ruis 3J 57
Flamborough St. E14 . . . . .6A 86
Flamborough Wlk. E14 . . . .*6A 86*
   (off Flamborough St.)
Flamingo Ct. SE8 . . . .*7C 104*
   (off Hamilton St.)
   SE17 . . . .*5C 102*
   (off Crampton St.)
Flamingo Gdns. UB5: N'olt 3C 76
Flamstead Gdns. RM9: Dag 7C 72
Flamstead Ho. SW3 . . . .*5C 16*
   (off Cale St.)
Flamsteed Rd. RM9: Dag 7C 72
Flamsteed Av. HA9: Wemb 6G 61
Flamsteed Rd. SE7 . . . . .5C 106

Flanaghan Apts. *E3* 4B *86*
    (off Portia Way)
Flanchford Rd. W12 . . . . .3B *98*
Flanders Ct. E17 . . . . .7A *50*
Flanders Cres. SW17 . . . . .7D *136*
Flanders Mans. W4 . . . . .4B *98*
Flanders Rd. E6 . . . . .2D *88*
    W4 . . . . .4A *98*
Flanders Way E9 . . . . .6K *67*
Flandrian Cl. EN3: Enf L 1J *25*
Flank St. E1 . . . . .7G *85*
Flannery Ct. SE16 . . . . .3H *103*
Flansham Ho. E14 . . . . .6B *86*
    (off Clemence St.)
Flask Wlk. NW3 . . . . .4A *64*
Flatford Ho. SE6 . . . . .4E *140*
Flather Cl. SW16 . . . . .5G *137*
Flat Iron Sq. SE1 . . . . .5D *14*
    (off Southwark Bri. Rd.)
Flatiron Yd. SE1 . . . . .5D *14*
    (off Ayres St.)
Flavell M. SE10 . . . . .5G *105*
Flaxen Cl. E4 . . . . .3J *35*
Flaxen Rd. E4 . . . . .3J *35*
Flaxley Ho. SW1 . . . . .5J *17*
    (part of Abbots Mnr.)
Flaxley Rd. SM4: Mord 7K *153*
Flaxman Cl. DA17: Belv 4G *109*
    (off Hoddesdon Rd.)
    W1 . . . . .1C **12** (6H **83**)
    WC1 . . . . .2D **6**
    (off Flaxman Ter.)
Flaxman Ho. SE1 . . . . .3B *102*
    (off London Rd.)
    W4 . . . . .5A *98*
    (off Devonshire St.)
Flaxman Rd. SE5 . . . . .3B *120*
Flaxman Sports Cen. 2C *120*
Flaxman Ter. WC1 . . . . . . .2D **6** (3H **83**)
Flaxton Rd. SE18 . . . . .7H *107*
Flecker Cl. HA7: Stan 5E *26*
Flecker Ho. SE5 . . . . .7C *102*
    (off Lomond Gro.)
Fleece Dr. N9 . . . . .4B *34*
Fleece Rd. KT6: Surb 1C *162*
Fleece Wlk. N7 . . . . .6J *65*
Fleeming Cl. E17 . . . . .2B *50*
Fleeming Rd. E17 . . . . .2B *50*
Fleetbank Ho. EC4 . . . . .1K *13*
    (off Salisbury Sq.)
Fleet Cl. HA4: Ruis 6E *38*
    KT8: W Mole 5D *148*
Fleetfield WC1 . . . . .1F *7*
    (off Birkenhead St.)
Fleet Ho. E14 . . . . .7A *86*
    (off Victory Pl.)
Fleet La. KT8: W Mole 6D *148*
Fleet Pl. EC4 . . . . .7A **8** (6B **84**)
Fleet Rd. IG11: Bark 1F *89*
    NW3 . . . . .5C *64*
Fleetside KT8: W Mole 5D *148*
Fleet Sq. WC1 . . . . .2H **7** (3K **83**)
Fleet St. EC4 . . . . .1J **13** (6A **84**)
Fleetway WC1 . . . . .1F *7*
    (off Birkenhead St.)
Fleetway W. UB6: G'frd 2B *78*
Fleetwood Cl. CRO: C'don 3F *169*
    E16 . . . . .5B *88*
    KT9: Chess 7D *162*
Fleetwood Ct. E6 . . . . .5D *88*
    (off Evelyn Dennington Rd.)
    TW19: Stanw 6A *110*
    (off Douglas Rd.)
Fleetwood Rd. KT1: King T 3H *151*
    NW10 .5C *62*
Fleetwood Sq. KT1: King T 3H *151*
Fleetwood St. N16 . . . . .2E *66*
Fleming N8 . . . .
    (off Boyton Cl.)
Fleming Cl. SW10 . . . . . .6A **4**, 5H **13**, 6A *16*
Fleming Ct. CRO: Wadd 5A *168*
    W2 . . . . .5A **4**

Fleming Dr. N21 . . . . .5E *22*
Fleming Ho. HA9: Wemb 3J *61*
    (off Barnhill Rd.)
    N4 . . . . .1C *66*
    SE16 . . . . .2G *103*
    (off George Row)
    SW17 . . . . .3B *136*
Fleming Lodge W9 . . . . .5J *81*
    (off Admiral Wlk.)
Fleming Mead CR4: Mitc 7C *136*
Fleming Rd. SE17 . . . . .6B *102*
    UB1: S'hall 6F *77*
Fleming Wlk. NW9 . . . . .3A *44*
Fleming Way SE28 . . . . .7D *90*
    TW7: Isle 4K *113*
Flemming Av. HA4: Ruis 1K *57*
Flempton Rd. E10 . . . . .1A *68*
Fletcher Bldgs. WC2 . . . . .1F *13*
    (off Martlett Ct.)
Fletcher Cl. E6 . . . . .6F *89*
Fletcher Ct. NW9 . . . . .3A *44*
Fletcher Ho. N1 . . . . .1E *84*
    (off Nuttall St.)
    SE15 .7J *103*
    (off Clifton Way)
Fletcher La. E10 . . . . .7E *50*
Fletcher Path SE8 . . . . .7C *104*
Fletcher Rd. W4 . . . . .3J *97*
Fletchers Cl. BR2: Broml 4K *159*
Fletcher St. E1 . . . . .7G *85*
Fletching Apts. E3 . . . . .4B *86*
    (off Siyah Gdn.)
Fletching Rd. E5 . . . . .3J *67*
    SE7 .6A *106*
Fletton Rd. N11 . . . . .7D *32*
Fleur de Lis St. E1 . . . .4H **9** (4F **85**)
Fleur Gates SW19 . . . . .7F *117*
Flexmere Gdns. N17 . . . . .1D *48*
Flexmere Rd. N17 . . . . .1D *48*
Flight App. NW9 . . . . .2B *44*
Flight Ho. N1 . . . . .1E *84*
    (off Phillipp St.)
Flimwell Cl. BR1: Broml 5G *141*
Flinders Ho. E1 . . . . .1H *103*
    (off Green Bank)
Flint Cl. BR6: Chels 6K *173*
    CRO: C'don 6K *155*
    E15 . . . . .7H *69*
Flintlock Cl. E1 . . . . .6H *85*
    TW19: Stanw M 7B *174*
Flintmill Cres. SE3 . . . . .2C *124*
Flinton St. SE17 . . . . .5E *102*
Flint St. SE17 . . . . .4D *102*
Flip Out
    Brent Cross 1D *62*
    East Ham 1C *88*
    Wandsworth 1K *135*
Flitcroft St. WC2 . . . . .1D **12** (6H **83**)
Flitton Ho. N1 . . . . .7B *66*
    (off The Sutton Est.)
Floathaven Cl. SE28 . . . . .1A *108*
Flock Mill Pl. SW18 . . . . .1K *135*
Flockton St. SE16 . . . . .2G *103*
Flodden Rd. SE5 . . . . .1C *120*
Flood La. TW1: Twick 1A *132*
Flood Pas. SE18 . . . . .3C *106*
Flood St. SW3 . . . . .6D **16** (5C **100**)
Flood Wlk. SW3 . . . . . . .7D **16** (6C **100**)
Flora Cl. E14 . . . . .6D *86*
    HA7: Stan 3K *27*
Flora Gdns. RM6: Chad H 6C *54*
    W6 . . . . .4D *98*
    (off Albion Gdns.)
Flora Ho. E3 . . . . .1C *86*
    (off Garrison Rd.)
Floral Ct. WC2 . . . . . . .2F **13** (7J **83**)
Floral Pl. N1 . . . . .5D *66*
Floral St. WC2 . . . . . . .2E **12** (7J **83**)
Flora St. DA17: Belv 5F *109*
Florence Av. EN2: Enf 3H *23*
    SM4: Mord 5A *154*
Florence Cantwell Wlk. N19 . . . . .7J *47*
    (off Jessie Blythe La.)

Florence Cl. KT2: King T 5F *133*
    KT12: Walt T 7K *147*
Florence Ct. E11 . . . . .4K *51*
    N1 . . . . .7B *66*
    (off Florence St.)
    SW19 . . . . .6G *135*
    W9 . . . . .3A *82*
    (off Maida Vale)
Florence Dr. EN2: Enf 3H *23*
Florence Elson Cl. E12 . . . . .4E *70*
Florence Gdns. RM6: Chad H 7C *54*
    W4 . . . . .6J *97*
Florence Ho. KT2: King T 7F *133*
    (off Florence Rd.)
    SE16 . . . . .5H *103*
    (off Rotherhithe New Rd.)
    W11 . . . . .7F *81*
    (off St Ann's Rd.)
Florence Mans. NW4 . . . . .5D *44*
    (off Vivian Av.)
    SW6 .1H *117*
    (off Rostrevor Rd.)
Florence Nightingale Mus.
    . . . . .7G **13** (2K **101**)
Florence Rd. BR1: Broml 1J *159*
    BR3: Beck 2A *158*
    CR2: Sande 7D *168*
    E6 . . . . .1A *88*
    E13 . . . . .2J *87*
    KT2: King T 7F *133*
    KT12: Walt T 7K *147*
    N4 . . . . .7K *47*
    (not continuous)
    SE2 .4C *108*
    SE14 . . . . .1B *122*
    SW19 . . . . .6K *135*
    TW13: Felt 1K *129*
    UB2: S'hall 4B *94*
    W4 . . . . .3K *97*
    W5 . . . . .7E *78*
Florence Root Ho. IG4: Ilf 5C *52*
Florence Sq. E3 . . . . .4D *86*
Florence St. E16 . . . . .4H *87*
    N1 . . . . .7B *66*
    NW4 . . . . .4E *44*
Florence Ter. SE14 . . . . .1B *122*
    SW15 . . . . .3A *134*
Florence Way SW12 . . . . .1D *136*
Florey Lodge W9 . . . . .5J *81*
    (off Admiral Wlk.)
Florey Sq. N21 . . . . .5E *22*
Florfield Pas. E8 . . . . .6H *67*
    (off Reading La.)
Florfield Rd. E8 . . . . .6H *67*
Florian SE5 . . . . .1E *120*
Florian Av. SM1: Sutt 4B *166*
Florian Ct. E16 . . . . .5J *87*
    (off Hastings Rd.)
Florian Rd. SW15 . . . . .4G *117*
Florida Cl. WD23: B Hea 2C *26*
Florida Ct. BR2: Broml 4H *159*
    (off Westmoreland Rd.)
Florida Rd. CR7: Thor H 1B *156*
Florida St. E2 . . . . .3G *85*
Florin Ct. EC1 . . . . .5C *8*
    N18 . . . . .4K *33*
    SE1 . . . . .7J *15*
    (off Tanner St.)
Floris Pl. SW4 . . . . .3G *119*
Floriston Av. UB10: Hil 7E *56*
Floriston Cl. HA7: Stan 1B *42*
Floriston Ct. UB5: N'olt 5F *59*
Floriston Gdns. HA7: Stan 1B *42*
Florys Ct. SW19 . . . . .1G *135*
Floss St. SW15 . . . . .2E *116*
Flotilla Ho. E16 . . . . .2K *105*
    (off Cable St.)
    SW18 . . . . .3A *118*
Flounder Ho. SE8 . . . . .7D *104*
    (off Creative Rd.)
Flower & Dean Wlk. E1 . . . .6K **9** (5F **85**)
Flowerdown Ct. HA4: Eastc 6J *39*
    (off Lidgould Gro.)

Flower La. NW7 . . . . .5G *29*
Flower M. NW11 . . . . .6G *45*
Flower Pot Cl. N15 . . . . .6F *49*
Flowers Av. HA4: Eastc, Ruis 6J *39*
Flowers Cl. NW2 . . . . .3C *62*
Flowersmead SW17 . . . . .2E *136*
Flowers M. N19 . . . . .2G *65*
The Flower Wlk. SW7 . . . .6A **10** (2A **100**)
Floyd Rd. SE7 . . . . .5A *106*
Floyer Cl. TW10: Rich 5F *115*
Fludyer St. SE13 . . . . .4G *123*
Flutemakers M. SW4 . . . . .5H *119*
Flying Angel Ho. E16 . . . . .7K *87*
    (off Victoria Dock Rd.)
Flynn Ct. E14 . . . . .7C *86*
    (off Garford St.)
Foley Ho. E1 . . . . .6J *85*
    (off Tarling St.)
Foley St. W1 . . . . .6A **6** (5G **83**)
Folgate St. E1 . . . . .5H **9** (5E **84**)
    (not continuous)
Foliot Ho. N1 . . . . .2K *83*
    (off Priory Grn. Est.)
Foliot St. W12 . . . . .6B *80*
Folkestone Ct. UB5: N'olt 5F *59*
    (off Newmarket Av.)
Folkestone Ho. SE17 . . . . .5E *102*
    (off Upnor Way)
Folkestone Rd. E6 . . . . .2E *88*
    E17 . . . . .4D *50*
    N18 . . . . .4B *34*
Folkingham La. NW9 . . . . .1K *43*
Folkington Cnr. N12 . . . . .5C *30*
Folland NW9 . . . . .2B *44*
    (off Hundred Acre)
Follett Ho. SW10 . . . . .7B *100*
    (off Worlds End Est.)
Follett St. E14 . . . . .6E *86*
Follingham Ct. N1 . . . . .2D **9**
    (off Drysdale Pl.)
Folly Brook & Darland's Lake
    Nature Reserve 3B *30*
Folly La. E4 . . . . .6G *35*
    E17 . . . . .1A *50*
Folly M. W11 . . . . .6H *81*
Folly Wall E14 . . . . .2E *104*
Fonda Ct. E14 . . . . .7C *86*
    (off Premiere Pl.)
Fondant Ct. E3 . . . . .2D *86*
    (off Taylor Pl.)
Fontaine Ho. E17 . . . . .4C *50*
    (off Hoe St.)
Fontaine Rd. SW16 . . . . .7K *137*
Fontayne Av. RM1: Rom 2K *55*
Fontenelle SE5 . . . . .1E *120*
Fontenoy Ho. SE11 . . . . .4B *102*
    (off Kennington La.)
Fontenoy Rd. SW12 . . . . .2F *137*
Fonteyne Gdns. IG8: Wfd G 2B *52*
Fonthill Cl. SE20 . . . . .2G *157*
Fonthill Ho. SW1 . . . . .5K *17*
    (part of Abbots Mnr.)
    W14 . . . . .3G *99*
    (off Russell Rd.)
Fonthill M. N4 . . . . .2K *65*
Fonthill Rd. N4 . . . . .1K *65*
Font Hills N2 . . . . .2A *46*
Footbury Way SW15 . . . . .7C *116*
Fontmell Cl. TW15: Ashf 5C *128*
Fontmell Pk. TW15: Ashf 5B *128*
Fontwell Cl. HA3: Hrw W 7D *26*
    UB5: N'olt 6E *58*
Fontwell Dr. BR2: Broml 5E *160*
Football La. HA1: Harr 1K *59*
The Footpath SW15 . . . . .6C *116*
FOOTS CRAY 6C *144*
Foots Cray High St. DA14: Sidc . . .6C *144*
Foots Cray La. DA14: Sidc 1C *144*
Foots Cray Meadows 4D *144*
Footscray Rd. SE9 . . . . .6E *124*
Forber Ho. E2 . . . . .3J *85*
    (off Cornwall Av.)

Forbes Cl. NW2 . . . . .3C 62
Forbes Ho. E7 . . . . .5A 70
(off Romford Rd.)
W4 . . . . .5G 97
(off Stonehill Rd.)
Forbes St. E1 . . . . .6G 85
Forbes Way HA4: Ruis 2K 57
Forburg Rd. N16 . . . . .1G 67
Fordbridge Ct. TW15: Ashf 6A 128
Fordbridge Pk. TW16: Sun 6H 147
Fordbridge Rd. TW15: Ashf 6A 128
TW16: Sun 6G 147
TW17: Shep 6G 147
FORDBRIDGE RDBT. 6A 128
Ford Cl. CR7: Thor H 5B 156
E3 . . . . .2A 86
HA1: Harr 7H 41
TW15: Ashf 6A 128
TW17: Shep 4C 146
Forde Av. BR1: Broml 3A 160
Fordel Rd. SE6 . . . . .1E 140
Ford End IG8: Wfd G 6E 36
Fordgate Bus. Pk.
DA17: Belv 2J 109
Fordham KT1: King T 2G 151
(off Excelsior Cl.)
Fordham Cl. EN4: Cockf 3H 21
KT4: Wor Pk 1D 164
Fordham Ho. SE14 . . . . .7A 104
(off Angus St.)
Fordham Rd. EN4: Cockf 3G 21
Fordham St. E1 . . . . .6G 85
Fordhook Av. W5 . . . . .1F 97
Ford Ho. EN5: New Bar 5E 20
Fordie Ho. SW1 . . . . .2F 17
(off Sloane St.)
Ford Ind. Pk. RM9: Dag 4H 91
Fordingley Rd. W9 . . . . .3H 81
Fordington Ho. SE26 . . . . .3G 139
Fordington Rd. N6 . . . . .5D 46
Ford Lodge RM7: Rom 4K 55
Fordmill Rd. SE6 . . . . .2C 140
Ford Rd. E3 . . . . .2B 86
RM9: Dag 7F 73
RM10: Dag 7F 73
TW15: Ashf 4B 128
Fords Gro. N21 . . . . .1H 33
Fords Pk. Rd. E16 . . . . .5J 87
Fords Pl. HA6: Nwood 2J 39
Ford Sq. E1 . . . . .5H 85
Ford St. E3 . . . . .1A 86
E16 . . . . .6H 87
Fordview Ind. Est.
RM13: Rain 3K 91
Fordwich Cl. BR6: Orp 7K 161
Fordwych Rd. NW2 . . . . .4G 63
Fordyce Rd. SE13 . . . . .6E 122
Fordyke Rd. RM8: Dag 2F 73
Foreign St. SE5 . . . . .2B 120
Foreland Ct. NW4 . . . . .1F 45
Foreland Ho. W11 . . . . .7G 81
(off Walmer Rd.)
Foreland St. SE18 . . . . .4H 107
Forelle Way SM5: Cars 7D 166
Foreman Cl. TW1: Twick 1K 131
Foreman Ho. SE4 . . . . .4K 121
(off Billingford Cl.)
Foreshore SE8 . . . . .4B 104
The Forest E11 . . . . .4G 51
Forest App. E4 . . . . .1B 36
IG8: Wfd G 7D 36
Forest Av. E4 . . . . .1B 36
IG7: Chig 5K 37
Forest Bus. Pk. E10 . . . . .7K 49
Forest Cl. BR7: Chst 1E 160
E11 . . . . .5J 51
IG8: Wfd G 3E 36
N10 . . . . .1F 47
NW6 . . . . .7G 63
Forest Ct. E4 . . . . .1C 36
E11 . . . . .4G 51
N12 . . . . .5E 30

Forest Cft. SE23 . . . . .2H 139
FORESTDALE 7B 170
Forestdale N14 . . . . .4C 32
The Forestdale Cen. 7B 170
Forest Dene Ct. SM2: Sutt 6A 166
Forest Dr. BR2: Kes 4C 172
BR3: Beck 7B 158
E12 . . . . .3B 70
IG8: Wfd G 7A 36
TW16: Sun 7H 129
Forest Dr. E. E11 . . . . .7F 51
Forest Dr. W. E11 . . . . .7E 50
Forest Edge IG9: Buck H 4F 37
Forester Ho. E14 . . . . .7A 86
(off Victory Pl.)
Forester Rd. SE15 . . . . .3H 121
Foresters Cl. SM6: W'gton 7H 167
Foresters Cres. DA7: Bex 4H 127
Foresters Dr. E17 . . . . .4F 51
SM6: W'gton 7H 167
Forest Gdns. N17 . . . . .2F 49
FOREST GATE 5J 69
Forest Ga. NW9 . . . . .4A 44
Forest Gate Learning Zone 4J 69
(off Woodford Rd.)
Forest Ga. Retreat E7 . . . . .5J 69
(off Odessa Rd.)
Forest Glade E4 . . . . .4B 36
E11 . . . . .6G 51
Forest Gro. E8 . . . . .6F 67
Forest Hgts. IG9: Buck H 2D 36
FOREST HILL 2J 139
Forest Hill Bus. Cen. SE23 . . . . . . .2J 139
(off Clyde Va.)
Forest Hill Ind. Est. SE23 . . . . .2J 139
Forest Hill Pools 2J 139
Forest Hill Rd. SE22 . . . . .5H 121
SE23 .5H 121
Forest Hill School Sports Cen. . . .3K 139
Forestholme Cl. SE23 . . . . .2J 139
Forest Ind. Pk. IG6: Ilf 1J 53
Forest La. E7 . . . . .5G 69
E15 . . . . .5G 69
IG7: Chig 5K 37
Forest Lodge SE23 . . . . .3J 139
(off Dartmouth Rd.)
Forest Mt. Rd. IG8: Wfd G 7A 36
Forest Point E7 . . . . .5K 69
(off Windsor Rd.)
Fore St. EC2 . . . . .6D 8 (5C 84)
HA5: Eastc 4H 39
N9 . . . . .4B 34
N18 . . . . .6A 34
Fore St. Av. EC2 . . . . .6E 8 (5D 84)
Forest Ridge
BR2: Kes 4C 172
BR3: Beck 3C 158
Forest Ri. E17 . . . . .3F 51
Forest Rd. E7 . . . . .4J 69
E8 . . . . .6F 67
E11 . . . . .7F 51
E17 . . . . .4A 50
IG6: Chig, Ilf 2H 53
IG8: Wfd G 3D 36
N9 . . . . .1C 34
N17 . . . . .4J 49
RM7: Mawney 3H 55
SM3: Sutt 1J 165
TW9: Kew 7G 97
TW13: Felt 2A 130
Forest Side E4 . . . . .1C 36
E7 . . . . .4K 69
IG9: Buck H 1F 37
KT4: Wor Pk 1R 164
Forest St. E7 . . . . .5J 69
Forest Ter. IG7: Chig 5K 37
Forest Trad. Est. E17 . . . . .3K 49
Forest Vw. E4 . . . . .7K 25, 1B 36
E11 . . . . .7H 51
Forest Vw. Av. E10 . . . . .5F 51
Forest Vw. Rd. E12 . . . . .4C 70
E17 . . . . .1E 50
Forest Wlk. N10 . . . . .1F 47

Forest Way BR5: St M Cry 5K 161
DA15: Sidc 7H 125
IG8: Wfd G 4E 36
N19 . . . . .2G 65
Forfar Rd. N22 . . . . .1B 48
SW11 .1E 118
Forge Cl. BR2: Hayes 1J 171
UB3: Harl 6F 93
Forge Cotts. W5 . . . . .1D 96
Forge Dr. KT10: Clay 7A 162
Forge La. HA6: Nwood 1G 39
SM3: Cheam 7G 165
TW10: Ham 1E 132
TW13: Hanw 5C 130
TW16: Sun 3J 147
Forge M. CR0: Addtn 5C 170
TW16: Sun 3J 147
(off Forge La.)
Forge Pl. NW1 . . . . .6E 64
Forge Sq. E14 . . . . .4D 104
Forlong Path UB5: N'olt 6C 58
(off Cowings Mead)
Forman Pl. N16 . . . . .4F 67
(off Woolwich Mnr. Way)
Formby Av. HA7: Stan 3C 42
Formby Cl. N7 . . . . .5A 66
(off Morgan Rd.)
Formosa Ho. E1 . . . . .4A 86
(off Ernest St.)
Formosa St. W9 . . . . .4K 81
Formunt Cl. E16 . . . . .5H 87
Forres Gdns. NW11 . . . . .6J 45
Forrester Path SE26 . . . . .4J 139
Forresters Apts. IG11: Bark 7G 71
(off Linton Rd.)
Forrester Way E15 . . . . .6F 69
Forrest Gdns. SW16 . . . . .3K 155
Forris Av. UB3: Hayes 1H 93
Forset Ct. W2 . . . . .7D 4
(off Edgware Rd.)
Forset St. W1 . . . . .7D 4 (6C 82)
(not continuous)
Forstal Cl. BR2: Broml 3J 159
Forster Cl. IG8: Wfd G 7A 36
Forster Ho. BR1: Broml 4F 141
SW17 .3B 136
(off Grosvenor Way)
Forster Rd. BR3: Beck 3A 158
E17 . . . . .6A 50
N17 . . . . .3F 49
SW2 . . . . .7J 119
Forsters Cl. RM6: Chad H 6F 55
Forsters Way UB4: Yead 6K 75
Forston Apartments SW11 . . . . . . .4C 118
(off Monarch Square)
Forston St. N1 . . . . .2C 84
Forsyte Cres. SE19 . . . . .1E 156
Forsyte Ho. SW3 . . . . .6D 16
Forsythe Shades Ct. BR3: Beck . . .1E 158
Forsyth Gdns. SE17 . . . . .6B 102
Forsyth Ho. E9 . . . . .7J 67
(off Frampton Pk. Rd.)
SW1 . . . . .5B 18
(off Tachbrook St.)
Forsythia Cl. IG1: Ilf 5F 71
Forsyth Pl. EN1: Enf 5K 23
Forterie Gdns. IG3: Bark, Ilf 3A 72
Fortescue Av. E8 . . . . .7H 67
TW2: Twick 3G 131
Fortescue Rd. HA8: Edg 1K 43
SW19 .7B 136
Fortess Gro. NW5 . . . . .5G 65
Fortess Rd. NW5 . . . . .5F 65
Fortess Wlk. NW5 . . . . .5F 65
Fortess Yd. NW5 . . . . .4F 65
Forte St. SE18 . . . . .1C 124
(off Tellson Av.)
Forthbridge Rd. SW11 . . . . .4E 118
Forth Ho. E3 .2B 86
(off Tredegar Rd.)
Fortis Cl. E16 . . . . .6A 88
Fortis Ct. N10 . . . . .3E 46

FORTIS GREEN 4D 46
Fortis Grn. N2 . . . . .4C 46
N10 . . . . .4C 46
Fortis Grn. Av. N2 . . . . .3D 46
Fortis Grn. Rd. N10 . . . . .3E 46
Fortismere Av. N10 . . . . .3E 46
Fortius Apts. E3 . . . . .2C 86
(off Tredegar La.)
Fortius Wlk. E20 . . . . .6E 68
Fortnam Rd. N19 . . . . .2H 65
Fortnum's Acre HA7: Stan 6E 26
Fort Rd. SE1 .4F 103
UB5: N'olt 7E 58
Fortrose Cl. E14 . . . . .6F 87
Fortrose Gdns. SW2 . . . . .1J 137
(not continuous)
Fort St. E1 . . . . .6H 9 (5E 84)
E16 . . . . .1K 105
Fortuna Cl. N7 . . . . .6K 65
Fortuna Ho. E20 . . . . .5D 68
(off Scarlet Cl.)
Fortune Av. HA8: Edg 1H 43
Fortune Ct. E8 . . . . .7F 67
(off Queensbridge Rd.)
IG11: Bark 2C 90
Fortune Ga. Rd. NW10 . . . . .1A 80
FORTUNE GREEN 5J 63
Fortune Grn. Rd. NW6 . . . . .4J 63
Fortune Ho. EC1 . . . . .4D 8
(off Fortune St.)
SE11 . . . . .4J 19
Fortune Pl. SE1 . . . . .5F 103
Fortunes Mead UB5: N'olt 6C 58
Fortune St. EC1 . . . . .4D 8 (4C 84)
Fortunes Wlk. E20 . . . . .5E 68
Fortune Theatre 1F 13
(off Russell St.)
Fortune Wlk. SE28 . . . . .3H 107
(off Broadwater Rd.)
Fortune Way NW10 . . . . .3C 80
Forty Acre La. E16 . . . . .5J 87
Forty Av. HA9: Wemb 3F 61
Forty Cl. HA9: Wemb 3F 61
Forty Footpath SW14 . . . . .3J 115
Forty Foot Way SE9 . . . . .7G 125
FORTY HILL .1K 23
Forty Hill EN2: Enf 1K 23
Forty La. HA9: Wemb 2H 61
The Forum KT8: W Mole 4F 149
Forum Cl. E3 . . . . .1C 86
Forum Ho. HA9: Wemb 4G 61
Forum Magnum Sq. SE1 . . . . .6H 13
(off York Rd.)
Forumside HA8: Edg 6B 28
Forum Way HA8: Edg 6B 28
Forval Cl. CR4: Mitc 5D 154
The Forward Bus. Cen. E16 . . . . . . .4F 87
Forward Dr. HA3: W'stone 4K 41
Fosbrooke Ho. SW8 . . . . .7J 101
(off Davidson Gdns.)
Fosbury M. W2 . . . . .7K 81
Foscote Ct. W9 . . . . .4J 81
(off Amberley Rd.)
Foscote M. W9 . . . . .4J 81
Foscote Rd. NW4 . . . . .6D 44
Foskett Ho. N2 . . . . .2B 46
(off The Grange)
Foskett M. E8 . . . . .5F 67
Foskett Rd. SW6 . . . . .2H 117
Foss Av. CR0: Wadd 5A 168
Fossdene Rd. SE7 . . . . .5K 105
Fossdyke Cl. UB4: Yead 5C 76
Fosset Lodge DA7: Bex 1J 127
Fosse Way W13 . . . . .5A 78
Foss Ho. NW8 . . . . .2K 81
(off Carlton Hill)
Fossil Cl. SE1 . . . . .7G 15
(off Long La.)
Fossil Rd. SE13 . . . . .3C 122
Fossington Rd.
DA17: Belv 4D 108
Foss Rd. SW17 . . . . .4B 136
Fossway RM8: Dag 2C 72

Foster Ct. *E16*	.7H **87**	
	(off Tarling Rd.)	
NW1	.7G **65**	
	(off Royal College St.)	
NW4	.4E **44**	
Foster Ho. SE14	.1B **122**	
Foster La. EC2	.7C **6** (6C **84**)	
Foster Rd. E13	.4J **87**	
W3	.7A **80**	
W4	.5K **97**	
Fosters Cl. BR7: Chst	.5D **142**	
E18	.1K **51**	
Foster St. NW4	.4E **44**	
Foster's Way SW18	.1K **135**	
Foster Wlk. NW4	.4E **44**	
Fothergill Cl. E13	.2J **87**	
Fothergill Dr. N21	.5D **22**	
Fotheringham Rd. EN1: Enf	.4A **24**	
	(not continuous)	
Foubert's Pl. W1	.1A **12** (6G **83**)	
Foulden Rd. N16	.4F **67**	
Foulden Ter. N16	.4F **67**	
Foulis Ter. SW7	.5B **16** (5B **100**)	
Foulser Rd. SW17	.3D **136**	
Foulsham Rd.		
CR7: Thor H	.3C **156**	
Foundation Pl. *SE9*	.5E **124**	
	(off Archery Rd.)	
Founder Cl. E6	.6F **89**	
Founders Cl. UB5: N'olt	.3D **76**	
Founders Ct. EC2	.7E **8**	
Founders Gdns. SE19	.7C **138**	
Founders Ho. *SW1*	.6C **18**	
	(off Aylesford St.)	
Foundling Ct. *WC1*	.3E **6**	
	(off Brunswick Cen.)	
The Foundling Mus.	.3F **7**	
The Foundry *EC2*	.2H **9**	
	(off Dereham Pl.)	
Foundry Cl. SE16	.1A **104**	
Foundry Ho. *E14*	.5D **86**	
	(off Morris Rd.)	
E15	.6F **69**	
	(off Forrester Way)	
SW8	.1F **119**	
	(off Lockington Rd.)	
Foundry M. E17	.3E **50**	
NW1	.3B **6** (4G **83**)	
SW13	.2B **116**	
TW3: Houn	.4F **113**	
Foundry Pl. *E1*	.5J **85**	
	(off Jubilee St.)	
SW18	.7K **117**	
Fountain Cl. E5	.4H **67**	
SE18	.5F **107**	
UB8: Hil	.5E **74**	
Fountain Ct. DA15: Sidc	.6B **126**	
EC4	.2J **13** (7A **84**)	
SE23	.2K **139**	
SW1	.4J **17**	
	(off Buckingham Pal. Rd.)	
W11	.2F **99**	
	(off Clearwater Ter.)	
Fountain Dr. SE19	.4F **139**	
SM5: Cars	.7D **166**	
Fountain Ho. CR4: Mitc	.2D **154**	
E2	.3J **9**	
	(off Redchurch St.)	
NW6	.7G **63**	
SE16	.2G **103**	
	(off Bermondsey Wall E.)	
SW6	.2A **118**	
W1	.4G **11**	
	(off Park St.)	
Fountain M. *N5*	.4C **66**	
	(off Highbury Grange)	
NW3	.6D **64**	
Fountain Park Way W12	.7E **80**	
Fountain Pl. SW9	.1A **120**	
Fountain Rd. CR7: Thor H	.3C **156**	
SW17	.5B **136**	
FOUNTAIN RDBT.	.4A **152**	

The Fountains *N3*	.7E **30**
	(off Ballards La.)
Fountains Av. TW13: Hanw	.3D **130**
Fountains Cl. TW13: Hanw	.2D **130**
	(not continuous)
Fountains Cres. N14	.7D **22**
Fountain Sq. SW1	.3K **17** (4F **101**)
Fountayne Bus. Cen. N15	.4G **49**
Fountayne Rd. N15	.4G **49**
N16	.2G **67**
Fount St. SW8	.7H **101**
Fouracre *NW1*	.2A **6**
	(off Stanhope St.)
Fouracre Path SE25	.6E **156**
Four Acres N12	.3E **30**
Fouracres EN3: Enf H	.1F **25**
Four Casson Sq. SE1	.5H **13** (1K **101**)
Fourland Wlk. HA8: Edg	.6D **28**
Fourlands Ter. E1	.5J **9** (5F **85**)
Fourscore Mans. *E8*	.7G **67**
	(off Shrubland Rd.)
Four Seasons Cl. E3	.2C **86**
Four Seasons Cres. SM3: Sutt	.2H **165**
Four Seasons Ter. UB7: W Dray	.2C **92**
Four Sq. Ct. TW3: Houn	.6E **112**
Fourth Av. E12	.4D **70**
RM7: Rush G	.1K **73**
UB3: Hayes	.1H **93**
W10	.4G **81**
Fourth Cross Rd. TW2: Twick	.2H **131**
Fourth Way HA9: Wemb	.4H **61**
The Four Wents E4	.1A **36**
Fovant Ct. SW8	.2G **119**
Fowey Av. IG4: Ilf	.5B **52**
Fowey Cl. E1	.1H **103**
Fowey Ho. SE11	.5K **19**
Fowey Pl. SM2: Sutt	.7J **165**
Fowler Cl. SW11	.3B **118**
Fowler Ho. *N15*	.5D **48**
	(off South Gro.)
Fowler Rd. CR4: Mitc	.2E **154**
E7	.4J **69**
N1	.1B **84**
Fowlers Cl. DA14: Sidc	.5E **144**
Fowlers M. *N19*	.2G **65**
	(off Holloway Rd.)
Fowler's Wlk. W5	.4D **78**
Fowler Way UB10: Uxb	.2A **74**
Fownes St. SW11	.3C **118**
Fox & Knot St. EC1	.5B **8**
Foxberry Rd. SE4	.3A **122**
Foxborough Gdns. SE4	.5C **122**
Foxbourne Rd. SW17	.2E **136**
Foxbury Av. BR7: Chst	.6H **143**
Foxbury Cl. BR1: Broml	.6K **141**
Foxbury Rd. BR1: Broml	.6J **141**
Fox Cl. BR6: Chels	.5K **173**
E1	.4J **85**
E16	.5J **87**
Foxcombe CR0: New Ad	.6D **170**
	(not continuous)
Foxcombe Cl. E6	.2B **88**
Foxcombe Rd. SW15	.1C **134**
Foxcote SE5	.5E **102**
Foxcroft *WC1*	.1H **7**
	(off Penton Ri.)
Foxcroft Rd. SE18	.1F **125**
Foxdene Cl. E18	.3K **51**
Foxearth Spur CR2: Sels	.7J **169**
Foxes Dale BR2: Broml	.3F **159**
SE3	.3J **123**
Foxfield *NW1*	.1F **83**
	(off Arlington Rd.)
Foxfield Rd. BR6: Orp	.2H **173**
Foxglove Cl. DA15: Sidc	.6A **126**
N9	.1D **34**
UB1: S'hall	.7C **76**
UB7: W Dray	.2A **92**
Foxglove Cl. *E3*	.2C **86**
	(off Four Seasons Cl.)
HA0: Wemb	.2E **78**
Foxglove Gdns. E11	.4A **52**
Foxglove La. KT9: Chess	.4G **163**

Foxglove Path *SE28*	.1J **107**
	(off Martins Pl.)
Foxglove Rd. RM7: Rush G	.2K **73**
Foxglove St. W12	.7B **80**
Foxglove Way SM6: W'gton	.1F **167**
Fox Gro. KT12: Walt T	.7K **147**
Foxgrove N14	.3D **32**
Foxgrove Av. BR3: Beck	.7D **140**
Foxgrove Rd. BR3: Beck	.7D **140**
Foxham Rd. N19	.3H **65**
Fox Hill SE19	.7F **139**
Fox Hill Gdns. SE19	.7F **139**
Foxhole Rd. SE9	.5C **124**
Fox Hollow Cl. SE18	.5J **107**
Fox Hollow Dr. DA7: Bex	.3D **126**
Foxholt Gdns. NW10	.7J **61**
Foxhome Cl. BR7: Chst	.6E **142**
Fox Ho. Rd. DA17: Belv	.5H **109**
	(not continuous)
Foxlands Cres. RM10: Dag	.5J **73**
Foxlands La. RM10: Dag	.5K **73**
Foxlands Rd. RM10: Dag	.5J **73**
Fox La. BR2: Kes	.5K **171**
N13	.2E **32**
W5	.4E **78**
Foxleas Ct. BR1: Broml	.7G **141**
Foxlees HA0: Wemb	.4A **60**
Foxley Cl. E8	.5G **67**
Foxley Ct. SM2: Sutt	.7A **166**
Foxley Ho. *E3*	.3D **86**
	(off Bow Rd.)
Foxley Mews N20	.2G **31**
Foxley Rd. CR7: Thor H	.4B **156**
SW9	.7A **102**
Foxley Sq. SW9	.7B **102**
Foxmead Cl. EN2: Enf	.3E **22**
Foxmore St. SW11	.1D **118**
Fox Rd. E16	.5H **87**
Fox's Path CR4: Mitc	.2C **154**
Fox's Yd. E2	.3K **9**
Foxton Gro. CR4: Mitc	.2B **154**
Foxton Ho. *E16*	.2E **106**
	(off Albert Rd.)
Foxton M. TW10: Rich	.6E **114**
Foxton Way SM3: Sutt	.1J **165**
Foxwarren KT10: Clay	.7A **162**
Foxwell M. SE4	.3A **122**
Foxwell St. SE4	.3A **122**
Foxwood Cl. NW7	.4F **29**
TW13: Felt	.3K **129**
Foxwood Grn. Cl. EN1: Enf	.6K **23**
Fox Wood Nature Reserve	.4E **78**
Foxwood Rd. SE3	.4H **123**
Foyle Rd. N17	.1G **49**
SE3	.6H **105**
Framfield Cl. N12	.3D **30**
Framfield Ct. *EN1: Enf*	.6K **23**
	(off Queen Anne's Gdns.)
Framfield Rd. CR4: Mitc	.7E **136**
N5	.5B **66**
W7	.6J **77**
Framlingham Cl. E5	.2J **67**
Framlingham Ct. *RM6: Chad H*	.5B **54**
	(off Norwich Cres.)
Framlingham Cres. SE9	.4C **142**
Frampton *NW1*	.7H **65**
	(off Wrotham Rd.)
Frampton Cl. IG6: Ilf	.4H **53**
SM2: Sutt	.7J **165**
Frampton Ct. *W3*	.2J **97**
	(off Avenue Rd.)
Frampton Ho. *NW8*	.4B **4**
	(off Frampton St.)
Frampton Pk. Est. E9	.7J **67**
Frampton Pk. Rd. E9	.6J **67**
Frampton Rd.	
TW4: Houn	.5C **112**
Frampton St. NW8	.4B **4** (4B **82**)
Frampton Ter. SE9	.3F **143**
Francemary Rd. SE4	.5C **122**
Frances Cl. E17	.6C **50**
SE25	.3F **157**
Frances Rd. E4	.6H **35**

Frances St. SE18	.3D **106**
Frances Wharf E14	.6B **86**
Franche Ct. Rd. SW17	.3A **136**
Francis & Dick James Cl. NW7	.7B **30**
Francis Av. DA7: Bex	.2G **127**
IG1: Ilf	.2H **71**
TW13: Felt	.3J **129**
Francis Bacon Ct. *SE16*	.4H **103**
	(off Galleywall Rd.)
Francis Barber Cl. SW16	.5K **137**
Francis Bentley M. SW4	.3G **119**
Franciscan Rd. SW17	.5D **136**
Francis Chichester Way SW11	.1E **118**
Francis Cl. E14	.4F **105**
KT19: Ewe	.4K **163**
TW17: Shep	.4C **146**
Francis Ct. EC1	.5A **8**
KT5: Surb	.4E **150**
	(off Cranes Pk. Av.)
NW7	.5G **29**
	(off Watford Way)
SE14	.6K **103**
	(off Myers La.)
Francis Gro. SW19	.6H **135**
Francis Harvey Way SE8	.1B **122**
Francis Ho. *N1*	.1E **84**
	(off Colville Est.)
SW10	.7K **99**
	(off Coleridge Gdns.)
SW18	.4A **118**
	(off Eltringham St.)
Francis M. SE12	.7J **123**
Francis Pl. *N6*	.7F **47**
	(off Shepherd's Cl.)
Francis Rd. CR0: C'don	.7B **156**
E10	.1E **68**
HA1: Harr	.5A **42**
HA5: Eastc	.5A **40**
IG1: Ilf	.2H **71**
N2	.4D **46**
SM6: W'gton	.6G **167**
TW4: Houn	.2B **112**
UB6: G'frd	.2B **78**
Francis St. E15	.5G **69**
IG1: Ilf	.2H **71**
SW1	.3A **18** (4G **101**)
Francis Ter. N19	.3G **65**
Francis Ter. M. N19	.3G **65**
Francis Wlk. N1	.1K **83**
Franck House *EC1*	.2B **8**
	(off Goswell Road)
Francklyn Gdns. HA8: Edg	.3B **28**
Franco Av. NW9	.1B **44**
Franconia Rd. SW4	.5H **119**
Frank Bailey Wlk. E12	.6E **70**
Frank Beswick Ho. *SW6*	.6H **99**
	(off Clem Attlee Ct.)
Frank Burton Cl. SE7	.5K **105**
Frank Dixon Cl. SE21	.7E **120**
Frank Dixon Way SE21	.1E **138**
Frankfurt Rd. SE24	.5C **120**
Frank Godley Ct. DA14: Sidc	.5B **144**
Frankham Ho. *SE8*	.7C **104**
	(off Frankham St.)
Frankham St. SE8	.7C **104**
Frank Ho. *SW8*	.7J **101**
	(off Wyvil Rd.)
Frankland Cl. IG8: Wfd G	.5F **37**
SE16	.3H **103**
Frankland Rd. E4	.5H **35**
SW7	.2A **16** (3B **100**)
Franklin Bldg. E14	.2C **104**
Franklin Cl. KT1: King T	.3G **151**
N20	.7F **21**
SE13	.1D **122**
SE27	.3B **138**
Franklin Cotts. HA7: Stan	.4G **27**
Franklin Cres. CR4: Mitc	.4G **155**
Franklin Ho. BR2: Broml	.3G **159**
E1	.1H **103**
	(off Watts St.)
E14	.6F **87**
	(off E. India Dock Rd.)

Franklin Ho. NW6 . . . . .3J 81
(off Carlton Va.)
Franklin Ind. Est. SE20 . . . . .1J 157
(off Franklin Rd.)
Franklin Pas. SE9 . . . . .3C 124
Franklin Pl. SE13 . . . . .1D 122
Franklin Rd. DA7: Bex 1E 126
SE20 . . . . .7J 139
Franklins M. HA2: Harr 2G 59
Franklin Sq. W14 . . . . .5H 99
Franklin's Row SW3 . . . .5F 17 (5D 100)
Franklin St. E3 . . . . .3D 86
N15 . . . . .6E 48
Franklin Way CRO: Wadd 7J 155
Franklyn Rd. KT12: Walt T 6J 147
NW10 . . . . .6B 62
Frank M. SE1 . . . . .4H 103
Franks Av. KT3: N Mald 4J 151
Frank Soskice Ho. SW6 . . . . .6H 99
(off Clem Attlee Ct.)
Frank St. E13 . . . . .4J 87
Frankswood Av. BR5: Pet W 5F 161
UB7: Yiew 6B 74
Frank Towell Ct. TW14: Felt 7J 111
Frank Whipple Pl. E14 . . . . .6A 86
(off Repton St.)
Frank Whymark Ho. SE16 . . . . . . .2J 103
(off Rupack St.)
Franlaw Cres. N13 . . . . .4H 33
Fransfield Gro. SE26 . . . . .3H 139
Frans Hals Ct. E14 . . . . .3F 105
Franshams WD23: B Hea 2D 26
(off Hartsbourne Rd.)
Frant Cl. SE20 . . . . .7J 139
Franthorne Way SE6 . . . . .2D 140
Frant Rd. CR7: Thor H 5B 156
Fraserburgh Ho. E3 . . . . .2B 86
(off Vernon Rd.)
Fraser Cl. DA5: Bexl 1J 145
E6 . . . . .6C 88
Fraser Ct. E14 . . . . .5E 104
(off Ferry St.)
SE1 . . . . .7D 14
SW11 . . . . .1C 118
(off Surrey La. Est.)
Fraser Ho. TW8: Bford 5F 97
Fraser Rd. DA8: Erith 5K 109
E17 . . . . .5D 50
N9 . . . . .3C 34
UB6: G'frd 1B 78
Fraser St. W4 . . . . .5A 98
Frating Cres. IG8: Wfd G 6E 36
Frazer Av. HA4: Ruis 5A 58
Frazer Nash Cl. TW7: Isle 1K 113
Frazier St. SE1 . . . . . .7J 13 (2A 102)
Frean St. SE16 . . . . .3G 103
Frearson Ho. WC1 . . . . .1H 7
(off Penton Ri.)
Freda Corbett Cl. SE15 . . . . .7G 103
Freda St. SE16 . . . . . . .7K 15 (3G 103)
Frederica Ct. SW2 . . . . .1B 138
Frederica Rd. E4 . . . . .1A 36
Frederica St. N7 . . . . .7K 65
Frederick Charrington Ho. E1 . . . .4J 85
(off Wickford St.)
Frederick Cl. SM1: Sutt 4H 165
W2 . . . . .2D 10 (7D 82)
Frederick Cl. SW3 . . . . .4F 17
(off Duke of York Sq.)
Frederick Cres. EN3: Enf H 2D 24
SW9 . . . . .7B 102
Frederick Dobson Ho. W11 . . . . . .7G 81
(off Cowling Cl.)
Frederick Gdns. CRO. C'don 6B 156
SM1: Sutt 5H 165
Frederick Ho. SE18 . . . . .4C 106
(off Pett St.)
Frederick Pl. N8 . . . . .6H 47
(off Crouch Hall Rd.)
SE18 . . . . .5F 107
Frederick Rd. RM13: Rain 2K 91
SE17 . . . . .6B 102
SM1: Sutt 5H 165

Frederick's Pl. EC2 . . . . .1E 14 (6D 84)
Fredericks Pl. N12 . . . . .4F 31
Frederick Sq. SE16 . . . . .7A 86
(off Sovereign Cres.)
Frederick's Row EC1 . . . . .1A 8 (3B 84)
Frederick St. WC1 . . . . . .2G 7 (3K 83)
Frederick Ter. E8 . . . . .7F 67
Frederick Vs. W7 . . . . .1J 95
(off Lwr. Boston Rd.)
Frederic M. SW1 . . . . .7F 11
Frederic St. E17 . . . . .5A 50
Fredora Av. UB4: Hayes 4H 75
Fred Styles Ho. SE7 . . . . .6A 106
Fred Tibble Ct. RM9: Dag 4E 72
Fred White Wlk. N7 . . . . .6J 65
Freedom Cl. E17 . . . . .4A 50
Freedom Rd. N17 . . . . .2D 48
Freedom St. SW11 . . . . .2D 118
Freegrove Rd. N7 . . . . .5J 65
(not continuous)
Freehold Ind. Cen. TW4: Houn . . .5A 112
Freeland Ct. DA15: Sidc 3A 144
Freeland Pk. NW4 . . . . .2G 45
Freeland Rd. W5 . . . . .7F 79
Freelands Av. CR2: Sels 7K 169
Freelands Gro. BR1: Broml 1K 159
Freelands Rd. BR1: Broml 1K 159
Freeling Ho. NW8 . . . . .1B 82
(off Dorman Way)
Freeling St. N1 . . . . .7K 65
(Carnoustie Dr.)
N1 . . . . .7J 65
(Pembroke St.)
Freeman Cl. TW17: Shep 4G 147
UB5: N'olt 7C 58
Freeman Ct. N7 . . . . .3J 65
SW16 . . . . .2J 155
Freeman Dr. KT8: W Mole 3D 148
Freeman Ho. SE11 . . . . .4B 102
(off George Mathers Rd.)
Freeman Rd. SM4: Mord 5B 154
Freemans La. UB3: Hayes 7G 75
Freemantle Av. EN3: Pond E 5E 24
Freemantle St. SE17 . . . . .5E 102
Freeman Wlk. SE9 . . . . .5A 124
Freemasons' Hall 7F 7
Freemasons Pl. CRO: C'don 1E 168
(off Freemasons Rd.)
Freemasons Rd. CRO: C'don 1E 168
E16 . . . . .5K 87
Freesia Cl. BR6: Chels 5K 173
Freethorpe Cl. SE19 . . . . .7D 138
Free Trade Wharf E1 . . . . .7K 85
Freezeland Way UB10: Hil 6D 56
Freight La. N1 . . . . .1H 65
Freightliners City Farm 6A 66
Freke Rd. SW11 . . . . .3E 118
Fremantle Ho. E1 . . . . .4H 85
(off Somerford St.)
Fremantle Rd. DA17: Belv 4G 109
IG6: Ilf 2F 53
Fremantle Way UB3: Hayes 7H 75
Fremont St. E9 . . . . .1H 85
(not continuous)
French Horn Yd. WC1 . . . . .6G 7
French Ordinary Ct. EC3 . . . . .2H 15
French Pl. E1 . . . . .2H 9 (3E 84)
French St. TW16: Sun 2A 148
Frendsbury Rd. SE4 . . . . .4A 122
Frensham Cl. UB1: S'hall 4D 76
Frensham Ct. SW19 . . . . .3A 154
Frensham Dr. CRO: New Ad 7E 170
SW15 . . . . .3B 134
Frensham Rd. SE9 . . . . .2H 143
Frensham St. SE15 . . . . .6G 103
Frere St. SW11 . . . . .2C 118
Fresham Ho. BR2: Broml 3H 159
(off Durham Rd.)
Freshfield Av. E8 . . . . .7F 67
Freshfield Cl. SE13 . . . . .4F 123
Freshfield Dr. N14 . . . . .7A 22
Freshfields CRO: C'don 1B 170
Freshford St. SW18 . . . . .3A 136

Fresh Mill La. UB1: S'hall 4E 76
Freshwater Cl. SW17 . . . . .6E 136
Freshwater Ct. UB1: S'hall 3E 76
W1 . . . . .6D 4
(off Crawford St.)
Freshwater Rd. RM8: Dag 1D 72
SW17 . . . . .6E 136
Freshwell Av. RM6: Chad H 4C 54
Fresh Wharf Est. IG11: Bark 2F 89
Fresh Wharf Rd. IG11: Bark 1F 89
Freshwood Cl. BR3: Beck 1D 158
Freshwood Way SM6: W'gton 7F 167
Freston Gdns. EN4: Cockf 5K 21
Freston Pk. N3 . . . . .2H 45
Freston Rd. W10 . . . . .7F 81
W11 . . . . .7F 81
Freswick Ho. SE8 . . . . .4A 104
(off Chilton Gro.)
Freta Rd. DA6: Bex 5F 127
Freud Mus. .6A 64
Frewell Ho. EC1 . . . . .5J 7
(off Bourne Est.)
Frewin Rd. SW18 . . . . .1B 136
Friar M. SE27 . . . . .3B 138
Friar Rd. BR5: St M Cry 5K 161
EN2: Enf .1F 23
UB4: Yead 4B 76
Friars Av. N20 . . . . .3H 31
SW15 . . . . .3B 134
Friars Cl. E4 . . . . .3K 35
IG1: Ilf 1H 71
SE1 . . . . .5B 14
UB5: N'olt 3B 76
Friars Ct. E17 . . . . .1B 50
RM7: Rush G 6K 55
SM6: W'gton 4F 167
Friars Gdns. W3 . . . . .6K 79
Friarsgate NW10 . . . . .2H 79
Friars Ga. Cl. IG8: Wfd G 4D 36
Friars La. TW9: Rich 5D 114
Friars Mead E14 . . . . .3E 104
Friars M. SE9 . . . . .5E 124
Friars Mt. Ho. E2 . . . . .2J 9
(off Rochelle St.)
Friars Pl. La. W3 . . . . .7K 79
Friars Rd. E6 . . . . .1B 88
Friars Stile Pl. TW10: Rich 6E 114
Friars Stile Rd. TW10: Rich 6E 114
Friar St. EC4 . . . . .1B 14 (6B 84)
Friars Wlk. N14 . . . . .7A 22
SE2 . . . . .5D 108
Friars Way W3 . . . . .6K 79
Friars Wood CRO: Sels 7A 170
Friary Cl. N12 . . . . .5H 31
Friary Ct. SW1 . . . . .5B 12
Friary Est. SE15 . . . . .6G 103
(not continuous)
Friary La. IG8: Wfd G 4D 36
Friary Pk. W3 . . . . .6K 79
Friary Pk. Ct. W3 . . . . .6J 79
Friary Rd. N12 . . . . .4G 31
N20 . . . . .4G 31
SE15 . . . . .7G 103
W3 . . . . .6J 79
Friary Way N12 . . . . .4H 31
FRIDAY HILL 2B 36
Friday Hill E4 . . . . .2B 36
Friday Hill E. E4 . . . . .3B 36
Friday Hill W. E4 . . . . .2B 36
Friday Rd. CR4: Mitc 7D 136
DA8: Erith 5B 110
Friday St. EC4 . . . . .2C 14 (7C 84)
Frideswide Pl. NW5 . . . . .5G 65
Friendly Pl. SE13 . . . . .1D 122
Friendly St. SE8 . . . . .2C 122
Friendly St. M. SE8 . . . . .2C 122
Friendship Ho. SE1 . . . . .7B 14
(off Belvedere Pl.)
Friendship Wlk. UB5: N'olt 3B 76
Friendship Way E15 . . . . .1E 86
Friends Rd. CRO: C'don 3D 168
Friend St. EC1 . . . . .1A 8 (3B 84)
FRIERN BARNET 5J 31

Friern Barnet La. N11 . . . . .2G 31
N20 . . . . .2G 31
Friern Barnet Rd. N11 . . . . .5J 31
Friern Bri. Retail Pk. 6A 32
Friern Ct. N20 . . . . .3G 31
Friern Mt. Dr. N20 . . . . .7F 21
Friern Pk. N12 . . . . .5F 31
Friern Rd. SE22 . . . . .7G 121
(not continuous)
Friern Watch Av. N12 . . . . .4F 31
Frigate Ho. E14 . . . . .4E 104
(off Stebondale St.)
Frigate M. SE8 . . . . .6C 104
Frimley Av. SM6: W'gton 5J 167
Frimley Cl. CRO: New Ad 7E 170
SW19 . . . . .2G 135
Frimley Ct. DA14: Sidc 5C 144
Frimley Cres. CRO: New Ad 7E 170
Frimley Gdns. CR4: Mitc 3C 154
Frimley Rd. IG3: Ilf 3J 71
KT9: Chess 5D 162
Frimley St. E1 . . . . .4K 85
(off Frimley Way)
Frimley Way E1 . . . . .4K 85
Fringewood Cl. HA6: Nwood 1D 38
Frinstead Ho. W10 . . . . .7F 81
(off Freston Rd.)
Frinsted Rd. DA8: Erith 7K 109
Frinton Cl. W13 . . . . .5B 78
(off Hardwick Grn.)
Frinton Dr. IG8: Wfd G 7A 36
Frinton M. IG2: Ilf 6E 52
Frinton Rd. DA14: Sidc 2E 144
E6 . . . . .3B 88
N15 . . . . .6E 48
SW17 . . . . .6E 136
Friston St. SW6 . . . . .2K 117
Friswell Pl. DA6: Bex 4G 127
Fritham Cl. KT3: N Mald 6A 152
Frith Ct. NW7 . . . . .7B 30
Frith Ho. NW8 . . . . .4B 4
(off Frampton St.)
Frith La. NW7 . . . . .7B 30
Frith Rd. CRO: C'don 2C 168
E11 . . . . .4E 68
Frith St. W1 . . . . .1C 12 (6H 83)
Frithville Ct. W12 . . . . .1E 98
(off Frithville Gdns.)
Frithville Gdns. W12 . . . . .1E 98
Frizlands La. RM10: Dag 2H 73
Frobisher Cl. HA5: Pinn 7B 40
Frobisher Ct. NW9 . . . . .2A 44
SE8 . . . . .5A 104
(off Evelyn St.)
SE10 . . . . .6F 105
(off Old Woolwich Rd.)
SE23 . . . . .2H 139
SM3: Cheam 7G 165
W12 . . . . .2E 98
(off Lime Gro.)
Frobisher Cres. EC2 . . . . .5D 8
(off Silk St.)
TW19: Stanw 7A 110
Frobisher Gdns. E10 . . . . .7D 50
TW19: Stanw 7A 110
Frobisher Ho. E1 . . . . .1H 103
(off Watts St.)
SW1 . . . . .7C 18
(off Dolphin Sq.)
Frobisher M. EN2: Enf 4J 23
Frobisher Pas. E14 . . . . .1C 104
Frobisher Pl. SE15 . . . . .1J 121
Frobisher Rd. E6 . . . . .6D 88
N8 . . . . .4A 48
Frobisher St. SE10 . . . . .6G 105
Frobisher Yd. E16 . . . . .7G 89
Froebel College 6B 116
Frog La. RM13: Rain 6K 91
Frogley Rd. SE22 . . . . .4F 121
Frogmore SW18 . . . . .5J 117
Frogmore Av. UB4: Hayes 4G 75
Frogmore Cl. SM3: Cheam 3F 165
Frogmore Ct. UB2: S'hall 4D 94

Frogmore Gdns.—Gaisford St.

Frogmore Gdns. SM3: Cheam 4G 165
UB4: Hayes 4G 75
Frogmore Ind. Est. N5 5C 66
NW10 3J 79
UB3: Hayes 2G 93
Frognal NW3 4A 64
Frognal Av. DA14: Sidc 6A 144
HA1: Harr 4K 41
Frognal Cl. NW3 5A 64
FROGNAL CORNER 6K 143
Frognal Ct. NW3 6A 64
Frognal Gdns. NW3 4A 64
Frognal La. NW3 5K 63
Frognal Pde. NW3 6A 64
Frognal Pl. DA14: Sidc 6A 144
Frognal Ri. NW3 3A 64
Frognal Way NW3 4A 64
Frogwell Cl. N15 6D 48
Froissart Rd. SE9 5B 124
Frome Ho. SE15 4H 121
Frome Rd. N22 3B 48
Frome St. N1 2C 84
Fromondes Rd. SM3: Cheam 5G 165
Fromows Cnr. W4 5J 97
Frontenac NW10 7D 62
Frontier Works N17 6K 33
Frost Ct. NW9 2A 44
(off Salk Cl.)
Frostic Wlk. E1 6K 9 (5G 85)
Froude St. SW8 2F 119
Fruen Rd. TW14: Felt 7H 111
Fryatt Rd. N17 7J 33
(not continuous)
Fryday Gro. M. SW12 7G 119
(off Weir Rd.)
Frye Ct. E3 3B 86
(off Benworth St.)
Frye Ho. E20 6E 68
(off Penny Brookes St.)
Fryent Cl. NW9 6G 43
Fryent Country Park 7G 43
Fryent Cres. NW9 6A 44
Fryent Flds. NW9 6A 44
Fryent Gro. NW9 6A 44
Fryent Way NW9 5G 43
Fryers Vw. SE4 4K 121
(off Frendsbury Rd.)
Fry Ho. E6 7A 70
Frying Pan All. E1 6J 9
Fry La. HA8: Edg 4A 28
Fry Rd. E6 7B 70
NW10 1B 80
Frys Ct. SE10 6E 104
(off Durnford St.)
Fryston Av. CR0: C'don 2G 169
Fuchsia Cl. RM7: Rush G 2K 73
Fuchsia St. SE2 5B 108
Fulbeck Dr. NW9 1A 44
Fulbeck Ho. N7 6K 65
(off Sutterton St.)
Fulbeck Rd. N19 4G 65
Fulbeck Wlk. HA8: Edg 2C 28
Fulbeck Way HA2: Harr 2G 41
Fulbourn KT1: King T 2G 151
(off Eureka Rd.)
Fulbourne Rd. E17 1E 50
Fulbourne St. E1 5H 85
Fulbrook M. N19 4G 65
Fulcher Ho. N1 1E 84
(off Colville Est.)
SE8 5B 104
Fulford Ho. KT19: Ewe 7K 163
Fulford Rd. KT19: Ewe 7K 163
Fulford St. SE16 2H 103
FULHAM 1G 117
FULHAM BROADWAY 7J 99
Fulham B'way. SW6 7J 99
Fulham B'way. Shop. Cen. 7J 99
Fulham Bus. Exchange SW6 1A 118
(off The Boulevard)
Fulham Cl. UB10: Hil 4E 74
Fulham Ct. SW6 1J 117
Fulham FC 1F 117
Fulham High St. SW6 2G 117
Fulham Island SW6 7J 99
(off Farm La.)
Fulham Palace 2G 117
Fulham Pal. Rd. SW6 5E 98
W6 5E 98
Fulham Pk. Gdns. SW6 2H 117
Fulham Pk. Rd. SW6 2H 117
Fulham Pools 6G 99
Fulham Rd. SW3 7A 16 (7K 99)
SW6 2G 117
(not continuous)
SW10 7A 16 (7K 99)
Fullbrooks Av. KT4: Wor Pk 1B 164
Fuller Cl. BR6: Chels 5K 173
E2 4G 85
(off Cheshire St.)
WD23: Bush 1C 26
Fuller Ct. N8 5H 47
Fuller Rd. RM8: Dag 3B 72
Fullers Av. IG8: Wfd G 7C 36
KT6: Surb 2F 163
Fullers Cl. RM5: Col R 1J 55
Fuller's Griffin Brewery 6B 98
Fullers La. RM5: Col R 1J 55
Fullers Rd. E18 7C 36
Fuller St. NW4 4E 44
Fullers Way Nth. KT6: Surb 3F 163
Fullers Way Sth. KT9: Chess 4E 162
Fuller's Wood CR0: C'don 5C 170
Fullerton Av. RM8: Dag 1E 72
Fullerton Ct. TW11: Tedd 6A 132
Fullerton Rd. CR0: C'don 7F 157
SM5: Cars 7C 166
SW18 5K 117
Fuller Way UB3: Harl 5H 93
Fullwell Av. IG5: Ilf 1D 52
IG6: Ilf 1F 53
FULLWELL CROSS 2G 53
FULLWELL CROSS 2H 53
Fullwell Cross Leisure Cen. 2G 53
Fullwell Pde. IG5: Ilf 1E 52
Fullwood's M. N1 1F 9 (3D 84)
Fulmar Cl. KT5: Surb 6F 151
Fulmar Ho. SE16 4K 103
(off Tawny Way)
Fulmead St. SW6 1K 117
Fulmer Cl. TW12: Hamp 5C 130
Fulmer Ho. NW8 4D 4
(off Mallory St.)
UB8: Uxb 6A 56
Fulmer Rd. E16 5B 88
Fulmer Way W13 3B 96
Fulneck Pl. E1 4J 85
Fulready Rd. E10 5F 51
Fulstone Cl. TW4: Houn 4D 112
Fulthorp Rd. SE3 2H 123
Fulton M. W2 7A 82
Fulton Rd. HA9: Wemb 3G 61
FULWELL 4H 131
Fulwell Ct. IG5: Ilf 1E 52
UB1: S'hall 7G 77
(off Baird Av.)
Fulwell Golf Course 4H 131
Fulwell Pk. Av. TW2: Twick 2F 131
Fulwell Rd. TW11: Tedd 4H 131
Fulwood Av. HA0: Wemb 2F 79
Fulwood Cl. UB3: Hayes 6H 75
Fulwood Ct. HA3: Kenton 6A 42
Fulwood Gdns. TW1: Twick 6K 113
Fulwood Pl. WC1 6H 7 (5K 83)
Fulwood Wlk. SW19 1G 135
Funky Footprints Nature Reserve 6C 146
Furber St. W6 3D 98
Furham Feild HA5: Hat E 7A 26
Furley Ho. SE15 7G 103
(off Peckham Pk. Rd.)
Furley Rd. SE15 7G 103
Furlong Av. CR4: Mitc 3C 154
Furlong Cl. CR0: C'don 1H 169
SM6: W'gton 1F 167
Furlong Rd. N7 6A 66
Furlow Ho. NW9 3C 44
Furmage St. SW18 7K 117
Furneaux Av. SE27 5B 138
Furness Ho. SW1 5J 17
(part of Abbots Mnr.)
Furness Rd. HA2: Harr 7F 41
NW10 2C 80
SM4: Mord 6K 153
SW6 2K 117
Furnival Ct. E3 2C 86
(off Four Seasons Cl.)
Furnival Mans. W1 6A 6
(off Wells St.)
Furnival St. EC4 7J 7 (6A 84)
Furrow Ho. E4 6K 35
Furrow La. E9 5J 67
Fursby Av. N3 6D 30
Fursecroft W1 7E 4
Furtherfield Cl. CR0: C'don 6A 156
Further Grn. Rd. SE6 7G 123
FURZEDOWN 5F 137
Furzedown Dr. SW17 5F 137
Furzedown Recreation Cen. 5F 137
Furzedown Rd. SW17 5F 137
Furze Farm Cl. RM6: Chad H 2E 54
Furzefield Cl. BR7: Chst 6F 143
Furzefield Rd. SE3 6K 105
Furzeground Way UB11: Stock P 1E 92
Furzeham Rd. UB7: W Dray 2A 92
Furze Rd. CR7: Thor H 3C 156
Furze St. E3 5C 86
Furzewood TW16: Sun 1J 147
The Fusilier Museum 7F 85
Fusiliers Way TW4: Houn 3A 112
(not continuous)
Fusion Apts. SE14 6A 104
(off Moulding La.)
Fye Foot La. EC4 2C 14
(off Queen Victoria St.)
Fyfe Apts. N8 3K 47
Fyfe Way BR1: Broml 2J 159
Fyfield N4 2A 66
(off Six Acres Est.)
Fyfield Cl. BR2: Broml 4F 159
Fyfield Ct. E7 6J 69
Fyfield Ho. E6 1C 88
(off Ron Leighton Way)
Fyfield Rd. E17 3F 51
EN1: Enf 3K 23
IG8: Wfd G 7F 37
SW9 3A 120
Fynes St. SW1 3C 18 (4H 101)

G

Gable Cl. HA5: Hat E 1E 40
Gable Ct. SE26 4H 139
Gable M. BR2: Broml 2C 172
The Gables BR1: Broml 7K 141
HA9: Wemb 3G 61
IG11: Bark 6G 71
N10 3E 46
(off Fortis Grn.)
Gables Av. TW15: Ashf 5B 128
Gables Cl. SE5 1E 120
SE12 1J 141
Gables Lodge EN4: Had W 1F 21
Gabriel Cl. TW13: Hanw 4C 130
Gabriel Ct. E1 5A 86
(off Elsa Street)
NW9 2A 44
Gabriel Ho. N1 1B 84
(off Islington Grn.)
SE11 3G 19 (4K 101)
SE16 3B 104
(off Odessa St.)
Gabrielle Cl. HA9: Wemb 3F 61
Gabrielle Ct. NW3 6B 64
Gabriel M. NW2 2H 63
Gabriel's M. BR3: Beck 1K 157
Gabriel St. SE23 7K 121
Gabriels Wharf SE1 4J 13 (1A 102)
Gad Cl. E13 3K 87
Gaddesden Av. HA9: Wemb 6F 61
Gaddesden Ho. EC1 2F 9
(off Cranwood St.)
Gadebridge Ho. SW3 5C 16
(off Cale St.)
Gade Cl. UB3: Hayes 1K 93
Gadesden Rd. KT19: Ewe 6J 163
Gadsbury Cl. NW9 6B 44
Gadsden Ho. W10 4G 81
(off Hazlewood Cres.)
Gadwall Cl. E16 6K 87
Gadwall Ho. NW9 6C 44
(off Perryfield Way)
Gadwall Way SE28 2H 107
Gage Brown Ho. W10 6F 81
(off Bridge Cl.)
Gage M. CR2: S Croy 5B 168
Gage Rd. E16 5G 87
Gage St. WC1 5F 7 (5J 83)
Gainford Ho. E2 3H 85
(off Ellsworth St.)
Gainford St. N1 1A 84
Gainsboro Gdns. UB6: G'frd 5J 59
Gainsborough Av. E12 5E 70
Gainsborough Cl. BR3: Beck 7C 140
KT10: Esh 7J 149
Gainsborough Ct. BR2: Broml 4A 160
KT19: Ewe 6B 164
N12 5E 30
SE16 5H 103
(off Stubbs Dr.)
SE21 2E 138
W4 5H 97
(off Chaseley Dr.)
W12 2E 98
Gainsborough Gdns. HA8: Edg 2F 43
NW3 3B 64
NW11 7H 45
TW7: Isle 5H 113
Gainsborough Ho. E14 2C 104
(off Cassilis Rd.)
E14 7A 86
(off Victory Pl.)
EN1: Enf 5B 24
RM8: Dag 4B 72
(off Longbridge Rd.)
SW1 4D 18
(off Erasmus St.)
Gainsborough Lodge HA1: Harr 5K 41
(off Hindes Rd.)
Gainsborough Mans. W14 6G 99
(off Queen's Club Gdns.)
Gainsborough M. SE26 3H 139
Gainsborough Rd. E11 7G 51
E15 3G 87
IG8: Wfd G 6H 37
KT3: N Mald 6K 151
N12 5E 30
RM8: Dag 4B 72
TW9: Rich 2F 115
UB4: Hayes 2E 74
W4 4B 98
Gainsborough Sq. DA6: Bex 3D 126
Gainsborough St. E9 6B 68
Gainsborough Studios E. N1 1D 84
(off Poole St.)
Gainsborough Studios Nth. N1 1D 84
(off Poole St.)
Gainsborough Studios Sth. N1 1D 84
(off Poole St.)
Gainsborough Studios W. N1 1D 84
(off Poole St.)
Gainsborough Ter. SM2: Sutt 7H 165
(off Belmont Ri.)
Gainsborough Twr. UB5: N'olt 2B 76
(off Academy Gdns.)
Gainsfield Ct. E11 3G 69
Gainsford Rd. E17 4B 50
Gainsford St. SE1 6J 15 (2F 103)
Gairloch Ho. NW1 7H 65
(off Stratford Vs.)
Gairloch Rd. SE5 2E 120
Gaisford St. NW5 6G 65

Gaitskell Ct. SW11 . . . . .2C 118
Gaitskell Ho. E6 . . . . .1B 88
  E17 . . . . .3D 50
  SE17 .6E 102
                    (off Villa St.)
Gaitskell Rd. SE9 . . . . .1G 143
Gaitskell Way SE1 . . . . .6C 14
                  (off Weller St.)
Gala Bingo
  Surrey Quays 3K 103
  Tooting 5C 136
Gala Ct. CR7: Thor H 5A 156
Galahad M. E3 . . . . .2B 86
Galahad Rd. BR1: Broml 4J 141
  N9 . . . . .3B 34
Galata Rd. SW13 . . . . .7C 98
Galatea Sq. SE15 . . . . .3H 121
Galaxy Bldg. E14 . . . . .4C 104
                (off Crews St.)
Galaxy Ho. EC2 . . . . .3F 9
               (off Leonard St.)
Galba Ct. TW8: Bford 7D 96
Galbraith St. E14 . . . . .3E 104
Galdana Av. EN5: New Bar 3F 21
Galeborough Av. IG8: Wfd G 7A 36
Gale Cl. CR4: Mitc 3B 154
  TW12: Hamp 6C 130
Galena Arches W6 . . . . .4D 98
              (off Galena Rd.)
Galena Hgts. E20 . . . . .6E 68
            (off Mirabelle Gdns.)
Galena Ho. SE18 . . . . .5K 107
            (off Grosmont Rd.)
Galena Rd. W6 . . . . .4D 98
Galen Pl. WC1 . . . . .6F 7 (5J 83)
Galesbury Rd. SW18 . . . . .6A 118
Gales Gdns. E2 . . . . .3H 85
Gale St. E3 . . . . .5C 86
  RM9: Dag 5C 72
Gales Way IG8: Wfd G 7H 37
Galgate Cl. SW19 . . . . .1F 135
Gallants Farm Rd. EN4: E Barn . . .7H 21
Galleon Cl. DA8: Erith 4K 109
  SE16 . . . . .2K 103
Galleon Ho. E14 . . . . .4E 104
           (off Glengarnock Av.)
Galleons Dr. IG11: Bark 3A 90
Galleons Vw. E14 . . . . .2E 104
Galleria Ct. SE15 . . . . .6F 103
The Galleria Shop. Mall 2J 51
The Galleries NW8 . . . . .1A 4
            (off Abbey Rd.)
The Gallery 1G 89
          (off Clockhouse Av.)
The Gallery E20 . . . . .6E 68
        (within Westfield Shop. Cen.)
  SE14 . . . . .7B 104
           (off New Cross Rd.)
Gallery Apts. E1 . . . . .6J 85
           (off Commercial Rd.)
  SE1 .7G 15
           (off Lamb Wlk.)
The Gallery at London Glassblowing
  . . . . .6G 15
Gallery By The Pool 3J 103
Gallery Ct. E17 . . . . .2E 50
           (off Fulbourne Rd.)
  SE1 .7E 14
           (off Pilgrimage St.)
  SW10 . . . . .6A 100
           (off Gunter Gro.)
Gallery Gdns. UB5: N'olt 2B 76
Gallery Ho. E8 . . . . .6H 67
           (off Hackney Rd.)
Gallery Rd. SE21 . . . . .1D 138
The Galley E16 . . . . .7F 89
Galleymead Rd. SL3: Poyle 4A 174
Galleywall Rd. SE16 . . . . .4H 103
Galleywall Rd. Trad. Est. SE16 . . .4H 103
Galleywood Ho. W10 . . . . .5E 80
           (off Sutton Way)
Galliard Cl. N9 . . . . .6D 24
Galliard Ct. N9 . . . . .6B 24

Galliard Rd. N9 . . . . .1B 34
Galia Rd. N5 . . . . .5B 66
Gallica Ct. SM1: Sutt 1K 165
Gallions Cl. IG11: Bark 3A 90
Gallions Reach Shop. Pk. E6 . . . . .5G 89
Gallions Rd. E16 . . . . .7F 89
  SE7 . . . . .4K 105
           (not continuous)
GALLIONS RDBT. 7F 89
Gallions Vw. Rd. SE28 . . . . .2J 107
Gallipoli Pl. RM9: Dag 1B 90
Gallon Cl. SE7 . . . . .4A 106
Gallosson Rd. SE18 . . . . .4J 107
Galloway Path CR0: C'don 4D 168
Galloway Rd. W12 . . . . .1C 98
Gallus Cl. N21 . . . . .6E 22
Gallus Sq. SE3 . . . . .3K 123
Galpins Rd. CR7: Thor H 5J 155
Galsworthy Av. E14 . . . . .6A 86
  RM6: Chad H 7B 54
Galsworthy Cl. NW2 . . . . .4G 63
  SE28 . . . . .1B 108
Galsworthy Cres. SE3 . . . . .7A 106
Galsworthy Ho. W11 . . . . .6G 81
           (off Elgin Cres.)
Galsworthy Rd. KT2: King T 7H 133
  NW2 . . . . .4G 63
Galsworthy Ter. N16 . . . . .3D 66
Galton Ct. NW9 . . . . .3A 44
           (off Joslin Av.)
Galton St. W10 . . . . .3G 81
Galva Cl. EN4: Cockf 4K 21
Galvani Way CR0: Wadd 1K 167
Galveston Ho. E1 . . . . .4A 86
           (off Harford St.)
Galveston Rd. SW15 . . . . .5H 117
Galway Cl. SE16 . . . . .5H 103
           (off Masters Dr.)
Galway Ho. E1 . . . . .5K 85
           (off White Horse La.)
  EC1 .2D 8
Galway St. EC1 . . . . .2D 8 (3C 84)
Gambado
  Beckenham 6C 140
  Chelsea 1A 118
           (off Station Ct.)
Gambetta St. SW8 . . . . .2F 119
Gambia St. SE1 . . . . .5B 14 (1B 102)
Gambier Ho. EC1 . . . . .2D 8
           (off Mora St.)
Gamble Ho. SW17 . . . . .4C 136
Games Rd. EN4: Cockf 3H 21
Gamlen Rd. SW15 . . . . .4F 117
Gamma Ct. CR0: C'don 1D 168
          (off Sydenham Rd.)
Gamuel Cl. E17 . . . . .6C 50
Gander Grn. Cres. TW12: Hamp . . .1E 148
Gander Grn. La. SM1: Sutt 3H 165
  SM3: Cheam 2G 165
Gandhi Cl. E17 . . . . .6C 50
Gandolfi St. SE15 . . . . .6E 102
Ganley Ct. SW11 . . . . .3B 118
          (off Winstanley Est.)
Ganton St. W1 . . . . .2A 12 (7G 83)
GANTS HILL 6E 52
GANTS HILL 6E 52
Gantshill Cres. IG2: Ilf 5E 52
Gap Rd. SW19 . . . . .5J 135
Garage Rd. W3 . . . . .6G 79
Garand Ct. N7 . . . . .5K 65
Garbett Ho. SE17 . . . . .6B 102
          (off Doddington Gro.)
Garbutt Pl. W1 . . . . .5H 5 (5E 82)
Garda Ho. SE10 . . . . .4G 105
           (off Cable Wlk.)
Garden Av. CR4: Mitc 7F 137
  DA7: Bex 3F 127
Garden City HA8: Edg 6B 28
Garden Cl. E4 . . . . .5H 35
  HA4: Ruis 2G 57
  KT3: N Mald 4A 152

Garden Cl. SE12 . . . . .3K 141
  SM6: W'gton 5J 167
  SW15 . . . . .7D 116
  TW12: Hamp 5D 130
  TW15: Ashf 6E 128
  UB5: N'olt 1C 76
Garden Ct. CR0: C'don 2F 169
  EC4 .2J 13
  HA7: Stan 5H 27
  N12 .5E 30
  NW8 .1A 4
           (off Garden Rd.)
  TW9: Kew 1F 115
  TW12: Hamp 5D 130
  W4 . . . . .3J 97
  W11 . . . . .7G 81
          (off Clarendon Rd.)
Gardener Gro. TW13: Hanw 2D 130
Gardeners Cl. N11 . . . . .2K 31
  SE9 . . . . .3C 142
Gardeners Rd. CR0: C'don 1B 168
The Garden Halls WC1 . . . .2E 6 (3J 83)
Garden Ho. N2 . . . . .2B 46
           (off The Grange)
  NW6 . . . . .2K 81
          (off Oxford Rd.)
  SW7 . . . . .3K 99
         (off Cornwall Gdns.)
The Garden Ho's. W6 . . . . .6F 99
          (off Bothwell St.)
Gardenia Rd. BR1: Broml 3E 160
  EN1: Enf 6K 23
Gardenia Way IG8: Wfd G 6D 36
Garden La. BR1: Broml 6K 141
  SW2 . . . . .1K 137
Garden M. SE10 . . . . .4G 105
  W2 . . . . .7J 81
The Garden Mus. 2G 19 (3K 101)
Garden Pl. E8 . . . . .1F 85
Garden Rd. BR1: Broml 7K 141
  KT12: Walt T 6A 148
  NW8 . . . . .1A 4 (3A 82)
  SE20 . . . . .1J 157
  TW9: Rich 3G 115
Garden Row SE1 . . . . .3B 102
Garden Royal SW15 . . . . .6F 117
The Gardens BR3: Beck 1E 158
  E5 . . . . .7F 49
  HA1: Harr 6G 41
  HA5: Pinn 6D 40
  N8 . . . . .4J 47
           (not continuous)
  SE22 . . . . .4G 121
  TW14: Felt 5F 111
Garden Sq. SW1 . . . . . . .6H 17 (5E 100)
Garden St. E1 . . . . .5K 85
Garden Ter. SW1 . . . . . . .5C 18 (5H 101)
  SW7 . . . . .7D 10
Garden Wlk. BR3: Beck 1B 158
  EC2 . . . . .2G 9 (3E 84)
Gdn. Way NW10 . . . . .6J 61
Gardiner Av. NW2 . . . . .5E 62
Gardiner Cl. EN3: Pond E 6E 24
  RM8: Dag 4D 72
Gardiner Ct. CR2: S Croy 6D 168
Gardiner Ho. SW11 . . . . .1C 118
Gardner Cl. E11 . . . . .6K 51
Gardner Ct. EC1 . . . . .3A 8
          (off Brewery Sq.)
  N5 . . . . .4C 66
Gardner Ho. TW13: Hanw 2D 130
  UB1: S'hall 7D 76
         (off The Broadway)
Gardner Ind. Est. BR3: Beck 5B 140
Gardner Pl. TW14: Felt 6K 111
Gardner Rd. E13 . . . . .4K 87
Gardners La. EC4 . . . . . . .2C 14 (7C 84)
Gardnor Rd. NW3 . . . . .4B 64
Gard St. EC1 . . . . .1B 8 (3B 84)
Garendon Gdns. SM4: Mord 7K 153
Garendon Rd. SM4: Mord 7K 153
Garenne Ct. E4 . . . . .1K 35
Gareth Cl. KT4: Wor Pk 2F 165

Gareth Ct. SW16 . . . . .3H 137
Gareth Dr. N9 . . . . .2B 34
Gareth Gro. BR1: Broml 4J 141
Garfield EN2: Enf 5J 23
           (off London Rd.)
Garfield Ct. NW6 . . . . .7G 63
          (off Willesden La.)
Garfield M. SW11 . . . . .3E 118
Garfield Rd. E4 . . . . .1A 36
  E13 .4H 87
  EN3: Pond E 4D 24
  SW11 . . . . .3E 118
  SW19 . . . . .5A 136
  TW1: Twick 1A 132
Garford St. E14 . . . . .7C 86
Garganey Ct. NW10 . . . . .6K 61
           (off Elgar Av.)
Garganey Wlk. SE28 . . . . .7C 90
Garibaldi St. SE18 . . . . .4J 107
Garland Cl. SE11 . . . . .3C 102
Garland Ct. E14 . . . . .7C 86
           (off Premiere Pl.)
  SE17 . . . . .4C 102
           (off Wansey St.)
Garland Dr. TW3: Houn 2G 113
Garland Ho. KT2: King T 1E 150
           (off Skerne Rd.)
  UB7: W Dray 2B 92
Garland Rd. HA7: Stan 1E 42
  SE18 . . . . .7H 107
Garlands Ct. CR0: C'don 4D 168
          (off Chatsworth Rd.)
Garlands Ho. NW8 . . . . .2A 82
           (off Carlton Hill)
Garlands La. HA1: Harr 1A 59
Garlick Hill EC4 . . . . .2D 14 (7C 84)
Garlies Rd. SE23 . . . . .3A 140
Garlinge Ho. SW9 . . . . .1A 120
          (off Gosling Way)
Garlinge Rd. NW2 . . . . .6H 63
Garman Cl. N18 . . . . .5J 33
Garman Rd. N17 . . . . .7C 34
           (not continuous)
Garnault M. EC1 . . . . .2K 7
Garnault Pl. EC1 . . . . .2K 7 (3A 84)
Garnault Rd. EN1: Enf 1A 24
Garner Cl. RM8: Dag 1D 72
Garner Ct. TW19: Stanw 6A 110
           (off Douglas Rd.)
Garner Rd. E17 . . . . .1E 50
Garner St. E2 . . . . .2G 85
Garnet Ho. E1 . . . . .1J 103
           (off Garnet St.)
Garnet Pl. UB7: Yiew 1A 92
Garnet Rd. CR7: Thor H 4C 156
  NW10 . . . . .6A 62
Garnet St. E1 . . . . .7J 85
Garnett Cl. SE9 . . . . .3D 124
Garnett Rd. NW3 . . . . .5D 64
Garnett Way E17 . . . . .1A 50
          (off McEntee Av.)
Garnet Wlk. E6 . . . . .5C 88
Garnham Cl. N16 . . . . .2F 67
Garnham St. N16 . . . . .2F 67
Garnies Cl. SE15 . . . . .7F 103
Garrad's Rd. SW16 . . . . .3H 137
Garrard Cl. BR7: Chst 5F 143
  DA7: Bex 3G 127
Garrard Wlk. NW10 . . . . .6A 62
Garratt Cl. CR0: Bedd 4J 167
  CR7: Thor H 2C 156
Garratt Ct. SW18 . . . . .7K 117
Garratt La. SW17 . . . . .6K 117
  SW18 . . . . .6K 117
Garratt Rd. HA8: Edg 7B 28
Garratts Rd. WD23: Bush 1B 26
Garratt Ter. SW17 . . . . .4C 136
Garraway Ct. SW13 . . . . .7E 98
           (off Wyatt Dr.)
Garratt Cl. W3 . . . . .5K 79
Garrett Ho. SE1 . . . . .6A 14
          (off Burrows M.)
Garrett St. EC1 . . . . .3D 8 (4C 84)

Garrick Av.—Genotin Ter.

Garrick Av. NW11 . . . 6G 45
Garrick Cl. SW18 . . . 4A 118
TW9: Rich . . . 5D 114
W5 . . . 4E 78
Garrick Ct. *E8* . . . *7F 67*
(off Jacaranda Gro.)
Garrick Cres. CR0: C'don . . . 2E 168
Garrick Dr. NW4 . . . 2E 44
SE28 . . . 3H 107
Garrick Gdns. KT8: W Mole . . . 3E 148
Garrick Ho. *KT1: King T* . . . *4E 150*
(off Surbiton Rd.)
W1 . . . 5J 11
W4 . . . 6A 98
Garrick Ind. Cen. NW9 . . . 5B 44
Garrick Pk. NW4 . . . 2F 45
Garrick Rd. NW9 . . . 6B 44
TW9: Rich . . . 2G 115
UB6: G'frd . . . 4F 77
Garricks Ho. *KT1: King T* . . . *2D 150*
(off Wadbrook St.)
Garrick St. WC2 . . . 2E 12 (7J 83)
Garrick Theatre . . . *3E 12*
(off Charing Cross Rd.)
Garrick Way NW4 . . . 4F 45
Garrick Yd. WC2 . . . 2E 12
Garrison Cl. SE18 . . . 7E 106
TW4: Houn . . . 5D 112
Garrison La. KT9: Chess . . . 7D 162
Garrison Rd. E3 . . . 1C 86
Garrison Sq. SW1 . . . 5H 17 (5E 100)
Garrowsfield EN5: Barn . . . 6C 20
Garry Way RM1: Rom . . . 1K 55
Garsdale Cl. N11 . . . 6K 31
Garsdale Ter. *W14* . . . *5H 99*
(off Aisgill Av.)
Garside Cl. SE28 . . . 3H 107
TW12: Hamp . . . 6F 131
Garside Ct. TW11: Hamp W . . . 1C 150
Garsington M. SE4 . . . 3B 122
Garson Ho. *W2* . . . *2A 10*
(off Gloucester Ter.)
Garston Ho. *N1* . . . *7B 66*
(off The Sutton Est.)
Garter Way SE16 . . . 2K 103
The Garth HA3: Kenton . . . 6F 43
TW12: Hamp H . . . 6F 131
Garth Cl. HA4: Ruis . . . 1B 58
KT2: King T . . . 5F 133
SM4: Mord . . . 7F 153
Garth Ct. *HA1: Harr* . . . *6K 41*
(off Northwick Pk. Rd.)
W4 . . . 5K 97
Garth Ho. NW2 . . . 2H 63
Garth M. W5 . . . 4E 78
Garthorne Rd. SE23 . . . 7K 121
Garthorne Road Nature Reserve . . . 7K 121
Garth Rd. KT2: King T . . . 5F 133
NW2 . . . 2H 63
SM4: Mord . . . 6E 152
W4 . . . 5K 97
The Garth Rd. Ind. Cen.
SM4: Mord . . . 1F 165
Garthside TW10: Ham . . . 5E 132
Garthway N12 . . . 6H 31
Gartmoor Gdns. SW19 . . . 1H 135
Gartmore Rd. IG3: Ilf . . . 2K 71
Garton Pl. SW18 . . . 6A 118
Gartons Cl. EN3: Pond E . . . 4D 24
Gartons Way SW11 . . . 3A 118
Garvary Rd. E16 . . . 6K 87
Garway Ct. *E3* . . . *2C 86*
(off Matilda Gdns.)
Garway Rd. W2 . . . 6K 81
Garwood Cl. N17 . . . 1H 49
Gascoigne Cl. N17 . . . 1F 49
Gascoigne Gdns. IG8: Wfd G . . . 7B 36
Gascoigne Pl. E2 . . . 1J 9 (3F 85)
(not continuous)
Gascoigne Rd. CR0: New Ad . . . 7F 171
IG11: Bark . . . 1G 89
Gascony Av. NW6 . . . 7J 63
Gascony Pl. W12 . . . 1F 99
Gascoyne Ho. E9 . . . 7A 68
Gascoyne Rd. E9 . . . 7K 67
Gaselee St. *E14* . . . *1E 104*
(off Baffin Way)
Gasholder Pk. . . . 1H 83
Gaskarth Rd. HA8: Edg . . . 1J 43
SW12 . . . 6F 119
Gaskell Ct. SE20 . . . 7K 139
Gaskell Rd. N6 . . . 6D 46
Gaskell St. SW4 . . . 2J 119
Gaskin St. N1 . . . 1B 84
Gaspar Cl. SW5 . . . 4K 99
Gaspar M. SW5 . . . 4K 99
Gassiot Rd. SW17 . . . 4D 136
Gassiot Way SM1: Sutt . . . 3B 166
Gasson Ho. *SE14* . . . *6K 103*
(off John Williams Cl.)
Gastein Rd. W6 . . . 6F 99
Gastigny Ho. EC1 . . . 2D 8
Gaston Bell Cl. TW9: Rich . . . 3F 115
Gaston Bri. Rd. TW17: Shep . . . 6F 147
Gaston Rd. CR4: Mitc . . . 3E 154
Gaston Way TW17: Shep . . . 5F 147
Gataker Ho. *SE16* . . . *3H 103*
(off Slippers Pl.)
Gataker St. SE16 . . . 3H 103
Gatcombe Ct. BR3: Beck . . . 7C 140
Gatcombe Ho. SE22 . . . 3E 120
Gatcombe M. W5 . . . 7F 79
Gatcombe Rd. E16 . . . 1J 105
N19 . . . 3H 65
Gatcombe Way EN4: Cockf . . . 3J 21
Gateacre Ct. DA14: Sidc . . . 4B 144
The Gate Cen. TW8: Bford . . . 7A 96
Gate Cinema . . . *1J 99*
(off Notting Hill Ga.)
The Gatefold Bldg. UB3: Hayes . . . 3G 93
Gateforth St. NW8 . . . 4C 4 (4C 82)
Gate Hill Ct. *W11* . . . *1H 99*
(off Ladbroke Ter.)
Gate Ho. *E3* . . . *1A 86*
(off Gunmakers La.)
N1 . . . *7D 66*
(off Ufton Rd.)
NW6 . . . *2K 81*
(off Oxford Rd.)
Gatehouse Cl. KT2: King T . . . 7J 133
Gatehouse Sq. SE1 . . . 4D 14
Gateley Ho. *SE4* . . . *4K 121*
(off Coston Wlk.)
Gateley Rd. SW9 . . . 3K 119
Gate Lodge *W9* . . . *5J 81*
(off Admiral Wlk.)
Gately Ct. SE15 . . . 7F 103
Gate M. SW7 . . . 7D 10
Gater Dr. EN2: Enf . . . 1J 23
Gatesborough St. EC2 . . . 3G 9 (4E 84)
Gates Cnr. Cl. E18 . . . 1J 51
Gates Ct. SE17 . . . 5C 102
Gatesden WC1 . . . 2G 7 (3J 83)
Gates Grn. Rd. BR2: Kes . . . 3H 171
BR4: W W'ck . . . 3H 171
Gateside Rd. SW17 . . . 3D 136
Gatestone Ct. *SE19* . . . *6E 138*
(off Central Hill)
Gatestone Rd. SE19 . . . 6E 138
Gate St. WC2 . . . 7G 7 (6K 83)
The Gate Theatre . . . *1J 99*
(off Pembridge Rd.)
Gateway SE17 . . . 6C 102
Gateway Apartments E17 . . . 5C 50
Gateway Arc. *N1* . . . *2B 84*
(off Upper St.)
Gateway Bus. Cen. SE26 . . . 6A 140
SE28 . . . 3H 107
Gateway Ct. *IG2: Ilf* . . . *6E 52*
(off Parham Dr.)
Gateway Ho. IG11: Bark . . . 1G 89
Gateway Ind. Est. NW10 . . . 3B 80
Gateway M. E8 . . . 5F 67
N11 . . . 6B 32
Gateway Retail Pk. . . . 4F 89
Gateway Rd. E10 . . . 3D 68
Gateways *KT6: Surb* . . . *5E 150*
(off Surbiton Hill Rd.)
The Gateways SW3 . . . 4D 16 (4C 100)
TW9: Rich . . . *4D 114*
(off Park La.)
Gateways Ct. SM6: W'gton . . . 5F 167
Gateway Sq. N18 . . . 6D 34
Gatfield Gro. TW13: Hanw . . . 2E 130
Gatfield Ho. TW13: Hanw . . . 2D 130
Gathorne Rd. N22 . . . 2A 48
Gathorne St. E2 . . . 2K 85
Gatley Av. KT19: Ewe . . . 5H 163
Gatliff Cl. SW1 . . . 6H 17
Gatliff Rd. SW1 . . . 6J 17 (5F 101)
Gatling Rd. SE2 . . . 5A 108
Gatonby St. SE15 . . . 1F 121
Gatting Cl. HA8: Edg . . . 7D 28
Gatting Way UB8: Uxb . . . 6A 56
Gattis Wharf *N1* . . . *2J 83*
(off New Wharf Rd.)
Gatton Cl. SM2: Sutt . . . 7K 165
Gatton Rd. SW17 . . . 4C 136
Gattons Way DA14: Sidc . . . 4F 145
Gatward Cl. N21 . . . 6G 23
Gatward Grn. N9 . . . 2A 34
Gatward Pl. IG11: Bark . . . 3K 89
Gatwick Ho. *E14* . . . *6B 86*
(off Clemence St.)
Gatwick Rd. SW18 . . . 7H 117
Gauden Cl. SW4 . . . 3H 119
Gauden Rd. SW4 . . . 2H 119
Gaudi Apts. *N8* . . . *3K 47*
(off Gt. Amwell La.)
Gaugin Ct. *SE16* . . . *5H 103*
(off Stubbs Dr.)
Gaugin Sq. E1 . . . 7G 85
Gaumont Pl. SW2 . . . 2J 137
Gaumont Ter. *W12* . . . *2E 98*
(off Lime Gro.)
Gaumont Twr. *E8* . . . *6F 67*
(off Dalston Sq.)
Gauntlet *NW9* . . . *2B 44*
(off Five Acre)
Gauntlet Cl. UB5: N'olt . . . 7C 58
Gauntlett Ct. HA0: Wemb . . . 5B 60
Gauntlett Rd. SM1: Sutt . . . 5B 166
Gaunt St. SE1 . . . 3C 102
Gautrey Rd. SE15 . . . 2J 121
Gautrey Sq. E6 . . . 6D 88
Gavel St. SE17 . . . 4D 102
Gaverick M. E14 . . . 4C 104
Gavestone Cres. SE12 . . . 7A 124
Gavestone Rd. SE12 . . . 7K 123
Gaviller Pl. E5 . . . 4H 67
Gavina Cl. SM4: Mord . . . 5C 154
Gavin Ho. SE18 . . . 4J 107
Gawain Wlk. N9 . . . 3B 34
Gawber St. E2 . . . 3J 85
Gawsworth Cl. E15 . . . 5H 69
Gawthorne Ct. E3 . . . 2C 86
Gay Cl. NW2 . . . 5D 62
Gaydon Ho. *W2* . . . *5K 81*
(off Bourne Ter.)
Gaydon La. NW9 . . . 1A 44
Gayfere Pl. *SE25* . . . *2E 156*
(off Grange Hill)
Gayfere Rd. IG5: Ilf . . . 3D 52
KT17: Ewe . . . 5C 164
Gayfere St. SW1 . . . 2E 18 (3J 101)
Gayford Rd. W12 . . . 2B 98
Gay Gdns. RM10: Dag . . . 4J 73
Gay Ho. N16 . . . 5E 66
Gayhurst *SE17* . . . *6D 102*
(off Hopwood Rd.)
Gayhurst Ct. UB5: N'olt . . . 3A 76
Gayhurst Ho. *NW8* . . . *3C 4*
(off Mallory St.)
Gayhurst Rd. E8 . . . 7G 67
Gaylor Rd. UB5: N'olt . . . 5D 58
Gaymead *NW8* . . . *1K 81*
(off Abbey Rd.)
Gaynesford Rd. SE23 . . . 2K 139
SM5: Cars . . . 7D 166
Gaynes Hill Rd. IG8: Wfd G . . . 6H 37
Gay Rd. E15 . . . 2F 87
Gaysham Av. IG2: Ilf . . . 5E 52
Gaysham Hall IG5: Ilf . . . 3F 53
Gaysley Ho. SE11 . . . 4J 19
Gay St. SW15 . . . 3F 117
Gayton *HA1: Harr* . . . *7J 41*
(off Grove Hill)
Gayton Ct. HA1: Harr . . . 6K 41
Gayton Cres. NW3 . . . 4B 64
Gayton Ho. *E3* . . . *4C 86*
(off Chiltern Rd.)
Gayton Rd. HA1: Harr . . . 6K 41
NW3 . . . 4B 64
SE2 . . . 3C 108
Gayville Rd. SW11 . . . 6D 118
Gaywood Cl. SW2 . . . 1K 137
Gaywood Rd. E17 . . . 3C 50
Gaywood St. SE1 . . . 3B 102
Gaza St. SE17 . . . 5B 102
Gazelle Ho. E15 . . . 6G 69
Gean Ct. E11 . . . 4F 69
N11 . . . *6B 32*
(off Cline Rd.)
Geariesville Gdns. IG6: Ilf . . . 4F 53
Gearing Cl. SW17 . . . 4E 136
Geary Rd. NW10 . . . 5C 62
Geary St. N7 . . . 5K 65
Geddes Pl. *DA6: Bex* . . . *4G 127*
(off Arnsberg Way)
Gedeney Rd. N17 . . . 1C 48
Gedling Ct. *SE1* . . . *7K 15*
(off Sweeney Cres.)
Gedling Pl. SE1 . . . 7K 15 (3F 103)
Geere Rd. E15 . . . 1H 87
Gees Ct. W1 . . . 1H 11 (6E 82)
Gee St. EC1 . . . 3C 8 (4C 84)
Geffery's Ct. SE9 . . . 3C 142
Geffrye Ct. N1 . . . 2E 84
Geffrye Est. N1 . . . 2E 84
Geffrye Mus. . . . 1J 9 (2F 85)
Geffrye St. E2 . . . 1J 9 (2F 85)
Geldart Rd. SE15 . . . 7H 103
Geldeston Rd. E5 . . . 2G 67
Gellatly Rd. SE14 . . . 2J 121
Gell Cl. UB10: Ick . . . 3B 56
Gelsthorpe Rd. RM5: Col R . . . 1H 55
Gem Ct. *SE10* . . . *7D 104*
(off Merryweather Pl.)
Gemini Apts. *E1* . . . *3K 9*
(off Sclater St.)
Gemini Bus. Cen. E16 . . . 4F 87
Gemini Bus. Est. SE14 . . . 5K 103
Gemini Bus. Pk. E6 . . . 5H 89
Gemini Ct. *E1* . . . *7G 85*
(off Vaughan Way)
Gemini Gro. UB5: N'olt . . . 3C 76
Gemini Ho. *E3* . . . *1C 86*
(off Garrison Rd.)
Gemini Pl. TW15: Ashf . . . 6G 129
Genas Cl. IG6: Ilf . . . 1F 53
General Gordon Pl. SE18 . . . 4F 107
General Gordon Sq. *SE18* . . . *4F 107*
(off Woolwich New Rd.)
General Wolfe Rd. SE10 . . . 1F 123
Genesis Bus. Pk. NW10 . . . 2H 79
Genesis Cl. TW19: Stanw . . . 1B 128
Genesta Rd. SE18 . . . 6F 107
Geneva Cl. TW17: Shep . . . 2G 147
Geneva Ct. NW9 . . . 5B 44
Geneva Dr. SW9 . . . 4A 120
Geneva Gdns. RM6: Chad H . . . 5E 54
Geneva Rd. CR7: Thor H . . . 5C 156
KT1: King T . . . 4E 150
Genever Cl. E4 . . . 5H 35
Genista Rd. N18 . . . 5C 34
Genoa Av. SW15 . . . 5E 116
Genoa Ho. *E1* . . . *4K 85*
(off Ernest St.)
SW18 . . . 3A 118
Genoa Rd. SE20 . . . 1J 157
Genotin Rd. EN1: Enf . . . 3J 23
Genotin Ter. EN1: Enf . . . 3J 23

Gentlemans Row EN2: Enf 3H 23
Gentry Gdns. E13 . . . . .4J 87
Geoff Cade Way E3 . . . . .5B 86
Geoffrey Chaucer Way E3 . . . . . . .5B 86
Geoffrey Cl. SE5 . . . . .2C 120
Geoffrey Cl. SE4 . . . . .2B 122
Geoffrey Gdns. E6 . . . . .2C 88
Geoffrey Ho. SE1 . . . . .7F 15
(off Pardoner St.)
Geoffrey Jones Ct. NW10 . . . . .1C 80
Geoffrey Rd. SE4 . . . . .3B 122
George V Av. HA5: Pinn 2D 40
George V Cl. HA5: Pinn 3E 40
George V Way UB6: G'frd 1B 78
George Beard Rd. SE8 . . . . .4B 104
George Belt Ho. E2 . . . . .3K 85
(off Smart St.)
George Comberton Wlk. E12 . . . . .5E 70
George Ct. TW15: Ashf 4B 128
(off Church Rd.)
UB3: Hayes 5H 75
WC2 . . . . .3F 13
George Cres. N10 . . . . .7K 31
George Davies Lodge IG6: Ilf 5G 53
(off Veronique Gdns.)
George Downing Est. N16 . . . . . . .2F 67
George Eliot Ho. SE17 . . . . .5C 102
(off Thrush St.)
SW1 . . . . .4B 18
(off Vauxhall Bri. Rd.)
George Elliston Ho. SE1 . . . . .5G 103
(off Old Kent Rd.)
George Eyre Ho. NW8 . . . . .2B 82
(off Cochrane St.)
George Furness Ho. NW10 . . . . . .6D 62
(off Grange Rd.)
George Gange Way HA3: W'stone . .3J 41
George Gillett Ct. EC1 . . . . .3D 8
George Groves Rd. SE20 . . . . . . .1G 157
George Hilsdon Ct. E14 . . . . .6A 86
(off Repton St.)
George Ho. NW6 . . . . .2H 81
(off Albert Rd.)
George Hudson Twr. E15 . . . . .2D 86
(off High St.)
George Inn Yd. SE1 . . . . .5E 14 (1D 102)
George La. BR2: Hayes 1K 171
E18 . . . . .2J 51
SE6 .6D 122
SE13 .6D 122
George Lansbury Ho. E3 . . . . .3B 86
(off Bow Rd.)
N22 . . . . .1A 48
(off Progress Way)
NW10 . . . . .7A 62
George Leybourne Ho. E1 . . . . . . .7G 85
(off Fletcher St.)
George Lindgren Ho. SW6 . . . . . . .7H 99
(off Clem Attlee Ct.)
George Loveless Ho. E2 . . . . .1K 9
(off Diss St.)
George Lowe Ct. W2 . . . . .5K 81
(off Bourne Ter.)
George Mathers Rd. SE11 . . . . . . .4B 102
George M. EN2: Enf 3J 23
NW1 . . . . .2B 6
SW9 .2A 120
George Padmore Ho. E8 . . . . .1G 85
(off Brougham Rd.)
George Peabody Ct. NW1 . . . . .5C 4
(off Burne St.)
George Peabody St. E13 . . . . .2A 88
George Pl. N17 . . . . .3E 48
George Potter Ho. SW11 . . . . .2B 118
(off George Potter Way)
George Potter Way SW11 . . . . . . .2B 118
George Rd. E4 . . . . .6H 35
KT2: King T 7H 133
KT3: N Mald 4B 152
George Row SE16 . . . . .2G 103
George Scott Ho. E1 . . . . .6K 85
(off W. Arbour St.)
George Sq. SW19 . . . . .3J 153

George's Rd. N7 . . . . .5K 65
George's Sq. SW6 . . . . .6H 99
(off North End Rd.)
George St. CRO: C'don 2C 168
E16 . . . . .6H 87
IG11: Bark 7G 71
TW3: Houn 2D 112
TW9: Rich 5D 114
UB2: S'hall 4C 94
W1 . . . . .7E 4 (6D 82)
W7 . . . . .1J 95
Georgetown Cl. SE19 . . . . .5E 138
George Vale Ho. E2 . . . . .2G 85
(off Mansford St.)
George Vw. Ho. SW18 . . . . .1K 135
(off Knaresborough Dr.)
Georgeville Gdns. IG6: Ilf 4F 53
George Walter Ct. SE16 . . . . .4J 103
(off Millender Wlk.)
George Wyver Cl. SW19 . . . . .7G 117
George Yd. EC3 . . . . . . .1F 15 (6D 84)
W1 . . . . .2H 11 (7E 82)
Georgia Ct. SE16 . . . . .3G 103
(off Priter Rd.)
Georgiana St. NW1 . . . . .1G 83
Georgian Cl. BR2: Hayes 1K 171
HA7: Stan 7F 27
UB10: Ick 4A 56
Georgian Ct. CRO: C'don 1D 168
(off Cross Rd.)
E9 . . . . .1J 85
EN5: New Bar 4F 21
HA9: Wemb 6G 61
N3 . . . . .1H 45
NW4 .5D 44
SW16 . . . . .4J 137
Georgian Ho. E16 . . . . .1J 105
(off Capulet M.)
N1 . . . . .1E 84
(off Hertford Rd.)
Georgian Way HA1: Harr 2H 59
Georgia Rd. CR7: Thor H 1B 156
KT3: N Mald 4J 151
Georgina Gdns. E2 . . . . . .1K 9 (3F 85)
Geotgette Ct. SW18 . . . . .5K 117
(off Courthouse Way)
Geraint Rd. BR1: Broml 4J 141
Geraldine Rd. SW18 . . . . .5A 118
W4 . . . . .6G 97
Geraldine St. SE11 . . . . . .2K 19 (3B 102)
Gerald M. SW1 . . . . .3H 17
Gerald Pl. E8 . . . . .6F 67
(off Dalston Sq.)
Gerald Rd. E16 . . . . .4H 87
RM8: Dag 1F 73
SW1 . . . . .3H 17 (4E 100)
Gerard Av. TW4: Houn 7E 112
Gerard Gdns. RM13: Rain 2K 91
Gerard Pl. E9 . . . . .7K 67
Gerard Rd. HA1: Harr 6A 42
SW13 . . . . .1B 116
Gerards Cl. SE16 . . . . .5J 103
Gerards Pl. SW4 . . . . .4H 119
Gerda Rd. SE9 . . . . .2G 143
Germander Way E15 . . . . .3G 87
Gernigan Ho. SW18 . . . . .6B 118
Gernon Rd. E3 . . . . .2A 86
Geron Way NW2 . . . . .1D 62
Gerrard Gdns. HA5: Eastc 5J 39
Gerrard Ho. SE14 . . . . .7J 103
(off Briant St.)
Gerrard Pl. W1 . . . . .2D 12 (7H 83)
Gerrard Rd. N1 . . . . .2B 84
Gerrards Cl. N14 . . . . .5B 22
Gerrards St. W5 . . . . .3D 96
Gerrard St. W1 . . . . .2D 12 (7H 83)
Gerrard Way SE3 . . . . .4A 124
Gerridge Ct. SE1 . . . . .1K 19
(off Gerridge St.)
Gerridge St. SE1 . . . . . . .1K 19 (3A 102)
Gerry Raffles Sq. E15 . . . . .6F 69
Gertrude Rd. DA17: Belv 4G 109

Gertrude St. SW10 . . . . . . .7A 16 (6A 100)
Gervase Cl. HA9: Wemb 3J 61
Gervase Rd. HA8: Edg 1J 43
Gervase St. SE15 . . . . .7H 103
Gervis Ct. TW7: Isle 7G 95
Ghent St. SE6 . . . . .2C 140
Ghent Way E8 . . . . .6F 67
The Gherkin 1H 15
Giant Arches Rd. SE24 . . . . .7C 120
Giant Tree Hill WD23: B Hea 1C 26
Gibbfield Cl. RM6: Chad H 3E 54
Gibbings Ho. SE1 . . . . .7B 14
(off King James St.)
Gibbins Rd. E15 . . . . .7E 68
Gibbon Ho. NW8 . . . . .4B 4
(off Fisherton St.)
Gibbon Rd. KT2: King T 1E 150
SE15 . . . . .2J 121
W3 . . . . .7A 80
Gibbons M. NW11 . . . . .5H 45
Gibbon's Rents SE1 . . . . .5G 15
Gibbon Rd. NW10 . . . . .6A 62
Gibbon Wlk. SW15 . . . . .4C 116
Gibbs Av. SE19 . . . . .5D 138
Gibbs Cl. SE19 . . . . .6D 138
Gibbs Grn. HA8: Edg 4D 28
W14 .5H 99
(not continuous)
Gibbs Ho. BR1: Broml 1H 159
(off Longfield)
Gibbs La. E2 . . . . .2G 85
Gibb's Rd. N18 . . . . .4D 34
Gibbs Sq. SE19 . . . . .5D 138
Gibney Ter. BR1: Broml 4H 141
Gibraltar Wlk. E2 . . . . .2K 9
Gibson Cl. E1 . . . . .4J 85
KT9: Chess 5C 162
N21 .6F 23
TW7: Isle 3J 113
Gibson Cl. SE9 . . . . .5A 124
Gibson Gdns. N16 . . . . .2F 67
Gibson Ho. SM1: Sutt 4J 165
Gibson M. TW1: Twick 6C 114
Gibson Rd. RM8: Dag 1C 72
SE11 . . . . .4H 19 (4K 101)
SM1: Sutt 5K 165
UB10: Ick 4B 56
Gibsons Hill SW16 . . . . .7A 138
(not continuous)
Gibsons Pl. TW8: Bford 6D 96
(off Sidney Gdns.)
Gibson Sq. N1 . . . . .1A 84
Gibson Sq. Gdns. 1A 84
(off Gibson Sq.)
Gibson St. SE10 . . . . .5G 105
Gideon Cl. DA17: Belv 4H 109
HA8: Edg 6B 28
Gideon M. W5 . . . . .2D 96
Gideon Rd. SW11 . . . . .3E 118
Gielgud Theatre 2C 12
(off Shaftesbury Av.)
Giesbach Rd. N19 . . . . .2H 65
Giffard Rd. N18 . . . . .6K 33
Giffin Sq. Mkt. 7C 104
(off Giffin St.)
Giffin St. SE8 . . . . .7C 104
Gifford Gdns. W7 . . . . .5H 77
Gifford Ho. SE10 . . . . .5F 105
(off Eastney St.)
SW1 .6A 18
(off Churchill Gdns.)
Gifford Rd. NW10 . . . . .7A 62
Gifford St. N1 . . . . .7J 65
Gift La. E15 . . . . .1G 87
GIGGSHILL 7A 150
Giggs Hill BR5: St P 2K 161
Giggs Hill Gdns. KT7: T Ditt 1A 162
Giggs Hill Rd. KT7: T Ditt 7A 150
GILBERT BRI. 5D 8
(off Wood St.)
Gilbert Cl. SE18 . . . . .1D 124
SW19 . . . . .1K 153
(off Morden Rd.)

Gilbert Ct. W5 . . . . .6F 79
(off Green Va.)
Gilbert Gro. HA8: Edg 1K 43
Gilbert Ho. E2 . . . . .3K 85
(off Usk St.)
E17 .3E 50
EC2 .5D 8
SE8 .6C 104
SW1 .6K 17
(off Churchill Gdns.)
SW8 .7J 101
(off Wyvil Rd.)
SW13 . . . . .7D 98
(off Trinity Chu. Rd.)
Gilbert Pl. WC1 . . . . .6E 6 (5J 83)
Gilbert Rd. BR1: Broml 7J 141
DA17: Belv 3G 109
HA5: Pinn 4B 40
SE11 . . . . .4K 19 (4A 102)
SW19 . . . . .7A 136
UB9: Hare 2A 38
Gilbert Scott Bldg. SW15 . . . . .6G 117
Gilbert Scott Cl. HAO: Wemb 5D 60
Gilbert Scott Ho. W14 . . . . .4H 99
(off Warwick La.)
Gilbert Sheldon Ho. W2 . . . . .5B 4
(off Edgware Rd.)
Gilbertson Ho. E14 . . . . .3C 104
(off Mellish St.)
Gilbert St. E15 . . . . .4G 69
TW3: Houn 3G 113
W1 . . . . .1H 11 (6E 82)
Gilbert Way CRO: Wadd 2K 167
Gilbert White Cl. UB6: G'frd 1A 78
Gilbey Cl. UB10: Ick 4D 56
Gilbey Ho. NW1 . . . . .7F 65
Gilbey Rd. SW17 . . . . .4C 136
Gilbeys Yd. NW1 . . . . .7E 64
Gilbourne Rd. SE18 . . . . .6K 107
Gilby Ho. E9 . . . . .6K 67
Gilda Av. EN3: Pond E 5F 25
Gilda Ct. NW7 . . . . .1C 44
Gilda Cres. N16 . . . . .1G 67
Gildea Cl. HA5: Hat E 1E 40
Gildea St. W1 . . . . .6K 5 (5F 83)
Gilden Cres. NW5 . . . . .5E 64
Gildersome St. SE18 . . . . .6E 106
Gilders Rd. KT9: Chess 7F 163
Giles Coppice SE19 . . . . .4F 139
Giles Cres. UB10: Uxb 1B 74
(off St Andrews Rd.)
Giles Ho. E15 . . . . .6F 69
(off Forrester Way)
W11 .6J 81
(off Westbourne Gro.)
Gilesmead SE5 . . . . .1D 120
Gilford Ho. IG1: Ilf 2F 71
(off Clements Rd.)
Gilfrid Cl. UB8: Hil 6D 74
Gilkes Cres. SE21 . . . . .6E 120
Gilkes Pl. SE21 . . . . .6E 120
Gillan Ct. SE12 . . . . .3K 141
Gillan Grn. WD23: B Hea 2B 26
Gillards M. E17 . . . . .4C 50
Gillards Way E17 . . . . .4C 50
Gill Av. E16 . . . . .6J 87
Gillender St. E3 . . . . .4E 86
E14 .4E 86
Gillespie Pk. Local Nature Reserve . . .3A 66
Gillespie Rd. N5 . . . . .3A 66
Gillett Av. E6 . . . . .2C 88
GILLETTE CORNER 7A 96
Gillett Ho. N8 . . . . .3J 47
(off Campsfield Rd.)
Gillett Pl. N16 . . . . .5E 66
Gillett Rd. CR7: Thor H 4D 156
Gillett Sq. N16 . . . . .5E 66
(off Gillett St.)
Gillett St. N16 . . . . .5E 66
Gillfoot NW1 . . . . .1A 6
(off Hampstead Rd.)
Gillham Ter. N17 . . . . .6B 34
Gillian Ho. HA3: Hrw W 6D 26

Gillian Lynne Theatre 7F 7
(off Parker St.)
Gillian Pk. Rd. SM3: Sutt 1H 165
Gillian St. SE13 . . . . .5D 122
Gillies Ho. NW6 . . . . .7B 64
(off Hilgrove Rd.)
Gillies St. NW5 . . . . .5E 64
Gilling Ct. NW3 . . . . .6C 64
Gillingham M. SW1 . . . . .3A 18 (4G 101)
Gillingham Rd. NW2 . . . . .3G 63
Gillingham Row SW1 . . . .3A 18 (4G 101)
Gillingham St. SW1 . . . . .3A 18 (4G 101)
Gillings Ct. EN5: Barn 4B 20
(off Wood St.)
Gillison Wlk. SE16 . . . . .3H 103
Gillis Sq. SW15 . . . . .6C 116
Gillman Dr. E15 . . . . .1H 87
Gilman Ho. E2 . . . . .2G 85
(off Pritchard's Rd.)
Gillray Ho. SW10 . . . . .6B 100
(off Ann La.)
Gill St. E14 . . . . .6B 86
Gillum Cl. EN4: E Barn 1J 31
Gilman Ho. N1 . . . . .7A 66
(off Drummond Way)
Gilmore Cl. UB10: Ick 3C 56
Gilmore Ct. N11 . . . . .5J 31
Gilmore Cres. TW15: Ashf 5C 128
Gilmore Rd. SE13 . . . . .4F 123
Gilmour Ho. NW9 . . . . .2C 44
Gilpin Av. SW14 . . . . .4K 115
Gilpin Cl. CR4: Mitc 2C 154
W2 . . . . .5A 4
(off Porteus Rd.)
Gilpin Cres. N18 . . . . .5A 34
TW2: Whitt 7F 113
Gilpin Rd. E5 . . . . .4A 68
Gilpin Way UB3: Harl 7F 93
Gilray Ho. W2 . . . . .2A 10
(off Gloucester Ter.)
Gilsland Pl. CR7: Thor H 4D 156
Gilsland Rd. CR7: Thor H 4D 156
Gilson Pl. N10 . . . . .7J 31
Gilstead Rd. SW6 . . . . .2K 117
Gilston Rd. SW10 . . . . . .7A 16 (5A 100)
Gilton Rd. SE6 . . . . .3G 141
Giltspur St. EC1 . . . . . . .7B 8 (6B 84)
Gilwell Cl. E4 . . . . .4J 25
Gilwell La. E4 . . . . .4K 25
(not continuous)
GILWELL PARK 4K 25
Gilwell Pk. E4 . . . . .3K 25
Ginger Apts. SE1 . . . . .6K 15
(off Cayenne Ct.)
Ginsburg Yd. NW3 . . . . .4A 64
Gippeswyck Cl. HA5: Pinn 1B 40
Gipsy Hill SE19 . . . . .4E 138
Gipsy La. SW15 . . . . .3D 116
Gipsy Rd. DA16: Well 7D 108
SE27 . . . . .4C 138
Gipsy Rd. Gdns. SE27 . . . . .4C 138
Giralda Cl. E16 . . . . .5B 88
Giraud St. E14 . . . . .6D 86
Girdler's Rd. W14 . . . . .4F 99
Girdlestone Wlk. N19 . . . . .2G 65
Girdwood Rd. SW18 . . . . .7G 117
Girling Ho. N1 . . . . .1E 84
(off Colville Est.)
Girling Way TW14: Felt 3J 111
Gironde Rd. SW6 . . . . .7H 99
Girtin Ho. UB5: N'olt 2B 76
(off Academy Gdns.)
Girton Av. NW9 . . . . .3G 43
Girton Cl. UB5: N'olt 6G 59
Girton Gdns. CR0: C'don 3C 170
Girton Rd. SE26 . . . . .5K 139
UB5: N'olt 6G 59
Girton Vs. W10 . . . . .6F 81
Gisbourne Cl. SM6: Bedd 3H 167
Gisburn Ho. SE15 . . . . .6G 103
(off Friary Est.)
Gisburn Rd. N8 . . . . .4K 47
Gissing Wlk. N1 . . . . .7A 66

Gittens Cl. BR1: Broml 4H 141
Given Wilson Wlk. E13 . . . . .2H 87
Giverny Ho. SE16 . . . . .2K 103
(off Water Gdns. Sq.)
Glacier Ho. SW11 . . . . .7H 101
(off Ponton Rd.)
Glacier Pl. E2 . . . . .2H 85
(off Clare St.)
Glacier Way HA0: Wemb 2D 78
Gladbeck Way EN2: Enf 4G 23
Gladding Rd. E12 . . . . .4B 70
The Glade BR1: Broml 2B 160
BR4: W W'ck 3D 170
CR0: C'don 5K 157
E8 . . . . .6G 67
EN2: Enf 3F 23
IG5: Ilf 1D 52
IG8: Wfd G 3E 36
KT17: Ewe 6C 164
N12 . . . . .3G 31
N21 . . . . .6E 22
SE7 .7A 106
SM2: Cheam 7G 165
W12 .2D 98
(off Coningham Rd.)
Glade Apts. E14 . . . . .4E 104
(off Stebondale St.)
Glade Cl. KT6: Surb 2D 162
Glade Ct. IG5: Ilf 1D 52
Glade Gdns. CR0: C'don 7A 158
Glade La. UB2: S'hall 2F 95
Glade Path SE1 . . . . .2B 102
(off Blackfriars Rd.)
The Glades 2J 159
The Glades KT6: Surb 7E 150
Gladeside CR0: C'don 6K 157
N21 . . . . .6E 22
Gladeside Cl. KT9: Chess 7D 162
Gladesmore Community
School & Sports Cen. 5G 49
Gladesmore Rd. N15 . . . . .6F 49
Glades Pl. BR1: Broml 2J 159
Gladeswood Rd. DA17: Belv 4H 109
Gladwin Ho. NW1 . . . . .2B 6
(off Werrington St.)
Gladiator St. SE23 . . . . .7A 122
Glading Ter. N16 . . . . .3F 67
Gladioli Cl. TW12: Hamp 6E 130
Gladsaxe Ho. SM1: Sutt 4K 165
Gladsdale Dr. HA5: Eastc 4J 39
Gladsmuir Rd. EN5: Barn 2B 20
N19 . . . . .1G 65
Gladstone Av. E12 . . . . .7C 70
N22 . . . . .2A 48
TW2: Twick 1H 131
TW14: Felt 6J 111
Gladstone Ct. NW6 . . . . .7A 64
(off Fairfax Rd.)
SW1 .4D 18
(off Regency St.)
Gladstone Ct. Bus. Cen. SW8 . . . .1F 119
(off Pagden St.)
Gladstone Gdns. TW3: Houn 1G 113
Gladstone Ho. CR4: Mitc 2D 154
E14 . . . . .6C 86
(off E. India Dock Rd.)
Gladstone M. N22 . . . . .2A 48
NW6 .7H 63
(off Cavendish Rd.)
SE20 . . . . .7J 139
Gladstone Pde. NW2 . . . . .2E 62
Gladstone Pk. Gdns. NW2 . . . . . .4D 62
Gladstone Pl. E3 . . . . .2B 86
EN5: Barn 4A 20
KT8: E Mos 5J 149
Gladstone Rd. BR6: Farnb 5G 173
CR0: C'don 7D 156
IG9: Buck H 1F 37
KT1: King T 3G 151
KT6: Surb 2D 162
SW19 . . . . .7J 135
UB2: S'hall 2C 94
W4 . . . . .3K 97
Gladstone St. SE1 . . . . .3B 102

Gladstone Ter. SE27 . . . . .5C 138
(off Bentons La.)
SW8 .1F 119
Gladstone Way HA3: W'stone 3J 41
Gladwell Rd. BR1: Broml 6J 141
N8 . . . . .6K 47
Gladwin Ho. NW1 . . . . .1B 6
(off Werrington St.)
Gladwyn Rd. SW15 . . . . .3F 117
Gladys Cl. BR1: Broml 2H 141
Gladys Dimson Ho. E7 . . . . .5H 69
Gladys Rd. NW6 . . . . .7J 63
Glaisher St. SE8 . . . . .6C 104
Glamis Ct. W3 . . . . .2H 97
Glamis Cres. UB3: Harl 3E 92
Glamis Pl. E1 . . . . .7J 85
Glamis Rd. E1 . . . . .7J 85
Glamis Way UB5: N'olt 6G 59
Glamorgan Cl. CR4: Mitc 3J 155
Glamorgan Ct. W7 . . . . .5K 77
(off Copley Cl.)
Glamorgan Rd. KT1: Hamp W . . .7C 132
Glandford Way RM6: Chad H 5B 54
Glanfield Rd. BR3: Beck 4B 158
Glanleam Rd. HA7: Stan 4J 27
Glanville M. HA7: Stan 5F 27
Glanville Rd. BR2: Broml 3K 159
SW2 . . . . .5J 119
Glasbrook Av. TW2: Whitt 1D 130
Glasbrook Rd. SE9 . . . . .7B 124
Glaserton Rd. N16 . . . . .7E 48
Glasford St. SW17 . . . . .6D 136
Glasfryn Ct. HA2: Harr 2H 59
(off Roxeth Hill)
Glasfryn Ho. HA2: Harr 2H 59
(off Roxeth Hill)
Glasgow Ho. W9 . . . . .2K 81
(off Maida Vale)
Glasgow Rd. E13 . . . . .2K 87
N18 . . . . .5C 34
Glasgow Ter. SW1 . . . . . .6A 18 (5G 101)
Glasier Ct. E15 . . . . .7G 69
Glaskin M. E9 . . . . .6A 68
Glass Blowers Ho. E14 . . . . .6F 87
(off Valencia Cl.)
The Glass Bldg. NW1 . . . . .1F 83
(off Jamestown Rd.)
Glassaxe Ho. SM1: Sutt 3A 78
Glass Foundry Yd. E13 . . . . .5K 87
(off Denmark St.)
Glasshill St. SE1 . . . . . . .6B 14 (2B 102)
Glass Ho. WC2 . . . . .1E 12
(off Shaftesbury Av.)
The Glass Ho. SE1 . . . . .7G 15
(off Royal Oak Yd.)
Glasshouse Cl. UB8: Hil 5D 74
Glasshouse Flds. E1 . . . . .7K 85
(not continuous)
Glasshouse Gdns. E20 . . . . .7E 68
Glasshouse Gdns. Development
E20 . . . . .7D 68
Glasshouse St. W1 . . . . .3B 12 (7G 83)
Glasshouse Wlk.
SE11 . . . . .5F 19 (5J 101)
Glasshouse Yd. EC1 . . . . .4C 8 (4C 84)
Glasslyn Rd. N8 . . . . .5H 47
Glassmill La. BR2: Broml 2H 159
Glass Mill Leisure Cen. 3E 122
Glass St. E2 . . . . .4H 85
Glassworks Studios E2 . . . . .1H 9
(off Basing Pl.)
Glass Yd. SE18 . . . . .3E 106
Glastonbury Av. IG8: Wfd G 7G 37
Glastonbury Ct. SE14 . . . . .7J 103
(off Farrow La.)
Glastonbury Ho. SE12 . . . . .5K 123
(off Wantage Rd.)
SW1 .5J 17
(part of Abbots Mnr.)
Glastonbury Pl. E1 . . . . .6J 85
Glastonbury Rd. N9 . . . . .1B 34
SM4: Mord 7J 153
Glastonbury St. NW6 . . . . .5H 63

Glaston Cl. W5 . . . . .1D 96
(off Grange Rd.)
Glaucus St. E3 . . . . .5D 86
Glazbury Rd. W14 . . . . .4G 99
Glazebrook Cl. SE21 . . . . .2D 138
Glazebrook Rd. TW11: Tedd 7K 131
The Glebe BR7: Chst 1G 161
KT4: Wor Pk 1B 164
SE3 . . . . .3G 123
SW16 . . . . .4H 137
UB7: W Dray 4B 92
Glebe Av. CR4: Mitc 2C 154
EN2: Enf 2G 23
HA3: Kenton 4E 42
HA4: Ruis 6K 57
IG8: Wfd G 6D 36
UB10: Ick 3C 56
W4 . . . . .5A 98
Glebe Cl. UB10: Ick 4E 56
W4 . . . . .5A 98
Glebe Cotts. TW13: Hanw 3E 130
(off Twickenham Rd.)
Glebe Ct. CR4: Mitc 3D 154
E3 . . . . .3D 86
(off Rainhill Way)
HA7: Stan 5H 27
N13 . . . . .3F 33
SE3 . . . . .3G 123
W5 . . . . .1D 96
W7 . . . . .7H 77
Glebe Cres. HA3: Kenton 3E 42
NW4 .4E 44
Glebe Farm Bus. Pk. BR2: Kes . . .7B 172
Glebe Gdns. KT3: N Mald 7A 152
Glebe Ho. SE16 . . . . .3H 103
(off Slippers Pl.)
Glebe Ho. Dr. BR2: Hayes 1K 171
Glebe Hyrst SE19 . . . . .4E 138
Glebe Knoll BR2: Broml 2H 159
Glebeland Gdns. TW17: Shep 6E 146
Glebelands E10 . . . . .2D 68
KT8: W Mole 5F 149
Glebelands Av. E18 . . . . .2J 51
IG2: Ilf 7H 53
Glebelands Cl. N12 . . . . .1B 46
SE5 .3E 120
Glebe Ter. W4: Felt 1J 129
Glebe M. DA15: Sidc 6K 125
Glebe Path CR4: Mitc 3D 154
Glebe Pl. SW3 . . . . .7C 16 (6C 100)
Glebe Rd. BR1: Broml 1J 159
E8 . . . . .7F 67
HA7: Stan 5H 27
N3 . . . . .1A 46
N8 . . . . .4K 47
NW10 . . . . .6C 62
RM10: Dag 6H 73
SM2: Cheam 7G 165
SM5: Cars 6D 166
SW13 . . . . .2C 116
UB3: Hayes 1H 93
Glebe Side TW1: Twick 6K 113
Glebe Sq. CR4: Mitc 3D 154
Glebe St. W4 . . . . .5A 98
Glebe Ter. W4 . . . . .5A 98
Glebe Way BR4: W W'ck 2E 170
IG8: Wfd G 5F 37
TW13: Hanw 3E 130
Gledhow Gdns. SW5 . . . . .4A 100
Gledstanes Rd. W14 . . . . .5G 99
Gledwood Av. UB4: Hayes 5H 75
Gledwood Ct. UB4: Hayes 5H 75
Gledwood Cres. UB4: Hayes 5H 75
Gledwood Dr. UB4: Hayes 5H 75
Gledwood Gdns. UB4: Hayes 5H 75
Gleed Av. WD23: B Hea 2C 26
Gleeson Dr. BR6: Chels 5K 173
Glegg Pl. SW15 . . . . .4F 117
The Glen BR2: Broml 2G 159
BR6: Farnb 3D 172
CR0: C'don 3K 169
EN2: Enf 4G 23
HA5: Eastc 5K 39

The Glen HA5: Pinn 7C 40
  HA9: Wemb 4E 60
  UB2: S'hall 5D 94
Glenaffric Av. E14 . . . .4E 104
Glen Albyn Rd. SW19 . . . .2F 135
Glenallan Ho. W14 . . . .4H 99
  (off North End Cres.)
Glenalla Rd. HA4: Ruis 7H 39
Glenalmond Ho. TW15: Ashf 3A 128
Glenalmond Rd. HA3: Kenton 4E 42
Glenalvon Way SE18 . . . .4C 106
Glena Mt. SM1: Sutt 4A 166
Glenarm Rd. E5 . . . .4J 67
Glen Av. TW15: Ashf 4C 128
Glenavon Cl. KT10: Clay 6A 162
Glenavon Ct. KT4: Wor Pk 2D 164
Glenavon Lodge BR3: Beck 7C 140
Glenavon Rd. E15 . . . .7G 69
Glenbarr Cl. SE9 . . . .3F 125
Glenbow Rd. BR1: Broml 6G 141
Glenbrook Nth. EN2: Enf 4E 22
Glenbrook Rd. NW6 . . . .5J 63
Glenbrook Sth. EN2: Enf 4E 22
Glenbuck Ct. KT6: Surb 6E 150
Glenbuck Rd. KT6: Surb 6D 150
Glenburnie Rd. SW17 . . . .3D 136
Glencairn Dr. W5 . . . .4C 78
Glencairne Cl. E16 . . . .5B 88
Glencairn Rd. SW16 . . . .1J 155
Glencar Ct. SE19 . . . .6B 138
Glen Cl. TW17: Shep 4C 146
Glencoe Av. IG2: Ilf 7H 53
Glencoe Dr. RM10: Dag 4G 73
Glencoe Mans. SW9 . . . .7A 102
  (off Mowll St.)
Glencoe Rd. UB4: Yead 5B 76
Glen Ct. BR1: Broml 7H 141
  (off Bromley Av.)
  DA15: Sidc 4A 144
Glen Cres. IG8: Wfd G 6E 36
Glendale Av. HA8: Edg 4A 28
  N22 . . . .7F 33
  RM6: Chad H 7C 54
Glendale Cl. SE9 . . . .3E 124
Glendale Dr. SW19 . . . .5H 135
Glendale Gdns. HA9: Wemb 1D 60
Glendale M. BR3: Beck 1D 158
Glendale Rd. DA8: Erith 4J 109
Glendale Way SE28 . . . .7C 90
Glendall St. SW9 . . . .4K 119
Glendarvon St. SW15 . . . .3F 117
Glendevon Cl. HA8: Edg 3C 28
Glendish Rd. N17 . . . .1H 49
Glendor Gdns. NW7 . . . .4E 28
Glendower Gdns. SW14 . . . .3A 90
Glendower Pl. SW7 . . . .3A 16 (4B 100)
Glendower Rd. E4 . . . .1A 36
  SW14 . . . .3K 115
Glendown Ho. E8 . . . .5G 67
Glendown Rd. SE2 . . . .5A 108
Glendun Ct. W3 . . . .7A 80
Glendun Rd. W3 . . . .7A 80
Gleneagle M. SW16 . . . .5H 137
Gleneagle Rd. SW16 . . . .5H 137
Gleneagles HA7: Stan 7G 27
  W13 . . . .5B 78
  (off Malvern Way)
Gleneagles Cl. BR6: Orp 1H 173
  SE16 . . . .5H 103
Gleneagles Grn. BR6: Orp 1H 173
Gleneagles Twr. UB1: S'hall 6G 77
  (off Fleming Rd.)
Gleneldon M. SW16 . . . .4J 137
Gleneldon Rd. SW16 . . . .4J 137
Glenelg Rd. SW2 . . . .5J 119
Glenesk Rd. SE9 . . . .3E 124
Glenfarg Rd. SE6 . . . .1E 140
Glenfield Cres. HA4: Ruis 7F 39
Glenfield Rd. SW12 . . . .1G 137
  TW15: Ashf 6D 128
  W13 . . . .2B 96
Glenfield Ter. W13 . . . .2B 96
Glenfinlas Way SE5 . . . .7B 102

Glenforth St. SE10 . . . .5H 105
Glengall Bus. Cen. SE15 . . . .6F 103
Glengall Gro. E14 . . . .3D 104
Glengall Pas. NW6 . . . .1J 81
  (off Priory Pk. Rd.)
Glengall Rd. DA7: Bex 3E 126
  HA8: Edg 3C 28
  IG8: Wfd G 6D 36
  NW6 . . . .1H 81
  SE15 . . . .5F 103
Glengall Ter. SE15 . . . .6F 103
Glen Gdns. CR0: Wadd 3A 168
Glengariff Mans. SW9 . . . .7A 102
  (off Sth. Island Pl.)
Glengarnock Av. E14 . . . .4E 104
Glengarry Rd. SE22 . . . .5E 120
Glenham Dr. IG2: Ilf 5F 53
Glenhead Cl. SE9 . . . .3F 125
Glenhill Cl. N3 . . . .2J 45
Glen Ho. E16 . . . .1E 106
  (off Storey St.)
Glenhouse Rd. SE9 . . . .5E 124
Glenhurst BR3: Beck 1E 158
Glenhurst Av. DA5: Bexl 1F 145
  HA4: Ruis 7E 38
  NW5 . . . .4E 64
Glenhurst Ct. SE19 . . . .5F 139
Glenhurst Ri. SE19 . . . .7C 138
Glenhurst Rd. N12 . . . .5G 31
  TW8: Bford 6C 96
Glenilla Rd. NW3 . . . .6C 64
Glenister Gdns. UB3: Hayes 2K 93
Glenister Ho. UB3: Hayes 1K 93
  (off Avondale Dr.)
Glenister Pk. Rd. SW16 . . . .7H 137
Glenister Rd. SE10 . . . .5H 105
Glenister St. E16 . . . .1E 106
Glenkerry Ho. E14 . . . .6E 86
  (off Burcham St.)
Glenlea Rd. SE9 . . . .5D 124
Glenloch Rd. EN3: Enf H 2D 24
  NW3 . . . .6C 64
Glenluce Rd. SE3 . . . .6J 105
Glenlyon Rd. SE9 . . . .5E 124
Glenmead IG9: Buck H 1F 37
Glenmere Av. NW7 . . . .7H 29
Glenmere Row SE12 . . . .6J 123
Glen M. E17 . . . .5B 50
Glenmill TW12: Hamp 5D 130
Glenmore Lawns W13 . . . .6A 78
Glenmore Lodge BR3: Beck 1D 158
Glenmore Pde. HA0: Wemb 1E 78
Glenmore Rd. DA16: Well 7K 107
  NW3 . . . .6C 64
Glenmore Way IG11: Bark 2A 90
Glenmount Path SE18 . . . .5G 107
Glennie Ct. SE22 . . . .1G 139
Glennie Rd. SE27 . . . .3A 138
Glenny Rd. IG11: Bark 6G 71
Glenorchy Cl. UB4: Yead 5C 76
Glenpark Ct. W13 . . . .7A 78
Glenparke Rd. E7 . . . .6K 69
Glenridding NW1 . . . .1B 6
  (off Ampthill Est.)
Glen Ri. IG8: Wfd G 6E 36
Glen Rd. E13 . . . .4A 88
  E17 . . . .5B 50
  KT9: Chess 4F 163
Glen Rd. End SM6: W'gton 7F 167
Glenrosa St. SW6 . . . .2A 118
Glenrose Ct. DA14: Sidc 5B 144
  SE1 . . . .7G 15
  (off Long La.)
Glenroy St. W12 . . . .6E 80
Glensdale Rd. SE4 . . . .3B 122
Glenshaw Mans. SW9 . . . .7A 102
  (off Brixton Rd.)
Glenshiel Rd. SE9 . . . .5E 124
Glentanner Way SW17 . . . .3B 136
Glen Ter. E14 . . . .2E 104
  (off Manchester Rd.)
Glentham Gdns. SW13 . . . .6D 98
Glentham Rd. SW13 . . . .6C 98

Glenthorne Av. CR0: C'don 1H 169
Glenthorne Cl. SM3: Sutt 1J 165
  UB10: Hil 3C 74
Glenthorne Gdns. IG6: Ilf 3E 52
  SM3: Sutt 1J 165
Glenthorne M. W6 . . . .4D 98
Glenthorne Rd. E17 . . . .5A 50
  KT1: King T 4F 151
  N11 . . . .5J 31
  W6 . . . .4D 98
Glenthorpe Av. SW15 . . . .4C 116
Glenthorpe Gdns. HA7: Stan 3E 26
Glenthorpe Rd. SM4: Mord 5F 153
Glenton M. SE15 . . . .2J 121
Glenton Rd. SE13 . . . .4G 123
Glentrammon Av. BR6: Chels 6K 173
Glentrammon Cl. BR6: Chels 5K 173
Glentrammon Gdns.
  BR6: Chels 6K 173
Glentrammon Rd. BR6: Chels 6K 173
Glentworth St. NW1 . . . .4F 5 (4D 82)
Glenure Rd. SE9 . . . .5E 124
Glenvern Ct. TW7: Isle 2A 114
  (off White Lodge Cl.)
Glenview SE2 . . . .6D 108
Glenview Rd. BR1: Broml 2B 160
Glenville Av. EN2: Enf 1H 23
Glenville Gro. SE8 . . . .7B 104
Glenville M. Ind. Est. SW18 . . . .7J 117
Glenville Rd. KT2: King T 1G 151
Glen Wlk. TW7: Isle 5H 113
  (not continuous)
Glenwood Av. NW9 . . . .1A 62
Glenwood Cl. HA1: Harr 5K 41
Glenwood Ct. DA14: Sidc 4A 144
Glenwood Gdns. IG2: Ilf 5E 52
Glenwood Gro. NW9 . . . .1J 61
Glenwood Rd. KT17: Ewe 6C 164
  N15 . . . .5B 48
  NW7 . . . .3F 29
  SE6 . . . .1B 140
  TW3: Houn 3H 113
Glenwood Way CR0: C'don 6K 157
Glenworth Av. E14 . . . .4F 105
Gliddon Dr. E5 . . . .4H 67
Gliddon Rd. W14 . . . .4G 99
Glimpsing Grn. DA18: Erith 3E 108
Glisson Rd. UB10: Hil 2C 74
Global App. E3 . . . .2E 86
Globe Apts. SE8 . . . .6B 104
  (off Evelyn St.)
Globe Ho. E14 . . . .6G 87
Globe Pond Rd. SE16 . . . .1A 104
Globe Rd. E1 . . . .3J 85
  E2 . . . .3J 85
  E15 . . . .5H 69
  IG8: Wfd G 6F 37
Globe St. SE1 . . . .7E 14 (3D 102)
Globe Ter. E2 . . . .3J 85
GLOBE TOWN 3K 85
Globe Town Mkt. 3K 85
Globe Vw. EC4 . . . .2C 14
  (off High Timber St.)
Globe Wharf SE16 . . . .7K 85
Globe Yd. W1 . . . .1J 11
Glossop Rd. CR2: Sande 7D 168
Gloster Ridley Ct. E14 . . . .6B 86
  (off St Anne's Row)
Gloster Rd. KT3: N Mald 4A 152
Gloucester W14 . . . .4H 99
  (off Kensington Village)
Gloucester Arc. SW7 . . . .4A 100
Gloucester Av. DA15: Sidc 2J 143
  DA16: Well 4K 125
  NW1 . . . .7E 64
Gloucester Cir. SE10 . . . .7E 104
Gloucester Cl. KT7: T Ditt 1A 162
  NW10 . . . .7K 61
Gloucester Ct.
  CR4: Mitc 5J 155
  EC3 . . . .3H 15 (7E 84)

Gloucester Ct. HA1: Harr 3J 41
  NW11 . . . .7H 45
  (off Golders Grn. Rd.)
  SE1 . . . .5F 103
  (off Rolls Rd.)
  SE1 . . . .7B 14
  (Swan St.)
  SE22 . . . .1G 139
  TW9: Kew 7G 97
  W7 . . . .5K 77
  (off Copley Cl.)
Gloucester Cres. NW1 . . . .1F 83
  TW18: Staines 6A 128
Gloucester Dr. N4 . . . .2B 66
  NW11 . . . .4J 45
Gloucester Gdns. EN4: Cockf 4K 21
  IG1: Ilf 7C 52
  NW11 . . . .7H 45
  SM1: Sutt 2K 165
  W2 . . . .6A 82
Gloucester Ga. NW1 . . . .2F 83
  (not continuous)
GLOUCESTER GA. BRI. 1F 83
  (off Gloucester Gate)
Gloucester Ga. M. NW1 . . . .2F 83
Gloucester Gro. HA8: Edg 1K 43
Gloucester Ho. E16 . . . .1J 105
  (off Gatcombe Rd.)
  NW6 . . . .2J 81
  (off Cambridge Rd.)
  SW9 . . . .7A 102
  TW10: Rich 5J 115
Gloucester M. E10 . . . .7C 50
  W2 . . . .1A 10 (6A 82)
Gloucester M. W. W2 . . . .6A 82
Gloucester Pde. DA15: Sidc 5A 126
  UB3: Harl 3E 92
Gloucester Pk. Apts. SW7 . . . .4A 100
  (off Ashburn Pl.)
Gloucester Pl. NW1 . . . .4E 4 (4D 82)
  W1 . . . .4E 4 (4D 82)
Gloucester Pl. M. W1 . . . .6F 5 (5D 82)
Gloucester Rd. CR0: C'don 1D 168
  DA17: Belv 5F 109
  E10 . . . .7C 50
  E11 . . . .5K 51
  E12 . . . .3D 70
  E17 . . . .2K 49
  EN2: Enf 1H 23
  EN5: New Bar 5E 20
  HA1: Harr 5J 41
  KT1: King T 2G 151
  N17 . . . .2D 48
  N18 . . . .5A 34
  SW7 . . . .4A 16 (3A 100)
  TW2: Twick 1G 131
  TW4: Houn 4C 112
  TW9: Kew 7G 97
  TW11: Tedd 5J 131
  TW12: Hamp 7F 131
  TW13: Felt 1A 130
  W3 . . . .2J 97
  W5 . . . .2C 96
Gloucester Sq. E2 . . . .1G 85
  W2 . . . .1B 10 (6B 82)
  (not continuous)
Gloucester St. SW1 . . . .6A 18 (5G 101)
Gloucester Ter. N14 . . . .1C 32
  (off Crown La.)
  W2 . . . .1A 10 (6K 81)
Gloucester Wlk. W8 . . . .2J 99
Gloucester Way EC1 . . . .2K 7 (3A 84)
Glover Cl. SE2 . . . .4C 108
Glover Dr. N18 . . . .6D 34
Glover Ho. NW6 . . . .7A 64
  (off Harben Rd.)
  SE15 . . . .4H 121
Glover Rd. HA5: Pinn 6B 40
Glovers Gro. HA4: Ruis 7D 38
Gloxinia Wlk. TW12: Hamp 6E 130
Glycena Rd. SW11 . . . .3D 118
Glyn Av. EN4: E Barn 4G 21
Glyn Cl. SE25 . . . .2E 156

Glyn Ct. HA7: Stan 6G 27
  SW16 .3A 138
Glyndale Grange SM2: Sutt 6K 165
Glyndebourne Ct. UB5: N'olt 3A 76
  (off Canberra Dr.)
Glyndebourne Pk. BR6: Farnb 2F 173
Glynde M. SW3 . . . . .2D 16
Glynde Reach WC1 . . . . .2F 7
Glynde Rd. DA7: Bex 3D 126
Glynde St. SE4 . . . . .6B 122
Glyndon Rd. SE18 . . . . .4G 107
  (not continuous)
Glyn Dr. DA14: Sidc 4B 144
Glynfield Rd. NW10 . . . . .7A 62
Glyn Mans. W14 . . . . .4G 99
  (off Hammersmith Rd.)
Glynne Rd. N22 . . . . .2A 48
Glyn Rd. E5 . . . . .4K 67
  EN3: Pond E 4D 24
  KT4: Wor Pk 2F 165
Glyn St. SE11 . . . . .6G 19 (5K 101)
Glynswood Pl. HA6: Nwood 1D 38
Glynwood Ct. SE23 . . . . .2J 139
Goals Soccer Cen.
  Bexleyheath 3F 127
  Chingford 6H 35
  Dagenham 1D 90
  Eltham .6A 124
  Gillette Corner 6K 95
  Hayes 1A 94
  Heathrow 4E 92
  Ruislip 5B 58
  Sutton .3F 165
  Tolworth 2J 163
  Wimbledon 3C 152
Go Ape!
  Alexandra Palace 2H 47
  Battersea Park 1D 118
  Trent Park 3K 21
Goater's All. SW6 . . . . .7H 99
  (off Dawes Rd.)
GOAT HO. BRI. 3G 157
Goat La. EN1: Enf 1A 24
Goat Rd. CR4: Cars, Mitc 7D 154
Goat Wharf TW8: Bford 6E 96
Gobions Av. RM5: Col R 1K 55
Goby Ho. SE8 . . . . .7D 104
  (off Creative Rd.)
Godalming Av. SM6: W'gton 5J 167
Godalming Rd. E14 . . . . .5D 86
Godbold Rd. E15 . . . . .4G 87
Goddard Cl. TW17: Shep 3B 146
Goddard Ct. HA3: Kenton 2A 42
Goddard Ho. SE11 . . . . .4B 102
  (off George Mathers Rd.)
Goddard Pl. N19 . . . . .3G 65
Goddard Rd. BR3: Beck 4K 157
Goddards Way IG1: Ilf 1H 71
Goddarts Ho. E17 . . . . .3C 50
Goddington La. BR6: Chels 3K 173
Godfree Ct. SE1 . . . . .6E 14
  (off Long La.)
Godfrey Av. TW2: Whitt 7H 113
  UB5: N'olt 1C 76
Godfrey Hill SE18 . . . . .4C 106
Godfrey Ho. EC1 . . . . .2E 8
Godfrey Pl. E2 . . . . .2J 9
  (off Austin St.)
Godfrey Rd. SE18 . . . . .4D 106
Godfrey St. E15 . . . . .2E 86
  SW3 . . . . .5D 16 (5C 100)
Godfrey Way TW4: Houn 7C 112
Goding St. SE11 . . . . .5F 19 (5J 101)
Godley Cl. SE14 . . . . .1J 121
Godley Rd. SW18 . . . . .1B 136
Godliman St. EC4 . . . . . . .1B 14 (6B 84)
Godman Rd. SE15 . . . . .2H 121
Godolphin Cl. N13 . . . . .6G 33
Godolphin Ho. NW3 . . . . .7C 64
  (off Fellows Rd.)
Godolphin Pl. W3 . . . . .7K 79
Godolphin Rd. W12 . . . . .1D 98
  (not continuous)

Godric Cres. CR0: New Ad 7F 171
Godson Rd. CR0: Wadd 3A 168
Godson St. N1 . . . . .2A 84
Godson Yd. NW6 . . . . .3J 81
Godstone Ho. SE1 . . . . .7F 15
  (off Pardoner St.)
Godstone Rd. SM1: Sutt 4A 166
  TW1: Twick 6B 114
Godstow Rd. SE2 . . . . .2B 108
Godward Sq. E1 . . . . .4K 85
Godwin Cl. E4 . . . . .1K 25
  KT19: Ewe 6J 163
  N1 . . . . .2C 84
Godwin Ct. NW1 . . . . .2G 83
  (off Chalton St.)
Godwin Ho. E2 . . . . .2F 85
  (off Thurtle Rd.)
  SE1 . . . . .5J 15
  (off Still Wlk.)
Godwin Rd. BR2: Broml 3A 160
  E7 . . . . .4K 69
Goffers Rd. SE3 . . . . .1G 123
Goffs Rd. TW15: Ashf 6F 129
Goidel Cl. SM6: Bedd 4H 167
Golborne Gdns. W10 . . . . .4G 81
  (not continuous)
Golborne M. W10 . . . . .5G 81
Golborne Rd. W10 . . . . .5G 81
Golda Cl. EN5: Barn 6A 20
Golday Rd. N3 . . . . .2H 45
Goldbeaters Gro. HA8: Edg 6F 29
Goldbeaters Ho. W1 . . . . .1D 12
  (off Manette St.)
Goldcliff Cl. SM4: Mord 7J 153
Goldcrest Cl. E16 . . . . .5B 88
  SE28 . . . . .7C 90
Goldcrest M. N16 . . . . .2E 67
  W5 . . . . .5D 78
Goldcrest Way CR0: New Ad 7F 171
  WD23: Bush 1B 26
Golden Anchor House SE10 . . . . . . .3J 105
  (off Latimer Square)
Golden Bus. Pk. E10 . . . . .1A 68
Golden Ct. EN4: E Barn 4H 21
  TW7: Isle 2H 113
  TW9: Rich 5D 114
Golden Cres. UB3: Hayes 1H 93
Golden Cross M. W11 . . . . .6H 81
  (off Portobello Rd.)
Golden Hinde 4E 14 (1D 102)
Golden Hind Pl. SE8 . . . . .4B 104
  (off Grove St.)
Golden Jubilee Bridges 5G 13
Golden La. BR4: W W'ck 3E 170
  EC1 . . . . .3C 8 (4C 84)
Golden La. Campus EC1 . . . . .4D 8
Golden La. Est. EC1 . . . . . . .4C 8 (4C 84)
Golden Lane Sport & Fitness Centre
  . . . . .4C 8
Golden Mnr. W7 . . . . .7J 77
Golden M. SE20 . . . . .1J 157
Golden Mile Ho. TW8: Bford 5E 96
  (off Clayponds La.)
Golden Pde. E17 . . . . .3E 50
  (off Wood St.)
Golden Plover Cl. E16 . . . . .6J 87
Golden Sq. W1 . . . . .2B 12 (7G 83)
Golden Yd. NW3 . . . . .4A 64
  (off Holly M.)
Golders Cl. HA8: Edg 5C 28
Golders Ct. NW11 . . . . .7H 45
Golders Gdns. NW11 . . . . .7G 45
GOLDERS GREEN 6G 45
Golders Grn. Crematorium 7J 45
Golders Grn. Cres. NW11 . . . . .7H 45
Golders Grn. Rd. NW11 . . . . .6G 45
Golderslea NW11 . . . . .1J 63
Golders Mnr. Dr. NW11 . . . . .6F 45
Golders Pk. Cl. NW11 . . . . .1J 63
Golders Ri. NW4 . . . . .5E 45
Golders Way NW11 . . . . .7H 45
Golderton NW4 . . . . .4D 44
  (off Prince of Wales Cl.)

Goldfinch Ct. E3 . . . . .2C 86
  (off Four Seasons Cl.)
Goldfinch Rd. SE28 . . . . .3H 107
Goldhawk Ho. NW9 . . . . .2C 44
Goldhawk M. W12 . . . . .2D 98
Goldhawk Rd. W6 . . . . .4B 98
  W12 . . . . .4B 98
Goldhaze Cl. IG8: Wfd G 7F 37
Gold Hill HA8: Edg 6E 28
Goldhurst Ho. W6 . . . . .6E 98
Goldhurst Mans. NW6 . . . . .6A 64
  (off Goldhurst Ter.)
Goldhurst Ter. NW6 . . . . .7K 63
Goldie Ho. N19 . . . . .7H 47
Golding Cl. KT9: Chess 6C 162
  N18 . . . . .6J 33
Golding Ct. IG1: Ilf 3E 70
Golding Ho. NW9 . . . . .2C 44
Golding St. E1 . . . . .6G 85
  (not continuous)
Golding Ter. E1 . . . . .5H 85
  (off Rope Wlk. Gdns.)
  SW11 .2E 118
Goldington Bldgs. NW1 . . . . .1H 83
  (off Royal College St.)
Goldington Cres. NW1 . . . . .2H 83
Goldington St. NW1 . . . . .2H 83
Gold La. HA8: Edg 6E 28
Goldman Cl. E2 . . . . .3K 9 (4G 85)
Goldney Rd. W9 . . . . .4J 81
Goldrill Dr. N11 . . . . .2K 31
Goldsboro' Rd. SW8 . . . . .1H 119
Goldsborough Cres. E4 . . . . .2J 35
Goldsborough Ho. E14 . . . . .5D 104
  (off St Davids Sq.)
Goldsdown Cl. EN3: Enf H 2F 25
Goldsdown Rd. EN3: Enf H 2E 24
Goldsmid St. SE18 . . . . .5J 107
Goldsmith Av. E12 . . . . .6C 70
  NW9 . . . . .5A 44
  RM7: Rush G 7G 55
  W3 . . . . .7K 79
Goldsmith Cl. HA2: Harr 1E 58
Goldsmith Ct. WC2 . . . . .7F 7
  (off Stukeley St.)
Goldsmith Est. SE15 . . . . .1G 121
Goldsmith La. NW9 . . . . .4H 43
Goldsmith Rd. E10 . . . . .1C 68
  E17 . . . . .2K 49
  N11 . . . . .5J 31
  SE15 .1G 121
  W3 . . . . .1K 97
Goldsmith's Bldgs. W3 . . . . .1K 97
Goldsmith's Cl. W3 . . . . .1K 97
Goldsmiths College 1A 122
Goldsmith's Pl. NW6 . . . . .1K 81
  (off Springfield La.)
Goldsmith's Row E2 . . . . .2G 85
Goldsmith's Sq. E2 . . . . .2G 85
Goldsmith St. EC2 . . . . . . .7D 8 (6C 84)
Goldsworthy Gdns. SE16 . . . . .5J 103
Goldthorpe NW1 . . . . .1G 83
  (off Camden St.)
Goldwell Ho. SE22 . . . . .3E 120
  (off Quorn Rd.)
Goldwell Rd. CR7: Thor H 4K 155
Goldwin Cl. SE14 . . . . .1J 121
Goldwing Cl. E16 . . . . .6J 87
Golf Cl. CR7: Thor H 1A 156
  HA7: Stan 7H 27
Golf Club Dr. KT2: King T 7K 133
Golfe Rd. IG1: Ilf 3H 71
Golf Kingdom
  Barking .5F 55
Golf Rd. BR1: Broml 3E 160
  W5 . . . . .6F 79
Golf Side TW2: Twick 3H 131
Golfside Cl. KT3: N Mald 2A 152
  N20 . . . . .3H 31
Gollogly Ter. SE7 . . . . .5A 106
Gomer Gdns. TW11: Tedd 6A 132
Gomer Pl. TW11: Tedd 6A 132
Gomm Rd. SE16 . . . . .3J 103

Gomshall Av. SM6: W'gton 5J 167
Gondar Gdns. NW6 . . . . .5H 63
Gonson St. SE8 . . . . .6D 104
Gonston Cl. SW19 . . . . .2G 135
Gonville Cres. UB5: N'olt 6F 59
Gonville Rd. CR7: Thor H 5K 155
Gonville St. SW6 . . . . .3G 117
Gooch Ho. E5 . . . . .3H 67
  EC1 . . . . .5J 7
  (off Portpool La.)
  SW11 . . . . .7H 101
  (off Malthouse Rd.)
Goodall Ho. SE4 . . . . .4K 121
Goodall Rd. E11 . . . . .3E 68
Goodchild Rd. N4 . . . . .1C 66
Gooden Ct. HA1: Harr 3J 59
Goodenough Rd. SW19 . . . . .7H 135
Goodey Rd. IG11: Bark 7K 71
Goodfaith Ho. E14 . . . . .7D 86
  (off Simpson's Rd.)
Goodge Pl. W1 . . . . .6B 6 (5G 83)
Goodge St. W1 . . . . .6B 6 (5G 83)
Goodhall Cl. HA7: Stan 6F 27
Goodhall St. NW10 . . . . .3B 80
  (not continuous)
Goodhart Pl. E14 . . . . .7A 86
Goodhart Way BR4: W W'ck 7G 159
Goodhew Rd. CR0: C'don 6G 157
Goodhope Ho. E14 . . . . .7D 86
  (off Poplar High St.)
Gooding Cl. KT3: N Mald 4J 151
Goodinge Cl. N7 . . . . .6J 65
Goodinge Rd. N7 . . . . .6J 65
Gooding Ho. SE7 . . . . .5A 106
Goodman Cres. CR0: C'don 6B 156
  SW2 . . . . .2J 137
Goodman Rd. E10 . . . . .7E 50
Goodman's Ct. E1 . . . . . . .2J 15 (7F 85)
Goodmans Ct. HA0: Wemb 4D 60
Goodman's Stile E1 . . . . .6G 85
Goodmans Yd. E1 . . . . .2J 15 (7F 85)
GOODMAYES 2A 72
Goodmayes Av. IG3: Ilf 1A 72
Goodmayes La. IG3: Ilf 4A 72
Goodmayes Lodge
  RM8: Dag 4A 72
Goodmayes Retail Pk. 1B 72
Goodmayes Rd. IG3: Ilf 1A 72
Goodrich Ct. W10 . . . . .6F 81
Goodrich Ho. E2 . . . . .2J 85
  (off Sewardstone Rd.)
Goodrich Rd. SE22 . . . . .6F 121
Goodridge Ho. E4 . . . . .7K 35
Goodson Ho. SM4: Mord 7A 154
  (off Green La.)
Goodson Rd. NW10 . . . . .7A 62
Goodspeed Ho. E14 . . . . .7D 86
  (off Simpson's Rd.)
Goods Way N1 . . . . .2J 83
Goodway Gdns. E14 . . . . .6F 87
Goodwill Dr. HA2: Harr 1E 58
Goodwill Ho. E14 . . . . .7D 86
  (off Simpson's Rd.)
Goodwin Cl. CR4: Mitc 3B 154
  SE16 . . . . .3F 103
Goodwin Ct. EN4: E Barn 6H 21
  N8 . . . . .3J 47
  (off Campsbourne Rd.)
  SW19 . . . . .7C 136
Goodwin Dr. DA14: Sidc 3D 144
Goodwin Gdns. CR0: Wadd 6B 168
Goodwin Ho. N9 . . . . .1D 34
Goodwin Rd. CR0: Wadd 5B 168
  N9 . . . . .1E 34
  W12 . . . . .2C 98
Goodwins Ct. WC2 . . . . . . .2E 12 (7J 83)
Goodwin St. N4 . . . . .2A 66
Goodwood Cl. HA7: Stan 5H 27
  SM4: Mord 4J 153
Goodwood Ct. W1 . . . . .5K 5
  (off Devonshire St.)
Goodwood Dr. UB5: N'olt 6E 58

Goodwood Ho. *SE14* 7A **104**
    (off Goodwood Rd.)
Goodwood Pde. BR3: Beck 4A **158**
Goodwood Rd. SE14 . . . . .7A **104**
Goodwyn Av. NW7 . . . . .5F **29**
Goodwyns Va. N10 . . . . .1E **46**
Goodyear Ho. *N2* 2B **46**
    (off The Grange)
Goodyear Pl. SE5 . . . . .6C **102**
Goodyer Ho. *SW1* 5C **18**
    (off Tachbrook St.)
Goodyers Gdns. NW4 . . . . .5F **45**
Goosander Way SE28 . . . . .3H **107**
Gooseacre La. HA3: Kenton 5D **42**
Goose Grn. Trad. Est.
   SE22 . . . . .4F **121**
Gooseley La. E6 . . . . .4F **89**
    (Claps Ga. La.)
   E6 . . . . .3E **88**
    (Folkestone Rd.)
Goosens Cl. SM1: Sutt 5A **166**
Goose Sq. E6 . . . . .6D **88**
Gophir La. EC4 . . . . .2E **14** (7D **84**)
Gopsall St. N1 . . . . .1D **84**
Gordian Apts. *SE10* 4G **105**
    (off Cable Wlk.)
Gordon Av. E4 . . . . .6B **36**
   HA7: Stan 7E **26**
   SW14 .4A **116**
   TW1: Twick 5A **114**
Gordonbrock Rd. SE4 . . . . .5C **122**
Gordon Cl. E17 . . . . .6C **50**
   N19 . . . . .1G **65**
Gordon Cotts. *W8* 2K **99**
    (off Dukes La.)
Gordon Ct. HA8: Edg 5A **28**
Gordon Cres. CRO: C'don 1D **168**
   UB3: Hayes 4J **93**
Gordondale Rd. SW19 . . . . .2J **135**
Gordon Dr. TW17: Shep 7F **147**
Gordon Gdns. HA8: Edg 2H **43**
Gordon Gro. SE5 . . . . .2B **120**
Gordon Hill EN2: Enf 1H **23**
Gordon Ho. *E1* 7J **85**
    (off Glamis Rd.)
   SW1 . . . . .2B **18**
    (off Greencoat Pl.)
   W5 . . . . .3E **78**
Gordon Ho. Rd. NW5 . . . . .4E **64**
Gordon Mans. *W14* 3F **99**
    (off Addison Gdns.)
   WC1 . . . . .4C **6**
    (off Torrington Pl.)
Gordon Pl. W8 . . . . .2J **99**
Gordon Rd. BR3: Beck 3B **158**
   DA15: Sidc 5J **125**
   DA17: Belv 4J **109**
   E4 . . . . .1B **36**
   E11 . . . . .6J **51**
   E15 . . . . .4E **68**
   E18 . . . . .1K **51**
   EN2: Enf 1H **23**
   HA3: W'stone 3J **41**
   IG1: Ilf 3H **71**
   IG11: Bark 1J **89**
   KT2: King T 1F **151**
   KT5: Surb 7F **151**
   N3 . . . . .7C **30**
   N9 . . . . .2C **34**
   N11 . . . . .7C **32**
   RM6: Chad H 6F **55**
   SE15 . . . . .2H **121**
   SM5: Cars 6D **166**
   TW3: Houn 4G **113**
   TW9: Rich 2F **115**
   TW15: Ashf 3A **128**
   TW17: Shep 6F **147**
   UB2: S'hall 4C **94**
   UB7: Yiew 7A **74**
   W4 . . . . .6H **97**
   W5 . . . . .7B **78**
   W13 . . . . .7B **78**
Gordon Sq. WC1 . . . . .3C **6** (4H **83**)

Gordon St. E13 . . . . .3J **87**
   WC1 . . . . .3C **6** (4H **83**)
Gordon Way BR1: Broml 1J **159**
   EN5: Barn 4C **20**
Gore Ct. NW9 . . . . .5G **43**
Gorefield Ho. *NW6* 2J **81**
    (off Gorefield Pl.)
Gorefield Pl. NW6 . . . . .2J **81**
Gore Ho. *N1* 7A **66**
    (off Drummond Way)
Gore Rd. E9 . . . . .1J **85**
   SW20 . . . . .2E **152**
GORESBROOK INTERCHANGE . . .2F **91**
Goresbrook Rd. RM9: Dag 1B **90**
Gore St. SW7 . . . . .3A **100**
Gorham Ho. *SE16* 2K **103**
    (off Wolfe Cres.)
Gorham Pl. W11 . . . . .7G **81**
Goring Cl. RM5: Col R 1J **55**
Goring Gdns. RM8: Dag 4C **72**
Goring Rd. N11 . . . . .6D **32**
   RM10: Dag 6K **73**
Goring St. EC3 . . . . .7H **9**
Goring Way UB6: G'frd 2G **77**
Gorleston Rd. N15 . . . . .5D **48**
Gorleston St. W14 . . . . .4G **99**
    (not continuous)
Gorman Rd. SE18 . . . . .4D **106**
Gorringe Pk. Av. CR4: Mitc 7D **136**
Gorse Cl. E16 . . . . .6J **87**
Gorsefield Ho. *E14* 7C **86**
    (off E. India Dock Rd.)
Gorse Ri. SW17 . . . . .5E **136**
Gorse Rd. CR0: C'don 4C **170**
Gorse Wlk. UB7: Yiew 6A **74**
Gorseway RM7: Rush G 1K **73**, 2K **73**
Gorst Rd. NW10 . . . . .4J **79**
   SW11 . . . . .6D **118**
Gorsuch Pl. E2 . . . . .1J **9** (3F **85**)
Gorsuch St. E2 . . . . .1J **9** (2F **85**)
Gosberton Rd. SW12 . . . . .1D **136**
Gosbury Hill KT9: Chess 4E **162**
Gosfield Rd. RM8: Dag 2G **73**
Gosfield St. W1 . . . . .6A **6** (5G **83**)
Gosford Gdns. IG4: Ilf 5D **52**
Gosford Ho. *E3* 2B **86**
    (off Tredegar Rd.)
Goshawk Ct. NW9 . . . . .7B **44**
Goshawk Gdns. UB4: Hayes 3G **75**
Goslett Yd. WC2 . . . . . . .1D **12** (6H **83**)
Gosling Cl. UB6: G'frd 3E **76**
Gosling Ho. *E1* 7J **85**
    (off Sutton St.)
Gosling Way SW9 . . . . .1A **120**
Gospatrick Rd. N17 . . . . .7H **33**
GOSPEL OAK 4E **64**
Gosport Rd. E17 . . . . .5B **50**
Gosport Wlk. N17 . . . . .4H **49**
Gossage Rd. SE18 . . . . .5H **107**
   UB10: Uxb 7B **56**
Gossamer Gdns. E2 . . . . .2H **85**
Gosse Ct. *N1* 1E **84**
    (off Downham Rd.)
Gosset St. E2 . . . . .1K **9** (3F **85**)
Gosshill Rd. BR7: Chst 2E **160**
Gossington Cl. BR7: Chst 4F **143**
Gosterwood St. SE8 . . . . .6A **104**
Gostling Rd. TW2: Whitt 1E **130**
Goston Gdns. CR7: Thor H 3A **156**
Goston Ga. *SW8* 1K **119**
    (off Hampson Way)
Goswell Pl. EC1 . . . . .2B **8**
Goswell Rd. EC1 . . . . .1A **8** (2B **84**)
Gothenburg Cl. *SE8* 4A **104**
    (off Bailey St.)
Gothic Cotts. *EN2: Enf* 2H **23**
    (off Chase Grn. Av.)
Gothic Ct. *SE5* 7C **102**
    (off Wyndham Rd.)
   UB3: Harl 6F **93**
Gothic Rd. TW2: Twick 2H **131**
Gottfried M. NW5 . . . . .4G **65**
Goudhurst Rd. BR1: Broml 5G **141**

Gough Ho. *KT1: King T* 2E **150**
    (off Eden St.)
   N1 . . . . .1B **84**
    (off Windsor St.)
Gough Rd. E15 . . . . .4H **69**
   EN1: Enf 2C **24**
Gough Sq. EC4 . . . . .1K **13** (6A **84**)
Gough St. WC1 . . . . .3H **7** (4K **83**)
Gough Wlk. E14 . . . . .6C **86**
Goulden Ho. SW11 . . . . .2C **118**
Goulden Ho. App. SW11 . . . . .2C **118**
Goulding Gdns.
   CR7: Thor H 2C **156**
Gouldman Ho. *E1* 4J **85**
    (off Wyllen Cl.)
Gould Rd. TW2: Twick 1J **131**
   TW14: Felt 7G **111**
GOULDS GREEN 5D **74**
Gould's Grn. UB8: Hil 7D **74**
Gould Ter. E8 . . . . .5H **67**
Gould Way HA8: Edg 7C **28**
Goulston St. E1 . . . . .7J **9** (6F **85**)
Goulton Rd. E5 . . . . .4H **67**
Gourley Pl. N15 . . . . .5E **48**
Gourley St. N15 . . . . .5E **48**
Gourock Rd. SE9 . . . . .5E **124**
Govan St. E2 . . . . .1G **85**
Govett Av. TW17: Shep 5E **146**
Govier Cl. E15 . . . . .7G **69**
Gowan Av. SW6 . . . . .1G **117**
Gowan Ho. *E2* 2K **9**
    (off Chambord St.)
Gowan Rd. NW10 . . . . .6D **62**
Gower Cl. SW4 . . . . .6G **119**
Gower Ct. WC1 . . . . .3C **6** (4H **83**)
Gower Ho. E17 . . . . .3D **50**
   SE17 .5C **102**
    (off Morecambe St.)
Gower M. WC1 . . . . .6D **6** (5H **83**)
Gower M. Mans. *WC1* 5D **6**
    (off Gower M.)
Gower Pl. WC1 . . . . .3B **6** (4H **83**)
Gower Rd. E7 . . . . .6J **69**
   TW7: Isle 6K **95**
Gower St. WC1 . . . . .3B **6** (4G **83**)
Gower's Wlk. E1 . . . . .6G **85**
Gowland Pl. BR3: Beck 2B **158**
Gowlett Rd. SE15 . . . . .3G **121**
Gowlland Cl. CR0: C'don 7G **157**
Gowrie Rd. SW11 . . . . .3E **118**
Graburn Way KT8: E Mos 3H **149**
Grace Av. DA7: Bex 2F **127**
Grace Bus. Cen. CR4: Mitc 6D **154**
Gracechurch St. EC3 . . . .2F **15** (7D **84**)
Grace Cl. HA8: Edg 1J **43**
   SE9 .3B **142**
Grace Ct. *CR0: C'don* 3B **168**
    (off Waddon Rd.)
   SM2: Sutt 7K **165**
Gracedale Rd. SW16 . . . . .5F **137**
Gracefield Gdns. SW16 . . . . .3J **137**
Gracehill *E1* 5J **85**
    (off Hannibal Rd.)
Grace Ho. SE11 . . . . .7H **19**
Grace Jones Cl. E8 . . . . .6G **67**
Grace M. BR3: Beck 6C **140**
   SE20 .2J **157**
    (off Marlow Rd.)
Grace Path SE26 . . . . .4J **139**
Grace Pl. E3 . . . . .3D **86**
Grace Rd. CR0: C'don 6C **156**
Graces All. E1 . . . . .7G **85**
Grace's M. SE5 . . . . .2D **120**
Graces M. NW8 . . . . .2A **82**
Grace's Rd. SE5 . . . . .2E **120**
Grace St. E3 . . . . .3D **86**
The Gradient SE26 . . . . .4G **139**
Graduate Pl. SE1 . . . . .7F **15**
Graeme Rd. EN1: Enf 2J **23**
Graemesdyke Av. SW14 . . . . .3H **115**
Grafton Chambers *NW1* 2D **6**
    (off Grafton Pl.)

Grafton Cl. KT4: Wor Pk 3A **164**
   TW4: Houn 1C **130**
   W13 . . . . .6A **78**
Grafton Ct. TW14: Bedf 1F **129**
Grafton Cres. NW1 . . . . .6F **65**
Grafton Gdns. N4 . . . . .6C **48**
   RM8: Dag 2E **72**
Grafton Ho. *E3* 3C **86**
    (off Wellington Way)
   SE8 . . . . .5B **104**
Grafton M. W1 . . . . .4A **6** (4G **83**)
Grafton Pk. Rd. KT4: Wor Pk 2A **164**
Grafton Pl. NW1 . . . . .2D **6** (3H **83**)
Grafton Rd. CR0: C'don 1A **168**
   EN2: Enf 3E **22**
   HA1: Harr 5G **41**
   KT3: N Mald 3A **152**
   KT4: Wor Pk 3K **163**
   NW5 . . . . .5E **64**
   RM8: Dag 2E **72**
   W3 . . . . .7J **79**
The Graftons NW2 . . . . .3J **63**
Grafton Sq. SW4 . . . . .3G **119**
Grafton St. W1 . . . . .3K **11** (7F **83**)
   TW5: Hrow . . . . .not complete (Tr. . .)
Grafton Ter. NW5 . . . . .5D **64**
Grafton Way KT8: W Mole 4D **148**
   W1 . . . . .4A **6** (4G **83**)
    (not continuous)
   WC1 . . . . .4A **6** (4G **83**)
Grafton Yd. NW5 . . . . .6F **65**
Graham Av. CR4: Mitc 1E **154**
   W13 . . . . .2B **96**
Graham Cl. CR0: C'don 2C **170**
Graham Ct. *SE14* 6K **103**
    (off Myers La.)
   UB5: N'olt 5C **58**
GRAHAME PARK 1A **44**
Grahame Pk. Way NW7 . . . . .7G **29**
   NW9 . . . . .2B **44**
Grahame White Ho. HA3: Kenton . .3D **42**
Grahame Gdns. KT6: Surb 1E **162**
Graham Ho. *N9* 1D **34**
    (off Cumberland Rd.)
Graham Lodge NW4 . . . . .6D **44**
Graham Mans. *IG11: Bark* 7A **72**
    (off Lansbury Av.)
Graham Rd. CR4: Mitc 1E **154**
   DA6: Bex 4F **127**
   E8 . . . . .6G **67**
   E13 . . . . .4J **87**
   HA3: W'stone 3J **41**
   N15 . . . . .3B **48**
   NW4 . . . . .6D **44**
   SW19 . . . . .7H **135**
   TW12: Hamp H 4E **130**
   W4 . . . . .3K **97**
Graham Ter. *DA15: Sidc* 6B **126**
    (off Westerham Dr.)
   SW1 . . . . .4G **17** (4E **100**)
Grail Rd. SE6 . . . . .2G **141**
Grainger Cl. UB5: N'olt 5F **59**
Grainger Ct. SE5 . . . . .7C **102**
Grainger Rd. N22 . . . . .1C **48**
   TW7: Isle 2K **113**
The Grainstore E16 . . . . .7J **87**
Gramer Cl. E11 . . . . .2F **69**
Gramophone La. UB3: Hayes 2G **93**
Grampian Cl. BR6: St M Cry 6K **161**
   SM2: Sutt 7A **166**
   UB3: Harl 7F **93**
Grampian Gdns. NW2 . . . . .1G **63**
The Grampians *W6* 2F **99**
    (off Shepherd's Bush Rd.)
Gramsci Way SE6 . . . . .3D **140**
Granada St. SW17 . . . . .5D **136**
Granard Av. SW15 . . . . .5D **116**
Granard Bus. Cen. NW7 . . . . .6F **29**
Granard Ho. E9 . . . . .6K **67**
Granard Rd. SW12 . . . . .7D **118**
Granary Cl. N9 . . . . .7D **24**
Granary Ct. E15 . . . . .6F **69**
    (off Millstone Cl.)

Granary Mans.—Gravel Hill

Granary Mans. SE28 2G 107
Granary Rd. E1 4H 85
Granary Sq. N1 1J 83
Granary St. NW1 1H 83
Granby Pl. *SE1* *7J 13*
(off Lwr. Marsh)
Granby Rd. SE9 2D 124
Granby St. E2 3K 9 (4G 85)
(not continuous)
Granby Ter. NW1 1A 6 (2G 83)
Grand Arc. N12 5F 31
Grand Av. EC1 5B 8 (5B 84)
(not continuous)
HA9: Wemb 5G 61
KT5: Surb 5H 151
N10 4E 46
Grand Av. E. HA9: Wemb 5H 61
Grand Canal Apts. *N1* *1E 84*
(off De Beauvoir Cres.)
Grand Canal Av. SE16 4A 104
Grand Courts RM8: Dag 3E 72
Grand Depot Rd. SE18 5E 106
Grand Dr. SW20 2E 152
UB2: S'hall 2G 95
Granden Rd. SW16 2J 155
Grandfield Ct. W4 6K 97
Grandison Rd. KT4: Wor Pk 2E 164
SW11 5D 118
Grand Junc. Wharf E2 3K 85
N1 2C 84
Grand Pde. HA9: Wemb 2G 61
KT6: Surb 1G 163
N4 5B 48
SW14 *4J 115*
(off Up. Richmond Rd. W.)
Grand Pde. M. SW15 5G 117
Grand Regent Twr. *E2* *3K 85*
(off Palmer's Rd.)
Grandstand Way UB5: N'olt 5D 58
Grand Twr. *SW15* *5G 117*
(off Plaza Gdns.)
Grand Union Cen. *W10* *4F 81*
(off West Row)
Grand Union Cl. W9 5H 81
Grand Union Cres. E8 1G 85
Grand Union Ent. Pk. UB2: S'hall 3E 94
Grand Union Hgts. HA0: Wemb 1D 78
Grand Union Ho. *N1* *1E 84*
(off Hertford Rd.)
Grand Union Ind. Est. NW10 2H 79
Grand Union Village UB5: N'olt 3D 76
Grand Union Wlk. *NW1* *7F 65*
(off Kentish Town Rd.)
Grand Union Way UB2: S'hall 2E 94
Grand Vitesse Ind. Cen. *SE1* *5B 14*
(off Gt. Suffolk St.)
Grand Wlk. E1 4A 86
Granfield St. SW11 1B 118
The Grange CR0: C'don 2B 170
E17 *5A 50*
(off Lynmouth Rd.)
HA0: Wemb 7G 61
KT3: N Mald 5B 152
KT4: Wor Pk 4K 163
N2 2B 46
N20 1F 31
(Grangeview Rd.)
N20 1G 31
(Oxford Gdns.)
SE1 3F 103
SW19 6F 135
W3 2H 97
W4 5H 97
W13 5C 78
W14 4H 99
Grange Av. EN4: E Barn 1H 31
HA7: Stan 2B 42
IG8: Wfd G 6D 36
N12 5F 31
N20 7B 20
SE25 2E 156
TW2: Twick 2J 131
Grangecliffe Gdns. SE25 2E 156
Grange Cl. DA15: Sidc 3A 144
HA8: Edg 5D 28
IG8: Wfd G 7D 36
KT8: W Mole 4F 149
TW5: Hest 6D 94
UB3: Hayes 5G 75
Grange Ct. HA1: Harr 4K 59
HA5: Pinn 3C 40
NW10 *3A 62*
(off Neasden La.)
SM2: Sutt 7K 165
SM6: W'gton 3F 167
TW17: Shep 4C 146
UB5: N'olt 2A 76
WC2 1H 13 (6K 83)
Grangecourt Rd. N16 1E 66
Grange Cres. SE28 6C 90
Grangedale Cl. HA6: Nwood 1G 39
Grange Dr. BR7: Chst 6C 142
Grange Farm Cl. HA2: Harr 2G 59
Grangefield *NW1* *7H 65*
(off Marquis Rd.)
Grange Gdns. HA5: Pinn 3C 40
N14 1C 32
NW3 3K 63
SE25 2E 156
Grange Gro. N1 6C 66
Grange Hill HA8: Edg 5D 28
SE25 2E 156
Grangehill Pl. SE9 3D 124
Grangehill Rd. SE9 4D 124
Grange Ho. NW10 7D 62
SE1 3F 103
Grange La. SE21 2F 139
Grange Lodge SW19 6F 135
Grange Mans. KT17: Ewe 7B 164
Grange M. N21 6G 23
TW13: Felt 4J 129
Grangemill Rd. SE6 3C 140
Grangemill Way SE6 2C 140
GRANGE PARK 6G 23
Grange Pk. W5 1E 96
Grange Pk. Av. N21 6H 23
Grange Pk. Pl. SW20 7D 134
Grange Pk. Rd. CR7: Thor H 4D 156
E10 1D 68
Grange Pl. NW6 7J 63
Grange Rd. BR6: Orp 2H 173
CR2: S Croy 7C 168
CR7: Thor H 4D 156
E10 1C 68
E13 3H 87
E17 5A 50
(not continuous)
HA1: Harr 5A 42
HA2: Harr 2H 59
HA8: Edg 6E 28
IG1: Ilf 4F 71
KT1: King T 3E 150
KT8: W Mole 4F 149
KT9: Chess 4E 162
N6 6E 46
N17 6B 34
N18 6B 34
NW10 6D 62
SE1 3E 102
SE19 4D 156
SE25 4D 156
SM2: Sutt 7J 165
SW13 1C 116
UB1: S'hall 2C 94
UB3: Hayes 6G 75
W4 5H 97
W5 1D 96
Grange St. N1 1D 84
Grange Va. SM2: Sutt 7K 165
Grange Vw. Rd. N20 1F 31
Grange Wlk. SE1 3E 102
Grange Wlk. M. *SE1* *3E 102*
(off Grange Wlk.)
Grangeway IG8: Wfd G 4F 37
N12 4E 30
NW6 7J 63
The Grangeway N21 6G 23
Grangeway Gdns. IG4: Ilf 5C 52
Grangewood DA5: Bexl 1F 145
Grangewood Cl. HA5: Eastc 5J 39
Grangewood Dr. TW16: Sun 7H 129
Grangewood La. BR3: Beck 6B 140
Grangewood St. E6 1B 88
Grangewood Ter. SE25 2D 156
Grange Yd. SE1 3F 103
Granham Gdns. N9 2A 34
Granite Apts. E15 6G 69
SE10 5G 105
Granite St. SE18 5K 107
Granleigh Rd. E11 2G 69
Gransden Av. E8 7H 67
Gransden Ho. SE8 5B 104
Gransden Rd. W12 2B 98
Grant Av. KT12: Walt T 5A 148
Grantbridge St. N1 2B 84
Grantchester *KT1: King T* *2G 151*
(off St Peters Rd.)
Grantchester Cl. HA1: Harr 3K 59
Grant Cl. DA17: Belv 5F 109
N14 7B 22
N17 2E 48
TW17: Shep 6D 146
Grant Ct. *E4* *1K 35*
(off The Ridgeway)
NW9 *2B 44*
(off Hazel Cl.)
Grantham Cl. HA8: Edg 3K 27
Grantham Ct. KT2: King T 5D 132
RM6: Chad H 7F 55
SE16 *2K 103*
(off Eleanor Cl.)
Grantham Gdns. RM6: Chad H 6F 55
Grantham Ho. E14 6G 87
SE15 *6G 103*
(off Friary Est.)
TW16: Sun 7G 129
UB5: N'olt *3D 76*
(off Taywood Rd.)
Grantham Pl. W1 5J 11 (1F 101)
Grantham Rd. E12 4E 70
SW9 2J 119
W4 7A 98
Grant Ho. *E17* *4C 50*
(off High St.)
SW9 *1K 119*
(off Liberty St.)
Grantley Ho. *SE14* *6K 103*
(off Myers La.)
Grantley Rd. TW4: Cran 2A 112
Grantley St. E1 3K 85
Grant Mus. of Zoology 4C 6 (4H 83)
Grantock Rd. E17 1F 51
Granton Rd. DA14: Sidc 6C 144
IG3: Ilf 1A 72
SW16 1G 155
Grant Pl. CR0: C'don 1F 169
Grant Rd. CR0: C'don 1F 169
HA3: W'stone 3K 41
SW11 4B 118
Grants Cl. NW7 7K 29
Grants Quay Wharf EC3 3F 15 (7D 84)
Grant St. E13 3J 87
N1 2A 84
Grant Ter. *N16* *7G 49*
(off Castlewood Rd.)
Grantully Rd. W9 3K 81
Grant Way TW7: Isle 6A 96
Granville Arc. SW9 4A 120
Granville Av. N9 3D 34
TW3: Houn 5E 112
TW13: Felt 2J 129
Granville Cl. CR0: C'don 2E 168
Granville Ct. N1 1E 84
N4 6K 47
SE14 *7A 104*
(off Nynehead St.)
Granville Gdns. SW16 1K 155
W5 1F 97
Granville Gro. SE13 3E 122
Granville Ho. *E14* *6C 86*
(off E. India Dock Rd.)
Granville Mans. *W12* *2E 98*
(off Shepherd's Bush Grn.)
Granville M. DA14: Sidc 4A 144
Granville Pk. SE13 3E 122
Granville Pl. HA5: Pinn 3B 40
N12 7F 31
SW6 7K 99
W1 1G 11 (6E 82)
Granville Point NW2 2H 63
Granville Rd. DA14: Sidc 4A 144
DA16: Well 3C 126
E17 6D 50
E18 2K 51
EN5: Barn 4A 20
IG1: Ilf 1F 71
N4 6K 47
N12 7F 31
N13 6E 32
N22 1B 48
NW2 2H 63
NW6 2J 81
(not continuous)
SW18 7H 117
SW19 7J 135
UB3: Harl 4H 93
UB10: Hil 6D 56
Granville Sq. SE15 7E 102
WC1 2H 7 (3K 83)
Granville St. WC1 2H 7 (3K 83)
Granwood Ct. TW7: Isle 1J 113
Grape St. WC2 7E 6 (6J 83)
The Graphite Apts. *N1* *1E 8*
(off Provost St.)
Graphite Point *E2* *3K 85*
(off Palmer's Rd.)
Graphite Sq. SE11 5G 19 (5K 101)
Grapsome Cl. KT9: Chess 7C 162
Grasdene Rd. SE18 7A 108
Grasgarth Cl. W3 7J 79
Grasmere *NW1* *2K 5*
(off Osnaburgh St.)
Grasmere Av. BR6: Farnb 3F 173
HA4: Ruis 7E 38
HA9: Wemb 7C 42
SW15 4K 133
SW19 3J 153
TW3: Houn 6F 113
W3 7K 79
Grasmere Cl. TW14: Felt 1H 129
Grasmere Ct. N22 6E 32
SE26 5G 139
SM2: Sutt 6A 166
SW13 *6C 98*
(off Verdun Rd.)
Grasmere Gdns. BR6: Farnb 3F 173
HA3: W'stone 2A 42
IG4: Ilf 5D 52
Grasmere Point *SE15* *7J 103*
(off Old Kent Rd.)
Grasmere Rd. BR1: Broml 1H 159
BR6: Farnb 3F 173
DA7: Bex 2J 127
E13 2J 87
N10 1F 47
N17 6B 34
SE25 6H 157
SW16 5J 137
Grasshaven Way SE28 1K 107
(not continuous)
Grassington Cl. N11 6K 31
Grassington Rd. DA14: Sidc 4A 144
Grassmount SE23 2H 139
Grass Pk. N3 1H 45
Grassway SM6: W'gton 4G 167
Grasvenor Av. EN5: Barn 5D 20
Gratton Rd. W14 3G 99
Gratton Ter. NW2 3F 63
Gravel Hill CR0: Addtn 6K 169
DA6: Bex 4H 127
N3 2H 45
UB8: Uxb 5A 56

Gravel Hill Cl. DA6: Bex 5H 127
Gravel La. E1 . . . . .7J 9 (6F 85)
Gravel Pit La. SE9 . . . . .5F 125
Gravel Pit Way BR6: Orp 2K 173
Gravel Rd. BR2: Broml 3C 172
  TW2: Twick 1J 131
Gravelwood Cl. BR7: Chst 3G 143
Gravely Ho. SE8 . . . . .4A 104
  (off Chilton Gro.)
Gravenel Gdns. SW17 . . . . .5C 136
  (off Nutwell St.)
Graveney Gro. SE20 . . . . .7J 139
Graveney Rd. SW17 . . . . .4C 136
Gravesend Rd. W12 . . . . .7C 80
Gravesham Way BR3: Beck 7B 158
Gray Av. RM8: Dag 1F 73
Gray Ct. E1 . . . . .5A 86
  HA5: Pinn 4C 40
Grayham Cres. KT3: N Mald 4K 151
Grayham Rd. KT3: N Mald 4K 151
Gray Ho. SE17 . . . . .5C 102
  (off King & Queen St.)
Grayland Cl. BR1: Broml 1B 160
Grayling Cl. E16 . . . . .4G 87
Grayling Ct. W5 . . . . .1D 96
  (off Grange Rd.)
Grayling Rd. N16 . . . . .2D 66
Grayling Sq. E2 . . . . .3G 85
  (off Nelson Gdns.)
Grayscroft Rd. SW16 . . . . .7H 137
Grays Farm Rd. BR5: St P 7B 144
Grayshott Rd. SW11 . . . . .2E 118
Gray's Inn 5H 7 (5K 83)
Gray's Inn Bldgs. EC1 . . . . .4J 7
  (off Rosebery Av.)
Gray's Inn Pl. WC1 . . . . .6H 7 (5K 83)
Gray's Inn Rd. WC1 . . . . . . .1F 7 (3J 83)
Gray's Inn Sq. WC1 . . . . . . .5J 7 (5K 83)
Grays La. TW15: Ashf 4D 128
Grayson Ho. EC1 . . . . .2D 8
Grays Rd. UB10: Uxb 7A 56
Grays Ter. E7 . . . . .6A 70
Grayston Ho. SE3 . . . . .4A 124
Gray St. SE1 . . . . .7K 13 (2A 102)
Grayswood Gdns. SW20 . . . . .2D 152
Grayswood Point SW15 . . . . .1C 134
Gray's Yd. W1 . . . . .1H 11
Graywood Ct. N12 . . . . .7F 31
Grazebrook Rd. N16 . . . . .2D 66
Grazeley Cl. DA6: Bex 5J 127
Grazeley Ct. SE19 . . . . .5E 138
Gt. Acre Cl. SW4 . . . . .4H 119
Gt. Amwell La. N8 . . . . .3K 47
Gt. Arthur Ho. EC1 . . . . .4C 8
  (off Golden La. Est.)
Gt. Bell All. EC2 . . . . .7E 8 (6D 84)
Great Benty UB7: W Dray 4A 92
Gt. Brownings SE21 . . . . .4F 139
Gt. Bushey Dr. N20 . . . . .1E 30
Gt. Cambridge Ind. Est. EN1: Enf . . .5C 24
GREAT CAMBRIDGE JUNC. 4J 33
  N9 . . . . .4J 33
  N17 . . . . .5J 33
  N18 . . . . .4J 33
Gt. Castle St. W1 . . . . .7K 5 (6F 83)
Gt. Central Av. HA4: Ruis 5A 58
Gt. Central St. NW1 . . . . . .5E 4 (5D 82)
Gt. Central War HA9: Wemb 4J 61
  NW10 . . . . .5A 62
Gt. Chapel St. W1 . . . . . .7C 6 (6H 83)
Gt. Chart St. SW11 . . . . .4B 118
Gt. Chertsey Rd. TW2: Twick 3D 130
  TW13: Hanw, Twick 3D 130
  W4 . . . . .1J 115
  (not continuous)
Gt. Church La. W6 . . . . .4F 99
Gt. College St. SW1 . . . . .1E 18 (3J 101)
Great Ct. WC1 . . . . .2F 7
  (off Cromer St.)
Gt. Cross Av. SE10 . . . . .7F 105
Gt. Cumberland M. W1 . . .1E 10 (6D 82)
Gt. Cumberland Pl. W1 . . .7E 4 (6D 82)

Gt. Dover St. SE1 . . . . . . .7D 14 (2C 102)
Greatdown Rd. W7 . . . . .4K 77
Gt. Eastern Ent. Cen. E14 . . . . .2D 104
Gt. Eastern Mkt. 6E 68
  (within Westfield Shop. Cen.)
Gt. Eastern Rd. E15 . . . . .7F 69
Gt. Eastern St. EC2 . . . . . .2G 9 (3E 84)
Gt. Eastern Wlk. EC2 . . . . .6H 9
Gt. Elms Rd. BR2: Broml 4A 160
Greater London Ho. NW1 . . . . .2G 83
  (off Hampstead Rd.)
Great Fld. NW9 . . . . .1A 44
Greatfield NW5 . . . . .5G 65
Greatfield Av. E6 . . . . .4D 88
Greatfield Cl. N19 . . . . .4G 65
  SE4 .4C 122
Greatfields Dr. UB8: Hil 5C 74
Greatfields Rd. IG11: Bark 1H 89
Gt. Fleete Way IG11: Bark 2C 90
Gt. Galley Cl. IG11: Bark 3B 90
Gt. Gatton Cl. CR0: C'don 7A 158
Gt. George St. SW1 . . . . . .7D 12 (2H 101)
Gt. Guildford Bus. Sq.
  SE1 . . . . .5C 14 (1C 102)
Gt. Guildford St. SE1 . . . .4C 14 (1C 102)
Great Hall SW11 . . . . .1E 118
  (off Battersea Pk. Rd.)
Greatham Wlk. SW15 . . . . .1C 134
Gt. Harry Dr. SE9 . . . . .3E 142
Gt. James St. WC1 . . . . . . .5G 7 (5K 83)
Gt. Marlborough St. W1 . . .1A 12 (6G 83)
Gt. Maze Pond SE1 . . . . . .6F 15 (2D 102)
Gt. Mill Apts. E2 . . . . .1F 85
  (off Whiston Rd.)
Gt. Minster Ho. SW1 . . . . .3D 18
  (off Marsham St.)
Gt. Newport St. WC2 . . . . .2E 12 (7J 83)
Gt. New St. EC4 . . . . .7K 7
  (off New Fetter La.)
Great Nth. Leisure Pk. N12 . . . . . . .7G 31
Great Nth. Rd. EN5: Barn . . .1C 20, 2C 20
  EN5: New Bar 5D 20
  N2 . . . . .5C 46
  N6 . . . . .5C 46
Great Nth. Way NW4 . . . . .2D 44
Greatorex Ho. E1 . . . . .5G 85
  (off Greatorex St.)
Greatorex St. E1 . . . . .5G 85
Gt. Ormond St. WC1 . . . . . .5F 7 (5J 83)
Gt. Owl Rd. IG7: Chig 3K 37
Gt. Percy St. WC1 . . . . . . .1H 7 (3K 83)
Gt. Peter St. SW1 . . . . . . .2C 18 (3H 101)
Gt. Portland St. W1 . . . . . . .4K 5 (4F 83)
Gt. Pulteney St. W1 . . . . . .2B 12 (7G 83)
Gt. Queen St. WC2 . . . . . . .1F 13 (6J 83)
Gt. Russell Mans. WC1 . . . . .6E 6
  (off Gt. Russell St.)
Gt. Russell St. WC1 . . . . . . .7D 6 (6H 83)
Gt. St Helen's EC3 . . . . . . .7G 9 (6E 84)
Gt. St Thomas Apostle
  EC4 . . . . .2D 14 (7C 84)
Gt. Scotland Yd. SW1 . . . . .5E 12 (1J 101)
Gt. Smith St. SW1 . . . . . . .1D 18 (3H 101)
Great Sth. W. Rd. TW4: Houn 4H 111
  TW14: Bedf, Felt 7E 110
Great Spilmans SE22 . . . . .5E 120
Great Strand NW9 . . . . .1B 44
Gt. Suffolk St. SE1 . . . . . .5B 14 (1B 102)
Gt. Sutton St. EC1 . . . . . . .4B 8 (4B 84)
Gt. Swan All. EC2 . . . . .7E 8 (6D 84)
Great Thrift BR5: Pet W 4G 161
Gt. Titchfield St. W1 . . . . . .4K 5 (4F 83)
Gt. Tower St. EC3 . . . . .2G 15 (7E 84)
Gt. Trinity La. EC4 . . . . . . .2D 14 (7C 84)
Gt. Turnstile WC1 . . . . .6H 7 (5K 83)
Gt. Turnstile Ho. WC1 . . . . .6H 7
  (off Great Turnstile)
Gt. Western Ind. Pk. UB2: S'hall 2F 95
Gt. Western Rd. W2 . . . . .5H 81
  W9 . . . . .5H 81
  W11 .5H 81

Gt. West Rd. TW5: Hest 2B 112
  TW7: Bford, Isle 2B 112
  TW8: Bford 2B 112
  W4 . . . . .5H 97
  (Cedars Rd.)
  W4 . . . . .6B 98
  (Dorchester Gro.)
  W6 . . . . .6B 98
Great W. Trad. Est. TW8: Bford 6B 96
Gt. Winchester St. EC2 . . . .7F 9 (6D 84)
Gt. Windmill St. W1 . . . . . .2C 12 (7H 83)
Greatwood BR7: Chst 7E 142
Great Yd. SE1 . . . . .6H 15
Greaves Cl. IG11: Bark 7H 71
Greaves Cotts. E14 . . . . .5A 86
  (off Maroon St.)
Greaves Pl. SW17 . . . . .4C 136
Greaves Twr. SW10 . . . . .7A 100
  (off Worlds End Est.)
Grebe Av. UB4: Yead 6B 76
Grebe Cl. E7 . . . . .5H 69
  E17 . . . . .7F 35
  IG11: Bark 4A 90
Grebe Ct. E14 . . . . .2E 104
  (off River Barge Cl.)
  SE8 .6B 104
  (off Dorking Cl.)
  SM1: Sutt 5H 165
Grebe Ter. KT1: King T 3E 150
Grecian Cres. SE19 . . . . .6B 138
Greek Cl. W1 . . . . .1D 12 (6H 83)
Greek St. W1 . . . . .1D 12 (6H 83)
The Green BR1: Broml 3J 141
  (not continuous)
  BR2: Hayes 7J 159
  BR5: St P 7B 144
  CR0: Sels 7B 170
  DA7: Bex 1G 127
  DA14: Sidc 4A 144
  DA16: Well 4J 125
  E4 . . . . .1K 35
  E11 .6K 51
  E15 .6G 69
  HA0: Wemb 2A 60
  IG8: Wfd G 5D 36
  IG9: Buck H 1E 36
  KT3: N Mald 3K 151
  N9 . . . . .2B 34
  N14 .2C 32
  N17 .6H 33
  N21 .7F 23
  SM1: Sutt 3K 165
  SM4: Mord 4G 153
  SM5: Cars 4E 166
  SM6: W'gton 2E 166
  SW14 . . . . .3J 115
  SW19 . . . . .5F 135
  TW2: Twick 1J 131
  TW5: Hest 6E 94
  TW9: Rich 5D 114
  TW13: Felt 2K 129
  TW17: Shep 4G 147
  UB2: S'hall 3C 94
  UB7: W Dray 3A 92
  UB10: Ick 2E 56
  W3 . . . . .6A 80
  W5 . . . . .1D 96
  UB5: N'olt 5D 58
Greenacre Cl. EN5: Barn 1C 20
  N3 . . . . .3C 44
Greenacre Gdns. E17 . . . . .4E 50
Greenacre Pl. SM6: W'gton 2F 167
Green Acres CR0: C'don 3F 169
  DA14: Sidc 4A 144
Greenacres N3 . . . . .2H 45
  SE9 .6E 124
  WD23: B Hea 2C 26
Greenacres Av. UB10: Ick 3B 56
Greenacres Cl. BR6: Farnb 4G 173
Greenacres Dr. HA7: Stan 6G 27
Greenacres Ho. SW18 . . . . .1K 135
  (off Knaresborough Dr.)
Greenacre Sq. SE16 . . . . .2K 103
Greenacre Wlk. N14 . . . . .3C 32

Greenan Ct. E2 . . . . .3K 85
  (off Meath Cres.)
Grn. Arbour Ct. EC1 . . . . .7A 8
Green Av. NW7 . . . . .4E 28
  W13 .3B 96
Greenaway Gdns. NW3 . . . . .4K 63
Greenaway Ho. NW8 . . . . .1A 82
  (off Boundary Rd.)
  WC1 .2J 7
Greenaway Ter. TW19: Stanw 1A 128
  (off Victory Cl.)
Green Bank E1 . . . . .1H 103
  N12 .4E 30
Greenbank Av. HA0: Wemb 5A 60
Greenbank Cl. E4 . . . . .2K 35
Greenbank Ct. TW7: Isle 2K 113
  (off Lanadron Cl.)
Greenbank Cres. NW4 . . . . .4G 45
Greenbank Lodge BR7: Chst 2E 160
  (off Forest Cl.)
Greenbanks HA1: Harr 4J 59
Greenbanks Cl. SE13 . . . . .3D 122
Greenbay Rd. SE7 . . . . .7B 106
Greenberry St. NW8 . . . . . .1C 4 (2C 82)
Greenbrook Av. EN4: Had W 1F 21
Green Cl. BR2: Broml 3G 159
  NW9 .6J 43
  NW11 . . . . .7A 46
  SM5: Cars 2D 166
  TW13: Hanw 5C 130
Greencoat Mans. SW1 . . . . .2B 18
  (off Greencoat Row)
Greencoat Pl. SW1 . . . . . . .3B 18 (4G 101)
Greencoat Row SW1 . . . . . .2B 18 (3G 101)
Green Ct. TW16: Sun 6H 129
Greencourt Av. CR0: C'don 2H 169
  HA8: Edg 1H 43
Greencourt Gdns. CR0: C'don 1H 169
Greencourt Ho. E1 . . . . .4K 85
  (off Mile End Rd.)
Greencourt Rd. BR5: Pet W 5H 161
Greencrest Pl. NW2 . . . . .3C 62
Greencroft HA8: Edg 5D 28
Greencroft Av. HA4: Ruis 2A 58
Greencroft Cl. E6 . . . . .5B 88
Greencroft Gdns. EN1: Enf 3K 23
  NW6 .7K 63
Greencroft Rd. TW5: Hest 1D 112
Green Dale SE5 . . . . .4D 120
  SE22 .5E 120
Greendale NW7 . . . . .4F 29
Grn. Dale Cl. SE22 . . . . .5E 120
Grn. Dragon Ct. SE1 . . . . .4E 14
Grn. Dragon Ho. CR0: C'don 3C 168
  (off High St.)
  WC2 .7F 7
  (off Stukeley St.)
Grn. Dragon La. N21 . . . . .6F 23
  TW8: Bford 5E 96
Grn. Dragon Yd. E1 . . . . . . .6K 9 (5G 85)
Green Dr. UB1: S'hall 1E 94
Greene Ct. SE14 . . . . .6K 103
  (off Samuel Cl.)
Greene Ho. SE1 . . . . .3D 102
  (off Burbage Cl.)
Green End KT9: Chess 4E 162
  N21 .2G 33
Greenend Rd. W4 . . . . .2A 98
Greener Ct. CR0: C'don 6C 156
  (off Goodman Cres.)
Greener Ho. SW4 . . . . .3H 119
Grn. Farm Cl. BR6: Chels 5K 173
Greenfell Mans. SE8 . . . . .6D 104
Green Ferry Way E17 . . . . .4K 49
Greenfield Av. KT5: Surb 7H 151
Greenfield Cl. SE9 . . . . .3C 142
Greenfield Dr. BR1: Broml 2A 160
  N2 . . . . .4D 46
Greenfield Gdns. BR5: Pet W 7H 161
  NW2 .2G 63
  RM9: Dag 1D 90
Greenfield Ho. SW19 . . . . .1F 135

Greenfield Pl. UB3: Hayes 7H 75
Greenfield Rd. DA2: Wilm 5K 145
  E1 ....5G 85
  N15 ....5E 48
  RM9: Dag 1C 90
Greenfields UB1: S'hall 6E 76
Greenfield Way HA2: Harr 3F 41
GREENFORD 3E 76
Greenford Av. UB1: S'hall 7D 76
  W7 ....4J 77
Greenford Bus. Cen. UB6: G'frd 7H 59
Greenford Gdns. UB6: G'frd 3F 77
GREENFORD GREEN 6J 59
Greenford Ind. Est. UB6: G'frd 7F 59
Greenford Pk. UB6: G'frd 7H 59
Greenford Rd. HA1: Harr 2H 77
  SM1: Sutt 4K 165
  (not continuous)
  UB1: S'hall 7G 77
  UB6: G'frd 2H 77
GREENFORD RDBT. 2H 77
Greenford Sports Cen. 3E 76
Green Gdns. BR6: Farnb 5G 173
Greengate UB6: G'frd 6B 60
Greengate Lodge E13 ....2K 87
  (off Hollybush St.)
Greengate Pde. IG2: Ilf 6H 53
Greengate St. E13 ....2K 87
Greenhalgh Wlk. N2 ....4A 46
Greenham Cl. SE1 ....7J 13 (2A 102)
Greenham Cres. E4 ....6G 35
Greenham Ho. E9 ....1J 85
  (off Templecombe Rd.)
  TW7: Isle 3H 113
Greenham Rd. N10 ....2E 46
Greenhaven Dr. SE28 ....6B 90
Green Hedges TW1: Twick 5C 114
Greenheys Cl. HA6: Nwood 1G 39
Greenheys Dr. E18 ....3H 51
GREENHILL 5J 41
Greenhill HA9: Wemb 2H 61
  IG9: Buck H 1F 37
  NW3 ....4B 64
  SE18 ....5D 106
  SM1: Sutt 2A 166
Greenhill Ct. EN5: New Bar 5E 20
  SE18 ....5D 106
Greenhill Gdns. UB5: N'olt 2D 76
Greenhill Gro. E12 ....4C 70
Greenhill Pde. EN5: New Bar 5E 20
Greenhill Pk. EN5: New Bar 5E 20
  NW10 ....1A 80
Greenhill Rd. HA1: Harr 6J 41
  NW10 ....1A 80
Greenhill's Rents EC1 ....5A 8 (5B 84)
Greenhills Ter. N1 ....6D 66
Greenhill Ter. SE18 ....5D 106
  UB5: N'olt 2D 76
Greenhill Way HA1: Harr 6J 41
  HA9: Wemb 2H 61
Greenhithe Cl. DA15: Sidc 7J 125
Greenholm Rd. SE9 ....5F 125
Green Hundred Rd. SE15 ....6G 103
Greenhurst Rd. SE27 ....5A 138
Greening St. SE2 ....4C 108
Greenland Cres. UB2: S'hall 3A 94
Greenland Ho. E1 ....4A 86
  (off Ernest St.)
Greenland M. SE8 ....5K 103
Greenland Pl. NW1 ....1F 83
Greenland Quay SE16 ....4K 103
Greenland Rd. EN5: Barn 6A 20
  NW1 ....1G 83
Greenlands KT19: Ewe 5H 163
Greenlands La. NW4 ....1D 44
Greenland St. NW1 ....1F 83
Greenland Way CR0: Bedd 7H 155
Green La. BR7: Chst 1F 143
  CR7: Thor H 7K 137
  HA1: Harr 3J 59
  HA7: Stan 4G 27
  HA8: Edg 4A 28
  (not continuous)

Green La. IG1: Ilf 2H 71
  IG3: Ilf 2H 71
  KT3: N Mald 5J 151
  KT4: Wor Pk 1C 164
  KT8: W Mole 5F 149
  KT9: Chess 7D 162
  NW4 ....4F 45
  RM8: Dag 2H 71
  SE9 ....1F 143
  SE20 ....7K 139
  SM4: Mord 6J 153
  (Central Rd.)
  SM4: Mord 7E 152
  (Lwr. Morden La.)
  SW16 ....7K 137
  TW4: Houn 3K 111
  TW13: Hanw 5C 130
  TW16: Sun 7H 129
  TW17: Shep 6E 146
  UB8: Hil 5E 74
  W7 ....2J 95
Green La. Bus. Pk. SE9 ....2E 142
Green La. Cotts. HA7: Stan 4G 27
Green La. Gdns.
  CR7: Thor H 2C 156
Green Lanes KT19: Ewe 7A 164
  N4 ....1C 66
  N8 ....3B 48
  N13 ....6E 32
  N15 ....3B 48
  N16 ....1C 66
  N21 ....3F 33
Grn. Lanes Wlk. N4 ....1C 66
Greenlaw Ct. W5 ....6D 78
  (off Mount Pk. Rd.)
Greenlaw Gdns. KT3: N Mald 7B 152
Greenlawn La. TW8: Bford 4D 96
Green Lawns HA4: Ruis 1A 58
Greenlawns N12 ....6E 30
Green Leaf Av. SM6: Bedd 4H 167
Greenleaf Cl. SW2 ....7A 120
Greenleafe Dr. IG6: Ilf 3F 53
Greenleaf Rd. E6 ....1A 88
  E17 ....3B 50
Greenleaf Way HA3: W'stone 3K 41
Greenlea Pk. SW19 ....7B 136
Green Leas KT1: King T 3E 150
  (off Mill St.)
Green Leas Cl. TW16: Sun 6H 129
Greenleaves Ct. TW15: Ashf 6D 128
Greenlink Wlk. TW9: Kew 1H 115
Green Man Gdns. W13 ....7A 78
Green Man La. TW14: Felt 4J 111
  (not continuous)
  W13 ....7A 78
Green Man Pas. W13 ....7B 78
  (not continuous)
GREEN MAN RDBT. 7H 51
Greenman St. N1 ....7C 66
Greenmead DA18: Erith 3E 108
Greenmead Cl. SE25 ....5G 157
Green M. N1 ....3D 84
Green Moor Link N21 ....7G 23
Greenmoor Rd. EN3: Enf H 2D 24
Greenoak Pl. EN4: Cockf 2J 21
Green Oaks UB2: S'hall 4B 94
Greenoak Way SW19 ....4F 135
Greenock Rd. SW16 ....1H 155
  W3 ....3H 97
Greeno Cres. TW17: Shep 5C 146
Green Pde. TW3: Houn 5F 113
Green Pk. 6K 11 (2F 101)
Greenpark Ct. HA0: Wemb 7C 60
Green Pk. Way UB6: G'frd 1J 77
Green Pt. SE10 ....2G 105
Green Point E15 ....6G 69
Grn. Pond Cl. E17 ....3B 50
Grn. Pond Rd. E17 ....3A 50
Green Rd. N14 ....6A 22
  N20 ....3F 31
Green Rd. Nth. EN3: Pond E 4F 25

Greenfield Pl. TW8: Bford 5E 96
  (off Clayponds La.)
Greenroof Way SE10 ....3H 105
Green's Ct. W1 ....2C 12
  W11 ....1H 99
  (off Lansdowne M.)
Green's End SE18 ....4F 107
Greenshank Cl. E17 ....7F 35
Greenshank Ho. NW9 ....6B 44
Greenshaw School Sports Cen. 2A 166
Greenshields Ind. Est. E16 ....2J 105
Greenside DA5: Bexl 1E 144
  RM8: Dag 1C 72
Greenside Cl. N20 ....2G 31
  SE6 ....2F 141
Greenside Rd. CR0: C'don 7A 156
  W12 ....3C 98
Greenslade Rd. IG11: Bark 7H 71
Greenstead Av. IG8: Wfd G 7F 37
Greenstead Cl. IG8: Wfd G 6F 37
Greenstead Gdns. IG8: Wfd G 6F 37
  SW15 ....5D 116
Greensted Rd. IG10: Lough 1H 37
Greenstone M. E11 ....6J 51
Green St. E7 ....6K 69
  E13 ....6K 69
  EN3: Brim, Enf H 2D 24
  TW16: Sun 1J 147
  W1 ....2G 11 (7E 82)
GREEN STREET GREEN 6K 173
Greenstreet Hill SE14 ....2K 121
Green Ter. EC1 ....2K 7 (3A 84)
Green Va. DA6: Bex 5D 126
  W5 ....6F 79
Greenvale Rd. SE9 ....4D 124
Green Verges HA7: Stan 7J 27
Green Vw. KT9: Chess 7F 163
Greenview Av. BR3: Beck 6A 158
  CR0: C'don 6A 158
Greenview Cl. W3 ....1A 98
Greenview Ct. TW15: Ashf 4B 128
Greenview Dr. SW20 ....3E 152
Green Wlk. HA4: Ruis 1H 57
  IG8: Wfd G 6H 37
  IG10: Lough 1H 37
  NW4 ....5F 45
  SE1 ....3E 102
  TW12: Hamp 6D 130
  UB2: S'hall 5E 94
The Green Wlk. E4 ....1A 36
Green Way BR2: Broml 6C 160
  SE9 ....5B 124
  TW16: Sun 4J 147
Greenway HA3: Kenton 1C 86
  E3 ....4E 88
  HA3: Kenton 5E 42
  HA5: Pinn 2K 39
  IG8: Wfd G 5F 37
  N14 ....2D 32
  N20 ....2D 30
  RM8: Dag 2D 30
  SM6: W'gton 4G 167
  SW20 ....4E 152
  UB4: Yead 3J 75
The Greenway HA3: W'stone 1J 41
  HA5: Pinn 6D 40
  NW9 ....2K 43
  TW4: Houn 4D 112
  UB8: Uxb 2A 74
  UB10: Ick 2D 56
Greenway Av. E17 ....4F 51
Greenway Cl. N4 ....2C 66
  N11 ....6K 31
  N15 ....4F 49
  N20 ....2D 30
  NW9 ....2K 43
Greenway Cl. IG1: Ilf 1E 70
Greenway Gdns. CR0: C'don 3B 170
  HA3: W'stone 2J 41
  NW9 ....2K 43
  UB6: G'frd 3E 76
Greenways BR3: Beck 3C 158

The Greenways TW1: Twick 6A 114
Greenways Dr. TW4: Houn 4C 112
Greenwell St. W1 ....4K 5 (4F 83)
GREENWICH 7E 104
Greenwich Bus. Pk. SE10 ....7D 104
The Greenwich Cen. 5H 105
  (off Lambarde Sq.)
Greenwich Chu. St. SE10 ....6E 104
Greenwich Ct. E1 ....6H 85
  (off Cavell St.)
Greenwich Cres. E6 ....5C 88
GREENWICH FOOT TUNNEL 5E 104
Greenwich Hgts. SE18 ....7C 106
Greenwich High Rd. SE10 ....1D 122
Greenwich Ho. SE13 ....6F 123
Greenwich Mkt. SE10 ....6E 104
GREENWICH MILLENNIUM
  VILLAGE 3H 105
Greenwich Pk. 7F 105
Greenwich Pk. St. SE10 ....6F 105
Greenwich Peninsula Ecology Pk. 3J 105
Greenwich Peninsula Golf Driving Range 3J 105
Greenwich Picturehouse 7E 104
Greenwich Quay SE8 ....6D 104
Greenwich Shop. Pk. 4K 105
Greenwich Sth. St. SE10 ....1D 122
Greenwich Theatre 7E 104
Greenwich Tourist Information Centre 6E 104
Greenwich Vw. Pl. E14 ....3D 104
Greenwich Yacht Club 3J 105
Greenwood NW5 ....5G 65
  (off Osney Cres.)
Greenwood Av. EN3: Enf H 2F 25
  RM10: Dag 4H 73
Greenwood Bus. Cen. CR0: C'don 7F 157
Greenwood Cl. BR5: Pet W 6J 161
  DA15: Sidc 2A 144
  KT7: T Ditt 1A 162
  SM4: Mord 4G 153
  UB3: Hayes 1J 93
  WD23: B Hea 1D 26
Greenwood Dr. E4 ....5A 36
Greenwood Gdns. IG6: Ilf 1G 53
  N13 ....3G 33
Greenwood Ho. EC1 ....2J 7
  (off Rosebery Av.)
  N22 ....1K 47
  SE4 ....4K 121
Greenwood La. TW12: Hamp H 5F 131
Greenwood Mans. IG11: Bark 7A 72
  (off Lansbury Av.)
Greenwood Pk. KT2: King T 7A 134
Greenwood Pl. NW5 ....5F 65
Greenwood Rd. CR0: C'don 7B 156
  CR4: Mitc 3H 155
  DA5: Bexl 4K 145
  E8 ....6G 67
  E13 ....2H 87
  KT7: T Ditt 1A 162
  TW7: Isle 3K 113
The Greenwoods HA2: Harr 3G 59
Greenwood Ter. NW10 ....1K 79
Greenwood Theatre 2D 102
Grn. Wrythe Cres. SM5: Cars 1C 166
Grn. Wrythe La. SM5: Cars 6B 154
Green Yd. WC1 ....3H 7 (4K 83)
The Green Yd. EC3 ....1G 15
Greer Rd. HA3: Hrw W 1G 41
Greet Ho. SE1 ....7K 13
Greet St. SE1 ....5K 13 (1A 102)
Greg Cl. E10 ....6E 50
Gregor M. SE3 ....7J 105
Gregory Cl. BR2: Broml 4G 159
Gregory Cres. SE9 ....7B 124
Gregory Pl. W8 ....2K 99
Gregory Rd. RM6: Chad H 4D 54
  UB2: S'hall 3E 94
Grehan M. SE14 ....8B 104
Greig Cl. N8 ....5J 47
Greig Ter. SE17 ....6B 102

Grenaby Av. CR0: C'don 7D 156
Grenaby Rd. CR0: C'don 7D 156
Grenada Ho. E14 . . . . .7B 86
    (off Limehouse C'way.)
Grenada Rd. SE7 . . . . .7A 106
Grenade St. E14 . . . . .7B 86
Grenadier St. E16 . . . . .1E 106
Grena Gdns. TW9: Rich 4F 115
Grenard Cl. SE15 . . . . .7G 103
Grena Rd. TW9: Rich 4F 115
Grendon Gdns. HA9: Wemb 2G 61
Grendon Ho. E9 . . . . .7J 67
    (off Shore Pl.)
N1 . . . . .2K 83
    (off Calshot St.)
Grendon Lodge HA8: Edg 2D 28
Grendon St. NW8 . . . . . . .3C 4 (4C 82)
Grenfell Ct. E3 . . . . .4D 86
    (off Barry Blandford Way)
NW7 . . . . .6J 29
Grenfell Gdns. HA3: Kenton 7E 42
IG3: Ilf 5K 53
Grenfell Ho. SE5 . . . . .7C 102
Grenfell Rd. CR4: Mitc 6D 136
W11 . . . . .7F 81
Grenfell Wlk. W11 . . . . .7F 81
Grenier Apts. SE15 . . . . .7H 103
Grennell Cl. SM1: Sutt 2B 166
Grennell Rd. SM1: Sutt 2A 166
Grenoble Gdns. N13 . . . . .6F 33
Grenville Cl. KT5: Surb 1J 163
N3 . . . . .1G 45
Grenville Ct. W13 . . . . .5B 78
Grenville Gdns. IG8: Wfd G 1A 52
Grenville Ho. E3 . . . . .2A 86
    (off Arbery Rd.)
SE8 . . . . .6C 104
    (off New King St.)
SW1 . . . . .7C 18
    (off Dolphin Sq.)
Grenville M. N19 . . . . .1J 65
SW7 . . . . .4A 100
TW12: Hamp H 5F 131
Grenville Pl. NW7 . . . . .5E 28
SW7 . . . . .3A 100
Grenville Rd. N19 . . . . .1J 65
Grenville St. WC1 . . . . .4F 7 (4J 83)
Gresham Av. N20 . . . . .4J 31
Gresham Cl. DA5: Bexl 6E 126
EN2: Enf .3H 23
Gresham Dr. RM6: Chad H 5B 54
Gresham Gdns. NW11 . . . . .1G 63
Gresham Lodge E17 . . . . .5D 50
Gresham Pl. E3 . . . . .5C 86
N19 . . . . .2H 65
Gresham Rd. BR3: Beck 2A 158
E6 . . . . .2D 88
E16 . . . . .6K 87
HA8: Edg 6A 28
NW10 . . . . .5K 61
SE25 . . . . .4G 157
SW9 . . . . .3A 120
TW3: Houn 1G 113
TW12: Hamp 6E 130
UB10: Hil 2C 74
Gresham St. EC2 . . . . .7C 8 (6C 84)
Gresham Way SW19 . . . . .3K 135
Gresham Way Ind. Est. SW19 . . . .3K 135
    (off Gresham Way)
Gresley Cl. E17 . . . . .6A 50
N15 . . . . .4D 48
Gresley Rd. N19 . . . . .1G 65
Gressenhall Rd. SW18 . . . . .6H 117
Gresse St. W1 . . . . .6C 6 (6H 83)
Gresswell Cl. DA14: Sidc 3A 144
Greswell St. SW6 . . . . .1F 117
Gretton Ho. E2 . . . . .3J 85
    (off Globe Rd.)
Gretton Rd. N17 . . . . .7A 34
Greville Cl. TW1: Twick 7B 114
Greville Ct. E5 . . . . .3H 67
    (off Napoleon Rd.)
HA1: Harr .4J 59

Greville Hall NW6 . . . . .2K 81
Greville Ho. SW1 . . . . .1G 17
    (off Kinnerton St.)
Greville Lodge E13 . . . . .1K 87
HA8: Edg 4C 28
    (off Broadhurst Av.)
N12 . . . . .5E 30
Greville M. NW6 . . . . .1K 81
    (off Greville Rd.)
Greville Pl. NW6 . . . . .2K 81
Greville Rd. E17 . . . . .4E 50
NW6 . . . . .2K 81
TW10: Rich 6F 115
Greville St. EC1 . . . . .6J 7 (5A 84)
    (not continuous)
Grey Cl. NW11 . . . . .6A 46
Greycoat Gdns. SW1 . . . . .2C 18
    (off Greycoat St.)
Greycoat Pl. SW1 . . . . . . .2C 18 (3H 101)
Greycoat St. SW1 . . . . . . .2C 18 (3H 101)
Greycot Rd. BR3: Beck 5C 140
Grey Eagle St. E1 . . . . .4K 9 (4F 85)
Greyfell Cl. HA7: Stan 5G 27
Greyfriars SE26 . . . . .3G 139
    (off Wells Pk. Rd.)
Greyfriars Pas. EC1 . . . . . . .7B 8 (6B 84)
Greyhound Ct. WC2 . . . . . .2H 13 (7K 83)
Greyhound Hill NW4 . . . . .3C 44
Greyhound La. SW16 . . . . .6H 137
Greyhound Mans. W6 . . . . .6G 99
    (off Greyhound Rd.)
Greyhound Rd. N17 . . . . .3E 48
NW10 . . . . .3D 80
SM1: Sutt 5A 166
W6 . . . . .6F 99
W14 . . . . .6F 99
Greyhound Ter. SW16 . . . . .1G 155
Grey Ho. W12 . . . . .7D 80
    (off White City Est.)
Greyladies Gdns. SE10 . . . . .2E 122
Greys Pk. Cl. BR2: Kes 5B 172
Greystead Rd. SE23 . . . . .7J 121
Greystoke Av. HA5: Pinn 3E 40
Greystoke Ct. W5 . . . . .4E 78
Greystoke Dr. HA4: Ruis 6D 38
Greystoke Gdns. EN2: Enf 4C 22
W5 . . . . .4E 78
Greystoke Ho. SE15 . . . . .6G 103
    (off Peckham Pk. Rd.)
W5 . . . . .4E 78
Greystoke Lodge W5 . . . . .4F 79
    (off Hanger La.)
Greystoke Pk. Ter. W5 . . . . .3D 78
Greystoke Pl. EC4 . . . . . . .7J 7 (6A 84)
Greystone Gdns. HA3: Kenton 6C 42
IG6: Ilf 2G 53
Greyswood St. SW16 . . . . .6F 137
Grey Turner Ho. W12 . . . . .6C 80
Grierson Ho. SW16 . . . . .4G 137
Grierson Rd. SE23 . . . . .7K 121
Griffen Ct. BR3: Beck 1D 158
Griffin Cen. TW14: Felt 5K 111
The Griffin Cen. KT1: King T 2D 150
    (off Market Pl.)
Griffin Cl. NW10 . . . . .5D 62
Griffin Ct. TW8: Bford 6E 96
W4 . . . . .5B 98
Griffin Ho. CR0: C'don 7B 156
E14 . . . . .6D 86
    (off Ricardo St.)
N1 . . . . .1E 84
    (off Halcomb St.)
W6 . . . . .4F 99
    (off Hammersmith Rd.)
Griffin Mnr. Way SE28 . . . . .3H 107
Griffin M. SW12 . . . . .1G 137
Griffin Pk. 6D 96
Griffin Rd. N17 . . . . .2E 48
SE18 . . . . .5H 107
Griffins Cl. N21 . . . . .7J 23
Griffin Way TW16: Sun 2J 147
Griffith Cl. E17 . . . . .1F 51
RM8: Dag 7C 54

Griffiths Cl. KT4: Wor Pk 2D 164
Griffiths Rd. SW19 . . . . .7J 135
Griggs App. IG1: Ilf 2G 71
Griggs Cl. IG3: Ilf 4J 71
Griggs Ct. SE1 . . . . .3E 102
    (off Grigg's Pl.)
Grigg's Pl. SE1 . . . . .3E 102
Griggs Rd. E10 . . . . .6E 50
Grilse Cl. N9 . . . . .4C 34
Grimaldi Ho. N1 . . . . .2K 83
    (off Calshot St.)
Grimsby Gro. E16 . . . . .2F 107
Grimsby St. E2 . . . . .4K 9 (4F 85)
Grim's Ditch 5A 26
Grim's Dyke Golf Course 5A 26
Grimsdyke Rd. HA5: Hat E 1D 40
Grimsel Path SE5 . . . . .7B 102
Grimshaw Cl. N6 . . . . .7E 46
Grimston Rd. SW6 . . . . .2H 117
Grimthorpe Ho. EC1 . . . . .3A 8
Grimwade Av. CR0: C'don 3G 169
Grimwade Cl. SE15 . . . . .3J 121
Grimwood Rd. TW1: Twick 7K 113
Grindall Cl. CR0: Wadd 4B 168
Grindall Ho. E1 . . . . .4H 85
    (off Darling Row)
Grindal St. SE1 . . . . .7J 13 (2A 102)
Grindleford Av. N11 . . . . .2K 31
Grindley Gdns. CR0: C'don 6F 157
Grindley Ho. E3 . . . . .5B 86
    (off Leopold St.)
Grinling Pl. SE8 . . . . .6C 104
Grinstead Rd. SE8 . . . . .5A 104
Grisedale NW1 . . . . .1A 6
    (off Cumberland Mkt.)
Grittleton Av. HA9: Wemb 6H 61
Grittleton Rd. W9 . . . . .4J 81
Grizedale Ter. SE23 . . . . .2H 139
Grocer's Hall Ct. EC2 . . . . . .1E 14 (6D 84)
Grocer's Hall Gdns. EC2 . . . . .1E 14
Grogan Cl. TW12: Hamp 6D 130
Groombridge Cl. DA16: Well 5A 126
Groombridge Ho. SE17 . . . . .5E 102
    (off Upnor Way)
Groombridge Rd. E9 . . . . .7K 67
Groom Cl. BR2: Broml 4K 159
Groom Cres. SW18 . . . . .7B 118
Groome Ho. SE11 . . . . .4H 19 (4K 101)
Groomfield Cl. SW17 . . . . .4E 136
Groom Pl. SW1 . . . . .1H 17 (3E 100)
Grooms Dr. HA5: Eastc 5J 39
Grosmont Rd. SE18 . . . . .5K 107
Grosse Way SW15 . . . . .6D 116
Grosvenor Av. HA2: Harr 6F 41
N5 . . . . .5C 66
SM5: Cars 6D 166
SW14 . . . . .3A 116
TW10: Rich 5E 114
UB4: Hayes 2H 75
Grosvenor Cotts. SW1 . . . .3G 17 (4E 100)
Grosvenor Ct. E10 . . . . .1D 68
E14 . . . . .3D 104
    (off Wharf La.)
N14 . . . . .7B 22
NW6 . . . . .1F 81
NW7 . . . . .5E 28
    (off Hale La.)
SE5 . . . . .6C 102
SM2: Sutt 6K 165
SM4: Mord 4J 153
TW11: Tedd 6A 132
W3 . . . . .1G 97
W5 . . . . .7E 78
    (off The Grove)
W14 . . . . .3F 99
    (off Irving Rd.)
Grosvenor Ct. Mans. W2 . . . . .1E 10
    (off Edgware Rd.)
Grosvenor Cres. NW9 . . . . .4G 43
SW1 . . . . .7H 11 (2E 100)
UB10: Hil .7D 56
Grosvenor Cres. M.
SW1 . . . . .7G 11 (2E 100)

Grosvenor Est. SW1 . . . . . .3D 18 (4H 101)
Grosvenor Gdns. E6 . . . . .3B 88
IG8: Wfd G 6D 36
KT2: King T 6D 132
N10 . . . . .3G 47
N14 . . . . .4C 22
NW2 . . . . .6E 62
NW11 . . . . .6H 45
SM6: W'gton 7G 167
SW1 . . . . .1J 17 (3F 101)
SW14 . . . . .3A 116
Grosvenor Gdns. M. E. SW1 . . . . . .1K 17
Grosvenor Gdns. M. Nth. SW1 . . . .2J 17
Grosvenor Gdns. M. Sth. SW1 . . . .2K 17
Grosvenor Ga. SW1 . . . . . .3G 11 (7E 82)
Grosvenor Hill SW19 . . . . .6G 135
W1 .2J 11 (7F 83)
Grosvenor Hill Ct. W1 . . . . .2J 11
    (off Bourdon St.)
Grosvenor Ho. SM1: Sutt 5K 165
    (off West St.)
Grosvenor Pde. W5 . . . . .1G 97
    (off Uxbridge Rd.)
Grosvenor Pk. SE5 . . . . .7C 102
Grosvenor Pk. Rd. E17 . . . . .5C 50
Grosvenor Ri. E. E17 . . . . .5D 50
Grosvenor Rd. BR4: W W'ck 1D 170
BR5: St M Cry 3J 161
DA6: Bex .5D 126
DA17: Belv 6G 109
E6 . . . . .1B 88
E7 . . . . .6K 69
E10 . . . . .1E 68
E11 . . . . .5K 51
IG1: Ilf 3G 71
N3 . . . . .7C 30
N9 . . . . .1C 34
N10 . . . . .1F 47
RM7: Rush G 7K 55
RM8: Dag .1F 73
SE25 . . . . .4F 157
SM6: W'gton 6F 167
SW1 . . . . .7J 17 (6F 101)
TW1: Twick 1A 132
TW3: Houn 2D 112
TW8: Bford 6D 96
TW10: Rich 5E 114
UB2: S'hall 3D 94
W4 . . . . .5H 97
W7 . . . . .1A 96
Grosvenor Sq. W1 . . . . . . .2H 11 (7E 82)
SW1 . . . . .2J 11 (7F 83)
Grosvenor Studios SW1 . . . . .3G 17
    (off Eaton Ter.)
Grosvenor Ter. SE5 . . . . .7C 102
Grosvenor Va. HA4: Ruis 2H 57
Grosvenor Vale Stadium 2H 57
Grosvenor Way E5 . . . . .2J 67
W7 . . . . .3B 136
Grosvenor Wharf Rd. E14 . . . . .4F 105
Grotes Bldgs. SE3 . . . . .2G 123
Grote's Pl. SE3 . . . . .2G 123
Groton Rd. SW18 . . . . .2K 135
Grotto Ct. SE1 . . . . .6B 14 (2B 102)
Grotto Pas. W1 . . . . .5H 5 (5E 82)
Grotto Rd. TW1: Twick 2K 131
THE GROVE 1G 139
The Grove BR4: W W'ck 3D 170
DA6: Bex .4D 126
DA14: Sidc 5E 144
E15 . . . . .6G 69
EN2: Enf .2F 23
HA1: Harr .7J 41
HA7: Stan .2F 27
HA8: Edg .4C 28
KT12: Walt T 7K 147
N3 . . . . .1J 45
N4 . . . . .7K 47
N6 . . . . .1E 64
N8 . . . . .5J 47
N13 . . . . .4F 33
    (not continuous)

The Grove NW9 . . . . .5K 43
NW11 .7G 45
TW1: Twick 6B 114
TW7: Isle 1J 113
TW11: Tedd 4A 132
UB6: G'frd 6G 77
UB10: Ick 5C 56
W5 . . . . .1D 96
Grove Av. HA5: Pinn 4C 40
N3 . . . . .7D 30
N10 . . . . .2G 47
SM1: Sutt 6J 165
TW1: Twick 1K 131
W7 . . . . .7J 77
Grovebury Cl. DA8: Erith 6K 109
Grovebury Ct. DA6: Bex 5H 127
N14 . . . . .7C 22
Grovebury Rd. SE2 . . . . .2B 108
Grove Cl. BR2: Hayes 2J 171
KT1: King T 4F 151
N14 . . . . .7B 22
SE23 . . . . .1A 140
TW13: Hanw 4C 130
UB10: Ick 5C 56
Grove Cotts. SW3 . . . . .7D 16
W4 . . . . .6A 98
Grove Ct. EN5: Barn 3C 20
(off Hadley Ridge)
KT1: King T 3E 150
(off Grove Cres.)
KT8: E Mos 5H 149
NW8 . . . . .1A 4
SE15 . . . . .7E 102
(off Peckham Rd.)
SW10 . . . . .6A 16
(off Drayton Gdns.)
TW3: Houn 4E 112
W5 . . . . .1E 96
Grove Cres. E18 . . . . .2H 51
KT1: King T 3E 150
KT12: Walt T 7K 147
NW9 . . . . .4J 43
TW13: Hanw 4C 130
Grove Cres. Rd. E15 . . . . .6F 69
Grovedale Rd. N19 . . . . .2H 65
Grove Dwellings E1 . . . . .5J 85
Grove End E18 . . . . .2H 51
NW5 . . . . .4F 65
Grove End Gdns. NW8 . . . . .2B 82
Grove End Ho. NW8 . . . . .2A 4
Grove End La. KT10: Esh 7H 149
Grove End Rd. NW8 . . . .1A 4 (2B 82)
Grove Farm Retail Pk. 7C 54
Grovefield N11 . . . . .4A 32
(off Coppies Gro.)
Grove Footpath KT5: Surb 4E 150
Grove Gdns. EN3: Enf W 1E 24
NW4 . . . . .5C 44
NW8 . . . . .2D 4 (3C 82)
RM10: Dag 3J 73
TW10: Rich 6F 115
TW11: Tedd 4A 132
Grove Grn. Rd. E11 . . . . .3E 68
Grove Hall Ct. E3 . . . . .2C 86
(off Jebb St.)
NW8 . . . . .1A 4 (3A 82)
Grove Hill E18 . . . . .2H 51
HA1: Harr 7J 41
Grovehill Ct. BR1: Broml 6H 141
Grove Hill Rd. HA1: Harr 7K 41
SE5 .3E 120
Grove Ho. N3 . . . . .3F 45
SW3 .7D 16
(off Chelsea Mnr. St.)
Grove Ho. Rd. N8 . . . . .4J 47
Groveland Av. SW16 . . . . .7K 137
Groveland Ct. EC4 . . . . .1D 14
Groveland Rd. BR3: Beck 3B 158
Grovelands KT1: King T 4D 150
(off Palace Rd.)
KT8: W Mole 4E 148
Grovelands Cl. HA2: Harr 3F 59
SE5 .2E 120

Grovelands Ct. N14 . . . . .7C 22
Grovelands Rd. BR5: St P 7A 144
N13 . . . . .4E 32
N15 . . . . .6G 49
Groveland Way KT3: N Mald 5J 151
Grove La. KT1: King T 4E 150
SE5 .1D 120
UB8: Hil 4B 74
Grove La. Ter. SE5 . . . . .2D 120
Groveley Rd.
TW13: Felt 5H 129
TW16: Sun 5G 129
Grove Mans. W6 . . . . .2E 98
(off Hammersmith Gro.)
Grove M. W6 . . . . .3E 98
Grove Mill Pl. SM5: Cars 3E 166
The Grove Nature Reserve 4B 74
GROVE PARK
SE12 . . . . .3K 141
W4 . . . . .1J 115
Grove Pk. E11 . . . . .6K 51
NW9 . . . . .4J 43
SE5 .2E 120
Grove Pk. Av. E4 . . . . .7J 35
GROVE PK. BRI. 7J 97
Grove Pk. Gdns. W4 . . . . .7H 97
Grove Pk. M. W4 . . . . .7J 97
Grove Pk. Nature Reserve 1H 141
Grove Pk. Rd. N15 . . . . .4E 48
SE9 .3A 142
W4 . . . . .7H 97
Grove Pk. Ter. W4 . . . . .7H 97
Grove Pas. E2 . . . . .2H 85
Grove Pl. IG11: Bark 7G 71
NW3 . . . . .3B 64
SE9 .6D 124
SW12 . . . . .7F 119
W3 . . . . .1J 97
Grove Rd. SE13 . . . . .2D 122
Grover Ho. SE11 . . . . . .6H 19 (5K 101)
Grover Rd. CR4: Mitc 3E 154
(not continuous)
CR7: Thor H 4A 156
DA7: Bex 4J 127
DA17: Belv 6F 109
E3 . . . . .1K 85
E4 . . . . .4K 35
E11 . . . . .7H 51
E17 . . . . .6D 50
E18 . . . . .2H 51
EN4: Cockf 3H 21
HA5: Pinn 5D 40
HA8: Edg 6B 28
KT6: Surb 5D 150
KT8: E Mos 4H 149
N11 . . . . .5A 32
N12 . . . . .5G 31
N15 . . . . .4E 48
NW2 . . . . .6E 62
RM6: Chad H 7B 54
SM1: Sutt 6J 165
SW13 . . . . .2B 116
SW19 . . . . .7A 136
TW2: Twick 3H 131
TW3: Houn 4E 112
TW7: Isle 1J 113
TW9: Rich 6F 115
TW17: Shep 6E 146
UB8: Uxb 7A 56
W3 . . . . .1J 97
W5 . . . . .7D 78
Groveside Cl. SM5: Cars 2C 166
W3 . . . . .5G 79
Groveside Ct. SW11 . . . . .2B 118
Grovestile Rd. E4 . . . . .2B 36
Grovestile Waye TW14: Bedf 7F 111
Grove St. N18 . . . . .5A 34
SE8 .4B 104
Grove Ter. NW5 . . . . .3F 65
TW11: Tedd 4A 132
UB1: S'hall 7E 76
Grove Ter. M. NW5 . . . . .3F 65

Grove Va. BR7: Chst 6E 142
SE22 . . . . .4F 121
Grove Vs. E14 . . . . .7D 86
Grove Way HA9: Wemb 5H 61
KT10: Esh 7G 149
UB8: Uxb 7A 56
Groveway RM8: Dag 3D 72
SW9 .1K 119
Grovewood TW9: Kew 1G 115
Grove Wood Cl. BR1: Broml 3E 160
Grovewood Pl. IG8: Wfd G 6J 37
Grummant Rd. SE15 . . . . .1F 121
Grundy St. E14 . . . . .6D 86
Gruneisen Rd. N3 . . . . .7E 30
Grunwick Cl. NW2 . . . . .5C 62
Gtec Ho. E15 . . . . .2F 87
(off Canning Rd.)
Guardhouse Way NW7 . . . . .5A 30
Guardian Apts. E3 . . . . .4B 86
(off Kevtar Gdn.)
Guardian Av. NW9 . . . . .3A 44
Guardian Ct. SE12 . . . . .5G 123
Guards Memorial 5D 12 (1H 101)
The Guards' Mus. 7B 12 (2G 101)
Gubyon Av. SE24 . . . . .5B 120
Guerin Sq. E3 . . . . .3B 86
Guernsey Cl. TW5: Hest 7E 94
Guernsey Gro. SE24 . . . . .7C 120
Guernsey Ho. EN3: Enf W 1E 24
(off Eastfield Rd.)
N1 . . . . .6C 66
(off Channel Island Est.)
Guernsey Rd. E11 . . . . .1F 69
Guglielmo Marconi M. E3 . . . . . . .2B 86
Guibal Rd. SE12 . . . . .7K 123
Guildersfield Rd. SW16 . . . . .7J 137
Guildford Av. TW13: Felt 2A 130
Guildford Ct. SW8 . . . . .7J 101
(off Guildford Rd.)
Guildford Gro. SE10 . . . . .1D 122
Guildford Rd. CR0: C'don 6D 156
E6 . . . . .6D 88
E17 . . . . .1E 50
IG3: Ilf 2J 71
SW8 .1J 119
Guildford Way SM6: W'gton 5J 167
Guildhall 7E 8
Guildhall Art Gallery 7E 8
(off Aldermanbury)
Guildhall Bldgs. EC2 . . . . .7E 8
Guildhall College 6H 85
Guildhall Offices EC2 . . . . .7D 8
Guildhall Yd. EC2 . . . . . .7D 8 (6C 84)
Guildhouse St. SW1 . . . .3A 18 (4G 101)
Guildown Av. N12 . . . . .4E 30
Guild Rd. SE7 . . . . .6B 106
Guildsway E17 . . . . .1B 50
Guilford Av. KT5: Surb 5F 151
Guilford Pl. WC1 . . . . . .4G 7 (4K 83)
Guilford St. WC1 . . . . . .4E 6 (4J 83)
Guilfoyle NW9 . . . . .2B 44
Guillemot Ct. SE8 . . . . .6B 104
(off Alexandra Cl.)
Guillemot Pl. N22 . . . . .2K 47
Guinea Cl. E1 . . . . .7G 85
(off Royal Mint St.)
Guinea Ct. E1 . . . . .6A 86
(off Repton St.)
Guinness Cl. E9 . . . . .7A 68
UB3: Harl 3F 93
Guinness Ct. CR0: C'don 1D 169
E1 . . . . .1J 15
EC1 . . . . .2D 8
SE1 .6G 15
SW3 . . . . .4E 16 (4D 100)
Guinness Sq. SE1 . . . . .4E 102
Guinness Trust SW3 . . . . .4E 16
(off Cadogan St.)
Guinness Trust Bldgs. SE11 . . . . .5B 102
W6 . . . . .5E 98
(off Fulham Pal. Rd.)
The Guinness Trust Est. N16 . . . . .1E 66
Guion Rd. SW6 . . . . .2H 117

Gulland Wlk. N1 . . . . .6C 66
(off Church Rd.)
Gullane Ho. E3 . . . . .2B 86
(off Shetland Rd.)
Gulliver Cl. UB5: N'olt 1D 76
Gulliver Rd. DA15: Sidc 2H 143
Gulliver's Ho. EC1 . . . . .4C 8
Gulliver St. SE16 . . . . .3A 104
Gullivers Wlk. SE8 . . . . .4B 104
Gulston Wlk. SW3 . . . . .4F 17
Gumleigh Rd. W5 . . . . .4C 96
Gumley Gdns. TW7: Isle 3A 114
Gumping Rd. BR5: Farnb 2G 173
Gundulf St. SE11 . . . . .4A 102
Gundulph Rd. BR2: Broml 3A 160
Gun Ho. E1 . . . . .1H 103
(off Wapping High St.)
Gunmakers La. E3 . . . . .1A 86
Gun M. IG9: Buck H 4G 37
Gunnel Ct. E3 . . . . .3E 86
(off Bolinder Way)
Gunnell Cl. CR0: C'don 6G 157
SE25 . . . . .6G 157
(off Backley Gdns.)
SE26 . . . . .4G 139
Gunner La. SE18 . . . . .5E 106
GUNNERSBURY 5H 97
Gunnersbury Av. W3 . . . . .1F 97
W4 . . . . .1F 97
W5 . . . . .1F 97
Gunnersbury Cl. W4 . . . . .5H 97
Gunnersbury Ct. W3 . . . . .2H 97
Gunnersbury Cres. W3 . . . . .2G 97
Gunnersbury Dr. W5 . . . . .2F 97
Gunnersbury Gdns. W3 . . . . .2G 97
Gunnersbury La. W3 . . . . .3G 97
Gunnersbury Mnr. W5 . . . . .1F 97
Gunnersbury M. W4 . . . . .5H 97
GUNNERSBURY PARK 3G 97
Gunnersbury Pk. Mus. 3G 97
Gunnersbury Triangle Nature Reserve
. . . . .4J 97
Gunners Gro. E4 . . . . .3K 35
Gunners Rd. SW18 . . . . .2B 136
Gunnery Ter. SE18 . . . . .3G 107
Gunning St. SE18 . . . . .4J 107
Gunpowder Sq. EC4 . . . . .7K 7
(off E. Harding St.)
Gunstor Rd. N16 . . . . .4E 66
Gun St. E1 . . . . .6J 9 (5F 85)
Gunter Gro. HA8: Edg 1K 43
SW10 . . . . .6A 100
Gunter Hall Studios SW10 . . . . . .6A 100
(off Gunter Gro.)
Gunterstone Rd. W14 . . . . .4G 99
Gunthorpe St. E1 . . . . . .6K 9 (5F 85)
Gunton M. SE13 . . . . .5F 123
Gunton Rd. E5 . . . . .3H 67
SW17 . . . . .6E 136
Gunwhale Cl. SE16 . . . . .1K 103
Gun Wharf E1 . . . . .1J 103
(off Wapping High St.)
Gunyard M. SE18 . . . . .7C 106
Gurdon Ho. E14 . . . . .6C 86
(off Dod St.)
Gurdon Rd. SE7 . . . . .5J 105
Gurdwara Sri Guru Singh Sabha
Southall 3C 94
Gurnard Cl. UB7: Yiew 7A 74
Gurnell Gro. W13 . . . . .4K 77
Gurnell Leisure Cen. 3K 77
Gurney Cl. E15 . . . . .5G 69
E17 . . . . .1K 49
IG11: Bark 6F 71
Gurney Cres. CR0: C'don 1K 167
Gurney Dr. N2 . . . . .4A 46
Gurney Ho. E2 . . . . .2G 85
(off Goldsmiths Row)
UB3: Harl 5G 69
Gurney Rd. E15 . . . . .5G 69
SM5: Cars 4E 166
SW6 .3A 118
UB5: N'olt 3K 75

Gutenberg Ct. SE1 . . . . 3F 103
(off Grange Rd.)
Guthridge Cl. E14 . . . . 5C 86
Guthrie Cl. SE1 . . . . 7K 13
Guthrie St. SW3 . . . . 5C 16 (5B 100)
Gutter La. EC2 . . . . 7C 8 (6C 84)
Guyatt Gdns. CR4: Mitc 2E 154
Guy Barnett Gro. SE3 . . . . 3J 123
Guy Rd. SM6: Bedd 3H 167
Guyscliff Rd. SE13 . . . . 5E 122
Guys Retreat IG9: Buck H 1F 37
Guy St. SE1 . . . . 6F 15 (2D 102)
Guy Townsley Sq. E3 . . . . .5D 86
Gwalior Ho. N14 . . . . 6B 22
Gwalior Rd. SW15 . . . . 4F 117
Gwendolen Av. SW15 . . . . 4F 117
Gwendolen Cl. SW15 . . . . 5F 117
Gwendolen Ho. TW19: Stanw 1A 128
(off Yeoman Dr.)
Gwendoline Av. E13 . . . . 1K 87
Gwendwr Rd. W14 . . . . 5G 99
Gweneth Cotts. HA8: Edg 6B 28
Gwen Morris Ho. SE5 . . . . .7C 102
Gwent Ct. SE16 . . . . .1K 103
(off Rotherhithe St.)
Gwillim Cl. DA15: Sidc 5A 126
Gwilym Maries Ho. E2 . . . . .3H 85
(off Blythe St.)
Gwydor Rd. BR3: Beck 3K 157
Gwydyr Rd. BR2: Broml 3H 159
Gwyn Cl. SW6 . . . . .7A 100
Gwynne Av. CR0: C'don 7K 157
Gwynne Cl. W4 . . . . .6B 98
Gwynne Ho. E1 . . . . .5H 85
(off Turner St.)
SW1 . . . . .5G 17
(off Lwr. Sloane St.)
WC1 .2J 7
(off Lloyd Baker St.)
Gwynne Pk. Av. IG8: Wfd G 6J 37
Gwynne Pl. WC1 . . . . . .2H 7 (3K 83)
Gwynne Rd. SW11 . . . . 2B 118
Gylcote Cl. SE5 . . . . .4D 120
Gyles Pk. HA7: Stan 1C 42
Gyllyngdune Gdns. IG3: Ilf 2K 71
The Gym
  Bloomsbury 4E 6 (4J 83)
  Holborn Circus 6K 7
  Hounslow 3F 113
  Kingsbury 5G 43
  London Monument 7D 84
  Walworth Road 5C 102
The Gymnasium N1 . . . . .2J 83
GYPSY CORNER 5K 79

H

Haarlem Rd. W14 . . . . .3F 99
Haberdasher Est. N1 . . . . .1F 9 (3D 84)
Haberdasher Pl. N1 . . . . . .1F 9 (3D 84)
Haberdashers St. SE14 . . . . .3K 121
Haberdasher St. N1 . . . . .1F 9 (3D 84)
Habitat Cl. SE15 . . . . 2H 121
Habitat Sq. SE10 . . . . .3H 105
(off Teal St.)
Haccombe Rd. SW19 . . . . .6A 136
HACKBRIDGE 1E 166
Hackbridge Pk. Gdns.
  SM5: Cars 2D 166
Hackbridge Rd. SM6: W'gton . . .2E 166
Hackford Rd. SW9 . . . . 1K 119
Hackford Wlk. SW9 . . . . .1A 120
Hackington Cres. BR3: Beck 6C 140
HACKNEY 6H 67
Hackney City Farm 2G 85
Hackney Empire Theatre 6H 67
Hackney Fashion Hub E9 . . . . . .6J 67
Hackney Gro. E8 . . . . .6H 67
Hackney Marshes Cen. 4B 68
Hackney Mus. 6H 67
Hackney Picturehouse 6H 67
(off Mare St.)

Hackney Rd. E2 . . . . .2J 9 (3F 85)
Hackney University Technical College
 . . . . .1H 9 (3E 84)
HACKNEY WICK 6B 68
HACKNEY WICK 6A 68
Hackworth Point E3 . . . . .3D 86
(off Rainhill Way)
Hacon Sq. E8 . . . . .7H 67
(off Mare St.)
Hadar Cl. N20 . . . . .1D 30
Hadden Rd. SE28 . . . . .3J 107
Hadden Way UB6: G'frd 6H 59
Haddington Rd. BR1: Broml 3F 141
Haddo Ho. SE10 . . . . .6D 104
(off Haddo St.)
Haddon Cl. EN1: Enf 6B 24
  KT3: N Mald 5B 152
Haddon Cl. NW4 . . . . 3E 44
  W3 . . . . .7B 80
Haddonfield SE8 . . . . .4K 103
Haddon Gro. DA15: Sidc 7K 125
Haddon Rd. SM1: Sutt 4K 165
(not continuous)
Haddo St. SE10 . . . . .6D 104
Haden La. N11 . . . . .4B 32
Hadfield Cl. UB1: S'hall 3D 76
Hadfield Ho. E1 . . . . 6G 85
(off Ellen St.)
Hadleigh Cl. E1 . . . . 4J 85
  HA2: Harr 4E 58
  SW20 . . . . .2H 153
Hadleigh Cl. E4 . . . . .1B 36
  NW2 . . . . .6E 62
Hadleigh Ho. E1 . . . . .4J 85
(off Hadleigh Cl.)
Hadleigh Lodge IG8: Wfd G 6D 36
(off Snakes La. W.)
Hadleigh Rd. N9 . . . . .7C 24
Hadleigh St. E2 . . . . .3J 85
Hadleigh Wlk. E6 . . . . .6C 88
HADLEY 3C 20
Hadley Cl. N21 . . . . .6F 23
Hadley Comn.
  EN5: Barn, New Bar 2D 20
  N16 . . . . .1G 67
  SL3: Poyle 4A 174
(off Coleridge Cres.)
Hadley Gdns. UB2: S'hall 5D 94
  W4 . . . . .5K 97
Hadley Grn. EN5: Barn 2C 20
Hadley Grn. Rd. EN5: Barn 2C 20
Hadley Grn. W. EN5: Barn 2C 20
Hadley Gro. EN5: Barn 2B 20
Hadley Highstone EN5: Barn 1C 20
Hadley M. EN5: Barn 3C 20
Hadley Pde. EN5: Barn 3B 20
(off High St.)
Hadley Ridge EN5: Barn 3C 20
Hadley Rd. CR4: Mitc 4H 155
  DA17: Belv 4F 109
  EN2: Enf 1A 22
  EN4: Had W 1K 21
  EN5: New Bar 2E 20
Hadley St. NW1 . . . . .6F 65
(not continuous)
Hadley Way N21 . . . . .6F 23
HADLEY WOOD 1F 21
Hadley Wood Golf Course 1H 21
Hadley Wood Lawn Tennis Club 1F 21
Hadley Wood Nature Reserve 2F 21
Hadley Wood Rd. EN4: Cockf 2F 21
  EN5: Cockf, New Bar 2F 21
Hadlow Ho. SE17 . . . . .5E 102
(off Kinglake Est.)
Hadlow Pl. SE19 . . . . .7G 139
Hadlow Rd. DA14: Sidc 4A 144
  DA16: Well 2B 126
Hadrian Cl. E3 . . . . .1C 86
(off Garrison Rd.)
  TW19: Stanw 7A 110
Hadrian Ct. SM2: Sutt 7K 165

Hadrian Est. E2 . . . . .2G 85
Hadrian M. CR4: Mitc 3F 155
  N7 . . . . .7K 65
Hadrians Ride EN1: Enf 5A 24
Hadrian St. SE10 . . . . .5G 105
Hadrian Way TW19: Stanw 7A 110
(not continuous)
Hadstock Ho. NW1 . . . . .1D 6
(off Ossulston St.)
Hadyn Pk. Ct. W12 . . . . .2C 98
(off Curwen Rd.)
Hadyn Pk. Rd. W12 . . . . .2C 98
Hafer Rd. SW11 . . . . .4D 118
Hafton Rd. SE6 . . . . .1G 141
Haggard Rd.
  TW1: Twick 7B 114
Hagger Ct. E17 . . . . .3F 51
HAGGERSTON 7F 67
Haggerston Rd. E8 . . . . .7F 67
Haggerston Studios E8 . . . . .1F 85
(off Kingsland Rd.)
Hague St. E2 . . . . .3G 85
Ha Ha Rd. SE18 . . . . .6D 106
Haider Cl. NW2 . . . . .2F 63
Haig Ho. E2 . . . . .1K 9
(off Shipton St.)
Haig Pl. SM4: Mord 6J 153
Haig Rd. HA7: Stan 5H 27
  UB8: Hil 5D 74
Haig Rd. E. E13 . . . . .3A 88
Haig Rd. W. E13 . . . . .3A 88
Haigville Gdns. IG6: Ilf 4F 53
Hailes Cl. CR0: Bedd 2H 167
  SW19 . . . . .6A 136
Haileybury Av. EN1: Enf 6A 24
Hailey Rd. DA18: Erith 2G 109
Hailey Rd. Bus. Pk.
  DA18: Erith 2G 109
Hailing M. BR2: Broml 3K 159
(off Wendover Rd.)
Hailsham Av. SW2 . . . . .2K 137
Hailsham Cl. KT6: Surb 7D 150
Hailsham Dr. HA1: Harr 3H 41
Hailsham Ho. NW8 . . . . .4C 4
(off Salisbury St.)
Hailsham Rd. SW17 . . . . .6E 136
Hailsham Ter. N18 . . . . .5J 33
Haimo Rd. SE9 . . . . .5B 124
Hainault Bri. Pde. IG1: Ilf 2F 71
(off Hainault St.)
Hainault Ct. E17 . . . . .4F 51
(off Forest Ri.)
Hainault Gore RM6: Chad H 5E 54
Hainault Rd. E11 . . . . .1E 68
  RM5: Col R, Rom 2J 55
  RM6: Chad H 1B 54
(Forest Rd.)
  RM6: Chad H 6B 55
(Sylvan Av.)
Hainault St. IG1: Ilf 2G 71
  SE9 . . . . .1F 143
Haines Cl. N1 . . . . .7E 66
Haines Ho. SW11 . . . . .7H 101
(off Ponton Rd.)
Haines St. SW11 . . . . .7G 101
Hainford Cl. SE4 . . . . .4K 121
Haining Cl. W4 . . . . .5G 97
Hainthorpe Rd. SE27 . . . . .3B 138
Hainton Cl. E1 . . . . .6H 85
Halberd M. E5 . . . . .2H 67
Halbutt Gdns. RM9: Dag 3F 73
Halbutt St. RM9: Dag 4F 73
Halcomb St. N1 . . . . .1E 84
Halcot Av. DA6: Bex 5H 127
Halcrow St. E1 . . . . .5H 85
Halcyon EN1: Enf 5K 23
(off Private Rd.)
Halcyon Cl. SW13 . . . . .3C 116
Halcyon Wharf E1 . . . . .1G 103
(off Hermitage Wall)
Haldane Cl. N10 . . . . .7A 32
Haldane Pl. SW18 . . . . .1K 135

Haldane Rd. E6 . . . . .3B 88
  SE28 . . . . .7D 90
  SW6 . . . . .7H 99
  UB1: S'hall 7G 77
Haldan Rd. E4 . . . . .6K 35
Haldon Rd. SW18 . . . . .6H 117
THE HALE 5E 28
The Hale E4 . . . . .7A 36
  N17 . . . . .3G 49
Hale Cl. BR6: Farnb 4G 173
  E4 . . . . .3K 35
  HA8: Edg 5D 28
Hale Dr. NW7 . . . . .6D 28
HALE END 6B 36
Hale End Cl. HA4: Ruis 6J 39
Hale End Rd. E4 . . . . .6A 36
  E17 . . . . .1E 50
  IG8: Wfd G 7A 36
Halefield Rd. N17 . . . . .1H 49
Hale Gdns. N17 . . . . .4G 49
  W3 . . . . .1G 97
Hale Gro. Gdns. NW7 . . . . .5F 29
Hale Ho. SW1 . . . . .5D 18
(off Lindsay Sq.)
Hale La. HA8: Edg 5C 28
  NW7 . . . . .5E 28
Hale Path SE27 . . . . .4B 138
Hale Rd. E6 . . . . .4C 88
  N17 . . . . .3G 49
Halesowen Rd. SM4: Mord 7K 153
Hales Prior N1 . . . . .1G 7
(off Calshot St.)
Hales St. SE8 . . . . .7C 104
Hale St. E14 . . . . .7D 86
Halesworth Cl. E5 . . . . .2J 67
Halesworth Rd. SE13 . . . . .3D 122
Hale Wlk. W7 . . . . .5J 77
Haley Rd. NW4 . . . . .6E 44
Half Acre HA7: Stan 5H 27
  TW8: Bford 6D 96
Half Acre Rd. W7 . . . . .1J 95
Half Moon Ct. CR0: C'don 7B 156
  EC1 . . . . .6C 8
Half Moon Cres. N1 . . . . .2K 83
(not continuous)
Half Moon La. SE24 . . . . .6C 120
Half Moon Pas. E1 . . . .1K 15 (6F 85)
(not continuous)
Half Moon St. W1 . . . .4K 11 (1F 101)
Halford Cl. HA8: Edg 2H 43
Halford Pl. W7 . . . . .1K 95
Halford Rd. E10 . . . . .5F 51
  SW6 . . . . .6J 99
  TW10: Rich 5E 114
  UB10: Ick 4C 56
Halfway St. DA15: Sidc 7H 125
Haliburton Rd. TW1: Twick 5A 114
Haliday Ho. N1 . . . . .6D 66
(off Mildmay St.)
Halidon Cl. E9 . . . . .5J 67
Halifax NW9 . . . . .2B 44
Halifax Cl. TW11: Tedd 6J 131
Halifax Rd. EN2: Enf 2H 23
  UB6: G'frd 1F 77
Halifax St. SE26 . . . . .3H 139
Halifield Dr. DA17: Belv 3E 108
Haling Down Pas. CR8: Purl 7C 168
Haling Gro. CR2: S Croy 7C 168
Haling Pk. Gdns. CR2: S Croy . . .6B 168
Haling Pk. Rd. CR2: S Croy 5B 168
Haling Rd. CR2: S Croy 6D 168
Haliwell Ho. NW6 . . . . .1K 81
(off Mortimer Cres.)
Halkett Ho. E2 . . . . .1J 85
(off Waterloo Gdns.)
Halkin Arc. SW1 . . . . . .1F 17 (3D 100)
Halkin M. SW1 . . . . . . .1G 17 (3E 100)
Halkin Pl. SW1 . . . . . . .1G 17 (3E 100)
Halkin St. SW1 . . . . . .7H 11 (2E 100)
The Hall SE3 . . . . .3J 123
Hallam Cl. BR7: Chst 5D 142

Hallam Ct. W1 .....5K 5
(off Hallam St.)
Hallam Gdns. HA5: Hat E 1C 40
Hallam Ho. SW1 .....6B 18
(off Churchill Gdns.)
Hallam M. W1 .....5K 5 (5F 83)
Hallam Rd. N15 .....4B 48
SW13 .....3D 116
Hallam St. W1 .....4K 5 (5F 83)
Hallane Ho. SE27 .....5C 138
Hall Apts. E3 .....5B 86
(off Geoff Cade Way)
Hall Cl. W5 .....5E 78
Hall Ct. TW11: Tedd 5K 131
Hall Dr. SE26 .....5J 139
W7 .....6J 77
Halley Gdns. SE13 .....4F 123
Halley Ho. E2 .....2G 85
(off Pritchards Rd.)
SE10 .....5H 105
(off Armitage Rd.)
Halley Rd. E7 .....6A 70
E12 .....6A 70
Halley St. E14 .....5A 86
Hall Farm Cl. HA7: Stan 4G 27
Hall Farm Dr. TW2: Whitt 7H 113
Hallfield Est. W2 .....6A 82
(not continuous)
Hall Gdns. E4 .....4G 35
Hall Ga. NW8 .....1A 4 (3B 82)
The Halliards KT12: Walt T 6J 147
Halliday Ho. E1 .....6G 85
(off Christian St.)
Halliday Sq. UB2: S'hall 1H 95
Halliford Cl. TW17: Shep 4F 147
Halliford Rd. TW16: Sun 5G 147
TW17: Shep 5G 147
Halliford St. N1 .....7C 66
Hallingbury Ct. E17 .....3D 50
Halling Ho. SE1 .....7F 15
(off Long La.)
Hallings Wharf Studios E15 .....1F 87
Hallington Ct. HA8: Edg 4A 28
(off Brannigan Way)
Halliwell Ct. SE22 .....5G 121
Halliwell Rd. SW2 .....6K 119
Halliwick Ct. Pde. N12 .....6J 31
(off Woodhouse Rd.)
Halliwick Rd. N10 .....1E 46
HALL LANE 5E 34
Hall La. E4 .....5F 35
NW4 .....1C 44
UB3: Harl 7F 93
Hallmark Ho. E14 .....5C 86
(off Ursula Gould Way)
Hallmark Trad. Est. HA9: Wemb 4J 61
Hallmead Rd. SM1: Sutt 3K 165
Hall Oak Wlk. NW6 .....6H 63
Hallowell Av. CRO: Bedd 4J 167
Hallowell Cl. CR4: Mitc 3E 154
Hallowell Gdns. CR7: Thor H 2C 156
Hallowell Rd. HA6: Nwood 1G 39
Hallowfield Way CR4: Mitc 3B 154
Hallows Gro. TW16: Sun 5H 129
Hall Pl. W2 .....4A 4 (4B 82)
(not continuous)
Hall Place & Gdns. 6J 127
Hall Pl. Cres. DA5: Bexl 5J 127
Hall Place Sports Pavilion 6J 127
Hall Rd. E6 .....1D 88
E15 .....4F 69
NW8 .....1A 4 (3A 82)
RM6: Chad H 6C 54
SM6: W'gton 7F 167
TW7: Isle 5H 113
Hallside Rd. EN1: Enf 1A 24
Halls Ter. UB10: Hil 4D 74
Hall St. EC1 .....1B 8 (3B 84)
N12 .....5F 31
Hallsville Rd. E16 .....6H 87
Hallswelle Pde. NW11 .....5H 45
Hallswelle Rd. NW11 .....5H 45
Hall Twr. W2 .....5B 4

Hall Vw. SE9 .....2B 142
Hallywell Cres. E6 .....5D 88
Halo E15 .....1E 86
Halons Rd. SE9 .....7E 124
Halpin Building SE10 .....3J 105
(off Rennie Street)
Halpin Pl. SE17 .....4D 102
Halsbrook Rd. SE3 .....3A 124
Halsbury Cl. HA7: Stan 4G 27
Halsbury Ct. HA7: Stan 5G 27
Halsbury Ho. N7 .....4K 65
(off Biddestone Rd.)
Halsbury Rd. W12 .....1D 98
Halsbury Rd. E. UB5: N'olt 4G 59
Halsbury Rd. W. UB5: N'olt 5F 59
Halsend UB3: Hayes 1K 93
Halsey Ho. WC1 .....6G 7
(off Red Lion Sq.)
Halsey M. SW3 .....3E 16 (4D 100)
Halsey St. SW3 .....3E 16 (4D 100)
Halsham Cres. IG11: Bark 5K 71
Halsmere Rd. SE5 .....1B 120
Halstead Cl. CRO: C'don 3C 168
Halstead Ct. E17 .....7B 50
N1 .....1F 9
(off Murray Gro.)
Halstead Gdns. N21 .....1J 33
Halstead Rd. E11 .....5J 51
EN1: Enf 4K 23
N21 .....1H 33
Halston Cl. SW11 .....6D 118
Halstow Rd. NW10 .....3F 81
SE10 .....5J 105
Halsway UB3: Hayes 1J 93
Halton Cl. N11 .....6J 31
Halton Ct. SE3 .....3K 123
Halton Cross St. N1 .....1B 84
Halton Ho. N1 .....7C 66
(off Halton Rd.)
Halton Mans. N1 .....7C 66
Halton Pl. N1 .....1C 84
Halton Rd. N1 .....7B 66
Halt Robin La. DA17: Belv 4H 109
Halt Robin Rd. DA17: Belv 4G 109
(not continuous)
Halyard Ho. E14 .....3E 104
(off Manchester Rd.)
Halyard Pl. E16 .....2K 105
Halyard St. RM9: Dag 4E 90
The Ham TW8: Bford 7C 96
Hamara Ghar E13 .....1A 88
Hambalt Rd. SW4 .....5G 119
Hamble Cl. HA4: Ruis 2G 57
Hambledon SE17 .....6D 102
(off Villa St.)
Hambledon Cl. UB8: Hil 4D 74
Hambledon Ct. SE22 .....4E 120
W5 .....7E 78
Hambledon Gdns. SE25 .....3F 157
Hambledon Pl. SE21 .....1E 138
Hambledon Rd. SW18 .....7H 117
Hambledon Rd. DA15: Sidc 7H 125
Hamble Dr. UB3: Hayes 7H 75
Hamblehyrst BR3: Beck 2D 158
Hamble St. SW6 .....3K 117
Hambleton Cl. KT4: Wor Pk 2E 164
Hamble Wlk. UB5: N'olt 2E 76
(off Brabazon Rd.)
Hambley Ho. SE16 .....4H 103
(off Camilla Rd.)
Hamblin Ho. UB1: S'hall 7C 76
(off The Broadway)
Hambridge Way SW2 .....7A 120
Hambro Av. BR2: Hayes 1J 171
Hambrook Rd. SE25 .....3H 157
Hambro Rd. SW16 .....6H 137
Hambrough Ho. UB4: Yead 5A 76
Hambrough Rd. UB1: S'hall 1C 94
Ham Cl. TW10: Ham 3D 132
(not continuous)
Ham Common 4E 132
Ham Comn. TW10: Ham 3D 132

Ham Ct. NW9 .....2A 44
Ham Cft. Cl. TW13: Felt 3J 129
Hamden Cres. RM10: Dag 3H 73
Hamel Cl. HA3: Kenton 4D 42
Hamella Ho. E9 .....5A 68
(off Sadler Pl.)
Hameway E6 .....3E 88
Ham Farm Rd. TW10: Ham 4D 132
Ham Flds. TW10: Ham 3B 132
Hamfrith Rd. E15 .....6H 69
Ham Ga. Av. TW10: Ham 3D 132
Ham House & Garden 1C 132
Hamilton Av. IG6: Ilf 4F 53
KT6: Surb 2G 163
N9 .....7B 24
RM1: Rom 2K 55
SM3: Cheam 2G 165
Hamilton Cl. EN4: Cockf 4H 21
HA7: Stan 2D 26
N17 .....3F 49
NW8 .....2A 4 (3B 82)
SE16 .....2A 104
TW11: Tedd 6B 132
TW13: Felt 5H 129
Hamilton Cl. CRO: C'don 1G 169
SE6 .....1H 141
SW15 .....3G 117
TW3: Houn 4F 113
(off Hanworth Rd.)
W5 .....7E 78
W9 .....3A 82
(off Maida Vale)
Hamilton Cres. HA2: Harr 3D 58
N13 .....4F 33
TW3: Houn 5F 113
Hamilton Gdns. NW8 .....1A 4 (3A 82)
Hamilton Hall NW8 .....2A 82
(off Hamilton Ter.)
Hamilton Ho. E3 .....3B 86
(off British St.)
E14 .....5D 104
(off St Davids Sq.)
E14 .....7B 86
(off Victory Pl.)
NW8 .....1A 4
W4 .....6A 98
W8 .....2K 99
(off Vicarage Ga.)
Hamilton La. N5 .....4B 66
Hamilton Lodge E1 .....4J 85
(off Cleveland Gro.)
Hamilton M. SW18 .....1J 135
SW19 .....7J 135
W1 .....6J 11 (2F 101)
Hamilton Pde. TW13: Felt 4H 129
Hamilton Pk. N5 .....4B 66
Hamilton Pk. W. N5 .....4B 66
Hamilton Pl. N19 .....3H 65
TW16: Sun 7K 129
W1 .....5H 11 (1E 100)
Hamilton Rd. CR7: Thor H 3D 156
DA7: Bex 2E 126
DA15: Sidc 4A 144
E15 .....3G 87
E17 .....2A 50
EN4: Cockf 4H 21
HA1: Harr 5J 41
IG1: Ilf 4F 71
N2 .....3A 46
N9 .....7B 24
NW10 .....5C 62
NW11 .....7F 45
SE27 .....4D 138
SW19 .....7K 135
TW2: Twick 1J 131
TW8: Bford 6D 96
TW13: Felt 4H 129
UB1: S'hall 1D 94
UB3: Hayes 7K 75
W4 .....2A 98
W5 .....7E 78
Hamilton Rd. Ind. Est. SE27 .....4D 138
Hamilton Rd. M. SW19 .....7K 135

Hamilton Sq. N12 .....6G 31
SE1 .....6F 15 (2D 102)
Hamilton St. SE8 .....6C 104
Hamilton Ter. NW8 .....2A 4 (2K 81)
Hamilton Way N3 .....6D 30
N13 .....4G 33
SM6: W'gton 7H 167
Ham Lands Nature Reserve 2A 132
Hamlea Cl. SE12 .....5J 123
The Hamlet SE5 .....3D 120
Hamlet Cl. RM5: Col R 1G 55
SE6 .....7D 122
SE13 .....4G 123
Hamlet Ct. E3 .....3C 86
(off Tomlin's Gro.)
EN1: Enf 5K 23
SE11 .....5B 102
(off Opal St.)
W6 .....4C 98
Hamlet Gdns. W6 .....4C 98
Hamlet Ind. Est. E9 .....7C 68
Hamlet Intl. Ind. Est. DA8: Erith 5K 109
Hamlet Lodge UB10: Hil 6D 56
Hamlet M. SE21 .....1D 138
Hamleton Ter. RM9: Dag 7C 72
(off Flamstead Rd.)
Hamlet Rd. RM5: Col R 1G 55
SE19 .....7F 139
Hamlet Sq. NW2 .....3G 63
Hamlets Way E3 .....4B 86
Hamlet Way SE1 .....6F 15 (2D 102)
Hamlin Cres. HA5: Eastc 5A 40
Hamlyn Cl. HA8: Edg 3K 27
Hamlyn Gdns. SE19 .....7E 138
Hamlyn Ho. TW13: Felt 1K 129
Hammelton Ct. BR1: Broml 1H 159
(off London Rd.)
Hammelton Rd. BR1: Broml 1H 159
Hammerfield Ho. SW3 .....5D 16
(off Cale St.)
Hammers La. NW7 .....5H 29
Hammersley Ho. SE14 .....7J 103
(off Pomeroy St.)
Hammersley Rd. E16 .....5J 87
HAMMERSMITH 4E 98
Hammersmith Apollo 5E 98
HAMMERSMITH BRI. 6D 98
Hammersmith Bri. Rd. W6 .....5E 98
HAMMERSMITH BROADWAY 4E 98
Hammersmith B'way. W6 .....4E 98
Hammersmith Emb. W6 .....6E 98
Hammersmith Fitness & Squash Cen.
.....4F 99
(off Chalk Hill Rd.)
HAMMERSMITH FLYOVER 5E 98
Hammersmith Flyover W6 .....5E 98
Hammersmith Gro. W6 .....2E 98
Hammersmith Information Centre
.....4E 98
(within The Broadway Cen.)
Hammersmith Rd. W6 .....4F 99
W14 .....4F 99
Hammersmith Ter. W6 .....5C 98
Hammett Cl. UB4: Yead 5B 76
Hammett St. EC3 .....2J 15 (7F 85)
Hammond Av. CR4: Mitc 2F 155
Hammond Cl. EN5: Barn 5B 20
TW12: Hamp 1E 148
UB6: G'frd 5H 59
Hammond Ct. E10 .....2D 68
(off Leyton Grange Est.)
SE11 .....5J 19
(off Hotspur St.)
Hammond Ho. E14 .....3C 104
(off Tiller Rd.)
SE14 .....7D 103
(off Lubbock St.)
Hammond Lodge W9 .....5J 81
(off Admiral Wlk.)
Hammond Rd. EN1: Enf 2C 24
UB2: S'hall 3C 94
Hammonds Cl. RM8: Dag 3C 72
Hammond St. NW5 .....6G 65

Hammond Way SE28 ....7B 90	Hampton Ct. Rd. KT1: Hamp W ..3K 149	Handel Pl. NW10 ....6K 61	Hanover Ho. E14 ....1B 104

Hammond Way SE28 ....7B 90
Hamond Cl. CR2: S Croy 7B 168
Hamonde Cl. HA8: Edg 2C 28
Hamond Sq. N1 ....2E 84
Ham Pk. Rd. E7 ....7H 69
  E15 ....7H 69
Hampden Av. BR3: Beck 2A 158
Hampden Cl. NW1 ....2H 83
Hampden Cl. N10 ....7K 31
Hampden Gurney St. W1 ..1E 10 (6D 82)
Hampden Ho. SW9 ....2A 120
  (off Overton Rd.)
Hampden La. N17 ....1F 49
Hampden Rd. BR3: Beck 2A 158
  HA3: Hrw W 1G 41
  KT1: King T 3G 151
  N8 ....4A 48
  N10 ....7K 31
  N17 ....1G 49
  N19 ....2H 65
  RM5: Col R 1H 55
Hampden Sq. N14 ....1A 32
Hampden Way N14 ....1A 32
Hampshire Cl. N18 ....5C 34
Hampshire Hog La. W6 ....5D 98
Hampshire Rd. N22 ....7E 32
Hampshire St. NW5 ....6H 65
Hampson Way SW8 ....1K 119
HAMPSTEAD 4B 64
Hampstead Av. IG8: Wfd G 7K 37
Hampstead Cl. SE28 ....1B 108
Hampstead Gdns. NW11 ....6J 45
  RM6: Chad H 5B 54
HAMPSTEAD GARDEN SUBURB ..5A 46
Hampstead Ga. NW3 ....5A 64
Hampstead Golf Course 7B 46
Hampstead Grn. NW3 ....5C 64
Hampstead Gro. NW3 ....3A 64
Hampstead Heath 2B 64
Hampstead Hgts. N2 ....3A 46
Hampstead High St. NW3 ......4B 64
Hampstead Hill Gdns. NW3 ....4B 64
Hampstead Ho. NW1 ....2A 6
  (off William Rd.)
Hampstead La. N6 ....1B 64
  NW3 ....1B 64
Hampstead Lodge NW1 ....5C 4
  (off Bell St.)
Hampstead M. BR3: Beck 4D 158
Hampstead Mus. 4B 64
  (off New End Sq.)
Hampstead Rd. NW1 ...1A 6 (2G 83)
Hampstead Sq. NW3 ....3A 64
Hampstead Theatre 7B 64
Hampstead Wlk. E3 ....1B 86
Hampstead Way NW11 ....5K 45
Hampstead W. NW6 ....6J 63
HAMPTON 1F 149
Hampton & Richmond Borough FC
  ....1F 149
Hampton Bus. Pk. TW13: Hanw .3G 130
Hampton Cl. N11 ....5A 32
  NW6 ....3J 81
  SW20 ....7E 134
HAMPTON COURT 4J 149
HAMPTON COURT 3J 149
Hampton Ct. N1 ....6B 66
  N22 ....1G 47
  SE14 ....7A 104
  (off Batavia Rd.)
  SE16 ....7K 85
  (off King & Queen Wharf)
Hampton Ct. Av. KT8: E Mos ..6H 149
HAMPTON CT. BRI. 4J 149
Hampton Ct. Cres.
  KT8: E Mos 3H 149
Hampton Ct. Est. KT7: T Ditt ..4J 149
Hampton Ct. M. KT8: E Mos ...4J 149
  (off Feltham Av.)
Hampton Court Palace 4K 149
Hampton Court Palace Golf Course
  ....5C 150
Hampton Ct. Pde. KT8: E Mos ..4J 149

Hampton Ct. Rd. KT1: Hamp W ..3K 149
  KT8: E Mos 3K 149
  TW12: E Mos, Hamp 2G 149
Hampton Ct. Way KT7: T Ditt ..7J 149
  KT8: E Mos 7J 149
Hampton Golf Course 3E 130
Hampton Grange BR1: Broml ..7A 142
HAMPTON HILL 5G 131
Hampton Hill Bus. Pk.
  TW12: Hamp H 5G 131
  (off High St.)
Hampton Hill Theatre 5G 131
Hampton Ho. DA7: Bex 2H 127
  (off Erith Rd.)
  SW8 ....7G 101
  (off Ascalon St.)
Hampton La. TW13: Hanw 4C 130
Hampton M. EN3: Enf H 3D 24
  NW10 ....3K 79
  WD23: B Hea 1B 26
Hampton Open Air Pool 7G 131
Hampton Ri. HA3: Kenton 6E 42
Hampton Rd. CR0: C'don 6C 156
  E4 ....5G 35
  E7 ....5K 69
  E11 ....1F 69
  HA7: Stan 3D 26
  IG1: Ilf 4G 71
  KT4: Wor Pk 2C 164
  TW2: Twick 3H 131
  TW11: Tedd 5H 131
  TW12: Hamp H 5H 131
Hampton Rd. E. TW13: Hanw ..4D 130
Hampton Rd. Ind. Pk.
  CR0: C'don 6C 156
Hampton Rd. W. TW13: Hanw ..3C 130
Hampton Sports & Fitness Cen. ..5E 130
Hampton St. SE1 ....4C 102
  SE17 ....4B 102
HAMPTON WICK 1C 150
Hampton Youth Project
  (Sports Hall) 6D 130
Ham Ridings TW10: Ham 5F 133
Hamshades Cl. DA15: Sidc 3K 143
Hamston Ho. W8 ....3K 99
  (off Kensington Ct. Pl.)
Ham St. TW10: Ham 1B 132
Ham Vw. CR0: C'don 6A 158
Ham Yd. W1 ....2C 12 (7H 83)
Hanah Ct. SW19 ....7F 135
Hanameel St. E16 ....1K 105
Hana M. E5 ....4H 67
Hanbury Cl. NW4 ....3E 44
Hanbury Ct. HA1: Harr 6K 41
Hanbury Dr. E11 ....7H 51
  N21 ....5E 22
Hanbury Ho. E1 ....5G 85
  (off Hanbury St.)
  SW8 ....7J 101
  (off Regent's Bri. Gdns.)
Hanbury M. CR0: C'don 1A 170
  N1 ....1C 84
Hanbury Rd. N17 ....2H 49
  W3 ....2H 97
Hanbury St. E1 ....5K 9 (5F 85)
Hanbury Wlk. DA5: Bexl 3K 145
Hancock Nunn Ho. NW3 ....6D 64
  (off Fellows Rd.)
Hancock Rd. E3 ....3E 86
  SE19 ....6D 138
Handa Wlk. N1 ....6D 66
Hand Axe Yd. WC1 ....3J 83
Hand Ct. WC1 ....6H 7 (5K 83)
Handcroft Rd. CR0: C'don 7B 156
Handel & Hendrix in London ..2J 11
  (off Brook St.)
Handel Bus. Cen. SW8 ....7E 18 (6J 101)
Handel Cl. HA8: Edg 6A 28
Handel Mans. SW13 ....7E 98
  WC1 ....3F 7
  (off Handel St.)
Handel Pde. HA8: Edg 7B 28
  (off Whitchurch La.)

Handel Pl. NW10 ....6K 61
Handel St. WC1 ....3E 6 (4J 83)
Handel Way HA8: Edg 7B 28
Handen Rd. SE12 ....5G 123
Handforth Rd. IG1: Ilf 3F 71
  SW9 ....7A 102
Handley Dr. SE3 ....3K 123
Handley Gro. NW2 ....3F 63
Handley Page Rd.
  IG11: Bark 4A 90
  SM6: W'gton 7K 167
Handley Rd. E9 ....7J 67
Handowe Cl. NW4 ....4C 44
Handside Cl. KT4: Wor Pk 1F 165
Hands Wlk. E16 ....6J 87
Handsworth Av. E4 ....6A 36
Handsworth Rd. N17 ....3D 48
Handtrough Way IG11: Bark ...2F 89
Handyside St. N1 ....1H 83
Hanford Cl. SW18 ....1J 135
Hanford Row SW19 ....6E 134
Hanger Cl. W5 ....4F 79
Hanger Grn. W5 ....4G 79
HANGER HILL 4F 79
HANGER LANE 3E 78
Hanger La. W5 ....2E 78
Hanger Va. La. W5 ....6F 79
  (not continuous)
Hanger Vw. Way W3 ....6G 79
Hanging Sword All. EC4 ....1K 13
Hankey Ho. SE1 ....7F 15
  (off Hankey Pl.)
Hankey Pl. SE1 ....7F 15 (2D 102)
Hankins Ho. SE10 ....3J 105
  (off Peartree Way)
Hankins La. NW7 ....1E 28
Hanley Gdns. N4 ....1K 65
Hanley Pl. BR3: Beck 7C 140
Hanley Rd. N4 ....1J 65
Hanmer Wlk. N7 ....2K 65
Hannaford Wlk. E3 ....4D 86
Hannah Barlow Ho. SW8 .....1K 119
Hannah Bldg. E1 ....6H 85
  (off Watney St.)
Hannah Cl. BR3: Beck 3E 158
  NW10 ....4J 61
Hannah Ct. E15 ....2H 87
Hannah Mary Way SE1 ....4G 103
Hannah M. SM6: W'gton 7G 167
Hannay Ho. SW15 ....6G 117
Hannay La. N8 ....7H 47
Hannay Wlk. SW16 ....2H 137
Hannell Rd. SW6 ....7G 99
Hannen Rd. SE27 ....3B 138
Hannibal Rd. E1 ....5J 85
  TW19: Stanw 7A 110
Hannibal Way CR0: Wadd 5K 167
Hannington Rd. SW4 ....3F 119
Hanno Cl. SM6: W'gton 7H 167
Hanover Av. E16 ....1J 105
  TW13: Felt 1J 129
Hanover Circ. UB3: Hayes 6E 74
Hanover Cl.
  SM3: Cheam 4G 165
  TW9: Kew 7G 97
  TW15: Ashf 4A 128
Hanover Ct. E8 ....6D 64
  (off Stean St.)
  HA4: Ruis 3J 57
  NW9 ....3A 44
  SE19 ....7G 139
  (off Anerley Rd.)
  SW15 ....4B 116
  W12 ....1C 98
  (off Uxbridge Rd.)
Hanover Dr. BR7: Chst 4G 143
Hanover Flats W1 ....2H 11
  (off Binney St.)
Hanover Gdns. IG6: Ilf 1G 53
  SE11 ....6A 102
Hanover Ga. NW1 .....2D 4 (3C 82)
Hanover Ga. Mans.
  NW1 ....3D 4 (4C 82)

Hanover Ho. E14 ....1B 104
  (off Westferry Cir.)
  NW8 ....2C 82
  (off St John's Wood High St.)
  SE16 ....2K 103
  (off Dominion Dr.)
  SW9 ....3A 120
Hanover Mans. SW2 ....5A 120
  (off Barnwell Rd.)
Hanover Mead NW11 ....5G 45
Hanover Pk. SE15 ....1G 121
Hanover Pl. E3 ....3B 86
  WC2 ....1F 13 (6J 83)
Hanover Rd. N15 ....4F 49
  NW10 ....7E 62
  SW19 ....7A 136
Hanover Sq. W1 ....1K 11 (6F 83)
Hanover Steps W2 ....1D 10
Hanover St. CR0: C'don 3B 168
  W1 ....1K 11 (6F 83)
Hanover Ter. NW1 ......2E 4 (3D 82)
  TW7: Isle 1A 114
Hanover Ter. M. NW1 ..2D 4 (3C 82)
Hanover Trad. Est. N7 ....5J 65
Hanover Way DA6: Bex 3D 126
Hanover W. Ind. Est. NW10 ...3K 79
Hanover Yd. N1 ....2C 84
  (off Noel Rd.)
Hansa Cl. UB2: S'hall 3A 94
Hansard M. W14 ....2F 99
Hansart Way EN2: Enf 1F 23
Hanscomb M. SW4 ....4G 119
Hans Cres. SW1 ....1E 16 (3D 100)
Hanseatic Wlk. EC4 ....3E 14
Hanselin Cl. HA7: Stan 5E 26
Hansel Rd. NW6 ....3J 81
Hansen Dr. N21 ....5E 22
Hanshaw Dr. HA8: Edg 1K 43
Hansler Ct. SW19 ....1G 135
  (off Princes Way)
Hansler Gro. KT8: E Mos 4H 149
Hansler Rd. SE22 ....5F 121
Hansol Rd. DA6: Bex 5E 126
Hansom M. SE11 ......5H 19 (5K 101)
Hansom Ter. BR1: Broml 1K 159
  (off Freelands Gro.)
Hanson Cl. BR3: Beck 6D 140
  SW12 ....7F 119
  SW14 ....3J 115
  UB7: W Dray 3B 92
Hanson Ct. E17 ....6D 50
Hanson Gdns. UB1: S'hall 2C 94
Hanson Ho. E1 ....7G 85
  (off Pinchin St.)
Hanson St. W1 ....5A 6 (5G 83)
Hans Pl. SW1 ....1F 17 (3D 100)
Hans Rd. SW3 ....1E 16 (3D 100)
Hans St. SW1 ....2F 17 (3D 100)
Hanway Pl. W1 ....7C 6 (6H 83)
Hanway Rd. W7 ....6H 77
Hanway St. W1 ....7C 6 (6H 83)
HANWELL 1K 95
Hanwell Ho. W2 ....5J 81
  (off Gt. Western Rd.)
HANWORTH 4B 130
Hanworth Air Pk. Leisure Cen. ..2B 130
Hanworth Ho. SE5 ....7B 102
Hanworth Rd. TW3: Houn 1C 130
  TW4: Houn 1C 130
  TW12: Hamp 4D 130
  TW13: Felt 1K 129
  TW16: Sun 7J 129
  (not continuous)
Hanworth Ter. TW3: Houn 4F 113
Hanworth Trad. Est.
  TW13: Hanw 3C 130
Hapgood Cl. UB6: G'frd 5H 59
Harad's Pl. E1 ....7G 85
Harbans Ct. SL3: Poyle 4A 174
Harben Pde. NW3 ....7A 64
  (off Finchley Rd.)
Harben Rd. NW6 ....7A 64

Harberson Rd.—Harold Pinter Theatre

Harberson Rd. E15 .... 1H 87
SW12 .... 1F 137
Harberton Rd. N19 .... 1G 65
Harbet Rd. E4 .... 5F 35
N18 .... 5F 35
W2 .... 6B 4 (5B 82)
Harbex Cl. DA5: Bexl 7H 127
Harbinger Rd. E14 .... 4D 104
Harbledown Ho. SE1 .... 7E 14
(off Manciple St.)
Harbledown Rd. SW6 .... 1J 117
Harbord Cl. SE5 .... 2D 120
Harbord Ho. SE16 .... 4K 103
(off Cope St.)
Harbord St. SW6 .... 1F 117
Harborough Av. DA15: Sidc 7J 125
Harborough Ho. UB5: N'olt 3D 76
(off Taywood Rd.)
Harborough Rd. SW16 .... 4K 137
Harbour Av. SW10 .... 1A 118
Harbour Cl. CR4: Mitc 1E 154
Harbour Club
Chelsea 2A 118
Kensington 4K 99
(off Point West)
Notting Hill 5J 81
Harbour Exchange Sq. E14 .... 2D 104
Harbour Quay E14 .... 1E 104
Harbour Reach SW6 .... 1A 118
Harbour Rd. SE5 .... 3C 120
Harbourside Ct. SE8 .... 4A 104
(off Plough Way)
Harbour Way E14 .... 2C 104
Harbour Yd. SW10 .... 1A 118
Harbridge Av. SW15 .... 7B 116
Harbury Rd. SM5: Cars 7C 166
Harbut Rd. SW11 .... 4B 118
Harbutt Rd. HA9: Wemb 4G 61
Harcombe Rd. N16 .... 3E 66
Harcourt Av.
DA15: Sidc 6C 126
E12 .... 4D 70
HA8: Edg 3D 28
SM6: W'gton 4F 167
Harcourt Bldgs. EC4 .... 2J 13
Harcourt Cl. TW7: Isle 3A 114
Harcourt Fld. SM6: W'gton 4F 167
Harcourt Ho. W1 .... 7J 5
Harcourt Lodge
SM6: W'gton 4F 167
Harcourt Rd. CR7: Thor H 6K 155
DA6: Bex 4E 126
E15 .... 2H 87
N22 .... 1H 47
SE4 .... 3B 122
SM6: W'gton 4F 167
SW19 .... 7J 135
Harcourt St. W1 .... 6D 4 (5C 82)
Harcourt Ter. SW10 .... 5K 99
Hardcastle Cl. CR0: C'don 6G 157
Hardcastle Ho. SE14 .... 1A 122
(off Loring Rd.)
Hardcourts Cl. BR4: W W'ck 3D 170
Hardegray Cl. SM2: Sutt 7J 165
Hardel Ri. SW2 .... 1B 138
Hardel Wlk. SW2 .... 7A 120
Harden Ct. SE7 .... 4C 106
Harden Ho. SE5 .... 2E 120
Harden's Manorway SE7 .... 3B 106
(not continuous)
Harders Rd. SE15 .... 2H 121
Hardess St. SE24 .... 3C 120
Hardie Cl. NW10 .... 5K 61
Hardie Rd. RM10: Dag 3J 73
Harding Cl. CR0: C'don 3F 169
SE17 .... 6C 102
Harding Dr. RM8: Dag 1E 72
Hardinge Cl. UB8: Hil 5D 74
Hardinge Cres. SE18 .... 3G 107
Hardinge La. E1 .... 6J 85
(not continuous)
Hardinge Rd. N18 .... 6K 33
NW10 .... 1D 80
Hardinge St. E1 .... 7J 85
(Johnson St.)
E1 .... 6J 85
(Steel's La.)
Harding Ho. SW13 .... 6D 98
(off Wyatt Dr.)
UB3: Hayes 6K 75
Harding Rd. DA7: Bex 2F 127
Harding's Cl. KT2: King T 1F 151
Hardings La. SE20 .... 6K 139
Hardington NW1 .... 7E 64
(off Belmont St.)
Hardman Rd. KT2: King T 2E 150
SE7 .... 5K 105
Hardwick Cl. HA7: Stan 5H 27
Hardwick Ct. DA8: Erith 6K 109
Hardwicke Av. TW5: Hest 1E 112
Hardwicke M. WC1 .... 2H 7
Hardwicke Rd. N13 .... 6D 32
TW10: Ham 4C 132
W4 .... 4K 97
Hardwicke St. IG11: Bark 1G 89
Hardwick Grn. W13 .... 5B 78
Hardwick Ho. NW8 .... 3D 4
(off Lilestone St.)
Hardwick Pl. SW16 .... 7G 137
Hardwicks Sq. SW18 .... 5J 117
Hardwick St. EC1 .... 2K 7 (3A 84)
Hardwidge St. SE1 .... 6G 15 (2E 102)
Hardy Av. E16 .... 1J 105
HA4: Ruis 5K 57
Hardy Cl. EN5: Barn 6B 20
HA5: Pinn 7B 40
SE16 .... 2K 103
Hardy Cotts. SE10 .... 6F 105
Hardy Ho. SW4 .... 7G 119
SW17 .... 3B 136
(off Grosvenor Way)
SW18 .... 7K 117
Hardying Ho. E17 .... 4A 50
Hardy Pas. N22 .... 1K 47
Hardy Rd. E4 .... 6G 35
SE3 .... 7H 105
SW19 .... 7K 135
Hardy's M. KT8: E Mos 4J 149
Hardy Way EN2: Enf 1F 23
Hare & Billet Rd. SE3 .... 1F 123
Harebell Dr. E6 .... 5E 88
Harecastle Cl. UB4: Yead 4C 76
Hare Ct. EC4 .... 1J 13
Harecourt Rd. N1 .... 6C 66
Harecroft La. UB10: Ick 3E 56
Haredale Ho. SE16 .... 2G 103
(off East La.)
Haredale Rd. SE24 .... 4C 120
Haredon Cl. SE23 .... 7K 121
HAREFIELD 1A 38
Harefield Cl. EN2: Enf 1F 23
Harefield Grn. NW7 .... 6K 29
Harefield M. SE4 .... 3B 122
Harefield Rd. DA14: Sidc 3D 144
N8 .... 5H 47
SE4 .... 3B 122
SW16 .... 7K 137
UB8: Uxb 5A 56
Hare Marsh E2 .... 4G 85
Harepit Cl. CR2: S Croy 7B 168
Hare Pl. EC4 .... 1K 13
(off Fleet St.)
Hare Row E2 .... 2H 85
Haresfield Rd. RM10: Dag 6G 73
Hare St. SE18 .... 3E 106
Hare Wlk. N1 .... 2E 84
(not continuous)
Harewood Av. NW1 .... 4D 4 (4C 82)
NW7 .... 6B 30
UB5: N'olt 7D 58
Harewood Cl. UB5: N'olt 7D 58
Harewood Dr. IG5: Ilf 2D 52
Harewood Pl. W1 .... 1K 11 (6F 83)
Harewood Rd. CR2: S Croy 6E 168
SW19 .... 6C 136
TW7: Isle 7K 95
Harewood Row NW1 .... 5D 4 (5C 82)
Harewood Ter. UB2: S'hall 4D 94
Harfield Gdns. SE5 .... 3E 120
Harfield Rd. TW16: Sun 2B 148
Harfleur Ct. SE11 .... 4B 102
(off Opal St.)
Harford Cl. E4 .... 7J 25
Harford Ho. SE5 .... 6C 102
(off Bethwin Rd.)
W11 .... 5H 81
Harford M. N19 .... 3H 65
Harford Rd. E4 .... 7J 25
Harford St. E1 .... 4A 86
Harford Wlk. N2 .... 4B 46
Harfst Way BR8: Swan 7J 145
Hargood Cl. HA3: Kenton 6E 42
Hargood Rd. SE3 .... 1A 124
Hargrave Mans. N19 .... 2H 65
Hargrave Pk. N19 .... 2G 65
Hargrave Pl. N7 .... 5H 65
Hargrave Rd. N19 .... 2G 65
Hargraves Ho. W12 .... 7D 80
(off White City Est.)
Hargreaves Ct. E3 .... 3E 86
(off Bolinder Way)
Hargwyne St. SW9 .... 3K 119
Hari Cl. UB5: N'olt 5F 59
Haringey Independent Cinema 4C 48
Haringey Pk. N8 .... 6J 47
Haringey Pas. N8 .... 4A 48
Haringey Rd. N8 .... 4J 47
Harington Ter. N9 .... 3J 33
N18 .... 3J 33
Harkett Cl. HA3: W'stone 2K 41
Harkett Ct. HA3: W'stone 2K 41
Harkness Ct. SM1: Sutt 1K 165
(off Cleeve Way)
Harkness Ho. E1 .... 6G 85
(off Christian St.)
Harland Av. CR0: C'don 3F 169
DA15: Sidc 3H 143
Harland Cl. SW19 .... 3K 153
Harland Rd. SE12 .... 7J 123
Harlands Gro. BR6: Farnb 4F 173
Harlech Gdns. HA5: Pinn 7B 40
TW5: Hest 6A 94
Harlech Rd. N14 .... 3D 32
Harlech Twr. W3 .... 2J 97
Harlequin Av. TW8: Bford 6A 96
Harlequin Cl. IG11: Bark 4A 90
TW7: Isle 5J 113
UB4: Yead 5B 76
Harlequin Ct. E1 .... 7G 85
(off Thomas More St.)
NW10 .... 6K 61
(off Mitchellbrook Way)
W5 .... 7C 78
Harlequin FC 7J 113
Harlequin Ho. DA18: Erith 3E 108
(off Kale Rd.)
Harlequin Rd. TW11: Tedd 7B 132
Harlescott Rd. SE15 .... 4K 121
HARLESDEN 2B 80
Harlesden Gdns. NW10 .... 1B 80
Harlesden La. NW10 .... 1C 80
Harlesden Plaza NW10 .... 2B 80
Harlesden Rd. NW10 .... 1C 80
Harleston Cl. E5 .... 2J 67
Harley Cl. HA0: Wemb 6D 60
Harley Ct. E11 .... 7J 51
HA1: Harr 4H 41
N20 .... 3F 31
Harley Cres. HA1: Harr 4H 41
Harleyford BR1: Broml 1K 159
Harleyford Ct. SE11 .... 7G 19
Harleyford Mnr. W3 .... 1J 97
(off Edgecote Cl.)
Harleyford Rd. SE11 .... 7G 19 (6K 101)
Harleyford St. SE11 .... 7J 19 (6A 102)
Harley Gdns.
BR6: Orp 4J 173
SW10 .... 5A 100
Harley Gro. E3 .... 3B 86
Harley Ho. E11 .... 7F 51
E14 .... 6B 86
(off Frances Wharf)
NW1 .... 4H 5
Harley Pl. W1 .... 6J 5 (5F 83)
Harley Rd. HA1: Harr 4H 41
NW3 .... 7B 64
NW10 .... 2A 80
Harley St. W1 .... 4J 5 (4F 83)
Harley Vs. NW10 .... 2A 80
Harlie Ct. SE6 .... 6C 122
Harling Ct. SW11 .... 2D 118
Harlinger St. SE18 .... 3C 106
HARLINGTON 6F 93
Harlington Cl. UB3: Harl 7E 92
HARLINGTON CORNER 1F 111
Harlington Rd. DA7: Bex 3E 126
UB8: Hil 3C 74
Harlington Rd. E. TW13: Felt 7K 111
TW14: Felt 7K 111
Harlington Rd. W. TW14: Felt 6K 111
The Harlington Sports Cen. 4F 93
(off Pinkwell La.)
Harlington Young People's Cen. 4F 93
Harlow Mans. IG11: Bark 7F 71
(off Whiting Av.)
Harlow Rd. N13 .... 3J 33
Harlyn Dr. HA5: Eastc 3K 39
Harlynwood SE5 .... 7C 102
(off Wyndham Rd.)
Harman Av. IG8: Wfd G 6C 36
Harman Cl. E4 .... 4A 36
NW2 .... 3G 63
SE1 .... 5G 103
Harman Dr. DA15: Sidc 6K 125
NW2 .... 3G 63
Harman Ri. IG3: Ilf 4J 71
Harman Rd. EN1: Enf 5A 24
HARMONDSWORTH 2E 174
Harmondsworth La.
UB7: Harm, Sip 6A 92
Harmondsworth Moor Waterside 2C 174
Harmondsworth Moor Waterside Vis. Cen.
.... 2C 174
Harmondsworth Rd. UB7: W Dray 5A 92
Harmon Ho. SE8 .... 4B 104
Harmont Ho. W1 .... 6J 5
(off Harley St.)
Harmony Apts. BR1: Broml 2J 159
(off High St.)
Harmony Cl. NW11 .... 5G 45
(not continuous)
SM6: W'gton 7J 167
Harmony Pl. SE1 .... 5F 103
SE8 .... 6D 104
(off Dancers Way)
Harmony Ter. HA2: Harr 1F 59
Harmony Way BR1: Broml 2J 159
NW4 .... 4E 44
Harmood Gro. NW1 .... 7F 65
Harmood Ho. NW1 .... 7F 65
(off Harmood St.)
Harmood Pl. NW1 .... 7F 65
Harmood St. NW1 .... 6F 65
Harmsworth M. SE11 .... 2K 19 (3B 102)
Harmsworth St. SE17 .... 6K 19 (5B 102)
Harmsworth Way N20 .... 1C 30
Harold Av. DA17: Belv 5F 109
UB3: Hayes 3H 93
Harold Ct. SE16 .... 2K 103
(off Christopher Cl.)
Harold Est. SE1 .... 3E 102
Harold Gibbons Ct. SE7 .... 6A 106
Harold Ho. E2 .... 2K 85
(off Mace St.)
Harold Laski Ho. EC1 .... 2B 8
(off Percival St.)
Harold Maddison Ho. SE17 .... 5B 102
(off Penton Pl.)
Harold Mugford Ter. E6 .... 6E 88
(off Pearl Cl.)
Harold Pinter Theatre 3C 12
(off Panton St.)

Harold Pl.—Harvey Ho.

Harold Pl. SE11 6J 19 (5A 102)
Harold Rd. E4 4K 35
E11 1G 69
E13 1K 87
IG8: Wfd G 1J 51
N8 5K 47
N15 5F 49
NW10 3K 79
SE19 7D 138
SM1: Sutt 4B 166
Haroldstone Rd. E17 5K 49
Harold Wilson Ho. SE28 1B 108
SW6 6H 99
(off Clem Attlee Ct.)
Harp All. EC4 7A 8 (6B 84)
The Harp Bus. Cen. NW2 2C 62
Harpenden Rd. E12 2A 70
SE27 3B 138
Harpenmead Point NW2 2H 63
Harper Cl. N14 5B 22
Harper Ho. SW9 3B 120
Harper M. SW17 3A 136
Harper Rd. E6 6D 88
SE1 7C 14 (3C 102)
Harper's Yd. N17 1F 49
Harpers Yd. TW7: Isle 2J 113
(off Rennels Way)
Harp Island Cl. NW10 2K 61
Harp La. EC3 3G 15 (7E 84)
Harpley Sq. E1 4K 85
Harpour Rd. IG11: Bark 6G 71
Harp Rd. W7 4K 77
Harpsden St. SW11 1E 118
Harpur M. WC1 5G 7 (5K 83)
Harpur St. WC1 5G 7 (5K 83)
Harraden Rd. SE3 1A 124
Harrier Av. E11 6K 51
The Harrier Cen. 6K 163
Harrier Ct. TW4: Houn 3C 112
Harrier M. SE28 2H 107
Harrier Rd. NW9 2A 44
Harriers Cl. W5 7E 78
Harrier Way E6 5D 88
Harries Rd. UB4: Yead 4A 76
Harriet Cl. E8 1G 85
Harriet Ct. SE14 7J 103
(off Pomeroy St.)
Harriet Gdns. CR0: C'don 2G 169
Harriet Ho. SW6 7K 99
(off Wandon Rd.)
Harriet M. DA16: Well 2B 126
Harriet St. SW1 7F 11 (2D 100)
Harriet Tubman Cl. SW2 7K 119
Harriet Wlk.
SW1 7F 11 (2D 100)
Harriet Way WD23: Bush 1C 26
HARRINGAY 5B 48
Harringay Gdns. N8 4B 48
Harringay Rd. N15 5B 48
(not continuous)
Harrington Cl. CR0: Bedd 2J 167
NW10 3K 61
Harrington Ct. CR0: C'don 2D 168
SW7 3B 16
(off Harrington Rd.)
W10 3H 81
Harrington Gdns. SW7 4K 99
Harrington Hill E5 1H 67
Harrington Ho. NW1 1A 6
(off Harrington St.)
UB10: Ick 4D 56
Harrington Rd. E11 1G 69
SE25 4G 157
SW7 3A 16 (4B 100)
Harrington Sq. NW1 2G 83
Harrington St. NW1 1A 6 (2G 83)
(not continuous)
Harrington Way SE18 3B 106
Harriott Cl. SE10 4H 105
Harriott Ho. E1 5J 85
(off Jamaica St.)
Harris Bldgs. E1 6G 85
(off Burslem St.)
Harris Cl. EN2: Enf 1G 23
N11 5J 31
TW3: Houn 1E 112
Harris Ct. HA9: Wemb 3F 61
Harris Ho. E3 3C 86
(off Alfred St.)
E11 1G 69
SW9 3A 120
(off St James's Cres.)
Harris Lodge SE6 1E 140
Harrison Cl. N20 1H 31
RM7: Mawney 3G 55
Harrison Ct. E18 1J 51
(off Queen Mary Av.)
Harrison Dr. BR1: Broml 4E 160
Harrison Ho. E1 6H 85
SE17 5D 102
(off Brandon St.)
Harrison Rd. NW10 1K 79
RM10: Dag 6H 73
Harrisons Ct. SE14 6K 103
(off Myers La.)
Harrison's Ri. CR0: Wadd 3B 168
Harrison St. WC1 2F 7 (3J 83)
Harrison Way TW17: Shep 5D 146
Harris Rd. DA7: Bex 1E 126
RM9: Dag 5F 73
Harris Sports Cen. 5J 121
Harris St. E17 7B 50
SE5 7D 102
Harris Way TW16: Sun 1G 147
Harrod Ct. NW9 4J 43
Harrods 1E 16 (3D 100)
Harrogate Ct. N11 6K 31
SE12 7J 123
SE26 3G 139
(off Droitwich Cl.)
Harrold Ho. NW3 7B 64
Harrold Rd. RM8: Dag 5B 72
Harrovian Bus. Village HA1: Harr 7J 41
HARROW 6J 41
Harrow Arts Cen. 7A 26
Harrow Av. EN1: Enf 6A 24
Harroway Rd. SW11 2B 118
Harrow Borough FC 4D 58
Harrowby Ho. W1 7E 4
(off Harrowby St.)
Harrowby St. W1 7D 4 (6C 82)
Harrow Central Mosque 4K 41
Harrow Cl. KT9: Chess 7D 162
Harrow Club W10 7F 81
Harrowdene Cl. HA0: Wemb 4D 60
Harrowdene Gdns.
TW11: Tedd 6A 132
Harrowdene Rd. HA0: Wemb 3D 60
Harrow Dr. N9 1A 34
Harrowes Meade HA8: Edg 3B 28
Harrow Flds. Gdns. HA1: Harr 3J 59
Harrow Gdns. KT8: E Mos 3H 149
Harrowgate Ho. E9 6K 67
Harrowgate Rd. E9 6A 68
Harrow Grn. E11 3G 69
Harrow High School Sports Cen. 6A 42
Harrow Hill Golf Course 7K 41
Harrow La. E14 7D 86
Harrow Leisure Cen. 3K 41
Harrow Lodge NW8 3A 4
(off Northwick Ter.)
Harrow Mnr. Way SE28 7C 90
Harrow Manorway SE2 1C 108
Harrow Mus. 3G 41
HARROW ON THE HILL 1J 59
Harrow Pk. HA1: Harr 2J 59
Harrow Pl. E1 7H 9 (6E 84)
HARROW ROAD 7H 61
Harrow Rd. E6 1C 88
E11 3G 69
HA0: Wemb 4K 59
HA9: Wemb 5G 61
IG1: Ilf 4G 71
IG11: Bark 1J 89
NW10 3D 80
SM5: Cars 6C 166
Harrow Rd. TW14: Bedf 2C 128
W2 6A 4 (5A 82)
(not continuous)
W9 4F 81
W10 4G 81
HARROW RD. BRI. 5A 82
Harrow School Golf Course 2K 59
Harrow Sports Hall 7A 42
Harrow St. NW1 5D 4
Harrow Vw. HA1: Harr 2G 41
HA2: Harr 2G 41
UB3: Hayes 6J 75
UB10: Hil 3E 74
Harrow Vw. Rd. W5 4B 78
Harrow Vw. W. HA2: Harr 3G 41
Harrow Way TW17: Shep 2E 146
HARROW WEALD 1J 41
Harrow Weald Lawn Tennis Club 1J 41
Harrow Weald Pk. HA3: Hrw W 6C 26
Harry Cl. CR0: C'don 6C 156
Harry Cole Ct. SE17 5D 102
(off Thurlow St.)
Harry Day M. SE27 3C 138
Harry Hinkins Ho. SE17 5C 102
(off Bronti Cl.)
Harry Lambourn Ho. SE15 7H 103
(off Gervase St.)
Harry Zeital Way E5 2J 67
Harston Wlk. E3 4D 86
Hartcliff Ct. W7 2K 95
Hart Cl. CR0: C'don 3B 168
Hart Ct. E6 7E 70
Harte Rd. TW3: Houn 2D 112
Hartfield Av. UB5: N'olt 2K 75
Hartfield Cres. BR4: W W'ck 3J 171
SW19 7H 135
Hartfield Gro. SE20 1J 157
Hartfield Ho. UB5: N'olt 2K 75
(off Hartfield Av.)
Hartfield Rd. BR4: W W'ck 4J 171
KT9: Chess 5D 162
SW19 7H 135
Hartfield Ter. E3 2C 86
Hartford Av. HA3: Kenton 3A 42
Hartford Rd. DA5: Bexl 6G 127
KT19: Ewe 6H 163
Hart Gro. UB1: S'hall 5E 76
W5 1G 97
Hart Gro. Ct. W5 1G 97
Hartham Cl. N7 5J 65
TW7: Isle 1A 114
Hartham Rd. N7 5J 65
N17 2F 49
TW7: Isle 1K 113
Harting Rd. SE9 3C 142
Hartington Cl. BR6: Farnb 5G 173
HA1: Harr 4J 59
Hartington Ct. SW8 1J 119
W4 7H 97
Hartington Ho. SW1 5D 18
(off Drummond Ga.)
Hartington Rd. E16 6K 87
E17 6A 50
SW8 1J 119
TW1: Twick 7B 114
UB2: S'hall 3C 94
W4 7H 97
W13 7B 78
Hartismere Rd. SW6 7H 99
Hartlake Rd. E9 6K 67
Hartland NW1 1G 83
(off Royal College St.)
Hartland Cl. HA8: Edg 2B 28
N21 6H 23
Hartland Ct. N11 5J 31
(off Hartland Rd.)
Hartland Dr. HA4: Ruis 3K 57
HA8: Edg 2B 28
Hartland Rd. E15 7H 69
N11 5J 31
NW1 7F 65
NW6 2H 81
SM4: Mord 7J 153
Hartland Rd. TW7: Isle 3A 114
TW12: Hamp H 4F 131
The Hartlands TW5: Cran 6K 93
Hartlands Cl. DA5: Bexl 6F 127
Hartland Way CR0: C'don 3A 170
SM4: Mord 7H 153
Hartlepool Ct. E16 1F 107
Hartley Av. E6 1C 88
NW7 5G 29
Hartley Cl. BR1: Broml 2D 160
NW7 5G 29
Hartley Ho. SE1 4F 103
(off Longfield Est.)
Hartley Rd. CR0: C'don 7C 156
DA16: Well 7C 108
E11 1H 69
Hartley St. E2 3J 85
(not continuous)
Hart Lodge EN5: Barn 3B 20
Hartmann Rd. E16 1B 106
Hartnoll St. N7 5K 65
Harton Cl. BR1: Broml 1B 160
Harton Lodge SE8 1C 122
(off Harton St.)
Harton Rd. N9 2C 34
Harton St. SE8 1C 122
Hartop Point SW6 7G 99
(off Pellant Rd.)
Hartsbourne Av. WD23: B Hea 2B 26
Hartsbourne Cl. WD23: B Hea 2C 26
Hartsbourne Country Club & Golf Course
2B 26
Hartsbourne Ct. UB1: S'hall 6G 77
(off Fleming Rd.)
Hartsbourne Pk. WD23: B Hea 2D 26
Hartsbourne Rd. WD23: B Hea 2C 26
Harts Gro. IG8: Wfd G 5D 36
Hartshill Cl. UB10: Hil 7D 56
Hartshorn All. EC3 1H 15
Hartshorn Gdns. E6 4E 88
Hart's La. SE14 1A 122
Harts La. IG11: Bark 6F 71
Hartslock Dr. SE2 2D 108
Hartsmead Rd. SE9 2D 142
Hart Sq. SM4: Mord 6J 153
Hart St. EC3 2H 15 (7E 84)
Hartsway EN3: Pond E 4D 24
Hartswood Gdns. W12 3B 98
Hartswood Grn. WD23: B Hea 2C 26
Hartswood Rd. W12 2B 98
Hartsworth Cl. E13 2H 87
Hartville Rd. SE18 4J 107
Hartwell Cl. SW2 1K 137
Hartwell Dr. E4 6K 35
Hartwell Ho. SE7 5K 105
(off Troughton Rd.)
Hartwell St. E8 6F 67
Harvard Ct. NW6 5K 63
Harvard Hill W4 6H 97
Harvard Ho. SE17 6B 102
(off Doddington Gro.)
Harvard La. W4 5J 97
Harvard Rd. SE13 5E 122
TW7: Isle 1J 113
W4 5H 97
Harvel Cl. BR5: St P 3K 161
Harvel Cres. SE2 5D 108
Harvest Bank Rd. BR4: W W'ck 3H 171
Harvest Ct. RM13: Rain 2K 91
(off Broadis Way)
TW17: Shep 4C 146
Harvesters Cl. TW7: Isle 5H 113
Harvest La. KT7: T Ditt 6A 150
Harvest Rd. TW13: Felt 4J 129
Harvey Cl. NW9 2A 44
Harvey Ct. E17 5C 50
Harvey Dr. TW12: Hamp 1F 149
Harvey Gdns. E11 1H 69
SE7 5A 106
Harvey Ho. E1 4H 85
(off Brady St.)
N1 1D 84
(off Colville Est.)

Harvey Ho. RM6: Chad H 4D **54**
SW1 . . . . .6D **18**
    (off Aylesford St.)
TW8: Bford 5E **96**
Harvey Lodge W9 . . . . .5J **81**
    (off Admiral Wlk.)
Harvey M. N8 . . . . .5K **47**
    (off Harvey Rd.)
Harvey Rd. E11 . . . . .1G **69**
IG1: Ilf 5F **71**
KT12: Walt T 7H **147**
N8 . . . . .5K **47**
SE5 .1D **120**
    (not continuous)
TW4: Houn 7D **112**
UB5: N'olt 7A **58**
UB10: Hil 2C **74**
Harvey's Bldgs. WC2 . . . .3F **13** (7J **83**)
Harveys La. RM7: Rush G 2K **73**
Harvey St. N1 . . . . .1D **84**
Harvil Ct. NW9 . . . . .3A **44**
    (off Mornington Cl.)
Harvil Rd. DA14: Sidc 5E **144**
Harvil Rd. IG9: Hare 6A **38**
UB10: Ick 6A **38**
Harvington Wlk. E8 . . . . .7G **67**
Harvist Est. N7 . . . . .4A **66**
Harvist Rd. NW6 . . . . .2F **81**
Harwell Cl. HA4: Ruis 1F **57**
Harwell Pas. N2 . . . . .4D **46**
Harwicke Ho. E3 . . . . .3D **86**
    (off Bow Rd.)
Harwood Av. BR1: Broml 2K **159**
CR4: Mitc 3C **154**
Harwood Cl. HA0: Wemb 4D **60**
N12 . . . . .6H **31**
Harwood Ct. N1 . . . . .1D **84**
    (off Colville Est.)
SW15 . . . . .4E **116**
Harwood Dr. UB10: Hil 1B **74**
Harwood M. SW6 . . . . .7J **99**
Harwood Point SE16 . . . . .2B **104**
Harwood Rd. SW6 . . . . .7J **99**
Harwoods Yd. N21 . . . . .7F **23**
Harwood Ter. SW6 . . . . .1K **117**
    (off Love Wlk.)
Hascombe Ter. SE5 . . . . .2D **120**
Haselbury Rd. N9 . . . . .4K **33**
N18 . . . . .4K **33**
Haseley End SE23 . . . . .7J **121**
Haselrigge Rd. SW4 . . . . .4H **119**
Haseltine Rd. SE26 . . . . .4B **140**
Haskard Rd. RM9: Dag 4D **72**
Hasker St. SW3 . . . . . .3D **16** (4C **100**)
Haslam Av. SM3: Sutt 1G **165**
Haslam Cl. N1 . . . . .7A **66**
UB10: Ick 2E **56**
Haslam Cl. N11 . . . . .4A **32**
Haslam Ho. N1 . . . . .7C **66**
    (off Canonbury Rd.)
Haslam St. SE15 . . . . .7F **103**
Haslemere Av. CR4: Mitc 2B **154**
EN4: E Barn 1J **31**
NW4 . . . . .6F **45**
SW18 . . . . .2K **135**
TW5: Cran 2A **112**
W7 . . . . .3A **96**
W13 . . . . .3A **96**
Haslemere Bus. Cen. EN1: Enf 4C **24**
Haslemere Cl. SM6: W'gton 5J **167**
TW12: Hamp 5D **130**
Haslemere Gdns. N3 . . . . .3H **45**
The Haslemere Heathrow Est.
  TW4: Cran 2K **111**
Haslemere Ind. Est. SW18 . . . . . .2K **135**
Haslemere Rd.
  CR7: Thor H 5B **156**
  DA7: Bex 2F **127**
  IG3: Ilf 2K **71**
  N8 . . . . .7H **47**
  N21 .2G **33**
Hasler Cl. SE28 . . . . .7B **90**

Haslers Wharf E3 . . . . .1A **86**
    (off Old Ford Rd.)
Haslett Rd. TW17: Shep 2G **147**
Hasluck Gdns. EN5: New Bar 6E **20**
Hassard St. E2 . . . . .1K **9** (2F **85**)
Hassendean Rd. SE3 . . . . .7K **105**
Hassett Rd. E9 . . . . .6K **67**
Hassocks Cl. SE26 . . . . .3H **139**
Hassocks Rd. SW16 . . . . .1H **155**
Hassock Wood BR2: Kes 4B **172**
Hassop Rd. NW2 . . . . .4F **63**
Hassop Wlk. SE9 . . . . .4C **142**
Hasted Rd. SE7 . . . . .5B **106**
Haste Hill Golf Course 2G **39**
Hastings Av. IG6: Ilf 4G **53**
Hastings Cl. EN5: New Bar 4F **21**
HA0: Wemb 4C **60**
SE15 .7G **103**
Hastings Ct. TW11: Tedd 5H **131**
Hastings Dr. KT6: Surb 6C **150**
Hastings Ho. EN3: Enf H 2D **24**
SE18 .4D **106**
    (off Mulgrave Rd.)
W12 . . . . .7D **80**
    (off White City Est.)
W13 . . . . .7B **78**
WC1 . . . . .2E **6**
    (off Hastings St.)
Hastings Pl. CR0: C'don 1F **169**
    (off Hastings Rd.)
Hastings Rd. BR2: Broml 1C **172**
  CR0: C'don 1F **169**
  E16 . . . . .5J **87**
  N11 .5B **32**
  N17 .3D **48**
  W13 .7B **78**
Hastings St. SE18 . . . . .3G **107**
  WC1 . . . . .2E **6** (3J **83**)
Hastingwood Ct. E17 . . . . .5D **50**
Hastoe Cl. UB4: Yead 4C **76**
Hasty Cl. CR4: Mitc 1F **155**
Hat & Mitre Ct. EC1 . . . . .4B **8**
The Hatch EN3: Enf H 1E **24**
Hatcham Mews Bus. Cen. SE14 . .1K **121**
    (off Hatcham Pk. Rd.)
Hatcham Pk. M. SE14 . . . . .1K **121**
Hatcham Pk. Rd. SE14 . . . . .1K **121**
Hatchard Rd. N19 . . . . .2H **65**
Hatchcroft NW4 . . . . .3D **44**
HATCH END 7A **26**
Hatch End Lawn Tennis Club 6A **26**
Hatch End Swimming Pool 7A **26**
Hatchers M. SE1 . . . . .7H **15**
Hatchett Rd. TW14: Bedf 1E **128**
Hatchfield Ho. N15 . . . . .6E **48**
    (off Albert Rd.)
Hatch Gro. RM6: Chad H 4E **54**
Hatch La. E4 . . . . .4A **36**
  UB7: Harm 3E **174**
Hatch Pl. KT2: King T 5F **133**
Hatch Rd. SW16 . . . . .2J **155**
Hatch Side IG7: Chig 5K **37**
Hatchwood Cl. IG8: Wfd G 4C **36**
Hatcliffe Almshouses SE10 . . . . .5G **105**
    (off Tuskar St.)
Hatcliffe Cl. SE3 . . . . .3H **123**
Hatcliffe St. SE10 . . . . .5H **105**
Hatfeild Cl. CR4: Mitc 4B **154**
Hatfeild Mead SM4: Mord 5J **153**
Hatfield Cl. IG6: Ilf 3F **53**
  SE14 . . . . .7K **103**
Hatfield Ct. SE3 . . . . .7J **105**
  UB5: N'olt 3A **76**
    (off Canberra Dr.)
Hatfield Ho. EC1 . . . . .4C **8**
  SE10 . . . . .7D **104**
Hatfield M. RM9: Dag 7E **72**
Hatfield Rd. E15 . . . . .5G **69**
  RM9: Dag 6E **72**
  W4 . . . . .3A **98**
  W13 . . . . .1A **96**
Hatfields SE1 . . . . .4K **13** (1A **102**)

Hathaway Cl. BR2: Broml 1D **172**
  HA4: Ruis 4H **57**
  HA7: Stan 5F **27**
Hathaway Cres. E12 . . . . .6D **70**
Hathaway Gdns. RM6: Chad H 5D **54**
  W13 . . . . .5A **78**
Hathaway Ho. N1 . . . . .2E **84**
Hathaway Rd. CR0: C'don 7B **156**
Hatherleigh Cl. KT9: Chess 5D **162**
  NW7 .6A **30**
  SM4: Mord 4J **153**
Hatherleigh Rd. HA4: Ruis 2J **57**
Hatherley Ct. W2 . . . . .6K **81**
    (off Hatherley Gro.)
Hatherley Cres. DA14: Sidc 2A **144**
Hatherley Gdns. E6 . . . . .3B **88**
  N8 . . . . .6J **47**
Hatherley Gro. W2 . . . . .6K **81**
Hatherley Ho. E17 . . . . .4C **50**
Hatherley M. E17 . . . . .4C **50**
Hatherley Rd. DA14: Sidc 4A **144**
  E17 .4B **50**
  TW9: Kew 1F **115**
Hatherley St. SW1 . . . .4B **18** (4G **101**)
Hathern Gdns. SE9 . . . . .4E **142**
Hatherop Rd. TW12: Hamp 7D **130**
Hathersage Ct. N1 . . . . .5D **66**
Hathorne Cl. SE15 . . . . .2H **121**
Hathway St. SE14 . . . . .2K **121**
Hathway Ter. SE14 . . . . .2K **121**
    (off Hathway St.)
Hatley Av. IG6: Ilf 4G **53**
Hatley Cl. N11 . . . . .5J **31**
Hatley Rd. N4 . . . . .2K **65**
Hatteraick St. SE16 . . . . .2J **103**
Hattersfield Cl. DA17: Belv 4F **109**
HATTON 4H **111**
Hatton Cl. SE18 . . . . .7H **107**
HATTON CROSS 4H **111**
Hatton Cross Cen.
  TW6: H'row A 3H **111**
Hatton Gdn. EC1 . . . . . . .5K **7** (5A **84**)
Hatton Gdns. CR4: Mitc 5D **154**
Hatton Grn. TW14: Felt 4J **111**
Hatton Ho. E1 . . . . .7G **85**
    (off Hindmarsh Cl.)
  KT1: King T 2F **151**
    (off Victoria Rd.)
Hatton Pl. EC1 . . . . .5K **7** (5A **84**)
Hatton Rd. CR0: C'don 1A **168**
  HA0: Wemb 1E **78**
  TW14: Bedf, Felt 7E **110**
Hatton Rd. Sth. TW14: Felt 4H **111**
Hatton Row NW8 . . . . .4B **4**
Hatton St. NW8 . . . . . . .4B **4** (4B **82**)
Hatton Wlk. EN2: Enf 3J **23**
Hatton Wall EC1 . . . . . . .5K **7** (5A **84**)
Haughmond N12 . . . . .4E **30**
Haunch of Venison Yd.
  W1 . . . . .1J **11** (6F **83**)
Hauteville Ct. Gdns. W6 . . . . .3B **98**
    (off South Side)
Havana Rd. SW19 . . . . .2J **135**
Havanna Dr. NW11 . . . . .5G **45**
Havannah St. E14 . . . . .2C **104**
Havant Rd. E17 . . . . .3E **50**
Havelock Cl. W12 . . . . .7D **80**
Havelock Ct. UB2: S'hall 3D **94**
    (off Havelock Rd.)
Havelock Ho. SE1 . . . . .4F **103**
    (off Fort Rd.)
  SE23 . . . . .1J **139**
Havelock Pl. HA1: Harr 6J **41**
Havelock Rd. BR2: Broml 4A **160**
  CR0: C'don 2E **168**
  DA17: Belv 4F **109**
  HA3: W'stone 3J **41**
  N17 .2G **49**
  SW19 . . . . .5A **136**
  UB2: S'hall 3C **94**
Havelock St. IG1: Ilf 2F **71**
  N1 . . . . .1J **83**

Havelock Ter. SW8 . . . . .1F **119**
Havelock Ter. Arches SW8 . . . . . . .1F **119**
    (off Havelock Ter.)
Havelock Wlk. SE23 . . . . .1J **139**
The Haven TW9: Rich 3G **115**
  TW16: Sun 7J **129**
Haven Cl. DA14: Sidc 6C **144**
  SE9 .3D **142**
  SW19 . . . . .3F **135**
  UB4: Hayes 4G **75**
Haven Ct. BR3: Beck 2E **158**
  KT5: Surb 6F **151**
Haven Grn. W5 . . . . .6D **78**
Haven Grn. Ct. W5 . . . . .6D **78**
Havenhurst Ri. EN2: Enf 2F **23**
Haven La. W5 . . . . .6E **78**
Haven Lodge EN1: Enf 6K **23**
    (off Village Rd.)
SE18 . . . . .4F **107**
    (off Vincent Rd.)
Haven M. E3 . . . . .5B **86**
  N1 . . . . .7A **66**
Haven Pl. W5 . . . . .7D **78**
Havenpool NW8 . . . . .1K **81**
    (off Abbey Rd.)
Haven St. TW15: Ashf 4D **128**
Haven St. NW1 . . . . .7F **65**
Haven Way SE1 . . . . .3F **103**
Havenwood HA9: Wemb 3H **61**
Haverfield Gdns. TW9: Kew 7G **97**
Haverfield Rd. E3 . . . . .3A **86**
Haverford Way HA8: Edg 1F **43**
Haverhill Rd. E4 . . . . .1K **35**
  SW12 . . . . .1G **137**
Havering NW1 . . . . .7F **65**
    (off Castlehaven Rd.)
Havering Dr. RM1: Rom 4K **55**
Havering Gdns. RM6: Chad H 5C **54**
Havering Mus. 5K **55**
Havering Rd. RM1: Rom 3K **55**
Havering St. E1 . . . . .6K **85**
Havering Way IG11: Bark 3B **90**
Haversham Cl. TW1: Twick 6D **114**
Haversham Ct. UB6: G'frd 6K **59**
Haversham Pl. N6 . . . . .2D **64**
Haverstock Cl. HA1: Harr 7G **41**
Haverstock Hill NW3 . . . . .5C **64**
Haverstock Pl. N1 . . . . .1B **8**
    (off Haverstock St.)
Haverstock Rd. NW5 . . . . .5E **64**
Haverstock St. N1 . . . . . . .1B **8** (2B **84**)
Haverthwaite Rd. BR6: Orp 2H **173**
Havilland M. W12 . . . . .2D **98**
Havil St. SE5 . . . . .7E **102**
Havisham Apts. E15 . . . . .6F **69**
    (off Grove Cres. Rd.)
Havisham Ho. SE16 . . . . .2G **103**
Havisham Pl. SE19 . . . . .7B **138**
Hawarden Gro. SE24 . . . . .7C **120**
Hawarden Hill NW2 . . . . .3C **62**
Hawarden Rd. E17 . . . . .4K **49**
Hawbridge Rd. E11 . . . . .1F **69**
Hawbush Ct. RM6: Ilf 4B **54**
Hawes Ho. E17 . . . . .4K **49**
Hawes La. BR4: W W'ck 1E **170**
Hawes Rd. BR1: Broml 1K **159**
    (not continuous)
  N18 .6C **34**
Hawes St. N1 . . . . .7B **66**
Haweswater Ho. TW7: Isle 5K **113**
Hawfinch Ho. NW9 . . . . .7B **44**
Hawgood St. E3 . . . . .5C **86**
Hawkdene E4 . . . . .6J **25**
Hawke Cl. UB4: Yead 4K **75**
    (off Perth Av.)
Hawke Ho. E1 . . . . .4K **85**
    (off Ernest St.)
Hawke Pk. Rd. N22 . . . . .3B **48**
Hawke Pl. SE16 . . . . .2K **103**
Hawker NW9 . . . . .1B **44**
    (off Everglade Strand)
Hawker Ct. E3 . . . . .3E **86**
    (off Bolinder Way)

Hawker Ct.—Hazel La.

Hawker Ct. KT1: King T 2F 151
(off Church Rd.)
Hawke Rd. SE19 . . . . 6D 138
Hawker Pl. E17 . . . . 2E 50
Hawker Rd. CR0: Wadd 6A 168
Hawkesbury Rd. SW15 . . . . 5D 116
Hawkesfield Rd. SE23 . . . . 2A 140
Hawkesley Cl. TW1: Twick 4A 132
Hawkes Rd. CR4: Mitc 1D 154
TW14: Felt 7J 111
Hawkesworth Cl. HA6: Nwood 1G 39
Hawkes Yd. KT7: T Ditt 6K 149
Hawke Twr. SE14 . . . . 6A 104
Hawkewood Rd. TW16: Sun 3J 147
Hawkfield Ct. TW7: Isle 2J 113
Hawkhurst Gdns. KT9: Chess 4E 162
Hawkhurst Rd. SW16 . . . . 1H 155
Hawkhurst Way BR4: W W'ck 2D 170
KT3: N Mald 5K 151
Hawkinge N17 . . . . 2D 48
(off Gloucester Rd.)
Hawkins Cl. HA1: Harr 7H 41
NW7 . . . . 5E 28
Hawkins Ct. SE18 . . . . 4C 106
Hawkins Ho. SE8 . . . . 6C 104
(off New King St.)
SW1 . . . . 7B 18
(off Dolphin Sq.)
Hawkins Rd. NW10 . . . . 7A 62
TW11: Tedd 6B 132
Hawkins Ter. SE7 . . . . 5C 106
Hawkins Way SE6 . . . . 5C 140
Hawkley Gdns. SE27 . . . . 2B 138
Hawkridge Cl. RM6: Chad H 6C 54
Hawksbrook La. BR3: Beck 6D 158
Hawkshaw Cl. SW2 . . . . 7J 119
Hawkshead NW1 . . . . 1A 6
Hawkshead Cl. BR1: Broml 7G 141
Hawkshead Rd. NW10 . . . . 7B 62
W4 . . . . 2A 98
Hawkslade Rd. SE15 . . . . 5K 121
Hawksley Rd. N16 . . . . 3E 66
Hawks M. SE10 . . . . 7E 104
Hawksmoor Cl. E6 . . . . 6C 88
SE18 . . . . 5J 107
Hawksmoor Gro. BR2: Broml 6B 160
Hawksmoor M. E1 . . . . 7H 85
Hawksmoor Pl. E2 . . . . 3K 9
(off Cheshire St.)
Hawksmoor St. W6 . . . . 6F 99
Hawksmouth E4 . . . . 7K 25
Hawks Pas. KT1: King T 2F 151
(off London Rd.)
Hawks Rd. KT1: King T 2F 151
Hawkstone Rd. SE16 . . . . 4J 103
Hawksworth Ho. BR1: Broml 2J 159
Hawkwell Ct. E4 . . . . 3K 35
Hawkwell Ho. RM8: Dag 1G 73
Hawkwell Wlk. N1 . . . . 1C 84
(off Maldon Cl.)
Hawkwood Cres. E4 . . . . 6J 25
Hawkwood La. BR7: Chst 1G 161
Hawkwood Mt. E5 . . . . 1H 67
Hawlands Dr. HA5: Pinn 7C 40
Hawley Cl. TW12: Hamp 6D 130
Hawley Cres. NW1 . . . . 7F 65
Hawley M. NW1 . . . . 7F 65
Hawley Rd. N18 . . . . 5E 34
NW1 . . . . 7F 65
(not continuous)
Hawley St. NW1 . . . . 7F 65
Hawley Way TW15: Ashf 5C 128
Hawstead Rd. SE6 . . . . 6D 122
Hawsted IG9: Buck H 1E 36
Hawthorn Av. CR7: Thor H 1B 156
E3 . . . . 1B 86
N13 . . . . 5D 32
The Hawthorn Cen. HA1: Harr 5K 41
Hawthorn Cl. BR5: Pet W 6H 161
TW5: Cran 7K 93
TW12: Hamp 5E 130
Hawthorn Cotts. DA16: Well 3A 126
(off Hook La.)
Hawthorn Ct. HA5: Pinn 2A 40
(off Rickmansworth Rd.)
TW9: Kew 1H 115
TW15: Ashf 7E 128
Hawthorn Cres. IG5: Ilf 1D 52
SW17 . . . . 5E 136
Hawthornden Cl. N12 . . . . 6H 31
Hawthorndene Cl. BR2: Hayes 2H 171
Hawthorndene Rd. BR2: Hayes 2H 171
Hawthorn Dr. BR4: W W'ck 4G 171
HA2: Harr 6E 40
Hawthorne Av. CR4: Mitc 2B 154
HA3: Kenton 6A 42
HA4: Ruis 6K 39
SM5: Cars 7E 166
Hawthorne Cl. BR1: Broml 3D 160
N1 . . . . 6E 66
SM1: Sutt 2A 166
Hawthorne Ct. HA6: Nwood 2J 39
W5 . . . . 1E 96
Hawthorne Cres. SE10 . . . . 5H 105
UB7: W Dray 2B 92
Hawthorne Gro. NW9 . . . . 7J 43
Hawthorne Ho. N15 . . . . 5G 49
SW1 . . . . 6B 18
(off Churchill Gdns.)
Hawthorne M. UB6: G'frd 6G 77
Hawthorne Pl. UB3: Hayes 7H 75
Hawthorne Rd. BR1: Broml 3C 160
E17 . . . . 3C 50
N18 . . . . 6A 34
Hawthorne Way N9 . . . . 2A 34
Hawthorn Farm Av. UB5: N'olt 1C 76
Hawthorn Gdns. W5 . . . . 3D 96
Hawthorn Gro. EN2: Enf 1J 23
SE20 . . . . 7H 139
Hawthorn Hatch TW8: Bford 7B 96
Hawthorn Ho. E15 . . . . 6F 69
(off Forrester Way)
SE16 . . . . 2A 104
(off Blondin Way)
Hawthorn M. NW7 . . . . 1G 45
Hawthorn Pl. DA8: Erith 5J 109
Hawthorn Rd. DA6: Bex 4F 127
IG9: Buck H 4G 37
N8 . . . . 3H 47
NW10 . . . . 7C 62
SM1: Sutt 6C 166
SM6: W'gton 7F 167
TW8: Bford 7B 96
TW13: Felt 1J 129
Hawthorns CR2: S Croy 4C 168
(off Bramley Hill)
IG8: Wfd G 3D 36
The Hawthorns KT17: Ewe 7B 164
SL3: Poyle 4A 174
Hawthorn Ter. DA15: Sidc 5K 125
Hawthorn Wlk. W10 . . . . 4G 81
Hawthorn Way TW17: Shep 4F 147
Hawtrey Av. UB5: N'olt 2B 76
Hawtrey Dr. HA4: Ruis 7J 39
Hawtrey Rd. NW3 . . . . 7C 64
Haxted Rd. BR1: Broml 1K 159
Hay Cl. E15 . . . . 7G 69
Haycroft Gdns. NW10 . . . . 1C 80
Haycroft Rd. KT6: Surb 2D 162
SW2 . . . . 5J 119
Hay Currie St. E14 . . . . 6D 86
Hayday Rd. E16 . . . . 5J 87
(not continuous)
Hayden Ct. TW13: Felt 4G 129
Hayden Piper Ho. SW3 . . . . 7E 16
(off Caversham St.)
Haydens M. W3 . . . . 6J 79
Hayden's Pl. W11 . . . . 6H 81
Hayden Twr. SW8 . . . . 7H 101
Hayden Way RM5: Col R 2J 55
Haydock Av. UB5: N'olt 6E 58
Haydock Grn. UB5: N'olt 6E 58
Haydock Grn. Flats UB5: N'olt 6E 58
(off Haydock Grn.)
Haydon Cl. EN1: Enf 6K 23
NW9 . . . . 4J 43
Haydon Ct. NW9 . . . . 4J 43
Haydon Dr. HA5: Eastc 4J 39
Haydon Pk. Rd. SW19 . . . . 5J 135
Haydon Rd. RM8: Dag 2C 72
Haydons Rd. SW19 . . . . 5K 135
Haydon St. EC3 . . . . 2J 15 (7F 85)
Haydon Wlk. E1 . . . . 1K 15 (6F 85)
Haydon Way SW11 . . . . 4B 118
Hay Dr. CR4: Mitc 2C 154
HAYES
BR2 . . . . 1J 171
UB3 . . . . 6G 75
Hayes & Yeading United FC 1A 94
Hayes Bri. Retail Pk. 7A 76
Hayes Chase BR4: W W'ck 6F 159
Hayes Cl. BR2: Hayes 2J 171
Hayes Ct. BR2: Hayes 3J 171
HA0: Wemb 1E 78
SE5 . . . . 7C 102
(off Camberwell New Rd.)
SW2 . . . . 1J 137
Hayes Cres. NW11 . . . . 5H 45
SM3: Cheam 4F 165
HAYES END 4F 75
Hayes End Cl. UB4: Hayes 4F 75
Hayes End Dr. UB4: Hayes 4F 75
Hayes End Rd. UB4: Hayes 4F 75
Hayesens Ho. SW17 . . . . 4A 136
Hayesford Pk. Dr. BR2: Broml 5H 159
Hayes Gdn. BR2: Hayes 1J 171
Hayes Gro. SE22 . . . . 3F 121
Hayes Hill BR2: Hayes 1G 171
Hayes Hill Rd. BR2: Hayes 1H 171
Hayes La. BR2: Broml, Hayes 5K 159
BR3: Beck 3E 158
Hayes Mead Rd. BR2: Hayes 1G 171
Hayes Metro Cen. UB4: Yead 7A 76
Hayes M. SE8 . . . . 1B 122
Hayes Pk. Lodge UB4: Hayes 4F 75
Hayes Pl. NW1 . . . . 4D 4 (4C 82)
Hayes Rd. BR2: Broml 4J 159
UB2: S'hall 4K 93
Hayes St. BR2: Hayes 1K 171
HAYES TOWN 2H 93
Hayes Way BR3: Beck 4E 158
Hayes Wood Av. BR2: Hayes 1K 171
Hayfield Pas. E1 . . . . 4J 85
Hayfield Yd. E1 . . . . 4J 85
Haygarth Pl. SW19 . . . . 5F 135
Haygreen Cl. KT2: King T 6H 133
Hay Hill W1 . . . . 3K 11 (7F 83)
Hayhurst Ct. N1 . . . . 1B 84
(off Dibden St.)
Hayland Cl. NW9 . . . . 4K 43
Haylands Ct. TW8: Bford 6C 96
Hay La. NW9 . . . . 4J 43
Hayles Bldgs. SE11 . . . . 4B 102
(off Elliotts Row)
Hayles St. SE11 . . . . 4B 102
Haylett Gdns. KT1: King T 4D 150
Hayling Av. TW13: Felt 3J 129
Hayling Cl. N16 . . . . 5E 66
Hayling Ct. SM3: Cheam 4E 164
Hayling Way HA8: Edg 4A 28
Haymaker Cl. UB10: Uxb 7B 56
Hayman Cres. UB4: Hayes 2F 75
Haymans Point SE11 . . . . . 5G 19 (4K 101)
Hayman St. N1 . . . . 7B 66
Haymarket SW1 . . . . 3C 12 (7H 83)
Haymarket Arc. SW1 . . . . 3C 12
Haymarket Ct. E8 . . . . 7F 67
(off Jacaranda Gro.)
Haymarket Theatre Royal 3D 12
(off Haymarket)
Haymer Gdns. KT4: Wor Pk 3C 164
Haymerle Ho. SE15 . . . . 6G 103
(off Haymerle Rd.)
Haymerle Rd. SE15 . . . . 6G 103
Hay M. NW3 . . . . 6D 64
Haymill Cl. UB6: G'frd 3K 77
Hayne Ho. W11 . . . . 1G 99
(off Penzance Pl.)
Hayne Rd. BR3: Beck 2B 158
Haynes Cl. N11 . . . . 3K 31
N17 . . . . 7C 34
SE3 . . . . 3G 123
Haynes Dr. N9 . . . . 3C 34
Haynes La. SE19 . . . . 6E 138
Haynes Rd. HA0: Wemb 7E 60
Hayne St. EC1 . . . . 5B 8 (5B 84)
Haynt Wlk. SW20 . . . . 3G 153
Hayre Dr. UB2: S'hall 5C 94
Hay's Ct. SE16 . . . . 2J 103
(off Rotherhithe St.)
Hay's Galleria SE1 . . . . . . 4G 15 (1E 102)
Hays La. SE1 . . . . 4G 15 (1E 102)
Haysleigh Gdns. SE20 . . . . 2G 157
Hay's M. W1 . . . . 4J 11 (1F 101)
Haysoms Cl. RM1: Rom 4K 55
Haystall Cl. UB4: Hayes 2G 75
Hay St. E2 . . . . 1G 85
Hayter Ct. E11 . . . . 2K 69
Hayter Rd. SW2 . . . . 5J 119
Hayton Cl. E8 . . . . 6F 67
Hayward Cl. DA1: Cray 5K 127
SW19 . . . . 7K 135
Hayward Ct. SW9 . . . . 2J 119
(off Studley Rd.)
Hayward Gallery 5H 13 (1K 101)
Hayward Gdns. SW15 . . . . 6E 116
Hayward Ho. N1 . . . . 2A 84
(off Penton St.)
Hayward M. SE4 . . . . 5B 122
Hayward Rd. KT7: T Ditt 7K 149
N20 . . . . 2F 31
Haywards Cl. RM6: Chad H 5B 54
Hayward's Pl. EC1 . . . . 3A 8 (4B 84)
Haywood Cl. HA5: Pinn 2B 40
Haywood Lodge N11 . . . . 6D 32
(off York Rd.)
Haywood Ri. BR6: Orp 5J 173
Haywood Rd. BR2: Broml 4B 160
Hazel Av. UB7: W Dray 3C 92
Hazel Bank SE25 . . . . 2E 156
Hazelbank KT5: Surb 1J 163
Hazelbank Rd. SE6 . . . . 2F 141
Hazelbourne Rd. SW12 . . . . 6F 119
Hazelbury Cl. SW19 . . . . 2J 153
Hazelbury Grn. N9 . . . . 3K 33
Hazelbury La. N9 . . . . 3K 33
Hazel Cl. CR0: C'don 7K 157
CR4: Mitc 4H 155
N13 . . . . 3J 33
N19 . . . . 2G 65
NW9 . . . . 2A 44
SE15 . . . . 2G 121
(off Bournemouth Cl.)
TW2: Whitt 7G 113
TW8: Bford 7B 96
Hazel Ct. W5 . . . . 7E 78
Hazelcroft HA5: Hat E 6A 26
Hazelcroft Cl. UB10: Hil 7B 56
Hazeldean Rd. NW10 . . . . 7K 61
Hazeldene Dr. HA5: Pinn 3A 40
Hazeldene Gdns. UB10: Hil 1E 74
Hazeldene Rd. DA16: Well 2C 126
IG3: Ilf 2B 72
Hazeldon Rd. SE4 . . . . 5A 122
Hazeleigh Gdns. IG8: Wfd G 5H 37
Hazel Gdns. HA8: Edg 4C 28
Hazelgreen Cl. N21 . . . . 1G 33
Hazel Gro. BR6: Farnb 2F 173
EN1: Enf 6B 24
HA0: Wemb 1E 78
RM6: Chad H 3E 54
SE26 . . . . 4K 139
TW13: Felt 1J 129
Hazel Ho. E3 . . . . 1B 86
(off Barge La.)
Hazelhurst BR3: Beck 1F 159
Hazelhurst Ct. SE6 . . . . 5E 140
(off Beckenham Hill Rd.)
Hazelhurst Rd. SW17 . . . . 4A 136
Hazel La. IG6: Ilf 6K 37
SE10 . . . . 5H 105
TW10: Ham 2E 132

A-Z London 293

Hazell Cres. RM5: Col R 1H 55
Hazellville Rd. N19 . . . . .7H 47
Hazelmere Cl. TW14: Felt 6G 111
UB5: N'olt 2D 76
Hazelmere Ct. SW2 . . . . .1K 137
Hazelmere Dr. UB5: N'olt 2D 76
Hazelmere Rd. BR5: Pet W 4G 161
NW6 . . . . .1H 81
UB5: N'olt 2D 76
Hazelmere Wlk. UB5: N'olt 2D 76
(not continuous)
Hazelmere Way BR2: Hayes 6J 159
Hazel M. N22 . . . . .3A 48
(off High Rd.)
Hazel Rd. E15 . . . . .5G 69
NW10 . . . . .3D 80
(not continuous)
Hazeltree La. UB5: N'olt 3C 76
Hazel Wlk. BR2: Broml 6E 160
Hazel Way E4 . . . . .6G 35
SE1 . . . . .4F 103
Hazelwood Av. SM4: Mord 4K 153
Hazelwood Cl. W5 . . . . .2E 96
Hazelwood Ct. KT6: Surb 6E 150
N13 .4F 33
(off Hazelwood La.)
NW10 . . . . .3A 62
Hazelwood Cres. N13 . . . . .4F 33
Hazelwood Dr. HA5: Pinn 2K 39
TW16: Sun 3J 147
Hazelwood Ho. SE8 . . . . .4A 104
TW16: Sun 1J 147
Hazelwood Ho's. BR2: Broml . . .3G 159
Hazelwood La. N13 . . . . .4F 33
Hazelwood Rd. E17 . . . . .5A 50
EN1: Enf 6A 24
Hazelwood Sports Club 7H 23
Hazlebury Rd. SW6 . . . . .2K 117
Hazledean Rd. CR0: C'don 2D 168
Hazledene Rd. W4 . . . . .6J 97
Hazlemere Gdns. KT4: Wor Pk . . .1C 164
Hazlewell Rd. SW15 . . . . .5E 116
Hazlewood Cl. E5 . . . . .3A 68
HA2: Harr 4F 41
Hazlewood Cres. W10 . . . . .4G 81
Hazlewood M. SW9 . . . . .3J 119
Hazlewood Twr. W10 . . . . .4G 81
(off Golborne Gdns.)
Hazlitt Cl. TW13: Hanw 4C 130
Hazlitt M. W14 . . . . .3G 99
Hazlitt Rd. W14 . . . . .3G 99
Heacham Av. UB10: Ick 3E 56
Headbourne Ho. E17 . . . . .3A 50
(off Sutherland Rd.)
SE1 . . . . .7F 15 (3D 102)
Headcorn Pl. CR7: Thor H 4K 155
Headcorn Rd. BR1: Broml 5H 141
CR7: Thor H 4K 155
N17 . . . . .7A 34
Headfort Pl. SW1 . . . . . . .7H 11 (2E 100)
Headingley Dr. BR3: Beck 6C 140
Headington Ct. CR0: C'don 4C 168
(off Tanfield Rd.)
Headington Rd. SW18 . . . . .2A 136
Headlam Rd. SW4 . . . . .6H 119
(not continuous)
Headlam St. E1 . . . . .4H 85
Headley App. IG2: Ilf 5F 53
Headley Av. SM6: W'gton 5K 167
Headley Cl. KT19: Ewe 6G 163
Headley Ct. SE26 . . . . .5J 139
Headley Dr. CR0: New Ad 7D 170
IG2: Ilf 6F 53
Headley M. SW18 . . . . .5K 117
Head's M. W11 . . . . .6J 81
HEADSTONE 4G 41
Headstone Dr. HA1: Harr 3H 41
HA3: W'stone 3J 41
Headstone Gdns. HA2: Harr 4G 41
Headstone La. HA2: Harr 4E 40
HA3: Hrw W 7A 26
Headstone Manor 3G 41
Headstone Pde. HA1: Harr 4H 41

Headstone Rd. HA1: Harr 5J 41
Head St. E1 . . . . .6K 85
(not continuous)
Headway Cl. TW10: Ham 4C 132
Headway Gdns. E17 . . . . .1C 50
Heald St. SE14 . . . . .1C 122
Healey Ho. E3 . . . . .4C 86
(off Wellington Way)
SW9 . . . . .7A 102
Healey St. NW1 . . . . .6F 65
Healy Ct. EN5: Barn 6A 20
Healy Dr. BR6: Orp 4K 173
Hearne Rd. W4 . . . . .6G 97
Hearn Pl. SW16 . . . . .4A 138
Hearn Ri. UB5: N'olt 1B 76
Hearn's Bldgs. SE17 . . . . .4D 102
Hearnshaw St. E14 . . . . .6A 86
Hearn St. EC2 . . . . .4H 9 (4E 84)
Hearnville Rd. SW12 . . . . .1E 136
The Heart KT12: Walt T 7J 147
The Heath W7 . . . . .1J 95
Heatham Pk. TW2: Twick 7K 113
Heath Av. DA7: Bex 6D 108
Heathbourne Rd. HA7: Stan 2D 26
WD23: B Hea 1D 26
Heath Brow NW3 . . . . .3A 64
Heath Bus. Cen. TW3: Houn 4G 113
Heath Cl. CR2: S Croy 6B 168
NW11 . . . . .7K 45
UB3: Harl 7F 93
W5 .4F 79
Heathcock Ct. WC2 . . . . .3F 13
(off Exchange Ct.)
Heathcote Av. IG5: Ilf 2D 52
Heathcote Ct. IG5: Ilf 1D 52
(not continuous)
Heathcote Ga. SW6 . . . . .3J 117
Heathcote Gro. E4 . . . . .3K 35
Heathcote Rd. TW1: Twick 6B 114
Heathcote St. WC1 . . . . . . .3G 7 (4K 83)
Heath Ct. CR0: C'don 4D 168
(off Heathfield Rd.)
SE9 .1G 143
TW4: Houn 4D 112
UB8: Uxb 7A 56
Heath Cft. NW11 . . . . .1K 63
Heathcroft W5 . . . . .4F 79
Heathcroft Av. TW16: Sun 7H 129
Heathcroft Gdns. E17 . . . . .1F 51
Heathdale Av. TW4: Houn 3C 112
Heathdene Dr. DA17: Belv 4H 109
Heathdene Rd. SM6: W'gton 7F 167
SW16 . . . . .7K 137
Heath Dr. NW3 . . . . .4K 63
SM2: Sutt 7A 166
SW20 . . . . .4E 152
Heathedge SE26 . . . . .2H 139
Heath End Rd. DA5: Bexl 1K 145
Heather Av. RM1: Rom 2K 55
Heatherbank BR7: Chst 2E 160
SE9 .2D 124
Heather Cl. E6 . . . . .6E 88
N7 .3K 65
RM1: Rom 1K 55
SE13 . . . . .7F 123
SW8 . . . . .3F 119
TW7: Isle 5H 113
TW12: Hamp 1D 148
UB8: Hil 5B 74
Heather Ct. DA14: Sidc 6D 144
Heatherdale Cl. KT2: King T 6G 133
Heatherdene Cl. CR4: Mitc 4B 154
N12 .7F 31
Heather Dr. EN2: Enf 2G 23
RM1: Rom 2K 55
Heatherfold Way HA5: Eastc 3H 39
Heather Gdns. NW11 . . . . .6G 45
RM1: Rom 2K 55
SM2: Sutt 6J 165
Heather Glen RM1: Rom 2K 55
Heather Ho. E14 . . . . .6E 86
(off Dee St.)
Heatherlands TW16: Sun 6J 129

Heather La. UB7: Yiew 6A 74
Heatherlea Gro. KT4: Wor Pk 1D 164
Heatherley Cl. E5 . . . . .3G 67
Heatherley Dr. IG5: Ilf 3C 52
Heather Pk. Dr. HA0: Wemb 7G 61
Heather Pk. Pde. HA0: Wemb 7F 61
(off Heather Pk. Dr.)
Heather Rd. E4 . . . . .6G 35
NW2 . . . . .2B 62
SE12 . . . . .2J 141
The Heathers TW19: Stanw 7B 110
Heatherset Gdns. SW16 . . . . .7K 137
Heatherside Rd. DA14: Sidc 3C 144
KT19: Ewe 7K 163
Heatherton Ter. N3 . . . . .2K 45
Heather Wlk. HA8: Edg 5C 28
TW2: Whitt 7E 112
(off Stephenson Rd.)
W10 .4G 81
Heather Way CR2: Sels 7K 169
HA7: Stan 6E 26
RM1: Rom 2K 55
Heatherwood Cl. E12 . . . . .2A 70
Heatherwood Dr. UB4: Hayes 2F 75
Heathfield BR7: Chst 6G 143
E4 .3K 35
HA1: Harr 7K 41
Heathfield Av. SW18 . . . . .7B 118
Heathfield Cl. BR2: Kes 5A 172
E16 .5B 88
Heathfield Ct. E3 . . . . .2C 86
(off Tredegar Rd.)
SE14 . . . . .7J 103
SE20 . . . . .7J 139
TW15: Ashf 3A 128
W4 .5K 97
Heathfield Dr. CR4: Mitc 1C 154
Heathfield Gdns. CR0: C'don 4D 168
NW11 . . . . .6F 45
SE3 . . . . .2G 123
(off Baizdon Rd.)
SW18 . . . . .6B 118
W4 .5J 97
Heathfield Ho. SE3 . . . . .2G 123
Heathfield La. BR7: Chst 6G 143
Heathfield Nth. TW2: Twick 7J 113
Heathfield Pk. NW2 . . . . .6E 62
Heathfield Pk. Dr. RM6: Chad H . . .5B 54
Heathfield Ri. HA4: Ruis 7E 38
Heathfield Rd. BR1: Broml 7H 141
BR2: Kes 5A 172
CR0: C'don 4D 168
DA6: Bex 4F 127
SW18 . . . . .6A 118
W3 .2H 97
Heathfields Ct. TW4: Houn 5C 112
Heathfield Sth. TW2: Twick 7K 113
Heathfield Sq. SW18 . . . . .7B 118
Heathfield Ter. SE18 . . . . .6J 107
W4 .5J 97
Heathfield Va. CR2: Sels 7K 169
Heath Gdns. TW1: Twick 1K 131
Heathgate NW11 . . . . .6K 45
Heathgate Pl. NW3 . . . . .5D 64
Heath Gro. SE20 . . . . .7J 139
TW16: Sun 7H 129
Heath Ho. DA15: Sidc 4K 143
Heath Hurst Rd. NW3 . . . . .4C 64
Heathhurst Rd. CR2: Sande 7E 168
Heathland Rd. N16 . . . . .1E 66
Heathlands Cl. TW1: Twick 2K 131
TW16: Sun 2J 147
Heathlands Way TW4: Houn 5C 112
Heath La. SE3 . . . . .2F 123
(not continuous)
Heathlee Rd. SE3 . . . . .4H 123
Heathley End BR7: Chst 6G 143
Heath Lodge WD23: B Hea 1D 26
Heathmans Rd. SW6 . . . . .1H 117
Heath Mead SW19 . . . . .3F 135
Heath Pk. Dr. BR1: Broml 3C 160
Heath Pas. NW3 . . . . .2K 63
Heath Pl. E3 . . . . .4B 86

Heathpool Ct. E1 . . . . .4H 85
Heath Ri. BR2: Hayes 6H 159
SW15 . . . . .6F 117
Heath Rd. CR7: Thor H 3C 156
DA5: Bexl 1J 145
HA1: Harr 7G 41
RM6: Chad H 7D 54
SW8 . . . . .2F 119
TW1: Twick 1K 131
TW2: Twick 1K 131
TW3: Houn, Isle 4F 113
TW7: Isle 4F 113
UB10: Hil 4E 74
Heath Robinson Mus. 4B 40
Heathrow Blvd. UB7: Sip 7B 92
(not continuous)
TW4: Houn 3K 111
Heathrow Causeway Cen.
. . . . .3D 110
Heathrow Central Tourist Info. Cen.
. . . . .3D 110
Heathrow Cl. UB7: Lford 4C 174
Heathrow Gateway TW4: Houn . . .7C 112
Heathrow Interchange UB4: Yead . . .1A 94
Heathrow Intl. Trad. Est.
TW4: Houn 3K 111
Heathrow Prologis Pk. UB3: Harl . . .3D 92
Heath Royal SW15 . . . . .6F 117
Heaths Cl. EN1: Enf 2K 23
Heath Side BR5: Pet W 1G 173
NW3 . . . . .4B 64
Heathside NW11 . . . . .1J 63
SE13 . . . . .2E 122
TW4: Houn 7D 112
Heathside Av. DA7: Bex 1E 126
Heathside Cl. IG2: Ilf 5H 53
Heathstan Rd. W12 . . . . .6C 80
Heath St. NW3 . . . . .4A 64
Heath Ter. RM6: Chad H 7D 54
Heath Vw. N2 . . . . .4A 46
Heathview Gdns. SW15 . . . . .7E 116
Heathview Rd. CR7: Thor H 4A 156
Heath Vs. NW3 . . . . .3B 64
SE18 . . . . .5K 107
Heathville Rd. N19 . . . . .7J 47
Heathwall St. SW11 . . . . .3D 118
HEATHWAY 1G 91
Heath Way DA8: Erith 1J 127
Heathway CR0: C'don 3B 170
IG8: Wfd G 5F 37
RM9: Dag 3F 73
RM10: Dag 3F 73
SE3 . . . . .7J 105
UB2: S'hall 4B 94
Heathway Ct. NW3 . . . . .2J 63
Heathway Ind. Est. RM10: Dag . . .4H 73
Heathwood Gdns. SE7 . . . . .4C 106
Heathwood Point SE23 . . . . .3K 139
Heathwood Wlk. DA5: Bexl 1K 145
Heaton Cl. E4 . . . . .3K 35
Heaton Ho. SW10 . . . . .6A 100
(off Fulham Rd.)
Heaton Rd. CR4: Mitc 7E 136
SE15 . . . . .2H 121
Heaven Tree Cl. N1 . . . . .6C 66
Heaver Rd. SW11 . . . . .3B 118
Heaverham Ct. SE18 . . . . .5H 107
Heavitree Rd. SE18 . . . . .5H 107
(not continuous)
Hebden St. E2 . . . . .1F 85
SW8 . . . . .7H 101
Hebden Ter. N17 . . . . .6K 33
Hebdon Rd. SW17 . . . . .3C 136
Heber Mans. W14 . . . . .6H 99
(off Queen's Club Gdns.)
Heber Rd. NW2 . . . . .5F 63
SE22 . . . . .6F 121
Hebrides Cl. E1 . . . . .5A 86
(off Ocean Est.)
Hebron Rd. W6 . . . . .3E 98
Hecham Cl. E17 . . . . .2A 50

Heckfield Pl. SW6 . . . . 7J 99
Heckford Cl. SE18 . . . . 5J 107
Heckford Ho. E14 . . . . 6D 86
(off Grundy St.)
Heckford St. E1 . . . . 7K 85
Heckford St. Bus. Cen. E1 . . . . 7K 85
(off Heckford St.)
Hector NW9 . . . . 1B 44
(off Five Acre)
Hector Cl. N9 . . . . 2B 34
Hector Ct. SW9 . . . . 7A 102
(off Caldwell St.)
Hector Ho. E2 . . . . 2H 85
(off Old Bethnal Grn. Rd.)
Hector St. SE18 . . . . 4J 107
Heddington Gro. N7 . . . . 5K 65
Heddon Cl. TW7: Isle 4A 114
Heddon Ct. Av. EN4: Cockf 5J 21
Heddon Ct. Pde. EN4: Cockf . . . 5K 21
Heddon Rd. EN4: Cockf 5J 21
Heddon St. W1 . . . . . 2A 12 (7G 83)
Hedera Pl. TW4: Houn 4D 112
Hedgegate Ct. W11 . . . . 6H 81
(off Powis Ter.)
Hedge Hill EN2: Enf 1G 23
Hedge La. N13 . . . . 3G 33
Hedgeley IG4: Ilf 4D 52
Hedgemans Rd. RM9: Dag 7D 72
Hedgemans Way RM9: Dag . . . 6E 72
Hedgerley Gdns. UB6: G'frd . . . 2G 77
Hedgerow Ct. E6 . . . . 1D 88
(off Nelson St.)
Hedgers Gro. E9 . . . . 6A 68
Hedger St. SE11 . . . . 4B 102
Hedges Cl. TW14: Felt 6K 111
Hedge Wlk. SE6 . . . . 5D 140
Hedgewood Gdns. IG5: Ilf 5E 52
Hedgley M. SE12 . . . . 5H 123
Hedgley St. SE12 . . . . 5H 123
Hedingham Cl. N1 . . . . 7C 66
Hedingham Ho. KT2: King T . . . 1E 150
(off Royal Quarter)
Hedingham Rd. RM8: Dag 5B 72
Hedley Cl. RM1: Rom 5K 55
Hedley Ho. E14 . . . . 3E 104
(off Stewart St.)
Hedley Rd. TW2: Whitt 7E 112
Hedley Row N5 . . . . 5D 66
Hedsor Ho. E2 . . . . 3J 9
(off Ligonier St.)
Heenan Cl. IG11: Bark 6G 71
Heene Rd. EN2: Enf 1J 23
Heer M. E2 . . . . 2G 85
(off Hackney Rd.)
Hega Ho. E14 . . . . 6E 86
(off Ullin St.)
Heidegger Cres. SW13 . . . . 7D 98
Heigham Rd. E6 . . . . 7C 70
Heighton Gdns. CR0: Wadd . . . 5B 168
The Heights BR3: Beck 7E 140
(not continuous)
SE7 . . . . 5A 106
UB5: N'olt 5D 58
Heights Cl. SW20 . . . . 7D 134
Heiron St. SE17 . . . . 6B 102
Helby Rd. SW4 . . . . 6H 119
Heldar Ct. SE1 . . . . . . 7F 15 (2D 102)
Helder Gro. SE12 . . . . 7H 123
Helder St. CR2: S Croy 6D 168
Heldmann Cl. TW3: Houn 4H 113
Helegan Cl. BR6: Chels 4K 173
Helena Cl. SW19 . . . . 7F 117
Helena Ct. NW6 . . . . 7K 63
(off Compayne Gdns.)
W5 . . . . 5D 78
Helena Pl. E9 . . . . 1H 85
Helena Rd. E13 . . . . 2H 87
E17 . . . . 5C 50
NW10 . . . . 5D 62
W5 . . . . 5D 78
Helena Sq. SE16 . . . . 7A 86
(off Sovereign Cres.)
Helen Av. TW14: Felt 7K 111

Helen Cl. KT8: W Mole 4F 149
N2 . . . . 3A 46
Helen Gladstone Ho. SE1 . . . . . . 6A 14
(off Surrey Row)
Helen Ho. E2 . . . . 2H 85
(off Old Bethnal Grn. Rd.)
Helen Peele Cotts. SE16 . . . . . . 3J 103
(off Lower Rd.)
Helenslea Av. NW11 . . . . 1J 63
Helen's Pl. E2 . . . . 3J 85
Helen St. SE18 . . . . 4F 107
Helen Taylor Ho. SE16 . . . . 3G 103
(off Evelyn Lowe Est.)
Helford Cl. HA4: Ruis 2G 57
Helgiford Gdns. TW16: Sun 7G 129
Heligan Ho. SE16 . . . . 2K 103
(off Water Gdns. Sq.)
The Helios 7E 80
Helios Rd. SM6: W'gton 1E 166
Helios Way EN5: Barn 5C 20
Heliport Ind. Est. SW11 . . . . 2B 118
Helix Cl. W11 . . . . 1F 99
(off Swanscombe Rd.)
Helix Gdns. SW2 . . . . 6K 119
Helix Rd. SW2 . . . . 6K 119
Helix Ter. SW19 . . . . 2F 135
Hellings St. E1 . . . . 1G 103
The Helm E16 . . . . 7F 89
Helme Cl. SW19 . . . . 5H 135
Helmet Row EC1 . . . . 2D 8 (4C 84)
Helmore Rd. IG11: Bark 7K 71
Helmsdale Apartments SW11 . . . 4C 118
(off Monarch Square)
Helmsdale Cl. UB4: Yead 4C 76
Helmsdale Ho. NW6 . . . . 2K 81
(off Carlton Vale)
Helmsdale Rd. SW16 . . . . 1H 155
Helmsley Pl. E8 . . . . 7H 67
Helmsley St. E8 . . . . 7H 67
Helperby Rd. NW10 . . . . 7A 62
Helsby Ct. NW8 . . . . 3A 4
(off Pollitt Dr.)
Helsinki Sq. SE16 . . . . 3A 104
Helston NW1 . . . . 1G 83
(off Camden St.)
Helston Cl. HA5: Hat E 1D 40
Helston Ct. N15 . . . . 5E 48
(off Culvert Rd.)
Helston Ho. SE11 . . . . 5K 19
(off Kennings Way)
Helvetia St. SE6 . . . . 2B 140
Helwys Cl. E4 . . . . 6J 35
Hemans St. SW8 . . . . 7H 101
Hemans St. Est. SW8 . . . . 7J 101
Hemberton Rd. SW9 . . . . 3J 119
Hemery Rd. UB6: G'frd 5H 59
Hemingford Cl. N12 . . . . 5G 31
Hemingford Rd. N1 . . . . 1K 83
SM3: Cheam 4E 164
Heming Rd. HA8: Edg 7C 28
Hemington Av. N11 . . . . 5J 31
Hemingway Cl. NW5 . . . . 4E 64
Hemlock Cl. SW16 . . . . 2G 155
Hemlock Ho. SE16 . . . . 3A 104
Hemlock Rd. W12 . . . . 7B 80
(not continuous)
Hemmen La. UB3: Hayes 6H 75
Hemming Cl. TW12: Hamp 1E 148
Hemmings Cl. DA14: Sidc 2B 144
Hemmings Mead KT19: Ewe . . . 6J 163
Hemming St. E1 . . . . 4G 85
Hempstead Cl. IG9: Buck H 2D 36
Hempstead Rd. E17 . . . . 3F 51
Hemp Wlk. SE17 . . . . 4D 102
Hemsby Rd. KT9: Chess 6F 163
Hemstal Rd. NW6 . . . . 7J 63
Hemsted Rd. DA8: Erith 7K 109
Hemswell Dr. NW9 . . . . 1A 44
Hemsworth Ct. N1 . . . . 2E 84
Hemsworth St. N1 . . . . 2E 84
Hemus Pl. SW3 . . . . . 6D 16 (5C 100)
Hen & Chicken Ct. EC4 . . . . 1J 13
(off Fleet St.)

Hen & Chickens Theatre 6B 66
(off St Paul's Rd.)
Henchman St. W12 . . . . 6B 80
Hendale Av. NW4 . . . . 3D 44
Henderson Cl. NW10 . . . . 6J 61
Henderson Ct. N12 . . . . 4E 30
NW3 . . . . 5C 64
(off Fitzjohn's Av.)
SE14 . . . . 6K 103
(off Myers La.)
Henderson Dr. NW8 . . . . . . 3A 4 (4B 82)
Henderson Ho. RM10: Dag 3G 73
(off Kershaw Rd.)
Henderson Rd. CR0: C'don 6D 156
E7 . . . . 6A 70
N9 . . . . 1C 34
SW18 . . . . 7C 118
UB4: Yead 3J 75
Hendfield Ct. SM6: W'gton 6F 167
Hendham Rd. SW17 . . . . 2C 136
HENDON 4E 44
Hendon Av. N3 . . . . 1G 45
Hendon Crematorium 1F 45
Hendon FC 4D 58
Hendon Golf Course 7K 29
Hendon Hall Ct. NW4 . . . . 3F 45
Hendon Ho. NW4 . . . . 5F 45
Hendon La. N3 . . . . 3G 45
Hendon Leisure Cen. 7F 45
Hendon Lodge NW4 . . . . 3D 44
Hendon Pk. Mans. NW4 . . . . 5E 44
Hendon Pk. Row NW11 . . . . 6H 45
Hendon Rd. N9 . . . . 2B 34
Hendon St. SE10 . . . . 3H 105
Hendon Ter. TW15: Ashf 6F 129
Hendon Way NW2 . . . . 7F 45
NW4 . . . . 6D 44
Hendon Wood La. NW7 . . . . 1G 29
Hendre Ho. SE1 . . . . 4E 102
(off Hendre Rd.)
Hendren Cl. UB6: G'frd 5H 59
Hendre Rd. SE1 . . . . 4E 102
Hendrick Av. SW12 . . . . 7D 118
Heneage La. EC3 . . . . 1H 15 (6E 84)
Heneage Pl. EC3 . . . . 1H 15 (6E 84)
Heneage St. E1 . . . . 5K 9 (5F 85)
Henfield Cl. DA5: Bexl 6G 127
N19 . . . . 1G 65
Henfield Rd. SW19 . . . . 1H 153
Hengelo Gdns. CR4: Mitc 4B 154
Hengest Av. KT10: Surb 3A 162
Hengist Rd. DA8: Erith 7H 109
SE12 . . . . 7K 123
Hengist Way BR2: Broml 4G 159
SM6: W'gton 7H 167
Hengrave Rd. SE23 . . . . 6J 121
Hengrove Ct. DA5: Bexl 1E 144
Hengrove Cres. TW15: Ashf 3A 128
Henham Ct. RM5: Col R 1J 55
Henley Av. SM3: Cheam 3G 165
Henley Cl. SE16 . . . . 2J 103
(off St Marychurch St.)
TW7: Isle 1K 113
UB6: G'frd 2G 77
Henley Ct. N14 . . . . 7B 22
NW2 . . . . 6F 63
Henley Dr. KT2: King T 7B 134
SE1 . . . . 4F 103
Henley Gdns. HA5: Eastc 3K 39
RM6: Chad H 5E 54
Henley Hgts. N1 . . . . 7K 65
(off Caledonian Rd.)
Henley Ho. E2 . . . . 3K 9
(off Swanfield St.)
Henley Prior N1 . . . . 1G 7
(off Affleck St.)
Henley Rd. E16 . . . . 2D 106
IG1: Ilf 4G 71
N18 . . . . 4K 33
NW10 . . . . 1E 80
Henley St. SW11 . . . . 2E 118
Henley Way TW13: Hanw 5B 130
Henlow Pl. TW10: Ham 2D 132

HENLYS CORNER 4H 45
HENLYS RDBT. 2A 112
Hennel Cl. SE23 . . . . 3J 139
Hennessey M. RM8: Dag 1E 72
Hennessy Ct. E10 . . . . 6E 50
Hennessy Rd. N9 . . . . 2D 34
Henniker Gdns. E6 . . . . 3B 88
Henniker M. SW3 . . . . . 7A 16 (6B 100)
Henniker Point E15 . . . . 5G 69
(off Leytonstone Rd.)
Henniker Rd. E15 . . . . 5F 69
Henningham Rd. N17 . . . . 1D 48
Henning St. SW11 . . . . 1C 118
Henrietta Barnet Wlk. NW11 . . . . 6J 45
Henrietta Cl. SE8 . . . . 6C 104
Henrietta Ct. TW1: Twick 7C 114
(off Richmond Rd.)
Henrietta Gdns. N21 . . . . 1F 33
Henrietta Ho. N15 . . . . 6E 48
(off St Ann's Rd.)
W6 . . . . 5E 98
(off Queen Caroline St.)
Henrietta M. WC1 . . . . 3F 7 (4J 83)
Henrietta Pl. W1 . . . . 1J 11 (6F 83)
Henrietta St. WC2 . . . 2F 13 (7J 83)
Henriques St. E1 . . . . 6G 85
Henry Addlington Cl. E6 . . . . 5F 89
Henry Chester Bldg. SW15 . . . . . 2E 116
Henry Cl. EN2: Enf 1K 23
Henry Cooper Way SE9 . . . . 3B 142
Henry Ct. HA7: Stan 7J 27
Henry Darlot Dr. NW7 . . . . 6A 30
Henry Dent Cl. SE5 . . . . 3D 120
Henry Dickens Ct. W11 . . . . 7F 81
Henry Doulton Dr. SW17 . . . . 4E 136
Henry Hatch Ct. SM2: Sutt 7A 166
Henry Ho. SE1 . . . . . 5J 13 (1A 102)
SW8 . . . . 7J 101
(off Wyvil Rd.)
Henry Hudson Apts. SE10 . . . . . . 5G 105
(off Banning St.)
Henry Jackson Rd. SW15 . . . . . . 3F 117
Henry Macaulay Av.
KT2: King T 1D 150
Henry Moore Ct.
SW3 . . . . 6C 16 (5C 100)
Henry Peters Dr. TW11: Tedd . . . 5J 131
(off Somerset Gdns.)
Henry Purcell Ho. E16 . . . . 1K 105
(off Evelyn Rd.)
Henry Rd. E6 . . . . 2C 88
EN4: E Barn 5G 21
N4 . . . . 1C 66
SW9 . . . . 1A 120
Henrys Av. IG8: Wfd G 5C 36
Henryson Rd. SE4 . . . . 5C 122
Henry St. BR1: Broml 1K 159
Henry's Wlk. IG6: Ilf 1H 53
Henry Tate M. SW16 . . . . 5K 137
Henry Wise Ho. SW1 . . . . 4B 18
(off Vauxhall Bri. Rd.)
Hensford Gdns. SE26 . . . . 4H 139
Henshall Point E3 . . . . 3D 86
(off Bromley High St.)
Henshall St. N1 . . . . 6D 66
Henshawe Rd. RM8: Dag 3D 72
Henshaw St. SE17 . . . . 4D 102
Henslowe Rd. SE22 . . . . 5G 121
Henslow Ho. SE15 . . . . 7G 103
(off Peckham Pk. Rd.)
Henson Av. NW2 . . . . 5E 62
Henson Cl. BR6: Farnb 2F 173
Henson Path HA3: Kenton 3D 42
Henson Pl. UB5: N'olt 1A 76
Henson Rd. RM8: Dag 1E 72
Henstridge Pl. NW8 . . . . 1C 82
Henty Cl. SW11 . . . . 7C 100
Henty Wlk. SW15 . . . . 5D 116
Henville Rd. BR1: Broml 1K 159
Henwick Rd. SE9 . . . . 3B 124
Henwood Side IG8: Wfd G 6J 37
Hepburn Gdns. BR2: Hayes 1G 171

Hepburn M. SW11 . . . . .5D 118
Hepburn Pl. W3 . . . . .7H 79
Hepdon M. SW17 . . . . .5B 136
Hepple Cl. TW7: Isle 2B 114
Hepplestone Cl. SW15 . . . . .6D 116
Hepscott Rd. E9 . . . . .6C 68
Hepworth Ct. N1 . . . . .1B 84
(off Gaskin St.)
NW3 . . . . .5C 64
SM3: Sutt 1J 165
SW1 . . . . .6J 17 (5F 101)
Hepworth Gdns. IG11: Bark 5A 72
Hepworth Rd. SW16 . . . . .7J 137
Hepworth Way KT12: Walt T 7H 147
Hera Av. EN5: Barn 5C 20
Heracles NW9 . . . . .1B 44
(off Five Acre)
Hera Ct. E14 . . . . .4C 104
(off Homer Dr.)
Herald Gdns. SM6: W'gton 2F 167
Herald's Pl. SE11 . . . . . .3K 19 (4B 102)
Herald St. E2 . . . . .4H 85
Herbal Hill EC1 . . . . .4K 7 (4A 84)
Herbal Hill Gdns. EC1 . . . . .4K 7
(off Herbal Hill)
Herbal Pl. EC1 . . . . .4K 7
Herbert Ct. KT5: Surb 6F 151
Herbert Cres. SW1 . . . . . .1F 17 (3D 100)
Herbert Gdns. NW10 . . . . .2D 80
RM6: Chad H 7D 54
W4 . . . . .6H 97
Herbert Ho. E1 . . . . .7J 9
(off Old Castle St.)
Herbert M. SW2 . . . . .6A 120
Herbert Morrison Ho. SW6 . . . . . . .6H 99
(off Clem Attlee Ct.)
Herbert Pl. SE18 . . . . .6F 107
TW7: Isle 2H 113
Herbert Rd. BR2: Broml 5B 160
DA7: Bex 2E 126
E12 . . . . .4C 70
E17 . . . . .7B 50
IG3: Ilf 2J 71
KT1: King T 3F 151
N11 . . . . .7D 32
N15 . . . . .5F 49
NW9 . . . . .6C 44
SE18 . . . . .7E 106
(not continuous)
SW19 .7H 135
(not continuous)
UB1: S'hall 1D 94
Herbert St. E13 . . . . .2J 87
Herbrand Est. WC1 . . . . .3E 6 (4J 83)
Herbrand St. WC1 . . . . . .3E 6 (4J 83)
Hercies Rd. UB10: Hil 7B 56
Hercules Ct. SE14 . . . . .6A 104
Hercules Ho. E14 . . . . .6G 87
Hercules Pl. N7 . . . . .3J 65
(not continuous)
Hercules Rd. SE1 . . . . . . .2H 19 (3K 101)
Hercules St. N7 . . . . .3J 65
Hercules Wharf E14 . . . . .7G 87
(off Orchard Pl.)
Hercules Yd. N7 . . . . .3J 65
Here E. E20 .5C 68
Hereford Av. EN4: E Barn 1J 31
Hereford Bldgs. SW3 . . . . .7B 16
(off Old Church St.)
Hereford Ct. HA1: Harr 4J 41
SM2: Sutt 7J 165
W7 . . . . .5K 77
(off Copley Cl.)
Hereford Gdns. HA5: Pinn 5C 40
IG1: Ilf .7C 52
SE13 .5G 123
TW2: Twick 1G 131
Hereford Ho. N18 . . . . .5C 34
(off Cameron Cl.)
NW6 . . . . .2J 81
(off Carlton Vale)

Hereford Ho. SW3 . . . . .1D 16
(off Ovington Gdns.)
SW10 . . . . .7K 99
(off Fulham Rd.)
Hereford Mans. W2 . . . . .6J 81
(off Hereford Rd.)
Hereford M. W2 . . . . .6J 81
Hereford Pl. SE14 . . . . .7B 104
Hereford Retreat SE15 . . . . .7G 103
Hereford Rd. E3 . . . . .2B 86
E11 . . . . .5K 51
TW13: Felt 1A 130
W2 . . . . .6J 81
W3 . . . . .7H 79
W5 . . . . .3C 96
Hereford Sq. SW7 . . . . .4A 100
Hereford St. E2 . . . . .4G 85
Hereford Way KT9: Chess 5C 162
Herent Dr. IG5: Ilf 4C 52
Herent Gdns. IG5: Ilf 4D 52
Hereward Gdns. N13 . . . . .5F 33
Hereward Rd. SW17 . . . . .4D 136
Herga Cl. HA1: Harr 3J 59
Herga Rd. HA3: W'stone 4K 41
Heriot Av. E4 . . . . .2H 35
Heriot Rd. NW4 . . . . .5E 44
Heriots Cl. HA7: Stan 4F 27
Heritage Av. NW9 . . . . .3B 44
Heritage Cl. SW9 . . . . .3B 120
TW16: Sun 1J 147
Heritage Ct. SE8 . . . . .5K 103
Heritage Hill BR2: Kes 5A 172
Heritage La. NW6 . . . . .6J 63
Heritage Pl. SW18 . . . . .1A 136
TW8: Bford 5F 97
(off Heritage Wlk.)
Heritage Vw. HA1: Harr 3K 59
Heritage Wlk. TW8: Bford 5F 97
(off Kew Bri. Rd.)
Herlwyn Av. HA4: Ruis 2G 57
Herlwyn Gdns. SW17 . . . . .4D 136
Her Majesty's Theatre 4C 12
(off Haymarket)
Herm Cl. TW7: Isle 7G 95
Hermes Cl. EN5: Barn 5C 20
W9 . . . . .4J 81
Hermes Ct. SW2 . . . . .6K 119
SW9 . . . . .1A 120
(off Southey Rd.)
Hermes St. N1 . . . . .1J 7 (2A 84)
Hermes Wlk. UB5: N'olt 2E 76
Herm Ho. EN3: Enf W 1E 24
N1 . . . . .6C 66
(off Clifton Rd.)
Hermiston Av. N8 . . . . .5J 47
The Hermitage KT1: King T 4D 150
SE13 .2E 122
SE23 . . . . .1J 139
SW13 .1B 116
TW10: Rich 5E 114
TW13: Felt 3H 129
UB8: Uxb 6A 56
Hermitage Cl. E18 . . . . .4H 51
EN2: Enf 2G 23
KT10: Clay 6A 162
SE2 . . . . .3C 108
TW17: Shep 4C 146
Hermitage Ct. E1 . . . . .1G 103
(off Knighten St.)
E18 . . . . .4J 51
NW2 . . . . .3J 63
Hermitage Gdns. NW2 . . . . .3J 63
SE19 .7C 138
Hermitage Grn. SW16 . . . . .1J 155
Hermitage Ho. N1 . . . . .2B 84
(off Gerrard Rd.)
Hermitage La. CR0: C'don 7G 157
N18 . . . . .5J 33
NW2 . . . . .3J 63
SE25 . . . . .6G 157
SW16 .7K 137
Hermitage Moorings E1 . . . . .1G 103
Hermitage Path SW16 . . . . .1J 155

Hermitage Rd. N4 . . . . .7B 48
N15 . . . . .7B 48
SE19 .7C 138
Hermitage Row E8 . . . . .5G 67
Hermitage St. W2 . . . . .6A 4 (5B 82)
Hermitage Vs. SW6 . . . . .6J 99
(off Lillie Rd.)
Hermitage Wlk. E18 . . . . .4H 51
Hermitage Wall E1 . . . . .1G 103
Hermitage Waterside E1 . . . . .1G 103
(off Thomas More St.)
Hermitage Way HA7: Stan 1A 42
Hermit Pl. NW6 . . . . .1K 81
Hermit Rd. E16 . . . . .5H 87
Hermit St. EC1 . . . . .1A 8 (3B 84)
Hermon Gro. UB3: Hayes 1J 93
Hermon Hill E11 . . . . .5J 51
E18 . . . . .5J 51
Herndon Rd. SW18 . . . . .5A 118
Herne Cl. NW10 . . . . .5K 61
UB3: Hayes 6H 75
WD23: Bush 1C 26
Herne Ct. WD23: Bush 1B 26
HERNE HILL 5C 120
Herne Hill SE24 . . . . .6C 120
Herne Hill Rd. SE24 . . . . .6B 120
(off Railton Rd.)
Herne Hill Rd. SE24 . . . . .3C 120
Herne Hill Velodrome 6D 120
Herne M. N18 . . . . .4B 34
Herne Pl. SE24 . . . . .5B 120
Herne Rd. KT6: Surb 2D 162
Heron Cl. E17 . . . . .2B 50
IG9: Buck H 1D 36
NW10 . . . . .6A 62
SM1: Sutt 5H 165
Heron Ct. BR2: Broml 4A 160
E14 . . . . .3E 104
(off New Union Cl.)
HA4: Ruis 2F 57
KT1: King T 3E 150
NW9 . . . . .2A 44
TW19: Stanw 1A 128
Heron Cres. DA14: Sidc 3J 143
Herondale Av. SW18 . . . . .1B 136
Heron Dr. N4 . . . . .2C 66
Herongate N1 . . . . .1C 84
(off Ridgewell Cl.)
Herongate Rd. E12 . . . . .2A 70
Heron Hill DA17: Belv 5F 109
Heron Ho. DA14: Sidc 3B 144
E3 . . . . .1B 86
(off Sycamore Av.)
E6 . . . . .7C 70
NW8 . . . . .1C 4
(off Newcourt St.)
SW11 .7C 100
(off Searles Cl.)
W13 . . . . .4A 78
Heron Ind. Est. E15 . . . . .2D 86
Heron Mead EN3: Enf L 1H 25
Heron M. IG1: Ilf 2F 71
Heron Pl. E16 . . . . .1A 106
(off Bramwell Way)
SE16 . . . . .1A 104
W1 . . . . .7H 5
(off Thayer St.)
Heron Quay E14 . . . . .1C 104
Heron Rd. CR0: C'don 2E 168
SE24 . . . . .4C 120
TW1: Twick 4A 114
The Herons E11 . . . . .6H 51
Heronsforde W13 . . . . .6C 78
Heronsgate HA8: Edg 5B 28
Heron's Lea N6 . . . . .6D 46
Heronslea Dr. HA7: Stan 5K 27
Heron's Pl. TW7: Isle 3B 114
Heron Tower 7H 9
Herons Ri. EN4: E Barn 4H 21
Heron Tower 7H 9
Heron Trad. Est. W3 . . . . .5H 79
Heron Vw. TW8: Bford 7C 96
(off Commerce Rd.)

Heron Way SM6: W'gton 7H 167
TW14: Felt 4J 111
Heronway IG8: Wfd G 4F 37
Herrick Ct. W3 . . . . .3J 97
(off Bollo Bri. Rd.)
Herrick Ho. N16 . . . . .4D 66
(off Howard Rd.)
SE5 . . . . .7D 102
(off Elmington Est.)
Herrick Rd. N5 . . . . .3C 66
Herries St. W10 . . . . .2G 81
Herringham Rd. SE7 . . . . .3A 106
Herron Cl. BR2: Broml 4H 159
Herrongate Cl. EN1: Enf 2A 24
Hersant Cl. NW10 . . . . .1C 80
Herschell M. SE5 . . . . .3C 120
Herschell Rd. SE23 . . . . .7A 122
Hersham Cl. SW15 . . . . .7C 116
Hershell Ct. SW14 . . . . .4H 115
Hertford Av. SW14 . . . . .5K 115
Hertford Cl. EN4: Cockf 3G 21
Hertford Ct. E6 . . . . .3D 88
N13 . . . . .3F 33
Hertford Ho. UB5: N'olt 4D 76
Hertford Lock Ho. E3 . . . . .1B 86
(off Parnell Rd.)
Hertford Pl. W1 . . . . .4B 6 (4G 83)
Hertford Rd. EN3: Enf H, Enf W 3D 24
EN4: Cockf 3F 21
IG2: Ilf 6J 53
IG11: Bark 7E 70
N1 . . . . .1E 84
(not continuous)
N2 . . . . .3C 46
N9 . . . . .2C 34
Hertford St. W1 . . . . .5J 11 (1F 101)
Hertford Wlk. DA17: Belv 5G 109
Hertford Way CR4: Mitc 4J 155
Hertford Wharf N1 . . . . .1E 84
(off Hertford Rd.)
Hertslet Rd. N7 . . . . .3K 65
Hertsmere Rd. E14 . . . . .1C 104
Hertswood Ct. EN5: Barn 4B 20
Hervey Cl. N3 . . . . .1J 45
Hervey Pk. Rd. E17 . . . . .4A 50
Hervey Rd. SE3 . . . . .1K 123
Hervey Way N3 . . . . .1J 45
Hesa Rd. UB3: Hayes 6J 75
Hesewall Cl. SW4 . . . . .2G 119
Hesketh Pl. W11 . . . . .7G 81
Hesketh Rd. E7 . . . . .3J 69
Heslop Rd. SW12 . . . . .1D 136
Hesper M. SW5 . . . . .4K 99
Hesperus Cres. E14 . . . . .4D 104
Hessel Rd. W13 . . . . .2A 96
Hessel St. E1 . . . . .6H 85
Hestercombe Av. SW6 . . . . .2G 117
Hesterman Way CR0: Wadd 1K 167
Hester Rd. N18 . . . . .5B 34
SW11 .7C 100
Hester Ter. TW9: Rich 3G 115
Hestia Ho. SE1 . . . . .7G 15
HESTON 7E 94
Heston Av. TW5: Hest 6C 94
The Heston Cen. TW5: Cran 5A 94
Heston Community Sports Hall 7E 94
Heston Grange TW5: Hest 6D 94
Heston Grange La. TW5: Hest 6D 94
Heston Ho. SE8 . . . . .1C 122
Heston Ind. Mall TW5: Hest 7D 94
Heston Phoenix Distribution Pk.
TW5: Hest 6A 94
Heston Pool .6D 94
Heston Rd. TW5: Hest 6E 94
HESTON SERVICE AREA 6B 94
Heston St. SE14 . . . . .1C 122
Hetherington Rd. SW4 . . . . .4J 119
TW17: Shep 2E 146
Hetherington Way UB10: Ick 4A 56
Hethpool Ho. W2 . . . . .4A 4
Hetley Gdns. SE19 . . . . .7F 139
Hetley Rd. W12 . . . . .1D 98

Heton Gdns. NW4 . . . . .4D **44**
Hevelius Cl. SE10 . . . . .5H **105**
Hever Cft. SE9 . . . . .4E **142**
Hever Gdns. BR1: Broml 2E **160**
Heverham Rd. SE18 . . . . .4J **107**
Hever Ho. SE15 . . . . .6K **103**
(off Lovelinch Cl.)
Hever Pl. KT8: E Mos 3G **149**
Heversham Ho. SE15 . . . . .6J **103**
Heversham Rd. DA7: Bex 2G **127**
Hevingham Dr. RM6: Chad H 5C **54**
Hevingham Vw. SE26 . . . . .5H **139**
Hewens Rd. UB4: Hil 4E **74**
UB10: Hil 4E **74**
Hewer St. W10 . . . . .5F **81**
Hewett Cl. HA7: Stan 4G **27**
Hewett Rd. RM8: Dag 5D **72**
Hewetts Quay IG11: Bark 1F **89**
Hewett St. EC2 . . . . .4H **9** (4E **84**)
Hewish Rd. N18 . . . . .4K **33**
Hewison St. E3 . . . . .2B **86**
Hewitt Av. N22 . . . . .2B **48**
Hewitt Cl. CR0: C'don 3C **170**
Hewitt Rd. N8 . . . . .5A **48**
Hewlett Ho. SW8 . . . . .7F **101**
(off Havelock St.)
Hewlett Rd. E3 . . . . .2A **86**
Hewson Way SE17 . . . . .4C **102**
The Hexagon N6 . . . . .1D **64**
Hexagon Bus. Cen. UB4: Yead 7A **76**
Hexal Rd. SE6 . . . . .3G **141**
Hexham Gdns. TW7: Isle 7A **96**
UB5: N'olt 5D **58**
Hexham Rd. EN5: New Bar 4E **20**
SE27 . . . . .2C **138**
SM4: Mord 1K **165**
Heybourne Cres. NW9 . . . . .1A **44**
Heybourne Rd. N17 . . . . .7C **34**
Heybridge NW1 . . . . .6F **65**
(off Lewis St.)
Heybridge Av. SW16 . . . . .7J **137**
Heybridge Dr. IG6: Ilf 2H **53**
Heybridge Way E10 . . . . .7A **50**
Heydon Ct. BR4: W W'ck 2G **171**
(off Deer Pk. Way)
Heydon Ho. SE14 . . . . .1J **121**
(off Kender St.)
Heyford Av. SW8 . . . . .7J **101**
SW20 . . . . .3H **153**
Heyford Rd. CR4: Mitc 2C **154**
Heyford Ter. SW8 . . . . .7J **101**
(off Old Sth. Lambeth Rd.)
Heygate St. SE17 . . . . .4C **102**
Heylyn Sq. E3 . . . . .3B **86**
Heynes Rd. RM8: Dag 4C **72**
Heysham La. NW3 . . . . .3K **63**
Heysham Rd. N15 . . . . .6D **48**
Heythorp St. SW18 . . . . .1H **135**
Heythrop Dr. UB10: Ick 4B **56**
Heywood Av. NW9 . . . . .1A **44**
Heywood Ct. HA7: Stan 5H **27**
Heywood Ho. SE14 . . . . .6K **103**
(off Myers La.)
Heyworth Rd. E5 . . . . .4H **67**
E15 .5H **69**
Hibbert Ho. E14 . . . . .3C **104**
(off Tiller Rd.)
Hibbert Rd. E17 . . . . .7B **50**
HA3: W'stone 2K **41**
Hibbert St. SW11 . . . . .3B **118**
Hibernia Gdns. TW3: Houn 4E **112**
Hibernia Point SE2 . . . . .2D **108**
(off Wolvercote Rd.)
Hibernia Rd. TW3: Houn 4E **112**
Hibiscus Cl. HA8: Edg 4D **28**
Hibiscus Ho. E17 . . . . .7D **158**
TW13: Felt 1J **129**
Hibiscus Lodge E15 . . . . .7G **69**
(off Glenavon Rd.)
Hichisson Rd. SE15 . . . . .5J **121**
Hicken Rd. SW2 . . . . .5K **119**
Hickes Ho. NW6 . . . . .7B **64**
Hickey's Almshouses TW9: Rich . .4F **115**

Hickin Cl. SE7 . . . . .4B **106**
Hickin St. E14 . . . . .3E **104**
Hickleton NW1 . . . . .1G **83**
(off Camden St.)
Hickling Ho. SE16 . . . . .3H **103**
(off Slippers Pl.)
Hickling Rd. IG1: Ilf 5F **71**
Hickman Av. E4 . . . . .6K **35**
Hickman Cl. E16 . . . . .5B **88**
Hickman Rd. RM6: Chad H 7C **54**
Hickman Wlk. SE18 . . . . .5E **106**
(off Brumwell Av.)
Hickmore Wlk. SW4 . . . . .3H **119**
Hickory Cl. N9 . . . . .7B **24**
Hicks Av. UB6: G'frd 3H **77**
Hicks Bolton Ho. NW6 . . . . .2H **81**
(off Denmark Ho.)
Hicks Cl. SW11 . . . . .3C **118**
Hicks Ct. RM10: Dag 3H **73**
Hicks Gallery 5J **135**
Hicks Ho. SE16 . . . . .3G **103**
(off Spa Rd.)
Hicks St. SE8 . . . . .5A **104**
Hidcote Apts. SW11 . . . . .4C **118**
(off Danvers Av.)
Hidcote Gdns. SW20 . . . . .3D **152**
Hidden Cl. KT8: W Mole 4G **149**
Hide Cl. SE8 . . . . .6E **88**
Hide Pl. SW1 . . . . .4C **18** (4H **101**)
Hider Cl. SE3 . . . . .7A **106**
Hide Rd. HA1: Harr 4G **41**
Hides St. N7 . . . . .6K **65**
Hide Twr. SW1 . . . . .4C **18**
(off Regency St.)
Hierro Ct. E1 . . . . .5A **86**
(off Ocean Est.)
Higgins Ho. N1 . . . . .1E **84**
(off Colville Est.)
Higginson Ho. NW3 . . . . .7D **64**
(off Fellows Rd.)
Higgins Wlk. TW12: Hamp 6C **130**
(off Abbott Cl.)
Higgs Ind. Est. SE24 . . . . .3B **120**
High Acres EN2: Enf 3G **23**
HIGHAM HILL 2A **50**
Higham Hill Rd. E17 . . . . .1A **50**
Higham M. UB5: N'olt 4D **76**
Higham Path E17 . . . . .3A **50**
Higham Pl. E17 . . . . .3A **50**
Higham Rd. IG8: Wfd G 6D **36**
N17 .3D **48**
The Highams E17 . . . . .1E **50**
Highams Ct. E4 . . . . .3K **35**
Highams Lodge Bus. Cen. E17 . . . .3K **49**
HIGHAMS PARK 6A **36**
Higham Sta. Av. E4 . . . . .6H **35**
Higham St. E17 . . . . .3A **50**
High Ashton KT2: King T 7H **133**
Highbanks Cl. DA16: Well 7B **108**
Highbanks Rd. HA5: Hat E 6A **26**
Highbank Way N8 . . . . .6A **48**
HIGH BARNET 2A **20**
Highbarrow Rd. CR0: C'don 1G **169**
High Beech CR2: S Croy 7E **168**
N21 .6E **22**
High Beeches DA14: Sidc 5E **144**
High Birch Ct. EN4: E Barn 4H **21**
(off Park Rd.)
High Bri. SE10 . . . . .5F **105**
Highbridge Ct. SE14 . . . . .7J **103**
(off Farrow La.)
Highbridge Rd. IG11: Bark 1F **89**
High Bri. Wharf SE10 . . . . .5F **105**
(off High Bri.)
Highbrook Rd. SE3 . . . . .3B **124**
High Broom Cres. BR4: W W'ck . . .7D **158**
HIGHBURY 4B **66**
Highbury Av. CR7: Thor H 2A **156**
Highbury Cl. BR4: W W'ck 2D **170**
KT3: N Mald 4J **151**
HIGHBURY CORNER 6B **66**
Highbury Cres. N5 . . . . .5B **66**
Highbury Est. N5 . . . . .5C **66**

Highbury Gdns. IG3: Ilf 2J **71**
N7 . . . . .5A **66**
Highbury Grange N5 . . . . .4C **66**
Highbury Gro. N5 . . . . .5B **66**
Highbury Gro. Ct. N5 . . . . .6C **66**
Highbury Hill N5 . . . . .3A **66**
Highbury Leisure Centre 6B **66**
Highbury Mans. N1 . . . . .7B **66**
(off Upper St.)
Highbury New Pk. N5 . . . . .5C **66**
Highbury Pk. N5 . . . . .3B **66**
Highbury Pl. N5 . . . . .6B **66**
Highbury Quad. N5 . . . . .3B **66**
Highbury Rd. SW19 . . . . .5G **135**
Highbury Sq. N14 . . . . .1B **32**
Highbury Stadium Sq. N5 . . . . .3B **66**
Highbury Sta. Rd. N1 . . . . .6A **66**
Highbury Ter. N5 . . . . .5B **66**
Highbury Ter. M. N5 . . . . .5B **66**
High Cedar Dr. SW20 . . . . .7E **134**
Highclere Rd. KT3: N Mald 3K **151**
Highclere St. SE26 . . . . .4A **140**
Highcliffe W13 . . . . .6B **78**
(off Clivedon Ct.)
Highcliffe Dr. SW15 . . . . .6B **116**
Highcliffe Gdns. IG4: Ilf 5C **52**
Highcombe SE7 . . . . .6K **105**
Highcombe Cl. SE9 . . . . .1B **142**
High Coombe Pl. KT2: King T 6K **133**
Highcroft NW9 . . . . .5A **44**
Highcroft Av. HA0: Wemb 7G **61**
Highcroft Est. N19 . . . . .7J **47**
Highcroft Gdns. NW11 . . . . .6H **45**
Highcroft Rd. N19 . . . . .7J **47**
The High Cross Cen. N15 . . . . .4G **49**
High Cross Rd. N17 . . . . .3G **49**
Highcross Way SW15 . . . . .1C **134**
Highdaun Dr. SW16 . . . . .4K **155**
Highdown KT4: Wor Pk 2A **164**
Highdown Rd. SW15 . . . . .6D **116**
High Dr. KT3: N Mald 1J **151**
High Elms IG8: Wfd G 5D **36**
High Elms Country Pk. 7H **173**
High Elms Golf Course 7G **173**
High Elms Rd. BR6: Downe 7G **173**
Highfield WD23: B Hea 2D **26**
Highfield Av. BR6: Chels 5K **173**
DA8: Erith 6H **109**
HA5: Pinn 5D **40**
HA9: Wemb 3F **61**
NW9 . . . . .5J **43**
NW11 . . . . .7F **45**
UB6: G'frd 5J **59**
Highfield Cl. HA6: Nwood 1G **39**
KT6: Surb 1C **162**
N22 .1A **48**
NW9 . . . . .5J **43**
SE13 . . . . .6F **123**
Highfield Ct. N14 . . . . .6B **22**
NW11 . . . . .6G **45**
Highfield Cres. HA6: Nwood 1G **39**
Highfield Dr. BR2: Broml 4G **159**
BR4: W W'ck 2D **170**
KT19: Ewe 6B **164**
UB10: Ick 4A **56**
Highfield Gdns. NW11 . . . . .6G **45**
Highfield Hill SE19 . . . . .7D **138**
Highfield M. NW6 . . . . .7K **63**
(off Compayne Gdns.)
Highfield Rd. BR1: Broml 4D **160**
BR7: Chst 3K **161**
DA6: Bex 5F **127**
HA6: Nwood 1G **39**
IG8: Wfd G 7H **37**
KT5: Surb 7J **151**
KT12: Walt T 7J **147**
N21 .2G **33**
NW11 . . . . .6G **45**
SM1: Sutt 5C **166**
TW7: Isle 1K **113**
TW13: Felt 2J **129**
TW16: Sun 5H **147**
W3 .5H **79**

Highfields SM1: Sutt 2J **165**
Highfields Gro. N6 . . . . .1D **64**
High Foleys KT10: Clay 7B **162**
High Gables BR2: Broml 2G **159**
HIGHGATE 6E **46**
Highgate Av. N6 . . . . .7F **47**
Highgate Cemetery 1E **64**
Highgate Cl. N6 . . . . .7E **46**
Highgate Edge N2 . . . . .5C **46**
Highgate Golf Course 6C **46**
Highgate Hgts. N6 . . . . .6G **47**
Highgate High St. N6 . . . . .1E **64**
Highgate Hill N6 . . . . .1F **65**
N19 . . . . .1F **65**
Highgate Ho. SE26 . . . . .3G **139**
Highgate Rd. NW5 . . . . .3E **64**
Highgate Spinney N8 . . . . .6H **47**
Highgate Wlk. SE23 . . . . .2J **139**
Highgate W. Hill N6 . . . . .1E **64**
High Gro. BR1: Broml 1B **160**
SE18 . . . . .7H **107**
Highgrove Cl. BR7: Chst 1C **160**
N11 .5K **31**
Highgrove Ct. BR3: Beck 7C **140**
SM1: Sutt 6J **165**
Highgrove Ho. HA4: Ruis 6J **39**
Highgrove M. SM5: Cars 3D **166**
Highgrove Pool & Fitness Cen. 6J **39**
Highgrove Rd. RM8: Dag 5C **72**
Highgrove Ter. E4 . . . . .2A **36**
Highgrove Way HA4: Ruis 6J **39**
High Hill Est. E5 . . . . .1H **67**
High Hill Ferry E5 . . . . .1H **67**
High Holborn WC1 . . . . .7E **6** (6J **83**)
High Ho. M. N16 . . . . .2E **66**
W7 .2J **95**
Highland Cotts. SM6: W'gton 4G **167**
Highland Ct. BR1: Broml 1H **159**
E18 .1K **51**
Highland Cft. BR3: Beck 5D **140**
Highland Dr. WD23: Bush 1A **26**
Highland Pk. TW13: Felt 4H **129**
Highland Rd. BR1: Broml 1H **159**
BR2: Broml 1H **159**
DA6: Bex 5G **127**
HA6: Nwood 2H **39**
SE19 . . . . .6E **138**
Highlands N20 . . . . .2G **31**
The Highlands EN5: New Bar 4D **20**
HA8: Edg 2H **43**
Highlands Av. N21 . . . . .5E **22**
W3 .7J **79**
Highlands Cl. N4 . . . . .7J **47**
TW3: Houn 1F **113**
Highlands Ct. SE19 . . . . .6E **138**
Highlands Gdns. IG1: Ilf 1D **70**
Highlands Heath SW15 . . . . .7E **116**
Highlands Rd. EN5: New Bar 5D **20**
Highland St. E15 . . . . .2D **86**
HIGHLANDS VILLAGE 5E **22**
Highland Ter. SE13 . . . . .3D **122**
(off Algernon Rd.)
Highland Vw. Pk. Homes 1D **174**
High La. W7 . . . . .5H **77**
Highlawn Hall HA1: Harr 3J **59**
Highlever Rd. W10 . . . . .7F **29**
High Level Dr. SE26 . . . . .4G **139**
Highlever Rd. W10 . . . . .5E **80**
High Mead BR4: W W'ck 2F **171**
HA1: Harr 5J **41**
Highmead SE18 . . . . .7K **107**
Highmead Cres. HA0: Wemb 7F **61**
High Mdw. Cl. HA5: Eastc 4A **40**
Highmeadow Cres. NW9 . . . . .5K **43**
High Meads Rd. E16 . . . . .6B **88**
Highmore Rd. SE3 . . . . .7G **105**
High Mt. NW4 . . . . .6C **44**
High Oaks EN2: Enf 1E **22**
The High Pde. SW16 . . . . .3J **137**
High Pk. Av. TW9: Kew 1G **115**
High Pk. Rd. TW9: Kew 1G **115**
High Path SW19 . . . . .1K **153**

High Point N6 . . . . .7E **46**
  SE9 . . . . .3F **143**
High Ridge N10 . . . . .1F **47**
High Rd. E18 . . . . .1J **51**
  HA0: Wemb 5D **60**
  HA3: Hrw W 7D **26**
  HA5: Eastc 6J **39**
  HA9: Wemb 5D **60**
  IG1: Ilf .3F **71**
    (not continuous)
  IG3: Ilf .1K **71**
  IG7: Chig 5K **37**
  IG9: Buck H 2E **36**
  N11 . . . . .5A **32**
  N15 . . . . .4F **49**
  N17 . . . . .2F **49**
  N22 . . . . .7E **32**
  NW10 . . . . .6A **62**
  RM6: Chad H 7D **54**
  UB4: Hayes 5G **75**
  UB10: Ick 3D **56**
  WD23: B Hea 1C **26**
High Rd. E. Finchley N2 . . . . .1B **46**
High Rd. Leyton E10 . . . . .6D **50**
  E15 . . . . .2D **68**
High Rd. Leytonstone E11 . . . . . . .3G **69**
  E15 . . . . .4G **69**
High Rd. Nth. Finchley N12 . . . . . .3F **31**
    (not continuous)
High Rd. Whetstone N20 . . . . .7F **21**
High Rd. Woodford Grn. E18 . . . . .1J **51**
  IG8: Wfd G 6C **36**
High Sheldon N6 . . . . .6D **46**
Highshore Rd. SE15 . . . . .2F **121**
    (not continuous)
Highstead Cres. DA8: Erith 1K **127**
Highstone Av. E11 . . . . .6J **51**
Highstone Ct. E11 . . . . .6H **51**
    (off New Wanstead)
Highstone Mans. NW1 . . . . .7G **65**
    (off Camden Rd.)
High St. BR1: Broml 2J **159**
    (not continuous)
  BR3: Beck 2C **158**
  BR4: W W'ck 1D **170**
  BR6: Chels 7K **173**
  BR6: Farnb 5F **173**
  BR6: Orp 2K **173**
  BR7: Chst 6F **143**
  CR0: C'don 3C **168**
  CR7: Thor H 4C **156**
  E11 . . . . .5J **51**
  E13 . . . . .2J **87**
  E15 . . . . .2E **86**
  E17 . . . . .5A **50**
  EN3: Pond E 6D **24**
  EN5: Barn 3B **20**
  HA1: Harr 1J **59**
  HA3: Hrw W, W'stone 2J **41**
  HA4: Ruis 7G **39**
  HA5: Pinn 3C **40**
  HA6: Nwood 1H **39**
  HA8: Edg 6B **28**
  HA9: Wemb 4F **61**
  IG6: Ilf 3G **53**
  KT1: Hamp W 1C **150**
  KT1: King T 3D **150**
  KT3: N Mald 4A **152**
  KT7: T Ditt 6A **150**
  KT8: W Mole 4E **148**
  KT12: Walt T 7J **147**
  KT17: Ewe 7B **164**
  N8 . . . . .4J **47**
  N14 . . . . .1C **32**
  NW7 .5J **29**
  RM1: Rom 5K **55**
  SE20 .6J **139**
  SE25 .4F **157**
  SM1: Sutt 4K **165**
  SM3: Cheam 6G **165**
  SM5: Cars 5E **166**
  SW19 . . . . .5F **135**
  TW2: Whitt 7G **113**

High St. TW3: Houn 3F **113**
  TW5: Cran 1J **111**
  TW8: Bford 7C **96**
  TW11: Tedd 5K **131**
  TW12: Hamp, Hamp H 1G **149**
  TW13: Felt 3H **129**
  TW17: Shep 6D **146**
  TW19: Stanw 6A **110**
  UB1: S'hall 1D **94**
  UB3: Harl 6F **93**
  UB7: Harm 2E **174**
  UB7: Yiew 7A **74**
  UB8: Uxb 1A **74**
  W3 . . . . .1H **97**
  W5 . . . . .1D **96**
High St. Colliers Wood SW19 . . . . .7B **136**
High St. Harlesden NW10 . . . . .2B **80**
High St. M. SW19 . . . . .5G **135**
High St. Nth. E6 . . . . .1C **88**
  E12 . . . . .5C **70**
High St. Sth. E6 . . . . .2D **88**
High Timber St. EC4 . . . . .2C **14** (7C **84**)
High Tor Cl. BR1: Broml 7K **141**
High Tor Vw. SE28 . . . . .1J **107**
High Trees CR0: C'don 1A **170**
  EN4: E Barn 5H **21**
  N20 . . . . .3F **31**
  SW2 .1A **138**
Hightrees Ct. W7 . . . . .7J **77**
Hightrees Ho. SW12 . . . . .6E **118**
High Vw. HA5: Pinn 4A **40**
Highview N6 . . . . .6G **47**
  NW7 .3E **28**
  UB5: N'olt 3C **76**
High Vw. HA8: Edg 4D **28**
  SM6: W'gton 5K **167**
High Vw. Cl. SE19 . . . . .2F **157**
High Vw. Ct. HA3: Hrw W 7D **26**
Highview Gdns. HA8: Edg 4D **28**
  N3 . . . . .3G **45**
  N11 . . . . .5B **32**
Highview Ho. RM6: Chad H 4E **54**
Highview Lodge EN2: Enf 3G **23**
    (off The Ridgeway)
High Vw. Pde. IG4: Ilf 5D **52**
High Vw. Rd. E18 . . . . .2H **51**
  SE19 .6D **138**
Highview Rd. DA14: Sidc 4B **144**
  W13 . . . . .5A **78**
The Highway E1 . . . . .7G **85**
  HA7: Stan 1K **41**
  SM2: Sutt 7A **166**
The Highway Trad. Cen. E1 . . . . . .7K **85**
    (off Heckford St.)
Highwood BR2: Broml 3F **159**
Highwood Av. N12 . . . . .4F **31**
Highwood Cl. BR6: Farnb 2G **173**
  SE22 .1G **139**
Highwood Ct. EN5: New Bar 5D **20**
  N12 . . . . .3F **31**
Highwood Dr. BR6: Farnb 2G **173**
Highwood Gdns. IG5: Ilf 5D **52**
Highwood Gro. NW7 . . . . .5E **28**
HIGHWOOD HILL 3G **29**
Highwood Hill NW7 . . . . .2G **29**
Highwood Rd. N19 . . . . .3J **65**
High Worple HA2: Harr 7D **40**
Highworth Rd. N11 . . . . .6C **32**
Highworth St. NW1 . . . . .5D **4**
Hi-Gloss Cen. SE8 . . . . .5A **104**
Hilary Av. CR4: Mitc 3E **154**
Hilary Cl. DA8: Erith 1H **127**
  SW6 .7K **99**
Hilary Dennis Ct. E11 . . . . .4J **51**
Hilary M. SE1 . . . . .2C **102**
Hilary Rd. W12 . . . . .6B **80**
    (not continuous)
Hilberry Cl. WD23: Bush 1A **26**
Hilbert Rd. SM3: Cheam 3F **165**
Hilborough Cl. SW19 . . . . .7A **136**
Hilborough Ct. E8 . . . . .7F **67**
Hilborough Way BR6: Farnb 5H **173**
Hilda Ct. KT6: Surb 7D **150**

Hilda Lockert Wlk. SW9 . . . . .2B **120**
    (off Loughborough Rd.)
Hilda Rd. E6 . . . . .7B **70**
  E16 . . . . .4G **87**
  UB2: S'hall 2G **95**
Hilda Ter. SW9 . . . . .2A **120**
Hilda Va. Cl. BR6: Farnb 4F **173**
Hilda Va. Rd. BR6: Farnb 4E **172**
Hildenborough Gdns.
  BR1: Broml 6G **141**
Hildenborough Ho. BR3: Beck 7B **140**
    (off Bethersden Cl.)
Hildenlea Pl. BR2: Broml 2F **159**
Hilderley Ho. KT1: King T 2F **151**
    (off Winery La.)
Hildreth St. SW12 . . . . .1F **137**
Hildreth St. M. SW12 . . . . .1F **137**
Hildyard Rd. SW6 . . . . .6J **99**
Hiley Rd. NW10 . . . . .3E **80**
Hilgrove Rd. NW6 . . . . .7A **64**
Hiliary Gdns. HA7: Stan 2C **42**
Hillary N8 .3J **47**
    (off Boyton Cl.)
Hillary Ct. W12 . . . . .2E **98**
    (off Titmuss St.)
Hillary Cres. KT12: Walt T 7A **148**
Hillary Dr. TW7: Isle 5K **113**
Hillary Rd. UB2: S'hall 3E **94**
Hillary Ri. EN5: New Bar 4D **20**
Hillbeck Cl. SE15 . . . . .7J **103**
    (not continuous)
Hillbeck Way UB6: G'frd 1H **77**
Hillborne Cl. UB3: Harl 5J **93**
Hillbrook Rd. SW17 . . . . .3D **136**
Hill Brow BR1: Broml 1B **160**
Hillbrow KT3: N Mald 3B **152**
Hillbrow Cl. DA5: Bexl 4K **145**
Hillbrow Rd. BR1: Broml 7G **141**
Hillbury Av. HA3: Kenton 5B **42**
Hillbury Rd. SW17 . . . . .3F **137**
Hill Cl. BR7: Chst 5F **143**
  HA1: Harr 3J **59**
  HA7: Stan 4G **27**
  NW2 .3D **62**
  NW11 . . . . .6J **45**
Hillcote Av. SW16 . . . . .7A **138**
Hill Ct. EN4: E Barn 4H **21**
  UB5: N'olt 5E **58**
  W5 . . . . .4F **79**
Hillcourt Av. N12 . . . . .6E **30**
Hillcourt Est. N16 . . . . .1D **66**
Hillcourt Rd. SE22 . . . . .6H **121**
Hill Cres. DA5: Bexl 1J **145**
  HA1: Harr 5A **42**
  KT4: Wor Pk 2E **164**
  KT5: Surb 5F **151**
  N20 . . . . .2E **30**
Hill Crest DA15: Sidc 7A **126**
  KT5: Surb 7E **150**
Hillcrest N6 . . . . .7E **46**
  N21 . . . . .7F **23**
  SE24 .4D **120**
  W11 . . . . .7H **81**
    (off St John's Gdns.)
Hillcrest Av. HA5: Pinn 4B **40**
  HA8: Edg 4C **28**
  NW11 . . . . .5H **45**
Hillcrest Cl. BR3: Beck 6B **158**
  SE26 .4G **139**
Hillcrest Ct. RM5: Col R 1K **55**
  SM2: Sutt 7B **166**
    (off Eaton Rd.)
Hillcrest Gdns. KT10: Hin W 3A **162**
  N3 . . . . .4G **45**
  NW2 .3C **62**
Hillcrest Rd. BR1: Broml 5J **141**
  BR6: Chels 2K **173**
  E17 . . . . .2F **51**
  E18 . . . . .2H **51**
  W3 . . . . .1H **97**
  W5 . . . . .5E **78**

Hillcrest Vw. BR3: Beck 6B **158**
Hillcroft Av. HA5: Pinn 6D **40**
Hillcroft Cres. HA4: Ruis 3B **58**
  HA9: Wemb 4F **61**
  W5 . . . . .6D **78**
Hillcroft Rd. E6 . . . . .5F **89**
Hillcroome Rd. SM2: Sutt 6B **166**
Hillcross Av. SM4: Mord 6F **153**
Hilldale Rd. SM1: Sutt 4H **165**
Hilldown Ct. SW16 . . . . .7J **137**
Hilldown Rd. BR2: Hayes 1G **171**
  SW16 . . . . .7J **137**
Hill Dr. NW9 . . . . .1J **61**
  SW16 . . . . .3K **155**
Hilldrop Cres. N7 . . . . .5H **65**
Hilldrop Est. N7 . . . . .5H **65**
    (not continuous)
Hilldrop La. N7 . . . . .5H **65**
Hilldrop Rd. BR1: Broml 6K **141**
  N7 . . . . .5H **65**
Hill End BR6: Orp 2K **173**
Hillend SE18 . . . . .1E **124**
Hillend Green NW7 . . . . .4K **29**
Hillersden Ho. SW1 . . . . .5J **17**
    (off Ebury Bri. Rd.)
Hillersdon Av. HA8: Edg 5A **28**
  SW13 . . . . .2C **116**
Hillery Cl. SE17 . . . . .4D **102**
Hill Farm Cotts. HA4: Ruis 7E **38**
Hill Farm Rd. UB10: Ick 4F **57**
  W10 .5E **80**
Hillfield Av. HA0: Wemb 7E **60**
  N8 . . . . .5J **47**
  NW9 .5A **44**
  SM4: Mord 6C **154**
Hillfield Cl. HA2: Harr 4G **41**
Hillfield Ct. NW3 . . . . .5C **64**
Hillfield Ho. N5 . . . . .5C **66**
Hillfield M. N8 . . . . .4K **47**
Hillfield Pde. SM4: Mord 6B **154**
Hillfield Pk. N10 . . . . .4F **47**
  N21 . . . . .2F **33**
Hill Fld. Rd. TW12: Hamp 7D **130**
Hillfoot Av. RM5: Col R 1J **55**
Hillfoot Rd. RM5: Col R 1J **55**
Hillgate Pl. SW12 . . . . .7F **119**
  W8 . . . . .1J **99**
Hillgate St. W8 . . . . .1J **99**
Hill Ga. Wlk. N6 . . . . .6G **47**
Hill Gro. RM1: Rom 3K **55**
  TW13: Hanw 2D **130**
Hill Ho. BR2: Broml 2H **159**
  E5 . . . . .2J **67**
    (off Harrington Hill)
  N19 . . . . .2G **65**
    (off Highgate Hill)
  SE28 .1H **107**
Hill Ho. Apts. N1 . . . . .1H **7**
    (off Pentonville Rd.)
Hill Ho. Av. HA7: Stan 7E **26**
Hill Ho. Cl. N21 . . . . .7F **23**
Hill Ho. Dr. TW12: Hamp 1E **148**
Hill Ho. M. BR2: Broml 2H **159**
Hill Ho. Rd. SW16 . . . . .5K **137**
Hilliard Ho. E1 . . . . .1H **103**
    (off Prusom St.)
Hilliard Rd. HA6: Nwood 1H **39**
Hilliards Ct. E1 . . . . .1J **103**
Hillier Cl. EN5: New Bar 6E **20**
Hillier Gdns. CR0: Wadd 5A **168**
Hillier Ho. NW1 . . . . .7H **65**
    (off Camden Sq.)
Hillier Lodge TW11: Tedd 5H **131**
Hillier Pl. KT9: Chess 6D **162**
Hillier Rd. SW11 . . . . .6D **118**
Hilliers Av. UB8: Hil 3C **74**
Hilliers La. CR0: Bedd 3J **167**
HILLINGDON 3C **74**
Hillingdon Athletic Club 5F **39**
Hillingdon Athletics Stadium 6A **56**
Hillingdon Av. TW19: Stanw 1A **128**

HILLINGDON CIRCUS 6D 56
Hillingdon Ct. HA3: Kenton 4D 42
Hillingdon Cycle Circuit 1A 94
Hillingdon Golf Course 2B 74
HILLINGDON HEATH 4D 74
Hillingdon Hill UB10: Hil 2A 74
Hillingdon Pde. UB10: Hil 4D 74
  (off Uxbridge Rd.)
Hillingdon Rd. DA7: Bex 2J 127
  UB8: Uxb 1A 74
  UB10: Uxb 1A 74
Hillingdon Sports & Leisure Complex
  . . . . .6A 56
Hillingdon St. SE17 . . . . .6B 102
Hillington Gdns.
  IG8: Wfd G 2B 52
Hill La. HA4: Ruis 1E 56
Hillman Cl. UB8: Uxb 5A 56
Hillman Dr. W10 . . . . .4E 80
Hillman St. E8 . . . . .6H 67
Hillmarton Rd. N7 . . . . .5J 65
Hillmarton Ter. N7 . . . . .5J 65
  (off Hillmarton Rd.)
Hillmead Dr. SW9 . . . . .4B 120
Hillmore Ct. SE13 . . . . .3F 123
  (off Belmont Hill)
Hillmore Gro. SE26 . . . . .5A 140
Hill Path SW16 . . . . .5K 137
Hillreach SE18 . . . . .5D 106
Hill Ri. HA4: Ruis 1E 56
  KT10: Hin W 2B 162
  N9 . . . . .6C 24
  NW11 . . . . .4K 45
  SE23 . . . . .1H 139
  TW10: Rich 5D 114
  UB6: G'frd 7G 59
Hillrise KT12: Walt T 7H 147
Hillrise Mans. N19 . . . . .7J 47
  (off Warltersville Rd.)
Hillrise Rd. N19 . . . . .7J 47
Hill Rd. CR4: Mitc 1F 155
  HA0: Wemb 3B 60
  HA1: Harr 5A 42
  HA5: Pinn 5C 40
  N10 . . . . .1D 46
  NW8 . . . . .2A 82
  SM1: Sutt 5K 165
  SM5: Cars 6C 166
Hillsboro' Rd. SE22 . . . . .5E 120
Hillsborough Ct. NW6 . . . . .1K 81
  (off Mortimer Cres.)
Hillsgrove Cl. DA16: Well 7C 108
HILLSIDE .4J 109
Hillside DA8: Erith 4J 109
  EN5: New Bar 5F 21
  N8 . . . . .6H 47
  NW5 . . . . .3E 64
  NW9 . . . . .4K 43
  NW10 . . . . .7J 61
  SE10 . . . . .7F 105
  (off Croom's Hill)
  SW19 . . . . .6F 135
Hillside Av. HA9: Wemb 4F 61
  IG8: Wfd G 6F 37
  N11 . . . . .6J 31
  SE10 . . . . .1E 122
Hillside Cl. IG8: Wfd G 5F 37
  NW8 . . . . .2K 81
  SM4: Mord 4G 153
Hillside Cres. HA2: Harr 1G 59
  HA6: Nwood 1J 39
Hillside Dr. HA8: Edg 6B 28
Hillside Gdns. E17 . . . . .3F 51
  EN5: Barn 4B 20
  HA3: Kenton 7E 42
  HA6: Nwood 1J 39
  HA8: Edg 4A 28
  N6 . . . . .6F 47
  N11 . . . . .6B 32
  SM6: W'gton 7G 167
  SW2 . . . . .2A 138
Hillside Gro. N14 . . . . .7C 22
  NW7 . . . . .7H 29

Hillside Ho. CR0: Wadd 4B 168
  (off Duppas Av.)
Hillside La. BR2: Hayes 2H 171
  (not continuous)
Hillside Mans. EN5: Barn 4C 20
Hillside Pas. SW2 . . . . .2K 137
Hillside Ri. HA6: Nwood 1J 39
Hillside Rd. BR2: Broml 3H 159
  CR0: Wadd 5B 168
  HA5: Pinn 1K 39
  HA6: Nwood 1J 39
  KT5: Surb 4F 151
  N15 . . . . .7E 48
  SM2: Sutt 7H 165
  SW2 . . . . .2K 137
  UB1: S'hall 4E 76
  W5 . . . . .5E 78
Hills La. HA6: Nwood 1G 39
Hillsleigh Rd. W8 . . . . .1H 99
Hill M. W5 .7E 78
Hills Pl. W1 . . . . .1A 12 (6G 83)
Hills Rd. IG9: Buck H 1E 36
Hillstone Ct. E3 . . . . .4D 86
  (off Empson St.)
Hillstowe St. E5 . . . . .3J 67
Hill St. TW9: Rich 5D 114
  W1 . . . . .4H 11 (1E 100)
Hill Top NW11 . . . . .4K 45
  SM3: Sutt 7H 153
  SM4: Mord 6J 153
Hilltop E17 .3D 50
Hilltop Av. NW10 . . . . .7J 61
  (not continuous)
Hilltop Ct. NW8 . . . . .7A 64
  (off Alexandra Rd.)
Hilltop Gdns. BR6: Orp 2J 173
  NW4 . . . . .2D 44
Hilltop Ho. N6 . . . . .7H 47
Hilltop Rd. NW6 . . . . .7J 63
Hill Top Vw. IG8: Wfd G 6J 37
Hilltop Way HA7: Stan 3F 27
Hill Vw. NW3 . . . . .1D 82
  (off Ainger Rd.)
Hillview SW20 . . . . .7D 134
Hillview Av. HA3: Kenton 5E 42
Hillview Cl. HA9: Wemb 2F 61
Hillview Cres. BR6: Orp 1J 173
  IG1: Ilf 6D 52
Hill Vw. Dr. DA16: Well 2J 125
  SE28 . . . . .1J 107
Hill Vw. Gdns. NW9 . . . . .5K 43
Hillview Gdns. HA2: Harr 3E 40
  NW4 . . . . .4F 45
Hill Vw. Rd. KT10: Clay 7A 162
  TW1: Twick 6A 114
Hillview Rd. BR6: Orp 1K 173
  BR7: Chst 5E 142
  HA5: Hat E 1D 40
  NW7 . . . . .4A 30
  SM1: Sutt 3A 166
Hillway N6 .2E 64
  NW9 . . . . .1A 62
Hill-Wood Ho. NW1 . . . . .1B 6
  (off Polygon Rd.)
Hillworth BR3: Beck 2D 158
Hillworth Rd. SW2 . . . . .7A 120
Hillyard Ho. SW9 . . . . .1A 120
Hillyard Pl. SW20 . . . . .7D 134
Hillyard Rd. W7 . . . . .5J 77
Hillyard St. SW9 . . . . .1A 120
Hillyfield E17 . . . . .2A 50
Hillyfield Cl. E9 . . . . .5A 68
Hilly Flds. Cres. SE4 . . . . .3C 122
  SE13 . . . . .3C 122
Hilsea Point SW15 . . . . .1D 134
Hilsea St. E5 . . . . .4J 67
Hilton Av. N12 . . . . .5G 31
Hilton Ho. SE4 . . . . .4K 121
  W13 . . . . .6C 78
Hilversum Cres. SE22 . . . . .5E 120
Himalaya Palace Cinema 1D 94
Himley Rd. SW17 . . . . .5C 136

Hinchinbrook Ho. NW6 . . . . .1K 81
  (off Mortimer Cres.)
Hinchley Cl. KT10: Hin W 4A 162
Hinchley Dr. KT10: Hin W 3A 162
Hinchley Mnr. KT10: Hin W 3A 162
Hinchley Way KT10: Hin W 3A 162
HINCHLEY WOOD 4G 121
Hinckley Rd. SE15 . . . . .4G 121
Hind Ct. EC4 . . . . .1K 13 (6A 84)
Hind Cres. DA8: Erith 6K 109
Hinde Ho. W1 . . . . .7H 5
  (off Hinde St.)
Hinde M. W1 . . . . .7H 5
Hindes Rd. HA1: Harr 5H 41
Hinde St. W1 . . . . .7H 5 (6E 82)
Hind Gro. E14 . . . . .6C 86
Hindhead Cl. N16 . . . . .1E 66
  UB8: Hil .5D 74
Hindhead Gdns. UB5: N'olt 1C 76
Hindhead Point SW15 . . . . .1D 134
Hindhead Way SM6: W'gton 5J 167
Hind Ho. N7 . . . . .4A 66
  SE14 . . . . .6K 103
  (off Myers La.)
Hindle Ho. E8 . . . . .5F 67
Hindlip Ho. SW8 . . . . .1H 119
Hindmans Rd. SE22 . . . . .5G 121
Hindmans Way RM9: Dag 4F 91
Hindmarsh Cl. E1 . . . . .7G 85
Hindon Ct. SW1 . . . . .3A 18
Hindrey Rd. E5 . . . . .5H 67
Hindsley's Pl. SE23 . . . . .2J 139
Hinkler Rd. HA3: Kenton 3D 42
Hinksey Path SE2 . . . . .2D 108
Hinstock NW6 . . . . .1K 81
  (off Belsize Rd.)
Hinstock Rd. SE18 . . . . .6G 107
Hinton Av. TW4: Houn 4B 112
Hinton Cl. SE9 . . . . .1C 142
Hinton Ct. E10 . . . . .2D 68
  (off Leyton Grange Est.)
Hinton Rd. N18 . . . . .4K 33
  SE24 . . . . .3C 120
  SM6: W'gton 6G 167
  SW9 . . . . .3B 120
Hippisley Ct. TW7: Isle 3K 113
Hippodrome M. W11 . . . . .7G 81
Hippodrome Pl. W11 . . . . .7G 81
Hiroshima Prom. SE7 . . . . .3A 106
Hirst Cl. SW1 . . . . .7J 17 (6F 101)
Hirst Cres. HA9: Wemb 3E 60
Hitcham Rd. E17 . . . . .7B 50
Hitchcock Cl. TW17: Shep 3B 146
Hitchcock La. E20 . . . . .6E 68
Hitchin La. HA7: Stan 7J 27
Hitchin Rd. HA7: Stan 7K 27
Hitchin Sq. E3 . . . . .2A 86
Hitch St. RM9: Dag 3E 90
Hithe Gro. SE16 . . . . .3J 103
Hitherbroom Rd. UB3: Hayes 1J 93
Hither Farm Rd. SE3 . . . . .3A 124
Hitherfield Rd. RM8: Dag 2E 72
  SW16 . . . . .2K 137
HITHER GREEN 6F 123
Hither Green Crematorium 2H 141
Hither Grn. La. SE13 . . . . .5E 122
Hithermoor Rd. TW19: Stanw M . .7B 174
Hitherwell Dr. HA3: Hrw W 1H 41
Hitherwood Ct. NW9 . . . . .2A 44
  (off Charcot Rd.)
Hitherwood Dr. SE19 . . . . .4F 139
Hittard Ct. SE17 . . . . .6D 102
  (off Red Lion Row)
The Hive 1E 40
Hive Cl. WD23: B Hea 2C 26
The Hive Football & Fitness Cen. . .1E 42
Hive Rd. WD23: B Hea 2C 26
HMP Belmarsh 2J 107
HMP Brixton 6J 119
HMP Isis 6K 107
HMP Pentonville 6K 65
HMP Thameside 3J 107
HMP Wandsworth 7B 118

HMP Wormwood Scrubs 6C 80
HMS Belfast 4G 15 (1E 102)
HMYOI Feltham 3F 129
Hoadly Ho. SE1 . . . . .5C 14
  (off Union St.)
Hoadly Rd. SW16 . . . . .3H 137
Hobart Cl. N20 . . . . .2H 31
  UB4: Yead 4B 76
Hobart Ct. CR2: S Croy 5D 168
  (off Sth Pk. Hill Rd.)
  IG8: Wfd G 4C 36
Hobart Dr. UB4: Yead 4B 76
Hobart Gdns. CR7: Thor H 3D 156
Hobart La. UB4: Yead 4B 76
Hobart Pl. SW1 . . . . .1J 17 (3F 101)
  TW10: Rich 7F 115
Hobart Rd. IG6: Ilf 2G 53
  KT4: Wor Pk 3D 164
  RM9: Dag 4D 72
  UB4: Yead 4B 76
Hobbayne Rd. W7 . . . . .6H 77
Hobbes Wlk. SW15 . . . . .5D 116
Hobbs Ct. SE1 . . . . .6K 15
  (off Mill St.)
Hobbs Grn. N2 . . . . .3A 46
Hobbs M. IG3: Ilf 2K 71
Hobbs Pl. N1 . . . . .1E 84
Hobbs Pl. Est. N1 . . . . .2E 84
  (off Hobbs Pl.)
Hobbs Rd. SE27 . . . . .4C 138
Hobby Ho. SE1 . . . . .4H 103
Hobday St. EN3: Pond E 5E 24
Hobday St. E14 . . . . .6D 86
Hobhouse Ct. SW1 . . . . .3D 12
  (off Suffolk St.)
Hobill Wlk. KT5: Surb 6F 151
Hoblands End BR7: Chst 6J 143
Hobson's Pl. E1 . . . . .5G 85
Hobury St. SW10 . . . . . . .7A 16 (6A 100)
Hocker St. E2 . . . . .2J 9 (3F 85)
Hockett Cl. SE8 . . . . .4B 104
  (off Grove St.)
Hockington Ct. EN5: New Bar 4E 20
Hockley Av. E6 . . . . .2C 88
Hockley Ct. E18 . . . . .1J 51
Hockley M. IG11: Bark 3J 89
Hockliffe Ho. W10 . . . . .5E 80
  (off Sutton Way)
Hockney Ct. SE16 . . . . .5H 103
  (off Rossetti Rd.)
Hocroft Av. NW2 . . . . .3H 63
Hocroft Ct. NW2 . . . . .3H 63
Hocroft Rd. NW2 . . . . .4H 63
Hocroft Wlk. NW2 . . . . .3H 63
Hodder Dr. UB6: G'frd 2K 77
Hoddesdon Rd. DA17: Belv 5G 109
Hodes Row NW3 . . . . .4E 64
Hodford Rd. NW11 . . . . .1H 63
Hodgkin Cl. SE28 . . . . .7D 90
Hodgkins Cl. SE5 . . . . .7D 102
  (off Dobson Wlk.)
Hodgkins M. HA7: Stan 5G 27
Hodister Cl. SE5 . . . . .7C 102
Hodnet Gro. SE16 . . . . .4K 103
Hodson Cl. HA2: Harr 3D 58
Hoecroft Ct. EN3: Enf W 1D 24
  (off Hoe La.)
Hoe La. EN1: Enf 1B 24
  EN3: Enf W 1C 24
Hoe St. E17 . . . . .4C 50
Hoever Ho. SE6 . . . . .4E 140
Hoey Ct. E3 . . . . .4D 86
  (off Barry Blandford Way)
Hoffmann Gdns. CR2: Sels 7H 169
Hoffman Sq. N1 . . . . .1F 9
Hofland Rd. W14 . . . . .3K 49
Hofland Rd. W14 . . . . .3G 99
Hogan M. W2 . . . . .5A 4 (5A 82)
Hogan Way E5 . . . . .2G 67
Hogarth Av. TW15: Ashf 6E 128
Hogarth Bus. Pk. W4 . . . . .6A 98
Hogarth Cl. E16 . . . . .5B 88
  W5 . . . . .5E 78

Hogarth Ct. E1 . . . . .6G 85
(off Batty St.)
NW1 .7G 65
(off St Pancras Way)
SE19 .4F 139
TW5: Hest 7C 94
Hogarth Cres. CR0: C'don 7C 156
SW19 . . . . .1B 154
Hogarth Gdns. TW5: Hest 7E 94
The Hogarth Health Club 4B 98
Hogarth Hill NW11 . . . . .4H 45
Hogarth Ho. EC1 . . . . .6C 8
(off Bartholomew Cl.)
SW1 .4D 18
(off Erasmus St.)
UB5: N'olt 2B 76
(off Gallery Gdns.)
Hogarth Ind. Est. NW10 . . . . .4C 80
Hogarth La. W4 . . . . .6A 98
Hogarth Pl. SW5 . . . . .4K 99
(off Hogarth Rd.)
Hogarth Rd. HA8: Edg 2G 43
RM8: Dag 5B 72
SW5 .4K 99
HOGARTH RDBT. 6A 98
Hogarth's House 6A 98
(off Hogarth La.)
Hogarth Way TW12: Hamp 1G 149
Hog Hill Rd. RM5: Col R 1F 55
Hogsmill Ho. KT1: King T 3F 151
(off Vineyard Cl.)
Hogsmill La. KT1: King T 3F 151
Hogsmill Local Nature Reserve . . .5H 163
Hogsmill Wlk. KT1: King T 3E 150
(off Penrhyn Rd.)
Hogsmill Way KT19: Ewe 5J 163
Holbeach Cl. NW9 . . . . .1A 44
Holbeach Gdns. DA15: Sidc 6J 125
Holbeach M. SW12 . . . . .1F 137
Holbeach Rd. SE6 . . . . .7C 122
Holbeck Rd. W13 . . . . .1B 96
Holbeck Row SE15 . . . . .7G 103
Holbein Ho. SW1 . . . . .5G 17
(off Holbein M.)
Holbein M. SW1 . . . . . .5G 17 (5E 100)
Holbein Pl. SW1 . . . . .4G 17 (4E 100)
Holbein Ter. RM8: Dag 4C 72
(off Marlborough Rd.)
Holberton Gdns. NW10 . . . . .3D 80
HOLBORN 7F 7 (6J 83)
Holborn EC1 . . . . .6J 7 (5A 84)
Holborn Bars EC1 . . . . .6J 7
(off Holborn)
Holborn Cir. EC1 . . . . .6K 7 (5A 84)
Holborn Cl. NW7 . . . . .4G 29
Holborn Ho. W12 . . . . .6D 80
Holborn Pl. WC1 . . . . . .6G 7 (5K 83)
Holborn Rd. E13 . . . . .4K 87
Holborn Viaduct EC1 . . . .6K 7 (5B 84)
Holborn Way CR4: Mitc 2D 154
Holbrook Cl. EN1: Enf 1A 24
N19 .1F 65
Holbrooke Ct. N7 . . . . .4J 65
Holbrooke Pl. TW10: Rich 5D 114
Holbrook Ho. BR7: Chst 1H 161
Holbrook La. BR7: Chst 7H 143
Holbrook Rd. E15 . . . . .2H 87
Holbrook Way BR2: Broml 6D 160
Holburne Cl. SE3 . . . . .1A 124
Holburne Gdns. SE3 . . . . .1B 124
Holburne Rd. SE3 . . . . .1A 124
Holcombe Hill NW7 . . . . .3H 29
Holcombe Ho. SW9 . . . . .3J 119
(off Landor Rd.)
Holcombe Pl. SE4 . . . . .3A 122
(off St Asaph Rd.)
Holcombe Rd. IG1: Ilf 7E 52
N17 .3F 49
Holcombe St. W6 . . . . .4D 98
Holcote Cl. DA17: Belv 3E 108
Holcroft Ct. W1 . . . . .5A 6
Holcroft Ho. SW11 . . . . .3B 118
Holcroft Rd. E9 . . . . .7J 67

Holden Av. N12 . . . . .5E 30
NW9 .1J 61
Holdenby Rd. SE4 . . . . .5A 122
Holden Cl. RM8: Dag 3B 72
Holden Ho. N1 . . . . .1C 84
(off Prebend St.)
SE8 .7C 104
Holdenhurst Av. N12 . . . . .7F 31
Holden Point E15 . . . . .6F 69
(off Waddington St.)
Holden Rd. N12 . . . . .5E 30
Holden St. SW11 . . . . .2E 118
Holder Cl. N3 . . . . .7E 30
Holdernesse Cl. TW7: Isle 1A 114
Holdernesse Rd. SW17 . . . . .3D 136
Holderness Ho. SE5 . . . . .3E 120
Holderness Way SE27 . . . . .5B 138
HOLDERS HILL 2F 45
Holder's Hill Av. NW4 . . . . .2F 45
HOLDERS HILL CIR. 7B 30
Holders Hill Cres. NW4 . . . . .2F 45
Holders Hill Dr. NW4 . . . . .3F 45
Holder's Hill Gdns. NW4 . . . . .2G 45
Holders Hill Pde. NW7 . . . . .1G 45
Holders Hill Rd. NW4 . . . . .2F 45
NW7 .2F 45
Holford Ho. SE16 . . . . .4H 103
(off Camilla Rd.)
WC1 . . . . .1H 7
(off Gt. Percy St.)
Holford M. WC1 . . . . .1J 7
Holford Pl. WC1 . . . . . .1H 7 (3K 83)
Holford Rd. NW3 . . . . .3A 64
Holford St. WC1 . . . . . .1J 7 (3K 83)
Holford Way SW15 . . . . .6C 116
Holford Yd. WC1 . . . . .1J 7
(off Cruikshank St.)
Holgate Av. SW11 . . . . .3B 118
Holgate Gdns. RM10: Dag 6G 73
Holgate Rd. RM10: Dag 5G 73
Holgate St. SE7 . . . . .3B 106
Holinser Ter. N5 . . . . .1D 96
Hollam Ho. N8 . . . . .4K 47
Hollar Ho. SM2: Sutt 7J 165
SW20 . . . . .1B 152
Holland Cl. BR2: Hayes 2H 171
EN5: New Bar 7G 21
HA7: Stan 5G 27
RM7: Rom 5J 55
Holland Ct. E17 . . . . .4E 50
(off Evelyn Rd.)
KT6: Surb 7D 150
NW7 .6H 29
Holland Dr. SE23 . . . . .3A 140
Holland Dwellings WC2 . . . . .7F 7
(off Newton St.)
Holland Gdns. SE9: Sidc 1H 143
TW8: Bford 6E 96
W14 .3G 99
Hollandgreen Pl. W8 . . . . .3J 99
Holland Gro. SW9 . . . . .7A 102
Holland Ho. E4 . . . . .4K 35
NW10 . . . . .2D 80
(off Holland Rd.)
HOLLAND PARK 1H 99
Holland Pk. 2H 99
Holland Pk. W11 . . . . .1G 99
Holland Pk. Av. IG3: Ilf 6J 53
W11 .2G 99
Holland Pk. Ct. W14 . . . . .2G 99
(off Holland Pk. Gdns.)
Holland Pk. Gdns. W14 . . . . .2G 99
Holland Pk. Mans. W14 . . . . .1G 99
(off Holland Pk. Gdns.)
Holland Pk. M. W11 . . . . .1G 99
Holland Pk. Rd. W14 . . . . .3H 99
Holland Pk. Ter. W11 . . . . .1G 99
(off Portland Rd.)
Holland Pk. Theatre (Open Air) . . .2H 99
Holland Pas. N1 . . . . .1C 84
(off Basire St.)

Holland Pl. W8 . . . . .2K 99
(off Kensington Chu. St.)
Holland Pl. Chambers W8 . . . . . . .2K 99
(off Holland Pl.)
Holland Ri. Ho. SW9 . . . . .7K 101
(off Clapham Rd.)
Holland Rd. E6 . . . . .1D 88
E15 . . . . .3G 87
HA0: Wemb 6D 60
NW10 . . . . .1C 80
SE25 .5G 157
W14 .2F 99
The Hollands KT4: Wor Pk 1B 164
TW13: Hanw 4B 130
Holland St. SE1 . . . . . .4B 14 (1B 102)
W8 . . . . .2J 99
Holland Vs. Rd. W14 . . . . .2G 99
Holland Wlk. HA7: Stan 5F 27
N19 . . . . .1H 65
(off Calverley Gro.)
N19 . . . . .1H 65
(Up. Holloway)
W8 . . . . .1H 99
Holland Way BR2: Hayes 2H 171
Hollar Rd. N16 . . . . .3F 67
Hollen St. W1 . . . . .7C 6 (6H 83)
Holles Cl. TW12: Hamp 6E 130
Holles Ho. SW9 . . . . .2A 120
Holles St. W1 . . . . .7K 5 (6F 83)
Hollickwood Av. N12 . . . . .6J 31
Holliday Sq. SW11 . . . . .3B 118
(off Fowler Cl.)
Hollidge Way RM10: Dag 7H 73
The Hollies E11 . . . . .5J 51
(off New Wanstead)
HA3: W'stone 4A 42
N20 . . . . .1G 31
Hollies Av. DA15: Sidc 2K 143
Hollies Cl. SW16 . . . . .6A 138
TW1: Twick 2K 131
Hollies End NW7 . . . . .5H 29
Hollies Rd. W5 . . . . .4C 96
Hollies Way SW12 . . . . .7E 118
Holligrave Rd. BR1: Broml 1J 159
Hollingbourne Av. DA7: Bex 1F 127
Hollingbourne Gdns. W13 . . . . . . .5B 78
Hollingbourne Rd. SE24 . . . . .5C 120
Hollingsworth Ct. KT6: Surb 7D 150
Hollingsworth Rd. CR0: C'don 6H 169
Hollington Cl. KT8: W Mole 4D 148
Hollington Cres. KT3: N Mald 6B 152
Hollington Rd. E6 . . . . .3D 88
N17 . . . . .2G 49
Hollingworth Cl. KT8: W Mole 4D 148
Hollingworth Rd. BR5: Pet W 6F 161
Hollins Ho. N7 . . . . .4J 65
Hollisfield WC1 . . . . .2F 7
(off Cromer St.)
Hollister Ho. NW6 . . . . .3J 81
(off Kilburn Pk. Rd.)
Hollman Gdns. SW16 . . . . .6B 138
The Hollow IG8: Wfd G 4C 36
HOLLOWAY 3J 65
Holloway Cl. UB7: Harm 5A 92
Holloway Ho. NW2 . . . . .3E 62
(off Stoll Cl.)
Holloway La. UB7: Harm, W Dray . .2E 174
Holloway Rd. E6 . . . . .3D 88
E11 . . . . .3F 69
N7 . . . . .4K 65
N19 . . . . .2H 65
Holloway St. TW3: Houn 3F 113
Hollowfield Wlk. UB5: N'olt 6C 58
The Hollows TW8: Bford 6F 97
Holly Av. HA7: Stan 2E 42
KT12: Walt T 7B 148
TW12: Hamp 5E 130
Hollyberry La. NW3 . . . . .4A 64
Hollybrake Cl. BR7: Chst 7H 143
Hollybush Cl. E11 . . . . .5J 51
HA3: Hrw W 1J 41
Hollybush Gdns. E2 . . . . .3H 85

Holly Bush Hill NW3 . . . . .4A 64
Hollybush Hill E11 . . . . .6H 51
Hollybush Ho. E2 . . . . .3H 85
Holly Bush La. TW12: Hamp 7D 130
Hollybush Pl. E2 . . . . .3H 85
Hollybush Rd. KT2: King T 5E 132
Holly Bush Steps NW3 . . . . .4A 64
(off Holly Mt.)
Hollybush St. E13 . . . . .3K 87
Holly Bush Va. NW3 . . . . .4A 64
Hollybush Wlk. SW9 . . . . .4B 120
Holly Cl. BR3: Beck 4E 158
IG9: Buck H 3G 37
KT19: Eps 7K 163
SM6: W'gton 7F 167
TW13: Hanw 5C 130
TW16: Sun 3K 147
Holly Cott. M. UB8: Hil 5C 74
Holly Ct. DA14: Sidc 4B 144
(off Sidcup Hill)
N15 . . . . .4E 48
SE10 .3H 105
SM2: Sutt 7J 165
Holly Cres. BR3: Beck 5B 158
IG8: Wfd G 7A 36
Hollycroft Av. HA9: Wemb 2F 61
NW3 .3J 63
Hollycroft Cl. CR2: S Croy 5E 168
UB7: Sip 6C 92
Hollycroft Gdns. UB7: Sip 6C 92
Hollydale Cl. UB5: N'olt 4F 59
Hollydale Dr. BR2: Broml 3D 172
Hollydale Rd. SE15 . . . . .1J 121
Hollydene BR2: Broml 1H 159
(off Beckenham La.)
SE13 .6F 123
SE15 .1H 121
Hollydown Way E11 . . . . .3F 69
Holly Dr. E4 . . . . .7J 25
Holly Farm Rd. UB2: S'hall 5C 94
Hollyfield Av. N11 . . . . .5J 31
Hollyfield Rd. KT5: Surb 7F 151
Holly Gdns. DA7: Bex 4J 127
UB7: W Dray 2B 92
Holly Gro. HA5: Pinn 1C 40
NW9 .7J 43
SE15 .2F 121
Hollygrove WD23: Bush 1C 26
Hollygrove Cl. TW3: Houn 4D 112
Holly Hedge Ter. SE13 . . . . .5F 123
Holly Hill N21 . . . . .6E 22
NW3 .4A 64
Holly Hill Rd. DA8: Erith 5H 109
DA17: Belv, Erith 5H 109
Holly Ho. TW8: Bford 6C 96
W10 .4G 81
(off Hawthorn Wlk.)
Holly La. IG3: Ilf 2A 72
Holly Lodge HA1: Harr 5H 41
W8 . . . . .2J 99
(off Thornwood Gdns.)
Holly Lodge Gdns. N6 . . . . .2E 64
Holly Lodge Mans. N6 . . . . .2E 64
Hollymead SM5: Cars 3D 166
Holly M. SW10 . . . . .6A 16 (5A 100)
Holly Mt. NW3 . . . . .4A 64
Hollymount Cl. SE10 . . . . .1E 122
Holly Pde. TW13: Felt 3H 129
(off High St.)
Holly Pk. N3 . . . . .3H 45
N4 . . . . .7J 47
(not continuous)
Holly Pk. Est. N4 . . . . .7K 47
Holly Pk. Gdns. N3 . . . . .3J 45
Holly Pk. Rd. N11 . . . . .5K 31
W7 . . . . .1K 95
Holly Pl. NW3 . . . . .4A 64
(off Holly Berry La.)
Holly Rd. E11 . . . . .7H 51
TW1: Twick 1K 131
TW3: Houn 4F 113
TW12: Hamp H 6G 131
W4 . . . . .4K 97

Holly St. E8 . . . . .7F 67
Holly Ter. N6 . . . . .1E 64
Holly Tree Cl. SW19 . . . . .1F 135
Holly Tree Cres. SM5: Cars 1D 166
Holly Tree Ho. SE4 . . . . .3B 122
　　　　　　(off Brockley Rd.)
Hollytree Pde. DA14: Sidc 6C 144
　　　　　　(off Sidcup Hill)
Hollyview Cl. NW4 . . . . .6C 44
Holly Village N6 . . . . .2F 65
Holly Vs. W6 . . . . .3D 98
　　　　　　(off Wellesley Av.)
Holly Wlk. EN2: Enf 3H 23
　　NW3 . . . . .4A 64
Holly Way CR4: Mitc 4H 155
Hollywood Bowl
　　Dagenham 1E 90
　　Finchley 7G 31
　　The O2 . . . . .1G 105
　　Surrey Quays 3K 103
　　Tolworth 2H 163
Hollywood Ct. SW10 . . . . .6A 100
　　　　　　(off Hollywood Rd.)
　　W5 .7F 79
Hollywood Gdns. UB4: Yead 6K 75
Hollywood M. SW10 . . . . .6A 100
Hollywood Rd. E4 . . . . .5F 35
　　SW10 . . . . .6A 100
Hollywood Way IG8: Wfd G 7A 36
Holman Cl. KT17: Ewe 7C 164
Holman Dr. UB2: S'hall 1H 95
Holman Ho. E2 . . . . .3K 85
　　　　　　(off Roman Rd.)
Holman Hunt Ho. W6 . . . . .5G 99
　　　　　　(off Field Rd.)
Holman Rd. KT19: Ewe 5J 163
　　SW11 . . . . .2B 118
Holmbank Dr. TW17: Shep 4G 147
Holmbridge Gdns.
　　EN3: Pond E 4E 24
Holmbrook NW1 . . . . .2G 83
　　　　　　(off Eversholt St.)
Holmbrook Dr. NW4 . . . . .5F 45
Holmbury Ct. CR2: S Croy 5E 168
　　SW17 . . . . .3D 136
　　SW19 . . . . .7C 136
Holmbury Gdns. UB3: Hayes 1H 93
Holmbury Gro. CR0: Sels 7B 170
Holmbury Ho. SE24 . . . . .5B 120
Holmbury Mnr. DA14: Sidc 4A 144
Holmbury Pk. BR1: Broml 7C 142
Holmbury Vw. E5 . . . . .1H 67
Holmbush Rd. SW15 . . . . .6G 117
Holmcote Gdns. N5 . . . . .5C 66
Holm Cl. SE12 . . . . .3K 141
Holmcroft Ho. E17 . . . . .4D 50
Holmcroft Way BR2: Broml 5D 160
Holmdale Gdns. NW4 . . . . .5F 45
Holmdale Rd. BR7: Chst 5G 143
　　NW6 . . . . .5J 63
Holmdale Ter. N15 . . . . .6E 48
Holmdene N12 . . . . .5E 30
Holmdene Av. HA2: Harr 3F 41
　　NW7 . . . . .6H 29
　　SE24 . . . . .5C 120
Holmdene Cl. BR3: Beck 2E 158
Holmdene Ct. BR1: Broml 3C 160
Holmead Rd. SW6 . . . . .7K 99
Holmebury Cl. WD23: B Hea 2D 26
Holme Ct. TW7: Isle 3A 114
Holmefield Ho. W10 . . . . .4G 81
　　　　　　(off Hazlewood Cres.)
Holme Ho. SE15 . . . . .7H 103
　　　　　　(off Studholme St.)
Holme Lacey Rd. SE12 . . . . .6H 123
Holmeoak Av. RM13: Rain 2K 91
Holme Rd. E6 . . . . .1C 88
Holmes Av. E17 . . . . .3B 50
Holmes Cl. SE22 . . . . .4G 121
Holmesdale Av. SW14 . . . . .3H 115
Holmesdale Cl. SE25 . . . . .3F 157
Holmesdale Ho. NW6 . . . . .1J 81
　　　　　　(off Kilburn Vale)

Holmesdale Rd. CR0: C'don 5D 156
　　DA7: Bex 2D 126
　　N6 . . . . .7F 47
　　SE25 . . . . .5D 156
　　TW9: Kew 1F 115
　　TW11: Tedd 7C 132
Holmesdale Rd. SE23 . . . . .6A 122
Holmes Pl. SW10 . . . . .6A 100
Holmes Rd. NW5 . . . . .5F 65
　　SW19 . . . . .7A 136
　　TW1: Twick 2K 131
Holmes Ter. SE1 . . . . .6J 13
Holmeswood SM2: Sutt 6K 165
Holmeswood Ct. N2 . . . . .2A 48
Holme Way HA7: Stan 6E 26
Holmewood Gdns. SW2 . . . . .7K 119
Holmewood Rd. SE25 . . . . .3E 156
　　SW2 . . . . .7K 119
Holmfield Av. NW4 . . . . .5F 45
Holmfield Cl. NW3 . . . . .5C 64
Holm Gro. UB10: Hil 7C 56
Holmhurst SE13 . . . . .6F 123
Holmhurst Rd. DA17: Belv 5H 109
Holmlea Ct. CR0: C'don 4D 168
　　　　　　(off Chatsworth Rd.)
Holmleigh Ct. EN3: Pond E 4D 24
Holmleigh Rd. N16 . . . . .1E 66
Holmleigh Rd. Est. N16 . . . . .1E 66
Holm Oak Cl. SW15 . . . . .6H 117
Holm Oak M. SW4 . . . . .5J 119
Holmoaks Ho. BR3: Beck 2E 158
Holmsdale Ho. E14 . . . . .7D 86
　　　　　　(off Poplar High St.)
　　N11 .4A 32
　　　　　　(off Coppies Gro.)
Holmshaw Cl. SE26 . . . . .4A 140
Holmside Rd. SW12 . . . . .6E 118
Holmsley Cl. KT3: N Mald 6B 152
Holmsley Ho. SW15 . . . . .7B 116
　　　　　　(off Tangley Gro.)
Holmstall Av. HA8: Edg 3J 43
Holmstall Pde. HA8: Edg 2J 43
Holmstead Ct. CR2: S Croy 5D 168
Holm Wlk. SE3 . . . . .2J 123
Holmwood Cl. HA2: Harr 3G 41
　　SM2: Cheam 7F 165
　　UB5: N'olt 6F 59
Holmwood Gdns. N3 . . . . .2J 45
　　SM6: W'gton 6F 167
Holmwood Gro. NW7 . . . . .5E 28
Holmwood Rd. IG3: Ilf 2J 71
　　KT9: Chess 5D 162
　　SM2: Cheam 7E 164
Holmwood Vs. SE7 . . . . .5J 105
Holne Chase N2 . . . . .6A 46
　　SM4: Mord 6H 153
Holness Rd. E15 . . . . .6H 69
The Holocaust Memorial Garden
　　. . . . . .6F 11 (2D 100)
Holroyd Rd. KT10: Clay 7A 162
　　SW15 . . . . .4E 116
Holsgrove Ho. W3 . . . . .1A 98
Holst Cl. SE1 . . . . .1J 19
　　　　　　(off Kennington Rd.)
Holstein Way DA18: Erith 3D 108
Holst Ho. W12 . . . . .6D 80
　　　　　　(off Du Cane Rd.)
Holst Mans. SW13 . . . . .6E 98
Holstock Rd. IG1: Ilf 2G 71
Holst Rd. W3 . . . . .5J 79
Holsworth Cl. HA2: Harr 5G 41
Holsworthy Ho. E3 . . . . .3D 86
　　　　　　(off Talwin St.)
Holsworthy Sq. WC1 . . . . .4H 7
Holsworthy Way KT9: Chess 5C 162
The Holt SM4: Mord 4J 153
　　SM6: W'gton 4G 167
Holt Cl. BR7: Chst 5D 142
　　DA14: Sidc 4E 144
　　N10 .4E 46
　　SE28 . . . . .7B 90
Holt Ct. SE10 . . . . .6E 104
　　　　　　(off Horseferry Pl.)

Holt Ho. SW2 . . . . .6A 120
Holton St. E1 . . . . .4K 85
Holt Rd. E16 . . . . .1C 106
　　HA0: Wemb 3B 60
Holtwhite Av. EN2: Enf 2H 23
Holtwhite's Hill EN2: Enf 1G 23
Holwell Pl. HA5: Pinn 4C 40
Holwood Est. BR2: Kes 6C 172
Holwood Pk. Av. BR6: Farnb 4D 172
Holwood Pl. SW4 . . . . .4H 119
Holybourne Av. SW15 . . . . .7C 116
Holycross Cl. SM4: Mord 7J 153
Holyhead Cl. E6 . . . . .5D 88
Holyhead Ct. KT1: King T 4D 150
　　　　　　(off Anglesea Rd.)
Holyoake Ct. SE16 . . . . .2B 104
Holyoake Ho. W5 . . . . .4C 78
Holyoake Wlk. N2 . . . . .3A 46
　　W5 .4C 78
Holyoak Rd. SE11 . . . . .4B 102
Holyport Rd. SW6 . . . . .7F 99
Holyrood Av. HA2: Harr 4C 58
Holyrood Ct. NW1 . . . . .1F 83
　　　　　　(off Gloucester Av.)
Holyrood Gdns. HA8: Edg 3H 43
Holyrood M. E16 . . . . .1J 105
Holyrood Rd. EN5: New Bar 6F 21
Holyrood St. SE1 . . . . .5G 15 (1E 102)
Holywell Cen. EC2 . . . . .3G 9
　　　　　　(off Phipp St.)
Holywell Cl. BR6: Chels 4K 173
　　SE3 .6J 105
　　SE16 . . . . .5H 103
　　TW19: Stanw 1A 128
Holywell La. EC2 . . . . .3H 9 (4E 84)
Holywell Row EC2 . . . . . .4G 9 (4E 84)
Holywell Way TW19: Stanw 1A 128
Homan Ct. N12 . . . . .4G 31
Homebush Ho. E4 . . . . .7J 25
Homecedars Ho. WD23: B Hea . . .1C 26
Home Cl. SM5: Cars 2D 166
　　UB5: N'olt 3D 76
Home Ct. KT6: Surb 5D 150
Homecroft Rd. N22 . . . . .1C 48
　　SE26 . . . . .5J 139
Home Farm Cl. KT7: T Ditt 7K 149
　　TW17: Shep 4G 147
Homefarm Rd. W7 . . . . .6J 77
Homefield SM4: Mord 4J 153
Homefield Av. IG2: Ilf 5J 53
Homefield Cl. NW10 . . . . .6J 61
　　UB4: Yead 4B 76
Homefield Gdns. CR4: Mitc 2A 154
　　N2 . . . . .3B 46
Homefield Ho. SE23 . . . . .3J 139
Homefield M. BR3: Beck 1C 158
Homefield Pk. SM1: Sutt 6K 165
Homefield Pl. CR0: C'don 2F 169
Homefield Rd. BR1: Broml 1A 160
　　HA0: Wemb 4A 60
　　HA8: Edg 6E 28
　　KT12: Walt T 7C 148
　　SW19 . . . . .6F 135
　　W4 . . . . .5B 98
Homefield St. N1 . . . . . .1G 9 (2E 84)
Homefirs Ho. HA9: Wemb 3F 61
Home Gdns. RM10: Dag 3J 73
Homeheather Ho. IG4: Ilf 5D 52
Home Lea BR6: Orp 5K 173
Homelands Dr. SE19 . . . . .7E 138
Home Lea BR6: Chels 5K 173
Homeleigh Cl. SW16 . . . . .3J 137
Homeleigh Ct. SW16 . . . . .3J 137
Homeleigh Rd. SE15 . . . . .5K 121
Home Mead HA7: Stan 1C 42
Home Mdw. M. SE22 . . . . .5G 121
Homemead Rd. BR2: Broml 5D 160
　　CR0: C'don 6G 155
Home Pk. KT1: E Mos 5B 150
Home Pk. Ct. KT1: King T 4D 150
　　　　　　(off Palace Rd.)
Home Pk. Pde. KT1: Hamp W 2D 150
　　　　　　(off High St.)
Home Pk. Rd. SW19 . . . . .4H 135

Home Pk. Ter. KT1: Hamp W 2D 150
　　　　　　(off Hampton Ct. Rd.)
Home Pk. Wlk. KT1: King T 4D 150
Homer Cl. DA7: Bex 1J 127
Homer Dr. E14 . . . . .4C 104
Homer Rd. SW11 . . . . .2C 118
Homer Rd. CR0: C'don 6K 157
　　E9 . . . . .6A 68
Homer Row W1 . . . . .6D 4 (5C 82)
Homersham Rd. KT1: King T 2G 151
Homer St. W1 . . . . .6D 4 (5C 82)
HOMERTON 5K 67
Homerton Gro. E9 . . . . .5K 67
Homerton High St. E9 . . . . .5K 67
Homerton Rd. E9 . . . . .5A 68
Homerton Row E9 . . . . .5J 67
Homerton Ter. E9 . . . . .6J 67
　　　　　　(not continuous)
Homesdale Cl. E11 . . . . .5J 51
Homesdale Rd. BR1: Broml 4A 160
　　BR2: Broml 4A 160
　　BR5: Pet W 7J 161
Homesfield NW11 . . . . .5J 45
Homestall Rd. SE22 . . . . .5J 121
Homestead Cl. EN5: New Bar 5D 20
Homestead Paddock N14 . . . . . . .5A 22
Homestead Pk. NW2 . . . . .3B 62
Homestead Rd. RM8: Dag 2F 73
　　SW6 .7H 99
The Homesteads N11 . . . . .4A 32
Homevale Cl. BR2: Hayes 7H 159
Homewalk Ho. SE26 . . . . .4H 139
Homewaters Av. TW16: Sun 1H 147
Homewillow Cl. N21 . . . . .6G 23
Homewood Cl. TW12: Hamp 6D 130
Homewood Cres. BR7: Chst 6J 143
Homewoods SW12 . . . . .7G 119
Homildon Ho. SE26 . . . . .3G 139
Honduras St. EC1 . . . . . . .3C 8 (4C 84)
Honeybourne Rd. NW6 . . . . .5K 63
Honeybrook Rd. SW12 . . . . .7G 119
Honey Cl. RM10: Dag 6H 73
Honeycroft Hill UB10: Uxb 7A 56
Honeyden Rd. DA14: Sidc 6E 144
Honeyfield M. SE23 . . . . .3K 139
Honeyghan Ct. SE17 . . . . .5E 102
　　　　　　(off Sedan Way)
Honey Hill UB10: Uxb 7B 56
Honey La. EC2 . . . . .1D 14
Honey La. Ho. SW10 . . . . .6K 99
　　　　　　(off Finborough Rd.)
Honeyman Cl. NW6 . . . . .7F 63
Honeymead N8 . . . . .3J 47
　　　　　　(off Campsfield Rd.)
Honey M. RM7: Rom 5J 55
　　SE27 . . . . .4C 138
　　　　　　(off Norwood High St.)
Honeypot Bus. Cen. HA7: Stan . . .1E 42
Honeypot Cl. NW9 . . . . .4F 43
Honeypot La. HA7: Stan 7J 27
　　NW9 .1D 42
Honeysett Rd. N17 . . . . .2F 49
Honeysuckle Cl. UB1: S'hall 7C 76
Honeysuckle Cl. IG1: Ilf 6F 71
　　IG9: Buck H 3G 37
Honeysuckle Gdns. CR0: C'don . . .7K 157
　　E17 . . . . .3C 50
Honeysuckle La. N22 . . . . .2C 48
Honeywell Rd. SW11 . . . . .6D 118
Honeywood Ho. SE15 . . . . .1G 121
　　　　　　(off Goldsmith Rd.)
Honeywood Mus. 5D 166
Honeywood Rd. NW10 . . . . .2B 80
　　TW7: Isle 4A 114
Honeywood Wlk. SM5: Cars 4D 166
Honister Cl. HA7: Stan 1B 42
Honister Gdns. HA7: Stan 7G 27
Honister Pl. HA7: Stan 1B 42
Honiton Gdns. NW7 . . . . .7A 30
　　SE15 . . . . .2J 121
　　　　　　(off Gibbon Rd.)
Honiton Ho. EN3: Pond E 3E 24

Honiton Rd. DA16: Well 2K 125
  NW6 .2H 81
  RM7: Rom 6K 55
Honley Rd. SE6 . . . . .7D 122
Honnor Gdns. TW7: Isle 2H 113
HONOR OAK 6J 121
Honor Oak Crematorium 5K 121
HONOR OAK PARK 7A 122
Honor Oak Pk. SE23 . . . . .6J 121
Honor Oak Ri. SE23 . . . . .6J 121
Honor Oak Rd. SE23 . . . . .1J 139
Honour Gdns. RM8: Dag 4A 72
Honour Lea Av. E20 . . . . .5D 68
Hood Av. N14 . . . . .6A 22
  SW14 . . . . .5J 115
Hood Cl. CR0: C'don 1B 168
Hoodcote Gdns. N21 . . . . .7G 23
Hood Ct. EC4 . . . . .1K 13
Hood Ho. SE5 . . . . .4E 102
   (off Elmington Est.)
  SW1 . . . . .6C 18
   (off Dolphin Sq.)
Hood Point SE16 . . . . .2B 104
   (off Rotherhithe St.)
Hood Rd. SW20 . . . . .7B 134
Hood Wlk. RM7: Mawney 1H 55
HOOK 4D 162
The Hook EN5: New Bar 6G 21
Hooke Ct. SE10 . . . . .1E 122
   (off Winforton St.)
Hooke Ho. E3 . . . . .2A 86
   (off Gernon Rd.)
Hookers Rd. E17 . . . . .3K 49
Hook Farm Rd. BR2: Broml 5B 160
Hookham Ct. SW8 . . . . .1H 119
Hooking Grn. HA2: Harr 5F 41
HOOK JUNC. 3E 162
Hook La. DA16: Well 4K 125
Hook Ri. Nth. KT6: Surb 3E 162
Hook Ri. Sth. KT6: Surb 3E 162
Hook Ri. Sth. Ind. Pk. KT6: Surb . .3E 162
Hook Rd. KT6: Surb 2E 162
  KT9: Chess 5D 162
  KT19: Eps, Ewe 7J 163
Hooks Cl. SE15 . . . . .1H 121
Hooks Hall Dr. RM10: Dag 3J 73
Hookstone Way IG8: Wfd G 7G 37
Hook Wlk. HA8: Edg 6D 28
Hool Cl. NW9 . . . . .5J 43
Hooper Dr. UB8: Hil 5D 74
Hooper Ho. TW15: Ashf 3A 128
Hooper Rd. E16 . . . . .6J 87
Hooper's Ct. SW3 . . . . . .7E 10 (2D 100)
Hooper's M. W3 . . . . .1J 97
Hoopers M. WD23: Bush 1A 26
Hooper Sq. E1 . . . . .6G 85
   (off Hooper St.)
Hooper St. E1 . . . . .6G 85
Hoopers Yd. NW6 . . . . .1H 81
   (off Kimberley Rd.)
Hoop La. NW11 . . . . .7H 45
Hop Cl. HA0: Wemb 5A 60
   (off Brewery Cl.)
Hope Cl. IG8: Wfd G 6F 37
  N1 . . . . .6C 66
  NW4 . . . . .2E 44
  RM6: Chad H 4D 54
  SE12 . . . . .3K 141
  SM1: Sutt 5A 166
  TW8: Bford 5E 96
Hope Ct. NW10 . . . . .3F 81
   (off Chamberlayne Rd.)
  SE1 . . . . .5G 103
   (off Avocet Cl.)
Hopedale Rd. SE7 . . . . .6K 105
Hopefield Av. NW6 . . . . .2G 81
Hope Gdns. W3 . . . . .2H 97
Hope Ho. CR0: C'don 4E 168
   (off Steep Hill)
Hope La. SE9 . . . . .2F 143
Hope Pk. BR1: Broml 7H 141
Hopes Cl. TW5: Hest 6E 94
Hope Sq. EC2 . . . . .6G 9

Hope St. E14 . . . . .6G 87
  SW11 . . . . .3B 118
Hopetown St. E1 . . . . . . .6K 9 (5F 85)
Hopewell St. SE5 . . . . .7D 102
Hopewell Yd. SE5 . . . . .7D 102
   (off Hopewell St.)
Hope Wharf SE16 . . . . .2J 103
Hop Gdns. WC2 . . . . . .3E 12 (7J 83)
Hopgood St. W12 . . . . .1E 98
Hopground Ho. E20 . . . . .6E 68
   (off De Coubertin St.)
Hopkins Cl. N10 . . . . .7K 31
Hopkins Ho. E14 . . . . .6C 86
   (off Canton St.)
Hopkins M. E15 . . . . .1H 87
Hopkinsons Pl. NW1 . . . . .1E 82
Hopkins Rd. E10 . . . . .7D 50
Hopkins St. W1 . . . . . .1B 12 (6G 83)
Hoppers Rd. N13 . . . . .2F 33
  N21 . . . . .2F 33
Hoppett Rd. E4 . . . . .2B 36
Hopping La. N1 . . . . .6B 66
Hoppingwood Av. KT3: N Mald . .3A 152
Hoppner Rd. UB4: Hayes 2F 75
Hopps Ct. NW9 . . . . .2A 44
   (off Salk Cl.)
Hops Ho. E17 . . . . .5B 50
   (off Old Brewery Way)
Hop St. SE10 . . . . .4H 105
Hopton Ct. BR2: Hayes 1K 171
Hopton Gdns. KT3: N Mald 6C 152
Hopton Rd. SE18 . . . . .3F 107
  SW16 . . . . .5J 137
Hopton's Gdns. SE1 . . . . .4B 14
Hopton St. SE1 . . . . . . .3A 14 (7B 84)
Hoptree Cl. N12 . . . . .5E 30
Hopwood Cl. SW17 . . . . .3A 136
Hopwood Rd. SE17 . . . . .6D 102
Hopwood Wlk. E8 . . . . .7G 67
Horace Av. RM7: Rush G 1J 73
Horace Bldg. SW11 . . . . .7F 101
Horace Jones Ho. SE1 . . . . .5J 15
   (off Duchess Wlk.)
Horace Rd. E7 . . . . .4K 69
  IG6: Ilf 3G 53
  KT1: King T 3F 151
Horatio Ct. SE16 . . . . .1J 103
   (off Rotherhithe St.)
Horatio Ho. E2 . . . . .2F 85
   (off Horatio St.)
  W6 . . . . .5F 99
   (off Fulham Pal. Rd.)
Horatio Pl. E14 . . . . .1E 104
   (off Managers St.)
  SW19 . . . . .1J 153
Horatio St. E2 . . . . .2F 85
Horatius Way CR0: Wadd 5K 167
Horbury Cres. W11 . . . . .7J 81
Horbury M. W11 . . . . .7H 81
Horder Rd. SW6 . . . . .1G 117
Hordle Prom. Sth. SE15 . . . . . . .7F 103
   (off Quarley Way)
Horizon Bldg. E14 . . . . .7C 86
   (off Hertsmere Rd.)
Horizon Bus. Cen. N9 . . . . .2E 34
   (off Goodwin Rd.)
Horizon Ct. SM2: Cheam 7G 165
   (off Up. Mulgrave Rd.)
Horizon Ho. SW18 . . . . .3A 118
   (off Juniper Ct.)
Horizon Ind. Est. SE15 . . . . .6G 103
Horle Wlk. SE5 . . . . .2B 120
Horley Cl. DA6: Bex 5G 127
Horley Rd. SE9 . . . . .4C 142
Hormead Rd. W9 . . . . .4H 81
Hornbeam Cl. IG1: Ilf 5H 71
  IG9: Buck H 3G 37
  IG11: Bark 3A 90
  NW7 . . . . .3G 29
  SE11 . . . . .3J 19 (4A 102)
  UB5: N'olt 5D 58
Hornbeam Cres. TW8: Bford 7B 96
Hornbeam Gdns. KT3: N Mald . . .6C 152

Hornbeam Gro. E4 . . . . .3B 36
Hornbeam Ho. IG9: Buck H 3H 37
Hornbeam La. DA7: Bex 2J 127
Hornbeam Rd. IG9: Buck H 3G 37
  UB4: Yead 5A 76
Hornbeam Sq. E3 . . . . .1B 86
Hornbeams Ri. N11 . . . . .6K 31
Hornbeam Ter. SM5: Cars 1C 166
Hornbeam Wlk. TW10: Rich 2F 133
Hornbeam Way BR2: Broml 6E 160
Hornbean Ho. E15 . . . . .3G 87
   (off Manor Rd.)
Hornblower Cl. SE16 . . . . .3A 104
Hornbuckle Cl. HA2: Harr 2H 59
Hornby Cl. NW3 . . . . .7B 64
Hornby Ct. NW10 . . . . .6B 62
Hornby Ho. SE11 . . . . .7J 19
Horncastle Cl. SE12 . . . . .7J 123
Horncastle Rd. SE12 . . . . .7J 123
Hornchurch N17 . . . . .2D 48
   (off Gloucester Rd.)
Hornchurch Cl. KT2: King T 4D 132
Horndean Cl. SW15 . . . . .1C 134
Horndon Cl. RM5: Col R 1J 55
Horndon Grn. RM5: Col R 1J 55
Horndon Rd. RM5: Col R 1J 55
Horner Ho. N1 . . . . .1E 84
   (off Nuttall St.)
Horner La. CR4: Mitc 2B 154
Horne Rd. TW17: Shep 4C 146
Horner Sq. E1 . . . . .5J 9
   (within Old Spitalfields Mkt.)
Hornet Way E6 . . . . .5H 89
Horne Way SW15 . . . . .2E 116
Hornfair Rd. SE7 . . . . .6A 106
Horniman Dr. SE23 . . . . .1H 139
Horniman Gdns. 1H 139
Horniman Mus. 1H 139
Horning Cl. SE9 . . . . .4C 142
Horn La. IG8: Wfd G 6D 36
  SE10 . . . . .5J 105
   (not continuous)
  W3 . . . . .7J 79
   (not continuous)
Horn Link Way SE10 . . . . .4J 105
HORN PARK 5K 123
Horn Pk. Cl. SE12 . . . . .5K 123
Horn Pk. La. SE12 . . . . .5K 123
Hornscroft Cl. IG11: Bark 7J 71
Horns End Pl. HA5: Eastc 4A 40
HORNSEY 4J 47
Hornsey Cricket Club 5H 47
Hornsey La. N6 . . . . .1F 65
Hornsey La. Est. N19 . . . . .7H 47
Hornsey La. Gdns. N6 . . . . .7G 47
Hornsey Pk. Rd. N8 . . . . .3K 47
Hornsey Ri. N19 . . . . .7H 47
Hornsey Ri. Gdns. N19 . . . . .7H 47
Hornsey Rd. N7 . . . . .1J 65
  N19 .1J 65
Hornsey St. N7 . . . . .5K 65
HORNSEY VALE 5K 47
Hornshay St. SE15 . . . . .6J 103
Horns Rd. IG2: Ilf 5G 53
  IG6: Ilf 4H 53
Hornton Ct. W8 . . . . .2J 99
   (off Kensington High St.)
Hornton Pl. W8 . . . . .2K 99
Hornton St. W8 . . . . .2J 99
Horsa Rd. DA8: Erith 7H 109
  SE12 . . . . .7A 124
Horse & Dolphin Yd. W1 . . . . . . .2D 12
Horsebridge Cl. RM9: Dag 1E 90
Horsecroft Rd. HA8: Edg 7E 28
Horse Fair KT1: King T 2D 150
Horseferry Pl. SE10 . . . . .6E 104
Horseferry Rd. E14 . . . . .7A 86
  SW1 . . . . .2C 18 (3H 101)
Horseferry Rd. Est. SW1 . . . . . . .2C 18
Horse Guards Av. SW1 . . .5E 12 (1J 101)
Horse Guards Parade 5E 12 (1H 101)
Horse Guards Rd. SW1 . . .5D 12 (1H 101)
Horse Leaze E6 . . . . .6E 88

Horseley Ct. E1 . . . . .5A 86
Horsell Rd. BR5: St P 7B 144
  N5 . . . . .5A 66
   (not continuous)
Horselydown La. SE1 . . . .6J 15 (2F 103)
Horselydown Mans. SE1 . . . . . . .6J 15
   (off Lafone St.)
Horsemongers M. SE1 . . . . .7D 14
Horsenden Av. UB6: G'frd 5K 59
Horsenden Cres. UB6: G'frd 5K 59
Horsenden Hill Footgolf Cen. 6A 60
Horsenden Hill Golf Course 7A 60
Horsenden La. Nth. UB6: G'frd . . .6J 59
Horsenden La. Sth. UB6: G'frd . . .1A 78
Horse Ride SW1 . . . . . .5C 12 (1G 101)
Horseshoe Cl. E14 . . . . .5E 104
  NW2 . . . . .2D 62
Horseshoe Ct. EC1 . . . . .3B 8
   (off Brewhouse Yd.)
Horseshoe Cres. UB5: N'olt 2E 76
Horseshoe Dr. UB8: Hil 6C 74
Horse Shoe Grn. SM1: Sutt 2K 165
Horseshoe La. EN2: Enf 3H 23
  N20 .1A 30
Horseshoe M. SW2 . . . . .4J 119
Horseshoe Wharf SE1 . . . . .4E 14
   (off Clink St.)
Horse Yd. N1 . . . . .1B 84
   (off Essex Rd.)
Horsfeld Gdns. SE9 . . . . .5C 124
Horsfeld Rd. SE9 . . . . .5B 124
Horsfield Ho. N1 . . . . .7C 66
   (off Northampton St.)
Horsford Rd. SW2 . . . . .5K 119
Horsham Av. N12 . . . . .5H 31
Horsham Ct. N17 . . . . .1G 49
   (off Lansdowne Rd.)
Horsham Rd. DA6: Bex 5G 127
  TW14: Bedf 6E 110
Horsley Cl. SW1 . . . . .4D 18
   (off Vincent St.)
Horsley Dr. CR0: New Ad 7E 170
  KT2: King T 5D 132
Horsley Rd. BR1: Broml 1K 159
  E4 . . . . .2K 35
Horsley St. SE17 . . . . .6D 102
Horsman Ho. SE5 . . . . .6C 102
   (off Bethwin Rd.)
Horsman St. SE5 . . . . .6C 102
Horsmonden Cl. BR6: Orp 7K 161
Horsmonden Rd. SE4 . . . . .5B 122
Horsnell Close SE5 . . . . .7D 102
Hortensia Ho. SW10 . . . . .7A 100
   (off Gunter Gro.)
Hortensia Rd. SW10 . . . . .7A 100
Horticultural Pl. W4 . . . . .5K 97
Horton Av. NW2 . . . . .4G 63
Horton Bri. Rd. UB7: View 1B 92
Horton Cl. UB7: View 1C 92
Horton Country Pk.
  Local Nature Reserve 7G 163
Horton Halls SW17 . . . . .3B 136
Horton Ho. SE15 . . . . .6J 103
  SW8 . . . . .7K 101
  W6 . . . . .5G 99
   (off Field Rd.)
Horton Ind. Pk. UB7: View 1B 92
Horton La. KT19: Eps 7H 163
Horton Pde. UB7: View 1A 92
Horton Pk. Golf Course 7J 163
Horton Rd. E8 . . . . .6H 67
  SL3: Poyle 6A 174
  TW19: Stanw M 7A 174
  UB7: View 1A 92
  UB11: Stock P 1A 92
Horton Rd. Ind. Est. UB7: View . . .1B 92
Horton Way CR0: C'don 5K 157
Hortus Rd. E4 . . . . .2K 35
  UB2: S'hall 2D 94
Horwood Ho. E2 . . . . .3H 85
   (off Pott Cl.)
  NW8 .3D 4
   (off Paveley St.)

Hosack Rd. SW17 . . . . .2E **136**
Hoser Av. SE12 . . . . .2J **141**
Hosier La. EC1 . . . . .6A **8** (5B **84**)
Hoskins Cl. E16 . . . . .6A **88**
   UB3: Harl 5H **93**
Hoskins St. SE10 . . . . .5F **105**
Hospital Bri. Rd.
   TW2: Twick, Whitt 7F **113**
HOSPITAL BRIDGE RDBT. 2F **131**
Hospital Rd. E9 . . . . .5K **67**
   E11 . . . . .5F **51**
   TW3: Houn 3E **112**
Hospital Way SE13 . . . . .7F **123**
Hotham Cl. KT8: W Mole 3E **148**
Hotham Rd. SW15 . . . . .3E **116**
   SW19 . . . . .7A **136**
Hotham Rd. M. SW19 . . . . .7A **136**
Hotham St. E15 . . . . .1G **87**
Hothfield Pl. SE16 . . . . .3J **103**
Hotspur Ind. Est. N17 . . . . .6C **34**
Hotspur Rd. UB5: N'olt 2E **76**
Hotspur St. SE11 . . . . .5J **19** (4A **102**)
Houblon Rd. TW10: Rich 5E **114**
Houghton Cl. E8 . . . . .6F **67**
   TW12: Hamp 6C **130**
Houghton Ct. *EC1* *4C 8*
             (off Glasshouse Yd.)
Houghton Rd. N15 . . . . .4F **49**
Houghton Sq. *SW9* 2J **119**
              (off Clapham Rd.)
Houghton St. WC2 . . . . . .1H **13** (6K **83**)
              (not continuous)
Houlder Cres. CR0: Wadd 6B **168**
Houlton Ho. *SW3* *5E 16*
              (off Walpole St.)
Houlton Pl. *E3* *4B 86*
             (off Hamlets Way)
Houndsden Rd. N21 . . . . .6E **22**
Houndsditch EC3 . . . . . . .7H **9** (6E **84**)
Houndsfield Rd. N9 . . . . .7C **24**
HOUNSLOW 3F **113**
Hounslow & District Indoor Bowls Club
                    . . . . .2D **112**
Hounslow Av. TW3: Houn 5F **113**
Hounslow Bus. Pk.
   TW3: Houn 4E **112**
Hounslow Cen. TW3: Houn 3F **113**
Hounslow Gdns. TW3: Houn 5F **113**
Hounslow Heath
   Local Nature Reserve 6C **112**
Hounslow Rd. TW2: Whitt 6E **112**
   TW13: Hanw 4B **130**
   TW14: Felt 1K **129**
Hounslow Urban Farm 5J **111**
HOUNSLOW WEST 3C **112**
The Household Cavalry Mus.
         . . . . .5D **12** (1H **101**)
The House Mill 3E **86**
House of Illustration 1J **83**
Houses of Parliament 1F **19** (3J **101**)
Houston Bus. Pk.
   UB4: Yead 1A **94**
Houston Pl. KT10: Esh 7J **149**
Houston Rd.
   KT6: Surb .6B **150**
   SE23 . . . . .2A **140**
Houstoun Ct. TW5: Hest 7D **94**
Hove Av. E17 . . . . .5B **50**
Hoveden Rd. NW2 . . . . .5G **63**
Hove Gdns. SM1: Sutt 1K **165**
Hove St. *SE15* *7J 103*
              (off Culmore Rd.)
Hoveton Rd. SE28 . . . . .6C **90**
Hoveton Way IG6: Ilf 1F **53**
Howard Av. DA5: Bexl 1C **144**
Howard Bldg. SW11 . . . . . .7J **17** (6F **101**)
Howard Cl. N11 . . . . .2K **31**
   NW2 . . . . .4G **63**
   TW12: Hamp 7G **131**
   TW16: Sun 6H **129**
   W3 . . . . .6H **79**
   WD23: B Hea 1D **26**
Howard Ct. IG11: Bark 1H **89**

Howard Ho. *E16* *1K 105*
              (off Wesley Av.)
   SE8 . . . .*6B 104*
              (off Evelyn St.)
   SW1 . . . .*6B 18*
              (off Dolphin Sq.)
   SW9 . . . .*3B 120*
             (off Barrington Rd.)
   W1 . . . .*4K 5*
              (off Cleveland St.)
Howard M. N5 . . . . .4B **66**
Howard Rd. BR1: Broml 7J **141**
   E6 . . . . .2D **88**
   E11 . . . . .3G **69**
   E17 . . . . .3C **50**
   HA7: Stan .1D **42**
   IG1: Ilf 4F **71**
   IG11: Bark 1H **89**
   KT3: N Mald 3A **152**
   KT5: Surb .6F **151**
   N15 . . . . .6E **48**
   N16 . . . . .4D **66**
   NW2 . . . . .4F **63**
   SE20 . . . . .1J **157**
   SE25 . . . . .5G **157**
   TW7: Isle .3K **113**
   UB1: S'hall 6F **77**
Howards Cl. HA5: Pinn 2K **39**
Howards Crest Cl. BR3: Beck 2E **158**
Howard's La. SW15 . . . . .4D **116**
Howards Rd. E13 . . . . .3J **87**
Howard St. KT7: T Ditt 7B **150**
Howard Wlk. N2 . . . . .4A **46**
Howard Way EN5: Barn 5A **20**
Howarth Rd. SE2 . . . . .5A **108**
Howberry Cl. HA8: Edg 6J **27**
Howberry Rd. CR7: Thor H 1D **156**
   HA7: Stan .6J **27**
   HA8: Edg 6J **27**
Howbury Rd. SE15 . . . . .3J **121**
Howcroft Cres. N3 . . . . .7D **30**
Howcroft Ho. *E3* *3B 86*
             (off Benworth St.)
Howcroft La. UB6: G'frd 3H **77**
Howden Cl. SE28 . . . . .7D **90**
Howden Rd. SE25 . . . . .2F **157**
Howden St. SE15 . . . . .3G **121**
Howe Cl. RM7: Mawney 1G **55**
Howell Cl. RM6: Chad H 5D **54**
Howell Ct. E10 . . . . .7D **50**
Howell Wlk. SE1 . . . . .4B **102**
Howerd Way SE18 . . . . .1C **124**
              (not continuous)
Howes Cl. N3 . . . . .3J **45**
Howeth Ct. *N11* *6J 31*
              (off Ribblesdale Av.)
Howfield Pl. N17 . . . . .3F **49**
Howgate Rd. SW14 . . . . .3K **115**
Howick Pl. SW1 . . . . . . .2B **18** (3G **101**)
Howie St. SW11 . . . . .7C **100**
Howitt Cl. N16 . . . . .4E **66**
   NW3 . . . . .6C **64**
Howitt Rd. NW3 . . . . .6C **64**
Howland Est. SE16 . . . . .3J **103**
Howland Ho. SW16 . . . . .3J **137**
Howland M. E. W1 . . . . . . .5B **6** (5G **83**)
Howland St. W1 . . . . .5A **6** (5G **83**)
Howland Way SE16 . . . . .2A **104**
Howlett Apts. *N1* *7J 65*
              (off Caledonian Rd.)
Howletts La. HA4: Ruis 5E **38**
Howlett's Rd. SE24 . . . . .6C **120**
Howley Pl. W2 . . . . .5A **4** (5A **82**)
Howley Rd. CR0: C'don 3B **168**
Howsman Rd. SW13 . . . . .6C **98**
Howson Rd. SE4 . . . . .4A **122**
Howson Ter. TW10: Rich 6E **114**
How's St. E2 .2F **85**
Howton Pl. WD23: B Hea 1C **26**
HOXTON 2E **84**
Hoxton Hall Theatre 2E **84**
              (off Hoxton St.)
Hoxton Mkt. N1 . . . . .2G **9**

Hoxton Sq. N1 . . . . .2G **9** (3E **84**)
Hoxton St. N1 . . . . .2H **9** (1E **84**)
Hoylake Cres. UB10: Ick 2C **56**
Hoylake Gdns. CR4: Mitc 3G **155**
   HA4: Ruis .1K **57**
Hoylake Rd. W3 . . . . .6A **80**
Hoyland Cl. SE15 . . . . .7H **103**
Hoyle Rd. SW17 . . . . .5C **136**
Hoy St. E16 .6H **87**
HQS Wellington 3J **13**
The Hub
   Westminster 1F **5** (2D **82**)
Hubbard Ct. IG10: Lough 1H **37**
Hubbard Dr. KT9: Chess 6D **162**
Hubbard Ho. *SW10* *7B 100*
             (off World's End Pas.)
Hubbard Rd. SE27 . . . . .4C **138**
Hubbards Cl. UB8: Hil 6D **74**
Hubbard St. E15 . . . . .1G **87**
Hubbinet Ind. Est.
   RM7: Mawney 3J **55**
Huberd Ho. *SE1* *7F 15*
              (off Manciple St.)
Hubert Gro. SW9 . . . . .3J **119**
Hubert Ho. *NW8* *4C 4*
              (off Ashbridge St.)
Hubert Rd. E6 . . . . .3B **88**
Hucknall Ct. *NW8* *3A 4*
             (off Cunningham Pl.)
Huddart St. E3 . . . . .5B **86**
              (not continuous)
Huddleston Cl. E2 . . . . .2J **85**
Huddlestone Rd. E7 . . . . .4H **69**
   NW2 . . . . .6D **62**
Huddleston Rd. N7 . . . . .3G **65**
Hudson *NW9* *1B 44*
              (off Five Acre)
Hudson Apts. N8 . . . . .3K **47**
Hudson Bldg. *E1* *6K 9*
              (off Chicksand St.)
Hudson Cl. E15 . . . . .1J **87**
   W12 . . . . .7D **80**
Hudson Ct. *E14* *5C 104*
              (off Maritime Quay)
   SW19 . . . . .1A **154**
Hudson Gdns. BR6: Chels 6K **173**
Hudson Ho. *SW10* *7A 100*
              (off Hortensia Rd.)
   W11 . . . .*6G 81*
              (off Ladbroke Gro.)
Hudson Pl. SE18 . . . . .5G **107**
Hudson Rd. DA7: Bex 2F **127**
   UB3: Harl .6F **93**
Hudson's Pl. SW1 . . . . . .3A **18** (4F **101**)
Hudson Way E16 . . . . .7G **89**
   N9 . . . . .3D **34**
   NW2 . . . . .3F **63**
Hugero Point SE10 . . . . .3J **105**
Huggin Cl. EC4 . . . . .2D **14**
Huggin Hill EC4 . . . . .2C **14** (7C **84**)
Huggins Ho. *E3* *3C 86*
              (off Alfred St.)
Huggins Pl. SW2 . . . . .1K **137**
Hughan Rd. E15 . . . . .5F **69**
Hugh Astor Ct. *SE1* *7B 14*
              (off Keyworth St.)
Hugh Clark Ho. *W13* *1A 96*
              (off Singapore Rd.)
Hugh Cubitt Ho. *N1* *2K 83*
              (off Collier St.)
Hugh Dalton Av. SW6 . . . . .6H **99**
Hughenden Av. HA3: Kenton 5B **42**
Hughenden Gdns. UB5: N'olt 3A **76**
              (not continuous)
Hughenden Ho. NW8 . . . . .3C **4**
Hughenden Rd. KT4: Wor Pk 7C **152**
Hughenden EN5: New Bar 4E **20**
Hughendon Cl. UB3: Hayes 7H **75**
             (off Chamberlain Cl.)
Hughendon Ter. E15 . . . . .4E **68**
Hughes Cl. N12 . . . . .5F **31**
Hughes Ct. N7 . . . . .5H **65**
Hughes Ho. *E2* *3J 85*
              (off Sceptre Ho.)

Hughes Ho. *E3* *3C 86*
             (off Trevithick Way)
   SE5 . . . .*1C 120*
              (off Flodden Rd.)
   SE8 . . . .*6C 104*
              (off Benbow St.)
   SE17 . . . .*4B 102*
              (off Peacock St.)
Hughes Mans. E1 . . . . .4G **85**
Hughes Rd. TW15: Ashf 7E **128**
   UB3: Hayes 7K **75**
Hughes Ter. *SW9* *3B 120*
              (off Styles Gdns.)
Hughes Wlk. CR0: C'don 7C **156**
Hugh Gaitskell Cl. SW6 . . . . .6H **99**
Hugh Gaitskell Ho. N16 . . . . .2F **67**
Hugh Herland Ho. KT1: King T 3E **150**
Hugh M. SW1 . . . . .4K **17** (4F **101**)
Hugh Platt Ho. *E2* *2H 85*
              (off Patriot Sq.)
Hugh St. SW1 . . . . .4K **17** (4F **101**)
Hugo Ho. *SW1* *1F 17*
              (off Sloane St.)
Hugon Rd. SW6 . . . . .3K **117**
Hugo Rd. N19 . . . . .4G **65**
Huguenot Dr. N13 . . . . .5F **33**
Huguenot Pl. E1 . . . . .5K **9** (5F **85**)
   SW18 . . . . .5A **118**
Huguenot Sq. SE15 . . . . .3H **121**
Hullbridge M. N1 . . . . .1D **84**
Hull Cl. SE16 . . . . .2K **103**
Hull Pl. E16 .1G **107**
Hull St. EC1 . . . . .2C **8** (3C **84**)
Hulme Pl. SE1 . . . . .7D **14** (2C **102**)
Hulse Av. IG11: Bark 6H **71**
   RM7: Mawney 1H **55**
Hulse Ter. IG1: Ilf 6G **71**
Hult Intl. Studios *E1* *6G 85*
              (off Alder St.)
Hult Twr. *E1* *6G 85*
              (off Alder St.)
Hulverston Cl. SM2: Sutt 7K **165**
Humber Cl. UB7: W Dray 1A **92**
Humber Ct. *W7* *6H 77*
              (off Hobbayne Rd.)
Humber Dr. W10 . . . . .4F **81**
Humber Rd. NW2 . . . . .2D **62**
   SE3 . . . . .6H **105**
Humberstone Rd. E13 . . . . .3A **88**
Humberton Cl. E9 . . . . .5A **68**
Humber Trad. Est. NW2 . . . . .2D **62**
Humbolt Rd. W6 . . . . .6G **99**
Hume Ct. *N1* *7B 66*
              (off Hawes St.)
Hume Ho. *W11* *1F 99*
              (off Queensdale Cres.)
Humes Av. W7 . . . . .3J **95**
Hume Ter. E16 . . . . .5K **87**
Hume Way HA4: Ruis 6J **39**
Humphrey Cl. IG5: Ilf 1D **52**
Humphrey St. SE1 . . . . .5F **103**
Humphries Cl. RM9: Dag 4F **73**
Humphry Repton Way HA9: Wemb . .4G **61**
Hundred Acre NW9 . . . . .2B **44**
Hungerdown E4 . . . . .1K **35**
Hungerford Ho. *SW1* *7B 18*
              (off Churchill Gdns.)
Hungerford La. WC2 . . . . .4F **13**
              (not continuous)
Hungerford Rd. N7 . . . . .6H **65**
Hungerford St. E1 . . . . .6H **85**
Hunsdon Cl. RM9: Dag 6E **72**
Hunsdon Rd. SE14 . . . . .7K **103**
Hunslett St. E2 . . . . .3J **85**
Hunstanton Ho. *NW1* *5D 4*
              (off Cosway St.)
Hunston Rd. SM4: Mord 1K **165**
Hunt Cl. W11 .1F **99**
Hunt Cl. N14 .7A **22**
   RM7: Rush G 6K **55**
              (off Union Rd.)
   UB5: N'olt .2B **76**
              (off Gallery Gdns.)

Hunter Cl. SE1 . . . . .3D 102
  SM6: W'gton 7J 167
  SW12 . . . . .1E 136
Hunter Ho. SE1 . . . . .7B 14
      (off King James St.)
  SW5 . . . . .5J 99
     (off Old Brompton Rd.)
  SW8 .7H 101
       (off Fount St.)
  TW13: Felt 1J 129
       (off Hazel Rd.)
  WC1 . . . . .3F 7
      (off Hunter St.)
Hunterian Mus. 1H 13 (6K 83)
Hunter Lodge W9 . . . . .5J 81
     (off Admiral Wlk.)
Hunter Rd. CR7: Thor H 3D 156
  IG1: Ilf 5F 71
  SW20 . . . . .1E 152
Hunters Cl. DA5: Bexl 3K 145
Hunters Ct. TW9: Rich 5D 114
Hunters Gro. BR6: Farnb 4G 173
  HA3: Kenton 4C 42
  UB3: Hayes 1J 93
Hunters Hall Rd. RM10: Dag 4G 73
Hunters Hill HA4: Ruis 3A 58
Hunters Mdw. SE19 . . . . .4E 138
Hunter's Rd. KT9: Chess 3E 162
Hunters Sq. RM10: Dag 4G 73
Hunter St. WC1 . . . . . . .3F 7 (4J 83)
Hunter's Way CRO: C'don 4E 168
Hunters Way EN2: Enf 1F 23
Hunter Wlk. E13 . . . . .2J 87
Huntingdon Cl. CR4: Mitc 3J 155
  UB5: N'olt 6E 58
Huntingdon Gdns.
  KT4: Wor Pk 3E 164
  W4 . . . . .7J 97
Huntingdon Rd. N2 . . . . .3C 46
  N9 . . . . .2D 34
Huntingdon St. E16 . . . . .6H 87
  N1 . . . . .7K 65
Huntingfield CRO: Sels 7B 170
Huntingfield Rd. SW15 . . . . . . .4C 116
Hunting Ga. Cl. EN2: Enf 3F 23
Hunting Ga. Dr. KT9: Chess 7E 162
Hunting Ga. M. SM1: Sutt 3K 165
  TW2: Twick 1J 131
Hunting Pl. TW5: Hest 6D 94
Huntings Farm IG1: Ilf 2J 71
Huntings Rd. RM10: Dag 6G 73
Huntington Cl. DA5: Bexl 1H 145
Huntington Ho. SW11 . . . . .7F 101
     (off Palmer Rd.)
Huntley Cl. SE10 . . . . .5G 105
  TW19: Stanw 7A 110
Huntley St. WC1 . . . . . . .4B 6 (4G 83)
Huntley Way SW20 . . . . .2C 152
Huntloe Ho. SE14 . . . . .1J 121
      (off Kender St.)
Huntly Dr. N3 . . . . .6D 30
Huntly Rd. SE25 . . . . .4E 156
Hunton St. E1 . . . . .4K 9 (5G 85)
Hunt Rd. UB2: S'hall 3E 94
Hunt's Cl. SE3 . . . . .2J 123
Hunt's Ct. WC2 . . . . . .3D 12 (7H 83)
Huntshaw Ho. E3 . . . . .3D 86
     (off Devons Rd.)
Hunts La. E15 . . . . .2E 86
Huntsmans Cl. TW13: Felt 4K 129
Huntsman St. SE17 . . . . .4E 102
Hunts Mead EN3: Enf H 3E 24
Hunts Mead Cl. BR7: Chst 7D 142
Huntsmoor Rd.
  KT19: Ewe 5K 163
Huntspill St. SW17 . . . . .3A 136
Hunts Slip Rd. SE21 . . . . .3E 138
Huntsworth M. NW1 . . .3E 4 (4D 82)
Hurdwick Ho. NW1 . . . . .2G 83
    (off Harrington Sq.)
Hurdwick Pl. NW1 . . . . .2G 83
    (off Hampstead Rd.)
Hurleston Ho. SE8 . . . . .5B 104

Hurley Ct. SW17 . . . . .6E 136
     (off Mitcham Rd.)
  W5 . . . . .6C 78
Hurley Cres. SE16 . . . . .2K 103
Hurley Ho. SE11 . . . . . .4K 19 (4B 102)
  UB7: W Dray 2B 92
     (off Park Lodge Av.)
Hurley Rd. UB6: G'frd 6F 77
HURLINGHAM 3K 117
Hurlingham Bus. Pk. SW6 . . . . .3J 117
The Hurlingham Club 3J 117
Hurlingham Ct. SW6 . . . . .3H 117
Hurlingham Gdns. SW6 . . . . . . .3H 117
Hurlingham Pk. 2H 117
Hurlingham Retail Pk. 3K 117
Hurlingham Rd. DA7: Bex 7F 109
  SW6 .2H 117
Hurlingham Sq. SW6 . . . . .3J 117
Hurlingham Yacht Club 3G 117
Hurlock St. N5 . . . . .3B 66
Hurlstone Rd. SE25 . . . . .5E 156
Hurn Cl. TW4: Houn 2B 112
Hurn Ct. Rd. TW4: Houn 2B 112
Huron Cl. BR6: Chels 6J 173
Huron Rd. SW17 . . . . .2E 136
Hurrell Dr. HA2: Harr 3G 41
Hurren Cl. SE3 . . . . .3G 123
Hurricane Rd. SM6: W'gton 7J 167
Hurricane Trad. Cen. NW9 . . . . .1C 44
Hurry Cl. E15 . . . . .7G 69
Hurst Av. E4 . . . . .4H 35
  N6 . . . . .6G 47
Hurstbourne KT10: Clay 6A 162
Hurstbourne Gdns. IG11: Bark . . .6J 71
Hurstbourne Ho. SW15 . . . . .6B 116
     (off Tangley Gro.)
Hurstbourne Rd. SE23 . . . . . . .1A 140
Hurst Cl. BR2: Hayes 1H 171
  E4 . . . . .3H 35
  KT9: Chess 5G 163
  NW11 . . . . .6K 45
  UB5: N'olt 6D 58
Hurstcombe IG9: Buck H 2D 36
Hurst Cl. DA15: Sidc 2A 144
  E6 . . . . .5B 88
     (off Tollgate Rd.)
  IG8: Wfd G 6E 36
     (off Snakes La. W.)
Hurstcourt Rd. SM1: Sutt 2K 165
Hurstdene Av. BR2: Hayes 1H 171
Hurstdene Gdns. N15 . . . . .7E 48
Hurstfield BR2: Broml 5J 159
Hurstfield Cres. UB4: Hayes 4G 75
Hurstfield Rd. KT8: W Mole 3E 148
Hurst Gro. KT12: Walt T 7H 147
Hurst Ho. WC1 . . . . .1H 7
      (off Penton Ri.)
Hurst La. KT8: E Mos 4G 149
  SE2 .5D 108
Hurst La. Est. SE2 . . . . .5D 108
Hurstleigh Gdns. IG5: Ilf 1D 52
Hurstmead Ct. HA8: Edg 4C 28
HURST PARK 2G 149
Hurst Pl. HA6: Nwood 1D 38
Hurst Pool 3F 149
Hurst Ri. EN5: New Bar 3D 20
Hurst Rd. CRO: C'don 5D 168
  DA5: Bexl 1D 144
  DA8: Erith 1J 127
  DA15: Bexl, Sidc 2A 144
  E17 .3D 50
  IG9: Buck H 1G 37
  KT8: W Mole, E Mos 3F 149
  KT12: Walt T 5A 148
  N21 .1F 33
Hurst Springs DA5: Bexl 1E 144
Hurst St. SE24 . . . . .6B 120
Hurst Vw. Rd. CR2: S Croy 7E 168
Hurst Way CR2: S Croy 6C 168
Hurstway Rd. W11 . . . . .7F 81
     (off Hurstway Wlk.)
Hurstway Wlk. W11 . . . . .7F 81

Hurstwood Av. DA5: Bexl 1E 144
  E18 . . . . .4K 51
Hurstwood Ct. N12 . . . . .6H 31
  NW11 . . . . .4H 45
     (off Finchley Rd.)
Hurstwood Dr. BR1: Broml 3D 160
Hurstwood Rd. NW11 . . . . .4G 45
Hurtwood Rd. KT12: Walt T 7D 148
Husborne Ho. SE8 . . . . .4A 104
     (off Chilton Gro.)
Huson Cl. NW3 . . . . .7C 64
Hussain Cl. HA1: Harr 4K 59
Hussars Cl. TW4: Houn 3C 112
Husseywell Cres. BR2: Hayes . . .1J 171
Hutchings St. E14 . . . . .2C 104
Hutchings Wlk. NW11 . . . . .4K 45
Hutchings Wharf E14 . . . . .2C 104
     (off Hutchings St.)
Hutchins Cl. E15 . . . . .7E 68
Hutchinson Ct. RM6: Chad H 4D 54
Hutchinson Ho. NW3 . . . . .7D 64
  SE14 . . . . .7J 103
Hutchinson Ter. HA9: Wemb 3D 60
Hutchins Rd. SE28 . . . . .7A 90
Hutton Cl. IG8: Wfd G 6E 36
  UB6: G'frd 5H 59
Hutton Ct. N4 . . . . .1K 65
     (off Victoria Rd.)
  N9 . . . . .7D 24
     (off Tramway Av.)
  W5 . . . . .5B 78
Hutton Gdns. HA3: Hrw W 7B 26
Hutton Gro. N12 . . . . .5E 30
Hutton La. HA3: Hrw W 7B 26
Hutton M. SW15 . . . . .5D 116
Hutton Row HA8: Edg 7D 28
Hutton St. EC4 . . . . . . .2K 13 (6B 84)
Hutton Wlk. HA3: Hrw W 7B 26
Huxbear St. SE4 . . . . .5B 122
Huxley Cl. UB5: N'olt 2C 76
  UB8: Cowl 4A 74
Huxley Dr. RM6: Chad H 7B 54
Huxley Gdns. NW10 . . . . .3F 79
Huxley Ho. NW8 . . . . .4B 4
    (off Fisherton St.)
Huxley Pde. N18 . . . . .5J 33
Huxley Pl. N13 . . . . .3G 33
Huxley Rd. DA16: Well 3K 125
  E10 . . . . .2E 68
  N18 . . . . .4J 33
Huxley Sayze N18 . . . . .5J 33
Huxley Sth. N18 . . . . .5J 33
Huxley St. W10 . . . . .3G 81
Hyacinth Cl. IG1: Ilf 6F 71
  TW12: Hamp 6E 130
Hyacinth Dr. UB10: Uxb 7A 56
Hyacinth Ho. E17 . . . . .3D 50
      (off Vine St.)
Hyacinth Rd. SW15 . . . . .1C 134
Hybrid Ho. W3 . . . . .1A 98
THE HYDE 5B 44
The Hyde NW9 . . . . .4A 44
     (not continuous)
Hyde Cl. E13 . . . . .2J 87
  EN5: Barn 3C 20
  TW15: Ashf 6G 129
Hyde Ct. N20 . . . . .3G 31
Hyde Cres. NW9 . . . . .5A 44
Hyde Est. Rd. NW9 . . . . .5B 44
Hyde Farm M. SW12 . . . . .1H 137
Hydefield Cl. N21 . . . . .1J 33
Hydefield Ct. N9 . . . . .2K 33
Hyde Ho. E3 . . . . .5C 86
      (off Furze St.)
  TW3: Houn 3G 113
  UB8: Uxb 6A 56
  W13 . . . . .1A 96
    (off Singapore Rd.)
The Hyde Ind. Est. NW9 . . . . .5B 44
Hyde La. SW11 . . . . .1C 118
Hyde Pk. 4D 10 (1D 100)
Hyde Pk. Av. N21 . . . . .2H 33
Hyde Park Barracks 7D 10

HYDE PARK CORNER 2F 101
Hyde Pk. Cnr. W1 . . . . .6H 11 (2E 100)
Hyde Pk. Cres. W2 . . . . . .1C 10 (6C 82)
Hyde Pk. Gdns. N21 . . . . .1H 33
  W2 . . . . .2B 10 (7B 82)
     (not continuous)
Hyde Pk. Gdns. M. W2 . . .2B 10 (7B 82)
Hyde Pk. Ga. SW7 . . . . .2A 100
     (not continuous)
Hyde Pk. Ga. M. SW7 . . . . .2A 100
Hyde Pk. Mans. NW1 . . . . .6C 4
     (off Cabbell St.)
Hyde Pk. Pl. W2 . . . . . . .2D 10 (7C 82)
Hyde Pk. Sq. W2 . . . . . .1C 10 (6C 82)
Hyde Pk. Sq. M. W2 . . . . .1C 10
Hyde Pk. St. W2 . . . . . .1C 10 (6C 82)
Hyde Pk. Towers W2 . . . . .7A 82
Hyderabad Way E15 . . . . .7G 69
Hyde Rd. DA7: Bex 2F 127
  N1 . . . . .1E 84
  TW10: Rich 5F 115
Hydeside Gdns. N9 . . . . .2A 34
Hyde's Pl. N1 . . . . .7B 66
Hyde St. SE8 . . . . .6C 104
Hyde Ter. TW15: Ashf 6G 129
Hydethorpe Av. N9 . . . . .2A 34
Hydethorpe Rd. SW12 . . . . .1G 137
Hyde Va. SE10 . . . . .7E 104
Hyde Wlk. SM4: Mord 7J 153
Hyde Way N9 . . . . .2A 34
  UB3: Harl 4H 93
Hydon Cl. N11 . . . . .5J 31
The Hydra Bldg. EC1 . . . . .2K 7
Hylands Rd. E17 . . . . .2F 51
Hyltons Ho. E17 . . . . .2F 51
Hylton St. SE18 . . . . .4K 107
Hyndewood SE23 . . . . .3K 139
Hyndman Ho. RM10: Dag 3G 73
     (off Kershaw Rd.)
Hyndman St. SE15 . . . . .6H 103
Hynton Rd. RM8: Dag 2C 72
Hyperion Ct. E16 . . . . .5J 87
     (off Robertson Rd.)
Hyperion Ho. E3 . . . . .2A 86
     (off Arbery Rd.)
  SW2 .6K 119
Hyrstdene CR2: S Croy 4B 168
Hyson Rd. SE16 . . . . .5H 103
Hythe Av. DA7: Bex 7E 108
Hythe Cl. N18 . . . . .4B 34
Hythe Ho. SE16 . . . . .2J 103
     (off Swan Rd.)
  W6 . . . . .4E 98
    (off Shepherd's Bush Rd.)
Hythe Rd. CR7: Thor H 2D 156
  KT6: Surb 6E 150
  NW10 . . . . .3B 80
Hythe Rd. Ind. Est. NW10 . . . . . . .3C 80

I

Ian Bowater Ct. N1 . . . . .1F 9
      (off East Rd.)
Ian Ct. SE23 . . . . .2J 139
Ian Sq. EN3: Enf H 1E 24
Ibberton Ho. SW8 . . . . .7K 101
     (off Meadow Rd.)
  W14 . . . . .3G 99
     (off Russell Rd.)
Ibbotson Av. E16 . . . . .6H 87
Ibbott St. E1 . . . . .4J 85
Iberia Ho. N19 . . . . .7H 47
Iberian Av. SM6: Bedd 4H 167
Ibex Ho. E15 . . . . .5G 69
     (off Forest La.)
Ibis Ct. BR3: Beck 1F 159
    (off Albemarle Rd.)
  SE8 . . . . .6B 104
     (off Edward Pl.)
Ibis La. W4 . . . . .1J 115
Ibis Way UB4: Yead 6B 76
Ibrox Ct. IG9: Buck H 2F 37
Ibscott Cl. RM10: Dag 6J 73

Ibsley Gdns. SW15 . . . . .1C **134**
Ibsley Way EN4: Cockf 5H **21**
ICA Cinema *4D 12*
(within ICA)
Icarus Ho. *E3* *3B 86*
(off British St.)
ICA Theatre *4D 12*
(within ICA)
Iceland Rd. E3 . . . . .1C **86**
Iceland Wharf SE16 . . . . .4A **104**
Iceni Ct. *E3* *1B 86*
(off Parnell Rd.)
IG9: Buck H 1E **36**
Ice Wharf N1 . . . . .2J **83**
Ice Wharf Marina *N1* *2J 83*
(off New Wharf Rd.)
The Ice Works NW1 . . . . .7F **65**
(off Jamestown Rd.)
Ickburgh Est. E5 . . . . .2H **67**
Ickburgh Rd. E5 . . . . .3H **67**
ICKENHAM 3D **56**
Ickenham Cl. HA4: Ruis 2F **57**
Ickenham Grn. UB10: Ick 1D **56**
Ickenham Rd. HA4: Ruis 2E **56**
Ickleton Rd. SE9 . . . . .4C **142**
Icknield Dr. IG2: Ilf 5F **53**
Icknield Ho. *SW3* *5D 16*
(off Cale St.)
Ickworth Pk. Rd. E17 . . . . .4A **50**
Icon Apts. *SE1* *7G 15*
(off Cluny Pl.)
Icona Point *E15* *1E 86*
(off Warton Rd.)
Icon College of Technology &
Management *6G 85*
(off Adler St.)
Iconia Ho. BR2: Broml 4A **160**
Idaho Bldg. *SE13* 1D **122**
(off Deal's Gateway)
Ida Rd. N15 . . . . .4D **48**
Ida St. E14 .6E **86**
(not continuous)
Ide Mans. *E1* *7K 85*
(off Cable St.)
Iden Cl. BR2: Broml 3G **159**
Idlecombe Rd. SW17 . . . . .6E **136**
Idmiston Rd. E15 . . . . .4H **69**
KT4: Wor Pk 7B **152**
SE27 . . . . .3C **138**
Idmiston Sq. KT4: Wor Pk 7B **152**
Idol La. EC3 . . . . .3G **15** (7E **84**)
Idonia St. SE8 . . . . .7C **104**
Iffley Cl. UB8: Uxb 7A **56**
Iffley Rd. W6 . . . . .3D **98**
Ifield Ho. *SE17* *5E 102*
(off Madron St.)
Ifield Rd. SW10 . . . . .6K **99**
Ifor Evans Pl. E1 . . . . .4K **85**
Ightham Ho. *BR3: Beck* 7B **140**
(off Bethersden Cl.)
SE17 . . . .*4E 102*
(off Beckway St.)
Ightham Rd. DA8: Erith 7G **109**
Ikon Ho. *E1* *7J 85*
(off Devonport St.)
Ilbert St. W10 . . . . .3F **81**
Ilchester Gdns. W2 . . . . .7K **81**
Ilchester Mans. *W8* *3J 99*
(off Abingdon Rd.)
Ilchester Pl. W14 . . . . .3H **99**
Ilchester Rd. RM8: Dag 5B **72**
Ildersly Gro. SE21 . . . . .2D **138**
Ilderton Rd. SE15 . . . . .5J **103**
SE16 . . . . .5J **103**
Ilderton Wharf *SE15* *6J 103*
(off Rollins St.)
Ilex Cl. TW16: Sun 2A **148**
Ilex Rd. NW10 . . . . .6B **62**
Ilex Way SW16 . . . . .5A **138**
ILFORD 3F **71**
Ilford Bldg. IG1: Ilf 3E **70**
Ilford Golf Course 1D **70**
Ilford Hill IG1: Ilf 3E **70**

Ilford Ho. *N1* *6D 66*
(off Dove Rd.)
Ilford La. IG1: Ilf 3F **71**
Ilford Sports Club 2J **71**
Ilfracombe Flats *SE1* 6D **14**
(off Marshalsea Rd.)
Ilfracombe Gdns. RM6: Chad H . . .7B **54**
Ilfracombe Rd. BR1: Broml 3H **141**
Iliffe St. SE17 . . . . .5B **102**
Iliffe Yd. *SE17* *5B 102*
(off Crampton St.)
Ilkeston Ct. *E5* *4K 67*
(off Overbury St.)
Ilkley Cl. SE19 . . . . .6D **138**
Ilkley Rd. E16 . . . . .5A **88**
Illingworth Cl. CR4: Mitc 3B **154**
Illingworth Way EN1: Enf 5K **23**
Illumina Ho. *SW18* *5J 117*
(off Broomhill Rd.)
Ilmington Rd. HA3: Kenton 6D **42**
Ilminster Gdns. SW11 . . . . .4C **118**
Ilsley Ct. SW8 . . . . .2G **119**
Image Ct. RM7: Rush G 6K **55**
Images IG2: Ilf 6E **52**
Imani Mans. *SW11* 2B **118**
IMAX (BFI) 5J **13** (1A **102**)
Imber Cl. N14 . . . . .7B **22**
Imber Court 7H **149**
Imber Cross KT7: T Ditt 6K **149**
Imber Gro. KT10: Esh 7H **149**
Imber Pk. Rd. KT10: Esh 7H **149**
Imber St. N1 . . . . .1D **84**
Impact Bus. Pk. UB6: G'frd 2B **78**
Impact Ct. SE20 . . . . .2H **157**
Impact Ho. CR0: C'don 3C **168**
Imperial Av. N16 . . . . .4E **66**
Imperial Cl. HA2: Harr 6E **40**
NW2 . . . . .5D **62**
Imperial College London
Charing Cross Campus 6F **99**
Chelsea & Westminster Campus
. . . . .6A **100**
(within Chelsea & Westminster Hospital)
Hammersmith Campus 6C **80**
Royal Brompton Campus,
Emmanuel Kaye 6C **16**
Guy Scadding Bldg. 5C **16**
St Mary's Campus 7B **4**
Sth. Kensington Campus
. . . . .1A **16** (3B **100**)
Ennismore Gdns. M. 1B **16**
Kensington Gore . . .1A **16** (3B **100**)
Imperial Coll. Rd. SW7 . .2A **16** (3B **100**)
Imperial Ct. HA2: Harr 7E **40**
N6 . . . . .6G **47**
N20 . . . . .3F **31**
NW8 . . . .*2C 82*
(off Prince Albert Rd.)
SE11 . . . . .6J **19** (5A **102**)
Imperial Cres. SW6 . . . . .2A **118**
Imperial Dr. HA2: Harr 7E **40**
Imperial Gdns. CR4: Mitc 3F **155**
Imperial Gro.
EN4: Had W 1E **20**
Imperial Hgts. *E18* *1J 51*
(off Queen Mary Av.)
Imperial Ho. *E3* *3A 86*
(off Grove Rd.)
E14 . . . .*7B 86*
(off Victory Pl.)
Imperial M. E6 . . . . .2B **88**
SW9 . . . .*4K 119*
(off Brighton Ter.)
Imperial Pl. BR7: Chst 1E **160**
Imperial Rd. N22 . . . . .7D **32**
SW6 . . . . .1K **117**
TW14: Felt 7G **111**
Imperial Sq. SW6 . . . . .1K **117**
Imperial St. E3 . . . . .3E **86**
Imperial War Mus. London
All Saints Annexe *3K 19*
(off Austral St.)
Main Museum 2K **19** (3A **102**)

Imperial Way BR7: Chst 3G **143**
CR0: Wadd 6K **167**
HA3: Kenton 6E **42**
Imperial Wharf *E2* 2H **85**
(off Darwen Pl.)
SW6 . . . . .2A **118**
Imperium Ho. *E1* *6H 85*
(off Cannon St. Rd.)
Imre Cl. W12 . . . . .1D **98**
Inca Dr. SE9 . . . . .7F **125**
Inca Ter. N15 . . . . .3B **48**
Inchmery Rd. SE6 . . . . .2D **140**
Inchwood BR4: Addtn 4D **170**
Independence Ho. *SW19* 1B **154**
(off Chapter Way)
Independent Ind. Est. UB7: Yiew . . .1A **92**
Independent Pl. E8 . . . . .5F **67**
Independents Rd. SE3 . . . . .3H **123**
Inderwick Rd. N8 . . . . .5K **47**
Indescon Ct. E14 . . . . .2D **104**
Indescon Sq. E14 . . . . .2C **104**
India Gdns. UB5: N'olt 7A **58**
India House .2G **13**
(off Aldwych)
Indiana Bldg. *SE13* 1C **122**
(off Deal's Gateway)
India Pl. WC2 . . . . .2G **13**
India St. EC3 . . . . .1J **15** (6F **85**)
India Way SW15 . . . . .6C **116**
W12 . . . . .7D **80**
Indigo at the O2 . . . . .1G **105**
Indigo M. E14 . . . . .7E **86**
N16 . . . . .3D **66**
Indigo Wlk. N2 . . . . .4D **46**
N6 . . . . .4D **46**
Indus Ct. *SE15* 7F **103**
(off Amstel Ct.)
Indus Rd. SE7 . . . . .7A **106**
Infirmary Ct. SW3 . . . . .7F **17**
Inforum M. SE15 . . . . .7G **103**
Infrastructure Way IG11: Bark 3D **90**
Ingal Rd. E13 . . . . .4J **87**
Ingate Pl. SW8 . . . . .1F **119**
Ingatestone Rd. E12 . . . . .1A **70**
IG8: Wfd G 7E **36**
SE25 . . . . .4H **157**
Ingelow Ho. *W8* *2K 99*
(off Holland St.)
Ingelow Rd. SW8 . . . . .2F **119**
Ingersoll Rd. EN3: Enf W 1D **24**
W12 . . . . .1D **98**
Ingestre Pl. W1 . . . . .1B **12** (6G **83**)
Ingestre Rd. E7 . . . . .4J **69**
NW5 . . . . .4F **65**
Ingham Cl. CR2: Sels 7K **169**
Ingham Rd. CR2: Sels 7J **169**
NW6 . . . . .4J **63**
Inglebert St. EC1 . . . . .1J **7** (3A **84**)
Ingleborough St. SW9 . . . . .2A **120**
Ingleby Dr. HA1: Harr 3H **59**
Ingleby Rd. IG1: Ilf 1F **71**
N7 . . . . .3J **65**
RM10: Dag 6H **73**
Ingleby Way BR7: Chst 5E **142**
SM6: W'gton 7H **167**
Ingle Cl. HA5: Pinn 3C **40**
Ingledene Cl. NW4 . . . . .6C **44**
Ingledew Rd. SE18 . . . . .5H **107**
Inglefield Sq. *E1* *1H 103*
(off Prusom St.)
Inglehurst Gdns. IG4: Ilf 5D **52**
Inglemere Rd. CR4: Mitc 7D **136**
SE23 . . . . .3K **139**
Ingle M. EC1 . . . . .1J **7** (3A **84**)
Inglesham Wlk. E9 . . . . .6B **68**
Ingleside SL3: Poyle 4A **174**
Ingleside Cl. BR3: Beck 7C **140**
Ingleside Gro. SE3 . . . . .6H **105**
Inglethorpe St. SW6 . . . . .1F **117**
Ingleton Av. DA16: Well 5A **126**
Ingleton Rd. N18 . . . . .6B **34**
SM5: Cars 7C **166**
Ingleton St. SW9 . . . . .2A **120**

Ingleway N12 . . . . .6G **31**
Inglewood BR7: Chst 6H **143**
CR0: Sels 7A **170**
Inglewood Cl. E14 . . . . .4C **104**
Inglewood Copse BR1: Broml 2C **160**
Inglewood Ct. BR1: Broml 7G **141**
SE27 . . . . .5C **138**
(off Elder Rd.)
Inglewood Rd. DA7: Bex 4K **127**
NW6 . . . . .5J **63**
Inglis Barracks NW7 . . . . .6A **30**
Inglis Rd. CR0: C'don 1F **169**
W5 . . . . .7F **79**
Inglis St. SE5 . . . . .1B **120**
Inglis Way NW7 . . . . .6A **30**
Ingoldisthorpe Gro. SE15 . . . . .6F **103**
Ingot Twr. *E14* *5C 86*
(off Ursula Gould Way)
Ingram Av. NW11 . . . . .7A **46**
Ingram Cl. HA7: Stan 5H **27**
SE11 . . . . .3H **19** (4K **101**)
Ingram Ct. CR0: C'don 1B **168**
Ingram Ho. E3 . . . . .1A **86**
Ingram Rd. CR7: Thor H 1C **156**
N2 . . . . .4C **46**
Ingram Way UB6: G'frd 1H **77**
Ingrave Rd. RM1: Rom 4K **55**
Ingrave St. SW11 . . . . .3B **118**
Ingrebourne Apts. SW6 . . . . .3K **117**
Ingrebourne Ct. E4 . . . . .3J **35**
Ingrebourne Ho. *BR1: Broml* 5F **141**
(off Brangbourne Rd.)
NW8 . . . .*5B 4*
(off Broadley St.)
Ingress St. W4 . . . . .5A **98**
Inigo Jones Rd. SE7 . . . . .7C **106**
Inigo Pl. WC2 . . . . .2E **12**
Ink Bldg. W10 . . . . .5F **81**
Inkerman Rd. NW5 . . . . .6F **65**
Inkerman Ter. *W8* *3J 99*
(off Allen St.)
Inks Grn. E4 . . . . .5K **35**
Inkster Ho. SW11 . . . . .3C **118**
Inkwell Cl. N12 . . . . .3F **31**
Ink Works Ct. *SE1* *7H 15*
(off Bell Yd. M.)
Inman Rd. NW10 . . . . .1A **80**
SW18 . . . . .7A **118**
Inmans Row IG8: Wfd G 4D **36**
Inner Circ. NW1 . . . . .2G **5** (3E **82**)
Inner Ct. SW3 . . . . .7C **16** (6C **100**)
Innerd Ct. *CR0: C'don* *6C 156*
(off Harry Cl.)
Inner Pk. Rd. SW19 . . . . .1F **135**
Inner Ring E. TW6: H'row A 3D **110**
Inner Ring W. TW6: H'row A 3C **110**
Inner Temple La. EC4 . . . . .1J **13**
Innes Cl. SW20 . . . . .2G **153**
Innes Gdns. SW15 . . . . .6D **116**
Innes St. SE15 . . . . .7E **102**
Innes Yd. CR0: C'don 3C **168**
Innis Ho. *SE17* *5E 102*
(off East St.)
Inniskilling Rd. E13 . . . . .2A **88**
Innova Ct. CR0: C'don 1E **168**
Innova Pas. *E1* *3J 9*
(off Sclater St.)
The Innovation Cen. E14 . . . . .2E **104**
(off Marsh Wall)
Innovation Cl. HA0: Wemb 1E **78**
Inns of Court & City Yeomanry Mus.
. . . . .6H **7** (5K **83**)
Insignia Point E20 . . . . .5E **68**
Inskip Cl. E10 . . . . .2D **68**
Inskip Rd. RM8: Dag 1D **72**
Insley Ho. *E3* *3D 86*
(off Bow Rd.)
The Institute for Arts in Therapy &
Education 1B **84**
(off Britannia Row)
Institute of Archaeology Collections
. . . . .4H **83**

Institute of Commonwealth Studies
. . . . .5D 6
Institute of Contemporary Arts (ICA)
. . . . .5D 12
Institute of Germanic & Romance Studies
. . . . .5D 6
Institute of Ophthalmology 2E 8
                              (off Peerless St.)
The Institute of Psychoanalysis 4J 81
                                 (off Elgin Av.)
Institute Pl. E8 . . . . .5H 67
Instituto Cervantes 1J 13
                              (off Devereux Ct.)
Integer Gdns. E11 . . . . .7F 51
The Interchange NW1 . . . . .7F 65
                            (off Camden Lock Pl.)
Interface Ho. TW3: Houn 3E 112
                               (off Staines Rd.)
Intl. Av. TW5: Cran 5A 94
Intl. Bus. Pk. E15 . . . . .1F 87
Intl. Hall 4F 7
Intl. Ho. E1 . . . . .3K 15
                          (off St Katharine's Way)
TW8: Bford 5E 96
                              (off Gt. West Rd.)
THE INTERNATIONAL QUARTER . . .6E 68
Intl. Sq. E20 . . . . .6E 68
                          (within Westfield Shop. Cen.)
Intl. Trad. Est. UB2: S'hall 3K 93
Intl. Way E20 . . . . .6E 68
TW16: Sun 1G 147
Inverary Pl. SE18 . . . . .6H 107
Inver Cl. E5 . . . . .2J 67
Inverclyde Gdns. RM6: Chad H 4C 54
                                 (not continuous)
Inver Ct. W2 . . . . .6K 81
W6 . . . . .3C 98
Inveresk Gdns. KT4: Wor Pk 3C 164
Inverforth Cl. NW3 . . . . .2A 64
Inverforth Rd. N11 . . . . .5A 32
Invergarry Ho. NW6 . . . . .2K 81
                               (off Carlton Vale)
Inverine Rd. SE7 . . . . .5K 105
Invermead Cl. W6 . . . . .3C 98
Invermore Pl. SE18 . . . . .4G 107
Inverness Av. EN1: Enf 1K 23
Inverness Ct. SE6 . . . . .1H 141
Inverness Gdns. W8 . . . . .1K 99
Inverness M. E16 . . . . .1G 107
W2 . . . . .7K 81
Inverness Pl. W2 . . . . .7K 81
Inverness Rd. KT4: Wor Pk 1F 165
N18 . . . . .5C 34
TW3: Houn 4D 112
UB2: S'hall 4C 94
Inverness St. NW1 . . . . .1F 83
Inverness Ter. W2 . . . . .6K 81
Inverton Rd. SE15 . . . . .4K 121
The Invicta Cen. IG11: Bark 1A 90
Invicta Cl. BR7: Chst 5E 142
E3 . . . . .5C 86
TW14: Felt 1H 129
Invicta Gro. UB5: N'olt 3D 76
Invicta Pde. DA14: Sidc 4B 144
Invicta Plaza SE1 . . . . . . .4A 14 (1B 102)
Invicta Rd. SE3 . . . . .7J 105
Inville Rd. SE17 . . . . .5D 102
                                 (not continuous)
Inville Wlk. SE17 . . . . .5D 102
Invito IG2: Ilf 6E 52
Inwen Ct. SE8 . . . . .5A 104
                                 (not continuous)
Inwood Av. TW3: Houn 3G 113
Inwood Bus. Pk. TW3: Houn 4F 113
Inwood Cl. CRO: C'don 2A 170
Inwood Ct. NW1 . . . . .7G 65
                              (off Rochester Sq.)
Inwood Ho. N1 . . . . .1B 84
                                (off Elliott's Pl.)
Inwood Rd. TW3: Houn 4F 113
Inworth St. SW11 . . . . .2C 118
Inworth Wlk. N1 . . . . .1C 84
                               (off Popham St.)

IO Centre SE18 . . . . .3G 107
                                 (not continuous)
Iona Cl. SE6 . . . . .7C 122
SM4: Mord 7K 153
Ion Ct. E2 . . . . .2G 85
Ionian Bldg. E14 . . . . .7A 86
                                 (off Narrow St.)
Ionian Ho. E1 . . . . .4K 85
                                (off Duckett St.)
Ion Sq. E2 . . . . .2G 85
IO Trade Cen. CRO: Bedd 4K 167
Ipsden Bldgs. SE1 . . . . .5K 13
Ipswich Rd. SW17 . . . . .6E 136
Ira Ct. SE27 . . . . .2B 138
Ireland Cl. E6 . . . . .5D 88
Ireland Pl. N22 . . . . .7D 32
Ireland Yd. EC4 . . . . .1B 14 (6B 84)
Irene M. W7 . . . . .1K 95
                              (off Uxbridge Rd.)
Irene Rd. BR6: Orp 7K 161
SW6 . . . . .1J 117
Ireton Cl. N10 . . . . .7K 31
Ireton Ho. SW15 . . . . .5G 117
                              (off Stamford Sq.)
Ireton St. E3 . . . . .4C 86
Iris Av. DA5: Bexl 5E 126
Iris Cl. CRO: C'don 1K 169
E6 . . . . .5C 88
KT6: Surb 7F 151
N14 .7C 22
Iris Ct. SE14 . . . . .1J 121
                                 (off Briant St.)
Iris Cres. DA7: Bex 6F 109
Iris Gdns. KT7: T Ditt 7J 149
Iris M. TW4: Houn 6E 112
Iris Rd. KT19: Ewe 5H 163
Iris Wlk. HA8: Edg 4D 28
Iris Way E4 . . . . .6G 35
Irkdale Av. EN1: Enf 1A 24
Iron Bri. Cl. NW10 . . . . .5A 62
Ironbridge Cl. UB2: S'hall 1G 95
Iron Bri. Rd. Nth. UB11: Stock P . . .2C 92
Iron Bri. Rd. Sth. UB7: W Dray 2C 92
Iron Mill Pl. SW18 . . . . .6K 117
Iron Mill Rd. SW18 . . . . .6K 117
Ironmonger La. EC2 . . . . . . .1D 14 (6C 84)
Ironmonger Pas. EC1 . . . . .2D 8
                            (off Ironmonger Row)
Ironmonger Row EC1 . . . . . .2D 8 (3C 84)
Ironmonger Row Baths 2C 8
Ironmongers Pl. E14 . . . . .4C 104
Ironside Cl. SE16 . . . . .2K 103
Ironside Ct. CR2: S Croy 6D 168
TW11: Hamp W 1C 150
Ironside Ho. E9 . . . . .4A 68
Irons Way RM5: Col R 1J 55
Iron Works E3 . . . . .1C 86
The Ironworks N1 . . . . .2J 83
                              (off Albion Wlk.)
Ironworks Way E13 . . . . .2B 88
Irvine Av. HA3: Kenton 3A 42
Irvine Cl. E14 . . . . .5D 86
N20 .2H 31
Irvine Ct. W1 . . . . .4B 6
                               (off Whitfield St.)
Irvine Ho. N7 . . . . .6K 65
                             (off Caledonian Rd.)
Irvine Way BR6: Orp 7K 161
Irving Av. UB5: N'olt 1B 76
Irving Gro. SW9 . . . . .2K 119
Irving Ho. SE17 . . . . .5B 102
                            (off Doddington Gro.)
Irving Mans. W14 . . . . .6G 99
                            (off Queen's Club Gdns.)
Irving M. N1 . . . . .6C 66
Irving Rd. W14 . . . . .3F 99
Irving St. WC2 . . . . .3D 12 (7H 83)
Irving Way NW9 . . . . .5G 44
Irwell Cl. W7 . . . . .6H 77
                              (off Hobbayne Rd.)
Irwell Est. SE16 . . . . .3J 103
Irwin Av. SE18 . . . . .7J 107

Irwin Cl. NW7 . . . . .5B 30
UB10: Ick 3C 56
Irwin Gdns. NW10 . . . . .1D 80
Isaac Way SE1 . . . . .6D 14
                              (off Sanctuary St.)
Isabel Hill Cl. TW12: Hamp 1F 149
Isabella Cl. N14 . . . . .7B 22
Isabella Ct. TW10: Rich 6F 115
                               (off Kingsmead)
Isabella Dr. BR6: Farnb 4G 173
Isabella Ho. SE11 . . . . .5K 19
W6 . . . . .5E 98
                          (off Queen Caroline St.)
Isabella M. N1 . . . . .6E 66
Isabella Pl. KT2: King T 5F 133
Isabella Plantation Garden 3H 133
Isabella Rd. E9 . . . . .5J 67
Isabella St. SE1 . . . . .5A 14 (1B 102)
Isabel St. SW9 . . . . .1K 119
Isambard M. E14 . . . . .3E 104
Isambard Pl. SE16 . . . . .1J 103
Isel Way SE22 . . . . .5E 120
Isham Rd. SW16 . . . . .2J 155
Isis Cl. HA4: Ruis 6E 38
SW15 . . . . .4E 116
Isis Ct. W4 . . . . .7H 97
Isis Ho. N18 . . . . .6A 34
NW8 . . . . .4B 4
                              (off Church St. Est.)
SE20 . . . . .7G 139
Isis St. SW18 . . . . .2A 136
The Island KT7: T Ditt 6A 150
UB7: Lford 3D 174
Island Apts. N1 . . . . .1C 84
Island Barn Reservoir Sailing Club
. . . . .6F 149
Island Farm Av. KT8: W Mole 5D 148
Island Farm Rd. KT8: W Mole 5D 148
Island Ho. E3 . . . . .3E 86
Island Rd. CR4: Mitc 7D 136
SE16 . . . . .4K 103
Island Row E14 . . . . .6B 86
Islay Gdns. TW4: Houn 5B 112
Islay Wlk. N1 . . . . .6C 66
                             (off Douglas Rd. Sth.)
Isleden Ho. N1 . . . . .1C 84
                               (off Prebend St.)
Isledon Rd. N7 . . . . .3A 66
ISLEWORTH 3A 66
Islehurst Cl. BR7: Chst 1E 160
ISLE OF DOGS 2D 104
ISLEWORTH 3E 114
Isleworth Ait Nature Reserve 3B 114
Isleworth Bus. Complex TW7: Isle . . .2K 113
Isleworth Prom. TW1: Twick 4B 114
Isleworth Recreation Cen. 4K 113
Isley Ct. E14 . . . . .4E 86
                                (off Teviot St.)
SW8 . . . . .2G 119
ISLINGTON 7B 66
Islington Bus. Cen. N1 . . . . .1C 84
                              (off Coleman Flds.)
Islington Crematorium 1D 46
The Islington Ecology Cen. 3A 84
Islington Grn. N1 . . . . .1B 84
                                 (not continuous)
Islington High St. N1 . . . . .2A 84
                                 (not continuous)
Islington Mus. 2A 8 (3B 84)
Islington Pk. M. N1 . . . . .7B 66
Islington Pk. St. N1 . . . . .7A 66
Islington Pl. N1 . . . . .1A 84
Islington Sq. N1 . . . . .1B 84
Islington Tennis Cen. 6J 65
Islip Gdns. HA8: Edg 7E 28
UB5: N'olt 7C 58
Islip Mnr. Rd. UB5: N'olt 7C 58
Islip St. NW5 . . . . .5G 65
Ismailia Rd. E7 . . . . .7K 69
Ismaili Cen. 3B 16
Isobel Ho. HA1: Harr 5K 41
Isobel Pl. N15 . . . . .4F 49

Isola Ct. N1 . . . . .1C 84
                               (off Popham Rd.)
Isom Cl. E13 . . . . .3K 87
Issa Rd. TW3: Houn 4D 112
Issigonis Ho. W3 . . . . .1B 98
                                 (off Cowley Rd.)
Istra Ho. E20 . . . . .5E 68
                                (off Logan Cl.)
Itaska Cotts. WD23: B Hea 1D 26
Ithell Ct. HA0: Wemb 5D 60
Ivanhoe Cl. UB8: Cowl 5A 74
Ivanhoe Dr. HA3: Kenton 3A 42
Ivanhoe Ho. E3 . . . . .2A 86
                                (off Grove Rd.)
Ivanhoe Rd. SE5 . . . . .3F 121
TW4: Houn 3B 112
Ivaro Ct. RM5: Col R 1J 55
Ivatt Pl. W14 . . . . .5H 99
Ivatt Way N17 . . . . .3B 48
Iveagh Av. NW10 . . . . .2G 79
Iveagh Cl. E9 . . . . .1K 85
HA6: Nwood 1D 38
NW10 . . . . .2G 79
Iveagh Ct. BR3: Beck 3E 158
E1 . . . . .1J 15
Iveagh Ho. SW9 . . . . .2B 120
SW10 . . . . .7A 100
                                (off King's Rd.)
Iveagh Ter. NW10 . . . . .2G 79
                                (off Iveagh Av.)
Ivedon Rd. DA16: Well 2C 126
Ive Farm Cl. E10 . . . . .2C 68
Ive Farm La. E10 . . . . .2C 68
Iveley Rd. SW4 . . . . .2G 119
Ivere Dr. EN5: New Bar 6E 20
Iver Ho. N1 . . . . .1E 84
                               (off Halcomb St.)
Iverhurst Cl. DA6: Bex 5D 126
Iverna Ct. W8 . . . . .3J 99
Iverna Gdns. TW14: Felt 5F 111
W8 . . . . .3J 99
Iverson Rd. NW6 . . . . .6H 63
Ivers Way CRO: New Ad 7D 170
Ives Rd. E16 . . . . .5G 87
Ives St. SW3 . . . . .3D 16 (4C 100)
Ivestor Ter. SE23 . . . . .7J 121
Ivimey St. E2 . . . . .3G 85
Ivinghoe Cl. EN1: Enf 1K 23
Ivinghoe Ho. N7 . . . . .5H 65
Ivinghoe Rd. RM8: Dag 5B 72
Ivo Pl. N19 . . . . .3H 65
Ivor Ct. N8 . . . . .6J 47
NW1 . . . . .3E 4
                               (off Gloucester Pl.)
Ivor Gro. SE9 . . . . .1F 143
The Ivories N1 . . . . .7C 66
                             (off Northampton St.)
Ivor Pl. NW1 . . . . .4E 4 (4D 82)
Ivor St. NW1 . . . . .7G 65
Ivory Ct. E18 . . . . .1J 51
TW13: Felt 1J 129
Ivorydown BR1: Broml 4J 141
Ivory Ho. E1 . . . . .3K 15 (1F 103)
Ivory Pl. W11 . . . . .7G 81
                               (off Treadgold St.)
Ivory Sq. SW11 . . . . .3A 118
Ivybridge Cl. TW1: Twick 7A 114
UB8: Uxb 3A 74
Ivybridge Ct. BR7: Chst 1E 160
                                 (off Old Hill)
NW1 . . . . .7F 65
                                (off Lewis St.)
Ivybridge La. WC2 . . . . . .3F 13 (7J 83)
Ivy Bri. Retail Pk. 5K 113
Ivychurch Cl. SE20 . . . . .7J 139
Ivychurch La. SE17 . . . . .5F 103
Ivy Cl. HA2: Harr 4D 58
HA5: Eastc 7A 40
TW16: Sun 2A 148
Ivy Cotts. E14 . . . . .7E 86
UB10: Hil 3C 74
Ivy Ct. SE16 . . . . .5G 103
                                (off Argyle Way)

Ivy Cres. W4 .4J 97
Ivydale Rd. SE15 . . . . .3K 121
   SM5: Cars 2D 166
Ivyday Gro. SW16 . . . . .3K 137
Ivydene KT8: W Mole 5D 148
Ivydene Cl. SM1: Sutt 4A 166
Ivydene Ct. IG9: Buck H 2F 37
   (off Queen's Rd.)
Ivy Gdns. CR4: Mitc 3H 155
   N8 . . . . .6J 47
Ivy Ho. Rd. UB10: Ick 3D 56
Ivyhouse Rd. RM9: Dag 6D 72
Ivy La. TW4: Houn 4D 112
Ivy Lodge W11 . . . . .1J 99
   (off Notting Hill Ga.)
Ivymount Rd. SE27 . . . . .3A 138
Ivy Rd. E16 .6J 87
   E17 . . . . .6C 50
   KT6: Surb 1G 163
   N14 . . . . .7B 22
   NW2 . . . . .4E 62
   SE4 . . . . .4B 122
   SW17 . . . . .5C 136
   TW3: Houn 4F 113
Ivy St. N1 . . . . .2E 84
Ivy Wlk. HA6: Nwood 1G 39
   RM9: Dag 6E 72
Ixworth Pl. SW3 . . . . .5C 16 (5C 100)
Izane Rd. DA6: Bex 4F 127

J

Jacana Ct. E1 . . . . .3K 15
   (off Star Pl.)
Jacaranda Cl. KT3: N Mald 3A 152
Jacaranda Gro. E8 . . . . .7F 67
Jackass La. BR2: Kes 5K 171
Jack Barnett Way N22 . . . . .2K 47
Jack Clow Rd. E15 . . . . .2G 87
Jack Cook Ho. IG11: Bark 7F 71
Jack Cornwell St. E12 . . . . .4E 70
Jack Dash Way E6 . . . . .4C 88
Jack Dimmer Cl. SW16 . . . . .2G 155
Jackets La. HA6: Nwood 1D 38
Jack Goodchild Way
   KT1: King T 3H 151
Jack Jones Way RM9: Dag 1F 91
Jacklin Grn. IG8: Wfd G 4D 36
Jackman Ho. E1 . . . . .1H 103
   (off Watts St.)
Jackman M. NW2 . . . . .3A 62
Jackman St. E8 . . . . .1H 85
Jacks Farm Way E4 . . . . .6K 35
Jackson & Joseph Bldg. E1 . . . . . . .5K 9
   (off Princelet St.)
Jackson Cl. E9 . . . . .7J 67
   UB10: Uxb 7A 56
Jackson Ct. E7 . . . . .6K 69
Jackson Ho. N11 . . . . .5B 32
Jackson Rd. BR2: Broml 2D 172
   EN4: E Barn 6H 21
   IG11: Bark 1H 89
   N7 . . . . .4K 65
   UB10: Uxb 7A 56
Jacksons La. N6 . . . . .7E 46
Jacksons Lane Theatre 6F 47
   (off Archway Rd.)
Jacksons Pl. CR0: C'don 1D 168
Jackson St. SE18 . . . . .6E 106
Jackson's Way CR0: C'don 3C 170
Jackson Way UB2: S'hall 2F 95
Jacks Pl. E1 . . . . .5J 9
   (off Corbet Pl.)
Jack the Ripper Mus. 7G 85
Jack Walker Ct. N5 . . . . .4B 66
Jacob Ho. DA18: Erith 2D 108
   (off Kale Rd.)
Jacobin Lodge N7 . . . . .5J 65
Jacob Mans. E1 . . . . .6H 85
   (off Commercial Rd.)
Jacob M. HA7: Stan 2F 27
Jacobs Cl. RM10: Dag 4H 73

Jacobs Ct. E1 . . . . .6G 85
   (off Plumber's Row)
Jacobs Ho. E13 . . . . .3A 88
   (off New City Rd.)
Jacobs Island Ho. SE16 . . . . .3F 103
   (off Spa Rd.)
Jacobs M. SW15 . . . . .4G 117
Jacob St. SE1 . . . . .6K 15 (2G 103)
Jacob's Well M. W1 . . . . . .6H 5 (5E 82)
Jacotts Ho. W10 . . . . .4E 80
   (off Sutton Way)
Jacquard Ct. SW18 . . . . .5K 117
   (off Courthouse Way)
Jacqueline Cl. UB5: N'olt 1C 76
Jacqueline Creft Ter. N6 . . . . .6E 46
   (off Grange Rd.)
Jacqueline Ho. NW1 . . . . .1D 82
   (off Regent's Pk. Rd.)
Jacqueline Vs. E17 . . . . .5E 50
   (off Shernhall St.)
Jade Cl. E16 . . . . .6B 88
   NW2 . . . . .7F 45
   RM8: Dag 1C 72
Jade Ter. NW6 . . . . .7A 64
Jaffe Rd. IG1: Ilf 1H 71
Jaffray Pl. SE27 . . . . .4B 138
Jaffray Rd.
   BR2: Broml 4B 160
Jaggard Way SW12 . . . . .7D 118
Jagger Ho. SW11 . . . . .1D 118
   (off Rosenau Rd.)
Jago Cl. SE18 . . . . .6G 107
Jago Wlk. SE5 . . . . .7D 102
Jake Russell Wlk. E16 . . . . .7A 88
Jamaica Rd. CR7: Thor H 6B 156
   SE1 . . . . .7K 15 (2F 103)
   SE16 . . . . .7K 15 (2F 103)
Jamaica St. E1 . . . . .6J 85
James Allens School Swimming Pool
   . . . . .5E 120
James Anderson Ct. E2 . . . . .2E 84
   (off Kingsland Rd.)
James Av. NW2 . . . . .5E 62
   RM8: Dag 1F 73
James Bedford Cl. HA5: Pinn 2A 40
James Boswell Cl. SW16 . . . . .4K 137
James Brine Ho. E2 . . . . .1K 9
   (off Ravenscroft St.)
James Campbell Ho. E2 . . . . .2J 85
   (off Old Ford Rd.)
James Clavell Sq. SE18 . . . . .3F 107
James Cl. E13 . . . . .2J 87
   NW11 . . . . .6G 45
James Collins Cl. W9 . . . . .4H 81
James Ct. HA6: Nwood 1H 39
   N1 . . . . .1C 84
   (off Raynor Pl.)
   NW9 . . . . .2A 44
   UB5: N'olt 2C 76
   (off Church Rd.)
James Docherty Ho. E2 . . . . .2H 85
   (off Patriot Sq.)
James Dudson Ct. NW10 . . . . .7J 61
James East. CR4: Mitc 2D 154
James Gdns. N22 . . . . .7G 33
James Hammett Ho. E2 . . . . .1K 9
   (off Ravenscroft St.)
James Hill Ho. W10 . . . . .4G 81
   (off Kensal Rd.)
James Ho. E1 . . . . .4A 86
   (off Solebay St.)
   SE16 . . . . .2K 103
   (off Wolfe Cres.)
   SW8 . . . . .7J 101
   (off Wyvil Rd.)
   W10 . . . . .4G 81
James Joyce Wlk. SE24 . . . . .4B 120
James La. E10 . . . . .7E 50
   E11 . . . . .7F 51
James Leal Cen.
   Woodford 5G 37
James Lighthill Ho. WC1 . . . . .1H 7
   (off Penton Ri.)

James Lind Ho. SE8 . . . . .4B 104
   (off Grove St.)
James Middleton Ho. E2 . . . . .3H 85
   (off Middleton St.)
James Morgan M. N1 . . . . .1C 84
James Newman Ct. SE9 . . . . .3E 142
Jameson Cl. W3 . . . . .2J 97
Jameson Ct. E2 . . . . .2J 85
   (off Russia La.)
Jameson Ho. SE11 . . . . .5G 19
   (off Glasshouse Wlk.)
Jameson Lodge N6 . . . . .6G 47
Jameson St. W8 . . . . .1J 99
James Pl. N17 . . . . .1F 49
James Riley Point E15 . . . . .1E 86
   (off Carpenters Rd.)
James's Cotts. TW9: Kew 7G 97
James Stewart Ho. NW6 . . . . .7H 63
James St.
   EN1: Enf 5A 24
   IG11: Bark 7G 71
   TW3: Houn 3H 113
   W1 . . . . .1H 11 (6E 82)
   WC2 . . . . .1F 13 (7J 83)
James Stroud Ho. SE17 . . . . .5C 102
   (off Walworth Pl.)
James Ter. SW14 . . . . .3K 115
   (off Church Path)
Jameston Lodge HA4: Ruis 1H 57
Jamestown Rd. NW1 . . . . .1F 83
Jamestown Way E14 . . . . .7F 87
James Voller Way E1 . . . . .6J 85
James Yd. E4 . . . . .6A 36
The Jam Factory SE1 . . . . .3E 102
   (off Green Wlk.)
Jamieson Ho. TW4: Houn 6D 112
Jamilah Ho. E16 . . . . .7E 88
   (off University Way)
Jamuna Cl. E14 . . . . .5A 86
Jane Austen Hall E16 . . . . .1K 105
   (off Wesley Av.)
Jane Austen Ho. SW1 . . . . .6A 18
   (off Churchill Gdns.)
Jane Seymour Ct. SE9 . . . . .7H 125
Jane St. E1 .6H 85
Janet Adegoke Swimming Pool 7C 80
Janeway Pl. SE16 . . . . .2H 103
Janeway St. SE16 . . . . .2G 103
Janice M. IG1: Ilf 2F 71
Jansen Wlk. SW11 . . . . .3B 118
Janson Cl. E15 . . . . .5G 69
   NW10 . . . . .3A 62
Janson Rd. E15 . . . . .5G 69
Jansons Rd. N15 . . . . .3E 48
Japan Cres. N4 . . . . .7K 47
Japan Rd. RM6: Chad H 6D 54
Jaquard Ct. E2 . . . . .2J 85
   (off Bishop's Way)
Jardine Rd. E1 . . . . .7K 85
Jarman Ho. E1 . . . . .5J 85
   (off Jubilee St.)
   SE16 . . . . .4K 103
   (off Hawkstone Rd.)
Jarret Ho. E3 . . . . .3C 86
   (off Bow Rd.)
Jarrett Cl. SW2 . . . . .1B 138
Jarrow Cl. SM4: Mord 5K 153
Jarrow Rd. N17 . . . . .4H 49
   RM6: Chad H 6C 54
   SE16 . . . . .4J 103
Jarrow Way E9 . . . . .4B 68
Jarvis Cl.
   EN5: Barn 5A 20
   IG11: Bark 1H 89
Jarvis Ho. SE15 . . . . .1G 121
   (off Goldsmith Rd.)
Jarvis Rd. CR2: S Croy 6D 168
   SE22 . . . . .4E 120
Jashoda Ho. SE18 . . . . .5E 106
   (off Connaught M.)
Jasmin Cl. HA6: Nwood 1H 39
Jasmin Ct. SE12 . . . . .6J 123

Jasmine Cl. BR6: Farnb 2F 173
   IG1: Ilf 5F 71
   UB1: S'hall 7C 76
Jasmine Ct. SW19 . . . . .5J 135
Jasmine Gdns. CR0: C'don 3D 170
   HA2: Harr 2E 58
Jasmine Gro. SE20 . . . . .1H 157
Jasmine Ho. SW18 . . . . .3A 118
Jasmine Rd. RM7: Rush G 2K 73
Jasmine Sq. E3 . . . . .1B 86
   (off Hawthorn Av.)
Jasmine Ter. UB7: W Dray 2C 92
Jasmine Way KT8: E Mos 4J 149
Jasmin Lodge SE16 . . . . .5H 103
   (off Sherwood Gdns.)
Jasmin Rd. KT19: Ewe 5H 163
Jason Cl. SW9 . . . . .1A 120
   (off Southey Rd.)
   W1 . . . . .7H 5
Jason Wlk. SE9 . . . . .4E 142
Jasper Av. W7 . . . . .2K 95
Jasper Cl. EN3: Enf W 1D 24
Jasper Pas. SE19 . . . . .6F 139
Jasper Rd. E16 . . . . .6B 88
   SE19 . . . . .5F 139
Jasper Wlk. N1 . . . . .3D 84
Java Ho. E14 . . . . .6G 87
Java Wharf SE1 . . . . .6K 15
   (off Shad Thames)
Javelin Ct. HA7: Stan 5G 27
   (off William Dr.)
Javelin Way UB5: N'olt 3B 76
Jaycroft EN2: Enf 1F 23
Jay Gdns. BR7: Chst 4D 142
Jay Ho. E3 . . . . .1B 86
   (off Hawthorn Av.)
Jay M. SM5: Cars 3D 166
   SW7 . . . . .7A 10 (2A 100)
Jays St. N1 .1K 83
Jazzfern Ter. HA0: Wemb 5A 60
Jean Batten Cl. SM6: W'gton 7K 167
The Jean Brown Indoor Arena 1H 53
Jean Darling Ho. SW10 . . . . .6B 100
   (off Milman's St.)
Jean Ho. SW17 . . . . .5C 136
Jeanne Court E14 . . . . .5A 86
   (off Pechora Way)
Jean Pardies Ho. E1 . . . . .5J 85
   (off Jubilee St.)
Jebb Av. SW2 . . . . .6J 119
   (not continuous)
Jebb St. E3 .2C 86
Jedburgh Rd. E13 . . . . .3A 88
Jedburgh St. SW11 . . . . .4E 118
Jeddo M. W12 . . . . .2B 98
Jeddo Rd. W12 . . . . .2B 98
Jeeyas Apts. E16 . . . . .5H 87
Jefferson Bldg. E14 . . . . .2C 104
Jefferson Cl. IG2: Ilf 5F 53
   W13 . . . . .3B 96
Jefferson Ho. TW8: Bford 6E 96
   UB7: W Dray 2B 92
   (off Park Lodge Av.)
Jefferson Pl. BR2: Broml 6B 160
Jefferson Plaza E3 . . . . .4E 86
   (off Hannaford Wlk.)
Jefferson Wlk. SE18 . . . . .6E 106
Jeffrey Row SE12 . . . . .5K 123
Jeffrey's Pl. NW1 . . . . .7G 65
Jeffreys Rd. EN3: Brim 4F 25
   SW4 . . . . .2J 119
Jeffrey's St. NW1 . . . . .7G 65
Jeffreys Wlk. SW4 . . . . .2J 119
Jeffs Cl. TW12: Hamp 6F 131
Jeffs Rd. SM1: Sutt 4H 165
Jeger Av. E2 .1F 85
Jeken Rd. SE9 . . . . .4A 124
Jelf Rd. SW2 . . . . .5A 120
Jelico Point SE16 . . . . .2B 104
   (off Rotherhithe St.)
Jellicoe Gdns. HA7: Stan 6E 26
Jellicoe Ho. E2 . . . . .2G 85
   (off Ropley St.)

Jellicoe Rd. E13 . . . . .4J 87
N17 . . . . .7J 33
Jemma Knowles Cl. SW2 . . . . . .1A 138
(off Tulse Hill)
Jemmett Cl. KT2: King T 1H 151
Jemotts Ct. SE14 . . . . .6K 103
(off Myers La.)
Jem Paterson Ct. HA1: Harr 4J 59
Jengar Cl. SM1: Sutt 4K 165
Jenkins La. IG11: Bark 2G 89
Jenkinson Ho. E2 . . . . .3K 85
(off Usk St.)
Jenkins Rd. E13 . . . . .4K 87
Jenner Av. W3 . . . . .5K 79
Jenner Cl. DA14: Sidc 4A 144
Jenner Ct. N21 . . . . .5D 22
(off Pennington Dr.)
Jenner Ho. WC1 . . . . .3F 7
(off Hunter St.)
Jenner Pl. SW13 . . . . .6D 98
Jenner Rd. N16 . . . . .3F 67
Jennett Rd. CRO: Wadd 3A 168
Jennifer Ho. E14 . . . . .6E 86
SE11 . . . . .4K 19
(off Reedworth St.)
Jennifer Rd. BR1: Broml 3H 141
Jenningsbury Ho. SW3 . . . . . . .5D 16
(off Cale St.)
Jennings Cl. KT6: Surb 7C 150
RM8: Dag 1E 72
Jennings Ho. SE10 . . . . .5F 105
(off Old Woolwich Rd.)
Jennings Rd. SE22 . . . . .6F 121
Jennings Way EN5: Barn 3A 20
Jenningtree Way DA17: Belv 2J 109
Jenny Hammond Cl. E11 . . . . . .3H 69
Jensen Ho. E3 . . . . .4C 86
(off Wellington Way)
Jenson Hgts. N1 . . . . .7K 65
(off Caledonian Rd.)
Jenson Way SE19 . . . . .7F 139
Jenton Av. DA7: Bex 1E 126
Jephson Cl. SW4 . . . . .2J 119
Jephson Ho. SE17 . . . . .6B 102
(off Doddington Gro.)
Jephson Rd. E7 . . . . .7A 70
Jephson St. SE5 . . . . .1D 120
Jephtha Rd. SW18 . . . . .6J 117
Jeppos La. CR4: Mitc 4D 154
Jepson Ho. SW6 . . . . .1K 117
(off Pearscroft Rd.)
Jerdan Ho. SW6 . . . . .7J 99
(off North End Rd.)
Jerdan Pl. SW6 . . . . .7J 99
Jeremiah St. E14 . . . . .6D 86
Jeremy Bentham Ho. E2 . . . . . .3G 85
(off Mansford St.)
Jeremy's Grn. N18 . . . . .4C 34
Jermyn St. SW1 . . . . . .4A 12 (1G 101)
Jermyn Street Theatre 3C 12
(off Jermyn St.)
Jerningham Av. IG5: Ilf 2F 53
Jerningham Ct. SE14 . . . . .1A 122
Jerningham Rd. SE14 . . . . .2A 122
Jerome Cres. NW8 . . . . . .3C 4 (4C 82)
Jerome Ho. KT1: Hamp W 2D 150
(off Old Bridge St.)
NW1 . . . . .5D 4
(off Lisson Gro.)
SW7 . . . . .3A 16
(off Glendower Pl.)
Jerome Pl. KT1: King T 2D 150
(off Wadbrook St.)
Jerome St. E1 . . . . .5J 9 (4F 85)
Jerome Twr. W3 . . . . .2H 97
Jerrard St. SE13 . . . . .3D 122
Jerrold St. N1 . . . . .1H 9 (2E 84)
Jersey Av. HA7: Stan 2B 42
Jersey Dr. BR5: Pet W 6H 161
Jersey Ho. EN3: Enf W 1E 24
(off Eastfield Rd.)
N1 . . . . .6C 66
(off Jersey Rd.)

Jersey Rd. E11 . . . . .1F 69
E16 . . . . .6A 88
IG1: Ilf 4F 71
N1 . . . . .6C 66
SW17 . . . . .6F 137
TW3: Houn 1F 113
TW5: Hest, Isle 1F 113
TW7: Isle 7H 95
W7 . . . . .2A 96
Jerusalem Pas. EC1 . . . .4A 8 (4B 84)
Jervis Ct. RM10: Dag 6H 73
SE10 . . . . .1E 122
(off Blissett St.)
W1 . . . . .1K 11
Jervis Rd. SW6 . . . . .6H 99
Jerviston Gdns. SW16 . . . . .6A 138
Jerwood Space Art Gallery 6C 14
Jesmond Av. HA9: Wemb 6F 61
Jesmond Cl. CR4: Mitc 3F 155
Jesmond Dene NW3 . . . . .6A 64
Jesmond Rd. CRO: C'don 7F 157
Jesmond Way HA7: Stan 5K 27
Jessam Av. E5 . . . . .1H 67
Jessamine Rd. W7 . . . . .1K 95
Jessel Ho. SW1 . . . . .3D 18
(off Page St.)
WC1 . . . . .2E 6
(off Judd St.)
Jessel Mans. W14 . . . . .6G 99
(off Queen's Club Gdns.)
Jesse Rd. E10 . . . . .1E 68
Jessett Cl. DA8: Erith 4K 109
Jessica Rd. SW18 . . . . .6A 118
Jessie Blythe La. N19 . . . . .7J 47
Jessie Duffett Ho. SE5 . . . . .7C 102
(off Pitman St.)
Jessie Wood Ct. SW9 . . . . .7A 102
(off Caldwell St.)
Jessiman Ter. TW17: Shep 5C 146
Jesson Ho. SE17 . . . . .4D 102
(off Orb St.)
Jessop Av. UB2: S'hall 4D 94
Jessop Ct. N1 . . . . .2B 84
Jessop Ho. W4 . . . . .4K 97
(off Kirton Cl.)
Jessop Lodge CRO: C'don 2C 168
(off Tamworth Rd.)
Jessop Pl. W7 . . . . .3J 95
Jessop Rd. SE24 . . . . .4B 120
Jessop Sq. E14 . . . . .1C 104
Jessops Way CRO: Bedd, Mitc . . .6G 155
Jessup Cl. SE18 . . . . .4G 107
Jetstar Way UB5: N'olt 3C 76
Jevington Way SE12 . . . . .1K 141
Jevons Ho. NW8 . . . . .7B 64
(off Hilgrove Rd.)
Jewel Rd. E17 . . . . .3C 50
Jewel Sq. E1 . . . . .7H 85
Jewel Tower 1E 18
(off College M.)
Jewish Mus. 1F 83
Jewry St. EC3 . . . . .1J 15 (6F 85)
Jew's Row SW18 . . . . .4K 117
Jews' Wlk. SE26 . . . . .4H 139
Jeymer Av. NW2 . . . . .5D 62
Jeymer Dr. UB6: G'frd 1F 77
(not continuous)
Jeypore Rd. SW18 . . . . .7A 118
Jeypore Rd. Pas. SW18 . . . . . . .6A 118
Jhumat Pl. IG1: Ilf 3E 70
(off Roden St.)
Jigger Mast Ho. SE18 . . . . .3E 106
Jillian Cl. TW12: Hamp 7E 130
Jim Bradley Cl. SE18 . . . . .4E 106
Jim Griffiths Ho. SW6 . . . . .6H 99
(off Clem Attlee Ct.)
Jim Veal Dr. N7 . . . . .6J 65
Joan Cres. SE9 . . . . .7B 124
Joan Gdns. RM8: Dag 2E 72
Joanna Ho. W6 . . . . .5E 98
(off Queen Caroline St.)
Joan Rd. RM8: Dag 2E 72

Joan St. SE1 . . . . .5A 14 (1B 102)
Job Drain Pl. IG11: Bark 2A 90
Jocelin Ho. N1 . . . . .1K 83
(off Barnsbury Est.)
Jocelyn Rd. TW9: Rich 3E 114
Jocelyn St. SE15 . . . . .1G 121
Jockey's Flds. WC1 . . . . . .5H 7 (5K 83)
Jodane St. SE8 . . . . .4B 104
Jodrell Cl. TW7: Isle 1A 114
Jodrell Rd. E3 . . . . .1B 86
Joe Hunte Ct. SE27 . . . . .5B 138
Joel St. HA5: Eastc 3J 39
HA6: Nwood 2J 39
Johanna St. SE1 . . . . . . .7J 13 (2A 102)
John Adams Ct. N9 . . . . .2A 34
John Adam St. WC2 . . . . .3F 13 (7J 83)
John Aird Ct. W2 . . . . .5A 4
(not continuous)
John Archer Way SW18 . . . . . . .6B 118
John Ashby Cl. SW2 . . . . .6J 119
John Austin Cl. KT2: King T 1F 151
John Baird Ct. SE26 . . . . .4J 139
John Barker Ct. NW6 . . . . .7G 63
John Barnes Wlk. E15 . . . . .6H 69
John Bell Twr. E. E3 . . . . .2C 86
(off Pancras Way)
John Bell Twr. W. E3 . . . . .2C 86
(off Pancras Way)
John Betts' Ho. W12 . . . . .3B 98
John Bond Ho. E3 . . . . .2B 86
(off Wright's Rd.)
John Bowles Ct. E1 . . . . .7K 85
(off Schoolhouse La.)
John Bradshaw Ho. N14 . . . . . . .1C 32
John Brent Ho. SE8 . . . . .4K 103
(off Haddonfield)
John Buck Ho. NW10 . . . . .1B 80
John Bull Pl. W4 . . . . .4H 97
John Burns Dr. IG11: Bark 7J 71
John Campbell Rd. N16 . . . . . . .5E 66
John Carpenter St. EC4 . . .2A 14 (7B 84)
John Cartwright Ho. E2 . . . . .3H 85
(off Old Bethnal Grn. Rd.)
John Crane St. SE17 . . . . .6D 102
John Donne Way SE10 . . . . .7D 104
(off Norman Rd.)
John Drinkwater Cl. E11 . . . . . . .7H 51
John Fearon Wlk. W10 . . . . .3G 81
(off Dart St.)
John Fielden Ho. E2 . . . . .3H 85
(off Canrobert St.)
John Fisher St. E1 . . . . . . .2K 15 (7G 85)
John Goddard Way TW13: Felt . . .2K 129
John Gooch Dr. EN2: Enf 1G 23
John Harrison Way SE10 . . . . . . .3H 105
John Horner M. N1 . . . . .2C 84
John Hunter Av. SW17 . . . . .3C 136
John Islip St. SW1 . . . . . .5D 18 (4H 101)
John Kaye Ct. TW17: Shep 5C 146
John Keats Ho. N22 . . . . .7E 32
John Keats Lodge EN2: Enf 1J 23
John Kennedy Ct. N1 . . . . .6D 66
(off Newington Grn. Rd.)
John Kennedy Ho. SE16 . . . . . . .4K 103
(off Rotherhithe Old Rd.)
John Knight Lodge SW6 . . . . . . .7J 99
John Lamb Ct. HA3: W'stone 1J 41
John McDonald Ho. E14 . . . . . . .3E 104
(off Glengall Gro.)
John McKenna Wlk. SE16 . . . . . .3G 103
John Masefield Ho. N15 . . . . . . .6D 48
(off Fladbury Rd.)
John Maurice Cl. SE17 . . . . .4D 102
John Nash M. E14 . . . . .6A 86
(off Commercial Rd.)
John Newton Ct. DA16: Well 3B 126
Johnny Andrews Ho. E1 . . . . .6K 85
(off Boulcott St.)
John Orwell Sports Cen. 1H 103
John Parker Cl. RM10: Dag 7H 73
John Parker Sq. SW11 . . . . .3B 118
John Parry Ct. N1 . . . . .2E 84
(off Hare Wlk.)

John Penn Ho. SE14 . . . . .7B 104
(off Amersham Va.)
John Penn St. SE13 . . . . .1D 122
John Penry Ho. SE1 . . . . .5G 103
(off Marlborough Gro.)
John Perrin Pl. HA3: Kenton 7E 42
John Prince's St. W1 . . . . .7K 5 (6F 83)
John Pritchard Ho. E1 . . . . .4G 85
(off Buxton St.)
John Ratcliffe Ho. NW6 . . . . .3J 81
(off Chippenham Gdns.)
John Rennie Wlk. E1 . . . . .7H 85
John Riley Ho. E3 . . . . .5B 86
(off Geoffrey Chaucer Way)
John Roll Way SE16 . . . . .3G 103
John Ruskin St. SE5 . . . . .7B 102
John's Av. NW4 . . . . .4E 44
John Sayer Cl. IG11: Bark 3K 89
John's Cl. TW15: Ashf 4E 128
John Scurr Ho. E14 . . . . .6A 86
(off Ratcliffe La.)
John Sessions Sq. E1 . . . . .7K 9
(off Alie St.)
John Silkin La. SE8 . . . . .5K 103
John's La. SM4: Mord 5A 154
John's M. WC1 . . . . .4H 7 (4K 83)
John Smith Av. SW6 . . . . .7H 99
John Smith M. E14 . . . . .7F 87
Johnson Cl. E8 . . . . .1G 85
Johnson Ct. SE9 . . . . .4A 124
Johnson Ho. E2 . . . . .3G 85
(off Roberta St.)
NW1 . . . . .2G 83
(off Cranleigh St.)
NW3 . . . . .7D 64
(off Adelaide Rd.)
SW1 . . . . .1H 17
(off Cundy St.)
SW8 . . . . .7H 101
(off Wandsworth Rd.)
W8 . . . . .2J 99
(off Campden Hill)
Johnson Lock Ct. E1 . . . . .5A 86
Johnson Lodge W9 . . . . .5J 81
(off Admiral Wlk.)
Johnson Mans. W14 . . . . .6G 99
(off Queen's Club Gdns.)
Johnson Rd. BR2: Broml 5B 160
CRO: C'don 7D 156
NW10 . . . . .1K 79
TW5: Hest 7A 94
Johnsons Cl. SM5: Cars 2D 166
Johnson's Ct. EC4 . . . . .6A 84
Johnsons Dr. TW12: Hamp 1G 149
Johnsons Ind. Est. UB3: Hayes . . .2H 93
Johnson's Pl. SW1 . . . . .6A 18 (5G 101)
Johnson St. E1 . . . . .7J 85
UB2: S'hall 3A 94
Johnsons Way NW10 . . . . .4H 79
John Spencer Sq. N1 . . . . .6B 66
John's Pl. E1 . . . . .6H 85
John's Ter. CRO: C'don 1E 168
Johnston Cl. SW9 . . . . .1K 119
Johnston Ct. E10 . . . . .3D 68
Johnstone Ho. SE13 . . . . .3F 123
(off Belmont Hill)
Johnstone Rd. E6 . . . . .3D 88
Johnston Rd. IG8: Wfd G 6D 36
Johnston Ter. NW2 . . . . .3F 63
John Strachey Ho. SW6 . . . . .6H 99
(off Clem Attlee Ct.)
John St. E15 . . . . .1H 87
EN1: Enf 5A 24
SE25 . . . . .4G 157
TW3: Houn 2C 112
WC1 . . . . .4H 7 (4K 83)
John Strype Ct. E10 . . . . .1D 68
John Trundle Ct. EC2 . . . . .5C 8
John Trundle Highwalk EC2 . . . . .5C 8
(off Aldersgate St.)
John Tucker Ho. E14 . . . . .3C 104
(off Mellish St.)
John Watkin Cl. KT19: Eps 7H 163

John Wesley Cl. E6 . . . . .3D 88
John Wesley Ct. TW1: Twick 1A 132
John Wesley Highwalk EC2 . . . . . . .6C 8
    (off Aldersgate St.)
John Wetherby Ct. E15 . . . . .2D 86
    (off High St.)
John Wetherby Ct. E. E15 . . . . .2D 86
    (off High St.)
John Wetherby Ct. W. E15 . . . . .2D 86
    (off High St.)
John Wheatley Ho. SW6 . . . . .6H 99
    (off Clem Attlee Ct.)
John Williams Cl. KT2: King T 1D 150
SE14 . . . . .6K 103
John Wilson St. SE18 . . . . .3E 106
John Woolley Cl. SE13 . . . . .4G 123
Joiners Arms Yd. SE5 . . . . .1D 120
Joiners M. E11 . . . . .3G 69
Joiners Pl. N5 . . . . .4D 66
Joiner St. SE1 . . . . .5F 15 (1D 102)
Joiners Yd. N1 . . . . .1F 7
    (off Caledonia St.)
Jolles Ho. E3 . . . . .3D 86
    (off Bromley High St.)
Jolly M. SW16 . . . . .2G 155
Jollys La. HA2: Harr 1H 59
UB4: Yead 5B 76
Jonathan St. SE11 . . . . .5G 19 (5K 101)
Jones Ho. E14 . . . . .6F 87
    (off Blair St.)
Jones M. SW15 . . . . .4G 117
Jones Rd. E13 . . . . .4K 87
Jones St. W1 . . . . .3J 11 (7F 83)
Jones Wlk. TW10: Rich 6F 115
Jonquil Gdns. TW12: Hamp 6E 130
Jonson Cl. CR4: Mitc 4F 155
UB4: Hayes 5J 75
Jonson Ho. SE1 . . . . .3D 102
    (off Burbage Cl.)
Jonzen Wlk. E14 . . . . .6C 86
Jordan Cl. HA2: Harr 3D 58
Jordan Ct. SW15 . . . . .4F 117
Jordan Ho. N1 . . . . .1D 84
    (off Colville Est.)
SE4 . . . . .4K 121
    (off St Norbert Rd.)
Jordan Rd. UB6: G'frd 1B 78
Jordans Cl. RM10: Dag 4H 73
TW7: Isle 1J 113
Jordans Ho. NW8 . . . . .3C 4
    (off Capland St.)
Jordans M. TW2: Twick 2J 131
Joscoyne Ho. E1 . . . . .6H 85
    (off Philpot St.)
Joseph Av. W3 . . . . .6K 79
Joseph Cl. N4 . . . . .2B 66
Joseph Conrad Ho. SW1 . . . . .4B 18
    (off Tachbrook St.)
Joseph Ct. N16 . . . . .6E 48
    (off Amhurst Pk.)
Joseph Hardcastle Cl. SE14 . . . .7K 103
Josephine Av. SW2 . . . . .5K 119
Joseph Irwin Ho. E14 . . . . .7B 86
    (off Gill St.)
Joseph Lister Ct. E7 . . . . .7J 69
Joseph M. N7 . . . . .6A 66
    (off Westbourne Rd.)
SE15 . . . . .5K 121
Joseph Powell Cl. SW12 . . . . . . .6G 119
Joseph Priestley Ho. E2 . . . . .3H 85
    (off Canrobert St.)
Joseph Ray Rd. E11 . . . . .2G 69
Joseph St. E3 . . . . .4B 86
Joseph Trotter Cl. EC1 . . . . .2K 7
Joshua Cl.
CR2: S Croy 7B 168
N10 . . . . .7A 32
Joshua Pedley Ho. E3 . . . . .2C 86
Joshua St. E14 . . . . .6E 86
Josiah Dr. UB10: Ick 2E 56
Joslin Av. NW9 . . . . .3A 44
Joslings Cl. W12 . . . . .7C 80
Joslyn Cl. EN3: Enf L 1H 25

Jossiline Ct. E3 . . . . .2A 86
    (off Ford St.)
Joubert Mans. SW3 . . . . .5D 16
    (off Jubilee Pl.)
Joubert St. SW11 . . . . .2D 118
Jowett St. SE15 . . . . .7F 103
Jowitt Ho. E2 . . . . .3K 85
    (off Morpeth St.)
Joyce Av. N18 . . . . .5A 34
Joyce Butler Ho. N22 . . . . .1K 47
Joyce Dawson Way SE28 . . . . . . .7A 90
Joyce Latimore Ct. N9 . . . . .3C 34
    (off Colthurst Dr.)
Joyce Page Cl. SE7 . . . . .6B 106
Joyce Wlk. SW2 . . . . .6A 120
JOYDENS WOOD 4K 145
Joydens Wood 4H 145
Joydon Dr. RM6: Chad H 6B 54
Joyners Cl. RM9: Dag 4F 73
Joy of Life Fountain 1E 100
Joystone Ct. EN4: E Barn 4H 21
    (off Park Rd.)
Jubb Powell Ho. N15 . . . . .6E 48
The Jubilee SE10 . . . . .7D 104
Jubilee Av. E4 . . . . .6K 35
RM7: Rom 5H 55
TW2: Whitt 1G 131
Jubilee Bldgs. NW8 . . . . .1B 82
Jubilee Cl. HA5: Pinn 2A 40
KT1: Hamp W 1D 150
NW9 . . . . .6K 43
NW10 .2A 80
RM7: Rom 5H 55
Jubilee Country Pk. 4F 161
Jubilee Country Pk.
    Local Nature Reserve 5F 161
Jubilee Ct. BR4: W W'ck 1E 170
E16 . . . . .6H 87
    (off Silvertown Sq.)
E18 . . . . .1J 51
HA3: Kenton 7E 42
N10 . . . . .3E 46
SE10 .6D 104
    (off Dowells St.)
TW3: Houn 3F 113
    (off Bristow Rd.)
Jubilee Cres. E14 . . . . .3E 104
N9 . . . . .1B 34
Jubilee Dr. HA4: Ruis 4B 58
Jubilee Gdns. UB1: S'hall 5E 76
Jubilee Hall Gym 2F 13
    (within Jubilee Hall)
Jubilee Hgts. SE10 . . . . .1E 122
    (off Parkside Av.)
Jubilee Ho. HA7: Stan 5J 27
SE11 . . . . .4K 19
    (off Reedworth St.)
WC1 . . . . .3G 7
Jubilee La. W5 . . . . .6E 78
Jubilee Mans. E1 . . . . .6J 85
    (off Jubilee St.)
Jubilee Mkt. 2F 13
    (off Covent Gdn.)
Jubilee Mkt. IG8: Wfd G 6F 37
WC2 . . . . .2F 13
Jubilee Pde. IG8: Wfd G 6F 37
Jubilee Pl. SW3 . . . . . .5D 16 (5C 100)
Jubilee Pl. Shop. Mall 1D 104
    (off Bank St.)
Jubilee Rd. SM3: Cheam 7F 165
UB6: G'frd 1B 78
Jubilee St. E1 . . . . .6J 85
Jubilee Vs. KT10: Esh 7H 149
Jubilee Walkway SE1 . . . .3B 14 (7B 84)
Jubilee Way DA14: Sidc 2A 144
KT9: Chess 4G 163
SW19 . . . . .1K 153
TW14: Felt 1J 129
Jubilee Way Training Track 3H 163
Jubilee Yd. SE1 . . . . .6J 15
Judd Apts. N8 . . . . .3K 47
    (off Gt. Amwell La.)

Judd St. WC1 . . . . .2E 6 (3J 83)
Jude St. E16 . . . . .6H 87
Judge Heath La. UB3: Hayes 6E 74
UB8: Hil 6E 74
Judges Wlk. NW3 . . . . .3A 64
Juer St. SW11 . . . . .7C 100
Juett Lodge SE10 . . . . .4J 105
    (off Peartree Way)
Jules Thorn Av. EN1: Enf 4B 24
Julia Ct. E17 . . . . .5D 50
Julia Gdns. IG11: Bark 2D 90
Julia Garfield M. E16 . . . . .1K 105
    (not continuous)
Juliana Cl. N2 . . . . .2A 46
Julian Av. W3 . . . . .7H 79
Julian Cl. EN5: New Bar 3E 20
Julian Ct. NW1 . . . . .7G 65
    (off Rochester Sq.)
Julian Hill HA1: Harr 2J 59
Julian Ho. SE21 . . . . .4E 138
Julian Pl. E14 . . . . .5D 104
Julian Taylor Path SE23 . . . . .2H 139
Julia Scurr St. E3 . . . . .5C 86
Julia St. NW5 . . . . .4E 64
Julien Rd. W5 . . . . .3C 96
Juliet Ho. N1 . . . . .2E 84
    (off Arden Est.)
Juliette Rd. E13 . . . . .2J 87
Julius Caesar Way HA7: Stan 3J 27
Julius Ho. E14 . . . . .6F 87
    (off E. India Dock Rd.)
Julius Nyerere Cl. N1 . . . . .1K 83
    (off Copenhagen St.)
Junction App. SE13 . . . . .3E 122
SW11 . . . . .3C 118
Junction M. W2 . . . . . . .7C 4 (6C 82)
Junction Pl. W2 . . . . .7A 4
Junction Rd. CR2: S Croy 5D 168
E13 . . . . .2K 87
HA1: Harr 6H 41
    (not continuous)
N9 . . . . .1B 34
N17 . . . . .3G 49
N19 . . . . .4G 65
TW8: Bford 4C 96
TW15: Ashf 5E 128
W5 . . . . .4C 96
Junction Rd. E. RM6: Chad H 7E 54
Junction Rd. W RM6: Chad H 7E 54
The Junction Shop. Cen. 4C 118
Jungle Falls Adventure Golf 4B 22
Juniper Cl. EN5: Barn 5A 20
HA2: Harr 2F 59
HA9: Wemb 5G 61
KT9: Chess 5F 163
TW13: Felt 3K 129
Juniper Ct. HA3: Hrw W 1K 41
HA6: Nwood 1J 39
KT8: W Mole 4F 149
RM6: Chad H 6B 54
TW3: Houn 4F 113
    (off Grove Rd.)
W8 . . . . .3K 99
    (off St Mary's Pl.)
Juniper Cres. NW1 . . . . .7E 64
Juniper Dr. SW18 . . . . .4A 118
Juniper Gdns. SW16 . . . . .1G 155
TW16: Sun 6H 129
Juniper Ho. SE14 . . . . .7J 103
TW9: Kew 1H 115
W10 . . . . .4G 81
    (off Fourth Av.)
Juniper La. E6 . . . . .5C 88
Juniper Rd. IG1: Ilf 3E 70
Juniper St. E1 . . . . .7J 85
Juniper Way UB3: Hayes 7F 75
Juno Ct. SW9 . . . . .7A 102
    (off Caldwell St.)
Juno Ho. E3 . . . . .1C 86
    (off Garrison Rd.)
Juno Way SE14 . . . . .6K 103
Juno Way Ind. Est. SE14 . . . . .6K 103

Jupiter Ct. E3 . . . . .2C 86
    (off Four Seasons Cl.)
SW9 . . . . .7A 102
    (off Caldwell St.)
UB5: N'olt 3B 76
    (off Seasprite Cl.)
Jupiter Hgts. UB10: Uxb 1B 74
Jupiter Ho. E14 . . . . .5D 104
    (off St Davids Sq.)
E16 . . . . .6H 87
    (off Turner St.)
HA2: Harr 1E 58
Jupiter Way N7 . . . . .6K 65
Jupp Rd. E15 . . . . .7F 69
Jupp Rd. W. E15 . . . . .1F 87
Jura Ho. SE16 . . . . .4K 103
    (off Plough Way)
Jurassic Encounter 3C 152
Jurston Ct. SE1 . . . . .7K 13
Justice Apts. E1 . . . . .6K 85
    (off Aylward St.)
Justice Wlk. SW3 . . . . . .7C 16 (6C 100)
Justin Cl. TW8: Bford 7D 96
Justines Pl. E2 . . . . .3K 85
Justin Pl. N22 . . . . .7E 32
Justin Plaza CR4: Mitc 4C 154
Justin Rd. E4 . . . . .6G 35
Jute La. EN3: Brim 2F 25
Jutland Cl. N19 . . . . .1J 65
Jutland Ho. SE5 . . . . .2C 120
SE18 .4C 106
    (off Prospect Va.)
Jutland Rd. E13 . . . . .4J 87
SE6 . . . . .7E 122
Jutsums Av. RM7: Rom 6H 55
Jutsums Ct. RM7: Rom 6H 55
Jutsums La. RM7: Rom, Rush G . . .6H 55
Juxon Cl. HA3: Hrw W 1F 41
Juxon Ho. EC4 . . . . .1B 14
    (off St Paul's Chyd.)
Juxon St. SE11 . . . . .3H 19 (4K 101)
JVC Bus. Pk. NW2 . . . . .1C 62

K

Kaduna Cl. HA5: Eastc 5J 39
Kaine Pl. CR0: C'don 7A 158
Kaleidoscope Ho. E20 . . . . .5E 68
    (off Mirabelle Gdns.)
Kale Rd. DA18: Erith 2D 108
Kambala Rd. SW11 . . . . .3B 118
Kamen Ho. SE1 . . . . .5G 15
    (off Magdalen St.)
Kamrans Pl. HA8: Edg 2F 43
Kane Ct. SE10 . . . . .4J 105
    (off Peartree Way)
Kangley Bri. Rd. SE26 . . . . .6B 140
Kangley Bus. Cen. SE26 . . . . .5B 140
Kaplan Dr. N21 . . . . .5E 22
Kapuvar Cl. SE15 . . . . .2G 121
Karachi Ho. E15 . . . . .6G 69
    (off Well St.)
Kara Way NW2 . . . . .4F 63
Karen Cl. BR1: Broml 1H 159
Karen Ter. E11 . . . . .2H 69
Karenza Ct. HA9: Wemb 7C 42
Kariba Cl. N9 . . . . .3D 34
Karim M. E17 . . . . .4A 50
Karma Way HA2: Harr 1E 58
Karner Ho. E20 . . . . .5D 68
    (off Logan Cl.)
Karoline Gdns. IG8: G'frd 2H 77
Kashgar Rd. SE18 . . . . .4K 107
Kashmir Rd. SE7 . . . . .7B 106
Kassala Rd. SW11 . . . . .1D 118
Katella Trad. Est.
IG11: Bark 3J 89
Katharine Ho. CR0: C'don 3C 168
    (off Katharine St.)
Katharine St. CR0: C'don 3C 168
Katherine Bell Twr. E3 . . . . .2C 86
    (off Pancras Way)

Katherine Cl. N4 . . . . .7C **48**
  NW7 . . . . .7K **29**
  SE16 .1K **103**
Katherine Ct. SE23 . . . . .1H **139**
Katherine Gdns. SE9 . . . . .4B **124**
Katherine Ho. W10 . . . . .4G **81**
  (off Portobello Rd.)
Katherine Rd. E6 . . . . .5A **70**
  E7 . . . . .5A **70**
  TW1: Twick 1A **132**
Katherine Sq. W11 . . . . .1G **99**
Kathleen Av. HA0: Wemb 7E **60**
  W3 . . . . .5J **79**
Kathleen Godfree Ct. SW19 . . . . .6J **135**
Kathleen Rd. SW11 . . . . .3D **118**
Katial House EC1 . . . . .1B **8**
  (off Goswell Road)
Kavan Gdns. TW5: Cran 7J **93**
Kavsan Pl. TW5: Cran 7J **93**
Kayani Av. N4 . . . . .1C **66**
Kayani Ho. E16 . . . . .6K **87**
  (off Burrard Rd.)
Kayemoor Rd. SM2: Sutt 6B **166**
Kay Rd. SW9 . . . . .2J **119**
Kays Ter. E18 . . . . .1H **51**
Kay St. DA16: Well 1B **126**
  E2 . . . . .2G **85**
  E15 . . . . .3F **69**
  (off New Mount St.)
Kean Cres. RM8: Dag 1E **72**
Kean Ho. SE17 . . . . .6B **102**
  TW1: Twick 6D **114**
  (off Arosa Rd.)
Kean St. WC2 . . . . .1G **13** (6K **83**)
Keatley Grn. E4 . . . . .6G **35**
Keats CRO: C'don 1C **168**
  (off Saffron Central Sq.)
Keats Apts. E3 . . . . .4B **86**
  (off Wraxall Rd.)
Keats Av. E16 . . . . .1K **105**
Keats Cl. E11 . . . . .5K **51**
  EN3: Pond E 5E **24**
  NW3 . . . . .4C **64**
  SE1 . . . . .4F **103**
  SE7 . . . . .7A **106**
  SW19 . . . . .6B **136**
  UB4: Hayes 5J **75**
Keats Est. N16 . . . . .2F **67**
  (off Kyverdale Rd.)
Keats Gro. NW3 . . . . .4C **64**
Keats House 4C **64**
Keats Ho. E2 . . . . .3J **85**
  (off Roman Rd.)
  HA2: Harr 2J **59**
  SE5 . . . . .7C **102**
  (off Elmington Est.)
  SW1 . . . . .7K **17**
Keats Pde. N9 . . . . .2B **34**
  (off Church St.)
Keats Pl. EC2 . . . . .6E **8**
  (off Moorfields)
Keats Rd. DA16: Well 1J **125**
  DA17: Belv 3J **109**
  E10 . . . . .7D **50**
Keats Way CRO: C'don 6J **157**
  UB6: G'frd 5F **77**
  UB7: W Dray 4B **92**
Kebbell Ter. E7 . . . . .5K **69**
  (off Claremont Rd.)
Keble Cl. KT4: Wor Pk 1B **164**
  UB5: N'olt 5G **59**
Keble Pl. SW13 . . . . .6D **98**
Keble St. SW17 . . . . .4A **136**
Kebony Cl. UB7: W Dray 2C **92**
Kechill Gdns. BR2: Hayes 7J **159**
Kedeston Ct. SM1: Sutt 1K **165**
Kedge Ho. E14 . . . . .3C **104**
  (off Tiller Rd.)
Kedleston Dr. BR5: St M Cry 5K **161**
Kedleston Wlk. E2 . . . . .3H **85**
Kedyngton Ho. HA8: Edg 2J **43**
  (off Burnt Oak B'way.)
Keeble Cl. SE18 . . . . .6F **107**

Keedonwood Rd. BR1: Broml 5G **141**
Keel Cl. IG11: Bark 2C **90**
  N18 . . . . .6K **33**
  SE16 .1K **103**
Keel Ct. E14 . . . . .7F **87**
  (off Newport Av.)
Keele Ho. RM8: Dag 4A **72**
Keeley Rd. CRO: C'don 2C **168**
Keeley St. WC2 . . . . .1G **13** (6K **83**)
Keeling Ho. E2 . . . . .2H **85**
  (off Claredale St.)
Keeling Rd. SE9 . . . . .5B **124**
Keelson Ho. E14 . . . . .3C **104**
  (off Mellish St.)
Keely Cl. EN4: E Barn 5H **21**
Keemor Cl. SE18 . . . . .7E **106**
Keens Cl. SW16 . . . . .5H **137**
Keens Rd. CRO: C'don 4C **168**
Keen's Yd. N1 . . . . .6B **66**
The Keep KT2: King T 6F **133**
  SE3 . . . . .2J **123**
Keepers Ct. CR2: S Croy 5C **168**
  (off Warham Rd.)
Keepers M. TW11: Tedd 6C **132**
Keepier Wharf E14 . . . . .7K **85**
  (off Narrow St.)
Keeping Ct. BR2: Broml 3J **159**
  (off St Mark's Sq.)
Keeton's Rd. SE16 . . . . .3H **103**
  (not continuous)
Keevil Dr. SW19 . . . . .7F **117**
Keibs Way SE17 . . . . .5E **102**
Keighley Cl. N7 . . . . .5J **65**
Keightley Dr. SE9 . . . . .1G **143**
Keilder Cl. UB10: Hil 2C **74**
Keildon Rd. SW11 . . . . .4D **118**
Keiller Ho. E16 . . . . .1D **106**
  (off Kennard St.)
The Keir SW19 . . . . .5E **134**
Keir Hardie Est. E5 . . . . .1H **67**
Keir Hardie Ho. N19 . . . . .7H **47**
  NW10 .7B **62**
  W6 . . . . .6F **99**
  (off Fulham Pal. Rd.)
Keir Hardie Way IG11: Bark 7A **72**
  UB4: Yead 3J **75**
Keirin Rd. E20 . . . . .5D **68**
Keith Connor Cl. SW8 . . . . .3F **119**
Keith Gro. W12 . . . . .2C **98**
Keith Ho. NW6 . . . . .2K **81**
  (off Carlton Vale)
  SW8 . . . . .7J **101**
  (off Wheatsheaf La.)
Keith Pk. Rd. UB10: Uxb 7B **56**
Keith Rd. E17 . . . . .1B **50**
  IG11: Bark 2H **89**
  UB3: Hayes 3G **93**
Kelbrook Rd. SE3 . . . . .2C **124**
Kelby Ho. N7 . . . . .6K **65**
  (off Sutterton St.)
Kelby Path SE9 . . . . .3F **143**
Kelceda Cl. NW2 . . . . .2C **62**
Kelday Hgts. E1 . . . . .6H **85**
  (off Spencer Way)
Kelf Gro. UB3: Hayes 6H **75**
Kelfield Ct. W10 . . . . .6F **81**
Kelfield Gdns. W10 . . . . .6E **80**
Kelfield M. W10 . . . . .6F **81**
Kelland Cl. N8 . . . . .5H **47**
Kelland Rd. E13 . . . . .4J **87**
Kellaway Rd. SE3 . . . . .2B **124**
Keller Cres. E12 . . . . .4B **70**
Kellerton Rd. SE13 . . . . .5G **123**
Kellet Ho's. WC1 . . . . .2F **7**
  (off Tankerton St.)
Kellett Ho. N1 . . . . .1E **84**
  (off Colville Est.)
Kellett Rd. SW2 . . . . .4A **120**
Kelling Gdns. CRO: C'don 7B **156**
Kellino St. SW17 . . . . .4D **136**
Kellner Rd. SE28 . . . . .3K **107**
Kellogg Twr.
  UB6: G'frd 5J **59**

Kellow Ho. SE1 . . . . .6E **14**
  (off Tennis St.)
Kell St. SE1 . . . . .7B **14** (3B **102**)
Kelly Av. SE15 . . . . .7F **103**
Kelly Cl. NW10 . . . . .3K **61**
  TW17: Shep 2G **147**
Kelly Ct. E14 . . . . .7C **86**
  (off Garford St.)
Kelly M. W9 . . . . .5H **81**
Kelly Rd. NW7 . . . . .6F **65**
Kelly Ter. E17 . . . . .4C **50**
Kelly Way RM6: Chad H 5E **54**
Kelmore Gro. SE22 . . . . .4G **121**
Kelmscott Cl. E17 . . . . .1B **50**
Kelmscott Gdns. W12 . . . . .3C **98**
Kelmscott House 5D **98**
Kelmscott Rd. SW11 . . . . .5C **118**
Kelross Pas. N5 . . . . .4C **66**
Kelross Rd. N5 . . . . .4C **66**
Kelsall Cl. SE3 . . . . .2K **123**
Kelsall M. TW9: Kew 1H **115**
Kelsey Cl. KT9: Chess 7D **162**
Kelsey Ga. BR3: Beck 2D **158**
Kelsey La. BR3: Beck 2C **158**
Kelsey Pk. Av. BR3: Beck 2D **158**
Kelsey Pk. Rd. BR3: Beck 2C **158**
Kelsey Sq. BR3: Beck 2C **158**
Kelsey St. E2 . . . . .4G **85**
Kelsey Way BR3: Beck 3C **158**
Kelson Ho. E14 . . . . .3E **104**
  E16 . . . . .2K **105**
Kelso Pl. W8 . . . . .3K **99**
Kelso Rd. SM5: Cars 7A **154**
Kelston Rd. IG6: Ilf 2F **53**
Kelvedon Cl. KT2: King T 6G **133**
Kelvedon Ho. SW8 . . . . .1J **119**
Kelvedon Rd. SW6 . . . . .7H **99**
Kelvedon Way IG8: Wfd G 6J **37**
Kelvin Av. N13 . . . . .6E **32**
  TW11: Tedd 6J **131**
Kelvinbrook KT8: W Mole 3F **149**
Kelvin Cl. KT19: Ewe 6G **163**
Kelvin Ct. SE20 . . . . .1H **157**
  TW7: Isle 2J **113**
  W11 . . . . .7J **81**
  (off Kensington Pk. Rd.)
Kelvin Cres. HA3: Hrw W 7D **26**
Kelvin Dr. TW1: Twick 6B **114**
Kelvin Gdns. CRO: Wadd 7J **155**
  UB1: S'hall 6E **76**
Kelvin Gro. KT9: Chess 3D **162**
  SE26 .3H **139**
Kelvington Cl. CRO: C'don 7A **158**
Kelvington Rd. SE15 . . . . .5K **121**
Kelvin Ho. SE26 . . . . .4B **140**
  (off Worsley Bri. Rd.)
Kelvin Ind. Est. UB6: G'frd 7F **59**
Kelvin Pde. BR6: Orp 1J **173**
Kelvin Rd. DA16: Well 3A **126**
  N5 . . . . .4C **66**
Kelway Ho. W14 . . . . .5H **99**
Kember St. N1 . . . . .7K **65**
Kemble Dr. BR2: Broml 3C **172**
Kemble Ho. SW9 . . . . .3B **120**
  (off Barrington Rd.)
Kemble Rd. CRO: Wadd 3B **168**
  N17 . . . . .1G **49**
  SE23 .1K **139**
Kemble St. WC2 . . . . .1G **13** (6K **83**)
Kemerton Rd. BR3: Beck 2D **158**
  CRO: C'don 7F **157**
  SE5 . . . . .3C **120**
Kemey's St. E9 . . . . .5A **68**
Kemmel Rd. RM9: Dag 1B **90**
Kemnal Rd. BR7: Chst 4H **143**
Kemp NW9 .1B **44**
  (off Quakers Course)
Kemp Ct. SW8 . . . . .7J **101**
  (off Hartington Rd.)
Kempe Ho. SE1 . . . . .3D **102**
  (off Burbage Cl.)
Kempe Rd. NW6 . . . . .2F **81**

Kemp Gdns. CRO: C'don 6C **156**
Kemp Ho. E2 . . . . .2K **85**
  (off Sewardstone Rd.)
  E6 . . . . .6E **70**
  W1 . . . . .2C **12**
  (off Berwick St.)
Kempis Way SE22 . . . . .5E **120**
Kemplay Rd. NW3 . . . . .4B **64**
Kemp Rd. RM8: Dag 1D **72**
Kemps Ct. W1 . . . . .1B **12**
  (off Hopkins St.)
Kemps Dr. E14 . . . . .7C **86**
  HA6: Nwood 1H **39**
Kempsford Gdns. SW5 . . . . .5J **99**
Kempsford Rd. SE11 . . . .4K **19** (4B **102**)
  (not continuous)
Kemps Gdns. SE13 . . . . .5E **122**
Kempshott Rd. SW16 . . . . .7H **137**
Kempson Rd. SW6 . . . . .1J **117**
Kempthorne Rd. SE8 . . . . .4B **104**
Kempton Av.
  TW16: Sun 1K **147**
  UB5: N'olt 6E **58**
Kempton Cl. DA8: Erith 6J **109**
  UB10: Ick 4E **56**
Kempton Ct. E1 . . . . .5H **85**
  TW16: Sun 1K **147**
Kempton Ga. Bus. Cen.
  TW12: Hamp 1D **148**
Kempton Ho. N1 . . . . .1E **84**
  (off Hoxton St.)
Kempton Nature Reserve 6B **130**
Kempton Pk. Racecourse 7K **129**
Kempton Rd. E6 . . . . .1D **88**
The Kemptons TW15: Ashf 2C **128**
Kempton Wlk. CRO: C'don 6A **158**
Kempt St. SE18 . . . . .6E **106**
Kemsing Cl. BR2: Hayes 2H **171**
  CR7: Thor H 4C **156**
  DA5: Bexl 7E **126**
Kemsing Ho. SE1 . . . . .7F **15**
  (off Long La.)
Kemsing Rd. SE10 . . . . .5J **105**
Kemsley SE13 . . . . .5D **122**
Kemsley Ct. W13 . . . . .1C **96**
Kenbrook Ho. NW5 . . . . .5G **65**
  W14 . . . . .3H **99**
Kenbury Cl. UB10: Ick 3C **56**
Kenbury Gdns. SE5 . . . . .2C **120**
Kenbury Mans. SE5 . . . . .2C **120**
  (off Kenbury St.)
Kenbury St. SE5 . . . . .2C **120**
Kenchester Cl. SW8 . . . . .7J **101**
Kencot Way DA18: Erith 2F **109**
Kendal NW1 .1K **5**
  (off Augustus St.)
Kendal Av. IG11: Bark 1J **89**
  N18 . . . . .4J **33**
  W3 . . . . .4G **79**
Kendal Cl. IG8: Wfd G 2C **36**
  N20 . . . . .2H **31**
  SW9 .7B **102**
  TW14: Felt 1H **129**
  UB4: Hayes 2G **75**
Kendal Ct. W3 . . . . .5G **79**
Kendale Rd. BR1: Broml 5G **141**
Kendal Gdns. N18 . . . . .4J **33**
  SM1: Sutt 2A **166**
Kendal Ho. E9 . . . . .1J **85**
  N1 . . . . .2K **83**
  (off Priory Grn. Est.)
  SE20 .2G **157**
  (off Derwent Rd.)
Kendall Av. BR3: Beck 2A **158**
  CR2: Sande 7D **168**
Kendall Ct. DA15: Sidc 3A **144**
  SW19 . . . . .6B **136**
Kendall Ho. W14 . . . . .4H **99**
  (off Warwick La.)
Kendall Lodge BR1: Broml 1K **159**
  (off Willow Tree Wlk.)
Kendall Mnr. HA6: Nwood 1D **38**
Kendall Pl. W1 . . . . .6G **5** (5E **82**)

Kendall Rd. BR3: Beck 2A 158
  SE18 . . . . .1C 124
  TW7: Isle 2A 114
Kendalmere Cl. N10 . . . . .1F 47
Kendal Pde. N18 . . . . .4J 33
Kendal Pl. SW15 . . . . .5H 117
Kendal Rd. NW10 . . . . .4C 62
Kendal Steps W2 . . . . .1D 10
Kendal St. W2 . . . . .1D 10 (6C 82)
Kender Est. SE14 . . . . .1J 121
  (off Queen's Rd.)
Kender St. SE14 . . . . .7J 103
Kendoa Rd. SW4 . . . . .4H 119
Kendon Cl. E11 . . . . .5K 51
Kendon Ho. E15 . . . . .7F 69
  (off Bryant St.)
Kendra Hall Rd. CR2: S Croy 7B 168
Kendrey Gdns. TW2: Whitt 7J 113
Kendrick Ct. SE15 . . . . .1H 121
  (off Colmore M.)
Kendrick M. SW7 . . . .3A 16 (4B 100)
Kendrick Pl. SW7 . . . .4A 16 (4B 100)
Kenelm Cl. HA1: Harr 3A 60
Kenerne Dr. EN5: Barn 5B 20
KEN FRIAR BRI. 4A 66
Kenilford Rd. SW12 . . . . .7F 119
Kenilworth Av. E17 . . . . .2C 50
  HA2: Harr 4D 58
  SW19 . . . . .5J 135
Kenilworth Ct. SW15 . . . . .3G 117
  (off Lwr. Richmond Rd.)
Kenilworth Cres. EN1: Enf 1K 23
Kenilworth Gdns. IG3: Ilf 2K 71
  SE18 . . . . .2F 125
  UB1: S'hall 3D 76
  UB4: Hayes 5H 75
Kenilworth Rd. BR5: Pet W 6G 161
  E3 .2A 86
  HA8: Edg 3D 28
  KT17: Ewe 5C 164
  NW6 . . . . .1H 81
  SE20 . . . . .1K 157
  TW15: Ashf 3A 128
  W5 .1E 96
Kenley N17 . . . . .2D 48
  (off Gloucester Rd.)
Kenley Av. NW9 . . . . .1A 44
Kenley Cl. BR7: Chst 3J 161
  DA5: Bexl 7G 127
  EN4: E Barn 4H 21
Kenley Gdns. CR7: Thor H 4B 156
Kenley Pl. UB10: Uxb 1A 74
Kenley Rd. KT1: King T 2H 151
  SW19 . . . . .2J 153
  TW1: Twick 6B 114
Kenley Wlk. SM3: Cheam 4F 165
  W11 . . . . .7G 81
Kenlor Rd. SW17 . . . . .5B 136
Kenmare Cl. UB10: Ick 2F 57
Kenmare Dr. CR4: Mitc 7D 136
  N17 . . . . .2F 49
Kenmare Gdns. N13 . . . . .4H 33
Kenmare Rd. CR7: Thor H 6A 156
Kenmere Gdns. HA0: Wemb 1G 79
Kenmere Rd. DA16: Well 2C 126
Kenmont Gdns. NW10 . . . . .3D 80
  (not continuous)
Kenmore Av. HA3: Kenton, W'stone .4A 42
Kenmore Cl. TW9: Kew 7G 97
Kenmore Cl. NW6 . . . . .7K 63
  (off Acol Rd.)
Kenmore Cres. UB4: Hayes 3H 75
Kenmore Gdns. HA8: Edg 2H 43
Kenmore Rd. HA3: Kenton 3D 42
  UB4: Hayes 5H 67
Kenmure Yd. E8 . . . . .5H 67
Kennacraig Cl. E16 . . . . .1J 105
Kennard Ho. SW11 . . . . .2E 118
Kennard Rd. E15 . . . . .7F 69
  N11 . . . . .5J 31
Kennard St. E16 . . . . .1D 106
  SW11 . . . . .1E 118
Kennedy Av. EN3: Pond E 6D 24

Kennedy Cl. BR5: Pet W 1H 173
  CR4: Mitc 1E 154
  E13 . . . . .2J 87
Kennedy Cl. TW15: Ashf 5E 128
  WD23: B Hea 2C 26
Kennedy Cox Ho. E16 . . . . .5H 87
  (off Burke St.)
Kennedy Ho. SE11 . . . . .5G 19
  (off Vauxhall Wlk.)
Kennedy Path W7 . . . . .4K 77
Kennedy Rd. IG11: Bark 1J 89
  W7 .5J 77
Kennedy Wlk. SE17 . . . . .4D 102
  (off Elsted St.)
Kennet Cl. E17 . . . . .3F 51
  SW11 . . . . .4B 118
Kennet Ct. W9 . . . . .5J 81
  (off Elmfield Way)
Kenneth Av. IG1: Ilf 4F 71
Kenneth Campbell Ho. NW8 . . . . . .3B 4
  (off Orchardson St.)
Kenneth Chambers Ct. IG8: Wfd G . .6H 37
Kenneth Ct. SE11 . . . .3K 19 (4A 102)
Kenneth Cres. NW2 . . . . .5D 62
Kenneth Gdns. HA7: Stan 6F 27
Kenneth More Rd. IG1: Ilf 3F 71
Kenneth More Theatre 3F 71
Kennet Ho. NW8 . . . . .4B 4
  (off Church St. Est.)
Kennet Rd. RM6: Chad H 7D 54
Kenneth Robbins Ho. N17 . . . . .7C 34
Kenneth Way W5 . . . . .7F 79
Kenneth Younger Ho. SW6 . . . . . . .6H 99
  (off Clem Attlee Ct.)
Kennet Rd. TW7: Isle 3K 113
  W9 .4H 81
Kennet Sq. CR4: Mitc 1C 154
Kennet St. E1 . . . . .1G 103
Kennett Ct. W4 . . . . .7H 97
Kennett Dr. UB4: Yead 5C 76
Kennett Wharf La. EC4 . . . .3D 14 (7C 84)
KENNINGHALL 5D 34
Kenninghall Rd. E5 . . . . .3G 67
  N18 . . . . .5D 34
Kenning Ho. N1 . . . . .1E 84
  (off Colville Est.)
Kenning St. SE16 . . . . .2J 103
Kenning Ter. N1 . . . . .1E 84
Kennings Way SE11 . . . .5K 19 (5A 102)
Kennington Grn. SE11 . . .6J 19 (5A 102)
KENNINGTON 7K 19 (6A 102)
Kennington Grn. SE11 . . .6J 19 (5A 102)
Kennington La. SE11 . . . .6G 19 (5K 101)
KENNINGTON OVAL 6A 102
Kennington Oval SE11 . . .7H 19 (6K 101)
Kennington Pal. Ct. SE11 . . . . .5J 19
Kennington Pk. Gdns.
  SE11 . . . . .7K 19 (6B 102)
Kennington Pk. Ho. SE11 . . . . .6K 19
Kennington Pk. Pl. SE11 . .7K 19 (6A 102)
Kennington Pk. Rd. SE11 . .7K 19 (6A 102)
Kennington Rd. SE1 . . . .1J 19 (3A 102)
  SE11 . . . . .1J 19 (3A 102)
Kennistoun Ho. NW5 . . . . .5G 65
Kennoldes SE21 . . . . .2D 138
  (off Croxted Rd.)
Kenny Dr. SM5: Cars 7E 166
Kennyland Ct. NW4 . . . . .6D 44
  (off Hendon Way)
Kenrick Pl. W1 . . . . .6G 5 (5E 82)
KENSAL GREEN 3E 80
Kensal Ho. W10 . . . . .4F 81
  (off Ladbroke Gro.)
KENSAL RISE 2F 81
Kensal Rd. W10 . . . . .4G 81
KENSAL TOWN 4G 81
Kensal Wharf W10 . . . . .4F 81
KENSINGTON 3J 99
Kensington Arc. W8 . . . . .2K 99
  (off Kensington High St.)
Kensington Av. CR7: Thor H 1A 156
  E12 . . . . .6C 70

Kensington Bus. Cen. SW3 . . . . . . .1D 16
Kensington Cen. W14 . . . . .4G 99
  (not continuous)
Kensington Chu. Ct. W8 . . . . .2K 99
Kensington Chu. St. W8 . . . . .1J 99
Kensington Chu. Wlk. W8 . . . . .2K 99
  (not continuous)
Kensington Cl. N11 . . . . .6K 31
Kensington Ct. SE16 . . . . .1K 103
  (off King & Queen Wharf)
  W8 .2K 99
Kensington Ct. Gdns. W8 . . . . .3K 99
  (off Kensington Ct. Pl.)
Kensington Ct. Mans. W8 . . . . .2K 99
  (off Kensington Ct.)
Kensington Ct. M. W8 . . . . .3K 99
  (off Kensington Ct. Pl.)
Kensington Ct. Pl. W8 . . . . .3K 99
Kensington Dr. IG8: Wfd G 2B 52
Kensington Gdns. 4A 10 (1A 100)
Kensington Gdns. IG1: Ilf 1D 70
  KT1: King T 3D 150
Kensington Gdns. Sq. W2 . . . . .6K 81
Kensington Ga. W8 . . . . .3A 100
Kensington Gore SW7 . . .7A 10 (2A 100)
Kensington Hall Gdns. W14 . . . . . .5H 99
Kensington Hgts. HA1: Harr 6K 41
  (off Sheepcote Rd.)
  W8 .1J 99
Kensington High St. W8 . . . . .3H 99
  W14 . . . . .3H 99
Kensington Ho. IG8: Wfd G 7K 37
  SW11 . . . . .7F 101
  (off Palmer Rd.)
  UB7: W Dray 2B 92
  (off Park Lodge Av.)
  W8 .2K 99
  (off Kensington Ct.)
  W14 . . . . .2F 99
Kensington Leisure Cen. 7G 81
Kensington Mall W8 . . . . .1J 99
Kensington Mans. SW5 . . . . .5J 99
  (off Trebovir Rd.)
Kensington Palace 1K 99
Kensington Pal. Gdns. W8 . . . . .1K 99
Kensington Pk. Gdns. W11 . . . . . . .7H 81
Kensington Pk. M. W11 . . . . .6H 81
Kensington Pk. Rd. W11 . . . . .6H 81
Kensington Pl. W8 . . . . .1J 99
Kensington Rd. RM7: Rom 6J 55
  SW7 . . . . .2A 100
  UB5: N'olt 3E 76
  W8 .2K 99
Kensington Sq. W8 . . . . .3K 99
Kensington Ter. CR2: S Croy 7D 168
Kensington Village W14 . . . . .4H 99
Kensington W. W14 . . . . .4G 99
Kensworth Ho. EC1 . . . . .2F 9
  (off Cranwood St.)
Kent Av. DA16: Well 5K 125
  RM9: Dag 4G 91
  W13 . . . . .5B 78
Kent Bldg. E14 . . . . .6G 87
Kent Cl. BR6: Chels 6J 173
  CR4: Mitc 4J 155
Kent Ct. E2 . . . . .2F 85
  NW9 . . . . .2A 44
Kent Dr. EN4: Cockf 4K 21
  TW11: Tedd 5J 131
Kentford Way UB5: N'olt 1C 76
Kent Gdns. HA4: Ruis 6J 39
  W13 . . . . .5B 78
Kent Ga. Way CR0: Addtn 6B 170
Kent Ho. SE1 . . . . .5F 103
  SW1 . . . . .5C 18
  (off Aylesford St.)
  W4 .5A 98
  (off Devonshire St.)
  W8 .2K 99
  (off Kensington Ct.)
  W11 . . . . .1H 99
  (off Boyne Ter. M.)
Kent Ho. La. BR3: Beck 6A 140

Kent Ho. Rd. BR3: Beck 1K 157
  SE26 . . . . .5A 140
Kent House Station Approach
  BR3: Beck 1A 158
Kentish Bldgs. SE1 . . . . .5E 14 (2D 102)
Kentish Pl. SE2 . . . . .3A 108
Kentish Rd. DA17: Belv 4G 109
KENTISH TOWN 5F 65
Kentish Town Ind. Est. NW5 . . . . . .5F 65
Kentish Town Rd. NW1 . . . . .7F 65
  NW5 . . . . .7F 65
Kentish Town Sports Cen. 6F 65
Kentish Way BR1: Broml 2K 159
  BR2: Broml 2K 159
Kentlea Rd. SE28 . . . . .2J 107
Kentmere Ho. SE15 . . . . .6J 103
Kentmere Mans. W5 . . . . .4B 78
Kentmere Rd. SE18 . . . . .4J 107
KENTON .5C 42
Kenton Av. HA1: Harr 7K 41
  TW16: Sun 2B 148
  UB1: S'hall 7E 76
Kenton Ct. HA3: Kenton 6B 42
  SE26 . . . . .4A 140
  (off Adamsrill Rd.)
  TW1: Twick 6D 114
  W14 . . . . .3H 99
Kentone Ct. SE25 . . . . .4H 157
Kenton Gdns. HA3: Kenton 5C 42
Kenton Ho. E1 . . . . .4J 85
  (off Mantus Cl.)
Kentonian Cl. HA3: Kenton 5B 42
Kenton La.
  HA3: Hrw W, Kenton, W'stone
  . . . . .6E 26
Kenton Pk. Av. HA3: Kenton 5D 42
Kenton Pk. Cl. HA3: Kenton 4C 42
Kenton Pk. Cres. HA3: Kenton 4D 42
Kenton Pk. Mans. HA3: Kenton 5C 42
  (off Kenton Rd.)
Kenton Pk. Pde. HA3: Kenton 5C 42
Kenton Pk. Rd. HA3: Kenton 4C 42
Kenton Rd. E9 . . . . .6K 67
  HA1: Harr 7K 41
  HA3: Kenton 6A 42
Kenton St. WC1 . . . . .3E 6 (4J 83)
Kenton Way UB4: Hayes 3G 75
Kent Pk. Ind. Est. SE15 . . . . .6H 103
Kent Pas. NW1 . . . . .3E 4 (4D 82)
Kent Rd.
  BR4: W W'ck 1D 170
  KT1: King T 3D 150
  KT8: E Mos 4G 149
  N21 . . . . .1J 33
  RM10: Dag 5H 73
  TW9: Kew 7G 97
  W4 .3J 97
Kent's Pas. TW12: Hamp 1D 148
Kent St. E2 . . . . .2F 85
  E13 . . . . .3A 88
Kent Ter. NW1 . . . . .2D 4 (3C 82)
Kent Vw. Gdns. IG3: Ilf 2J 71
Kent Wlk. SW9 . . . . .4B 120
Kent Way KT6: Surb 3E 162
Kentwell Cl. SE4 . . . . .4A 122
Kent Wharf SE8 . . . . .7D 104
  (off Creekside)
Kentwode Grn. SW13 . . . . .7C 98
Kent Yd. SW7 . . . . .7D 10 (2C 100)
Kenver Av. N12 . . . . .6G 31
Kenward Rd. SE9 . . . . .5A 124
Kenward Way SW11 . . . . .2E 118
Ken Way HA9: Wemb 3J 61
Kenway RM5: Col R 2J 55
Kenway Rd. SW5 . . . . .4K 99
Ken Wilson Ho. E2 . . . . .2G 85
  (off Pritchards St.)
Kenwood Av. N14 . . . . .5C 22
Kenwood Cl. NW3 . . . . .1B 64
  UB7: Sip 6C 92
Kenwood Ct. NW9 . . . . .4J 43
  (off Elmwood Cres.)
Kenwood Dr. BR3: Beck 3E 158

Kenwood Gdns. E18 . . . . .3K 51
  IG2: Ilf .5E 52
  IG5: Ilf .4E 52
Kenwood House 1C 64
Kenwood Ho. SW9 . . . . .4B 120
Kenwood Pl. N6 . . . . .1D 64
Kenwood Rd. N6 . . . . .6D 46
  N9 . . . . .1B 34
Kenworthy Rd. E9 . . . . .5A 68
Kenwrick Ho. N1 . . . . .1K 83
       (off Barnsbury Est.)
Kenwyn Dr. NW2 . . . . .2A 62
Kenwyn Lodge N2 . . . . .4D 46
Kenwyn Rd. SW4 . . . . .4H 119
  SW20 .1E 152
Kenya Rd. SE7 . . . . .7B 106
Kenyngton Ct. TW16: Sun 5J 129
Kenyngton Dr. TW16: Sun 5J 129
Kenyngton Pl. HA3: Kenton 5C 42
Kenyon Ho. SE5 . . . . .7C 102
      (off Camberwell Rd.)
Kenyon Mans. W14 . . . . .6G 99
     (off Queen's Club Gdns.)
Kenyon St. SW6 . . . . .1F 117
Keogh Rd. E15 . . . . .6G 69
Kepler Ho. SE10 . . . . .5H 105
      (off Armitage Rd.)
Kepler Rd. SW4 . . . . .4J 119
Keppel Ho. SE8 . . . . .5B 104
  SW3 . . . . .4C 16
      (off Elystan St.)
Keppel Rd. E6 . . . . .7D 70
  RM9: Dag 4E 72
Keppel Row SE1 . . . . . .5C 14 (1C 102)
Keppel St. WC1 . . . . .5D 6 (5H 83)
Kepplestone M. BR3: Beck 2E 158
Kerbela St. E2 . . . . .3K 9 (4G 85)
Kerbey St. E14 . . . . .6D 86
Kerfield Cres. SE5 . . . . .1D 120
Kerfield Pl. SE5 . . . . .1D 120
Kerlin Vw. SW16 . . . . .2G 155
Kerr Cl. CR2: Sels 7A 170
Kerridge Ct. N1 . . . . .6E 66
      (off Balls Pond Rd.)
Kerrier Ho. SW10 . . . . .7A 100
      (off Stadium St.)
Kerrington Ct. W10 . . . . .4G 81
      (off Wornington Rd.)
  W12 . . . . .2E 98
      (off Uxbridge Rd.)
Kerris Ho. SE11 . . . . .5K 19
      (off Tavy Cl.)
Kerrison Pl. W5 . . . . .1D 96
Kerrison Rd. E15 . . . . .1F 87
  SW11 .3C 118
  W5 . . . . .1D 96
Kerrison Vs. W5 . . . . .1D 96
Kerry Av. HA7: Stan 4H 27
Kerry Cl. E16 . . . . .6K 87
  N13 . . . . .2E 32
Kerry Ct. HA7: Stan 4J 27
Kerry Ho. E1 . . . . .6J 85
      (off Sidney St.)
Kerry Path SE14 . . . . .6B 104
Kerry Rd. SE14 . . . . .6B 104
Kerscott Ho. E3 . . . . .3D 86
      (off Rainhill Way)
Kersey Gdns. SE9 . . . . .4C 142
Kersfield Ho. SW15 . . . . .6F 117
Kersfield Rd. SW15 . . . . .6F 117
Kershaw Cl. SW18 . . . . .6B 118
Kershaw Rd. RM10: Dag 3G 73
Kersley M. SW11 . . . . .1D 118
Kersley Rd. N16 . . . . .2E 66
Kersley St. SW11 . . . . .2D 118
Kerstin Cl. UB3: Hayes 7H 75
Kerswell Cl. N15 . . . . .5E 48
Kerwick Cl. N7 . . . . .7J 65
Keslake Mans. NW10 . . . . .2F 81
      (off Station Ter.)
Keslake Rd. NW6 . . . . .2F 81
Kessock Cl. N17 . . . . .5H 49
Kestlake Rd. DA5: Bexl 6C 126

KESTON 5A 172
Keston Av. BR2: Kes 5A 172
Keston Cl. DA16: Well 7C 108
  N18 . . . . .3J 33
Keston Ct. DA5: Bexl 7F 127
  KT5: Surb 5F 151
      (off Cranes Pk.)
Keston Gdns. BR2: Kes 4A 172
Keston Ho. SE17 . . . . .5E 102
      (off Kinglake Est.)
KESTON MARK 4C 172
KESTON MARK 3C 172
Keston Pk. Cl. BR2: Kes 3D 172
Keston Rd. CR7: Thor H 6A 156
  N17 . . . . .3D 48
  SE15 . . . . .3G 121
Keston Windmill 5B 172
Kestrel Av. E6 . . . . .5C 88
  SE24 . . . . .5B 120
Kestrel Cl. KT2: King T 4D 132
  NW9 . . . . .2A 44
  NW10 . . . . .5K 61
Kestrel Ct. CR2: S Croy 6C 168
  E3 . . . . .2C 86
     (off Four Seasons Cl.)
  E17 . . . . .2K 49
  HA4: Ruis 2G 57
  SM6: W'gton 5G 167
Kestrel Ho. EC1 . . . . .1C 8
      (off Pickard St.)
  EN3: Pond E 5F 25
  SE10 . . . . .1E 122
      (off Parkside Av.)
Kestrel Pl. SE14 . . . . .6A 104
Kestrel Way CR0: New Ad 7F 171
  UB3: Hayes 2F 93
Keswick Av. SW15 . . . . .5A 134
  SW19 .2J 153
  TW17: Shep 3G 147
Keswick B'way. SW15 . . . . .5H 117
     (off Up. Richmond Rd.)
Keswick Cl. SM1: Sutt 4A 166
Keswick Ct. BR2: Broml 4H 159
  SE6 . . . . .1H 141
  SE13 . . . . .5D 122
Keswick Gdns. HA4: Ruis 6F 39
  HA9: Wemb 4E 60
  IG4: Ilf .4C 52
Keswick Ho. SE5 . . . . .2C 120
Keswick M. W5 . . . . .1E 96
Keswick Rd. BR4: W W'ck 2G 171
  BR6: Orp 1K 173
  DA7: Bex 2G 127
  SW15 .5G 117
  TW2: Whitt 6G 113
Ketch St. IG11: Bark 1H 89
Kettering Ct. CR7: Thor H 4C 156
Kettering St. SW16 . . . . .6G 137
Kett Gdns. SW2 . . . . .5K 119
Kettlebaston Rd. E10 . . . . .1B 68
Kettleby Ho. SW9 . . . . .3B 120
      (off Barrington Rd.)
Kettlewell Cl. N11 . . . . .6K 31
Ketton Ho. W10 . . . . .4E 80
      (off Sutton Way)
Kevan Ct. E17 . . . . .4C 50
Kevan Ho. SE5 . . . . .7C 102
Kevelioc Rd. N17 . . . . .1C 48
Kevin Cl. TW4: Houn 2B 112
Kevington Cl. BR5: St P 4K 161
Kevington Dr. BR5: St P 4K 161
  BR7: Chst 4K 161
Kevtar Gdn. E3 . . . . .3B 86
      (off Violet Rd.)
KEW 7F 97
KEW BRIDGE 6G 97
Kew Bri. Arches TW9: Kew 6G 97
Kew Bri. Ct. W4 . . . . .5G 97
Kew Bri. Distribution Cen.
  TW8: Bford 5F 97
KEW BRIDGE JUNCTION 5F 97
Kew Bri. Rd. TW8: Bford 6F 97
Kew Ct. KT2: King T 1E 150
Kew Cres. SM3: Cheam 3G 165

Kew Foot Rd. TW9: Rich 4E 114
Kew Gdns. 7E 96
Kew Gdns. Rd. TW9: Kew 7F 97
KEW GREEN 7G 97
Kew Grn. TW9: Kew 6F 97
Kew Mdw. Path TW9: Kew 2J 115
      (Clifford Av.)
  TW9: Kew 2H 115
      (Magnolia Ct.)
Kew Palace .7E 96
Kew Retail Pk.
  Kew 1H 115
Kew Riverside Pk. TW9: Kew 7H 97
Kew Rd. TW9: Kew, Rich 6G 97
Key Cl. E1 . . . . .4J 85
Keyes Ho. SW1 . . . . .6C 18
      (off Dolphin Sq.)
Keyes Rd. NW2 . . . . .5F 63
Keyham Ho. W2 . . . . .5J 81
     (off Westbourne Pk. Rd.)
Key Ho. SE11 . . . . .7K 19 (6A 102)
Keymer Pl. E14 . . . . .6B 86
Keymer Rd. SW2 . . . . .2K 137
Keynes Cl. N2 . . . . .4D 46
Keynes Ct. SE28 . . . . .7B 90
      (off Attlee Rd.)
Keynsham Av. IG8: Wfd G 4B 36
Keynsham Gdns. SE9 . . . . .5C 124
Keynsham Rd. SE9 . . . . .5B 124
  SM4: Mord 1K 165
Keynsham Wlk. SM4: Mord 1K 165
Keys Ct. CR0: C'don 3D 168
      (off Beech Ho. Rd.)
Keyse Rd. SE1 . . . . .3F 103
Keysham Av. TW5: Cran 1J 111
Keystone Cres. N1 . . . . . . .1F 7 (2J 83)
Key W. Ct. IG7: Chig 4K 37
Keywood Dr. TW16: Sun 6J 129
Keyworth Cl. E5 . . . . .4A 68
Keyworth Pl. SE1 . . . . .7B 14
Keyworth St. SE1 . . . . . .7B 14 (3B 102)
Kezia M. SE8 . . . . .5A 104
Kezia St. SE8 . . . . .5A 104
Khalsa Ct. N22 . . . . .1B 48
Khama Rd. SW17 . . . . .4C 136
Khartoum Rd. E13 . . . . .3K 87
  IG1: Ilf .5F 71
  SW17 .4B 136
Khyber Rd. SW11 . . . . .2C 118
The Kia Oval 7H 19 (6K 101)
Kibble Cl. RM6: Chad H 7C 54
Kibworth St. SW8 . . . . .7K 101
Kidbulabous 1G 147
KIDBROOKE 2K 123
Kidbrooke Est. SE3 . . . . .3A 124
Kidbrooke Gdns. SE3 . . . . .2J 123
Kidbrooke Green Nature Reserve
  . . . . .3A 124
Kidbrooke Gro. SE3 . . . . .1J 123
Kidbrooke La. SE9 . . . . .4C 124
Kidbrooke Pk. Cl. SE3 . . . . .1K 123
Kidbrooke Pk. Rd. SE3 . . . . .1K 123
Kidbrooke Way SE3 . . . . .2K 123
Kidderminster Pl. CR0: C'don 1B 168
Kidderminster Rd. CR0: C'don 1B 168
Kidderpore Av. NW3 . . . . .4J 63
Kidderpore Gdns. NW3 . . . . .4J 63
Kidd Pl. SE7 . . . . .5C 106
Kidspace
  Croydon 6A 168
Kiebs Way SE17 . . . . .5D 102
Kiffen St. EC2 . . . . .3F 9 (4D 84)
Kilberry Cl. TW7: Isle 1H 113
Kilbrennan Ho. E14 . . . . .6E 86
      (off Findhorn St.)
KILBURN 2H 81
Kilburn Bri. NW6 . . . . .1J 81
Kilburn Ga. NW6 . . . . .2K 81
Kilburn High Rd. NW6 . . . . .7H 63
Kilburn Ho. NW6 . . . . .2J 81
      (off Malvern Pl.)
Kilburn La. W9 . . . . .3F 81
  W10 . . . . .3F 81

Kilburn Pk. Rd. NW6 . . . . .3J 81
Kilburn Pl. NW6 . . . . .1J 81
Kilburn Priory NW6 . . . . .1K 81
Kilburn Sq. NW6 . . . . .1J 81
Kilburn Va. NW6 . . . . .1K 81
Kilburn Va. Est. NW6 . . . . .1K 81
      (off Kilburn Vale)
Kilby Ct. SE10 . . . . .3H 105
     (off Greenroof Way)
Kildare Cl. HA4: Ruis 1A 58
Kildare Ct. W2 . . . . .6J 81
      (off Kildare Ter.)
Kildare Gdns. W2 . . . . .6J 81
Kildare Rd. E16 . . . . .5J 87
Kildare Ter. W2 . . . . .6J 81
Kildare Wlk. E14 . . . . .6C 86
Kildoran Rd. SW2 . . . . .5J 119
Kildowan Rd. IG3: Ilf 1A 72
Kilgour Rd. SE23 . . . . .6A 122
Kilkie St. SW6 . . . . .2A 118
Killarney Rd. SW18 . . . . .6A 118
Kilburns Mill Cl. SM6: W'gton 2F 167
Killearn Rd. SE6 . . . . .1F 141
Killester Gdns. KT4: Wor Pk 4D 164
Killick Ho. SM1: Sutt 4J 165
Killick M. SM3: Cheam 6G 165
Killick St. N1 . . . . .1G 7 (2K 83)
Killieser Av. SW2 . . . . .2J 137
Killigarth Ct. DA14: Sidc 4A 144
Killigrew Ho. TW16: Sun 7G 129
Killip Cl. E16 . . . . .6H 87
Killoran Ho. E14 . . . . .3E 104
      (off Galbraith St.)
Killowen Av. UB5: N'olt 5G 59
Killowen Rd. E9 . . . . .6K 67
Killyon Rd. SW8 . . . . .2G 119
Killyon Ter. SW8 . . . . .2G 119
Kilmaine Rd. SW6 . . . . .7G 99
Kilmarnock Gdns. RM8: Dag 3C 72
Kilmarsh Rd. W6 . . . . .4E 98
Kilmartin Av. SW16 . . . . .3A 156
Kilmartin Rd. IG3: Ilf 2A 72
Kilmington Rd. SW13 . . . . .6C 98
Kilmiston Av. TW17: Shep 6E 146
Kilmiston Ho. TW17: Shep 6E 146
Kilmore Ho. E14 . . . . .6D 86
      (off Vesey Path)
Kilmorey Gdns. TW1: Twick 5B 114
Kilmorey Rd. TW1: Twick 4B 114
Kilmorie Rd. SE23 . . . . .1A 140
Kilmuir Ho. SW1 . . . . .4H 17
      (off Bury St.)
Kiln Cinema .7H 63
Kiln Cl. UB3: Harl 6F 93
Kiln Ct. E14 .7B 86
      (off Newell St.)
Kilner Ho. E16 . . . . .5K 87
     (off Freemasons Rd.)
  SE11 . . . . .7J 19
Kilner St. E14 . . . . .5C 86
Kiln Ho. E1 . . . . .5K 85
      (off Duckett St.)
  UB2: S'hall 3E 94
      (off Lockwood Rd.)
Kiln M. SW17 . . . . .5B 136
Kiln Pl. NW5 .5E 64
Kilnside KT10: Clay 7A 162
Kiln Theatre .7H 63
Kilpatrick Way UB4: Yead 5C 76
Kilravock St. W10 . . . . .3G 81
Kilronan W3 .6K 79
Kilross Rd. TW14: Bedf 1F 129
Kilsby Wlk. RM9: Dag 6B 72
Kilsha Rd. KT12: Walt T 6A 148
Kimbell Gdns. SW6 . . . . .1G 117
Kimbell Pl. SE3 . . . . .4A 124
Kimber Ct. SE1 . . . . .2H 8
      (off Long La.)
Kimberley Av. E6 . . . . .2C 88
  IG2: Ilf .7H 53
  RM7: Rom 6J 55
  SE15 . . . . .2H 121

Kimberley Ct. NW6 . . . . .1G 81
(off Kimberley Rd.)
Kimberley Dr. DA14: Sidc 2D 144
Kimberley Gdns. EN1: Enf 3A 24
N4 . . . . .5B 48
Kimberley Ga. BR1: Broml 7G 141
Kimberley Ho. E14 . . . . .3E 104
(off Galbraith St.)
Kimberley Rd. BR3: Beck 2K 157
CRO: C'don 6B 156
E4 .1B 36
E11 .2F 69
E16 .4H 87
E17 .1A 50
N17 .2G 49
N18 .6C 34
NW6 . . . . .1G 81
SW9 . . . . .2J 119
Kimberley Wlk. KT12: Walt T 7K 147
Kimberley Way E4 . . . . .1B 36
Kimber Pl. TW4: Houn 7D 112
(Conway Rd.)
TW4: Houn 4D 112
(Marryat Cl.)
Kimber Rd. SW18 . . . . .7J 117
Kimble Cres. WD23: Bush 1B 26
Kimble Ho. NW8 . . . . .3D 4
Kimble Rd. SW19 . . . . .6B 136
Kimbolton Cl. SE12 . . . . .6H 123
Kimbolton Ct. SW3 . . . . .4C 16
(off Fulham Rd.)
Kimbolton Row SW3 . . . . .4C 16
(off Fulham Rd.)
Kimmeridge Gdns. SE9 . . . . .4C 142
Kimmeridge Rd. SE9 . . . . .4C 142
Kimmins Ct. SE16 . . . . .7K 15
(off Old Jamaica Rd.)
Kimpton Ho. SW15 . . . . .7C 116
Kimpton Ind. Est. SM3: Sutt 2H 165
Kimpton Link Bus. Cen.
SM3: Sutt 2H 165
Kimpton Pk. Way SM1: Sutt 2G 165
SM3: Sutt 2G 165
Kimpton Rd. SE5 . . . . .1D 120
SM3: Sutt 2H 165
Kimpton Trade & Bus. Cen.
SM3: Sutt 2H 165
Kinburn St. SE16 . . . . .2K 103
Kincaid Rd. SE15 . . . . .7H 103
Kincardine Gdns. W9 . . . . .4J 81
(off Harrow Rd.)
Kincha Lodge KT2: King T 1F 151
(off Elm Rd.)
Kinch Gro. HA9: Wemb 7F 43
Kinder Cl. SE28 . . . . .7D 90
Kinder Ho. N1 . . . . .2D 84
(off Cranston Est.)
Kindersley Ho. E1 . . . . .6G 85
(off Pinchin St.)
Kinder St. E1 . . . . .6H 85
Kinderton Cl. N14 . . . . .1B 32
Kinefold Ho. N7 . . . . .6J 65
(off York Way Est.)
Kinesis Gym & Fitness Cen. 4C 124
(off Well Hall Rd.)
Kinfauns Rd. IG3: Ilf 1A 72
SW2 . . . . .2A 138
King Alfred Av. SE6 . . . . .4C 140
(not continuous)
King & Queen Cl. SE9 . . . . .4C 142
King & Queen St. SE17 . . . . .5C 102
King & Queen Wharf SE16 . . . . . . .7K 85
King Arthur Cl. SE15 . . . . .7J 103
KING CHARLES I ISLAND 4E 12
King Charles Ct. SE17 . . . . .6B 102
(off Royal Rd.)
King Charles Cres. KT5: Surb 7F 151
King Charles Ho. SW6 . . . . .7K 99
(off Wandon Rd.)
King Charles Rd. KT5: Surb 5F 151
King Charles's Ct. SE10 . . . . .6E 104
(off Park Row)
King Charles St. SW1 . . . .6D 12 (2H 101)

King Charles Ter. E1 . . . . .7H 85
(off Sovereign Cl.)
King Charles Wlk. SW19 . . . . .1G 135
King Ct. E10 . . . . .7D 50
Kingcup Cl. CRO: C'don 7K 157
King David La. E1 . . . . .7J 85
Kingdom St. W2 . . . . .5A 82
Kingdon Ho. E14 . . . . .3E 104
(off Galbraith St.)
Kingdon Rd. NW6 . . . . .6J 63
King Edward Bldg. EC1 . . . . .7B 8
(off King Edward St.)
King Edward Ct. HA9: Wemb 5E 60
(off Elm Rd.)
King Edward Dr. KT9: Chess 3E 162
King Edward Mans. E8 . . . . .1H 85
(off Mare St.)
King Edward M. SW13 . . . . .1C 116
King Edward Rd. E10 . . . . .1E 68
E17 .3A 50
EN5: New Bar 4D 20
King Edward's Gdns. W3 . . . . .1G 97
King Edward's Mans. SW6 . . . . .7J 99
(off Fulham Rd.)
King Edward's Pl. W3 . . . . .1G 97
King Edward's Rd. E9 . . . . .1H 85
EN3: Pond E 4E 24
HA4: Ruis 1F 57
N9 .7C 24
King Edwards Rd. IG11: Bark 1H 89
King Edward St. EC1 . . . . .7C 8 (6C 84)
King Edward the Third M. SE16 . . . .2H 103
King Edward Wlk. SE1 . . .1K 19 (3A 102)
Kingfield Rd. W5 . . . . .4D 78
Kingfield St. E14 . . . . .4E 104
Kingfisher Av. E11 . . . . .6K 51
Kingfisher Cl. HA3: Hrw W 7E 26
HA6: Nwood 1D 38
SE28 . . . . .7C 90
Kingfisher Ct. CRO: C'don 3C 168
(off Wandle Rd.)
E14 . . . . .2E 104
(off River Barge Cl.)
EN2: Enf 1E 22
KT8: E Mos 4J 149
SE1 . . . . .7D 14
(off Swan St.)
SM1: Sutt 5H 165
SW19 . . . . .2F 135
TW3: Houn 5F 113
TW7: Isle 2H 113
Kingfisher Dr. TW10: Ham 4B 132
Kingfisher Hgts. E16 . . . . .1A 106
(off Bramwell Way)
N17 .3H 49
(off Waterside Way)
Kingfisher Ho. SW18 . . . . .3A 118
W14 . . . . .3H 99
(off Melbury Rd.)
Kingfisher Leisure Cen.
Kingston upon Thames 2E 150
Kingfisher M. SE13 . . . . .4D 122
Kingfisher Pl. N22 . . . . .2K 47
Kingfisher Sq. SE8 . . . . .6B 104
(off Clyde St.)
Kingfisher St. E6 . . . . .5C 88
Kingfisher Wlk. NW9 . . . . .2A 44
Kingfisher Way BR3: Beck 5K 157
NW10 . . . . .6K 61
King Frederick IX Twr. SE16 . . . . . .3B 104
King Gdns. CRO: Wadd 5B 168
King George IV Ct. SE17 . . . . .5D 102
(off Dawes St.)
King George VI Av. CR4: Mitc 4D 154
King George VI Memorial
. . . . .5C 12 (1H 101)
King George Av. E16 . . . . .6A 88
IG2: Ilf 5H 53
King George Cr. RM7: Mawney 3J 55
TW16: Sun 5G 129
King George Cres. HA0: Wemb 5D 60
King George M. SW17 . . . . .5D 136

King George Sailing Club 6J 25
King George's Dr. UB1: S'hall 5D 76
King George's Field 3G 163
King George Sq. TW10: Rich 6F 115
King George's Trad. Est.
KT9: Chess 4G 163
King George St. SE10 . . . . .7E 104
King George Way E4 . . . . .4J 25
Kingham Cl. SW18 . . . . .7A 118
W11 . . . . .2G 99
King Harolds Way DA7: Belv, Bex . .7D 108
DA17: Belv 7D 108
King Henry Lodge E4 . . . . .4H 35
HA2: Harr 1J 59
King Henry M. BR6: Chels 5K 173
HA2: Harr 1J 59
King Henry's Dr. CRO: New Ad 7D 170
King Henry's Reach W6 . . . . .6E 98
King Henry's Rd. KT1: King T 3H 151
NW3 . . . . .7C 64
King Henry's Stairs E1 . . . . .1H 103
King Henry St. N16 . . . . .5E 66
King Henry's Wlk. N1 . . . . .6E 66
King Henry Ter. E1 . . . . .7H 85
(off Sovereign Cl.)
Kinghorn St. EC1 . . . . .6C 8 (5C 84)
King Ho. W12 . . . . .6D 80
Kingisholt Ct. NW10 . . . . .3F 81
(off Wellington Rd.)
King James Ct. SE1 . . . . .7B 14
King James St. SE1 . . . . . .7B 14 (2B 102)
King John Ct. EC2 . . . . . . .3H 9 (4E 84)
King John St. E1 . . . . .5K 85
King John's Wlk. SE9 . . . . .7C 124
Kinglake Est. SE17 . . . . .5E 102
Kinglake St. SE17 . . . . .5E 102
(not continuous)
Kinglet Cl. E7 . . . . .6J 69
Kingly Ct. W1 . . . . .2B 12
Kingly St. W1 . . . . .1A 12 (6G 83)
Kings Arbour UB2: S'hall 5C 94
King's Arms All. TW8: Bford 6D 96
Kings Arms Ct. E1 . . . . .5G 85
Kings Arms Yd. EC2 . . . . .7E 8 (6D 84)
Kingsash Dr. UB4: Yead 4C 76
King's Av. IG8: Wfd G 6E 36
IG9: Buck H 6E 36
(The Broadway)
IG9: Buck H 2G 37
(Langfords)
N10 .3E 46
SM5: Cars 7C 166
TW16: Sun 5H 129
UB6: G'frd 5F 77
Kings Av. BR1: Broml 6H 141
KT3: N Mald 4A 152
N21 .1G 33
RM6: Chad H 6F 55
SW4 . . . . .1H 137
SW12 . . . . .1H 137
TW3: Houn 1F 113
W5 .6D 78
King's Bench St. SE1 . . . .6B 14 (2B 102)
King's Bench Wlk. EC4 . . . .1K 13 (6A 84)
King's Blvd. N1 . . . . .2J 83
Kingsbridge Av. W3 . . . . .2F 97
Kingsbridge Ct. E14 . . . . .3C 104
(off Dockers Tanner Rd.)
NW1 . . . . .7F 65
(off Castlehaven Rd.)
Kingsbridge Cres. UB1: S'hall 5D 76
Kingsbridge Dr. NW7 . . . . .7A 30
Kingsbridge Rd. IG11: Bark 2H 89
KT12: Walt T 7K 147
SM4: Mord 6F 153
UB2: S'hall 4D 94
W10 . . . . .6E 80
Kingsbridge Way UB4: Hayes 3G 75
Kingsbridge Wharf IG11: Bark 3J 89
KINGSBURY 5H 43
Kingsbury Circ. NW9 . . . . .5G 43
KINGSBURY GREEN 6K 43

Kingsbury Rd. N1 . . . . .6E 66
NW9 . . . . .5G 43
Kingsbury Ter. N1 . . . . .6E 66
Kingsbury Trad. Est. NW9 . . . . .6K 43
Kings Chase KT8: E Mos 3G 149
Kings Chase Vw. EN2: Enf 2F 23
Kingsclere Cl. SW15 . . . . .7C 116
Kingsclere Ct. N12 . . . . .5H 31
Kingsclere Pl. EN2: Enf 2H 23
Kingscliffe Gdns. SW19 . . . . .1H 135
King's Cl. DA1: Cray 4K 127
NW4 . . . . .4F 45
Kings Cl. E10 . . . . .7D 50
KT7: T Ditt 6A 150
KT12: Walt T 7K 147
TW18: Staines 7A 128
The King's Club 6E 134
Kings Coll. Ct. NW3 . . . . .7C 64
King's College London
Denmark Hill Campus 2D 120
Guy's Campus 5E 14
(within Guy's Hospital)
Institute of Psychiatry,
De Crespigny Park 2D 120
Maughan Library 7J 7 (6A 84)
St Thomas' Campus -
Lambeth Pal. Rd. 2F 19
St Thomas' House 1G 19
Strand Campus 2H 13 (7K 83)
Waterloo Campus . . .5J 13 (1A 102)
King's Coll. Rd. NW3 . . . . .7C 64
Kings Coll. Rd. HA4: Ruis 6H 39
King's College School of Medicine &
Dentistry 2C 120
Kingscote Rd. CRO: C'don 7H 157
KT3: N Mald 3K 151
W4 .3K 97
Kingscote St. EC4 . . . . . . .2A 14 (7B 84)
King's Ct. E13 . . . . .1K 87
SE1 . . . . .6B 14 (2B 102)
Kings Ct. HA9: Wemb 3H 61
IG9: Buck H 2G 37
N7 . . . . .7K 65
(off Caledonian Rd.)
NW8 . . . . .1D 82
(off Prince Albert Rd.)
W6 .4C 98
Kings Ct. Mans. SW6 . . . . .1H 117
(off Fulham Rd.)
Kings Ct. M. KT8: E Mos 5H 149
Kings Ct. Nth. SW3 . . . . .6C 16 (5C 100)
Kingscourt Rd. SW16 . . . . .3H 137
Kings Ct. Sth. SW3 . . . . .6C 16
King's Cres. N4 . . . . .3C 66
Kings Cres. Est. N4 . . . . .2C 66
Kingscroft SW4 . . . . .6J 119
Kingscroft Rd. NW2 . . . . .6H 63
KING'S CROSS 2J 83
King's Cross Bri. N1 . . . . .1F 7
King's Cross Rd. WC1 . . . .1G 7 (3K 83)
King's Cross Sq. N1 . . . . .1E 6
(off Euston Rd.)
Kingsdale Gdns. W11 . . . . .1F 99
Kingsdale Rd. SE18 . . . . .7K 107
SE20 . . . . .7K 139
Kingsdown Av. CR2: S Croy 7C 168
W3 .7A 80
W13 . . . . .2B 96
Kingsdown Cl. SE16 . . . . .5H 103
(off Masters Dr.)
W10 . . . . .6F 81
Kingsdowne Rd. KT6: Surb 7E 150
Kingsdown Ho. E8 . . . . .5G 67
Kingsdown Point SW2 . . . . .2A 138
Kingsdown Rd. E11 . . . . .3G 69
N19 .2J 65
SM3: Cheam 5G 165
Kingsdown Way BR2: Hayes 7J 159
King's Dr. HA8: Edg 4A 28
Kings Dr. HA9: Wemb 2H 61
KT5: Surb 7G 151
KT7: T Ditt 7B 150
TW11: Tedd 5H 131

Kingsend—Kingsway

Kingsend HA4: Ruis 1F **57**
Kingsend Ct. HA4: Ruis 1G **57**
Kings Farm E17 1D **50**
Kings Farm Av. TW10: Rich 4G **115**
Kingsfield Av. HA2: Harr 4F **41**
Kingsfield Ho. SE9 3B **142**
Kingsfield Rd. HA1: Harr 7H **41**
Kingsfield Ter. HA1: Harr 7H **41**
Kingsford St. NW5 5D **64**
Kingsford Way E6 5D **88**
King's Gdns. NW6 7J **63**
Kings Gdns. IG1: Ilf 1H **71**
KT12: Walt T 7K **147**
Kings Gth. M. SE23 2J **139**
Kingsgate HA9: Wemb 3J **61**
Kingsgate Av. N3 3J **45**
Kingsgate Bus. Cen. *KT2: King T* *1E* ***150***
(off Kingsgate Rd.)
Kingsgate Cl. DA7: Bex 1E **126**
Kingsgate Est. N1 6E **66**
Kingsgate Ho. SW9 1A **120**
Kingsgate Mans. *WC1* *6G* ***7***
(off Red Lion Sq.)
Kings Ga. M. *N8* *5K* ***47***
(off Spencer Rd.)
Kingsgate Pde. SW1 2B **18**
Kingsgate Pl. NW6 7J **63**
Kingsgate Rd. KT1: King T 1E **150**
KT2: King T 1E **150**
NW6 7J **63**
Kings Ga. Wlk. *SW1* *1B* ***18***
(off Victoria St.)
Kings Grange HA4: Ruis 1H **57**
Kingsground SE9 7B **124**
King's Gro. SE15 7H **103**
(not continuous)
Kingsgrove Cl. DA14: Sidc 4K **143**
Kings Hall Leisure Cen. 5J **67**
Kings Hall M. SE13 3E **122**
Kings Hall Rd. BR3: Beck 7A **140**
Kings Head Hill E4 7J **25**
Kingshead Ho. NW7 4J **29**
Kings Head Pas. *SW4* *4H* ***119***
(off Clapham Pk. Rd.)
Kings Head Theatre *1B* ***84***
(off Upper St.)
King's Head Yd. SE1 5E **14** (1D **102**)
King's Highway SE18 6J **107**
Kingshill Av. HA3: Kenton 4B **42**
KT4: Wor Pk 7C **152**
UB4: Hayes, Yead 3G **75**
UB5: N'olt 3G **75**
Kingshill Cl. UB4: Hayes 3J **75**
Kingshill Ct. EN5: Barn 4B **20**
Kingshill Dr. HA3: Kenton 2B **42**
Kingshold Rd. E9 7J **67**
Kingsholm Gdns. SE9 4B **124**
King's Ho. *SW10* *7A* ***16***
(off King's Rd.)
Kings Ho. *SW8* *7J* ***101***
(off Sth. Lambeth Rd.)
King's Ho. Studios *SW10* *7A* ***16***
(off Lamont Rd. Pas.)
Kingshurst Rd. SE12 7J **123**
Kingside SE18 3C **106**
Kings Keep BR2: Broml 2G **159**
KT1: King T 4E **150**
SW15 5F **117**
KINGSLAND 6E **66**
Kingsland NW8 1C **82**
Kingsland Basin 1E **84**
Kingsland Grn. E8 6E **66**
Kingsland High St. E8 6F **67**
Kingsland Pas. E8 6E **66**
Kingsland Rd. E2 2H **9** (3E **84**)
E8 3E **84**
E13 3A **88**
Kingsland Shop. Cen. 6F **67**
Kings La. SM1: Sutt 6B **166**
Kingslawn Cl. SW15 5D **116**
Kingslee Ct. SM2: Sutt 7K **165**
Kingsleigh Cl. TW8: Bford 6D **96**
Kingsleigh Pl. CR4: Mitc 3D **154**
Kingsleigh Wlk. BR2: Broml 4H **159**
Kingsley Av. SM1: Sutt 4B **166**
TW3: Houn 2G **113**
UB1: S'hall 7E **76**
W13 5A **78**
Kingsley Cl. N2 5A **46**
RM10: Dag 4H **73**
Kingsley Ct. DA6: Bex 4G **127**
HA8: Edg 3C **28**
KT4: Wor Pk *2B* ***164***
(off The Avenue)
NW2 6D **62**
Kingsley Dr. KT4: Wor Pk 2B **164**
Kingsley Flats *SE1* *4E* ***102***
(off Old Kent Rd.)
Kingsley Gdns. E4 5H **35**
Kingsley Ho. *SW3* *6B* ***100***
(off Beaufort St.)
W14 *4G* ***99***
(off Avonmore Pl.)
Kingsley Mans. *W14* *6G* ***99***
(off Greyhound Rd.)
Kingsley M. BR7: Chst 6F **143**
E1 7H **85**
W8 3K **99**
Kingsley Pl. N6 7E **46**
Kingsley Rd. BR6: Chels 7K **173**
CR0: C'don 1A **168**
E7 7J **69**
E17 2E **50**
HA2: Harr 4G **59**
HA5: Pinn 4D **40**
IG6: Ilf 1G **53**
N13 4F **33**
NW6 1H **81**
SW19 5K **135**
TW3: Houn 1F **113**
Kingsley St. SW11 3D **118**
Kingsley Way N2 5A **46**
Kingsley Wood Dr. SE9 3D **142**
Kings Lodge *HA4: Ruis* *1G* ***57***
(off Pembroke Rd.)
N12 6F **31**
Kingslyn Cres. SE19 1E **156**
Kings Mall W6 4E **98**
Kingsman Pde. SE18 3D **106**
Kings Mans. *SW3* *7C* ***16***
(off Lawrence St.)
Kingsman St. SE18 3D **106**
Kingsmead EN5: New Bar 4D **20**
TW10: Rich 6F **115**
Kingsmead Av. CR4: Mitc 3G **155**
KT4: Wor Pk 2D **164**
KT6: Surb 2G **163**
N9 1C **34**
NW9 7K **43**
TW16: Sun 2A **148**
Kingsmead Cl. DA15: Sidc 2A **144**
KT19: Ewe 7K **163**
TW11: Tedd 6B **132**
Kingsmead Cotts. BR2: Broml 1C **172**
Kingsmead Ct. N6 7H **47**
Kingsmead Dr. UB5: N'olt 7D **58**
Kingsmead Ho. E9 4A **68**
Kingsmead Lodge SM2: Sutt 6B **166**
Kingsmeadow 3G **151**
Kingsmeadow Athletics Cen. 3G **151**
Kingsmead Rd. SW2 2A **138**
Kingsmead Way E9 4A **68**
Kingsmere Cl. SW15 3F **117**
Kingsmere Pk. NW9 1H **61**
Kingsmere Pl. N16 1D **66**
Kingsmere Rd. SW19 2F **135**
King's M. SW4 5J **119**
WC1 4H **7** (4K **83**)
Kingsmill *NW8* *2B* ***82***
(off Kingsmill Ter.)
Kingsmill Bus. Pk. KT1: King T 3F **151**
Kingsmill Gdns. RM9: Dag 5F **73**
Kingsmill Ho. *SW3* *5D* ***16***
(off Cale St.)
Kingsmill Rd. RM9: Dag 5F **73**
Kingsmill Ter. NW8 2B **82**
Kingsnorth Ho. W10 6F **81**
Kingsnympton Pk.
KT2: King T 7H **133**
Kings Oak RM7: Mawney 3G **55**
King's Orchard SE9 6C **124**
King's Paddock TW12: Hamp 1G **149**
King's Pde. *SM5: Cars* *3D* ***166***
(off Wrythe La.)
Kings Pde. N17 3F **49**
NW10 1E **80**
W12 3C **98**
Kingspark Bus. Cen.
KT3: N Mald 4J **151**
Kingspark Ct. E18 3J **51**
King's Pas. KT2: King T 1D **150**
Kings Pas. E11 7G **51**
KT1: King T 2D **150**
Kings Place 2J **83**
King's Pl. SE1 7C **14**
W4 5J **97**
Kings Pl. IG9: Buck H 2F **37**
King Sq. EC1 2C **8** (3C **84**)
Kings Quarter Apts. *N1* *1K* ***83***
(off Copenhagen St.)
King's Quay *SW10* *1A* ***118***
(off Chelsea Harbour Dr.)
Kings Reach Twr. SE1 4A **14**
Kings Ride Ga. TW10: Rich 4G **115**
Kingsridge SW19 2G **135**
King's Rd. BR6: Orp 4K **173**
E6 1A **88**
KT2: King T 7E **132**
KT6: Surb 1C **162**
N17 1F **49**
SW3 6D **16** (7K **99**)
SW6 7K **99**
SW10 7A **16** (7K **99**)
SW19 6J **135**
TW11: Tedd 5H **131**
UB7: W Dray 2B **92**
Kings Rd. CR4: Mitc 3E **154**
E4 1A **36**
E11 7G **51**
EN5: Barn 3A **20**
HA2: Harr 2D **58**
IG11: Bark 7G **71**
KT12: Walt T 7K **147**
N18 5B **34**
N22 1K **47**
NW10 7D **62**
SE25 3G **157**
SW14 3K **115**
TW1: Twick 6B **114**
TW10: Rich 6F **115**
TW13: Felt 1A **130**
W5 5D **78**
King's Scholars' Pas. SW1 2A **18**
King Stairs Cl. SE16 2H **103**
King's Ter. NW1 1G **83**
TW7: Isle 4A **114**
Kingsthorpe Rd. SE26 4K **139**
Kingston Av. SM3: Cheam 3G **165**
TW14: Felt 6G **111**
UB7: Yiew 7B **74**
(Ash Gro.)
UB7: Yiew 1B **92**
(Whitethorn Av.)
KINGSTON BRI. 2D **150**
Kingston Bus. Cen.
KT9: Chess 3E **162**
Kingston By-Pass KT6: Surb 3D **162**
Kingston By-Pass Rd.
KT10: Hin W, Surb 3A **162**
Kingston Cl. RM6: Chad H 3E **54**
(not continuous)
TW11: Tedd 6B **132**
UB5: N'olt 1D **76**
Kingston Crematorium 3G **151**
Kingston Cres. BR3: Beck 1B **158**
Kingston Gdns. CR0: Bedd 3J **167**
Kingston Hall Rd. KT1: King T 3D **150**
Kingston Hill KT2: King T 1G **151**
Kingston Hill Av. RM6: Chad H 3E **54**
Kingston Hill Pl. KT2: King T 4J **133**
Kingston Ho. *KT1: King T* *4D* ***150***
(off Surbiton Rd.)
NW1 *1G* ***83***
(off Camden St.)
NW6 7G **63**
Kingston Ho. E. *SW7* *7C* ***10***
(off Prince's Ga.)
Kingston Ho. Est. KT6: Surb 6B **150**
Kingston Ho. Nth. *SW7* *7C* ***10***
(off Prince's Ga.)
Kingston Ho. Sth. *SW7* *7C* ***10***
(off Ennismore Gdns.)
Kingstonian FC 3G **163**
Kingston La. TW11: Tedd 5A **132**
UB7: W Dray 2B **92**
UB8: Hil 3A **74**
Kingston Lodge KT3: N Mald 4A **152**
Kingston Mans. *SW9* *1K* ***119***
(off Clapham Rd.)
Kingston Mus. 2E **150**
Kingston Pl. HA3: Hrw W 7E **26**
Kingston Rd. EN4: E Barn 5G **21**
IG1: Ilf 4F **71**
KT1: King T 3H **151**
KT3: N Mald 3H **151**
KT4: Wor Pk 2H **163**
KT5: Surb 2H **163**
KT17: Ewe 7B **164**
KT19: Ewe 2H **163**
N9 2B **34**
SW15 2C **134**
SW19 2C **134**
(Norstead Pl.)
SW19 2H **153**
(Rothesay Av.)
SW20 2F **153**
TW11: Tedd 5B **132**
TW15: Ashf 6A **128**
UB2: S'hall 2D **94**
Kingston Sq. SE19 5D **138**
Kingston University
Kingston Hill Campus 5K **133**
Knights Pk. Campus 3E **150**
Penrhyn Road Campus 4E **150**
Reg Bailey Bldg. 3D **150**
Roehampton Vale Cen. 3B **134**
KINGSTON UPON THAMES 2D **150**
Kingston upon Thames
Tourist Information Centre 2D **150**
KINGSTON VALE 4A **134**
Kingston Va. SW15 4K **133**
Kingstown St. NW1 1E **82**
(not continuous)
King St. E13 4J **87**
EC2 1D **14** (6C **84**)
N2 3B **46**
N17 1F **49**
SW1 5B **12** (1G **101**)
TW1: Twick 1A **132**
TW9: Rich 5D **114**
UB2: S'hall 3C **94**
W3 1J **97**
W6 4C **98**
WC2 2E **12** (7J **83**)
King St. Cloisters *W6* *4D* ***98***
(off King St.)
King St. M. N2 3B **46**
King St. Pde. *TW1: Twick* *1A* ***132***
(off King St.)
Kings Wlk. Shop. Cen.
Chelsea 5E **16** (5D **100**)
Kingswater Pl. SW11 7C **100**
King's Way CR0: Wadd 5K **167**
Kings Way HA1: Harr 4J **41**
Kingsway BR4: W W'ck 3G **171**
BR5: Pet W 5H **161**
EN3: Pond E 5C **24**
HA9: Wemb 4E **60**
IG8: Wfd G 5F **37**
KT3: N Mald 4E **152**
N12 6F **31**
SW14 3H **115**

Kingsway—Knightswood Ct.

Kingsway TW19: Stanw 1A 128
UB3: Hayes 5E 74
WC2 . . . . 7G 7 (6K 83)
Kingsway Bus. Pk. TW12: Hamp . . 1D 148
Kingsway Cres. HA2: Harr 4G 41
Kingsway Est. N18 . . . . 6E 34
Kingsway Mans. WC1 . . . . 5G 7
(off Red Lion Sq.)
Kingsway Pde. N16 . . . . 3D 66
(off Albion Rd.)
Kingsway Pl. EC1 . . . . 3K 7
(off Sans Wlk.)
Kingsway Rd. SM3: Cheam 7G 165
Kingswear Rd. HA4: Ruis 2J 57
NW5 . . . . 3F 65
King's Wharf SE10 . . . . 6D 104
(off Wood Wharf)
Kings Wharf E8 . . . . 1E 84
(off Kingsland Rd.)
Kingswood E2 . . . . 2J 85
(off Cyprus St.)
Kingswood Av. BR2: Broml 3G 159
CR7: Thor H 5A 156
DA17: Belv 4F 109
NW6 . . . . 1G 81
TW3: Houn 1D 112
TW12: Hamp 6F 131
Kingswood Cl. BR6: Orp 7J 161
EN1: Enf 5K 23
KT3: N Mald 6B 152
KT6: Surb 7E 150
N20 . . . . 7F 21
SW8 . . . . 7J 101
TW15: Ashf 5F 129
Kingswood Ct. E4 . . . . 5H 35
NW6 . . . . 7J 63
(off West End La.)
SE13 . . . . 6F 123
TW10: Rich 5F 115
Kingswood Dr. SE19 . . . . 4E 138
SM2: Sutt 7K 165
SM5: Cars 1D 166
Kingswood Est. SE21 . . . . 4E 138
Kingswood Hgts. E18 . . . . 1J 51
(off Queen Mary Av.)
Kingswood M. N15 . . . . 4B 48
Kingswood Pk. N3 . . . . 2H 45
Kingswood Pl. SE13 . . . . 4G 123
UB4: Hayes 5G 75
Kingswood Rd. BR2: Broml 4F 159
E11 . . . . 7G 51
HA9: Wemb 3G 61
IG3: Ilf 1A 72
SE20 . . . . 6J 139
SW2 . . . . 6J 119
SW19 . . . . 7H 135
W4 . . . . 3J 97
Kingswood Ter. W4 . . . . 3J 97
Kingswood Way SM6: W'gton 5J 167
Kingsworth Cl. BR3: Beck 5A 158
Kingsworthy Cl. KT1: King T 3F 151
Kings Yd. SW15 . . . . 3E 116
(off Lwr. Richmond Rd.)
Kingthorpe Rd. NW10 . . . . 7K 61
Kingthorpe Ter. NW10 . . . . 6K 61
Kington Ho. NW6 . . . . 1K 81
(off Mortimer Cres.)
Kingward Ho. E1 . . . . 5G 85
(off Hanbury St.)
King Wardrobe Apts. EC4 . . . . 1B 14
(off Carter La.)
Kingweston Cl. NW2 . . . . 3G 63
King William IV Gdns. SE20 . . . . 6J 139
King William La. SE10 . . . . 5G 105
King William's Ct. SE10 . . . . 6F 105
(off Park Row)
King William St. EC4 . . . . 1F 15 (6D 84)
King William Wlk. SE10 . . . . 6E 104
(not continuous)
Kingwood Gdns. E1 . . . . 1K 15
(off Piazza Wlk.)
Kingwood Rd. SW6 . . . . 1G 117
Kinlet Rd. SE18 . . . . 1G 125
Kinloch Dr. NW9 . . . . 7K 43
Kinloch St. N7 . . . . 3K 65
Kinloss Ct. N3 . . . . 4H 45
Kinloss Gdns. N3 . . . . 3H 45
Kinloss Rd. SM5: Cars 7A 154
Kinnaird Av. BR1: Broml 6H 141
W4 . . . . 7J 97
Kinnaird Cl. BR1: Broml 6H 141
Kinnaird Ho. SE17 . . . . 4D 102
Kinnaird Way IG8: Wfd G 6J 37
Kinnear Apts. N8 . . . . 3K 47
Kinnear Rd. W12 . . . . 2B 98
Kinnerton Pl. Nth. SW1 . . . . 7F 11
Kinnerton Pl. Sth. SW1 . . . . 7F 11
Kinnerton St. SW1 . . . . 7G 11 (2E 100)
Kinnerton Yd. SW1 . . . . 7G 11
Kinnoul Rd. W6 . . . . 6G 99
Kino Bermondsey 7H 15
(off Bermondsey Sq.)
Kinross Av. KT4: Wor Pk 2C 164
Kinross Cl. HA3: Kenton 5F 43
HA8: Edg 2C 28
TW16: Sun 5H 129
Kinross Ct. BR1: Broml 1H 159
(off Highland Rd.)
SE6 . . . . 1H 141
Kinross Dr. TW16: Sun 5H 129
Kinross Ho. N1 . . . . 1K 83
(off Bemerton Est.)
Kinross Ter. E17 . . . . 2B 50
Kinsale Cl. NW7 . . . . 6A 30
Kinsale Rd. SE15 . . . . 3G 121
Kinsella Gdns. SW19 . . . . 5D 134
Kinsham Ho. E2 . . . . 4G 85
(off Ramsey St.)
Kinsheron Pl. KT8: E Mos 4G 149
Kintore Way SE1 . . . . 4F 103
Kintyre Cl. SW16 . . . . 2K 155
Kintyre Ct. SW2 . . . . 7J 119
Kintyre Ho. E14 . . . . 1E 104
(off Coldharbour)
Kinveachy Gdns. SE7 . . . . 5C 106
Kinver Ho. N19 . . . . 2H 65
Kinver Rd. SE26 . . . . 4J 139
Kipling Ct. W7 . . . . 7K 77
Kipling Dr. SW19 . . . . 6B 136
Kipling Est. SE1 . . . . 7F 15 (2D 102)
Kipling Ho. N19 . . . . 1J 65
(off Charles St.)
SE5 . . . . 7D 102
(off Elmington Est.)
Kipling Pl. HA7: Stan 6E 26
Kipling Rd. DA7: Bex 1E 126
Kipling St. SE1 . . . . 7F 15 (2D 102)
Kipling Ter. N9 . . . . 3J 33
Kipling Twr. W3 . . . . 3J 97
(off Palmerston Rd.)
Kippington Dr. SE9 . . . . 1B 142
Kira Bldg. E3 . . . . 3B 86
Kiran Apts. E1 . . . . 6K 9
(off Chicksand St.)
Kirby Cl. KT19: Ewe 5B 164
Kirby Est. SE16 . . . . 3H 103
UB7: Yiew 7A 74
Kirby Gro. SE1 . . . . 6G 15 (2E 102)
Kirby St. EC1 . . . . 5K 7 (5A 84)
Kirby Way KT12: Walt T 6A 148
UB8: Hil 4B 74
Kirchen Rd. W13 . . . . 7B 78
Kirkby Apts. E3 . . . . 5B 86
(off St Paul's Way)
Kirkby Cl. N11 . . . . 6K 31
Kirkdale SE26 . . . . 2H 139
Kirkdale Cnr. SE26 . . . . 4J 139
Kirkdale Rd. E11 . . . . 1G 69
Kirkeby Ho. EC1 . . . . 5J 7
(off Leather La.)
Kirkfield Cl. W13 . . . . 1B 96
Kirkham Apts. IG11: Bark 7G 71
(off Linton Rd.)
Kirkham Rd. E6 . . . . 6C 88
Kirkham St. SE18 . . . . 6J 107
Kirk Ho. HA9: Wemb 3E 60
Kirkland Av. IG5: Ilf 2E 52
Kirkland Cl. DA15: Sidc 6J 125
Kirkland Dr. EN2: Enf 1H 23
Kirkland Ho. E14 . . . . 5D 104
(off St Davids Sq.)
E14 . . . . 5D 104
(off Westferry Rd.)
Kirkland Ter. BR3: Beck 6C 140
Kirkland Wlk. E8 . . . . 6F 67
Kirk La. SE18 . . . . 6G 107
Kirkleas Rd. KT6: Surb 1E 162
Kirklees Rd. CR7: Thor H 5A 156
RM8: Dag 5C 72
Kirkley Rd. SW19 . . . . 1J 153
Kirkman Pl. W1 . . . . 6C 6
Kirkmichael Rd. E14 . . . . 6E 86
Kirk Ri. SM1: Sutt 3K 165
Kirk Rd. E17 . . . . 6B 50
Kirkside Rd. SE3 . . . . 6J 105
Kirk's Place 5B 86
Kirkstall Av. N17 . . . . 4D 48
Kirkstall Gdns. SW2 . . . . 1J 137
Kirkstall Ho. SW1 . . . . 5J 17
(part of Abbots Mnr.)
Kirkstall Rd. SW2 . . . . 1H 137
Kirkstead Ct. E5 . . . . 4K 67
Kirksted Rd. SM4: Mord 1K 165
Kirkstone NW1 . . . . 1A 6
(off Harrington St.)
Kirkstone Way BR1: Broml 7G 141
Kirk St. WC1 . . . . 4G 7
Kirkton Rd. N15 . . . . 4E 48
Kirkwall Pl. E2 . . . . 3J 85
Kirkwood Pl. NW1 . . . . 7E 64
Kirkwood Rd. SE15 . . . . 2H 121
Kirn Rd. W13 . . . . 7B 78
Kirrane Cl. KT3: N Mald 5B 152
Kirtley Ho. SW8 . . . . 1G 119
Kirtley Rd. SE26 . . . . 4A 140
Kirtling St. SW11 . . . . 7G 101
Kirton Cl. W4 . . . . 4K 97
Kirton Gdns. E2 . . . . 2K 9 (3F 85)
(not continuous)
Kirton Lodge SW18 . . . . 6K 117
Kirton Rd. E13 . . . . 2A 88
Kirton Wlk. HA8: Edg 7D 28
Kirwyn Way SE5 . . . . 7B 102
Kitcat Ter. E3 . . . . 3C 86
Kitchen Ct. E10 . . . . 2D 68
Kitchener Ho. SE18 . . . . 7E 106
Kitchener Rd. CR7: Thor H 3D 156
E7 . . . . 6K 69
E17 . . . . 1D 50
N2 . . . . 3C 46
N17 . . . . 3E 48
RM10: Dag 6H 73
Kite Ho. SE1 . . . . 4H 103
SE3 . . . . 4K 123
Kite Pl. E2 . . . . 3G 85
(off Warner Pl.)
Kite Yd. SW11 . . . . 1D 118
(off Cambridge Rd.)
Kitley Gdns. SE19 . . . . 1F 157
Kitson Rd. SE5 . . . . 7D 102
SW13 . . . . 1C 116
Kittiwake Ct. SE1 . . . . 7D 14
(off Gt. Dover St.)
SE8 . . . . 6B 104
(off Abinger Gro.)
Kittiwake Pl. SM1: Sutt 5H 165
Kittiwake Rd. UB5: N'olt 3B 76
Kittiwake Way UB4: Yead 5B 76
Kitto Rd. SE14 . . . . 2K 121
Kitts End Rd. EN5: Barn 1C 20
Kiver Rd. N19 . . . . 2H 65
Klea Av. SW4 . . . . 6G 119
Kleine Wharf N1 . . . . 1E 84
Klein's Wharf E14 . . . . 3C 104
(off Westferry Rd.)
Knapdale Cl. SE23 . . . . 2H 139
Knapmill Rd. SE6 . . . . 2C 140
Knapmill Way SE6 . . . . 2D 140
Knapp Cl. NW10 . . . . 6A 62
Knapp Rd. E3 . . . . 4C 86
TW15: Ashf 4B 128
Knapton M. SW17 . . . . 6E 136
Knaresborough Dr. SW18 . . . . 1K 135
Knaresborough Pl. SW5 . . . . 4K 99
Knatchbull Rd. NW10 . . . . 1K 79
SE5 . . . . 2B 120
Knebworth Av. E17 . . . . 1C 50
Knebworth Cl. EN5: New Bar 4E 20
Knebworth Ho. SW8 . . . . 2H 119
Knebworth Rd. N16 . . . . 4E 66
Knee Hill SE2 . . . . 4C 108
Knee Hill Cres. SE2 . . . . 4C 108
Kneller Gdns. TW7: Isle 6H 113
Kneller Ho. UB5: N'olt 2B 76
(off Academy Gdns.)
Kneller Rd. KT3: N Mald 7A 152
SE4 . . . . 4A 122
TW2: Whitt 6G 113
Knevett Ter. TW3: Houn 4E 112
Knight Cl. RM8: Dag 2C 72
Knight Ct. E4 . . . . 1K 35
(off The Ridgeway)
N15 . . . . 5E 48
Knighten St. E1 . . . . 1H 103
Knighthead Point E14 . . . . 2C 104
Knight Ho. SE17 . . . . 4E 102
(off Tatum St.)
Knightland Rd. E5 . . . . 2H 67
Knightleas Ct. NW2 . . . . 6E 62
Knightleys Ct. E10 . . . . 1A 68
(off Wellington Rd.)
Knightley Wlk. SW18 . . . . 4J 117
Knighton Cl. CR2: S Croy 7B 168
IG8: Wfd G 4E 36
RM7: Rom 6K 55
Knighton Dr. IG8: Wfd G 4E 36
Knighton Grn. IG9: Buck H 2E 36
Knighton La. IG9: Buck H 2E 36
Knighton Pk. Rd. SE26 . . . . 5K 139
Knighton Pl. IG9: Buck H 2E 36
(off Knighton La.)
Knighton Rd. E7 . . . . 3J 69
RM7: Rom 6J 55
Knightrider Ct. EC4 . . . . 2B 14
Knightrider St. EC4 . . . . 2B 14 (6B 84)
Knights Arc. SW1 . . . . 7E 10
Knights Av. W5 . . . . 2E 96
KNIGHTSBRIDGE 7D 10 (2C 100)
Knightsbridge SW1 . . . . 7D 10 (2D 100)
SW7 . . . . 7D 10 (2D 100)
The Knightsbridge Apts. SW7 . . . . 7E 10
(off Knightsbridge)
Knightsbridge Ct. BR2: Broml 6C 160
(off Wells Vw. Dr.)
SW1 . . . . 7F 11
Knightsbridge Gdns. RM7: Rom 5K 55
Knightsbridge Grn. SW1 . . . . 7E 10 (2D 100)
(not continuous)
Knights Cl. E9 . . . . 5J 67
KT8: W Mole 5D 148
The Knights Community Stadium 4J 165
Knightscote Cl. UB9: Hare 2A 38
Knights Ct. BR1: Broml 3H 141
KT1: King T 3E 150
WD23: B Hea 1C 26
Knights Hill SE27 . . . . 5B 138
Knight's Hill Sq. SE27 . . . . 4B 138
Knight's Ho. SW10 . . . . 7A 100
(off Hortensia Rd.)
W14 . . . . 5H 99
(off Baron's Ct. Rd.)
Knights Ho. SW8 . . . . 7J 101
(off Sth. Lambeth Rd.)
Knight's Pk. KT1: King T 3E 150
Knight's Pl. TW2: Twick 1J 131
Knight's Rd. E16 . . . . 2J 105
Knights Rd. HA7: Stan 4H 27
Knights Twr. SE8 . . . . 5C 104
Knight's Wlk. SE11 . . . . 4K 19 (4B 102)
(not continuous)
Knightswood Cl. HA8: Edg 2D 28
Knightswood Ct. N6 . . . . 7H 47

Knightswood Ho. N12 ......6F 31
Knightwood Cres. KT3: N Mald ...6A 152
Knivet Rd. SW6 ....6J 99
Knockholt Rd. SE9 ....5B 124
The Knole SE9 ....4E 142
Knole Cl. CR0: C'don 6J 157
Knole Ct. UB5: N'olt 3A 76
  (off Broomcroft Av.)
Knole Ga. DA15: Sidc 3J 143
The Knoll BR2: Hayes 2J 171
  BR3: Beck 1D 158
  HA1: Harr 1K 59
  HA5: Pinn 2B 40
  W13 ....5C 78
Knoll Ct. SE19 ....5F 139
  (off Farquhar Rd.)
Knoll Cres. HA6: Nwood 2G 39
  (not continuous)
Knoll Dr. N14 ....7K 21
Knoll Ho. NW8 ....2A 82
  (off Carlton Hill)
Knollmead KT5: Surb 1J 163
Knoll Ri. BR6: Orp 1K 173
Knoll Rd. DA5: Bexl 7G 127
  DA14: Sidc 5B 144
  SW18 ....5A 118
Knolls Cl. KT4: Wor Pk 3D 164
Knollys Cl. SW16 ....3A 138
Knolly's Ho. WC1 . . . . .3E 6
  (off Tavistock Pl.)
Knollys Rd. SW16 ....3K 137
Knot Ho. SE1 ....5J 15
  (off Brewery Sq.)
Knotley Way BR4: W W'ck ...2D 170
Knottisford St. E2 ....3J 85
Knotts Grn. M. E10 ....6D 50
Knotts Grn. Rd. E10 ....6D 50
Knowland M. CR7: Thor H ...4D 156
Knowiden Ho. E1 . . . . .7J 85
  (off Cable St.)
Knowle Av. DA7: Bex 7E 108
Knowle Cl. SW9 ....3A 120
Knowledge Cl. SW16 ......3K 155
Knowle Rd. BR2: Broml 2D 172
  TW2: Twick 1J 131
Knowles Cl. UB7: Yiew 1A 92
Knowles Ct. HA1: Harr 6K 41
Knowles Hill Cres. SE13 ....5F 123
Knowles Ho. SW18 ....6K 117
  (off Neville Gill Cl.)
Knowles Wlk. SW4 ....3G 119
Knowles Wharf NW1 . . . . . . .1G 83
  (off St Pancras Way)
Knowlton Grn. BR2: Broml ...5H 159
Knowlton Ho. SW9 ....1A 120
  (off Cowley Rd.)
Knowl Wood La. BR6: Farnb ...2E 172
Knowsley Av. UB1: S'hall 1F 95
Knowsley Rd. SW11 ....2D 118
Knox Cl. SW4 ....2J 119
Knox Rd. E7 ....6H 69
Knox St. W1 ....5E 4 (5D 82)
Knoyle Ho. W14 ....3G 99
  (off Russell Rd.)
Knoyle St. SE14 ....6A 104
Koblenz Ho. N8 . . . . .3J 47
  (off Newland Rd.)
Kohat Rd. SW19 ....5K 135
Koops Mill M. SE1 ....7K 15 (3F 103)
Korda Cl. TW17: Shep 3B 146
Kossuth St. SE10 ....5G 105
Kotata Ho. E20 . . . . .6E 68
  (off Ravens Wlk.)
Kotree Way SE1 ....4G 103
Kramer M. SW5 ....5J 99
Kreedman Wlk. E8 ....5G 67
Kreisel Wlk. TW9: Kew 6F 97
Kristina Ct. SM2: Sutt 6J 165
  (off Overton Rd.)
Krithia Rd. RM9: Dag 1B 90
Krupnik Pl. EC2 . . . . .3H 9
  (shown as Curtain Pl.)
Kuala Gdns. SW16 ....1K 155

Kubrick Bus. Est. E7 ....4K 69
  (off Station App.)
Kuhn Way E7 ....5J 69
Kurdish Mus. 4C 98
Kwame M. E16 . . . . .7F 89
  (off University Way)
Kwesi M. SE27 ....5A 138
Kydbrook Cl. BR5: Pet W 7G 161
Kyle Ho. NW6 ....1J 81
Kylemore Cl. E6 ....2B 88
Kylemore Rd. NW6 ....7J 63
Kylestrome Ho. SW1 ....4H 17
  (off Cundy St.)
Kymberley Rd. HA1: Harr 6J 41
Kymes Ct. HA2: Harr 2H 59
Kynance Gdns. HA7: Stan 1C 42
Kynance M. SW7 ....3K 99
Kynance Pl. SW7 ....3A 100
Kynaston Av. CR7: Thor H 5C 156
  N16 ....3F 67
Kynaston Cl. HA3: Hrw W 7C 26
Kynaston Cres. CR7: Thor H ...5C 156
Kynaston Rd. BR1: Broml 5J 141
  CR7: Thor H 5C 156
  EN2: Enf 1J 23
  N16 ....3E 66
Kynaston Wood HA3: Hrw W ...7C 26
Kynersley Cl. SM5: Cars 3D 166
Kynoch Rd. N18 ....4D 34
Kyrle Rd. SW11 ....6E 118
Kyverdale Rd. N16 ....7F 49

L

Laban Cen. 6D 104
Laban Wlk. SE8 ....6D 104
  (off Copperas St.)
The Laboratory Spa & Health Club ...3G 47
Laboratory Sq. SE18 ....3F 107
Laburnham Cl. EN5: Barn 3C 20
Laburnum Av. N9 ....2A 34
  N17 ....7J 33
  SM1: Sutt 3C 166
  UB7: Yiew 7B 74
Laburnum Cl. E4 ....6G 35
  HA0: Wemb 1G 79
  N11 ....6K 31
  SE15 ....7J 103
Laburnum Ct. E2 ....1F 85
  HA1: Harr 5F 41
  HA7: Stan 4H 27
  SE16 ....2J 103
  (off Albion St.)
Laburnum Cres. TW16: Sun ...1K 147
Laburnum Gdns. CR0: C'don ...7K 157
  N21 ....2H 33
Laburnum Gro. HA4: Ruis 6F 39
  KT3: N Mald 2K 151
  N21 ....2H 33
  NW9 ....7J 43
  TW3: Houn 4D 112
  UB1: S'hall 4D 76
Laburnum Ho. BR2: Broml ...1F 159
  RM10: Dag 2G 73
Laburnum La. E2 ....2F 85
Laburnum Lodge N3 ....2H 45
Laburnum Pl. SE9 ....5E 124
Laburnum Rd. CR4: Mitc 2E 154
  SW19 ....7A 136
  UB3: Hay 4H 93
The Laburnums E6 ....4C 88
Laburnum St. E2 ....1F 85
Laburnum Way BR2: Broml ...7E 160
  TW19: Stanw 1B 128
Labyrinth Twr. E8 . . . . .6F 67
  (off Dalston Sq.)
Lacebark Cl. DA15: Sidc 7K 125
Lace Cl. SM6: W'gton 2F 167
Lace Ct. E1 . . . . .5K 85
  (off Master's St.)
Lacewing Cl. E13 ....3J 87
Lacey Cl. N9 ....2B 34

Lacey Dr. HA8: Edg 4K 27
  RM8: Dag 3C 72
  TW12: Hamp 1D 148
Lacey Gro. UB10: Uxb 2A 74
Lacey M. E3 ....2C 86
Lacine Cl. SE16 ....2K 103
  (off Christopher Cl.)
Lackington St. EC2 .....5F 9 (5D 84)
Lackland Ho. SE1 ....5F 103
  (off Rowcross St.)
Lacland Ho. SW10 ....7B 100
  (off Worlds End Est.)
Lacock Cl. SW19 ....6A 136
Lacock Ct. W13 ....1A 96
Lacon Ho. WC1 . . . . .5G 7
  (off Theobald's Rd.)
Lacon Rd. SE22 ....4G 121
Lacrosse Way SW16 ....1H 155
Ladas Rd. SW15 ....4F 117
Ladas Rd. SE27 ....4C 138
Ladbroke Ct. E1 ....6F 85
Ladbroke Cres. W11 ....6G 81
Ladbroke Gdns. W11 ....7H 81
Ladbroke Gro. W10 ....4F 81
  W11 ....4F 81
Ladbroke Gro. Ho. W11 .....7H 81
  (off Ladbroke Gro.)
Ladbroke Grove Memorial 4F 81
Ladbroke M. W11 ....1G 99
Ladbroke Rd. EN1: Enf 6A 24
  W11 ....1H 99
Ladbroke Sq. W11 ....7H 81
Ladbroke Ter. W11 ....7H 81
Ladbroke Wlk. W11 ....1H 99
Ladbrook Cl. BR1: Broml 6G 141
  HA5: Pinn 5D 40
Ladbrooke Cres. DA14: Sidc ...3D 144
Ladbrook Rd. SE25 ....4D 156
Ladderstile Ride 5H 133
Ladderswood Way N11 .....5B 32
Ladlands SE22 ....7G 121
Lady Anne Ct. E18 . . . . .1J 51
  (off Queen Mary Av.)
Lady Aylesford Av. HA7: Stan ...5F 27
Lady Booth Rd. KT1: King T ...2E 150
Lady Craig Ct. UB8: Hil 5D 74
Ladycroft Gdns. BR6: Farnb ...5G 173
Ladycroft Rd. SE13 ....3D 122
Ladycroft Wlk. HA7: Stan 1D 42
Ladycroft Way BR6: Farnb ...5G 173
Lady Dock Path SE16 ......2A 104
Lady Elizabeth Ho. SW14 ....3J 115
Ladyfern Ho. E3 . . . . .5C 86
  (off Gail St.)
Lady Florence Ctyd. SE8 . . . . .7C 104
  (off Reginald Sq.)
Lady Forsdyke Way KT19: Eps ...7G 163
Ladygate La. HA4: Ruis 6D 38
Lady Harewood Way
  KT19: Eps 7G 163
Lady Hay KT4: Wor Pk 2B 164
Lady Jane Ct. KT2: King T 2F 151
  (off Cambridge Rd.)
Lady Margaret Ho. SE17 .....6D 102
  (off Queen's Row)
Lady Margaret Rd. N19 .....4G 65
  NW5 ....5G 65
  UB1: S'hall 7D 76
Lady May Ho. SE5 . . . . .7C 102
  (off Pitman St.)
Lady Micos Almshouses E1 . . . . .6J 85
  (off Aylward St.)
Lady Sarah Cohen Ho. N11 . . . . .6J 31
  (off Asher Loftus Way)
Lady Shaw Ct. N13 ....2E 32
Ladyship Ter. SE22 ....7G 121
Ladysmith Av. E6 ....2C 88
  IG2: Ilf 7J 53
Ladysmith Cl. NW7 ....7H 29
Ladysmith Rd. E16 ....3H 87
  EN1: Enf 3K 23
  (not continuous)

Ladysmith Rd. HA3: W'stone ...2J 41
  N17 ....2G 49
  N18 ....5C 34
  SE9 ....6E 124
Lady Somerset Rd. NW5 .....4F 65
LADYWELL 5D 122
Ladywell Arena (Running Track) ...6C 122
Ladywell Cl. SE4 ....5C 122
Ladywell Hgts. SE4 ....6B 122
Ladywell Rd. SE13 ....5C 122
Ladywell St. E15 ....1H 87
Ladywell Water Twr. SE4 .....5C 122
Ladywood Av. BR5: Pet W 5J 161
Ladywood Rd. KT6: Surb 2G 163
Lafone Av. TW13: Felt 2A 130
Lafone St. SE1 ....6J 15 (2F 103)
Lagado M. SE16 ....1K 103
Lagonier Apts. SE1 . . . . .6B 14
  (off Surrey Row)
Lagonda Ho. E3 . . . . .4C 86
  (off Tidworth Rd.)
Lagonier Ho. EC1 . . . . .2D 8
  (off Ironmonger Row)
Laidlaw Dr. N21 ....5E 22
Laing Dean UB5: N'olt 1A 76
Laing Ho. SE5 ....7C 102
Laings Av. CR4: Mitc 2D 154
Lainlock Pl. TW3: Houn 1F 113
Lainson St. SW18 ....7J 117
Lairdale Cl. SE21 ....1C 138
Laird Ho. SE5 ....7C 102
  (off Redcar St.)
Lairs Cl. N7 ....5J 65
Lait Ho. BR3: Beck 1D 158
Laitwood Rd. SW12 ....1F 137
Lakanal SE5 . . . . .1E 120
  (off Sceaux Gdns.)
The Lake WD23: B Hea 1C 26
Lake Av. BR1: Broml 6J 141
Lake Bus. Cen. N17 ....7B 34
Lake Cl. RM8: Dag 3D 72
  SW19 ....5H 135
Lakedale Ct. IG11: Bark 4B 90
Lakedale Rd. SE18 ....6J 107
Lake Dr. WD23: B Hea 2C 26
Lake Farm Country Pk. 1G 93
Lakefield Cl. SE20 ....7H 139
Lakefield Rd. N22 ....2B 48
Lake Gdns. RM10: Dag 5G 73
  SM6: W'gton 3F 167
  TW10: Ham 2B 132
Lakehall Gdns. CR7: Thor H ...5B 156
Lakehall Rd. CR7: Thor H 5B 156
Lake Ho. SE1 . . . . .7C 14
  (off Southwark Bri. Rd.)
Lake Ho. Rd. E11 ....3J 69
Lakehurst Rd. KT19: Ewe 5A 164
Lakeland Cl. HA3: Hrw W 6C 26
Lakenham Pl. E3 ....4B 86
Lakenheath N14 ....5B 22
Laker Cl. SW4 ....1J 119
Laker Ho. E16 ....2K 105
Laker Ind. Est. BR3: Beck 5A 140
Lake Rd. CR0: C'don 2B 170
  E10 ....7D 50
  RM6: Chad H 4D 54
  RM9: Dag 3H 91
  SW19 ....5H 135
Laker Pl. SW15 ....6G 117
Lakeside BR3: Beck 3D 158
  EN2: Enf 4C 22
  KT2: King T 7H 133
  KT19: Ewe 6A 164
  N3 ....2K 45
  SM6: W'gton 4F 167
  W13 ....6C 78
Lakeside Av. IG4: Ilf 4B 52
  SE28 ....1A 108
Lakeside Cl. DA15: Sidc 5C 126
  HA4: Ruis 4F 39
  SE25 ....2G 157
Lakeside Ct. N4 ....2C 66
Lakeside Cres. EN4: E Barn ...5J 21

Lakeside Dr. BR2: Broml 3C 172
  NW10 . . . . .3F 79
Lakeside Ind. Est. SL3: Coln 2B 174
Lakeside Rd. N13 . . . . .4E 32
  SL0: Rich P 3A 174
  SL3: Coln, Rich P 3A 174
  W14 . . . . .3F 99
Lakeside Ter. EC2 . . . . .5D 8
Lakeside Way HA9: Wemb 4G 61
Lakes Rd. BR2: Kes 5A 172
Lakeswood Rd. BR5: Pet W 6F 161
Lake Vw. HA8: Edg 5A 28
Lakeview Ct. SE28 . . . . .7B 90
Lake Vw. Est. E3 . . . . .2A 86
Lakeview Rd. DA16: Well 4B 126
  SE27 . . . . .5A 138
Lake Vw. Ter. N18 . . . . .4A 34
    (off Sweet Briar Wlk.)
Lakin Cl. SM5: Cars 4E 166
Lakis Cl. NW3 . . . . .4A 64
Laleham Av. NW7 . . . . .3E 28
Laleham Ct. SM1: Sutt 5A 166
Laleham Ho. E2 . . . . .3J 9
    (off Camlet St.)
Laleham Rd. SE6 . . . . .7E 122
  TW17: Shep 4B 146
Lalor St. SW6 . . . . .2G 117
Lambarde Av. SE9 . . . . .4E 142
Lambarde Sq. SE10 . . . . .5H 105
Lambard Ho. SE10 . . . . .7E 104
    (off Langdale Rd.)
Lamb Cl. UB5: N'olt 3C 76
Lamb Ct. E14 . . . . .7A 86
    (off Narrow St.)
Lamberhurst Ho. SE15 . . . . . . .6J 103
Lamberhurst Rd. RM8: Dag 1F 73
  SE27 . . . . .4A 138
Lambert Av. TW9: Rich 3G 115
Lambert Ct. DA8: Erith 6J 109
    (off Park Cres.)
Lambert Ho. SW11 . . . . .3B 118
    (off Gartons Way)
Lambert Jones M. EC2 . . . . .5C 8
Lambert Lodge TW8: Bford 5D 96
    (off Layton Rd.)
Lambert M. N12 . . . . .5F 31
    (off Lambert Way)
Lambert Rd. E16 . . . . .6K 87
  N12 . . . . .5G 31
  SW2 . . . . .5J 119
Lambert's Pl. CR0: C'don 1D 168
Lamberts Rd. KT5: Surb 5E 150
Lambert St. N1 . . . . .7A 66
Lambert Wlk. HA9: Wemb 3E 60
Lambert Way N12 . . . . .5F 31
LAMBETH 3G 19 (4K 101)
Lambeth Bri. SW1 . . . . . .3F 19 (4J 101)
Lambeth Crematorium 4A 136
Lambeth High St.
  SE1 . . . . .4G 19 (4K 101)
Lambeth Hill EC4 . . . . . .2C 14 (7C 84)
Lambeth Palace 2G 19 (3K 101)
Lambeth Pal. Rd.
  SE1 . . . . .2G 19 (3K 101)
Lambeth Rd. CR0: C'don 7A 156
  SE1 . . . . .3G 19 (4K 101)
  SE11 . . . . .3G 19 (4K 101)
Lambeth Towers SE11 . . . . .2J 19
Lambeth Wlk. SE11 . . . .4H 19 (4K 101)
    (not continuous)
Lambfold Ho. N7 . . . . .6J 65
    (off North Rd.)
Lamb Ho. SE5 . . . . .7C 102
    (off Elmington Est.)
  SE10 . . . . .6E 104
    (off Haddo St.)
Lambkins M. E17 . . . . .4E 50
Lamb La. E8 . . . . .7H 67
Lamble St. NW5 . . . . .5E 64
Lambley Rd. RM9: Dag 6B 72
Lambolle Pl. NW3 . . . . .6C 64
Lambolle Rd. NW3 . . . . .6C 64
Lamborne Pl. UB10: Ick 3D 56

Lambourn Cl. CR2: S Croy 7B 168
  NW5 . . . . .4G 65
  W7 . . . . .2K 95
Lambourne Av. SW19 . . . . .4H 135
Lambourne Ct. IG8: Wfd G 7F 37
Lambourne Gdns. E4 . . . . .2H 35
  EN1: Enf 2A 24
  IG11: Bark 7K 71
Lambourne Gro. SE16 . . . . .5K 103
Lambourne Ho. NW8 . . . . .5B 4
    (off Broadley St.)
  SE20 . . . . .1G 157
Lambourne Pl. SE3 . . . . .1K 123
Lambourne Rd. E11 . . . . .7E 50
  IG3: Ilf 2J 71
  IG11: Bark 7J 71
Lambourn Gro. KT1: King T 2H 151
Lambourn Rd. SW4 . . . . .3F 119
Lambrook Ho. SE15 . . . . .1G 121
Lambrook Ter. SW6 . . . . .1G 117
Lamb's Bldgs. EC1 . . . . . .4E 8 (4D 84)
Lamb's Cl. N9 . . . . .2B 34
Lamb's Conduit Pas.
  WC1 . . . . .5G 7 (5K 83)
Lamb's Conduit St. WC1 . . . .4G 7 (4K 83)
    (not continuous)
Lambscroft Av. SE9 . . . . .3A 142
Lambs Mdw. IG8: Wfd G 2B 52
Lamb's M. N1 . . . . .1B 84
Lambs Pas. EC1 . . . . . . .5E 8 (4D 84)
Lambs Ter. N9 . . . . .2J 33
Lamb St. E1 . . . . .5J 9 (5F 85)
Lamb's Wlk. EN2: Enf 2H 23
Lambton M. N19 . . . . .1J 65
    (off Lambton Rd.)
Lambton Pl. W11 . . . . .7H 81
Lambton Rd. N19 . . . . .1J 65
  SW20 . . . . .1E 152
Lamb Wlk. SE1 . . . . . . .7G 15 (2E 102)
Lamerock Rd. BR1: Broml 4H 141
Lamerton Rd. IG6: Ilf 2F 53
Lamerton St. SE8 . . . . .6C 104
Lamford Cl. N17 . . . . .7J 33
Lamington St. W6 . . . . .4D 98
Lamlash St. SE11 . . . . .4B 102
Lamley Ho. SE10 . . . . .7D 104
    (off Ashburnham Pl.)
Lammas Av. CR4: Mitc 2E 154
Lammas Grn. SE26 . . . . .3H 139
Lammas Pk. Gdns. W5 . . . . . . .1C 96
Lammas Pk. Rd. W5 . . . . .2D 96
Lammas Rd. E9 . . . . .7K 67
  E10 . . . . .2A 68
  TW10: Ham 4C 132
Lammermoor Rd. SW12 . . . . . . .7F 119
Lamont Rd. SW10 . . . . .7A 16 (6B 100)
Lamont Rd. Pas. SW10 . . . . . . .7A 16
LAMORBEY 1K 143
Lamorbey Cl. DA15: Sidc 1K 143
Lamorbey Pk. 1B 144
Lamorna Cl. BR6: Orp 7K 161
  E17 . . . . .2E 50
Lamorna Gro. HA7: Stan 1D 42
Lampard Gro. N16 . . . . .1F 67
Lampern Sq. E2 . . . . .3G 85
Lampeter Cl. NW9 . . . . .6A 44
Lampeter Sq. W6 . . . . .6G 99
Lamplighter Cl. E1 . . . . .4J 85
Lampmead Rd. SE12 . . . . .5H 123
Lamp Office Ct. WC1 . . . . .4G 7
Lamport Cl. SE18 . . . . .4D 106
LAMPTON 1F 113
Lampton Av. TW3: Houn 1F 113
Lampton Ct. TW3: Houn 1F 113
Lampton Ho. Cl. SW19 . . . . . . .4F 135
Lampton Pk. Rd. TW3: Houn 2F 113
Lampton Rd. TW3: Houn 2F 113
Lanacre Av. NW9 . . . . .1K 43
Lanadron Cl. TW7: Isle 2K 113
Lanain Ct. SE12 . . . . .7H 123
Lanark Cl. W5 . . . . .5C 78
Lanark Ct. UB5: N'olt 5E 58
    (off Newmarket Av.)

Lanark Ho. SE1 . . . . .5G 103
    (off Old Kent Rd.)
Lanark Mans. W9 . . . . .4A 82
    (off Lanark Rd.)
  W12 . . . . .2E 98
    (off Pennard Rd.)
Lanark M. W9 . . . . .3A 82
Lanark Pl. W9 . . . . .3A 4 (4A 82)
Lanark Rd. W9 . . . . .2K 81
Lanark Sq. E14 . . . . .3D 104
Lanata Wlk. UB4: Yead 4B 76
    (off Alba Cl.)
Lanbury Rd. SE15 . . . . .4K 121
Lancashire Ct. W1 . . . . .2K 11 (7F 83)
Lancaster Av. CR4: Mitc 5J 155
  E18 . . . . .4K 51
  EN4: Had W 1F 21
  IG11: Bark 7J 71
  SE27 . . . . .2B 138
  SW19 . . . . .5F 135
Lancaster Cl. BR2: Broml 4H 159
  KT2: King T 5D 132
  N1 . . . . .7E 66
  N17 . . . . .7B 34
  NW9 . . . . .7G 29
  TW15: Ashf 4A 128
  TW19: Stanw 6A 110
  W2 . . . . .7K 81
    (off St Petersburgh Pl.)
Lancaster Cotts. TW10: Rich 6E 114
Lancaster Ct. KT12: Walt T 7J 147
  SE27 . . . . .2B 138
  SM2: Sutt 7J 165
    (off Mulgrave Rd.)
  SW6 . . . . .7H 99
  TW19: Stanw 1A 128
  W2 . . . . .2A 10
    (off Lancaster Ga.)
Lancaster Dr. E14 . . . . .1E 104
  NW3 . . . . .6C 64
Lancaster Gdns. BR1: Broml 5C 160
  KT2: King T 5D 132
  SW19 . . . . .5G 135
  W13 . . . . .2B 96
Lancaster Ga. W2 . . . . . .2A 10 (7A 82)
Lancaster Gro. NW3 . . . . .6B 64
Lancaster Hall E16 . . . . .1J 105
    (off Wesley Av.)
Lancaster House 6A 12
Lancaster Ho. E11 . . . . .2H 69
  EN2: Enf 1J 23
  RM8: Dag 4B 72
  TW7: Isle 7K 95
Lancaster Lodge W11 . . . . .6G 81
    (off Lancaster Rd.)
Lancaster M. SW18 . . . . .5K 117
  TW10: Rich 6E 114
  W2 . . . . .2A 10 (7A 82)
Lancaster Pk. TW10: Rich 5E 114
Lancaster Pl. IG1: Ilf 5G 71
  SW19 . . . . .5F 135
  TW1: Twick 6A 114
  TW4: Houn 2A 112
  WC2 . . . . .2G 13 (7K 83)
Lancaster Rd. E7 . . . . .7J 69
  E11 . . . . .2G 69
  E17 . . . . .2K 49
  EN2: Enf 1J 23
  EN4: E Barn 5G 21
  HA2: Harr 5E 40
  N4 . . . . .7K 47
  N11 . . . . .6C 32
  N18 . . . . .5A 34
  NW10 . . . . .5C 62
  SE25 . . . . .2F 157
  SW19 . . . . .5F 135
  UB1: S'hall 7C 76
  UB5: N'olt 6D 59
  W11 . . . . .6G 81
Lancaster Rd. Ind. Est.
  EN4: E Barn 5G 21
Lancaster Stables NW3 . . . . . . .6C 64
Lancaster St. SE1 . . . . .7A 14 (2B 102)

Lancaster Ter. W2 . . . . . .2A 10 (7B 82)
Lancaster Wlk. UB3: Hayes 6E 74
  W2 . . . . .3A 10 (1A 100)
Lancaster Way KT4: Wor Pk 7D 152
Lancastrian Rd. SM6: W'gton 7J 167
Lancefield Ho. SE15 . . . . .4H 121
Lancefield St. W10 . . . . .3H 81
Lancell St. N16 . . . . .2E 66
Lancelot Av. HA0: Wemb 4D 60
Lancelot Cres. HA0: Wemb 4D 60
Lancelot Gdns. EN4: E Barn 7K 21
Lancelot Pl. SW7 . . . . . .7E 10 (2D 100)
Lancelot Rd. DA16: Well 4A 126
  HA0: Wemb 4D 60
Lance Rd. HA1: Harr 7G 41
Lancer Sq. W8 . . . . .2K 99
    (off Kensington Chu. St.)
Lancey Cl. SE7 . . . . .4C 106
Lanchester Ct. W2 . . . . .1E 10
    (off Seymour St.)
Lanchester Rd. N6 . . . . .5D 46
Landale Ho. SE16 . . . . .3H 103
    (off Lower Rd.)
Landau Apts. SW6 . . . . .6J 99
Landau Ct. CR2: S Croy 5C 168
    (off Warham Rd.)
Landcroft Rd. SE22 . . . . .5F 121
Landells Rd. SE22 . . . . .6F 121
Landford Rd. SW15 . . . . .3E 116
Landgrove Rd. SW19 . . . . .5J 135
Landing Waiters Ho. E14 . . . . . . .6F 87
    (off New Village Av.)
Landin Ho. E14 . . . . .6C 86
    (off Thomas Rd.)
Landleys Fld. N7 . . . . .5H 65
    (off Long Mdw.)
Landmann Ho. SE16 . . . . .4H 103
    (off Rennie Est.)
Landmann Point SE10 . . . . .3J 105
Landmann Way SE14 . . . . .5K 103
Landmark Arts Cen. 5B 132
Landmark Commercial Cen. N18 . .6K 33
Landmark East Twr. E14 . . . . . . .2C 104
    (off Marsh Wall)
Landmark Hgts. E5 . . . . .4A 68
Landmark Ho. W6 . . . . .5E 98
    (off Hammersmith Bri. Rd.)
Landmark Pl. UB10: Hil 2D 74
Landmark Sq. E14 . . . . .2C 104
Landmark West Twr. E14 . . . . . .2C 104
    (off Marsh Wall)
Landon Pl. SW1 . . . . . . .1E 16 (3D 100)
Landon's Cl. E14 . . . . .1E 104
Landon Wlk. E14 . . . . .7D 86
Landon Way TW15: Ashf 6D 128
Landor Ho. SE5 . . . . .7D 102
    (off Elmington Est.)
  W2 . . . . .5J 81
    (off Westbourne Pk. Rd.)
Landor Rd. SW9 . . . . .3J 119
Landor Space 3J 119
Landor Wlk. W12 . . . . .2C 98
Landra Gdns. N21 . . . . .6G 23
Landrake NW1 . . . . .1G 83
    (off Plender St.)
Landridge Dr. EN1: Enf 1C 24
Landridge Rd. SW6 . . . . .2H 117
Landrock Rd. N8 . . . . .6J 47
Landscape Rd. IG8: Wfd G 7E 36
Landsdown Cl. EN5: New Bar 4F 21
Landsdowne Ct. N19 . . . . .1J 65
    (off Fairbridge Rd.)

Landseer Av. E12 . . . . .5E **70**
Landseer Cl. HA8: Edg 2G **43**
   SW19 .1A **154**
Landseer Ct. UB4: Hayes 2F **75**
Landseer Ho. NW8 . . . . .3B **4**
   (off Frampton St.)
   SW1 . . . . .4D **18**
   (off Herrick St.)
   SW11 .1E **118**
   UB5: N'olt 2B **76**
   (off Parkfield Dr.)
Landseer Rd. EN1: Enf 5B **24**
   KT3: N Mald 7K **151**
   N19 . . . . .3J **65**
   (not continuous)
   SM1: Sutt 6J **165**
Landstead Rd. SE18 . . . . .7H **107**
Landulph Ho. SE11 . . . . .5K **19**
   (off Kennings Way)
Landward Ct. W1 . . . . .7D **4**
   (off Harrowby St.)
The Lane NW8 . . . . .2A **82**
   SE3 . . . . .3J **123**
Lane Cl. NW2 . . . . .3D **62**
La. End DA7: Bex 3H **127**
   SW15 .6F **117**
Lane Gdns. WD23: B Hea 1D **26**
Lane M. E12 . . . . .3D **70**
Lanercost Cl. SW2 . . . . .2A **138**
Lanercost Gdns. N14 . . . . .7D **22**
Lanercost Rd. SW2 . . . . .2A **138**
Lanesborough Ct. N1 . . . . .1G **9**
   (off Fanshaw St.)
Lanesborough Pl. SW1 . . . . .6H **11**
Lanesborough Way SW17 . . . . .3B **136**
Laneside BR7: Chst 5F **143**
   HA8: Edg 5D **28**
Laneside Av. RM8: Dag 7F **55**
Laneway SW15 . . . . .5D **116**
Laney Ho. EC1 . . . . .5J **7**
   (off Leather La.)
Lanfranc Ct. HA1: Harr 3K **59**
Lanfranc Rd. E3 . . . . .2A **86**
Lanfrey Pl. W14 . . . . .5H **99**
Langan Ho. E14 . . . . .6B **86**
   (off Keymer Pl.)
Langbourne Av. N6 . . . . .2E **64**
Langbourne Ct. E17 . . . . .6A **50**
Langbourne Mans. N6 . . . . .2E **64**
Langbourne Pl. E14 . . . . .5D **104**
Langbourne Way KT10: Clay 6A **162**
Lanbrook Rd. SE3 . . . . .3B **124**
Langcroft Cl. SM5: Cars 3D **166**
Langdale NW1 . . . . .1A **6**
   (off Stanhope St.)
Langdale Av. CR4: Mitc 3D **154**
Langdale Cl. BR6: Farnb 3F **173**
   RM8: Dag 1C **72**
   SE17 . . . . .6C **102**
   SW14 .4H **115**
Langdale Cres. DA7: Bex 7G **109**
Langdale Dr. UB4: Hayes 2G **75**
Langdale Gdns. UB6: G'frd 3B **78**
Langdale Ho. SW1 . . . . .6A **18**
   (off Churchill Gdns.)
Langdale Pde. CR4: Mitc 3D **154**
Langdale Rd. CR7: Thor H 4A **156**
   SE10 . . . . .7E **104**
Langdale St. E1 . . . . .6H **85**
Langdon Ct. EC1 . . . . .1B **8**
   (off City Rd.)
   NW10 .1A **80**
Langdon Cres. E6 . . . . .2E **88**
Langdon Dr. NW9 . . . . .1J **61**
Langdon Ho. E14 . . . . .6E **86**
   (off Ida St.)
Langdon Pk. TW11: Tedd 7C **132**
Langdon Pk. Rd. N6 . . . . .7G **47**
Langdon Pl. SW14 . . . . .3J **115**
Langdon Rd. BR2: Broml 3K **159**
   E6 . . . . .1E **88**
   SM4: Mord 5A **154**
Langdons Ct. UB2: S'hall 3E **94**

Langdon Shaw DA14: Sidc 5K **143**
Langdon Wlk. SM4: Mord 5A **154**
Langdon Way SE1 . . . . .4G **103**
Langford Cl. E8 . . . . .5G **67**
   N15 . . . . .6E **48**
   NW8 . . . . .2A **82**
   W3 . . . . .2H **97**
Langford Ct. NW8 . . . . .2A **82**
   (off Abbey Rd.)
Langford Cres. EN4: Cockf 4J **21**
Langford Grn. SE5 . . . . .3E **120**
Langford Ho. SE8 . . . . .6C **104**
Langford M. N1 . . . . .7A **66**
   SW11 .4B **118**
   (off St John's Hill)
Langford Pl. DA14: Sidc 3A **144**
   NW8 . . . . .2A **82**
Langford Rd. EN4: Cockf 4J **21**
   IG8: Wfd G 6F **37**
   SW6 . . . . .2K **117**
Langfords IG9: Buck H 2G **37**
Langham Cl. BR2: Broml 2C **172**
   N15 . . . . .3B **48**
   (off Langham Rd.)
Langham Ct. HA4: Ruis 5K **57**
   NW4 . . . . .5F **45**
   SW20 .2E **152**
Langham Dr. RM6: Chad H 6B **54**
Langham Gdns. HA0: Wemb 2C **60**
   HA8: Edg 7D **28**
   N21 . . . . .5F **23**
   TW10: Ham 4C **132**
   W13 . . . . .7B **78**
Langham Ho. E15 . . . . .6F **69**
   (off Forrester Way)
Langham Ho. Cl. TW10: Ham 4D **132**
Langham Mans. SW5 . . . . .5K **99**
   (off Earl's Ct. Sq.)
Langham Pk. Pl. BR2: Broml 4H **159**
Langham Pl. N15 . . . . .3B **48**
   W1 . . . . .6K **5** (5F **83**)
   W4 . . . . .6A **98**
Langham Rd. HA8: Edg 6D **28**
   N15 . . . . .3B **48**
   SW20 .1E **152**
   TW11: Tedd 5B **132**
Langham St. W1 . . . . .6K **5** (5F **83**)
Langhedge Cl. N18 . . . . .6A **34**
Langhedge La. N18 . . . . .6A **34**
Langhedge La. Ind. Est. N18 . . . . . .6A **34**
Langholme WD23: Bush 1B **26**
Langholm Dr. TW2: Twick 7J **113**
Langhorne Ct. NW8 . . . . .7B **64**
   (off Dorman Way)
Langhorne Rd. RM10: Dag 7G **73**
Langhorne St. SE18 . . . . .7D **106**
Lang Ho. SW8 . . . . .7J **101**
   (off Hartington Rd.)
   TW19: Stanw 1A **128**
Langland Cres. HA7: Stan 2D **42**
Langland Dr. HA5: Pinn 1C **40**
Langland Gdns. CR0: C'don 2B **170**
   NW3 . . . . .5K **63**
Langland Ho. SE5 . . . . .7D **102**
   (off Edmund St.)
Langler Rd. NW10 . . . . .2E **80**
Langley Av. HA4: Ruis 2K **57**
   KT4: Wor Pk 1F **165**
   KT6: Surb 1D **162**
Langley Ct. WC2 . . . . .2E **12** (7J **83**)
Langley Cres. E11 . . . . .7A **52**
   HA8: Edg 3D **28**
   RM9: Dag 7C **72**
   UB3: Harl 7H **93**
Langley Dr. E11 . . . . .7K **51**
   W3 . . . . .2H **97**
Langley Gdns. BR2: Broml 4A **160**
   BR5: Pet W 6F **161**
   RM9: Dag 7D **72**
Langley Gro. KT3: N Mald 2A **152**
Langley Ho. W2 . . . . .5J **81**
   (off Alfred Rd.)

Langley La. SW8 . . . . . . .7F **19** (6K **101**)
Langley Mans. SW8 . . . . .7F **19**
Langley M. RM9: Dag 7D **72**
Langley Pk. NW7 . . . . .6F **29**
Langley Pk. Golf Course 6F **159**
Langley Pk. Rd. SM1: Sutt 5A **166**
   SM2: Sutt 5A **166**
Langley Pk. Sports Cen. 6E **158**
Langley Rd. BR3: Beck 4A **158**
   DA16: Well 6C **108**
   KT6: Surb 7E **150**
   SW19 .1H **153**
   TW7: Isle 2K **113**
Langley Row EN5: Barn 1C **20**
Langley St. WC2 . . . . .1E **12** (6J **83**)
Langley Way BR4: W W'ck 1F **171**
Langmead Dr. WD23: B Hea 1D **26**
Langmead Ho. E3 . . . . .3D **86**
   (off Bruce Rd.)
Langmead St. SE27 . . . . .4B **138**
Langmore Cl. DA6: Bex 3D **126**
Langmore Ho. E1 . . . . .6G **85**
   (off Stutfield St.)
Langport Ct. KT12: Walt T 7A **148**
Langport Ho. SW9 . . . . .2B **120**
Langridge M. TW12: Hamp 6D **130**
Langroyd Rd. SW17 . . . . .2D **136**
Langside Av. SW15 . . . . .4C **116**
Langside Cres. N14 . . . . .3C **32**
Langstone Mews UB1: S'hall 1E **94**
Langstone Way NW7 . . . . .7A **30**
Langston Hughes Cl. SE24 . . . . . . .4B **120**
Lang St. E1 .4J **85**
Langthorn Ct. EC2 . . . . .7E **8** (6D **84**)
Langthorne Ct. BR1: Broml 4E **140**
Langthorne Ho. E3 . . . . .3B **86**
   (off Merchant St.)
   UB3: Harl 4G **93**
Langthorne Rd. E11 . . . . .3E **68**
   (not continuous)
Langthorne St. SW6 . . . . .7F **99**
Langton Av. E6 . . . . .3E **88**
   N20 . . . . .7F **21**
Langton Cl. WC1 . . . . .3H **7** (4K **83**)
Langton Ho. SE11 . . . . .3H **19**
Langton Pl. SW18 . . . . .1J **135**
Langton Ri. SE23 . . . . .7H **121**
Langton Rd. HA3: Hrw W 7B **26**
   KT8: W Mole 4G **149**
   NW2 . . . . .3E **62**
   SW9 . . . . .7B **102**
Langton St. SW10 . . . . .6A **100**
Langton Way CR0: C'don 3E **168**
   SE3 . . . . .1H **123**
Langtry Ct. TW7: Isle 2K **113**
Langtry Ho. KT2: King T 1G **151**
   (off London Rd.)
Langtry Pl. SW6 . . . . .6J **99**
Langtry Rd. NW8 . . . . .1K **81**
   UB5: N'olt 2B **76**
Langtry Wlk. NW8 . . . . .1K **81**
Langwood Chase
   TW11: Tedd 6C **132**
Langworth Dr. UB4: Yead 6K **75**
Lanhill Rd. W9 . . . . .4J **81**
Lanier Rd. SE13 . . . . .6F **123**
Lanigan Dr. TW3: Houn 5F **113**
Lankaster Gdns. N2 . . . . .1B **46**
Lankers Dr. HA2: Harr 6D **40**
Lankton Cl. BR3: Beck 1E **158**
Lannock Rd. UB3: Hayes 1H **93**
Lannoy Point SW6 . . . . .7G **99**
   (off Pellant Rd.)
Lannoy Rd. SE9 . . . . .1G **143**
Lanrick Rd. E14 . . . . .6F **87**
Lanridge Rd. SE2 . . . . .3D **108**
Lansbury Av. IG11: Bark 7A **72**
   N18 . . . . .5J **33**
   RM6: Chad H 5E **54**
   TW14: Felt 6K **111**
Lansbury Cl. NW10 . . . . .5J **61**
Lansbury Ct. SE28 . . . . .7B **90**
   (off Saunders Way)

Lansbury Dr. UB4: Hayes 2G **75**
Lansbury Est. E14 . . . . .6D **86**
Lansbury Gdns. E14 . . . . .6F **87**
Lansbury Rd. EN3: Enf H 1E **24**
Lansbury Way N18 . . . . .5K **33**
Lanscombe Wlk. SW8 . . . . .1J **119**
Lansdell Ho. SW2 . . . . .6A **120**
Lansdell Rd. CR4: Mitc 2E **154**
Lansdowne Av. BR6: Farnb 1F **173**
   DA7: Bex 7D **108**
Lansdowne Cl. KT6: Surb 2H **163**
   SW20 .7F **135**
   TW1: Twick 1K **131**
Lansdowne Ct. IG5: Ilf 3C **52**
   KT4: Wor Pk 2C **164**
   W11 . . . . .7G **81**
   (off Lansdowne Ri.)
Lansdowne Cres. W11 . . . . .7G **81**
Lansdowne Dr. E8 . . . . .6G **67**
Lansdowne Gdns. SW8 . . . . .1J **119**
Lansdowne Grn. SW8 . . . . .1J **119**
Lansdowne Gro. NW10 . . . . .4A **62**
Lansdowne Hill SE27 . . . . .3B **138**
Lansdowne Ho. W11 . . . . .1H **99**
   (off Ladbroke Rd.)
Lansdowne La. SE7 . . . . .6B **106**
Lansdowne M. SE7 . . . . .5B **106**
   W11 . . . . .1H **99**
Lansdowne Pl. SE1 . . . . .3D **102**
   SE19 . . . . .7F **139**
Lansdowne Ri. W11 . . . . .7G **81**
Lansdowne Rd. BR1: Broml 7J **141**
   CR0: C'don 2D **168**
   E4 . . . . .2H **35**
   E11 . . . . .2H **69**
   E17 . . . . .6C **50**
   E18 . . . . .3J **51**
   HA1: Harr 7J **41**
   HA7: Stan 6H **27**
   IG3: Ilf .1K **71**
   KT19: Ewe 7J **163**
   N3 . . . . .7D **30**
   N10 . . . . .2G **47**
   N17 . . . . .1F **49**
   SW20 .7E **134**
   TW3: Houn 3F **113**
   UB8: Hil 6E **74**
   W11 . . . . .7G **81**
Lansdowne Row W1 . . . . .4K **11** (1F **101**)
Lansdowne Ter. WC1 . . . . . . .4F **7** (4J **83**)
Lansdowne Wlk. W11 . . . . .1H **99**
Lansdowne Way SW8 . . . . .1H **119**
Lansdowne Wood Cl. SE27 . . . . . . .3B **138**
Lansdowne Workshops SE7 . . . . . .5A **106**
Lansdown Rd. DA14: Sidc 3B **144**
   E7 . . . . .7A **70**
Lansfield Av. N18 . . . . .4B **34**
Lanson Apts. SW11 . . . . .7F **101**
Lantan Hgts. E20 . . . . .7E **68**
Lantern SE1 . . . . .6C **14**
   (off Lant St.)
Lantern Cl. BR6: Farnb 4F **173**
   HA0: Wemb 5D **60**
   SW15 .4C **116**
Lantern Ho. UB3: Harl 3E **92**
   (off Nine Acres Cl.)
Lanterns Way E14 . . . . .2C **104**
Lantern Way UB7: W Dray 2A **92**
Lant Ho. SE1 . . . . .7C **14**
   (off Toulmin St.)
Lantry Ct. W3 . . . . .1H **97**
Lant St. SE1 . . . . .6C **14** (2C **102**)
Lanvanor Rd. SE15 . . . . .2J **121**
Lanward Apts. N1 . . . . .7K **65**
   (off Caledonian Rd.)
Lanyard Ho. SE8 . . . . .4B **104**
Lapford Cl. W9 . . . . .4H **81**
Lapis Cl. NW10 . . . . .3G **79**
Lapis M. E15 . . . . .1E **86**
Lapponum Wlk. UB4: Yead 4B **76**
Lapse Wood Wlk. SE23 . . . . .1H **139**
Lapstone Gdns.
   HA3: Kenton 6C **42**

Lapwing Ct. KT6: Surb 3G 163
SE1 ....7D 14
(off Swan St.)
Lapwing Ter. E7 ....5B 70
Lapwing Twr. SE8 ....6B 104
(off Taylor Cl.)
Lapwing Way UB4: Yead 6B 76
Lapworth N11 ....4A 32
(off Coppies Gro.)
Lapworth Ct. W2 ....5K 81
(off Delamere Ter.)
Lara Cl. KT9: Chess 7E 162
SE13 ....6E 122
Larbert Rd. SW16 ....7G 137
Larch Av. W3 ....1A 98
Larch Cl. E13 ....4K 87
N11 ....7K 31
N19 ....2G 65
SE8 ....6B 104
SW12 ....2F 137
Larch Ct. SE1 ....7G 15
(off Royal Oak Yd.)
W9 ....5J 81
(off Admiral Wlk.)
Larch Cres. KT19: Ewe 6H 163
UB4: Yead 4A 76
Larch Dene BR6: Farnb 2E 172
Larch Dr. W4 ....5G 97
The Larches N13 ....3H 33
UB10: Hil 3D 74
Larches Av. SW14 ....4K 115
Larch Grn. NW9 ....1A 44
Larch Gro. DA15: Sidc 1K 143
Larch Ho. BR2: Broml 1G 159
SE16 ....2J 103
(off Ainsty Est.)
UB4: Yead 5A 76
W10 ....4G 81
(off Rowan Wlk.)
Larch Rd. E10 ....1C 68
NW2 ....4E 62
Larch Tree Way CRO: C'don ...3C 170
Larchvale Ct. SM2: Sutt 7K 165
Larch Way BR2: Broml 7E 160
Larchwood Ho. UB7: W Dray ...2B 92
(off Park Lodge Av.)
Larchwood Rd. SE9 ....2F 143
Larcombe Cl. CRO: C'don 4F 169
Larcombe Cl. SM2: Sutt 7K 165
(off Worcester Rd.)
Larcom St. SE17 ....4C 102
Larden Rd. W3 ....1A 98
Largewood Av. KT6: Surb 2G 163
Lariat Apts. SE10 ....4G 105
(off Cable Wlk.)
Larissa St. SE17 ....5D 102
Larkbere Rd. SE26 ....4A 140
Lark Ct. NW9 ....1A 44
(off Lanacre Av.)
Larken Cl. WD23: Bush 1B 26
Larken Dr. WD23: Bush 1B 26
Larkfield Av. HA3: Kenton 3B 42
Larkfield Cl. BR2: Hayes 2H 171
Larkfield Rd. DA14: Sidc 3K 143
TW9: Rich 4E 114
Larkhall La. SW4 ....2H 119
Larkhall Ri. SW4 ....3G 119
(not continuous)
Larkham Cl. TW13: Felt 3G 129
Lark Row E2 ....1J 85
Larksfield Gro. EN1: Enf 1C 24
Larks Gro. IG11: Bark 7J 71
Larkshall Ct. RM7: Mawney 2J 55
Larkshall Cres. E4 ....4K 35
Larkshall Rd. E4 ....5K 35
Larkspur Cl. E6 ....5C 88
HA4: Ruis 7E 38
N17 ....7J 33
NW9 ....5H 43
Larkspur Gro. HA8: Edg 4D 28
Larkspur Lodge DA14: Sidc ...3B 144
Larkspur Way KT19: Ewe 5J 163
Larkswood Ct. E4 ....5A 36

Larkswood Ri. HA5: Eastc 4A 40
Larkswood Rd. E4 ....4H 35
Lark Way SM5: Cars 7C 154
Larkway Cl. NW9 ....4K 43
Larkwood Av. SE10 ....1E 122
Larnach Rd. W6 ....6F 99
Larne Rd. HA4: Ruis 7H 39
Larpent Av. SW15 ....5E 116
Larson Wlk. E14 ....3C 104
Larwood Cl. UB6: G'frd 5H 59
Lascar Cl. TW3: Houn 3D 112
Lascar Wharf Bldg. E14 ......6A 86
(off Parnham St.)
Lascelles Av. HA1: Harr 7H 41
Lascelles Cl. E11 ....2F 69
Lascelles Ho. NW1 ....4D 4
Lascotts Rd. N22 ....6E 32
Laseron Ho. N15 ....4F 49
(off Tottenham Grn. E.)
Laserquest
Romford 2F 55
Las Palmas Est. TW17: Shep ..7E 146
Lassa Rd. SE9 ....5C 124
Lassell St. SE10 ....5F 105
Lasseter Pl. SE3 ....6H 105
Latchett Rd. E18 ....1K 51
Latchingdon Cl. E17 ....4K 49
Latchingdon Gdns. IG8: Wfd G .6H 37
Latchmere Cl. TW10: Ham 5E 132
Latchmere La. KT2: King T 6F 133
TW10: Ham 6F 133
Latchmere Leisure Cen. 2D 118
Latchmere Pas. SW11 ....2C 118
Latchmere Pl. TW15: Ashf 2A 128
Latchmere Rd. KT2: King T 7E 132
SW11 ....2D 118
Latchmere St. SW11 ....2D 118
Lateward Rd. TW8: Bford 6D 96
Latham Cl. E6 ....5C 88
TW1: Twick 7A 114
Latham Ct. N11 ....6D 32
(off Brownlow Rd.)
SW5 ....4J 99
(off W. Cromwell Rd.)
UB5: N'olt 3B 76
(off Delta Gro.)
Latham Ho. E1 ....6K 85
(off Chudleigh St.)
Latham Rd. DA6: Bex 5G 127
TW1: Twick 7K 113
Latham's Way CRO: Wadd 1K 167
Lathkill Cl. EN1: Enf 7B 24
Lathkill Ct. BR3: Beck 1B 158
Lathom Rd. E6 ....7C 70
Lathom Rd. E6 ....1D 88
Latimer Cl. HA5: Pinn 1A 40
KT4: Wor Pk 4D 164
Latimer Ct. BR2: Broml 4H 159
(off Durham Rd.)
Latimer Gdns. HA5: Pinn 1A 40
Latimer Ho. E9 ....6K 67
W11 ....7H 81
(off Kensington Pk. Rd.)
Latimer Ind. Est. W10 ....6E 80
Latimer Pl. W10 ....6E 80
Latimer Rd. CRO: C'don 3B 168
E7 ....4K 69
EN5: New Bar 3E 20
N15 ....6E 48
SW19 ....6K 135
TW11: Tedd 5K 131
W10 ....5E 80
(not continuous)
Latimer Square SE10 ....3J 105
Latitude Apts. CRO: C'don ...3D 168
(off Fairfield Rd.)
Latitude Ct. E16 ....7G 89
Latitude Ho. NW1 ....1F 83
(off Oval Rd.)
Latona Ct. SW9 ....7A 102
(off Caldwell St.)
Latona Rd. SE15 ....6G 103
La Tourne Gdns. BR6: Farnb ..3G 173

Lattimer Pl. W4 ....7A 98
Latton Cl. KT12: Walt T 7C 148
Latvia Cl. SE17 ....5C 102
(off Macleod St.)
Latymer Ct. W6 ....4F 99
Latymer Gdns. N3 ....2G 45
Latymer Rd. N9 ....1A 34
Latymer Way N9 ....2K 33
Laubin Cl. TW1: Twick 4B 114
Lauder Cl. UB5: N'olt 2B 76
Lauder Ct. N14 ....7D 22
Lauderdale Dr. TW10: Ham 3D 132
Lauderdale House 1F 65
Lauderdale Ho. SW9 ....1A 120
Lauderdale House Community Arts Cen.
......................1F 65
(within Lauderdale House)
Lauderdale Mans. W9 ....3K 81
(off Lauderdale Rd.)
Lauderdale Pde. W9 ....4K 81
Lauderdale Pl. EC2 ....5C 8
(off Beech St.)
Lauderdale Rd. W9 ....3K 81
Lauderdale Twr. EC2 ....5C 8
Laud St. CRO: C'don 3C 168
SE11 ....5G 19 (5K 101)
Laugan Wlk. SE17 ....5C 102
Laughton Rd. UB5: N'olt 1B 76
Launcelot Rd. BR1: Broml 4J 141
Launcelot St. SE1 .....7J 13 (2A 102)
Launceston Gdns. UB6: G'frd .1C 78
Launceston Pl. W8 ....3A 100
Launceston Rd. UB6: G'frd 1C 78
Launch St. E14 ....3E 104
Launders Ga. W3 ....2H 97
Laundress La. N16 ....3G 67
Laundry Cl. CRO: C'don 7D 156
Laundry La. N1 ....1C 84
Laundry M. SE23 ....7A 122
Laundry Rd. W6 ....6G 99
Launton Dr. DA6: Bex 4D 126
Laura Cl. E11 ....5A 52
EN1: Enf 5K 23
Lauradale Rd. N2 ....4D 46
Laura Pl. E5 ....4J 67
Laura Ter. N4 ....2B 66
Laurel Apts. SE17 ....4E 102
(off Townsend St.)
Laurel Av. TW1: Twick 1K 131
Laurel Bank N12 ....4F 31
Laurel Bank Gdns. SW6 ......2H 117
Laurel Bank Rd. EN2: Enf 1H 23
Laurel Bank Vs. W7 ....2J 95
(off Lwr. Boston Rd.)
Laurel Cl. DA14: Sidc 3A 144
N19 ....2G 65
SW17 ....5C 136
Laurel Ct. CR2: S Croy 4E 168
(off South Pk. Hill Rd.)
HA0: Wemb 2E 78
SE1 ....3D 102
(off Garland Cl.)
Laurel Cres. CRO: C'don 3C 170
RM7: Rush G 1K 73
Laurel Dr. N21 ....7F 23
Laurel Gdns. BR1: Broml 4C 160
E4 ....7J 25
NW7 ....3E 28
TW4: Houn 4C 112
TW15: Ashf 5E 128
W7 ....1J 95
Laurel Gro. SE20 ....7J 139
SE26 ....4K 139
Laurel Ho. BR2: Broml 1G 159
E3 ....4A 86
(off Hornbeam Sq.)
SE8 ....6B 104
Laurel La. UB7: W Dray 4A 92
Laurel Mnr. SM2: Sutt 7A 166
Laurel M. SE5 ....3C 120
(off Harbour Rd.)
Laurel Pk. HA3: Hrw W 7E 26

Laurel Rd. SW13 ....2C 116
SW20 ....1D 152
TW12: Hamp H 5H 131
The Laurels BR1: Broml 1K 159
BR2: Broml 4J 159
IG9: Buck H 1F 37
NW10 ....1D 80
SW9 ....7B 102
(off Langton Rd.)
WD23: B Hea 2D 26
Laurel St. E8 ....6F 67
Laurel Vw. N12 ....3E 30
Laurel Way E18 ....4H 51
N20 ....3D 30
Laurence Calvert Cl. IG11: Bark ...2J 89
Laurence Ct. E10 ....7D 50
W11 ....7G 81
(off Lansdowne Rd.)
Laurence M. W12 ....2C 98
Laurence Pountney Hill
EC4 ....2E 14 (7D 84)
Laurence Pountney La.
EC4 ....2E 14 (7D 84)
Laurence Rd. TW3: Houn 3G 113
Laurie Gro. SE14 ....1A 122
Laurie Ho. SE1 ....3B 102
(off St George's Rd.)
W8 ....1J 99
(off Airlie Gdns.)
Laurie Rd. W7 ....5J 77
Laurier Rd. CRO: C'don 7F 157
NW5 ....3F 65
Laurimel Cl. HA7: Stan 6G 27
Laurino Pl. WD23: B Hea 2B 26
Lauriston Ho. E9 ....7J 67
(off Lauriston Rd.)
Lauriston Rd. E9 ....7J 67
SW19 ....6F 135
Lausanne Rd. N8 ....4A 48
SE15 ....1J 121
Laval Ho. TW8: Bford 5E 96
(off Ealing Rd.)
Lavell St. N16 ....4D 66
Lavender Av. CR4: Mitc 1C 154
KT4: Wor Pk 3E 164
NW9 ....1J 61
Lavender Cl. BR2: Broml 6C 160
E4 ....4H 35
SM5: Cars 4F 167
SW3 ....7B 16 (6B 100)
Lavender Cl. KT8: W Mole 3F 149
SM2: Sutt 7A 166
TW14: Felt 6K 111
Lavender Gdns. EN2: Enf 1G 23
HA3: Hrw W 6D 26
SW11 ....4D 118
Lavender Gro. CR4: Mitc 1C 154
E8 ....7G 67
Lavender Hill EN2: Enf 1F 23
SW11 ....4C 118
Lavender Ho. SE16 ....1K 103
(off Rotherhithe St.)
TW9: Kew 1H 115
Lavender M. TW12: Hamp H ...6G 131
Lavender Pl. IG1: Ilf 5F 71
Lavender Pond Nature Pk. ...1A 104
Lavender Ri. UB7: W Dray 2C 92
Lavender Rd. CRO: C'don 6K 155
EN2: Enf 1J 23
KT19: Ewe 5H 163
SE16 ....1A 104
SM1: Sutt 4B 166
SM5: Cars 4E 166
SW11 ....3B 118
UB8: Hil 5B 74
Lavender Sq. SW9 ....1K 119
(off Printers Rd.)
Lavender St. E15 ....6G 69
Lavender Sweep SW11 ....4D 118
Lavender Ter. SW11 ....3C 118
Lavender Va. SM6: W'gton 6H 167
Lavender Wlk. CR4: Mitc 3E 154
SW11 ....4D 118

Lavender Way CRO: C'don 6K 157
Lavendon Ho. NW8 . . . . .3D 4
(off Paveley St.)
Lavengro Rd. SE27 . . . . .2C 138
Lavenham Rd. SW18 . . . . .2H 135
Lavernock Rd. DA7: Bex 2G 127
Lavers Rd. N16 . . . . .3E 66
Laverstoke Gdns. SW15 . . . . .7B 116
Laverton M. SW5 . . . . .4K 99
Laverton Pl. SW5 . . . . .4K 99
Lavette Ho. E3 . . . . .3C 86
(off Rainhill Way)
Lavidge Rd. SE9 . . . . .2C 142
Lavina Gro. N1 . . . . .2K 83
Lavington Cl. E9 . . . . .6B 68
Lavington Rd. CRO: Bedd 3K 167
W13 . . . . .2B 96
Lavington St. SE1 . . . . . . .5B 14 (1B 102)
Lavisham Ho. BR1: Broml 5K 141
Lawdons Gdns. CRO: Wadd 4B 168
Lawes Ho. W10 . . . . .3H 81
(off Lancefield St.)
Lawes Way IG11: Bark 3K 89
Lawford Rd. N1 . . . . .7E 66
NW5 . . . . .6G 65
W4 . . . . .7J 97
Lawfords Wharf NW1 . . . . .7G 65
(off Lyme St.)
Law Ho. IG11: Bark 2A 90
Lawless Ho. E14 . . . . .7E 86
(off Bazely St.)
Lawless St. E14 . . . . .7D 86
Lawley Ho. TW1: Twick 6D 114
Lawley Rd. N14 . . . . .7A 22
Lawley St. E5 . . . . .4J 67
Lawlor Cl. TW16: Sun 1K 147
The Lawn UB2: S'hall 5E 94
Lawn Cl. BR1: Broml 6K 141
HA4: Ruis 3H 57
KT3: N Mald 2A 152
N9 . . . . .7A 24
Lawn Cres. TW9: Kew 2G 115
Lawn Farm Gro. RM6: Chad H 4E 54
Lawnfield Ct. NW6 . . . . .7F 63
(off Coverdale Rd.)
Lawn Gdns. W7 . . . . .1J 95
Lawn Ho. Cl. E14 . . . . .2E 104
Lawn La. SW8 . . . . .7F 19 (6K 101)
Lawn Rd. BR3: Beck 7B 140
NW3 . . . . .5D 64
The Lawns DA14: Sidc 4B 144
E4 . . . . .5H 35
HA5: Hat E 7A 26
SE3 . . . . .3H 123
SE19 . . . . .1D 156
SM2: Cheam 7G 165
SW19 . . . . .5H 135
Lawns Cl. HA9: Wemb 2F 61
Lawnside SE3 . . . . .4H 123
Lawns Way RM5: Col R 1J 55
Lawnswood EN5: Barn 5B 20
Lawn Ter. SE3 . . . . .3G 123
Lawn Va. HA5: Pinn 2C 40
Lawrence Av. E12 . . . . .4E 70
E17 . . . . .1K 49
KT3: N Mald 6K 151
N13 . . . . .4G 33
NW7 . . . . .4F 29
NW10 . . . . .1K 79
Lawrence Bldgs. N16 . . . . .3F 67
Lawrence Campe Cl. N20 . . . . .3G 31
Lawrence Cl. E3 . . . . .3C 86
N15 . . . . .4E 48
W12 . . . . .7D 80
Lawrence Ct. N10 . . . . .3G 47
N16 . . . . .3F 67
(off Smalley Rd. Est.)
NW7 . . . . .5F 29
SE6 . . . . .6C 122
W3 . . . . .3J 97
(off Stanley Rd.)
Lawrence Cres. HA8: Edg 2G 43
RM10: Dag 3H 73

Lawrence Dr. UB10: Ick 4E 56
Lawrence Est. TW4: Houn 4A 112
Lawrence Gdns. NW7 . . . . .3G 29
Lawrence Gro. UB10: Uxb 2A 74
Lawrence Hill E4 . . . . .2H 35
Lawrence Ho. NW1 . . . . .7F 65
(off Hawley Cres.)
SW1 . . . . .4D 18
(off Cureton St.)
Lawrence La. EC2 . . . . .7D 8 (6C 84)
Lawrence Mans. SW3 . . . . .7C 16
(off Lordship Pl.)
Lawrence M. SW8 . . . . .7J 101
SW15 . . . . .4E 116
Lawrence Pde. TW7: Isle 3B 114
(off Lower Sq.)
Lawrence Pl. N1 . . . . .1J 83
(off Brydon Wlk.)
Lawrence Rd. BR4: W W'ck 4J 171
DA8: Erith 7H 109
E6 . . . . .1C 88
E13 . . . . .1K 87
HA5: Pinn 6B 40
N15 . . . . .4E 48
N18 . . . . .4C 34
(not continuous)
SE25 . . . . .4F 157
TW4: Houn 4A 112
TW10: Ham 4C 132
TW12: Hamp 7D 130
UB4: Hayes 2E 74
W5 . . . . .4D 96
Lawrence St. E16 . . . . .5H 87
NW7 . . . . .5G 29
SW3 . . . . .7C 16 (6C 100)
Lawrence Trad. Est. SE10 . . . . .4G 105
Lawrence Way NW10 . . . . .3J 61
Lawrence Weaver Cl.
SM4: Mord 6J 153
Lawrence Yd. N15 . . . . .4E 48
Lawrie Ho. SW19 . . . . .5K 135
(off Durnsford Rd.)
Lawrie Pk. Av. SE26 . . . . .5H 139
Lawrie Pk. Cres. SE26 . . . . .5H 139
Lawrie Pk. Gdns. SE26 . . . . .4H 139
Lawrie Pk. Rd. SE26 . . . . .6H 139
Laws Cl. SE25 . . . . .4D 156
Lawson Cl. E16 . . . . .5A 88
IG1: Ilf .5H 71
SW19 . . . . .3F 135
Lawson Ct. KT6: Surb 7D 150
N4 . . . . .1K 65
(off Lorne Rd.)
N11 . . . . .6B 32
(off Ring Way)
Lawson Gdns. HA5: Eastc 3K 39
Lawson Ho. SE18 . . . . .6E 106
(off Nightingale Pl.)
W12 . . . . .7D 80
(off White City Est.)
Lawson Rd. EN3: Enf H 1D 24
UB1: S'hall 4E 76
Lawson Ter. SE15 . . . . .4J 121
Law St. SE1 . . . . .3D 102
Lawton Rd. E3 . . . . .3A 86
(not continuous)
E10 . . . . .1E 68
EN4: Cockf 3G 21
Laxcon Cl. NW10 . . . . .5K 61
Laxey Rd. BR6: Chels 6K 173
Laxfield Ct. E8 . . . . .1G 85
(off Pownall Rd.)
Laxford Ho. SW1 . . . . .4H 17
(off Cundy St.)
Laxley Cl. SE5 . . . . .7B 102
Laxton Ct. CR7: Thor H 4C 156
Laxton Pl. NW1 . . . . .3K 5 (4F 83)
Layard Rd. CR7: Thor H 2D 156
EN1: Enf 1A 24
SE16 . . . . .4H 103
Layard Sq. SE16 . . . . .4H 103
Laybourne Ho. E14 . . . . .2C 104
(off Admirals Way)

Laybrook Lodge E18 . . . . .4H 51
Laycock St. N1 . . . . .6A 66
Layer Gdns. W3 . . . . .7G 79
Layfield Cl. NW4 . . . . .7D 44
Layfield Cres. NW4 . . . . .7D 44
Layfield Ho. SE10 . . . . .5J 105
(off Kemsing Rd.)
Layfield Rd. NW4 . . . . .7D 44
Layhams Rd. BR2: Kes 4G 171
BR4: W W'ck 4G 171
Laymarsh Cl. DA17: Belv 3F 109
Laymead Cl. UB5: N'olt 6C 58
Laystall Ct. WC1 . . . . .4J 7
(off Mt. Pleasant)
Laystall St. EC1 . . . . .4J 7 (4A 84)
Layton Ct. TW8: Bford 5D 96
Layton Cres. CRO: Wadd 5A 168
Layton Pl. TW9: Kew 1G 115
Layton Rd. TW3: Houn 4F 113
TW8: Bford 5D 96
Layton's La. TW16: Sun 2H 147
Layzell Wlk. SE9 . . . . .1B 142
Lazar Wlk. N7 . . . . .2K 65
Lazenby Ct. WC2 . . . . .2E 12
Leabank Cl. HA1: Harr 3J 59
Leabank Sq. E9 . . . . .6C 68
Leabank Vw. N15 . . . . .6G 49
Lea Bon Ct. E15 . . . . .1H 87
(off Plaistow Gro.)
Leabourne Rd. N16 . . . . .7G 49
LEA BRIDGE 3K 67
Lea Bri. Ind. Cen. E10 . . . . .1A 68
Lea Bri. Rd. E5 . . . . .3J 67
E10 . . . . .7C 50
E17 . . . . .5C 50
Lea Cl. TW2: Whitt 7D 112
Lea Ct. E4 .2K 35
E13 . . . . .3J 87
N15 . . . . .4G 49
Lea Cres. HA4: Ruis 4H 57
Leacroft Av. SW12 . . . . .7D 118
Leacroft Cl. N21 . . . . .2G 33
UB7: Yiew 6A 74
Leadale Av. E4 . . . . .2H 35
Leadale Rd. N15 . . . . .6G 49
N16 . . . . .6G 49
Leadbeaters Cl. N11 . . . . .5J 31
Leadbetter Ct. NW10 . . . . .7K 61
(off Melville Rd.)
Leadenhall Mkt. 1G 15 (6E 84)
Leadenhall Pl. EC3 . . . . .1G 15 (6E 84)
Leadenhall St. EC3 . . . . .1G 15 (6E 84)
Leadenham Ct. E3 . . . . .4C 86
Leader Av. E12 . . . . .5E 70
The Leadings HA9: Wemb 3J 61
Leadmill La. E20 . . . . .4D 68
Leaf Cl. HA6: Nwood 1F 39
KT7: T Ditt 5J 149
Leaf Gro. SE27 . . . . .5A 138
Leaf Ho. HA1: Harr 5K 41
(off Catherine Pl.)
Leafield Cl. NW6 . . . . .6B 138
Leafield La. DA14: Sidc 3F 145
Leafield Rd. SM1: Sutt 2J 165
SW20 . . . . .3H 153
Leaf Wlk. N7 . . . . .4H 65
Leafy Gro. BR2: Kes 5A 172
Leafy Oak Rd. SE12 . . . . .4A 142
Leafy Way CRO: C'don 2F 169
Lea Gdns. HA9: Wemb 4F 61
Leagrave St. E5 . . . . .3J 67
Lea Hall Gdns. E10 . . . . .1C 68
Lea Hall Rd. E10 . . . . .1C 68
Leaholme Way
HA4: Ruis 6E 38
Lea Ho. NW8 . . . . .4C 4
(off Salisbury St.)
Leahurst Rd. SE13 . . . . .5F 123
LEA INTERCHANGE 5C 68
Leake Ct. SE1 . . . . .7H 13 (2K 101)
Leake St. SE1 . . . . .6H 13 (2K 101)
(not continuous)
Lealand Rd. N15 . . . . .6F 49

Leamington Av. BR1: Broml 5A 142
BR6: Orp 4J 173
E17 . . . . .5C 50
SM4: Mord 4G 153
Leamington Cl. BR1: Broml 4A 142
E12 . . . . .5C 70
TW3: Houn 5G 113
Leamington Ct. SE3 . . . . .6G 105
Leamington Cres. HA2: Harr 3C 58
Leamington Gdns. IG3: Ilf 2K 71
Leamington Ho. HA8: Edg 5A 28
W11 . . . . .5H 81
(off Tavistock Rd.)
Leamington Pk. W3 . . . . .5K 79
Leamington Pl. HA2: Harr 4H 75
Leamington Rd. UB2: S'hall 4B 94
Leamington Rd. Vs. W11 . . . . .5H 81
Leamore Ct. E2 . . . . .3K 85
Leamore St. W6 . . . . .4E 98
LEAMOUTH 7G 87
Leamouth Rd. E6 . . . . .5C 88
E14 . . . . .6F 87
Leander Ct. E9 . . . . .7K 67
(off Lauriston Rd.)
KT6: Surb 7D 150
NW9 . . . . .1A 44
SE8 . . . . .1C 122
Leander Rd. CR7: Thor H 4K 155
SW2 . . . . .6K 119
UB5: N'olt 2E 76
Lea Pk. Trad. Est. E10 . . . . .7B 50
Learner Dr. HA2: Harr 2E 58
Lea Rd. BR3: Beck 2C 158
EN2: Enf 1J 23
UB2: S'hall 4C 94
Learoyd Gdns. E6 . . . . .7E 88
Leary Ho. SE11 . . . . .5K 101
Leas Cl. KT9: Chess 7F 163
Leas Dale SE9 . . . . .3E 142
Leas Grn. BR7: Chst 6K 143
Leaside Av. N10 . . . . .3E 46
Leaside Bus. Cen. EN3: Brim 2G 25
Leaside Ct. UB10: Hil 3D 74
Leaside Mans. N10 . . . . .3E 46
(off Fortis Grn.)
Leaside Rd. E5 . . . . .1J 67
Leasowes Rd. E10 . . . . .1C 68
Lea Sq. E3 .1B 86
Leatherbottle Grn. DA18: Erith 3F 109
Leather Bottle La. DA17: Belv 4E 108
Leather Cl. CR4: Mitc 2E 154
Leatherdale St. E1 . . . . .3K 85
Leather Gdns. E15 . . . . .1G 87
Leatherhead Cl. N16 . . . . .1F 67
Leatherhead Rd. KT9: Chess 7D 162
Leather La. EC1 . . . . .5J 7 (5A 84)
(not continuous)
The Leather Mkt. SE1 . . . . .7G 15
Leathermarket Ct. SE1 . . . .7G 15 (2E 102)
Leathermarket St. SE1 . . . .7G 15 (2E 102)
Leather Pl. SE1 . . . . .3E 102
(off Crimscott St.)
Leather Rd. SE16 . . . . .4K 103
Leathersellers Cl. EN5: Barn 3B 20
(off The Avenue)
Leather St. E1 . . . . .7K 85
Leathsail Rd. HA2: Harr 3F 59
Leathwaite Rd. SW11 . . . . .4D 118
Leathwell Rd. SE8 . . . . .2D 122
Lea Va. DA1: Cray 4K 127
Lea Valley Bus. Pk. E10 . . . . .2A 68
Lea Valley Rd. E4 . . . . .5F 25
EN3: Pond E 5F 25
Lea Valley Trad. Est. N18 . . . . .6E 34
Lea Valley Viaduct N18 . . . . .5E 34
Leaveland Cl. BR3: Beck 4C 158
Leaver Gdns. UB6: G'frd 2H 77
Leavesden Rd. HA7: Stan 6F 27
Leaves Grn. Rd. BR2: Kes 7B 172
Lea Vw. Ho. E5 . . . . .1H 67
Leaway E10 . . . . .1K 67
Lebanon Av. TW13: Hanw 5B 130
Lebanon Ct. TW1: Twick 7B 114

Lebanon Gdns. SW18 . . . . .6J 117
Lebanon Pk. TW1: Twick 7B 114
Lebanon Rd. CRO: C'don 1E 168
  SW18 . . . . .5J 117
Lebus Ho. NW8 . . . . .1C 4
  (off Cochrane St.)
Lebus St. N17 . . . . .3H 49
Le Chateau CRO: C'don 3D 168
  (off Chatsworth Rd.)
Lechmere App. IG8: Wfd G 2A 52
Lechmere Av. IG8: Wfd G 2B 52
Lechmere Rd. NW2 . . . . .6D 62
Leckford Rd. SW18 . . . . .2A 136
Leckhampton Pl. SW2 . . . . .7A 120
Leckwith Av. DA7: Bex 6E 108
Lecky St. SW7 . . . . . .5A 16 (5B 100)
Leconfield Av. SW13 . . . . .3B 116
Leconfield Ho. SE5 . . . . .4E 120
Leconfield Rd. N5 . . . . .4D 66
Leda Av. EN3: Enf W 1E 24
Leda Ct. SW9 . . . . .1A 102
  (off Caldwell St.)
Ledam Ho. EC1 . . . . .5J 7
  (off Bourne Est.)
Leda Rd. SE18 . . . . .3D 106
Ledbury Ho. SE22 . . . . .3E 120
  W11 .6H 81
  (off Colville Rd.)
Ledbury M. Nth. W11 . . . . .7J 81
Ledbury M. W. W11 . . . . .7J 81
Ledbury Pl. CRO: C'don 4D 168
Ledbury Rd. CRO: C'don 4D 168
  W11 .6H 81
Ledbury St. SE15 . . . . .7G 103
Ledger M. E17 . . . . .6C 50
Ledrington Rd. SE19 . . . . .6G 139
Ledway Dr. HA9: Wemb 7F 43
LEE 6J 123
Lee Av. RM6: Chad H 6E 54
Lee Bri. SE13 . . . . .3E 122
Leechcroft Av. DA15: Sidc 5K 125
Leechcroft Rd.
  SM6: W'gton 3E 166
Lee Chu. St. SE13 . . . . .4G 123
Lee Cl. E17 . . . . .1K 49
  EN5: New Bar 4F 21
Lee Conservancy Rd. E9 . . . . .5B 68
Lee Ct. E3 . . . . .4E 86
  (off Navigation Rd.)
  SE13 . . . . .4F 123
  (off Lee High Rd.)
Leecroft Rd. EN5: Barn 5B 20
Leeds Ct. EC1 . . . . .3A 8
  (off St John St.)
Leeds Pl. N4 . . . . .1K 65
Leeds Rd. IG1: Ilf 1H 71
Leeds St. N18 . . . . .5B 34
Leefern Rd. W12 . . . . .2C 98
Leegate SE12 . . . . .5H 123
Lee Gro. IG7: Chig 2K 37
Lee High Rd. SE12 . . . . .3E 122
  SE13 . . . . .3E 122
Leeke St. WC1 . . . . . . .1G 7 (3K 83)
Leeland Rd. W13 . . . . .1A 96
Leeland Ter. W13 . . . . .1A 96
Leeland Way NW10 . . . . .4B 62
Lee M. BR3: Beck 3A 158
Leemount Ho. NW4 . . . . .4F 45
Lee Pk. SE3 . . . . .4H 123
Lee Pk. Way N9 . . . . .4E 34
  N18 .4E 34
Leerdam Dr. E14 . . . . .3E 104
Lee Rd. EN1: Enf 6B 24
  NW7 .7A 30
  SE3 .3H 123
  SW19 . . . . .1K 153
  UB6: G'frd 1C 78
The Lees CRO: C'don 2B 170
Lees Av. HA6: Nwood 1H 39
Lees Ct. W1 . . . . .2G 11
  (off Lees Pl.)

Lees Ho. SE17 . . . . .5D 102
  (off Inville Rd.)
Leeside EN5: Barn 5B 20
Leeside Ct. SE16 . . . . .1K 103
  (off Rotherhithe St.)
Leeside Cres. NW11 . . . . .6G 45
Leeside Ind. Est. N17 . . . . .7D 34
Leeside Rd. N17 . . . . .6C 34
Leeside Works N17 . . . . .7D 34
Leeson Ho. TW1: Twick 7B 114
Leeson Rd. SE24 . . . . .4A 120
Leesons Hill BR5: St P 3J 161
  BR7: Chst 3J 161
Leeson's Way BR5: St P 2K 161
Lees Pde. UB10: Hil 4D 74
Lees Pl. W1 . . . . .2G 11 (7E 82)
Lee St. E8 . . . . .1F 85
Lee Ter. SE3 . . . . .3G 123
  SE13 . . . . .3G 123
Lee Valley Athletics Cen. 1E 34
Lee Valley Golf Course 7F 25
Lee Valley Hockey & Tennis Cen.
  . . . . .4D 68
Lee Valley Ice Cen. 2K 67
Lee Valley Pk. 7E 34
Lee Valley Technopark N17 . . . . . . .3G 49
Lee Valley VeloPark 5D 68
Leeve Ho. W10 . . . . .3H 81
  (off Lancefield St.)
Lee Vw. EN2: Enf 1G 23
Leeward Ct. E1 . . . . .1G 103
  SE8 .4A 104
  (off Yeoman St.)
Leeward Gdns. SW19 . . . . .5G 135
Leeward Ho. N1 . . . . .1E 84
  (off Halcomb St.)
Leeway SE8 . . . . .5B 104
Leeway Cl. HA5: Hat E 1D 40
The Leeways SM3: Cheam 6G 165
Leewood Cl. SE12 . . . . .6J 123
Lefa Bus. & Ind. Pk. DA14: Sidc . . .6D 144
Lefevre Wlk. E3 . . . . .2C 86
Leff Ho. NW6 . . . . .1G 81
Lefroy Ho. SE1 . . . . .7C 14
  (off Southwark Bri. Rd.)
Lefroy Rd. W12 . . . . .2B 98
Left Side N14 . . . . .1C 32
  (off Statione Pde.)
Legacy Bldg. SW11 . . . . .6H 101
Legacy Wharf E15 . . . . .2D 86
Legard Rd. N5 . . . . .3B 66
Legatt Rd. SE9 . . . . .5B 124
Leggatt Rd. E15 . . . . .2E 86
Legge St. SE13 . . . . .5E 122
Leghorn Rd. NW10 . . . . .2B 80
  SE18 . . . . .5H 107
Legion Cl. N1 . . . . .7A 66
Legion Ct. SM4: Mord 6J 153
Legion Rd. UB6: G'frd 1G 77
Legion Ter. E3 . . . . .1B 86
Legion Way N12 . . . . .7H 31
Leg O'Mutton Reservoir
  Local Nature Reserve 7B 98
Legon Av. RM7: Rush G 1J 73
Legrace Av. TW4: Houn 2B 112
Leicester Av. CR4: Mitc 4J 155
Leicester Cl. KT4: Wor Pk 4E 164
Leicester Ct. TW1: Twick 6D 114
  (off Clevedon Rd.)
  W9 . . . . .5J 81
  (off Elmfield Way)
  WC2 .2D 12
Leicester Flds. 3D 12
Leicester Gdns. IG3: Ilf 7J 53
Leicester Ho. N18 . . . . .5C 34
  (off Cavendish Cl.)
  SW9 .4B 120
  (off Loughborough Rd.)
Leicester M. N2 . . . . .3C 46
Leicester Pl. WC2 . . . . .2D 12 (7H 83)
Leicester Rd. CRO: C'don 1E 156
  E11 . . . . .5K 51

Leicester Rd. EN5: New Bar 5E 20
  N2 . . . . .3C 46
  NW10 . . . . .7K 61
Leicester Sq. WC2 . . . . .3D 12 (7H 83)
Leicester Square Theatre 2D 12
  (off Leicester Pl.)
Leicester St. WC2 . . . . .2D 12 (7H 83)
The Leigh KT2: King T 7A 134
Leigham Av. SW16 . . . . .3J 137
Leigham Cl. SW16 . . . . .3K 137
Leigham Ct. SM6: W'gton 6G 167
Leigham Ct. Rd. SW16 . . . . .2J 137
Leigham Dr. TW7: Isle 7J 95
Leigham Hall Pde. SW16 . . . . .3J 137
  (off Streatham High Rd.)
Leigham Va. SW2 . . . . .3K 137
  SW16 . . . . .3K 137
Leigh Av. IG4: Ilf 4B 52
Leigh Cl. KT3: N Mald 4J 151
Leigh Cl. Ind. Est. KT3: N Mald 4K 151
Leigh Ct. HA2: Harr 1J 59
  W14 .4H 99
  (off Avonmore Rd.)
Leigh Cres. CRO: New Ad 7D 170
Leigh Gdns. NW10 . . . . .2E 80
Leigh Hunt Dr. N14 . . . . .1C 32
Leigh Orchard Cl. SW16 . . . . .3K 137
Leigh Pl. DA16: Well 2A 126
  EC1 . . . . .5J 7 (5A 84)
  TW13: Felt 1A 130
Leigh Rd. E6 . . . . .6E 70
  E10 . . . . .7E 50
  N5 . . . . .4B 66
  TW3: Houn 4H 113
Leigh St. WC1 . . . . .2E 6 (3J 83)
Leighton Av. E12 . . . . .5E 70
  HA5: Pinn 3C 40
Leighton Cl. HA8: Edg 2G 43
Leighton Cres. NW5 . . . . .5G 65
  NW10 . . . . .2D 80
Leighton Gdns. CRO: C'don 1B 168
  NW10 . . . . .2D 80
Leighton Gro. NW5 . . . . .5G 65
Leighton Ho. SW1 . . . . .4D 18
  (off Herrick St.)
Leighton House Mus. 3H 99
Leighton Mans. W14 . . . . .6G 99
  (off Greyhound Rd.)
Leighton Pl. NW5 . . . . .5G 65
Leighton Rd. EN1: Enf 5A 24
  HA3: Hrw W 2H 41
  NW5 .5G 65
  W13 .2A 96
Leighton St. CRO: C'don 1B 168
Leila Parnell Pl. SE7 . . . . .6A 106
Leinster Av. SW14 . . . . .3J 115
Leinster Gdns. W2 . . . . .6A 82
Leinster M. EN5: Barn 3B 20
  W2 . . . . .7A 82
Leinster Pl. W2 . . . . .6A 82
Leinster Rd. N10 . . . . .4F 47
Leinster Sq. W2 . . . . .6J 81
  (not continuous)
Leinster Ter. W2 . . . . .7A 82
Leirum St. N1 . . . . .1K 83
Leisure Way N12 . . . . .7G 31
Leisure W. 2K 129
Leitch Ho. NW8 . . . . .7B 64
  (off Hilgrove Rd.)
Leith Cl. NW9 . . . . .1K 61
Leithcote Gdns. SW16 . . . . .4K 137
Leithcote Path SW16 . . . . .3K 137
Leith Hill BR5: St P 1K 161
Leith Hill Grn. BR5: St P 1K 161
Leith Mans. W9 . . . . .3K 81
  (off Grantully Rd.)
Leith Rd. N22 . . . . .1B 48
Leith Towers SM2: Sutt 7K 165
Leith Yd. NW6 . . . . .1J 81
  (off Quex Rd.)
Lela Av. TW4: Houn 2A 112
Lelitia Cl. E8 . . . . .1G 85
Lely Ho. UB5: N'olt 2B 76
  (off Academy Gdns.)

Leman St. E1 . . . . .7K 9 (6F 85)
Le Mare Ter. E3 . . . . .5C 86
Lemark Cl. HA7: Stan 6H 27
Le May Av. SE12 . . . . .3K 141
Lemmon Rd. SE10 . . . . .6G 105
Lemna Rd. E11 . . . . .7H 51
Le Moal Ho. E1 . . . . .5J 85
  (off Stepney Way)
Lemonade Bldg. IG11: Bark 7G 71
  (off Ripple Rd.)
Lemon Gro. TW13: Felt 1J 129
Lemon Tree Ho. E3 . . . . .3B 86
  (off Bow Rd.)
Lemonwell Dr. SE9 . . . . .5G 125
Lemsford Cl. N15 . . . . .6G 49
Lemsford Ct. N4 . . . . .2C 66
Lemuel St. SW18 . . . . .6A 118
Lena Cres. N9 . . . . .2D 34
Lena Gdns. W6 . . . . .3E 98
Lena Kennedy Cl. E4 . . . . .6K 35
Lenanton Steps E14 . . . . .2C 104
  (off Manilla St.)
Len Bishop Ct. E1 . . . . .7K 85
  (off Schoolhouse La.)
Len Clifton Ho. SE18 . . . . .4D 106
  (off Cambridge Barracks Rd.)
Lendal Ter. SW4 . . . . .3H 119
Lendy Pl. TW16: Sun 4J 147
Leneiby Rd. KT6: Surb 1G 163
Len Freeman Pl. SW6 . . . . .6H 99
Lenham Ho. SE1 . . . . .7F 15
  (off Staple St.)
Lenham Rd. CR7: Thor H 2D 156
  DA7: Bex 6F 109
  SE12 . . . . .4H 123
  SM1: Sutt 4K 165
Lennard Av. BR4: W W'ck 2G 171
Lennard Cl. BR4: W W'ck 2G 171
Lennard Rd. BR2: Broml 1D 172
  BR3: Beck 6K 139
  CRO: C'don 1C 168
  SE20 . . . . .6K 139
Lennon Rd. NW2 . . . . .5E 62
Lennox Gdns. CRO: Wadd 4B 168
  IG1: Ilf 1D 70
  NW10 . . . . .4B 62
  SW1 . . . . .2E 16 (3D 100)
Lennox Gdns. M.
  . . . . .2E 16 (3D 100)
Lennox Ho. DA17: Belv 3G 109
  (off Ambrooke Rd.)
  TW1: Twick 6D 114
  (off Clevedon Rd.)
Lennox Rd. E17 . . . . .6B 50
  N4 . . . . .2K 65
  SW9 .1B 120
Lenor Cl. DA6: Bex 4E 126
Lensbury Av. SW6 . . . . .2A 118
Lensbury Way SE2 . . . . .3C 108
Lens Rd. E7 . . . . .7A 70
Len Taylor Cl. UB4: Hayes 4G 75
Lenthall Ho. SW1 . . . . .6B 18
  (off Churchill Gdns.)
Lenthall Rd. E8 . . . . .7G 67
Lenthorp Rd. SE10 . . . . .4H 105
Lentmead Rd. BR1: Broml 3H 141
Lenton Path SE18 . . . . .6H 107
Lenton Ri. TW9: Rich 3E 114
Lenton St. SE18 . . . . .4H 107
Lenton Ter. N4 . . . . .2A 66
Len Williams Ct. NW6 . . . . .2J 81
Leo Ct. TW8: Bford 7D 96
Leof Cres. SE6 . . . . .5D 140
Leominster Rd. SM4: Mord 6A 154
Leominster Wlk.
  SM4: Mord 6A 154
Leonard Av. RM7: Rush G 1K 73
  SM4: Mord 5A 154
Leonard Cir. EC2 . . . . . . .3F 9 (4D 84)
Leonard Ct. HA3: Hrw W 1J 41
  W8 . . . . .3J 99
  WC1 . . . . .3D 6 (4H 83)
Leonard Pl. N16 . . . . .4E 66

Leonard Rd. E4 . . . . .6H **35**
E7 . . . . .4J **69**
N9 . . . . .3A **34**
SW16 . . . . .1G **155**
UB2: S'hall 3B **94**
Leonard Robbins Path SE28 . . . .7B **90**
(off Tawney Rd.)
Leonard St. E16 . . . . .1C **106**
EC2 . . . . .3F **9** (4D **84**)
Leon Ho. CRO: C'don 3C **168**
Leonora Ho. W9 . . . . .4A **82**
(off Lanark Rd.)
Leonora Tyson M. SE21 . . . . .2D **138**
Leontine Cl. SE15 . . . . .7G **103**
Leopards Ct. EC1 . . . . .5J **7**
Leopold Av. SW19 . . . . .5H **135**
Leopold Bldgs. E2 . . . . .1J **9**
(off Columbia Rd.)
Leopold M. E9 . . . . .1J **85**
Leopold Rd. E17 . . . . .5C **50**
N2 .3B **46**
N18 . . . . .5C **34**
NW10 . . . . .7A **62**
SW19 . . . . .4H **135**
W5 .1F **97**
Leopold St. E3 . . . . .5B **86**
Leopold Ter. SW19 . . . . .5H **135**
Leo St. SE15 . . . . .7H **103**
Leo Yd. EC1 . . . . .4B **8**
Leppoc Rd. SW4 . . . . .5H **119**
Leroy St. SE1 . . . . .4E **102**
Lerry Cl. W14 . . . . .6H **99**
Lerwick Ct. EN1: Enf 5K **23**
Lescombe Cl. SE23 . . . . .3A **140**
Lescombe Rd. SE23 . . . . .3A **140**
Lescot Pl. BR2: Broml 6C **160**
Lesley Cl. DA5: Bexl 7H **127**
Lesley Ct. SW1 . . . . .2C **18**
(off Strutton Ground)
Leslie Foster Cl. IG11: Bark 2K **89**
Leslie Gdns. SM2: Sutt 6J **165**
Leslie Gro. CRO: C'don 1E **168**
Leslie Gro. Pl. CRO: C'don 1E **168**
Leslie Ho. SW8 . . . . .7J **101**
(off Wheatsheaf La.)
Leslie Pk. Rd. CRO: C'don 1E **168**
Leslie Prince Ct. SE5 . . . . .7D **102**
Leslie Rd. E11 . . . . .4E **68**
E16 .6K **87**
N2 .3B **46**
Leslie Smith Sq. SE18 . . . . .6E **106**
Lesnes Abbey 4D **108**
Lesnes Abbey Woods 4D **108**
Lesney Av. E20 . . . . .5C **68**
Lesney Farm Est. DA8: Erith 7K **109**
Lesney Pk. DA8: Erith 6K **109**
Lesney Pk. Rd. DA8: Erith 6K **109**
Lessar Av. SW4 . . . . .6G **119**
Lessingham Av. IG5: Ilf 3E **52**
SW17 . . . . .4D **136**
Lessing St. SE23 . . . . .7A **122**
Lessington Av. RM7: Rom 6J **55**
Lessness Av. DA7: Bex 7D **108**
LESSNESS HEATH 5G **109**
Lessness Pk. DA17: Belv 5F **109**
Lessness Rd. DA17: Belv 6G **109**
SM4: Mord 6A **154**
Lester Av. E15 . . . . .4G **87**
Lester Ct. E3 . . . . .3D **86**
(off Bruce Rd.)
Lestock Cl. SE25 . . . . .3G **157**
(off Manor Rd.)
Leswin Pl. N16 . . . . .3F **67**
Leswin Rd. N16 . . . . .3F **67**
Letchford Gdns. NW10 . . . . .3C **80**
Letchford Ho. E3 . . . . .2C **86**
(off Thomas Fyre Dr.)
Letchford M. NW10 . . . . .3C **80**
Letchford Ter. HA3: Hrw W 1F **41**
Letchmore Ho. W10 . . . . .4E **80**
(off Sutton Way)
Letchworth Av. TW14: Felt 7H **111**
Letchworth Cl. BR2: Broml 5J **159**

Letchworth Dr. BR2: Broml 5J **159**
Letchworth Rd. HA7: Stan 7K **27**
Letchworth St. SW17 . . . . .4D **136**
Lethbridge Cl. SE10 . . . . .1E **122**
Letterstone Rd. SW6 . . . . .7H **99**
Lettice St. SW6 . . . . .1H **117**
Lett Rd. E15 . . . . .7F **69**
SW9 . . . . .1K **119**
Lettsom St. SE5 . . . . .2E **120**
Lettsom Wlk. E13 . . . . .2J **87**
Leucha Rd. E17 . . . . .5A **50**
Levana Cl. SW19 . . . . .1G **135**
Levant Ho. E1 . . . . .4K **85**
(off Ernest St.)
Levehurst Ho. SE27 . . . . .5C **138**
Levendale Rd. SE23 . . . . .2A **140**
Levenhurst Way SW4 . . . . .2J **119**
Leven Rd. E14 . . . . .5E **86**
Leven Way UB3: Hayes 6G **75**
Leverett St. SW3 . . . . .3D **16** (4C **100**)
Leverholme Gdns. SE9 . . . . .4E **142**
Leverington Pl. N1 . . . . . .2F **9** (3D **84**)
Leverson St. SW16 . . . . .6G **137**
Leverstock Ho. SW3 . . . . .5D **16**
(off Cale St.)
Lever St. EC1 . . . . .2B **8** (3B **84**)
Leverton Cl. N22 . . . . .1K **47**
Leverton Pl. NW5 . . . . .5G **65**
Leverton St. NW5 . . . . .5G **65**
The Levett Buildging EC1 . . . . .5B **84**
(off Little Britain)
Levett Gdns. IG3: Ilf 4K **71**
Levett Rd. IG11: Bark 6J **71**
Levett Square TW9: Kew 7H **97**
Levine Gdns. IG11: Bark 2D **90**
Levison Way N19 . . . . .1H **65**
Levita Ho. NW1 . . . . .1D **6**
(not continuous)
Levyne Ct. EC1 . . . . .3J **7**
(off Pine St.)
Lewen Cl. CRO: C'don 1D **168**
Lewes Cl. UB5: N'olt 6E **58**
Lewes Ct. CR4: Mitc 3D **154**
(off Chatsworth Pl.)
Lewesdon Cl. SW19 . . . . .1F **135**
Lewes Ho. SE1 . . . . .6H **15**
(off Druid St.)
SE15 . . . . .6G **103**
(off Friary Est.)
Lewes Rd. BR1: Broml 2B **160**
N12 .5H **31**
Leweston Pl. N16 . . . . .7F **49**
Lew Evans Ho. SE22 . . . . .5G **121**
Lewey Ho. E3 . . . . .4B **86**
(off Joseph St.)
Lewgars Av. NW9 . . . . .6J **43**
Lewing Cl. BR6: Orp 1J **173**
Lewington Apts. SE16 . . . . .4J **103**
(off Alpine Rd.)
Lewington Cen. SE16 . . . . .4J **103**
(off Alpine Rd.)
Lewin Rd. DA6: Bex 4E **126**
SW14 . . . . .3K **115**
SW16 . . . . .6H **137**
Lewin Ter. TW14: Bedf 7F **111**
Lewis Av. E17 . . . . .1C **50**
Lewis Cl. N14 . . . . .7B **22**
Lewis Ct. SE16 . . . . .5H **103**
(off Stubbs Dr.)
Lewis Cres. NW10 . . . . .5K **61**
Lewis Cubitt Pk. 1J **83**
Lewis Cubitt Sq. N1 . . . . .1J **83**
Lewis Cubitt Wlk. N1 . . . . .1J **83**
Lewis Gdns. N2 . . . . .2B **46**
N16 .6F **49**
Lewis Gro. SE13 . . . . .3E **122**
LEWISHAM 3E **122**
Lewisham Cen. 4E **122**
Lewisham Hgts. SE23 . . . . .1J **139**
Lewisham High St. SE13 . . . . .3E **122**
(not continuous)
Lewisham Hill SE13 . . . . .2E **122**
Lewisham Indoor Bowls Cen. 5B **140**

Lewisham Lions Cen. 5J **103**
Lewisham Model Mkt. 4E **122**
(off Lewisham High St.)
Lewisham Pk. SE13 . . . . .5E **122**
Lewisham Rd. SE13 . . . . .1D **122**
Lewisham St. SW1 . . . . .7D **12** (2H **101**)
Lewisham Way SE4 . . . . .1B **122**
SE14 . . . . .1B **122**
Lewis Ho. E14 . . . . .1E **104**
(off Coldharbour)
N1 . . . . .6B **66**
(off Canonbury Rd.)
Lewis M. BR7: Chst 5D **142**
Lewis Pl. E8 . . . . .5G **67**
Lewis Rd. CR4: Mitc 2B **154**
DA14: Sidc 3C **144**
DA16: Well 3C **126**
SM1: Sutt 4K **165**
TW10: Rich 5D **114**
UB1: S'hall 2C **94**
Lewis Silkin Ho. SE15 . . . . .6J **103**
(off Lovelinch Cl.)
Lewis Sports & Leisure Cen. 1F **157**
(not continuous)
Lewis St. NW1 . . . . .7F **65**
(not continuous)
Lewiston Cl. KT4: Wor Pk 7D **152**
Lewis Way RM10: Dag 6H **73**
Lexden Dr. RM6: Chad H 6B **54**
Lexden Rd. CR4: Mitc 4H **155**
W3 . . . . .7H **79**
Lexham Apts. EC1 . . . . . .3F **9** (4D **84**)
Lexham Gdns. W8 . . . . .4J **99**
Lexham Gdns. M. W8 . . . . .3K **99**
Lexham Ho. W8 . . . . .4J **99**
(off Lexham Gdns.)
Lexham M. W8 . . . . .4J **99**
Lexham Wlk. W8 . . . . .3K **99**
Lexington Apts. EC1 . . . . .3F **9** (4D **84**)
Lexington Bldg. E3 . . . . .2C **86**
Lexington Ho. UB7: W Dray 2B **92**
(off Park Lodge Av.)
Lexington Pl. KT1: Hamp W 7D **132**
Lexington St. W1 . . . . .2B **12** (7G **83**)
Lexington Way EN5: Barn 4A **20**
Lexton Gdns. SW12 . . . . .1H **137**
Leyborne Av. W13 . . . . .2B **96**
Leyborne Pk. TW9: Kew 1G **115**
Leybourne Cl. BR2: Broml 6J **159**
Leybourne Ho. E14 . . . . .6B **86**
(off Dod St.)
SE15 . . . . .6J **103**
Leybourne Rd. E11 . . . . .1H **69**
NW1 .7F **65**
NW9 . . . . .5G **43**
UB10: Hil 1E **74**
Leybourne St. NW1 . . . . .7F **65**
Leyburn Gdns. CRO: C'don 2E **168**
Leybridge Ct. SE12 . . . . .5J **123**
Leyburn Cl. E17 . . . . .4D **50**
Leyburn Gro. N18 . . . . .6B **34**
Leyburn Rd. N18 . . . . .6B **34**
Leydenhatch La.
BR8: Swan 7J **145**
Leyden Mans. N19 . . . . .7J **47**
Leyden St. E1 . . . . .6J **9** (5F **85**)
Leygreen Cl. SE16 . . . . .1K **103**
Leyes Rd. E16 . . . . .6B **88**
Leyfield KT4: Wor Pk 1A **164**
Ley Ho. SE1 . . . . .7C **14**
(off Scovell Rd.)
Leyland Av. EN3: Enf H 2F **25**
Leyland Court SE15 . . . . .7F **103**
(off Shield Street)
Leyland Gdns. IG8: Wfd G 5F **37**
Leyland Ho. E14 . . . . .7D **86**
(off Hale St.)
Leyland Rd. SE12 . . . . .5J **123**
Leylands SW18 . . . . .6H **117**
Leylands La. TW19: Stanw M 7A **174**
(not continuous)
Leylang Rd. SE14 . . . . .7K **103**
The Leys HA3: Kenton 6F **43**
N2 . . . . .4A **46**
Leys Av. RM10: Dag 1J **91**

Leys Cl. HA1: Harr 5H **41**
RM10: Dag 7J **73**
Leys Ct. SW9 . . . . .2A **120**
Leysdown Av. DA7: Bex 4J **127**
Leysdown Ho. SE17 . . . . .5E **102**
(off Madron St.)
Leysdown Rd. SE9 . . . . .2C **142**
Leysfield Rd. W12 . . . . .3C **98**
Leys Gdns. EN4: Cockf 5K **21**
Leyspring Rd. E11 . . . . .1H **69**
Leys Rd. E. EN3: Enf H 1F **25**
Leys Rd. W. EN3: Enf H 1F **25**
Leys Sq. N3 . . . . .1K **45**
Ley St. IG1: Ilf 2F **71**
IG2: Ilf 2G **71**
Leyswood Dr. IG2: Ilf 5J **53**
Leythe Rd. W3 . . . . .2J **97**
LEYTON 2E **68**
Leyton Bus. Cen. E10 . . . . .2C **68**
Leyton Ct. SE23 . . . . .1J **139**
Leyton Grange E10 . . . . .1C **68**
Leyton Grn. Rd. E10 . . . . .6E **50**
Leyton Grn. Twr. E10 . . . . .6E **50**
(off Leyton Grn. Rd.)
Leyton Ho. E2 . . . . .2J **9**
(off Calvert Av.)
Leyton Ind. Village E10 . . . . .7K **49**
Leyton Leisure Cen. 7E **50**
Leyton Link Est. E10 . . . . .7A **50**
Leyton Mills E10 . . . . .3E **68**
Leyton Orient FC 3D **68**
Leyton Pk. Rd. E10 . . . . .3E **68**
Leyton Rd. E15 . . . . .5E **68**
SW19 . . . . .7A **136**
LEYTONSTONE 1G **69**
Leytonstone Ho. E11 . . . . .7H **51**
(off Hanbury Dr.)
Leytonstone Leisure Cen. 2G **69**
Leytonstone Rd. E15 . . . . .6G **69**
Leyton Way E11 . . . . .7G **51**
Leywick St. E15 . . . . .2G **87**
Lezayre Rd. BR6: Chels 6K **173**
Lianne Gro. SE9 . . . . .3A **142**
Liardet St. SE14 . . . . .6A **104**
Libari Mans. E20 . . . . .5E **68**
(off Victory Pde.)
Liberal Jewish Synagogue . . .2B **4** (3B **82**)
Liberia Rd. N5 . . . . .6B **66**
Liberty Av. SW19 . . . . .1B **154**
Liberty Bri. Rd. E15 . . . . .5E **68**
E20 .5E **68**
Liberty Cen. HA0: Wemb 1F **79**
Liberty Cl. KT4: Wor Pk 1E **164**
N18 .4A **34**
Liberty Ct. BR1: Broml 3B **160**
IG11: Bark 2B **90**
Liberty Ho. CR7: Thor H 5A **156**
(off Thornton Rd.)
E1 . . . . .7G **85**
(off Ensign St.)
E13 .2J **87**
Liberty M. N22 . . . . .1B **48**
SW12 . . . . .6F **119**
Liberty Point CRO: C'don 7G **157**
(off Blackhorse La.)
Liberty St. SW9 . . . . .1K **119**
Libra Mans. E3 . . . . .2B **86**
(off Libra Rd.)
Libra Rd. E3 . . . . .1B **86**
E13 .2J **87**
The Library & Mus. of Freemasonry
. . . . .7F **7**
(in Freemasons' Hall)
Library Ct. N17 . . . . .3F **49**
Library Mans. W12 . . . . .2E **98**
(off Pennard Rd.)
Library M. TW12: Hamp H 6G **131**
Library Pde. NW10 . . . . .1A **80**
(off Craven Pk. Rd.)
Library Sq. E1 . . . . .7H **85**
Library Sq. E1 . . . . .4A **86**
Library St. SE1 . . . . .7A **14** (2B **102**)
Library Way TW2: Whitt 7G **113**

Libro Ct. E4 . . . . .4H **35**
Lichfield Cl. EN4: Cockf 3J **21**
Lichfield Ct. KT6: Surb 5E **150**
   (off Claremont Rd.)
  TW9: Rich 5E **114**
Lichfield Gdns. TW9: Rich 4E **114**
Lichfield Gro. N3 . . . . .1J **45**
Lichfield La. TW2: Whitt 1G **131**
Lichfield Rd. E3 . . . . .3A **86**
  E6 . . . . .3B **88**
  HA6: Nwood 3J **39**
  IG8: Wfd G 4B **36**
  N9 . . . . .2B **34**
  NW2 .4G **63**
  RM8: Dag 4B **72**
  TW4: Houn 3A **112**
  TW9: Kew 2B **114**
Lichfield Ter. TW9: Rich 5E **114**
   (off Sheen Rd.)
Lichlade Cl. BR6: Orp 4K **173**
Lickey Ho. W14 . . . . .6H **99**
   (off North End Rd.)
Lidcote Gdns. SW9 . . . . .2K **119**
Liddall Way UB7: Yiew 1B **92**
Liddell Cl. HA3: Kenton 3D **42**
Liddell Gdns. NW10 . . . . .2E **80**
Liddell Pl. NW6 . . . . .6J **63**
Liddell Rd. NW6 . . . . .6J **63**
Liddiard Ho. W11 . . . . .7G **81**
   (off Lansdowne Rd.)
Lidding Rd. HA3: Kenton 5D **42**
Liddington Rd. E15 . . . . .1H **87**
Liddon Rd. BR1: Broml 3A **160**
  E13 . . . . .3K **87**
Liden Cl. E17 . . . . .7B **50**
Lidfield Rd. N16 . . . . .4D **66**
Lidgate Rd. SE15 . . . . .7F **103**
Lidgould Gro. HA4: Ruis 6J **39**
Lidiard Rd. SW18 . . . . .2A **136**
Lidlington Pl. NW1 . . . . .2G **83**
Lido Sq. N17 . . . . .2D **48**
Lidyard Rd. N19 . . . . .1G **65**
Lifeboat Station
  Chiswick 7B **98**
The Lifestyle Club @ Charlton . . .7B **106**
Liffler Rd. SE18 . . . . .5J **107**
Liffords Pl. SW13 . . . . .2B **116**
Lifford St. SW15 . . . . .4F **117**
Lightcliffe Rd. N13 . . . . .4F **33**
Lighterage Ct. TW8: Bford 6E **96**
Lighter Cl. SE16 . . . . .4A **104**
Lighterman Ho. E14 . . . . .7E **86**
Lighterman M. E1 . . . . .6K **85**
Lighterman Point E14 . . . . .6F **87**
   (off New Village Av.)
Lightermans Rd. E14 . . . . .2C **104**
Lightermans Wlk. SW18 . . . . . . .4J **117**
Lightfoot Rd. N8 . . . . .5J **47**
Lightfoot Vs. N1 . . . . .7A **66**
   (off Augustas La.)
Light Horse Ct. SW3 . . . . .6G **17**
The Lighthouse 7C **102**
Lighthouse Apts. E1 . . . . .6J **85**
   (off Commercial Rd.)
Lighthouse View SE10 . . . . .1G **105**
Lightley Cl. HA0: Wemb 1E **78**
Ligonier St. E2 . . . . .3J **9** (4F **85**)
Lilac Cl. E4 . . . . .6G **35**
Lilac Ct. E13 . . . . .1A **88**
  TW11: Tedd 4K **131**
Lilac Gdns. CR0: C'don 3C **170**
  RM7: Rush G 1K **73**
  UB3: Hayes 6G **75**
  W5 . . . . .3D **96**
Lilac Ho. SE4 . . . . .3C **122**
Lilac La. E2 . . . . .3K **85**
Lilac M. N22 . . . . .3A **48**
   (off High Rd.)
Lilac Pl. SE11 . . . . .4G **19** (4K **101**)
  UB7: Yiew 7B **74**
Lilac St. W12 . . . . .7C **80**
Lilah M. BR2: Broml 2G **159**
Lilburne Gdns. SE9 . . . . .5C **124**

Lilburne Rd. SE9 . . . . .5C **124**
Lilburne Wlk. NW10 . . . . .6J **61**
Lile Cres. W7 . . . . .5J **77**
Lilestone Ho. NW8 . . . . .3B **4**
   (off Frampton St.)
Lilestone St. NW8 . . . . . . .3C **4** (4C **82**)
Lilford Ho. SE5 . . . . .2C **120**
Lilford Rd. SE5 . . . . .2B **120**
Lilian Barker Cl. SE12 . . . . .5J **123**
Lilian Board Way UB6: G'frd 5H **59**
Lilian Cl. N16 . . . . .3E **66**
Lilian Gdns. IG8: Wfd G 1K **51**
Lilian Knowles Ho. E1 . . . . .6J **9**
   (off Crispin St.)
Lilian Rd. SW16 . . . . .1G **155**
Lilium M. E10 . . . . .7C **50**
Lillechurch Rd. RM8: Dag 6B **72**
Lilleshall Rd. SM4: Mord 6B **154**
Lilley Cl. E1 . . . . .1G **103**
Lilley La. NW7 . . . . .5E **28**
Lillian Av. W3 . . . . .2G **97**
Lillian Rd. SW13 . . . . .6C **98**
Lillie Bri. Dpt. W14 . . . . .5H **99**
   (off Aisgill Av.)
Lillie Mans. SW6 . . . . .6G **99**
   (off Lillie Rd.)
Lillie Rd. SW6 . . . . .6G **99**
Lillie Road Fitness Cen. 7F **99**
Lillieshall Rd. SW4 . . . . .3F **119**
Lillie Sq. SW6 . . . . .6J **99**
Lillie Yd. SW6 . . . . .6J **99**
Lillingston Ho. N7 . . . . .4A **66**
Lillington Gdns. Est. SW1 . . . . . .4B **18**
Lilliput Av. UB5: N'olt 1C **76**
Lilliput Ct. SE12 . . . . .5K **123**
Lilliput Rd. E15 . . . . .1G **87**
  RM7: Rush G 7K **55**
Lily Cl. HA5: Pinn 2A **40**
  W14 . . . . .4F **99**
Lily Gdns. HA0: Wemb 2C **78**
Lily M. SE11 . . . . .4B **102**
Lily Nichols Ho. E16 . . . . .1B **106**
   (off Connaught Rd.)
Lily Pl. EC1 . . . . .5K **7** (5A **84**)
Lily Rd. E17 . . . . .6C **50**
Lilyville Rd. SW6 . . . . .1H **117**
Lily Way N13 . . . . .5D **32**
Limasol St. SE16 . . . . .3F **103**
Limborough Ho. E14 . . . . .5C **86**
   (off Thomas Rd.)
Limburg Av. RM8: Dag 7F **55**
Limburg Rd. SW11 . . . . .4C **118**
Lime Av. UB7: Yiew 7B **74**
Limeburner La. EC4 . . . . .1A **14** (6B **84**)
Lime Cl. BR1: Broml 4C **160**
  E1 . . . . .1G **103**
  HA3: W'stone 2A **42**
  HA5: Eastc 3H **39**
  IG9: Buck H 2G **37**
  RM7: Rom 5J **55**
  SM5: Cars 2D **166**
Lime Ct. CR4: Mitc 2B **154**
  E11 . . . . .2G **69**
   (off Trinity Cl.)
  E17 . . . . .5E **50**
  HA1: Harr 6K **41**
   (off Gayton Rd.)
  HA4: Ruis 7K **39**
  SE9 . . . . .2F **143**
Lime Cres. TW16: Sun 2A **148**
Limecroft Cl. KT19: Ewe 7K **163**
Limedene Cl. HA5: Pinn 1B **40**
Lime Gro. BR6: Farnb 2F **173**
  DA15: Sidc 6K **125**
  E4 . . . . .6G **35**
  HA4: Ruis 6F **39**
  KT3: N Mald 3K **151**
  N20 . . . . .1C **30**
  TW1: Twick 6K **113**
  UB3: Hayes 7F **75**
  W12 . . . . .2E **98**
Limeharbour E14 . . . . .3D **104**
LIMEHOUSE 6B **86**

Lime Ho. TW9: Kew 1H **115**
Limehouse C'way. E14 . . . . .7B **86**
Lime Ho. Ct. E14 . . . . .6B **86**
   (off Wharf La.)
Limehouse Ct. E14 . . . . .6C **86**
Limehouse Cut E14 . . . . .5A **86**
   (off Morris Rd.)
Limehouse Flds. Est. E14 . . . . . . .5A **86**
Limehouse Link E14 . . . . .6A **86**
Limehouse Lodge E5 . . . . .2J **67**
   (off Harry Zeital Way)
Lime Kiln Dr. SE7 . . . . .6K **105**
Limekiln Pl. SE19 . . . . .7F **139**
Limekiln Wharf E14 . . . . .7B **86**
Limelight Ho. SE11 . . . . .4B **102**
   (off Dugard Way)
Lime Lodge TW16: Sun 7H **129**
   (off Forest Dr.)
Lime Quay E14 . . . . .4E **86**
Limerick Cl. SW12 . . . . .7G **119**
Limerick M. N2 . . . . .3C **46**
Lime Row DA18: Erith 3F **109**
Limerston St.
  SW10 . . . . .7A **16** (6A **100**)
The Limes BR2: Broml 2C **172**
  KT8: W Mole 4F **149**
  SW18 . . . . .6J **117**
  W2 . . . . .7J **81**
Limes Av. CR0: Wadd 3A **168**
  E11 . . . . .4K **51**
  N12 . . . . .4F **31**
  NW7 .6F **29**
  NW11 . . . . .7G **45**
  SE20 .7H **139**
  SM5: Cars 1D **166**
  SW13 . . . . .2B **116**
The Limes Av. N11 . . . . .5A **32**
Limes Cl. N11 . . . . .5B **32**
  TW15: Ashf 5C **128**
Limes Ct. BR3: Beck 2D **158**
  NW6 .7G **63**
   (off Brondesbury Pk.)
Limesdale Gdns. HA8: Edg 2J **43**
Limes Fld. Rd. SW13 . . . . .3A **116**
Limesford Rd. SE15 . . . . .4K **121**
Limes Gdns. SW18 . . . . .6J **117**
Limes Gro. SE13 . . . . .4E **122**
Limes Pl. CR0: C'don 7D **156**
Limes Rd. BR3: Beck 2D **158**
  CR0: C'don 7D **156**
Limes Row BR6: Farnb 5F **173**
Limestone Wlk. DA18: Erith 2D **108**
Lime St. E17 . . . . .4A **50**
  EC3 . . . . .2G **15** (7E **84**)
Lime St. Pas. EC3 . . . . . .1G **15** (6E **84**)
Lime St. Sq. EC3 . . . . . . .1G **15** (6E **84**)
Limes Wlk. SE15 . . . . .4J **121**
  W5 . . . . .2D **96**
Lime Ter. W7 . . . . .7J **77**
Lime Tree Av. KT7: T Ditt 7H **149**
  KT10: Esh 7H **149**
Lime Tree Cl. E18 . . . . .4A **52**
Lime Tree Ct. CR2: S Croy 6C **168**
  E3 . . . . .5C **86**
   (off Whitehorn St.)
  SE17 .5C **102**
   (off Walworth Rd.)
Lime Tree Gro. CR0: C'don 3B **170**
Lime Tree Pl. CR4: Mitc 1F **155**
Lime Tree Rd. TW5: Hest 1F **113**
Limetree Ter. DA16: Well 3A **126**
  SE6 . . . . .1B **140**
Lime Tree Wlk.
  BR4: W W'ck 4H **171**
  EN2: Enf 1H **23**
  WD23: B Hea 1D **26**
Limetree Wlk. SW17 . . . . .5E **136**
Lime View Apts. E14 . . . . .6A **86**
   (off Commerical Rd.)
Lime Wlk. E15 . . . . .1G **87**
  KT8: E Mos 4K **149**

Lime Wood Cl. BR3: Beck 5E **158**
  E17 . . . . .4B **50**
  W13 . . . . .6B **78**
Limewood Cl. IG4: Ilf 5D **52**
Limewood M. SE20 . . . . .7G **139**
   (off Lullington Rd.)
Limewood Rd. DA8: Erith 7J **109**
Limpsfield Av. CR7: Thor H 5K **155**
  SW19 . . . . .2F **135**
Limscott Ho. E3 . . . . .3D **86**
   (off Bruce Rd.)
Linacre Cl. SE15 . . . . .3H **121**
Linacre Ct. W6 . . . . .5F **99**
Linacre Rd. NW2 . . . . .6D **62**
Linale Ho. N1 . . . . .1E **8**
Linberry Wlk. SE8 . . . . .4B **104**
Linchmere Rd. SE12 . . . . .7H **123**
Lincoln Apartments W12 . . . . .7E **80**
   (off Fountain Park Way)
Lincoln Av. N14 . . . . .3B **32**
  RM7: Rush G 2K **73**
  SW19 . . . . .3F **135**
  TW2: Twick 2G **131**
Lincoln Cl. HA2: Harr 5D **40**
  SE25 .6G **157**
  UB6: G'frd 1G **77**
Lincoln Ct. CR2: S Croy 5C **168**
   (off Warham Rd.)
  IG2: Ilf 6G **53**
  N16 . . . . .7D **48**
  SE12 .3K **141**
Lincoln Cres. EN1: Enf 5K **23**
Lincoln Gdns. IG1: Ilf 7C **52**
Lincoln Grn. Rd. BR5: St M Cry . .5K **161**
Lincoln Ho. SE5 . . . . .7A **102**
  SW3 .2D **100**
  TW8: Bford 5D **96**
   (off Ealing Rd.)
Lincoln M. N15 . . . . .4C **48**
  NW6 .1H **81**
  SE21 .2D **138**
Lincoln Pde. HA9: Wemb 1E **60**
  N2 . . . . .3C **46**
   (off Lincoln Rd.)
Lincoln Plaza E14 . . . . .2D **104**
   (off Lightermans Rd.)
Lincoln Rd. CR4: Mitc 5J **155**
  DA14: Sidc 5B **144**
  E7 . . . . .6B **70**
  E13 . . . . .4K **87**
  E18 . . . . .1J **51**
  EN1: Enf 4K **23**
  EN3: Pond E 5B **24**
  HA0: Wemb 6D **60**
  HA2: Harr 5D **40**
  HA6: Nwood 3H **39**
  KT3: N Mald 3J **151**
  KT4: Wor Pk 1D **164**
  N2 . . . . .3C **46**
  SE25 .3H **157**
  TW13: Hanw 3D **130**
The Lincolns NW7 . . . . .3G **29**
Lincoln's Inn Flds. WC2 . . . .7G **7** (6K **83**)
Lincoln's Inn Hall 7H **7** (6K **83**)
Lincoln St. E11 . . . . .2G **69**
  SW3 . . . . .4E **16** (4D **100**)
Lincoln Ter. SM2: Sutt 7J **165**
Lincoln Way EN1: Enf 5C **24**
  TW16: Sun 1G **147**
Lincombe Rd. BR1: Broml 3H **141**
Lindal Cl. E18 . . . . .1H **51**
Lindal Cres. EN2: Enf 4D **22**
Lindale Cl. IG4: Ilf 5D **52**
The Lindales N17 . . . . .6B **34**
   (off Grasmere Rd.)
Lindal Rd. SE4 . . . . .5B **122**
Lindbergh Rd. SM6: W'gton 7J **167**
Linden Av. CR7: Thor H 4B **156**
  EN1: Enf 1B **24**
  HA4: Ruis 1J **57**
  HA9: Wemb 5F **61**
  NW10 . . . . .2F **81**
  TW3: Houn 5F **113**

Linden Cl. HA4: Ruis 1J 57
HA7: Stan 5G 27
KT7: T Ditt 7K 149
N14 . . . . .6B 22
Linden Ct. DA14: Sidc 4J 143
SE20 . . . . .7H 139
(off Anerley Pk.)
W12 . . . . .1E 98
Linden Cres. IG8: Wfd G 6E 36
KT1: King T 2F 151
UB6: G'frd 6K 59
Lindenfield BR7: Chst 2F 161
Linden Gdns. EN1: Enf 1B 24
W2 . . . . .7J 81
W4 . . . . .5A 98
Linden Gro. KT3: N Mald 3A 152
SE15 .3H 121
SE26 .6J 139
TW11: Tedd 5K 131
Linden Ho. SE8 . . . . .6B 104
(off Abinger Gro.)
TW12: Hamp 6E 130
Linden Lawns HA9: Wemb 4F 61
Linden Lea N2 . . . . .5A 46
Linden Leas BR4: W W'ck 2F 171
Linden Mans. N6 . . . . .1F 65
(off Hornsey La.)
Linden M. N1 . . . . .5D 66
W2 . . . . .7J 81
Linden Pl. CR4: Mitc 4C 154
Linden Rd. N10 . . . . .4F 47
N11 . . . . .2J 31
N15 . . . . .4C 48
TW12: Hamp 7E 130
The Lindens CR0: New Ad 6E 170
E17 . . . . .4D 50
(off Prospect Hill)
N12 . . . . .5G 31
W4 . . . . .1J 115
Linden St. RM7: Rom 4K 55
Linden Wlk. N19 . . . . .2G 65
Linden Way N14 . . . . .6B 22
TW17: Shep 5E 146
Linder's Field
Local Nature Reserve 1G 37
Lindeth Cl. HA7: Stan 6G 27
Lindfield Gdns. NW3 . . . . .5K 63
Lindfield Rd. CR0: C'don 6F 157
W5 . . . . .4C 78
Lindfield St. E14 . . . . .6C 86
Lindhill Cl. EN3: Enf H 2E 24
Lindholme Ct. NW9 . . . . .1A 44
(off Pageant Av.)
Lindie Gdns. UB8: Uxb 7A 56
Lindisfarne Ct. HA8: Edg 4A 28
Lindisfarne Rd. RM8: Dag 3C 72
SW20 . . . . .7C 134
Lindisfarne Way E9 . . . . .4A 68
Lindley Cl.
KT1: Hamp W 1C 150
Lindley Est. SE15 . . . . .7G 103
Lindley Ho. E1 . . . . .5J 85
(off Lindley St.)
SE15 .7G 103
(off Peckham Pk. Rd.)
Lindley Pl. TW9: Kew 1G 115
Lindley Rd. E10 . . . . .2E 68
Lindley St. E1 . . . . .5J 85
Lindop Ho. E1 . . . . .4A 86
(off Mile End Rd.)
Lindore Rd. SW11 . . . . .4D 118
Lindores Rd. SM5: Cars 7A 154
Lindo St. SE15 . . . . .2J 121
Lind Rd. SM1: Sutt 5A 166
Lindrop St. SW6 . . . . .2A 118
Lindsay Cl. KT9: Chess 7E 162
TW19: Stanw 5A 110
Lindsay Ct. CR0: C'don 4D 168
(off Eden Rd.)
SE13 .3D 122
(off Loampit Va.)
SW11 .1B 118
(off Battersea High St.)

Lindsay Dr. HA3: Kenton 6E 42
TW17: Shep 6F 147
Lindsay Ho. SW7 . . . . .3A 100
(off Gloucester Rd.)
Lindsay Rd. KT4: Wor Pk 2D 164
TW12: Hamp H 4F 131
Lindsay Sq. SW1 . . . . .5D 18 (5H 101)
Lindsell St. SE10 . . . . .1E 122
Lindsey Cl. BR1: Broml 3B 160
CR4: Mitc 4J 155
Lindsey Ct. N13 . . . . .3F 33
(off Green Lanes)
Lindsey Gdns. TW14: Bedf 7F 111
Lindsey Ho. W5 . . . . .4D 96
Lindsey M. N1 . . . . .7C 66
Lindsey Rd. RM8: Dag 4C 72
Lindsey St. EC1 . . . . .5B 8 (5B 84)
Lind St. SE8 . . . . .2C 122
Lindum Rd. TW11: Tedd 7C 132
Lindway SE27 . . . . .5B 138
Lindwood Cl. E6 . . . . .6D 88
Linear Pk. 6H 101
The Linen Ho. W10 . . . . .2G 81
Linen M. N12 . . . . .2B 98
Liner Ho. E16 . . . . .2A 106
Linfield WC1 . . . . .2G 7
(off Sidmouth St.)
Linfield Cl. NW4 . . . . .3E 44
Linford Christie Stadium 5C 80
Linford Ho. E2 . . . . .1G 85
(off Whiston Rd.)
E16 . . . . .5J 87
(off Hammersley Rd.)
Linford Rd. E17 . . . . .3E 50
Linford St. SW8 . . . . .1G 119
Linford St. Bus. Est. SW8 . . . . . . .1G 119
(off Linford St.)
Lingard Av. NW9 . . . . .2A 44
Lingard Ho. E14 . . . . .3E 104
(off Marshfield St.)
Lingards Rd. SE13 . . . . .4E 122
Lingey Cl. DA15: Sidc 2K 143
Lingfield Apts. E4 . . . . .7J 35
Lingfield Cl. EN1: Enf 6K 23
HA6: Nwood 1G 39
Lingfield Ct. UB5: N'olt 2E 76
Lingfield Cres. SE9 . . . . .4H 125
Lingfield Gdns. N9 . . . . .7C 24
Lingfield Ho. SE1 . . . . .7B 14
Lingfield Rd. KT4: Wor Pk 3E 164
SW19 .5F 135
Lingham Ct. SW9 . . . . .2J 119
Lingham St. SW9 . . . . .2J 119
Lingholm Way EN5: Barn 5A 20
Ling Rd. DA8: Erith 6J 109
E16 . . . . .5J 87
Lingrove Gdns. IG9: Buck H 2E 36
Lings Coppice SE21 . . . . .2D 138
Lingwell Rd. SW17 . . . . .3C 136
Lingwood DA7: Bex 2H 127
Lingwood Ct. N2 . . . . .3C 46
(off Norfolk Cl.)
Lingwood Gdns. TW7: Isle 7J 95
Lingwood Rd. E5 . . . . .7G 49
Linhope St. NW1 . . . . . .3E 4 (4D 82)
The Link EN3: Enf H 1F 25
HA0: Wemb 1C 60
HA5: Eastc 7A 40
NW2 . . . . .1C 62
SE9 . . . . .3E 142
(off William Barefoot Dr.)
UB5: N'olt 5D 58
W3 . . . . .6H 79
Linkenholt Mans. W6 . . . . .4B 98
(off Stamford Brook Av.)
Linkfield BR2: Hayes 6J 159
KT8: W Mole 3F 149
Linkfield Rd. TW7: Isle 2K 113
Link Ho. E3 . . . . .3D 86
W10 . . . . .6F 81
(off Kingsdown Cl.)
Link La. SM6: W'gton 6H 167

Linklea Cl. NW9 . . . . .7F 29
Link Rd. E1 . . . . .2K 15 (7G 85)
N11 . . . . .4K 31
RM9: Dag 2H 91
SM6: W'gton 1E 166
TW14: Felt 7H 111
The Links E17 . . . . .4A 50
Links Av. SM4: Mord 4J 153
Linkscroft Av. TW15: Ashf 6D 128
Links Dr. N20 . . . . .1D 30
Links Gdns. SW16 . . . . .7A 138
Linkside KT3: N Mald 2A 152
N12 . . . . .6D 30
Linkside Av. EN2: Enf 3E 22
Linkside Gdns. EN2: Enf 3E 22
Links Rd. BR4: W W'ck 1E 170
IG8: Wfd G 5D 36
NW2 . . . . .2B 62
SW17 .6E 136
TW15: Ashf 5A 128
W3 . . . . .6G 79
Links Side EN2: Enf 3E 22
Link St. E9 . . . . .6J 67
Links Vw. N3 . . . . .7C 30
Linksview N2 . . . . .5D 46
(off Great Nth. Rd.)
Links Vw. Cl. HA7: Stan 7F 27
Linksview Ct.
TW12: Hamp H 4H 131
Links Vw. Rd. CR0: C'don 3C 170
TW12: Hamp H 5G 131
Links Way BR3: Beck 6C 158
Linksway HA6: Nwood 1E 38
NW4 . . . . .2F 45
Links Yd. E1 . . . . .5K 9
Link Way BR2: Broml 7C 160
HA5: Pinn 1B 40
TW10: Ham 2B 132
Linkway N4 . . . . .7C 48
RM8: Dag 4C 72
SW20 .3D 152
The Linkway EN5: Barn 6E 20
Linkwood Wlk. NW1 . . . . .7H 65
Linley Cl. SM1: Sutt 4A 166
Linley Cres. RM7: Mawney 3H 55
Linley Rd. N17 . . . . .2E 48
Linnell Cl. NW11 . . . . .6K 45
Linnell Dr. NW11 . . . . .6K 45
Linnell Ho. E1 . . . . .5J 9
(off Folgate St.)
NW8 . . . . .1A 82
(off Ainsworth Way)
Linnell Rd. N18 . . . . .5B 34
SE5 . . . . .2E 120
Linnet Cl. N9 . . . . .1E 34
SE28 .7C 90
WD23: Bush 1B 26
Linnet St. SW15 . . . . .6E 116
Linnet M. SW12 . . . . .7E 118
Linnet Cl. E4 . . . . .4K 35
Linom Rd. SW4 . . . . .4J 119
Linscott Rd. E5 . . . . .4J 67
Linsdell Rd. IG11: Bark 1G 89
Linsey Ct. E10 . . . . .1C 68
(off Grange Rd.)
Linsey St. SE16 . . . . .4G 103
(not continuous)
Linslade Cl. HA5: Eastc 4K 39
TW4: Houn 5C 112
Linslade Ho. E2 . . . . .1G 85
NW8 . . . . .4C 4
(off Paveley St.)
Linslade Rd. BR6: Chels 6K 173
Linstead St. NW6 . . . . .7J 63
Linstead Way SW18 . . . . .7G 117
Linsted Ct. SE9 . . . . .6J 125
Lintaine Cl. W6 . . . . .6G 99
Linthorpe Av. HA0: Wemb 6C 60
Linthorpe Rd. EN4: Cockf 3H 21
N16 . . . . .7E 48
Linton Cl. CR4: Mitc 7D 154
DA16: Well 1B 126
SE7 . . . . .5A 106

Linton Ct. NW1 . . . . .7G 65
(off Agar Gro.)
RM1: Rom 2K 55
Linton Gdns. E6 . . . . .6C 88
Linton Gro. SE27 . . . . .5B 138
Linton Ho. E3 . . . . .5C 86
(off St Paul's Way)
Linton Rd. IG11: Bark 7G 71
Linton St. N1 . . . . .1C 84
(not continuous)
Lintott Ct. TW19: Stanw 6A 110
Linver Rd. SW6 . . . . .2J 117
Linwood Cl. SE5 . . . . .2F 121
Linwood Cres. EN1: Enf 1B 24
Linzee Rd. N8 . . . . .4J 47
Lion Apts. SE16 . . . . .5H 103
(off Rotherhithe New Rd.)
Lion Av. TW1: Twick 1K 131
Lion Cl. SE4 . . . . .6C 122
TW17: Shep 3A 146
Lion Ct. E1 . . . . .7K 85
(off The Highway)
N1 . . . . .1K 83
(off Copenhagen St.)
SE1 . . . . .5G 15
(off Magdalen St.)
Lionel Gdns. SE9 . . . . .5B 124
Lionel Mans. W14 . . . . .3F 99
(off Haarlem Rd.)
Lionel M. W10 . . . . .5G 81
Lionel Rd. SE9 . . . . .5B 124
Lionel Rd. Nth. TW8: Bford 3E 96
Lionel Rd. Sth. TW8: Bford 5F 97
Liongate Ent. Pk. CR4: Mitc 4B 154
Lion Ga. Gdns. TW9: Rich 3F 115
Lion Ga. M. SW18 . . . . .7J 117
Liongate M. KT8: E Mos 3K 149
Lion Head Ct. CR0: C'don 4C 168
(off St Andrew's Rd.)
Lion Mills E2 . . . . .2G 85
Lion Pk. Av. KT9: Chess 4G 163
Lion Rd. CR0: C'don 5C 156
DA6: Bex 4E 126
E6 . . . . .5D 88
N9 . . . . .2B 34
TW1: Twick 1K 131
Lions Cl. SE9 . . . . .3A 142
Lion Way TW8: Bford 7D 96
Lion Wharf Rd. TW7: Isle 3B 114
Lion Yd. SW4 . . . . .4H 119
Liphook Cres. SE23 . . . . .7J 121
Lipton Cl. SE28 . . . . .7C 90
Lipton Rd. E1 . . . . .6K 85
Lisbon Av. TW2: Twick 2G 131
Lisbon Cl. E17 . . . . .2B 50
Lisburne Rd. NW3 . . . . .4D 64
Lisford St. SE15 . . . . .1F 121
Lisgar Ter. W14 . . . . .4H 99
Liskeard Cl. BR7: Chst 6G 143
Liskeard Gdns. SE3 . . . . .1J 123
Liskeard Ho. SE11 . . . . .5K 19
(off Kennings Way)
Lisle Cl. SW17 . . . . .4F 137
Lisle Cl. NW2 . . . . .3G 63
Lisle St. WC2 . . . . .2D 12 (7H 83)
Lismore SW19 . . . . .5H 135
(off Woodside)
Lismore Boulevard NW9 . . . . .3B 44
Lismore Cir. NW5 . . . . .5E 64
Lismore Cl. TW7: Isle 2A 114
Lismore Rd. CR2: S Croy 6E 168
N17 . . . . .3D 48
Lismore Wlk. N1 . . . . .6C 66
(off Clephane Rd. Nth.)
Lissant Cl. KT6: Surb 7D 150
Lisselton Ho. NW4 . . . . .4F 45
(off Belle Vue Est.)
Lissenden Gdns. NW5 . . . . .4E 64
(not continuous)
Lissenden Mans. NW5 . . . . .4E 64
Lisson Grn. Est. NW8 . . . . .3C 4
(off Tresham Cres.)
LISSON GROVE 5B 4 (5C 82)

Lisson Gro. NW1 . . . . .3B 4 (4B 82)
  NW8 . . . . .3B 4 (4B 82)
Lisson Ho. NW1 . . . . .5C 4
  (off Lisson St.)
Lisson St. NW1 . . . . . . .5C 4 (5C 82)
Lister Cl. CR4: Mitc 1C 154
  W3 .5K 79
Lister Cl. HA1: Harr 7B 42
  N16 . . . . .2E 66
  NW9 . . . . .2A 44
Lister Gdns. N18 . . . . .5H 33
Listergate St. SW15 . . . . . . .4E 116
Lister Ho. E1 . . . . .5G 85
  (off Lomas St.)
  HA9: Wemb 3J 61
  (off Barnhill Rd.)
  UB3: Harl 4G 93
Lister Lodge W9 . . . . .5J 81
  (off Admiral Wlk.)
Lister Rd. E11 . . . . .1G 69
Lister Wlk. SE28 . . . . .7D 90
Liston Rd. N17 . . . . .1G 49
  SW4 . . . . .3G 119
Liston Way IG8: Wfd G 7F 37
Listowel Cl. SW9 . . . . .7A 102
Listowel Rd. RM10: Dag 3G 73
Listria Pk. N16 . . . . .2E 66
Litcham Ho. E1 . . . . .3K 85
  (off Longnor Rd.)
Litchfield Av. E15 . . . . .6G 69
  SM4: Mord 7H 153
Litchfield Ct. E17 . . . . .6C 50
Litchfield Gdns. NW10 . . . . . . .6C 62
Litchfield Rd. SM1: Sutt 4A 166
Litchfield St. WC2 . . . . .2D 12 (7H 83)
Litchfield Way NW11 . . . . .5K 45
Lithgow's Rd. TW6: H'row A . .4G 111
Lithos Rd. NW3 . . . . .6K 63
Litten Nature Reserve 3G 77
Lit. Acre BR3: Beck 3C 158
Lit. Albany St. NW1 . . . . .3K 5
Little Angel Theatre 1B 84
  (off Dagmar Ter.)
Lit. Argyll St. W1 . . . . . .1A 12 (6G 83)
Lit. Benty UB7: W Dray 1E 174
Lit. Birches DA15: Sidc 2J 143
The Lit. Boltons SW5 . . . . .5K 99
  SW10 . . . . .5K 99
Lit. Bornes SE21 . . . . .4E 138
Littlebourne SE13 . . . . .7G 123
Littlebourne Ho. SE17 . . . . . . .5E 102
  (off Upnor Way)
Lit. Brights Rd. DA17: Belv 2H 109
Lit. Britain EC1 . . . . .6B 8 (5B 84)
Littlebrook Cl. CR0: C'don 6K 157
Lit. Brownings SE23 . . . . .2H 139
Littlebury Rd. SW4 . . . . .3H 119
Lit. Bury St. N9 . . . . .1J 33
Lit. Bushey La. WD23: Bush 1C 26
Lit. Cedars N12 . . . . .4F 31
Lit. Chelsea Ho. SW10 . . . . . . .6A 100
  (off Edith Gro.)
Lit. Chester St. SW1 . . . .1J 17 (3F 101)
Lit. Cloisters SW1 . . . . .1E 18 (3J 101)
Lit. College La. EC4 . . . . .2E 14
  (off College St.)
Lit. College St. SW1 . . . .1E 18 (3J 101)
Littlecombe SE7 . . . . .6K 105
Littlecombe Cl. SW15 . . . . .6F 117
Little Comn. HA7: Stan 3F 27
Littlecote Cl. SW19 . . . . .7G 117
Littlecote Pl. HA5: Hat E 1C 40
Lit. Cottage Pl. SE10 . . . . .7D 104
Little Ct. BR4: W W'ck 2G 171
Littlecroft SE9 . . . . .3E 124
Littledale SE2 . . . . .6A 108
Lit. Dean's Yd. SW1 . . . . .1E 18
Lit. Dimocks SW12 . . . . .2F 137
Lit. Dorrit Ct. SE1 . . . . .6D 14 (2C 102)
LITTLE EALING 3D 96
Lit. Ealing La. W5 . . . . .4C 96
Lit. Edward St. NW1 . . . .1K 5 (3F 83)
Lit. Elms UB3: Harl 7F 93

Lit. Essex St. WC2 . . . . .2J 13
Lit. Ferry Rd. TW1: Twick 1B 132
Littlefield Cl. KT1: King T 2E 150
  N19 . . . . .4G 65
Littlefield Ho. KT1: King T 2E 150
  (off Littlefield Cl.)
Littlefield Rd. HA8: Edg 7D 28
Lit. Friday Rd. E4 . . . . .2B 36
Lit. Gearies IG6: Ilf 4F 53
Lit. George St. SW1 . . . . .7E 12 (2J 101)
Lit. Grange UB6: G'frd 3A 78
Little Grn. TW9: Rich 4D 114
Lit. Green St. NW5 . . . . .4F 65
Littlegrove EN4: E Barn 6H 21
Lit. Halliards KT12: Walt T 6J 147
LITTLE HEATH 5B 54
Lit. Heath RM6: Chad H 4B 54
  SE7 . . . . .6C 106
Lit. Heath Rd. DA7: Bex 1F 127
Littleheath Rd. CR2: Sels 7H 169
Little Holland House 7D 166
Lit. Holt E11 . . . . .5J 51
LITTLE ILFORD 5D 70
Lit. Ilford La. E12 . . . . .4D 70
Littlejohn Rd. W7 . . . . .6K 77
Lit. Larkins EN5: Barn 6B 20
Lit. London Cl. UB8: Hil 5D 74
Lit. London Ct. SE1 . . . . .7K 15
  (off Wolseley St.)
Lit. Marlborough St. W1 . . . . . . .1A 12
Littlemede SE9 . . . . .3D 142
Littlemoor Rd. IG1: Ilf 3H 71
Littlemore Rd. SE2 . . . . .2A 108
Lit. Moss La. HA5: Pinn 2C 40
Lit. Newport St. WC2 . . . .2D 12 (7H 83)
Lit. New St. EC4 . . . . . . .7K 7 (6A 84)
Lit. Oaks Cl. TW17: Shep 4B 146
Lit. Orchard Cl. HA5: Pinn 2C 40
Lit. Park Dr. TW13: Felt 2C 130
Lit. Park Gdns. EN2: Enf 2H 23
Lit. Pluckett's Way IG9: Buck H . . .1G 37
Lit. Portland St. W1 . . . . .7K 5 (6G 83)
Lit. Potters WD23: Bush 1C 26
Lit. Queen's Rd. TW11: Tedd . . .6K 131
Lit. Redlands BR1: Broml 2C 160
Little Rd. UB3: Hayes 2H 93
Littlers Cl. SW19 . . . . .1B 154
Lit. Russell St. WC1 . . . . .6E 6 (5J 83)
Lit. St James's St. SW1 . .5A 12 (1G 101)
Lit. St Leonard's SW14 . . . . . . .3J 115
Lit. Sanctuary SW1 . . . . .7D 12 (2H 101)
Lit. Smith St. SW1 . . . . .1D 18 (3H 101)
Lit. Somerset St. E1 . . . .1J 15 (6F 85)
Lit. South St. SE5 . . . . .1E 120
LITTLE STANMORE 7A 28
Littlestone Cl. BR3: Beck 6C 140
Lit. Strand NW9 . . . . .2B 44
Lit. Thames Wlk. SE8 . . . . .6D 104
  (off Dancers Way)
Lit. Thrift BR5: Pet W 4G 161
Lit. Titchfield St. W1 . . . .6A 6 (5G 83)
LITTLETON 3C 146
Littleton Av. E4 . . . . .1C 36
LITTLETON COMMON 7E 128
Littleton Cres. HA1: Harr 2K 59
Littleton Ho. SW1 . . . . .6A 18
  (off Lupus St.)
Littleton La. TW17: Shep 7A 146
Littleton Rd. HA1: Harr 2K 59
  TW15: Ashf 7E 128
Littleton St. SW18 . . . . .2A 136
Lit. Trinity La. EC4 . . . . .2D 14 (7C 84)
Lit. Turnstile WC1 . . . . . .6G 7 (5K 83)
LITTLE VENICE 5A 82
Little Venice Sports Cen. . . .5A 4 (5B 82)
Littlewood SE13 . . . . .6E 122
Littlewood Cl. W13 . . . . .3B 96
Littleworth Av. KT10: Esh 6H 149
Littleworth Bus. Cen. DA5: Bexl . .1H 145
Livermere Ct. E8 . . . . .1F 85
  (off Queensbridge Rd.)
Livermere Rd. E8 . . . . .1F 85
Liverpool Gro. SE17 . . . . .5C 102

Liverpool Rd. CR7: Thor H 3C 156
  E10 . . . . .6E 50
  E16 . . . . .5G 87
  KT2: King T 7G 133
  N1 .5A 66
  N7 .5A 66
  W5 .2D 96
Liverpool St. EC2 . . . . . .6G 9 (5E 84)
Livery Stables Cl. BR2: Broml . . .3B 172
Livesey Cl. KT1: King T 3F 151
  SE28 . . . . .3G 107
Livesey Pl. SE15 . . . . .6G 103
Livingstone Ct. E10 . . . . .6E 50
  EN5: Barn 2B 20
  (off Church La.)
  HA3: W'stone 3K 41
Livingstone Ho. NW10 . . . . . . .7K 61
  SE5 . . . . .7C 102
  (off Wyndham Rd.)
Livingstone Lodge W9 . . . . .5J 81
  (off Admiral Wlk.)
Livingstone Mans. W14 . . . . . . .6G 99
  (off Queen's Club Gdns.)
Livingstone Pl. E14 . . . . .5E 104
Livingstone Rd. CR7: Thor H 2C 156
  E17 . . . . .6D 50
  N13 . . . . .6D 32
  SW11 . . . . .3B 118
  TW3: Houn 4G 113
  UB1: S'hall 7B 76
LivingWell Health Club
  London Heathrow Hilton 6E 110
  Wembley 4G 61
Livonia St. W1 . . . . .1B 12 (6G 83)
Lizard St. EC1 . . . . .2D 8 (3C 84)
Lizban St. SE3 . . . . .7K 105
Lizmans Ter. W8 . . . . .3J 99
  (off Earl's Ct. Rd.)
Llandovery Ho. E14 . . . . .2E 104
  (off Chipka St.)
Llanelly Rd. NW2 . . . . .2H 63
Llanover Rd. HA9: Wemb 3D 60
  SE18 . . . . .6E 106
Llanthony Rd. SM4: Mord 5B 154
Llanvanor Rd. NW2 . . . . .2H 63
Llewellyn Ct. SE20 . . . . .1J 157
Llewellyn Mans. W14 . . . . .4G 99
  (off Hammersmith Rd.)
Llewellyn St. SE16 . . . . .2G 103
Lloyd Av. SW16 . . . . .1J 155
Lloyd Baker St. WC1 . . . .2H 7 (3K 83)
  (not continuous)
Lloyd Ct. HA5: Pinn 5B 40
  SW11 . . . . .2D 118
  (off Roydon Cl.)
Lloyd Ho. BR3: Beck 6D 140
  CR0: C'don 1D 168
  (off Tavistock Rd.)
Lloyd M. EN3: Enf L 1H 25
Lloyd Pk. 2C 50
Lloyd Pk. Av. CR0: C'don 4F 169
Lloyd Pk. Ho. E17 . . . . .3C 50
Lloyd Rd. E6 . . . . .1D 88
  E17 . . . . .4K 49
  KT4: Wor Pk 3E 164
  RM9: Dag 7F 73
Lloyd's Av. EC3 . . . . .1H 15 (6E 84)
Lloyd's Building 1G 15 (6E 84)
Lloyd's Pl. SE3 . . . . .2G 123
Lloyd Sq. WC1 . . . . .1J 7 (3A 84)
Lloyd's Row EC1 . . . . . . .2K 7 (3A 84)
Lloyd St. WC1 . . . . .1J 7 (3A 84)
Lloyds Way BR3: Beck 5A 158
Lloyds Wharf SE1 . . . . .6K 15
Lloyd Thomas Ct. N22 . . . . .7E 32
Lloyd Vs. E6 . . . . .4C 88
  SE4 . . . . .2C 122
Loampit Hill SE13 . . . . .2C 122
Loampit Rd. DA8: Erith 6J 109
LOAMPIT VALE 3E 122
Loampit Va. SE13 . . . . .3D 122
Loanda Cl. E8 . . . . .1F 85
Loats Rd. SW2 . . . . .6J 119

Lobelia Cl. E6 . . . . .5C 88
Locarno Ct. SW16 . . . . .5G 137
Locarno Rd. UB6: G'frd 4H 77
  W3 .1J 97
Lochaber Rd. SE13 . . . . .4G 123
Lochaline St. W6 . . . . .6E 98
Lochan Cl. UB4: Yead 4C 76
Loch Cres. HA8: Edg 4A 28
Lochinvar St. SW12 . . . . .7F 119
Lochleven Ho. N2 . . . . .2B 46
  (off The Grange)
Lochmere Cl. DA8: Erith 6H 109
Lochmore Ho. SW1 . . . . .4H 17
  (off Cundy St.)
Lochnagar St. E14 . . . . .5E 86
Lockbridge Ct. W9 . . . . .5J 81
  (off Woodfield Rd.)
The Lock Bldg. E15 . . . . .2E 86
Lock Chase SE3 . . . . .3G 123
Lock Cl. UB2: S'hall 2G 95
Lock Cotts. UB1: S'hall 2H 95
Lock Ct. E5 . . . . .2K 67
Locke Hgts. N1 . . . . .7K 65
  (off Caledonian Rd.)
Locke Ho. SW8 . . . . .1G 119
  (off Wadhurst Rd.)
Lockes End E17 . . . . .4E 50
Lockesfield Pl. E14 . . . . .5D 104
Lockesley Dr. BR5: St M Cry 6K 161
Lockesley Sq. KT6: Surb 6D 150
Locket Rd. HA3: W'stone 3J 41
Locket Rd. M. HA3: W'stone 2J 41
Lockfield Av. EN3: Brim 2F 25
Lockgate Cl. E9 . . . . .5B 68
Lockhart Cl. EN3: Pond E 5C 24
  N7 .6K 65
Lockhart St. E3 . . . . .4B 86
The Lockhouse NW1 . . . . .1E 82
Lockhurst St. E5 . . . . .4K 67
Lockie Pl. SE25 . . . . .3G 157
Lockier Wlk. HA9: Wemb 3D 60
Lockington Rd. SW8 . . . . .1F 119
Lock Keepers Hgts. SE16 . . . . . .3K 103
  (off Brunswick Quay)
Lockmead Rd. N15 . . . . .6G 49
  SE13 . . . . .3E 122
Lock M. NW1 . . . . .6H 65
  (off Northpoint Sq.)
Lock Mill Apts. E2 . . . . .1F 85
  (off Whiston Rd.)
Lock Rd. TW10: Ham 4C 132
Lock Side E14 . . . . .7A 86
  (off Narrow St.)
Lock Side Way E16 . . . . .7G 89
Locks La. CR4: Mitc 1E 154
Locksley Est. E14 . . . . .6B 86
Locksley Ho. E15 . . . . .6F 69
  (off Forrester Way)
Locksley St. E14 . . . . .5B 86
Locksmeade Rd. TW10: Ham 4C 132
Locksons Cl. E14 . . . . .5D 86
Lockswood Cl. EN4: Cockf 4J 21
Lockton St. W10 . . . . .7F 81
  (off Bramley Rd.)
Lock Vw. Ct. E14 . . . . .7A 86
  (off Narrow St.)
Lockwell Rd. RM10: Dag 3G 73
Lockwood Cl. SE26 . . . . .4K 139
Lockwood Ho. E5 . . . . .2J 67
  SE11 . . . . .7J 19 (6A 102)
Lockwood Ind. Pk. N17 . . . . . . .3H 49
Lockwood Pl. E4 . . . . .6H 35
Lockwood Sq. SE16 . . . . .3H 103
Lockwood Way E17 . . . . .2A 49
  KT9: Chess 5G 163
Lockworks Ho. E17 . . . . .4K 49
  (off Wickford Way)
Lockyer Est. SE1 . . . . .7F 15
  (not continuous)

Lockyer Ho. *SE10* *5H 105*
  (off Armitage Rd.)
  SW8 . . . .*7H 101*
  (off Wandsworth Rd.)
  SW15 .3F 117
Lockyer M. EN3: Enf L 1J 25
Lockyer St. SE1 . . . . . .7F 15 (2D 102)
Locomotive Dr. TW14: Felt 1J 129
Locton Grn. E3 . . . . .1B 86
Loddiges Ho. E9 . . . . .7J 67
Loddiges Rd. E9 . . . . .7J 67
Loddon Ho. *NW8* 4B 4
  (off Church St. Est.)
Loder St. SE15 . . . . .7J 103
The Lodge *W12* 2F 99
  (off Richmond Way)
Lodge Av. CR0: Wadd 3A 168
  HA3: Kenton 4E 42
  RM8: Dag 6B 72
  RM9: Dag 1A 90
  SW14 . . . . .3A 116
LODGE AVENUE FLYOVER JUNC. . . .1A 90
Lodge Cl. HA8: Edg 6A 28
  N18 .5H 33
  SM6: W'gton 1E 166
  TW7: Isle 1B 114
Lodge Ct. *HA0: Wemb* 5E 60
  (off Station Gro.)
Lodge Dr. N13 . . . . .4F 33
Lodge Gdns. BR3: Beck 5B 158
Lodge Hill DA16: Well 7B 108
  IG4: Ilf 4C 52
  SE2 . . . . .7B 108
Lodgehill Pk. Cl. HA2: Harr 2F 59
Lodge La. CR0: New Ad 6C 170
  DA5: Bexl 6D 126
  N12 .5F 31
  RM5: Col R 1G 55
Lodge M. N5 . . . . .4C 66
Lodge Pl. SM1: Sutt 5K 165
Lodge Rd. BR1: Broml 7A 142
  CR0: C'don 6B 156
  NW4 . . . . .4E 44
  NW8 . . . . .2B 4 (3B 82)
  SM6: W'gton 5F 167
Lodge Vs. IG8: Wfd G 6C 36
Lodge Way TW15: Ashf 2A 128
  TW17: Shep 2E 146
Lodore Gdns. NW9 . . . . .5A 44
Lodore Grn. UB10: Ick 3A 56
Lodore St. E14 . . . . .6E 86
The Loft W12 . . . . .7J 9
Loft Ho. *E1* . . . .
  (off Middlesex St.)
Lofthouse Pl. KT9: Chess 6C 162
Loftie St. SE16 . . . . .2G 103
Lofting Ho. *N1* 7A 66
  (off Liverpool Rd.)
Lofting Rd. N1 . . . . .7K 65
Lofts on the Park E9 . . . . .6K 67
  (off Cassland Rd.)
Loftus Road 1D 98
Loftus Rd. IG11: Bark 6G 71
  W12 .1D 98
Loftus Vs. *W12* 1D 98
  (off Loftus Rd.)
Logan E. E20 . . . . .5E 68
  EN3: Enf H 1E 24
  TW4: Houn 3D 112
Logan M. RM1: Rom 5K 55
  W8 .4J 99
Logan Pl. W8 . . . . .4J 99
Logan Rd. HA9: Wemb 2D 60
  N9 . . . . .2C 34
The Log Cabin 3C 96
  (off Northfield Av.)
Loggetts SE21 . . . . .2E 138
Logs Hill BR1: Broml 7C 142
  BR7: Chst 7C 142
Logs Hill Cl. BR7: Chst 1C 160
Lohmann Ho. SE11 . . . . .7J 19
Lois Dr. TW17: Shep 5D 146
Lolesworth Cl. E1 . . . . . .6J 9 (5F 85)

Lolland Ho. SE7 . . . . .4C 106
Lollard St. SE11 . . . . . .3H 19 (4K 101)
  (not continuous)
Loman St. SE1 . . . . . . .6B 14 (2B 102)
Lomas Cl. CR0: New Ad 7E 170
Lomas Dr. E8 . . . . .7F 67
Lomas St. E1 . . . . .5G 85
Lombard Av. EN3: Enf H 1D 24
  IG3: Ilf 1J 71
Lombard Bus. Pk. CR0: C'don . . .7K 155
  SW19 . . . . .2K 153
Lombard Ct. EC3 . . . . .2F 15 (7D 84)
  RM7: Rom 4J 55
  W3 . . . . .1H 97
Lombard La. EC4 . . . . .1K 13 (6A 84)
Lombard Pl. E3 . . . . .2A 86
Lombard Rd. N11 . . . . .5A 32
  SW11 . . . . .2B 118
  SW19 . . . . .2K 153
LOMBARD RDBT. 7K 155
Lombard St. EC3 . . . . .1F 15 (6D 84)
Lombard Trad. Est. SE7 . . . . . . .4K 105
Lombard Wall SE7 . . . . .3K 105
Lombard Wharf SW11 . . . . .2B 118
Lombardy Cl. IG6: Ilf 7K 37
Lombardy Pl. W2 . . . . .7K 81
Lombardy Retail Pk. 7K 75
Lomond Cl. HA0: Wemb 7F 61
  N15 .5E 48
Lomond Gdns. CR2: Sels 7A 170
Lomond Gro. SE5 . . . . .7D 102
Lomond Ho. SE5 . . . . .7D 102
Loncroft Rd. SE5 . . . . .6F 103
Londesborough Rd. N16 . . . . . . .4E 66
Londinium Twr. *E1* 2K 15
  (off W. Tenter St.)
LONDON 4E 12 (1J 101)
London Aquatics Cen.
  Queen Elizabeth Olympic Pk.
  . . . . .7E 68
London Bri. EC4 . . . . . .3F 15 (7D 84)
  SE1 . . . . .4F 15 (1D 102)
London Bridge Experience 4F 15
  (off Tooley St.)
London Bri. St. SE1 . . .5F 15 (1D 102)
London Bri. Wlk. *SE1* 4F 15
  (off Duke St. Hill)
London Broncos RLFC 1E 42
London Buddhist Cen. 3J 85
  (off Roman Rd.)
London Business School . .3E 4 (4D 82)
London Canal Mus. 2J 83
London Central Markets 6A 8
London Central Mosque . .2D 4 (3C 82)
London City College 5J 13
  (off Waterloo Rd.)
London Coliseum 3E 12
  (off St Martin's La.)
The London College of Fashion
  John Prince's St. 7K 5 (6F 83)
  Mare St. 7J 67
Londonderry Pde. DA8: Erith 7K 109
London Designer Outlet
  HA9: Wemb 4G 61
London Dock E1 . . . . .7G 85
London Dungeon 6G 13 (2K 101)
London E. Leisure Pk. RM9: Dag . . .1E 90
London Eye 6G 13 (2K 101)
London Fazal Mosque 7H 117
London Flds. East Side E8 . . . . . .7H 67
London Fields Lido 7H 67
London Flds. West Side E8 . . . . . .7G 67
London Film Mus. 2F 13
London Fruit Exchange *E1* 6J 9
  (off Brushfield St.)
LONDON GATEWAY SERVICE AREA
  . . . . .1D 28
London Group Bus. Pk. NW2 . . . .1J 62
London Ho. *EC1* 6C 8
  (off Aldersgate St.)
  NW8 . . . . .2C 82
  (off Avenue Rd.)
  WC1 . . . . .3G 7 (4K 83)

The London Ind. Pk. E6 . . . . .5F 89
  (not continuous)
London Information Centre 7H 83
  (off Leicester Sq.)
London International Gallery of
  Children's Art 1F 65
  (within Waterloo Pk. Cen.)
London Irish RFC 3H 147
London La. BR1: Broml 7H 141
  E8 . . . . .7H 67
London Marathon Community Track
  . . . . .1D 86
London Master Bakers Almshouses
  E10 .6D 50
London Mercantile Court . . .7J 7 (6A 84)
London Metropolitan Archives . . .3K 7
London Metropolitan University
  London City Campus,
    Calcutta House & Goulston St.
    . . . . .7K 9 (6F 85)
    Central House 7K 9
    Commercial Rd. 6G 85
    Moorgate 6E 8
  North London Campus,
    Eden Grove 5K 65
    Stapleton House 5K 65
    Tower Bldg. & Graduate Cen.
    . . . . .5A 66
London M. *W2* 7B 4 (6B 82)
London Mill Apts. *E2* 1F 85
  (off Whiston Rd.)
London Mithraeum 1E 14
London Motorcycle Mus. 3G 77
London Oxford St. Youth Hostel . . .1B 12
  (off Noel St.)
The London Palace 4C 102
  (within Elephant & Castle Shopping
  Centre)
London Palladium 1A 12
  (off Argyll St.)
London Pavilion 3C 12
  (off Piccadilly Circus)
London Plane Ho. E15 . . . . .3G 87
  (off Teasel Way)
London Regatta Cen. 7B 88
London Rd. BR1: Broml 7H 141
  CR0: C'don 7B 156
  CR4: Mitc 5C 154
    (Brookfields Av.)
  CR4: Mitc 7E 154
    (Mill Grn. Rd.)
  CR7: Thor H 1K 155
  DA1: Bexl, Cray 5K 127
  E13 .2J 87
  EN2: Enf 3J 23
  HA1: Harr 2J 59
  HA7: Stan 5H 27
  HA9: Wemb 5E 60
  IG11: Bark 7F 71
  KT2: King T 2F 151
  KT17: Ewe 7B 164
  RM6: Chad H 6G 55
  RM7: Chad H, Rom 6G 55
  SE1 . . . . .7A 14 (3B 102)
  SE23 . . . . .1H 139
  SM3: Cheam 3F 165
  SM4: Mord 5J 153
  SM6: W'gton 4F 167
  SW16 . . . . .1K 155
  SW17 . . . . .7D 136
  TW1: Twick 7A 114
  TW3: Houn 3G 113
  TW7: Bford, Isle 2K 113
  TW7: Isle, Twick 5A 114
  TW8: Bford 2K 113
  TW14: Bedf 2A 128
  TW15: Ashf 2A 128
LONDON ROAD RDBT. 6A 114
London School of
  Economics & Political
  Science 1G 13 (6K 83)
London Scottish FC 3D 114
London Scottish Golf Course 3D 134

London Shootlighters Gym 4G 79
London South Bank University
  Keyworth St. 7B 14 (3B 102)
  London Rd. 7A 14
  Southwark Campus . . .7B 14 (3B 102)
London South Bank University Technopark
  . . . . .3B 102
  (off London Rd.)
London's Roman Amphitheatre . . .7E 8
  (off Aldermanbury)
London Stadium
  Queen Elizabeth Olympic Pk. . . .7D 68
London Stile W4 . . . . .5G 97
London Stock Exchange 7C 8
London St. EC3 . . . . . . .2H 15 (7E 84)
  W2 . . . . .7A 4 (6B 82)
The London Telecom Tower
  . . . . .5A 6 (5G 83)
London Ter. E2 . . . . .2G 85
London Transport Mus. . . .2F 13 (7J 83)
London Transport Mus. Depot 2G 97
London Trocadero 2C 12 (7H 83)
London Underwriting Cen. 2H 15
London Wall EC2 . . . . . .6D 8 (5C 84)
London Wall Bldgs. EC2 . . . . . . .6F 9
London Wall Pl. EC2 . . . . .6D 8
London Wetland Cen. 1D 116
London Wetland Cen. Vis. Cen. . . .1D 116
London Wharf *E2* 1H 85
  (off Wharf Pl.)
London Zoo 2E 82
LONESOME 1G 155
Lonesome Cvn. Site 1F 155
Lonesome Way SW16 . . . . .1F 155
Long Acre WC2 . . . . . . .2E 12 (7J 83)
Long Acre Cl. W13 . . . . .5A 78
Longacre Pl. SM5: Cars 6E 166
Longacre Rd. E17 . . . . .1F 51
Longbeach Rd. SW11 . . . . .3D 118
Longberrys NW2 . . . . .3H 63
Longboat Row UB1: S'hall 6D 76
Longbow Apts. *E3* 4B 86
  (off St Clements Av.)
Longbow Ho. *EC1* 5E 8
  (off Chiswell St.)
Longbridge Ho. *E16* 7F 89
  (off University Way)
  RM8: Dag 4B 72
  (off Longbridge Rd.)
Longbridge Rd. IG11: Bark 6H 71
  RM8: Dag 6H 71
Longbridge Way SE13 . . . . .5E 122
Longcourt M. E11 . . . . .4A 52
Longcroft SE9 . . . . .3D 142
Longcrofte Rd. HA8: Edg 7J 27
Long Deacon Rd. E4 . . . . .1B 36
LONG DITTON 1C 162
Longdon Wood BR2: Kes 3C 172
Longdown Rd. SE6 . . . . .4C 140
Long Dr. HA4: Ruis 5A 58
  UB6: G'frd 1F 77
  UB7: W Dray 2A 92
  W3 . . . . .6A 80
Long Elmes HA3: Hrw W 1F 41
Longfellow Rd. E17 . . . . .6B 50
  KT4: Wor Pk 2C 164
Longfellow Way SE1 . . . . .4F 103
Long Fld. NW9 . . . . .7F 29
Longfield BR1: Broml 1H 159
Longfield Av. E17 . . . . .4A 50
  HA9: Wemb 1E 60
  NW7 . . . . .7H 29
  SM6: W'gton 1E 166
  W5 . . . . .7C 78
Longfield Cres. SE26 . . . . .3J 139
Longfield Dr. CR4: Mitc 1C 154
  SW14 . . . . .5H 115
Longfield Est. SE1 . . . . .4F 103
Longfield Ho. E17 . . . . .5B 50
  W5 . . . . .7C 78
Longfield Rd. W5 . . . . .6C 78
Longfield St. SW18 . . . . .7J 117
Longfield Wlk. W5 . . . . .6C 78

LONGFORD 4C 174
Longford Av. TW14: Felt 6G 111
  TW19: Stanw 1A 128
  UB1: S'hall 7F 77
LONGFORD CIR. 4C 174
Longford Cl. TW12: Hamp H 4E 130
  TW13: Hanw 3C 130
  UB4: Yead 7B 76
Longford Ct. E5 . . . . .4K 67
           (off Pedro St.)
  KT19: Ewe 4J 163
  NW4 .4F 45
  TW12: Hamp H 6F 131
  UB1: S'hall 1E 94
         (off Uxbridge Rd.)
Longford Gdns. SM1: Sutt 3A 166
  UB4: Yead 7B 76
Longford Ho. BR1: Broml 5F 141
     (off Brangbourne Rd.)
  E1 . . . . .6J 85
         (off Jubilee St.)
  TW12: Hamp H 4E 130
Longford Ind. Est. TW12: Hamp . .6F 131
LONGFORDMOOR 4B 174
Longford Rd. TW2: Whitt 1E 130
Longford St. NW1 . . . . . . .3K 5 (4F 83)
Longford Way TW19: Stanw 1A 128
Longhayes Av. RM6: Chad H 4D 54
Longhayes Ct. RM6: Chad H 4D 54
Longheath Gdns. CRO: C'don 5J 157
Longhedge Ho. SE26 . . . . .4G 139
     (off High Level Dr.)
Long Hedges TW3: Houn 2E 112
Longhedge St. SW11 . . . . .2E 118
Longhill Rd. SE6 . . . . .2F 141
Longhook Gdns. UB5: N'olt 2J 75
Longhope Cl. SE15 . . . . .6E 102
Longhurst Ho. W10 . . . . .3H 81
     (off Lancefield St.)
Longhurst Rd. CRO: C'don 6H 157
  SE13 . . . . .5F 123
Longitude Apts. CRO: C'don 2D 168
    (off Addiscombe Gro.)
Longland Ct. E9 . . . . .5A 68
        (off Mabley St.)
  SE1 .5G 103
Longland Dr. N20 . . . . .3E 30
LONGLANDS 3G 143
Longlands Ct. CR4: Mitc 1E 154
  DA15: Sidc 2K 143
  W11 .7H 81
Longlands Pk. Cres.
  DA15: Sidc 3J 143
Longlands Rd. DA15: Sidc 3J 143
Long La. CRO: C'don 6J 157
  DA7: Bex 7D 108
  EC1 . . . . .6B 8 (5B 84)
  N2 . . . . .7E 30
  N3 . . . . .7E 30
  SE1 . . . . .7E 14 (2D 102)
  TW19: Stanw 2B 128
  UB10: Hil, Ick 3C 74
Longleat Ho. SW1 . . . . .5C 18
     (off Rampayne St.)
Longleat Rd. EN1: Enf 5K 23
Longleat Way TW14: Bedf 7F 111
Longleigh Ho. SE5 . . . . .1E 120
     (off Peckham Rd.)
Longleigh La. DA7: Bex 6C 108
  SE2 .6C 108
Long Lents Ho. NW10 . . . . .1K 79
    (off Shrewsbury Rd.)
Longley Av. HA0: Wemb 1F 79
Longley Cl. SW8 . . . . .1J 119
Longley Rd. CRO: C'don 7B 156
  HA1: Harr 5G 41
  SW17 . . . . .6C 136
Long Leys E4 . . . . .6J 35
Longley St. SE1 . . . . .4G 103
Longley Way NW2 . . . . .3E 62
Longman Ho. E2 . . . . .2K 85
        (off Mace St.)

Longman Ho. E8 . . . . .1F 85
    (off Haggerston Rd.)
Longmans M. SW20 . . . . .2G 153
Long Mark Rd. E16 . . . . .5B 88
Longmarsh La. SE28 . . . . .1J 107
Long Mead NW9 . . . . .1B 44
Longmead BR7: Chst 2E 160
Longmead Dr. DA14: Sidc 2D 144
Longmead Ho. SE27 . . . . .5C 138
Long Mdw. NW5 . . . . .5H 65
Long Mdw. Cl. BR4: W W'ck 7E 158
Longmeadow Rd. DA15: Sidc 1J 143
Longmead Rd. KT7: T Ditt 7J 149
  SW17 . . . . .5D 136
  UB3: Hayes 7H 75
Long Mill SE10 . . . . .1D 122
    (off Greenwich High Rd.)
Longmoore St. SW1 . . . . .4A 18 (4G 101)
Longmoor Point SW15 . . . . .1D 134
       (off Norley Va.)
Longmore Av. EN4: E Barn 6F 21
  EN5: New Bar 6F 21
Longmore Gdns. Est. SW1 . . . . . .4B 18
Longnor Est. E1 . . . . .3K 85
Longnor Rd. E1 . . . . .3K 85
Long Pond Rd. SE3 . . . . .1G 123
Longreach Ct. IG11: Bark 2H 89
Long Reach Rd. IG11: Bark 4K 89
Longridge Ho. SE1 . . . . .3C 102
Longridge La. UB1: S'hall 6F 77
Longridge Rd. IG11: Bark 7G 71
  SW5 .4J 99
Long Ridges N2 . . . . .3E 46
        (off Fortis Grn.)
Long Rd. SW4 . . . . .4F 119
Long's Ct. WC2 . . . . .3D 12
Longs Ct. TW9: Rich 4F 115
Longshaw Rd. E4 . . . . .3A 36
Longshore SE8 . . . . .4B 104
Longshott Cl. SW5 . . . . .4J 99
    (off W. Cromwell Rd.)
Longstaff Cres. SW18 . . . . .6J 117
Longstaff Rd. SW18 . . . . .6J 117
Longstone Av. NW10 . . . . .7B 62
Longstone Ct. SE1 . . . . .7E 14
    (off Gt. Dover St.)
Longstone Rd. SW17 . . . . .5F 137
Long St. E2 . . . . .1J 9 (3F 85)
Longthornton Rd. SW16 . . . . .2G 155
Longthorpe Ct. W6 . . . . .4C 98
Longton Av. SE26 . . . . .4H 139
Longton Gro. SE26 . . . . .4H 139
Longview Vs. RM5: Col R 1F 55
Longview Way RM5: Col R 1K 55
Longville Rd. SE11 . . . . .4B 102
Long Wlk. KT3: N Mald 3J 151
  SE1 .3E 102
  SE18 .6F 107
  SW13 . . . . .2A 116
Longwalk Rd. UB11: Stock P 1D 92
Long Wall E15 . . . . .3F 87
Longwater Ho. KT1: King T 3D 150
    (off Portsmouth Rd.)
Longwood Bus. Pk. TW16: Sun . . .5H 147
Longwood Dr. SW15 . . . . .6C 116
Longwood Gdns. IG5: Ilf 4D 52
  IG6: Ilf 4D 52
Longworth Cl. SE28 . . . . .6D 90
Long Yd. WC1 . . . . .4G 7 (4K 83)
The Loning NW9 . . . . .4A 44
Lonsdale Av. E6 . . . . .4B 88
  HA9: Wemb 5E 60
  RM7: Rom 6J 55
Lonsdale Cl. E6 . . . . .4C 88
  HA5: Hat E 1C 40
  HA8: Edg 5A 28
  SE9 .3B 142
  UB8: Hil 5E 74
Lonsdale Ct. KT6: Surb 7D 150
Lonsdale Cres. IG2: Ilf 6F 53
Lonsdale Dr. EN2: Enf 4C 22
Lonsdale Dr. Nth. EN2: Enf 5D 22
Lonsdale Gdns. CR7: Thor H 4K 155

Lonsdale Ho. W11 . . . . .6H 81
    (off Lonsdale Rd.)
Lonsdale M. TW9: Kew 1G 115
  W11 . . . . .6H 81
     (off Colville M.)
Lonsdale Pl. N1 . . . . .7A 66
Lonsdale Rd. DA7: Bex 2F 127
  E11 . . . . .6H 51
  NW6 .2H 81
  SE25 . . . . .4H 157
  SW13 . . . . .6C 98
  UB2: S'hall 3B 94
  W4 . . . . .4B 98
  W11 . . . . .6H 81
Lonsdale Road Reservoir
  Local Nature Reserve 7B 98
Lonsdale Sq. N1 . . . . .7A 66
Lonsdale Yd. W11 . . . . .7J 81
Loobert Rd. N15 . . . . .3E 48
Looe Gdns. IG6: Ilf 3F 53
Lookout Lane E14 . . . . .6G 87
Loop Cl. SE10 . . . . .4G 105
    (off Telegraph Av.)
Loop Rd. BR7: Chst 6G 143
Lopen Rd. N18 . . . . .4K 33
Lopez Ho. SW9 . . . . .3J 119
Lorac Cl. SM2: Sutt 7J 165
Loraine Cl. EN3: Pond E 5D 24
Loraine Cotts. N7 . . . . .4K 65
Loraine Ct. BR7: Chst 5F 143
Loraine Ho. SM6: W'gton 4F 167
Loraine Rd. N7 . . . . .4K 65
  W4 . . . . .6H 97
Lord Admiral's Vw. SE18 . . . . . . .4D 106
     (off Frances St.)
Lord Amory Way E14 . . . . .2E 104
Lord Av. IG5: Ilf 4D 52
Lord Chancellor Wlk. KT2: King T . .1J 151
Lord Ct. IG5: Ilf 4D 52
Lordell Pl. SW19 . . . . .6E 134
Lorden Wlk. E2 . . . . .2K 9 (3G 85)
Lord Gdns. IG5: Ilf 4D 52
Lord Graham M. N18 . . . . .5B 34
Lord Hills Bri. W2 . . . . .5K 81
Lord Hills Rd. W2 . . . . .5K 81
Lord Holland La. SW9 . . . . .2A 120
Lord Kensington Ho. W14 . . . . .4H 99
    (off Radnor Ter.)
Lord Knyvetts Ct. TW19: Stanw . . .6A 110
Lord Napier Pl. W6 . . . . .5C 98
Lord Nth. St. SW1 . . . . . .2E 18 (3J 101)
Lord Roberts M. SW6 . . . . .7K 99
Lord Robert's Ter. SE18 . . . . .5E 106
Lord's 2B 4 (3B 82)
Lords Cl. SE21 . . . . .2C 138
  TW13: Hanw 2C 130
Lordship Gro. N16 . . . . .2D 66
Lordship La. N17 . . . . .1D 48
  N22 . . . . .2A 48
  SE22 . . . . .4F 121
Lordship La. Est. SE21 . . . . .7G 121
Lordship Pk. N16 . . . . .2C 66
Lordship Pk. M. N16 . . . . .2C 66
Lordship Pl. SW3 . . . . . .7C 16 (6C 100)
Lordship Rd. N16 . . . . .1D 66
  UB5: N'olt 7C 58
Lordship Ter. N16 . . . . .2D 66
Lordsmead Rd. N17 . . . . .1E 48
Lord St. E16 . . . . .1C 106
Lords Vw. NW8 . . . . .2C 4 (3B 82)
     (not continuous)
Lordswood Cl. DA6: Bex 5E 126
Lord Warwick St. SE18 . . . . .3D 106
Loreburn Ho. N7 . . . . .4K 65
Lorenzo Ho. IG3: Ilf 6A 54
Lorenzo St. WC1 . . . . .1G 7 (3K 83)
Loretto Gdns. HA3: Kenton 4E 42
Lorian Cl. N12 . . . . .4E 30
Lorimer Row BR2: Broml 6B 160
Loring Rd. N20 . . . . .2H 31
  SE14 . . . . .1A 122
  TW7: Isle 2K 113
Loris Rd. W6 . . . . .3E 98

Lorn Ct. SW9 . . . . .2A 120
Lorne Av. CRO: C'don 7K 157
Lorne Cl. NW8 . . . . .2D 4 (3C 82)
Lorne Gdns. CRO: C'don 7K 157
  E11 . . . . .4A 52
  W11 . . . . .2F 99
Lorne Ho. E1 . . . . .5A 86
    (off Ben Jonson Rd.)
Lorne Rd. E7 . . . . .4K 69
  E17 . . . . .5C 50
  HA3: W'stone 2K 41
  N4 . . . . .1K 65
  TW10: Rich 5F 115
Lorne Ter. N3 . . . . .2H 45
Lorn Rd. SW9 . . . . .2K 119
Lorraine Ct. NW1 . . . . .7F 65
Lorraine Pk. HA3: Hrw W 7D 26
Lorrimore Rd. SE17 . . . . .6B 102
Lorrimore Sq. SE17 . . . . .6B 102
Lorton Ho. NW6 . . . . .1J 81
    (off Kilburn Vale)
Lost Theatre 1H 119
Lothair Rd. W5 . . . . .2D 96
Lothair Rd. Nth. N4 . . . . .6B 48
Lothair Rd. Sth. N4 . . . . .7A 48
Lothbury EC2 . . . . .7E 8 (6D 84)
Lothian Av. UB4: Yead 5K 75
Lothian Cl. HA0: Wemb 3A 60
Lothian Rd. SW9 . . . . .1B 120
Lothrop St. W10 . . . . .3G 81
Lots Rd. SW10 . . . . .7A 100
Lotus Cl. SE21 . . . . .3D 138
Lotus M. N19 . . . . .2J 65
Loubet St. SW17 . . . . .6D 136
Loudoun Av. IG6: Ilf 5F 53
Loudoun Rd. NW8 . . . . .1A 82
Loudwater Cl. TW16: Sun 4J 147
Loudwater Rd. TW16: Sun 4J 147
Loughborough Est. SW9 . . . . .3B 120
Loughborough Ho. RM8: Dag 4A 72
    (off Academy Way)
Loughborough Pk. SW9 . . . . .4B 120
Loughborough Rd. SW9 . . . . .2A 120
Loughborough St. SE11 . .5H 19 (5K 101)
Lough Rd. N7 . . . . .5K 65
Loughton Way IG9: Buck H 1G 37
Louisa Cl. E9 . . . . .1K 85
Louisa Ct. TW2: Twick 2J 131
Louisa Gdns. E1 . . . . .4K 85
Louisa Ho. IG3: Ilf 6A 54
Louisa Oakes Cl. E4 . . . . .4G 35
Louisa St. E1 . . . . .4K 85
Louise Aumonier Wlk. N19 . . . . . . .7J 47
   (off Jessie Blythe La.)
Louise Bennett Cl. SE24 . . . . .4B 120
Louise Cl. E11 . . . . .5K 51
  N22 . . . . .1A 48
Louise De Marillac Ho. E1 . . . . . . .5J 85
     (off Smithy St.)
Louise Rd. E15 . . . . .6G 69
Louise White Ho. N19 . . . . .1H 65
Louis Gdns. BR7: Chst 4D 142
Louis M. N10 . . . . .1F 47
Louisville Rd. SW17 . . . . .3E 136
Lourdes Cl. SE13 . . . . .3F 123
Lousada Lodge N14 . . . . .6B 22
     (off Avenue Rd.)
Louvaine Rd. SW11 . . . . .4B 118
Lovage App. E6 . . . . .5C 88
Lovat Cl. E14 . . . . .6B 86
  NW2 .3B 62
Lovat La. EC3 . . . . .2G 15 (7E 84)
Lovatt Cl. HA8: Edg 6C 28
Lovatt Ct. SW12 . . . . .1F 137
Lovatt Dr. HA4: Ruis 5J 39
Lovat Wlk. TW5: Hest 7C 94
Loveday Rd. W13 . . . . .2B 96
Lovegrove St. SE1 . . . . .5G 103
Lovegrove Wlk. E14 . . . . .1E 104
Lovegrove Way N20 . . . . .2G 31
Lovejoy Ct. SE11 . . . . .6A 102
     (off Pownell Ter.)

Lovekyn Cl.—Lulworth Dr.

Lovekyn Cl. KT2: King T 2E **150**
Lovelace Av. BR2: Broml 6E **160**
Lovelace Gdns. IG11: Bark 4A **72**
KT6: Surb 7D **150**
Lovelace Grn. SE9 3D **124**
Lovelace Ho. W13 7B **78**
Lovelace Rd. EN4: E Barn 7H **21**
KT6: Surb 7C **150**
SE21 2C **138**
Lovelace St. E8 1F **85**
Lovelace Vs. *KT7: T Ditt 7B **150***
(off Portsmouth Rd.)
Loveland Ct. *SE1 7K **15***
(off Jamaica Rd.)
Loveland Mans. *IG11: Bark 7K **71***
(off Upney La.)
Love La. BR1: Broml 3K **159**
CR4: Mitc 3C **154**
(not continuous)
DA5: Bexl 6F **127**
EC2 7D **8** (6C **84**)
HA5: Pinn 2B **40**
IG8: Wfd G 6J **37**
KT6: Surb 2C **162**
N17 7A **34**
SE18 4F **107**
SE25 3H **157**
SM1: Sutt 6H **165**
SM3: Cheam, Sutt 6G **165**
SM4: Mord 7J **153**
Lovel Av. DA16: Well 2A **126**
Lovelinch Cl. SE15 6J **103**
Lovell Ho. *E8 1G **85***
(off Shrubland Rd.)
Lovell Pl. SE16 3A **104**
Lovell Rd. TW10: Ham 3C **132**
UB1: S'hall 6F **77**
Loveridge M. NW6 6H **63**
Loveridge Rd. NW6 6H **63**
Lovers Wlk. N3 7D **30**
NW7 6C **30**
SE10 6F **105**
Lovers' Wlk. W1 4G **11** (1E **100**)
Lovett Dr. SM5: Cars 7A **154**
Lovett's Pl. SW18 4K **117**
Lovett Way NW10 5J **61**
Love Wlk. SE5 2D **120**
Lovibond La. *SE10 7D **104***
(off Norman Rd.)
Lovibonds Av. BR6: Farnb 4F **173**
UB7: Yiew 6B **74**
Lowbrook Rd. IG1: Ilf 4F **71**
Low Cross Wood La. SE21 3F **139**
Lowdell Cl. UB7: Yiew 6A **74**
Lowden Rd. N9 1C **34**
SE24 4B **120**
UB1: S'hall 7C **76**
Lowder Ho. *E1 1H **103***
(off Wapping La.)
Lowe Av. E16 5J **87**
Lowell Ho. *SE5 7C **102***
(off Wyndham Est.)
Lowell St. E14 6A **86**
Lowen Rd. RM13: Rain 2K **91**
Lwr. Addiscombe Rd.
CR0: C'don 1E **168**
Lwr. Addison Gdns. W14 2G **99**
Lwr. Ash Est. TW17: Shep 6H **147**
Lwr. Belgrave St. SW1 2J **17** (3F **101**)
Lwr. Boston Rd. W7 1J **95**
Lwr. Broad St. RM10: Dag 1G **91**
Lower Camden BR7: Chst 7D **142**
Lwr. Church St. CR0: C'don 2B **168**
LOWER CLAPTON 4H **67**
Lwr. Clapton Rd. E5 3H **67**
Lwr. Clarendon Wlk. *W11 6G **81***
(off Clarendon Rd.)
Lwr. Common Sth. SW15 3D **116**
Lwr. Coombe St. CR0: C'don 4C **168**
Lwr. Downs Rd. SW20 1F **153**
Lwr. Drayton Pl. CR0: C'don 2B **168**
LOWER EDMONTON 2B **34**
LOWER FELTHAM 3J **129**
Lower Fosters *NW4 5E **44***
(off New Brent St.)
Lwr. George St. TW9: Rich 5D **114**
Lwr. Gravel Rd. BR2: Broml 1C **172**
Lower Grn. Gdns. KT4: Wor Pk 1C **164**
Lower Grn. W. CR4: Mitc 3C **154**
Lwr. Grosvenor Pl. SW1 1K **17** (3F **101**)
Lower Gro. Rd. TW10: Rich 6F **115**
LOWER HALLIFORD 7F **147**
Lwr. Hall La. E4 5F **35**
(not continuous)
Lwr. Hampton Rd. TW16: Sun 3A **148**
Lwr. Ham Rd. KT2: King T 5D **132**
LOWER HOLLOWAY 5K **65**
Lwr. Hook Bus. Pk. BR6: Downe 7D **172**
Lwr. James St. W1 2B **12** (7G **83**)
Lwr. John St. W1 2B **12** (7G **83**)
Lwr. Kenwood Av. EN2: Enf 5D **22**
Lwr. King's Rd. KT2: King T 1E **150**
Lwr. Lea Crossing E14 7G **87**
E16 7G **87**
Lwr. Maidstone Rd. N11 6B **32**
Lwr. Mall W6 5D **98**
Lwr. Mardyke Av. RM13: Rain 2J **91**
Lwr. Marsh SE1 7J **13** (2A **102**)
Lwr. Marsh La. KT1: King T 4F **151**
Lwr. Merton Ri. NW3 7C **64**
Lower Mill KT17: Ewe 7B **164**
Lwr. Morden La. SM4: Mord 6E **152**
Lwr. Mortlake Rd. TW9: Rich 4E **114**
Lwr. New Change Pas. *EC4 1D **14***
(off One New Change)
Lower Pk. Rd. DA17: Belv 4G **109**
N11 5B **32**
Lwr. Park Trad. Est. NW10 4J **79**
LOWER PLACE 2J **79**
Lower Pl. Bus. Cen. *NW10 2K **79***
(off Steele Rd.)
Lwr. Queen's Rd. IG9: Buck H 2G **37**
Lwr. Richmond Rd. SW14 3G **115**
SW15 3D **116**
TW9: Rich 3G **115**
Lower Rd. DA8: Erith 3H **109**
DA17: Belv 3H **109**
HA2: Harr 1H **59**
SE1 6J **13** (2A **102**)
SE8 4K **103**
SE16 2J **103**
(not continuous)
SM1: Sutt 4A **166**
Lwr. Robert St. *WC2 3F **13***
(off Robert St.)
Lwr. Sand Hills KT6: Surb 7C **150**
Lwr. Sloane St. SW1 4G **17** (4E **100**)
Lower Sq. TW7: Isle 3B **114**
The Lower Sq. *SM1: Sutt 5K **165***
(off St Nicholas Way)
Lwr. Stable St. *N1 1J **83***
(off Stable Street)
Lower Strand NW9 2B **44**
Lwr. Sunbury Rd. TW12: Hamp 2D **148**
LOWER SYDENHAM 4K **139**
Lwr. Sydenham Ind. Est. SE26 5B **140**
Lwr. Teddington Rd.
KT1: Hamp W 1D **150**
Lower Ter. NW3 3A **64**
*SE27 5B **138***
(off Woodcote Pl.)
Lwr. Thames St. EC3 3F **15** (7D **84**)
Lowerwood Ct. *W11 6G **81***
(off Westbourne Pk. Rd.)
Lwr. Wood Rd. KT10: Clay 6B **162**
Lowestoft Cl. *E5 2J **67***
(off Theydon Rd.)
Lowestoft M. E16 2F **107**
Loweswater Cl. HA9: Wemb 2D **60**
Loweswater Ho. E3 4B **86**
Lowfield Rd. NW6 7J **63**
W3 6H **79**
Low Hall Cl. E4 7J **25**
Low Hall La. E17 6A **50**
Low Hall Mnr. Bus. Cen. E17 6A **50**
Lowick Rd. HA1: Harr 4J **41**
Lowlands Gdns. RM7: Rom 6H **55**
Lowlands Rd. HA1: Harr 6J **41**
HA5: Eastc 7A **40**
Lowman Rd. N7 4K **65**
Lownde M. SW16 2J **137**
Lowndes Cl. SW1 2H **17** (3E **100**)
Lowndes Ct. SW1 1F **17** (3D **100**)
*W1 1A **12***
(off Carnaby St.)
Lowndes Lodge *SW1 1F **17***
(off Cadogan Pl.)
Lowndes M. SW16 2J **137**
Lowndes Pl. SW1 2G **17** (3E **100**)
Lowndes Sq. SW1 7F **11** (2D **100**)
Lowndes St. SW1 1F **17** (3E **100**)
Lownds Ct. BR1: Broml 2J **159**
Lowood Ct. *SE19 5F **139***
(off Farquhar Rd.)
Lowood Ho. *E1 7J **85***
(off Bewley St.)
Lowood St. E1 7H **85**
Lowry Cl. DA8: Erith 4K **109**
Lowry Ct. *SE16 5H **103***
(off Stubbs Dr.)
Lowry Cres. CR4: Mitc 2C **154**
Lowry Ho. *E14 2C **104***
(off Cassilis Rd.)
*N17 1F **49***
(off Pembury Rd.)
*W3 3J **97***
(off Palmerston Rd.)
Lowry Rd. RM8: Dag 5B **72**
Lowshoe La. RM5: Col R 1G **55**
Lowswood Cl. HA6: Nwood 1E **38**
Lowther Dr. EN2: Enf 4D **22**
Lowther Hill SE23 7A **122**
Lowther Ho. *SW1 6B **18***
(off Churchill Gdns.)
Lowther Rd. E17 2A **50**
HA7: Stan 3F **43**
KT2: King T 1F **151**
N7 5A **66**
SW13 1B **116**
Lowth Rd. SE5 1C **120**
LOXFORD 5G **71**
Loxford Av. E6 2B **88**
Loxford Gdns. N5 4B **66**
Loxford La. IG1: Ilf 5G **71**
IG3: Ilf 5G **71**
Loxford Rd. IG11: Bark 6F **71**
Loxford Ter. IG11: Bark 6G **71**
Loxham Rd. E4 7J **35**
Loxham St. WC1 2F **7** (3J **83**)
Loxley Cl. SE26 5K **139**
Loxley Ho. HA9: Wemb 3E **60**
Loxley Rd. SW18 1B **136**
TW12: Hamp 4D **130**
Loxton Rd. SE23 1K **139**
Loxwood Cl. TW14: Bedf 1F **129**
Loxwood Rd. N17 3E **48**
LSO St Lukes *3D 8*
(off Old St.)
Lubbock Ho. *E14 7D **86***
(off Poplar High St.)
Lubbock Rd. BR7: Chst 7D **142**
Lubbock St. SE14 7J **103**
Lucan Ho. *N1 1D **84***
(off Colville Est.)
Lucan Pl. SW3 4C **16** (4C **100**)
Lucan Rd. EN5: Barn 3B **20**
Lucas Av. E13 1K **87**
HA2: Harr 2E **58**
Lucas Cl. NW10 7C **62**
Lucas Ct. SE26 5A **140**
SW11 1E **118**
Lucas Gdns. N2 2A **46**
Lucas Ho. *SW10 7K **99***
(off Coleridge Gdns.)
*WC1 2E **6***
(off Tonbridge St.)
Lucas Rd. SE20 6J **139**
Lucas Sq. NW11 6J **45**
Lucas St. SE8 1C **122**
Lucent Ho. *SW18 5J **117***
(off Hardwicks Sq.)
Lucerne Cl. N13 3D **32**
Lucerne Ct. DA18: Erith 3E **108**
Lucerne Gro. E17 4F **51**
Lucerne M. W8 1J **99**
Lucerne Rd. BR6: Orp 1K **173**
CR7: Thor H 5B **156**
N5 4B **66**
Lucey Rd. SE16 3G **103**
Lucey Way SE16 3G **103**
Lucia Hgts. *E20 5E **68***
(off Logan Cl.)
Lucie Av. TW15: Ashf 6D **128**
Lucien Rd. SW17 4E **136**
SW19 2K **135**
Lucinda Ct. E17 2K **49**
EN1: Enf 4K **23**
Lucknow St. SE18 7J **107**
Lucorn Cl. SE12 6H **123**
Luctons Av. IG9: Buck H 1F **37**
Lucy Brown Ho. SE1 5D **14**
Lucy Cres. W3 5J **79**
Lucy Gdns. RM8: Dag 3F **73**
Luddesdon Rd. DA8: Erith 7G **109**
Ludford Cl. CR0: Wadd 3B **168**
Ludgate B'way. EC4 1A **14** (6B **84**)
Ludgate Cir. EC4 1A **14** (6B **84**)
Ludgate Hill EC4 1A **14** (6B **84**)
Ludgate Sq. EC4 1B **14** (6B **84**)
Ludham NW5 5D **64**
Ludham Cl. IG6: Ilf 1G **53**
SE28 6C **90**
Ludlow Cl. BR2: Broml 3J **159**
HA2: Harr 4D **58**
Ludlow Ct. W3 2J **97**
Ludlow Rd. TW13: Felt 4J **129**
W5 4C **78**
Ludlow St. EC1 3C **8** (4C **84**)
Ludlow Way N2 4A **46**
Ludovick Wlk. SW15 4A **116**
Ludwell Ho. *W14 3G **99***
(off Russell Rd.)
Ludwick M. SE14 7A **104**
Luff Ct. *E3 5C **86***
(off Shelmerdine Cl.)
Luffield Rd. SE2 3B **108**
Luffman Rd. SE12 3K **141**
Lugard Ho. *W12 1D **98***
(off Bloemfontein Rd.)
Lugard Rd. SE15 2H **121**
Lugg App. E12 3E **70**
Luke Allsopp Sq. RM10: Dag 3H **73**
Luke Ho. *E1 6H **85***
(off Tillman St.)
Lukes Cl. NW2 2C **62**
Luke St. EC2 3G **9** (4E **84**)
Lukin Cres. E4 3A **36**
Lukin St. E1 6J **85**
Luli Ct. SE14 6B **104**
Lullingstone Cl. BR5: St P 7B **144**
Lullingstone Cres. BR5: St P 7A **144**
Lullingstone Ho. *SE15 6J **103***
(off Lovelinch Cl.)
Lullingstone La. SE13 6F **123**
Lullingstone Rd. DA17: Belv 6F **109**
Lullington Gth. BR1: Broml 7G **141**
N12 5C **30**
Lullington Rd. RM9: Dag 7E **72**
SE20 7G **139**
Lulot Gdns. N19 2F **65**
Lulsgate M. E3 4B **86**
Lulworth *NW1 7H **65***
(off Wrotham Rd.)
*SE17 5D **102***
(off Portland St.)
Lulworth Av. HA9: Wemb 7C **42**
TW5: Hest 1F **113**
Lulworth Cl. HA2: Harr 3D **58**
Lulworth Ct. *N1 7E **66***
(off St Peter's Way)
Lulworth Cres. CR4: Mitc 2C **154**
Lulworth Dr. HA5: Pinn 6B **40**

328 A-Z London

Lulworth Gdns. HA2: Harr 2C 58
Lulworth Ho. SW8 . . . . .7K 101
Lulworth Rd. DA16: Well 2K 125
  SE9 . . . . .2C 142
  SE15 . . . . .2H 121
Lulworth Waye UB4: Yead 6K 75
Lumen Rd. HA9: Wemb 2D 60
Lumiere Apts. SW11 . . . . .4B 118
The Lumiere Bldg. E7 . . . . .5B 70
  (off Romford Rd.)
Lumiere Ct. SW17 . . . . .2E 136
Lumina Bldgs. E14 . . . . .1E 104
  (off Prestons Rd.)
Lumina Bus. Pk. EN1: Enf 5B 24
Lumina Loft Apts. SE1 . . . . .7H 15
  (off Tower Bri. Rd.)
Lumina Way EN1: Enf 5B 24
Luminosity Ct. W13 . . . . .7B 78
Lumley Cl. DA17: Belv 5G 109
Lumley Ct. WC2 . . . . . . .3F 13 (7J 83)
Lumley Flats SW1 . . . . .5G 17
  (off Holbein Pl.)
Lumley Gdns. SM3: Cheam 5G 165
Lumley Rd. SM3: Cheam 5G 165
Lumley St. W1 . . . . . . .1H 11 (6E 82)
Lumsdon NW8 . . . . .1K 81
  (off Abbey Rd.)
Luna Ho. SE16 . . . . .2G 103
Lunan Ho. E3 . . . . .2B 86
  (off Shetland Rd.)
Lunaria Ho. E20 . . . . .5E 68
  (off Elis Way)
Luna Rd. CR7: Thor H 3C 156
Lund Point E15 . . . . .1E 86
Lundy Dr. UB3: Harl 4G 93
Lundy Wlk. N1 . . . . .6C 66
Lunham Rd. SE19 . . . . .6E 138
Luntley Pl. E1 . . . . .6K 9
  (off Chicksand St.)
Lupin Cl. CR0: C'don 1K 169
  RM7: Rush G 2K 73
  SW2 . . . . .2B 138
  UB7: W Dray 1E 174
Lupin Cres. IG1: Ilf 6F 71
Lupin M. E17 . . . . .3E 50
Lupino Ct. SE11 . . . . . . .3H 19 (4K 101)
Lupin Point SE1 . . . . .7K 15
Lupton Cl. SE12 . . . . .3K 141
Lupton St. NW5 . . . . .4G 65
  (not continuous)
Lupus St. SW1 . . . . .6K 17 (5F 101)
Luraida Wharf E14 . . . . .5F 105
Lurgan Av. W6 . . . . .6F 99
Lurline Gdns. SW11 . . . . .1E 118
Luscombe Ct. BR2: Broml 2G 159
Luscombe Way SW8 . . . . .7J 101
Lushington Ho.
  KT12: Walt T 6A 148
Lushington Rd. NW10 . . . . .2D 80
  SE6 . . . . .4D 140
Lushington Ter. E8 . . . . .5G 67
Lutea Ho. SM2: Sutt 7A 166
  (off Walnut M.)
Luther Cl. HA8: Edg 2D 28
Luther King Cl. E17 . . . . .6B 50
Luther M. TW11: Tedd 5K 131
Luther Rd. TW11: Tedd 5K 131
Luton Ho. E13 . . . . .4J 87
  (off Luton Rd.)
Luton Pl. SE10 . . . . .7E 104
Luton Rd. DA14: Sidc 3C 144
  E13 . . . . .4J 87
  E17 . . . . .3B 50
Luton St. NW8 . . . . .4B 4 (4B 82)
Lutton Ter. NW3 . . . . .4A 64
  (off Lakis Cl.)
Luttrell Av. SW15 . . . . .5D 116
Lutwyche M. SE6 . . . . .2B 140
Lutwyche Rd. SE6 . . . . .2B 140
Lutyens Ho. SW1 . . . . .6B 18
  (off Churchill Gdns.)
Lux Apts. SW18 . . . . .5J 117
  (off Broomhill Rd.)

Luxborough Ho. W1 . . . . .5G 5
  (off Luxborough St.)
Luxborough La. IG7: Chig 3H 37
Luxborough St. W1 . . . . . .5G 5 (5E 82)
Luxborough Twr. W1 . . . . .5G 5
  The Lux Bldg.
  RM7: Rush G 6K 55
Luxembourg M. E15 . . . . .5G 69
Luxemburg Gdns. W6 . . . . .4F 99
Luxfield Rd. SE9 . . . . .1C 142
Luxford St. SE16 . . . . .4K 103
Luxmore St. SE4 . . . . .1B 122
Luxor St. SE5 . . . . .3C 120
Lyall Av. SE21 . . . . .4E 138
Lyall M. SW1 . . . . .2G 17 (3E 100)
Lyall M. W. SW1 . . . . . . .2G 17 (3E 100)
Lyall St. SW1 . . . . .2G 17 (3E 100)
Lyal Rd. E3 . . . . .2A 86
Lycett Pl. W12 . . . . .2C 98
Lyceum Theatre 2G 13
Lychgate Cl. N12 . . . . .5G 31
Lychgate Mnr. HA1: Harr 7J 41
Lych Ga. Wlk. UB3: Hayes 7H 75
  (not continuous)
Lyconby Gdns. CR0: C'don 7A 158
Lydd Cl. DA14: Sidc 3J 143
Lydden Ct. SE9 . . . . .6J 125
Lydden Gro. SW18 . . . . .7K 117
Lydden Rd. SW18 . . . . .7K 117
Lydd Rd. DA7: Bex 7F 109
Lydeard Rd. E6 . . . . .7D 70
Lydford NW1 .1G 83
  (off Royal College St.)
Lydford Cl. N16 . . . . .5E 66
  (off Pellerin Rd.)
Lydford Rd. N15 . . . . .5D 48
  NW2 . . . . .6E 62
  W9 . . . . .4H 81
Lydhurst Av. SW2 . . . . .2K 137
Lydia Cl. KT1: King T 3E 150
  (off Grove Cres.)
  N12 . . . . .6F 31
Lydney Cl. SW19 . . . . .2G 135
Lydon Rd. SW4 . . . . .3G 119
Lydstep Rd. BR7: Chst 4E 142
Lyell St. E14 .6G 87
Lyford Rd. SW18 . . . . .7B 118
Lyford St. SE7 . . . . .4C 106
Lygon Ho. E2 .1K 9
  (off Gosset St.)
  SW6 . . . . .1G 117
  (off Fulham Pal. Rd.)
Lygon Pl. SW1 . . . . . . .2J 17 (3F 101)
Lyham Cl. SW2 . . . . .6J 119
Lyham Rd. SW2 . . . . .5J 119
Lyle Cl. CR4: Mitc 7E 154
Lyle Ct. SM4: Mord 6B 154
Lyly Ho. SE1 .3D 102
  (off Burbage Cl.)
Lyme Farm Rd. SE12 . . . . .4J 123
Lyme Gro. E9 . . . . .7J 67
Lyme Gro. Ho. E9 . . . . .7J 67
  (off Lyme Gro.)
Lymer Av. SE19 . . . . .5F 139
Lyme Rd. DA16: Well 1B 126
Lymescote Gdns. SM1: Sutt 2J 165
Lyme St. NW1 . . . . .7G 65
Lyme Ter. NW1 . . . . .7G 65
Lyminge Cl. DA14: Sidc 4K 143
Lyminge Gdns. SW18 . . . . .1C 136
Lymington Av. N22 . . . . .2A 48
Lymington Cl. E6 . . . . .5D 88
  SW16 . . . . .2H 155
Lymington Ct. SM1: Sutt 3K 165
Lymington Dr. HA4: Ruis 2F 57
Lymington Lodge E14 . . . . .3F 105
  (off Schooner Cl.)
Lymington Rd. NW6 . . . . .6K 63
  RM8: Dag 1D 72
Lyminster Cl. UB4: Yead 5C 76
Lympne N17 .2D 48
  (off Gloucester Rd.)

Lympstone Gdns. SE15 . . . . .7G 103
Lynbridge Gdns. N13 . . . . .4G 33
Lynbrook Cl.
  RM13: Rain 2K 91
Lynbrook Gro. SE15 . . . . .7E 102
Lynch Cl. SE3 . . . . .2H 123
Lynch Wlk. SE8 . . . . .6B 104
  (off Prince St.)
Lyncott Cres. SW4 . . . . .4F 119
Lyncourt SE3 . . . . .2F 123
Lyncroft Av. HA5: Pinn 5C 40
Lyncroft Gdns. NW6 . . . . .5J 63
  TW3: Houn 5G 113
  W13 . . . . .2C 96
Lyncroft Mans. NW6 . . . . .5J 63
Lyndale KT7: T Ditt 7J 149
  NW2 . . . . .4H 63
Lyndale Av. NW2 . . . . .3H 63
Lyndale Cl. SE3 . . . . .6H 105
Lyndale Rd. Ind. Est. SE2 . . . . .3C 108
Lynde Ho. KT12: Walt T 6A 148
  SW4 . . . . .3H 119
Lynden Ho. E1 . . . . .3K 85
  (off Westfield Way)
Lynden Hyrst CR0: C'don 2F 169
Lyndhurst Av. HA5: Pinn 1K 39
  KT5: Surb 1H 163
  N12 . . . . .6J 31
  NW7 . . . . .6F 29
  SW16 . . . . .2H 155
  TW2: Whitt 1D 130
  TW16: Sun 3J 147
  UB1: S'hall 1F 95
Lyndhurst Cl. BR6: Farnb 4F 173
  CR0: C'don 3F 169
  DA7: Bex 3H 127
  NW10 . . . . .3K 61
Lyndhurst Ct. E18 . . . . .1J 51
  NW8 . . . . .1B 82
  (off Finchley Rd.)
  SM2: Sutt 7J 165
  (off Grange Rd.)
Lyndhurst Dr. E10 . . . . .7E 50
  KT3: N Mald 7A 152
  HA5: Pinn 1K 39
  IG2: Ilf 6H 53
  IG11: Bark 6J 71
  N3 . . . . .1G 45
  NW3 . . . . .5B 64
Lyndhurst Gro. SE15 . . . . .2E 120
Lyndhurst Lodge E14 . . . . .4F 105
  (off Millennium Dr.)
Lyndhurst Ri. IG7: Chig 4K 37
Lyndhurst Rd. CR7: Thor H 4A 156
  DA7: Bex 3H 127
  E4 . . . . .7K 35
  N18 . . . . .4B 34
  N22 . . . . .6F 33
  NW3 . . . . .5B 64
  UB6: G'frd 4F 77
Lyndhurst Sq. SE15 . . . . .1F 121
Lyndhurst Ter. NW3 . . . . .5B 64
Lyndhurst Way SE15 . . . . .1F 121
  SM2: Sutt 7J 165
Lyndon Av. DA15: Sidc 5K 125
  SM6: W'gton 3E 166
Lyndon Ho. E18 . . . . .1J 51
  (off Queen Mary Av.)
Lyndon Rd. DA17: Belv 4G 109
Lyndon Yd. SW17 . . . . .4A 136
Lyne Cres. E17 . . . . .1B 50
Lynegrove Av. TW15: Ashf 5E 128
Lyneham Dr. NW9 . . . . .1A 44
Lyneham Wlk. E5 . . . . .5A 68
  HA5: Eastc 3H 39
Lynette Av. SW4 . . . . .6F 119
Lynford Cl. HA8: Edg 1J 43
  NW4 . . . . .4E 68
Lynford Ct. CR0: C'don 4E 168
  (off Coombe Rd.)
Lynford French Ho. SE17 . . . . .5C 102
  (off Thrush St.)

Lynford Gdns. HA8: Edg 3C 28
  IG3: Ilf 2K 71
  SE13 . . . . .1A 34
Lynford Ter. N9 . . . . .1A 34
Lynhurst Cres. UB10: Hil 7F 56
Lynhurst Rd. UB10: Hil 7E 56
Lynmere Rd. DA16: Well 2B 126
Lyn M. E3 . . . . .3B 86
Lyn Rd. N16 . . . . .4E 66
Lynmouth Av. EN1: Enf 6A 24
  SM4: Mord 6F 153
Lynmouth Av. Gdns. 1F 165
Lynmouth Dr. HA4: Ruis 2K 57
Lynmouth Gdns.
  TW5: Hest 7B 94
  UB6: G'frd 1B 78
Lynmouth Rd. E17 . . . . .6A 50
  N2 . . . . .3D 46
  N16 . . . . .1F 67
  UB6: G'frd 1B 78
Lynn Cl. HA3: Hrw W 2H 41
  TW15: Ashf 5F 129
Lynne Cl. BR6: Chels 6K 173
  SE23 . . . . .7B 122
Lynne Ct. CR2: S Croy 4E 168
  (off Birdhurst Rd.)
  NW6 . . . . .7K 63
  (off Priory Rd.)
Lynnett Ct. E9 . . . . .6A 68
  (off Annis Rd.)
Lynnett Rd. RM8: Dag 2D 72
Lynne Way UB5: N'olt 2B 76
Lynn Ho. SE15 . . . . .6H 103
  (off Friary Est.)
Lynn M. E11 . . . . .2G 69
Lynn Rd. E11 .2G 69
  IG2: Ilf 7H 53
  SW12 . . . . .7F 119
Lynn St. EN2: Enf 1J 23
Lynscott Way CR2: S Croy 7B 168
Lynstead Cl. BR3: Beck 2A 158
Lynsted Cl. BR1: Broml 2A 160
  DA6: Bex 5H 127
Lynsted Gdns. SE9 . . . . .4B 124
Lynton Av. N12 . . . . .4G 31
  NW9 . . . . .4B 44
  RM7: Mawney 1G 55
  W13 . . . . .6A 78
Lynton Cl. KT9: Chess 4E 162
  NW10 . . . . .5A 62
  TW7: Isle 4K 113
Lynton Cres. IG2: Ilf 6F 53
Lynton Est. SE1 . . . . .4G 103
Lynton Gdns. EN1: Enf 7K 23
  N11 . . . . .6C 32
Lynton Grange N2 . . . . .3D 46
Lynton Ho. IG1: Ilf 2G 71
  (off High Rd.)
  W2 . . . . .6A 82
  (off Hallfield Est.)
Lynton Mans. SE1 . . . . .1J 19
  (off Westminster Bri. Rd.)
Lynton Mead N20 . . . . .3D 30
Lynton Rd. CR0: C'don 6A 156
  E4 . . . . .5J 35
  HA2: Harr 2C 58
  KT3: N Mald 5K 151
  N8 . . . . .5H 47
  (not continuous)
  NW6 . . . . .2H 81
  SE1 . . . . .4F 103
  W3 . . . . .7G 79
Lynton Ter. W3 . . . . .6J 79
Lynton Wlk. UB4: Hayes 3G 75
Lynwood Cl. E18 . . . . .1A 52
  HA2: Harr 3C 58
Lynwood Ct. KT1: King T 2H 151
Lynwood Dr.
  HA6: Nwood 1H 39
  KT4: Wor Pk 2C 164
Lynwood Gdns. CR0: Wadd 4K 167
  UB1: S'hall 6D 76
Lynwood Gro. BR6: Orp 7J 161
  N21 . . . . .1F 33

Lynwood Rd. KT7: T Ditt 2A **162**
SW17 . . . . .3D **136**
W5 . . . . .3D **78**
Lynx Way E16 . . . . .7B **88**
Lyon Bus. Pk. IG11: Bark 2J **89**
Lyon Ct. HA4: Ruis 1H **57**
Lyon Ho. NW8 . . . . .4C **4**
(off Broadley St.)
Lyon Ind. Est. NW2 . . . . .2D **62**
Lyon Meade HA7: Stan 1C **42**
Lyon Pk. Av. HA0: Wemb 6E **60**
(not continuous)
Lyon Rd. HA1: Harr 6K **41**
SW19 . . . . .1A **154**
LYONSDOWN 5F **21**
Lyonsdown Av.
EN5: New Bar 6F **21**
Lyonsdown Rd.
EN5: New Bar 6F **21**
Lyons Pl. HA7: Stan 3D **26**
NW8 . . . . .4A **4** (4B **82**)
Lyon St. N1 . . . . .7K **65**
Lyons Wlk. W14 . . . . .4G **99**
Lyon Way UB6: G'frd 1J **77**
Lyoth Rd. BR5: Farnb 2G **173**
Lyric Ct. E8 . . . . .7F **67**
(off Holly St.)
Lyric Dr. UB6: G'frd 4F **77**
Lyric M. SE26 . . . . .4J **139**
Lyric Rd. SW13 . . . . .1B **116**
Lyric Sq. W6 . . . . .4E **98**
(off King St.)
Lyric Theatre
Hammersmith 4E **98**
Westminster 2C **12**
(off Shaftesbury Av.)
Lysander NW9 . . . . .1B **44**
Lysander Gdns. KT6: Surb 6F **151**
Lysander Gro. N19 . . . . .1H **65**
Lysander Ho. E2 . . . . .2H **85**
(off Temple St.)
Lysander M. N19 . . . . .1G **65**
Lysander Rd. CR0: Wadd 6K **167**
HA4: Ruis 2F **57**
Lysander Way BR6: Farnb 3G **173**
Lysia Ct. SW6 . . . . .7F **99**
(off Lysia St.)
Lysias Rd. SW12 . . . . .6F **119**
Lysia St. SW6 . . . . .7F **99**
Lysons Wlk. SW15 . . . . .4C **116**
Lytchet Rd. BR1: Broml 7J **141**
Lytchet Way EN3: Enf H 1D **24**
Lytchgate Cl.
CR2: S Croy 7E **168**
Lytcott Dr. KT8: W Mole 3D **148**
Lytcott Gro. SE22 . . . . .5E **120**
Lytham Cl. SE28 . . . . .6E **90**
Lytham Gro. W5 . . . . .3F **79**
Lytham St. SE17 . . . . .5D **102**
Lyttelton Cl. NW3 . . . . .7C **64**
Lyttelton Ct. N2 . . . . .5A **46**
Lyttelton Ho. E9 . . . . .7J **67**
(off Well St.)
Lyttelton Rd. E10 . . . . .3D **68**
N2 . . . . .5A **46**
Lyttelton Theatre 4H **13**
(within National Theatre)
Lyttleton Ct. UB4: Yead 4A **76**
(off Dunedin Way)
Lyttleton Rd. N8 . . . . .3A **48**
Lytton Av. EN3: Enf L 1F **25**
N13 . . . . .2F **33**
Lytton Cl. N2 . . . . .6B **46**
UB5: N'olt 7D **58**
Lytton Ct. WC1 . . . . .6F **7**
(off Barter St.)
Lytton Gdns. SM6: Bedd 4H **167**
Lytton Gro. SW15 . . . . .5F **117**
Lytton Rd. E11 . . . . .7G **51**
EN5: New Bar 4F **21**
HA5: Pinn 1C **40**
Lytton Strachey Path SE28 . . . . .7B **90**
Lytton Ter. E12 . . . . .6D **70**

Lyveden Rd. SE3 . . . . .7K **105**
SW17 . . . . .6D **136**

M

Mabbett Ho. SE18 . . . . .6E **106**
(off Nightingale Pl.)
Mabel Evetts Ct. UB3: Hayes 7K **75**
Maberley Cres. SE19 . . . . .7G **139**
Maberley Rd. BR3: Beck 3K **157**
SE19 . . . . .1F **157**
Mabledon Pl. WC1 . . . . .2D **6** (3H **83**)
Mablethorpe Rd. SW6 . . . . .7G **99**
Mabley St. E9 . . . . .5A **68**
Mablin Lodge IG9: Buck H 1F **37**
McAdam Dr. EN2: Enf 2G **23**
McAllister Gro. IG11: Bark 3A **90**
Macaret Cl. N20 . . . . .7E **20**
Macarthur Cl. DA8: Erith 5K **109**
E7 . . . . .6J **69**
HA9: Wemb 6H **61**
Macarthur Ter. SE7 . . . . .6B **106**
Macartney Ho. SE10 . . . . .7F **105**
(off Chesterfield Wlk.)
SW9 . . . . .1A **120**
(off Gosling Way)
Macaulay Ct. SW4 . . . . .3F **119**
Macaulay Rd. E6 . . . . .2B **88**
SW4 . . . . .3F **119**
Macaulay Sq. SW4 . . . . .4F **119**
Macaulay Wlk. SW9 . . . . .1K **119**
(off Lett Rd.)
Macaulay Way SE28 . . . . .1B **108**
McAuley Cl. SE1 . . . . .1J **19** (3A **102**)
SE9 . . . . .5F **125**
Macaulay Ho. W10 . . . . .5G **81**
(off Portobello Rd.)
Macauley M. SE13 . . . . .2E **122**
McAusland Ho. E3 . . . . .2B **86**
(off Wright's Rd.)
Macbean St. SE18 . . . . .3F **107**
Macbeth Ho. N1 . . . . .2E **84**
Macbeth St. W6 . . . . .5D **98**
McBride Ho. E3 . . . . .2B **86**
(off Libra Rd.)
McCabe Ct. E16 . . . . .5H **87**
(off Barking Rd.)
McCall Cl. SW4 . . . . .2J **119**
McCall Cres. SE7 . . . . .5C **106**
McCall Ho. N7 . . . . .4J **65**
McCarthy Rd. TW13: Hanw 5B **130**
Macclesfield Apts. N1 . . . . .1D **84**
(off Branch Pl.)
Macclesfield Ho. EC1 . . . . .2C **8**
(off Central St.)
Macclesfield Rd. EC1 . . .1C **8** (3C **84**)
SE25 . . . . .5J **157**
Macclesfield St. W1 . . . .2D **12** (7H **83**)
McCoid Way SE1 . . . . .7C **14** (2C **102**)
McCrone M. NW3 . . . . .6B **64**
McCullum Rd. E3 . . . . .1B **86**
McDermott Cl. SW11 . . . . .3C **118**
McDermott Rd. SE15 . . . . .3G **121**
Macdonald Av.
RM10: Dag 3H **73**
Macdonald Ho. SW11 . . . . .2E **118**
(off Dagnall St.)
McDonald Ho. NW6 . . . . .3J **81**
(off Malvern Rd.)
Macdonald Rd. E7 . . . . .4J **69**
E17 . . . . .2E **50**
(not continuous)
N11 . . . . .5J **31**
N19 . . . . .2G **65**
McDonough Cl. KT9: Chess 4E **162**
McDougall Ct. TW9: Rich 2G **115**
McDowall Cl. E16 . . . . .5H **87**
McDowall Rd. SE5 . . . . .1C **120**
Macduff Rd. SW11 . . . . .1E **118**
Mace Cl. E1 . . . . .1H **103**
Mace Ho. TW7: Isle 1B **114**
McEntee Av. E17 . . . . .1A **50**

Mace St. E2 . . . . .2K **85**
McEwan Ho. E3 . . . . .2B **86**
(off Roman Rd.)
McEwen Way E15 . . . . .1F **87**
(off Rokeby St.)
Macey Ho. SW11 . . . . .1C **118**
Macey St. SE10 . . . . .6E **104**
(off Thames St.)
McFadden Ct. E10 . . . . .3D **68**
(off Buckingham Rd.)
Macfarland Gro. SE15 . . . . .7E **102**
Macfarlane La. TW7: Isle 6K **95**
Macfarlane Rd. W12 . . . . .1E **98**
Macfarren Pl. NW1 . . . . .4H **5** (4E **82**)
Macfarron Ho. W10 . . . . .3G **81**
(off Parry Rd.)
McGlashon Ho. E1 . . . . .4K **9**
(off Hunton St.)
McGrath Rd. E15 . . . . .5H **69**
McGregor Ct. N1 . . . . .1H **9**
Macgregor Rd. E16 . . . . .5A **88**
McGregor Rd. W11 . . . . .6H **81**
Machell Rd. SE15 . . . . .3J **121**
McIndoe Ct. N1 . . . . .1D **84**
(off Sherborne St.)
McIntosh Cl. RM1: Rom 3K **55**
SM6: W'gton 7J **167**
Macintosh Ho. W1 . . . . .5H **5**
(off Beaumont St.)
McIntosh Ho. SE16 . . . . .4J **103**
(off Millender Wlk.)
McIntosh Rd. RM1: Rom 3K **55**
McIntyre Ct. SE18 . . . . .4C **106**
(off Prospect Va.)
Mackay Ho. W12 . . . . .7D **80**
(off White City Est.)
Mackay Rd. SW4 . . . . .3F **119**
McKay Rd. SW20 . . . . .7D **134**
McKeever Ho. E16 . . . . .5J **87**
(off Hammersley Rd.)
McKellar Cl. WD23: B Hea 2B **26**
McKenna Ho. E3 . . . . .2B **86**
(off Wright's Rd.)
Mackennal St. NW8 . . . . .2C **82**
Mackenzie Cl. W12 . . . . .7D **80**
Mackenzie Ho. N8 . . . . .4J **47**
(off Pembroke Rd.)
NW2 . . . . .3C **62**
Mackenzie Rd. BR3: Beck 2J **157**
N7 . . . . .6K **65**
Mackenzie Wlk. E14 . . . . .1C **104**
McKerrell Rd. SE15 . . . . .1G **121**
Mackeson Rd. NW3 . . . . .4D **64**
Mackie Ho. SW2 . . . . .7A **120**
McKillop Way DA14: Sidc 7C **144**
Mackintosh La. E9 . . . . .5K **67**
Mackintosh St.
BR2: Broml 6B **160**
Macklin St. WC2 . . . . . .7F **7** (6J **83**)
Mackonochie Ho. EC1 . . . . .5J **7**
(off Baldwins Gdns.)
Mackrow Wlk. E14 . . . . .7E **86**
Mack's Rd. SE16 . . . . .4G **103**
Mackworth Ho. NW1 . . . . .1A **6**
(off Augustus St.)
Mackworth St. NW1 . . . .1A **6** (3G **83**)
McLaren Ho. SE1 . . . . .7A **14**
(off St Georges Cir.)
Maclaren M. SW15 . . . . .4E **116**
Maclean Rd. SE23 . . . . .6A **122**
Macleod Ct. SE22 . . . . .1G **139**
Macleod Rd. N21 . . . . .5D **22**
McLeod Rd. SE2 . . . . .4B **108**
McLeod's M. SW7 . . . . .4K **99**
McLeod St. SE17 . . . . .5C **102**
Maclise Ho. SW1 . . . . .4E **18**
(off Marsham St.)
Maclise Rd. W14 . . . . .3G **99**
Macmillan Cl. HA2: Harr 1E **58**
UB6: G'frd 4H **77**
Macmillan Ho. NW8 . . . . .2D **4**
(off Lorne Cl.)

McMillan Ho. SE4 . . . . .3A **122**
(off Arica Rd.)
SE14 . . . . .1A **122**
McMillan St. SE8 . . . . .6C **104**
McMillan Student Village
SE8 . . . . .6C **104**
Macmillan Way SW17 . . . . .4F **137**
McNair Rd. UB2: S'hall 3F **95**
Macnamara Ho. SW10 . . . . .7B **100**
(off Worlds End Est.)
McNeil Rd. SE5 . . . . .2E **120**
McNicol Dr. NW10 . . . . .2J **79**
Macoma Rd. SE18 . . . . .6H **107**
Macoma Ter. SE18 . . . . .6H **107**
Maconochies Rd. E14 . . . . .5D **104**
Macquarie Way E14 . . . . .4D **104**
McRae La. CR4: Mitc 7D **154**
Macready Ho. W1 . . . . .6E **4**
(off Crawford St.)
Macready Pl. N7 . . . . .4J **65**
(not continuous)
Mcready Rd. N20 . . . . .2G **31**
Macrea Ho. E3 . . . . .3B **86**
(off Bow Rd.)
Macroom Ho. W9 . . . . .3H **81**
(off Macroom Rd.)
Macroom Rd. W9 . . . . .3H **81**
Macs Ho. E17 . . . . .3D **50**
Mac's Pl. EC4 . . . . .7J **7**
Madame Tussaud's 4G **5** (4E **82**)
Mada Rd. BR6: Farnb 3F **173**
Maddams St. E3 . . . . .4D **86**
Madderfields Ct. N11 . . . . .1H **47**
Maddison Cl. N2 . . . . .2A **46**
TW11: Tedd 6K **131**
Maddison Ct. E16 . . . . .5J **87**
(off Hastings Rd.)
Maddocks Cl. DA14: Sidc 5E **144**
Maddocks Ho. E1 . . . . .7H **85**
(off Cornwall St.)
Maddock Way SE17 . . . . .6B **102**
Maddox St. W1 . . . . . . .2K **11** (7F **83**)
Madeira Av. BR1: Broml 7G **141**
Madeira Gro. IG8: Wfd G 6F **37**
Madeira Rd. CR4: Mitc 4D **154**
E11 . . . . .1F **69**
N13 . . . . .4G **33**
SW16 . . . . .5J **137**
Madeira St. E14 . . . . .5D **86**
Madeira Twr. SW11 . . . . .7H **101**
Madeleine Cl.
RM6: Chad H 6C **54**
Madeleine Ct. HA7: Stan 7K **27**
(off Letchworth Rd.)
Madeley Rd. W5 . . . . .6D **78**
Madeline Gro. IG1: Ilf 5H **71**
Madeline Rd. SE20 . . . . .7G **139**
Madge Gill Way E6 . . . . .1C **88**
(off High St. Nth.)
Madinah Rd. E8 . . . . .6G **67**
The Madison SE1 . . . . .6E **14**
(off Long La.)
Madison Bldg. SE10 . . . . .1D **122**
(off Blackheath Rd.)
Madison Cl. SM2: Sutt 7B **166**
Madison Ct. RM10: Dag 6H **73**
Madison Cres. DA7: Bex 7C **108**
Madison Gdns. BR2: Broml 3H **159**
DA7: Bex 7C **108**
Madison Ho. E14 . . . . .7B **86**
(off Victory Pl.)
Madison Way E20 . . . . .5D **68**
Madoc Cl. NW2 . . . . .2J **63**
Madras Pl. N7 . . . . .6A **66**
Madras Rd. IG1: Ilf 4F **71**
Madrid Rd. SW13 . . . . .1C **116**
Madrigal La. SE5 . . . . .7B **102**
Madron St. SE17 . . . . .5E **102**
Mafeking Av. E6 . . . . .2C **88**
IG2: Ilf .7H **53**
TW8: Bford 6E **96**

Mafeking Rd. E16 . . . . .4H 87
EN1: Enf 3A 24
N17 . . . . .1K 69
Magazine Ga. W2 . . . . .4D 10 (1C 100)
Magdala Av. N19 . . . . .2G 65
Magdala Rd. CR2: S Croy 7D 168
TW7: Isle 3A 114
Magdalene Cl. SE15 . . . . .2H 121
Magdalene Gdns. E6 . . . . .4E 88
N20 . . . . .1J 31
Magdalene Rd. TW17: Shep 4B 146
Magdalene Ho. E16 . . . . .1K 105
(off Keats Av.)
Magdalen M. NW3 . . . . .6A 64
(off Frognal)
Magdalen Pas. E1 . . . . .2K 15 (7F 85)
Magdalen Rd. SW18 . . . . .1A 136
Magdalen St.
SE1 . . . . .5G 15 (1E 102)
Magee St. SE11 . . . . . .7J 19 (6A 102)
Magellan Blvd. E16 . . . . .7G 89
Magellan Ct. NW10 . . . . .7K 61
(off Brentfield Rd.)
Magellan Ho. E1 . . . . .4K 85
(off Ernest St.)
Magellan Pl. E14 . . . . .4C 104
Magic Circle .3B 6
(off Stephenson Way)
Magistrates' Court
Barkingside 3G 53
Belmarsh 2J 107
Bexley 4G 127
Bromley 1H 159
City of London 1E 14
Croydon 3D 168
Ealing .1A 96
(off Green Man La.)
Hendon 6B 44
Highbury Corner 6A 66
Lavender Hill 3D 118
Stratford 7F 69
Thames 3C 86
Westminster 5D 4 (5C 82)
Willesden 6B 62
Wimbledon 6J 135
Magna Sq. SW14 . . . . .3J 115
(off Moore Cl.)
Magnaville Rd. WD23: B Hea 1D 26
Magnet Rd. HA9: Wemb 2D 60
Magnin Cl. E8 . . . . .1G 85
Magnolia Cl. E10 . . . . .2C 68
KT2: King T 6H 133
Magnolia Ct. HA3: Kenton 7J 165
SM2: Sutt 7J 165
(off Grange Rd.)
SM6: W'gton 5F 167
TW9: Kew 1H 115
TW13: Felt 1J 129
(off Plum Cl.)
UB5: N'olt 4C 76
UB10: Hil 6D 56
Magnolia Gdns. E10 . . . . .2C 68
HA8: Edg 4D 28
Magnolia Ho. SE8 . . . . .6B 104
(off Evelyn Rd.)
TW16: Sun 7H 129
Magnolia Lodge E4 . . . . .3J 35
W8 . . . . .3K 99
(off St Mary's Ga.)
Magnolia Pl. HA2: Harr 2H 41
SW4 .5J 119
W5 . . . . .5D 78
Magnolia Rd. W4 . . . . .6H 97
Magnolia St. UB7: W Dray 4A 92
Magnolia Way KT19: Ewe 5J 163
Magnolia Wharf W4 . . . . .6G 97
Magpie All. EC4 . . . . . . .1K 13 (6A 84)
Magpie Cl. E7 . . . . .5H 69
EN1: Enf 1B 24
Magpie Cl. SW9 . . . . .3A 44
Magpie Hall Cl. BR2: Broml 6C 160
Magpie Hall La. BR2: Broml 5D 160
Magpie Hall Rd. WD23: B Hea 2D 26

Magpie Ho. E3 . . . . .1B 86
(off Sycamore Av.)
Magpie Pl. SE14 . . . . .6A 104
Magri Wlk. E1 . . . . .5J 85
Maguire Apts. E3 . . . . .5B 86
(off Geoff Cade Way)
Maguire Dr. TW10: Ham 4C 132
Maguire St. SE1 . . . . . .6K 15 (2F 103)
Maha Bldg. E3 . . . . .3C 86
(off Merchant St.)
Mahatma Gandhi Ind. Est. SE24 . .4B 120
Mahlon Av. HA4: Ruis 5K 57
(not continuous)
Mahogany Cl. SE16 . . . . .1A 104
Mahon Cl. EN1: Enf 1A 24
Mahoney Ho. SE14 . . . . .1B 122
(off Heald St.)
Maibeth Gdns. BR3: Beck 4A 158
Maida Av. E4 . . . . .7J 25
W2 . . . . .4A 4 (5A 82)
MAIDA HILL 4H 81
Maida Rd. DA17: Belv 3G 109
MAIDA VALE 4K 81
Maida Va. W9 . . . . .3A 4 (2K 81)
Maida Way E4 . . . . .7J 25
Maiden Erlegh Av. DA5: Bexl 1E 144
Maiden La. NW1 . . . . .7H 65
SE1 . . . . .5D 14 (1C 102)
WC2 . . . . .3F 13 (7J 83)
Maiden Pl. NW5 . . . . .3G 65
Maiden Rd. E15 . . . . .7G 69
Maidenstone Hill SE10 . . . . .1E 122
Maids of Honour Row
TW9: Rich 5D 114
Maidstone Av. RM5: Col R 2J 55
Maidstone Bldgs. M.
SE1 . . . . .5D 14 (1C 102)
Maidstone Ho. E14 . . . . .6D 86
(off Carmen St.)
Maidstone Rd.
DA14: Sidc, Swan 6D 144
N11 . . . . .6B 32
Mailcoach Yd. E2 . . . . . .1H 9 (3E 84)
Main Av. EN1: Enf 5A 24
Main Dr. HA9: Wemb 3D 60
Main Mill SE10 . . . . .7D 104
(off Greenwich High St.)
Mainridge Rd. BR7: Chst 4E 142
Main Rd. DA14: Sidc 3H 143
Main St. TW13: Hanw 5B 130
Mainwaring Ct. CR4: Mitc 2E 154
Mais Ho. SE26 . . . . .2H 139
Maismore St. SE15 . . . . .6G 103
The Maisonettes SM1: Sutt 5H 165
Maison Ho. N20 . . . . .1F 31
Maitland Cl. SE10 . . . . .7D 104
TW4: Houn 3D 112
Maitland Ct. W2 . . . . .2A 10
(off Lancaster Ter.)
Maitland Ho. E2 . . . . .2J 85
(off Waterloo Gdns.)
SW1 . . . . .7A 18
(off Churchill Gdns.)
Maitland Pk. Est. NW3 . . . . .6D 64
Maitland Pk. Rd. NW3 . . . . .6D 64
Maitland Pk. Vs. NW3 . . . . .6D 64
Maitland Pl. E5 . . . . .4H 67
Maitland Rd. E15 . . . . .6H 69
SE26 .6K 139
Maitland Yd. W13 . . . . .1A 96
Maize Row E14 . . . . .7B 86
Majendie Rd. SE18 . . . . .5H 107
Majestic Way CR4: Mitc 2D 154
Major Cl. SW9 . . . . .3B 120
Major Draper St. SE18 . . . . .3F 107
Major Rd. E15 . . . . .5F 69
SE16 .3G 103
Makepeace Av. N6 . . . . .2E 64
Makepeace Mans. N6 . . . . .2E 64
Makepeace Rd. E11 . . . . .4J 51
UB5: N'olt 2C 76
Makers' Yd. E20 . . . . .6C 68
Makinen Ho. IG9: Buck H 1F 37

Makins St. SW3 . . . . . .4D 16 (4C 100)
Malabar Ct. W12 . . . . .7D 80
(off India Way)
Malabar St. E14 . . . . .2C 104
Malam Ct. SE11 . . . . . .4J 19 (4A 102)
Malam Gdns. E14 . . . . .7D 86
Malbrook Rd. SW15 . . . . .4D 116
Malcolm Cl. SE20 . . . . .7J 139
Malcolm Ct. E7 . . . . .6H 69
HA7: Stan 5H 27
NW4 . . . . .6C 44
Malcolm Cres. NW4 . . . . .6C 44
Malcolm Dr. KT6: Surb 1E 162
Malcolm Ho. N1 . . . . .2E 84
(off Arden Est.)
Malcolm Pl. E2 . . . . .4J 85
Malcolm Rd. E1 . . . . .4J 85
SE20 .7J 139
SE25 .6G 157
SW19 . . . . .6G 135
UB10: Ick 4B 56
Malcolm Sargent Ho. E16 . . . . .1K 105
(off Evelyn Rd.)
Malcolmson Ho. SW1 . . . . .6C 18
(off Aylesford St.)
Malcolms Way N14 . . . . .5B 22
Malcolm Way E11 . . . . .5J 51
Malden Av. SE25 . . . . .4H 157
UB6: G'frd 5J 59
Malden Cl. KT3: N Mald 3D 152
N4 . . . . .6C 48
Malden Cres. NW1 . . . . .6E 64
MALDEN GREEN 1C 164
Malden Golf Course 2A 152
Malden Grn. Av. KT4: Wor Pk 1B 164
Malden Grn. M. KT4: Wor Pk 1C 164
Malden Hill KT3: N Mald 3B 152
Malden Hill Gdns.
KT3: N Mald 3B 152
MALDEN JUNC. 5B 152
Malden Pk. KT3: N Mald 6B 152
Malden Pl. NW5 . . . . .5E 64
Malden Rd. KT3: N Mald 5A 152
KT4: Wor Pk 6B 152
NW5 . . . . .5D 64
SM3: Cheam 4F 165
Malden Way KT3: N Mald 6K 151
Maldon & District Society
of Model Engineers 1A 162
Maldon Cl. E15 . . . . .5G 69
N1 . . . . .1C 84
SE5 . . . . .3E 120
Maldon Ct. E6 . . . . .1E 88
SM6: W'gton 5G 167
Maldon Rd. N9 . . . . .3A 34
RM7: Rush G 7J 55
SM6: W'gton 5F 167
W3 . . . . .7J 79
Maldon Wlk. IG8: Wfd G 6F 37
Malet Pl. WC1 . . . . . . .4C 6 (4H 83)
Malet St. WC1 . . . . . . .4C 6 (4H 83)
Maley Av. SE27 . . . . .2B 138
Malford Ct. E18 . . . . .2J 51
Malford Gro. E18 . . . . .4H 51
Malfort Rd. SE5 . . . . .3E 120
Malham Cl. N11 . . . . .6K 31
Malham Rd. SE23 . . . . .1K 139
Malham Rd. Ind. Est. SE23 . . . . . .1K 139
Malham Ter. N18 . . . . .5C 34
Malibu Cl. SE26 . . . . .3H 139
The Mall BR1: Broml 3J 159
CR0: C'don 2C 168
DA6: Bex 4G 127
E15 . . . . .7F 69
HA3: Kenton 6F 43
KT6: Surb 5D 150
N14 . . . . .3D 32
RM10: Dag 6G 73
SW1 . . . . .6B 12 (2G 101)
SW14 .5J 115
TW8: Bford 6D 96
W5 . . . . .7E 78
Mallams M. SW9 . . . . .3B 120

Mallard Cl. E9 . . . . .6B 68
EN5: New Bar 6G 21
NW6 . . . . .2J 81
TW2: Whitt 7E 112
W7 . . . . .2J 95
Mallard Ct. E17 . . . . .3F 51
Mallard Ho. NW8 . . . . .2C 82
(off Bridgeman St.)
SW6 . . . . .1A 118
(off Station Ct.)
Mallard Path SE28 . . . . .3H 107
Mallard Pl. N22 . . . . .2K 47
TW1: Twick 3A 132
Mallard Point E3 . . . . .3D 86
(off Rainhill Way)
Mallards E11 . . . . .7J 51
(off Blake Hall Rd.)
Mallards Rd. IG8: Wfd G 7E 36
IG11: Bark 4A 90
Mallard Wlk. BR3: Beck 5K 157
DA14: Sidc 6C 144
Mallard Way NW9 . . . . .7J 43
SM6: W'gton 7G 167
Mall Chambers W8 . . . . .1J 99
(off Kensington Mall)
Mallet Dr. UB5: N'olt 5D 58
Mallet Rd. SE13 . . . . .6F 123
Mall Galleries 4D 12
Malling SE13 . . . . .5D 122
Malling Cl. CR0: C'don 6J 157
Malling Gdns. SM4: Mord 6A 154
Malling Way BR2: Hayes 7H 159
Mallinson Rd. CR0: Bedd 3H 167
SW11 . . . . .5C 118
Mallinson Sports Cen. 7D 46
Mallon Gdns. E1 . . . . .7K 9
(off Commercial St.)
Mallord St. SW3 . . . . . .7B 16 (6B 100)
Mallory Bldgs. EC1 . . . . .4A 8
(off St John St.)
Mallory Cl. E14 . . . . .5D 86
SE4 . . . . .4A 122
Mallory Ct. N17 . . . . .6A 34
(off Cannon Rd.)
SE12 .7K 123
Mallory Gdns. EN4: E Barn 7K 21
Mallory St. NW8 . . . . . . .3D 4 (4C 82)
Mallory Way SE3 . . . . .4K 123
Mallow Cl. CR0: C'don 1K 169
Mallow Mead NW7 . . . . .7B 30
The Mallows UB10: Ick 3D 56
Mallow St. EC1 . . . . . . .3E 8 (4D 84)
Mall Rd. W6 .5D 98
Mall Vs. W6 .5D 98
(off Mall Rd.)
Malmains Cl. BR3: Beck 4F 159
Malmains Way BR3: Beck 4E 158
Malmesbury E2 . . . . .2J 85
(off Cyprus St.)
Malmesbury Cl. HA5: Eastc 4H 39
Malmesbury Rd. E3 . . . . .3B 86
E16 . . . . .5G 87
E18 . . . . .1H 51
SM4: Mord 7A 154
Malmesbury Ter. E16 . . . . .5H 87
Malmo Twr. SE8 . . . . .4A 104
Malmsey Ho. SE11 . . . . .5H 19 (5K 101)
Malmsmead Ho. E9 . . . . .5B 68
(off Homerton Rd.)
Malory Cl. BR3: Beck 2A 158
Malpas Dr. HA5: Pinn 5B 40
Malpas Rd. E8 . . . . .5H 67
RM9: Dag 6D 72
SE4 . . . . .2B 122
Malswick Cl. SE15 . . . . .7E 102
(off Tower Mill Rd.)
Malta Rd. E10 . . . . .1C 68
Malta St. EC1 . . . . .3A 8 (4B 84)
Maltby Cl. BR6: Orp 1K 173
Maltby Dr. EN1: Enf 1C 24
Maltby Ho. SE1 . . . . .7J 15
(off Maltby St.)
SE3 . . . . .4A 124

Maltby Rd. KT9: Chess 6G 163
Maltby St. SE1 . . . .7J 15 (2F 103)
Malt Ho. E17 . . . .5B 50
(off Old Brewery Way)
Malthouse Ct. TW8: Bford 6E 96
(off High St.)
Malthouse Dr. TW13: Hanw . . .5B 130
W4 . . . .6B 98
Malthouse Pas. SW13 . . . .2B 116
(off Clevelands Gdns.)
Malthouse Rd. SW11 . . . .7H 101
Malthus Path SE28 . . . .1C 108
Malting Ho. E14 . . . .7B 86
(off Oak La.)
The Maltings BR6: Orp 1K 173
W4 . . . .5G 97
(off Spring Gro.)
Maltings Cl. E3 . . . .3E 86
SW13 . . . .2B 116
Maltings Lodge W4 . . . .6A 98
(off Corney Reach Way)
Maltings M. DA15: Sidc 3A 144
Maltings Pl. SE1 . . . .7H 15
SW6 . . . .1K 117
Malting Way TW7: Isle 3K 113
Malton M. SE18 . . . .6J 107
W10 . . . .6G 81
Malton Rd. W10 . . . .6G 81
Malton St. SE18 . . . .6J 107
Maltravers St. WC2 . . .2H 13 (7K 83)
Malt St. SE1 . . . .6G 103
Malva Cl. SW18 . . . .5K 117
Malvern Av. DA7: Bex 7E 108
E4 . . . .7A 36
HA2: Harr 3C 58
Malvern Cl. CR4: Mitc 3G 155
KT6: Surb 1E 162
SE20 . . . .2G 157
UB10: Ick 2C 56
W10 . . . .5H 81
Malvern Cl. SM2: Sutt 7J 165
SW7 . . . .3B 16
W12 . . . .2C 98
(off Hadyn Pk. Rd.)
Malvern Dr. IG3: Bark, Ilf 4K 71
IG8: Wfd G 5F 37
TW13: Hanw 5B 130
Malvern Gdns. HA3: Kenton . . .4E 42
NW2 . . . .2G 63
Malvern Ho. N16 . . . .1F 67
SE17 . . . .5D 102
(off Liverpool Gro.)
Malvern M. NW6 . . . .3J 81
Malvern Pl. NW6 . . . .3H 81
Malvern Rd. CR7: Thor H 4A 156
E6 . . . .1C 88
E8 . . . .7G 67
E11 . . . .2G 69
KT6: Surb 2E 162
N8 . . . .3K 47
N17 . . . .3G 49
NW6 . . . .2H 81
(not continuous)
TW12: Hamp 7E 130
UB3: Harl 7G 93
Malvern Ter. N1 . . . .1A 84
N9 . . . .1A 34
Malvern Way W13 . . . .5B 78
Malwood Rd. SW12 . . . .6F 119
The Malyons TW17: Shep 6F 147
Malyons Rd. SE13 . . . .6D 122
Malyons Ter. SE13 . . . .5D 122
Managers St. E14 . . . .1E 104
Manaton Cl. SE15 . . . .3H 121
Manaton Cres.
UB1: S'hall 6E 76
Manbey Gro. E15 . . . .6G 69
Manbey M. E15 . . . .6G 69
Manbey Pk. Rd. E15 . . . .6G 69
Manbey Rd. E15 . . . .6G 69
Manbey St. E15 . . . .6G 69
Manbre Rd. W6 . . . .6E 98

Manbrough Av. E6 . . . .3D 88
Manby Wlk. E17 . . . .5A 50
Manchester Ct. E16 . . . .6K 87
(off Garvary Rd.)
Manchester Dr. W10 . . . .4G 81
Manchester Gro. E14 . . . .5E 104
Manchester Ho. SE17 . . . .5C 102
(off East Cl.)
Manchester M. W1 . . . .6G 5
Manchester Rd. CR7: Thor H . . .3C 156
E14 . . . .5E 104
N15 . . . .6D 48
Manchester Sq. W1 . . .7G 5 (6E 82)
Manchester St. W1 . . .5G 5 (5E 82)
Manchester Way RM10: Dag 4H 73
Manchuria Rd. SW11 . . . .6E 118
Manciple St. SE1 . . . .7E 14 (2D 102)
Mancroft Ct. NW8 . . . .1B 82
(off St John's Wood Pk.)
Mandalay Rd. SW4 . . . .5G 119
Mandara Pl. SE8 . . . .4A 104
(off Yeoman St.)
Mandarin Ct. NW10 . . . .6K 61
(off Mitchellbrook Way)
SE8 . . . .6B 104
Mandarin St. E14 . . . .7C 86
Mandarin Way UB4: Yead 6B 76
Mandarin Wharf N1 . . . .1E 84
(off De Beauvoir Cres.)
Mandela Cl. NW10 . . . .7J 61
W12 . . . .7D 80
Mandela Ho. E2 . . . .2J 9
(off Virginia Rd.)
SE5 . . . .2B 120
Mandela Rd. E16 . . . .6J 87
Mandela St. NW1 . . . .1G 83
SW9 . . . .7A 102
(not continuous)
Mandela Way SE1 . . . .4E 102
Mandeley M. E11 . . . .1H 69
Mandel Ho. SW18 . . . .4J 117
Manderley W14 . . . .3H 99
(off Oakwood La.)
Mandeville Cl. SE3 . . . .7H 105
SW20 . . . .7G 135
Mandeville Ct. E4 . . . .5F 35
Mandeville Dr. KT6: Surb 1D 162
Mandeville Ho. SE1 . . . .5F 103
(off Rolls Rd.)
SW4 . . . .5G 119
Mandeville M. SW4 . . . .4J 119
Mandeville Pl. W1 . . .7H 5 (6E 82)
Mandeville Rd. N14 . . . .2A 32
TW7: Isle 2A 114
TW17: Shep 5C 146
UB5: N'olt 7E 58
Mandeville St. E5 . . . .3A 68
Mandrake Rd. SW17 . . . .3D 136
Mandrake Way E15 . . . .7G 69
Mandrell Rd. SW2 . . . .5J 119
Manesty Ct. N14 . . . .7C 22
(off Ivy Rd.)
Manet Gdns. W3 . . . .7A 80
Manette St. W1 . . .1D 12 (6H 83)
Manfred Rd. SW15 . . . .5H 117
Manger Rd. N7 . . . .6J 65
Mangold Way DA18: Erith . . .3D 108
Manhattan Bldg. E3 . . . .2C 86
Manhattan Bus. Pk. W5 . . . .3E 78
Manhattan Loft Gdns. E20 . . . .6E 68
Manilla Ct. RM6: Chad H . . .6B 54
(off Quarles Pk. Rd.)
Manilla St. E14 . . . .2C 104
Manilla Wlk. SE10 . . . .4G 105
Manister Rd. SE2 . . . .3A 108
Manitoba Ct. SE16 . . . .2J 103
(off Canada Est.)
Manitoba Gdns. BR6: Chels . .6K 173
Manley Ct. N16 . . . .3F 67
Manley Ho. SE11 . . .5J 19 (5A 102)
Manley St. NW1 . . . .1E 82
Manna Ho. E20 . . . .6E 68
(off Glade Wlk.)

Mannan Ho. E3 . . . .2B 86
(off Roman Rd.)
Mann Cl. CR0: C'don 3C 168
Manneby Prior N1 . . . .1H 7
(off Cumming St.)
Mannequin Ho. E17 . . . .3K 49
Manning Ct. SE28 . . . .1B 108
(off Titmuss Av.)
Manning Gdns. CR0: C'don . . .7H 157
HA3: Kenton 7D 42
Manning Ho. W11 . . . .6G 81
(off Westbourne Pk. Rd.)
Manning Pl. TW10: Rich 6F 115
Manning Rd. E17 . . . .5A 50
RM10: Dag 6G 73
Manningford Cl. EC1 . . .1A 8 (3B 84)
Manningtree Cl. SW19 . . . .1G 135
Manningtree Rd. HA4: Ruis . . .4K 57
Manningtree St. E1 . . . .6G 85
Mannin Rd. RM6: Chad H 7B 54
Mannock Cl. NW9 . . . .3K 43
Mannock M. E18 . . . .1A 52
Mannock Rd. N22 . . . .3B 48
Mann's Cl. TW7: Isle 5K 113
Manns Rd. HA8: Edg 6B 28
Manns Ter. SE27 . . . .3C 138
Manny Shinwell Ho. SW6 . . . .6H 99
(off Clem Attlee Ct.)
Manoel Rd. TW2: Twick 2G 131
The Manor IG8: Wfd G 7K 37
Manor Av. SE4 . . . .2B 122
TW4: Houn 3B 112
UB5: N'olt 7D 58
Manorbrook SE3 . . . .4J 123
MANOR CIRCUS 3G 115
Manor Cl. DA1: Cray 4K 127
E17 . . . .1A 50
EN5: Barn 4B 20
HA4: Ruis 1K 57
KT4: Wor Pk 1A 164
NW7 . . . .5E 28
NW9 . . . .5H 43
RM10: Dag 6K 73
Manor Cotts. HA6: Nwood 1H 39
N2 . . . .2A 46
(off Manor Cotts. App.)
Manor Cotts. App. N2 . . . .2A 46
Manor Ct. BR4: W W'ck . . .1D 170
DA7: Bex 4H 127
E4 . . . .1B 36
E10 . . . .1D 68
HA1: Harr 6K 41
HA9: Wemb 5E 60
IG11: Bark 7K 71
KT2: King T 1G 151
KT8: W Mole 4E 148
N2 . . . .5D 46
N14 . . . .2C 32
N20 . . . .3J 31
(off York Way)
SM5: Cars 3E 166
SW2 . . . .5K 119
SW3 . . . .6D 16
(off Hemus Pl.)
SW6 . . . .1K 117
SW16 . . . .3J 137
TW2: Twick 2G 131
W3 . . . .4G 97
Manor Ct. Rd. W7 . . . .7J 77
Manor Cres. KT5: Surb 6G 151
Manor Dene SE28 . . . .6C 90
Manordene Cl. KT7: T Ditt . . .1A 162
Manordene Rd. SE28 . . . .6C 90
Manor Dr. HA9: Wemb 4F 61
KT5: Surb 6F 151
KT10: Hin W 2A 162
KT19: Ewe 6A 164
N14 . . . .1A 32
N20 . . . .4J 31
NW7 . . . .5E 28
TW13: Hanw 5B 130
TW16: Sun 2J 147

The Manor Dr. KT4: Wor Pk . . .1A 164
Manor Dr. Nth. KT3: N Mald . . .7K 151
KT4: Wor Pk 1A 164
Manor Est. SE16 . . . .4H 103
Manor Farm 7G 39
Mnr. Farm Av. TW17: Shep . . .6D 146
Mnr. Farm Cl. KT4: Wor Pk . . .1A 164
Mnr. Farm Ct. E6 . . . .3D 88
Mnr. Farm Dr. E4 . . . .3B 36
Mnr. Farm Rd. HA0: Wemb 2D 78
SW16 . . . .2A 156
Manorfield Cl. N19 . . . .4G 65
(off Fulbrook M.)
Manor Flds. SW15 . . . .6F 117
Manorfields Cl. BR7: Chst 3K 161
Manor Gdns. CR2: S Croy 6F 169
HA4: Ruis 3J 65
N7 . . . .3J 65
SW4 . . . .2G 119
(off Larkhall Ri.)
SW20 . . . .2H 153
TW9: Rich 4F 115
TW12: Hamp 7F 131
TW16: Sun 1J 147
W3 . . . .4G 97
W4 . . . .5A 98
Manor Ga. UB5: N'olt 7C 58
Manor Gro. BR3: Beck 2D 158
SE15 . . . .6J 103
TW9: Rich 4G 115
Mnr. Hall Av. NW4 . . . .2F 45
Mnr. Hall Dr. NW4 . . . .2F 45
Manorhall Gdns. E10 . . . .1C 68
MANOR HOUSE 7D 48
MANOR HOUSE 7C 48
Manor Ho. NW1 . . . .4A 4
(off Lisson Gro.)
UB2: S'hall 3C 94
Manor Ho. Ct. TW17: Shep . . .7D 146
W9 . . . .4A 82
(off Warrington Gdns.)
Manor Ho. Dr. HA6: Nwood . . .1D 38
NW6 . . . .7F 63
Manor Ho. Est. HA7: Stan . . .6G 27
Manor Ho. Gdn. E11 . . . .6K 51
Manor Ho. Way TW7: Isle 3B 114
Manor La. SE12 . . . .5G 123
SE13 . . . .5G 123
SM1: Sutt 5A 166
TW13: Felt 2J 129
TW16: Sun 2J 147
UB3: Harl 6F 93
Manor La. Ter. SE13 . . . .4G 123
Manor Lodge NW6 . . . .7F 63
(off Willesden La.)
Manor M. NW6 . . . .2J 81
(off Cambridge Av.)
SE4 . . . .2B 122
Mnr. Mt. SE23 . . . .1J 139
Manor Pde. HA1: Harr 6K 41
N16 . . . .2F 67
NW10 . . . .2B 80
(off High St. Harlesden)
MANOR PARK 4B 70
Manor Pk. BR7: Chst 2H 161
SE13 . . . .5F 123
TW9: Rich 4F 115
TW13: Felt 2J 129
Manor Pk. Cl. BR4: W W'ck . .1D 170
Manor Pk. Crematorium 4A 70
Manor Pk. Cres. HA8: Edg 6B 28
Manor Pk. Dr. HA2: Harr 3F 41
Manor Pk. Gdns. HA8: Edg . . .5B 28
Manor Pk. Pde. SE13 . . . .4F 123
(off Lee High Rd.)
Manor Pk. Rd. BR4: W W'ck . . .1D 170
BR7: Chst 1G 161
E12 . . . .4B 70
(not continuous)
N2 . . . .3A 46
NW10 . . . .1B 80
SM1: Sutt 5A 166

Manor Pl. BR1: Broml 1C **160**
 BR7: Chst 2H **161**
 CR4: Mitc 3G **155**
 KT12: Walt T 7H **147**
  (not continuous)
 SE17 . . . . .5B **102**
 SM1: Sutt 4K **165**
 TW14: Felt 1J **129**
Manor Rd. BR3: Beck 2D **158**
 BR4: W W'ck 2D **170**
 CR4: Mitc 4G **155**
 DA1: Cray 4K **127**
 DA5: Bexl 1H **145**
 DA15: Sidc 3K **143**
 E10 .7C **50**
 E15 .2G **87**
 E16 .2G **87**
 E17 .2A **50**
 EN2: Enf 2H **23**
 EN5: Barn 4B **20**
 HA1: Harr 6A **42**
 HA4: Ruis 1F **57**
 IG7: Chig 6J **37**
 IG8: Wfd G 6J **37**
 IG11: Bark 6K **71**
 KT8: E Mos 4H **149**
 KT12: Walt T 7H **147**
 N16 .2D **66**
 N17 .1G **49**
 N22 .6D **32**
 RM6: Chad H 6D **54**
 RM10: Dag 6J **73**
 SE25 . . . . .4G **157**
 SM2: Cheam 7H **165**
 SM6: W'gton 4F **167**
 SW20 . . . . .2H **153**
 TW2: Twick 2G **131**
 TW9: Rich 4G **115**
 TW11: Tedd 5A **132**
  (not continuous)
 TW15: Ashf 5B **128**
 UB3: Hayes 6J **75**
 W13 .7A **78**
Manor Rd. Ho. HA1: Harr 6A **42**
Manor Rd. Nth. KT7: T Ditt 3A **162**
 KT10: Hin W, T Ditt
  . . . . .3A **162**, 3A **162**
 SM6: W'gton 4F **167**
Manorside EN5: Barn 4B **20**
Manorside Cl. SE2 . . . . .4C **108**
Manor Sq. RM8: Dag 2C **72**
Manor Vw. TW8: Bford 5C **96**
Manor Vw. N3 . . . . .2K **45**
Mnr. Way BR2: Broml 6C **160**
 BR3: Beck 2C **158**
 BR5: Pet W 4G **161**
 CR2: S Croy 6E **168**
 CR4: Mitc 3G **155**
 DA5: Bexl 1G **145**
 DA7: Bex 3K **127**
 E4 . . . . .4A **36**
 HA2: Harr 4F **41**
 HA4: Ruis 7G **39**
 KT4: Wor Pk 1A **164**
 NW9 . . . . .4A **44**
 RM13: Rain 4K **91**
 SE3 .4H **123**
 SE23 . . . . .7J **121**
 UB2: S'hall 4B **94**
Manorway EN1: Enf 7K **23**
 IG8: Wfd G 5F **37**
The Manor Way SM6: W'gton 4F **167**
Manor Way Bus. Cen.
 RM13: Rain 5K **91**
Manor Waye UB8: Uxb 1A **74**
Manpreet Ct. E12 . . . . .5D **70**
Manresa Rd. SW3 . . . . . .6C **16** (5C **100**)
Mansard Beeches SW17 . . . . .5E **136**
Mansard Cl. HA5: Pinn 3B **40**
Mansbridge Ho. SW8 . . . . .1F **119**
  (off Patcham Ter.)
Manse Cl. UB3: Harl 6F **93**
Mansel Gro. E17 . . . . .1C **50**

Mansell Rd. UB6: G'frd 5F **77**
 W3 . . . . .2K **97**
Mansell St. E1 . . . . . . .1K **15** (6F **85**)
Mansel Rd. SW19 . . . . .6G **135**
Manser Ct. RM13: Rain 3K **91**
Mansergh Cl. SE18 . . . . .7C **106**
Manse Rd. N16 . . . . .3F **67**
Manser Rd. RM13: Rain 3K **91**
Mansfield Av.
 EN4: E Barn 6J **21**
 HA4: Ruis 1K **57**
 N15 .4D **48**
Mansfield Cl. N9 . . . . .6B **24**
Mansfield Ct. E2 . . . . .1F **85**
  (off Whiston Rd.)
 SE15 . . . . .7F **103**
  (off Sumner Rd.)
Mansfield Dr. UB4: Hayes 4G **75**
Mansfield Hgts. N2 . . . . .5C **46**
Mansfield Hill E4 . . . . .7J **25**
Mansfield Ho. N1 . . . . .1E **84**
  (off Halcomb St.)
Mansfield M. W1 . . . . .6J **5** (5F **83**)
Mansfield Pl. CR2: S Croy 6D **168**
 NW3 . . . . .4A **64**
Mansfield Rd. CR2: S Croy 6D **168**
 E11 .6K **51**
 E17 .4B **50**
 IG1: Ilf 2E **70**
 KT9: Chess 5C **162**
 NW3 . . . . .5D **64**
 W3 . . . . .4H **79**
Mansfield St. W1 . . . . .6J **5** (5F **83**)
Mansford St. E2 . . . . .2G **85**
Manship Rd. CR4: Mitc 7E **136**
Mansion Cl. SW9 . . . . .1A **120**
  (not continuous)
Mansion Gdns. NW3 . . . . .3K **63**
Mansion House
 London 1E **14** (6D **84**)
Mansion Ho. Dr. HA7: Stan 2D **26**
Mansion Ho. Pl. EC4 . . .1E **14** (6D **84**)
Mansion Ho. St. EC4 . . . . .1E **14**
Mansion Lock Ho. NW1 . . . . .7F **65**
  (off Hawley Cres.)
The Mansions SW5 . . . . .5K **99**
  (Earl's Ct. Rd.)
 SW5 . . . . .5K **99**
  (off Old Brompton Rd.)
Mansion Vw. E15 . . . . .1F **87**
  (off High St.)
Manson Ho. N1 . . . . .7A **66**
  (off Drummond Way)
Manson M. SW7 . . . . .4A **16** (4B **100**)
Manson Pl. SW7 . . . . .4A **16** (4B **100**)
Mansted Gdns. RM6: Chad H 7C **54**
Manston N17 . . . . .2D **48**
  (off Adams Rd.)
 NW1 .7G **65**
  (off Agar Gro.)
Manston Av. UB2: S'hall 4E **94**
Manston Cl. SE20 . . . . .1J **157**
Manston Ct. E20 . . . . .1B **50**
Manstone Rd. NW2 . . . . .5G **63**
Manston Gro. KT2: King T 5D **132**
Manston Ho. W14 . . . . .3G **99**
  (off Russell Rd.)
Manthorpe Rd. SE18 . . . . .5G **107**
Mantilla Rd. SW17 . . . . .4E **136**
Mantle Cl. SW18 . . . . .6K **117**
  (off Mapleton Rd.)
Mantle Rd. SE4 . . . . .3A **122**
Mantlet Cl. SW16 . . . . .7G **137**
Mantle Way E15 . . . . .7G **69**
Manton Av. W7 . . . . .2K **95**
Manton Cl. UB3: Hayes 7G **75**
Manton Rd. EN3: Enf L 1H **25**
 SE2 .4A **108**
Manton Way EN3: Enf L 1J **25**
Mantua St. SW11 . . . . .3B **118**
Mantus Cl. E1 . . . . .4J **85**
Mantus Rd. E1 . . . . .4J **85**
Manuka Cl. W7 . . . . .1A **96**

Manuka Hgts. E20 . . . . .5E **68**
  (off Napa Cl.)
Manus Way N20 . . . . .2F **31**
Manville Gdns. SW17 . . . . .3F **137**
Manville Rd. SW17 . . . . .2E **136**
Manwell La. IG11: Bark 4A **90**
Manwood Rd. SE4 . . . . .5B **122**
Manwood St. E16 . . . . .1D **106**
Manygate La. TW17: Shep 7E **146**
Manygate Pk. TW17: Shep 6F **147**
  (off Mitre Cl.)
Manygates SW12 . . . . .2F **137**
Mapesbury Ct. NW2 . . . . .5G **63**
Mapesbury M. NW4 . . . . .6C **44**
Mapesbury Rd. NW2 . . . . .7G **63**
Mapeshill Pl. NW2 . . . . .6E **62**
Mapes Ho. NW6 . . . . .7G **63**
Mape St. E2 . . . . .4H **85**
  (not continuous)
Maple Av. E4 . . . . .5G **35**
 HA2: Harr 2F **59**
 UB7: Yiew 7A **74**
 W3 . . . . .1A **98**
Maple Cl. BR5: Pet W 5H **161**
 CR4: Mitc 1F **155**
 HA4: Ruis 6K **39**
 IG9: Buck H 3G **37**
 N3 . . . . .6D **30**
 N16 .6G **49**
 SW4 . . . . .6H **119**
 TW12: Hamp 6D **130**
 UB4: Yead 3B **76**
Maple Ct. CR0: C'don 4C **168**
  (off Lwr. Coombe St.)
 CR0: C'don 3J **157**
  (off The Waldrons)
 E3 . . . . .2C **86**
  (off Four Seasons Cl.)
 E6 . . . . .5E **88**
 KT3: N Mald 3K **151**
 SE6 .1D **140**
 TW15: Ashf 7F **129**
Maple Cres. DA15: Sidc 6A **126**
Maplecroft Cl. E6 . . . . .6B **88**
Mapledale Av. CR0: C'don 2G **169**
Mapledene BR7: Chst 6G **143**
Mapledene Est. E8 . . . . .7G **67**
Mapledene Rd. E8 . . . . .7F **67**
Maple Gdns. HA8: Edg 7F **29**
 TW19: Stanw 2A **128**
Maple Gro. NW9 . . . . .7J **43**
 TW8: Bford 7B **96**
 UB1: S'hall 5D **76**
 W5 . . . . .3D **96**
Maple Gro. Bus. Cen.
 TW4: Houn 4A **112**
Maple Ho. E17 . . . . .3D **50**
 HA9: Wemb 4G **61**
  (off Empire Way)
 KT1: King T 5E **150**
  (off Maple Rd.)
 N19 .3G **65**
 SE8 .7B **104**
  (off Idonia St.)
 TW9: Kew 1H **115**
Maplehurst BR2: Broml 2G **159**
Maplehurst Cl. KT1: King T 4E **150**
Maple Ind. Est. TW13: Felt 3J **129**
Maple Leaf Dr. DA15: Sidc 1K **143**
Mapleleafe Gdns. IG6: Ilf 3F **53**
Maple Leaf Sq. SE16 . . . . .2K **103**
Maple Lodge W8 . . . . .3K **99**
  (off Abbots Wlk.)
Maple M. NW6 . . . . .2K **81**
 SE16 . . . . .2K **103**
 SW16 . . . . .5K **137**
Maple Pl. N17 . . . . .7B **34**
 UB7: Yiew 1A **92**
 W1 . . . . .5B **6** (4G **83**)
Maple Rd. E11 . . . . .6G **51**
 KT6: Surb 6D **150**
 SE20 . . . . .1H **157**
 UB4: Yead 3A **76**

The Maples KT1: Hamp W 7C **132**
 KT10: Clay 7A **162**
Maples Pl. E1 . . . . .5H **85**
Maplestead Rd. RM9: Dag 1B **90**
 SW2 .7K **119**
Maple St. E2 . . . . .2H **85**
 RM7: Rom 4J **55**
 W1 . . . . .5A **6** (5G **83**)
Maplethorpe Rd. CR7: Thor H 4A **156**
Mapleton Cl. BR2: Broml 6J **159**
Mapleton Cres. EN3: Enf W 1D **24**
 SW18 . . . . .6K **117**
Mapleton Rd. E4 . . . . .3K **35**
 EN1: Enf 2C **24**
 SW18 . . . . .6J **117**
  (not continuous)
Maple Tree Pl. SE3 . . . . .1C **124**
Maple Wlk. W10 . . . . .3F **81**
Maple Way SE13 . . . . .2A **104**
 TW13: Felt 3J **129**
Maplewood Apts. N4 . . . . .7C **48**
  (off Katherine Cl.)
Maplewood Ct. TW15: Ashf 4A **128**
Maplin Cl. N21 . . . . .6E **22**
Maplin Ho. SE2 . . . . .2D **108**
  (off Wolvercote Rd.)
Maplin Rd. E16 . . . . .6J **87**
Maplin St. E3 . . . . .3B **86**
Mapperley Cl. E11 . . . . .6H **51**
Mapperley Dr. IG8: Wfd G 7B **36**
Marabou Cl. E12 . . . . .5C **70**
Mara Ho. E20 . . . . .5D **68**
  (off Victory Pde.)
Maran Way DA18: Erith 2D **108**
Maraschino Apartment
 CR0: C'don 1D **168**
  (off Cherry Orchard Rd.)
Marathon Ho. NW1 . . . . .5E **4**
  (off Marylebone Rd.)
Marathon Way SE28 . . . . .2K **107**
Marbaix Gdns. TW7: Isle 1H **113**
Marban Rd. W9 . . . . .3H **81**
Marble Arch 2F **11**
MARBLE ARCH 7D **82**
Marble Arch W1 . . . . .2E **10** (7D **82**)
Marble Arch Apts. W1 . . . . .7E **4**
  (off Harrowby St.)
Marble Cl. W3 . . . . .1H **97**
Marble Dr. NW2 . . . . .1F **63**
Marble Hill Cl. TW1: Twick 7B **114**
Marble Hill Gdns. TW1: Twick 7B **114**
Marble Hill House 7C **114**
Marble Ho. SE18 . . . . .5K **107**
 W9 . . . . .4H **81**
Marble Quay E1 . . . . .4K **15** (1G **103**)
Marbles Ho. SE5 . . . . .6C **102**
  (off Grosvenor Ter.)
Marbrook Ct. SE12 . . . . .3A **142**
Marcella Rd. SW9 . . . . .2A **120**
Marcellina Way BR6: Orp 3J **173**
March NW9 . . . . .1B **44**
  (off Long Mead)
Marchant Cl. NW7 . . . . .6F **29**
Marchant Ho. N1 . . . . .1E **84**
  (off Halcomb St.)
Marchant Rd. E11 . . . . .2F **69**
Marchant St. SE14 . . . . .6A **104**
Marchbank Rd. W14 . . . . .6H **99**
March Ct. SW15 . . . . .4D **116**
Marchmont Gdns. TW10: Rich 5F **115**
Marchmont Rd.
 SM6: W'gton 7G **167**
 TW10: Rich 5F **115**
Marchmont St. WC1 . . . . .3E **6** (4J **83**)
March Rd. TW1: Twick 7A **114**
Marchside Cl. TW5: Hest 1B **112**
Marchwood Cl. SE5 . . . . .7E **102**
Marchwood Cres. W5 . . . . .6C **78**
Marcia Cl. SE1 . . . . .4E **102**
  (off Marcia Rd.)
Marcia Rd. SE1 . . . . .4E **102**
Marcilly Rd. SW18 . . . . .5B **118**
Marco Dr. HA5: Hat E 1D **40**

Marcon Ct. *E8* 5H *67*
   (off Amhurst Rd.)
Marconi Pl. N11 . . . . .4A **32**
Marconi Rd. E10 . . . . .1C **68**
Marconi Way UB1: S'hall 6F **77**
Marcon Pl. E8 . . . . .6H **67**
Marco Rd. W6 . . . . .3E **98**
Marcourt Lawns W5 . . . . .4E **78**
Marcus Ct. E15 . . . . .1G **87**
Marcus Garvey M. SE22 . . . . .6H **121**
Marcus Garvey Way SE24 . . . . . . .4A **120**
Marcus St. E15 . . . . .1H **87**
   SW18 . . . . .6K **117**
Marcus Ter. SW18 . . . . .6K **117**
Mardale Ct. NW7 . . . . .7H **29**
Mardale Dr. NW9 . . . . .5K **43**
Mardell Rd. CR0: C'don 5K **157**
Marden Av. BR2: Hayes 6J **159**
Marden Cres. CR0: C'don 6K **155**
   DA5: Bexl 5J **127**
Marden Ho. E8 . . . . .5H **67**
Marden Rd. CR0: C'don 6K **155**
   N17 . . . . .2E **48**
Marden Sq. SE16 . . . . .3H **103**
Marder Rd. W13 . . . . .2A **96**
Mardyke Cl. RM13: Rain 2J **91**
Mardyke Ho. *SE17* 4D *102*
   (off Mason St.)
Marechal Niel Av. DA15: Sidc 3H **143**
Marechal Niel Pde. *DA14: Sidc* . . .3H *143*
   (off Main Rd.)
Maresby Ho. E4 . . . . .2J **35**
Maresfield CR0: C'don 3E **168**
Maresfield Gdns. NW3 . . . . .5A **64**
Mare St. E8 .5H **67**
Marfleet Cl. SM5: Cars 2C **166**
Margaret Av. E4 . . . . .6J **25**
Margaret Bondfield Av.
   IG11: Bark 7A **72**
Margaret Bondfield Ho. *E3* 2A *86*
   (off Driffield Rd.)
Margaret Ct. EN4: E Barn 4G **21**
   W1 . . . . .7A **6**
Margaret Gardner Dr. SE9 . . . . . . .2D **142**
Margaret Herbison Ho. *SW6* 6H *99*
   (off Clem Attlee Ct.)
Margaret Ho. *W6* 5E *98*
   (off Queen Caroline St.)
Margaret Ingram Cl. SW6 . . . . . . .6H **99**
Margaret Lockwood Cl.
   KT1: King T 4F **151**
Margaret McMillan Ho. E16 . . . . . .6A **88**
Margaret Rd. DA5: Bexl 6D **126**
   E11 . . . . .6G **51**
   EN4: E Barn 4G **21**
   N16 . . . . .1F **67**
Margaret Rutherford Pl. SW12 . . .1G **137**
Margarets Ct. HA8: Edg 5C **28**
Margaret St. W1 . . . . .7K 5 (6F **83**)
Margaretta Ter. SW3 . . . .7C 16 (6C **100**)
Margaretting Rd. E12 . . . . .1A **70**
Margaret Way IG4: Ilf 6C **52**
Margaret White Ho. *NW1* 1D *6*
   (off Chalton St.)
Margate Rd. SW2 . . . . .5J **119**
Margerie Ct. *E2* 2H *85*
   (off Esker Pl.)
Margery Fry Ct. N7 . . . . .3J **65**
Margery Pk. Rd. E7 . . . . .6J **69**
Margery Rd. RM8: Dag 3D **72**
Margery St. WC1 . . . . .2J 7 (3A **84**)
Margery Ter. E7 . . . . .6J *69*
   (off Margery Pk. Rd.)
Margin Dr. SW19 . . . . .5F **135**
Margravine Gdns. W6 . . . . .5F **99**
Margravine Rd. W6 . . . . .5F **99**
Marham Dr. NW9 . . . . .1A **44**
Marham Gdns. SM4: Mord 6A **154**
   SW18 . . . . .1C **136**
Mar Ho. NW9 . . . . .3K **43**
Maria St. SE1 . . . . .4H **103**
Maria Ct. SE25 . . . . .2E **156**
Marian Cl. UB4: Yead 4B **76**

Marian Ct. E9 . . . . .5J **67**
   SM1: Sutt 5K **165**
Marian Gdns. BR1: Broml 7A **142**
Marianne Cl. SE5 . . . . .1E **120**
Marianne North Gallery 2F **115**
Marian Pl. E2 . . . . .2H **85**
Marian Rd. SW16 . . . . .1G **155**
Marian St. E2 . . . . .2H **85**
Marian Way NW10 . . . . .7B **62**
Maria Ter. E1 . . . . .5K **85**
Maria Theresa Cl. KT3: N Mald . . .5K **151**
Maribor *SE10* 7E *104*
   (off Burney St.)
Maricas Av. HA3: Hrw W 1H **41**
Marie Curie SE5 . . . . .1F **121**
Marie Lloyd Gdns. N19 . . . . .7J **47**
Marie Lloyd Ho. *N1* 1E *8*
   (off Murray Gro.)
Marie Lloyd Wlk. E8 . . . . .6F **67**
Marien Cl. E4 . . . . .5A **36**
Mariette Way SM6: W'gton 7J **167**
Marigold All. SE1 . . . . .3A 14 (7B **84**)
Marigold Cl. UB1: S'hall 7C **76**
Marigold Rd. N17 . . . . .7D **34**
Marigold St. SE16 . . . . .2H **103**
Marina Av. KT3: N Mald 5D **152**
Marina Cl. BR2: Broml 3J **159**
Marina Ct. *E3* 3B *86*
   (off Alfred St.)
Marina Dr. DA16: Well 2J **125**
Marina Gdns. RM7: Rom 5J **55**
Marina One *N1* 2J *83*
   (off New Wharf Rd.)
Marina Pl. KT1: Hamp W 1D **150**
Marina Point *E14* 3D *104*
   (off Lanark Sq.)
   SW6 . . . . .2A **118**
Marina Way TW11: Tedd 7D **132**
Marine Ct. E11 . . . . .2G **69**
Marine Dr. IG11: Bark 4A **90**
   SE18 . . . . .4D **106**
Marinefield Rd. SW6 . . . . .2K **117**
Marinel Ho. SE5 . . . . .7C **102**
Mariner Bus. Cen. CR0: Wadd . . .5A **168**
Mariner Gdns. TW10: Ham 3C **132**
Mariner Rd. E12 . . . . .4E **70**
Mariners Cl. EN4: E Barn 5G **21**
Mariners M. E14 . . . . .4F **105**
Mariners Pl. *SE16* 4A *104*
   (off Plough Way)
Marine St. SE16 . . . . .3G **103**
Marine Twr. *SE8* 6B *104*
   (off Abinger Gro.)
Marion Av. TW17: Shep 5D **146**
Marion Gro. IG8: Wfd G 5B **36**
Marion Ho. *NW1* 1D *82*
   (off Regent's Pk. Rd.)
Marion M. SE21 . . . . .3D **138**
Marion Rd. CR7: Thor H 5C **156**
   NW7 . . . . .5H **29**
Marischal Rd. SE13 . . . . .3F **123**
Maritime Ho. SE18 . . . . .4F **107**
Maritime Quay E14 . . . . .5C **104**
Maritime St. E3 . . . . .4B **86**
   SE16 . . . . .3K **103**
Marius Mans. SW17 . . . . .2E **136**
Marius Rd. SW17 . . . . .2E **136**
Marjorie Gro. SW11 . . . . .4D **118**
Marjorie M. E1 . . . . .6K **85**
Mark Av. E4 .6J **25**
Mark Cl. DA7: Bex 1E **126**
   UB1: S'hall 7F **77**
Marke Cl. BR2: Kes 4C **172**
The Market SM1: Sutt 1A **166**
   SM5: Cars 1A **166**
Market App. W12 . . . . .2E **98**
Market Chambers *EN2: Enf* 3J *23*
   (off Church St.)
Market Ct. W1 . . . . .7A **6**
Market Dr. W4 . . . . .7A **98**
Market Entrance SW8 . . . . .7G **101**

Market Est. N7 . . . . .6J **65**
Market Hall N22 . . . . .2A **48**
Market Hill SE18 . . . . .3E **106**
Market La. HA8: Edg 1J **43**
   W12 . . . . .2E **98**
Market Link RM1: Rom 4K **55**
Market M.
   W1 . . . . .5J 11 (1F **101**)
Market Pde. *BR1: Broml* 1J *159*
   (off East St.)
   DA14: Sidc 4B **144**
   E10 . . . . .6E **50**
   (off High Rd. Leyton)
   E17 . . . . .3B *50*
   (off Higham Hill Rd.)
   N9 . . . . .2B *34*
   (off Winchester Rd.)
   N16 . . . . .1G *67*
   (off Oldhill St.)
   SE25 . . . . .4G **157**
   TW13: Hanw 3C **130**
Market Pav. E10 . . . . .3C **68**
Market Pl. DA6: Bex 4G **127**
   EN2: Enf .3J **23**
   KT1: King T 2D **150**
   N2 . . . . .3B **46**
   SE16 . . . . .4G **103**
   (not continuous)
   TW8: Bford 7C **96**
   UB1: S'hall 1D **94**
   W1 . . . . .7A 6 (6G **83**)
   W3 . . . . .1J **97**
The Market Pl. NW11 . . . . .4A **46**
Market Rd. N7 . . . . .6J **65**
   TW9: Rich 3G **115**
Market Row SW9 . . . . .4A **120**
Market Sq. BR1: Broml 2J **159**
   (not continuous)
   E14 . . . . .6D **86**
   KT1: King T 2D *150*
   (off Market Pl.)
The Market Square *N9* 2C *34*
   (within Edmonton Grn. Shop. Cen.)
Market St. E1 . . . . .5J 9 (5F **85**)
   E6 . . . . .2D **88**
   SE18 . . . . .4E **106**
Market Ter. *TW8: Bford* 6E *96*
   (off Albany Rd.)
Market Trad. Est. UB2: S'hall 4K **93**
Mkt. Way E14 . . . . .6D **86**
   NW10 : Wemb 5E **60**
Market Yd. SE8 . . . . .7C **104**
Market Yd. M. SE1 . . . . . . .7G 15 (2E **102**)
Markfield Beam Engine & Mus. . . .5G **49**
Markfield Gdns. E4 . . . . .7J **25**
Markfield Rd. N15 . . . . .4G **49**
Markham Ho. *RM10: Dag* 3G *73*
   (off Uvedale Rd.)
Markham Pl. SW3 . . . . .5E 16 (5D **100**)
Markham Sq. SW3 . . . . .5E 16 (5D **100**)
Markham St. SE17 . . . . .5E **102**
   SW3 . . . . .5D 16 (5C **100**)
Markhole Cl. TW12: Hamp 7D **130**
Mark Ho. *E2* 2K *85*
   (off Sewardstone Rd.)
Markhouse Av. E17 . . . . .6A **50**
Markhouse Pas. *E17* 6B *50*
   (off Downsfield Rd.)
Markhouse Rd. E17 . . . . .6B **50**
Markland Ho. *W10* 7F *81*
   (off Darfield Way)
Mark La. EC3 . . . . .2H 15 (7E **84**)
Mark Lodge *EN4: Cockf* 4H *21*
   (off Edgeworth Rd.)
Markmanor Av. E17 . . . . .7A **50**
Mark Sq. EC2 . . . . .3D **84**
Marksbury Av. TW9: Rich 3G **115**
MARKS GATE 1J **55**
Mark Sq. EC2 . . . . .3G 9 (4E **84**)
Marks Rd. RM7: Rom 5J **55**
   (not continuous)
Markstone Ho. *SE1* 7A *14*
   (off Lancaster St.)

Mark St. E15 . . . . .7G **69**
   EC2 . . . . .3G 9 (4E **84**)
Mark Twain Dr. NW2 . . . . .4D **62**
Mark Wade Cl. E12 . . . . .1B **70**
Markway TW16: Sun 2A **148**
Markwell Cl. SE26 . . . . .4H **139**
Markyate Ho. *W10* 4E *80*
   (off Sutton Way)
Markyate Rd. RM8: Dag 5B **72**
Marland Ho. *SW1* 1F *17*
   (off Sloane St.)
Marlands Rd. IG5: Ilf 3C **52**
Marlborough *SW19* 1F *135*
   (off Inner Pk. Rd.)
   W9 . . . . .3A *82*
   (off Maida Vale)
Marlborough Av. E8 . . . . .1G **85**
   (not continuous)
   HA4: Ruis 6E **38**
   HA8: Edg 3C **28**
   N14 . . . . .3B **32**
Marlborough Cl. BR6: Orp 6K **161**
   N20 . . . . .3J **31**
   SE17 . . . . .4C **102**
   SW19 . . . . .6C **136**
Marlborough Ct. *CR2: S Croy* 4E *168*
   (off Birdhurst Rd.)
   EN1: Enf .5K **23**
   HA1: Harr 4H **41**
   HA6: Nwood 1H **39**
   IG9: Buck H 2F **37**
   N17 . . . . .1G *49*
   (off Kemble Rd.)
   SM6: W'gton 7G **167**
   W1 . . . . .1B *12*
   (off Carnaby St.)
   W8 . . . . .4J *99*
   (off Pembroke Rd.)
Marlborough Cres. UB3: Harl 7F **93**
   W4 . . . . .3K **97**
Marlborough Dr. IG5: Ilf 3C **52**
Marlborough Flats SW3 . . . . .3D **16**
Marlborough Gdns. KT6: Surb 7D **150**
   N20 . . . . .3J **31**
Marlborough Ga. Ho. *W2* 2A *10*
   (off Elms M.)
Marlborough Gro. SE1 . . . . .5G **103**
Marlborough Hill HA1: Harr 4H **41**
   NW8 . . . . .2A **82**
Marlborough House 5B 12 (1G **101**)
Marlborough Ho. *E16* 1J *105*
   (off Hardy Av.)
   UB7: W Dray 2B *92*
   (off Park Lodge Av.)
Marlborough La. SE7 . . . . .6A **106**
Marlborough Lodge *NW8* 2A *82*
   (off Hamilton Ter.)
Marlborough Mans. *NW6* 5K *63*
   (off Canon Hill)
Marlborough M. SW2 . . . . .4K **119**
Marlborough Pde. UB10: Hil 4D **74**
Marlborough Pk. Av. DA15: Sidc . .7A **126**
Marlborough Pl. NW8 . . . . .2A **82**
Marlborough Rd. BR2: Broml 4A **160**
   CR2: S Croy 7C **168**
   DA7: Bex 3D **126**
   E4 . . . . .6J **35**
   E7 . . . . .7A **70**
   E15 . . . . .4G **69**
   E18 . . . . .2J **51**
   N9 . . . . .1B **34**
   N19 . . . . .2H **65**
   N22 . . . . .7D **32**
   RM7: Mawney 4G **55**
   RM8: Dag 4B **72**
   SE18 . . . . .4F **107**
   SE28 . . . . .3G **107**
   SM1: Sutt 3J **165**
   SW1 . . . . .5B 12 (1G **101**)
   SW19 . . . . .6C **136**
   TW7: Isle 1B **114**
   TW10: Rich 6F **115**
   TW12: Hamp 6E **130**

Marlborough Rd. TW13: Felt . . .2B 130
  TW15: Ashf 5A 128
  UB2: S'hall 3A 94
  UB10: Hil 4D 74
  W4 . . . . .5J 97
  W5 . . . . .2D 96
Marlborough St. SW3 . . . .4C 16 (4C 100)
Marlborough Yd. N19 . . . .2H 65
Marlbury NW8 . . . . .1K 81
  (off Abbey Rd.)
Marler Rd. SE23 . . . . . . .1A 140
Marley Av. DA7: Bex 6D 108
Marley Cl. N15 . . . . .4B 48
  UB6: G'frd 3E 76
Marley Ho. E16 . . . . .7F 89
  (off University Way)
  W11 . . . . .7F 81
  (off St Ann's Rd.)
Marley St. SE16 . . . . . . .4K 103
Marley Wlk. NW2 . . . . . . .5E 62
Marl Fld. Cl. KT4: Wor Pk . .1C 164
Marlin Cl. TW16: Sun 6G 129
Marling Ct. TW12: Hamp . .6D 130
Marlingdene Cl. TW12: Hamp . .6E 130
MARLING PARK 7D 130
Marlings Cl. BR7: Chst 4J 161
Marlings Pk. Av. BR7: Chst . .4J 161
Marlin Pk. TW14: Felt 5K 111
Marlins Cl. SM1: Sutt 5A 166
Marloes Cl. HA0: Wemb . . .4D 60
Marloes Rd. W8 . . . . . . .3K 99
Marlow Cl. SE20 . . . . . . .3H 157
Marlow Cl. N14 . . . . .7B 22
  NW6 . . . . .7F 63
  NW9 . . . . .3B 44
Marlow Cres. TW1: Twick . .6K 113
Marlow Dr. SM3: Cheam . . .2F 165
Marlowe Cl. BR7: Chst 6H 143
  IG6: Ilf 1G 53
Marlowe Ct. SE19 . . . . . .5F 139
  SW3 . . . . .4D 16
  (off Petyward)
Marlowe Gdns. SE9 . . . . .6E 124
Marlowe Ho. IG8: W'fd G . .7K 37
  KT1: King T 4D 150
  (off Portsmouth Rd.)
Marlowe Path SE8 . . . . . .6C 104
Marlowe Rd. E17 . . . . . . .4E 50
The Marlowes DA1: Cray . . .4K 127
  NW8 . . . . .1B 82
Marlowe Sq. CR4: Mitc . . .4G 155
Marlowe Way CR0: Bedd . .2J 167
Marlow Gdns. UB3: Harl . . .3F 93
Marlow Ho. E2 . . . . .2J 9
  (off Calvert Av.)
  KT5: Surb 5E 150
  (off Cranes Pk.)
  SE1 . . . . .3C 86
  (off Abbey St.)
  TW11: Tedd 4A 132
  W2 . . . . .6K 81
  (off Hallfield Est.)
Marlow Rd. E6 . . . . .3D 88
  RM8: Dag 1E 72
  SE20 . . . . .3H 157
  UB2: S'hall 3D 94
Marlow Way SE16 . . . . . .2K 103
  (off Virginia Rd.)
Marl Rd. SW18 . . . . .4A 118
Marlston NW1 . . . . .2K 5
Marlton St. SE10 . . . . . . .5H 105
Marlu Ct. SE14 . . . . .1K 121
  (off Hatcham Pk. M.)
Marlu Ho. SE14 . . . . .1K 121
  (off Hatcham Pk. M.)
Marlwood Cl. DA15: Sidc . .2J 143
Marmadon Rd. SE18 . . . . .4K 107
Marmara Apts. E16 . . . . . .7J 87
  (off Western Gateway)
Marmion App. E4 . . . . . . .4H 35
Marmion Av. E4 . . . . .4G 35
Marmion Cl. E4 . . . . .4G 35

Marmion M. SW11 . . . . . .3E 118
Marmion Rd. SW11 . . . . .4E 118
Marmont Rd. SE15 . . . . . .1G 121
Marmora Rd. SE22 . . . . . .6J 121
Marmot Rd. TW4: Houn . . .3B 112
Marne Av. DA16: Well 3A 126
  N11 . . . . .4A 32
Marnell Way TW4: Houn . . .3B 112
Marne Rd. RM9: Dag 1B 90
Marner Point E3 . . . . .4E 86
Marney St. W10 . . . . .3G 81
Marney Rd. SW11 . . . . . .4E 118
Marnfield Cres. SW2 . . . . .1A 138
Marnham Av. NW2 . . . . . .4G 63
Marnham Cl. HA0: Wemb . .5C 60
Marnham Cres. UB6: G'frd . .3F 77
Marnock Ho. SE17 . . . . . .5D 102
  (off Brandon St.)
Marnock Rd. SE4 . . . . . . .5B 122
Maroon St. E14 . . . . .5A 86
Maroons Way SE6 . . . . . .5C 140
Marquee Ct. W8 . . . . .2K 99
  (off Kensington Chu. St.)
Marquee Towers SW16 . . .7K 137
Marquess Hgts. E18 . . . . .1K 51
Marquess Rd. N1 . . . . . . .6D 66
Marquis Cl. HA0: Wemb . . .7F 61
Marquis Ct. IG11: Bark 5J 71
  KT1: King T 4D 150
  (off Anglesea Rd.)
  N4 . . . . .1K 65
  (off Marquis Rd.)
  TW19: Stanw 1A 128
Marquis Rd. N4 . . . . .1K 65
  N22 . . . . .6E 32
  NW1 . . . . .6H 65
Marrabon Cl. DA15: Sidc . . .1A 144
Marrick Cl. SW15 . . . . . . .4C 116
Marrick Ho. NW6 . . . . . . .1K 81
  (off Mortimer Cres.)
Marriett Ho. SE6 . . . . . . .4E 140
Marrilyne Av. EN3: Enf L . . .1G 25
Marriner Ct. UB3: Hayes . . .7G 75
  (off Barra Hall Ct.)
Marriott Cl. TW14: Felt 6F 111
Marriott Rd. E15 . . . . .1G 87
  EN5: Barn 3A 20
  N4 . . . . .1K 65
  N10 . . . . .1D 46
Marriotts Cl. NW9 . . . . . . .6B 44
Marryat Cl. TW4: Houn 4D 112
Marryat Ho. SW1 . . . . . . .6A 18
  (off Churchill Gdns.)
Marryat Pl. SW19 . . . . . . .4G 135
Marryat Rd. SW19 . . . . . .5F 135
Marryat Sq. SW6 . . . . . . .1G 117
Marsala Rd. SE13 . . . . . . .4D 122
Marsalis Ho. E3 . . . . .3C 86
  (off Rainhill Way)
Marsault Ct. TW9: Rich 4E 114
  (off Kew Foot Rd.)
Marsden Rd. N9 . . . . .2C 34
  SE15 . . . . .3F 121
Marsden St. NW5 . . . . . . .6E 64
Marsden Way BR6: Orp . . .4K 173
Marshall Bldg. W2 . . . . . . .6A 4
  (off Hermitage St.)
Marshall Cl. HA1: Harr 7H 41
  SW18 . . . . .6A 118
  TW4: Houn 5D 112
Marshall Cl. NW6 . . . . . . .7F 63
  (off Coverdale Rd.)
  SE20 . . . . .7H 139
  (off Anerley Rd.)
Marshall Dr. UB4: Hayes . . .5H 75
Marshall Est. NW7 . . . . . . .4H 29
Marshall Ho. N1 . . . . .2D 84
  (off Cranston St.)
  SE1 . . . . .3E 102
  (off Page's Wlk.)
  SE17 . . . . .5D 102
  (off East St.)
Marshall Path SE28 . . . . . .7B 90

Marshall Rd. E10 . . . . . . .3D 68
  N17 . . . . .1D 48
Marshalls Cl. N11 . . . . . . .4A 32
Marshalls Dr. RM1: Rom . . .3K 55
Marshalls Gro. SE18 . . . . .4C 106
Marshall's Pl. SE16 . . . . . .3F 103
Marshall's Rd. SM1: Sutt . . .4K 165
Marshall St. NW10 . . . . . .7K 61
  W1 . . . . . . .1B 12 (6G 83)
Marshall Street Leisure Cen.
  . . . . .1B 12 (6G 83)
Marshalsea Rd. SE1 . . .6D 14 (2C 102)
Marsham Cl. BR7: Chst 5F 143
Marsham Ct. SW1 . . . .3D 18 (4H 101)
  SW11 . . . . .2D 18 (3H 101)
Marsh Av. CR4: Mitc 2D 154
Marshbrook Cl. SE3 . . . . . .3B 124
The Marsh Cen. E1 . . . . . . .7K 9
  (off Whitechapel High St.)
Marsh Cl. NW7 . . . . .3G 29
Marsh Ct. E8 . . . . .6G 67
  SE17 . . . . .5D 102
  (off Thurlow St.)
  SW19 . . . . .1A 154
Marsh Dr. NW9 . . . . .6B 44
Marsh Farm Rd. TW2: Twick . .1K 131
Marshfield St. E14 . . . . . . .3E 104
Marshgate Bus. Cen. E15 . .1E 86
Marshgate La. E15 . . . . . .1D 86
  . . . . .2C 68
Marshgate Path SE28 . . . . .3G 107
Marsh Grn. Rd. RM10: Dag . .1G 91
Marsh Hall HA9: Wemb 3F 61
Marsh Hill E9 . . . . .5A 68
Marsh Ho. SW1 . . . . .6D 18
  (off Aylesford St.)
  SW8 . . . . .1G 119
Marsh La. E10 . . . . .2B 68
  HA7: Stan 5H 27
  N17 . . . . .7C 34
  NW7 . . . . .3F 29
Marsh Rd. HA0: Wemb 3D 78
  HA5: Pinn 4C 40
Marshside Cl. N9 . . . . . . .1D 34
Marsh St. E14 . . . . .4D 104
Marsh Wall E14 . . . . .1C 104
Marsh Way RM13: Rain 3K 91
Marshwood Apartments SW11 . .4C 118
  (off Eckstein Road)
Marshwood Ho. NW6 . . . . .1J 81
  (off Kilburn Vale)
Marsland Cl. SE17 . . . . . . .5B 102
Marsom Ho. N1 . . . . .1E 8
  (off Provost St.)
Marston Av. KT9: Chess 6E 162
  RM10: Dag 2G 73
Marston Cl. NW6 . . . . .7A 64
  RM10: Dag 3G 73
Marston Ho. SW9 . . . . . . .2A 120
Marston Rd. IG5: Ilf 1C 52
  TW11: Tedd 5B 132
Marston Way SE19 . . . . . .7B 138
Marsworth Av. HA5: Pinn . . .1B 40
Marsworth Cl. UB4: Yead . . .5C 76
Marsworth Ho. E2 . . . . . . .1G 85
  (off Whiston Rd.)
  HA0: Wemb 1E 78
Martaban Rd. N16 . . . . . . .2F 67
Martara M. SE17 . . . . .5C 102
Marta Rose Ct. SE20 . . . . .2H 157
  (off Wadhurst Cl.)
Martello St. E8 . . . . .7H 67
Martello Ter. E8 . . . . .7H 67
Martell Rd. SE21 . . . . .3D 138
Martel Pl. E8 . . . . .6F 67
Marten Rd. E17 . . . . .2C 50
Martens Av. DA7: Bex 4H 127
Martens Cl. DA7: Bex 4J 127
Martha Ct. IG6: Ilf 1F 53
  SE28 . . . . .7D 90
Martha Rd. E15 . . . . .6G 69
Martha's Bldgs. EC1 . . .3E 8 (4D 84)

Martha St. E1 . . . . .6J 85
Marthorne Cres. HA3: Hrw W . .2H 41
Martin Bowes Rd. SE9 . . . .3D 124
Martinbridge Trad. Est. EN1: Enf . .5B 24
Martin Cl. N9 . . . . .1E 34
  UB10: Uxb 2A 74
Martin Cl. CR2: S Croy 5E 168
  (off Birdhurst Rd.)
  E14 . . . . .2E 104
  (off River Barge Cl.)
Martin Cres. CR0: C'don 1A 168
Martindale SW14 . . . . . . .5J 115
Martindale Av. BR6: Chels . . .5K 173
  E16 . . . . .7J 87
  (off Poplar High St.)
Martin Dale Ind. Est. EN1: Enf . .3C 24
Martindale Rd. SW12 . . . . .7F 119
  TW4: Houn 3C 112
Martin Dene DA6: Bex 5F 127
Martin Dr. UB5: N'olt 5D 58
Martineau Cl. TW1: Twick . .4B 114
Martineau Est. E1 . . . . . . .7J 85
Martineau Ho. SW1 . . . . . .6A 18
  (off Churchill Gdns.)
Martineau M. N5 . . . . . . .4B 66
Martineau Rd. N5 . . . . . . .4B 66
Martineau Sq. E1 . . . . . . .7G 85
Martingale Cl. TW16: Sun . . .4J 147
Martingale Ho. E1 . . . . . . .1H 103
  (off Raine St.)
Martingales Cl. TW10: Ham . . .3D 132
Martin Gdns. RM8: Dag 4C 72
Martin Gro. SM4: Mord 3J 153
Martin Ho. E3 . . . . .3B 86
  (off Old Ford Rd.)
  SE1 . . . . .3C 102
  SW8 . . . . .7J 101
  (off Wyvil Rd.)
Martin Kinggett Gdns. RM9: Dag . .1E 90
Martin La. EC4 . . . . . .2F 15 (7D 84)
  (not continuous)
Martin Ri. DA6: Bex 5F 127
Martin Rd. RM8: Dag 4C 72
The Martins HA9: Wemb 3F 61
  SE26 . . . . .5H 139
Martins Cl. BR4: W W'ck . . .1F 171
Martin's Mt. EN5: New Bar . . .4D 20
Martins Pl. SE28 . . . . .1J 107
Martin's Rd. BR2: Broml 2G 159
Martins St. SE28 . . . . .1J 107
Martins Wlk. N10 . . . . .1E 46
  N22 . . . . .3A 48
  SE28 . . . . .1J 107
Martin Way SM4: Mord 2F 153
  SW20 . . . . .2F 153
Martlesham N17 . . . . .2E 48
  (off Adams Rd.)
Martlesham Wlk. NW9 . . . . .2A 44
Martlett Ct. WC2 . . . .1F 13 (6J 83)
Martley Dr. IG2: Ilf 5F 53
Martock Cl. HA3: W'stone . . .4A 42
Martock Gdns. N11 . . . . . .5J 31
Marton Cl. SE6 . . . . .3C 140
Marton Rd. N16 . . . . .2E 66
Martynside NW9 . . . . .1B 44
Martys Yd. NW3 . . . . .4B 64
Marula Ho. E1 . . . . .6G 85
  (off Boulevard Walkway)
Marvel Av. UB4: Hayes 5J 75
Marvell Ct. RM6: Chad H . . .6B 54
  (off Quarles Pk. Rd.)
Marvell Ho. SE5 . . . . .7D 102
  (off Camberwell Rd.)
Marvels Cl. SE12 . . . . .2K 141
Marvels La. SE12 . . . . .2K 141
Marville Rd. SW6 . . . . .7H 99
Marvin St. E8 . . . . .6H 67
Marwell Cl. BR4: W W'ck . . .2H 171
Marwood Cl. DA16: Well 3B 126
Marwood Dr. NW7 . . . . . . .7A 30
Marwood Square N10 . . . . .4E 46

Mary Adelaide Cl. SW15	4A 134
Mary Ann Gdns. SE8	6C 104
Maryatt Av. HA2: Harr	2F 59
Marybank SE18	4D 106
Mary Bayly Ho. W11	1G 99
(off Wilsham St.)	
Mary Cl. HA7: Stan	4F 43
Mary Datchelor Cl. SE5	1D 120
Mary Datchelor Ho. SE5	1D 120
(off Grove La.)	
Maryfield Cl. DA5: Bexl	3K 145
Mary Flux Ct. SW5	5K 99
(off Bramham Gdns.)	
Mary Grn. NW8	1K 81
Mary Holben Ho. SW16	5G 137
Mary Ho. W6	5E 98
(off Queen Caroline St.)	
Mary Jones Ct. E14	7C 86
(off Garford St.)	
Maryland Ind. Est. E15	5G 69
Maryland Pk. E15	5G 69
(not continuous)	
Maryland Point E15	6G 69
(off The Grove)	
Maryland Rd. CR7: Thor H	1B 156
E15	5F 69
N22	6E 32
Maryland Sq. E15	5G 69
Marylands Rd. W9	4J 81
(not continuous)	
Maryland St. E15	5F 69
Maryland Wlk. N1	1C 84
(off Popham St.)	
Maryland Way TW16: Sun	2J 147
Mary Lawrenson Pl. SE3	7J 105
MARYLEBONE	5H 5 (5E 82)
Marylebone Cricket Club	2B 4
MARYLEBONE FLYOVER	5C 82
Marylebone Fly-Over W2	6B 4 (5B 82)
Marylebone Gdns. TW9: Rich	4G 115
Marylebone High St. W1	5H 5 (5E 82)
Marylebone La. W1	6H 5 (5E 82)
Marylebone M. W1	6J 5 (5F 83)
Marylebone Pas. W1	7B 6 (6G 83)
Marylebone Rd. NW1	5D 4 (5C 82)
Marylebone St. W1	6H 5 (5E 82)
Mary Le Bow Way E3	5D 86
Marylee Way SE11	4H 19 (4K 101)
Mary Macarthur Ho. E2	3K 85
(off Warley St.)	
RM10: Dag	3G 73
(off Wythenshawe Rd.)	
W6	6G 99
Mary Neuner Rd. N8	3K 47
N22	3K 47
Maryon Gro. SE7	4C 106
Maryon Ho. NW6	7A 64
(off Goldhurst Ter.)	
Maryon M. NW3	4C 64
Maryon Rd. SE7	4C 106
SE18	4C 106
Mary Peters Dr. UB6: G'frd	5H 59
Mary Pl. W11	7G 81
Mary Rose Cl. TW12: Hamp	1E 148
Mary Rose Mall E6	5D 88
Mary Rose Sq. SE16	4A 104
(off Cary Av.)	
Maryrose Way N20	1G 31
Marys Ct. NW1	3D 4
Mary Seacole Cl. E8	1F 85
Mary Seacole Ho. W6	3C 98
(off Invermead Cl.)	
Mary Smith Ct. SW5	4J 99
(off Trebovir Rd.)	
Marysmith Ho. SW1	5D 18
(off Cureton St.)	
Mary's Ter. TW1: Twick	7A 114
Mary St. E16	5H 87
N1	1C 84
Mary Ter. NW1	1F 83
Maryville DA16: Well	2K 125
Mary Wallace Theatre	1A 132
Mary Wharrie Ho. NW3	7D 64
(off Fellows Rd.)	
Marzell Ho. W14	5H 99
(off North End Rd.)	
Marzena Ct. TW3: Houn	6G 113
Masbro' Rd. W14	3F 99
Mascalls Cl. SE7	6A 106
Mascalls Rd. SE7	6A 106
Mascotte Rd. SW15	4F 117
Mascotts Cl. NW2	3D 62
Masefield Av. HA7: Stan	5E 26
UB1: S'hall	7E 76
Masefield Cl. EN5: New Bar	4F 21
KT6: Surb	7D 150
Masefield Cres. N14	5B 22
Masefield Gdns. E6	4E 88
Masefield Ho. NW6	3J 81
(off Stafford Rd.)	
Masefield La. UB4: Yead	4K 75
Masefield Rd. TW12: Hamp	4D 130
Masefield Vw. BR6: Farnb	3G 173
Masefield Way TW19: Stanw	1B 128
Masey M. SW2	5A 120
Masham Ho. DA18: Erith	2D 108
(off Kale Rd.)	
Mashie Rd. W3	6A 80
Mashiters Hill RM1: Rom	1K 55
Masjid La. E14	5B 86
Maskall Cl. SW2	1A 138
Maskani Wlk. SW16	7G 137
Maskell Rd. SW17	3A 136
Maskelyne Cl. SW11	1C 118
Mason Cl. DA7: Bex	3H 127
E16	7J 87
SE16	5G 103
SW20	1F 153
TW12: Hamp	1D 148
Mason Ho. E9	7J 67
(off Frampton Pk. Rd.)	
SE1	4G 103
(off Simms Rd.)	
Mason Rd. IG8: Wfd G	4B 36
SM1: Sutt	5K 165
Masonry Ho. SE14	1K 121
(off Fishers Ct.)	
Mason's Arms M. W1	1K 11 (6F 83)
Mason's Av. CR0: C'don	3C 168
EC2	7E 8 (6D 84)
Masons Av. HA3: W'stone	4K 41
Masons Grn. La. W3	4G 79
W5	4G 79
Masons Hill BR1: Broml	3J 159
BR2: Broml	3K 159
SE18	4F 107
Masons Pl. CR4: Mitc	1D 154
EC1	1B 8 (3C 84)
Mason St. SE17	4D 102
Mason's Yd. SW1	4B 12 (1G 101)
SW19	5F 135
Masons Yd. EC1	1B 8 (3B 84)
Massey Cl. N11	5A 32
Massey Ct. E6	1A 88
(off Florence Rd.)	
Massie Rd. E8	6G 67
Massingberd Way SW17	4F 137
Massinger St. SE17	4E 102
Massingham St. E1	4K 85
Masson Av. HA4: Ruis	6A 58
Masson Ho. TW8: Bford	6F 97
The Mast E16	7G 89
Mast Cl. SE16	4A 104
(off Boat Lifter Way)	
Master Gunner Pl. SE18	7C 106
Masterhead Ho. E16	2K 105
(off Royal Crest Av.)	
Masterman Ho. SE5	7D 102
(off Elmington Est.)	
Masterman Rd. E6	3C 88
Masters Cl. SW16	6G 137
Masters Dr. SE16	5H 103
Masters Lodge E1	6J 85
(off Johnson St.)	
Masters St. E1	5K 85
Mast Ho. Ter. E14	4C 104
(not continuous)	
Mastmaker Cl. E14	2C 104
Mastmaker Rd. E14	2C 104
Mast Quay SE18	3D 106
Mast St. IG11: Bark	1H 89
MASWELL PARK	5G 113
Maswell Pk. Cres. TW3: Houn	5G 113
Maswell Pk. Rd. TW3: Houn	5F 113
Matcham Ct. TW1: Twick	6D 114
(off Clevedon Rd.)	
Matcham Rd. E11	3G 69
Match Ct. E3	2C 86
(off Blondin St.)	
Matching Ct. E3	3B 86
(off Merchant St.)	
Matchless Dr. SE18	7E 106
The Material Store UB3: Hayes	3G 93
(off Material Wlk.)	
Material Wlk. UB3: Hayes	2G 93
Matfield Cl. BR2: Broml	5J 159
Matfield Rd. DA17: Belv	6G 109
Matha Ct. BR1: Broml	1A 160
Matham Gro. SE22	4F 121
Matham Rd. KT8: E Mos	5H 149
Matheson Lang Ho. SE1	7J 13
Matheson Rd. W14	4H 99
Mathews Av. E6	2E 88
Mathews Pk. Av. E15	6H 69
Mathews Yd. WC2	1E 12 (6J 83)
Mathieson Ct. SE1	7B 14
(off King James St.)	
Mathison Ho. SW10	7A 100
(off Coleridge Gdns.)	
Matilda Cl. SE19	7D 138
Matilda Gdns. E3	2C 86
Matilda Ho. E1	1G 103
(off St Katherine's Way)	
Matilda St. N1	1K 83
Matisse Ct. EC1	3E 8
Matisse Rd. TW3: Houn	3F 113
Matlock Cl. EN5: Barn	5A 20
SE24	4C 120
Matlock Ct. NW8	2A 82
(off Abbey Rd.)	
SE5	4D 120
W11	7J 81
(off Kensington Pk. Rd.)	
Matlock Cres. SM3: Cheam	4G 165
Matlock Gdns. SM3: Cheam	4G 165
Matlock Ho. E15	4F 69
(off Forrester Way)	
Matlock Pl. SM3: Cheam	4G 165
Matlock Rd. E10	6E 50
Matlock St. E14	6A 86
Matlock Way KT3: N Mald	1K 151
Maton Ho. SW6	7H 99
(off Estcourt Rd.)	
Matrimony Pl. SW8	2G 119
Matson Ct. IG8: Wfd G	7B 36
Matson Ho. SE16	3H 103
Matthew Cl. W10	4F 81
Matthew Ct. CR4: Mitc	5H 155
E17	3E 50
Matthew Parker St. SW1	7D 12 (2H 101)
Matthews Cl. HA9: Wemb	3G 61
Matthews Ho. E14	5C 86
(off Burgess St.)	
Matthews Rd. UB6: G'frd	5H 59
Matthews St. SW11	2D 118
Matthews Wlk. E17	1E 50
(off Chingford Rd.)	
Matthews Yd. CR0: C'don	3C 168
(off Surrey St.)	
Matthias Apts. N1	7D 66
(off Northchurch Rd.)	
Matthias Ct. TW10: Rich	5E 114
Matthias Rd. N16	5E 66
Mattison Rd. N4	6A 48
Mattock La. W5	1B 96
W13	1B 96
Maud Cashmore Way SE18	3D 106
Maud Chadburn Pl. SW4	6F 119
Maude Ho. E2	2G 85
(off Ropley St.)	
Maude Rd. E17	5A 50
SE5	1E 120
Maudesville Cottages W7	1J 95
Maude Ter. E17	5A 50
Maud Gdns. E13	1H 87
IG11: Bark	2K 89
Maudlins Grn. E1	4K 15 (1G 103)
Maud Rd. E10	3E 68
E13	2H 87
Maudslay Rd. SE9	3D 124
Maudsley Ho. TW8: Bford	5E 96
Maud St. E16	5H 87
Maud Wilkes Cl. NW5	5G 65
Maugham Way W3	3J 97
Mauleverer Rd. SW2	5J 119
Maundeby Wlk. NW10	6A 62
Maunder Rd. W7	1K 95
Maunsel St. SW1	3C 18 (4H 101)
Maureen Campbell Ct.	
TW17: Shep	5D 146
(off Harrison Way)	
Maureen Ct. BR3: Beck	2J 157
Maurer Ct. SE10	3H 105
Mauretania Bldg. E1	7K 85
(off Jardine Rd.)	
Maurice Av. N22	2B 48
Maurice Browne Av. NW7	6A 30
Maurice Ct. E1	3K 85
N22	1K 47
TW8: Bford	7D 96
Maurice Drummond Ho. SE10	1D 122
(off Catherine Gro.)	
Maurice St. W12	6D 80
Maurice Wlk. NW11	4A 46
Maurier Cl. NW5	1A 76
Mauritius Rd. SE10	4G 105
Maury Rd. N16	2G 67
Mauveine Gdns. TW3: Houn	4E 112
Mavelstone Cl. BR1: Broml	1C 160
Mavelstone Rd. BR1: Broml	1B 160
Maverton Rd. E3	1C 86
Mavery Ct. BR1: Broml	7H 141
(off Bromley Av.)	
Mavis Av. KT19: Ewe	5A 164
Mavis Cl. KT19: Ewe	5A 164
Mavis Wlk. E6	5C 88
(off Greenwich Cres.)	
Mavor Ho. N1	1K 83
(off Barnsbury Est.)	
Mawbey Ho. SE1	5G 103
Mawbey Pl. SE1	5G 103
Mawbey Rd. SE1	5F 103
Mawbey St. SW8	7J 101
Mawdley Ho. SE1	7A 14
MAWNEY	3H 55
Mawney Cl. RM7: Mawney	2H 55
Mawney Rd. RM7: Mawney, Rom	2H 55
Mawson Cl. SW20	2G 153
Mawson Ct. N1	1D 84
(off Gopsall St.)	
Mawson Ho. EC1	5J 7
(off Baldwins Gdns.)	
Mawson La. W4	6B 98
Maxden Ct. SE15	3F 121
Maxey Gdns. RM9: Dag	4E 72
Maxey Rd. RM9: Dag	4E 72
SE18	4G 107
Maxfield Cl. N20	7F 21
Maxilla Wlk. W10	6F 81
Maxim Apts. BR2: Broml	4K 159
(off Tiger La.)	
Maximfeldt Rd. DA8: Erith	5K 109
Maxim Rd. DA8: Erith	4K 109
N21	6F 23
Maxted Pk. HA1: Harr	7J 41
Maxted Rd. SE15	3F 121
Maxwell Cl. CR0: Wadd	1J 167
UB3: Hayes	7J 75
Maxwell Ct. SE22	1G 139
SW4	5H 119
Maxwell Gdns. BR6: Orp	3K 173

Maxwell Rd. DA16: Well 3K 125
HA6: Nwood 1F 39
RM7: Rush G 6K 55
SW6 .7K 99
TW15: Ashf 6E 128
UB7: W Dray 4B 92
Maxwelton Av. NW7 . . . . .5E 28
Maxwelton Cl. NW7 . . . . .5E 28
Maya Angelou Ct. E4 . . . . .4K 35
Maya Apts. E20 . . . . .5E 68
(off Victory Pde.)
Maya Cl. SE15 . . . . .2H 121
Mayall Cl. EN3: Enf L 1H 25
Mayall Rd. SE24 . . . . .5B 120
Maya Pl. N11 . . . . .7C 32
Maya Rd. N2 . . . . .4A 46
Maybank Av. E18 . . . . .2K 51
HA0: Wemb 5K 59
Maybank Gdns. HA5: Eastc 5J 39
Maybank Rd. E18 . . . . .1K 51
May Bate Av. KT2: King T 1D 150
Maybells Commercial Est.
IG11: Bark 2D 90
Mayberry Ct. BR3: Beck 7B 140
(off Copers Cope Rd.)
Mayberry Pl. KT5: Surb 7F 151
Maybourne Cl. SE26 . . . . .6H 139
Maybury Cl. BR5: Pet W 5F 161
EN1: Enf 1C 24
Maybury Ct. CR2: S Croy 5B 168
(off Haling Pk. Rd.)
HA1: Harr 6H 41
W1 . . . . .6H 5
(off Marylebone St.)
Maybury Gdns. NW10 . . . . .6D 62
Maybury M. N6 . . . . .7G 47
Maybury Rd. E13 . . . . .4A 88
IG11: Bark 2K 89
Maybury St. SW17 . . . . .5C 136
Maychurch Cl. HA7: Stan 7J 27
May Cl. KT9: Chess 6F 163
May Ct. SW19 . . . . .1A 154
(off Pincott Rd.)
Maycroft HA5: Pinn 2K 39
Maycross Av. SM4: Mord 4H 153
Mayday Gdns. SE3 . . . . .2C 124
Mayday Rd. CR7: Thor H 6B 156
Maydeb Cl. RM6: Chad H 6F 55
Maydew Ho. SE16 . . . . .4J 103
(off Abbeyfield Est.)
Maydwell Ho. E14 . . . . .5C 86
(off Thomas Rd.)
Mayerne Rd. SE9 . . . . .5B 124
Mayesbrook Pk. Arena 5A 72
Mayesbrook Rd. IG3: Ilf 3A 72
IG11: Bark 1K 89
RM8: Dag 3A 72
Mayes Cl. CR0: New Ad 7F 171
Mayesford Rd. RM6: Chad H 7C 54
Mayes Rd. N22 . . . . .2K 47
Mayeswood Rd. SE12 . . . . .4A 142
MAYFAIR 3J 11 (7F 83)
Mayfair Av. DA7: Bex 1D 126
IG1: Ilf 2D 70
KT4: Wor Pk 1C 164
RM6: Chad H 6D 54
TW2: Whitt 7G 113
Mayfair Cl. BR3: Beck 1D 158
KT6: Surb 1E 162
Mayfair Ct. HA8: Edg 5A 28
Mayfair Gdns. IG8: Wfd G 7D 36
N17 .6H 33
Mayfair M. NW1 . . . . .7D 64
(off Regents Pk. Rd.)
SW12 . . . . .1F 137
Mayfair Pl. W1 . . . . . . .4K 11 (1F 101)
Mayfair Row W1 . . . . .1F 101
Mayfair Ter. N14 . . . . .7C 22
Mayfield DA7: Bex 3F 127
HA3: Kenton 5B 42
IG8: Wfd G 6D 36
N12 .4F 31

Mayfield Av. N14 . . . . .2C 32
W4 . . . . .4A 98
W13 .3B 96
Mayfield Cl. E8 . . . . .6F 67
KT7: T Ditt 1B 162
SE20 . . . . .1H 157
SW4 .5H 119
TW15: Ashf 6D 128
UB10: Hil 3D 74
Mayfield Cres. CR7: Thor H 4K 155
N9 . . . . .6C 24
Mayfield Dr. HA5: Pinn 4D 40
Mayfield Gdns. NW4 . . . . .6F 45
W7 . . . . .6H 77
Mayfield Ho. E2 . . . . .2H 85
(off Cambridge Heath Rd.)
Mayfield Mans. SW15 . . . . .5H 117
Mayfield Rd. BR1: Broml 5C 160
CR2: Sande 7D 168
CR7: Thor H 4K 155
DA17: Belv 4J 109
E4 . . . . .2K 35
E8 . . . . .7F 67
E13 .4H 87
E17 .2A 50
EN3: Enf H 2E 24
N8 . . . . .5K 47
RM8: Dag 1C 72
SM2: Sutt 6B 166
SW19 . . . . .1H 153
W3 . . . . .7H 79
W12 .2A 98
Mayfield Rd. Flats N8 . . . . .6K 47
Mayfields HA9: Wemb 2G 61
Mayfields Cl. HA9: Wemb 2G 61
Mayfield Vs. DA14: Sidc 6C 144
Mayflower Cl. HA4: Ruis 6E 38
SE16 . . . . .4K 103
Mayflower Ho. E14 . . . . .2C 104
(off Westferry Rd.)
IG11: Bark 1H 89
(off Westbury Rd.)
Mayflower Rd. SW9 . . . . .3J 119
Mayflower St. SE16 . . . . .2J 103
Mayfly Cl. HA5: Eastc 7A 40
Mayfly Gdns. UB5: N'olt 3B 76
Mayford NW1 . . . . .2G 83
(not continuous)
Mayford Cl. BR3: Beck 3K 157
SW12 . . . . .7D 118
Mayford Rd. SW12 . . . . .7D 118
May Gdns. HA0: Wemb 3C 78
Maygood Ho. N1 . . . . .2K 83
(off Maygood St.)
Maygood St. N1 . . . . .2A 84
Maygrove Rd. NW6 . . . . .6H 63
Mayhew Cl. E4 . . . . .3H 35
Mayhew Ct. SE5 . . . . .4D 120
Mayhill Cl. SE15 . . . . .7E 102
(off Tower Mill Rd.)
Mayhill Rd. EN5: Barn 6B 20
SE7 .6K 105
May Ho. E3 . . . . .2C 86
(off Thomas Fyre Dr.)
Mayland Mans. IG11: Bark 7F 71
(off Whiting Av.)
Maylands Dr. DA14: Sidc 3D 144
UB8: Uxb 6A 56
Maylands Ho. SW3 . . . . .4D 16
(off Cale St.)
May La. HA3: Kenton 7F 43
Maylie Ho. SE16 . . . . .2H 103
(off Marigold St.)
Maynard Cl. N15 . . . . .5E 48
SW6 .7K 99
Maynard Path E17 . . . . .5E 50
Maynard Rd. E17 . . . . .5E 50
Maynards Quay E1 . . . . .7J 85
Mayne Ct. SE26 . . . . .5H 139
Maynooth Gdns. SM5: Cars 7D 154
Mayo Cl. W13 . . . . .3B 96
Mayo Ho. E1 . . . . .5J 85
(off Lindley St.)

Mayola Rd. E5 . . . . .4J 67
Mayo Rd. CR0: C'don 5D 156
KT12: Walt T 7J 147
NW10 . . . . .6A 62
The Mayor's & City of London Court
. . . . .7E 8
Mayow Rd. SE23 . . . . .4K 139
SE26 . . . . .4K 139
Mayplace Cl. DA7: Bex 3H 127
Mayplace La. SE18 . . . . .6F 107
(not continuous)
Mayplace Rd. E. DA1: Cray 3J 127
DA7: Bex 3H 127
Mayplace Rd. W. DA7: Bex 4G 127
MAYPOLE 1K 145
Maypole Ct. UB2: S'hall 2D 94
(off Merrick Rd.)
May Rd. E4 . . . . .6H 35
E13 .2J 87
TW2: Twick 1J 131
Mayroyd Av. KT6: Surb 2G 163
Maysoule Rd. SW11 . . . . .4B 118
Mays Rd. TW11: Tedd 5H 131
Mayston M. SE10 . . . . .5J 105
(off Ormiston Rd.)
May St. W14 . . . . .5H 99
(Kelway Ho.)
W14 .5H 99
(Orchard Sq.)
Mayswood Gdns. RM10: Dag 6J 73
Maythorne Cotts. SE13 . . . . .5F 123
Mayton St. N7 . . . . .3K 65
Maytree Cl. HA8: Edg 3D 28
Maytree Ct. CR4: Mitc 3E 154
UB5: N'olt 3C 76
Maytree Gdns. W5 . . . . .2D 96
May Tree Ho. SE4 . . . . .3B 122
(off Wickham Rd.)
Maytree La. HA7: Stan 7F 27
Maytree Wlk. SW2 . . . . .2A 138
Mayville Est. N16 . . . . .5E 66
Mayville Rd. E11 . . . . .2G 69
(not continuous)
IG1: Ilf 5F 71
May Wlk. E13 . . . . .2K 87
Mayward Ho. SE5 . . . . .1E 120
(off Peckham Rd.)
Maywood Cl. BR3: Beck 7D 140
May Wynne Ho. E16 . . . . .7K 87
(off Murray Sq.)
Mazal Ct. KT8: W Mole 4F 149
Maze Hill SE3 . . . . .7H 105
SE10 . . . . .6G 105
Maze Hill Lodge SE10 . . . . .6F 105
(off Park Vista)
Mazenod Av. NW6 . . . . .7J 63
Maze Rd. TW9: Kew 7G 97
MCC Cricket Mus. & Tours
. . . . .2A 4 (3B 82)
The Mead BR3: Beck 1E 158
BR4: W W'ck 1F 171
N2 . . . . .2A 46
SM6: W'gton 6H 167
UB10: Ick 2C 56
W13 .5B 78
Meadbank Studios SW11 . . . . .7C 100
(off Parkgate Rd.)
Mead Cl. HA3: Hrw W 1H 41
NW1 .6E 64
Mead Ct. NW9 . . . . .5J 43
Mead Cres. E4 . . . . .4K 35
SM1: Sutt 3C 166
Meadcroft Rd. SE11 . . . . . . .7K 19 (6B 102)
(not continuous)
SE17 . . . . .6B 102
Meade Cl. W4 . . . . .6G 97
Meade Ho. E14 . . . . .6G 87
(off Lyell St.)

Meade M. SW1 . . . . .5D 18
(off Causton St.)
Meader Ct. SE14 . . . . .7K 103
Mead Fld. HA2: Harr 3D 58
Meadfield HA8: Edg 2C 28
(not continuous)
Meadfield Grn. HA8: Edg 2C 28
Meadfoot Rd. SW16 . . . . .7G 137
Meadgate Av. IG8: Wfd G 5H 37
Mead Gro. RM6: Chad H 3D 54
Mead Ho. W11 . . . . .1H 99
(off Ladbroke Rd.)
Mead Ho. La. UB4: Hayes 4F 75
Meadhurst Club 5H 129
Meadhurst Pk. TW16: Sun 6G 129
Meadlands Dr. TW10: Ham 2D 132
Mead Lodge W4 . . . . .2K 97
The Meadow BR7: Chst 6G 143
N10 .3E 46
Meadow Av. CR0: C'don 6K 157
Mdw. Bank N21 . . . . .6E 22
Meadowbank KT5: Surb 6F 151
NW3 .7D 64
SE3 .3H 123
Meadowbank Cl. SW6 . . . . .7E 98
TW7: Isle 1J 113
Meadowbank Gdns. TW5: Cran 1J 111
Meadowbank Rd. NW9 . . . . .7K 43
Meadowbridge Ct. CR0: C'don 5D 156
(off Princess Rd.)
Meadowbrook Cl. SL3: Poyle 4A 174
Meadowbrook Ct. TW7: Isle 3J 113
BR7: Chst 5F 143
DA6: Bex 5F 127
E4 . . . . .1J 35
E9 . . . . .6B 68
EN3: Enf W 1F 25
EN5: Barn 6C 20
HA4: Ruis 6H 39
IG11: Bark 7A 72
KT10: Hin W 3A 162
SE6 .5C 140
SM1: Sutt 2A 166
SW20 . . . . .4E 152
TW4: Houn 6E 112
TW10: Ham 1E 132
UB5: N'olt 2E 76
Meadow Cl. E16 . . . . .1A 106
(off Booth Rd.)
N1 . . . . .2E 84
TW4: Houn 6F 113
Meadowcourt Rd. SE3 . . . . .4H 123
Meadowcroft BR1: Broml 3D 160
W4 . . . . .5G 97
(off Brooks Av.)
Meadowcroft Cl. E10 . . . . .7D 50
N13 .2F 33
Meadowcroft M. E1 . . . . .7G 85
(off Cable St.)
SE6 .6D 122
Meadowcroft Rd. N13 . . . . .2F 33
Meadow Dr. N10 . . . . .3F 47
NW4 .2E 44
Meadowford Cl. SE28 . . . . .7A 90
Meadow Gdns. HA8: Edg 6C 28
Meadow Gth. NW10 . . . . .6J 61
Meadow Ga. HA2: Harr 3F 59
Meadowgate Cl. NW7 . . . . .5G 29
Meadow Hill KT3: N Mald 6A 152
Meadow La. SE12 . . . . .3K 141
Meadowlark Ho. NW9 . . . . .7B 44
Meadowlea Cl. UB7: Harm 2E 174
Meadow M. SW8 . . . . .6K 101
Meadow Pl. SW8 . . . . .7J 101
W4 . . . . .7A 98
Meadow Rd.
BR2: Broml 2G 159
HA5: Pinn 4B 40
IG11: Bark 7K 71
RM7: Rush G 1J 73
RM9: Dag 6F 73
SM1: Sutt 4C 166
SW8 . . . . .7H 19 (7K 101)

Meadow Rd. SW19 . . . . .7A **136**
  TW13: Felt 2C **130**
  TW15: Ashf 5F **129**
  UB1: S'hall 7D **76**
Meadow Row SE1 . . . . .3C **102**
The Meadows E4 . . . . .4A **36**
Meadows Cl. E10 . . . . .2C **68**
Meadows Ct. DA14: Sidc 6B **144**
Meadows End TW16: Sun 1J **147**
Meadowside SE3 . . . . .4A **124**
  SE9 . . . . .4A **124**
  TW1: Twick 7D **114**
Meadow Stile CR0: C'don 3C **168**
Mdws. Way SE4 . . . . .3A **122**
Meadowsweet Cl. E16 . . . . .5B **88**
  SW20 . . . . .4E **152**
Meadow Vw. DA15: Sidc 7B **126**
  HA1: Harr 1J **59**
  TW19: Stanw M 7A **174**
Meadow Vw. Rd. CR7: Thor H . .5B **156**
  SW20 . . . . .4E **152**
  UB4: Hayes 4F **75**
Meadowview Rd. DA5: Bexl 6E **126**
  KT19: Ewe 7A **164**
  SE6 . . . . .5B **140**
Meadow Wlk. E18 . . . . .4J **51**
  KT17: Ewe 7B **164**
  KT19: Ewe 6A **164**
  RM9: Dag 6F **73**
  SM6: W'gton 3F **167**
Mdw. Way BR6: Farnb 3E **172**
  HA4: Ruis 6K **39**
  HA9: Wemb 4D **60**
  KT9: Chess 5E **162**
  NW9 . . . . .5K **43**
The Meadow Way HA3: Hrw W . .1J **41**
Meadow Ways TW5: Hest 6C **94**
Meadow Works EN5: New Bar . . .6E **20**
Mead Path SW17 . . . . .4A **136**
Mead Pl. CR0: C'don 1C **168**
  E9 . . . . .6J **67**
Mead Plat NW10 . . . . .6J **61**
Mead Rd. BR7: Chst 6G **143**
  HA8: Edg 6B **28**
  TW10: Ham 3C **132**
Mead Row SE1 . . . . .1J **19** (3H **102**)
The Meads HA8: Edg 6E **28**
  SM3: Cheam 3G **165**
  SM4: Mord 5C **154**
  UB8: Cowl 4A **74**
Meads Ct. E15 . . . . .6H **69**
Meadside Cl. BR3: Beck 1A **158**
Meads La. IG3: Ilf 7J **53**
Meads Rd. EN3: Enf H 1F **25**
  N22 . . . . .2B **48**
Mead Ter. HA9: Wemb 4D **60**
Meadvale Rd. CR0: C'don 7F **157**
  W5 . . . . .4B **78**
Mead Way BR2: Hayes 6H **159**
  CR0: C'don 2A **170**
  HA4: Ruis 6F **39**
Meadway BR3: Beck 1E **158**
  EN5: Barn, New Bar 4D **20**
  IG3: Bark, Ilf 4J **71**
  IG8: Wfd G 5F **37**
  KT5: Surb 1J **163**
  N14 . . . . .2C **32**
  NW11 . . . . .6J **45**
  SW20 . . . . .4E **152**
  TW2: Twick 1H **131**
  TW15: Ashf 4C **128**
The Meadway IG9: Buck H 1G **37**
  SE3 . . . . .2F **123**
Meadway Cl. EN5: Barn 4D **20**
  HA5: Hat E 6A **26**
  NW11 . . . . .6K **45**
Meadway Ct. RM8: Dag 2F **73**
  TW11: Tedd 5C **132**
  W5 . . . . .4F **79**
Meadway Gdns. HA4: Ruis 6F **39**
Meadway Ga. NW11 . . . . .6J **45**
Meaford Way SE20 . . . . .7H **139**
Meakin Est. SE1 . . . . .3E **102**

Meander Ho. E20 . . . . .5D **68**
               (off Logan Cl.)
Meanley Rd. E12 . . . . .4C **70**
Meard St. W1 . . . . . . .1C **12** (6H **83**)
           (not continuous)
Mears Cl. E1 . . . . .5G **85**
           (off Settles St.)
Meath Cres. E2 . . . . .3K **85**
Meath Ho. SE24 . . . . .6B **120**
           (off Dulwich Rd.)
Meath Rd. E15 . . . . .2H **87**
  IG1: Ilf 3G **71**
Meath St. SW11 . . . . .1F **119**
Mecca Bingo
  Camden 1F **83**
          (off Arlington Rd.)
  Catford .7D **122**
  Croydon 2C **168**
  Dagenham 1E **90**
  Hayes 6J **75**
  Morden .7A **154**
  Wood Green 2A **48**
          (off Lordship La.)
Mecklenburgh Pl. WC1 . . . .3G **7** (4K **83**)
Mecklenburgh Sq. WC1 . . . .3G **7** (4K **83**)
Mecklenburgh St. WC1 . . . .3G **7** (4K **83**)
Medals Way E20 . . . . .5E **68**
Medburn St. NW1 . . . . .2H **83**
Medcroft Gdns. SW14 . . . . .4J **115**
Medebourne Cl. SE3 . . . . .3J **123**
Mede Ho. BR1: Broml 5K **141**
           (off Pike Cl.)
Medesenge Way N13 . . . . .6G **33**
Medfield St. SW15 . . . . .7C **116**
Medhurst Cl. E3 . . . . .2A **86**
           (not continuous)
Medhurst Dr. BR1: Broml 5G **141**
Median Rd. E5 . . . . .5J **67**
Medici Cl. IG3: Ilf 6A **54**
           (not continuous)
Medina Gro. N7 . . . . .3A **66**
Medina Pl. E14 . . . . .5C **86**
Medina Rd. N7 . . . . .3A **66**
Medland Cl. SM6: W'gton 1E **166**
Medland Ho. E14 . . . . .7A **86**
Medlar Cl. UB5: N'olt 2B **76**
Medlar Ho. DA15: Sidc 3A **144**
Medlar St. SE5 . . . . .1C **120**
Medley Rd. NW6 . . . . .6J **63**
Medora Rd. RM7: Rom 4K **55**
  SW2 . . . . .7K **119**
Medusa Rd. SE6 . . . . .6D **122**
Medway Bldgs. E3 . . . . .2A **86**
          (off Medway Rd.)
Medway Cl. CR0: C'don 6J **157**
  IG1: Ilf 5G **71**
  RM7: Mawney 1H **55**
Medway Ct. NW11 . . . . .6K **45**
  WC1 . . . . .2E **6**
           (off Judd St.)
Medway Dr. UB6: G'frd 2K **77**
Medway Gdns. HA0: Wemb 4A **60**
Medway Ho. KT2: King T 1D **150**
  NW8 . . . . .4C **4**
          (off Penfold St.)
  SE1 . . . . .7F **15**
          (off Hankey Pl.)
Medway M. E3 . . . . .2A **86**
Medway Pde. UB6: G'frd 2K **77**
Medway Rd. E3 . . . . .2A **86**
Medway St.
  SW1 . . . . .2D **18** (3H **101**)
Medwin St. SW4 . . . . .4K **119**
Meerbrook Rd. SE3 . . . . .3A **124**
Meeson Rd. E15 . . . . .7H **69**
Meeson St. E5 . . . . .4A **68**
Meeson's Wharf E15 . . . . .2E **86**
Meeting Fld. Path E9 . . . . .6J **67**
Meeting Ho. All. E1 . . . . .1H **103**
Meeting Ho. La. SE15 . . . . .1H **121**
Megan Ct. SE14 . . . . .7J **103**
          (off Pomeroy St.)
Megelish M. UB1: S'hall 3E **76**

Mehetabel Rd. E9 . . . . .5J **67**
Meister Cl. IG1: Ilf 1H **71**
Melancholy Wlk.
  TW10: Ham 2C **132**
Melanda Cl. BR7: Chst 5D **142**
Melanie Cl. DA7: Bex 1E **126**
Melba Way SE13 . . . . .1D **122**
Melbourne Av. HA5: Pinn 3F **41**
  N13 . . . . .6E **32**
  W13 . . . . .1A **96**
Melbourne Cl. BR6: Orp 7J **161**
  SE20 . . . . .7G **139**
  SM6: W'gton 5G **167**
  UB10: Ick 4C **56**
Melbourne Ct. E5 . . . . .4A **68**
         (off Daubeney Rd.)
  N10 . . . . .7A **32**
  W9 . . . . .4A **82**
         (off Randolph Av.)
Melbourne Gdns. RM6: Chad H . .5E **54**
Melbourne Gro. SE22 . . . . .4E **120**
Melbourne Ho. UB4: Yead 4A **76**
  W8 . . . . .1J **99**
        (off Kensington Pl.)
Melbourne Mans. W14 . . . . .6G **99**
         (off Musard Rd.)
Melbourne M. SE6 . . . . .7E **122**
  SW9 . . . . .1A **120**
Melbourne Pl. WC2 . . . .1H **13** (6K **83**)
Melbourne Rd. E6 . . . . .2D **88**
  E10 . . . . .7D **50**
  E17 . . . . .4A **50**
  IG1: Ilf 1F **71**
  SM6: W'gton 5F **167**
  SW19 . . . . .1J **153**
  TW11: Tedd 6C **132**
Melbourne Sq. SW9 . . . . .1A **120**
Melbourne Ter. SW6 . . . . .7K **99**
         (off Moore Pk. Rd.)
Melbourne Way EN1: Enf 6A **24**
Melbourne Yd. SE19 . . . . .6E **138**
Melbray M. SW6 . . . . .2H **117**
Melbreak Ho. SE22 . . . . .3E **120**
Melbury Av. UB2: S'hall 3F **95**
Melbury Ct. BR7: Chst 6C **142**
  KT10: Clay 6B **162**
Melbury Ct. W8 . . . . .3H **99**
Melbury Dr. SE5 . . . . .7E **102**
Melbury Gdns. SW20 . . . . .1D **152**
Melbury Ho. SW8 . . . . .7K **101**
         (off Richborne Ter.)
Melbury Rd. HA3: Kenton 5F **43**
  W14 . . . . .3H **99**
Melchester W11 . . . . .6H **81**
         (off Ledbury Rd.)
Melchester Ho. N19 . . . . .3H **65**
         (off Wedmore St.)
Melcombe Ct. NW1 . . . . .5E **4**
         (off Melcombe Pl.)
Melcombe Ho. SW8 . . . . .7K **101**
         (off Dorset Rd.)
Melcombe Pl. NW1 . . . . . . .5E **4** (5D **82**)
Melcombe Regis Ct. W1 . . . . .6H **5**
         (off Weymouth St.)
Melcombe St. NW1 . . . . . .4F **5** (4D **82**)
Meldex Cl. NW7 . . . . .6K **29**
Meldon Cl. SW6 . . . . .1K **117**
Meldone Cl. KT5: Surb 7H **151**
Meldrum Rd. IG3: Ilf 2A **72**
Melford Av. IG11: Bark 6J **71**
Melford Cl. KT9: Chess 5F **163**
Melford Ct. SE1 . . . . .3E **102**
         (off Fendall St.)
  SE22 . . . . .1G **139**
         (not continuous)
Melford Pas. SE22 . . . . .7G **121**
Melford Rd. E6 . . . . .4D **88**
  E11 . . . . .2G **69**
  E17 . . . . .4A **50**
  IG1: Ilf 2H **71**
  SE22 . . . . .7G **121**

Melfort Av. CR7: Thor H 3B **156**
Melfort Rd. CR7: Thor H 3B **156**
Melgund Rd. N5 . . . . .5A **66**
Melina Cl. UB3: Hayes 5F **75**
Melina Ct. NW8 . . . . .2A **4**
  SW15 . . . . .3C **116**
Melina Pl. NW8 . . . . .2A **4** (3B **82**)
Melina Rd. W12 . . . . .2D **98**
Melior Ct. N6 . . . . .6G **47**
Melior Pl. SE1 . . . . .6G **15** (2E **102**)
Melior St. SE1 . . . . .6G **15** (2E **102**)
Mellor Rd. SE6 . . . . .2F **141**
Melier Cl. CR0: Bedd 3J **167**
Meller Ho. E20 . . . . .6E **68**
         (off Champions Wlk.)
Mellifont Cl. SM5: Cars 7B **154**
Melling Dr. EN1: Enf 1B **24**
Melling St. SE18 . . . . .6J **107**
Mellish Cl. IG11: Bark 1K **89**
  N20 . . . . .2G **31**
Mellish Flats E10 . . . . .7C **50**
Mellish Gdns. IG8: Wfd G 5D **36**
Mellish Ho. E1 . . . . .6H **85**
         (off Varden St.)
Mellish Ind. Est. SE18 . . . . .3B **106**
Mellish St. E14 . . . . .3C **104**
Mellison Rd. SW17 . . . . .5C **136**
Melliss Av. TW9: Kew 1H **115**
Mellitus St. W12 . . . . .5B **80**
Mellor Cl. KT12: Walt T 7D **148**
Mellow La. E. UB4: Hayes 3E **74**
Mellow La. W. UB10: Hil 3E **74**
Mellows Rd. IG5: Ilf 3D **52**
  SM6: W'gton 5H **167**
Mells Cres. SE9 . . . . .4D **142**
Mell St. SE10 . . . . .5G **105**
Melody La. N5 . . . . .5C **66**
Melody Rd. SW18 . . . . .5A **118**
Melon Pl. W8 . . . . .2J **99**
Melon Rd. E11 . . . . .3G **69**
  SE15 . . . . .1G **121**
Melrose Av. CR4: Mitc 7F **137**
  DA1: Cray 7K **127**
  N22 . . . . .2A **48**
  NW2 . . . . .5D **62**
  SW16 . . . . .3K **155**
  SW19 . . . . .2H **135**
  TW2: Whitt 7F **113**
  UB6: G'frd 2F **77**
Melrose Cl. SE12 . . . . .1J **141**
  UB4: Hayes 5J **75**
  UB6: G'frd 2F **77**
Melrose Ct. W13 . . . . .1A **96**
         (off Williams Rd.)
Melrose Cres. BR6: Orp 4H **173**
Melrose Dr. UB1: S'hall 1E **94**
Melrose Gdns. HA8: Edg 3H **43**
  KT3: N Mald 3K **151**
  W6 . . . . .3E **98**
Melrose Ho. NW6 . . . . .3J **81**
         (off Carlton Vale)
  SW1 . . . . .5J **17**
        (part of Abbots Mnr.)
Melrose Rd. HA5: Pinn 4D **40**
  SW13 . . . . .2B **116**
  SW18 . . . . .6H **117**
  SW19 . . . . .2J **153**
  W3 . . . . .3J **97**
Melrose Ter. W6 . . . . .3E **98**
Melrose Tudor SM6: W'gton 5J **167**
         (off Plough La.)
Melsa Rd. SM4: Mord 6A **154**
Meltham Dr. HA4: Ruis 3A **58**
Melthorpe Gdns. SE3 . . . . .1C **124**
Melton Cl. HA4: Ruis 1A **58**
Melton Ct. SM2: Sutt 7A **166**
  SW7 . . . . .4B **16** (4B **100**)
  SW1 . . . . .2B **6** (3G **83**)
Melville Av.
  CR2: S Croy 5F **169**
  SW20 . . . . .7C **134**
  UB6: G'frd 5K **59**
Melville Cl. UB10: Ick 2F **57**

Melville Ct.—Merton Hall Rd.

Melville Ct. SE8 ....4A **104**
W4 ....*5G* ***97***
(*off Haining Cl.*)
W12 ....*3D* ***98***
(*off Goldhawk Rd.*)
Melville Gdns. N13 ....5G **33**
Melville Ho. EN5: New Bar 5G **21**
Melville Pl. N1 ....7C **66**
Melville Rd. DA14: Sidc 2C **144**
E17 ....3B **50**
NW10 ....7K **61**
RM5: Col R 1H **55**
SW13 ....1C **116**
Melville Vs. Rd. W3 ....1J **97**
Melvin Rd. SE20 ....1J **157**
Melwood Ho. *E1* *6H* ***85***
(*off Watney Mkt.*)
Melyn Cl. N7 ....4G **65**
Memel Ct. EC1 ....4C **8**
Memel St. EC1 ....4C **8** (4C **84**)
Memess Path SE18 ....6E **106**
Memorial Av. E15 ....3G **87**
Memorial Cl. TW5: Hest 6D **94**
Memorial Hgts. IG2: Ilf 6H **53**
Menai Pl. *E3* *2C* ***86***
(*off Blondin St.*)
Menard Ct. *EC1* *2D* ***8***
(*off Galway St.*)
Mendez Way SW15 ....6C **116**
Mendham Ho. *SE1* *7G* ***15***
(*off Cluny Pl.*)
Mendip Cl. KT4: Wor Pk 1E **164**
SE26 ....4J **139**
UB3: Harl 7F **93**
Mendip Ct. *SE14* *6J* ***103***
(*off Avonley Rd.*)
SW11 ....3A **118**
Mendip Dr. NW2 ....2G **63**
Mendip Ho. *N9* *2B* ***34***
(*within Edmonton Grn. Shop. Cen.*)
Mendip Ho's. *E2* *3J* ***85***
(*off Welwyn St.*)
Mendip Rd. DA7: Bex 1K **127**
IG2: Ilf 5J **53**
SW11 ....3A **118**
Mendora Rd. SW6 ....7G **99**
Menelik Rd. NW2 ....4G **63**
Menier Chocolate Factory ***5D 14***
(off Southwark St.)
Menlo Gdns. SE19 ....7D **138**
Menlo Lodge *N13* *3E* ***32***
(*off Crothall Cl.*)
Menon Dr. N9 ....3C **34**
Menotti St. E2 ....4G **85**
Menteath Ho. *E14* *6C* ***86***
(*off Dod St.*)
Mentmore Cl. HA3: Kenton 6C **42**
Mentmore Ter. E8 ....7H **67**
Mentone Mans. *SW10* *7K* ***99***
(*off Fulham Rd.*)
Meon Ct. TW7: Isle 2J **113**
Meon Rd. W3 ....2J **97**
Meopham Rd. CR4: Mitc 1G **155**
Mepham Cres. HA3: Hrw W 7B **26**
Mepham Gdns. HA3: Hrw W 7B **26**
Mepham St. SE1 ....5H **13** (1A **102**)
Mera Dr. DA7: Bex 4G **127**
Meranti Ho. *E1* *6G* ***85***
(*off Goodman's Stile*)
Merantun Way SW19 ....1K **153**
Merbury Cl. SE13 ....5E **122**
SE28 ....1H **107**
Merbury Rd. SE28 ....1H **107**
Mercator Pl. E14 ....5C **104**
Mercator Rd. SE13 ....4F **123**
Mercer Bldg. *EC2* *3H* ***9***
(*off New Inn Yd.*)
Mercer Cl. KT7: T Ditt 7K **149**
Mercer Ct. E1 ....5A **86**
Mercer Ho. *SW1* *5J* ***17***
(*off Ebury Bri. Rd.*)
SW8 ....*1F* ***119***
(*off Gladstone Ter.*)
Merceron Ho's. *E2* *3J* ***85***
(*off Globe Rd.*)
Merceron St. E1 ....4H **85**
Mercer Pl. HA5: Pinn 2A **40**
Mercers Cl. SE10 ....4H **105**
Mercer's Cotts. *E1* *6A* ***86***
(*off White Horse Rd.*)
Mercers M. N19 ....3H **65**
Mercers Pl. W6 ....4F **99**
Mercers Rd. N19 ....3H **65**
(not continuous)
Mercer St. WC2 ....1E **12** (6J **83**)
Mercer Wlk. *WC2* *1E* ***12***
(*off Mercer St.*)
Merchant Cl. KT19: Ewe 5K **163**
Merchant Ct. *E1* *1J* ***103***
(*off Wapping Wall*)
Merchant Ho. *E14* *3D* ***104***
(*off Selsdon Way*)
Merchant Ind. Ter. NW10 ....4J **79**
Merchant Navy Memorial **3H 15** (**7F 85**)
Merchants Cl. SE25 ....4G **157**
Merchants Ho. *E14* *6F* ***87***
(*off New Village Av.*)
E15 ....*6F* ***69***
(*off Forrester Way*)
SE10 ....*5F* ***105***
(*off Collington St.*)
Merchants Lodge *E17* *4C* ***50***
(*off Westbury Rd.*)
Merchant Sq. W2 ....6B **4**
Merchant Square East W2 ....6B **4**
Merchant Square West W2 ....6B **4**
Merchants Row *SE10* *5F* ***105***
(*off Hoskins St.*)
Merchant St. E3 ....3B **86**
Merchiston Rd. SE6 ....2F **141**
Merchland Rd. SE9 ....1G **143**
Mercia Gro. SE13 ....4E **122**
Mercia Ho. *SE5* *2C* ***120***
(*off Denmark Rd.*)
TW15: Ashf 1E **146**
Mercier Ct. *E16* *1A* ***106***
(*off Starboard Way*)
Mercier Rd. SW15 ....5G **117**
Mercury *NW9* *1B* ***44***
(*off Quakers Course*)
Mercury Cen. TW14: Felt 5J **111**
Mercury Ct. *E14* *4C* ***104***
(*off Homer Dr.*)
SW9 ....*1A* ***120***
(*off Southey Rd.*)
Mercury Ho. *E3* *1C* ***86***
(*off Garrison Rd.*)
E16 ....*6H* ***87***
(*off Jude St.*)
TW8: Bford *6C* ***96***
(*off Glenhurst Rd.*)
W5 ....4F **79**
Mercury Rd. TW8: Bford 6C **96**
Mercury Way SE14 ....6K **103**
Mercy Ter. SE13 ....5D **122**
Merebank La. CR0: Wadd 5K **167**
Mere Cl. BR6: Farnb 2E **172**
SW15 ....7F **117**
Meredith Av. NW2 ....5E **62**
Meredith Cl. HA5: Pinn 1B **40**
Meredith Ho. N16 ....5E **66**
Meredith M. SE4 ....4B **122**
Meredith St. E13 ....3J **87**
EC1 ....2A **8** (3B **84**)
Meredith Wlk. *RM8: Dag* *1E* ***72***
(*off Ellis Av.*)
Meredyth Rd. SW13 ....2C **116**
Mere End CR0: C'don 7K **157**
Mere Rd. SE2 ....2D **108**
TW17: Shep 6D **146**
Mereside BR6: Farnb 2E **172**
Mereside Pk. TW15: Ashf 4E **128**
Meretone Cl. SE4 ....4A **122**
Mereton Mans. *SE8* *1C* ***122***
(*off Brookmill Rd.*)
Merevale Cres. SM4: Mord 6A **154**
Mereway Rd. TW2: Twick 1H **131**
Merewood Cl. BR1: Broml 2E **160**
Merewood Gdns. CR0: C'don 7K **157**
Merewood Rd. DA7: Bex 2J **127**
Mereworth Cl. BR2: Broml 5H **159**
Mereworth Dr. SE18 ....7F **107**
Mereworth Ho. SE15 ....6J **103**
Merganser Ct. *E1* *3K* ***15***
(*off Star Pl.*)
SE8 ....*6B* ***104***
(*off Edward St.*)
Merganser Gdns. SE28 ....3H **107**
Meriden Cl. BR1: Broml 7B **142**
IG6: Ilf 1G **53**
Meriden Ct. SW3 ....6C **16**
Meriden Ho. *N1* *1E* ***84***
(*off Wilmer Gdns.*)
Merideth Ct. KT1: King T 2F **151**
Meridia Ct. *E15* *1E* ***86***
(*off Biggerstaff Rd.*)
Meridian Bus. Pk. EN3: Pond E 6F **25**
Meridian Cl. NW7 ....4E **28**
Meridian Ct. *SE15* *7H* ***103***
(*off Gervase St.*)
SE16 ....*2G* ***103***
(*off East La.*)
UB4: Yead 4A **76**
Meridian Ga. E14 ....2D **104**
Meridian Ho. *NW1* *7G* ***65***
(*off Baynes St.*)
SE10 ....*4G* ***105***
(*off Azof St.*)
SE10 ....*7E* ***104***
(*off Royal Hill*)
SW18 ....*4A* ***118***
(*off Juniper Dr.*)
Meridian Pl. E14 ....2D **104**
Meridian Point SE8 ....6D **104**
Meridian Rd. SE7 ....7B **106**
Meridian Sq. E15 ....7F **69**
Meridian Trad. Est. SE7 ....4K **105**
Meridian Wlk. N17 ....6K **33**
Meridian Water Development N18 ....6E **34**
Meridian Way EN3: Pond E 4D **34**
N9 ....4D **34**
N18 ....5D **34**
Merifield Rd. SE9 ....4A **124**
Merino Cl. E11 ....4A **52**
SM6: W'gton 2E **166**
Merino Ct. *EC1* *2D* ***8***
(*off Lever St.*)
Merino Pl. DA15: Sidc 6A **126**
Merioneth Ct. *W7* *5K* ***77***
(*off Copley Cl.*)
Merita Ho. *E1* *1G* ***103***
(*off Nesham St.*)
Merivale Rd. HA1: Harr 7G **41**
SW15 ....4G **117**
Merle Mans. *E20* *6E* ***68***
(*off Glade Wlk.*)
Merlewood Dr. BR7: Chst 1D **160**
Merley Ct. NW9 ....1J **61**
Merlin *NW9* *1B* ***44***
(*off Near Acre*)
Merlin Cl. CR0: C'don 4E **168**
CR4: Mitc 3C **154**
SM6: W'gton 6K **167**
UB5: N'olt 3A **76**
Merlin Ct. BR2: Broml 3H **159**
HA4: Ruis 2F **57**
HA7: Stan *5G* ***27***
(*off William Dr.*)
SE3 ....4K **123**
Merlin Cres. HA8: Edg 1F **43**
Merlin Gdns. BR1: Broml 3J **141**
Merling Cl. KT9: Chess 5C **162**
Merlin Gro. BR3: Beck 4B **158**
Merlin Hgts. *N17* *3H* ***49***
(*off Daneland Wlk.*)
Merlin Ho. EN3: Pond E 5E **24**
Merlin Rd. DA16: Well 4A **126**
E12 ....2B **70**
Merlin Rd. Nth. DA16: Well 4A **126**
Merlins Av. HA2: Harr 3D **58**
Merlins Ct. *WC1* *2J* ***7***
(*off Margery St.*)
Merlin St. WC1 ....2J **7** (3A **84**)
Mermaid Ct. *E8* *7F* ***67***
(*off Celandine Dr.*)
SE1 ....6E **14** (2D **102**)
SE16 ....1B **104**
Mermaid Ho. *E14* *7E* ***86***
(*off Bazely St.*)
Mermaid Twr. *SE8* *6B* ***104***
(*off Abinger Gro.*)
Meroe Ct. N16 ....2E **66**
Mero Way NW7 ....7B **30**
Merredene St. SW2 ....6K **119**
Merriam Av. E9 ....6B **68**
Merriam Cl. E4 ....5K **35**
Merrick Rd. UB2: S'hall 2D **94**
Merrick Sq. SE1 ....7E **14** (3D **102**)
Merridene N21 ....6G **23**
Merrielands Cres. RM9: Dag 2F **91**
Merrielands Retail Pk. 1F **91**
Merrilands Rd. KT4: Wor Pk 1E **164**
Merrilees Rd. DA15: Sidc 7J **125**
Merrilyn Cl. KT10: Clay 6A **162**
Merriman Rd. SE3 ....1A **124**
Merrington Rd. SW6 ....6J **99**
Merrion Av. HA7: Stan 5J **27**
Merrion Ct. *HA4: Ruis* *1H* ***57***
(*off Pembroke Rd.*)
Merritt Gdns. KT9: Chess 6C **162**
Merritt Rd. SE4 ....5B **122**
Merrivale N14 ....6C **22**
NW1 ....*1G* ***83***
(*off Camden St.*)
Merrivale Av. IG4: Ilf 4B **52**
Merrivale M. HA8: Edg 1J **43**
Merrow Bldgs. *SE1* *6B* ***14***
(*off Rushworth St.*)
Merrow Ct. CR4: Mitc 2B **154**
Merrow Rd. SM2: Cheam 7F **165**
Merrow St. SE17 ....5D **102**
Merrow Wlk. SE17 ....5D **102**
Merrow Way CR0: New Ad 6E **170**
Merrydown Way BR7: Chst 1C **160**
Merryfield SE3 ....2H **123**
Merryfield Ct. SW11 ....2D **118**
Merryfield Gdns. HA7: Stan 5H **27**
Merryfield Ho. *SE9* *3A* ***142***
(*off Grove Pk. Rd.*)
Merryfields UB8: Uxb 2A **74**
Merryfields Way SE6 ....7D **122**
MERRY HILL 1A **26**
Merryhill Cl. E4 ....7J **25**
Merry Hill Mt. WD23: Bush 1A **26**
Merry Hill Rd. WD23: Bush 1A **26**
Merryhills Ct. N14 ....5B **22**
Merryhills Dr. EN2: Enf 4C **22**
Merryweather Ct. KT3: N Mald 5A **152**
N19 ....3G **65**
Merryweather Pl. SE10 ....7D **104**
Mersea Ho. IG11: Bark 6F **71**
Mersey Ct. *KT2: King T* *1D* ***150***
(*off Samuel Gray Gdns.*)
Mersey Rd. E17 ....3B **50**
Mersey Wlk. UB5: N'olt 2E **76**
Mersham Dr. NW9 ....5G **43**
Mersham Pl. *CR7: Thor H* *2D* ***156***
(*off Livingstone Rd.*)
SE20 ....1H **157**
Mersham Rd. CR7: Thor H 3D **156**
Merten Rd. RM6: Chad H 7E **54**
Merthyr Ter. SW13 ....6D **98**
MERTON 7A **136**
Merton Abbey Mills SW19 ....1A **154**
Merton Av. UB5: N'olt 5G **59**
UB10: Hil 7D **56**
W4 ....4B **98**
Merton Ct. DA16: Well 2B **126**
IG1: Ilf 6C **52**
Merton Gdns. BR5: Pet W 5F **161**
Merton Hall Gdns. SW20 ....1G **153**
Merton Hall Rd. SW19 ....7G **135**

Merton High St. SW19 . . . . . . .7K 135
Merton Ind. Pk. SW19 . . . . .1K 153
Merton La. N6 . . . . .2D 64
Merton Lodge EN5: New Bar 5F 21
Merton Mans. SW20 . . . . .2F 153
MERTON PARK 2J 153
Merton Pk. Pde. SW19 . . . . .1H 153
Merton Pl. SW19 . . . . .1A 154
(off Nelson Gro. Rd.)
Merton Ri. NW3 . . . . .7C 64
Merton Rd. E17 . . . . .5E 50
EN2: Enf 1J 23
HA2: Harr 1G 59
IG3: Ilf 7K 53
IG11: Bark 7K 71
SE25 . . . . .5F 157
SW18 . . . . .6J 117
SW19 . . . . .7K 135
Merton's Intergenerational Cen. . . .2F 155
Merton Way KT8: W Mole 4F 149
UB10: Hil 7D 56
Mertoun Ter. W1 . . . . .7E 4
(off Seymour Pl.)
Merttins Rd. SE15 . . . . .5K 121
Meru Cl. NW5 . . . . .4E 64
Mervan Rd. SW2 . . . . .4A 120
Mervyn Av. SE9 . . . . .3G 143
Mervyn Rd. TW17: Shep 7E 146
W13 . . . . .3A 96
Messaline Av. W3 . . . . .6J 79
Messenger Ct. SE16 . . . . .3G 103
(off Spa Rd.)
Messent Rd. SE9 . . . . .5A 124
Messeter Pl. SE9 . . . . .6E 124
Messina Av. NW6 . . . . .7J 63
Messina Way RM9: Dag 2F 91
Messiter Ho. N1 . . . . .1K 83
(off Barnsbury Est.)
Messom M. TW1: Twick 1A 132
Metcalfe Ct. SE10 . . . . .3H 105
Metcalf Rd. TW15: Ashf 5D 128
Metcalf Wlk. TW13: Hanw 4C 130
Meteor St. SW11 . . . . .4E 118
Meteor Way SM6: W'gton 7J 167
Methley St. SE11 . . . . .6K 19 (5A 102)
Methuen Cl. HA8: Edg 7B 28
Methuen Pk. N10 . . . . .3F 47
Methuen Rd. DA6: Bex 4F 127
DA17: Belv 4H 109
HA8: Edg 7B 28
Methven Ct. N9 . . . . .3B 34
(off The Broadway)
Methwold Rd. W10 . . . . .5F 81
Metro Bus. Cen. SE26 . . . . .6B 140
Metro Central Hgts. SE1 . . . . . .3C 102
(off Newington C'way.)
Metro Golf Cen. 7K 29
Metro Ind. Cen. TW7: Isle 2J 113
Metropolis SE11 . . . . .3B 102
(off Oswin St.)
Metropolis Plaza E3 . . . . .4A 86
(off Copperfield Rd.)
Metropolitan Bldg. SW10 . . . . . . .7A 100
Metropolitan Bus. Cen. N1 . . . . .7E 66
(off Enfield Rd.)
The Metropolitan Cen. UB6: G'frd . . .1F 77
Metropolitan Cl. E14 . . . . .5C 86
Metropolitan Cres. SW4 . . . . .5H 119
Metropolitan Ho. TW8: Bford 6F 97
Metropolitan Police FC 6H 149
Metropolitan Sta. Bldgs. W6 . . . .4E 98
(off Beadon Rd.)
Metropolitan Wharf E1 . . . . .1J 103
Metro Trad. Est. HA9: Wemb 4H 61
The Mews DA14: Sidc 4A 144
IG4: Ilf 5B 52
N1 . . . . .1C 84
N8 . . . . .3A 48
RM1: Rom 4K 55
TW1: Twick 6B 114
TW12: Hamp H 6G 131
Mews Pl. IG8: Wfd G 4D 36
Mews St. E1 . . . . . . .4K 15 (1G 103)

Mexborough NW1 . . . . .1G 83
Mexfield Rd. SW15 . . . . .5H 117
Meyer Grn. EN1: Enf 1B 24
Meyer Rd. DA8: Erith 6K 109
Meymott St. SE1 . . . . . .5A 14 (1B 102)
Meynell Cres. E9 . . . . .7K 67
Meynell Gdns. E9 . . . . .7K 67
Meynell Rd. E9 . . . . .7K 67
Meyrick Ho. E14 . . . . .5C 86
(off Burgess St.)
Meyrick Rd. NW10 . . . . .6C 62
SW11 . . . . .3B 118
MFA Bowl
Lewisham 3E 122
Miah Ter. E1 . . . . .1G 103
Miall Wlk. SE26 . . . . .4A 140
Mia M. N13 . . . . .5F 33
Mica Ho. N1 . . . . .7A 66
Micawber Av. UB8: Hil 4C 74
Micawber Ct. N1 . . . . .1D 8
(off Windsor Ter.)
Micawber Ho. SE16 . . . . .2G 103
(off Llewellyn St.)
Micawber St. N1 . . . . .1D 8 (3C 84)
Michael Cliffe Ho. EC1 . . . . .2A 8
Michael Cl. E3 . . . . .4B 86
The Michael Edwards Studio Theatre
. . . . .6E 104
(within Cutty Sark)
Michael Faraday Ho. SE17 . . . . . .5E 102
(off Beaconsfield Rd.)
Michael Gaynor Cl. W7 . . . . .1K 95
Michael Haines Ho. SW9 . . . . . .7A 102
(off Sth. Island Pl.)
Michael Manley Ind. Est. SW8 . . .1G 119
Michaelmas Cl. SW20 . . . . .3E 152
Michael Rd. E11 . . . . .1G 69
SE25 . . . . .3E 156
SW6 . . . . .1K 117
Michael Robbins Way NW7 . . . . .5B 30
Michaels Cl. SE13 . . . . .4G 123
Michael Stewart Ho. SW6 . . . . . .6H 99
(off Clem Attlee Ct.)
Michelangelo Ct. SE16 . . . . .5H 103
(off Stubbs Dr.)
Micheldever Rd. SE12 . . . . .6G 123
Micheltham Gdns. TW1: Twick . . .3K 131
Michelle Ct. BR1: Broml 1H 159
(off Blyth Rd.)
N12 . . . . .5F 31
W3 . . . . .1F 97
Michelsdale Dr. TW9: Rich 4E 114
Michelson Ho. SE11 . . . . .4H 19
Michel's Row TW9: Rich 4E 114
(off Michelsdale Dr.)
Michel Wlk. SE18 . . . . .5F 107
Michigan Av. E12 . . . . .4D 70
Michigan Bldg. E14 . . . . .1F 105
(off Biscayne Av.)
Michigan Ho. E14 . . . . .3C 104
Michleham Down N12 . . . . .4C 30
Mickledore NW1 . . . . .1B 6
(off Ampthill Est.)
Mickleham Cl. BR5: St P 2K 161
Mickleham Gdns. SM3: Cheam . . .6G 165
Mickleham Rd. BR5: St P 1K 161
Mickleham Way CR0: New Ad 7F 171
Micklethwaite Rd. SW6 . . . . .6J 99
Micklewood Ho. W2 . . . . .5J 81
(off Westbourne Pk. Rd.)
Midas Bus. Cen. RM10: Dag 4H 73
Midas Metropolitan Ind. Est.
SM4: Mord 7E 152
MID BECKTON 5D 88
Midcroft HA4: Ruis 1G 57
Middle Dartrey Wlk. SW10 . . . . .7A 100
(off Worlds End Est.)
Middle Dene NW7 . . . . .3E 28
Middlefield NW8 . . . . .1B 82
Middlefielde W13 . . . . .5B 78
Middlefield Gdns. IG2: Ilf 6F 53
Middle Grn. Cl. KT5: Surb 6F 151
Middleham Gdns. N18 . . . . .6B 34

Middleham Rd. N18 . . . . .6B 34
Middle La. N8 . . . . .5J 47
TW11: Tedd 6K 131
Middle La. M. N8 . . . . .5J 47
Middle Mill Halls of Residence
KT1: King T 3F 151
(off Pemberton Row)
Middle New St. EC4 . . . . .7K 7
(off Pemberton Row)
Middle Pk. Av. SE9 . . . . .6B 124
Middle Path HA2: Harr 1H 59
Middle Rd. E13 . . . . .2J 87
EN4: E Barn 6H 21
HA2: Harr 2H 59
SW16 . . . . .2H 155
Middle Row W10 . . . . .4G 81
Middlesborough Rd. N18 . . . . .6B 34
The Middlesex Bldg. E1 . . . . .7H 9
(off Artillery La.)
Middlesex Bus. Cen. UB2: S'hall . . .2E 94
Middlesex CCC 1B 4 (3B 82)
Middlesex Cl. UB1: S'hall 4F 77
Middlesex Ct. HA1: Harr 5K 41
TW8: Bford 5C 96
(off Glenhurst Rd.)
W4 . . . . .4B 98
Middlesex Filter Beds Nature Reserve
. . . . .3K 67
Middlesex Guildhall 7E 12
(off Lit. George St.)
Middlesex Ho. HA0: Wemb 1D 78
Middlesex Pas. EC1 . . . . .6B 8
Middlesex Pl. E9 . . . . .6J 67
(off Elsdale St.)
Middlesex Rd. CR4: Mitc 5J 155
Middlesex St. E1 . . . . .6H 9 (5E 84)
Middlesex University
Archway Campus 1G 65
Hendon Campus 4D 44
Middlesex Wharf E5 . . . . .2J 67
Middle St. CR0: C'don 2C 168
(not continuous)
EC1 . . . . .5C 8 (5C 84)
Middle Temple Hall 7A 84
Middle Temple La. EC4 . . . .1J 13 (6A 84)
Middleton Av. DA14: Sidc 6B 144
E4 . . . . .4G 35
UB6: G'frd 2H 77
Middleton Cl. E4 . . . . .3G 35
Middleton Dr. HA5: Eastc 3J 39
SE16 . . . . .2K 103
Middleton Gdns. IG2: Ilf 6F 53
Middleton Gro. IG11: Bark 3A 90
N7 . . . . .5J 65
Middleton Ho. E8 . . . . .7G 67
SE1 . . . . .7D 14
(off Burbage Cl.)
SW1 . . . . .4D 18
(off Causton St.)
Middleton M. N7 . . . . .5J 65
Middleton Pl. W1 . . . . .6A 6
Middleton Rd. E8 . . . . .7F 67
NW11 . . . . .7J 45
SM4: Mord, Cars 6K 153
SM5: Cars 6A 154
UB3: Hayes 5F 75
Middleton St. E2 . . . . .3H 85
Middleton Way SE13 . . . . .4F 123
Middle Way DA18: Erith 3E 108
SW16 . . . . .2H 155
UB4: Yead 4A 76
Middleway NW11 . . . . .5K 45
The Middle Way
HA3: W'stone 2K 41
Middle Yd. SE1 . . . . . . .4G 15 (1E 102)
Midfield Av. DA7: Bex 3J 127
Midfield Pde. DA7: Bex 3J 127
Midfield Way BR5: St P 7A 144
Midford Ho. NW4 . . . . .4F 45
(off Belle Vue Est.)
Midford Pl. W1 . . . . .4B 6 (4G 83)
Midholm HA9: Wemb 1G 61
NW11 . . . . .4K 45
Midholm Cl. NW11 . . . . .4K 45

Midholm Rd. CR0: C'don 2A 170
Midhope Ho. WC1 . . . . .2F 7
(off Midhope St.)
Midhope St. WC1 . . . . . . .2F 7 (3J 83)
Midhurst SE26 . . . . .6J 139
Midhurst Av. CR0: C'don 7A 156
N10 . . . . .3E 46
(off Hill 1E 74
Midhurst Gdns. UB10: Hil 1E 74
Midhurst Hill DA6: Bex 6G 127
Midhurst Ho. E14 . . . . .6B 86
(off Salmon La.)
Midhurst Pde. N10 . . . . .3E 46
(off Fortis Grn.)
Midhurst Rd. W13 . . . . .2A 96
Midhurst Way E5 . . . . .4G 67
Midland Goods Shed N1 . . . . . . .1J 83
(off Handyside St.)
Midland Pde. NW6 . . . . .6K 63
Midland Pl. E14 . . . . .5E 104
Midland Rd. E10 . . . . .7E 50
NW1 . . . . .1D 6 (2H 83)
Midland Ter. NW2 . . . . .3F 63
NW10 . . . . .4A 80
Midleton Rd. KT3: N Mald 3J 151
Midlothian Rd. E3 . . . . .4B 86
(off Burdett Rd.)
Midmoor Rd. SW12 . . . . .1G 137
SW19 . . . . .1F 153
Midnight Av. SE5 . . . . .7B 102
Midship Cl. SE16 . . . . .1K 103
Midship Point E14 . . . . .2C 104
(off The Quarterdeck)
Midstrath Rd. NW10 . . . . .4A 62
Midsummer Av. TW4: Houn 4D 112
Midway SM3: Sutt 7H 153
Midway Ho. EC1 . . . . .1A 8
Midwinter Cl. DA16: Well 3A 126
Midwood Cl. NW2 . . . . .3D 62
Miers Cl. E6 . . . . .1E 88
Mighell Av. IG4: Ilf 5B 52
Mikardo Ct. E14 . . . . .7E 86
(off Poplar High St.)
Milan Ct. N11 . . . . .1H 47
Milan Rd. UB1: S'hall 2D 94
Milborne Gro. SW10 . . . . . .6A 16 (5A 100)
Milborne St. E9 . . . . .6J 67
Milborough Cres. SE12 . . . . .6G 123
Milbourne Ho. KT1: King T 1G 151
(off Coombe Rd.)
Milbourne Pl. KT19: Ewe 4K 163
Milburn Dr. UB7: Yiew 7A 74
Milcote St. SE1 . . . . .7A 14 (2B 102)
Mildenhall Rd. E5 . . . . .4J 67
Mildmay Av. N1 . . . . .6D 66
Mildmay Gro. Sth. N1 . . . . .5D 66
Mildmay Gro. Sth. N1 . . . . .5D 66
Mildmay Pk. N1 . . . . .5D 66
Mildmay Pl. N16 . . . . .5E 66
Mildmay Rd. IG1: Ilf 3F 71
N1 . . . . .5D 66
RM7: Rom 5J 55
Mildmay St. N1 . . . . .6D 66
Mildred Av. UB3: Harl 4F 93
UB5: N'olt 5F 59
Mildred Ct. CR0: C'don 1G 169
Mildred Rd. DA8: Erith 5K 109
Mildrose Ct. NW6 . . . . .3J 81
(off Malvern M.)
Mildura Ct. N8 . . . . .4K 47
MILE END 4B 86
The Mile End E17 . . . . .1K 49
Mile End Pk. 2A 86
Mile End Pk. Leisure Cen. 5A 86
Mile End Pl. E1 . . . . .4K 85
Mile End Rd. E1 . . . . .5J 85
E3 . . . . .5J 85
Mile End Stadium 5B 86
Mile Rd. SM6: Bedd, W'gton 1F 167
(not continuous)
Miles Bldgs. NW1 . . . . .5C 4
(off Penfold Pl.)
Miles Cl. SE28 . . . . .1H 107

Miles Ct. *CRO: C'don* 2B **168**
E1 . . . . .6H **85**
(off Cuthbert Rd.)
Miles Dr. SE28 . . . . .1J **107**
Miles Ho. *SE10* 5G **105**
(off Tuskar St.)
Miles Lodge *E15* 5F **69**
(off Colegrave Rd.)
HA1: Harr 5H **41**
Milespit Hill NW7 . . . . .5J **29**
Miles Pl. KT5: Surb 4F **151**
NW8 . . . . .5B **4**
Miles Rd. CR4: Mitc 3C **154**
N8 . . . . .3J **47**
Miles St. SW8 . . . . .7E **18** (6J **101**)
(not continuous)
Milestone Cl. N9 . . . . .2B **34**
SM2: Sutt 6B **166**
Milestone Ct. E10 . . . . .7D **50**
MILESTONE GREEN 4J **115**
Milestone Ho. *KT1: King T* 3D **150**
(off Surbiton Rd.)
Milestone Rd. SE19 . . . . .6F **139**
Miles Way N20 . . . . .2H **31**
Milfoil St. W12 . . . . .7C **80**
Milford Cl. SE2 . . . . .6E **108**
Milford Ct. UB1: S'hall 1E **94**
Milford Gdns.
CRO: C'don 5J **157**
HA0: Wemb 4D **60**
HA8: Edg 7B **28**
Milford Gro. SM1: Sutt 4A **166**
Milford La. WC2 . . . . .2H **13** (7A **84**)
Milford M. SW16 . . . . .3K **137**
Milford Rd. UB1: S'hall 7E **76**
W13 . . . . .1B **96**
Milford Towers SE6 . . . . .7D **122**
Milk St. BR1: Broml 6K **141**
E16 . . . . .1F **107**
EC2 . . . . .7D **8** (6C **84**)
Milkwell Gdns. IG8: Wfd G 7E **36**
Milkwell Yd. SE5 . . . . .1C **120**
Milkwood Rd. SE24 . . . . .5B **120**
Milk Yd. E1 . . . . .7J **85**
Millais Av. E12 . . . . .5E **70**
Millais Ct. *UB5: N'olt* 2B **76**
(off Academy Gdns.)
Millais Cres. KT19: Ewe 5A **164**
Millais Gdns. HA8: Edg 2G **43**
Millais Ho. *SW1* 4E **18**
(off Marsham St.)
Millais Rd. E11 . . . . .4E **68**
EN1: Enf 5A **24**
KT3: N Mald 7A **152**
Millais Way KT19: Ewe 4J **163**
Millard Cl. N16 . . . . .5E **66**
Millard Rd. SE8 . . . . .5B **104**
Millbank SM6: W'gton 5H **167**
SW1 . . . . .2E **18** (3J **101**)
Millbank Ct. SW1 . . . . .4J **101**
Millbank Twr. SW1 . . . . . .4E **18** (4J **101**)
Millbank Way SE12 . . . . .5J **123**
Millbourne Rd.
TW13: Hanw 4C **130**
Mill Bridge EN5: Barn 6C **20**
Millbroke M. IG8: Wfd G 6B **36**
Millbrook Av. DA16: Well 4H **125**
Millbrooke Ct. *SW15* 5G **117**
(off Keswick Rd.)
Millbrook Gdns. RM6: Chad H 6F **55**
Millbrook Ho. *SE15* 6G **103**
(off Peckham Pk. Rd.)
Millbrook Pk. NW7 . . . . .6B **30**
Millbrook Pas. SW9 . . . . .3B **120**
Millbrook Pl. *NW1* 2G **83**
(off Hampstead Rd.)
Millbrook Rd. N9 . . . . .1C **34**
SW9 .3B **120**
Mill Cl. NW7 . . . . .1G **45**
SM5: Cars 2E **166**
Mill Cnr. EN5: Barn 1C **20**

Mill Ct. E5 . . . . .2J **67**
E10 . . . . .3E **68**
SE28 . . . . .7B **90**
(off Titmuss Av.)
Millcroft Ho. *SE6* 4E **140**
(off Melfield Gdns.)
Mill Dr. HA4: Ruis 7F **39**
Millender Wlk. *SE16* 4J **103**
(off New Rotherhithe Rd.)
MILLENNIUM BRIDGE 3C **14** (7C **84**)
Millennium Bri. Ho. EC4 . . . . .2C **14**
(off Up. Thames St.)
Millennium Bus. Cen. NW2 . . . . . .2D **62**
The Millennium Cen. 4K **73**
Millennium Cl. E16 . . . . .6K **87**
Millennium Dr. E14 . . . . .4F **105**
Millennium Ho. E17 . . . . .5K **49**
SW15 . . . . .5G **117**
(off Plaza Gdns.)
Millennium Pl. E2 . . . . .2H **85**
Millennium Sq. SE1 . . . .6K **15** (2F **103**)
Millennium Way SE10 . . . . .2G **105**
Miller Av. EN3: Enf L 1H **25**
Miller Cl. BR1: Broml 5K **141**
CR4: Mitc 7D **154**
HA5: Pinn 2A **40**
RM5: Col R 1G **55**
Miller Ct. DA7: Bex 3J **127**
Miller Ho. *E1* 5K **85**
(off Shandy St.)
W10 . . . . .4H **81**
(off Harrow Rd.)
Miller Rd. CRO: C'don 1K **167**
SW19 . . . . .6B **136**
Miller's Av. E8 . . . . .5F **67**
Millers Cl. NW7 . . . . .4H **29**
Millers Ct. *HA0: Wemb* 2E **78**
(off Vicars Bri. Cl.)
Millers Grn. Cl. EN2: Enf 3G **23**
Miller's House Visitor Centre 3E **86**
(off Three Mill La.)
Millers Mdw. Cl. SE3 . . . . .4H **123**
Millers Row E20 . . . . .5D **68**
Miller's Ter. E8 . . . . .5F **67**
Miller St. NW1 . . . . .2G **83**
(not continuous)
Millers Way W6 . . . . .2E **98**
Millers Wharf Ho. *E1* 5K **15**
(off St Katherine's Way)
Millers Yd. N3 . . . . .1K **45**
Mille Wlk. SE1 . . . . .5K **13** (1A **102**)
Milles Sq. SW9 . . . . .4A **120**
Millet Rd. UB6: G'frd 2F **77**
Mill Farm Av. TW16: Sun 7G **129**
Mill Farm Bus. Pk. TW4: Houn 7C **112**
Mill Farm Cl. HA5: Pinn 2A **40**
Mill Farm Cres. TW4: Houn 1C **130**
Millfield KT1: King T 3F **151**
N4 . . . . .2A **66**
TW16: Sun 1F **147**
Millfield Av. E17 . . . . .1A **50**
Millfield La. N6 . . . . .1C **64**
Millfield Pl. N6 . . . . .2E **64**
Millfield Rd. HA8: Edg 2J **43**
TW4: Houn 1C **130**
Millfields Rd. E5 . . . . .4J **67**
Millfield Theatre 4J **33**
Mill Gdns. SE26 . . . . .3H **139**
Mill Grn. CR4: Mitc 7E **154**
Mill Grn. Bus. Pk. CR4: Mitc 7E **154**
Mill Grn. Rd. CR4: Mitc 7D **154**
Millgrove St. SW11 . . . . .1E **118**
Millharbour E14 . . . . .2D **104**
Millhaven Cl. RM6: Chad H 6B **54**
MILL HILL .5F **29**
Mill Hill SW13 . . . . .2C **116**
MILL HILL CIR. 5G **29**
Mill Hill Cir. NW7 . . . . .5G **29**
Mill Hill Golf Course 2F **29**
Mill Hill Gro. W3 . . . . .1J **97**
Mill Hill Ind. Est. NW7 . . . . .6G **29**
Mill Hill Old Railway Nature Reserve
. . . . .6D **28**

Mill Hill Rd. SW13 . . . . .2C **116**
W3 . . . . .2H **97**
Mill Hill School Sports Cen. 4H **29**
Mill Hill Ter. W3 . . . . .1H **97**
Mill Ho. IG8: Wfd G 5C **36**
Millhouse Pl. SE27 . . . . .4B **138**
Millicent Fawcett Ct. N17 . . . . .1F **49**
Millicent Gro. N13 . . . . .5G **33**
Millicent Preston Ho. *IG11: Bark* . .1H **89**
(off Ripple Rd.)
Millicent Rd. E10 . . . . .1B **68**
Milligan St. E14 . . . . .7B **86**
Milliner Ho. *SW10* 7A **100**
(off Hortensia Rd.)
Milliners Ho. *SE1* 7H **15**
(off Bermondsey St.)
SW18 . . . . .4J **117**
Milling Rd. HA8: Edg 7E **28**
Millington Ho. N16 . . . . .3D **66**
Millington Rd. UB3: Harl 3G **93**
Mill La. CR0: Wadd 3K **167**
E4 . . . . .3J **25**
IG8: Wfd G 5C **36**
KT17: Ewe 7B **164**
NW6 . . . . .5H **63**
RM6: Chad H 6E **54**
SE8 . . . . .1C **122**
(off Deptford Bri.)
SE18 .5E **106**
SM5: Cars 4D **166**
Mill La. Trad. Est. CR0: Wadd 3K **167**
Millman Ct. *WC1* 4G **7**
(off Millman St.)
Millman M. WC1 . . . . .4G **7** (4K **83**)
Millman Pl. *WC1* 4G **7**
(off Millman St.)
Millman Rd. E16 . . . . .7D **88**
Millman St. WC1 . . . . .4G **7** (4K **83**)
Millmarsh La. EN3: Brim 2F **25**
Millmead Ind. Cen. N17 . . . . .2H **49**
Mill Mead Rd. N17 . . . . .3H **49**
MILL MEADS 2F **87**
Mill Pl. BR7: Chst 1E **160**
E14 . . . . .6A **86**
KT1: King T 3F **151**
Mill Plat TW7: Isle 2A **114**
(not continuous)
Mill Plat Av. TW7: Isle 2A **114**
Mill Pond Cl. SW8 . . . . .7H **101**
Millpond Est. SE16 . . . . .2H **103**
Millpond Pl. SM5: Cars 3E **166**
Mill Ridge HA8: Edg 5A **28**
Mill River Trad. Est. EN3: Pond E . .3F **25**
Mill Rd. DA8: Erith 7J **109**
E16 . . . . .1K **105**
IG1: Ilf .3E **70**
SW19 . . . . .7A **136**
TW2: Twick 2G **131**
Mill Row DA5: Bexl 1H **145**
N1 . . . . .1E **84**
Mills Cl. UB10: Hil 2C **74**
Mills Ct. EC2 . . . . .3G **9**
Mills Gro. E14 . . . . .6E **86**
NW4 . . . . .3F **45**
Millshott Cl. SW6 . . . . .1E **116**
Mills Ho. *SW8* 1G **119**
(off Thessaly Rd.)
Millside SM5: Cars 2D **166**
Millside Pl. TW7: Isle 2B **114**
Millson Cl. N20 . . . . .2G **31**
Mills Row W4 . . . . .4K **97**
Millstone Cl. E15 . . . . .6F **69**
Millstream Cl. N13 . . . . .5F **33**
Millstream Ho. *SE16* 2H **103**
(off Jamaica Rd.)
Millstream Rd. SE1 . . . . .7J **15** (2F **103**)
Mill St. KT1: King T 3E **150**
SE1 . . . . .7K **15** (2F **103**)
W1 . . . . .2A **12** (7F **83**)
Mills Yd. SW6 . . . . .3K **117**
The Mill Trad. Est. NW10 . . . . .3J **79**
Mill Va. BR2: Broml 2H **159**

Mill Vw. Cl. KT17: Ewe 7B **164**
Mill Vw. Gdns. CR0: C'don 3K **169**
MILLWALL 4D **104**
Millwall Dock Rd. E14 . . . . .3C **104**
Millwall FC 5J **103**
Millwall Pk. 4E **104**
Mill Way TW14: Felt 5K **111**
Millway NW7 . . . . .4F **29**
Millway Gdns. UB5: N'olt 6D **58**
Millwood Rd. TW3: Houn 5G **113**
Millwood St. W10 . . . . .5G **81**
Mill Yd. E1 . . . . .7G **85**
Mill Yd. Ind. Est. HA8: Edg 1H **43**
Milman Cl. HA5: Pinn 3B **40**
Milman Rd. NW6 . . . . .2F **81**
Milman's Ho. *SW10* 6B **100**
(off Milman's St.)
Milman's St. SW10 . . . . .6B **100**
Milne Ct. E18 . . . . .1J **51**
Milne Gdns. SE9 . . . . .5C **124**
Milne Ho. *SE18* 4D **106**
(off Ogilby St.)
Milner Ct. *SE15* 7F **103**
(off Colegrove Rd.)
Milner Dr. TW2: Whitt 7H **113**
Milner Pl. N1 . . . . .1A **84**
SE1 . . . . .6H **13** (2K **101**)
SM5: Cars 4E **166**
Milner Rd. CR7: Thor H 3D **156**
E15 . . . . .3G **87**
KT1: King T 3D **150**
RM8: Dag 2C **72**
SM4: Mord 5B **154**
SW19 . . . . .1K **153**
Milner Sq. N1 . . . . .7B **66**
Milner St. SW3 . . . . .3E **16** (4D **100**)
Milnthorpe Rd. W4 . . . . .6K **97**
Milo Gdns. SE22 . . . . .6F **121**
Milo Rd. SE22 . . . . .6F **121**
Milrood Ho. *E1* 5K **85**
(off Stepney Grn.)
Milroy Wlk. SE1 . . . . .4A **14** (1B **102**)
Milson Rd. W14 . . . . .3F **99**
Milstead Ho. E5 . . . . .5H **67**
Milton Av. CR0: C'don 7D **156**
E6 . . . . .7B **70**
EN5: Barn 5C **20**
N6 . . . . .7G **47**
NW9 . . . . .3J **43**
NW10 . . . . .1J **79**
SM1: Sutt 3B **166**
Milton Cl. N2 . . . . .5A **46**
SE1 . . . . .4F **103**
SM1: Sutt 3B **166**
UB4: Hayes 6J **75**
Milton Ct. E17 . . . . .4C **50**
EC2 . . . . .5E **8** (5D **84**)
RM6: Chad H 7C **54**
SE14 .6B **104**
(not continuous)
SW18 . . . . .5J **117**
TW2: Twick 3J **131**
UB10: Ick 3D **56**
Milton Court Concert Hall 5E **8**
(off Milton Ct.)
Milton Ct. Rd. SE14 . . . . .6A **104**
Milton Cres. IG2: Ilf 7F **53**
Milton Dr. TW17: Shep 4A **146**
Milton Gdn. Est. N16 . . . . .4D **66**
Milton Gdns. TW19: Stanw 1B **128**
Milton Gro. N11 . . . . .5B **32**
N16 . . . . .4D **66**
Milton Ho. *E2* 3J **85**
(off Roman Rd.)
E17 . . . . .4C **50**
SE5 . . . . .7D **102**
(off Elmington Est.)
SM1: Sutt 3J **165**
Milton Lodge DA14: Sidc 4A **144**
TW1: Twick 7K **113**
Milton Mans. *W14* 6G **99**
(off Queen's Club Gdns.)

Milton Pk.—Monarch Ho.

Milton Pk. N6 .7G 47
Milton Rd. CR0: C'don .7D 156
CR4: Mitc .7E 136
DA16: Well .1K 125
DA17: Belv .4G 109
E17 .4C 50
HA1: Harr .4J 41
N6 .7G 47
N15 .4B 48
NW7 .5H 29
NW9 .7C 44
SE24 .5B 120
SM1: Sutt .3J 165
SM6: W'gton .6G 167
SW14 .3K 115
SW19 .6A 136
TW12: Hamp .7E 130
UB10: Ick .4D 56
W3 .1K 97
W7 .7K 77
Milton St. EC2 .5E 8 (5D 84)
Milton Way UB7: W Dray .4B 92
Milverton Dr. UB10: Ick .4E 56
Milverton Gdns. IG3: Ilf .2K 71
Milverton Ho. SE6 .3A 140
Milverton Pl. BR1: Broml .5A 142
Milverton Rd. NW6 .7E 62
Milverton St. SE11 .6K 19 (5A 102)
Milverton Way SE9 .4E 142
Milward St. E1 .5H 85
Milward Wlk. SE18 .6E 106
Mimosa Ho. *E20* .*5E 68*
(off Liberty Bri. Rd.)
UB4: Yead .5A 76
Mimosa Lodge NW10 .5B 62
Mimosa Rd. UB4: Yead .5A 76
Mimosa St. SW6 .1H 117
Minard Rd. SE6 .7G 123
Mina Rd. SE17 .5E 102
SW19 .1J 153
Mina Ter. N9 .7B 24
Minchenden Ct. N14 .2C 32
Minchenden Cres. N14 .3B 32
Minchin Ho. *E14* .*6C 86*
(off Dod St.)
Mincing La. EC3 .2G 15 (7E 84)
Minden Gdns. IG11: Bark .3B 90
Minden Rd. SE20 .1H 157
SM3: Sutt .2G 165
Minehead Rd. HA2: Harr .3E 58
SW16 .5K 137
Mineral Cl. EN5: Barn .6A 20
Mineral St. SE18 .4J 107
Minera M. SW1 .3G 17 (4E 100)
Minerva Cl. DA14: Sidc .3J 143
SW9 .7A 102
TW19: Stanw M .7B 174
Minerva Ct. *EC1* .*4K 7*
(off Bowling Grn. La.)
Minerva Lodge N7 .6K 65
Minerva Rd. E4 .7J 35
KT1: King T .2F 151
NW10 .4J 79
Minerva St. E2 .2H 85
Minerva Wlk. EC1 .7B 8 (6B 84)
Minerva Way EN5: Barn .5C 20
Minet Av. NW10 .2A 80
Minet Country Pk. .2A 94
Minet Dr. UB3: Hayes .1J 93
Minet Gdns. NW10 .2A 80
UB3: Hayes .1K 93
Minet Rd. SW9 .2B 120
Minford Gdns. W14 .2F 99
Minford Ho. *W14* .*2F 99*
(off Minford Gdns.)
Mingard Wlk. N7 .2K 65
Ming St. E14 .7C 86
Minimax Cl. TW14: Felt .6J 111
Minima Yacht Club .*3D 150*
(off High St.)
Ministry Way SE9 .2D 142
Miniver Pl. EC4 .2D 14
Mink Ct. TW4: Houn .2A 112
Minnie Baldock St. E16 .6H 87
Minniedale KT5: Surb .5F 151
Minnow St. SE17 .4E 102
Minnow Wlk. SE17 .4E 102
Minories EC3 .1J 15 (6F 85)
Minotaur Dr. EN5: Barn .5C 20
Minshaw Ct. DA14: Sidc .4K 143
Minshill St. SW8 .1H 119
Minshull Pl. BR3: Beck .7C 140
Minson Rd. E9 .1K 85
Minstead Gdns. SW15 .7B 116
Minstead Way KT3: N Mald .6A 152
Minster Av. SM1: Sutt .2J 165
Minster Ct. EC3 .2H 15
W5 .4E 78
Minster Dr. CR0: C'don .4E 168
Minster Gdns. KT8: W Mole .4D 148
Minsterley Av. TW17: Shep .4G 147
Minster Pavement *EC3* .*2H 15*
(off Mincing La.)
Minster Rd. BR1: Broml .7K 141
NW2 .5G 63
Minster Wlk. N8 .4J 47
Minstrel Gdns. KT5: Surb .4F 151
Mint Bus. Pk. E16 .5K 87
Mint Cl. UB10: Hil .3D 74
Mintern Cl. N13 .3G 33
Minterne Av. UB2: S'hall .4E 94
Minterne Rd. HA3: Kenton .5F 43
Minterne Waye UB4: Yead .6A 76
Mintern St. N1 .2D 84
Minter Rd. IG11: Bark .4A 90
Minton Apts. SW8 .7J 101
Minton Ho. SE11 .3J 19
Minton M. NW6 .6K 63
Mint Rd. SM6: W'gton .4F 167
Mint St. *E2* .*4H 85*
(off Three Colts La.)
SE1 .6C 14 (2C 102)
Mint Wlk. CR0: C'don .3C 168
Mirabelle Gdns. E20 .5E 68
Mirabel Rd. SW6 .7H 99
Mira Ho. *E20* .*5E 68*
(off Prize Wlk.)
Miranda Cl. E1 .5J 85
Miranda Ct. W3 .6F 79
Miranda Ho. *N1* .*1G 9*
(off Crondall St.)
Miranda Rd. N19 .1G 65
Mirfield St. SE7 .4B 106
Miriam Rd. SE18 .5J 107
Mirravale Trad. Est. RM8: Dag .7E 54
Mirren Cl. HA2: Harr .4D 58
Mirror Path SE9 .3A 142
Misbourne Rd. UB10: Hil .1C 74
Missenden *SE17* .*5D 102*
(off Roland Way)
Missenden Cl. TW14: Felt .1H 129
Missenden Gdns. SM4: Mord .6A 154
Missenden Ho. NW8 .3C 4
The Mission *E14* .*6B 86*
(off Commercial Rd.)
Mission Gro. E17 .5A 50
Mission Pl. SE15 .1G 121
Mission Sq. TW8: Bford .6E 96
Missouri Ct. HA5: Eastc .6A 40
Mistletoe Cl. CR0: C'don .1K 169
Mistral SE5 .1E 120
Misty's Fld. KT12: Walt T .7A 148
Mitali Pas. E1 .6G 85
MITCHAM .3D 154
Mitcham Gdn. Village CR4: Mitc .5E 154
Mitcham Golf Course .5E 154
Mitcham Ho. SE5 .1C 120
Mitcham Ind. Est. CR4: Mitc .1E 154
Mitcham La. SW16 .6G 137
Mitcham Pk. CR4: Mitc .4C 154
Mitcham Rd. CR0: C'don .6J 155
E6 .3C 88
IG3: Ilf .7K 53
SW17 .5D 136
Mitchell *NW9* .*1B 44*
(off Quakers Course)
Mitchellbrook Way NW10 .6K 61
Mitchell Cl. DA17: Belv .3J 109
RM8: Dag .3C 72
SE2 .4C 108
Mitchell Ho. *N1* .*7B 66*
(off College Cross)
W12 .*7D 80*
(off White City Est.)
Mitchell Rd. BR6: Orp .4K 173
N13 .5H 33
Mitchell's Pl. *SE21* .*6E 120*
(off Aysgarth Rd.)
Mitchell St. EC1 .3C 8 (4C 84)
(not continuous)
Mitchell Wlk. *E6* .*5C 88*
(off Allhallows Rd.)
E6 .5D 88
(Elmley Cl.)
Mitchell Way BR1: Broml .1J 159
NW10 .6J 61
Mitchison Ct. *TW16: Sun* .*1J 147*
(off Downside)
Mitchison Rd. N1 .6D 66
Mitchley Rd. N17 .3G 49
Mitford Bldgs. *SW6* .*7J 99*
(off Dawes Rd.)
Mitford Cl. KT9: Chess .6C 162
Mitford Rd. N19 .2J 65
The Mitre E14 .7B 86
Mitre Av. E17 .3C 50
Mitre Bri. Ind. Pk. W10 .4D 80
(not continuous)
Mitre Cl. BR2: Broml .2H 159
SM2: Sutt .7A 166
TW17: Shep .6F 147
Mitre Ho. *SW3* .*5E 16*
(off King's Rd.)
Mitre Pas. *EC3* .*1H 15*
(off Mitre Sq.)
SE10 .2G 105
Mitre Rd. E15 .2G 87
SE1 .6K 13 (2A 102)
Mitre Sq. EC3 .1H 15 (6E 84)
Mitre St. EC3 .1H 15 (6E 84)
Mitre Way W10 .4D 80
Mitre Yd. SW3 .3D 16 (4C 100)
Mitten Ho. *SE8* .*7D 104*
(off Creative Rd.)
Mizen Ct. *E14* .*2C 104*
(off Alpha Gro.)
Mizzen Mast Ho. SE18 .3D 106
Mizzen St. IG11: Bark .1H 89
The Moat KT3: N Mald .1A 152
Moat Cl. BR6: Chels .6K 173
Moat Ct. DA15: Sidc .3K 143
SE9 .6D 124
Moat Cres. N3 .3K 45
Moat Cft. DA16: Well .3C 126
Moat Dr. E13 .2A 88
HA1: Harr .4G 41
HA4: Ruis .7G 39
Moat Farm Rd. UB5: N'olt .6D 58
Moatfield NW6 .7G 63
Moatlands Ho. *WC1* .*2F 7*
(off Cromer St.)
Moat La. KT8: E Mos .3K 149
The Moat Lodge HA2: Harr .2J 59
Moat Pl. SW9 .3K 119
W3 .6H 79
Moat Side EN3: Pond E .4E 24
TW13: Hanw .4A 130
Moberly Rd. SW4 .7H 119
Moberly Sports Cen. .3F 81
Mobil Ct. *WC2* .*1H 13*
(off Clement's Inn)
MOBY DICK .4E 54
Mocatta Ho. *E1* .*4H 85*
(off Brady St.)
Mocha Ct. *E3* .*2D 86*
(off Taylor Pl.)
MoDA .2B 44
Modbury Gdns. NW5 .6E 64
Modder Pl. SW15 .4F 117
Model Cotts. SW14 .4J 115
W13 .2B 96
Model Farm Cl. SE9 .3C 142
Modena Ho. *E14* .*6G 87*
(off Lyell St.)
Modern Ct. EC4 .7A 8
Modling Ho. *E2* .*2K 85*
(off Mace St.)
Moelwyn N7 .5H 65
Moelyn M. HA1: Harr .5A 42
Moffat Ct. SW19 .5J 135
Moffat Ho. SE5 .7C 102
Moffat Rd. CR7: Thor H .2C 156
N13 .6D 32
SW17 .4D 136
Mogden La. TW7: Isle .5K 113
Mogul Bldg. *E15* .*5E 68*
(off Property Row)
Mohammedi Pk. UB5: N'olt .1E 76
Mohawk Ho. *E3* .*2A 86*
(off Gernon Rd.)
Mohmmad Khan Rd. E11 .1H 69
Moineau *NW9* .*1B 44*
(off Long Mead)
Moira Cl. N17 .2E 48
Moira Ho. *SW9* .*1A 120*
(off Gosling Way)
Moira Rd. SE9 .4D 124
Mokswell Ct. N10 .1E 46
Molasses Ho. *SW11* .*3A 118*
(off Clove Hitch Quay)
Molasses Row SW11 .3A 118
Mole Abbey Gdns. KT8: W Mole .3F 149
Mole Ct. KT19: Ewe .4J 163
Mole Ho. *NW8* .*4B 4*
(off Church St. Est.)
Molember Ct. KT8: E Mos .4J 149
Molember Rd. KT8: E Mos .5J 149
Mole Pl. KT8: W Mole .4F 149
Molescroft SE9 .3G 143
Molesey Av. KT8: W Mole .5D 148
Molesey Dr. SM3: Cheam .2G 165
Molesey Heath
Local Nature Reserve .6E 148
Molesey Pk. Av. KT8: W Mole .5F 149
Molesey Pk. Cl. KT8: E Mos .5G 149
Molesey Pk. Rd.
KT8: W Mole, E Mos .5F 149
Molesey Rd. KT8: W Mole .5C 148
KT12: Walt T .7C 148
Molesford Rd. SW6 .1J 117
Molesham Cl. KT8: W Mole .3F 149
Molesham Way KT8: W Mole .3F 149
Molesworth Ho. *SE17* .*6B 102*
(off Brandon Est.)
Molesworth St. SE13 .4E 122
Moliner Ct. BR3: Beck .7C 140
Mollis Ho. *E3* .*5C 86*
(off Gale St.)
Mollison Av.
EN3: Brim, Enf L, Enf W, Pond E .4F 25
Mollison Dr. SM6: W'gton .7H 167
Mollison Sq. *SM6: W'gton* .*7H 167*
(off Mollison Dr.)
Mollison Way HA8: Edg .2F 43
Molly Huggins Cl. SW12 .7G 119
Molten Ct. *SE14* .*6B 104*
(off Moulding La.)
Molton Ho. *N1* .*1K 83*
(off Barnsbury Est.)
Molyneux Dr. SW17 .4F 137
Molyneux St. W1 .6D 4 (5C 82)
Monarch Cl.
BR4: W W'ck .4H 171
TW14: Felt .7G 111
Monarch Ct. *HA7: Stan* .*7J 27*
(off Howard Rd.)
N2 .5B 46
Monarch Dr. E16 .5B 88
UB3: Hayes .7H 75
Monarch Ho. *W8* .*3J 99*
(off Kensington High St.)

Monarch M.—Moordown

Monarch M. E17 . . . . .6D **50**
SW16 .5A **138**
Monarch Pde. CR4: Mitc 2D **154**
Monarch Pl. IG9: Buck H 2F **37**
Monarch Point SW6 . . . . .2A **118**
Monarch Rd. DA17: Belv 3G **109**
Monarch Sq. SW11 . . . . .4C **118**
Monarchs Way HA4: Ruis 1F **57**
Monarch Way IG2: Ilf 6H **53**
Mona Rd. SE15 . . . . .2J **121**
Monastery Gdns. EN2: Enf 2J **23**
Mona St. E16 . . . . .5H **87**
Monaveen Gdns. KT8: W Mole 3F **149**
Monck Ho. *SE1* *7D **14***
(off Cole St.)
Moncks Row SW18 . . . . .6H **117**
Monck St. SW1 . . . . .2D **18** (3H **101**)
Monckton Ct. *W14* *3H **99***
(off Strangways Ter.)
Monclar Rd. SE5 . . . . .4D **120**
Moncorvo Cl. SW7 . . . . . . .7C **10** (2C **100**)
Moncrieff Cl. E6 . . . . .6C **88**
Moncrieff Pl. SE15 . . . . .2G **121**
Moncrieff St. SE15 . . . . .2G **121**
Monday All. *N16* *2F **67***
(off High St.)
Mondial Way UB3: Harl 7E **92**
Mondragon Ho. *SW8* *1J **119***
(off Guildford Rd.)
Monega Rd. E7 . . . . .6A **70**
E12 . . . . .6A **70**
Monet Ct. *SE16* *5H **103***
(off Stubbs Dr.)
Moneyer Ho. *N1* *1E **8***
(off Provost St.)
Money La. UB7: W Dray 3A **92**
Mongers Almshouses *E9* *7K **67***
(off Church Cres.)
Monica Ct. EN1: Enf 5K **23**
Monica James Ho. DA14: Sidc 3A **144**
Monica Shaw Ct. *NW1* *1D **6***
(off Purchese St.)
Monier Rd. E3 . . . . .7C **68**
Monivea Rd. BR3: Beck 7B **140**
Monk Ct. W12 . . . . .1C **98**
Monk Dr. E16 . . . . .7J **87**
MONKEN HADLEY 2C **20**
Monkfrith Av. N14 . . . . .6A **22**
Monkfrith Cl. N14 . . . . .7A **22**
Monkfrith Way N14 . . . . .7K **21**
Monkham's Av. IG8: Wfd G 5E **36**
Monkham's Dr. IG8: Wfd G 5E **36**
Monkham's La. IG8: Wfd G 5D **36**
IG9: Buck H 3E **36**
Monkleigh Rd. SM4: Mord 3G **153**
Monks Av. EN5: New Bar 6F **21**
KT8: W Mole 5D **148**
Monks Cl. EN2: Enf 2H **23**
HA2: Harr 2F **59**
HA4: Ruis 4B **58**
SE2 . . . . .4D **108**
Monks Cres. KT12: Walt T 7K **147**
Monksdene Gdns. SM1: Sutt 3K **165**
Monks Dr. W3 . . . . .5G **79**
Monksfarm Pl. SE2 . . . . .2B **108**
MONKS ORCHARD 7A **158**
Monks Orchard Rd. BR3: Beck 1C **170**
Monks Pk. HA9: Wemb 6H **61**
Monks Pk. Gdns. HA9: Wemb 7H **61**
Monks Rd. EN2: Enf 2G **23**
Monk St. SE18 . . . . .4E **106**
Monks Way BR3: Beck 6C **158**
BR5: Farnb 1G **173**
NW11 . . . . .4H **45**
UB7: Harm 6A **92**
Monkswood Gdns. IG5: Ilf 3E **52**
Monkton Ho. E5 . . . . .5H **67**
SE16 . . . .*2K **103***
(off Wolfe Cres.)
Monkton Rd. DA16: Well 2K **125**
Monkton St. SE11 . . . . .3K **19** (4A **102**)
Monkville Av. NW11 . . . . .4H **45**
Monkville Pde. NW11 . . . . .4H **45**
Monkwell Sq. EC2 . . . . .6D **8** (5C **84**)
Monmouth Av. E18 . . . . .3K **51**
KT1: Hamp W 7C **132**
Monmouth Cl. CR4: Mitc 4J **155**
DA16: Well 4A **126**
W4 . . . . .3J **97**
Monmouth Ct. *W7* *5K **77***
(off Copley Cl.)
Monmouth Gro. TW8: Bford 4E **96**
Monmouth Pl. *W2* *6K **81***
(off Monmouth Rd.)
Monmouth Rd. E6 . . . . .3D **88**
N9 . . . . .2C **34**
RM9: Dag 5F **73**
UB3: Harl 4G **93**
W2 . . . . .6J **81**
Monmouth St. WC2 . . . . . . .1E **12** (6J **83**)
Monnery Rd. N19 . . . . .3G **65**
Monnow Rd. SE1 . . . . .5G **103**
Mono La. TW13: Felt 2K **129**
Monolulu Ct. *SE17* *5D **102***
(off East St.)
Monoux Almshouses E17 . . . . .4D **50**
Monoux Gro. E17 . . . . .1C **50**
Monro Ct. E16 . . . . .4H **87**
Monroe Cres. EN1: Enf 1C **24**
Monroe Dr. SW14 . . . . .5H **115**
Monroe Ho. *NW8* *2D **4***
(off Lorne Cl.)
Monro Gdns. HA3: Hrw W 7D **26**
Monro Way E5 . . . . .4G **67**
Monsell Ct. N4 . . . . .3B **66**
Monsell Rd. N4 . . . . .3A **66**
Monsey Pl. E1 . . . . .4A **86**
Monson Rd. NW10 . . . . .2C **80**
SE14 . . . . .7K **103**
Mons Way BR2: Broml 6C **160**
Montacute Rd. CR0: New Ad 7E **170**
SE6 . . . . .7B **122**
SM4: Mord 6B **154**
WD23: B Hea 1E **26**
Montagu Ct. *W1* *6F **5***
(off Montagu Pl.)
Montagu Cres. N18 . . . . .4C **34**
Montague Av. SE4 . . . . .4B **122**
W7 . . . . .1K **95**
Montague Cl. EN5: Barn 4C **20**
KT12: Walt T 7K **147**
SE1 . . . . .4E **14** (1D **102**)
Montague Ct. DA15: Sidc 3A **144**
N7 . . . .*7A **66***
(off St Clements St.)
Montague Gdns. W3 . . . . .7G **79**
Montague Ho. *E16* *1K **105***
(off Wesley Av.)
IG3: Ilf .1A **72**
N1 . . . .*1E **84***
(off Halcomb St.)
Montague M. *E3* *3B **86***
(off Tredegar Ter.)
SE20 . . . . .6J **139**
Montague Pas. UB8: Uxb 7A **56**
Montague Pl. WC1 . . . . .5D **6** (5H **83**)
Montague Rd. CR0: C'don 1B **168**
E8 . . . . .5G **67**
E11 . . . . .2H **69**
N8 . . . . .5K **47**
N15 . . . . .4G **49**
SW19 .7K **135**
TW3: Houn 3F **113**
TW10: Rich 6E **114**
UB2: S'hall 4C **94**
UB8: Uxb 7A **56**
W7 . . . . .1K **95**
W13 . . . . .6B **78**
Montague Sq. SE15 . . . . .7J **103**
Montague St. EC1 . . . . .6C **8** (5C **84**)
WC1 . . . . .5E **6** (5J **83**)
Montague Ter. BR2: Broml 4H **159**
Montague Walks HA0: Wemb 1F **79**
Montague Waye UB2: S'hall 3C **94**
Montagu Gdns. N18 . . . . .4C **34**
SM6: W'gton 4G **167**
Montagu Ind. Est. N18 . . . . .4D **34**
Montagu Mans. W1 . . . . .5F **5** (5D **82**)
Montagu M. Nth. W1 . . . . . . .6F **5** (5D **82**)
Montagu M. Sth. W1 . . . . . . .7F **5** (6D **82**)
Montagu M. W. W1 . . . . .7F **5** (6D **82**)
Montagu Pl. W1 . . . . .6E **4** (5D **82**)
Montagu Rd. N9 . . . . .4C **34**
N18 . . . . .5C **34**
NW4 . . . . .6C **44**
Montagu Row W1 . . . . .6F **5** (5D **82**)
Montagu Sq. W1 . . . . .6F **5** (5D **82**)
Montagu St. W1 . . . . .7F **5** (6D **82**)
Montaigne Cl. SW1 . . . . . .4D **18** (4H **101**)
Montalt Rd. IG8: Wfd G 4C **36**
Montana *HA9: Wemb* *4G **61***
(off Exhibition Way)
Montana Bldg. *SE13* *1D **122***
(off Deal's Gateway)
Montana Gdns. SE26 . . . . .5B **140**
SM1: Sutt 5A **166**
Montana Rd. SW17 . . . . .3E **136**
SW20 .1E **152**
Montanaro Ct. *N1* *1C **84***
(off Coleman Flds.)
Montbelle Rd. SE9 . . . . .3F **143**
Montcalm Cl.
BR2: Hayes 6J **159**
UB4: Yead 3K **75**
Montcalm Ho. E14 . . . . .4B **104**
Montcalm Rd. SE7 . . . . .7B **106**
Montclare St. E2 . . . . .3J **9** (4F **85**)
Monteagle Av. IG11: Bark 6G **71**
Monteagle Ct. N1 . . . . .2E **84**
Monteagle Way E5 . . . . .3G **67**
SE15 . . . . .3H **121**
Montefiore Ct. N16 . . . . .1F **67**
Montefiore St. SW8 . . . . .2F **119**
Montego Cl. SE24 . . . . .4A **120**
Montem Rd. KT3: N Mald 4A **152**
SE23 . . . . .7B **122**
Montem St. N4 . . . . .1K **65**
Montenotte Rd. N8 . . . . .5G **47**
Monterey Apts. N15 . . . . .5D **48**
Monterey Cl. DA5: Bexl 2J **145**
NW7 . . . .*5F **29***
(off The Broadway)
UB10: Hil 7C **56**
Monterey Studios W10 . . . . .2G **81**
Montesole Ct. HA5: Pinn 2A **40**
Montevetro SW11 . . . . .1B **118**
Montfichet Rd. E20 . . . . .7E **68**
Montford Pl. E15 . . . . .2E **86**
SE11 . . . . .6J **19** (5A **102**)
Montford Rd. TW16: Sun 4J **147**
Montfort Ho. *E2* *3J **85***
(off Victoria Pk. Sq.)
E14 . . . .*3E **104***
(off Galbraith St.)
Montfort Pl. SW19 . . . . .1F **135**
Montgolfier Wlk. UB5: N'olt 3C **76**
Montgomerie M. SE23 . . . . .7J **121**
Montgomery Cl. CR4: Mitc 4J **155**
DA15: Sidc 6K **125**
Montgomery Ct. *CR2: S Croy* *5E **168***
(off Birdhurst Rd.)
W4 . . . . .7J **97**
Montgomery Gdns. SM2: Sutt 7B **166**
Montgomery Ho. *UB5: N'olt* *3D **76***
(off Taywood Rd.)
W2 . . . .*6A **4***
(off Harrow Rd.)
Montgomery Lodge *E1* *4J **85***
(off Cleveland Gro.)
Montgomery Rd. HA8: Edg 6A **28**
W4 . . . . .4J **97**
Montgomery Sq. E14 . . . . .1D **104**
Montgomery St. E14 . . . . .1D **104**
Montholme Rd. SW11 . . . . .6D **118**
Monthope Rd. E1 . . . . .6K **9** (5G **85**)
Montolieu Gdns. SW15 . . . . .5D **116**
Montpelier Av. DA5: Bexl 7D **126**
W5 . . . . .5C **78**
Montpelier Cl. UB10: Hil 1C **74**
Montpelier Ct. *BR2: Broml* *4H **159***
(off Westmoreland Rd.)
W5 . . . . .5D **78**
Montpelier Gdns. E6 . . . . .3B **88**
RM6: Chad H 7C **54**
Montpelier Gro. NW5 . . . . .5G **65**
Montpelier M. SW7 . . . . .1D **16** (3C **100**)
Montpelier Pl. E1 . . . . .6J **85**
SW7 . . . . .1D **16** (3C **100**)
Montpelier Ri. HA9: Wemb 1D **60**
NW11 . . . . .7G **45**
(not continuous)
Montpelier Rd. N3 . . . . .1A **46**
SE15 . . . . .1H **121**
SM1: Sutt 4A **166**
W5 . . . . .5D **78**
Montpelier Row SE3 . . . . .2H **123**
TW1: Twick 7C **114**
Montpelier Sq. SW7 . . . . .7D **10** (2C **100**)
Montpelier St. SW7 . . . . . .1D **16** (3C **100**)
Montpelier Ter. SW7 . . . . .7D **10** (2C **100**)
Montpelier Va. SE3 . . . . .2H **123**
Montpelier Wlk. SW7 . . . .1D **16** (3C **100**)
Montpelier Way NW11 . . . . .7G **45**
Montpellier Ct. KT12: Walt T 6J **147**
Montrave Rd. SE20 . . . . .6J **139**
Montreal Ho. *SE16* *2K **103***
(off Maple M.)
UB4: Yead *3K **75***
(off Ayles Rd.)
Montreal Pl. WC2 . . . . . . .2G **13** (7K **83**)
Montreal Rd. IG1: Ilf 7G **53**
Montrell Rd. SW2 . . . . .1J **137**
Montrose Av. DA15: Sidc 7A **126**
DA16: Well 3H **125**
HA8: Edg 2J **43**
NW6 . . . . .2G **81**
TW2: Whitt 7F **113**
Montrose Cl. DA16: Well 3K **125**
IG8: Wfd G 4D **36**
TW15: Ashf 6E **128**
Montrose Ct. HA1: Harr 5F **41**
NW9 . . . . .2J **43**
NW11 . . . . .4H **45**
SE6 . . . . .2H **141**
SW7 . . . . .7B **10** (2B **100**)
Montrose Cres. HA0: Wemb 6E **60**
N12 . . . . .6F **31**
Montrose Gdns. CR4: Mitc 2D **154**
SM1: Sutt 2K **165**
Montrose Ho. E14 . . . . .3C **104**
SW1 . . . .*7H **11***
(off Montrose Pl.)
Montrose Pl. SW1 . . . . . . .7H **11** (2E **100**)
Montrose Rd. HA3: W'stone 2J **41**
TW14: Bedf 6F **111**
Montrose Wlk. HA7: Stan 6G **27**
Montrose Way SE23 . . . . .1K **139**
Montserrat Av. IG8: Wfd G 7A **36**
Montserrat Cl. SE19 . . . . .5D **138**
Montserrat Rd. SW15 . . . . .4G **117**
The Monument 3F **15** (7D **84**)
Monument Gdns. SE13 . . . . .5E **122**
Monument St. EC3 . . . . .2F **15** (7D **84**)
Monument Way N15 . . . . .3F **49**
N17 . . . . .3F **49**
Monza St. E1 . . . . .7J **85**
Moodkee St. SE16 . . . . .3J **103**
Moody Rd. SE15 . . . . .1F **121**
Moody St. E1 . . . . .3K **85**
Moon Ct. SE12 . . . . .4J **123**
Moon Ho. HA1: Harr 4J **41**
Moon La. EN5: Barn 3C **20**
Moonlight Dr. SE23 . . . . .7H **121**
Moonraker Point *SE1* *6B **14***
(off Pocock St.)
Moon St. N1 . . . . .1B **84**
Moorcroft HA8: Edg 1H **43**
Moorcroft Gdns. BR2: Broml 5C **160**
Moorcroft La. UB8: Hil 5C **74**
Moorcroft Rd. SW16 . . . . .3J **137**
Moorcroft Way HA5: Pinn 5C **40**
Moordown SE18 . . . . .7F **107**

Moore Cl.—Morse Cl.

Moore Cl. CR4: Mitc 2F 155
SW14 3J 115
Moore Ct. HA0: Wemb 6E 60
HA7: Stan 1D 42
N1 1B 84
(off Gaskin St.)
Moore Cres. RM9: Dag 1B 90
Moorefield Rd. N17 2F 49
Moorehead Way SE3 3J 123
Moore Ho. *E1 7J 85*
(off Cable St.)
E2 3J 85
(off Roman Rd.)
E14 2C 104
N8 4J 47
(off Pembroke Rd.)
SE10 5H 105
(off Armitage Rd.)
SW1 6J 17
Mooreland Rd. BR1: Broml 7H 141
Moore Pk. Rd. SW6 7J 99
Moore Rd. SE19 6C 138
Moore St. SW3 3E 16 (4D 100)
Moore Wlk. E7 4J 69
Moore Way SM2: Sutt 7J 165
Moorey Cl. E15 1H 87
Moorfield Av. W5 4D 78
Moorfield Rd. EN3: Enf H 1D 24
KT9: Chess 5E 162
UB8: Cowl 6A 74
Moorfields EC2 6E 8 (5D 84)
Moorfields Highwalk *EC2 6E 8*
(off New Union St.)
Moorgate EC2 7E 8 (6D 84)
Moorgate Pl. EC2 7E 8
Moorgreen Ho. EC1 1A 8
Moorhen Dr. NW9 6B 44
Moorhen Ho. *E3 1B 86*
(off Old Ford Rd.)
Moorhouse NW9 1B 44
Moorhouse Rd. HA3: Kenton 3D 42
W2 6J 81
The Moorings *E16 5A 88*
(off Prince Regent La.)
Moorings Ho. TW8: Bford 7C 96
MOOR JUNC. 3C 174
Moorland Cl. RM5: Col R 1H 55
TW2: Whitt 7E 112
Moorland Rd. SW9 4B 120
UB7: Harm 2D 174
Moorlands UB5: N'olt 1C 76
Moorlands Av. NW7 6J 29
Moor La. EC2 6E 8 (5D 84)
(not continuous)
KT9: Chess 4E 162
UB7: Harm 2D 174
Moormead Dr. KT19: Ewe 5A 164
Moor Mead Rd. TW1: Twick 6A 114
Moor Pk. Gdns. KT2: King T 7A 134
Moor Pl. EC2 6E 8 (5D 84)
Moorside Rd. BR1: Broml 3G 141
Moor St. W1 1D 12 (6H 83)
Moot Ct. NW9 5G 43
Moran Ho. *E1 1H 103*
(off Wapping La.)
Morant Pl. N22 1K 47
Morant St. E14 7C 86
Mora Rd. NW2 4E 62
Mora St. EC1 2D 8 (3C 84)
Morat St. SW9 1K 119
Moravian Cl. SW10 7A 16 (6B 100)
Moravian Pl. SW10 6B 100
Moravian St. E2 2J 85
Moray Av. UB3: Hayes 1H 93
Moray Cl. HA8: Edg 2C 28
RM1: Rom 1K 55
Moray Ct. *CR2: S Croy 5C 168*
(off Warham Rd.)
Moray Ho. *E1 4A 86*
(off Harford St.)
Moray M. N7 2K 65
Moray Rd. N4 2K 65
Moray Way RM1: Rom 1K 55
Mordaunt Gdns. RM9: Dag 7E 72
Mordaunt Ho. *NW10 1K 79*
(off Stracey Rd.)
Mordaunt Rd. NW10 1K 79
Mordaunt St. SW9 3K 119
MORDEN 3K 153
Morden Ct. SM4: Mord 4K 153
Morden Ct. Pde. SM4: Mord 4K 153
Morden Gdns. CR4: Mitc 4B 154
UB6: G'frd 5K 59
Morden Hall Pk. 3A 154
Morden Hall Rd. SM4: Mord 3K 153
Morden Hill SE13 2E 122
Morden Ho. SM4: Mord 4J 153
Morden La. SE13 2E 122
Morden Leisure Centre 5H 153
MORDEN PARK 6G 153
Morden Rd. CR4: Mitc 4A 154
RM6: Chad H 7E 54
SE3 2J 123
SM4: Mord 4A 154
SW19 1K 153
Morden Rd. M. SE3 2J 123
Morden St. SE13 1D 122
Morden Way SM3: Sutt 7J 153
Morden Wharf *SE10 3G 105*
(off Morden Wharf Rd.)
Morden Wharf Rd. SE10 3G 105
Mordern Ho. NW1 3D 4
Mordon Rd. IG3: Ilf 7K 53
Morea M. N5 5C 66
Morecambe Cl. E1 5K 85
Morecambe Gdns. HA7: Stan 4J 27
Morecambe St. SE17 4C 102
Morecambe Ter. *N18 4J 33*
(off Gt. Cambridge Rd.)
More Cl. E16 6H 87
W14 4F 99
Morecoombe Cl. KT2: King T 7H 133
More Copper Ho. *SE1 5G 15*
(off Magdalen St.)
Moree Way N18 4B 34
Moreland Cotts. *E3 2C 86*
(off Fairfield Rd.)
Moreland Ct. NW2 3J 63
Moreland St. EC1 1B 8 (3B 84)
Moreland Way E4 3J 35
Morella Rd. SW12 7D 118
Morell Cl. EN5: New Bar 3F 21
Morello Av. UB8: Hil 5D 74
Morel M. RM8: Dag 1D 72
More London Pl. SE1 5G 15 (1E 102)
(not continuous)
More London Riverside
SE1 5H 15 (1E 102)
(not continuous)
Moremead Rd. SE6 4B 140
Morena St. SE6 7D 122
Moreno Ho. *E2 2H 85*
(off Esker Pl.)
Moresby Av. KT5: Surb 7H 151
Moresby Rd. E5 1H 67
Moresby Wlk. SW8 2G 119
More's Gdn. SW3 7B 16
Moreton Av. TW7: Isle 1J 113
Moreton Cl. E5 2H 67
N15 6D 48
NW7 6K 29
SW1 5B 18
Moreton Gdns. IG8: Wfd G 5H 37
Moreton Ho. SE16 3H 103
Moreton Pl. SW1 5B 18 (5G 101)
Moreton Rd. CR2: S Croy 5D 168
KT4: Wor Pk 2C 164
N15 6D 48
Moretons HA1: Harr 1J 59
Moreton St. SW1 5B 18 (5G 101)
Moreton Ter. SW1 5B 18 (5G 101)
Moreton Ter. M. Nth.
SW1 5B 18 (5G 101)
Moreton Ter. M. Sth.
SW1 5B 18 (5G 101)
Moreton Twr. W3 1H 97
Morford Cl. HA4: Ruis 7K 39
Morford Way HA4: Ruis 7K 39
Morgan Av. E17 4F 51
Morgan Cl. RM10: Dag 7G 73
Morgan Ct. SM5: Cars 4D 166
TW15: Ashf 5D 128
Morgan Cres. RM8: Dag 1E 72
Morgan Ho. *SW1 4B 18*
(off Vauxhall Bri. Rd.)
SW8 1G 119
(off Wadhurst Rd.)
Morgan Mans. *N7 5A 66*
(off Morgan Rd.)
Morgan Rd. BR1: Broml 7J 141
N7 5A 66
W10 5H 81
Morgan's La. UB3: Hayes 5F 75
Morgans La. *SE1 5G 15*
(off Tooley St.)
Morgan St. E3 3A 86
(not continuous)
E16 5H 87
Morgan Wlk. BR3: Beck 4D 158
Morgan Way IG8: Wfd G 6H 37
Moriarty Cl. BR1: Broml 4E 160
Moriatry Cl. N7 4J 65
Morie St. SW18 5K 117
Morieux Rd. E10 1B 68
Moring Rd. SW17 4E 136
Morkyns Wlk. SE21 3E 138
Morland Av. CR0: C'don 1E 168
Morland Cl. CR4: Mitc 3C 154
NW11 1K 63
TW12: Hamp 5D 130
Morland Ct. *W12 2D 98*
(off Coningham Rd.)
Morland Est. E8 7G 67
Morland Gdns. NW10 7K 61
UB1: S'hall 1F 95
Morland Ho. *NW1 1B 6*
(off Werrington St.)
NW6 1J 81
SW1 3E 18
(off Marsham St.)
W11 6G 81
(off Lancaster Rd.)
Morland M. N1 7A 66
Morland Pl. N15 4E 48
Morland Rd. CR0: C'don 1E 168
E17 5K 49
HA3: Kenton 5E 42
IG1: Ilf 2F 71
RM10: Dag 7G 73
SE20 6K 139
SM1: Sutt 5A 166
Morley Av. E4 7A 36
N18 4B 34
N22 2A 48
Morley Cl. BR6: Farnb 2F 173
Morley Ct. BR2: Broml 4H 159
E4 5G 35
Morley Cres. HA4: Ruis 2A 58
HA8: Edg 2D 28
Morley Cres. E. HA7: Stan 2C 42
Morley Cres. W. HA7: Stan 3C 42
Morley Hill EN2: Enf 1J 23
Morley Ho. *SE15 7F 103*
(off Commercial Way)
Morley Rd. BR7: Chst 1G 161
E10 1E 68
E15 2H 87
IG11: Bark 1H 89
RM6: Chad H 5E 54
SE13 4E 122
SM3: Sutt 1H 165
TW1: Twick 6D 114
Morley St. SE1 1K 19 (3A 102)
Morna Rd. SE5 2C 120
Morning La. E9 6J 67
Morningside Rd. KT4: Wor Pk 2E 164
Mornington Av. BR1: Broml 3A 160
IG1: Ilf 7E 52
W14 4H 99
Mornington Av. Mans. *W14 4H 99*
(off Mornington Av.)
Mornington Cl. IG8: Wfd G 4D 36
NW9 3A 44
Mornington Ct. DA5: Bexl 1K 145
NW1 2G 83
(off Mornington Cres.)
Mornington Cres. NW1 2G 83
TW5: Cran 1K 111
Mornington Gro. E3 3C 86
Mornington M. SE5 1C 120
Mornington Pl. NW1 2G 83
SE8 7B 104
(off Mornington Rd.)
Mornington Rd. E4 7K 25, 1A 36
E11 7H 51
IG8: Wfd G 4C 36
SE8 7B 104
TW15: Ashf 5E 128
UB6: G'frd 5F 77
Mornington St. NW1 2F 83
Mornington Ter. NW1 1F 83
Mornington Wlk. TW10: Ham 4C 132
Moro Apts. *E14 6C 86*
(off New Festival Av.)
Morocco St. SE1 7G 15 (2E 102)
Morocco Wharf *E1 1H 103*
(off Wapping High St.)
Morpeth Gro. E9 1K 85
Morpeth Mans. *SW1 2A 18*
(off Morpeth Ter.)
Morpeth Rd. E9 1K 85
Morpeth St. E2 3J 85
Morpeth Ter. SW1 2A 18 (3G 101)
Morpeth Wlk. N17 7C 34
Morphou Rd. NW7 6B 30
Morrab Gdns. IG3: Ilf 3K 71
Morrel Ct. *E2 2G 85*
(off Goldsmiths Row)
Morrells Yd. *SE11 5K 19*
(off Cleaver St.)
Morris Av. E12 5D 70
UB8: Uxb 6A 56
Morris Blitz Ct. N16 4F 67
Morris Cl. BR6: Orp 3J 173
CR0: C'don 5A 158
Morris Ct. E4 3J 35
Morris Dr. DA17: Erith 4J 109
Morris Gdns. SW18 7J 117
Morris Ho. *E2 3J 85*
(off Roman Rd.)
NW8 4C 4
(off Salisbury St.)
W3 2B 98
Morrish Rd. SW2 7J 119
Morris M. SW19 5A 136
Morrison Av. E4 6H 35
N17 3E 48
Morrison Bldgs. Nth. *E1 6G 85*
(off Commercial Rd.)
Morrison Ct. *EN5: Barn 4B 20*
(off Manor Way)
N12 7H 31
SW1 1D 18
(off Gt. Smith St.)
Morrison Ho. *SW2 1A 138*
(off Tulse Hill)
Morrison Rd. IG11: Bark 2E 90
RM9: Bark, Dag 2E 90
SW9 2A 120
UB4: Yead 3K 75
Morrison St. SW11 3E 118
Morris Pl. N4 2A 66
Morris Rd. E14 5D 86
E15 4G 69
RM8: Dag 2F 73
TW7: Isle 3K 113
Morriss Ho. *SE16 2H 103*
(off Cherry Gdn. St.)
Morris St. E1 6H 85
Morritt Ho. *HA0: Wemb 5D 60*
(off Talbot Rd.)
Morse Cl. E13 3J 87

344 A-Z London

Morshead Mans. *W9* 3J *81*
(off Morshead Rd.)
Morshead Rd. W9 . . . . .3J *81*
Morson Rd. EN3: Pond E 6F *25*
Morston Gdns. SE9 . . . . .4D *142*
Mortain Ho. *SE16* 4H *103*
(off Roseberry St.)
Morten Cl. SW4 . . . . .6H *119*
Morteyne Rd. N17 . . . . .1D *48*
Mortgramit Sq. SE18 . . . . .3E *106*
Mortham St. E15 . . . . .1G *87*
Mortimer Cl. NW2 . . . . .2H *63*
SW16 . . . . .2H *137*
Mortimer Ct. *NW8* 1A *4*
(off Abbey Rd.)
Mortimer Cres. KT4: Wor Pk 3K *163*
NW6 . . . . .1K *81*
Mortimer Dr. EN1: Enf 5K *23*
Mortimer Est. *NW6* 1K *81*
(off Mortimer Pl.)
Mortimer Ho. W11 . . . . .1F *99*
W14 . . . . .4G *99*
(off North End Rd.)
Mortimer Mkt. WC1 . . . . . .4B *6* (4G *83*)
Mortimer Pl. NW6 . . . . .1K *81*
Mortimer Rd. CR4: Mitc 1D *154*
DA8: Erith 6K *109*
E6 . . . . .3D *88*
N1 . . . . .7E *66*
(not continuous)
NW10 . . . . .3E *80*
W13 . . . . .6C *78*
Mortimer Sq. W11 . . . . .7F *81*
Mortimer St. W1 . . . . .7K *5* (6G *83*)
Mortimer Ter. NW5 . . . . .4F *65*
MORTLAKE 3K *115*
Mortlake Cl. CR0: Bedd 3J *167*
Mortlake Crematorium 2H *115*
Mortlake Dr. CR4: Mitc 1C *154*
Mortlake High St. SW14 . . . . . . .3K *115*
Mortlake Rd. E16 . . . . .6K *87*
IG1: Ilf 4G *71*
TW9: Kew, Rich 7G *97*
Mortlake Ter. *TW9: Kew* 7G *97*
(off Mortlake Rd.)
Mortlock Cl. SE15 . . . . .1H *121*
Mortlock Ct. E7 . . . . .4B *70*
Morton Apts. *E16* 7G *89*
(off Lock Side Way)
Morton Cl. E1 . . . . .6J *85*
SM6: W'gton 7K *167*
UB8: Hil 4B *74*
Morton Ct. UB5: N'olt 5G *59*
Morton Cres. N14 . . . . .4C *32*
Morton Gdns.
SM6: W'gton 5G *167*
Morton Ho. SE17 . . . . .6B *102*
Morton M. SW5 . . . . .4K *99*
Morton Pl. SE1 . . . . .2J *19* (3A *102*)
Morton Rd. E15 . . . . .7H *69*
N1 . . . . .7C *66*
SM4: Mord 5B *154*
Morton Way N14 . . . . .3B *32*
Morvale Cl. DA17: Belv 4F *109*
Morval Rd. SW2 . . . . .5A *120*
Morven Rd. SW17 . . . . .3D *136*
Morville Ho. *SW18* 6B *118*
(off Fitzhugh Gro.)
Morville St. E3 . . . . .2C *86*
Morwell St. WC1 . . . . .6C *6* (5H *83*)
Moscow Mans. *SW5* 4J *99*
(off Cromwell Rd.)
Moscow Pl. W2 . . . . .7K *81*
Moscow Rd. W2 . . . . .7J *81*
Mosedale *NW1* 2K *5*
(off Cumberland Mkt.)
Moseley Row SE10 . . . . .4H *105*
Moselle Av. N22 . . . . .2A *48*
Moselle Cl. N8 . . . . .3K *47*
Moselle Ho. *N17* 7A *34*
(off William St.)
Moselle Pl. N17 . . . . .7A *34*
Moselle St. N17 . . . . .7A *34*

Mosque Ter. *E1* 5G *85*
(off Whitechapel Rd.)
Mosque Twr. *E1* 5G *85*
(off Fieldgate St.)
E3 . . . . .2A *86*
(off Ford St.)
Mosquito Cl. SM6: W'gton . .7J *167*
Mossborough Cl. N12 . . . . .6E *30*
Mossbury Rd. SW11 . . . . .3C *118*
Moss Cl. E1 . . . . .5G *85*
HA5: Pinn 2D *40*
N9 . . . . .1B *34*
Mossdown Cl. DA17: Belv 4G *109*
Mossford Cl. IG6: Ilf 3F *53*
Mossford Grn. IG6: Ilf 3F *53*
Mossford La. IG6: Ilf 2F *53*
Mossford St. E3 . . . . .4B *86*
Moss Gdns. CR2: Sels 7K *169*
TW13: Felt 2J *129*
Moss Hall Ct. N12 . . . . .6E *30*
Moss Hall Cres. N12 . . . . .6E *30*
Moss Hall Gro. N12 . . . . .6E *30*
Mossington Gdns. SE16 . . . . . . .4J *103*
Moss La. HA5: Pinn 1C *40*
Mosslea Rd. BR2: Broml 5B *160*
BR6: Farnb 3G *173*
SE20 . . . . .6J *139*
(not continuous)
Mossop St. SW3 . . . . .3D *16* (4C *100*)
Moss Rd. RM10: Dag 7G *73*
Mossville Gdns. SM4: Mord 3H *153*
Mosswell Ho. N10 . . . . .1E *46*
Moston Cl. UB3: Harl 5H *93*
Mostyn Av. HA9: Wemb 5F *61*
Mostyn Gdns. NW10 . . . . .3F *81*
Mostyn Gro. E3 . . . . .2C *86*
Mostyn Rd. HA8: Edg 7F *29*
SW9 . . . . .1A *120*
SW19 . . . . .1H *153*
Mosul Way BR2: Broml 6C *160*
Motcomb St. SW1 . . . . . .1G *17* (3E *100*)
Moth Cl. SM6: W'gton 7J *167*
Mothers Sq. E5 . . . . .4H *67*
Motley Av. EC2 . . . . .4G *9*
MOTSPUR PARK 6C *152*
Motspur Pk. KT3: N Mald 6B *152*
MOTTINGHAM 2C *142*
Mottingham Gdns. SE9 . . . . .1B *142*
Mottingham La. SE9 . . . . .1A *142*
SE12 . . . . .1A *142*
Mottingham Rd. N9 . . . . .6E *24*
SE9 .2C *142*
Mottisfont Rd. SE2 . . . . .3A *108*
Mottistone Gro. SM2: Sutt 7K *165*
Motts La. RM8: Dag 2F *73*
Mott St. E4 . . . . .1K *25*
Moulding La. SE14 . . . . .6A *104*
Moules Ct. SE5 . . . . .7C *102*
Moulins Rd. E9 . . . . .7J *67*
Moulsford Ho. N7 . . . . .5H *65*
W2 . . . . .5J *81*
(off Westbourne Pk. Rd.)
Moulton Av. TW3: Houn 2C *112*
The Mound SE9 . . . . .3E *142*
Moundfield Rd. N16 . . . . .6G *49*
Mounsey Ho. *W10* 3G *81*
(off Third Av.)
The Mount BR1: Broml 1C *160*
CR2: S Croy 5C *168*
(off Warham Rd.)
DA6: Bex 5H *127*
E5 . . . . .2H *67*
(not continuous)
HA9: Wemb 2H *61*
KT3: N Mald 3B *152*
KT4: Wor Pk 4D *164*
N20 .2F *31*
NW3 . . . . .3A *64*
UB5: N'olt 5F *59*
W3 . . . . .1J *97*
W8 . . . . .1J *99*
(off Bedford Gdns.)
Mountacre Cl. SE26 . . . . .4F *139*

Mt. Adon Pk. SE22 . . . . .7G *121*
Montague Pl. E14 . . . . .7E *86*
Mountain Ho. SE11 . . . . .4H *19* (4K *101*)
Mt. Angelus Rd. SW15 . . . . .7B *116*
Mt. Ararat Rd. TW10: Rich 5E *114*
Mt. Arlington *BR2: Broml* 2G *159*
(off Park Hill Rd.)
Mt. Ash Rd. SE26 . . . . .3H *139*
Mount Av. E4 . . . . .3H *35*
UB1: S'hall 6E *76*
W5 . . . . .5C *78*
Mountbatten Cl. SE18 . . . . .6J *107*
SE19 . . . . .5E *138*
Mountbatten Ct. IG9: Buck H 2G *37*
SE16 . . . . .1J *103*
(off Rotherhithe St.)
Mountbatten Gdns. BR3: Beck . . .4A *158*
Mountbatten Ho. *N6* 7E *46*
(off Hillcrest)
Mountbatten M. SW18 . . . . .7A *118*
Mountbel Rd. HA7: Stan 1A *42*
Mt. Carmel Chambers *W8* 2J *99*
(off Dukes La.)
Mount Cl. BR1: Broml 1C *160*
EN4: Cockf 4K *21*
SM5: Cars 7E *166*
W5 . . . . .5C *78*
Mountcombe Cl. KT6: Surb 7E *150*
Mount Ct. BR4: W W'ck 2G *171*
SW15 . . . . .3G *117*
Mt. Culver Av. DA14: Sidc 6D *144*
Mount Dr. DA6: Bex 5E *126*
HA2: Harr 5D *40*
HA9: Wemb 2J *61*
Mounteagl Gdns. SW16 . . . . . . .3K *137*
Mt. Eaton Ct. *W5* 5C *78*
(off Mount Av.)
Mt. Echo Av. E4 . . . . .2J *35*
Mt. Echo Dr. E4 . . . . .1J *35*
Mt. Ephraim La. SW16 . . . . .3H *137*
Mt. Ephraim Rd. SW16 . . . . .3H *137*
Mount Felix KT12: Walt T 7H *147*
Mountfield Cl. SE6 . . . . .7F *123*
Mountfield Rd. E6 . . . . .2E *88*
N3 . . . . .3H *45*
W5 . . . . .6D *78*
Mountfield Ter. SE6 . . . . .7F *123*
Mountford Mans. *SW11* 1E *118*
(off Battersea Pk. Rd.)
Mountfort Cres. N1 . . . . .7A *66*
Mountfort Ho. *N1* 7A *66*
(off Barnsbury Sq.)
Mountfort Ter. N1 . . . . .7A *66*
Mount Gdns. SE26 . . . . .3H *139*
Mount Gro. HA8: Edg 3D *28*
Mountgrove Rd. N5 . . . . .3B *66*
Mount Holme KT7: T Ditt 7B *150*
Mounthurst Rd. BR2: Hayes 7H *159*
Mountington Pk. Cl. HA3: Kenton . .6D *42*
Mountjoy Cl. *EC2* 6D *8*
(off Monkwell Sq.)
SE2 . . . . .2B *108*
Mountjoy Ho. EC2 . . . . .6C *8*
Mount Lodge N6 . . . . .6G *47*
Mount M. TW12: Hamp 1F *149*
Mount Mills EC1 . . . . . . .2B *8* (3B *84*)
Mt. Nod Rd. SW16 . . . . .3K *137*
Mt. Olive Ct. W7 . . . . .2J *95*
Mount Pde. EN4: Cockf 4H *21*
Mount Pk. SM5: Cars 7E *166*
Mount Pk. Av. CR2: S Croy 7B *168*
HA1: Harr 2H *59*
Mount Pk. Cres. W5 . . . . .6D *78*
Mount Pk. Rd. HA1: Harr 3H *59*
HA5: Eastc 5J *39*
W5 . . . . .5D *78*
Mount Pl. W3 . . . . .1H *97*
Mt. Pleasant EN4: Cockf 4H *21*
HA0: Wemb 1E *78*
HA4: Ruis 2A *58*
IG1: Ilf 1G *71*
SE27 . . . . .4C *138*
WC1 . . . . .4J *7* (4A *84*)

Mt. Pleasant Cotts. *N14* 7C *22*
(off The Wells)
Mt. Pleasant Cres. N4 . . . . .1K *65*
Mt. Pleasant Hill E5 . . . . .2H *67*
Mt. Pleasant La. E5 . . . . .1H *67*
Mt. Pleasant M. *N4* 1K *65*
(off Mt. Pleasant Cres.)
Mt. Pleasant Pl. SE18 . . . . .4H *107*
Mt. Pleasant Rd. E17 . . . . .2A *50*
KT3: N Mald 3J *151*
N17 .2E *48*
NW10 . . . . .7E *62*
SE13 . . . . .6D *122*
W5 . . . . .4C *78*
Mt. Pleasant Vs. N4 . . . . .7K *47*
Mt. Pleasant Wlk. DA5: Bexl 5J *127*
Mount Rd. CR4: Mitc 2B *154*
DA6: Bex 5D *126*
EN4: E Barn 5H *21*
KT3: N Mald 3K *151*
KT9: Chess 5F *163*
NW2 . . . . .3D *62*
NW4 . . . . .6C *44*
RM8: Dag 1F *73*
SE19 . . . . .6D *138*
SW19 . . . . .2J *135*
TW13: Hanw 3C *130*
UB3: Hayes 2J *93*
Mount Row W1 . . . . .3J *11* (7F *83*)
Mountsfield Ct. SE13 . . . . .6F *123*
Mountsfield Ho. *SE10* 1E *122*
(off Primrose Way)
Mountside HA7: Stan 1A *42*
Mounts Pond Rd. SE3 . . . . .2F *123*
(not continuous)
The Mount Sq. NW3 . . . . .3A *64*
Mt. Stewart Av. HA3: Kenton 7D *42*
Mount St. W1 . . . . .3G *11* (7E *82*)
Mount St. M. W1 . . . . . . .3J *11* (7F *83*)
Mountstuart Ct. TW11: Hamp W . .1B *150*
Mount Ter. E1 . . . . .5H *85*
Mount Vernon NW3 . . . . .4A *64*
Mount Vw. EN2: Enf 1E *22*
NW7 . . . . .3E *28*
UB2: S'hall 4B *94*
W5 . . . . .4D *78*
Mountview Cl. NW11 . . . . .1K *63*
Mountview Ct. N8 . . . . .4B *48*
Mount Vw. Rd. E4 . . . . . . .7K *25*, 1A *36*
KT10: Clay 7B *162*
N4 . . . . .7J *47*
NW9 . . . . .5K *43*
Mountview Rd.
BR6: Orp, St M Cry 7K *161*
(not continuous)
Mount Vs. SE27 . . . . .3B *138*
Mount Way SM5: Cars 7E *166*
Mountwood KT8: W Mole 3F *149*
MOVERS LANE 2J *89*
Movers La. IG11: Bark 1H *89*
Mowat Ct. *KT4: Wor Pk* 2B *164*
(off The Avenue)
Mowatt Cl. N19 . . . . .1H *65*
Mowbray Cl. N22 . . . . .1A *48*
SE19 . . . . .7F *139*
Mowbray Gdns. UB5: N'olt 1E *76*
Mowbray Ho. *N2* 2B *46*
(off The Grange)
Mowbray Pde. HA8: Edg 4B *28*
Mowbray Rd. EN5: New Bar 5F *21*
HA8: Edg 4B *28*
NW6 . . . . .7G *63*
SE19 . . . . .1F *157*
TW10: Ham 3C *132*
Mowbrays Cl. RM5: Col R 1J *55*
Mowbrays Rd. RM5: Col R 2J *55*
Mowlem St. E2 . . . . .2H *85*
Mowlem Trad. Est. N17 . . . . .7D *34*
Mowll St. SW9 . . . . .7A *102*
Moxon Cl. E13 . . . . .2H *87*
Moxon Pl. UB10: Uxb 1B *74*
Moxon St. EN5: Barn 3C *20*
W1 . . . . .6G *5* (5E *82*)

Moye Cl. E2 . . . . .2G 85
Moyers Rd. E10 . . . . .7E 50
Moy La. SE18 . . . . .5F 107
Moylan Rd. W6 . . . . .6G 99
Moyle Ho. DA17: Belv 2H 109
    SW1 . . . . .6B 18
        (off Churchill Gdns.)
Moyne Ho. SW9 . . . . .5B 120
Moyne Pl. NW10 . . . . .2G 79
Moynihan Dr. N21 . . . . .5D 22
Moys Cl. CRO: C'don 6J 155
Moyser Rd. SW16 . . . . .5F 137
Mozart St. W10 . . . . .3H 81
Mozart Ter. SW1 . . . . . . .4H 17 (4E 100)
MTV Europe 7F 65
Muchelney Rd. SM4: Mord 6A 154
Mudchute Park & Farm 4E 104
Mudlarks Blvd. SE10 . . . . .3H 105
Mudlarks Way SE10 . . . . .3J 105
Muggeridge Cl. CR2: S Croy 5D 168
Muggeridge Rd. RM10: Dag 4H 73
Muirdown Av. SW14 . . . . .4K 115
Muir Dr. SW18 . . . . .6C 118
Muirfield W3 . . . . .6A 80
Muirfield Cl. SE16 . . . . .5H 103
Muirfield Cres. E14 . . . . .3D 104
Muirhead Quay
    IG11: Bark 2G 89
Muirkirk Rd. SE6 . . . . .1E 140
Muir Rd. E5 . . . . .3G 67
Muir St. E16 . . . . .1C 106
        (not continuous)
Mulberry Apts. N4 . . . . .1C 66
        (off Coster Av.)
Mulberry Av. TW19: Stanw 1A 128
Mulberry Cl. E4 . . . . .2H 35
    EN4: E Barn 4G 21
    N8 . . . . .5J 47
    NW3 . . . . .4B 64
    NW4 . . . . .3E 44
    SE7 . . . . .6B 106
    SE22 .5G 121
    SW3 . . . . .6B 100
        (off Beaufort St.)
    SW16 .4G 137
    TW13: Felt 3K 129
    UB5: N'olt 2C 76
Mulberry Ct. DA1: Cray 5K 127
    E11 . . . . .4F 69
        (off Langthorne Rd.)
    EC1 . . . . .2B 8
        (off Tompion St.)
    IG11: Bark 6K 71
    KT6: Surb 7D 150
    N2 . . . . .3C 46
        (off Bedford Rd.)
    SW3 . . . . .7B 16 (6B 100)
        (not continuous)
    TW1: Twick 3K 131
    W9 . . . . .3H 81
        (off Ashmore Rd.)
Mulberry Cres. TW8: Bford 7B 96
    UB7: W Dray 2C 92
Mulberry Ho. BR2: Broml 1G 159
    E2 . . . . .3J 85
        (off Victoria Pk. Sq.)
    SE8 . . . . .6B 104
    SE10 .1E 122
        (off Parkside Av.)
Mulberry Housing Co-operative
    SE1 . . . . .4K 13
Mulberry La. CRO: C'don 1F 169
Mulberry M. SE14 . . . . .1B 122
    SM6: W'gton 6G 167
Mulberry Pde. UB7: W Dray 3C 92
Mulberry Pl. E14 . . . . .7B 86
        (off Clove Cres.)
    HA2: Harr 2H 41
    SE9 . . . . .4B 124
    W6 . . . . .5C 98
Mulberry Rd. E8 . . . . .7F 67
Mulberry St. E1 . . . . .6G 85
Mulberry Tree M. W4 . . . . .2J 97

Mulberry Trees TW17: Shep 7F 147
Mulberry Wlk. SW3 . . . . . .7B 16 (6B 100)
Mulberry Way DA17: Belv 2J 109
    E18 . . . . .2K 51
    IG6: Ilf .4G 53
Mulgrave Ct. SM2: Sutt 6K 165
        (off Mulgrave Rd.)
Mulgrave Rd. CRO: C'don 3D 168
    HA1: Harr 2A 60
    NW10 . . . . .4B 62
    SE18 .4D 106
    SM2: Sutt 7H 165
    SW6 . . . . .6H 99
    W5 . . . . .3D 78
Mulholland Cl. CR4: Mitc 2F 155
Mulkern Rd. N19 . . . . .1H 65
        (not continuous)
Mullards Cl. CR4: Mitc 1D 166
Mullen Twr. WC1 . . . . .4J 7
        (off Mt. Pleasant)
Mullet Gdns. E2 . . . . .3G 85
Mulletsfield WC1 . . . . .2F 7
        (off Cromer St.)
Mull Ho. E3 . . . . .2B 86
        (off Stafford Rd.)
Mulligans Apts. NW6 . . . . .7J 63
        (off Kilburn High Rd.)
Mullins Path SW14 . . . . .3K 115
Mullins Pl. SW4 . . . . .7J 119
Mullion Cl. HA3: Hrw W 1F 41
Mull Wlk. N1 . . . . .6C 66
        (off Clephane Rd.)
Mulready Ho. SW1 . . . . .4E 18
        (off Marsham St.)
Mulready St. NW8 . . . . . .4C 4 (4C 82)
Multi Way W3 . . . . .2A 98
Multon Ho. E9 . . . . .1J 67
Multon Rd. SW18 . . . . .7B 118
Mulvaney Way SE1 . . . . . .7F 15 (2D 102)
        (not continuous)
Mumford Mills SE10 . . . . .1D 122
        (off Greenwich High Rd.)
Mumford Rd. SE24 . . . . .5B 120
Muncaster Cl. TW15: Ashf 4C 128
Muncaster Rd. SW11 . . . . .5D 118
    TW15: Ashf 5D 128
Muncies M. SE6 . . . . .2E 140
Mundania Ct. SE22 . . . . .6H 121
Mundania Rd. SE22 . . . . .6H 121
Munday Ho. SE1 . . . . .3D 102
        (off Burbage Cl.)
Munday Rd. E16 . . . . .7J 87
Munden Ho. E3 . . . . .3D 86
        (off Bromley High St.)
Munden St. W14 . . . . .4G 99
Mundford Rd. E5 . . . . .2J 67
Mundon Gdns. IG1: Ilf 1H 71
Mund St. W14 . . . . .5H 99
Mundy Ho. W10 . . . . .3G 81
        (off Dart St.)
Mundy St. N1 . . . . .1G 9 (3E 84)
Mungo Pk. Cl. WD23: B Hea 2B 26
Munkenbeck Bldg. W2 . . . . .6A 4
        (off Hermitage St.)
Munnery Way BR6: Farnb 3E 172
Munnings Gdns. TW7: Isle 5H 113
Munnings Ho. E16 . . . . .1K 105
        (off Portsmouth M.)
Munro Dr. N11 . . . . .6B 32
Munro Ho. SE1 . . . . .7J 13 (2A 102)
Munro M. W10 . . . . .5G 81
        (not continuous)
Munro Ter. SW10 . . . . .7B 100
Munslow Gdns. SM1: Sutt 4B 166
Munster Av. TW4: Houn 5C 112
Munster Ct. SW6 . . . . .2H 117
    TW11: Tedd 6C 132
Munster Gdns. N13 . . . . .4G 33
Munster M. SW6 . . . . .7G 99
Munster Rd. SW6 . . . . .7G 99
    TW11: Tedd 6B 132
Munster Sq. NW1 . . . . . . .2K 5 (3F 83)
Munster Ter. E13 . . . . .3A 88

Munton Rd. SE17 . . . . .4C 102
Muratori Ho. WC1 . . . . .2J 7
        (off Margery St.)
Murchison Av. DA5: Bexl 1D 144
Murchison Ho. W10 . . . . .5G 81
        (off Ladbroke Gro.)
Murchison Rd. E10 . . . . .2E 68
Murdoch Ho. SE16 . . . . .3J 103
        (off Moodkee St.)
Murdock Cl. E16 . . . . .6H 87
Murdock St. SE15 . . . . .6H 103
Murfett Cl. SW19 . . . . .2G 135
Muriel St. N1 . . . . .2K 83
        (not continuous)
Murillo Rd. SE13 . . . . .4F 123
Muro Ct. SE1 . . . . .7B 14
        (off Milcote St.)
Murphy Ho. SE1 . . . . .7B 14
        (off Borough Rd.)
Murphy St. SE1 . . . . .7J 13 (2A 102)
Murrain Rd. N4 . . . . .2C 66
Murray Av. BR1: Broml 3K 159
    TW3: Houn 5F 113
Murray Cl. SE28 . . . . .1J 107
Murray Ct. E3 . . . . .5B 86
        (off Geoff Cade Way)
    HA1: Harr 6K 41
    TW2: Twick 2H 131
    W7 . . . . .2J 95
Murray Cres. HA5: Pinn 1B 40
Murray Gro. N1 . . . . .1D 8 (2C 84)
Murray Ho. SE18 . . . . .4D 106
        (off Rideout St.)
Murray M. NW1 . . . . .7H 65
Murray Rd. HA6: Nwood 1G 39
    SW19 . . . . .6F 135
    TW10: Ham 2B 132
    W5 . . . . .4C 96
Murray Sq. E16 . . . . .6J 87
Murray St. NW1 . . . . .7G 65
Murrays Yd. SE18 . . . . .4F 107
Murray Ter. NW3 . . . . .4A 64
    W5 . . . . .4D 96
Mursell Est. SW8 . . . . .1K 119
Musard Rd. W6 . . . . .6G 99
    W14 . . . . .6G 99
Musbury St. E1 . . . . .6J 85
Muscal W6 . . . . .6G 99
        (off Field Rd.)
Muscatel Pl. SE5 . . . . .1E 120
Muschamp Rd. SE15 . . . . .3F 121
    SM5: Cars 2C 166
Muscott Ho. E2 . . . . .1G 85
        (off Whiston Rd.)
Muscovy Ho. DA18: Erith 2E 108
        (off Kale Rd.)
Muscovy St. EC3 . . . . . . .2H 15 (7E 84)
Museum Chambers WC1 . . . . .6E 6
        (off Bury Pl.)
Museum Ho. E2 . . . . .3J 85
        (off Burnham St.)
Museum La. SW7 . . . . .2B 16 (3B 100)
Museum Mans. WC1 . . . . .6E 6
        (off Gt. Russell St.)
Mus. of Brands,
    Packaging & Advertising 6G 81
        (off Lancaster Rd.)
Mus. of Comedy 6E 6
Mus. of Croydon 3C 168
        (off High St.)
Mus. of Domestic Design & Architecture
    . . . . .2B 44
Mus. of London 6C 8 (5C 84)
Mus. of London Docklands 7C 86
Mus. of Richmond 5D 114
Mus. of The Order of St John 4B 84
Mus. of Water & Steam 5F 97
Mus. of Wimbledon 6G 135
Museum Pas. E2 . . . . .3J 85
Museum St. WC1 . . . . . . .6E 6 (5J 83)
Mus. Way W3 . . . . .2G 97
Musgrave Cl. EN4: Had W 1F 21
Musgrave Ct. SW11 . . . . .1C 118

Musgrave Cres. SW6 . . . . .7J 99
Musgrave Rd. TW7: Isle 1K 113
Musgrove Rd. SE14 . . . . .1K 121
The Musical Mus. 6E 96
Musjid Rd. SW11 . . . . .2B 118
Musket Cl. EN4: E Barn 6G 21
Musquash Way TW4: Houn 2A 112
Mustang Ho. N1 . . . . .6B 66
        (off Canonbury Rd.)
Muston Rd. E5 . . . . .2H 67
Mustow Pl. SW6 . . . . .2H 117
Muswell Av. N10 . . . . .1F 47
MUSWELL HILL 3F 47
Muswell Hill N10 . . . . .3F 47
Muswell Hill B'way. N10 . . . . .3F 47
Muswell Hill Golf Course 1G 47
Muswell Hill Pl. N10 . . . . .4F 47
Muswell Hill Rd. N6 . . . . .6E 46
    N10 . . . . .6E 46
Muswell M. N10 . . . . .3F 47
Muswell Rd. N10 . . . . .3F 47
Mutrix Rd. NW6 . . . . .1J 81
Mutton Pl. NW1 . . . . .6E 64
Muybridge Rd.
    KT3: N Mald 2J 151
Muybridge Yd.
    KT5: Surb 7F 151
Myatt Rd. SW9 . . . . .1B 120
Myatts Fld. Sth. SW9 . . . . .2A 120
Mycenae Rd. SE3 . . . . .7J 105
Myddelton Av. EN1: Enf 1K 23
Myddelton Cl. EN1: Enf 1A 24
Myddelton Gdns. N21 . . . . .7H 23
Myddelton Pk. N20 . . . . .3G 31
Myddelton Pas. EC1 . . . . .1K 7 (3A 84)
Myddelton Rd. N8 . . . . .4J 47
        (not continuous)
Myddelton Sq. EC1 . . . . . .1K 7 (3A 84)
Myddelton St. EC1 . . . . . .2K 7 (3A 84)
Myddelton Av. N4 . . . . .2C 66
Myddleton Cl. HA7: Stan 2F 27
Myddleton Ho. N1 . . . . .1J 7
Myddleton M. N22 . . . . .7D 32
Myddleton Rd. N22 . . . . .7D 32
Myers Ho. SE5 . . . . .7C 102
        (off Bethwin Rd.)
Myers La. SE14 . . . . .6K 103
Myers Wlk. E14 . . . . .1E 104
Myles Cl. SE16 . . . . .3J 103
        (off Neptune St.)
Mylis Cl. SE26 . . . . .4H 139
Mylius Cl. SE14 . . . . .7J 103
Mylne Cl. W6 . . . . .5C 98
Mylne St. EC1 . . . . .1J 7 (2A 84)
Myra St. SE2 . . . . .4A 108
Myrdle Ct. E1 . . . . .6G 85
        (off Myrdle St.)
Myrdle St. E1 . . . . .5G 85
Myrna Cl. SW19 . . . . .7C 136
Myron Pl. SE13 . . . . .3E 122
Myrtleberry Cl. E8 . . . . .6F 67
        (off Beechwood Rd.)
Myrtle Cl. EN4: E Barn 1J 31
    UB7: W Dray 3B 92
    UB8: Hil 5B 74
Myrtledene Rd. SE2 . . . . .5A 108
Myrtle Gdns. W7 . . . . .1J 95
Myrtle Gro. EN2: Enf 1J 23
    KT3: N Mald 2J 151
Myrtle Rd. CRO: C'don 3D 168
    E6 . . . . .1D 88
    E17 . . . . .6A 50
    IG1: Ilf 2F 71
    N13 . . . . .3H 33
    SM1: Sutt 5A 166
    TW3: Houn 2G 113
    TW12: Hamp H 6G 131
    W3 . . . . .1J 97
Myrtle Wlk. N1 . . . . .1G 9 (2E 84)
Mysore Rd. SW11 . . . . .3D 118
Myton Rd. SE21 . . . . .3D 138

N

Mytton Ho. *SW8* 7K *101*
(off St Stephens Ter.)

N1 Shop. Cen. 2A 84
Nacton Ct. *RM6: Chad H* 5C *54*
(off Hevingham Dr.)
Nadine Cl. SM6: W'gton 7G 167
Nadine St. SE7 . . . . .5A 106
Nagasaki Wlk. SE7 . . . . .3K 105
Nagle Cl. E17 . . . . .2F 51
NAG'S HEAD 3J 65
Nags Head Ct. EC1 . . . . .4D 8
Nags Head La. DA16: Well 3B 126
Nags Head Rd.
 EN3: Pond E 4D 24
Nags Head Shop. Cen. 4K 65
Nainby Ho. SE11 . . . . .4J 19
Nairne Gro. SE24 . . . . .5D 120
Nairn Rd. HA4: Ruis 6A 58
Nairn St. E14 . . . . .5E 86
Naldera Gdns. SE3 . . . . .6J 105
Nallhead Rd. TW13: Hanw 5A 130
Nalton Ho. *NW6* 7A *64*
(off Belsize Rd.)
Namba Roy Cl. SW16 . . . . .4K 137
Namco Funscape
 Romford 6K 55
Namton Dr. CR7: Thor H 4K 155
Nankin St. E14 . . . . .6C 86
Nansen Ho. *NW10* 7K *61*
(off Stonebridge Pk.)
Nansen Rd. SW11 . . . . .3E 118
Nansen Village N12 . . . . .4E 30
Nant Ct. NW2 . . . . .2H 63
Nantes Cl. SW18 . . . . .4A 118
Nantes Pas. E1 . . . . .5J 9 (5F 85)
Nant Rd. NW2 . . . . .2H 63
Nant St. E2 . . . . .3H 85
Naomi St. SE8 . . . . .4A 104
Naoroji St. WC1 . . . . .2J 7 (3A 84)
Napa Cl. E20 . . . . .5C 68
Napier NW9 . . . . .1B 44
Napier Av. E14 . . . . .5C 104
 SW6 . . . . .3H 117
Napier Cl. SE8 . . . . .7B 104
 UB7: W Dray 3B 92
 W14 . . . . .3G 99
Napier Ct. *BR2: Broml* 4K *159*
(off Napier Rd.)
 N1 . . . . .2D *84*
(off Cropley St.)
 SE12 . . . . .3K 141
 SW6 . . . . .3H *117*
(off Ranelagh Gdns.)
 UB4: Yead 4A *76*
(off Dunedin Way)
Napier Gro. N1 . . . . .2C 84
Napier Ho. *E3* 3C *86*
(off Campbell Rd.)
 SE17 . . . . .6B *102*
(off Cooks Rd.)
 W3 . . . . .1A 98
Napier Lodge TW15: Ashf 6F 129
Napier Pl. W14 . . . . .3H 99
Napier Rd. BR2: Broml 4K 159
 CR2: S Croy 7D 168
 DA17: Belv 4F 109
 E6 . . . . .1E 88
 E11 . . . . .4G 69
 E15 . . . . .2C 87
(not continuous)
 EN3: Pond E 5E 24
 HA0: Wemb 6D 60
 N17 . . . . .3E 48
 NW10 . . . . .3D 80
 SE25 . . . . .4H 157
 TW7: Isle 4A 114
 TW15: Ashf 7F 129
 W14 . . . . .3H 99

Napier St. *SE8* 7B *104*
(off Napier Cl.)
Napier Ter. N1 . . . . .7B 66
Napier Wlk. TW15: Ashf 7F 129
Napoleon La. SE18 . . . . .7D 106
Napoleon Rd. E5 . . . . .3H 67
 TW1: Twick 7B 114
Napoleon Cl. UB4: Yead 4C 76
Nara SE13 . . . . .2D 122
Narbonne Av. SW4 . . . . .5G 119
Narborough Cl. UB10: Ick 2E 56
Narborough St. SW6 . . . . .2K 117
Narcissus Rd. NW6 . . . . .5J 63
Nardini *NW9* 1B *44*
(off Long Mead)
Naresby Fold HA7: Stan 6H 27
Nares Cl. TW19: Stanw 1A 128
Narev Dr. EN4: E Barn 5H 21
Narford Rd. E5 . . . . .3G 67
Narrowboat Av. TW8: Bford 7C 96
Narrow Boat Cl. SE28 . . . . .2H 107
Narrow St. E14 . . . . .7A 86
 W3 . . . . .1H 97
Narrow Way BR2: Broml 6C 160
Narvic Ho. SE5 . . . . .2C 120
Narwhal Inuit Art Gallery 5K 97
Nascot St. W12 . . . . .6E 80
Naseby Cl. NW6 . . . . .7A 64
 TW7: Isle 1J 113
Naseby Ct. DA14: Sidc 4K 143
Naseby Rd. IG5: Ilf 1D 52
 RM10: Dag 3G 73
 SE19 . . . . .6D 138
NASH 6J 171
Nash Cl. SM1: Sutt 3B 166
Nash Ct. HA3: Kenton 6B 42
Nashe Ho. *SE1* 3D *102*
(off Burbage Cl.)
Nash Grn. BR1: Broml 6J 141
Nash Ho. *E14* 2C *104*
(off Alpha Gro.)
 E17 . . . . .3D 50
 NW1 . . . . .2F *83*
(off Park Village E.)
 SW1 . . . . .6K *17*
(off Lupus St.)
Nash La. BR2: Kes 7J 171
Nash Pl. E14 . . . . .1D 104
Nash Rd. N9 . . . . .2D 34
 RM6: Chad H 4D 54
 SE4 . . . . .4A 122
Nash St. NW1 . . . . .1K 5 (3F 83)
Nash Way HA3: Kenton 6B 42
Nasmyth St. W6 . . . . .3D 98
Nassau Path SE28 . . . . .1C 108
Nassau Rd. SW13 . . . . .1B 116
Nassau St. W1 . . . . .6A 6 (5G 83)
Nassington Rd. NW3 . . . . .4D 64
Natalie Cl. TW14: Bedf 7F 111
Natalie M. N22 . . . . .6D 32
 TW2: Twick 3H 131
Natal Rd. CR7: Thor H 3D 156
 IG1: Ilf 4F 71
 N11 . . . . .6D 32
 SW16 . . . . .6H 137
Natasha M. SE15 . . . . .4J 121
Nathan Ct. *N9* 7D *24*
(off Causeyware Rd.)
Nathan Ho. *SE11* 4K *19*
(off Reedworth St.)
Nathaniel Cl. E1 . . . . .6K 9 (5F 85)
Nathaniel Ct. E17 . . . . .7A 50
Nathans Rd. HA0: Wemb 1C 60
Nathan Way SE28 . . . . .4J 107
The National Archives 7H 97
National Army Mus. . . .7F 17 (6D 100)
National Gallery 3D 12 (7H 83)
National Maritime Mus. 6F 105
National Portrait Gallery 3D 12
National Tennis Cen. 5A 116
National Ter. *SE16* 2H *103*
(off Bermondsey Wall E.)
National Theatre 4H 13 (1A 102)

National Works TW4: Houn 3D 112
Nation Way E4 . . . . .1K 35
Natural History Mus. . . .2A 16 (3B 100)
Nature Gdn. 5J *103*
(off Bramcote Gro.)
Nautical Dr. E16 . . . . .1D 106
Nautical Ho. *SW18* 4A *118*
(off Juniper Dr.)
Nauticus Wlk. E14 . . . . .4D 104
The Nautilus Bldg. *EC1* 1K *7*
(off Myddelton Pas.)
Naval Ho. *E14* 7F *87*
(off Quixley St.)
 SE18 . . . . .3F 107
Naval Row E14 . . . . .7E 86
Naval Wlk. BR1: Broml 2J *159*
(off High St.)
Navarino Gro. E8 . . . . .6G 67
Navarino Mans. E8 . . . . .6G 67
Navarino Rd. E8 . . . . .6G 67
Navarre Rd. E6 . . . . .2C 88
 SW9 . . . . .1B 120
Navarre St. E2 . . . . .3J 9 (4F 85)
Navenby Wlk. E3 . . . . .4C 86
Navestock Cl. E4 . . . . .3K 35
Navestock Cres. IG8: Wfd G 7F 37
Navigation Cl. E16 . . . . .7G 89
Navigation Dr. EN3: Enf L 1H 25
Navigation Ho. *SE16* 4A *104*
(off Grand Canal Av.)
Navigation Rd. E3 . . . . .4E 86
Navigator Dr. UB2: S'hall 2G 95
Navigator Pk. UB2: S'hall 4A 94
Navigator Sq. N19 . . . . .2G 65
Navy St. SW4 . . . . .3H 119
Naxos Bldg. E14 . . . . .2B 104
Nayim Pl. E8 . . . . .5H 67
Nayland Ho. SE6 . . . . .4E 140
Naylor Bldg. E. *E1* 6G *85*
(off Assam St.)
Naylor Bldg. W. *E1* 6G *85*
(off Adler St.)
Naylor Gro. EN3: Pond E 5E 24
Naylor Ho. *SE17* 4D *102*
(off Flint St.)
 W10 . . . . .3G *81*
(off Dart St.)
Naylor Rd. N20 . . . . .2F 31
 SE15 . . . . .7H 103
Nazareth Gdns. SE15 . . . . .2H 121
Nazrul St. E2 . . . . .1J 9 (3F 85)
NCR Bus. Cen. NW10 . . . . .5A 62
Neagle Ho. *NW2* 3E *62*
(off Stoll Cl.)
Neal Av. UB1: S'hall 4D 76
Neal Cl. HA6: Nwood 1J 39
Nealden St. SW9 . . . . .3K 119
Neale Cl. N2 . . . . .3A 46
Neal St. SE10 . . . . .3H 105
 WC2 . . . . .1E 12 (6J 83)
Neal's Yd. WC2 . . . . .1E 12 (6J 83)
Neap Ct. *E3* 4E *86*
(off Navigation Rd.)
Near Acre NW9 . . . . .1B 44
NEASDEN .3A 62
Neasden Cl. NW10 . . . . .5A 62
NEASDEN JUNC. 4A 62
Neasden La. NW10 . . . . .3A 62
Neasden La. Nth. NW10 . . . . .3K 61
Neasham Rd. RM8: Dag 5B 72
Neate Ho. *SW1* 6B *18*
(off Lupus St.)
Neate St. SE5 . . . . .6E 102
Neath Gdns. SM4: Mord 6A 154
Neathouse Pl. SW1 . . . .3A 18 (4G 101)
Neats Acre HA4: Ruis 7F 39
Neatscourt Rd. E6 . . . . .5B 88
Nebraska Bldg. *SE13* 1D *122*
(off Deal's Gateway)
Nebraska St. SE1 . . . . . . .7E 14 (2D 102)
Nebula Ct. *E13* 2J *87*
(off Umbriel Pl.)

Neckinger SE16 . . . . .7K 15 (3F 103)
Neckinger Est. SE16 . . . . .3F 103
Neckinger St. SE1 . . . . . .7K 15 (2F 103)
Nectarine Way SE13 . . . . .2D 122
Needham Ho. SE11 . . . . .4J 19
Needham Rd. W11 . . . . .6J 81
Needham Ter. NW2 . . . . .3F 63
Needleman Cl. NW9 . . . . .2A 44
Needleman St. SE16 . . . . .2K 103
Needwood Ho. N4 . . . . .1C 66
Neela Cl. UB10: Ick 4D 56
Neeld Cres. HA9: Wemb 5G 61
 NW4 . . . . .5D 44
Neeld Pde. HA9: Wemb 5F 61
Neeld Pl. W9 . . . . .5H 81
Neil Cl. TW15: Ashf 5E 128
Neil Wates Cres. SW2 . . . . .1A 138
Neilgarde Rd. SE6 . . . . .7C 122
Nelia Rd. W6 . . . . .6F 99
Nelldale Rd. SE16 . . . . .4J 103
Nellgrove Rd. UB10: Hil 4D 74
Nell Gwynn Av. TW17: Shep 6F 147
Nell Gwynn Ho. SW3 . . . .4D 16 (4C 100)
Nellie Cressall Way E3 . . . . .5B 86
Nello James Gdns. SE27 . . . . .4D 138
Nelson Arc. *SE10* 6E *104*
(off Nelson Rd.)
Nelson Cl. CR0: C'don 1B 168
 KT12: Walt T 7K 147
 NW6 . . . . .3J 81
 RM7: Mawney 1H 55
 TW14: Felt 1H 129
 UB10: Hil 3D 74
Nelson Ct. *SE16* 1J *103*
(off Brunel Rd.)
Nelson Gdns. E2 . . . . .3G 85
 TW3: Houn 6E 112
Nelson Gro. Rd. SW19 . . . . .1K 153
Nelson Ho. *SW1* 7B *18*
(off Dolphin Sq.)
Nelson La. UB10: Hil 3D 74
Nelson Mandela Cl. N10 . . . . .2E 46
Nelson Mandela Ho. N16 . . . . .2G 67
Nelson Mandela Rd. SE3 . . . . .3A 124
Nelson Pas. EC1 . . . . .1D 8 (3C 84)
Nelson Rd. BR2: Broml 4A 160
 DA14: Sidc 4A 144
 DA17: Belv 5F 109
 E4 . . . . .6J 35
 E11 . . . . .4J 51
 EN3: Pond E 6E 24
 HA1: Harr 1H 59
 HA7: Stan 6H 27
 KT3: N Mald 5K 151
 N8 . . . . .5K 47
 N9 . . . . .2C 34
 N15 . . . . .4E 48
 SE10 . . . . .6E 104
 SW19 . . . . .7K 135
 TW2: Whitt 7F 113
 TW3: Houn 6E 112
 TW6: H'row A 1B 110
 TW15: Ashf 5A 128
 UB10: Hil 3D 74
Nelson Rd. M. SW19 . . . . .7K *135*
(off Nelson Rd.)
Nelson's Column 4E 12 (1J 101)
Nelson Sq. SE1 . . . . .6A 14 (2B 102)
Nelson's Row SW4 . . . . .4H 119
Nelson St. E1 . . . . .6H 85
 E6 . . . . .2D 88
(not continuous)
 E16 . . . . .6H 87
Nelsons Yd. *NW1* 2G *83*
(off Mornington Cres.)
Nelson Ter. N1 . . . . .1B 8 (2B 84)
Nelson Trad. Est. SW19 . . . . .1K 153
Nelson Wlk. E3 . . . . .4D 86
 KT19: Eps 7G 163
 SE16 . . . . .1A 104
Nemoure Rd. W3 . . . . .7J 79
Nemus Apts. SE8 . . . . .4K 103

Nene Gdns. TW13: Hanw 3D 130
Nene Rd. TW6: H'row A 1D 110
NENE ROAD RDBT. 1D 110
Nepaul Rd. SW11 . . . . .2C 118
Nepean St. SW15 . . . . .6C 116
Neptune Ct. E14 . . . . .4C 104
  (off Homer Dr.)
E16 . . . . .5J 87
  (off Hammersley Rd.)
Neptune Development SE8 . . . . . .5A 104
Neptune Ho. E3 . . . . .1C 86
  (off Garrison Rd.)
SE16 . . . . .3J 103
  (off Moodkee St.)
Neptune Rd. HA1: Harr 6H 41
TW6: H'row A 1F 111
Neptune St. SE16 . . . . .3J 103
Neptune Wlk. DA8: Erith 4K 109
Nero Ct. TW8: Bford 7D 96
Nero Ho. E20 . . . . .6E 68
  (off Anthems Way)
Neroli Ho. E1 . . . . .1K 15
  (off Blvd. Walkway)
Nesbit Ct. SE17 . . . . .6B 102
  (off Cook's Rd.)
Nesbit Rd. SE9 . . . . .4B 124
Nesbitt Cl. SE3 . . . . .3G 123
Nesbitts All. EN5: Barn 3C 20
Nesbitt Sq. SE19 . . . . .7E 138
Nesham Ho. N1 . . . . .1E 84
  (off Hoxton St.)
Nesham St. E1 . . . . .1G 85
Ness St. SE16 . . . . .3G 103
Nesta Rd. IG8: Wfd G 6B 36
Nestles Av. UB3: Hayes 3H 93
Nestor Av. N21 . . . . .6G 23
Nestor Ho. E2 . . . . .2H 85
  (off Old Bethnal Grn. Rd.)
Netheravon Rd. W4 . . . . .4B 98
W7 . . . . .1K 95
Netheravon Rd. Sth. W4 . . . . .5B 98
Netherbury Rd. W5 . . . . .3D 96
Netherby Gdns. EN2: Enf 4D 22
Netherby Rd. SE23 . . . . .7J 121
Nether Cl. N3 . . . . .7D 30
Nethercott Ho. E3 . . . . .3D 86
  (off Bruce Rd.)
Nethercourt Av. N3 . . . . .6D 30
Netherfield Gdns. IG11: Bark 6H 71
Netherfield Rd. N12 . . . . .5E 30
SW17 . . . . .3E 136
Netherford Rd. SW4 . . . . .2G 119
Netherhall Gdns. NW3 . . . . .6A 64
Netherhall Way NW3 . . . . .5A 64
Netherheys Dr. CR2: S Croy 7B 168
Netherlands Rd. EN5: New Bar 6G 21
Netherleigh Cl. N6 . . . . .1F 65
Nether St. N3 . . . . .7D 30
N12 . . . . .5F 31
  (not continuous)
Netherton Gro. SW10 . . . . .6A 100
Netherton Rd. N15 . . . . .6D 48
TW1: Twick 5A 114
Netherwood N2 . . . . .2B 46
Netherwood Pl. W14 . . . . .3F 99
  (off Netherwood Rd.)
Netherwood Rd. W14 . . . . .3F 99
Netherwood St. NW6 . . . . .7H 63
Nethewode Ct. DA17: Belv 3H 109
  (off Lower Pk. Rd.)
Netley SE5 . . . . .1E 120
  (off Redbridge Gdns.)
Netley Cl. CR0: New Ad 7E 170
SM3: Cheam 5F 165
Netley Dr. KT12: Walt T 7D 148
Netley Gdns. SM4: Mord 7A 154
Netley Rd. E17 . . . . .5B 50
IG2: Ilf .5H 53
SM4: Mord 7A 154
TW8: Bford 6E 96
Netley St. NW1 . . . . .2A 6 (3G 83)
Nettlecombe NW1 . . . . .7H 65
  (off Agar Gro.)

Nettleden Av. HA9: Wemb 6G 61
Nettleden Ho. SW3 . . . . .4D 16
  (off Cale St.)
Nettlefold Pl. SE27 . . . . .3B 138
TW16: Sun 5J 147
Nettlefold Wlk. KT12: Walt T 7H 147
Nettlestead Cl. BR3: Beck 7B 140
Nettleton Ct. EC2 . . . . .6C 8
  (off London Wall)
Nettleton Rd. SE14 . . . . .1K 121
TW6: H'row A 1D 110
UB10: Ick 4B 56
Nettlewood Rd. SW16 . . . . .7H 137
Neuchatel Rd. SE6 . . . . .2B 140
Neutron Twr. E14 . . . . .7F 87
Nevada Bldg. SE10 . . . . .1D 122
  (off Blackheath Rd.)
Nevada Cl. KT3: N Mald 4J 151
Nevada St. SE10 . . . . .6E 104
Nevern Mans. SW5 . . . . .5J 99
  (off Warwick Rd.)
Nevern Pl. SW5 . . . . .4J 99
Nevern Rd. SW5 . . . . .4J 99
Nevern Sq. SW5 . . . . .4J 99
Nevil Ho. SW9 . . . . .2B 120
  (off Loughborough Est.)
Nevill Ct. SW10 . . . . .7A 100
  (off Edith Ter.)
Neville Av. KT3: N Mald 1K 151
Neville Cl. DA15: Sidc 4K 143
E11 . . . . .3H 69
NW1 . . . . .2H 83
NW6 . . . . .2H 81
SE15 . . . . .1G 121
TW3: Houn 2F 113
W3 . . . . .2J 97
Neville Ct. NW8 . . . . .1A 4
Neville Dr. N2 . . . . .6A 46
Neville Gdns. RM8: Dag 3D 72
Neville Gill Cl. SW18 . . . . .6J 117
Neville Ho. N11 . . . . .4K 31
N22 . . . . .1K 47
  (off Neville Pl.)
NW6 . . . . .2H 81
  (off Denmark Rd.)
Neville Ho. Yd. KT1: King T 2E 150
Neville Pl. N22 . . . . .1K 47
Neville Rd. CR0: C'don 7D 156
E7 . . . . .7J 69
IG6: Ilf 1G 53
KT1: King T 2G 151
NW6 . . . . .2H 81
RM8: Dag 3D 72
TW10: Ham 3C 132
W5 . . . . .4D 78
Nevilles Ct. NW2 . . . . .3C 62
Neville St. SW7 . . . . .5A 16 (5B 100)
Neville Ter. . . . .
SW7 . . . . .5A 16 (5B 100)
Neville Wlk. SM5: Cars 7C 154
Nevill La. EC4 . . . . .7K 7
Nevill Rd. N16 . . . . .4E 66
Nevin Dr. E4 . . . . .1J 35
Nevin Ho. UB3: Harl 3E 92
Nevinson Cl. SW18 . . . . .6B 118
Nevis Cl. E13 . . . . .2K 87
Nevis Rd. SW17 . . . . .2E 136
Nevitt Ho. N1 . . . . .2D 84
  (off Cranston Est.)
New Acres Rd. SE28 . . . . .2J 107
NEW ADDINGTON 7F 171
Newall Ct. UB10: Uxb 1B 74
Newall Ho. SE1 . . . . .3C 102
  (off Bath Ter.)
Newall Rd. TW6: H'row A 1E 110
Newark Cres. NW10 . . . . .3K 79
Newark Ho. SW9 . . . . .2B 120
Newark Knok E6 . . . . .6E 88
Newark Rd. CR2: S Croy 6D 168
Newark St. E1 . . . . .5H 85
  (not continuous)
Newark Way NW4 . . . . .4C 44
New Ash Cl. N2 . . . . .3B 46

New Atlas Wharf E14 . . . . .3C 104
  (off Arnhem Pl.)
New Baltic Wharf SE8 . . . . .5A 104
  (off Evelyn St.)
New Barn Cl. SM6: W'gton 6K 167
NEW BARNET 4G 21
New Barn Rd. BR8: Swan 7K 145
New Barns Av. CR4: Mitc 4H 155
New Barn St. E13 . . . . .4J 87
New Barns Way IG7: Chig 3K 37
Newbeck Cl. BR3: Beck 7B 140
NEW BECKENHAM 6B 140
New Bentham Ct. N1 . . . . .7C 66
  (off Ecclesbourne Rd.)
Newberry M. SW4 . . . . .4J 119
Newberry Ho. N1 . . . . .7C 66
  (off Northampton St.)
Newbold Cotts. E1 . . . . .6J 85
Newbolt Av. SM3: Cheam 5E 164
Newbolt Ho. SE17 . . . . .5D 102
  (off Brandon St.)
Newbolt Rd. HA7: Stan 5E 26
New Bond St. W1 . . . . .1J 11 (6F 83)
Newborough Grn. KT3: N Mald 4K 151
New Brent St. NW4 . . . . .5E 44
Newbridge Point SE23 . . . . .3K 139
  (off Windrush La.)
New Bri. St. EC4 . . . . .1A 14 (6B 84)
New Broad St. EC2 . . . . .6G 9 (5E 84)
New Broadway TW12: Hamp H 5H 131
UB10: Hil 3D 74
W5 . . . . .7D 78
New Broadway Bldgs. W5 . . . . .7D 78
Newburgh Rd. W3 . . . . .1J 97
Newburgh St. W1 . . . . .1B 12 (6G 83)
New Burlington M. W1 . . . . .2A 12 (7G 83)
New Burlington Pl. W1 . . . . .2A 12 (7G 83)
New Burlington St. W1 . . . . .2A 12 (7G 83)
Newburn Ho. SE11 . . . . .5H 19
  (off Newburn St.)
Newburn St. SE11 . . . . .5H 19 (5K 101)
Newbury Cl. RM10: Dag 2G 73
UB5: N'olt 6D 58
Newbury Ct. DA14: Sidc 4K 143
E5 . . . . .5A 68
  (off Daubeney Rd.)
Newbury Gdns. KT19: Ewe 4B 164
Newbury Ho. N22 . . . . .1J 47
SW9 . . . . .2B 120
W2 . . . . .6K 81
  (off Hallfield Est.)
Newbury M. NW5 . . . . .6E 64
NEWBURY PARK 5H 53
Newbury Rd. BR2: Broml 3J 159
E4 . . . . .6K 35
IG2: Ilf 6J 53
TW6: H'row A 1B 110
Newbury Way UB5: N'olt 6C 58
The New Bus. Cen. NW10 . . . . .3B 80
New Butt La. SE8 . . . . .7C 104
New Butt La. Nth. SE8 . . . . .7C 104
  (off Hales St.)
Newby NW1 . . . . .2A 6
  (off Robert St.)
Newby Cl. EN1: Enf 2K 23
Newby Ho. E14 . . . . .7E 86
  (off Newby Pl.)
Newby Pl. E14 . . . . .7E 86
Newby St. SW8 . . . . .3F 119
New Caledonian Mkt. . . . .
  (off Bermondsey Sq.)
New Caledonian Wharf SE16 . . . . . . .3B 104
Newcastle Cl. EC4 . . . . .7A 8 (6B 84)
Newcastle Ct. EC4 . . . . .2D 14
  (off College Hill)
Newcastle Ho. W1 . . . . .5G 5
  (off Luxborough St.)
Newcastle Pl. W2 . . . . .5B 4 (5B 82)
Newcastle Row EC1 . . . . . . .4K 7 (4A 84)
New Cavendish St. W1 . . . . .6H 5 (5E 82)
New Century Ho. E16 . . . . .6H 87
  (off Jude St.)

New Change EC4 . . . . .1C 14 (6C 84)
New Change Pas. EC4 . . . . .1C 14
  (off New Change)
New Chapel Sq. TW13: Felt 1K 129
New Charles St. EC1 . . . . . . .1B 8 (3B 84)
NEW CHARLTON 4A 106
New Chiswick Pool 7A 98
New Church Rd. SE5 . . . . .7C 102
  (not continuous)
New City Rd. E13 . . . . .3A 88
New Claremont Apts. SE1 . . . . .4F 103
  (off Setchell Rd.)
New Clocktower Pl. N7 . . . . .6J 65
New Cl. SW19 . . . . .3A 154
TW13: Hanw 5C 130
New Colebrooke Ct. SM5: Cars 7D 166
New College Ct. NW3 . . . . .6A 64
  (off College Cres.)
New College M. N1 . . . . .7A 66
New College Pde. NW3 . . . . .6B 64
  (off Finchley Rd.)
Newcombe Gdns. SW16 . . . . .4J 137
TW4: Houn 4D 112
Newcombe Ho. E5 . . . . .3H 67
Newcombe Pk. HA0: Wemb 1F 79
NW7 . . . . .5F 29
Newcombe Ri. UB7: Yiew 6A 74
Newcombe St. W8 . . . . .1J 99
Newcomen Rd. E11 . . . . .3H 69
SW11 . . . . .3B 118
Newcomen St. SE1 . . . . . . .6E 14 (2D 102)
New Compton St. WC2 . . . . .1D 12 (6H 83)
New Concordia Wharf . . . .
SE1 . . . . .6K 15 (2G 103)
New Ct. EC4 . . . . .2J 13
UB5: N'olt 5F 59
Newcourt Ho. E2 . . . . .3H 85
  (off Pott St.)
Newcourt St. NW8 . . . . .1C 4 (2C 82)
New Covent Garden Market 7H 101
New Crane Pl. E1 . . . . .1J 103
New Crane Wharf E1 . . . . .1J 103
  (off New Crane Rd.)
New Cres. Yd. NW10 . . . . .2B 80
Newcroft Cl. UB8: Hil 5B 74
Newcroft Ho. CR0: C'don 2F 169
  (off Homefield Rd.)
NEW CROSS 7B 104
NEW CROSS 1B 122
NEW CROSS GATE 1K 121
NEW CROSS GATE 1K 121
New Cross Rd. SE14 . . . . .7J 103
Newdales Cl. N9 . . . . .2B 34
Newdene Av. UB5: N'olt 2B 76
Newdigate Ho. E14 . . . . .6B 86
  (off Norbiton Rd.)
New Diorama Theatre 4F 83
New Drum St. E1 . . . . .7K 9
  (off Buckle St.)
Newell St. E14 . . . . .6B 86
NEW ELTHAM 2G 143
New End NW3 . . . . .3A 64
New End Sq. NW3 . . . . .4B 64
New England Ind. Est. . . . .
IG11: Bark 2G 89
Newent Cl. SE15 . . . . .7E 102
SM5: Cars 1D 166
New Era Est. N1 . . . . .1E 84
  (off Halcomb St.)
New Era Ho. N1 . . . . .1E 84
  (off Halcomb St.)
New Farm Av. BR2: Broml 4J 159
New Farm La. HA6: Nwood 1G 39
New Ferry App. SE18 . . . . .3E 106
New Festival Av. E14 . . . . .6C 86
New Fetter La. EC4 . . . . .7K 7 (6A 84)
Newfield Cl. TW12: Hamp 1E 148
Newfield Ri. NW2 . . . . .3C 62
New Forest La. IG7: Chig 6K 37
Newgale Gdns. HA8: Edg 1F 43
New Gdn. Dr. UB7: W Dray 2A 92
Newgate CR0: C'don 1C 168
Newgate Cl. TW13: Hanw 2C 130

Newgate St. E4 .....3B 36
(not continuous)
EC1 .....7B 8 (6B 84)
New Globe Wlk. SE1 .....4C 14 (1C 102)
New Goulston St. E1 .....7J 9 (6F 85)
New Grn. Pl. SE19 .....6E 138
New Gun Wharf E3 .....1A 86
(off Gunmaker's La.)
Newhall Ct. N1 .....1C 84
(off Popham Rd.)
Newham Academy of Music 1C 88
Newham City Farm 6B 88
Newham Dockside E16 .....7C 88
Newham Leisure Cen. 4A 88
Newham's Row SE1 .....7H 15 (3E 102)
Newham Way E6 .....5A 88
E16 .....5H 87
Newhaven Cl. UB3: Harl 4H 93
Newhaven Cres. TW15: Ashf 5F 129
Newhaven Gdns. SE9 .....4B 124
Newhaven La. E16 .....4H 87
Newhaven Rd. SE25 .....5D 156
New Heston Rd. TW5: Hest 7D 94
New Hope Cl. NW10 .....3D 80
New Horizons Ct. TW8: Bford 6A 96
Newhouse Av. RM6: Chad H 3D 54
Newhouse Cl. KT3: N Mald 7A 152
Newhouse Wlk. SM4: Mord 7A 154
Newick Cl. DA5: Bexl 6H 127
Newick Rd. E5 .....4H 67
Newing Grn. BR1: Broml 7B 142
NEWINGTON 3C 102
Newington Barrow Way N7 .....3K 65
Newington Butts SE1 .....4B 102
SE11 .....4B 102
Newington C'way. SE1 .....7C 14 (3B 102)
Newington Ct. N16 .....4C 66
(off Green Lanes)
Newington Ct. Bus. Cen. SE1 .....7C 14
Newington Grn. N1 .....5D 66
N16 .....5D 66
Newington Grn. Community Gdns.
.....5D 66
(off Newington Grn.)
Newington Grn. Mans. N16 .....5D 66
Newington Grn. Rd. N1 .....6D 66
Newington Ind. Est. SE17 .....4B 102
New Inn B'way. EC2 .....3H 9 (4E 84)
New Inn Pas. WC2 .....1H 13
New Inn Sq. EC2 .....3H 9
New Inn St. EC2 .....3H 9 (4E 84)
New Inn Yd. EC2 .....3H 9 (4E 84)
New Jubilee Ct. IG8: Wfd G 7D 36
New Jubilee Wharf E1 .....1J 103
(off Wapping Wall)
New Kelvin Av. TW11: Tedd 6J 131
New Kent Rd. SE1 .....3C 102
New Kings Rd. SW6 .....2H 117
New King St. SE8 .....6C 104
Newland Cl. EC1 .....2E 8
HA9: Wemb 2G 61
Newland Dr. EN1: Enf 1C 24
Newland Gdns. W13 .....2A 96
Newland Ho. N8 .....3J 47
(off Newland Rd.)
SE14 .....6K 103
(off John Williams Cl.)
Newland Rd. N8 .....3J 47
NEWLANDS
HA8 .....3K 27
SE23 .....5K 121
Newlands HA1: Harr 1J 59
NW1 .....1A 6
(off Harrington St.)
The Newlands KT7: T Ditt 7J 149
SM6: W'gton 7G 167
Newlands Av. KT7: T Ditt 7J 149
Newlands Cl. HA0: Wemb 6C 60
HA8: Edg 3K 27
UB2: S'hall 5C 94
Newlands Cl. SE9 .....6E 124
Newlands Dr. SL3: Poyle 6A 174
Newlands Pk. SE26 .....6J 139

Newlands Pl. EN5: Barn 5A 20
Newlands Quay E1 .....7J 85
Newlands Rd. IG8: Wfd G 2C 36
SW16 .....2J 155
Newland St. E16 .....1C 106
Newlands Way KT9: Chess 5C 162
Newlands Woods CR0: Sels 7B 170
Newling Cl. E6 .....6D 88
New London Performing Arts Cen.
.....4F 47
New London St. EC3 .....2H 15
New Lydenburg Commercial Est.
SE7 .....3A 106
New Lydenburg St. SE7 .....3A 106
Newlyn NW1 .....1G 83
(off Plender St.)
Newlyn Cl. BR6: Chels 4K 173
UB8: Hil 5C 74
Newlyn Gdns. HA2: Harr 7D 40
Newlyn Ho. HA5: Hat E 1D 40
Newlyn Rd. DA16: Well 2K 125
EN5: Barn 4C 20
N17 .....1F 49
NEW MALDEN 4A 152
Newman Cl. NW10 .....6D 62
SE26 .....4J 139
Newman Ct. BR1: Broml 1J 159
(off North St.)
TW15: Ashf 6D 128
Newman Ho. SE1 .....3B 102
Newman Pas. W1 .....6B 6 (5G 83)
Newman Rd. BR1: Broml 1J 159
CR0: C'don 1K 167
E13 .....3K 87
E17 .....5K 49
UB3: Hayes 7K 75
Newman Rd. Ind. Est.
CR0: C'don 7K 155
Newman's Ct. EC3 .....1F 15
Newmans La. KT6: Surb 6D 150
Newman's Row WC2 .....6H 7 (5K 83)
Newmarsh Rd. SE28 .....1K 107
Newmill Ho. E3 .....4E 86
New Mill Rd. SW11 .....6H 101
Newminster Rd. SM4: Mord 6A 154
New Mossford Way IG6: Ilf 4G 53
New Mt. St. E15 .....7F 69
Newnes Path SW15 .....4D 116
Newnham Av. HA4: Ruis 1A 58
Newnham Cl. CR7: Thor H 2C 156
UB5: N'olt 6G 59
Newnham Gdns. UB5: N'olt 6G 59
Newnham Grn. N22 .....1A 48
(off Highfield Cl.)
Newnham Lodge DA17: Belv 5G 109
(off Erith Rd.)
Newnham M. N22 .....7F 33
Newnham Rd. N22 .....1K 47
Newnhams Cl. BR1: Broml 3D 160
Newnham Ter. SE1 .....1J 19 (3A 102)
Newnham Way HA3: Kenton 5E 42
New Nth. Pl. EC2 .....3G 9 (4E 84)
New Nth. Rd. IG6: Ilf 1G 53
N1 .....1F 9 (7C 66)
New Nth. St. WC1 .....5G 7 (5K 83)
Newnton Cl. N4 .....7D 48
New Oak Rd. N2 .....2A 46
New Orleans Wlk. N19 .....7H 47
New Oxford St. WC1 .....7D 6 (6H 83)
New Pde. TW15: Ashf 4B 128
UB7: Yiew 1A 92
New Paragon Wlk. SE17 .....4D 102
New Pk. Av. N13 .....3H 33
New Pk. Cl. UB5: N'olt 6C 58
New Pk. Est. N18 .....5D 34
New Pk. Ho. N13 .....4E 32
New Pk. Pde. SW2 .....7J 119
(off New Pk. Rd.)

New Pk. Rd. SW2 .....1H 137
TW15: Ashf 5E 128
New Pl. CR0: Addtn 6C 170
New Pl. Sq. SE16 .....3H 103
New Plaistow Rd. E15 .....1G 87
New Pond Pde. HA4: Ruis 3J 57
Newport Av. E13 .....4K 87
E14 .....7B 86
Newport Ct. WC2 .....2D 12 (7H 83)
Newport Ho. E3 .....3A 86
(off Strahan Rd.)
Newport Lodge EN1: Enf 5K 23
(off Village Rd.)
Newport Pl. WC2 .....2D 12 (7H 83)
Newport Rd. E10 .....2E 68
E17 .....4A 50
SW13 .....1C 116
TW6: H'row A 1C 110
UB4: Hayes 5F 75
W3 .....2J 97
Newport St. SE11 .....4G 19 (4K 101)
Newport Street Gallery 3H 19 (4K 101)
New Priory Ct. NW6 .....7J 63
(off Mazenod Av.)
New Providence Wharf E14 .....1F 105
Newquay Cres. HA2: Harr 2C 58
Newquay Ho. SE11 .....5J 19 (5A 102)
Newquay Rd. SE6 .....2D 140
New Quebec St. W1 .....1F 11 (6D 82)
New Ride SW7 .....6C 10 (2C 100)
New River Av. N8 .....3K 47
New River Ct. N5 .....4C 66
New River Cres. N13 .....4G 33
New River Head EC1 .....1K 7 (3A 84)
New River Sports & Fitness Cen. 7G 33
New River Wlk. N1 .....6C 66
(not continuous)
New River Way N4 .....7D 48
New Rd. CR4: Mitc 1D 166
DA16: Well 2B 126
E1 .....5H 85
E4 .....4J 35
HA1: Harr 4K 59
IG3: Ilf 2J 71
KT2: King T 7G 133
KT8: W Mole 4E 148
N8 .....5J 47
N9 .....2C 34
N17 .....1F 49
N22 .....1C 48
NW7 .....7B 30
RM9: Dag 2G 91
RM10: Dag 2G 91
RM13: Rain 2G 91
SE2 .....4D 108
TW3: Houn 4F 113
TW8: Bford 6D 96
TW10: Ham 4C 132
TW13: Hanw 5C 130
TW14: Bedf 6F 111
TW14: Felt 1K 129
TW17: Shep 3C 146
UB3: Harl 7E 92
UB8: Hil 4E 74
New Rd. Hill BR2: Kes 7C 172
BR6: Downe 7C 172
New Rochford St. NW5 .....5D 64
New Row WC2 .....3E 62
WC2 .....2E 12 (7J 83)
Newry Rd. TW1: Twick 5A 114
Newsam Av. N15 .....5D 48
New Scotland Yard 6F 13
Newsholme Dr. N21 .....5E 22
NEW SOUTHGATE 5A 32
New Southgate Crematorium 3A 32
New Southgate Ind. Est. N11 .....5B 32
New Spitalfields Mkt. E10 .....3C 68
New Spring Gdns. Wlk.
SE11 .....6F 19 (5J 101)
New Sq. TW14: Bedf 1E 128
WC2 .....7J 7 (6A 84)
New Sq. Pk. TW14: Bedf 1E 128
New Sq. Pas. WC2 .....7J 7

Newstead Av. BR6: Orp 3H 173
Newstead Cl. N12 .....6H 31
Newstead Ct. UB5: N'olt 3C 76
Newstead Ho. N1 .....2A 84
(off Tolpuddle St.)
Newstead Rd. SE12 .....7H 123
Newstead Wlk. SM5: Cars 7A 154
Newstead Way SW19 .....4F 135
New St. EC2 .....6H 9 (5E 84)
New St. Hill BR1: Broml 5K 141
New St. Sq. EC4 .....7K 7 (6A 84)
(not continuous)
Newton Av. N10 .....1E 46
W3 .....2J 97
Newton Cl. E17 .....6A 50
HA2: Harr 2E 58
E13 .....5C 86
NW6 .....7A 64
(off Fairfax Rd.)
SW17 .....3B 136
(off Grosvenor Way)
W8 .....2J 99
(off Kensington Chu. St.)
Newton Gro. W4 .....4A 98
Newton Ho. E1 .....7H 85
(off Cornwall St.)
E17 .....3D 50
(off Prospect Hill)
EN3: Enf H 3E 24
NW8 .....1K 81
(off Abbey Rd.)
SE20 .....7K 139
Newton Ind. Est. RM6: Chad H 4D 54
Newton Lodge SE10 .....3H 105
(off Teal St.)
Newton Mans. W14 .....6G 99
(off Queen's Club Gdns.)
Newton Pk. Pl. BR7: Chst 7D 142
Newton Pl. E14 .....4C 104
Newton Rd. DA16: Well 3A 126
E15 .....5F 69
HA0: Wemb 7F 61
HA3: Hrw W 2J 41
N15 .....5G 49
NW2 .....4E 62
SW19 .....7G 135
TW7: Isle 2K 113
W2 .....6K 81
Newton St. WC2 .....7F 7 (6J 83)
Newton's Yd. SW18 .....5J 117
Newton Ter. BR2: Broml 6B 160
Newton Wlk. HA8: Edg 1H 43
Newton Way N18 .....5H 33
New Tower Bldgs. E1 .....1H 103
Newtown St. SW11 .....1F 119
New Trinity Rd. N2 .....3B 46
New Turnstile WC1 .....6G 7
New Union Cl. E14 .....3E 104
New Union Sq. SW11 .....6H 101
New Union St. EC2 .....6E 8 (5D 84)
New Village Av. E14 .....6F 87
New Wanstead E11 .....6H 51
New Warren La. SE18 .....3F 107
New Way Rd. NW9 .....4A 44
New West End Synagogue 7K 81
(off St Petersburgh Pl.)
New Wharf Rd. N1 .....2J 83
New Willow Ho. E13 .....2J 87
(off Plaistow Rd.)
NEWYEARS GREEN 7B 38
New Years Grn. La. UB9: Hare 6A 38
New Zealand Av. KT12: Walt T 7H 147
New Zealand Way W12 .....7D 80
Nexus Apts. BR1: Broml 3K 159
(off Elmfield Rd.)
Nexus Cl. TW14: Felt 5J 111
Nexus Ct. E11 .....5J 68
NW6 .....3J 81
Niagara Av. W5 .....4C 96
Niagara Cl. N1 .....2C 84
Niagra Ct. SE16 .....3J 103
(off Canada Est.)
Nibthwaite Rd. HA1: Harr 5J 41

Nice Bus. Pk. SE15 . . . . .6H 103
Nicholas Cl. UB6: G'frd 2F 77
Nicholas Ct. E13 . . . . .3K 87
 N7 . . . . .5K 65
 SE12 . . . . .1J 141
 W4 . . . . .6A 98
  (off Corney Reach Way)
Nicholas Gdns. W5 . . . . .2D 96
Nicholas La. EC4 . . . . .2F 15 (7D 84)
  (not continuous)
Nicholas M. W4 . . . . .6A 98
Nicholas Pas. EC4 . . . . .2F 15
Nicholas Rd. CR0: Bedd 4J 167
 E1 . . . . .4J 85
 RM8: Dag .2F 73
 W11 . . . . .7F 81
Nicholas Stacey Ho. SE7 . . . . .5K 105
  (off Frank Burton Cl.)
Nicholas Way HA6: N'wood 1E 38
Nicholay Rd. N19 . . . . .1H 65
  (not continuous)
Nichol Cl. N14 . . . . .1C 32
Nicholes Rd. TW3: Houn 4E 112
Nichol La. BR1: Broml 7J 141
Nicholl Ho. N4 . . . . .1C 66
Nicholls Av. UB8: Hil 4C 74
Nichollsfield Wlk. N7 . . . . .5K 65
Nicholls M. SW16 . . . . .4J 137
Nicholls Point E15 . . . . .1J 87
  (off Park Gro.)
Nicholl St. E2 . . . . .1G 85
Nichols Cl. KT9: Chess 6C 162
 N4 . . . . .1A 66
  (off Osborne Rd.)
Nichols Ct. E2 . . . . .2F 85
Nichols Grn. W5 . . . . .5E 78
Nicholson Ct. E17 . . . . .4K 49
 N17 . . . . .3F 49
Nicholson Ho. SE17 . . . . .5D 102
Nicholson M. KT1: King T 4E 150
Nicholson Rd. CR0: C'don 1F 169
Nicholson Sq. E3 . . . . .3E 86
  (off Bolinder Way)
Nicholson St. SE1 . . . . . . .5A 14 (1B 102)
Nicholson Wlk. UB10: Uxb 1A 74
Nickelby Apts. E15 . . . . .6F 69
  (off Grove Cres. Rd.)
Nickelby Cl. SE28 . . . . .6C 90
Nickelby Cl. UB8: Hil 6D 74
Nickelby Ho. SE16 . . . . .7K 15
  (off Parkers Row)
 W11 . . . . .1F 99
  (off St Ann's Rd.)
Nickols Wlk. SW18 . . . . .4K 117
Nicola Cl. CR2: S Croy 6C 168
 HA3: Hrw W 2H 41
Nicola Ter. DA7: Bex 1E 126
Nicol Cl. TW1: Twick 6B 114
Nicoll Cir. NW7 . . . . .6B 30
Nicoll Ct. N10 . . . . .7A 32
 NW10 . . . . .1A 80
Nicoll Pl. NW4 . . . . .6D 44
Nicoll Rd. NW10 . . . . .1A 80
Nicolson NW9 . . . . .1A 44
Nicolson Dr.
 WD23: B Hea 1B 26
Nicosia Rd. SW18 . . . . .7C 118
Niederwald Rd. SE26 . . . . .4A 140
Nield Rd. UB3: Hayes 2H 93
Nigel Cl. UB5: N'olt 1C 76
Nigel Ct. N3 . . . . .7E 30
Nigel Fisher Way
 KT9: Chess 7C 162
Nigel Ho. EC1 . . . . .5J 7
  (off Portpool La.)
Nigel M. IG1: Ilf 4F 71
Nigel Playfair Av. W6 . . . . .4D 98
Nigel Rd. E7 . . . . .5A 70
 SE15 . . . . .3G 121
Nigeria Rd. SE7 . . . . .7A 106
Nighthawk NW9 . . . . .1B 44
Nightingale Av. E4 . . . . .5B 36
 HA1: Harr .7B 42

Nightingale Cl. E4 . . . . .4A 36
 HA5: Eastc 5A 40
 SM5: Cars 2E 166
 W4 . . . . .6J 97
Nightingale Ct. BR2: Broml 2G 159
 E14 . . . . .2E 104
  (off Ovex Cl.)
 HA1: Harr .6K 41
 N4 . . . . .2K 65
  (off Tollington Pk.)
 SM1: Sutt .5A 166
Nightingale Dr. KT19: Ewe 6H 163
Nightingale Gro. SE13 . . . . .5F 123
Nightingale Hgts. SE18 . . . . .6E 107
Nightingale Ho. E1 . . . . .1G 103
  (off Thomas More St.)
 E2 . . . . .1E 84
  (off Kingsland Rd.)
 NW8 . . . . .4C 4
  (off Samford St.)
 SE18 . . . . .5E 106
  (off Connaught La.)
 UB7: W Dray 2B 92
 W12 . . . . .6E 80
  (off Du Cane Rd.)
Nightingale La. BR1: Broml 2A 160
 E11 . . . . .4K 51
 N8 . . . . .4J 47
 SW4 . . . . .7D 118
 SW12 . . . . .7D 118
 TW10: Rich 7E 114
Nightingale Lodge W9 . . . . .5J 81
  (off Admiral Wlk.)
Nightingale M. E3 . . . . .2K 85
 E11 . . . . .5J 51
 KT1: King T 3D 150
  (off South La.)
 SE11 . . . . .3K 19 (4B 102)
Nightingale Pl. SE18 . . . . .6E 106
 SW10 . . . . .7A 16 (6A 100)
Nightingale Rd. BR5: Pet W 6G 161
 E5 . . . . .3H 67
 KT8: W Mole 5F 149
 KT12: Walt T 7A 148
 N1 . . . . .6C 66
 N9 . . . . .6D 24
 N22 . . . . .2J 47
 NW10 . . . . .2B 80
 SM5: Cars 3D 166
 TW12: Hamp 5E 130
 W7 . . . . .1K 95
The Nightingales TW19: Stanw 1B 128
Nightingale Sq. SW12 . . . . .7E 118
Nightingale Va. SE18 . . . . .6E 106
Nightingale Wlk. N1 . . . . .6C 66
 SW4 . . . . .6F 119
Nightingale Way E6 . . . . .5C 88
Nihill Pl. CR0: C'don 1F 169
Nile Cl. N16 .3F 67
Nile Dr. N9 .2D 34
Nile Ho. N1 .1E 8
  (off Nile St.)
Nile Path SE18 . . . . .6E 106
Nile Rd. E13 . . . . .2A 88
Nile St. N1 . . . . .1D 8 (3C 84)
Nile Ter. SE15 . . . . .5F 103
Nimegen Way SE22 . . . . .5E 120
Nimmo Dr. WD23: B Hea 1C 26
Nimrod NW9 . . . . .1A 44
Nimrod Cl. UB5: N'olt 3B 76
Nimrod Ho. E16 . . . . .5K 87
  (off Vanguard Cl.)
Nimrod Pas. N1 . . . . .6E 66
Nimrod Rd. SW16 . . . . .6F 137
Nina Mackay Cl. E15 . . . . .1G 87
Nine Acres Cl. E12 . . . . .5C 70
 UB3: Harl .3E 92
NINE ELMS 7H 101
Nine Elms Cl. TW14: Felt 1H 129
Nine Elms La. SW8 . . . . .6H 101
 SW11 . . . . .7C 18 (7G 101)
Nineteenth Rd. CR4: Mitc 4J 155
Ninhams Wood BR6: Farnb 4E 172

Ninth Av. UB3: Hayes 7J 75
Nipper All. KT1: King T 2E 150
  (off Clarence St.)
Nipponzan Myohoji Peace Pagoda
 . . . . .6D 100
Nisbet Ho. E9 . . . . .5K 67
Nisbett Wlk. DA14: Sidc 4A 144
Nita Ct. SE12 . . . . .1J 141
Nithdale Rd. SE18 . . . . .7F 107
Nithsdale Gro. UB10: Ick 3E 56
Niton Cl. EN5: Barn 6A 20
Niton Rd. TW9: Rich 3G 115
Niton St. SW6 . . . . .7F 99
Niveda Cl. W12 . . . . .2C 98
Noah Cl. EN3: Enf W 1D 24
Noah's Yd. N1 . . . . .2J 83
Nobel Cl. NW9 . . . . .2K 43
Nobel Dr. UB3: Harl 1F 111
Nobel Ho. SE5 . . . . .2C 120
Nobel Rd. N18 . . . . .4D 34
Noble Cnr. TW5: Hest 1E 112
Noble Ct. CR4: Mitc 2B 154
 E1 . . . . .7H 85
Noblefield Hgts. N2 . . . . .5C 46
Noble M. N16 . . . . .3D 66
  (off Albion Rd.)
Noble St. EC2 . . . . .7C 8 (6C 84)
Noble Yd. N1 . . . . .2C 84
  (off Camden Pas.)
Nocavia Ho. SW6 . . . . .2A 118
  (off Townmead Rd.)
Noel NW9 . . . . .1A 44
Noel Cl. CR0: C'don 7D 156
 TW4: Houn 3D 112
Noel Coward Ho. SW1 . . . . .4B 18
  (off Vauxhall Bri. Rd.)
Noel Coward Theatre 2E 12
  (off St Martin's La.)
Noel Ho. NW6 . . . . .7B 64
  (off Harben Rd.)
NOEL PARK .2B 48
Noel Pk. Rd. N22 . . . . .2A 48
Noel Rd. E6 .4C 88
 N1 . . . . .2B 84
 W3 . . . . .7G 79
Noel Sq. RM8: Dag 4C 72
 TW11: Tedd 5K 131
Noel St. W1 . . . . .1B 12 (6G 83)
Noel Ter. DA14: Sidc 4B 144
 SE23 . . . . .2J 139
Noko W10 . . . . .3F 81
Nolands Cl. RM5: Col R 2J 55
Nolan Mans. E20 . . . . .5D 68
  (off Honour Lea Av.)
Nolan Way E5 . . . . .4G 67
Noll Ho. N7 .2K 65
  (off Tomlins Wlk.)
Nolton Pl. HA8: Edg 1F 43
Nonsuch Ho. SW19 . . . . .1B 154
  (off Chapter Way)
Nonsuch Pl. SM3: Cheam 7F 165
  (off Ewell Rd.)
Nonsuch Wlk. SM2: Cheam 7F 165
Nook Apts. E1 . . . . .1K 15
  (off Scarborough St.)
Nora Gdns. NW4 . . . . .4F 45
Nora Leverton Ct. NW1 . . . . .7G 65
  (off Randolph St.)
Norbiton 2G 151
Norbiton Av. KT1: King T 1G 151
Norbiton Comn. Rd. KT1: King T . . .3H 151
Norbiton Hall KT2: King T 2F 151
Norbiton Ho. NW1 . . . . .1G 83
  (off Camden St.)
Norbiton Rd. E14 . . . . .6B 86
Norbreck Gdns. NW10 . . . . .3F 79
Norbreck Pde. NW10 . . . . .3E 78
Norbroke St. W12 . . . . .7B 80
Norburn St. W10 . . . . .5G 81
NORBURY 1K 155
Norbury Av. CR7: Thor H 1K 155
 SW16 . . . . .1K 155
 TW3: Houn 4H 113

Norbury Cl. SW16 . . . . .1A 156
Norbury Ct. Rd. SW16 . . . . .3J 155
Norbury Cres. SW16 . . . . .1K 155
Norbury Cross SW16 . . . . .3J 155
Norbury Gdns. RM6: Chad H 5D 54
Norbury Gro. NW7 . . . . .3F 29
Norbury Hill SW16 . . . . .7A 138
Norbury Ri. SW16 . . . . .3J 155
Norbury Rd. CR7: Thor H 2C 156
 E4 . . . . .5H 35
 TW13: Felt 3H 129
Norbury Trad. Est. SW16 . . . . .2K 155
Norcombe Gdns.
 HA3: Kenton 6C 42
Norcombe Ho. N19 . . . . .3H 65
  (off Wedmore St.)
Norcott Cl. UB4: Yead 4A 76
Norcott Rd. N16 . . . . .2G 67
Norcroft Gdns. SE22 . . . . .7G 121
Norcutt Rd. TW2: Twick 1J 131
Nordenfeldt Rd. DA8: Erith 5K 109
Norden Ho. E2 . . . . .3H 85
  (off Pott St.)
Norfield Rd. DA2: Wilm 4J 145
Norfolk Apts. E4 . . . . .7J 35
Norfolk Av. N13 . . . . .6G 33
 N15 . . . . .6F 49
Norfolk Cl. EN4: Cockf 4K 21
 N2 . . . . .3C 46
 N13 . . . . .6G 33
 TW1: Twick 6B 114
Norfolk Ct. EN5: Barn 4B 20
 RM6: Chad H 5B 54
  (off Norwich Cres.)
Norfolk Cres. DA15: Sidc 7J 125
 W2 . . . . .7C 4 (6C 82)
Norfolk Gdns. DA7: Bex 1F 127
Norfolk Ho. BR2: Broml 4H 159
  (off Westmoreland Rd.)
 EC4 . . . . .2C 14
 SE8 . . . . .1C 122
  (off Brookmill Rd.)
 SE20 . . . . .1J 157
 SW1 . . . . .3D 18
  (off Page St.)
Norfolk Ho. Rd. SW16 . . . . .3H 137
Norfolk Mans. SW11 . . . . .1D 118
  (off Prince of Wales Dr.)
Norfolk M. W10 . . . . .5G 81
  (off Blagrove Rd.)
Norfolk Pl. DA16: Well 2A 126
 W2 . . . . .7B 4 (6B 82)
  (not continuous)
Norfolk Rd. CR7: Thor H 3C 156
 E6 . . . . .1D 88
 E17 . . . . .2K 49
 EN3: Pond E 6C 24
 EN5: New Bar 3D 20
 HA1: Harr .5F 41
 IG3: Ilf 1J 71
 IG11: Bark 7J 71
 NW8 . . . . .1B 82
 NW10 . . . . .7A 62
 RM7: Rom .6J 55
 RM10: Dag 5H 73
 SW19 . . . . .7C 136
 TW13: Felt 1A 130
 UB8: Uxb .6A 56
Norfolk Row SE1 . . . . .3G 19 (4K 101)
Norfolk Sq. W2 . . . . .1B 10 (6B 82)
Norfolk Sq. M. W2 . . . . .1B 10
Norfolk St. E7 . . . . .5J 69
Norfolk Ter. W6 . . . . .5G 99
Norgrove St. SW12 . . . . .7E 118
Norhyrst Av. SE25 . . . . .3F 157
Norland Ho. W11 . . . . .1F 99
  (off Queensdale Cres.)
Norland Pl. W11 . . . . .1G 99
Norland Rd. W11 . . . . .1F 99
  (not continuous)
Norlands Cres. BR7: Chst 1F 161
Norlands Ga. BR7: Chst 1F 161
Norland Sq. W11 . . . . .1G 99

Norland Sq. Mans.—Nth. Lodge Cl.

Norland Sq. Mans. *W11* *1G 99*
(off Norland Sq.)
Norlem Ct. *SE8* *4A 104*
(off Seafarer Way)
Norley Va. SW15 1C **134**
Norlington Rd. E10 1E **68**
E11 1E **68**
Norman Av. N22 1B **48**
TW1: Twick 7C **114**
TW13: Hanw 2C **130**
UB1: S'hall 7C **76**
Norman Butler Ho. *W10* *4G 81*
(off Ladbroke Gro.)
Normanby Cl. SW15 5H **117**
Normanby Rd. NW10 4B **62**
Norman Cl. BR6: Farnb 3G **173**
N22 1C **48**
RM5: Col R 1H **55**
Norman Ct. IG2: Ilf 7H **53**
N3 *1J 45*
(off Nether St.)
N4 7A **48**
NW10 7C **62**
W13 *1B 96*
(off Kirkfield Cl.)
Norman Cres. HA5: Pinn 1A **40**
TW5: Hest 7B **94**
Normand Gdns. *W14* *6G 99*
(off Greyhound Rd.)
Normand Mans. *W14* *6G 99*
(off Normand M.)
Normand M. W14 6G **99**
Normand Rd. W14 6H **99**
Normandy Av. EN5: Barn 5C **20**
Normandy Cl. SE26 3A **140**
Normandy Dr. UB3: Hayes 6E **74**
Normandy Ho. *E14* *2E 104*
(off Plevna St.)
EN2: Enf 1H **23**
Normandy Pl. W12 1F **99**
Normandy Rd. SW9 1A **120**
Normandy Ter. E16 6K **87**
Normandy Way DA8: Erith 1K **127**
Norman Gro. E3 2A **86**
The Norman Hay Trad. Est.
UB7: Sip 7B **92**
Norman Ho. *SE1* *7H 15*
(off Riley Rd.)
SW8 *7J 101*
(off Wyvil Rd.)
TW13: Hanw *2D 130*
(off Watermill Way)
Normanhurst TW15: Ashf 5C **128**
Normanhurst Av. DA7: Bex 1D **126**
Normanhurst Dr. TW1: Twick 5A **114**
Normanhurst Rd. SW2 2K **137**
Norman Leddy Memorial Gdns. 6H **75**
Norman Pk. Athletics Track 6K **159**
Norman Rd. CR7: Thor H 5B **156**
DA17: Belv 3H **109**
(not continuous)
E6 4D **88**
E11 2F **69**
IG1: Ilf 5F **71**
N15 5F **49**
SE10 7D **104**
SM1: Sutt 5J **165**
SW19 7A **136**
TW15: Ashf 6F **129**
Norman's Cl. NW10 6K **61**
Normans Cl. UB8: Hil 5B **74**
Normansfield Av.
TW11: Tedd 7C **132**
Normanshire Dr. E4 4H **35**
Norman's Mead NW10 6K **61**
Norman St. EC1 2D **8** (3C **84**)
Norman Ter. NW6 5H **63**
Normanton Av. SW19 2J **135**
Normanton Ct. *CR2: S Croy* *5E 168*
(off Croham Rd.)
Normanton Pk. E4 2B **36**
Normanton Rd. CR2: S Croy 5E **168**
Normanton St. SE23 2K **139**
Norman Way N14 2D **32**
W3 5H **79**
Normington Cl. SW16 5A **138**
Norrice Lea N2 5B **46**
Norris *NW9* *1B 44*
(off Withers Mead)
Norris Ho. *E9* *1J 85*
(off Handley Rd.)
N1 *1E 84*
(off Colville Est.)
SE8 *5B 104*
(off Grove St.)
TW7: Isle 2A **114**
Norris St. SW1 3C **12** (7H **83**)
Norroy Rd. SW15 4F **117**
Norry's Cl. EN4: Cockf 4J **21**
Norry's Rd. EN4: Cockf 4J **21**
Norseman Cl. IG3: Ilf 1B **72**
Norseman Way UB6: G'frd 1F **77**
Norstead Pl. SW15 2C **134**
Nth. Access Rd. E17 6K **49**
North Acre NW9 1A **44**
NORTH ACTON 4K **79**
Nth. Acton Bus. Pk. W3 5K **79**
Nth. Acton Rd. NW10 2K **79**
Northall Rd. DA7: Bex 2J **127**
Northampton Gro. N1 5D **66**
Northampton Pk. N1 6C **66**
Northampton Rd.
CR0: C'don 2G **169**
EC1 3K **7** (4A **84**)
EN3: Pond E 4F **25**
Northampton Row EC1 3K **7**
Northampton Sq. EC1 2A **8** (3B **84**)
Northampton St. N1 7C **66**
Northanger Rd. SW16 6J **137**
Nth. Audley St. W1 1G **11** (7E **82**)
North Av. HA2: Harr 6F **41**
N18 4B **34**
SM5: Cars 7E **166**
TW9: Kew 1G **115**
UB1: S'hall 7D **76**
UB3: Hayes 7J **75**
W13 5B **78**
Northaw Ho. *W10* *4E 80*
(off Sutton Way)
Nth. Bank NW8 2C **4** (3C **82**)
Northbank Rd. E17 2E **50**
NORTH BECKTON 5D **88**
Nth. Birkbeck Rd. E11 3F **69**
Nth. Block *SE1* *6H 13*
(off Chicheley St.)
Northborough Rd. SW16 3H **155**
Northbourne BR2: Hayes 7J **159**
Northbourne Rd. SW4 5H **119**
Northbrook Dr. HA6: Nwood 1G **39**
Northbrook Rd. CR0: C'don 5D **156**
EN5: Barn 6B **20**
IG1: Ilf 2E **70**
N22 7D **32**
SE13 5G **123**
Northburgh St. EC1 4B **8** (4B **84**)
Northbury Cl. IG11: Bark 7G **71**
Nth. Carriage Dr. W2 2C **10**
NORTH CHEAM 3E **164**
Northchurch SE17 5D **102**
(not continuous)
Northchurch Ho. *E2* *1G 85*
(off Whiston Rd.)
Northchurch Rd. HA9: Wemb 6G **61**
N1 7D **66**
(not continuous)
Northchurch Ter. N1 7E **66**
Nth. Circular Rd. E4 6G **35**
E12 3E **70**
E18 2H **51**
IG1: Ilf 2D **70**
IG11: Bark 2D **70**
N3 4H **45**
N12 4H **45**
N13 5F **33**
NW2 3A **62**
NW4 7E **44**
Nth. Circular Rd. NW10 2F **79**
NW11 7E **44**
Northcliffe Cl. KT4: Wor Pk 3A **164**
Northcliffe Dr. N20 1C **30**
North Cl. DA6: Bex 4D **126**
RM10: Dag 1G **91**
SM4: Mord 4G **153**
TW14: Bedf 6F **111**
The Nth. Colonnade E14 1C **104**
(not continuous)
North Comn. Rd. UB8: Uxb 5A **56**
W5 7E **78**
Northcote HA5: Pinn 2A **40**
Northcote Av. KT5: Surb 7H **151**
TW7: Isle 5A **114**
UB1: S'hall 7C **76**
W5 7E **78**
Northcote Rd. CR0: C'don 6D **156**
DA14: Sidc 4J **143**
E17 4A **50**
KT3: N Mald 3J **151**
NW10 7A **62**
SW11 5C **118**
TW1: Twick 5A **114**
Northcott Av. N22 1J **47**
Nth. Countess Rd. E17 2B **50**
North Ct. *BR1: Broml* *1K 159*
(off Palace Gro.)
SE24 3B **120**
SW1 *2E 18*
(off Gt. Peter St.)
W1 5B **6** (5G **83**)
NORTH CRAY 5E **144**
Nth. Cray Rd. DA5: Bexl 1H **145**
DA14: Sidc 6E **144**
North Cray Woods 4D **144**
North Cres. E16 4F **87**
N3 2H **45**
WC1 5C **6** (5H **83**)
Northcroft Ct. W12 2C **98**
Northcroft Rd. KT19: Ewe 7A **164**
W13 2B **96**
Nth. Crofts SE23 1H **139**
Northcroft Ter. W13 2B **96**
Nth. Cross Rd. IG6: Ilf 4G **53**
SE22 5F **121**
Northdale Ct. SE25 3F **157**
North Dene NW7 3E **28**
TW3: Houn 1F **113**
Northdene Gdns. N15 6F **49**
Northdown Cl. HA4: Ruis 3H **57**
Northdown Gdns. IG2: Ilf 5J **53**
Northdown Rd. DA16: Well 2B **126**
Northdown St. N1 1G **7** (2J **83**)
North Dr. BR3: Beck 4D **158**
BR6: Orp 4J **173**
HA4: Ruis 7G **39**
SW16 4G **137**
TW3: Houn 2G **113**
Nth. E. Surrey Crematorium 6E **152**
NORTH END 2A **64**
Nth. End CR0: C'don 2C **168**
IG9: Buck H 1F **37**
NW3 2A **64**
Nth. End Av. NW3 2A **64**
Nth. End Cres. W14 4H **99**
Nth. End Ho. W14 4G **99**
Nth. End La. BR6: Downe 7F **173**
Nth. End Pde. *W14* *4G 99*
(off North End Rd.)
Nth. End Rd. HA9: Wemb 3G **61**
NW11 1J **63**
SW6 4G **99**
W14 4G **99**
Nth. End Way NW3 2A **64**
Northern Av. N9 2K **33**
Northernhay Wlk. SM4: Mord 4G **153**
Northern Hgts. *N8* *7H 47*
(off Crescent Rd.)
Northern Perimeter Rd.
TW6: H'row A 1D **110**
Northern Perimeter Rd. (W.)
TW6: H'row A 4E **174**
Northern Rd. E13 2K **87**
Northesk Ho. *E1* *4H 85*
(off Tent St.)
Nth. Eyot Gdns. W6 5B **98**
Northey St. E14 7A **86**
NORTH FELTHAM 6K **111**
Nth. Feltham Trad. Est.
TW14: Felt 5K **111**
Northfield Av. HA5: Pinn 4B **40**
W5 1B **96**
W13 1B **96**
Northfield Cl. BR1: Broml 1C **160**
UB3: Harl 3H **93**
Northfield Cres. SM3: Cheam 4G **165**
Northfield Gdns. RM9: Dag 4F **73**
Northfield Ho. SE15 6G **103**
Northfield Pde. UB3: Harl 3G **93**
Northfield Pk. UB3: Harl 3H **93**
Northfield Path RM9: Dag 4F **73**
Northfield Recreation Ground W5 4B **96**
Northfield Rd. E6 7D **70**
EN3: Pond E 5C **24**
EN4: Cockf 3H **21**
N16 7E **48**
RM9: Dag 4F **73**
TW5: Hest 6B **94**
W13 2B **96**
NORTHFIELDS 3B **96**
Northfields SW18 4J **117**
Northfields Ind. Est. HA0: Wemb 1G **79**
Northfields Prospect Bus. Cen.
SW18 4J **117**
Northfields Rd. W3 5H **79**
NORTH FINCHLEY 5F **31**
Northfleet Ho. *SE1* *6E 14*
(off Tennis St.)
Northflock St. SE16 2G **103**
Nth. Flower Wlk. W2 3A **10**
North Gdn. E14 1B **104**
North Gdns. SW19 7B **136**
North Ga. NW8 1C **4**
Northgate HA6: Nwood 1E **38**
Northgate Bus. Cen. EN1: Enf 3C **24**
Northgate Ct. SW9 3A **120**
Northgate Dr. NW9 6A **44**
Northgate Ho. *E14* *7C 86*
(off E. India Dock Rd.)
Northgate Ind. Pk. RM5: Col R 1F **55**
Northgate Rd. IG11: Bark 3C **90**
North Gates *N12* *1A 46*
(off Bow La.)
The Nth. Glade DA5: Bexl 7F **127**
Nth. Gower St. NW1 2B **6** (3G **83**)
North Grn. NW9 7F **29**
North Gro. N6 7E **46**
N15 5D **48**
NORTH HARROW 5F **41**
Nth. Hatton Rd. TW6: H'row A 1F **111**
Nth. Hill N6 6D **46**
North Hill Av. N6 6E **46**
NORTH HILLINGDON 7E **56**
North Ho. SE8 5B **104**
Nth. Hyde Gdns. UB3: Harl, Hayes 4J **93**
Nth. Hyde La. TW5: Hest 5C **94**
UB2: S'hall 5B **94**
Nth. Hyde Rd. UB3: Harl, Hayes 3G **93**
Nth. Hyde Wharf UB2: S'hall 4A **94**
Northiam N12 4D **30**
(not continuous)
WC1 *2F 7*
(off Cromer St.)
Northiam St. E9 1H **85**
Northington St. WC1 4H **7** (4K **83**)
NORTH KENSINGTON 5E **80**
Northlands Av. BR6: Orp 4J **173**
Northlands St. SE5 2C **120**
North La. TW11: Tedd 6K **131**
Northleigh Ho. *E3* *3D 86*
(off Powis Rd.)
Nth. Lodge *E16* *1K 105*
(off Wesley Av.)
EN5: New Bar 5F **21**
Nth. Lodge Cl. SW15 5F **117**

Nth. London Bus. Pk. N11 . . . . .2K **31**
Nth. Mall N9 .2C **34**
 (within Edmonton Grn. Shop. Cen.)
SW18 . . . . .5K **117**
 (off Southside Shop. Cen.)
North M. WC1 . . . . .4H 7 (4K **83**)
North Middlesex Golf Course . . .3G **31**
North Mill Apts. E8 . . . . .1F **85**
 (off Lovelace St.)
North Mt. N20 . . . . .2F **31**
 (off High Rd.)
Northolm HA8: Edg 4E **28**
Northolme Gdns. HA8: Edg 1G **43**
Northolme Ri. BR6: Orp 2J **173**
Northolme Rd. N5 . . . . .4C **66**
NORTHOLT 7E **58**
Northolt N17 . . . . .2E **48**
 (off Griffin Rd.)
Northolt Av. HA4: Ruis 5K **57**
Northolt Gdns. UB6: G'frd 5K **59**
Northolt Golf Course 2C **76**
Northolt Leisure Cen. 6E **58**
Northolt Rd. HA2: Harr 4F **59**
 TW6: H'row A 1A **110**
 (not continuous)
Northolt Trad. Est. UB5: N'olt . . .7F **59**
Northover BR1: Broml 3H **141**
North Pde. HA8: Edg 2G **43**
 KT9: Chess 5F **163**
 UB1: S'hall 6E **76**
 (off North Rd.)
North Pk. SE9 . . . . .6D **124**
North Pas. SW18 . . . . .5J **117**
North Pl. CR4: Mitc 7D **136**
 TW11: Tedd 6K **131**
North Point N8 . . . . .5K **47**
Northpoint Cl. SM1: Sutt 3A **166**
Northpoint Ho. N1 . . . . .6D **66**
 (off Essex Rd.)
Northpoint Sq. NW1 . . . . .6H **65**
Nth. Pole La. BR2: Kes 6H **171**
Nth. Pole Rd. W10 . . . . .5E **80**
Northport St. N1 . . . . .1D **84**
 (off North Row)
Nth. Ride W2 . . . . .3C 10 (7C **82**)
North Ri. W2 . . . . .1D 10 (6C **82**)
North Rd. BR1: Broml 1K **159**
 BR4: W W'ck 1D **170**
 DA17: Belv 3H **109**
 HA1: Harr 7A **42**
 HA8: Edg 1H **43**
 IG3: Ilf 2J **71**
 KT6: Surb 6D **150**
 N6 . . . . .7E **46**
 N7 . . . . .6J **65**
 N9 . . . . .1C **34**
 RM6: Chad H 5E **54**
 SE18 . . . . .4J **107**
 SW19 . . . . .6A **136**
 TW8: Bford 6E **96**
 TW9: Kew, Rich 3G **115**
 TW14: Bedf 6F **111**
 UB1: S'hall 6E **76**
 UB3: Hayes 5F **75**
 UB7: W Dray 3B **92**
 W5 . . . . .3D **96**
Northrop Rd. TW6: H'row A 1G **111**
Nth. Row W1 . . . . .2F 11 (7D **82**)
Nth. Row Bldgs. W1 . . . . .2G **11**
 (off North Row)
Nth. Several SE3 . . . . .2F **123**
NORTH SHEEN 3G **115**
Northside Rd. BR1: Broml 1J **159**
Northside Studios E8 . . . . .1H **85**
 (off Andrew's Rd.)
Nth. Side Wandsworth Comn.
 SW18 . . . . .5B **118**
Northspur Rd. SM1: Sutt 3J **165**
North Sq. N9 . . . . .2C **34**
 (off New Rd.)
 NW11 . . . . .5J **45**
Nth. Stand N5 . . . . .3B **66**
Northstead Rd. SW2 . . . . .2A **138**

North St. BR1: Broml 1J **159**
 DA7: Bex 4G **127**
 E13 . . . . .2K **87**
 IG11: Bark 6F **71**
 NW4 .5E **44**
 RM1: Rom 3K **55**
 RM5: Rom 3K **55**
 SM5: Cars 3D **166**
 SW4 .3G **119**
 TW7: Isle 3A **114**
North St. Pas. E13 . . . . .2K **87**
Nth. Tenter St. E1 . . . . . .1K 15 (6F **85**)
North Ter. SW3 . . . . .2C 16 (3C **100**)
 WC2 .4E **12**
Northumberland All. EC3 . . .1H 15 (6E **84**)
 (not continuous)
Northumberland Av. DA16: Well . . .4H **125**
 E12 . . . . .1A **70**
 EN1: Enf 1C **24**
 TW7: Isle 1K **113**
 WC2 . . . . .4E 12 (1J **101**)
 TW19: Stanw 6A **110**
Northumberland Cres.
 TW14: Felt 6G **111**
Northumberland Gdns.
 BR1: Broml 4E **160**
 CR4: Mitc 5H **155**
 N9 . . . . .3A **34**
 TW7: Isle 7A **96**
Northumberland Gro. N17 . . . . . .7C **34**
NORTHUMBERLAND HEATH 7J **109**
Northumberland Ho. IG8: Wfd G . . .7K **37**
 SW1 .4E **12**
 (off Northumberland Av.)
Northumberland Pk. DA8: Erith . . .7J **109**
 N17 .7A **34**
Northumberland Pk. Ind. Est. N17 . . .7C **34**
Northumberland Pk. School Sports Cen.
 . . . . .7B **34**
Northumberland Pl. TW10: Rich . . .5D **114**
 W2 . . . . .6J **81**
Northumberland Rd. E6 . . . . .6C **88**
 E17 . . . . .7C **50**
 EN5: New Bar 6F **21**
 HA2: Harr 5D **40**
Northumberland Way DA8: Erith . . .1J **127**
Northumbria St. E14 . . . . .6C **86**
Nth. Verbena Gdns. W6 . . . . .5C **98**
North Vw. HA5: Eastc 7A **40**
 SW19 . . . . .5E **134**
 W5 . . . . .4C **78**
North Vw. Cvn. Site 1A **54**
Northview Cres. NW10 . . . . .4B **62**
North Vw. Dr. IG8: Wfd G 2D **52**
Northview Pde. N7 . . . . .3J **65**
North Vw. Rd. N8 . . . . .4H **47**
North Vs. NW1 . . . . .6H **65**
North Wlk. CR0: New Ad 6D **170**
 (not continuous)
Northwall Rd. E20 . . . . .5C **68**
Nth. Way HA5: Pinn 4B **40**
 N9 . . . . .2E **34**
 N11 .6B **32**
 NW9 .3H **43**
 UB10: Uxb 7A **56**
Northway NW11 . . . . .5K **45**
 SM4: Mord 3G **153**
 SM6: W'gton 4G **167**
Northway Cir. NW7 . . . . .4E **28**
Northway Ct. NW7 . . . . .4E **28**
Northway Cres. NW7 . . . . .4E **28**
Northway Gdns. 5K **45**
Northway Ho. N20 . . . . .1F **31**
Northway Rd. CR0: C'don 6F **157**
 SE5 .3C **120**
Northways NW3 . . . . .7B **64**
 (off College Cres.)
Northways Pde. NW3 . . . . .7B **64**
 (off College Cres.)
Northweald La. KT2: King T 5D **132**
NORTH WEMBLEY 3D **60**

Northwest Pl. N1 . . . . .2A **84**
Nth. Wharf E14 . . . . .1E **104**
 (off Coldharbour)
Nth. Wharf Rd. W2 . . . . . . .6A 4 (5B **82**)
Northwick Av. HA3: Kenton 6A **42**
Northwick Circ. HA3: Kenton 6C **42**
Northwick Cl. HA1: Harr 1B **60**
 NW8 . . . . .3A 4 (4B **82**)
Northwick Ho. NW8 . . . . .3A **4**
Northwick Pk. Playgolf 1A **60**
Northwick Pk. Rd. HA1: Harr 6K **41**
NORTHWICK PARK RDBT. 7A **42**
Northwick Rd. HA0: Wemb 1D **78**
Northwick Ter. NW8 . . . . . . .3A 4 (4B **82**)
Northwick Wlk. HA1: Harr 7K **41**
Northwold Dr. HA5: Pinn 2A **40**
Northwold Rd. E5 . . . . .2F **67**
 N16 .2F **67**
NORTHWOOD 1H **39**
The Northwood Club 2H **39**
Nth. Wood Ct. SE25 . . . . .3G **157**
Northwood Est. E5 . . . . .2G **67**
Northwood Gdns. IG5: Ilf 4E **52**
 N12 .5G **31**
 UB6: G'frd 5K **59**
Northwood Golf Course 1F **39**
Northwood Hall N6 . . . . .7G **47**
NORTHWOOD HILLS 2J **39**
NORTHWOOD HILLS CIR. 1J **39**
Northwood Ho. KT2: King T 2G **151**
 (off Coombe Rd.)
 SE27 . . . . .4D **138**
Northwood Pl. DA18: Erith 3F **109**
Northwood Rd. CR7: Thor H 2B **156**
 N6 . . . . .7F **47**
 SE23 . . . . .1B **140**
 SM5: Cars 6E **166**
 TW6: H'row A 4E **174**
 UB9: Hare 1A **38**
Northwood Way HA6: Nwood 1J **39**
 SE19 . . . . .6D **138**
 UB9: Hare 1A **38**
NORTH WOOLWICH 2E **106**
Nth. Woolwich Rd. E16 . . . . .1H **105**
Nth. Worple Way SW14 . . . . .3K **115**
Norton Av. KT5: Surb 7H **151**
Norton Cl. E4 . . . . .5H **35**
 EN1: Enf 2C **24**
Norton Ct. BR3: Beck 1B **158**
Norton Folgate E1 . . . . . . .5H 9 (5E **84**)
Norton Folgate Ho. E1 . . . . .5J **9**
 (off Puma Ct.)
Norton Gdns. SW16 . . . . .2J **155**
Norton Ho. E1 . . . . .6H **85**
 (off Bigland St.)
 E2 . . . . .2K **85**
 (off Mace St.)
 SW1 .2D **18**
 (off Arneway St.)
 SW9 . . . . .2K **119**
 (off Aytoun Rd.)
Norton Rd. E10 . . . . .1B **68**
 HA0: Wemb 6D **60**
 RM10: Dag 6K **73**
Norval Grn. SW9 . . . . .2A **120**
Norval Rd. HA0: Wemb 2B **60**
Norway Ga. SE16 . . . . .3A **104**
Norway Ho. N1 . . . . .1E **84**
 (off Hertford Rd.)
Norway Pl. E14 . . . . .6B **86**
Norway St. SE10 . . . . .6D **104**
Norway Wharf E14 . . . . .6B **86**
Norwegian War Memorial
 . . . . .5D 10 (1C **100**)
Norwich Cres. RM6: Chad H 5B **54**
Norwich Ho. E14 . . . . .6D **86**
 (off Cordelia St.)
 IG3: Ilf 1A **72**
Norwich Pl. DA6: Bex 4G **127**
Norwich Rd. CR7: Thor H 3C **156**
 E7 . . . . .5J **69**
 HA6: Nwood 3H **39**
 UB6: G'frd 1F **77**

Norwich St. EC4 . . . . .7J 7 (6A **84**)
Norwich Wlk. HA8: Edg 7D **28**
NORWOOD 6E **138**
Norwood Av. HA0: Wemb 1F **79**
 RM7: Rush G 7K **55**
Norwood Cl. NW2 . . . . .3G **63**
 TW2: Twick 2H **131**
 UB2: S'hall 4E **94**
Norwood Dr. HA2: Harr 6D **40**
Norwood Gdns. UB2: S'hall 4D **94**
 UB4: Yead 4A **76**
NORWOOD GREEN 4D **94**
Norwood Grn. Rd. UB2: S'hall 4E **94**
Norwood High St. SE27 . . . . .3B **138**
Norwood Ho. E14 . . . . .7D **86**
 (off Poplar High St.)
NORWOOD NEW TOWN 6C **138**
Norwood Pk. Rd. SE27 . . . . .5C **138**
Norwood Rd. SE24 . . . . .1B **138**
 SE27 . . . . .2B **138**
 TW5: Hest 6A **94**
 UB2: S'hall 3C **94**
Norwood Ter. UB2: S'hall 4F **95**
Notley Pl. SW4 . . . . .7J **119**
Notley St. SE5 . . . . .7D **102**
Notson Rd. SE25 . . . . .4H **157**
Notting Barn Rd. W10 . . . . .4F **81**
Nottingdale Sq. W11 . . . . .1G **99**
Nottingham Av. E16 . . . . .5A **88**
Nottingham Ct. WC2 . . . . .1E 12 (6J **83**)
 (off Shorts Gdns.)
Nottingham Ho. WC2 . . . . .2E **12**
 (off Shorts Gdns.)
Nottingham Pl. W1 . . . . .4G 5 (5E **82**)
Nottingham Rd. CR2: S Croy 4C **168**
 E10 . . . . .6E **50**
 SW17 . . . . .1D **136**
 TW7: Isle 2K **113**
Nottingham St. W1 . . . . . . .5G 5 (5E **82**)
Nottingham Ter. NW1 . . . . .4G **5**
NOTTING HILL 7H **81**
Notting Hill Ga. W11 . . . . .1J **99**
Nottingwood Ho. W11 . . . . .7G **81**
 (off Clarendon Rd.)
Nova Bldg. E14 . . . . .4C **104**
Nova Ct. E. E14 . . . . .1E **104**
 (off Yabsley St.)
Nova Ct. W. E14 . . . . .1E **104**
 (off Yabsley St.)
Nova M. SM3: Sutt 1G **165**
Novar Cl. BR6: Orp 7K **161**
Nova Rd. CR0: C'don 1B **168**
Novar Rd. SE9 . . . . .1G **143**
Novello Ct. N1 . . . . .1C **84**
 (off Dibden St.)
Novello St. SW6 . . . . .1J **117**
Novello Theatre 2G **13**
 (off Aldwych)
Novem Ho. E1 . . . . .6K **9**
 (off Chicksand St.)
Nowell Rd. SW13 . . . . .6C **98**
Nower Ct. HA5: Pinn 4D **40**
Nower Hill HA5: Pinn 4D **40**
Noyna Rd. SW17 . . . . .3D **136**
Nubia Way BR1: Broml 3G **141**
Nucleus Apts. SW15 . . . . .7F **117**
 (off W. Hill)
Nuding Cl. SE13 . . . . .3C **122**
Nuffield Ct. TW5: Hest 7D **94**
Nuffield Health
 Baker Street 2J **23**
 Battersea 2D **118**
 (within Latchmere Leisure Cen.)
 Bloomsbury 3G **7**
 (off Mecklenburgh Pl.)
 Bromley 5K **159**
 Cannon Street 3E **14**
 Cheam 7G **165**
 Chingford 4K **35**
 Chislehurst 5J **143**
 Covent Garden 1F **13**
 (off Endell St.)
 Ealing 7D **78**
 (within Ealing Broadway Cen.)

Nuffield Health
Friern Barnet 5K 31
Fulham 1F 117
Hendon 5E 44
Ilford 3F 71
    (off Clements Rd.)
Islington 1B 84
Kingston upon Thames,
  Richmond Rd. 1E 150
Merton Abbey 1B 154
    (off Watermill Way)
Norbury 2K 155
Paddington 5A 82
Purley Way 6A 168
Romford 5K 55
Stockley Park 7E 74
Sunbury 1J 147
Surbiton 6C 150
Surrey Street 3C 168
    (off Surrey St.)
Sydney Rd. 4J 23
Twickenham 7J 113
Wandsworth 7K 117
Wandsworth,
  Southside Shop. Cen. . . .5J 117
Willesden Green 7E 62
Wimbledon 6H 135
Nuffield Lodge N6 . . . . .6G 47
W9 . . . . .5J 81
    (off Admiral Wlk.)
Nugent Rd. N19 . . . . .1J 65
SE25 . . . . .3F 157
Nugents Ct. HA5: Pinn 1C 40
Nugent's Pk. HA5: Hat E 1C 40
Nugent Ter. NW8 . . . . .2A 82
Numa Ct. TW8: Bford 7D 96
No. 1 St. SE18 . . . . .3F 107
No. One EC1 . . . . . . .4D 8 (4C 84)
Nun Ct. EC2 . . . . .7E 8
Nuneaton Rd. RM9: Dag 7E 72
NUNHEAD 3H 121
Nunhead Cemetery
  Local Nature Reserve 4J 121
Nunhead Cres. SE15 . . . . . . .3H 121
Nunhead Est. SE15 . . . . .4H 121
Nunhead Grn. SE15 . . . . .3H 121
Nunhead Gro. SE15 . . . . .3H 121
Nunhead La. SE15 . . . . .3H 121
Nunhead Pas. SE15 . . . . .3G 121
Nunnington Cl. SE9 . . . . .3C 142
Nunns Rd. EN2: Enf 2H 23
Nupton Dr. EN5: Barn 6A 20
Nurse Cl. HA8: Edg 1J 43
Nursery App. N12 . . . . .6H 31
Nursery Av. CRO: C'don 2K 169
  DA7: Bex 3F 127
  N3 . . . . .2A 46
Nursery Cl. BR6: Orp 7K 161
  CRO: C'don 2K 169
  EN3: Enf H 1E 24
  IG8: Wfd G 5E 36
  RM6: Chad H 6D 54
  SE4 . . . . .2B 122
  SW15 . . . . .4F 117
  TW14: Felt 7K 111
    (not continuous)
Nursery Ct. N17 . . . . .7A 34
  W13 . . . . .5A 78
Nursery Gdns. BR7: Chst 6F 143
  EN3: Enf H 1E 24
  TW4: Houn 5D 112
  TW12: Hamp 4D 130
  TW16: Sun 2H 147
Nursery La. E2 . . . . .1F 85
  E7 . . . . .6J 69
  UB8: Cowl 4A 74
  W10 . . . . .5E 80
Nurserymans Rd. N11 . . . . . . .2K 31
Nursery Rd. CR4: Mitc 3C 154
  CR7: Thor H 4D 156
  E9 . . . . .6J 67
  HA5: Pinn 3A 40
  N2 . . . . .1B 46

Nursery Rd. N14 . . . . .7B 22
  SM1: Sutt 4A 166
  SW9 . . . . .4K 119
  SW19 . . . . .7G 135
    (Elm Gro.)
  SW19 . . . . .2K 153
    (Parkleigh Rd.)
  TW16: Sun 2G 147
Nursery Row EN5: Barn 3B 20
  SE17 . . . . .4D 102
Nursery St. N17 . . . . .7A 34
Nursery Wlk. NW4 . . . . .3E 44
  RM7: Rush G 7K 55
Nursery Waye UB8: Uxb 1A 74
Nurstead Rd. DA8: Erith 7G 109
Nutbourne St. W10 . . . . .3G 81
Nutbrook St. SE15 . . . . .3G 121
Nutbrowne Rd. RM9: Dag 1F 91
Nutcroft Rd. SE15 . . . . .7H 103
Nutfield Cl. N18 . . . . .6B 34
  SM5: Cars 3C 166
Nutfield Ct. BR1: Broml 3J 159
Nutfield Gdns. IG3: Ilf 2K 71
  UB5: N'olt 2A 76
Nutfield Rd. CR7: Thor H 4B 156
  E15 . . . . .4E 68
  NW2 . . . . .3C 62
  SE22 . . . . .4F 121
Nutfield Way BR6: Farnb 2F 173
Nutford Pl. W1 . . . . .7D 4 (6D 82)
Nuthatch Cl. TW19: Stanw 1B 128
Nuthatch Gdns. SE28 . . . . . . .2H 107
    (not continuous)
Nuthatch M. IG5: Ilf 1D 52
Nuthatch Row KT10: Clay 6A 162
Nuthurst Av. SW2 . . . . .2K 137
Nutkin Wlk. UB8: Uxb 7A 56
Nutley Ter. NW3 . . . . .6A 64
Nutmead Cl. DA5: Bexl 1J 145
Nutmeg Cl. E16 . . . . .4G 87
Nutmeg La. E14 . . . . .6F 87
Nuttall St. N1 . . . . .2E 84
Nutter La. E11 . . . . .6A 52
Nutt Gro. HA8: Edg 2J 27
Nutt St. SE15 . . . . .7F 103
Nutty La. TW17: Shep 3E 146
Nutwell St. SW17 . . . . .5C 136
Nuxley Rd. DA17: Belv 6F 109
Nyanza St. SE18 . . . . .6H 107
Nye Bevan Est. E5 . . . . .3K 67
Nye Bevan Ho. *SW6* 7H 99
    (off St Thomas's Way)
Nyland Ct. *SE8* 4A 104
    (off Naomi St.)
Nylands Av. TW9: Kew 1G 115
Nymans Gdns. SW20 . . . . .3D 152
Nynehead St. SE14 . . . . .7A 104
Nyon Gro. SE6 . . . . .2B 140
Nyssa Cl. IG8: Wfd G 6J 37
Nyton Cl. N19 . . . . .1J 65

The O2 . . . . .1G 105
O2 Brixton Academy 3A 120
O2 Cen. 6A 64
2 Forum Kentish Town 5F 65
O2 Shepherd's Bush Empire Theatre
  . . . . .2E 98
Oak Apple Ct. SE12 . . . . .1J 141
Oak Av. CRO: C'don 1C 170
  EN2: Enf 1E 22
  N8 . . . . .4J 47
  N10 . . . . .7A 32
  N17 . . . . .7J 33
  TW5: Hest 7B 94
  TW12: Hamp 5C 130
  UB7: W Dray 3C 92
  UB10: Ick 2D 56
Oak Avenue
  Local Nature Reserve 5C 130
Oak Bank CRO: New Ad 6E 170

Oakbank Av. KT12: Walt T 7D 148
Oakbank Gro. SE24 . . . . .4C 120
Oakbank Ho. *TW8: Bford* 7C 96
    (off High St.)
Oakbrook Cl. BR1: Broml 4K 141
Oakbury Rd. SW6 . . . . .2K 117
Oak Cl. N14 . . . . .7A 22
  SM1: Sutt 2A 166
Oakcombe Cl. KT3: N Mald 1A 152
Oak Cott. Cl. SE6 . . . . .1H 141
Oak Cotts. W7 . . . . .2J 95
Oak Ct. *SE15* 7F 103
    (off Sumner Rd.)
Oak Cres. E16 . . . . .5G 87
Oakcroft Bus. Cen. KT9: Chess . .4F 163
Oakcroft Cl. HA5: Pinn 2K 39
Oakcroft Rd. KT9: Chess 4F 163
  SE13 . . . . .2F 123
Oakcroft Vs. KT9: Chess 4F 163
Oakdale N14 . . . . .1A 32
Oakdale Av. HA3: Kenton 5E 42
  HA6: Nwood 2J 39
Oakdale Cl. E4 . . . . .5K 35
Oakdale Gdns. E4 . . . . .5K 35
Oakdale Rd. E7 . . . . .7K 69
  E11 . . . . .2F 69
  E18 . . . . .2K 51
  KT19: Ewe 7K 163
  N4 . . . . .6C 48
  SE15 . . . . .3J 121
  SW16 . . . . .5J 137
Oakdale Way CR4: Mitc 7E 154
Oak Dene W13 . . . . .5B 78
Oakdene SE15 . . . . .1H 121
Oakdene Av. BR7: Chst 5E 142
  DA8: Erith 6J 109
  KT7: T Ditt 1A 162
Oakdene Cl. HA5: Hat E 1D 40
Oakdene Dr. KT5: Surb 7J 151
Oakdene M. SM3: Sutt 1H 165
Oakdene Pk. N3 . . . . .7C 30
Oakdene Rd. BR5: St M Cry 5K 161
  UB10: Hil 2D 74
Oakden St. SE11 . . . . . .3K 19 (4A 102)
Oake Cl. SW15 . . . . .5G 117
Oakeford Ho. *W14* 3G 99
    (off Russell Rd.)
Oakenholt Ho. SE2 . . . . .1D 108
Oakenshaw Cl. KT6: Surb 7E 150
Oakes Cl. E6 . . . . .6D 88
Oakeshott Av. N6 . . . . .2E 64
Oakes M. *E14* 5E 86
    (off Nairn St.)
Oakey La. SE1 . . . . . .1J 19 (3A 102)
Oakfield E4 . . . . .5J 35
Oakfield Av. HA3: Kenton 3B 42
Oakfield Cl. HA4: Ruis 6H 39
  KT3: N Mald 5B 152
Oakfield Ct. N8 . . . . .7J 47
  NW2 . . . . .7F 45
Oakfield Gdns. BR3: Beck 5D 158
  N18 . . . . .4K 33
  SE19 . . . . .5E 138
    (not continuous)
  SM5: Cars 1C 166
  UB6: G'frd 4H 77
Oakfield Ho. *E3* 3C 86
    (off Gale St.)
Oakfield La. BR2: Kes 4A 172
Oakfield Lodge *IG1: Ilf* 3F 71
    (off Albert Rd.)
Oakfield Rd. CRO: C'don 1C 168
  E6 . . . . .1C 88
  E17 . . . . .2A 50
  IG1: Ilf 3F 71
  N3 . . . . .1K 45
  N4 . . . . .6A 48
  N14 . . . . .2D 32
  SE20 . . . . .7H 139
  SW19 . . . . .3F 135
  TW15: Ashf 5D 128
Oakfield Rd. Ind. Est. SE20 . . . .7H 139
Oakfields Rd. NW11 . . . . .6G 45

Oakfield St. SW10 . . . . .6A 100
Oakford Rd. NW5 . . . . .4G 65
Oak Gdns. CRO: C'don 2C 170
  HA8: Edg 2J 43
Oak Glade HA6: Nwood 1D 38
Oak Gro. BR4: W W'ck 1E 170
  HA4: Ruis 7K 39
  NW2 . . . . .4G 63
  TW16: Sun 7K 129
Oak Gro. Rd. SE20 . . . . .1J 157
Oakhall Ct. E11 . . . . .6K 51
  TW16: Sun 5H 129
Oakhall Dr. TW16: Sun 5H 129
Oak Hall Rd. E11 . . . . .6K 51
Oakhampton Cl. EN4: Cockf 3J 21
  SE6 . . . . .2B 140
Oakham Dr. BR2: Broml 4H 159
Oakham Ho. *W10* 4E 80
    (off Sutton Way)
Oakhampton Rd. NW7 . . . . .7A 30
Oak Hill IG8: Wfd G 7A 36
  KT6: Surb 7E 150
Oakhill KT10: Clay 6A 162
Oakhill Av. HA5: Pinn 2C 40
  NW3 . . . . .4K 63
Oak Hill Cl. IG8: Wfd G 7A 36
Oak Hill Ct. IG8: Wfd G 7A 36
Oakhill Ct. SE23 . . . . .6J 121
  SW19 . . . . .7F 135
Oak Hill Cres. IG8: Wfd G 7A 36
  KT6: Surb 7E 150
Oak Hill Dr. KT6: Surb 7E 150
Oak Hill Gdns. IG8: Wfd G 1G 51
Oak Hill Gro. KT6: Surb 6E 150
Oak Hill Pk. NW3 . . . . .4K 63
Oak Hill Pk. M. NW3 . . . . .4A 64
Oak Hill Path KT6: Surb 6E 150
Oakhill Pl. SW15 . . . . .5J 117
Oak Hill Rd. KT6: Surb 6E 150
Oakhill Rd. BR3: Beck 2E 158
  BR6: Orp 1K 173
  SM1: Sutt 3K 165
  SW15 . . . . .5H 117
  SW16 . . . . .1K 155
Oak Hill Way NW3 . . . . .4K 63
    (not continuous)
Oak Hill Woods Nature Reserve 5J 21
Oak Ho. *E14* 2E 104
    (off Stewart St.)
  N2 . . . . .2B 46
  RM7: Rom 5K 55
  TW9: Kew 1H 115
  W10 . . . . .4G 81
    (off Sycamore Wlk.)
Oakhouse Rd. DA6: Bex 5G 127
Oakhurst Av. DA7: Bex 7E 108
  EN4: E Barn 7H 21
Oakhurst Cl. BR7: Chst 1D 160
  E17 . . . . .4G 51
  IG6: Ilf 1G 53
  KT2: King T 6F 133
  TW11: Tedd 5J 131
Oakhurst Ct. *E17* 4G 51
    (off Woodford New Rd.)
Oakhurst Gdns. DA7: Bex 7E 108
  E4 . . . . .1C 36
  E17 . . . . .4G 51
Oakhurst Gro. SE22 . . . . .4G 121
Oakhurst Rd. KT19: Ewe 6J 163
Oakington Av. HA2: Harr 7E 40
  HA9: Wemb 3F 61
  UB3: Harl 4F 93
Oakington Cl. TW16: Sun 2A 148
Oakington Ct. EN2: Enf 2G 23
Oakington Dr. TW16: Sun 2A 148
Oakington Mnr. Dr.
  HA9: Wemb 5G 61
Oakington Rd. W9 . . . . .4J 81
Oakington Way N8 . . . . .7J 47
Oakland Pl.
  IG9: Buck H 2D 36
Oakland Quay E14 . . . . .3D 104
Oakland Rd. E15 . . . . .4F 69

Oaklands BR3: Beck 1D **158**
   N21 .2E **32**
   W13 .5A **78**
Oaklands Av. BR4: W W'ck 3D **170**
   CR7: Thor H 4A **156**
   DA15: Sidc 7K **125**
   KT10: Esh 7H **149**
   N9 . . . . .6C **24**
   TW7: Isle 6K **95**
Oaklands Cl. BR5: Pet W 6J **161**
   DA6: Bex 5F **127**
   HA0: Wemb 5D **60**
   KT9: Chess 4C **162**
Oaklands Ct. HA0: Wemb 5D **60**
   NW10 . . . . .1A **80**
            (off Nicoll Rd.)
   SE20 . . . . .7J **139**
         (off Chestnut Gro.)
Oaklands Dr. TW2: Whitt 7G **113**
Oaklands Est. SW4 . . . . .6G **119**
Oaklands Gro. W12 . . . . .1C **98**
Oaklands M. NW2 . . . . .4F **63**
         (off Oaklands Rd.)
Oaklands Pk. Av. IG1: Ilf 2G **71**
Oaklands Pas. NW2 . . . . .4F **63**
         (off Oaklands Rd.)
Oaklands Pl. SW4 . . . . .4G **119**
Oaklands Rd. BR1: Broml 7G **141**
   DA6: Bex 4F **127**
   N20 .7C **20**
   NW2 . . . . .4F **63**
   SW14 . . . . .3K **115**
   W7 .2K **95**
         (not continuous)
   W13 .2K **95**
Oaklands Way SM6: W'gton . . .7H **167**
Oakland Way KT19: Ewe 6A **164**
Oak La. E14 . . . . .7B **86**
   IG8: Wfd G 4C **36**
   N2 . . . . .2B **46**
   N11 .6C **32**
   TW1: Twick 7A **114**
   TW7: Isle 4J **113**
Oakleafe Gdns. IG6: Ilf 3F **53**
Oaklea Lodge IG3: Ilf 3A **72**
Oaklea Pas. KT1: King T 3D **150**
Oakleigh Av. HA8: Edg 2H **43**
   KT6: Surb 1G **163**
   N20 .2G **31**
Oakleigh Cl. N20 . . . . .3J **31**
Oakleigh Ct. EN4: E Barn 6H **21**
   HA8: Edg 2J **43**
   N1 . . . . .1E **8**
   UB1: S'hall 1D **94**
Oakleigh Cres. N20 . . . . .2H **31**
Oakleigh Gdns. BR6: Orp 4J **173**
   HA8: Edg 5A **28**
   N20 .1F **31**
Oakleigh M. N20 . . . . .1F **31**
OAKLEIGH PARK 1F **31**
Oakleigh Pk. Av.
   BR7: Chst 1E **160**
Oakleigh Pk. Lawn Tennis & Squash Club
   . . . . .2G **31**
Oakleigh Pk. Nth. N20 . . . . .1G **31**
Oakleigh Pk. Sth. N20 . . . . .7H **21**
Oakleigh Rd. UB10: Hil 7E **56**
Oakleigh Rd. Nth. N20 . . . . .2G **31**
Oakleigh Rd. Sth. N11 . . . . .3K **31**
Oakleigh Way CR4: Mitc 1F **155**
   KT6: Surb 1G **163**
Oakley Av. CR0: Bedd 4K **167**
   IG11: Bark 7K **71**
   W5 . . . . .7G **79**
Oakley Cl. E4 . . . . .3K **35**
   E6 . . . . .6C **88**
   TW7: Isle 1H **113**
   W7 . . . . .7J **77**
Oakley Ct. CR4: Mitc 7E **154**
Oakley Cres. EC1 . . . . .2B **84**
Oakley Dr. BR2: Broml 3C **172**
   SE9 .1H **143**
   SE13 . . . . .6F **123**

Oakley Gdns. N8 . . . . .5K **47**
   SW3 . . . . .7D **16** (6C **100**)
Oakley Grange HA1: Harr 2H **59**
Oakley Ho. SE11 . . . . .4J **19**
           (off Hotspur St.)
   SW1 . . . . .2F **17** (4D **100**)
   W5 . . . . .7G **79**
Oakley M. EN2: Enf 2F **23**
Oakley Pk. DA5: Bexl 7C **126**
Oakley Pl. SE1 . . . . .5F **103**
Oakley Rd. BR2: Broml 3C **172**
   HA1: Harr 6J **41**
   N1 . . . . .7D **66**
   SE25 . . . . .5H **157**
Oakley Sq. NW1 . . . . .2G **83**
Oakley St. SW3 . . . . . .7C **16** (6C **100**)
Oakley Studios SW3 . . . . .7C **16**
        (off Up. Cheyne Row)
Oakley Wlk. W6 . . . . .6F **99**
Oakley Yd. E2 . . . . .3K **9** (4F **85**)
Oak Lock M. W4 . . . . .5A **98**
Oak Lodge E11 . . . . .6J **51**
   SM1: Sutt 4A **166**
   TW16: Sun 7H **129**
           (off Forest Dr.)
   W8 . . . . .3K **99**
           (off Chantry Sq.)
Oak Lodge Cl. HA7: Stan 5H **27**
Oak Lodge Dr. BR4: W W'ck 7D **158**
Oaklodge Way NW7 . . . . .5G **29**
Oakman Ho. SW19 . . . . .1F **135**
Oakmead Av. BR2: Hayes 6J **159**
Oakmead Ct. HA7: Stan 4H **27**
Oakmeade HA5: Hat E 6A **26**
Oakmead Gdns. HA8: Edg 4E **28**
Oakmead Pl. CR4: Mitc 1C **154**
Oakmead Rd. CR0: C'don 6H **155**
   SW12 . . . . .1E **136**
Oakmede EN5: Barn 4A **20**
Oakmere Rd. SE2 . . . . .6A **108**
Oakmont Pl. BR6: Orp 1H **173**
Oak Pk. Gdns. SW19 . . . . .1F **135**
Oak Pk. M. N16 . . . . .3F **67**
Oak Pl. SW18 . . . . .5K **117**
Oakridge Dr. N2 . . . . .3B **46**
Oakridge La. BR1: Broml 5F **141**
Oakridge Rd. BR1: Broml 4F **141**
Oak Ri. IG9: Buck H 3G **37**
Oak Rd. BR6: Chels 7K **173**
   DA8: Erith 7J **109**
   KT3: N Mald 2K **151**
   W5 . . . . .7D **78**
Oak Row SW16 . . . . .2G **155**
The Oaks BR2: Broml 6E **160**
   EN2: Enf 3G **23**
   HA4: Ruis 7F **39**
   IG8: Wfd G 6B **36**
   N12 .4E **30**
   NW6 .7F **63**
       (off Brondesbury Rd.)
   NW10 . . . . .7D **62**
   SE18 . . . . .5G **107**
   SM4: Mord 4G **153**
   TW13: Felt 2B **130**
   UB4: Hayes 2E **74**
Oaks Av. KT4: Wor Pk 3D **164**
   RM5: Col R 2J **55**
   SE19 . . . . .5E **138**
   TW13: Felt 2C **130**
The Oaks Cvn. Pk. 3C **162**
Oaksford Av. SE26 . . . . .3H **139**
Oaks Gro. E4 . . . . .2B **36**
Oakshade Rd.
   BR1: Broml 4F **141**
Oakshaw Rd. SW18 . . . . .7K **117**
Oakshott Ct. NW1 . . . . . .1C **6** (2H **83**)
         (not continuous)
Oakside Cl. IG6: Ilf 2H **53**
Oakside Ter. NW10 . . . . .3K **61**
Oaks La. CR0: C'don 3H **169**
   IG2: Ilf 5J **53**
Oaks Pavilion M. SE19 . . . . .5E **138**
Oak Sq. SW9 . . . . .2K **119**

Oaks Rd. CR0: C'don 5H **169**
   TW19: Stanw 5A **110**
Oak St. RM7: Rom 5J **55**
Oaks Way KT6: Surb 1D **162**
   SM5: Cars 7D **166**
Oakthorpe Ct. N13 . . . . .5H **33**
Oakthorpe Est. N13 . . . . .5H **33**
Oakthorpe Rd. N13 . . . . .5F **33**
Oaktree Av. N13 . . . . .3G **33**
Oak Tree Cl. HA7: Stan 7H **27**
   KT19: Ewe 6H **163**
   W5 . . . . .6C **78**
Oak Tree Ct. UB5: N'olt 2A **76**
   W3 . . . . .7H **79**
Oak Tree Dell NW9 . . . . .5J **43**
Oak Tree Dr. N20 . . . . .1E **30**
Oak Tree Gdns. BR1: Broml 5K **141**
Oaktree Gdns. SE9 . . . . .3F **143**
Oaktree Gro. IG1: Ilf 5H **71**
Oak Tree Ho. W9 . . . . .4J **81**
          (off Shirland Rd.)
Oak Tree M. NW2 . . . . .6C **62**
Oak Tree Rd. NW8 . . . . . .2B **4** (3C **82**)
Oakview Apts. SM1: Sutt 4B **166**
Oakview Gdns. N2 . . . . .4B **46**
Oakview Gro. CR0: C'don 1A **170**
Oakview Lodge NW11 . . . . .7H **45**
        (off Beechcroft Av.)
Oakview Rd. SE6 . . . . .5D **140**
Oak Village NW5 . . . . .4E **64**
Oak Vs. NW11 . . . . .6H **45**
        (off Hendon Pk. Row)
Oakville Ho. SE16 . . . . .2K **103**
          (off Dominion Dr.)
Oak Wlk. SM6: W'gton 1E **166**
           (off Helios Rd.)
Oak Way CR0: C'don 6K **157**
   N14 .7A **22**
   TW14: Felt 1G **129**
   W3 . . . . .1A **98**
Oakway BR2: Broml 2F **159**
   SW20 . . . . .4E **152**
Oakway Cl. DA5: Bexl 6E **126**
Oakways SE9 . . . . .6F **125**
OAKWOOD 4C **22**
Oakwood SM6: W'gton 7F **167**
Oakwood Av. BR2: Broml 3K **159**
   BR3: Beck 2E **158**
   CR4: Mitc 1B **154**
   N14 .7C **22**
   UB1: S'hall 7E **76**
Oakwood Bus. Pk. NW10 . . . . . .4K **79**
Oakwood Cl. BR7: Chst 6D **142**
   IG8: Wfd G 6H **37**
   N14 .6B **22**
   SE13 . . . . .6F **123**
Oakwood Ct. E6 . . . . .1C **88**
   HA1: Harr 4H **41**
   W14 .3H **99**
Oakwood Cres. N21 . . . . .6D **22**
   UB6: G'frd 6A **60**
Oakwood Dr. DA7: Bex 4J **127**
   HA8: Edg 6D **28**
   SE19 . . . . .6D **138**
Oakwood Gdns. BR6: Farnb 2G **173**
   IG3: Ilf 2K **71**
   SM1: Sutt 2J **165**
Oakwood Ho. E9 . . . . .6J **67**
        (off Frampton Pk. Rd.)
Oakwood La. W14 . . . . .3H **99**
Oakwood Lodge N14 . . . . .6B **22**
          (off Avenue Rd.)
Oakwood Mans. W14 . . . . .3H **99**
        (off Oakwood Ct.)
Oakwood Pde. N14 . . . . .5B **22**
Oakwood Pk. Rd. N14 . . . . .7C **22**
Oakwood Pl. CR0: C'don 6A **156**
Oakwood Rd. BR6: Farnb 2G **173**
   CR0: C'don 6A **156**
   HA5: Pinn 2K **39**
   NW11 . . . . .4J **45**
   SW20 . . . . .1C **152**
Oakwood Vw. N14 . . . . .6C **22**

Oakworth Rd. W10 . . . . .5E **80**
Oarsman Pl. KT8: E Mos 4J **149**
The Oasis BR1: Broml 2A **160**
Oasis Academy Sports Hall 1E **24**
Oasis Sports Cen. 7E **6** (6J **83**)
Oast Ct. E14 . . . . .7B **86**
          (off Newell St.)
Oast Lodge W4 . . . . .7A **98**
      (off Corney Reach Way)
Oates Cl. BR2: Broml 3F **159**
Oatfield Ho. N15 . . . . .6E **48**
           (off Perry Ct.)
Oatfield Rd. BR6: Orp 1K **173**
Oatland Ri. E17 . . . . .2A **50**
Oatlands Dr. KT13: Weyb 7G **147**
Oatlands Rd. EN3: Enf H 1D **24**
Oat La. EC2 . . . . .7C **8** (6C **84**)
Oatwell Ho. SW3 . . . . .4D **16**
           (off Cale St.)
Oban Cl. E13 . . . . .4A **88**
Oban Ho. E14 . . . . .6E **87**
           (off Oban St.)
   IG11: Bark 2H **89**
Oban Rd. E13 . . . . .3A **88**
   SE25 . . . . .4D **156**
Oban St. E14 . . . . .6F **87**
Oberon Cl. E6 . . . . .7B **70**
Oberon Ho. N1 . . . . .2E **84**
          (off Arden St.)
Oberon Way TW17: Shep 3A **146**
Oberstein Rd. SW11 . . . . .4B **118**
Oborne Cl. SE24 . . . . .5B **120**
O'Brien Ho. E2 . . . . .2K **85**
         (off Roman Rd.)
Observatory Gdns. W8 . . . . .2J **99**
Observatory M. E14 . . . . .4F **105**
Observatory Rd. SW7 . . .2A **16** (3B **100**)
   SW14 . . . . .4J **115**
Observer Cl. NW9 . . . . .3A **44**
Occupation La. SE18 . . . . .1F **125**
   W5 . . . . .4D **96**
Occupation Rd. KT19: Ewe 7K **163**
   SE17 . . . . .5C **102**
   W13 .2B **96**
Ocean Est. E1 . . . . .5A **86**
         (Ben Jonson Rd.)
   E1 . . . . .4K **85**
           (Ernest St.)
Oceanis Apts. E16 . . . . .7J **87**
         (off Seagull La.)
Ocean St. E1 . . . . .5K **85**
Ocean Wharf E14 . . . . .2B **104**
Ockbrook E1 . . . . .5J **85**
         (off Hannibal Rd.)
Ockendon M. N1 . . . . .6D **66**
Ockendon Rd. N1 . . . . .6D **66**
Ockham Bldg. SE16 . . . . .3F **103**
           (off Arts La.)
Ockham Dr. BR5: St P 7A **144**
   UB6: G'frd 7G **59**
Ockley Ct. DA14: Sidc 3J **143**
   SM1: Sutt 4A **166**
Ockley Rd. CR0: C'don 7K **155**
   SW16 . . . . .4J **137**
The Octagon SW10 . . . . .7K **99**
        (off Coleridge Gdns.)
Octagon Arc. EC2 . . . . . . .6G **9** (5E **84**)
Octagon Ct. SE16 . . . . .1K **103**
        (off Rotherhithe St.)
Octavia Cl. CR4: Mitc 5C **154**
Octavia Ho. SW1 . . . . .2C **18**
         (off Medway St.)
   W10 .4G **81**
Octavia M. W9 . . . . .4H **81**
Octavia Rd. TW7: Isle 3J **113**
Octavia St. SW11 . . . . .1C **118**
Octavia Way SE28 . . . . .7B **90**
Octavius St. SE8 . . . . .7C **104**
October Pl. NW4 . . . . .3F **45**
Odard Rd. KT8: W Mole 4E **148**
Oddmark Ho. IG11: Bark 2H **89**
Odelia Ct. E15 . . . . .1E **86**
        (off Biggerstaff Rd.)

Odell Cl. IG11: Bark 7K **71**
Odell Ho. E14 . . . . .6C **86**
    (off New Festival Av.)
Odell Wlk. SE13 . . . . .3E **122**
The Odeon IG11: Bark 7H **71**
Odeon Cinema
  Beckenham 2C **158**
  Camden Town 1F **83**
    (off Parkway)
  Covent Gdn. 3D **12**
    (off Shaftesbury Av.)
  Edmonton 7E **24**
  Greenwich 4H **105**
  Haymarket, Panton St. 3D **12**
    (off Panton St.)
  Holloway 3J **65**
  IMAX (BFI) 5J **13** (1A **102**)
  Kingston upon Thames 2E **150**
    (within The Rotunda Cen.)
  Leicester Sq. 3D **12**
    (off Leicester Sq.)
  Putney 3G **117**
  Richmond upon Thames,
    Hill Street 5D **114**
    Red Lion Street 5D **114**
  South Woodford 3J **137**
  Streatham 3J **137**
  Surrey Quays 3K **103**
  Swiss Cottage 7B **64**
  Tottenham Ct. Rd. 6C **6**
    (off Tottenham Ct. Rd.)
  Uxbridge 7A **56**
  Whiteleys 6K **81**
  Wimbledon 6H **135**
Odeon Ct. E16 . . . . .5J **87**
NW10 . . . . .1A **80**
    (off St Albans Rd.)
Odeon Pde. N7 . . . . .3J **65**
    (off Holloway Rd.)
SE9 . . . . .4C **124**
    (off Well Hall Rd.)
UB6: G'frd .6B **60**
    (off Allendale Rd.)
Odessa Rd. E7 . . . . .3H **69**
NW10 . . . . .2C **80**
Odessa St. SE16 . . . . .2B **104**
Odessa Wharf SE16 . . . . .3B **104**
    (off Odessa St.)
Odessey Ho. E15 . . . . .6F **69**
    (off Leyton Rd.)
Odette Duval Ho. E1 . . . . .5J **85**
    (off Stepney Way)
Odger St. SW11 . . . . .2D **118**
Odhams Wlk. WC2 . . . . . .1F **13** (6J **83**)
Odin Ho. SE5 . . . . .2D **120**
O'Donnell Ct. WC1 . . . . . . .3F **7** (4J **83**)
O'Driscoll Ho. W12 . . . . .6D **80**
Odyssey Bus. Pk. HA4: Ruis 5K **57**
Offa's Mead E9 . . . . .4B **68**
Offenbach Ho. E2 . . . . .2K **85**
    (off Mace St.)
Offenham Rd. SE9 . . . . .4D **142**
SW9 . . . . .1A **120**
Offers Ct. KT1: King T 3F **151**
Offerton Rd. SW4 . . . . .3G **119**
Offham Ho. SE17 . . . . .4E **102**
    (off Beckway St.)
Offham Slope N12 . . . . .5C **30**
Offley Pl. TW7: Isle 2H **113**
Offley Rd. SW9 . . . . .7A **102**
Offord Cl. N17 . . . . .6B **34**
Offord Rd. N1 . . . . .7K **65**
Offord St. N1 . . . . .7K **65**
Ogden Ho. TW13: Hanw 3C **130**
Ogilby St. SE18 . . . . .4D **106**
Ogilvie Ho. E1 . . . . .6K **85**
    (off Stepney C'way.)
Oglander Rd. SE15 . . . . .4F **121**
Ogle St. W1 . . . . .5A **6** (5G **83**)
Oglethorpe Rd. RM10: Dag 3F **73**
O'Gorman Ho. SW10 . . . . .7A **100**
    (off King's Rd.)
O'Grady Ho. E17 . . . . .3D **50**

Ohio Bldg. SE13 . . . . .1D **122**
    (off Deal's Gateway)
Ohio Rd. E13 . . . . .4H **87**
Oil Mill La. W6 . . . . .5C **98**
Okeburn Rd. SW17 . . . . .5E **136**
Okehampton Cl. N12 . . . . .5G **31**
Okehampton Cres. DA16: Well 1B **126**
Okehampton Rd. NW10 . . . . .1E **80**
Olaf Ct. W8 .2J **99**
    (off Kensington Chu. St.)
Olaf St. W11 . . . . .7F **81**
Old Abbey La. SE16 . . . . .3F **103**
    (off Vauban St.)
Oldacre M. SW12 . . . . .7E **118**
The Old Aeroworks NW8 . . . . .4B **4**
    (off Hatton St.)
Old Bailey 7B **8** (6B **84**)
Old Bailey EC4 . . . . .1B **14** (6B **84**)
Old Barge Ho. All. SE1 . . . . .3K **13**
Old Barn Cl. SM2: Cheam 7G **165**
Old Barn Way DA7: Bex 3K **127**
Old Barracks W8 . . . . .2K **99**
Old Barrack Yd. SW1 . . . . . .7G **11** (2E **100**)
    (not continuous)
Old Barrowfield E15 . . . . .1G **87**
Old Bellgate Pl. E14 . . . . .3C **104**
Oldberry Rd. HA8: Edg 6E **28**
Old Bethnal Grn. Rd. E2 . . . . .3G **85**
Old Bexley Bus. Pk. DA5: Bexl 7H **127**
Old Bexley La. DA5: Bexl, Dart 2K **145**
Old Billingsgate Mkt. EC3 . . . . .3F **15**
Old Billingsgate Wlk. EC3 . . .3G **15** (7E **84**)
Old Bond St. W1 . . . . .3A **12** (7G **83**)
Oldborough Rd. HA0: Wemb 3C **60**
OLD BRENTFORD 7D **96**
Old Brewer's Yd. WC2 . . . .1E **12** (6J **83**)
Old Brewery M. NW3 . . . . .4B **64**
Old Brewery Way E17 . . . . .5B **50**
Old Bri. Cl. UB5: N'olt 2E **76**
Old Bridge St. KT1: Hamp W 2D **150**
Old Broad St. EC2 . . . . . . .7F **9** (6D **84**)
Old Bromley Rd. BR1: Broml 5F **141**
Old Brompton Rd. SW5 . . . . .5J **99**
SW7 . . . . .4A **16** (5J **99**)
Old Bldgs. WC2 . . . . .7J **7**
Old Burlington St. W1 . . . .2A **12** (7G **83**)
Oldbury Ct. E9 . . . . .5A **68**
    (off Mabley St.)
Oldbury Ho. W2 . . . . .5K **81**
    (off Harrow Rd.)
Oldbury Pl. W1 . . . . .5H **5** (5E **82**)
Oldbury Rd. EN1: Enf 2B **24**
Old Canal M. SE15 . . . . .5F **103**
    (off Trafalgar Av.)
Old Castle St. E1 . . . . .7J **9** (6F **85**)
Old Cavendish St. W1 . . . . . .7J **5** (6F **83**)
Old Change Ct. EC4 . . . . .1C **14**
Old Chapel Pl. SW9 . . . . .2A **120**
Old Charlton Rd. TW17: Shep 5E **146**
Old Chelsea M. SW3 . . . . . .7C **16** (6C **100**)
Old Chiswick Yd. W4 . . . . .6A **98**
    (off Pumping Sta. Rd.)
Old Church Ct. N11 . . . . .5A **32**
Oldchurch Gdns. RM7: Rush G 7K **55**
Old Church La. HA7: Stan 5G **27**
NW9 . . . . .2K **61**
UB6: G'frd .3A **78**
Oldchurch Ri. RM7: Rush G 7K **55**
Old Church Rd. E1 . . . . .6K **85**
E4 . . . . .4H **35**
Oldchurch Rd. RM7: Rush G 7K **55**
Old Church St. SW3 . . . . .6B **16** (5B **100**)
Old Claygate La. KT10: Clay 6A **162**
Old Clem Sq. SE18 . . . . .6E **106**
    (off Woolwich Comn.)
Old Coal Yd. SE28 . . . . .4H **107**
Old College Ct. DA17: Belv 5G **109**
Old Compton St. W1 . . . . .2C **12** (7H **83**)
Old Cople La. SE19 . . . . .7F **139**
Old Cote Dr. TW5: Hest 6E **94**
Old Ct. Ho. W8 . . . . .2K **99**
    (off Old Court Pl.)

Old Ct. Pl. W8 . . . . .2K **99**
The Old Ctyd. BR1: Broml 1K **159**
Old Curiosity Shop 7G **7**
    (off Portsmouth St.)
Old Dairy N15 . . . . .6E **48**
Old Dairy Gro. UB2: S'hall 5E **94**
Old Dairy La. HA4: Ruis 4K **57**
Old Dairy M. NW5 . . . . .6F **65**
SW4 . . . . .4J **119**
    (off Tintern St.)
SW12 . . . . .1E **136**
Old Dairy Sq. N21 . . . . .7F **23**
    (off Wade Hill)
Old Deer M. 2C **114**
Old Deer Pk. Gdns. TW9: Rich 3E **114**
Old Devonshire Rd. SW12 . . . . .7F **119**
Old Dock Cl. TW9: Kew 6G **97**
Old Dover Rd. SE3 . . . . .7J **105**
Oldegate Ho. E6 . . . . .7B **70**
Old Farm Av. DA15: Sidc 1H **143**
N14 . . . . .7B **22**
Old Farm Cl. SW17 . . . . .2C **136**
TW4: Houn 4D **112**
Old Farm La. SW9 . . . . .5K **135**
Old Farm Pas. TW12: Hamp 1G **149**
Old Farm Rd. N2 . . . . .1B **46**
TW12: Hamp 6D **130**
UB7: W Dray 2A **92**
Old Farm Rd. E. DA15: Sidc 2A **144**
Old Farm Rd. W. DA15: Sidc 2A **143**
Oldfield Cl. BR1: Broml 4D **160**
HA7: Stan .5F **27**
UB6: G'frd .5J **59**
Oldfield Ct. KT5: Surb 4F **151**
    (off Cranes Pk. Cres.)
Old Fld. Cl. SM1: Sutt 4K **165**
Oldfield Gro. SE16 . . . . .4K **103**
Oldfield Ho. W4 . . . . .5A **98**
    (off Devonshire Rd.)
Oldfield La. Nth. UB6: G'frd 2H **77**
Oldfield La. Sth. UB6: G'frd 4G **77**
Oldfield M. N6 . . . . .7G **47**
Oldfield Rd. BR1: Broml 4D **160**
DA7: Bex .2E **126**
N16 . . . . .3E **66**
NW10 . . . . .7B **62**
SW19 . . . . .6G **135**
TW12: Hamp 1D **148**
W3 . . . . .2B **98**
Oldfields Cir. UB5: N'olt 6G **59**
Oldfields Rd. SM1: Sutt 3H **165**
The Old Fire Station SE18 . . . . .7F **107**
Old Fish St. Hill EC4 . . . . .2C **14**
    (off Queen Victoria St.)
Old Fleet La. EC4 . . . . .7A **8** (6B **84**)
Old Fold Cl. EN5: Barn 1C **20**
Old Fold La. EN5: Barn 1C **20**
Old Fold Manor Golf Course 1B **20**
Old Fold Vw. EN5: Barn 3A **20**
OLD FORD .1B **86**
OLD FORD .1C **86**
Old Ford Rd. E2 . . . . .3J **85**
E3 . . . . .2A **86**
Old Ford Trading Cen. E3 . . . . .1C **86**
    (off Maverton Rd.)
Old Forge Cl. HA7: Stan 4F **27**
Old Forge Cres. TW17: Shep 6D **146**
Old Forge Rd. EN1: Enf 1A **24**
N19 . . . . .2H **65**
Old Forge Way DA14: Sidc 4B **144**
Old Gloucester St. WC1 . . . .5F **7** (5J **83**)
The Old Goods Yd. W2 . . . . .5A **82**
Old Hall Cl. HA5: Pinn 1C **40**
Old Hall Dr. HA5: Pinn 1C **40**
Oldham Ter. W3 . . . . .1J **97**
    (not continuous)
Old Hatch Mnr. HA4: Ruis 7H **39**
Old Highwayman Pl. SW15 . . . . . . .1D **134**
Old Hill BR6: Downe 6H **173**
BR7: Chst .1E **160**
Oldhill St. N16 . . . . .1G **67**
Old Homesdale Rd. BR2: Broml 4A **160**

Old Hospital Cl. SW12 . . . . .1D **136**
Old Ho. Cl. SW19 . . . . .5G **135**
Old Ho. Gdns. TW1: Twick 6C **114**
Old Howlett's La. HA4: Ruis 6F **39**
OLD ISLEWORTH 3B **114**
Old Jamaica Bus. Est.
    SE16 . . . . .7K **15** (3F **103**)
Old Jamaica Rd. SE16 . . . .7K **15** (3G **103**)
Old James St. SE15 . . . . .3H **121**
Old Jewry EC2 . . . . .1E **14** (6D **84**)
Old Kenton La. NW9 . . . . .5H **43**
Old Kent Rd. SE1 . . . . .4E **102**
    SE15 . . . . .4E **102**
Old Kingston Rd. KT4: Wor Pk 2J **163**
Old Laundry BR7: Chst 1G **161**
Old Library Ct. HA4: Ruis 2J **57**
Old Library Ho. E3 . . . . .2A **86**
    (off Roman Rd.)
Old Lodge Pl. TW1: Twick 6B **114**
Old Lodge Way HA7: Stan 5F **27**
Old London Rd.
    DA14: Sidc, Swan 7G **145**
    KT2: King T 2E **150**
Old Lyonian Sports Club 5G **41**
Old Maidstone Rd. DA14: Sidc 7F **145**
OLD MALDEN 1A **164**
Old Malden La. KT4: Wor Pk 2K **163**
Old Manor Dr. TW7: Isle 6G **113**
Old Manor Ho. M. TW17: Shep 3C **146**
Old Manor Rd. UB2: S'hall 4B **94**
Old Manor Way BR7: Chst 5D **142**
    DA7: Bex 1K **127**
Old Manor Yd. SW5 . . . . .4K **99**
Old Mkt. Ct. SM1: Sutt 4K **165**
Old Mkt. Sq. E2 . . . . .1J **9** (3F **85**)
Old Marylebone Rd. NW1 . .6D **4** (5C **82**)
Oldmead Ho. RM10: Dag 6H **73**
Old M. HA1: Harr 5J **41**
Old Mill Cl. E18 . . . . .3A **52**
Old Mill Pl. RM7: Rom 6K **55**
Old Mill Rd. SE18 . . . . .6H **107**
Old Mitre Ct. EC4 . . . . .1K **13** (6A **84**)
Old Montague St. E1 . . . . . .6K **9** (5G **85**)
Old Nichol St. E2 . . . . .3J **9** (4F **85**)
Old North St. WC1 . . . . .5G **7**
Old Nursery Ct. E2 . . . . .2F **85**
    (off Dawson St.)
Old Nursery Pl. TW15: Ashf 5D **128**
Old Oak Cl. KT9: Chess 4F **163**
OLD OAK COMMON 5A **80**
Old Oak Comn. La. NW10 . . . . .5A **80**
Old Oak La. NW10 . . . . .3A **80**
Old Oak Rd. W3 . . . . .7B **80**
The Old Operating Theatre
    Mus. & Herb Garret 5F **15**
Old Orchard TW16: Sun 2A **148**
The Old Orchard NW3 . . . . .4D **64**
Old Orchard Cl. EN4: Had W 1G **21**
    UB8: Hil 6C **74**
Old Palace La. TW9: Rich 5C **114**
Old Palace Rd. CRO: C'don 3B **168**
Old Palace Ter. TW9: Rich 5D **114**
Old Palace Yd. SW1 . . . . .1E **18** (3J **101**)
    TW9: Rich 5C **114**
Old Paradise St. SE11 . . . .3G **19** (4K **101**)
Old Pk. Av. EN2: Enf 4H **23**
    SW12 . . . . .6E **118**
Old Pk. Gro. EN2: Enf 4H **23**
Old Pk. La. W1 . . . . .5J **11** (1F **101**)
Old Pk. M. TW5: Hest 7D **94**
Old Pk. Ridings N21 . . . . .6G **23**
Old Pk. Rd. EN2: Enf 3J **23**
    N13 . . . . .4E **32**
    SE2 . . . . .5A **108**
Old Pk. Rd. Sth. EN2: Enf 4G **23**
Old Pk. Vw. EN2: Enf 3F **23**
Old Pearson St. SE10 . . . . .7D **104**
Old Perry St. BR7: Chst 6J **143**
Old Police Station M. SE20 . . . . . . .7K **139**
The Old Police Stn. SW17 . . . . .2D **136**
Old Post Office La. SE3 . . . . .3K **123**

Old Post Office Wlk. KT6: Surb 6D 150
   (off Victoria Rd.)
Old Pound Cl. TW7: Isle 1A 114
Old Pye St. SW1 . . . . .1C 18 (3H 101)
Old Pye St. Est. SW1 . . . . .2C 18
   (off Old Pye St.)
Old Quebec St. W1 . . . . . . .1F 11 (6D 82)
   (not continuous)
Old Queen St. SW1 . . . . . .7D 12 (2H 101)
Old Rectory Gdns. HA8: Edg 6B 28
Old Redding HA3: Hrw W 5A 26
Old Red Lion Theatre 1K 7
   (off St John St.)
Oldridge Rd. SW12 . . . . .7E 118
Old Rd. DA1: Cray 5K 127
  EN3: Enf H 1D 24
  SE13 .4G 123
Old Rope Wlk. TW16: Sun 3K 147
Old Royal Free Pl. N1 . . . . .1A 84
Old Royal Free Sq. N1 . . . . .1A 84
Old Royal Naval College 5F 105
Old Ruislip Rd. UB5: N'olt 2A 76
The Old School WC1 . . . . .5H 7
   (off Princeton St.)
Old School Cl. BR3: Beck 2K 157
  SE10 .3G 105
  SW19 .2J 153
Old School Ct. N17 . . . . .3F 49
Old School Cres. E7 . . . . .6J 69
Old School Pl. CR0: Wadd 4A 168
Old School Rd. UB8: Hil 4B 74
Old Schools La. KT17: Ewe 7B 164
Old School Sq. E14 . . . . .6C 86
   (off Pelling St.)
  KT7: T Ditt 6K 149
Old School Ter. SM3: Cheam 7F 165
Old Seacoal La. EC4 . . . . . .7A 8 (6B 84)
The Old Sessions Ho. EC1 . . .4A 8 (4B 84)
Old Slade La. SL0: Rich P 1A 174
  SL3: Coln 1A 174
Old Sth. Cl. HA5: Pinn 1B 40
Old Sth. Lambeth Rd. SW8 . . . . . . .7J 101
Old Speech Room Gallery 1J 59
Old Spitalfields Market 5J 9 (5F 85)
Old Sq. WC2 . . . . .7J 7 (6K 83)
Old Stable M. N5 . . . . .3C 66
Old Stable Row SE18 . . . . .4E 106
   (off Woolwich New Rd.)
Old Stables Ct. SE5 . . . . .1C 120
   (off Camberwell New Rd.)
Old Station Gdns. TW11: Tedd 6A 132
   (off Victoria Rd.)
Old Station Ho. SE17 . . . . .5C 102
Old Station Rd. UB3: Harl 3H 93
Old Station Way SW4 . . . . .3H 119
   (off Voltaire Road)
The Old Station Yd. E17 . . . . .4E 50
Oldstead Rd. BR1: Broml 4E 140
Old Stn. Way SW4 . . . . .3H 119
   (off Voltaire Rd.)
Old Stockley Rd. UB7: W Dray 2D 92
OLD STREET 3F 9 (4D 84)
Old St. E13 .2K 87
  EC1 . . . . .3C 8 (4C 84)
Old St. Yd. EC1 . . . . .3E 8
Old Studio Cl. CR0: C'don 7D 156
Old Sungate Cotts. RM5: Col R 1F 55
Old Sun Wharf E14 . . . . .7A 86
   (off Narrow St.)
Old Swan Wharf SW11 . . . . .1B 118
Old Swan Yd. SM5: Cars 4D 166
Old Theatre Ct. SE1 . . . . .4D 14
  SW4 .3G 119
Old Town Hall Apts. SE16 . . . . .3F 103
Old Tramyard SE18 . . . . .4J 107
Old Twelve Cl. W7 . . . . .4J 77
The Old Vic Theatre 2K 13
The Old Vinyl Factory UB3: Hayes . . .2G 93
Old Watercress Wlk. SM5: Cars 4E 166
Old Willow Cl. E3 . . . . .3C 86
Old Woolwich Rd. SE10 . . . . .6F 105
Old York Rd. SW18 . . . . .5K 117

Oleander Cl. BR6: Farnb 5H 173
Oleander Ho. SE15 . . . . .5F 103
O'Leary Sq. E1 . . . . .5J 85
Olga St. E3 .2A 86
Olinda Rd. N16 . . . . .6F 49
Oliphant St. E14 . . . . .7E 86
   (off Bullivant St.)
  W10 . . . . .3F 81
Olive Blythe Ho. W10 . . . . .4G 81
   (off Ladbroke Gro.)
Olive Ct. E5 .2J 67
   (off Woodmill Rd.)
  N1 . . . . .1A 84
   (off Liverpool Rd.)
Olive Gro. N15 . . . . .4C 48
Olive Haines Lodge SW15 . . . . .5H 117
Olive Ho. EC1 .3K 7
   (off Bowling Grn. La.)
Oliver Av. SE25 . . . . .3F 157
Oliver Bus. Pk. NW10 . . . . .2J 79
Oliver Cl. W4 . . . . .6H 97
Oliver Ct. SE18 . . . . .4G 107
Oliver Gdns. E6 . . . . .5C 88
Oliver Goldsmith Est. SE15 . . . . . . .1G 121
Oliver Gro. SE25 . . . . .4F 157
Oliver Ho. SE14 . . . . .2G 121
   (off New Cross Rd.)
  SE16 .2G 103
   (off George Row)
  SW8 . . . . .7J 101
   (off Wyvil Rd.)
Oliver M. SE15 . . . . .2G 121
Olive Rd. E13 . . . . .3A 88
  NW2 . . . . .4D 62
  SW19 .7A 136
  W5 . . . . .3D 96
Oliver Rd. E10 . . . . .2D 68
  E17 . . . . .5E 50
  KT3: N Mald 2J 151
  NW10 .2J 79
  SM1: Sutt 4B 166
Olivers Row N8 . . . . .6J 47
Olivers Wharf E1 . . . . .1H 103
   (off Wapping High St.)
Olivers Yd. EC1 . . . . .3F 9 (4D 84)
Olive St. RM7: Rom 5K 55
Olive Tree Ho. SE15 . . . . .6J 103
   (off Sharratt St.)
Olivette St. SW15 . . . . .3F 117
Olive Waite Ho. NW6 . . . . .7J 63
Olivia Ct. CR0: C'don 7C 156
   (off Whitehorse Rd.)
  EN2: Enf 1H 23
   (off Chase Side)
Olivia M. HA3: Hrw W 7D 26
Olivier Theatre 4H 13
   (within National Theatre)
Ollerton Grn. E3 . . . . .1B 86
Ollerton Rd. N11 . . . . .5C 32
Olley Cl. SM6: W'gton 7J 167
Ollgar Cl. W12 . . . . .1B 98
Olliffe St. E14 . . . . .3E 104
Olmar St. SE1 . . . . .6G 103
Olmstead Cl. N10 . . . . .4E 46
Olney Ho. NW8 . . . . .3D 4
   (off Tresham Cres.)
Olney Rd. SE17 . . . . .6B 102
   (not continuous)
Olron Cres. DA6: Bex 5D 126
Olven Rd. SE18 . . . . .6G 107
Olveston Wlk. SM5: Cars 6B 154
Olwen M. HA5: Pinn 2B 40
Olyffe Av. DA16: Well 1A 144
Olyffe Dr. BR3: Beck 1E 158
Olympia 3G 99
Olympia Ind. Est. N22 . . . . .3K 47
Olympia M. W2 . . . . .7K 81
Olympian Ct. E3 . . . . .2C 86
   (off Wick La.)
  E14 . . . . .4C 104
   (off Homer Dr.)
Olympian Way SE10 . . . . .1G 105
   (not continuous)

Olympia Way W14 . . . . .3G 99
Olympic Ho. N16 . . . . .4F 67
Olympic M. SW18 . . . . .5A 118
Olympic Pk. Av. E20 . . . . .5D 68
Olympic Way HA9: Wemb 3G 61
  UB6: G'frd 1G 77
Olympus Gro. N22 . . . . .1A 48
Olympus Sq. E5 . . . . .3G 67
O'Mahoney Ct. SW17 . . . . .3A 136
Oman Av. NW2 . . . . .4E 62
Oman Way E14 . . . . .6A 86
O'Meara St. SE1 . . . . .5D 14 (1C 102)
Omega Ct. E14 . . . . .3D 104
Omega Pl. RM7: Rom 5K 55
Omega Ho. SW10 . . . . .7A 100
   (off King's Rd.)
Omega Pl. N1 .1F 7
Omega St. SE14 . . . . .1C 122
Omega Works E3 . . . . .7C 68
Ommaney Rd. SE14 . . . . .1K 121
Omnibus Ho. N22 . . . . .2A 48
   (off Lordship La.)
Omnibus Way E17 . . . . .2C 50
Omnium Ct. WC1 . . . . .5G 7
   (off Princeton St.)
Ondine Rd. SE15 . . . . .4F 121
One Blackfriars SE1 . . . . .4A 14
One Casson Sq. SE1 . . . . .5H 13
   (off Casson Sq.)
Onedin Ct. E1 .7G 85
   (off Ensign St.)
Onega Ga. SE16 . . . . .3A 104
One Hyde Pk. SW1 . . . . . .7E 10 (2D 100)
O'Neill Ho. NW8 . . . . .18 4
   (off Cochrane St.)
O'Neill Path SE18 . . . . .6E 106
One Lillie Sq. SW6 . . . . .6J 99
One New Change 1C 14 (6C 84)
One Owen St. EC1 . . . . .1A 8
   (off Goswell St.)
One Southbank Pl. SE1 . . . . .6H 13
   (off York Rd.)
One The Elephant SE1 . . . . .4B 102
   (off Brook Dr.)
One Tree Cl. SE23 . . . . .6J 121
One Tree Hill
  Local Nature Reserve 6J 121
Ongar Cl. RM6: Chad H 5C 54
Ongar Rd. SW6 . . . . .6J 99
Onra Rd. E17 .7C 50
Onslow Av. TW10: Rich 5E 114
Onslow Cl. E4 . . . . .2K 35
  KT7: T Ditt 7J 149
  W10 . . . . .3H 81
Onslow Ct. SW10 . . . . .6A 16
Onslow Cres. BR7: Chst 1F 161
  SW7 . . . . .4B 16 (4B 100)
Onslow Dr. DA14: Sidc 2D 144
Onslow Gdns. E18 . . . . .3K 51
  KT7: T Ditt 7J 149
  N10 . . . . .5F 47
  N21 . . . . .5E 22
  SM6: W'gton 6G 167
  SW7 . . . . .4A 16 (4B 100)
Onslow M. KT2: King T 1F 151
   (off Acre Rd.)
Onslow M. E. SW7 . . . . . . .4A 16 (4B 100)
Onslow M. W. SW7 . . . . . . .4A 16 (4B 100)
Onslow Pde. N14 . . . . .1A 32
Onslow Rd.
  CR0: C'don 7K 155
  KT3: N Mald 4C 152
  TW10: Rich 5E 114
Onslow Sq. SW7 . . . . .3B 16 (4B 100)
Onslow St. EC1 . . . . .4K 7 (4A 84)
Onslow Way KT7: T Ditt 7J 149
Ontario Point SE16 . . . . .2J 103
   (off Surrey Quays Rd.)
Ontario St. SE1 . . . . .3B 102
Ontario Twr. E14 . . . . .7F 87
Ontario Way E14 . . . . .7C 86
   (not continuous)
Onyx M. E15 .6H 69

Opal Apts. W2 . . . . .6J 81
   (off Hereford Rd.)
Opal Cl. E16 .6B 88
Opal Cl. E15 .1E 86
Opal M. IG1: Ilf 2F 71
  NW6 . . . . .1H 81
Opal St. SE11 . . . . .5K 19 (5B 102)
Open Air Stage 1C 64
Openshaw Rd. SE2 . . . . .4B 108
Openview SW18 . . . . .1A 136
Opera Ct. N19 . . . . .3H 65
   (off Wedmore St.)
Ophelia Gdns. NW2 . . . . .3G 63
Ophelia Ho. W6 . . . . .5F 99
   (off Fulham Pal. Rd.)
Ophir Ter. SE15 . . . . .1G 121
Opie Ho. NW8 . . . . .2C 82
   (off Townshend Est.)
Opossum Way TW4: Houn 3A 112
Oppenheim Rd. SE13 . . . . .2E 122
Oppidan Apts. NW6 . . . . .7J 63
   (off Netherwood St.)
Oppidans Rd. NW3 . . . . .7D 64
Opulens Pl. HA6: Nwood 1E 38
Orange Ct. La. BR6: Downe 7E 172
Orange Gro. E11 . . . . .3G 69
Orange Hill Rd. HA8: Edg 7D 28
Orange Pl. SE16 . . . . .3J 103
The Orangery TW10: Ham 2C 132
The Orangery Gallery 2H 99
Orangery La. SE9 . . . . .5D 124
Orange St. WC2 . . . . .3D 12 (7H 83)
Orange Tree Ct. SE5 . . . . .7E 102
   (off Havil St.)
Orange Tree Theatre 4E 114
Orange Yd. W1 . . . . .1D 12
Oransay Rd. N1 . . . . .6C 66
Oratory La. SW3 . . . . .5B 16 (5B 100)
Orbain Rd. SW6 . . . . .7G 99
Orbel St. SW11 . . . . .1C 118
Orbis Wharf SW11 . . . . .3B 118
Orbital Cen. IG8: Wfd G 2B 52
Orb St. SE17 . . . . .4D 102
The Orchard KT17: Ewe 7B 164
  N14 . . . . .5A 22
  N20 . . . . .1E 30
  N21 . . . . .6J 23
  NW11 . . . . .5J 45
  SE3 . . . . .2F 123
  TW3: Houn 2G 113
  W4 . . . . .4K 97
  W5 . . . . .5D 78
   (off Montpelier Rd.)
Orchard Av. CR0: C'don 2A 170
  CR4: Mitc 1E 166
  DA17: Belv 6E 108
  KT3: N Mald 2A 152
  KT7: T Ditt 1A 162
  N3 . . . . .3J 45
  N14 . . . . .6B 22
  N20 . . . . .2G 31
  TW5: Hest 7C 94
  TW14: Felt 5F 111
  TW15: Ashf 6E 128
  UB1: S'hall 1D 94
Orchard Bus. Cen. SE26 . . . . .5B 140
Orchard Cl. DA7: Bex 1E 126
  E4 . . . . .4H 35
  E11 . . . . .4K 51
  HA0: Wemb 1E 78
  HA4: Ruis 7E 38
  HA8: Edg 6K 27
  KT6: Surb 1B 162
  KT12: Walt T 7K 147
  KT19: Ewe 6H 163
  N1 . . . . .7C 66
  NW2 . . . . .3C 62
  SE23 .6J 121
  SW20 .4E 152
  TW15: Ashf 6E 128
  UB5: N'olt 6G 59
  W10 . . . . .5H 81
  WD23: B Hea 1C 26

Orchard Cotts. KT2: King T 1F **151**
UB3: Hayes 2G **93**
Orchard Ct. E10 ....1D **68**
EN5: New Bar 3E **20**
HA8: Edg 5A **28**
KT4: Wor Pk 1C **164**
KT12: Walt T 7H **147**
(off Bridge St.)
N14 ....6B **22**
SE26 ....4B **140**
SM6: W'gton 5F **167**
TW2: Twick 2H **131**
TW7: Isle 1H **113**
UB7: Lford 3D **174**
UB8: Uxb 2A **74**
(off The Greenway)
W1 ....7G **5**
(off Fitzhardinge St.)
Orchard Cres. EN1: Enf 1A **24**
HA8: Edg 5D **28**
Orchard Dr. HA8: Edg 5A **28**
SE3 ....2F **123**
TW17: Shep 3G **147**
Orchard Farm Av.
KT8: E Mos 6H **149**
Orchard Gdns. KT9: Chess 4E **162**
SM1: Sutt 5J **165**
Orchard Ga. KT10: Esh 7H **149**
NW9 ....4A **44**
UB6: G'frd 6B **60**
Orchard Grn. BR6: Orp 2J **173**
Orchard Gro. BR6: Orp 2K **173**
CR0: C'don 7A **158**
HA3: Kenton 5F **43**
HA8: Edg 1G **43**
SE20 ....7G **139**
Orchard Hill DA1: Cray 5K **127**
SE13 ....2D **122**
SM5: Cars 5D **166**
Orchard Ho. SE5 ....1C **120**
(off County Gro.)
SE16 ....3J **103**
SW6 ....7H **99**
(off Varna Rd.)
W12 ....1C **98**
Orchard La. IG8: Wfd G 4F **37**
KT8: E Mos 6H **149**
SW20 ....1D **152**
Orchardleigh Av.
EN3: Enf H 2D **24**
Orchard Mead Ho. NW2 ....6J **23**
Orchardmede N21 ....6J **23**
Orchard M. N1 ....7D **66**
N6 ....7F **47**
SW17 ....3A **136**
Orchard Pl. BR2: Kes 7A **172**
E5 ....5H **67**
E14 ....6F **87**
(not continuous)
N17 ....7A **34**
W4 ....4A **98**
Orchard Ri. CR0: C'don 1A **170**
HA5: Eastc 3H **39**
KT2: King T 1J **151**
TW10: Rich 4F **115**
Orchard Ri. E. DA15: Sidc 5K **125**
Orchard Ri. W. DA15: Sidc 5J **125**
Orchard Rd. BR1: Broml 1A **160**
BR6: Farnb 5F **173**
CR4: Mitc 1E **166**
DA14: Sidc 4J **143**
DA16: Well 3B **126**
DA17: Belv 4G **109**
EN3: Pond E 5D **24**
EN5: Barn 4C **20**
KT1: King T 2E **150**
KT9: Chess 4E **162**
N6 ....7F **47**
RM7: Mawney 1H **55**
RM10: Dag 1G **91**
SE3 ....2G **123**
SE18 ....4H **107**
SM1: Sutt 5J **165**

Orchard Rd. TW1: Twick 5A **114**
TW4: Houn 5D **112**
TW8: Bford 6C **96**
TW9: Rich 3G **115**
TW12: Hamp 7D **130**
TW13: Felt 1J **129**
TW16: Sun 7K **129**
UB3: Hayes 7J **75**
Orchardson Ho. NW8 ....4A **4**
Orchardson St. NW8 ....4A 4 (4B **82**)
Orchard Sq. SW1 ....5H 17 (5E **100**)
W14 ....5H **99**
Orchard St. E17 ....4A **50**
W1 ....1G 11 (6E **82**)
Orchard Studios W6 ....4F **99**
(off Brook Grn.)
Orchard Ter. EN1: Enf 6B **24**
NW10 ....4B **62**
Orchard Vs. DA14: Sidc 6C **144**
Orchard Wlk. KT2: King T 1G **151**
(off Gordon Rd.)
Orchard Way BR3: Beck 7C **158**
(Monks Orchard Rd.)
BR3: Beck 1A **170**
(Orchard Av.)
CR0: C'don 1A **170**
EN1: Enf 3K **23**
SM1: Sutt 4B **166**
TW15: Ashf 2B **128**
Orchard Waye UB8: Uxb 2A **74**
Orchard Wharf E14 ....7G **87**
(off Orchard Pl.)
Orchestra Ct. HA8: Edg 7C **28**
Orchid Cl. E6 ....5C **88**
KT9: Chess 7C **162**
SE13 ....5F **123**
UB1: S'hall 7C **76**
Orchid Ct. HA9: Wemb 2E **60**
Orchid Gdns. TW3: Houn 4D **112**
Orchid Grange N14 ....7B **22**
Orchid M. NW10 ....1K **79**
Orchid Rd. N14 ....7B **22**
Orchid St. W12 ....7C **80**
Orde NW9 ....1B **44**
Orde Hall St. WC1 ....4G 7 (4K **83**)
Ordell Ct. E3 ....2B **86**
(off Ordell Rd.)
Ordell Rd. E3 ....2B **86**
Ordnance Ct. TW13: Felt 2J **129**
Ordnance Cres. SE10 ....2G **105**
Ordnance Dock Pl.
UB2: S'hall 4B **94**
Ordnance Hill NW8 ....1B **82**
Ordnance M. NW8 ....2B **82**
Ordnance Rd. E16 ....5H **87**
SE18 ....6E **106**
Oregano Cl. UB7: Yiew 6A **74**
Oregano Dr. E14 ....6F **87**
Oregon Av. E12 ....4D **70**
Oregon Bldg. SE13 ....1D **122**
(off Deal's Gateway)
Oregon Cl. KT3: N Mald 4J **151**
Oregon M. W5 ....5C **78**
Oregon Sq. BR6: Orp 1H **173**
O'reilly St. SE1 ....4F **103**
(off Willow Wlk.)
Orestes M. NW6 ....5J **63**
Orford Ct. HA7: Stan 6H **27**
SE27 ....2B **138**
Orford Gdns. TW1: Twick 2K **131**
Orford Rd. E17 ....5C **50**
E18 ....3K **51**
SE6 ....3D **140**
ORGAN CROSSROADS 7C **164**
Organ La. E4 ....2K **35**
Oriana Ho. E10 ....2D **68**
(off Grange Pk. Rd.)
E14 ....7B **86**
(off Victory Pl.)
Oriel Cl. CR4: Mitc 4H **155**
Oriel Ct. CR0: C'don 1D **168**
NW3 ....4A **64**
Oriel Dr. SW13 ....6E **98**

Oriel Gdns. IG5: Ilf 3D **52**
Oriel Ho. NW6 ....1J **81**
(off Priory Pk. Rd.)
RM7: Rom 6K **55**
Oriel M. E18 ....2J **51**
Oriel Pl. NW3 ....4A **64**
(off Heath St.)
Oriel Rd. E9 ....6K **67**
Oriel Way UB5: N'olt 7F **59**
Oriens M. E20 ....5E **68**
Oriental Rd. E16 ....1B **106**
Oriental St. E14 ....7C **86**
(off Pennyfields)
Orient Ho. SW6 ....1A **118**
(off Station Ct.)
Orient Ind. Pk. E10 ....2C **68**
Orient St. SE11 ....4B **102**
Orient Way E5 ....3K **67**
E10 ....1A **68**
Orient Wharf E1 ....1H **103**
(off Wapping High St.)
Origin Bus. Pk. NW10 ....3G **79**
Oriole Way SE28 ....7B **90**
Orion E14 ....4C **104**
(off Crews St.)
Orion Bus. Cen. SE14 ....5K **103**
The Orion Cen. CR0: Bedd 2J **167**
Orion Ho. E1 ....4H **85**
(off Coventry Rd.)
Orion M. SM4: Mord 4J **153**
Orion Pk. RM9: Dag 2F **91**
Orion Rd. N11 ....7K **31**
Orissa Rd. SE18 ....5J **107**
Orkney Ct. E1 ....5A **86**
(off Ocean Est.)
Orkney Ho. N1 ....1K **83**
(off Bemerton Est.)
Orkney St. SW11 ....2E **118**
Orlando Rd. SW4 ....3G **119**
Orleans Ct. TW1: Twick 7B **114**
Orleans House Gallery 1B **132**
Orleans Pk. School Sports Cen. ...7B **114**
TW1: Twick 7B **114**
Orleston M. N7 ....6A **66**
Orleston Rd. N7 ....6A **66**
Orley Ct. HA1: Harr 4K **59**
Orley Farm Rd. HA1: Harr 3J **59**
Orlop St. SE10 ....5G **105**
Ormanton Rd. SE26 ....4G **139**
Orme Ct. W2 ....7K **81**
Orme Ct. M. W2 ....7K **81**
(off Orme La.)
Orme Ho. E8 ....1F **85**
Orme La. W2 ....7K **81**
Ormeley Rd. SW12 ....1F **137**
Orme Rd. KT1: King T 2H **151**
SM1: Sutt 6K **165**
Ormerod Gdns. CR4: Mitc 2E **154**
Ormesby Cl. SE28 ....7D **90**
Ormesby Way HA3: Kenton 6F **43**
Orme Sq. W2 ....7K **81**
Ormiston Gro. W12 ....1D **98**
Ormiston Rd. SE10 ....5J **105**
Ormond Av. TW10: Rich 5D **114**
TW12: Hamp 1F **149**
Ormond Cl. WC1 ....5F 7 (5J **83**)
Ormond Cres. TW12: Hamp 1F **149**
Ormond Dr. TW12: Hamp 7F **131**
Ormonde Av. BR6: Farnb 2G **173**
Ormonde Ct. NW8 ....1D **82**
(off St Edmund's Cl.)
SW15 ....4E **116**
Ormonde Ga. SW3 ......6F 17 (5D **100**)
(not continuous)
Ormonde Mans. WC1 ....7F **7**
(off Southampton Row)
Ormonde Pl. SW1 ......4G 17 (4E **100**)
Ormonde Ri. IG9: Buck H 1F **37**
Ormonde Rd. SW14 ....3J **115**
Ormonde Ter. NW8 ....1D **82**
Ormond Ho. N16 ....2D **66**
Ormond M. WC1 ....4F 7 (4J **83**)

Ormond Rd. N19 ....1J **65**
TW10: Rich 5D **114**
Ormond Yd. SW1 ....4B 12 (1G **101**)
Ormrod Ct. W11 ....6G **81**
(off Westbourne Pk. Rd.)
Ormsby SM2: Sutt 7K **165**
Ormsby Gdns. UB6: G'frd 2G **77**
Ormsby Lodge W4 ....3A **98**
Ormsby Pl. N16 ....3F **67**
Ormsby Point SE18 ....4F **107**
(off Vincent Rd.)
Ormsby St. E2 ....2F **85**
Ormside St. SE15 ....6J **103**
Ornan Rd. NW3 ....5C **64**
Orpen Ho. SW5 ....4J **99**
(off Trebovir Rd.)
Orpen Wlk. N16 ....3E **66**
Orpheus Ho. W10 ....4H **81**
(off Harrow Rd.)
Orpheus St. SE5 ....1D **120**
ORPINGTON 1K **173**
Orpington Gdns. N18 ....3K **33**
Orpington Golf Cen. 7E **144**
Orpington Mans. N21 ....1G **33**
Orpington Rd. BR7: Chst 3J **161**
N21 ....1G **33**
Orpwood Cl. TW12: Hamp 6D **130**
Orsett M. W2 ....6K **81**
(not continuous)
Orsett St. SE11 ....5H 19 (5K **101**)
Orsett Ter. IG8: Wfd G 7F **37**
W2 ....6K **81**
Orsman Rd. N1 ....1E **84**
Orton Gro. EN1: Enf 1B **24**
Orton Pl. SW19 ....7K **135**
Orton St. E1 ....1G **103**
Orville Rd. SW11 ....2B **118**
Orwell Cl. RM13: Rain 5K **91**
UB3: Hayes 7G **75**
Orwell Ct. E8 ....1G **85**
(off Pownall Rd.)
N5 ....4C **66**
SE13 ....3D **122**
SW17 ....3B **136**
(off Grosvenor Way)
Orwell Rd. E13 ....2A **88**
Osbaldeston Rd. N16 ....2G **67**
Osberton Rd. SE12 ....5J **123**
Osbert St. SW1 ....4C 18 (4H **101**)
Osborn Cl. E8 ....1G **85**
Osborne Av. TW19: Stanw 1A **128**
Osborne Cl. BR3: Beck 4A **158**
EN4: Cockf 3J **21**
TW13: Hanw 5B **130**
Osborne Ct. E10 ....7D **50**
HA2: Harr 4F **41**
W5 ....5E **78**
Osborne Gdns. CR7: Thor H 2C **156**
Osborne Gro. E17 ....4B **50**
Osborne Ho. E16 ....1J **105**
(off Wesley Av.)
Osborne M. E17 ....4B **50**
Osborne Pl. SM1: Sutt 5B **166**
Osborne Rd. CR7: Thor H 2C **156**
DA17: Belv 5F **109**
E7 ....5K **69**
E9 ....6B **68**
E10 ....2D **68**
EN3: Enf H 2F **25**
IG9: Buck H 1E **36**
KT2: King T 7E **132**
KT12: Walt T 7J **147**
N4 ....1A **66**
N13 ....3F **33**
NW2 ....6D **62**
RM9: Dag 5F **73**
TW3: Houn 3D **112**
UB1: S'hall 6G **77**
W3 ....3H **97**
Osborne Sq. RM9: Dag 4F **73**
Osborne Ter. SW17 ....5D **136**
(off Church La.)
Osborne Way KT9: Chess 5F **163**

Osborn Gdns. NW7 . . . . .7A 30
Osborn La. SE23 . . . . .7A 122
Osborn St. E1 . . . . .6K 9 (5F 85)
Osborn Ter. SE3 . . . . .4H 123
Osbourne Ho. IG8: Wfd G 7K 37
  TW2: Twick 2G 131
Oscar Ct. SE16 . . . . .2A 104
Oscar Faber Pl. N1 . . . . .7E 66
Oscar St. SE8 . . . . .2C 122
  (not continuous)
Oseney Cres. NW5 . . . . .5G 65
Osgood Av. BR6: Chels 5K 173
Osgood Gdns. BR6: Chels 5K 173
OSIDGE 1A 32
Osidge La. N14 . . . . .1K 31
Osier Cl. BR6: Farnb 4F 173
Osier Ct. E1 .4K 85
  (off Osier St.)
  RM7: Rom 6K 55
  TW8: Bford 6E 96
  (off Ealing Rd.)
Osier Cres. N10 . . . . .1D 46
Osier Ho. SE16 . . . . .3A 104
Osier La. SE10 . . . . .3H 105
Osier M. W4 . . . . .6A 98
Osiers Ct. KT1: King T 1D 150
  (off Steadfast Rd.)
Osiers Rd. SW18 . . . . .4J 117
Osiers Twr. SW18 . . . . .4J 117
  (off Enterprise Way)
Osier St. E1 .4J 85
Osier Way CR4: Mitc 5D 154
  E10 . . . . .3D 68
Oslac Rd. SE6 . . . . .5D 140
Oslo Ct. NW8 . . . . .2C 82
  (off Prince Albert Rd.)
Oslo Ho. E9 .6B 68
  (off Felstead St.)
  SE5 . . . . .2C 120
  (off Carew St.)
Oslo Sq. SE16 . . . . .3A 104
Oslo Twr. SE8 . . . . .4A 104
  (off Naomi St.)
Osman Cl. N15 . . . . .6D 48
Osmani Youth Cen. 5G 85
Osman Rd. N9 . . . . .3B 34
  W6 . . . . .3E 98
Osmington Ho. SW8 . . . . .7K 101
  (off Dorset Rd.)
Osmond Cl. HA2: Harr 2G 59
Osmond Gdns.
  SM6: W'gton 5G 167
Osmunda Ct. E1 . . . . .6G 85
  (off Myrtle St.)
Osmund St. W12 . . . . .5B 80
Osnaburgh St. NW1 . . . . . .4K 5 (4F 83)
  (Euston St.)
  NW1 . . . . .2K 5
  (Robert St.)
Osnaburgh Ter. NW1 . . . . .3K 5 (4F 83)
Osney Ho. SE2 . . . . .2D 108
Osney Wlk. SM5: Cars 6B 154
Osprey NW9 . . . . .1B 44
Osprey Cl. BR2: Broml 1C 172
  E6 . . . . .5C 88
  E11 . . . . .4J 51
  E17 . . . . .7F 35
  SM1: Sutt 5H 165
  UB7: W Dray 2A 92
Osprey Ct. BR3: Beck 7C 140
  CR0: C'don 3C 168
  (off Innes Yd.)
  E1 . . . . .3K 15
  (off Star Pl.)
Osprey Est. SE16 . . . . .4K 103
Osprey Ho. E14 . . . . .7A 86
  (off Victory Pl.)
  SE1 . . . . .3B 102
  (off Lynton Rd.)
Osprey La. HA2: Harr 2F 59
Osprey M. EN3: Pond E 5D 24
Ospringe Cl. SE20 . . . . .7J 139
Ospringe Ct. SE9 . . . . .6H 125

Ospringe Ho. SE1 . . . . .6K 13
  (off Wootton St.)
Ospringe Rd. NW5 . . . . .4G 65
Osram Ct. W6 . . . . .3E 98
Osram Rd. HA9: Wemb 3D 60
Osric Path N1 . . . . .2E 84
Ossel Ct. SE10 . . . . .4G 105
Ossian M. N4 . . . . .7K 47
Ossian Rd. N4 . . . . .7K 47
OSSIE GARVIN RDBT. 7K 75
Ossington Bldgs. W1 . . . . .5G 5 (5E 82)
Ossington Cl. W2 . . . . .7J 81
Ossington St. W2 . . . . .7J 81
Ossory Rd. SE1 . . . . .6G 103
Ossulston St. NW1 . . . . . . .1D 6 (2H 83)
Ossulton Pl. N2 . . . . .3A 46
Ossulton Way N2 . . . . .4A 46
Ostade Rd. SW2 . . . . .7K 119
Ostell Cres. EN3: Enf L 1H 25
Ostend Pl. SE1 . . . . .4C 102
Osten M. SW7 . . . . .3K 99
OSTERLEY 7H 95
Osterley Av. TW7: Isle 7H 95
Osterley Cl. BR5: St P 1K 161
Osterley Ct. TW7: Isle 1H 113
  UB5: N'olt 3A 76
  (off Canberra Dr.)
Osterley Cres. TW7: Isle 1J 113
Osterley Gdns. CR7: Thor H 2C 156
  UB2: S'hall 2G 95
Osterley Ho. E14 . . . . .6D 86
  (off Giraud St.)
Osterley La. TW7: Isle 4G 95
  UB2: S'hall 5E 94
Osterley Lodge TW7: Isle 7J 95
  (off Church Rd.)
Osterley Pk. .6G 95
Osterley Pk. & House 6G 95
Osterley Pk. Rd. UB2: S'hall 3D 94
Osterley Pk. Vw. Rd. W7 . . . . .2J 95
Osterley Rd. N16 . . . . .4E 66
  TW7: Isle .7J 95
Osterley Sports & Athletics Cen. 7J 95
Osterley Sports Club 3G 95
Osterley Views UB2: S'hall 1F 95
Oster Ter. E17 . . . . .5K 49
Ostlers Dr. TW15: Ashf 5E 128
Ostliffe Rd. N13 . . . . .5H 33
Oswald Bldg. SW11 . . . . .6F 101
Oswald's Mead E9 . . . . .4A 68
Oswald St. E5 . . . . .3K 67
Oswald Ter. NW2 . . . . .3E 62
Osward CR0: Sels 7B 170
  (not continuous)
Osward Pl. N9 . . . . .2C 34
Osward Rd. SW17 . . . . .2D 136
Oswell Ho. E1 . . . . .1H 103
  (off Farthing Flds.)
Oswin St. SE11 . . . . .4B 102
Oswyth Rd. SE5 . . . . .2E 120
Otford Cl. BR1: Broml 3E 160
  DA5: Bexl 6H 127
  SE20 . . . . .1J 157
Otford Cres. SE4 . . . . .6B 122
Otford Ho. SE1 . . . . .7F 15
  (off Staple St.)
  SE15 . . . . .6J 103
  (off Lovelinch Cl.)
Othello Cl. SE11 . . . . .5K 19 (5B 102)
The Other Place Theatre 1A 18
  (off Palace St.)
Otho Ct. TW8: Bford 7D 96
Otley App. IG2: Ilf 6F 53
Otley Dr. IG2: Ilf 5F 53
Otley Ho. N5 .3A 66
Otley Rd. E16 . . . . .6A 88
Otley Ter. E5 .3K 67
Ottawa Gdns. RM10: Dag 7K 73
Ottawa Ho. SE16 . . . . .2J 103
  (off Province Dr.)
  UB4: Yead 3K 75
  (off Ayles Rd.)

Ottaway St. E5 . . . . .3G 67
Otterbourne Rd. CR0: C'don 2C 168
  E4 . . . . .3A 36
Otterburn Gdns. TW7: Isle 7A 96
Otterburn Ho. SE5 . . . . .7C 102
  (off Sultan St.)
Otterburn St. SW17 . . . . .6D 136
Otter Cl. E15 .1E 86
Otterden Cl. BR6: Orp 3J 173
Otterden St. SE6 . . . . .4C 140
Otterden Ter. SE1 . . . . .4F 103
  (off Lynton Rd.)
Otter Dr. SM5: Cars 1D 166
Otterfield Rd. UB7: Yiew 7A 74
Otter Rd. UB6: G'frd 4G 77
Otter Way UB7: Yiew 1A 92
Ottley Dr. SE3 . . . . .4A 124
Otto Cl. SE26 . . . . .3H 139
Otto Dr. UB2: S'hall 3E 94
Otto St. SE17 . . . . .6B 102
Ott's Yd. N19 . . . . .4G 65
  (off Southcote Rd.)
Otway Gdns. WD23: Bush 1D 26
Oulton Cl. E5 .2J 67
  SE28 . . . . .6C 90
Oulton Cres. IG11: Bark 5K 71
Oulton Rd. N15 . . . . .5D 48
Our Lady's Cl. SE19 . . . . .6D 138
Ouseley Rd. SW12 . . . . .1D 136
Outer Circ.
  NW1 . . . . .1D 4, 1J 5 (2C 82)
Outgate Rd. NW10 . . . . .7B 62
Outram Pl. N1 .1J 83
Outram Rd. CR0: C'don 2F 169
  E6 . . . . .1C 88
  N22 . . . . .1H 47
Outwich St. EC3 . . . . .7H 9
Outwood Ho. SW2 . . . . .7K 119
  (off Deepdene Gdns.)
The Oval
  Surrey CCC 7H 19 (6K 101)
The Oval DA15: Sidc 7A 126
  E2 . . . . .2H 85
Oval Ct. HA8: Edg 7D 28
Ovalhouse 6A 102
Oval Ho. CR0: C'don 1E 168
  (off Oval Rd.)
Oval Mans. SE11 . . . . .7H 19 (6K 101)
Oval PI. SW8 .7K 101
Oval Rd. CR0: C'don 2D 168
  NW1 . . . . .1F 83
Oval Rd. Nth. RM10: Dag 1H 91
Oval Rd. Sth. RM10: Dag 2H 91
Oval Way SE11 . . . . .6H 19 (5K 101)
Ovanna M. E1 . . . . .6E 66
Overbrae BR3: Beck 6C 140
Overbrook Wlk. HA8: Edg 7B 28
  (not continuous)
Overbury Av. BR3: Beck 3D 158
Overbury Rd. N15 . . . . .6D 48
Overbury St. E5 . . . . .4K 67
Overcliff Rd. SE13 . . . . .3C 122
Overcourt Cl. DA15: Sidc 6B 126
Overdale Av. KT3: N Mald 2J 151
Overdale Rd. W5 . . . . .3C 96
Overdown Rd. SE6 . . . . .4C 140
Overhill Rd. SE22 . . . . .7G 121
Overhill Way BR3: Beck 5F 159
Overlea Rd. E5 . . . . .7G 49
Overmead DA15: Sidc 7H 125
Oversley Ho. W2 . . . . .5J 81
  (off Alfred Rd.)
Overstand Cl. BR3: Beck 5C 158
Overstone Gdns.
  CR0: C'don 7B 158
Overstone Ho. E14 . . . . .6C 86
  (off E. India Dock Rd.)
Overstone Rd. W6 . . . . .3E 98
Overstrand Mans. SW11 . . . . .1D 118
Overton Cl. NW10 . . . . .6J 61
  TW7: Isle .1K 113
Overton Ct. E11 . . . . .7J 51
  SM2: Sutt .7J 165

Overton Dr. E11 . . . . .7J 51
  RM6: Chad H 7C 54
Overton Ho. SW15 . . . . .7B 116
  (off Tangley Gro.)
Overton Rd. E10 . . . . .1A 68
  N14 . . . . .5D 22
  SE2 . . . . .3C 108
  SM2: Sutt .6J 165
  SW9 . . . . .2A 120
Overton Rd. E. SE2 . . . . .3D 108
Overton's Yd. CR0: C'don 3C 168
Overy Ho. SE1 . . . . .7A 14 (2B 102)
Ovesdon Av. HA2: Harr 1D 58
Ovett Cl. SE19 . . . . .6E 138
Ovex Cl. E14 .2E 104
Ovington Ct. SW3 . . . . .2D 16
  (off Brompton Rd.)
Ovington Gdns. SW3 . . . . .2D 16 (3C 100)
Ovington M. SW3 . . . . .2D 16
Ovington Sq. SW3 . . . . . . .2D 16 (3C 100)
Ovington St. SW3 . . . . .3D 16 (4C 100)
Owen Cl. CR0: C'don 6D 156
  SE28 . . . . .1C 108
  TW16: Sun 1G 147
  UB5: N'olt 6C 58
  (Arnold Rd.)
  UB5: N'olt .3K 75
  (Attlee Rd.)
Owen Gdns. IG8: Wfd G 6H 37
Owen Ho. TW1: Twick 7B 114
  TW14: Felt 7J 111
Owenite St. SE2 . . . . .4B 108
Owen Mans. W14 . . . . .6G 99
  (off Queen's Club Gdns.)
Owen Rd. N13 . . . . .5H 33
  UB4: Yead 3K 75
Owens M. E11 . . . . .2G 69
Owen's Row EC1 . . . . .1A 8 (3B 84)
Owen St. EC1 . . . . .1A 8 (2B 84)
Owens Way SE23 . . . . .7A 122
Owen Wlk. SE20 . . . . .1G 157
Owen Way NW10 . . . . .6J 61
Owgan Cl. SE5 . . . . .7D 102
Oxberry Av. SW6 . . . . .2G 117
Oxborough Ho. SW18 . . . . .4A 118
  (off Eltringham St.)
Oxendon St. SW1 . . . . .3C 12 (7H 83)
Oxenford St. SE15 . . . . .3F 121
Oxenham Ho. SE8 . . . . .6C 104
  (off Benbow St.)
Oxenholme NW1 . . . . .1A 6
  (off Hampstead Rd.)
Oxenpark Av. HA9: Wemb 7E 42
Oxestall's Rd. SE8 . . . . .5A 104
Oxford & Cambridge Mans. NW1 . . .6D 4
  (off Old Marylebone Rd.)
Oxford Av. N14 . . . . .1B 32
  SW20 . . . . .2G 153
  TW5: Hest .5E 94
  UB3: Harl .7H 93
Oxford Cir. W1 . . . . .1A 12
Oxford Cir. Av. W1 . . . . . . .1A 12 (6G 83)
Oxford Cir. CR4: Mitc 3G 155
  N9 . . . . .2C 34
  TW15: Ashf 7F 128
Oxford Ct. EC4 . . . . .2E 14
  KT6: Surb .5E 150
  (off Avenue Elmers)
  TW13: Hanw 4B 130
  W3 . . . . .6G 79
  W4 . . . . .5H 97
  W7 . . . . .5K 77
  (off Copley Cl.)
  W9 . . . . .5J 81
  (off Elmfield Way)
Oxford Cres. KT3: N Mald 6K 151
Oxford Dr. HA4: Ruis 2A 58
  SE1 . . . . .5G 15 (1E 102)
Oxford Gdns. N20 . . . . .1G 31
  N21 . . . . .7H 23
  W4 . . . . .5G 97
  W10 . . . . .6E 80
Oxford Ga. W6 . . . . .4F 99

Oxford Ho. BR2: Broml 6B 160
   (off Wells Vw. Dr.)
E3 . . . . .5B 86
   (off William Whiffin Sq.)
NW6 . . . . .2J 81
   (off Oxford Rd.)
RM8: Dag 4A 72
Oxford M. DA5: Bexl 7G 127
Oxford Pl. NW10 . . . . .3K 61
   (off Press Rd.)
Oxford Rd. DA14: Sidc 5B 144
E15 . . . . .6F 69
   (not continuous)
EN3: Pond E 5C 24
HA1: Harr 6G 41
HA3: W'stone 3K 41
IG1: Ilf 5G 71
IG8: Wfd G 5G 37
N4 . . . . .1A 66
N9 . . . . .2C 34
NW6 . . . . .2J 81
SE19 .6D 138
SM5: Cars 6C 166
SM6: W'gton 5G 167
SW15 . . . . .4G 117
TW11: Tedd 5H 131
W5 . . . . .7D 78
Oxford Rd. Nth. W4 . . . . .5H 97
Oxford Rd. Sth. W4 . . . . .5G 97
Oxford Row TW16: Sun 3A 148
Oxford Sq. W2 . . .2J 10 (6C 82)
Oxford St. W1 . . . . .1G 11 (6E 82)
Oxford Ter. NW6 . . . . .2K 81
   (off Oxford Vw.)
Oxford Wlk. UB1: S'hall 1D 94
Oxford Way TW13: Hanw 4B 130
Oxgate Cen. NW2 . . . . .2D 62
Oxgate Ct. NW2 . . . . .2C 62
Oxgate Ct. Pde. NW2 . . . . .2C 62
Oxgate Gdns. NW2 . . . . .3D 62
Oxgate La. NW2 . . . . .2D 62
Oxgate Pde. NW2 . . . . .2C 62
Oxhawth Cres. BR2: Broml 5E 160
Oxhey La. HA3: Hrw W 5A 26
HA5: Hat E 5A 26
Oxleas E6 . . . . .6F 89
Oxleas Cl. DA16: Well 2H 125
Oxleay Rd. HA2: Harr 1E 58
Oxleigh Cl. KT3: N Mald 3A 152
Oxley Cl. SE1 . . . . .5F 103
Oxley Sq. E3 . . . . .4D 86
   (off Truman Wlk.)
Oxleys Rd. NW2 . . . . .3G 62
Oxlip Cl. CR0: C'don 1K 169
Oxlow La. RM9: Dag 4F 73
RM10: Dag 4F 73
Oxonian St. SE22 . . . . .4F 121
Oxo Tower Wharf 3K 13 (7A 84)
Oxted Cl. CR4: Mitc 3B 154
Oxtoby Way SW16 . . . . .1H 155
The Oxygen E16 . . . . .7J 87
OYO Bus. Units
DA17: Belv 2J 109
RM9: Dag 4F 91
Oystercatcher Cl. E16 . . . . .6K 87
Oyster Cl. EN5: Barn 6B 20
Oyster Ct. SE17 . . . . .4C 102
   (off Crampton St.)
Oystergate Wlk. EC4 . . . . .3E 14
Oyster M. E7 . . . . .6B 70
Oyster Row E1 . . . . .6J 85
Oyster Wharf SW11 . . . . .2B 118
Ozolins Way E16 . . . . .6J 87

P

Pablo Neruda Cl. SE24 . . . . . . .4B 120
Pace Pl. E1 . . . . .6H 85
Pacific Bldg. E15 . . . . .5F 87
   (off Property Row)
Pacific Cl. TW14: Felt 1H 129
Pacific Ct. E1 . . . . .5J 85

Pacific Ho. E1 . . . . .4K 85
   (off Ernest St.)
Pacific M. SW9 . . . . .4A 120
Pacific Rd. E16 . . . . .6J 87
Pacific Wharf SE16 . . . . .1K 103
Packenham Ho. E2 . . . . .1K 9
   (off Wellington Row)
W10 .7F 81
   (off Shalfleet Dr.)
Packham Ct. KT4: Wor Pk 3E 164
Packington Rd. W3 . . . . .3J 97
Packington Sq. N1 . . . . .1C 84
   (not continuous)
Packington St. N1 . . . . .1B 84
Packmores Rd. SE9 . . . . .5H 125
Packwell Pl. TW5: Hest 6A 94
Padbury SE17 . . . . .5E 102
   (off Bagshot St.)
Padbury Cl. TW14: Bedf 1F 129
Padbury Ct. E2 . . . .2K 9 (3F 85)
Padbury Ho. NW8 . . . . .3D 4
   (off Tresham Cres.)
Padbury Oaks UB7: Lford 4C 174
Padcroft Rd. UB7: Yiew 1A 92
Paddenswick Rd. W6 . . . . .3C 98
PADDINGTON 7A 4 (6B 82)
Paddington Cl. UB4: Yead 4B 76
Paddington Ct. W7 . . . . .5K 77
   (off Copley Cl.)
Paddington Gdns. W2 . .6A 4 (5B 82)
Paddington Grn. W2 . . .5A 4 (5B 82)
Paddington Sports Club 4K 81
Paddington St. W1 . . .5G 5 (5E 82)
The Paddock N10 . . . . .3E 46
NW9 .5G 43
UB10: Ick 4D 56
Paddock Cl. BR6: Farnb 4F 173
KT4: Wor Pk 1A 164
SE3 .2J 123
SE26 . . . . .4K 139
UB5: N'olt 2E 76
Paddock Gdns. SE19 . . . . .6E 138
Paddock Lodge EN1: Enf 5K 23
   (off Village Rd.)
Paddock Mobile Home Pk. 7C 172
Paddock Rd. DA6: Bex 4E 126
HA4: Ruis 3B 58
NW2 .3C 62
The Paddocks CR0: Addtn 6C 170
EN4: Cockf 3J 21
HA9: Wemb 2H 61
W5 . . . . .3D 96
   (off Popes La.)
Paddocks Cl. HA2: Harr 4F 59
Paddocks Grn. NW9 . . . . .1H 61
Paddock Way BR7: Chst 7H 143
SW15 . . . . .7E 116
Padelford La. HA7: Stan 2F 27
Padfield Ct. HA9: Wemb 3F 61
Padfield Rd. SE5 . . . . .3C 120
Padley Cl. KT9: Chess 5F 163
Padnall Ct. RM6: Chad H 3D 54
Padnall Rd. RM6: Chad H 3D 54
Padstone Ho. E3 . . . . .3D 86
   (off Talwin St.)
Padstow Rd. EN2: Enf 1G 23
Padstow Wlk. TW14: Felt 1H 129
Padua Rd. SE20 . . . . .1J 157
Pagden St. SW8 . . . . .1F 119
Pageant Av. NW9 . . . . .1K 43
Pageant Cres. SE16 . . . . .1A 104
Pageantmaster Ct. EC4 . . . . . . .1A 14
Pageant Wlk. CR0: C'don 3E 168
Page Av. HA9: Wemb 3J 61
Page Cl. HA3: Kenton 6F 43
RM9: Dag 5E 72
TW12: Hamp 6C 130
Page Cl. NW7 . . . . .7J 29
Page Cres. CR0: Wadd 5B 168
Page Grn. Rd. N15 . . . . .5G 49

Page Grn. Ter. N15 . . . . .5F 49
Page Heath La. BR1: Broml 3B 160
Page Heath Vs. BR1: Broml 3B 160
Page High N22 . . . . .2A 48
   (off Lymington Av.)
Page Ho. SE10 . . . . .6E 104
   (off Welland St.)
Pagehurst Rd. CR0: C'don 7H 157
Page Mdw. NW7 . . . . .7J 29
Page M. SW11 . . . . .2E 118
Page Rd. TW14: Bedf 6F 111
Pages Hill N10 . . . . .2E 46
Pages La. N10 . . . . .2E 46
Page St. NW7 . . . . .1C 44
SW1 . . . . .3D 18 (4H 101)
Page's Wlk. SE1 . . . . .4E 102
Pages Yd. W4 . . . . .6B 98
Paget Av. SM1: Sutt 3B 166
Paget Cl. TW12: Hamp H 4H 131
Paget Gdns. BR7: Chst 1F 161
Paget Ho. E2 . . . . .2J 85
   (off Bishop's Way)
Paget La. TW7: Isle 3H 113
Paget Pl. KT2: King T 6J 133
KT7: T Ditt 1A 162
Paget Ri. SE18 . . . . .6E 106
Paget Rd. IG1: Ilf 4F 71
N16 .1D 66
UB10: Hil 4E 74
Paget St. EC1 . . . . .1A 8 (3B 84)
Paget Ter. SE18 . . . . .6F 107
Pagham Ho. W10 . . . . .4E 80
   (off Sutton Way)
Pagin Ho. N15 . . . . .5E 48
   (off Braemar Rd.)
Pagitts Gro. EN4: Had W 1E 20
Pagnell St. SE14 . . . . .7B 104
Pagoda Av. TW9: Rich 3F 115
Pagoda Gdns. SE3 . . . . .2F 123
Pagoda Gro. SE27 . . . . .2C 138
Paignton Rd. HA4: Ruis 3J 57
N15 .6E 48
Paines Cl. HA5: Pinn 3C 40
Paines La. HA5: Pinn 1C 40
Pain's Cl. CR4: Mitc 2F 155
Painsthorpe Rd. N16 . . . . .3E 66
Painted Hall 6F 105
Painters M. SE16 . . . . .4G 103
Painters Rd. IG2: Ilf 3K 53
Paisley Rd. N22 . . . . .1B 48
SM5: Cars 1B 166
Paisley Ter. SM5: Cars 7B 154
Pakefield M. SW2 . . . . .1K 137
Pakeman Ho. SE1 . . . . .6B 14
   (off Surrey Row)
Pakeman St. N7 . . . . .3K 65
Pakenham Cl. SW12 . . . . .1E 136
Pakenham St. WC1 . . . . . .2H 7 (3K 83)
Pakington Ho. SW9 . . . . .2J 119
   (off Stockwell Gdns. Est.)
Palace Arts Way HA9: Wemb . . .4G 61
Palace Av. W8 . . . . .2K 99
Palace Cl. E9 . . . . .6B 68
Palace Ct. BR1: Broml 1K 159
   (off Palace Gro.)
HA3: Kenton 6E 42
NW3 .5K 63
W2 . . . . .7K 81
   (not continuous)
Palace Ct. Gdns. N10 . . . . .3G 47
Palace Exchange 4J 23
Palace Gdns. IG9: Buck H 1G 37
Palace Gdns. M. W8 . . . . .1K 99
Palace Gdns. Shop. Cen. 4J 23
Palace Gdns. Ter. W8 . . . . .1J 99
Palace Ga. W8 . . . . .3A 100
Palace Gates M. N8 . . . . .4J 47
Palace Gates Rd. N22 . . . . .1H 47
Palace Grn. CR0: Sels 7B 170
W8 . . . . .1K 99
Palace Gro. BR1: Broml 1K 159
SE19 .7F 139

Palace Mans. KT1: King T 4D 150
   (off Palace Rd.)
W14 .4G 99
   (off Hammersmith Rd.)
Palace M. E17 . . . . .4B 50
SW1 .4H 17
SW6 .7H 99
Palace Pde. E17 . . . . .4B 50
Palace Pl. SW1 . . . . . .1A 18 (3G 101)
Palace Pl. Mans. W8 . . . . .2K 99
   (off Kensington Ct.)
Palace Rd. BR1: Broml 1K 159
HA4: Ruis 4C 58
KT1: King T 4D 150
KT8: E Mos 3G 149
N8 . . . . .5H 47
   (not continuous)
N11 .7D 32
SE19 .7F 139
SW2 .1K 137
SE19 .7F 139
Palace Sq. SE19 . . . . .7F 139
Palace St. SW1 . . . . . .1A 18 (3G 101)
Palace Superbowl 4C 102
   (within Elephant & Castle Shop. Cen.)
Palace Theatre 1D 12
   (off Shaftesbury Av.)
Palace Vw. BR1: Broml 3K 159
   (not continuous)
CR0: C'don 4B 170
SE12 . . . . .2J 141
Palace Vw. Rd. E4 . . . . .5J 35
Pal. Wharf W6 . . . . .7E 98
   (off Rainville Rd.)
Palamos Rd. E10 . . . . .1C 68
Palatine Av. N16 . . . . .4E 66
Palatine Rd. N16 . . . . .4E 66
Palazzo Apts. N1 . . . . .7E 66
   (off Ardleigh Rd.)
Palemead Cl. SW6 . . . . .1F 117
Palermo Rd. NW10 . . . . .2C 80
Palestine Gro. SW19 . . . . .1B 154
Palestra Ho. SE1 . . . . .5A 14
   (off Blackfriars Rd.)
Palewell Comn. Dr. SW14 . . . . .5K 115
Palewell Pk. SW14 . . . . .5K 115
Palfrey Pl. SW8 . . . . .7K 101
Palgrave Av. UB1: S'hall 7E 76
Palgrave Ct.
TW11: Hamp W 7C 132
Palgrave Gdns. NW1 . . . . .3D 4 (4C 82)
Palgrave Ho. SE5 . . . . .7C 102
   (off Wyndham Est.)
TW2: Whitt 7G 113
Palgrave Rd. W12 . . . . .3B 98
Palissy St. E2 . . . . .2J 9 (3F 85)
   (not continuous)
Palladian Gdns. W4 . . . . .6A 98
Palladino Ho. SW17 . . . . .5C 136
   (off Laurel Cl.)
Palladio Ct. SW18 . . . . .6K 117
   (off Mapleton Cres.)
Palladium Ct. E8 . . . . .7F 67
   (off Queensbridge Rd.)
Pallant Ho. SE1 . . . . .3D 102
   (off Tabard St.)
Pallant Way BR6: Farnb 3E 172
Pallet Way SE18 . . . . .1C 124
Palliser Ct. W14 . . . . .5G 99
   (off Palliser Rd.)
Palliser Ho. E1 . . . . .4K 85
   (off Ernest St.)
SE10 . . . . .6F 105
   (off Trafalgar Rd.)
Palliser Rd. W14 . . . . .5G 99
Pallister Ter. SW15 . . . . .3B 134
Pall Mall SW1 . . . . . . .5B 12 (1G 101)
Pall Mall E. SW1 . . . . . .4D 12 (1H 101)
Pall Mall Pl. SW1 . . . . .5B 12
Palmadium Cl. N13 . . . . .3F 33
Palmar Cres. DA7: Bex 3G 127
Palmar Rd. DA7: Bex 2G 127
Palm Av. DA14: Sidc 6D 144
Palm Cl. E10 . . . . .3D 68

Palm Ct. SE15 . . . . .7F 103
(off Garnies Cl.)
Palmeira Rd. DA7: Bex 3D 126
Palmer Av. SM3: Cheam 4E 164
Palmer Cl. BR4: W W'ck 3F 171
TW5: Hest 1E 112
UB5: N'olt 6C 58
Palmer Cres. KT1: King T 3E 150
Palmer Dr. BR1: Broml 4F 161
Palmer Gdns. EN5: Barn 5A 20
Palmer Ho. SE14 . . . . .7K 103
(off Lubbock St.)
Palmer Pl. N7 . . . . .5A 66
Palmer Rd. E13 . . . . .4K 87
RM8: Dag 1D 72
SW11 . . . . .7F 101
Palmer's Ct. N11 . . . . .5B 32
(off Palmer's Rd.)
PALMERS GREEN 3F 33
Palmers Gro. KT8: W Mole 4E 148
Palmers La. EN1: Enf 1C 24
EN3: Enf H 1C 24
Palmer's Rd. E2 . . . . .2K 85
N11 . . . . .5B 32
Palmers Rd. SW14 . . . . .3J 115
SW16 . . . . .2K 155
Palmerston Cen. HA3: W'stone . . .3K 41
Palmerston Ct. E3 . . . . .2K 85
(off Old Ford Rd.)
IG9: Buck H 1F 37
KT6: Surb 7D 150
Palmerston Cres. N13 . . . . .5E 32
SE18 . . . . .6G 107
Palmerston Gro. SW19 . . . . .7J 135
Palmerston Ho. SE1 . . . . .7J 13
(off Westminster Bri. Rd.)
W8 . . . . .6G 99
(off Kensington Pl.)
Palmerston Mans. W14 . . . . .6G 99
(off Queen's Club Gdns.)
Palmerston Rd. BR6: Farnb 4G 173
CRO: C'don 5D 156
E7 . . . . .6K 69
E17 . . . . .3B 50
HA3: W'stone 3J 41
IG9: Buck H 2E 36
N22 . . . . .7E 32
NW6 .7H 63
(not continuous)
SM1: Sutt 5A 166
SM5: Cars 4D 166
SW14 . . . . .4J 115
SW19 . . . . .7J 135
TW2: Twick 6J 113
TW3: Houn 1G 113
W3 . . . . .3J 97
Palmerston Way SW8 . . . . .7F 101
Palmer St. SW1 . . . . . . .1C 18 (3H 101)
(not continuous)
Palmers Wharf KT1: King T 2D 150
(off Emms Pas.)
Palm Gro. W5 . . . . .3E 96
Palm Rd. RM7: Rom 5J 55
Palomino Cl. UB4: Hayes 2F 75
Palyn Ho. EC1 . . . . .2D 8
(off Radnor St.)
Pamela Ct. N12 . . . . .6E 30
Pamela Gdns. HA5: Eastc 5K 39
Pamela St. E8 . . . . .1F 85
Pampisford Rd. CR2: S Croy 7B 168
Pams Way KT19: Ewe 5K 163
Panama Ho. E1 . . . . .5K 85
(off Beaumont Sq.)
Panavia Ct. NW9 . . . . .2B 44
Pancras La. EC4 . . . . . .1E 14 (6C 84)
Pancras Rd. N1 . . . . . . .1E 6 (2J 83)
NW1 .2H 83
Pancras Sq. N1 . . . . .2J 83
Pancras Square Leisure Cen. . . .2J 83
Pancras Way E3 . . . . .2C 86
Pandangle Ho. E8 . . . . .1F 85
(off Kingsland Rd.)
Pandian Way NW1 . . . . .6H 65

Pandora Ct. E16 . . . . .5J 87
(off Robertson Rd.)
Pandora Rd. NW6 . . . . .6J 63
Panfield M. IG2: Ilf 6E 52
Panfield Rd. SE2 . . . . .3A 108
Pangbourne NW1 . . . . .2A 6
(off Stanhope St.)
Pangbourne Av. W10 . . . . .5E 80
Pangbourne Dr. HA7: Stan 5J 27
Panhard Pl. UB1: S'hall 7F 77
Pank Av. EN5: New Bar 5F 21
Pankhurst Av. E3 . . . . .5D 86
E16 . . . . .1K 105
Pankhurst Cl. SE14 . . . . .7K 103
TW7: Isle 3K 113
Pankhurst Ho. W12 . . . . .6D 80
Pankhurst Rd. KT12: Walt T 7A 148
Panmuir Rd. SW20 . . . . .1D 152
Panmure Cl. N5 . . . . .4B 66
Panmure Ct. SE26 . . . . .3H 139
UB1: S'hall 6G 77
(off Osborne Rd.)
Panmure Rd. SE26 . . . . .3H 139
Pannells Ct. TW5: Hest 6E 94
Panorama Ct. N6 . . . . .6G 47
Panoramic Twr. E14 . . . . .6D 86
(off Burcham St.)
Pan Peninsula Sq. E14 . . . . .2D 104
Pansy Gdns. W12 . . . . .7C 80
Panther Dr. NW10 . . . . .5K 61
The Pantiles BR1: Broml 3C 160
DA7: Bex 7F 109
NW11 . . . . .4H 45
WD23: B Hea 1C 26
Pantiles Cl. N13 . . . . .5G 33
Panton Cl. CRO: C'don 1B 168
Panton St. SW1 . . . . . . .3C 12 (7H 83)
Panyer All. EC1 . . . . .7C 8
(off Newgate St.)
Panyers Gdns. RM10: Dag 3H 73
Paper Bldgs. EC4 . . . . .2K 13
Papermill Cl. SM5: Cars 4E 166
Papermill Pl. E17 . . . . .2A 50
Paper Mill Wharf E14 . . . . .7A 86
Papillons Wlk. SE3 . . . . .2J 123
Papworth Gdns. N7 . . . . .5K 65
Papworth Way SW2 . . . . .7A 120
Papyrus Ho. N1 . . . . .1C 8
Parabola Ct. KT8: E Mos 4G 149
The Parade CRO: C'don 6J 155
KT2: King T 2E 150
(off London Rd.)
KT4: Wor Pk 4B 164
N4 . . . . .1A 66
SE4 . . . . .2B 122
(off Up. Brockley Rd.)
SE26 . . . . .3H 139
(off Wells Pk. Rd.)
SM1: Sutt 3H 165
SM5: Cars 3H 165
(off Beynon Rd.)
SW11 . . . . .7D 100
TW12: Hamp H 5H 131
TW16: Sun 7H 129
UB6: G'frd 5B 60
Parade Gdns. E4 . . . . .7J 35
Parade Ground Path SE18 . . . . . .7D 106
Parade Mans. NW4 . . . . .5D 44
Parade M. SE27 . . . . .2B 138
Paradise Gdns. W6 . . . . .4D 98
Paradise Pas. N7 . . . . .5A 66
Paradise Path SE28 . . . . .1A 108
Paradise Pl. SE18 . . . . .4C 106
Paradise Rd. SW4 . . . . .2J 119
TW9: Rich 5D 114
Paradise Row E2 . . . . .3H 85
Paradise St. SE16 . . . . .2H 103
Paradise Wlk. SW3 . . . . .7F 17 (6D 100)
Paragon TW8: Bford 5C 96
(off Boston Pk. Rd.)
The Paragon SE3 . . . . .2H 123
Paragon Cl. E16 . . . . .6J 87
Paragon Gro. KT5: Surb 6F 151

Paragon M. SE1 . . . . .4D 102
SW8 .6K 101
Paragon Pl. KT5: Surb 6F 151
SE3 . . . . .2H 123
Paragon Rd. E9 . . . . .6J 67
Paramount Bldg. EC1 . . . . .3A 8
(off St John St.)
Paramount Ct. WC1 . . . . .4B 6
Parbury Ri. KT9: Chess 6E 162
Parbury Rd. SE23 . . . . .6A 122
Parchment Cl. CR4: Mitc 7E 154
Parchmore Rd. CR7: Thor H 2B 156
Parchmore Way CR7: Thor H 2B 156
Pardoe Rd. E10 . . . . .7D 50
Pardoner Ho. SE1 . . . . .3D 102
(off Pardoner St.)
Pardoner St. SE1 . . . . . .7F 15 (3D 102)
(not continuous)
Pardon St. EC1 . . . . .3B 8 (4B 84)
Parent Shop. Mall 2J 51
(off Marlborough Rd.)
Parfett St. E1 . . . . .5G 85
(not continuous)
Parfitt Cl. NW3 . . . . .1A 64
Parfrey St. W6 . . . . .6E 98
Pargraves Ct. HA9: Wemb 2G 61
Parham Dr. IG2: Ilf 6F 53
Parham Way N10 . . . . .2G 47
Paris Corte SE13 . . . . .3D 122
(off Loampit Va.)
Paris Gdn. SE1 . . . . .4A 14 (1B 102)
Parish Ct. KT6: Surb 5E 150
Parish Ga. Dr. DA15: Sidc 6J 125
Parish La. SE20 . . . . .6K 139
Parish M. SE20 . . . . .7K 139
Paris Ho. E2 . . . . .2H 85
(off Old Bethnal Grn. Rd.)
Parish Wharf Pl. SE18 . . . . .4C 106
Parison Cl. TW9: Rich 3G 115
The Park DA14: Sidc 5A 144
HA1: Harr 1J 59
N6 . . . . .6E 46
NW11 . . . . .1K 63
SE23 . . . . .1J 139
SM5: Cars 5D 166
W5 . . . . .1D 96
Park App. DA16: Well 4B 126
SE16 . . . . .3H 103
Park Av. BR1: Broml 6H 141
BR4: W W'ck 2E 170
BR6: Chels 2K 173
BR6: Farnb 3D 172
CR4: Mitc 7F 137
E6 . . . . .1E 88
E15 . . . . .6G 69
EN1: Enf 5J 23
HA4: Ruis 6F 39
IG1: Ilf 1E 70
IG8: Wfd G 5E 36
IG11: Bark 6G 71
N3 . . . . .1K 45
N13 . . . . .3F 33
N18 . . . . .4B 34
N22 . . . . .2J 47
NW2 .5D 62
NW10 . . . . .2F 79
(Brent Cres., not continuous)
NW10 . . . . .5D 62
(Park Av. Nth.)
NW11 . . . . .1K 63
SM5: Cars 6E 166
SW14 . . . . .4K 115
TW3: Houn 6F 113
TW17: Shep 3G 147
UB1: S'hall 2D 94
Park Av. E. KT17: Ewe 6C 164
Park Av. M. CR4: Mitc 7F 137
Park Av. Nth. N8 . . . . .3H 47
NW10 . . . . .5D 62
Park Av. Rd. N17 . . . . .7C 34
Park Av. Sth. N8 . . . . .4H 47
Park Av. W. KT17: Ewe 6C 164
Park Central SE17 . . . . .4C 102

Park Central Bldg. E3 . . . . .2C 86
Park Chase HA9: Wemb 4F 61
Park Cl. E9 . . . . .1J 85
HA3: Hrw W 1J 41
KT2: King T 1G 151
N12 . . . . .3G 31
NW2 .3D 62
NW10 . . . . .3F 79
SM5: Cars 6D 166
SW1 . . . . .7E 10 (2D 100)
TW3: Houn 5G 113
TW12: Hamp 1G 149
W4 . . . . .6K 97
W14 . . . . .3H 99
The Park Club
Acton 1A 98
Park Cl. CR2: S Croy 5C 168
(off Warham Rd.)
E4 . . . . .2K 35
E17 . . . . .5D 50
HA3: Kenton 7E 42
HA9: Wemb 5E 60
KT1: Hamp W 1C 150
KT3: N Mald 4K 151
N11 . . . . .7C 32
N17 . . . . .7B 34
SE21 . . . . .3C 138
SE26 . . . . .5H 139
SM6: W'gton 5J 167
SW11 . . . . .1F 119
UB8: Uxb 1A 74
W6 . . . . .4C 98
Park Cres. DA8: Erith 6J 109
EN2: Enf 4J 23
HA3: Hrw W 1J 41
N3 . . . . .7F 31
TW2: Twick 1H 131
W1 . . . . .4J 5 (4F 83)
Park Cres. M. E. W1 . . . .4K 5 (4F 83)
Park Cres. M. W. W1 . . . .4J 5 (4F 83)
Park Cres. Rd. DA8: Erith 6K 109
Park Cft. HA8: Edg 1J 43
Parkcroft Rd. SE12 . . . . .7H 123
Parkdale N11 . . . . .6C 32
Parkdale Cres. KT4: Wor Pk 3K 163
Parkdale Rd. SE18 . . . . .5J 107
Park Dr. HA2: Harr 7E 40
HA3: Hrw W 6C 26
N21 . . . . .6H 23
NW11 . . . . .1K 63
RM1: Rom 4K 55
RM10: Dag 3J 73
SE7 . . . . .6C 106
SW14 . . . . .5K 115
W3 . . . . .3G 97
Park Dwellings NW3 . . . . .5D 64
Park E. Bldg. E3 . . . . .2C 86
(off Fairfield Rd.)
Park End BR1: Broml 1H 159
NW3 .4C 64
Parker Bldg. SE16 . . . . .7K 15
(off Old Jamaica Rd.)
Parker Cl. E16 . . . . .1C 106
SM5: Cars 6D 166
Parker Ct. N1 . . . . .1C 84
(off Basire St.)
Parker Ho. E14 . . . . .2C 104
(off Admirals Way)
Parker M. WC2 . . . . .7F 7 (6J 83)
Parke Rd. SW13 . . . . .1C 116
TW16: Sun 4J 147
Parker Rd. CRO: C'don 4C 168
Parkers Row SE1 . . . . . .7K 15 (2G 103)
Parker St. E16 . . . . .1C 106
WC2 . . . . .7F 7 (6J 83)
Parkes St. E20 . . . . .6C 68
Park Farm Cl. HA5: Eastc 5K 39
N2 . . . . .3A 46
Park Farm Ct. UB3: Hayes 7G 75
Park Farm Rd.
BR1: Broml 1B 160
KT2: King T 7E 132
Parkfield TW7: Isle 1J 113

Parkfield Av. HA2: Harr 2G 41
SW14 . . . . .4A 116
TW13: Felt 3J 129
UB5: N'olt 2B 76
UB10: Hil 3D 74
Parkfield Cl. HA8: Edg 6C 28
UB5: N'olt 2C 76
Parkfield Ct. SE14 . . . . .1B 122
(off Parkfield Rd.)
Parkfield Cres. HA2: Harr 2G 41
HA4: Ruis 2C 58
TW13: Felt 3J 129
Parkfield Dr. UB5: N'olt 2B 76
Parkfield Gdns. HA2: Harr 3F 41
Parkfield Ho. HA2: Harr 1F 41
Parkfield Ind. Est. SW11 . . . . . .2E 118
Parkfield Pde. TW13: Felt 3J 129
Parkfield Rd. HA2: Harr 3G 59
NW10 . . . . .7D 62
SE14 . . . . .1B 122
SW4 . . . . .6H 119
(not continuous)
TW13: Felt 3J 129
UB5: N'olt 2C 76
UB10: Ick 2D 56
Parkfields CR0: C'don 1B 170
SW15 . . . . .4E 116
Parkfields Av. NW9 . . . . .1K 61
SW20 . . . . .1D 152
Parkfields Cl. SM5: Cars 4E 166
Parkfields Rd. KT2: King T 5F 133
Parkfield St. N1 . . . . .2A 84
Parkfield Way BR2: Broml 6D 160
Park Gdns. DA8: Erith 4K 109
E10 . . . . .1C 68
KT2: King T 5F 133
NW9 . . . . .3H 43
Park Ga. N2 . . . . .3B 46
N21 . . . . .7E 22
W5 . . . . .5D 78
Parkgate N1 . . . . .1D 84
(off Southgate Rd.)
SE3 . . . . .3H 123
Parkgate Av. EN4: Had W 1F 21
Parkgate Cl. KT2: King T 6H 133
Park Ga. Ct. TW12: Hamp H 6G 131
Parkgate Cres. EN4: Had W 1F 21
Parkgate Gdns. SW14 . . . . . .5K 115
Parkgate M. N6 . . . . .7G 47
Parkgate Rd. SM6: W'gton 5E 166
SW11 . . . . .7C 100
Park Gates HA2: Harr 4E 58
Park Gro. BR1: Broml 1K 159
DA7: Bex 4J 127
E15 . . . . .1J 87
HA8: Edg 5A 28
N11 . . . . .7C 32
Park Gro. Rd. E11 . . . . .2G 69
Park Hall SE10 . . . . .7F 105
(off Croom's Hill)
Park Hall Rd. N2 . . . . .4C 46
SE21 . . . . .3C 138
Park Hall Trad. Est. SE21 . . . .3C 138
Parkham Ct. BR2: Broml 2G 159
Parkham St. SW11 . . . . .1C 118
Park Hgts. Ct. E14 . . . . .6B 86
(off Wharf La.)
Park Hill BR1: Broml 4C 160
SE23 . . . . .2H 139
SM5: Cars 6C 166
SW4 . . . . .5H 119
TW10: Rich 6F 115
W5 . . . . .5D 78
Park Hill Cl. SM5: Cars 5C 166
Park Hill Ct. SW17 . . . . .3D 136
Park Hill M. CR2: S Croy 5D 168
Park Hill Rd. BR2: Broml 2G 159
CR0: C'don 2E 168
SM6: W'gton 7F 167
Parkhill Rd. DA5: Bexl 7F 127
DA14: Sidc 3H 143
DA15: Sidc 3H 143

Parkhill Rd. E4 . . . . .1K 35
NW3 . . . . .5D 64
Parkhill Wlk. NW3 . . . . .5D 64
Parkholme Rd. E8 . . . . .6G 67
Park Ho. E9 . . . . .7J 67
(off Shore Rd.)
N21 . . . . .7E 22
SE5 . . . . .1D 120
(off Camberwell Grn.)
W1 . . . . .1G 11
Park Ho. Gdns. TW1: Twick 5C 114
Park Ho. Pas. N6 . . . . .7E 46
Parkhouse St. SE5 . . . . .7D 102
Parkhurst Ct. N7 . . . . .4J 65
Parkhurst Gdns. DA5: Bexl 7G 127
Parkhurst Rd. DA5: Bexl 7G 127
E12 . . . . .4E 70
E17 . . . . .4A 50
N7 . . . . .4J 65
N11 . . . . .5K 31
N17 . . . . .2G 49
N22 . . . . .6E 32
SM1: Sutt 4B 166
Parkinson Ct. N1 . . . . .2F 9
(off Charles Sq. Est.)
Parkinson Ho. E9 . . . . .7J 67
(off Frampton Pk. Rd.)
SW1 . . . . .5C 18
(off Tachbrook St.)
Parkland Ct. E15 . . . . .5G 69
(off Maryland Pk.)
W14 . . . . .2G 99
(off Holland Pk. Av.)
Parkland Gdns. SW19 . . . . . .1F 135
Parkland Gro. TW15: Ashf 3C 128
Parkland Mead BR1: Broml 3F 161
(not continuous)
Parkland M. BR7: Chst 7H 143
Parkland Rd. IG8: Wfd G 7E 36
N22 . . . . .2K 47
TW15: Ashf 4C 128
Parklands KT5: Surb 5F 151
N6 . . . . .7F 47
Parklands Cl. EN4: Had W 1G 21
IG2: Ilf 7G 53
SW14 . . . . .5J 115
Parklands Ct. TW5: Hest 2B 112
Parklands Dr. N3 . . . . .3G 45
Parklands Gro. TW7: Isle 1K 113
Parklands Pde. TW5: Hest 2B 112
(off Parklands Ct.)
Parklands Rd. SW16 . . . . . . .5F 137
Parklands Way KT4: Wor Pk 2A 164
Parkland Wlk.
Local Nature Reserve 7J 47
Park La. CR0: C'don 3D 168
E15 . . . . .1F 87
HA2: Harr 3F 59
HA7: Stan 3F 27
HA9: Wemb 5E 60
N9 . . . . .3K 33
(not continuous)
N17 . . . . .7A 34
(not continuous)
RM6: Chad H 6D 54
SM3: Cheam 6G 165
SM5: Cars 4E 166
SM6: W'gton 5E 166
TW5: Cran 7J 93
TW9: Rich 4D 114
TW11: Tedd 6K 131
UB4: Hayes 5G 75
W1 . . . . .2F 11 (7D 82)
Park La. Cl. N17 . . . . .7B 34
Park La. Mans. CR0: C'don 3D 168
(off Park La.)
PARK LANGLEY 4E 158
The Parklangley Club 4E 158
Parklangley Tennis Club 4E 158
Parklea Cl. NW9 . . . . .1A 44
Park Lee Ct. N16 . . . . .7E 48
Parkleigh Rd. SW19 . . . . . . .2K 153
Parkleys TW10: Ham 4D 132

Parkleys Pde. TW10: Ham 4D 132
Park Lodge NW8 . . . . .7B 64
W14 . . . . .3H 99
(off Melbury Rd.)
Park Lodge Av. UB7: W Dray 2B 92
Park Lofts SW2 . . . . .5J 119
(off Lyham Rd.)
Park Lorne NW8 . . . . .2D 4
(off Park Rd.)
Park Mnr. SM2: Sutt 7A 166
(off Christchurch Pk.)
Park Mans. NW4 . . . . .5D 44
NW8 . . . . .2C 82
(off Allitsen Rd.)
SW1 . . . . .7E 10
(off Knightsbridge)
SW8 . . . . .7F 19 (6J 101)
SW11 . . . . .1D 118
(off Prince of Wales Dr.)
Park Mead DA15: Sidc 5B 126
HA2: Harr 3F 59
Parkmead SW15 . . . . .6D 116
Parkmead Cl. CR0: C'don 6K 157
Parkmead Gdns. NW7 . . . . . . .6G 29
Park M. BR7: Chst 6F 143
N8 . . . . .6J 47
SE10 . . . . .5H 105
SE24 . . . . .7C 120
TW19: Stanw 7B 110
W10 . . . . .2G 81
Parkmore Cl. IG8: Wfd G 4D 36
Park Pde. NW10 . . . . .2B 80
UB3: Hayes 6G 75
W3 . . . . .3G 97
Park Piazza SE13 . . . . .6F 123
Park Pl. BR1: Broml 1K 159
(off Park Rd.)
E14 . . . . .1C 104
HA9: Wemb 4F 61
N1 . . . . .7D 66
(off Downham Rd.)
SW1 . . . . . . .5A 12 (1A 101)
TW12: Hamp H 6G 131
W3 . . . . .4G 97
W5 . . . . .1D 96
Park Pl. Dr. W3 . . . . .3G 97
Park Pl. Vs. W2 . . . . . .5A 4 (5A 82)
Park Ridings N8 . . . . .3A 48
Park Ri. HA3: Hrw W 1J 41
SE23 . . . . .1A 140
Park Ri. Rd. SE23 . . . . .1A 140
Park Rd. BR1: Broml 1K 159
BR3: Beck 7B 140
BR7: Chst 6F 143
E6 . . . . .1A 88
E10 . . . . .1C 68
E12 . . . . .1K 69
E15 . . . . .1J 87
E17 . . . . .5B 50
EN4: Barn 4G 21
EN5: Barn 4C 20
HA0: Wemb 6E 60
IG1: Ilf 3H 71
KT1: Hamp W 1C 150
KT2: King T 5F 133
KT3: N Mald 4K 151
KT5: Surb 6F 151
KT8: E Mos 4G 149
N2 . . . . .3B 46
N8 . . . . .4G 47
N11 . . . . .7C 32
N14 . . . . .1C 32
N15 . . . . .4B 48
N18 . . . . .4B 34
NW1 . . . . .2D 4 (4D 82)
NW4 . . . . .7C 44
NW8 . . . . .2D 4 (3C 82)
NW9 . . . . .7K 43
NW10 . . . . .1A 80
SE25 . . . . .4E 156
SM3: Cheam 6G 165
SM6: W'gton 5F 167
(Clifton Rd.)

Park Rd. SM6: W'gton 2F 167
(Elmwood Cl.)
SW19 . . . . .6B 136
TW1: Twick 6C 114
TW3: Houn 5F 113
TW7: Isle 1B 114
TW10: Rich 6F 115
TW11: Tedd 6K 131
TW12: Hamp H 4F 131
TW13: Hanw 4B 130
TW15: Ashf 5D 128
TW16: Sun 1H 147
UB4: Hayes 5G 75
UB8: Uxb 1A 74
W4 . . . . .7J 97
W7 . . . . .7K 77
Park Rd. E. UB10: Uxb 2A 74
W3 . . . . .2H 97
Park Rd. Ho. KT2: King T 7G 133
Park Rd. Nth. W3 . . . . .2H 97
W4 . . . . .5K 97
Park Rd. Pools & Fitness 5H 47
Park Row SE10 . . . . .6F 105
PARK ROYAL 3H 79
Park Royal NW10 . . . . .3G 79
PARK ROYAL JUNC. 1G 79
Park Royal Metro Cen. NW10 . . .4H 79
Park Royal Rd. NW10 . . . . . . .3J 79
W3 . . . . .3J 79
Park St James NW8 . . . . .1D 82
(off St James's Ter. M.)
Parkshot TW9: Rich 4D 114
Park Side NW2 . . . . .3C 62
Parkside DA14: Sidc 2B 144
IG9: Buck H 2E 36
N3 . . . . .1K 45
NW7 . . . . .6H 29
SE3 . . . . .7H 105
SM3: Cheam 6G 165
SW1 . . . . .6F 11
SW19 . . . . .3F 135
TW12: Hamp H 5H 131
UB3: Hayes 7G 75
W3 . . . . .1A 98
W5 . . . . .7E 78
Parkside Av. BR1: Broml 4C 160
DA7: Bex 2K 127
RM1: Rom 3K 55
SE10 . . . . .1E 122
SW19 . . . . .5F 135
Parkside Bus. Est. SE8 . . . . . .6A 104
(not continuous)
Parkside Cl. SE20 . . . . .7J 139
Parkside Ct. E11 . . . . .6J 51
(off Wanstead Pl.)
E16 . . . . .2A 106
(off Booth Rd.)
N22 . . . . .6E 32
Parkside Cres. KT5: Surb 6J 151
N7 . . . . .3A 66
Parkside Cross DA7: Bex 2K 127
Parkside Dr. HA8: Edg 3B 28
Parkside Est. E9 . . . . .1J 85
(not continuous)
Parkside Gdns. EN4: E Barn 1J 31
SW19 . . . . .4F 135
Parkside Ho. RM10: Dag 3J 73
Parkside Lodge DA17: Belv 5J 109
Parkside Rd. DA17: Belv 4H 109
SW11 . . . . .1E 118
TW3: Houn 5F 113
Parkside Sq. E14 . . . . .4E 104
SE10 . . . . .1E 122
Parkside Ter. BR6: Farnb 3F 173
(off Willow Wlk.)
N18 . . . . .4J 33
Parkside Way HA2: Harr 4F 41
Parks Info. Cen. 4D 10 (1C 100)
Park Sth. SW11 . . . . .1E 118
(off Austin Rd.)
Park Sq. E. NW1 . . . . .3J 5 (4F 83)
Park Sq. M. NW1 . . . . .4J 5 (4F 83)
Park Sq. W. NW1 . . . . .3J 5 (4F 83)

Parkstead Rd. SW15 . . . . .5C 116
Park Steps W2 . . . . .2D 10
Parkstone Av. N18 . . . . .6A 34
Parkstone Rd. E17 . . . . .3E 50
  SE15 . . . . .2G 121
Park St. CR0: C'don 2C 168
  SE1 . . . . .4C 14 (1C 102)
  SW6 . . . . .1A 118
  TW11: Tedd 6J 131
  W1 . . . . .2G 11 (7E 82)
Park Ter. EN3: Enf H 1F 25
  KT4: Wor Pk 1C 164
  SE3 . . . . .3A 124
  SM5: Cars 3C 166
Park Theatre 2A 66
Parkthorne Cl. HA2: Harr 6F 41
Parkthorne Dr. HA2: Harr 6E 40
Parkthorne Rd. SW12 . . . . . . .7H 119
Park Towers W1 . . . . .5J 11
  (off Brick St.)
Park Vw. HA5: Hat E 1D 40
  HA9: Wemb 5H 61
  IG7: Chig 3H 37
  KT3: N Mald 3B 152
  N5 . . . . .4C 66
  N21 . . . . .7E 22
  RM6: Chad H 6D 54
  SE8 . . . . .5K 103
  (off Trundleys Rd.)
  UB7: Yiew 7A 74
  W3 . . . . .5J 79
Parkview UB6: G'frd 3A 78
  (off Perivale La.)
Park View Academy Sports Cen. . . .4C 48
Park Vw. Apts. SE16 . . . . .3H 103
  (off Banyard Rd.)
Parkview Apts. E14 . . . . .6D 86
  (off Chrisp St.)
Parkview Cl. SM5: Cars 7D 166
Park Vw. Ct. E3 . . . . .5C 86
  N12 . . . . .4H 31
  SE12 . . . . .3A 142
  SE20 . . . . .1H 157
Parkview Ct. HA3: Hrw W 7D 26
  IG2: Ilf 6J 53
  SW6 . . . . .2G 117
  SW18 . . . . .6J 117
Park Vw. Cres. N11 . . . . .4A 32
Parkview Cres. KT4: Wor Pk 7E 152
Park Vw. Est. E2 . . . . .2K 85
Park Vw. Gdns. IG4: Ilf 4D 52
  N22 . . . . .1A 48
  NW4 . . . . .5E 44
Park Vw. Ho. E4 . . . . .5H 35
  SE24 . . . . .6B 120
  (off Hurst St.)
Parkview Ho. N9 . . . . .7C 24
Park Vw. Mans. E20 . . . . .5D 68
  (off Olympic Pk. Av.)
  N4 . . . . .6B 48
Park Vw. M. SW9 . . . . .2K 119
Park View Road 3C 126
Park Vw. Rd. DA16: Well 3C 126
  N3 . . . . .1K 45
  N17 . . . . .3G 49
  NW10 . . . . .4B 62
  UB1: S'hall 1E 94
  UB8: Hil 6B 74
  W5 . . . . .5E 78
Parkview Rd. CR0: C'don 1G 169
  SE9 . . . . .1F 143
Park Village E. NW1 . . . . .1K 5 (2F 83)
Park Village W. NW1 . . . . .2F 83
Park Vs. RM6: Chad H 6D 54
Parkville Rd. SW6 . . . . .7H 99
Park Vista SE10 . . . . .6F 105
Park Wlk. N6 . . . . .7E 46
  SE10 . . . . .7F 105
  SW10 . . . . .7A 16 (6A 100)
Park Way EN2: Enf 2F 23
  HA4: Ruis 1J 57
  HA8: Edg 1H 43

Park Way KT8: W Mole 3F 149
  N20 . . . . .4J 31
  NW11 . . . . .5G 45
  TW14: Felt 7K 111
  W3 . . . . .3G 97
Parkway DA18: Erith 3E 108
  IG3: Ilf 3K 71
  IG8: Wfd G 5F 37
  N14 . . . . .2D 32
  NW1 . . . . .1F 83
  SW20 . . . . .4F 153
  UB10: Hil 7C 56
The Parkway TW5: Cran 5J 93
Park Way Cl. HA4: Ruis 1H 57
Parkway Cres. E15 . . . . .5E 68
Parkway Trad. Est. TW5: Hest 6A 94
Park W. W2 . . . . .7D 4
Park W. Bldg. E3 . . . . .2C 86
Park W. Pl. W2 . . . . .7D 4 (6C 82)
Park Wharf SE8 . . . . .5A 104
  (off Evelyn St.)
Parkwood BR3: Beck 7C 140
  N20 . . . . .3K 31
  NW8 . . . . .1D 82
  (off St Edmund's Ter.)
Parkwood Av. KT10: Esh 7G 149
Park Wood Ct. HA4: Ruis 4E 38
Parkwood Flats N20 . . . . .3J 31
Parkwood Gro. TW16: Sun 3J 147
Parkwood M. N6 . . . . .6F 47
Parkwood Rd. DA5: Bexl 7F 127
  SW19 . . . . .5H 135
  TW7: Isle 1K 113
Parliament Ct. E1 . . . . .6H 9
Parliament Hill 3D 64
Parliament Hill NW3 . . . . .4C 64
Parliament Hill Fields 3E 64
Parliament Hill Lido 4E 64
Parliament Hill Mans. NW5 . . . . .4E 64
Parliament M. SW14 . . . . .2J 115
Parliament Sq. SW1 . . . . .7E 12 (2J 101)
Parliament St. SW1 . . . . .6E 12 (2J 101)
Parliament Vw. SE1 . . . . .3G 19 (4K 101)
Parma Cres. SW11 . . . . .4D 118
Parmiter St. E2 . . . . .2H 85
Parmoor Ct. EC1 . . . . .3C 8
Parndon Ho. IG10: Lough 1H 37
Parnell Cl. HA8: Edg 4C 28
  W12 . . . . .3D 98
Parnell Ho. WC1 . . . . . .6D 6 (5H 83)
Parnell Ho. N1 . . . . .6B 66
  (off Canonbury Rd.)
Parnell Rd. E3 . . . . .1B 86
Parnell Way HA3: Stan 1B 42
Parnham Cl. BR1: Broml 3F 161
Parnham St. E14 . . . . .6A 86
  (not continuous)
Parolles Rd. N19 . . . . .1G 65
Paroma Rd. DA17: Belv 4G 109
Parr Cl. N9 . . . . .4C 34
  N18 . . . . .4C 34
Parr Ct. N1 . . . . .2D 84
  (off New North Rd.)
  TW13: Hanw 4A 130
Parr Ho. E16 . . . . .1K 105
  (off Beaulieu Av.)
Parrington Ho. SW4 . . . . .6H 119
Parr Rd. E6 . . . . .1B 88
  HA7: Stan 1D 42
Parrs Cl. CR2: Sande 7D 168
Parr St. N1 . . . . .2D 84
Parrs Way W6 . . . . .6E 98
Parry Av. E6 . . . . .6D 88
Parry Cl. KT17: Ewe 7D 164
Parry Ho. E1 . . . . .1H 103
  (off Green Bank)
Parry Pl. SE18 . . . . .4F 107
Parry Rd. SE25 . . . . .3E 156
  W10 . . . . .3G 81
Parry St. SW8 . . . . . . .7F 19 (6J 101)
Parsifal Rd. NW6 . . . . .5J 63
Parsley Gdns. CR0: C'don 1K 169

Parsloes Av. RM9: Dag 4D 72
Parsonage Cl. UB3: Hayes 6H 75
Parsonage Gdns. EN2: Enf 2H 23
Parsonage La. DA14: Sidc 4F 145
  EN1: Enf 2H 23
  EN2: Enf 2H 23
Parsonage Manorway DA17: Belv . . .6G 109
Parsonage St. E14 . . . . .4E 104
Parsons Cl. SM1: Sutt 3K 165
Parsons Cres. HA8: Edg 3B 28
Parsons Ga. M. SW6 . . . . .2J 117
PARSONS GREEN 2H 117
Parson's Grn. SW6 . . . . .1J 117
Parson's Grn. La. SW6 . . . . .1J 117
Parson's Gro. HA8: Edg 3B 28
Parsons Ho. W2 . . . . .4A 4
  (off Powis St.)
Parsons Lodge NW6 . . . . .7K 63
  (off Priory Rd.)
Parson's Mead CR0: C'don 1B 168
Parsons Mead KT8: E Mos 3G 149
Parson's M. SW18 . . . . .5A 118
Parson's Rd. E13 . . . . .2A 88
Parson St. NW4 . . . . .4E 44
Parthenia Dr. TW7: Isle 3A 114
Parthenia Rd. SW6 . . . . .1J 117
Partingdale La. NW7 . . . . .5A 30
Partington Cl. N19 . . . . .1H 65
Partington Ct. E16 . . . . .5B 88
  EN5: Barn 6A 20
  HA7: Stan 4K 27
  UB10: Uxb 1B 74
  WD23: Bush 1B 26
Partridge Ct. EC1 . . . . .3A 8
Partridge Dr. BR6: Farnb 3G 173
Partridge Grn. SE9 . . . . .3E 142
Partridge Ho. E3 . . . . .2B 86
  (off Stafford Rd.)
Partridge Rd. DA14: Sidc 3J 143
  TW12: Hamp 6D 130
Partridge Sq. E6 . . . . .5C 88
Partridge Way N22 . . . . .1J 47
Pasadena Cl. UB3: Hayes 2J 93
Pasadena Cl. Trad. Est.
  UB3: Hayes 2K 93
Pascall Ho. SE17 . . . . .6C 102
  (off Draco St.)
Pascal M. SE19 . . . . .7G 139
Pascal Rd. UB1: S'hall 6F 77
Pascal St. SW8 . . . . .7H 101
Pascoe Rd. SE13 . . . . .5F 123
Pasley Cl. SE17 . . . . .5B 102
Pasquier Rd. E17 . . . . .3A 50
The Passage TW9: Rich 5E 114
Passey Pl. SE9 . . . . .6D 124
Passfield Dr. E14 . . . . .5D 86
Passfield Hall WC1 . . . . .3D 6
  (off Endsleigh Pl.)
Passfield Path SE28 . . . . .7B 90
Passfields SE6 . . . . .3D 140
  W14 . . . . .5H 99
  (off Star Rd.)
Passing All. EC1 . . . . .4B 8
Passingham Ho. TW5: Hest 6E 94
Passmore Ct. E14 . . . . .6C 86
  (off New Festival Av.)
Passmore Edwards Ho. N11 . . . . .6C 32
Passmore Gdns. N11 . . . . .6C 32
Passmore Ho. E2 . . . . .1F 85
  (off Kingsland Rd.)
Passmore St. SW1 . . . . .5G 17 (5E 100)
Pastel Ct. E1 . . . . .5K 85
  (off Shandy St.)
Pasteur Cl. NW9 . . . . .2A 44
Pasteur Ct. HA1: Harr 1B 60
Pasteur Gdns. N18 . . . . .5G 33
Paston Cl. E5 . . . . .3K 67
  SM6: W'gton 3G 167
Paston Cres. SE12 . . . . .7K 123
Pastor Ct. N6 . . . . .6G 47
Pastor St. SE11 . . . . .4B 102
Pasture Cl. HA0: Wemb 3B 60

Pasture Rd. HA0: Wemb 2B 60
  RM9: Dag 5F 73
  SE6 . . . . .1H 141
The Pastures N20 . . . . .1C 30
Pastures Mead UB10: Hil 6C 56
Pastures Path E11 . . . . .1H 69
Patcham Ter. SW8 . . . . .1F 119
Patch Cl. UB10: Uxb 1B 74
Patching Way UB4: Yead 5C 76
Patent Ho. E14 . . . . .5D 86
  (off Morris Rd.)
Paternoster La. EC4 . . . . . .1B 14 (6B 84)
Paternoster Row EC4 . . . . .1C 14 (6C 84)
Paternoster Sq. EC4 . . . . .1B 14 (6B 84)
Paterson Cl. EC1 . . . . .2E 8
Pater St. W8 . . . . .3J 99
Pates Mnr. Dr. TW14: Bedf 7F 111
The Path SW19 . . . . .1K 153
Pathfield Rd. SW16 . . . . .6H 137
Patience Rd. SW11 . . . . .2C 118
Patina Mans. E20 . . . . .5E 68
  (off Mirabelle Gdns.)
Patio Cl. SW4 . . . . .6H 119
Patmore Est. SW8 . . . . .1G 119
Patmore Ho. N16 . . . . .5E 66
Patmore St. SW8 . . . . .1G 119
Patmos Lodge SW9 . . . . .1B 120
  (off Elliott Rd.)
Patmos Rd. SW9 . . . . .7B 102
Paton Cl. E3 . . . . .3C 86
Paton Ho. SW9 . . . . .2K 119
  (off Stockwell Rd.)
Paton St. EC1 . . . . .2C 8 (3C 84)
Patricia Ct. BR7: Chst 1H 161
  DA16: Well 7B 108
Patrick Coman Ho. EC1 . . . . .2A 8
  (off St John St.)
Patrick Connolly Gdns. E3 . . . . . .3D 86
Patrick Ct. SE1 . . . . .7B 14
  (off Webber St.)
Patrick Cres. RM8: Dag 1E 72
Patrick Pas. SW11 . . . . .2C 118
Patrick Rd. E13 . . . . .3A 88
Patriot Sq. E2 . . . . .2H 85
Patrol Pl. SE6 . . . . .6D 122
Patroni Ct. E15 . . . . .3G 87
  (off Durban Rd.)
Pat Shaw Ho. E1 . . . . .4K 85
  (off Globe Rd.)
Patshull Pl. NW5 . . . . .6G 65
Patshull Rd. NW5 . . . . .6G 65
Patten All. TW10: Rich 5D 114
Pattenden Rd. SE6 . . . . .1B 140
Patten Ho. N4 . . . . .1C 66
Patten Rd. SW18 . . . . .7C 118
Patterdale NW1 . . . . .2K 5
  (off Osnaburgh St.)
Patterdale Cl. BR1: Broml 6H 141
Patterdale Rd. SE15 . . . . .7J 103
Patterson Ct. SE19 . . . . .7F 139
Patterson Rd. SE19 . . . . .6F 139
Pattina Wlk. SE16 . . . . .1A 104
  (off Silver Wlk.)
Pattison Ho. E1 . . . . .6K 85
  (off Wellesley St.)
  SE1 . . . . .6D 14
  (off Redcross Way)
Pattison Rd. NW2 . . . . .3J 63
Pattison Wlk. SE18 . . . . .5G 107
Paul Byrne Ho. N2 . . . . .3A 46
Paul Cl. E15 . . . . .1G 87
Paul Ct. N18 . . . . .4B 34
  (off Fairfield Rd.)
  RM7: Rom 5J 55
Paul Daisley Ct. NW6 . . . . .7G 63
  (off Christchurch Av.)
Paulet Rd. SE5 . . . . .2B 120
Paulet Way NW10 . . . . .7A 62
Paul Gdns. CR0: C'don 2F 169
Paulhan Rd. HA3: Kenton 4D 42
Paul Ho. W10 . . . . .4G 81
  (off Ladbroke Gro.)

Paulin Dr. N21 7F **23**
Pauline Cres. TW2: Whitt 1G **131**
Pauline Ho. *E1* *5G* ***85***
(off Old Montague St.)
Paul Julius Cl. E14 7F **87**
Paul Robeson Cl. E6 3E **88**
Paul Robeson Ho. *WC1* *1H* ***7***
(off Penton Ri.)
The Paul Robeson Theatre 3F **113**
Paul St. E15 1G **87**
EC2 4F **9** (4D **84**)
Paul's Wlk. EC4 2B **14** (7C **84**)
Paultons Ho. *SW3* *7B* ***16***
(off Paultons Sq.)
Paultons Sq. SW3 7B **16** (6B **100**)
Paultons St. SW3 7B **16** (6B **100**)
Pauntley St. N19 1G **65**
Pavan Ct. *E2* *3J* ***85***
(off Sceptre Rd.)
Paved Ct. TW9: Rich 5D **114**
Paveley Ct. *NW7* *7B* ***30***
(off Langstone Way)
Paveley Dr. SW11 7C **100**
Paveley Ho. *N1* *2K* ***83***
(off Priory Grn. Est.)
Paveley St. NW8 2C **4** (3C **82**)
The Pavement *E11* *1E* ***68***
(off Hainault Rd.)
SW4 4G **119**
SW19 *6H* ***135***
(off Worple Rd.)
TW7: Isle *3A* ***114***
(off South St.)
TW11: Tedd 7B **132**
W5 3E **96**
Pavement M. RM6: Chad H 7D **54**
Pavement Sq. CR0: C'don 1G **169**
Pavers Way E3 2K **85**
Pavet Cl. RM10: Dag 6H **73**
The Pavilion SW8 7H **101**
Pavilion Apts. NW8 2B **4** (3B **82**)
Pavilion Ct. *NW6* *3J* ***81***
(off Stafford Rd.)
Pavilion La. BR3: Beck 6B **140**
Pavilion Leisure Cen. 2J **159**
Pavilion Lodge HA2: Harr 1H **59**
Pavilion M. N3 3J **45**
Pavilion Pde. *W12* *6E* ***80***
(off Wood La.)
Pavilion Rd. IG1: Ilf 7D **52**
SW1 7F **11** (3D **100**)
SW3 1F **17** (4D **100**)
TW11: Tedd 7K **131**
The Pavilion Sports & Fitness Club
3G **149**
Pavilion Sq. SW17 3D **136**
Pavilion St. E13 2A **88**
SW1 2F **17** (3D **100**)
Pavilion Ter. IG2: Ilf 5J **53**
W12 *6E* ***80***
(off Wood La.)
Pavilion Wlk. E10 2C **68**
Pavilion Way HA4: Ruis 2A **58**
HA8: Edg 7C **28**
SE10 2G **105**
Pavillion Ho. *SE16* *2K* ***103***
(off Water Gdns. Sq.)
Pavillion M. *N4* *2K* ***65***
(off Tollington Pl.)
Pawleyne Cl. SE20 7J **139**
Pawsey Cl. E13 1K **87**
Pawsons Rd. CR0: C'don 6C **156**
Paxfold HA7: Stan 5J **27**
Paxford Rd. HA0: Wemb 2B **60**
Paxton Cl. KT12: Walt T 7A **148**
TW9: Kew 2F **115**
Paxton Ct. *CR4: Mitc* *2D* ***154***
(off Armfield Cres.)
N7 *6A* ***66***
(off Westbourne Rd.)
SE12 3A **142**
SE26 *4A* ***140***
(off Adamsrill Rd.)
Paxton Ho. *SE17* *5D* ***102***
(off Morecambe St.)
SE25 4F **157**
Paxton M. *SE19* *7E* ***138***
(off Westow St.)
Paxton Pl. SE27 4E **138**
Paxton Point SE10 7D **104**
Paxton Rd. BR1: Broml 7J **141**
SE23 3A **140**
W4 6A **98**
Paxton Ter. SW1 7K **17** (6F **101**)
Paymal Ho. *E1* *5J* ***85***
(off Stepney Way)
Payne Cl. IG11: Bark 7J **71**
Payne Ho. *N1* *1K* ***83***
(off Barnsbury Est.)
Paynell Ct. SE3 3G **123**
Payne Rd. E3 2D **86**
Paynesfield Av. SW14 3K **115**
Paynesfield Rd. WD23: B Hea 1E **26**
Payne St. SE8 7B **104**
Paynes Wlk. W6 6G **99**
Payzes Gdns. IG8: Wfd G 6C **36**
Peaberry Ct. NW4 3C **44**
Peabody Av. SW1 5J **17** (5F **101**)
Peabody Bldgs. *E1* *7G* ***85***
(off John Fisher St.)
EC1 *4D* ***8***
(off Banner St.)
SW3 7C **16**
Peabody Cl. CR0: C'don 1J **169**
SE10 1D **122**
SW1 7K **17** (5F **101**)
Peabody Cotts. N17 1E **48**
Peabody Ct. *EC1* *4D* ***8***
(off Roscoe St.)
SE5 *1D* ***120***
(off Kimpton Rd.)
Peabody Est. *E1* *7K* ***85***
(off Brodlove La.)
E2 *2H* ***85***
(off Minerva St.)
EC1 *4D* ***8***
(off Dufferin St.)
EC1 *4K* ***7***
(off Farringdon La.)
N1 1C **84**
SE1 5K **13** (1A **102**)
(Duchy St.)
SE1 6D **14**
(Marshalsea Rd.)
SE1 5C **14** (1C **102**)
(Southwark St.)
SE5 *1D* ***120***
(off Camberwell Grn.)
SE24 7B **120**
SW1 3B **18**
SW3 7D **16** (6C **100**)
SW6 *6J* ***99***
(off Lillie Rd.)
SW11 4C **118**
W6 5E **98**
W10 5E **80**
Peabody Hill SE21 1B **138**
Peabody Ho. *N1* *1C* ***84***
(off Greenman St.)
Peabody Sq. *N1* *1C* ***84***
(off Peabody Est.)
SE1 7A **14** (2B **102**)
(not continuous)
Peabody Ter. *EC1* *4K* ***7***
(off Farringdon La.)
Peabody Twr. *EC1* *4D* ***8***
(off Golden La.)
Peabody Trust SE17 4D **102**
Peabody Yd. N1 1C **84**
Peace Cl. N14 5A **22**
SE25 4E **156**
UB6: G'frd 1H **77**
Peace Ct. *SE1* *5G* ***103***
(off Harmony Pl.)
Peace Gro. HA9: Wemb 3H **61**
Peace St. SE18 6E **106**
Peaches Cl. SM2: Cheam 7G **165**
Peachey Ho. *SW18* *4A* ***118***
(off Eltringham St.)
Peachey La. UB8: Cowl 5A **74**
Peach Gro. E11 3F **69**
Peach Rd. TW13: Felt 1J **129**
W10 3F **81**
Peach Tree Av. UB7: Yiew 6B **74**
Peachtree Cl. EN1: Enf 2B **24**
IG6: Ilf 1F **53**
Peachum Rd. SE3 6H **105**
Peachwalk M. E3 2K **85**
Peachy Cl. HA8: Edg 6B **28**
Peacock Av. TW14: Bedf 1F **129**
Peacock Cl. E4 7G **35**
NW7 5B **30**
RM8: Dag 1C **72**
Peacock Ho. *SE5* *1E* ***120***
(off St Giles Rd.)
Peacock Ind. Est. N17 7A **34**
Peacock Pl. N1 6A **66**
Peacock St. SE17 4B **102**
Peacock Theatre *1G* ***13***
(off Portugal St.)
Peacock Wlk. N6 7F **47**
Peacock Yd. *SE17* *5B* ***102***
(off Iliffe St.)
The Peak SE26 3J **139**
Peaketon Av. IG4: Ilf 4B **52**
Peak Hill SE26 4J **139**
Peak Hill Av. SE26 4J **139**
Peak Hill Gdns. SE26 4J **139**
Peal Gdns. W13 4A **78**
Peall Rd. CR0: C'don 6K **155**
Peall Rd. Ind. Est.
CR0: C'don 6K **155**
Pearce Cl. CR4: Mitc 2E **154**
Pearcefield Av. SE23 1J **139**
Pearce Ho. *SW1* *4D* ***18***
(off Causton St.)
Pear Cl. NW9 4K **43**
SE14 7A **104**
Pear Ct. *SE15* *7F* ***103***
(off Thruxton Way)
Pearcroft Rd. E11 2F **69**
Peardon St. SW8 2F **119**
Peareswood Gdns. HA7: Stan 1D **42**
Pearfield Rd. SE23 3A **140**
Pearing Cl. KT4: Wor Pk 2F **165**
Pearl Cl. CR7: Thor H 2D **156**
E6 6E **88**
NW2 7F **45**
Pearl Rd. E17 3C **50**
Pearl St. E1 1H **103**
Pearmain Cl. TW17: Shep 5D **146**
Pearmain Ct. *W6* *3D* ***98***
(off Vinery Way)
Pearman St. SE1 1K **19** (3A **102**)
Pear Pl. SE1 6J **13** (2A **102**)
Pear Rd. E11 3F **69**
Pears Av. TW17: Shep 3G **147**
Pearscroft Ct. SW6 1K **117**
Pearscroft Rd. SW6 1K **117**
Pearse St. SE15 6E **102**
Pearson Cl. EN5: New Bar 3E **20**
SE5 *1C* ***120***
(off Camberwell New Rd.)
Pearson M. *SW4* *3H* ***119***
(off Edgeley Rd.)
Pearson's Av. SE14 1C **122**
Pearson Sq. W1 6B **6** (5G **83**)
Pearson St. E2 2F **85**
Pearson Way CR4: Mitc 1E **154**
Pears Rd. TW3: Houn 3G **113**
Peartree SE26 5A **140**
Pear Tree Av. UB7: Yiew 6B **74**
Peartree Av. SW17 3A **136**
Pear Tree Cl. BR2: Broml 5B **160**
CR4: Mitc 2C **154**
E2 1F **85**
KT9: Chess 5G **163**
KT19: Eps 7K **163**
Peartree Cl. DA8: Erith 1K **127**
Pear Tree Ct. E18 1K **51**
EC1 4K **7** (4A **84**)
SE26 3B **140**
Peartree Gdns. RM7: Mawney 2H **55**
RM8: Dag 4B **72**
Pear Tree Ho. SE4 3B **122**
Pear Tree La. RM13: Rain 2K **91**
Peartree La. E1 7J **85**
Pear Tree Rd. TW15: Ashf 5E **128**
Peartree Rd. EN1: Enf 3K **23**
Peartrees UB7: Yiew 7A **74**
Pear Tree St. EC1 3B **8** (4C **84**)
Peartree Way SE10 4J **105**
Peary Ho. NW10 7K **61**
Peary Pl. E2 3J **85**
Peasmead Ter. E4 4K **35**
Peatfield Cl. DA15: Sidc 3J **143**
Pebble Way *W3* *1H* ***97***
(off Steyne Rd.)
Pebworth Rd. HA1: Harr 2A **60**
Pechora Way E14 5A **86**
Peckarmans Wood SE26 3G **139**
Peckett Sq. N5 4C **66**
Peckford Pl. SW9 2A **120**
PECKHAM 1G **121**
Peckham Gro. SE15 7E **102**
Peckham High St. SE15 1G **121**
Peckham Hill St. SE15 7G **103**
Peckham Pk. Rd. SE15 7G **103**
Peckhamplex 2G **121**
Peckham Pulse Leisure Cen. 1G **121**
Peckham Rd. SE5 1E **120**
SE15 1E **120**
Peckham Rye SE15 3G **121**
SE22 4G **121**
Peckham Sq. SE15 1G **121**
Pecks Yd. *E1* *5J* ***9***
(off Hanbury St.)
Peckwater St. NW5 5G **65**
Pedlar's Wlk. N7 5K **65**
Pedley Rd. RM8: Dag 1C **72**
Pedley St. E1 4G **85**
Pedro St. E5 3K **67**
Pedworth Gdns. SE16 4J **103**
Peebles Ct. *UB1: S'hall* *6G* ***77***
(off Haldane Rd.)
Peebles Ho. *NW6* *2K* ***81***
(off Carlton Vale)
Peek Cres. SW19 5F **135**
Peel Cl. E4 2J **35**
N9 3B **34**
Peel Dr. IG5: Ilf 3C **52**
NW9 3B **44**
Peel Gro. E2 2J **85**
Peel Pas. W8 1J **99**
Peel Pl. IG5: Ilf 2C **52**
SE18 1D **124**
SW6 6J **99**
Peel Pct. NW6 2J **81**
Peel Rd. BR6: Farnb 5G **173**
E18 1H **51**
HA3: W'stone 3K **41**
HA9: Wemb 3D **60**
Peel Square NW9 3C **44**
Peel St. W8 1J **99**
Peel Way UB8: Hil 5A **74**
Peerglow Est. EN3: Pond E 5D **24**
Peerless St. EC1 2E **8** (3D **84**)
Pegamoid Rd. N18 3D **34**
Pegasus Cl. N16 4D **66**
Pegasus Ct. KT1: King T 3D **150**
N21 7H **23**
NW10 *3D* ***80***
(off Trenmar Gdns.)
TW8: Bford 5F **97**
W3 *6J* ***79***
(off Horn La.)
Pegasus Ho. *E1* *4K* ***85***
(off Beaumont Sq.)
E13 3K **87**
Pegasus Pl. SE11 7J **19** (6A **102**)
SW6 1J **117**
Pegasus Rd. CR0: Wadd 6A **168**

Pegasus Way N11 . . . . .6A 32
Peggotty Way UB8: Hil 6D 74
Pegg Rd. TW5: Hest 7B 94
Pegler Sq. SE3 . . . . .3K 123
Pegley Gdns. SE12 . . . . .2J 141
Pegswood Ct. E1 . . . . .7G 85
(off Cable St.)
Pegwell St. SE18 . . . . .7J 107
Pekin Cl. E14 . . . . .6C 86
(off Pekin St.)
Pekin St. E14 . . . . .6C 86
Pelabon Ho. TW1: Twick 6D 114
(off Clevedon Rd.)
Peldon Cl. IG8: Wfd G 7F 37
Peldon Ct. TW9: Rich 4F 115
Peldon Pas. TW10: Rich 4F 115
Peldon Wlk. N1 . . . . .1B 84
(off Popham St.)
Pelham Av. IG11: Bark 1K 89
Pelham Cl. SE5 . . . . .3E 120
Pelham Cotts. DA5: Bexl 1H 145
Pelham Ct. DA14: Sidc 3A 144
SW3 . . . . .4C 16
(off Fulham Rd.)
Pelham Cres. SW7 . . . .4C 16 (4C 100)
Pelham Ho. SW1 . . . . .2D 18
(off Gt. Peter St.)
W14 . . . . .4H 99
(off Mornington Av.)
Pelham Pl. SW7 . . . .4C 16 (4C 100)
W13 . . . . .4K 77
Pelham Rd. BR3: Beck 2J 157
DA7: Bex 3G 127
E18 . . . . .3K 51
IG1: Ilf 2H 71
N15 . . . . .4F 49
N22 . . . . .2A 48
SW19 . . . . .7J 135
Pelham St. SW7 . . . .3B 16 (4B 100)
Pelican Dr. HA2: Harr 2F 59
Pelican Est. SE15 . . . . .1F 121
Pelican Ho. SE5 . . . . .1F 121
SE8 . . . . .4B 104
Pelican Pas. E1 . . . . .4J 85
Pelican Wlk. SW9 . . . . .4B 120
Pelican Wharf E1 . . . . .1J 103
(off Wapping Wall)
Pelier St. SE17 . . . . .6C 102
Pelinore Rd. SE6 . . . . .2G 141
Pella Ho. SE11 . . . . . .5H 19 (5K 101)
Pellant Rd. SW6 . . . . .7G 99
Pellatt Gro. N22 . . . . .1A 48
Pellatt Rd. HA9: Wemb 2D 60
SE22 .5F 121
Pellerin Rd. N16 . . . . .5E 66
Pellew Ho. E1 . . . . .4H 85
(off Somerford St.)
Pellings Cl. BR2: Broml 3G 159
Pelling St. E14 . . . . .6C 86
Pellipar Cl. N13 . . . . .3F 33
Pellipar Gdns. SE18 . . . . .5D 106
Pellipar Rd. SE18 . . . . .5D 106
Pellow Cl. EN5: Barn 6C 20
Pelt St. SE8 . . . . .4A 104
Pelly Rd. E13 . . . . .1J 87
(not continuous)
Peloton Av. E20 . . . . .5D 68
Pelter St. E2 . . . . .1J 9 (3F 85)
Pelton Rd. SE10 . . . . .5G 105
Pembar Av. E17 . . . . .3A 50
Pemberley Chase KT19: Ewe . . .5H 163
Pemberley Cl. KT19: Ewe 5H 163
Pemberley Ho. KT19: Ewe 5H 163
(off Pemberley Chase)
Pember Rd. NW10 . . . . .3F 81
Pemberton Cl. TW19: Stanw 1A 128
Pemberton Ct. E1 . . . . .3K 85
(off Portelet Rd.)
EN1: Enf 2K 23
Pemberton Gdns. N19 . . . . .3G 65
RM6: Chad H 5E 54
Pemberton Ho. SE26 . . . . .4G 139
(off High Level Dr.)

Pemberton Pl. E8 . . . . .7H 67
Pemberton Rd. KT8: E Mos 4G 149
N4 . . . . .5A 48
Pemberton Row EC4 . . . .7K 7 (6A 84)
Pemberton Ter. N19 . . . . .3G 65
Pembridge Av. TW2: Whitt 1D 130
Pembridge Cres. W11 . . . . .7J 81
Pembridge Gdns. W2 . . . . .7J 81
Pembridge M. W11 . . . . .7J 81
Pembridge Pl. SW15 . . . . .5J 117
W2 . . . . .7J 81
Pembridge Rd. W11 . . . . .7J 81
Pembridge Sq. W2 . . . . .7J 81
Pembridge Studios W11 . . . . . . .7J 81
(off Pembridge Vs.)
Pembridge Vs. W2 . . . . .7J 81
W11 . . . . .7J 81
(off Kensington Village)
Pembroke W14 . . . . .4H 99
(off Prusom St.)
Pembroke Av. EN1: Enf 1C 24
HA3: Kenton 3A 42
HA5: Pinn 1B 58
KT5: Surb 5H 151
N1 . . . . .1J 83
Pembroke Bldgs. NW10 . . . . . . .3C 80
Pembroke Bus. Cen. BR8: Swan . .7K 145
The Pembroke Cen. HA4: Ruis . . .1H 57
Pembroke Cl. SW1 . . . .7H 11 (2E 100)
Pembroke Cotts. W8 . . . . .3J 99
(off Pembroke Sq.)
Pembroke Ct. W7 . . . . .6K 77
(off Copley Cl.)
W8 . . . . .3J 99
(off Sth. Edwardes Sq.)
Pembroke Gdns. HA4: Ruis 1H 57
RM10: Dag 3H 73
SW14 . . . . .4H 115
W8 . . . . .4H 99
Pembroke Gdns. Cl. W8 . . . . . . .3J 99
Pembroke Hall NW4 . . . . .3E 44
(off Mulberry Cl.)
Pembroke Ho. RM8: Dag 5A 72
SW1 . . . . .2G 17
(off Chesham St.)
W2 . . . . .6K 81
(off Hallfield Est.)
W3 . . . . .2J 97
(off Park Rd. E.)
Pembroke Lodge HA7: Stan 6J 27
Pembroke Mans. NW6 . . . . .6A 64
(off Canfield Gdns.)
Pembroke M. E3 . . . . .3A 86
N10 . . . . .1E 46
W8 . . . . .3J 99
Pembroke Pde. DA8: Erith 5J 109
Pembroke Pl. HA8: Edg 7B 28
TW7: Isle 2J 113
W8 . . . . .3J 99
Pembroke Rd. BR1: Broml 2A 160
CR4: Mitc 2E 154
DA8: Erith 5J 109
E6 . . . . .5D 88
E17 . . . . .5D 50
HA4: Ruis 1G 57
HA9: Wemb 3D 60
IG3: Ilf 1K 71
N8 . . . . .4J 47
N10 . . . . .1E 46
N13 . . . . .3H 33
N15 . . . . .5F 49
SE25 .4E 156
UB6: G'frd 4F 77
W8 . . . . .4H 99
Pembroke Sq. W8 . . . . .3J 99
Pembroke St. N1 . . . . .7J 65
(not continuous)
Pembroke Studios W8 . . . . .3H 99
Pembroke Ter. NW8 . . . . .1B 82
(off Queen's Ter.)
Pembroke Vs. TW9: Rich 4D 114
W8 . . . . .4J 99
Pembroke Wlk. W8 . . . . .4J 99
Pembroke Way UB3: Harl 3E 92

Pembrook M. SW11 . . . . .4B 118
Pembry Cl. SW9 . . . . .1A 120
Pembury Av. KT4: Wor Pk 1C 164
Pembury Cl. BR2: Hayes 7H 159
E5 . . . . .5H 67
Pembury Ct. UB3: Harl 6F 93
Pembury Cres. DA14: Sidc 2E 144
Pembury Pl. E5 . . . . .5H 67
Pembury Rd. DA7: Bex 7E 108
E5 . . . . .5H 67
N17 . . . . .1F 49
SE25 .4G 157
Pemdevon Rd. CR0: C'don 7A 156
Pemell Cl. E1 . . . . .4J 85
Pemell Ho. E1 . . . . .4J 85
(off Pemell Cl.)
Pemerich Cl. UB3: Harl 5H 93
Penally Pl. N1 . . . . .1D 84
Penang Ho. E1 . . . . .1H 103
(off Prusom St.)
Penang St. E1 . . . . .1H 103
Penarth Cen. SE15 . . . . .6J 103
Penarth Ct. SM2: Sutt 7A 166
Penarth St. SE15 . . . . .6J 103
Penberth Rd. SE6 . . . . .2E 140
Pencombe M. W11 . . . . .7H 81
Pencraig Way SE15 . . . . .6H 103
Pendall Cl. EN4: E Barn 4H 21
Penda Rd. DA8: Erith 7H 109
Pendarves Rd. SW20 . . . . .1E 152
Penda's Mead E9 . . . . .4A 68
Pendell Av. UB3: Harl 7H 93
Pendennis Ho. SE8 . . . . .4A 104
Pendennis Rd. N17 . . . . .3D 48
SW16 . . . . .4J 137
Penderel Rd.
TW3: Houn 5E 112
Penderry Ri. SE6 . . . . .2F 141
Penderyn Way N7 . . . . .4H 65
Pendlebury Ct. KT5: Surb 4E 150
(off Cranes Pk.)
Pendle Ct. UB10: Hil 1D 74
Pendle Ho. SE26 . . . . .3G 139
Pendle Rd. SW16 . . . . .6F 137
Pendlestone Rd. E17 . . . . .5D 50
Pendlewood Cl. W5 . . . . .5C 78
Pendley Ho. E2 . . . . .1G 85
(off Whiston Rd.)
Pendolino Way NW10 . . . . .7G 61
Pendragon Rd.
BR1: Broml 3H 141
Pendragon Wlk. NW9 . . . . .6A 44
Pendrell Ho. WC2 . . . . .1D 12
(off New Compton St.)
Pendrell Rd. SE4 . . . . .2A 122
Pendrell St. SE18 . . . . .6H 107
Pendulum M. E8 . . . . .5F 67
Penerley Rd. SE6 . . . . .1D 140
Penfield Ct. NW9 . . . . .3A 44
(off Tanner Cl.)
Penfield Lodge W9 . . . . .5J 81
(off Admiral Wlk.)
Penfields Ho. N7 . . . . .6J 65
(off York Way Est.)
Penfold Cl. CR0: Wadd 3A 168
Penfold La. DA5: Bexl 2D 144
(not continuous)
Penfold Pl. NW1 . . . . .5C 4 (5C 82)
Penfold Rd. N9 . . . . .1E 34
Penfold St. NW1 . . . . .4B 4 (4B 82)
NW8 . . . . .4B 4 (4B 82)
Penford Gdns. SE9 . . . . .3B 124
Penford St. SE5 . . . . .2B 120
Pengarth Rd. DA5: Bexl 5D 126
PENGE 7J 139
Penge Ho. SW11 . . . . .3B 118
Penge La. SE20 . . . . .7J 139
Pengelly Apts. E14 . . . . .5D 104
(off Bartlett M.)

Penge Rd. E13 . . . . .1A 88
SE20 .3G 157
SE25 .3G 157
Penhale Cl. BR6: Chels 4K 173
Penhall Rd. SE7 . . . . .4B 106
Penhill Rd. DA5: Bexl 6C 126
Penhurst Mans. SW6 . . . . .1H 117
(off Rostrevor Rd.)
Penhurst Pl. SE1 . . . . .1H 19
Penhurst Rd. IG6: Ilf 1F 53
Penifather La. UB6: G'frd 3H 77
Peninsula Apts. N1 . . . . .1C 84
(off Basire St.)
W2 . . . . .6C 4
(off Praed St.)
Peninsula Ct. E14 . . . . .3D 104
(off E. Ferry Rd.)
N1 . . . . .1C 84
(off Basire St.)
Peninsula Hgts. SE1 . . .5F 19 (5J 101)
Peninsular Cl. NW7 . . . . .5B 30
TW14: Felt 6F 111
Peninsular Pk. 4J 105
Peninsular Pk. Rd. SE7 . . . . .4J 105
Peninsula Sq. SE10 . . . . .2G 105
Penistone Rd. SW16 . . . . .7J 137
Penketh Dr. HA1: Harr 3H 59
Penley Ct. WC2 . . . . . . .2H 13 (7K 83)
Penmayne Ho. SE11 . . . . .5K 19
(off Kennings Way)
Penmon Rd. SE2 . . . . .3A 108
Pennack Rd. SE15 . . . . .6F 103
Penn Almshouses SE10 . . . . .1E 122
(off Greenwich Sth. St.)
Pennant M. W8 . . . . .4K 99
Pennant Ter. E17 . . . . .2B 50
Pennard Mans. W12 . . . . .2E 98
(off Goldhawk Rd.)
Pennard Rd. W12 . . . . .2E 98
The Pennards TW16: Sun 3A 148
Penn Cl. HA3: Kenton 4C 42
UB6: G'frd 2F 77
Penn Ct. NW9 . . . . .3K 43
Penner Cl. SW19 . . . . .2G 135
Penners Gdns. KT6: Surb 7E 150
Pennethorne Cl. E9 . . . . .1J 85
Pennethorne Ho. SW11 . . . . .3B 118
Pennethorne Rd. SE15 . . . . .7H 103
Penn Gdns. BR7: Chst 2F 161
RM5: Col R 1G 55
Penn Ho. NW8 . . . . .4C 4
(off Mallory St.)
Pennine Dr. NW2 . . . . .2F 63
Pennine Ho. N9 . . . . .3B 34
(off Plevna Rd.)
Pennine La. NW2 . . . . .2G 63
Pennine Pde. NW2 . . . . .2G 63
Pennine Way DA7: Bex 1K 127
UB3: Harl 7F 93
Pennington Cl. SE27 . . . . .4D 138
Pennington Ct. SE16 . . . . .1A 104
Pennington Dr. N21 . . . . .5D 22
Pennington Lodge KT5: Surb 5E 150
(off Cranes Dr.)
Pennington St. E1 . . . . .7H 85
Pennington Way SE12 . . . . .2K 141
Penniston Cl. N17 . . . . .2C 48
Penniwell Cl. HA8: Edg 4A 28
Penn La. DA5: Bexl 5D 126
Penn Rd. N7 . . . . .5J 65
Penn St. N1 . . . . .1D 84
Penny Brookes St. E20 . . . . .6E 68
Penny Cl. E4 . . . . .3B 36
Pennycroft CR0: Sels 7A 170
Penny Farthing M.
TW12: Hamp H 6G 131
Pennyfather La. EN2: Enf 3H 23
Pennyfields E14 . . . . .7C 86
(not continuous)
Penny Flds. Ho. SE8 . . . . .1B 122
(off Francis Harvey Way)
Pennyford Ct. NW8 . . . . .3A 4
(off St John's Wood Rd.)

Penny La. TW17: Shep 7G 147
Penny M. SW12 . . . . .7F 119
Pennymoor Wlk. W9 . . . . .4H 81
    (off Fernhead Rd.)
Penny Rd. NW10 . . . . .3H 79
Penny Royal SM6: W'gton 6H 167
Pennyroyal Av. E6 . . . . .6E 88
Pennyroyal Dr. UB7: W Dray . . .2B 92
Penpoll Rd. E8 . . . . .6H 67
Penpool La. DA16: Well 3B 126
Penrhyn Av. E17 . . . . .1B 50
Penrhyn Cres. E17 . . . . .1C 50
    SW14 . . . . .4J 115
Penrhyn Gdns. KT1: King T 4D 150
Penrhyn Gro. E17 . . . . .1C 50
Penrhyn Rd. KT1: King T 4E 150
Penrith Cl. BR3: Beck 1D 158
    SW15 . . . . .5G 117
    UB8: Uxb 7A 56
Penrith Pl. SE27 . . . . .2B 138
Penrith Rd. CR7: Thor H 2C 156
    KT3: N Mald 4K 151
    N15 .5D 48
Penrith St. SW16 . . . . .6G 137
Penrose Ct. SW12 . . . . .1E 136
Penrose Gdns. NW3 . . . . .4J 63
Penrose Gro. SE17 . . . . .5C 102
Penrose Ho. N21 . . . . .5E 22
    SE17 . . . . .5C 102
Penrose St. SE17 . . . . .5C 102
Penrose Way SE10 . . . . .1G 105
Penryn Ho. SE11 . . . . .5B 102
    (off Seaton Cl.)
Penryn St. NW1 . . . . .2H 83
Penry St. SE1 . . . . .4E 102
Pensbury Pl. SW8 . . . . .2G 119
Pensbury St. SW8 . . . . .2G 119
Pensford Av. TW9: Kew 2G 115
Penshurst NW5 . . . . .6E 64
Penshurst Av. DA15: Sidc 6A 126
Penshurst Gdns. HA8: Edg 5C 28
Penshurst Grn. BR2: Broml . . .5H 159
Penshurst Ho. SE15 . . . . .6J 103
    (off Lovelinch Cl.)
Penshurst Rd. CR7: Thor H 5B 156
    DA7: Bex 1F 127
    E9 . . . . .7K 67
    N17 .7A 34
Penshurst Wlk. BR2: Broml . . .5H 159
Penshurst Way SM2: Sutt 7J 165
Pensilver Cl. EN4: E Barn 4H 21
Penstemon Cl. N3 . . . . .6D 30
Penstock Footpath N8 . . . . .3K 47
Pentagram Yd. W11 . . . . .6J 81
    (off Needham Rd.)
Pentavia Retail Pk. 7G 29
Pentelow Gdns. TW14: Felt 6J 111
Pentire Rd. E17 . . . . .1F 51
Pentland Av. HA8: Edg 2C 28
    TW17: Shep 5C 146
Pentland Cl. N9 . . . . .2D 34
    NW11 . . . . .2G 63
Pentland Gdns. SW18 . . . . .6A 118
Pentland Pl. UB5: N'olt 1C 76
Pentland Rd. NW6 . . . . .3J 81
Pentlands Cl. CR4: Mitc 3F 155
Pentland St. SW18 . . . . .6A 118
Pentland Way UB10: Ick 3E 56
Pentlow St. SW15 . . . . .3E 116
Pentlow Way IG9: Buck H 1H 37
Pentney Rd. E4 . . . . .1A 36
    SW12 . . . . .1G 137
    SW19 . . . . .1G 153
Penton Gro. N1 . . . . .2A 84
Penton Ho. N1 . . . . .1J 7
    (off Pentonville Rd.)
    SE2 . . . . .1D 108
Penton Pl. SE17 . . . . .5B 102
Penton Ri. WC1 . . . . .1H 7 (3K 83)
Penton St. N1 . . . . .2A 84
PENTONVILLE 2K 83
Pentonville Rd. N1 . . .1F 7 (2J 83)
Pentrich Av. EN1: Enf 1B 24

Pentridge St. SE15 . . . . .7F 103
Pentyre Av. N18 . . . . .5J 33
Penwerris Av. TW7: Isle 7G 95
Penwerris Ct. TW5: Hest 7G 95
Penwith Rd. SW18 . . . . .2J 135
Penwood Ct. HA5: Pinn 4D 40
Penwood Ho. SW15 . . . . .6B 116
Penwortham Ct. N22 . . . . .2A 48
    (off Mayes Rd.)
Penwortham Rd. SW16 . . . . . . .6F 137
Penylan Pl. HA8: Edg 7B 28
Penywern Rd. SW5 . . . . .5J 99
Penzance Pl. W11 . . . . .1G 99
Penzance St. W11 . . . . .1G 99
Peony Ct. IG8: Wfd G 7B 36
    SW10 . . . . .7A 16 (6A 100)
Peony Gdns. W12 . . . . .7C 80
Peperfield WC1 . . . . .2G 7
    (off Cromer St.)
Pepler Ho. W10 . . . . .4G 81
    (off Wornington Rd.)
Pepler M. SE5 . . . . .5F 103
Peploe Rd. NW6 . . . . .2F 81
Peplow Cl. UB7: Yiew 1A 92
Pepper Cl. E6 . . . . .5D 88
Peppercorn Cl. CR7: Thor H . . .2D 156
Peppermead Sq. SE13 . . . . .5C 122
Peppermint Cl. CR0: C'don 7J 155
Peppermint Pl. E11 . . . . .3G 69
Pepper St. E14 . . . . .3D 104
    SE1 . . . . .6C 14 (2C 102)
Peppie Cl. N16 . . . . .2E 66
Pepys Cl. UB10: Ick 4D 56
Pepys Cres. E16 . . . . .1J 105
    EN5: Barn 5A 20
Pepys Ho. E2 . . . . .3J 85
    (off Kirkwall Pl.)
Pepys Ri. BR6: Orp 1K 173
Pepys Rd. SE14 . . . . .1K 121
    SW20 . . . . .1E 152
Pepys St. EC3 . . . . .2H 15 (7E 84)
Perceval Av. NW3 . . . . .5C 64
Perceval Ct. UB5: N'olt 5E 58
Perceval Ho. W5 . . . . .7C 78
Percheron Cl. TW7: Isle 3K 113
Perch St. E8 . . . . .4F 67
Percival Av. NW9 . . . . .2B 44
Percival Ct. N17 . . . . .7A 34
    Percival Gdns. RM6: Chad H . . .6C 54
Percival Ho. EC1 . . . . .5B 84
    (off Bartholomew Cl.)
Percival M. SE11 . . . . . .7G 19 (6K 101)
Percival Rd. BR6: Farnb 2F 173
    EN1: Enf 4A 24
    SW14 . . . . .4J 115
    TW13: Felt 2H 129
Percival St. EC1 . . . . .3A 8 (4B 84)
Percival Way KT19: Ewe 4K 163
Percy Av. TW15: Ashf 5C 128
Percy Bilton Ct. TW5: Hest 1F 113
    (off Skinners La.)
Percy Bryant Rd. TW16: Sun . . .7G 129
Percy Bush Rd.
    UB7: W Dray 3B 92
Percy Cir. WC1 . . . . .1H 7 (3K 83)
Percy Gdns. EN3: Pond E 5E 24
    KT4: Wor Pk 1K 163
    TW7: Isle 3B 114
    UB4: Hayes 3G 75
Percy Laurie Ho. SW15 . . . . . . .4F 117
    (off Nursery Cl.)
Percy M. W1 . . . . .6C 6
Percy Pas. W1 . . . . .6C 6
Percy Rd. CR4: Mitc 7E 154
    DA7: Bex 2E 126
    E11 .7G 51
    E16 .5G 87
    IG3: Ilf 7A 54
    N12 . . . . .5F 31
    N21 .7H 23
    RM7: Mawney 3H 55
    SE20 . . . . .1K 157
    SE25 . . . . .5G 157

Percy Rd. TW2: Whitt 1F 131
    TW7: Isle 4A 114
    TW12: Hamp 7E 130
    W12 .2C 98
Percy St. W1 . . . . .6C 6 (5H 83)
Percy Ter. BR1: Broml 3F 161
Percy Way TW2: Whitt 1G 131
Percy Yd. WC1 . . . . .1H 7 (3K 83)
Peregrine Cl. NW10 . . . . .5K 61
Peregrine Ct. DA16: Well 1K 125
    SE8 . . . . .6C 104
    (off Edward St.)
    SW16 . . . . .4K 137
Peregrine Gdns. CR0: C'don . . .2A 170
Peregrine Ho. EC1 . . . . .1B 8
Peregrine Rd. N17 . . . . .7H 33
    TW16: Sun 2H 147
Peregrine Way SW19 . . . . .7E 134
Perendale Dr. TW17: Shep 1E 146
Perham Rd. W14 . . . . .5G 99
Peridot Ct. E2 . . . . .2J 9
    (off Virginia Rd.)
Peridot St. E6 . . . . .5C 88
Perifield SE21 . . . . .1C 138
Perilla Ho. E1 . . . . .1K 15
Perimeade Rd. UB6: G'frd 2C 78
Periton Rd. SE9 . . . . .4B 124
PERIVALE .1C 78
Perivale Gdns. W13 . . . . .4B 78
Perivale Grange UB6: G'frd 3A 78
Perivale La. UB6: G'frd 3A 78
Perivale Lodge UB6: G'frd 3A 78
    (off Perivale La.)
Perivale New Bus. Cen.
    UB6: G'frd 2C 78
Perivale Pk. UB6: G'frd 2B 78
Perivale Pk. Athletics Track 3J 77
Perivale Pk. Golf Course 3J 77
Perivale Wood
    Local Nature Reserve 1K 77
Periwood Cres. UB6: G'frd 1A 78
Perkin Cl. HA0: Wemb 5G 60
    TW3: Houn 4E 112
Perkins Cl. TW15: Ashf 5B 128
Perkins Ct. TW15: Ashf 5B 128
Perkin's Rents SW1 . . . . .2C 18 (3H 101)
Perkins Rd. IG2: Ilf 5H 53
Perkins Sq. SE1 . . . . . . .4D 14 (1C 102)
Perks Cl. SE3 . . . . .3G 123
Perkyn Sq. N17 . . . . .3H 49
Perley Ho. E3 . . . . .5B 86
    (off Weatherley Cl.)
Perpins Rd. SE9 . . . . .6J 125
Perran Rd. SW2 . . . . .1B 138
Perran St. NW5 . . . . .6F 65
Perrers Rd. W6 . . . . .4D 98
Perrin Apts. N1 . . . . .7J 65
    (off Caledonian Rd.)
Perrin Cl. TW15: Ashf 5B 128
    WD23: B Hea 1D 26
Perrin Ct. TW15: Ashf 5B 128
Perring Est. E3 . . . . .5C 86
    (off Gale St.)
Perrin Ho. NW6 . . . . .3J 81
Perrin Rd. HA0: Wemb 4B 60
Perrin's Ct. NW3 . . . . .4A 64
Perrin's La. NW3 . . . . .4A 64
Perrin's Wlk. NW3 . . . . .4A 64
Perronet Ho. SE1 . . . . .3B 102
    (off Princess St.)
Perrott St. SE18 . . . . .4G 107
Perry Av. W3 . . . . .6K 79
Perry Cl. IG2: Ilf 6H 53
    RM13: Rain 2K 91
    UB8: Hil 6D 74
Perry Ct. E14 . . . . .5C 104
    (off Maritime Quay)
    KT2: King T 2E 150
    (off Old London Rd.)
    N15 .6E 48

Perryfield Way NW9 . . . . .6B 44
    TW10: Ham 3B 132
Perry Gdns. N9 . . . . .3J 33
Perry Gth. UB5: N'olt 1A 76
Perry Hall Rd. BR6: St M Cry . . .6K 161
Perry Hill SE6 . . . . .3B 140
Perry How KT4: Wor Pk 1B 164
Perry Lodge E12 . . . . .1B 70
Perryman Ho. IG11: Bark 1G 89
    (off The Shaftesburys)
Perrymans Farm Rd. IG2: Ilf . . .6H 53
Perry Mead EN2: Enf 2G 23
Perrymead St. SW6 . . . . .1J 117
Perryn Ct. TW1: Twick 6A 114
Perryn Ho. W3 . . . . .7A 80
Perryn Rd. SE16 . . . . .3H 103
    W3 . . . . .1K 97
Perry Ri. SE23 . . . . .3A 140
Perry Rd. RM9: Dag 5F 91
Perry's Pl. W1 . . . . .7C 6 (6H 83)
Perry St. BR7: Chst 6H 143
    DA1: Cray 4K 127
Perry St. Gdns. BR7: Chst 6J 143
Perry St. Shaw BR7: Chst 7J 143
Perry Va. SE23 . . . . .2J 139
Persant Rd. SE6 . . . . .2G 141
Perseverance Pl. SW9 . . . . .7A 102
    TW9: Rich 4E 114
Perseverance Works E2 . . . . .1H 9
    (off Kingsland Rd.)
Pershore Cl. IG2: Ilf 5F 53
Pershore Gro. SM5: Cars 6B 154
Pershore Ho. W13 . . . . .1A 96
    (off Singapore Rd.)
Pert Cl. N10 . . . . .7A 32
Perth Av. NW9 . . . . .7K 43
    UB4: Yead 4G 76
Perth Cl. SE5 . . . . .4D 120
    SW20 . . . . .2B 152
    UB5: N'olt 5E 58
Perth Ho. N1 . . . . .7K 65
    (off Bemerton Est.)
Perth Rd. BR3: Beck 2E 158
    E10 . . . . .1A 68
    E13 . . . . .2K 87
    IG2: Ilf 6E 52
    IG11: Bark 2H 89
    N4 . . . . .1A 66
    N22 .1B 48
Perth Ter. IG2: Ilf 7G 53
Peruvian Wharf E16 . . . . .1J 105
Perwell Av. HA2: Harr 1D 58
Perystreete SE23 . . . . .2J 139
Petavel Rd. TW11: Tedd 6J 131
Peter Av. NW10 . . . . .7D 62
Peter Best Ho. E1 . . . . .6H 85
    (off Nelson St.)
Peterboat Cl. SE10 . . . . .4G 105
Peterborough Ct. EC4 . . . .1K 13 (6A 84)
Peterborough Gdns. IG1: Ilf 7C 52
Peterborough M. SW6 . . . . .2J 117
Peterborough Rd. E10 . . . . .5E 50
    HA1: Harr 1J 59
    SM5: Cars 6C 154
    SW6 . . . . .2J 117
Peterborough Vs. SW6 . . . . .1K 117
Peter Butler Ho. SE1 . . . . .7K 15
    (off Wolseley St.)
Peterchurch Ho. SE15 . . . . .6H 103
    (off Commercial Way)
Petergate SW11 . . . . .4A 118
Peter Harrison Planetarium 7F 105
Peterhead Ct. UB1: S'hall 6G 77
    (off Osborne Rd.)
Peter Heathfield Ho. E15 . . . . . .1F 87
    (off Wise Rd.)
Peter Hills Ho. SE16 . . . . .4G 103
    (off Alexis St.)
Peter Ho. SW8 . . . . .7J 101
    (off Luscombe Way)
Peter James Bus. Cen.
    UB3: Hayes 2J 93
Peter James Ent. Cen. NW10 . . .3J 79

Peter Kennedy Ct. CR0: C'don 6B 158
Peterley Bus. Cen. E2 . . . . .2H 85
Peter Lyell Cl. HA4: Ruis 2K 57
Peter May Sports Cen. 7K 35
Peter Pan Statue 4A 10 (1B 100)
Peters Cl. DA16: Well 2J 125
   HA7: Stan 6J 27
   RM8: Dag 1D 72
Peters Ct. W2 . . . . .6K 81
                        (off Porchester Rd.)
Petersfield Cl. N18 . . . . .5H 33
Petersfield Ri. SW15 . . . . .1D 134
Petersfield Rd. W3 . . . . .2J 97
Petersgate KT2: King T 6J 133
                           (off Warren Rd.)
PETERSHAM 1E 132
Petersham Cl. SM1: Sutt 5J 165
   TW10: Ham 2D 132
Petersham Dr. BR5: St P 2K 161
Petersham Gdns. BR5: St P 2K 161
Petersham Ho. SW7 . . . . .3A 16
                        (off Kendrick M.)
Petersham La. SW7 . . . . .3A 100
Petersham M. SW7 . . . . .3A 100
Petersham Pl. SW7 . . . . .3A 100
Petersham Rd.
   TW10: Rich, Ham 6D 114
Petersham Ter. CR0: Bedd 3J 167
                        (off Richmond Grn.)
Peter's Hill EC4 . . . . .2C 14 (7C 84)
Peter Shore Ct. E1 . . . . .5K 85
                        (off Beaumont Sq.)
Peter's La. EC1 . . . . .5B 8 (5B 84)
                              (not continuous)
Peter's Path SE26 . . . . .4H 139
Peterstone Rd. SE2 . . . . .2B 108
Peterstow Cl. SW19 . . . . .2G 135
Peter St. W1 . . . . .2C 12 (7H 83)
Peterwood Pk. CR0: Wadd 2K 167
Peterwood Way
   CR0: Wadd 2K 167
Petherton Ct. HA1: Harr 6K 41
                           (off Gayton Rd.)
   NW10 .1F 81
                         (off Tiverton Rd.)
Petherton Rd. N5 . . . . .5C 66
Petiver Cl. E9 . . . . .7J 67
Petley Rd. W6 . . . . .6F 99
Peto Pl. NW1 . . . . .3K 5 (4F 83)
Peto St. Nth. E16 . . . . .6H 87
Petra Way E16 . . . . .5H 87
Petrie Cl. NW2 . . . . .6G 63
Petrie Ho. SE18 . . . . .6E 106
                      (off Woolwich Comn.)
Petrie Mus. of Egyptian Archaeology
   . . . . .4C 6 (4H 83)
Petros Gdns. NW3 . . . . .6K 63
Pettacre Cl. SE28 . . . . .3G 107
Petticoat Lane Market . . .7J 9 (5E 84)
Petticoat Sq. E1 . . . . . . .7J 9 (6F 85)
Petticoat Twr. E1 . . . . .7J 9
Pettits Cl. RM1: Rom 2K 55
Pettits La. Nth. RM1: Rom 1K 55
Pettits Pl. RM10: Dag 5G 73
Pettits Rd. RM10: Dag 5G 73
Pettiward Cl. SW15 . . . . .4E 116
Pettley Gdns. RM7: Rom 5K 55
Pettman Cres. SE28 . . . . .3H 107
Pettsgrove Av. HA0: Wemb 5C 60
Pett's Hill UB5: N'olt 5F 59
Petts La. TW17: Shep 4C 146
Pett St. SE18 . . . . .4C 106
PETTS WOOD 5H 161
Petts Wood Rd.
   BR5: Pet W 5G 161
Petty France SW1 . . . .1B 18 (3G 101)
Petty Wales EC3 . . . . . . .3H 15 (7E 84)
Petworth Cl. UB5: N'olt 7D 58
Petworth Gdns. SW20 . . . . .3D 152
   UB10: Hil 1E 74
Petworth Ho. DA6: Bex 5G 127
   N12 . . . . .5H 31
Petworth St. SW11 . . . . .1C 118
Petyt Pl. SW3 . . . . .6C 100
Petyward SW3 . . . . . . .4D 16 (4C 100)
Pevensey Av. EN1: Enf 2K 23
   N11 . . . . .5C 32
Pevensey Cl. TW7: Isle 7G 95
Pevensey Cl. TW16 . . . . .3A 138
   W3 . . . . .2H 97
Pevensey Ho. E1 . . . . .5K 85
                        (off Ben Jonson Rd.)
Pevensey Rd. E7 . . . . .4H 69
   SW17 . . . . .4B 136
   TW13: Felt 1C 130
Peverel E6 . . . . .6E 88
Peverel Ho. RM10: Dag 2F 73
Peverett Cl. N11 . . . . .5A 32
Peveril Dr. TW11: Tedd 5H 131
Peveril Ho. SE1 . . . . .3D 102
                         (off Rephidim St.)
Pewsey Cl. E4 . . . . .5H 35
Peyton Pl. SE10 . . . . .7E 104
Pharamond NW2 . . . . .6F 63
Pharaoh Cl. CR4: Mitc 7D 154
Pheasant Cl. E16 . . . . .6K 87
Pheasantry Ho. SW3 . . . . .5D 16
                              (off Jubilee Pl.)
The Pheasantry Welcome Cen. . . .1K 149
Phelps La. NW7 . . . . .5B 30
Phelps Lodge N1 . . . . .1K 83
Phelp St. SE17 . . . . .6D 102
Phelps Way UB3: Harl 4H 93
Phene St. SW3 . . . . .7D 16 (6C 100)
Philadelphia Cl. SW10 . . . . .7A 100
                             (off Uverdale Rd.)
Philbeach Gdns. SW5 . . . . .5J 99
Phil Brown Pl. SW8 . . . . .3F 119
                      (off Daley Thompson Way)
Philchurch Pl. E1 . . . . .6G 85
Philia Ho. NW1 . . . . .7G 65
                                (off Farrier St.)
Philimore Cl. SE18 . . . . .5J 107
Philip Av. RM7: Rush G 1K 73
Philip Cl. RM7: Rush G 1K 73
Philip Ct. W2 . . . . .5A 4
                                (off Hall Pl.)
Philip Gdns. CR0: C'don 2B 170
Philip Ho. NW6 . . . . .1K 81
                           (off Mortimer Pl.)
Philip Jones Ct. N4 . . . . .1K 65
Philip La. N15 . . . . .4D 48
Philip Mole Ho. W9 . . . . .4J 81
                        (off Chippenham Rd.)
Philipot Path SE9 . . . . .6D 124
Philippa Gdns. SE9 . . . . .5B 124
Philip Rd. N15 . . . . .4D 48
   TW18: Staines 6A 128
Philips Cl. SM5: Cars 1E 166
Philip Sq. SW8 . . . . .2F 119
Philip St. E13 . . . . .4J 87
Philip Wlk. SE15 . . . . .3G 121
                              (not continuous)
Phillimore Ct. W8 . . . . .2J 99
                         (off Kensington High St.)
Phillimore Gdns. NW10 . . . . .1E 80
   W3 . . . . .1G 97
   W8 . . . . .2J 99
Phillimore Gdns. Cl. W8 . . . . .3J 99
Phillimore Pl. W8 . . . . .2J 99
Phillimore Ter. W8 . . . . .3J 99
                                (off Allen St.)
Phillimore Wlk. W8 . . . . .3J 99
Phillip Ho. E1 . . . . .6K 9
                           (off Heneage St.)
Phillipp St. N1 . . . . .1E 84
Phillips Cl. HA8: Edg 6B 28
Philpot La. EC3 . . . . . . .2G 15 (7E 84)
Philpot Path IG1: Ilf 3G 71
Philpots Cl. UB7: View 7A 74
Philpot Sq. SW6 . . . . .3K 117
Philpot St. E1 . . . . .6H 85
Phineas Pett Rd. SE9 . . . . .3C 124
Phipps Bri. Rd. CR4: Mitc 3B 154
   SW19 . . . . .2A 154
Phipps Hatch La. EN2: Enf 1H 23
Phipps Ho. SE7 . . . . .5K 105
                         (off Woolwich Rd.)
   W12 . . . . .7D 80
                         (off White City Est.)
Phipp's M. SW1 . . . . .2K 17
                      (off Buckingham Palace Rd.)
Phipp St. EC2 . . . . .3G 9 (4E 84)
Phoebeth Rd. SE4 . . . . .5C 122
Phoebe Wlk. E16 . . . . .6K 87
Phoenix Av. SE10 . . . . .2G 105
Phoenix Cen. 7J 167
Phoenix Cinema 4C 46
Phoenix Cl. BR4: W W'ck 2F 171
   CR4: Mitc 3B 154
   E8 . . . . .1F 85
   E17 . . . . .2B 50
   W12 . . . . .7D 80
Phoenix Ct. CR2: S Croy 5F 169
   E1 . . . . .4H 85
                         (off Buckhurst St.)
   E4 . . . . .3J 35
   E14 . . . . .4C 104
   KT3: N Mald 3B 152
   NW1 . . . . .1D 6
                          (off Purchese St.)
   SE14 .6A 104
                            (off Chipley St.)
   TW3: Houn 3E 112
   TW4: Houn 5B 112
   TW8: Bford 5E 96
   TW13: Felt 4G 129
Phoenix Dr. BR2: Kes 4B 172
Phoenix Fitness Centre 7C 80
Phoenix Hgts. E. E14 . . . . .2C 104
                                (off Byng St.)
Phoenix Hgts. W. E14 . . . . .2C 104
                         (off Mastmaker Ct.)
Phoenix Ind. Est. HA1: Harr 4K 41
Phoenix Lodge Mans. W6 . . . . . . .4F 99
                             (off Brook Grn.)
Phoenix Pk. NW2 . . . . .2C 62
Phoenix Pl. WC1 . . . . . . .3H 7 (4K 83)
Phoenix Point SE28 . . . . .1C 108
Phoenix Rd. NW1 . . . . . .1C 6 (2H 83)
   SE20 .6J 139
Phoenix St. WC2 . . . . . . .1D 12 (6H 83)
Phoenix Theatre 1D 12
                         (off Charing Cross Rd.)
Phoenix Trad. Est. UB6: G'frd 1C 78
Phoenix Trad. Pk. TW8: Bford 5D 96
Phoenix Way E16 . . . . .4H 87
                              (off Barking Rd.)
   SW18 . . . . .5A 118
   TW5: Hest 6B 94
Phoenix Wharf E1 . . . . .1H 103
                        (off Wapping High St.)
Phoenix Wharf Rd. SE1 . . . . .7K 15
Phoenix Works HA5: Hat E 1D 40
Phoenix Yd. WC1 . . . . .2H 7
Photographers' Gallery 1A 12
                            (off Ramillies St.)
Phyllis Av. KT3: N Mald 5D 152
Phyllis Hodges Ho. NW1 . . . . .1C 6
                         (off Aldenham St.)
Phyllis Ho. CR0: Wadd 4B 168
                              (off Ashley La.)
Phyppe Way E17 . . . . .5E 50
Physical Energy Statue . .5A 10 (1A 100)
Physic Pl. SW3 . . . . . . .7E 16 (6D 100)
Piano La. N16 . . . . .3D 66
Piano Works IG11: Bark 7G 71
                                (off Ripple Rd.)
Piano Yd. NW5 . . . . .5F 65
The Piazza UB8: Uxb 7A 56
   WC2 . . . . .2F 13
                              (not continuous)
Piazza Wlk. E1 . . . . . . .1K 15 (6G 85)
Picardy Ho. EN2: Enf 1H 23
Picardy Manorway DA17: Belv . . .3H 109
Picardy Rd. DA17: Belv 5G 109
Picardy St. DA17: Belv 3G 109
Piccadilly W1 . . . . .5K 11 (1F 101)
Piccadilly Arc. SW1 . . . . .4A 12
Piccadilly Circus 3C 12 (7H 83)
Piccadilly Ct. N7 . . . . .6K 65
                           (off Caledonian Rd.)
Piccadilly Pl. W1 . . . . .3B 12
Piccadilly Theatre 2B 12
                              (off Denman St.)
Pickard Cl. N14 . . . . .1C 32
Pickard Gdns. E3 . . . . .5B 86
Pickard St. EC1 . . . . .1B 8 (3B 84)
Pickering Av. E6 . . . . .2E 88
Pickering Cl. E9 . . . . .7K 67
Pickering Gdns. CR0: C'don 6F 157
   N11 . . . . .6K 31
Pickering Ho. W2 . . . . .6A 82
                           (off Hallfield Est.)
   W5 . . . . .4C 96
                             (off Windmill Rd.)
Pickering La. BR5: Farnb 1H 173
Pickering M. W2 . . . . .6K 81
Pickering Pl. SW1 . . . . .5B 12
Pickering Rd. IG11: Bark 6G 71
Pickering St. N1 . . . . .1B 84
Pickets Cl. WD23: B Hea 1C 26
Pickets St. SW12 . . . . .7F 119
Pickett Cft. HA7: Stan 1D 42
Picketts Lock La. N9 . . . . .2D 34
Picketts Lock La. Ind. Est. N9 . . . .2F 35
Picketts Ter. SE22 . . . . .5G 121
Pickford Cl. DA7: Bex 2E 126
Pickford La. DA7: Bex 2E 126
Pickford Rd. DA7: Bex 2E 126
Pickfords Wharf N1 . . . . .2C 84
   SE1 . . . . .4E 14 (1D 102)
Pickhurst Grn. BR2: Hayes 7H 159
Pickhurst La. BR2: Hayes 5G 159
   BR4: W W'ck 5G 159
Pickhurst Mead BR2: Hayes 7H 159
Pickhurst Pk. BR2: Broml 5G 159
Pickhurst Ri. BR4: W W'ck 7E 158
Pickle M. SW9 . . . . .7A 102
Pickle Sq. SE1 . . . . .3E 102
                            (off The Tannery)
Pickwick Cl. TW4: Houn 5C 112
Pickwick Ct. SE9 . . . . .1C 142
Pickwick Ho. SE16 . . . . .2G 103
                           (off George Row)
   W11 . . . . .1F 99
                              (off St Ann's Rd.)
Pickwick M. N18 . . . . .4K 33
Pickwick Pl. HA1: Harr 7J 41
Pickwick Rd. SE21 . . . . .7D 120
Pickwick St. SE1 . . . . . .7C 14 (2C 102)
Pickwick Way BR7: Chst 6G 143
Pickworth Cl. SW8 . . . . .7J 101
Picton Pl. KT6: Surb 1G 163
   W1 . . . . .1H 11 (6E 82)
Picton St. SE5 . . . . .7D 102
Picture Ho. SW16 . . . . .2J 137
Picturehouse Central 2C 12
                         (off Shaftesbury Av.)
Picture House Mews E17 . . . . .4F 51
Pied Bull Cl. WC1 . . . . .6E 6
                                (off Bury Pl.)
Pied Bull Yd. N1 . . . . .1B 84
                           (off Theberton St.)
   WC1 . . . . .6E 6
Piedmont Rd. SE18 . . . . .5H 107
                              (not continuous)
PIELD HEATH 4B 74
Pield Heath Av. UB8: Hil 4C 74
Pield Heath Rd.
   UB8: Cowl, Hil 4A 74
Pierce Campion Cl. E17 . . . . .3B 50
Pier Head E1 . . . . .1H 103
                              (not continuous)
Pierhead Wharf E1 . . . . .1H 103
                        (off Wapping High St.)
Pier Ho. SW3 . . . . .7D 16 (6C 100)
Pieris Ho. TW13: Felt 2J 129
                                (off High St.)
Piermont Grn. SE22 . . . . .5H 121
Piermont Pl. BR1: Broml 2C 160
Piermont Rd. SE22 . . . . .5H 121

Pier Pde. *E16* 1E **106**
       (off Pier Rd.)
Pierpoint Bldg. E14 . . . . .2B **104**
Pierrepoint Rd. W3 . . . . .7H **79**
Pierrepont Arc. *N1* 2B **84**
       (off Islington High St.)
Pierrepont Row *N1* 2B **84**
       (off Camden Pas.)
Pier Rd. E16 . . . . .1E **106**
  TW14: Felt 5K **111**
Pier St. E14 . . . . .4E **104**
       (not continuous)
Pier Ter. SW18 . . . . .4K **117**
Pier Wlk. SE10 . . . . .2G **105**
Pier Way SE28 . . . . .2G **107**
Pietra Lara Bldg. *EC1* 3C **8**
       (off Pear Tree St.)
Pigeon La. TW12: Hamp 4E **130**
Piggott Ho. *E2* 2K **85**
       (off Sewardstone Rd.)
Pigott St. E14 . . . . .6C **86**
Pike Cl. BR1: Broml 5K **141**
  UB10: Uxb 1B **74**
Pike Cres. TW15: Ashf 4B **128**
Pikemans Ct. *SW5* 4J **99**
       (off W. Cromwell Rd.)
Pike Rd. NW7 . . . . .4E **28**
Pike's End HA5: Eastc 4K **39**
Pikestone Cl. UB4: Yead 4C **76**
Pikethorne SE23 . . . . .2K **139**
Pilgrimage St.
  SE1 . . . . .7E **14** (2D **102**)
Pilgrim Cl. SM4: Mord 7K **153**
Pilgrim Hill SE27 . . . . .4C **138**
Pilgrim Ho. *SE1* 3D **102**
       (off Tabard St.)
  SE16 . . . . .2J **103**
       (off Brunel Rd.)
Pilgrims Cloisters SE5 . . . . .7E **102**
       (off Sedgmoor Pl.)
Pilgrims Cl. N13 . . . . .4E **32**
  UB5: N'olt 5G **59**
Pilgrims Cnr. *NW6* 2J **81**
       (off Chichester Rd.)
Pilgrims Ct. EN1: Enf 2J **23**
Pilgrim's La. NW3 . . . . .4B **64**
Pilgrims M. E14 . . . . .7G **87**
Pilgrim's Pl. NW3 . . . . .4B **64**
Pilgrims Ri. EN4: E Barn 5H **21**
Pilgrim St. EC4 . . . . .1A **14** (6B **84**)
Pilgrim's Way HA9: Wemb 1H **61**
Pilgrims Way CR2: S Croy 6F **169**
  E6 . . . . .1C **88**
  N19 . . . . .1H **65**
Pilkington Rd. BR6: Farnb 3G **173**
  SE15 .2H **121**
Pill Box Studios *E2* 4H **85**
       (off Coventry Rd.)
Pillford Ho. *SE11* 3G **19**
       (off Old Paradise St.)
Pillions La. UB4: Hayes 4F **75**
Pilot Cl. SE8 . . . . .6B **104**
Pilot Ind. Cen. NW10 . . . . .4K **79**
Pilot Wlk. SE10 . . . . .2H **105**
Pilsdon Cl. SW19 . . . . .1F **135**
The Pilton Est. CR0: C'don 2B **168**
Pilton Gdns. SM4: Mord 6K **153**
Pilton Pl. SE17 . . . . .5C **102**
Pimento Ct. W5 . . . . .3D **96**
PIMLICO 6B **18** (5G **101**)
Pimlico Ho. *SW1* 5J **17**
       (off Ebury Bri. Rd.)
Pimlico Rd. SW1 . . . . .5G **17** (5E **100**)
Pimlico Sq. SW1 . . . . .5G **17** (5E **100**)
Pimlico Wlk. N1 . . . . .1G **9**
Pimp Hall Nature Reserve 2A **36**
Pinchbeck Rd. BR6: Chels 6K **173**
Pinchin & Johnsons Yd. *E1* 7G **85**
       (off Pinchin St.)
Pinchin St. E1 . . . . .7G **85**
Pincombe Ho. *SE17* 5D **102**
       (off Orb St.)
Pincott Pl. SE4 . . . . .3K **121**

Pincott Rd. DA6: Bex 5G **127**
  SW19 .7A **136**
Pindar St. EC2 . . . . .5G **9** (5E **84**)
Pindock M. W9 . . . . .4K **81**
Pindoria M. E1 . . . . .4J **9**
Pineapple Ct. SW1 . . . . .1B **18**
Pine Av. BR4: W W'ck 1D **170**
  E15 . . . . .5F **69**
Pine Cl. E10 . . . . .2D **68**
  HA7: Stan 4G **27**
  N14 . . . . .7B **22**
  N19 . . . . .2G **65**
  SE20 . . . . .1J **157**
Pine Coombe CR0: C'don 4K **169**
Pine Ct. N21 . . . . .5E **22**
  UB5: N'olt 4C **76**
Pinecrest Gdns. BR6: Farnb 4F **173**
Pinecroft Ct. DA16: Well 7A **108**
Pinecroft Cres. EN5: Barn 4B **20**
Pinedene SE15 . . . . .1H **121**
Pinefield Cl. E14 . . . . .7C **86**
Pine Gdns. HA4: Ruis 1K **57**
  KT5: Surb 6G **151**
Pine Glade BR6: Farnb 4D **172**
Pine Gro. N4 . . . . .2J **65**
  N20 . . . . .1C **30**
  SW19 .5H **135**
Pine Ho. *E3* 1A **86**
       (off Barge La.)
  SE16 .2J **103**
       (off Ainsty Est.)
  W10 . . . . .4G **81**
       (off Droop St.)
Pinehurst Ct. *W11* 6H **81**
       (off Colville Gdns.)
Pinehurst Wlk. BR6: Orp 1H **173**
Pinelands Cl. SE3 . . . . .7H **105**
Pinemartin Cl. NW2 . . . . .3E **62**
Pine M. NW10 . . . . .2F **81**
       (off Clifford Gdns.)
Pine Needle La. HA6: Nwood 1H **39**
Pine Pl. UB4: Hayes 4H **75**
Pine Ridge SM5: Cars 7E **166**
Pineridge Ct. EN5: Barn 4A **20**
Pine Rd. N11 . . . . .2K **31**
  NW2 . . . . .4E **62**
The Pines IG8: Wfd G 3C **36**
  KT9: Chess 3E **162**
  N14 . . . . .5B **22**
  SE19 . . . . .6B **138**
  TW16: Sun 3J **147**
Pines Rd. BR1: Broml 2C **160**
Pine St. EC1 . . . . .3K **7** (4A **84**)
Pine Tree Cl. TW2: Whitt 7F **113**
  TW5: Cran 1K **111**
Pine Tree Lodge BR2: Broml 4H **159**
Pine Tree Way SE13 . . . . .3D **122**
Pineview Ct. E4 . . . . .1K **35**
Pine Wlk. KT5: Surb 6G **151**
Pine Wood TW16: Sun 1J **147**
Pinewood Av. DA15: Sidc 1J **143**
  HA5: Hat E 6A **26**
  UB8: Hill 6B **74**
Pinewood Cl. BR6: Orp 1H **173**
  CR0: C'don 3A **170**
  HA5: Hat E 6A **26**
Pinewood Ct. EN2: Enf 3G **23**
  SW4 . . . . .6H **119**
Pinewood Dr. BR6: Orp 5J **173**
Pinewood Gdns. TW11: Tedd 5B **132**
Pinewood Gro. W5 . . . . .6C **78**
Pinewood Lodge WD23: B Hea 1C **26**
Pinewood Pl. DA2: Wilm 2K **145**
  KT19: Ewe 4K **163**
Pinewood Rd. BR2: Broml 4J **159**
  SE2 . . . . .6D **108**
  TW13: Felt 3K **129**
Pinfold Rd. SW16 . . . . .4J **137**
Pinglestone Cl. UB7: Harm 7A **92**
Pinkcoat Cl. TW13: Felt 3K **129**
Pinkerton Pl. SW16 . . . . .4H **137**
Pinkham Mans. W4 . . . . .5G **97**

Pinkham Way N11 . . . . .7K **31**
Pinkwell Av. UB3: Harl 4F **93**
Pinkwell La. UB3: Harl 4E **92**
Pinley Gdns. RM9: Dag 1B **90**
Pinnace Ho. E14 . . . . .3E **104**
       (off Manchester Rd.)
The Pinnacle 1G **15**
The Pinnacle RM6: Chad H 6E **54**
       (off High Rd.)
Pinnacle Apts. *CR0: C'don* 1C **168**
       (off Saffron Central Sq.)
Pinnacle Cl. N10 . . . . .3F **47**
Pinnacle Hill DA7: Bex 4H **127**
Pinnacle Hill Nth. DA7: Bex 4H **127**
Pinnacle Ho. *EN1: Enf* 3K **23**
       (off Colman Pde.)
  NW9 . . . . .2A **44**
       (off Heritage Av.)
  SW18 .4A **118**
Pinnacle Pl. HA7: Stan 4G **27**
Pinnacle Way *E14* 6A **86**
       (off Commercial Rd.)
Pinnata Cl. EN2: Enf 1H **23**
Pinnell Rd. SE9 . . . . .4B **124**
PINNER 4C **40**
Pinner Cl. HA5: Pinn 4E **40**
  NW8 . . . . .3A **4**
PINNER GREEN 2A **40**
Pinner Grn. HA5: Pinn 2A **40**
Pinner Gro. HA5: Pinn 4C **40**
Pinner Hill HA5: Pinn 1K **39**
Pinner Hill Farm HA5: Pinn 1K **39**
Pinner Hill Golf Course 1A **40**
Pinner Hill Rd. HA5: Pinn 1K **39**
Pinner Pk. .1E **40**
Pinner Pk. HA5: Pinn 2E **40**
Pinner Pk. Av. HA2: Harr 3F **41**
Pinner Pk. Gdns. HA2: Harr 2G **41**
Pinner Rd. HA1: Harr 4E **40**
  HA2: Harr 4E **40**
  HA5: Pinn 4D **40**
  HA6: Nwood, Pinn 1H **39**
Pinners Cl. SM5: Cars 2C **166**
Pinner Vw. HA1: Harr 4G **41**
  HA2: Harr 3G **41**
PINNERWOOD PARK 1A **40**
Pinn Way HA4: Ruis 7F **39**
Pintail Cl. E6 . . . . .5C **88**
Pintail Ct. *SE8* 6B **104**
       (off Pilot Cl.)
Pintail Rd. IG8: Wfd G 7E **36**
Pintail Way UB4: Yead 5B **76**
Pinter Ho. *SW9* 2J **119**
       (off Grantham Rd.)
Pintle Pl. E3 . . . . .3E **86**
Pinto Twr. SW8 . . . . .7J **101**
Pinto Way SE3 . . . . .4K **123**
The Pioneer Cen. SE15 . . . . .1J **121**
Pioneer Cl. E14 . . . . .5D **86**
Pioneer Ct. *E16* 5J **87**
       (off Hammersley Rd.)
Pioneer Ho. *WC1* 1G **7**
       (off Britannia St.)
Pioneer Pl. CR0: Sels 7C **170**
Pioneer Point IG1: Ilf 3F **71**
Pioneers Ind. Pk. CR0: Bedd 1J **167**
Pioneer St. SE15 . . . . .1G **121**
Pioneer Way W12 . . . . .6D **80**
The Piper Bldg. SW6 . . . . .3K **117**
Piper Cl. N7 . . . . .6K **65**
Piper Rd. KT1: King T 3G **151**
Piper's Gdns. CR0: C'don 7A **158**
Pipers Grn. NW9 . . . . .5J **43**
Pipers Grn. La. HA8: Edg 3K **27**
       (not continuous)
Pipers Ho. *SE10* 5F **105**
       (off Collington St.)
Piper Way IG1: Ilf 1H **71**
Pipewell Rd. SM5: Cars 6C **154**
Pipit Dr. SW15 . . . . .6E **116**
Pippenhall SE9 . . . . .6F **125**
Pippin Cl. CR0: C'don 1B **170**
  NW2 . . . . .3C **62**
  TW13: Hanw 3D **130**

Pippin Ct. *SW8* 7G **19**
       (off Vauxhall Gro.)
Pippin Ho. *W10* 7F **81**
       (off Freston Rd.)
Pippin Mans. *E20* 5E **68**
       (off Mirabelle Gdns.)
Pippins Cl. UB7: W Dray 3A **92**
Pippins Ct. TW15: Ashf 6D **128**
Pique M. *E1* 7K **85**
       (off Glasshouse Flds.)
Piquet Rd. SE20 . . . . .2J **157**
Pirbright Cres. CR0: New Ad 6E **170**
Pirbright Rd. SW18 . . . . .1H **135**
Pirie Cl. SE5 . . . . .3D **120**
Pirie St. E16 . . . . .1K **105**
Pirin Cl. E4 .4H **35**
Pisces Ct. HA8: Edg 7B **28**
Pissaro Ho. *N1* 7A **66**
       (off Augustas La.)
Pitcairn Cl. RM7: Mawney 4G **55**
Pitcairn Ho. E9 . . . . .7J **67**
Pitcairn Rd. CR4: Mitc 7D **136**
Pitcairn's Path HA2: Harr 3G **59**
Pitcher La. TW15: Ashf 4B **128**
Pitchford St. E15 . . . . .7F **69**
Pitfield Cres. SE28 . . . . .1A **108**
Pitfield Est. N1 . . . . .1G **9** (3E **84**)
Pitfield St. N1 . . . . .1G **9** (3E **84**)
Pitfield Way EN3: Enf H 1D **24**
  NW10 . . . . .6J **61**
Pitfold Cl. SE12 . . . . .6K **123**
Pitfold Rd. SE12 . . . . .6J **123**
Pitlake CR0: C'don 2B **168**
Pitlochry Ho. SE27 . . . . .2B **138**
       (off Elmcourt Rd.)
Pitman Bldg. *SE16* 7K **15**
       (off Old Jamaica Rd.)
Pitman Ho. SE8 . . . . .1C **122**
Pitman St. SE5 . . . . .7C **102**
Pitmaston Ho. *SE13* 2E **122**
       (off Lewisham Rd.)
Pitmaston Rd. SE13 . . . . .2E **122**
Pitsea Pl. E1 . . . . .6K **85**
Pitsea St. E1 . . . . .6K **85**
Pitshanger La. W5 . . . . .4B **78**
Pitshanger Manor House & Gallery
  . . . . .1D **96**
Pitt Cres. SW19 . . . . .4K **135**
Pittman Gdns. IG1: Ilf 5G **71**
Pitt Rd. BR6: Farnb 4G **173**
  CR0: C'don 5C **156**
  CR7: Thor H 5C **156**
Pitt's Head M. W1 . . . . .5H **11** (1E **100**)
Pittsmead Av. BR2: Hayes 7J **159**
Pitt St. W8 .2J **99**
Pittville Gdns. SE25 . . . . .3G **157**
Pitwell M. E8 . . . . .6G **67**
Pixfield Ct. *BR2: Broml* 2H **159**
       (off Beckenham La.)
Pixley St. E14 . . . . .6B **86**
Pixton Way CR0: Sels 7A **170**
The Place 3H **83**
The Place SE1 . . . . .5F **15** (1D **102**)
Place Farm Av. BR6: Orp 1H **173**
Plaisterers Highwalk *EC2* 6C **8**
       (off London Wall)
PLAISTOW
  BR1 . . . . .7J **141**
  E13 . . . . .2J **87**
Plaistow Gro. BR1: Broml 7K **141**
  E15 . . . . .1H **87**
Plaistow La. BR1: Broml 7J **141**
Plaistow Pk. Rd. E13 . . . . .2K **87**
       (not continuous)
Plaistow Rd. E13 . . . . .1H **87**
  E15 . . . . .1H **87**
Plaistow Wharf E16 . . . . .2J **105**
Plamer Cl. NW9 . . . . .2A **44**
Plane Ho. BR2: Broml 2G **159**
Plane St. SE26 . . . . .3H **139**
Planetree Ct. *W6* 4F **99**
       (off Brook Grn.)
Plane Tree Cres. TW13: Felt 3K **129**

Plane Tree Ho.—Ponton Rd.

Plane Tree Ho. *SE8* 6A 104
(off Etta St.)
W8 2H 99
(off Duchess of Bedford's Wlk.)
Plane Tree Wlk. N2 3C 46
SE19 6E 138
Plantagenet Cl. KT4: Wor Pk 4K 163
Plantagenet Gdns. RM6: Chad H 7D 54
Plantagenet Ho. *SE18* 3D 106
(off Leda Rd.)
Plantagenet Pl. RM6: Chad H 7D 54
Plantagenet Rd. EN5: New Bar 4F 21
Plantain Gdns. *E11* 3F 69
(off Hollydown Way)
Plantain Pl. SE1 6E 14 (2D 102)
The Plantation SE3 2J 123
Plantation Cl. SW4 5J 119
Plantation La. EC3 2G 15
Plantation Pl. EC3 2G 15
Plantation Wharf SW11 3A 118
Plants & People Exhibition 7F 97
Plasel Ct. *E13* 1K 87
(off Pawsey Cl.)
PLASHET 6C 70
Plashet Gro. E6 1A 88
Plashet Rd. E13 1J 87
Plassy Rd. SE6 7D 122
Plate Ho. *E14* 5D 104
(off Burrells Wharf Sq.)
Platform Theatre 1J 83
Platina St. EC2 3F 9
Platinum Ct. *E1* 4J 85
(off Cephas Av.)
RM7: Mawney 3H 55
Platinum M. N15 5F 49
Plato Rd. SW2 4J 119
The Platt SW15 3F 117
Platt Halls NW9 2B 44
Platt's Eyot TW12: Hamp 2E 148
Platt's La. NW3 4J 63
Platts Rd. EN3: Enf H 1D 24
Platt St. NW1 2H 83
Plawsfield Rd. BR3: Beck 1K 157
Plaxdale Ho. *SE17* 4E 102
(off Congreve St.)
Plaxtol Cl. BR1: Broml 1A 160
Plaxtol Rd. DA8: Erith 7G 109
Plaxton Ct. E11 3H 69
Playfair Ho. *E14* 6C 86
(off Saracen St.)
Playfair Mans. *W14* 6G 99
(off Queen's Club Gdns.)
Playfair St. W6 5E 98
Playfield Av. RM5: Col R 1J 55
Playfield Cres. SE22 5F 121
Playfield Rd. HA8: Edg 2J 43
Playford Rd. N4 2K 65
(not continuous)
Playgreen Way SE6 3C 140
Playground Cl. BR3: Beck 2K 157
Playground Gdns. *E2* 2J 9
(off Rochelle St.)
Playhouse Ct. *SE1* 6C 14
(off Southwark Bri. Rd.)
Playhouse Theatre 4F 13
(off Northumberland Av.)
Playhouse Yd. EC4 1A 14 (6B 84)
Plaza Bus. Cen. EN3: Brim 2G 25
Plaza Gdns. SW15 5G 117
Plaza Hgts. E10 3E 68
Plaza Pde. *HA0: Wemb* 6E 60
(off Ealing Rd.)
NW6 2K 81
Plaza Wlk. NW9 3J 43
The Pleasance SW15 4D 116
Pleasance Rd. SW15 5D 116
Pleasance Theatre 6J 65
(off Carpenters M.)
Pleasant Gro. CR0: C'don 3B 170
Pleasant Pl. N1 7B 66
Pleasant Row NW1 1F 83
Pleasant Vw. Pl. BR6: Farnb 5F 173
Pleasant Way HA0: Wemb 2C 78
Pleasaunce Mans. *SE10* 5J 105
(off Halstow Rd.)
Plender Ct. *NW1* 1G 83
(off College Pl.)
Plender St. NW1 1G 83
Pleshey Rd. N7 4H 65
Plesman Way SM6: W'gton 7J 167
Plessey Bldg. *E14* 6C 86
(off Dod St.)
Plevna Cres. N15 6E 48
Plevna Rd. N9 3B 34
TW12: Hamp 1F 149
Plevna St. E14 3E 104
Pleydell Av. SE19 7F 139
W6 4B 98
Pleydell Ct. *EC4* 1K 13
(off Pleydell St.)
Pleydell Est. EC1 2D 8
Pleydell Gdns. *SE19* 6F 139
(off Anerley Hill)
Pleydell Ho. *EC4* 1K 13
(off Pleydell St.)
Pleydell St. EC4 1K 13
Plimley Pl. *W12* 2F 99
(off Shepherd's Bush Pl.)
Plimsoll Cl. E14 6D 86
Plimsoll Rd. N4 3A 66
Plough Cl. NW10 3D 80
Plough Ct. EC3 2F 15 (7D 84)
RM13: Rain 2K 91
(off Broadis Way)
Plough Farm Cl. HA4: Ruis 6F 39
Plough La. CR8: Purl 7J 167
SE22 6F 121
SM6: Bedd 4J 167
SW17 5K 135
SW19 5K 135
TW11: Tedd 5A 132
Plough La. Cl. SM6: Bedd 5J 167
Ploughmans Cl. NW1 1H 83
Ploughmans End TW7: Isle 5H 113
Plough M. SW11 4B 118
Plough Pl. EC4 7K 7 (6A 84)
Plough Rd. KT19: Ewe 7K 163
SW11 3B 118
Plough St. E1 7K 9
Plough Ter. SW11 4B 118
Plough Way SE16 4K 103
Plough Yd. EC2 4H 9 (4E 84)
Plover Ho. *SW9* 7A 102
(off Brixton Rd.)
Plover Way SE16 3A 104
UB4: Yead 6B 76
Plowden Bldgs. EC4 2J 13
Plowman Cl. N18 5J 33
Plowman Way RM8: Dag 1C 72
Plumber's Row E1 5G 85
Plumbridge St. SE10 1E 122
Plum Cl. TW13: Felt 1J 129
Plume Ho. *SE10* 6D 104
(off Creek Rd.)
Plum Gth. TW8: Bford 4D 96
Plum La. RM13: Rain 2K 91
SE18 7F 107
Plummer La. CR4: Mitc 2D 154
Plummer Rd. SW4 7H 119
Plumpton Cl. UB5: N'olt 6E 58
Plumpton Way SM5: Cars 3C 166
PLUMSTEAD 4J 107
PLUMSTEAD COMMON 6F 107
Plumstead Comn. Rd. SE18 6F 107
Plumstead High St. SE18 4H 107
Plumstead Rd. SE18 4F 107
(not continuous)
Plumtree Cl. RM10: Dag 6H 73
SM6: W'gton 7H 167
Plumtree Ct. EC4 7A 8 (6B 84)
Plum Tree M. SW16 6J 137
Plymen Ho. KT8: W Mole 5E 148
Plymouth Ct. *KT5: Surb* 4E 150
(off Cranes Pk. Av.)
Plymouth Ho. *IG11: Bark* 7A 72
(off Margaret Bondfield Av.)
Plymouth Ho. *SE10* 1D 122
(off Devonshire Dr.)
Plymouth Rd. BR1: Broml 1K 159
E16 5J 87
Plymouth Ter. *NW2* 6E 62
(off Sidmouth Rd.)
Plymouth Wharf E14 4F 105
Plympton Av. NW6 7H 63
Plympton Cl. DA17: Belv 3E 108
Plympton Pl. NW8 4C 4 (4C 82)
Plympton Rd. NW6 7H 63
Plympton St. NW8 4C 4 (4C 82)
Plymstock Rd. DA16: Well 7C 108
Pocklington Cl. NW9 2A 44
W12 3C 98
(off Ashchurch Pk. Vs.)
Pocklington Ct. SW15 1C 134
Pocklington Lodge W12 3C 98
Pocock Av. UB7: W Dray 3B 92
Pocock St. SE1 6A 14 (2B 102)
Podmore Rd. SW18 4A 118
Poet Ct. *E1* 5K 85
(off Shandy St.)
Poets Ct. SE25 4G 157
W3 1J 97
Poet's Rd. N5 5D 66
Poets Way HA1: Harr 4J 41
The Point *E17* 4C 50
(off Tower M.)
HA4: Ruis 4J 57
W2 6A 4
Pointalls Cl. N3 2A 46
Point Cl. SE10 1E 122
Pointer Cl. SE28 6D 90
Pointers Cl. E14 5D 104
Pointers Cotts. TW10: Ham 2C 132
Point Hill SE10 7E 104
Point Pl. HA9: Wemb 7H 61
Point Pleasant SW18 4J 117
Point Ter. *E7* 5K 69
(off Claremont Rd.)
Point W. SW7 4K 99
Point Wharf TW8: Bford 7E 96
Point Wharf La. TW8: Bford 7D 96
Poland St. W1 1B 12 (6G 83)
Polar Pk. UB7: Harm 7B 92
Poldo Ho. *SE10* 4G 105
(off Cable Wlk.)
Polebrook Rd. SE3 3A 124
Pole Cat All. BR2: Hayes 2H 171
Polecroft La. SE6 2B 140
The Polehamptons
TW12: Hamp 7G 131
Pole Hill Rd. E4 7K 25
UB4: Hayes 4D 74
UB10: Hil 4D 74
Polesden Gdns. SW20 2D 152
Polesworth Ho. *W2* 5J 81
(off Alfred Rd.)
Polesworth Rd. RM9: Dag 7D 72
Police Sta. La. WD23: Bush 1A 26
POLISH WAR MEMORIAL 7A 58
Polka Theatre for Children 6K 135
Pollard Cl. E16 7J 87
N7 4K 65
Pollard Ho. KT4: Wor Pk 4E 164
N1 1G 7
(off Northdown St.)
SE16 3F 103
(off Spa Rd.)
Pollard Rd. N20 2H 31
SM4: Mord 5B 154
Pollard Row E2 3G 85
Pollards Cres. SW16 3J 155
Pollards Hill E. SW16 3K 155
Pollards Hill Nth. SW16 3J 155
Pollards Hill Sth. SW16 3J 155
Pollards Hill W. SW16 3K 155
Pollard St. E2 3G 85
Pollards Wood Rd. SW16 3J 155
Pollard Wlk. DA14: Sidc 6C 144
Pollen St. W1 1A 12 (6G 83)
Pollitt Dr. NW8 3B 4 (4B 82)
Pollock Ho. *W10* 4G 81
(off Kensal Rd.)
Pollock's Toy Mus. 5B 6 (5G 83)
Polo M. BR7: Chst 5H 143
Polperro Cl. BR6: St M Cry 6K 161
Polperro Ho. *W2* 5J 81
(off Westbourne Pk. Rd.)
Polperro M. SE11 3K 19 (4B 102)
Polsted Rd. SE6 7B 122
Polthorne Est. *SE18* 4H 107
(off Polthorne Gro.)
Polthorne Gro. SE18 4G 107
Polworth Rd. SW16 5J 137
Polychrome Ct. *SE1* 7A 14
(off Waterloo Rd.)
Polydamas Cl. E3 2C 86
The Polygon *NW8* 1B 82
(off Avenue Rd.)
SW4 4G 119
Polygon Bus. Cen. SL3: Poyle 5A 174
Polygon Rd. NW1 1C 6 (2H 83)
(not continuous)
Polytechnic St. SE18 4E 106
Pomell Way E1 7K 9 (6F 85)
Pomeroy Cl. TW1: Twick 4B 114
Pomeroy Ho. *E2* 2K 85
(off St James's Av.)
W11 6G 81
(off Lancaster Rd.)
Pomeroy St. SE14 7J 103
Pomfret Pl. *E14* 7E 86
(off Bullivant St.)
Pomfret Rd. SE5 3B 120
Pomoja La. N19 2J 65
Pomona Ho. *SE8* 4A 104
(off Evelyn St.)
Pompadour Way IG11: Bark 2B 90
Pond Cl. N12 6H 31
SE3 2J 123
Pond Cott. La. BR4: W W'ck 1C 170
Pond Cotts. SE21 1E 138
PONDERS END 5D 24
Ponders End Ind. Est.
EN3: Pond E 5F 25
Ponder St. N7 7K 65
Pond Farm Est. E5 3J 67
Pondfield Ho. SE27 5C 138
Pondfield Rd. BR2: Hayes 1G 171
BR6: Farnb 3F 173
RM10: Dag 5H 73
Pond Grn. HA4: Ruis 2G 57
Pond Hill Gdns. SM3: Cheam 6G 165
Pond Ho. HA7: Stan 6G 27
SW3 4C 16 (4C 100)
Pond Lees Cl. RM10: Dag 7K 73
Pond Mead SE21 6D 120
Pond Path BR7: Chst 6F 143
Pond Pl. SW3 4C 16 (4C 100)
Pond Rd. E15 2G 87
SE3 2H 123
Pondside Av. KT4: Wor Pk 1E 164
Pondside Cl. UB3: Harl 6F 93
Pond Sq. N6 1E 64
Pond St. NW3 5C 64
Pond Way TW11: Tedd 6C 132
Pondwood Ri. BR6: Orp 7J 161
Ponler St. E1 6H 85
Ponsard Rd. NW10 3D 80
Ponsford St. E9 6J 67
Ponsonby Ho. *E2* 2J 85
(off Bishop's Way)
Ponsonby Pl. SW1 5D 18 (5H 101)
Ponsonby Rd. SW15 7D 116
Ponsonby Ter. SW1 5D 18 (5H 101)
Ponsonby Vs. *E2* 2J 85
(off Lark Row)
Pontefract Ct. *UB5: N'olt* 5F 59
(off Newmarket Av.)
Pontefract Rd. BR1: Broml 5H 141
Pontes Av. TW3: Houn 4D 112
Pontifex Apts. *SE1* 4E 14
(off Stoney St.)
Ponton Rd. SW11 7C 18 (6H 101)

Pontoon Reach E16 . . . . .1B **106**
Pont St. SW1 . . . . .2E **16** (3D **100**)
Pont St. M. SW1 . . . . .2E **16** (3D **100**)
Pontypool PI. SE1 . . . . . .6A **14** (2B **102**)
Pooja Ct. NW1 . . . . .7G **65**
(off Agar Gro.)
Pool Cl. BR3: Beck 5C **140**
KT8: W Mole 5D **148**
Pool Ct. SE6 . . . . .2C **140**
Poole Cl. HA4: Ruis 2G **57**
Poole Ct. N1 . . . . .7E **66**
(off St Peter's Way)
TW4: Houn 2C **112**
Poole Ct. Rd. TW4: Houn 2C **112**
Poole Ho. SE11 . . . . .2H **19**
Poole La. TW19: Stanw 7B **110**
POOL END 5C **146**
Poole Rd. E9 . . . . .6K **67**
KT19: Ewe 6K **163**
Pooles Bldgs. WC1 . . . . .4J **7**
Pooles Cotts. TW10: Ham 2D **132**
Pooles La. RM9: Dag 2E **90**
SW10 . . . . .7A **100**
Pooles Pk. N4 . . . . .2A **66**
Poole St. N1 . . . . .1D **84**
Poole Way UB4: Hayes 3G **75**
Pooley Dr. SW14 . . . . .3J **115**
Pooley Ho. E1 . . . . .3K **85**
E18 . . . . .1J **51**
Pool Ho. NW8 . . . . .5C **4**
(off Penfold St.)
Poolmans St. SE16 . . . . .2K **103**
Pool Rd. HA1: Harr 7H **41**
KT8: W Mole 5D **148**
Poolsford Rd. NW9 . . . . .4A **44**
Poolside Manor 1H **45**
Pools on the Pk. 4D **114**
Pool St. E20 . . . . .7E **68**
Poonah St. E1 . . . . .6J **85**
Pope Cl. SW19 . . . . .6B **136**
TW14: Felt 1H **129**
Pope Ho. SE5 . . . . .7D **102**
(off Elmington Est.)
SE16 . . . . .4H **103**
(off Manor Est.)
Pope Rd. BR2: Broml 5B **160**
Popes Av. TW2: Twick 2J **131**
Popes Ct. TW2: Twick 2J **131**
Popes Dr. N3 . . . . .1J **45**
Popes Gro. CR0: C'don 3B **170**
TW1: Twick 2K **131**
TW2: Twick 2K **131**
Pope's Head All. EC3 . . . .1F **15** (6D **84**)
Popes La. W5 . . . . .3D **96**
Pope's Rd. SW9 . . . . .3A **120**
Pope St. SE1 . . . . .7H **15** (2E **102**)
Popham Cl. TW13: Hanw 3D **130**
Popham Gdns. TW9: Rich 3G **115**
Popham Rd. N1 . . . . .1C **84**
Popham St. N1 . . . . .1B **84**
(not continuous)
Pop in Commercial Cen.
HA9: Wemb 5H **61**
Popinjays Row SM3: Cheam 5F **165**
(off Netley Cl.)
POPLAR 7D **86**
Poplar Av. BR6: Farnb 2F **173**
CR4: Mitc 1D **154**
UB2: S'hall 3F **95**
UB7: Yiew 7B **74**
Poplar Baths Leisure Cen. 7D **86**
Poplar Bath St. E14 . . . . .6D **86**
Poplar Bus. Pk. E14 . . . . .7E **86**
Poplar Cl. E9 . . . . .5B **68**
HA5: Pinn 1B **40**
SL3: Poyle 4A **174**
Poplar Ct. SW19 . . . . .5J **135**
TW1: Twick 6C **114**
UB5: N'olt 2A **76**
Poplar Cres. KT19: Ewe 6J **163**
Poplar Farm Cl. KT19: Ewe 6J **163**
Poplar Gdns. KT3: N Mald 2K **151**

Poplar Gro. HA9: Wemb 3J **61**
KT3: N Mald 2K **151**
N11 .6K **31**
W6 . . . . .2E **98**
Poplar High St. E14 . . . . .7D **86**
Poplar Ho. SE4 . . . . .4B **122**
(off Wickham Rd.)
SE16 . . . . .2K **103**
(off Woodland Cres.)
Poplar M. W12 . . . . .1E **98**
Poplar Mt. DA17: Belv 4H **109**
Poplar Pl. SE28 . . . . .7C **90**
UB3: Hayes 7J **75**
W2 . . . . .7K **81**
Poplar Rd. KT10: Surb 3B **162**
SE24 . . . . .4C **120**
SM3: Sutt 1H **165**
SW19 . . . . .2J **153**
TW15: Ashf 5E **128**
Poplar Rd. Sth. SW19 . . . . .3J **153**
The Poplars N14 . . . . .5A **22**
Poplars Av. NW2 . . . . .6E **62**
Poplars Cl. HA4: Ruis 1G **57**
Poplars Rd. E17 . . . . .6D **50**
Poplar St. RM7: Rom 4J **55**
Poplar Vw. HA9: Wemb 2D **60**
Poplar Wlk. CR0: C'don 2C **168**
SE24 . . . . .3C **120**
(not continuous)
Poplar Way IG6: Ilf 4G **53**
TW13: Felt 3J **129**
Poppins Cl. KT12: Walt T 5A **148**
Poppins Ct. EC4 . . . . . .1A **14** (6B **84**)
Poppleton Rd. E11 . . . . .6G **51**
Poppy Cl. DA17: Belv 3H **109**
EN5: New Bar 6F **21**
SM6: W'gton 1E **166**
UB5: N'olt 6D **58**
UB7: W Dray 3B **92**
Poppy Dr. EN3: Pond E 4C **24**
Poppy La. CR0: C'don 7J **157**
Poppy M. SE22 . . . . .5G **121**
Poppy Pl. SE13 . . . . .6F **123**
Porchester Cl. SE5 . . . . .4C **120**
Porchester Ct. W2 . . . . .7K **81**
(off Porchester Gdns.)
Porchester Gdns. W2 . . . . .7K **81**
Porchester Gdns. M. W2 . . . . .6K **81**
Porchester Ga. W2 . . . . .7K **81**
(off Bayswater Rd.)
Porchester Ho. E1 . . . . .6H **85**
(off Philpot St.)
Porchester Leisure Cen. 6K **81**
Porchester Mead
BR3: Beck 6D **140**
Porchester Pl. W2 . . . . . . .1D **10** (6C **82**)
Porchester Rd. KT1: King T 2H **151**
W2 . . . . .6K **81**
Porchester Sq. W2 . . . . .6K **81**
Porchester Sq. M. W2 . . . . .6K **81**
Porchester Ter. W2 . . . . .7A **82**
Porchester Ter. Nth. W2 . . . . .6K **81**
Porch Way N20 . . . . .3J **31**
Porcupine Cl. SE9 . . . . .2C **142**
Porden Rd. SW2 . . . . .4K **119**
Porlock Av. HA2: Harr 1G **59**
Porlock Ho. SE26 . . . . .3G **139**
Porlock Rd. EN1: Enf 7A **24**
Porlock St. SE1 . . . . .6F **15** (2D **102**)
Porrington Cl. BR7: Chst 1D **160**
Portal Cl. HA4: Ruis 4J **57**
SE27 . . . . .3A **138**
UB10: Uxb 7A **56**
Portal Way W3 . . . . .5K **79**
Portbury Cl. SE15 . . . . .1G **121**
Port Cres. E13 . . . . .4K **87**
Portcullis Ho. SW1 . . . . .7E **12**
Portcullis Lodge Rd. EN1: Enf . .3J **23**
Port East Apts. E14 . . . . .7C **86**
(off Hertsmere Rd.)
Portelet Cl. N1 . . . . .1E **84**
(off De Beauvoir Est.)
Portelet Rd. E1 . . . . .3K **85**

Porten Ho's. W14 . . . . .3G **99**
(off Porten Rd.)
Porten Rd. W14 . . . . .3G **99**
Porter Rd. E6 . . . . .6D **88**
Porters & Walters Almshouses
N22 .7E **32**
(off Nightingale Rd.)
Porters Av. RM8: Dag 6B **72**
RM9: Dag 6B **72**
The Porters Lodge SW10 . . . . . . .7A **100**
(off Coleridge Gdns.)
Porters M. RM9: Dag 6B **72**
Porter Sq. N19 . . . . .1J **65**
Porter St. SE1 . . . . .4D **14** (1C **102**)
W1 . . . . .5F **5** (5D **82**)
Porters Wlk. E1 . . . . .7H **85**
Porters Way N12 . . . . .6H **31**
UB7: W Dray 3B **92**
Porteus Pl. SW4 . . . . .3G **119**
Porteus Rd. W2 . . . . .5A **4** (5A **82**)
Portfleet Pl. N1 . . . . .1E **84**
(off De Beauvoir Rd.)
Portgate Cl. W9 . . . . .4H **81**
Porthallow Cl. BR6: Chels 4K **173**
Porthcawe Rd. SE26 . . . . .4A **140**
Porthkerry Av. DA16: Well 4A **126**
Port Ho. E14 . . . . .5D **104**
(off Burrells Wharf Sq.)
Portia Ct. IG11: Bark 7A **72**
SE11 . . . . .5B **102**
(off Opal St.)
Portia Way E3 . . . . .4B **86**
The Porticos SW3 . . . . .7A **16**
Portinscale Rd. SW15 . . . . .5G **117**
Portishead Ho. W2 . . . . .5J **81**
(off Westbourne Pk. Rd.)
Portland Av. DA15: Sidc 6A **126**
KT3: N Mald 7B **152**
N16 .7F **49**
Portland Cl. KT4: Wor Pk 7D **152**
RM6: Chad H 5E **54**
Portland Commercial Est.
IG11: Bark 2C **90**
Portland Cotts. CR0: Bedd 7H **155**
Portland Ct. N1 . . . . .7E **66**
(off St Peter's Way)
SE1 . . . . .7E **14**
(off Gt. Dover St.)
SE14 . . . . .6A **104**
(off Whitcher Cl.)
Portland Cres. HA7: Stan 2D **42**
SE9 . . . . .2C **142**
TW13: Felt 4F **129**
UB6: G'frd 4F **77**
Portland Dr. EN2: Enf 1K **23**
Portland Gdns. N4 . . . . .6B **48**
RM6: Chad H 5D **54**
Portland Gro. SW8 . . . . .1K **119**
Portland Ho. SW1 . . . . .1A **18**
SW15 . . . . .5F **117**
Portland Mans. W14 . . . . .4H **99**
(off Addison Bri. Pl.)
Portland M. W1 . . . . .1B **12** (6G **83**)
Portland Pl. SE25 . . . . .4G **157**
(off Sth. Norwood Hill)
W1 . . . . .4J **5** (5F **83**)
Portland Ri. N4 . . . . .1B **66**
(not continuous)
Portland Rd. BR1: Broml 4A **142**
CR4: Mitc 2C **154**
KT1: King T 3E **150**
N15 .4F **49**
SE9 . . . . .2C **142**
SE25 . . . . .4G **157**
TW15: Ashf 3A **128**
UB2: S'hall 3D **94**
UB4: Hayes 3G **75**
W11 . . . . .7G **81**
Portland Sq. E1 . . . . .1H **103**
Portland St. SE17 . . . . .5D **102**
Portland Ter. HA8: Edg 7B **28**
TW9: Rich 4D **114**
Portland Wlk. SE17 . . . . .6D **102**

Portman Av. SW14 . . . . .3K **115**
Portman Cl. DA5: Bexl 1K **145**
DA7: Bex 3E **126**
W1 . . . . .7F **5** (6D **82**)
Portman Dr. IG8: Wfd G 2B **52**
Portman Gdns. NW9 . . . . .2K **43**
UB10: Hil 7C **56**
Portman Ga. NW1 . . . . .4D **4** (4C **82**)
Portman Mans. W1 . . . . .5F **5**
(off Chiltern St.)
Portman M. Sth. W1 . . . . . .1G **11** (6E **82**)
Portman Pl. E2 . . . . .3J **85**
Portman Rd. KT1: King T 2F **151**
Portman Sq. W1 . . . . .7G **5** (6E **82**)
Portman St. W1 . . . . .1G **11** (6E **82**)
Portman Towers W1 . . . . . .7F **5** (6D **82**)
Portmeadow Wlk. SE2 . . . . .2D **108**
Portmeers Cl. E17 . . . . .6B **50**
Portnall Ho. W9 . . . . .3H **81**
(off Portnall Rd.)
Portnall Rd. W9 . . . . .2H **81**
Portnoi Cl. RM1: Rom 2K **55**
Portobello Ct. W11 . . . . .6H **81**
Portobello Grn. W10 . . . . .5G **81**
(off Portobello Rd.)
Portobello Ho. BR2: Broml 6B **160**
Portobello Lofts W10 . . . . .4G **81**
(off Kensal Rd.)
Portobello Mkt. 6H **81**
Portobello M. W11 . . . . .7J **81**
Portobello Rd. W10 . . . . .5G **81**
W11 . . . . .6H **81**
Portobello Road Market 7H **81**
(off Portobello Rd.)
Porton Ct. KT6: Surb 6C **150**
Portpool La. EC1 . . . . .5J **7** (5A **84**)
Portree Cl. N22 . . . . .7E **32**
Portree St. E14 . . . . .6F **87**
Portrush Ct. UB1: S'hall 6G **77**
(off Whitecote Rd.)
Portsdown HA8: Edg 5B **28**
Portsdown Av. NW11 . . . . .6H **45**
Portsdown M. NW11 . . . . .6H **45**
Portsea Hall W2 . . . . .1D **10**
(off Portsea Pl.)
Portsea M. W2 . . . . .1D **10**
Portsea Pl. W2 . . . . .1D **10** (6C **82**)
Portslade Rd. SW8 . . . . .2G **119**
Portsmouth Av. KT7: T Ditt 7A **150**
Portsmouth M. E16 . . . . .1K **105**
Portsmouth Rd.
KT1: King T 7A **150**
KT6: Surb 7A **150**
KT7: T Ditt 1A **162**
SW15 . . . . .7D **116**
Portsmouth St. WC2 . . . . .1G **13** (6K **83**)
Portsoken Pav. EC3 . . . . .1J **15**
(off Aldgate Sq.)
Portsoken St. E1 . . . . .2J **15** (7F **85**)
Portswood Pl. SW15 . . . . .6B **116**
Portugal Gdns. TW2: Twick 2G **131**
Portugal St. WC2 . . . . . . .1G **13** (6K **83**)
Portway E15 . . . . .1H **87**
Portway Gdns. SE18 . . . . .7B **106**
Pory Ho. SE11 . . . . .4H **19** (4K **101**)
Poseidon Ct. E14 . . . . .4C **104**
(off Homer Dr.)
POSK 4C **98**
(off King St.)
Postal Cl. DA5: Bexl 7H **127**
The Postal Mus. 3H **7** (4K **83**)
The Postern EC2 . . . . .6D **8**
Postern Grn. EN2: Enf 2F **23**
Post La. TW2: Twick 1H **131**
Postmark Development
EC1 . . . . .3H **7** (4K **83**)
Postmasters Lodge HA5: Pinn . . .7C **40**
Postmill Cl. CR0: C'don 3J **169**
Post Office App. E7 . . . . .5K **69**
Post Office Ct. EC3 . . . . .1F **15**
(off King William St.)
Post Office Way SW11 . . . . .1H **101**
Post Rd. UB2: S'hall 3F **95**

Postway M. IG1: Ilf 3F 71
(not continuous)
Potager Pl. CR0: Bedd ...3H 167
Potier St. SE1 ....3D 102
Potter Cl. CR4: Mitc 2F 155
  SE2 ....5A 108
  SE15 ....7E 102
Potter Ho. E1 ....5K 85
(off Beaufort Gdns.)
The Potteries EN5: Barn 5D 20
Potterne Cl. SW19 ....7F 117
Potters Cl. CR0: C'don 1A 170
Potters Cl. SM1: Sutt 6H 165
(off Rosebery Rd.)
Pottersfield EN1: Enf 4K 23
(off Lincoln Rd.)
Potters Flds. SE1 ......5H 15 (1E 102)
Potters Gro. KT3: N Mald 4J 151
Potters Hgts. Cl. HA5: Pinn ...1K 39
Potter's La. SW16 ....6H 137
Potters La. EN5: New Bar 4D 20
Potters Lodge E14 ....5E 104
(off Ferry St.)
Potter's Rd. EN5: New Bar 4E 20
Potters Rd. SW6 ....2A 118
  UB2: S'hall 3E 94
Potters Row E20 ....5D 68
(off Keirin Rd.)
Potter St. HA5: Pinn 1K 39
  HA6: Nwood 1J 39
Potter St. Hill HA5: Pinn 1K 39
Pottery Café 1H 117
(off Fulham Rd.)
Pottery Cl. SE25 ....3G 157
Pottery Ga. N11 ....6C 32
Pottery La. W11 ....1G 99
Pottery M. SW6 ....2H 117
Pottery Rd. DA5: Bexl 2J 145
  TW8: Bford 6E 96
Pottery St. SE16 ....2H 103
Pott St. E2 ....3H 85
Poulett Gdns. TW1: Twick 1A 132
Poulett Rd. E6 ....2D 88
Poulter Pk. 6C 154
Poulters Wood BR2: Kes 5B 172
Poulton Av. SM1: Sutt 3B 166
Poulton Cl. E8 ....6H 67
Poulton Ho. W3 ....5K 79
(off Victoria Rd.)
Poultry EC2 ....1E 14 (6D 84)
Pound Cl. BR6: Orp 2H 173
  KT6: Surb 1C 162
Pound Ct. Dr. BR6: Orp 2H 173
Pound Farm Cl. KT10: Esh 7G 149
Pound Grn. DA5: Bexl 7G 127
Pound La. NW10 ....6C 62
Pound Pk. Rd. SE7 ....4B 106
Pound Path E3 ....2K 85
(off Stoneway Wlk.)
Pound Pl. SE9 ....6E 124
Pound St. SM5: Cars 5D 166
Pound Way RM7: Chst 7G 143
Pountney Rd. SW11 ....3E 118
POVEREST 4K 161
Poverest Rd. BR5: St M Cry ...5K 161
Povey Ho. SE17 ....4E 102
(off Beckway St.)
Powder Mill La. TW2: Whitt 7D 112
Powell Cl. HA8: Edg 6A 28
  KT9: Chess 5D 162
Powell Ct. CR2: S Croy 4B 168
(off Bramley Hill)
  E17 ....3D 50
Powell Dr. E4 ....4J 25
Powell Gdns. RM10: Dag 4G 73
Powell Ho. EN1: Enf 4K 23
(off Dunstan Rd.)
  W2 ....2A 10
(off Gloucester Ter.)
Powell Rd. E5 ....3H 67
  IG9: Buck H 1F 37
Powell's Wlk. W4 ....6A 98
Powergate Bus. Pk. NW10 .....3K 79

The Powerhouse 2G 93
Powerhouse La. UB3: Hayes 2G 93
Powerleague
  Battersea 7G 101
  Colney Hatch 7K 31
  Croydon 6K 167
  Ilford 1K 53
  Mill Hill 1H 29
  Newham 3G 89
  Tottenham 6C 34
  Wembley 4G 61
Power Rd. W4 ....4G 97
Powers Ct. TW1: Twick 7D 114
Powerscroft Rd. DA14: Sidc 6C 144
(not continuous)
  E5 ....4J 67
Powis Ct. W11 ....6H 81
(off Powis Gdns.)
  WD23: B Hea 1C 26
(off Rutherford Way)
Powis Gdns. NW11 ....7H 45
  W11 ....6H 81
Powis Ho. WC2 ....7F 7
(off Macklin St.)
Powis M. W11 ....6H 81
Powis Pl. WC1 ....4F 7 (4J 83)
Powis Rd. E3 ....3D 86
Powis Sq. W11 ....6H 81
(not continuous)
Powis St. SE18 ....3E 106
Powis Ter. W11 ....6H 81
Powlesland Ct. E1 ....6A 86
(off White Horse Rd.)
Powlett Ho. NW1 ....6F 65
(off Powlett Pl.)
Powlett Pl. NW1 ....7F 64
Pownall Gdns. TW3: Houn 4F 113
Pownall Rd. E8 ....1F 85
  TW3: Houn 4F 113
Pownell Ter. SE11 ....6A 102
Pownsett Ter. IG1: Ilf 5G 71
Powster Rd. BR1: Broml 5J 141
Powys Cl. DA7: Bex 6D 108
Powys Ct. N11 ....5D 32
Powys La. N13 ....4D 32
  N14 ....4D 32
POYLE 4A 174
Poyle Ind. Est. SL3: Poyle 6A 174
Poyle New Cotts. SL3: Poyle 6A 174
Poyle Technical Cen.
  SL3: Poyle 5A 174
Poyle Trad. Est. SL3: Poyle 6A 174
Poynders Ct. SW4 ....6G 119
Poynders Gdns. SW4 ......7G 119
Poynders Pde. SW4 ....6H 119
Poynders Rd. SW4 ....6G 119
The Poynings SL0: Rich P 1A 174
Poynings Rd. N19 ....3G 65
Poynings Way N12 ....5D 30
Poyntell Cres. BR7: Chst 1H 161
Poynter Cl. UB5: N'olt 2B 76
(off Gallery Gdns.)
Poynter Ho. NW8 ....3A 4
(off Fisherton St.)
  W11 ....1F 99
(off Queensdale Cres.)
Poynter Rd. EN1: Enf 5B 24
Poynton Rd. N17 ....2G 49
Poyntz Rd. SW11 ....2D 118
Poyser St. E2 ....2H 85
Prado Path TW1: Twick 1K 131
(off Laurel Av.)
Praed M. W2 ....7B 4 (6B 82)
Praed St. W2 ....1A 10 (6B 82)
Pragel St. E13 ....2A 88
Pragnell Rd. SE12 ....2K 141
Prague Pl. SW2 ....5J 119
Prah Rd. N4 ....2A 66
Prairie Bldg. E15 ....5F 69
(off Property Row)
Prairie St. SW8 ....2E 118
Praline Ct. E3 ....2D 86
(off Taylor Pl.)

Pratt M. NW1 ....1G 83
Pratts Pas. KT1: King T 2E 150
Pratt St. NW1 ....1G 83
Pratt Wlk. SE11 ......3H 19 (4K 101)
Prayle Gro. NW2 ....1F 63
Preachers Ct. EC1 ....5B 8
(off Charterhouse Sq.)
Prebend Gdns. W4 ....4B 98
  W6 ....4B 98
(not continuous)
Prebend Mans. W4 ....4B 98
(off Chiswick High Rd.)
Prebend St. N1 ....1C 84
The Precinct N1 ....1C 84
Precinct Rd. UB3: Hayes 7J 75
The Precincts SM4: Mord 6J 153
Premier Cnr. W9 ....2H 81
Premier Ct. EN3: Enf W 1D 24
Premiere Pl. E14 ....7C 86
Premier Ho. N1 ....7B 66
(off Waterloo Ter.)
Premier Pk. NW10 ....1H 79
(not continuous)
Premier Pk. Rd. NW10 .....2H 79
Premier Pl. SW15 ....4G 117
Prendergast Rd. SE3 ......3G 123
Prentice Ct. SW19 ....5H 135
Prentis Rd. SW16 ....4H 137
Prentiss Ct. SE7 ....4B 106
Presburg Rd. KT3: N Mald 5A 152
Presburg St. E5 ....3K 67
Prescelly Pl. HA8: Edg 1F 43
Prescot St. E1 ....2K 15 (7F 85)
Prescott Av. BR5: Pet W 6F 161
Prescott Cl. SW16 ....7J 137
Prescott Ho. SE17 ....6B 102
(off Hillingdon St.)
Prescott Pl. SW4 ....3H 119
Presentation M. SW2 .....2A 138
Preshaw Cres. CR4: Mitc 3C 154
President Dr. E1 ....1H 103
President Ho. EC1 ......2B 8 (3B 84)
President Quay E1 ....4K 15
President St. EC1 ....1C 8
Prespa Cl. N9 ....2D 34
Press Ct. SE1 ....5G 103
Press Ho. BR5: Pet W 5G 161
  E1 ....5K 85
(off Trafalgar Gdns.)
  NW10 ....3K 61
Pressing La. UB3: Hayes 3G 93
Press Rd. NW10 ....3K 61
Prestage Way E14 ....7E 86
Prestbury Rd. E7 ....7A 70
Prestbury Sq. SE9 ....4D 142
Prested Rd. SW11 ....4C 118
Prestige Ho. N20 ....1F 31
(off Acton Wlk.)
Prestige Way NW4 ....5E 44
PRESTON 1E 60
Preston Av. E4 ....6A 36
Preston Cl. SE1 ....4E 102
  TW2: Twick 3J 131
Preston Ct. DA14: Sidc 4K 143
(off The Crescent)
  EN5: New Bar 4F 21
Preston Dr. DA7: Bex 1D 126
  E11 ....5A 52
  KT19: Ewe 6A 164
Preston Gdns. IG1: Ilf 6C 52
  NW10 ....6B 62
Preston Hill HA3: Kenton 7E 42
Preston Ho. RM10: Dag 3G 73
(off Uvedale Rd.)
  SE1 ....4E 102
(off Preston Cl.)
  SE1 ....7J 15
(off St Saviour's Est.)
Preston Pl. NW2 ....6C 62
  TW10: Rich 5E 114
Preston Rd. E11 ....6G 51
  HA3: Kenton 1E 60
  HA9: Wemb 1E 60

Preston Rd. SE19 ....6B 138
  SW20 ....7B 134
  TW17: Shep 5C 146
Preston's Rd. E14 ....7E 86
Prestons Rd. BR2: Hayes 3J 171
Preston St. E2 ....2K 85
Preston Waye HA3: Kenton 1E 60
Prestwich Ter. SW4 ....5G 119
Prestwick Cl. UB2: S'hall 5C 94
Prestwick Ct. UB1: S'hall 7G 77
(off Baird Av.)
Prestwood Av. HA3: Kenton 4B 42
Prestwood Cl. HA3: Kenton 4B 42
  SE18 ....6A 108
Prestwood Gdns. CR0: C'don 7C 156
Prestwood Ho. SE16 ......3H 103
(off Drummond Rd.)
Prestwood St. N1 ....1D 8 (2C 84)
Pretoria Av. E17 ....4A 50
Pretoria Cres. E4 ....1K 35
Pretoria Rd. E4 ....1K 35
  E11 ....1F 69
  E16 ....4H 87
  IG1: Ilf 5F 71
  N17 ....7A 34
  RM7: Rom 4J 55
  SW16 ....6F 137
Pretoria Rd. Nth. N18 .....6A 34
Prevost Rd. N11 ....2K 31
Priam Ho. E2 ....2H 85
(off Old Bethnal Grn. Rd.)
Price Cl. SW17 ....3D 136
Price Ho. N1 ....1C 84
(off Britannia Row)
Price Rd. CR0: Wadd 5B 168
Prices Cl. NW7 ....6B 30
Price's Ct. SW11 ....3B 118
Price's M. N1 ....1K 83
Price's St. SE1 ....5B 14 (1B 102)
Price Way TW12: Hamp 6C 130
Prichard Cl. N7 ....5K 65
Prichard Ho. SE11 ....4J 19
(off Kennington Rd.)
Pricklers Hill EN5: New Bar 6E 20
Prickley Wood BR2: Hayes 1H 171
Priddy's Yd. CR0: C'don 2C 168
Prideaux Ho. WC1 ....1H 7
(off Prideaux Pl.)
Prideaux Pl. W3 ....7K 79
  WC1 ....1H 7 (3K 83)
Pridham Rd. SW9 ....3J 119
Pridham Rd. CR7: Thor H 4D 156
Priest Cl. TW12: Hamp 4E 130
Priestfield Rd. SE23 ......3A 140
Priestlands Pk. Rd. DA15: Sidc 3K 143
Priestley Cl. N16 ....7F 49
Priestley Gdns. RM6: Chad H 6B 54
Priestley Ho. EC1 ....3D 8
(off Old St.)
  HA9: Wemb 3J 61
(off Barnhill Rd.)
Priestley Rd. CR4: Mitc 2E 154
Priestley Way E17 ....3K 49
  NW2 ....1C 62
Priestman Point E3 ......3D 86
(off Rainhill Way)
Priests Av. RM1: Rom 2K 55
Priests Bri. SW14 ....3A 116
  SW15 ....3A 116
Priest's Ct. EC2 ....7C 8
Prima Rd. SW9 ....7A 102
Prime Meridian Line 7F 105
Prime Meridian Wlk. E14 .....7F 87
Primeplace M. CR7: Thor H 2C 156
Primezone M. N8 ....6J 47
Primrose Av. EN2: Enf 1J 23
  RM6: Chad H 7B 54
Primrose Cl. E3 ....2C 86
  HA2: Harr 3D 58
  N3 ....2K 45
  SE6 ....5E 140
  SM6: W'gton 7F 155

Primrose Ct. NW8 . . . . .2D **82**
           (off Prince Albert Rd.)
SW12 . . . . .7H **119**
Primrose Gdns. HA4: Ruis 5A **58**
NW3 . . . . .6C **64**
WD23: Bush 1A **26**
PRIMROSE HILL 1E **82**
Primrose Hill EC4 . . . . .1K **13** (6A **84**)
Primrose Hill Ct. NW3 . . . . .7D **64**
Primrose Hill Rd. NW3 . . . . .7D **64**
Primrose Hill Studios NW1 . . . . . .1E **82**
Primrose Ho. SE15 . . . . .1G **121**
          (off Peckham Hill St.)
SE16 . . . . .2A **104**
            (off Blondin Way)
Primrose La. CR0: C'don 1J **169**
Primrose Mans. SW11 . . . . .1E **118**
Primrose M. NW1 . . . . .7D **64**
         (off Sharpleshall St.)
SE3 . . . . .7J **105**
Primrose Pl. TW7: Isle 2K **113**
Primrose Rd. E10 . . . . .1D **68**
E18 . . . . .2K **51**
Primrose Sq. E9 . . . . .7J **67**
Primrose St. EC2 . . . . . .5G **9** (5E **84**)
Primrose Wlk. KT17: Ewe 7B **164**
SE14 . . . . .7A **104**
Primrose Way HA0: Wemb 2D **78**
SE10 . . . . .2E **122**
Primula St. W12 . . . . .6C **80**
Prince Albert Ct. NW8 . . . . .1D **82**
         (off Prince Albert Rd.)
TW16: Sun 7H **129**
Prince Albert Mews SW11 . . . . . .7C **100**
Prince Albert Rd. NW1 . . . . .1C **4** (3C **82**)
NW8 . . . . .1C **4** (3C **82**)
Prince Arthur M. NW3 . . . . .4A **64**
Prince Arthur Rd. NW3 . . . . .5A **64**
Prince Charles Cinema 2D **12**
         (off Leicester Pl.)
Prince Charles Dr. NW4 . . . . .7E **44**
Prince Charles Rd. SE3 . . . . .2H **123**
Prince Charles Way SM6: W'gton . . .3F **167**
Prince Consort Dr. BR7: Chst 1H **161**
Prince Consort Rd. SW7 . . . .1A **16** (3A **100**)
Princedale Rd. W11 . . . . .1G **99**
Prince Edward Mans. W2 . . . . .7J **81**
         (off Moscow Rd.)
Prince Edward Rd. E9 . . . . .6B **68**
Prince Edward Theatre 1D **12**
        (off Old Compton St.)
Prince George Av. N14 . . . . .5C **22**
Prince George Ho. N16 . . . . .4E **66**
Prince George's Av. SW20 . . . . .2E **152**
Prince George's Rd. SW19 . . . . .1B **154**
Prince Henry Rd. SE7 . . . . .7B **106**
Prince Imperial Rd. BR7: Chst . . .1F **161**
SE18 . . . . .1D **124**
Prince John Rd. SE9 . . . . .5C **124**
Princelet St. E1 . . . . .5K **9** (5F **85**)
Prince of Orange Ct. SE16 . . . . . .3J **103**
           (off Lower Rd.)
Prince of Orange La. SE10 . . . . . .7E **104**
Prince of Wales Ct. NW4 . . . . .4D **44**
Prince of Wales Dr. SW8 . . . . .7F **101**
SW11 . . . . .1C **118**
Prince of Wales Mans. SW11 . . . .1E **118**
Prince of Wales Pas. NW1 . . . . . . .2A **6**
Prince of Wales Rd. E16 . . . . .6A **88**
NW5 . . . . .6E **64**
SE3 . . . . .2H **123**
SM1: Sutt 2B **166**
Prince of Wales Ter. W4 . . . . .5A **98**
W8 . . . . .2K **99**
Prince of Wales Theatre 3C **12**
         (off Coventry St.)
Prince Regent Ct. NW8 . . . . .2C **82**
           (off Avenue Rd.)
SE16 . . . . .7A **86**
          (off Edward Sq.)
Prince Regent La. E13 . . . . .3K **87**
E16 . . . . .3K **87**
Prince Regent M. NW1 . . . . .2A **6**

Prince Regent Rd. TW3: Houn . . .3F **113**
Prince Rd. SE25 . . . . .5E **156**
Prince Rupert Rd. SE9 . . . . .4D **124**
Princes Arc. SW1 . . . . .4B **12**
Prince's Av. UB6: G'frd 6F **77**
Princes Av. BR5: Pet W 5J **161**
IG8: Wfd G 4E **36**
KT6: Surb 1G **163**
N3 . . . . .1J **45**
N10 . . . . .3F **47**
N13 . . . . .5F **33**
N22 . . . . .1H **47**
NW9 . . . . .4G **43**
SM5: Cars 7D **166**
W3 . . . . .3G **97**
Princes Cir. WC2 . . . . . . .7E **6** (6J **83**)
Prince's Cl. TW11: Tedd 4H **131**
Princes Cl. DA14: Sidc 3D **144**
HA8: Edg 5B **28**
N4 . . . . .1B **66**
NW9 . . . . .4G **43**
SW4 . . . . .3G **119**
Prince's Ct. SE16 . . . . .3B **104**
SW3 . . . . .1E **16**
         (off Brompton Rd.)
Princes Ct. HA9: Wemb 5E **60**
Princes Ct. Bus. Cen. E1 . . . . .7H **85**
Princes Dr. HA1: Harr 3J **41**
Prince's Gdns. SW7 . . . .1B **16** (3B **100**)
Princes Gdns. W3 . . . . .5G **79**
W5 . . . . .4C **78**
Prince's Ga. SW7 . . . . . .1B **16** (2B **100**)
         (not continuous)
Prince's Ga. Ct. SW7 . . . .7B **10** (2B **100**)
Prince's Ga. M. SW7 . . . .1B **16** (3B **100**)
Princes Ho. W11 . . . . .7H **81**
Princes La. N10 . . . . .3F **47**
Prince's M. W2 . . . . .7K **81**
Princes M. TW3: Houn 4E **112**
W6 . . . . .5D **98**
           (off Down Pl.)
Princes Pde. NW11 . . . . .6G **45**
        (off Golders Grn. Rd.)
Princes Pk. Av. NW11 . . . . .6G **45**
UB3: Hayes 7F **75**
Princes Pk. Circ. UB3: Hayes 7F **75**
Princes Pk. Cl. UB3: Hayes 7F **75**
Princes Pk. La. UB3: Hayes 7F **75**
Princes Pk. Pde. UB3: Hayes 7F **75**
Princes Pl. SW1 . . . . .4B **12**
W11 . . . . .1G **99**
Prince's Plain BR2: Broml 7C **160**
Prince's Ri. SE13 . . . . .2E **122**
Princes Riverside Rd. SE16 . . . . .1K **103**
Prince's Rd. SW19 . . . . .6J **135**
TW11: Tedd 4H **131**
Princes Rd. IG6: Ilf 4H **53**
IG9: Buck H 2F **37**
KT2: King T 7G **133**
N18 . . . . .4D **34**
SE20 . . . . .6K **139**
SW14 . . . . .3K **115**
TW9: Kew 1F **115**
TW10: Rich 5F **115**
TW13: Felt 2H **129**
TW15: Ashf 5B **128**
W13 . . . . .1B **96**
Princessa Ct. EN2: Enf 5J **23**
Princess Alice Ho. W10 . . . . .4E **80**
Princess Alice Way SE28 . . . . . .2H **107**
Princess Av. HA9: Wemb 2E **60**
Princess Cl. SE28 . . . . .6D **90**
Princess Ct. KT1: King T 3F **151**
         (off Horace Rd.)
N6 . . . . .7G **47**
NW6 . . . . .6K **63**
        (off Compayne Gdns.)
W1 . . . . .6E **4**
         (off Bryanston Pl.)
W2 . . . . .7K **81**
          (off Queensway)
Princess Cres. N4 . . . . .2B **66**
Princess La. HA4: Ruis 1G **57**

Princess Louise Bldg. SE8 . . . . . .7C **104**
           (off Hales St.)
Princess Louise Cl. W2 . . . .5B **4** (5B **82**)
Princess Louise Wlk. W10 . . . . . .5F **81**
Princess Mary Ho. SW1 . . . . .3D **18**
         (off Vincent St.)
Princess May Rd. N16 . . . . .4E **66**
Princess M. KT1: King T 3F **151**
NW3 . . . . .5B **64**
Princess Pde. BR6: Farnb 3E **172**
RM10: Dag 2G **91**
Princess Pk. Mnr. N11 . . . . .5K **31**
Princess Sq. SW2 . . . . .7K **81**
         (not continuous)
Princess Rd. CR0: C'don 6C **156**
NW1 . . . . .1E **82**
NW6 . . . . .2J **81**
Princess St. SE1 . . . . .3B **102**
Prince's St. EC2 . . . . . . .1E **14** (6D **84**)
Princes St. DA7: Bex 3F **127**
N17 . . . . .6K **33**
SM1: Sutt 4B **166**
TW9: Rich 5E **114**
W1 . . . . .1K **11** (6F **83**)
Princes Ter. E13 . . . . .1K **87**
Prince's Twr. SE16 . . . . .2J **103**
         (off Elephant La.)
Prince St. SE8 . . . . .6B **104**
Princes Way BR4: W W'ck 4H **171**
CR0: Wadd 5K **167**
HA4: Ruis 4C **58**
IG9: Buck H 2F **37**
SW19 . . . . .7F **117**
W3 . . . . .3G **97**
Prince's Yd. W11 . . . . .1G **99**
Princethorpe Ho. W2 . . . . .5K **81**
        (off Woodchester Sq.)
Princethorpe Rd. SE26 . . . . .4K **139**
Princeton Ct. SW15 . . . . .3F **117**
Princeton M. KT2: King T 1G **151**
Princeton St. WC1 . . . . . . .6G **7** (5K **83**)
Prince William Ct. TW15: Ashf . . .5B **128**
        (off Clarendon Rd.)
Principal Cl. N14 . . . . .1B **32**
Principal Pl. EC2 . . . . .4H **9**
Principal Sq. E9 . . . . .5K **67**
Pringle Gdns. SW16 . . . . .4G **137**
         (not continuous)
Printers Inn Ct. EC4 . . . . .6A **84**
Printers M. E3 . . . . .1A **86**
Printers Rd. SW9 . . . . .1K **119**
Printer St. EC4 . . . . .7K **7** (6A **84**)
Printing Ho. La.
UB3: Hayes 2G **93**
Printing Ho. Yd. E2 . . . . .1H **9** (3E **84**)
Printon Ho. E14 . . . . .5B **86**
         (off Wallwood St.)
The Print Room 6J **81**
         (off Hereford Rd.)
Print Room at the Coronet 1G **99**
        (off Notting Hill Ga.)
Print Village SE15 . . . . .2F **121**
Printwork Apts. SE1 . . . . .7G **15**
          (off Long La.)
SE5 . . . . .2C **120**
        (off Coldharbour La.)
Priolo Rd. SE7 . . . . .5A **106**
Prior Av. SM2: Sutt 7C **166**
Prior Bolton St. N1 . . . . .6B **66**
Prior Ct. KT8: W Mole 5D **148**
Prioress Ho. E3 . . . . .3D **86**
        (off Bromley High St.)
Prioress Rd. SE27 . . . . .3B **138**
Prioress St. SE1 . . . . .3E **102**
Prior Rd. IG1: Ilf 3E **70**
The Priors NW3 . . . . .3B **64**
Priors Cft. E17 . . . . .2A **50**
Priors Farm La. UB5: N'olt 6C **58**
Priors Fld. UB5: N'olt 6C **58**
Priors Gdns. HA4: Ruis 5A **58**
Priors Mead EN1: Enf 1K **23**
Prior St. SE10 . . . . .7E **104**
Priors Wood KT10: Hin W 2A **162**

The Priory CR0: Wadd 4A **168**
N8 . . . . .4H **47**
SE3 . . . . .3H **123**
The Priory Apts. SE6 . . . . .1D **140**
Priory Av. BR5: Pet W 6H **161**
E4 . . . . .3G **35**
E17 . . . . .5C **50**
HA0: Wemb 4K **59**
N8 . . . . .4H **47**
SM3: Cheam 4F **165**
W4 . . . . .4A **98**
Priory Cl. BR3: Beck 3A **158**
BR7: Chst 1D **160**
E4 . . . . .3G **35**
E18 . . . . .1J **51**
HA0: Wemb 4K **59**
HA4: Ruis 1H **57**
HA7: Stan 3E **26**
N3 . . . . .1H **45**
N14 . . . . .5A **22**
N20 . . . . .1C **30**
SW19 . . . . .1K **153**
TW12: Hamp 1D **148**
TW16: Sun 7J **129**
UB3: Hayes 7K **75**
Priory Ct. E6 . . . . .1A **88**
E9 . . . . .5K **67**
E17 . . . . .2B **50**
EC4 . . . . .1B **14**
          (off Pilgrim St.)
HA0: Wemb 2E **78**
KT1: King T 3E **150**
        (off Denmark Rd.)
KT17: Ewe 7B **164**
SM3: Cheam 4G **165**
SW8 . . . . .1H **119**
TW3: Houn 3F **113**
WD23: Bush 1B **26**
        (off Sparrows Herne)
Priory Ct. Est. E17 . . . . .2B **50**
Priory Cres. HA0: Wemb 3A **60**
SE19 . . . . .7C **138**
SM3: Cheam 4F **165**
Priory Dr. HA7: Stan 3E **26**
SE2 . . . . .5D **108**
Priory Fld. Dr. HA8: Edg 4C **28**
Priory Gdns. HA0: Wemb 4A **60**
N6 . . . . .6F **47**
NW10 . . . . .3E **78**
SE25 . . . . .4F **157**
SW13 . . . . .3B **116**
TW12: Hamp 7D **130**
TW15: Ashf 5F **129**
W4 . . . . .4A **98**
W5 . . . . .3E **78**
Priory Grange N2 . . . . .3D **46**
          (off Fortis Grn.)
Priory Grn. N1 . . . . .2K **83**
Priory Grn. Est. N1 . . . . .2K **83**
Priory Gro. EN5: Barn 5D **20**
SW8 . . . . .1J **119**
Priory Hgts. N1 . . . . .2K **8**
          (off Wynford Rd.)
Priory Hill HA0: Wemb 4A **60**
Priory Ho. E1 . . . . .5J **9**
           (off Folgate St.)
EC1 . . . . .3A **8**
         (off Sans Wlk.)
SW1 . . . . .5C **18**
        (off Rampayne St.)
Priory La. KT8: W Mole 4F **149**
SW15 . . . . .6A **116**
Priory Leas SE9 . . . . .1C **142**
Priory Lodge W4 . . . . .5G **97**
        (off Kew Bri. Ct.)
Priory Mans. SW10 . . . . .5A **100**
        (off Drayton Gdns.)
Priory M. SW8 . . . . .1J **119**
Priory Pk. HA8: Edg 4C **28**
SE3 . . . . .3H **123**
Priory Pk. Rd. HA0: Wemb 4A **60**
NW6 . . . . .1H **81**
Priory Retail Pk. 7B **136**

Priory Rd. CR0: C'don 7A 156
E6 . . . . .1B 88
IG11: Bark 7H 71
KT9: Chess 3E 162
N8 . . . . .4G 47
NW6 . . . . .1K 81
SM3: Cheam 4F 165
SW19 . . . . .7B 136
TW3: Houn 5G 113
TW9: Kew 6G 97
TW12: Hamp 7D 130
W4 . . . . .3K 97
Priory St. E3 . . . . .3D 86
Priory Ter. NW6 . . . . .1K 81
TW16: Sun 7J 129
Priory Vw. WD23: B Hea 1D 26
Priory Vs. N11 . . . . .5J 31
(off Colney Hatch La.)
Priory Wlk. SW10 . . . . .5A 100
TW16: Sun 7J 129
Priory Way HA2: Harr 4F 41
UB2: S'hall 3B 94
UB7: Harm 6A 92
Priscilla Cl. N15 . . . . .5C 48
Pritchard Ho. E2 . . . . .2H 85
(off Ada Pl.)
Pritchard's Rd. E2 . . . . .1G 85
Priter Rd. SE16 . . . . .3G 103
Priter Rd. Hostel SE16 . . . . .3G 103
(off Dockley Rd.)
Priter Way SE16 . . . . .3G 103
Private Rd. EN1: Enf 5J 23
Prize Wlk. E20 . . . . .5E 68
Probert Rd. SW2 . . . . .5A 120
Probyn Ho. SW1 . . . . .3D 18
(off Page St.)
Probyn Rd. SW2 . . . . .2B 138
Procter Ho. SE1 . . . . .5G 103
(off Avondale Sq.)
SE5 . . . . .7D 102
(off Picton St.)
Procter St. WC1 . . . . .6G 7 (5K 83)
Proctor Cl. CR4: Mitc 1E 154
Proctors Cl. TW14: Felt 1J 129
Progress Bus. Pk. CR0: Wadd 2K 167
The Progress Cen. EN3: Pond E 3E 24
Progress Way CR0: Wadd 2K 167
EN1: Enf 5B 24
N22 . . . . .1A 48
Project Pk. E16 . . . . .4F 87
Project Rd. IG11: Bark 4B 90
Prologis Pk. CR0: Bedd 7H 155
E3 . . . . .4E 86
TW4: Houn 4A 112
The Promenade HA8: Edg 5B 28
W4 . . . . .2A 116
Promenade App. Rd. W4 . . . . .7A 98
Propeller Cres. CR0: Wadd 5A 168
Propeller Way NW4 . . . . .3C 44
Prospect Cl. DA17: Belv 4G 109
HA4: Ruis 7B 40
SE26 . . . . .4H 139
TW3: Houn 1D 112
Prospect Cotts. SW18 . . . . .4J 117
Prospect Cres. TW2: Whitt 6G 113
Prospect Hill E17 . . . . .4D 50
Prospect Ho. E3 . . . . .3C 86
(off Campbell Rd.)
E17 . . . . .3E 50
(off Prospect Hill)
N1 . . . . .2A 84
(off Donegal St.)
SE1 . . . . .3B 102
(off Gaywood St.)
SE16 . . . . .3G 103
(off Frean St.)
SW19 . . . . .1B 154
(off Chapter Way)
W10 . . . . .6F 81
(off Bridge Cl.)
Prospect Pl. BR2: Broml 3K 159
E1 . . . . .1J 103
(not continuous)

Prospect Pl. N2 . . . . .4B 46
N7 . . . . .4J 65
NW2 . . . . .7K 33
NW2 . . . . .3H 63
NW3 . . . . .4A 64
RM5: Col R 2J 55
SE8 . . . . .6B 104
(off Evelyn St.)
SW11 . . . . .7F 101
SW20 . . . . .7D 134
W4 . . . . .5K 97
Prospect Quay SW18 . . . . .4J 117
(off Lightermans Wlk.)
Prospect Ring N2 . . . . .3B 46
Prospect Rd. EN5: New Bar 4D 20
IG8: Wfd G 6F 37
KT6: Surb 6C 150
NW2 . . . . .3H 63
Prospect Row E15 . . . . .5E 68
Prospect Row Ho's. E15 . . . . .5E 68
(off Property Row)
Prospect St. SE16 . . . . .3H 103
Prospectus Pl. CR2: S Croy 6C 168
Prospect Va. SE18 . . . . .4C 106
Prospero Ho. E1 . . . . .2J 15
(off Portsoken St.)
Prospero Rd. N19 . . . . .1H 65
Protea Cl. E16 . . . . .4H 87
Protea Pl. E9 . . . . .7J 67
(off Lyme Gro.)
Protheroe Ho. N17 . . . . .3F 49
Prothero Gdns. NW4 . . . . .5D 44
Prothero Ho. NW10 . . . . .7K 61
(off Fawood Av.)
Prothero Rd. SW6 . . . . .7G 99
Proton Twr. E14 . . . . .7F 87
Proud Ho. E1 . . . . .6H 85
(off Amazon St.)
Prout Gro. NW10 . . . . .4A 62
Prout Rd. E5 . . . . .3H 67
Provence St. N1 . . . . .2C 84
Providence Av. HA2: Harr 1E 58
Providence Cl. E9 . . . . .1K 85
Providence Ct. W1 . . . . .2H 11 (7E 82)
Providence Ho. E14 . . . . .6B 86
(off Three Colt St.)
Providence La. UB3: Harl 7F 93
Providence Pl. N1 . . . . .1B 84
RM5: Col R 1F 55
SE10 . . . . .5G 105
Providence Rd. UB7: Yiew 1A 92
Providence Row N1 . . . . .2K 83
(off Pentonville Rd.)
Providence Row Cl. E2 . . . . .3H 85
Providence Sq. SE1 . . . . .6K 15 (2G 103)
Providence Twr. E14 . . . . .7F 87
(off Fairmont Av.)
SE16 . . . . .2G 103
(off Bermondsey Wall W.)
Providence Yd. E2 . . . . .1K 9
(off Ezra St.)
Provident Ind. Est. UB3: Hayes 2J 93
Province Dr. SE16 . . . . .2J 103
Province Sq. E14 . . . . .1E 104
(off Blackwall Way)
Provincial Ter. SE20 . . . . .7K 139
Provost Ct. NW3 . . . . .6D 64
(off Eton Rd.)
Provost Est. N1 . . . . .1E 8
Provost Rd. NW3 . . . . .7D 64
Provost St. N1 . . . . .1E 8 (2D 84)
Provost Way RM8: Dag 4A 72
Prowse Av. WD23: B Hea 1B 26
Prowse Cl. N18 . . . . .5B 34
(off Lord Graham M.)
Prowse Pl. NW1 . . . . .7G 65
Proyers Path HA1: Harr 7B 42
Prudence La. BR6: Farnb 4E 172
Pruden Cl. N14 . . . . .2B 32
Prudent Pas. EC2 . . . . .7D 8
Prusom's Island E1 . . . . .1J 103
(off Wapping High St.)

Prusom St. E1 . . . . .1H 103
Pryce Ho. E3 . . . . .3C 86
(off Campbell Rd.)
Puccinia Ct. TW19: Stanw 1A 128
(off Yeoman Dr.)
Pucknells Cl. BR8: Swan 7J 145
Pudding La. EC3 . . . . .3F 15 (7D 84)
Pudding Mill La. E15 . . . . .1D 86
Puddle Dock EC4 . . . . .2A 14 (7B 84)
(not continuous)
Puffin Cl. BR3: Beck 5K 157
IG11: Bark 3B 90
Pugin Cl. SW19 . . . . .4K 135
Pugin Ct. N1 . . . . .7A 66
(off Liverpool Rd.)
Pulborough Rd. SW18 . . . . .7H 117
Pulborough Way TW4: Houn 4A 112
Pulford Rd. N15 . . . . .6D 48
Pulham Av. N2 . . . . .4A 46
Pulham Ho. SW8 . . . . .7K 101
(off Dorset Rd.)
Pullen's Bldgs. SE17 . . . . .5B 102
(off Iliffe St.)
Puller Rd. EN5: Barn 2B 20
Pulleyns Av. E6 . . . . .3C 88
Pullman Ct. SW2 . . . . .1J 137
Pullman Gdns. SW15 . . . . .6E 116
Pullman M. SE12 . . . . .3K 141
Pullman Pl. SE9 . . . . .5C 124
Pulross Rd. SW9 . . . . .3K 119
Pulse Apts. NW6 . . . . .5K 63
(off Lymington Rd.)
Pulse Ct. RM7: Rush G 6K 55
Pulsford Close TW1: Twick 7K 113
Pulteney Cl. E3 . . . . .1B 86
TW7: Isle 3A 114
Pulteney Gdns. E18 . . . . .3J 51
Pulteney Rd. E18 . . . . .3K 51
Pulteney Ter. N1 . . . . .1K 83
(not continuous)
Pultney St. N1 . . . . .1K 83
Pulton Ho. SE4 . . . . .4A 122
(off Turnham Rd.)
Pulton Pl. SW6 . . . . .7J 99
Puma Ct. E1 . . . . .5J 9 (5F 85)
Pump All. TW8: Bford 7D 96
Pump Cl. UB5: N'olt 2E 76
Pump Ct. EC4 . . . . .1J 13 (6A 84)
The Pumphouse N8 . . . . .4K 47
Pump Ho. Cl. BR2: Broml 2G 159
SE16 . . . . .2J 103
Pump Ho. Cres. TW8: Bford 5C 96
Pump House Gallery 7E 100
Pump Ho. La. SW11 . . . . .7G 101
Pump Ho. M. E1 . . . . .7G 85
(off Hooper St.)
Pumping Ho. E14 . . . . .7F 87
(off Naval Row)
Pumping Station Rd. W4 . . . . .7A 98
Pump La. SE14 . . . . .7J 103
UB3: Hayes 2J 93
Pump Pail Nth. CR0: C'don 3C 168
Pump Pail Sth. CR0: C'don 3C 168
Punchard Cres. EN3: Enf L 1J 25
Punderson's Gdns. E2 . . . . .3H 85
Punjab La. UB1: S'hall 1D 94
Purbeck Av. KT3: N Mald 6B 152
Purbeck Dr. NW2 . . . . .2F 63
Purbeck Gdns. SE26 . . . . .5B 140
Purbeck Ho. SW8 . . . . .7K 101
(off Bolney St.)
Purbrook Est. SE1 . . . . .7H 15 (2E 102)
Purbrook St. SE1 . . . . .7H 15 (3E 102)
Purcell Cres. SW6 . . . . .7F 99
Purcell Ho. EN1: Enf 1B 24
SW10 . . . . .6B 100
(off Milman's St.)
Purcell Mans. W14 . . . . .6G 99
(off Queen's Club Gdns.)
Purcell M. NW10 . . . . .7A 62
Purcell Rd. UB6: G'frd 5F 77
Purcell Room 4H 13
(in Southbank Cen.)

Purcells Av. HA8: Edg 5B 28
Purcell St. N1 . . . . .2E 84
Purchese St. NW1 . . . . .1D 6 (2H 83)
Purday Ho. W10 . . . . .3G 81
(off Bruckner St.)
Purdon Ho. SE15 . . . . .1G 121
(off Oliver Goldsmith Est.)
Purdy Ct. KT4: Wor Pk 2C 164
Purdy St. E3 . . . . .4D 86
PureGym
Aldgate .7J 9
Bayswater 7K 81
(off Moscow Pl.)
Canary Wharf 7C 86
Croydon 2C 168
(off Crown Hill)
East India Dock 7E 86
(off Clove Cres.)
Edgware 6B 28
Finchley 2K 45
Hallam St. 5K 5
(off Hallam St.)
Hammersmith Palais 4E 98
Holborn .5G 7
(off Theobald's Rd.)
Limehouse 6A 86
London Wall 6E 8
Marylebone,
Balcombe St. 5E 4 (5D 82)
Muswell Hill 4F 47
New Barnet 4G 21
Northolt .1E 76
Piccadilly 4C 12
(off Regent St.)
Putney .4G 117
St Pauls .6C 8
(off Little Britain)
Southgate 1C 32
South Kensington . . .3C 16 (4C 100)
Sydenham 4J 139
Tower Hill 2J 15
Wembley 5E 60
Purelake M. SE13 . . . . .3F 123
(off Marischal Rd.)
Purkis Cl. UB8: Hil 7E 74
Purland Cl. RM8: Dag 1F 73
Purland Rd. SE28 . . . . .2K 107
(not continuous)
Purleigh Av. IG8: Wfd G 6H 37
Purley Av. NW2 . . . . .2G 63
Purley Cl. IG5: Ilf 2E 52
Purley Pl. N1 . . . . .7B 66
Purley Rd. CR2: S Croy 7D 168
N9 . . . . .3K 33
Purley Vw. Ter. CR2: S Croy 7D 168
(off Sanderstead Rd.)
Purley Way CR0: C'don, Wadd 7K 155
The Purley Way Cen. 2A 168
Purley Way Cres. CR0: C'don 7K 155
Purneys Rd. SE9 . . . . .4B 124
Purrett Rd. SE18 . . . . .5K 107
Purser Ho. SW2 . . . . .6A 120
Pursers Cross Rd. SW6 . . . . .1H 117
Pursewardens Cl. W13 . . . . .1C 96
Pursley Rd. NW7 . . . . .7J 29
Purves Rd. NW10 . . . . .3D 80
Purvis Ho. CR0: C'don 7D 156
Pusey Ho. E14 . . . . .6C 86
(off Saracen St.)
Puteaux Ho. E2 . . . . .2K 85
(off Mace St.)
PUTNEY 4F 117
Putney Arts Theatre 4F 117
PUTNEY BRI. 3G 117
Putney Bri. App. SW6 . . . . .3G 117
Putney Bri. Rd. SW15 . . . . .4G 117
SW18 . . . . .4G 117
Putney Comn. SW15 . . . . .3E 116
Putney Exchange (Shop. Cen.) 4F 117
Putney Gdns. RM6: Chad H 5B 54
PUTNEY HEATH 6E 116
Putney Heath SW15 . . . . .7D 116
Putney Heath La. SW15 . . . . .6F 117

Putney High St.—Queen's Gdns.

Putney High St. SW15 … 4F 117
Putney Hill SW15 … 7F 117
(not continuous)
Putney Leisure Cen. … 4E 116
Putney Pk. Av. SW15 … 4C 116
Putney Pk. La. SW15 … 4D 116
(not continuous)
PUTNEY VALE … 3C 134
Putney Va. Crematorium … 2D 134
Putney Wharf SW15 … 3G 117
Putt in the Pk. … 4H 117
Pycroft Way N9 … 4A 34
Pyecombe Cnr. N12 … 4C 30
Pylbrook Rd. SM1: Sutt … 3J 165
Pylon Way CR0: Bedd … 1J 167
Pym Cl. EN4: E Barn … 5G 21
Pymers Mead SE21 … 1C 138
Pymmes Brook Dr.
EN4: E Barn … 4H 21
Pymmes Brook Ho. N10 … 7K 31
Pymmes Cl. N13 … 5E 32
N17 … 1H 49
Pymmes Gdns. Nth. N9 … 3A 34
Pymmes Gdns. Sth. N9 … 3A 34
Pymmes Grn. Rd. N11 … 4A 32
Pymmes Rd. N13 … 6D 32
Pynchester Cl. UB10: Ick … 2C 56
Pyne Rd. KT6: Surb … 1G 163
Pyne Ter. SW19 … 1G 135
(off Windlesham Gro.)
Pynfolds SE16 … 2H 103
Pynham Cl. SE2 … 3B 108
Pynnacles Cl. HA7: Stan … 5G 27
Pynnersmead SE24 … 5C 120
Pyramid Ct. KT1: King T … 2F 151
(off Cambridge Rd.)
Pyramid Ho. TW4: Houn … 2C 112
Pyrford Ho. SW9 … 4B 120
Pyrland Rd. N5 … 5D 66
TW10: Rich … 6F 115
Pyrmont Gro. SE27 … 3B 138
Pyrmont Rd. W4 … 6G 97
Pytchley Cres. SE19 … 6C 138
Pytchley Rd. SE22 … 3E 120

Q

The Q Bldg. E15 … 6G 69
(off The Grove)
QPR Training Academy & Sports Complex … 3H 95
Quad Ct. SE1 … 3E 102
(off Grigg's Pl.)
The Quadrangle E15 … 6G 69
SE24 … 5C 120
SW6 … 7G 99
SW10 … 1A 118
W2 … 7C 4 (6C 82)
Quadrangle Cl. SE1 … 4E 102
Quadrangle M. HA7: Stan … 7H 27
The Quadrant DA7: Bex … 7D 108
HA2: Harr … 3H 41
HA8: Edg … 6B 28
(off Manor Pk. Cres.)
SM2: Sutt … 6A 166
SW20 … 1G 153
TW9: Rich … 4D 114
W10 … 3F 81
Quadrant Arc. W1 … 3B 12
Quadrant Bus. Cen. NW6 … 1G 81
Quadrant Cl. NW4 … 5D 44
Quadrant Ct. HA9: Wemb … 4F 61
Quadrant Gro. NW5 … 5D 64
Quadrant Ho. E1 … 7G 85
(off Nesham St.)
E15 … 3G 87
(off Durban Rd.)
SE1 … 4A 14
Quadrant Rd. CR7: Thor H … 4B 156
TW9: Rich … 4D 114
Quadrant Wlk. E14 … 3D 104
(off Lanterns Way)
Quad Rd. HA9: Wemb … 3D 60
Quaggy Wlk. SE3 … 4J 123
Quain Mans. W14 … 6G 99
(off Queen's Club Gdns.)
Quainton St. NW10 … 3K 61
Quaker Ct. E1 … 4J 9
(off Quaker St.)
EC1 … 3E 8
Quaker La. UB2: S'hall … 3E 94
Quakers Course NW9 … 1B 44
Quakers La. TW7: Isle … 7A 96
Quakers Pl. E7 … 5B 70
Quaker St. E1 … 4J 9 (4F 85)
Quakers Wlk. N21 … 5J 23
Quality Ct. WC2 … 7J 7
Quant Bldg. E17 … 4C 50
Quantock Cl. UB3: Harl … 7F 93
Quantock Dr. KT4: Wor Pk … 2E 164
Quantock Gdns. NW2 … 2F 63
Quantock Ho. N16 … 1F 67
Quantock M. SE15 … 2G 121
Quantum Ct. E1 … 7J 85
(off King David La.)
Quarles Pk. Rd. RM6: Chad H … 6B 54
Quarrendon St. SW6 … 2J 117
Quarr Rd. SM5: Cars … 6B 154
Quarry Pk. Rd. SM1: Sutt … 6H 165
Quarry Ri. SM1: Sutt … 6H 165
Quarry Rd. SW18 … 6A 118
The Quarterdeck E14 … 2C 104
Quarter Ho. SW18 … 4A 118
Quartermaster La. NW7 … 5B 30
Quarters Apts. CR0: C'don … 2D 168
(off Wellesley Rd.)
Quartz Apts. SE14 … 6A 104
(off Moulding La.)
Quartz Ho. HA2: Harr … 1E 58
Quastel Ho. SE1 … 7E 14
(off Long La.)
Quatre Ports E4 … 5A 36
Quay Ho. E14 … 2C 104
(off Admirals Way)
Quayle Cres. N20 … 2F 31
Quay Rd. IG11: Bark … 1F 89
Quayside Cotts. E1 … 4K 15
(off Mews St.)
Quayside Ct. SE16 … 1K 103
(off Abbotshade Rd.)
Quayside Ho. E14 … 1B 104
E16 … 6H 87
(off Tarling Rd.)
TW8: Bford … 6F 97
W10 … 4G 81
Quayside Wlk. KT1: King T … 2D 150
(off Wadbrook St.)
Quay Vw. Apts. E14 … 3C 104
(off Arden Cres.)
Quebec M. W1 … 1F 11 (6D 82)
Quebec Rd. IG1: Ilf … 7F 53
IG2: Ilf … 7F 53
UB4: Yead … 6A 76
Quebec Way SE16 … 2K 103
Quebec Wharf E8 … 1E 84
(off Kingsland Rd.)
E14 … 6B 86
Quedgeley Ct. SE15 … 6F 103
(off Ebley Cl.)
Queen Adelaide Ct. SE20 … 6J 139
Queen Adelaide Rd. SE20 … 6J 139
Queen Alexandra Mans. WC1 … 2E 6
(off Bidborough St.)
Queen Alexandra's Ct. SW19 … 5H 135
Queen Anne Alcove … 3A 10
Queen Anne Av.
BR2: Broml … 3H 159
Queen Anne Ga. DA7: Bex … 3D 126
Queen Anne Ho. E16 … 1J 105
(off Hardy Av.)
Queen Anne M. W1 … 6K 5 (5F 83)
Queen Anne Rd. E9 … 6K 67
Queen Anne's Cl. TW2: Twick … 3H 131
Queen Anne's Ct. SE10 … 5F 105
(off Park Row)
Queen Anne's Gdns. CR4: Mitc … 3D 154
EN1: Enf … 6K 23
W4 … 3A 98
W5 … 2E 96
Queen Anne's Ga. SW1 … 7C 12 (2H 101)
Queen Anne's Gro. EN1: Enf … 7J 23
W4 … 3A 98
W5 … 2E 96
Queen Anne's Pl. EN1: Enf … 6K 23
Queen Annes Sq. SE1 … 4G 103
(off Monnow Rd.)
Queen Anne St. W1 … 7J 5 (6F 83)
Queen Anne's Wlk. WC1 … 4F 7
Queen Anne Ter. E1 … 7H 85
(off Sovereign Cl.)
Queenborough Gdns. BR7: Chst … 6H 143
IG2: Ilf … 4E 52
Queen Caroline's Temple
… 5A 10 (1B 100)
Queen Caroline St. W6 … 5E 98
Queen Catherine Ho. SW6 … 7K 99
(off Wandon Rd.)
Queen Charlotte's Cottage … 2D 114
Queen Ct. WC1 … 4F 7
(off Queen Sq.)
Queen Elizabeth II Stadium … 2A 24
Queen Elizabeth Bldgs. EC4 … 2J 13
Queen Elizabeth Ct. EN5: Barn … 3D 20
Queen Elizabeth Gdns.
SM4: Mord … 4J 153
Queen Elizabeth Hall … 4H 13 (1K 101)
Queen Elizabeth Ho. SW12 … 7E 118
Queen Elizabeth Leisure Cen. … 4C 20
Queen Elizabeth II Conference Cen.
… 7D 12 (2H 101)
Queen Elizabeth Olympic Pk. … 7D 68
Queen Elizabeth Rd. E17 … 3A 50
KT2: King T … 2F 151
Queen Elizabeth's Cl. N16 … 2D 66
Queen Elizabeth's Coll. SE10 … 7E 104
Queen Elizabeth's Dr.
CR0: New Ad … 7F 171
N14 … 1D 32
Queen Elizabeth's Hunting Lodge … 1C 36
Queen Elizabeth St. SE1 … 6J 15 (2E 102)
Queen Elizabeth's Wlk. N16 … 1D 66
SM6: Bedd … 4H 167
Queen Elizabeth Wlk. SW13 … 1C 116
Queenhithe EC4 … 2D 14 (7C 84)
Queen Isabella Way EC1 … 7B 8
Queen Margaret Flats E2 … 3H 85
(off St Jude's Rd.)
Queen Margaret's Gro. N1 … 5E 66
Queen Mary Av. E18 … 1J 51
SM4: Mord … 5F 153
Queen Mary Cl. KT6: Surb … 3G 163
Queen Mary Ct. TW19: Stanw … 1A 128
Queen Mary Ho. E16 … 1K 105
(off Wesley Av.)
E18 … 1K 51
Queen Mary Rd. SE19 … 6B 138
TW17: Shep … 2E 146
Queen Mary's Av. SM5: Cars … 7D 166
Queen Marys Bldgs. SW1 … 3B 18
(off Stillington St.)
Queen Mary's Ct. SE10 … 6F 105
(off Park Row)
Queen Mary's Ho. SW15 … 6C 116
Queen Mary University of London
Charterhouse Sq. … 4B 8 (4B 84)
Lincoln's Inn Flds. Campus … 7G 7
(off Remnant St.)
Mile End Campus … 4A 86
W. Smithfield Campus … 6B 8
Queen Mother Memorial … 5C 12
The Queen Mother Sports Cen. … 3A 18
Queen of Denmark Ct. SE16 … 3B 104
Queens Acre SM3: Cheam … 7F 165
Queen's Av. UB6: G'frd … 6F 77
Queens Av. HA7: Stan … 3C 42
IG8: Wfd G … 5E 36
N3 … 7F 31
N10 … 3E 46
Queens Av. N20 … 2G 31
N21 … 1G 33
TW13: Hanw … 4A 130
Queensberry Ho. TW9: Rich … 5C 114
Queensberry M. W.
SW7 … 3A 16 (4B 100)
Queensberry Pl. E12 … 5B 70
SW7 … 3A 16 (4B 100)
TW9: Rich … 5D 114
(off Friars La.)
Queensberry Way SW7 … 3A 16 (4B 100)
Queensborough Ct. N3 … 4H 45
(off Tillingbourne Gdns.)
Queensborough M. W2 … 7A 82
Queensborough Pas. W2 … 7A 82
(off Queensborough M.)
Queensborough Studios W2 … 7A 82
(off Queensborough M.)
Queensborough Ter. W2 … 7K 81
Queensbridge Ct. E2 … 1F 85
(off Queensbridge Rd.)
Queensbridge Pk. TW7: Isle … 5J 113
Queensbridge Rd. E2 … 6F 67
E8 … 6F 67
Queensbridge Sports & Community Cen.
… 7F 67
QUEENSBURY … 3E 42
Queensbury Circ. Pde.
HA3: Kenton … 3E 42
HA7: Kenton … 3E 42
Queensbury Rd. HA0: Wemb … 2F 79
NW9 … 7K 43
Queensbury Sta. Pde. HA8: Edg … 3F 43
Queensbury St. N1 … 7C 66
Queen's Cir. SW11 … 7F 101
Queens Cl. HA8: Edg … 5B 28
SM6: W'gton … 5F 167
Queen's Club Gdns. W14 … 6G 99
The Queen's Club (Tennis Courts) … 5G 99
Queens Club Ter. W14 … 6H 99
(off Normand Rd.)
Queen's Ct. NW8 … 2B 82
(off Queen's Ter.)
Queens Ct. CR2: S Croy … 5C 168
(off Warham Rd.)
CR7: Thor H … 5A 156
E11 … 7G 51
HA3: Kenton … 2B 42
IG9: Buck H … 2G 37
NW6 … 5K 63
NW11 … 5H 45
SE16 … 7K 15
SE23 … 2J 139
TW10: Rich … 6F 115
W2 … 7K 81
(off Queensway)
Queenscourt HA9: Wemb … 4E 60
Queen's Cres. NW5 … 6E 64
TW10: Rich … 5F 115
Queenscroft Rd. SE9 … 5B 124
Queensdale Cres. W11 … 1F 99
(not continuous)
Queensdale Pl. W11 … 1G 99
Queensdale Rd. W11 … 1F 99
Queensdale Wlk. W11 … 1G 99
The Queen's Diamond Jubilee Galleries
… 1E 18 (3J 101)
Queensdown Rd. E5 … 4H 67
Queen's Dr. KT5: Surb … 7G 151
KT7: T Ditt … 6A 150
N4 … 2B 66
Queens Dr. E10 … 7C 50
W3 … 6F 79
W5 … 6F 79
Queen's Elm Pde. SW3 … 5B 16
(off Old Church St.)
Queen's Elm Sq. SW3 … 6B 16 (5B 100)
Queensferry Wlk. N17 … 4H 49
Queensfield Ct. SM3: Cheam … 4E 164
Queen's Gallery … 7K 11 (2F 101)
Queen's Gdns. NW4 … 5E 44
RM13: Rain … 2K 91
TW5: Hest … 1C 112

A-Z London 373

Queen's Gdns.—Radley Gdns.

Queen's Gdns. W2 7A 82
W5 4C 78
Queen's Ga. SW7 7A 10 (2A 100)
Queensgate Ct. N12 5E 30
Queen's Ga. Gdns. SW7 3A 100
Queens Ga. Gdns. BR7: Chst 1H 161
SW15 4D 116
Queensgate Ho. *E3* *2B 86*
(off Hereford Rd.)
Queen's Ga. M. SW7 3A 100
Queensgate M. BR3: Beck 1A 158
Queen's Ga. Pl. SW7 3A 100
Queensgate Pl. NW6 7J 63
Queen's Ga. Pl. M. SW7 2A 16 (3A 100)
Queen's Ga. Ter. SW7 1A 16 (3A 100)
Queens Ga. Vs. E9 7A 68
Queen's Gro. NW8 1B 82
Queens Gro. Rd. E4 1A 36
Queen's Gro. Studios NW8 1B 82
Queen's Head Pas. EC4 7C 8 (6C 84)
Queen's Head St. N1 1B 84
Queen's Head Yd. SE1 5E 14
The Queen's House *6F 105*
(within National Maritime Mus.)
Queens Ho. *SE17* *6D 102*
(off Merrow St.)
SW8 *7J 101*
(off Sth. Lambeth Rd.)
TW11: Tedd 6K 131
W2 *7K 81*
(off Queensway)
Queenshurst Sq. KT2: King T 1E 150
Queen's Ice & Bowl 7K 81
Queen's Keep TW1: Twick 6C 114
Queensland Av. N18 6H 33
SW19 1K 153
Queensland Cl. E17 2B 50
Queensland Ho. *E16* *1E 106*
(off Rymill St.)
Queensland Rd. N7 4A 66
Queens La. N10 3F 47
Queen's Mans. *W6* *4F 99*
(off Brook Grn.)
Queen's Mkt. E13 1A 88
Queens Mead HA8: Edg 6A 28
Queensmead NW8 1B 82
Queens Mead Rd. BR2: Broml 2H 159
Queensmead Sports Cen. 5B 58
Queensmere Cl. SW19 2F 135
Queensmere Ct. SW13 7B 98
Queensmere Rd. SW19 2F 135
Queen's M. W2 7K 81
Queensmill Rd. SW6 7F 99
Queen's Pde. *N11* *5J 31*
(off Friern Barnet Rd.)
NW2 *6E 62*
(off Willesden La.)
Queens Pde. N8 4B 48
NW4 *5E 44*
(off Queens Rd.)
W5 6F 79
Queen's Pde. Cl. N11 5J 31
QUEENS PARK 2G 81
Queens Pk. Ct. W10 3F 81
Queen's Pk. Gdns. TW13: Felt 3H 129
Queen's Pk. Rangers FC 1D 98
Queens Pas. BR7: Chst 6F 143
Queens Pl. SM4: Mord 4J 153
Queen's Prom. KT1: King T, Surb 4D 150
Queen Sq. WC1 4F 7 (4J 83)
Queen Sq. Pl. WC1 4F 7
Queen's Quay *EC4* *2C 14*
(off Up. Thames St.)
Queens Reach KT1: King T 2D 150
KT8: E Mos 4J 149
Queens Ride SW13 3C 116
Queens Ri. TW10: Rich 6F 115
Queen's Rd. CR4: Mitc 3B 154
DA16: Well 2B 126
E17 6B 50
EN1: Enf 4K 23
IG9: Buck H 2E 36
KT7: T Ditt 5K 149
Queen's Rd. SE14 1H 121
SE15 1H 121
SW14 3K 115
TW3: Houn 3F 113
TW10: Rich 7F 115
TW11: Tedd 6K 131
TW12: Hamp H 4F 131
TW13: Felt 1K 129
W5 6E 78
Queens Rd. BR1: Broml 2J 159
BR3: Beck 2A 158
BR7: Chst 6F 143
CR0: C'don 6B 156
E11 7F 51
E13 1K 87
EN5: Barn 3A 20
IG11: Bark 6G 71
KT2: King T 7G 133
KT3: N Mald 4B 152
N3 1A 46
N9 3C 34
N11 7D 32
NW4 5E 44
SM4: Mord 4J 153
SM6: W'gton 5F 167
SW19 6H 135
TW1: Twick 1A 132
UB2: S'hall 2B 94
UB3: Hayes 6G 75
UB7: W Dray 2B 92
Queens Rd. Est. EN5: Barn 3A 20
Queens Rd. W. E13 2J 87
Queen's Row SE17 6D 102
Queens St. TW15: Ashf 4B 128
Queen's Ter. E13 1K 87
NW8 1B 82
Queens Ter. *E1* *4J 85*
(off Cephas St.)
KT7: T Ditt *6A 150*
(off Queens Dr.)
TW7: Isle 4A 114
Queen's Ter. Cotts. W7 2J 95
Queen's Theatre *2C 12*
(off Shaftesbury Av.)
Queensthorpe M. SE26 4K 139
Queensthorpe Rd. SE26 4K 139
Queen's Tower *1A 16*
(within Impertial College London)
Queenstown M. SW8 2F 119
Queenstown Rd. SW8 1F 119
SW11 7J 17 (6F 101)
Queen St. CR0: C'don 4C 168
DA7: Bex 3F 127
EC4 2D 14 (7C 84)
(not continuous)
N17 6K 33
RM7: Rom 6K 55
W1 4J 11 (1F 101)
Queen St. Pl. EC4 2D 14 (7C 84)
Queensville Rd. SW12 7H 119
Queen's Wlk. N5 5B 66
SW1 5A 12 (1G 101)
TW15: Ashf 4A 128
W5 4C 78
Queens Wlk. E4 1A 36
HA1: Harr 4J 41
HA4: Ruis 2A 58
NW9 2J 61
The Queen's Wlk. SE1 4H 13 (1K 101)
Queens Wlk. Ter. HA4: Ruis 3A 58
Queen's Way NW4 5E 44
Queens Way TW13: Hanw 4A 130
Queensway BR4: W W'ck 3G 171
BR5: Pet W 5G 161
CR0: Wadd 6K 167
EN3: Pond E 4C 24
TW16: Sun 2K 147
W2 6K 81
Queensway Bus. Cen.
EN3: Pond E 4C 24
Queensway Ind. Est. EN3: Pond E 4D 24
Queensway M. *SE6* *4E 140*
(off Whitefoot La.)
Queenswell Av. N20 3H 31
Queenswood Av. CR7: Thor H 5A 156
E17 1E 50
SM6: Bedd 4H 167
TW3: Houn 2D 112
TW12: Hamp 6F 131
Queenswood Ct. KT2: King T 1G 151
SE27 4D 138
SW4 5J 119
Queenswood Gdns. E11 1K 69
Queenswood Pk. N3 2G 45
Queens Wood Rd. N10 6F 47
Queenswood Rd. DA15: Sidc 5K 125
SE23 3K 139
Queen's Yd. WC1 4B 6 (5G 83)
Queens Yd. E9 6C 68
QUEEN VICTORIA 4F 165
Queen Victoria Av. HA0: Wemb 7D 60
Queen Victoria Memorial
7A 12 (2G 101)
Queen Victoria Seaman's Rest
E14 *6D 86*
(off E. India Dock Rd.)
Queen Victoria Statue 1K 99
Queen Victoria St. EC4 2A 14 (7B 84)
Queen Victoria Ter. *E1* *7H 85*
(off Sovereign Cl.)
Quemerford Rd. N7 5K 65
Quendon Ho. *W10* *4E 80*
(off Sutton Way)
Quenington Ct. SE15 6F 103
Quentin Ho. *SE1* *6A 14*
(off Chaplin Cl.)
Quentin Pl. SE13 3G 123
Quentin Rd. SE13 3G 123
Quernmore Cl. BR1: Broml 6J 141
Quernmore Rd. BR1: Broml 6J 141
N4 6A 48
Querrin St. SW6 2A 118
The Quest *W11* *7G 81*
(off Clarendon Rd.)
Quested Ct. *E8* *5H 67*
(off Brett Rd.)
The Questors Theatre 7C 78
Quex Ct. *NW6* *1K 81*
(off West End La.)
Quex M. NW6 1J 81
Quex Rd. NW6 1J 81
Quiberon Ct. *E13* *1J 87*
(off Pelly Rd.)
TW16: Sun 3J 147
Quick Rd. W4 5A 98
Quicks Rd. SW19 7K 135
Quick St. N1 2B 84
Quick St. M. N1 2B 84
Quickswood NW3 7C 64
Quiet Nook BR2: Hayes 3B 172
Quill Ho. *E2* *3K 9*
(off Cheshire St.)
Quill La. SW15 4F 117
Quill St. N4 3A 66
W5 3E 78
Quilp St. SE1 6C 14 (2C 102)
(not continuous)
Quilters Pl. SE9 1G 143
Quilter St. E2 1K 9 (3G 85)
SE18 5K 107
Quilting Ct. *SE16* *2K 103*
(off Garter Way)
Quince Ho. *SE13* *2D 122*
(off Quince Rd.)
Quince Rd. SE13 2D 122
Quinn Cl. E2 2J 85
Quinnell Cl. SE18 5K 107
Quinta Dr. EN5: Barn 5A 20
Quintain Ho. *KT1: King T* *2D 150*
(off Wood St.)
The Quintet KT12: Walt T 7J 147
Quintin Av. SW20 1H 153
Quintin Cl. HA5: Eastc 4K 39
Quinton Cl. BR3: Beck 3E 158
SM6: W'gton 4F 167
TW5: Cran 7K 93
Quinton Ct. *SE16* *4A 104*
(off Plough Way)
Quinton Ho. *SW8* *7J 101*
(off Wyvil Rd.)
Quinton Rd. KT7: T Ditt 1A 162
Quinton St. SW18 2A 136
Quixley St. E14 7F 87
Quorn Rd. SE22 4E 120

R

Rabbit Row W8 1J 99
Rabbits Rd. E12 4C 70
Rabournmead Dr.
UB5: N'olt 5C 58
Raby Rd. KT3: N Mald 4K 151
Raby St. E14 6A 86
Raccoon Way TW4: Houn 2A 112
Rachel Cl. IG6: Ilf 3H 53
Racine *SE5* *1E 120*
(off Sceaux Gdns.)
Rackham Cl. DA16: Well 2B 126
Rackham M. SW16 6G 137
Rackstraw Ho. NW3 7D 64
Racton Rd. SW6 6J 99
RADA
Chenies St. *5C 6*
(off Chenies St.)
Gower St. 5C 6
RADA Studios *5C 6*
(off Chenies St.)
Radbourne Av. W5 4C 96
Radbourne Cl. E5 4K 67
Radbourne Ct. HA3: Kenton 6B 42
Radbourne Cres. E17 2F 51
Radbourne Rd. SW12 7G 119
Radcliff Ct. *E3* *4B 86*
(off Jospeh St.)
Radcliffe Av. EN2: Enf 1H 23
NW10 2C 80
Radcliffe Gdns. SM5: Cars 7C 166
Radcliffe Ho. *SE16* *4H 103*
(off Anchor St.)
SE20 1G 157
Radcliffe M. TW12: Hamp H 5G 131
Radcliffe Path SW8 2F 119
Radcliffe Rd. CR0: C'don 2F 169
HA3: W'stone 2A 42
N21 1G 33
SE1 3E 102
Radcliffe Sq. SW15 6F 117
Radcliffe Way UB5: N'olt 3B 76
Radcot Point SE23 3K 139
Radcot St. SE11 6K 19 (5A 102)
Raddington Rd. W10 5G 81
Raddon Twr. *E8* *6F 67*
(off Dalston Sq.)
Radfield Way DA15: Sidc 7H 125
Radford Ct. *SE15* *7H 103*
(off Old Kent Rd.)
Radford Est. NW10 3A 80
Radford Ho. *E14* *5D 86*
(off St Leonard's Rd.)
N7 5K 65
Radford Rd. SE13 6E 122
Radford Way IG11: Bark 3K 89
Radio La. RM8: Dag 3B 72
Radipole Rd. SW6 1H 117
Radisson Ct. *SE1* *7G 15*
(off Long La.)
Radius Apts. *N1* *1G 7*
(off Omega Pl.)
Radius Pk. TW14: Felt 4H 111
Radland Rd. E16 6H 87
Radleigh Pl. BR3: Beck 6C 140
Radlet Av. SE26 3H 139
Radlett Cl. E7 6H 69
Radlett Pl. NW8 1C 82
Radley Av. IG3: Bark, Ilf 4A 72
Radley Cl. TW14: Felt 1H 129
Radley Ct. SE16 2K 103
Radley Gdns. HA3: Kenton 4E 42

374 A-Z London

Radley Ho. NW1 . . . . .3E *4*
(off Gloucester Pl.)
SE2 . . . . .2D *108*
(off Wolvercote Rd.)
Radley M. W8 . . . . .3J *99*
Radley Rd. N17 . . . . .2E *48*
Radley's La. E18 . . . . .2J *51*
Radleys Mead RM10: Dag 6H *73*
Radley Sq. E5 . . . . .2J *67*
Radley Ter. E16 . . . . .5H *87*
(off Hermit Rd.)
Radlix Rd. E10 . . . . .1C *68*
Radnor Av. DA16: Well 5B *126*
HA1: Harr 5J *41*
Radnor Cl. BR7: Chst 6J *143*
CR4: Mitc 4J *155*
Radnor Ct. HA3: Hrw W 1K *41*
W7 . . . . .6K *77*
(off Copley Cl.)
Radnor Cres. IG4: Ilf 5D *52*
SE18 . . . . .7A *108*
Radnor Gdns. EN1: Enf 1K *23*
TW1: Twick 2K *131*
Radnor Gro. UB10: Hil 2C *74*
Radnor Ho. EC1 . . . . .2D *8*
(off Radnor St.)
SW16 . . . . .2K *155*
Radnor Lodge W2 . . . . .1B *10*
(off Sussex Pl.)
Radnor M. W2 . . . . .1B (6B *82*)
Radnor Pl. W2 . . . . .1C *10* (6C *82*)
Radnor Rd. HA1: Harr 5H *41*
NW6 . . . . .1G *81*
SE15 .7G *103*
TW1: Twick 1K *131*
Radnor St. EC1 . . . . .2D *8* (3C *84*)
Radnor Ter. SM2: Sutt 7J *165*
W14 . . . . .4H *99*
Radnor Wlk. CR0: C'don 6A *158*
E14 . . . . .4C *104*
(off Barnsdale Av.)
SW3 . . . . .6D *16* (5C *100*)
Radnor Way NW10 . . . . .4H *79*
Radstock Av. HA3: Kenton 3A *42*
Radstock Cl. N11 . . . . .6K *31*
Radstock St. SW11 . . . . .7C *100*
(not continuous)
Radway Ho. W2 . . . . .5J *81*
(off Alfred Rd.)
Raeburn Av. KT5: Surb 1H *163*
Raeburn Cl. KT1: Hamp W 7D *132*
NW11 . . . . .6A *46*
Raeburn Ho. UB5: N'olt 2B *76*
(off Academy Gdns.)
Raeburn Rd. DA15: Sidc 6J *125*
HA8: Edg 1G *43*
UB4: Hayes 2F *75*
Raeburn St. SW2 . . . . .4J *119*
RAF Bomber Command Memorial
St. 6J *11* (2F *101*)
Raffles Ho. NW4 . . . . .4D *44*
Rafford Way BR1: Broml 2K *159*
RAF Mus. London 2C *44*
RAF Uxbridge,
Battle of Britain Bunker 1B *74*
Ragged School Mus. 5A *86*
Raggleswood BR7: Chst 1E *160*
Raglan Cl. TW4: Houn 5D *112*
Raglan Ct.
CR2: S Croy 5B *168*
E17 . . . . .5E *50*
HA9: Wemb 4F *61*
SE12 . . . . .5J *123*
Raglan Rd. BR2: Broml 4A *160*
DA17: Belv 4F *109*
E17 . . . . .5E *50*
EN1: Enf 7A *24*
SE18 . . . . .5G *107*
Raglan St. NW5 . . . . .6F *65*
Raglan Ter. HA2: Harr 4F *59*
Raglan Way UB5: N'olt 6G *59*
Ragley Cl. W3 . . . . .2J *97*
Ragwort Ct. SE26 . . . . .5H *139*

Rahere Ct. E1 . . . . .4A *86*
(off Toby La.)
Raider Cl. RM7: Mawney 1G *55*
Railey M. NW5 . . . . .5G *65*
Railshead Rd. TW1: Isle 4B *114*
TW7: Isle 4B *114*
Railton Rd. SE24 . . . . .4A *120*
Railway App. HA1: Harr 4K *41*
HA3: Harr 4K *41*
N4 . . . . .6A *48*
RM7: Rush G 6K *55*
SE1 . . . . .5F *15* (1D *102*)
SM6: W'gton 5F *167*
TW1: Twick 7A *114*
Railway Arches E1 . . . . .6K *85*
(off Barnardo St.)
E1 . . . . .7H *85*
(off Chapman St.)
E1 . . . . .1J *9*
(off Cremer St.)
E2 . . . . .2F *85*
(off Geffrye St.)
E2 . . . . .1F *85*
(off Laburnum St.)
E3 . . . . .4B *86*
(off Cantrell Rd.)
E7 . . . . .4J *69*
(off Winchelsea Rd.)
E8 . . . . .7H *67*
(off Martello Ter.)
E8 . . . . .7H *67*
(off Mentmore Ter.)
E10 . . . . .1E *68*
E11 . . . . .1F *69*
(off Grove Grn. Rd.)
E16 . . . . .1J *105*
W6 . . . . .3E *98*
W12 . . . . .2E *98*
(off Shepherd's Bush Mkt.)
Railway Av. SE16 . . . . .2J *103*
(not continuous)
Railway Children Wlk.
BR1: Broml 2J *141*
Railway Cotts. E15 . . . . .2G *87*
(off Baker's Row)
SW19 . . . . .4K *135*
W6 . . . . .2E *98*
(off Sulgrave Rd.)
Railway Fields
Local Nature Reserve 6B *48*
Railway Gro. SE14 . . . . .7B *104*
Railway M. W10 . . . . .6G *81*
Railway Pas. TW11: Tedd 6A *132*
Railway Pl. DA17: Belv 3G *109*
Railway Ri. SE22 . . . . .4E *120*
Railway Rd. TW11: Tedd 4J *131*
Railway Side SW13 . . . . .3A *116*
Railway Sidings Rd. SE16 . . . . . .3G *103*
Railway Sta. Bri. E7 . . . . .5K *69*
Railway St. N1 . . . . .2J *83*
RM6: Chad H 7C *54*
Railway Ter. E17 . . . . .1E *50*
SE13 . . . . .5D *122*
TW13: Felt 1J *129*
Railway Wharf KT1: King T 1D *150*
(off Thames Side)
Rainbird Cl. HA0: Wemb 2C *78*
Rainborough Cl. NW10 . . . . .6J *61*
Rainbow Av. E14 . . . . .5D *104*
Rainbow Ct. SE14 . . . . .6A *104*
(off Chipley St.)
Rainbow Ind. Est. SW20 . . . . .2D *152*
UB7: Yiew 7A *74*
Rainbow Quay SE16 . . . . .3A *104*
(not continuous)
Rainbow St. SE5 . . . . .7E *102*
Raine Gdns. IG8: Wfd G 4D *36*
Rainer Apartment CR0: C'don . .1D *168*
(off Cherry Orchard Rd.)
Raines Ct. N16 . . . . .2F *67*
Raine St. E1 . . . . .1H *103*
Rainham Cl. SE9 . . . . .6J *125*
SW11 . . . . .6C *118*

Rainham Ho. NW1 . . . . .1G *83*
(off Bayham Pl.)
Rainham Rd. NW10 . . . . .3E *80*
Rainham Rd. Nth. RM10: Dag 2G *73*
Rainham Rd. Sth. RM10: Dag 4H *73*
Rainhill Way E3 . . . . .3C *86*
(not continuous)
Rainsborough Av. SE8 . . . . .4A *104*
Rainsborough Ho. SW15 . . . . .5G *117*
(off Stamford Sq.)
Rainsborough Sq. SW6 . . . . .6J *99*
Rainsford Cl. HA7: Stan 5H *27*
Rainsford Rd. NW10 . . . . .3G *79*
Rainsford St. W2 . . . . .7C *4* (6C *82*)
Rainton Rd. SE7 . . . . .5J *105*
Rainville Rd. W6 . . . . .6E *98*
Raisins Hill HA5: Eastc 3A *40*
Raith Av. N14 . . . . .3C *32*
Rajsee Apts. E2 . . . . .3G *85*
(off Bethnal Grn. Rd.)
Raleana Rd. E14 . . . . .1E *104*
Raleigh Av. SM6: Bedd 4H *167*
UB4: Yead 5K *75*
Raleigh Cl. HA4: Ruis 2H *57*
HA5: Pinn 7B *40*
NW4 . . . . .5E *44*
Raleigh Ct. BR3: Beck 1D *158*
SE8 . . . . .5A *104*
(off Evelyn St.)
SE16 . . . . .1K *103*
(off Clarence M.)
SM6: W'gton 6F *167*
W12 . . . . .2E *98*
(off Scott's Rd.)
W13 . . . . .5B *78*
Raleigh Dr. KT5: Surb 1J *163*
N20 . . . . .3H *31*
Raleigh Gdns. CR4: Mitc 3D *154*
(not continuous)
SW2 .6K *119*
Raleigh Ho. BR1: Broml 1J *159*
(off Hammelton Rd.)
CR0: C'don 7K *155*
(off Mitcham Rd.)
E14 . . . . .2D *104*
(off Admirals Way)
SW1 . . . . .7C *18*
(off Dolphin Sq.)
Raleigh M. BR6: Chels 5K *173*
N1 . . . . .1B *84*
(off Packington St.)
Raleigh Rd. EN2: Enf 4J *23*
N8 . . . . .4A *48*
SE20 . . . . .7K *139*
TW9: Rich 3F *115*
TW13: Felt 3H *129*
UB2: S'hall 5C *94*
Raleigh St. N1 . . . . .1B *84*
Raleigh Way N14 . . . . .1C *32*
TW13: Hanw 5A *130*
Rali La. E4 .1A *36*
Rally Bldg. E17 . . . . .5B *50*
Ralph Bayer Ct. E3 . . . . .5C *86*
(off Geoff Cade Way)
Ralph Brook Ct. N1 . . . . .1F *9*
(off Chart St.)
Ralph Ct. W2 . . . . .6K *81*
(off Queensway)
Ralph Perring Ct. BR3: Beck 4C *158*
Ralston St. SW3 . . . . .6E *16* (5D *100*)
Ramac Ind. Est. SE7 . . . . .4K *105*
Rama Cl. SW16 . . . . .7J *137*
Rama Ct. HA1: Harr 2J *59*
Ramac Way SE7 . . . . .4K *105*
Rama La. SE19 . . . . .7F *139*
Ramar Ho. E1 . . . . .5G *85*
(off Hanbury St.)
Rambert 4J *13*
(off Upper Ground)
Rambler Cl. SW16 . . . . .4G *137*
Rame Cl. SW17 . . . . .5E *136*
Ramilles Cl. SW2 . . . . .6J *119*
Ramillies Pl. W1 . . . . .1A *12* (6G *83*)

Ramillies Rd. DA15: Sidc 6B *126*
NW7 . . . . .2F *29*
W4 . . . . .4K *97*
Ramillies St. W1 . . . . .1A *12* (6G *83*)
Ramones Ter. CR4: Mitc 4J *155*
(off Yorkshire Rd.)
Rampart St. E1 . . . . .6H *85*
Ram Pas. KT1: King T 2D *150*
Rampayne St. SW1 . . . . . .5C *18* (5H *101*)
Ram Pl. E9 .6J *67*
Rampton Cl. E4 . . . . .3H *35*
Ram Quarter SW18 . . . . .5K *117*
Ramsay Ho. NW8 . . . . .2C *82*
(off Townshend Est.)
Ramsay M. SW3 . . . . .7C *16* (6C *100*)
Ramsay Rd. E7 . . . . .4G *69*
W3 . . . . .3J *97*
Ramscroft Cl. N9 . . . . .7K *23*
Ramsdale Rd. SW17 . . . . .5E *136*
Ramsden Dr. RM5: Col R 1G *55*
Ramsden Rd. DA8: Erith 7K *109*
N11 . . . . .5J *31*
SW12 . . . . .6E *118*
Ramsey Cl. NW9 . . . . .6B *44*
UB6: G'frd 5H *59*
Ramsey Ct. CR0: C'don 2B *168*
(off Church St.)
Ramsey Ho. SW9 . . . . .7A *102*
Ramsey Rd. CR7: Thor H 6K *155*
Ramsey St. E2 . . . . .4G *85*
Ramsey Wlk. N1 . . . . .6D *66*
Ramsey Way N14 . . . . .7B *22*
Ramsfort Ho. SE16 . . . . .4H *103*
(off Camilla Rd.)
Ramsgate Cl. E16 . . . . .1K *105*
Ramsgate St. E8 . . . . .6F *67*
Ramsgill App. IG2: Ilf 4K *53*
Ramsgill Dr. IG2: Ilf 5K *53*
Rams Gro. RM6: Chad H 4E *54*
Ram St. SW18 . . . . .5K *117*
Ram Twr. SW18 . . . . .5K *117*
Ramus Dr. UB4: Yead 4B *76*
Ramuswood Av. BR6: Chels 5J *173*
Rancliffe Gdns. SE9 . . . . .4C *124*
Rancliffe Rd. E6 . . . . .2C *88*
Randall Av. NW2 . . . . .2A *62*
Randall Cl. DA8: Erith 6J *109*
SW11 . . . . .1C *118*
Randall Ct. NW7 . . . . .7H *29*
Randall Pl. SE10 . . . . .7E *104*
Randall Rd. SE11 . . . . .4G *19* (5K *101*)
Randall Row SE11 . . . . . .4G *19* (4K *101*)
Randalls Rents SE16 . . . . .3B *104*
(off Gulliver St.)
Randell's Rd. N1 . . . . .1J *83*
Randisbourne Gdns. SE6 . . . . . . .3D *140*
Randle Rd. TW10: Ham 4C *132*
Randlesdown Rd. SE6 . . . . .4C *140*
(not continuous)
Randolph App. E16 . . . . .6A *88*
Randolph Av. W9 . . . . .4A *4* (2K *81*)
Randolph Cl. DA7: Bex 3J *127*
KT2: King T 5J *133*
Randolph Cres. W9 . . . . .4A *82*
Randolph Gdns. NW6 . . . . .2K *81*
Randolph Gro. RM6: Chad H 5C *54*
Randolph M. W9 . . . . .4A *82*
Randolph Rd.
BR2: Broml 1D *172*
E17 . . . . .5D *50*
UB1: S'hall 2D *94*
W9 . . . . .4A *82*
Randolph St. NW1 . . . . .7G *65*
Randon Cl. HA2: Harr 2F *41*
Ranelagh Av. SW6 . . . . .3H *117*
SW13 . . . . .2C *116*
Ranelagh Bri. W2 . . . . .5K *81*
Ranelagh Cl. HA8: Edg 4B *28*
Ranelagh Cotts. SW1 . . . . .5J *17*
(off Ebury Bri. Rd.)
Ranelagh Dr. HA8: Edg 4B *28*
TW1: Twick 4B *114*

Ranelagh Gdns. E11 . . . . .5A **52**
   IG1: Ilf 1D **70**
   SW6 . . . . .7J **97**
     (not continuous)
   W4 . . . . .7J **97**
   W6 . . . . .4B **98**
Ranelagh Gdns. Mans. SW6 . . . . .3G **117**
    (off Ranelagh Gdns.)
Ranelagh Gro. SW1 . . . . . .5H 17 (5E **100**)
Ranelagh Ho. SW3 . . . . .5E **16**
     (off Elystan Pl.)
Ranelagh M. W5 . . . . .2D **96**
Ranelagh Pl. KT3: N Mald 5A **152**
Ranelagh Rd. E6 . . . . .1E **88**
   E11 . . . . .4G **69**
   E15 . . . . .2G **87**
   HA0: Wemb 6D **60**
   N17 . . . . .3E **48**
   N22 . . . . .1K **47**
   NW10 . . . . .2B **80**
   SW1 . . . . .6B 18 (5G **101**)
   UB1: S'hall 1B **94**
   W5 . . . . .2D **96**
Ranfurly Rd. SM1: Sutt 2J **165**
Rangbourne Ho. N7 . . . . .5J **65**
Rangefield Rd. BR1: Broml 5G **141**
Rangemoor Rd. N15 . . . . .5F **49**
Ranger's House 1F **123**
Ranger's Rd. E4 . . . . .1B **36**
Rangers Sq. SE10 . . . . .1F **123**
Range Way TW17: Shep 7C **146**
Rangeworth Pl. DA15: Sidc 3K **143**
Rangoon St. EC3 . . . . .1J **15**
Rankin Cl. NW9 . . . . .3A **44**
Rankine Ho. SE1 . . . . .3C **102**
     (off Bath Ter.)
Ranleigh Gdns. DA7: Bex 7F **109**
Ranmere St. SW12 . . . . .1F **137**
Ranmoor Cl. HA1: Harr 4H **41**
Ranmoor Gdns. HA1: Harr 4H **41**
Ranmore Av. CR0: C'don 3F **169**
Ranmore Cl. KT6: Surb 5D **150**
Ranmore Path BR5: St M Cry 4K **161**
Ranmore Rd. SM2: Cheam 7F **165**
Rannoch Cl. HA8: Edg 2C **28**
Rannoch Rd. W6 . . . . .6E **98**
Rannock Av. NW9 . . . . .7K **43**
Ransome's Dock Bus. Cen.
   SW11 . . . . .7C **100**
Ransom Rd. SE7 . . . . .4A **106**
Ranston St. NW1 . . . . .5C 4 (5C **82**)
Ranulf Rd. NW2 . . . . .4H **63**
Ranwell Cl. E3 . . . . .1B **86**
Ranwell Ho. E3 . . . . .1B **86**
     (off Ranwell Cl.)
Ranworth Rd. N9 . . . . .2D **34**
Ranyard Cl. KT9: Chess 3F **163**
Raphael Cl. KT1: King T 4D **150**
Raphael Ct. SE16 . . . . .5H **103**
     (off Stubbs Dr.)
Raphael Dr. KT7: T Ditt 7K **149**
Raphael Ho. IG1: Ilf 2G **71**
Raphael St. SW7 . . . . . .7E 10 (2D **100**)
Raphen Apts. E3 . . . . .2A **86**
     (off Medway Rd.)
Rapley Ho. E2 . . . . .2K **9**
     (off Turin St.)
Raquel Ct. SE1 . . . . .6G **15**
     (off Snowfields)
Rashleigh Ct. SW8 . . . . .2F **119**
Rashleigh Ho. WC1 . . . . .2E **6**
     (off Thanet St.)
Rashleigh St. SW8 . . . . .2F **119**
     (off Peardon St.)
Rasper Rd. N20 . . . . .2F **31**
Rastell Av. SW2 . . . . .2H **137**
RATCLIFF .5A **86**
Ratcliffe Cl. SE12 . . . . .7J **123**
Ratcliffe Cl. SE1 . . . . .7D **14**
     (off Gt. Dover St.)
Ratcliffe Cross St. E1 . . . . .6K **85**
Ratcliffe Ho. E14 . . . . .6A **86**
     (off Barnes St.)

Ratcliffe La. E14 . . . . .6A **86**
Ratcliffe Orchard E1 . . . . .7K **85**
Ratcliff Rd. E7 . . . . .5A **70**
Rathbone Ho. E16 . . . . .6H **87**
     (off Rathbone St.)
   NW6 . . . . .1J **81**
Rathbone Mkt. E16 . . . . .5H **87**
Rathbone Pl. W1 . . . . . . .6C 6 (5H **83**)
Rathbone Sq. CR0: C'don 4C **168**
   W1 . . . . .7C 6 (6G **83**)
Rathbone St. E16 . . . . .6H **87**
   W1 . . . . .6B 6 (5G **83**)
Rathcoole Av. N8 . . . . .5K **47**
Rathcoole Gdns. N8 . . . . .5K **47**
Rathfern Rd. SE6 . . . . .1B **140**
Rathgar Av. W13 . . . . .1B **96**
Rathgar Cl. N3 . . . . .2H **45**
Rathgar Rd. SW9 . . . . .3B **120**
Rathmell Dr. SW4 . . . . .6H **119**
Rathmore Rd. SE7 . . . . .5K **105**
Rathone Ct. E2 . . . . .3K **85**
     (off Meath Cres.)
Rathore Cl. RM6: Chad H 5D **54**
Rattray Ct. SE6 . . . . .2H **141**
Rattray Rd. SW2 . . . . .4A **120**
Raul Rd. SE15 . . . . .2G **121**
Raveley St. NW5 . . . . .4G **65**
     (not continuous)
Ravel Ho. SW11 . . . . .3B **118**
     (off York Place)
Raven Cl. NW9 . . . . .2A **44**
   RM7: Rush G 7G **55**
Ravendale Rd. TW16: Sun 2H **147**
Ravenet St. SW8 . . . . .1F **119**
   SW11 . . . . .1F **119**
     (not continuous)
Ravenfield Rd. SW17 . . . . .3D **136**
Ravenhill Rd. E13 . . . . .2A **88**
Raven Ho. SE16 . . . . .4K **103**
     (off Tawny Way)
Ravenings Pde. IG3: Ilf 1A **72**
Ravenna Rd. SW15 . . . . .5F **117**
Ravenor Ct. UB6: G'frd 4F **77**
Ravenor Pk. Rd. UB6: G'frd 3F **77**
Raven Rd. E18 . . . . .2A **52**
Raven Row E1 . . . . .5H **85**
Raven Row Contemporary Art Cen.
     . . . . .5F **85**
Ravensbourne Apts. SW6 . . . . . . .3A **118**
     (off Central Av.)
Ravensbourne Av. BR2: Broml 7F **141**
   BR3: Beck 7F **141**
   TW19: Stanw 1A **128**
Ravensbourne Ct. SE6 . . . . .7C **122**
Ravensbourne Gdns. IG5: Ilf 1E **52**
   W13 . . . . .5B **78**
Ravensbourne Ho. BR1: Broml 5F **141**
   E15 . . . . .6F **69**
     (off Forrester Way)
   NW8 . . . . .5C **4**
     (off Broadley St.)
Ravensbourne Mans. SE8 . . . . . . .6C **104**
     (off Berthon St.)
Ravensbourne Pk. SE6 . . . . .7C **122**
Ravensbourne Pk. Cres. SE6 . . . . .7B **122**
Ravensbourne Pl. SE8 . . . . .1C **122**
   SE13 . . . . .2D **122**
Ravensbourne Rd. BR1: Broml 3J **159**
   SE6 . . . . .7B **122**
   TW1: Twick 6C **114**
Ravensbourne Ter.
   TW19: Stanw 1A **128**
Ravensbury Av. SM4: Mord 5A **154**
Ravensbury Ct. CR4: Mitc 4B **154**
     (off Ravensbury Gro.)
Ravensbury Gro. CR4: Mitc 4B **154**
Ravensbury La. CR4: Mitc 4B **154**
Ravensbury Path CR4: Mitc 4B **154**
Ravensbury Rd. BR5: St P 3K **161**
   SW18 . . . . .2K **135**
Ravensbury Ter. SW18 . . . . .2K **135**
Ravenscar NW1 . . . . .1G **83**
     (off Bayham St.)

Ravenscar Rd. BR1: Broml 4G **141**
   KT6: Surb 2F **163**
Ravens Cl. BR2: Broml 2H **159**
   EN1: Enf .2K **23**
   KT6: Surb 6D **150**
Ravens Ct. KT1: King T 5D **150**
     (off Uxbridge Rd.)
Ravenscourt TW16: Sun 1H **147**
Ravenscourt Av. W6 . . . . .4C **98**
Ravenscourt Cl. HA4: Ruis 7E **38**
Ravenscourt Gdns. W6 . . . . .4C **98**
Ravenscourt Pk. EN5: Barn 4A **20**
   W6 . . . . .3C **98**
Ravenscourt Pk. Mans. W6 . . . . . .3D **98**
     (off Paddenswick Rd.)
Ravenscourt Pl. W6 . . . . .4D **98**
Ravenscourt Rd. W6 . . . . .4D **98**
Ravenscourt Sq. W6 . . . . .3C **98**
Ravenscraig Rd. N11 . . . . .4B **32**
Ravenscroft Av. HA9: Wemb 1E **60**
   NW11 . . . . .7H **45**
     (not continuous)
Ravenscroft Cl. E16 . . . . .5J **87**
Ravenscroft Cotts. EN5: New Bar . .4D **20**
Ravenscroft Cres. SE9 . . . . .3D **142**
Ravenscroft Pk. EN5: Barn 3A **20**
Ravenscroft Rd. BR3: Beck 2J **157**
   E16 . . . . .5J **87**
   W4 . . . . .4J **97**
Ravenscroft St. E2 . . . . .1K 9 (2F **85**)
Ravensdale Av. N12 . . . . .4F **31**
Ravensdale Gdns. SE19 . . . . .7D **138**
   TW4: Houn 3C **112**
Ravensdale Ind. Est. N16 . . . . .6G **49**
Ravensdale Mans. N8 . . . . .6J **47**
     (off Haringey Pk.)
Ravensdale Rd. N16 . . . . .7F **49**
   TW4: Houn 3C **112**
Ravens Dene BR7: Chst 6J **142**
Ravensdon St. SE11 . . . . .6K 19 (5A **102**)
Ravensfield Cl. RM9: Dag 4D **72**
Ravensfield Gdns. KT19: Ewe 5A **164**
Ravens Ga. M. BR2: Broml 2G **159**
Ravenshaw St. NW6 . . . . .5H **63**
Ravenshill BR7: Chst 1F **161**
Ravenshurst Av. NW4 . . . . .4E **44**
Ravenside KT1: King T 5D **150**
     (off Portsmouth Rd.)
Ravenside Cl. N18 . . . . .5E **34**
Ravenside Retail Pk.
   London 5E **34**
Ravenslea Rd. SW12 . . . . .7D **118**
Ravensleigh Gdns. BR1: Broml 5K **141**
Ravensmead Rd. BR2: Broml 7F **141**
Ravensmede Way W4 . . . . .4B **98**
Ravens M. SE12 . . . . .5J **123**
Ravenstone SE17 . . . . .5E **102**
Ravenstone Rd. N8 . . . . .3A **48**
   NW9 . . . . .6B **44**
Ravenstone St. SW12 . . . . .1E **136**
Ravens Way SE12 . . . . .5J **123**
Ravenswood DA5: Bexl 1E **144**
Ravenswood Av. BR4: W W'ck 1E **170**
   KT6: Surb 2F **163**
Ravenswood Ct. KT2: King T 6H **133**
   W3 . . . . .3J **97**
     (off Bassington Rd.)
Ravenswood Cres. BR4: W W'ck . .1E **170**
   HA2: Harr 2D **58**
Ravenswood Ind. Est. E17 . . . . . . .4E **50**
Ravenswood Rd. CR0: Wadd 3B **168**
   E17 . . . . .4E **50**
   SW12 . . . . .7F **119**
Ravensworth Cl. SW6 . . . . .7J **99**
     (off Fulham Rd.)
Ravensworth Rd. NW10 . . . . .3D **80**
   SE9 . . . . .3D **142**
Raven Wharf SE1 . . . . .6J **15**
     (off Lafone St.)
Ravey St. EC2 . . . . .3G 9 (4E **84**)
Ravine Gro. SE18 . . . . .6J **107**

Ravine Way SW11 . . . . .6H **101**
Rav Pinter Cl. N16 . . . . .7E **48**
Rawchester Cl. SW18 . . . . .1H **135**
Rawlings Cl. BR3: Beck 5E **158**
   BR6: Chels 5K **173**
Rawlings Cres. HA9: Wemb 3H **61**
Rawlings St. SW3 . . . . . .3E 16 (4D **100**)
Rawlins Cl. CR2: Sels 7B **170**
   N3 . . . . .3G **45**
Rawlinson Ct. NW2 . . . . .7E **44**
Rawlinson Ho. SE13 . . . . .4F **123**
     (off Mercator Rd.)
Rawlinson Ter. N17 . . . . .3F **49**
Rawnsley Av. CR4: Mitc 5B **154**
Rawreth Wlk. N1 . . . . .1C **84**
     (off Basire St.)
Rawson St. SW11 . . . . .1E **118**
     (not continuous)
Rawsthorne Cl. E16 . . . . .1D **106**
Rawsthorne Ct. TW4: Houn 4D **112**
Rawstone Wlk. E13 . . . . .2J **87**
Rawstorne Pl. EC1 . . . . . . .1A 8 (3B **84**)
Rawstorne St. EC1 . . . . . . .1A 8 (3B **84**)
     (not continuous)
Raybell Ct. TW7: Isle 2K **113**
Rayburne Ct. IG9: Buck H 1F **37**
   W14 . . . . .3G **99**
Ray Cl. KT9: Chess 6C **162**
Raydean Rd. EN5: New Bar 5E **20**
Raydons Gdns. RM9: Dag 5E **72**
Raydons Rd. RM9: Dag 5E **72**
Raydon St. N19 . . . . .2F **65**
Rayfield Cl. BR2: Broml 6C **160**
Rayford Av. SE12 . . . . .7H **123**
Ray Gdns. HA7: Stan 5G **27**
   IG11: Bark 2A **90**
Ray Gunter Ho. SE17 . . . . .5B **102**
     (off Marsland Cl.)
Ray Ho. N1 . . . . .1E **84**
     (off Colville Est.)
   W10 . . . . .6F **81**
     (off Cambridge Gdns.)
Rayleas Cl. SE18 . . . . .1F **125**
Rayleigh Av. TW11: Tedd 6J **131**
Rayleigh Cl. N13 . . . . .3J **33**
Rayleigh Ct. KT1: King T 2G **151**
   N22 . . . . .1C **48**
Rayleigh Ri. CR2: S Croy 6E **168**
Rayleigh Rd. E16 . . . . .1K **105**
   IG8: Wfd G 6F **37**
   N13 . . . . .3H **33**
   SW19 . . . . .1H **153**
Ray Lodge Rd. IG8: Wfd G 6F **37**
Ray Massey Way E6 . . . . .1C **88**
     (off High St. Nth.)
Raymead Av. CR7: Thor H 5A **156**
Raymede Towers W10 . . . . .5F **81**
     (off Treverton St.)
Raymere Gdns. SE18 . . . . .7H **107**
Raymond Av. E18 . . . . .3H **51**
   W13 . . . . .3A **96**
Raymond Bldgs. WC1 . . . . .5H 7 (5K **83**)
Raymond Chadburn Ho. E7 . . . . . .4K **69**
Raymond Cl. SE26 . . . . .5J **139**
   SL3: Poyle 4A **174**
Raymond Ct. N10 . . . . .7A **32**
Raymond Postgate Ct. SE28 . . . . .7B **90**
Raymond Rd. BR3: Beck 4A **158**
   E13 . . . . .1A **88**
   IG2: Ilf 7H **53**
   SW19 . . . . .6G **135**
Raymond Way KT10: Clay 6A **162**
Raymouth Rd. SE16 . . . . .4H **103**
Raynald Ho. SW16 . . . . .3J **137**
Rayne Ct. E18 . . . . .4H **51**
Rayne Ho. SW12 . . . . .6E **118**
   W9 . . . . .4K **81**
     (off Delaware Rd.)
Rayner Cl. SM5: Cars 5D **166**
Rayner Ct. W12 . . . . .2E **98**
     (off Bamborough Gdns.)
Rayners Cl. HA0: Wemb 5D **60**
Rayners Cres. UB5: N'olt 3K **75**

Rayners Gdns. UB5: N'olt 2K **75**
RAYNERS LANE 1D **58**
Rayners La. HA2: Harr 1E **58**
  HA5: Pinn 5D **40**
Rayners Rd. SW15 . . . . .5G **117**
Rayners Ter. E14 . . . . .6A **86**
  (off Carr St.)
Rayner Towers E10 . . . . .7C **50**
  (off Albany Rd.)
Raynes Av. E11 . . . . .7A **52**
RAYNES PARK 4E **152**
RAYNES PK. BRI. 2E **152**
Raynes Pk. School Sports Cen. . .3D **152**
Raynham W2 . . . . .7D **4**
  (off Norfolk Cres.)
Raynham Av. N18 . . . . .6B **34**
Raynham Ho. E1 . . . . .4K **85**
  (off Harpley Sq.)
Raynham Rd. N18 . . . . .5B **34**
  W6 . . . . .4D **98**
Raynham Ter. N18 . . . . .5B **34**
Raynor Cl. UB1: S'hall 1D **94**
Raynor Pl. N1 . . . . .7C **66**
Raynton Cl. HA2: Harr 1C **58**
  UB4: Hayes 4H **75**
Raynton Dr. UB4: Hayes 4H **75**
Rayon Cl. SM6: W'gton 2E **166**
Ray Rd. KT8: W Mole 5F **149**
Rays Av. N18 . . . . .4D **34**
Rays Rd. BR4: W W'ck 7E **158**
  N18 . . . . .4D **34**
Ray St. EC1 . . . . .4K **7** (4A **84**)
RAY ST. BRI. 4K **7**
Ray Wlk. N7 . . . . .2K **65**
Raywood Cl. UB3: Harl 7E **92**
Raywood Mans. E20 . . . . .6E **68**
  (off West Pk. Wlk.)
Razia M. E12 . . . . .5D **70**
Reachview Cl. NW1 . . . . .7G **65**
Read Cl. KT7: T Ditt 7A **150**
Read Ct. E17 . . . . .6C **50**
Reade Cl. W3 . . . . .3J **97**
  (off Stanley Rd.)
Reader Ho. SE5 . . . . .1C **120**
  (off Badsworth St.)
Read Ho. SE11 . . . . .7J **19**
  SE20 . . . . .7H **139**
  (off Anerley Pk.)
Reading Cl. SE22 . . . . .6G **121**
Reading Ho. SE15 . . . . .6G **103**
  (off Friary Est.)
  W2 . . . . .6A **82**
  (off Hallfield Est.)
Reading La. E8 . . . . .6H **67**
Reading Rd. SM1: Sutt 5A **166**
  UB5: N'olt 5F **59**
Readman Ct. SE20 . . . . .1H **157**
Reads Cl. IG1: Ilf 3F **71**
Ream Apts. SE23 . . . . .2J **139**
  (off Clyde Ter.)
Reapers Cl. NW1 . . . . .1H **83**
Reapers Way TW7: Isle 5H **113**
Reardon Ct. N21 . . . . .2G **33**
Reardon Ho. E1 . . . . .1H **103**
  (off Reardon St.)
Reardon Path E1 . . . . .1H **103**
  (not continuous)
Reardon St. E1 . . . . .1H **103**
Reaston St. SE14 . . . . .7K **103**
Rebecca Cl. DA14: Sidc 4B **144**
Rebecca Ho. E3 . . . . .4B **86**
  (off Brokesley St.)
  N12 . . . . .4E **30**
  (off Woodside Pk. Rd.)
Reckitt Rd. W4 . . . . .5A **98**
Record St. SE15 . . . . .6J **103**
Record Wlk. UB3: Hayes 2G **93**
Recovery St. SW17 . . . . .5C **136**
Recreation Av. RM7: Rom 5J **55**
Recreation Rd. BR2: Broml 2H **159**
  DA15: Sidc 3J **143**
  SE26 . . . . .4K **139**
  UB2: S'hall 4C **94**

Recreation Way CR4: Mitc 3H **155**
Rector St. N1 . . . . .1C **84**
Rectory Bus. Cen. DA14: Sidc 4B **144**
Rectory Chambers SW3 . . . . .7C **16**
  (off Old Church St.)
Rectory Cl. DA14: Sidc 4B **144**
  E4 . . . . .3H **35**
  HA7: Stan 5G **27**
  KT6: Surb 1C **162**
  N3 . . . . .1H **45**
  SW20 . . . . .3E **152**
  TW17: Shep 3C **146**
Rectory Ct. E18 . . . . .1H **51**
  SM6: W'gton 4G **167**
  TW13: Felt 4A **130**
Rectory Cres. E11 . . . . .6A **52**
  (not continuous)
Rectory Farm 1A **112**
Rectory Farm Rd. EN2: Enf 1E **22**
  (not continuous)
Rectory Field 7K **105**
Rectory Fld. Cres. SE7 . . . . .7A **106**
Rectory Gdns. BR3: Beck 1C **158**
  (off Rectory Rd.)
  N8 . . . . .4J **47**
  SW4 . . . . .3G **119**
  UB5: N'olt 1D **76**
Rectory Grn. BR3: Beck 1B **158**
Rectory Gro. CR0: C'don 2B **168**
  SW4 . . . . .3G **119**
  TW12: Hamp 4D **130**
Rectory La. DA14: Sidc 4B **144**
  HA7: Stan 5G **27**
  HA8: Edg 6B **28**
  KT6: Surb 1B **162**
  SM6: W'gton 4G **167**
  SW17 . . . . .6E **136**
Rectory Orchard SW19 . . . . .4G **135**
Rectory Pk. Av. UB5: N'olt 3D **76**
Rectory Pl. SE18 . . . . .4E **106**
Rectory Rd. BR2: Kes 7B **172**
  BR3: Beck 1C **158**
  E12 . . . . .5D **70**
  E17 . . . . .4D **50**
  N16 . . . . .2F **67**
  RM10: Dag 6H **73**
  SM1: Sutt 3J **165**
  SW13 . . . . .2C **116**
  TW4: Cran 2A **112**
  UB2: S'hall 3D **94**
  UB3: Hayes 6J **75**
  W3 . . . . .1H **97**
Rectory Sq. E1 . . . . .5K **85**
Rectory Way UB10: Ick 2D **56**
Reculver Ho. SE15 . . . . .6J **103**
  (off Lovelinch Cl.)
Reculver M. N18 . . . . .4B **34**
Reculver Rd. SE16 . . . . .5K **103**
Red Anchor Cl. SW3 . . . . .6B **100**
Redan Pl. W2 . . . . .6K **81**
Redan St. W14 . . . . .3F **99**
Redan Ter. SE5 . . . . .2B **120**
Red Barracks Rd. SE18 . . . . .4D **106**
Redberry Gro. SE26 . . . . .3J **139**
Redbourne Av. N3 . . . . .1J **45**
Redbourne Dr. SE28 . . . . .6D **90**
  (not continuous)
Redbourne Ho. E14 . . . . .6B **86**
  (off Norbiton Rd.)
Redbourn Ho. W10 . . . . .4E **80**
  (off Sutton Way)
REDBRIDGE 6C **52**
Redbridge Ent. Cen. IG1: Ilf 2G **71**
Redbridge Foyer IG1: Ilf 2G **71**
  (off Sylvan Rd.)
Redbridge Gdns. SE5 . . . . .7E **102**
Redbridge Ho. E16 . . . . .7F **89**
  (off University Way)
Redbridge La. E. IG4: Ilf 6B **52**
Redbridge La. W. E11 . . . . .6K **51**
REDBRIDGE RDBT. 6B **52**
Redbridge Sports & Leisure Cen. . .1H **53**
Redburn Ind. Est. EN3: Pond E 6E **24**

Redburn St. SW3 . . . . .7E **16** (6D **100**)
Redcar Cl. UB5: N'olt 5F **59**
Redcar St. SE5 . . . . .7C **102**
Redcastle Cl. E1 . . . . .7J **85**
Red Cedars Rd. BR6: Orp 7J **161**
Redchurch St. E2 . . . . .3J **9** (4F **85**)
Redcliffe Cl. SW5 . . . . .5K **99**
  (off Old Brompton Rd.)
Redcliffe Ct. E5 . . . . .3H **67**
  (off Napoleon Rd.)
Redcliffe Gdns. IG1: Ilf 1E **70**
  SW5 . . . . .5K **99**
  SW10 . . . . .5K **99**
  W4 . . . . .7H **97**
Redcliffe M. SW10 . . . . .5K **99**
Redcliffe Pl. SW10 . . . . .6A **100**
Redcliffe Rd. SW10 . . . . .5A **100**
Redcliffe Sq. SW10 . . . . .5K **99**
Redcliffe St. SW10 . . . . .6K **99**
Redclose Av. SM4: Mord 5J **153**
Redclyffe Rd. E6 . . . . .1A **88**
Redclyf Ho. E1 . . . . .4J **85**
  (off Cephas St.)
Redcourt CR0: C'don 3E **168**
Red Cow La. EC1 . . . . .3C **8** (4C **84**)
Redcroft Rd. UB1: S'hall 7G **77**
Red Cross Cotts. SE1 . . . . .6D **14**
  (off Ayres St.)
Redcross Way SE1 . . . . . . .6D **14** (2C **102**)
Redding Ho. SE18 . . . . .3C **106**
The Reddings NW7 . . . . .3G **29**
Reddings Cl. NW7 . . . . .4G **29**
Reddins Rd. SE15 . . . . .6G **103**
Reddons Rd. BR3: Beck 7A **140**
Redenham Ho. SW15 . . . . .7C **116**
  (off Ellisfield Dr.)
Rede Pl. W2 . . . . .6J **81**
Redesdale Gdns. TW7: Isle 7A **96**
Redesdale St. SW3 . . . . . . .7D **16** (6C **100**)
Redfern Av. TW4: Houn 7E **112**
Redfern Ho. E13 . . . . .1H **87**
  (off Redriffe Rd.)
  NW8 . . . . .1B **82**
  (off Dorman Way)
Redfern Rd. NW10 . . . . .7A **62**
  SE6 . . . . .7E **122**
Redfield La. SW5 . . . . .4J **99**
Redfield M. SW5 . . . . .4K **99**
Redford Av. CR7: Thor H 4K **155**
  SM6: W'gton 6J **167**
Redford Cl. TW13: Felt 2H **129**
Redford Wlk. N1 . . . . .1C **84**
  (off Popham St.)
Redgate Dr. BR2: Hayes 2K **171**
Redgate Ter. SW15 . . . . .6F **117**
Redgrave Cl. CR0: C'don 6F **157**
Redgrave Rd. SW15 . . . . .3F **117**
Redgrave Ter. E2 . . . . .3G **85**
  (off Derbyshire St.)
Red Hill BR7: Chst 5F **143**
Redhill Cl. SW2 . . . . .2A **138**
Redhill Dr. HA8: Edg 2H **43**
Redhill St. NW1 . . . . .1K **5** (2F **83**)
Red House 4E **126**
Red Ho. La. DA6: Bex 4D **126**
Redhouse Rd. CR0: C'don 6H **155**
Red Ho. Sq. N1 . . . . .7C **66**
Redif Ho. RM10: Dag 4H **73**
Redington Gdns. NW3 . . . . .4K **63**
Redington Ho. N1 . . . . .2K **83**
  (off Priory Grn. Est.)
Redington Rd. NW3 . . . . .3K **63**
Redknap Ho. TW10: Ham 3C **132**
Redland Gdns. KT8: W Mole 4D **148**
Redlands N15 . . . . .4D **48**
  TW11: Tedd 6A **132**
The Redlands BR3: Beck 2D **158**
Redlands Ct. BR1: Broml 7H **141**
Redlands Rd. EN3: Enf H 1F **25**
Redlands Way SW2 . . . . .7K **119**
Red La. KT10: Clay 6A **162**
Redleaf Cl. DA17: Belv 6G **109**
Redleaves Av. TW15: Ashf 6D **128**

Redlees Cl. TW7: Isle 4A **114**
Red Leys UB8: Uxb 7A **56**
Red Lion Bus. Pk. KT6: Surb 3F **163**
Red Lion Cl. SE17 . . . . .6D **102**
  (off Red Lion Row)
Red Lion Ct. EC4 . . . . .1K **13** (6A **84**)
  SE1 . . . . .4D **14** (1C **102**)
  TW3: Houn 3F **113**
  (off Alexandra Rd.)
Red Lion Hill N2 . . . . .2B **46**
  (not continuous)
Red Lion La. SE18 . . . . .7E **106**
Red Lion Pde. HA5: Pinn 3C **40**
Red Lion Pl. SE18 . . . . .1E **124**
Red Lion Rd. KT6: Surb 2F **163**
Red Lion Row SE17 . . . . .6C **102**
Red Lion Sq. SW18 . . . . .5J **117**
  WC1 . . . . .6G **7** (5K **83**)
Red Lion St. TW9: Rich 5D **114**
  WC1 . . . . .5G **7** (5K **83**)
Red Lion Wlk. TW3: Houn 3F **113**
  (off High St.)
Red Lion Yd. W1 . . . . .4H **11**
Red Lodge BR4: W W'ck 1E **170**
Red Lodge Cres. DA5: Bexl 3K **145**
Red Lodge Rd. BR4: W W'ck 1E **170**
  DA5: Bexl 3K **145**
Redlynch Ct. W14 . . . . .2G **99**
  (off Addison Cres.)
Redlynch Ho. SW9 . . . . .1A **120**
  (off Gosling Way)
Redman Cl. UB5: N'olt 2A **76**
Redman Ho. EC1 . . . . .5J **7**
  (off Bourne Est.)
  SE1 . . . . .7D **14**
  (off Borough High St.)
Redman's Rd. E1 . . . . .5J **85**
Redmead La. E1 . . . . .1G **103**
Redmead Rd. UB3: Harl 4G **93**
Redmill Ho. E1 . . . . .4H **85**
  (off Headlam St.)
Redmond Ho. N1 . . . . .1K **83**
  (off Barnsbury Est.)
Redmore Rd. W6 . . . . .4D **98**
Red Oak Cl. BR6: Farnb 3F **173**
  CR0: C'don 2C **170**
Redo Ho. E12 . . . . .5E **70**
  (off Dore Av.)
Red Path E9 . . . . .6A **68**
Redpath Way SE10 . . . . .2G **105**
Red Pl. W1 . . . . .2G **11** (7E **82**)
Redpoll Way DA18: Erith 3D **108**
Red Post Hill SE21 . . . . .4D **120**
  SE24 . . . . .4D **120**
Red Post Ho. E6 . . . . .7B **70**
Redriffe Rd. E13 . . . . .1H **87**
Redriff Est. SE16 . . . . .3B **104**
Redriff Rd. RM7: Mawney 2H **55**
  SE16 . . . . .4K **103**
Redroofs Cl. BR3: Beck 1D **158**
Redrose Trad. Cen. EN4: E Barn . . .5G **21**
RED ROVER 4C **116**
Redrup Ho. SE14 . . . . .6K **103**
  (off John Williams Cl.)
Redruth Cl. N22 . . . . .7E **32**
Redruth Gdns. KT10: Clay 7A **162**
Redruth Ho. SM2: Sutt 7K **165**
Redruth Rd. E9 . . . . .1J **85**
Redsan Cl. CR2: S Croy 7D **168**
Redshank Ho. SE1 . . . . .5F **103**
  (off Avocet Cl.)
Red Sq. N16 . . . . .3D **66**
Redstart Cl. E6 . . . . .5C **88**
  SE14 . . . . .7A **104**
Redstart Mans. IG1: Ilf 3E **70**
  (off Mill Rd.)
Redston Rd. N8 . . . . .4H **47**
Redvers Rd. N22 . . . . .2A **48**
Redvers St. N1 . . . . .1H **9** (3E **84**)
Redwald Rd. E5 . . . . .4K **67**
Redway Dr. TW2: Whitt 7G **113**
Redwing Ct. SE1 . . . . .7D **14**
  (off Swan Ra.)

Redwing M. SE5 . . . . .2C 120
Redwing Path SE28 . . . . .2H 107
Redwing Rd. SM6: W'gton 7J 167
Redwood Cl. DA15: Sidc 1A 144
  E3 . . . . .2C 86
  N14 . . . . .7C 22
  SE16 . . . . .1A 104
  UB10: Hil 2D 74
Redwood Ct. KT6: Surb 7D 150
  N19 . . . . .7H 47
  NW6 . . . . .7G 63
  UB5: N'olt 3C 76
Redwood Est. TW5: Cran 6K 93
Redwood Gdns. E4 . . . . .6J 25
Redwood Gro. W5 . . . . .3B 96
Redwood Ho. EC1 . . . . .2C 8
  (off Bollinder Pl.)
  HA9: Wemb 4G 61
  (off Empire Way)
Redwood Mans. W8 . . . . .3K 99
  (off Chantry Sq.)
Redwood M. SW4 . . . . .3F 119
  TW15: Ashf 7F 129
  (off Staines Rd. W.)
Redwoods SW15 . . . . .1C 134
Redwoods Cl. IG9: Buck H 2E 36
Redwood Wlk. KT6: Surb 1D 162
Redwood Way EN5: Barn 5A 20
Reece M. SW7 . . . . .3A 16 (4B 100)
Reed Av. BR6: Orp 3J 173
Reed Cl. E16 . . . . .5J 87
  SE12 . . . . .5J 123
Reede Gdns. RM10: Dag 5H 73
Reede Rd. RM10: Dag 6G 73
Reede Way RM10: Dag 6H 73
Reedham Cl. N17 . . . . .4H 49
Reedham St. SE15 . . . . .2G 121
Reedholm Vs. N16 . . . . .4D 66
Reed Ho. SW19 . . . . .4K 135
Reed Pl. SW4 . . . . .4H 119
Reed Rd. N17 . . . . .2F 49
Reedsfield Cl. TW15: Ashf 3D 128
Reedsfield Rd. TW15: Ashf 4D 128
Reed's Pl. NW1 . . . . .7G 65
Reedworth St. SE11 . . . .4K 19 (4A 102)
Reef Ho. E14 . . . . .3E 104
  (off Manchester St.)
Reef St. RM9: Dag 3E 90
Reenglass Rd. HA7: Stan 4J 27
Rees Dr. HA7: Stan 4K 27
Rees Gdns. CRO: C'don 6F 157
Reesland Cl. E12 . . . . .6E 70
Rees St. N1 . . . . .1C 84
Reeves Av. NW9 . . . . .7K 43
Reeves Cnr. CRO: C'don 2B 168
Reeves Ho. SE1 . . . . .7J 13
  (off Baylis Rd.)
Reeves M. W1 . . . . .3G 11 (7E 82)
Reeves Rd. E3 . . . . .4D 86
  SE18 . . . . .6F 107
Reference Ho. NW9 . . . . .3B 44
The Reflection E16 . . . . .2F 107
  (off Woolwich Mnr. Way)
Reflection Ho. E2 . . . . .4G 85
  (off Cheshire St.)
Reflex Apts. BR2: Broml 4K 159
  (off Wheeler Pl.)
Reform Row N17 . . . . .2F 49
Reform St. SW11 . . . . .2D 118
Regal Bldg. W10 . . . . .3F 81
Regal Cl. E1 . . . . .5G 85
  W5 . . . . .5D 78
Regal Ct. CR4: Mitc 3D 154
  N18 . . . . .5A 34
  NW6 . . . . .2H 81
  (off Malvern Rd.)
  SW6 . . . . .7J 99
  (off Dawes Rd.)
Regal Cres. SM6: W'gton 3F 167
Regal Dr. N11 . . . . .5A 32
Regal Ho. IG2: Ilf 6H 53
The Regal Ho. SW6 . . . . .2A 118

Regalia Cl. E16 . . . . .2K 105
Regalia Point E2 . . . . .3K 85
  (off Palmer's Rd.)
Regal La. NW1 . . . . .1E 82
Regal Pl. E3 . . . . .3B 86
  SW6 . . . . .7K 99
Regal Row SE15 . . . . .1J 121
Regal Way HA3: Kenton 6E 42
Regal Wharf Apts. N1 . . . . .1E 84
  (off De Beauvoir Cres.)
Regan Ho. N18 . . . . .6A 34
Regan Way N1 . . . . .1G 9 (2E 84)
Regatta Ho. TW11: Tedd 4A 132
Regatta La. W6 . . . . .6E 98
Regatta Point E14 . . . . .2C 104
  (off Westferry Rd.)
TW8: Bford 6F 97
Regency Cl. TW12: Hamp 5D 130
  E3 . . . . .2B 86
  (off Norman Gro.)
  E9 . . . . .1J 85
  (off Park Cl.)
  E18 . . . . .2J 51
  EN1: Enf .5J 23
  HA7: Stan 7J 27
  (off Unwin Way)
  SE8 . . . . .7B 104
  (off Glenville Gro.)
  SM1: Sutt 4A 166
  TW11: Tedd 6B 132
Regency Cres. NW4 . . . . .2F 45
Regency Dr. HA4: Ruis 1G 57
Regency Gdns. KT12: Walt T 7A 148
Regency Ho. E16 . . . . .1J 105
  (off Pepys Cres.)
  N3 . . . . .2H 45
  SW1 . . . . .3D 18
  (off Regency St.)
  SW6 . . . . .1A 118
  (off The Boulevard)
Regency Lawn NW5 . . . . .3F 65
Regency Lodge IG9: Buck H 2G 37
  NW3 . . . . .7B 64
  (off Adelaide Rd.)
Regency M. BR3: Beck 1E 158
  NW10 . . . . .6C 62
  SW9 . . . . .7B 102
  TW7: Isle 5J 113
Regency Pde. NW3 . . . . .7B 64
  (off Finchley Rd.)
Regency Pl. SW1 . . . . .3D 18 (4H 101)
Regency St. NW10 . . . . .4A 80
  SW1 . . . . .3D 18 (4H 101)
Regency Ter. SW7 . . . . .5A 16
Regency Wlk. CR0: C'don 6B 158
  TW10: Rich 5E 114
  (off The Vineyard)
Regency Way DA6: Bex 3D 126
Regeneration House 1J 83
Regeneration Rd. SE16 . . . . .4K 103
Regent Av. UB10: Hil 7D 56
Regent Bus. Cen. UB3: Hayes 2K 93
Regent Cl. HA3: Kenton 6E 42
  N12 . . . . .5F 31
  TW4: Cran 1K 111
Regent Ct. N3 . . . . .7E 30
  N20 . . . . .2G 31
  NW6 . . . . .7H 63
  (off Cavendish Rd.)
  NW8 . . . . .2C 4
  W6 . . . . .3D 98
  (off Vinery Way)
  W8 . . . . .3K 99
  (off Wright's La.)
Regent Gdns. IG3: Ilf 7A 54
Regent Ho. W14 . . . . .4G 99
  (off Windsor Way)
Regent Pde. SM2: Sutt 6A 166
Regent Pl. CR0: C'don 1F 169
  SW19 . . . . .5A 136
  W1 . . . . .2B 12 (7G 83)

Regent Rd. KT5: Surb 5F 151
  SE24 . . . . .6B 120
Regents Av. N13 . . . . .5F 33
Regent's Bri. Gdns. SW8 . . . . .7J 101
Regents Canal Ho. E14 . . . . .6A 86
  (off Commercial Rd.)
Regents Cl. CR2: S Croy 6E 168
  HA8: Edg 4K 27
  UB4: Hayes 5H 75
Regents Ct. BR1: Broml 7H 141
  E8 . . . . .1G 85
  HA5: Pinn 2B 40
  KT2: King T 1E 150
  (off Sopwith Way)
Regents Dr. BR2: Kes 5B 172
  IG8: Wfd G 6K 37
Regents Ga. Ho. E14 . . . . .7A 86
  (off Horseferry Rd.)
Regents Ho. E3 . . . . .5C 86
  (off Bow Common La.)
Regents M. NW8 . . . . .2A 82
REGENT'S PARK 2K 5 (3F 83)
Regent's Pk. 1F 5 (2D 82)
Regent's Pk. Barracks 1K 5
Regent's Pk. Est. NW1 . . . . .1A 6
Regent's Pk. Gdns. M. NW1 . . . . . .1D 82
Regent's Pk. Ho. NW8 . . . . .2D 4
  (off Park Rd.)
Regent's Pk. Open Air Theatre
  . . . . .2G 5 (3E 82)
Regent's Pk. Rd. NW1 . . . . .7D 64
  (not continuous)
  N3 . . . . .3H 45
Regent's Pk. Ter. NW1 . . . . .1F 83
Regents Pl. SE3 . . . . .2J 123
Regents Pl. NW1 . . . . .3A 6 (4G 83)
Regent's Pl. Plaza NW1 . . . . .4G 83
Regents Plaza NW6 . . . . .2K 81
  (off Kilburn High Rd.)
Regent's Row E8 . . . . .1G 85
Regents Studios E8 . . . . .1H 85
Regent St. NW10 . . . . .3F 81
  SW1 . . . . .3C 12 (7H 83)
  W1 . . . . .7K 5 (6F 83)
  W4 . . . . .5G 97
Regent Street Cinema 7K 5 (6F 83)
Regent's University London
  . . . . .3F 5 (4D 82)
Regents Wharf E2 . . . . .1H 85
  (off Wharf Pl.)
  N1 . . . . .2K 83
Regent Ter. SW8 . . . . .6J 101
Regiment Hill NW7 . . . . .6B 30
Regina Cl. EN5: Barn 3A 20
Regina Ho. SE20 . . . . .1K 157
Reginald Ellingworth St.
  RM9: Dag 1B 90
Reginald Pl. SE8 . . . . .7C 104
  (off Deptford High St.)
Reginald Rd. E7 . . . . .7J 69
  HA6: Nwood 1H 39
  SE8 . . . . .7C 104
Reginald Sorenson Ho. E11 . . . . . . .7F 51
Reginald Sq. SE8 . . . . .7C 104
Regina Point SE16 . . . . .3J 103
  (off Canada Est.)
Regina Rd. N4 . . . . .1A 65
  SE25 . . . . .3G 157
  UB2: S'hall 4C 94
  W13 . . . . .1A 96
Regina Ter. W13 . . . . .1B 96
Regis Ct. CR4: Mitc 1C 154
  N8 . . . . .4K 47
  NW1 . . . . .5E 4
  (off Melcombe Pl.)
Regis Ho. W1 . . . . .5H 5
  (off Beaumont St.)
Regis Pl. SW2 . . . . .4K 119
Regis Rd. NW5 . . . . .5F 65
Regnart Bldgs. NW1 . . . . .3B 6

Regnas Ho. E15 . . . . .6H 69
  (off Carnarvon Rd.)
Regnolruf Ct. KT12: Walt T 7J 147
Regnum Apts. E1 . . . . .4J 9
  (off Wheler St.)
Reid Bldg. E3 . . . . .4B 86
  (off Eric St.)
Reid Cl. HA5: Eastc 4J 39
  UB3: Hayes 6G 75
Reidhaven Rd. SE18 . . . . .4J 107
Reigate Av. SM1: Sutt 1J 165
Reigate Rd. BR1: Broml 3H 141
  IG3: Ilf 2K 71
Reigate Way SM6: W'gton 5J 167
Reighton Rd. E5 . . . . .3G 67
Reindeer Cl. E13 . . . . .1J 87
Reinickendorf Av. SE9 . . . . .6G 125
Reis Pl. N15 . . . . .4F 49
  (off Blenheim Rd.)
Reizel Cl. N16 . . . . .1F 67
Relay Rd. W12 . . . . .7F 81
Relf Rd. SE15 . . . . .3G 121
Reliance Arc. SW9 . . . . .4A 120
Reliance Wharf N1 . . . . .1E 84
Relko Gdns. SM1: Sutt 5B 166
Relton M. SW7 . . . . .1D 16 (3C 100)
Rembrandt Cl. E14 . . . . .3F 105
  SW1 . . . . .4G 17
Rembrandt Ct. KT19: Ewe 6B 164
  SE16 . . . . .5H 103
  (off Stubbs Dr.)
Rembrandt Rd. HA8: Edg 2G 43
  SE13 . . . . .4G 123
Reminder La. SE10 . . . . .3H 105
  (not continuous)
Remington Rd. E6 . . . . .6C 88
  N15 . . . . .6D 48
Remington St. N1 . . . . . . .1B 8 (2B 84)
Remnant St. WC2 . . . . . . .7G 7 (6K 83)
Remsted Ho. NW6 . . . . .1K 81
  (off Mortimer Cres.)
The Remus Bldg. EC1 . . . . .2K 7
  (off Hardwick St.)
Remus Rd. E3 . . . . .7C 68
Renaissance Ct. SM1: Sutt 1A 166
  TW3: Houn 3G 113
  (off Prince Regent Rd.)
Renaissance Sq. W4 . . . . .6A 98
Renaissance Wlk. SE10 . . . . .3H 105
  (off Teal St.)
Renbold Ho. SE10 . . . . .1E 122
  (off Blissett St.)
Rendalls HA1: Harr 1J 59
  (off Grove Hill)
Rendel Apts. E16 . . . . .7D 88
  (off Lock Side Way)
Rendle Cl. CRO: C'don 5F 157
Rendle Ho. W10 . . . . .4G 81
  (off Wornington Rd.)
Rendlesham Rd. E5 . . . . .4G 67
  EN2: Enf .1G 23
Renforth St. SE16 . . . . .3J 103
Renfrew Way
  TW17: Shep 7C 146
Renfrew Cl. E6 . . . . .7E 88
Renfrew Ct. TW4: Houn 2C 112
Renfrew Ho. E17 . . . . .2B 50
  NW6 . . . . .2K 81
  (off Carlton Vale)
Renfrew Rd. KT2: King T 7H 133
  SE11 . . . . .3K 19 (4B 102)
  TW4: Houn 2B 112
Renmuir St. SW17 . . . . .6D 136
Rennell St. SE13 . . . . .3E 122
Rennels Way TW7: Isle 2J 113
Renness Rd. E17 . . . . .3A 50
Rennets Cl. SE9 . . . . .5J 125
Rennets Wood Rd. SE9 . . . . .5H 125
Rennie Cotts. E1 . . . . .4J 85
  (off Pemell Cl.)
Rennie Ct. EN3: Enf L 1H 25
  SE1 . . . . .4A 14
Rennie Est. SE16 . . . . .4H 103

Rennie Ho.—Richmond Ter.

Rennie Ho. SE1 . . . . 3C 102
(off Bath Ter.)
Rennie St. SE1 . . . . 4A 14 (1B 102)
(not continuous)
SE10 . . . . 3J 105
Renoir Ct. SE16 . . . . 5H 103
(off Stubbs Dr.)
The Renovation E16 . . . . 2F 107
(off Woolwich Mnr. Way)
Renown Cl. CR0: C'don 1B 168
RM7: Mawney 1G 55
Rensburg Rd. E17 . . . . 5K 49
Renshaw Cl. DA17: Belv 6F 109
SE6 . . . . 7C 122
Renters Av. NW4 . . . . 6E 44
Renton Cl. SW2 . . . . 6K 119
Renwick Dr. BR2: Broml 6B 160
Renwick Ind. Est.
IG11: Bark 2B 90
Renwick Rd. IG11: Bark 4B 90
Repens Way UB4: Yead 4B 76
Rephidim St. SE1 . . . . 3E 102
Replingham Rd. SW18 . . . . 1H 135
Reporton Rd. SW6 . . . . 7G 99
Repository Rd. SE18 . . . . 6D 106
Repton Av. HA0: Wemb 4C 60
UB3: Harl 4F 93
Repton Cl. SM5: Cars 5C 166
Repton Ct. BR1: Broml 6B 142
BR3: Beck 1D 158
Repton Gro. IG5: Ilf 1D 52
Repton Ho. E4 . . . . 6K 35
E16 . . . . 2K 105
(off Royal Crest Av.)
SW1 . . . . 4B 18
(off Charlwood St.)
REPTON PARK 7K 37
Repton Rd. BR6: Chels 3K 173
HA3: Kenton 4F 43
Repton St. E14 . . . . 6A 86
Repulse Cl. RM5: Col R 1G 55
Reservoir Cl. CR7: Thor H 3D 156
Reservoir Rd. HA4: Ruis 4E 38
N14 . . . . 5B 22
SE4 . . . . 2A 122
Reservoir Studios E1 . . . . 6K 85
(off Cable St.)
Reservoir Way NW10 . . . . 7C 62
Resham Cl. UB2: S'hall 3A 94
Residence Twr. N4 . . . . 7C 48
(off Goodchild Rd.)
Resolution Plaza E1 . . . . 7K 9
Resolution Wlk. SE18 . . . . 3D 106
Resolution Way SE8 . . . . 7C 104
(off Deptford High St.)
Restell Cl. SE3 . . . . 6G 105
Restmor Way SM6: W'gton 2E 166
Reston Pl. SW7 . . . . 2A 100
Restons Cres. SE9 . . . . 6H 125
Restoration Sq. SW11 . . . . 1B 118
Restormel Cl. TW3: Houn 5E 112
Restormel Ho. SE11 . . . . 4J 19
Retcar Pl. N19 . . . . 2F 65
Retford St. N1 . . . . 1H 9 (2E 84)
Retingham Way E4 . . . . 2J 35
Retles Ct. HA1: Harr 7J 41
The Retreat CR7: Thor H 4D 156
HA2: Harr 7E 40
KT4: Wor Pk 2D 164
KT5: Surb 6F 151
NW9 . . . . 5K 43
SW14 . . . . 3A 116
Retreat Cl. HA3: Kenton 5C 42
Retreat Ho. E9 . . . . 6J 67
The Retreat Mobile Home Pk. 2D 36
Retreat Pl. E9 . . . . 6J 67
Retreat Rd. TW9: Rich 5D 114
Reubens Ct. W4 . . . . 5H 97
(off Chaseley Dr.)
Reuters Plaza E14 . . . . 1D 104
(off The South Colonnade)
Reveley Sq. SE16 . . . . 2A 104
Revell Ri. SE18 . . . . 6K 107
Revell Rd. KT1: King T 2H 151
SM1: Sutt 6H 165
Revelon Rd. SE4 . . . . 4A 122
Revelstoke Rd. SW18 . . . . 2H 135
Reventlow Rd. SE9 . . . . 1G 143
Reverdy Rd. SE1 . . . . 4G 103
Reverend Cl. HA2: Harr 3F 59
Revesby Rd. SM5: Cars 6B 154
Review Lodge RM10: Dag 1H 91
Review Rd. NW2 . . . . 2B 62
RM10: Dag 1H 91
Revolution Karting 5B 86
Rewell St. SW6 . . . . 7A 100
Rewley Rd. SM5: Cars 6B 154
Rex Av. TW15: Ashf 6C 128
Rex Cl. RM5: Col R 1H 55
Rex Pl. W1 . . . . 3H 11 (7E 82)
Reydon Av. E11 . . . . 5A 52
Reynard Cl. BR1: Broml 3E 160
SE4 . . . . 3A 122
Reynard Dr. SE19 . . . . 7F 139
Reynard Pl. SE14 . . . . 6A 104
Reynardson Rd. N17 . . . . 7H 33
Reynard Way TW8: Bford 5C 96
Reynolah Gdns. SE7 . . . . 5K 105
Reynolds Av. E12 . . . . 5E 70
KT9: Chess 7E 162
RM6: Chad H 7C 54
Reynolds Cl. NW11 . . . . 7K 45
SM5: Cars 1D 166
SW19 . . . . 1B 154
Reynolds Ct. RM6: Chad H 3D 54
Reynolds Dr. HA8: Edg 3F 43
Reynolds Ho. E2 . . . . 2J 85
(off Approach Rd.)
NW8 . . . . 2B 82
(off Wellington Rd.)
SW1 . . . . 4D 18
(off Erasmus St.)
Reynolds Pl. SE3 . . . . 7K 105
TW10: Rich 6F 115
Reynolds Rd. KT3: N Mald 7K 151
SE15 . . . . 4J 121
UB4: Yead 4A 76
W4 . . . . 3J 97
Reynolds Sports Cen. 2G 97
Reynolds Way CR0: C'don 4E 168
Rheidol M. N1 . . . . 2C 84
Rheidol Ter. N1 . . . . 1C 84
Rheingold Way SM6: W'gton 7J 167
Rhein Ho. N8 . . . . 3J 47
(off Campsfield Rd.)
Rheola Cl. N17 . . . . 1F 49
Rhoda St. E2 . . . . 3K 9 (4F 85)
Rhodes Av. N22 . . . . 1G 47
Rhodes Ho. N1 . . . . 1E 8
(off Provost St.)
Rhodesia Rd. E11 . . . . 2F 69
SW9 . . . . 2J 119
Rhodes Moorhouse Ct.
SM4: Mord 6J 153
Rhodes St. N7 . . . . 5K 65
Rhodeswell Rd. E14 . . . . 5A 86
(not continuous)
Rhodium Ct. E14 . . . . 5C 86
(off Thomas Rd.)
Rhodrons Av. KT9: Chess 5E 162
Rhondda Gro. E3 . . . . 3A 86
RHS Lawrence Hall 2C 18 (3H 101)
RHS Lindley Hall 3C 18
Rhyl Rd. UB6: G'frd 2K 77
Rhyl St. NW5 . . . . 6E 64
Rhys Av. N11 . . . . 7C 32
Rialto Rd. CR4: Mitc 2E 154
Ribble Cl. IG8: Wfd G 6F 37
Ribblesdale Av. N11 . . . . 6K 31
UB5: N'olt 6F 59
Ribblesdale Ho. NW6 . . . . 1J 81
(off Kilburn Vale)
Ribblesdale Rd. N8 . . . . 4K 47
SW16 . . . . 6F 137
Ribbon Dance M. SE5 . . . . 1D 120
Ribbons Wlk. E20 . . . . 5E 68
Ribchester Av. UB6: G'frd 3K 77
Ribston Cl. BR2: Broml 1D 172
Ricardo Path SE28 . . . . 1C 108
Ricardo St. E14 . . . . 6D 86
Ricards Rd. SW19 . . . . 5H 135
Riccall Ct. NW9 . . . . 1A 44
(off Pageant Av.)
Rice Pde. BR5: Pet W 5H 161
Riceyman Ho. WC1 . . . . 2J 7
(off Lloyd Baker St.)
Richard Anderson Ct. SE14 . . . . 7K 103
(off Monson Rd.)
Richard Burbidge Mans. SW13 . . . . 6E 98
(off Brasenose Dr.)
Richard Burton Ct. IG9: Buck H 2F 37
(off Palmerston Rd.)
Richard Challoner Sports Cen. . . . 7K 151
Richard Cl. SE18 . . . . 4C 106
Richard Fell Ho. E12 . . . . 4E 70
(off Walton Rd.)
Richard Fielden Ho. E1 . . . . 3A 86
Richard Ho. SE16 . . . . 4J 103
(off Silwood St.)
Richard Ho. Dr. E16 . . . . 6B 88
Richard Neale Ho. E1 . . . . 7H 85
(off Cornwall St.)
Richard Neve Ho. SE18 . . . . 4J 107
(off Plumstead High St.)
The Richard Robert Residence
E15 . . . . 6F 69
(off Salway Rd.)
Richard Ryan Pl. RM9: Dag 1E 90
Richards Av. RM7: Rom 6J 55
Richards Cl. HA1: Harr 5A 42
UB3: Harl 6F 93
UB10: Hil 1C 74
WD23: Bush 1C 26
Richards Fld. KT19: Ewe 7K 163
Richard Sharples Ct. SM2: Sutt 7A 166
Richardson Cl. E8 . . . . 1F 85
Richardson Ct. SW4 . . . . 2J 119
(off Studley Rd.)
Richardson Gdns. RM10: Dag 6H 73
Richardson Rd. E15 . . . . 2G 87
Richardson's M. W1 . . . . 4A 6
Richard's Pl. SW3 . . . . 3D 16 (4C 100)
Richards Pl. E17 . . . . 3C 50
Richard St. E1 . . . . 6H 85
Richard Tress Way E3 . . . . 4B 86
Richbell WC1 . . . . 5F 7
(off Boswell St.)
Richbell Pl. WC1 . . . . 5G 7 (5K 83)
Richborne Ter. SW8 . . . . 7K 101
Richborough Ho. SE15 . . . . 6J 103
(off Sharratt St.)
Richborough Rd. NW2 . . . . 4G 63
Richbourne Ct. W1 . . . . 7D 4
(off Harrowby St.)
Richens Cl. TW3: Houn 2H 113
Riches Rd. IG1: Ilf 2G 71
Richfield Rd. WD23: Bush 1B 26
Richford Ga. W6 . . . . 3E 98
Richford Rd. E15 . . . . 1H 87
Richford St. W6 . . . . 2E 98
Rich Ind. Est. SE1 . . . . 4E 102
SE15 . . . . 6H 103
Richland Ho. SE15 . . . . 1G 121
(off Goldsmith Rd.)
Richlands Av. KT17: Ewe 4C 164
Rich La. SW5 . . . . 5K 99
Richman Ho. SE8 . . . . 5B 104
(off Grove St.)
Richmix Sq. E1 . . . . 3K 9
(off Bethnal Grn. Rd.)
RICHMOND 5D 114
Richmond, The American
International University in London
Kensington Campus,
Ansdell Street 3K 99
(off Ansdell St.)
St Albans Grove 3K 99
Young Street 2K 99
Richmond Hill Campus 7E 114
Richmond & London Scottish RUFC
. . . . 3D 114
Richmond Athletic Ground 3D 114
Richmond Av. E4 . . . . 5A 36
N1 . . . . 1K 83
NW10 . . . . 6E 62
SW20 . . . . 1G 153
TW14: Felt 6G 111
UB10: Hil 6D 56
RICHMOND BRI. 6D 114
Richmond Bldgs. W1 . . . . 1C 12 (6H 83)
RICHMOND CIRCUS 4E 114
Richmond Cl. E17 . . . . 6B 50
Richmond Cotts. W14 . . . . 4G 99
(off Hammersmith Rd.)
Richmond Ct. CR4: Mitc 3B 154
E8 . . . . 7H 67
(off Mare St.)
HA9: Wemb 3F 61
N11 . . . . 6K 31
(off Pickering Gdns.)
NW6 . . . . 7F 63
(off Willesden La.)
SW1 . . . . 7F 11
(off Sloane St.)
W14 . . . . 4G 99
(off Hammersmith Rd.)
Richmond Cres. E4 . . . . 5A 36
N1 . . . . 1K 83
N9 . . . . 1B 34
Richmond Cricket Ground 3E 114
Richmond Dr. IG8: Wfd G 7K 37
TW17: Shep 6F 147
Richmond FC 3D 114
Richmond Gdns. HA3: Hrw W 7E 26
NW4 . . . . 5C 44
Richmond Golf Course
Surrey 2E 132
Richmond Grn. CR0: Bedd 3J 167
Richmond Gro. KT5: Surb 6F 151
N1 . . . . 7B 66
(not continuous)
Richmond Hill TW10: Rich 6E 114
Richmond Hill Ct. TW10: Rich 6E 114
Richmond Ho. E3 . . . . 5C 86
(off Bow Common La.)
NW1 . . . . 1K 5
(off Park Village E.)
SE17 . . . . 5D 102
(off Portland St.)
Richmond Mans. SW5 . . . . 5K 99
(off Old Brompton Rd.)
TW1: Twick 6D 114
Richmond M. SE6 . . . . 1D 140
TW11: Tedd 5K 131
W1 . . . . 1C 12 (6H 83)
Richmond Olympus Gym & Squash Club
Richmond 4D 114
Richmond Pde. TW1: Twick 6C 114
(off Richmond Rd.)
Richmond Pk. 1G 133
Richmond Pk. Golf Course 7A 116
Richmond Pk. Rd. KT2: King T 1E 150
SW14 . . . . 5J 115
Richmond Pl. SE18 . . . . 4G 107
Richmond Rd. CR0: Bedd 3J 167
CR7: Thor H 3B 156
E4 . . . . 1A 36
E7 . . . . 5K 69
E8 . . . . 7F 67
E11 . . . . 2F 69
EN5: New Bar 5E 20
IG1: Ilf 3G 71
KT2: King T 5D 132
N2 . . . . 2A 46
N11 . . . . 6D 32
N15 . . . . 6E 48
SW20 . . . . 1D 152
TW1: Twick 7B 114
TW7: Isle 3A 114
W5 . . . . 2E 96
Richmond St. E13 . . . . 2J 87
Richmond Ter. SW1 . . . . 6E 12 (2J 101)

A-Z London 379

Richmond Theatre 4D 114
Richmond Way E11 . . . . .2J 69
  W12 .2F 99
  W14 .3F 99
Richmount Gdns. SE3 . . . . .3J 123
Rich St. E14 . . . . .7B 86
Rickard Cl. NW4 . . . . .4D 44
  SW2 .1A 138
Rickards Cl. KT6: Surb 2E 162
Rickett St. SW6 . . . . .6J 99
Rickman Ho. E1 . . . . .3J 85
  (off Rickman St.)
Rickman St. E1 . . . . .4J 85
Rickmansworth Rd. HA5: Pinn . . .2K 39
  HA6: Nwood 1F 39
Rick Roberts Way E15 . . . . .1E 86
Rickthorne Rd. N19 . . . . .2J 65
Rickyard Path SE9 . . . . .4C 124
Riddell Ct. SE5 . . . . .5F 103
  (off Albany Rd.)
Ridding La. UB6: G'frd 5K 59
Riddons Rd. SE12 . . . . .3A 142
The Ride EN3: Pond E 3D 24
  TW8: Bford 3B 96
Rideout St. SE18 . . . . .4D 106
Rider Cl. DA15: Sidc 6J 125
Riders Twr. E17 . . . . .5B 50
  (off Track St.)
Rideway Dr. W3 . . . . .3G 97
Ridgdale St. E3 . . . . .2D 86
The Ridge BR6: Orp 2H 173
  DA5: Bexl 7F 127
  EN5: Barn 5C 20
  KT5: Surb 5G 151
  TW2: Whitt 7H 113
Ridge Av. N21 . . . . .7H 23
Ridgebrook Rd. SE3 . . . . .3B 124
Ridge Cl. NW4 . . . . .2F 45
  NW9 .4K 43
  SE28 . . . . .2H 107
Ridge Ct. SE22 . . . . .7G 121
Ridge Crest EN2: Enf 1E 22
Ridgecroft Cl. DA5: Bexl 1J 145
Ridge Hill NW11 . . . . .1G 63
Ridgemead Ct. N14 . . . . .2D 32
Ridgemont Gdns. HA8: Edg 4D 28
Ridgemount Av. CRO: C'don 1K 169
Ridgemount Cl. SE20 . . . . .7H 139
Ridgemount Gdns. EN2: Enf 3G 23
Ridge Rd. CR4: Mitc 7F 137
  N8 . . . . .6K 47
  N21 .1H 33
  NW2 .3H 63
  SM3: Sutt 1G 165
  (not continuous)
Ridges Yd. CRO: C'don 3B 168
Ridgeview Cl. EN5: Barn 6A 20
Ridgeview Rd. N20 . . . . .3E 30
Ridge Way SE19 . . . . .6E 138
  TW13: Hanw 3C 130
Ridgeway BR2: Hayes 2J 171
  IG8: Wfd G 4F 37
The Ridgeway CRO: Wadd 3K 167
  E4 . . . . .2J 35
  EN2: Enf 1E 22
  HA2: Harr 5D 40
  (not continuous)
  HA3: Kenton 6C 42
  HA4: Ruis 7J 39
  HA7: Stan 6H 27
  KT12: Walt T 7H 147
  N3 . . . . .7E 30
  N11 .4J 31
  N14 .2D 32
  NW7 .3H 29
  NW9 .4K 43
  NW11 . . . . .7G 45
  W3 . . . . .3G 97
Ridgeway Av. EN4: E Barn 6J 21
Ridgeway Cres. BR6: Orp 3J 173
Ridgeway Cres. Gdns. BR6: Orp . .2J 173
Ridgeway Dr. BR1: Broml 4K 141
Ridgeway E. DA15: Sidc 5K 125

Ridgeway Gdns. IG4: Ilf 5C 52
  N6 . . . . .7G 47
Ridgeway Rd. TW7: Isle 7J 95
Ridgeway Rd. Nth. TW7: Isle 6J 95
Ridgeway Wlk. UB5: N'olt 6C 58
  (off Cowings Mead)
Ridgeway W. DA15: Sidc 5J 125
Ridgewell Cl. N1 . . . . .1C 84
  RM10: Dag 1H 91
  SE26 . . . . .4B 140
Ridgmount Gdns. WC1 . . .5C 6 (5H 83)
Ridgmount Pl. WC1 . . . . .5C 6 (5H 83)
Ridgmount Rd. SW18 . . . . .5K 117
Ridgmount St. WC1 . . . . .5C 6 (5H 83)
Ridgway SW19 . . . . .7E 134
  TW10: Rich 6E 114
The Ridgway SM2: Sutt 7B 166
Ridgway Ct. SW19 . . . . .6F 135
Ridgway Gdns. SW19 . . . . .7F 135
Ridgway Pl. SW19 . . . . .6G 135
Riding Ho. St. W1 . . . . . . .6K 5 (5F 83)
The Ridings E11 . . . . .5J 51
  EN4: E Barn 7G 21
  KT5: Surb 5G 151
  KT17: Ewe 7B 164
  TW16: Sun 1J 147
  W5 . . . . .4F 79
Ridings Av. N21 . . . . .4G 23
Ridings Cl. N6 . . . . .7G 47
Ridings La. UB4: Hayes 2F 75
Ridler Rd. EN1: Enf 1K 23
Ridley Av. W13 . . . . .3B 96
Ridley Cl. IG11: Bark 7K 71
Ridley Ct. SW16 . . . . .6J 137
Ridley Ho. SW1 . . . . .2D 18
  (off Monck St.)
Ridley Rd. BR2: Broml 3H 159
  DA16: Well 1B 126
  E7 . . . . .4A 70
  E8 . . . . .5F 67
  NW10 . . . . .2C 80
  SW19 . . . . .7K 135
Ridsdale Rd. SE20 . . . . .7H 139
Riefield Rd. SE9 . . . . .4G 125
Riesco Dr. CRO: C'don 6J 169
Riffel Rd. NW2 . . . . .5E 62
Rifle St. E14 . . . . .5D 86
Riga M. E1 . . . . .7K 9
Rigault Rd. SW6 . . . . .2G 117
Rigby Cl. CRO: Wadd 3A 168
Rigby La. UB3: Hayes 2E 92
Rigby M. IG1: Ilf 2F 71
Rigden St. E14 . . . . .6D 86
Rigeley Rd. NW10 . . . . .3C 80
Rigg App. E10 . . . . .1K 67
Rigge Pl. SW4 . . . . .4H 119
Riggindale Rd. SW16 . . . . .5H 137
Riley Ho. E3 . . . . .4C 86
  (off Ireton St.)
  SW10 . . . . .7B 100
  (off Riley St.)
Riley Rd. EN3: Enf W 1D 24
  SE1 . . . . .7H 15 (3F 103)
Riley St. SW10 . . . . .6B 100
Rill Ct. IG11: Bark 2G 89
  (off Spring Pl.)
Rill Ho. SE5 . . . . .7D 102
  (off Harris St.)
Rill La. HA8: Edg 6E 28
Rima Ho. SW3 . . . . .7A 16
  (off Callow St.)
Rinaldo Rd. SW12 . . . . .7F 119
The Ring SW7 . . . . .7B 10 (2B 100)
  W2 . . . . .2C 10 (7B 82)
Ring Cl. BR1: Broml 7K 141
Ring Ct. SE1 . . . . .6A 14
  (off The Cut)
Ringcroft St. N7 . . . . .5A 66
Ringcross Youth Cen. 5K 65
  (off Lough Rd.)

Ringers Ct. BR1: Broml 3J 159
  (off Ringers Rd.)
Ringers Rd. BR1: Broml 3J 159
Ringford Rd. SW18 . . . . .5H 117
Ring Ho. E1 . . . . .7J 85
  (off Sage St.)
Ringles Ct. E6 . . . . .1D 88
Ringlet Cl. E16 . . . . .5K 87
Ringlewell Cl. EN1: Enf 2C 24
Ringmer Av. SW6 . . . . .1G 117
Ringmer Gdns. N19 . . . . .2J 65
Ringmer Pl. N21 . . . . .5J 23
Ringmer Way BR1: Broml 5C 160
Ringmore Ri. SE23 . . . . .7H 121
Ringmore Vw. SE23 . . . . .7H 121
Ring Rd. W12 . . . . .1E 98
  (not continuous)
Ringsfield Ho. SE17 . . . . .5C 102
  (off Bronti Cl.)
Ringside Ct. SE28 . . . . .1C 108
Ringslade Rd. N22 . . . . .2K 47
Ringstead Rd. SE6 . . . . .7D 122
  SM1: Sutt 4B 166
Ring Way N11 . . . . .6B 32
Ringway UB2: S'hall 5B 94
Ringwold Cl. BR3: Beck 7A 140
Ringwood Av. CRO: C'don 7J 155
  N2 . . . . .2D 46
Ringwood Cl. HA5: Pinn 3A 40
Ringwood Gdns. E14 . . . . .4C 104
  SW15 . . . . .1C 134
Ringwood Rd. E17 . . . . .6B 50
Ringwood Way N21 . . . . .1G 33
  TW12: Hamp H 4E 130
Rio Cinema 5F 66
  (off Kingsland High St.)
Ripley Bldgs. SE1 . . . . .6B 14
  (off Rushworth St.)
Ripley Cl. BR1: Broml 5D 160
  CRO: New Ad 6E 170
Ripley Ct. CR4: Mitc 2B 154
Ripley Gdns. SM1: Sutt 4A 166
  SW14 . . . . .3K 115
Ripley Ho. SW1 . . . . .7A 18
  (off Churchill Gdns.)
Ripley M. E11 . . . . .6G 51
Ripley Rd. DA17: Belv 4G 109
  E16 . . . . .6A 88
  EN2: Enf 1H 23
  IG3: Ilf 2K 71
  TW12: Hamp 7E 130
Ripley Vs. W5 . . . . .6C 78
Ripon Cl. UB5: N'olt 5C 58
Ripon Ct. N11 . . . . .5A 32
  (off Ribblesdale Av.)
Ripon Gdns. IG1: Ilf 6C 52
  KT9: Chess 5D 162
Ripon Rd. N9 . . . . .7C 24
  N17 .3D 48
  SE18 . . . . .6F 107
Rippersley Rd. DA16: Well 1A 126
The Ripple Nature Reserve 3B 90
Ripple Rd. IG11: Bark, Dag 7G 71
  RM9: Dag 1B 90
RIPPLESIDE 1B 90
Rippleside Commercial Est.
  IG11: Bark 2C 90
Ripplevale Gro. N1 . . . . .7K 65
Rippolson Rd. SE18 . . . . .5K 107
Ripston Rd. TW15: Ashf 5F 129
Risborough Cl. N10 . . . . .3F 47
Risborough Dr. KT4: Wor Pk 7C 152
Risborough Ho. NW8 . . . . .3D 4
  (off Mallory St.)
Risborough St. SE1 . . . . .6B 14 (2B 102)
Risdon Ho. SE16 . . . . .2J 103
  (off Risdon St.)
Risdon St. SE16 . . . . .3J 103
The Rise DA5: Bexl 7C 126
  E11 . . . . .5J 51
  HA8: Edg 5C 28
  IG9: Buck H 1G 37

The Rise N13 . . . . .4F 33
  NW7 .6G 29
  NW10 . . . . .4K 61
  UB6: G'frd 5A 60
  UB10: Hil 2B 74
Risedale Rd. DA7: Bex 3J 127
Riseholme Ct. E9 . . . . .6B 68
Riseldine Rd. SE23 . . . . .6A 122
RISE PARK 2K 55
Rise Pk. Pde. RM1: Rom 2K 55
Risinghill St. N1 . . . . .2K 83
Risingholme Cl. HA3: Hrw W 1J 41
  WD23: Bush 1A 26
Risingholme Rd. HA3: Hrw W 2J 41
The Risings E17 . . . . .4F 51
Rising Sun Ct. EC1 . . . . .5B 8
Risley Av. N17 . . . . .1C 48
Risley Cl. SM4: Mord 5K 153
Rita Rd. SW8 . . . . .6J 101
Ritches Rd. N15 . . . . .5C 48
Ritchie Ho. E14 . . . . .6F 87
  (off Blair St.)
  N19 . . . . .1H 65
  SE16 . . . . .3J 103
  (off Howland Est.)
Ritchie Rd. CRO: C'don 6H 157
Ritchie St. N1 . . . . .2A 84
Ritchings Av. E17 . . . . .4A 50
Ritherdon Rd. SW17 . . . . .2E 136
Ritson Ho. N1 . . . . .1K 83
  (off Barnsbury Est.)
Ritson Rd. E8 . . . . .6G 67
Ritter St. SE18 . . . . .6E 106
Ritz Pde. W5 . . . . .4F 79
Ritzy Picturehouse 4A 120
  (off Coldharbour La.)
The Riva Bldg. SE13 . . . . .4F 123
Rivaz Pl. E9 . . . . .6J 67
Riven Ct. W2 . . . . .6K 81
  (off Inverness Ter.)
Rivenhall Gdns. E18 . . . . .4H 51
River App. HA8: Edg 1J 43
RIVER ASH ESTATE 7H 147
River Av. KT7: T Ditt 7A 150
  N13 .3G 33
River Av. Ind. Est. N13 . . . . .5F 33
River Bank KT7: T Ditt 5K 149
  KT8: E Mos 3J 149
  N21 .7H 23
  TW12: Hamp 3E 148
Riverbank Rd. BR1: Broml 3J 141
Riverbank Way SM6: W'gton 1E 166
  TW8: Bford 6C 96
River Barge Cl. E14 . . . . .2E 104
River Brent Bus. Pk. W7 . . . . .3J 95
River Cl. E11 . . . . .6A 52
  HA4: Ruis 6H 39
  UB2: S'hall 2G 95
River Ct. KT6: Surb 5D 150
  (off Portsmouth Rd.)
  SE1 . . . . .3A 14 (7B 84)
  TW17: Shep 7E 146
Rivercourt Rd. W6 . . . . .4D 98
River Crane Way TW13: Hanw . . .2D 130
  (off Watermill Way)
Riverdale SE13 . . . . .4E 122
Riverdale Cl. IG11: Bark 4B 90
Riverdale Ct. N21 . . . . .5J 23
Riverdale Dr. SW18 . . . . .1K 135
Riverdale Gdns. TW1: Twick 6C 114
Riverdale Rd. DA5: Bexl 7F 127
  DA8: Erith 5H 109
  SE18 . . . . .5K 107
  TW1: Twick 6C 114
  TW13: Hanw 4C 130
Riverdale Shop. Cen. 3E 122
Riverdene HA8: Edg 3D 28
Riverdene Rd. IG1: Ilf 3E 70
Riverfleet WC1 . . . . .1H 7
  (off Birkenhead St.)
Riverford Ho. W2 . . . . .5J 81
  (off Westbourne Pk. Rd.)

River Front EN1: Enf 3K 23
River Gdns. SM5: Cars 2E 166
TW14: Felt 5K 111
River Gdns. Bus. Cen.
TW14: Felt 5K 111
River Gdns. Wlk. SE10 . . . . .5G 105
River Gro. Pk. BR3: Beck 1B 158
Riverhead Cl. E17 . . . . .2K 49
River Hgts. E15 . . . . .1E 86
N17 . . . . .1F 49
Riverhill KT4: Wor Pk 2K 163
Riverhill M. KT4: Wor Pk 3K 163
Riverhill Mobile Home Pk. 2K 163
Riverholme Dr. KT19: Ewe 7K 163
Riverhope Mans. SE18 . . . . .3C 106
River Ho. SE26 . . . . .3H 139
Riverhouse Barn 7H 147
River La. TW10: Ham 7D 114
Riverleigh Ct. E4 . . . . .5G 35
Riverlight Quay SW11 . . . .7B 18 (6G 101)
River Lodge SW1 . . . . .7B 18
(off Grosvenor Rd.)
Rivermead KT1: King T 5D 150
KT8: E Mos 3G 149
Rivermead Cl. TW11: Tedd 5B 132
Rivermead Ct. SW6 . . . . .3H 117
Rivermead Ho. E9 . . . . .5A 68
TW16: Sun 3A 148
(off Thames St.)
Rivermead Rd. N18 . . . . .6E 34
Rivermeads Av. TW2: Twick 3E 130
River Mill One SE13 . . . . .3E 122
(off Station Rd.)
River Mill Two SE13 . . . . .3E 122
(off Station Rd.)
River Mt. KT12: Walt T 7H 147
Rivernook Cl. KT12: Walt T 5A 148
River Pk. Gdns. BR2: Broml 7F 141
River Pk. Rd. N22 . . . . .2K 47
River Pl. N1 . . . . .7C 66
River Reach TW11: Tedd 5C 132
River Rd. IG9: Buck H 1H 37
IG11: Bark 2J 89
River Rd. Bus. Pk. IG11: Bark 3K 89
Rivers Apts. N17 . . . . .6A 34
(off Cannon Rd.)
Riversdale Gdns. N22 . . . . .1A 48
Riversdale Rd. KT7: T Ditt 5A 150
N5 . . . . .3B 66
RM5: Col R 1H 55
Riversfield Rd. EN1: Enf 3K 23
Rivers Ho. TW7: Isle 4B 114
(off Richmond Rd.)
TW8: Bford 5G 97
(off Aitman Dr.)
Riverside E3 . . . . .1C 86
NW4 . . . . .7D 44
SE7 . . . . .3K 105
SW11 .7C 100
TW1: Twick 1B 132
TW9: Rich 5D 114
TW10: Rich 5D 114
TW16: Sun 2B 148
TW17: Shep 7G 147
W6 . . . . .6E 98
WC1 . . . . .1F 7
The Riverside KT8: E Mos 3H 149
Riverside Apts. N4 . . . . .7D 48
(off Goodchild Rd.)
N13 . . . . .5E 32
Riverside Arts Cen. 3A 148
Riverside Av. KT8: E Mos 5H 149
Riverside Bus. Cen. SW18 . . . . .1K 135
Riverside Bus. Pk. SW19 . . . . . . .1A 154
Riverside Cl. E5 . . . . .1J 67
KT1: King T 4D 150
RM1: Rom 4K 55
SM6: W'gton 3F 167
W7 . . . . .4J 77
Riverside Cotts. IG11: Bark 2H 89
Riverside Ct. E4 . . . . .6H 25
SE3 . . . . .4H 123

Riverside Ct. SW8 . . . . . . .7D 18 (6H 101)
TW7: Isle 2K 113
(off Woodlands Rd.)
TW14: Felt 7G 111
Riverside Dr. CR4: Mitc 5C 154
NW11 .6G 45
TW10: Ham 3B 132
W4 . . . . .7K 97
Riverside Gdns. EN2: Enf 2H 23
HA0: Wemb 2E 78
N3 . . . . .3G 45
W6 . . . . .5D 98
Riverside Ho. N1 . . . . .7C 66
(off Canonbury St.)
Riverside Ind. Est. EN3: Pond E 6F 25
IG11: Bark 3A 90
Riverside Mans. E1 . . . . .1J 103
(off Milk Yd.)
Riverside M. CR0: Bedd 3J 167
Riverside Pl. N11 . . . . .3B 32
TW19: Stanw 6A 110
Riverside Rd. DA14: Sidc 3E 144
E15 . . . . .2E 86
N15 . . . . .6G 49
SW17 .4K 135
TW19: Stanw 5A 110
Riverside Sq. N18 . . . . .6E 34
Riverside Studios 5E 98
Riverside Twr. SW6 . . . . .2A 118
(off The Boulevard)
Riverside Vs. KT6: Surb 6C 150
Riverside Wlk. BR4: W W'ck 1D 170
EN5: Barn 6A 20
(not continuous)
KT1: King T 3D 150
N12 . . . . .6D 30
(not continuous)
TW7: Isle 3J 113
Riverside Wharf E3 . . . . .1C 86
Riverside Works IG11: Bark 7F 71
Riverside Yd. SW17 . . . . .4A 136
Riverstone Cl. HA2: Harr 1H 59
Riverstone Ct. KT2: King T 1F 151
River St. EC1 . . . . .1J 7 (3A 84)
River St. M. EC1 . . . . .1J 7
River Ter. EC2 . . . . .3G 13
River Thames Vis. Cen. 6D 114
Riverton Cl. W9 . . . . .3H 81
River Twr. SW8 . . . . .7E 18 (6J 101)
River Vw. EN2: Enf 3H 23
Riverview Ct. E14 . . . . .3B 104
River Vw. Gdns. TW1: Twick 2K 131
Riverview Gdns. SW13 . . . . .6D 98
Riverview Gro. W4 . . . . .6H 97
River Vw. Hgts. SE16 . . . . .2G 103
(off Bermondsey Wall W.)
River Vw. M. CR0: Bedd 3J 167
Riverview Pk. SE6 . . . . .2C 140
Riverview Rd. KT19: Ewe 4J 163
W4 . . . . .7H 97
Riverview Wlk. SE6 . . . . .3B 140
River Wlk. E4 . . . . .7K 35
KT12: Walt T 6J 147
W6 . . . . .7E 98
(not continuous)
Riverwalk SW1 . . . . .5J 101
Riverwalk Apts. SW6 . . . . .3A 118
(off Central Av.)
Riverwalk Bus. Pk. EN3: Brim 4G 25
Riverwalk Rd. EN3: Brim 4G 25
River Way BR3: Beck 1C 170
KT19: Ewe 5K 163
SE10 .3H 105
TW2: Twick 2F 131
Riverway N13 . . . . .5F 33
River Wharf Bus. Pk.
DA17: Belv 1K 109
Riverwood La. BR7: Chst 1H 161
Rivet Ho. SE1 . . . . .5F 103
(off Cooper's Rd.)
Riviera Ct. E1 . . . . .1G 103
(off St Katharine's Way)
Rivington Av. IG8: Wfd G 2B 52

Rivington Ct. NW10 . . . . .1C 80
RM10: Dag 6H 73
Rivington Cres. NW7 . . . . .7G 29
Rivington Pl. EC2 . . . . .2H 9 (3E 84)
Rivington St. EC2 . . . . .2G 9 (3E 84)
Rivington Wlk. E8 . . . . .1G 85
Rivulet Apts. N4 . . . . .7D 48
Rivulet Rd. N17 . . . . .7H 33
Rixon Ho. SE18 . . . . .6F 107
Rixon St. N7 . . . . .3A 66
Rixsen Rd. E12 . . . . .5C 70
Roach Rd. E3 . . . . .7C 68
Roads Pl. N19 . . . . .2J 65
Roan Gdns. CR4: Mitc 1D 154
Roan St. SE10 . . . . .6E 104
Robarts Cl. HA5: Eastc 5K 39
Robbins Hall EN3: Pond E 6E 24
Robb Rd. HA7: Stan 6F 27
Robert Adam St. W1 . . . . . . .7G 5 (6E 82)
Roberta St. E2 . . . . .3G 85
Robert Bell Ho. SE16 . . . . .4G 103
(off Rouel Rd.)
Robert Burns Ho. N17 . . . . .7C 34
(off Northumberland Pk.)
Robert Burns M. SE24 . . . . .5B 120
Robert Clack Leisure Cen. 1G 73
Robert Cl. W9 . . . . .4A 4 (4A 82)
Robert Ct. SE15 . . . . .2G 121
Robert Dashwood Way
SE17 .4C 102
Robert Gentry Ho. W14 . . . . .5G 99
(off Gledstanes Rd.)
Robert Jones Ho. SE16 . . . . .4G 103
(off Rouel Rd.)
Robert Keen Cl. SE15 . . . . .1G 121
Robert Lewis Ho. IG11: Bark 4B 90
Robert Lowe Cl. SE14 . . . . .7K 103
Robert Morton Ho. NW8 . . . . .7A 64
Roberton Dr. BR1: Broml 1A 160
Robert Owen Ho. E2 . . . . .1K 9
(off Baroness Rd.)
N22 . . . . .1A 48
(off Progress Way)
SW6 . . . . .1F 117
Robert Runcie Ct. SW2 . . . . .4K 119
Roberts All. W5 . . . . .2D 96
Robertsbridge Rd. SM5: Cars 1A 166
Roberts Cl. CR7: Thor H 3D 156
IG11: Bark 6G 71
(off Tanner St.)
SE9 . . . . .1H 143
SE16 .2K 103
SM3: Cheam 7F 165
UB7: Yiew 1A 92
Roberts Ct. KT9: Chess 5D 162
N1 . . . . .1B 84
(off Essex Rd.)
NW10 .6A 62
SE20 .1J 157
(off Maple Rd.)
Roberts M. SW1 . . . . .1G 17 (3E 100)
Robertson Gro. SW17 . . . . .5C 136
Robertson Rd. E16 . . . . .5J 87
Robertson St. SW8 . . . . .3F 119
Roberts Pl. EC1 . . . . .3K 7 (4A 84)
RM10: Dag 6G 73
Roberts Sq. SE13 . . . . .4E 122
Roberts Rd. DA17: Belv 5G 109
E17 . . . . .1D 50
Robert St. CR0: C'don 3C 168
E16 . . . . .4E 88
NW1 . . . . .2K 5 (3F 83)
SE18 .5H 107
(not continuous)
WC2 . . . . .3F 13 (7J 83)
Robert Sutton Ho. E1 . . . . .6J 85
(off Tarling St.)
Robeson St. E3 . . . . .5B 86
Robina Cl. DA6: Bex 4D 126
HA6: Nwood 1H 39
Robin Cl. NW7 . . . . .3F 29
RM5: Col R 1K 55
TW12: Hamp 5C 130

Robin Ct. E14 . . . . .2E 104
SE16 .4G 103
SM6: W'gton 5G 167
Robin Cres. E6 . . . . .5B 88
Robin Gro. HA3: Kenton 6F 43
N6 . . . . .2E 64
TW8: Bford 6C 96
Robin Hill Dr. BR7: Chst 6C 142
ROBIN HOOD 3A 134
Robinhood Cl. CR4: Mitc 3G 155
Robin Hood Ct. EC4 . . . . .7K 7
(off Shoe La.)
Robin Hood Dr. HA3: Hrw W 7E 26
Robin Hood Gdns. E14 . . . . .7E 86
(off Woolmore St.)
Robin Hood Grn. BR5: St M Cry . . .5K 161
Robin Hood La. DA6: Bex 5E 126
E14 . . . . .7E 86
SM1: Sutt 5J 165
SW15 .3A 134
Robin Hood La. CR4: Mitc 3G 155
Robin Hood Rd. SW19 . . . . .5C 134
SW20 .3A 134
Robin Hood Way SW15 . . . . .3A 134
SW20 .3A 134
UB6: G'frd 6K 59
Robin Ho. NW8 . . . . .2C 82
(off Newcourt St.)
Robin Howard Dance Theatre
(The Place) 2D 6
(off Duke's Rd.)
Robinia Cl. SE20 . . . . .1G 157
(off Sycamore Gro.)
Robinia Cres. E10 . . . . .2D 68
Robinia Ho. SE16 . . . . .2A 104
(off Blondin Way)
Robin La. NW4 . . . . .3F 45
Robins Ct. BR3: Beck 2F 158
Robins Ct. CR2: S Croy 4E 168
(off Birdhurst Rd.)
SE12 .3A 142
Robinscroft M. SE10 . . . . .1E 122
Robins Gro. BR4: W W'ck 3J 171
Robinson Cl. E11 . . . . .3G 69
EN2: Enf 3H 23
Robinson Ct. CR7: Thor H 6B 156
N1 . . . . .1B 84
(off St Mary's Path)
TW9: Rich 4F 115
Robinson Cres. WD23: B Hea 1B 26
Robinson Ho. E14 . . . . .5C 86
W10 . . . . .6F 81
(off Bramley Rd.)
Robinson Rd. E2 . . . . .2J 85
RM10: Dag 4G 73
SE1 . . . . .4A 14 (1B 102)
SW17 .6C 136
Robinson's Cl. W13 . . . . .5A 78
Robinson St. SW3 . . . . .7E 16 (6D 100)
Robinson Way SE14 . . . . .7K 103
Robinswood Gdns. E17 . . . . .1B 50
Robinwood M. N5 . . . . .5B 66
Robinwood Gro. UB8: Hil 4B 74
Robinwood Pl. SW15 . . . . .4K 133
Robsart St. SW9 . . . . .2K 119
Robson Av. NW10 . . . . .7C 62
Robson Cl. E6 . . . . .6C 88
EN2: Enf 2G 23
Robson Ho. SE27 . . . . .3C 138
Roby Ho. EC1 . . . . .3C 8
(off Mitchell St.)
Roca Ct. E11 . . . . .5J 51
Rocastle Rd. SE4 . . . . .5A 122
Roch Av. HA8: Edg 2F 43
Rochdale Rd. E17 . . . . .7C 50
SE2 . . . . .5B 108
Rochdale Way SE8 . . . . .7C 104
(not continuous)
Roche Ho. E14 . . . . .7B 86
(off Beccles St.)
Rochelle Cl. SW11 . . . . .4B 118
Rochelle St. E2 . . . . .2J 9 (3F 85)
(not continuous)

Rochemont Wlk. *E8* 1G **85**
............................(off Pownell Rd.)
Roche Rd. SW16 ....1K **155**
Rochester Av. BR1: Broml ...2K **159**
E13 ....1A **88**
TW13: Felt 2H **129**
Rochester Cl. DA15: Sidc 6B **126**
EN1: Enf 1K **23**
SW16 ....7J **137**
Rochester Ct. *E2* 4H **85**
.............................(off Wilmot St.)
NW1 ....7G **65**
.........................(off Rochester Sq.)
Rochester Dr. DA5: Bexl 6F **127**
HA5: Pinn 5B **40**
Rochester Gdns. CRO: C'don ..3E **168**
IG1: IIf 7D **52**
Rochester Ho. *SE1* 7F **15**
..........................(off Manciple St.)
SE15 ....6J **103**
...........................(off Sharratt St.)
Rochester M. NW1 ....7G **65**
W5 ....4C **96**
Rochester Pde. TW13: Felt ...2J **129**
Rochester Pl. NW1 ....6G **65**
Rochester Rd. HA6: Nwood ...3H **39**
NW1 ....6G **65**
SM5: Cars 4D **166**
Rochester Row SW1 ...3B **18** (4G **101**)
Rochester Sq. NW1 ....7G **65**
Rochester St. SW1 ...2C **18** (3H **101**)
Rochester Ter. NW1 ....7G **65**
Rochester Wlk. SE1 ...4E **14** (1D **102**)
Rochester Way DA1: Dart 7K **127**
SE3 ....1K **123**
SE9 ....3D **124**
Rochester Way Relief Rd. SE3 ..1K **123**
Roche Wlk. SM5: Cars 6B **154**
Rochford *N17* 2E **48**
.............................(off Griffin Rd.)
Rochford Av. RM6: Chad H 5C **54**
Rochford Cl. E6 ....2B **88**
Rochford Wlk. E8 ....7G **67**
Rochford Way CRO: C'don 6J **155**
Rochfort Ho. SE8 ....5B **104**
Rock Av. SW14 ....3K **115**
Rockbourne M. SE23 ....1K **139**
Rockbourne Rd. SE23 ....1K **139**
Rock Cl. CR4: Mitc 2B **154**
Rockell's Pl. SE22 ....6H **121**
Rockfield Ho. *NW4* 4F **45**
.........................(off Belle Vue Est.)
SE10 ....6E **104**
............................(off Welland St.)
Rockford Av. UB6: G'frd 2A **78**
Rock Gdns. RM10: Dag 5H **73**
Rock Gro. Way SE16 ....4G **103**
...............................(not continuous)
Rockhall Rd. NW2 ....4F **63**
Rockhall Way NW2 ....3F **63**
Rockhampton Cl. SE27 ....4A **138**
Rockhampton Rd. CR2: S Croy ..6E **168**
SE27 ....4A **138**
Rock Hill SE26 ....4F **139**
...............................(not continuous)
Rockingham Cl. SW15 ....4B **116**
Rockingham St. SE1 ....3C **102**
Rockland Rd. SW15 ....4G **117**
Rocklands Dr. CR2: S Croy 6D **168**
HA7: Stan 2B **42**
Rockley Ct. *W14* 2F **99**
............................(off Rockley Rd.)
Rockley Rd. W14 ....2F **99**
Rockmount Rd. SE18 ....5K **107**
SE19 ....6D **138**
Rocks La. SW13 ....1C **116**
Rock St. N4 ....2A **66**
Rockware Av. UB6: G'frd 1H **77**
Rockware Av. Bus. Cen.
UB6: G'frd 1H **77**
Rockwell Gdns. SE19 ....5E **138**
Rockwell Rd. RM10: Dag 5H **73**
Rockwood Pl. W12 ....2E **98**

Rocliffe St. N1 ....2B **84**
Rocombe Cres. SE23 ....7J **121**
Rocque Ho. *SW6* 7H **99**
...........................(off Estcourt Rd.)
Rocque La. SE3 ....3H **123**
Rodale Mans. SW18 ....6K **117**
Rodborough Ct. *W9* 4J **81**
.............................(off Hermes St.)
Rodborough Rd. NW11 ....1J **63**
Rodd Est. TW17: Shep 5E **146**
Roden Cl. N6 ....7H **47**
Roden Gdns. CRO: C'don 6E **156**
Rodenhurst Rd. SW4 ....6G **119**
Roden St. IG1: IIf 3E **70**
N7 ....3K **65**
Roden Way *IG1: IIf* 3E **70**
..............................(off Roden St.)
Roderick Ho. SE16 ....4J **103**
.........................(off Raymouth Rd.)
Roderick Rd. NW3 ....4D **64**
Rodgers Ho. SW4 ....7H **119**
........................(off Clapham Pk. Est.)
Rodin Ct. N1 ....1B **84**
.............................(off Essex Rd.)
Roding Av. IG8: Wfd G 6H **37**
Roding Ho. *N1* 1A **84**
.........................(off Barnsbury Est.)
Roding La. IG7: Chig 2K **37**
IG9: Buck H 1G **37**
Roding La. Nth. IG8: Wfd G ...6H **37**
Roding La. Sth. IG4: IIf, Wfd G ..4B **52**
...............................(not continuous)
Roding M. E1 ....1G **103**
The Rodings IG8: Wfd G 6F **37**
Roding Rd. E5 ....4K **67**
E6 ....5F **89**
The Rodings IG8: Wfd G 6F **37**
Roding Trad. Est. IG11: Bark 7F **71**
Roding Valley Meadows Nature Reserve
....1K **37**
Roding Vw. IG9: Buck H 1G **37**
Rodmarton St. W1 ...6F **5** (5D **82**)
Rodmell *WC1* 2F **7**
............................(off Regent Sq.)
Rodmell Cl. UB4: Yead 4C **76**
Rodmell Slope N12 ....5C **30**
Rodmere St. SE10 ....5G **105**
Rodmill La. SW2 ....7J **119**
Rodney Cl. CRO: C'don 1B **168**
HA5: Pinn 7C **40**
KT3: N Mald 5A **152**
Rodney Ct. EN5: Barn 3C **20**
W9 ....3A **4** (4A **82**)
Rodney Gdns. BR4: W W'ck 4J **171**
HA5: Eastc 5K **39**
Rodney Ho. *E14* 4J **103**
.............................(off Cahir St.)
N1 ....2K **83**
.............................(off Donegal St.)
SW1 ....6B **18**
.............................(off Dolphin Sq.)
W11 ....7J **81**
.........................(off Pembridge Cres.)
Rodney Pl. E17 ....2A **50**
SE17 ....4C **102**
SW19 ....1A **154**
Rodney Point SE16 ....2B **104**
.........................(off Rotherhithe St.)
Rodney Rd. CR4: Mitc 3C **154**
E11 ....4K **51**
KT3: N Mald 5A **152**
SE17 ....4C **102**
...............................(not continuous)
TW2: Whitt 1H **131**
Rodney St. N1 ....1H **7** (2K **83**)
Rodney Way RM7: Mawney 1H **55**
SL3: Poyle 4A **174**
Rodway Rd. BR1: Broml 1K **159**
SW15 ....7C **116**
Rodwell Cl. HA4: Ruis 1A **58**
Rodwell Pl. HA8: Edg 6B **28**
Rodwell Rd. SE22 ....6F **121**
Roe NW9 ....7G **29**

Roebourne Way E16 ....1E **106**
Roebuck Cl. N17 ....6A **34**
TW13: Felt 4K **129**
Roebuck Hgts. IG9: Buck H 1F **37**
Roebuck La. IG9: Buck H 1F **37**
Roebuck Rd. KT9: Chess 5G **163**
Roedean Av. EN3: Enf H 1D **24**
Roedean Cl. EN3: Enf H 1D **24**
Roedean Cres. SW15 ....6A **116**
Roe End NW9 ....4J **43**
ROE GREEN 4J **43**
Roe Grn. NW9 ....5J **43**
ROEHAMPTON 7C **116**
Roehampton Cl. SW15 ....4C **116**
Roehampton Dr. BR7: Chst 6G **143**
Roehampton Ga. SW15 ....6A **116**
Roehampton Golf Course 4B **116**
Roehampton High St. SW15 ...7C **116**
Roehampton Ho. RM8: Dag 5A **72**
ROEHAMPTON LANE 1D **134**
Roehampton La. SW15 ....4C **116**
Roehampton Sport & Fitness Cen.
....7C **116**

Roehampton University
Digby Stuart College 5C **116**
Main Site 5C **116**
Southlands College 5C **116**
Whitelands Site 7C **116**
Roehampton Va. SW15 ....3B **134**
Roe La. NW9 ....4H **43**
Roesel Pl. BR5: Pet W 5F **161**
Roe Way SM6: W'gton 6J **167**
Roffe Gdns. RM8: Dag 1E **72**
Roffey St. E14 ....2E **104**
Roffo Cl. SE17 ....6D **102**
.........................(off Boundary La.)
Rogan Ho. SW8 ....1F **119**
.........................(off St Joseph's St.)
Rogate Ho. E5 ....3G **67**
Roger Dowley Ct. E2 ....2J **85**
Roger Harriss Almshouses E15 ..1H **87**
.................................(off Gift La.)
Roger Reede's Almshouses
RM1: Rom 4K **55**
Rogers Ct. *E14* 7C **86**
.........................(off Premiere Pl.)
Rogers Est. E2 ....3J **85**
...............................(not continuous)
Rogers Gdns. RM10: Dag 5G **73**
Roger's Ho. RM10: Dag 5G **73**
Rogers Rd. E16 ....6H **87**
RM10: Dag 5G **73**
SW17 ....4B **136**
Rogers Ruff HA6: Nwood 1E **38**
Roger St. WC1 ....4H **7** (4K **83**)
Rogers Wlk. N12 ....3E **30**
Rohere Ho. EC1 ....1C **8** (3C **84**)
Rojack Rd. SE23 ....1K **139**
Rokeby Gdns. IG8: Wfd G 1J **51**
Rokeby Ho. *SW12* 7F **119**
.........................(off Lochinvar St.)
WC1 ....4G **7**
.......................(off Lamb's Conduit St.)
Rokeby Pl. SW20 ....7D **134**
Rokeby Rd. HA1: Harr 3H **41**
SE4 ....2B **122**
Rokeby St. E15 ....1F **87**
Rokell Ho. *BR3: Beck* 5D **140**
.........................(off Beckenham Hill Rd.)
Roker Pk. Av. UB10: Ick 4A **56**
Rokesby Cl. DA16: Well 2H **125**
Rokesby Pl. HA0: Wemb 5D **60**
Rokesly Av. N8 ....5J **47**
Rokewood Apts. BR3: Beck 1C **158**
Roland Gdns. SW7 ...5A **16** (5A **100**)
SW10 ....5A **16**
Roland Ho. *SW7* 5A **16**
.........................(off Old Brompton Rd.)
Roland Mans. *SW7* 5A **100**
.........................(off Old Brompton Rd.)
Roland M. E1 ....5K **85**

Roland Rd. E17 ....4F **51**
Roland Way KT4: Wor Pk 2B **164**
SE17 ....5D **102**
SW7 ....5A **16** (5A **100**)
Roles Gro. RM6: Chad H 4D **54**
Rolfe Cl. EN4: E Barn 4H **21**
Rolfe Ter. SE18 ....5F **107**
Rolinsden Way BR2: Kes 5B **172**
Rollerbowl 2F **55**
Rollesby Rd. KT9: Chess 6G **163**
Rollesby Way SE28 ....6C **90**
Rolleston Av. BR5: Pet W 6F **161**
Rolleston Cl. BR5: Pet W 7F **161**
Rolleston Rd. CR2: S Croy 7D **168**
Roll Gdns. IG2: IIf 5E **52**
Rolling Mills M. E14 ....6A **86**
Rollins Ho. SE15 ....6J **103**
.............................(off Rollins St.)
Rollins St. SE15 ....6J **103**
Rollit Cres. TW3: Houn 5E **112**
Rollit St. N7 ....5A **66**
Rolls Bldgs. EC4 ....7J **7** (6A **84**)
Rollscourt Av. SE24 ....5C **120**
Rolls Pk. Av. E4 ....5H **35**
Rolls Pk. Rd. E4 ....5J **35**
Rolls Rd. SE1 ....5F **103**
Rolls Royce Cl. SM6: W'gton ...7J **167**
Rolt St. SE8 ....6A **104**
...............................(not continuous)
Rolvenden Gdns. BR1: Broml ...7B **142**
Rolvenden Pl. N17 ....1G **49**
Roma Corte SE13 ....3D **122**
.............................(off Elmira St.)
Romana Ct. CRO: C'don 2F **169**
Roman Apts. *E8* 1H **7**
.............................(off Silesia Bldgs.)
Roman Cl. RM13: Rain 2K **91**
TW14: Felt 5A **112**
W3 ....2H **97**
Roman Ct. N7 ....6K **65**
Romanfield Rd. SW2 ....7K **119**
Roman Ho. EC2 ....6D **8**
RM13: Rain 2K **91**
Romanhurst Av. BR2: Broml ...4G **159**
Romanhurst Gdns. BR2: Broml ..4G **159**
Roman Ind. Est. CRO: C'don ...7E **156**
Roman Ri. SE19 ....6D **138**
Roman Rd. E2 ....3J **85**
E3 ....2A **86**
E6 ....4B **88**
IG1: IIf 6F **71**
N10 ....7A **32**
NW2 ....2E **62**
.............................(Edgware Rd.)
NW2 ....3E **62**
.............................(Temple Rd.)
W4 ....4A **98**
Roman Rd. Mkt. 1B **86**
.............................(off Roman Rd.)
Roman Sq. SE28 ....1A **108**
Roman Way CRO: C'don 2B **168**
EN1: Enf 5A **24**
N7 ....6K **65**
SE15 ....7J **103**
Roman Way Ind. Est. *N7* 7K **65**
.........................(off Roman Way)
Romany Gdns. E17 ....1A **50**
SM3: Sutt 7J **153**
Romany Ri. BR5: Farnb 1G **173**
Roma Read Cl. SW15 ....7D **116**
Roma Rd. E17 ....3A **50**
Romayne Ho. SW4 ....3H **119**
Romberg Rd. SW17 ....3E **136**
Romborough Gdns. SE13 ......5E **122**
Romborough Way SE13 ....5E **122**
Romero Cl. SW9 ....3K **119**
Romeyn Rd. SW16 ....3K **137**
ROMFORD 5K **55**
Romford Greyhound Stadium ..6J **55**
Romford Rd. E7 ....6G **69**
E12 ....5A **70**

Romford Rd. E15 . . . . .6G **69**
 RM5: Col R 1E **54**
Romford St. E1 . . . . .5G **85**
Romilly Ho. W11 . . . . .7G **81**
 (off Wilsham St.)
Romilly Rd. N4 . . . . .2B **66**
Romilly St. W1 . . . . .2D **12** (7H **83**)
Romily Cl. SW6 . . . . .2H **117**
Rommany Rd. SE27 . . . . .4D **138**
 (not continuous)
Romney Cl. HA2: Harr 7E **40**
 KT9: Chess 4E **162**
 N17 . . . . .1H **49**
 NW11 . . . . .1A **64**
 SE14 . . . . .7J **103**
 TW15: Ashf 5E **128**
Romney Ct. NW3 . . . . .6C **64**
 UB5: N'olt 2B **76**
 (off Parkfield Dr.)
 W12 . . . . .2F **99**
 (off Shepherd's Bush Grn.)
Romney Dr. BR1: Broml 7B **142**
 HA2: Harr 7E **40**
Romney Gdns. DA7: Bex 1F **127**
Romney Ho. SW1 . . . . .2E **18**
 (off Marsham St.)
Romney M. W1 . . . . . . .5G **5** (5E **82**)
Romney Pde. UB4: Hayes 2F **75**
Romney Rd. KT3: N Mald 6K **151**
 SE10 . . . . .6F **105**
 UB4: Hayes 2F **75**
Romney Row NW2 . . . . .2F **63**
 (off Brent Ter.)
Romney St. SW1 . . . . . . .2E **18** (3J **101**)
Romola Rd. SE24 . . . . .1B **138**
Romsey Cl. BR6: Farnb 4F **173**
Romsey Gdns. RM9: Dag 1D **90**
Romsey Rd. RM9: Dag 1D **90**
 W13 . . . . .7A **78**
Romside Pl. RM7: Rom 4K **55**
Romulus Ct. TW8: Bford 7D **96**
Ronald Av. E15 . . . . .3G **87**
Ronald Buckingham Ct. SE16 . . . .2J **103**
 (off Kenning St.)
Ronald Cl. BR3: Beck 4B **158**
Ronald Ct. EN5: New Bar 3E **20**
Ronaldshay N4 . . . . .7A **48**
Ronalds Rd. BR1: Broml 1J **159**
 N5 . . . . .5A **66**
 (not continuous)
Ronaldstone Rd. DA15: Sidc 6J **125**
Ronald St. E1 . . . . .6J **85**
Rona Rd. NW3 . . . . .4E **64**
Ronart St. HA3: W'stone 3K **41**
Rona Wlk. N1 . . . . .6D **66**
Rondel Ct. DA5: Bexl 6E **126**
Rondu Rd. NW2 . . . . .5G **63**
Ronelean Rd. KT6: Surb 2F **163**
Ron Grn. Ct. DA8: Erith 6K **109**
Ron Leighton Way E6 . . . . .1C **88**
Ronnie La. E12 . . . . .4E **70**
 (not continuous)
Ron Todd Cl. RM10: Dag 1G **91**
Ronver Rd. SE12 . . . . .7H **123**
Rood La. EC3 . . . . . . .2G **15** (7E **84**)
The Roof Ter. Apts. EC1 . . . . .4B **8**
 (off Gt. Sutton St.)
Rookby Ct. N21 . . . . .2G **33**
Rook Cl. HA9: Wemb 3H **61**
Rookeries Cl. TW13: Felt 3K **129**
Rookery Cl. NW9 . . . . .5B **44**
Rookery Ct. E10 . . . . .3D **68**
Rookery Cres. RM10: Dag 7H **73**
Rookery Dr. BR7: Chst 1E **160**
Rookery La. BR2: Broml 6B **160**
Rookery Rd. SW4 . . . . .4G **119**
Rookery Way NW9 . . . . .5B **44**
Rooke Way SE10 . . . . .5H **105**
Rookfield Av. N10 . . . . .4G **47**
Rookfield Cl. N10 . . . . .4G **47**
Rooksmead Rd. TW16: Sun 2H **147**
Rooks Ter. UB7: W Dray 2A **92**
Rookstone Rd. SW17 . . . . .5D **136**

Rook Wlk. E6 . . . . .6B **88**
Rookwood Av. KT3: N Mald 4C **152**
 SM6: Bedd 4H **167**
Rookwood Gdns. E4 . . . . .2C **36**
Rookwood Ho. IG11: Bark 2H **89**
Rookwood Rd. N16 . . . . .7F **49**
Rookwood Way E3 . . . . .7C **68**
Roosevelt Memorial 2H **11** (7E **82**)
Roosevelt Way RM10: Dag 6K **73**
Rootes Dr. W10 . . . . .5F **81**
Ropemaker Rd. SE16 . . . . .2A **104**
Ropemaker's Flds. E14 . . . . .7B **86**
Ropemaker St. EC2 . . . . .5E **8** (5D **84**)
Roper Cres. TW16: Sun 1J **147**
Roper La. SE1 . . . . . . .7H **15** (2E **102**)
Ropers Av. E4 . . . . .5J **35**
Ropers Orchard SW3 . . . . .6C **100**
 (off Danvers St.)
Roper St. SE9 . . . . .5D **124**
Ropers Wlk. SW2 . . . . .7A **120**
Roper Way CR4: Mitc 2E **154**
Ropery Bus. Pk. SE7 . . . . .4A **106**
Ropery St. E3 . . . . .4B **86**
Rope St. SE16 . . . . .4A **104**
Rope Ter. E16 . . . . .2K **105**
Rope Wlk. TW16: Sun 3A **148**
Ropewalk Gdns. E1 . . . . .6G **85**
Ropewalk M. E8 . . . . .7G **67**
The Ropeworks IG11: Bark 1G **89**
Ropley St. E2 . . . . .2G **85**
Rosa Alba M. N5 . . . . .4C **66**
Rosa Av. TW15: Ashf 4C **128**
Rosalind Ct. IG11: Bark 7A **72**
 (off Meadow Rd.)
Rosalind Ho. N1 . . . . .2E **84**
 (off Arden Est.)
Rosaline Rd. SW6 . . . . .7G **99**
Rosaline Ter. SW6 . . . . .7G **99**
 (off Rosaline Rd.)
Rosa M. E17 . . . . .3B **50**
Rosamond St. SE26 . . . . .3H **139**
Rosamund Cl. CR2: S Croy 4D **168**
Rosamun St. UB2: S'hall 4C **94**
Rosa Parks Ho. SE17 . . . . .4C **102**
 (off Munton Rd.)
Rosary Cl. TW3: Houn 2C **112**
Rosary Gdns. SW7 . . . . .4A **100**
 TW15: Ashf 4D **128**
Rosaville Rd. SW6 . . . . .7H **99**
Roscoe St. EC1 . . . . . . .4D **8** (4C **84**)
 (not continuous)
Roscoe St. Est. EC1 . . . . .4D **8** (4C **84**)
Roscoff Cl. HA8: Edg 1J **43**
Rosea Apts. SW11 . . . . .4C **118**
 (off Danvers Av.)
Roseacre Cl. SM1: Sutt 2A **166**
 TW17: Shep 5C **146**
 W13 . . . . .5B **78**
Roseacre Rd. DA16: Well 3B **126**
Rose All. EC2 . . . . .6H **9**
 (off Bishopsgate)
 SE1 . . . . .4D **14** (1C **102**)
Rose & Crown Cl. EC2 . . . . .7D **8**
Rose & Crown M. TW7: Isle 1A **114**
Rose & Crown Yd.
 SW1 . . . . .4B **12** (1G **101**)
Rose Apts. SE11 . . . . .7K **19**
Roseary Cl. UB7: W Dray 4A **92**
Rose Av. CR4: Mitc 1D **154**
 E18 . . . . .2K **51**
 SM4: Mord 5A **154**
Rosebank SE20 . . . . .7H **139**
 SW6 . . . . .7F **98**
 W3 . . . . .6K **79**
Rosebank Av. HA0: Wemb 4K **59**
Rosebank Cl. N12 . . . . .5H **31**
 TW11: Tedd 6A **132**
Rosebank Gdns. E3 . . . . .2B **86**
 W3 . . . . .6K **79**
Rosebank Gdns. Nth. E3 . . . . .2B **86**
Rosebank Gro. E17 . . . . .3B **50**
Rosebank Rd. E17 . . . . .6D **50**
 W7 . . . . .2J **95**

Rosebank Vs. E17 . . . . .4C **50**
Rosebank Wlk. NW1 . . . . .7H **65**
 SE18 . . . . .4C **106**
Rosebank Way W3 . . . . .6K **79**
Rose Bates Dr. NW9 . . . . .4G **43**
Rosebay Dr. N17 . . . . .2F **49**
Rosebay Ho. E3 . . . . .5C **86**
 (off Hawgood St.)
Roseberry Dr. HA8: Edg 2C **28**
Roseberry Gdns. BR6: Orp 3J **173**
 N4 . . . . .6B **48**
Roseberry Mans. N1 . . . . .1J **83**
 (off Tapper Wlk.)
Roseberry M. SW2 . . . . .6J **119**
Roseberry Pl. E8 . . . . .6F **67**
Roseberry St. SE16 . . . . .4H **103**
Rosebery Av. CR7: Thor H 2C **156**
 DA15: Sidc 7J **125**
 E12 . . . . .6C **70**
 EC1 . . . . .4J **7** (4A **84**)
 HA2: Harr 4C **58**
 KT3: N Mald 2B **152**
 N17 . . . . .2G **49**
Rosebery Cl. SM4: Mord 6F **153**
Rosebery Ct. EC1 . . . . .3J **7**
 (off Rosebery Av.)
 W1 . . . . .4J **11**
 (off Charles St.)
Rosebery Gdns. N8 . . . . .5J **47**
 SM1: Sutt 4K **165**
 W13 . . . . .6A **78**
Rosebery Ho. E2 . . . . .2J **85**
 (off Sewardstone Rd.)
Rosebery Ind. Pk. N17 . . . . .2H **49**
Rosebery M. N10 . . . . .2G **47**
 SW2 . . . . .6J **119**
Rosebery Pl. NW7 . . . . .7G **29**
Rosebery Rd. KT1: King T 2H **151**
 N10 . . . . .2G **47**
 SM1: Sutt 6H **165**
 SW2 . . . . .6J **119**
 TW3: Houn 5G **113**
 WD23: Bush 1A **26**
Rosebery Sq. EC1 . . . . .4J **7**
 KT1: King T 2H **151**
Rosebine Av. TW2: Twick 7H **113**
Rosebury Rd. SW6 . . . . .2K **117**
Rosebury Sq. IG8: Wfd G 7K **37**
Rosebury Va. HA4: Ruis 2J **57**
Rose Bush Ct. NW3 . . . . .5D **64**
Rose Ct. E1 . . . . .6K **9**
 E8 . . . . .7F **67**
 (off Richmond Rd.)
 HA0: Wemb 2E **78**
 (off Vicars Bri. Cl.)
 HA2: Harr 2G **59**
 N1 . . . . .18 **84**
 (off Collin's Yd.)
 SE8 . . . . .4K **103**
Rosecourt Rd. CR0: C'don 6K **155**
Rosecrest Ct. N15 . . . . .4F **49**
Rosecroft N14 . . . . .2D **32**
Rosecroft Av. NW3 . . . . .3J **63**
Rosecroft Gdns. NW2 . . . . .3C **62**
 TW2: Twick 1H **131**
Rosecroft Rd. UB1: S'hall 4E **76**
Rosecroft Wlk. HA0: Wemb 5D **60**
 HA5: Pinn 5B **40**
Rose Dale BR6: Farnb 2F **173**
Rosedale Av. UB3: Hayes 5F **75**
Rosedale Cl. HA7: Stan 6G **27**
 SE2 . . . . .3B **108**
 W7 . . . . .2K **95**
Rosedale Ct. HA1: Harr 4K **59**
 N5 . . . . .4B **66**
Rosedale Dr. RM9: Dag 7B **72**
Rosedale Gdns. RM9: Dag 7B **72**
Rosedale Ho. N16 . . . . .1D **66**
Rosedale Pl. CR0: C'don 7K **157**
Rosedale Rd. E7 . . . . .5A **70**
 KT17: Ewe 5C **164**
 RM1: Rom 2J **55**
 RM9: Dag 7B **72**
 TW9: Rich 3E **114**

Rosedale Ter. W6 . . . . .3D **99**
 (off Dalling Rd.)
Rosedene NW6 . . . . .1F **81**
Rosedene Av. CR0: C'don 7J **155**
 SM4: Mord 5J **153**
 SW16 . . . . .3K **137**
 UB6: G'frd 3E **76**
Rosedene Ct. HA4: Ruis 1G **57**
Rosedene Gdns. IG2: Ilf 4E **52**
Rosedene Ter. E10 . . . . .2D **68**
Rosedew Rd. W6 . . . . .6F **99**
Rose End KT4: Wor Pk 1F **165**
Rosefield Cl. SM5: Cars 5C **166**
Rosefield Gdns. E14 . . . . .7C **86**
Roseford Ct. W12 . . . . .2F **99**
 (off Shepherd's Bush Grn.)
Rose Gdn. Cl. HA8: Edg 6K **27**
Rose Gdns. TW13: Felt 2J **129**
 UB1: S'hall 4E **76**
 W5 . . . . .3D **96**
Rosegate Ho. E3 . . . . .2B **86**
 (off Hereford Rd.)
Rose Glen NW9 . . . . .4K **43**
 RM7: Rush G 1K **73**
Rosehart M. W11 . . . . .6J **81**
Rose Hatch Av. RM6: Chad H 3D **54**
Roseheath Rd. TW4: Houn 5D **112**
ROSEHILL 7A **154**
Rose Hill SM1: Sutt 2K **165**
Rosehill KT10: Clay 6A **162**
 TW12: Hamp 1E **148**
Rosehill Av. SM1: Sutt 1A **166**
Rosehill Ct. SM4: Mord 7A **154**
 (off St Helier Av.)
Rosehill Ct. Pde. SM4: Mord 7A **154**
 (off St Helier Av.)
Rosehill Gdns. SM1: Sutt 2K **165**
 UB6: G'frd 5K **59**
Rose Hill Pk. W. SM1: Sutt 1A **166**
Rosehill Rd. SW18 . . . . .6A **118**
ROSE HILL RDBT. 7A **154**
Rose Joan M. NW6 . . . . .4J **63**
Rosekey Ct. SE8 . . . . .7B **104**
 (off Baildon St.)
Roseland Cl. N17 . . . . .7J **33**
Rose La. RM6: Chad H 3D **54**
Rose Lawn WD23: B Hea 1B **26**
Roseleigh Av. N5 . . . . .4B **66**
Roseleigh Cl. TW1: Twick 6D **114**
Rose Lipman Bldg. 1E **84**
Rosemary Av. EN2: Enf 1K **23**
 KT8: W Mole 3E **148**
 N3 . . . . .2K **45**
 N9 . . . . .1C **34**
 TW4: Houn 2B **112**
Rosemary Branch Theatre 1D **84**
 (off Rosemary St.)
Rosemary Cl. CR0: C'don 6J **155**
 UB8: Hil 5C **74**
Rosemary Ct. SE8 . . . . .6B **104**
 (off Dorking Cl.)
 SE15 . . . . .7E **102**
Rosemary Dr. E14 . . . . .6F **87**
 IG4: Ilf 5B **52**
Rosemary Gdns. KT9: Chess 4E **162**
 RM8: Dag 1F **73**
 SW14 . . . . .3J **115**
Rosemary Ho. N1 . . . . .1D **84**
 (off Colville Est.)
 NW10 . . . . .1D **80**
 (off Uffington Rd.)
Rosemary La. SW14 . . . . .3J **115**
Rosemary Rd. DA16: Well 1K **125**
 SE15 . . . . .7F **103**
 SW17 . . . . .3A **136**
Rosemary St. N1 . . . . .1D **84**
Rosemary Works N1 . . . . .1D **84**
 (off Branch Pl.)
Rosemead Av. CR4: Mitc 3G **155**
 HA9: Wemb 5E **60**
 TW13: Felt 2H **129**
Rosemead Cl. KT6: Surb 1G **163**
Rosemere Pl. BR2: Broml 4G **159**

Rose M. N18 . . . . .4C **34**
Rosemont Av. N12 . . . . .6F **31**
Rosemont Ct. W3 . . . . .1H **97**
            (off Rosemont Rd.)
Rosemont Rd. HA0: Wemb 1E **78**
  KT3: N Mald 3J **151**
  NW3 . . . . .6A **64**
  TW10: Rich 6E **114**
  W3 . . . . .7H **79**
Rosemoor Ho. W13 . . . . .1A **96**
            (off Broadway)
Rosemoor St. SW3 . . . . .4E **16** (4D **100**)
Rosemount SM6: W'gton 6G **167**
           (off Clarendon Rd.)
Rosemount Cl. IG8: Wfd G 6J **37**
Rosemount Dr. BR1: Broml 4D **160**
Rosemount Point SE23 . . . . .3K **139**
Rosemount Rd. W13 . . . . .6A **78**
Rosenau Cres. SW11 . . . . .1D **118**
Rosenau Rd. SW11 . . . . .1C **118**
Rosenburg Rd. W3 . . . . .2H **97**
Rosendale Rd. SE21 . . . . .7C **120**
  SE24 . . . . .7C **120**
Roseneath Av. N21 . . . . .1G **33**
Roseneath Pl. SW16 . . . . .4K **137**
          (off Curtis Fld. Rd.)
Roseneath Rd. SW11 . . . . .6E **118**
Roseneath Wlk. EN1: Enf 4K **23**
Rosen's Wlk. HA8: Edg 3C **28**
Rosenthal Rd. SE6 . . . . .6D **122**
Rosenthorpe Rd. SE15 . . . . .5K **121**
Rose Pk. Cl. UB4: Yead 5A **76**
Rosepark Ct. IG5: Ilf 2D **52**
Rose Pl. N8 . . . . .6J **47**
Rose Playhouse 4D **14**
            (off Park St.)
Roserton St. E14 . . . . .2E **104**
The Rosery CR0: C'don 6K **157**
The Roses IG8: Wfd G 7C **36**
Rose Sq. SW3 . . .5B **16** (5B **100**)
Rose Stapleton Ter. SE1 . . . . .3E **102**
          (off Page's Wlk.)
Rose St. EC4 . . . . .7B **8** (6B **84**)
  WC2 . . . . .2E **12** (7J **83**)
          (not continuous)
Rose Theatre
  Kingston 2D **150**
  Sidcup 1B **144**
Rosethorn Cl. SW12 . . . . .7H **119**
Rose Tree M. IG8: Wfd G 6H **37**
Rosetree Pl. TW12: Hamp 7E **130**
Rosetta Cl. SW8 . . . . .7J **101**
          (off Kenchester Cl.)
Rosetta Ct. SE19 . . . . .7E **138**
Rosetti Ter. RM8: Dag 4B **72**
          (off Marlborough Rd.)
Roseveare Rd. SE12 . . . . .4A **142**
Roseville N21 . . . . .1F **33**
             (off The Green)
Roseville Av. TW3: Houn 5E **112**
Roseville Rd. UB3: Harl 5J **93**
Rosevine Rd. SW20 . . . . .1E **152**
Rose Wlk. BR4: W W'ck 2E **170**
  KT5: Surb 5H **151**
Rose Way HA8: Edg 4D **28**
  SE12 . . . . .5J **123**
Roseway SE21 . . . . .6D **120**
Rosewell Cl. SE20 . . . . .7H **139**
Rosewood KT7: T Ditt 2A **162**
Rosewood Av. UB6: G'frd 5A **60**
Rosewood Cl. DA14: Sidc 3C **144**
Rosewood Ct. BR1: Broml 1A **160**
  E11 . . . . .4F **69**
  KT2: King T 7G **133**
  RM6: Chad H 5C **54**
Rosewood Dr. TW17: Shep 5B **146**
Rosewood Gdns. SE13 . . . . .2E **122**
Rosewood Gro. SM1: Sutt 2A **166**
Rosewood Ho. SW8 . . . .7G **19** (6K **101**)
Rosewood Sq. W12 . . . . .6C **80**
Rosher Cl. E15 . . . . .7F **69**
Roshni Ho. SW17 . . . . .6C **136**
Rosina St. E9 . . . . .6K **67**

Rosing Apts. BR2: Broml 4A **160**
         (off Homesdale Rd.)
Roskeen Ct. SW20 . . . . .7E **134**
Roskell Rd. SW15 . . . . .3F **117**
Rosler Bldg. SE1 . . . . .5C **14**
            (off Ewer St.)
Roslin Ho. E1 . . . . .7K **85**
         (off Brodlove La.)
Roslin Rd. W3 . . . . .3H **97**
Roslin Way BR1: Broml 5J **141**
Roslyn Cl. CR4: Mitc 2B **154**
Roslyn Rd. N15 . . . . .5D **48**
Rosmead Rd. W11 . . . . .7G **81**
Rosoman Pl. EC1 . . . . . . .3K **7** (4A **84**)
Rosoman St. EC1 . . . . . . .2K **7** (3A **84**)
Rossall Cres. NW10 . . . . .3F **79**
Ross Apts. E16 . . . . .7J **87**
            (off Seagull La.)
Ross Av. RM8: Dag 1F **73**
Ross Cl. HA3: Hrw W 7B **26**
  UB3: Harl 4F **93**
  UB5: N'olt 4H **59**
Ross Ct. E5 . . . . .4H **67**
          (off Napoleon Rd.)
  NW9 .3A **44**
  SW15 . . . . .7F **117**
  W13 . . . . .5B **78**
         (off Cleveland Rd.)
Rosscourt Mans. SW1 . . . . .1A **18**
         (off Buckingham Pal. Rd.)
Rossdale SM1: Sutt 5C **166**
Rossdale Dr. N9 . . . . .6D **24**
  NW9 .1J **61**
Rossdale Rd. SW15 . . . . .4E **116**
Rosse Gdns. SE13 . . . . .6F **123**
Rosse M. SE3 . . . . .1K **123**
Rossendale St. E5 . . . . .2H **67**
Rossendale Way NW1 . . . . .7G **65**
Rossetti CR0: C'don 1C **168**
         (off Saffron Central Sq.)
Rossetti Ct. WC1 . . . . .5C **6**
          (off Ridgmount Pl.)
Rossetti Gdn. Mans. SW3 . . . . . . .7E **16**
Rossetti Ho. SW1 . . . . .4D **18**
           (off Erasmus St.)
Rossetti M. NW8 . . . . .1B **82**
Rossetti Rd. SE16 . . . . .5H **103**
Rossetti Studios SW3 . . . . .7D **16**
            (off Flood St.)
Ross Haven Pl. HA6: Nwood 1H **39**
Ross Ho. E1 . . . . .1H **103**
           (off Prusom St.)
Rossignol Gdns. SM5: Cars 2E **166**
Rossindel Rd. TW3: Houn 5E **112**
Rossington Cl. EN1: Enf 1C **24**
Rossington St. E5 . . . . .2G **67**
Rossiter Cl. SE19 . . . . .7C **138**
Rossiter Fids. EN5: Barn 6B **20**
Rossiter Gro. SW9 . . . . .3A **120**
Rossiter Rd. SW12 . . . . .1F **137**
Rossland Cl. DA6: Bex 5H **127**
Rosslyn Av. E4 . . . . .2C **36**
  EN4: E Barn 6H **21**
  RM8: Dag 7F **55**
  SW13 . . . . .3A **116**
  TW14: Felt 6J **111**
Rosslyn Cl. BR4: W W'ck 3F **171**
  TW16: Sun 6G **129**
  UB3: Hayes 5F **75**
Rosslyn Cres. HA1: Harr 4K **41**
  HA9: Wemb 4E **60**
Rosslyn Gdns. HA9: Wemb 3E **60**
Rosslyn Hill NW3 . . . . .4B **64**
Rosslyn Mans. NW6 . . . . .7A **64**
          (off Goldhurst Ter.)
Rosslyn M. NW3 . . . . .4B **64**
Rosslyn Pk. M. NW3 . . . . .5B **64**
Rosslyn Rd. E17 . . . . .4E **50**
  IG11: Bark 7H **71**
  TW1: Twick 6C **114**
Rossmore Cl. EN3: Pond E 4E **24**
  NW1 . . . . .4D **4**
          (off Rossmore Rd.)

Rossmore Ct. NW1 . . . . . . .3E **4** (4D **82**)
Rossmore Rd. NW1 . . . . . .4D **4** (4C **82**)
Ross Pde. SM6: W'gton 6F **167**
Ross Rd. SE25 . . . . .3D **156**
  SM6: W'gton 5G **167**
  TW2: Whitt 1F **131**
Ross Wlk. SE27 . . . . .3D **138**
Ross Way E14 . . . . .6A **86**
  SE9 . . . . .3C **124**
Rosswood Gdns. SM6: W'gton . . .6G **167**
Rostella Rd. SW17 . . . . .4B **136**
Rostrevor Av. N15 . . . . .6F **49**
Rostrevor Gdns. UB2: S'hall 5C **94**
  UB3: Hayes 1G **93**
Rostrevor Mans. SW6 . . . . .1H **117**
          (off Rostrevor Rd.)
Rostrevor M. SW6 . . . . .1H **117**
Rostrevor Rd. SW6 . . . . .1H **117**
  SW19 . . . . .5J **135**
Roswell Apts. E3 . . . . .5B **86**
          (off Joseph St.)
Rotary St. SE1 . . . . .7A **14** (3B **102**)
Rothay NW1 . . . . .1K **5**
           (off Albany St.)
Rothbury Cotts. SE10 . . . . .4G **105**
          (off Maritius Rd.)
Rothbury Gdns. TW7: Isle 7A **96**
Rothbury Rd. E9 . . . . .7B **68**
Rothbury Wlk. N17 . . . . .7B **34**
Rotheley Ho. E9 . . . . .7J **67**
          (off Balcorne St.)
Rotherfield Ct. N1 . . . . .7D **66**
          (off Rotherfield St.)
Rotherfield Rd. SM5: Cars 4E **166**
  EN3: Enf 1C **66**
Rotherham Wlk. SE1 . . . . .5A **14**
Rotherhithe Av. SW16 . . . . .6H **137**
ROTHERHITHE 2J **103**
Rotherhithe Bus. Est. SE16 . . . . .4H **103**
Rotherhithe New Rd. SE16 . . . . . .5H **103**
Rotherhithe Old Rd. SE16 . . . . . .4K **103**
Rotherhithe Sands Film Studios . . .2J **103**
          (off Tunnel Rd.)
ROTHERHITHE TUNNEL 1K **103**
Rother Ho. SE15 . . . . .4H **121**
Rotherwick Hill W5 . . . . .4F **79**
Rotherwick Ho. E1 . . . . .7G **85**
         (off Thomas More St.)
Rotherwick Rd. NW11 . . . . .7J **45**
Rotherwood Cl. SW20 . . . . .1G **153**
Rotherwood Rd. SW15 . . . . .3F **117**
Rothery St. N1 . . . . .1B **84**
          (off St Marys Path)
Rothery Ter. SW9 . . . . .7B **102**
           (off Foxley Rd.)
Rothesay Av. SW20 . . . . .2G **153**
  TW10: Rich 4H **115**
  UB6: G'frd 6G **59**
          (not continuous)
Rothesay Ct. SE6 . . . . .2H **141**
          (off Cumberland Pl.)
  SE11 .7J **19**
  SE12 .3K **141**
Rothesay Rd. SE25 . . . . .4D **156**
Rothley Ct. NW8 . . . . .3A **4**
        (off St John's Wood Rd.)
Rothsay Rd. E7 . . . . .7A **70**
Rothsay St. SE1 . . . . .3E **102**
Rothsay Wlk. E14 . . . . .4C **104**
          (off Charnwood Gdns.)
Rothschild Ho. TW8: Bford 6F **97**
Rothschild Rd. W4 . . . . .4J **97**
Rothschild St. SE27 . . . . .4B **138**
Roth Wlk. N7 . . . . .2K **65**
Rothwell Cl. HA1: Harr 5K **41**
Rothwell Gdns. RM9: Dag 7C **72**
Rothwell Ho. TW5: Hest 6E **94**
Rothwell Rd. RM9: Dag 1C **90**
Rothwell St. NW1 . . . . .1D **82**
Rotten Row NW3 . . . . .1A **64**
  SW7 . . . . .6B **10** (2B **100**)
Rotterdam Dr. E14 . . . . .3E **104**

The Rotunda RM7: Rom 5K **55**
         (off Yew Tree Gdns.)
  SW10 . . . . .7A **100**
The Rotunda Cen. 2E **150**
Rotunda Cl. BR1: Broml 5K **141**
           (off Burnt Ash La.)
Rouel Rd. SE16 . . . . .4G **103**
Rougemont Av. SM4: Mord 6J **153**
Roundabout Ho.
  HA6: Nwood 1J **39**
Roundacre SW19 . . . . .2F **135**
Roundaway Rd. IG5: Ilf 1D **52**
Roundel Cl. SE4 . . . . .4B **122**
Round Gro. CR0: C'don 7K **157**
Roundhay Cl. SE23 . . . . .2K **139**
Roundhedge Way EN2: Enf 1E **22**
Round Hill SE26 . . . . .2J **139**
          (not continuous)
Roundhill Dr. EN2: Enf 4E **22**
The Roundhouse 7E **64**
Roundhouse La. E20 . . . . .6E **68**
         (off International Way)
ROUNDSHAW 7J **167**
Roundshaw Downs
  Local Nature Reserve 7K **167**
Roundtable Rd. BR1: Broml 3H **141**
Roundtree Rd. HA0: Wemb 5B **60**
The Roundway KT10: Clay 6A **162**
  N17 . . . . .1C **48**
Roundways HA4: Ruis 3H **57**
Roundwood BR7: Chst 2F **161**
Roundwood Av. UB11: Stock P 1E **92**
Roundwood Cl. HA4: Ruis 7F **39**
Roundwood Ct. E2 . . . . .3K **85**
Roundwood Rd. NW10 . . . . .6B **62**
Rounton Rd. E3 . . . . .4C **86**
Roupell Ho. KT2: King T 7F **133**
          (off Florence Rd.)
Roupell Rd. SW2 . . . . .1K **137**
Roupell St. SE1 . . . . .5K **13** (1A **102**)
Rousden St. NW1 . . . . .7G **65**
Rouse Gdns. SE21 . . . . .4E **138**
Rous Rd. IG9: Buck H 1H **37**
Routemaster Cl. E13 . . . . .3K **87**
Routh Ct. TW14: Bedf 1F **129**
Routh Rd. SW18 . . . . .7C **118**
Routh St. E6 . . . . .5D **88**
Rover Ho. N1 . . . . .1E **84**
          (off Whitmore Est.)
Rowallan Rd. SW6 . . . . .7G **99**
Rowallen Pde. RM8: Dag 1C **72**
Rowan N10 . . . . .2F **47**
Rowan Av. E4 . . . . .6G **35**
  NW9 .7G **29**
Rowan Cl. HA0: Wemb 3A **60**
  HA7: Stan 6E **26**
  IG1: Ilf 5H **71**
  KT3: N Mald 2A **152**
  SW16 . . . . .1G **155**
  W5 . . . . .2E **96**
Rowan Ct. E13 . . . . .2K **87**
            (off High St.)
  SE15 .7F **103**
          (off Garnies Cl.)
  SW11 . . . . .6D **118**
Rowan Cres. SW16 . . . . .1G **155**
Rowan Dr. NW9 . . . . .3C **44**
Rowan Gdns. CR0: C'don 3F **169**
Rowan Ho. BR2: Broml 2G **159**
  DA14: Sidc 3K **143**
  E3 . . . . .1B **86**
          (off Hornbeam Sq.)
  IG1: Ilf 5H **71**
  SE16 . . . . .2K **103**
         (off Woodland Cres.)
Rowan Lodge W8 . . . . .3K **99**
           (off Chantry Sq.)
Rowan Pl. UB3: Hayes 7H **75**
Rowan Rd. DA7: Bex 3E **126**
  SW16 . . . . .2G **155**
  TW8: Bford 7B **96**
  UB7: W Dray 4A **92**
  W6 . . . . .4F **99**

The Rowans N13 . . . . .3G 33
  TW16: Sun 5H 129
Rowans Tenpin 2A 66
Rowan Ter. SW19 . . . . .7G 135
  W6 . . . . .4F 99
Rowantree Cl. N21 . . . . .1J 33
Rowantree Rd. EN2: Enf 2G 23
  N21 . . . . .1J 33
Rowan Wlk. BR2: Broml 3D 172
  EN5: New Bar 5E 20
  N2 .5A 46
  N19 . . . . .2G 65
  W10 . . . . .4G 81
Rowan Way RM6: Chad H 3C 54
Rowanwood Av. DA15: Sidc 1A 144
Rowanwood M. EN2: Enf 2G 23
Rowben Cl. N20 . . . . .1E 30
Rowberry Cl. SW6 . . . . .7E 98
Rowcross St. SE1 . . . . .5F 103
Rowdell Rd. UB5: N'olt 1E 76
Rowden Pde. E4 . . . . .6H 35
              (off Chingford Rd.)
Rowden Pk. Gdns. E4 . . . . .7H 35
Rowden Rd. BR3: Beck 1A 158
  E4 .6J 35
  KT19: Ewe 4H 163
Rowditch La. SW11 . . . . .2E 118
Rowdon Av. NW10 . . . . .7D 62
Rowdown Cres. CR0: New Ad . . .7F 171
Rowdowns Rd. RM9: Dag 1F 91
Rowe Gdns. IG11: Bark 2K 89
Rowe Ho. E9 . . . . .6J 67
Rowe La. E9 . . . . .5J 67
Rowena Cres. SW11 . . . . .2C 118
Rowenhurst Mans. NW6 . . . . .6A 64
              (off Canfield Gdns.)
Rowe Wlk. HA2: Harr 3E 58
Rowfant Rd. SW17 . . . . .1E 136
Rowhill Rd. E5 . . . . .4H 67
Rowington Cl. W2 . . . . .5K 81
Rowland Av. HA3: Kenton 3C 42
Rowland Ct. E16 . . . . .4H 87
Rowland Gro. SE26 . . . . .3H 139
           (not continuous)
Rowland Hill Almshouses
  TW15: Ashf 5C 128
          (off Feltham Hill Rd.)
Rowland Hill Av. N17 . . . . .7H 33
Rowland Hill Ho. SE1 . . . .6A 14 (2B 102)
Rowland Hill St. NW3 . . . . .5C 64
Rowlands Av. HA5: Hat E 5A 26
Rowlands Cl. N6 . . . . .6E 46
  NW7 . . . . .7H 29
Rowlands Rd. RM8: Dag 2F 73
Rowland Way SW19 . . . . .1K 153
  TW15: Ashf 7F 129
Rowley Av. DA15: Sidc 7B 126
Rowley Cl. HA0: Wemb 7F 61
Rowley Ct. EN1: Enf 5K 23
          (off Wellington Rd.)
Rowley Gdns. N4 . . . . .7C 48
Rowley Ho. SE8 . . . . .5C 104
          (off Watergate St.)
Rowley Ind. Pk. W3 . . . . .3H 97
Rowley Rd. N15 . . . . .5C 48
Rowley Way NW8 . . . . .1K 81
Rowlheys Pl. UB7: W Dray 3A 92
Rowlls Rd. KT1: King T 3F 151
Rowney Gdns. RM9: Dag 6C 72
Rowney Rd. RM9: Dag 6B 72
Rowntree Clifford Cl. E13 . . . . . . .4J 87
Rowntree Cl. NW6 . . . . .6J 63
Rowntree M. E17 . . . . .1B 50
Rowntree Path SE28 . . . . .1B 108
Rowntree Rd. TW2: Twick 1J 131
Rowse Cl. E15 . . . . .1E 86
Rowsley Av. NW4 . . . . .3E 44
Rowstock Gdns. N7 . . . . .5H 65
Rowton Rd. SE18 . . . . .7G 107
Roxborough Av. HA1: Harr 7H 41
  TW7: Isle 7K 95
Roxborough Hgts. HA1: Harr 6J 41
          (off College Rd.)

Roxborough Pk. HA1: Harr 7J 41
Roxborough Rd. HA1: Harr 5H 41
Roxbourne Cl. UB5: N'olt 6B 58
Roxbourne Pk. Miniature Railway
  . . . . .2B 58
Roxburghe Mans. W8 . . . . .2K 99
          (off Kensington Ct.)
Roxburgh Pl. BR1: Broml 1C 160
Roxburgh Rd. SE27 . . . . .5B 138
Roxburn Way HA4: Ruis 3H 57
Roxby Pl. SW6 . . . . .6J 99
ROXETH 2H 59
Roxeth Ct. TW15: Ashf 5C 128
Roxeth Grn. Av.
  HA2: Harr 3F 59
  UB5: N'olt 5E 58
Roxeth Gro. HA2: Harr 4F 59
Roxeth Hill HA2: Harr 2H 59
Roxford Cl. TW17: Shep 5G 147
Roxford Ho. E3 . . . . .4D 86
            (off Devas St.)
Roxley Rd. SE13 . . . . .6D 122
Roxton Gdns. CR0: Addtn 5C 170
Roxwell NW1 . . . . .6F 65
           (off Hartland Rd.)
Roxwell Rd. IG11: Bark 2A 90
  W12 . . . . .2C 98
Roxwell Trad. Pk. E10 . . . . .7A 50
Roxwell Way IG8: Wfd G 7F 37
Roxy Av. RM6: Chad H 7C 54
Royal Academy of Arts
  (Burlington House) . . .3A 12 (7G 83)
Royal Academy of Music 4H 5 (4E 82)
Royal Academy of Music Mus. 4H 5
            (off York Ga.)
Royal Academy Schools 7G 83
Royal Air Force Memorial 1J 101
Royal Albert Hall 7A 10 (2B 100)
ROYAL ALBERT RDBT. 7C 88
        (on Royal Albert Way)
Royal Albert Way E16 . . . . .7B 88
Royal Anglian Way RM8: Dag 1E 72
Royal Arc. W1 . . . . .3A 12
Royal Archer SE14 . . . . .7K 103
          (off Egmont St.)
ROYAL ARSENAL WEST 3F 107
Royal Av. KT4: Wor Pk 2A 164
  SW3 . . . . .5E 16 (5D 100)
Royal Av. Ho. SW3 . . . . .5E 16
            (off Royal Av.)
Royal Ballet School 1F 13
             (off Floral St.)
Royal Belgrave Ho. SW1 . . . . . . .4K 17
            (off Hugh St.)
Royal Blackheath Golf Course 7D 124
Royal Botanic Gdns.
  Kew 1E 114
Royal Brass Foundry 3F 107
Royal Carriage M. SE18 . . . . .3F 107
Royal Cir. SE27 . . . . .3A 138
Royal Cl. BR6: Farnb 4F 173
  IG3: Ilf 7A 54
  KT4: Wor Pk 2A 164
  N16 .1E 66
  SE8 . . . . .6B 104
  SW19 . . . . .3F 135
  UB8: Hil 6B 74
Royal College of Art
  Battersea 7C 100
          (off Parkgate Rd.)
  Kensington 7A 10 (2B 100)
Royal College of Music . . .1A 16 (3B 100)
Royal College of Nursing 7K 5
           (off Dean's M.)
Royal College of Obstetricians &
  Gynaecologists 3E 4 (4D 82)
Royal College of Physicians 3K 5
Royal College of Physicians Mus.
  . . . . .3K 5 (4F 83)
Royal College of Surgeons 7H 7
Royal Coll. St. NW1 . . . . .7G 65
Royal Connaught Apts. E16 . . . . .1B 106
          (off Connaught Rd.)

Royal Ct. EC3 . . . . .1F 15
            (off Cornhill)
  EN1: Enf 6K 23
  HA4: Ruis 6J 39
  SE9 . . . . .1D 142
  SE16 . . . . .3B 104
Royal Courts of Justice 1H 13
Royal Court Theatre 4D 16
            (off Sloane Sq.)
Royal Cres. HA4: Ruis 4C 58
  IG2: Ilf 6H 53
  W11 .1F 99
Royal Cres. M. W11 . . . . .1F 99
Royal Crest Av. E16 . . . . .2K 105
Royal Docks Rd. E6 . . . . .6F 89
  IG11: Bark 6F 89
Royal Dr. N11 . . . . .5K 31
          (not continuous)
Royal Duchess M. SW12 . . . . . . .7F 119
Royale Leisure Pk. W3 . . . . .4G 79
Royal Engineers Way NW7 . . . . . .6B 30
Royal Epping Forest Golf Course . . .6K 25
Royal Exchange 1F 15 (6D 84)
Royal Exchange Av. EC3 . . . . .1F 15
Royal Exchange Bldgs. EC3 . . . . . .1F 15
Royal Festival Hall 5H 13 (1K 101)
Royal Gdns. W7 . . . . .3A 96
Royal Geographical Society 7A 10
Royal George M. SE5 . . . . .4D 120
Royal Herbert Pavilions SE18 . . . .1D 124
Royal Hill SE10 . . . . .7E 104
Royal Hill Ct. SE10 . . . . .7E 104
         (off Greenwich High St.)
Royal Holloway (University of London)
  Gower Street 5D 6
Royal Hospital Chelsea 5E 100
Royal Hospital Chelsea Great Hall
  . . . . .6F 17 (5D 100)
Royal Hospital Chelsea Mus.
  . . . . .6G 17 (5E 100)
Royal Hospital Rd. SW3 . .7E 16 (6D 100)
Royal Institution 3A 12 (7G 83)
Royal La. UB7: Yiew 5B 74
  UB8: Hil 5B 74
Royal Langford Apts. NW6 . . . . . . .2K 81
            (off Greville Rd.)
Royal London Bldgs. SE15 . . . . . .6H 103
          (off Old Kent Rd.)
The Royal London Est. N17 . . . . . .6C 34
Royal London Hospital Archives & Mus.
  . . . . .5J 85
           (off Newark St.)
Royal London Ind. Est. NW10 . . . . .2K 79
The Royal Mews 1K 17 (2F 101)
Royal M. KT8: E Mos 3J 149
  SW1 . . . . .1K 17 (3F 101)
Royal Mid-Surrey Golf Course 3D 114
Royal Mint Ct. EC3 . . . . . .3K 15 (7F 85)
Royal Mint Pl. E1 . . . . . .2K 15 (7G 85)
Royal Mint St. E1 . . . . . .2K 15 (7G 85)
Royal Naval Pl. SE14 . . . . .7B 104
Royal Oak Ct. N1 . . . . .1G 9
            (off Pitfield St.)
Royal Oak M. TW11: Tedd 5A 132
Royal Oak Pl. SE22 . . . . .6H 121
Royal Oak Rd. DA6: Bex 5F 127
          (not continuous)
  E8 . . . . .6H 67
Royal Oak Yd. SE1 . . . . .7G 15 (2E 102)
Royal Observatory Greenwich 7G 105
Royal Opera Arc.
  SW1 . . . . .4C 12 (1H 101)
Royal Opera House 1F 13 (6J 83)
Royal Orchard Cl. SW18 . . . . . . .7G 117
Royal Pde. BR7: Chst 7G 143
  RM10: Dag 6H 73
  SE3 . . . . .2H 123
  SW6 . . . . .7G 99
  TW9: Kew 1G 115
          (off Station App.)
  W5 .3E 78
Royal Pde. M. BR7: Chst 7G 143
            (off Royal Pde.)

Royal Pde. M. SE3 . . . . .2H 123
           (off Royal Pde.)
Royal Pl. SE10 . . . . .7E 104
Royal Quarter KT2: King T 1E 150
Royal Quay Rd. E16 . . . . .7F 89
Royal Rd. DA14: Sidc 3D 144
  E16 .6B 88
  SE17 . . . . .6B 102
  TW11: Tedd 5H 131
Royal Route HA9: Wemb 4F 61
Royal St. SE1 . . . . .1H 19 (3K 101)
Royal Thames Wlk. KT7: T Ditt 1A 162
Royal Twr. Lodge E1 . . . . .3K 15
          (off Cartwright St.)
Royalty Mans. W1 . . . . .1C 12
            (off Meard St.)
Royalty M. W1 . . . . . . .1C 12 (6H 83)
Royalty Studios W11 . . . . .6G 81
          (off Lancaster Rd.)
Royal Veterinary College 1H 83
Royal Victoria Dock E16 . . . . .7K 87
Royal Victoria Gdns. SE16 . . . . . .4A 104
          (off Whiting Way)
Royal Victoria Patriotic Bldg.
  SW18 . . . . .6B 118
Royal Victoria Pl. E16 . . . . .1K 105
Royal Victoria Sq. E16 . . . . .7K 87
Royal Victor Pl. E3 . . . . .2K 85
Royal Wlk. SM6: W'gton 2F 167
Royal Westminster Lodge SW1 . . .3C 18
          (off Elverton St.)
Royal Wharf E16 . . . . .2K 105
Royal Wharf Wlk. E16 . . . . .2K 105
Royal Wimbledon Golf Course 5D 134
Royce Av. NW9 . . . . .2C 44
Roycraft Av. IG11: Bark 2K 89
Roycroft Cl. IG11: Bark 2K 89
Roycroft Cl. E18 . . . . .1K 51
  SW2 . . . . .1A 138
Roydene Rd. SE18 . . . . .6J 107
Roydon Cl. IG10: Lough 1H 37
  SW11 . . . . .2D 118
Roy Gdns. IG2: Ilf 4J 53
Roy Gro. TW12: Hamp 6F 131
Royle Bldg. N1 . . . . .2C 84
           (off Wenlock Rd.)
Royle Cres. W13 . . . . .4A 78
Royley Ho. EC1 . . . . .3D 8
            (off Old St.)
Roymount Ct. TW2: Twick 3J 131
Roy Rd. HA6: Nwood 1H 39
Roy Sq. E14 . . . . .7A 86
Royston Av. E4 . . . . .5H 35
  SM1: Sutt 3B 166
  SM6: Bedd 4H 167
Royston Ct. KT12: Walt T 7J 147
  TW5: Cran 1K 111
Royston Ct. E13 . . . . .1J 87
          (off Stopford Rd.)
  SE24 . . . . .6C 120
  TW9: Kew 1F 115
  W8 .1J 99
         (off Kensington Chu. St.)
Royston Gdns. IG1: Ilf 6B 52
Royston Ho. N11 . . . . .4J 31
  SE15 . . . . .6H 103
            (off Friary Est.)
Royston Pde. IG1: Ilf 6B 52
Royston Pk. Rd. HA5: Hat E 5A 26
Royston Rd. SE20 . . . . .1K 157
  TW10: Rich 5E 114
The Roystons KT5: Surb 5H 151
Royston St. E2 . . . . .2J 85
Rozel Ct. N1 . . . . .1E 84
Rozel Rd. SW4 . . . . .3G 119
Rozel Ter. CR0: C'don 3C 168
           (off Church Rd.)
RQ33 SW18 . . . . .4J 117
Rubastic Rd. UB2: S'hall 3A 94
Rubens Gdns. SE22 . . . . .7G 121
          (off Lordship La.)
Rubens Pl. SW4 . . . . .4J 119
Rubens Rd. UB5: N'olt 2A 76

Rubens St. SE6 . . . . .2B 140
Rubicon Cl. N1 . . . . .1J 83
Ruby Cl. E5 .3K 67
Ruby Ct. E15 . . . . .1E 86
(off Warton Rd.)
RM8: Dag 1G 73
(off Emerald Gdns.)
Ruby Mews N13 . . . . .5D 32
Ruby Rd. E17 . . . . .3C 50
Ruby St. NW10 . . . . .7J 61
SE15 . . . . .6H 103
Ruby Triangle SE15 . . . . .6H 103
Ruby Way NW9 . . . . .1B 44
Ruckholt Cl. E10 . . . . .3D 68
Ruckholt Rd. E10 . . . . .4C 68
Rucklidge Av. NW10 . . . . .2B 80
Rudall Cres. NW3 . . . . .4B 64
Rudbeck Ho. SE15 . . . . .7G 103
(off Peckham Pk. Rd.)
Ruddington Cl. E5 . . . . .4A 68
Ruddock Cl. HA8: Edg 7D 28
Ruddstreet Cl. SE18 . . . . .4F 107
Ruddy Way NW7 . . . . .6G 29
Rudge Ho. SE16 . . . . .3G 103
(off Jamaica Rd.)
Rudgwick Ct. SE18 . . . . .4C 106
(off Woodville St.)
Rudgwick Ter. NW8 . . . . .1C 82
Rudland Rd. DA7: Bex 3H 127
Rudloe Rd. SW12 . . . . .7G 119
Rudolf Pl. SW8 . . . . .7F 19 (6J 101)
Rudolph Rd. E13 . . . . .2H 87
NW6 . . . . .2J 81
Rudstone Ho. E3 . . . . .3D 86
(off Bromley High St.)
Rudyard Ct. SE1 . . . . .7F 15
(off Long La.)
Rudyard Gro. NW7 . . . . .6D 28
Ruegg Ho. SE18 . . . . .6E 106
(off Woolwich Comn.)
The Ruffetts CR2: Sels 7H 169
Ruffetts Cl. CR2: Sels 7H 169
Ruffle Cl. UB7: W Dray 2A 92
Rufford Cl. HA3: Kenton 6A 42
Rufford St. N1 . . . . .1J 83
Rufford St. M. N1 . . . . .7J 65
Rufford Twr. W3 . . . . .1H 97
Rufforth Ct. NW9 . . . . .1A 44
(off Pageant Av.)
Rufus Bus. Cen. SW18 . . . . .2K 135
Rufus Cl. HA4: Ruis 3C 58
Rufus Ho. SE1 . . . . .7K 15
(off St Saviour's Est.)
Rufus St. N1 . . . . .2G 9 (3E 84)
Rugby Av. HA0: Wemb 5B 60
N9 . . . . .1A 34
UB6: G'frd 6H 59
Rugby Cl. HA1: Harr 4J 41
Rugby Gdns. RM9: Dag 6C 72
Rugby Mans. W14 . . . . .4G 99
(off Bishop King's Rd.)
Rugby Rd. NW9 . . . . .4H 43
RM9: Dag 7B 72
TW1: Twick 5J 113
W4 . . . . .2A 98
Rugby St. WC1 . . . . .4G 7 (4K 83)
Rugg St. E14 .7C 86
Rugless Ho. E14 . . . . .2E 104
(off E. Ferry Rd.)
Rugmere NW1 . . . . .7E 64
(off Ferdinand St.)
RUISLIP 1G 57
Ruislip Cl. UB6: G'frd 4F 77
RUISLIP COMMON 4E 38
Ruislip Ct. HA4: Ruis 2H 57
RUISLIP GARDENS 3J 57
Ruislip Golf Course 2E 56
Ruislip Lido 4F 39
Ruislip Lido Railway 4F 39
Ruislip Lido Woodlands Cen. 4F 39
RUISLIP MANOR 2J 57
Ruislip Rd. UB5: N'olt 1A 76
UB6: G'frd 3E 76

Ruislip Rd. E. UB6: G'frd 4H 77
W7 . . . . .4J 77
W13 . . . . .4H 77
Ruislip Social Club 2H 57
(off Cranley Dr.)
Ruislip St. SW17 . . . . .4D 136
Ruislip Woods 3E 38
Rumball Ho. SE5 . . . . .7E 102
(off Harris St.)
Rumbold Rd. SW6 . . . . .7K 99
Rum Cl. E1 . . . . .7J 85
Rumford Ho. SE1 . . . . .3C 102
(off Tiverton St.)
Rumsey Cl. TW12: Hamp 6D 130
Rumsey M. N4 . . . . .3B 66
Rumsey Rd. SW9 . . . . .3K 119
Runacres Ct. SE17 . . . . .5C 102
Runbury Circ. NW9 . . . . .2K 61
Runcie Ct. IG6: Ilf 4H 53
Runcorn Cl. N17 . . . . .4H 49
Runcorn Pl. W11 . . . . .7G 81
Rundell Cres. NW4 . . . . .5D 44
Rundell Twr. SW8 . . . . .1K 119
Runes Cl. CR4: Mitc 4B 154
Runnel Ct. IG11: Bark 2G 89
(off Spring Pl.)
Runnelfield HA1: Harr 3J 59
Running Horse Yd. TW8: Bford 6E 96
Runnymede SW19 . . . . .1A 154
Runnymede Cl. TW2: Whitt 6F 113
Runnymede Ct. SM6: W'gton 6F 167
SW15 . . . . .1C 134
Runnymede Cres. SW16 . . . . .1H 155
Runnymede Gdns. TW2: Whitt 6F 113
UB6: G'frd 2J 77
Runnymede Ho. E9 . . . . .4A 68
Runnymede Rd. TW2: Whitt 6F 113
The Runway HA4: Ruis 5K 57
Runway Cl. NW9 . . . . .2K 43
Rupack St. SE16 . . . . .2J 103
Rupert Av. HA9: Wemb 5E 60
Rupert Ct. KT8: W Mole 4E 148
(off St Peter's Rd.)
W1 . . . . .2C 12 (7H 83)
Rupert Gdns. SW9 . . . . .2B 120
Rupert Ho. SE11 . . . . . . .4K 19 (4A 102)
SW5 . . . . .4J 99
(off Nevern Sq.)
Rupert Rd. N19 . . . . .3H 65
(not continuous)
NW6 . . . . .2H 81
W4 . . . . .3A 98
Rupert St. W1 . . . . .2C 12 (7H 83)
Rural Way SW16 . . . . .7F 137
Rusbridge Cl. E8 . . . . .5G 67
Ruscoe Rd. E16 . . . . .6H 87
Ruscombe NW1 . . . . .1F 83
(off Delancey St.)
Ruscombe Way TW14: Felt 7H 111
Ruscus Rd. E17 . . . . .1D 50
The Rush SW19 . . . . .1H 153
(off Watery La.)
Rusham Rd. SW12 . . . . .6D 118
Rushbridge Cl. CR0: C'don 6C 156
Rushbrook Cres. E17 . . . . .1B 50
Rushbrook Rd. SE9 . . . . .2G 143
Rushbury Ct. TW12: Hamp 1E 148
Rush Comn. M. SW2 . . . . .7K 119
Rushcroft Rd. E4 . . . . .7J 35
SW2 . . . . .4A 120
Rushcutters Ct. SE16 . . . . .4A 104
(off Boat Lifter Way)
Rushden Cl. SE19 . . . . .7D 138
Rushdene SE2 . . . . .3D 108
(not continuous)
Rushdene Av. EN4: E Barn 7H 21
Rushdene Cl. UB5: N'olt 2A 76
Rushdene Cres. UB5: N'olt 2K 75
Rushdene Rd. HA5: Eastc 6B 40
Rushden Gdns. IG5: Ilf 2E 52
NW7 . . . . .6K 29
Rushen Wlk. SM5: Cars 1B 166
Rushett Cl. KT7: T Ditt 1B 162

Rushett Rd. KT7: T Ditt 7B 150
Rushey Cl. KT3: N Mald 4K 151
Rushey Grn. SE6 . . . . .7D 122
Rushey Hill EN2: Enf 4E 22
Rushey Mead SE4 . . . . .5C 122
Rushford Rd. SE4 . . . . .6B 122
RUSH GREEN 1K 73
Rush Grn. Gdns. RM7: Rush G 1J 73
Rush Grn. Rd. RM7: Rush G 1H 73
Rushgrove Av. NW9 . . . . .5A 44
Rushgrove Ct. NW9 . . . . .5A 44
Rushgrove Pde. NW9 . . . . .5A 44
Rushgrove St. SE18 . . . . .4D 106
Rush Hill M. SW11 . . . . .3E 118
(off Rush Hill Rd.)
Rush Hill Rd. SW11 . . . . .3E 118
Rushley Cl. BR2: Kes 4B 172
Rushmead 3H 85
TW10: Ham 3B 132
Rushmead Cl. CR0: C'don 4F 169
HA8: Edg .2C 28
Rushmere Ct. KT4: Wor Pk 2C 164
Rushmere Pl. SW19 . . . . .5F 135
Rushmon Pl. SM3: Cheam 6G 165
Rushmon Vs. KT3: N Mald 4B 152
Rushmoor Cl. HA5: Eastc 4K 39
Rushmoor Cl. BR1: Broml 3C 160
Rushmore Cres. E5 . . . . .4K 67
Rushmore Ho. SW15 . . . . .7C 116
W14 . . . . .3G 99
(off Russell Rd.)
Rushmore Rd. E5 . . . . .4J 67
(not continuous)
Rusholme Av. RM10: Dag 3G 73
Rusholme Gro. SE19 . . . . .5E 138
Rusholme Rd. SW15 . . . . .6F 117
Rushout Av. HA3: Kenton 6B 42
Rushton Ho. SW8 . . . . .2H 119
Rushton St. N1 . . . . .2D 84
Rushworth St. SE1 . . . . .6B 14 (2B 102)
Rushy Mdw. La. SM5: Cars 2C 166
Ruskin Av. DA16: Well 2A 126
E12 . . . . .6C 70
TW9: Kew .7G 97
TW14: Felt 6H 111
Ruskin Cl. NW11 . . . . .6K 45
Ruskin Ct. N21 . . . . .7E 22
SE5 . . . . .3D 120
(off Champion Hill)
Ruskin Dr. BR6: Orp 3J 173
DA16: Well 3A 126
KT4: Wor Pk 2D 164
Ruskin Gdns. HA3: Kenton 5F 43
W5 . . . . .4D 78
Ruskin Gro. DA16: Well 2A 126
Ruskin Ho. SW1 . . . . .5D 18
(off Herrick St.)
Ruskin Mans. W14 . . . . .6H 99
(off Queen's Club Gdns.)
Ruskin Pde. CR2: S Croy 5D 168
(off Selsdon Rd.)
HA8: Edg .4A 28
Ruskin Pk. Ho. SE5 . . . . .3D 120
Ruskin Rd. CR0: C'don 2B 168
DA17: Belv 4G 109
N17 . . . . .1F 49
SM5: Cars 5D 166
TW7: Isle .3K 113
UB1: S'hall 7C 76
Ruskin Sq. CR0: C'don 2D 168
Ruskin Wlk. BR2: Broml 6D 160
N9 . . . . .2B 34
SE24 . . . . .5C 120
Ruskin Way SW19 . . . . .1B 154
Rusland Av. BR6: Orp 3H 173
Rusland Hgts. HA1: Harr 4J 41
Rusland Pk. Rd. HA1: Harr 4J 41
Rusper Cl. HA7: Stan 4H 27
NW2 . . . . .3E 62

Rusper Ct. SW9 . . . . .2J 119
(off Clapham Rd.)
Rusper Rd. N17 . . . . .3C 48
N22 . . . . .2B 48
RM9: Dag .6C 72
Russell Av. N22 . . . . .2A 48
Russell Chambers WC1 . . . . .6F 7
(off Bury Pl.)
Russell Cl. BR3: Beck 3E 158
DA7: Bex .4G 127
HA4: Ruis .2A 58
NW10 . . . . .7J 61
SE7 . . . . .7A 106
W4 . . . . .6B 98
Russell Cl. E10 . . . . .7D 50
EN5: New Bar 4F 21
N14 . . . . .6C 22
SE15 . . . . .2H 121
(off Heaton Rd.)
SM6: W'gton 5G 167
(off Ross Rd.)
SW1 . . . . .5B 12
SW16 . . . . .5K 137
WC1 . . . . .4E 6
Russell Flint Ho. E16 . . . . .1K 105
(off Pankhurst Av.)
Russell Gdns. IG2: Ilf 7H 53
N20 . . . . .2H 31
NW11 . . . . .6G 45
TW10: Ham 2C 132
UB7: Sip .5C 92
W14 . . . . .3G 99
Russell Gdns. M. W14 . . . . .2G 99
Russell Gro. NW7 . . . . .5F 29
SW9 . . . . .7A 102
Russell Ho. BR2: Broml 6C 160
(off Wells Vw. Dr.)
E14 . . . . .6C 86
(off Saracen St.)
SW1 . . . . .5A 18
(off Cambridge St.)
Russell Kerr Cl. W4 . . . . .7J 97
Russell La. N20 . . . . .2H 31
Russell Lodge E4 . . . . .2K 35
SE1 . . . . .3D 102
(off Spurgeon St.)
Russell Mans. WC1 . . . . .5F 7
(off Southampton Row)
Russell Mead HA3: Hrw W 1K 41
Russell Pde. NW11 . . . . .6G 45
(off Golders Grn. Rd.)
Russell Pl. NW3 . . . . .5C 64
SE16 . . . . .3A 104
SM2: Sutt .7K 165
Russell Rd. CR4: Mitc 3C 154
E4 . . . . .4G 35
E10 . . . . .6D 50
E16 . . . . .6J 87
E17 . . . . .3B 50
EN1: Enf 1A 24
IG9: Buck H 1E 36
KT12: Walt T 6J 147
N8 . . . . .6H 47
N13 . . . . .6E 32
N15 . . . . .5E 48
N20 . . . . .2H 31
NW9 . . . . .6B 44
SW19 . . . . .7J 135
TW2: Twick 6K 113
TW17: Shep 7E 146
UB5: N'olt .5G 59
W14 . . . . .3G 99
Russell's Footpath SW16 . . . . .5J 137
Russell Sq. WC1 . . . . .4E 6 (5J 83)
Russell Sq. Mans. WC1 . . . . .5F 7
(off Southampton Row)
Russell St. WC2 . . . . .2F 13 (7J 83)
Russell's Wharf Flats W10 . . . . .4H 81
Russell Wlk. TW10: Rich 6F 115
Russell Yd. SW15 . . . . .4G 117
Russet Av. TW17: Shep 3G 147
Russet Cl. UB10: Hil 4E 74

Russet Cres. N7 . . . . .5K **65**
Russet Dr. CR0: C'don 1A **170**
Russets Cl. E4 . . . . .4A **36**
Russett Way SE13 . . . . .2D **122**
Russia Dock Rd. SE16 . . . . .1A **104**
Russia La. E2 . . . . .2J **85**
Russia Row EC2 . . . . . .1D **14** (6C **84**)
Russia Wlk. SE16 . . . . .2A **104**
Russington Rd. TW17: Shep 6F **147**
Rusthall Av. W4 . . . . .4K **97**
Rusthall Cl. CR0: C'don 6J **157**
Rustic Av. SW16 . . . . .7F **137**
Rustic Pl. HA0: Wemb 4D **60**
Rustic Wlk. E16 . . . . .6K **87**
(off Lambert Rd.)
Rustington Wlk. SM4: Mord 7H **153**
Ruston Av. KT5: Surb 7H **151**
Ruston Gdns. N14 . . . . .6K **21**
Ruston M. W11 . . . . .6G **81**
Ruston Rd. SE18 . . . . .3C **106**
Ruston St. E3 . . . . .1B **86**
Rust Sq. SE5 . . . . .7D **102**
Rutford Rd. SW16 . . . . .5J **137**
Ruth Cl. HA7: Stan 4F **43**
Ruth Ct. E3 . . . . .2A **86**
Rutherford Cl. SM2: Sutt 6B **166**
UB8: Hil 4B **74**
Rutherford Ho. E1 . . . . .4H **85**
(off Brady St.)
HA9: Wemb 3J **61**
(off Barnhill Rd.)
SW11 . . . . .2D **118**
(off Battersea Pk. Rd.)
Rutherford St. SW1 . . . . .3C **18** (4H **101**)
Rutherford Twr. UB1: S'hall 6F **77**
Rutherford Way HA9: Wemb 3G **61**
WD23: B Hea 1C **26**
Rutherglen Rd. SE2 . . . . .6A **108**
Rutherwyke Cl. KT17: Ewe 6C **164**
Ruth Ho. W10 . . . . .4G **81**
(off Kensal Rd.)
Ruthin Cl. NW9 . . . . .6A **44**
Ruthin Rd. SE3 . . . . .6J **105**
Ruthven St. E9 . . . . .1K **85**
Rutland Av. DA15: Sidc 7A **126**
Rutland Cl. DA5: Bexl 2D **144**
KT9: Chess 6F **163**
SW14 . . . . .3H **115**
SW19 . . . . .7C **136**
Rutland Ct. BR7: Chst 1E **160**
EN3: Pond E 5C **24**
KT1: King T 4D **150**
(off Palace Rd.)
SE5 .4D **120**
SE9 .2G **143**
SW7 .7D **10**
W3 . . . . .6G **79**
Rutland Dr. SM4: Mord 6H **153**
TW10: Ham 1D **132**
Rutland Gdns. CR0: C'don 4E **168**
N4 . . . . .6B **48**
RM8: Dag 5C **72**
SW7 . . . . .7D **10** (2C **100**)
W13 .5A **78**
Rutland Gdns. M. SW7 . .7D **10** (2C **100**)
Rutland Ga. BR2: Broml 4H **159**
DA17: Belv 5H **109**
SW7 . . . . .7D **10** (2C **100**)
Rutland Ga. M. SW7 . . . . .7C **10**
Rutland Gro. W6 . . . . .5D **98**
Rutland Ho. NW10 . . . . .3C **80**
UB5: N'olt 6E **58**
(off The Farmlands)
W8 .3K **99**
(off Marloes Rd.)
Rutland M. NW8 . . . . .1K **81**
Rutland M. E. SW7 . . . . .1C **16**
Rutland M. Sth. SW7 . . . . .1C **16**
Rutland M. W. SW7 . . . . .1C **16**
Rutland Pk. NW2 . . . . .6E **62**
SE6 .2B **140**
Rutland Pk. Gdns. NW2 . . . . .6E **62**
(off Rutland Pk.)

Rutland Pk. Mans. NW2 . . . . .6E **62**
Rutland Pl. EC1 . . . . . . .5B **8** (4B **84**)
WD23: B Hea 1C **26**
Rutland Rd. E7 . . . . .7B **70**
E9 . . . . .1K **85**
E11 .5K **51**
E17 .6C **50**
HA1: Harr 6G **41**
IG1: Ilf 3F **71**
SW19 . . . . .7C **136**
TW2: Twick 2H **131**
UB1: S'hall 5E **76**
UB3: Harl 4F **93**
Rutland St. SW7 . . . . . . .1D **16** (3C **100**)
Rutland Wlk. SE6 . . . . .2B **140**
Rutley Cl. SE17 . . . . .6B **102**
Rutlish Rd. SW19 . . . . .1J **153**
Rutter Gdns. CR4: Mitc 4A **154**
Rutters Cl. UB7: W Dray 2C **92**
The Rutts WD23: B Hea 1C **26**
Rutt's Ter. SE14 . . . . .1K **121**
Ruvigny Gdns. SW15 . . . . .3F **117**
Ruxbury Ct. TW15: Ashf 3A **128**
RUXLEY .7D **144**
Ruxley Cl. DA14: Sidc 6D **144**
KT19: Ewe 5H **163**
Ruxley Cnr. Ind. Est. DA14: Sidc . .6D **144**
Ruxley Ct. KT19: Ewe 5J **163**
Ruxley Cres. KT10: Clay 6B **162**
Ruxley Gdns. TW17: Shep 5E **146**
Ruxley La. KT19: Ewe 6H **163**
Ruxley M. KT19: Ewe 5H **163**
Ruxley Pk. Golf Course 7D **144**
Ruxley Ridge KT10: Clay 7A **162**
Ruxley Towers KT10: Clay 7A **162**
Ryalls Ct. N20 . . . . .3J **31**
Ryan Cl. HA4: Ruis 1K **57**
SE3 .4A **124**
Ryan Ct. RM7: Rom 6J **55**
SW16 . . . . .7J **137**
Ryan Dr. TW8: Bford 6A **96**
Ryarsh Cres. BR6: Orp 4J **173**
Rycott Path SE22 . . . . .7G **121**
Rycroft Way N17 . . . . .3F **49**
Ryculff Sq. SE3 . . . . .2H **123**
Rydal Cl. NW4 . . . . .1G **45**
Rydal Ct. HA8: Edg 5A **28**
HA9: Wemb 7F **43**
Rydal Cres. UB6: G'frd 3B **78**
Rydal Dr. BR4: W W'ck 2G **171**
DA7: Bex 1G **127**
Rydal Gdns. HA9: Wemb 1C **60**
NW9 .5A **44**
SW15 . . . . .5A **134**
TW3: Houn 6F **113**
Rydal Mt. BR2: Broml 4H **159**
Rydal Rd. SW16 . . . . .4H **137**
Rydal Water NW1 . . . . . . .2A **6** (3G **83**)
Rydal Way EN3: Pond E 6D **24**
HA4: Ruis 4A **58**
Ryde Ho. NW6 . . . . .1J **81**
(off Priory Pk. Rd.)
Rydens Ho. SE9 . . . . .3A **142**
Rydens Rd. KT12: Walt T 7C **148**
Ryde Pl. TW1: Twick 6D **114**
Ryder Av. E10 . . . . .7D **50**
Ryder Cl. BR1: Broml 5K **141**
Ryder Ct. E10 . . . . .2D **68**
SW1 .4B **12**
Ryder Dr. SE16 . . . . .5H **103**
Ryder Ho. E1 . . . . .4J **85**
(off Colebert Av.)
Ryder M. E9 . . . . .5J **67**
Ryder's Ter. NW8 . . . . .2A **82**
Ryder St. SW1 . . . . . . .4B **12** (1G **101**)
Ryde Va. Rd. SW12 . . . . .2G **137**
Rydon M. SW19 . . . . .7E **134**
Rydons Cl. SE9 . . . . .3C **124**
Rydon St. N1 . . . . .1C **84**
Rydston Cl. N7 . . . . .7J **65**
The Rye N14 . . . . .7C **22**
Rye Cl. DA5: Bexl 6H **127**
Ryecotes Mead SE21 . . . . .1E **138**

Ryecroft Av. IG5: Ilf 2F **53**
TW2: Whitt 7F **113**
Ryecroft Rd. BR5: Pet W 6H **161**
SE13 . . . . .5E **122**
SW16 . . . . .6A **138**
Ryecroft St. SW6 . . . . .1K **117**
Ryedale SE22 . . . . .6H **121**
Ryefield Av. UB10: Hil 7D **56**
Ryefield Cl. HA6: Nwood 2J **39**
Ryefield Cres. HA6: Nwood 2J **39**
Ryefield Pde. HA6: Nwood 2J **39**
(off Joel St.)
Ryefield Path SW15 . . . . .1C **134**
Ryefield Rd. SE19 . . . . .6C **138**
Ryegates SE15 . . . . .2H **121**
(off Caulfield Rd.)
Rye Hill Pk. SE15 . . . . .4J **121**
Rye Ho. SE16 . . . . .2J **103**
(off Swan Rd.)
SW1 .5J **17**
(off Ebury Bri. Rd.)
Ryeland Blvd. SW18 . . . . .5K **117**
Ryeland Cl. UB7: Yiew 6A **74**
Ryelands Cres. SE12 . . . . .6A **124**
Rye La. SE15 . . . . .1G **121**
Rye Mans. E20 . . . . .5E **68**
(off Napa Cl.)
Rye Pas. SE15 . . . . .3G **121**
Rye Rd. SE15 . . . . .4K **121**
Rye Wlk. SW15 . . . . .5F **117**
Rye Way HA8: Edg 6A **28**
Ryfold Rd. SW19 . . . . .3J **135**
Ryhope Rd. N11 . . . . .4A **32**
Ryland Cl. TW13: Felt 4H **129**
Rylandes Rd. NW2 . . . . .3C **62**
Ryland Rd. NW5 . . . . .6F **65**
Rylett Cres. W12 . . . . .2B **98**
Rylett Rd. W12 . . . . .2B **98**
Rylston Rd. N13 . . . . .3J **33**
SW6 .6H **99**
Rymer Rd. CR0: C'don 7E **156**
Rymer St. SE24 . . . . .6B **120**
Rymill St. E16 . . . . .1E **106**
Rysbrack St. SW3 . . . . .1E **16** (3D **100**)
Rythe Bank Cl. KT7: T Ditt 7B **150**
Rythe Cl. KT9: Chess 7C **162**
Rythe Ct. KT7: T Ditt 7A **150**

S

Saatchi Gallery 5F **17** (5D **100**)
Sabah Ct. TW15: Ashf 4C **128**
Sabella Cl. E3 . . . . .2B **86**
Sabine Rd. SW11 . . . . .3D **118**
Sable Cl. TW4: Houn 3A **112**
Sable Ho. E20 . . . . .5D **68**
(off Scarlet Cl.)
Sable St. N1 . . . . .7B **66**
Sach Rd. E5 . . . . .2H **67**
Sackett Rd. IG11: Bark 4A **90**
Sackville Av. BR2: Hayes 1J **171**
Sackville Cl. HA2: Harr 3H **59**
Sackville Gdns. IG1: Ilf 1D **70**
Sackville Ho. SW16 . . . . .3J **137**
Sackville St. W1 . . . . . . .3B **12** (7G **83**)
Saddleback La. W7 . . . . .3J **95**
Saddlebrook Pk.
TW16: Sun 7G **129**
Saddle M. CR0: C'don 7C **156**
Saddlers Cl. HA5: Hat E 6A **26**
Saddlers Ho. E17 . . . . .5B **50**
(off Track St.)
E20 .5E **68**
(off Ribbons Wlk.)
Saddlers M. HA0: Wemb 4K **59**
KT1: Hamp W 1C **150**
SW8 .1J **119**
Saddlers Pl. TW3: Houn 3G **113**
Saddlescombe Way N12 . . . . .5D **30**
Saddle Yd. W1 . . . . . . .4J **11** (1F **101**)
Sadler Cl. CR4: Mitc 2D **154**

Sadler Hgts. N1 . . . . .7K **65**
(off Caledonian Rd.)
Sadler Ho. E3 . . . . .3D **86**
(off Bromley High St.)
EC1 .1K **7**
(off Spa Grn. Est.)
Sadler Pl. E9 . . . . .5A **68**
Sadlers Ct. SE1 . . . . .7G **15**
Sadlers Ga. M. SW15 . . . . .3E **116**
Sadlers Ride KT8: W Mole 2G **149**
Sadler's Wells Theatre 1K **7** (3A **84**)
Safara Ho. SE5 . . . . .1E **120**
(off Dalwood St.)
Safari Cinema 5K **41**
Saffron Av. E14 . . . . .7F **87**
Saffron Central Sq. CR0: C'don . . .1C **168**
Saffron Cl. CR0: C'don 6J **155**
NW11 . . . . .6H **45**
Saffron Ct. E15 . . . . .5G **69**
(off Maryland Pk.)
TW14: Bedf 7E **110**
Saffron Hill EC1 . . . . .5K **7** (5A **84**)
Saffron Ho. SM2: Sutt 7K **165**
TW9: Kew 1H **115**
Saffron M. SW19 . . . . .7G **135**
Saffron Rd. RM5: Col R 2K **55**
Saffron St. EC1 . . . . .5K **7** (5A **84**)
Saffron Way KT6: Surb 1D **162**
Saffron Wharf SE1 . . . . .6K **15**
(off Shad Thames)
Sage Cl. E6 . . . . .5D **88**
Sage M. SE22 . . . . .5F **121**
Sage St. E1 . . . . .7J **85**
Sage Way WC1 . . . . .2G **7**
Sage Yd. KT6: Surb 1F **163**
Sahara Ct. UB1: S'hall 7C **76**
Saigasso Cl. E16 . . . . .6B **88**
Sailacre Ho. SE10 . . . . .5H **105**
Sail Cl. E14 . . . . .7F **87**
(off Newport Av.)
Sailmakers Ct. SW6 . . . . .3A **118**
Sailors Ho. E14 . . . . .6F **87**
(off Deauville Cl.)
Sail St. SE11 . . . . .3H **19** (4K **101**)
Saimet NW9 . . . . .7G **29**
(off Wiggins Mead)
Sainfoin Rd. SW17 . . . . .2E **136**
Sainsbury Rd. SE19 . . . . .5E **138**
Sainsbury Wing 3D **12**
(within National Gallery)
St Agatha's Dr. KT2: King T 6F **133**
St Agatha's Gro. SM5: Cars 1D **166**
St Agnes Cl. E9 . . . . .1J **85**
St Agnes Ho. E3 . . . . .2C **86**
(off Ordell Rd.)
St Agnes Pl. SE11 . . . . . .7K **19** (6B **102**)
St Agnes Quad. SE11 . . . . .6A **102**
St Agnes Well EC1 . . . . .3F **9**
St Aidans Cl. IG11: Bark 2B **90**
St Aidan's Rd. SE22 . . . . .6H **121**
W13 . . . . .2B **96**
St Alban's Av. E6 . . . . .3D **88**
W4 . . . . .4K **97**
St Albans Av. TW13: Hanw 5B **130**
St Albans Cl. NW11 . . . . .1J **63**
St Albans Ct. EC2 . . . . .6D **8**
St Alban's Cres. IG8: Wfd G 7D **36**
N22 .1A **48**
St Albans Farm TW14: Houn 5A **112**
St Alban's Gdns. TW11: Tedd 5A **132**
St Alban's Gro. SM5: Cars 7C **154**
W8 . . . . .3K **99**
St Albans La. NW11 . . . . .1J **63**
St Albans Mans. W8 . . . . .3K **99**
(off Kensington Ct. Pl.)
St Alban's Pl. N1 . . . . .1B **84**
St Alban's Rd. IG8: Wfd G 7D **36**
KT2: King T 6E **132**
SM1: Sutt 4H **165**
St Albans Rd. EN5: Barn 1A **20**
IG3: Ilf 1K **71**
NW5 . . . . .3E **64**
NW10 . . . . .1A **80**

St Alban's St.—St Francis' Ho.

St Alban's St. SW1 . . . . 3C 12 (7H 83)
St Albans Studios W8 . . . . 3K 99
(off St Albans Gro.)
St Albans Ter. W6 . . . . 6G 99
St Albans Vs. NW5 . . . . 3E 64
St Alfege Pas. SE10 . . . . 6E 104
St Alfege Rd. SE7 . . . . 6B 106
St Alphage Ct. NW9 . . . . 3K 43
St Alphage Gdn. EC2 . . . . . . 6D 8 (5C 84)
St Alphage Highwalk EC2 . . . . 6D 8
St Alphage Wlk. HA8: Edg 2J 43
St Alphege Rd. N9 . . . . 7D 24
St Alphonsus Rd. SW4 . . . . 4G 119
St Amunds Cl. SE6 . . . . 4C 140
St Andrew's Av. HA0: Wemb 4A 60
St Andrews Chambers W1 . . . . 6B 6
(off Wells St.)
St Andrew's Cl. HA4: Ruis 2B 58
HA7: Stan 2C 42
N12 . . . . 4F 31
NW2 . . . . 3D 62
TW7: Isle 1J 113
TW17: Shep 4F 147
St Andrews Cl. KT7: T Ditt 1B 162
SE16 . . . . 5H 103
SE28 . . . . 6D 90
SW19 . . . . 6K 135
St Andrew's Ct. SW18 . . . . 2A 136
St Andrews Ct. E17 . . . . 2A 50
SM1: Sutt 3C 166
St Andrews Dr. HA7: Stan 1C 42
St Andrew's Gro. N16 . . . . 1D 66
St Andrew's Hill EC4 . . . . . 2B 14 (6B 84)
(not continuous)
St Andrews Ho. RM8: Dag 4A 72
SE16 . . . . 3H 103
(off Southwark Pk. Rd.)
St Andrews Mans. W1 . . . . 6G 5
(off Dorset St.)
W14 . . . . 6G 99
(off St Andrew's Rd.)
St Andrew's M. N16 . . . . 1E 66
SE3 . . . . 7J 105
St Andrews M. SW12 . . . . 1H 137
St Andrew's Pl. NW1 . . . . . . 3K 5 (4F 83)
St Andrew's Rd. CR0: C'don 4C 168
DA14: Sidc 3D 144
E11 . . . . 6G 51
E13 . . . . 3K 87
E17 . . . . 2K 49
EN1: Enf 3J 23
IG1: Ilf 7D 52
KT6: Surb 6D 150
N9 . . . . 7D 24
NW9 . . . . 1K 61
NW10 . . . . 6D 62
NW11 . . . . 6H 45
RM7: Rom 6K 55
SM5: Cars 3C 166
UB10: Uxb 1A 74
W3 . . . . 7A 80
W14 . . . . 6G 99
St Andrews Rd. W7 . . . . 2J 95
St Andrew's Sq. KT6: Surb 6D 150
St Andrews Sq. W11 . . . . 6G 81
St Andrew's Twr. UB1: S'hall 7G 77
(off Baird Av.)
St Andrew St. EC4 . . . . 6K 7 (5A 84)
St Andrews Way E3 . . . . 4D 86
St Andrew's Wharf SE1 . . . . 2F 103
St Anna Rd. EN5: Barn 5A 20
St Anne's Cl. N6 . . . . 3E 64
St Anne's Ct. BR4: W W'ck 4G 171
NW6 . . . . 1G 81
W1 . . . . 1C 12 (6H 83)
St Anne's Flats NW1 . . . . 1C 6
(off Doric Way)
St Anne's Gdns. NW10 . . . . 3F 79
St Annes M. SW20 . . . . 7F 135
St Anne's Pas. E14 . . . . 6B 86
St Anne's Rd. E11 . . . . 2F 69
HA0: Wemb 5D 60
St Anne's Row E14 . . . . 6B 86
St Anne's Trad. Est. E14 . . . . 6B 86
(off St Anne's Row)
St Anne St. E14 . . . . 6B 86
St Ann's IG11: Bark 1G 89
St Ann's Ct. NW4 . . . . 3D 44
St Ann's Cres. SW18 . . . . 6K 117
St Ann's Gdns. NW5 . . . . 6E 64
St Ann's Hill SW18 . . . . 5K 117
St Ann's Ho. WC1 . . . . 2J 7
(off Margery St.)
St Ann's La. SW1 . . . . 2D 18 (3H 101)
St Ann's Pk. Rd. SW18 . . . . 6A 118
St Ann's Pas. SW13 . . . . 3A 116
St Ann's Rd. HA1: Harr 6J 41
IG11: Bark 1G 89
N9 . . . . 2A 34
N15 . . . . 5B 48
SW13 . . . . 2B 116
W11 . . . . 7F 81
St Ann's Shop. Cen. 6J 41
St Ann's St. SW1 . . . . 1D 18 (3H 101)
St Ann's Ter. NW8 . . . . 2B 82
St Ann's Vs. W11 . . . . 1F 99
St Ann's Way CR2: S Croy 6B 168
St Anselms Ct. SW16 . . . . 5J 137
St Anselm's Pl. W1 . . . . 2J 11 (7F 83)
St Anselm's Rd. UB3: Hayes 2H 93
St Anthony's Av. IG8: Wfd G 6F 37
St Anthony's Cl. E1 . . . . 1G 103
E9 . . . . 6B 68
(off Wallis Rd.)
SW17 . . . . 2C 136
St Anthony's Ct. BR6: Farnb 2F 173
SW17 . . . . 2E 136
St Anthony's Flats NW1 . . . . 2H 83
(off Aldenham St.)
St Anthony's Way TW14: Felt 4H 111
St Antony's Rd. E7 . . . . 7K 69
St Arvan's Cl. CR0: C'don 3E 168
St Asaph Rd. SE4 . . . . 3K 121
St Aubins Ct. N1 . . . . 1D 84
St Aubyn's Av. SW19 . . . . 5H 135
TW3: Houn 5E 112
St Aubyn's Cl. BR6: Orp 3K 173
St Aubyn's Gdns. BR6: Orp 2K 173
St Aubyn's Rd. SE19 . . . . 6F 139
St Audrey Av. DA7: Bex 2G 127
St Augustine's Av. BR2: Broml 5C 160
CR2: S Croy 6C 168
HA9: Wemb 3E 60
W5 . . . . 2E 78
St Augustine's Ct. SE1 . . . . 5H 103
(off Lynton Rd.)
St Augustine's Ho. NW1 . . . . 1C 6
(off Werrington St.)
St Augustine's Mans. SW1 . . . . 4B 18
(off Bloomburg St.)
St Augustine's Path N5 . . . . 4C 66
St Augustine's Rd. DA17: Belv 4F 109
NW1 . . . . 7H 65
St Augustine's Sports Cen. 2J 81
St Austell Cl. HA8: Edg 2F 43
St Austell Rd. SE13 . . . . 2E 122
St Awdry's Rd. IG11: Bark 7H 71
St Awdry's Wlk. IG11: Bark 7G 71
St Barnabas Cl. BR3: Beck 2E 158
SE22 . . . . 5E 120
St Barnabas Ct. HA3: Hrw W 1G 41
St Barnabas Gdns. KT8: W Mole . . 5E 148
St Barnabas M. SW1 . . . . 5H 17
St Barnabas Rd. CR4: Mitc 7E 136
E17 . . . . 6C 50
IG8: Wfd G 1K 51
SM1: Sutt 5B 166
St Barnabas St. SW1 . . . . . 5H 17 (5E 100)
St Barnabas Ter. E9 . . . . 5K 67
St Barnabas Vs. SW8 . . . . 1J 119
St Bartholomew's Cl. SE26 . . . . . . 4H 139
St Bartholomew's Ct. E6 . . . . 2C 88
(off St Bartholomew's Rd.)
St Bartholomew's Hospital Mus. 6B 8
St Bartholomew's Rd. E6 . . . . 2D 88
St Benedict's Cl. SW17 . . . . 5E 136
St Benet's Cl. SW17 . . . . 2C 136
St Benet's Gro. SM5: Cars 7A 154
St Benet's Pl. EC3 . . . . 2F 15 (7D 84)
St Bernards CR0: C'don 3E 168
St Bernard's Cl. SE27 . . . . 4D 138
St Bernards Ho. E14 . . . . 3E 104
(off Galbraith St.)
St Bernard's Rd. E6 . . . . 1B 88
St Blaise Av. BR1: Broml 2K 159
St Botolph Row EC3 . . . . . . 1J 15 (6F 85)
St Botolphs E1 . . . . 7J 9
(off St Botolph St.)
St Botolph St. EC3 . . . . 7J 9 (6F 85)
St Brelades Ct. N1 . . . . 1E 84
St Bride's Av. EC4 . . . . 1A 14
HA8: Edg 1F 43
St Bride's Church 1A 14 (6B 84)
St Brides Cl. DA18: Erith 2D 108
St Bride's Crypt Mus. 1A 14
(off Fleet St.)
St Bride's Ho. E3 . . . . 2C 86
(off Ordell Rd.)
St Bride's Pas. EC4 . . . . 1A 14
St Bride St. EC4 . . . . 7A 8 (6B 84)
St Catherine's Apts. E3 . . . . 3D 86
(off Bow Rd.)
St Catherine's Cl. SW17 . . . . 2C 136
SW20 . . . . 5E 152
St Catherines Cl. KT9: Chess 6D 162
St Catherine's Ct. W4 . . . . 3A 98
St Catherines Ct. TW13: Felt 1J 129
St Catherine's Dr. SE14 . . . . 2K 121
St Catherine's Farm Ct.
HA4: Ruis 6E 38
St Catherines M. SW3 . . . . 3E 16 (4D 100)
St Catherine's Rd. E4 . . . . 2H 35
HA4: Ruis 6F 39
St Cecilia Pl. SE3 . . . . 5J 105
St Cecilia's Cl. SM3: Sutt 1G 165
St Chads Cl. KT6: Surb 7C 150
St Chad's Gdns. RM6: Chad H 7E 54
St Chad's Pl. WC1 . . . . 1F 7 (3J 83)
St Chad's Rd. RM6: Chad H 7E 54
St Chad's St. WC1 . . . . 1F 7 (3J 83)
(not continuous)
St Charles Pl. W10 . . . . 5G 81
St Charles Sq. W10 . . . . 5F 81
St Chloe's Ho. E3 . . . . 2C 86
(off Ordell Rd.)
St Christopher Rd. UB8: Cowl 6A 74
St Christopher's Cl. TW7: Isle 1J 113
St Christophers Dr. UB3: Hayes 7K 75
St Christopher's Gdns.
CR7: Thor H 3A 156
St Christopher's Ho. NW1 . . . . 2G 83
(off Bridgeway St.)
St Christopher's M. SM6: W'gton . . 5G 167
St Christopher's Pl. W1 . . . . 7H 5 (6E 82)
St Clair Cl. IG5: Ilf 2D 52
St Clair Dr. KT4: Wor Pk 3D 164
St Clair Ho. E3 . . . . 3B 86
(off British St.)
St Clair Rd. E13 . . . . 2K 87
St Clair's Rd. CR0: C'don 2E 168
St Clare Bus. Pk. TW12: Hamp H . . 6G 131
St Clare St. EC3 . . . . 1J 15 (6F 85)
St Clements Av. E3 . . . . 3B 86
St Clement's Ct. EC4 . . . . 2F 15
N7 . . . . 6A 66
St Clements Ct. SE14 . . . . 6K 103
(off Myers La.)
W11 . . . . 7F 81
(off Stoneleigh St.)
St Clement's Development E3 . . . . 3B 86
St Clement's Hgts. SE26 . . . . 4G 139
St Clements Ho. E1 . . . . 6J 9
(off Leyden St.)
St Clement's La. WC2 . . . . 1G 13 (6K 83)
St Clements Mans. SW6 . . . . 6F 99
(off Lillie Rd.)
St Clements St. N7 . . . . 6A 66
St Clements Yd. SE22 . . . . 4F 121
St Cloud Rd. SE27 . . . . 4C 138
St Columba's Ct. E15 . . . . 4G 69
(off Janson Rd.)
St Columbas Ho. E17 . . . . 4D 50
St Columb's Ho. W10 . . . . 5G 81
(off Blagrove Rd.)
St Crispin's Cl. NW3 . . . . 4C 64
UB1: S'hall 6D 76
St Cross St. EC1 . . . . 5K 7 (5A 84)
St Cuthbert's Rd. NW2 . . . . 6H 63
St Cuthberts Rd. N13 . . . . 6F 33
St Cyprian's St. SW17 . . . . 4D 136
St David's Cl. BR4: W W'ck 7D 158
HA9: Wemb 3J 61
St Davids Cl. SE16 . . . . 5H 103
(off Masters Dr.)
St David's Ct. BR1: Broml 3F 161
E17 . . . . 3E 50
St Davids Ct. TW15: Ashf 2B 128
St David's Dr. HA8: Edg 1F 43
St Davids M. E3 . . . . 3A 86
(off Morgan St.)
E18 . . . . 1J 51
St David's Pl. NW4 . . . . 7D 44
St Davids Sq. E14 . . . . 5D 104
St Denis Rd. SE27 . . . . 4D 138
St Dionis Rd. SW6 . . . . 2H 117
St Domingo Ho. SE18 . . . . 3D 106
(off Leda Rd.)
St Donatt's Rd. SE14 . . . . 1B 122
ST DUNSTAN'S 6H 165
St Dunstan's All. EC3 . . . . 2G 15
St Dunstans Av. W3 . . . . 7K 79
St Dunstan's Cl. UB3: Harl 5H 93
St Dunstan's Ct. EC4 . . . . . 1K 13 (6A 84)
St Dunstan's Enterprises 1C 140
St Dunstan's Gdns. W3 . . . . 7K 79
St Dunstan's Hill SM1: Sutt 5G 165
St Dunstans Hill EC3 . . . . . 3G 15 (7E 84)
St Dunstan's Ho. WC2 . . . . 1J 13
(off Chancery La.)
St Dunstan's La. BR3: Beck 6E 158
EC3 . . . . 3G 15 (7E 84)
St Dunstans M. E1 . . . . 5A 86
(off White Horse Rd.)
St Dunstan's Rd. E7 . . . . 6K 69
SE25 . . . . 4F 157
TW4: Cran 2K 111
(not continuous)
TW13: Felt 3H 129
W6 . . . . 5F 99
W7 . . . . 2J 95
St Edmund's Av. HA4: Ruis 6F 39
St Edmund's Cl. NW8 . . . . 1D 82
SW17 . . . . 2C 136
St Edmunds Cl. DA18: Erith 2D 108
St Edmund's Ct. NW8 . . . . 1D 82
(off St Edmund's Ter.)
St Edmunds Ct. CR0: C'don 2B 168
St Edmunds Dr. HA7: Stan 1A 42
St Edmund's La. TW2: Whitt 7F 113
St Edmund's Rd. IG1: Ilf 6D 52
N9 . . . . 7B 24
St Edmunds Sq. SW13 . . . . 6E 98
St Edmund's Ter. NW8 . . . . 1C 82
St Edward's Cl. NW11 . . . . 6J 45
St Edwards Ct. NW11 . . . . 6J 45
St Edwards Way RM1: Rom 5K 55
St Egberts Way E4 . . . . 1K 35
St Elmo Rd. W12 . . . . 1B 98
St Elmos Rd. SE16 . . . . 2A 104
St Erkenwald M. IG11: Bark 1H 89
St Erkenwald Rd. IG11: Bark 1H 89
St Ermin's Hill SW1 . . . . 1C 18
St Ervan's Rd. W10 . . . . 5H 81
St Eugene Ct. NW6 . . . . 1G 81
(off Salusbury Rd.)
St Faith's Cl. EN2: Enf 1H 23
St Faith's Rd. SE21 . . . . 1B 138
St Fidelis Rd. DA8: Erith 4K 109
St Fillans Rd. SE6 . . . . 1E 140
St Francis Cl. BR5: Pet W 6J 161
St Francis' Ho. NW1 . . . . 2H 83
(off Bridgeway St.)

St Francis Pl. SW12 . . . . .6F 119
St Francis Rd. DA8: Erith 4K 109
  SE22 . . . . .4E 120
St Francis Way IG1: Ilf 4H 71
St Frideswide's M. E14 . . . . .6E 86
St Gabriel's Cl. E11 . . . . .2K 69
  E14 .5D 86
St Gabriels Ct. N11 . . . . .7C 32
St Gabriels Mnr. SE5 . . . . .1B 120
            (off Cormont Rd.)
St Gabriels Rd. NW2 . . . . .5F 63
St Gabriel Wlk. SE1 . . . . .4B 102
        (off Elephant & Castle)
St George's Av. E7 . . . . .7K 69
  N7 . . . . .4H 65
  NW9 .4K 43
  UB1: S'hall 7D 76
  W5 . . . . .2D 96
St George's Bldgs. SE1 . . . . . . .3B 102
         (off St George's Rd.)
St George's Cir. SE1 . . . . .7A 14 (3B 102)
St George's Cl. HA0: Wemb 3A 60
  NW11 . . . . .6H 45
  SW8 .1G 119
St Georges Cl. SE28 . . . . .6D 90
St George's Ct. E6 . . . . .4D 88
  SE1 .3B 102
           (off Garden Row)
  SW1 .5A 18
         (off St George's Dr.)
  SW3 .3C 16
          (off Brompton Rd.)
  SW7 . . . . .3A 100
  SW15 . . . . .4H 117
St Georges Ct. E17 . . . . .5F 51
  EC4 . . . . .7A 8 (6B 84)
  HA3: Kenton 6A 42
          (off Kenton Rd.)
St George's Dr. SW1 . . . .4K 17 (4F 101)
  UB10: Ick 3B 56
ST GEORGE'S FIELD 7C 82
St George's Flds. W2 . . . .1D 10 (6C 82)
St George's Gdns. KT6: Surb . . .2H 163
St George's Gro. SW17 . . . . . . .3B 136
St George's Ho. NW1 . . . . .2H 83
         (off Bridgeway St.)
St George's Ho. SW11 . . . . .1E 118
     (off Charlotte Despard Av.)
St George's Ind. Est. KT2: King T . .5D 132
  N22 . . . . .7G 33
St George's La. EC3 . . . . .2F 15
St George's Leisure Cen. 7H 85
St George's Mans. SW1 . . . . .5D 18
          (off Causton St.)
St George's M. NW1 . . . . .7D 64
  SE1 . . . . .1K 19
  SE8 .4B 104
St Georges Pde. SE6 . . . . .2B 140
          (off Perry Hill)
St George's Pl. TW1: Twick 1A 132
St George's Rd. BR1: Broml 2D 160
  BR3: Beck 1D 158
  BR5: Pet W 6H 161
  CR4: Mitc 3F 155
  DA14: Sidc 6D 144
  E7 . . . . .7K 69
  E10 . . . . .3E 68
  EN1: Enf 1A 24
  IG1: Ilf 7D 52
  KT2: King T 7G 133
  N13 . . . . .3E 32
  NW11 . . . . .6H 45
  RM9: Dag 5E 72
  SE1 . . . . .1K 19 (3A 102)
  SM6: W'gton 5F 167
  SW19 . . . . .7H 135
         (not continuous)
  TW1: Twick 5B 114
  TW13: Hanw 4B 130
  W4 . . . . .2K 97
  W7 . . . . .1K 95
St George's Rd. TW9: Rich 3F 115
St George's Rd. W. BR1: Broml . . .1C 160

St George's Shop. & Leisure Cen. . . .6J 41
St George's Sq. E7 . . . . .7K 69
  KT3: N Mald 3A 152
  SE8 .4B 104
         (not continuous)
  SW1 . . . . .5C 18 (5H 101)
St Georges Sq. E14 . . . . .7A 86
St George's Sq. M. SW1 . . .6C 18 (5H 101)
St George's Ter. E6 . . . . .3C 88
         (off Masterman Rd.)
  NW1 .7D 64
  SE15 .7G 103
        (off Peckham Hill St.)
St George St. W1 . . . . .1K 11 (7F 83)
St George's University of London . . .5B 136
St George's Wlk. CR0: C'don 3C 168
St George's Way SE15 . . . . .6E 102
St George's Wharf SE1 . . . . .6K 15
         (off Shad Thames)
St George Wharf SW8 . . . .7E 18 (6J 101)
St Gerards Cl. SW4 . . . . .5G 119
St German's Pl. SE3 . . . . .1J 123
St German's Rd. SE23 . . . . .1A 140
St Giles Av. RM10: Dag 7H 73
  UB10: Ick 4E 56
St Giles Churchyard EC2 . . .6D 8 (5C 84)
St Giles Cir. W1 . . . . .7D 6 (6H 83)
St Giles Cl. BR6: Farnb 5H 173
  RM10: Dag 7H 73
  TW5: Hest 7C 94
St Giles High St. WC2 . . . . .7D 6 (6H 83)
St Giles Ho. EN5: New Bar 4F 21
  SE5 .1E 120
St Giles Pas. WC2 . . . . .1D 12
St Giles Rd. SE5 . . . . .7E 102
St Giles Sq. WC2 . . . . .7D 6 (6H 83)
St Giles Ter. EC2 . . . . .6D 8
          (off Wood St.)
St Giles Twr. SE5 . . . . .1E 120
          (off Gables Cl.)
St Gilles Ho. E2 . . . . .2K 85
           (off Mace St.)
St Gothard Rd. SE27 . . . . .4D 138
          (not continuous)
St Gregory Cl. HA4: Ruis 4A 58
St Helena Ho. WC1 . . . . .2J 7
          (off Margery St.)
St Helena Rd. SE16 . . . . .4K 103
St Helena St. WC1 . . . . .2J 7 (3A 84)
St Helena Ter. TW9: Rich 5D 114
St Helens KT7: T Ditt 7K 149
St Helen's Cl. KT4: Wor Pk 1C 164
St Helens Ct. UB8: Cowl 5A 74
St Helen's Cres. SW16 . . . . .1K 155
St Helens Gdns. W10 . . . . .5F 81
St Helens Pl. EC3 . . . . .7G 9 (6E 84)
St Helens Pl. E10 . . . . .7A 50
St Helen's Rd. DA18: Erith 2D 108
  IG1: Ilf 6D 52
  SW16 . . . . .1K 155
  W13 . . . . .1B 96
ST HELIER 7C 154
St Helier Av. SM4: Mord 7A 154
St Helier Ct. N1 . . . . .1E 84
       (off De Beauvoir Est.)
  SE16 .2K 103
         (off Poolmans St.)
St Helier's Av. TW3: Houn 5E 112
St Helier's Rd. E10 . . . . .6E 50
St Henera's Ct. BR1: Broml 3E 160
          (off Brady Dr.)
St Hilary's Ct. BR1: Broml 3F 161
St Hilda's Av. TW15: Ashf 5A 128
St Hilda's Cl. NW6 . . . . .7F 63
  SW17 . . . . .2C 136
St Hilda's Rd. SW13 . . . . .6D 98
St Hilda's Wharf E1 . . . . .1J 103
       (off Wapping High St.)
St Hubert's Ho. E14 . . . . .3C 104
          (off Janet St.)
St Hughes Cl. SW17 . . . . .2C 136
St Hugh's Rd. SE20 . . . . .1H 157
St Ives Pl. E14 . . . . .5E 86

St Ivian Ct. N10 . . . . .2E 46
St James Apts. E17 . . . . .5A 50
         (off Pretoria Av.)
St James Av. N20 . . . . .3H 31
  SM1: Sutt 5J 165
  W13 . . . . .1A 96
St James Cl. EN4: E Barn 4G 21
  HA4: Ruis 2A 58
  KT3: N Mald 5B 152
  N20 . . . . .3H 31
St James Ct. CR0: C'don 7B 156
  E2 . . . . .3G 85
        (off Bethnal Grn. Rd.)
  E12 . . . . .2A 70
  SE3 .1K 123
St James' Ct. SW1 . . . . . .1B 18 (3G 101)
St James Gdns. RM6: Chad H 4B 54
St James' Gdns. HA0: Wemb 7D 60
St James Ga. IG9: Buck H 1F 37
St James Gro. SW11 . . . . .2D 118
St James Hall N1 . . . . .1C 84
          (off Prebend St.)
St James Ind. M. SE1 . . . . .5G 103
St James Mans. SE1 . . . . .1J 19
          (off McAuley Cl.)
St James' Mans. NW6 . . . . .7J 63
         (off West End La.)
St James M. E14 . . . . .3E 104
  E17 . . . . .5A 50
St James Path E17 . . . . .5A 50
St James Residences W1 . . . . . . .2C 12
          (off Brewer St.)
St James Rd. CR4: Mitc 7E 136
  SM1: Sutt 5J 165
  SM5: Cars 3C 166
St James' Rd. E15 . . . . .5H 69
  KT6: Surb 6D 150
  N9 . . . . .2C 34
ST JAMES'S 4B 12 (1H 101)
St James's SE14 . . . . .1A 122
St James's App. EC2 . . . . .4G 9 (4E 84)
St James's Av. BR3: Beck 3A 158
  E2 . . . . .2J 85
  TW12: Hamp H 5G 131
St James's Chambers SW1 . . . . . .4B 12
         (off Jermyn St.)
St James's Cl. NW8 . . . . .1D 82
       (off St James's Ter. M.)
  SE18 .5G 107
  SW17 . . . . .2D 136
St James's Cotts. TW9: Rich 5D 114
St James's Ct. HA1: Harr 6A 42
  KT1: King T 3E 150
  N18 . . . . .5B 34
          (off Fore St.)
St James's Cres. SW9 . . . . .3A 120
St James's Dr. SW12 . . . . .1D 136
  SW17 . . . . .1D 136
St James's Gdns. W11 . . . . .1G 99
         (not continuous)
St James's Ho. SE1 . . . . .4G 103
        (off Strathnairn St.)
St James's La. N10 . . . . .4F 47
St James's Mkt. SW1 . . . .3C 12 (7H 83)
St James's Palace 6B 12 (2G 101)
St James's Pk. 6C 12 (2H 101)
St James's Pk. CR0: C'don 7C 156
St James's Pas. EC3 . . . . .1H 15
St James's Rd. CR0: C'don 7C 156
  SE1 . . . . .5A 12 (1G 101)
St James's Rd. CR0: C'don 7C 156
  KT1: King T 2D 150
  SE1 . . . . .6G 103
  SE16 .3G 103
  TW12: Hamp H 5F 131
St James's Sq. SW1 . . . .4B 12 (1G 101)
St James's St. E17 . . . . .5A 50
  SW1 . . . . .4A 12 (1G 101)
St James's Ter. NW8 . . . . .1D 82
       (off Prince Albert Rd.)
St James's Ter. M. NW8 . . . . .1D 82
St James St. W6 . . . . .5E 98
St James's Wlk. EC1 . . . . .3A 8 (4B 84)
St James Ter. SW12 . . . . .1E 136

St James Way DA14: Sidc 5E 144
St Jeromes Gro. UB3: Hayes 6E 74
St Joan's Ho. NW1 . . . . .1C 6
          (off Phoenix Rd.)
St Joan's Rd. N9 . . . . .2A 34
St John Fisher Rd.
  DA18: Erith 3D 108
ST JOHNS 2C 122
St John's Av. N11 . . . . .5J 31
  NW10 .1B 80
  SW15 . . . . .5F 117
St Johns Chu. Rd. E9 . . . . .5J 67
St John's Cl. HA9: Wemb 5E 60
  N20 . . . . .3F 31
          (off Rasper Rd.)
  SW6 . . . . .7J 99
St Johns Cl. N14 . . . . .6B 22
St John's Cotts. SE20 . . . . .7J 139
St John's Ct. DA8: Erith 4K 109
  E1 . . . . .1H 103
         (off Scandrett St.)
  HA1: Harr 6K 41
  HA6: Nwood 1G 39
         (off Murray Rd.)
  IG9: Buck H 1E 36
  KT1: King T 4E 150
         (off Beaufort Rd.)
  N4 . . . . .2B 66
  SE13 .2E 122
  TW7: Isle 2K 113
  W6 . . . . .4D 98
        (off Glenthorne Rd.)
St Johns Ct. SW10 . . . . .7A 100
        (off Ashburnham Rd.)
St John's Cres. SW9 . . . . .3A 120
St Johns Dr. SW18 . . . . .1K 135
St John's Est. N1 . . . . .2D 84
  SE1 . . . . .6J 15
St John's Gdns. W11 . . . . .7G 81
St John's Gate 4A 8
St John's Gro. N19 . . . . .2G 65
  SW13 . . . . .2B 116
  TW9: Rich 4E 114
St John's Hill SW11 . . . . .5B 118
St John's Hill Gro. SW11 . . . . . . .4B 118
St John's Ho. E14 . . . . .4E 104
          (off Pier St.)
St Johns Ho. SE17 . . . . .6D 102
          (off Lytham St.)
St John's La. EC1 . . . . .4A 8 (4B 84)
St John Lodge NW3 . . . . .7C 64
        (off King Henry's Rd.)
St John's Mans. EC1 . . . . .1A 8
          (off St John St.)
St John's M. KT1: Hamp W 2C 150
  W11 . . . . .6H 81
St John Smith Square 2E 18
St John's Pde. DA14: Sidc 4A 144
         (off Sidcup High St.)
St John's Pk. SE3 . . . . .7H 105
St John's Pk. Mans. N19 . . . . .3G 65
St John's Pas. SW19 . . . . .6G 135
St John's Path EC1 . . . . .4A 8
St Johns Pathway SE23 . . . . .1J 139
St John's Pl. EC1 . . . . .4A 8 (4B 84)
St John's Rd. BR5: Pet W 6H 161
  CR0: C'don 3B 168
  DA8: Erith 5K 109
  DA14: Sidc 4B 144
         (not continuous)
  DA16: Well 3B 126
  E4 . . . . .4J 35
  E6 . . . . .1C 88
  E16 . . . . .6J 87
  E17 . . . . .2D 50
  HA1: Harr 6K 41
  HA9: Wemb 4D 60
  IG2: Ilf 7H 53
  IG11: Bark 1J 89
  KT1: Hamp W 2C 150
  KT3: N Mald 3J 151
  KT8: E Mos 4H 149

St John's Rd. N15 . . . . .6E 48
  NW11 .6H 45
  SE20 .6J 139
  SM1: Sutt 2K 165
  SM5: Cars 3C 166
  SW11 . . . . .4C 118
  SW19 . . . . .7G 135
  TW7: Isle 2K 113
  TW9: Rich 4E 114
  TW13: Hanw 4C 130
  UB2: S'hall 3C 94
St John's Sq. EC1 . . . . .4A 8 (4B 84)
St John's Ter. E7 . . . . .6K 69
  SE18 . . . . .6G 107
  SW15 . . . . .3A 134
        (off Kingston Va.)
  W10 . . . . .4F 81
St John St. EC1 . . . . .1K 7 (2A 84)
St John's Va. SE8 . . . . .2C 122
St John's Vs. N11 . . . . .5J 31
        (off Friern Barnet Rd.)
  N19 . . . . .2H 65
  W8 . . . . .3K 99
        (off St Mary's Pl.)
St John's Way N19 . . . . .2G 65
ST JOHN'S WOOD 1A 4 (2B 82)
St John's Wood Ct. NW8 . . . . .2B 4
St John's Wood High St.
  NW8 . . . . .1C 4 (2B 82)
St John's Wood Pk. NW8 . . . . .1B 82
St John's Wood Rd. NW8 . . .3A 4 (4B 82)
St John's Wood Ter. NW8 . . . . .2B 82
St Josephs Almshouses W6 . . . . . . .4F 99
        (off Brook Grn.)
St Joseph's Cl. BR6: Orp 4K 173
  W10 . . . . .5G 81
St Joseph's College Sports Cen. . .6B 138
St Joseph's Cotts. SW3 . . . . .4E 16
        (off Cadogan St.)
St Josephs Ct. SE2 . . . . .6D 108
  SE7 .6K 105
St Joseph's Dr. UB1: S'hall 1C 94
St Joseph's Flats NW1 . . . . .1C 6
        (off Drummond Cres.)
St Joseph's Gro. NW4 . . . . .4D 44
St Joseph's Ho. W6 . . . . .4F 99
        (off Brook Grn.)
St Joseph's Rd. N9 . . . . .7C 24
St Joseph's St. SW8 . . . . .1F 119
St Joseph's Va. SE3 . . . . .3F 123
St Judes Ct. IG8: Wfd G 7H 37
St Jude's Rd. E2 . . . . .2H 85
St Jude St. N16 . . . . .5E 66
St Julian's Cl. SW16 . . . . .4A 138
St Julian's Farm Rd. SE27 . . . . . . .4A 138
St Julian's Rd. NW6 . . . . .1J 81
St Katharine Docks 3K 15
St Katharine's Pct. NW1 . . . . .2F 83
St Katharine's Way E1 . . . .4K 15 (1F 103)
        (not continuous)
St Katharine's Yacht Haven 1F 103
        (off St Katharine's Way)
St Katherine's Rd. DA18: Erith . . .2D 108
St Katherine's Row EC3 . . . . .2H 15
St Katherines Wlk. W11 . . . . .1F 99
St Keverne Rd. SE9 . . . . .4C 142
St Kilda Rd. BR6: Orp 1K 173
  W13 . . . . .1A 96
St Kilda's Rd. HA1: Harr 6J 41
  N16 . . . . .1D 66
St Kitts Ter. SE19 . . . . .5E 138
St Laurence Cl. NW6 . . . . .1F 81
St Lawrence Bus. Cen.
  TW13: Felt 2K 129
St Lawrence Cl. HA8: Edg 7A 28
St Lawrence Cotts. E14 . . . . .1E 104
        (off St Lawrence St.)
St Lawrence Ct. N1 . . . . .7D 66
St Lawrence Dr. HA5: Eastc 5K 39
St Lawrence Ho. SE1 . . . . .7H 15
        (off Purbrook St.)
St Lawrence St. E14 . . . . .1E 104
St Lawrence Ter. W10 . . . . .5G 81

St Lawrence Way SW9 . . . . .1A 120
St Leger Ct. NW6 . . . . .7F 63
        (off Coverdale Rd.)
St Leonard M. N1 . . . . .2E 84
        (off Hoxton St.)
St Leonard's Av. E4 . . . . .6A 36
  HA3: Kenton 5C 42
St Leonard's Cl. DA16: Well 3A 126
St Leonard's Ct. N1 . . . . .1F 9
St Leonards Ct. SW14 . . . . .3J 115
St Leonard's Gdns. IG1: Ilf 5G 71
  TW5: Hest 7C 94
St Leonard's Ri. BR6: Orp 4J 173
St Leonard's Rd. CR0: Wadd 3B 168
  E14 . . . . .5D 86
        (not continuous)
  KT6: Surb 5D 150
  KT7: T Ditt 6A 150
  KT10: Clay 6A 162
  NW10 .4K 79
  SW14 . . . . .3H 115
  W13 . . . . .7C 78
        (not continuous)
St Leonards Sq. KT6: Surb 5D 150
  NW5 . . . . .6E 64
St Leonard's St. E3 . . . . .3D 86
St Leonard's Studios SW3 . . . . .6E 16
        (off Smith St.)
St Leonard's Ter. SW3 . . . .6E 16 (5D 100)
St Leonard's Wlk. SW16 . . . . .7K 137
St Loo Av. SW3 . . . . .7D 16 (6C 100)
St Loo Ct. SW3 . . . . .7D 16
        (off St Loo Av.)
St Louis Rd. SE27 . . . . .4D 138
St Loy's Rd. N17 . . . . .2E 48
St Lucia Dr. E15 . . . . .1H 87
St Luke Cl. UB8: Cowl 6A 74
ST LUKE'S 3D 8 (4C 84)
St Luke's Av. EN2: Enf 1J 23
  IG1: Ilf .5F 71
  SW4 .4H 119
St Luke's Cl. EC1 . . . . . . .3D 8 (4C 84)
  SE25 . . . . .6H 157
St Lukes Ct. E10 . . . . .7D 50
        (off Capworth St.)
  W11 . . . . .6H 81
        (off St Luke's Rd.)
St Luke's Est. EC1 . . . . . .2E 8 (3D 84)
St Luke's M. W11 . . . . .6H 81
St Lukes M. E14 . . . . .2C 104
        (off Strafford St.)
St Luke's Pas. KT2: King T 1F 151
St Luke's Path IG1: Ilf 5F 71
St Luke's Rd. UB10: Uxb 1A 74
  W11 . . . . .5H 81
St Luke's Sq. E16 . . . . .6H 87
St Luke's St. SW3 . . . . . . .5D 16 (5C 100)
St Luke's Yd. W9 . . . . .2H 81
        (not continuous)
St Malo Av. N9 . . . . .3D 34
ST MARGARETS 6B 114
St Margaret's IG11: Bark 1H 89
  KT2: King T 5J 133
St Margaret's Av. DA15: Sidc 3H 143
  HA2: Harr 3G 59
  N15 . . . . .4B 48
  N20 . . . . .1F 31
  SM3: Cheam 3G 165
  TW15: Ashf 5D 128
St Margarets Av. UB8: Hil 4C 74
St Margarets Bus. Cen.
  TW1: Twick 6B 114
St Margaret's Cl. EC2 . . . . .6D 84
St Margaret's Ct. N11 . . . . .4K 31
St Margarets Ct. SE1 . . . .5D 14 (1C 102)
  SW15 . . . . .4D 116
St Margaret's Cres. SW15 . . . . . . .5D 116
St Margaret's Dr. TW1: Twick 5B 114
St Margaret's Gro. E11 . . . . .3H 69
  SE18 . . . . .6G 107
  TW1: Twick 6A 114
St Margaret's Ho. NW1 . . . . .1C 6
        (off Polygon Rd.)

St Margaret's La. W8 . . . . .3K 99
St Margaret's M. KT2: King T 5J 133
St Margaret's Pas. SE13 . . . . .3G 123
        (not continuous)
St Margarets Path SE18 . . . . .5G 107
St Margaret's Rd. E12 . . . . .2A 70
  HA4: Ruis 6F 39
  HA8: Edg 5C 28
  N17 . . . . .3E 48
  NW10 .3E 80
  W7 . . . . .2J 95
St Margarets Rd. BR3: Beck 4K 157
  SE4 . . . . .4B 122
        (not continuous)
  TW1: Twick 6B 114
  TW7: Isle, Twick 4B 114
ST MARGARETS RDBT. 6B 114
St Margaret's Sports Cen. 1A 26
St Margaret's Ter. SE18 . . . . .5G 107
St Margaret St. SW1 . . . .7E 12 (2J 101)
St Mark's Cl. EN5: New Bar 3E 20
  SE10 .7E 104
  W11 . . . . .6G 81
St Marks Cl. HA1: Harr 7B 42
  SW6 . . . . .1J 117
St Marks Ct. NW8 . . . . .2A 82
        (off Abercorn Pl.)
  W7 . . . . .2J 95
        (off Lwr. Boston Rd.)
St Mark's Cres. NW1 . . . . .1E 82
St Mark's Ga. E9 . . . . .7B 68
St Mark's Gro. SW10 . . . . .7K 99
St Mark's Hill KT6: Surb 6E 150
St Marks Ho. SE17 . . . . .6D 102
        (off Lytham St.)
St Marks Ind. Est. E16 . . . . .1B 106
St Mark's Pl. RM10: Dag 6G 73
  SW19 . . . . .6H 135
  W11 . . . . .6G 81
St Mark's Ri. E8 . . . . .5F 67
St Mark's Rd. BR2: Broml 3J 159
  SE25 .4G 157
  TW11: Tedd 7B 132
  W5 . . . . .1E 96
  W7 . . . . .2J 95
  W10 . . . . .6F 81
  W11 . . . . .6G 81
St Marks Rd. CR4: Mitc 2D 154
  EN1: Enf 6A 24
St Mark's Sq. BR2: Broml 3J 159
  NW1 . . . . .1E 82
St Mark St. E1 . . . . .1K 15 (6F 85)
St Mark's Vs. N4 . . . . .2K 65
        (off Moray Rd.)
St Martin Cl. UB8: Cowl 6A 74
St Martin-in-the-Fields Church 3E 12
St Martin-in-the-Fields Chu. Pth.
  WC2 .3E 12
        (off St Martin's Pl.)
St Martin's Almshouses NW1 . . . . .1G 83
St Martin's App. HA4: Ruis 7G 39
St Martin's Av. E6 . . . . .2B 88
St Martin's Cl. DA18: Erith 2D 108
  EN1: Enf 1C 24
  NW1 . . . . .1G 83
St Martin's Ct. EC4 . . . . .7C 8
        (off Newgate St.)
  WC2 . . . . .2E 12 (7J 83)
St Martins Ct. N1 . . . . .7E 84
        (off De Beauvoir Est.)
St Martin's Ctyd. WC2 . . . . .2E 12
        (off Up. St Martin's La.)
St Martins Est. SW2 . . . . .1A 138
St Martin's Ho. NW1 . . . . .1C 6
        (off Polygon Rd.)
St Martin's La. BR3: Beck 5D 158
  WC2 . . . . .2E 12 (7J 83)
St Martin's Le-Grand EC1 . . .7C 8 (6E 84)
St Martin's Pl. WC2 . . . . . .3E 12 (7J 83)
St Martin's Rd. N9 . . . . .2C 34
  SW9 .2K 119
St Martin's St. WC2 . . . . . .3D 12 (7H 83)
        (not continuous)

St Martin's Theatre 2E 12
        (off West St.)
St Martins Way SW17 . . . . .3A 136
St Mary Abbot's Ct. W14 . . . . .3H 99
        (off Warwick Gdns.)
St Mary Abbot's Pl. W8 . . . . .3H 99
St Mary Abbot's Ter. W14 . . . . .3H 99
St Mary at Hill EC3 . . . . . . .3G 15 (7E 84)
St Mary Av. SM6: W'gton 3E 166
St Mary Axe EC3 . . . . .1G 15 (6E 84)
St Marychurch St. SE16 . . . . .2J 103
St Mary Graces Cl. E1 . . . .3K 15 (7F 85)
St Marylebone Cl. NW10 . . . . .1A 80
St Marylebone Crematorium 3K 45
St Mary le-Park Ct. SW11 . . . . .7C 100
        (off Parkgate Rd.)
St Mary Magdalene Cres. SE18 . . .3E 106
St Mary Magdalene Gdns. N7 . . . . .6A 66
St Mary Newington Cl. SE17 . . . . . .5E 102
        (off Surrey Sq.)
St Mary Rd. E17 . . . . .4C 50
St Mary's IG11: Bark 1H 89
St Mary's App. E12 . . . . .5D 70
St Mary's Av. BR2: Broml 3G 159
  E11 . . . . .7K 51
  N3 . . . . .2G 45
  TW11: Tedd 6K 131
St Mary's Av. Central UB2: S'hall . .4F 95
St Mary's Av. Nth. UB2: S'hall 4F 95
St Mary's Av. Sth. UB2: S'hall 4F 95
St Mary's Cl. KT9: Chess 7F 163
  KT17: Ewe 7B 164
  N17 . . . . .1G 49
  TW16: Sun 4J 147
St Mary's Community Gdn. 2F 85
        (off Appleby St.)
St Mary's Copse KT4: Wor Pk 2A 164
St Mary's Ct. E3 . . . . .3D 86
        (off Bow Rd.)
  E6 . . . . .4D 88
  KT3: N Mald 3A 152
  SE7 . . . . .7B 106
  SM6: W'gton 4G 167
  W5 . . . . .2D 96
  W6 . . . . .3B 98
St Mary's Cres. NW4 . . . . .3D 44
  TW7: Isle 7H 95
  UB3: Hayes 7H 75
St Mary's Dr. TW14: Bedf 7E 110
St Mary's Est. SE16 . . . . .2J 103
        (off Elephant La.)
St Mary's Flats NW1 . . . . .1C 6
        (off Drummond Cres.)
St Mary's Gdns. SE11 . . . .3K 19 (4A 102)
St Mary's Ga. W8 . . . . .3K 99
St Mary's Grn. N2 . . . . .2A 46
St Mary's Gro. N1 . . . . .6B 66
  SW13 . . . . .3D 116
  TW9: Rich 4F 115
  W4 . . . . .6H 97
St Mary's Ho. N1 . . . . .1B 84
        (off St Mary's Path)
St Mary's Mans. W2 . . . . . . .5A 4 (5B 82)
St Mary's M. NW6 . . . . .7K 63
St Marys M. TW10: Ham 2C 132
St Mary's Path N1 . . . . .1B 84
St Mary's Pl. SE9 . . . . .6E 124
  W5 . . . . .2D 96
  W8 . . . . .3K 99
St Mary's Rd. DA5: Bexl 1J 145
  E10 . . . . .3E 68
  E13 . . . . .2K 87
  EN4: E Barn 7J 21
  IG1: Ilf .2G 71
  KT4: Wor Pk 2A 164
  KT6: Surb 7C 150
        (St Chads Cl.)
  KT6: Surb 6D 150
        (Victoria Rd.)
  KT8: E Mos 5H 149
  N8 . . . . .4J 47
  N9 . . . . .1C 34
        (not continuous)

St Mary's Rd. NW10 ......1A 80
  NW11 ......7G 45
  SE15 ......1J 121
  SE25 ......3E 156
  SW19 ......5G 135
  UB3: Hayes 7H 75
St Marys Rd. W5 ......2D 96
St Mary's Sq. W2 ......5A 4 (5B 82)
  W5 ......2D 96
St Mary's Ter. W2 ......5A 4 (5B 82)
St Mary's Twr. EC1 ......4D 8
  (off Fortune St.)
St Mary St. SE18 ......4D 106
St Mary's University College 3K 131
St Mary's University College Sports Cen.
  ......4K 131
St Mary's Vw. HA3: Kenton 5C 42
St Mary's Wlk. SE11 ......3K 19 (4A 102)
  UB3: Hayes 7H 75
St Mary's Way IG7: Chig 5K 37
St Matthew Cl. UB8: Cowl 6A 74
St Matthew's Av. KT6: Surb 1E 162
St Matthew's Ct. TW15: Ashf 4C 128
  (off Feltham Rd.)
St Matthews Ct. E10 ......7D 50
  N10 ......3E 46
  SE1 ......3C 102
  (off Meadow Row)
St Matthew's Dr. BR1: Broml 3D 160
St Matthews Ho. SE17 ......6D 102
  (off Phelp St.)
St Matthew's Lodge NW1 ......2G 83
  (off Oakley Sq.)
St Matthew's Rd. SW2 ......4K 119
  W5 ......1E 96
St Matthew's Row E2 ......3G 85
St Matthew St. SW1 ......2C 18 (3H 101)
St Matthias Cl. NW9 ......5B 44
St Maur Rd. SW6 ......1H 117
St Meddens BR7: Chst 7H 143
St Mellion Cl. SE28 ......6D 90
St Merryn Cl. SE18 ......7H 107
St Merryn Ct. BR3: Beck 7C 140
St Michael's All. EC3 ......1F 15 (6D 84)
St Michael's Av. HA9: Wemb 6G 61
  N9 ......7D 24
St Michael's Cl. BR1: Broml 3D 160
  DA18: Erith 2D 108
  KT4: Wor Pk 2B 164
  N3 ......2H 45
  N12 ......5H 31
St Michaels Cl. E16 ......5B 88
St Michael's Cl. CR0: C'don 1C 168
  (off Poplar Wlk.)
  SE1 ......7D 14
  (off Trinity St.)
St Michaels Ct. E14 ......5E 86
  (off St Leonard's Rd.)
St Michael's Cres. HA5: Pinn 6C 40
St Michael's Flats NW1 ......1C 6
  (off Aldenham St.)
St Michael's Gdns. W10 ......5G 81
St Michael's M. SW1 ......4G 17 (4E 100)
St Michael's Ri. DA16: Well 1B 126
St Michael's Rd. CR0: C'don 1C 168
  DA16: Well 3B 126
  NW2 ......4E 62
  SM6: W'gton 6G 167
  SW9 ......2K 119
  TW15: Ashf 5C 128
St Michael's St. W2 ......7B 4 (6B 82)
St Michael's Ter. N22 ......1J 47
St Michaels Ter. N6 ......1E 64
  (off South Gro.)
St Mildred's Ct. EC2 ......1E 14 (6D 84)
St Mildreds Rd. SE6 ......7G 123
  SE12 ......7G 123
St Mirren Cl. EN5: New Bar 5F 21
St Nicholas Cen. 5K 165
St Nicholas Cl. UB8: Cowl 6A 74
St Nicholas Ct. KT1: King T 4E 150
  (off Surbiton Rd.)
St Nicholas Dr. TW17: Shep 7C 146

St Nicholas' Flats NW1 ......1C 6
  (off Werrington St.)
St Nicholas Glebe SW17 ......5E 136
St Nicholas Ho. SE8 ......6C 104
  (off Deptford Grn.)
St Nicholas M. KT7: T Ditt 6K 149
St Nicholas Rd. KT7: T Ditt 6K 149
  SE18 ......5K 107
  SM1: Sutt 5K 165
St Nicholas St. SE8 ......1B 122
St Nicholas Way SM1: Sutt 4K 165
St Nicolas La. BR7: Chst 1C 160
St Ninian's Ct. N20 ......3J 31
St Norbert Grn. SE4 ......4A 122
St Norbert Rd. SE4 ......5K 121
St Olaf Ho. SE1 ......4F 15
St Olaf's Rd. SW6 ......7G 99
St Olaf Stairs SE1 ......4F 15
St Olave's Cl. EC2 ......1E 14 (6D 84)
St Olave's Est. SE1 ......6H 15 (2E 102)
St Olave's Gdns. SE11 ......3J 19 (4A 102)
St Olaves Ho. SE11 ......3J 19
  (off Walnut Tree Wlk.)
St Olave's Mans. SE11 ......3J 19
St Olave's Rd. E6 ......1E 88
St Olaves Wlk. SW16 ......2G 155
St Olav's Sq. SE16 ......2J 103
St Onge Pde. EN1: Enf 3J 23
  (off Southbury Rd.)
St Oswald's Pl. SE11 ......6G 19 (5K 101)
St Oswald's Rd. SW16 ......1B 156
St Oswalds Studios SW6 ......6J 99
  (off Sedlescombe Rd.)
St Oswulf St. SW1 ......4D 18 (4H 101)
St Owen Ho. SE1 ......3E 102
  (off St Saviour's Est.)
ST PANCRAS 2F 7 (3J 83)
St Pancras Commercial Cen. NW1 ......1G 83
  (off Pratt St.)
St Pancras Ct. N2 ......2B 46
St Pancras Gardens 2H 83
St Pancras Gdns. NW1 ......2H 83
  (off Pancras Rd.)
St Pancras Way NW1 ......7G 65
St Patrick's Ct. IG8: Wfd G 7B 36
St Paul Cl. UB8: Cowl 5A 74
St Paulinus Ct. DA1: Cray 4K 127
  (off Manor Rd.)
St Paul's All. EC4 ......1B 14
  (off St Paul's Chyd.)
St Paul's Av. HA3: Kenton 4F 43
  NW2 ......6E 62
  SE16 ......1K 103
St Paul's Bldgs. EC1 ......3B 8
  (off Dallington St.)
St Paul's Cathedral 1B 14 (6C 84)
St Paul's Churchyard EC4 ......1B 14 (6B 84)
St Paul's Cl. KT9: Chess 4D 162
  SM5: Cars 1C 166
  TW3: Houn 2C 112
  TW15: Ashf 5E 128
  UB3: Harl 5F 93
  W5 ......2F 97
St Pauls Cl. SE7 ......5B 106
St Pauls Ct. TW4: Houn 3C 112
St Pauls Cl. SW4 ......5H 119
St Pauls Ctyd. SE8 ......7C 104
  (off Crossfield St.)
ST PAUL'S CRAY 2K 161
St Paul's Cray Rd. BR7: Chst 1H 161
St Paul's Cres. NW1 ......7H 65
  (not continuous)
St Pauls Ho. SE7 ......7C 104
  (off Market Yd.)
St Paul's M. NW1 ......7H 65
St Paul's Pl. N1 ......6D 66
St Paul's Ri. N13 ......6G 33
St Paul's Rd. CR7: Thor H 3C 156
  DA8: Erith 7J 109
  IG11: Bark 1G 89
  N1 ......6B 66
  N17 ......7B 34

St Paul's Rd. TW8: Bford 6D 96
  TW9: Rich 3F 115
St Paul's Shrubbery N1 ......6D 66
St Paul's Sq. BR2: Broml 2H 159
St Paul's Studios W14 ......5G 99
  (off Talgarth Rd.)
St Pauls Ter. SE17 ......6B 102
St Paul St. N1 ......1C 84
  (not continuous)
St Pauls Vw. Apts. EC1 ......2J 7
  (off Amwell St.)
St Paul's Wlk. KT2: King T 7G 133
St Paul's Way E3 ......5B 86
  N3 ......7E 30
St Paul's Wood Hill BR5: St P 2J 161
St Peter's All. EC3 ......1F 15
  (off Gracechurch St.)
St Peter's Av. E2 ......2G 85
  E17 ......4G 51
  N18 ......4B 34
St Petersburgh M. W2 ......7K 81
St Petersburgh Pl. W2 ......7K 81
St Peter's Cen. E1 ......1H 103
  (off Reardon St.)
St Peter's Chu. Ct. N1 ......1B 84
  (off St Peter's St.)
St Peter's Cl. BR7: Chst 7H 143
  E2 ......2G 85
  HA4: Ruis 2B 58
  IG2: Ilf 4J 53
  SW17 ......2C 136
St Peters Cl. TW4: Houn 5E 44
  WC1 ......2F 7
  (off Seaford St.)
St Peters Cl. E1 ......4J 85
  (off Cephas St.)
  KT8: W Mole 4E 148
  SE12 ......5H 123
St Peter's Gdns. SE27 ......3A 138
St Peter's Gro. W6 ......4C 98
St Peters Ho. WC1 ......2F 7
  (off Regent Sq.)
St Peters Ho. SE17 ......6D 102
St Peters M. N4 ......5B 48
  N8 ......5A 48
St Peter's Path E17 ......3G 51
St Peters Pl. W9 ......4K 81
St Peter's Rd. CR0: C'don 4D 168
  KT1: King T 2G 151
  KT8: W Mole 4E 148
  N9 ......1C 34
  TW1: Twick 5B 114
  UB1: S'hall 5E 76
  W6 ......5C 98
St Peters Rd. UB8: Cowl 5A 74
St Peter's Sq. E2 ......2G 85
  W6 ......4B 98
St Peter's St. CR2: S Croy 5D 168
  N1 ......1B 84
St Peter's St. M. N1 ......2B 84
  (off St Peters St.)
St Peter's Ter. SW6 ......7H 99
St Peter's Vs. W6 ......4C 98
St Peter's Way N1 ......7E 66
  W5 ......5D 78
St Peters Way UB3: Harl 5F 93
St Peter's Wharf W4 ......5C 98
St Philip Ho. WC1 ......2J 7
  (off Lloyd Baker St.)
St Philip Sq. SW8 ......2F 119
St Philip's Ga. KT4: Wor Pk 2D 164
St Philip's Rd. E8 ......6G 67
St Philips Rd. KT6: Surb 6D 150
St Philip's Way N1 ......1C 84
St Quentin Ho. SW18 ......6B 118
St Quentin Rd. DA16: Well 3K 125
St Quintin Av. W10 ......5E 80
St Quintin Gdns. W10 ......5E 80
St Quintin Ho. W10 ......5F 81
  (off Princess Louise Wlk.)

St Quintin Rd. E13 ......3K 87
St Quintin Vw. W10 ......5E 80
St Raphael's Way NW10 ......5J 61
St Regis Cl. N10 ......2F 47
St Regis Hgts. NW3 ......3K 63
St Richard's Ho. NW1 ......1C 6
  (off Eversholt St.)
St Ronan's Cl. EN4: Had W 1G 21
St Ronan's Cres. IG8: Wfd G 7D 36
St Rule St. SW8 ......2G 119
St Saviours Ct. HA1: Harr 5J 41
  N22 ......2H 47
St Saviour's Est. SE1 ......7J 15 (2F 103)
St Saviour's Rd. CR0: C'don 6B 156
  SW2 ......5K 119
St Saviour's Wharf SE1 ......6K 15
  (off Mill St.)
  SE1 ......6K 15
  (off Shad Thames)
Saints Cl. SE27 ......4B 138
Saints Dr. E7 ......5B 70
St Silas Pl. NW5 ......6E 64
St Simon's Av. SW15 ......5E 116
Saints M. CR4: Mitc 3C 154
St Stephen's Av. E17 ......5E 50
  W12 ......1D 98
  (not continuous)
  W13 ......6B 78
St Stephen's Cl. E17 ......5D 50
  NW8 ......1C 82
  UB1: S'hall 5E 76
St Stephens Cl. NW5 ......5D 64
  (off Malden Rd.)
St Stephen's Cl. EN1: Enf 6K 23
  (off Park Av.)
St Stephens Cl. N8 ......6K 47
  W13 ......6B 78
St Stephens Cres. CR7: Thor H 3A 156
  W2 ......6J 81
St Stephen's Gdns. SW15 ......5H 117
  TW1: Twick 6C 114
  W2 ......6J 81
  (not continuous)
St Stephens Gro. SE13 ......3E 122
St Stephens Ho. SE17 ......6D 102
  (off Lytham St.)
St Stephen's M. W2 ......5J 81
St Stephens Pde. E7 ......7A 70
St Stephen's Pas. TW1: Twick 6C 114
St Stephen's Rd. E3 ......1A 86
  E6 ......7A 70
  E17 ......5D 50
  EN5: Barn 5B 20
  TW3: Houn 6E 112
  UB7: Yiew 1A 92
  W13 ......6B 78
St Stephen's Row EC4 ......1E 14
St Stephen's Ter. SW8 ......7H 101
St Stephen's Wlk. SW7 ......4A 100
  (off Southwell Gdns.)
St Swithins La. EC4 ......2E 14 (7D 84)
St Swithun's Rd. SE13 ......6F 123
St Theresa's Cl. E9 ......4C 68
St Theresa's Rd. TW14: Felt 4H 111
St Thomas Cl. K16: Surb 1F 163
St Thomas Cl. DA5: Bexl 7G 127
  E10 ......7D 50
  (off Lake Rd.)
  HA5: Pinn 1C 40
  NW1 ......7G 65
  (off Wrotham Rd.)
St Thomas Dr. BR5: Farnb 1G 173
St Thomas' Dr. HA5: Pinn 1C 40
St Thomas Gdns. IG1: Ilf 6G 71
St Thomas Ho. E1 ......6K 85
  (off W. Arbour St.)
St Thomas M. SW18 ......5J 117
St Thomas Rd. DA17: Belv 2J 109
  E16 ......6J 87
  N14 ......7C 22
  W4 ......6J 97
St Thomas's Gdns. NW5 ......6E 64
St Thomas's M. SE7 ......4C 106

St Thomas's Pl. E9 ....7J 67
St Thomas's Rd. N4 ....2A 66
  NW10 ....1A 80
St Thomas's Sq. E9 ....7J 67
St Thomas St. SE1 ....5F 15 (1D 102)
St Thomas's Way SW6 ....7H 99
St Timothys M. BR1: Broml 1K 159
St Ursula Gro. HA5: Pinn 5B 40
St Ursula Rd. UB1: S'hall 6E 76
St Valery Pl. TW5: Hest 7B 94
St Vincent Cl. SE27 ....5B 138
St Vincent De Paul Ho. E1 ....5J 85
  (off Jubilee St.)
St Vincent Ho. SE1 ....3F 103
  (off St Saviour's Est.)
St Vincent Rd. TW2: Whitt 6G 113
St Vincent's La. NW7 ....4K 29
St Vincent St. W1 ....6H 5 (5E 82)
St Wilfrid's Cl. EN4: E Barn 5H 21
St Wilfrid's Rd. EN4: E Barn 5G 21
St Williams Ct. N1 ....7J 65
St Winefride's Av. E12 ....5D 70
St Winifred's Rd. TW11: Tedd 6B 132
Sakura Dr. N22 ....1H 47
Salamanca Pl. IG11: Bark 2B 90
  SE1 ....4G 19 (4K 101)
Salamanca Sq. SE1 ....4G 19
  (off Salamanca Pl.)
Salamanca St. SE1 ....4G 19 (4K 101)
  SE11 ....4G 19 (4K 101)
Salamander Cl. KT2: King T 5C 132
Salamander Quay
  KT1: Hamp W 1D 150
Salcombe Ct. E14 ....5E 86
  (off St Ives Pl.)
Salcombe Dr. RM6: Chad H 6F 55
  SM4: Mord 1F 165
Salcombe Gdns. NW7 ....6K 29
Salcombe Rd. E17 ....7B 50
  N16 ....5E 66
  TW15: Ashf 3A 128
Salcombe Vs. TW10: Rich 5E 114
Salcombe Way HA4: Ruis 2J 57
  UB4: Hayes 3F 75
Salcroft Rd. CRO: Bedd 3J 167
  SW11 ....5C 118
Salehurst Cl. HA3: Kenton 5E 42
Salehurst Rd. SE4 ....6B 122
Salem Pl. CRO: C'don 3C 168
Salem Rd. W2 ....7K 81
Salento Cl. N3 ....7D 30
Sale Pl. W2 ....6C 4 (5C 82)
Sale St. E2 ....4G 85
Salford Ho. E14 ....4E 104
  (off Seyssel St.)
Salford Rd. SW2 ....1H 137
Salhouse Cl. SE28 ....6C 90
Salisbury Av. IG11: Bark 7H 71
  N3 ....3H 45
  SM1: Sutt 6H 165
Salisbury Cl. KT4: Wor Pk 3B 164
  SE17 ....4D 102
Salisbury Ct. E9 ....5A 68
  (off Mabley St.)
  EC4 ....1A 14 (6B 84)
  EN2: Enf 4J 23
  (off London Rd.)
  SE16 ....3G 103
  (off Stork's Rd.)
  SM5: Cars 5D 166
  UB5: N'olt 5F 59
  (off Newmarket Av.)
Salisbury Gdns. IG9: Buck H 2G 37
  SW19 ....7G 135
Salisbury Hall Gdns. E4 ....6H 35
Salisbury Ho. E14 ....6D 86
  (off Hobday St.)
  EC2 ....6F 9
  (off London Wall)
  HA7: Stan 6F 27
  N1 ....1B 84
  (off St Mary's Path)
  SM6: W'gton 5F 167

Salisbury Ho. SW1 ....5D 18
  (off Drummond Ga.)
  SW9 ....7A 102
  (off Cranmer Rd.)
Salisbury Mans. N15 ....5B 48
Salisbury M. SW6 ....7H 99
Salisbury Pas. SW6 ....7H 99
  (off Dawes Rd.)
Salisbury Pavement SW6 ....7H 99
  (off Dawes Rd.)
Salisbury Pl. SW9 ....7B 102
  W1 ....5E 4 (5D 82)
Salisbury Prom. N8 ....5B 48
Salisbury Rd. BR2: Broml 5C 160
  DA5: Bexl 1G 145
  E4 ....3H 35
  E7 ....6J 69
  E10 ....2E 68
  E12 ....5B 70
  E17 ....5E 50
  EN5: Barn 3B 20
  HA1: Harr 5H 41
  HA5: Eastc 4J 39
  IG3: Ilf 2J 71
  KT3: N Mald 3K 151
  KT4: Wor Pk 4K 163
  N4 ....5B 48
  N22 ....1B 48
  RM10: Dag 6H 73
  SE25 ....6G 157
  SM5: Cars 6D 166
  SW19 ....7G 135
  TW4: Houn 3A 112
  TW6: H'row A 6E 110
  (not continuous)
  TW9: Rich 4E 114
  TW13: Felt 1A 130
  UB2: S'hall 4C 94
  W13 ....2B 96
Salisbury Sq. EC4 ....1K 13 (6A 84)
Salisbury St. NW8 ....4C 4 (4C 82)
  W3 ....2J 97
Salisbury Ter. SE15 ....3J 121
Salisbury Wlk. N19 ....2G 65
Salix Cl. TW16: Sun 7K 129
Salix Ct. N3 ....6D 30
Salix La. IG8: Wfd G 1C 52
Salk Cl. NW9 ....2A 44
Salliesfield TW2: Whitt 6H 113
Sally Murray Cl. E12 ....4E 70
Salmen Rd. E13 ....2H 87
Salmond Cl. HA7: Stan 6F 27
Salmon La. E14 ....6A 86
Salmon M. NW6 ....5J 63
Salmon Rd. DA17: Belv 5G 109
Salmons Rd. KT9: Chess 6E 162
  N9 ....1B 34
Salmon St. E14 ....6B 86
  NW9 ....1H 61
Salomons Rd. E13 ....5A 88
Salop Rd. E17 ....6K 49
Salsabil Apts. E3 ....4B 86
Saltash Cl. SM1: Sutt 4H 165
Saltash Rd. DA16: Well 1C 126
  IG6: Ilf 1H 53
Saltcoats Rd. W4 ....2A 98
Saltcroft Cl. HA9: Wemb 1H 61
Saltdene N4 ....1K 65
Salter Cl. HA2: Harr 4D 58
Salterford Rd. SW17 ....6E 136
Saltern Ct. IG11: Bark 3B 90
  (off Galleons Dr.)
Salter Rd. SE16 ....1K 103
Salters Ct. EC4 ....1D 14
Salter's Hall Ct. EC4 ....2E 14
Salter's Hill SE19 ....5D 138
Salters Rd. E17 ....4F 51
  W10 ....4F 81
Salters Row N1 ....6D 66
  (off Tilney Gdns.)
Salter St. E14 ....7B 86
  (not continuous)
  NW10 ....3C 80

Salterton Rd. N7 ....3K 65
Salt Hill Cl. UB8: Uxb 5A 56
Salting St. IG11: Bark 1H 89
Saltley Cl. E6 ....6C 88
Salton Cl. N3 ....2J 45
Salton Sq. E14 ....6B 86
Saltoun Rd. SW2 ....4A 120
Saltram Cl. N15 ....4F 49
Saltram Cres. W9 ....3H 81
Saltwell St. E14 ....7C 86
Saltwood Gro. SE17 ....5D 102
Saltwood Ho. SE15 ....6J 103
  (off Lovelinch Cl.)
Salusbury Rd. NW6 ....1G 81
Salus Ct. CRO: C'don 4C 168
  (off Parker Rd.)
Salutation Rd. SE10 ....4G 105
Salvador SW17 ....5D 136
Salvia Gdns. UB6: G'frd 2A 78
Salvin Rd. SW15 ....3F 117
Salway Cl. IG8: Wfd G 7D 36
Salway Pl. E15 ....6F 69
Salway Rd. E15 ....6F 69
Samantha Cl. E17 ....7B 50
Samaras Mans. E20 ....5E 68
  (off Liberty Bri. Rd.)
Sam Bartram Cl. SE7 ....5A 106
The Sambourne Family Home 3J 99
  (off Stafford Ter.)
Sambroke Sq. EN4: E Barn 4G 21
Sambrooke Ct. EN1: Enf 6K 23
Sambrook Ho. E1 ....5J 85
  (off Jubilee St.)
Sambrook M. SE6 ....1D 140
Samels Cl. W6 ....5C 98
Samford Ho. N1 ....1A 84
  (off Barnsbury Est.)
Samford St. NW8 ....4C 4 (4B 82)
Samira Cl. E17 ....6C 50
Sam King Wlk. SE5 ....7D 102
  (off Edmund St.)
Sammi Cl. CR7: Thor H 4C 156
Samos Rd. SE20 ....2H 157
Samphire Hgts. E20 ....5E 68
  (off Napa Cl.)
Sampson Av. EN5: Barn 5A 20
Sampson Cl. DA17: Belv 3D 108
Sampson Ct. TW17: Shep 5E 146
Sampson Ho. SE1 ....4A 14 (1B 102)
Sampson St. E1 ....1G 103
Samson St. E13 ....2A 88
Samuda Est. E14 ....3E 104
Samuel Cl. E8 ....1F 85
  HA7: Stan 2F 27
  SE14 ....6K 103
  SE18 ....4C 106
Samuel Ct. N1 ....2G 9
  (off Pitfield St.)
Samuel Ferguson Pl. IG11: Bark 2K 89
Samuel Gray Gdns.
  KT2: King T 1D 150
Samuel Johnson Cl. SW16 ....4K 137
Samuel Jones Ct. SE15 ....7E 102
Samuel Lewis Bldgs. N1 ....6A 66
Samuel Lewis Trust Dwellings E8 ....5G 67
  (off Amhurst Rd.)
  N16 ....6E 48
  SW3 ....4C 16 (4C 100)
  SW6 ....7J 99
  (off Vanston Pl.)
  W14 ....1H 99
  (off Lisgar Ter.)
Samuel Lewis Trust Est. SE5 ....1C 120
  (off Warner Rd.)
Samuel Richardson Ho. W14 ....4H 99
  (off North End Cres.)
Samuel's Cl. W6 ....4E 98
Samuelson Pl. TW7: Isle 2J 113

Samuel St. E8 ....1F 85
  SE15 ....7F 103
  SE14 ....4D 106
Samuel Wallis Lodge SE3 ....3H 123
  (off Banning St.)
  SE10 ....4G 105
  (off Banning St.)
Sanchia Ct. E2 ....3G 85
  (off Wellington Row)
Sancroft Cl. NW2 ....3D 62
Sancroft Ho. SE11 ....5H 19
Sancroft Rd. HA3: W'stone 2K 41
Sancroft St. SE11 ....5H 19 (5K 101)
The Sanctuary DA5: Bexl 6D 126
  SM4: Mord 6J 153
  SW1 ....1D 18
Sanctuary M. E8 ....6F 67
Sanctuary Rd. TW6: H'row A 6C 110
Sanctuary St. SE1 ....6D 14 (2C 102)
Sandale Cl. N16 ....3D 66
Sandall Cl. W5 ....4E 78
Sandall Ho. E3 ....2A 86
Sandall Rd. NW5 ....6G 65
  W5 ....4E 78
Sandal Rd. KT3: N Mald 5K 151
  N18 ....5B 34
Sandal St. E15 ....1G 87
Sandalwood Cl. E1 ....4A 86
Sandalwood Dr. HA4: Ruis 7E 38
Sandalwood Ho. DA15: Sidc 2K 143
Sandalwood Mans. W8 ....3K 99
  (off Stone Hall Gdns.)
Sandalwood Rd. TW13: Felt 3K 129
Sandbach Pl. SE18 ....4G 107
Sandbanks TW14: Felt 1G 129
Sandbourne NW8 ....1K 81
  (off Abbey Rd.)
  W11 ....6J 81
  (off Dartmouth Cl.)
Sandbourne Av. SW19 ....2K 153
Sandbourne Rd. SE4 ....2A 122
Sandbrook Cl. NW7 ....6E 28
Sandbrook Rd. N16 ....3E 66
Sandby Ct. NW10 ....3D 80
  (off Plough Cl.)
Sandby Grn. SE9 ....3C 124
Sandby Ho. NW6 ....1J 81
Sandcliff Rd. DA8: Erith 4K 109
Sandcroft Cl. N13 ....6G 33
Sandell's Av. TW15: Ashf 4E 128
Sandell St. SE1 ....6J 13 (2A 102)
Sanderling Cl. SE8 ....6B 104
  (off Abinger Gro.)
  SE28 ....7C 90
Sanderling Lodge E1 ....3K 15
  (off Star Pl.)
Sanders Cl. TW12: Hamp H 5G 131
Sanders Ho. WC1 ....1J 7
  (off Gt. Percy St.)
Sanders La. NW7 ....7K 29
  (Bittacy Ri.)
  NW7 ....7A 30
  (Grants Cl.)
  TW4: Houn 5D 112
Sanderson Bldg. NW2 ....2E 62
Sanderson Cl. NW5 ....4F 65
Sanderson Ho. E16 ....5J 87
  (off Hammersley Rd.)
  SE8 ....5B 104
  (off Grove St.)
Sandersons La. W4 ....5K 97
  (off Chiswick High Rd.)
Sanderson Sq. BR1: Broml 3E 160
Sanderstead Av. NW2 ....2G 63
Sanderstead Cl. SW12 ....7G 119
Sanderstead Rd.
  CR2: Sande, S Croy 7D 168
  E10 ....1A 68
Sanders Way N19 ....1H 65
Sandes Ct. CR7: Thor H 3C 156
Sandfield WC1 ....2F 7
  (off Cromer St.)
Sandfield Gdns. CR7: Thor H 3B 156

Sandfield Pas. CR7: Thor H 3C **156**
Sandfield Pl. CR7: Thor H 3C **156**
Sandfield Rd. CR7: Thor H 3B **156**
Sandford Av. N22 . . . . .1C **48**
Sandford Cl. E6 . . . . .4D **88**
Sandford Rd. EN5: New Bar 3E **20**
   N16 . . . . .1E **66**
Sandridge Rd. BR2: Broml 3J **159**
   DA7: Bex 4E **126**
   E6 .3C **88**
Sandford St. SW6 . . . . .7K **99**
Sandgate Cl. RM7: Rush G 7J **55**
Sandgate Ho. E5 . . . . .5H **67**
   W5 .5C **78**
Sandgate La. SW18 . . . . .1C **136**
Sandgate Rd. DA16: Well 7C **108**
Sandgate St. SE15 . . . . .6H **103**
Sandgate Trad. Est. SE15 . . . . .6H **103**
   (off Sandgate St.)
Sandham Cl. SW4 . . . . .1J **119**
Sandham Point SE18 . . . . .4F **107**
   (off Vincent Rd.)
Sandhills SM6: Bedd 4H **167**
The Sandhills SW10 . . . . .7A **16**
   (off Limerston St.)
Sandhills Mdw. TW17: Shep 7E **146**
Sandhurst Av. HA2: Harr 6F **41**
   KT5: Surb 7H **151**
Sandhurst Cl. CR2: Sande 7E **168**
   NW9 . . . . .3G **43**
Sandhurst Ct. SW2 . . . . .4J **119**
Sandhurst Dr. IG3: Bark, Ilf 4K **71**
Sandhurst Ho. E1 . . . . .5J **85**
   (off Wolsy St.)
   E17 . . . . .1B **50**
   (off Robinswood Gdns.)
Sandhurst Mkt. SE6 . . . . .1E **140**
   (off Sandhurst Rd.)
Sandhurst Rd. BR6: Chels 3K **173**
   DA5: Bexl 5D **126**
   DA15: Sidc 3K **143**
   N9 .6D **24**
   NW9 . . . . .3G **43**
   SE6 . . . . .1F **141**
Sandhurst Way CR2: Sande 7E **168**
Sandifer Dr. NW2 . . . . .3F **63**
Sandiford Rd. SM3: Sutt 2H **165**
Sandiland Cres. BR2: Hayes 2H **171**
Sandilands CRO: C'don 2G **169**
Sandilands Rd. SW6 . . . . .1K **117**
Sandison St. SE15 . . . . .3G **121**
Sandland St. WC1 . . . . . .6H **7** (5K **83**)
Sandling Ri. SE9 . . . . .3E **142**
The Sandlings N22 . . . . .2A **48**
Sandlings Cl. SE15 . . . . .2H **121**
Sandmartin Way SM6: W'gton . . .1E **166**
Sandmere Rd. SW4 . . . . .4J **119**
Sandon Cl. KT10: Esh 7H **149**
Sandover Ho. SE16 . . . . .3G **103**
   (off Spa Rd.)
Sandow Cres. UB3: Hayes 3H **93**
Sandown Av. RM10: Dag 6J **73**
Sandown Cl. TW5: Cran 1J **111**
Sandown Ct. HA7: Stan 5H **27**
   RM10: Dag 6J **73**
   (off Sandown Av.)
   SE26 . . . . .3H **139**
   SM2: Sutt 7K **165**
Sandown Dr. SM5: Cars 7E **166**
Sandown Rd. SE25 . . . . .5H **157**
Sandown Way UB5: N'olt 6C **58**
Sandpiper Cl. E17 . . . . .7E **34**
   SE16 . . . . .2B **104**
Sandpiper Ct. E1 . . . . .7G **85**
   (off Thomas More St.)
   E14 . . . . .3E **104**
   (off New Union Cl.)
   SE8 . . . . .2J **103**
   (off Edward Pl.)
Sandpiper Dr. HA2: Harr 2F **59**
Sandpiper Rd. SM1: Sutt 5H **165**
Sandpiper Ter. IG5: Ilf 3F **53**
Sandpit Pl. SE7 . . . . .5C **106**

Sandpit Rd. BR1: Broml 5G **141**
Sandpits Rd. CRO: C'don 4K **169**
   TW10: Ham 2D **132**
Sandra Cl. N22 . . . . .1C **48**
   TW3: Houn 5F **113**
Sandra Ct. CR4: Mitc 6D **136**
Sandridge Cl. HA1: Harr 4J **41**
Sandridge St. N19 . . . . .2G **65**
Sandringham Av. SW20 . . . . . . .1G **153**
Sandringham Bldgs. SE17 . . . . .4D **102**
   (off Balfour St.)
Sandringham Cl. EN1: Enf 2K **23**
   IG6: Ilf 3G **53**
   SW19 . . . . .1F **135**
Sandringham Ct. DA15: Sidc 6K **125**
   KT2: King T 1E **150**
   (off Skerne Wlk.)
   SE16 . . . . .1K **103**
   (off King & Queen Wharf)
   UB10: Hil 4E **74**
   W1 .1B **12**
   (off Dufour's Pl.)
   W9 .3A **82**
   (off Maida Vale)
Sandringham Cres. HA2: Harr . . .2E **58**
Sandringham Dr. DA2: Wilm 2K **145**
   DA16: Well 2J **125**
   TW15: Ashf 4A **128**
Sandringham Flats WC2 . . . . . . .2D **12**
   (off Charing Cross Rd.)
Sandringham Gdns. IG6: Ilf 3G **53**
   KT8: W Mole 4E **148**
   N8 .6J **47**
   N12 . . . . .6G **31**
   TW5: Cran 1J **111**
Sandringham Ho. SE1 . . . . .1E **102**
   (off Potters Flds.)
   W14 . . . . .4G **99**
   (off Windsor Way)
Sandringham M. TW12: Hamp . . .1D **148**
Sandringham Rd.
   BR1: Broml 5J **141**
   CR7: Thor H 5C **156**
   E7 .5A **70**
   E8 .5F **67**
   E10 . . . . .6F **51**
   IG11: Bark 5K **71**
   KT4: Wor Pk 3C **164**
   N22 . . . . .3C **48**
   NW2 . . . . .6D **62**
   NW11 . . . . .7G **45**
   TW6: H'row A 5A **110**
   UB5: N'olt 7E **58**
Sandrock Pl. CRO: C'don 4K **169**
Sandrock Rd. SE13 . . . . .3C **122**
SANDS END 1A **118**
Sand's End La. SW6 . . . . .1K **117**
Sandstone La. E16 . . . . .7K **87**
Sandstone Pl. N19 . . . . .2F **65**
Sandstone Rd. SE12 . . . . .2K **141**
Sands Way IG8: Wfd G 6J **37**
Sandtoft Rd. SE7 . . . . .6K **105**
Sandwell Cres. NW6 . . . . .6J **63**
Sandwich Ho. SE16 . . . . .2J **103**
   (off Swan Rd.)
   WC1 . . . . .2E **6**
   (off Sandwich St.)
Sandwich St. WC1 . . . . . .2E **6** (3J **83**)
Sandwick Cl. NW7 . . . . .7H **29**
Sandy Bury BR6: Orp 3H **173**
Sandycombe Rd.
   TW9: Kew, Rich 3F **115**
   TW14: Felt 1J **129**
Sandycoombe Rd. TW1: Twick . . .6C **114**
Sandycroft SE2 . . . . .6A **108**
Sandy Dr. TW14: Felt 1G **129**
Sandy Hill Av. SE18 . . . . .5F **107**
Sandy Hill Rd. SE18 . . . . .5F **107**
   SM6: W'gton 7G **167**
Sandyhill Rd. IG1: Ilf 4F **71**
Sandy Ho. IG11: Bark 4A **90**

Sandy La. BR5: St P 7D **144**
   BR6: Orp 7K **161**
   CR4: Mitc 1E **154**
   DA14: Sidc 7D **144**
   HA3: Kenton 6F **43**
   KT1: Hamp W 7A **132**
   KT12: Walt T 6K **147**
   SM2: Cheam 7G **165**
   SM6: W'gton 6H **167**
   TW10: Ham 2C **132**
   TW11: Hamp W, Tedd 7A **132**
Sandy La. Nth. SM6: W'gton 6H **167**
Sandy La. Sth. SM6: W'gton 7G **167**
Sandymount Av. HA7: Stan 5H **27**
Sandy Ridge BR7: Chst 6E **142**
Sandy Rd. DA8: Erith 5J **109**
   NW3 . . . . .2K **63**
Sandys Row E1 . . . . .6H **9** (5E **84**)
Sandy Way CRO: C'don 3B **170**
   KT12: Walt T 7H **147**
Sanford La. N16 . . . . .3F **67**
Sanford St. SE14 . . . . .6A **104**
Sanford Ter. N16 . . . . .3F **67**
Sanford Wlk. N16 . . . . .2F **67**
   SE14 . . . . .6A **104**
Sangam Cl. UB2: S'hall 3C **94**
Sanger Av. KT9: Chess 5E **162**
Sangley Rd. SE6 . . . . .7D **122**
   SE25 . . . . .4E **156**
Sangora Rd. SW11 . . . . .4B **118**
Sankey Ho. E2 . . . . .2J **85**
   (off St James's Av.)
Sansom Rd. E11 . . . . .2H **69**
Sansom St. SE5 . . . . .1D **120**
San Wlk. EC1 . . . . .3K **7** (4A **84**)
Santa Maria Ct. E1 . . . . .5A **86**
   (off Ocean Est.)
Santi Ho. SE17 . . . . .4C **102**
   (off Browning St.)
Santiago Ct. E1 . . . . .5A **86**
   (off Ocean Est.)
Santina Apartment CRO: C'don . . .1D **168**
   (off Cherry Orchard Rd.)
Santley Ho. SE1 . . . . . .7K **13** (2A **102**)
Santley St. SW4 . . . . .4K **119**
Santos Rd. SW18 . . . . .5J **117**
The Santway HA7: Stan 5D **26**
Sapcote Trad. Cen. NW10 . . . . .6B **62**
Saperton Wlk. SE11 . . . . .3H **19**
Saphire Ct. E15 . . . . .1E **86**
   (off Warton Rd.)
Saphora Cl. BR6: Farnb 5H **173**
Sapperton Ct. EC1 . . . . .3C **8**
Sapperton Ho. W2 . . . . .5J **81**
   (off Westbourne Pk. Rd.)
Sapphire Cl. E6 . . . . .6E **88**
   RM8: Dag 1C **72**
Sapphire Ct. E1 . . . . .7G **85**
   (off Cable St.)
Sapphire Rd. NW10 . . . . .7J **61**
   SE8 . . . . .4A **104**
Saracen Cl. CRO: C'don 6D **156**
Saracens FC 7K **29**
Saracens Head Yd. EC3 . . . . . . .1J **15**
Saracen St. E14 . . . . .6C **86**
Sarah Ct. UB5: N'olt 1D **76**
Sarah Ho. E1 . . . . .6H **85**
   (off Commercial Rd.)
Sarah Swift Ho. SE1 . . . . .6F **15**
   (off Kipling St.)
Sara La. Ct. N1 . . . . .2E **84**
   (off Stanway St.)
Saratoga Rd. E5 . . . . .4J **67**
Sara Turnbull Ho. SE18 . . . . . . .4D **106**
Saravia Ct. SE13 . . . . .6G **123**
Sardinia St. WC2 . . . . . .1G **13** (6K **83**)
Sarita Cl. HA3: Hrw W 2H **41**
Sarjant Path SW19 . . . . .2F **135**
   (off Blincoe Cl.)
Sarjeant Ct. BR4: W W'ck 2F **171**
   (off Bencurtis Pk.)
Sark Cl. TW5: Hest 7E **94**
Sark Ho. EN3: Enf W 1E **24**

Sark Twr. SE28 . . . . .2G **107**
Sark Wlk. E16 . . . . .6K **87**
Sarnes Ct. N11 . . . . .4A **32**
   (off Oakleigh Rd. Sth.)
Sarnesfield Ho. SE15 . . . . .6H **103**
   (off Pencraig Way)
Sarnesfield Rd. EN2: Enf 4J **23**
Sarratt Ho. W10 . . . . .5E **80**
   (off Sutton Way)
Sarre Rd. NW2 . . . . .5H **63**
Sarsen Av. TW3: Houn 2E **112**
Sarsfield Rd. SW12 . . . . .2D **136**
Sarsfield Rd. UB6: G'frd 2B **78**
Sartor Rd. SE15 . . . . .4K **121**
Sarum Ho. W11 . . . . .7H **81**
   (off Portobello Rd.)
Sarum Ter. E3 . . . . .4B **86**
Saskia M. SE15 . . . . .2H **121**
Sassoon NW9 . . . . .1B **44**
Satanita Cl. E16 . . . . .6B **88**
Satchell Mead NW9 . . . . .1B **44**
Satchwell Rd. E2 . . . . . . .2K **9** (3G **85**)
Satchwell St. E2 . . . . . . .2K **9** (3G **85**)
Satin Ho. E1 . . . . .1K **15**
Sattar M. N16 . . . . .3D **66**
Saturn Ho. E3 . . . . .1C **86**
   (off Garrison Rd.)
   E15 . . . . .1F **87**
   (off High St.)
Sauls Grn. E11 . . . . .3G **69**
Saundby Ho. SE3 . . . . .4K **123**
Saunders Apts. E3 . . . . .3C **86**
   (off Marchant St.)
Saunders Cl. E14 . . . . .7B **86**
   (off Limehouse C'way.)
   IG1: Ilf 1H **71**
Saunders Ho. SE16 . . . . .2K **103**
   (off Quebec Way)
Saunders Ness Rd. E14 . . . . . . .5E **104**
Saunders Rd. SE18 . . . . .5K **107**
   UB10: Uxb 7B **56**
Saunders St. SE11 . . . . .3J **19** (4A **102**)
Saunders Way SE28 . . . . .7B **90**
   HA2: Wemb 5B **60**
Saunton Av. UB3: Harl 7H **93**
Saunton Ct. UB1: S'hall 7G **77**
   (off Haldane Rd.)
Savage Gdns. E6 . . . . .6D **88**
   EC3 . . . . .2H **15** (7E **84**)
   (not continuous)
Savannah Cl. SE15 . . . . .7F **103**
Savera Cl. UB2: S'hall 3A **94**
Savernake Ct. HA7: Stan 6G **27**
Savernake Ho. N4 . . . . .7C **48**
Savernake Rd. N9 . . . . .6B **24**
   NW3 . . . . .4D **64**
Savery Dr. KT6: Surb 7B **150**
Savile Cl. KT3: N Mald 5A **152**
   KT7: T Ditt 7K **149**
Savile Gdns. CRO: C'don 2F **169**
Savile Row W1 . . . . .2A **12** (7G **83**)
Saville Cres. TW15: Ashf 6F **129**
Saville Rd. E16 . . . . .1C **106**
   RM6: Chad H 6F **55**
   TW1: Twick 1K **131**
   W4 .3K **97**
Saville Row BR2: Hayes 1H **171**
   EN3: Enf H 2E **24**
Savill Gdns. SW20 . . . . .3C **152**
Savill Ho. E16 . . . . .1F **107**
   (off Robert St.)
   SW4 . . . . .6H **119**
Savill Row IG8: Wfd G 6C **36**
Savin Lodge SM2: Sutt 7A **166**
   (off Walnut M.)
Savona Cl. SW19 . . . . .7F **135**
Savona Ho. SW8 . . . . .7G **101**
   (off Savona St.)
Savona St. SW8 . . . . .7G **101**
Savoy Av. UB3: Harl 5G **93**
Savoy Bldgs. WC2 . . . . .3G **13**
Savoy Chapel 3G **13**
SAVOY CIRCUS 7B **80**

Savoy Cl. E15 . . . . 1G 87
  HA8: Edg . . . 5B 28
Savoy Ct. HA2: Harr . . . 5F 41
  NW3 . . . 3A 64
  SW5 . . . 4J 99
    (off Cromwell Rd.)
  WC2 . . . 3F 13 (7K 83)
Savoy Hill WC2 . . . 3G 13 (7K 83)
Savoy M. SW9 . . . 3J 119
Savoy Pde. EN1: Enf . . . 3K 23
Savoy Pl. W12 . . . 1F 99
  WC2 . . . 3F 13 (7J 83)
Savoy Row WC2 . . . 2G 13
Savoy St. WC2 . . . 3G 13 (7K 83)
Savoy Steps WC2 . . . 3G 13
Savoy Theatre . . . 3F 13
    (off Strand)
Savoy Way WC2 . . . 3G 13
Sawbill Cl. UB4: Yead . . . 5B 76
Sawkins Cl. SW19 . . . 2G 135
Sawley Rd. W12 . . . 1C 98
Saw Mill Way N16 . . . 6G 49
Sawmill Yd. E3 . . . 1A 86
Sawtry Cl. SM5: Cars . . . 7C 154
Sawyer Cl. N9 . . . 2B 34
Sawyer Ct. NW10 . . . 7K 61
Sawyers Apartments SW11 . . . 4C 118
    (off Danvers Avenue)
Sawyers Cl. RM10: Dag . . . 6J 73
Sawyer's Hill TW10: Rich . . . 7F 115
Sawyers Lawn W13 . . . 6A 78
Sawyer St. SE1 . . . 6C 14 (2C 102)
Saxby Rd. SW2 . . . 7J 119
Saxham Rd. IG11: Bark . . . 2J 89
Saxlingham Rd. E4 . . . 3A 36
Saxon Av. TW13: Hanw . . . 2C 130
Saxonbury Av. TW10: Sun . . . 3K 147
Saxonbury Cl. CR4: Mitc . . . 3B 154
Saxonbury Ct. N7 . . . 5J 65
Saxonbury Gdns. KT6: Surb . . . 1C 162
Saxon Bus. Cen. SW19 . . . 2A 154
Saxon Chase N8 . . . 6K 47
Saxon Cl. E17 . . . 7C 50
  KT6: Surb . . . 6D 150
  UB8: Hil . . . 5B 74
Saxon Ct. N1 . . . 1J 83
Saxon Dr. W3 . . . 6G 79
Saxonfield Cl. SW2 . . . 7K 119
Saxon Gdns. UB1: S'hall . . . 7C 76
Saxon Hall W2 . . . 7K 81
    (off Palace Ct.)
Saxon Ho. E1 . . . 6K 9
    (off Thrawl St.)
  KT1: King T . . . 4F 151
  SM6: W'gton . . . 1E 166
    (off London Rd.)
  TW13: Hanw . . . 2D 130
Saxon Lea Ct. E3 . . . 2A 86
    (off Saxon Rd.)
Saxon Lodge CR0: C'don . . . 1C 168
    (off Tavistock Rd.)
Saxon Rd. BR1: Broml . . . 7H 141
  E3 . . . 2B 86
  E6 . . . 4D 88
  HA9: Wemb . . . 3J 61
  IG1: Ilf . . . 6F 71
  KT2: King T . . . 1E 150
  N22 . . . 1B 48
  SE25 . . . 5D 156
  TW15: Ashf . . . 6F 129
  UB1: S'hall . . . 7C 76
Saxon Ter. SE6 . . . 2B 140
Saxon Wlk. DA14: Sidc . . . 6C 144
Saxon Way N14 . . . 6C 22
  UB7: Harm . . . 2D 174
Saxon Way Ind. Est. UB7: Harm . . . 2D 174
Saxony Pde. UB3: Hayes . . . 5E 74
Saxton Cl. SE13 . . . 3F 123
Saxton Pl. KT8: W Mole . . . 4D 148
Sayers Ct. W5 . . . 2D 96
Sayers Ho. N2 . . . 2B 46
    (off The Grange)
Sayer St. SE17 . . . 4C 102

Sayer's Wlk. TW10: Rich . . . 7F 115
Sayesbury La. N18 . . . 5B 34
Sayes Cl. SE8 . . . 6B 104
Sayes Ct. St. SE8 . . . 6B 104
Scadbury Pk. . . . 7K 143
Scads Hill Cl. BR6: Pet W . . . 6K 161
Scafell NW1 . . . 1A 6
    (off Stanhope St.)
Scala . . . 1F 7
Scala St. W1 . . . 5B 6 (5G 83)
Scales Rd. N17 . . . 3F 49
The Scalpel . . . 1G 15
Scampston M. W10 . . . 6F 81
Scandrett St. E1 . . . 1H 103
Scarab Cl. E16 . . . 7H 87
Scarba Wlk. N1 . . . 6D 66
    (off Essex Rd.)
Scarborough Rd. E11 . . . 1F 69
  N4 . . . 7A 48
  N9 . . . 7D 24
  TW6: H'row A . . . 6E 110
Scarborough St. E1 . . . 1K 15 (6F 85)
Scarbrook Rd. CR0: C'don . . . 3C 168
Scarle Rd. HA0: Wemb . . . 6D 60
Scarlet Cl. E20 . . . 5D 68
Scarlet Rd. SE6 . . . 3G 141
Scarlette Mnr. Way SW2 . . . 7A 120
Scarlet Wlk. EN3: Pond E . . . 5E 24
Scarsbrook Rd. SE3 . . . 3B 124
Scarsdale Pl. W8 . . . 3K 99
Scarsdale Rd. HA2: Harr . . . 3G 59
Scarsdale Studios W8 . . . 3J 99
    (off Stratford Rd.)
Scarsdale Vs. W8 . . . 3J 99
Scarth Rd. SW13 . . . 3B 116
Scawen Cl. SM5: Cars . . . 4E 166
Scawen Rd. SE8 . . . 5A 104
Scawfell St. E2 . . . 2F 85
Scaynes Link N12 . . . 4D 30
Sceaux Gdns. SE5 . . . 1E 120
Scena Way SE5 . . . 7C 102
Sceptre Ct. EC3 . . . 3K 15
    (off Tower Hill)
Sceptre Ho. E1 . . . 4J 85
    (off Malcolm Rd.)
Sceptre Rd. E2 . . . 3J 85
Schafer Ho. NW1 . . . 2A 6 (3G 83)
Schofield Wlk. SE3 . . . 7J 105
Scholars Cl. EN5: Barn . . . 4B 20
Scholars Ho. NW6 . . . 1J 81
    (off Glengall Rd.)
Scholars Pl. N16 . . . 3E 66
Scholars Rd. E4 . . . 1A 36
  SW12 . . . 1G 137
Scholars Vw. KT7: T Ditt . . . 7J 149
Scholars Way RM8: Dag . . . 4A 72
Scholefield Rd. N19 . . . 2H 65
Scholey Ho. SW11 . . . 3C 118
Schomberg Ho. SW1 . . . 3D 18
    (off Page St.)
Schonfeld Sq. N16 . . . 2D 66
School All. TW1: Twick . . . 1A 132
School App. E2 . . . 1H 9
  UB4: Hayes . . . 4H 75
Schoolbank Rd. SE10 . . . 3H 105
Schoolbell M. E3 . . . 2A 86
Schoolgate Dr. SM4: Mord . . . 5K 153
School Ho. SE1 . . . 4E 102
    (off Page's Wlk.)
School Ho. La. NW7 . . . 6B 30
  TW11: Tedd . . . 7B 132
Schoolhouse La. E1 . . . 7K 85
Schoolhouse Yd. SE18 . . . 5F 107
School La. DA16: Well . . . 3B 126
  HA5: Pinn . . . 4C 40
  KT1: Hamp W . . . 1C 150
  KT6: Surb . . . 1F 163
  SE23 . . . 2H 139
  TW17: Shep . . . 6D 146
  WD23: Bush . . . 1A 26
School M. E1 . . . 7H 85
    (off Hawksmoor M.)
School Nook E5 . . . 2K 67

School of Oriental & African Studies
  Vernon Sq. Campus . . . 1H 7 (3K 83)
The School of Pharmacy . . . 3F 7
School Pas. KT1: King T . . . 2F 151
  UB1: S'hall . . . 7D 76
School Rd. BR7: Chst . . . 1G 161
  E12 . . . 4D 70
  KT1: Hamp W . . . 1C 150
  KT8: E Mos . . . 4H 149
  NW10 . . . 4A 79
  RM10: Dag . . . 1G 91
  TW3: Houn . . . 3G 113
  TW12: Hamp H . . . 6G 131
  TW15: Ashf . . . 6D 128
  UB7: Harm . . . 2E 174
School Rd. Av. TW12: Hamp H . . . 6G 131
SCHOOL ROAD JUNC. . . . 7D 128
School Sq. SE10 . . . 3H 105
School Wlk. TW16: Sun . . . 4H 147
School Way N12 . . . 6G 31
  RM8: Dag . . . 3C 72
Schooner Cl. E14 . . . 3F 105
  IG11: Bark . . . 3B 90
  SE16 . . . 2K 103
Schooner Rd. E16 . . . 2K 105
Schubert Rd. SW15 . . . 5H 117
Schurlock Pl. TW2: Twick . . . 2J 131
Schwartz Wharf E9 . . . 7C 68
Science Mus. . . . 2B 16 (3B 100)
Sclater St. E1 . . . 3J 9 (4F 85)
Scoble Pl. N16 . . . 4F 67
Scoles Cres. SW2 . . . 1B 138
The Scoop . . . 5H 15 (1E 102)
Scope Way KT1: King T . . . 4E 150
The Score Complex
  Leyton . . . 3D 68
Scoresby St. SE1 . . . 5A 14 (1B 102)
Scorton Av. UB6: G'frd . . . 2A 78
Scorton Ho. N1 . . . 2E 84
    (off Whitmore Est.)
Scotch Comn. W13 . . . 5A 78
SCOTCH HOUSE . . . 2D 100
Scoter Cl. IG8: Wfd G . . . 7E 36
Scoter Ct. SE8 . . . 6B 104
    (off Abinger Gro.)
Scot Gro. HA5: Pinn . . . 1B 40
Scotia Bldg. E1 . . . 7K 85
    (off Jardine Rd.)
Scotia Ct. SE16 . . . 2J 103
    (off Canada Est.)
Scotia Rd. SW2 . . . 7A 120
Scotland Grn. N17 . . . 2F 49
Scotland Grn. Rd. EN3: Pond E . . . 5E 24
Scotland Grn. Rd. Nth.
  EN3: Pond E . . . 4E 24
Scotland Pl. SW1 . . . 5E 12 (1J 101)
Scotland Rd. IG9: Buck H . . . 1F 37
Scotney Cl. BR6: Farnb . . . 4E 172
Scotney Ho. E9 . . . 6J 67
Scots Cl. TW19: Stanw . . . 1A 128
Scotsdale Cl. BR5: Pet W . . . 4J 161
  SM3: Cheam . . . 7G 165
Scotsdale Rd. SE12 . . . 5K 123
Scotson Ho. SE11 . . . 4J 19
Scotswood Cl. EC1 . . . 3K 7 (4A 84)
Scotswood Wlk. N17 . . . 7B 34
Scott Av. SW15 . . . 6G 117
Scott Cl. KT19: Ewe . . . 5J 163
  SW16 . . . 1K 155
  UB7: W Dray . . . 4B 92
Scott Ct. W3 . . . 2K 97
Scott Cres. HA2: Harr . . . 1F 59
Scott Ellis Gdns. NW8 . . . 2A 4 (3B 82)
Scott Farm Cl. KT7: T Ditt . . . 1B 162
Scott Gdns. TW5: Hest . . . 7B 94
Scott Ho. DA17: Belv . . . 5F 109
  E13 . . . 2J 87
    (off Queens Rd. W.)
  E14 . . . 2C 104
    (off Admirals Way)
  N7 . . . 6K 65
    (off Caledonian Rd.)

Scott Ho. N18 . . . 5B 34
    (off Woolmer Rd.)
  NW8 . . . 4C 4
    (off Broadley St.)
  NW10 . . . 7K 61
    (off Stonebridge Pk.)
  SE8 . . . 5B 104
    (off Grove St.)
Scott Lidgett Cres. SE16 . . . 2G 103
Scott Rd. HA8: Edg . . . 2H 43
Scott Russell Pl. E14 . . . 5D 104
Scotts Av. BR2: Broml . . . 2F 159
  TW16: Sun . . . 7G 129
Scotts Ct. W12 . . . 2E 98
    (off Scott's Rd.)
Scotts Dr. TW12: Hamp . . . 7F 131
Scotts Farm Rd. KT19: Ewe . . . 6J 163
Scott's La. BR2: Broml . . . 3F 159
Scotts Pas. SE18 . . . 4F 107
Scott's Rd. E10 . . . 1E 68
  UB2: S'hall . . . 3A 94
  W12 . . . 2D 98
Scotts Rd. BR1: Broml . . . 7J 141
Scott's Sufferance Wharf SE1 . . . 7K 15
Scotts Ter. SE9 . . . 2C 142
Scotts Way TW16: Sun . . . 7G 129
Scott's Yd. EC4 . . . 2E 14 (7D 84)
Scott Trimmer Way TW3: Houn . . . 2C 112
Scottwell Dr. NW9 . . . 5B 44
Scoulding Ho. E14 . . . 3C 104
    (off Mellish St.)
Scoulding Rd. E16 . . . 6J 87
Scouler St. E14 . . . 7E 86
Scout App. NW10 . . . 4A 62
Scout La. SW4 . . . 3G 119
Scout Pk. . . . 7C 32
Scout Way NW7 . . . 4E 28
Scovell Cres. SE1 . . . 7C 14
Scovell Rd. SE1 . . . 7C 14 (2C 102)
Scrattons Farm Eco-Park . . . 2E 90
Scrattons Ter. IG11: Bark . . . 2D 90
Screenworks N5 . . . 5C 66
Scrimgeour Pl. N4 . . . 1C 66
Scriven Ct. E8 . . . 1F 85
Scriven St. E8 . . . 1F 85
Scrooby St. SE6 . . . 6D 122
Scrope Ho. EC1 . . . 5J 7
    (off Bourne Est.)
Scrubs La. NW10 . . . 3C 80
  W10 . . . 3C 80
Scrutton Cl. SW12 . . . 7H 119
Scrutton St. EC2 . . . 4G 9 (4E 84)
Scudamore La. NW9 . . . 4J 43
Sculpture Ho. E1 . . . 5K 85
    (off Duckett St.)
Scutari Rd. SE22 . . . 5J 121
Scylla Cres. TW6: H'row A . . . 7D 110
    (not continuous)
Scylla Rd. SE15 . . . 3G 121
    (not continuous)
  TW6: H'row A . . . 6D 110
Seaborne Wharf E3 . . . 5C 86
    (off Invicta Cl.)
Seabright St. E2 . . . 3H 85
Seabrook Dr. BR4: W W'ck . . . 2G 171
Seabrook Gdns. RM7: Rush G . . . 7G 55
Seabrook Rd. RM8: Dag . . . 3D 72
Seaburn Ct. RM13: Rain . . . 2K 91
Seacole Cl. W3 . . . 6K 79
Seacole Lodge N21 . . . 5E 22
    (off Pennington Dr.)
Sea Containers Ho. SE1 . . . 3K 13
Seacon Twr. E14 . . . 2B 104
Seacourt Rd. SE2 . . . 2D 108
Seafarer Way SE16 . . . 4A 104
Seafield Rd. N11 . . . 4C 32
Seaford Cl. HA4: Ruis . . . 1F 57
Seaford Ho. SE16 . . . 2J 103
    (off Swan Rd.)
Seaford Rd. E17 . . . 3D 50
  EN1: Enf . . . 4K 23
  N15 . . . 5D 48

Seaford Rd. TW6: H'row A 5A **110**
W13 . . . . .1B **96**
Seaford St. WC1 . . . . .2F 7 (3J **83**)
Seaforth Av. KT3: N Mald 5D **152**
Seaforth Cres. N5 . . . . .5C **66**
Seaforth Gdns. IG8: Wfd G 5F **37**
KT19: Ewe 4B **164**
N21 . . . . .7E **22**
Seaforth Pl. SW1 . . . . .1B **18**
Seager Pl. SE8 . . . . .1C **122**
(off Deptford Bri.)
Seagrave Cl. E1 . . . . .5K **85**
Seagrave Lodge SW6 . . . . .6J **99**
(off Seagrave Rd.)
Seagrave Rd. SW6 . . . . .6J **99**
Seagry Rd. E11 . . . . .7J **51**
Seagull Cl. IG11: Bark 3A **90**
Seagull La. E16 . . . . .7J **87**
Seahorse Sailing Club 2K **61**
Sealand Rd. TW6: H'row A 6C **110**
Sealand Wlk. UB5: N'olt 3B **76**
Seal Ho. SE1 . . . . .7F **15**
(off Weston St.)
Sea Life
London 6G 13 (2K **101**)
Seal St. E8 . . . . .4F **67**
Searle Ho. NW8 . . . . .1C **82**
(off Cecil Gro.)
SW11 . . . . .1E **118**
(off Macduff Rd.)
Searle Pl. N4 . . . . .1K **65**
Searles Cl. SW11 . . . . .7C **100**
Searles Dr. E6 . . . . .5F **89**
Searles Rd. SE1 . . . . .4D **102**
Searson Ho. SE17 . . . . .4B **102**
(off Canterbury Pl.)
Sears St. SE5 . . . . .7D **102**
Seasalter Ho. SW9 . . . . .1A **120**
(off Gosling Way)
Seasons Cl. W7 . . . . .1K **95**
Seasons Ho. E20 . . . . .6E **68**
(off Mirabelle Gdns.)
Seasprite Cl. UB5: N'olt 3B **76**
Seaton Av. IG3: Ilf 5K **71**
Seaton Cl. E13 . . . . .4J **87**
SE11 . . . . .5K 19 (5A **102**)
SW15 . . . . .1D **134**
TW2: Whitt 6H **113**
Seaton Dr. TW15: Ashf 2A **128**
Seaton Gdns. HA4: Ruis 3H **57**
Seaton Point E5 . . . . .4G **67**
Seaton Rd. CR4: Mitc 2C **154**
DA16: Well 7C **108**
HA0: Wemb 2E **78**
TW2: Whitt 6G **113**
UB3: Harl 4F **93**
Seaton Sq. NW7 . . . . .7A **30**
Seaton St. N18 . . . . .5B **34**
Seawall Ct. IG11: Bark 2G **89**
(off Dock Rd.)
Sebastian Ct. IG11: Bark 1K **89**
Sebastian Ho. N1 . . . . .1G **9**
(off Hoxton St.)
Sebastian St. EC1 . . . . . .2B 8 (3B **84**)
Sebastopol Rd. N9 . . . . .4B **34**
Sebbon St. N1 . . . . .7B **66**
Sebergham Gro. NW7 . . . . .7H **29**
Sebert Rd. E7 . . . . .5K **69**
Sebright Ho. E2 . . . . .2G **85**
(off Coate St.)
Sebright Pas. E2 . . . . .2G **85**
Sebright Rd. EN5: Barn 2A **20**
Secker Cres. HA3: Hrw W 1G **41**
Secker Ho. SW9 . . . . .2B **120**
(off Loughborough Est.)
Secker St. SE1 . . . . . . .5J 13 (1A **102**)
Second Av. E12 . . . . .4C **70**
E13 . . . . .3J **87**
E17 . . . . .5C **50**
EN1: Enf 5A **24**
HA9: Wemb 2D **60**
KT12: Walt T 6K **147**
N18 . . . . .4D **34**

Second Av. NW4 . . . . .4F **45**
RM6: Chad H 5C **54**
RM10: Dag 2H **91**
SW14 . . . . .3A **116**
UB3: Hayes 1H **93**
W3 . . . . .1B **98**
W10 . . . . .4G **81**
Second Cl. KT8: W Mole 4G **149**
Second Cross Rd. TW2: Twick . . .2J **131**
Second Way HA9: Wemb 4H **61**
Sedan Way SE17 . . . . .5E **102**
Sedcombe Cl. DA14: Sidc 4B **144**
Sedcote Rd. EN3: Pond E 5D **24**
Sedding St. SW1 . . . . .3G 17 (4E **100**)
Sedding Studios SW1 . . . . .3G **17**
(off Sedding St.)
Seddon Highwalk EC2 . . . . .5C **8**
(off Aldersgate St.)
Seddon Ho. EC2 . . . . .5C **8**
Seddon Rd. SM4: Mord 5B **154**
Seddon St. WC1 . . . . . .2H 7 (3K **83**)
Sedgebrook Rd. SE3 . . . . .2B **124**
Sedgecombe Av. HA3: Kenton . . .5C **42**
Sedgefield Ct. UB5: N'olt 5F **59**
(off Newmarket Av.)
Sedgeford Rd. W12 . . . . .1B **98**
Sedge Gdns. IG11: Bark 3A **90**
Sedgehill Rd. SE6 . . . . .4C **140**
Sedgemere Av. N2 . . . . .3A **46**
Sedgemere Rd. SE2 . . . . .3C **108**
Sedgemoor Dr. RM10: Dag 4G **73**
Sedge Rd. N17 . . . . .7D **34**
Sedgeway SE6 . . . . .1H **141**
Sedgewood Cl. BR2: Hayes 7H **159**
Sedgmoor Pl. SE5 . . . . .7E **102**
Sedgwick Av. UB10: Hil 7D **56**
Sedgwick Ho. E3 . . . . .5C **86**
(off Gale St.)
Sedgwick Rd. E10 . . . . .2E **68**
Sedgwick St. E9 . . . . .5K **67**
Sedleigh Rd. SW18 . . . . .6H **117**
Sedlescombe Rd. SW6 . . . . .6J **99**
Sedley Cl. EN1: Enf 1C **24**
Sedley Ct. SE26 . . . . .2H **139**
Sedley Ho. SE11 . . . . .5H **19**
(off Newburn St.)
Sedley Pl. W1 . . . . .1J 11 (6F **83**)
Sedona Ho. E20 . . . . .6D **68**
(off Victory Pde.)
Sedum Cl. NW9 . . . . .5H **43**
Sedum M. EN2: Enf 2F **23**
Seeley Dr. SE21 . . . . .4E **138**
Seelig Av. NW9 . . . . .7C **44**
Seely Rd. SW17 . . . . .6E **136**
Seetha Ho. IG1: Ilf 2H **71**
(off High Rd.)
Seething La. EC3 . . . . . .2H 15 (7E **84**)
SEETHING WELLS 6C **150**
Seething Wells La. KT6: Surb 6C **150**
Sefton Av. HA3: Hrw W 2H **41**
NW7 . . . . .5E **28**
Sefton Cl. BR5: St M Cry 4K **161**
Sefton Ct. EN2: Enf 2G **23**
TW3: Houn 1F **113**
Sefton Rd. BR5: St M Cry 4K **161**
CR0: C'don 1G **169**
Sefton St. SW15 . . . . .3E **116**
Segal Cl. SE23 . . . . .7A **122**
Sekforde St. EC1 . . . . . . .4A 8 (4B **84**)
Sekhon Ter. TW13: Hanw 3E **130**
Selah Dr. BR8: Swan 7J **145**
Selan Gdns. UB4: Yead 5K **75**
Selbie Av. NW10 . . . . .5B **62**
Selborne Av. DA5: Bexl 1E **144**
E12 . . . . .4E **70**
Selborne Gdns. NW4 . . . . .4C **44**
UB6: G'frd 2A **78**
Selborne Rd. CR0: C'don 3E **168**
DA14: Sidc 4B **144**
E17 . . . . .5B **50**
IG1: Ilf 2E **70**
KT3: N Mald 2A **152**
N14 . . . . .3D **32**

Selborne Rd. N22 . . . . .1K **47**
SE5 . . . . .2D **120**
Selborne Wlk. E17 . . . . .5B **50**
Selborne Wlk. Shop. Cen. 4B **50**
Selbourne Av. KT6: Surb 2F **163**
Selbourne Ho. SE1 . . . . .7E **14**
The Selby Cen. 6K **33**
Selby Chase HA4: Ruis 2K **57**
Selby Cl. BR7: Chst 6E **142**
E6 . . . . .5C **88**
KT9: Chess 7E **162**
Selby Gdns. UB1: S'hall 4E **76**
Selby Grn. SM5: Cars 7C **154**
Selby Rd. E11 . . . . .3G **69**
E13 . . . . .5K **87**
N17 . . . . .7K **33**
SE20 . . . . .2G **157**
SM5: Cars 7C **154**
TW15: Ashf 6E **128**
W5 . . . . .4B **78**
Selby Sq. W10 . . . . .3G **81**
(off Dowland St.)
Selby St. E1 . . . . .4G **85**
Selcroft Ho. SE10 . . . . .5H **105**
(off Glenister Rd.)
Selden Ho. SE15 . . . . .2J **121**
(off Selden Rd.)
Selden Rd. SE15 . . . . .2J **121**
Selden Wlk. N7 . . . . .2K **65**
Seldon Ho. SW1 . . . . .6A **18**
(off Churchill Gdns.)
SW8 .7G **101**
(off Stewart's Rd.)
Selfridges 1H **11**
SELHURST 6E **156**
Selhurst Cl. SW19 . . . . .1F **135**
Selhurst New Rd. SE25 . . . . .6E **156**
Selhurst Pk. 4E **156**
Selhurst Pl. SE25 . . . . .6E **156**
Selhurst Rd. N9 . . . . .3J **33**
SE25 . . . . .6E **156**
Selig Ct. NW11 . . . . .7G **45**
Selina Ho. NW8 . . . . .3B **4**
(off Frampton St.)
Selinas La. RM8: Dag 7E **54**
Selkirk Ho. N1 . . . . .1K **83**
(off Bingfield St.)
Selkirk Rd. SW17 . . . . .4C **136**
TW2: Twick 2G **131**
Sellers Hall Cl. N3 . . . . .7D **30**
Sellincourt Rd. SW17 . . . . .5C **136**
Sellindge Cl. BR3: Beck 7B **140**
Sellons Av. NW10 . . . . .1B **80**
Sellwood Dr. EN5: Barn 5A **20**
Selman Ho. E9 . . . . .6A **68**
SELSDON 7J **169**
Selsdon Av. CR2: S Croy 6D **168**
Selsdon Cl. KT6: Surb 5E **150**
RM5: Col R 1J **55**
Selsdon Pk. Rd. CR0: Sels 7K **169**
CR2: Sels 7K **169**
Selsdon Rd. CR2: S Croy 5D **168**
E11 . . . . .7J **51**
E13 . . . . .1A **88**
NW2 .2B **62**
SE27 . . . . .3A **138**
Selsdon Way E14 . . . . .3D **104**
Selsea Pl. N16 . . . . .5E **66**
Selsey WC1 . . . . .2F **7**
(off Tavistock Pl.)
Selsey Cres. DA16: Well 1D **126**
Selsey St. E14 . . . . .5C **86**
Selvage La. NW7 . . . . .5E **28**
Selway Cl. HA5: Eastc 4K **39**
Selway Ho. SW8 . . . . .1J **119**
(off Sth. Lambeth Rd.)
Selwood Pl. SW7 . . . . . .5A 16 (5B **100**)
Selwood Rd. CR0: C'don 2H **169**
KT9: Chess 4D **162**
SM3: Sutt 1H **165**
Selwood St. SW2 . . . . .7A **120**
Selwood Ter. SW7 . . . . . .5A 16 (5B **100**)
Selworthy Cl. E11 . . . . .5J **51**

Selworthy Ho. SW11 . . . . .1B **118**
(off Battersea Church Rd.)
Selworthy Rd. SE6 . . . . .3B **140**
Selwyn Av. E4 . . . . .6K **35**
IG3: Ilf 6K **53**
TW9: Rich 3E **114**
Selwyn Cl. TW4: Houn 4C **112**
Selwyn Ct. E17 . . . . .5C **50**
(off Yunus Khan Cl.)
HA8: Edg 7C **28**
HA9: Wemb 3J **61**
SE3 .3H **123**
TW10: Rich 5F **115**
(off Church Rd.)
Selwyn Cres. DA16: Well 3B **126**
Selwyn Rd. E3 . . . . .2B **86**
E13 . . . . .1K **87**
KT3: N Mald 5K **151**
NW10 .7A **62**
Semley Ga. E9 . . . . .6B **68**
(not continuous)
Semley Ho. SW1 . . . . .4J **17**
(off Semley Pl.)
Semley Pl. SW1 . . . . . . .4H 17 (4E **100**)
SW16 . . . . .2J **155**
Senate St. SE15 . . . . .2J **121**
Senators Lodge E3 . . . . .2A **86**
(off Roman Rd.)
Senator Wlk. SE28 . . . . .3H **107**
Sendall Ct. SW11 . . . . .3B **118**
(off Winstanley Rd.)
Seneca Rd. CR7: Thor H 4C **156**
Sener Ct. CR2: S Croy 6C **168**
Senga Rd. SM6: W'gton 1E **166**
Senhouse Rd. SM3: Cheam 3F **165**
Senior St. W2 . . . . .5K **81**
Senlac Rd. SE12 . . . . .1K **141**
Sennen Rd. EN1: Enf 7A **24**
Sennen Wlk. SE9 . . . . .3C **142**
Senrab St. E1 . . . . .6K **85**
Sentamu Cl. SE24 . . . . .1B **138**
Sentinel Bldg. E15 . . . . .5F **69**
(off Property Row)
Sentinel Cl. UB5: N'olt 4C **76**
Sentinel Sq. NW4 . . . . .4E **44**
September Ct. UB1: S'hall 1F **95**
(off Dormer's Wells La.)
September Way HA7: Stan 6G **27**
Septimus Pl. EN1: Enf 5B **24**
Sequoia Cl. WD23: B Hea 1C **26**
Sequoia Gdns. BR6: Orp 7K **161**
Sequoia Pk. HA5: Hat E 6A **26**
Serap Ct. CR0: C'don 4D **168**
(off Dean Rd.)
Seraph Ct. EC1 . . . . .1C **8**
(off Moreland St.)
Serbin Cl. E10 . . . . .7E **50**
Serenaders Rd. SW9 . . . . .2A **120**
Serenity Apts. E17 . . . . .5D **50**
SW11 . . . . .4C **118**
(off Monarch Sq.)
Serenity Cl. HA2: Harr 2F **59**
Seren Pk. Gdns. SE3 . . . . .6G **105**
Sergeant Ind. Est. SW18 . . . . . . .6K **117**
Serica Ct. SE10 . . . . .7E **104**
Serjeants Inn EC4 . . . . . .1K 13 (6A **84**)
Serlby Ct. W14 . . . . .3H **99**
(off Somerset Sq.)
Serle St. WC2 . . . . .7H 7 (6K **83**)
Sermon La. EC4 . . . . .1C **14**
The Serpentine 5D 10 (1C **100**)
Serpentine Cl. RM6: Chad H 7C **54**
Serpentine Ct. SE16 . . . . .2K **103**
(off Christopher Cl.)
Serpentine Gallery 6A 10 (2B **100**)
The Serpentine Lido 1C **100**
Serpentine Rd. W2 . . . . .5C 10 (1C **100**)
Serpentine Sackler Gallery
. . . . .4B 10 (1B **100**)
Serviden Dr. BR1: Broml 1B **160**
Servite Ho. BR3: Beck 1B **158**
KT4: Wor Pk 2B **164**
(off The Avenue)

Servite Ho. *N14* *5A 22*
    (off Bramley Rd.)
Servius Ct. TW8: Bford 7D **96**
Setchell Rd. SE1 . . . . .4F **103**
Setchell Way SE1 . . . . .4F **103**
Seth St. SE16 . . . . .2J **103**
Seton Gdns. RM9: Dag 7C **72**
Settle Point E13 . . . . .2J **87**
Settlers Ct. E14 . . . . .7F **87**
Settles St. E1 . . . . .5G **85**
Settrington Rd. SW6 . . . . .2K **117**
Seven Acres SM5: Cars 2C **166**
Seven Dials WC2 . . . . . .1E **12** (6J **83**)
Seven Dials Ct. *WC2* *1E 12*
    (off Shorts Gdns.)
Sevenex Pde. HA9: Wemb 5E **60**
Seven Islands Leisure Cen. . . .3J **103**
SEVEN KINGS 1K **71**
Seven Kings Rd. IG3: Ilf 1J **71**
Seven Kings Way KT2: King T 1E **150**
Sevenoaks Cl. DA7: Bex 4H **127**
Sevenoaks Cl. HA6: N'wood 1E **38**
Sevenoaks Rd. BR6: Chels, Orp . .5K **173**
  BR6: Prat B 7K **173**
  SE4 . . . . .6A **122**
Sevenoaks Way BR5: St P 7C **144**
  DA14: Sidc 7C **144**
Seven Sea Gdns. E3 . . . . .5D **86**
Sevenseas Rd.
  TW6: H'row A 6E **110**
SEVEN SISTERS 5F **49**
Seven Sisters Rd. N4 . . . . .2A **66**
  N7 . . . . .3K **65**
  N15 .7C **48**
Seven Stars Cnr. W12 . . . . .3C **98**
Seven Stars Yd. E1 . . . . .5K **9**
Seventeen *SM1: Sutt* *6A 166*
    (off Sutton Ct. Rd.)
Seventh Av. E12 . . . . .4D **70**
  UB3: Hayes 1J **93**
Seven Ways Pde. IG2: Ilf 5E **52**
Severin Ct. *SE17* *5E 102*
    (off East St.)
Severnake Ct. E14 . . . . .4C **104**
Severn Av. W10 . . . . .3G **81**
Severn Ct. *KT2: King T* *1D 150*
    (off John Williams Cl.)
Severn Dr. KT10: Hin W 2A **162**
Severn Ho. SW18 . . . . .4J **117**
    (off Enterprise Way)
Severn Way NW10 . . . . .5B **62**
Severus Ho. UB3: Hayes 6F **75**
Severus Rd. SW11 . . . . .4C **118**
Seville Ho. *E1* *1G 103*
    (off Wapping High St.)
Seville M. N1 . . . . .7E **66**
Seville St. SW1 . . . . .7F **11** (2D **100**)
Sevington Rd. NW4 . . . . .6D **44**
Sevington St. W9 . . . . .4K **81**
Seward Rd. BR3: Beck 2K **157**
  W7 . . . . .2A **96**
SEWARDSTONE 1K **25**
Sewardstone Cl. E4 . . . . .1K **25**
Sewardstone Gdns. E4 . . . . .5J **25**
Sewardstone Rd. E2 . . . . .2J **85**
  E4 . . . . .7J **25**
Seward St. EC1 . . . . .3B **8** (3B **84**)
Sewdley St. E5 . . . . .3K **67**
Sewell Rd. SE2 . . . . .3A **108**
Sewell St. E13 . . . . .3J **87**
Sextant Av. E14 . . . . .4F **105**
Sexton Ct. *E14* *7F 87*
    (off Newport Av.)
Sextons Ho. *SE10* *6E 104*
    (off Bardsley La.)
Seymer Rd. RM1: Rom 3K **55**
Seymore M. *SE14* *7B 104*
    (off New Cross Rd.)
Seymour Av. KT17: Ewe 7E **164**
  N17 . . . . .2G **49**
  SM4: Mord 7F **153**
Seymour Cl. HA5: Hat E 1D **40**
  KT8: E Mos 5G **149**

Seymour Ct. E4 . . . . .2C **36**
  KT1: Hamp W 1D **150**
  N10 . . . . .2E **46**
  N21 . . . . .6E **22**
  NW2 .2D **62**
Seymour Dr. BR2: Broml 1D **172**
Seymour Gdns. HA4: Ruis 1B **58**
  IG1: Ilf 1D **70**
  KT5: Surb 5F **151**
  SE4 .3A **122**
  TW1: Twick 7B **114**
  TW13: Hanw 4A **130**
Seymour Ho. *E16* *1J 105*
    (off De Quincey M.)
  NW1 . . . .*1D 6*
    (off Churchway)
  SM2: Sutt *6K 165*
    (off Mulgrave Rd.)
  WC1 . . . .*3E 6*
    (off Tavistock Pl.)
Seymour Leisure Cen. 6E **4** (5D **82**)
Seymour M. W1 . . . . .7G **5** (6E **82**)
Seymour Pl. SE25 . . . . .4F **157**
  W1 . . . . .6E **4** (5D **82**)
Seymour Rd. CR4: Mitc 7E **154**
  E4 . . . . .1J **35**
  E6 . . . . .2B **88**
  E10 . . . . .1B **68**
  KT1: Hamp W 1D **150**
  KT8: W Mole, E Mos 5G **149**
  N3 . . . . .7E **30**
  N8 . . . . .5A **48**
  N9 . . . . .2C **34**
  SM5: Cars 5E **166**
  SW18 . . . . .7H **117**
  SW19 . . . . .3F **135**
  TW12: Hamp H 5G **131**
  W4 . . . . .4J **97**
Seymour St. SE18 . . . . .3D **107**
  W1 . . . . .1E **10** (6D **82**)
  W2 . . . . .1E **10** (6D **82**)
Seymour Ter. SE20 . . . . .1H **157**
Seymour Vs. SE20 . . . . .1H **157**
Seymour Wlk. SW10 . . . . .6A **100**
Seymour Way TW16: Sun 7H **129**
Seyssel St. E14 . . . . .4E **104**
Shaa Rd. W3 . . . . .7K **79**
Shabana Rd. W12 . . . . .1D **98**
Shackelgate La. TW11: Tedd 4J **131**
Shackleton Cl. SE23 . . . . .2H **139**
Shackleton Ct. *E14* *5C 104*
    (off Maritime Quay)
  TW19: Stanw *6A 110*
    (off Whitley Cl.)
  W12 . . . .*2D 98*
    (off Scott's Rd.)
Shackleton Ho. CR0: Wadd 1K **167**
  E1 . . . .*1J 103*
    (off Prusom St.)
  NW10 . . . . .7K **61**
Shackleton Rd. UB1: S'hall 7D **76**
Shackleton Way E16 . . . . .7G **89**
SHACKLEWELL 4F **67**
Shacklewell Grn. E8 . . . . .4F **67**
Shacklewell Ho. E8 . . . . .4F **67**
Shacklewell La. E8 . . . . .5F **67**
  N16 . . . . .4F **67**
Shacklewell Rd. N16 . . . . .4F **67**
Shacklewell Row E8 . . . . .4F **67**
Shacklewell St. E2 . . . . . .2K **9** (3F **85**)
Shadbolt Av. E4 . . . . .5H **35**
Shadbolt Cl. KT4: Wor Pk 2B **164**
Shad Thames SE1 . . . . . .5J **15** (1F **103**)
    (Anchor Brewhouse)
  SE1 . . . . .7K **15** (2F **103**)
    (Jamaica Rd.)
SHADWELL 7H **85**
Shadwell Ct. UB5: N'olt 2D **76**
Shadwell Dr. UB5: N'olt 3D **76**
Shadwell Gdns. E1 . . . . .7J **85**
Shadwell Pierhead E1 . . . . .7J **85**
Shadwell Pl. *E1* *7J 85*
    (off Sutton St.)

Shady Bush Cl. WD23: Bush 1B **26**
Shaef Way TW11: Tedd 7A **132**
Shafter Rd. RM10: Dag 6J **73**
Shaftesbury Av. EN3: Enf H 2E **24**
  EN5: New Bar 4F **21**
  HA2: Harr 1F **59**
  HA3: Kenton 5D **42**
  TW14: Felt 6J **111**
  UB2: S'hall 4E **94**
  W1 . . . . .3C **12** (7H **83**)
  WC1 . . . . .7E **6** (6J **83**)
  WC2 . . . . .7E **6** (6J **83**)
Shaftesbury Barnet Harriers 1E **44**
Shaftesbury Cen. *W10* *4F 81*
    (off Barlby Rd.)
Shaftesbury Circ. HA2: Harr 1G **59**
Shaftesbury Ct. *E6* *6E 88*
    (off Sapphire Cl.)
  N1 . . . .*2D 84*
    (off Shaftesbury St.)
  SE1 . . . .*3D 102*
    (off Alderney M.)
  SE5 .4D **120**
  SW16 . . . . .3H **137**
Shaftesbury Cres.
  TW18: Staines 7A **128**
Shaftesbury Gdns. NW10 . . . . . . .4A **80**
Shaftesbury Lodge *E14* *6D 86*
    (off Upper Nth. St.)
Shaftesbury M. SW4 . . . . .5G **119**
  W8 . . . . .3J **99**
Shaftesbury Pde. HA2: Harr 1G **59**
Shaftesbury Pl. *EC2* *6C 8*
    (off London Wall)
  W14 . . . .*4H 99*
    (off Warwick Rd.)
Shaftesbury Point *E13* *2J 87*
    (off High St.)
Shaftesbury Rd. BR3: Beck 2B **158**
  E4 . . . . .1A **36**
  E7 . . . . .7A **70**
  E10 . . . . .1C **68**
  E17 . . . . .6D **50**
  N18 . . . . .6K **33**
  N19 . . . . .1J **65**
  SM5: Cars 7B **154**
  TW9: Rich 3E **114**
Shaftesbury Row *SE8* *7C 104*
    (off Speedwell St.)
The Shaftesburys IG11: Bark 2G **89**
Shaftesbury St. N1 . . . . .2C **84**
    (not continuous)
Shaftesbury Theatre 7E **6**
    (off Shaftesbury Av.)
Shaftesbury Vs. *W8* *3J 99*
    (off Allen St.)
Shaftesbury Way TW2: Twick 3H **131**
Shaftesbury Waye UB4: Yead 5A **76**
Shafto M. SW1 . . . . .2F **17** (3D **100**)
Shafton M. E9 . . . . .1K **85**
Shafton Rd. E9 . . . . .1K **85**
Shafts Ct. EC3 . . . . .1G **15** (6E **84**)
Shaftswood Ct. SW17 . . . . .3D **136**
    (off Lynwood Rd.)
Shahjalal Ho. *E2* *2G 85*
    (off Pritchards Rd.)
Shakespeare Av. N11 . . . . .5B **32**
  NW10 . . . . .1K **79**
  TW14: Felt 6J **111**
  UB4: Hayes, Yead 6J **75**
    (not continuous)
  UB4: Yead 4K **75**
Shakespeare Cl. HA3: Kenton 7G **43**
Shakespeare Ct. EN5: New Bar . . .3E **20**
  HA3: Kenton 6F **43**
  NW6 . . . .*7A 64*
    (off Fairfax Rd.)
Shakespeare Cres. E12 . . . . .6D **70**
Shakespeare Dr. HA3: Kenton 6F **43**
Shakespeare Gdns. N2 . . . . .4D **46**
Shakespeare Ho. *E9* *7J 67*
    (off Lyme Gro.)
  N14 . . . . .2C **32**

Shakespeare Rd. DA7: Bex 1E **126**
  E17 . . . . .2K **49**
  N3 . . . . .1J **45**
  NW7 .4G **29**
  NW10 . . . . .1K **79**
  SE24 . . . . .5B **120**
  W3 . . . . .1J **97**
  W7 . . . . .7K **77**
Shakespeare's Globe & Exhibition
  . . . . .4C **14** (1C **102**)
Shakespeare Twr. EC2 . . . . .5D **8**
Shakespeare Way TW13: Hanw . . .4A **130**
Shakspeare M. N16 . . . . .4E **66**
Shakspeare Wlk. N16 . . . . .4E **66**
Shalbourne Sq. E9 . . . . .6B **68**
Shalcomb St. SW10 . . . . .6A **100**
Shalden Ho. SW15 . . . . .6B **116**
Shaldon Dr. HA4: Ruis 3A **58**
  SM4: Mord 5G **153**
Shaldon Rd. HA8: Edg 2F **43**
Shallfleet Dr. W10 . . . . .7F **81**
Shalford Cl. BR6: Farnb 4G **173**
Shalford Ct. N1 . . . . .2B **84**
Shalford Ho. SE1 . . . . .3D **102**
Shalimar Gdns. W3 . . . . .7J **79**
Shalimar Rd. W3 . . . . .7J **79**
Shallons Rd. SE9 . . . . .4F **143**
Shalstone Rd. SW14 . . . . .3H **115**
Shalston Vs. KT6: Surb 6F **151**
Shamrock Ho. *SE26* *4G 139*
    (off Talisman Sq.)
Shamrock Rd. CR0: C'don 6K **155**
Shamrock St. SW4 . . . . .3H **119**
Shamrock Way N14 . . . . .1A **32**
Shandon Rd. SW4 . . . . .6G **119**
Shand St. SE1 . . . . .6H **15** (2E **102**)
Shandy St. E1 . . . . .5K **85**
Shan Ho. *WC1* *4G 7*
    (off Millman St.)
Shanklin Ho. E17 . . . . .2B **50**
Shanklin Rd. N8 . . . . .5H **47**
  N15 . . . . .4G **49**
Shannon Cl. NW2 . . . . .3F **63**
  UB2: S'hall 5B **94**
Shannon Commercial Cen.
  KT3: N Mald 4C **152**
SHANNON CORNER 4C **152**
Shannon Cnr. Retail Pk. 4C **152**
Shannon Ct. *CR0: C'don* *1C 168*
    (off Tavistock Rd.)
  N16 . . . . .3E **66**
  SE15 . . . .*7F 103*
    (off Garnies Cl.)
Shannon Gro. SW9 . . . . .4K **119**
Shannon M. SE3 . . . . .4H **123**
Shannon Pl. NW8 . . . . .2C **82**
Shannon Way BR3: Beck 6D **140**
Shanti Cl. SW18 . . . . .1J **135**
Shap Cres. SM5: Cars 1D **166**
Shapland Way N13 . . . . .5E **32**
Shapwick Cl. N11 . . . . .5J **31**
The Shard 5F **15** (1D **102**)
Shardcroft Av. SE24 . . . . .5B **120**
Shardeloes Rd. SE4 . . . . .3B **122**
  SE14 . . . . .2B **122**
Shard's Sq. SE15 . . . . .6G **103**
Sharland Cl. CR7: Thor H 6A **156**
Sharman Ct. DA14: Sidc 4A **144**
Sharman Way E3 . . . . .5D **86**
Sharnbrooke Cl. DA16: Well 3C **126**
Sharnbrook Ho. W14 . . . . .6J **99**
Sharon Cl. KT6: Surb 1C **162**
Sharon Ct. *CR2: S Croy* *5C 168*
    (off Warham Rd.)
Sharon Gdns. E9 . . . . .1J **85**
Sharon Rd. EN3: Enf H 2F **25**
  W4 . . . . .5K **97**
Sharpe Cl. W7 . . . . .5K **77**
Sharp Ho. SW8 . . . . .3E **119**
  TW1: Twick 6D **114**
Sharpleshall St. NW1 . . . . .7D **64**
Sharpley Ct. *SE1* *6A 14*
    (off Pocock St.)

Sharpness Cl. UB4: Yead 5C 76
Sharp's La. HA4: Ruis 7F 39
Sharratt St. SE15 . . . . 6J 103
Sharsted St. SE17 . . . .6K 19 (5B 102)
Sharvel La. UB5: N'olt 1J 75
Sharwood WC1 . . . . .1H 7
(off Penton Ri.)
Shaver's Pl. SW1 . . . . .3C 12
The Shaw BR7: Chst 7G 143
Shaw Av. IG11: Bark 2E 90
Shawbrooke Rd. SE9 . . . . .5A 124
Shawbury Cl. NW9 . . . . .1A 44
Shawbury Rd. SE22 . . . . .5F 121
Shaw Cl. SE28 . . . . .1B 108
TW19: Stanw 1A 128
WD23: B Hea 2D 26
Shaw Ct. SM4: Mord 7A 154
Shaw Cres. E14 . . . . .5A 86
Shaw Dr. KT12: Walt T 7A 148
Shawfield Ct. UB7: W Dray 3A 92
Shawfield Pk. BR1: Broml 2B 160
Shawfield St. SW3 . . . .6D 16 (5C 100)
Shawford Ct. SW15 . . . . .7C 116
Shawford Rd. KT19: Ewe 6K 163
Shaw Gdns. IG11: Bark 2E 90
Shaw Ho. DA17: Belv 5F 109
E16 . . . . .1E 106
(off Claremont St.)
Shaw Path BR1: Broml 3H 141
Shaw Pl. N2 . . . . .3E 46
Shaw Rd. BR1: Broml 3H 141
EN3: Enf H 1E 24
SE22 . . . . .4E 120
Shaws Cotts. SE23 . . . . .3A 140
Shaw Sq. E17 . . . . .1A 50
Shaw Theatre 2D 6 (3H 83)
Shaw Way SM6: W'gton 7J 167
Shead Ct. E1 . . . . .6H 85
(off James Voller Way)
Shearing Dr. SM5: Cars 7A 154
Shearling Way N7 . . . . .6J 65
Shearman Rd. SE3 . . . . .4H 123
THE SHEARS 7G 129
Shears Ct. TW16: Sun 7G 129
Shears La. TW16 . . . . .7J 137
Shearsmith Ho. E1 . . . . .7G 85
(off Hindmarsh Cl.)
Shears Way TW16: Sun 1G 147
Shearwater Cl. IG11: Bark 3A 90
Shearwater Ct. E1 . . . . .3K 15
(off Star Pl.)
SE8 . . . . .6B 104
(off Abinger Gro.)
Shearwater Dr. NW9 . . . . .7C 44
Shearwater Rd. SM1: Sutt 5H 165
Shearwater Way UB4: Yead 6B 76
Sheath Cotts. KT7: T Ditt 6B 150
(off Ferry Rd.)
Sheaveshill Av. NW9 . . . . .4A 44
Sheaveshill Ct. NW9 . . . . .4K 43
Sheaveshill Pde. NW9 . . . . .4A 44
(off Sheaveshill Av.)
Sheba Ct. N17 . . . . .6B 34
(off Altair Cl.)
Sheba Pl. E1 . . . . .4K 9 (4F 85)
Sheen Comn. Dr. TW10: Rich . . .4G 115
Sheen Ct. TW10: Rich 4G 115
Sheen Ct. Rd. TW10: Rich 4G 115
Sheendale Rd. TW9: Rich 4F 115
Sheenewood SE26 . . . . .4H 139
Sheen Ga. Gdns. SW14 . . . . . .4J 115
Sheen Gro. N1 . . . . .1A 84
Sheen La. SW14 . . . . .5J 115
Sheen Pk. TW9: Rich 4F 115
Sheen Rd. BR5: St M Cry 4K 161
TW9: Rich 5E 114
TW10: Rich 5E 114
Sheen Way SM6: W'gton 5K 167
Sheen Wood SW14 . . . . .5J 115
Sheepcote Cl. TW5: Cran 7J 93
Sheepcote La. SW11 . . . . .2D 118
Sheepcote Rd. HA1: Harr 6K 41

Sheepcotes Rd. RM6: Chad H 4E 54
Sheephouse Way KT3: N Mald . . .1K 163
Sheep La. E8 . . . . .1H 85
Sheep Wlk. TW17: Shep 7B 146
Sheep Wlk. M. SW19 . . . . .6F 135
Sheerness M. E16 . . . . .2F 107
Sheerwater Rd. E16 . . . . .5B 88
Sheffield Rd. TW6: H'row A 6E 110
Sheffield Sq. E3 . . . . .3B 86
Sheffield St. WC2 . . . .1G 13 (6K 83)
Sheffield Ter. W8 . . . . .1J 99
Sheffield Way TW6: H'row A 5F 111
Shelbourne Cl. HA5: Pinn 3D 40
Shelbourne Pl. BR3: Beck 7B 140
Shelbourne Rd. N17 . . . . .2H 49
Shelburne Dr. TW4: Houn 6E 112
Shelburne Rd. N7 . . . . .4K 65
Shelbury Cl. DA14: Sidc 3A 144
Shelbury Rd. SE22 . . . . .5H 121
Sheldon Av. IG5: Ilf 2F 53
N2 . . . . .6D 46
N6 . . . . .7C 46
Sheldon Cl. SE12 . . . . .5K 123
SE20 . . . . .1H 157
Sheldon Ct. EN5: New Bar 4E 20
RM7: Rush G 6K 55
(off Union Rd.)
SW8 . . . . .7J 101
(off Lansdowne Grn.)
Sheldon Ho. N1 . . . . .1E 84
(off Kingsland Rd.)
Sheldon Pl. E2 . . . . .2G 85
(not continuous)
Sheldon Rd. DA7: Bex 1F 127
N18 . . . . .4K 33
NW2 . . . . .4F 63
RM9: Dag 7E 72
Sheldon Sq. W2 . . . .6A 4 (5A 82)
Sheldon St. CR0: C'don 3C 168
Sheldrake Cl. E16 . . . . .1D 106
Sheldrake Ho. SE16 . . . . .4K 103
(off Tawny Way)
Sheldrake Pl. W8 . . . . .2J 99
Sheldrick Cl. SW19 . . . . .2B 154
Shelduck Cl. E15 . . . . .5H 69
Shelduck Ct. SE8 . . . . .6B 104
(off Pilot Cl.)
Sheldwich Ter. BR2: Broml 6C 160
Shelford KT1: King T 2G 151
Shelford Pl. N16 . . . . .3D 66
Shelford Rd. EN5: Barn 6A 20
Shelgate Rd. SW11 . . . . .5C 118
Shell Cl. BR2: Broml 6C 160
Shellduck Cl. NW9 . . . . .2A 44
Shelley N8 . . . . .3J 47
(off Boyton Rd.)
Shelley Av. E12 . . . . .6C 70
UB6: G'frd 3H 77
Shelley Cl. BR6: Orp 3J 173
HA8: Edg 4B 28
SE15 . . . . .2H 121
UB4: Hayes 5J 75
UB6: G'frd 3H 77
Shelley Ct. E10 . . . . .7D 50
(off Skelton's La.)
E11 . . . . .4K 51
(off Makepeace Rd.)
N19 . . . . .1K 65
SW3 . . . . .7F 17
(off Tite St.)
Shelley Cres. TW5: Hest 1B 112
UB1: S'hall 6D 76
Shelley Dr. DA16: Well 1J 125
Shelley Gdns. HA0: Wemb 2C 60
Shelley Ho. E2 . . . . .3J 85
(off Cornwall Av.)
N16 . . . . .4E 66
SE17 . . . . .5C 102
(off Browning St.)
SW1 . . . . .7B 18
(off Churchill Gdns.)
Shelley Lodge EN2: Enf 1J 23

Shelley Pl. N1 . . . . .1B 84
Shelley Rd. NW10 . . . . .1K 79
Shelley Way SW19 . . . . .5B 136
Shellness Rd. E5 . . . . .5H 67
Shell Rd. SE13 . . . . .3D 122
Shell Twr. SE1 . . . . .6H 13
Shellwood Rd. SW11 . . . . .2D 118
Shelmerdine Cl. E3 . . . . .5C 86
Shelson Av. TW13: Felt 3H 129
Shelson Pde. TW13: Felt 3H 129
Shelton Rd. SW19 . . . . .1J 153
Shelton St. WC2 . . . . . .1E 12 (6J 83)
(not continuous)
Shene Ho. EC1 . . . . .5J 7
(off Bourne Est.)
Shene Sports & Fitness Cen. 4A 116
Shenfield Ho. SE18 . . . . .1B 124
(off Portway Gdns.)
Shenfield Rd. IG8: Wfd G 7E 36
Shenfield St. N1 . . . . . .1H 9 (2E 84)
(not continuous)
Shenley Av. HA4: Ruis 2H 57
Shenley Rd. SE5 . . . . .1E 120
TW5: Hest 1C 112
Shenstone W13 . . . . .1C 96
Shenstone Cl. DA1: Cray 4K 127
Shenstone Ho. SW16 . . . . .5G 137
Shephard's Ho. BR7: Chst 1H 161
Shepherd Cl. TW13: Hanw 4C 130
Shepherdess Pl. N1 . . . .1D 8 (3C 84)
Shepherdess Wlk. N1 . . . .1D 8 (2C 84)
Shepherd Ho. E14 . . . . .6D 86
(off Annabel Cl.)
E16 . . . . .7F 89
(off University Way)
Shepherd Mkt. W1 . . . .4J 11 (1F 101)
SHEPHERD'S BUSH 2E 98
Shepherd's Bush Empire Theatre . . .2E 98
Shepherd's Bush Grn. W12 . . . . .2E 98
Shepherd's Bush Mkt. W12 . . . . .2E 98
(not continuous)
Shepherd's Bush Pl. W12 . . . . . . .2F 99
Shepherd's Bush Rd. W6 . . . . . .4E 98
Shepherd's Cl. BR6: Orp 3K 173
N6 . . . . .6F 47
Shepherds Cl. HA7: Stan 5F 27
(not continuous)
RM6: Chad H 5D 54
TW17: Shep 6D 146
W1 . . . . .2G 11
(off Lees Pl.)
Shepherds Ct. W12 . . . . .2F 99
(off Shepherd's Bush Grn.)
Shepherds Grn. BR7: Chst 7H 143
Shepherd's Hill N6 . . . . .6F 47
Shepherds La. E9 . . . . .6K 67
SE28 . . . . .1J 107
Shepherds Leas SE9 . . . . .4G 125
Shepherds Path UB5: N'olt 6C 58
(off Arnold Rd.)
Shepherds Pl. W1 . . . .2G 11 (7E 82)
Shepherd St. W1 . . . . . .5J 11 (1F 101)
Shepherd's Wlk. NW3 . . . . .4B 64
Shepherds Wlk. NW2 . . . . .2C 62
WD23: B Hea 2C 26
Shepherds Way CR2: Sels 7K 169
Shepiston La. UB3: Harl 4D 92
Shepley Cl. SM5: Cars 3E 166
Shepley Ct. EN1: Enf 1C 24
KT1: King T 4E 150
Sheppard Dr. SE16 . . . . .5H 103
Sheppard Ho. E2 . . . . .2G 85
(off Warner Pl.)
SW2 . . . . .1A 138
Sheppards Coll. BR1: Broml 1J 159
(off London Rd.)
Sheppard St. E16 . . . . .4H 87
SHEPPERTON 6D 146
Shepperton Bus. Pk.
TW17: Shep 5E 146
Shepperton Ct. TW17: Shep 6D 146
Shepperton Ct. Dr.
TW17: Shep 5D 146

Shepperton Film Studios 3B 146
SHEPPERTON GREEN 4C 146
Shepperton Marina
TW17: Shep 6G 147
Shepperton Rd. BR5: Pet W 6G 161
N1 . . . . .1C 84
TW18: Lale, Shep 4A 146
Sheppey Gdns. RM9: Dag 7C 72
Sheppey Rd. RM9: Dag 7B 72
Shepton Ho's. E2 . . . . .3J 85
(off Welwyn St.)
Sherard Ct. N7 . . . . .3J 65
Sherard Ho. E9 . . . . .7J 67
(off Frampton Pk. Rd.)
Sherard Rd. SE9 . . . . .5C 124
Sheraton Bus. Cen. UB6: G'frd . . .2B 78
Sheraton Ho. SW1 . . . . .7K 17
(off Churchill Gdns.)
Sheraton St. W1 . . . . .1C 12 (6H 83)
Sherborne NW1 . . . . .7H 65
(off Agar Gro.)
Sherborne Av. EN3: Enf H 2D 24
UB2: S'hall 4E 94
Sherborne Cl. SL3: Poyle 4A 174
UB4: Yead 6A 76
Sherborne Cres. SM5: Cars 7C 154
Sherborne Gdns. NW9 . . . . .3G 43
W13 . . . . .5B 78
Sherborne Ho. SW1 . . . . .5K 17
(part of Abbots Mnr.)
SW8 . . . . .7K 101
(off Bolney St.)
Sherborne La. EC4 . . . . . .2E 14 (7D 84)
Sherborne Rd.
BR5: St M Cry 4K 161
KT9: Chess 5E 162
SM3: Sutt 2J 165
TW14: Bedf 1F 129
(not continuous)
Sherborne St. N1 . . . . .1D 84
Sherboro Rd. N15 . . . . .6F 49
Sherbourne Ct. SM2: Sutt 6A 166
SW5 . . . . .4K 99
(off Cromwell Rd.)
Sherbourne Gdns. TW17: Shep . . .7G 147
Sherbourne Pl. HA7: Stan 6F 27
Sherbrooke Cl. DA6: Bex 4G 127
Sherbrooke Ho. E2 . . . . .2J 85
(off Bonner Rd.)
SW1 . . . . .2D 18
(off Monck St.)
Sherbrooke Rd. SW6 . . . . .7G 99
Sherbrooke Ter. SW6 . . . . .7G 99
(off Sherbrooke Rd.)
Sherbrooke Way KT4: Wor Pk . . .7D 152
Sherbrook Gdns. N21 . . . . .7G 23
Sherbrook Ho. SE16 . . . . .2J 103
(off Albatross Way)
Shere Cl. KT9: Chess 5D 162
Sheredan Rd. E4 . . . . .5A 36
Shere Ho. SE1 . . . . .7E 14
Shere Rd. IG2: Ilf 5E 52
Sherfield Cl. KT3: N Mald 4H 151
Sherfield Gdns. SW15 . . . . .6B 116
Sherfield Rd. UB3: Hayes 6G 75
Sheridan Bldgs. WC2 . . . . .1F 13
(off Martlett Ct.)
Sheridan Cl. UB10: Hil 4E 74
Sheridan Ct. CR0: C'don 4E 168
(off Coombe Rd.)
HA1: Harr 6H 41
NW6 . . . . .7A 64
(off Belsize Rd.)
SW5 . . . . .4K 99
(off Barkston Gdns.)
TW4: Houn 5C 112
UB5: N'olt 5F 59
W7 . . . . .7K 77
(off Milton Rd.)
Sheridan Cres. BR7: Chst 2F 161
Sheridan Gdns. HA3: Kenton 6D 42
Sheridan Hgts. E1 . . . . .6H 85
(off Watney St.)

Sheridan Ho. *SE11* 4K *19*
    (off Wincott St.)
Sheridan Lodge *BR2: Broml* 4A *160*
    (off Homesdale Rd.)
Sheridan M. E11 . . . . .6K 51
Sheridan Pl. BR1: Broml 2B 160
   SW13 . . . . .3B 116
   TW12: Hamp 1F 149
Sheridan Rd. DA7: Bex 3E 126
   DA17: Belv 4G 109
   E7 . . . . .3H 69
   E12 . . . . .5C 70
   SW19 . . . . .1H 153
   TW10: Ham 3C 132
Sheridan Ter. UB5: N'olt 5F 59
Sheridan Wlk. NW11 . . . . .6J 45
   SM5: Cars 5D 166
Sheridan Way BR3: Beck 1B 158
Sheriden Pl. HA1: Harr 7J 41
Sheringham NW8 . . . . .1B 82
Sheringham Av. E12 . . . . .4D 70
   N14 . . . . .5C 22
   RM7: Rom 6J 55
   TW2: Whitt 1D 130
Sheringham Ct. *TW13: Felt* 3J *129*
    (off Sheringham Av.)
   UB3: Hayes 2H 93
Sheringham Dr. IG11: Bark 5K 71
Sheringham Ho. NW1 . . . . .5C 4
Sheringham Rd. N7 . . . . .6K 65
   SE20 . . . . .3J 157
Sheringham Twr. UB1: S'hall 7F 77
Sherington Av. HA5: Hat E 7A 26
Sherington Rd. SE7 . . . . .6K 105
Sherland Rd. TW1: Twick 1K 131
Sherleys Ct. HA4: Ruis 2G 57
Sherlies Av. BR6: Orp 2J 173
Sherlock Cl. SW16 . . . . .2K 155
Sherlock Ct. *NW8* 1B *82*
    (off Dorman Way)
Sherlock Holmes Mus. 4F 5
Sherlock M. W1 . . . . .5G 5 (5E 82)
Sherman Av. KT12: Walt T 5A 148
Sherman Gdns.
   RM6: Chad H 6C 54
Sherman Ho. *E14* 6E *86*
    (off Dee St.)
   UB3: Harl 3E *92*
    (off Nine Acres Cl.)
Sherman Rd. BR1: Broml 1J 159
Shernhall St. E17 . . . . .3E 50
Sherrard Rd. E7 . . . . .6A 70
   E12 . . . . .6A 70
Sherrards Way
   EN5: Barn 5D 20
Sherren Ho. E1 . . . . .4J 85
Sherrick Grn. Rd. NW10 . . . . .5D 62
Sherriff Ct. *NW6* 6J *63*
    (off Sherriff Rd.)
Sherriff Rd. NW6 . . . . .6J 63
Sherringham Av. N17 . . . . .2G 49
   TW13: Felt 3J 129
Sherringham Ct. *E16* 6H *87*
    (off Silvertown Sq.)
Sherrington Ct. *E16* 5H *87*
    (off Rathbone St.)
Sherrin Rd. E10 . . . . .4D 68
Sherrock Gdns. NW4 . . . . .4D 44
Sherry M. IG11: Bark 7H 71
Sherston Ct. *SE1* 4B *102*
    (off Newington Butts)
   WC1 . . . . .2J 7
Sherwin Ho. SE11 . . . . .7J 19
Sherwin Rd. SE14 . . . . .1K 121
Sherwood
   KT6: Surb 2D 162
   NW6 . . . . .7G 63
Sherwood Av. E18 . . . . .3K 51
   HA4: Ruis 6G 39
   SW16 .7H 137
   UB4: Yead 4K 75
   UB6: G'frd 6J 59

Sherwood Cl. DA5: Bexl 6C 126
   E17 . . . . .2B 50
   SW13 . . . . .3D 116
   W13 . . . . .1B 96
Sherwood Ct. *CR2: S Croy* 5C *168*
    (off Nottingham Rd.)
   HA2: Harr 2F 59
   SW11 . . . . .3A 118
Sherwood Ct. *W1* 6E *4*
    (off Bryanston Pl.)
Sherwood Gdns. E14 . . . . .4C 104
   IG11: Bark 7H 71
   SE16 . . . . .5G 103
Sherwood Rd.
   CR0: C'don 7H 157
   DA16: Well 2J 125
   HA2: Harr 2G 59
   IG6: Ilf 4H 53
   NW4 . . . . .3E 44
   SW19 . . . . .7H 135
   TW12: Hamp H 5G 131
Sherwood St. N20 . . . . .3G 31
   W1 . . . . .2B 12 (7G 83)
Sherwood Ter. *E16* 6A *88*
    (off Bingley Rd.)
   N20 . . . . .3G 31
Sherwood Way BR4: W W'ck 2E 170
Shetland Ho. DA17: Belv 2H 109
Shetland Rd. E3 . . . . .2B 86
   TW6: H'row A 6E 110
Shield Dr. TW8: Bford 6A 96
Shieldhall St. SE2 . . . . .4C 108
Shield Rd. TW15: Ashf 4E 128
Shield St. SE15 . . . . .7F 103
Shifford Path SE23 . . . . .3K 139
Shillaker Ct. W3 . . . . .1B 98
Shillibeer Pl. *W1* 6D 4
Shillingford Cl. NW7 . . . . .7A 30
Shillingford Ho. *E3* 3D *86*
    (off Talwin St.)
Shillingford St. N1 . . . . .7B 66
Shilling Pl. W7 . . . . .2A 96
Shillingshaw Lodge *E16* 6J *87*
    (off Butchers Rd.)
Shillingstone Ho. *W14* 3G *99*
    (off Russell Rd.)
Shinfield St. W12 . . . . .6E 80
Shinglewell Rd. DA8: Erith 7G 109
Shingly Pl. E4 . . . . .1K 35
Shinners Cl. SE25 . . . . .5G 157
Ship All. W4 . . . . .6G 97
Ship & Mermaid Row
   SE1 . . . . .6F 15 (2D 102)
Shipbuilding Way E13 . . . . .2B 88
Shipka Rd. SW12 . . . . .1F 137
Shiplake Ho. *E2* 2J *9*
    (off Arnold Cir.)
Ship La. SW14 . . . . .3J 115
Shipman Rd. E16 . . . . .6K 87
   SE23 . . . . .2K 139
Ship St. SE8 . . . . .1C 122
Ship Tavern Pas. EC3 . . . . .2G 15 (7E 84)
Shipton Cl. RM8: Dag 3D 72
Shipton Ho. *E2* 1K *9*
    (off Shipton St.)
Shipton Rd. UB10: Ick 4B 56
Shipton St. E2 . . . . .1K 9 (2F 85)
Shipwright Rd. SE16 . . . . .2A 104
Shipwright St. E16 . . . . .2K 105
Shipwright Yd. SE1 . . . . . .5G 15 (1E 102)
Ship Yd. E14 . . . . .5D 104
Shirburn Cl. SE23 . . . . .7J 121
Shirebrook Rd. SE3 . . . . .3B 124
Shire Ct.
   DA18: Erith 3D 108
   KT17: Ewe 7B 164
Shirehall Cl. NW4 . . . . .6F 45
Shirehall Gdns. NW4 . . . . .6F 45
Shirehall La. NW4 . . . . .6F 45

Shirehall Pk. NW4 . . . . .5F 45
Shire Horse Way TW7: Isle 3K 113
Shire Ho. *E3* .3D *86*
    (off Talwin St.)
   EC1 . . . . .4E *8*
    (off Lambs Pas.)
Shire La. BR2: Kes 7C 172
   BR6: Chels, Downe 7F 173
    (not continuous)
The Shire London Golf Course 1A 20
Shire M. TW2: Whitt 6G 113
Shire Pl. SW18 . . . . .7A 118
   TW8: Bford 7D 96
The Shires TW10: Ham 4E 132
Shirland M. W9 . . . . .3H 81
Shirland Rd. W9 . . . . .3H 81
Shirlbutt St. E14 . . . . .7D 86
Shirley Cl. SW16 . . . . .7J 137
Shirley Cres. BR3: Beck 4A 158
Shirley Dr. TW3: Houn 5G 113
Shirley Gdns. IG11: Bark 6J 71
   W7 . . . . .1K 95
Shirley Gro. N9 . . . . .7D 24
   SW11 . . . . .3E 118
Shirley Hgts. SM6: W'gton 7G 167
Shirley Hills Rd.
   CR0: C'don 5J 169
Shirley Ho. *SE5* 7D *102*
    (off Picton St.)
Shirley Ho. Dr. SE7 . . . . .7A 106
SHIRLEY OAKS 1K 169
Shirley Oaks Rd. CR0: C'don 1K 169
Shirley Pk. CR0: C'don 2J 169
Shirley Pk. Golf Course 2H 169
Shirley Pk. Rd. CR0: C'don 1H 169
Shirley Rd. CR0: C'don 7H 157
   DA15: Sidc 3J 143
   E15 . . . . .7G 69
   EN2: Enf .3H 23
   SM6: W'gton 7G 167
   W4 . . . . .2K 97
The Shirley Sherwood
   Gallery of Botanical Art 2F 115
Shirley St. E16 . . . . .6H 87
Shirley Way CR0: C'don 3A 170
Shirley Windmill 3J 169
Shirlock Rd. NW3 . . . . .4D 64
Shirwell Cl. NW7 . . . . .7A 30
Shobden Rd. N17 . . . . .1D 48
Shobroke Cl. NW2 . . . . .3E 62
Shoebury Rd. E6 . . . . .7D 70
Shoelands Ct. NW9 . . . . .3K 43
Shoe La. EC4 . . . . .7K 7 (6A 84)
Sholto Rd. TW6: H'row A 5B 110
Shona Ho. E13 . . . . .5A 88
Shooters Av. HA3: Kenton 4C 42
SHOOTERS HILL 1E 124
Shooters Hill DA16: Well 1D 124
   SE18 . . . . .1D 124
Shooters Hill Golf Course 1G 125
Shooters Hill Rd. SE3 . . . . .1F 123
   SE10 . . . . .1F 123
   SE18 . . . . .1F 123
Shooters Rd. EN2: Enf 1G 23
Shoot Up Hill NW2 . . . . .5G 63
The Shopping Hall E6 . . . . .1C 88
Shore Bus. Cen. E9 . . . . .7J 67
Shore Cl. TW12: Hamp 6C 130
   TW14: Felt 7J 111
Shoredicche Cl. UB10: Ick 3B 56
SHOREDITCH 1G 9 (3E 84)
Shoreditch Ct. *E8* 7F *67*
    (off Queensbridge Rd.)
Shoreditch High St. E1 . . . . .4H 9 (4E 84)

Shoreditch Ho. BR2: Broml 6C 160
   N1 . . . . .2F 9
Shore Gro. TW13: Hanw 2E 130
Shoreham Cl. CR0: C'don 6J 157
   DA5: Bexl 1D 144
   SW18 . . . . .5K 117
Shoreham Rd. E.
   TW6: H'row A 5A 110
Shoreham Rd. W.
   TW6: H'row A 5A 110
Shoreham Way BR2: Hayes 6J 159
Shore Ho. SW8 . . . . .3F 119
Shore M. *E9* .7J *67*
    (off Shore Rd.)
Shore Pl. E9 . . . . .7J 67
Shore Point IG9: Buck H 2E 36
Shore Rd. E9 . . . . .7J 67
Shore Way *SW9* 2A *120*
    (off Crowhurst Cl.)
Shorncliffe Rd. SE1 . . . . .5F 103
Shorndean St. SE6 . . . . .1E 140
Shorne Cl. DA15: Sidc 6B 126
Shornefield Cl. BR1: Broml 3E 160
Shornells Way SE2 . . . . .4C 108
Short Blue Pl. IG11: Bark 7G 71
Shortcroft Rd. KT17: Ewe 7B 164
Shortcrofts Rd. RM9: Dag 6F 73
Shorter St. E1 . . . . .2J 15 (7F 85)
Shortgate N12 . . . . .4C 30
Short Hedges TW3: Houn 1E 112
Short Hill HA1: Harr 1J 59
SHORTLANDS 2G 159
Shortlands UB3: Harl 6F 93
   W6 . . . . .4F 99
Shortlands Cl. DA17: Belv 3F 109
   N18 . . . . .3J 33
Shortlands Gdns.
   BR2: Broml 2G 159
Shortlands Golf Course 1G 159
Shortlands Gro. BR2: Broml 3F 159
Shortlands Rd. BR2: Broml 3F 159
   E10 . . . . .7D 50
   KT2: King T 7F 133
Short La. TW19: Stanw 7B 110
Short Path SE18 . . . . .6E 107
Short Rd. E11 . . . . .2G 69
   TW6: H'row A 6A 110
   W4 . . . . .6A 98
Shorts Cft. NW9 . . . . .4H 43
Shorts Gdns. WC2 . . . . . . .1E 12 (6J 83)
Shorts Rd. SM5: Cars 4C 166
Short St. *NW4* 4E *44*
    (off Foster St.)
   SE1 . . . . .6K 13 (2A *102*)
Short Wall E15 . . . . .3E 86
Short Way SE9 . . . . .3C 124
   TW2: Whitt 7G 113
Shortway N12 . . . . .6H 31
Shotfield SM6: W'gton 6F 167
Shott Cl. SM1: Sutt 5A 166
Shottendane Rd. SW6 . . . . .1J 117
Shottery Cl. SE9 . . . . .3C 142
Shottfield Av. SW14 . . . . .4A 116
Shottsford *W2* 6J *81*
    (off Talbot Rd.)
Shoulder of Mutton All. E14 . . . . . .7A 86
Shouldham St. W1 . . . . . . .6D 4 (5C 82)
Showcase Cinema 3H 89
Showers Way UB3: Hayes 1J 93
Shrapnel Cl. SE18 . . . . .7C 106
Shrapnel Rd. SE9 . . . . .3D 124
Shrek's Adventure! 6G 13 (2K 101)
Shrewsbury Av. HA3: Kenton 4E 42
   SW14 . . . . .4J 115
Shrewsbury Cl. KT6: Surb 2E 162
Shrewsbury Ct. EC1 . . . . .4D 8
Shrewsbury Ho. SW3 . . . . .7C 16
   SW8 . . . . .7H 19
Shrewsbury La. SE18 . . . . .1F 125
Shrewsbury M. *W2* 5J *81*
    (off Chepstow Rd.)

Shrewsbury Rd.—Simone Cl.

Shrewsbury Rd. BR3: Beck 3A 158
E7 5B 70
N11 6B 32
NW10 1K 79
SM5: Cars 6C 154
TW6: H'row A 6E 110
(not continuous)
W2 6J 81
Shrewsbury St. W10 4E 80
Shrewsbury Wlk. *TW7: Isle* 3A 114
(off Magdala Rd.)
Shrewton Rd. SW17 7D 136
Shri Swaminarayan Mandir
London 6K 61
Shroffold Rd. BR1: Broml 4G 141
Shropshire Cl. CR4: Mitc 4J 155
Shropshire Ct. *W7* 6K 77
(off Copley Cl.)
Shropshire Ho. *N18* 5C 34
(off Cavendish Cl.)
Shropshire Pl. WC1 4C 6 (4G 83)
Shropshire Rd. N22 7E 32
Shroton St. NW1 5D 4 (5C 82)
The Shrubberies E18 2J 51
The Shrubbery E11 5K 51
KT6: Surb 1E 162
Shrubbery Cl. N1 1C 84
Shrubbery Gdns. N21 7G 23
Shrubbery Rd. N9 3B 34
SW16 4J 137
UB1: S'hall 1D 94
Shrubland Gro. KT4: Wor Pk 3E 164
Shrubland Rd. E8 1F 85
E10 7C 50
E17 5C 50
Shrublands Av. CR0: C'don 3C 170
Shrublands Cl. N20 1G 31
SE26 3J 139
Shrubsall Cl. SE9 1C 142
Shuna Wlk. N1 6D 66
Shurland Av. EN4: E Barn 6G 21
Shurland Gdns. SE15 7F 103
Shurlock Dr. BR6: Farnb 4G 173
Shushan Cl. N16 7E 48
Shuters Sq. W14 5H 99
Shuttle Cl. DA15: Sidc 7K 125
Shuttlemead DA5: Bexl 7F 127
Shuttle St. E1 4G 85
Shuttleworth Rd. SW11 2C 118
Siamese M. N3 1J 45
Siani M. N8 4B 48
Sibella Rd. SW4 2H 119
Sibley Cl. BR1: Broml 5C 160
DA6: Bex 5E 126
Sibley Ct. BR2: Broml 2F 159
UB8: Hil 5E 74
Sibley Gro. E12 7C 70
Sibthorpe Rd. SE12 6K 123
Sibthorp Rd. CR4: Mitc 2D 154
Sibton Rd. SM5: Cars 7C 154
Sicilian Av. WC1 6F 7
Sickle Cnr. RM9: Dag 4H 91
Sidbury St. SW6 1G 117
SIDCUP 4A 144
Sidcup By-Pass
BR7: Chst 3H 143
Sidcup Family Golf 3G 143
Sidcup Golf Course 1B 144
Sidcup High St.
DA14: Sidc 4A 144
Sidcup Hill DA14: Sidc 4B 144
Sidcup Hill Gdns.
DA14: Sidc 5C 144
Sidcup Leisure Cen. 2A 144
Sidcup Place 5A 144
Sidcup Pl. DA14: Sidc 5A 144
Sidcup Rd. SE9 1D 142
SE12 6A 124
Sidcup Technology Cen.
DA14: Sidc 5D 144
Siddeley Dr. TW4: Houn 3C 112
Siddeley Rd. E17 2E 50
Siddons La. NW1 4F 5 (4D 82)
Siddons Rd. CR0: Wadd 3A 168
N17 1G 49
SE23 2A 140
Sidewood Rd. SE9 1H 143
Sidford Ho. SE1 2H 19
Sidford Pl. SE1 2H 19 (3A 102)
Sidgwick Ho. *SW9* 2K 119
(off Stockwell Rd.)
Sidi Ct. N15 3B 48
The Sidings E11 1E 68
The Sidings Apts. E16 2E 106
Sidings M. N7 3A 66
Siding St. E20 1D 86
Sidlaw Ho. N16 1F 67
Sidmouth Av. TW7: Isle 2J 113
Sidmouth Dr. HA4: Ruis 3J 57
Sidmouth Ho. *SE15* 7G 103
(off Lindsey Est.)
W1 7D 4
(off Cato St.)
Sidmouth M. WC1 2G 7 (3K 83)
Sidmouth Pde. NW2 7E 62
Sidmouth Rd. DA16: Well 7C 108
E10 3E 68
NW2 7E 62
Sidmouth St. WC1 2F 7 (3J 83)
Sidney Av. N13 5E 32
Sidney Boyd Ct. NW6 7J 63
Sidney Elson Way E6 2E 88
Sidney Est. E1 6J 85
(Bromhead St.)
E1 5J 85
(Lindley St.)
Sidney Gdns. TW8: Bford 6D 96
Sidney Godley (VC) Ho. *E2* 3J 85
(off Digby St.)
Sidney Gro. EC1 1A 8 (2B 84)
Sidney Ho. *E2* 2K 85
(off Old Ford Rd.)
Sidney Miller Ct. *W3* 1H 97
(off Crown St.)
Sidney Rd. BR3: Beck 2A 158
E7 3J 69
HA2: Harr 3G 41
KT12: Walt T 7J 147
N22 7E 32
SE25 5G 157
SW9 2K 119
TW1: Twick 6A 114
Sidney Sq. E1 5J 85
Sidney St. E1 5H 85
(not continuous)
Sidney Webb Ho. *SE1* 3D 102
(off Tabard St.)
Sidonie Apts. *SW11* 4C 118
(off Danvers Av.)
Sidworth St. E8 7H 67
Siebert Rd. SE3 6J 105
Siege Ho. *E1* 6H 85
(off Sidney St.)
Siemens Brothers Way E16 7J 87
Siemens Rd. SE18 3B 106
Sienna SE28 3A 108
Sienna Alto *SE13* 3E 122
(off Cornmill La.)
Sienna Cl. KT9: Chess 6D 162
Sienna Ho. *E20* 6D 68
(off Victory Pde.)
Sienna Ter. NW2 2C 62
Sigdon Pas. E8 5G 67
Sigdon Rd. E8 5G 67
The Sigers HA5: Eastc 6K 39
Sigmund Freud Statue 6B 64
Signal Ho. *E8* 7H 67
(off Martello Ter.)
SE1 7C 14
(off Gt. Suffolk St.)
Signal Wlk. E4 6K 35
Signmakers Yd. *NW1* 1F 83
(off Delancey St.)
Sigrist Sq. KT2: King T 1E 150
Sikorski Mus. 7B 10 (2B 100)
Silbury Av. CR4: Mitc 1C 154
Silbury Ho. SE26 3G 139
Silbury St. N1 1E 8 (3D 84)
Silchester Ct.
CR7: Thor H 4A 156
TW15: Ashf 2A 128
Silchester Rd. W10 6F 81
Silecroft Rd. DA7: Bex 1G 127
Silesia Bldgs. E8 7H 67
Silex St. SE1 7B 14 (2B 102)
Silicon Bus. Cen.
UB6: G'frd 2C 78
Silicon M. E3 1C 86
Silicon Way N1 2F 9
Silk Cl. SE12 5J 123
Silk Ct. *E2* 3G 85
(off Squirries St.)
Silkfield Rd. NW9 5A 44
Silk Ho. E1 1K 15
(Leman St.)
E1 5K 85
(off Trafalgar Gdns.)
Silk Ho. *E2* 2F 85
(off How's St.)
NW9 3K 43
Silkin M. SE15 7G 103
Silk M. SE11 5K 19
Silk Mills Pas. SE13 2D 122
Silk Mills Path SE13 2E 122
(not continuous)
Silk Mills Sq. E9 6B 68
Silk Rd. SM6: W'gton 2E 166
Silks Ct. E11 1H 69
Silkstream Pde. HA8: Edg 1J 43
Silkstream Rd. HA8: Edg 1J 43
Silk St. EC2 5D 8 (5C 84)
Silk Weaver Way E2 2H 85
Sillitoe Ho. *N1* 1D 84
(off Colville Est.)
Silsoe Ho. NW1 2F 83
Silsoe Rd. N22 2K 47
Silverbeck Way
TW19: Stanw M 7B 174
Silver Birch Av. E4 5G 35
Silver Birch Cl. DA2: Wilm 4K 145
N11 6K 31
SE6 3B 140
SE28 1A 108
UB10: Ick 4A 56
Silver Birch Gdns. E6 4D 88
Silverbirch Wlk. NW3 6D 64
Silverburn Ho. *SW9* 1B 120
(off Lothian Rd.)
Silvercliffe Gdns. EN4: E Barn 4H 21
Silver Cl. HA3: Hrw W 7C 26
SE14 7A 104
Silver Cres. W4 4H 97
Silverdale EN2: Enf 4D 22
NW1 1A 6
(off Harrington St.)
SE26 4J 139
Silverdale Av. IG2: Ilf 5J 53
The Silverdale Cen. HA0: Wemb 1F 79
Silverdale Cl. SM1: Sutt 4H 165
UB5: N'olt 5D 58
W7 1J 95
Silverdale Ct. EC1 3B 8
Silverdale Dr. SE9 2C 142
TW16: Sun 2K 147
Silverdale Factory Cen.
UB3: Hayes 3J 93
Silverdale Gdns. UB3: Hayes 2J 93
Silverdale Ind. Est.
UB3: Hayes 2J 93
Silverdale Rd. BR5: Pet W 4G 161
DA7: Bex 2H 127
E4 6A 36
UB3: Hayes 2H 93
Silverdene *N12* 6E 30
(off Thyra Gro.)
Silvergate KT19: Ewe 5J 163
Silverhall St. TW7: Isle 3A 114
Silverholme Cl. HA3: Kenton 7E 42
Silver Jubilee Way
TW4: Cran 2K 111
Silverland St. E16 1D 106
Silver La. BR4: W W'ck 2F 171
Silverleigh Rd.
CR7: Thor H 4K 155
Silver Mead E18 1J 51
Silvermere Dr. N18 6E 34
Silvermere Rd. SE6 7D 122
Silver Pl. W1 2B 12 (6G 83)
Silver Rd. SE13 3D 122
W12 7F 81
Silvers *IG9: Buck H* 1F 37
(off Palmerston Rd.)
Silver Spring Cl. DA8: Erith 6H 109
Silverston Way HA7: Stan 6H 27
Silver St. EN1: Enf 3J 23
N18 4J 33
Silverthorn *NW8* 1K 81
(off Abbey Rd.)
Silverthorne Loft Apts. *SE5* 6D 102
(off Albany Rd.)
Silverthorne Rd. SW8 2F 119
Silverthorn Gdns. E4 2H 35
Silverton Rd. W6 6F 99
SILVERTOWN 1A 106
Silvertown Quay Development
E16 1A 106
Silvertown Sq. E16 6H 87
Silvertown Viaduct E16 6H 87
Silvertown Way E16 6G 87
(Clarkson Rd.)
E16 1J 105
(Hanover Av.)
Silvertree La. UB6: G'frd 3H 77
Silver Wlk. SE16 1A 104
Silver Way RM7: Mawney 3H 55
UB10: Hil 2D 74
Silver Wing Ind. Est.
CR0: Wadd 6K 167
Silverwood Cl. BR3: Beck 7C 140
CR0: Sels 7B 170
HA6: Nwood 1E 38
Silverwood Pl. SE10 1E 122
Silverworks Cl. NW9 3K 43
Silvester Ho. *E1* 6H 85
(off Varden St.)
E2 3J 85
(off Sceptre Rd.)
W11 6H 81
(off Basing St.)
Silvester Rd. SE22 5F 121
Silvester St. SE1 7E 14 (2D 102)
Silvocea Way E14 6F 87
Silwood Est. SE16 4J 103
Silwood St. *SE16* 4J 103
(off Rotherhithe New Rd.)
Simkins Cl. SW2 4J 119
Simla Ct. *N7* 7J 65
(off Brewery Rd.)
Simla Ho. *SE1* 7F 15
(off Kipling Est.)
Simmonds Ct. *SW5* 4K 99
(off Earl's Ct. Gdns.)
Simmonds Ho. *TW8: Bford* 5E 96
(off Clayponds La.)
Simmons Cl. KT9: Chess 6C 162
N20 2H 31
Simmons Dr. RM8: Dag 3E 72
Simmons La. E4 2A 36
Simmons Way N20 2H 31
Simms Cl. SM5: Cars 2C 166
Simms Gdns. N2 2A 46
Simms Rd. SE1 4G 103
Simnel Rd. SE12 7K 123
Simon Cl. W11 7H 81
Simon Ct. *W9* 3J 81
(off Saltram Cres.)
Simonds Rd. E10 2C 68
Simone Cl. BR1: Broml 1B 160

A-Z London 399

Simone Ct. SE26 . . . . .3J 139
Simons Ct. N16 . . . . .2F 67
Simons Wlk. E15 . . . . .5F 69
Simpson Cl. CRO: C'don 5C 156
N21 . . . . .5D 22
Simpson Dr. W3 . . . . .6K 79
Simpson Ho. NW8 . . . . . .20 4 (4C 82)
SE11 . . . . .6g 19 (5K 101)
Simpson Rd. TW4: Houn 6D 112
TW10: Ham 4C 132
Simpson's Rd. BR1: Broml 3J 159
E14 . . . . .7D 86
Simpson St. SW11 . . . . .2C 118
Simpson Way KT6: Surb 6C 150
Simrose Ct. SW18 . . . . .5J 117
Sim St. N4 . . . . .2C 66
Sims Wlk. SE3 . . . . .4H 123
Sinclair Cl. CRO: C'don 2E 168
Sinclair Dr. SM2: Sutt 7K 165
Sinclair Gdns. W14 . . . . .2F 99
Sinclair Gro. NW11 . . . . .6F 45
Sinclair Ho. E15 . . . . .6F 69
(off Leyton Rd.)
WC1 . . . . .2E 6
(off Sandwich St.)
Sinclair Mans. W12 . . . . .2F 99
(off Richmond Way)
Sinclair Pl. SE4 . . . . .6C 122
Sinclair Rd. E4 . . . . .5G 35
W14 . . . . .2F 99
Sinclairs Ho. E3 . . . . .2B 86
(off St Stephen's Rd.)
Sinclare Cl. Enf 1A 24
Sindercombe M. W12 . . . . .3C 98
Singapore Rd. W13 . . . . .1A 96
Singer M. SW4 . . . . .2J 119
Singer St. EC2 . . . . . .2F 9 (3D 84)
Singleton Cl. CRO: C'don 7C 156
SW17 . . . . .7D 136
Singleton Rd. RM9: Dag 5F 73
Singleton Scarp N12 . . . . .5D 30
Sinnott Rd. E17 . . . . .1K 49
Siobhan Davies Dance Studios . . .3B 102
(off St George's Rd.)
Sion Ct. TW1: Twick 1B 132
Sion Rd. TW1: Twick 1B 132
Sippets Ct. IG1: Ilf 1H 71
SIPSON 6C 92
Sipson Cl. UB7: Sip 6C 92
Sipson La. UB3: Harl 6C 92
UB7: Sip 6C 92
Sipson Rd. UB7: Sip, W Dray 3B 92
(not continuous)
Sipson Way UB7: Sip 7C 92
Sir Abraham Dawes Cotts.
SW15 . . . . .4G 117
Sir Alexander Cl. W3 . . . . .1B 98
Sir Alexander Rd. W3 . . . . .1B 98
Sir Christopher France Ho.
E1 . . . . .3A 86
Sir Cyril Black Way SW19 . . . . .7J 135
Sirdar Rd. CR4: Mitc 6E 136
N22 . . . . .3B 48
W11 . . . . .7F 81
Sireen Apts. E3 . . . . .4B 86
Sir Francis Drake Ct. SE10 . . . . . .5F 105
Sirinham Point SW8 . . . . .7H 19
Sirius Bldg. E1 . . . . .7K 85
(off Jardine Rd.)
Sirius Ho. SE16 . . . . .4A 104
(off Seafarer Way)
Sir James Black Ho. SE5 . . . . . .2D 120
(off Coldharbour La.)
Sir John Kirk Cl. SE5 . . . . .7C 102
Sir John Lyon Ho. EC4 . . . . .2C 14
(off High Timber St.)
Sir John Morden Wlk. SE3 . . . . . .2J 123
Sir John Soane's Mus. 7G 7 (6K 83)
Sir Nicholas Garrow Ho. W10 . . . . .4G 81
(off Kensal Rd.)
Sir Oswald Stoll Mans. SW6 . . . . . .7K 99
(off Fulham Rd.)

Sir Simon Milton Sq.
SW1 . . . . .2K 17 (3F 101)
SIR STEVE REDGRAVE BRIDGE 7F 89
Sir Walter Raleigh Ct.
SE10 . . . . .5G 105
Sir William Powell's Almshouses
SW6 . . . . .2G 117
Sise La. EC4 . . . . .1E 14 (6D 84)
Siskin Ho. SE16 . . . . .4K 103
(off Tawny Way)
Siskin Pl. UB4: Yead 5A 76
Sisley Rd. IG11: Bark 1J 89
Sispara Gdns. SW18 . . . . .6H 117
Sissinghurst Cl. BR1: Broml 5G 141
Sissinghurst Ho. SE15 . . . . .6J 103
(off Sharratt St.)
Sissinghurst Rd. CRO: C'don 7G 157
Sissulu Ct. E6 . . . . .1A 88
Sister Mabel's Way SE15 . . . . .7G 103
Sisters Av. SW11 . . . . .3D 118
Sistova Rd. SW12 . . . . .1F 137
Sisulu Pl. SW9 . . . . .3A 120
Sitarey Ct. W12 . . . . .1D 98
Sitka Ho. SE16 . . . . .2E 104
Sittingbourne Av. EN1: Enf 6J 23
Sitwell Gro. HA7: Stan 5E 26
Siverst Cl. UB5: N'olt 6F 59
Sivill Ho. E2 . . . . .1K 9
(off Columbia Rd.)
Siviter Way RM10: Dag 7H 73
Siward Rd. BR2: Broml 3K 159
N17 . . . . .1D 48
SW17 . . . . .3A 136
Six Acres Est. N4 . . . . .2K 65
Six Bridges Ind. Est. SE1 . . . . .5G 103
(not continuous)
Sixpenny Ct. IG11: Bark 6G 71
Sixth Av. E12 . . . . .4D 70
UB3: Hayes 1H 93
W10 . . . . .3G 81
Sixth Cross Rd. TW2: Twick 3G 131
Siyah Gdn. E3 . . . . .3B 86
Skardu Rd. NW2 . . . . .5G 63
Skeena Hill SW18 . . . . .7G 117
Skeffington Rd. E6 . . . . .1D 88
Skeffington St. SE18 . . . . .3G 107
Skeggs Ho. E14 . . . . .3E 104
(off Glengall St.)
Skegness Ho. N7 . . . . .7K 65
(off Sutterton St.)
Skelbrook St. SW18 . . . . .2A 136
Skelgill Rd. SW15 . . . . .4H 117
Skelley Rd. E15 . . . . .7H 69
Skelton Cl. E8 . . . . .6F 67
Skelton Lodge SE10 . . . . .3J 105
(off Billingshurst Way)
Skelton Rd. E7 . . . . .6J 69
Skelton's La. E10 . . . . .7D 50
Skelwith Rd. W6 . . . . .6E 98
Skenfrith Ho. SE15 . . . . .6H 103
(off Commercial Way)
Skerne Rd. KT2: King T 1D 150
Skerne Wlk. KT2: King T 1D 150
Sketch Apts. E1 . . . . .5K 85
(off Shandy St.)
Sketchley Gdns. SE16 . . . . .5K 103
Sketty Rd. EN1: Enf 3A 24
Skieasy 2K 115
Skiers St. E15 . . . . .1G 87
Skiffington Cl. SW2 . . . . .1A 138
Skillen Lodge HA5: Pinn 1B 40
Skinner Ct. E3 . . . . .4D 86
(off Barry Blandford Way)
Skinner Pl. SW1 . . . . .4G 17
Skinners Ct. N13 . . . . .4F 33
Skinners La. EC4 . . . . . . .2D 14 (7C 84)
TW5: Hest 1F 113
Skinner's Row SE10 . . . . .1D 122
Skinner St. EC1 . . . . .2K 7 (3A 84)
Skip La. UB9: Hare 1A 56
Skipper Cl. IG11: Bark 1G 89
Skipsea Ho. SW18 . . . . .6C 118

Skipsey Av. E6 . . . . .3D 88
Skipton Cl. N11 . . . . .6K 31
Skipton Dr. UB3: Harl 3E 92
Skipton Ho. SE4 . . . . .4A 122
Skipwith Ho. EC1 . . . . .5J 7
(off Bourne Est.)
Skipworth Rd. E9 . . . . .1J 85
Skua Ct. SE8 . . . . .6B 104
(off Dorking Cl.)
Skye La. HA8: Edg 4A 28
Sky Gdn. Wlk. EC3 . . . . .2G 15
(off Philpot La.)
Skylark Cl. RM13: Rain 2K 91
SE1 . . . . .7D 14
(off Swan St.)
SW15 . . . . .6E 116
Skyline Apts. N4 . . . . .2F 67
(off Devan Gro.)
Skyline Ct. CRO: C'don 3D 168
(off Park La.)
SE1 . . . . .3F 103
Skyline Plaza Bldg. E1 . . . . .6G 85
(off Commercial Rd.)
Skylines E14 . . . . .2E 104
Skylines Village E14 . . . . .2E 104
Sky Peals Rd.
IG8: Wfd G 7A 36
Skyport Dr. UB7: Harm 3E 174
Sky Studios E16 . . . . .2E 106
Skyvan Cl. TW6: H'row A 5E 110
Skyview Apts. CRO: C'don 2C 168
(off Park St.)
Sky View Tower E15 . . . . .2D 86
(off High Street)
Skyway 14 SL3: Poyle 6A 174
The Slade SE18 . . . . .6J 107
Sladebrook Rd. SE3 . . . . .3B 124
Slade Ct. EN5: New Bar 3E 20
Sladedale Rd. SE18 . . . . .5J 107
Slade Ho. TW4: Houn 6D 112
Sladen Pl. E5 . . . . .4H 67
Slades Cl. EN2: Enf 3F 23
Slades Dr. BR7: Chst 3G 143
Slades Gdns. EN2: Enf 2F 23
Slades Hill EN2: Enf 3F 23
Slades Ri. EN2: Enf 3F 23
Slade Twr. E10 . . . . .2C 68
(off Leyton Grange Est.)
Slade Wlk. SE17 . . . . .6B 102
Slade Way CR4: Mitc 1E 154
Slagrove Pl. SE13 . . . . .5C 122
Slaidburn St. SW10 . . . . .6A 100
Slaithwaite Rd. SE13 . . . . .4E 122
Slaney Cl. NW10 . . . . .7E 62
Slaney Pl. N7 . . . . .5A 66
Slate Ho. E14 . . . . .4C 86
(off Keymer Pl.)
Slater Cl. SE18 . . . . .5E 106
Slater M. SW4 . . . . .3G 119
(off Grafton Sq.)
Slatter NW9 .7G 29
Slattery Rd. TW13: Felt 1B 130
Sleaford Ho. E3 . . . . .4C 86
(off Fern St.)
Sleaford Ind. Est. SW8 . . . . .7G 101
Sleaford St. SW8 . . . . .7G 101
Sleat Ho. E3 .2B 86
(off Saxon Rd.)
Sledmere Ct. TW14: Bedf 1G 129
Sleigh Ho. E2 . . . . .3J 85
(off Bacton St.)
The Slide 7D 68
Slievemore Cl. SW4 . . . . .3H 119
Sligo Ho. E1 .4K 85
(off Beaumont Gro.)
Slindon Ct. N16 . . . . .3F 67
Slingsby Pl. WC2 . . . . .2E 12 (7J 83)
Slippers Pl. SE16 . . . . .3H 103
Slipway Ho. E14 . . . . .5D 104
(off Burrells Wharf Sq.)
Sloane Av. SW3 . . . . .4D 16 (4C 100)
Sloane Av. Mans. SW3 . . . .4E 16 (4D 100)

Sloane Ct. TW7: Isle 1J 113
Sloane Ct. E.
SW3 . . . . .5G 17 (5E 100)
Sloane Ct. W.
SW3 . . . . .5G 17 (5E 100)
Sloane Gdns. BR6: Farnb 3G 173
SW1 . . . . .4G 17 (4E 100)
Sloane Ga. Mans. SW1 . . . . .3G 17
(off D'Oyley St.)
Sloane Ho. E9 . . . . .7J 67
(off Loddiges Rd.)
Sloane M. N8 .5J 47
Sloane Sq. SW1 . . . . .4G 17 (4E 100)
Sloane St. SW1 . . . . .7F 11 (2D 100)
Sloane Ter. SW1 . . . . .3G 17 (4E 100)
Sloane Ter. Mans. SW1 . . . . .3G 17
(off Sloane Ter.)
Sloane Wlk. CRO: C'don 6B 158
Slocum Cl. SE28 . . . . .7C 90
Slough La. NW9 . . . . .5J 43
Sly St. E1 . . . . .6H 85
Smaldon Cl. UB7: W Dray 3C 92
Smallberry Av. TW7: Isle 2K 113
Smallbrook M. W2 . . . . . . .1A 10 (6B 82)
Smalley Cl. N16 . . . . .3F 67
Smalley Rd. Est. N16 . . . . .3F 67
(off Smalley Cl.)
Smallwood Rd. SW17 . . . . .4B 136
Smarden Cl. DA17: Belv 5G 109
Smarden Gro. SE9 . . . . .4D 142
Smart's Pl. N18 . . . . .5B 34
WC2 . . . . .7F 7 (6J 83)
Smart St. E2 .3K 85
Smead Way SE13 . . . . .3D 122
Smeaton Cl. KT9: Chess 6D 162
Smeaton Ct. SE1 . . . . .3C 102
Smeaton Rd. IG8: Wfd G 5J 37
SW18 . . . . .7J 117
Smeaton St. E1 . . . . .1H 103
Smedley St. SW4 . . . . .2H 119
SW8 . . . . .2H 119
Smeed Rd. E3 . . . . .7C 68
Smikle Ct. SE14 . . . . .1K 121
(off Hatcham Pk. M.)
Smiles Pl. SE13 . . . . .2E 122
Smith Cl. SE16 . . . . .1K 103
Smithfield Ct. E1 . . . . .7G 85
(off Cable St.)
Smithfield Market 6A 8
Smithfield Sq. N8 . . . . .4J 47
Smithfield St. EC1 . . . . . . .6A 8 (5B 84)
Smith Hill TW8: Bford 6E 96
Smithies Rd. SE2 . . . . .4B 108
Smith's Ct. W1 . . . . .2B 12
Smithson Rd. N17 . . . . .1D 48
Smiths Point E13 . . . . .1J 87
(off Brooks Rd.)
Smith Sq. SW1 . . . . .2E 18 (3J 101)
Smiths Sq. W6 . . . . .5F 99
Smith St. KT5: Surb 6F 151
SW3 . . . . .5E 16 (5D 100)
Smiths Yd. CRO: C'don 3C 168
(off St George's Wlk.)
SW18 . . . . .2A 136
Smith Ter. SW3 . . . . .6E 16 (5D 100)
Smithwood Cl. SW19 . . . . .1G 135
Smithy La. TW3: Houn 3F 113
Smithy St. E1 . . . . .5J 85
Smock Wlk. CRO: C'don 6C 156
Smokehouse Yd. EC1 . . . . .5B 8
(off St John St.)
Smoothfield Ct. TW3: Houn 4E 112
Smugglers Way SW18 . . . . .4K 117
Smugglers Yd. W12 . . . . .1D 98
(off Devonport Rd.)
Smyrk's Rd. SE17 . . . . .5E 102
Smyrna Mans. NW6 . . . . .7J 63
(off Smyrna Rd.)
Smyrna Rd. NW6 . . . . .7J 63
Smythe Cl. N9 . . . . .3B 34
Smythe St. E14 . . . . .7D 86
Snag La. BR6: Prat B 7J 173

Snakes La. N14 . . . . .3A **22**
Snakes La. E.
  IG8: Buck H, Wfd G 6F **37**
Snakes La. W. IG8: Wfd G 5D **36**
Snakey La. TW13: Felt 4J **129**
SNARESBROOK 5J **51**
Snaresbrook Dr. HA7: Stan 4J **27**
Snaresbrook Hall E18 . . . . .4J **51**
Snaresbrook Ho. E18 . . . . .4H **51**
Snaresbrook Rd. E11 . . . . .4G **51**
Snarsgate St. W10 . . . . .5E **80**
Sneath Av. NW11 . . . . .7H **45**
Snells Pk. N18 . . . . .6A **34**
Sneyd Rd. NW2 . . . . .4E **62**
Snowberry Cl. E15 . . . . .4F **69**
  EN5: Barn 3C **20**
Snowbury Rd. Sw6 . . . . .2K **117**
Snowden Av. UB10: Hil 2D **74**
Snowden St. EC2 . . . . . . .4G **9** (4E **84**)
Snowdon Aviary 1D **82**
  (in London Zoo)
Snowdon Cres. UB3: Harl 3E **92**
Snowdon Dr. NW9 . . . . .6A **44**
Snowdon Rd. TW6: H'row A 6E **110**
Snowdown Cl. SE20 . . . . .1K **157**
Snowdrop Cl. TW12: Hamp 6E **130**
Snowdrop Ct. RM13: Rain 2J **91**
Snowdrop M. HA5: Pinn 2A **40**
Snow Hill EC1 . . . . .6A **8** (5B **84**)
Snow Hill Ct. EC1 . . . . . .7B **8** (6B **84**)
Snowman Ho. NW6 . . . . .1K **81**
Snowsfields SE1 . . . . . .6F **15** (2D **102**)
Snowshill Rd. E12 . . . . .5C **70**
Snowy Fielder Waye
  TW7: Isle 2B **114**
Soames Pl. EN4: Had W 2E **20**
Soames St. SE15 . . . . .3F **121**
Soames Wlk. KT3: N Mald 1A **152**
Soane Cl. W5 . . . . .2D **96**
Soane Ct. NW1 . . . . .7G **65**
  (off St Pancras Way)
Soane Ct. SE17 . . . . .5D **102**
  (off Roland Way)
Soane Sq. HA7: Stan 3D **26**
Soap Ho. La. TW8: Bford 7E **96**
Sobell Leisure Cen. 3K **65**
Sobraon Ho. KT2: King T 1F **150**
  (off Elm Rd.)
Socket La. BR2: Hayes 6K **159**
Soda Studios E8 . . . . .1F **85**
  (off Kingsland Rd.)
SOHO 1C **12** (6G **83**)
Soho Ho. W12 . . . . .7E **80**
Soho Sq. W1 . . . . .7C **6** (6H **83**)
Soho St. W1 . . . . .7C **6** (6H **83**)
Soho Theatre 1C **12**
  (off Dean St.)
Sojourner Truth Cl. E8 . . . . .6H **67**
Sola Ct. CR0: C'don 1D **168**
  (off Sydenham Rd.)
Solander Gdns. E1 . . . . .7H **85**
  (off Cable St.)
  E1 .7J **85**
  (The Highway)
Solar Ct. N3 . . . . .7E **30**
  SE16 . . . . .2G **103**
  (off Chambers St.)
Solar Ho. E6 . . . . .5E **88**
  E15 . . . . .6G **69**
  (off Romford Rd.)
Solarium Ct. SE1 . . . . .4F **103**
  (off Alscot Rd.)
Soldene Ct. N7 . . . . .6K **65**
Solebay St. E1 . . . . .4A **86**
Solent Ct. SW16 . . . . .2K **155**
Solent Ho. E1 . . . . .5A **86**
  (off Ben Jonson Rd.)
Solent Ri. E13 . . . . .3J **87**
Solent Rd. NW6 . . . . .5J **63**
Soley M. WC1 . . . . .1J **7** (3A **84**)
Solna Av. SW15 . . . . .5E **116**
Solna Rd. N21 . . . . .1J **33**

Solomon Av. N9 . . . . .4B **34**
Solomons Ct. N12 . . . . .7F **31**
Solomon's Pas. SE15 . . . . .4H **121**
Solomon Way E1 . . . . .5A **86**
Solon New Rd. SW4 . . . . .4J **119**
Solon New Rd. Est. SW4 . . . . .4J **119**
Solon Rd. SW2 . . . . .4J **119**
Solway Cl. E8 . . . . .6F **67**
  (off Queensbridge Rd.)
  TW4: Houn 3C **112**
Solway Ho. E1 . . . . .4K **85**
  (off Ernest St.)
Solway Rd. N22 . . . . .1B **48**
  SE22 . . . . .4G **121**
Somaford Gro. EN4: E Barn 6G **21**
Somali Rd. NW2 . . . . .5H **63**
Sombourne Ho. SW15 . . . . .7C **116**
  (off Fontley Way)
Somerby Rd. IG11: Bark 7H **71**
Somercoates Cl. EN4: Cockf . . .3H **21**
Somer Ct. SW6 . . . . .6J **99**
  (off Anselm Rd.)
Somerfield Rd. N4 . . . . .2B **66**
  (not continuous)
Somerfield St. SE16 . . . . .5K **103**
Somerford Cl. HA5: Eastc 4J **39**
Somerford Gro. N16 . . . . .4F **67**
  N17 . . . . .7B **34**
  (not continuous)
Somerford Gro. Est. N16 . . . . . .4F **67**
Somerford St. E1 . . . . .4H **85**
Somerford Way SE16 . . . . .2A **104**
Somerhill Av. DA15: Sidc 7B **126**
Somerhill Rd. DA16: Well 2B **126**
Somerleyton Pas. SW9 . . . . . . .4B **120**
Somerleyton Rd. SW9 . . . . .4A **120**
Somersby Gdns. IG4: Ilf 5D **52**
Somers Cl. NW1 . . . . .2H **83**
Somers Cres.
  W2 . . . . .1C **10** (6C **82**)
Somerset Av. DA16: Well 5K **125**
  KT9: Chess 4D **162**
  SW20 . . . . .2D **152**
Somerset Cl. IG8: Wfd G 1J **51**
  KT3: N Mald 6A **152**
  N17 . . . . .2D **48**
  SM3: Wor Pk 4E **164**
Somerset Ct. IG9: Buck H 2F **37**
  NW1 . . . . .1C **6** (2H **83**)
  TW11: Tedd 5J **131**
  W7 .6K **77**
  (off Copley Cl.)
Somerset Est. SW11 . . . . .1B **118**
Somerset Gdns. HA0: Wemb . . .5C **60**
  N6 .7E **46**
  N17 . . . . .7K **33**
  SE13 . . . . .2D **122**
  SW16 . . . . .3K **155**
  TW11: Tedd 5J **131**
Somerset Hall N17 . . . . .7K **33**
Somerset House 2G **13** (7K **83**)
Somerset Ho. SW19 . . . . .3F **135**
Somerset Lodge TW8: Bford . . .6D **96**
Somerset Rd. E17 . . . . .5C **50**
  EN5: New Bar 5E **20**
  HA1: Harr 5G **41**
  KT1: King T 2F **151**
  N17 . . . . .3F **49**
  N18 . . . . .5A **34**
  NW4 . . . . .4E **44**
  SW19 . . . . .3F **135**
  TW8: Bford 6C **96**
  TW11: Tedd 5J **131**
  UB1: S'hall 5D **76**
  W4 .3K **97**
  W13 . . . . .1B **96**
Somerset Sq. W14 . . . . .2G **99**
Somerset Waye TW5: Hest 6C **94**
Somersham Rd. DA7: Bex 2E **126**
Somers Pl. SW2 . . . . .7K **119**
Somers Rd. E17 . . . . .4B **50**
  SW2 . . . . .6K **119**

Somerston Ho. NW1 . . . . .1G **83**
  (off St Pancras Way)
SOMERS TOWN 1C **6** (2H **83**)
Somers Town Community Sports Cen.
  . . . . .2H **83**
Somerton Av. TW9: Rich 3H **115**
Somerton Ho. WC1 . . . . .2D **6**
Somerton Rd. NW2 . . . . .3F **63**
  SE15 . . . . .4H **121**
Somertrees Av. SE12 . . . . .2K **141**
Somervell Rd. HA2: Harr 5D **58**
Somerville Av. SW13 . . . . .6D **98**
Somerville Cl. SW9 . . . . .1K **119**
Somerville Point SE16 . . . . .2B **104**
Somerville Rd. RM6: Chad H . . .6C **54**
  SE20 . . . . .7K **139**
Sonderburg Rd. N7 . . . . .2K **65**
Sondes St. SE17 . . . . .6D **102**
Sonesta Apts. SE15 . . . . .1H **121**
Songhurst Cl. CR0: C'don 6K **155**
Sonia Ct. HA1: Harr 6K **41**
  HA8: Edg 7A **28**
Sonia Gdns. N12 . . . . .4F **31**
  NW10 . . . . .4B **62**
  TW5: Hest 7E **94**
Sonning Gdns. TW12: Hamp . . .6C **130**
Sonning Ho. E2 . . . . .2J **9**
  (off Swanfield St.)
Sonning Rd. SE25 . . . . .6G **157**
Soper Cl. E4 . . . . .5G **35**
  SE23 . . . . .1K **139**
Soper M. EN3: Enf L 1H **25**
Sophia Cl. N7 . . . . .6K **65**
Sophia Ho. W6 . . . . .5E **98**
  (off Queen Caroline St.)
Sophia Rd. E10 . . . . .1D **68**
  E16 .6K **87**
Sophia Sq. SE16 . . . . .7A **86**
  (off Sovereign Cres.)
Sophora Ho. SW11 . . . . .7F **101**
Soprano Ct. E15 . . . . .1H **87**
  (off Plaistow Rd.)
Soprano Way KT10: Surb 3B **162**
Sopwith NW9 . . . . .7G **29**
Sopwith Av. E17 . . . . .4K **49**
  KT9: Chess 5E **162**
Sopwith Cl. KT2: King T 5F **133**
Sopwith Rd. TW5: Hest 7A **94**
Sopwith Way KT2: King T 1E **150**
  SW11 . . . . .7J **17** (7F **101**)
Sorbus Ct. EN2: Enf 2G **23**
Sorensen Ct. E10 . . . . .2D **68**
  (off Leyton Grange Est.)
Sorrel Cl. SE28 . . . . .1A **108**
Sorrel Gdns. E6 . . . . .5C **88**
Sorrel La. E14 . . . . .6F **87**
Sorrell Cl. SE14 . . . . .7A **104**
  SW9 . . . . .2A **120**
Sorrel Mead NW9 . . . . .7C **44**
Sorrento Rd. SM1: Sutt 3K **165**
Sotheby Rd. N5 . . . . .3B **66**
Sotheran Cl. E8 . . . . .1G **85**
Sotherby Lodge E2 . . . . .2J **85**
  (off Sewardstone Rd.)
Sotheron Pl. SW6 . . . . .7K **99**
Soudan Rd. SW11 . . . . .1D **118**
Souldern Rd. W14 . . . . .3F **99**
Soul St. SE6 . . . . .1E **140**
Sounding All. E3 . . . . .1C **86**
Sth. Access Rd. E17 . . . . .7A **50**
Southacre W2 . . . . .1C **10**
  (off Hyde Pk. Cres.)
Southacre Way HA5: Pinn 1A **40**
SOUTH ACTON 2J **97**
Sth. Africa Rd. W12 . . . . .1D **98**
SOUTHALL 1D **94**
Southall Ct. UB1: S'hall 7D **76**
Southall Ent. Cen. UB2: S'hall . . .2K **93**
SOUTHALL GREEN 3C **94**
Southall La. TW5: Cran 6K **93**
  UB2: S'hall 6K **93**
Southall Pl. SE1 . . . . .7E **14** (2D **102**)

Southall Sports Cen. 1C **94**
Southall Waterside UB1: S'hall . . .2B **94**
Southam Ho. W10 . . . . .4G **81**
  (off Southam St.)
Southampton Bldgs.
  WC2 . . . . .6J **7** (5A **84**)
Southampton Gdns.
  CR4: Mitc 5J **155**
Southampton M. E16 . . . . .1K **105**
Southampton Pl. WC1 . . . .6F **7** (5J **83**)
Southampton Rd. NW5 . . . . . . .5D **64**
Southampton Rd. E.
  TW6: H'row A 6B **110**
Southampton Rd. W.
  TW6: H'row A 6A **110**
Southampton Row
  WC1 . . . . .5F **7** (5J **83**)
Southampton St. WC2 . . .2F **13** (7J **83**)
Southampton Way
  SE5 . . . . .7D **102**
  SE15 . . . . .7E **102**
Southam St. W10 . . . . .4G **81**
Sth. Audley St. W1 . . . . . .3H **11** (7E **82**)
South Av. E4 . . . . .7J **25**
  SM5: Cars 7E **166**
  TW9: Kew 2G **115**
  UB1: S'hall 7D **76**
Sth. Av. Gdns. UB1: S'hall 7D **76**
Sth. Bank
  KT6: Surb 6E **150**
  SE1 . . . . .4G **13** (1K **101**)
Southbank KT7: T Ditt 7B **150**
Southbank Bus. Cen.
  SW11 . . . . .1D **118**
Southbank Cen. 4H **13** (1K **101**)
Sth. Bank Ter. KT6: Surb 6E **150**
SOUTH BARNET 1K **31**
SOUTH BEDDINGTON 6H **167**
Sth. Birkbeck Rd. E11 . . . . .3F **69**
Sth. Black Lion La. W6 . . . . .5C **98**
Sth. Block SE1 . . . . .7G **13**
  (off Belvedere Rd.)
Sth. Bolton Gdns. SW5 . . . . . . .5K **99**
SOUTHBOROUGH
  BR2 . . . . .5D **160**
  KT6 .1E **162**
Southborough Cl. KT6: Surb 1D **162**
Southborough Ho. SE17 . . . . . . .5E **102**
  (off Kinglake Est.)
Southborough La. BR2: Broml . . .5C **160**
Southborough Rd. BR1: Broml . . .3C **160**
  E9 . . . . .1K **85**
  KT6: Surb 1E **162**
Southbourne BR2: Hayes 7J **159**
Southbourne Av. NW9 . . . . .2J **43**
Southbourne Cl. HA5: Pinn 7C **40**
Southbourne Cl. NW9 . . . . .2J **43**
Southbourne Cres. NW4 . . . . . . .4G **45**
Southbourne Gdns.
  HA4: Ruis 1K **57**
  IG1: Ilf 5G **71**
  SE12 . . . . .5K **123**
Southbridge Pl. CR0: C'don 4C **168**
Southbridge Rd. CR0: C'don 4C **168**
Southbridge Way UB2: S'hall . . .2C **94**
SOUTH BROMLEY 7E **86**
Southbrook M. SE12 . . . . .6H **123**
Southbrook Rd. SE12 . . . . .6H **123**
  SW16 . . . . .1J **155**
Southbury NW8 . . . . .1A **82**
  (off Loudoun Rd.)
Southbury Av. EN1: Enf 4B **24**
Southbury Leisure Cen. 3B **24**
Southbury Rd. EN1: Enf 3K **23**
  EN3: Pond E 3K **23**
Sth. Carriage Dr.
  SW7 . . . . .7B **10** (2B **100**)
SOUTH CHINGFORD 6G **35**
Southchurch Ct. E6 . . . . .2D **88**
  (off High St. Sth.)
Southchurch Rd. E6 . . . . .2D **88**
South City Ct. SE15 . . . . .7E **102**

South Cl. DA6: Bex 4D **126**
  EN5: Barn 3C **20**
  HA5: Pinn 7D **40**
  N6 . . . . .6F **47**
  RM10: Dag 1G **91**
  SM4: Mord 6J **153**
  TW2: Twick 3E **130**
  UB7: W Dray 3B **92**
The Sth. Colonnade E14 . . . . .1C **104**
  (not continuous)
Southcombe St. W14 . . . . .4G **99**
South Comn. Rd. UB8: Uxb 6A **56**
Southcote Av. KT5: Surb 7H **151**
  TW13: Felt 2H **129**
Southcote Ri. HA4: Ruis 7F **39**
Southcote Rd. E17 . . . . .5K **49**
  N19 . . . . .4G **65**
  SE25 . . . . .5H **157**
Southcott Ho. E3 . . . . .3D **86**
  (off Devons Rd.)
  W9 . . . . .4A **82**
  (off Clifton Gdns.)
Southcott M. NW8 . . . . .2C **82**
Southcott Rd. TW11: Hamp W 1C **150**
Sth. Countess Rd. E17 . . . . .3B **50**
South Cres. E16 . . . . .4F **87**
  WC1 . . . . .6C **6** (5H **83**)
Sth. Crescent M. WC1 . . . . .4J **83**
Southcroft Av. BR4: W W'ck 2E **170**
  DA16: Well 3J **125**
Southcroft Rd. BR6: Orp 3J **173**
  SW16 . . . . .6E **136**
  SW17 . . . . .6E **136**
Sth. Cross Rd. IG6: Ilf 5G **53**
Sth. Croxted Rd. SE21 . . . . .3D **138**
SOUTH CROYDON 5D **168**
South Croydon Sports Club 5E **168**
Southdean Gdns. SW19 . . . . .2H **135**
South Dene NW7 . . . . .3E **28**
Southdene Cl. N11 . . . . .3A **32**
Southdown Av. W7 . . . . .3A **96**
Southdown Cres. HA2: Harr 1G **59**
  IG2: Ilf 5J **53**
Southdown Dr. SW20 . . . . .7F **135**
Southdown Rd. SM5: Cars 7E **166**
  SW20 . . . . .1F **153**
South Dr. BR6: Orp 5J **173**
  HA4: Ruis 1G **57**
Sth. Ealing Rd. W5 . . . . .2D **96**
Sth. Eastern Av. N9 . . . . .3A **34**
Sth. Eaton Pl. SW1 . . . . .3H **17** (4E **100**)
Sth. Eden Pk. Rd. BR3: Beck 6D **158**
Sth. Edwardes Sq. W8 . . . . .3H **99**
SOUTHEND 4F **141**
Sth. End CR0: C'don 4C **168**
  CR2: S Croy 4C **168**
  W8 . . . . .3K **99**
Sth. End Cl. NW3 . . . . .4C **64**
Southend Cl. SE9 . . . . .6F **125**
Southend Cres. SE9 . . . . .6F **125**
Sth. End Grn. NW3 . . . . .4C **64**
Southend La. SE6 . . . . .4B **140**
  SE26 . . . . .4B **140**
Sth. End Rd. NW3 . . . . .4C **64**
Southend Rd. BR3: Beck 1C **158**
  E4 . . . . .5F **35**
  E6 . . . . .7D **70**
  E17 . . . . .1D **50**
  E18 . . . . .1J **51**
  IG8: Wfd G 2A **52**
Sth. End Row W8 . . . . .3K **99**
Southern Av. SE25 . . . . .3F **157**
  TW14: Felt 1J **129**
Southern Cotts.
  TW19: Stanw M 7B **174**
Southerngate Way SE14 . . . . .7A **104**
Southern Gro. E3 . . . . .3B **86**
Southern Perimeter Rd.
  TW6: H'row A, Stanw
  . . . . .5A **110**, 7C **174**
  (not continuous)
Southern Pl. HA1: Harr 4K **59**

Southern Rd. E13 . . . . .2K **87**
  N2 . . . . .4D **46**
Southern Row W10 . . . . .4G **81**
Southern St. N1 . . . . .2K **83**
Southern Ter. W12 . . . . .1E **98**
Southern Way RM7: Rom 6G **55**
  SE10 . . . . .4H **105**
Southernwood Retail Pk. 5F **103**
Southerton Rd. W6 . . . . .4E **98**
Sth. Esk Rd. E7 . . . . .6A **70**
Southey Ho. SE17 . . . . .5C **102**
  (off Browning St.)
Southey M. E16 . . . . .1J **105**
Southey Rd. N15 . . . . .5E **48**
  SW9 . . . . .1A **120**
  SW19 . . . . .7J **135**
Southey St. SE20 . . . . .7K **139**
Southfield EN5: Barn 6A **20**
Southfield Cl. UB8: Hil 4C **74**
Southfield Cotts. W7 . . . . .2K **95**
Southfield Ct. E11 . . . . .3H **69**
Southfield Gdns. TW1: Twick 4K **131**
Southfield Pk. HA2: Harr 4F **41**
Southfield Rd. BR7: Chst 3K **161**
  EN3: Pond E 6C **24**
  N17 . . . . .2E **48**
  W4 . . . . .2K **97**
SOUTHFIELDS 1H **135**
Southfields KT8: E Mos 6J **149**
  NW4 . . . . .3D **44**
Southfields Av. TW15: Ashf 6D **128**
Southfields Ct. SM1: Sutt 2J **165**
Southfields M. SW18 . . . . .6J **117**
Southfields Pas. SW18 . . . . .6J **117**
Southfields Rd. SW18 . . . . .6J **117**
Southfleet NW5 . . . . .6E **64**
Southfleet Rd. BR6: Orp 3J **173**
South Gdns.
  HA9: Wemb 2G **61**
  SE17 . . . . .4C **102**
  SW19 . . . . .7B **136**
SOUTHGATE 1C **32**
Southgate Av. TW13: Felt 4F **129**
SOUTHGATE CIR. 1C **32**
Southgate Ct. N1 . . . . .7D **66**
  (off Downham Rd.)
Southgate Gro. N1 . . . . .7D **66**
Southgate Hockey Cen. 3A **22**
Southgate Leisure Cen. 7C **22**
Southgate Rd. N1 . . . . .1D **84**
Sth. Gipsy Rd. DA16: Well 3D **126**
The Sth. Glade DA5: Bexl 1F **145**
South Grn. NW9 . . . . .1A **44**
  (off Parklea Cl.)
South Gro. E17 . . . . .5B **50**
  N6 . . . . .1E **64**
  N15 . . . . .5D **48**
South Gro. Ho. N6 . . . . .1E **64**
SOUTH HACKNEY 1K **85**
SOUTH HAMPSTEAD 7A **64**
SOUTH HARROW 3G **59**
Sth. Harrow Ind. Est.
  HA2: Harr 2G **59**
South Herts Golf Course 1D **30**
Sth. Hill BR7: Chst 6D **142**
  HA6: Nwood 1G **39**
Sth. Hill Av. HA1: Harr 3G **59**
  HA2: Harr 3G **59**
Sth. Hill Gro. HA1: Harr 4J **59**
Sth. Hill Pk. NW3 . . . . .4C **64**
Sth. Hill Pk. Gdns. NW3 . . . . .3C **64**
Sth. Hill Rd. BR2: Broml 3G **159**
Southholme Cl. SE19 . . . . .1E **156**
SOUTH HORNCHURCH 2K **91**
Southill Ct. BR2: Broml 5H **159**
Southill La. HA5: Eastc 4K **39**
Southill Rd. BR7: Chst 7C **142**
Southill St. E14 . . . . .6D **86**
Sth. Island Pl. SW9 . . . . .7K **101**
SOUTH KENSINGTON 4B **100**
Sth. Kensington Sta. Arc. SW7 . . . .3B **16**
  (off Pelham St.)

SOUTH LAMBETH 7J **101**
Sth. Lambeth Pl.
  SW8 . . . . .7F **19** (6J **101**)
Sth. Lambeth Rd.
  SW8 . . . . .7F **19** (6J **101**)
Southland Rd. SE18 . . . . .7K **107**
Southlands Av. BR6: Orp 4H **173**
Southlands College
  Roehampton University 5C **116**
Southlands Dr. SW19 . . . . .2F **135**
Southlands Gro. BR1: Broml 3C **160**
Southlands Rd.
  BR1: Broml 3A **160**
  BR2: Broml 5H **159**
Southland Way TW3: Houn 5H **113**
South La. KT1: King T 3D **150**
  KT3: N Mald 4K **151**
South La. W. KT3: N Mald 4K **151**
Sth. Lodge E16 . . . . .1K **105**
  (off Audley Dr.)
  NW8 . . . . .1A **4** (2B **82**)
  SW7 . . . . .7D **10**
  (off Knightsbridge)
  TW2: Whitt 6G **113**
Sth. Lodge Av. CR4: Mitc 4J **155**
Sth. Lodge Cres. EN2: Enf 4C **22**
  (not continuous)
Sth. Lodge Dr. N14 . . . . .4C **22**
Sth. London Crematorium 2G **155**
South London Gallery 1E **120**
South London Theatre 3B **138**
  (off Norwood High St.)
Sth. Mall N9 . . . . .3B **34**
  (off Plevna Rd.)
  SW18 . . . . .6K **117**
South Mead KT19: Ewe 7B **164**
  NW9 . . . . .1B **44**
Southmead Gdns.
  TW11: Tedd 6A **132**
Southmead Rd. SW19 . . . . .1G **135**
Southmere Boating Cen. 2C **108**
Southmere Dr. SE2 . . . . .2D **108**
Southmere House E15 . . . . .2D **86**
  (off Highland Street)
Sth. Mill Apts. E2 . . . . .1F **85**
  (off Hebden St.)
Sth. Molton La. W1 . . . . .1J **11** (6F **83**)
Sth. Molton Rd. E16 . . . . .6J **87**
Sth. Molton St. W1 . . . . .1J **11** (6F **83**)
Southmoor Way E9 . . . . .6B **68**
South Mt. N20 . . . . .2F **31**
  (off High Rd.)
SOUTH NORWOOD 4F **157**
South Norwood Country Pk. 4J **157**
South Norwood Country Pk.
  Vis. Cen. 4H **157**
Sth. Norwood Hill SE25 . . . . .1E **156**
South Norwood Leisure Cen. 5H **157**
Sth. Oak Rd. SW16 . . . . .4K **137**
Southold Ri. SE9 . . . . .3D **142**
Southolm St. SW11 . . . . .1F **119**
Southover BR1: Broml 5J **141**
  N12 . . . . .3D **30**
South Pde. HA8: Edg 2G **43**
  SM6: W'gton 6G **167**
  SW3 . . . . .5B **16** (5B **100**)
  W4 . . . . .4K **97**
South Pk. Ct. BR3: Beck 7C **140**
South Pk. Cres. IG1: Ilf 3H **71**
  SE6 . . . . .1G **141**
South Pk. Dr. IG3: Ilf 2J **71**
  IG11: Bark 5J **71**
South Pk. Gro.
  KT3: N Mald 4J **151**
South Pk. Hill Rd.
  CR2: S Croy 5D **168**
South Pk. M. SW6 . . . . .3K **117**
South Pk. Rd. IG1: Ilf 3H **71**
  SW19 . . . . .6J **135**
South Pk. Ter. IG1: Ilf 3J **71**
South Pk. Vs. IG3: Ilf 4J **71**
South Pk. Way HA4: Ruis 6A **58**

South Pl. EC2 . . . . .5F **9** (5D **84**)
  EN3: Pond E 5D **24**
  KT5: Surb 7F **151**
South Pl. M. EC2 . . . . .6F **9** (5D **84**)
Southport Rd. SE18 . . . . .4H **107**
Sth. Quay Plaza E14 . . . . .2D **104**
Sth. Quay Sq. E14 . . . . .2D **104**
Southridge Pl. SW20 . . . . .7F **135**
South Ri. SM5: Cars 7C **166**
  W2 . . . . .2D **10**
Sth. Ri. Way SE18 . . . . .5H **107**
South Rd. HA1: Harr 1A **60**
  HA8: Edg 1H **43**
  N9 . . . . .1B **34**
  RM6: Chad H 5C **54**
  (Dunmow Cl.)
  RM6: Chad H 6E **54**
  (Mill La.)
  SE23 . . . . .2K **139**
  SW19 . . . . .6A **136**
  TW2: Twick 3H **131**
  TW5: Hest 6B **94**
  TW12: Hamp 6C **130**
  TW13: Hanw 5B **130**
  UB1: S'hall 2D **94**
  UB7: W Dray 3C **92**
  W5 . . . . .4D **96**
Sth. Row SE3 . . . . .2H **123**
SOUTH RUISLIP 4A **58**
Southsea Rd. KT1: King T 4E **150**
South Sea St. SE16 . . . . .3B **104**
Sth. Side N15 . . . . .4F **49**
  W6 . . . . .3B **98**
Southside N7 . . . . .4H **65**
Southside Cl. UB10: Uxb 7A **56**
Southside Comn. SW19 . . . . .6E **134**
Southside Halls SW7 . . . . .1B **16**
  (off Prince's Gdns.)
Southside House 6E **134**
Southside Ind. Est. SW8 . . . . .1G **119**
  (off Havelock Ter.)
Southside Shop. Cen. 6K **117**
Southspring DA15: Sidc 7H **125**
South Sq. NW11 . . . . .6K **45**
  WC1 . . . . .6J **7** (5A **84**)
Sth. Stand N5 . . . . .4B **66**
South St. BR1: Broml 2J **159**
  EN3: Pond E 5D **24**
  RM1: Rom 5K **55**
  RM13: Rain 2J **91**
  TW7: Isle 3A **114**
  W1 . . . . .4H **11** (1E **100**)
South St. Studios BR1: Broml 2J **159**
  (off South Cl.)
Sth. Tenter St. E1 . . . . . . .2K **15** (7F **85**)
South Ter. KT6: Surb 6E **150**
  SW7 . . . . .3C **16** (4C **100**)
SOUTH TOTTENHAM 5F **49**
South Va. HA1: Harr 4J **59**
  SE19 . . . . .6E **138**
Southvale Rd. SE3 . . . . .2G **123**
South Vw. BR1: Broml 2A **160**
  SW19 . . . . .6F **135**
Southview Av. NW10 . . . . .5B **62**
South Vw. Cl. DA5: Bexl 6F **127**
Southview Cl. SW17 . . . . .5E **136**
South Vw. Ct. SE19 . . . . .7C **138**
Southview Cres. IG2: Ilf 6F **53**
South Vw. Dr. E18 . . . . .3K **51**
Southview Gdns.
  SM6: W'gton 7G **167**
Southview Pde. RM13: Rain 3K **91**
South Vw. Rd.
  HA5: Pinn 1K **39**
  N8 . . . . .3H **47**
Southview Rd. BR1: Broml 4F **141**
South Vs. NW1 . . . . .6H **65**
Southville SW8 . . . . .1H **119**
Southville Cl. KT19: Ewe 7K **163**
  TW14: Bedf, Felt 1G **129**
  (not continuous)
Southville Cres. TW14: Felt 1G **129**

Southville Rd. KT7: T Ditt 7A 150
  TW14: Felt 1G 129
South Wlk. BR4: W W'ck 3G 171
  UB3: Hayes 5F 75
SOUTHWARK 5A 14 (1B 102)
Southwark Bri. SE1 . . . . . .3D 14 (7C 84)
Southwark Bri. Bus. Cen. SE1 . . . .5D 14
  (off Southwark Bri. Rd.)
Southwark Bri. Rd. SE1 . . .7B 14 (3B 102)
Southwark Cathedral 4E 14 (1D 102)
Southwark Pk. 3H 103
Southwark Pk. Est. SE16 . . . . . . .4H 103
  (off Southwark Pk. Rd.)
Southwark Pk. Rd. SE16 . . . . .4F 103
Southwark Pk. Sports Cen. Track
  . . . . .4J 103
Southwark Pk. Sports Complex
  . . . . .4J 103
Southwark Pl. BR1: Broml 3D 160
Southwark Playhouse 3C 102
  (off Newington C'way)
Southwark St George's RC Cathedral
  . . . . .1K 19 (3A 102)
Southwark St. SE1 . . . . .4A 14 (1B 102)
Southwater Cl. BR3: Beck 7D 140
  E14 . . . . .6B 86
Sth. Way CRO: C'don 3A 170
  HA2: Harr 4E 40
  HA9: Wemb 5G 61
  N9 . . . . .2D 34
  N11 . . . . .6B 32
Southway BR2: Hayes 7J 159
  N20 . . . . .2D 30
  NW11 . . . . .6K 45
  SM6: W'gton 4G 167
  SW20 . . . . .5E 152
Southway Cl. W12 . . . . .2D 98
Southwell Av. SE18: N'olt 6E 58
Southwell Gdns. SW7 . . . . .4A 100
Southwell Gro. Rd. E11 . . . . .2G 69
Southwell Ho. SE16 . . . . .4H 103
  (off Anchor St.)
Southwell Rd. CRO: C'don 6A 156
  HA3: Kenton 6D 42
  SE5 .3C 120
Sth. Western Rd. TW1: Twick . . .6A 114
Sth. W. India Dock Entrance
  E14 . . . . .2E 104
Sth. W. Middlesex Crematorium . . .1C 130
Southwest Rd. E11 . . . . .1F 69
Sth. Wharf Rd. W2 . . . . . .7A 4 (6B 82)
Southwick M. W2 . . . . . . .7B 4 (6B 82)
Southwick Pl. W2 . . . . . .1C 10 (6C 82)
Southwick St. W2 . . . . . . .7C 4 (6C 82)
Southwick Yd. W2 . . . . .1C 10
SOUTH WIMBLEDON 6K 135
Southwold Dr. IG11: Bark 5A 72
Southwold Mans. W9 . . . . .3J 81
  (off Widley Rd.)
Southwold Rd. DA5: Bexl 6H 127
  E5 . . . . .2H 67
Southwood Av. KT2: King T 1J 151
  N6 . . . . .7E 47
Southwood Cl. BR1: Broml 4D 160
  KT4: Wor Pk 1F 165
Southwood Ct. EC1 . . . . .2A 8
  (off Wynyatt St.)
  NW11 . . . . .5K 45
Southwood Dr. KT5: Surb 7J 151
SOUTH WOODFORD 2J 51
Sth. Woodford to Barking Relief Rd.
  E11 . . . . .5B 52
Southwood Gdns. IG2: Ilf 4F 53
  KT10: Hin Wd 3A 162
Southwood Hall N6 . . . . .6F 47
Southwood Hgts. N6 . . . . .7F 47
Southwood Ho. W11 . . . . .7G 81
  (off Avondale Pk. Rd.)
Southwood La. N6 . . . . .7E 46
Southwood Lawn Rd. N6 . . . . . . .7E 46
Southwood Mans. N6 . . . . .6E 46
  (off Southwood La.)

Southwood Pk. N6 . . . . .7E 46
Southwood Rd. SE9 . . . . .2F 143
  SE28 .1B 108
Southwood Smith Ho. E2 . . . . . . .3H 85
  (off Florida St.)
Southwood Smith St. N1 . . . . .1B 84
Sth. Worple Av. SW14 . . . . .3A 116
Sth. Worple Way SW14 . . . . .3K 115
Southwyck Ho. SW9 . . . . .4B 120
Soval Ct. HA6: Nwood 1F 39
Sovereign Bus. Cen.
  EN3: Brim 3G 25
Sovereign Cl. E1 . . . . .7H 85
  HA4: Ruis 1G 57
  W5 . . . . .5C 78
Sovereign Ct. CR2: S Croy 5C 168
  (off Warham Rd.)
  HA6: Nwood 1J 39
  HA7: Stan 7J 27
  KT8: W Mole 4D 148
  TW3: Houn 3E 112
  W8 . . . . .3K 99
  (off Wright's La.)
Sovereign Cres. SE16 . . . . .7A 86
Sovereign Gro. HA0: Wemb 3D 60
Sovereign Ho. E1 . . . . .4H 85
  (off Cambridge Heath Rd.)
  SE18 .3D 106
  (off Leda Rd.)
  TW15: Ashf 4A 128
Sovereign M. E2 . . . . .2F 85
  EN4: Cockf 3J 21
Sovereign Pk. NW10 . . . . .4H 79
Sovereign Pk. Trad. Est. NW10 . . .4H 79
Sovereign Pl. HA1: Harr 5K 41
Sovereign Rd. IG11: Bark 3C 90
Sowerby Cl. SE9 . . . . .5D 124
The Spa at Beckenham 1B 158
Spa Bus. Pk. SE16 . . . . .3G 103
The Space Arts Cen. 4C 104
  (off Westferry Rd.)
Space Bus. Pk. NW10 . . . . .3H 79
Spaces Bus. Cen. SW8 . . . . .1G 119
Space Waye TW14: Felt 5J 111
Spa Cl. SE25 . . . . .1E 156
Spa Ct. SE16 . . . . .3G 103
  SW16 .4K 137
Spafield St. EC1 . . . . .3J 7 (4A 84)
Spa Grn. Est. EC1 . . . . . . .1K 7 (3B 84)
Spa Hill SE19 . . . . .1D 156
Spalding Cl. HA8: Edg 7F 29
Spalding Ho. SE4 . . . . .4A 122
Spalding Rd. NW4 . . . . .7E 44
  SW17 . . . . .5F 137
Spanby Rd. E3 . . . . .4C 86
Spaniards Cl. NW11 . . . . .1B 64
Spaniards End NW3 . . . . .1A 64
Spaniards Rd. NW3 . . . . .2A 64
Spanish Pl. W1 . . . . .7H 5 (6E 82)
Spanish Rd. SW18 . . . . .5A 118
Spanswick Lodge N15 . . . . .4B 48
Spare St. SE17 . . . . .4C 102
Sparkbridge Rd. HA1: Harr 4J 41
Sparkes Cl. BR2: Broml 4K 159
Sparkes Cotts. SW1 . . . . .4G 17
Sparkford Gdns. N11 . . . . .5K 31
Sparkford Ho. SW11 . . . . .1B 118
  (off Battersea Church Rd.)
Sparks Cl. RM8: Dag 2D 72
  TW12: Hamp 6C 130
  W3 . . . . .6K 79
Spa Rd. SE16 . . . . .3F 103
Sparrick's Row SE1 . . . . .6F 15 (2D 102)
Sparrow Cl. TW12: Hamp 6C 130
Sparrow Dr. BR5: Farnb 1G 173
Sparrow Ho. E1 . . . . .4J 85
  (off Cephas Av.)

Sparrow's Farm Leisure Cen. 7G 125
Sparrows Herne WD23: Bush 1A 26
Sparrows La. SE9 . . . . .7G 125
Sparrows Way WD23: Bush 1B 26
Sparsholt Cl. IG11: Bark 1J 89
  (off St John's Rd.)
Sparsholt Rd. IG11: Bark 1J 89
  N19 . . . . .1K 65
Spartan Cl. SM6: W'gton 7J 167
Sparta St. SE10 . . . . .1E 122
Speakers' Corner 2F 11 (7D 82)
Speakers Ct. CRO: C'don 1D 168
Speakman Ho. SE4 . . . . .3A 122
  (off Arica Rd.)
Spearman Ho. E14 . . . . .6E 86
  (off Upper Nth. St.)
Spearman St. SE18 . . . . .6E 106
Spear M. SW5 . . . . .4J 99
Spearpoint Gdns. IG2: Ilf 5K 53
Spears Rd. N19 . . . . .1J 65
Speart La. TW5: Hest 7C 94
Spectacle Works E13 . . . . .3A 88
The Spectrum Bldg. N1 . . . . .1F 9
  (off East Rd.)
Spectrum Pl. SE17 . . . . .6D 102
  (off Lytham St.)
Spectrum Twr. IG1: Ilf 2G 71
  (off Hainault St.)
Spectrum Way SW18 . . . . .5J 117
Spedan Cl. NW3 . . . . .3A 64
Speechly M. E8 . . . . .5F 67
Speedbird Way UB7: Harm 3C 174
Speed Highwalk EC2 . . . . .5D 8
  (off Silk St.)
Speed Ho. EC2 . . . . .5D 8
Speedway Ind. Est.
  UB3: Hayes 2F 93
Speedwell Ho. N12 . . . . .4E 30
Speedwell St. SE8 . . . . .7C 104
Speedy Pl. WC1 . . . . .2E 6
Speer Rd. KT7: T Ditt 6K 149
Speirs Cl. KT3: N Mald 6B 152
Speirs Gardens RM8: Dag 1E 72
Spekehill SE9 . . . . .3D 142
Speke Rd. CR7: Thor H 2D 156
Speke's Monument
  . . . . .4A 10 (1A 100)
Speldhurst Cl. BR2: Broml 5H 159
Speldhurst Rd. E9 . . . . .7K 67
  W4 . . . . .3K 97
Spellbrook Wlk. N1 . . . . .1C 84
Spelman Ho. E1 . . . . .6K 9
  (off Spelman St.)
Spelman St. E1 . . . . .5K 9 (5G 85)
  (not continuous)
Spelthorne Gro. TW16: Sun 7H 129
Spelthorne La.
  TW15: Ashf 1E 146
Spence Cl. SE16 . . . . .2B 104
Spencer Av. N13 . . . . .6E 32
  UB4: Hayes 5J 75
Spencer Cl. BR6: Orp 2J 173
  IG8: Wfd G 5F 37
  N3 . . . . .2J 45
  NW10 . . . . .3F 79
Spencer Ct. BR6: Farnb 5G 173
  NW8 .2A 82
  (off Marlborough Pl.)
  SW20 .1D 152
Spencer Ctyd. N3 . . . . .2H 45
  (off Regents Pk. Rd.)
Spencer Dr. N2 . . . . .6A 46
Spencer Gdns. SE9 . . . . .5D 124
  SW14 .5J 115
Spencer Hill SW19 . . . . .6G 135
Spencer Hill Rd. SW19 . . . . .7G 135
Spencer House 5A 12
Spencer Mans. W14 . . . . .6G 99
  (off Queen's Club Gdns.)
Spencer M. SW8 . . . . .1K 119
  (off Lansdowne Way)
  W6 . . . . .6G 99

SPENCER PARK 5B 118
Spencer Pk. KT8: E Mos 5G 149
  SW18 .5B 118
Spencer Pl. CRO: C'don 7D 156
  N1 . . . . .7B 66
Spencer Ri. NW5 . . . . .4F 65
Spencer Rd. BR1: Broml 7H 141
  CR2: S Croy 5E 168
  CR4: Mitc 3E 154
  (Commonside E.)
  CR4: Mitc 7E 154
  (Wood St.)
  E6 . . . . .1B 88
  E17 . . . . .2E 50
  HA0: Wemb 2C 60
  HA3: W'stone 2J 41
  IG3: Ilf 1K 71
  KT8: E Mos 4G 149
  N8 . . . . .5K 47
  (not continuous)
  N11 . . . . .4A 32
  N17 . . . . .1G 49
  RM13: Rain 3K 91
  SW18 .4B 118
  SW20 .1D 152
  TW2: Twick 3J 131
  TW7: Isle 1G 113
  W3 . . . . .1J 97
  W4 . . . . .7J 97
Spencer St. EC1 . . . . .2A 8 (3B 84)
  UB2: S'hall 2B 94
Spencer Wlk. NW3 . . . . .4B 64
  SW15 .4F 117
Spencer Way E1 . . . . .6H 85
Spencer Yd. SE3 . . . . .2H 123
  (off Tranquil Va.)
Spenlow Ho. SE16 . . . . .3G 103
  (off Jamaica Rd.)
Spenser Gro. N16 . . . . .5E 66
Spenser M. SE21 . . . . .2D 138
Spenser Rd. SE24 . . . . .5B 120
Spenser St.
  SW1 . . . . .1B 18 (3G 101)
Spens Ho. WC1 . . . . .4G 7
  (off Lamb's Conduit St.)
Spensley Wlk. N16 . . . . .3D 66
Speranza St. SE18 . . . . .5K 107
Sperling Rd. N17 . . . . .2E 48
Spert St. E14 . . . . .7A 86
Speyside N14 . . . . .6B 22
Spey St. E14 . . . . .5E 86
Spey Way RM1: Rom 1K 55
Spezia Rd. NW10 . . . . .2C 80
The Sphere E16 . . . . .6H 87
  (off Hallsville Rd.)
Sphinx Way EN5: Barn 5C 20
Spice Cl. E1 . . . . .7G 85
Spice Quay Hgts.
  SE1 . . . . .5K 15 (1F 103)
Spicer Cl. KT12: Walt T 6A 148
  SW9 . . . . .2B 120
Spicer Ct. EN1: Enf 3K 23
Spice's Yd. CRO: C'don 4C 168
Spigurnell Rd. N17 . . . . .1D 48
Spikes Bri. Moorings
  UB4: Yead 7C 76
Spikes Bri. Rd. UB1: S'hall 6C 76
Spindle Cl. SE18 . . . . .3C 106
Spindle M. BR6: Farnb 4F 173
Spindlewood Gdns.
  CRO: C'don 4E 168
Spindrift Av. E14 . . . . .4C 104
Spinel Cl. SE18 . . . . .5K 107
Spinnaker Cl. IG11: Bark 3B 90
Spinnaker Ct. KT1: Hamp W 1D 150
  (off Becketts Pl.)
Spinnaker Ho. E14 . . . . .2C 104
  (off Byng St.)
  E16 . . . . .2K 105
  (off Waypoint Way)
  SW18 .4A 118
  (off Juniper Dr.)

Spinnells Rd. HA2: Harr 1D 58
Spinner Ho. E8 . . . . .1F 85
   (off Lovelace St.)
The Spinney DA14: Sidc 5E 144
  EN5: New Bar 2E 20
  HA0: Wemb 3A 60
  HA7: Stan 4K 27
  N21 . . . . .7F 23
  SM3: Cheam 4E 164
  SW13 . . . . .7D 98
  SW16 . . . . .3G 137
  TW16: Sun 1J 147
Spinney Cl. BR3: Beck 4D 158
  KT3: N Mald 5A 152
  KT4: Wor Pk 2B 164
  UB7: View 7A 74
Spinney Dr. TW14: Bedf 7E 110
Spinney Gdns. RM9: Dag 5E 72
  SE19 . . . . .5F 139
Spinney Oak BR1: Broml 2C 160
The Spinneys BR1: Broml 2D 160
Spinning Wheel Way
  SM6: W'gton 2E 166
Spire Ct. BR3: Beck 2D 158
   (off Crescent Rd.)
Spire Ho. W2 . . . . .7A 82
   (off Lancaster Ga.)
The Spires Shop. Cen. 3B 20
Spirit Quay E1 . . . . .1G 103
SPITALFIELDS 5J 9 (5F 85)
Spitalfields City Farm 4G 85
Spital Sq. E1 . . . . .5H 9 (5E 84)
Spital St. E1 . . . . .5K 9 (5G 85)
Spital Yd. E1 . . . . .5H 9 (5E 84)
Spitfire Bldg. N1 . . . . .2K 83
   (off Collier St.)
Spitfire Bus. Pk. CR0: Wadd 6A 168
The Spitfire Est. TW5: Cran 5A 94
Spitfire Rd. SM6: W'gton 7J 167
  TW6: H'row A 6E 110
Spitfire Way TW5: Cran 5A 94
Splendour Wlk. SE16 . . . . .5J 103
   (off Verney Rd.)
Spode Ho. SE11 . . . . .2J 19
Spode Wlk. NW6 . . . . .5K 63
Spondon Rd. N15 . . . . .4G 49
Spoonbill Way UB4: Yead 5B 76
Spooner Ho. TW5: Hest 6E 94
Spooners M3 . . . . .1K 97
Spooner Wlk. SM6: W'gton 5J 167
Sporle Rd. Ct. SW11 . . . . .3B 118
Sports Academy (LSBU) 3B 102
   (off London Rd.)
Sportsbank St. SE6 . . . . .7E 122
Sports Direct Fitness
  Croydon 7A 168
  Epsom 4K 163
SportsDock 7F 89
Sportsman Pl. E2 . . . . .1G 85
Spottiswood Ct. CR0: C'don 6C 156
   (off Harry Cl.)
Spottons Gro. N17 . . . . .1C 48
Spout Hill CR0: Addtn 5C 170
Spout La. TW19: Stanw M 7B 174
Spout La. Nth.
  TW19: Stanw M 7C 174
Spratt Hall Rd. E11 . . . . .6J 51
Spray La. TW2: Whitt 6J 113
Spray St. SE18 . . . . .4F 107
Spreighton Rd.
  KT8: W Mole 4F 149
Spriggs Ho. N1 . . . . .7B 66
   (off Canonbury Rd.)
Sprimont Pl. SW3 . . . . .5E 16 (5D 100)
Springall St. SE15 . . . . .7H 103
Springalls Wharf SE16 . . . . .2G 103
   (off Bermondsey Wall W.)
Spring Apts. CR0: C'don 2D 168
   (off Addiscombe Gro.)
  E14 . . . . .4E 104
   (off Stebondale St.)
Springbank N21 . . . . .6E 22

Springbank Rd. SE13 . . . . .6F 123
Springbank Wlk. NW1 . . . . .7H 65
Springbourne Ct.
  BR3: Beck 1E 158
Spring Bri. M. W5 . . . . .7D 78
Spring Bri. Rd. W5 . . . . .7D 78
Spring Cl. EN5: Barn 5A 20
  RM8: Dag 1D 72
Springclose La.
  SM3: Cheam 6G 165
Spring Cnr. TW13: Felt 3J 129
Spring Cotts. KT6: Surb 5D 150
Spring Ct. KT17: Ewe 7B 164
  NW6 .6H 63
  W7 . . . . .7H 77
Spring Ct. Rd. EN2: Enf 1F 23
Springcroft Av. N2 . . . . .4D 46
Springdale M. N16 . . . . .4D 66
Springdale Rd. N16 . . . . .4D 66
Spring Dr. HA5: Eastc 6J 39
Springer Ct. E3 . . . . .4E 86
   (off Navigation Rd.)
Springett Ho. SW2 . . . . .5A 120
   (off St Matthews Rd.)
Springfield E5 . . . . .1H 67
  SE25 . . . . .3G 157
  WD23: B Hea 1C 26
Springfield Av. N10 . . . . .3G 47
  SW20 . . . . .3H 153
  TW12: Hamp 6F 131
Springfield Cl. HA7: Stan 3F 27
  N12 . . . . .5E 30
Springfield Ct. IG1: Ilf 5F 71
  KT1: King T 3E 150
   (off Springfield Rd.)
  NW3 .7C 64
   (off Eton Av.)
  SM6: W'gton 5F 167
Springfield Dr. IG2: Ilf 5G 53
Springfield Gdns.
  BR1: Broml 4D 160
  BR4: W W'ck 2D 170
  E5 . . . . .1H 67
  HA4: Ruis 1K 57
  IG8: Wfd G 7F 37
  NW9 .5K 43
Springfield Gro. SE7 . . . . .6A 106
  TW16: Sun 1H 147
Springfield La. NW6 . . . . .1K 81
Springfield Mt. NW9 . . . . .5A 44
Springfield Pde. M. N13 . . . . .4F 33
Springfield Pk. 2B 136
Springfield Pl.
  KT3: N Mald 4J 151
Springfield Ri. SE26 . . . . .3H 139
Springfield Rd.
  BR1: Broml 4D 160
  CR7: Thor H 1C 156
  DA7: Bex 4H 127
  DA16: Well 3B 126
  E4 . . . . .1B 36
  E6 . . . . .7D 70
  E15 . . . . .3G 87
  E17 . . . . .6B 50
  HA1: Harr 6J 41
  KT1: King T 3E 150
  N11 . . . . .5A 32
  N15 . . . . .4G 49
  NW8 .1A 82
  SE26 . . . . .5H 139
  SM6: W'gton 5F 167
  SW19 . . . . .5H 135
  TW2: Whitt 1E 130
  TW11: Tedd 5A 132
  TW15: Ashf 5B 128
  UB4: Yead 1A 94
  W7 . . . . .1J 95
Springfields EN5: New Bar 5E 20
   (off Somerset Rd.)
Springfield Wlk. BR6: Orp 1H 173
   (off Place Farm Av.)
  NW6 .1K 81

Spring Gdns. IG8: Wfd G 7F 37
  KT8: W Mole 5F 149
  N5 . . . . .5C 66
  RM7: Rom 5J 55
  SM6: W'gton 5G 167
  SW1 . . . . .4D 12 (1H 101)
   (not continuous)
Spring Gdns. Bus. Pk.
  RM7: Rom 6J 55
SPRING GROVE 1J 113
Spring Gro. CR4: Mitc 1E 154
  SE19 . . . . .7F 139
  TW12: Hamp 1F 149
  W4 . . . . .5G 97
  W7 . . . . .7J 77
Spring Gro. Cres. TW3: Houn 1G 113
Spring Gro. Rd.
  TW3: Houn, Isle 1F 113
  TW7: Isle 1F 113
  TW10: Rich 5F 115
SpringHealth Leisure Club
  Richmond 4D 114
   (within Pools on the Pk.)
Spring Hill E5 . . . . .7G 49
  SE26 . . . . .4J 139
Springhill Cl. SE5 . . . . .3D 120
Spring Ho. E17 . . . . .2E 50
   (off Fulbourne Rd.)
  WC1 . . . . .2J 7
Springhurst Cl. CR0: C'don 4B 170
Spring Lake HA7: Stan 4G 27
Spring La. E5 . . . . .7H 49
  N10 . . . . .3E 46
  SE25 . . . . .6H 157
Spring M. KT17: Ewe 7B 164
  SE11 . . . . .5G 19 (5K 101)
  TW9: Rich 4E 114
   (off Rosedale Rd.)
  W1 . . . . .5F 5 (5D 82)
SPRING PARK 3C 170
Spring Pk. Av. CR0: C'don 2K 169
Spring Pk. Dr. N4 . . . . .1C 66
Springpark Dr. BR3: Beck 3E 158
Spring Pk. Rd. CR0: C'don 2K 169
Spring Pas. SW15 . . . . .3F 117
Spring Path NW3 . . . . .5B 64
Spring Pl. IG11: Bark 2G 89
  N3 . . . . .3J 45
  NW5 .5F 65
Springpond Rd. RM9: Dag 5E 72
Spring Prom. UB7: W Dray 2B 92
Springrice Rd. SE13 . . . . .6F 123
Spring Rd. TW13: Felt 3H 129
Springs Cl. TW19: Stanw 1A 128
Spring Shaw Rd. BR5: St P 7A 144
Spring St. W2 . . . . .1A 10 (6B 82)
Spring Ter. TW9: Rich 5E 114
Spring Tide Cl. SE15 . . . . .1H 121
Spring Va. DA7: Bex 4H 127
Springvale Av. TW8: Bford 5D 96
Springvale Ter. W14 . . . . .3F 99
Spring Villa Pk. HA8: Edg 7B 28
Spring Villa Rd. HA8: Edg 7B 28
Spring Wlk. E1 . . . . .5G 85
Springwater WC1 . . . . .5G 7
Springwater Cl. SE18 . . . . .1E 124
Spring Way SE5 . . . . .1C 120
Springway HA1: Harr 7H 41
Springwell Av. NW10 . . . . .1B 80
Springwell Cl. SW16 . . . . .4K 137
Springwell Rd. SW16 . . . . .4A 138
  TW4: Houn 2B 112
  TW5: Hest 2B 112
Springwood Cl. E3 . . . . .2C 86
Springwood Ct. CR2: S Croy 4E 168
   (off Birdhurst Rd.)
Springwood Cres. HA8: Edg 2B 28
Sproggit Ind. Est. TW19: Stanw . . .6B 110
Sprowston M. E7 . . . . .6J 69
Sprowston Rd. E7 . . . . .5J 69
Spruce Cl. W5 . . . . .3E 96
Sprucedale Gdns. CR0: C'don 4K 169

Spruce Hills Rd. E17 . . . . .2E 50
Spruce Ho. SE16 . . . . .2K 103
   (off Woodland Cres.)
Spruce Pk. BR2: Broml 4H 159
Sprules Rd. SE4 . . . . .2A 122
Spurfield KT8: W Mole 3F 149
Spurgeon Av. SE19 . . . . .1D 156
Spurgeon Rd. SE19 . . . . .1D 156
Spurgeon St. SE1 . . . . .3D 102
Spurling Rd. RM9: Dag 6F 73
  SE22 . . . . .4F 121
Spurrell Av. DA5: Bexl 4K 145
Spur Rd. BR6: Orp 2K 173
  HA8: Edg 4K 27
  N15 . . . . .4D 48
  SE1 . . . . .6J 13 (2A 102)
  SW1 . . . . .7A 12 (2G 101)
  TW7: Isle 7B 96
  TW14: Felt 4K 111
Spurstowe Rd. E8 . . . . .6H 67
Spurstowe Ter. E8 . . . . .5G 67
Spurway Pde. IG2: Ilf 5D 52
   (off Woodford Av.)
The Square E10 . . . . .3E 68
  IG1: Ilf 7E 52
  IG8: Wfd G 5D 36
  RM8: Dag 1E 72
  SM5: Cars 5E 166
  TW9: Rich 5D 114
  UB3: S'hall 4A 94
  UB7: Lford 4C 174
  UB11: Stock P 1F 93
  W6 . . . . .5E 98
Square of Fame 4G 61
   (off Arena Sq.)
Square Rigger Row SW11 . . . . . . .3A 118
Squarey St. SW17 . . . . .3A 136
Squire Gdns. NW8 . . . . .2A 4
   (off Grove End Rd.)
The Squires RM7: Rom 6J 55
Squire's Bri. Rd. TW17: Shep 4B 146
Squires Ct. SW4 . . . . .1J 119
  SW19 . . . . .4J 135
Squires La. N3 . . . . .2K 45
Squires Mt. NW3 . . . . .3B 64
Squire's Rd. TW17: Shep 4C 146
Squires Wlk. TW15: Ashf 7F 129
   (not continuous)
Squires Way DA2: Wilm 4K 145
Squires Wood Dr.
  BR7: Chst 7C 142
Squirrel Cl. TW4: Houn 3A 112
Squirrel M. W13 . . . . .7K 77
The Squirrels HA5: Pinn 3D 40
  SE13 . . . . .3F 123
Squirrels Cl. BR6: Orp 1J 173
  N12 . . . . .4F 31
  UB10: Hil 7C 56
Squirrels Ct. KT4: Wor Pk 2B 164
   (off The Avenue)
Squirrels Drey BR2: Broml 2G 159
   (off Park Hill Rd.)
Squirrels Grn. KT4: Wor Pk 2B 164
Squirrel's La. IG9: Buck H 3G 37
Squirrels Trad. Est.
  UB3: Hayes 3H 93
Squirries St. E2 . . . . .3G 85
The SSE Arena Wembley 4G 61
SS Robin .7K 87
Stable Cl. KT2: King T 6F 133
  UB5: N'olt 2E 76
Stable Ct. EC1 . . . . .4B 8
   (off Clerkenwell Rd.)
Stable La. DA5: Bexl 2H 145
Stable M. NW5 . . . . .6F 65
  SE6 . . . . .1G 141
  TW1: Twick 1K 131
Stable Pl. N4 . . . . .2B 66
The Stables IG9: Buck H 1F 37
Stables End BR6: Farnb 3G 173
Stables Gallery & Arts Cen. 3C 62

Stables Lodge—Stanley Rd.

Stables Lodge *E8* 7H ***67***
(off Mare St.)
The Stables Mkt. NW1 7F **65**
Stables M. SE27 5C **138**
Stables Row E11 5J **51**
Stable St. N1 1J **83**
SE18 5F **107**
Stables Way SE11 5J **19** (5A **102**)
Stables Yd. SW18 6J **117**
Stable Vs. BR1: Broml 6B **142**
Stable Wlk. *E1* *6G* ***85***
(off Boulevard Walkway)
N2 1B **46**
Stable Way W10 6E **80**
Stable Yd. SW1 6A **12**
SW15 3E **116**
The Stableyard SW9 2K **119**
Stableyard M. TW11: Tedd 6K **131**
Stable Yd. Rd. SW1 6B **12** (2G **101**)
(not continuous)
Staburn Ct. HA8: Edg 2J **43**
Stacey Av. N18 4D **34**
Stacey Cl. E10 5F **51**
Stacey St. N7 3A **66**
WC2 1D **12** (6H **83**)
Stack Ho. *SW1* *4H* ***17***
(off Cundy St.)
Stackhouse St. SW3 1E **16**
Stacy Path SE5 7E **102**
Staddon Cl. BR3: Beck 4A **158**
Stadium Bus. Cen.
HA9: Wemb 3H **61**
Stadium M. N5 3A **66**
Stadium Retail Pk. 3G **61**
Stadium Rd. SE18 7C **106**
Stadium Rd. E. NW4 7D **44**
Stadium St. SW10 7A **100**
Stadium Way HA9: Wemb 4F **61**
Staffa Rd. E10 1A **68**
Stafford Cl. E17 6B **50**
(not continuous)
N14 5B **22**
NW6 3J **81**
SM3: Cheam 6G **165**
Stafford Ct. DA5: Bexl 7F **127**
SW8 7J **101**
W7 *6K* ***77***
(off Copley Cl.)
W8 3J **99**
Stafford Cripps Ho. *E2* *3J* ***85***
(off Globe Rd.)
SW6 *6H* ***99***
(off Clem Attlee Ct.)
Stafford Cross Bus. Pk.
CR0: Wadd 5K **167**
Stafford Gdns. CR0: Wadd 5K **167**
Stafford Ho. *SE1* *5F* ***103***
(off Cooper's Rd.)
Stafford Mans. *SW1* *1A* ***18***
(off Stafford Pl.)
SW4 4J **119**
SW11 *7D* ***100***
(off Albert Bri. Rd.)
W14 *3F* ***99***
(off Haarlem Rd.)
Stafford Pl. SW1 1A **18** (3G **101**)
TW10: Rich 7F **115**
Stafford Rd.
CR0: Wadd 4A **168**
DA14: Sidc 4J **143**
E3 2B **86**
E7 7A **70**
HA3: Hrw W 7B **26**
HA4: Ruis 4H **57**
KT3: N Mald 3J **151**
NW6 3J **81**
SM6: W'gton 6G **167**
Staffordshire St. SE15 1G **121**
Stafford St. W1 4A **12** (1G **101**)
Stafford Ter. W8 3J **99**
Staff St. EC1 2F **9** (3D **84**)
Stag Cl. HA8: Edg 2H **43**
Stag Ct. *KT2: King T* *1G* ***151***
(off Coombe Rd.)
STAG LANE 2B **134**
Stag La. HA8: Edg 2H **43**
IG9: Buck H 2E **36**
NW9 2H **43**
SW15 3B **134**
Stags Way TW7: Isle 6K **95**
Stainbank Rd. CR4: Mitc 3F **155**
Stainby Cl. UB7: W Dray 3A **92**
Stainby Rd. N15 4F **49**
Staines Av. SM3: Cheam 2F **165**
Staines Rd. IG1: Ilf 5G **71**
TW2: Twick 3E **130**
TW3: Houn 3F **113**
TW4: Houn 7F **111**
TW14: Bedf, Felt 1C **128**
Staines Rd. E. TW16: Sun 7J **129**
Staines Rd. W.
TW15: Ashf 6D **128**
TW16: Sun 6D **128**
Staines Wlk. DA14: Sidc 6C **144**
Stainford Cl. TW15: Ashf 5F **129**
Stainforth Rd. E17 4C **50**
IG2: Ilf 7H **53**
Staining La. EC2 7D **8** (6C **84**)
Stainmore Cl. BR7: Chst 1H **161**
Stainsbury St. E2 2J **85**
Stainsby Rd. E14 6C **86**
Stainton Rd. EN3: Enf H 1D **24**
SE6 6F **123**
Staith Ct. *E3* *3E* ***86***
(off Bolinder Way)
Stalbridge Flats *W1* *1H* ***11***
(off Lumley St.)
Stalbridge Ho. *NW1* *1A* ***6***
(off Hampstead Rd.)
Stalbridge St. NW1 5D **4** (5C **82**)
Stalham St. SE16 3H **103**
Stalham Way IG6: Ilf 1F **53**
Stambourne Way
BR4: W W'ck 2E **170**
SE19 7E **138**
Stambourne Woodland Wlk.
SE19 7E **138**
Stamford Bridge 7K **99**
Stamford Bri. Studios *SW6* *7K* ***99***
(off Wandon Rd.)
Stamford Brook Arches W6 4C **98**
Stamford Brook Av. W6 3B **98**
Stamford Brook Gdns. W6 3B **98**
Stamford Brook Mans. *W6* *4B* ***98***
(off Goldhawk Rd.)
Stamford Brook Rd. W6 3B **98**
Stamford Bldgs. *SW8* *7J* ***101***
(off Meadow Pl.)
Stamford Cl. HA3: Hrw W 7D **26**
N15 4G **49**
NW3 *3A* ***64***
(off Heath St.)
UB1: S'hall 7E **76**
Stamford Cotts. *SW10* *7K* ***99***
(off Billing St.)
Stamford Ct. W6 4C **98**
Stamford Dr. BR2: Broml 4H **159**
Stamford Gdns. RM9: Dag 7C **72**
Stamford Ga. SW6 7K **99**
Stamford Ga. Ho. *SW6* *7K* ***99***
(off Stamford Ga.)
Stamford Gro. E. N16 1G **67**
Stamford Gro. W. N16 1G **67**
STAMFORD HILL 1F **67**
Stamford Hill N16 2F **67**
Stamford Lodge N16 7F **49**
Stamford Rd. E6 1C **88**
N1 7E **66**
N15 5G **49**
RM9: Dag 1B **90**
Stamford Sq. SW15 5G **117**
Stamford St. SE1 5J **13** (1A **102**)
Stamp Pl. E2 1J **9** (2F **85**)
Stanard Cl. N16 7E **48**
Stanborough Cl.
TW12: Hamp 6D **130**
Stanborough Ho. *E3* *4D* ***86***
(off Empson St.)
Stanborough Pas. E8 6F **67**
Stanborough Rd.
TW3: Houn 3H **113**
Stanbridge Pl. N21 2G **33**
Stanbridge Rd. SW15 3E **116**
Stanbrook Rd. SE2 2B **108**
Stanbury Ct. NW3 6D **64**
Stanbury Rd. SE15 1H **121**
(not continuous)
Stancroft NW9 5A **44**
Standale Gro. HA4: Ruis 5E **38**
Standard Ind. Est. E16 2D **106**
Standard Pl. EC2 2H **9**
Standard Rd. DA6: Bex 4E **126**
DA17: Belv 5G **109**
NW10 4J **79**
TW4: Houn 3C **112**
Standcumbe Ct. BR3: Beck 5B **158**
Standen Rd. SW18 7H **117**
Standfield Gdns.
RM10: Dag 6G **73**
Standfield Rd. RM10: Dag 5G **73**
Standish Ho. *W6* *4C* ***98***
(off St Peter's Gro.)
Standish Rd. W6 4C **98**
Standlake Point SE23 3K **139**
Stane Cl. SW19 7K **135**
Stane Gro. SW9 2J **119**
Stanesgate Ho. *SE15* *7G* ***103***
(off Friary Est.)
Stane Way SE18 7B **106**
Stanfield Ho. *NW8* *3B* ***4***
(off Frampton St.)
UB5: N'olt *2B* ***76***
(off Academy Gdns.)
Stanfield Rd. E3 2A **86**
Stanford Cl. HA4: Ruis 6E **38**
IG8: Wfd G 5H **37**
RM7: Rom 6H **55**
TW12: Hamp 6D **130**
Stanford Ct. SW6 1K **117**
W8 *3K* ***99***
(off Cornwall Gdns.)
Stanford M. E8 5G **67**
Stanford Pl. SE17 4E **102**
Stanford Rd. N11 5J **31**
SW16 2H **155**
W8 3K **99**
Stanford St. SW1 4C **18** (4H **101**)
Stanford Way SW16 2H **155**
Stangate SE1 1H **19**
Stangate Gdns. HA7: Stan 4G **27**
Stangate Lodge N21 6E **22**
Stanger Rd. SE25 4G **157**
Stanhill Cotts. DA2: Wilm 7K **145**
Stanhope Av. BR2: Hayes 1H **171**
HA3: Hrw W 1H **41**
N3 3H **45**
Stanhope Cl. SE16 2K **103**
Stanhope Gdns. IG1: Ilf 1D **70**
N4 6B **48**
N6 6F **47**
NW7 5G **29**
RM8: Dag 3F **73**
SW7 3A **16** (4A **100**)
Stanhope Ga. W1 5H **11** (1E **100**)
Stanhope Gro.
BR3: Beck 5B **158**
Stanhope Ho. *N11* *4A* ***32***
(off Coppies Gro.)
SE8 *7B* ***104***
(off Adolphus St.)
Stanhope M. E. SW7 3A **16** (4A **100**)
Stanhope M. Sth. SW7 4A **100**
Stanhope M. W. SW7 4A **100**
Stanhope Pde. NW1 1A **6** (3G **83**)
Stanhope Pk. Rd.
UB6: G'frd 4G **77**
Stanhope Pl. W2 1E **10** (7D **82**)
Stanhope Rd.
CR0: C'don 3E **168**
DA7: Bex 2E **126**
DA15: Sidc 4A **144**
E17 5D **50**
EN5: Barn 6A **20**
N6 6G **47**
N12 5F **31**
RM8: Dag 2F **73**
SM5: Cars 7E **166**
UB6: G'frd 5G **77**
Stanhope Row W1 5J **11** (1F **101**)
Stanhope St. NW1 1A **6** (2G **83**)
Stanhope Ter.
TW2: Twick 7K **113**
W2 2B **10** (7B **82**)
Stanier Cl. W14 5H **99**
Stanier Ho. *SW6* *1A* ***118***
(off Station Ct.)
Stanlake M. W12 1E **98**
Stanlake Rd. W12 1E **98**
Stanlake Vs. W12 1E **98**
Stanley Av. BR3: Beck 2E **158**
HA0: Wemb 7E **60**
IG11: Bark 2K **89**
KT3: N Mald 5C **152**
RM8: Dag 1F **73**
UB6: G'frd 1G **77**
Stanley Bri. Studios *SW6* *7K* ***99***
(off King's Rd.)
Stanley Cl. HA0: Wemb 7E **60**
SE9 1G **143**
SW8 6K **101**
Stanley Cohen Ho. *EC1* *4C* ***8***
(off Golden La.)
Stanley Ct. SM2: Sutt 7K **165**
SM5: Cars 7E **166**
W5 5C **78**
Stanley Cres. W11 7H **81**
Stanleycroft Cl. TW7: Isle 1J **113**
Stanley Gdns. CR4: Mitc 6E **136**
NW2 5E **62**
SM6: W'gton 6G **167**
W3 2A **98**
W11 7H **81**
Stanley Gdns. M. *W11* *7H* ***81***
(off Kensington Pk. Rd.)
Stanley Gdns. Rd.
TW11: Tedd 5J **131**
Stanley Gro. CR0: C'don 6A **156**
SW8 2E **118**
Stanley Holloway Ct. *E16* *6J* ***87***
(off Coolfin Rd.)
Stanley Ho. *E14* *6C* ***86***
(off Saracen St.)
SW10 *7A* ***100***
(off Coleridge Gdns.)
Stanley Mans. *SW10* *7A* ***16***
(off Park Wlk.)
Stanley M. *SW10* *7A* ***100***
(off Coleridge Gdns.)
Stanley Pk. Dr. HA0: Wemb 1F **79**
Stanley Pk. Rd.
SM5: Cars 7C **166**
SM6: W'gton 6F **167**
Stanley Picker Gallery ***3E 150***
(off Springfield Rd.)
Stanley Rd.
BR2: Broml 4K **159**
BR6: Orp 1K **173**
CR0: C'don 7A **156**
CR4: Mitc 7E **136**
DA14: Sidc 3A **144**
E4 1A **36**
E10 6D **50**
E12 5C **70**
E18 1H **51**
EN1: Enf 3K **23**
HA2: Harr 2G **59**
HA6: Nwood 1J **39**
HA9: Wemb 6F **61**

Stanley Rd. IG1: Ilf 2H **71**
  N2 . . . . .3B **46**
  N9 . . . . .1A **34**
  N10 . . . . .7A **32**
  N11 . . . . .6C **30**
  N15 . . . . .4B **48**
  NW9 .7C **44**
  SM2: Sutt 6K **165**
  SM4: Mord 4J **153**
  SM5: Cars 7E **166**
  SW14 . . . . .4H **115**
  SW19 . . . . .6J **135**
  TW2: Twick 3H **131**
  TW3: Houn 4G **113**
  TW11: Tedd 4J **131**
  TW15: Ashf 5A **128**
  UB1: S'hall 7C **76**
  W3 . . . . .3J **97**
Stanley Sq. SM5: Cars 7D **166**
Stanley St. SE8 . . . . .7B **104**
Stanley Studios SW10 . . . . .7A **16**
             (off Park Wlk.)
Stanley Ter. DA6: Bex 4G **127**
  N19 . . . . .2J **65**
Stanliff Ho. E14 . . . . .3C **104**
Stanmer St. SW11 . . . . .1C **118**
STANMORE 5G **27**
Stanmore & Edgware Golf Cen. . .3J **27**
Stanmore Commo
  Local Nature Reserve 2E **26**
Stanmore Country Pk. &
  Local Nature Reserve 3H **27**
Stanmore Gdns. SM1: Sutt 3A **166**
  TW9: Rich 3F **115**
Stanmore Golf Course 7G **27**
Stanmore Hill HA7: Stan 3F **27**
Stanmore Lodge
  HA7: Stan 4G **27**
Stanmore Pl. NW1 . . . . .1F **83**
Stanmore Rd. DA17: Belv 4J **109**
  E11 . . . . .1H **69**
  N15 . . . . .4B **48**
  TW9: Rich 3F **115**
Stanmore St. N1 . . . . .1K **83**
Stanmore Ter. BR3: Beck 2C **158**
             (off Fox Cl.)
Stannard Cotts. E1 . . . . .4J **85**
         (off Stannard Rd.)
Stannard Ct. SE6 . . . . .1D **140**
Stannard Ho. SW19 . . . . .4A **136**
Stannard M. E8 . . . . .6G **67**
         (off Stannard Rd.)
Stannard Rd. E8 . . . . .6G **67**
Stannary Pl. SE11 . . . . . .6K **19** (5A **102**)
Stannary St. SE11 . . . . . .7K **19** (6A **102**)
Stannet Way
  SM6: W'gton 4G **167**
Stansbury Sq. W10 . . . . .3G **81**
Stansfeld Ho. SE1 . . . . .4F **103**
         (off Longfield Est.)
Stansfeld Rd. E6 . . . . .5B **88**
  E16 . . . . .5B **88**
Stansfield Rd. SW9 . . . . .3K **119**
  TW4: Cran 2K **111**
Stansgate Rd.
  RM10: Dag 2G **73**
Stanstead WC1 . . . . .2F **7**
         (off Tavistock Pl.)
Stanstead Cl. BR2: Broml 5H **159**
Stanstead Gro. SE6 . . . . .1B **140**
Stanstead Ho. E3 . . . . .4E **86**
         (off Devas St.)
Stanstead Mnr. SM1: Sutt 6J **165**
Stanstead Rd. E11 . . . . .5K **51**
  SE6 .1A **140**
  SE23 . . . . .1K **139**
Stansted Cres. DA5: Bexl 1D **144**
Stansted Rd.
  TW6: H'row A 6B **110**
Stanswood Gdns. SE5 . . . . .7E **102**
Stanthorpe Cl. SW16 . . . . .5J **137**
Stanthorpe Rd. SW16 . . . . .5J **137**
Stanton Av. TW11: Tedd 6J **131**

Stanton Cl. KT4: Wor Pk 1F **165**
  KT19: Ewe 5H **163**
Stanton Ct. CR2: S Croy 5E **168**
         (off Birdhurst Ri.)
Stanton Ho. SE10 . . . . .6E **104**
         (off Thames St.)
  SE16 . . . . .2B **104**
         (off Rotherhithe St.)
Stanton Rd. CR0: C'don 7C **156**
  SE26 . . . . .4B **140**
  SW13 . . . . .2B **116**
  SW20 . . . . .1F **153**
Stanton Sq. SE26 . . . . .4B **140**
Stanton Way SE26 . . . . .4B **140**
Stanway Ct. N1 . . . . .1H **9**
         (off Shenfield St.)
Stanway Gdns. HA8: Edg 5D **28**
  W3 . . . . .1G **97**
Stanway St. N1 . . . . .2E **84**
STANWELL 6A **110**
Stanwell Cl. TW19: Stanw 6A **110**
Stanwell Moor Rd.
  TW19: Staines, Stanw M 7C **174**
  UB7: Lford 7C **174**
Stanwell Rd. TW14: Bedf 7D **110**
  TW15: Ashf 2A **128**
Stanwick Rd. W14 . . . . .4H **99**
Stanworth Ct. TW5: Hest 7D **94**
Stanworth St.
  SE1 . . . . .7J **15** (3F **103**)
Stanyhurst SE23 . . . . .1A **140**
Stapenhill Rd.
  HA0: Wemb 3B **60**
Staple Cl. DA5: Bexl 3K **145**
Staplefield Cl. SW2 . . . . .1J **137**
Stapleford N17 . . . . .2E **48**
         (off Willan Rd.)
Stapleford Av. IG2: Ilf 5J **53**
Stapleford Cl. E4 . . . . .3K **35**
  KT1: King T 2G **151**
  SW19 . . . . .7G **117**
Stapleford Rd. HA0: Wemb 7D **60**
  SM5: Cars 7C **166**
Staple Inn WC1 . . . . .6J **7**
Staple Inn Bldgs. WC1 . . . .6J **7** (5A **84**)
Staples Cl. SE16 . . . . .1A **104**
STAPLES CORNER 1D **62**
Staples Cnr. Bus. Pk.
  NW2 .1D **62**
Staples Cnr. Retail Pk. 1D **62**
Staples Ho. E6 . . . . .6E **88**
         (off Savage Gdns.)
Staple St. SE1 . . . . .7F **15** (2D **102**)
Stapleton Gdns. CR0: Wadd 5A **168**
Stapleton Hall Rd. N4 . . . . .1K **65**
Stapleton Ho. E2 . . . . .3H **85**
         (off Ellsworth St.)
Stapleton Rd. BR6: Orp 4K **173**
  DA7: Bex 7F **109**
  SW17 . . . . .3E **136**
Stapleton Vs. N16 . . . . .4E **66**
         (off Wordsworth Rd.)
Stapley Rd. DA17: Belv 5G **109**
Stapylton Rd. EN5: Barn 3B **20**
Star All. EC3 . . . . .2H **15**
Star & Garter Hill
  TW10: Rich 1E **132**
Starboard Way E14 . . . . .3C **104**
  E16 . . . . .1A **106**
Starbuck Cl. SE9 . . . . .7E **124**
Star Bus. Cen.
  RM13: Rain 5K **91**
Starch Ho. La. IG6: Ilf 2H **53**
Star Cl. EN3: Pond E 6D **24**
Starcross St. NW1 . . . . .2B **6** (3G **83**)
Starfield Rd. W12 . . . . .2C **98**
Star Hill DA1: Cray 5K **127**
Star La. E16 . . . . .4G **87**
Starley Cl. E17 . . . . .1F **51**
Starlight Way
  TW6: H'row A 5E **110**

Starling Cl. CR0: C'don 6A **158**
  HA5: Pinn 3A **40**
  IG9: Buck H 1D **36**
Starling Ho. NW8 . . . . .2C **82**
         (off Charlbert St.)
Starling M. KT5: Surb 6F **151**
Starling Wlk.
  TW12: Hamp 5C **130**
Starmans Cl. RM9: Dag 1E **90**
Star Path UB5: N'olt 2E **76**
         (off Brabazon Rd.)
Star Pl. E1 . . . . .3K **15** (7F **85**)
Star Rd. TW7: Isle 2H **113**
  UB10: Hil 4E **74**
  W14 .6H **99**
Star St. W2 . . . . .7B **4** (6C **82**)
Starts Cl. BR6: Farnb 3E **172**
Starts Hill Av. BR6: Farnb 4F **173**
Starts Hill Rd.
  BR6: Farnb 3E **172**
Starveall Cl.
  UB7: W Dray 3B **92**
Star Wharf NW1 . . . . .1G **83**
         (off St Pancras Way)
Star Yd. WC2 . . . . .7J **7** (6A **84**)
State Farm Av.
  BR6: Farnb 4F **173**
Staten Bldg. E3 . . . . .2K **86**
         (off Fairfield Rd.)
Staten Gdns. TW1: Twick 1K **131**
State Pde. IG6: Ilf 2G **53**
Statham St. N19 . . . . .3J **65**
         (off Alexander Rd.)
Statham Gro. N16 . . . . .4D **66**
  N18 . . . . .5K **33**
Statham Ho. SW8 . . . . .1G **119**
         (off Wadhurst Rd.)
Station App. BR1: Broml 3J **159**
         (off High St.)
  BR2: Hayes 1J **171**
  BR3: Beck 1C **158**
  BR4: W W'ck 7E **158**
  BR6: Orp 2K **173**
  BR7: Chst 6C **142**
         (Bennetts Copse)
  BR7: Chst 1E **160**
         (Vale Rd.)
  CR2: Sande 7D **168**
  DA5: Bexl 1G **145**
  DA7: Bex 2J **127**
         (Barnehurst Rd.)
  DA7: Bex 2E **126**
         (Percy Rd.)
  DA16: Well 2A **126**
  E4 . . . . .6A **36**
  E7 . . . . .4J **69**
  E11 . . . . .5J **51**
  E17 . . . . .5C **50**
  E18 . . . . .2K **51**
  EN5: New Bar 4F **21**
  HA0: Wemb 5G **60**
  HA1: Harr 7J **41**
  HA4: Ruis 5K **57**
         (Mahlon Av.)
  HA4: Ruis 1G **57**
         (Pembroke Rd.)
  HA5: Pinn 3C **40**
  IG8: Wfd G 6E **36**
  IG9: Buck H 4G **37**
  KT1: King T 1G **151**
  KT4: Wor Pk 1C **164**
  KT17: Ewe 7B **164**
  KT19: Ewe 5C **164**
  N11 . . . . .5A **32**
  N12 . . . . .4E **30**
  N16 . . . . .2F **67**
         (off Stamford Hill)
  NW1 . . . . .4F **5** (4D **82**)
  NW10 . . . . .3B **80**
  NW11 . . . . .7F **45**
  SE9 .2G **143**
         (Bercta Rd.)

Station App.
  SE9 .1D **142**
         (Crossmead)
  SE12 .6J **123**
         (off Burnt Ash Hill)
  SE26 . . . . .5B **140**
  SM2: Cheam 7G **165**
  SM5: Cars 4D **166**
  SW6 .3G **117**
  SW14 . . . . .3J **115**
  SW16 . . . . .6H **137**
         (Estreham Rd.)
  SW16 . . . . .5H **137**
         (Gleneagle Rd.)
  SW20 . . . . .2D **152**
  TW8: Bford 6C **96**
         (off Sidney Gdns.)
  TW9: Kew 1G **115**
  TW12: Hamp 1E **148**
  TW15: Ashf 4B **128**
  TW16: Sun 1J **147**
  TW17: Shep 5E **146**
  UB3: Hayes 3H **93**
  UB6: G'frd 7G **59**
  UB7: View 1A **92**
  W7 . . . . .1J **95**
Station App. Nth.
  DA15: Sidc 2A **144**
Station App. Rd.
  SE1 . . . . .7H **13** (2A **102**)
  W4 . . . . .7J **97**
Station App. Sth DA15: Sidc 2A **144**
         (off Jubilee Way)
Station App. Southside SE9 . . . .1D **142**
Station Arc. W1 . . . . .4K **5**
         (off Gt. Portland St.)
Station Av. KT3: N Mald 3A **152**
  KT19: Ewe 7A **164**
  SW9 .3B **120**
  TW9: Kew 1G **115**
Station Bldgs. KT1: King T 2E **150**
         (off Fife Rd.)
Station Chambers E6 . . . . .7C **70**
         (off High St. Nth.)
Station Cl. N3 . . . . .1J **45**
  N12 . . . . .4E **30**
  TW12: Hamp 1F **149**
Station Cotts. BR6: Orp 2K **173**
Station Ct. N15 . . . . .5F **49**
  SW6 .1A **118**
Station Cres. HA0: Wemb 6B **60**
  N15 . . . . .4D **48**
  SE3 . . . . .5J **105**
  TW15: Ashf 4A **128**
Stationer's Hall Ct.
  EC4 . . . . .1B **14** (6B **84**)
Station Est. BR3: Beck 3K **157**
  E18 . . . . .2K **51**
Station Est. Rd. TW14: Felt 1K **129**
Station Gdns. W4 . . . . .7J **97**
Station Garage M. SW16 . . . . . .6H **137**
Station Gro. HA0: Wemb 6E **60**
Sta. Hill BR2: Hayes 2J **171**
Station Ho. SE8 . . . . .7C **104**
         (off Deptford High St.)
Station Ho. M. N9 . . . . .4B **34**
Station M. Ter. SE3 . . . . .5J **105**
Station Pde.
  BR1: Broml 1J **159**
         (off Tweedy Rd.)
  DA15: Sidc 2A **144**
  E5 . . . . .3H **67**
         (off Up. Clapton Rd.)
  E6 . . . . .7C **70**
  E11 . . . . .5J **51**
  E13 . . . . .1A **88**
         (off Green St.)
  EN4: Cockf 4K **21**
  HA2: Harr 4F **59**
  HA3: Kenton 2A **42**
  HA4: Ruis 2F **57**
  HA8: Edg 7K **27**

Station Pde.
IG9: Buck H 4G **37**
IG11: Bark 7G **71**
N14 .1C **32**
NW2 .6E **62**
RM9: Dag 6G **73**
SM2: Sutt 6A **166**
(off High St.)
SW12 . . . . .1E **136**
TW9: Kew 1G **115**
TW14: Felt 1K **129**
TW15: Ashf 4B **128**
UB5: N'olt 4F **59**
(Accock Gro.)
UB5: N'olt 7E **58**
(Court Farm Rd.)
W3 . . . . .6G **79**
W4 . . . . .7J **97**
W5 . . . . .1F **97**
Station Pas. E18 . . . . .2K **51**
E20 .6E **68**
SE15 . . . . .1J **121**
Station Path SW6 . . . . .3H **117**
Station Pl. N4 . . . . .2A **66**
Station Ri. SE27 . . . . .2B **138**
Station Rd.
BR1: Broml 1J **159**
BR2: Broml 2G **159**
BR4: W W'ck 1E **170**
BR6: Orp 2K **173**
CR0: C'don 1C **168**
DA7: Bex 3E **126**
DA15: Sidc 2A **144**
DA17: Belv 3G **109**
E4 . . . . .1A **36**
E7 . . . . .4J **69**
E12 .4C **70**
E17 .6A **50**
EN5: New Bar 5E **20**
HA1: Harr 4K **41**
HA2: Harr 5F **41**
HA8: Edg 6B **28**
IG1: Ilf 3F **71**
IG6: Ilf 3H **53**
KT1: Hamp W 1C **150**
KT2: King T 1G **151**
KT3: N Mald 5D **152**
KT7: T Ditt 7K **149**
KT9: Chess 5E **162**
N3 . . . . .1J **45**
N11 .5A **32**
N17 .3G **49**
N19 .3G **65**
N21 .1G **33**
N22 .2J **47**
(not continuous)
NW4 .6C **44**
NW7 .6F **29**
NW10 . . . . .2B **80**
RM6: Chad H, Dag 7D **54**
SE13 . . . . .3E **122**
SE20 . . . . .6J **139**
SE25 . . . . .4F **157**
SM5: Cars 4D **166**
SW13 . . . . .2B **116**
SW19 . . . . .1A **154**
TW1: Twick 1K **131**
TW3: Houn 4F **113**
TW11: Tedd 6A **132**
TW12: Hamp 1E **148**
TW15: Ashf 4B **128**
TW16: Sun 6J **147**
TW17: Shep 5E **146**
UB3: Harl, Hayes 4G **93**
(not continuous)
UB7: W Dray 2A **92**
W5 . . . . .1F **97**
W7 . . . . .1J **95**
Station Rd. Nth. DA17: Belv . . .3H **109**
Station Sq. BR5: Pet W 5G **161**
Station St. E15 . . . . .7F **69**
E16 .1F **107**

Station Ter. NW10 . . . . .2F **81**
SE5 .1C **120**
Station Vw. UB6: G'frd 1H **77**
Station Wlk. W11 . . . . .7F **81**
(off Bramley Rd.)
Station Way IG9: Buck H 4F **37**
SE15 . . . . .2G **121**
SE18 . . . . .3F **107**
SM3: Cheam 6G **165**
Station Yd. HA4: Ruis 2E **56**
TW1: Twick 7A **114**
Staton Ct. E10 . . . . .7D **50**
(off Kings Cl.)
Staunton Ho. SE17 . . . . .4E **102**
(off Wansey St.)
Staunton Rd. KT2: King T 6E **132**
Staunton St. SE8 . . . . .6B **104**
Stave Hill Ecological Pk. 2A **104**
Staveley NW1 . . . . .1A **6**
(off Varndell St.)
Staveley Cl. E9 . . . . .5J **67**
N7 . . . . .4J **65**
SE15 . . . . .1H **121**
Staveley Ct. E11 . . . . .5J **51**
Staveley Gdns. W4 . . . . .1K **115**
Staveley Rd. TW15: Ashf 6F **129**
W4 . . . . .6J **97**
Stavers Ho. E3 . . . . .2B **86**
(off Tredegar Rd.)
Staverton Pl. BR1: Broml 4D **160**
Staverton Rd. NW2 . . . . .7E **62**
Stave Yd. Rd. SE16 . . . . .1A **104**
Stavordale Lodge W14 . . . . . . .3H **99**
(off Melbury Rd.)
Stavordale Rd. N5 . . . . .4B **66**
SM5: Cars 7A **154**
Stayner's Rd. E1 . . . . .4K **85**
Stayton Rd. SM1: Sutt 3J **165**
Stead Cl. BR7: Chst 5E **142**
Steadfast Rd. KT1: King T 1D **150**
Steadman Ct. EC1 . . . . .3D **8**
(off Old l)
Steadman Ho. RM10: Dag 3G **73**
(off Uvedale Rd.)
Stead St. SE17 . . . . .4D **102**
Steam Farm La. TW14: Felt 4H **111**
Stean St. E8 . . . . .1F **85**
Stebbing Ho. W11 . . . . .1F **99**
(off Queensdale Cres.)
Stebbing Way IG11: Bark 2A **90**
Stebondale St. E14 . . . . .4E **104**
Stedham Pl. WC1 . . . . .7E **6**
Stedman Cl.
DA5: Bexl 3K **145**
UB10: Ick 3C **56**
Steedman St. SE17 . . . . .4C **102**
Steeds Rd. N10 . . . . .1D **46**
Steele Ct. TW11: Tedd 7C **132**
Steele Ho. E15 . . . . .2G **87**
(off Eve Rd.)
Steele Rd. E11 . . . . .4G **69**
N17 .3E **48**
NW10 . . . . .2J **79**
TW7: Isle 4A **114**
W4 . . . . .3J **97**
Steele's M. Nth. NW3 . . . . .6D **64**
Steele's M. Sth. NW3 . . . . .6D **64**
Steele's Rd. NW3 . . . . .6D **64**
Steele's Studios NW3 . . . . .6D **64**
Steele Wlk. DA8: Erith 7H **109**
Steel's La. E1 . . . . .6J **85**
Steelyard Pas. EC4 . . . . .3E **14**
Steen Way SE22 . . . . .5E **120**
Steep Cl. BR6: Chels 6K **173**
Steep Hill CR0: C'don 4E **168**
SW16 . . . . .3H **137**
Steeple Cl. SW6 . . . . .2G **117**
SW19 . . . . .5G **135**
Steeple Ct. E1 . . . . .4H **85**
Steeplestone Cl. N18 . . . . .5H **33**
Steeple Wlk. N1 . . . . .1C **84**
(off New Nth. Rd.)

Steerforth St. SW18 . . . . .2A **136**
Steering Cl. N9 . . . . .1D **34**
Steers Mead CR4: Mitc 1D **154**
Steers Way SE16 . . . . .2A **104**
Stelfox Ho. WC1 . . . . .1H **7**
(off Penton Ri.)
Stella Cl. UB8: Hil 5D **74**
Stellar Ho. N17 . . . . .6A **34**
Stella Rd. SW17 . . . . .6D **136**
Stelling Rd. DA8: Erith 7K **109**
Stellman Cl. E5 . . . . .3G **67**
Stembridge Rd. SE20 . . . . .2H **157**
Stephan Cl. E8 . . . . .1G **85**
Stephen Cl. BR6: Orp 3J **173**
Stephendale Rd. SW6 . . . . .3K **117**
Stephendale Yd. SW6 . . . . .3K **117**
(off Stephendale Rd.)
Stephen Fox Ho. W4 . . . . .5A **98**
(off Chiswick La.)
Stephen Jewers Gdns.
IG11: Bark 7K **71**
Stephen M. W1 . . . . . .6C **6** (5H **83**)
Stephen Pl. SW4 . . . . .3G **119**
Stephen Rd. DA7: Bex 3J **127**
Stephens Cl. E16 . . . . .4H **87**
SE4 .3A **122**
Stephens Lodge N12 . . . . .3F **31**
(off Woodside La.)
Stephenson Cl. DA16: Well 2A **126**
E3 . . . . .3D **86**
Stephenson Ct. SM2: Cheam . . .7G **165**
(off Station App.)
Stephenson Ho. SE1 . . . . .3C **102**
Stephenson Rd. E17 . . . . .5A **50**
TW2: Whitt 7E **112**
W7 . . . . .6K **77**
Stephenson St. E16 . . . . .4G **87**
NW10 . . . . .3A **80**
Stephenson Way
NW1 . . . . .3B **6** (4G **83**)
Stephen's Rd. E15 . . . . .1G **87**
Stephen St. W1 . . . . . .6C **6** (5H **83**)
STEPNEY 5K **85**
Stepney C'way. E1 . . . . .6K **85**
Stepney City Apts. E1 . . . . .5J **85**
Stepney City Farm 5K **85**
Stepney Cl. CR4: Mitc 1E **154**
Stepney Grn. E1 . . . . .5J **85**
Stepney Grn. Ct. E1 . . . . .5K **85**
(off Stepney Grn.)
Stepney High St. E1 . . . . .5K **85**
Stepney Way E1 . . . . .5H **85**
Sterling Av. HA8: Edg 4A **28**
Sterling Cl. NW10 . . . . .7C **62**
Sterling Gdns. SE14 . . . . .6A **104**
Sterling Ind. Est.
RM10: Dag 4H **73**
Sterling Pl. W5 . . . . .4E **96**
Sterling Rd.
DA7: Bex 4H **127**
EN2: Enf 1J **23**
Sterling St. SW7 . . . .1D **16** (3C **100**)
Sterling Way N7 . . . . .6K **65**
N18 .4J **33**
The Sternberg Cen. 3J **45**
Stern Cl. IG11: Bark 2C **90**
Stern Ct. E3 . . . . .3E **86**
(off Culvert Dr.)
Sterndale Rd. W14 . . . . .3F **99**
Sterne St. W12 . . . . .2F **99**
Sternhall La. SE15 . . . . .3G **121**
Sternhold Av. SW2 . . . . .2H **137**
Sterry Cres. RM10: Dag 5G **73**
Sterry Dr. KT7: T Ditt 6J **149**
KT19: Ewe 4A **164**
Sterry Gdns. RM10: Dag 6G **73**
Sterry Rd. IG11: Bark 1K **89**
RM10: Dag 4G **73**
Sterry St. SE1 . . . . . .7E **14** (2D **102**)
Steucers La. SE23 . . . . .1A **140**
Stevannie Ct.
DA17: Belv 5F **109**

Steve Biko Ct. W10 . . . . .4F **81**
(off St John's Ter.)
Steve Biko La. SE6 . . . . .4C **140**
Steve Biko Lodge E13 . . . . .2J **87**
(off London Rd.)
Steve Biko Rd. N7 . . . . .3A **66**
Steve Biko Way TW3: Houn 3E **112**
Stevedale Rd. DA16: Well 2C **126**
Stevedore St. E1 . . . . .1H **103**
Stevenage Rd. E6 . . . . .6E **70**
SW6 . . . . .7F **99**
Stevens Av. E9 . . . . .6J **67**
Stevens Cl. BR3: Beck 6C **140**
DA5: Bexl 4K **145**
HA5: Eastc 5A **40**
TW12: Hamp 6D **130**
Stevens Grn. WD23: B Hea 1B **26**
Stevens La. KT10: Clay 7A **162**
Stevenson Cl.
EN5: New Bar 7G **21**
Stevenson Ct.
CR4: Mitc 3C **154**
SE6 .2H **141**
Stevenson Cres. SE16 . . . . .5G **103**
Stevenson Ho. NW8 . . . . .1A **82**
(off Boundary Rd.)
Stevens Rd. RM8: Dag 2C **72**
Stevens St. SE1 . . . . .7H **15** (3E **102**)
Steventon Rd. W12 . . . . .7B **80**
Steward Ho. E3 . . . . .3C **86**
(off Trevithick Way)
Stewards Holte Wlk. N11 . . . . . .4A **32**
Steward St. E1 . . . . . . .6H **9** (5E **84**)
Stewart Av. TW17: Shep 4C **146**
Stewart Cl. BR7: Chst 5F **143**
NW9 .6J **43**
TW12: Hamp 6C **130**
Stewart Ho. KT1: King T 3F **151**
Stewart Quay UB3: Hayes 2G **93**
Stewart Rainbird Ho. E12 . . . . . .5E **70**
(off Parkhurst Rd.)
Stewart Rd. E15 . . . . .4F **69**
Stewartsby Cl. N18 . . . . .5H **33**
Stewart's Gro. SW3 . . . .5B **16** (5B **100**)
Stewart's Pl. SW2 . . . . .6K **119**
Stewart's Rd. SW8 . . . . .7G **101**
Stewart St. E14 . . . . .2E **104**
Stew La. EC4 . . . . . . .2C **14** (7C **84**)
Steyne Horn La. W3 . . . . .1H **97**
Steyne Ho. W3 . . . . .1J **97**
(off Narrow St.)
Steyne Rd. W3 . . . . .1H **97**
Steyning Gro. SE9 . . . . .4D **142**
Steynings Way N12 . . . . .5D **30**
Steyning Way TW4: Houn 4A **112**
Steynton Av. DA5: Bexl 2D **144**
Stibbington Ho. NW1 . . . . .2G **83**
(off Cranleigh St.)
Stickland Rd. DA17: Belv 4G **109**
Stickle Ho. SE8 . . . . .7D **104**
(off Creative Rd.)
Stickleton Cl. UB6: G'frd 3F **77**
Stifford Ho. E1 . . . . .5J **85**
(off Stepney Way)
Stilecroft Gdns. HA0: Wemb 3B **60**
Stile Hall Gdns. W4 . . . . .5G **97**
Stile Hall Mans. W4 . . . . .5G **97**
(off Wellesley Rd.)
Stile Hall Pde. W4 . . . . .5G **97**
Stileman Ho. E3 . . . . .5B **86**
(off Ackroyd St.)
Stile Path TW16: Sun 3J **147**
Stiles Cl. BR2: Broml 6D **160**
DA8: Erith 5H **109**
Stillingfleet Rd. SW13 . . . . .6C **98**
Stillington St.
SW1 . . . . .3B **18** (4G **101**)
Stillness Rd. SE23 . . . . .6A **122**
Still Wlk. SE1 . . . . .5H **15**
Stilwell Cl. BR5: St P 7B **144**
Stilwell Dr. UB8: Hil 4B **74**
STILWELL RDBT. 7C **74**

Stipularis Dr. UB4: Yead 4B **76**
Stirling Av. HA5: Pinn 1B **58**
  SM6: W'gton 7J **167**
  TW17: Shep 3G **147**
Stirling Cl. DA14: Sidc 4J **143**
  SW16 . . . . .1H **155**
Stirling Ct. *EC1* *3A 8*
  (off St John St.)
  W13 . . . . .7B **78**
Stirling Gro. TW3: Houn 2G **113**
Stirling Rd. E13 . . . . .2K **87**
  E17 . . . . .3A **50**
  HA3: W'stone 3K **41**
  N17 . . . . .1G **49**
  N22 . . . . .1B **48**
  SW9 . . . . .2J **119**
  TW2: Whitt 7E **112**
  TW6: H'row A 6B **110**
  UB3: Hayes 7K **75**
  W3 . . . . .3H **97**
Stirling Rd. Path E17 . . . . .3A **50**
Stirling Wlk. KT5: Surb 6H **151**
Stirling Way CR0: Bedd 7J **155**
Stiven Cres. HA2: Harr 3D **58**
Stockbeck NW1 . . . . .18 **6**
  (off Ampthill Est.)
Stockbridge Ho. SW18 . . . . .4A **118**
  (off Eltringham St.)
Stockbury Rd. CR0: C'don 6J **157**
Stockdale Rd. RM8: Dag 2F **73**
Stockdove Way
  UB6: G'frd 3K **77**
Stocker Gdns. RM9: Dag 7C **72**
Stockfield Rd. SW16 . . . . .3K **137**
Stockford Av. NW7 . . . . .7A **30**
Stockholm Apts. NW1 . . . . .7E **64**
  (off Chalk Farm Rd.)
Stockholm Ho. E1 . . . . .7G **85**
  (off Swedenborg Gdns.)
Stockholm Rd. SE16 . . . . .5J **103**
Stockholm Way E1 . . . . .1G **103**
Stockhurst Cl. SW15 . . . . .2E **116**
Stockingswater La.
  EN3: Brim 2G **25**
Stockland Rd. RM7: Rom 6K **55**
Stockleigh Hall NW8 . . . . .2C **82**
  (off Prince Albert Rd.)
Stockley Cl. UB7: W Dray 2D **92**
Stockley Country Pk. 7C **74**
Stockley Farm Rd.
  UB7: W Dray 3D **92**
STOCKLEY PARK 1D **92**
Stockley Pk. Golf Course 7E **74**
Stockley Rd.
  UB7: W Dray 4D **92**
  UB8: Hil 6C **74**
  UB11: Stock P 6C **74**
Stock Orchard Cres. N7 . . . . .5K **65**
Stock Orchard St. N7 . . . . .5K **65**
Stockport Rd. SW16 . . . . .1H **155**
Stocksfield Rd. E17 . . . . .3E **50**
Stocks Pl. E14 . . . . .7B **86**
  UB10: Hil 1C **74**
Stock St. E13 . . . . .2J **87**
Stockton Cl. EN5: New Bar 4F **21**
Stockton Ct. SW1 . . . . .2C **18**
  (off Greycoat St.)
Stockton Gdns. N17 . . . . .7H **33**
  NW7 . . . . .3F **29**
Stockton Ho. E2 . . . . .3H **85**
  (off Ellsworth St.)
  HA2: Harr 1E **58**
Stockton Rd. N17 . . . . .7H **33**
  N18 . . . . .6B **34**
STOCKWELL 2K **119**
Stockwell Av. SW9 . . . . .3K **119**
Stockwell Cl.
  BR1: Broml 2K **159**
  HA8: Edg 2J **43**
Stockwell Gdns. SW9 . . . . .1K **119**
Stockwell Gdns. Est. SW9 . . . . . .2J **119**
Stockwell Grn. SW9 . . . . .2K **119**

Stockwell Grn. Ct. SW9 . . . . .2K **119**
Stockwell La. SW9 . . . . .2K **119**
Stockwell Pk. Cres. SW9 . . . . . . .2K **119**
Stockwell Pk. Est. SW9 . . . . .2K **119**
Stockwell Pk. Rd. SW9 . . . . .1K **119**
Stockwell Pk. Wlk. SW9 . . . . .3A **120**
Stockwell Rd. SW9 . . . . .1K **119**
Stockwell St. SE10 . . . . .6E **104**
Stockwell Ter. SW9 . . . . .1K **119**
Stodart Rd. SE20 . . . . .1J **157**
Stoddart Ho. SW8 . . . . . .7H **19** (6K **101**)
Stodmarsh Ho. SW9 . . . .*1A 120*
  (off Cowley Rd.)
Stofield Gdns. SE9 . . . . .3B **142**
Stoford Cl. SW19 . . . . .7G **117**
Stokenchurch St. SW6 . . . . .1K **117**
STOKE NEWINGTON 3F **67**
Stoke Newington Chu. St.
  N16 . . . . .3D **66**
Stoke Newington Comn.
  N16 . . . . .3F **67**
Stoke Newington High St.
  N16 . . . . .3F **67**
Stoke Newington Rd. N16 . . . . . . .5F **67**
Stoke Pl. NW10 . . . . .3B **80**
Stoke Rd. KT2: King T 7J **133**
Stokesby Rd. KT9: Chess 6F **163**
Stokes Cotts. IG6: Ilf 1G **53**
Stokes Ct. N2 . . . . .4C **46**
Stokes Field
  Local Nature Reserve 2B **162**
Stokesley St. W12 . . . . .6B **80**
Stokes M. TW11: Tedd 5A **132**
Stokes Rd. CR0: C'don 6K **157**
  E6 .4C **88**
Stokley Ct. N8 . . . . .4J **47**
Stoll Cl. NW2 . . . . .3E **62**
Stoms Path SE6 . . . . .5C **140**
  (off Maroons Way)
Stonard Rd. N13 . . . . .3F **33**
  RM8: Dag 5B **72**
Stondon Pk. SE23 . . . . .6A **122**
Stondon Wlk. E6 . . . . .2B **88**
Stonebanks KT12: Walt T 7J **147**
STONEBRIDGE 1K **79**
Stonebridge Cen. N15 . . . . .5F **49**
Stonebridge Gdns. 1F **85**
  (off Arbutus St.)
Stonebridge M. SE19 . . . . .7D **138**
Stonebridge Pk. NW10 . . . . .7K **61**
Stonebridge Rd. N15 . . . . .5F **49**
Stonebridge Way
  HA9: Wemb 6H **61**
Stone Bldgs. WC2 . . . . .6H **7**
Stonechat M. SW15 . . . . .4C **116**
Stonechat Sq. E6 . . . . .5C **88**
Stone Cl. RM8: Dag 2F **73**
  SW4 . . . . .2G **119**
  UB7: Yiew 1B **92**
Stonecot Cl. SM3: Sutt 1G **165**
Stonecot Hill SM3: Sutt 1G **165**
Stone Cres. TW14: Felt 7H **111**
Stonecroft Rd. DA8: Erith 7J **109**
Stonecroft Way CR0: C'don 7J **155**
Stonecrop Cl. NW9 . . . . .3K **43**
Stonecutter St. EC4 . . . . . .7A **8** (6B **84**)
Stonefield N4 . . . . .2K **65**
Stonefield Cl. DA7: Bex 3G **127**
  HA4: Ruis 5C **58**
Stonefield Mans. N1 . . . . .1A **84**
  (off Cloudesley St.)
Stonefield St. N1 . . . . .1A **84**
Stonefield Way
  HA4: Ruis 4C **58**
  SE7 . . . . .7B **106**
STONEGROVE 4A **28**
Stonegrove HA8: Edg 4K **27**
Stone Gro. Ct. HA8: Edg 5A **28**
Stonegrove Gdns. HA8: Edg 5K **27**
Stone Hall W8 . . . . .3K **99**
  (off Stone Hall Gdns.)

Stonehall Av. IG1: Ilf 6C **52**
Stone Hall Gdns. W8 . . . . .3K **99**
Stone Hall Pl. W8 . . . . .3K **99**
Stone Hall Rd. N21 . . . . .7E **22**
Stoneham Rd. N11 . . . . .5B **32**
Stonehill Cl. SW14 . . . . .5K **115**
Stonehill Ct. E4 . . . . .7J **25**
STONEHILL GREEN 7J **145**
Stonehill Grn. DA2: Wilm 7J **145**
Stonehill Rd. SW14 . . . . .5J **115**
  W4 .5G **97**
Stonehills Ct. SE21 . . . . .3E **138**
Stonehill Woods Pk.
  DA14: Sidc 6H **145**
Stonehorse Rd. EN3: Pond E 5D **24**
Stonehouse NW1 . . . . .1G **83**
  (off Plender St.)
Stonehouse Ho. W2 . . . . .5J **81**
  (off Westbourne Pk. Rd.)
Stone Lake Ind. Pk. SE7 . . . . .4A **106**
Stone Lake Retail Pk. SE7 . . . . . .4A **106**
STONELEIGH 5C **164**
Stoneleigh Av. EN1: Enf 1C **24**
  KT4: Wor Pk 4C **164**
Stoneleigh B'way.
  KT17: Ewe 5C **164**
Stoneleigh Cl. IG5: Ilf 3C **52**
Stoneleigh Cres. KT19: Ewe 5B **164**
Stoneleigh M. E3 . . . . .2A **86**
Stoneleigh Pk. Av.
  CR0: C'don 6K **157**
Stoneleigh Pk. Rd.
  KT4: Wor Pk 6B **164**
  KT19: Ewe 6B **164**
Stoneleigh Pl. W11 . . . . .7F **81**
Stoneleigh Rd. BR1: Broml 3F **161**
  IG5: Ilf 3C **52**
  N17 . . . . .3F **49**
  SM5: Cars 7C **154**
Stoneleigh St. W11 . . . . .7F **81**
Stoneleigh Ter. N19 . . . . .2F **65**
Stonell's Rd. SW11 . . . . .6D **118**
Stonemason Ct. SE1 . . . . .7C **14**
  (off Borough Rd.)
Stonemason Ho. SE14 . . . . .1K **121**
  (off Fishers Ct.)
Stonemasons Cl. N15 . . . . .4D **48**
Stonemasons Yd. SW18 . . . . .7B **118**
Stonenest St. N4 . . . . .1K **65**
Stone Pk. Av. BR3: Beck 4C **158**
Stone Pl. KT4: Wor Pk 2C **164**
Stone Rd. BR2: Broml 5H **159**
Stones End St. SE1 . . . . .7C **14** (2C **102**)
Stonewall E6 . . . . .5E **88**
Stoneway Wlk. E3 . . . . .2K **85**
Stone Well Rd.
  TW19: Stanw 1A **128**
Stonewold Ct. W5 . . . . .6D **78**
Stoney All. SE18 . . . . .2E **124**
Stoneyard La. E14 . . . . .7D **86**
Stoneycroft Cl. SE12 . . . . .7H **123**
Stoneycroft Rd. IG8: Wfd G 6H **37**
Stoneydeep TW11: Tedd 4A **132**
Stoneydown E17 . . . . .4A **50**
Stoneydown Av. E17 . . . . .4A **50**
Stoneydown Ho. E17 . . . . .4A **50**
  (off Stoneydown)
Stoneyfields Gdns. HA8: Edg 4E **28**
Stoneyfields La.
  HA8: Edg 5D **28**
Stoney La. E1 . . . . .7H **9** (6F **85**)
  SE19 . . . . .6E **139**
Stoney St. SE1 . . . . .4E **14** (1D **102**)
Stonhouse St. SW4 . . . . .4H **119**
Stonor Rd. W14 . . . . .4H **99**
Stonycroft Cl. EN3: Enf H 2F **25**
Stopes St. SE15 . . . . .7F **103**
Stopford Rd. E13 . . . . .1J **87**
  SE17 . . . . .5B **102**
Stopher Ho. SE1 . . . . .7B **14**
  (off Webber St.)
Storehouse M. E14 . . . . .7C **86**

Storer Dr. DA16: Well 3B **126**
Store Rd. E16 . . . . .2E **106**
Storers Quay E14 . . . . .4F **105**
Store St. E15 . . . . .5F **69**
  WC1 . . . . .6C **6** (5H **83**)
Storey Cl. UB10: Ick 3E **56**
Storey Ct. NW8 . . . . .2A **4**
Storey Ho. E14 . . . . .7D **86**
  (off Cottage St.)
Storey Rd. E17 . . . . .4B **50**
  N6 .6D **46**
Storey's Ga. SW1 . . . . . .7D **12** (2H **101**)
Storey St. E16 . . . . .1E **106**
Stories M. SE5 . . . . .2E **120**
Stories Rd. SE5 . . . . .3E **120**
Stork Rd. E7 . . . . .6H **69**
Storksmead Rd. HA8: Edg 7F **29**
Stork's Rd. SE16 . . . . .3G **103**
Stormont Lawn Tennis & Squash Club
  . . . . .5D **46**
Stormont Rd. N6 . . . . .7D **46**
  SW11 . . . . .3E **118**
Stormont Way KT9: Chess 5C **162**
Stormount Dr. UB3: Harl 2E **92**
Storrington WC1 . . . . .2F **7**
  (off Regent Sq.)
Storrington Rd. CR0: C'don 1F **169**
Storth Oaks Mead
  BR7: Chst 5D **142**
Story St. N1 . . . . .7K **65**
Stothard Ho. E1 . . . . .4J **85**
  (off Amiel St.)
Stothard Pl. E1 . . . . .5H **9** (5E **84**)
Stothard St. E1 . . . . .4J **85**
Stott Cl. SW18 . . . . .6B **118**
Stoughton Av.
  SM3: Cheam 5F **165**
Stoughton Cl. SE11 . . . . .4H **19** (4K **101**)
  SW15 . . . . .1C **134**
Stour Av. UB2: S'hall 3E **94**
Stourcliffe Cl. W1 . . . . . . .1E **10** (6D **82**)
Stourcliffe St. W1 . . . . . . .1E **10** (6D **82**)
Stour Cl. BR2: Kes 4A **172**
Stourhead Cl. SW19 . . . . .7F **117**
Stourhead Gdns. SW20 . . . . .3C **152**
Stourhead Ho. SW1 . . . . .5C **18**
  (off Tachbrook St.)
Stour Rd. E3 . . . . .7C **68**
  RM10: Dag 2G **73**
Stourton Av. TW13: Hanw 4D **130**
Stowage SE8 . . . . .6C **104**
Stow Cres. E17 . . . . .7F **35**
Stowe Cres. HA4: Ruis 6D **38**
Stowe Gdns. N9 . . . . .1A **34**
Stowe Ho. NW11 . . . . .6A **46**
Stowell Ho. N8 . . . . .4J **47**
  (off Pembroke Rd.)
Stowe Pl. N15 . . . . .3E **48**
Stowe Rd. W12 . . . . .2D **98**
Stowting Rd. BR6: Orp 4J **173**
Stox Mead HA3: Hrw W 1H **41**
Stracey Rd. E7 . . . . .4J **69**
  NW10 . . . . .1K **79**
Strachan Pl. SW19 . . . . .6E **134**
Stradbroke Dr. IG7: Chig 6K **37**
Stradbroke Gro. IG5: Ilf 3C **52**
  IG9: Buck H 1G **37**
Stradbroke Pk. IG7: Chig 6K **37**
Stradbroke Rd. N5 . . . . .4C **66**
Stradbrook Cl. HA2: Harr 3D **58**
Stradella Rd. SE24 . . . . .6C **120**
Strafford Av. IG5: Ilf 2E **52**
Strafford Ho. SE8 . . . . .5B **104**
  (off Grove St.)
Strafford Rd. EN5: Barn 3B **20**
  TW1: Twick 7A **114**
  TW3: Houn 3D **112**
  W3 .2J **97**
Strafford St. E14 . . . . .2C **104**
Strahan Rd. E3 . . . . .3A **86**
The Straight UB1: S'hall 2B **94**
Straightsmouth SE10 . . . . .7E **104**

Strait Rd. E6 . . . . .7C 88
Strakers Rd. SE15 . . . . .4H 121
Strale Ho. N1 . . . . .1E 84
(off Whitmore Est.)
Strand WC2 . . . . .3F 13 (7J 83)
Strand Ct. SE18 . . . . .5K 107
Strand Dr. TW9: Kew 7H 97
Strand E. Twr. E15 . . . . .2E 86
Strandfield Cl. SE18 . . . . .5J 107
Strand Ho. BR2: Broml 6B 160
(off Wells Vw. Dr.)
SE28 . . . . .1H 107
Strand La. WC2 . . . . . . .2H 13 (7K 83)
STRAND ON THE GREEN 6G 97
Strand on the Grn. W4 . . . . .6G 97
Strand Pl. N18 . . . . .4K 33
Strand School App. W4 . . . . .6G 97
Strang Ho. N1 . . . . .1C 84
Strangways Ter. W14 . . . . .3H 99
Stranraer Way N1 . . . . .7J 65
TW6: H'row A 6A 110
Strasburg Rd. SW11 . . . . .1E 118
Strata SE1 . . . . .4C 102
(off Walworth Rd.)
Strata Ct. KT12: Walt T 7H 147
Strata Rd. DA8: Erith 5J 109
Stratfield Pk. Cl. N21 . . . . .7G 23
STRATFORD 7F 69
Stratford Av. UB10: Hil 2B 74
The Stratford Cen. 7F 69
Stratford Circus
(Performing Arts Cen.) 6F 69
Stratford Cl. IG11: Bark 7A 72
RM10: Dag 7J 73
Stratford Ct. KT3: N Mald 4K 151
Stratford Eye E15 . . . . .6F 69
Stratford Gro. SW15 . . . . .4F 117
Stratford Ho. Av.
BR1: Broml 3C 160
STRATFORD NEW TOWN 6F 69
The Stratford Office Village
E15 .7G 69
(off Romford Rd.)
Stratford One E20 . . . . .6D 68
Stratford Picturehouse 6F 69
Stratford Pl. E20 . . . . .6E 68
(within Westfield Shop. Cen.)
W1 . . . . .1J 11 (6F 83)
Stratford Rd. CR7: Thor H 4A 156
E13 . . . . .1H 87
(not continuous)
NW4 . . . . .4F 45
TW6: H'row A 6D 110
UB2: S'hall 4C 94
UB4: Yead 4K 75
W8 . . . . .3J 99
Stratford Studios W8 . . . . .3J 99
Stratford Vs. NW1 . . . . .7G 65
Stratford Workshops E15 . . . . . . .1F 87
(off Burford Rd.)
Strathan Cl. SW18 . . . . .6G 117
Strathaven Rd. SE12 . . . . .6K 123
Strathblaine Rd. SW11 . . . . . . .5B 118
Strathbrook Rd. SW16 . . . . .7K 137
Strathcona Rd. HA9: Wemb 2D 60
Strathdale SW16 . . . . .5K 137
Strathdon Dr. SW17 . . . . .3B 136
Strathearn Av. TW2: Whitt 1J 131
UB3: Harl 7H 93
Strathearn Ho. W2 . . . . .2C 10
(off Strathern Pl.)
Strathearn Pl. W2 . . . .1C 10 (6C 82)
Strathearn Rd.
SM1: Sutt 5J 165
SW19 . . . . .5J 135
Stratheden Pde. SE3 . . . . .7J 105
Stratheden Rd. SE3 . . . . .1J 123
Strathfield Gdns.
IG11: Bark 6H 71
Strathleven Rd. SW2 . . . . .5J 119
Strathmore Ct. NW8 . . . . .1C 4
(off Park Rd.)

Strathmore Gdns. HA8: Edg 2H 43
N3 . . . . .1K 45
W8 . . . . .1J 99
Strathmore Rd. CRO: C'don 7D 156
SW19 . . . . .3J 135
TW11: Tedd 4J 131
Strathnairn St. SE1 . . . . .4G 103
(not continuous)
Strathray Gdns. NW3 . . . . .6C 64
Strath Ter. SW11 . . . . .4C 118
Strathville Rd. SW18 . . . . .2J 135
(not continuous)
Strathyre Av. SW16 . . . . .3A 156
Stratosphere Twr. E15 . . . . .7F 69
(off Gt. Eastern Rd.)
Stratton Cl. DA7: Bex 3E 126
HA8: Edg 6A 28
SW19 . . . . .2J 153
TW3: Houn 1E 112
Stratton Ct. HA5: Hat E 1D 40
(off Devonshire Rd.)
N1 .7E 66
(off Hertford Rd.)
Strattondale St. E14 . . . . .3E 104
Stratton Dr. IG11: Bark 5J 71
Stratton Gdns. UB1: S'hall 6D 76
Stratton Rd. DA7: Bex 3E 126
SW19 . . . . .2J 153
TW16: Sun 2H 147
Stratton St. W1 . . . . . .4K 11 (1F 101)
Strauss Rd. W4 . . . . .2K 97
Strawberry Flds.
BR6: Farnb 5F 173
STRAWBERRY HILL 3K 131
Strawberry Hill 3K 131
Strawberry Hill
KT9: Chess 6D 162
TW1: Twick 3K 131
Strawberry Hill Cl.
TW1: Twick 3K 131
Strawberry Hill Golf Course 3J 131
Strawberry Hill Rd.
TW1: Twick 3K 131
Strawberry La. SM5: Cars 3E 166
Strawberry Ter. N10 . . . . .1D 46
Strawberry Va. N2 . . . . .1B 46
TW1: Twick 3A 132
(not continuous)
Streakes Fld. Rd. NW2 . . . . .2C 62
Streamdale SE2 . . . . .6B 108
Stream La. HA8: Edg 5C 28
Streamline Ct. SE22 . . . . .1G 139
(off Streamline M.)
Streamline M. SE22 . . . . .1G 139
Streamside Cl. BR2: Broml 4J 159
N9 . . . . .1A 34
Streamway DA17: Belv 6G 109
Streatfeild Av. E6 . . . . .1D 88
Streatfield Rd. HA3: Kenton 3C 42
STREATHAM 3J 137
Streatham Cl. SW16 . . . . .2J 137
STREATHAM COMMON 6H 137
Streatham Comn. Nth.
SW16 . . . . .5J 137
Streatham Comn. Sth.
SW16 . . . . .6J 137
Streatham Ct. SW16 . . . . .3J 137
Streatham High Rd. SW16 . . . . . .4J 137
STREATHAM HILL 2J 137
Streatham Hill SW2 . . . . .2J 137
STREATHAM PARK 5G 137
Streatham Pl. SW2 . . . . .7J 119
Streatham Rd. CR4: Mitc 1E 154
SW16 . . . . .1E 154
Streatham St. WC1 . . . . .7E 6 (6J 83)
STREATHAM VALE 7G 137
Streatham Va. SW16 . . . . .1G 155
Streathbourne Rd. SW17 . . . . . . .2E 136
Streatley Pl. NW3 . . . . .4A 64
Streatley Rd. NW6 . . . . .7H 63
The Street E20 . . . . .6E 68
(within Westfield Shop. Cen.)

Streeters La. SM6: Bedd 3H 167
Streetfield M. SE3 . . . . .3J 123
Streetwater E20 . . . . .7C 68
Streimer Rd. E15 . . . . .2E 86
Strelley Way W3 . . . . .7A 80
Stretton Mans. SE8 . . . . .5C 104
Stretton Rd. CRO: C'don 7E 156
TW10: Ham 2C 132
Strickland Ct. SE15 . . . . .3G 121
Strickland Ho. E2 . . . . .2K 9
(off Chambord St.)
Strickland Row SW18 . . . . .7B 118
Strickland St. SE8 . . . . .2C 122
Strickland Way BR6: Orp 4K 173
Stride Rd. E13 . . . . .2H 87
Strimon Cl. N9 . . . . .2D 34
Stringer Ho. N1 . . . . .1E 84
(off Whitmore Est.)
Strode Cl. N10 . . . . .7K 31
Strode Rd. E7 . . . . .4J 69
N17 . . . . .2E 48
NW10 . . . . .6C 62
SW6 . . . . .7G 99
Strome Ho. NW6 . . . . .2K 81
(off Carlton Vale)
Stromness Wlk. W3 . . . . .1J 97
Strone Rd. E7 . . . . .6A 70
E12 . . . . .6A 70
Strone Way UB4: Yead 4C 76
Strongbow Cres. SE9 . . . . .5D 124
Strongbow Rd. SE9 . . . . .5D 124
Strongbridge Cl. HA2: Harr 1E 58
Stronsa Rd. W12 . . . . .2B 98
Strood Av. RM7: Rush G 1K 73
Strood Ho. SE1 . . . . .7F 15
(off Staple St.)
Stroud Cres. SW15 . . . . .3C 134
Stroudes Cl. KT4: Wor Pk 7A 152
Stroud Fld. UB5: N'olt 6C 58
Stroud Ga. HA2: Harr 4F 59
STROUD GREEN 7K 47
Stroud Grn. Gdns.
CRO: C'don 7J 157
Stroud Grn. Rd. N4 . . . . .1K 65
Stroud Grn. Way
CRO: C'don 7H 157
Stroudley Ho. SW8 . . . . .1G 119
Stroudley Wlk. E3 . . . . .3D 86
Stroud Rd. SE25 . . . . .6G 157
SW19 . . . . .3J 135
Stroud's Cl. RM6: Chad H 5B 54
Stroud Way TW15: Ashf 6D 128
Strouts Pl. E2 . . . . .1J 9 (3F 85)
Strudwick Ct. SW4 . . . . .1J 119
(off Binfield Rd.)
Strutton Ct. SW1 . . . . .2C 18
(off Gt. Peter St.)
Strutton Ground SW1 . . . .1C 18 (3H 101)
Strype St. E1 . . . . .6J 9 (5F 85)
Stuart Av.
BR2: Hayes 1J 171
HA2: Harr 3D 58
KT12: Walt T 7K 147
NW9 . . . . .7C 44
W5 . . . . .2F 97
Stuart Cl. UB10: Hil 6C 56
Stuart Ct. CRO: C'don 3B 168
(off St John's Rd.)
Stuart Cres. CRO: C'don 3B 170
N22 . . . . .1K 47
UB3: Hayes 6E 74
Stuart Evans Cl.
DA16: Well 3C 126
Stuart Gro. TW11: Tedd 5J 131
Stuart Ho. E9 . . . . .1K 105
(off Queen Anne Rd.)
E16 . . . . .1K 105
(off Beaulieu Av.)
W14 . . . . .4G 99
(off Windsor Way)
Stuart Mantle Way DA8: Erith 7K 109
(not continuous)

Stuart Mill Ho. N1 . . . . .1G 7
(off Killick St.)
Stuart Pl. CR4: Mitc 1D 154
Stuart Rd. CR7: Thor H 4C 156
DA16: Well 1B 126
EN4: E Barn 7H 21
HA3: W'stone 3K 41
IG11: Bark 7K 71
NW6 . . . . .3J 81
SE15 . . . . .4J 121
SW19 . . . . .3J 135
TW10: Ham 2B 132
W3 . . . . .1J 97
Stuart Twr. W9 . . . . .3A 82
(off Maida Vale)
Stubbs Cl. NW9 . . . . .5J 43
Stubbs Ct. W4 . . . . .5H 97
(off Chaseley Dr.)
Stubbs Dr. SE16 . . . . .5H 103
Stubbs Ho. E2 . . . . .3K 85
(off Bonner St.)
SW1 . . . . .4D 18
(off Erasmus St.)
Stubbs M. RM8: Dag 4B 72
(off Marlborough Rd.)
Stubbs Point E13 . . . . .4K 87
Stubbs Way SW19 . . . . .1B 154
Stucley Pl. NW1 . . . . .7F 65
Stucley Rd. TW5: Hest 7G 95
Studdridge St. SW6 . . . . .2J 117
Studd St. N1 . . . . .1B 84
Studholme Ct. NW3 . . . . .4J 63
Studholme St. SE15 . . . . .7H 103
Studio La. W5 . . . . .1D 96
Studio M. NW4 . . . . .4E 44
Studio Pl. SW1 . . . . .7F 11
Studio Plaza 7J 147
The Studios SW4 . . . . .4G 119
(off Crescent La.)
W8 . . . . .1J 99
(off Edge St.)
Studios Rd. TW17: Shep 3B 146
Studland SE17 . . . . .5D 102
(off Portland St.)
Studland Cl. DA15: Sidc 3K 143
Studland Rd. KT2: King T 6E 132
SE26 . . . . .5K 139
W7 . . . . .6H 77
Studland St. W6 . . . . .4D 98
Studley Av. E4 . . . . .7A 36
Studley Cl. E5 . . . . .5A 68
Studley Ct. DA14: Sidc 5B 144
E14 . . . . .7F 87
(off Jamestown Way)
Studley Dr. IG4: Ilf 6B 52
Studley Est. SW4 . . . . .1J 119
Studley Grange Rd. W7 . . . . .2J 95
Studley Rd. E7 . . . . .6K 69
RM9: Dag 7D 72
SW4 . . . . .1J 119
Stukeley Rd. E7 . . . . .7K 69
Stukeley St. WC2 . . . . . .7F 7 (6J 83)
Stumps Hill La.
BR3: Beck 6C 140
Stunell Ho. SE14 . . . . .6K 103
(off John Williams Cl.)
Sturdee Ho. E2 . . . . .2G 85
(off Horatio St.)
Sturdy Ho. E3 . . . . .2A 86
(off Gernon Rd.)
Sturdy Rd. SE15 . . . . .2H 121
Sturge Av. E17 . . . . .2D 50
Sturgeon Rd. SE17 . . . . .5C 102
Sturges Fld. BR7: Chst 6H 143
Sturgess Av. NW4 . . . . .7D 44
Sturge St.
SE1 . . . . .6C 14 (2C 102)
Sturmer Way N7 . . . . .5K 65
Sturminster NW1 . . . . .7H 65
(off Agar Gro.)
Sturminster Cl. UB4: Yead 6A 76

Sturminster Ho. *SW8* 7K *101*
   (off Dorset Rd.)
Sturrock Cl. N15 . . . . .4D 48
Sturry St. E14 . . . . .6D 86
Sturts Apts. *N1* 1D *84*
   (off Branch Pl.)
Sturt St. N1 . . . . .1D 8 (2C 84)
Stutfield St. E1 . . . . .6G 85
Stuttle Ho. *E1* 4K *9*
   (off Buxton St.)
Styles Gdns. SW9 . . . . .3B 120
Styles Ho. SE1 . . . . .6A 14
Styles Way BR3: Beck 4E 158
Stylus Ho. E1 . . . . .6J 85
Success Ho. *SE1* 5F *103*
   (off Cooper's Rd.)
Succession Wlk. E3 . . . . .7C 68
Sudbourne Rd. SW2 . . . . .5J 119
Sudbrooke Rd. SW12 . . . . .6D 118
Sudbrook Gdns.
   TW10: Ham 3D 132
Sudbrook La. TW10: Ham 1E 132
SUDBURY 5B 60
Sudbury E6 . . . . .5E 88
Sudbury Av. HA0: Wemb 3C 60
Sudbury Ct. *SW8* 1H *119*
   (off Allen Edwards Dr.)
Sudbury Ct. Dr. HA1: Harr 3K 59
Sudbury Ct. Rd. HA1: Harr 3K 59
Sudbury Cres.
   BR1: Broml 6J 141
   HA0: Wemb 5B 60
Sudbury Cft. HA0: Wemb 4K 59
Sudbury Gdns. CR0: C'don 4E 168
Sudbury Golf Course 7C 60
Sudbury Hgts. Av.
   UB6: G'frd 5K 59
Sudbury Hill HA1: Harr 2J 59
Sudbury Hill Cl.
   HA0: Wemb 4K 59
Sudbury Ho. SW18 . . . . .5K 117
Sudbury Rd. IG11: Bark 5K 71
Sudeley Ct. *E17* 1B *50*
   (off Broughton Pl.)
Sudeley St. N1 . . . . .2B 84
Sudlow Rd. SW18 . . . . .5J 117
Sudrey St. SE1 . . . . . . .7C 14 (2C 102)
Suez Av. UB6: G'frd 2K 77
Suez Rd. EN3: Brim 4F 25
SUFFIELD HATCH 4K 35
Suffield Ho. *SE17* 5B *102*
   (off Berryfield Rd.)
Suffield Rd. E4 . . . . .3J 35
   N15 . . . . .5F 49
   SE20 . . . . .2J 157
Suffolk Cl. E10 . . . . .7C 50
   IG3: Ilf 6J 53
   RM6: Chad H 6C 54
Suffolk Ho. *CR0: C'don* 2D *168*
   (off George St.)
   SE20 . . . . .1K *157*
   (off Croydon Rd.)
Suffolk La. EC4 . . . . . . .2E 14 (7D 84)
Suffolk Pk. Rd. E17 . . . . .4A 50
Suffolk Pl. SE2 . . . . .5C 108
   SW1 . . . . .4D 12 (1H 101)
Suffolk Rd.
   DA14: Sidc 6C 144
   E13 . . . . .3J 87
   EN3: Pond E 5C 24
   HA2: Harr 6D 40
   IG3: Ilf 6J 53
   IG11: Bark 7H 71
   KT4: Wor Pk 2B 164
   N15 . . . . .5D 48
   NW10 . . . . .7A 62
   RM10: Dag 5J 73
   SE25 . . . . .4F 157
   SW13 . . . . .7B 98
Suffolk St. E7 . . . . .4J 69
   SW1 . . . . .3D 12 (7H 83)
Sugar Bakers Ct. EC3 . . . . .1H 15

Sugar Ho. *E1* 1K *15*
   (off Leman St.)
Sugar Ho. Island Development
   E15 . . . . .2E 86
Sugar Ho. La. E15 . . . . .2E 86
Sugar La. SE16 . . . . .2G 103
Sugar Loaf Wlk. E2 . . . . .3J 85
Sugar Quay EC3 . . . . .3H 15
Sugar Quay Wlk.
   EC3 . . . . .3H 15 (7E 84)
Sugden Rd.
   KT7: T Ditt 1B 162
   SW11 . . . . .3E 118
Sugden Way IG11: Bark 2K 89
Sulby Ho. *SE4* 4A *122*
   (off Turnham Rd.)
Sulgrave Gdns. W6 . . . . .2E 98
Sulgrave Rd. W6 . . . . .3E 98
Sulina Rd. SW2 . . . . .7J 119
Sulivan Ct. SW6 . . . . .2J 117
Sulivan Ent. Cen. SW6 . . . . .3K 117
Sulivan Rd. SW6 . . . . .3J 117
Sulkin Ho. *E2* 3K *85*
   (off Knottisford St.)
Sullivan Av. E16 . . . . .5B 88
Sullivan Cl. KT8: W Mole 3F 149
   SW11 . . . . .3C 118
   UB4: Yead 5A 76
Sullivan Ct. *E3* 4B *86*
   (off Eric St.)
   N16 . . . . .7F 49
   SW5 . . . . .4J *99*
   (off Earls Ct. Rd.)
Sullivan Cres. UB9: Hare 2A 38
Sullivan Dr. SE9: Sidc 1H 143
Sullivan Ho. *SE11* 4H *19*
   (off Vauxhall St.)
   SW1 . . . . .7K *17*
   (off Churchill Gdns.)
Sullivan Rd. SE11 . . . . . .3K 19 (4A 102)
Sullivan Row BR2: Broml 6B 160
Sullivans Reach
   KT12: Walt T 7H 147
Sultan Ho. *SE1* 5G *103*
   (off St James's Rd.)
Sultan Rd. E11 . . . . .4K 51
Sultan St. BR3: Beck 2K 157
   SE5 . . . . .7C 102
Sultan Ter. N22 . . . . .2A 48
Sumatra Rd. NW6 . . . . .5J 63
Sumburgh Rd. SW12 . . . . .6E 118
Sumeria Ct. *SE16* 4J *103*
   (off Rotherhithe New Rd.)
Summer Av. KT8: E Mos 5J 149
Summerbee Ho. *SW18* 4A *118*
   (off Eltringham St.)
Summercourt Rd. E1 . . . . .6J 85
Summer Dr. UB7: W Dray 2B 92
Summerene Cl. SW16 . . . . .7G 137
Summerfield *BR1: Broml* 1K *159*
   (off Freelands Rd.)
Summerfield Av. NW6 . . . . .2G 81
Summerfield La. KT6: Surb 2D 162
Summerfield Rd. W5 . . . . .4B 78
Summerfields Av. N12 . . . . .6H 31
Summerfield St. SE12 . . . . .7H 123
Summer Gdns. KT8: E Mos 5J 149
   UB10: Ick 2E 56
Summer Gro. BR4: W W'ck 2G 171
Summer Hill BR7: Chst 2E 160
Summerhill Cl. BR6: Orp 3J 173
Summerhill Gro. EN1: Enf 6K 23
Summerhill Rd. N15 . . . . .4D 48
Summerhill Vs. *BR7: Chst* 1E *160*
   (off Susan Wood)
Summerhill Way CR4: Mitc 1E 154
Summerhouse Av.
   TW5: Hest 1C 112
Summerhouse Dr. DA2: Wilm 4K 145
   DA5: Bexl, Dart 4K 145
   HA7: Stan 5E 26

Summerhouse La. UB7: Harm 2E 174
Summerhouse Rd. N16 . . . . .2E 66
Summerland Gdns. N10 . . . . .3F 47
Summerland Grange N10 . . . . . . .3F 47
Summerlands Av. W3 . . . . .7J 79
Summerlands Lodge
   BR6: Farnb 4E 172
Summerlee Av. N2 . . . . .4D 46
Summerlee Gdns. N2 . . . . .4D 46
Summerley St. SW18 . . . . .2K 135
Summer Rd. KT7: T Ditt 5J 149
   KT8: E Mos 5H 149
   (not continuous)
Summersby Rd. N6 . . . . .6F 47
Summers Cl. HA9: Wemb 1H 61
   SM2: Sutt 7J 165
Summerskill Cl. SE15 . . . . .3H 121
Summerskille Cl. N9 . . . . .3C 34
Summers La. N12 . . . . .7G 31
Summers Row N12 . . . . .6H 31
Summers St. EC1 . . . . . . .4J 7 (4A 84)
Summerstown SW17 . . . . .3A 136
Summerton Ho. *E16* 2A *106*
   (off Starboard Way)
Summerton Way SE28 . . . . .6D 90
Summer Trees TW16: Sun 1K 147
Summerville Gdns.
   SM1: Sutt 6H 165
Summerwood Rd.
   TW7: Isle 5K 113
Summit Av. NW9 . . . . .5K 43
Summit Bus. Pk. TW16: Sun 7J 129
Summit Cl. HA8: Edg 7B 28
   N14 . . . . .2B 32
   NW9 . . . . .4K 43
Summit Ct. NW2 . . . . .5G 63
Summit Dr. IG8: Wfd G 2B 52
Summit Est. N16 . . . . .7G 49
Summit Ho. BR4: W W'ck 2E 170
Summit Rd. E17 . . . . .4D 50
   UB5: N'olt 7E 58
Summit Way N14 . . . . .2A 32
   SE19 . . . . .7E 138
Sumner Av. SE15 . . . . .1F 121
Sumner Bldgs. SE1 . . . . .4C 14
Sumner Cl. BR6: Farnb 4G 173
Sumner Ct. SW8 . . . . .7J 101
Sumner Est. SE15 . . . . .7F 103
Sumner Gdns. CR0: C'don 1A 168
Sumner Ho. *E3* 5D *86*
   (off Watts Gro.)
Sumner Pl. SW7 . . . . .4B 16 (4B 100)
Sumner Pl. M.
   SW7 . . . . .4B 16 (4B 100)
Sumner Rd. CR0: C'don 1A 168
   HA1: Harr 7G 41
   SE15 . . . . .6F 103
Sumner Rd. Sth.
   CR0: C'don 1A 168
Sumner St. SE1 . . . . .4B 14 (1B 102)
Sumpter Cl. NW3 . . . . .6A 64
Sun All. TW9: Rich 4E 114
Sunbeam Cres. W10 . . . . .4E 80
Sunbeam Rd. NW10 . . . . .4J 79
Sunbeam Way NW10 . . . . .4K 79
Sunbird Wlk. *HA2: Harr* 2F *59*
   (off Sandpiper Dr.)
SUNBURY 3A 148
Sunbury Av. NW7 . . . . .5E 28
   SW14 . . . . .4K 115
Sunbury Av. Pas. SW14 . . . . .4A 116
Sunbury Bus. Cen.
   TW16: Sun 1H 147
Sunbury Cl. KT12: Walt T 6J 147
SUNBURY COMMON 7H 129
Sunbury Ct. Island
   TW16: Sun 3B 148
Sunbury Ct. M. TW16: Sun 2B 148
Sunbury Ct. Rd. TW16: Sun 2A 148
Sunbury Cres. TW13: Felt 4H 129

SUNBURY CROSS 7J 129
Sunbury Cross Cen.
   TW16: Sun 7H 129
The Sunbury Embroidery Gallery
   . . . . .3K 147
Sunbury Gdns. NW7 . . . . .5E 28
Sunbury Golf Course 4F 147
Sunbury Ho. *E2* 2J *9*
   (off Swanfield St.)
   SE14 . . . . .6K *103*
   (off Myers La.)
   TW16: Sun 1B *147*
   (off Brooklands Cl.)
Sunbury La. KT12: Walt T 6J 147
   SW11 . . . . .1B 118
   (not continuous)
Sunbury Leisure Cen. 1H 147
Sunburylock Ait
   KT12: Walt T 4K 147
Sunbury Pk. Walled Garden 3K 147
Sunbury Rd. SM3: Cheam 3F 165
   TW13: Felt 3H 129
Sunbury St. SE18 . . . . .3D 106
Sunbury Way TW13: Hanw 5A 130
Sunbury Workshops *E2* 2J *9*
   (off Swanfield St.)
Sun Ct. *E3* 4E *86*
   (off Navigation Rd.)
   EC3 . . . . .1F 15
Suncroft Pl. SE26 . . . . .3J 139
Sundeala Cl. *TW16: Sun* 7J *129*
   (off Hanworth Rd.)
Sunderland Ct. SE22 . . . . .7G 121
   TW19: Stanw 6A *110*
   (off Whitley Cl.)
Sunderland Ho. *W2* 5J *81*
   (off Westbourne Pk. Rd.)
Sunderland Mt. SE23 . . . . .2K 139
Sunderland Point E16 . . . . .1G 107
Sunderland Rd. SE23 . . . . .1K 139
   W5 .3D 96
Sunderland Ter. W2 . . . . .6K 81
Sunderland Way E12 . . . . .2B 70
Sundew Av. W12 . . . . .7C 80
Sundew Cl. W12 . . . . .7C 80
Sundew Ct. *HA0: Wemb* 2E *78*
   (off Elmore Cl.)
Sundial Av. SE25 . . . . .3F 157
Sundial Ct. *EC1* 5E *8*
   (off Chiswell St.)
Sundorne Rd. SE7 . . . . .5A 106
Sundown Rd. TW15: Ashf 5E 128
Sundra Wlk. E1 . . . . .4K 85
SUNDRIDGE 6K 141
Sundridge Av. BR1: Broml 1B 160
   BR7: Chst 1B 160
   DA16: Well 2H 125
Sundridge Ho. *E9* 7K *67*
   (off Church Cres.)
Sundridge Pde. BR1: Broml 7K 141
SUNDRIDGE PARK 7K 141
Sundridge Pk. Golf Course 6K 141
Sundridge Park Mansions
   BR1: Broml 6B 142
Sundridge Pl. CR0: C'don 1G 169
Sundridge Rd. CR0: C'don 7F 157
Sunfields Pl. SE3 . . . . .7K 105
Sunflower Ct. NW2 . . . . .2H 63
   RM13: Rain 2J 91
Sunflower Mews HA7: Stan 5E 26
Sungate Cotts.
   RM5: Col R 1F 55
Sun Ga. Ho. KT3: N Mald 4B 152
Sunguard Ct. SE1 . . . . . . .4A 14 (1B 102)
SUN-IN-THE-SANDS 7K 105
Sunken Rd. CR0: C'don 5J 169
Sunkist Way
   SM6: W'gton 7J 167
Sunland Av. DA6: Bex 4E 126
Sun La. SE3 . . . . .7K 105
Sunleigh Rd. HA0: Wemb 1E 78
Sunley Gdns. UB6: G'frd 1A 78

Sun Life Trad. Est.
TW14: Felt 3J **111**
Sunlight Cl. SW19 . . . . .6A **136**
Sunlight M. SW6 . . . . .2K **117**
Sunlight Sq. E2 . . . . .3H **85**
Sunmead Rd. TW16: Sun 3J **147**
Sunna Gdns. TW16: Sun 2K **147**
Sunniholme Ct. CR2: S Croy 5C **168**
. . . . (off Warham Rd.)
Sunningdale N14 . . . . .5C **32**
W13 . . . . .5B **78**
. . . . (off Hardwick Grn.)
Sunningdale Av. HA4: Ruis 1A **58**
IG11: Bark 1H **89**
TW13: Hanw 2C **130**
W3 .7A **80**
Sunningdale Cl. E6 . . . . .3D **88**
HA7: Stan 6F **27**
KT6: Surb 2E **162**
SE16 . . . . .5H **103**
SE28 . . . . .6E **90**
Sunningdale Gdns. NW9 . . . . . .5J **43**
W8 .3J **99**
. . . . (off Stratford Rd.)
Sunningdale Lodge HA8: Edg . . .5A **28**
. . . . (off Stonegrove)
Sunningdale Rd.
BR1: Broml 4C **160**
SM1: Sutt 3H **165**
Sunningfields Cres. NW4 . . . . . .2D **44**
Sunningfields Rd. NW4 . . . . . . .2D **44**
Sunninghill Ct. W3 . . . . .2J **97**
Sunninghill Rd. SE13 . . . . .2D **122**
Sunny Bank SE25 . . . . .3G **157**
Sunny Cres. NW10 . . . . .7J **61**
Sunnycroft Rd. SE25 . . . . .3G **157**
TW3: Houn 2F **113**
UB1: S'hall 5E **76**
Sunnydale BR6: Farnb 2E **172**
Sunnydale Gdns. NW7 . . . . .6E **28**
Sunnydale Rd. SE12 . . . . .5K **123**
Sunnydene Av. E4 . . . . .5A **36**
HA4: Ruis 1J **57**
Sunnydene Gdns. HA0: Wemb . . .6C **60**
Sunnydene St. SE26 . . . . .4A **140**
Sunnyfield NW7 . . . . .4G **29**
Sunnyfield Rd. BR7: Chst 3K **161**
Sunny Gdns. Pde. NW4 . . . . . . .2D **44**
Sunny Gdns. Rd. NW4 . . . . .2D **44**
Sunny Hill NW4 . . . . .3D **44**
Sunnyhill Cl. E5 . . . . .4A **68**
Sunnyhill Rd. SW16 . . . . .4J **137**
Sunnyhurst Cl. SM1: Sutt 3J **165**
Sunnymead Av. CR4: Mitc 3H **155**
Sunnymead Rd. NW9 . . . . .7K **43**
SW15 . . . . .5D **116**
Sunnymede Av.
KT19: Ewe 7A **164**
Sunnymede Dr. IG2: Ilf 5F **53**
IG6: Ilf 5F **53**
Sunny M. NW1 . . . . .7E **64**
Sunny Nook Gdns.
CR2: S Croy 6D **168**
Sunny Pl. NW4 . . . . .4E **44**
The Sunny Rd. EN3: Enf H 1E **24**
Sunnyside KT12: Walt T 5A **148**
NW2 . . . . .3H **63**
SE6 . . . . .7B **122**
. . . . (off Blythe Hill)
SW19 . . . . .6G **135**
Sunnyside Dr. E4 . . . . .7K **25**
Sunnyside Ho's. NW2 . . . . .3H **63**
. . . . (off Sunnyside)
Sunnyside Pas. SW19 . . . . .6G **135**
Sunnyside Pl. SW19 . . . . .6G **135**
Sunnyside Rd. E10 . . . . .1C **68**
IG1: Ilf 3G **71**
N19 .7H **47**
TW11: Tedd 4H **131**
W5 .1D **96**
Sunnyside Rd. E. N9 . . . . .3B **34**
Sunnyside Rd. Nth. N9 . . . . .3A **34**

Sunnyside Rd. Sth. N9 . . . . .3A **34**
Sunnyside Ter. NW9 . . . . .3K **43**
Sunny Vw. NW9 . . . . .5K **43**
Sunny Way N12 . . . . .7H **31**
Sun Pas. SE16 . . . . .3G **103**
. . . . (off Old Jamaica Rd.)
Sunray Av. BR2: Broml 6C **160**
KT5: Surb 1H **163**
SE24 . . . . .4D **120**
Sunrise Cl. E20 . . . . .5E **68**
TW13: Hanw 3D **130**
Sunrise Vw. NW7 . . . . .6G **29**
Sun Rd. W14 . . . . .5H **99**
Sunset Av. E4 . . . . .1J **35**
IG8: Wfd G 4C **36**
Sunset Ct. IG8: Wfd G 7F **37**
Sunset Gdns. SE25 . . . . .2F **157**
Sunset Lodge NW10 . . . . .7E **62**
. . . . (off Hanover Rd.)
Sunset Rd. SE5 . . . . .4C **120**
SE28 . . . . .1A **108**
SW19 . . . . .5D **134**
Sunset Vw. EN5: Barn 2B **20**
Sunshine Way CR4: Mitc 2D **154**
Sun St. EC2 . . . . .5F **9** (5D **84**)
. . . . (Finsbury Sq.)
EC2 . . . . .5G **9** (5E **84**)
. . . . (Primrose St.)
Sun St. Pas. EC2 . . . . .6G **9** (5E **84**)
Sun Wlk. E1 . . . . .3K **15** (7F **85**)
Sunwell Cl. SE15 . . . . .1H **121**
Sun Wharf SE8 . . . . .7D **104**
. . . . (off Creekside)
Superior Dr. BR6: Chels 6K **173**
Supreme Court 2J **101**
Supreme Point E16 . . . . .5J **87**
. . . . (off Butchers Rd.)
SURBITON 6D **150**
Surbiton Ct. KT6: Surb 6C **150**
Surbiton Cres. KT1: King T 4E **150**
Surbiton Golf Course 4B **162**
Surbiton Hall Cl. KT1: King T 4E **150**
Surbiton Hill Pk. KT5: Surb 5F **151**
Surbiton Hill Rd. KT6: Surb 4E **150**
Surbiton Pde. KT6: Surb 6E **150**
Surbiton Plaza KT6: Surb 6D **150**
. . . . (off St Mary's Rd.)
Surbiton Raceway 3K **163**
Surbiton Rd. KT1: King T 4D **150**
Surlingham Cl. SE28 . . . . .7D **90**
Surma Cl. E1 . . . . .4H **85**
Surmans Cl. RM9: Dag 1C **90**
Surrendale Pl. W9 . . . . .4J **81**
Surrey Canal Rd. SE14 . . . . .6J **103**
Surrey Canal Trade Pk.
SE14 . . . . .6K **103**
Surrey Cl. N3 . . . . .3G **45**
Surrey County Cricket Club
. . . . .7H **19** (6K **101**)
Surrey Cres. W4 . . . . .5G **97**
Surrey Docks Farm 2B **104**
Surrey Docks Watersports Cen.
. . . . .3A **104**
Surrey Gdns. N4 . . . . .6C **48**
Surrey Gro. SE17 . . . . .5E **102**
SM1: Sutt 3B **166**
Surrey Ho. CR0: C'don 3C **168**
. . . . (off Surrey St.)
SE16 . . . . .1K **103**
. . . . (off Rotherhithe St.)
Surrey La. SW11 . . . . .1C **118**
Surrey La. Est. SW11 . . . . .1C **118**
Surrey M. SE27 . . . . .4E **138**
Surrey Mt. SE23 . . . . .1H **139**
Surrey Quays Rd. SE16 . . . . . . .3J **103**
Surrey Quays Shop. Cen. SE16 . . .3K **103**
Surrey Rd.
BR4: W W'ck 1D **170**
HA1: Harr 5G **41**
IG11: Bark 7J **71**
RM10: Dag 5H **73**
SE15 . . . . .5K **121**

Surrey Row SE1 . . . . .6A **14** (2B **102**)
Surrey Sq. SE17 . . . . .5E **102**
Surrey Steps WC2 . . . . .2B **12**
. . . . (off Surrey St.)
Surrey St. CR0: C'don 2C **168**
E13 .3K **87**
WC2 . . . . .2H **13** (7K **83**)
Surrey Ter. SE17 . . . . .5E **102**
Surrey Water Rd. SE16 . . . . .1K **103**
Surridge Ct. SW9 . . . . .2J **119**
. . . . (off Clapham Rd.)
Surridge Gdns. SE19 . . . . .6D **138**
Surr St. N7 . . . . .5J **65**
Surry Crescent UB6: G'frd 3E **76**
Surry Basin KT2: King T 1E **150**
Susan Cl.
RM7: Mawney 3J **55**
Susan Constant Ct. E14 . . . . .7F **87**
. . . . (off Newport Av.)
Susan Lawrence Ho. E3 . . . . .2A **86**
. . . . (off Zealand Rd.)
E12 .4E **70**
. . . . (off Walton Rd.)
Susannah St. E14 . . . . .6D **86**
Susan Rd. SE3 . . . . .2K **123**
Susan Wood BR7: Chst 1E **160**
Sussex Av. TW7: Isle 3J **113**
Sussex Cl. IG4: Ilf 5D **52**
KT3: N Mald 4A **152**
N19 .2J **65**
TW1: Twick 6B **114**
Sussex Ct. SE10 . . . . .6E **104**
. . . . (off Roan St.)
W2 .1A **10**
. . . . (off Spring St.)
Sussex Cres. UB5: N'olt 6E **58**
Sussex Gdns. KT9: Chess 6D **162**
N4 .5C **48**
N6 .5D **46**
W2 . . . . .2A **10** (7B **82**)
Sussex Ga. N6 . . . . .5D **46**
Sussex Ho. NW1 . . . . .2H **83**
. . . . (off Chalton St.)
Sussex Lodge W2 . . . . .1B **10**
. . . . (off Sussex Pl.)
Sussex Mans. SW7 . . . . .4A **16**
WC2 . . . . .2F **13**
. . . . (off Maiden La.)
Sussex M. SE6 . . . . .7C **122**
Sussex M. E. W2 . . . . .1B **10**
Sussex M. W. W2 . . . . .2B **10** (7B **82**)
Sussex Pl.
KT3: N Mald 4A **152**
NW1 . . . . .3E **4** (4D **82**)
Sussex Pl. W2 . . . . . . .1B **10** (6B **82**)
W6 .5E **98**
Sussex Ring N12 . . . . .5D **30**
Sussex Rd. BR4: W W'ck 1D **170**
CR2: S Croy 6D **168**
CR4: Mitc 5J **155**
DA8: Erith 7H **109**
DA14: Sidc 5B **144**
E6 .1E **88**
HA1: Harr 5G **41**
KT3: N Mald 4A **152**
SM5: Cars 6D **166**
UB2: S'hall 3B **94**
UB10: Ick 4E **56**
Sussex Sq. W2 . . . . . . .2B **10** (7B **82**)
Sussex St. E13 . . . . .3K **87**
SW1 . . . . .6K **17** (5F **101**)
Sussex Ter. SE20 . . . . .7J **139**
. . . . (off Graveney Gro.)
Sussex Way EN4: Cockt 5K **21**
N7 .2J **65**
N19 .1H **65**
. . . . (not continuous)
Sutcliffe Cl. NW11 . . . . .5K **45**
Sutcliffe Ho. UB3: Hayes 6J **75**
Sutcliffe Pk. Athletics Track 5A **124**
Sutcliffe Rd. DA16: Well 2C **126**
SE18 . . . . .6J **107**

Sutherland Av. BR5: St M Cry 6K **161**
DA16: Well 4J **125**
TW16: Sun 2H **147**
UB3: Hayes 4J **93**
W9 .4J **81**
W13 . . . . .6B **78**
Sutherland Cl. EN5: Barn 4B **20**
Sutherland Ct. N16 . . . . .3D **66**
NW9 . . . . .5H **43**
W9 .4J **81**
. . . . (off Marylands Rd.)
Sutherland Dr. SW19 . . . . .1B **154**
Sutherland Gdns.
KT4: Wor Pk 1D **164**
SW14 . . . . .3A **116**
TW16: Sun 2H **147**
Sutherland Gro. SW18 . . . . .6G **117**
TW11: Tedd 5J **131**
Sutherland Ho. IG8: Wfd G 7K **37**
W8 .3K **99**
Sutherland Pl. W2 . . . . .6J **81**
Sutherland Rd. CR0: C'don 7A **156**
DA17: Belv 3G **109**
E3 .2B **86**
E17 . . . . .2K **49**
N9 .1C **34**
N17 . . . . .7B **34**
UB1: S'hall 6D **76**
W4 .6A **98**
W13 . . . . .6A **78**
Sutherland Rd. Path E17 . . . . . . .3K **49**
Sutherland Row
SW1 . . . . .5K **17** (5F **101**)
Sutherland Sq. SE17 . . . . .5C **102**
Sutherland St.
SW1 . . . . .5J **17** (5F **101**)
Sutherland Wlk. SE17 . . . . .5C **102**
Sutlej Rd. SE7 . . . . .7A **106**
Sutterton St. N7 . . . . .6K **65**
SUTTON 5K **165**
Sutton Cl. BR3: Beck 1C **158**
HA5: Eastc 5J **39**
IG10: Lough 1H **37**
W4 .6J **97**
. . . . (off Sutton La. Sth.)
Sutton Comn. Rd. SM1: Sutt 7H **153**
SM3: Sutt 7H **153**
Sutton Ct. KT8: W Mole 5G **149**
SE19 . . . . .7F **139**
SM2: Sutt 6A **166**
W4 .6J **97**
W5 .1E **96**
Sutton Ct. Rd. E13 . . . . .3A **88**
SM1: Sutt 6A **166**
UB10: Hil 1D **74**
W4 .7J **97**
Sutton Cres. EN5: Barn 5A **20**
Sutton Dene TW3: Houn 1F **113**
Sutton Ecology Centre 4D **166**
Sutton Est. EC1 . . . . .2F **9**
SW3 . . . . .5D **16** (5C **100**)
W10 . . . . .5E **80**
The Sutton Est. N1 . . . . .7B **66**
Sutton Gdns. CR0: C'don 5F **157**
IG11: Bark 1J **89**
. . . . (off Sutton Rd.)
Sutton Grn. IG11: Bark 1J **89**
. . . . (off Sutton Rd.)
Sutton Gro. SM1: Sutt 4B **166**
Sutton Hall Rd.
TW5: Hest 7E **94**
Sutton Hgts. SM2: Sutt 7B **166**
Sutton La. EC1 . . . . .4B **8**
. . . . (off Gt. Sutton St.)
TW3: Houn 3D **112**
Sutton La. Nth. W4 . . . . .5J **97**
Sutton La. Sth. W4 . . . . .6J **97**
Sutton Pde. NW4 . . . . .4E **44**
. . . . (off Church Rd.)
Sutton Pk. Rd. SM1: Sutt 6K **165**
Sutton Pl. E9 . . . . .5J **67**
Sutton Plaza SM1: Sutt 6A **166**

Sutton Rd. E13 . . . . .4H 87
  E17 . . . . .1K 49
  IG11: Bark 2J 89
  N10 . . . . .1E 46
  TW5: Hest 1E 112
Sutton Row W1 . . . . .7D 6 (6H 83)
Suttons Bus. Pk.
  RM13: Rain 3K 91
Sutton Sports Village 1K 165
Sutton Sq. E9 . . . . .5J 67
  TW5: Hest 1D 112
Sutton St. E1 . . . . .7J 85
Sutton's Way EC1 . . . . .4D 8
Suttons Wharf E2 . . . . .3K 85
Sutton Tennis Academy 1K 165
Sutton United FC 4J 165
Sutton Wlk.
  SE1 . . . . .5H 13 (1K 101)
Sutton Way TW5: Hest 1D 112
  W10 . . . . .4E 80
Swaby Rd. SW18 . . . . .1A 136
Swaffam Ct. RM6: Chad H 6C 54
Swaffham Way N22 . . . . .7G 33
Swaffield Rd. SW18 . . . . .7K 117
Swain Cl. SW16 . . . . .6F 137
Swain Rd. CR7: Thor H 5C 156
Swains Cl. UB7: W Dray 2A 92
Swain's La. N6 . . . . .1E 64
Swainson Rd. W3 . . . . .2B 98
Swains Rd. SW17 . . . . .7D 136
Swain St. NW8 . . . . .3C 4 (4C 82)
Swakeleys Dr. UB10: Ick 4C 56
Swakeleys Rd. UB10: Ick 4A 56
SWAKELEYS RDBT. 4A 56
Swalecliffe Rd.
  DA17: Belv 5H 109
Swaledale Cl. N11 . . . . .6K 31
Swallands Rd. SE6 . . . . .3C 140
                (not continuous)
Swallow Cl. DA8: Erith 1K 127
  SE14 .1K 121
  WD23: Bush 1B 26
Swallow Ct. HA4: Ruis 1A 58
  IG2: Ilf 5F 53
  SE1 . . . . .7D 14
                (off Swan St.)
  SE12 .7J 123
  W9 . . . . .5J 81
           (off Admiral Wlk.)
Swallow Dr. NW10 . . . . .6K 61
  UB5: N'olt 2E 76
Swallowfield NW1 . . . . .2K 5
           (off Munster Sq.)
Swallowfield Rd. SE7 . . . . .5A 106
Swallowfield Way UB3: Hayes 2F 93
Swallow Gdns. SW16 . . . . .5H 137
Swallow Ho. NW8 . . . . .2C 82
             (off Allitsen Rd.)
Swallow Pk. Cl. KT6: Surb 3F 163
Swallow Pas. W1 . . . . .1K 11
            (off Swallow Pl.)
Swallow Pl. E14 . . . . .6B 86
           (off Newell St.)
  W1 . . . . .1K 11 (6F 83)
Swallows Cl. SM1: Sutt 3J 165
Swallow St. E6 . . . . .5C 88
  W1 . . . . .3B 12 (7G 83)
Swallowtail Ho. E20 . . . . .5E 68
           (off Sunrise Cl.)
THE SWAN 2E 170
Swanage Ct. N1 . . . . .7E 66
           (off Hertford Rd.)
Swanage Ho. SW8 . . . . .7K 101
            (off Dorset Rd.)
Swanage Rd. E4 . . . . .7K 35
  SW18 . . . . .6A 118
Swanage Waye UB4: Yead 6A 76
Swan & Pike Rd. EN3: Enf L 1H 25
Swan App. E6 . . . . .5C 88
Swanbourne Ho. NW8 . . . . .3C 4
           (off Capland St.)
Swanbridge Rd. DA7: Bex . . .1G 127

The Swan Cen. SW17 . . . . .3K 135
Swan Cl. CR0: C'don 7E 156
  E17 . . . . .1A 50
  KT12: Walt T 7H 147
  TW13: Hanw 4C 130
Swan Ct. E1 . . . . .3K 15
                (off Star Pl.)
  E14 . . . . .6B 86
             (off Agnes St.)
  HA4: Ruis 1J 57
  SW3 . . . . .6D 16 (5C 100)
  SW6 . . . . .7J 99
           (off Fulham Rd.)
  TW7: Isle 3B 114
           (off Swan St.)
Swandon Way SW18 . . . . .4K 117
Swan Dr. NW9 . . . . .2A 44
Swanfield St. E2 . . . . . . .2J 9 (3F 85)
Swan Ho. E15 . . . . .7G 69
           (off Broadway)
  EN3: Pond E 5D 24
  N1 . . . . .7D 66
           (off Oakley Rd.)
Swan Island TW1: Twick 3A 132
Swan La. EC4 . . . . .3F 15 (7D 84)
  N4 . . . . .1C 66
  N20 . . . . .3F 31
Swanley Ho. SE17 . . . . .5E 102
          (off Kinglake Est.)
Swanley Rd. DA16: Well 1C 126
Swan Mead SE1 . . . . .3E 102
Swan M. CR4: Mitc 1D 154
  RM7: Mawney 4H 55
  SW6 .1H 117
  SW9 .2K 119
Swann Ct. TW7: Isle 3A 114
           (off South St.)
Swanne Ho. SE10 . . . . .7E 104
          (off Gloucester Cir.)
Swannell Way NW2 . . . . .1F 63
Swan Pas. E1 . . . . .3K 15
Swan Path KT1: King T 3F 151
Swan Pl. SW13 . . . . .2B 116
Swan Rd. SE16 . . . . .2J 103
  SE18 .3B 106
  TW13: Hanw 5C 130
  UB1: S'hall 6F 77
  UB7: W Dray 2A 92
The Swan Sanctuary 6G 147
Swanscombe Ho. W11 . . . . .1F 99
           (off St Ann's Rd.)
Swanscombe Rd. W4 . . . . .5A 98
  W11 . . . . .1F 99
          (off Fishguard Way)
Swansea Ct. E16 . . . . .1F 107
          (off Fishguard Way)
Swansea Rd. EN3: Pond E 4D 24
  TW14: Felt 6E 110
Swansland Gdns. E17 . . . . .1A 50
Swansmere Cl. KT12: Walt T 7A 148
Swan St.
  SE1 . . . . .7D 14 (3C 102)
  TW7: Isle 3B 114
Swanton Ct. SE13 . . . . .3D 122
Swanton Gdns. SW19 . . . . .1F 135
Swanton Rd. DA8: Erith 7G 109
Swan Wlk.
  SW3 . . . . .7E 16 (6D 100)
  TW17: Shep 7G 147
Swan Way EN3: Enf H 2E 24
Swanwick Cl. SW15 . . . . .7B 116
Swan Yd. N1 . . . . .6B 66
Sward Rd. BR5: St M Cry 6K 161
Swathling Ho. SW15 . . . . .6B 116
         (off Tunworth Cres.)
Swaton Rd. E3 . . . . .4C 86
Swaylands Rd. DA17: Belv 6G 109
Swaythling Cl. N18 . . . . .4C 34
Swedeland Ct. E1 . . . . .6H 9
Swedenborg Gdns. E1 . . . . .7H 85
Sweden Ga. SE16 . . . . .3A 104
Swedish Quays SE16 . . . . .3A 104
          (not continuous)

Sweeney Cres. SE1 . . . . .7K 15 (2F 103)
Sweetbriar Av.
  SM5: Cars 1D 166
Sweet Briar Grn. N9 . . . . .3A 34
Sweet Briar Gro. N9 . . . . .3A 34
Sweet Briar Wlk. N18 . . . . .4A 34
Sweetcroft La. UB10: Hil 7B 56
Sweetmans Av. HA5: Pinn 3B 40
Sweets Way N20 . . . . .2G 31
Swell Cl. E17 . . . . .6C 50
Swetenham Wlk. SE18 . . . . .5G 107
Swete St. E13 . . . . .2J 87
Sweyn Pl. SE3 . . . . .2J 123
Swift Cl. E17 . . . . .7F 35
  HA2: Harr 2F 59
  SE28 . . . . .7B 90
  UB3: Hayes 6H 75
Swift Ct. SM2: Sutt 7K 165
Swift Ho. SE3 . . . . .1B 86
          (off Old Ford Rd.)
  NW6 . . . . .2H 81
           (off Albert Rd.)
Swift La. SE13 . . . . .4G 123
Swift Lodge W9 . . . . .5J 81
          (off Admiral Wlk.)
Swift Rd. TW13: Hanw 3C 130
  UB2: S'hall 3E 94
Swiftsden Way BR1: Broml 6G 141
Swiftstone Twr. SE10 . . . . .3J 105
Swift St. SW6 . . . . .1H 117
Swimmers La. E2 . . . . .1F 85
Swinbrook Rd. W10 . . . . .5G 81
Swinburne Ct. SE5 . . . . .4D 120
         (off Basingdon Way)
Swinburne Cres. CR0: C'don 6J 157
Swinburne Ho. E2 . . . . .3J 85
         (off Roman Rd.)
Swinburne Rd. SW15 . . . . .4C 116
Swinderby Rd. HA0: Wemb 6E 60
Swindon Cl. IG3: Ilf 2J 71
Swindon Rd.
  TW6: H'row A 5E 110
Swindon St. W12 . . . . .1D 98
Swinfield Cl. TW13: Hanw 3C 130
Swinford Gdns. SW9 . . . . .3B 120
Swingate La. SE18 . . . . .6J 107
Swingfield Ho. E9 . . . . .1J 85
         (off Templecombe Rd.)
Swinley Ho. NW1 . . . . .1K 5
          (off Redhill St.)
Swinnerton St. E9 . . . . .5A 68
Swinson Ho. N11 . . . . .5B 32
Swinton Cl. HA9: Wemb 1H 61
Swinton Pl. WC1 . . . . .1G 7 (3K 83)
Swinton St. WC1 . . . . .1G 7 (3K 83)
Swires Shaw BR2: Kes 4B 172
SWISS COTTAGE 7B 64
Swiss Cottage Sports Cen. 7B 64
Swiss Ct. W1 . . . . .3D 12
Swiss Ter. NW6 . . . . .7B 64
Switch Ho. E14 . . . . .7F 87
Swithland Gdns. SE9 . . . . .4E 142
Swyncombe Av. W5 . . . . .4B 96
Swynford Gdns. NW4 . . . . .4C 44
Sybil M. N4 . . . . .6B 48
Sybil Phoenix Cl. SE8 . . . . .5K 103
Sybil Thorndike Casson Ho.
  SW5 . . . . .5J 99
         (off Kramer M.)
Sycamore Av.
  DA15: Sidc 6K 125
  E3 . . . . .1B 86
  UB3: Hayes 7G 75
  W5 . . . . .3D 96
Sycamore Cl.
  CR2: S Croy 5E 168
  E16 . . . . .4F 87
  EN4: E Barn 6G 21
  HA8: Edg 4D 28
  KT19: Ewe 5H 163

Sycamore Cl. N9 . . . . .4B 34
  SE9 . . . . .2C 142
  SM5: Cars 4D 166
  TW13: Felt 3J 129
  UB5: N'olt 1C 76
  UB7: Yiew 7B 74
  W3 . . . . .1A 98
Sycamore Ct. DA8: Erith 5K 109
         (off Sandcliff Rd.)
  E7 . . . . .6J 69
  KT3: N Mald 3A 152
  NW6 . . . . .1J 81
         (off Bransdale Cl.)
  SE1 . . . . .7G 15
          (off Royal Oak Yd.)
  TW4: Houn 4C 112
Sycamore Gdns. CR4: Mitc 2B 154
  N15 . . . . .4F 49
  W6 . . . . .2D 98
Sycamore Gro. KT3: N Mald 3K 151
  NW9 . . . . .7J 43
  SE6 . . . . .6E 122
  SE20 .1G 157
Sycamore Hill N11 . . . . .6K 31
Sycamore Ho. BR2: Broml 2G 159
  IG9: Buck H 2G 37
  N2 . . . . .2B 46
         (off The Grange)
  SE16 .2K 103
        (off Woodland Cres.)
  W6 . . . . .2D 98
Sycamore Lodge BR6: Orp 2K 173
  TW16: Sun 7H 129
  W8 . . . . .3K 99
         (off Stone Hall Pl.)
Sycamore M. DA8: Erith 5K 109
         (off St John's Rd.)
  SW4 . . . . .3G 119
Sycamore Path E17 . . . . .6D 50
         (off Poplars Rd.)
Sycamore Pl. BR1: Broml 3E 160
Sycamore Rd. SW19 . . . . .6E 134
Sycamore St. EC1 . . . . . .4C 8 (4C 84)
Sycamore Wlk. IG6: Ilf 4G 53
  W10 . . . . .4G 81
Sycamore Way CR7: Thor H 5A 156
  TW11: Tedd 6C 132
Sydcote SE21 . . . . .1C 138
SYDENHAM 4J 139
Sydenham Av. N21 . . . . .5E 22
  SE26 . . . . .5H 139
Sydenham Cotts. SE12 . . . . .2A 142
Sydenham Ct. CR0: C'don 1D 168
         (off Sydenham Rd.)
Sydenham Hill SE23 . . . . .1H 139
  SE26 . . . . .4F 139
Sydenham Hill Wood &
  Cox's Walk Nature Reserve
                    . . . . . .2G 139
Sydenham Pk. SE26 . . . . .3J 139
Sydenham Pk. Mans. SE26 . . . . .3J 139
         (off Sydenham Pk.)
Sydenham Pk. Rd. SE26 . . . . .3J 139
Sydenham Pl. SE27 . . . . .3B 138
Sydenham Ri. SE23 . . . . .2H 139
Sydenham Rd.
  CR0: C'don 1C 168
  SE26 . . . . .4J 139
Sydenham Stn. App.
                    . . . . . .4J 139
Sydmons Ct. SE23 . . . . .7J 121
Sydner M. N16 . . . . .4F 67
Sydner Rd. N16 . . . . .4F 67
Sydney Chapman Way
  EN5: Barn 2C 20
Sydney Cl. SW3 . . . . . . .4B 16 (4B 100)
  UB4: Yead 4A 76
Sydney Cres.
  TW15: Ashf 6D 128
Sydney Gro. NW4 . . . . .5E 44
Sydney M. SW3 . . . . . . .4B 16 (4B 100)
Sydney Pl. SW7 . . . . . . .4B 16 (4B 100)

Sydney Rd. DA6: Bex 4D **126**
  DA14: Sidc 4J **143**
  E11 ....6K **51**
  EN2: Enf 4J **23**
  IG6: Ilf 2G **53**
  IG8: Wfd G 4D **36**
  N8 ....4A **48**
  N10 ....1E **46**
  SE2 ....3C **108**
  SM1: Sutt 4J **165**
  SW20 ....2F **153**
  TW9: Rich 4E **114**
  TW11: Tedd 5K **131**
  TW14: Felt 1J **129**
  W13 ....1A **96**
Sydney Russell Leisure Cen. 5E **72**
Sydney St. SW3 ......5C **16** (5C **100**)
Sylva Cotts. SE8 ....1C **122**
Sylvana Cl. UB10: Hil 1B **74**
Sylvan Av. N3 ....2J **45**
  N22 ....7E **32**
  NW7 ....6F **29**
  RM6: Chad H 6F **55**
Sylvan Ct. N12 ....3E **30**
  NW6 ....1K **81**
  (off Abbey Rd.)
Sylvan Est. SE19 ....1F **157**
Sylvan Gdns. KT6: Surb 7D **150**
Sylvan Gro. NW2 ....4F **63**
  SE15 ....6H **103**
Sylvan Hill SE19 ....1E **156**
Sylvan Rd. E7 ....6K **69**
  E11 ....5J **51**
  E17 ....5C **50**
  IG1: Ilf 2G **71**
  SE19 ....1F **157**
Sylvan Ter. SE15 ....6H **103**
  (off Sylvan Gro.)
Sylvan Wlk. BR1: Broml 3D **160**
Sylvan Way BR4: W W'ck 4G **171**
  RM8: Dag 4B **72**
Sylverdale Rd. CR0: C'don 3B **168**
Sylvester Av. BR7: Chst 6D **142**
Sylvester Path E8 ....6H **67**
Sylvester Rd. E8 ....6H **67**
  E17 ....7B **50**
  HA0: Wemb 5C **60**
  N2 ....2A **46**
Sylvestrian Leisure Cen. 4G **51**
Sylvestrus Cl. KT1: King T 1G **151**
Sylvia Ct. HA9: Wemb 7H **61**
  N1 ....2D **84**
  (off Wenlock St.)
Sylvia Gdns. HA9: Wemb 7H **61**
Sylvia Pankhurst Ho.
  RM10: Dag 3G **73**
  (off Wythenshawe Rd.)
Sylvia Pankhurst St. E16 ......6H **87**
Symes M. NW1 ....2G **83**
Symington Ho. SE1 ....3D **102**
  (off Deverell St.)
Symington M. E9 ....5K **67**
Symister M. N1 ....2G **9**
Symons Cl. SE15 ....2J **121**
Symons St. SW3 ......4F **17** (4D **100**)
Symphony Cl. HA8: Edg 7C **28**
Symphony M. W10 ....3G **81**
Syon Ct. E11 ....5K **51**
Syon Ga. Way TW8: Bford 7A **96**
Syon House 1C **114**
Syon La. TW7: Isle 6J **95**
Syon Lodge SE12 ....7J **123**
Syon Pk. 1B **114**
Syon Pk. Gdns. TW7: Isle 7K **95**
Syringa Ho. SE4 ....3B **122**

T

Tabard Ct. E14 ....6E **86**
  (off Lodore St.)
Tabard Gdn. Est. SE1 ......7E **14** (3D **102**)

Tabard Ho. SE1 ....7F **15**
  (off Manciple St.)
Tabard St. SE1 ......6D **14** (2D **102**)
Tabard Theatre 4A **98**
The Tabernacle 6H **81**
  (off Powis Sq.)
Tabernacle Av. E13 ....4J **87**
Tabernacle Gdns. E2 ....2J **9**
  (off Hackney Rd.)
Tabernacle St. EC2 ......4F **9** (4D **84**)
Tableer Av. SW4 ....5G **119**
Tabley Rd. N7 ....4J **65**
Tabor Ct. SM3: Cheam 6G **165**
Tabor Gdns.
  SM3: Cheam 6H **165**
Tabor Gro. SW19 ....7H **135**
Tabor Rd. W6 ....3D **98**
Tachbrook Est.
  SW1 ......6C **18** (5H **101**)
Tachbrook M.
  SW1 ......3A **18** (4G **101**)
Tachbrook Rd. TW14: Felt 7H **111**
  UB2: S'hall 4B **94**
  UB7: W Dray 1A **92**
Tachbrook St. SW1 ...4B **18** (4G **101**)
Tack M. SE4 ....3C **122**
Tadema Ho. NW8 ....4B **4**
Tadema Rd. SW10 ....7A **100**
Tadlow KT1: King T 3G **151**
  (off Washington Rd.)
Tadmor Cl. TW16: Sun 4H **147**
Tadmor St. W12 ....1F **99**
Tadworth Av.
  KT3: N Mald 4B **152**
Tadworth Ho. SE1 ....7A **14**
Tadworth Rd. NW2 ....2C **62**
Taeping St. E14 ....4D **104**
Taffeta Ho. E20 ....6E **68**
  (off De Coubertin St.)
Taff Ho. KT2: King T 1D **150**
  (off Henry Macaulay Av.)
Taffrail Ho. E14 ....5D **104**
  (off Burrells Wharf Sq.)
Taffy's How CR4: Mitc 3C **154**
Taft Way E3 ....3D **86**
Taggs Ho. KT1: King T 2D **150**
  (off Market Sq.)
Taggs Island TW12: Hamp 2H **149**
Tagore Cl. HA3: W'stone 3K **41**
Tagwright Ho. N1 ....1E **8**
  (off Westland Pl.)
Tailor Ho. WC1 ....4F **7**
  (off Colonnade)
Tailworth St. E1 ....6K **9**
  (off Chicksand St.)
Tait Ct. E3 ....1B **86**
  (off St Stephen's Rd.)
  SW8 ....1J **119**
  (off Lansdowne Grn.)
Tait Ho. SE1 ....5K **13**
  (off Greet St.)
Tait Rd. CR0: C'don 7E **156**
Tait Rd. Ind. Est. CR0: C'don 7E **156**
  (off Tait Rd.)
Tait St. E1 ....6H **85**
Taj Apts. E1 ....5K **9**
  (off Brick La.)
Takeley Cl. RM5: Col R 2K **55**
Takhar M. SW11 ....2C **118**
Tala Cl. KT6: Surb 3F **163**
Talacre Community Sports Cen.
  ....6E **64**
Talacre Rd. NW5 ....6E **64**
Talbot Av. N2 ....3B **46**
Talbot Cl. CR4: Mitc 4G **155**
  N15 ....4F **49**
Talbot Ct. EC3 ....2F **15**
  NW9 ....3K **61**
Talbot Cres. NW4 ....5C **44**
Talbot Gdns. IG3: Ilf 2A **72**
Talbot Gro. Ho. W11 ....6G **81**
  (off Lancaster Rd.)

Talbot Ho. E14 ....6D **86**
  (off Girauld St.)
  N7 ....3A **66**
  SW11 ....3B **118**
  (off York Place)
Talbot Pl. SE3 ....2G **123**
Talbot Rd. CR7: Thor H 4D **156**
  E6 ....2E **88**
  E7 ....4J **69**
  HA0: Wemb 6D **60**
  HA3: W'stone 2K **41**
  N6 ....6E **46**
  N15 ....4F **49**
  N22 ....2G **47**
  RM9: Dag 6F **73**
  SE22 ....4E **120**
  SM5: Cars 5E **166**
  TW2: Twick 1J **131**
  TW7: Isle 4A **114**
  TW15: Ashf 5A **128**
  UB2: S'hall 4C **94**
  W2 ....6H **81**
  W11 ....6H **81**
  W13 ....1A **96**
Talbot Sq. W2 ......1B **10** (6B **82**)
Talbot Wlk. NW10 ....6A **62**
  W11 ....6G **81**
  (off St Mark's Rd.)
Talbot Yd. SE1 ......5E **14** (1D **102**)
Talcott Path SW2 ....1A **138**
Talehangers Cl.
  DA6: Bex 4D **126**
Talfourd Pl. SE15 ....1F **121**
Talfourd Rd. SE15 ....1F **121**
Talgarth Mans. W14 ....5G **99**
  (off Talgarth Rd.)
Talgarth Rd. W6 ....5F **99**
  W14 ....5F **99**
Talgarth Wlk. NW9 ....5A **44**
Talia Ho. E14 ....3E **104**
  (off Manchester Rd.)
Talina Cen. SW6 ....1A **118**
Talisman Cl. IG3: Ilf 1B **72**
Talisman Sq. SE26 ....4G **139**
Talisman Way HA9: Wemb 3F **61**
Tallack Cl. HA3: Hrw W 7D **26**
Tallack Rd. E10 ....1B **68**
Tall Elms Cl. BR2: Broml 5H **159**
Talleyrand Ho. SE5 ....2C **120**
  (off Lilford Rd.)
Tallis Cl. E16 ....6K **87**
Tallis Gro. SE7 ....6K **105**
Tallis St. EC4 ......2K **13** (7A **84**)
Tallis Vw. NW10 ....6K **61**
Tallow Cl. RM9: Dag 7D **72**
Tallow Rd. TW8: Bford 6C **96**
Tall Trees SW16 ....3K **155**
Talma Gdns. TW2: Twick 6J **113**
Talmage Cl. SE23 ....7J **121**
Talman Gro. HA7: Stan 6J **27**
Talma Rd. SW2 ....4A **120**
Talwin St. E3 ....3D **86**
Tamar Cl. E3 ....1B **86**
Tamar Ho. E14 ....2E **104**
  (off Plevna St.)
  SE11 ....5K **19**
  (off Kennington La.)
Tamarind Ct. SE1 ....6K **15**
  W8 ....3K **99**
  (off Stone Hall Gdns.)
Tamarind Ho. SE15 ....7G **103**
  (off Reddins Rd.)
Tamarind Yd. E1 ....1G **103**
  (off Kennet St.)
Tamarisk Sq. W12 ....7B **80**
Tamar Sq. IG8: Wfd G 6E **36**
Tamar St. SE7 ....3C **106**
Tamar Way N17 ....3F **49**
Tamesis Gdns. KT4: Wor Pk 2A **164**
Tamian Ind. Est. TW4: Houn 4A **112**
Tamian Way TW4: Houn 4A **112**

Tamworth Av. IG8: Wfd G 6B **36**
Tamworth La. CR4: Mitc 2F **155**
Tamworth Pk. CR4: Mitc 4F **155**
Tamworth Pl. CR0: C'don 2C **168**
Tamworth Rd.
  CR0: C'don 2B **168**
Tamworth St. SW6 ....6J **99**
Tancred Rd. N4 ....6B **48**
Tandem Cen. 1B **154**
Tandem Ho. E17 ....5B **50**
  (off Track St.)
Tandem Way SW19 ....1B **154**
Tandridge Dr. BR6: Orp 1H **173**
Tandridge Pl. BR6: Orp 1H **173**
Tanfield Av. NW2 ....4B **62**
Tanfield Rd. CR0: C'don 4C **168**
Tangerine Ho. SE1 ....7F **15**
  (off Long La.)
Tangier Rd. TW10: Rich 4G **115**
Tangleberry Cl. BR1: Broml 4D **160**
Tangle Tree Cl. N3 ....2K **45**
Tanglewood Cl.
  CR0: C'don 3J **169**
  HA7: Stan 2D **26**
  UB10: Hil 4C **74**
Tanglewood Way TW13: Felt 3K **129**
Tangley Gro. SW15 ....6B **116**
Tangley Pk. Rd.
  TW12: Hamp 6D **130**
Tanglyn Av. TW17: Shep 5D **146**
Tangmere N17 ....2D **48**
  (off Willan Rd.)
  WC1 ....2G **7**
  (off Sidmouth St.)
Tangmere Cres. UB10: Uxb 1A **74**
Tangmere Gdns. UB5: N'olt 2A **76**
Tangmere Gro. KT2: King T 5D **132**
Tangmere Way NW9 ....2A **44**
Tan Ho. E9 ....5A **68**
  (off Sadler Pl.)
Tanhouse Fld. NW5 ....5H **65**
  (off Torriano Av.)
Tanhurst Ho. SW2 ....7K **119**
  (off Redlands Way)
Tanhurst Wlk. SE2 ....3D **108**
  (off Alsike Rd.)
Tankerton Ho's. WC1 ....2F **7**
  (off Tankerton St.)
Tankerton Rd. KT6: Surb 2F **163**
Tankerton St. WC1 ......2F **7** (3J **83**)
Tankerton Ter. CR0: C'don 6K **155**
Tankerville Ct.
  TW3: Houn 3G **113**
Tankerville Rd. SW16 ....7H **137**
Tankridge Rd. NW2 ....2D **62**
Tanner Cl. NW9 ....2A **44**
Tanner Ho. E1 ....5K **85**
  (off White Horse La.)
  SE1 ....7H **15**
  (off Tanner St.)
The Tanneries E1 ....4J **85**
  (off Cephas Av.)
Tanner Point E13 ....1J **87**
  (off Pelly Rd.)
Tanners Cl. KT12: Walt T 6K **147**
Tanners End La. N18 ....4K **33**
Tanner's Hill SE8 ....1B **122**
Tanners La. IG6: Ilf 3G **53**
Tanners M. SE8 ....1B **122**
  (off Tanner's Hill)
Tanner St. IG11: Bark 6G **71**
  SE1 ....7H **15** (2E **102**)
Tanners Yd. E2 ....2H **85**
  (off Treadway St.)
The Tannery SE1 ....3E **102**
  (Grange Rd.)
  SE1 ....6H **15**
  (off Black Swan Yd.)
Tannery Cl. BR3: Beck 5K **157**
  RM10: Dag 1J **85**
Tannery Ho. E1 ....5G **85**
  (off Deal St.)

Tannery Sq. *SE1* 3E **102**
    (off Tannery Way)
Tannery Way *SE1* 3F **103**
Tannington Ter. *N5* 3B **66**
Tannoy Sq. *SE27* 4D **138**
Tannsfield Rd. *SE26* 5K **139**
Tansley Cl. *N7* 5H **65**
Tanswell St. *SE1* 7J **13** (2A **102**)
Tansy Cl. *E6* 6E **88**
Tantallon Rd. *SW12* 1E **136**
Tant Av. *E16* 6H **87**
Tantony Gro.
    RM6: Chad H 3D **54**
Tanworth Gdns.
    HA5: Pinn 2K **39**
Tanyard Ho. *TW8*: Bford 7C **96**
    (off High St.)
Tan Yd. La. *DA5*: Bexl 7G **127**
Tanza Rd. *NW3* 4D **64**
Tapestry Apts. *N1* 1H **83**
Tapestry Bldg. *EC2* 6H **9**
    (off New St.)
Tapestry Cl. *SM2*: Sutt 7K **165**
Tapley Cl. *E14* 6E **86**
Tapley Ho. *SE1* 7K **15**
    (off Wolseley St.)
Taplow *NW3* 7B **64**
    SE17 . . . . .5D **102**
    (off Thurlow St.)
Taplow Ct. *CR4*: Mitc 4C **154**
Taplow Ho. *E2* 2J **9**
    (off Palissy St.)
Taplow Rd. *N13* 4H **33**
Taplow St. *N1* 1D **8** (2C **84**)
Tapper Wlk. *N1* 1J **83**
Tappesfield Rd. *SE15* 3J **121**
Tapping Cl.
    KT2: King T 7G **133**
Tapp St. *E1* 4H **85**
Tapster St.
    EN5: Barn 3C **20**
Tara Arts Cen. 1K **135**
Tara Ct. *BR3*: Beck 2D **158**
Tara Ho. *E14* 4C **104**
    (off Deptford Ferry Rd.)
Tara M. *N8* 6J **47**
Taransay Wlk. *N1* 6D **66**
Tarbert M. *N15* 5E **48**
Tarbert Rd. *SE22* 5E **120**
Tarbert Wlk. *E1* 7J **85**
Tarbuck Ho. *SE10* 4G **105**
    (off Manilla Wlk.)
Target Cl. *TW14*: Felt 6G **111**
Target Ho. *W13* 1B **96**
    (off Sherwood Cl.)
TARGET RDBT. 1D **76**
Tariff Cres. *SE8* 4B **104**
Tariff Rd. *N17* 6B **34**
Tarleton Ct. *N22* 2A **48**
Tarleton Gdns. *SE23* 2H **139**
Tarling Cl. *DA14*: Sidc 3B **144**
Tarling Rd. *E16* 6H **87**
    N2 .2A **46**
Tarling St. *E1* 6H **85**
Tarling St. Est. *E1* 6J **85**
Tarmac Way
    UB7: Harm 3C **174**
Tarnbank *EN2*: Enf 5D **22**
Tarnbrook Ct. *SW1* 4G **17**
    (off Holbein Pl.)
The Tarns *NW1* 1A **6**
    (off Varndell St.)
Tarn St. *SE1* 3C **102**
Tarnwood Pk. *SE9* 7D **124**
Tarplett Ho. *SE14* 6K **103**
    (off John Williams Cl.)
Tarquin Ho. *SE26* 4G **139**
    (off High Level Dr.)
Tarragon Cl. *SE14* 7A **104**
Tarragon Ct. *IG1*: Ilf 2J **71**
Tarragon Gro. *SE26* 6K **139**
Tarranbrae *NW6* 7G **63**

Tarrant Ho. *E2* 3J **85**
    (off Roman Rd.)
    W14 . . . . .3G **99**
    (off Russell Rd.)
Tarrant Pl. *W1* 6E **4** (5D **82**)
Tarrington Cl. *SW16* 3H **137**
Tartan Ho. *E14* 6E **86**
    (off Dee St.)
Tarver Rd. *SE17* 5B **102**
Tarves Way *SE10* 7D **104**
    (Lit. Cottage Pl.)
    SE10 . . . . .7D **104**
    (Norman Rd.)
Taryn Gro. *BR1*: Broml 3D **160**
Tash Pl. *N11* 5A **32**
Tasker Cl. *UB3*: Harl 7E **92**
Tasker Ho. *E14* 5B **86**
    (off Wallwood St.)
    IG11: Bark 2H **89**
Tasker Lodge *W8* 2J **99**
    (off Campden Hill)
Tasker Rd. *NW3* 5D **64**
Tasman Ct. *E14* 4D **104**
    (off Westferry Rd.)
    TW16: Sun 7G **129**
Tasman Ho. *E1* 1H **103**
    (off Clegg St.)
Tasmania Ter. *N18* 6H **33**
Tasman Rd. *SW9* 3J **119**
Tasman Wlk. *E16* 6B **88**
Tasso Rd. *W6* 6G **99**
Tasso Yd. *W6* 6G **99**
    (off Tasso Rd.)
Tatam Rd. *NW10* 7K **61**
Tatchbury Ho. *SW15* 6B **116**
    (off Tunworth Cres.)
Tate Apts. *E1* 6H **85**
    (off Sly St.)
Tate Britain 4E **18** (4J **101**)
Tate Ho. *E2* 2K **85**
    (off Mace St.)
Tate Modern 4B **14** (1B **102**)
Tate Rd. *E16* 1D **106**
    (not continuous)
    SM1: Sutt 5J **165**
Tatham Pl. *NW8* 2B **82**
Tatnell Rd. *SE23* 6A **122**
Tatsfield Ho. *SE1* 7F **15**
    (off Pardoner St.)
Tattersall Cl. *SE9* 5C **124**
Tatton Cl.
    SM5: W'gton 1E **166**
Tatton Cres. *N16* 7F **49**
Tatum St. *SE17* 4D **102**
Tauheed Cl. *N4* 2C **66**
Taunton Av. *SW20* 2D **152**
    TW3: Houn 2G **113**
Taunton Cl. *DA7*: Bex 2K **127**
    SM3: Sutt 1J **165**
Taunton Dr. *EN2*: Enf 3F **23**
    N2 .2A **46**
Taunton Ho. *W2* 6A **82**
    (off Hallfield Est.)
Taunton M. *NW1* 4E **4** (4D **82**)
Taunton Pl. *NW1* 3E **4** (4D **82**)
Taunton Rd.
    SE12 . . . . .5G **123**
    UB6: G'frd 1F **77**
Taunton Way *HA7*: Stan 2E **42**
Tavern Cl. *SM5*: Cars 7C **154**
Tavern Ct. *SE1* 3C **102**
    (off New Kent Rd.)
Taverners Cl. *W11* 1G **99**
Taverners Ct. *E3* 3A **86**
    (off Grove Rd.)
Taverner Sq. *N5* 4C **66**
Taverners Way *E4* 1B **36**
Tavern La. *SW9* 2A **120**
Tavern Quay *SE16* 4A **104**
Tavistock Av. *E17* 3K **49**
    NW7 . . . . .7A **30**
    UB6: G'frd 2A **78**

Tavistock Cl. *N16* 5E **66**
    TW18: Staines 7A **128**
Tavistock Ct. *CR0*: C'don 1D **168**
    (off Tavistock Rd.)
    WC1 . . . . .3D **6**
    (off Tavistock Sq.)
    WC2 . . . . .7J **83**
    (off Tavistock Street)
Tavistock Cres. *CR4*: Mitc 4J **155**
    W11 . . . . .5H **81**
    (not continuous)
Tavistock Gdns. *IG3*: Ilf 4J **71**
Tavistock Ga. *CR0*: C'don 1D **168**
Tavistock Gro.
    CR0: C'don 7D **156**
Tavistock Ho. *IG8*: Wfd G 6K **37**
    W11 . . . . .3D **6** (4H **83**)
Tavistock M. *N19* 3J **65**
    (off Tavistock Ter.)
    W11 . . . . .6H **81**
Tavistock Pl. *N14* 6A **22**
    WC1 . . . . .3E **6** (4J **83**)
Tavistock Rd. *BR2*: Broml 4H **159**
    CR0: C'don 1D **168**
    DA16: Well 1C **126**
    E7 .4H **69**
    E15 . . . . .6H **69**
    E18 . . . . .3J **51**
    HA8: Edg 1G **43**
    N4 .6D **48**
    NW10 . . . . .2B **80**
    SM5: Cars 1B **166**
    UB7: Yiew 1A **92**
    UB10: Ick 5F **57**
    W11 . . . . .6H **81**
    (not continuous)
Tavistock Sq. *WC1* 3D **6** (4H **83**)
Tavistock St. *WC2* 2F **13** (7J **83**)
Tavistock Ter. *N19* 3H **65**
Tavistock Twr. *SE16* 3A **104**
Tavistock Wlk.
    SM5: Cars 1B **166**
Tavistock Youth Cen. 2B **80**
    (off Tavistock Rd.)
Taviton St. *WC1* 3C **6** (4H **83**)
Tavy Bri. *SE2* 2C **108**
Tavy Cl. *SE11* 5K **19**
Tawney Rd. *SE28* 7B **90**
Tawny Cl. *TW13*: Felt 3J **129**
    W13 . . . . .1B **96**
Tawny Way *SE16* 4K **103**
Tayben Av. *TW2*: Twick 6J **113**
Tayberry Ho. *E20* 6D **68**
    (off Ravens Wlk.)
Taybridge Rd. *SW11* 3E **118**
Tay Bldgs. *SE1* 7G **15**
Tayburn Cl. *E14* 6E **86**
Tay Cty. *E2* 3K **85**
    (off Meath Cres.)
    SE1 . . . . .7G **15**
    (off Decima St.)
Tayfield Cl. *UB10*: Ick 3F **57**
Tay Ho. *E3* 2B **86**
    (off St Stephen's Rd.)
Tayler Cl. *NW8* 1B **82**
Taylor Av. *TW9*: Kew 2H **115**
Taylor Cl. *BR6*: Orp 4K **173**
    N17 . . . . .7B **34**
    SE8 . . . . .6B **104**
    TW3: Houn 1G **113**
    TW12: Hamp H 5G **131**
Taylor Ct. *SE20* 2J **157**
    (off Elmers End Rd.)
Taylor Ho. *E14* 7C **86**
    (off Storehouse M.)
Taylor Pl. *E3* 2D **86**
Taylor Rd. *CR4*: Mitc 7C **136**
    SM6: W'gton 5F **167**
Taylors Bldgs. *SE18* 4F **107**
Taylors Cl. *DA14*: Sidc 3K **143**
Taylors Ct. *TW13*: Felt 2J **129**
Taylors Grn. *W3* 6A **80**

Taylor's La. *SE26* 4H **139**
Taylors La. *EN5*: Barn 1C **20**
    NW10 . . . . .6A **62**
Taylors Mead *NW7* 5H **29**
Taylors Yd. *E1* 4K **9**
    (off Brick La.)
Taymount Grange *SE23* 2J **139**
Taymount Ri. *SE23* 2J **139**
Tayport Cl. *N1* 7J **65**
Tayside Cl. *SE5* 4D **120**
Tayside Dr. *HA8*: Edg 3C **28**
Taywood Rd. *UB5*: N'olt 4D **76**
Tazzeta Ho. *E20* 5E **68**
    (off Victory Pde.)
Teak Cl. *SE16* 1A **104**
Tealby Ct. *N7* 6K **65**
Teal Cl. *E16* 5B **88**
Teal Ct. *E1* 3K **15**
    (off Star Pl.)
    NW10 . . . . .6K **61**
    SE8 . . . . .6B **104**
    (off Taylor Cl.)
    SM6: W'gton 5G **167**
Teal Dr. *HA6*: Nwood 1E **38**
Teale St. *E2* 2G **85**
Tealing Dr. *KT19*: Ewe 4K **163**
Teal Pl. *SM1*: Sutt 5H **165**
Teal St. *SE10* 3H **105**
TeamSport Indoor Karting
    Southwark 3H **103**
Teamsport Karting
    Edmonton 4E **34**
Teasel Cl. *CR0*: C'don 1K **169**
Teasel Cres. *SE28* 1J **107**
Teasel Way *E15* 3G **87**
Tea Trade Wharf *SE1* 6K **15**
    (off Shad Thames)
Tea Tree Cl. *TW15*: Ashf 5E **128**
Tebworth Rd. *N17* 7A **34**
The Technology Pk.
    NW9 . . . . .3A **44**
Teck Cl. *TW7*: Isle 2A **114**
Tedder Cl.
    HA4: Ruis 5J **57**
    KT9: Chess 5C **162**
    UB10: Uxb 7B **56**
Tedder Rd. *CR2*: Sels 7J **169**
TEDDINGTON 5A **132**
Teddington Bus. Pk.
    TW11: Tedd 6K **131**
    (off Station Rd.)
TEDDINGTON LOCK 4B **132**
Teddington Lock *TW10*: Ham 4B **132**
Teddington Pk. *TW11*: Tedd 5K **131**
Teddington Pk. Rd.
    TW11: Tedd 4K **131**
Teddington Pool & Fitness Cen.
    . . . . .5A **132**
Teddington Riverside
    TW11: Tedd 5B **132**
Teddington Sports Cen. 6D **132**
Ted Hennem Ho. *RM10*: Dag 3H **73**
Ted Roberts Ho. *E2* 2H **85**
    (off Parmiter St.)
Tedworth Gdns. *SW3* 6E **16** (5D **100**)
Tedworth Sq. *SW3* 6E **16** (5D **100**)
The Tee *W3* 6A **80**
Tees Av. *UB6*: G'frd 2J **77**
Tees Ct. *W7* 6H **77**
    (off Hanway Rd.)
Teesdale Av. *TW7*: Isle 1A **114**
Teesdale Cl. *E2* 2G **85**
Teesdale Gdns. *SE25* 2E **156**
    TW7: Isle 1A **114**
Teesdale Rd. *E11* 6H **51**
Teesdale St. *E2* 2H **85**
Teesdale Yd. *E2* 2H **85**
    (off Teesdale St.)
Teeswater Ct. *DA18*: Erith 3D **108**
Teevan Cl. *CR0*: C'don 7G **157**
Teevan Rd. *CR0*: C'don 1G **169**
Tegan Cl. *SM2*: Sutt 7J **165**

Teign M. SE9 . . . . .2C **142**
Teignmouth Cl. HA8: Edg 2F **43**
  SW4 . . . . .4H **119**
Teignmouth Gdns.
  UB6: G'frd 2A **78**
Teignmouth Pde. UB6: G'frd 2A **78**
Teignmouth Rd.
  DA16: Well 2C **126**
  NW2 . . . . .5F **63**
Telcon Way SE10 . . . . .4G **105**
Telcote Way HA4: Ruis 7A **40**
Telegraph Av. NW9 . . . . .3A **44**
  SE10 . . . . .4G **105**
Telegraph Hill NW3 . . . . .3K **63**
Telegraph La.
  KT10: Clay 4A **162**
Telegraph M. IG3: Ilf 1A **72**
Telegraph Path
  BR7: Chst 5F **143**
Telegraph Pl. E14 . . . . .4D **104**
Telegraph Rd. SW15 . . . . .7D **116**
Telegraph St. EC2 . . . . .7E **8** (6D **84**)
Telemann Sq. SE3 . . . . .4K **123**
Telephone Pl. SW6 . . . . .6H **99**
Telfer Cl. W3 . . . . .2J **97**
Telfer Ho. EC1 .2B **8**
Telferscot Rd. SW12 . . . . .1H **137**
Telford Av. SW2 . . . . .1H **137**
Telford Cl. E17 . . . . .7A **50**
  SE19 . . . . .6F **139**
Telford Dr. KT12: Walt T 7A **148**
Telford Ho. SE1 . . . . .3C **102**
               (off Tiverton St.)
Telford Rd. N11 . . . . .5B **32**
  NW9 . . . . .6C **44**
  SE9 . . . . .2H **143**
  TW2: Whitt 7E **112**
  UB1: S'hall 7F **77**
  W10 . . . . .5G **81**
Telfords Yd. E1 . . . . .7G **85**
Telford Ter.
  SW1 . . . . .7A **18** (6G **101**)
Telford Way UB4: Yead 5C **76**
  W3 . . . . .5A **80**
Telham Rd. E6 . . . . .2E **88**
Tell Gro. SE22 . . . . .4F **121**
Teilson Av. SE18 . . . . .1B **124**
Telscombe Cl. BR6: Orp 2J **173**
Temair Ho. SE10 . . . . .7D **104**
             (off Tarves Way)
Temeraire Pl. TW8: Bford 5F **97**
Temeraire St. SE16 . . . . .2J **103**
Tempelhof Av. NW4 . . . . .7E **44**
Temperley Rd. SW12 . . . . .7E **118**
Templar Ct. NW8 . . . . .2A **4**
  RM7: Mawney 4H **55**
Templar Dr. SE28 . . . . .6D **90**
Templar Ho. E15 . . . . .6F **69**
              (off Leyton Rd.)
  HA2: Harr 2G **59**
  NW2 . . . . .6H **63**
Templar Pl. TW12: Hamp 7E **130**
Templars Av. NW11 . . . . .6H **45**
Templars Cres. N3 . . . . .2J **45**
Templars Dr. HA3: Hrw W 6C **26**
Templars Ho. E16 . . . . .7F **89**
           (off University Way)
Templar St. SE5 . . . . .2B **120**
Temple Av. CR0: C'don 2B **170**
  EC4 . . . . .2K **13** (7A **84**)
  N20 . . . . .7G **21**
  RM8: Dag 1G **73**
Temple Bar 1J **13** (6A **84**)
Temple Bar Gate 1B **14 8**
         (off Paternoster Sq.)
Temple Chambers EC4 . . . . .2K **13**
Temple Cl. E11 . . . . .7G **51**
  N3 . . . . .2H **45**
  SE28 . . . . .3G **107**
Templecombe Rd. E9 . . . . .1J **85**
Templecombe Way
  SM4: Mord 5G **153**

Temple Ct. E1 . . . . .5K **85**
            (off Rectory Sq.)
  SW8 . . . . .7J **101**
         (off Thorncroft St.)
Templecroft TW15: Ashf 6F **129**
Temple Dwellings E2 . . . . .2H **85**
             (off Temple St.)
TEMPLE FORTUNE 5H **45**
Temple Fortune Hill NW11 . . . . . .5J **45**
Temple Fortune La. NW11 . . . . . . .6H **45**
Temple Fortune Pde. NW11 . . . . .5H **45**
Temple Gdns. EC4 . . . . .2J **13**
  N21 . . . . .2G **33**
  NW11 . . . . .6H **45**
  RM8: Dag 3D **72**
Temple Gro. EN2: Enf 2G **23**
  NW11 . . . . .6J **45**
Temple Hall Ct. E4 . . . . .2A **36**
Temple La. EC4 . . . . . . .1K **13** (6A **84**)
Templeman Rd. W7 . . . . .5K **77**
Temple Mead Cl.
  HA7: Stan 6G **27**
Templemead Cl. W3 . . . . .6A **80**
Templemead Ho. E9 . . . . .4A **68**
TEMPLE MILLS 4D **68**
Temple Mills La. E10 . . . . .4D **68**
  E15 . . . . .5E **68**
  E20 . . . . .4E **68**
Temple Pde. EN5: New Bar 7G **21**
          (off Netherlands Rd.)
Temple Pk. UB8: Hil 3D **74**
Temple Pl. WC2 . . . . . . .2H **13** (7K **83**)
Temple Rd. CR0: C'don 4D **168**
  E6 . . . . .1C **88**
  N8 . . . . .4K **47**
  NW2 . . . . .4E **62**
  TW3: Houn 4F **113**
  TW9: Rich 2F **115**
  W4 . . . . .3J **97**
  W5 . . . . .3D **96**
Temple Sheen SW14 . . . . .4J **115**
Temple Sheen Rd. SW14 . . . . . . .4H **115**
Temple St. E2 . . . . .2H **85**
Temple Ter. N22 . . . . .2A **48**
           (off Vincent Rd.)
Templeton Av. E4 . . . . .4H **35**
Templeton Cl. N15 . . . . .6D **48**
  N16 . . . . .5E **66**
  SE19 . . . . .1D **156**
Templeton Ct. EN3: Enf W 1D **24**
Templeton Pl. SW5 . . . . .4J **99**
Templeton Rd. N15 . . . . .6D **48**
Temple Way SM1: Sutt 3B **166**
Temple W. M. SE11 . . . . .3B **102**
Templewood W13 . . . . .5B **78**
Templewood Av. NW3 . . . . .3K **63**
Templewood Gdns. NW3 . . . . .3K **63**
Templewood Point NW2 . . . . .2H **63**
         (off Granville Rd.)
Temple Yd. E2 . . . . .2H **85**
            (off Temple St.)
Tempo Ho. UB5: N'olt 3B **76**
Tempsford Cl. EN2: Enf 2H **23**
Tempsford Ct. HA1: Harr 6K **41**
Tempus Apts. EC1 . . . . .1A **8**
           (off Goswell Rd.)
Tempus Ct. E18 . . . . .1J **51**
Tempus Wharf SE16 . . . . .2G **103**
    (off Bermondsey Wall W.)
Temsford Cl. HA2: Harr 2G **41**
Tenbury Cl. E7 . . . . .5B **70**
Tenbury Ct. SW2 . . . . .1H **137**
Tenby Av. HA3: Kenton 2B **42**
Tenby Cl. N15 . . . . .4F **49**
  RM6: Chad H 6E **54**
Tenby Ct. E17 . . . . .5A **50**
Tenby Gdns. UB5: N'olt 6E **58**
Tenby Ho. UB3: Harl 3E **92**
  W2 . . . . .6A **82**
            (off Hallfield Est.)
Tenby Mans. W1 . . . . .5H **5**
         (off Nottingham St.)

Tenby Rd. DA16: Well 1D **126**
  E17 . . . . .5A **50**
  EN3: Pond E 4D **24**
  HA8: Edg .1F **43**
  RM6: Chad H 6E **54**
Tench St. E1 . . . . .1H **103**
Tenda Rd. SE16 . . . . .4H **103**
Tendring Way
  RM6: Chad H 5C **54**
Tenham Av. SW2 . . . . .1H **137**
Tenison Ct. W1 . . . . .2A **12** (7G **83**)
Tenison Way SE1 . . . . .5J **13**
Tenniel Cl. W2 . . . . .7A **82**
Tennis Ct. La. KT8: E Mos 3K **149**
Tennison Rd. SE25 . . . . .4F **157**
Tennis St. SE1 . . . . .6E **14** (2D **102**)
Tennyson Rd.
  EN1: Enf .1K **23**
Tennyson Cl. CR0: C'don 1C **168**
Tennyson Av. E11 . . . . .7J **51**
  E12 . . . . .7C **70**
  KT3: N Mald 5D **152**
  NW9 . . . . .3J **43**
  TW1: Twick 1K **131**
Tennyson Cl. DA16: Well 1J **125**
  EN3: Pond E 5E **24**
  TW14: Felt 6H **111**
Tennyson Ct. NW1 . . . . .4E **4**
             (off Dorset Sq.)
Tennyson Ho. DA17: Belv 5F **109**
  N8 . . . . .3J **47**
            (off Boyton Cl.)
  SE17 . . . . .5C **102**
           (off Browning St.)
Tennyson Mans. SW3 . . . . .7C **16**
            (off Lordship Pl.)
  W14 . . . . .6H **99**
        (off Queen's Club Gdns.)
Tennyson Rd. E10 . . . . .1D **68**
  E15 . . . . .7G **69**
  E17 . . . . .6B **50**
  NW6 . . . . .1H **81**
  NW7 . . . . .5H **29**
  SE20 . . . . .7K **139**
  SW19 . . . . .6A **136**
  TW3: Houn 2G **113**
  TW15: Ashf 5A **128**
  W7 . . . . .7K **77**
Tennyson St. SW8 . . . . .2F **119**
Tenpin
  Acton 4G **79**
  Bexleyheath 4F **127**
  Croydon .2K **167**
  Feltham 2K **129**
  Kingston upon Thames 2E **150**
    (within The Rotunda Cen.)
Tensing Rd. UB2: S'hall 3E **94**
Tentelow La. UB2: S'hall 5E **94**
Tenterden Cl. NW4 . . . . .3F **45**
  SE9 . . . . .4D **142**
Tenterden Dr. NW4 . . . . .3F **45**
Tenterden Gdns. CR0: C'don 7G **157**
  NW4 . . . . .3F **45**
Tenterden Gro. NW4 . . . . .3F **45**
Tenterden Ho. SE17 . . . . .5E **102**
           (off Surrey Gro.)
Tenterden Rd. CR0: C'don 7G **157**
  N17 . . . . .7A **34**
  RM8: Dag 2F **73**
Tenterden St. W1 . . . . . .1K **11** (6F **83**)
Tenter Ground E1 . . . . .6J **9** (5F **85**)
Tent Peg La. BR5: Pet W 5G **161**
Tent St. E1 .4H **85**
Tenzing Ct. E14 . . . . .5D **86**
            (off Hillary M.)
Tequila Wharf E14 . . . . .6A **86**
Tera 40 UB6: G'frd 7G **59**
Terborch Way SE22 . . . . .5E **120**
Tercelet Ter. NW3 . . . . .4A **64**
Teredo St. SE16 . . . . .3K **103**
Terence Ct. DA17: Belv 6F **109**
           (off Nuxley Rd.)

Terence McMillan Stadium 4A **88**
Terence Messenger Twr. E10 . . . .2D **68**
            (off Alpine Rd.)
Teresa M. E17 . . . . .4C **50**
Teresa Wlk. N10 . . . . .5F **47**
Terling Cl. E11 . . . . .3H **69**
Terling Ho. W10 . . . . .5E **80**
           (off Sutton Way)
Terling Rd. RM8: Dag 2G **73**
Terling Wlk. N1 . . . . .1C **84**
           (off Popham St.)
TERMINAL 4 RDBT. 6E **110**
TERMINAL 5 RDBT. 5C **174**
Terminal Ho. HA7: Stan 5J **27**
Terminus Pl.
  SW1 . . . . .2K **17** (3F **101**)
The Terrace E2 . . . . .3J **85**
          (off Old Ford Rd.)
  E4 . . . . .3B **36**
           (off Newgate St.)
  EC4 . . . . .1K **13**
  IG8: Wfd G 6D **36**
  N3 . . . . .2H **45**
  NW6 . . . . .1J **81**
  SE8 . . . . .4B **104**
           (off Longshore)
  SE23 . . . . .7A **122**
  SW13 . . . . .2A **116**
Terrace Apts. N5 . . . . .5A **66**
Terrace Gdns. SW13 . . . . .2B **116**
Terrace La. TW10: Rich 6E **114**
Terrace Rd. E9 . . . . .7J **67**
  E13 . . . . .2J **87**
  KT12: Walt T 7J **147**
The Terraces E2 . . . . .2G **85**
           (off Garner St.)
  NW8 . . . . .2B **82**
          (off Queen's Ter.)
Terrace Wlk. RM9: Dag 5E **72**
  SW11 . . . . .7H **17** (7D **100**)
Terrano Ho. TW9: Kew 1H **97**
Terrapin Rd. SW17 . . . . .3F **137**
Terretts Pl. N1 . . . . .7B **66**
           (off Upper St.)
Terrick Rd. N22 . . . . .1J **47**
Terrick St. W12 . . . . .6D **80**
Terrilands HA5: Pinn 3D **40**
Territorial Ho. SE11 . . . . .4K **19**
Terront Rd. N15 . . . . .4C **48**
Terry Spinks Pl. E16 . . . . .5H **87**
          (off Barking Rd.)
Tersha St. TW9: Rich 4F **115**
Tesla Ct. W3 . . . . .2A **98**
Tessa Sanderson Pl. SW8 . . . . . . .3F **119**
    (off Daley Thompson Way)
Tessa Sanderson Way
  UB6: G'frd 5H **59**
Testerton Rd. W11 . . . . .7F **81**
        (off Hurstway Wlk.)
Testerton Wlk. W11 . . . . .7F **81**
Testwood Ct. W7 . . . . .7J **77**
Tetbury Pl. N1 . . . . .1B **84**
Tetcott Rd. SW10 . . . . .7A **100**
           (not continuous)
Tetherdown N10 . . . . .3E **46**
Tetty Way BR1: Broml 2J **159**
Tevatree Ho. SE1 . . . . .5G **103**
         (off Old Kent Rd.)
Teversham La. SW8 . . . . .1J **119**
Teviot Cl. DA16: Well 1B **126**
Teviot Est. E14 . . . . .5D **86**
Teviot St. E14 . . . . .5E **86**
Tewkesbury Av. HA5: Pinn 5C **40**
  SE23 . . . . .1H **139**
Tewkesbury Cl. EN4: E Barn 4G **21**
  N15 . . . . .6D **48**
Tewkesbury Gdns. NW9 . . . . .3H **43**
Tewkesbury Rd. N15 . . . . .6D **48**
  SM5: Cars 1B **166**
  W13 . . . . .1A **96**
Tewkesbury Ter. N11 . . . . .6B **32**
Tewson Rd. SE18 . . . . .5J **107**

Texryte Ho. *N1* 1D *84*
   (off Southgate Rd.)
Textile Ho. *E1* 5K *85*
   (off Duckett St.)
Teynham Av. EN1: Enf 6J 23
Teynham Ct. BR3: Beck 3D 158
Teynham Grn. BR2: Broml 5J 159
Teynton Ter. N17 . . . . .1C 48
Thackeray Av. N17 . . . . .2G 49
Thackeray Cl. SW19 . . . . .7F 135
   TW7: Isle 2A 114
   UB8: Hil 6D 74
Thackeray Ct. NW6 . . . . .7A *64*
   (off Fairfax Rd.)
   SW3 .5C *16*
   (off Elystan Pl.)
   W5 . . . . .6F *79*
   (off Hanger Va. La.)
   W14 .3G *99*
   (off Blythe Rd.)
Thackeray Dr. RM6: Chad H 7A *54*
Thackeray Ho. WC1 . . . . .3E *6*
Thackeray Lodge TW14: Bedf . . .6F *111*
Thackeray M. E8 . . . . .6G *67*
Thackeray Rd. E6 . . . . .2B *88*
   SW8 .2F *119*
Thackeray St. W8 . . . . .3K *99*
Thackery Ct. EC1 . . . . .5A *8*
   (off Turnmill St.)
Thackrah Cl. N2 . . . . .2A *46*
   (off Simms Gdns.)
Thakeham Cl. SE26 . . . . .4H *139*
Thalia Cl. SE10 . . . . .6F *105*
Thalia Ct. E8 . . . . .7F *67*
   (off Albion Dr.)
Thame Rd. SE16 . . . . .2K *103*
Thames Av. KT4: Wor Pk 1E *164*
   RM9: Dag, Rain 4H *91*
   SW10 . . . . .1A *118*
   UB6: G'frd 2K *77*
Thames Bank SW14 . . . . .2J *115*
Thamesbank Pl. SE28 . . . . .6C *90*
Thames Barrier 2B *106*
Thames Barrier Ind. Area SE18 . .3B *106*
   (off Faraday Way)
Thames Barrier Info. Cen. 3B *106*
Thames Barrier Pk. 2A *106*
Thamesbrook SW3 . . . . .6C *16*
Thames Circ. E14 . . . . .4C *104*
Thames Cl. TW12: Hamp 2F *149*
Thames Cotts. KT7: T Ditt 6B *150*
Thames Ct. KT8: W Mole 2F *149*
   NW6 .2H *81*
   (off Albert Rd.)
   SE15 .7F *103*
   (off Daniel Gdns.)
   W7 . . . . .6J *77*
   (off Hanway Rd.)
Thames Cres. W4 . . . . .7A *98*
THAMES DITTON 6A *150*
Thames Ditton Youth Cen. 7A *150*
Thames Dr. HA4: Ruis 6E *38*
Thames Exchange Bldg. EC4 . . . .3D 14
Thames Eyot TW1: Twick 1A *132*
Thamesfield Ct. TW17: Shep 7E *146*
Thamesfield M. TW17: Shep 7E *146*
Thamesgate Cl. TW10: Ham 4B *132*
Thames Gateway RM9: Dag 2F *91*
   RM13: Rain 2F *91*
Thames Gateway Pk. RM9: Dag . . .3F *91*
Thames Haven KT6: Surb 5D *150*
Thames Hgts. SE1 . . . . .6J *15*
   (off Gainsford St.)
Thames Ho. EC4 . . . . .2D 14
   (off Queen St. Pl.)
   KT1: King T 4D *150*
   (off Surbiton Rd.)
   SW1 .4J *101*
   (off Millbank)
Thameside KT8: W Mole 3F *149*
   TW11: Tedd 7D *132*

Thameside Ind. Est. E16 . . . . . . .2B *106*
Thameside Pl.
   KT1: Hamp W 1D *150*
Thameside Wlk. SE28 . . . . .6A *90*
Thames Innovation Cen.
   DA18: Erith 2F *109*
THAMES LOCK 3A *148*
Thamesmead KT12: Walt T 6J *147*
THAMESMEAD CENTRAL 1A *108*
THAMESMEAD EAST 2F *109*
THAMESMEAD NORTH 6D *90*
Thames Mdw.
   KT8: W Mole 2E *148*
   TW17: Shep 7F *147*
THAMESMEAD SOUTH 2D *108*
THAMESMEAD SOUTH WEST . . .2K *107*
THAMESMEAD WEST 3G *107*
Thamesmere Dr. SE28 . . . . .7A *90*
Thamesmere Leisure Cen. 7A *90*
Thames Path SE10 . . . . .3J *105*
Thames Pl. SW15 . . . . .3F *117*
Thames Point SW6 . . . . .2A *118*
Thamespoint TW11: Tedd 7D *132*
Thames Police Mus. 1H *103*
Thames Quay E14 . . . . .2D *104*
   SW10 . . . . .1A *118*
   (off Chelsea Harbour)
Thames Reach KT1: Hamp W 1D *150*
   SE28 .2J *107*
   W6 . . . . .6E *98*
   (off Rainville Rd.)
Thames Rd. E16 . . . . .1B *106*
   IG11: Bark 3K 89
   W4 . . . . .6G 97
Thames Rd. Ind. Est. E16 . . . . . .1B *106*
Thames Side KT1: King T 1D *150*
   KT7: T Ditt 6B *150*
Thames St. KT1: King T 2D *150*
   KT12: Walt T 7H *147*
   SE10 .6D *104*
   TW12: Hamp 1F *149*
   TW16: Sun 4J *147*
Thames Tunnel Mills SE16 . . . . .2J *103*
Thamesvale Cl. TW3: Houn 3E *112*
Thames Vw. *IG1: Ilf* 2G *71*
   (off Axon Pl.)
Thamesview Bus. Cen.
   RM13: Rain 5K *91*
Thamesview Ho's.
   KT12: Walt T 6J *147*
Thames Vw. Lodge IG11: Bark . . .3J *89*
Thames Village W4 . . . . .1J *115*
Thames Wlk. *KT12: Walt T* 7J *147*
   (off Manor Rd.)
   SW11 . . . . .7C *100*
Thames Wharf Studios W6 . . . . .6E *98*
   (off Rainville Rd.)
Thanescroft Gdns. CR0: C'don . . .3E *168*
Thanet Ct. W3 . . . . .6G *79*
Thanet Dr. BR2: Kes 3B *172*
Thanet Ho. *CR0: C'don* 4C *168*
   (off Coombe Rd.)
   WC1 .2E *6*
   (off Thanet St.)
Thanet Lodge NW2 . . . . .6G *63*
   (off Mapesbury Rd.)
Thanet Pl. CR0: C'don 4C *168*
Thanet Rd. DA5: Bexl 7G *127*
Thanet St. WC1 . . . . .2E *6* (3J *83*)
Thanet Wharf SE8 . . . . .6D *104*
   (off Copperas St.)
Thane Vs. N7 . . . . .3K 65
Thane Works N7 . . . . .3K 65
Thanington Ct. SE9 . . . . .6J *125*
Thant Cl. E10 . . . . .3D 68
Tharp Rd. SM6: W'gton 5H *167*
Thatcham Ct. N20 . . . . .7F 21
Thatcham Gdns. N20 . . . . .7F 21
Thatcher Cl. UB7: W Dray 2A 92
Thatchers Way TW7: Isle 5H *113*
Thatches Gro. RM6: Chad H 4E 54

Thavie's Inn EC4 . . . . .7K 7 (6A *84*)
Thaxted Ct. *N1* 1F *9*
   (off Murray Gro.)
Thaxted Ho. RM10: Dag 7H 73
   SE16 .4J *103*
   (off Abbeyfield Est.)
Thaxted Pl. SW20 . . . . .7F *135*
Thaxted Rd. IG9: Buck H 1H 37
   SE9 .3G *143*
Thaxton Pl. E4 . . . . .1A 36
Thaxton Rd. W14 . . . . .6H 99
Thayers Farm Rd. BR3: Beck 1A *158*
Thayer St. W1 . . . . .6H 5 (6E *82*)
The Theatre 5C *68*
Theatre Bldg. *E3* 3C *86*
   (off Paton Cl.)
Theatre Pl. *SE8* 7C *104*
   (off Speedwell St.)
Theatre-Rites 7A *14*
   (off Blackfriars Rd.)
Theatre Royal
   Drury Lane 2G 13
   (off Catherine St.)
   Haymarket 3D 12
   (off Haymarket)
   Stratford East 7F 69
Theatre Sq. E15 . . . . .6F 69
Theatre St. SW11 . . . . .3D *118*
Theatre Vw. Apts. *SE1* 6K *13*
   (off Short St.)
Theatro Technis 1G *83*
   (off Crowndale Rd.)
Theatro Twr. SE8 . . . . .6C *104*
Theberton St. N1 . . . . .1A *84*
Theed St. SE1 . . . . .5K 13 (1A *102*)
Thelbridge Ho. *E3* 3D *86*
   (off Bruce Rd.)
Thelma Gdns. SE3 . . . . .1B *124*
Thelma Gro. TW11: Tedd 6A *132*
Theobald Cres. HA3: Hrw W 1G 41
Theobald Rd. CR0: C'don 2B *168*
   E17 . . . . .7B 50
Theobalds Av. N12 . . . . .4F 31
Theobalds Ct. N4 . . . . .3C 66
Theobald's Rd. WC1 . . . .5G 7 (5K *83*)
Theobald St. SE1 . . . . .3D *102*
Theodora Way HA5: Eastc 3H 39
Theodor Ct. NW9 . . . . .2K 43
Theodore Ct. SE13 . . . . .6F *123*
Theodore Rd. SE13 . . . . .6F *123*
Therapia La. CR0: Bedd 7H *155*
   CR0: C'don 6J *155*
Therapia Rd. SE22 . . . . .6J *121*
Theresa Rd. W6 . . . . .4C *98*
Therfield Ct. N4 . . . . .2C 66
Thermopylae Ga. E14 . . . . .4D *104*
Theseus Wlk. N1 . . . . .1B *8*
Thesiger Rd. SE20 . . . . .7K *139*
Thessaly Ho. *SW8* 7G *101*
   (off Thessaly Rd.)
Thessaly Rd. SW8 . . . . .7G *101*
   (not continuous)
Thesus Ho. *E14* 6E *86*
   (off Blair St.)
Thetford Cl. N13 . . . . .6G 33
Thetford Gdns. RM9: Dag 7E 72
Thetford Ho. *SE1* 7J *15*
   (off St Saviour's Est.)
Thetford Rd. KT3: N Mald 6K *151*
   RM9: Dag 7D 72
   TW15: Ashf 4A *128*
Thetis Ter. TW9: Kew 6G 97
Theven St. E1 . . . . .4J 85
Theydon Gro. IG8: Wfd G 6F 37
Theydon Rd. E5 . . . . .2J 67
Theydon St. E17 . . . . .7B 50
The Thicket UB7: Yiew 6A 74
Thicket Cres. SM1: Sutt 4A 166
Thicket Gro. RM9: Dag 6C 72
   SE20 .7G *139*
Thicket Rd. SE20 . . . . .7G *139*
   SM1: Sutt 4A 166

Thimble Cres. SM6: W'gton 2E *166*
Third Av. E12 . . . . .4C 70
   E13 . . . . .3J 87
   E17 . . . . .5C 50
   EN1: Enf 5A 24
   HA9: Wemb 2D 60
   RM6: Chad H 6C 54
   RM10: Dag 1H 91
   UB3: Hayes 1H 93
   W3 . . . . .1B 98
   W10 .3G 81
Third Cl. KT8: W Mole 4G *149*
Third Cross Rd.
   TW2: Twick 2H *131*
Third Way HA9: Wemb 4H 61
Thirleby Rd. HA8: Edg 1K 43
   NW7 .5B 30
   SW1 . . . . .2B 18 (3G *101*)
Thirlestane Ct. N10 . . . . .2E 46
Thirlmere NW1 . . . . .1K *5*
   (off Cumberland Mkt.)
Thirlmere Av. UB6: G'frd 3C 78
Thirlmere Gdns. HA9: Wemb 1C 60
Thirlmere Ho. *N16* 4D *66*
   (off Howard Rd.)
   TW7: Isle 5K *113*
Thirlmere Ri. BR1: Broml 6H *141*
Thirlmere Rd. DA7: Bex 1J *127*
   N10 .1F 47
   SW16 . . . . .4H *137*
Thirsk Cl. UB5: N'olt 6E *58*
Thirsk Rd. CR4: Mitc 7E *136*
   SE25 .4D *156*
   SW11 . . . . .3E *118*
Thirty Casson Sq. *SE1* 5H *13*
   (off Casson Sq.)
Thirza Ho. *E1* 6J *85*
   (off Devonport St.)
Thistlebrook SE2 . . . . .3C *108*
Thistlebrook Ind. Est. SE2 . . . . . .3C *108*
Thistle Ct. SE12 . . . . .2J *141*
Thistlecroft Gdns.
   HA7: Stan 1D *42*
Thistledene KT7: T Ditt 6J *149*
Thistledene Av. HA2: Harr 3C *58*
Thistlefield Cl. DA5: Bexl 1D *144*
Thistle Gro. SW10 . . . . . .6A *16* (5A *100*)
Thistle Ho. *E14* 6E *86*
   (off Dee St.)
Thistlemead BR7: Chst 2F *161*
Thistleton Ho. NW9 . . . . .3B 44
Thistlewaite Rd. E5 . . . . .3H 67
Thistleworth Cl. TW7: Isle 7H 95
Thistleworth Marine TW7: Isle . . .4B *114*
   (off Railshead Rd.)
Thistley Cl. N12 . . . . .6H 31
Thistley Ct. SE8 . . . . .6D *104*
Thomas a Beckett Cl.
   HA0: Wemb 4K *59*
Thomas Baines Rd. SW11 . . . . . .3B *118*
Thomas Burt Ho. *E2* 3H *85*
   (off Canrobert St.)
Thomas Coulter House *E16* 2K *105*
   (off Shipwright Street)
Thomas Ct. IG6: Ilf 4G 53
Thomas Cribb M. E6 . . . . .6E *88*
Thomas Darby Ct. *W11* 6G 81
   (off Lancaster Rd.)
Thomas Dean Rd. SE26 . . . . . . .4B *140*
Thomas Dinwiddy Rd. SE12 . . . . .2K *141*
Thomas Doyle St.
   SE1 . . . . .7A *14* (3B *102*)
Thomas Dr. UB8: Uxb 6A 56
Thomas Earle Ho. *W14* 4H *99*
   (off Warwick La.)
Thomas England Ho. *RM7: Rom* . . .6K *55*
   (off Waterloo Gdns.)
Thomas Frye Ct. *E15* 2D *86*
   (off High St.)

Thomas Fyre Dr. E3 . . . . .2C **86**
Thomas Hardy Ho. N22 . . . . .7E **32**
Thomas Hardy M. SW16 . . . . . .5G **137**
Thomas Hewlett Ho.
  HA1: Harr 4J **59**
Thomas Hollywood Ho. E2 . . . . . .2J **85**
    (off Approach Rd.)
Thomas Ho. SM2: Sutt 7K **165**
Thomas Jacomb Pl. E17 . . . . .4B **50**
Thomas Joseph Ho. SE4 . . . . . . .5K **121**
    (off St Norbert Rd.)
Thomas La. SE6 . . . . .7C **122**
Thomas Lodge E17 . . . . .5D **50**
Thomas More Highwalk EC2 . . . . .6C **8**
    (off Aldersgate St.)
Thomas More Ho. EC2 . . . . .6C **8**
  HA4: Ruis 1G **57**
Thomas More Sq. E1 . . . . .7G **85**
Thomas More St. E1 . . . . .7G **85**
Thomas More Way N2 . . . . .3A **46**
Thomas Neal's Cen. 1E **12** (6J **83**)
Thomas Pl. W8 . . . . .3K **99**
Thomas Rd. E14 . . . . .6B **86**
Thomas Rd. Ind. Est. E14 . . . . . .5C **86**
    (not continuous)
Thomas Spencer Hall of Residence
  SE18 . . . . .4E **106**
    (off Grand Depot Rd.)
Thomas St. SE18 . . . . .4F **107**
Thomas Tallis Sports Cen. 3K **123**
Thomas Twr. E8 . . . . .6F **67**
    (off Dalston Sq.)
Thomas Turner Path
  CRO: C'don 2C **168**
    (off George St.)
Thomas Wall Cl. SM1: Sutt 5K **165**
Thomas Watson Cott. Homes
  EN5: Barn 4B **20**
    (off Leecroft Rd.)
Thompson Av. TW9: Rich 3G **115**
Thompson Cl. IG1: Ilf 2G **71**
  SM3: Sutt 1J **165**
Thompson Ho. SE14 . . . . .6K **103**
    (off John Williams Cl.)
  W10 .4G **81**
    (off Wornington Rd.)
Thompson Rd. RM9: Dag 3F **73**
  SE22 . . . . .6F **121**
  TW3: Houn 4F **113**
  UB10: Uxb 7A **56**
Thompson's Av. SE5 . . . . .7C **102**
Thomson Cres. CRO: C'don 1A **168**
Thomson Ho. E14 . . . . .6C **86**
    (off Saracen St.)
  SE17 . . . . .4E **102**
    (off Tatum St.)
  SW1 .6D **18**
  UB1: S'hall 7C **76**
    (off The Broadway)
Thomson Rd. HA3: W'stone 3J **41**
Thonrey Cl. NW9 . . . . .3B **44**
Thorburn Ho. SW1 . . . . .7F **11**
    (off Kinnerton St.)
Thorburn Sq. SE1 . . . . .4G **103**
Thorburn Way SW19 . . . . .1B **154**
Thoresby St. N1 . . . . .1D **8** (3C **84**)
Thorkhill Gdns.
  KT7: T Ditt 1A **162**
Thorkhill Rd. KT7: T Ditt 1A **162**
Thornaby Gdns. N18 . . . . .6B **34**
Thornaby Ho. E2 . . . . .3H **85**
    (off Canrobert St.)
Thorn Apts. E3 . . . . .5C **86**
    (off St Paul's Way)
Thorn Av. WD23: B Hea 1E **26**
Thornbill Ho. SE15 . . . . .7G **103**
    (off Bird in Bush Rd.)
Thornbury NW4 . . . . .4D **44**
    (off Prince of Wales Cl.)
Thornbury Av. TW7: Isle 7H **95**
Thornbury Cl. N16 . . . . .5E **66**
  NW7 .7A **30**

Thornbury Ct. CR2: S Croy 5D **168**
    (off Blunt Rd.)
  TW7: Isle 7J **95**
  W11 .7J **81**
    (off Chepstow Vs.)
Thornbury Lodge EN2: Enf 3G **23**
Thornbury Rd. SW2 . . . . .6J **119**
  TW7: Isle 7H **95**
Thornbury Sq. N6 . . . . .1G **65**
Thornbury Way E17 . . . . .1B **50**
Thornby Rd. E5 . . . . .3J **67**
Thorncliffe Rd. SW2 . . . . .6J **119**
  UB2: S'hall 5D **94**
Thorn Cl. BR2: Broml 6E **160**
  UB5: N'olt 3D **76**
Thorncombe Rd. SE22 . . . . .5E **120**
Thorncroft Rd. SM1: Sutt 5K **165**
Thorncroft St. SW8 . . . . .7J **101**
Thorndean St. SW18 . . . . .2A **136**
Thorndene Av. N11 . . . . .1K **31**
Thorndike Av. UB5: N'olt 1B **76**
Thorndike Cl. SW10 . . . . .7A **100**
Thorndike Ho. SW1 . . . . .5C **18**
    (off Vauxhall Bri. Rd.)
Thorndike Rd. N1 . . . . .6D **66**
Thorndike St. SW1 . . . .4C **18** (4H **101**)
Thorndon Cl. BR5: St P 2K **161**
Thorndon Gdns. KT19: Ewe 5A **164**
Thorndon Rd. BR5: St P 2K **161**
Thorne Cl. DA8: Erith 6H **109**
  E11 . . . . .4F **69**
  E16 . . . . .6J **87**
  KT10: Clay 7A **162**
  TW15: Ashf 7E **128**
Thorne Ho. E2 . . . . .3J **85**
    (off Roman Rd.)
  E14 . . . . .3E **104**
    (off Launch St.)
Thorneloe Gdns. CRO: Wadd 5A **168**
Thorne Pas. SW13 . . . . .2A **116**
Thorne Rd. SW8 . . . . .7J **101**
Thornes Cl. BR3: Beck 3E **158**
Thornes Ho. SW11 . . . . .7H **101**
    (off Ponton Rd.)
Thorne St. SW13 . . . . .3A **116**
Thornet Wood Rd.
  BR1: Broml 3E **160**
Thornewill Ho. E1 . . . . .7J **85**
    (off Cable St.)
Thorney Cl. W8 . . . . .2A **100**
    (off Palace Ga.)
Thorney Cres. SW11 . . . . .7B **100**
Thorneycroft Cl.
  KT12: Walt T 6A **148**
Thorneycroft Rd. N20 . . . . .2G **31**
Thorney Hedge Rd. W4 . . . . .4H **97**
Thorney St.
  SW1 . . . . .3E **18** (4J **101**)
Thornfield Av. NW7 . . . . .1G **45**
Thornfield Ct. NW7 . . . . .7B **30**
Thornfield Ho. E14 . . . . .7C **86**
    (off Rosefield Gdns.)
Thornfield Pde. NW7 . . . . .7B **30**
    (off Holders Hill Rd.)
Thornfield Rd. W12 . . . . .2D **98**
    (not continuous)
Thornford Rd. SE13 . . . . .5E **122**
Thorngate Rd. W9 . . . . .4J **81**
Thorngrove Rd. E13 . . . . .1K **87**
Thornham Gro. E15 . . . . .5F **69**
Thornham Ind. Est. E15 . . . . .5F **69**
Thornham St. SE10 . . . . .6D **104**
Thornhaugh M. WC1 . . . .4D **6** (4H **83**)
Thornhaugh St. WC1 . . . .4D **6** (4H **83**)
Thornhill Av. KT6: Surb 2E **162**
  SE18 . . . . .7J **107**
THORNHILL BRI. 2K **83**
    (off Caledonian Rd.)
Thornhill Bri. Wharf N1 . . . . .1K **83**
Thornhill Cres. N1 . . . . .7K **65**
Thornhill Gdns. E10 . . . . .2D **68**
  IG11: Bark 7J **71**

Thornhill Gro. N1 . . . . .7K **65**
Thornhill Ho. W4 . . . . .5A **98**
    (off Wood St.)
Thornhill Ho's. N1 . . . . .7A **66**
    (off Thornhill Rd.)
Thornhill M. SW15 . . . . .4H **117**
Thornhill Rd. CRO: C'don 7C **156**
  E10 . . . . .2D **68**
  KT6: Surb 2E **162**
  N1 . . . . .7A **66**
  UB10: Ick 4B **56**
Thornhill Sq. N1 . . . . .7K **65**
Thornhill Way TW17: Shep 5C **146**
Thornicroft Ho. SW9 . . . . .2K **119**
    (off Stockwell Rd.)
Thornlaw Rd. SE27 . . . . .4A **138**
Thornley Cl. N17 . . . . .7B **34**
Thornley Dr. HA2: Harr 2F **59**
Thornley Pl. SE10 . . . . .5G **105**
Thornsbeach Rd. SE6 . . . . .1E **140**
Thornsett Pl. SE20 . . . . .2H **157**
Thornsett Rd. SE20 . . . . .2H **157**
  SW18 . . . . .1K **135**
Thornsett Ter. SE20 . . . . .2H **157**
    (off Croydon Rd.)
Thorn Ter. SE15 . . . . .3J **121**
Thornton Av. CRO: C'don 6K **155**
  SW2 . . . . .1H **137**
  UB7: W Dray 3B **92**
  W4 . . . . .4A **98**
Thornton Cl. UB7: W Dray 3B **92**
Thornton Dene BR3: Beck 2C **158**
Thornton Gdns. SW12 . . . . .1H **137**
THORNTON HEATH 4C **156**
Thornton Heath Leisure Cen. 4C **156**
THORNTON HEATH POND 5A **156**
Thornton Hill SW19 . . . . .7G **135**
Thornton Ho. SE17 . . . . .4E **102**
    (off Townsend St.)
Thornton Pl. W1 . . . . .5F **5** (5D **82**)
Thornton Rd. BR1: Broml 5J **141**
  CRO: C'don 7K **155**
  CR7: Thor H 7K **155**
  DA17: Belv 4H **109**
  E11 . . . . .2F **69**
  EN5: Barn 3B **20**
  IG1: Ilf 4F **71**
  N18 . . . . .3D **34**
  SM5: Cars 1B **166**
  SW12 . . . . .7H **119**
  SW14 . . . . .4K **115**
  SW19 . . . . .6F **135**
Thornton Rd. E. SW19 . . . . .6F **135**
Thornton Rd. Ind. Est.
  CRO: C'don 6K **155**
Thornton Row CR7: Thor H 5A **156**
Thornton's Farm Av.
  RM7: Rush G 1J **73**
Thornton St. E20 . . . . .7D **68**
  SW9 . . . . .2A **120**
Thornton Way NW11 . . . . .5K **45**
Thorntree Ct. W5 . . . . .5E **78**
Thorntree Rd. SE7 . . . . .5B **106**
Thornville Gro. CR4: Mitc 2B **154**
Thornville St. SE8 . . . . .1C **122**
Thornwell Ct. W7 . . . . .2J **95**
    (off Lwr. Boston Rd.)
Thornwood Cl. E18 . . . . .2K **51**
Thornwood Gdns. W8 . . . . .2J **99**
Thornwood Ho. IG9: Buck H 1H **37**
Thornwood Lodge W8 . . . . .2J **99**
    (off Thornwood Gdns.)
Thornwood Rd. SE13 . . . . .5G **123**
Thornycroft Ho. W4 . . . . .5A **98**
    (off Fraser St.)
Thorogood Gdns. E15 . . . . .5G **69**
Thorogood Way RM13: Rain 1K **91**
Thorold Ho. SE1 . . . . .6C **14**
    (off Pepper St.)
Thorold Rd. IG1: Ilf 2F **71**
  N22 . . . . .7D **32**
Thorparch Rd. SW8 . . . . .1H **119**

Thorpebank Rd. W12 . . . . .1C **98**
Thorpe Cl. BR6: Orp 2J **173**
  SE26 . . . . .4K **139**
  W10 .6G **81**
Thorpe Ct. EN2: Enf 3G **23**
Thorpe Cres. E17 . . . . .2B **50**
Thorpedale Gdns. IG2: Ilf 4E **52**
  IG6: Ilf 4E **52**
Thorpedale Rd. N4 . . . . .2J **65**
Thorpe Hall Rd. E17 . . . . .1E **50**
Thorpe Ho. N1 . . . . .1K **83**
    (off Barnsbury Est.)
Thorpe Rd. E6 . . . . .1D **88**
  E7 . . . . .4H **69**
  E17 . . . . .2E **50**
  IG11: Bark 7H **71**
  KT2: King T 7E **132**
  N15 . . . . .6E **48**
Thorpewood Av. SE26 . . . . .2H **139**
Thorpland Av. UB10: Ick 3E **56**
Thorsden Way SE19 . . . . .5E **138**
Thorverton Rd. NW2 . . . . .3G **63**
Thoydon Rd. E3 . . . . .2A **86**
Thrale Rd. SW16 . . . . .4G **137**
Thrale St. SE1 . . . . . .5D **14** (1C **102**)
Thrasher Cl. E8 . . . . .1F **85**
Thrawl St. E1 . . . . .6K **9** (5F **85**)
Thrayle Ho. SW9 . . . . .3K **119**
    (off Benedict Rd.)
Threadgold Ho. N1 . . . . .6D **66**
    (off Dovercourt Est.)
Threadneedle St. EC2 . . .1F **15** (6D **84**)
Threadneedle Wlk. EC2 . . . . .1F **15**
Thread St. SM6: W'gton 2E **166**
Three Angels Cl.
  SM6: W'gton 5K **167**
Three Bridges Bus. Cen.
  UB2: S'hall 2G **95**
Three Colt Cnr. E2 . . . . .3K **9**
Three Colts La. E2 . . . . .4H **85**
Three Colt St. E14 . . . . .6B **86**
Three Corners DA7: Bex 2H **127**
Three Cranes Wlk. EC4 . . . . .3D **14**
Three Cups Yd. WC1 . . . . .6H **7**
Three Kings Yd. W1 . . . . . .2J **11** (7F **83**)
Three Meadows M.
  HA3: Hrw W 1K **41**
Three Mill La. E3 . . . . .3E **86**
Three Mills Studios 3E **86**
Three Oak La. SE1 . . . . .6J **15** (2F **103**)
Three Oaks Cl. UB10: Ick 3B **56**
Three Quays EC3 . . . . .3H **15**
Three Quays Wlk. EC3 . . .3H **15** (7E **84**)
Threshers Pl. W11 . . . . .7G **81**
Thriftwood SE26 . . . . .3J **139**
Thrigby Rd. KT9: Chess 6F **163**
Thring Ho. SW9 . . . . .2K **119**
    (off Stockwell Rd.)
Throckmorton Rd. E16 . . . . .6K **87**
Throgmorton Av. EC2 . . . .7F **9** (6D **84**)
    (not continuous)
Throgmorton St. EC2 . . . .7F **9** (6D **84**)
Throwley Cl. SE2 . . . . .3C **108**
    (not continuous)
Throwley Rd. SM1: Sutt 5K **165**
Throwley Way SM1: Sutt 4K **165**
Thrupp Cl. CR4: Mitc 2F **155**
Thrush Grn. HA2: Harr 4E **40**
Thrush St. SE17 . . . . .5C **102**
Thunderer St. E13 . . . . .2A **88**
Thunderer Wlk. SE18 . . . . .3F **107**
Thurbarn Rd. SE6 . . . . .5D **140**
Thurland Ho. SE16 . . . . .4H **103**
    (off Camilla Rd.)
Thurland Rd. SE16 . . . . .3G **103**
Thurlby Cl. HA1: Harr 6A **42**
  IG8: Wfd G 5J **37**
Thurlby Cft. NW4 . . . . .5E **44**
    (off Mulberry Cl.)
Thurlby Rd. HA0: Wemb 6D **60**
  SE27 . . . . .4A **138**
Thurleigh Av. SW12 . . . . .6E **118**

Thurleigh Ct. SW12 . . . . .6E 118
Thurleigh Rd. SW12 . . . . .7D 118
Thurleston Av. SM4: Mord 5G 153
Thurlestone Av. IG3: Bark, Ilf 4K 71
N12 . . . . .6J 31
Thurlestone Cl. TW17: Shep 6E 146
Thurlestone Cl. UB1: S'hall 6F 77
(off Howard Rd.)
Thurlestone Pde. TW17: Shep 6E 146
(off High St.)
Thurlestone Rd. SE27 . . . . .3A 138
Thurloe Cl. SW7 . . . . . .3C 16 (4C 100)
Thurloe Ct. SW3 . . . . .4C 16
(off Fulham Rd.)
Thurloe Pl. SW7 . . . . . .3B 16 (4B 100)
Thurloe Pl. M. SW7 . . . . .3B 16
Thurloe Sq. SW7 . . . . . .3C 16 (4C 100)
Thurloe St. SW7 . . . . . .3B 16 (4B 100)
Thurlow Cl. E4 . . . . .6K 35
Thurlow Gdns. HA0: Wemb 5D 60
Thurlow Hill SE21 . . . . .1C 138
Thurlow Ho. SW16 . . . . .3J 137
Thurlow Pk. Rd. SE21 . . . . .2B 138
Thurlow Rd. NW3 . . . . .5B 64
W7 . . . . .2A 96
Thurlow St. SE17 . . . . .5D 102
(not continuous)
Thurlow Ter. NW5 . . . . .5E 64
Thurlow Wlk. SE17 . . . . .5E 102
(not continuous)
Thurlstone Rd. HA4: Ruis 3J 57
Thurnby Ct. TW2: Twick 3J 131
Thurnscoe NW1 . . . . .1G 83
(off Pratt St.)
Thursland Rd. DA14: Sidc 5E 144
Thursley Cres. CR0: New Ad 7E 170
Thursley Gdns. SW19 . . . . .2F 135
Thursley Ho. SW2 . . . . .7K 119
(off Holmewood Gdns.)
Thursley Rd. SE9 . . . . .3D 142
Thurso Ho. NW6 . . . . .2K 81
Thurso St. SW17 . . . . .4B 136
Thurstan Dwellings WC2 . . . . .7F 7
(off Newton St.)
Thurstan Rd. SW20 . . . . .7D 134
Thurstan St. SW6 . . . . .1A 118
Thurston Ho. BR3: Beck 6D 140
N1 . . . . .1K 83
(off Barnsbury Est.)
Thurston Rd. SE13 . . . . .2D 122
UB1: S'hall 6D 76
Thurtle Rd. E2 . . . . .1F 85
Thwaite Cl. DA8: Erith 6J 109
Thyer Cl. BR6: Farnb 4G 173
Thyme Cl. SE3 . . . . .3A 124
Thyme Ct. NW7 . . . . .1G 45
Thyme Wlk. E5 . . . . .4K 67
Thyra Gro. N12 . . . . .6E 30
Tibbatt's Rd. E3 . . . . .4D 86
Tibbenham Pl. SE6 . . . . .2C 140
Tibbenham Wlk. E13 . . . . .2H 87
Tibberton Sq. N1 . . . . .1C 84
Tibbet's Cl. SW19 . . . . .1F 135
TIBBET'S CORNER 7F 117
Tibbet's Ride SW15 . . . . .7F 117
Tiber Cl. E3 . . . . .1C 86
Tiber Gdns. N1 . . . . .1J 83
Ticehurst Cl. BR5: St P 7A 144
Ticehurst Rd. SE23 . . . . .2A 140
Tickford Cl. SE2 . . . . .2C 108
Tickford Ho. NW8 . . . . .2C 4 (3C 82)
Tidal Basin Rd. E16 . . . . .7H 87
(not continuous)
Tidbury Ct. SW8 . . . . .7G 101
(off Stewart's Rd.)
Tide Cl. CR4: Mitc 1E 154
Tideham Ho. SE28 . . . . .1H 107
Tidelea Twr. SE28 . . . . .2G 107
Tidemill Sq. SE10 . . . . .4G 105
Tidemill Way SE8 . . . . .7C 104
Tidenham Gdns.
CR0: C'don 3E 168

Tideside Ct. SE18 . . . . .3C 106
Tideslea Path SE28 . . . . .1H 107
Tideswell Rd. CR0: C'don 3J 170
SW15 .4E 116
Tidewalters Ho. E14 . . . . .6F 87
(off Blair St.)
Tideway Cl. TW10: Ham 4B 132
Tideway Ct. SE16 . . . . .1K 103
Tideway Ho. E14 . . . . .2C 104
(off Strafford St.)
E17 . . . . .4K 49
Tideway Wlk. SW11 . . .7B 18 (6G 101)
Tidey St. E3 . . . . .5C 86
Tidford Rd. DA16: Well 2K 125
Tidlock Ho. SE28 . . . . .2H 107
Tidworth Rd. E3 . . . . .4C 86
Tiepigs La.
BR2: Hayes 2G 171
BR4: W W'ck 2G 171
Tierney Cl. CR0: C'don 2E 168
Tierney La. W6 . . . . .6E 98
Tierney Rd. SW2 . . . . .1J 137
Tiffany Hgts. SW18 . . . . .7J 117
Tiffin Girls Community Sports Cen.
. . . . .6E 132
Tiffin Sports Cen. 2F 151
Tiger Cl. IG11: Bark 2B 90
Tiger Ho. WC1 . . . . .2D 6
(off Burton St.)
Tiger La. BR2: Broml 4K 159
Tiger Way E5 . . . . .4H 67
Tiggap Ho. SE10 . . . . .4G 105
Tigris Cl. N9 . . . . .2D 34
Tilbrook Rd. SE3 . . . . .3A 124
Tilbury Cl. HA5: Hat E 1D 40
SE15 .7F 103
Tilbury Ho. SE14 . . . . .6K 103
(off Myers La.)
Tilbury Rd. E6 . . . . .2D 88
E10 . . . . .7E 50
Tildesley Rd. SW15 . . . . .6E 116
Tile Farm Rd.
BR6: Orp 3H 173
Tile Ho. N1 . . . . .1J 83
(off Beaconsfield Rd.)
Tilehurst NW1 . . . . .2K 5
(off Lit. Albany St.)
Tilehurst Point SE2 . . . . .2C 108
(not continuous)
Tilehurst Rd. SM3: Cheam 5G 165
SW18 .1B 136
Tile Kiln La. DA5: Bexl 2J 145
N6 . . . . .1F 65
N13 . . . . .5H 33
UB9: Hare 7D 38
Tile Kiln Studios N6 . . . . .1G 47
Tileyard Rd. N7 . . . . .7J 65
Tilford Av. CR0: New Ad 7E 170
Tilford Gdns. SW19 . . . . .1F 135
Tilford Ho. SW2 . . . . .7K 119
(off Holmewood Gdns.)
Tilia Cl. SM1: Sutt 5H 165
Tilia Rd. E5 . . . . .4H 67
Tilia Wlk. SW9 . . . . .4B 120
Tiller Ho. N1 . . . . .1E 84
(off Whitmore Est.)
UB2: S'hall 3E 94
(off Lockwood Rd.)
Tiller Leisure Cen. 3C 104
Tiller Rd. E14 . . . . .3C 104
Tillett Cl. NW10 . . . . .6J 61
Tillett Sq. SE16 . . . . .2A 104
Tillett Way E2 . . . . .3G 85
Tilley Rd. TW13: Felt 1J 129
Tillingbourne Gdns. N3 . . . . .3H 45
Tillingbourne Grn.
BR5: St M Cry 4K 161, 5K 161
Tillingbourne Way N3 . . . . .4H 45
Tillingham Way N12 . . . . .4D 30
Tilling Rd. NW2 . . . . .1E 62
Tillings Cl. SE5 . . . . .1C 120

Tilling Way HA9: Wemb 2D 60
Tillman St. E1 . . . . .6H 85
Tilloch St. N1 . . . . .7K 65
Tillotson Ct. SW8 . . . . .7H 101
(off Wandsworth Rd.)
Tillotson Rd. HA3: Hrw W 7A 26
IG1: Ilf .7E 52
N9 . . . . .2A 34
Tilney Ct. EC1 . . . . .3D 8 (4C 84)
IG9: Buck H 2D 36
Tilney Dr. IG9: Buck H 2D 36
Tilney Gdns. N1 . . . . .6D 66
Tilney Rd. RM9: Dag 6F 73
UB2: S'hall 4A 94
Tilney St. W1 . . . . . .4H 11 (1E 100)
Tilson Cl. SE5 . . . . .7E 102
Tilson Gdns. SW2 . . . . .7J 119
Tilson Ho. SW2 . . . . .7J 119
Tilson Rd. N17 . . . . .1G 49
Tilston Bright Sq.
SE2 . . . . .3C 108
Tilston Cl. E11 . . . . .3H 69
Tiltman Pl. N7 . . . . .3K 65
Tilton St. SW6 . . . . .6G 99
The Tiltwood W3 . . . . .7J 79
Tilt Yd. App. SE9 . . . . .6D 124
Timber Cl. BR7: Chst 2E 160
Timbercroft KT19: Ewe 4A 164
Timbercroft La. SE18 . . . . .6J 107
Timberdene NW4 . . . . .2F 45
Timberdene Av. IG6: Ilf 1G 53
Timberland Cl. SE15 . . . . .7G 103
Timberland Rd. E1 . . . . .6H 85
Timberley Ct. DA14: Sidc 5K 143
Timber Mill Way SW4 . . . . .3H 119
Timber Pond Rd. SE16 . . . . .1K 103
The Timbers
SM3: Cheam 6G 165
Timberslip Dr.
SM6: W'gton 7H 167
Timber St. EC1 . . . . . .3C 8 (4C 84)
Timber Wharf E2 . . . . .1F 85
Timberwharf Rd. N16 . . . . .6G 49
Timber Wharves Est. E14 . . . . . . .4C 104
(off Copeland Dr.)
The Timber Yd. N1 . . . . .2H 9
(off Drysdale St.)
Timberyard M. KT4: Wor Pk 2D 164
Timbrell Pl. SE16 . . . . .1B 104
Time Sq. E8 . . . . .5F 67
Times Sq. E1 . . . . .6G 85
SM1: Sutt 5K 165
Timians Way BR1: Broml 4K 141
Timmins Apts. E2 . . . . .3K 85
Timms Cl. BR1: Broml 4D 160
Timor Ho. E1 . . . . .4A 86
(off Duckett St.)
Timothy Cl. DA6: Bex 5E 126
SW4 . . . . .5G 119
Timothy Ho. DA18: Erith 2E 108
(off Kale Rd.)
Timothy Pl. KT8: W Mole 5D 148
Timpberley Ct. SW19 . . . . .1G 135
Timsbury Wlk. SW15 . . . . .1C 134
Tina Ct. SE6 . . . . .7B 122
Tindal St. SW9 . . . . .1B 120
Tinderbox All. SW14 . . . . .3K 115
Tinderbox Ho. SE8 . . . . .7C 104
(off Octavius St.)
Tinniswood Cl. N5 . . . . .5A 66
Tinsley Cl. SE25 . . . . .3H 157
Tinsley Rd. E1 . . . . .5J 85
Tintagel Ct. EC1 . . . . .3A 8
(off St John St.)
Tintagel Cres. SE22 . . . . .4F 121
Tintagel Dr. HA7: Stan 4J 27
Tintagel Gdns. SE22 . . . . .4F 121
Tintern Av. NW9 . . . . .3H 43
Tintern Cl. SW15 . . . . .5G 117
SW19 .6A 136
Tintern Ct. W13 . . . . .7A 78
Tintern Gdns. N14 . . . . .7D 22

Tintern Ho. NW1 . . . . .1K 5
(off Augustus St.)
SW1 . . . . .4J 17
(part of Abbots Mnr.)
Tintern Path NW9 . . . . .6A 44
(off Fryent Gro.)
Tintern Rd. N22 . . . . .1C 48
SM5: Cars 1B 166
Tintern St. SW4 . . . . .4J 119
Tintern Way HA2: Harr 1F 59
Tinto Rd. E16 . . . . .4J 87
Tinworth Ct. SE17 . . . . .6B 102
(off Royal Rd.)
Tinworth St. SE11 . . . . .5F 19 (5J 101)
Tippett Ct. E6 . . . . .2D 88
Tippetts Cl. EN2: Enf 1H 23
Tippler Wlk. E15 . . . . .5F 69
Tipthorpe Rd. SW11 . . . . .3E 118
Tipton Dr. CR0: C'don 4E 168
Tiptree NW1 . . . . .7F 65
(off Castlehaven Rd.)
Tiptree Cl. E4 . . . . .3K 35
Tiptree Cres. IG5: Ilf 3E 52
Tiptree Dr. EN2: Enf 4J 23
Tiptree Rd. HA4: Ruis 4K 57
Tirlemont Rd. CR2: S Croy 7C 168
Tirrell Rd. CR0: C'don 6C 156
Tisbury Ct. W1 . . . . .2C 12
Tisbury Rd. SW16 . . . . .2J 155
Tisdall Ho. SE17 . . . . .4D 102
(off Barlow St.)
Tisdall Pl. SE17 . . . . .4D 102
Tissington Ct. SE16 . . . . .4J 103
Titan Bus. Est. SE8 . . . . .7C 104
(off Ffinch St.)
Titan Ct. TW8: Bford 5F 97
Titan Ho. E20 . . . . .5E 68
(off Napa Cl.)
Titanium Point E2 . . . . .3K 85
(off Palmer's Rd.)
Titchborne Row W2 . . . .1D 10 (6C 82)
Titchfield Rd. NW8 . . . . .1C 82
SM5: Cars 1B 166
Titchfield Wlk. SM5: Cars 7B 154
Titchwell Rd. SW18 . . . . .1B 136
Tite St. SW3 . . . . .6E 16 (5D 100)
Tithe Barn Cl. KT2: King T 1F 151
The Tithe Barn Way UB5: N'olt . . .2K 75
Tithe Cl. KT12: Walt T 6K 147
NW7 . . . . .1C 44
UB4: Hayes 5H 75
Tithe Farm Av. HA2: Harr 3E 58
Tithe Farm Cl. HA2: Harr 3E 58
The Tithe Social Club 2E 58
Tithe Wlk. NW7 . . . . .1C 44
Titian Av. WD23: B Hea 1D 26
Tithe Hgts. E20 . . . . .5D 68
(off Scarlet Cl.)
Titley Cl. E4 . . . . .5H 35
Titmus Cl. UB8: Hil 6E 74
Titmuss Av. SE28 . . . . .7B 90
Titmuss St. W12 . . . . .2E 98
Tivendale N8 . . . . .3J 47
Tiverton Av. IG5: Ilf 3E 52
Tiverton Cl. CR0: C'don 7F 157
Tiverton Dr. SE9 . . . . .1G 143
Tiverton Ho. EN3: Enf H 3E 24
Tiverton Rd.
HA0: Wemb 2E 78
HA4: Ruis 3J 57
HA8: Edg 2F 43
N15 . . . . .6D 48
N18 . . . . .5K 33
NW10 . . . . .1F 81
TW3: Houn 2G 113
Tiverton St. SE1 . . . . .3C 102
Tiverton Way KT9: Chess 5D 162
NW7 . . . . .7A 30
Tivoli Ct. SE16 . . . . .1B 104
Tivoli Gdns. SE18 . . . . .4C 106
(not continuous)
Tivoli M. E14 . . . . .6B 86

Tivoli Rd. N8 . . . . .5H 47
SE27 . . . . .5C 138
TW4: Houn 4C 112
Tivoli Way E14 . . . . .6B 86
Tizzard Gro. SE3 . . . . .4K 123
Toad La. TW4: Houn 4C 112
Tobacco Dock 7H 85
Tobago St. E14 . . . . .2C 104
Tobin Cl. NW3 . . . . .7C 64
Toby Ct. N9 . . . . .7D 24
(off Tramway Av.)
Toby La. E1 . . . . .4A 86
Toby Way KT5: Surb 2H 163
Todber Ho. W14 . . . . .3G 99
(off Russell Rd.)
Todd Ho. N2 . . . . .2B 46
(off The Grange)
Todds Wlk. N7 . . . . .2K 65
Todhunter Ter. EN5: New Bar 4D 20
Token Ho. CRO: C'don 3C 168
(off Robert St.)
Tokenhouse Yd. EC2 . . . . . .7E 8 (6D 84)
Token Yd. SW15 . . . . .4G 117
TOKYNGTON 6H 61
Tokyngton Av. HA9: Wemb 6G 61
Toland Sq. SW15 . . . . .5C 116
Tolcairn Ct. DA17: Belv 5G 109
Tolcarne Dr. HA5: Eastc 2J 39
Tolchurch W11 . . . . .2E 6
(off Dartmouth Cl.)
Toley Av. HA9: Wemb 7E 42
Tolhurst Dr. W10 . . . . .3G 81
Tollard Ho. W14 . . . . .3H 99
(off Kensington High St.)
Toll Bar Ct. SM2: Sutt 7K 165
Tollbridge Cl. W10 . . . . .4G 81
Tollesbury Gdns. IG6: Ilf 3H 53
Tollet St. E1 . . . . .4K 85
Tollgate Ct.
CR2: S Croy 5D 168
Tollgate Dr. SE21 . . . . .2E 138
UB4: Yead 7B 76
Tollgate Gdns. NW6 . . . . .2K 81
(off Oxford Rd.)
Tollgate Ho. NW6 . . . . .2K 81
(off Tollgate Gdns.)
Tollgate Lodge BR7: Chst 1E 160
(off Caveside Cl.)
Tollgate Rd. E6 . . . . .5A 88
E16 . . . . .5A 88
Tollgate Sq. 5D 88
Tollhouse Way N19 . . . . .2G 65
Tollington Pk. N4 . . . . .2K 65
Tollington Pl. N4 . . . . .2K 65
Tollington Rd. N7 . . . . .4K 65
Tollington Way N7 . . . . .3J 65
Tolmers Sq. NW1 . . . . . . .3B 6 (4G 83)
(not continuous)
Tolpaide Ho. SE11 . . . . .4J 19
Tolpuddle Av. E13 . . . . .1A 88
Tolpuddle St. N1 . . . . .2A 84
Tolsford Rd. E5 . . . . .5H 67
Tolson Rd. TW7: Isle 3A 114
Tolverne Rd. SW20 . . . . .1E 152
TOLWORTH 2H 163
Tolworth B'way. KT6: Surb 1H 163
Tolworth Cl. KT6: Surb 1H 163
Tolworth Gdns. RM6: Chad H 5D 54
TOLWORTH JUNC.
(TOBY JUG) 2H 163
Tolworth Pde. RM6: Chad H 5E 54
Tolworth Pk. Rd. KT6: Surb 2F 163
Tolworth Recreation Cen. 3F 163
Tolworth Ri. Nth. KT5: Surb 1H 163
Tolworth Ri. Sth. KT5: Surb 2E 163
Tolworth Rd. KT6: Surb 2E 162
Tolworth Twr. KT6: Surb 2H 163
Tomahawk Gdns. UB5: N'olt 3B 76
Tomblin M. SW16 . . . . .2G 155
Tom Coombs Cl. SE9 . . . . .4C 124
Tom Cribb Rd. SE28 . . . . .3G 107
Tom Groves Cl. E15 . . . . .5F 69

Tom Hood Cl. E15 . . . . .5F 69
Tom Jenkinson Rd. E16 . . . . .1J 105
Tomkyns Ho. SE11 . . . . .3J 19
Tomline Ho. SE1 . . . . .5C 14
(off Union St.)
Tomlins All. TW1: Twick 1A 132
Tomlin's Gro. E3 . . . . .3C 86
Tomlinson Cl. E2 . . . . .2K 9 (3F 85)
W4 . . . . .5H 97
Tomlins Orchard IG11: Bark 1G 89
Tomlins Ter. E14 . . . . .6A 86
Tomlins Wlk. N7 . . . . .2K 65
Tom Mann Cl. IG11: Bark 1J 89
Tommy Flowers M. NW7 . . . . .5A 30
Tom Nolan Cl. E15 . . . . .2G 87
Tompion Ho. EC1 . . . . .3B 8
(off Percival St.)
Tompion St. EC1 . . . . .2A 8 (3B 84)
(not continuous)
Tom Smith Cl. SE10 . . . . .6G 105
Tomson Ho. SE1 . . . . .7J 15
(off St Saviour's Est.)
Tomswood Ct. IG6: Ilf 1G 53
Tomswood Hill IG6: Ilf 1F 53, 6K 37
Tomswood Rd. IG7: Chig 6K 37
Tom Williams Ho. SW6 . . . . .6H 99
(off Clem Attlee Ct.)
Tonbridge Cres. HA3: Kenton 4E 42
Tonbridge Ho's. WC1 . . . . .2E 6
(off Tonbridge St.)
Tonbridge Rd. KT8: W Mole 4D 148
Tonbridge St. WC1 . . . . . . .1E 6 (3J 83)
Tonbridge Wlk. WC1 . . . . .1E 6
Toneborough NW8 . . . . .1K 81
(off Abbey Rd.)
Tonfield Rd. SM3: Sutt 1H 165
Tonge Cl. BR3: Beck 5C 158
Tonsley Hill SW18 . . . . .5K 117
Tonsley Pl. SW18 . . . . .5K 117
Tonsley Rd. SW18 . . . . .5K 117
Tonsley St. SW18 . . . . .5K 117
Tonstall Rd. CR4: Mitc 2E 154
Tony Cannell M. E3 . . . . .3B 86
Tony Law Ho. SE20 . . . . .1H 157
Tony Rawson Way RM10: Dag 3J 73
Tooke Cl. HA5: Pinn 1C 40
Tookey Cl. HA3: Kenton 7F 43
Took's Ct. EC4 . . . . .7J 7 (6A 84)
Tooley St. SE1 . . . . .4F 15 (1D 102)
Toorack Rd.
HA3: Hrw W 2H 41
TOOTING .5C 136
TOOTING BEC 3D 136
Tooting Bec Gdns. SW16 . . . . .4H 137
(not continuous)
Tooting Bec Lido 4G 137
Tooting Bec Rd. SW16 . . . . .3E 136
SW17 . . . . .3E 136
Tooting B'way. SW17 . . . . .5C 136
TOOTING GRAVENEY 6D 136
Tooting Gro. SW17 . . . . .5C 136
Tooting High St. SW17 . . . . .6C 136
Tooting Leisure Cen. 4B 136
Tooting Mkt. SW17 . . . . .4D 136
Tootswood Rd. BR2: Broml 5G 159
Topaz Ct. E11 . . . . .1G 69
Topaz Wlk. NW2 . . . . .7F 45
Topcliffe Dr. BR6: Farnb 4H 173
Topham Ho. SE10 . . . . .7E 104
(off Prior St.)
Topham Sq. N17 . . . . .1C 48
Topham St. EC1 . . . . .3J 7 (4A 84)
Topham Yard SW19 . . . . .1K 153
Top Ho. Ri. E4 . . . . .7K 25
Topiary Sq. TW9: Rich 3F 115
Topley St. SE9 . . . . .4A 124
Topmast Point E14 . . . . .2C 104
Top Pk. BR3: Beck 5G 159
Topp Wlk. NW2 . . . . .2E 62
Topsfield Cl. N8 . . . . .5H 47
Topsfield Pde. N8 . . . . .5J 47
(off Tottenham La.)

Topsfield Rd. N8 . . . . .5J 47
Topsham Rd. SW17 . . . . .3D 136
Tora Ct. IG9: Buck H 2F 37
Torbay Ct. NW1 . . . . .7F 65
Torbay Mans. NW6 . . . . .1H 81
(off Willesden La.)
Torbay Rd. HA2: Harr 2C 58
NW6 .7H 63
Torbay St. NW1 . . . . .7F 65
Torbitt Way IG2: Ilf 5K 53
Torbridge Cl. HA8: Edg 7K 27
Torbrook Cl. DA5: Bexl 6E 126
Tor Ct. W8 .2J 99
Torcross Dr. SE23 . . . . .2J 139
Torcross Rd. HA4: Ruis 3K 57
Toreno Mansion E20 . . . . .5D 68
(off Olympic Pk. Av.)
Tor Gdns. W8 . . . . .2J 99
Tor Gro. SE28 . . . . .1J 107
Tor Ho. N6 .6F 47
Tormead Cl. SM1: Sutt 6J 165
Tormount Rd. SE18 . . . . .6J 107
Tornay Ho. E9 . . . . .7J 67
N1 . . . . .2K 83
(off Priory Grn. Est.)
Toronto Av. E12 . . . . .4D 70
Toronto Ho. SE16 . . . . .2K 103
Toronto Rd. IG1: Ilf 1F 71
Torquay Ct. E14 . . . . .5E 86
(off St Ives Pl.)
Torquay Gdns. IG4: Ilf 4B 52
Torquay St. W2 . . . . .5K 81
Torrance Cl. SE7 . . . . .6B 106
Torrens Ct. SE5 . . . . .3D 120
Torrens Rd. E15 . . . . .6H 69
SW2 .5K 119
Torrens Sq. E15 . . . . .6H 69
Torrens St. EC1 . . . . .2A 84
Torrent Lodge SE10 . . . . .7D 104
(off Merryweather Pl.)
Torres Sq. E14 . . . . .5C 104
Torre Vista SE13 . . . . .3E 122
(off Loampit Va.)
Torre Wlk. SM5: Cars 1C 166
Torrey Dr. SW9 . . . . .2A 120
Torriano Av. NW5 . . . . .5H 65
Torriano Cotts. NW5 . . . . .5G 65
Torriano M. NW5 . . . . .5G 65
Torridge Gdns. SE15 . . . . .4J 121
Torridge Rd. CR7: Thor H 5B 156
Torridon Ho. NW6 . . . . .2K 81
(off Randolph Gdns.)
Torridon Rd. SE6 . . . . .7F 123
SE13 .7F 123
Torrington Av. N12 . . . . .5G 31
Torrington Cl. N12 . . . . .4G 31
Torrington Ct. SE26 . . . . .5A 140
(off Crystal Palace Pk. Rd.)
Torrington Dr. HA2: Harr 4F 59
Torrington Gdns. N11 . . . . .6B 32
UB6: G'frd 1C 78
Torrington Gro. N12 . . . . .5H 31
Torrington Pk. N12 . . . . .5F 31
Torrington Pl. E1 . . . . .1C 103
WC1 . . . . .5C 6 (5H 83)
Torrington Rd. E18 . . . . .3J 51
HA4: Ruis 3H 57
RM8: Dag 1F 73
UB6: G'frd 1C 78
Torrington Sq. CR0: C'don 7D 156
WC1 . . . . .4D 6 (4H 83)
Torrington Way
SM4: Mord 6J 153
Tor Rd. DA16: Well 1C 126
Tortington Ho. SE15 . . . . .7G 103
(off Friary Est.)
Torver Rd. HA1: Harr 4J 41
Torver Way BR6: Orp 3H 173
Torwood Rd. SW15 . . . . .5C 116
Tothill Ho. SW1 . . . . .3D 18
(off Page St.)

Tothill St. SW1 . . . . .7D 12 (2H 101)
Totnes Rd. DA16: Well 7B 108
Totnes Vs. N11 . . . . .5B 32
(off Telford Rd.)
Totnes Wlk. N2 . . . . .4B 46
Tottan Ter. E1 . . . . .6K 85
Tottenhall NW1 . . . . .7E 64
(off Ferdinand St.)
Tottenhall Rd. N13 . . . . .6F 33
TOTTENHAM 2F 49
Tottenham Community Sports Cen.
. . . . .1F 49
Tottenham Ct. Rd. W1 . . . .4B 6 (4G 83)
Tottenham Ent. Cen. N17 . . . . .2F 49
Tottenham Grn. E. N15 . . . . .4F 49
(not continuous)
Tottenham Green Pools & Fitness . .4F 49
TOTTENHAM HALE 2G 49
TOTTENHAM HALE GYRATORY
. . . . .4G 49
Tottenham Hale Retail Pk. 4G 49
Tottenham Hotspur FC 7A 34
Tottenham La. N8 . . . . .6J 47
Tottenham M. W1 . . . . .5B 6 (5G 83)
Tottenham Rd. N1 . . . . .6E 66
Tottenham St. W1 . . . . .6B 6 (5G 83)
Totterdown St. SW17 . . . . .4D 136
TOTTERIDGE 1C 30
Totteridge Comn. N20 . . . . .2H 29
Totteridge Fields
Local Nature Reserve 1H 29
Totteridge Grn. N20 . . . . .2D 30
Totteridge Ho. SW11 . . . . .2B 118
(off Yelverton Rd.)
Totteridge La. N20 . . . . .2D 30
Totteridge Village N20 . . . . .1B 30
Totternhoe Cl. HA3: Kenton 5C 42
Totters Cl. SE17 . . . . .6D 102
(off Westmorland Rd.)
Totton Rd. CR7: Thor H 3A 156
Toucan Cl. NW10 . . . . .3G 79
Touchard Ho. N1 . . . . .2F 9
Toulmin St. SE1 . . . . .7C 14 (2C 102)
Toulon St. SE5 . . . . .7C 102
Toulouse Ct. SE16 . . . . .5H 103
(off Rossetti Rd.)
Tounson Ct. SW1 . . . . .4D 18
(off Montaigne Cl.)
Tourers Ho. E17 . . . . .5B 50
(off Track St.)
Tournay Rd. SW6 . . . . .7H 99
Tour Pas. SW11 . . . . .4A 118
Toussaint Wlk. SE16 . . . . .3G 103
Tovil Cl. SE20 . . . . .2H 157
Tovy Ho. SE1 . . . . .5G 103
(off Avondale Sq.)
Towcester Rd. E3 . . . . .4D 86
The Tower SE1 . . . . .5J 15
(off Potters Flds.)
SW8 . . . . .7E 18 (6J 101)
TW8: Bford 5D 96
(off Ealing Rd.)
Tower 42 . . . . .7G 9 (6E 84)
TOWER BRIDGE 5J 15 (1F 103)
Tower Bri. App.
E1 . . . . .4J 15 (1F 103)
Tower Bri. Bus. Complex
SE16 .3G 103
Tower Bri. Bus. Sq. SE16 . . . . .4H 103
Tower Bridge Exhibition 4J 15
Tower Bri. M. HA1: Harr 4K 59
Tower Bri. Plaza
SE1 . . . . .5J 15 (1F 103)
Tower Bri. Rd. SE1 . . . . . .7H 15 (3E 102)
Tower Bri. Sq. SE1 . . . . .6J 15
Tower Bri. Wharf
E1 . . . . .5K 15 (1G 103)
Tower Bldgs. E1 . . . . .1H 103
(off Brewhouse La.)
Tower Cl. BR6: Orp 2K 173
NW3 . . . . .5B 64
SE20 .7H 139

Tower Ct. DA17: Belv 4J 109
E5 . . . . .7F 49
N1 . . . . . . .7C 66
(off Canonbury St.)
NW8 . . . . .2C 82
(off Mackennal St.)
WC2 . . . . . .1E 12
Tower Gdns. KT10: Clay 7A 162
Tower Gdns. Rd. N17 . . . . .1C 48
Towergate SE1 . . . . . .4E 102
(off Page's Wlk.)
Towergate Cl. UB8: Uxb 5A 56
Towergate Ho. E3 . . . . . . .2B 86
(off Ordell Rd.)
Tower Hamlets Rd. E7 . . . . .4H 69
E17 . . . . . .3C 50
TOWER HILL 3J 15 (7F 85)
Twr. Hill EC3 . . . . .3J 15 (7F 85)
Tower Hill Ct. DA17: Erith 4J 109
(off Tower Ct.)
Tower Hill Memorial . .3H 15 (7F 85)
Tower Hill Ter. EC3 . . . . .3H 15
Tower Ho. E1 . . . . . .5G 85
(off Fieldgate St.)
SE13 . . . . . . .3E 122
Tower La. HA9: Wemb 3D 60
Tower Mans. SE1 . . . . . .3F 103
(off Grange Rd.)
Tower M. E5 . . . . .4A 68
E17 . . . . . .4C 50
Tower Mill Rd. SE15 . . . .7F 102
The Tower of London 3J 15 (7F 85)
Tower of London Jewel House 7F 85
Tower of London Welcome Centre
. . . . .3H 15 (7E 84)
Tower Pier EC3 . . . . .3H 15 (7E 84)
Tower Pl. EC3 . . . . .3H 15 (7E 84)
Tower Pl. E. EC3 . . . . .3H 15
(off Lwr. Thames St.)
Tower Pl. W. EC3 . . . . .3H 15
(off Lwr. Thames St.)
Tower Point EN2: Enf 4J 23
Tower Ri. TW9: Rich 3E 114
Tower Rd. BR6: Orp 2K 173
DA7: Bex 4G 127
DA17: Belv 4J 109
NW10 . . . . . .7C 62
TW1: Twick 3K 131
Towers Av. UB10: Hil 3E 74
Towers Bus. Pk. HA9: Wemb 4J 61
(off Carey Way)
Towers Ct. UB10: Hil 3E 74
Towers Pl. TW9: Rich 5E 114
Towers Rd. HA5: Pinn 1C 40
UB1: S'hall 4E 76
Tower St. WC2 . . . . .1E 12 (6J 83)
Tower Ter. N22 . . . . .2K 47
Tower Vw. CR0: C'don 7A 158
WD23: B Hea 1D 26
Tower Wlk. SE1 . . . . .4E 102
(off Leroy St.)
Tower Wharf SE1 . . . . .6J 15
(off Tooley St.)
Tower Workshops SE1 . . . .7J 15
Towfield Ct. TW13: Hanw 2D 130
Towfield Rd. TW13: Hanw 2D 130
The Town EN2: Enf 3J 23
Towncourt Cres.
BR5: Pet W 5G 161
Towncourt La. BR5: Pet W 6H 161
Town Ct. Path N4 . . . . .1C 66
Townend Ct. BR1: Broml 1H 159
Town End Pde. KT1: King T 3D 150
(off High St.)
Towney Mead UB5: N'olt 2D 76
Towney Mead Ct. UB5: N'olt 2D 76
Townfield Rd. UB3: Hayes 1H 93
Townfield Sq. UB3: Hayes 7H 75
Town Fld. Way TW7: Isle 2A 114
Town Hall App. N16 . . . . .4D 66
(off Albion Rd.)
Town Hall App. Rd. N15 . . . .4F 49

Town Hall Av. W4 . . . . .5K 97
Town Hall Rd. SW11 . . . .3D 118
Townholm Cres. W7 . . . . .3K 95
Townhouse M. W12 . . . .2D 98
Town La. TW19: Stanw 1A 128
Townley Ct. E15 . . . . .6H 69
Townley Rd. DA6: Bex 5F 127
SE22 . . . . . .5E 120
Townley St. SE17 . . . . .5D 102
(not continuous)
Townmead Bus. Cen. SW6 . . . .3A 118
Town Mdw. TW8: Bford 6D 96
Town Mdw. Rd. TW8: Bford 7D 96
Townmead Rd. SW6 . . . .3K 117
TW9: Kew 2H 115
Town Quay IG11: Bark 1F 89
Town Quay Wharf IG11: Bark 1F 89
Town Rd. N9 . . . . . .2C 34
Townsend Av. N14 . . . . .4C 32
Townsend Ho. SE1 . . . . .4G 103
(off Strathnairn St.)
Townsend Ind. Est. NW10 . . . .2J 79
Townsend La. NW9 . . . . .7K 43
Townsend M. SW18 . . . .2A 136
Townsend Rd. N15 . . . . .5F 49
SE3 . . . . . .4A 124
TW15: Ashf 5A 128
UB1: S'hall 1C 94
Townsend St. SE17 . . . . .4E 102
Townsend Way HA6: Nwood 1H 39
Townsend Yd. N6 . . . . .1F 65
Townshend Cl. DA14: Sidc 6B 144
Townshend Ct. NW8 . . . . .2C 82
(off Townshend Rd.)
Townshend Est. NW8 . . . . .2C 82
Townshend Rd. BR7: Chst 5F 143
NW8 . . . . . .1C 82
(not continuous)
TW9: Rich 4F 115
Townshend Ter. TW9: Rich 4F 115
Towns Ho. SW4 . . . . . .3H 119
Towpath KT12: Walt T 5J 147
TW17: Shep 7B 146
Towpath Rd. N18 . . . . .6E 34
Towpath Wlk. E9 . . . . .5B 68
Towpath Way CR0: C'don 6F 157
Towton M. N11 . . . . . .6C 32
Towton Rd. SE27 . . . . .2C 138
Toye Av. N20 . . . . . .2G 31
Toynbec Cl. BR7: Chst 4F 143
Toynbee Rd. SW20 . . . .1G 153
Toynbee St. E1 . . . . .6J 9 (5F 85)
Toynbee Studios 7K 9
Toyne Way N6 . . . . .6D 46
Tracey Av. NW2 . . . . .5E 62
Tracey Bellamy Ct. E14 . . . . .6A 86
(off Repton St.)
Track St. E17 . . . . .5B 50
Tracy Cl. HA7: Stan 7H 27
Tracy Ho. E3 . . . . . .3B 86
(off Mile End Rd.)
Trade City Bus. Pk. TW16: Sun 1G 147
Trade Cl. N13 . . . . .4F 33
Trader Rd. E6 . . . . . .6F 89
Tradescant Ho. E9 . . . . .7J 67
(off Frampton Pk. Rd.)
Tradescant Rd. SW8 . . . . .7J 101
Tradewind Hgts. SE16 . . . .1K 103
(off Rotherhithe St.)
Tradewinds Ct. E1 . . . . .7G 85
Trading Est. Rd. NW10 . . . .4J 79
Trafalgar Av.
KT4: Wor Pk 1F 165
N17 . . . . . .6K 33
SE15 . . . . . .5F 103

Trafalgar Bldg. KT2: King T 1D 150
(off Henry Macaulay Av.)
Trafalgar Bus. Cen. IG11: Bark 4K 89
Trafalgar Chambers SW3 . . . . . .5B 16
(off South Pde.)
Trafalgar Cl. SE16 . . . . .3A 104
Trafalgar Cl. E1 . . . . .1J 103
(off Wapping Wall)
Trafalgar Gdns. E1 . . . . .5K 85
W8 . . . . . .3K 99
Trafalgar Gro. SE10 . . . . .6F 105
Trafalgar Ho. SE17 . . . . .5C 102
(off Bronti Cl.)
SW18 . . . . . .4A 118
Trafalgar M. E9 . . . . .6B 68
Trafalgar Pl. E11 . . . . .4J 51
N18 . . . . . .5B 34
Trafalgar Point N1 . . . . .7D 66
(off Downham Rd.)
Trafalgar Quarters SE10 . . . . . .6F 105
(off Park Row)
Trafalgar Rd. SE10 . . . . .6F 105
SW19 . . . . . .7K 135
TW2: Twick 2H 131
Trafalgar Square 4D 12 (1H 101)
Trafalgar Sq. SW1 . . . .4D 12 (1H 101)
WC2 . . . . . .4D 12 (1H 101)
Trafalgar St. SE17 . . . . .5D 102
Trafalgar Studios 4E 12
(off Whitehall)
Trafalgar Ter. HA1: Harr 1J 59
Trafalgar Trad. Est. EN3: Brim 4F 25
Trafalgar Way CR0: Wadd 2A 168
E14 . . . . . .1E 104
Trafford Ho. N1 . . . . . .2D 84
(off Cranston Est.)
Trafford Rd. CR7: Thor H 5K 155
Trafford Way BR3: Beck 6C 140
Traherne Lodge
TW11: Tedd 5K 131
Trahorn Cl. E1 . . . . .4H 85
Trail St. E17 . . . . .5B 50
Traitors' Gate 4J 15
Tralee Ct. SE16 . . . . .5H 103
(off Masters Dr.)
Tram Cl. SE24 . . . . .3B 120
(off Milkwood Rd.)
The Tramlink SW19 . . . .2A 154
The Tramsheds CR0: Bedd 7H 155
Tramway Av. E15 . . . . .7G 69
N9 . . . . . .7C 24
Tramway Cl. SE20 . . . .1J 157
Tramway Cl. E1 . . . . .5A 86
Tramway Path CR4: Mitc 4C 154
(not continuous)
Tranby M. E9 . . . . .5K 67
(off Brooksby's Wlk.)
Tranley M. NW3 . . . . .4C 64
(off Fleet Rd.)
Tranmere Ct. SM2: Sutt 7A 166
Tranmere Rd. N9 . . . . .7A 24
SW18 . . . . . .2A 136
TW2: Whitt 7F 113
Tranquil La. HA2: Harr 1F 59
Tranquil Pas. SE3 . . . . .2H 123
(off Montpelier Va.)
Tranquil Va. SE3 . . . . .2G 123
Transenna Works N1 . . . . . .6B 66
(off Laycock St.)
Transept St. NW1 . . . .6D 4 (5C 82)
Transmere Cl. BR5: Pet W 6G 161
Transmere Rd.
BR5: Pet W 6G 161
Transom Cl. SE16 . . . . .4A 104
Transom Sq. E14 . . . . .5D 104
Transport Av. TW8: Bford 5A 96
Tranton Rd. SE16 . . . . .3G 103
Trappes Ho. SE16 . . . . .4H 103
(off Camilla Rd.)
Traps La. KT3: N Mald 1A 152
Traq Motor Racing 6G 155
Travellers Path E6 . . . . .1B 88

Travellers Way TW4: Cran 2A 112
Travers Cl. E17 . . . . .1K 49
Travers Ho. SE10 . . . . .6F 105
(off Trafalgar Gro.)
Travers Rd. N7 . . . . .3A 66
Trays Hill Cl. N19 . . . . .7G 47
Treacy Cl. WD23: B Hea 2B 26
Treadgold Ho. W11 . . . . .7F 81
(off Bomore Rd.)
Treadgold St. W11 . . . . .7F 81
Treadway St. E2 . . . . .2H 85
Treasury Cl. SM6: W'gton 5H 167
Treasury M. DA5: Bexl 7H 127
Treasury Pas. SW1 . . . . .6E 12
Treaty Cen. 3F 113
Treaty St. N1 . . . . .1K 83
Trebeck St. W1 . . . . .4J 11 (1F 101)
Trebovir Rd. SW5 . . . . .5J 99
Treby St. E3 . . . . .4B 86
Trecastle Way N7 . . . . .4H 65
Tredegar Ho. E3 . . . . . .3C 86
(off Bow Rd.)
Tredegar M. E3 . . . . .3B 86
Tredegar Rd. E3 . . . . .2B 86
N11 . . . . . .7C 32
Tredegar Sq. E3 . . . . .3B 86
Tredegar Ter. E3 . . . . .3B 86
Trederwen Rd. E8 . . . . .1G 85
Tredown Rd. SE26 . . . . .5J 139
Tredwell Cl. BR2: Broml 4C 160
SW2 . . . . . .2K 137
Tredwell Rd. SE27 . . . . .4B 138
Treebank Gdns. W7 . . . . .7J 77
Tree Cl. TW10: Ham 1D 132
Treen Av. SW13 . . . . .3B 116
Tree Rd. E16 . . . . .6A 88
Treeside Cl. UB7: W Dray 4A 92
Treeside Pl. N10 . . . . .4F 47
Treetop Ct. CR7: Thor H 5C 156
Tree Top M. RM10: Dag 6K 73
Treetop M. NW6 . . . . .7G 63
Treetops Cl. SE2 . . . . .5E 108
Tree Vw. Cl. SE19 . . . . .1E 156
Treewall Gdns.
BR1: Broml 4K 141
Trefgarne Rd. RM10: Dag 2G 73
Trefil Wlk. N7 . . . . .4J 65
Trefoil Ho. DA18: Erith 2E 108
(off Kale Rd.)
SE10 . . . . . .4G 105
Trefoil Rd. SW18 . . . . .5A 118
Trefusis Ct. TW5: Cran 1K 111
Tregaron Av. N8 . . . . . .6J 47
Tregaron Gdns.
KT3: N Mald 4A 152
Tregarvon Rd. SW11 . . . .4E 118
Tregenna Av. HA2: Harr 4E 58
Tregenna Cl. N14 . . . . .5B 22
Tregenna Ct. HA2: Harr 4E 58
Tregonwell Ter. SE9 . . . . .4F 143
Tregony Rd.
BR6: Chels 4K 173
Trego Rd. E9 . . . . .7C 68
Tregothnan Rd. SW9 . . . .3J 119
Tregunter Rd. SW10 . . . .6K 99
Trehearn Rd. IG6: Ilf 1H 53
Treherne Ct. SW17 . . . . .4E 136
Trehern Rd. SW14 . . . .3K 115
Trehurst St. E5 . . . . .5A 68
Trelawney Est. E9 . . . . .6J 67
Trelawney Ho. SE1 . . . . .5C 14
(off Union St.)
Trelawney Rd. IG6: Ilf 1H 53
Trelawn Rd. E10 . . . . .3E 68
SW2 . . . . . .5A 120
Trelawny Cl. E17 . . . . .4D 50
Trellick Twr. W10 . . . . .4H 81
(off Golborne Rd.)
Trellis Ho. SW19 . . . . .7A 136
Trellis Sq. E3 . . . . .3B 86
Treloar Gdns. SE19 . . . .6D 138
Tremadoc Rd. SW4 . . . .4H 119

Tremaine Cl.—Troughton Rd.

Tremaine Cl. SE4 2C **122**
Tremaine Rd. SE20 2H **157**
Trematon Bldg. *N1* *2J* ***83***
(off Trematon Wlk.)
Trematon Ho. *SE11* *5K* ***19***
(off Kennings Way)
Trematon M. N1 2J **83**
Trematon Pl. TW11: Tedd 7C **132**
Trematon Wlk. *N1* *2J* ***83***
(off Trematon M.)
Tremelo Grn. RM8: Dag 1E **72**
Tremlett Gro. N19 3G **65**
Tremlett M. N19 3G **65**
Trenance Gdns. IG3: Ilf 3A **72**
Trenchard Av. HA4: Ruis 4K **57**
Trenchard Cl. HA7: Stan 6F **27**
NW9 1A **44**
Trenchard Ct. NW4 5C **44**
SM4: Mord 6J **153**
Trenchard St. SE10 5F **105**
Trenchold St. SW8 6J **101**
Trendell Ho. *E14* *6C* ***86***
(off Dod St.)
Trenear Cl. BR6: Chels 4K **173**
Trenholme Cl. SE20 7H **139**
Trenholme Rd. SE20 7H **139**
Trenholme Ter. SE20 7H **139**
Trenmar Gdns. NW10 3D **80**
Trent Av. W5 3C **96**
Trent Ct. *CR2: S Croy* *5C* ***168***
(off Nottingham Rd.)
E11 5J **51**
Trent Gdns. N14 6A **22**
Trentham Ho. W3 5K **79**
Trentham St. SW18 1J **135**
Trent Ho. KT2: King T 1D **150**
SE15 4J **121**
TRENT PARK 2A **22**
Trent Park 1K **21**
Trent Pk. EN4: Cockf 2B **22**
Trent Pk. Golf Course 4B **22**
Trent Rd. IG9: Buck H 1E **36**
SW2 5K **119**
Trent Way KT4: Wor Pk 3E **164**
UB4: Hayes 2G **75**
Trentwood Side EN2: Enf 3E **22**
Treport St. SW18 7K **117**
Tresco Cl. BR1: Broml 6G **141**
Trescoe Gdns. HA2: Harr 7C **40**
Tresco Gdns. IG3: Ilf 2A **72**
Tresco Ho. SE11 5J **19**
Tresco Rd. SE15 4H **121**
Tresham Cres. NW8 3D **4** (4C **82**)
Tresham Ho. *WC1* *5G* ***7***
(off Red Lion Sq.)
Tresham Rd. IG11: Bark 7K **71**
Tresham Wlk. E9 5J **67**
Tresidder Ho. SW4 7H **119**
Tresilian Av. N21 5E **22**
Tressell Cl. N1 7B **66**
Tressillian Cres. SE4 3C **122**
Tressillian Rd. SE4 4B **122**
Tress Pl. SE1 4A **14**
Trestis Cl. UB4: Yead 5B **76**
Treswell Rd. RM9: Dag 1E **90**
Tretawn Gdns. NW7 4F **29**
Tretawn Pk. NW7 4F **29**
Trevanion Rd. W14 4G **99**
Treve Av. HA1: Harr 7H **41**
Trevelyan Av. E12 4D **70**
Trevelyan Ct. KT3: N Mald 7A **152**
Trevelyan Cres.
HA3: Kenton 7D **42**
Trevelyan Gdns. NW10 1E **80**
Trevelyan Ho. *E2* *3K* ***85***
(off Morpeth St.)
SE5 *7B* ***102***
(off John Ruskin St.)
Trevelyan Rd. E15 4H **69**
SW17 5C **136**
Trevenna Ho. *SE23* *3K* ***139***
(off Dacres Rd.)
Trevera Ct. EN3: Pond E 4F **25**
Treveris St.
SE1 5B **14** (1B **102**)
Treversh Ct. BR1: Broml 1G **159**
Treverton St. W10 4F **81**
Treverton Towers *W10* *5F* ***81***
(off Treverton St.)
Treves Cl. N21 5E **22**
Treves Ho. *E1* *4G* ***85***
(off Vallance Rd.)
Treville St. SW15 7D **116**
Treviso Rd. SE23 2K **139**
Trevithick Cl. TW14: Felt 1H **129**
Trevithick Ho. *SE16* *4H* ***103***
(off Rennie Est.)
Trevithick St. SE8 6C **104**
Trevithick Way E3 3C **86**
Trevone Gdns. HA5: Pinn 6C **40**
Trevor Cl. BR2: Hayes 7H **159**
EN4: E Barn 6G **21**
HA3: Hrw W 7E **26**
TW7: Isle 5K **113**
UB5: N'olt 2A **76**
Trevor Cres. HA4: Ruis 4H **57**
Trevor Gdns. HA4: Ruis 4J **57**
HA8: Edg 1K **43**
UB5: N'olt 2A **76**
Trevor Pl.
SW7 7D **10** (2C **100**)
Trevor Rd. HA8: Edg 1K **43**
IG8: Wfd G 7D **36**
SW19 7G **135**
UB3: Hayes 2G **93**
Trevor Roper Cl. IG1: Ilf 2D **70**
Trevor Sq.
SW7 7E **10** (2D **100**)
Trevor St. SW7 7D **10** (2C **100**)
Trevor Wlk. *SW7* *7E* ***10***
(off Lancelot Pl.)
Trevose Ho. *SE11* *5H* ***19***
(off Orsett St.)
Trevose Rd. E17 1F **51**
Trewenna Dr.
KT9: Chess 5D **162**
Trewince Rd. SW20 1E **152**
Trewint St. SW18 2A **136**
Trewsbury Ho. SE2 1D **108**
Trewsbury Rd. SE26 5K **139**
Tria Apts. *E2* *3G* ***85***
(off Durant St.)
Triandra Way UB4: Yead 5B **76**
The Triangle *DA15: Sidc* *7A* ***126***
(off Burnt Oak La.)
E8 1H **85**
EC1 3B **8**
IG11: Bark 6G **71**
KT1: King T 2H **151**
N13 4E **32**
The Triangle Bus. Cen.
NW10 3B **80**
Triangle Cen. UB1: S'hall 1H **95**
Triangle Ct. E16 5B **88**
SE1 *5D* ***14***
(off Redcross Way)
Triangle Est. *SE11* *6J* ***19***
(off Kennington La.)
Triangle Ho. *SE1* *6J* ***15***
(off Three Oak La.)
Triangle Pas. EN4: E Barn 4F **21**
Triangle Pl. SW4 4H **119**
Triangle Rd. E8 1H **85**
Triangle Way W3 3G **97**
Triangle Works N9 2E **34**
Tribeca Apts. *E1* *6K* ***9***
(off Heneage St.)
Trickett Ho. SM2: Sutt 7K **165**
Trico Ho. *TW8: Bford* *5D* ***96***
(off Ealing Rd.)
Tricorn Ho. SE28 1J **107**
Trident Bus. Cen. SW17 5D **136**
Trident Gdns.
UB5: N'olt 3B **76**
Trident Ho. *E14* *6E* ***86***
(off Blair St.)
SE28 1H **107**
TW19: Stanw *7A* ***110***
(off Clare Rd.)
Trident Pl. *SW3* *7B* ***16***
(off Old Church St.)
Trident Point HA1: Harr 6H **41**
Trident St. SE16 4K **103**
Trident Way
UB2: S'hall 3K **93**
Trig La. EC4 2C **14** (7C **84**)
Trigon Rd. SW8 7K **101**
Trilby Rd. SE23 2K **139**
Trillo Ct. IG2: Ilf 7J **53**
Trimdon NW1 1G **83**
Trimmer Wlk.
TW8: Bford 6E **96**
Trim St. SE14 6B **104**
Trinder Gdns. N19 1J **65**
Trinder M. SW12 1E **136**
TW11: Tedd 5A **132**
Trinder Rd. EN5: Barn 5A **20**
N19 1J **65**
Tring Av. HA9: Wemb 6G **61**
UB1: S'hall 6D **76**
W5 1F **97**
Tring Cl. IG2: Ilf 5H **53**
Tring Ct. TW1: Twick 4A **132**
Trinidad Gdns. RM10: Dag 7K **73**
Trinidad Ho. *E14* *7B* ***86***
(off Gill St.)
Trinidad St. E14 7B **86**
Trinity Av. EN1: Enf 6A **24**
N2 3B **46**
Trinity Buoy Wharf E14 7G **87**
Trinity Chu. Pas. SW13 6D **98**
Trinity Chu. Rd. SW13 6D **98**
Trinity Chu. Sq.
SE1 7D **14** (3C **102**)
Trinity Cl.
BR2: Broml 1C **172**
CR2: Sande 7E **168**
E8 6F **67**
E11 2G **69**
NW3 4B **64**
SE13 4F **123**
SW4 4G **119**
TW4: Houn 4C **112**
Trinity Cotts. TW9: Rich 3F **115**
Trinity Ct. *BR1: Broml* *1H* ***159***
(off Highland Rd.)
CR0: C'don 2C **168**
EN2: Enf 2H **23**
N1 *1E* ***84***
(off Downham Rd.)
N18 6A **34**
NW2 5E **62**
SE7 4B **106**
SE8 *5A* ***104***
(off Evelyn St.)
SE25 6E **156**
SE26 3J **139**
SW9 3K **119**
W2 *6A* ***82***
(off Gloucester Ter.)
W9 *3H* ***81***
(off Croxley Rd.)
WC1 3G **7**
Trinity Cres. SW17 2D **136**
Trinity Dr. UB8: Hil 5E **74**
Trinity Gdns. E16 5H **87**
(not continuous)
SW9 4K **119**
Trinity Grn. E1 4J **85**
Trinity Gro. SE10 1E **122**
Trinity Hospital SE10 5F **105**
Trinity Ho. 2J **15**
Trinity Ho. RM8: Dag 5B **72**
SE1 *3C* ***102***
(off Bath Ter.)
W14 3H **99**
Trinity Laban ***6E 104***
(within Old Royal Naval College)
Trinity M. *E1* *5J* ***85***
(off Redman's Rd.)
SE20 1H **157**
W10 6F **81**
Trinity Pk. E4 6G **35**
Trinity Path SE26 3J **139**
(not continuous)
Trinity Pl. DA6: Bex 4F **127**
EC3 2J **15** (7F **85**)
Trinity Ri. SW2 1A **138**
Trinity Rd. IG6: Ilf 3G **53**
N2 3B **46**
N22 7D **32**
(not continuous)
SW17 4A **118**
SW18 4A **118**
SW19 6J **135**
Trinity Rd. TW9: Rich 3F **115**
UB1: S'hall 1C **94**
Trinity Sq. E14 6G **87**
EC3 3H **15** (7E **84**)
Trinity St. E16 5H **87**
EN2: Enf 2H **23**
SE1 7D **14** (2C **102**)
(not continuous)
Trinity Ter. IG9: Lough 1E **36**
Trinity Twr. *E1* *7G* ***85***
(off Vaughan Way)
E14 3D **104**
Trinity Wlk. NW3 6A **64**
Trinity Way E4 6G **35**
W3 7A **80**
Trio Pl. SE1 7D **14** (2C **102**)
Triptych Ho. *SE8* *7C* ***104***
(off Watson's St.)
Triscott Ho. UB3: Hayes 1J **93**
Tristan Ct. *SE8* *6B* ***104***
(off Dorking Cl.)
Tristan Sq. SE3 3G **123**
Tristram Cl. E17 3F **51**
Tristram Dr. N9 3B **34**
Tristram Rd. BR1: Broml 4H **141**
Triton Ct. *E16* *5J* ***87***
(off Robertson Rd.)
Triton Ho. *E14* *4D* ***104***
(off Cahir St.)
Triton Sq. NW1 3A **6** (4G **83**)
Triton St. NW1 3K **5** (4F **83**)
Tritton Av. CR0: Bedd 4J **167**
Tritton Rd. SE21 3D **138**
Triumph Cl. UB3: Harl 1E **110**
Triumph Ho. IG11: Bark 3A **90**
Triumph Rd. E6 6D **88**
Triumph Trad. Est. N17 6B **34**
Trocette Mans. *SE1* *3E* ***102***
(off Bermondsey St.)
Trojan Ct. NW6 7G **63**
Trojan Ind. Est.
NW10 6B **62**
Trojan M. SW19 7J **135**
Trojan Way
CR0: Wadd 3K **167**
Troon Cl. SE16 5H **103**
SE28 6D **90**
Troon Ho. *E1* *6A* ***86***
(off White Horse Rd.)
Troon St. E1 6A **86**
Tropical Ct. *W10* *3F* ***81***
(off Kilburn La.)
Trosley Rd. DA17: Belv 6G **109**
Trossachs Rd. SE22 5E **120**
Trothy Rd. SE1 4G **103**
Trotman Ho. *SE14* *1J* ***121***
(off Pomeroy St.)
Trott Rd. N10 7J **31**
Trott St. SW11 1C **118**
Trotwood Ho. *SE16* *2H* ***103***
(off Wilson Gro.)
Troubridge Sq. E17 3E **50**
Troughton Rd. SE7 5K **105**

Troutbeck NW1 . . . . .2K 5
Troutbeck Rd. SE14 . . .1A 122
Trout Rd. UB7: Yiew 7A 74
Trouville Rd. SW4 . . . . .6G 119
Trowbridge Est. E9 . . . . . . .6B 68
(off Osborne Rd.)
Trowbridge Ho. E9 . . . . . . .6B 68
(off Felstead St.)
Trowbridge Rd. E9 . . . . . . .6B 68
Trowlock Av. TW11: Tedd . . .6C 132
Trowlock Island
  TW11: Tedd 6D 132
Trowlock Way TW11: Tedd . . .6D 132
Troy Ct. SE18 . . . . .4F 107
  W8 .3J 99
  (off Kensington High St.)
Troy Ind. Est. HA1: Harr 5K 41
Troy Rd. SE19 . . . . .6D 138
Troy Town SE15 . . . . .3G 121
Trubshaw Rd. UB2: S'hall 3F 95
True Lovers Ct.
  HA6: Nwood 1F 39
Trueman Cl. HA8: Edg 7C 28
Truesdale Rd. E6 . . . . .6D 88
Truesdales UB10: Ick 2E 56
truGym
  Bromley 1J 159
  (off East St.)
Trulock Ct. N17 . . . . .7B 34
Trulock Rd. N17 . . . . .7B 34
Trumans Rd. N16 . . . . .5F 67
Truman Wlk. E3 . . . . .4D 86
Trumpers Way W7 . . . . .3J 95
Trumpington Rd. E7 . . . . .4H 69
Trump St. EC2 . . . .1D 14 (6C 84)
Trundle Ho. SE1 . . . . .6C 14
  (off Trundle St.)
Trundlers Way WD23: B Hea . . .1D 26
Trundle St.
  SE1 . . . . .6C 14 (2C 102)
Trundleys Rd. SE8 . . . . .5K 103
Trundley's Ter. SE8 . . . . .4K 103
Truro Gdns. IG1: Ilf 7C 52
Truro Ho. HA5: Hat E 1D 40
  W2 .5J 81
  (off Westbourne Pk. Rd.)
Truro Rd. E17 . . . . .4B 50
  N22 . . . . .7D 32
Truro St. NW5 . . . . .6E 64
Truro Way UB4: Hayes 3G 75
Truslove Rd. SE27 . . . . .5A 138
Trussley Rd. W6 . . . . .3E 98
Tryfan Cl. IG4: Ilf 5B 52
Tryon Cres. E9 . . . . .1J 85
Tryon St. SW3 . . . . .5E 16 (5D 100)
Trystings Cl.
  KT10: Clay 6A 162
Tuam Rd. SE18 . . . . .6H 107
Tubbenden Cl. BR6: Orp 3J 173
Tubbenden Dr. BR6: Orp 4H 173
Tubbenden La.
  BR6: Orp 4H 173
Tubbenden La. Sth.
  BR6: Farnb 5H 173
Tubbs Rd. NW10 . . . . .2B 80
Tucana Ct. E1 . . . . .3K 9
  (off Cygnet St.)
Tucana Hgts. E20 . . . . .5E 68
  (off Cheering La.)
Tucklow Wlk. SW15 . . . . .7B 116
Tudor Av.
  KT4: Wor Pk 3D 164
  TW12: Hamp 7E 130
Tudor Cl. BR7: Chst 1D 160
  HA5: Eastc 5J 39
  IG7: Chig 4K 37
  IG8: Wfd G 5E 36
  KT9: Chess 5E 162
  N6 .7G 47
  NW3 . . . . .5C 64
  NW7 . . . . .6H 29

Tudor Cl. NW9 . . . . .2J 61
  SM3: Cheam 5F 165
  SM6: W'gton 7G 167
  SW2 . . . . .6K 119
  TW12: Hamp H 5G 131
  TW15: Ashf 4A 128
Tudor Ct. DA14: Sidc 3A 144
  E17 .7B 50
  N1 . . . . .6E 66
  N22 . . . . .7D 32
  SE9 .4C 124
  SE16 . . . . .1K 103
  (off Princes Riverside Rd.)
  TW11: Tedd 6K 131
  TW13: Hanw 4A 130
  TW19: Stanw 6A 110
  W3 . . . . .2G 97
Tudor Ct. Nth. HA9: Wemb . . .5G 61
Tudor Ct. Sth. HA9: Wemb . . .5G 61
Tudor Cres. EN2: Enf 1H 23
Tudor Dr. KT2: King T 5D 132
  SM4: Mord 6F 153
Tudor Ent. Pk.
  HA1: Harr 3K 59
  HA3: W'stone 3H 41
Tudor Est. NW10 . . . . .2H 79
Tudor Gdns.
  BR4: W W'ck 3E 170
  HA3: Hrw W 2H 41
  NW9 . . . . .2J 61
  SW13 . . . . .3A 116
Tudor Gdns. TW1: Twick 1K 131
  W3 . . . . .5G 79
Tudor Gro. E9 . . . . .7J 67
  N20 . . . . .2H 31
Tudor Ho. E9 . . . . .7J 67
  E16 .1K 105
  (off Wesley Av.)
  HA5: Pinn 2A 40
  (off Pinner Hill Rd.)
  SE1 .5J 15
  W14 . . . . .4F 99
  (off Windsor Way)
Tudor M. E17 . . . . .4B 50
Tudor Pde. RM6: Chad H 7D 54
  SE9 .4C 124
Tudor Park Footgolf 3F 21
Tudor Pl. CR4: Mitc 7C 136
  IG9: Buck H 2H 37
  SE19 . . . . .7F 139
Tudor Rd. BR3: Beck 3E 158
  E4 . . . . .6J 35
  E6 . . . . .1A 88
  E9 . . . . .1H 85
  EN5: New Bar 3D 20
  HA3: Hrw W, W'stone 2H 41
  HA5: Pinn 2A 40
  IG11: Bark 1K 89
  KT2: King T 7G 133
  N9 . . . . .7C 24
  SE19 . . . . .7F 139
  SE25 . . . . .5H 157
  TW3: Houn 4H 113
  TW12: Hamp 7E 130
  TW15: Ashf 6F 129
  UB1: S'hall 7C 76
  UB3: Hayes 6F 75
Tudor Sq. UB3: Hayes 5F 75
Tudor Stacks SE24 . . . . .4C 120
Tudor St. EC4 . . . . . . .2K 13 (7A 84)
Tudor Wlk. DA5: Bexl 6E 126
Tudor Way BR5: Pet W 6H 161
  N14 .1C 32
  UB10: Hil 6C 56
  W3 . . . . .2G 97
Tudor Well Cl. HA7: Stan 5G 27
Tudor Works UB4: Yead 1A 94
Tudway Rd. SE3 . . . . .4A 124
Tufnell Ct. E3 . . . . .1B 86
  (off Old Ford Rd.)
TUFNELL PARK 4G 65
Tufnell Pk. Hall 3G 65

Tufnell Pk. Rd. N7 . . . . .4G 65
  N19 .4G 65
Tufton Ct. SW1 . . . . .2E 18
  (off Tufton St.)
Tufton Gdns. KT8: W Mole . . .2F 149
Tufton Rd. E4 . . . . .4H 35
Tufton St. SW1 . . . .1E 18 (3J 101)
Tugboat St. SE28 . . . . .2J 107
Tugela Rd. CR0: C'don 6D 156
Tugela St. SE6 . . . . .2B 140
Tugmutton Cl. BR6: Farnb 4F 173
Tulett Av. N20 . . . . .2G 31
Tulip Cl. CR0: C'don 1K 169
  E6 . . . . .5D 88
  TW12: Hamp 6D 130
  UB2: S'hall 2G 95
Tulip Gdns. E4 . . . . .3A 36
  IG1: Ilf 6F 71
Tullis Ho. E9 . . . . .7J 67
  (off Frampton Pk. Rd.)
Tull St. CR4: Mitc 7D 154
Tulse Cl. BR3: Beck 3E 158
TULSE HILL 1B 138
Tulse Hill SW2 . . . . .6A 120
Tulse Hill Est. SW2 . . . . .6A 120
Tulse Ho. SW2 . . . . .6A 120
Tulsemere Rd. SE27 . . . . .2C 138
Tumbling Bay
  KT12: Walt T 6J 147
Tummons Gdns. SE25 . . . . . . .2E 156
Tump Ho. SE28 . . . . .1J 107
Tunbridge Ho. EC1 . . . . .1K 7
Tuncombe Rd. N18 . . . . .4K 33
Tunis Rd. W12 . . . . .1E 98
Tunley Grn. E14 . . . . .5B 86
Tunley Rd. NW10 . . . . .1A 80
  SW17 . . . . .1E 136
Tunmarsh La. E13 . . . . .3K 87
Tunnan Leys E6 . . . . .6E 88
Tunnel App. E14 . . . . .7A 86
  SE10 . . . . .2G 105
  SE16 . . . . .2J 103
Tunnel Av. SE10 . . . . .2F 105
Tunnel Av. Trad. Est. SE10 . . .2F 105
Tunnel Gdns. N11 . . . . .7B 32
Tunnel Link Rd.
  TW6: H'row A 6C 110
Tunnel Rd. SE16 . . . . .2J 103
Tunnel Rd. E. TW6: H'row A . . .1D 110
Tunnel Rd. W.
  TW6: H'row A 1C 110
Tunstall Cl. BR6: Orp 4J 173
Tunstall Rd. CR0: C'don 1E 168
  SW9 . . . . .4A 120
Tunstall Wlk. TW8: Bford 6E 96
Tunstock Way
  DA17: Belv 3E 108
Tunworth Cl. NW9 . . . . .6J 43
Tunworth Cres. SW15 . . . . . . .6B 116
Tun Yd. SW8 . . . . .2F 119
  (off Peardon St.)
Tupelo Rd. E10 . . . . .2D 68
Tupman Ho. SE16 . . . . .2G 103
  (off Scott Lidgett Cres.)
Tuppy St. SE28 . . . . .3G 107
Turenne Cl. SW18 . . . . .4A 118
Turing St. E20 . . . . .7E 68
Turin Rd. N9 . . . . .7D 24
Turin St. E2 . . . . .2K 9 (3G 85)
Turkey Oak Cl. SE19 . . . . .1E 156
Turks Boatyard
  KT1: King T 1D 150
Turks Cl. UB8: Hil 3C 74
Turk's Head Yd.
  EC1 . . . . .5A 8 (5B 84)
Turk's Row SW3 . . . .5F 17 (5D 100)
Turle Rd. N4 . . . . .2K 65
  SW16 . . . . .2J 155
Turlewray Cl. N4 . . . . .1K 65
Turley Cl. E15 . . . . .1G 87
Turnagain La. EC4 . . . . .7A 8
Turnage Rd. RM8: Dag 1E 72

Turnant Rd. N17 . . . . .1C 48
Turnberry Cl. NW4 . . . . .2F 45
  SE16 . . . . .5H 103
Turnberry Quay E14 . . . . .3D 104
Turnberry Way BR6: Orp 1H 173
Turnbull Ho. N1 . . . . .1B 84
Turnbury Cl. SE28 . . . . .6D 90
Turnchapel M. SW4 . . . . .3F 119
Turner Av. CR4: Mitc 1D 154
  N15 .4E 48
  TW2: Twick 3G 131
Turner Cl. HA0: Wemb 6D 60
  NW11 . . . . .6K 45
  SW9 . . . . .7B 102
  UB4: Hayes 2E 74
Turner Ct. SE16 . . . . .2J 103
  (off Albion St.)
Turner Cres. CR0: C'don 6C 156
Turner Dr. NW11 . . . . .6K 45
Turner Ho. E14 . . . . .2C 104
  (off Cassilis Rd.)
  NW6 . . . . .5A 64
  (off Dresden Cl.)
  NW8 . . . . .2C 82
  (off Townshend Est.)
  SW1 .4D 18
  (off Herrick St.)
  TW1: Twick 6D 114
  (off Clevedon Rd.)
Turner M. SM2: Sutt 7K 165
Turner Pde. N1 . . . . .7A 66
  (off Barnsbury Pk.)
Turner Pl. SW11 . . . . .5C 118
Turner Rd. E17 . . . . .3E 50
  HA8: Edg 2E 42
  KT3: N Mald 7K 151
Turners Cl. N20 . . . . .3J 31
Turners Ct. E15 . . . . .4E 68
  (off Drapers Rd.)
  N15 .5D 48
Turners Mdw. Way
  BR3: Beck 1B 158
Turners Rd. E3 . . . . .5B 86
Turner St. E1 . . . . .5H 85
  E16 .6H 87
Turners Way CR0: Wadd 2A 168
Turners Wood NW11 . . . . .7A 46
Turneville Rd. W14 . . . . .6H 99
Turney Rd. SE21 . . . . .7C 120
TURNHAM GREEN 4A 98
Turnham Grn. Ter. W4 . . . . . . .4A 98
Turnham Grn. Ter. M.
  W4 . . . . .4A 98
Turnham Rd. SE4 . . . . .5A 122
Turnmill St. EC1 . . . .4A 8 (4B 84)
Turnour Ho. E1 . . . . .6H 85
  (off Walburgh St.)
Turnpike Cl. DA16: Well 3A 126
  SE8 .7B 104
Turnpike Ct. DA6: Bex 4D 126
Turnpike Ho. EC1 . . . .2B 8 (3B 84)
Turnpike La. N8 . . . . .4K 47
  SM1: Sutt 5A 166
  UB10: Uxb 3A 74
Turnpike Link CR0: C'don 2E 168
Turnpike M. N8 . . . . .3A 48
  (off Turnpike La.)
Turnpike Pde. N15 . . . . .3B 48
  (off Green Lanes)
Turnpike Way TW7: Isle 1A 114
Turnpin La. SE10 . . . . .6E 104
Turnstone Cl. E13 . . . . .3J 87
  NW9 . . . . .2A 44
  UB10: Ick 5D 56
Turnstone Ho. E1 . . . . .3K 15
  (off Star Pl.)
Turpentine La. SW1 . . .5K 17 (5F 101)
Turpin Cl. E1 . . . . .7K 85
Turpington Cl.
  BR2: Broml 7C 160
Turpington La.
  BR2: Broml 7C 160

Turpin Ho. SW11 . . . . .1F **119**
Turpin Rd. TW14: Felt 6H **111**
Turpin's La.
  IG8: Wfd G 5J **37**
Turpins Yd. NW2 . . . . .5F **63**
  SE10 .7E **104**
Turpin Way N19 . . . . .2H **65**
  SM6: W'gton 7F **167**
Turquand St. SE17 . . . . .4C **102**
Turret Gro. SW4 . . . . .3G **119**
Turton Rd. HA0: Wemb 5E **60**
Turville Ho. *NW8* *3C 4*
                  (off Grendon St.)
Turville St. E2 . . . . .3J **9** (4F **85**)
Tuscan Ho. *E2* *3J 85*
            (off Knottisford St.)
Tuscan Rd. SE18 . . . . .5H **107**
Tuscany Corte *SE13* *3D 122*
             (off Loampit Va.)
Tuscany Ho. E17 . . . . .2B **50**
  IG3: Ilf 6A **54**
Tuskar St. SE10 . . . . .6G **105**
Tussah Ho. *E2* *2J 85*
               (off Russia La.)
Tustin Est. SE15 . . . . .6J **103**
Tuttlebee La. IG9: Buck H 2D **36**
Tuttle Ho. *SW1* *6C 18*
             (off Aylesford St.)
Tweed Ct. *W7* *6J 77*
             (off Hanway Rd.)
Tweeddale Gro. UB10: Ick 3E **56**
Tweeddale Rd.
  SM5: Cars 1B **166**
Tweed Glen RM1: Rom 1K **55**
Tweed Grn. RM1: Rom 1K **55**
Tweedmouth Rd. E13 . . . . .2K **87**
Tweed Wlk. E14 . . . . .4E **86**
Tweed Way RM1: Rom 1K **55**
Tweedy Cl. EN1: Enf 5A **24**
Tweedy Rd. BR1: Broml 1J **159**
Tweezer's All. WC2 . . . . .2J **13**
Twelve Acre Ho. *E12* *3E 70*
           (off Grantham Rd.)
Twelvetrees Bus. Pk. E3 . . . . .4F **87**
Twelvetrees Cres. E3 . . . . .4E **86**
              (not continuous)
Twentyman Cl. IG8: Wfd G 5D **36**
TWICKENHAM 1A **132**
TWICKENHAM BRI. 5C **114**
Twickenham Cl.
  CR0: Bedd 3K **167**
Twickenham Gdns.
  HA3: Hrw W 7D **26**
  UB6: G'frd 5A **60**
Twickenham Mus. *1A 132*
          (off The Embankment)
Twickenham Rd. E11 . . . . .2E **68**
  TW7: Isle 5A **114**
  TW9: Rich 4C **114**
  TW11: Tedd 4A **132**
              (not continuous)
  TW13: Hanw 3D **130**
Twickenham Stadium 6J **113**
Twickenham Stoop 7J **113**
Twickenham Tourist Information Centre
  . . . .*1B 132*
              (off Church St.)
Twickenham Trad. Est.
  TW1: Twick 6K **113**
Twig Folly Cl. E2 . . . . .2K **85**
Twigg Cl. DA8: Erith 7K **109**
Twilley St. SW18 . . . . .7K **117**
Twill Way
  SM6: W'gton 2E **166**
Twin Bridges Bus. Pk.
  CR2: S Croy 6D **168**
Twine Cl. IG11: Bark 3B **90**
Twine Cl. E1 . . . . .7J **85**
Twineham Grn. N12 . . . . .4D **30**
Twine Ter. *E3* *4B 86*
             (off Ropery St.)
Twining Av. TW2: Twick 3G **131**

Twin Tumps Way
  SE28 .7A **90**
Twisden Rd. NW5 . . . . .4F **65**
Twist Ho. SE1 . . . . .3E **102**
Twitten Gro.
  BR1: Broml 3D **160**
Two Southbank Pl. *SE1* *6H 13*
              (off York Rd.)
Twybridge Way NW10 . . . . .7J **61**
Twycross M. SE10 . . . . .5G **105**
Twyford Abbey Rd.
  NW10 .3F **79**
Twyford Av. N2 . . . . .3D **46**
  W3 . . . . .7G **79**
Twyford Ct. HA0: Wemb 2E **78**
            (off Vicars Bri. Cl.)
  N10 . . . . .3E **46**
Twyford Cres. W3 . . . . .1G **97**
Twyford Ho. N5 . . . . .3B **66**
  N15 . . . .*6E 48*
             (off Chisley Rd.)
Twyford Pl. WC2 . . . . .7G **7** (6K **83**)
Twyford Rd. HA2: Harr 1F **59**
  IG1: Ilf 5G **71**
  SM5: Cars 1B **166**
Twyford Sports Cen. 1H **97**
Twyford St. N1 . . . . .1K **83**
Twynholm Mans. *SW6* *7G 99*
              (off Lillie Rd.)
Tyas Rd. E16 . . . . .4H **87**
Tyberry Rd. SW19 . . . . .3J **153**
Tyberry Rd. EN3: Enf H 3C **24**
Tyburn Ho. *NW8* *3B 4*
             (off Fisherton St.)
Tyburn La. HA1: Harr 7K **41**
Tyburn Tree (site of) 1F **11**
Tyburn Way W1 . . . . .2F **11** (7D **82**)
Tye La. BR6: Farnb 5G **173**
Tyers Est. SE1 . . . . .6G **15**
Tyer's Ga. SE1 . . . . .7G **15** (2E **102**)
Tyers St. SE11 . . . . .6G **19** (5K **101**)
Tyers Ter.
  SE11 . . . . .6G **19** (5K **101**)
Tyeshurst Cl. SE2 . . . . .5E **108**
Tygan Ho. *SM3: Cheam* *6G 165*
             (off The Broadway)
Tylecroft Rd. SW16 . . . . .2J **155**
Tylehurst Gdns.
  IG1: Ilf 5G **71**
Tyler Cl. DA8: Erith 7H **109**
  E2 . . . . .2F **85**
Tyler Ct. *SE17* *4D 102*
           (off New Paragon Wlk.)
Tyler Rd. UB2: S'hall 3F **95**
Tyler's Ct. W1 . . . . .1C **12**
Tylers Ct. E17 . . . . .4C **50**
             (off Westbury Rd.)
  HA0: Wemb 2E **78**
Tylers Path
  SM5: Cars 4D **166**
Tyler St. SE10 . . . . .5G **105**
              (not continuous)
Tylney Av. SE19 . . . . .5F **139**
              (not continuous)
Tylney Ho. *E1* *6H 85*
              (off Nelson St.)
Tylney Rd. BR1: Broml 2B **160**
  E7 . . . . .4A **70**
Tynamara *KT1: King T* *4D 150*
          (off Portsmouth Rd.)
Tynan Cl. TW14: Felt 1J **129**
Tyndale Ct. *E9* *6A 68*
            (off Brookfield Rd.)
  E14 . . . .*5D 104*
            (off Transom Sq.)
Tyndale Ho. *N1* *7B 66*
             (off Tyndale La.)
Tyndale La. N1 . . . . .7B **66**
Tyndale Mans. *N1* *7B 66*
             (off Upper St.)
Tyndale Ter. N1 . . . . .7B **66**

Tyndall Gdns. E10 . . . . .2E **68**
Tyndall Rd. DA16: Well 3K **125**
  E10 . . . . .2E **68**
Tyne Cl. *W7* *5J 77*
             (off Hanway Rd.)
Tyneham Cl. SW11 . . . . .3E **118**
Tyneham Rd. SW11 . . . . .2E **118**
Tyne Ho. KT2: King T 1D **150**
Tynemouth Cl. E6 . . . . .6F **89**
Tynemouth Dr.
  EN1: Enf 1B **24**
Tynemouth Rd.
  CR4: Mitc 7E **136**
  N15 . . . . .4F **49**
  SE18 .5J **107**
Tynemouth St. SW6 . . . . .2A **118**
Tyne St. E1 . . . . .7K **9** (6F **85**)
Tynne Ct. *E14* *4E 86*
              (off Teviot St.)
Tynsdale Rd. NW10 . . . . .7A **62**
Tynte Ct. *E9* *5A 68*
             (off Mabley St.)
Tynwald Ho. SE26 . . . . .3G **139**
Type St. E2 . . . . .2K **85**
Typhoon Way
  SM6: W'gton 7J **167**
Tyrawley Rd. SW6 . . . . .1K **117**
Tyre La. NW9 . . . . .4A **44**
Tyrell Cl. HA1: Harr 4J **59**
Tyrell Ct. SM5: Cars 4D **166**
Tyrell Ho. *BR3: Beck* *5D 140*
          (off Beckenham Hill Rd.)
Tyrian Pl. E1 . . . . .5G **85**
Tyrols Rd. SE23 . . . . .1K **139**
Tyrone Rd. E6 . . . . .2D **88**
Tyron Way DA14: Sidc 4J **143**
Tyrrell Av.
  DA16: Well 5A **126**
Tyrrell Ho. *SW1* *7B 18*
             (off Churchill Gdns.)
Tyrrell Rd. SE22 . . . . .4G **121**
Tyrrell Sq. CR4: Mitc 1C **154**
Tyrrel Way NW9 . . . . .7B **44**
Tyrwhitt Rd. SE4 . . . . .3C **122**
Tysoe St. EC1 . . . . .2K **7** (3A **84**)
Tyson Gdns. SE23 . . . . .7J **121**
Tyson Rd. SE23 . . . . .7J **121**
Tyssen Pas. E8 . . . . .6F **67**
Tyssen Rd. N16 . . . . .3F **67**
Tyssen St. E8 . . . . .6F **67**
  N1 . . . . .2E **84**
Tytherton *E2* *2J 85*
             (off Cyprus St.)
Tytherton Rd. N19 . . . . .3H **65**

U

UAL (London College of Fashion) 6H **7**
Uamvar St. E14 . . . . .5D **86**
Uber E17 . . . . .4B **50**
Uckfield Gro.
  CR4: Mitc 7E **136**
Udall St.
  SW1 . . . . .4B **18** (4G **101**)
Udimore Ho. *W10* *5E 80*
             (off Sutton Way)
Udney Pk. Rd. TW11: Tedd 6A **132**
Uffington Rd. NW10 . . . . .1C **80**
  SE27 .4A **138**
Ufford Cl. HA3: Hrw W 7A **26**
Ufford Rd. HA3: Hrw W 7A **26**
Ufford St. SE1 . . . . .6K **13** (2A **102**)
Ufton Cl. UB5: N'olt 3B **76**
Ufton Gro. N1 . . . . .7D **66**
Ufton Rd. N1 . . . . .7D **66**
              (not continuous)
Uhura Sq. N16 . . . . .3E **66**
Ujima Ct. SW16 . . . . .4J **137**
Ullathorne Rd. SW16 . . . . .4G **137**
Ulleswater Rd. N14 . . . . .3D **32**
Ullin St. E14 . . . . .5E **86**

Ullswater E18 . . . . .2J **51**
Ullswater Cl.
  BR1: Broml 7G **141**
  SW15 . . . . .4K **133**
  UB4: Hayes 2G **75**
Ullswater Ct. HA2: Harr 7E **40**
Ullswater Cres. SW15 . . . . .4K **133**
Ullswater Ho. *SE15* *6J 103*
            (off Hillbeck Cl.)
Ullswater Rd. SE27 . . . . .2B **138**
  SW13 .7C **98**
Ulster Gdns. N13 . . . . .4H **33**
Ulster Pl. NW1 . . . . .4J **5** (4F **83**)
Ulster Ter. NW1 . . . . .3H **5** (4F **83**)
Ulundi Rd. SE3 . . . . .6G **105**
Ulva Rd. SW15 . . . . .5F **117**
Ulverscroft Rd. SE22 . . . . .5F **121**
Ulverstone Rd. SE27 . . . . .2B **138**
Ulverston Rd. E17 . . . . .2F **51**
Ulysses Rd. NW6 . . . . .5H **63**
Umberston St. E1 . . . . .6G **85**
Umbria St. SW15 . . . . .6C **116**
Umbriel Pl. E13 . . . . .2J **87**
Umfreville Rd. N4 . . . . .6B **48**
Umpire Vw. HA1: Harr 5G **41**
Undercliff Rd. SE13 . . . . .3C **122**
UNDERHILL 5D **20**
Underhill EN5: Barn 5D **20**
Underhill Cl. EN5: Barn 5D **20**
Underhill Gdns. W5 . . . . .7C **78**
Underhill Ho. *E14* *5C 86*
             (off Burgess St.)
Underhill Pas. *NW1* *1F 83*
             (off Camden High St.)
Underhill Rd. SE22 . . . . .5G **121**
Underhill St. NW1 . . . . .1F **83**
Underne Av. N14 . . . . .2A **32**
Undershaft EC3 . . . . .1G **15** (6E **84**)
Undershaw Rd.
  BR1: Broml 3H **141**
The Underwood SE9 . . . . .2D **142**
Underwood CR0: New Ad 5E **170**
The Underwood Bldg. *EC1* *6C 8*
          (off Bartholomew Cl.)
Underwood Ct. *E10* *1D 68*
          (off Leyton Grange Est.)
Underwood Ho. *KT8: W Mole* *5E 148*
            (off Approach Rd.)
  W6 . . . .*3D 98*
           (off Sycamore Gdns.)
Underwood Rd. E1 . . . . .4G **85**
  E4 . . . . .5J **35**
  IG8: Wfd G 7F **37**
Underwood Row N1 . . . . . . .1D **8** (3C **84**)
Underwood St. N1 . . . . .1D **8** (3C **84**)
Undine Rd. E14 . . . . .4D **104**
Undine St. SW17 . . . . .5D **136**
Uneeda Dr.
  UB6: G'frd 1H **77**
Unex Twr. *E15* *7F 69*
             (off Station St.)
Unicorn Bldg. *E1* *7K 85*
             (off Jardine Rd.)
Unicorn Theatre 1E **102**
Unicorn Vw. EN5: Barn 6C **20**
Unicorn Works
  N17 . . . . .7D **34**
Union Cl. E11 . . . . .4F **69**
Union Cotts. E15 . . . . .7G **69**
Union Ct. EC2 . . . . .7G **9**
  SW4 . . . . .2J **119**
  TW9: Rich 5E **114**
  W9 . . . .*5J 81*
            (off Elmfield Way)
Union Dr. E1 . . . . .4K **85**
Union Gro. SW8 . . . . .2H **119**
Union Ho. CR0: C'don 7C **156**
  Union La. TW7: Isle 2A **114**
Union M. SW4 . . . . .2J **119**
Union Mills Apts. *E8* *1F 85*
             (off Samuel St.)
Union Pk. SE10 . . . . .5H **105**

Union Rd.
BR2: Broml 5B **160**
CR0: C'don 7C **156**
E17 .6B **50**
HA0: Wemb 6E **60**
N11 .6C **32**
RM7: Rush G 6K **55**
SW4 . . . . .2H **119**
SW8 . . . . .2H **119**
UB5: N'olt 2E **76**
Union Sq. N1 . . . . .1C **84**
Union St.
EN5: Barn 3B **20**
KT1: King T 2D **150**
SE1 . . . . .5A **14** (1B **102**)
Union Theatre 6B **14** (2B **102**)
Union Wlk. E2 . . . . . . .1H **9** (3E **84**)
Union Wharf N1 . . . . .1C **84**
(Arlington Av.)
N1 . . . . .2C **84**
(off Wenlock Rd.)
UB7: Yiew 1A **92**
(off Bentinck Rd.)
Union Yd. W1 . . . . . . .1K **11** (6F **83**)
Unitair Cen.
TW14: Bedf 6E **110**
United Dr. TW14: Felt 7H **111**
United Ho. SE16 . . . . .2J **103**
(off Brunel Rd.)
Unit Workshops E1 . . . . .6G **85**
(off Adler St.)
Unity Cl. CR0: New Ad 7D **170**
NW10 . . . . .6C **62**
SE19 . . . . .5C **138**
Unity Ct. SE1 . . . . .5F **103**
(off Fortune Pl.)
Unity M. NW1 . . . . .2H **83**
Unity Pl. E17 . . . . .3A **50**
Unity Ter.
HA2: Harr 1F **59**
Unity Trad. Est.
IG8: Wfd G 2B **52**
Unity Way
SE18 . . . . .3B **106**
Unity Wharf SE1 . . . . .6K **15**
(off Mill St.)
Universal Ho. UB1: S'hall 7C **76**
University Cl. NW7 . . . . .7G **29**
University College London
Art Mus. 3C **6**
(off Gower St.)
Department of Geological Collections
. . . . .4C **6**
(off Gower St.)
University College London
Bloomsbury Campus
. . . . .3C **6** (4H **83**)
The Institute of Cancer Research
. . . . .5A **100**
Institute of Neurology 4F **7**
(off Queen Sq.)
Slade School of Fine Art 3C **6**
(off Gower Ct.)
Wolfson Ho. 2B **6**
(off Stephenson Way)
University College London Medical School
Whittington Hospital Campus
. . . . .2G **65**
(within Whittington Hospital)
University Gdns. DA5: Bexl 7F **127**
University of East London
Docklands Campus 7E **88**
Stratford Campus 6G **69**
University of Greenwich
Avery Hill Campus 6G **125**
Greenwich Campus,
King William Wlk. 6F **105**
Maritime Greenwich Campus . .6E **104**
University of London
Birkbeck College 5D **6** (5H **83**)
Heythrop College 3K **99**
(off Kensington Sq.)
University of London
Institutes of Education & Advanced
Legal Studies 4D **6** (4H **83**)
School of Hygiene &
Tropical Medicine 5D **6**
School of Oriental &
African Studies 4D **6**
Senate House 5D **6** (5H **83**)
Warburg Institute 4D **6** (4H **83**)
University of London Observatory . .6G **29**
University of North London
Hornsey Rd. 4A **66**
Ladbrooke House 5C **66**
North London Campus,
Spring House 6A **66**
University of the Arts London
Camberwell College of Arts,
Peckham Rd. 1E **120**
Camberwell College of Arts,
Wilson Rd. 1E **120**
Chelsea College of Art & Design
. . . . .5D **18** (5H **101**)
London College of Communication
. . . . .4B **102**
London College of Fashion,
Curtain Rd. 3H **9**
London College of Fashion,
Golden La. 4C **8**
London College of Fashion,
Mare St. 7J **67**
Wimbledon College of Art 1G **153**
University of West London
Brentford Campus 5C **96**
Ealing Campus, Grove House . .1D **96**
Ealing Campus,
St Marys Road 1D **96**
Ealing Campus,
Spesom House 7C **78**
Ealing Campus, Vestry Hall . . .2D **96**
Ealing Campus,
Walpole House 7D **78**
University of Westminster
Cavendish Campus,
Hanson St. 5A **6** (5G **83**)
Cavendish Campus,
Lit. Titchfield St. 6A **6**
Harrow Campus 7A **42**
Marylebone Campus 5G **5** (5E **82**)
Regent Campus, Regent St. . . .7K **5**
Wells St. 7B **6**
University Pl. DA8: Erith 7J **109**
University Rd. SW19 . . . . .6B **136**
University St. WC1 . . . . .4B **6** (4G **83**)
University Way E16 . . . . .7E **88**
Unwin Av. TW14: Felt 5F **111**
Unwin Cl. SE15 . . . . .6G **103**
Unwin Cl. N2 . . . . .4C **46**
Unwin Mans. W14 . . . . .6H **99**
(off Queen's Club Gdns.)
Unwin Rd. SW7 . . . . .1A **16** (3B **100**)
TW7: Isle 3J **113**
Unwin Way HA7: Stan 7J **27**
Up at The O2 . . . . .1G **105**
Upbrook M. W2 . . . . . .1A **10** (6A **82**)
Upcerne Rd. SW10 . . . . .7A **100**
Upchurch Cl. SE20 . . . . .7H **139**
Upcott Ho. E3 . . . . .3D **86**
(off Bruce Rd.)
Upcott Ho. E9 . . . . .7J **67**
(off Frampton Pk. Rd.)
Upcroft Av. HA8: Edg 5D **28**
Updale Rd. DA14: Sidc 4K **143**
Upfield CR0: C'don 3H **169**
Upfield Rd. W7 . . . . .5K **77**
Upgrove Mnr. Way
SW2 . . . . .7A **120**
Uphall Rd. IG1: Ilf 5F **71**
Upham Pk. Rd. W4 . . . . .4A **98**
Uphill BR2: Broml 4H **159**
(off Westmoreland Rd.)
Uphill Dr. NW7 . . . . .5F **29**
NW9 . . . . .5J **43**

Uphill Gro. NW7 . . . . .4F **29**
Uphill Rd. NW7 . . . . .4F **29**
Upland M. SE22 . . . . .5G **121**
Upland Rd. CR2: S Croy 5D **168**
DA7: Bex 3F **127**
E13 . . . . .4J **87**
SE22 . . . . .5G **121**
(not continuous)
SM2: Sutt 7B **166**
The Uplands HA4: Ruis 1J **57**
Uplands BR3: Beck 2C **158**
Uplands Av. E17 . . . . .2K **49**
Uplands Bus. Pk. E17 . . . . .3K **49**
Uplands Cl. SE18 . . . . .5F **107**
SW14 . . . . .5H **115**
Uplands Ct. N21 . . . . .7F **23**
(off The Green)
Uplands End IG8: Wfd G 7H **37**
Uplands Pk. Rd. EN2: Enf 2F **23**
Uplands Rd. EN4: E Barn 1K **31**
IG8: Wfd G 7H **37**
N8 .5K **47**
RM6: Chad H 3D **54**
Uplands Way N21 . . . . .5F **23**
Upnall Ho. SE15 . . . . .6J **103**
Upney La. IG11: Bark 6J **71**
Upnor Way SE17 . . . . .5E **102**
Uppark Dr. IG2: Ilf 6G **53**
Up. Abbey Rd.
DA17: Belv 4F **109**
Up. Addison Gdns. W14 . . . . .2G **99**
Up. Bank St. E14 . . . . .1D **104**
(not continuous)
Up. Bardsey Wlk. N1 . . . . .6C **66**
(off Douglas Rd. Nth.)
Up. Belgrave St. SW1 . .1H **17** (3E **100**)
Up. Berenger Wlk.
SW10 . . . . .7B **100**
(off Worlds End Est.)
Up. Berkeley St. W1 . . . . .1E **10** (6D **82**)
Up. Beulah Hill SE19 . . . . .1E **156**
Up. Blantyre Wlk. SW10 . . . . . . .7B **100**
(off Worlds End Est.)
Up. Brighton Rd. KT6: Surb 6D **150**
Up. Brockley Rd. SE4 . . . . .3B **122**
(not continuous)
Up. Brook St. W1 . . . . . .2G **11** (7E **82**)
Upper Butts TW8: Bford 6C **96**
Up. Caldy Wlk. N1 . . . . .6C **66**
(off Caldy Wlk.)
Up. Camelford Wlk. W11 . . . . . . .6G **81**
Up. Cavendish Av. N3 . . . . .3J **45**
Up. Cheapside Pas. EC2 . . . . .1C **14**
(off Cheapside)
Up. Cheyne Row SW3 . . .7C **16** (6C **100**)
UPPER CLAPTON 2H **67**
Up. Clapton Rd. E5 . . . . .1H **67**
Up. Clarendon Wlk. W11 . . . . . . .6G **81**
(off Clarendon Rd.)
Up. Dartrey Wlk. SW10 . . . . .7A **100**
(off Worlds End Est.)
Up. Dengie Wlk. N1 . . . . .1C **84**
(off Baddow Wlk.)
Up. Dock Wlk. E16 . . . . .7G **89**
(off Frobisher Yd.)
UPPER EDMONTON 5B **34**
UPPER ELMERS END 5B **158**
Up. Elmers End Rd.
BR3: Beck 4A **158**
Up. Farm Rd. KT8: W Mole 4D **148**
Up. Feilde W1 . . . . .2G **11**
(off Park St.)
Upper Fosters NW4 . . . . .4E **44**
(off New Brent St.)
Up. Green E. CR4: Mitc 3D **154**
Up. Green W. CR4: Mitc 2D **154**
(not continuous)
Up. Grosvenor St. W1 . . . .3G **11** (7E **82**)
Up. Grotto Rd.
TW1: Twick 2K **131**
Up. Ground SE1 . . . . . .4J **13** (1A **102**)
Upper Gro. SE25 . . . . .4E **156**

Up. Grove Rd. DA17: Belv 6F **109**
Up. Gulland Wlk. N1 . . . . .7C **66**
(off Church Rd.)
UPPER HALLIFORD 4G **147**
Up. Halliford By-Pass
TW17: Shep 5G **147**
Up. Halliford Grn.
TW17: Shep 4G **147**
Up. Halliford Rd.
TW17: Shep 3G **147**
(not continuous)
Up. Hampstead Wlk. NW3 . . . . . . .4A **64**
Up. Ham Rd. KT2: King T 4D **132**
TW10: Ham 4D **132**
Up. Handa Wlk. N1 . . . . .6D **66**
(off Handa Wlk.)
Up. Hawkwell Wlk. N1 . . . . .1C **84**
(off Maldon Cl.)
UPPER HOLLOWAY 2G **65**
Up. Holly Hill Rd. DA17: Belv 5H **109**
Up. James St. W1 . . . . . .2B **12** (7G **83**)
Up. John St. W1 . . . . . . .2B **12** (7G **83**)
Up. Lismore Wlk. N1 . . . . .6C **66**
(off Clephane Rd.)
Up. Lodge W8 . . . . .1K **99**
(off Palace Grn.)
Up. Lodge M. TW12: Hamp H 6H **131**
Up. Mall W6 . . . . .5C **98**
(not continuous)
Up. Marsh SE1 . . . . . . .1H **19** (3K **101**)
Up. Montagu St. W1 . . . . .5E **4** (5D **82**)
Up. Mulgrave Rd. SM2: Cheam . . .7G **165**
Upper Nth. St. E14 . . . . .5C **86**
UPPER NORWOOD 1E **156**
Upper Pk. Rd. BR1: Broml 1K **159**
DA7: Belv 4H **109**
KT2: King T 6G **133**
N11 . . . . .5A **32**
NW3 . . . . .5D **64**
Up. Phillimore Gdns. W8 . . . . .2J **99**
Up. Ramsey Wlk. N1 . . . . .6D **66**
(off Ramsey Wlk.)
Up. Rawreth Wlk. N1 . . . . .1C **84**
(off Basire St.)
Up. Richmond Rd. SW15 . . . . . . .4B **116**
Up. Richmond Rd. W. SW14 . . . . .4G **115**
TW10: Rich 4G **115**
Upper Rd. E13 . . . . .3J **87**
SM6: W'gton 5H **167**
UPPER RUXLEY 7G **145**
Up. St Martin's La.
WC2 . . . . .2E **12** (7J **83**)
Up. Selsdon Rd.
CR2: Sande, Sels 7F **169**
Up. Sheridan Rd. DA17: Belv 4G **109**
UPPER SHIRLEY 4K **169**
Up. Shirley Rd. CR0: C'don 2J **169**
Upper Sq. TW7: Isle 3A **114**
Upper St. N1 . . . . .2A **84**
Up. Sunbury Rd. TW12: Hamp 1C **148**
Up. Sutton La. TW5: Hest 7E **94**
UPPER SYDENHAM 3H **139**
Up. Tachbrook St.
SW1 . . . . .3B **18** (4G **101**)
Up. Talbot Wlk. W11 . . . . .6G **81**
(off Talbot Wlk.)
Up. Teddington Rd.
KT1: Hamp W 7C **132**
Upper Ter. NW3 . . . . .3A **64**
Upper Thames St. EC4 . . . .2B **14** (7B **84**)
Up. Tollington Pk. N4 . . . . .1A **66**
(not continuous)
Upperton Rd. DA14: Sidc 5K **143**
Upperton Rd. E. E13 . . . . .3A **88**
Upperton Rd. W. E13 . . . . .3A **88**
UPPER TOOTING 4D **136**
Up. Tooting Pk. SW17 . . . . .2D **136**
Up. Tooting Rd. SW17 . . . . .4D **136**
Up. Town Rd. UB6: G'frd 4F **77**
Up. Tulse Hill SW2 . . . . .7K **119**
Up. Vernon Rd. SM1: Sutt 5B **166**
UPPER WALTHAMSTOW 4F **51**

Up. Walthamstow Rd. E17 . . . . .4E **50**
Up. Whistler Wlk. SW10 . . . . .7A **100**
   (off Worlds End Est.)
Up. Wickham La.
  DA16: Well 7B **108**
Up. Wimpole St. W1 . . . . . .5H **5** (5E **82**)
Up. Woburn Pl. WC1 . . . . . .2D **6** (3H **83**)
Uppingham Av.
  HA7: Stan 1B **42**
Upsdell Av. N13 . . . . .6F **33**
Upshire Ho. E17 . . . . .2B **50**
Upstairs at the Gatehouse Theatre
  . . . . .1E **64**
Upstall St. SE5 . . . . .1B **120**
UPTON
  DA6 . . . . .5D **126**
  E7 . . . . .7J **69**
Upton Av. E7 . . . . .7J **69**
Upton Cl. DA5: Bexl 6F **127**
  NW2 .3G **63**
Upton Ct. SE20 . . . . .7J **139**
   (off Blean Gro.)
Upton Dene SM2: Sutt 7K **165**
Upton Gdns. HA3: Kenton 5B **42**
Upton Hgts. E7 . . . . .7J **69**
Upton Ho. E9 . . . . .5A **68**
   (off Ward La.)
Upton La. E7 . . . . .7J **69**
Upton Lodge E7 . . . . .6J **69**
Upton Lodge Cl. WD23: Bush 1B **26**
UPTON PARK 1B **88**
Upton Pk. Boleyn Cinema 2B **88**
Upton Pk. Rd. E7 . . . . .7K **69**
Upton Rd. CR7: Thor H 2D **156**
  DA5: Bexl 4E **126**
  DA6: Bex 4E **126**
  N18 .5B **34**
  SE18 . . . . .6G **107**
  TW3: Houn 3E **112**
Upton Rd. Sth. DA5: Bexl 6F **127**
Upton Vs. DA6: Bex 4E **126**
Upway N12 . . . . .6H **31**
Upwey Ho. N1 . . . . .1E **84**
Upwood Rd. SE12 . . . . .6J **123**
  SW16 . . . . .1J **155**
Urbanest King's Cross N1 . . . . . . .1J **83**
Urban M. N4 . . . . .6B **48**
The Urdang 2K **7**
   (off Rosebery Av.)
Urlwin St. SE5 . . . . .6C **102**
Urlwin Wlk. SW9 . . . . .1A **120**
Urmston Dr. SW19 . . . . .1G **135**
Urmston Ho. E14 . . . . .4E **104**
   (off Seyssel St.)
Urquhart Ct. BR3: Beck 7B **140**
Ursa Mans. E20 . . . . .5E **68**
   (off Cheering La.)
Ursula Gould Way E14 . . . . .5C **86**
Ursula Lodges DA14: Sidc 5B **144**
Ursula M. N4 . . . . .1C **66**
Ursula St. SW11 . . . . .1C **118**
Urswick Gdns.
  RM9: Dag 7E **72**
Urswick Rd. E9 . . . . .5J **67**
  RM9: Dag 7D **72**
Usborne M. SW8 . . . . .7K **101**
Usher Hall NW4 . . . . .4D **44**
   (off The Burroughs)
Usher Rd. E3 . . . . .1B **86**
   (not continuous)
Usk Rd. SW11 . . . . .4A **118**
Usk St. E2 . . . . .3K **85**
Utah Bldg. SE13 . . . . .1D **122**
   (off Deal's Gateway)
Utopia Village NW1 . . . . .7E **64**
Uvedale Rd. EN2: Enf 5J **23**
  RM10: Dag 3G **73**
Uverdale Rd. SW10 . . . . .7A **100**
UXBRIDGE 1A **74**
Uxbridge Ct. KT1: King T 5D **150**
   (off Uxbridge Rd.)
Uxbridge Golf Course 2A **56**

Uxbridge Lido 6A **56**
Uxbridge Rd. HA3: Hrw W 7A **26**
  HA5: Hat E, Pinn 2A **40**
  HA7: Stan 7A **26**
  KT1: King T 4D **150**
  TW12: Hamp, Hamp H 4E **130**
  TW13: Felt 2A **130**
  UB1: S'hall 1E **94**
  UB4: Hayes, Yead 5G **75**
  UB10: Hil 3C **74**
  W3 . . . . .7E **78**
  W5 . . . . .7E **78**
  W7 . . . . .1K **95**
  W12 .1C **98**
  W13 .1B **96**
Uxbridge Rd. Retail Pk. 7A **76**
Uxbridge St. W8 . . . . .1J **99**
Uxendon Cres. HA9: Wemb 1E **60**
Uxendon Hill HA9: Wemb 1F **61**

V

Vaine Ho. E9 . . . . .6A **68**
Vaizeys Wharf SE7 . . . . .3K **105**
Valance Av. E4 . . . . .1B **36**
Valan Leas BR2: Broml 3G **159**
The Vale CRO: C'don 2K **169**
  HA4: Ruis 4A **58**
  IG8: Wfd G 7D **36**
  N10 .1E **46**
  N14 .7C **22**
  NW11 . . . . .3F **63**
  SW3 . . . . .7A **16** (6B **100**)
  TW5: Hest 6C **94**
  TW14: Felt 6K **111**
  TW16: Sun 6J **129**
  W3 . . . . .1K **97**
Vale Cl. BR6: Farnb 4E **172**
  N2 . . . . .3D **46**
  TW1: Twick 3A **132**
  W9 . . . . .3A **82**
Vale Cotts. SW15 . . . . .3A **134**
Vale Ct. EN5: New Bar 4E **20**
  W3 . . . . .1B **98**
  W9 . . . . .3A **82**
Vale Cres. SW15 . . . . .4A **134**
Vale Cft. HA5: Pinn 5C **40**
Vale Dr. EN5: Barn 4C **20**
Vale End SE22 . . . . .4F **121**
The Vale Est. W3 . . . . .1A **98**
Vale Farm Sports Cen. 4B **60**
Vale Gro. N4 . . . . .7C **48**
  W3 . . . . .2K **97**
Vale La. W3 . . . . .5G **79**
Vale Lodge SE23 . . . . .2J **139**
Vale Rd. EN5: New Bar 5E **20**
  W3 . . . . .1B **98**
  W9 . . . . .3A **82**
Valence Av. RM8: Dag 1D **72**
Valence Cir. RM8: Dag 3D **72**
Valence House Mus. 3E **72**
Valence Rd. DA8: Erith 7K **109**
Valence Wood Rd.
  RM8: Dag 3D **72**
Valencia Cl. E14 . . . . .6F **87**
Valencia Rd. HA7: Stan 4H **27**
Valencia Tower EC1 . . . . .1C **8**
   (off Bollinder Place)
Valentia Pl. SW9 . . . . .4A **120**
Valentina Av. NW9 . . . . .2B **44**
Valentine Av. DA5: Bexl 2E **144**
Valentine Ct. SE23 . . . . .2K **139**
   (not continuous)
Valentine Ho. E3 . . . . .1B **86**
   (off Garrison Rd.)
Valentine Pl. SE1 . . . . .6A **14** (2B **102**)
Valentine Rd. E9 . . . . .6K **67**
  HA2: Harr 3F **59**
Valentine Row SE1 . . . . . .7A **14** (2B **102**)
Valentines Mansion & Gdns. 7E **52**
Valentines Rd. IG1: Ilf 1F **71**
Valentine's Way
  RM7: Rush G 2K **73**
VALE OF HEALTH 3A **64**

Vale of Health NW3 . . . . .3B **64**
Vale Pde. SW15 . . . . .3A **134**
Valerian Wlk. N11 . . . . .2K **31**
Valerian Way E15 . . . . .3G **87**
Valerie Ct. SM2: Sutt 7K **165**
  WD23: Bush 1B **26**
Valerio M. N1 . . . . .6D **66**
Vale Ri. NW11 . . . . .1H **63**
Vale Rd. BR1: Broml 1E **160**
  CR4: Mitc 3H **155**
  E7 . . . . .6K **69**
  KT4: Wor Pk 3B **164**
  KT19: Ewe 4B **164**
  N4 . . . . .7C **48**
  SM1: Sutt 4K **165**
Vale Rd. Nth. KT6: Surb 2E **162**
Vale Rd. Sth. KT6: Surb 2E **162**
Vale Row N5 . . . . .3B **66**
Vale Royal N7 . . . . .7J **65**
Vale Royal Ho. WC2 . . . . .2D **12**
   (off Charing Cross Rd.)
Valery Pl. TW12: Hamp 7E **130**
Valeside Ct. EN5: New Bar 4E **20**
Vale St. SE27 . . . . .3D **138**
Valeswood Rd.
  BR1: Broml 5H **141**
Vale Ter. N4 . . . . .6C **48**
Valetta Gro. E13 . . . . .2J **87**
Valetta Ho. SW11 . . . . .7F **101**
Valetta Rd. W3 . . . . .2A **98**
Valette Ct. N10 . . . . .4F **47**
   (off St James's La.)
Valette Ho. E9 . . . . .6J **67**
Valette St. E9 . . . . .6J **67**
   (off Needleman St.)
Valiant Cl. RM7: Mawney 2H **55**
  UB5: N'olt 3B **76**
Valiant Ho. E14 . . . . .2E **104**
   (off Plevna St.)
  SE7 .5A **106**
Valiant Path NW9 . . . . .7F **29**
Valiant Way E6 . . . . .5D **88**
Vallance Rd. E1 . . . . .3G **85**
  E2 . . . . .3G **85**
  N22 .2G **47**
Vallentin Rd. E17 . . . . .4E **50**
The Valley 5A **106**
Valley Av. N12 . . . . .4G **31**
Valley Cl. HA5: Pinn 2K **39**
Valley Dr. NW9 . . . . .6G **43**
Valleyfield Rd. SW16 . . . . .5K **137**
Valley Flds. Cres. EN2: Enf 2F **23**
Valley Gdns.
  HA0: Wemb 7F **61**
  SW19 . . . . .7B **136**
Valley Gro. SE7 . . . . .5A **106**
Valley Leisure Pk. 1J **167**
Valleylink Est.
  EN3: Pond E 6F **25**
Valley M. TW1: Twick 2K **131**
Valley Point Ind. Est.
  CR0: Bedd 7J **155**
Valley Rd. BR2: Broml 2H **159**
  BR5: St P 7B **144**
  DA8: Erith 4J **109**
  DA17: Belv 4H **109**
  SW16 . . . . .5K **137**
  UB10: Uxb 2A **74**
Valley Side E4 . . . . .2H **35**
  SE7 .5B **106**
Valley Side Pde. E4 . . . . .2H **35**
Valley Vw. EN5: Barn 6B **20**
Valley Wlk. CR0: C'don 2J **169**
Valliers Wood Rd.
  DA15: Sidc 1J **143**
Vallings Pl. KT6: Surb 7B **150**
Vallis Way KT9: Chess 4D **162**
  W13 .5A **78**
Val McKenzie Av. N7 . . . . .3A **66**
Valmar Rd. SE5 . . . . .1C **120**
Valmar Trad. Est. SE5 . . . . .1C **120**
Valnay St. SW17 . . . . .5D **136**

Valognes Av. E17 . . . . .1A **50**
Valois Ho. SE1 . . . . .3F **103**
   (off St Saviour's Est.)
Valonia Gdns. SW18 . . . . .6H **117**
Vambery Rd. SE18 . . . . .6G **107**
Vamey Ct. BR1: Broml 3J **159**
V&A Mus. of Childhood 3J **85**
Vanbrough Cres.
  UB5: N'olt 1A **76**
Vanbrugh Castle SE10 . . . . .6G **105**
   (off Maze Hill)
Vanbrugh Cl. E16 . . . . .5B **88**
Vanbrugh Ct. SE11 . . . . .4K **19**
Vanbrugh Dr. KT12: Walt T 7A **148**
Vanbrugh Flds. SE3 . . . . .6H **105**
Vanbrugh Hill SE3 . . . . .5H **105**
  SE10 . . . . .5H **105**
Vanbrugh Ho. E9 . . . . .7J **67**
   (off Loddiges Rd.)
Vanbrugh M. E15 . . . . .4G **69**
  KT12: Walt T 7A **148**
Vanbrugh Pk. SE3 . . . . .7H **105**
Vanbrugh Pk. Rd. SE3 . . . . .7H **105**
Vanbrugh Pk. Rd. W. SE3 . . . . . .7H **105**
Vanbrugh Rd. W4 . . . . .3K **97**
Vanbrugh Ter. SE3 . . . . .1H **123**
Vanburgh Cl. BR6: Orp 1J **173**
Vanburgh Ho. E1 . . . . .5J **9**
   (off Folgate St.)
Vancouver Cl. BR6: Chels 4K **173**
Vancouver Ho. E1 . . . . .1H **103**
   (off Reardon Path)
  SE16 . . . . .2K **103**
   (off Needleman St.)
Vancouver Mans. HA8: Edg 1H **43**
Vancouver Rd. HA8: Edg 1H **43**
  SE23 . . . . .2A **140**
  TW10: Ham 4C **132**
  UB4: Yead 4K **75**
Vanderbilt Rd. SW18 . . . . .1K **135**
Vanderbilt Vs. W12 . . . . .2F **99**
   (off Sterne St.)
Vandervell Ct. W3 . . . . .2A **98**
   (off Amber Way)
Vanderville Gdns. N2 . . . . .2B **46**
Vandome Cl. E16 . . . . .6K **87**
Vandon Ct. SW1 . . . . .1B **18**
   (off Petty France)
Vandon Pas. SW1 . . . . . . .1B **18** (3G **101**)
Vandon St. SW1 . . . . .1B **18** (3G **101**)
Van Dyck Av.
  KT3: N Mald 7K **151**
Vandyke Cl. SW15 . . . . .7F **117**
Vandyke Cross SE9 . . . . .5C **124**
Vandy St. EC2 . . . . .4G **9** (4E **84**)
Vane Cl. HA3: Kenton 6F **43**
  NW3 .5B **64**
Vanessa Cl. DA17: Belv 5G **109**
Vanessa Way DA5: Bexl 3K **145**
Vane St. SW1 . . . . .3B **18** (4G **101**)
Vange Ho. W10 . . . . .5E **80**
   (off Sutton Way)
Van Gogh Cl. TW7: Isle 3A **114**
Van Gogh Ct. E14 . . . . .3F **105**
Vanguard NW9 . . . . .7F **29**
Vanguard Bldg. E14 . . . . .2B **104**
Vanguard Cl.
  CR0: C'don 1B **168**
  E16 . . . . .5J **87**
  RM7: Mawney 2G **55**
Vanguard Ct. SE5 . . . . .1E **120**
Vanguard Ho. E8 . . . . .7H **67**
Vanguard St. SE8 . . . . .1C **122**
Vanguard Way
  SM6: W'gton 7J **167**
  TW6: H'row A 2G **111**
Vanilla & Sesame Ct. SE1 . . . . . . .6K **15**
   (off Curlew St.)
Vanneck Sq. SW15 . . . . .5C **116**
Vanoc Gdns. BR1: Broml 4J **141**
Vanquish Cl. TW2: Whitt 7E **112**
Vansittart Rd. E7 . . . . .4H **69**

Vansittart St.—Vicarage Dr.

Vansittart St. SE14 7A 104
Vanstone Ct. N7 6A 66
(off Blackthorn Av.)
Vanston Pl. SW6 7J 99
Vantage Bldg. UB3: Hayes 3H 93
(off Station App.)
Vantage Ct. UB3: Harl 7G 93
Vantage M. E14 1E 104
(off Coldharbour)
Vantage Pl. TW14: Felt 6J 111
W8 3J 99
Vantage Point BR3: Beck 1F 159
(off Albemarle Rd.)
CR2: Sande 7D 168
EN5: Barn 4C 20
(off Victors Way)
Vantage W. TW8: Bford 4F 97
Vantrey Ho. SE11 4J 19
Vant Rd. SW17 5D 136
Varcoe Gdns.
UB3: Hayes 6F 75
Varcoe Rd. SE16 5H 103
Vardens Rd. SW11 4B 118
Varden St. E1 6H 85
Vardon Cl. W3 6K 79
Varley Dr. TW1: Isle 4B 114
Varley Ho. NW6 1J 81
SE1 3C 102
(off County St.)
Varley Pde. NW9 4A 44
Varley Rd. E16 6K 87
Varley Way CR4: Mitc 2B 154
Varna Rd. SW6 7G 99
TW12: Hamp 1F 149
Varndell St. NW1 1A 6 (3G 83)
Varnishers Yd. N1 1F 7
(off York Way)
Varsity Dr. TW1: Twick 5J 113
Varsity Row SW14 2J 115
Vartry Rd. N15 6D 48
Vascroft Est. NW10 4H 79
Vassall Ho. E3 3A 86
(off Antill Rd.)
Vassall Rd. SW9 7A 102
Vat Ho. SW8 7J 101
(off Rita Rd.)
Vauban Est. SE16 3F 103
Vauban St. SE16 3F 103
Vaudeville Theatre 3F 13
(off Strand)
Vaughan Almshouses
TW15: Ashf 5D 128
(off Feltham Hill Rd.)
Vaughan Av. NW4 5C 44
W6 4B 98
Vaughan Cl. TW12: Hamp 6C 130
Vaughan Est. E2 1J 9
Vaughan Gdns. IG1: Ilf 7D 52
Vaughan Ho. SE1 6A 14
(off Blackfriars Rd.)
SW4 7G 119
Vaughan Rd. DA16: Well 2K 125
E15 6H 69
HA1: Harr 6G 41
KT7: T Ditt 7B 150
SE5 2C 120
Vaughan St. SE16 2B 104
Vaughan Way E1 7G 85
Vaughan Williams Cl.
SE8 7C 104
Vaughn St. RM8: Dag 1E 72
VAUXHALL 5H 19 (6J 101)
Vauxhall Bri. SW1 6E 18 (5J 101)
Vauxhall Bri. Rd.
SW1 2A 18 (3G 101)
Vauxhall City Farm 6G 19
VAUXHALL CROSS 5J 101
Vauxhall Gdns.
CR2: S Croy 6C 168
Vauxhall Gro.
SW8 7G 19 (6K 101)
Vauxhall St. SE11 5H 19 (5K 101)
Vauxhall Wlk.
SE11 5G 19 (5K 101)
VauxWall East Climbing Centre 4K 101
VauxWall West Climbing Centre 7F 19
(off Sth. Lambeth Rd.)
Vawdrey Cl. E1 4J 85
Veals Mead CR4: Mitc 1C 154
Vectis Gdns. SW17 6F 137
Vectis Rd. SW17 6F 137
Veda Rd. SE13 4C 122
Vega Ho. E20 5E 68
(off Prize Wlk.)
Vega Rd. WD23: Bush 1B 26
Veitch Cl. TW14: Felt 7H 111
Veldene Way HA2: Harr 3D 58
Velde Way SE22 5E 120
Velletri Ho. E2 2K 85
(off Mace St.)
Vellum Ct. E17 2A 50
Vellum Dr. SM5: Cars 3E 166
Velodrome
Queen Elizabeth Olympic Pk. 5D 68
Velo Ho. E17 5B 50
(off Track St.)
Velo Pl. E20 5D 68
Velvet Ho. E2 2F 85
(off Whiston Rd.)
Venables Cl. RM10: Dag 4H 73
Venables St. NW8 5B 4 (4B 82)
Vencourt Pl. W6 4C 98
The Veneer Bldg. 2G 93
Venerable Ho. E3 4B 86
(off Portia Way)
Venetian Ho. E20 6D 68
(off Victory Pde.)
Venetian Rd. SE5 2C 120
Venetia Rd. N4 6B 48
W5 2D 96
Venice Corte SE13 3E 122
(off Elmira St.)
Venice Ct. SE5 7C 102
(off Bowyer St.)
Venice Ho. HA0: Wemb 1E 78
Venice Wlk. W2 5A 82
Venner Rd. SE26 6J 139
(not continuous)
Venners Cl. DA7: Bex 2K 127
Venn Ho. N1 1K 83
(off Barnsbury Est.)
Venn St. SW4 4G 119
Ventnor Av. HA7: Stan 1B 42
Ventnor Dr. N20 3E 30
Ventnor Gdns.
IG11: Bark 6J 71
Ventnor Rd. SE14 7K 103
SM2: Sutt 7K 165
Venture Cl. DA5: Bexl 7E 126
Venture Ct. SE1 7H 15
(off Market Yd. M.)
SE12 7J 123
Venture Ho. W10 6F 81
(off Bridge Cl.)
Venue St. E14 5E 86
Venus Ho. E3 1C 86
(off Garrison Rd.)
E14 4C 104
(off Westferry Rd.)
Venus M. CR4: Mitc 3C 154
Venus Rd. SE18 3D 106
Vera Av. N21 5F 23
Vera Ct. E3 3D 86
(off Grace Pl.)
Vera Lynn Cl. E7 4J 69
Vera Rd. SW6 1G 117
Verbena Cl.
E16 4H 87
UB7: W Dray 1E 174
Verbena Gdns. W6 5C 98
Verdant Ct. SE6 7G 123
(off Verdant La.)
Verdant La. SE6 7G 123
Verdayne Av.
CR0: C'don 2K 169
Verdi Cres. W10 2G 81
Verdon Roe Ct. E4 3J 35
Verdun Rd. SE18 6A 108
SW13 6C 98
Vere Ct. W2 6K 81
(off Westbourne Gdns.)
Vereker Dr. TW16: Sun 3J 147
Vereker Rd. W14 5G 99
Vere St. W1 1J 11 (6F 83)
Veridion Way
DA18: Erith 2F 109
Veritas Ho. DA14: Sidc 2A 144
(off Jubilee Way)
Verity Cl. W11 7G 81
Verity Ho. E3 3B 86
(off Merchant St.)
Vermeer Ct. E14 3F 105
Vermeer Gdns. SE15 4J 121
Vermilion Apts. E3 1A 86
(off Gunmaker's La.)
Vermont Cl. EN2: Enf 4G 23
Vermont Ho. E17 2B 50
Vermont Rd.
SE19 6D 138
SM1: Sutt 3K 165
SW18 6K 117
Verna Ho. E20 5E 68
(off Sunrise Cl.)
Verney Gdns. RM9: Dag 4E 72
Verney Ho. NW8 3B 4
Verney Rd. RM9: Dag 4E 72
(not continuous)
SE16 6G 103
Verney St. NW10 3K 61
Verney Way SE16 5H 103
Vernham Rd. SE18 6G 107
Vernon Av. E12 4D 70
IG8: Wfd G 7E 36
SW20 2F 153
Vernon Cl. KT19: Ewe 6J 163
TW19: Stanw 1A 128
Vernon Ct. HA7: Stan 1B 42
NW2 3H 63
W5 7C 78
Vernon Cres.
EN4: E Barn 6K 21
Vernon Dr. HA7: Stan 1A 42
Vernon Ho. SE11 6H 19
WC1 6F 7
(off Vernon Pl.)
Vernon Mans. W14 6H 99
(off Queen's Club Gdns.)
Vernon M. E17 5B 50
W14 4G 99
Vernon Pl. WC1 6F 7 (5J 83)
Vernon Ri. UB6: G'frd 5H 59
WC1 1H 7 (3K 83)
Vernon Rd. E3 2B 86
E11 1G 69
E15 7G 69
E17 5B 50
IG3: Ilf 1K 71
N8 3A 48
SM1: Sutt 5A 166
SW14 3K 115
TW13: Felt 2H 129
Vernon Sq. WC1 1H 7 (3K 83)
Vernon St. W14 4G 99
Vernon Yd. W11 7H 81
Veroan Rd. DA7: Bex 2E 126
Verona Ct. SE14 6K 103
(off Myers La.)
TW15: Ashf 4D 128
W4 5A 98
Verona Dr. KT6: Surb 2E 162
Verona Ho. CR4: Mitc 3F 155
(off Aventine Av.)
Verona Rd. E7 7J 69
Veronica Gdns. SW16 1G 155
Veronica Ho. E3 3D 86
(off Talwin St.)
SE4 3B 122
Veronica Rd. SW17 2F 137
Veronique Gdns. IG6: Ilf 5G 53
Verran Rd. SW12 7F 119
Versailles Rd. SE20 7G 139
Verulam Av. E17 6B 50
Verulam Bldgs. WC1 5H 7
Verulam Ct. NW9 7C 44
UB1: S'hall 6G 77
(off Haldane Rd.)
Verulam Ho. W6 2E 98
(off Hammersmith Gro.)
Verulam Rd. UB6: G'frd 4E 76
Verulam St. WC1 5J 7 (5A 84)
Vervian Ho. SE15 7G 103
(off Reddins Rd.)
Verwood Dr. EN4: Cockf 3J 21
Verwood Ho. SW8 7K 101
(off Cobbett St.)
Verwood Lodge E14 3F 105
(off Manchester Rd.)
Verwood Rd. HA2: Harr 2G 41
Veryan Ct. N8 5H 47
Vesage Ct. EC1 6K 7
Vesey Path E14 6D 86
Vespan Rd. W12 2C 98
Vespucci Court E14 5A 86
(off Oman Way)
Vesta Ct. SE1 7G 15
Vesta Ho. E3 1C 86
(off Garrison Rd.)
E20 5E 68
(off Liberty Bri. Rd.)
Vesta Rd. SE4 2A 122
Vestris Rd. SE23 2K 139
Vestry Ct. RM7: Rush G 6K 55
SW1 2D 18
(off Monck St.)
Vestry House Mus. 4D 50
Vestry M. SE5 1E 120
SW18 5B 118
Vestry Rd. E17 4D 50
SE5 1E 120
Vestry St. N1 1E 8 (3D 84)
Vesuvius Apts. E3 2B 86
(off Centurion La.)
Vevey St. SE6 2B 140
Veysey Gdns. RM10: Dag 3G 73
The Viaduct E18 2J 51
N10 4F 47
Viaduct Bldgs. EC1 6K 7 (5A 84)
Viaduct Gdns. SW11 7D 18 (6H 101)
(Ace Way)
SW11 7G 101
(Nine Elms La.)
Viaduct Pl. E2 3H 85
Viaduct Rd. N2 2B 46
Viaduct St. E2 3H 85
Vian St. SE13 3D 122
Viant Ho. NW10 7K 61
(off Fawood Av.)
Vibart Gdns. SW2 7K 119
Vibart Wlk. N1 1J 83
(off Outram Pl.)
Vibeca Apts. E1 6K 9
(off Chicksand St.)
Vibia Cl. TW19: Stanw 7A 110
Vicarage Av. SE3 7J 105
Vicarage Cl. DA8: Erith 6J 109
HA4: Ruis 7F 39
KT4: Wor Pk 1A 164
UB5: N'olt 7D 58
Vicarage Ct. BR3: Beck 3A 158
IG1: Ilf 5F 71
TW14: Bedf 7E 110
W8 2K 99
Vicarage Cres. SW11 1B 118
Vicarage Dr. BR3: Beck 1C 158
IG11: Bark 7G 71
SW14 5K 115

Vicarage Farm Ct. TW5: Hest 7D **94**
Vicarage Farm Rd.
  TW3: Houn 2C **112**
  TW5: Hest 1C **112**
Vicarage Flds. KT12: Walt T 6A **148**
Vicarage Fld. Shop. Cen. 7G **71**
Vicarage Gdns.
  CR4: Mitc 3C **154**
  SW14 .5J **115**
  W8 . . . . .1J **99**
Vicarage Ga. W8 . . . . .1K **99**
Vicarage Gro. SE5 . . . . .1D **120**
Vicarage Ho. *KT1: King T* *2F 151*
  (off Cambridge Rd.)
Vicarage La. E6 . . . . .3D **88**
  E15 . . . . .7G **69**
  IG1: Ilf .1H **71**
  KT17: Ewe 7C **164**
  (not continuous)
Vicarage M. NW9 . . . . .2K **61**
  W4 . . . .*6A 98*
  (off Bennett St.)
Vicarage Pde. N15 . . . . .4C **48**
Vicarage Pk. SE18 . . . . .5G **107**
Vicarage Path N8 . . . . .7J **47**
Vicarage Rd. CR0: Wadd 3A **168**
  DA5: Bexl 1H **145**
  E10 . . . . .7C **50**
  E15 . . . . .7H **69**
  IG8: Wfd G 7H **37**
Vicarage Rd. KT1: Hamp W 1C **150**
  KT1: King T 2D **150**
  N17 . . . . .1G **49**
  NW4 . . . . .6C **44**
  RM10: Dag 7H **73**
  SE18 .5G **107**
  (not continuous)
  SM1: Sutt 3K **165**
  SW14 .5J **115**
  TW2: Twick 2J **131**
  TW2: Whitt 6G **113**
  TW11: Tedd 5A **132**
  TW16: Sun 5H **129**
Vicarage Wlk.
  KT12: Walt T 7J **147**
  SW11 .1B **118**
Vicarage Way HA2: Harr 7E **40**
  NW10 .3K **61**
Vicars Bri. Cl. HA0: Wemb 2E **78**
Vicar's Cl. E9 . . . . .1J **85**
Vicars Cl. E15 . . . . .1J **87**
  EN1: Enf 2K **23**
Vicar's Hill SE13 . . . . .4D **122**
Vicars Moor La. N21 . . . . .7F **23**
Vicars Oak Rd. SE19 . . . . .6E **138**
Vicar's Rd. NW5 . . . . .5E **64**
Vicars Wlk. RM8: Dag 3B **72**
Vicary Ho. *EC1* *6C 8*
  (off Bartholomew Cl.)
Vicentia Ct. SW11 . . . . .3A **118**
Viceroy Cl. *N2* *4C 46*
  (off East End Rd.)
Viceroy Ct. CR0: C'don 1D **168**
  NW8 . . . .*2C 82*
  (off Prince Albert Rd.)
Viceroy Pde. *N2* *4C 46*
  (off High Rd.)
Viceroy Rd. SW8 . . . . .1J **119**
Vicinity Ho. *E14* *7C 86*
  (off Storehouse St.)
Vic Johnson Ho. *E3* *1B 86*
  (off Armagh Rd.)
Vickers Cl. SM6: W'gton 7K **167**
Vickers Ct. N17 . . . . .3H **49**
  SE20 .7K **139**
  TW19: Stanw *6A 110*
  (off Whitley Cl.)
Vickers Rd. DA8: Erith 5K **109**
Vickers Way TW4: Houn 5C **112**
Vickery Ct. *EC1* *3D 8*
  (off Mitchell St.)
Vickery's Wharf E14 . . . . .6C **86**

Victor Cazalet Ho. *N1* *1B 84*
  (off Gaskin St.)
Victor Gro. HA0: Wemb 7E **60**
Victor Ho. SE7 . . . . .4A **106**
Victoria & Albert Mus.
   . . . . .2B **16** (3B **100**)
Victoria Arc. *SW1* *2K 17*
  (off Victoria St.)
Victoria Av. E6 . . . . .1B **88**
  EC2 . . . . .6H **9** (5E **84**)
  EN4: E Barn 4G **21**
  HA9: Wemb 6H **61**
  KT6: Surb 6D **150**
  KT8: W Mole 3F **149**
  N3 . . . . .1H **45**
  SM6: W'gton 3E **166**
  TW3: Houn 5E **112**
  UB10: Hil 6D **56**
Victoria Bldgs. *E8* *1H 85*
  (off Mare St.)
Victoria Chambers *EC2* *3G 9*
  (off Paul St.)
Victoria Cl. EN4: E Barn 4G **21**
  HA1: Harr 6K **41**
  KT8: W Mole 3E **148**
  SE22 .5G **121**
  UB3: Hayes 6F **75**
Victoria Colonnade *WC1* *6F 7*
  (off Southampton Row)
Victoria Cotts. *E1* *5G 85*
  (off Deal St.)
  N10 . . . . .2E **46**
  TW9: Kew 1F **115**
Victoria Ct. E18 . . . . .3K **51**
  HA7: Stan *7J 27*
  (off Howard Rd.)
  HA9: Wemb 6G **61**
  SE1 . . . .*4E 102*
  (off Hendre Rd.)
  SE26 .6J **139**
  W3 . . . . .2G **97**
Victoria Cres. N15 . . . . .5E **48**
  SE19 .6E **138**
  SW19 .7H **135**
Victoria Dock Rd. E16 . . . . .7H **87**
Victoria Dr. SW19 . . . . .7F **117**
Victoria Emb.
  EC4 . . . . .6F **13** (7K **83**)
  SW1 . . . . .6F **13** (2J **101**)
  WC2 . . . . .6F **13** (2J **101**)
Victoria Embankment Gardens
  WC2 . . . . .4F **13**
Victoria Gdns. TW5: Hest 1C **112**
  W11 . . . . .1J **99**
Victoria Gro. N12 . . . . .5G **31**
  W8 . . . . .3A **100**
Victoria Gro. M. *W2* *7J 81*
Victoria Hall *E16* *1J 105*
  (off Wesley Av.)
Victoria Ho. E6 . . . . .6E **88**
  HA8: Edg 6C **28**
  SE16 . . . .*2J 103*
  (off Surrey Quays Rd.)
  SW1 . . . .*5J 17*
  (off Ebury St.)
  SW1 . . . .*3B 18*
  (off Francis St.)
  SW8 . . . .*7J 101*
  (off Sth. Lambeth Rd.)
Victoria Ind. Est. W3 . . . . .5A **80**
Victoria La. EN5: Barn 4C **20**
  UB3: Harl 5F **93**
Victoria Mans. NW10 . . . . .7D **62**
  SW8 . . . .*7J 101*
  (off Sth. Lambeth Rd.)
  W14 . . . .*6H 99*
  (off Queen's Club Gdns.)
Victoria M. E8 . . . . .6G **67**
  NW6 . . . . .1J **81**
  SW4 . . . . .4F **119**
  SW18 .1A **136**
  W11 . . . . .1J **99**

Victoria Mills Studios *E15* *1F 87*
  (off Burford Rd.)
Victorian Gro. N16 . . . . .4E **66**
Victorian Hgts. *SW8* *2F 119*
  (off Thackeray Rd.)
Victorian Rd. N16 . . . . .3E **66**
Victoria Palace Theatre *2A 18*
  (off Victoria St.)
Victoria Pde. SE10 . . . . .6D **104**
  TW9: Kew *1G 115*
  (off Sandycombe Rd.)
Victoria Pk. 1K **85**
Victoria Pk. Ct. *E9* *7J 67*
  (off Well St.)
Victoria Pk. Ind. Cen. *E9* *7C 68*
  (off Rothbury Rd.)
Victoria Pk. Rd. E9 . . . . .1J **85**
Victoria Pk. Sq. E2 . . . . .3J **85**
Victoria Pk. Studios *E9* *6J 67*
  (off Milborne St.)
Victoria Pas. NW8 . . . . .3B **4**
Victoria Pl. TW9: Rich 5D **114**
Victoria Pl. Shop. Cen. 3K **17**
Victoria Point *E13* *2J 87*
  (off Victoria Rd.)
Victoria Retail Pk.
  South Ruislip 5B **58**
Victoria Ri. *NW6* *7A 64*
  (off Hilgrove Rd.)
  SW4 . . . . .3F **119**
Victoria Road 5H **73**
Victoria Rd.
  BR2: Broml 5B **160**
  BR7: Chst 5E **142**
  CR4: Mitc 7C **136**
  DA6: Bex 4G **127**
  DA8: Erith 6K **109**
  DA15: Sidc 3K **143**
  E4 . . . . .1B **36**
  E11 . . . . .4G **69**
  E13 . . . . .2J **87**
  E17 . . . . .2E **50**
  E18 . . . . .2K **51**
  EN4: E Barn 4G **21**
  HA4: Ruis 1J **57**
  IG9: Buck H 2G **37**
  IG11: Bark 6F **71**
  KT1: King T 2F **151**
  KT6: Surb 6D **150**
  N4 . . . . .7K **47**
  N9 . . . . .4A **34**
  N15 . . . . .4G **49**
  N18 . . . . .4A **34**
  N22 . . . . .1G **47**
  NW4 . . . . .4E **44**
  NW6 . . . . .2H **81**
  NW7 . . . . .5G **29**
  NW10 .5K **79**
  RM10: Dag 5H **73**
  SM1: Sutt 5B **166**
  SW14 .3K **115**
  TW1: Twick 7B **114**
  TW11: Tedd 6A **132**
  TW13: Felt 1K **129**
  UB2: S'hall 3D **94**
  W3 . . . . .5K **79**
  W5 . . . . .5B **78**
  W8 . . . . .3A **100**
  WD23: Bush 1A **26**
Victoria Sq. SW1 . . . . . .1K **17** (3F **101**)
Victoria St.
  DA17: Belv 5F **109**
  E15 . . . . .7G **69**
  SW1 . . . . .2K **17** (3G **101**)
Victoria Ter. HA1: Harr 1J **59**
  N4 . . . . .1A **66**
  NW10 .4B **80**
  W5 . . . . .1D **96**
Victoria Vs. TW9: Rich 3F **115**
Victoria Way
  HA4: Ruis 5B **58**
  SE7 . . . . .5K **105**

Victoria Wharf *E2* *2K 85*
  (off Palmers Rd.)
  E14 . . . . .7A **86**
  SE8 . . . .*5B 104*
  (off Dragoon Rd.)
Victoria Works NW2 . . . . .2D **62**
Victoria Yd. E1 . . . . .6G **85**
Victor Rd. HA2: Harr 3G **41**
  NW10 .3D **80**
  SE20 .7K **139**
  TW11: Tedd 4J **131**
Victors Dr. TW12: Hamp 6C **130**
Victors Way EN5: Barn 3C **20**
Victor Vs. N9 . . . . .3J **33**
Victor Wlk. NW9 . . . . .2A **44**
Victor Wharf *SE1* *4E 14*
  (off Clink St.)
Victory Av. SM4: Mord 5A **154**
Victory Bus. Cen.
  TW7: Isle 4K **113**
Victory Cl. TW19: Stanw 1A **128**
Victory Ct. IG11: Bark 4B **90**
  W9 . . . .*4J 81*
  (off Hermes Cl.)
Victory M. UB2: S'hall 3C **94**
Victory Pde. E20 . . . . .6D **68**
  SE18 .3F **107**
Victory Pk. HA9: Wemb 3D **60**
Victory Pl. E14 . . . . .7A **86**
  SE17 .4D **102**
  SE19 .7E **138**
Victory Rd. E11 . . . . .4J **51**
  SW19 .7A **136**
Victory Rd. M. *SW19* *7A 136*
  (off Victory Rd.)
Victory Wlk. SE8 . . . . .1C **122**
Victory Way
  RM7: Mawney 2H **55**
  SE16 .2A **104**
  TW5: Cran 5A **94**
Vida Ho. SE8 . . . . .5K **103**
Video Cl. N4 . . . . .7K **47**
Vidler Cl. KT9: Chess 6C **162**
Vienna Cl. IG5: Ilf 2B **52**
The View SE2 . . . . .5E **108**
View Cl. HA1: Harr 4H **41**
  N6 . . . . .7D **46**
View Cres. N8 . . . . .5H **47**
Viewfield Cl. HA3: Kenton 7E **42**
Viewfield Rd.
  DA5: Bexl 1C **144**
  SW18 .6H **117**
Viewland Rd. SE18 . . . . .5K **107**
The View No. N6 . . . . .7D **46**
The View Tube 1D **86**
  (off Greenway)
Viga Rd. N21 . . . . .6F **23**
Vigers St. *NW10* *3D 80*
  (off Harrow Rd.)
Vigilant Cl. SE26 . . . . .4G **139**
Vignoles Rd. RM7: Rush G 7G **55**
Vigo St. W1 . . . . .3A **12** (7G **83**)
Viking Bus. Cen.
  RM7: Rush G 7J **55**
Viking Cl. E3 . . . . .2A **86**
Viking Ct. SW6 . . . . .6J **99**
Viking Gdns. E6 . . . . .4C **88**
Viking Ho. *SE5* *2C 120*
  (off Denmark Rd.)
  SE18 . . . .*4C 106*
  (off Pett St.)
Viking Pl. E10 . . . . .1B **68**
Viking Rd. UB1: S'hall 7C **76**
Viking Way DA8: Erith 3J **109**
Villacourt Rd. SE18 . . . . .7A **108**
The Village 1F **99**
The Village NW3 . . . . .2A **64**
  SE7 . . . . .6A **106**
Village Arc. E4 . . . . .1A **36**
Village Cl. E4 . . . . .5K **35**
  NW3 . . . .*5B 64*
  (off Belsize La.)

Village Ct. E17 . . . . .5D **50**
  SE3 .3G **123**
  (off Hurren Cl.)
Village Ctyd. SW11 . . . . .6F **101**
  (off Arches La.)
Village Ga. TW17: Shep 5D **146**
Village Hgts. IG8: Wfd G 5C **36**
Village M. NW9 . . . . .2K **61**
  SW18 . . . . .1H **135**
  (off Elsenham St.)
Village Mt. NW3 . . . . .4A **64**
  (off Perrins Ct.)
Village Pk. Cl. EN1: Enf 6K **23**
Village Rd. EN1: Enf 5K **23**
  N3 . . . . .2G **45**
Village Row SM2: Sutt 7J **165**
Village Way BR3: Beck 2C **158**
  HA5: Pinn 7C **40**
  IG6: Ilf 3G **53**
  NW10 . . . . .4K **61**
  SE21 . . . . .6D **120**
  TW15: Ashf 4B **128**
Village Way E. HA2: Harr 7E **40**
Villa Rd. SW9 . . . . .3A **120**
Villas on the Heath NW3 . . . . . . .3A **64**
Villas Rd. SE18 . . . . .5G **107**
Villa St. SE17 . . . . .5D **102**
Villa Wlk. SE17 . . . . .5D **102**
  (off Villa St.)
Villiers Av. KT5: Surb 5F **151**
  TW2: Whitt 1D **130**
Villiers Cl. E10 . . . . .2C **68**
  KT5: Surb 4F **151**
Villiers Ct. SW11 . . . . .1C **118**
  (off Battersea Bri. Rd.)
Villiers Gdns. E20 . . . . .5D **68**
Villiers Gro. SM2: Cheam 7F **165**
Villiers M. NW2 . . . . .6C **62**
Villiers Path KT6: Surb 5E **150**
Villiers Rd. BR3: Beck 2K **157**
  KT1: King T 4F **151**
  NW2 .6C **62**
  TW7: Isle 2J **113**
  UB1: S'hall 1D **94**
Villiers St. WC2 . . . . . . .3E **12** (1J **101**)
Vimy Cl. TW4: Houn 5D **112**
Vimy Ridge Ct. E3 . . . . .2B **86**
  (off Festubert Pl.)
Vincam Cl. TW2: Whitt 7E **112**
Vince Ct. N1 . . . . .2F **9** (3D **84**)
Vincennes Est. SE27 . . . . .4D **138**
Vincent Av. KT5: Surb 2J **163**
Vincent Cl. BR2: Broml 4K **159**
  DA15: Sidc 1J **143**
  EN5: New Bar 3E **20**
  SE16 . . . . .2A **104**
  UB7: Sip 6C **92**
Vincent Ct. HA6: Nwood 1H **39**
  N4 . . . . .1J **65**
  NW4 .4F **45**
  SW9 . . . . .1K **119**
  W1 . . . . .7E **4**
  (off Seymour Pl.)
Vincent Dr. TW17: Shep 3G **147**
  UB10: Uxb 1B **74**
Vincent Gdns. NW2 . . . . .3B **62**
Vincent Ho. SW1 . . . . .3D **18**
  (off Regency St.)
  SW1 .4C **18**
  (off Vincent Sq.)
Vincent M. E3 . . . . .2C **86**
Vincent Rd. CR0: C'don 7E **156**
  E4 . . . . .6A **36**
  HA0: Wemb 7F **61**
  KT1: King T 3G **151**
  N15 .4C **48**
  N22 .2A **48**
  RM9: Dag 7E **72**
  SE18 . . . . .4F **107**
  TW4: Houn 2B **112**
  TW7: Isle 1H **113**

Vincent Row
  TW12: Hamp H 6G **131**
Vincents Path UB5: N'olt 6C **58**
  (off Arnold Rd.)
Vincent Sq. N22 . . . . .2A **48**
  SW1 . . . . .3C **18** (4H **101**)
Vincent Sq. Mans. SW1 . . . . .3B **18**
  (off Walcott St.)
Vincent St. E16 . . . . .5H **87**
  SW1 . . . . .3C **18** (4H **101**)
Vincent's Yd. SW9 . . . . .1A **120**
  (off Alphabet M.)
Vincent Ter. N1 . . . . .2B **84**
Vince St. EC1 . . . . .2F **9** (3D **84**)
Vine Cl. E5 . . . . .4G **67**
  KT5: Surb 6F **151**
  SM1: Sutt 3A **166**
  TW19: Stanw M 7B **174**
  UB7: W Dray 4C **92**
Vine Cotts. E1 . . . . .6J **85**
  (off Sidney Sq.)
  W7 . . . . .1J **95**
Vine Ct. E1 . . . . .5G **85**
  HA3: Kenton 6E **42**
Vinegar All. E17 . . . . .4D **50**
Vinegar Gdns. IG1: Ilf 5G **71**
Vinegar St. E1 . . . . .1H **103**
Vinegar Yd. SE1 . . . . . . .6G **15** (2E **102**)
Vine Gro. UB10: Hil 7C **56**
Vine Hill EC1 . . . . .4J **7** (4A **84**)
Vine La.
  SE1 . . . . .5H **15** (1E **102**)
  UB10: Hil 1B **74**
Vine Pl. TW3: Houn 4F **113**
  W5 . . . . .1E **96**
  (off St Mark's Rd.)
Viner Cl. KT12: Walt T 6A **148**
The Vineries EN1: Enf 3K **23**
  N14 .6B **22**
  SE6 .1C **140**
Vineries Bank NW7 . . . . .5J **29**
Vineries Cl. RM9: Dag 6F **73**
  UB7: Sip 6C **92**
Vine Rd. BR6: Chels 6K **173**
  E15 .7H **69**
  KT8: E Mos 4G **149**
  SW13 . . . . .3B **116**
Viner Pl. E17 . . . . .4C **50**
The Vinery SW8 . . . . .7J **101**
  (off Regent's Bri. Gdns.)
Vinery Way W6 . . . . .3D **98**
Vines Av. N3 . . . . .1K **45**
Vine Sq. W14 . . . . .5H **99**
  (off Star Rd.)
Vine St. E17 . . . . .4D **50**
  EC3 . . . . .1J **15** (6F **85**)
  RM7: Rom 4J **55**
  W1 . . . . .3B **12** (7G **83**)
Vine St. Bri. EC1 . . . . . . .4K **7** (4A **84**)
The Vineyard
  TW10: Rich 5E **114**
Vine Yd. SE1 . . . . .6D **14**
Vineyard Cl. KT1: King T 3F **151**
  SE6 . . . . .1C **140**
Vineyard Gro. N3 . . . . .1K **45**
Vineyard Hill Rd.
  SW19 . . . . .4H **135**
Vineyard M. TW10: Rich 5E **114**
Vineyard Pas.
  TW10: Rich 5E **114**
Vineyard Path SW14 . . . . .3K **115**
Vineyard Rd. TW13: Felt 3J **129**
Vineyard Row
  KT1: Hamp W 1C **150**
The Vineyards TW13: Felt 3J **129**
  (off High St.)
  TW16: Sun 3J **147**
Vineyard Wlk. EC1 . . . . .3J **7** (4A **84**)
Viney Bank CR0: Sels 7B **170**
Viney Rd. SE13 . . . . .3D **122**
Vining St. SW9 . . . . .4A **120**

Vinlake Av. UB10: Ick 3B **56**
Vinson Cl. BR6: Orp 1K **173**
Vinson Ho. N1 . . . . .2D **84**
  (off Cranston Est.)
Vintage M. E4 . . . . .4H **35**
Vintage Yd.
  TW17: Shep 5C **146**
Vintner's Ct. EC4 . . . . . .3D **14** (7C **84**)
Vintner's Pl. EC4 . . . . . .3D **14** (7C **84**)
Vintry Ct. SE1 . . . . .7F **15**
  (off Porlock St.)
Vintry M. E17 . . . . .4C **50**
Vinyl Pl. UB3: Hayes 1F **93**
Viola Av. SE2 . . . . .4B **108**
  TW14: Felt 6A **112**
  TW19: Stanw 1A **128**
Viola Sq. W12 . . . . .7B **80**
Violet Av. EN2: Enf 1J **23**
  UB8: Hil 5B **74**
Violet Cl. E16 . . . . .4G **87**
  SE8 . . . . .6B **104**
  SM3: Sutt 1G **165**
  SM6: W'gton 1E **166**
Violet Ct. E15 . . . . .7G **69**
  (off Victoria St.)
  NW9 . . . . .1A **44**
Violet Gdns. CR0: Wadd 5B **168**
Violet Hill NW8 . . . . .2A **82**
Violet Hill Ho. NW8 . . . . .2A **82**
  (off Violet Hill)
Violet La. CR0: Wadd 6B **168**
Violet Rd. E3 . . . . .4D **86**
  E17 .6C **50**
  E18 .2K **51**
Violet St. E2 . . . . .4H **85**
Violet Ter.
  UB8: Hil 5C **74**
VIP Trading Est. SE7 . . . . .4A **106**
Virgil Pl. W1 . . . . .6E **4** (5D **82**)
Virgil St. SE1 . . . . .1H **19** (3K **101**)
Virgin Active
  Aldersgate 6C **8**
  (off Aldersgate St.)
  Bank 6D **84**
  Barbican 5C **8**
  (off Aldersgate St.)
  Broadgate 5G **9**
  Bromley 4B **160**
  Chelsea 6A **100**
  Chiswick 1A **116**
  Chiswick Pk. 4H **97**
  Cricklewood 3G **63**
  Crouch End 5J **47**
  (off Tottenham La.)
  Fulham Pools 6G **99**
  Hammersmith 4F **99**
  (off Hammersmith Rd.)
  Islington 2B **84**
  Kensington 2K **99**
  (off Old Court Pl.)
  Mansion Ho. 2D **14**
  (off Lit. Trinity La.)
  Mayfair 2F **11** (6E **82**)
  Mill Hill East 7B **30**
  Moorgate 4E **8** (4D **84**)
  Notting Hill 6G **81**
  Repton Park 7K **37**
  Smugglers Way 4K **117**
  Strand 7J **83**
  Streatham 3J **137**
  Swiss Cottage 6A **64**
  (within O2 Centre)
  Tower Bridge 2J **15**
  (off Haydon St.)
  The Twickenham Club 6J **113**
  Walbrook 7D **84**
  West London 1H **99**
  Wimbledon, Worple Rd. 6H **135**
Virginia Cl.
  BR2: Broml 3G **159**
  KT3: N Mald 4J **151**
  RM5: Col R 1J **55**

Virginia Ct. SE16 . . . . .2K **103**
  (off Eleanor Cl.)
  WC1 . . . . .3D **6**
  (off Burton St.)
Virginia Gdns. IG6: Ilf 2G **53**
Virginia Ho. E14 . . . . .7E **86**
  (off Newby Pl.)
  TW11: Tedd 5B **132**
Virginia Rd. CR7: Thor H 1B **156**
  E2 . . . . .2J **9** (3F **85**)
Virginia St. E1 . . . . .7G **85**
Virginia Wlk. SW2 . . . . .6K **119**
Viridian Apts. SW8 . . . . .7G **101**
Visage Apts. NW3 . . . . .7B **64**
  (off Winchester Rd.)
Viscount Cl. N11 . . . . .6A **32**
Viscount Ct. W2 . . . . .6J **81**
  (off Pembridge Vs.)
Viscount Dr. E6 . . . . .5D **88**
Viscount Gro. UB5: N'olt 3B **76**
Viscount M. BR7: Chst 6F **143**
Viscount Point SW19 . . . . .7J **135**
  (off The Broadway)
Viscount Rd. TW19: Stanw 1A **128**
Viscount St. EC1 . . . . . .4C **8** (4C **84**)
Viscount Way TW6: H'row A 4G **111**
Vision Ind. Pk. W3 . . . . .5H **79**
The Vista DA14: Sidc 5K **143**
  SE9 . . . . .6B **124**
Vista Av. EN3: Enf H 2E **24**
Vista Bldg. E3 . . . . .3B **86**
  (off Bow Rd.)
  SE18 . . . . .4E **106**
Vista Ct. E1 . . . . .5A **86**
  (off Ocean Est.)
Vista Dr. IG4: Ilf 5B **52**
Vista Ho. N4 . . . . .2A **66**
  SW19 . . . . .1B **154**
  (off Chapter Way)
Vista Way HA3: Kenton 6E **42**
Vistec Ho. CR0: C'don 7B **156**
Vita Apts. CR0: C'don 2D **168**
Vitae Apts. W6 . . . . .3C **98**
Vitali Cl. SW15 . . . . .6C **116**
Vittoria Ho. N1 . . . . .1K **83**
  (off High Rd.)
Viveash Cl. UB3: Hayes 3H **93**
Vivian Av. HA9: Wemb 5G **61**
  NW4 .5D **44**
Vivian Comma Cl. N4 . . . . .3B **66**
Vivian Ct. N12 . . . . .5E **30**
  W9 . . . . .2K **81**
Vivian Gdns. HA9: Wemb 5G **61**
Vivian Mans. NW4 . . . . .5D **44**
  (off Vivian Av.)
Vivian Rd. E3 . . . . .2A **86**
Vivian Sq. SE15 . . . . .3H **121**
Vivian Way N2 . . . . .5B **46**
Vivien Cl. KT9: Chess 7E **162**
Vivienne Cl. TW1: Twick 6D **114**
Vixen M. E8 . . . . .7F **67**
  (off Haggerston Rd.)
Voce Rd. SE18 . . . . .7H **107**
Voewood Cl.
  KT3: N Mald 6B **152**
Vogans Mill SE1 . . . . . . .6K **15** (2F **103**)
Vogler Ho. E1 . . . . .7J **85**
  (off Cable St.)
Vogue Ct. BR1: Broml 1K **159**
Vollasky Ho. E1 . . . . .5K **9**
  (off Daplyn St.)
Volta Cl. N9 . . . . .3D **34**
Voltaire Rd. SW4 . . . . .3H **119**
Voltaire Way UB3: Hayes 7G **75**
Volt Av. NW10 . . . . .3K **79**
Volta Way CR0: Wadd 1K **167**
Voluntary Pl. E11 . . . . .6J **51**
Vorley Rd. N19 . . . . .2G **65**
Voss Ct. SW16 . . . . .6J **137**
Voss St. E2 . . . . .3G **85**
Voyager Bus. Est. SE16 . . . . .3G **103**
  (off Spa Rd.)

Voyager Ct. *E16* 5J *87*
(off Hammersley Rd.)
Voyagers Cl. SE28 . . . . .6C *90*
Voysey Cl. N3 . . . . .3G *45*
Voysey Sq. E3 . . . . .4D *86*
Vue Cinema
  Acton .4G *79*
  Apollo 3C *12*
(off Regent St.)
  Bromley 3J *159*
  Croydon, High St. 3C *168*
  Croydon, Purley Way 1K *167*
  Dagenham 1E *90*
  Finchley Rd. 6A *64*
(within 02 Centre)
  Fulham Broadway 3J *99*
  Harrow 6J *41*
(within St George's Shop. & Leisure Cen.)
  Islington 2A *84*
  Leicester Square 2D *12*
(off Cranbourn St.)
  North Finchley 7G *31*
  Romford 6K *55*
  Shepherds Bush 2E *99*
  Stratford City 6E *68*
(in Shopping Cen.)
  Westfield 1E *98*
  Wood Green 2A *48*
Vulcan Cl. E6 . . . . .6E *88*
Vulcan Ga. EN2: Enf 2F *23*
Vulcan Rd. SE4 . . . . .2B *122*
Vulcan Sq. E14 . . . . .4D *104*
Vulcan Ter. SE4 . . . . .2B *122*
Vulcan Way N7 . . . . .6K *65*
  SM6: W'gton 7J *167*
Vulcan Wharf E15 . . . . .2D *86*
(off Cook's Rd.)
Vulliamy Cl. E4 . . . . .2A *36*
The Vyne DA7: Bex 3H *127*
Vyner Rd. W3 . . . . .7K *79*
Vyner St. E2 . . . . .1H *85*
Vyners Way UB10: Ick 5C *56*

W

Wadbrook St. KT1: King T 2D *150*
Wadding St. SE17 . . . . .4D *102*
Waddington Cl. EN1: Enf 4K *23*
Waddington Rd. E15 . . . . .5F *69*
Waddington St. E15 . . . . .6F *69*
Waddington Way SE19 . . . . .7C *138*
WADDON .3A *168*
Waddon Cl. CR0: Wadd 3A *168*
Waddon Ct. Rd.
  CR0: Wadd 3A *168*
Waddon Leisure Cen. 5A *168*
Waddon Marsh Way
  CR0: Wadd 1K *167*
Waddon New Rd.
  CR0: C'don 3B *168*
Waddon Pk. Av. CR0: Wadd 4A *168*
Waddon Rd.
  CR0: C'don, Wadd 3A *168*
Waddon Way CR0: Wadd 6A *168*
Wade Ct. N10 . . . . .7A *32*
Wade Ho. EN1: Enf 5J *23*
  SE1 .7K *15*
(off Parkers Row)
Wades Gro. N21 . . . . .7F *23*
Wades Hill N21 . . . . .6F *23*
Wades La. TW11: Tedd 5A *132*
Wadeson St. E2 . . . . .2H *85*
Wade's Pl. E14 . . . . .7D *86*
Wadeville Av. RM6: Chad H 6C *54*
Wadeville Cl. DA17: Belv 5G *109*
Wadham Av. E17 . . . . .7J *35*
Wadham Cl. TW17: Shep 7F *146*
Wadham Gdns. NW3 . . . . .1C *82*
  UB6: G'frd 6H *59*
Wadham Ho. N18 . . . . .5A *34*
Wadham M. SW14 . . . . .2J *115*

Wadham Rd. E17 . . . . .7J *35*
  SW15 . . . . .4G *117*
Wadhurst Cl. SE20 . . . . .2H *157*
Wadhurst Rd. SW8 . . . . .1G *119*
  W4 . . . . .3K *97*
Wadley Rd. E11 . . . . .7G *51*
Wadsworth Bus. Cen.
  UB6: G'frd 2C *78*
Wadsworth Cl.
  EN3: Pond E 5E *24*
  UB6: G'frd 2C *78*
Wadsworth Rd. UB6: G'frd 2B *78*
Wager St. E3 . . . . .4B *86*
WAGGONERS RDBT. 1K *111*
Waggon La. N17 . . . . .6B *34*
Waggon M. N14 . . . . .1B *32*
Waghorn Rd. E13 . . . . .1A *88*
  HA3: Kenton 3D *42*
Waghorn St. SE15 . . . . .3G *121*
Wagner M. KT6: Surb 5E *150*
(off Avenue Elmers)
Wagner St. SE15 . . . . .7J *103*
Wagstaff Gdns. RM9: Dag 7C *72*
Wagtail Cl. EN1: Enf 1C *24*
  NW9 .2A *44*
Wagtail Ct. SW15 . . . . .6E *116*
Wagtail Rd. TW6: H'row A 5C *174*
Wagtail Wlk. BR3: Beck 5E *158*
Waight's Ct. KT2: King T 1E *150*
Wainfleet Av. RM5: Col R 2J *55*
Wainford Cl. SW19 . . . . .1F *135*
Wainwright Gro. TW7: Isle 4H *113*
Wainwright Ho. E1 . . . . .1J *103*
(off Garnet St.)
Waite Davies Rd. SE12 . . . . .7H *123*
Waite Ho. W3 . . . . .1B *98*
Waite St. SE15 . . . . .6F *103*
Waithman St. EC4 . . . . .1A *14*
(off Black Friars La.)
Wakefield Ct. SE26 . . . . .6J *139*
Wakefield Gdns. IG1: Ilf 6C *52*
  SE19 . . . . .7E *138*
Wakefield Ho. SE15 . . . . .1G *121*
Wakefield M. WC1 . . . . .2F *7 (3J *83*)
  N15 .5F *49*
  TW10: Rich 5D *114*
Wakefield St. E6 . . . . .1B *88*
  N18 .5B *34*
  WC1 . . . . .2F *7 (3J *83*)
Wakeford Cl. DA5: Bexl 1D *144*
  SW4 . . . . .5G *119*
Wakehams Hill HA5: Pinn 3D *40*
Wakeham St. N1 . . . . .6D *66*
Wakehurst Rd. SW11 . . . . .5C *118*
Wakeling La. HA0: Wemb 3B *60*
Wakeling Rd. W7 . . . . .5K *77*
Wakeling St. E14 . . . . .6A *86*
Wakelin Ho. N1 . . . . .7B *66*
(off Sebbon St.)
Wakelin Rd. E15 . . . . .2G *87*
Wakeman Ho. NW10 . . . . .3F *81*
(off Wakeman Rd.)
Wakeman Rd. NW10 . . . . .3E *80*
Wakemans Hill Av. NW9 . . . . .5K *43*
Wakering Rd. IG11: Bark 6G *71*
(not continuous)
Wakerley Cl. E6 . . . . .6D *88*
Wakup Docklands 7J *87*
Wakley St. EC1 . . . . .1A *8* (3J *83*)
Walberswick St. SW8 . . . . .7J *101*
Walbrook EC4 . . . . .2E *14* (7D *84*)
(not continuous)
The Walbrook Bldg. EC4 . . . . .2E *14*
Walbrook Ct. N1 . . . . .2E *84*
(off Hemsworth St.)
Walbrook Ho. N9 . . . . .2D *34*
(off Huntingdon Rd.)
Walbrook Wharf EC4 . . . . .3D *14*
(off Cousin La.)
Walburgh St. E1 . . . . .6H *85*
Walcorde Av. SE17 . . . . .4C *102*

Walcot Gdns. SE11 . . . . .3J *19*
Walcot Rd. EN3: Brim 2G *25*
Walcot Sq. SE11 . . . . .3K *19* (4A *102*)
Walcott St. SW1 . . . . .3B *18* (4G *101*)
Waldair Ct. E16 . . . . .2F *107*
Waldeck Gro. SE27 . . . . .3B *138*
Waldeck Rd. N15 . . . . .4B *48*
  SW14 . . . . .3J *115*
  W4 . . . . .6G *97*
  W13 .6B *78*
Waldeck Ter. SW14 . . . . .3J *115*
(off Waldeck Rd.)
Waldegrave Ct. IG11: Bark 1H *89*
Waldegrave Gdns.
  TW1: Twick 2K *131*
Waldegrave Pk. TW1: Twick 4K *131*
Waldegrave Rd. BR1: Broml 4C *160*
  N8 . . . . .3A *48*
  RM8: Dag 2C *72*
  SE19 . . . . .7F *139*
  TW1: Twick 4K *131*
  TW11: Tedd 4K *131*
  W5 . . . . .7F *79*
Waldegrove CR0: C'don 3F *169*
Waldemar Av. SW6 . . . . .1G *117*
  W13 .1C *96*
Waldemar Rd. SW19 . . . . .5J *135*
Walden Av. BR7: Chst 4D *142*
  N13 .4H *33*
  RM13: Rain 2K *91*
Walden Cl. DA17: Belv 5F *109*
Walden Ct. SW8 . . . . .1H *119*
Walden Gdns. CR7: Thor H 3K *155*
Walden Ho. SW1 . . . . .4H *17*
(off Pimlico Rd.)
  SW11 . . . . .1E *118*
(off Dagnall St.)
Walden Pde. BR7: Chst 6D *142*
(not continuous)
Walden Rd. BR7: Chst 6D *142*
  N17 .1D *48*
Waldenshaw Rd. SE23 . . . . .1J *139*
Walden St. E1 . . . . .6H *85*
(not continuous)
Walden Way NW7 . . . . .6A *30*
Waldo Cl. SW4 . . . . .5G *119*
Waldo Ho. NW10 . . . . .3D *80*
(off Waldo Rd.)
Waldo Ind. Est. BR1: Broml 3B *160*
Waldo Pl. CR4: Mitc 7C *136*
Waldorf Cl. CR2: S Croy 7B *168*
Waldo Rd. BR1: Broml 3B *160*
  NW10 . . . . .3C *80*
Waldram Cres. SE23 . . . . .1J *139*
Waldram Pk. Rd. SE23 . . . . .1K *139*
Waldram Pl. SE23 . . . . .1J *139*
Waldrist Way DA18: Erith 3F *109*
Waldron Gdns. BR2: Broml 3F *159*
Waldronhyrst
  CR2: S Croy 4B *168*
Waldron M. SW3 . . . . . . .7B *16* (6B *100*)
Waldron Rd. HA1: Harr 1J *59*
  HA2: Harr 1J *59*
  SW18 . . . . .3A *136*
The Waldrons CR0: C'don 4B *168*
Waldron's Path CR2: S Croy 4C *168*
Waldrons Yd. HA2: Harr 2H *59*
Waldstock Rd. SE28 . . . . .7A *90*
Waleorde Rd. SE17 . . . . .5C *102*
Waleran Cl. HA7: Stan 5E *26*
Walerand Rd. SE13 . . . . .2E *122*
Waleran Flats SE1 . . . . .4E *102*
Wales Av. SM5: Cars 5C *166*
Wales Cl. SE15 . . . . .6H *103*
Wales Farm Rd. W3 . . . . .5K *79*
Wales Office 5E *12*
(off Whitehall)
Waleton Acres SM6: W'gton 6G *167*
Waley St. E1 . . . . .5A *86*
Walfield Av. N20 . . . . .7E *20*
Walford Ho. E1 . . . . .6H *85*
Walford Rd. N16 . . . . .4E *66*

Walfrey Gdns. RM9: Dag 7F *73*
WALHAM GREEN 1J *117*
Walham Grn. Ct. SW6 . . . . .7K *99*
(off Waterford Rd.)
Walham Gro. SW6 . . . . .7J *99*
Walham Ri. SW19 . . . . .6G *135*
Walham Yd. SW6 . . . . .7J *99*
The Walk N13 . . . . .3F *33*
(off Fox La.)
  TW16: Sun 7H *129*
Walkato Lodge IG9: Buck H 1F *37*
Walkden Rd. BR7: Chst 5E *142*
Walker Cl. CR0: New Ad 7E *170*
  N11 .4B *32*
  SE18 . . . . .4G *107*
  TW12: Hamp 6D *130*
  TW14: Felt 7H *111*
  W7 . . . . .1J *95*
Walker Ho. NW1 . . . . .1C *6* (2H *83*)
  SE16 .3B *104*
(off Redriff Est.)
Walker M. SW2 . . . . .5A *120*
Walker's Ct. W1 . . . . .2C *12*
Walkerscroft Mead SE21 . . . . .1C *138*
Walkers Lodge E14 . . . . .2E *104*
(off Manchester Rd.)
Walkers Pl. SW15 . . . . .4G *117*
The Walkie-Talkie 2G *15*
Walkinshaw Ct. N1 . . . . .7C *66*
(off Rotherfield St.)
The Walks N2 . . . . .3B *46*
Walkynscroft SE15 . . . . .2H *121*
(off Caulfield Rd.)
Wallace Bldg. NW8 . . . . .4B *4*
(off Penfold St.)
Wallace Cl. SE28 . . . . .7D *90*
  TW17: Shep 4F *147*
  UB10: Uxb 2A *74*
Wallace Collection 7G *5* (6E *82*)
Wallace Ct. NW1 . . . . .6D *4*
(off Old Marylebone Rd.)
  SE3 .4K *123*
Wallace Cres. SM5: Cars 5D *166*
Wallace Ho. N7 . . . . .6K *65*
(off Caledonian Rd.)
Wallace Rd. N1 . . . . .6C *66*
Wallace Way N19 . . . . .2H *65*
(off St John's Way)
  RM1: Rom 1K *55*
Wallasey Cres. UB10: Ick 2C *56*
Wallbrook Bus. Cen.
  TW4: Houn 3K *111*
Wallbutton Rd. SE4 . . . . .2A *122*
Wallcote Av. NW2 . . . . .1F *63*
Wall Ct. N4 . . . . .1K *65*
(off Stroud Grn. Rd.)
Walled Gdn. Cl. BR3: Beck 4D *158*
Walled Gdn. Ct. HA7: Stan 3D *26*
Wallenberg Pl. W1 . . . . .1F *11*
(off Gt. Cumberland Pl.)
WALLEND .1E *88*
Wall End Ct. E6 . . . . .1E *88*
(off Wall End Rd.)
Wall End Rd. E6 . . . . .7E *70*
Waller Dr. HA6: Nwood 2J *39*
Waller Rd. SE14 . . . . .1K *121*
Wallers Cl. IG8: Wfd G 6J *37*
  RM9: Dag 1E *90*
Waller Way SE10 . . . . .7D *104*
Wallflower St. W12 . . . . .7B *80*
Wallgrave Rd. SW5 . . . . .4K *99*
Wallingford Av. W10 . . . . .5F *81*
WALLINGTON 6F *167*
Wallington Cl. HA4: Ruis 6E *38*
Wallington Cnr. SM6: W'gton 4F *167*
(off Manor Rd. Nth.)
Wallington Ct. SM6: W'gton 6F *167*
(off Stanley Pk. Rd.)
WALLINGTON GREEN 4F *167*
Wallington Rd. IG3: Ilf 7K *53*
Wallington Sq.
  SM6: W'gton 6F *167*

Wallis All. SE1 . . . . .6D 14
Wallis Cl. SW11 . . . . .3B 118
Wallis Ho. HA4: Ruis 1F 57
   SE14 . . . . .1A 122
   TW8: Bford 5E 96
Wallis M. N8 . . . . .3A 48
   (off Courcy Rd.)
Wallis Rd. E9 . . . . .6B 68
   TW6: H'row A 5C 174
   UB1: S'hall 6F 77
Wallis's Cotts. SW2 . . . . .7J 119
Wallman Pl. N22 . . . . .1K 47
Wallorton Gdns. SW14 . . . . .4K 115
The Wallpaper Apts. N1 . . . . .7A 66
   (off Offord Rd.)
Wallside EC2 . . . . .6D 8
Wall St. N1 . . . . .6D 66
Wallwood Rd. E11 . . . . .7F 51
Wallwood St. E14 . . . . .5B 86
Walmar Cl. EN4: Had W 1G 21
Walmer Cl. BR6: Farnb 4H 173
   E4 . . . . .2J 35
   RM7: Mawney 2H 55
Walmer Ct. KT5: Surb 5E 150
   (off Cranes Pk.)
Walmer Gdns. W13 . . . . .2A 96
Walmer Ho. W10 . . . . .6F 81
   (off Bramley Rd.)
Walmer Pl. W1 . . . . .5E 4
Walmer Rd. W10 . . . . .6E 80
   W11 .7G 81
Walmer St. W1 . . . . .5E 4 (5D 82)
Walmer Ter. SE18 . . . . .4G 107
Walmgate Rd.
   UB6: G'frd 1B 78
Walmington Fold N12 . . . . .6D 30
Walm La. NW2 . . . . .6E 62
Walney Wlk. N1 . . . . .6C 66
Walnut Av. UB7: W Dray 3C 92
Walnut Cl. IG6: Ilf 4G 53
   SE8 . . . . .6B 104
   SM5: Cars 5D 166
   UB3: Hayes 7G 75
Walnut Ct. E17 . . . . .4E 50
   W5 .2E 96
   W8 . . . . .3K 99
   (off St Mary's La.)
Walnut Flds. KT17: Ewe 7B 164
Walnut Gdns. E15 . . . . .5G 69
Walnut Gro. EN1: Enf 5J 23
Walnut Ho. E3 . . . . .1B 86
   (off Barge La.)
Walnut M. N22 . . . . .3A 48
   (off High Rd.)
   SM2: Sutt 7A 166
Walnut Rd. E10 . . . . .2C 68
Walnut Tree Av. CR4: Mitc 3C 154
   (off De'Arn Gdns.)
Walnut Tree Cl. BR7: Chst 1H 161
   SW13 . . . . .1B 116
   TW17: Shep 3E 146
   UB10: Ick 4A 56
Walnut Tree Cotts. SW19 . . . . .5G 135
Walnut Tree Ho. SW10 . . . . .6K 99
   (off Tregunter Rd.)
Walnut Tree Rd. RM8: Dag 2E 72
   SE10 . . . . .5G 105
   (not continuous)
   TW5: Hest 6D 94
   TW8: Bford 6E 96
   TW17: Shep 2E 146
Walnut Tree Wlk.
   SE11 . . . . .3J 19 (4A 102)
Walnut Way HA4: Ruis 6A 58
   IG9: Buck H 3G 37
Walpole Av. TW9: Kew 2F 115
Walpole Cl. W13 . . . . .2C 96
Walpole Ct. NW6 . . . . .7A 64
   (off Fairfax Rd.)
   TW2: Twick 2J 131
   W14 .3F 99
   (off Blythe Rd.)

Walpole Cres. TW11: Tedd 5K 131
Walpole Gdns. TW2: Twick 2J 131
   W4 . . . . .5J 97
Walpole Ho. KT8: W Mole 5E 148
   (off Approach Rd.)
   SE1 .7J 13
   (off Westminster Bri. Rd.)
   SW15 . . . . .5G 117
   (off Plaza Gdns.)
Walpole Lodge W13 . . . . .1C 96
Walpole M. NW8 . . . . .1B 82
   SW19 . . . . .6B 136
Walpole Pl. SE18 . . . . .4F 107
   TW11: Tedd 5K 131
Walpole Rd. BR2: Broml 5B 160
   CR0: C'don 2D 168
   E6 . . . . .7A 70
   E17 .4A 50
   E18 .1H 51
   KT6: Surb 7E 150
   N17 .2C 48
   (not continuous)
   SW19 . . . . .6B 136
   TW2: Twick 2J 131
   TW11: Tedd 5K 131
Walpole St. SW3 . . . . .5E 16 (5D 100)
Walrond Av. HA9: Wemb 5E 60
Walsham Cl. N16 . . . . .1G 67
   SE28 . . . . .7D 90
Walsham Ho. SE14 . . . . .2K 121
   SE17 . . . . .5D 102
   (off Blackwood St.)
Walsham How Cl. E17 . . . . .5F 51
Walsham Rd. SE14 . . . . .2K 121
   TW14: Felt 7K 111
Walsingham NW8 . . . . .1B 82
Walsingham Gdns.
   KT19: Ewe 4A 164
Walsingham Lodge SW13 . . . . .1C 116
Walsingham Mans. SW6 . . . . .7K 99
   (off Fulham Rd.)
Walsingham Pk. BR7: Chst 2H 161
Walsingham Pl. SW4 . . . . .6E 118
Walsingham Rd. CR4: Mitc 5D 154
   E5 . . . . .3G 67
   EN2: Enf 4J 23
   W13 .1A 96
Walsingham Wlk. DA17: Belv 6G 109
Walston Ho. SW1 . . . . .5C 18
   (off Aylesford St.)
Walter Besant Ho. E1 . . . . .3K 85
   (off Bancroft Rd.)
Walter Ct. W3 . . . . .6J 79
   (off Lynton Ter.)
Walter Grn. Ho. SE15 . . . . .1J 121
   (off Lausanne Rd.)
Walter Ho. SW10 . . . . .7B 100
   (off Riley St.)
Walter Hurford Ho. E12 . . . . .4E 70
   (off Grantham Rd.)
Walter Langley Ct. SE16 . . . . .2J 103
   (off Brunel Rd.)
Walter Rodney Cl. E6 . . . . .6D 70
   (off Colchester Rd.)
Walter Savill Twr. E17 . . . . .6C 50
   (off Colchester Rd.)
Walters Cl. SE17 . . . . .4D 102
   (off Brandon St.)
   UB3: Hayes 2H 93
Walters Ho. N1 . . . . .1B 84
   (off Essex Rd.)
   SE17 . . . . .6B 102
   (off Otto St.)
Walter Sickert Hall N1 . . . . .1C 8
   (off Graham St.)
Walters Rd. EN3: Pond E 4D 24
   SE25 . . . . .4E 156
Walter St. E2 . . . . .3K 85
   KT2: King T 1E 150
Walters Way SE23 . . . . .6K 121
Walters Yd.
   BR1: Broml 2J 159
Walter Ter. E1 . . . . .6K 85

Walterton Rd. W9 . . . . .4H 81
Walter Wlk. HA8: Edg 6D 28
Waltham Av. NW9 . . . . .6G 43
   UB3: Harl 3E 92
Waltham Dr. HA8: Edg 2G 43
Waltham Forest Feel Good Centre
   . . . . .2D 50
Waltham Ho. NW8 . . . . .1A 82
Waltham Pk. Way E17 . . . . .1C 50
Waltham Rd. IG8: Wfd G 6H 37
   SM5: Cars 7B 154
   UB2: S'hall 3C 94
WALTHAMSTOW 3C 50
Walthamstow Av. E4 . . . . .6G 35
Walthamstow Bus. Cen.
   . . . . .2E 50
Walthamstow Leisure Cen. 6B 50
Walthamstow Marsh
   Nature Reserve 7H 49
Walthamstow Pumphouse Museum
   . . . . .6A 50
Waltham Way E4 . . . . .3G 35
Waltheof Av. N17 . . . . .1D 48
Waltheof Gdns. N17 . . . . .1D 48
Walton Av. HA2: Harr 5D 58
   HA9: Wemb 3H 61
   KT3: N Mald 4B 152
   SM3: Cheam 3H 165
WALTON BRI. 7G 147
Walton Bri. KT12: Walt T 7G 147
Walton Bri. Rd.
   TW17: Shep 7G 147
Walton Cl. E4 . . . . .5H 35
   E5 . . . . .3K 67
   (off Orient Way)
   HA1: Harr 4H 41
   NW2 .2D 62
   SW8 .7J 101
Walton Ct. CR2: S Croy 5C 168
   (off Warham Rd.)
   EN5: New Bar 5F 21
   NW6 .7A 64
   (off Fairfax Rd.)
Walton Cft. HA1: Harr 4J 59
Walton Dr. HA1: Harr 4H 41
   NW10 . . . . .6K 61
Walton Gdns. HA9: Wemb 2E 60
   TW13: Felt 4H 129
   W3 . . . . .5H 79
Walton Grn. CR0: New Ad 7D 170
Walton Ho. E2 . . . . .3K 9
   (off Montclare St.)
   E17 .3D 50
   NW1 .3K 5
   (off Longford St.)
   SW3 .2E 16
   (off Walton St.)
Walton La.
   KT13: Weyb 7F 147, 7G 147
   TW17: Shep 7F 147
WALTON-ON-THAMES 7J 147
WALTON-ON-THAMES Camping & Cvn. Site
   . . . . .7E 148
Walton Pl. SW3 . . . . . .1E 16 (3D 100)
Walton Rd. DA14: Sidc 2C 144
   E12 .4E 70
   (not continuous)
   E13 .2A 88
   HA1: Harr 4H 41
   KT8: W Mole, E Mos 4D 148
   KT12: Walt T 4D 148
   N15 .4F 49
   RM5: Col R 1F 55
Walton St. EN2: Enf 1J 23
   SW3 . . . . .3D 16 (4C 100)
Walton Vs. N1 . . . . .7E 66
   (off Downham Rd.)
Walton Way CR4: Mitc 4G 155
   W3 . . . . .5H 79
Walt Whitman Cl. SE24 . . . . .4B 120
WALWORTH 5C 102
Walworth Pl. SE17 . . . . .5C 102

Walworth Rd. SE1 . . . . .4C 102
   SE17 . . . . .4C 102
Walworth Sq. SE17 . . . . .4C 102
Walwyn Av. BR1: Broml 3B 160
Wanborough Dr. SW15 . . . . .1D 134
Wanderer Dr. IG11: Bark 3C 90
Wandle Apts. CR2: S Croy 5D 168
Wandle Bank CR0: Bedd 3J 167
   SW19 . . . . .7B 136
Wandle Ct. CR0: Bedd 3J 167
   KT19: Ewe 4J 163
Wandle Ct. Gdns.
   CR0: Bedd 3J 167
Wandle Ho. BR1: Broml 5F 141
   NW8 .5C 4
   (off Penfold St.)
Wandle Industrial Mus. 3D 154
Wandle Meadow Nature Pk. 5A 136
Wandle Pk. 2B 168
The Wandle Pk. Trad. Est.
   CR0: C'don 2B 168
Wandle Recreation Cen. 6K 117
Wandle Rd. CR0: Bedd 3J 167
   CR0: C'don 3C 168
   SM4: Mord 4A 154
   SM6: W'gton 3F 167
   SW17 . . . . .2C 136
Wandle Side CR0: Wadd 3K 167
   SM6: W'gton 3F 167
Wandle Trad. Est. CR4: Mitc 7D 154
Wandle Way CR4: Mitc 5D 154
   SW18 . . . . .1K 135
Wandon Rd. SW6 . . . . .7K 99
WANDSWORTH 5K 117
WANDSWORTH BRI. 3K 117
Wandsworth Bri. Rd. SW6 . . . . .1K 117
WANDSWORTH COMMON 1D 136
Wandsworth Comn. W. Side
   SW18 . . . . .5A 118
WANDSWORTH GYRATORY 5K 117
Wandsworth High St. SW18 . . . . . . .5J 117
Wandsworth Mus. 5J 117
Wandsworth Plain SW18 . . . . .5K 117
Wandsworth Rd. SW8 . . . . .7E 18 (3F 119)
Wangey Rd. RM6: Chad H 7D 54
Wangford Ho. SW9 . . . . .4B 120
   (off Loughborough Pk.)
Wanless Rd. SE24 . . . . .3C 120
Wanley Rd. SE5 . . . . .4D 120
Wanlip Rd. E13 . . . . .4K 87
Wannock Gdns. IG6: Ilf 1F 53
Wansbeck Ct. EN2: Enf 3G 23
   (off Waverley Rd.)
Wansbeck Rd. E9 . . . . .7B 68
Wansdown Pl. SW6 . . . . .7K 99
Wansey St. SE17 . . . . .4C 102
Wansford Rd. IG8: Wfd G 1A 52
WANSTEAD 6K 51
Wanstead Cl. BR1: Broml 2A 160
Wanstead Gdns. IG4: Ilf 6B 52
Wanstead Golf Course 7A 52
Wanstead La. IG1: Ilf 6B 52
Wanstead Leisure Cen. 6A 52
Wanstead Pk. Av. E12 . . . . .1B 70
Wanstead Pk. Rd. IG1: Ilf 6B 52
Wanstead Pl. E11 . . . . .6J 51
Wanstead Rd. BR1: Broml 2A 160
Wansunt Rd. DA5: Bexl 1J 145
Wantage Rd. SE12 . . . . .5H 123
Wantz Rd. RM10: Dag 4H 73
WAPPING 1H 103
Wapping Dock St. E1 . . . . .1H 103
Wapping High St. E1 . . . . .1G 103
Wapping La. E1 . . . . .7H 85
Wapping Wall E1 . . . . .1J 103
Waratah Dr. BR7: Chst 5D 142
Warbank La. KT2: King T 7B 134
Warbeck Rd. W12 . . . . .2D 98
Warberry Rd. N22 . . . . .1K 47
Warboys App. KT2: King T 6H 133
Warboys Cres. E4 . . . . .5K 35
Warboys Rd. KT2: King T 6H 133

Warburg Ct. NW9 . . . . .3A 44
(off Mornington Cl.)
Warburton Cl. HA3: Hrw W 6C 26
N1 . . . . .6E 66
(off Culford Rd.)
Warburton Cl. HA4: Ruis 2J 57
Warburton Ho. E8 . . . . .1H 85
(off Warburton St.)
Warburton Rd. E8 . . . . .1H 85
TW2: Whitt 1F 131
Warburton St. E8 . . . . .1H 85
Warburton Ter. E17 . . . . .2D 50
Wardalls Gro. SE14 . . . . .7J 103
Wardalls Ho. SE8 . . . . .6B 104
(off Staunton St.)
Ward Cl. CR2: S Croy 6E 168
DA8: Erith 6K 109
Wardell Cl. NW7 . . . . .7F 29
Wardell Fld. NW9 . . . . .1A 44
Wardell Ho. SE10 . . . . .6E 104
(off Welland St.)
Wardell M. SW4 . . . . .3F 119
Warden Av. HA2: Harr 1D 58
Warden Rd. NW5 . . . . .6E 64
Wardens Fld. Cl. BR6: Chels 6J 173
Wardens Gro. SE1 . . . . .5C 14 (1C 102)
Ward La. E9 . . . . .5A 68
Wardle St. E9 . . . . .5K 67
Wardley St. SW18 . . . . .7K 117
Wardo Av. SW6 . . . . .1G 117
Wardour M. W1 . . . . .1B 12
Wardour St. W1 . . . . . . .7B 6 (6G 83)
Ward Point SE11 . . . . .4J 19 (4A 102)
Ward Rd. E15 . . . . .1F 87
N19 . . . . .3G 65
SW19 . . . . .1A 154
The Wardrobe TW9: Rich 5D 114
(off Old Palace Yd.)
Wardrobe Pl. EC4 . . . . .1B 14
Wardrobe Ter. EC4 . . . . .2B 14
Wardroper Ho. SE1 . . . . .3B 102
(off St George's Rd.)
Wards Rd. IG2: Ilf 7H 53
Wards Wharf App. E16 . . . . .1B 106
Ware Ct. SM1: Sutt 4H 165
Wareham Cl.
TW3: Houn 4F 113
Wareham Ct. N1 . . . . .7E 66
(off Hertford Rd.)
Wareham Ho. SW8 . . . . .7K 101
Warehome M. E13 . . . . .4J 87
(off Jutland Rd.)
Warehouse Ct. SE18 . . . . .3F 107
Warehouse Way E16 . . . . .7K 87
Waremead Rd. IG2: Ilf 5F 53
Warepoint Dr. SE28 . . . . .2H 107
Warfield Rd. NW10 . . . . .3F 81
TW12: Hamp 1F 149
TW14: Felt 7G 111
Warfield Yd. NW10 . . . . .3F 81
(off Warfield Rd.)
Wargrave Av. N15 . . . . .6F 49
Wargrave Ho. E2 . . . . .2J 9
(off Navarre St.)
Wargrave Rd. HA2: Harr 3G 59
Warham Rd. CR2: S Croy 5B 168
HA3: W'stone 2K 41
N4 . . . . .5A 48
Warham St. SE5 . . . . .7B 102
Waring & Gillow Est.
W3 . . . . .4G 79
Waring Cl. BR6: Chels 6K 173
Waring Dr. BR6: Chels 6K 173
Waring Rd. DA14: Sidc 6C 144
Waring St. SE27 . . . . .4C 138
Warkworth Gdns.
TW7: Isle 7A 96
Warkworth Rd. N17 . . . . .7J 33
Warland Rd. SE18 . . . . .7H 107
Warley Av. RM8: Dag 7F 55
UB4: Hayes 6J 75
Warley Cl. E10 . . . . .1B 68

Warley Rd. IG5: Ilf 1E 52
IG8: Wfd G 7E 36
N9 . . . . .2D 34
UB4: Hayes 6J 75
Warley St. E2 . . . . .3K 85
Warlingham Ct. SE13 . . . . .6E 122
Warlingham Rd.
CR7: Thor H 4B 156
Warlock Rd. W9 . . . . .4H 81
Warlters Cl. N7 . . . . .4J 65
Warlters Rd. N7 . . . . .4J 65
Warltersville Mans. N19 . . . . .7J 47
Warltersville Rd. N19 . . . . .7J 47
War Memorial Sports Ground . . .4C 166
Warmington Cl. E5 . . . . .3K 67
Warmington Rd. SE24 . . . . .6C 120
Warmington St. E13 . . . . .4J 87
Warminster Gdns. SE25 . . . . .2G 157
Warminster Rd. SE25 . . . . .2F 157
Warminster Sq. SE25 . . . . .2G 157
Warminster Way CR4: Mitc 1F 155
Warmsworth NW1 . . . . .1G 83
(off Pratt St.)
Warmwell Av. NW9 . . . . .1A 44
Warndon St. SE16 . . . . .4K 103
Warneford Rd.
HA3: Kenton 3D 42
TW6: H'row A 5C 174
Warneford St. E9 . . . . .1H 85
Warne Pl. DA15: Sidc 6B 126
Warner Av. SM3: Cheam 2G 165
Warner Cl. E15 . . . . .5G 69
NW9 .7B 44
TW12: Hamp 5D 130
UB3: Harl 7F 93
Warner Ho. BR3: Beck 6D 140
NW8 .3A 82
SE13 . . . . .2D 122
(off Russett Way)
Warner Pl. E2 . . . . .2G 85
Warner Rd. BR1: Broml 7H 141
E17 . . . . .4A 50
N8 . . . . .4H 47
SE5 .1C 120
Warners Cl. IG8: Wfd G 5D 36
Warners La. KT2: King T 4D 132
Warners Path IG8: Wfd G 5D 36
Warner St. EC1 . . . . . . .4J 7 (4A 84)
Warner Ter. E14 . . . . .5D 86
(off Broomfield St.)
Warner Yd. EC1 . . . . .4J 7
Warnford Ct. EC2 . . . . .7F 9
(off Throgmorton Av.)
Warnford Ho. SW15 . . . . .6A 116
(off Tunworth Cres.)
Warnford Ind. Est. UB3: Hayes 2G 93
Warnford Rd.
BR6: Chels 5K 173
Warnham WC1 . . . . .2G 7
(off Sidmouth St.)
Warnham Ct. Rd. SM5: Cars 7D 166
Warnham Ho. SW2 . . . . .7K 119
(off Up. Tulse Hill)
Warnham Rd. N12 . . . . .5H 31
Warple M. W3 . . . . .2A 98
Warple Way W3 . . . . .2A 98
The Warren 2A 94
The Warren E12 . . . . .4C 70
KT4: Wor Pk 4K 163
TW5: Hest 7D 94
UB4: Hayes 6J 75
Warren Av.
BR1: Broml 7G 141
BR6: Chels 5K 173
CR2: Sels 7K 169
E10 . . . . .3E 68
TW10: Rich 4H 115
Warren Cl. DA6: Bex 5G 127
HA9: Wemb 2D 60
N9 . . . . .7E 24
SE21 . . . . .7C 120
UB4: Yead 5A 76

Warren Ct. BR3: Beck 7C 140
CR0: C'don 1E 168
N17 . . . . .3G 49
(off High Cross Rd.)
NW1 . . . . .3B 6
(off Warren St.)
SE7 .6A 106
W5 . . . . .5C 78
Warren Cres. N9 . . . . .7A 24
Warren Cutting KT2: King T 7K 133
Warrender Rd. N19 . . . . .3G 65
Warrender Way HA4: Ruis 7J 39
The Warren Dr. E11 . . . . .7A 52
Warren Dr. HA4: Ruis 7B 40
UB6: G'frd 4F 77
Warren Dr. Nth. KT5: Surb 1H 163
Warren Dr. Sth. KT5: Surb 1J 163
Warren Farm Cotts.
RM6: Chad H 4F 55
Warren Flds. HA7: Stan 4H 27
Warren Footpath TW1: Twick 1C 132
Warren Gdns. BR6: Chels 5K 173
E15 . . . . .5F 69
Warren Ho. E3 . . . . .3D 86
(off Bromley High St.)
N17 . . . . .3G 49
(off High Cross Rd.)
W14 . . . . .4H 99
Warren La. HA7: Stan 2F 27
SE18 . . . . .3F 107
Warren M. W1 . . . . . .4A 6 (4G 83)
Warren Pk. KT2: King T 6J 133
Warren Pk. Rd. SM1: Sutt 6B 166
Warren Pl. E1 . . . . .6K 85
(off Pitsea St.)
Warren Pond Rd. E4 . . . . .1C 36
Warren Ri. KT3: N Mald 1K 151
Warren Rd. BR2: Hayes 2J 171
BR6: Chels 5K 173
(not continuous)
CR0: C'don 1E 168
DA6: Bex 5G 127
DA14: Sidc 3C 144
E4 . . . . .2K 35
E10 . . . . .3E 68
E11 . . . . .6A 52
IG6: Ilf 5H 53
KT2: King T 6J 133
NW2 .2B 62
SW19 . . . . .6C 136
TW2: Whitt 6G 113
TW15: Ashf 7G 129
UB10: Ick 4A 56
WD23: B Hea 1B 26
Warren Sports Cen. 5F 55
Warrens Shawe La. HA8: Edg 2C 28
Warren Ter. RM6: Chad H 4D 54
Warren Wlk. SE7 . . . . .6A 106
Warren Way HA8: Edg 2H 43
Warren Wood Cl.
BR2: Hayes 2H 171
Warriner Dr. N9 . . . . .3B 34
Warriner Gdns. SW11 . . . . .1D 118
Warrington Ct. CR0: Wadd 3B 168
(off Warrington Rd.)
Warrington Cres. W9 . . . . .4A 82
Warrington Gdns. W9 . . . . .4A 82
(not continuous)
Warrington Rd. CR0: Wadd 3B 168
HA1: Harr 5J 41
RM8: Dag 2D 72
TW10: Rich 5D 114
Warrior Cl. SE28 . . . . .1H 107
Warrior Ct. SW9 . . . . .3B 120
(off Coldharbour Rd.)
Warrior Sq. E12 . . . . .4E 70
Warsaw Cl. HA4: Ruis 6K 57
Warspite Ho. E14 . . . . .4D 104
(off Cahir St.)
Warspite Rd. SE18 . . . . .3C 106

Warton Ct. E1 . . . . .7K 85
(off Cable St.)
W3 . . . . .3J 97
(off All Saints Rd.)
Warton Ho. E15 . . . . .1E 86
(off High St.)
Warton Rd. E15 . . . . .1E 86
Warwall E6 . . . . .6F 89
Warwark Ct. KT6: Surb 2E 162
Warwick W14 . . . . .4H 99
(off Kensington Village)
Warwick Av. HA2: Harr 4D 58
HA8: Edg 3C 28
W2 . . . . .4A 82
W9 . . . . .4K 81
Warwick Bldg. SW11 . . . . .6F 101
Warwick Chambers W8 . . . . .3J 99
(off Pater St.)
Warwick Cl. DA5: Bexl 7F 127
EN4: E Barn 5G 21
TW12: Hamp 7G 131
W8 . . . . .3J 99
(off Kensington High St.)
WD23: B Hea 1D 26
Warwick Cl. BR2: Broml 2G 159
EC4 . . . . .1B 14
(off Warwick La.)
EN5: New Bar 5E 20
(off Station Rd.)
HA1: Harr 3J 41
N11 . . . . .6C 32
UB5: N'olt 5E 58
(off Newmarket Av.)
W7 . . . . .6K 77
(off Copley Cl.)
WC1 . . . . .6H 7 (5K 83)
Warwick Cres. UB4: Hayes 4H 75
W2 . . . . .5A 82
Warwick Dene W5 . . . . .1E 96
Warwick Dr. SW15 . . . . .3D 116
Warwick Est. W2 . . . . .5A 82
Warwick Gdns. CR7: Thor H 3A 156
EN5: Barn 1C 20
IG1: Ilf 1F 71
KT7: T Ditt 5K 149
N4 . . . . .5C 48
W14 . . . . .3H 99
Warwick Gro. E5 . . . . .1H 67
KT5: Surb 7F 151
Warwick Ho. E16 . . . . .1J 105
(off Wesley Av.)
KT2: King T 1E 150
(off Acre Rd.)
SW9 .2A 120
Warwick Ho. St.
SW1 . . . . .4D 12 (1H 101)
Warwick La. EC4 . . . . . . .7B 8 (6B 84)
W14 . . . . .4H 99
Warwick Lodge TW2: Twick 3F 131
Warwick Mans. SW5 . . . . .4J 99
(off Cromwell Cres.)
Warwick Pde. HA3: Kenton 2B 42
Warwick Pas. EC4 . . . . .7B 8
(off Old Bailey)
Warwick Pl. KT7: T Ditt 6A 150
W5 . . . . .2D 96
W9 . . . . .5A 82
Warwick Pl. Nth.
SW1 . . . . .4A 18 (4G 101)
Warwick Rd.
CR7: Thor H 3A 156
DA14: Sidc 5B 144
DA16: Well 3C 126
E4 . . . . .5H 35
E11 . . . . .5K 51
E12 . . . . .5C 70
E15 . . . . .6H 69
E17 . . . . .1B 50
EN5: New Bar 4E 20
KT1: Hamp W 1C 150
KT3: N Mald 3J 151
KT7: T Ditt 5K 149

Warwick Rd. N11 . . . . .6C 32
  N18 . . . . .4K 33
  SE20 .3H 157
  SM1: Sutt 4A 166
  SW5 . . . . .4H 99
  TW2: Twick 1J 131
  TW4: Houn 3K 111
  TW15: Ashf 5A 128
  UB2: S'hall 3D 94
  UB7: W Dray 2A 92
  W5 . . . . .2D 96
  W14 . . . . .4H 99
Warwick Row SW1 . . . . . .1K 17 (3G 101)
Warwickshire Path SE8 . . . . . . .7B 104
Warwickshire Rd. N16 . . . . .4E 66
Warwick Sq. EC4 . . . . . . .7B 8 (6B 84)
  SW1 . . . . .5A 18 (5G 101)
              (not continuous)
Warwick Sq. M. SW1 . . .4A 18 (4G 101)
Warwick St. W1 . . . . .2B 12 (7G 83)
Warwick Ter. E17 . . . . .5F 51
              (off Lea Bri. Rd.)
  SE18 .6H 107
Warwick Way SW1 . . . . .5J 17 (5F 101)
Warwick Yd. EC1 . . . . . . .4D 8 (4C 84)
Wasdale NW1 . . . . .2K 5
              (off Cumberland Mkt.)
Washbourne Ct. N9 . . . . .2B 34
              (off Acton Cl.)
Washbourne Rd. NW10 . . . . .1K 79
Washington Av. E12 . . . . .4D 70
Washington Bldg. SE13 . . . . .1D 122
              (off Deal's Gateway)
Washington Cl. E3 . . . . .3D 86
Washington Ho. E17 . . . . .2B 50
  SW3 . . . . .7E 10
              (off Basil St.)
Washington Rd. E6 . . . . .7A 70
  E18 . . . . .2H 51
  KT1: King T 2G 151
  KT4: Wor Pk 2D 164
  SW13 .7C 98
  TW6: H'row A 6D 174
              (off Welland Rd.)
Wasp Rd. TW6: H'row A 5C 174
              (off Welland Rd.)
Wastdale Rd. SE23 . . . . .1K 139
The Watch N12 . . . . .4F 31
Watchfield Ct. W4 . . . . .5J 97
Watcombe Cotts.
  TW9: Kew 6G 97
Watcombe Pl. SE25 . . . . .5H 157
Watcombe Rd. SE25 . . . . .5H 157
              (off Knaresborough Dr.)
Waterbank Ho. SW18 . . . . .1K 135
Waterbank Rd. SE6 . . . . .3D 140
Waterbeach Rd.
  RM9: Dag 6C 72
Water Brook La. NW4 . . . . .5E 44
Watercress Pl. N1 . . . . .7E 66
Waterdale Rd. SE2 . . . . .6A 108
Waterden Ct. W11 . . . . .1G 99
Waterden Rd. E20 . . . . .5C 68
Waterer Ho. SE6 . . . . .4E 140
Waterer Ri. SM6: W'gton 6H 167
Waterfall Cl. N14 . . . . .3B 32
Waterfall Cotts. SW19 . . . . .6B 136
Waterfall Ho. SW2 . . . . .5A 120
              (off Brixton Water La.)
Waterfall Rd. N11 . . . . .4A 32
  N14 . . . . .4A 32
  SW19 .6B 136
Waterfall Ter. SW17 . . . . .6C 136
Waterfall Wlk. N14 . . . . .1A 32
Waterfield Cl. DA17: Belv 3G 109
  SE28 . . . . .1B 108
Waterfield Gdns. SE25 . . . . .4D 156
Waterford Ho. BR1: Broml 1J 159
              (off Newman Rd.)
  W11 . . . . .7H 81
              (off Kensington Pk. Rd.)
Waterford Point SW8 . . . . .7J 101
Waterford Rd. SW6 . . . . .7K 99

Waterfront Way NW10 . . . . .5D 62
Waterfront W6 . . . . .6E 98
Waterfront Dr. SW10 . . . . .1A 118
Waterfront Ho. E5 . . . . .2J 67
              (off Harry Zeital Way)
Waterfront Leisure Cen.
  Woolwich 3E 106
Waterfront M. N1 . . . . .2C 84
Waterfront Studios Bus. Cen.
  E16 . . . . .1H 105
              (off Dock Rd.)
The Water Gdns. W2 . . . .7D 4 (6C 82)
The Watergardens
  KT2: King T 6J 133
Water Gdns. HA7: Stan 6G 27
Water Gdns. Sq. SE16 . . . . .2K 103
Watergate EC4 . . . . .2A 14 (7B 84)
Watergate St. SE8 . . . . .6C 104
Watergate Wlk. WC2 . . . .4F 13 (1J 101)
Watergate Wlk. E14 . . . . .3D 104
Waterhall Av. E4 . . . . .4B 36
Waterhall Cl. E17 . . . . .1K 49
Waterhead NW1 . . . . .1A 6
              (off Varndell St.)
Waterhouse CRO: C'don 1C 168
              (off Saffron Central Sq.)
Waterhouse Cl. E16 . . . . .5B 88
  NW3 . . . . .5B 64
  W6 . . . . .4F 99
Waterhouse Sq. EC1 . . . .6J 7 (5A 84)
Water La. DA14: Sidc 2F 145
  E15 . . . . .6G 69
  EC3 . . . . .3H 15 (7E 84)
  IG3: Ilf 3J 71
  KT1: King T 1D 150
  N9 . . . . .1C 34
  NW1 . . . . .7F 65
  SE14 .7J 103
  TW1: Twick 1A 132
  TW9: Rich 5D 114
Water Lily Cl. UB2: S'hall 2G 95
Waterline Ho. W2 . . . . .6B 4
Waterloo Bri. WC2 . . . . .3G 13 (7K 83)
Waterloo Cl. E9 . . . . .5J 67
  TW14: Felt 1H 129
Waterloo East Theatre 5K 13
              (off Brad St.)
Waterloo Gdns. E2 . . . . .2J 85
  N1 . . . . .7B 66
  RM7: Rom 6K 55
Waterloo Pas. NW6 . . . . .7H 63
Waterloo Pl. SM5: Cars 3D 166
              (off Wrythe Grn.)
  SW1 . . . . .4C 12 (1H 101)
  TW9: Rich 4E 114
Waterloo Rd. E6 . . . . .7A 70
  E7 . . . . .5H 69
  E10 . . . . .7C 50
  IG6: Ilf 2G 53
  NW2 . . . . .1C 62
  RM7: Rom, Rush G 5K 55
  SE1 . . . . .4H 13 (1K 101)
  SM1: Sutt 5B 166
Waterloo Ter. N1 . . . . .7B 66
The Waterlow Bldg. E3 . . . . .5B 86
              (off Weatherley Cl.)
Waterlow Ct. NW11 . . . . .7K 45
Waterlow Pk. Cen. 1F 65
Waterlow Rd. N19 . . . . .1G 65
Waterman Bldg. E14 . . . . .2B 104
Waterman Ho. E15 . . . . .6F 69
              (off Forrester Way)
Watermans Art Cen., Cinema & Theatre
                      . . . . .6E 96
Watermans Cl. KT2: King T 7F 132
Watermans Ct. TW8: Bford 6D 96
              (off High St.)
Watermans Ho. E14 . . . . .6F 87
              (off New Village Av.)
Watermans M. W5 . . . . .7E 78
Waterman's Quay SW6 . . . . .2A 118

Waterman St. SW15 . . . . .3F 117
Watermans Wlk. SE16 . . . . .2A 104
Waterman Way E1 . . . . .1H 103
Watermark Ct. RM6: Chad H 6B 54
              (off Quarles Pk. Rd.)
Watermead TW14: Felt 1G 129
Watermead Ho. E9 . . . . .5A 68
Watermead La. SM5: Cars 7D 154
Watermead Lodge SE16 . . . . .1K 103
              (off Princes Riverside Rd.)
Watermeadow La. SW6 . . . . .2A 118
Watermead Rd. SE6 . . . . .4E 140
Watermead Way N17 . . . . .3H 49
Watermen's Sq. SE20 . . . . .7J 139
Watermen's Sq. SE20 . . . . .4J 121
Watermill Bus. Cen.
  EN3: Brim 2G 25
Watermill Cl. TW10: Ham 3C 132
Water Mill Ho. TW13: Hanw 2E 130
Watermill La. N18 . . . . .5K 33
Watermill Way SW19 . . . . .1A 154
  TW13: Hanw 2D 130
Watermint Quay N16 . . . . .7G 49
Water Rd. HA0: Wemb 1F 79
Water's Edge SW6 . . . . .1E 116
              (off Palemead Cl.)
Watersedge KT19: Ewe 4J 163
Watersfield Way HA8: Edg 7J 27
Waters Gdns. RM10: Dag 5G 73
Waterside BR3: Beck 1B 158
  E17 . . . . .6J 49
  N1 . . . . .2C 84
  UB7: Harm 3D 174
  W2 . . . . .6A 4
              (off Goodchild Rd.)
Waterside Av. BR3: Beck 5E 158
              (off Adamson Way)
Waterside Bus. Cen. TW7: Isle 4B 114
Waterside Cl. E3 . . . . .1B 86
  HA9: Wemb 3J 61
  IG11: Bark 4A 72
  KT6: Surb 2E 162
  SE16 . . . . .2G 103
  SE28 .1K 107
  TW17: Shep 1E 146
  UB5: N'olt 3D 76
Waterside Ct. SM5: Cars 3E 166
              (off Millpond Pl.)
Waterside Dr. KT12: Walt T 5J 147
Waterside Hgts. E16 . . . . .2A 106
              (off Booth Rd.)
Waterside Pl. NW1 . . . . .1E 82
Waterside Point SW11 . . . . .7C 100
Waterside Rd. UB2: S'hall 3E 94
Waterside Twr. SW6 . . . . .2A 118
              (off The Boulevard)
Waterside Trad. Cen. W7 . . . . .3J 95
Waterside Way N17 . . . . .3H 49
  SW17 .4A 136
Watersmeet Pl. N4 . . . . .1C 66
Watersmeet Way SE28 . . . . .6C 90
Waterson St. E2 . . . . .1H 9 (3E 84)
Waters Pl. SW15 . . . . .2E 116
Watersplash Cl.
  KT1: King T 3E 150
Watersplash La. TW5: Cran 5K 93
  UB3: Harl 4J 93
Watersplash Rd. TW17: Shep 5C 146
Watersreach Apts. N4 . . . . .1C 66
              (off Kayani Av.)
Waters Rd. KT1: King T 2H 151
  SE6 . . . . .3G 141
Waters Sq. KT1: King T 3H 151
Water St. WC2 . . . . .2J 13
Water Twr. Cl. UB8: Uxb 5A 56
Water Twr. Hill CRO: C'don 4D 168
Water Twr. Pl. N1 . . . . .1A 84
Waterview Cl. DA6: Bex 5D 126
Waterview Dr. SE10 . . . . .1F 105
Waterview Ho. E14 . . . . .5A 86
              (off Carr St.)

Waterway Av. SE13 . . . . .3D 122
Waterway Pk. UB3: Hayes 2E 92
Waterways Bus. Cen.
  EN3: Enf L 1G 25
Waterworks Cen. 2A 68
WATERWORKS CORNER 1G 51
Waterworks La. E5 . . . . .2K 67
Waterworks Nature Reserve 2A 68
Waterworks Rd. SW2 . . . . .6K 119
Waterworks Yd. CRO: C'don 3C 168
              (off Charles St.)
Watery La. DA14: Sidc 6B 144
  SW19 .2H 153
  SW20 .2H 153
  UB3: Harl 5F 93
  UB5: N'olt 2A 76
Wates Way CR4: Mitc 6D 154
Wateville Rd. N17 . . . . .1C 48
Watford By-Pass
  WD6: E'tree 1G 27
Watford Cl. SW11 . . . . .1C 118
Watford Rd. E16 . . . . .5J 87
  HA0: Wemb 2A 60
  HA1: Harr 7A 42
Watford Way NW4 . . . . .4C 44
  NW7 . . . . .4F 29
Watkin Rd. HA9: Wemb 3H 61
Watkins Cl. HA6: Nwood 1H 39
Watkins Ho. E14 . . . . .2E 104
              (off Manchester Rd.)
Watkinson Rd. N7 . . . . .6K 65
Watkins Way RM8: Dag 1E 72
WATLING .7E 28
Watling Av. HA8: Edg 1J 43
Watling Cl. EC4 . . . . .1D 14
Watling Farm Cl.
  HA7: Stan 1H 27
Watling Gdns. NW2 . . . . .6G 63
Watling Ga. NW9 . . . . .4A 44
Watling Ho. SE1 . . . . .4C 102
              (off New Kent Rd.)
Watlings Cl. CRO: C'don 6A 158
Watling St. DA1: Cray 5K 127
  DA6: Bex 4H 127
  DA7: Bex 4H 127
  EC4 . . . . .1D 14 (6C 84)
  SE15 . . . . .6E 102
Watlington Gro. SE26 . . . . .5A 140
Watney Cotts. SW14 . . . . .3J 115
Watney Mkt. E1 . . . . .6H 85
Watney Rd. SW14 . . . . .3J 115
Watney's Rd. CR4: Mitc 5H 155
Watney St. E1 . . . . .6H 85
Watson Av. E6 . . . . .7E 70
  SM3: Cheam 2G 165
Watson Cl. N16 . . . . .5D 66
  SW19 .6C 136
Watson Ct. E3 . . . . .3C 86
              (off Campbell Rd.)
Watson Ho. SW11 . . . . .7H 101
              (off Ponton Rd.)
Watsons Ho. N1 . . . . .1E 84
              (off Nuttall St.)
Watson's M. W1 . . . . .6D 4 (5C 82)
Watsons St. SE8 . . . . .7C 104
Watson St. E13 . . . . .2K 87
Watt Cl. W3 . . . . .2A 98
Watteau Sq. CRO: C'don 1A 168
Wattisfield Rd. E5 . . . . .3J 67
Watts Apts. SW8 . . . . .7J 101
              (off Cellini St.)
Watts Cl. N15 . . . . .5E 48
Wattsdown Cl. E13 . . . . .1J 87
Watts Gro. E3 . . . . .5C 86
Watts Ho. W10 . . . . .5G 81
              (off Wornington Rd.)
Watts La. BR7: Chst 1F 161
  TW11: Tedd 5A 132
Watts M. IG6: Ilf 3H 53
  SW16 .6H 137

Watts Rd. KT7: T Ditt 7A **150**
Watts St. E1 . . . . .1H **103**
SE15 . . . . .1F **121**
Wat Tyler Ho. N8 . . . . .3J **47**
(off Boyton Rd.)
Wat Tyler Rd. SE3 . . . . .2E **122**
SE10 . . . . .2E **122**
Wauthier Cl. N13 . . . . .5G **33**
Wave Ct. RM7: Rush G 6K **55**
Wavel Ct. CRO: C'don 5D **168**
(off Hurst Rd.)
E1 . . . . .1J **103**
(off Garnet St.)
Wavelengths Leisure Cen. 7C **104**
Wavell Dr. DA15: Sidc 6J **125**
Wavell Ho. N6 . . . . .6E **46**
(off Hillcrest)
Wavel M. N8 . . . . .4H **47**
NW6 . . . . .7K **63**
Wavel Pl. SE26 . . . . .4F **139**
Wavendon Av. W4 . . . . .5K **97**
Waveney Av. SE15 . . . . .4H **121**
Waveney Cl. E1 . . . . .1G **103**
Waveney Ho. SE15 . . . . .4H **121**
Waverley Av. E4 . . . . .4G **35**
E17 . . . . .3F **51**
HA9: Wemb 5F **61**
KT5: Surb 6H **151**
SM1: Sutt 2K **165**
TW2: Whitt 1D **130**
Waverley Cl. BR2: Broml 5B **160**
E18 . . . . .1A **52**
KT8: W Mole 5E **148**
UB3: Harl 4F **93**
Waverley Ct. EN2: Enf 3G **23**
NW3 . . . . .6D **64**
NW6 . . . . .7G **63**
SE26 . . . . .5J **139**
Waverley Cres. SE18 . . . . .5H **107**
Waverley Gdns. E6 . . . . .5C **88**
HA6: Nwood 1J **39**
IG6: Ilf 2G **53**
IG11: Bark 2J **89**
NW10 . . . . .2F **79**
Waverley Gro. N3 . . . . .3F **45**
Waverley Ind. Est. HA1: Harr 3H **41**
Waverley Lodge E15 . . . . .6G **69**
(off Litchfield Av.)
Waverley Pl. N4 . . . . .2B **66**
NW8 . . . . .2B **82**
Waverley Rd. E17 . . . . .3E **50**
E18 . . . . .1A **52**
EN2: Enf 3G **23**
HA2: Harr 5F **40**
KT17: Ewe 5D **164**
N8 . . . . .6J **47**
N17 . . . . .7C **34**
SE18 . . . . .5G **107**
SE25 . . . . .4H **157**
UB1: S'hall 7E **76**
Waverley Way SM5: Cars 6C **166**
Waverton Ho. E3 . . . . .1B **86**
Waverton Rd. SW18 . . . . .7A **118**
Waverton St. W1 . . . . . .4J **11** (1E **100**)
Wavertree Ct. SW2 . . . . .1J **137**
Wavertree Rd. E18 . . . . .2J **51**
SW2 . . . . .1K **137**
Waxham NW3 . . . . .5D **64**
Waxlow Cres. UB1: S'hall 6E **76**
Waxlow Ho. UB4: Yead 5B **76**
Waxlow Rd. NW10 . . . . .2J **79**
Waxlow Way UB5: N'olt 4D **76**
Waxwell Cl. HA5: Pinn 2B **40**
Waxwell Farm Ho. HA5: Pinn 2B **40**
Waxwell La. HA5: Pinn 2B **40**
Wayborne Gro. HA4: Ruis 6E **38**
Waye Av. TW5: Cran 1J **111**
Wayfarer Rd.
TW6: H'row A 5C **174**
UB5: N'olt 3B **76**
Wayfield Link SE9 . . . . .6H **125**
Wayford St. SW11 . . . . .2C **118**

Wayland Av. E8 . . . . .5G **67**
Wayland Ho. SW9 . . . . .2A **120**
(off Robsart St.)
Waylands UB3: Hayes 5F **75**
Waylands Mead BR3: Beck 1D **158**
Waylett Ho. SE11 . . . . .6J **19**
Waylett Pl. HAO: Wemb 4D **60**
SE27 . . . . .3B **138**
Wayman Ct. E8 . . . . .6H **67**
Wayne Cl. BR6: Orp 3K **173**
Wayne Kirkum Way NW6 . . . . . . .5H **63**
Waynflete Av. CRO: Wadd 3B **168**
Waynflete Ho. SE1 . . . . .5C **14**
(off Union St.)
Waynflete Sq. W10 . . . . .7F **81**
(not continuous)
Waynflete St. SW18 . . . . .2A **136**
Waypoint Way E16 . . . . .2K **105**
Wayside CRO: New Ad 6D **170**
NW11 . . . . .1G **63**
SW14 . . . . .5J **115**
Wayside Cl. N14 . . . . .6B **22**
Wayside Commercial Est.
IG11: Bark 1K **89**
Wayside Ct. HA9: Wemb 3G **61**
TW1: Twick 6C **114**
Wayside Gdns. RM10: Dag 5G **73**
Wayside Gro. SE9 . . . . .4D **142**
Wayside M. IG2: Ilf 5E **52**
WC1 WC1 . . . . .4H **7** (4K **83**)
The Weald BR7: Chst 6D **142**
Weald Cl. BR2: Broml 2C **172**
SE16 . . . . .5H **103**
Wealden Ho. E3 . . . . .3D **86**
(off Talwin St.)
Weald La. HA3: Hrw W 2H **41**
Weald Ri. HA3: Hrw W 7E **26**
Weald Rd. UB10: Hil 2C **74**
Weald Sq. E5 . . . . .2G **67**
WEALDSTONE 3J **41**
Wealdstone FC 2H **57**
Wealdstone Rd. SM3: Sutt 2H **165**
Weald Way RM7: Rom 6H **55**
UB4: Hayes 3G **75**
Wealdwood Gdns. HA5: Hat E 6A **26**
Weale Rd. E4 . . . . .3A **36**
Weall Ct. HA5: Pinn 4C **40**
Weardale Gdns. EN2: Enf 1J **23**
Weardale Rd. SE13 . . . . .4F **123**
Wearmouth Ho. E3 . . . . .4B **86**
(off Joseph St.)
Wear Pl. E2 . . . . .3H **85**
(not continuous)
Wearside Rd. SE13 . . . . .4D **122**
Weatherbury W2 . . . . .6J **81**
(off Talbot Rd.)
Weatherbury Ho. N19 . . . . .3H **65**
(off Wedmore St.)
Weatherley Cl. E3 . . . . .5B **86**
Weaver Cl. CRO: C'don 4F **169**
E6 .7F **89**
Weaver Ho. E1 . . . . .4G **85**
(off Pedley St.)
Weavers Almshouses E11 . . . . . . .6H **51**
(off Cambridge Rd.)
Weavers Cl. TW7: Isle 4J **113**
Weavers Ho. E11 . . . . .6J **51**
(off New Wanstead)
Weavers La. SE1 . . . . . .5H **15** (1E **102**)
Weavers Row E20 . . . . .5D **68**
Weavers Ter. SW6 . . . . .6J **99**
(off Micklethwaite Rd.)
Weaver St. E1 . . . . .4G **85**
(not continuous)
Weavers Way NW1 . . . . .1H **83**
Weaver Wlk. HA9: Wemb 4G **61**
SE27 . . . . .4C **138**
Webb Cl. W10 . . . . .4E **80**
Webb Ct. SE28 . . . . .7B **90**
(off Attlee Rd.)
Webber Ho. IG11: Bark 7G **71**
(off North St.)

Webber Path E14 . . . . .7E **86**
(off Bullivant St.)
Webber Row SE1 . . . . . .7K **13** (2B **102**)
Webber St. SE1 . . . . . . .6K **13** (2A **102**)
Webb Est. E5 . . . . .7G **49**
Webb Gdns. E13 . . . . .4J **87**
Webb Ho. E3 . . . . .3C **86**
(off Trevithick Way)
RM10: Dag 3G **73**
(off Kershaw Rd.)
SW8 . . . . .7H **101**
TW13: Hanw 3C **130**
Webb Pl. NW10 . . . . .3B **80**
Webb Rd. SE3 . . . . .6H **105**
Webbscroft Rd. RM10: Dag 4H **73**
Webb's Rd. SW11 . . . . .4D **118**
Webbs Rd. UB4: Yead 3K **75**
Webb St. SE1 . . . . .3E **102**
Webheath NW6 . . . . .7H **63**
(not continuous)
Webster Gdns. W5 . . . . .1D **96**
Webster Rd. E11 . . . . .3E **68**
SE16 . . . . .3G **103**
Weddell Ho. E1 . . . . .4K **85**
(off Duckett St.)
Wedderburn Ho. SW1 . . . . .5G **17**
(off Lwr. Sloane St.)
Wedderburn Rd. IG11: Bark 1J **89**
NW3 . . . . .5B **64**
Wedgewood Apts. SW8 . . . . .7J **101**
Wedgewood Ct. BR2: Broml 3H **159**
(off Cumberland Rd.)
DA5: Bexl 7G **127**
Wedgewood Ho. SW1 . . . . .6K **17**
(off Churchill Gdns.)
Wedgewood M. SW6 . . . . .2G **117**
W1 . . . . .1D **12** (6H **83**)
Wedgwood Ct. N7 . . . . .4K **65**
Wedgwood Ho. E2 . . . . .3K **85**
(off Warley St.)
SE11 . . . . .2J **19**
Wedgwood Wlk. NW6 . . . . .5K **63**
(off Dresden Cl.)
Wedgwood Way SE19 . . . . .7C **138**
Wedlake St. W10 . . . . .4G **81**
Wedmore Av. IG5: Ilf 1E **52**
Wedmore Gdns. N19 . . . . .2H **65**
Wedmore M. N19 . . . . .3H **65**
Wedmore Rd. UB6: G'frd 3H **77**
Wedmore St. N19 . . . . .3H **65**
Weech Rd. NW6 . . . . .4J **63**
Weedington Rd. NW5 . . . . .5E **64**
Weedon Ho. W12 . . . . .6C **80**
Weekley Sq. SW11 . . . . .3B **118**
Weigall Rd. SE12 . . . . .5J **123**
Weighhouse St. W1 . . . . .1H **11** (6E **82**)
Weightman Ho. SE16 . . . . .3G **103**
Weighton Rd. HA3: Hrw W 1H **41**
SE20 . . . . .2H **157**
Weihurst Ct. SM1: Sutt 5C **166**
Weihurst Gdns. SM1: Sutt 5B **166**
Weimar St. SW15 . . . . .3G **117**
Weirdale Av. N20 . . . . .2J **31**
Weir Hall Av. N18 . . . . .6J **33**
Weir Hall Gdns. N18 . . . . .5J **33**
Weir Hall Rd. N17 . . . . .5J **33**
N18 . . . . .5J **33**
Weir Rd. DA5: Bexl 7H **127**
KT12: Walt T 6J **147**
SW12 . . . . .7G **119**
SW19 . . . . .3K **135**
Weir's Pas. NW1 . . . . . .1D **6** (3H **83**)
Weiss Rd. SW15 . . . . .3F **117**
Welbeck Av. BR1: Broml 4J **141**
DA15: Sidc 1A **144**
UB4: Yead 4K **75**
Welbeck Cl. KT3: N Mald 5B **152**
KT17: Ewe 7C **164**
N12 . . . . .5G **31**
Welbeck Ct. UB4: Yead 4K **75**
W14 . . . . .4H **99**
(off Addison Bri. Pl.)

Welbeck Ho. W1 . . . . .7J **5**
(off Welbeck St.)
Welbeck Rd. E6 . . . . .3B **88**
EN4: E Barn 6H **21**
HA2: Harr 1F **59**
SM1: Sutt 2B **166**
SM5: Cars 2B **166**
Welbeck St. W1 . . . . . . .6H **5** (5E **82**)
Welbeck Vs. N21 . . . . .2H **33**
Welbeck Wlk.
SM5: Cars 1B **166**
Welbeck Way W1 . . . . . .7J **5** (6F **83**)
Welbury Ct. E8 . . . . .7E **66**
(off Kingsland Rd.)
Welby Ho. N19 . . . . .7H **47**
Welby St. SE5 . . . . .1B **120**
Welch Pl. HA5: Pinn 1A **40**
Welcome Ct. E17 . . . . .7C **50**
(off Saxon Cl.)
Weldin M. SW18 . . . . .5J **117**
(off Lebanon Rd.)
Weldon Cl. HA4: Ruis 6K **57**
Weldon Ct. N21 . . . . .5E **22**
(off Cockfosters Rd.)
KT8: W Mole 4D **148**
Weld Pl. N11 . . . . .5A **32**
(not continuous)
Weld Works M. SW2 . . . . .6K **119**
Welfare Rd. E15 . . . . .7G **69**
Welford Cl. E5 . . . . .3K **67**
Welford Ct. HA8: Edg 4K **27**
(off Lacey Dr.)
NW1 . . . . .7F **65**
(off Castlehaven Rd.)
SW8 . . . . .2G **119**
W9 . . . . .5J **81**
(off Elmfield Way)
Welford Ho. UB5: N'olt 4D **76**
(off Waxlow Way)
Welford Pl. SW19 . . . . .4G **135**
Welham Rd. SW16 . . . . .5E **136**
SW17 . . . . .5E **136**
Welhouse Rd. SM5: Cars 1C **166**
Wellacre Rd. HA3: Kenton 6B **42**
Wellan Cl. DA15: Sidc 5B **126**
Welland Ct. SE6 . . . . .2B **140**
(off Oakham Cl.)
Welland Gdns. UB6: G'frd 2K **77**
Welland Ho. SE15 . . . . .4J **121**
Welland M. E1 . . . . .1G **103**
Welland Rd.
BR1: Broml 2D **160**
Welland St. SE10 . . . . .6E **104**
Well App. EN5: Barn 5A **20**
Wellbrook Rd.
BR6: Farnb 4E **172**
Wellby Cl. N9 . . . . .1B **34**
Wellby Ct. E13 . . . . .1A **88**
Well Cl. HA4: Ruis 3C **58**
SW16 . . . . .4K **137**
Wellclose Sq. E1 . . . . .7G **85**
(not continuous)
Wellclose St. E1 . . . . .7G **85**
Wellcome Collection 3C **6**
The Wellcome Mus. 7H **7**
(within Royal College of Surgeons)
Well Cott. E11 . . . . .6A **52**
Well Ct. EC4 . . . . .1D **14** (6C **84**)
(not continuous)
Wellday Ho. E9 . . . . .6A **68**
(off Hedger's Gro.)
Welldon Ct. HA1: Harr 5J **41**
Welldon Cres. HA1: Harr 5J **41**
Weller Ct. W11 . . . . .1H **99**
(off Ladbroke Rd.)
Weller Ho. SE16 . . . . .2G **103**
(off George Row)
Weller M. BR2: Broml 4K **159**
EN2: Enf 1F **23**
Weller St. SE1 . . . . .6C **14** (2C **102**)

Welles Ct. E14 . . . . .7C **86**
(off Premiere Pl.)
Wellesley Av. W6 . . . . .3D **98**
Wellesley Cl. SE7 . . . . .5A **106**
Wellesley Ct. NW2 . . . . .2C **62**
SE1 .3C **102**
(off Rockingham St.)
SM3: Sutt 1G **165**
W9 .3A **82**
Wellesley Ct. Rd.
CR0: C'don 2D **168**
Wellesley Cres. TW2: Twick 2J **131**
Wellesley Gro. CR0: C'don 2D **168**
Wellesley Ho. NW1 . . . . .2D **6**
(off Wellesley Pl.)
SW1 . . . . .5J **17**
(off Ebury Bri. Rd.)
Wellesley Mans. W14 . . . . .5H **99**
(off Edith Vs.)
Wellesley Pde. TW2: Twick 3J **131**
Wellesley Pk. M.
EN2: Enf 2G **23**
Wellesley Pas. CR0: C'don 2C **168**
Wellesley Pl. NW1 . . . . .2C **6** (3H **83**)
NW5 .5E **64**
Wellesley Rd. CR0: C'don 1C **168**
E11 . . . . .5J **51**
E17 . . . . .6C **50**
HA1: Harr 5J **41**
IG1: Ilf 2F **71**
N22 . . . . .2A **48**
NW5 .5E **64**
SE18 .7E **106**
SM2: Sutt 6A **166**
(not continuous)
TW2: Twick 3H **131**
W4 . . . . .5G **97**
Wellesley St. E1 . . . . .5K **85**
Wellesley Ter. N1 . . . . . .1D **8** (3C **84**)
Wellfield Av. N10 . . . . .3F **47**
Wellfield Rd. SW16 . . . . .4J **137**
Wellfield Wlk. SW16 . . . . .4K **137**
Wellfit St. SE24 . . . . .3B **120**
Wellgarth UB6: G'frd 6B **60**
Wellgarth Rd. NW11 . . . . .1K **63**
Well Gro. N20 . . . . .1F **31**
Well Hall Pde. SE9 . . . . .4D **124**
Well Hall Rd. SE9 . . . . .3C **124**
WELL HALL RDBT. 4C **124**
Wellhouse La. EN5: Barn 4A **20**
Wellhouse Rd. BR3: Beck 4C **158**
Wellhurst Cl. BR6: Chels 7K **173**
WELLING 3B **126**
Welling High St.
DA16: Well 3B **126**
Wellings Ho. UB3: Hayes 1K **93**
Wellington N8 . . . . .4J **47**
(not continuous)
Wellington Arch 6H **11** (2E **100**)
Wellington Av. DA15: Sidc 6A **126**
E4 . . . . .2H **35**
HA5: Hat E 1D **40**
KT4: Wor Pk 3E **164**
N9 . . . . .3C **34**
N15 .6F **49**
TW3: Houn 5E **112**
Wellington Bldgs. E3 . . . . .3C **86**
(off Wellington Way)
SW1 . . . . .6H **17** (5E **100**)
Wellington Cl. KT12: Walt T 7H **147**
RM10: Dag 7J **73**
SE14 . . . . .1K **121**
W11 .6J **81**
Wellington Ct. NW8 . . . . .2B **82**
(off Wellington Rd.)
SW1 .7E **10**
(off Knightsbridge)
SW6 .1K **117**
(off Maltings Pl.)
TW12: Hamp H 5H **131**
TW15: Ashf 5A **128**
TW19: Stanw 7A **110**

Wellington Cres.
KT3: N Mald 3J **151**
Wellington Dr. RM10: Dag 7J **73**
Wellington Gdns. SE7 . . . . .6A **106**
TW2: Twick 4H **131**
Wellington Gro. SE10 . . . . .7F **105**
Wellington Ho. E16 . . . . .1J **105**
(off Pepys Cres.)
NW3 .6D **64**
(off Eton Rd.)
SE17 .6C **102**
(off Arnside St.)
UB5: N'olt 7E **58**
(off The Farmlands)
W5 . . . . .3E **78**
(off Waterloo Rd.)
Wellington Lodge SE1 . . . . .7A **14**
(off Waterloo Rd.)
Wellington Mans. E10 . . . . .1C **68**
SE7 .5A **106**
(off Wellington Gdns.)
W14 .6H **99**
(off Queen's Club Gdns.)
Wellington M. N7 . . . . .6K **65**
(off Roman Way)
SE7 .6A **106**
SE22 . . . . .4G **121**
SW16 . . . . .3H **137**
Wellington Monument
. . . . .6H **11** (2E **100**)
Wellington Mus. 6H **11** (2E **100**)
Wellington Pde. DA15: Sidc 5A **126**
Wellington Pk. Est. NW2 . . . . . . .2C **62**
Wellington Pas. E11 . . . . .5J **51**
Wellington Pl. N2 . . . . .5C **46**
NW8 . . . . .1B **4** (3B **82**)
Wellington Rd. BR2: Broml 4A **160**
CR0: C'don 7B **156**
DA5: Bexl 5D **126**
DA17: Belv 5F **109**
E6 . . . . .1D **88**
E7 . . . . .4H **69**
E10 .1A **68**
E11 . . . . .5J **51**
E17 . . . . .4A **50**
EN1: Enf 5K **23**
HA3: W'stone 3J **41**
HA5: Hat E 1D **40**
NW8 . . . . .1B **4** (2B **82**)
NW10 . . . . .3F **81**
SW19 . . . . .2J **135**
TW2: Twick 5H **131**
TW6: H'row A 6D **174**
(off Whittle Rd.)
TW12: Hamp H 5H **131**
TW14: Felt 5G **111**
TW15: Ashf 5A **128**
W5 . . . . .3C **96**
Wellington Rd. Nth.
TW4: Houn 3D **112**
Wellington Rd. Sth.
TW4: Houn 4D **112**
Wellington Row E2 . . . . . . .1K **9** (3F **85**)
Wellington Sq. N1 . . . . .1J **83**
SW3 . . . . .5E **16** (5D **100**)
Wellington St. SE18 . . . . .4E **106**
WC2 . . . . .2G **13** (7K **83**)
Wellington Ter. E1 . . . . .1H **103**
HA1: Harr 1H **59**
N8 . . . . .3A **48**
(off Turnpike La.)
W2 . . . . .7J **81**
Wellington Way E3 . . . . .3C **86**
Welling United FC 3C **126**
Welling Way DA16: Well 3G **125**
SE9 .3G **125**
Well La. SW14 . . . . .5J **115**
Wellmeadow Rd. SE6 . . . . .7G **123**
SE13 . . . . .6G **123**
(not continuous)
W7 . . . . .4A **96**
Wellow Wlk. SM5: Cars 1B **166**
Well Pl. NW3 . . . . .3B **64**

Well Rd. EN5: Barn 5A **20**
NW3 .3B **64**
The Wells N14 . . . . .7C **22**
Wellsborough M. SW20 . . . . .2G **153**
Wells Cl. CR2: S Croy 5E **168**
UB5: N'olt 3A **76**
Wells Ct. BR2: Broml 2F **159**
NW6 .2J **81**
(off Cambridge Av.)
Wells Dr. NW9 . . . . .1K **61**
Wells Gdns. IG1: Ilf 7C **52**
RM10: Dag 5H **73**
Wells Ga. Cl. IG8: Wfd G 4D **36**
Wells Ho. BR1: Broml 5K **141**
(off Pike Cl.)
EC1 . . . . .1K **7**
(off Spa Grn. Est.)
IG11: Bark 7A **72**
(off Margaret Bondfield Av.)
SE16 . . . . .3J **103**
(off Howland Est.)
W5 . . . . .7D **78**
(off Grove Rd.)
W10 .4G **81**
(off Wornington Rd.)
Wells Ho. Rd. NW10 . . . . .5A **80**
Wellside Cl. EN5: Barn 4A **20**
Wellside Gdns. SW14 . . . . .4J **115**
Wells La. TW3: Houn 3F **113**
Wells M. N11 . . . . .5C **32**
W1 . . . . .6B **6** (5G **83**)
Wellsmoor Gdns. BR1: Broml 3E **160**
Wells Pk. Rd. SE26 . . . . .3G **139**
Wells Path UB4: Hayes 3G **75**
Wells Pl. SW18 . . . . .7A **118**
Wellspring Cl. E14 . . . . .5E **86**
Wellspring Cres.
HA9: Wemb 3H **61**
Wellspring M. SE26 . . . . .3H **139**
Wells Ri. NW8 . . . . .1D **82**
Wells Rd. BR1: Broml 2D **160**
W12 .2E **98**
Wells Sq. WC1 . . . . .2G **7** (3K **83**)
Wells St. W1 . . . . .6A **6** (5G **83**)
Wellstead Av. N9 . . . . .7E **24**
Wellstead Rd. E6 . . . . .2E **88**
Wells Ter. N4 . . . . .2A **66**
Wellston Cres. N14 . . . . .6B **22**
Well St. E9 . . . . .7J **67**
E15 .6G **69**
Wells Vw. Dr.
BR2: Broml 6C **160**
Wells Way SE5 . . . . .6D **102**
SW7 . . . . .1A **16** (3B **100**)
Wells Yd. N7 . . . . .5A **66**
Well Wlk. NW3 . . . . .4B **64**
Wellwood Rd. IG3: Ilf 1A **72**
Welmar M. SW4 . . . . .4H **119**
(off Clapham Pk. Rd.)
Welsby Ct. W5 . . . . .5C **78**
Welsford St. SE1 . . . . .4G **103**
(not continuous)
Welsh Cl. E13 . . . . .3J **87**
Welsh Gdns. NW4 . . . . .4D **44**
Welsh Harp Reservoir 1B **62**
Welsh Ho. E1 . . . . .1H **103**
(off Wapping La.)
Welshpool Ho. E8 . . . . .1G **85**
(off Welshpool St.)
Welshpool St. E8 . . . . .1G **85**
(not continuous)
Welshside NW9 . . . . .6A **44**
(off Ruthin Cl.)
Welshside Wlk. NW9 . . . . .6A **44**
Welstead Ho. E1 . . . . .6H **85**
(off Cannon St. Rd.)
Welstead Way W4 . . . . .4B **98**
Weltje Rd. W6 . . . . .4C **98**
Welton Ct. SE5 . . . . .1E **120**
Welton Ho. E1 . . . . .5K **85**
(off Stepney Way)
Welton Rd. SE18 . . . . .7J **107**
Welwyn Av. TW14: Felt 6H **111**

Welwyn St. E2 . . . . .3J **85**
Welwyn Way UB4: Hayes 4G **75**
WEMBLEY 5E **60**
Wembley & Sudbury Tennis &
Squash Club 5D **60**
Wembley Commercial Cen.
HA9: Wemb 2D **60**
Wembley Hill Rd. HA9: Wemb 3F **61**
(East La.)
HA9: Wemb 5F **61**
(South Way)
Wembley Leisure Cen. 3G **61**
WEMBLEY PARK 4G **61**
Wembley Pk. Blvd. HA9: Wemb . . .5G **61**
Wembley Pk. Bus. Cen.
HA9: Wemb 4H **61**
Wembley Pk. Dr. HA9: Wemb 4F **61**
Wembley Pk. Ga. HA9: Wemb 4G **61**
Wembley Rd. TW12: Hamp 1E **148**
Wembley Sailing Club 2K **61**
Wembley Stadium 4G **61**
Wembley Stadium Ind. Est.
HA9: Wemb 4H **61**
Wembley Way HA9: Wemb 6H **61**
Wemborough Rd. HA7: Stan 1B **42**
Wembury M. N6 . . . . .7G **47**
Wembury Rd. N6 . . . . .7F **47**
Wemyss Rd. SE3 . . . . .2H **123**
Wendela Ct. HA1: Harr 2J **59**
Wendell M. W12 . . . . .2B **98**
Wendell Rd. W12 . . . . .3B **98**
Wenderholme CR2: S Croy 5D **168**
(off Sandpits Pk. Hill Rd.)
Wendle Ct. SW8 . . . . .7E **18** (6J **101**)
Wendle Sq. SW11 . . . . .1C **118**
Wendling NW5 . . . . .5D **64**
Wendling Rd. SM1: Sutt 1B **166**
Wendon St. E3 . . . . .1B **86**
Wendover SE17 . . . . .5E **102**
(not continuous)
Wendover Cl. UB4: Yead 4C **76**
Wendover Ct. BR2: Broml 3K **159**
(off Wendover Rd.)
NW2 .3J **63**
NW10 . . . . .4H **79**
W1 . . . . .6G **5**
(off Chiltern St.)
Wendover Dr. KT3: N Mald 6B **152**
Wendover Ho. W1 . . . . .6G **5**
(off Chiltern St.)
Wendover Rd. BR2: Broml 4K **159**
NW10 . . . . .2B **80**
SE9 .3B **124**
Wendover Way DA16: Well 5A **126**
Wendy Cl. EN1: Enf 6A **24**
Wendy Way HA0: Wemb 1E **78**
Wenham Ho. SW8 . . . . .7G **101**
Wenlake Ho. EC1 . . . . .3C **8**
(off Old St.)
Wenlock Barn Est. N1 . . . . .2D **84**
(off Wenlock St.)
Wenlock Ct. N1 . . . . .1F **9** (2D **84**)
Wenlock Gdns. NW4 . . . . .4D **44**
Wenlock M. E10 . . . . .7C **50**
Wenlock Rd. HA8: Edg 7C **28**
N1 . . . . .1D **8** (2C **84**)
Wenlock St. N1 . . . . .1D **8** (2C **84**)
Wennington Rd. E3 . . . . .2K **85**
Wensdale Ho. E5 . . . . .2G **67**
Wensley Av. IG8: Wfd G 7C **36**
Wensley Cl. N11 . . . . .6K **31**
SE9 .6D **124**
Wensleydale Av. IG5: Ilf 2C **52**
Wensleydale Gdns.
TW12: Hamp 7F **131**
Wensleydale Pas.
TW12: Hamp 1E **148**
Wensleydale Rd. TW12: Hamp . . .6E **130**
Wensley Rd. N18 . . . . .6C **34**
Wensum Pl. BR2: Hayes 7J **159**
Wentland Cl. SE6 . . . . .2F **141**
Wentland Rd. SE6 . . . . .2F **141**

Wentway Ct.—Western Beach Apts.

Wentway Ct. W13 . . . 4K 77
(off Ruislip Rd. E.)
Wentworth Av. N3 . . . 7D 30
Wentworth Cl. BR2: Hayes . . . 2J 171
BR6: Farnb . . . 5J 173
KT6: Surb . . . 2D 162
N3 . . . 7E 30
SE28 . . . 6D 90
SM4: Mord . . . 7J 153
TW15: Ashf . . . 4D 128
Wentworth Ct. SW1 . . . 6J 17 (5F 101)
SW18 . . . 6K 117
(off Garratt La.)
TW2: Twick . . . 3J 131
W6 . . . 6G 99
(off Paynes Wlk.)
Wentworth Cres. SE15 . . . 7G 103
UB3: Harl . . . 3F 93
Wentworth Dr. HA5: Eastc . . . 5J 39
TW6: H'row A . . . 5C 174
Wentworth Dwellings E1 . . . 7J 9
(off Wentworth St.)
Wentworth Flds. UB4: Hayes . . . 2F 75
Wentworth Gdns. N13 . . . 3G 33
Wentworth Hill HA9: Wemb . . . 1F 61
Wentworth Ho. IG8: Wfd G . . . 7K 37
Wentworth M. E3 . . . 4A 86
W3 . . . 6A 80
Wentworth Pk. N3 . . . 7D 30
Wentworth Pl. HA7: Stan . . . 6G 27
Wentworth Rd. CR0: C'don . . . 7A 156
E12 . . . 4B 70
EN5: Barn . . . 3A 20
NW11 . . . 6H 45
UB2: S'hall . . . 4A 94
Wentworth St. E1 . . . 7J 9 (6F 85)
Wentworth Way HA5: Pinn . . . 4C 40
Wenvoe Av. DA7: Bex . . . 2H 127
Wepham Cl. UB4: Yead . . . 5B 76
Wernbrook St. SE18 . . . 6G 107
Werndee Rd. SE25 . . . 4G 157
Werneth Hall Rd. IG5: Ilf . . . 3E 52
Werrington St. NW1 . . . 1B 6 (2G 83)
Werter Rd. SW15 . . . 4G 117
Wesleyan Pl. NW5 . . . 4F 65
Wesley Apts. SW8 . . . 1H 119
Wesley Av. E16 . . . 1J 105
NW10 . . . 3K 79
TW3: Houn . . . 2C 112
Wesley Cl. HA2: Harr . . . 2G 59
KT19: Ewe . . . 5J 163
N7 . . . 2K 65
SE17 . . . 4B 102
Wesley Ct. SE16 . . . 3H 103
Wesley Rd. E10 . . . 7E 50
NW10 . . . 1J 79
UB3: Hayes . . . 7J 75
Wesley's Chapel . . . 3F 9 (4D 84)
Wesley's House & Mus. of Methodism
. . . 3F 9 (4D 84)
Wesley Sq. W11 . . . 6G 81
Wesley St. W1 . . . 6H 5 (5E 82)
Wessex Av. SW19 . . . 3J 153
Wessex Cl. IG3: Ilf . . . 6J 53
KT1: King T . . . 1H 151
Wessex Ct. BR3: Beck . . . 1A 158
EN5: Barn . . . 4A 20
HA9: Wemb . . . 2F 61
TW19: Stanw . . . 6A 110
Wessex Dr. HA5: Hat E . . . 1C 40
Wessex Gdns. NW11 . . . 1G 63
Wessex Ho. SE1 . . . 5F 103
Wessex La. UB6: G'frd . . . 3H 77
Wessex St. E2 . . . 3J 85
Wessex Ter. CR4: Mitc . . . 5C 154
Wessex Wlk. DA2: Wilm . . . 2K 145
Wessex Way NW11 . . . 1G 63
Wesson Mead SE5 . . . 7C 102
(off Camberwell Rd.)
West 12 Shop. Cen. . . . 2F 99
Westacott UB4: Hayes . . . 5G 75
Westacott Cl. N19 . . . 1H 65
West Acre HA2: Harr . . . 2J 59
WEST ACTON . . . 6G 79
West App. BR5: Pet W . . . 5G 161
W. Arbour St. E1 . . . 6K 85
West Av. E17 . . . 4D 50
HA5: Pinn . . . 6D 40
N3 . . . 6D 30
NW4 . . . 5F 45
SM6: W'gton . . . 5J 167
UB1: S'hall . . . 7D 76
UB3: Hayes . . . 7H 75
West Av. Rd. E17 . . . 4C 50
W. Bank EN2: Enf . . . 2H 23
IG11: Bark . . . 1F 89
N16 . . . 7E 48
Westbank Rd. TW12: Hamp H . . . 6G 131
WEST BARNES . . . 5D 152
W. Barnes La. KT3: N Mald . . . 3D 152
SW20 . . . 3D 152
WEST BECKTON . . . 6B 88
WEST BEDFONT . . . 6B 110
Westbeech Rd. N22 . . . 3A 48
Westbere Dr. HA7: Stan . . . 5J 27
Westbere Rd. NW2 . . . 4G 63
W. Block SE1 . . . 7H 13
(off York Rd.)
Westbourne Apts. SW6 . . . 3K 117
Westbourne Av. SM3: Cheam . . . 2G 165
W3 . . . 6K 79
Westbourne Bri. W2 . . . 5A 82
Westbourne Cl. UB4: Yead . . . 4A 76
Westbourne Ct. W2 . . . 5A 82
Westbourne Cres.
W2 . . . 2A 10 (7B 82)
Westbourne Cres. M. W2 . . . 2A 10
Westbourne Dr. SE23 . . . 2K 139
Westbourne Gdns. W2 . . . 6K 81
WESTBOURNE GREEN . . . 5J 81
Westbourne Gro. W2 . . . 6J 81
W11 . . . 7H 81
Westbourne Gro. M. W11 . . . 6J 81
Westbourne Gro. Ter. W2 . . . 6K 81
Westbourne Ho. SW1 . . . 5J 17
(off Ebury Bri. Rd.)
TW5: Hest . . . 6E 94
Westbourne Pde. UB10: Hil . . . 4D 74
Westbourne Pk. Pas. W2 . . . 5J 81
(off Harrow Rd.)
Westbourne Pk. Rd. W2 . . . 5J 81
W11 . . . 6G 81
Westbourne Pk. Vs. W2 . . . 5J 81
Westbourne Pl. N9 . . . 3C 34
Westbourne Rd. CR0: C'don . . . 6F 157
DA7: Bex . . . 7D 108
N7 . . . 6K 65
SE26 . . . 6K 139
TW13: Felt . . . 3H 129
UB8: Hil . . . 4D 74
Westbourne St. W2 . . . 2A 10 (7B 82)
Westbourne Ter. SE23 . . . 2K 139
(off Westbourne Dr.)
W2 . . . 1A 10 (6A 82)
Westbourne Ter. M. W2 . . . 6A 82
Westbourne Ter. Rd. W2 . . . 5K 81
WESTBOURNE TER. RD. BRI. . . . 5A 82
(off Westbourne Ter. Rd.)
Westbridge Cl. W12 . . . 2C 98
Westbridge Ho. SW11 . . . 1C 118
(off Westbridge Rd.)
Westbridge Rd. SW11 . . . 1B 118
WEST BROMPTON . . . 6A 100
Westbrook Av. TW12: Hamp . . . 7D 130
Westbrook Cl. EN4: Cockf . . . 3G 21
Westbrook Cres. EN4: Cockf . . . 3G 21
Westbrooke Cres. DA16: Well . . . 3C 126
Westbrooke Rd. DA15: Sidc . . . 2H 143
DA16: Well . . . 3B 126
Westbrook Ho. E2 . . . 3J 85
(off Victoria Pk. Sq.)
Westbrook Rd. CR7: Thor H . . . 1D 156
SE3 . . . 1K 123
TW5: Hest . . . 7D 94
Westbrook Sq. EN4: Cockf . . . 3G 21
Westbury Av. HA0: Wemb . . . 7E 60
N22 . . . 3B 48
UB1: S'hall . . . 4E 76
Westbury Cl. HA4: Ruis . . . 7J 39
TW17: Shep . . . 6D 146
Westbury Ct. IG11: Bark . . . 1H 89
(off Ripple Rd.)
Westbury Gro. N12 . . . 6D 30
Westbury Ho. E17 . . . 4B 50
W11 . . . 5J 81
(off Aldridge Rd. Vs.)
Westbury La. IG9: Buck H . . . 2E 36
Westbury Lodge Cl. HA5: Pinn . . . 3B 40
Westbury Pde. SW12 . . . 6F 119
(off Balham Hill)
Westbury Pl. TW8: Bford . . . 6D 96
Westbury Rd. BR1: Broml . . . 1B 160
BR3: Beck . . . 3A 158
CR0: C'don . . . 6D 156
E7 . . . 6K 69
E17 . . . 4B 50
HA0: Wemb . . . 7E 60
IG1: Ilf . . . 2E 70
IG9: Buck H . . . 2F 37
IG11: Bark . . . 1H 89
KT3: N Mald . . . 4K 151
N11 . . . 6D 32
N12 . . . 6D 30
SE20 . . . 1K 157
TW13: Felt . . . 1B 130
W5 . . . 6E 78
Westbury Ter. E7 . . . 6K 69
Westbush Ct. W12 . . . 2D 98
(off Goldhawk M.)
W. Cadet Apts. SE18 . . . 7E 106
(off Langhorne St.)
W. Carriage Dr. W2 . . . 3C 10 (7C 82)
(Nth. Ride)
W2 . . . 6B 10 (2B 100)
(Rotten Row)
W. Carriage Ho. SE18 . . . 3F 107
(off Royal Carriage M.)
W. Central St. WC1 . . . 7E 6 (6J 83)
West Chantry HA3: Hrw W . . . 1F 41
Westchester Dr. NW4 . . . 3F 45
Westcliffe Apts. W2 . . . 6B 4 (5B 82)
West Cl. EN4: Cockf . . . 4K 21
HA9: Wemb . . . 1F 61
N9 . . . 3A 34
TW12: Hamp . . . 6C 130
TW15: Ashf . . . 4A 128
UB6: G'frd . . . 2G 77
Westcombe Av. CR0: C'don . . . 7J 155
Westcombe Ct. SE3 . . . 7H 105
Westcombe Dr. EN5: Barn . . . 5D 20
Westcombe Hill SE3 . . . 7J 105
SE10 . . . 5J 105
Westcombe Lodge Dr.
UB4: Hayes . . . 5G 75
Westcombe Pk. Rd. SE3 . . . 6G 105
West Comn. Rd.
BR2: Hayes, Kes . . . 1J 171
UB8: Uxb . . . 5A 56
Westcoombe Av. SW20 . . . 1B 152
Westcote Ri. HA4: Ruis . . . 7E 38
Westcote Rd. SW16 . . . 5G 137
West Cotts. NW6 . . . 5J 63
Westcott Cl. BR1: Broml . . . 5D 160
CR0: New Ad . . . 7D 170
N15 . . . 6F 49
Westcott Cres. W7 . . . 6J 77
Westcott Ho. E14 . . . 7C 86
Westcott Rd. SE17 . . . 6B 102
West Ct. E17 . . . 4C 50
HA0: Wemb . . . 2C 60
TW5: Isle . . . 7G 95
Westcroft Cl. EN3: Enf W . . . 1D 24
NW2 . . . 4G 63
Westcroft Est. NW2 . . . 4G 63
Westcroft Gdns.
SM4: Mord . . . 3H 153
Westcroft Leisure Cen. . . . 4E 166
Westcroft Rd. SM5: Cars . . . 4E 166
SM6: W'gton . . . 4E 166
Westcroft Sq. W6 . . . 4C 98
Westcroft Way NW2 . . . 4G 63
W. Cromwell Rd. SW5 . . . 5H 99
W14 . . . 5H 99
W. Cross Cen. TW8: Bford . . . 6A 96
W. Cross Route W10 . . . 7F 81
W. Cross Way TW8: Bford . . . 6B 96
Westdale Pas. SE18 . . . 6F 107
Westdale Rd. SE18 . . . 6F 107
Westdean Av. SE12 . . . 1K 141
Westdean Cl. SW18 . . . 6K 117
West Dene SM3: Cheam . . . 6G 165
Westdene CR0: C'don . . . 4D 168
(off Chatsworth Rd.)
Westdown Rd. E15 . . . 4E 68
SE6 . . . 7C 122
WEST DRAYTON . . . 2A 92
W. Drayton Pk. Av.
UB7: W Dray . . . 3A 92
W. Drayton Rd. UB8: Hil . . . 6D 74
West Dr. HA3: Hrw W . . . 6C 26
SM2: Cheam . . . 7F 165
SW16 . . . 4G 137
West Dr. Gdns.
HA3: Hrw W . . . 6C 26
WEST DULWICH . . . 2D 138
WEST EALING . . . 1B 96
W. Ealing Bus. Cen. W13 . . . 7A 78
W. Eaton Pl. SW1 . . . 3G 17 (4E 100)
W. Eaton Pl. M. SW1 . . . 2G 17
W. Ella Rd. NW10 . . . 7A 62
W. Elms Studios SW8 . . . 1G 119
WEST END . . . 2B 76
W. End Av. E10 . . . 5F 51
HA5: Pinn . . . 4B 40
W. End Cl. NW10 . . . 7J 61
W. End Ct. HA5: Pinn . . . 4B 40
NW6 . . . 7K 63
W. End Gdns. UB5: N'olt . . . 2A 76
W. End La. EN5: Barn . . . 4A 20
HA5: Pinn . . . 3B 40
NW6 . . . 5J 63
(not continuous)
UB3: Harl . . . 7E 92
W. End Quay W2 . . . 6B 4
W. End Rd. HA4: Ruis . . . 2G 57
UB1: S'hall . . . 1C 94
UB5: N'olt . . . 7A 58
Westerdale Ct. N5 . . . 4B 66
(off Hamilton Pk. W.)
Westerdale Rd. SE10 . . . 5J 105
Westerfield Rd. N15 . . . 5F 49
Westergate W5 . . . 5E 78
Westergate Ho. KT1: King T . . . 4D 150
(off Portsmouth Rd.)
Westergate Rd. SE2 . . . 6E 108
Westerham NW1 . . . 1G 83
(off Bayham St.)
Westerham Av. N9 . . . 3J 33
Westerham Dr. DA15: Sidc . . . 6B 126
Westerham Ho. SE1 . . . 3D 102
(off Law St.)
Westerham Lodge BR3: Beck . . . 7C 140
(off Park Rd.)
Westerham Rd. BR2: Kes . . . 6B 172
E10 . . . 7D 50
Westerley Cres. SE26 . . . 5B 140
Westerley Ware TW9: Kew . . . 6G 97
(off Kew Grn.)
Western Av. HA4: Ruis . . . 6D 56
NW11 . . . 6F 45
RM10: Dag . . . 6J 73
UB5: N'olt . . . 7A 58
UB6: G'frd . . . 7A 58
UB10: Hil, Uxb . . . 4A 56
W3 . . . 4F 79
W5 . . . 4F 79
Western Av. Bus. Pk. W3 . . . 4H 79
Western Beach Apts. E16 . . . 1J 105

Western Ct. N3 ....6D 30
  NW6 ....2H 81
  W3 ....6K 79
Western Clyd. EC2 ....7H 9
  (off Cutlers Gdns.)
Western Dr. TW17: Shep ..6F 147
Western Gdns. W5 ....7G 79
Western Gateway E16 ......7J 87
Western Intl. Mkt.
  UB2: S'hall 4K 93
Western La. SW12 ....7E 118
Western Mans. EN5: New Bar 5E 20
  (off Great Nth. Rd.)
Western M. W9 ....4H 81
Western Pde. EN5: New Bar 5D 20
Western Perimeter Rd.
  TW6: H'row A, Lford ...5C 174
Western Pl. SE16 ....2J 103
Western Rd. CR4: Mitc 1B 154
  E13 ....2A 88
  E17 ....5E 50
  N2 ....4D 46
  N22 ....2K 47
  NW10 ....4J 79
  SM1: Sutt 5J 165
  SW9 ....3A 120
  SW19 ....1B 154
  UB2: S'hall 4A 94
  W5 ....7D 78
Western Sq. N18 ....6D 34
Western Ter. W6 ....5C 98
Western Transit Shed N1 ...1J 83
Western Vw. UB3: Hayes ...2H 93
Westernville Gdns. IG2: Ilf ...7G 53
Western Wlk. KT1: King T 2E 150
  (off Eden Walk Shop. Cen.)
Western Way EN5: Barn 6D 20
  SE28 ....3H 107
WEST EWELL 7K 163
Westferry Cir. E14 ....1B 104
Westferry Rd. E14 ....7B 86
Westfield Av. E20 ....6D 68
Westfield Cl. EN3: Enf H 3F 25
  NW9 ....3J 43
  SM1: Sutt 4H 165
  SW10 ....7A 100
Westfield Ct. KT6: Surb ...5D 150
  (off Portsmouth Rd)
  NW10 ....3F 81
  (off Chamberlayne Rd.)
Westfield Dr. HA3: Kenton 4D 42
Westfield Gdns. HA3: Kenton 4D 42
  RM6: Chad H 6C 54
Westfield Ho. SE16 ....4H 103
  (off Rotherhithe New Rd.)
  SW10 ....7B 100
  (off Worlds End Est.)
Westfield La. HA3: Kenton 5D 42
Westfield Pk. HA5: Hat E 1J 40
Westfield Pk. Dr. IG8: Wfd G 6H 37
Westfield Rd. BR3: Beck 2B 158
  CR0: C'don 2B 168
  CR4: Mitc 2C 154
  DA7: Bex 3J 127
  KT6: Surb 5D 150
  KT12: Walt T 7C 148
  NW7 ....3E 28
  RM9: Dag 4E 72
  SM1: Sutt 4H 165
  W13 ....1A 96
Westfields SW13 ....3B 116
Westfields Av. SW13 ....3A 116
Westfield Shop. Cen.
  Stratford City 6E 68
  London 1E 98
Westfields Rd. W3 ....5H 79
Westfield St. SE18 ....3B 106
Westfield Way E1 ....3A 86
  HA4: Ruis 3G 57
West Gdn. Pl. W2 ...1D 10 (6C 82)
West Gdns. E1 ....7H 85
  SW17 ....6C 136

Westgate W5 ....3E 78
Westgate Apts. E16 ....7J 87
  (off Western Gateway)
Westgate Ct. SE12 ....1J 141
  (off Burnt Ash Hill)
  SW9 ....3A 120
  (off Canterbury Cres.)
Westgate Est. TW14: Bedf ...1D 128
Westgate Ho. TW7: Isle 2H 113
  TW8: Bford 5D 96
  (off Ealing Rd.)
Westgate M. W10 ....4G 81
  (off West Row)
Westgate Rd. BR3: Beck 1E 158
  SE25 ....4H 157
Westgate St. E8 ....1H 85
Westgate Ter. SW10 ....6K 99
Westglade Cl. HA3: Kenton ...5D 42
WEST GREEN 4B 48
West Grn. Pl. UB6: G'frd ...1H 77
West Grn. Rd. N15 ....4B 48
West Gro. IG8: Wfd G 6F 37
  SE10 ....1E 122
  SE17 ....4C 102
Westgrove La. SE10 ....1E 122
West Gro. Sq. SE17 ....4C 102
W. Halkin St. SW1 ...1G 17 (3E 100)
W. Hallowes SE9 ....1B 142
W. Hall Rd. TW9: Kew 1H 115
WEST HAM 1H 87
W. Ham La. E15 ....7F 69
West Ham Pk. E7 ....7J 69
WEST HAMPSTEAD 6K 63
W. Hampstead M. NW6 ....6K 63
West Ham Utd FC 1D 86
W. Handyside Canopy N1 ....1J 83
WEST HARROW 7G 41
W. Hatch Mnr. HA4: Ruis ...1H 57
Westhay Gdns. SW14 ......5H 115
WEST HEATH 6D 108
W. Heath Av. NW11 ....1J 63
W. Heath Cl. NW3 ....2J 63
W. Heath Dr. NW11 ....1J 63
W. Heath Gdns. NW3 ....2J 63
W. Heath Rd. NW3 ....2J 63
  SE2 ....6C 108
WEST HENDON 7C 44
W. Hendon B'way. NW9 ....6B 44
WEST HILL 6H 117
W. Hill CR2: Sande 7E 168
  HA2: Harr 2J 59
  HA9: Wemb 1F 61
  SW15 ....7F 117
  SW18 ....7F 117
W. Hill Ct. N6 ....3E 64
Westhill Ct. W11 ....7H 81
  (off Denbigh Rd.)
W. Hill Pk. N6 ....2D 64
  (not continuous)
W. Hill Rd. SW18 ....6H 117
W. Hill Way N20 ....1E 30
Westholm NW11 ....4K 45
West Holme DA8: Erith 1J 127
Westholme BR6: Orp 7J 161
Westholme Gdns.
  HA4: Ruis 1J 57
Westhope Ho. E2 ....4G 85
  (off Derbyshire St.)
Westhorne Av. SE9 ....5B 124
  SE12 ....7J 123
Westhorpe Gdns. NW4 ......3E 44
Westhorpe Rd. SW15 ....3E 116
West Ho. IG11: Bark 6F 71
West Ho. Cl. SW19 ....1G 135
West Ho. Cotts. HA5: Pinn 4B 40
Westhurst Dr. BR7: Chst 5F 143
W. India Av. E14 ....1C 104
W. India Dock Rd. E14 ......7B 86
W. India Ho. E14 ....7C 86
  (off W. India Dock Rd.)

WEST KENSINGTON 4G 99
W. Kensington Ct. W14 ......5H 99
  (off Edith Vs.)
W. Kensington Mans. W14 ....5H 99
  (off Beaumont Cres.)
WEST KILBURN 3H 81
Westking Pl. WC1 ...2G 7 (3K 83)
Westlake SE16 ....4J 103
  (off Rotherhithe New Rd.)
Westlake Cl. N13 ....3F 33
  UB4: Yead 4C 76
Westlake Rd. HA9: Wemb 2D 60
Westland Cl. TW19: Stanw 2A 110
Westland Cl. UB5: N'olt 3B 76
  (off Seasprite Cl.)
Westland Dr. BR2: Hayes 2H 171
Westland Ho. E16 ....1E 106
  (off Rymill St.)
Westland Pl. N1 ...1E 8 (3D 84)
Westlands Cl. UB3: Harl 4J 93
Westlands Ct. KT8: E Mos 4H 149
Westlands Est. UB3: Harl 3G 93
Westlands Ter. SW12 ....6G 119
West La. SE16 ....2H 103
Westlea Rd. W7 ....3A 96
Westleigh Av. SW15 ....5D 116
Westleigh Ct. CR2: S Croy 4E 168
  (off Birdhurst Rd.)
  E11 ....5J 51
  (off Nightingale La.)
Westleigh Dr. BR1: Broml 1C 160
Westleigh Gdns.
  HA8: Edg 1G 43
West Links HA0: Wemb 3D 78
Westlinton Cl. NW7 ....6B 30
W. Lodge E16 ....1J 105
  (off Britannia Ga.)
W. Lodge Av. W3 ....1G 97
W. Lodge Ct. W3 ....1G 97
W. London Crematorium 4D 80
West London Golf Course 1A 76
W. London Studios SW6 ......7K 99
  (off Fulham Rd.)
West London Synagogue
  (Reform) 1E 10
  (off Up. Berkeley St.)
Westmacott Dr. TW14: Felt 1H 129
Westmacott Ho. NW8 ....4B 4
  (off Hatton St.)
W. Mall N9 ....3B 34
  W8 ....1J 99
  (off Kensington Mall)
Westmark Point SW15 ......1D 134
  (off Norley Va.)
West Mead HA4: Ruis 4A 58
  KT19: Ewe 6A 164
Westmead SW15 ....6D 116
Westmead Cnr.
  SM5: Cars 4C 166
Westmead Ct. SE6 ....6C 122
Westmead Ho.
  SM1: Sutt 4B 166
Westmead Rd.
  SM1: Sutt 4B 166
Westmere Dr. NW7 ....3E 28
W. Mersea Cl. E16 ....1K 105
West M. N17 ....7C 34
  SW1 ....4A 18
West Middlesex Golf Course ...7G 77
WESTMINSTER ...7E 12 (2J 101)
Westminster Abbey ...7E 12 (3J 101)
Westminster Abbey Chapter House
  ....1E 18
  (within Abbey)
Westminster Abbey Museum ...3J 101
Westminster Abbey Pyx Chamber
  ....1E 18
  (within Westminster Abbey)
Westminster Av.
  CR7: Thor H 2B 156
Westminster Boating Base & Pier
  ....7C 18 (6H 101)

Westminster Bri.
  SW1 ....7F 13 (2J 101)
Westminster Bri. Ho. SE1 ....7A 14
  (off Lambeth Rd.)
Westminster Bri. Rd.
  SE1 ....7G 13 (2K 101)
Westminster Bus. Sq. SE11 ...7H 19
Westminster Cl. IG6: Ilf 2H 53
  TW11: Tedd 5A 132
  TW14: Felt 1J 129
Westminster Ct. E11 ....6K 51
  (off Cambridge Pk.)
  NW8 ....4A 4
  (off Aberdeen Pl.)
  SE16 ....1K 103
  (off King & Queen Wharf)
Westminster Dr. N13 ....5D 32
Westminster Gdns. E4 ....1B 36
  IG6: Ilf 2G 53
  IG11: Bark 2J 89
  SW1 ....3E 18
  (off Vincent St.)
Westminster Hall 7E 12
Westminster Ind. Est. SE18 ...3B 106
Westminster Mans. SW1 ......2D 18
  (off Gt. Smith St.)
Westminster Pal. Gdns. SW1 ...2C 18
Westminster RC Cathedral
  ....2A 18 (3G 101)
Westminster Rd. N9 ....1C 34
  SM1: Sutt 2B 166
  W7 ....1J 95
Westmoat Cl. BR3: Beck 7E 140
WEST MOLESEY 4E 148
Westmoor Gdns. EN3: Enf H ...2E 24
Westmoor Rd. EN3: Enf H 2E 24
Westmoor St. SE7 ....3A 106
Westmore Cl. SW15 ....5G 117
Westmoreland Av.
  DA16: Well 3J 125
Westmoreland Dr. SM2: Sutt ...7K 165
Westmoreland Ho. E16 ......1J 105
  (off Gatcombe Rd.)
  NW10 ....3C 80
Westmoreland Pl.
  BR1: Broml 3J 159
  SW1 ....6K 17 (5F 101)
  W5 ....5D 78
Westmoreland Rd.
  BR1: Broml 5G 159
  BR2: Broml 5G 159
  NW9 ....3F 43
  SE17 ....6D 102
  (not continuous)
  SW13 ....1B 116
Westmoreland St. W1 ...6H 5 (5E 82)
Westmoreland Ter.
  SE20 ....7H 139
  SW1 ....6K 17 (5F 101)
Westmoreland Wlk. SE17 ....6D 102
  (not continuous)
Westmorland Cl. E12 ....2B 70
  TW1: Twick 6B 114
Westmorland Ct.
  KT6: Surb 7D 150
Westmorland Rd. E17 ....6C 50
  HA1: Harr 5F 41
Westmorland Way CR4: Mitc ...4H 155
Westmount Cen. UB4: Yead 7B 76
Westmount Cl.
  KT4: Wor Pk 1E 164
Westmount Ct. W5 ....6F 79
Westmount Rd. SE9 ....2D 124
WEST NORWOOD 4C 138
West Norwood Crematorium ...3C 138
West Oak BR3: Beck 1F 159
Westoe Rd. N9 ....2C 34
W. Officers Apts. SE18 ......7E 106
Weston Av. KT7: T Ditt 7J 149
  KT8: W Mole 3C 148
Westonbirt Ct. SE15 ....6F 103
  (off Ebley Cl.)

Weston Ct. *KT1: King T* 3E **150**
            (off Grove Cres.)
N4 . . . . .3C **66**
N20 . . . . .7F **21**
            (off Farnham Cl.)
Weston Dr. HA7: Stan 1B **42**
W. One Ho. *W1* 6A **6**
            (off Wells St.)
Westone Mans. *IG11: Bark* 7K **71**
            (off Upney La.)
W. One Shop. Cen. 1H **11**
Weston Gdns. TW7: Isle 1J **113**
WESTON GREEN 7J **149**
Weston Grn. KT7: T Ditt 7J **149**
   RM9: Dag 4F **73**
Weston Grn. Rd. KT7: T Ditt 7J **149**
Weston Gro. BR1: Broml 1H **159**
Weston Ho. *E9* 1J **85**
         (off King Edward's St.)
NW6 . . . . .7G **63**
Weston Pk. KT1: King T 2E **150**
   KT7: T Ditt 7J **149**
N8 . . . . .6J **47**
Weston Ri. WC1 . . . . . . .1H **7** (3K **83**)
Weston Rd.
   BR1: Broml 7H **141**
   EN2: Enf 2J **23**
   RM9: Dag 4E **72**
   W4 . . . . .3J **97**
Weston St. SE1 . . . . .7F **15** (2E **102**)
            (not continuous)
Weston Wlk. E8 . . . . .7H **67**
Westover Hill NW3 . . . . .2J **63**
Westover Rd. SW18 . . . . .7A **118**
Westow Hill SE19 . . . . .6E **138**
Westow St. SE19 . . . . .6E **138**
West Pk. SE9 . . . . .2C **142**
Westpark W5 . . . . .6D **78**
West Pk. Av. TW9: Kew 1G **115**
West Pk. Cl. RM6: Chad H 5D **54**
   TW5: Hest 6D **94**
West Pk. Rd. TW9: Kew 1G **115**
   UB2: S'hall 1G **95**
W. Parkside SE10 . . . . .2G **105**
West Pk. Wlk. E20 . . . . .6E **68**
West Pl. SW19 . . . . .5E **134**
West Plaza TW15: Ashf 2A **128**
W. Point *E14* 7B **86**
          (off Grenade St.)
SE1 . . . . .5G **103**
Westpoint Apts. N8 . . . . .3K **47**
W. Point Cl. *TW4: Houn* 3D **112**
         (off Grosvenor Rd.)
Westpoint Trad. Est. W3 . . . . .5H **79**
Westpole Av. EN4: Cockf 4K **21**
Westport Cl. UB4: Yead 4A **76**
Westport Rd. E13 . . . . .4K **87**
Westport St. E1 . . . . .6A **86**
W. Poultry Av. EC1 . . . . . .6A **8** (5B **84**)
W. Quarters W12 . . . . .6C **80**
W. Quay SW10 . . . . .1A **118**
West Quay Dr. UB4: Yead 5C **76**
West Quay Wlk. E14 . . . . .3D **104**
West Ramp TW6: H'row A 1C **110**
West Reservoir Cen. 1C **66**
W. Ridge Gdns. UB6: G'frd 2G **77**
West Ri. W2 .2D **10**
West Rd. E15 . . . . .1H **87**
   EN4: E Barn 1K **31**
   KT2: King T 1J **151**
   N17 . . . . .6C **34**
   RM6: Chad H 6D **54**
   RM7: Rush G 7K **55**
   SE1 . . . . .6H **13** (2K **101**)
   SW3 . . . . .6F **17** (5D **100**)
   SW4 . . . . .5H **119**
   TW14: Bedf 6F **111**
   UB7: W Dray 3B **92**
   W5 . . . . .5E **78**
Westrovia Ct. *SW1* 4C **18**
         (off Moreton St.)
W. Row W10 . . . . .4G **81**

Westrow SW15 . . . . .6E **116**
Westrow Dr. IG11: Bark 5A **72**
Westrow Gdns. IG3: Ilf 2K **71**
WEST RUISLIP 2E **56**
W. Ruislip Ct. *HA4: Ruis* 2F **57**
         (off Ickenham Rd.)
W. Sheen Va. TW9: Rich 4F **115**
Westside N2 . . . . .3D **46**
   NW4 . . . . .2D **44**
Westside Apts. *IG1: Ilf* 3F **71**
         (off Roden St.)
W. Side Comm. SW19 . . . . .5E **134**
W. Side Ct. *TW16: Sun* 7G **129**
         (off Scotts Av.)
Westside Ct. *W9* 4J **81**
         (off Elgin Av.)
W. Smithfield EC1 . . . . .6A **8** (5B **84**)
W. Stand N5 . . . . .4B **66**
West St. BR1: Broml 1J **159**
   CR0: C'don 4C **168**
   DA7: Bex 3F **127**
   DA8: Erith 4K **109**
   E2 . . . . .2H **85**
   E11 . . . . .3G **69**
   E17 . . . . .5D **50**
   HA1: Harr 1H **59**
   SM1: Sutt 5K **165**
   SM5: Cars 3D **166**
   WC2 . . . . .1D **12** (6H **83**)
West St. La. SM5: Cars 4D **166**
West St. Pl. *CR0: C'don* 4C **168**
         (off West St.)
W. Temple Sheen SW14 . . . . .5H **115**
W. Tenter St. E1 . . . . . . .1K **15** (6F **85**)
West Ter. DA15: Sidc 1J **143**
W. Thamesmead Bus. Pk.
   SE28 .3J **107**
         (not continuous)
West Twr. *E14* 2D **104**
      (off Pan Peninsula Sq.)
SW10 . . . . .1B **118**
West Towers HA5: Pinn 5B **40**
Westvale M. W3 . . . . .2A **98**
West Vw. NW4 . . . . .4E **44**
   TW14: Bedf 7E **110**
W. View Apts. *N7* 7J **65**
         (off York Way)
Westview Cl. NW10 . . . . .5B **62**
   W7 . . . . .6J **77**
   W10 . . . . .6E **80**
Westview Ct. N20 . . . . .1F **31**
Westview Cres. N9 . . . . .7K **23**
Westview Dr. IG8: Wfd G 2B **52**
Westville Rd. KT7: T Ditt 1A **162**
   W12 . . . . .2C **98**
West Wlk. EN4: E Barn 7K **21**
   UB3: Hayes 1J **93**
   W5 . . . . .5E **78**
Westward Pde. *E14* 3D **104**
         (off Pepper St.)
Westward Rd. E4 . . . . .5G **35**
         (not continuous)
Westward Way HA3: Kenton 6E **42**
W. Warwick Pl. SW1 . . . .4A **18** (4G **101**)
W. Way BR4: W W'ck 1G **171**
   BR5: Pet W 5H **161**
   CR0: C'don 2A **170**
   HA4: Ruis 1H **57**
   HA5: Pinn 4B **40**
   HA8: Edg 6C **28**
   N18 . . . . .4J **33**
   NW10 .3K **61**
   TW5: Hest 1D **112**
   TW17: Shep 6D **146**
Westway SW20 . . . . .3D **152**
   W10 . . . . .5H **81**
   W12 . . . . .7B **80**
Westway Cl. SW20 . . . . .3D **152**
Westway Ct. UB5: N'olt 1E **76**
Westway Cross Shopping Park . . .1J **77**
Westway Est. W3 . . . . .5A **80**

W. Way Gdns.
   CR0: C'don 2K **169**
Westway Lodge *W9* 5J **81**
         (off Amberley Rd.)
W. Ways HA6: Nwood 2J **39**
Westways KT19: Ewe 4B **164**
Westway Sports Cen. 6F **81**
Westway Travellers Site *W12* 7F **81**
         (off Stable Way)
Westwell M. SW16 . . . . .6J **137**
Westwell Rd. SW16 . . . . .6J **137**
Westwell Rd. App. SW16 . . . . .6J **137**
Westwick KT1: King T 2G **151**
         (off Chesterton Ter.)
Westwick Gdns. TW4: Cran 2K **111**
   W14 . . . . .2F **99**
WEST WICKHAM 1E **170**
West Wickham Leisure Cen. 1E **170**
West Wintergarden 1D **104**
         (off Bank St.)
Westwood Av. HA2: Harr 4F **59**
   SE19 .1C **156**
Westwood Bus. Cen. NW10 . . . . . .4A **80**
Westwood Cl. BR1: Broml 2B **160**
   HA4: Ruis 6D **38**
Westwood Ct. *EN1: Enf* 6K **23**
         (off Village Rd.)
   HA0: Wemb 4B **60**
   UB6: G'frd 5H **59**
Westwood Gdns. SW13 . . . . .3B **116**
Westwood Hill SE26 . . . . .5G **139**
Westwood Ho. *W12* 1E **98**
         (off Wood La.)
Westwood La. DA15: Sidc 5A **126**
   DA16: Well 3K **125**
Westwood M. *E3* 3C **86**
         (off Addington Rd.)
Westwood Pk. SE23 . . . . .7H **121**
Westwood Pk. Trad. Est. W3 . . . . . .5H **79**
Westwood Pl. SE26 . . . . .4G **139**
Westwood Rd. E16 . . . . .1K **105**
   IG3: Ilf .1K **71**
   SW13 .3B **116**
West Woodside DA5: Bexl 7E **126**
Wetheral Dr. HA7: Stan 1B **42**
Wetherby Cl. UB5: N'olt 6F **59**
Wetherby Gdns. SW5 . . . . .4A **100**
Wetherby Mans. *SW5* 5K **99**
         (off Earls Ct. Sq.)
Wetherby M. SW5 . . . . .5K **99**
Wetherby Pl. SW7 . . . . .4A **100**
Wetherby Rd. EN2: Enf 1H **23**
Wetherby Way KT9: Chess 7E **162**
Wetherden St. E17 . . . . .7B **50**
Wetherell Rd. E9 . . . . .1K **85**
Wetherill Rd. N10 . . . . .1E **46**
Wevco Wharf SE15 . . . . .6H **103**
Wexford Ho. *E1* 5J **85**
         (off Sidney St.)
Wexford Rd. SW12 . . . . .7D **118**
Wexner Bldg. *E1* 6J **9**
         (off Strype St.)
Weybourne St. SW18 . . . . .2A **136**
Weybridge Ct. SE16 . . . . .5H **103**
Weybridge Point SW11 . . . . .2D **118**
Weybridge Rd. CR7: Thor H 4A **156**
Wey Ct. KT19: Ewe 4J **163**
Weydown Cl. SW19 . . . . .1G **135**
Weyhill Rd. E1 . . . . .6G **85**
Wey Ho. *NW8* 4B **4**
         (off Church St. Est.)
   UB5: N'olt 4D **76**
         (off Taywood Rd.)
Weylands Cl. KT12: Walt T 7D **148**
Weylond Rd. RM8: Dag 3F **73**
Weyman Rd. SE3 . . . . .1A **124**
The Weymarks N17 . . . . .6J **33**
Weymouth Av. NW7 . . . . .5F **29**
   W5 . . . . .3C **96**
Weymouth Cl. E6 . . . . .6F **89**
Weymouth Ct. E2 . . . . .2F **85**
   SM2: Sutt 7J **165**

Weymouth Ho. BR2: Broml 2H **159**
         (off Hill Ho. M.)
   SW8 . . . . .7K **101**
         (off Bolney St.)
Weymouth M. W1 . . . . .5J **5** (5F **83**)
Weymouth Pl. SE2 . . . . .3A **108**
Weymouth Rd. UB4: Hayes 3G **75**
Weymouth St. W1 . . . . .6H **5** (5E **82**)
Weymouth Ter. E2 . . . . . . .1K **9** (2F **85**)
Weymouth Vs. *N4* 2K **65**
         (off Moray Rd.)
Weymouth Wlk. HA7: Stan 6F **27**
Whadcoat St. N4 . . . . .2A **66**
Whaddon Ho. SE22 . . . . .3E **120**
Whalebone Av. RM6: Chad H 6F **55**
Whalebone Ct. EC2 . . . . .7E **8**
Whalebone Gro.
   RM6: Chad H 6F **55**
Whalebone La. E15 . . . . .7G **69**
Whalebone La. Nth.
   RM6: Chad H, Col R 1E **54**
Whalebone La. Sth.
   RM6: Chad H, Dag 7F **55**
   RM8: Dag 7F **55**
Whales Yd. *E15* 7G **69**
        (off West Ham La.)
The Wharf EC3 . . . . .4H **15** (1F **103**)
Wharldale Cl. N11 . . . . .6K **31**
Wharfdale Rd. N1 . . . . .2J **83**
Wharfedale Cl. E5 . . . . .4K **67**
Wharfedale Gdns.
   CR7: Thor H 4K **155**
Wharfedale Ho. *NW6* 1K **81**
         (off Kilburn Vale)
Wharfedale St. SW10 . . . . .5K **99**
Wharfedale W. N1 . . . . .2J **83**
        (off Wharfedale Rd.)
Wharf La. E14 . . . . .6B **86**
   TW1: Twick 1A **132**
Wharf Mill Apts. *E2* 1F **85**
         (off Laburnum St.)
Wharf Pl. E2 . . . . .1H **85**
Wharf Rd. E16 . . . . .1A **106**
   EN3: Pond E 6F **25**
   N1 . . . . .1C **8** (2C **84**)
         (City Rd.)
   N1 . . . . .1J **83**
         (York Way)
Wharf Rd. Ind. Est. EN3: Pond E . .6F **25**
Wharfside Point Nth. *E14* 7E **86**
        (off Poplar High St.)
Wharfside Point Sth. E14 . . . . .7E **86**
Wharfside Rd. E16 . . . . .5G **87**
Wharf St. E16 . . . . .5G **87**
   SE8 . . . . .5C **104**
Wharf Vw. Ct. *E14* 6E **86**
         (off Blair St.)
Wharncliffe Dr. UB1: S'hall 1H **95**
Wharncliffe Gdns. SE25 . . . . .2E **156**
Wharncliffe M. SW4 . . . . .6H **119**
Wharncliffe Rd. SE25 . . . . .2E **156**
Wharton Cl. NW10 . . . . .6A **62**
Wharton Cotts. WC1 . . . . . .2J **7** (3A **84**)
Wharton Rd. E2 . . . . .3K **85**
   SE1 . . . . .7F **15**
Wharton Rd.
   BR1: Broml 1K **159**
Wharton St. WC1 . . . . .2H **7** (3K **83**)
Whatcott's Yd. N16 . . . . .4E **66**
Whateley Rd. SE20 . . . . .7K **139**
   SE22 .5F **121**
Whatley Av. SW20 . . . . .3F **153**
Whatman Ho. *E14* 6B **86**
         (off Wallwood St.)
Whatman Rd. SE23 . . . . .7K **121**
Wheatcroft Ct. *SM1: Sutt* 1K **165**
         (off Cleeve Way)
Wheatfield Ho. *NW6* 3J **81**
        (off Kilburn Pk. Rd.)
Wheatfields E6 . . . . .6F **89**
   EN3: Enf H 1F **25**
Wheatfield Way KT1: King T 2E **150**

Wheathill Ho. SE20 . . . . .2H 157
   (off Penge Rd.)
Wheathill Rd. SE20 . . . . .3H 157
Wheatland Ho. SE22 . . . . .3E 120
Wheatlands TW5: Hest 6E 94
Wheatlands Rd. SW17 . . . . .3E 136
Wheatley Cl. NW4 . . . . .2C 44
Wheatley Ct. E3 . . . . .3D 86
   (off Bruce Rd.)
Wheatley Cres. UB3: Hayes 7J 75
Wheatley Gdns. N9 . . . . .2K 33
Wheatley Ho. SW15 . . . . .7C 116
   (off Ellisfield Dr)
Wheatley Mans. IG11: Bark 7A 72
   (off Lansbury Av.)
Wheatley M. KT8: E Mos 4H 149
Wheatley Rd. TW7: Isle 3K 113
Wheatley's Eyot
   TW16: Sun 5J 147
Wheatley St. W1 . . . . . .6H 5 (5E 82)
Wheat Sheaf Cl. E14 . . . . .4D 104
Wheatsheaf Cl.
   UB5: N'olt 5C 58
Wheatsheaf La. SW6 . . . . .7E 98
   SW8 . . . . .7J 101
Wheatsheaf Ter. SW6 . . . . .7H 99
Wheatstone Cl. CR4: Mitc 1C 154
Wheatstone Ho. SE1 . . . . .3C 102
   (off County St.)
Wheatstone Rd. DA8: Erith 5K 109
Wheeler Cl. IG8: Wfd G 6J 37
Wheeler Gdns. N1 . . . . .1J 83
   (off Outram Pl.)
Wheeler Pl. BR2: Broml 4K 159
Wheelers Cross IG11: Bark 2H 89
Wheelers Dr. HA4: Ruis 6E 38
Wheel Farm Dr. RM10: Dag 3J 73
Wheel Ho. E14 . . . . .5D 104
   (off Burrells Wharf Sq.)
   E17 . . . . .3K 49
Wheelock Cl. DA8: Erith 7H 109
Wheelwright St. N7 . . . . .7K 65
Whelan Rd. W3 . . . . .3H 97
Whelan Way SM6: Bedd 3H 167
Wheler Ho. E1 . . . . .4J 9
   (off Quaker St.)
Wheler St. E1 . . . . .4J 9 (4F 85)
Whellock Rd. W4 . . . . .3A 98
Whenman Av. DA5: Bexl 2J 145
Whernside Cl. SE28 . . . . .7C 90
WHETSTONE 2F 31
Whetstone Cl. N20 . . . . .2G 31
Whetstone Pk. WC2 . . . . .7G 7 (6K 83)
Whetstone Rd. SE3 . . . . .2A 124
Whewell Rd. N19 . . . . .2J 65
Whidborne Bldgs. WC1 . . . . .2F 7
   (off Whidborne St.)
Whidborne Cl. SE8 . . . . .2C 122
Whidborne St. WC1 . . . . .2F 7 (3J 83)
   (not continuous)
Whidbourne M. SW8 . . . . .1H 119
Whimbrel Cl. SE28 . . . . .7C 90
Whimbrel Way UB4: Yead 6B 76
Whinchat Rd. SE28 . . . . .3H 107
Whinfell Cl. SW16 . . . . .5H 137
Whinyates Rd. SE9 . . . . .3C 124
Whippendell Way
   BR5: St P 7B 144
Whippingham Ho. E3 . . . . .3B 86
   (off Merchant St.)
Whipps Cross E17 . . . . .5F 51
Whipps Cross Ho. E17 . . . . .5F 51
   (off Wood St.)
Whipps Cross Rd. E11 . . . . .5F 51
   (not continuous)
Whiskin St. EC1 . . . . . . .2A 8 (3B 84)
Whisperwood Cl.
   HA3: Hrw W 1J 41
Whistler Gdns. HA8: Edg 2F 43
Whistler M. RM8: Dag 5B 72
   (off Fitzstephen Rd.)
   SE15 . . . . .7F 103

Whistlers Av. SW11 . . . . .7B 100
Whistlers Gro.
   DA15: Sidc 7J 125
Whistler St. N5 . . . . .5B 66
Whistler Twr. SW10 . . . . .7A 100
   (off Worlds End Est.)
Whistler Wlk. SW10 . . . . .7B 100
Whiston Ho. N1 . . . . .7B 66
   (off Richmond Gro.)
Whiston Rd. E2 . . . . .2F 85
Whitacre M. SE11 . . . . . .6K 19 (5A 102)
Whitakers Lodge
   EN2: Enf 1J 23
Whitbread Cl. N17 . . . . .1G 49
Whitbread Ho. SW11 . . . . .7H 101
   (off Charles Clowes Wlk.)
Whitbread Rd. SE4 . . . . .4A 122
Whitburn Rd. SE13 . . . . .4D 122
Whitby Av. NW10 . . . . .3H 79
Whitby Ct. N7 . . . . .4J 65
Whitby Gdns. NW9 . . . . .3G 43
   SM1: Sutt 2B 166
Whitby Ho. NW8 . . . . .1A 82
   (off Boundary Rd.)
Whitby Pde. HA4: Ruis 2A 58
Whitby Rd. HA2: Harr 3G 59
   HA4: Ruis 3K 57
   SE18 . . . . .4D 106
   SM1: Sutt 2B 166
Whitby St. E1 . . . . .3J 9 (4F 85)
   (not continuous)
Whitcher Cl. SE14 . . . . .6A 104
Whitcher Pl. NW1 . . . . .6G 65
Whitchurch Av. HA8: Edg 7A 28
Whitchurch Cl. HA8: Edg 6A 28
Whitchurch Gdns. HA8: Edg 6A 28
Whitchurch Ho. W10 . . . . .6F 81
   (off Kingsdown Cl.)
Whitchurch La. HA8: Edg 7J 27
Whitchurch Pde. HA8: Edg 7B 28
Whitchurch Rd. W11 . . . . .7F 81
Whitcomb Ct. WC2 . . . . .3D 12
Whitcombe M. TW9: Kew 1H 115
Whitcomb St.
   WC2 . . . . .3D 12 (7H 83)
Whitcome M. TW9: Kew 1H 115
Whiteadder Way E14 . . . . .4D 104
Whitear Wlk. E15 . . . . .6F 69
Whitebarn La. RM10: Dag 1G 91
Whitebeam Av. BR2: Broml 7E 160
Whitebeam Cl. SW9 . . . . .7K 101
Whitebeam Ho. E15 . . . . .3G 87
   (off Teasel Way)
White Bear Pl. NW3 . . . . .4B 64
White Bear Yd. EC1 . . . . .4J 7
   (off Clerkenwell Rd.)
White Bri. Av. CR4: Mitc 3B 154
Whitebridge Cl.
   TW14: Felt 6H 111
White Butts Rd. HA4: Ruis 3B 58
WHITECHAPEL 7H 9
Whitechapel Art Gallery . . .7K 9 (6F 85)
Whitechapel High St.
   E1 . . . . .7K 9 (6F 85)
Whitechapel Rd. E1 . . . . . .7K 9 (6J 85)
Whitechapel Sports Cen. 5H 85
White Church La.
   E1 . . . . .7K 9 (6G 85)
White Church Pas. E1 . . . . .7K 9
   (off White Church La.)
WHITE CITY 7D 80
WHITE CITY 6E 80
White City Cl. W12 . . . . .7E 80
White City Est. W12 . . . . .7D 80
White City Rd. W12 . . . . .7E 80
White Collar Factory EC1 . . . . . . .3E 8
   (off Old St. Yd.)
White Conduit St. N1 . . . . .2A 84
Whitecote Rd. UB1: S'hall 6G 77
Whitecroft Cl. BR3: Beck 4F 159
Whitecroft Way
   BR3: Beck 5E 158

Whitecross Pl. EC2 . . . . . . .5F 9 (5D 84)
Whitecross St. EC1 . . . . . .3D 8 (4C 84)
Whitefield Av. NW2 . . . . .1E 62
Whitefield Cl. SW15 . . . . .6G 117
Whitefoot La. BR1: Broml 4E 140
   SE6 . . . . .4E 140
Whitefoot Ter. BR1: Broml 3H 141
Whitefriars Av.
   HA3: W'stone 2J 41
Whitefriars La. N12 . . . . .5G 31
Whitefriars Dr. HA3: Hrw W 2H 41
Whitefriars St.
   EC4 . . . . .1K 13 (6A 84)
Whitefriars Trad. Est.
   HA3: W'stone 3H 41
White Gables Ct.
   CR2: S Croy 5E 168
White Gdns. RM10: Dag 6G 73
Whitegate Gdns. HA3: Hrw W 7E 26
White Gates KT7: T Ditt 7A 150
Whitehall 6G 165
Whitehall SW1 . . . . .5E 12 (1J 101)
Whitehall Ct. SW1 . . . . . .5F 13 (1J 101)
   (not continuous)
Whitehall Cres. KT9: Chess 5D 162
Whitehall Gdns. E4 . . . . .1B 36
   SW1 . . . . .5E 12
   W3 . . . . .1G 97
   W4 . . . . .6H 97
Whitehall La. IG9: Buck H 2D 36
Whitehall Lodge N10 . . . . .2E 46
Whitehall Pk. N19 . . . . .1G 65
Whitehall Pk. Rd. W4 . . . . .6H 97
Whitehall Pl. E7 . . . . .5J 69
   SM6: W'gton 4F 167
   SW1 . . . . .5E 12 (1J 101)
Whitehall Rd. BR2: Broml 5B 160
   CR7: Thor H 5A 156
   E4 . . . . .2B 36
   HA1: Harr 7J 41
   IG8: Wfd G 2B 36
   W7 . . . . .2A 96
Whitehall St. N17 . . . . .7A 34
White Hart Av. SE18 . . . . .4K 107
   SE28 . . . . .4K 107
White Hart Cl. UB3: Harl 6F 93
White Hart Ct. EC2 . . . . .6G 9
White Hart La. N17 . . . . .7H 33
   N22 . . . . .1A 48
   NW10 . . . . .6B 62
   RM7: Col R, Mawney 1G 55
   SW13 . . . . .2A 116
White Hart Rd. SE18 . . . . .4J 107
WHITE HART RDBT. 2B 76
White Hart Slip BR1: Broml 2J 159
White Hart St. EC4 . . . . . .7B 8 (6B 84)
   SE11 . . . . .5K 19 (5A 102)
White Hart Triangle
   SE28 . . . . .2K 107
White Hart Triangle Bus. Pk.
   SE28 . . . . .2A 108
White Hart Yd.
   SE1 . . . . .5E 14 (1D 102)
Whitehaven Cl. BR2: Broml 4J 159
Whitehaven St. NW8 . . . . . .4C 4 (4C 82)
Whitehead Cl. N18 . . . . .5J 33
   SW18 . . . . .7A 118
Whiteheads Gro.
   SW3 . . . . .4D 16 (4C 100)
White Heart Av. UB8: Hil 5E 74
Whitehart Av. HA4: Ruis 7E 38
White Heather Ho. WC1 . . . . .2F 7
   (off Cromer St.)
White Heron M. TW11: Tedd 6K 131
White Horse All. EC1 . . . . .5A 8
White Horse Apts. N1 . . . . .1A 84
   (off Liverpool Rd.)
White Horse Hill BR7: Chst 4E 142
White Horse La. E1 . . . . .5K 85
Whitehorse La. SE25 . . . . .4D 156
White Horse M. EN3: Enf H 2E 24
Whitehorse M. SE1 . . . . . .1K 19 (3A 102)

White Horse Rd. E1 . . . . .6A 86
   (not continuous)
   E6 . . . . .3D 88
Whitehorse Rd. CR0: C'don 7C 156
   CR7: Thor H 7C 156
White Horse St.
   W1 . . . . .5K 11 (1F 101)
White Horse Yd. EC2 . . . . .7E 8 (6D 84)
The White Ho. NW1 . . . . .3K 5
White Ho. CR0: C'don 4D 168
   (off Coombe Rd.)
   SW4 . . . . .7H 119
   (off Clapham Pk. Est.)
   SW11 . . . . .1B 118
Whitehouse E10 . . . . .6E 50
   (off Leyton Grn. Rd.)
Whitehouse Apts. SE1 . . . . .1K 101
White Ho. Ct. N14 . . . . .2D 32
White Ho. Dr. HA7: Stan 4H 27
   IG8: Wfd G 6C 36
White Ho. La. EN2: Enf 1H 23
White Ho. M. E10 . . . . .6E 50
Whitehouse Way N14 . . . . .2A 32
White Kennett St. E1 . . . . . .7H 9 (6F 85)
Whitelands Cres. SW18 . . . . .7G 117
Whitelands Ho. SW3 . . . . .5F 17
   (off Cheltenham Ter.)
Whiteledges W13 . . . . .6C 78
Whitelegg Rd. E13 . . . . .2H 87
Whiteley Rd. SE19 . . . . .5D 138
Whiteleys Cen. 6K 81
Whiteleys Pde. UB10: Hil 4D 74
Whiteley's Way
   TW13: Hanw 3E 130
White Lion Cen. 1J 7
   (off White Lion St.)
White Lion Ct. EC3 . . . . .1G 15
   SE15 . . . . .6J 103
   TW7: Isle 3B 114
White Lion Hill EC4 . . . . .2B 14 (7B 84)
White Lion St. N1 . . . . .2A 84
White Lodge SE19 . . . . .7B 138
   W5 . . . . .5C 78
White Lodge Cl. N2 . . . . .6B 46
   SM2: Sutt 7A 166
   TW7: Isle 2A 114
White Lodge Ct.
   TW16: Sun 1A 148
White Lyon Ct. EC2 . . . . .5C 8
Whiteoak Ct. BR7: Chst 6E 142
White Oak Dr. BR3: Beck 2E 158
White Oak Gdns.
   DA15: Sidc 7K 125
Whiteoaks La. UB6: G'frd 3H 77
White Orchards HA7: Stan 5F 27
   N20 . . . . .1C 30
White Post La. E9 . . . . .7B 68
White Post St. SE15 . . . . .7J 103
White Rd. E15 . . . . .7G 69
White Rose Ct. E1 . . . . .6H 9
   (off Widegate St.)
Whiterose Trad. Est. EN4: E Barn . .5G 21
   (off Margaret Rd.)
Whites Av. IG2: Ilf 6J 53
Whites Grounds
   SE1 . . . . .7H 15 (2E 102)
White's Grounds Est.
   SE1 . . . . .6H 15
White's Mdw. BR1: Broml 4E 160
White's Row E1 . . . . .6J 9 (5F 85)
Whites Sq. SW4 . . . . .4H 119
Whitestile Rd. TW8: Bford 5C 96
Whitestone Cl. EN4: Had W 1H 21
Whitestone La. NW3 . . . . .3A 64
Whitestone Wlk. NW3 . . . . .3A 64
Whitestone Way
   CR0: Wadd 2A 168
White Swan M. W4 . . . . .5A 98
Whitethorn Av. UB7: Yiew 7A 74
Whitethorn Gdns.
   CR0: C'don 2H 169
   EN2: Enf 5J 23

Whitethorn Ho. E1 . . . . .1J 103
(off Prusom St.)
Whitethorn Pas. E3 . . . . .4C 86
(off Whitethorn St.)
Whitethorn Pl. UB7: Yiew 1B 92
Whitethorn St. E3 . . . . .5C 86
The White Tower 7F 85
White Twr. Way E1 . . . . .5A 86
Whitewebbs Way BR5: St P 1K 161
Whitfield Ct. IG1: Ilf 7D 52
SW20 . . . . .2F 153
Whitfield Ho. NW8 . . . . .4C 4
(off Salisbury St.)
Whitfield Pl. W1 . . . . .4A 6
Whitfield Rd. DA7: Bex 7F 109
E6 . . . . .7A 70
Whitfield St. W1 . . . . .4A 6 (4G 83)
Whitford Gdns.
CR4: Mitc 3D 154
Whitgift Av. CR2: S Croy 5B 168
Whitgift Cen. 2C 168
Whitgift Ct. CR2: S Croy 5C 168
(off Nottingham Rd.)
Whitgift Ho. SE11 . . . . . .3G 19 (4K 101)
SW11 . . . . .1C 118
Whitgift Sq. CR0: C'don 2C 168
Whitgift St. CR0: C'don 3C 168
SE11 . . . . .3G 19 (4K 101)
Whiting Av. IG11: Bark 7F 71
Whitings IG2: Ilf 5J 53
Whitings Rd. EN5: Barn 5A 20
Whitings Way E6 . . . . .5E 88
Whiting Way SE16 . . . . .4A 104
Whitland Rd. SM5: Cars 1B 166
Whitley Cl. TW19: Stanw 6A 110
Whitley Ho. SW1 . . . . .7B 18
(off Churchill Gdns.)
Whitley Rd. N17 . . . . .2E 48
Whitlock Dr. SW19 . . . . .7G 117
Whitman Ho. E2 . . . . .3J 85
(off Cornwall Av.)
Whitman Rd. E3 . . . . .4A 86
Whitmead Cl. CR2: S Croy 6E 168
Whitmore Bldg. SE16 . . . . .3F 103
(off Arts La.)
Whitmore Cl. N11 . . . . .5A 32
Whitmore Est. N1 . . . . .1E 84
Whitmore Gdns. NW10 . . . . .2E 80
Whitmore Ho. N1 . . . . .1E 84
(off Whitmore Est.)
Whitmore Rd. BR3: Beck 3B 158
HA1: Harr 7G 41
N1 . . . . .1E 84
Whitnell Way SW15 . . . . .5E 116
(not continuous)
Whitney Av. IG4: Ilf 4B 52
Whitney Rd. E10 . . . . .7D 50
Whitney Wlk. DA14: Sidc 6E 144
Whitstable Cl.
BR3: Beck 1B 158
HA4: Ruis 2G 57
Whitstable Ho. W10 . . . . .6F 81
(off Silchester Rd.)
Whitstable Pl. CR0: C'don 4C 168
Whitstone Av. W7 . . . . .6K 77
Whitstone La. BR3: Beck 5D 158
Whittaker Av. TW9: Rich 5D 114
Whittaker Pl. TW9: Rich 5D 114
(off Whittaker Av.)
Whittaker Rd. E6 . . . . .7A 70
SM3: Sutt 3H 165
Whittaker St. SW1 . . . . . .4G 17 (4E 100)
Whittaker Way SE1 . . . . .4G 103
Whitta Rd. E12 . . . . .4B 70
Whittell Gdns. SE26 . . . . .3J 139
Whittingham N17 . . . . .7C 34
Whittingham Ct. W4 . . . . .7A 98
Whittingstall Rd. SW6 . . . . .1H 117
Whittington Apts. E1 . . . . .6K 85
(off E. Arbour St.)
Whittington Av. EC3 . . . . . .1G 15 (6E 84)
UB4: Hayes 5H 75

Whittington Ct. N2 . . . . .5D 46
Whittington Ho. N19 . . . . .2H 65
(off Holloway Rd.)
Whittington M. N12 . . . . .4F 31
Whittington Rd. N22 . . . . .7D 32
Whittington Way HA5: Pinn 5C 40
Whittlebury Cl. SM5: Cars 7D 166
Whittlebury M. E. NW1 . . . . .7E 64
Whittlebury M. W. NW1 . . . . .7E 64
Whitt Cl. E17 . . . . .6A 50
UB1: S'hall 6F 77
Whittle Rd. TW5: Hest 7A 94
TW6: H'row A 6C 174
UB2: S'hall 2F 95
Whittlesea Cl. HA3: Hrw W 7B 26
Whittlesea Path
HA3: Hrw W 1G 41
Whittlesea Rd. HA3: Hrw W 7B 26
Whittlesey St.
SE1 . . . . .5J 13 (1A 102)
WHITTON 7G 113
Whitton NW3 . . . . .7D 64
Whitton Av. E. UB6: G'frd 5J 59
Whitton Av. W. UB5: N'olt 5F 59
UB6: G'frd 5F 59
Whitton Cl. UB6: G'frd 6B 60
Whitton Dene
TW3: Houn, Isle 5G 113
TW7: Isle 6H 113
Whitton Dr. UB6: G'frd 6A 60
Whitton Mnr. Rd.
TW7: Isle 6G 113
Whitton Rd. TW1: Twick 6K 113
TW2: Twick 6J 113
TW3: Houn 4F 113
WHITTON ROAD RDBT. 6K 113
Whitton Sports & Fitness Cen.
. . . . .2F 131
Whitton Wlk. E3 . . . . .3C 86
(not continuous)
Whitton Waye TW3: Houn 6E 112
Whitwell Rd. E13 . . . . .3J 87
Whitworth Ho. SE1 . . . . .3C 102
Whitworth Pl.
TW4: Houn 7C 112
Whitworth Rd. SE18 . . . . .7E 106
SE25 . . . . .3E 156
Whitworth St. SE10 . . . . .5G 105
Whorlton Rd. SE15 . . . . .3H 121
Whychcote Point NW2 . . . . .1E 62
(off Whitefield Av.)
Whymark Av. N22 . . . . .3A 48
Whytecroft TW5: Hest 7B 94
Whyte M. SM3: Cheam 7G 165
Whyteville Rd. E7 . . . . .6K 69
Whytlaw Ho. E3 . . . . .5B 86
(off Baythorne St.)
Wiblin M. NW5 . . . . .4F 65
Wickersley Rd. SW11 . . . . .2E 118
Wickers Oake SE19 . . . . .4F 139
Wicker St. E1 . . . . .6H 85
The Wicket CR0: Addtn 5C 170
Wicket Rd. UB6: G'frd 3A 78
The Wickets TW15: Ashf 4A 128
Wickfield Apts. E15 . . . . .6F 69
(off Grove Cres. Rd.)
Wickfield Ho. SE16 . . . . .2H 103
(off Wilson Gro.)
Wickford Ho. E1 . . . . .4J 85
(off Wickford St.)
Wickford St. E1 . . . . .4J 85
Wickford Way E17 . . . . .4K 49
Wickham Av. CR0: C'don 2A 170
SM3: Cheam 5E 164
Wickham Chase
BR4: W W'ck 1F 171
Wickham Cl. E1 . . . . .5J 85
EN3: Enf H 3C 24
KT3: N Mald 6B 152
Wickham Ct. KT5: Surb 5F 151
(off Cranes Pk.)

Wickham Cres. BR4: W W'ck 2E 170
Wickham Gdns. SE4 . . . . .3B 122
Wickham Ho. N1 . . . . .1E 84
(off Halcomb St.)
Wickham La. DA16: Well 5A 108
SE2 .5A 108
Wickham M. SE4 . . . . .2B 122
Wickham Noakes Ct.
BR3: Beck 1D 158
Wickham Rd. BR3: Beck 2D 158
CR0: C'don 2K 169
E4 . . . . .7K 35
HA3: Hrw W 2H 41
SE4 .4B 122
Wickham St. DA16: Well 2J 125
SE11 . . . . .5G 19 (5K 101)
Wickham Theatre Cen. 2F 171
Wickham Way BR3: Beck 4E 158
Wick Ho. KT1: Hamp W 1D 150
(off Station Rd.)
Wick La. E3 . . . . .1C 86
Wickliffe Av. N3 . . . . .2G 45
Wickliffe Gdns. HA9: Wemb 2H 61
Wicklow Ho. N16 . . . . .1F 67
Wicklow St. WC1 . . . . . . .1G 7 (3K 83)
Wick Rd. E9 . . . . .6K 67
TW11: Tedd 7B 132
Wicks Cl. SE9 . . . . .4B 142
Wicksteed Cl. DA5: Bexl 3K 145
Wicksteed Ho. SE1 . . . . .3C 102
TW8: Bford 5F 97
Wicks Way SE19 . . . . .6D 138
Wickway Ct. SE15 . . . . .6F 103
(off Cator St.)
Wickwood St. SE5 . . . . .2B 120
Widdenham Rd. N7 . . . . .4K 65
Widdicombe Av. HA2: Harr 2C 58
Widdin St. E15 . . . . .7G 69
Widecombe Gdns. IG4: Ilf 4C 52
Widecombe Rd. SE9 . . . . .3C 142
Widecombe Way N2 . . . . .5B 46
Wideford Dr.
RM7: Rush G 6K 55
Widegate St. E1 . . . . .6H 9 (5E 84)
Widenham Cl. HA5: Eastc 5A 40
Wide Way CR4: Mitc 3H 155
Widewing Cl. TW11: Tedd 7B 132
Widford NW1 . . . . .6F 65
(off Lewis St.)
Widford Ho. N1 . . . . .2B 84
(off Colebrooke Rd.)
Widgeon Cl. E16 . . . . .6K 87
Widgeon Rd. TW6: H'row A 5C 174
Widley Rd. W9 . . . . .3J 81
Widmer Ct. TW3: Houn 2C 112
WIDMORE 3A 160
WIDMORE GREEN 2B 160
Widmore Lodge Rd.
BR1: Broml 2B 160
Widmore Rd. BR1: Broml 2J 159
UB8: Hil 4D 74
Wigan Ho. E5 . . . . .1H 67
Wigeon Path SE28 . . . . .3H 107
Wigeon Way UB4: Yead 6B 76
Wiggins La. TW10: Ham 2C 132
Wiggins Mead NW9 . . . . .7G 29
Wigginton Av. HA9: Wemb 6H 61
Wight Ho. KT1: King T 3D 150
(off Portsmouth Rd.)
Wightman Rd. N4 . . . . .4A 48
N8 . . . . .4A 48
Wighton M. TW7: Isle 2J 113
Wigley Rd. TW13: Felt 2B 130
Wigmore Hall 7J 5
Wigmore Pl. E17 . . . . .3A 50
W1 . . . . .7J 5 (6F 83)
Wigmore Rd. SM5: Cars 2B 166
Wigmore St. W1 . . . . .7H 5 (6E 82)
Wigmore Wlk.
SM5: Cars 2B 166
Wigram Ho. E14 . . . . .7D 86
(off Wade's Pl.)

Wigram Rd. E11 . . . . .6A 52
Wigram Sq. E17 . . . . .3E 50
Wigston Cl. N18 . . . . .5K 33
Wigston Rd. E13 . . . . .4K 87
Wigton Gdns.
HA7: Stan 1E 42
Wigton Pl. SE11 . . . . .6K 19 (5A 102)
Wigton Rd. E17 . . . . .1B 50
Wilberforce Ct. BR2: Kes 7B 172
Wilberforce M. SW4 . . . . .4H 119
Wilberforce Rd. N4 . . . . .2B 66
NW9 .6C 44
Wilberforce Wlk. E15 . . . . .5G 69
Wilberforce Way SE25 . . . . .4F 157
SW19 . . . . .6F 135
Wilbraham Ho. SW8 . . . . .7J 101
(off Wandsworth Rd.)
Wilbraham Mans. SW1 . . . . .3G 17
(off Wilbraham Pl.)
Wilbraham Pl. SW1 . . . . . .3F 17 (4D 100)
Wilbrahams Almshouses
EN5: Barn 2C 20
Wilbrooke Pl. SE3 . . . . .1K 123
Wilbury Way N18 . . . . .5J 33
Wilby M. W11 . . . . .1H 99
Wilcox Cl. SW8 . . . . .7J 101
(not continuous)
Wilcox Gdns. TW17: Shep 3A 146
Wilcox Ho. E3 . . . . .5B 86
(off Ackroyd Dr.)
Wilcox Pl. SW1 . . . . .2B 18 (3G 101)
Wilcox Rd. SM1: Sutt 4K 165
SW8 .7J 101
TW11: Tedd 4H 131
Wildberry Cl. W7 . . . . .4A 96
Wildbore Ho. N1 . . . . .7A 66
(off Liverpool Rd.)
Wildcat Rd. TW6: H'row A 6C 174
(off Wayfarer Rd.)
Wild Ct. WC2 . . . . .1G 13 (6K 83)
Wildcroft Gdns. HA8: Edg 6J 27
Wildcroft Mnr. SW15 . . . . .7E 116
Wildcroft Rd. SW15 . . . . .7E 116
Wilde Cl. E8 . . . . .1G 85
Wilde Ho. W2 . . . . .2A 10
(off Gloucester Ter.)
Wilde Pl. N13 . . . . .6G 33
SW18 . . . . .7B 118
Wilder Cl. HA4: Ruis 1K 57
The Wilderness
KT8: W Mole, E Mos 5G 149
TW12: Hamp H 4F 131
Wildernesse Cl. HA8: Edg 4D 28
Wilderness Island
Local Nature Reserve 2E 166
The Wilderness
Local Nature Reserve 7F 101
(off Queenstown Rd.)
Wilderness M. SW4 . . . . .4F 119
Wilderness Rd. BR7: Chst 7F 143
Wilde Rd. DA8: Erith 7H 109
Wilderton Rd. N16 . . . . .7E 48
Wilder Wlk. W1 . . . . .3B 12
(off Glasshouse St.)
Wildfell Rd. SE6 . . . . .7D 122
Wild Goose Dr. SE14 . . . . .1J 121
Wild Hatch NW11 . . . . .6J 45
Wild's Rents SE1 . . . . .7G 15 (3E 102)
Wild St. WC2 . . . . .1F 13 (6J 83)
Wildwood Cl. SE12 . . . . .7H 123
Wildwood Gro. NW3 . . . . .1A 64
Wildwood Ri. NW11 . . . . .1A 64
Wildwood Rd. NW11 . . . . .6K 45
Wildwood Ter. NW3 . . . . .1A 64
Wilford Cl. EN2: Enf 3J 23
Wilford Rd. CR0: C'don 6C 156
Wilfred St. N15 . . . . .5D 48
(off South Gro.)
Wilfred Owen Cl. SW19 . . . . .6A 136
Wilfred St. SW1 . . . . .1A 18 (3G 101)
Wilfred Wood Ct. W6 . . . . .4E 98
(off Samuel's Cl.)

Wilfred Gdns.—Willow Lodge

Wilfrid Gdns. W3 5J 79
Wilkes Cl. NW7 6A 30
Wilkes Rd. TW8: Bford 6E 96
Wilkes St. E1 5K 9 (5F 85)
Wilkie Ho. SW1 5D 18
(off Cureton St.)
Wilkins Cl. CR4: Mitc 1C 154
UB3: Harl 5H 93
Wilkins Ho. SW1 7A 18
(off Churchill Gdns.)
Wilkinson Cl. NW2 2E 62
UB10: Hil 1D 74
Wilkinson Ct. SW17 4B 136
Wilkinson Gdns. SE25 1E 156
Wilkinson Ho. N1 2D 84
(off Cranston Est.)
Wilkinson Rd. E16 6A 88
Wilkinson St. SW8 7K 101
Wilkinson Way W4 2K 97
Wilkin St. NW5 6E 64
Wilkin St. M. NW5 6F 65
Wilks Gdns.
CR0: C'don 1A 170
Wilks Pl. N1 2E 84
Willan Rd. N17 2D 48
Willard St. SW8 3F 119
Willcocks Cl.
KT9: Chess 3E 162
Willcott Rd. W3 1H 97
Will Crooks Gdns. SE9 4A 124
Willen Fld. Rd. NW10 2J 79
Willenhall Av.
EN5: New Bar 6F 21
Willenhall Ct.
EN5: New Bar 6F 21
Willenhall Dr. UB3: Hayes 7G 75
Willenhall Rd. SE18 5F 107
Willersley Av.
BR6: Orp 3H 173
DA15: Sidc 1K 143
Willersley Cl. DA15: Sidc 1K 143
WILLESDEN 6C 62
WILLESDEN GREEN 6E 62
Willesden La. NW2 6E 62
NW6 6E 62
Willesden Section Ho. NW6 7F 63
(off Willesden La.)
Willesden Sports Cen. 1D 80
Willesden Sports Stadium 1D 80
Willes Rd. NW5 6F 65
Willett Cl. BR5: Pet W 6J 161
UB5: N'olt 3A 76
Willett Ho. E13 2K 87
(off Queens Rd. W.)
Willett Pl. CR7: Thor H 5A 156
Willett Rd. CR7: Thor H 5A 156
Willett Way BR5: Pet W 5H 161
William IV St.
WC2 3E 12 (7J 83)
William Allen Ho.
HA8: Edg 7A 28
William Ash Cl. RM9: Dag 6B 72
William Banfield Ho. SW6 2H 117
(off Munster Rd.)
William Barefoot Dr. SE9 4E 142
William Blake Ho. SW11 1C 118
William Bonney Est.
SW4 4H 119
William Booth Ho. E14 6C 86
(off Hind Gro.)
William Booth Rd. SE20 1G 157
William Carey Way
HA1: Harr 6J 41
William Caslon Ho. E2 2H 85
(off Patriot Sq.)
William Channing Ho. E2 3H 85
(off Canrobert St.)
William Cl. N2 2B 46
RM5: Col R 1J 55
SE7 5B 106
SE13 3E 122
UB2: S'hall 2G 95
William Cobbett Ho. W8 3K 99
(off Scarsdale Pl.)
William Congreve M. N1 1C 84
William Cotton Ct. E14 5C 86
(off Selsey St.)
William Ct. NW8 3A 82
SE10 1D 122
(off Greenwich High Rd.)
SE25 3F 157
(off Chalfont Rd.)
SW16 7K 137
(off Streatham High Rd.)
W5 5C 78
William Covell Cl.
EN2: Enf 1E 22
William Dr. HA7: Stan 6F 27
William Dromey Ct.
NW6 7H 63
William Dunbar Ho. NW6 2H 81
(off Albert Rd.)
William Dyce M. SW16 4H 137
William Ellis Way SE16 3G 103
(off St James's Rd.)
William Evans Ho. SE8 4K 103
(off Haddonfield)
William Farm La. SW15 3D 116
William Fenn Ho. E2 1K 9
(off Shipton Rd.)
William Foster La. DA16: Well 2A 126
William Fry Ho. E1 6K 85
(off W. Arbour St.)
William Gdns. SW15 5D 116
William Gibbs Ct. SW1 2C 18
(off Old Pye St.)
William Gunn Ho. NW3 5C 64
William Guy Gdns. E3 3D 86
William Harvey Ho. SW19 1G 135
(off Whitlock Dr.)
William Henry Wlk.
SW11 7C 18 (6H 101)
William Hope Cl.
IG11: Bark 2J 89
William Ho. BR1: Broml 3J 159
William Hunt Mans.
SW13 6E 98
William Margrie Cl. SE15 2G 121
William Marshall Cl. E17 6A 50
William M. N1 7E 66
SW1 7F 11 (2D 100)
William Morley Cl. E6 1B 88
William Morris Cl. E17 3B 50
William Morris Gallery 3C 50
William Morris Ho. W6 6F 99
William Morris Way SW6 3A 118
William Murdoch Rd.
E14 5F 87
William Owston Ct. E16 1C 106
(off Connaught Rd.)
William Parry House E16 2K 105
(off Shipwright Street)
William Perkin Ct.
UB6: G'frd 6J 59
William Pike Ho. RM7: Rom 6K 55
(off Waterloo Gdns.)
William Pl. E3 2B 86
William Rathbone Ho. E2 3H 85
(off Florida St.)
William Rd. NW1 2A 6 (3G 83)
SM1: Sutt 5A 166
SW19 7G 135
William Rushbrooke Ho. SE16 4G 103
(off Rouel Rd.)
Williams Av. E17 1B 50
William Saville Ho. NW6 2H 81
(off Denmark Rd.)
William's Bldgs. E2 4J 85
Williamsburg Plaza E14 7E 86
Williams Cl. N8 6H 47
SW6 7G 99
Williams Dr. TW3: Houn 4E 112
Williams Gro. KT6: Surb 6C 150
N22 1A 48
Williams Ho. E3 3C 86
(off Alfred St.)
E9 1H 85
(off King Edward's Rd.)
NW2 3E 62
(off Stoll Cl.)
SW1 4D 18
(off Montaigne Cl.)
William's La. SW14 3J 115
Williams La. SM4: Mord 5A 154
Williams M. SE4 6B 122
William Smith Ho. DA17: Belv 3G 109
(off Ambrooke Rd.)
E3 3C 86
(off Ireton St.)
Williamson Cl. SE10 5H 105
Williamson Ct. SE17 5C 102
Williamson Rd. N4 6B 48
Williamson St. N7 4J 65
William Sq. SE16 7A 86
(off Sovereign Cres.)
Williams Rd. UB2: S'hall 4C 94
W13 1A 96
Williams Ter. CR0: Wadd 6A 168
William St. E10 6D 50
IG11: Bark 7G 71
N17 7A 34
SM5: Cars 3C 166
SW1 7F 11 (2D 100)
Williams Way
DA2: Wilm 2K 145
HA0: Wemb 5B 60
William Whiffin Sq. E3 4B 86
William Wood Ho. SE26 3J 139
(off Shrublands Cl.)
Willifield Way NW11 4H 45
Willingale Cl.
IG8: Wfd G 6F 37
Willingdon Rd. N22 2B 48
Willingham Cl. NW5 5G 65
Willingham Ter. NW5 5G 65
Willingham Way
KT1: King T 3G 151
Willington Ct. E5 3A 68
Willington Rd. SW9 3J 119
Willis Av. SM2: Sutt 6C 166
Willis Ct. BR4: W W'ck 2F 171
CR7: Thor H 6A 156
Willis Ho. E14 7D 86
(off Hale St.)
Willis Rd. CR0: C'don 7C 156
DA8: Erith 4J 109
E15 2H 87
Willis St. E14 6D 86
Willis Yd. N14 7C 22
Will Miles Ct. SW19 7A 136
Willmore End SW19 1K 153
Willoughby Av.
CR0: Bedd 4K 167
UB10: Uxb 2A 74
Willoughby Dr. RM13: Rain 7K 73
Willoughby Gro. N17 7C 34
Willoughby Highwalk EC2 6E 8
(off Moor La.)
Willoughby Ho. E1 1H 103
(off Reardon Path)
EC2 5E 8
Willoughby La. BR1: Broml 7K 141
N17 6C 34
Willoughby M. N17 7C 34
SW4 4F 119
(off Cedars M.)
Willoughby Pk. Rd. N17 7C 34
Willoughby Pas. E14 1C 104
(off W. India Av.)
Willoughby Rd. KT2: King T 1F 151
N8 3A 48
NW3 4B 64
TW1: Twick 5C 114
(not continuous)
The Willoughbys SW14 3A 116
Willoughby St. WC1 6E 6
Willoughby Way SE7 4K 105
Willow Av. DA15: Sidc 6A 126
SW13 2B 116
UB7: Yiew 7B 74
Willow Bank SW6 3G 117
TW10: Ham 3B 132
Willowbank KT7: T Ditt 1A 162
Willowbay Cl. EN5: Barn 6A 20
Willow Bri. Rd. N1 6C 66
(not continuous)
Willowbrook TW12: Hamp H 5F 131
Willowbrook Est. SE15 7G 103
Willow Brook Rd. SE15 7F 103
Willowbrook Rd.
TW19: Stanw 2A 128
UB2: S'hall 3E 94
Willow Bus. Pk. SE26 3J 139
Willow Cl. BR2: Broml 5D 160
DA5: Bexl 6F 127
IG9: Buck H 3G 37
SE6 1H 141
TW8: Bford 6C 96
Willow Cotts. TW9: Kew 6G 97
TW13: Hanw 3C 130
Willow Ct. E11 2G 69
(off Trinity Cl.)
EC2 3G 9 (4E 84)
HA3: Hrw W 1K 41
HA8: Edg 4K 27
N12 4E 30
NW6 7G 63
SM6: W'gton 7F 167
(off Willow Rd.)
TW16: Sun 7G 129
(off Staines Rd. W.)
W4 7A 98
(off Corney Reach Way)
W9 5J 81
(off Admiral Wlk.)
Willowcourt Av. HA3: Kenton 5B 42
Willow Dene
HA5: Pinn 2B 40
WD23: B Hea 1D 26
Willowdene N6 7D 46
SE15 7H 103
Willowdene Cl. TW2: Whitt 7G 113
Willowdene Ct. N20 7F 21
(off High Rd. Whetstone)
Willow Dr. EN5: Barn 4B 20
Willow End KT6: Surb 1E 162
N20 2D 30
Willowfields Cl. SE18 5J 107
Willow Gdns.
HA4: Ruis 2H 57
TW3: Houn 1E 112
Willow Grange DA14: Sidc 3B 144
Willow Grn. NW9 1A 44
Willow Gro.
BR7: Chst 6E 142
E13 2J 87
HA4: Ruis 2H 57
Willowhayne Ct. KT12: Walt T 7K 147
(off Willowhayne Dr.)
Willowhayne Dr. KT12: Walt T 7K 147
Willowhayne Gdns.
KT4: Wor Pk 3E 164
Willow Ho. BR2: Broml 2G 159
SE1 4F 103
(off Curtis St.)
SE4 3A 122
(off Dragonfly Pl.)
W10 4F 81
(off Maple Wlk.)
Willow La. CR4: Mitc 5D 154
SE18 4D 106
Willow La. Bus. Pk. CR4: Mitc 6D 154
Willow La. Ind. Est.
CR4: Mitc 6D 154
Willow Lodge RM7: Rom 5K 55
SW6 1F 117
TW16: Sun 7H 129
(off Grangewood Dr.)

Willowmead Cl. W5 . . . . .4D 78
Willow Mt. CR0: C'don 3E 168
Willow Pl. SW1 . . . . . .3B 18 (4G 101)
Willow Rd. EN1: Enf 3K 23
  KT3: N Mald 4J 151
  NW3 .4B 64
  RM6: Chad H 6E 54
  SL3: Poyle 5A 174
  SM6: W'gton 7F 167
  W5 . . . . .2E 96
The Willows BR3: Beck 1C 158
  E6 . . . . .7D 70
  SE1 .4E 102
Willows Av. SM4: Mord 5K 153
Willows Cl. HA5: Pinn 2A 40
Willowside Ct. EN2: Enf 3G 23
Willows Ter. NW10 . . . . .2B 80
  (off Rucklidge Av.)
Willow St. E4 . . . . .1A 36
  EC2 . . . . .3G 9 (4E 84)
  RM7: Rom 4J 55
Willow Tree Cen. 5D 38
Willow Tree Cl. E3 . . . . .1B 86
  SW18 . . . . .1K 135
  UB4: Yead 4A 76
  UB5: N'olt 6D 58
Willowtree Cl. UB10: Ick 3E 56
Willow Tree Ct. DA14: Sidc 5A 144
  HA0: Wemb 5D 60
Willow Tree La. UB4: Yead 4A 76
WILLOW TREE RDBT. 5B 76
Willow Tree Wlk.
  BR1: Broml 1K 159
Willowtree Way
  CR7: Thor H 1A 156
Willow Va. BR7: Chst 6F 143
  W12 . . . . .1C 98
Willow Vw. SW19 . . . . .1B 154
Willow Wlk. BR6: Farnb 3F 173
  E17 . . . . .5B 50
  IG1: Ilf .2F 71
  N1 . . . . .2B 84
  N2 . . . . .2B 46
  N15 . . . . .4B 48
  N21 . . . . .6E 22
  SE1 .3E 102
  SM3: Sutt 3H 165
Willow Way HA0: Wemb 3A 60
  KT19: Ewe 6K 163
  N3 . . . . .7E 30
  SE26 .3J 139
  TW2: Twick 2F 131
  TW16: Sun 4J 147
  W11 . . . . .7F 81
Willow Wood Cres. SE25 . . . . . . .6E 156
Willow Wren Wharf UB2: S'hall . . .4K 93
Willrose Cres. SE2 . . . . .5B 108
Willsbridge Cl. SE15 . . . . .6F 103
Wills Cres. TW3: Houn 6F 113
Wills Gro. NW7 . . . . .5H 29
Will Wyatt Ct. N1 . . . . .2E 84
  (off Pitfield St.)
Wilman Gro. E8 . . . . .7G 67
Wilmar Cl. UB4: Hayes 4F 75
Wilmar Gdns. BR4: W W'ck 1D 170
Wilmcote Ho. W2 . . . . .5K 81
  (off Woodchester Sq.)
Wilment Ct. NW2 . . . . .3E 62
Wilmer Cl. KT2: King T 5F 133
Wilmer Cres. KT2: King T 5F 133
Wilmer Gdns. N1 . . . . .1E 84
  (not continuous)
Wilmer Ho. E3 . . . . .2A 86
  (off Daling Way)
Wilmer Lea Cl. E15 . . . . .7F 69
Wilmer Pl. N16 . . . . .2F 67
Wilmer Way N14 . . . . .5C 32
Wilmington Av. W4 . . . . .7K 97
Wilmington Ct. SW16 . . . . .7J 137
Wilmington Gdns. IG11: Bark 6H 71
Wilmington Sq. WC1 . . . . .2J 7 (3A 84)
  (not continuous)

Wilmington St. WC1 . . . . . .2J 7 (3A 84)
Wilmington Ter. SE16 . . . . .4H 103
  (off Camilla Rd.)
Wilmot Cl. N2 . . . . .2A 46
  SE15 .7G 103
Wilmot Ho. SE11 . . . . .4B 102
  (off George Mathers Rd.)
Wilmot Pl. NW1 . . . . .7G 65
  (not continuous)
  W7 . . . . .1J 95
Wilmot Rd. E10 . . . . .2D 68
  N17 . . . . .3D 48
  SM5: Cars 5D 166
Wilmot St. E2 . . . . .4H 85
Wilmount St. SE18 . . . . .4F 107
Wilna Rd. SW18 . . . . .7A 118
Wilsham St. W11 . . . . .1F 99
Wilshaw Cl. NW4 . . . . .3C 44
Wilshaw Ho. SE8 . . . . .7C 104
Wilshaw St. SE14 . . . . .1C 122
Wilsmere Dr.
  HA3: Hrw W 7D 26
  UB5: N'olt 6C 58
Wilson Av. CR4: Mitc 7C 136
Wilson Cl. CR2: S Croy 5D 168
  HA9: Wemb 7F 43
Wilson Ct. NW9 . . . . .2K 43
  RM7: Rush G 6K 55
  (off Union Rd.)
  SE28 .3G 107
Wilson Dr. HA9: Wemb 7F 43
Wilson Gdns. HA1: Harr 7G 41
Wilson Gro. SE16 . . . . .2H 103
Wilson Ho. NW6 . . . . .7A 64
  (off Goldhurst Ter.)
Wilson Rd. E6 . . . . .3B 88
  IG1: Ilf .7D 52
  KT9: Chess 6F 163
  SE5 . . . . .1E 120
Wilson's Av. N17 . . . . .2F 49
Wilson's Rd. W6 . . . . .5F 99
Wilson St. E17 . . . . .5C 50
  EC2 . . . . .5F 9 (5D 84)
  N21 . . . . .7F 23
Wilson Wlk. W4 . . . . .4B 98
  (off Prebend Gdns.)
Wilstone Cl. UB4: Yead 4C 76
Wiltern Ct. NW2 . . . . .6G 63
Wilthorne Gdns.
  RM10: Dag 7H 73
Wilton Av. W4 . . . . .5A 98
Wilton Cl. UB7: Harm 2E 174
Wilton Ct. E1 . . . . .6H 85
  (off Cavell St.)
Wilton Cres. SW1 . . . . . .7G 11 (2E 100)
  SW19 . . . . .1H 153
Wilton Dr. RM5: Col R 1J 55
Wilton Est. E8 . . . . .6G 67
Wilton Gdns.
  KT8: W Mole 3E 148
Wilton Gro.
  KT3: N Mald 6B 152
  SW19 . . . . .1H 153
Wilton Ho. CR2: S Croy 5C 168
  (off Nottingham Rd.)
Wilton M. E8 . . . . .6H 67
  SW1 . . . . .1H 17 (3E 100)
Wilton Pde. TW13: Felt 2J 129
Wilton Pl. E4 . . . . .6A 36
  HA1: Harr 6K 41
  SW1 . . . . .7G 11 (2E 100)
Wilton Plaza SW1 . . . . .3A 18
  (off Wilton Rd.)
Wilton Rd. EN4: Cockf 4J 21
  N10 . . . . .2E 46
  SE2 . . . . .4C 108
  SW1 . . . . .2K 17 (3F 101)
  SW19 . . . . .7C 136
  TW4: Houn 3B 112
Wilton Row SW1 . . . . . . .7G 11 (2E 100)
Wilton's Music Hall 7G 85
  (off Graces All.)

Wilton Sq. N1 . . . . .1D 84
Wilton St. SW1 . . . . . . .1J 17 (3F 101)
Wilton Ter. SW1 . . . . . .1G 17 (3E 100)
Wilton Vs. N1 . . . . .1D 84
  (off Wilton Sq.)
Wilton Way E8 . . . . .6G 67
Wiltshire Cl. NW7 . . . . .5G 29
  SW3 . . . . .3E 16 (4D 100)
Wiltshire Ct. CR2: S Croy 5C 168
  IG1: Ilf .6G 71
  N4 . . . . .1K 65
  (off Marquis Rd.)
Wiltshire Gdns. N4 . . . . .6C 48
  TW2: Twick 1G 131
Wiltshire La. HA5: Eastc 3H 39
Wiltshire Rd.
  BR6: Orp 7K 161
  CR7: Thor H 3A 156
  SW9 .3A 120
Wiltshire Row N1 . . . . .1D 84
Wilverley Cres.
  KT3: N Mald 6A 152
Wimbart Rd. SW2 . . . . .7K 119
WIMBLEDON 6G 135
Wimbledon All England Lawn Tennis &
  Croquet Club 4G 135
Wimbledon Bri. SW19 . . . . .6H 135
Wimbledon Cl. SW20 . . . . .7F 135
Wimbledon Common 4C 134
Wimbledon Common Golf Course
  . . . . .5D 134
Wimbledon Hill Rd. SW19 . . . . . . .6G 135
Wimbledon Lawn Tennis Mus.
  . . . . .3G 135
Wimbledon Leisure Cen. 6K 135
WIMBLEDON PARK 3J 135
Wimbledon Pk. Athletics Track
  . . . . .2H 135
Wimbledon Pk. Ct. SW19 . . . . . . .1H 135
Wimbledon Pk. Golf Course 3H 135
Wimbledon Pk. Rd.
  SW18 . . . . .2G 135
  SW19 . . . . .2G 135
Wimbledon Pk. Side SW19 . . . . . .3F 135
Wimbledon Pk. Watersports Cen.
  . . . . .2H 135
Wimbledon Rd. SW17 . . . . .4A 136
Wimbledon Stadium Bus. Cen.
  SW17 . . . . .3K 135
Wimbledon Theatre 7J 135
Wimbledon Windmill Mus. 3D 134
Wimbolt St. E2 . . . . .3G 85
Wimborne Av. BR5: St P 4K 161
  BR7: Chst 4K 161
  UB2: S'hall 4E 94
  UB4: Yead 6K 75
Wimborne Cl. IG9: Buck H 2E 36
  KT4: Wor Pk 1E 164
  SE12 .5H 123
Wimborne Ct. SW12 . . . . .3G 137
  UB5: N'olt 6E 58
Wimborne Dr. HA5: Pinn 7B 40
  NW9 . . . . .3G 43
Wimborne Gdns. W13 . . . . .5B 78
Wimborne Ho. E16 . . . . .7H 87
  (off Victoria Dock Rd.)
  NW1 . . . . .4D 4
  (off Harewood Av.)
  SW8 . . . . .7K 101
  (off Dorset Rd.)
  SW12 .3G 137
Wimborne Rd. N9 . . . . .2B 34
  N17 . . . . .2E 48
Wimborne Way BR3: Beck 3K 157
Wimbourne Ct. N1 . . . . .2D 84
  (off Wimbourne St.)
Wimbourne St. N1 . . . . .2D 84
Wimpole Cl. BR2: Broml 4A 160
  KT1: King T 2F 151
Wimpole M. W1 . . . . .5J 5 (5F 83)
Wimpole Rd. UB7: Yiew 1A 92
Wimpole St. W1 . . . . .6J 5 (5F 83)

Wimshurst Cl.
  CR0: Wadd 1J 167
Winans Wlk. SW9 . . . . .2A 120
Winant Ho. E14 . . . . .7D 86
  (off Simpson's Rd.)
Wincanton Ct. N11 . . . . .6K 31
  (off Martock Gdns.)
Wincanton Cres. UB5: N'olt 5E 58
Wincanton Gdns.
  IG6: Ilf .3F 53
Wincanton Rd. SW18 . . . . .7H 117
Winchcombe Rd.
  SM5: Cars 7B 154
Winchcomb Gdns. SE9 . . . . .3B 124
Winchelsea Av. DA7: Bex 7F 109
Winchelsea Cl. SW15 . . . . .5F 117
Winchelsea Ho. SE16 . . . . .2J 103
  (off Swan Rd.)
Winchelsea Rd. E7 . . . . .3J 69
  N17 . . . . .3E 48
  NW10 .1K 79
Winchelsey Ri.
  CR2: S Croy 6F 169
Winchendon Rd. SW6 . . . . .1H 117
  TW11: Tedd 4H 131
Winchester Av. NW6 . . . . .1G 81
  NW9 . . . . .3G 43
  TW5: Hest 6D 94
Winchester Bldgs. SE1 . . . . .6C 14
  (off Copperfield St.)
Winchester Cl. BR2: Broml 3D 160
  E6 . . . . .6D 88
  EN1: Enf 5K 23
  KT2: King T 7H 133
  SE17 .4B 102
  SL3: Poyle 4A 174
Winchester Ct. W8 . . . . .2J 99
  (off Vicarage Ga.)
Winchester Dr. HA5: Pinn 5B 40
Winchester Ho. E3 . . . . .3B 86
  (off Hamlets Way)
  E14 . . . . .6C 86
  (off New Festival Av.)
  IG11: Bark 7A 72
  (off Margaret Bondfield Av.)
  SE18 .7B 106
  (off Portway Gdns.)
  SW3 . . . . .7B 16
  SW9 .7A 102
  W2 . . . . .6A 82
  (off Hallfield Est.)
Winchester M. KT4: Wor Pk 2F 165
  NW3 . . . . .7B 64
  (off Winchester Rd.)
Winchester Palace 4E 14
  (off Stoney St.)
Winchester Pk. BR2: Broml 3H 159
Winchester Pl. E8 . . . . .5F 67
  N6 . . . . .1F 65
Winchester Rd.
  BR2: Broml 3H 159
  DA7: Bex 2D 126
  E4 . . . . .7K 35
  HA3: Kenton 4E 42
  HA6: Nwood 2H 39
  IG1: Ilf .3H 71
  KT12: Walt T 7J 147
  N6 . . . . .7F 47
  N9 . . . . .1A 34
  NW3 . . . . .7B 64
  TW1: Twick 6B 114
  TW13: Hanw 3D 130
  UB3: Harl 7G 93
Winchester Sq. SE1 . . . . .4E 14
  SE8 . . . . .4B 104
Winchester St. SW1 . . . . .5K 17 (5F 101)
  W3 . . . . .1J 97
Winchester Wlk. SE1 . . . . .4E 14 (1D 102)
  SW15 .5H 117
  (off Up. Richmond Rd.)
Winchester Wharf SE1 . . . . .4E 14
  (off Clink St.)

Winchet Wlk. CR0: C'don 6J **157**
Winchfield Cl.
  HA3: Kenton 6C **42**
Winchfield Ho. SW15 . . . . .6B **116**
Winchfield Rd. SE26 . . . . .5A **140**
Winch Ho. E14 . . . . .3D **104**
                (off Tiller Rd.)
  SW10 . . . . .7A **100**
              (off King's Rd.)
Winchilsea Cres. KT8: W Mole . .1C **148**
Winchilsea Ho. NW8 . . . . .2B **4**
        (off St John's Wood Rd.)
WINCHMORE HILL 7F **23**
Winchmore Hill Rd. N14 . . . . . . .1C **32**
  N21 .1C **32**
Winchmore School Sports Cen. . .2H **33**
Winchmore Vs. N21 . . . . .7F **23**
        (off Winchmore Hill Rd.)
Winchstone Cl. TW17: Shep 4B **146**
Winckley Cl.
  HA3: Kenton 5F **43**
Winckworth Ct. N1 . . . . .2F **9**
         (off Charles Sq. Est.)
Wincott Pde. SE11 . . . . .3K **19**
           (off Wincott St.)
Wincott St. SE11 . . . . . .4K **19** (4A **102**)
Wincrofts Dr. SE9 . . . . .4H **125**
Windall Cl. SE19 . . . . .1G **157**
Windborough Rd. SM5: Cars 7E **166**
Windermere NW1 . . . . .2K **5**
            (off Albany St.)
Windermere Av. HA4: Ruis 7A **40**
  HA9: Kenton, Wemb 7C **42**
  N3 . . . . .3J **45**
  NW6 .1G **81**
  SW19 . . . . .3K **153**
Windermere Cl. BR6: Farnb 3F **173**
  TW14: Felt 1H **129**
  TW19: Stanw 1A **128**
Windermere Ct. HA9: Wemb 7C **42**
  SM5: Cars 3E **166**
  SW13 . . . . .6B **98**
Windermere Gdns. IG4: Ilf 5C **52**
Windermere Gro.
  HA9: Wemb 1C **60**
Windermere Hall
  HA8: Edg 5A **28**
  EN5: New Bar 4E **20**
  TW7: Isle 5K **113**
Windermere Point SE15 . . . . .7J **103**
         (off Old Kent Rd.)
Windermere Rd.
  BR4: W W'ck 2G **171**
  CR0: C'don 1F **169**
  DA7: Bex 2J **127**
  N10 .1F **47**
  N19 .2G **65**
  SW15 . . . . .4A **134**
  SW16 . . . . .1G **155**
  UB1: S'hall 5D **76**
  W5 .3C **96**
Windermere Way
  UB7: Yiew 1A **92**
Winders Rd. SW11 . . . . .2C **118**
          (not continuous)
Windfield Cl. SE26 . . . . .4K **139**
Windham Rd. TW9: Rich 3F **115**
Winding Way
  RM8: Dag 3C **72**
Windlass Ho. E16 . . . . .2K **105**
        (off Schooner Rd.)
Windlass Pl. SE8 . . . . .4A **104**
Windlesham Gro. SW19 . . . . . . .1F **135**
Windlesham Ho. SE1 . . . . .5J **15**
        (off Duchess Wlk.)
Windlesham M.
  TW12: Hamp H 6G **131**
Windley Cl. SE23 . . . . .2J **139**
Windmill WC1 . . . . .5G **7**
        (off New North St.)
Windmill Av. UB2: S'hall 1G **95**

Windmill Bri. Ho. CR0: C'don 1E **168**
       (off Freemasons Rd.)
Windmill Bus. Village
  TW16: Sun 1G **147**
Windmill Cl. KT6: Surb 1C **162**
  SE1 .4G **103**
         (off Beatrice Rd.)
  SE13 . . . . .2E **122**
  TW16: Sun 7G **129**
Windmill Ct. E4 . . . . .2B **36**
  HA4: Ruis 1J **57**
  NW2 . . . . .6G **63**
  W5 .4C **96**
         (off Windmill Rd.)
Windmill Dr. BR2: Kes 4A **172**
  NW2 . . . . .3G **63**
  SW4 . . . . .5F **119**
Windmill Gdns. EN2: Enf 3F **23**
Windmill Grn. TW17: Shep 7G **147**
Windmill Gro. CR0: C'don 6C **156**
Windmill Hill EN2: Enf 3G **23**
  HA4: Ruis 7H **39**
  NW3 .3A **64**
Windmill Ho. E14 . . . . .4C **104**
  SE1 . . . . .5K **13**
        (off Windmill Wlk.)
Windmill La. E15 . . . . .6F **69**
  KT6: Surb 6B **150**
  TW7: Isle 3G **95**
  UB2: S'hall 1G **95**
  UB6: G'frd 6G **77**
  WD23: B Hea 1D **26**
Windmill M. W4 . . . . .4A **98**
Windmill Pas. W4 . . . . .4A **98**
Windmill Pl. UB2: S'hall 1G **95**
Windmill Ri. KT2: King T 7H **133**
Windmill Rd.
  CR0: C'don 7C **156**
  CR4: Mitc 5G **155**
  N18 .4J **33**
  SW18 . . . . .6B **118**
  SW19 . . . . .2D **134**
  TW8: Bford 4C **96**
  TW12: Hamp H 5F **131**
  TW16: Sun 1G **147**
  W4 .4A **98**
  W5 .4C **96**
Windmill Rd. W.
  TW16: Sun 2G **147**
Windmill Row SE11 . . . .6J **19** (5A **102**)
Windmill St. W1 . . . . .6C **6** (5H **83**)
         (not continuous)
  WD23: B Hea 1D **26**
Windmill Ter. TW17: Shep 7G **147**
Windmill Wlk.
  SE1 . . . . .5K **13** (1A **102**)
Windmill Way HA4: Ruis 1H **57**
Windmore Cl.
  HA0: Wemb 5A **60**
Windrose Cl. SE16 . . . . .2K **103**
Windrush KT3: N Mald 4H **151**
  SE28 . . . . .1B **108**
Windrush Cl. E8 . . . . .7G **67**
  N17 .1E **48**
  SW11 . . . . .4B **118**
  UB10: Ick 4B **56**
  W4 .1J **115**
Windrush Ho. NW8 . . . . .5B **4**
       (off Church St. Est.)
Windrush La. SE23 . . . . .3K **139**
Windrush Rd. NW10 . . . . .1K **79**
Windrush Sq. SW2 . . . . .4A **120**
Windsock Cl. SE16 . . . . .4B **104**
Windsock Way
  TW6: H'row A 5C **174**
Windsor Av. E17 . . . . .2A **50**
  HA8: Edg 4C **28**
  KT3: N Mald 5J **151**
  KT8: W Mole 3E **148**
  SM3: Cheam 3G **165**
  SW19 . . . . .1A **154**
  UB10: Hil 1D **74**

The Windsor Cen. N1 . . . . .1B **84**
         (off Windsor St.)
Windsor Cl. BR7: Chst 5F **143**
  HA2: Harr 3E **58**
  HA6: Nwood 2J **39**
  N3 . . . . .2G **45**
  SE27 . . . . .4C **138**
  TW6: H'row A 6D **174**
        (off Whittle Rd.)
  TW8: Bford 6B **96**
Windsor Cotts. SE14 . . . . .7B **104**
       (off Amersham Gro.)
Windsor Ct. E3 . . . . .2C **86**
         (off Mostyn Gro.)
  HA5: Pinn 3B **40**
  KT1: King T 4D **150**
         (off Palace Rd.)
  N11 .5J **31**
  N14 .7B **22**
  NW3 .4J **63**
  NW11 . . . . .6G **45**
        (off Golders Grn. Rd.)
  SE16 . . . . .7K **85**
       (off King & Queen Wharf)
  SW3 . . . . .5D **16**
         (off Jubilee Pl.)
  SW11 . . . . .2B **118**
  TW16: Sun 7J **129**
  W2 . . . . .7K **81**
        (off Moscow Rd.)
  W10 .6F **81**
        (off Bramley Rd.)
  WD23: Bush 1B **26**
        (off Catsey La.)
Windsor Cres. HA2: Harr 3E **58**
  HA9: Wemb 3H **61**
Windsor Dr.
  BR6: Chels 6K **173**
  EN4: E Barn 6J **21**
Windsor Gdns.
  CR0: Bedd 3J **167**
  UB3: Harl 3F **93**
  W9 . . . . .5J **81**
Windsor Gro. SE27 . . . . .4C **138**
Windsor Hall E16 . . . . .1K **105**
         (off Wesley Av.)
Windsor Ho. E2 . . . . .3K **85**
       (off Knottisford St.)
  E20 .5D **68**
        (off Peloton Av.)
  N1 . . . . .2C **84**
  NW1 .1K **5**
  NW2 . . . . .6G **63**
        (off Chatsworth Rd.)
  SW16 . . . . .2K **155**
  UB5: N'olt 6E **58**
       (off The Farmlands)
Windsor M. SE6 . . . . .1E **140**
  SE23 . . . . .1A **140**
Windsor Pk. Rd.
  UB3: Harl 7H **93**
Windsor Pl.
  SW1 . . . . .3B **18** (3G **101**)
Windsor Rd.
  CR7: Thor H 2B **156**
  DA6: Bex 4E **126**
  E4 . . . . .4J **35**
  E7 . . . . .5K **69**
  E10 .2D **68**
  E11 .1J **69**
  EN5: Barn 6A **20**
  HA3: Hrw W 1G **41**
  IG1: Ilf 4F **71**
  KT2: King T 7E **132**
  KT4: Wor Pk 2C **164**
  N3 . . . . .2G **45**
  N7 . . . . .3J **65**
  N13 .3F **33**
  N17 .2G **49**
  NW2 . . . . .6D **62**
  RM8: Dag 3E **72**
  TW4: Cran 2K **111**

Windsor Rd. TW9: Kew 2F **115**
  TW11: Tedd 5H **131**
  TW16: Sun 6J **129**
  UB2: S'hall 3D **94**
  W5 .7E **78**
         (not continuous)
The Windsors IG9: Buck H 2H **37**
Windsor St. N1 . . . . .1B **84**
Windsor Ter. N1 . . . . .1D **8** (3C **84**)
Windsor Wlk. SE5 . . . . .2D **120**
Windsor Way W14 . . . . .4F **99**
Windsor Wharf E9 . . . . .5B **68**
Windspoint Dr. SE15 . . . . .6H **103**
Windus M. N16 . . . . .1F **67**
Windus Rd. N16 . . . . .1F **67**
Windus Wlk. N16 . . . . .1F **67**
Windward Ct. E16 . . . . .7F **89**
        (off Gallions Rd.)
Windy Ridge BR1: Broml 1C **160**
Windy Ridge Cl.
  SW19 . . . . .5F **135**
Wine Cl. E1 . . . . .1J **103**
         (not continuous)
Wine Office Ct. EC4 . . . . . .7K **7** (6A **84**)
Winery La. KT1: King T 3F **151**
Winey Cl. KT9: Chess 7C **162**
Winford Ct. SE15 . . . . .1H **121**
Winford Ho. E3 . . . . .7B **68**
Winford Pde. UB1: S'hall 6F **77**
        (off Marconi Way)
Winforton St. SE10 . . . . .1E **122**
Winfrith Rd. SW18 . . . . .7A **118**
Wingate & Finchley FC 7G **31**
Wingate Cres. CR0: C'don 6J **155**
Wingate Ho. E3 . . . . .3D **86**
         (off Bruce Rd.)
Wingate Rd. DA14: Sidc 6C **144**
  IG1: Ilf 5F **71**
  W6 .3D **98**
Wingate Sq. SW4 . . . . .3G **119**
Wingfield Ct. DA15: Sidc 2K **143**
  E14 . . . . .7F **87**
        (off Newport Av.)
Wingfield Ho. E2 . . . . .2J **9**
        (off Virginia Rd.)
Wingfield M. SE15 . . . . .3G **121**
Wingfield Rd. E15 . . . . .4G **69**
  E17 .5D **50**
  KT2: King T 6F **133**
Wingfield St. SE15 . . . . .3G **121**
Wingfield Way
  HA4: Ruis 5K **57**
Wingford Rd. SW2 . . . . .6J **119**
Wingmore Rd. SE24 . . . . .3C **120**
Wingrad Ho. E1 . . . . .5J **85**
        (off Jubilee St.)
Wingrave Rd. W6 . . . . .6E **98**
Wingreen NW8 . . . . .1K **81**
        (off Abbey Rd.)
Wingrove E4 . . . . .7H **25**
Wingrove Ct. RM7: Rom 5J **55**
Wingrove Rd. SE6 . . . . .2G **141**
Wings Cl. SM1: Sutt 4J **165**
Wings Rd. TW6: H'row A 6C **174**
        (off Whittle Rd.)
Wing Yip Bus. Cen. NW2 . . . . . . .2D **62**
Winicotte Ho. W2 . . . . .5B **4**
       (off Paddington Grn.)
Winifred Pl. N12 . . . . .5F **31**
Winifred Rd.
  DA8: Erith 5K **109**
  RM8: Dag 2E **72**
  SW19 . . . . .1J **153**
  TW12: Hamp H 4E **130**
Winifred St. E16 . . . . .1D **106**
Winifred Ter.
  EN1: Enf 7A **24**
  E13 .2K **87**
  N22 .1A **48**
Winkfield Rd. E13 . . . . .2K **87**
  N22 .1A **48**
Winkley Ct. HA2: Harr 3E **58**
  N10 .4F **47**
        (off St James's La.)

Winkley St. E2 . . . . .2H **85**
Winkworth Cotts. *E1* 4J **85**
(off Cephas St.)
Winlaton Rd. BR1: Broml 4F **141**
Winmill Rd. RM8: Dag 3F **73**
Winn Comn. Rd. SE18 . . . . .6J **107**
Winnepeg Ho. *SE16* 2J **103**
(off Province Dr.)
Winnett St. W1 . . . . .2C **12** (7H **83**)
Winningales Ct. IG5: Ilf 2C **52**
Winnings Wlk. UB5: N'olt 6C **58**
Winnington Cl. N2 . . . . .6B **46**
Winnington Ho. *SE5* 7C **102**
(off Wyndham Est.)
W10 . . . . .4G **81**
(off Southern Row)
Winnington Rd. N2 . . . . .6B **46**
Winnipeg Dr. BR6: Chels 6K **173**
Winnock Rd. UB7: View 1A **92**
Winn Rd. SE12 . . . . .1J **141**
Winns Av. E17 . . . . .3B **50**
Winns M. N15 . . . . .4E **48**
Winns Ter. E17 . . . . .3C **50**
Winsbeach E17 . . . . .2F **51**
Winscombe Cres. W5 . . . . .4D **78**
Winscombe St. N19 . . . . .2F **65**
Winscombe Way
HA7: Stan 5F **27**
Winsford Rd. SE6 . . . . .3B **140**
Winsford Ter. N18 . . . . .5J **33**
Winsham Gro. SW11 . . . . .5E **118**
Winsham Ho. *NW1* 1D **6**
(off Churchway)
Winslade Rd. SW2 . . . . .5J **119**
Winslade Way SE6 . . . . .7D **122**
Winsland M. W2 . . . . .7A **4** (6B **82**)
Winsland St. W2 . . . . .7A **4** (6B **82**)
Winsley St. W1 . . . . .7B **6** (6G **83**)
Winslow SE17 . . . . .5E **102**
Winslow Cl.
HA5: Eastc 6K **39**
NW10 .3A **62**
Winslow Gro. E4 . . . . .2B **36**
Winslow Rd. W6 . . . . .6E **98**
Winslow Way TW13: Hanw 3B **130**
Winsmoor Ct. EN2: Enf 3G **23**
WINSOR PARK 5F **89**
Winsor Ter. E6 . . . . .5C **88**
Winstanley Est. SW11 . . . . .3B **118**
Winstanley Rd. SW11 . . . . .3B **118**
(not continuous)
Winstead Gdns. RM10: Dag 5J **73**
Winston Av. NW9 . . . . .7A **44**
Winston Cl.
HA3: Hrw W 6E **26**
KT8: E Mos 6H **149**
RM7: Mawney 4H **55**
Winston Ct. BR1: Broml 1H **159**
(off Widmore Rd.)
HA3: Hrw W 7A **26**
Winston Ho. *W13* 2A **96**
(off Balfour Rd.)
WC1 . . . . .3D **6**
Winston Rd. N16 . . . . .4D **66**
Winston Wlk. W4 . . . . .3K **97**
Winston Way IG1: Ilf 3F **71**
Winter Av. E6 . . . . .1C **88**
Winterborne Av. BR6: Orp 3H **173**
Winterbourne Ho. *W11* 7G **81**
(off Portland Rd.)
Winterbourne Rd. CR7: Thor H 4A **156**
RM8: Dag 2C **72**
SE6 . . . . .1B **140**
Winter Box Wlk.
TW10: Rich 5F **115**
Winterbrook Rd. SE24 . . . . .6C **120**
Winterburn Cl. N11 . . . . .6K **31**
Winterfold Cl. SW19 . . . . .2G **135**
Winter Gdns.
TW11: Tedd 4A **132**
Wintergreen Blvd.
UB7: W Dray 2B **92**

Wintergreen Cl. E6 . . . . .5C **88**
Winterleys NW6 . . . . .2H **81**
(off Denmark Rd.)
Winter Lodge *SE16* 5G **103**
(off Fern Wlk.)
Winter's Ct. E4 . . . . .3J **35**
Winterslow Ho. *SE5* 2C **120**
(off Flaxman Rd.)
Winterslow Rd. SW9 . . . . .1B **120**
Winters Rd. KT7: T Ditt 7B **150**
Winterstoke Gdns.
NW7 . . . . .5H **29**
Winterstoke Rd. SE6 . . . . .1B **140**
Winterton Ct. KT1: Hamp W 1D **150**
(off Lwr. Teddington Rd.)
SE20 . . . . .2G **157**
(off Deancross St.)
Winterton Pl. SW10 . . . . .7A **16** (6A **100**)
Winterwell Rd. SW2 . . . . .5J **119**
Winthorpe Rd. SW15 . . . . .4G **117**
Winthrop Ho. *W12* 7D **80**
(off White City Est.)
Winthrop St. E1 . . . . .5H **85**
Winthrop Wlk. *HA9: Wemb* 3E **60**
(off Everard Way)
Winton Av. N11 . . . . .7B **32**
Winton Cl. N9 . . . . .7E **24**
Winton Ct. N1 . . . . .2K **83**
(off Calshot St.)
Winton Gdns. HA8: Edg 7A **28**
Winton Rd. BR6: Farnb 4F **173**
Winton Way SW16 . . . . .5A **138**
Wireworks Ct. *SE1* 7C **14**
(off Gt. Suffolk St.)
Wirrall Ho. SE26 . . . . .3G **139**
Wirral Wood Cl. BR7: Chst 6E **142**
Wirra Rd. *TW6: H'row A* 5C **174**
(off Wayfarer Rd.)
Wisbeach Rd. CR0: C'don 5D **156**
Wisbech *N4* 1K **65**
(off Lorne Rd.)
Wisborough Rd. CR2: Sande 7F **169**
Wisden Ho.
SW8 . . . . .7H **19** (6K **101**)
Wisdom Ct. *TW7: Isle* 3A **114**
(off South St.)
Wisdons Cl. RM10: Dag 1H **73**
Wise La. NW7 . . . . .5H **29**
UB7: W Dray 4A **92**
Wiseman Rd. E10 . . . . .2C **68**
Wise Rd. E15 . . . . .1F **87**
Wiseton Rd. SW17 . . . . .1C **136**
Wishart Rd. SE3 . . . . .2B **124**
Wishaw Wlk. N13 . . . . .6D **32**
Wisley Ho. *SW1* 5C **18**
(off Rampayne St.)
Wisley Rd. BR5: St P 7A **144**
SW11 .5E **118**
Wistaria Cl. BR6: Farnb 2F **173**
Wisteria Apts. *E9* 6J **67**
(off Chatham Pl.)
Wisteria Cl. IG1: Ilf 5F **71**
NW7 . . . . .6G **29**
Wisteria Rd. SE13 . . . . .4F **123**
Wistow Ho. *E2* 1G **85**
(off Whiston Rd.)
Witanhurst La. N6 . . . . .1E **64**
Witan St. E2 . . . . .3H **85**
Witchwood Ho. SW9 . . . . .3A **120**
(off Gresham Rd.)
Witham Cl. E10 . . . . .3D **68**
SW17 .3D **136**
Witham Rd. RM10: Dag 5G **73**
SE20 . . . . .3J **157**
TW7: Isle 1H **113**
W13 . . . . .1A **96**
Witherby Cl. CR0: C'don 5E **168**
Witherington Rd. N5 . . . . .5A **66**
Withers Cl.
KT9: Chess 6C **162**
Withers Mead NW9 . . . . .1B **44**

Withers Pl. EC1 . . . . .3D **8** (4C **84**)
Witherston Way SE9 . . . . .2E **142**
Withycombe Rd.
SW19 .7F **117**
Withy Ho. *E1* 4K **85**
(off Globe Rd.)
Withy La. HA4: Ruis 5E **38**
Withy Mead E4 . . . . .3A **36**
Witley Ct. WC1 . . . . .4E **6**
Witley Cres. CR0: New Ad 6E **170**
Witley Gdns. UB2: S'hall 4D **94**
Witley Ho. SW2 . . . . .7J **119**
Witley Ind. Est.
UB2: S'hall 4D **94**
Witley Point SW15 . . . . .1D **134**
(off Wanborough Dr.)
Witley Rd. N19 . . . . .2G **65**
Witney Cl. UB10: Ick 4B **56**
Witney Path SE23 . . . . .3K **139**
Wittenham Way E4 . . . . .3A **36**
Wittering Cl. KT2: King T 5D **132**
Wittersham Rd.
BR1: Broml 5H **141**
Witts Ho. *KT1: King T* 3F **151**
(off Winery La.)
Wivenhoe Cl. SE15 . . . . .3H **121**
Wivenhoe Ct. TW3: Houn 4D **112**
Wivenhoe Rd.
IG11: Bark 2A **90**
Wiverton Rd. SE26 . . . . .6J **139**
Wiverton Twr. *E1* 7K **9**
(off Leman St.)
Wix Rd. RM9: Dag 1D **90**
Wix's La. SW4 . . . . .3F **119**
WLA Community Sports Cen. 1C **70**
Woburn *W13* 5B **78**
(off Clivedon Ct.)
Woburn Cl. SE28 . . . . .6D **90**
SW19 .6A **136**
Woburn Ct. CR0: C'don 1C **168**
E18 . . . . .2J **51**
SE16 .5H **103**
(off Masters Dr.)
WC1 . . . . .4E **6**
(off Bernard St.)
Woburn Mans. *WC1* 5C **6**
(off Torrington Pl.)
Woburn M. WC1 . . . . .4D **6** (4H **83**)
Woburn Pl. WC1 . . . . .4E **6** (4J **83**)
Woburn Rd.
CR0: C'don 1C **168**
SM5: Cars 1C **166**
Woburn Sq. WC1 . . . . .4D **6** (4H **83**)
(not continuous)
Woburn Twr. *UB5: N'olt* 3B **76**
(off Broomcroft Av.)
Woburn Wlk. WC1 . . . . .2D **6** (3H **83**)
Wodeham Gdns. E1 . . . . .5G **85**
Wodehouse Av. SE5 . . . . .1F **121**
Woffington Cl.
KT1: Hamp W 1C **150**
Wogan Ho. *W1* 6K **5**
(off Portland Pl.)
Woking Cl. SW15 . . . . .4B **116**
Wolcot Ho. *NW1* 1B **6**
(off Aldenham St.)
Woldham Pl. BR2: Broml 4A **160**
Woldham Rd.
BR2: Broml 4A **160**
Wolds Dr. BR6: Farnb 4E **172**
Wolfe Cl. BR2: Hayes 6J **159**
UB4: Yead 3K **75**
Wolfe Cres. SE7 . . . . .5B **106**
SE16 . . . . .2K **103**
Wolfe Ho. *W12* 7D **80**
(off White City Est.)
W14 . . . . .4H **99**
Wolferton Rd. E12 . . . . .4D **70**
Wolffe Gdns. E15 . . . . .6H **69**
Wolfington Rd. SE27 . . . . .4B **138**
Wolfram Cl. SE13 . . . . .5G **123**
Wolftencroft Cl. SW11 . . . . .3C **118**

Wollaston Cl. SE1 . . . . .4C **102**
Wollaton Ho. *N1* 2A **84**
(off Batchelor St.)
Wollett Ct. *NW1* 7G **65**
(off St Pancras Way)
Wollstonecraft St. N1 . . . . .1K **83**
Wolmer Cl. HA8: Edg 4B **28**
Wolmer Gdns.
HA8: Edg 3B **28**
Wolseley Av. SW19 . . . . .2J **135**
Wolseley Gdns. W4 . . . . .6H **97**
Wolseley Rd. CR4: Mitc 7E **154**
E7 . . . . .7K **69**
HA3: W'stone 3J **41**
N8 . . . . .6H **47**
N22 . . . . .1K **47**
RM7: Rush G 7K **55**
W4 . . . . .4J **97**
Wolseley St. SE1 . . . . .7K **15** (2G **103**)
Wolsey Av. E6 . . . . .3E **88**
E17 . . . . .3B **50**
KT7: T Ditt 5K **149**
Wolsey Cl. KT2: King T 1H **151**
KT4: Wor Pk 4C **164**
SE2 . . . . .2C **108**
SW20 .7D **134**
TW3: Houn 4G **113**
UB2: S'hall 3G **95**
Wolsey Ct. NW6 . . . . .7A **64**
SE9 . . . . .6D **124**
(off Court Rd.)
SW11 . . . . .1C **118**
(off Westbridge Rd.)
Wolsey Cres. CR0: New Ad 7E **170**
SM4: Mord 7G **153**
Wolsey Dr. KT2: King T 5E **132**
KT12: Walt T 7B **148**
Wolsey Gro. HA8: Edg 7E **28**
Wolsey M.
BR6: Chels 5K **173**
NW5 . . . . .6G **65**
Wolsey Rd.
EN1: Enf 2C **24**
KT8: E Mos 4H **149**
N1 . . . . .5D **66**
TW12: Hamp H 6F **131**
TW15: Ashf 4A **128**
TW16: Sun 7H **129**
Wolsey St. E1 . . . . .5J **85**
Wolsey Way KT9: Chess 5G **163**
Wolstenholme HA7: Stan 5G **27**
Wolstonbury N12 . . . . .5D **30**
Wolvercote Rd. SE2 . . . . .2D **108**
Wolverley St. E2 . . . . .3H **85**
Wolverton SE17 . . . . .5E **102**
(not continuous)
Wolverton Av. KT2: King T 1G **151**
Wolverton Gdns. W5 . . . . .7F **79**
W6 . . . . .4F **99**
Wolverton Rd.
HA7: Stan 6G **27**
Wolverton Way N14 . . . . .5B **22**
Wolves La. N13 . . . . .7F **33**
N22 . . . . .7F **33**
Womersley Rd. N8 . . . . .6K **47**
Wonersh Way
SM2: Cheam 7F **165**
Wonford Cl. KT2: King T 1A **152**
Wontner Cl. N1 . . . . .7C **66**
Wontner Rd. SW17 . . . . .2D **136**
Wooburn Cl. UB8: Hil 4D **74**
Woodall Av. EN3: Pond E 6E **24**
Woodall Cl. E14 . . . . .7D **86**
KT9: Chess 7C **162**
Woodall Rd. EN3: Pond E 6E **24**
Woodbank Rd.
BR1: Broml 3H **141**
Woodbastwick Rd. SE26 . . . . .5K **139**
Woodberry Av. HA2: Harr 4F **41**
N21 . . . . .2F **33**
Woodberry Cl. NW7 . . . . .7A **30**
TW16: Sun 6J **129**

Woodberry Cres. N10 . . . . .3F 47
Woodberry Down N4 . . . . .7C 48
Woodberry Down Est. N4 . . . . .7C 48
(not continuous)
Woodberry Gdns. N12 . . . . .6F 31
Woodberry Gro. DA5: Bexl 3K 145
N4 . . . . .7C 48
N12 . . . . .6F 31
Woodberry Way E4 . . . . .7K 25
N12 . . . . .6F 31
Woodbine Cl. TW2: Twick 2H 131
Woodbine Gro. EN2: Enf 1J 23
SE20 .7H 139
Woodbine La.
KT4: Wor Pk 3D 164
Woodbine Pl. E11 . . . . .6J 51
Woodbine Rd. DA15: Sidc 1J 143
Woodbines Av.
KT1: King T 3D 150
Woodbine Ter. E9 . . . . .6J 67
Woodborough Rd. SW15 . . . .4D 116
Woodbourne Av. SW16 . . . . . .3H 137
Woodbourne Cl. SW16 . . . . . . .3J 137
Woodbourne Gdns.
SM6: W'gton 7F 167
Woodbridge Cl. N7 . . . . .2K 65
NW2 . . . . .3C 62
Woodbridge Ct. IG8: Wfd G 7H 37
Woodbridge Ho. E11 . . . . .1H 69
Woodbridge Rd.
IG11: Bark 5K 71
Woodbridge St. EC1 . . . . .3A 8 (4B 84)
(not continuous)
Woodbridge Ter. RM6: Chad H 6B 54
Woodbrook Rd. SE2 . . . . .6A 108
Woodburn Cl. NW4 . . . . .5F 45
Woodbury Cl.
CR0: C'don 2F 169
E11 . . . . .4K 51
Woodbury Cres. IG5: Ilf 1D 52
Woodbury Gdns. SE12 . . . . . . .3K 141
Woodbury Ho. SE26 . . . . .3G 139
Woodbury Pk. Rd. W13 . . . . . . .4B 78
Woodbury Rd. E17 . . . . .4D 50
Woodbury St. SW17 . . . . .5C 136
Woodchester Ho. E14 . . . . .3D 104
(off Selsdon Way)
Woodchester Sq. W2 . . . . .5K 81
Woodchurch Cl.
DA14: Sidc 3H 143
Woodchurch Dr.
BR1: Broml 7B 142
Woodchurch Rd. NW6 . . . . .7J 63
Wood Cl. E2 . . . . .4G 85
HA1: Harr 7H 41
NW9 .7K 43
Woodclyffe Dr. BR7: Chst 2E 160
Woodcock Cl. TW6: H'row A . . .7C 174
Woodcock Ct. HA3: Kenton 7E 42
Woodcock Dell Av.
HA3: Kenton 7D 42
Woodcock Hill HA3: Kenton 5C 42
Woodcock Ho. E14 . . . . .5C 86
(off Burgess St.)
Woodcocks E16 . . . . .5A 88
Woodcombe Cres. SE23 . . . . .1J 139
Woodcote Av.
CR7: Thor H 4B 156
NW7 .6K 29
SM6: W'gton 7F 167
Woodcote Cl.
EN3: Pond E 6D 24
KT2: King T 5F 133
Woodcote Dr. BR6: Orp 1H 173
Woodcote Grn.
SM6: W'gton 7G 167
Woodcote Ho. SE8 . . . . .6B 104
(off Prince St.)
Woodcote M. SM6: W'gton 6F 167
Woodcote Pl. SE27 . . . . .5B 138
Woodcote Rd. E11 . . . . .7J 51
SM6: W'gton 6F 167

Woodcote Vs. SE27 . . . . .5C 138
(off Woodcote Pl.)
Wood Cres. W12 . . . . .7E 80
Wood Crest SM2: Sutt 7A 166
(off Christchurch Pk.)
Woodcroft N21 . . . . .1F 33
SE9 .3D 142
UB6: G'frd 6A 60
Woodcroft Av. HA7: Stan 1A 42
NW7 .6F 29
Woodcroft Cl. SE9 . . . . .6E 124
Woodcroft Cres. UB10: Hil 1D 74
Woodcroft M. SE8 . . . . .4A 104
Woodcroft Rd.
CR7: Thor H 5B 156
Wood Dr. BR7: Chst 6C 142
Woodedge Cl. E4 . . . . .1C 36
WOOD END 5H 75
Woodger Rd. W12 . . . . .2E 98
Woodget Cl. E6 . . . . .6C 88
Woodgrange Av.
EN1: Enf 6B 24
HA3: Kenton 5C 42
N12 . . . . .6G 31
W5 . . . . .1G 97
Woodgrange Cl.
HA3: Kenton 5D 42
Woodgrange Gdns.
EN1: Enf 6B 24
Woodgrange Ho. W5 . . . . .1F 97
(off Woodgrange Av.)
Woodgrange Mans.
HA3: Kenton 5C 42
Woodgrange Rd. E7 . . . . .5K 69
Woodgrange Ter. EN1: Enf 6B 24
WOOD GREEN 2K 47
Wood Grn. Animal Shelter 1B 48
(off Lordship La.)
Wood Grn. Hall N22 . . . . .2K 47
(off Station Rd.)
Wood Grn. Shop. City 2A 48
Woodhall NW1 . . . . .2G 5
(off Robert St.)
Woodhall Av. HA5: Pinn 1C 40
SE21 . . . . .3F 139
Woodhall Cl. UB8: Uxb 5A 56
Woodhall Dr. HA5: Pinn 1B 40
SE21 . . . . .3F 139
Woodhall Ga. HA5: Pinn 6A 22
Woodhall Ho. SW18 . . . . .6B 118
Woodham Ct. E18 . . . . .4H 51
Woodham Rd. SE6 . . . . .3E 140
Woodhatch Cl. E6 . . . . .5C 88
Woodhaven Gdns. IG6: Ilf 4G 53
Woodhayes Rd. SW19 . . . . .7E 134
Woodhead Dr. BR6: Orp 3J 173
Woodheyes Rd. NW10 . . . . .5K 61
Woodhill SE18 . . . . .4C 106
Woodhill Cres.
HA3: Kenton 6D 42
Wood Ho. NW6 . . . . .2H 81
(off Albert Rd.)
Woodhouse Av. UB6: G'frd 2K 77
Woodhouse Cl. SE22 . . . . .4G 121
UB3: Harl 3G 93
UB6: G'frd 1K 77
Woodhouse Gro. E12 . . . . .6C 70
Woodhouse Rd. E11 . . . . .3H 69
N12 . . . . .6G 31
Woodhurst Av. BR5: Pet W 6G 161
Woodhurst Rd. SE2 . . . . .5A 108
W3 . . . . .7J 79
Woodies La. KT3: N Mald 6K 151
Woodington Cl. SE9 . . . . .6E 124
Woodknoll Dr. BR7: Chst 1D 160
Woodland App. UB6: G'frd 6A 60
Woodland Cl.
IG8: Wfd G 3E 36
KT19: Ewe 6A 164
NW9 .6J 43
SE19 . . . . .6E 138
UB10: Ick 2D 56

WOODFORD GREEN 6D 36
Woodford Green Athletics Club
. . . . .6H 37
Woodford Hall Path E18 . . . . . .1H 51
Woodford Ho. E18 . . . . .4J 51
Woodford New Rd. E17 . . . . . . .4G 51
E18 .1G 51
IG8: Wfd G 1G 51
Woodford Pl. HA9: Wemb 1E 60
Woodford Rd. E7 . . . . .3K 69
E18 .4J 51
WOODFORD SIDE 5C 36
Woodford Trad. Est.
IG8: Wfd G 7B 52
WOODFORD WELLS 3E 36
Woodgate Av.
KT9: Chess 5D 162
Woodgate Dr. SW16 . . . . .7H 137

Woodland Ct. E11 . . . . .6J 51
(off New Wanstead)
N7 . . . . .6J 65
Woodland Cres. SE10 . . . . .6G 105
SE16 . . . . .2K 103
Woodland Gdns. N10 . . . . .5F 47
TW7: Isle 3J 113
Woodland Gro. SE10 . . . . .5G 105
Woodland Hill SE19 . . . . .6E 138
Woodland M. SE13 . . . . .3D 122
(off Loampit Hill)
SW16 . . . . .3J 137
Woodland Ri. N10 . . . . .4F 47
N22 . . . . .1J 47
UB6: G'frd 6A 60
Woodland Rd. CR7: Thor H 4A 156
E4 . . . . .1K 35
N11 .5A 32
SE19 . . . . .5E 138
WOODLANDS 3J 113
The Woodlands HA1: Harr 2J 59
HA7: Stan 5G 27
N5 . . . . .4C 66
N12 . . . . .6F 31
N14 .1A 32
SE13 . . . . .7F 123
SE19 . . . . .7C 138
SM6: W'gton 7F 167
SW9 .3B 102
(off Langton Rd.)
TW7: Isle 2K 113
Woodlands BR2: Broml 4H 159
DA6: Bex 5H 127
HA2: Harr 4E 40
NW11 . . . . .5G 45
SW20 . . . . .4E 152
Woodlands Av. DA15: Sidc 1J 143
E11 .1K 69
HA4: Ruis 7A 40
KT3: N Mald 1J 151
KT4: Wor Pk 2B 164
N3 . . . . .7F 31
RM6: Chad H 7E 54
W3 . . . . .1H 97
Woodlands Cl. BR1: Broml 2D 160
BR2: Broml 2A 160
KT10: Clay 7A 162
NW11 . . . . .5G 45
Woodlands Ct. BR1: Broml 1H 159
HA1: Harr 5K 41
KT12: Walt T 7K 147
NW10 .1F 81
(off Wrentham Av.)
SE23 . . . . .7H 121
Woodlands Dr. HA7: Stan 6E 26
TW16: Sun 2A 148
Woodlands Gdns. E17 . . . . .4G 51
Woodlands Ga. SW15 . . . . .5H 117
(off Woodlands Way)
Woodlands Gro. TW7: Isle 2J 113
Woodlands Hgts. SE3 . . . . .6H 105
(off Vanburgh Hill)
Woodlands Pde.
TW15: Ashf 6E 128
Woodlands Pk. DA5: Bexl 4K 145
Woodlands Pk. Rd. N15 . . . . . . .5B 48
SE10 . . . . .6G 105
(not continuous)
Woodlands Rd.
BR1: Broml 2C 160
BR6: Chels 6K 173
DA7: Bex 3E 126
E11 .2G 69
E17 .3E 50
EN2: Enf 1J 23
HA1: Harr 5K 41
IG1: Ilf 3G 71
KT6: Surb 7D 150
N9 . . . . .1D 34
SW13 . . . . .3B 116
TW7: Isle 3H 113
UB1: S'hall 1B 94
Woodlands St. SE13 . . . . .7F 123

The Wood End
SM6: W'gton 7F 167
Wood End UB3: Hayes 6G 75
Woodende SE19 . . . . .6C 138
SM1: Sutt 2A 166
Wood End Av. HA2: Harr 4F 59
UB5: N'olt 4F 59
Wood End Cl. UB5: N'olt 5H 59
Wood End Gdns.
UB5: N'olt 5G 59
Woodend Gdns. EN2: Enf 4D 22
WOOD END GREEN 5F 75
Wood End Grn. Rd.
UB3: Hayes 5F 75
Wood End La. UB5: N'olt 6F 59
Wood End Rd. HA1: Harr 4H 59
Woodend Rd. E17 . . . . .2E 50
Wood End Way
UB5: N'olt 5G 59
Wooder Gdns. E7 . . . . .4J 69
Wooderson Cl. SE25 . . . . .4E 156
Woodfall Av. EN5: Barn 5C 20
Woodfall Rd. N4 . . . . .2A 66
Woodfall St.
SW3 . . . . .6E 16 (5D 100)
Wood Farm Cl.
HA7: Stan 2G 27
Woodfarrs SE5 . . . . .4D 120
Wood Fld. NW3 . . . . .5D 64
Woodfield Av.
NA0: Wemb 3C 60
NW9 .4A 44
SM5: Cars 6E 166
SW16 . . . . .3H 137
W5 . . . . .4C 78
Woodfield Cl. EN1: Enf 4K 23
SE19 . . . . .7C 138
Woodfield Cres. W5 . . . . .4C 78
Woodfield Dr. EN4: E Barn 1K 31
Woodfield Gdns.
KT3: N Mald 5B 152
Woodfield Gro. SW16 . . . . .3H 137
Woodfield Ho. SE23 . . . . .3K 139
(off Dacres Rd.)
Woodfield La. SW16 . . . . .3H 137
Woodfield Pl. W9 . . . . .4H 81
Woodfield Ri. WD23: Bush 1C 26
Woodfield Rd. TW4: Cran 2K 111
W5 . . . . .4C 78
W9 . . . . .5H 81
Woodfield Way N11 . . . . .7C 32
WOODFORD 6F 37
Woodford Av. IG2: Ilf 5D 52
IG4: Ilf, Wfd G 3B 52
WOODFORD BRIDGE 6H 37
Woodford Bri. Rd.
IG4: Ilf 3B 52
Woodford Ct. W12 . . . . .2F 99
(off Shepherd's Bush Grn.)
Woodford Cres. HA5: Pinn 2K 39
Woodforde Cl. UB3: Harl 5F 93
Woodford Golf Course 5D 36

Woodlands Way SW15 . . . . . .5H 117
Woodland Ter. SE7 . . . . .4C 106
Woodland Wlk. BR1: Broml 4F 141
(not continuous)
KT19: Ewe 6G 163
NW3 .5C 64
SE10 . . . . .5G 105
Woodland Way
BR4: W W'ck 4D 170
BR5: Pet W 4G 161
CR0: C'don 1A 170
CR4: Mitc 7E 136
IG8: Wfd G 3E 36
KT5: Surb 2H 163
N21 .2F 33
NW7 . . . . .6G 29
SE2 . . . . .4D 108
SM4: Mord 4H 153
Wood La. HA4: Ruis 1F 57
HA7: Stan 3F 27
IG8: Wfd G 4C 36
N6 . . . . .6F 47
NW9 . . . . .7K 43
RM8: Dag 4C 72
RM9: Dag 4C 72
RM10: Dag 2G 73
TW7: Isle 6J 95
W12 .6E 80
Wood La. Studios W12 . . . . .6E 80
Woodlawn Cl. SW15 . . . . .5H 117
Woodlawn Cres.
TW2: Whitt 2F 131
Woodlawn Dr. TW13: Felt 2B 130
Woodlawn Rd. SW6 . . . . .7F 99
Woodlawns KT19: Ewe 7K 163
Woodlea Dr.
BR2: Broml 5G 159
Woodlea Rd. N16 . . . . .3E 66
Woodleigh E18 . . . . .1J 51
Woodleigh Av. N12 . . . . .6H 31
Woodleigh Gdns. SW16 . . . . .3J 137
Woodley Cl. SW17 . . . . .7D 136
Woodley La. SM5: Cars 3C 166
Wood Lodge Gdns.
BR1: Broml 7C 142
Wood Lodge La.
BR4: W W'ck 3E 170
Woodman M. TW9: Kew 1H 115
Woodman Pde. E16 . . . . .1E 106
(off Woodman St.)
Woodmans Gro. NW10 . . . . .5B 62
Woodman's M. W12 . . . . .5D 80
Woodmansterne Rd.
SM5: Cars 7C 166
SW16 . . . . .7G 137
Woodman St. E16 . . . . .1E 106
Wood Martyn Ct. BR6: Orp 2K 173
(off Orchard Gro.)
Wood Mead N17 . . . . .6B 34
Woodmere SE9 . . . . .1D 142
Woodmere Av. CR0: C'don 7J 157
Woodmere Cl.
CR0: C'don 7K 157
SW11 . . . . .3E 118
Woodmere Ct. N14 . . . . .7A 22
Woodmere Gdns.
CR0: C'don 7K 157
Woodmere Way
BR3: Beck 5F 159
Woodmill Cl. SW15 . . . . .6C 116
Woodmill Rd. E5 . . . . .2J 67
Woodmill St. SE16 . . . . .3F 103
Woodnook Rd. SW16 . . . . .5F 137
Woodpecker Cl.
HA3: Hrw W 1K 41
N9 .6C 24
WD23: Bush 1B 26
Woodpecker M. SE13 . . . . .4F 123
(off Freshfield Cl.)
Woodpecker Mt. CR0: Sels 7A 170
Woodpecker Rd. SE14 . . . . .6A 104
SE28 . . . . .7C 90

Woodquest Av. SE24 . . . . .5C 120
Wood Retreat SE18 . . . . .7H 107
Wood Ride BR5: Pet W 4H 161
EN4: Had W 1G 21
Woodridge Cl. EN2: Enf 1F 23
Woodridings Av.
HA5: Hat E 1D 40
Woodridings Cl.
HA5: Hat E 1C 40
Woodridings Ct. N22 . . . . .1H 47
Woodriffe Rd. E11 . . . . .7F 51
Wood Ri. HA5: Eastc 5J 39
Wood Rd. NW10 . . . . .7J 61
TW17: Shep 4C 146
Woodrow SE18 . . . . .4D 106
Woodrow Av. UB4: Hayes 5H 75
Woodrow Cl. UB6: G'frd 7B 60
Woodrow Ct. N17 . . . . .7C 34
SE5 .1C 120
(off Camberwell Sta. Rd.)
Woodrush Cl. SE14 . . . . .7A 104
Woodrush Way
RM6: Chad H 4D 54
The Woods UB10: Ick 4D 56
Wood's Bldgs. E1 . . . . .5H 85
(off Winthrop St.)
Woods Cl. TW3: Houn 3F 113
(off High St.)
Woodseer St. E1 . . . . .5K 9 (5F 85)
Woodsford SE17 . . . . .5D 102
(off Portland St.)
Woodsford Sq. W14 . . . . .2G 99
Woodshire Rd.
RM10: Dag 3H 73
Woods Ho. SW1 . . . . .6J 17 (5F 101)
SW8 . . . . .1G 119
(off Wadhurst Rd.)
WOODSIDE 6G 157
Woodside IG9: Buck H 2F 37
N10 .3E 46
NW11 . . . . .5J 45
SW19 . . . . .6H 135
Woodside Av. BR7: Chst 5G 143
HA0: Wemb 1E 78
KT10: Esh 7J 149
N6 . . . . .5D 46
N10 .5D 46
N12 .4E 30
SE25 . . . . .6H 157
Woodside Cl. DA7: Bex 4K 127
HA0: Wemb 1E 78
HA4: Ruis 6F 39
HA7: Stan 5G 27
KT5: Surb 7J 151
Woodside Ct. E12 . . . . .1A 70
N12 .4E 30
RM7: Mawney 4G 55
W5 . . . . .1E 96
Woodside Ct. Rd.
CR0: C'don 7G 157
Woodside Cres.
DA15: Sidc 3J 143
Woodside Dr. DA2: Wilm 4K 145
Woodside End
HA0: Wemb 1E 78
Woodside Gdns. E4 . . . . .6J 35
N17 .2E 48
Woodside Grange Rd. N12 . . . . . .4E 30
Woodside Grn. SE25 . . . . .6G 157
Woodside Gro. N12 . . . . .3F 31
Woodside Ho. SW19 . . . . .6H 135
Woodside La.
DA5: Bexl 6D 126
N12 .3F 31
Woodside M. SE22 . . . . .5F 121
Woodside Pde.
DA15: Sidc 3J 143
Woodside Pk. SE25 . . . . .6H 157
Woodside Pk. Av. E17 . . . . .4F 51
Woodside Pk. Rd. N12 . . . . .4E 30
Woodside Pl. HA0: Wemb 1E 78

Woodside Rd. BR1: Broml 5C 160
DA7: Bex 4K 127
DA15: Sidc 3J 143
E13 .4A 88
IG8: Wfd G 4D 36
KT2: King T 7E 132
KT3: N Mald 2K 151
N22 .7E 32
SE25 . . . . .6H 157
SM1: Sutt 3A 166
Woodside Way
CR0: C'don 6J 157
CR4: Mitc 1F 155
Woods M. W1 . . . . .2G 11 (7E 82)
Woodsome Rd. NW5 . . . . .3E 64
Woods Pl. SE1 . . . . .3E 102
Woodspring Rd. SW19 . . . . .2G 135
Woods Rd. SE15 . . . . .1H 121
Woodstar Ho. SE15 . . . . .7G 103
(off Reddins Rd.)
Woodstead Gro. HA8: Edg 6K 27
THE WOODSTOCK 7H 153
Woodstock Av. NW11 . . . . .7G 45
SM3: Sutt 7H 153
TW7: Isle 5A 114
UB1: S'hall 3D 76
W13 .3A 96
Woodstock Cl. DA5: Bexl 7F 127
HA7: Stan 2E 42
Woodstock Ct.
SE11 . . . . .5H 19 (5K 101)
SE12 . . . . .6J 123
Woodstock Cres. N9 . . . . .6C 24
Woodstock Dr. UB10: Ick 4A 56
Woodstock Gdns. BR3: Beck 1D 158
IG3: Ilf 2A 72
UB4: Hayes 5H 75
Woodstock Grange W5 . . . . .1E 96
Woodstock Gro. W12 . . . . .2F 99
Woodstock La. Nth.
KT6: Surb 2C 162
Woodstock La. Sth.
KT9: Chess 5B 162
KT10: Clay 5B 162
Woodstock M. W1 . . . . .6H 5
Woodstock Ri. SM3: Sutt 7H 153
Woodstock Rd. CR0: C'don 3D 168
E7 . . . . .7A 70
E17 .2F 51
HA0: Wemb 1F 79
N4 . . . . .1A 66
NW11 . . . . .7H 45
SM5: Cars 5E 166
W4 . . . . .4A 98
Woodstock St. W1 . . . . . . .1J 11 (6F 83)
Woodstock Studios W12 . . . . .2F 99
(off Woodstock Gro.)
Woodstock Ter. E14 . . . . .7D 86
Woodstock Way CR4: Mitc 2F 155
Woodstone Av. KT17: Ewe 5C 164
WOOD STREET 3E 50
Wood St. CR4: Mitc 7E 154
E17 .3E 50
EC2 . . . . .7D 8 (6C 84)
(not continuous)
EN5: Barn 4A 20
KT1: King T 2D 150
W4 . . . . .5A 98
Woodsyre SE26 . . . . .4F 139
Wood Ter. NW2 . . . . .3D 62
Woodthorpe Rd. SW15 . . . . .4D 116
TW15: Ashf 5A 128
Woodtree Cl. NW4 . . . . .2F 45
Wood Va. N10 . . . . .5G 47
SE23 . . . . .1H 139
Woodvale Av. SE25 . . . . .3F 157
Woodvale Ct. BR1: Broml 1K 159
(off Widmore Rd.)
Wood Va. Est. SE23 . . . . .7J 121
Woodvale Wlk. SE27 . . . . .5C 138
Woodvale Way NW11 . . . . .3F 63

Woodview Av. E4 . . . . .4K 35
Woodview Cl. BR6: Farnb 2G 173
N4 . . . . .7B 48
SW15 . . . . .4K 133
Wood Vw. M. RM1: Rom 1K 55
Woodview M. SE19 . . . . .1E 156
The Woodville W5 . . . . .6D 78
(off Woodville Rd.)
Woodville Cl. SE3 . . . . .1K 123
SE12 . . . . .5J 123
TW11: Tedd 4A 132
Woodville Ct. N14 . . . . .5B 22
SE10 . . . . .1E 122
(off Blissett St.)
SE19 . . . . .1F 157
Woodville Gdns. HA4: Ruis 7E 38
IG6: Ilf 3F 53
KT6: Surb 7D 150
NW11 . . . . .7F 45
W5 . . . . .6E 78
Woodville Gro. DA16: Well 3A 126
Woodville Ho. SE1 . . . . .3F 103
(off St Saviour's Est.)
Woodville Rd. CR7: Thor H 4C 156
E11 .1H 69
E17 .4B 50
E18 .2K 51
EN5: New Bar 3E 20
N16 .5E 66
NW6 . . . . .2H 81
NW11 . . . . .7F 45
SM4: Mord 4J 153
TW10: Ham 3B 132
W5 . . . . .6D 78
Woodville St. SE18 . . . . .4C 106
Woodward Av. NW4 . . . . .5C 44
Woodward Cl. KT10: Clay 6A 162
Woodwarde Rd. SE22 . . . . .6E 120
Woodward Gdns.
HA7: Stan 1E 26
RM9: Dag 7C 72
Woodward Rd. RM9: Dag 7B 72
Woodward's Footpath
TW2: Whitt 6G 113
Wood Way BR6: Farnb 2E 172
Woodway Cres.
HA1: Harr 6A 42
Woodwell St. SW18 . . . . .5A 118
Wood Wharf SE10 . . . . .6D 104
Wood Wharf Bus. Pk.
E14 . . . . .1D 104
Woodyard Cl. NW5 . . . . .5E 64
Woodyard La. SE21 . . . . .7E 120
Woodyates Rd. SE12 . . . . .6J 123
Woolacombe Rd. SE3 . . . . .1A 124
Woolacombe Way
UB3: Harl 4G 93
Woolcombes Ct. SE16 . . . . .1K 103
(off Princes Riverside Rd.)
Wooldridge Cl.
TW14: Bedf 1E 128
Wooler St. SE17 . . . . .5D 102
Woolf Cl. SE28 . . . . .1B 108
Woolf M. WC1 . . . . .3D 6
(off Burton Pl.)
Woolford Ct. SE5 . . . . .2C 120
(off Coldharbour La.)
Woolgar M. N16 . . . . .5E 66
(off Gillett St.)
Woollaston Rd. N4 . . . . .6B 48
Woolley Ho. SW9 . . . . .3B 120
(off Loughborough Rd.)
Woollon Ho. E1 . . . . .6J 85
(off Clark St.)
Woolmead Av. NW9 . . . . .7C 44
Woolmer Gdns. N18 . . . . .6B 34
Woolmer Rd. N18 . . . . .5B 34
Woolmore St. E14 . . . . .7E 86
Woolneigh St. SW6 . . . . .3K 117
Woolridge Way E9 . . . . .7J 67
Wool Rd. SW20 . . . . .6D 134
Woolstaplers Way SE16 . . . . .3G 103

Woolston Cl. E17 . . . . .2K 49
Woolstone Ho. E2 . . . . .1G 85
　(off Whiston Rd.)
Woolstone Rd. SE23 . . . . .2A 140
WOOLWICH 3D 106
The Woolwich Cen. 4E 106
　(off Wellington St.)
Woolwich Chu. St. SE18 . . . . .3C 106
Woolwich Comn. SE18 . . . . .6E 106
Woolwich Comn. Youth Club
　. . . . . .6E 106
Woolwich Dockyard Ind. Est.
　SE18 . . . . .3C 106
Woolwich High St. SE18 . . . . .3E 106
Woolwich Ho. UB3: Harl 3E 92
　(off Nine Acres Cl.)
Woolwich Mnr. Way E6 . . . . .4D 88
　E16 . . . . .2F 107
Woolwich New Rd. SE18 . . . . .5E 106
Woolwich Rd.
　DA6: Bex 3G 127
　DA7: Bex 3G 127
　DA17: Belv 5F 109
　SE2 . . . . .6D 108
　SE7 . . . . .5H 105
　SE10 . . . . .5H 105
Woolwich Trade Pk. SE28 . . . . .3H 107
Wooster Gdns. E14 . . . . .6F 87
Wooster M. HA2: Harr 3G 41
Wooster Pl. SE1 . . . . .4D 102
　(off Searles Rd.)
Wootton Gro. N3 . . . . .1J 45
Wootton St.
　SE1 . . . . .5K 13 (1A 102)
Worbeck Rd. SE20 . . . . .2H 157
Worcester Av. N17 . . . . .7B 34
Worcester Cl.
　CR0: C'don 2C 170
　CR4: Mitc 2E 154
　NW2 . . . . .3D 62
　SE20 . . . . .1G 157
Worcester Ct.
　HA1: Harr 3J 41
　KT4: Wor Pk 3A 164
　N12 . . . . .5E 30
　W7 . . . . .6K 77
　(off Copley Cl.)
　W9 . . . . .5J 81
　(off Elmfield Way)
Worcester Cres. IG8: Wfd G 5E 36
　NW7 . . . . .3F 29
Worcester Dr.
　TW15: Ashf 5D 128
　W4 . . . . .2A 98
Worcester Gdns. IG1: Ilf 7C 52
　KT4: Wor Pk 3A 164
　SW11 . . . . .5D 118
　(off Grandison Rd.)
　UB6: G'frd 6H 59
Worcester Ho. SE11 . . . . .2J 19
　(off Kennington Rd.)
　SW9 . . . . .7A 102
　(off Cranmer Rd.)
　W2 . . . . .6A 82
　(off Hallfield Est.)
Worcester M. NW6 . . . . .6K 63
WORCESTER PARK 1C 164
Worcester Pk. Rd.
　KT4: Wor Pk 3K 163
Worcester Point EC1 . . . . .3C 84
Worcester Rd. E12 . . . . .4D 70
　E17 . . . . .2K 49
　SM2: Sutt 7J 165
　SW19 . . . . .5H 135
Worcesters Av. EN1: Enf 1B 24
Wordsworth Av.
　E12 . . . . .7C 70
　E18 . . . . .3H 51
　UB6: G'frd 3H 77
Wordsworth Cl. HA1: Harr 7J 41
Wordsworth Dr.
　SM3: Cheam 4E 164

Wordsworth Ho. NW6 . . . . .3J 81
　(off Stafford Rd.)
　SE18 . . . . .6E 106
　(off Woolwich Comn.)
Wordsworth Mans. W14 . . . . .6H 99
　(off Queens Club Gdns.)
Wordsworth Pde. N8 . . . . .4B 48
Wordsworth Pl. NW5 . . . . .5D 64
Wordsworth Rd.
　DA16: Well 1J 125
　N16 . . . . .4E 66
　SE1 . . . . .4F 103
　SE20 . . . . .7K 139
　SM6: W'gton 6G 167
　TW12: Hamp 4D 130
Wordsworth Wlk. NW11 . . . . .4J 45
Wordsworth Way
　UB7: W Dray 4A 92
Worfield St. SW11 . . . . .7C 100
Worgan St. SE11 . . . . . . .5G 19 (5K 101)
　SE16 . . . . .4K 103
Worland Rd. E15 . . . . .7G 69
World Bus. Cen.
　TW6: H'row A 1E 110
World of Golf Cen.
　Croydon 5J 157
　New Malden 3C 152
World Rugby Mus. 6J 113
WORLD'S END 3E 22
Worlds End Est. SW10 . . . . .7B 100
World's End La.
　EN2: Enf 5E 22
　N21 . . . . .5E 22
Worlds End La. BR6: Chels 6K 173
World's End Pas. SW10 . . . . .7B 100
　(off Worlds End Est.)
World's End Pl. SW10 . . . . .7B 100
　(off Worlds End Est.)
Worleys Dr. BR6: Orp 4H 173
Worlidge St. W6 . . . . .5E 98
Worlingham Rd. SE22 . . . . .4F 121
Wormholt Rd. W12 . . . . .7C 80
Wormwood Scrubs Pk. 5B 80
Wormwood St. EC2 . . . . .7G 9 (6E 84)
Wormwood Rd. W10 . . . . .4G 81
　(not continuous)
Woronzow Rd. NW8 . . . . .1B 82
Worple Av. SW19 . . . . .7F 135
　TW7: Isle 5A 114
Worple Cl. HA2: Harr 1D 58
Worple Rd. SW19 . . . . .2E 152
　SW20 . . . . .2E 152
　TW7: Isle 4A 114
Worple Rd. M. SW19 . . . . .6H 135
Worple St. SW14 . . . . .3K 115
Worple Way HA2: Harr 1D 58
　TW10: Rich 5E 114
Worrall La. UB8: Uxb 7A 56
Worship St. EC2 . . . . .4F 9 (4D 84)
　(not continuous)
Worslade Rd. SW17 . . . . .4B 136
Worsley Bri. Rd.
　BR3: Beck 7C 140
　SE26 . . . . .4B 140
Worsley Grange
　BR7: Chst 6G 143
Worsley Gro. E5 . . . . .4G 67
Worsley Ho. SE23 . . . . .2J 139
Worsley Rd. E11 . . . . .4G 69
Worsopp Dr. SW4 . . . . .5G 119
Worth Cl. BR6: Orp 4J 173
Worthfield Cl.
　KT19: Ewe 7K 163
Worth Gro. SE17 . . . . .5D 102
Worthing Cl. E15 . . . . .1G 87
Worthing Rd. TW5: Hest 6D 94
Worthington Cl. CR4: Mitc 4F 155
Worthington Ho. EC1 . . . . .1K 7
　(off Myddelton Pas.)
Worthington Rd. KT6: Surb 1F 163
Wortley Rd. CR0: C'don 7A 156
　E6 . . . . .7B 70

Worton Ct. TW7: Isle 4J 113
Worton Gdns. TW7: Isle 2H 113
Worton Hall Ind. Est.
　TW7: Isle 4J 113
Worton Rd. TW7: Isle 4H 113
Worton Way TW3: Houn 2H 113
　TW7: Houn, Isle 2H 113
Wotton Ct. E14 . . . . .7F 87
　(off Jamestown Way)
Wotton Rd. NW2 . . . . .3E 62
　SE8 . . . . .6B 104
Wragby Rd. E16 . . . . .6A 88
Wragby Rd. E11 . . . . .3G 69
Wrampling Pl. N9 . . . . .1B 34
Wrangthorn Wlk.
　CR0: Wadd 4A 168
Wraxall Rd. E3 . . . . .4B 86
　(off Hamlets Way)
Wray Av. IG5: Ilf 3E 52
Wrayburn Ho. SE16 . . . . .2G 103
　(off Llewellyn St.)
Wray Cres. N4 . . . . .2J 65
Wrayfield Rd. SM3: Cheam 3F 165
Wray Rd. SM2: Cheam 7H 165
Wraysbury Cl.
　TW4: Houn 5C 112
Wrays Way UB4: Hayes 4G 75
Wrekin Rd. SE18 . . . . .7G 107
Wren Av. NW2 . . . . .4E 62
　NW10 . . . . .4B 62
　UB2: S'hall 4D 94
　UB10: Uxb 1B 74
Wren Cl. E16 . . . . .6H 87
　N9 . . . . .1E 34
　TW6: H'row A 6C 174
Wren Ct. CR0: C'don 4D 168
　(off Coombe Rd.)
Wren Cres. WD23: Bush 1B 26
Wren Gdns. RM9: Dag 5D 72
Wren Ho. E3 . . . . .2A 86
　(off Gernon Rd.)
　KT1: Hamp W 2D 150
　(off High St.)
　SW1 . . . . .6C 18
　(off Aylesford St.)
Wren Landing E14 . . . . .1C 104
Wren La. HA4: Ruis 6K 39
Wren M. SE11 . . . . . . .4H 19 (4K 101)
　SE13 . . . . .4G 123
Wren Path SE28 . . . . .3H 107
Wren Rd. DA14: Sidc 4C 144
　RM9: Dag 5D 72
　SE5 . . . . .1D 120
Wren's Av. TW15: Ashf 4E 128
Wren's Pk. Ho. E5 . . . . .2H 67
Wren St. WC1 . . . . .3H 7 (4K 83)
Wrentham Av. NW10 . . . . .2F 81
Wrenthorpe Rd.
　BR1: Broml 4G 141
Wren Vw. N6 . . . . .7G 47
Wrenwood Way
　HA5: Eastc 4K 39
Wrexham Rd. E3 . . . . .2C 86
Wricklemarsh Rd. SE3 . . . . .2K 123
　(not continuous)
Wrigglesworth St. SE14 . . . . .7K 103
Wright Cl. SE13 . . . . .4F 123
Wright Gdns.
　TW17: Shep 5C 146
Wright Rd. TW5: Hest 7A 94
Wrights All. SW19 . . . . .6E 134
Wrights Cl. RM10: Dag 4H 73
Wrights Grn. SW4 . . . . .4H 119
Wright's La. W8 . . . . .3K 99
Wrights Pl. NW10 . . . . .6J 61
Wright's Rd. E3 . . . . .2B 86
　(not continuous)
Wrights Rd. SE25 . . . . .3E 156
Wrights Row SM6: W'gton 4F 167
Wrights Wlk. SW14 . . . . .3K 115
Wright Way
　TW6: H'row A 5C 174

Wrigley Cl. E4 . . . . .5A 36
Writtle Ho. NW9 . . . . .2B 44
Wrotham Ho. BR3: Beck 7B 140
　(off Sellindge Cl.)
　SE1 . . . . .3D 102
　(off Law St.)
Wrotham Rd. DA16: Well 1C 126
　EN5: Barn 2B 20
　NW1 . . . . .7G 65
　W13 . . . . .1C 96
Wrottesley Rd. NW10 . . . . .2C 80
　SE18 . . . . .6G 107
Wroughton Rd. SW11 . . . . .5D 118
Wroughton Ter. NW4 . . . . .4D 44
Wroxall Rd. RM9: Dag 6C 72
Wroxham Gdns. N11 . . . . .7C 32
　N21 . . . . .2E 33
Wroxham Rd. SE28 . . . . .7D 90
Wroxham Way IG6: Ilf 1F 53
Wroxton Rd. SE15 . . . . .2J 121
THE WRYTHE 3D 166
Wrythe Grn. SM5: Cars 3D 166
Wrythe Grn. Rd.
　SM5: Cars 3D 166
Wrythe La. SM5: Cars 1A 166
Wulfstan St. W12 . . . . .5B 80
Wyatt Cl. SE16 . . . . .2B 104
　TW13: Felt 1B 130
　UB4: Hayes 5J 75
　WD23: Bush 1C 26
Wyatt Ct. HA0: Wemb 7E 60
　W3 . . . . .3J 97
　(off All Saints Rd.)
Wyatt Dr. SW13 . . . . .6D 98
Wyatt Ho. NW8 . . . . .4B 4
　(off Frampton St.)
　SE3 . . . . .2H 123
　TW1: Twick 6D 114
Wyatt Pk. Rd. SW2 . . . . .2J 137
Wyatt Point SE28 . . . . .2G 107
Wyatt Rd. E7 . . . . .6J 69
　N5 . . . . .3C 66
Wyatts La. E17 . . . . .3E 50
Wybert St. NW1 . . . . .3A 6 (4G 83)
Wyborne Ho. NW10 . . . . .7J 61
Wyborne Way NW10 . . . . .7J 61
Wyburn Av. EN5: Barn 3C 20
Wychcombe Studios
　NW3 . . . . .6D 64
Wyche Gro. CR2: S Croy 7D 168
Wych Elm Cl. KT2: King T 7F 133
Wych Elm Lodge
　BR1: Broml 7H 141
Wych Elm Pas. KT2: King T 7F 133
Wycherley Cl. SE3 . . . . .7H 105
Wycherley Cres.
　EN5: New Bar 6E 20
Wychwood Av.
　CR7: Thor H 3C 156
　HA8: Edg 6J 27
Wychwood Cl. HA8: Edg 6J 27
　TW16: Sun 6J 129
Wychwood End N6 . . . . .7G 47
Wychwood Gdns. IG5: Ilf 4D 52
Wychwood Way SE19 . . . . .6D 138
Wyclif Ct. EC1 . . . . .2A 8
　(off Wyclif St.)
Wycliffe Cl. DA16: Well 1K 125
Wycliffe Rd. SW11 . . . . .2E 118
　SW19 . . . . .6K 135
Wyclif St. EC1 . . . . .2A 8 (3B 84)
Wycombe Gdns. NW11 . . . . .2J 63
Wycombe Ho. NW8 . . . . .3C 4
　(off Grendon St.)
Wycombe Pl. SW18 . . . . .6A 118
Wycombe Rd.
　HA0: Wemb 1G 79
　IG2: Ilf 5D 52
　N17 . . . . .1G 49
Wycombe Sq. W8 . . . . .1H 99
Wydehurst Rd. CR0: C'don 7G 157
Wydell Cl. SM4: Mord 6F 153
Wydeville Mnr. Rd. SE12 . . . . .4K 141

Wye Cl. BR6: Orp 7K **161**
  HA4: Ruis 6E **38**
  TW15: Ashf 4D **128**
Wye Ct. W13 . . . . .5B **78**
  (off Malvern Way)
Wyemead Cres. E4 . . . . .2B **36**
Wye St. SW11 . . . . .2B **118**
Wyevale Cl. HA5: Eastc 3J **39**
Wyfields IG5: Ilf 1F **53**
Wyfold Ho. SE2 . . . . .2D **108**
  (off Wolvercote Rd.)
Wyfold Rd. SW6 . . . . .7G **99**
Wyhill Wlk. RM10: Dag 6J **73**
Wyke Cl. TW7: Isle 6K **95**
Wyke Gdns. W7 . . . . .3A **96**
Wyke Green Golf Course 6K **95**
Wykeham Av. RM9: Dag 6C **72**
Wykeham Cl.
  HA3: W'stone 1K **41**
  UB7: Sip 6C **92**
Wykeham Ct. NW4 . . . . .5E **44**
  (off Wykeham Rd.)
Wykeham Grn. RM9: Dag 6C **72**
Wykeham Hill HA9: Wemb 1F **61**
Wykeham Ho. SE1 . . . . .5C **14**
  (off Union St.)
Wykeham Ri. N20 . . . . .1B **30**
Wykeham Rd.
  HA3: Kenton 4B **42**
  NW4 . . . . .4E **44**
Wyke Rd. E3 . . . . .7C **68**
  SW20 . . . . .2E **152**
Wylchin Cl. HA5: Eastc 3H **39**
Wyldes Cl. NW11 . . . . .1A **64**
Wyldfield Gdns. N9 . . . . .2A **34**
Wyld Way
  HA9: Wemb 6H **61**
Wyleu St. SE23 . . . . .7A **122**
Wyllen Cl. E1 . . . . .4J **85**
Wymering Mans. W9 . . . . .3J **81**
  (off Wymering Rd.)
Wymering Rd. W9 . . . . .3J **81**
Wymondham Ct. NW8 . . . . .1B **82**
  (off Queensmead)
Wymond St. SW15 . . . . .3E **116**
Wynan Rd. E14 . . . . .5D **104**
Wynash Gdns. SM5: Cars 5C **166**
Wynaud Ct. N22 . . . . .6E **32**
Wyncham Av.
  DA15: Sidc 1J **143**
Wyncham Ho. DA15: Sidc 2A **144**
  (off Longlands Rd.)
Wynchgate HA3: Hrw W 7D **26**
  N14 .1C **32**
  N21 .1C **32**
  UB5: N'olt 5C **58**
Wyncroft Cl.
  BR1: Broml 3D **160**
Wyndale Av. NW9 . . . . .6G **43**
Wyndcliff Rd. SE7 . . . . .6K **105**
Wyndcroft Cl. EN2: Enf 3G **23**
Wyndham Apts. SE10 . . . . .5G **105**
Wyndham Cl.
  BR6: Farnb 1G **173**
  SM2: Sutt 7J **165**
Wyndham Ct. W7 . . . . .4A **96**
Wyndham Cres. N19 . . . . .3G **65**
  TW4: Houn 6E **112**
Wyndham Deedes Ho. E2 . . . . . . .2G **85**
  (off Hackney Rd.)
Wyndham Est. SE5 . . . . .7C **102**
Wyndham Ho. E14 . . . . .2D **104**
  (off Marsh Wall)
  SW1 .4G **17**
  (off Sloane Sq.)
Wyndham M. W1 . . . . .6E **4** (5D **82**)
Wyndham Pl. W1 . . . . .6E **4** (5D **82**)
Wyndham Rd. E6 . . . . .7B **70**
  EN4: E Barn 1J **31**
  KT2: King T 7F **133**
  SE5 .7C **102**
  W13 .3B **96**

Wyndhams Ct. E8 . . . . .7F **67**
  (off Celandine Dr.)
Wyndham's Theatre 2E **12**
  (off Charing Cross Rd.)
Wyndham St. W1 . . . . .5E **4** (5D **82**)
Wyndham Yd. W1 . . . . .6E **4** (5D **82**)
Wyndhurst Cl.
  CR2: S Croy 7B **168**
Wyneham Rd. SE24 . . . . .5D **120**
Wynell Rd. SE23 . . . . .3K **139**
Wynford Pl. DA17: Belv 6G **109**
Wynford Rd. N1 . . . . .2K **83**
Wynford Way SE9 . . . . .3D **142**
Wynlie Gdns. HA5: Pinn 2K **39**
Wynn Bri. Cl. IG8: Wfd G 1B **52**
Wynndale Rd. E18 . . . . .1K **51**
Wynne Rd. SW9 . . . . .2A **120**
Wynn's Av. DA15: Sidc 5K **125**
Wynnstay Gdns. W8 . . . . .3J **99**
Wynter St. SW11 . . . . .4A **118**
Wynton Gdns. SE25 . . . . .5F **157**
Wynton Pl. W3 . . . . .6H **79**
Wynyard Ho. SE11 . . . . .5H **19**
  (off Loughborough St.)
Wynyatt St. EC1 . . . . . . .2A **8** (3B **84**)
Wyre Gro. HA8: Edg 3C **28**
  UB3: Harl 4J **93**
Wyresdale Cres.
  UB6: G'frd 3K **77**
Wyteleaf Cl. HA4: Ruis 6E **38**
Wytham Ho. NW8 . . . . .4B **4**
  (off Church St. Est.)
Wythburn Ct. W1 . . . . .7E **4**
  (off Wythburn Pl.)
Wythburn Pl. W1 . . . . . .1E **10** (6D **82**)
Wythenshawe Rd.
  RM10: Dag 3G **73**
Wythens Wlk. SE9 . . . . .6F **125**
Wythes Cl. BR1: Broml 2D **160**
Wythes Rd. E16 . . . . .1C **106**
Wythfield Rd. SE9 . . . . .6D **124**
Wyvell Cl. CR0: C'don 7K **157**
Wyvenhoe Rd.
  HA2: Harr 4G **59**
Wyvern Est.
  KT3: N Mald 4C **152**
Wyvil Rd. SW8 . . . . .7J **101**
Wyvis St. E14 . . . . .5D **86**

X

Xylon Ho. KT4: Wor Pk 2D **164**

Y

Yabsley St. E14 . . . . .1E **104**
Yaldham Ho. SE1 . . . . .4E **102**
  (off Old Kent Rd.)
Yalding Rd. SE16 . . . . .3G **103**
Yale Cl. TW4: Houn 5D **112**
Yale Ct. NW6 . . . . .5K **63**
Yarborough Rd.
  SW19 . . . . .1B **154**
The Yard N1 . . . . .1F **7**
  (off Caledonia Rd.)
Yardley Cl. E4 . . . . .5J **25**
Yardley Ct. SM3: Cheam 4E **164**
Yardley La. E4 . . . . .5J **25**
Yardley St. WC1 . . . . . . .2J **7** (3A **84**)
  (not continuous)
Yardmaster Ho. CR0: C'don 1D **168**
Yarlington Ct. N11 . . . . .5K **31**
  (off Sparkford Gdns.)
Yarmouth Cres. N17 . . . . .5H **49**
Yarmouth Pl. W1 . . . . . .5J **11** (1F **101**)
Yarnfield Sq. SE15 . . . . .1G **121**
Yarnton Way
  DA18: Belv, Erith 3F **109**
  SE2 .2C **108**

Yarrell Mans. W14 . . . . .6H **99**
  (off Queen's Club Gdns.)
Yarrow Cres. E6 . . . . .5C **88**
Yarrow Ho. E14 . . . . .3E **104**
  (off Stewart St.)
  W10 .5E **80**
  (off Sutton Way)
Yateley St. SE18 . . . . .3B **106**
Yatesbury Ct. E5 . . . . .5A **68**
  (off Studley Cl.)
Yates Ct. NW2 . . . . .6F **63**
  (off Willesden La.)
  SE1 . . . . .7K **15**
  (off Abbey St.)
Yates Ho. E2 . . . . .3G **85**
  (off Roberta St.)
Yatton Ho. W10 . . . . .5E **80**
  (off Sutton Way)

YEADING 4A **76**
Yeading Av. HA2: Harr 2C **58**
Yeading Brook Meadows Nature Reserve
  . . . . .4J **75**
Yeading Ct. UB4: Yead 4A **76**
Yeading Fork UB4: Yead 5A **76**
Yeading Gdns.
  UB4: Yead 5K **75**
Yeading Ho. UB4: Yead 5B **76**
Yeading La. UB4: Yead 6K **75**
  UB5: N'olt 6K **75**
Yeading Wlk. HA2: Harr 5D **40**
Yeadon Ho. W10 . . . . .5E **80**
  (off Sutton Way)
Yeames Cl. W13 . . . . .6A **78**
Yearby Ho. W10 . . . . .4E **80**
  (off Sutton Way)
Yeate St. N1 . . . . .7D **66**
Yeatman Rd. N6 . . . . .6D **46**
Yeats Cl. NW10 . . . . .5A **62**
  SE13 . . . . .2F **123**
  W7 . . . . .7K **77**
Yeend Cl. KT8: W Mole 4E **148**
Yeldham Ho. W6 . . . . .5F **99**
  (off Yeldham Rd.)
Yeldham Rd. W6 . . . . .5F **99**
Yeldham Vs. W6 . . . . .5F **99**
  (off Yeldham Rd.)
Yellowhammer Ct. NW9 . . . . .2A **44**
  (off Eagle Dr.)
Yelverton Lodge TW1: Twick 7C **114**
  (off Richmond Rd.)
Yelverton Rd. SW11 . . . . .2B **118**
Ye Mkt. CR2: S Croy 5D **168**
  (off Selsdon Rd.)
Yenston Cl. SM4: Mord 6J **153**
Yeoman Cl. E6 . . . . .7F **89**
  SE27 . . . . .3B **138**
Yeoman Ct. E14 . . . . .4E **86**
  (off Tweed Wlk.)
  TW5: Hest 7D **94**
Yeoman Dr.
  TW19: Stanw 1A **128**
Yeoman Rd. UB5: N'olt 7C **58**
Yeomans Acre
  HA4: Ruis 6J **39**
Yeomans M. TW7: Isle 6H **113**
Yeoman's Row
  SW3 . . . . .2D **16** (3C **100**)
Yeoman St. SE8 . . . . .4A **104**
Yeomans Way
  EN3: Enf H 2D **24**
Yeoman's Yd. E1 . . . . .2K **15**
Yeo St. E3 . . . . .5D **86**
Yeovil Cl. BR6: Orp 2J **173**
Yeovil Ho. W10 . . . . .4E **80**
  (off Sutton Way)
Yeovilton Pl. KT2: King T 5C **132**
Yerbury Rd. N19 . . . . .3H **65**
  (not continuous)
Yester Dr. BR7: Chst 7C **142**
Yester Pk. BR7: Chst 7D **142**
Yester Rd. BR7: Chst 7C **142**
Yetev Lev Ct. E5 . . . . .1G **67**

Yew Av. UB7: Yiew 7A **74**
Yew Cl. IG9: Buck H 2G **37**
Yewdale Cl.
  BR1: Broml 6G **141**
Yewfield Rd.
  NW10 . . . . .6B **62**
Yew Gro. NW2 . . . . .4F **63**
Yew Ho. SE16 . . . . .2K **103**
  (off Woodland Cres.)
The Yews TW15: Ashf 4D **128**
Yewtree Av. RM10: Dag 5J **73**
Yew Tree Cl.
  DA16: Well 1A **126**
  KT4: Wor Pk 1A **164**
  N21 .7F **23**
  SE13 . . . . .3E **122**
Yewtree Cl. HA2: Harr 4F **41**
  N22 .1G **47**
Yew Tree Ct. NW11 . . . . .5H **45**
  (off Bridge La.)
  SM2: Sutt 7A **166**
  (off Walnut M.)
Yew Tree Gdns. RM6: Chad H 5E **54**
  RM7: Rom 5K **55**
Yew Tree Lodge HA4: Ruis 6J **39**
  RM7: Rom 5K **55**
  (off Yew Tree Gdns.)
  SW16 . . . . .4G **137**
Yew Tree Rd. BR3: Beck 3B **158**
  UB10: Uxb 1B **74**
  W12 .7B **80**
Yew Trees TW17: Shep 4B **146**
Yew Tree Wlk.
  TW4: Houn 5D **112**
Yew Tree Way
  CR0: Sels 7B **170**
Yew Wlk. HA1: Harr 1J **59**
YIEWSLEY 1A **92**
Yiewsley Ct. UB7: Yiew 1A **92**
YMCA
  German 7A **82**
  (off Craven Ter.)
  Hawker 5D **132**
  W. London, Uxbridge 1A **74**
Yoakley Rd. N16 . . . . .2E **66**
Yoga Way KT4: Wor Pk 2C **164**
Yoke Cl. N7 . . . . .6J **65**
Yolande Gdns. SE9 . . . . .5C **124**
Yonge Pk. N4 . . . . .3A **66**
York Av.
  DA15: Sidc 2J **143**
  HA7: Stan 1B **42**
  SW14 . . . . .5J **115**
  UB3: Hayes 5E **74**
  W7 . . . . .1J **95**
York Bri. NW1 . . . . .3G **5** (4E **82**)
York Bldgs.
  WC2 . . . . .3F **13** (7J **83**)
York Cl. E6 . . . . .6D **88**
  SE5 .2C **120**
  (off Lilford Rd.)
  SM4: Mord 4K **153**
  TW18: Staines 6A **128**
  W7 . . . . .1J **95**
York Ct. N14 . . . . .3D **32**
York Ga. N14 . . . . .7D **22**
  NW1 . . . . .4G **5** (4E **82**)
York Gro. SE15 . . . . .1J **121**
York Hall Leisure Cen. 2H **85**
York Hill SE27 . . . . .3B **138**
York Ho. E16 . . . . .1J **105**
  (off De Quincey M.)
  EN2: Enf 1J **23**
  HA9: Wemb 4G **61**
  KT2: King T 7F **133**
  (off Elm Rd.)
  SE1 . . . . .2H **19** (3K **101**)
  SW3 .5F **17**
  W1 . . . . .5E **4**
  (off York St.)
  W8 . . . . .2K **99**
  (off York Ho. Pl.)

York Ho. Pl. W8 . . . . .2K **99**
Yorkland Av.
  DA16: Well 3K **125**
York La. CR4: Mitc 2G **155**
Yorkley Ho. W10 . . . . .4E **80**
          (off Sutton Way)
York Mans. SE17 . . . . .5C **102**
          (off Browning St.)
  SW5 . . . . .5K **99**
          (off Earls Ct. Rd.)
  SW11 .1E **118**
       (off Prince of Wales Dr.)
  W1 . . . . .5G **5**
          (off Chiltern St.)
York M. IG1: Ilf 3E **70**
  NW5 . . . . .5F **65**
York Pde. NW9 . . . . .6C **44**
         (off W. Hendon B'way.)
  TW8: Bford 5D **96**
York Pl. IG1: Ilf 2E **70**
  RM10: Dag 6J **73**
  SW11 . . . . .3B **118**
  WC2 . . . . .3F **13**
York Pl. Mans. W1 . . . . .5F **5**
          (off Baker St.)
York Ri. BR6: Orp 2J **173**
  NW5 . . . . .3F **65**
York Rd. CR0: C'don 7A **156**
  E4 . . . . .4H **35**
  E7 . . . . .6J **69**
  E10 . . . . .3E **68**
  E17 . . . . .5K **49**
  EN5: New Bar 5F **21**
  HA6: Nwood 2J **39**
  IG1: Ilf 3E **70**
  KT2: King T 7F **133**
  N11 . . . . .6C **32**
  N18 . . . . .6C **34**
  N21 . . . . .7J **23**
  RM13: Rain 7K **73**
  SE1 . . . . .6H **13** (2K **101**)

York Rd. SM1: Sutt 6J **165**
  SM2: Sutt 6J **165**
  SW11 . . . . .4A **118**
  SW18 . . . . .4A **118**
  SW19 . . . . .6A **136**
  TW3: Houn 3F **113**
  TW8: Bford 5D **96**
  TW10: Rich 5F **115**
  TW11: Tedd 4J **131**
  W3 . . . . .6J **79**
  W5 . . . . .3C **96**
York Rd. Bus. Cen. SW11 . . . . . .2B **118**
Yorkshire Cl. N16 . . . . .3E **66**
Yorkshire Gdns. N18 . . . . .5C **34**
YORKSHIRE GREY 5B **124**
Yorkshire Grey Pl.
  NW3 .4A **64**
Yorkshire Grey Yd.
  WC1 . . . . .6G **7**
Yorkshire Rd.
  CR4: Mitc 5J **155**
  E14 . . . . .6A **86**
York Sq. E14 . . . . .6A **86**
York St. CR4: Mitc 7E **154**
  TW1: Twick 1A **132**
  W1 . . . . .6E **4** (5D **82**)
York St. Chambers W1 . . . . .6E **4**
          (off York St.)
York Ter. DA8: Erith 1J **127**
  EN2: Enf 1H **23**
  SE7 .4A **106**
          (off Gallon Cl.)
York Ter. E. NW1 . . . . . .4H **5** (4E **82**)
York Ter. W. NW1 . . . . . .4G **5** (4E **82**)
Yorkton St. E2 . . . . .2G **85**
York Way KT9: Chess 7E **162**
  N1 . . . . .1F **7** (2J **83**)
  N7 . . . . .6H **65**
  N20 . . . . .3J **31**
  TW13: Hanw 3D **130**
          (not continuous)

York Way Ct. N1 . . . . .1J **83**
        (not continuous)
York Way Est. N7 . . . . .6J **65**
Young Ct. NW6 . . . . .7G **63**
Youngmans Cl.
  EN2: Enf 1H **23**
Young Rd. E16 . . . . .6A **88**
Youngs Bldgs. EC1 . . . . .3D **8**
Youngs Ct. SW11 . . . . .1E **118**
Youngs Rd.
  IG2: Ilf 5H **53**
Young St. W8 . . . . .2K **99**
The Young Vic Theatre 6K **13**
Yoxall Ho. W10 . . . . .4E **80**
          (off Sutton Way)
Yoxford Ct. RM6: Chad H 5B **54**
Yoxley App. IG2: Ilf 6G **53**
Yoxley Dr. IG2: Ilf 6G **53**
Ypres Pl. RM9: Dag 1B **90**
Yukon Rd. SW12 . . . . .7F **119**
Yunus Khan Cl. E17 . . . . .5C **50**
Yvon Ho. SW11 . . . . .1E **118**
        (off Alexandra Av.)

Z

Zachary Ct. SW1 . . . . .4D **18**
        (off Montaigne Cl.)
Zachary Ho. SW9 . . . . .1K **119**
          (off Lett Rd.)
Zachary M. E3 . . . . .3B **86**
        (off Tredegar Sq.)
Zahra Ho. NW10 . . . . .3E **80**
        (off Harrow Rd.)
Zambezie Dr. N9 . . . . .3D **34**
Zampa Rd. SE16 . . . . .5J **103**
Zanara Ct. SE26 . . . . .5J **139**
Zander Ct. E2 . . . . .3G **85**
Zangwill Ho. NW6 . . . . .2H **81**
        (off Carlton Va.)

Zangwill Rd. SE3 . . . . .1B **124**
Zapotec Ho. SE8 . . . . .4K **103**
        (off Chilton Gro.)
Zealand Av. UB7: Harm 3E **174**
Zealand Ho. SE5 . . . . .2C **120**
        (off Denmark Rd.)
  SE18 . . . . .4C **106**
Zealand Rd. E3 . . . . .2A **86**
Zeller Ho. E20 . . . . .5D **68**
        (off Scarlet Cl.)
Zenith Cl. NW9 . . . . .3K **43**
Zenith Lodge N3 . . . . .7E **30**
Zennor Rd. SW12 . . . . .1G **137**
Zennor Rd. Ind. Est.
  SW12 . . . . .1G **137**
Zenobia Mans. W14 . . . . .6H **99**
        (off Queen's Club Gdns.)
Zenoria St. SE22 . . . . .4F **121**
Zermatt Rd. CR7: Thor H 4C **156**
Zetland Ho. W8 . . . . .3K **99**
        (off Marloes Rd.)
Zetland St. E14 . . . . .5D **86**
Zeus Ct. UB7: Yiew 1A **92**
The Zinc Bldg.
  SE13 . . . . .4G **123**
Zinnia Mans. E20 . . . . .6D **68**
        (off Olympic Pk. Av.)
Zion Ho. E1 . . . . .6J **85**
        (off Jubilee St.)
Zion Pl. CR7: Thor H 4D **156**
Zion Rd. CR7: Thor H 4D **156**
Zoar St. SE1 . . . . .4C **14** (1C **102**)
Zodiac Cl. HA8: Edg 7B **28**
Zodiac Ct.
  CR0: C'don 1B **168**
Zodiac Ho. E3 . . . . .4C **86**
        (off Wellington Way)
Zoffany St. N19 . . . . .2H **65**
Zona Ct. SE1 . . . . .3F **103**
        (off Grange Wlk.)
Zulu M. SW11 . . . . .2C **118**

HOSPITALS, HOSPICES and
selected HEALTHCARE FACILITIES
covered by this atlas.

N.B. Where it is not possible to name these facilities on the map,
the reference given is for the road in which they are situated.

ASHFORD HOSPITAL 2A **128**
London Road
ASHFORD
TW15 3AA
Tel: 01784 884488

BARKING HOSPITAL 7K **71**
Upney Lane
BARKING
IG11 9LX
Tel: 020 3644 2301

BARNES HOSPITAL 3A **116**
South Worple Way
LONDON
SW14 8SU
Tel: 020 3513 3663

BARNET HOSPITAL 4A **20**
Wellhouse Lane
BARNET
EN5 3DJ
Tel: 020 8216 4600

BECKENHAM BEACON 2B **158**
379 Croydon Road
BECKENHAM
BR3 3QL
Tel: 01689 863000

BETHLEM ROYAL HOSPITAL 7C **158**
Monks Orchard Road
BECKENHAM
BR3 3BX
Tel: 020 3228 6000

THE BLACKHEATH BMI HOSPITAL 3H **123**
40-42 Lee Terrace
LONDON
SE3 9UD
Tel: 020 8318 7722

THE BLACKHEATH BMI HOSPITAL
(OUTPATIENT DEPARTMENT) 3H **123**
Independents Road
LONDON
SE3 9LF
Tel: 020 8297 4500

BMI CAVELL HOSPITAL 2F **23**
Cavell Drive
ENFIELD
EN2 7PR
Tel: 020 8366 2122

BMI CITY MEDICAL 7G **9**
17 St Helen's Place
LONDON
EC3A 6DG
Tel: 0845 123 5380

BMI URGENT CARE CENTRE 3K **59**
The Clementine Hospital
Sudbury Hill
HARROW
HA1 3RX
Tel: 020 8872 3999

BRENT OLDER PEOPLE DAY HOSPITAL 1C **80**
341 Harlesden Road
LONDON
NW10 3RX
Tel: 020 8459 3562

BRIDGEWAYS DAY HOSPITAL 6C **160**
Turpington Lane
BROMLEY
BR2 8JA
Tel: 020 8629 4900

CAMDEN MEWS DAY HOSPITAL 7G **65**
1-5 Camden Mews
LONDON
NW1 9DB
Tel: 020 3317 4740

CASSEL HOSPITAL 4D **132**
1 Ham Common
RICHMOND
TW10 7JF
Tel: 020 8483 2900

CENTRAL MIDDLESEX HOSPITAL 3J **79**
Acton Lane
LONDON
NW10 7NS
Tel: 020 8965 5733

CHARING CROSS HOSPITAL 6F **99**
Fulham Palace Road
LONDON
W6 8RF
Tel: 020 3311 1234

CHASE FARM HOSPITAL 1F **23**
127 The Ridgeway
ENFIELD
EN2 8JL
Tel: 020 8375 2999

CHELSEA & WESTMINSTER HOSPITAL 7A **16** (6A **100**)
369 Fulham Road
LONDON
SW10 9NH
Tel: 020 3315 8000

THE CHILDREN'S HOSPITAL (LEWISHAM) 5D **122**
Lewisham University Hospital
Lewisham High Street
LONDON
SE13 6LH
Tel: 020 8333 3000

CHURCHILL CAMBIAN HOSPITAL 1K **19** (3A **102**)
Barkham Terrace
Lambeth Road
LONDON
SE1 7PW
Tel: 0800 138 1418

CITY & HACKNEY CENTRE FOR MENTAL HEALTH 5K **67**
Homerton Row
LONDON
E9 6SR
Tel: 020 8510 8117

CLAYPONDS HOSPITAL 4E **96**
Sterling Place
LONDON
W5 4RN
Tel: 020 8560 4011

CLEMENTINE CHURCHILL BMI HOSPITAL 2K **59**
Sudbury Hill
HARROW
HA1 3RX
Tel: 020 8872 3872

THE COBORN CENTRE FOR ADOLESCENT MENTAL HEALTH
....4B **88**
Glen Road
LONDON
E13 8SP
Tel: 020 7540 6789

CROMWELL BUPA HOSPITAL 4K **99**
162-178 Cromwell Road
LONDON
SW5 0TU
Tel: 020 7460 2000

CROYDON UNIVERSITY HOSPITAL 6B **156**
530 London Road
THORNTON HEATH
CR7 7YE
Tel: 020 8401 3000

CYGNET HOSPITAL, BECKTON 6E **88**
23 Tunnan Leys
LONDON
E6 6ZB
Tel: 020 7511 2299

CYGNET HOSPITAL, BLACKHEATH 1E **122**
80 Blackheath Hill
LONDON
SE10 8AD
Tel: 020 8694 2111

CYGNET LODGE 6E **122**
44 Lewisham Park
LONDON
SE13 6QZ
Tel: 020 8314 5123

DEMELZA HOSPICE CARE FOR CHILDREN 6D **124**
5 Wensley Close
LONDON
SE9 5AB
Tel: 020 8859 9800

DULWICH COMMUNITY HOSPITAL 4E **120**
East Dulwich Grove
LONDON
SE22 8PT
Tel: 020 3049 8800

EALING CYGNET HOSPITAL 5E **78**
22 Corfton Road
LONDON
W5 2HT
Tel: 020 8991 6699

EALING HOSPITAL 1H **95**
Uxbridge Road
SOUTHALL
UB1 3HW
Tel: 020 8967 5000

EAST HAM CARE CENTRE & DAY HOSPITAL 7B **70**
Shrewsbury Road
LONDON
E7 8QP
Tel: 020 8475 2001

EDGWARE COMMUNITY HOSPITAL 7C **28**
Burnt Oak Broadway
EDGWARE
HA8 0AD
Tel: 020 8952 2381

EDRIDGE ROAD COMMUNITY HEALTH CENTRE 3C **168**
Impact House
2 Edridge Road
CROYDON
CR0 1FE
Tel: 020 3040 0800

ELTHAM COMMUNITY HOSPITAL 6D **124**
Passey Place
LONDON
SE9 5DQ
Tel: 020 3049 0400

ERITH & DISTRICT HOSPITAL 6K **109**
Park Crescent
ERITH
DA8 3EE
Tel: 020 8308 3131

EVELINA CHILDREN'S HOSPITAL 1G **19**
St Thomas' Hospital
Westminster Bridge Road
LONDON
SE1 7EH
Tel: 020 7188 7188

THE FERGUSON CEN. 6A **50**
Low Hall Lane
LONDON
E17 8BE
Tel: 020 8521 5223

FINCHLEY MEMORIAL HOSPITAL 7F **31**
Granville Road
LONDON
N12 0JE
Tel: 020 8349 7500

FITZROY SQUARE HOSPITAL 4A **6** (4G **83**)
1 Fitzroy Square
LONDON
W1T 5HF
Tel: 0333 920 9135

GOODMAYES HOSPITAL 5A **54**
Barley Lane
ILFORD
IG3 8XJ
Tel: 0300 555 1200

GORDON HOSPITAL 4C **18** (4H **101**)
Bloomburg Street
LONDON
SW1V 2RH
Tel: 020 3315 8733

GRAYS COURT COMMUNITY HOSPITAL 7H **73**
John Parker Close
DAGENHAM
RM10 9SR
Tel: 020 3644 2762

GREAT ORMOND STREET HOSPITAL FOR CHILDREN
.... 4F **7** (4J **83**)
Great Ormond Street
LONDON
WC1N 3JH
Tel: 020 7405 9200

GREENWICH & BEXLEY COMMUNITY HOSPICE 5C **108**
185 Bostall Hill
LONDON
SE2 0GB
Tel: 020 8312 2244

GUY'S HOSPITAL 5F **15** (2D **102**)
Great Maze Pond
LONDON
SE1 9RT
Tel: 020 7188 7188

GUY'S NUFFIELD HOUSE 6E **14**
Guy's Hospital
LONDON
SE1 1YR
Tel: 020 7188 5292

HAMMERSMITH HOSPITAL 6C **80**
Du Cane Road
LONDON
W12 0HS
Tel: 020 3313 1000

THE HARLEY STREET CLINIC 5J **5** (5F **83**)
35 Weymouth Street
LONDON
W1G 8BJ
Tel: 020 3553 6106

HARLINGTON HOSPICE 5F **93**
St Peters Way
HAYES
UB3 5AB
Tel: 020 8759 0453

HARROW CYGNET HOSPITAL 2J **59**
London Road
HARROW
HA1 3JL
Tel: 020 8966 7000

HAVEN HOUSE CHILDREN'S HOSPICE 6C **36**
High Road
WOODFORD GREEN
IG8 9LB
Tel: 020 8505 9944

HAYES GROVE PRIORY HOSPITAL 2J **171**
Prestons Road
Hayes
BROMLEY
BR2 7AS
Tel: 020 8462 7722

HENDON BMI HOSPITAL 3E **44**
46-50 Sunny Gardens Road
LONDON
NW4 1RP
Tel: 020 8457 4500

HIGHGATE HOSPITAL 6D **46**
17- 19 View Road
LONDON
N6 4DJ
Tel: 020 8003 4518

HIGHGATE MENTAL HEALTH CENTRE 2F **65**
Dartmouth Park Hill
LONDON
N19 5NX
Tel: 020 7561 4000

HILLINGDON HOSPITAL 5B **74**
Pield Heath Road
UXBRIDGE
UB8 3NN
Tel: 01895 238282

THE HOLLY PRIVATE HOSPITAL 2E **36**
High Road
BUCKHURST HILL
IG9 5HX
Tel: 020 8505 3311

HOMERTON UNIVERSITY HOSPITAL 5K **67**
Homerton Row
LONDON
E9 6SR
Tel: 020 8510 5555

HOSPITAL FOR TROPICAL DISEASES 4B **6**
Mortimer Market
LONDON
WC1E 6JD
Tel: 020 3447 5959

HOSPITAL OF ST JOHN & ST ELIZABETH 2B **82**
60 Grove End Road
LONDON
NW8 9NH
Tel: 020 7806 4000

HUNTERCOMBE HOSPITAL ROEHAMPTON 7C **116**
Holybourne Avenue
LONDON
SW15 4JD
Tel: 020 8780 6155

JOHN HOWARD CENTRE 5A **68**
12 Kenworthy Road
LONDON
E9 5TD
Tel: 020 8510 2003

KING EDWARD VII'S HOSPITAL SISTER AGNES
.... 5H **5** (5E **82**)
5-10 Beaumont Street
LONDON
W1G 6AA
Tel: 020 7486 4411

KING GEORGE HOSPITAL 4A **54**
Barley Lane
ILFORD
IG3 8YB
Tel: 0330 400 4333

KING'S COLLEGE HOSPITAL 2D **120**
Denmark Hill
LONDON
SE5 9RS
Tel: 020 3299 9000

KING'S OAK BMI HOSPITAL 1F **23**
The Ridgeway
ENFIELD
EN2 8SD
Tel: 020 8370 9500

KINGSTON HOSPITAL 1H **151**
Galsworthy Road
KINGSTON UPON THAMES
KT2 7QB
Tel: 020 8546 7711

LAMBETH HOSPITAL 3K **119**
108 Landor Road
LONDON
SW9 9NU
Tel: 020 3228 6000

THE LISTER HOSPITAL 6J **17** (5F **101**)
Chelsea Bridge Road
LONDON
SW1W 8RH
Tel: 020 7730 4345

LONDON BRIDGE HOSPITAL 4F **15** (1D **102**)
27 Tooley Street
LONDON
SE1 2PR
Tel: 020 7407 3100

LONDON CLINIC 4H **5** (4E **82**)
20 Devonshire Place
LONDON
W1G 6BW
Tel: 020 7935 4444

LONDON EYE HOSPITAL 7J 5
4 Harley Street
LONDON
W1G 9PB
Tel: 020 7060 2602

LONDON INDEPENDENT BMI HOSPITAL 5K 85
1 Beaumont Square
LONDON
E1 4NL
Tel: 020 7780 2400

LONDON WELBECK HOSPITAL 6J 5
27 Welbeck Street
LONDON
W1G 8EN
Tel: 020 7224 2242

MARGARET CENTRE (HOSPICE) 6G 51
Whipps Cross University Hospital
Whipps Cross Road
LONDON
E11 1NR
Tel: 020 8539 5522

MARIE CURIE HOSPICE 5B 64
11 Lyndhurst Gardens
LONDON
NW3 5NS
Tel: 020 7853 3400

THE MAUDSLEY HOSPITAL 2D 120
Denmark Hill
LONDON
SE5 8AZ
Tel: 020 3228 6000

MEADOW HOUSE HOSPICE 2H 95
Uxbridge Road
SOUTHALL
UB1 3HW
Tel: 020 8967 5179

MEMORIAL HOSPITAL 2E 124
Shooters Hill
LONDON
SE18 3RG
Tel: 020 8836 8500

MILDMAY HOSPITAL 2J 9 (3F 85)
Austin Street
LONDON
E2 7NB
Tel: 0207 613 6300

MILE END HOSPITAL 4K 85
Bancroft Road
LONDON
E1 4DG
Tel: 020 3416 5000

MINOR INJURIES UNIT (GUY'S HOSPITAL) 2D 102
Great Maze Pond
LONDON
SE1 9RT
Tel: 020 7188 3879

MINOR INJURIES UNIT (ROEHAMPTON) 6C 116
Roehampton Lane
LONDON
SW15 5PN
Tel: 020 8487 6499

**MINOR INJURIES UNIT
(ST BARTHOLOMEW'S HOSPITAL)** 6B 8 (5B 84)
West Smithfield
LONDON
EC1A 7BE
Tel: 020 3465 8843

MOLESEY HOSPITAL 5E 148
High Street
WEST MOLESEY
KT8 2LU
Tel: 020 8941 4481

MOORFIELDS EYE HOSPITAL 2E 8 (3D 84)
162 City Road
LONDON
EC1V 2PD
Tel: 020 7253 3411

NATIONAL HOSPITAL FOR NEUROLOGY & NEUROSURGERY
....4F 7 (4J 83)
Queen Square
LONDON
WC1N 3BG
Tel: 020 3456 7890

NEWHAM CENTRE FOR MENTAL HEALTH 4B 88
Cherry Tree Way
Glen Road
LONDON
E13 8SP
Tel: 020 7540 4380

NEWHAM UNIVERSITY HOSPITAL 4A 88
Glen Road
LONDON
E13 8SL
Tel: 020 7476 4000

NEW VICTORIA HOSPITAL 1A 152
184 Coombe Lane West
KINGSTON UPON THAMES
KT2 7EG
Tel: 020 8949 9000

NHS WALK-IN CENTRE (ASHFORD) 2A 128
Ashford Hospital
London Road
ASHFORD
TW15 3AA
Tel: 01784 884000

NHS WALK-IN CENTRE (BARKING HOSPITAL) 7K 71
Upney Lane
BARKING
IG11 9LX
Tel: 020 8924 6262

NHS WALK-IN CENTRE (BELMONT HEALTH CENTRE) ...2A 42
516 Kenton Lane
HARROW
HA3 7LT
Tel: 020 8866 4100

NHS WALK-IN CENTRE (CLAPHAM JUNCTION) 3C 118
The Junction Health Centre
Arches 5-8, Clapham Junction Station
Grant Road
LONDON
SW11 2NU
Tel: 0333 200 1718

**NHS WALK-IN CENTRE
(CRICKLEWOOD HEALTH CENTRE)** 4F 63
Britannia Business Centre
Cricklewood Lane
LONDON
NW2 1DZ
Tel: 03000 334335

NHS WALK-IN CENTRE (EARL'S COURT) 4K 99
Earl's Court Health & Wellbeing Centre
2b Hogarth Road
LONDON
SW5 0PT
Tel: 020 7341 0300

NHS WALK-IN CENTRE (EDGWARE) 7C 28
Edgware Community Hospital
Burnt Oak Broadway
EDGWARE
HA8 0AD
Tel: 020 8732 6459

NHS WALK-IN CENTRE (FINCHLEY) 7F 31
Finchley Memorial Hospital
Granville Road
LONDON
N12 0JE
Tel: 020 8349 7470

NHS WALK-IN CENTRE (ISLE OF DOGS) 2C 104
Barkantine Practice
121 Westferry Road
LONDON
E14 8JH
Tel: 020 7510 4000

NHS WALK-IN CENTRE (PARSONS GREEN) 1J 117
5-7 Parsons Green
LONDON
SW6 4UL
Tel: 020 8102 4300

NHS WALK-IN CENTRE (PINNER) 3C 40
Pinn Medical Centre, The
37 Love Lane
PINNER
HA5 3EE
Tel: 020 8866 5766

NHS WALK-IN CENTRE (SOHO) 1C 12
1 Frith Street
LONDON
W1D 3HZ
Tel: 020 7534 6575

NHS WALK-IN CENTRE (TEDDINGTON) 6J 131
Teddington Memorial Hospital
Hampton Road
TEDDINGTON
TW11 0JL
Tel: 020 8714 4004

NHS WALK-IN CENTRE (THAMESMEAD) 2J 107
Thamesmead Health Centre
4-5 Thames Reach
LONDON
SE28 0NY
Tel: 020 8319 5880

NHS WALK-IN CENTRE (WEMBLEY) 6D 60
116 Chaplin Road
WEMBLEY
HA0 4UZ
Tel: 020 8795 6112

NIGHTINGALE HOSPITAL 5D 4 (5C 82)
11-19 Lisson Grove
LONDON
NW1 6SH
Tel: 020 7535 7705

NOAH'S ARK CHILDREN'S HOSPICE 4C 20
Beauchamp Court
10 Victors Way
BARNET
EN5 5TZ
Tel: 020 8449 8877

NORTH LONDON CLINIC 2B 34
15 Church Street
LONDON
N9 9DY
Tel: 020 8956 1234

NORTH LONDON HOSPICE (FINCHLEY) 3F 31
47 Woodside Avenue
LONDON
N12 8TT
Tel: 020 8343 8841

NORTH LONDON HOSPICE (WINCHMORE HILL) 3H 33
110 Barrowell Green
LONDON
N21 3AY
Tel: 020 8343 8841

NORTH LONDON PRIORY HOSPITAL 1D 32
The Bourne
LONDON
N14 6RA
Tel: 020 8882 8191

NORTH MIDDLESEX UNIVERSITY HOSPITAL 5K 33
Sterling Way
LONDON
N18 1QX
Tel: 020 8887 2000

NORTHWICK PARK HOSPITAL 7A 42
Watford Road
HARROW
HA1 3UJ
Tel: 020 8864 3232

OLD BROAD STREET PRIVATE MEDICAL CENTRE 7G 9
31 Old Broad Street
LONDON
EC2N 1HT
Tel: 020 7496 3522

ORPINGTON HOSPITAL 4K 173
Sevenoaks Road
ORPINGTON
BR6 9JU
Tel: 01689 863000

PARK ROYAL CENTRE (FOR MENTAL HEALTH) 2J 79
Central Way
LONDON
NW10 7NS
Tel: 020 8955 4400

PARKSIDE HOSPITAL 3F 135
53 Parkside
LONDON
SW19 5NX
Tel: 020 8971 8000

PEMBRIDGE PALLIATIVE CARE CENTRE 5F 81
St Charles Hospital
Exmoor Street
LONDON
W10 6DZ
Tel: 020 8102 5000

PORTLAND HOSPITAL FOR WOMEN & CHILDREN
....4K 5 (4F 83)
205-209 Great Portland Street
LONDON
W1W 5AH
Tel: 020 3131 5755

PRINCESS GRACE HOSPITAL 4G 5 (4E 82)
42-52 Nottingham Place
LONDON
W1U 5NY
Tel: 020 3130 6833

PRINCESS ROYAL UNIVERSITY HOSPITAL 3E 172
Farnborough Common
ORPINGTON
BR6 8ND
Tel: 01689 863000

PRIORY HOSPITAL ROEHAMPTON 4B 116
Priory Lane
LONDON
SW15 5JJ
Tel: 020 8876 8261

QUEEN CHARLOTTE'S & CHELSEA HOSPITAL 6C 80
Du Cane Road
LONDON
W12 0HS
Tel: 020 3313 1111

QUEEN ELIZABETH HOSPITAL 7C 106
Stadium Road
LONDON
SE18 4QH
Tel: 020 8836 6000

QUEEN MARY'S HOSPITAL FOR CHILDREN 1A 166
Wrythe Lane
CARSHALTON
SM5 1AA
Tel: 020 8296 2000

QUEEN MARY'S HOSPITAL, ROEHAMPTON 6C 116
Roehampton Lane
LONDON
SW15 5PN
Tel: 020 8487 6000

QUEEN MARY'S HOSPITAL, SIDCUP 6A 144
Frognal Avenue
SIDCUP
DA14 6LT
Tel: 020 8302 2678

QUEEN'S HOSPITAL 7K 55
Rom Valley Way
ROMFORD
RM7 0AG
Tel: 01708 435000

RICHARD DESMOND CHILDREN'S EYE CENTRE 2E 8
Moorfields Eye Hospital
3 Peerless Street
LONDON
EC1V 9EZ
Tel: 020 7253 3411

RICHARD HOUSE CHILDREN'S HOSPICE 7B 88
Richard House Drive
LONDON
E16 3RG
Tel: 020 7511 0222

RICHMOND ROYAL HOSPITAL 3E 114
Kew Foot Road
RICHMOND
TW9 2TE
Tel: 020 3513 3200

RODING SPIRE HOSPITAL 3B 52
Roding Lane South
ILFORD
IG4 5PZ
Tel: 020 3131 4324

ROYAL BROMPTON HOSPITAL 5C 16 (5C 100)
Sydney Street
LONDON
SW3 6NP
Tel: 020 7352 8121

ROYAL BROMPTON HOSPITAL (OUTPATIENTS)
....5B 16 (5B 100)
Fulham Road
LONDON
SW3 6HP
Tel: 020 7352 8121

ROYAL FREE HOSPITAL 5C 64
Pond Street
LONDON
NW3 2QG
Tel: 020 7794 0500

ROYAL HOSPITAL FOR NEURO-DISABILITY 6G 117
West Hill
LONDON
SW15 3SW
Tel: 020 8780 4500

THE ROYAL LONDON HOSPITAL 5H 85
Whitechapel Road
LONDON
E1 1FR
Tel: 020 3416 5000

ROYAL LONDON HOSPITAL FOR INTEGRATED MEDICINE
....5F 7 (4J 83)
Great Ormond Street
LONDON
WC1N 3HR
Tel: 020 3456 7890

THE ROYAL MARSDEN HOSPITAL 5B 16 (5B 100)
Fulham Road
LONDON
SW3 6JJ
Tel: 020 7352 8171

ROYAL NAT. ORTHOPAEDIC HOSPITAL 4K 5 (4F 83)
45-51 Bolsover Street
LONDON
W1W 5AQ
Tel: 020 3947 0100

ROYAL NAT. ORTHOPAEDIC HOSPITAL 2H 27
Brockley Hill
STANMORE
HA7 4LP
Tel: 020 8954 2300

ROYAL NATIONAL ENT and EASTMAN DENTAL HOSPITALS
....4C 6 (4H 83)
Huntley Street
LONDON
WC1E 6DG
Tel: 020 3456 7890

ST ANN'S HOSPITAL 5C 48
St Ann's Road
LONDON
N15 3TH
Tel: 020 8702 3000

ST ANTHONY'S HOSPITAL 1F 165
801 London Road
SUTTON
SM3 9DW
Tel: 020 8337 6691

ST BARTHOLOMEW'S HOSPITAL 6B 8 (5B 84)
West Smithfield
LONDON
EC1A 7BE
Tel: 020 3416 5000

ST BERNARD'S HOSPITAL 2H 95
Uxbridge Road
SOUTHALL
UB1 3EU
Tel: 020 8354 8354

ST CHARLES HOSPITAL 5F 81
Exmoor Street
LONDON
W10 6DZ
Tel: 020 8206 7343

ST CHRISTOPHER'S HOSPICE (SYDENHAM) 5J 139
51-59 Lawrie Park Road
LONDON
SE26 6DZ
Tel: 020 8768 4500

ST CHRISTOPHER'S HOSPISCARE (ORPINGTON) 4K **173**
Tregony Road
ORPINGTON
BR6 9XA
Tel: 01689 825755

ST EBBA'S 7J **163**
Hook Road
EPSOM
KT19 8QJ
Tel: 0300 555 5222

ST GEORGE'S HOSPITAL (TOOTING) 5B **136**
Blackshaw Road
LONDON
SW17 0QT
Tel: 020 8672 1255

ST HELIER HOSPITAL 1A **166**
Wrythe Lane
CARSHALTON
SM5 1AA
Tel: 020 8296 2000

ST JOHN'S HOSPICE 1A **4**
60 Grove End Road
LONDON
NW8 9NH
Tel: 020 7806 4040

ST JOSEPH'S HOSPICE 1H **85**
Mare Street
LONDON
E8 4SA
Tel: 020 8525 6000

ST LUKE'S HEALTHCARE FOR THE CLERGY 4A **6**
14 Fitzroy Square
LONDON
W1T 6HP
Tel: 020 7388 4954

ST LUKE'S HOSPICE 5D **42**
Kenton Road
HARROW
HA3 0YG
Tel: 020 8382 8000

ST MARK'S HOSPITAL (HARROW) 7B **42**
Watford Road
HARROW
HA1 3UJ
Tel: 020 8864 3232

ST MARY'S HOSPITAL 7B **4** (6B **82**)
Praed Street
LONDON
W2 1NY
Tel: 020 7886 6666

ST MICHAEL'S HOSPITAL 1J **23**
Gater Drive
ENFIELD
EN2 0JB
Tel: 020 8375 2894

ST PANCRAS HOSPITAL 1H **83**
4 St Pancras Way
LONDON
NW1 0PE
Tel: 020 3317 3500

ST RAPHAEL'S HOSPICE 2F **165**
London Road
SUTTON
SM3 9DX
Tel: 020 8099 7777

ST THOMAS' HOSPITAL 7G **13** (3K **101**)
Westminster Bridge Road
LONDON
SE1 7EH
Tel: 020 7188 7188

SHIRLEY OAKS BMI HOSPITAL 7J **157**
Poppy Lane
CROYDON
CR9 8AB
Tel: 020 8655 5500

SHOOTING STAR HOUSE, CHILDREN'S HOSPICE ...6D **130**
The Avenue
HAMPTON
TW12 3RA
Tel: 020 8783 2000

THE SLOANE BMI HOSPITAL 1F **159**
125 Albemarle Road
BECKENHAM
BR3 5HS
Tel: 020 8466 4000

SPIRE BUSHEY HOSPITAL 1E **26**
Heathbourne Road
Bushey Heath
BUSHEY
WD23 1RD
Tel: 020 3733 5424

SPRINGFIELD UNIVERSITY HOSPITAL 2C **136**
61 Glenburnie Road
LONDON
SW17 7DJ
Tel: 020 3513 5000

TEDDINGTON MEMORIAL HOSPITAL 6J **131**
Hampton Road
TEDDINGTON
TW11 0JL
Tel: 020 8714 4000

THORPE COOMBE HOSPITAL 3E **50**
714 Forest Road
LONDON
E17 3HP
Tel: 0300 555 1247

TOLWORTH HOSPITAL 2G **163**
Red Lion Road
SURBITON
KT6 7QU
Tel: 020 3513 5000

TOWER HAMLETS CENTRE FOR MENTAL HEALTH ...4K **85**
Bancroft Road
LONDON
E1 4DG
Tel: 020 8121 5001

TRINITY HOSPICE 4F **119**
30 Clapham Common North Side
LONDON
SW4 0RN
Tel: 020 7787 1000

UCH MACMILLAN CANCER CENTRE 4B **6** (4G **83**)
Huntley Street
LONDON
WC1E 6DH
Tel: 020 3456 7016

UNIVERSITY COLLEGE HOSPITAL 3B **6** (4G **83**)
235 Euston Road
LONDON
NW1 2BU
Tel: 020 3456 7890

UNIVERSITY COLLEGE HOSPITAL 4G **83**
25 Grafton Way
LONDON
WC1E 6DB
Tel: 020 3447 9400

UNIVERSITY COLLEGE HOSPITAL 6J **5** (5E **82**)
16-18 Westmoreland Street
LONDON
W1G 8PH
Tel: 020 3456 7890

UNIVERSITY HOSPITAL, LEWISHAM 5D **122**
Lewisham High Street
LONDON
SE13 6LH
Tel: 020 8333 3000

UPTON CENTRE 4E **126**
14 Upton Road
BEXLEYHEATH
DA6 8LQ
Tel: 020 8301 7900

URGENT CARE CENTRE
(ANGEL MEDICAL PRACTICE) 2A **84**
34 Ritchie Street
LONDON
N1 0DG
Tel: 020 7837 1663

URGENT CARE CENTRE (BARNET) 4A **20**
Barnet Hospital
Wellhouse Lane
BARNET
EN5 3DJ
Tel: 020 8216 4600

URGENT CARE CENTRE (BECKENHAM BEACON) 2B **158**
379 Croydon Road
BECKENHAM
BR3 3QL
Tel: 01689 866037

URGENT CARE CENTRE (CARSHALTON) 1B **166**
St Helier Hospital
Wrythe Lane
CARSHALTON
SM5 1AA
Tel: 020 8296 2000

URGENT CARE CENTRE
(CENTRAL MIDDLESEX HOSPITAL) 3J **79**
Acton Lane
LONDON .
NW10 7NS
Tel: 0333 999 2575

URGENT CARE CENTRE (CHASE FARM HOSPITAL) 1F **23**
The Ridgeway
ENFIELD
EN2 8JL
Tel: 020 8375 1010

URGENT CARE CENTRE
(CHELSEA & WESTMINSTER HOSPITAL) ...6A **100**
369 Fulham Road
LONDON
SW10 9NH
Tel: 020 3315 8000

URGENT CARE CENTRE (EALING) 2H **95**
Ealing Hospital
Uxbridge Road
SOUTHALL
UB1 3HW
Tel: 0333 999 2577

URGENT CARE CENTRE
(ERITH & DISTRICT HOSPITAL) 6K **109**
Park Crescent
ERITH
DA8 3EE
Tel: 01322 356116

URGENT CARE CENTRE (FULHAM) 5F **99**
Charing Cross Hospital
Fulham Palace Road
LONDON
W6 8RF
Tel: 020 8846 1005

URGENT CARE CENTRE
(HAMMERSMITH HOSPITAL) 6C **80**
Du Cane Road
LONDON
W12 0HS
Tel: 020 8383 4103

URGENT CARE CENTRE (HAMPSTEAD) 5C **64**
Royal Free Hospital
Pond Street
LONDON
NW3 2QG
Tel: 020 7794 0500

URGENT CARE CENTRE (HILLINGDON HOSPITAL) 5B **74**
Hillingdon Hospital
Pield Heath Road
UXBRIDGE
UB8 3NN
Tel: 01895 238282

URGENT CARE CENTRE
(HOMERTON UNIVERSITY HOSPITAL) 5K **67**
Homerton Row
LONDON
E9 6SR
Tel: 020 8510 5555

URGENT CARE CENTRE (KING GEORGE HOSPITAL) 4A **54**
Barley Lane
ILFORD
IG3 8YB
Tel: 020 8983 8000

URGENT CARE CENTRE (NEWHAM) 4A **88**
Newham University Hospital
Glen Road
LONDON
E13 8SL
Tel: 020 7476 4000

URGENT CARE CENTRE
(NORTH MIDDLESEX UNIVERSITY HOSPITAL) ...5K **33**
Bridport Road
LONDON
N18 1QX
Tel: 020 8887 2398

URGENT CARE CENTRE
(NORTHWICK PARK HOSPITAL) 7A **42**
Watford Road
HARROW
HA1 3UJ
Tel: 020 8869 3743

URGENT CARE CENTRE
(PRINCESS ROYAL UNIVERSITY HOSPITAL) 4E **172**
Farnborough Common
ORPINGTON
BR6 8ND
Tel: 01689 863050

URGENT CARE CENTRE
(QUEEN ELIZABETH HOSPITAL) 6C **106**
Stadium Road
LONDON
SE18 4QH
Tel: 020 8836 6846

URGENT CARE CENTRE (QUEEN'S HOSPITAL) 7K **55**
Rom Valley Way
ROMFORD
RM7 0AG
Tel: 01708 435000

URGENT CARE CENTRE (ST CHARLES CENTRE) 5F **81**
Exmoor Street
LONDON
W10 6DZ
Tel: 020 8102 5111

URGENT CARE CENTRE (ST GEORGE'S HOSPITAL) 5C **136**
Blackshaw Road
LONDON
SW17 0QT
Tel: 020 8672 1255

URGENT CARE CENTRE (ST MARY'S HOSPITAL) 6B **82**
Praed Street
LONDON
W2 1NY
Tel: 020 3312 5757

URGENT CARE CENTRE (SIDCUP) 6A **144**
Queen Mary's Hospital
Frognal Avenue
SIDCUP
DA14 6LT
Tel: 020 8308 5611

URGENT CARE CENTRE (THORNTON HEATH) 6B **156**
Croydon University Hospital
530 London Road
THORNTON HEATH
CR7 7YE
Tel: 020 8401 3000

URGENT CARE CENTRE
(UNIVERSITY COLLEGE HOSPITAL) 3B **6** (4G **83**)
235 Euston Road
LONDON
NW1 2BU
Tel: 020 3456 7890

URGENT CARE CENTRE
(UNIVERSITY HOSPITAL LEWISHAM) 5D **122**
Lewisham High Street
LONDON
SE13 6LH
Tel: 020 8333 3000

URGENT CARE CENTRE
(WEST MIDDLESEX UNIVERSITY HOSPITAL) ...2A **114**
Twickenham Road
ISLEWORTH
TW7 6AF
Tel: 020 8560 2121

URGENT CARE CENTRE
(WHIPPS CROSS UNIVERSITY HOSPITAL) 6F **51**
Whipps Cross Road
LONDON
E11 1NR
Tel: 0300 123 0808

URGENT CARE CENTRE
(WHITTINGTON HOSPITAL) 2G **65**
Magdala Avenue
LONDON
N19 5NF
Tel: 020 7272 3070

THE WELLINGTON HOSPITAL 1B **4** (3B **82**)
34 Circus Road
LONDON
NW8 9LE
Tel: 020 3733 6667

WESTERN EYE HOSPITAL 5E **4** (5D **82**)
153-173 Marylebone Road
LONDON
NW1 5QH
Tel: 020 7886 6666

WEST MIDDLESEX UNIVERSITY HOSPITAL 2A **114**
Twickenham Road
ISLEWORTH
TW7 6AF
Tel: 020 8560 2121

WEYMOUTH STREET HOSPITAL 5H **5**
42-46 Weymouth Street
LONDON
W1G 6NP
Tel: 020 7935 1200

WHIPPS CROSS UNIVERSITY HOSPITAL 5F **51**
Whipps Cross Road
LONDON
E11 1NR
Tel: 020 8539 5522

WHITTINGTON HOSPITAL 2G **65**
Magdala Avenue
LONDON
N19 5NF
Tel: 020 7272 3070

WILLESDEN CENTRE FOR HEALTH & CARE 7C **62**
Robson Avenue
LONDON
NW10 3RY
Tel: 020 8438 7006

THE WILSON HOSPITAL 4D **154**
Cranmer Road
MITCHAM
CR4 4LD
Tel: 020 8648 3021

WOODBURY UNIT 6G **51**
178 James Lane
LONDON
E11 1NR
Tel: 0300 555 1260

PUBLIC TRANSPORT
with their map square reference

A

Abbey Road (DLR) 2G 87
Abbey Wood (Rail & Crossrail) 3C 108
Acton Central (Overground) 1K 97
Acton Main Line (Rail & Crossrail) 6J 79
Acton Town (Underground) 2G 97
Addington Bus Station 6C 170
Addington Village Stop (London Tramlink) 6C 170
Addiscombe Stop (London Tramlink) 1G 169
Albany Park (Rail) 2D 144
Aldgate Bus Station 1J 15 (6F 85)
Aldgate East (Underground) 7K 9 (6F 85)
Aldgate (Underground) 1J 15 (6F 85)
Alexandra Palace (Rail) 2J 47
All Saints (DLR) 7D 86
Alperton (Underground) 1D 78
Ampere Way Stop (London Tramlink) 1K 167
Anerley (Rail & Overground) 1H 157
Angel (Underground) 2A 84
Archway Bus Station 2G 65
Archway (Underground) 2G 65
Arena Stop (London Tramlink) 5J 157
Arnos Grove (Underground) 5B 32
Arsenal (Underground) 3A 66
Ashford (Rail) 4B 128
Avenue Road Stop (London Tramlink) 2K 157

B

Baker Street (Underground) 4F 5 (4D 82)
Balham (Rail & Underground) 1F 137
Bankside Pier (River Bus & Tours) 3C 14 (7C 84)
Bank (Underground & DLR) 1E 14 (6D 84)
Barbican (Underground) 5C 8 (5C 84)
**Barking
     (Rail, Underground & Overground) 7G 71**
Barkingside (Underground) 3H 53
Barnehurst (Rail) 2J 127
Barnes Bridge (Rail) 2B 116
Barnes (Rail) 3C 116
Barons Court (Underground) 5G 99
Battersea Park (Rail) 7F 101
Battersea Power Pier (River Bus) 7K 17 (6G 101)
Bayswater (Underground) 7K 81
Beckenham Hill (Rail) 5E 140
**Beckenham Junction
     (Rail & London Tramlink) 1C 158**
Beckenham Road Stop (London Tramlink) 1A 158
Beckton (Underground) 5E 88
Beckton Park (DLR) 7D 88
Becontree (Underground) 6D 72
Beddington Lane Stop (London Tramlink) 6G 155
Belgrave Walk Stop (London Tramlink) 4B 154
Bellingham (Rail) 3D 140
Belsize Park (Underground) 5C 64
Belvedere (Rail) 3H 109
Bermondsey (Underground) 3G 103
Berrylands (Rail) 4H 151
Bethnal Green (Overground) 4H 85
Bethnal Green (Underground) 3J 85
Bexleyheath (Rail) 2E 126
Bexley (Rail) 1G 145
Bickley (Rail) 3C 160
Birkbeck (Rail & London Tramlink) 3J 157
Blackfriars Millennium Pier (River Bus) ...2B 14 (7B 84)
Blackfriars (Rail & Underground) 2A 14 (7B 84)
Blackheath (Rail) 3H 123
Blackhorse Lane Stop (London Tramlink) 7G 157
Blackhorse Road (Underground & Overground) ...4K 49
Blackwall Basin Moorings 1E 104
Blackwall (DLR) 7E 86
Bond Street (Underground & Crossrail) ...1J 11 (6E 82)
Borough (Underground) 7D 14 (2C 102)
Boston Manor (Underground) 4A 96
Bounds Green (Underground) 6C 32
Bow Church (Underground) 3C 86
Bowes Park (Rail) 7D 32
Bow Road (Underground) 3C 86
Brent Cross Bus Station 7E 44

Brent Cross (Underground) 7F 45
Brentford (Rail) 6C 96
Brimsdown (Rail) 3F 25
Brixton (Rail & Underground) 4A 120
Brockley (Rail & Overground) 3A 122
Bromley-by-Bow (Underground) 3D 86
Bromley North (Rail) 1J 159
Bromley South (Rail) 3J 159
Brondesbury (Overground) 7H 63
Brondesbury Park (Overground) 1G 81
Bruce Grove (Overground) 2F 49
Buckhurst Hill (Underground) 2G 37
Burnt Oak (Underground) 1J 43
Bush Hill Park (Overground) 6A 24

C

Cable Car 2H 105
Cadogan Pier (River Bus) 7D 16 (6C 100)
Caledonian Road & Barnsbury
     (Overground) 7K 65
Caledonian Road (Underground) 6K 65
Cambridge Heath (Overground) 2H 85
Camden Road (Overground) 7G 65
Camden Town (Underground) 1F 83
Canada Water Bus Station 2J 103
                                      (off Surrey Quays)
Canada Water (Underground & Overground) 2J 103
Canary Wharf (Crossrail) 1D 104
Canary Wharf Pier (River Bus) 1B 104
Canary Wharf (Underground & DLR) 1C 104
Canning Town Bus Station 6G 87
Canning Town (Underground) 6G 87
Canning Town (Underground & DLR) 6G 87
**Cannon Street
     (Rail & Underground) ....2E 14 (7D 84)**
Canonbury (Overground) 5C 66
Canons Park (Underground) 7K 27
Carshalton Beeches (Rail) 6D 166
Carshalton (Rail) 4D 166
Castle Bar Park (Rail) 5K 77
Catford Bridge (Rail) 7C 122
Catford (Rail) 7C 122
Centrale Stop (London Tramlink) 2C 168
Chadwell Heath (Rail & Crossrail) 7D 54
Chalk Farm (Underground) 7E 64
Chancery Lane (Underground) 6J 7 (5A 84)
Charing Cross (Rail & Underground) ...4E 12 (1J 101)
Charlton (Rail) 5A 106
Cheam (Rail) 7G 165
Chelsea Harbour Pier (River Bus) 1B 118
Chessington North (Rail) 5E 162
Chessington South (Rail) 7D 162
Chigwell (Underground) 3K 37
Chingford Bus Station 1B 36
Chingford (Overground) 1B 36
Chislehurst (Rail) 2E 160
Chiswick Park (Underground) 4J 97
Chiswick (Rail) 7J 97
Church Street Stop (London Tramlink) 2C 168
City Airport 1C 106
City Thameslink (Rail) 7A 8 (6B 84)
Clapham Common (Underground) 4G 119
Clapham High Street (Overground) 3H 119
Clapham Junction (Rail & Overground) 3C 118
Clapham North (Underground) 3J 119
Clapham South (Underground) 6F 119
Clapton (Overground) 2H 67
Clock House (Rail) 1A 158
Cockfosters (Underground) 4K 21
Colindale (Underground) 3A 44
Colliers Wood (Underground) 7B 136
Coombe Lane Stop
     (London Tramlink) 5J 169
Covent Garden (Underground) 2F 13 (7J 83)
Cricklewood (Rail) 4F 63
Crofton Park (Rail) 5B 122
Cromwell Road Bus Station 1E 150
Crossharbour (Underground & DLR) 3D 104
Crouch Hill (Overground) 7K 47
Crystal Palace (Rail & Overground) 6G 139
Custom House for ExCeL (DLR & Crossrail) 7K 87

Cutty Sark for Maritime Greenwich (DLR) 6E 104
Cyprus (DLR) 7E 88

D

Dagenham Dock (Rail) 2F 91
Dagenham East (Underground) 5J 73
Dagenham Heathway (Underground) 6F 73
Dalston Junction (Overground) 6F 67
Dalston Kingsland (Overground) 5E 66
Denmark Hill (Rail & Overground) 2D 120
Deptford Bridge (DLR) 1C 122
Deptford (Rail) 7C 104
Devons Road (DLR) 4D 86
Dollis Hill (Underground) 5C 62
Doubletree Docklands / Nelson Dock Pier
     (River Bus) 1B 104
Drayton Green (Rail) 6K 77
Drayton Park (Rail) 4A 66
Dundonald Road Stop (London Tramlink) 7H 135

E

Ealing Broadway (Rail, Underground & Crossrail) 7D 78
Ealing Common (Underground) 1F 97
Earl's Court (Underground) 4J 99
Earlsfield (Rail) 1A 136
East Acton (Underground) 6B 80
East Beckton Bus Station 6E 88
Eastcote (Underground) 7A 40
East Croydon Bus Station 2D 168
East Croydon (Rail & London Tramlink) 2D 168
East Dulwich (Rail) 4E 120
East Finchley (Underground) 4C 46
East Ham (Underground) 7C 70
East India (DLR) 7F 87
East Putney (Underground) 5G 117
Eden Park (Rail) 5C 158
Edgware Bus Station 6C 28
Edgware Road (Underground) 5C 4 (5C 82)
Edgware (Underground) 6C 28
Edmonton Bus Station 2C 34
Edmonton Green (Overground) 2B 34
Elephant & Castle (Rail & Underground) ...4C 102
Elmers End (Rail & London Tramlink) 4K 157
Elmstead Woods (Rail) 6C 142
Eltham (Rail) 5D 124
Elverson Road (DLR) 2D 122
Embankment Pier (River Bus & Tours) ...4G 13 (1J 101)
Embankment (Underground) 4F 13 (1J 101)
Emirates Air Line 2H 105
Emirates Greenwich Peninsula 2H 105
Emirates Royal Docks 7J 87
Enfield Chase (Rail) 3H 23
Enfield Town (Overground) 3K 23
Erith (Rail) 5K 109
Essex Road (Rail) 7C 66
Euston (Rail, Underground & Overground) ...2C 6 (3G 83)
Euston Square (Underground) 3B 6 (4G 83)
Ewell West (Rail) 7A 164

F

Fairfield Road Bus Station 2E 150
Fairlop (Underground) 1H 53
Falconwood (Rail) 4H 125
Farringdon
     (Rail, Underground & Crossrail) 5A 8 (5B 84)
Feltham (Rail) 1K 129
Fenchurch Street (Rail) 2J 15 (7F 85)
Festival Pier (River Tours) 4G 13 (1K 101)
Fieldway Stop (London Tramlink) 7D 170
Finchley Central (Underground) 1J 45
Finchley Road & Frognal (Overground) 5A 64
Finchley Road (Underground) 6A 64
Finsbury Park Interchange (Bus) 2A 66
Finsbury Park (Rail & Underground) 2A 66
Forest Gate (Rail & Crossrail) 5J 69
Forest Hill (Rail & Overground) 2J 139

Fulham Broadway (Underground) 7J 99
Fulwell (Rail) **4H 131**

G

Gallions Reach (DLR) 7F 89
Gants Hill (Underground) 6E 52
George Street Stop (London Tramlink) 2C 168
Gipsy Hill (Rail) **5E 138**
Gloucester Road (Underground) 4A 100
Golders Green (Underground) 1J 63
Goldhawk Road (Underground) 2E 98
Goodge Street (Underground) 5C 6 (5H 83)
Goodmayes (Rail & Crossrail) **1A 72**
Gordon Hill (Rail) **1G 23**
Gospel Oak (Overground) 4E 64
Grange Park (Rail) **5G 23**
Gravel Hill Stop (London Tramlink) 6A 170
Great Portland Street (Underground) 4K 5 (4F 83)
Greenford (Rail & Underground) **1H 77**
Greenland Pier (River Bus) 3B 104
Green Line Coach Station 4K 17
                                      (off Bulleid Way)
Green Park (Underground) 4K 11 (1F 101)
Greenwich Pier (River Bus & Tours) 5E 104
Greenwich (Rail & DLR) **7D 104**
Grove Park (Rail) **3K 141**
Gunnersbury (Underground & Overground) 5H 97

H

Hackbridge (Rail) **2F 167**
Hackney Central (Overground) 6H 67
Hackney Downs (Overground) 5H 67
Hackney Wick (Overground) 6C 68
Hadley Wood (Rail) **1F 21**
Haggerston (Overground) 1F 85
Hammersmith Bus Station 4E 98
Hammersmith (Underground) 4E 98
Hampstead Heath (Overground) 4C 64
Hampstead (Underground) 4A 64
Hampton Court (Rail) **4J 149**
Hampton (Rail) **1E 148**
Hampton Wick (Rail) **1C 150**
Hanger Lane (Underground) 3E 78
Hanwell (Rail & Crossrail) **7J 77**
Harlesden (Underground & Overground) 2K 79
Harringay Green Lanes (Overground) 6B 48
Harringay (Rail) **6A 48**
Harrington Road Stop (London Tramlink) 3J 157
Harrow & Wealdstone
        (Rail, Underground & Overground) **4J 41**
Harrow Bus Station 6J 41
Harrow-on-the-Hill (Rail & Underground) **6J 41**
Hatch End (Underground) 1E 40
Hatton Cross (Underground) 4H 111
Haydons Road (Rail) **5A 136**
Hayes & Harlington (Rail & Crossrail) **3H 93**
Hayes (Rail) **1J 171**
Headstone Lane (Overground) 1F 41
Heathrow Airport
        Terminals 2, 3 ....3C 110
        Terminal 4 ....5D 110
        Terminal 5 ....6D 174
Heathrow Central Bus Station 3D 110
Heathrow Central (Rail) **3C 110**
Heathrow Terminals 2 & 3
        (Rail, Underground & Crossrail) **3C 110**
Heathrow Terminal 4 (Rail) **6E 110**
Heathrow Terminal 4 (Underground & Crossrail) ..5E 110
Heathrow Terminal 5
        (Rail, Underground & Crossrail) **6D 174**
Hendon Central (Underground) 5D 44
Hendon (Rail) **6C 44**
Herne Hill (Rail) **6B 120**
Heron Quays (DLR) 1C 104
Highams Park (Rail) 6A 36
High Barnet (Underground) 4D 20
Highbury & Islington
        (Rail, Underground & Overground) **6B 66**
Highgate (Underground) 6F 47
High Street Kensington (Underground) 2K 99
Hillingdon (Underground) 5D 56
Hither Green (Rail) **6G 123**
Holborn (Underground) 6G 7 (6K 83)
Holland Park (Underground) 1H 99
Holloway Road (Underground) 5K 65

Homerton (Overground) 6K 67
Honor Oak Park
        (Rail & Overground) **6K 121**
Hornbeam Ho. 2A 104
Hornsey (Rail) **4K 47**
Hounslow Central (Underground) 3F 113
Hounslow East (Underground) 2G 113
Hounslow (Rail) **5F 113**
Hounslow West (Underground) 2C 112
Hoxton (Overground) 2F 85
Hyde Park Corner (Underground) 6H 11 (2E 100)

I

Ickenham (Underground) 4E 56
Ilford (Overground & Crossrail) 3E 70
Imperial Wharf (Overground) 1A 118
Island Gardens (DLR) 5E 104
Isleworth (Rail) **2K 113**

J

Jacobs Island Pier 2G 103
                              (off Bermondsey Wall W.)

K

Kempton Park (Rail) **7K 129**
Kennington (Underground) 5B 102
Kensal Green (Underground & Overground) 3E 80
Kensal Rise (Overground) 2F 81
Kensington Olympia
        (Rail, Underground & Overground) **3G 99**
Kent House (Rail) 1A 158
Kentish Town (Rail & Underground) **5G 65**
Kentish Town West (Overground) 6F 65
Kenton (Underground & Overground) 6B 42
Kew Bridge (Rail) **5F 97**
Kew Gardens (Underground & Overground) 1G 115
Kidbrooke (Rail) **3K 123**
Kilburn High Road (Overground) 1K 81
Kilburn Park (Underground) 2J 81
Kilburn (Underground) 6H 63
King George V (DLR) 1E 106
Kingsbury (Underground) 5G 43
King's Cross (Rail & Underground) .....**1E 6 (2J 83)**
King's Cross St Pancras
                                   ....1E 6 (3J 83)
Kingston (Rail) **1E 150**
Knightsbridge (Underground) 7F 11 (2D 100)

L

Ladbroke Grove (Underground) 6G 81
Ladywell (Rail) **5D 122**
Lambeth North (Underground) 1J 19 (3A 102)
Lancaster Gate (Underground) 2A 10 (7B 82)
Langdon Park (DLR) 6D 86
Latimer Road (Underground) 7F 81
Lea Bridge (Rail) **1A 68**
Lebanon Road Stop (London Tramlink) 2E 168
Lee (Rail) **6J 123**
Leicester Square (Underground) 2D 12 (7J 83)
Lewisham (Rail & DLR) **3E 122**
Leyton Midland Road (Overground) 7E 50
Leytonstone High Road (Overground) 2G 69
Leytonstone (Underground) 1G 69
Leyton (Underground) 3E 68
Limehouse (Rail & DLR) **6A 86**
Liverpool Street
        (Rail, Underground & Crossrail) ...**6G 9 (5E 84)**
Lloyd Park Stop (London Tramlink) 5F 169
London Bridge City Pier (River Bus) 4F 15 (1E 102)
London Bridge
        (Rail & Underground) ....**5F 15 (1D 102)**
London City Airport (Rail) **1C 106**
London City Airport (DLR) 1C 106
London Eye Millennium Pier
                   (River Bus & Tours) 6G 13 (2K 101)
London Fields (Overground) 7H 67
London Heathrow Airport
        Terminals 2, 3 ....3C 110
        Terminal 4 ....5D 110
        Terminal 5 ....6D 174
The London Heliport 2A 118

Loughborough Junction (Rail) 3B 120
Lower Sydenham (Rail) 5B 140

M

Maida Vale (Underground) 3K 81
Malden Manor (Rail) **7A 152**
Manor House (Underground) 7C 48
Manor Park (Rail & Crossrail) **4B 70**
Mansion House (Underground) 2D 14 (7C 84)
Marble Arch (Underground) 1F 11 (6D 82)
Maryland (Rail & Crossrail) **6G 69**
Marylebone (Rail & Underground) ......**4E 4 (4D 82)**
Masthouse Terrace Pier (River Bus) 5C 104
Maze Hill (Rail) **6G 105**
Meridian Water (Rail) **6D 34**
Merton Park Stop (London Tramlink) 1J 153
Mile End (Underground) 4B 86
Millbank Millennium Pier (River Bus) 4F 19 (4J 101)
Mill Hill Broadway Bus Station 6F 29
Mill Hill Broadway (Rail) **6F 29**
Mill Hill East (Underground) 7B 30
Mitcham Eastfields (Rail) **2E 154**
Mitcham Junction (Rail & London Tramlink) ...**5E 154**
Mitcham Stop (London Tramlink) 4C 154
Monument (Underground) 2F 15 (7D 84)
Moorgate (Rail & Underground) ....**6E 8 (5D 84)**
Morden Road Stop (London Tramlink) 2K 153
Morden South (Rail) **5J 153**
Morden (Underground) **5J 153**
Morden 3K 153
Mornington Crescent (Underground) 2G 83
Mortlake (Rail) **3J 115**
Motspur Park (Rail) **5D 152**
Mottingham (Rail) **1D 142**
Mudchute (DLR) 4D 104

N

Neasden (Underground) 5A 62
New Barnet (Rail) **5G 21**
New Beckenham (Rail) **7B 140**
Newbury Park (Underground) 6H 53
New Cross Gate (Rail & Overground) **7A 104**
New Cross (Rail & Overground) **7B 104**
New Eltham (Rail) **1F 143**
New Malden (Rail) **3A 152**
New Southgate (Rail) **5A 32**
Norbiton (Rail) 1G 151
Norbury (Rail) **1K 155**
North Dulwich (Rail) **5D 120**
North Ealing (Underground) 6F 79
Northfields (Underground) 3C 96
North Finchley Bus Station 5F 31
North Greenwich Pier (River Bus & Tours) 1H 105
North Greenwich (Underground) 2G 105
North Harrow (Underground) 5F 41
Northolt Park (Rail) **4F 59**
Northolt (Underground) 6E 58
North Sheen (Rail) **4G 115**
North Terminal (River Bus) 2E 106
Northumberland Park (Rail) **7C 34**
North Wembley (Underground & Overground) ...3D 60
Northwick Park (Underground) 7B 42
Northwood Hills (Underground) 2J 39
Norwood Junction (Rail & Overground) **4G 157**
Notting Hill Gate (Underground) 1J 99
Nunhead (Rail) **2J 121**

O

Oakleigh Park (Rail) **7G 21**
Oakwood (Underground) 5B 22
Old Street (Rail & Underground) ....**2F 9 (4D 84)**
Orpington (Rail) **2J 173**
Osterley (Underground) 7H 95
Oval (Underground) 6A 102
Oxford Circus (Underground) 1A 12 (6G 83)

P

Paddington (Rail, Underground & Crossrail) ....**7A 4 (6B 82)**
Palmers Green (Rail) **4E 32**
Park Royal (Underground) 4G 79
Parsons Green (Underground) 1J 117

Peckham Bus Station 1G 121
Peckham Rye (Rail & Overground) **2G 121**
Penge East (Rail) **6J 139**
Penge West (Rail & Overground) **6H 139**
Perivale (Underground) 2A 78
Petts Wood (Rail) **5G 161**
Phipps Bridge Stop (London Tramlink) 3B 154
Piccadilly Circus (Underground) 3C 12 (7H 83)
Pimlico (Underground) 5C 18 (5H 101)
Pinner (Underground) 4C 40
Plaistow (Underground) 2H 87
Plantation Wharf Pier (River Bus) 3K 118
Plumstead (Rail) **4H 107**
Ponders End (Rail) **5F 25**
Pontoon Dock (DLR) 1A 106
Poplar (DLR) 7D 86
Preston Road (Underground) 1E 60
Prince Regent (DLR) 7A 88
Pudding Mill Lane (DLR) 1D 86
Putney Bridge (Underground) 3H 117
Putney Pier (River Bus) 3G 117
Putney (Rail) **4G 117**

South Bermondsey (Rail) 5J 103
Southbury (Overground) , ...4C 24
South Croydon (Rail) **5D 168**
South Ealing (Underground) 3D 96
Southfields (Underground) 1H 135
Southgate (Underground) 1C 32
South Greenford (Rail) **3J 77**
South Hampstead (Overground) 7A 64
South Harrow (Underground) 3G 59
South Kensington (Underground) 3B 16 (4B 100)
South Kenton
     (Underground & Overground) 1C 60
South Merton (Rail) **3H 153**
South Quay (DLR) 2D 104
South Ruislip (Rail & Underground) **5A 58**
South Terminal (River Bus) 3E 106
South Tottenham (Overground) 5F 49
Southwark (Underground) 5A 14 (1B 102)
South Wimbledon (Underground) 7K 135
South Woodford (Underground) 2K 51
Stamford Brook (Underground) 4B 98
Stamford Hill (Overground) 7E 48
Stanmore (Underground) 4J 27
Star Lane (DLR) 4G 87
Stepney Green (Underground) 4K 85
Stockwell (Underground) 1J 119
Stoke Newington (Overground) 2F 67
Stonebridge Park (Underground & Overground) 7H 61
Stoneleigh (Rail) **5C 164**
Stratford Bus Station 7F 69
Stratford City Bus Station 6E 68
Stratford High Street (DLR) 1F 87
Stratford International (Rail & DLR) **6E 68**
Stratford (Rail, Underground, Overground, DLR & Crossrail)
    ....**7E 68**
Strawberry Hill (Rail) **3K 131**
Streatham Common (Rail) **6H 137**
Streatham Hill (Rail) **2J 137**
Streatham (Rail) **5H 137**
Sudbury & Harrow Road (Rail) **5B 60**
Sudbury Hill Harrow (Rail) **4J 59**
Sudbury Hill (Underground) 4J 59
Sudbury Town (Underground) 6B 60
Sunbury (Rail) **1J 147**
Sundridge Park (Rail) **7K 141**
Surbiton (Rail) **6E 150**
Surrey Quays (Overground) 4K 103
Sutton Common (Rail) **2K 165**
Sutton (Rail) **6A 166**
Swiss Cottage (Underground) 7B 64
Sydenham Hill (Rail) **3F 139**
Sydenham (Rail & Overground) **4J 139**
Syon Lane (Rail) **7A 96**

Upper Holloway (Overground) 2H 65
Upton Park (Underground) 1A 88

Vauxhall Bus Station 7E 18 (6J 101)
Vauxhall (Rail & Underground) ....**6F 19 (5J 101)**
Victoria Bus Station 2K 17 (3F 101)
Victoria Coach Station 4J 17 (4F 101)
Victoria (Rail & Underground) ....**3K 17 (4F 101)**

Queensbury (Underground) 3F 43
Queen's Park (Underground & Overground) 2H 81
Queens Road, Peckham (Rail & Overground) **1J 121**
Queenstown Road, Battersea (Rail) **1F 119**
Queensway (Underground) 7K 81

RAF Northolt Aerodrome 6H 57
Ravensbourne (Rail) **7F 141**
Ravenscourt Park (Underground) 4D 98
Rayners Lane (Underground) 7D 40
Raynes Park (Rail) **2E 152**
Rectory Road (Overground) 3F 67
Redbridge (Underground) 6B 52
Reeves Corner Stop (London Tramlink) 2B 168
Regent's Park (Underground) 4J 5 (4F 83)
Richmond (Rail, Underground & Overground) **4E 114**
Roding Valley (Underground) 4G 37
Rotherhithe (Overground) 2J 103
Royal Albert (DLR) 7C 88
Royal Oak (Underground) 5K 81
Royal Victoria (DLR) 7J 87
Royal Wharf Pier (River Bus) 2K 105
Ruislip Gardens (Underground) 4J 57
Ruislip Manor (Underground) 1J 57
Ruislip (Underground) 1G 57
Russell Square (Underground) 4E 6 (4J 83)

Waddon Marsh Stop (London Tramlink) 2A 168
Waddon (Rail) **4A 168**
Wallington (Rail) **6F 167**
Walthamstow Bus Station 4C 50
Walthamstow Central (Underground & Overground) ...5C 50
Walthamstow Queens Road (Overground) 5C 50
Wandle Park Stop (London Tramlink) 2A 168
Wandsworth Common (Rail) **1D 136**
Wandsworth Riverside Quarter Pier (River Bus) ...4J 117
Wandsworth Road (Overground) 2G 119
Wandsworth Town (Rail) **4K 117**
Wanstead Park (Overground) 4K 69
Wanstead (Underground) 6K 51
Wapping (Overground) 1J 103
Warren Street (Underground) 3A 6 (4G 83)
Warwick Avenue (Underground) 4A 82
Waterloo East (Rail) ....**5K 13 (1A 102)**
Waterloo (Rail & Underground) ....**6J 13 (2A 102)**
Wellesley Road Stop (London Tramlink) 2D 168
Welling (Rail) **2A 126**
Wembley Central (Rail, Underground & Overground) **5E 60**
Wembley Park (Underground) 3G 61
Wembley Stadium (Rail) **5F 61**
West Acton (Underground) 6G 79
Westbourne Park (Underground) 5H 81
West Brompton (Underground & Overground) 6J 99
Westcombe Park (Rail) **5J 105**
West Croydon Bus Station 1C 168
West Croydon (Rail, Overground & London Tramlink) ...**1C 168**
West Drayton (Rail & Crossrail) **1A 92**
West Dulwich (Rail) **2D 138**
West Ealing (Rail & Crossrail) **7B 78**
Westferry (DLR) 7C 86
Westfield London Bus Station 1E 98
West Finchley (Underground) 6E 30
West Ham (DLR) 3G 87
West Hampstead Thameslink (Rail) **6J 63**
West Hampstead (Underground & Overground) 6J 63
West Ham (Rail & Underground) **3G 87**
West Harrow (Underground) 6G 41
West India Quay (DLR) 7C 86
West Kensington (Underground) 5H 99
Westminster Millennium Pier
    (River Bus & Tours) 6F 13 (2J 101)
Westminster (Underground) 7F 13 (2J 101)
West Norwood (Rail) **4B 138**
West Ruislip (Rail & Underground) **2E 56**
West Silvertown (DLR) 1J 105
West Sutton (Rail) **4J 165**
West Wickham (Rail) **7E 158**
Whitechapel (Underground, Overground & Crossrail) ...5H 85
White City (Underground) 7E 80
White Hart Lane (Overground) 7A 34
Whitton (Rail) **7G 113**
Willesden Green (Underground) 6E 62
Willesden Junction (Underground & Overground) ...3B 80
Wimbledon Chase (Rail) **2G 153**
Wimbledon Park (Underground) 3J 135
Wimbledon (Rail, Underground & London Tramlink) ...**6H 135**
Winchmore Hill (Rail) **7G 23**
Woodford (Underground) 6E 36
Woodgrange Park (Overground) 5B 70
Wood Green (Underground) 2A 48
Wood Lane (Underground) 7E 80
Woodside Park (Underground) 4E 30
Woodside Stop (London Tramlink) 6H 157
Wood Street Walthamstow (Overground) 4F 51
Woolwich Arsenal Pier (River Bus) 3F 107
Woolwich Arsenal (Rail, DLR & Crossrail) **4F 107**
Woolwich Dockyard (Rail) **4D 106**
Worcester Park (Rail) **1C 164**

St George St Wharf Pier (River Bus) .....·. 6E 18 (6J 101)
St Helier (Rail) **6J 153**
St James's Park (Underground) 1C 18 (2H 101)
St James Street (Overground) 5A 50
St Johns (Rail) **2C 122**
St John's Wood (Underground) 2B 82
St Katharine's Pier (River Tours) 1F 103
St Margarets (Rail) **6B 114**
St Pancras International (Rail) 1E 6 (2J 83)
St Paul's (Underground) 7C 8 (6C 84)
Sanderstead (Rail) **7D 168**
Sandilands Stop (London Tramlink) 2F 169
Selhurst (Rail) **5E 156**
Seven Kings (Rail & Crossrail) **1J 71**
Seven Sisters (Underground & Overground) 5E 48
Shadwell (Underground & DLR) 7H 85
Shepherd's Bush Market (Underground) 1E 98
Shepherd's Bush (Rail, Underground & Overground) **2F 99**
Shepperton (Rail) **5E 146**
Shoreditch High Street (Overground) 3J 9 (4F 85)
Shortlands (Rail) **2G 159**
Sidcup (Rail) **2A 144**
Silver Street (Overground) 4A 34
Sloane Square (Underground) 4G 17 (4E 100)
Snaresbrook (Underground) 5J 51
South Acton (Overground) 3J 97
Southall (Rail & Crossrail) **2D 94**

Teddington (Rail) **6A 132**
Temple (Underground) 2J 13 (7K 83)
Thames Ditton (Rail) **7K 149**
Therapia Lane Stop (London Tramlink) 2A 168
Thornton Heath (Rail) **4C 156**
Tolworth (Rail) **2H 163**
Tooting Bec (Underground) 3E 136
Tooting Broadway (Underground) 5C 136
Tooting (Rail) **6D 136**
Tottenham Court Road
    (Underground & Crossrail) 7D 6 (6H 83)
Tottenham Hale Bus Station 3G 49
Tottenham Hale (Rail & Underground) **3H 49**
Totteridge & Whetstone (Underground) 2F 31
Tower Gateway (DLR) 2J 15 (7F 85)
Tower Hill (Underground) 2J 15 (7F 85)
Tower Millennium Pier
    (River Bus & Tours) 4H 15 (1E 102)
Tufnell Park (Underground) 4G 65
Tulse Hill (Rail) **2B 138**
Turnham Green (Underground) 4A 98
Turnpike Lane (Underground) 3B 48
Twickenham (Rail) **7A 114**

Upney (Underground) 7K 71
Upper Halliford (Rail) **2G 147**

London's Rail & Tube services

Key to lines and symbols

Bakerloo	
Central	
Circle	
District	limited service
Hammersmith & City	
Jubilee	
Metropolitan	
Northern	
Piccadilly	
Victoria	
Waterloo & City	
DLR	
London Overground	
London Trams	
TfL Rail	
Emirates Air Line cable car	

Chiltern Railways	
c2c	limited service
Gatwick Express	
Great Northern	
Great Western Railway	
Greater Anglia	peak hours only
Heathrow Express	
London Northwestern Railway	
South Western Railway	peak hours only
Southeastern	peak hours only
Southeastern high speed	peak hours and limited service
Southern	
Thameslink	peak hours only

◯	Interchange stations
◯-◯	Internal interchange
◯–◯	Under a 10 minute walk between stations
✈	Airport
⚓	Riverboat services
▭▭	Victoria Coach Station
Stratford	Station in both fare zones

tfl.gov.uk

nationalrail.co.uk

© Transport for London and Rail Delivery Group   May 2019

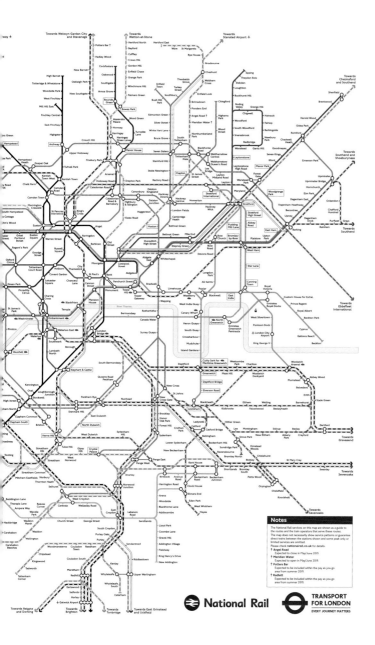

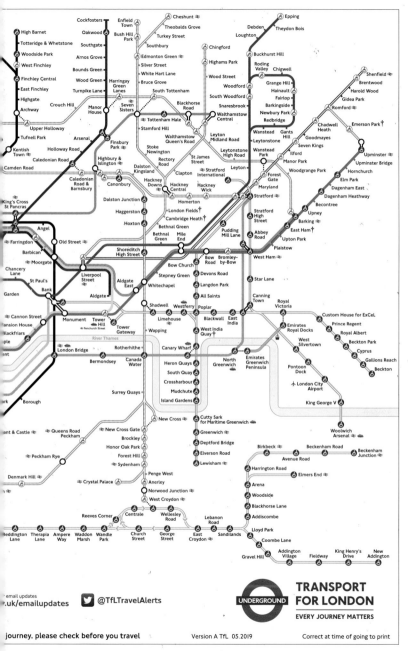

WEST END THEATRES

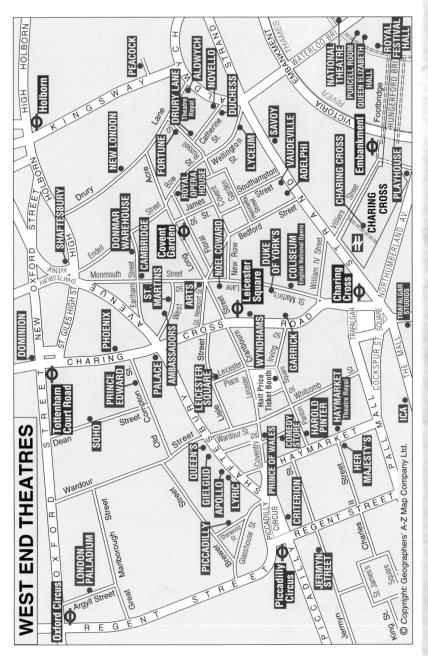